Computers, Data Processing, and the Law

Text and Cases

Computers, Data Processing, and the Law

Text and Cases

STEVEN L. MANDELL, D.B.A., J.D.

Certified Data Processor
Member of the Ohio Bar

WEST PUBLISHING COMPANY

St. Paul   New York   Los Angeles   San Francisco

COPYEDITING   Elaine Linden
COMPOSITION   Parkwood Composition Service, Inc.

COPYRIGHT © 1984 By WEST PUBLISHING CO.
      50 West Kellogg Boulevard
      P.O. Box 3526
      St. Paul, Minnesota 55165

Library of Congress Cataloging in Publication Data

Mandell, Steven L.
      Computers, data processing, and the law.

      Includes bibliographies and index.
      1. Computers—Law and legislation—United States.
Cases—I. Title.
KF390.5.C6M36   1984a   343.73′07800164   83-23369
ISBN 0-314-70624-0   347.3037800164

To the outstanding faculty at Toledo University College of Law

Contents

PART II:
Computer Systems Failures: Remedies   37

PART III:
Personnel, Consulting Services, and Facilities Management   61

PART V:
Computer Crime and Privacy   153

**PART VI:
Systems Design Considerations 199**

PART VII:
Computer Records In Court 231

PART VIII:
Computer Tax Considerations 249

Case Supplement   265

Preface

The information processing revolution has transformed our nation into a technologically based society. The computer will shortly become as commonplace as the telephone or television; estimates exceed 30 million units in use by the end of the decade. The dynamic nature of this area presents special problems for the courts in applying existing laws and principles to computer related facts. This book presents the current state of the law with respect to computers and data processing.

My journey through law school was far more focused than that of the traditional student. I had been a computer professor and professional for ten years and a well-established author of computer textbooks. Therefore, any course was reoriented in my mind to its relationship to computers and data processing. Recognizing the minimal knowledge of the law by computer professionals and the restricted expertise of lawyers regarding computers, I believed it necessary to prepare material that could satisfy the needs of both groups. This book is a result of that idea.

The book has been designed around the functional aspects of data-processing management to maximize its value to organizations. Two versions are available. The paperback college edition contains six parts:

   I. Acquiring Computer Hardware and Software: Contracting
  II. Computer System Failures: Remedies
 III. Personnel, Consulting Services, and Facilities Management
 IV. Writing Computer Programs for Sale
  V. Computer Crime and Privacy
 VI. Systems Design Considerations

and the hardback professional edition contains two additional parts:

 VII. Computer Records In Court
VIII. Computer Tax Considerations

as well as an appendix of almost 200 edited court opinions. The expanded version also serves as a primary research tool with the inclusion of a computer topic table of cases at the beginning of the case supplement. This index follows the outline of the material presented in the book and lists the appropriate cases, with page references, under each topic.

I have had the helpful counsel of several attorneys who have written widely on a variety of specific subjects. Professor Robert Holmes has been invaluable in the development of the contract material and deserves special recognition for his efforts on the first two parts. Professor Larry Kowalski was especially helpful concerning the tax implications that are often overlooked. Professor Marshall Leaffer has always provided sound counsel concerning copyright issues. In addition, I was fortunate to have three outstanding attorneys review the manuscript and provide insightful comments that greatly improved the material: Professor Lee G. Caldwell, Ms. Vivian Ann Maese, and Professor Michael A. Duggan.

It would be inappropriate to write this acknowledgment without specifically recognizing those law students who spent hours researching the case material: Kathryn Bates, Kelly Boseckerr, Dominic Graziano, Mary O'Reilly, Stephen Pennington, Douglas Powers, and Sharon Sampson.

My administrative assistant, Donna Pulschen, gave her heart, soul, and whip to the project, without which there would never have been a completed book. The many talents of Charles Caswell contributed greatly to this project. The final recognition goes to an outstanding young legal scholar, Gerald Laver, who must be given credit for any success that this book may experience, because of his editing and writing support.

West Publishing Company has never waivered in its support of this project. I would like to express my personal appreciation to all of the individuals involved for their professional style.

Computers, Data Processing, and the Law

Text and Cases

PART I

Acquiring Computer Hardware and Software: Contracting

Outline

INTRODUCTION[1]

Procuring computer hardware and software is much too complicated and important a decision to be made by one person. The best way to approach the problem is to form a team consisting of, at least, a tax expert, a lawyer, and, naturally, data-processing personnel. Since individuals or small businesspeople may find it too costly or impractical to establish such a procurement team, these people should, at the very least, seek the advice of data-processing experts regarding system specifications and a commercial lawyer regarding contracts. Each company has unique circumstances under which the procurement decision is made. It may be in the best interest of the particular company to purchase a computer, lease a computer, or employ a service bureau. Factors affecting this decision are the required size of the computer system, the functions to be performed, the system's cost, and many other system design considerations discussed elsewhere in this book.

HARDWARE PROCUREMENT METHODS

Leasing and purchasing hardware are the two basic methods for obtaining the use of in-house hardware. Both achieve the same end of placing sophisticated computer machinery totally within the user's control, but they achieve this by substantially different means. Some of the differences between leasing and purchasing computer hardware follow.

Leasing Hardware

Equipment leasing has been popular because of tax savings and cash-flow demands. It allows an organization to acquire the use of complex, expensive computer hardware without a large capital outlay. It is possible to lease a computer directly from the manufacturer or from a third-party leasing company that has already purchased the equipment, often at the user's specific request, from a manufacturer. Lease payments made to third parties are usually less than to manufacturers, due in part to the fact that leasing companies typically depreciate hardware over a longer period of time than do manufacturers. This may allow lower rates, but it also puts leasing companies in a financial bind if they become unable to lease the equipment for an extended period of time. Third-party leasing can be risky, so it is important for the acquisition team to examine carefully the financial stability, reliability, and integrity of the leasing company and the legal significance of the contracts involved. Consultation with others who have leased equipment from the prospective leasing company should be beneficial.

It should be kept in mind that there are basically two types of lease agreements—the "full payout" and the "nonfull payout." The distinction between these two is important. The full payout lease is usually considered a conditional sales agreement. After the lease term expires, usually five years, the user can often exercise an option to purchase the equipment for a minimal payment. The nonfull payout lease is usually for a term of from two to five years, after which the user must either renew the lease or return the equipment.

A lease is a special type of contract with such complex legal and tax implications that consultation with experts is necessary to apprise the user of his or her obligations. For maximum legal protection, the user should ensure that Article Two of the Uniform Commercial Code (UCC) governing sales transactions in goods applies to the lease. Article Two is most likely to be applied to leases that contain an option-to-purchase clause since they are, in effect, sales of goods. On whatever basis, most courts have had little difficulty treating computer leases as Article Two transactions in goods between the user and vendor.[2] If the user wants to ensure the applicability of Article Two, the user should negotiate a lease with an option-to-purchase clause or a clause specifying that the UCC is to control the transaction (discussed later in this chapter). Significant tax considerations are also involved in the sale/lease character of the transaction (see Part VIII).

Judging from many recent computer cases,[3] one aspect of computer leasing arrangements has been particularly troubling to computer users. Nearly all computer leases appear to contain what have euphemistically come to be called "hell-or-high-water" clauses, or waivers of defenses. These clauses require the user to make the required lease payments regardless of any problems that might develop with the system. Since the user has agreed to assume absolute liability for the financing lease payments, it makes no difference that contract defenses might exist against the computer vendor. The courts have somewhat mitigated the harsh effects of this policy against computer users by enabling the computer user to sue the vendor directly, even though a third-party lessor is technically the buyer. The user should realize from the start that it is more advantageous to join forces with the lessor against the vendor rather than to follow the more natural inclination to refuse to make payments on what is perceived as a bad investment.

Purchasing Hardware

Although the leasing of computer equipment is still widespread, the direct purchase of equipment is becoming increasingly popular. The rental agreement was favored in the past due to the large cash outlay required to purchase and the fear that hardware would quickly become obsolete. The last few years, however, have seen microprogramming and competition reduce the costs of hardware. Moreover, the purchase of equipment has the additional benefit of more certain Article Two protection.

The market for personal computers is expanding rapidly because of their ability to perform comparably to their main-frame counterparts at greatly reduced costs. Due to their initially low cost, they are almost always purchased rather than leased. Users and retailers, attracted by their low price, often overlook the myriad responsibilities, liabilities, and commitments that a computer acquisition entails. The retailer of the microcomputer may sell the equipment without the usual sales order clauses—integration, limitation of remedies and liabilities—that severely reduce the rights of a buyer who invests in a more expensive or complicated system (discussed later in this chapter). As a result, the buyer of a microcomputer is perhaps more likely to be fully protected by the Article Two implied-remedies provisions discussed in Part II. To be sure the buyer is protected, however, a close examination of the sales contract is essential. All of these legal issues are introduced later in this part and discussed in greater detail in Part II.

ACQUIRING COMPUTER SOFTWARE

In the past, hardware was the most costly part of the computer system. The software programming was supplied exclusively by the hardware manufacturer and was included in the price of the overall system. Advances in technology, along with increased competition, have provided users with more bargaining power to negotiate for a cheaper price. The labor costs of making the necessary software, however, have skyrocketed. Antitrust law now requires that applications software be "unbundled," that is, offered and priced separately from the hardware so that competitors have a meaningful opportunity to participate in the software market. These increased costs have made software an independently significant financial aspect of obtaining a computer system. Understanding how to acquire software intelligently is the goal of this section.

Defining Software

A universally accepted definition of software has, as yet, not been developed. It is a term used repeatedly by the data-processing industry, but it carries different meanings to different people. To some, software is merely the programming associated with a computer system. To others, particularly one court of law,

> "software" denotes the information loaded into the machine and directions given to the machine (usually by card or teleprompter) as to what it is to do and upon what command. "Software" is also frequently used to include "support"—that is, advice, assistance, counseling, and sometimes even expert engineering help furnished by the vendor in loading the machine for a certain program such as inventory control or preparation of payroll.[4]

Whether software is considered tangible or intangible is particularly important for tax purposes. Anyone procuring software should consult a tax expert prior to negotiating with vendors. Different software contract arrangements can create different tax situations. The distinction between tangible and intangible property becomes important in the areas of property taxation and income tax deductions.

Types of Software

Systems Software. Generally, there are two kinds of software included in a computer system. The first type, commonly known as systems software, consists of the instructions required for the machine to operate properly and the documentation that explains how the instructions work. Systems software "tells" the hardware how to move data from one device to another, which programs to load and execute, and what to do with the finished products. Systems software is almost always supplied by the manufacturer of the hardware and is included in the hardware agreement (rent, lease, or purchase). Because the systems software is an indispensable part of the hardware, it is invariably considered an Article Two "good."

Applications Software. Having found a promising computer hardware system and *before* committing him- or herself to buying the hardware, the user should investigate the availability of the second kind of software—applications software—and decide upon a suitable method of software procurement. An applications program is a set of instructions that tells the computer how to execute specific functions such as inventory control, payroll, and scheduling. The term "software" usually connotes applications programs. The compatibility of an applications program with a particular set of hardware may determine which system a user will acquire. System vendors often use the available applications programming as a major selling point of their hardware.

Software Procurement Methods

Bundled Systems. Most suppliers have application programs available for their hardware and often include these as a "bundled" package to be purchased along with the hardware, although antitrust law now requires that applications software be priced separately so that the user has the option of acquiring it elsewhere. A bundled system that includes hardware plus systems and applications software in one contract is generally a quick and easy method for an inexperienced user to acquire a system. Furthermore, the Article Two definition of goods should apply to the entire bundled system—both the hardware and software—since without the proper software, a computer is unable to perform the functions for which it was purchased. Therefore, most courts will probably rule that when a complete system is purchased in one contract, the software qualifies as an Article Two good. This should be true whether the vendor is supplying a preexisting packaged program or a program especially designed to meet the user's needs.

A bundled system would be particularly suited for a new computer user desiring to transfer standard procedures such as inventory, scheduling, or payroll from a manual system to a computer. A user acquiring a bundled system must still be cautious when negotiating with suppliers. Bundled systems often appear to be such simple and financially sound offerings that users overlook important issues. No matter how simple a supplier makes the procurement process appear, it is, nonetheless, a legally complex transaction. Legal and computer advice should be sought!

Software Packages. Another method for acquiring applications programs is the purchase of "packaged" or "canned" programs—preprogrammed disks or tapes that are compatible with the user's hardware, along with instructions for their use.

Software packages are a relatively new method of providing software for a computer system and are becoming increasingly popular. Software packages can be acquired from the manufacturer or an independent vendor; these have a minimal need for debugging. The copy of the program is usually licensed to the user. This is done to protect the proprietary rights of the program developer and to keep the program from being used or copied by an unauthorized third party (see Part IV on proprietary rights in software).

This method is most readily identified with the personal computer market. A computer user can go to the neighborhood computer store or department store and buy an applications program such as a word-processing or income tax program over the counter. Such a program is easy to obtain but is extremely inflexible in terms of the user's needs. Rather than adapting the program to the user's preexisting information system, the user must adapt the system to provide the information needed for that program in the prescribed format. The purchaser of such a canned program probably has less bargaining power than if he or she chose any other software procurement method. The warranty protection is likely to be comparable to that provided for other mass-produced products. For example, a limited warranty for replacement of defective programs within 90 days of purchase may be printed on the package or on a slip of paper inside the package. Unless the buyer supplies his or her own terms on a purchase order, as discussed in the section on the user's purchase order, the buyer has a basic choice of taking the deal or leaving it—there is no bargaining with the retailer over the terms of the warranty. The package method of procurement increases the user's chances of having the software treated as a good for purposes of UCC application if the sale is framed in terms of purchasing the tangible embodiment of the software.

Before negotiating with a software package supplier other than a retail store, a user should contact other customers and inquire about the reliability of the organization. Software suppliers can often be unstable organizations working with borderline capital and strict sales requirements because of the enormous costs of formulating, debugging, and selling the packages. The most reliable tips about the financial stability and integrity of a software supplier can be gleaned from previous customers. Firmly established software vendors often encourage customers to participate in user groups created and supported by the vendors. These groups provide feedback to the vendors on software problems and suggest possible improvements.

Software Development Contracts. Apart from manufacturer-supplied applications programs and prepackaged programs are the custom-designed programs used to perform specific functions peculiar to a user's operations. Whereas packaged programs are ready to be used with minimal debugging, software development contracts allow for the creation of programs from scratch. There are basically three methods of contracting for software development: body shop, cost plus, and fixed cost.[5]

The body-shop contract appears at first to be the least expensive of the three. It involves the contractor supplying the user with programmers who start developing the program. The user pays the contractor on a time-unit basis, that is, a certain amount per person-hour, person-day, or person-month spent on the project. It appears to be the most economical method at first because the user is paying directly for the amount of programming time actually spent on the project. However, if the programmers are inexperienced, the body-shop contract may end up costing more than the alternative methods. This method may actually encourage this result, since the contractor's profit comes from the surplus of the user's rate over the amount paid to the programmers. The contractor thus earns a greater profit by using lower-paid, and presumably less-qualified, programmers to do a lower-quality job over a longer period of time.

The cost-plus contractor also supplies programmers to the user, but a total cost is estimated before initiating the work. The cost-plus contract benefits the user as the total cost can be reliably estimated. Furthermore, more experienced programmers are usually provided.

In the fixed-cost contract, the contractor makes a bid of a specific dollar amount for the job. The fixed-cost contract benefits the user because the exact amount for the project can be budgeted. This method is usually the most expensive since the supplier must cushion the bid to ensure against any problems that may delay the project or escalate the costs.

Large organizations with extensive data-processing departments usually rely on their own in-house personnel to develop software. If software development by outside vendors is nevertheless required, it is absolutely essential that the appropriate computer specialists be consulted to evaluate the contract specifications.

Acquiring custom-designed applications programs warrants the utmost caution in negotiating with suppliers. The time schedule for payment and acceptable installation tests is particularly important. A user acquiring custom-designed programming should formulate a payment schedule whereby a payment is made as each phase of installation is completed, tested, and operating properly. This type of installment plan encourages the vendor/supplier to meet time schedules and also provides some bargaining leverage should problems arise. Custom-designed programming is more likely to develop problems and take longer to debug. Therefore, users should take this possibility into consideration when negotiating and include the appropriate clauses in the agreement for the user's protection.

As discussed later, the courts are more likely to rule that custom software is a common law service as opposed to an Article Two good. That interpretation, however, can be vigorously attacked by pointing out to the court that the end product of the programmer's services—that is, a tape or disk—is a movable object and hence fits the definition of UCC good. The user who wants UCC protection should help the judge visualize that something tangible and movable was purchased by specifying in the final contract that the user is buying a tape or disk containing the program, since the UCC drafters expressly intended that movable things to be specially manufactured in the future be considered UCC goods.[6]

Software Licenses. It is common practice in the computer industry for software suppliers to license a program rather than sell it outright. The single price paid for the license typically allows use of the program but with strict restrictions on the number of copies that can be made and used within the organization, along with strict prohibition against any use outside the organization. This allows others to use the program without the transfer of title and thus protects the ownership rights of the vendor. The user obtaining licensed software should be sure to include clauses in the agreement concerning ownership of the additions or changes that are made to the original programs. (For a better understanding of the implications of proprietary rights of programs, see Part IV, Writing Computer Programs for Sale.) Some doubt also arises as to the applicability of the UCC to licenses of software, as discussed in the following section.

Whether a user decides to use his or her own personnel for software development, to acquire a manufacturer's package, to hire an independent software development contractor, or to enter into a licensing agreement, there are nevertheless common factors important to the software procurement process. A basic knowledge of contract law is essential, as well as a basic knowledge of what ploys the hardware and software vendors are using in trying to have the user sign a contract prepared by the vendor's attorneys.

BASIC CONTRACT LAW

A contract is defined as "the total legal obligation which results from the parties' agreement."[7] An agreement is defined as "the bargain of the parties . . . as found in their language or by implication from other circumstances including course of dealing or usage of trade or course of performance. . . ."[8]

Contract law has taken centuries to develop. Much legislation has been passed and thousands of cases have been adjudicated, all of which have developed the law to its present state. This section is a cursory overview of contract and sales law and is not meant to take the place of legal assistance. It is provided here and in Part II so that the user may avoid undermining his or her legal position through dealings with the vendor and so that the user may better understand and communicate with legal counsel.

Contracting for hardware and software requires an understanding of basic contract and sales law principles. The lawyer on the acquisition team should give other team members a brief analysis of the following important contract principles: mutual assent (offer and acceptance), consideration, delivery, liabilities, and remedies.

The technical personnel, in turn, should provide the lawyer with a basic understanding of system design specifications (hardware and software), performance requirements, compatibility needs with current and future equipment, and other considerations relevant to the acquisition. Active input by all team members will result in the best possible contract.

The Uniform Commercial Code versus Common Law

The Uniform Commercial Code is a set of provisions proposed by legal experts to promote uniformity among the states in their legal treatment of commercial transactions. To date, 49 states, the Virgin Islands, and the District of Columbia have adopted Article Two of the UCC as the controlling sales law of their jurisdictions; Louisiana is the only state abstaining. Although slight differences still exist among the states, the UCC's uniformity makes a general analysis of contract law possible in those cases to which the UCC applies.

Unfortunately, Article Two of the UCC applies only to transactions in goods.[9] Article Two of the UCC is limited even further by certain sections that seem to apply only to contracts for the *sale* of goods.[10] If Article Two does not apply to a transaction, then the common law of contracts applies. The UCC is by far the better system since it is more modern and basically abolishes the concept of caveat emptor (a Latin legal maxim meaning "let the buyer beware"). Under Article Two, for example, the computer user is given implied warranty protection, whereas under the common law, buyer protection is not presumed or implied and therefore must be expressly negotiated and agreed upon in the final contract. Most computer suppliers will not assent to such negotiations.

For the UCC to apply to computer acquisitions, two main preconditions must be satisfied. First, the contract must be one for goods, not for services. As a general rule, the UCC is not applicable to contracts for services. Second, the contract must usually be for the *sale* of goods, although it is possible to apply Article Two to contracts for nonsales such as leases and licenses.[11]

Goods. For Article Two of the UCC to apply, a court must find that the subject matter of the contract was a good. Goods are defined as "all things (including specially manufactured goods) which are movable. . . ."[12] When the user acquires hardware, an Article Two good exists since the hardware is movable. When software is acquired along with the hardware, the courts appear to view all of the computer system acquisitions, including the software, as Article Two goods since the system as a whole is movable.[13]

On the other hand, when software is acquired separately from the hardware, considerable confusion exists as to whether Article Two applies. If a packaged or off-the-shelf program is acquired, such as a video game cartridge, it very likely will be considered an Article Two good since a movable disk or tape is purchased. But when a customized program is acquired, a court could rule that Article Two does not apply because considerable services are rendered to produce that particular program. In that case, it might appear to the court that the purchase was really a contract for services. Services are not movable since they have no physical existence.

Courts have applied two contradictory rules when faced with these customized program cases. First, the predominant factors rule is applied by some courts. According to this rule, the courts seek to determine whether the services-rendered aspect of the contract outweighs or dominates the goods-supplied aspect. If the services predominate, then Article Two does not apply. Hence, in most customized software transactions without a simultaneous hardware acquisition, courts are likely to consider the transaction to be a service and not a good. The cost of the goods supplied (a magnetic tape or disk) is incidental or insignificant when compared with the cost of the services rendered.

Second, the courts could employ the movable-end-product rule. Under this rule, the courts seek to determine whether the final product of the contract is movable. If it is, then Article Two goods exist. Since the end product of the programmers' labors is something movable—a magnetic tape or disk—customized programs are considered Article Two goods under the end-product rule.

Of the two rules, the movable-end-product rule is more logical since it gives effect to the "specially manufactured goods" language of Section 2-105(1). The drafters of the UCC seemed to intend specifically that a good is a good regardless of whether substantial services are required to create it.

The established methods for acquiring software discussed previously are all susceptible to UCC application if the buyer is able to characterize the transaction as the sale of the physical embodiment of the program. The buyer should be alert, however, to potential marketing practices by software vendors that might inhibit the application of Article Two. In all of the cases just described, the buyer is able to argue that a good exists because something movable (a tape or disk, for example) is being purchased. If the vendor is able to create the impression that nothing movable or tangible is being purchased, the vendor may convince a court that the UCC should not be applied since no goods are involved. For example, a vendor may rent the tape or disk to the user to make a copy, after which that particular tape or disk must be returned to the vendor. Similarly, the vendor may require that the buyer supply a blank tape or cartridge upon which the vendor will record the purchased program; or the vendor may rebate to the buyer the cost of the physical storage medium. In all of these cases, the vendor may be able to remove the tangible aspect of the transaction sufficiently to convince a court that the essence of the transaction is the transfer of pure information—an intangible. Likewise, many software vendors and buyers may be linked into a common data transmission network. If the vendor transmits a program directly from its computer to the buyer's computer via the data network, there is arguably no transaction in goods since the essence of what is transferred is ordered pulses through a communications medium. Although the issue of whether such a transmission is itself a movable thing may be debated, the buyer would nevertheless be unable to point to any physical thing that was transferred. The implication would again be that the buyer was purchasing intangible information, not a good.

In any event, the user should resolve all doubts about UCC application by specifying in the contract that the UCC will control the interpretation and application of the contract. This is discussed in greater detail in the purchase order section that follows.

Sales or Transactions. Article Two of the UCC applies only to contracts involving "transactions in goods."[14] Some sections of the UCC, however, speak in terms of "sales" of goods. Thus, a second issue that might determine the applicability of certain sections of Article Two of the UCC is whether a sale exists.[15] To have a sale under the UCC, title to the computer hardware must pass from the seller to the user for a price.[16] Clearly, if the computer system is sold outright, Article Two would apply. Problems arise, however, with rentals, leases, and licensing agreements. A true rental agreement for a set term with no option to purchase is not always considered to be a sale, and the user may therefore have no UCC protection. The user would then have to turn to the state's common law of contracts for any relief sought. If the system is not sold outright, the courts may apply one or more of several theories that would extend Article Two to nonsale contracts.

Leasing arrangements may be found to be, in effect, sales agreements in some situations so that Article Two applies. Most courts would probably not be sidetracked by the fact that the contract is technically a lease when the user is eventually to acquire title to the equipment. Under the economic reality test, a lease with an option to buy is treated as a sale of goods to the lessee, so most courts will apply Article Two. According to this view, a lease for a computer system should be treated as a UCC sale of goods if the lease is economically the equivalent of a sale.[17] To prove this, the lease between the user and supplier should feature a clause giving the user the option to purchase the system at the end of the lease period for a price below the fair market value of the equipment at that time.

A second method is known as the third-party beneficiary doctrine. In many transactions, the computer supplier will sell the computer system to a third party, typically a finance company, that will then lease the system to the user. Under the third-party beneficiary concept, the user is entitled to assert all remedies and rights that the supplier gave to the finance company since the user is the ultimate beneficiary of that sale-of-goods contract. Hence, if the supplier gives the finance company an express warranty in the contract of sale between them, the user is also given that remedy since the supplier and finance company intended that the user be the ultimate beneficiary of that contract.[18] The problem with this concept is that if the finance company is given few or no remedies by the supplier's form contract, then the user also receives the same minimal protection or none.

The user must insist upon negotiating the contract of sale between the supplier and the finance company in order to maximize the protection given to the finance company by the supplier in the sales contract. The user can then employ the third-party beneficiary doctrine for the user's benefit. Since the finance company, the true purchaser from the vendor, will usually negotiate little, if any, protection for the user, the third-party beneficiary rule may be of little value to the user unless the user obtains the finance company's permission to negotiate the contract for itself. Only then can the user's attorneys create a contract that will give the user some protection. If the finance company refuses to allow the user's attorneys to negotiate the terms of the sales contract with the supplier, the user should find another finance company that will.

A third method is known as the judicial extension of Article Two into nonsale areas. Comment 2 to UCC Section 2-313 allows the courts to extend Article Two to leases and licenses. Such an extension is supported by Section 2-102, which states that Article Two can apply to transactions in goods, a broader class than sales of goods. The term "transaction" includes sales but also includes nonsales such as leases and licenses.

A possible negative effect of considering the lease a conditional sales agreement is the tax result. If the transaction is considered to be a sales agreement and therefore a capital investment, the income tax and personal property tax consequences could be disastrous. A tax expert should therefore be consulted before deciding whether to lease or buy.

The Offer and Acceptance Process

The concept of mutual assent has often been called the manner in which the contracting parties come to a meeting of the minds. It has also been referred to simply as the offer and acceptance process. Mutual assent begins with one party offering to do something or to refrain from doing something if the other party agrees to a reciprocal obligation. Then, if the party to whom the offer is directed agrees to form a contract upon the terms of the first party's offer, an acceptance is made.

Whether the parties actually formed a contract depends upon whether a valid offer and acceptance occurred.[19] This, in turn, depends upon how closely the parties' offer and acceptance terms agreed. In contracting for computer hardware and software, if both parties sign the same written contract, agreement upon the same terms is shown so that offer and acceptance is clearly present. If the terms of the offer and acceptance are too dissimilar, then no contract was formed since there was no objectively expressed agreement even though both parties may have believed that a contract was formed. Before signing the final contract, the user should seek legal advice to determine the amount of protection he or she is receiving under the proposed terms and whether a valid contract will be formed.

Consideration

"Consideration" is the exchange of something of legal value for something that was bargained for. Usually, consideration in a sales agreement is the vendor's promise to deliver a good or service in exchange for the buyer's promise to pay an agreed amount of money for it. Hence, problems surrounding consideration are rarely present in sales agreements.

Some problems that occur with consideration involve attempts to modify the original contract. No new consideration is necessary to modify a contract governed by the UCC.[20] To modify a common law contract, however, additional consideration is required. For example, consider the case in which the initial contract specifies that the programmer will program the computer to perform inventory accounting functions, but after the contract has been formed, the buyer requests that an additional function such as inventory reordering be added. The programmer agrees to do so at no additional cost. Was a valid modification made? If the UCC applies, the answer is yes since no additional consideration is needed. If the common law applies, the answer is no since the buyer has given the programmer no added consideration for this additional program. An extra, say, $100 would have constituted sufficient consideration at common law. Therefore, when modifying existing computer contracts, the user would be well advised to have a lawyer review the modifications to be sure that the contract as changed is enforceable.

Statute of Frauds

The Statute of Frauds requires certain contracts to be reduced to writing and signed by at least the defendant in order to be enforced by a court. Specifically, contracts for the sale of land, surety contracts, *contracts for the sale of goods involving $500 or more,* and contracts in which performance will take longer than one year must be in writing and signed by the defendant. Because most contracts for computer hardware and software will be for goods costing more than $500, these agreements must be in writing to be enforceable in court.[21] The purpose of requiring a writing is to avoid perjury by witnesses and to prevent conflicting interpretations when the contract is challenged, as might occur with an oral contract. Reducing the agreement to writing and having it signed by the other party is thus a necessary step in contracting for hardware and software.

The general rule is that for a contract for the sale of goods to be enforceable, a writing must be signed by the party being sued. Certain exceptions to this rule exist, however. First, if both the buyer and seller are merchants, a writing sent by one party confirming an oral agreement satisfies the statute of frauds against the party to whom the confirmation is sent if that recipient does not object within ten days after the writing is received. Second, if payment for goods has been made and accepted, it is not necessary to also have a written contract to enforce the contract. The payment is sufficient to prove that an agreement existed between the parties. Third, the party being sued may admit in court proceedings that a contract for sale was made. Finally, if the goods are to be specially manufactured for the buyer and would not be suitable for sale to others in the ordinary course of the seller's business, a written contract may not be required. If the circumstances reasonably indicate that the goods are for the buyer and the seller has made a substantial beginning of their manufacture, no writing would be required. Thus, if a user orally agreed to have a software vendor design software to the user's specifications, the contract would be enforceable if the software would not be readily marketable to other buyers and if the vendor had made a substantial start on the creation of the software.

Another problem frequently occurring under the Statute of Frauds involves the modification of existing contracts. If the Statute of Frauds requires the original contract to be in writing and signed by the defendant, then the modified contract should also be reduced to writing and signed by the defendant to ensure enforcement of any changes by the courts.

The Parol Evidence Rule

The parol evidence rule is used by the courts as a means of protecting the sanctity and integrity of a written and signed contract. This rule provides that oral or written statements or representations made prior to the final written agreement are inadmissible in court if the purpose of such statements is to change or contradict the final written agreement.[22] Courts will not admit such evidence into the dispute since it is likely that the evidence may be perjured. The statements in the final written contract supersede any that were made before its signing. Once the parties begin to reduce their agreement to writing, great care must be taken to ensure that the final writing contains *all* the negotiated terms. Prior or contemporaneous oral or written statements may be admitted to supplement the writing only if the written agreement is incomplete or ambiguous.[23] Since salespersons often make oral promises about a computer's performance, it is extremely important for the prospective purchaser of hardware or software to understand this rule. These oral promises will be inadmissible as evidence in a legal dispute if they are not reduced to writing and incorporated into the final written contract.

The best method to protect the user from the parol evidence rule's harsh effects is to require that all representations concerning the equipment be put in writing and attached to the final sales contract. This is known as the "attach everything" rule. Moreover, all sales literature, correspondence, and all other items of significance should be attached to and, ideally, referenced in the final contract. Otherwise, the parol evidence rule, coupled with the supplier's integration clause (see the section on the contracting process), will prevent the admissibility into court of the supplier's representations.[24]

Express Warranties

Under Article Two of the UCC, express warranties are created when the seller makes any promise or affirmation of fact to the buyer that relates to the goods and is a basis of the bargain.[25] In this way, the seller warrants that the goods will conform to the affirmation or promise. An express warranty may be created by the supplier's use of a description, sample, or model in attempting to sell the goods, although the seller's contract terms will often attempt to limit or disclaim all such warranties (see the section on the contracting process). Express warranties are also found in the written contract, such as statements that defective equipment will be replaced or repaired for up to one year after delivery. A breach occurs if the goods fail to conform to the express warranty, in which case the buyer receives the right to a reduction in price of the goods as compensatory damages. The purchaser may also be entitled to additional or consequential damages for the amount of actual losses caused by the defective systems. (The contract may, however, limit these damages.) One drawback to the express warranty remedy is that the user must keep the defective equipment. Through breach-of-warranty litigation, the court can award compensatory damages amounting only to a reduction in the computer's purchase price commensurate with what it is worth in its defective state, as well as incidental and consequential damages, as discussed in the section on damages in Part II.[26]

Implied Warranties

Implied warranties are creatures of Article Two, which provides that a contract for the sale of goods automatically contains certain warranties that exist by operation of law. These warranties exist without any statement in the contract and without any effort to negotiate for them (assuming that the seller does not attempt to disclaim them in the manner permitted by the UCC (see the contracting process section)). An implied warranty need not be verbally made nor included in the written warranties of a contract to be effective. There are several types of implied warranties whenever a sale of goods has occurred. The two major types are introduced here but discussed in greater detail in Part II with the other UCC implied warranties.

Implied Warranty of Merchantability. The implied warranty of merchantability exists only if the seller is a merchant with respect to goods being sold. Vendors of data-processing systems are classified as merchants because they are in the business of selling computer systems on a repetitive basis. They therefore automatically warrant that their goods are merchantable. For goods to be merchantable, they must pass without objection in the trade under the contract description, be at least of average quality, and be fit for the ordinary purposes for the intended use of such goods.[27] In the case of a purchased computer system, an implied warranty of merchantability guarantees the user that the system will function properly for a reasonable period of time. The useful life of the system, its component parts, and trade custom are all factors in defining what is a reasonable time.

A breach of the implied warranty gives the user the right to sue for damages to recover losses caused by the defective equipment. As with express warranties, the user is stuck with the defective equipment but is entitled to sue for a price reduction (compensatory damages) as well as for consequential and incidental damages.[28]

Implied Warranty of Fitness for a Particular Purpose. Another important UCC implied warranty is that of fitness for a particular purpose.[29] This warranty is also created without negotiation and without an express statement in the contract. (If it is so stated, it becomes an express warranty.) To create this warranty, the user must first communicate to the supplier the particular purpose for which the product is needed. This may be done by sending the user's precise business requirements for which the computer is sought to the supplier. Then, the user must rely upon the supplier's judgment, skill, and expertise to select a suitable computer (hardware and software) to meet those particular needs. If the computer later fails to meet those needs, then the supplier has breached this implied warranty and is liable for any resulting damages. This warranty is very effective and potentially the most powerful protection the user has since it, in effect, guarantees that the installed computer system will meet the specific needs of each user who communicates those needs to the vendor and reasonably relies on the vendor's professed expertise to meet them. But, again, the violation of this warranty permits the user to recover only a reduction in price—the difference in values between the "perfect" computer promised and the "lemon" computer received—and possibly consequential and incidental damages. The user has still bought the lemon.

Remedies of Rejection and Revocation of Acceptance

UCC remedies include the right to reject a delivery of nonconforming goods[30] and the right to revoke acceptance of nonconforming goods.[31] The supplier has a duty to deliver and install a perfect computer, that is, one that complies with the contract's specifications. The buyer has a right to make a reasonable inspection of the computer before accepting the goods to be sure the computer complies (see Part II on acceptance). If a nonconforming or imperfect system is delivered or installed, the vendor must cure these defects upon demand by the buyer. If a cure is not made within a reasonable time, the user can notify the vendor that the goods are rejected and cancel the contract. Once a rejection notice is received by the supplier, the user is entitled to a full refund of the price paid as well as consequential and incidental damages for any losses incurred. This is the most desirable UCC remedy since the user is not stuck with a lemon as is the case with warranty protection.[32]

The UCC remedy known as the revocation of acceptance is another important remedy. It allows the user to cancel a computer contract whenever a hidden or latent defect that substantially impairs the value of the system appears after acceptance of the goods, provided that the vendor does not cure the defect.[33] The defect must have been difficult to discover at the time of delivery or installation. For example, if the computer's circuits all fail after thirteen months of use, that defect could be classified as latent or hidden if the defective condition existed at the time of acceptance but was not easily detectable. Once the user notifies the vendor of this problem, the vendor must cure or correct the problem free of charge. If the vendor does not do so, the contract can be cancelled (acceptance revoked) if the user revokes within a reasonable time after the defect was or should have been discovered. The user would then be entitled to a full refund plus consequential and incidental damages.[34] Again, this remedy is superior to warranty protection since the user does not have to keep and pay for a computer of inferior quality.

THE CONTRACTING PROCESS

Since the suppliers of computer systems are businesspeople, they like to minimize their risks and maximize their profits. This can be accomplished in a number of ways, some of which are discussed here and in the next part. The most important way that suppliers can accomplish the goals of profit maximization and risk minimization is by using the sales contract to eliminate many of the user's legal rights, especially those provided by the UCC, which have just been discussed. An analysis of how this is done follows.

Introduction

Too often, as an analysis of computer contracting cases dramatically illustrates, the user rushes into the contracting stage by signing the supplier's standard form (called a sales order) without documenting prior claims or promises made by the supplier's sales force and without realizing the legal significance of that sales order. Then something goes wrong—the user's expensive system does not function as the salespeople claimed it would. After futile efforts to have the system fixed by the supplier, the user visits a lawyer demanding justice. At that point, the attorney usually explains to the user that most of the rights and remedies were contracted away when the supplier's standard sales order was signed. The chances of a complete victory in court are minimal and the litigation would be expensive and protracted. This section focuses on how the user may avoid that result by taking action that will allow legal rights and remedies to survive the contracting process. The user will then have a meaningful opportunity to seek redress should the acquired computer system become seriously defective. Part II, in turn, focuses on what remedies are available. The user must bear in mind, however, that most of these remedies may not survive the contracting process if the user does not negotiate for a fair contract.

Before beginning negotiations, the user must either assemble a team of experts to assist in the acquisition or become sufficiently knowledgeable in these areas to protect him- or herself. A key member on the team is a computer specialist who must be able to read, speak, and comprehend the language of computers. This individual's function will be to define the precise computer needs of the user and then communicate those needs with unambiguous terminology to potential suppliers. But the computer specialist must also interpret and document all significant responses from the suppliers when describing the attributes of their systems and select those systems that are the most suitable. The failure to understand, record, or incorporate into the contract a supplier's promises or representations on the manner in which the installed system will operate may preclude subsequent legal action.

The lawyer on the team should have a specialty in sales and contract law with experience in handling computer law cases, if possible. One of his or her primary functions is to review the correspondence and the verbal (but documented) representations of the supplier's agents to ascertain what significant statements were made and to ensure that such statements are incorporated into the final contract. He or she must also be prepared to negotiate with the selected supplier a final contract that adequately protects the user. Finally, the lawyer must be prepared to enter the dispute when the system fails to perform up to expectations and negotiate a settlement or litigate.

If the computer is purchased for business use rather than personal use, then consulting a tax expert or a financial expert is recommended. Once such a team is assembled and the precise computer needs of the user are ascertained, negotiation and contracting processes can commence.

Negotiating with Sales Personnel

During negotiations, the user bears the initial responsibility of deciding what the user's computer needs are. These should be decided upon after a realistic appraisal of the user's business needs and desired price range. The user should then formulate a written outline of the proposed computer's anticipated uses, what computer specifications are desired, what the computer workload will be, and what the computer acceptance criteria will be. This information must be expressed in unambiguous terminology, then communicated to all potential suppliers during the preliminary negotiations, and eventually incorporated into the final contract. The user should then develop a negotiating strategy with the goal of obtaining the best system, *with legal protection,* for the lowest cost.

Once the supplier's representatives begin to call upon the user, ground rules for negotiating should be established. The most important of these is insisting that all significant representations of the salesperson be reduced to writing, dated, and signed. If the salesperson refuses to do so, the user should consider eliminating that supplier or salesperson from the list of vendor candidates. At the very least, the user should proceed with utmost caution in dealing with that supplier and salesperson, for it is likely that they will verbally promise a system that can do everything but deliver a system that can do very little. If the salesperson agrees to document these representations, then the user can proceed with some measure of assurance that he or she is dealing with a reputable supplier and salesperson. For example, if the salesperson verbally states that the installed system will have "an automatic footnoting capability" or can be "traded in at full purchase price within two years after purchase," then these promises should be reduced to writing and signed by the salesperson to be incorporated by reference in or attached to the final sales contract. To repeat, only by insisting on this documentation will the user obtain what is negotiated.

The more sophisticated suppliers have instructed their salespeople to close the deal as soon as possible after the negotiating has been completed by having the user sign the supplier's standard sales order. The second ground rule for the user is to refuse to sign such a document until the user's attorney has reviewed the form and the user has attached all the significant representations of the salesperson to it. Signing the form without legal advice is a grievous—often fatal—mistake since the form often contains several clauses in fine print that can create serious problems for the user. The sophisticated supplier has hired attorneys who are experts in computer or sales law to prepare standard forms. Those attorneys are being paid to protect the supplier, not the user, by designing a form that reduces the user's rights and remedies to almost nothing. The user will be at the mercy of the supplier and the supplier's troubleshooters when the system does not perform as promised. Hiring the best attorneys in the land after signing the standard sales order will be of little help to the user. The sales order should not be signed until the user understands its legal meaning, that is, (a) what rights it gives the user and (b) what rights and remedies for possible defects are taken away from the user.

Contracting with the Selected Supplier

As just noted, the typical sales order has been prepared to benefit and protect the supplier by effectively eliminating most of the user's rights and remedies. Legal advice will enable the user to ascertain the true meaning of the sales order's fine print and to negotiate for better protection. An explanation of the standard sales order is needed to understand how this form significantly reduces the rights and remedies of the user.

The Supplier's Sales Order. There are four standard clauses in sales orders that are caveat emptor situations for the user: the integration clause, the limitation-of-remedies/disclaimer-of-warranties clause, the limitation-of-damages clause, and the antimodification clause.

The Integration Clause. The typical integration clause is worded in the following manner:

> This written sales order contains the entire agreement between the parties; no statements, representations, warranties, or understandings have been made or exist which are not otherwise expressed in this written sales order and signed by both parties.

This clause serves several useful purposes for the supplier. The most important is to prevent all of the verbal representations made by the sales force from becoming part of the agreement. The only way for the user to avoid this result is to document the significant statements of the salesperson, then reduce those to a document signed by the user and the salesperson, and, finally, attach the writing to the final sales order or contract. Otherwise, the user has no legal right to expect that the delivered system will conform to those representations.

The integration clause enables the supplier to take full advantage of the parol evidence rule. This rule prevents the admissibility of testimony in court if the purpose of the testimony is to contradict, amend, or alter a written contract. For example, if the salesperson stated verbally that this system will "automatically footnote all pages," and after the system is installed this capacity is absent, the user's attempt to force the supplier to install that function through threatened or actual litigation will be futile. When the user takes the witness stand to testify about the verbal representations made by the salesperson concerning the missing function, the supplier's attorney will object to the admissibility of such testimony since the written contract does not say anything about an automatic footnote capability.

If the contract did not contain an integration clause, evidence concerning promised system capabilities not specified in the written contract could be submitted only if the court determined that the parties did *not* intend the written contract to be the complete and exclusive statement of their agreement and further found that the additional term, say, the footnoting capability, was *consistent* with the written contract. In the example presented here, a court could exclude any evidence of the promised footnoting capability because such a term would certainly have been included in the document if it was actually a part of the agreement. The user will lose solely because the verbal representations of the salesperson were not incorporated into the final written contract. On the other hand, in the appropriate circumstances, say, if the written contract was for a word processor, a court might find that the additional term was consistent with the written contract.

The evidence of the promised capability might then be admissible to explain or supplement what was intended in the written contract. With the integration clause, the user is effectively foreclosed from evading the parol evidence rule. First, the clause is a clear statement that the two parties *did* intend their writing to be the final and exclusive embodiment of their agreement. Second, since the clause states that no other terms were intended, any addition to the contract attempted by the user will be in conflict with the writing. Thus, unfortunately for the user, the use of the integration clause and the parol evidence rule will almost always combine to exclude all such testimony.

The Limitation-of-Remedies/Disclaimer-of-Warranties Clause. A second clause that is used by the suppliers in their sales orders, which has a more harmful effect on the buyer, is the limitation-of-remedies/disclaimer-of-warranties clause. The purpose of the following clause is to prevent the user from asserting significant UCC remedies:

> The supplier guarantees prompt repair and/or replacement without charge of any defective parts or workmanship found within 90 days after delivery. This remedy shall be the sole and exclusive remedy of the user. This remedy is given in lieu of all other remedies including, but not limited to, rejection, revocation of acceptance, express warranties, and all implied warranties including the warranty of merchantability and fitness for a particular purpose.

Most users would actually believe that the supplier is giving the user something of value—a 90-day express warranty. In reality, the supplier is eliminating the user's more extensive UCC protections. The UCC gives the user remedies and rights against the supplier for up to four years after the date of delivery. By using this clause in the sales order, the supplier has reduced its responsibilities to the repair of defects or replacement of parts for the first 90 days following the sale. If the system malfunctions after that, the user will bear the entire risk of a defective system.

To avoid the problems created by such a clause, the user should refuse to sign a contract containing it. Unfortunately, the clause has become a standard in the industry. Attempting to delete it from the contract through negotiation may be futile. The user should nevertheless try to negotiate for some meaningful protection, and if the supplier is unyielding, the user should refuse to sign the sales order unless the user is really desperate enough to forego the protection in order to get the system.

The Limitation-of-Damages Clause. The third clause found in almost all sales orders is the limitation-of-damages clause. The purpose of this clause is to reduce further the user's rights and remedies. Whereas the limitation-of-remedies/disclaimer-of-warranties clause limits the rights that might permit the user to seek damages, the limitation-of-damages clause permits the user to recover only for certain types of damages even if the supplier breaches one of its remaining duties to the user. The following clause, for example, typically prevents the user from suing the supplier for damages of any type and is used to supplement the limitation-of-remedies clause:

The supplier's duty to repair or replace defective systems for the first 90 days after delivery shall not include any liability for damages. The supplier shall not be responsible for damages of any type arising from the acquisition. This exclusion of liability includes lost profits, consequential, special, indirect, direct, or compensatory damages.

For example, what is the legal result if the user's newly installed computer system completely destroys all payroll and accounts receivable records on the sixtieth day after delivery? The supplier will claim that its sole obligation is to replace the defective system component. The supplier will not be responsible for any damages caused by the defective system. Any lost profits resulting from the lost accounts receivable and all costs incurred in reconstructing those records will be borne by the user. After all, the user signed the sales order and is getting exactly what he or she contracted for— an expensive system with very limited guarantees that it will work and with no right to sue for damages of any type if it does not.

What happens if the computer system destroys these records on the one hundred twentieth day after acquisition? Again, the supplier will claim that it cannot be sued for damages. In addition, the supplier could charge the user for the repair since the exclusive remedy of repair or replacement will have expired. After the 90-day warranty for repairs has expired, even the repairs are at the user's expense.

Again, the user should (a) attempt to delete such a clause through negotiation; (b) refuse to sign the sales order containing such a clause; or (c) sign the sales order only if the user is willing to forego the right to damages in order to make the purchase.

The user can request that the court declare that the sole remedy of repair or replacement has failed its essential purpose (discussed more fully in Part II) if the supplier's attempted repairs are unsuccessful.[35] But nonetheless, the user is acquiring an expensive and protracted lawsuit if the computer seriously malfunctions. The better tactic is to refuse to sign such a sales order and negotiate better protection for the user or to find a supplier who is willing to assume responsibility for potential failure of the system.

The Antimodification Clause. Another clause designed to protect the supplier is known as the antimodification clause. The purpose of this clause is to prevent the sales force, the programmers, or the troubleshooters of the supplier from creating any new warranties, remedies, or liability *after* the sales order has been signed by the user. A typical clause states:

> This sales order can be modified only by a written agreement signed by both the user and sales manager of the supplier.

The verbal representations made by the supplier's personnel after the execution of the sales order do not modify the contract, so no additional contractual remedies are created. The only way for a new remedy to be created is to request the sales manager of the supplier to sign a modified contract, an unlikely event.

The user should not sign a sales order that contains an antimodification clause unless the user is willing to be bound by it if and when problems develop. As stated earlier, the user should attempt to negotiate a new contract that is fair to both sides, and if the supplier refuses to negotiate on anything but the supplier's own terms, the user should consider finding a new supplier who will.

Conclusions: The Sales Order. After reviewing these clauses, the user should realize that signing the sales order severely reduces the user's rights and remedies. Litigating for damages after signing the standard sales order is an uphill battle. Successful litigation is possible only if the user can convince the court that the supplier has, in some way, breached the few obligations it has accepted. Clearly, the supplier has the advantage once the user makes the mistake of signing the sales order containing any of these clauses.

The User's Purchase Order. A good strategy for user protection is the use of a purchase order—the counterpart of a sales order. The purchasing departments of almost all corporations of any size use a purchase order that has been expertly developed by corporate attorneys seeking to maximize the protection afforded corporate buyers. There are six clauses in the typical corporate purchase order that can be used to protect the user of computer systems. These are discussed in the following pages.

The Only-My-Terms Clause. The "only-my-terms" clause is crucial to the user's protection. The purpose of this clause is to prevent the objectionable clauses of the supplier's sales order from becoming part of the contract:

> All terms and conditions of this purchase order shall become part of the contract between the user and supplier; the supplier's inconsistent or additional terms will never become part of this contract; the supplier's acceptance of any contract to acquire a computer system shall occur only when the supplier acknowledges this purchase order or delivers and installs a computer system in response to this purchase order.

This clause functions in two important ways. First, a court is clearly informed of the user's intent *not* to agree to a contract on the sales order's terms. Second, the court is informed of the user's intent to have the conduct of the supplier in delivering and installing the system act as an acceptance of the user's purchase order. This clause is absolutely essential to bind the supplier to the purchase order's terms even though the supplier may not expressly agree to be bound to the user's terms.

The UCC Remedies Clause. The second important clause in the user's purchase order is known as the UCC remedies clause:

> Regardless of whether goods are being sold or leased and regardless of whether services are being rendered, the user and supplier agree that both parties shall have available all of the Uniform Commercial Code rights, duties, and remedies, including, but not limited to, the rights of inspection, rejection, revocation of acceptance, and all implied and express warranties. The user and supplier specifically agree that these UCC rights, duties, and remedies shall apply to this contract even if the UCC would not otherwise apply. Specifically, the UCC shall apply to the present acquisition of the hardware, all present and future software

acquisitions, and all present and future training, support, and maintenance functions pertaining to the acquisition of the computer system.

The purpose of this clause is to ensure that the user enjoys the protection automatically given by the UCC by making such protection available to computer hardware leases and the selling of computer services such as programming, training, and maintenance. All doubts about whether the UCC applies are thereby dispelled. Insisting upon this clause is absolutely essential if the user wishes to maximize protection.

The Representations/Express Warranty Clause. The third clause, the express warranty/revocation-of-acceptance clause, enables all of the significant statements made by the supplier's personnel to become express warranties or representations that will keep the repair or cancellation remedies alive for up to four years after delivery or installation. A typical clause follows:

> During the negotiations between the supplier and the user, the supplier's agents made the following representations concerning the capabilities of the computer system which induced the user to acquire the system:
>
> [list the significant statements]
>
> The supplier and the user agree that if the computer system does not conform to these representations, the user has the option to revoke its acceptance of the entire system, to demand a cure, and to cancel the entire contract if no cure is made, and/or to sue for damages resulting from the nonconformity, including a refund of all payments plus liability for compensatory or consequential damages.

This clause is crucial since the UCC's express warranty and revocation provisions may not apply to all types of computer transactions. First, it resolves all doubts about whether these UCC rights and remedies apply to the user's situation. Second, the clause gives the user the opportunity to incorporate into the final contract all significant representations made by the supplier during the demonstration and negotiation stages of the acquisition process. The failure to incorporate the representations of the salesperson into the final contract allows the supplier to legally deliver a nonconforming system under the protection of the parol evidence rule/integration clause. Third, the clause gives the user the right to cancel the entire contract if the system cannot be installed according to the contract specifications or representations. Finally, the clause gives the user the right to sue for damages if the user elects to keep the malfunctioning system. The acquisition price can be reduced in proportion to the features that do not work and the user can recover consequential damages that result from those problems.

The Liquidated Damage Clause. Another clause that the user should consider inserting into the purchase order or final contract is the liquidated damage clause. This clause specifies in advance what damages the supplier will be liable for if the program or computer is not installed on time:

> In the event that all computer hardware [or specify each component] is not delivered, installed and operational by [date], the supplier agrees to reduce the price

or rental payments by [amount] per day, as liquidated damages, until the hardware is operational.

In the event that the program for [e.g., payroll] is not installed, tested, and operational by [date], the supplier agrees to reduce the price or rental payments by [amount] per day, as liquidated damages, until this program is operational.

[This clause should be repeated for each computer hardware component or for each program listed in the contract.]

This clause has numerous advantages. Most important, it encourages the supplier to provide top-quality service to ensure that computer-related deadlines are met. Next, it allows the user to avoid costly, protracted litigation by deducting these damages from the payment schedule, discussed in the partial payment clause section.

For liquidated damage clauses to be enforceable, the amount estimated for damages must be commensurate with the actual damages suffered as a result of system defects. Therefore, it is best when drafting the clause to specify liquidated damages for every program by estimating the cost of manually performing that function or of contracting performance of that function to another computer organization.

The Partial Payment Clause. Another clause that should be used to maximize protection is known as the payment-by-phase-of-completion clause:

The user shall pay the supplier the following amounts when the supplier completes each of the following tasks to the supplier's and user's mutual satisfaction:

(a) installation of [e.g., computer printer] [amount]

[list each item of hardware and its value or list price]

(b) installation of [e.g., payroll] program [amount]

[list each program or service to be performed and its value or list price]

With this clause, the user does not have to pay for the entire computer system unless it functions properly. Only those components that function according to the satisfaction of both parties must be paid for. The user has the leverage to demand corrections should some component malfunction immediately before acceptance and payment. The supplier thus has a strong incentive to fix the component in order to receive payment.

The Acceptance Criteria Clause. The final clause that the user should consider inserting into the purchase order or final contract is the performance, or acceptance criteria, clause:

The user preserves the right to reject the entire computer system or any component part until acceptance occurs. Acceptance shall not occur until after the supplier has demonstrated that the installed system can perform the specified functions to the mutual satisfaction of the user and supplier:

[list the performance test criteria]

This clause guarantees that the user can insist upon a computer system that is perfect (meeting the specifications listed in that clause). This right is important in preventing an acceptance of the equipment before the user has adequately tested and inspected it. As long as no acceptance has occurred, the UCC gives the user the right to reject the system, that is, to cancel the contract because of the supplier's failure to supply the promised quality. This clause becomes especially relevant in cases where it is debatable whether the user has accepted the system.

Conclusions: The Sales Order and the Purchase Order. After reviewing the various clauses found in the purchase order and sales order, the user should realize that protection must be negotiated for by demanding clauses that give some measure of protection to the user. Failure to do so results in the user bearing the entire risk of malfunctioning systems after the rather brief, limited express warranty given in the sales order expires. If the user is unable to comprehend "computerese" or "legalese," then experts should be hired to advise the user before the standard sales order is signed.

The Battle of the Forms. In reality, almost all sophisticated suppliers will insist upon using the sales order and almost all sophisticated users will insist upon using the purchase order. Thus, a battle of the forms has been created by commercial law attorneys, all of whom advise their clients: "Do not, under any circumstances, sign the other side's form!" What then are the possibilities for resolving this impasse? Several alternatives exist that place the user in a better position than if he or she simply signs the sales order without negotiating the critical terms:

a. a negotiated contract fair to both sides may be signed;

b. the user may try to negotiate, but give up and sign the sales order;

c. the supplier may give up and sign the purchase order; or

d. both may refuse to sign the other's form, but the computer system may be installed without a signed contract.

Negotiating a Fair Contract. The optimal solution is for both sides to negotiate a contract that allocates the risks fairly. Too often, suppliers have refused to do this. As the computer market has become more competitive, however, suppliers have to consider that there may be other suppliers who will provide more favorable terms to the user in order to get the sale.

The User Gives Up. The second possibility—the user signs the sales order—occurs far too often. Once the user signs the sales order, his or her rights and remedies are substantially reduced. The user then possesses only a few limited rights and remedies to rectify a seriously nonconforming computer system: whatever limited repair or replacement express warranties are offered by the seller, fraud,[36] mutual mistake,[37] unconscionability,[38] and failure of essential purpose[39] (all discussed in detail in Part II). If the user sues the supplier, the user's probability of success depends in large part on whether the representations made by the supplier's sales personnel were well documented, whether objectionable terms were negotiated from the final contract, and whether the circumstances surrounding the transaction were fair in the court's view.

The Supplier Gives Up. The third possibility—the supplier signs the purchase order—occurs rarely since most suppliers are sophisticated enough to realize the consequences. However, insisting that the final contract contain the purchase order terms is not always futile. First, many more unsophisticated suppliers (wholesalers and retailers) will frequently sign the purchase order to get the user's business. This occurs most often when the user explains to them that the purchase order system is the standard method of purchasing equipment in the corporate purchasing world, which is a misleading, but nonetheless true, statement. Most corporations have a policy that they will not issue a check for payment unless a purchase order has been previously issued by them. Second, sending the purchase order shows the supplier that the user is not an easy mark. This may motivate the supplier to take a negotiating posture if the sale is very important to the supplier. Finally, if the user sends the purchase order and the supplier fails to object in writing to that order and has not sent conflicting terms previously, a contract may be formed with the purchase order terms controlling.[40]

An Impasse. The final possibility—both sides refusing to sign the other side's form—involves a more extended solution. Different results may be reached, both under the common law and under the UCC, depending on which of several possible legal interpretations is applied.

Under the common law system, two possible results can occur. If the supplier had sent a sales order prior to the user's purchase order, a court under the common law "mirror-image" rule could hold that no contract was formed since it could not be assumed from the differing forms that either party intended to form a contract based on the other party's standard form. The mirror-image rule requires the acceptance to reflect exactly the terms of the offer in order to form a contract. This result might not seriously harm the prospective user because the court could rule that no contract existed and the user would therefore arguably be entitled to a full refund of any payments made and the supplier would get the malfunctioning system returned. The only disadvantage is that the user may not be able to sue the supplier under the contract for damages caused by the malfunctioning system. However, suing the supplier for the tort of fraud is a possible alternative method for recouping those damages if the supplier induced the user to enter into the transaction by making false claims about the computer.

If, on the other hand, the subsequent purchase order was sent and received and the system delivered and installed without any objection by the supplier, the court could rule that the purchase order was an offer (or a counteroffer if the supplier had previously sent a sales order or confirmation) and that the supplier accepted the offer (or counteroffer) by the supplier's actions. The user is thus protected by a contract that is formed solely on the terms of the purchase order. This result is more likely if the supplier never sent a sales order (or confirmation form with the supplier's terms). This fact pattern and legal result is known as the "last-shot" doctrine. The party who fires the last shot (sends the last form) under the common law system is likely to win. A court could declare the final contract to consist entirely of the terms in the last form sent before shipment or installation. The user in a common law situation should try to fire the last shot if a fair contract cannot be negotiated.

Depending on the situation, the results under the UCC should be different from those under the common law. If the user sends a purchase order and the supplier responds by supplying the system without interjecting its own form, the supplier's performance constitutes acceptance of the user's terms.[41] The contract is formed with the user's purchase order setting the terms. This result is the same as under the common law last-shot doctrine.

If each party sends a different form, neither of which is signed by the other party, the UCC states that neither the common law last-shot doctrine nor the mirror-image rule will apply. Rather, the UCC rules pertaining to the battle of the forms apply.[42]

The UCC provides that a definite acceptance or confirmation sent within a reasonable time in response to a previous offer or agreement operates to form a contract even though it states terms different from or additional to the previous offer or agreement's terms, unless the acceptance or confirmation is expressly made conditional on the other party's assent to the additional or different terms.[43] Assume that a user submits a purchase order to the supplier, then the supplier submits a sales order or confirmation to the user that agrees on terms of price and quantity but all other terms differ. The presence of an only-my-terms clause in the purchase order would prevent the formation of a contract on the terms of the sales order since the purchase order makes acceptance conditional upon the vendor's acceptance of the purchase order's terms. If, however, both parties performed the contract by delivering and accepting the computer system in spite of the lack of a written agreement, the UCC then instructs the court to examine the conduct of the parties.[44] If the computer system is shipped and installed by the supplier and if the installation is permitted by the user, then the conduct of the parties is sufficient to establish the existence of a contract since the parties acted in a manner consistent with the existence of a contract.

But what are the terms of the contract? First, the UCC instructs the court to examine both forms and extract only the consistent terms and discard all inconsistent terms. This canceling of conflicting terms is known as the "knock-out" rule. The price and specifications will probably be the only identical terms on both forms. Second, additional terms—terms that are not contained but also not contradicted in the other party's form—must be examined. Additional terms in the later forms are to be considered proposals to modify the contract but will *become* part of the contract under the additional terms rule unless:

a. one of the parties is not a merchant;

b. the party receiving the later form promptly objects to the terms;

c. the recipient already gave notice of objection to the terms *before* receiving the second form (for example, by using an only-my-terms clause in the *first* form); or

d. the new terms materially alter the terms of the first form.[45]

For example, if a supplier's sales order stated nothing about credit terms but the user's subsequent purchase order provided for 30 days' credit, the inconsistent terms rule would not apply since the sales order is silent on the issue of credit. Therefore, the additional terms rule controls, and the user would be entitled to 30 days' credit if:

a. the sales order contained no only-my-terms clause;

b. the user and supplier were both merchants;

c. the supplier did not promptly object to the credit terms; and

d. the addition of the credit term did not constitute a material change to the sales order.

This issue would be a question of fact for the judge or jury to decide. This would depend upon whether, under the surrounding circumstances including trade custom and usage, the other party would be surprised or suffer hardship by being subjected to such a term without express awareness of it.[46]

Three conflicting interpretations are possible for those terms that *conflict* with each other.[47] Most courts will probably rule that the knock-out rule should apply so that the conflicting terms cancel each other out and the UCC fills in the gap left by those terms.[48] Thus, if the supplier's form contains a valid disclaimer of all warranties but the user's purchase order contains a conflicting express warranty, neither term would become part of the contract. The UCC's implied warranties would fill the gap created by the knock-out of the warranty term, and the buyer would be at least minimally protected.

This result is not guaranteed, however, for at least one federal court in the much-criticized *Roto-Lith* case[49] refused to follow the inconsistent terms rule and held that a materially different second document is expressly conditional and thus not an acceptance of the original form. Instead, it was viewed as a counteroffer that was accepted by the other party's performance of the contract. If a court followed the *Roto-Lith* case, the terms contained in the second document would always control.

Yet another view is that the conflicting term in the second form does not knock out the first form's term but rather falls out itself so that the first form's term controls. According to this view, the knock-out rule does not apply to forms that serve as the offer and acceptance but only to *confirming* forms.[50]

This discussion represents only a sampling of the legal issues and uncertainties that trouble even the most astute sales law experts. It should be evident that legal counsel is a necessity for a successful computer acquisition.

Conclusions: The Contracting Process

To be protected from the supplier, the user must adopt the team approach to buying a computer system. First, an expert in computer systems and an expert in computer law or contract law must be retained. Second, the user must develop a negotiating strategy with these goals in mind:

a. precisely and unambiguously defining the user's computer needs and specifications;

b. communicating that information to the supplier;

c. documenting all significant representations of the supplier;

d. attaching all representations of the supplier to the sales order, the purchase order, and the final contract;

e. refusing to sign the proffered sales order;

f. insisting upon negotiating a fair contract;

g. using the purchase order to set up the last-shot doctrine or the knock-out rule at common law or the UCC remedies if no fair negotiated contract is possible;

h. following the advice of legal counsel to win the battle of the forms; and

i. documenting all events of significance!

COURT CASES

National Bank of North America v. DeLuxe Poster Co.[51] DeLuxe leased a system from Odyssey Systems in 1974. The lease contained hell-or-high-water and waiver-of-defense clauses and also stated that payment was due upon the signing of the lessor's acceptance form. A second contract was signed stating that the DeLuxe lease would not become effective until satisfactory equipment was delivered and installed.

Two days later only the lease requiring a cash payment to Odyssey was assigned to the National Bank of North America. The computer never performed properly. After making four monthly payments, DeLuxe stopped making payments to the bank. The bank sued, and DeLuxe defended on the ground that it was justified in not paying because the computer never worked.

The court ruled in favor of the bank, stating that (a) the waiver-of-defense clause in the lease means exactly that—any defense the user has can be asserted only against the manufacturer and not against the bank; (b) payments must continue to the bank regardless of whether the equipment functions because payments must be made "come hell or high water."

This case illustrates the reason why (a) computer lessees must seek expert legal assistance before signing any contract; (b) a commercial user should not sign a contract with these clauses because Article Two will not protect the buyer against a nonseller such as the bank; (c) commercial users get what they bargain for—in this instance, no protection when the computer malfunctioned.

National Cash Register Co. v. Marshall Savings and Loan Association.[52] Marshall contracted in April 1962 to purchase a computer system from NCR. The contract contained a hell-or-high-water clause—purchaser shall pay NCR's invoices when the computer is delivered, installed, and certified as being ready for use by NCR.

On May 18, 1964, NCR stated the computer had been delivered, installed, tested, and available for use. Marshall Savings and Loan promised prompt payment even though ten teller terminals had not been installed.

Six months later, new management took over at Marshall and notified NCR that the bill would not be paid until all equipment had been installed. NCR sued.

The appellate court ruled in favor of NCR because Marshall had promised to pay the bill in May immediately after NCR claimed the computer was installed and certified it as being ready for use.

This case is significant for two reasons. First, it demonstrates the importance of specifying in the contract precisely what the acceptance criteria will be before payment occurs and the importance of demanding exact compliance with those criteria by the supplier before payment occurs. Second, it shows the importance of assuring that the UCC applies to the transaction. The UCC did not apply to this case because the state of Illinois had not yet adopted the UCC when the parties signed the contract in April 1962. Had the UCC applied, the buyer would have probably been able to invoke the rejection or revocation of acceptance remedies (these are discussed in more detail in the next part).

Triangle Underwriters, Inc. v. Honeywell, Inc.[53] This case involved a dispute over malfunctioning customized programs. Triangle Underwriters attempted to sue on the basis of Honeywell's breach of implied and express UCC warranties. The initial issue was whether the UCC applied to the programs. The trial court held that the UCC did apply to the software.

Although the ideas or concepts involved in the custom-designed software remained Honeywell's intellectual property, Triangle was purchasing the product of these concepts. That product required efforts to produce, but it was a product nevertheless and, although consisting in part of intangible ideas, is more readily characterized as goods than services.

This case is very significant since it was the first to determine that the UCC applied to intellectual property. This result was brought about because (a) the final end product was found to be movable—a tape or disk—and (b) the software development process is not unlike other UCC goods transactions in which considerable services are involved such as the sale of a customized or specially engineered machine, tool, or die.

Computer Servicenters, Inc. v. Beacon Manufacturing Co.[54] Beacon orally contracted with Computer Servicenters "for performance of data-processing services" consisting of analysis, collection, storage, and reporting of manufacturing data. If the UCC statute of frauds applied to the transaction, as Beacon argued, no writing would be required to enforce the oral contract. However, the court found that the UCC did not apply since services, not goods, were involved. Beacon's suit for breach of the oral contract was therefore barred by the state's statute of frauds applicable to contracts for services.

This case is significant because it illustrates the problems that can result when care and attention are not paid in drafting a written contract. Computer Servicenters stated in a written proposal that they would provide "data processing services," to which Beacon orally agreed. Therefore, a court would be hard pressed to rule otherwise. Including the phrase "services" in the proposal precluded application of the UCC.

If the parties had specified that they were selling and buying a computer tape or disk containing instructions for the computer hardware, thus goods, albeit "specially manufactured goods" under Section 2-105(1), then the UCC protections could be invoked. Of course, in this case, Beacon lost out completely since it did not even insist on a binding written contract which would comply with the state's statute of frauds for service contracts.

IMPLICATIONS FOR ACTION

The following considerations should be kept in mind when a user wishes to acquire computer hardware:

Before contacting any vendors, assemble an acquisition team consisting preferably of a tax expert, a lawyer knowledgeable on UCC issues, and data-processing personnel. The small businessperson or individual desiring only a personal computer may want to seek advice from a data-processing expert regarding systems specifications and a lawyer regarding contracting.

With the aid of the team or outside consultant, prepare a feasibility study. The study should determine the system desired, the performance specifications, a time frame for the project, and all costs associated with the project.

Decide which method of acquiring a computer is best—rental, lease, or purchase. Each method's pros and cons should be kept in mind during the feasibility study.

If a decision is made to rent the equipment, some of the important factors to consider are the following:

a. What items are included in the rental price of the equipment: maintenance, a percentage of rental payments applicable to the purchase price, and so on?

b. What is the length of the rental period and possible extensions?

c. What trade-in allowances are associated with the rented equipment?

d. What are the manufacturer's commitments for upgrading the equipment or other changes during the term?

e. What is the manufacturer's policy regarding extra use charges (some rental agreements allow use of the equipment for a set time period such as 170 hours per month; any excess costs extra)?

In addition, be sure each party understands the definition of "installed and ready for use." (Equipment may otherwise be unusable while rent is being charged.) Finally, be aware of all factors involving software, that is, who supplies the programming and maintains it, whether programming is included in the rental costs, and so on.

If leasing computer equipment is decided upon, here are some important factors:

a. Make sure the lease contains detailed *performance standards*.

b. Be aware of the two kinds of leases (full payout versus nonfull payout) and of the legal implications of each.

c. Be aware of assignable leases, which allow the lessor to *assign the lease* to a third party such as a financial institution. This may remove any financial leverage the user might have should the equipment become inoperable.

d. Be aware of clauses that require rental payments regardless of circumstances (the hell-or-high-water clause).

e. Be aware that *rental* or *purchase option* in the lease may be found by the IRS to create a conditional sales agreement with concomitant tax implications.

f. Be knowledgeable about your responsibilities regarding *site preparation* such as power, supplies, and air conditioning. An oversight in this area could result in rent payments being due on an inoperable machine.

g. Be sure the lease contains a *maintenance* provision or accompanying maintenance contract. The user should at all times have repair personnel and a backup computer on call to guard against consequential damages if the machine needs to be repaired.

h. Carefully read the lease provisions regarding *rental charge increases.*

i. Try to negotiate some flexibility in the area of *alterations* and *additions* to the equipment. This will help protect against obsolescence should newer, more sophisticated peripherals become available prior to the termination of the agreement.

j. Be aware of the lease provisions regarding the termination policy of the lessor. Analyze the advantages and disadvantages of the short- and long-term lease arrangements.

The following are points to keep in mind if an outright purchase is decided upon:

a. Be aware of the tax implications of purchasing equipment.

b. Choose a reliable vendor. The best method of screening potential vendors is to contact the vendor's customers to inquire into the vendor's reliability and integrity.

c. Be aware of a computer owner's responsibilities (that is, liabilities for computer error, privacy, trade secrets, and the like).

d. All of the promotional materials, brochures, and representations made by sales representatives, as well as any terms included in the contract, are part of the contract's express warranties unless disclaimed in the contract.

e. The sale of the computer and program carries with it an implied warranty of merchantability. This can be disclaimed but only with language specified by the UCC.

f. If the buyer discussed his or her individual, specific needs with the computer representative and relied on the supplier's expertise in purchasing the computer, the implied warranty of fitness for a particular purpose would apply but can also be disclaimed with the language prescribed by the UCC.

There are two ways the computer buyer can protect against having to absorb the entire financial loss of a nonfunctional computer. First, include performance details in the contract such as input/output specifications, processing speed, functions to be performed, specific time frames for test runs of the different functions, and how test runs should be structured. The goal is to include *all* requirements of the computer's performance in the contract and not to rely on the verbal promises of the salesperson.

Second, refer back to the sales negotiations in the contract. It may be easier to get these express warranties included in the contract than to negotiate the implied warranty disclaimers out of the contract. Include a clause in the contract that refers to the performance capabilities discussed during negotiations. In addition to possibly creating express warranties, this will make it clear to the court, should problems arise, that there are other terms to the agreement not included in the contract. The court, with this reference, will be more willing to allow parol evidence to clarify these terms. For this approach to be effective, the buyer must document all meetings and the issues discussed. This approach may work even if the contract has an integration clause (disclaiming any statements made prior to the contract).

REFERENCES

1. Robert Holmes, Associate Professor of Legal Studies, Bowling Green State University, Bowling Green, Ohio, is responsible for the legal analysis contained in this chapter.

2. *See* Earman Oil Co. v. Burroughs Corp., 625 F.2d 1291 (5th Cir. 1980); Chatlos Systems, Inc. v. National Cash Register Corp., 479 F. Supp. 738 (D. N.J. 1979), *aff'd in part, remanded in part* 635 F.2d 1081 (3d Cir. 1980), *remand aff'd* 670 F.2d 1304 (3d Cir. 1982), *cert. dismissed* 102 S.Ct. 2918 (1982); Schatz Distributing Co. v. Olivetti Corp. of America, 7 Kan.App.2d 676, 647 P.2d 820 (1982); Uniflex, Inc. v. Olivetti Corp. of America, 86 A.D.2d 538, 445 N.Y.S.2d 993 (1982). *See also* discussion of the UCC's sale requirement in the section on sales or transactions. *Cf.* BarclaysAmerican/Leasing, Inc. v. Vista Chevrolet, Inc., 636 S.W.2d 769 (Tex. Ct. App. 1982).

3. *See, e.g.,* National Bank of America v. DeLuxe Poster Co., 51 A.D.2d 582, 378 N.Y.S.2d 462 (1976); Olivetti Leasing Corp. v. Mar-Mac Precision Corp., 117 Misc.2d 865, 459 N.Y.S.2d 399 (Sup. Ct. 1983). *Cf.* North American Corp. v. Allen, 636 S.W.2d 797 (Tex. Ct. App. 1982); Schepps Grocery Co. v. Burroughs Corp., 635 S.W.2d 606 (Tex. Ct. App. 1982).

4. Honeywell, Inc. v. Lithonia Lighting, Inc., 317 F. Supp. 406, 408 (N.D. Ga. 1970).

5. M. Wofsey, *Contracting for Software,* CLS 3-3, art. 1 (Bigelow, ed. 1981).

6. Uniform Commercial Code (UCC) 2-105(1) (1978).

7. UCC 1-201(11).

8. UCC 1-201(3).

9. UCC 2-102.

10. *E.g.,* the implied warranty of merchantability applies only to contracts for the sale of goods according to UCC 2-314(1). *See* J. White & R. Summers, *Handbook of the Law Under the Uniform Commercial Code* 22 (1980).

11. *E.g.,* comments of the UCC drafters allow the judiciary to extend all warranty provisions of Article Two to nonsale transactions such as a lease. UCC 2-313 comment 2.

12. UCC 2-105(1).

13. *E.g.,* Triangle Underwriters, Inc. v. Honeywell, Inc., 457 F. Supp. 765 (E.D. N.Y. 1978), *aff'd in part, rev'd in part* 604 F.2d 737 (2d Cir. 1979), *remand aff'd* 651 F.2d 132 (2d Cir. 1981).

14. UCC 2-102.

15. *See supra* note 10 and accompanying text.

16. UCC 2-106(1).

17. *See* Earman Oil Co. v. Burroughs Corp., 625 F.2d 1291 (5th Cir. 1980).

18. *Id.;* Uniflex Inc. v. Olivetti Corp. of America, 86 A.D.2d 538, 445 N.Y.S.2d 993 (1982).

19. *See* UCC 2-204, 2-207; Chelsea Industries, Inc. v. AccuRay Leasing Corp., 699 F.2d 58 (1st Cir. 1983); Textron, Inc. v. Teleoperator Systems Corp., 554 F. Supp. 315 (E.D. N.Y. 1983); Napasco International, Inc. v. Tymshare, Inc., 556 F. Supp. 654 (E.D. La. 1983); City University of New York v. Finalco, Inc., 93 A.D.2d 792, 461 N.Y.S.2d 830 (1983).

20. UCC 2-209(1). *But cf.* Flambeau Products Corp. v. Honeywell Information Systems, Inc., 111 Wis. 2d 317, 330 N.W.2d 228 (Wis. Ct. App. 1983) (accord and satisfaction not effected without consideration).

21. UCC 2-201. *See* DDP Microsystems v. Tilden Financial Corp., 88 A.D.2d 875, 451 N.Y.S.2d 778 (1982).

22. UCC 2-202.

23. *See* Diversified Environments, Inc. v. Olivetti Corp. of America, 461 F. Supp. 286 (M.D. Pa. 1978).

24. *See* Earman Oil Co. v. Burroughs Corp., 625 F.2d 1291 (5th Cir. 1980); APLications, Inc. v. Hewlett-Packard Co., 501 F. Supp. 129 (S.D. N.Y. 1980), *aff'd* 672 F.2d 1076 (2d Cir. 1982).

25. UCC 2-313.

26. UCC 2-714(2),(3). *See, e.g.,* Chatlos Systems, Inc. v. National Cash Register Corp., 479 F. Supp. 738 (D. N.J. 1979), *aff'd in part, remanded in part* 635 F.2d 1081 (3d Cir. 1980), *remand aff'd* 670 F.2d 1304 (3d Cir. 1982), *cert. dismissed* 102 S.Ct. 2918 (1982); Schatz Distributing Co. v. Olivetti Corp. of America, 7 Kan.App.2d 676, 647 P.2d 820 (1982).

27. UCC 2-314.

28. UCC 2-714(2),(3).

29. UCC 2-315.

30. UCC 2-601.

31. UCC 2-608.

32. *See* Carl Beasley Ford, Inc. v. Burroughs Corp., 361 F. Supp. 325 (E.D. Pa. 1973), *aff'd* 493 F.2d 1400 (3d Cir. 1974).

33. UCC 2-608.

34. UCC 2-711(1),(3); Jones, Morrison, Stalnaker, P.A. v. Contemporary Computer Services, Inc., 414 So. 2d 637 (Fla. Dist. Ct. App. 1982).

35. UCC 2-719(2). *See, e.g.,* Chatlos Systems, Inc. v. National Cash Register Corp., 479 F. Supp. 738 (D. N.J. 1979), *aff'd in part, remanded in part* 635 F.2d 1081 (3d

Cir. 1980), *remand aff'd* 670 F.2d 1304 (3d Cir. 1982), *cert. dismissed* 102 S.Ct. 2918 (1982).

36. *See* UCC 1-103.

37. *Id.*

38. UCC 2-302, 2-719(3).

39. UCC 2-719(2).

40. *See* UCC 2-206.

41. *Id.*

42. UCC 2-207. *See generally* J. White & R. Summers, *supra* note 10, at 24-39.

43. UCC 2-207(1).

44. UCC 2-207(3).

45. UCC 2-207(2).

46. UCC 2-207, comments 4, 5.

47. *See* UCC 2-207(3); J. White & R. Summers, *supra* note 10, at 28-31.

48. *See* UCC 2-207, comment 6; J. White & R. Summers, *supra* note 10, at 29, 30.

49. Roto-Lith v. F. P. Bartlett and Co., 297 F.2d 497 (1st Cir. 1962).

50. *See* J. White & R. Summers, *supra* note 10, at 29, 31.

51. 51 A.D.2d 582, 378 N.Y.S.2d 462 (1976).

52. 415 F.2d 1131 (7th Cir. 1969).

53. 457 F. Supp. 765 (E.D. N.Y. 1978), *aff'd in part, rev'd in part* 604 F.2d 737 (2d Cir. 1979), *remand aff'd* 651 F.2d 132 (2d Cir. 1981).

54. 328 F. Supp. 653 (D. S.C. 1970), *aff'd* 443 F.2d 906 (4th Cir. 1971).

PART II

Computer Systems Failures: Remedies

Outline

INTRODUCTION[1]

Rarely are computer systems installed without "bugs." Therefore, the prudent user must be informed of the available remedies should the system fail to perform as the supplier claimed it would. More important, to permit successful litigation, if ever necessary, the user must have paved the way by negotiating for the proper contract clauses and by documenting all significant representations of the supplier and all other significant events. Preparation for successful litigation must begin soon after the user has decided to acquire a computer system. Without laying that groundwork, the chances for successful litigation are minimal. This section focuses on what remedies are available when the computer system seriously malfunctions. These remedies are divided into two subsections: common law remedies and UCC remedies. Before discussing remedies, let us examine the distinction between Article Two of the UCC and the common law.

THE BATTLE OF COMPETING LEGAL SYSTEMS: CONTRACT LAW VERSUS SALES LAW

Unfortunately, the computer system acquisition effort becomes clouded because of the United States' dichotomous contract law system. Two competing systems of contract law exist side by side in every state except Louisiana. A battle between the common law of contract and the sales law or Uniform Commercial Code creates a preliminary choice of law issue in many contract disputes.

The Common Law

The common law is the system that was inherited from England when America was colonized; it has slowly evolved case by case in the last 280 years but is still somewhat anachronistic. This system features the policy of caveat emptor (let the buyer beware) and applies to all contracts that do not involve "transactions or sales of goods."[2] Leasing a computer system may be considered a common law transaction for purposes of some UCC remedies since it is not technically a sale, and acquiring programming services may be considered a common law transaction since services rather than goods are involved. Under the common law no warranty protection, no rejection, and no revocation-of-acceptance remedies exist unless the contract so specifies. The user can avoid the common law caveat emptor problem by inserting the UCC clauses in the contract stipulating that the UCC will apply or by negotiating express warranties in the contract and refusing to sign the supplier's sales order.

Article Two of the UCC

The UCC, on the other hand, is a modern system designed to deal with today's business world and the problems it creates. The UCC has been legislatively adopted in 49 states (all except Louisiana), the District of Columbia, and the Virgin Islands. It features a caveat venditor (let the seller beware) system, giving the buyer a wider range of effective remedies which usually apply to corporate buyers as well as to consumers. These UCC rights and remedies are listed here and explained in some detail in the following pages:

a. right to inspect the goods before payment in Sections 2-512 and 2-513;

b. right to reject the goods before payment and acceptance if the goods are nonconforming in Sections 2-601 to 2-605;

c. right to revoke acceptance of the goods if a promised cure was not made or if a latent defect was discovered in Section 2-608;

d. express warranty protection in Section 2-313;

e. implied warranty protection in Sections 2-312, 2-314, 2-315;

f. non-enforcement of unconscionable or unfair clauses in Sections 2-302 and 2-719(3); and

g. abolition of the repair or replacement remedy if that limited remedy fails in its essential purpose to give the buyer some minimal protection in Section 2-719(2).

REMEDIES

This section describes the common law remedies of mutual mistake and misrepresentation and the UCC remedies outlined previously.

The Common Law Remedies

Unfortunately, the common law of contracts provides few remedies that are not expressly agreed upon in the contract. This is the main reason for the common law being dubbed the "caveat emptor system." For the user to be fully protected under a common law contract, the contract clauses specified in Part I that protect the buyer must be negotiated for and expressly stated in the contract. If this cannot be accomplished, then the common law provides only two significant implied remedies: misrepresentation and mutual mistake. These common law remedies are also available under the UCC since the UCC is supplemented by all common law doctrines (including misrepresentation and mistake) that are not displaced by particular provisions of the Code.[3]

Mutual Mistake. The mutual mistake remedy is often overlooked but very useful. To prove mutual mistake, the user must be able to show that both the supplier and the user formed the contract under a mutual misunderstanding of present or past facts that are significant to the contract. In other words, the user must show that if the parties had known the real facts at the time of contracting, no contract would have been formed.[4] For example, the salesperson may claim that an existing packaged program to be used for the system is capable of handling all of the user's accounting needs (a frequently made claim). The supplier and user may honestly believe that to be the case. A few months later when the system is installed, that statement is found to be untrue for any one of several reasons; a mutual mistake of material fact was made. Therefore, both parties may have the right to terminate the transaction at that point.

The common law remedy for mutual mistake is known as the voidable or rescindable contract and is available at the option of either party. A court will order both parties restored to the status quo, that is, the supplier must return all payments made and the user must return the computer system. There are two problems with this remedy. First, to win, the user must document all of the representations made by the supplier's sales force. Second, the courts may not always award compensation for damages resulting from a defective system in a mutual mistake litigation. A refund of the payments made and cancellation of the contract is the most the user can usually expect from a mutual mistake lawsuit. At least, the user benefits by obtaining a full refund and not having to make any more payments for a lemon computer system. Another benefit is that settlement before litigation is more likely to occur under the mutual mistake concept than under the fraud concept.[5]

Misrepresentation. The misrepresentation remedy[6] has more advantages in terms of damages but is more difficult to prove than mutual mistake and usually provokes a fight since the user is assaulting the supplier's integrity. A more polite way to negotiate a settlement under the common law is the use of mutual mistake. But should that method fail or if contract recovery is otherwise unavailable, the user can argue fraud.[7] To prove fraud, the user, after having documented significant representations of the seller, must be able to demonstrate these elements:

a. a false statement was made by the supplier;

b. the falsity involves a fact important to the transaction;

c. the supplier either knew it was false or should have known it was false at the time of making it; and

d. detriment or injury to the user resulted from reliance on the falsity.

Once these factors are proven, the user may elect (a) to cancel the contract by returning the defective system and by demanding a refund of payments made and seek compensatory damages as well[8] or (b) to affirm the contract by keeping the system and sue for the tort of fraud to recover damages for losses resulting from the fraudulent contract. Recoverable damages include normal contract damages, that is, a reduction in the price of the defective system plus all consequential damages caused by the misrepresentations. These damages alone can involve substantial amounts of money. There is also a possibility of recovering punitive damages. Punitive damages are intended to punish the supplier for conduct that is deemed particularly reprehensible and therefore permit the judge or jury to consider how much money the supplier has in order to grant a recovery that will hurt the supplier.

An alternative form of representation action is that of negligent misrepresentation. This tort theory holds persons liable for false statements made unintentionally but with carelessness as to their truth, which caused harm to others who reasonably relied on the truth of the statements. The tort has traditionally been applied to persons who are in the business of supplying information for others to rely upon, such as stockbrokers or consumer magazines. In one recent case, an Illinois appellate court refused to apply this tort to hold the sellers of a computer and software package liable for the buyer's losses from the computer acquisition.[9] The vendors had assured the buyer that the hardware and software sold would meet the user's needs when in fact the hardware would not interface with the software. The court, expressing distaste for the idea of allowing parties to "circumvent their contractual remedies by suing in tort," refused to apply the tort of negligent misrepresentation because, first, the sellers were in the business of selling merchandise, not in the business of supplying information, and second, the information supplied was not offered for the guidance of the buyer in the buyer's dealings *with others*. Most courts would probably agree with the Illinois court and not apply the tort of negligent misrepresentation to a direct buyer–seller situation.

The UCC Remedies

Whereas the common law of contracts has failed to give users significant protection unless expressly stated in the contract, the UCC has by operation of law incorporated implied protection for the buyer into every contract for the sale of goods. The UCC has thus changed the contracting process from a caveat emptor to a caveat venditor situation. The sophisticated suppliers know this, so to minimize their liability or losses, sales orders reducing this buyer protection have been prepared by most suppliers in the industry. As we have stressed, to be protected, the user must avoid signing such a sales order and negotiate for clauses that make the UCC rights and remedies available to the buyer in all computer system transactions. The user must negotiate for this protection—the supplier will not *give* the user any protection beyond a limited 90-day warranty (or other short period of time). Let us examine the UCC rights and remedies to explore the extent of the implied protection. The user can, of course, negotiate for even greater protection by inserting express warranty clauses into the final contract.

The Rights of Inspection and Rejection. Implied in every UCC contract
is the right of inspection[10] needed to ascertain whether the delivered system conforms to the contract specifications and/or warranties. The right of inspection is guaranteed in every contract without the need for negotiation. This protection is thus said to be implied by operation of law in UCC contracts. The buyer can waive the inspection rights by signing a supplier sales order that requires the user to accept and pay for the system prior to a thorough inspection, such as by agreeing to a C.O.D. delivery term or to a delivery against negotiable documents of title.

After the inspection, the user has the absolute right to reject the computer system if it "fail[s] in any respect to conform to the contract." [11] This so-called perfect tender rule obligates the supplier to deliver and install a "perfect" computer system just as the user guarantees the payment of a "perfect" price. If the system is nonconforming "in any respect," the user must promptly notify the supplier of the defects, preferably in writing, and of the user's desire to reject the system. The supplier must be given a reasonable time in which to "cure" these defects.[12] If the supplier does not cure them within a reasonable time, the user may then cancel the contract by demanding a full refund of all prior payments and request that the system be removed. The user may also sue for damages.[13]

Incidentally, the user has two other important remedies available once the supplier has failed to make a satisfactory cure. After a valid rejection has been made, the user has the right to suspend all payments to the supplier under the adequate assurances rule until the defect is cured.[14] Second, the user has a security interest in the nonconforming system that is in its possession.[15] This means that the user may keep the nonconforming system until the user has recovered any losses or damages resulting from the prior payment of the price and any expenses reasonably incurred in inspection, receipt, transportation, care, and custody of the nonconforming system. The user may either hold the nonconforming system until reimbursement or resell the system at an auction or to a private buyer after first notifying the seller of the pending sale or auction. From the proceeds of the resale, the user can deduct his or her expenses, losses, damages, and a resale commission but then must forward the remainder (if any) to the supplier. The opportunity to resell the defective system to the highest bidder is a very important right since it gives the user tremendous leverage in negotiating a settlement with the supplier. Imagine the expression on the supplier's face when he or she reads the user's notice stating that due to the supplier's failure to cure the defect, the user is going to sell the defective system to the highest bidder to cover its losses and the supplier is welcome to bid!

The Problem of Acceptance. The supplier, knowing the importance of inspection and rejection rights to the user, will attempt to take them away. First, the supplier may try to persuade the user to sign the sales order, which eliminates these rights by stating that the "sole and exclusive right of the user is repair or replacement for 90 days after delivery." The prudent user should not sign such a sales order! Second, the supplier may, upon delivery of the computer hardware, attempt to have the user sign a statement that "the user has inspected the system and finds it to be conforming or accepts it as is." The user should likewise not sign this form (unless it is true) since once the user accepts the system, the right of rejection for an imperfect tender is lost.[16] In addition, once the user has accepted the system, the burden of persuasion rests with the buyer to prove any breach.[17]

An acceptance occurs by doing one of these acts:

a. signifying to the supplier that the system is conforming or that the user will keep the system even though it is nonconforming (for example, by signing the delivery form);

b. failing to make an effective rejection after having a reasonable opportunity to inspect (the user must inspect and, if necessary, reject as promptly as is possible under the circumstances); or

c. doing any act inconsistent with the supplier's ownership interest after purportedly rejecting the system (for example, using the system after rejecting it).

Until the system has been installed with all programs operating, few courts should find that the user has lost the right of rejection because the opportunity to make a reasonable inspection to determine the computer's quality does not exist until that time.[18] However, for the user to prevent any acceptance problems from arising, it is advisable to specify in the contract precisely what tests the system has to pass before the system is to be considered accepted.

The Right of Revocation of Acceptance. Another tremendously important remedy that is implied in all UCC contracts is the right to revoke a prior acceptance.[19] The UCC drafters realized that there are two situations in which the UCC buyer should be protected even after an acceptance has been made. Either (a) the acceptance occurred "on the reasonable assumption that its nonconformity would be cured and it has not been seasonably cured"; or (b) the acceptance occurred "without discovery of such nonconformity if [the] acceptance was reasonably induced either by the difficulty of discovery before acceptance or by the seller's assurances" (also known as the latent defect rule).

In addition, to be entitled to revoke a prior acceptance, the user must be able to prove that the nonconformity "substantially impairs the value" of the accepted system and that the revocation occurred "within a reasonable time after the buyer discovers or should have discovered" the nonconformity.[20] Therefore, the user must act as quickly as possible in discovering and in notifying the supplier in writing of all significant problems that may justify the use of the revocation-of-acceptance remedy.

Once it is proven that the promised cure did not occur or that a substantial latent defect existed at the time of acceptance, the user occupies the same legal position as if he or she had rejected the system earlier.[21] After notifying the supplier in writing of the intent to revoke acceptance, the user has several options:

a. negotiate a settlement by reducing the price of the system;

b. demand a prompt cure of the latent defect;

c. request that the seller remove the system after refunding all prior payments made and after paying all reasonable expenses incurred by the user; or

d. prepare to resell the system to the highest bidder under the security interest rules.

The right to revoke acceptance lasts for up to four years after the date of delivery according to the UCC statute of limitations[22] as long as the time period is reasonable upon the facts and nature of the defect. The user can, however, reduce this length of time to one year by signing a sales order to that effect.[23] Also, if the user substantially changes the system from its delivered condition, the right to revoke acceptance is lost.[24] The user should therefore allow only the supplier's personnel to install, modify, and maintain the system after delivery and until all bugs are out of the system. Once the user's personnel begin tinkering with a nonconforming system, the user may lose this valuable remedy since the user may no longer be able to prove that the supplier caused the nonconformity or latent defect. Initially, the user should not attempt to rescue a floundering system by making adjustments and repairs but should leave that responsibility to the supplier.

To illustrate the significance of the rejection or revocation-of-acceptance remedy, two noncomputer cases are quickly summarized. In *Sanborn v. Aranosian,*[25] a car dealer sold a new Fiat station wagon to a consumer. After it was driven for 17,000 miles, the court allowed the consumer to return it (to revoke its acceptance) for a *full* refund of the purchase price ($4,605) since the dealer was never able to fix it. Also, in *Ybarra v. Modern Trailer Sales, Inc.,*[26] the court allowed a consumer to revoke his acceptance of a mobile home after occupying it for nearly four years since the repeated repair efforts of the dealer did not cure the defects. In a recent computer case, a law firm that had revoked acceptance of a computer software package that did not perform as represented was held to be entitled as a matter of law to a full refund of the purchase price ($4,000) plus reasonable expenses incurred as a result of the breach.[27]

These cases dramatically illustrate that the right to revoke acceptance may be one of the most important remedies that the computer user has. The remedies of rejection and revocation of acceptance are also superior to UCC warranty protection, discussed next, because the breach of warranty remedies do not allow the buyer to return the defective system and regain the purchase price. The warranty remedies allow the user to obtain only a *reduction* in the price plus any damages incurred, but the user must keep the defective system since the contract cannot be canceled. Only the rejection or revocation-of-acceptance remedy permits a cancellation of the contract under the UCC.

The Express Warranty Remedy. The concept of express warranty is of grave concern to suppliers. Their use of the integration clause, the limitation-of-remedies clause, and the antimodification clause in their sales orders is designed to prevent the creation of broad express warranties and the additional liability they impose on the supplier. Instead, the supplier will most often give the user an extremely limited express warranty in the sales order; for example, the right to have defects repaired or replaced for the first 90 days after delivery. The user expects and should receive greater protection and therefore should not sign such a sales order.

Express warranties under the UCC are created in two ways: those stated in the contract (the free repair or replacement for the first 90 days after delivery) or those created by the statements or conduct of the supplier, which are a part of the "basis of the bargain."[28] It is, therefore, important to document all significant representations made by the supplier during demonstrations or negotiations and then incorporate them into the final contract.

For example, any description of the computer system made by the promotional literature or by the salesperson creates an express warranty.[29] Also, the act of demonstrating the computer system at a trade show or at another user's facility creates an express warranty that the system the user acquires will conform to the one demonstrated.[30] Unless these statements and events are written into the contract, the supplier's integration clause and the parol evidence rule may prevent these precontract express warranties from protecting the user. The sales order with an integration clause should therefore not be signed unless significant representations and events relied upon by the user are incorporated into the final contract.

Express warranties can also be created *after* the contract is formed since the UCC does not require any new consideration (exchange of legal value) to modify the contract[31] and since an express warranty may be a part of the basis of the bargain even after the contract is entered into.[32] For example, when the supplier's programmers or troubleshooters appear at the user's facility to install a new program or repair the computer system, they may make significant representations about the capabilities of that system or program, at least partly intended to prevent the user from exercising its right to call off the deal. Those representations can create express warranties. Therefore, the user should take great care to document those statements, reduce them to writing, and insist that the supplier's agent sign the writing at that time. Again, the supplier, being concerned about postcontract express warranties, probably inserted an antimodification clause into the sales order to prevent the creation of such warranties. The user should not sign a sales order with an antimodification clause unless the system is desired to the extent that the user will settle for less legal protection.

The supplier's limitation-of-remedies clause stating that there are no other express warranties except the repair or replacement warranty eliminates the user's protection from other express warranties. Again, the user should beware of a sales order with such disclaimer clauses.

The Implied Warranty of Merchantability. Whenever a merchant sells goods, the UCC creates an implied warranty of merchantability without the need for negotiation. This warranty guarantees that the goods sold are reasonably fit for their ordinary, intended uses and that they are of fair or average quality so that they would pass without objection within the trade or industry.[33] This basically means the goods must be of fair, average, or medium quality. The seller is not obligated to install the best quality system, nor is the buyer obligated to accept the installation of the lowest quality system.

The value to the user of the implied warranty of merchantability thus depends upon the court's view of the standard quality to be expected of a computer system. The application of this warranty requires the court to hear evidence on the average quality of similar computer systems. In the hands of courts that are sympathetic to users, this warranty could be a significant legal tool for imposing high-quality standards on the computer industry. Since this warranty guarantees only medium quality, it is of little value to the user who expects a guarantee of superior quality when spending large amounts of money to acquire a system. Therefore, the only sure way to protect the user is to negotiate for superior performance using the express warranty clause and to require performance testing before acceptance.

Even so, the user should not give up this limited protection by signing a supplier's sales order disclaiming this warranty without negotiation. The UCC requires that any disclaimer of this warranty by the seller be conspicuous, be in writing, and mention the word "merchantability" to be effective.[34] However, many courts will uphold a disclaimer of implied warranties even though it is not conspicuous if the buyer was actually aware of the disclaimer.[35] This occurred in a recent computer case in which the user's president testified that he read the disclaimer, tried to have it changed, was unable to do so, and then signed the contract anyway.[36] This leads to a curious result since, if the user has a disclaimer that is invalid because of inconspicuousness, that user appears to be better off if he does not read the fine print and try to negotiate the term. The problem with this view is, first, that the determination of conspicuousness is a close factual issue that cannot be determined without reading the disclaimer and, second, if the user decides that the clause is not conspicuous and takes a chance that a court will find it to be invalid but a court decides against him or her, the user is held to the disclaimer. The best policy is that followed by prudent businesspeople in every other type of transaction: Do not sign anything that you have not read, understood, and agreed to. This policy should be given no less consideration in the area of computer purchases.

The Implied Warranty of Fitness for a Particular Purpose. The implied warranty of fitness for a particular purpose affords the computer user a higher quality of protection than the implied warranty of merchantability. The warranty of fitness for a particular purpose is also implied in the UCC contract so that the user does not have to negotiate for it. It is created by the conduct of the parties. First, the supplier must have known the precise particular purpose for which the computer system was needed. So, the user should precisely define the specifications and functions needed and then communicate these in writing to the supplier. Second, the user must have relied upon the supplier's skill, judgment, or expertise in "selecting or furnishing suitable goods." This implied warranty of fitness guarantees that the goods selected or furnished by the supplier will suit the user's particular purposes.[37]

Thus, an implied warranty mandating a superior quality system can be created by communicating the high-quality specifications and desired functions to the supplier and requesting that the supplier select or furnish a system to meet those needs. The UCC actually gives the user the opportunity, in effect, to customize the implied warranty to fit its needs. This implied warranty affords the user significant protection without even having to negotiate for it in a UCC contract.

This warranty is *not,* however, a gimmick by which the user can, in every situation, throw the risk of proper selection onto the seller. For the warranty to be effective, the user must not only tell the seller what his or her needs are but the user must also actually rely upon the seller to provide the appropriate system. Actual reliance is another area in which the buyer can know too much. For example, if the buyer becomes involved in the selection process and insists upon a particular brand or style of computer, the buyer is not relying on the seller's expertise and no warranty exists.[38] Likewise, if the buyer is equally or more knowledgeable about computers than the vendor, there is no reliance.[39] A federal court recently used this rationale in dismissing a fraud claim (in which reliance is also a necessary element) brought by a computer purchaser who was more knowledgeable in computer science than the seller's representative and "much too knowledgeable to rely on publicity blurbs issued by the [seller]."[40]

Suppliers are also aware of the impact of this protection, however, so their sales orders attempt to disclaim the warranty clause to prevent its creation.[41] Disclaimers of the warranty of fitness must be in writing and conspicuous.[42] The same judicial disregard of nonconspicuousness when the buyer actually knows of the disclaimer applies as for the warranty of merchantability. Again, if the user wants this protection, he or she should not sign a sales order containing such a disclaimer.

The Implied Warranty of Title. If the computer system is being sold, the implied warranty of title guarantees that the supplier (a) owns the system, (b) has the right to sell it to the user, and (c) has no knowledge of any other persons claiming an interest in ownership of the system such as liens or security interests.[43] No negotiations or specific contract provisions are necessary to obtain this protection, although it is also susceptible to waiver by agreement. If the system is leased, the user also needs to be concerned about having the right to use the system for the lease period without any title claims from third parties, such as the manufacturer, for nonpayment by the lessor. Since this right is not necessarily related to rights of ownership, the user may wish to negotiate for an express warranty guaranteeing the quiet enjoyment or the exclusive right to use the system during the lease period.

This warranty may also be extremely helpful in preventing suppliers of software from claiming that a license existed rather than a sale. Before the supplier can prevent the user from acquiring title or ownership rights in software, the supplier must inform the user that the user is not acquiring title and only acquiring the right to use the software. For the license agreement to be effective, the user must agree to be a nonowner of the software. If the supplier delivers a software package without a formal contract stating that the package is merely licensed to the user, the user can claim that this warranty was violated if the supplier failed to deliver good title to the program.

The Implied Warranty Against Infringements. The last implied warranty protects the user against patent and copyright infringements.[44] The supplier who delivers the system is probably a merchant and thus implicitly guarantees that it has not violated a third party's patent, copyright, or trademark in designing, marketing, or installing the system. If a violation of a third party's intellectual property rights is later discovered by the user of the system, the user merely notifies the supplier of the problem. At this point, the supplier must pay any damages incurred by the user that arise out of the infringement. This warranty may also be disclaimed by the sales agreement. In addition, if the buyer has furnished specifications to the seller, the *buyer* must hold the *seller* harmless for any third party claims of infringement that might arise out of the seller's compliance with the buyer's specifications.

Failure of Essential Purpose. Failure of essential purpose[45] is the first UCC remedy provided to the unfortunate user who has signed the sales order featuring the integration clause, limitation-of-warranties, -remedies, and -damages clauses, and antimodification clauses. The only express remedy typically made available to the user in the sales order is the repair-or-replace remedy for a limited period of time. What then happens if the supplier is not able to satisfactorily repair or replace the system? Once the sole and exclusive remedy given to the user under the contract fails to provide any meaningful protection (that is, the system was not repaired or replacements did not work), all the normal remedies provided by the UCC apply to protect the user: rejection, revocation of acceptance, express warranties, and implied warranties. Computer users should derive substantial protection from this concept as long as the UCC applies to the transaction.

For example, in *Chatlos Systems, Inc. v. National Cash Register Corp.,*[46] the sales contract gave the user only a limited remedy of repair or replacement in lieu of all other warranties and remedies. The supplier continually tried to repair the system in order to get the promised functions working but was unsuccessful. When the user sued for breach of warranty, the supplier claimed that the user's sole contractual remedy was repair or replacement. The court, rejecting that notion, found that since that limited remedy's primary purpose was to provide the user with a working computer system and it had failed to do this, all other UCC warranties and remedies were resurrected to give the user some meaningful protection.

This remedy gives the user very significant protection. Once the user is able to establish that the supplier made several attempts to fix the system within the specified time period (for example, 90 days), the user can claim that the exclusive repair or replacement remedy failed to provide a working computer system within that period. Once that occurs, the user has all the UCC implied remedies available—rejection, revocation of acceptance, and implied warranties, as well as breach of the limited express warranty to repair or replace the system. This UCC provision is the most important remedy available to users who sign the supplier's sales order without reading or understanding the fine print.

Unconscionability. The UCC remedy of unconscionability[47] is difficult to define with precision, but it is important to discuss since courts are increasingly applying it to consumer buyers, to some non-UCC transactions, and to some isolated commercial buyers. Unconscionability, however, is basically a consumer remedy since consumers, due to their inexperience in the business world, are presumed to need protection from cunning or sharp business practices. Some courts apply it to transactions involving commercial buyers where one party has taken advantage of the other with an unfair written contract.[48] In computer transactions, this would mean that the sales order that attempts to unfairly limit remedies and to eliminate all liabilities could be declared unconscionable, deleted from the contract, and replaced with the UCC's implied remedies and unlimited liability. The UCC permits the court, after finding a contract or contract clause unconscionable, (a) to refuse to enforce the entire contract; (b) to refuse to enforce the unconscionable clauses; or (c) to limit the application of clauses to avoid an unconscionable result.[49] The UCC "gap-filler" terms and remedies may be applied to replace any terms declared unconscionable.

Unconscionability has taken on two separate meanings: procedural unconscionability (unfair surprise in the contract formation process) and substantive unconscionability (oppression or unfair terms).[50] Substantive unconscionability involves some fundamental unfairness about the contract terms themselves, commonly an unspoken deception as to what the buyer is getting for his or her money. Substantive unconscionability cases have largely centered on outrageous prices or excessive meddling with or reduction of the buyer's remedies.

A single unconscionability claim may use both meanings. For example, the computer user may be told that a contract contains the seller's standard terms but then may find out after he or she signed the sales order that the fine print on the reverse page eliminated *all* of his or her remedies and disclaimed any liability on the part of the seller.[51] Both the procedure and the substance of such a transaction are unfair.

Whether the court finds the supplier guilty of unconscionable conduct by contracting with its sales order ultimately depends on the following factors: (a) the degree of the user's computer and legal sophistication and ability to understand and negotiate the terms of the sales order, especially the limitation-of-remedies and liabilities clauses; (b) the relative bargaining power of the user and supplier; and (c) the conspicuousness of the limitation-of-remedies and liabilities clauses to the user.

The unconscionability remedy is a last-resort method for the consumer or user to eliminate the unfair clauses of the sales order that reduce the buyer's remedies to almost nothing. Unconscionability is *not* a legal doctrine that can be effectively planned for, even by the consumer. It involves a highly subjective judicial evaluation of the user's ability to comprehend the nature of the transaction, the extent of the user's obligations and rights, and the substance of what the parties bargained for. Thus, the more the user knows (or is presumed to know) about the law of contracts and about computers, the less likely the court is to relieve the user of the contract's harsh terms.

Commercial buyers find unconscionability even more difficult to prove. A first-time commercial buyer of computer hardware or software may be able to prove unconscionability if the buyer is completely ignorant of legal principles and the computer field. However, a sophisticated commercial user such as a bank or a Fortune 500 company with computer-experienced personnel could never prove unconscionability, since they are presumed to understand the legalese contained in the fine print and the nature of the risks involved and therefore are presumed to have contracted with the requisite knowledge to assume the risk for these clauses. The only conceivable way that commercial users can prove unconscionability is to show that the supplier would not negotiate the removal of the offensive clauses in the sales order. Thus, a contract of adhesion or a take-it-or-leave-it offer may be created, which may be illegal in some states.[52] However, none of the several computer cases located that have raised the issue of unconscionability have done so successfully.[53] Both consumer and commercial users would thus appear to be better off by negotiating the best contract possible or by claiming failure of essential purpose of limited remedies than by planning to prove unconscionability at a later date.

Damages. There are basically four categories of damages that may occur in breached contracts. The first to be considered is compensatory damages. Compensatory or direct damages are intended to compensate the user for the actual loss of the contract's value.

Compensatory damages for the remedies of mutual mistake, fraud, rejection, and revocation of acceptance can be established in two ways. First, the user can recover a full refund of the purchase price paid. Second, the user may "cover" under the UCC.[54] This allows the user to purchase a substitute system from another supplier whenever no delivery occurs or when a nonconforming delivery is rejected or acceptance revoked. The compensatory damages are then calculated by adding the purchase price paid (and to be refunded) to the additional cost of the covered goods. The additional cost is calculated by subtracting the price of the nondelivered or nonconforming goods from the price of the covered goods.

Compensatory damages for the remedies of express and implied warranties do not include a refund of the price. All that the buyer can expect to receive from a warranty claim is a price reduction. These compensatory damages are calculated by taking the difference between the value of the computer system if it had been in a perfect state as warranted (usually the contract price) and the value of the defective system actually received (usually the salvage or fair-market value).[55]

Recent court cases have illustrated a certain amount of judicial creativity in applying this formula to benefit the user where the user has executed a contract with disclaimers of liability. For example, in the case of *Schatz Distributing Co. v. Olivetti Corp. of America,*[56] the supplier's salesperson promised a computer system that would perform many functions that it could not do in reality. Since the user's attorney litigated only a warranty claim, the court applied the warranty damage formula but surprised everyone by claiming the computer was absolutely worthless—having $0 as a salvage value! Thus, this court in effect turned the warranty claim into a rejection or revocation claim for compensatory damages. Since the defective computer had no salvage value, the user received a full refund of the price paid in addition to keeping the defective computer. Although this case is quite interesting, one should not expect many courts to follow its novel approach to calculating warranty compensatory damages. Few courts would decide that a defective computer has no salvage value.

The *Chatlos* case[57] also indicates the extent to which courts may occasionally go out of their way to protect a user in a breach-of-warranty claim. NCR supplied a defective computer having a purchase price of $46,020. During the negotiations, the NCR salesperson claimed that the system could perform amazing feats of computing. The buyer bought the system under the belief that the system could perform as represented. When it was delivered, the only amazing aspect of the system was how badly it performed. After lengthy litigation and appeals, the trial court applied the warranty damages formula by ignoring the purchase price altogether. The court found that the fair-market value of the system promised to be delivered by NCR was $207,826.50 and the fair-market value of the defective system was $6,000, which left the user with compensatory damages of $201,826.50 for a computer system that cost only $46,020. Although the court was technically correct in its calculation of this amount as compensatory damages, it is not likely that courts would ignore the purchase price as part of the formula. Many courts would award the user only $40,020 in damages in this type of case (price of $46,020 less the salvage value of $6,000 = $40,020). In reality, the *Chatlos* court appears to have combined the warranty claim with consequential damages in spite of the fact that the contract executed by both parties excluded consequential damage, as determined by the first *Chatlos* appeal. Again, most courts will not do this unless the court is really upset with the supplier's conduct.

The next category, consequential damages,[58] is represented by such losses as downtime, lost profits, or increased expenses directly resulting from the defective computer system. The user may collect damages only for those losses that were reasonably foreseeable at the time of contracting. Suppliers, however, invariably insert into their standard contracts or sales orders a clause that eliminates their liability for consequential damages. Since a user could suffer substantial hardship from a supplier's breach of contract, the user should attempt to negotiate a contract that fairly allocates the risk of consequential damages. For example, the contract may require the seller, in the event of the system's malfunction, to supply additional equipment or pay for backup computer time purchased from other sources. Although suppliers usually consider this area nonnegotiable, an insistent user may be able to negotiate some concessions. If this approach fails, the user should then attempt to negotiate for a liquidated damage clause. The user should not sign the sales order without first attempting to negotiate some self-protection in this area.

A user can also take practical steps to minimize the amount of consequential losses suffered by, for example, duplicating sensitive data to prevent total loss of that data by a malfunctioning computer and arranging in advance to have backup systems available whenever the user's system is down.

The third type of damages, called liquidated damages,[59] may provide the user with some relief against supplier breaches. Liquidated damages are damages that the parties have agreed upon in the contract by stating the precise dollar amount for compensation in the event of a breach. For example, a late delivery or installation may be presumed to cost the user $100 per day, so the supplier will be liable for liquidated damages in that amount according to the contract. Liquidated damages are especially useful when it would otherwise be difficult to ascertain the precise dollar amount of such losses. The courts will usually uphold the liquidated damage clause and amounts except in cases where the court deems the amount to be excessive. Liquidated damages are illegal and unenforceable when they are not a realistic estimate of the potential damages that may result from a breach but are rather a stiff penalty imposed on a breaching party. Thus, these damages should be linked to the person-hour savings estimate that most computer salespeople supply in their sales pitch or to some other objectively ascertainable basis.

A fourth type of damages, incidental damages, compensate the buyer for expenses reasonably incurred in the user's handling of the defective computer system.[60] These expenses might include the expense of inspecting, transporting, and storing the defective system, as well as expenses and commissions paid to effect cover, or replacement, of the defective system.

COURT CASES

Kalil Bottling Co. v. Burroughs Corp.[61] Kalil first attempted to purchase a complete computer system from Burroughs for $40,168. After Kalil's credit application was denied, Burroughs sold the system to the National Equipment Co., which, in turn, leased it to Kalil without an option to purchase. The lease and the sales contract, both signed by Kalil, contained an integration clause and a limitation-of-liabilities and -remedies clause. The only remedy given in the contract (a standard Burroughs sales order) was the right to repair and replacement for one year after delivery. Soon after delivery, the computer system malfunctioned several times; a second computer was installed but it malfunctioned also. Moreover, Burroughs never installed all the software programs specified in the contract.

Kalil sued for fraud and breach of implied and express warranties, and the jury awarded $401,690 in damages (presumably $40,168 in compensatory damages as a refund of the price and $361,522 in consequential damages). On appeal, the court found that:

a. the allegations of fraud are not valid due to the integration clause, the parol evidence rule, and the user's failure to list any representations on the final contracts (the sales order);

b. the implied warranty claims are invalid due to the use of the limitation-of-remedies clause;

c. Section 2-719 protects the user here since the exclusive remedy of repair or replacement failed to protect the user (ruled for Kalil Bottling Company);

d. the issue of unconscionability of the contract clause was declared to be moot or not decided by the court since Section 2-719 adequately protected the user; and

e. the ability to recover consequential damages is available in Arizona after the seller refuses or is unable to repair or replace the defective system within a reasonable time.

The significance of this case is that the Arizona court (a) applied UCC law to a computer lease that did not contain an option-to-purchase clause; (b) found that once the supplier fails to repair or replace the system within a reasonable time, it breaches that express repair or replace warranty; and

(c) found that once the repair or replace warranty is breached, the limitation-of-damages clause is voided so that the user could sue for all damages (compensatory and consequential) caused by the failure to repair or replace the system within a reasonable time after the defect occurs.

This case dramatically demonstrates the usefulness of the UCC and of the failure-of-essential-purpose remedy in protecting a commercial computer user even in cases in which no sale of goods is involved. The case also illustrates the need to document all representations made by the sales force and attach them to the final contract, since the court threw out the fraud claim because the representations of the Burroughs salespeople were not specified in the sales order, which contained an integration clause.

Westfield Chemical Corp. v. Burroughs Corp.[62]

Westfield purchased a computer system from Burroughs in January 1971. The sales order gave the buyer the exclusive remedy of repair or replacement for one year after delivery, eliminated all other warranties and damage claims, and also contained an integration clause. After the computer system malfunctioned in some unexplained manner, the buyer filed suit for fraud and breach of implied and express warranty.

The trial court ruled in favor of Burroughs on all charges. The trial court found, and the finding was not appealed, that:

a. the breach-of-implied-warranty claim was invalid due to the valid limitation-of-remedy clause;

b. The limitation-of-remedy and -damage clauses are not unconscionable since the buyer was presumably a knowledgeable businessperson, suggesting that unconscionability is solely a *consumer* remedy in Massachusetts;

c. the repair or replacement express warranty had not failed its essential purpose since the user "could have returned the defective part for repair or replacement"; and

d. the claim of fraudulent misrepresentation by a salesperson stating that the system would provide substantial person-hour savings, which never materialized, is invalid since this representation was not attached to the contract, which had an integration clause.

This case illustrates that (a) some courts are reluctant to find contracts between businesspeople unconscionable; (b) the integration clause will at times prevent the proof of fraud unless all important representations made by the sales force are attached to the final contract; and (c) the user should document several unsuccessful attempts by the supplier to fix the defects in the computer system before going to court under Section 2-719 (the failure of the essential purposes of the exclusive repair or replacement remedy).

Chatlos Systems, Inc. v. National Cash Register Corp.[63]

Chatlos contacted NCR to purchase a computer system on credit. Since NCR decided not to extend credit, NCR sold the system to MidAtlantic National Bank, which leased it to Chatlos. The hardware was delivered in December, 1975, and NCR promised to have six customized programming functions operational by March, 1976. By that time, only one program (payroll) was operational. In June, Chatlos informed NCR that it wanted to cancel the contract, but NCR refused and started the programming work once again. By September, the state tax program was operational, but Chatlos's patience had expired; it demanded removal of the computer and filed suit. The contracts provided a limitation of damages so that consequential damages were not available and provided a limited remedy of repair or replacement. The trial court found in favor of Chatlos for $120,710, amounting to Chatlos's indebtedness on the transaction less the salvage value, $57,152, plus $63,558 in consequential damages. NCR appealed.

The appellate court decision is unique and quite interesting since it found:

a. the limitation-of-damages clause is not unconscionable since Chatlos Systems, Inc., is a sophisticated business manufacturing complex telecommunications systems, so it had some appreciation of computer systems and could not claim "unfair surprise" or a "linguistic maze" of legalese or computerese in the sales order;

b. NCR failed to program that hardware as warranted and breached the express warranty of providing "skillful and workmanlike" services in programming the hardware;

c. once the express repair or replace warranty fails its essential purpose, the limitation-of-consequential-damages clause is not automatically abolished (which is a different ruling than in the *Kalil* case);

d. Chatlos is precluded by the contract from receiving consequential damages and can recover only compensatory damages from NCR; and

e. the measure of compensatory damages is the value of the computer system as warranted to be (usually the price, which in this case is $46,020) less the value of the computer system in its defective state. (Interest incurred on the purchase price should not have been included in the purchase price applied by the trial court). In other words, Chatlos is stuck with the defective computer but can obtain a reduction in its price.

This case illustrates that:

a. the sale of the computer by the supplier to the financial institution that leases it to the user is a UCC sale of goods under the economic reality test;

b. courts are reluctant to declare clauses unconscionable where a sophisticated user is involved; that user is presumed to understand the legalese and computerese in the fine print of the sales order;

c. failure of the essential purpose under Section 3-719(2) does not always guarantee the right to sue for consequential damages but, at the least, it guarantees the right to sue for compensatory damages;

d. the lawsuit was caused by the failure to develop customized programs for the user; nonetheless, the court classified the failure to provide *customized computer programming services* as a UCC transaction, at least when hardware was also acquired; and

e. the breach-of-warranty remedy is not as effective as a rejection or revocation-of-acceptance remedy since all Chatlos received is a reduction in the price; the court ruled it must keep the defective system. If rejection or revocation of acceptance existed, then a full refund of the price would be awarded to the user.

One must wonder why Chatlos (a) did not vigorously pursue the revocation-of-acceptance remedy against NCR and (b) did not attempt to sue NCR on behalf of the system buyer—the MidAtlantic National Bank—for revocation of acceptance as well. Chatlos is stuck with a computer that does not work. This result was ameliorated considerably when the case was remanded on the issue of damages, which was later reappealed. In the later proceedings, the trial court found, with the appellate court concurring, that the actual compensatory damages were $201,826.50, notwithstanding the fact that the purchase price of the system was merely $46,020. The retrial and appellate courts, in effect, included consequential damages in this amount without so stating by inflating the real value of the computer system promised to $207,826.50 and deflating the salvage value of the defective system to $6,000.[64]

This case also illustrates why Chatlos should have requested the right to represent the bank in negotiating the bank's contract of purchase for the computer with Burroughs; then Chatlos could have acquired meaningful protection under the third-party beneficiary concept when it leased the system from the bank.

Triangle Underwriters, Inc. v. Honeywell, Inc.[65] Triangle leased a complete computer system from Honeywell—hardware, standard software programs, and customized software programs. Honeywell claimed the system was fully operational in December 1970. At that point, Triangle decided to purchase the system rather than lease it. Until September 1972, Honeywell worked on the system but could *never* get it to operate without substantial errors. Triangle filed suit in August 1975 for breach of UCC warranties and fraud. The court granted judgment for Honeywell without a trial on the ground that the statute of limitations for contract and negligence claims had expired.

The appellate court ruled that (a) the UCC applies to a leased computer system, but the UCC claims are barred by the four-year UCC statute of limitations since the suit was filed more than four years after the defective delivery (January 1971); (b) the fraud claim is valid since in New York it carries a six-year statute of limitations from the commission of the fraud; and (c) the case should be remanded to the trial court for trial on fraudulent misrepresentation by Honeywell's personnel.

At trial, the jury awarded Triangle $1,089,000 in damages, which included $1,000,000 for the termination of its business. The trial judge reduced this award to $35,000, the difference between the price paid and the computer's actual value to Triangle. The appellate court affirmed the $35,000 award.

This case shows (a) the importance of the common law fraud remedy to protect the user and (b) the necessity for the computer user to take prompt legal action against the supplier because of the UCC statute of limitations. It is also significant that (c) the court declared this contract to be a sale of goods even though it involved a considerable amount of computer programming services and training services on Honeywell's part and all defects occurred with the programming services.

Earman Oil Co. v. Burroughs Corp.[66] Earman originally signed a contract to purchase a Burroughs computer system, which contained the following standard clauses in the sales order: integration and limitation of remedies and liability. Five days later, Earman changed its mind and decided to lease the computer. New contracts were prepared, Burroughs selling the computer to National Equipment Rental Co., which simultaneously leased the computer system to Earman. A few months later, the system was installed and trouble started immediately, which Burroughs attempted unsuccessfully to remedy. After two years of frustration, Earman sued for breach of oral express warranties, implied warranties of fitness and merchantability, and fraud. Burroughs defended on the basis of the limitation-of-remedies clause and the integration clause.

The appellate court ruled in favor of Burroughs on all counts:

a. the integration clause prohibited the evidence of fraud from being introduced since the representations of the sales force were not contained in the written contract;

b. the UCC applied since the lease was in economic reality a sale of goods and, even if it was not, the third-party beneficiary doctrine applied to protect the user with all rights and remedies given by the supplier to the buyer, which were nothing of value in this case;

c. the limitation of liability and remedies are not unconscionable since Earman was a sophisticated business presumably knowledgeable about the terms of the sales order; and

d. the limitation-of-remedies clauses precluded Earman from proving any implied warranty since these were effectively disclaimed by the sales order.

This case illustrates that (a) unconscionability is difficult to establish if the user is a businessperson. As in previous cases, (b) the limitation-of-remedies clause was upheld, preventing implied warranty litigation; (c) the integration clause was effective to prevent fraud litigation; and (d) the sales order was signed without the user really understanding it.

Carl Beasley Ford, Inc. v. Burroughs Corp.[67] On June 19, 1969, Beasley Ford contracted to buy a computer system from Burroughs with 13 programs installed and operational by January 2, 1970. The equipment was delivered in October 1969; on January 2, 1970, only one program was operational. By June, the remaining programs were installed; however, all were defective in some manner and repeated attempts to cure the problem failed. Finally, after Beasley Ford's patience wore out, the buyer demanded the equipment be removed and sued for rejection and consequential damages. Burroughs defended by claiming, first, that the contract prevented consequential damages due to the limitation-of-remedies and -damages clauses and, second, that the equipment was already accepted so no rejection was possible.

The court ignored those defenses and awarded Beasley Ford $56,012 in damages—$35,000 in a refund of the purchase price and $21,012 in consequential damages. The court ruled that the rejection remedy was available whenever the tender was imperfect provided the acceptance had not yet occurred. The court further ruled that the acceptance did not occur until after the user had a reasonable opportunity for inspection of the completed system. Merely possessing the equipment for seven months while the Burroughs programmers "experimented" was not an acceptance. Mere physical custody of the computer should never be a UCC acceptance.

The significance of this case lies in several areas:

a. the court applied UCC remedies to the failure to install customized programming services included with the hardware;

b. the rejection remedy was preserved by the buyer by taking prompt action—giving notice of rejection and filing suit as soon as it became apparent that the completed program would not work;

c. the user is given a reasonable opportunity to inspect the completed system before the right of rejection is lost due to any acceptance; and

d. the rejection or revocation-of-acceptance remedy is preferable because it allows both the return of the equipment for a full refund and consequential damages.

IMPLICATIONS FOR ACTION

The computer user must realize that contract law concerning computer acquisition is quite complex. As we have emphasized, the initial step toward protecting the user is to develop a team approach. A lawyer with significant commercial law and trial experience must be on the team along with a computer specialist.

Next, the user must develop precise specifications and standards for acquiring the system before negotiations begin. In negotiations with the supplier, the user should have several goals in mind:

a. removing the objectionable terms of the sales order through negotiation;

b. documenting in writing all significant events and representations made by the supplier;

c. attaching those representations to the final contract; and

d. negotiating for a clause insuring that the UCC applies to the final contract.

Finally, the user should become knowledgeable about the remedies available so that after the contract is executed, the user will be able to take proper and reasonable action. Also, the user must document all of the supplier's attempts to fix or program the computer in order to set up the failure-of-essential-purpose remedy and the postcontract rejection or revocation-of-acceptance, as well as express warranty, remedies.

For the user who has already signed the sales order, all is not lost for it is still possible (a) to resurrect the UCC implied remedies under Section 2-719(2) after the repair or replacement remedy fails; (b) to claim unconscionability, especially where the user is a nonbusiness user, an unsophisticated business user, or perhaps where the supplier unfairly refused to negotiate the terms of the sales order; and (c) to pursue the common-law remedies of fraud or mutual mistake.

REFERENCES

1. Robert Holmes, Associate Professor of Legal Studies, Bowling Green State University, Bowling Green, Ohio, is responsible for the legal analysis contained in this chapter.

2. UCC 2-102.

3. UCC 1-103.

4. J. Calamari & J. Perillo, *The Law of Contracts* 299–311 (2d ed. 1977).

5. Note that a mutual rescission out of court for whatever reason must be assented to by both parties. *See* Cornell Industries, Inc. v. Colonial Bank, 162 Ga.App. 822, 293 S.E.2d 370 (1982).

6. J. Calamari & J. Perillo, *supra* note 4, at 277–98.

7. *See, e.g.,* APLications, Inc. v. Hewlett-Packard Co., 672 F.2d 1076 (2d Cir. 1982), *aff'g* 501 F. Supp. 129 (S.D. N.Y. 1980); Triangle Underwriters, Inc. v. Honeywell, Inc., 457 F. Supp. 765 (E.D. N.Y. 1978), *aff'd in part, rev'd in part* 604 F.2d 737 (2d Cir. 1979), *remand aff'd* 651 F.2d 132 (2d Cir. 1981); Cunard Line Limited v. Abney, 540 F. Supp. 657 (S.D. N.Y. 1982).

8. *See* UCC 2-721.

9. Black, Jackson, & Simmons Insurance Brokerage, Inc. v. International Business Machines Corp., 109 Ill.App.3d 132, 440 N.E.2d 282 (1982).

10. UCC 2-512, 2-513.

11. UCC 2-601. *See* Carl Beasley Ford, Inc. v. Burroughs Corp., 361 F. Supp. 325 (E.D. Pa. 1973), *aff'd* 493 F.2d 1400 (3d Cir. 1974).

12. UCC 2-508.

13. UCC 2-711(1).

14. UCC 2-609.

15. UCC 2-711(3).

16. UCC 2-606, 2-607(2).

17. UCC 2-607(4).

18. *See* Carl Beasley Ford, Inc. v. Burroughs Corp., 361 F. Supp. 325 (E.D. Pa. 1973), *aff'd* 493 F.2d 1400 (3d Cir. 1974).

19. UCC 2-608(1).

20. UCC 2-608(2).

21. UCC 2-608(3).

22. UCC 2-725.

23. UCC 2-725(1).

24. UCC 2-608(2).

25. 119 N.H. 969, 409 A.2d 1352 (1979).

26. 94 N.M. 249, 609 P.2d 331 (1980).

27. Jones, Morrison, Stalnaker, P.A. v. Contemporary Computer Services, Inc., 414 So. 2d 637 (Fla. Dist. Ct. App. 1982).

28. UCC 2-313.

29. UCC 2-313(1)(b).

30. UCC 2-313(1)(c).

31. UCC 2-209(1).

32. UCC 2-313, comment 7.

33. UCC 2-314.

34. UCC 2-316.

35. J. White & R. Summers, *Handbook of the Law under the Uniform Commercial Code* 444 (1980).

36. Office Supply Co. v. Basic/Four Corp., 538 F. Supp. 776 (E.D. Wis. 1982).

37. UCC 2-315.

38. UCC 2-315, comment 5; J. White & R. Summers, *supra* note 35, at 360.

39. J. White & R. Summers, *supra* note 35, at 360.

40. APLications, Inc. v. Hewlett-Packard Co., 672 F.2d 1076, 1077 (2d Cir. 1982), *aff'g* 501 F. Supp. 129 (S.D. N.Y. 1980).

41. *See* UCC 2-316.

42. UCC 2-316(2).

43. UCC 2-312(1).

44. UCC 2-312(3).

45. UCC 2-719(2).

46. 479 F. Supp. 738 (D. N.J. 1979), *aff'd in part, remanded in part* 635 F.2d 1081 (3d Cir. 1980), *remand aff'd* 670 F.2d 1304 (3d Cir. 1982), *cert. dismissed* 102 S.Ct. 2918 (1982).

47. UCC 2-302; 2-719(3).

48. *See, e.g.,* Wilson Trading Corp. v. David Ferguson Ltd., 23 N.Y.2d 398, 297 N.Y.S.2d 108, 244 N.E.2d 685 (1968).

49. UCC 2-302(1).

50. *See* J. White & R. Summers, *supra* note 35, at 151–52.

51. *Id.*

52. *See* Jefferson Credit Corp. v. Marcano, 60 Misc.2d 138, 302 N.Y.S.2d 390 (N.Y. City Civ. Ct. 1969).

53. *See, e.g.,* Earman Oil Co. v. Burroughs Corp., 625 F.2d 1291 (5th Cir. 1980); Office Supply Co. v. Basic/Four Corp., 538 F. Supp. 776 (E.D. Wis. 1982); Chatlos Systems, Inc. v. National Cash Register Corp., 479 F. Supp. 738 (D. N.J. 1979), *aff'd in part, remanded in part* 635 F.2d 1081 (3d Cir. 1980), *remand aff'd* 670 F.2d 1304 (3d Cir. 1982), *cert. dismissed* 102 S.Ct. 2918 (1982); Westfield Chemical Corp. v. Burroughs Corp., 6 CLSR 438, 21 UCC Rep. 1293 (Mass. Super. Ct. of Hampden County 1977). *But see* Horning v. Sycom, 556 F.Supp. 819 (E.D. Ky. 1983), where the court referred to unconscionability due to disparate bargaining power in refusing to relinquish its jurisdiction because of a forum selection clause in a computer form contract which represented the "best job of boiler-plating since the building of the Monitor." *Id.* at 821.

54. UCC 2-712.

55. UCC 2-714.

56. 7 Kan.App.2d 676, 647 P.2d 820 (1982).

57. Chatlos Systems, Inc. v. National Cash Register Corp., 670 F.2d 1304 (3d Cir. 1982), *cert. dismissed* 102 S.Ct. 2918 (1982) (*aff'g remand of* 479 F. Supp. 738 (D. N.J. 1979), *aff'd in part, remanded in part* 635 F.2d 1081 (3d Cir. 1980)).

58. UCC 2-715(2).

59. UCC 2-718.

60. UCC 2-715(1).

61. 127 Ariz. 278, 619 P.2d 1055 (Ct. App. 1980).

62. 6 CLSR 438, 21 UCC Rep. 1293 (Mass. Super. Ct. of Hampden County 1977).

63. 479 F. Supp. 738 (D. N.J. 1979), *aff'd in part, remanded in part* 635 F.2d 1081 (3d Cir. 1980), *remand aff'd* 670 F.2d 1304 (3d Cir. 1982), *cert. dismissed* 102 S.Ct. 2918 (1982).

64. 670 F.2d 1304 (3d Cir. 1982).

65. 457 F. Supp. 765 (E.D. N.Y. 1978), *aff'd in part, rev'd in part* 604 F.2d 737 (2d Cir. 1979), *remand aff'd* 651 F.2d 132 (2d Cir. 1981).

66. 625 F.2d 1291 (5th Cir. 1980).

67. 361 F. Supp. 325 (E.D. Pa. 1973), *aff'd* 493 F.2d 1400 (3d Cir. 1974).

PART III

Personnel, Consulting Services, and Facilities Management

INTRODUCTION

Hardware and software serve little purpose without skilled personnel to implement and run them. If data-processing personnel perform their jobs incorrectly or inefficiently, the resulting errors and disruptions may prove disastrous to the operation of the firm. Thus, close attention should be given to staffing a firm's computer operations.

A number of sources exist to help determine computer personnel requirements. If the employer already has some data-processing personnel, they can offer suggestions. Vendors or consultants may also lend their expertise. Using these combined resources, the employer should analyze the different skill levels and the number of persons required at each level to meet the processing load. Such an analysis should include a projection of how the staff will grow along with the data-processing needs.

A company considering implementation of a computer system must decide whether to maintain its own data-processing staff or hire another firm to perform this function. The company using its own personnel has the maximum amount of control over data-processing operations along with the entire legal responsibility. For example, if an employee's action in the course of employment causes injury to a third party, the injured third party may sue the employer for the employee's wrongful actions. In addition, the employer must weigh the likelihood of union activity by its computer employees and the attendant obligations, a legal area of considerable uncertainty at present. Furthermore, when the company maintains its own staff, increased operational costs may result. Thus, an in-house data-processing staff permits a company to have complete control over its operations but it also bears all the risks of the enterprise.

On the other hand, the company hiring another firm to perform data-processing functions foregoes some of its ability to control the daily operations while relieving itself of many of the risks and uncertainties. For example, if the contracted firm is considered an independent contractor, its negligent or otherwise wrongful acts committed against third parties may not be imputed to the hiring firm. A properly drafted contract will cause the contractor to absorb increased costs, permitting the hiring firm to treat its data-processing costs as a fixed, predictable expense. These aspects are considered in more detail in the section on facilities management contracts.

Throughout the process of investigating, designing, and implementing a new computer system, a firm may turn to outside experts for advice on various dilemmas that its own personnel are unable to handle. The need to hire computer consultants, felt especially by smaller firms, requires a firm to consider various legal issues. Among these are the protection of private information and the legal remedies available to deal with unsatisfactory consultant services.

ACQUIRING DATA-PROCESSING PERSONNEL

This section discusses hiring options, the determination of whether data-processing personnel have federal protection under the National Labor Relations Act (NLRA), and individual employment contracts for nonunion computer personnel.

Hiring Options

A firm that decides to hire its own data-processing personnel can turn to employees already in the firm, new personnel, or a combination of these two sources. The proper method depends on such factors as lead time, cost, and the type of functions that are to be performed by the new personnel. The existence of labor contracts requiring that union members not be replaced by nonunion employees will also significantly affect whether existing employees should be retrained to take on the new functions. (Part VI discusses labor law in detail.)

One possibility for acquiring personnel is retraining the present staff to perform the necessary data-processing functions. Workers displaced from their old jobs due to computerization or other highly motivated employees may provide a pool of loyal employees who have a well-developed knowledge of the business. In some cases, the employer may be forced by the terms of a preexisting collective bargaining agreement to retrain its present employees.

The employees' attitudes toward change are an important factor to be considered. Explaining how this change will affect them and their jobs is of paramount importance. Some employees may not want to be retrained. Their current job may be challenging enough or they may be fearful of learning the new technology of computers and programming. These considerations are particularly important in the labor law area. Employees of a company with a history of labor problems, for example, may feel especially threatened by such a major change in their jobs, perhaps concerned that they are not capable of higher-technology work and that it will provide an excuse for discharge.

A second option for acquiring computer-trained employees is to hire new personnel. This option has the advantage of providing trained employees who will be ready to take over the functions when the computers are installed. Potential disadvantages are that the new personnel may be unfamiliar with the business and its specific needs, may have little or no loyalty to the company, and must be oriented to the user's specific information system.

In the usual situation, the business will combine old employees with new employees. Even when the present employees are retrained, there will still be some positions they may not be able to fill. Similarly, new personnel may not be needed for some operational programming or maintenance functions.

There are certain behavioral stresses that occur when combining new and old employees. The old staff may have an authority hierarchy worked out that cannot readily accommodate the new employees. Establishing a new hierarchy will take time and may temporarily strain morale. The new staff will probably have more job skills and expertise and may hold more responsible positions than the original staff. Moreover, a new young manager may be the object of employee resentment. All of these factors may contribute to employee unrest and dissatisfaction. This may, in turn, lead to increased union activism, which must be handled with care and sound legal advice. Existing personnel policies and procedures may need to be altered to conform to organizational changes. If the employees are represented by a union, the employer must bargain with the union over any necessary changes. Massive reorganizations may render the old bargaining unit (that is, the class of employees represented by the union) inappropriate, depending on the nature and structure of their new positions.

The best way to cope with this adjustment period is to recognize in advance that there may be problems. Large-scale structural and operational changes may wreak havoc on the soundest of firms. Prudent managers and directors will recognize the risks and, if necessary, engage a system consultant and labor attorney qualified to advise on such situations. Reckless handling of a major corporate change may result in labor litigation, stockholder dissatisfaction, lower profits, or, in the extreme, director liability for damages suffered by the corporation as a result of poor management decisions that would not have been made by ordinary directors similarly situated.

Collective Bargaining by Computer Personnel

The National Labor Relations Act (NLRA) grants employees the right to engage in concerted activities for their mutual aid or protection.[1] These rights include, among others, the right to have a union represent them in bargaining over terms and conditions of employment with the employer and the right to strike. These rights are enforced in several ways. The employer is barred from restraining, threatening, or coercing employees in the exercise of these rights; from discriminating against employees on the basis of their involvement in or support of a union (or any nonunion activity that is concerted and for mutual aid or protection of employees); and from refusing to bargain in good faith with a union chosen by its employees to be their bargaining representative.[2]

The issue of whether these rights apply to computer personnel is vitally important to an employer who has entrusted or is considering entrusting vital functions or highly sensitive information to a computer system. For example, if the production process is to some degree controlled or monitored by computer, participation by computer personnel in a strike could effectively shut down the entire plant. Similarly, if the employer and union are in the midst of negotiating a new collective bargaining agreement, with the union clamoring for more wages and benefits, it can be extremely damaging to the employer's bargaining position if the union is able to produce the company's most sensitive data relating to its financial status, market growth projections, product line expansions, future proposals for wage scales, and so on. The employer's ability to avoid these situations is controlled by the label that the National Labor Relations Board (NLRB) and federal courts will place on the employer's computer personnel.

The analysis of whether a particular class of personnel is entitled to federal protection begins with the statute's definition of "employee" since every employee, as defined by the statute, enjoys these rights. The statute begins with a broad definition of "employee," stating that "the term 'employee' shall include any employee," but then proceeds to exclude from its definition broad classes of employees including agricultural laborers, domestic servants, and independent contractors.[3] Although the NLRA does not apply to railroad or government workers, other federal statutes provide comparable protection to railroad and federal employees, and individual states may provide similar protection to their own employees. Thus, although this book addresses the ordinary private-sector labor relations setting, the same concerns may apply to government or railroad computer personnel under their specialized regulatory framework.

For our purposes, the most significant express exclusion from the statutory definition of "employee" is the exclusion of "supervisors." This exclusion is significant to the employer in at least two ways. First, the supervisor label affects the courses of action available to the employer when the supervisor engages in certain types of conduct. The NLRA protects certain activities such as union organization and striking when engaged in by employees. The NLRA prohibits employers from, for example, firing an employee for trying to persuade other workers to join a union. Since a supervisor is not an employee under the Act, the supervisor enjoys no such protection. Therefore, if a supervisor tries to help organize employees into a union, there is nothing in the Act to prevent the employer from taking disciplinary action, including discharge, against that supervisor.

Second, the supervisor label affects the scope of the bargaining unit. When employees desire to unionize, one of the functions of the National Labor Relations Board is to establish an appropriate bargaining unit, that is, the class of employees to be represented by the union. When an election is held to determine whether the employees want to be represented by a particular union, all members of the bargaining unit are entitled to vote. If the NLRB establishes a bargaining unit that includes persons who are arguably supervisors, the employer or union may be able to persuade the NLRB or federal court to overturn the election on the ground that the bargaining unit set by the NLRB was improper.

The statutory definition of "supervisor" envisions that a supervisor must have some authority over *other employees,* not over the work of the employer in general.[4] The supervisor must be authorized to exercise discretion in directing the work of other employees, to hire or fire other employees, or to effectively recommend such actions by the employer. For an employer to argue that a particular person is a supervisor and therefore exempt from the NLRA's protection, the employer must be able to point to specific ways in which that person has authority on behalf of the employer to exert significant employment control over some other employee or employees.

A federal court in *Exxon Pipeline Co. v. NLRB,*[5] discussed in the court cases section, applied this standard to computer operators and found that supervision of a computer console, even coupled with the authority to direct another department to take action based on the computer-generated information, did not qualify the computer operators as supervisors. This is an extremely important principle given the ability of employers to centralize many decision-making functions through computerization. Before the computerization, the decision maker may have received decisional input from subordinate people and directed these people to act consistently with his or her decisions. In this situation, the decision maker was arguably a supervisor since he or she effectively directed and controlled the work of other people. After computerizaton of the information-gathering functions, the decision maker may be fulfilling the same organizational role as before but is no longer a supervisor in the labor law sense and is therefore arguably entitled to assert federal rights as an employee. This attitude by the courts reflects a view that the computer replaces the people who otherwise would have been supervised and rejects the view that the supervisor merely becomes a "computer-aided supervisor."

Two important points may be drawn in our search for a means by which computer personnel may be exempted from application of the federal labor laws. First, the NLRB and courts will apparently apply the same "supervisory" standard to computer personnel as to noncomputer personnel: To be a supervisor, the person must have *other employees* under his or her direct organizational control. It is not enough that the computer enables the person to do work that would otherwise be done by several people. Therefore, the computer operators, programmers, and other computer personnel without subordinate personnel will be subject to unionization (unless they fit into some other exception). The employer should therefore take precautions to minimize the attendant risks, such as developing strike contingency plans and protecting sensitive data.

Second, the interpretation given the term "supervisor" suggests the need for caution when deciding whether and in what manner to computerize certain organizational functions. By replacing the functions of lower-level personnel with a computer, the employer may also be stripping the supervisor of his or her supervisory status. If that former supervisor fulfills crucial operational functions or has access to sensitive information, this factor may be of critical importance in the system design decisions. Such a situation may require reconsideration of the entire change or at least a restructuring of the former supervisor's place in the organizational hierarchy.

Even if some computer personnel do not fit the supervisory exception, they may fit into one of the other exceptions applied by the NLRB and courts. The first such exception is that of managerial employees. The NLRB has historically implied this exception for executives who, although not supervisors, are in a position to formulate, determine, and effectuate management policies.[6] The Supreme Court has found this exception to be intended by Congress to exclude all managerial employees from the scope of the labor laws.[7]

The managerial employees' exception could be applied only to computer personnel who are part of the management team in the sense that they contribute to formulation of company policy or are empowered to direct the implementation of those policies. The head of the data-processing department, system analysts, or other highly skilled personnel may be managerial employees, first, if they participate in company decision making, but only to the extent that they provide input to the management team in relation to the information system's present or potential capabilities or, second, if they assume responsibility for making changes necessary to meet the company's objectives.

It should be noted that although in most cases, a managerial employee may already be excluded from the labor laws as a supervisor, this is not necessarily so. It is possible that a managerial employee will possess the necessary authority in the company's overall operations to be considered a managerial employee yet not have the necessary authority over particular employees to be a supervisor.

The managerial employee exception will prevent certain critical computer personnel from falling within the scope of the federal labor laws but only to the extent that the company utilizes and relies upon them in the formulation and implementation of company policy. As with the supervisory exception, the fact that the company labels an employee a manager will not be determinative. The NLRB and courts will instead look in great detail into the reality of the situation to see to what extent the company does in fact rely on the employee's input to company policies. Thus, it would be highly inadvisable to try to make computer employees look like managerial employees if the company does not intend to actually vest them with that authority.

Another implied exception to the labor laws' application, somewhat related to the managerial exception, is that of confidential employees. Confidential employees "assist and act in a confidential capacity to persons who exercise 'managerial' functions in the field of labor relations."[8] To establish the confidential-employee status of a person, two elements are required. First, that employee must have a confidential relationship with a managerial employee. Second, that confidential relationship must involve confidential information about the company's labor relations policies. Access to other types of confidential information (such as marketing, technological, or financial) does not qualify employees for confidential-employee status. The typical confidential employee envisioned by the NLRB and courts is the personal secretary of a labor relations manager. The rationale of the exception is that the manager should be able to go about his or her job without worrying that subordinates are revealing strategies and other labor-sensitive information to the union.[9]

The case of *Union Oil Co. v. NLRB*[10] typifies the problems that arise in applying the confidential-employee exception to computer personnel. In that case, the NLRB had included three computer operators within the bargaining unit of clerical employees. The computer operators were responsible for entering and extracting data concerning customers and personnel and some records of capital and operating expenses. Any requests for employee information came to the computer operators from the personnel supervisor through his personal secretary. The personnel supervisor used the data to resolve grievances and to negotiate labor contracts. The computer operators were supervised, however, by another supervisor responsible for computer operations. In upholding the NLRB's bargaining unit determination, the court rejected persuasive arguments by the employer that the computer operators should be regarded as confidential employees.

The employer contended that the computer operators had a confidential relationship with the personnel supervisor. This contention received strong support from the uncontested facts that his personal secretary was a confidential employee and that the computer operators performed duties previously carried out by the personal secretary. The court did not agree with the employer's contention, stating simply that the duties taken over by the computer operators were purely clerical in nature. The court did not elaborate on why the clerical nature of the duties was significant. The question remains why, if the handling of confidential labor information by the personal secretary makes him or her a confidential employee (whether the work is "purely clerical" or not), are not the computer operators also confidential employees when they assume that same function?

The court then cited the "more significant" fact that the computer operators were supervised by the computer operations supervisor, leading the court to conclude that since the computer operators acted as record custodians for persons who do not formulate or implement labor policy, they were not confidential employees with a labor relations nexus. This rationale is likewise open to some question since it seems to place undue emphasis on the way in which the employer set up the firm's supervisory hierarchy rather than focusing on the purpose of the exception, to protect the confidentiality of labor-related managerial information. For example, it may be inferred from the court's emphasis on the departmental lines that if the labor relations supervisor had his or her own computer operator in the department, that operator may have been a confidential employee even though his or her function may have been identical to those of the company operators. Such a distinction, although defensible in light of the traditional requirement that a confidential employee bear a direct confidential relationship to a labor relations manager, appears to serve the purpose of the exception poorly. The court's rationale appears to ignore the implications of a company's computerized central nervous system that contains all of the same confidential information that used to be pigeonholed into appropriate departments.

The court indicated one alternative means by which the computer operators might qualify as confidential employees. The court noted that prior NLRB decisions had afforded confidential status to employees with access to confidential information about anticipated changes from collective bargaining negotiations. The company contended that the operators' access to capital and expense records, as well as to personnel information that might be used in contract negotiations, entitled the operators to confidential status. The court held that since there had been no proof that the employees had access to the precise labor rates the employer was willing to pay, this general company information was insufficient to establish confidentiality in the labor sense. It may be inferred that in a case in which the operators, for example, ran test programs calculating the effects of potential wage rates that might be reached through negotiations with the union, confidential status might be justified.

One other aspect of the court's opinion deserves mention. The court called attention to the fact that the computerized employment data were distributed on a limited basis, since only five or six supervisory personnel were authorized to obtain it and the three operators were not allowed to extract information on their own. The court thus seemed to minimize the possibility that the operators would improperly use the sensitive information merely because such access would be unauthorized. Whether this presumption holds true, of course, depends on the practical safeguards used by the employer to prevent unauthorized access to sensitive information stored by the computer. The employer should therefore take such measures.

As with the previously discussed exceptions, it is inadvisable to try to create the appearance of confidential employee status if that status is not otherwise beneficial to the overall system design. It may be advisable, if it is consistent with the company's organizational needs, to treat labor-sensitive information separately from other stored information. For example, a special access code known only to labor relations personnel or specially designated computer personnel answerable to a labor relations manager may help to establish the required labor nexus between the persons with access to the confidential information and the labor relations manager.

The confidential employee exception at first glance is an appealing way to exclude computer personnel from labor law protection since its very purpose is to protect the confidentiality of the employer's labor-sensitive information, one of the primary employer concerns regarding unionization of computer operators. As applied by the NLRB and courts, however, the confidential employee exception is very narrow, and only in a rather specialized category of cases will it serve to exclude computer employees from labor law protection.

One partial exception may be applied to computer personnel. Professional employees, although endowed with the usual rights to organize, are treated specially in determining the appropriate bargaining unit. Professional employees are defined by federal statute as employees who engage in predominantly intellectual work, varied in character, as opposed to routine mental or physical work; consistently exercise discretion and judgment; produce work output that is not susceptible to standardization in a given period of time; and require advanced knowledge in a field of learning customarily acquired by a prolonged course of specialized intellectual instruction in an institution of higher learning as opposed to a general academic education, apprenticeship, or training in routine mental, manual, or physical processes.[11]

Professional employees are subject to the labor laws and enjoy all the rights and protections afforded to other employees. Professional employees may not, however, be included within the same bargaining unit as nonprofessional employees unless a majority of the professional employees vote to be so included.[12] Thus, professional employees may insist on having their own bargaining representative independently of the rank-and-file employees.

To qualify as a professional employee, a computer person must be highly educated and exercise independent judgment on an everyday basis. The technical training and primarily mental work of programmers is probably not enough. In one recent case, a federal court stated that "while the Board has previously determined that a systems analyst with wide discretion and significant amounts of technical training might be considered a 'professional employee' in certain situations, it has generally considered computer programmers to be technical and thus nonprofessional employees."[13]

An employer could try to create the appearance of professional employee status for certain sensitive positions by hiring only persons with the best possible educational credentials in that particular area. This is advisable, however, only if the employer is willing to compensate those employees commensurately with their qualifications and to require the actual exercise of those skills on an everyday basis, for two reasons.

First, professional employee classification will be made after intense scrutiny of job requirements, the employee's qualifications, and the nature of the actual duties. It does not matter that the highly specialized training required to be a professional employee might be desirable for the position if the actual work does not require those skills.

Second, it must be remembered that professional employees do enjoy organizational rights, and if they perceive that they are not being treated fairly by the employer, they have the legal right to choose to be represented by either their own union or the same union that represents other employees.

The professional employee classification is helpful to the employer of computer professionals who might qualify since the employer can legitimately try to insulate them from the effects of the unionization of the rest of the company by treating them as professionals. If the rest of the company is unionized or in the process of being organized, the professional employee exception may save a few positions of high responsibility, which otherwise would not have been within any of the absolute exceptions, from being included in the bargaining unit. If the employer has treated the computer professionals fairly so they feel that they do not need a union, then the computer professionals will probably choose to place their trust in the company as in the past rather than throw their lot in with the rank-and-file employees or choose their own union.

It is probably inevitable that some computer employees will be susceptible to unionization, that is, will not fall within any of the previously described exceptions. It is then their right to choose whether they will be represented by a union. Many very large employers have successfully avoided unionization for many years by maintaining fair personnel policies and excellent benefit programs. Once employees begin to think about organizing, however, any actions by the employer that might impermissibly influence their choice may result in sanctions by the NLRB. A labor lawyer should therefore be consulted before making any changes affecting personnel during a period of union-organizing activity.

Once computer personnel have chosen to be represented by a union, the employer is under a legal duty to bargain with the union about all terms and conditions of employment for those personnel. At this stage, the employer should be concerned about minimizing the risks of unionization identified earlier: protection of sensitive information and the threat of strikes.

Although protection of sensitive information is discussed generally elsewhere (see Parts IV and V), it is emphasized here that the disclosure of labor-sensitive information could undermine the firm's bargaining position. Examples of such information include data on the company's overall financial position, employees' personal information not otherwise available to the union, current wage–benefit information, and program runs calculating the effects of potential wage–benefit proposals. As with other sensitive information, access should be strictly monitored and controlled through the use of logs, secret access codes, physical security to prevent copies from leaving restricted areas, and so on. Access should be limited to a minimal number of persons who have a need to handle the data, preferably nonbargaining unit personnel if practicable (that is, supervisors, labor relations managers or their confidential employees, or nonunionized professional employees).

The risk of a debilitating strike is a serious one but it is the same type of risk that employers have had to deal with since the inception of federal labor laws. The right to strike has been considered the very essence of the employees' bargaining power. The Congress, courts, and the NLRB have uniformly held that this right outweighs contrary interests of the employer. The advent of the computer age has not changed this balancing of interests in favor of employees. The difference is simply that in the past, perhaps hundreds of workers would have had to go on strike to make an impact on the employer. When a business is dependent on its computer system for its most vital functions, however, a labor dispute or strike may be especially damaging. Now a handful of key computer employees may possess the same bargaining power as hundreds of production workers. The courts and NLRB have not modified, and are not likely to modify, their strike rules for employers of computer personnel merely because those employees are fortunate enough to enjoy greater bargaining leverage than the ordinary noncomputer employee. The employer must therefore, like noncomputer employers, take measures to minimize the potential for business losses due to strikes.

The first place the employer should look to minimize the strike potential is at the bargaining table. The employment contract should contain provisions aimed at preventing labor disputes. The contract should stipulate specific exclusive grievance procedures in advance, ending in binding arbitration or mediation of grievances. This grievance procedure should describe the different steps involved in resolving a grievance with set time frames for responses and persons to be included in the resolution (makeup of boards, independent arbitrators, and so on). An agreement not to strike should then also be made a part of the contract.

The employer should nevertheless have a contingency plan ready in case of a strike. This plan should identify the most essential data-processing functions that can be carried out only by the computer as well as those that can be delayed until the strike is over. In addition, there should be a current list of management personnel who are available and qualified to run the computers. If there is an insufficient number, the employer should check into sources of qualified replacement workers. The employer may also investigate the availability and cost of buying computer time on an emergency basis and, if feasible, contract ahead of time to use a compatible computer system with its personnel. Data and software backups should be maintained. The user's hardware and software vendors and consultants may be helpful in locating potential standby computer systems.

The Individual Employment Contract

If some or all of its computer employees are not unionized, the employer needs to consider setting some terms and conditions of employment for those employees. The employment relationship is considered a contractual one regardless of whether the parties ever sit down and work out specified terms. In the absence of an express contract to the contrary, the law implies an "at will" contract under which the employee agrees to perform services required of him or her by the employer and the employer agrees to pay for those services. The contract is terminable at the will of either party; that is, the employee may quit or be discharged at any time, for any reason (subject to certain labor and anti-discrimination statutes), without prior notice. It should be apparent that these sketchy implied contract terms do very little to protect the interests of either the employee or the employer. It is therefore almost always advisable to work out some express terms of employment setting out the nature of work to be performed, the agreed compensation, and perhaps a minimum term of employment. The same employee contract used for noncomputer personnel will serve as a starting point for the contract used for computer personnel. To deal with problems particularly acute in the current data-processing industry,[14] however, new provisions should be included such as noncompetition clauses, obligations to protect trade secrets and other confidential material, and specifications for ownership of employee-developed programs or innovations.

Noncompetition Clauses. In the highly competitive computer industry, new computer enterprises spring up rapidly. Noncompetition clauses are desirable to protect a company from the prospect of having its employees take customers, technological information, or marketing information with them when they leave the employer. These clauses generally provide that for a specific period of time after leaving the employer, the employee will not compete with the employer by starting his or her own business or by working for a competitor.

Courts generally view such clauses with some degree of disfavor for social policy reasons. Noncompetition clauses limit the employee's employment opportunities after the employment relationship has come to an end. Thus, while the employment relationship is technically ended and the employer is free of any obligation to the former employee, the former employee is still, by the terms of the contract, bound to refrain from seeking employment that allows him or her to enjoy the full benefit of his or her range of skills. Courts may view this situation to be not only unfair as applied to the individual employee but also socially undesirable in that human potential remains dormant and competition is artificially limited. Courts therefore tend to enforce anticompetition covenants only in limited types of cases.

Courts are more prone to enforce restrictive covenants when the promise is made in conjunction with the sale of an ownership interest in the company. When the departing employee is also the proprietor or a principal partner or shareholder, courts tend to view the covenant not to compete as an altogether legitimate means to protect the company from having its market torn between the departing owner and the remaining enterprise.[15]

Courts impose stricter requirements before they will enforce an anticompetition covenant against an employee who is not also an owner. First of all, some courts require that the employee's services be somehow unique or extraordinary so that the covenant is necessary to protect the employer from unfair competition or the disclosure of trade secrets. Second, courts require that the promise not to compete be made in exchange for some valuable consideration, that is, some return promise or legal obligation. If the covenant not to compete is made at the beginning of the employment relationship, there is generally no problem with consideration since the employer has given its promise to employ the employee, as well as any other promises made in the employment contract.

Problems with consideration may arise if the employer elicits the covenant after the employment relationship has begun. Some courts may find no consideration and thus invalidate the covenant since the employer has given up nothing in return for the covenant;[16] that is, the employer has agreed to do nothing more than it has already agreed to do. Other courts have found consideration, rendering the promise enforceable, by viewing the covenant as a condition to continued employment. These courts adopt the view that the employer has agreed to continue to employ the employee in exchange for the employee's covenant not to compete. This rationale applies, however, only if the employer was not under a preexisting obligation to continue employing the employee. The requirement of consideration to sustain an anticompetition covenant will vary from state to state, so local law should be researched and complied with. The safest course in accordance with general contract law principles, however, would be to have the employee agree to such covenants as part of the initial employment contract. If the employee has been working without such a covenant but the need for one has since been recognized, it may be prudent for the employer to return something of value in exchange for the promise, such as a promotion or increase in compensation.

Even if otherwise enforceable, these clauses are usually enforced only as long as the contract terms are reasonably related to the interest being protected, that is, as long as there are geographical and time limits on the agreement. A more stringent standard of reasonableness may be applied in the context of employee covenants than in ownership interest covenants. The court will not enforce covenants so restrictive that they effectively prevent the employee from finding employment.[17] Given the high mobility of personnel and rapid obsolescence of ideas in the industry, it may be to the employer's benefit to base the limitations on a time period, such as one year, rather than on a geographic area, such as within a 500-mile radius. Some courts, however, may refuse to enforce a restrictive covenant that contains no geographic limitation. If the employer is located in such a jurisdiction, a broader area and time period may be set while narrowing the scope of the restriction to work in the same data-processing field, such as health-care systems.

The effect that a court will give to an unreasonably broad covenant also varies from court to court.[18] Some courts will find that an overbroad covenant renders the entire covenant void and unenforceable. Others may enforce only the reasonably limited portion while still others will simply impose their own "reasonable" restrictions in place of the unreasonable ones. A definite trend can be seen in recent cases toward permitting courts to modify unreasonable, overly broad covenants to make them reasonable and enforceable. The individual state laws involved should be referred to since some states forbid covenants not to compete altogether while other courts vary significantly in their interpretations of such provisions.

Secrecy Provisions. The employment contract should expressly make clear the employee's duty to keep certain types of information confidential. This duty of secrecy may be critical in two respects. First is the protection of sensitive information that, if disclosed, would be damaging to the employer or the employer's customers.[19] Second is the proprietary nature of the employer's innovative ideas, which must be maintained through trade secrecy law.[20]

The first rationale is important in the purely competitive sense of protecting the company's customer lists, future products, marketing plans, and the like from disclosure to present or future competitors (including the employees themselves who may attempt to form their own competing enterprise). Moreover, the employer may have express or implied agreements to maintain the confidentiality of information in the employer's possession that belongs to a third party, such as customers or partners in a joint venture. The employer would be liable to the third party for any damages caused by an employee's unauthorized disclosure or use of the information. By making expressly clear the employee's duty to keep such information confidential, the employer lays the groundwork for either holding the employee liable in monetary damages for any loss attributable to the employee's breach of the agreement, using the breach as a ground for disciplinary action or discharge or, if detected early enough, bringing suit to prevent an unauthorized disclosure or use of the information.

The second rationale for including a secrecy provision in the employment contract is related to the trade secrecy protection afforded new ideas, discussed in greater detail in Part IV. In general, if the owner of unique or innovative information is able to convince the court that adequate precautions were taken to identify and safeguard such information as confidential, the courts will treat the information as the exclusive property of the party claiming ownership. Having stressed to employees that information labeled confidential must be treated as such, the employer will be in a better position to convince a court of its exclusive ownership of the information should the need arise to seek legal redress for the theft or misappropriation of such ideas.

It should be noted that the recitation of a duty of secrecy in an employment contract is only a first step toward protecting sensitive information. This provision gives the employee an initial notice that a secrecy duty exists and may aid in establishing legal liability against an employee or other person who misappropriates the information. But by the time the employer seeks legal recourse, the damage has been done. The employer, even if successful in a lawsuit, can realistically hope to recoup only a portion of its investment, regardless of the damages obtained, since any advantage that the information's confidentiality held is lost when the confidentiality is breached. Thus, the actual security of the information depends on how the employer follows up on its confidentiality and security programs by clearly labeling which information is confidential, restricting access to essential personnel, strictly monitoring use, and so on.

Even without an explicit contract provision on secrecy, if the employer can convince the court from other evidence of confidential treatment that the information qualifies for trade secret status, the employer may sue for damages or prevent, by means of an injunction, the use of misappropriated information. In addition, criminal charges may be brought for embezzlement or larceny of trade secrets. The inclusion of a secrecy clause in the employment contract can be instrumental in establishing the trade secret status of the information in court, the employee's duty to maintain its confidentiality, and the employee's state of mind or degree of intent regarding any breach of the duty of confidentiality.

Ownership of Employee-Developed Programs. To establish a claim to a trade secret or intellectual discovery as just outlined, the employer must be able to establish ownership of the relevant information. The typical non-computer production employee has no individual claim to the work product made while in the employ of another. In the rapid-growth computer industry with its high premium on innovative technologies, the work product is often intellectual rather than physical. This distinction has created problems in trying to determine ownership of the employee's work product. An all-too-real danger in the computer industry is that an employee, while working for a company, will make a new intellectual discovery or become privy to other information with a high potential for profit and try to turn a personal profit with the information. An employee contract should clearly define who has the rights to programs, ideas, and other intellectual discoveries made by employees while in the company's employ, both on company and non-company time. The contract should also include a provision whereby the employee agrees to disclose all intellectual discoveries capable of being used by the company. This type of clause informs the employee about the nature and duties of his or her relationship with the employer and may be instrumental in establishing the ownership of ideas when legal redress becomes necessary.

The ownership-of-ideas issue is another situation (like the anticompetition covenant) in which courts have been moved by the perceived fairness of the circumstances. At least one court has stated that since an employee cannot be deprived of the later use of the mental knowledge, experience, and skills the employee has acquired during his or her employment, an employee may have an interest in an innovation that he or she has developed that is at least equal to the employer's interest in it (see the court cases section). Employers should see that ownership-of-ideas clauses are carried out fairly for their employees. For example, a court would not be likely to to enforce such a provision against an employee who presented his or her ideas to the employer only to have the employer reject them.[21] Similarly, an innovation developed by an employee on the employee's own time and un-related to his or her normal work may not be regarded by a court as fairly claimable by the employer.

A provision that permits the company to have a first option to buy all employee innovations at an agreed price (or price formula) may be viewed more favorably by a court. If the company rejects the idea, then the employee would be free to develop the idea on his or her own time. Such a clause requires a great deal of accurate foresight by the employer about the potential of new ideas to avoid missing good opportunities, but it may encourage employees to bring their own ideas and pet projects to the company rather than squirrel them away for their own development and potential profit. The typical provision for absolute ownership by the employer may actually serve to encourage employees to secretly develop personal projects for themselves, and courts are not in unanimous agreement that the employees are wrong for doing so.

FACILITIES MANAGEMENT CONTRACTS

Facilities management refers to a contractual arrangement by which a completely independent third party provides complete on-site computer operations for a company. The facilities management company assumes responsibility for the day-to-day operation of the computer, design and implementation of new computer systems, and maintenance of application and system software.[22] The company may also be responsible for selection of hardware. Facilities management operations are common in governmental data-processing as well as in private-sector organizations that would rather not get involved with day-to-day management of their own data-processing operations.

In a typical facilities management agreement, the facilities management company takes control over the computer equipment or hardware (whether it is leased or owned) and a company's data-processing personnel (operations, programming, and system), who become employees of the facilities management company. In return, all computer needs are provided for by the facilities management company for a specified monthly fee. Many of the same considerations applicable to facilities management also apply to contracting for computer services, except that in the latter case, the service bureau will operate from its own facilities instead of the user's place of business.

The Decision to Contract

There are very important advantages and disadvantages to a facilities management service. Successfully implemented, the service can provide predictable cost outlays, qualified data-processing personnel and management resources, and significantly greater computer capacity. Potential disadvantages include loss of control over computer operations, security, and flexibility. The following sections discuss factors to consider before hiring a facilities management company.

Flexibility and Control. The use of facilities management will almost always result in some loss of flexibility—the ability to respond rapidly to an immediate or special need. This loss of flexibility and slower response time may be nothing more than an irritation under normal day-to-day operations, but if a financial opportunity depends on the immediate generation of information at an unusual time or in a different format, it can be very costly.

The user should anticipate a very real loss of control over data-processing activities. Even though the user may assign a highly trained expert to supervise the data-processing operations, as a practical matter, that person may have very little authority. The expert will have first responsibility, but no control over the data processing—he or she must go through the facilities management.

When a facilities management or service contract is entered into, both parties usually foresee that they will be able to work together to their mutual benefit. This ideal working relationship often breaks down even in ordinary circumstances, in which event the user could be left in an uncertain position if critical functions are in the hands of the computer service or management company. For example, in one case a hotel utilized an independent computerized reservation system and failed to pay its bill.[23] The reservation system began to tell potential customers that the hotel could not accommodate them although in reality it could. The hotel sued for actual and punitive damages on the basis of injurious falsehood. Although the hotel won at the trial level, the decision was reversed on appeal.

It may be possible to bargain for contract terms that provide the user with greater control. The desirability and likelihood of success of such a course of action is diminished, however, by the very nature and purpose of the facilities management contract. First, the primary reason for wanting to hire a facilities management company is to eliminate the need for having one's own computer operations personnel. Second, the facilities management team is able to do what it does because of its specialized personnel and cost-efficient procedures. Too much interference by the user could upset the effectiveness and diminish the value of the operation to both parties. The facilities management company may, for this reason, be understandably reluctant to give the user too much control over the day-to-day computer operations, at least not without an increase in the cost of the company's services.

Data-Processing Personnel. Facilities management services are specialized and may be able to provide services tailored to a user's particular field such as banking, engineering, or sales. This is an advantage to implementing a new computerized service—the facilities management will have the experts who will get the user's system on line and generate the information required. Once the system is operating properly, these high-priced experts are assigned to other clients until needed for modification of existing programs or development of new programs. A facilities management may already have developed a proprietary program that can be used as is or could be easily modified to meet a user's needs at a fraction of the cost of buying a program or hiring someone else to create it.

A disadvantage is signing over personnel and equipment to the facilities management firm. Once assigned, these personnel may be transferred or let go unless this is prohibited by the contract. This can be a detriment to the user since the new staff will probably not have as good an understanding of the business and its operations as the former employees.

The user should also consider the firm's obligations to its former employees when transferring to a facilities management operation. A Blue Cross/Blue Shield organization transferred its data-processing employees to a facilities management firm with assurances that their benefit programs would be unaffected.[24] As the new facilities management personnel became acquainted with the Blue Cross operations, however, all of the former Blue Cross personnel, by some coincidence, seemed to find themselves being discharged and thereby deprived of their pension benefits. A multimillion dollar lawsuit is now in progress against both the facilities management and Blue Cross. It should be noted that even if Blue Cross had nothing to do with the treatment of its former employees, it will have to pay a lot of money to prove that in court, if it can be proved at all. The user should try to avoid such situations by investigating the facilities management firm's labor relations background.

It should also be noted that if the user's former data-processing personnel were unionized and the facilities management rehires a sufficient number of them to do the same work, the facilities management firm may be obligated to bargain with the union as a successor employer.[25] If the facilities management has been nonunion and wishes to remain so, this factor may prevent the user from persuading the facilities management to retain the former employees. In either event the user would be obligated to bargain with the union over the impact of the change on its employees.

When the time comes to reassume management of the computer systems, the user may be faced with some formidable staff problems. Former employees may not wish to rejoin the staff or may have moved to other facilities management projects. The specialized staff of the facilities management company may have created software that is more complex than necessary, and specialized data-processing personnel may be required to keep it running, or it may need to be entirely rewritten. Software may have been tailored more to the particular configuration of hardware than to the user's information needs. The personnel left by the facilities management when the user reassumes control may not be experienced enough to maintain the system or to teach new staff, requiring additional outlays for qualified personnel. Thus, the potential user of a facilities management firm must be sure to factor into the user's cost-benefit analysis the potential outlay required after the contract to maintain the computer operations installed by the facilities management team.

Security. Having another company's employees on the premises will present special security problems. People with access to the information in a computer will, in most cases, have access to all of the user's confidential information. A security system will need to be developed to restrict access to trade secrets, confidential financial information, and other critical data. One possible solution is to assign only one person or a select few persons on the facilities management staff to be responsible for that information.

The facilities management, as part of its outside computer services, may have a competitor of the user as a client. This creates potential security problems that should be provided for in advance.

The insurance agent should also be consulted before making a final decision to use facilities management. Having nonemployees on the premises may require additional insurance at a higher cost.

Selecting Facilities Management Companies

If the user decides to use facilities management, specific companies should be investigated. The investigation should include the prior record of a company as well as interviews with its former and present customers. Facilities management companies reluctant to give the names of current or past customers or the names of only one or two should be considered suspect.

A second consideration is the financial stability of the facilities management company. Before entering a long-term business relationship with a facilities management company, with its special reliance of one party on the other, the user should be satisfied that the other party is stable enough to survive for the entire period. Otherwise, the user may be left not only with no one to fulfill the contract but also with no one to sue to recover any of the losses. If there are doubts about the capitalization or stability of a firm but the user wants to take a chance on it, such as with a relatively new but promising firm, the user should require the firm to provide a financially stable individual or company to underwrite or guarantee the firm's financial obligations. A certified financial statement along with credit reports, banks, and business associations should be consulted. Financial reporting services listing the company should be consulted. If the facilities management is publicly traded, the user may request a report from the Securities and Exchange Commission in Washington, D.C. If there is any question about the facilities management's financial stability that is not answered to the user's satisfaction, the firm should be dropped from consideration.

Contract Considerations

Once a facilities management company has been selected, the contract process begins. There are special problems associated with facilities management contracts that do not arise in nonoperation contract settings. First, the functions to be performed by the facilities management company must be precisely described. Second, it is necessary to establish a cost formula with performance standards and a system for measuring and monitoring performance. Third, the user must provide for turnover and turnback procedures for initiation of the contract and for termination or expiration; that is, transferring data-processing functions to the facilities management company and reassuming them at the end of the contract. Finally, there are considerations regarding the use of specific clauses in the contract that may work to the detriment of the user. These are all discussed next.

Key Functions. In facilities management, a variety of tasks and functions need to be performed by the company. Since it is impossible to define all tasks, let alone each step in a task, the user should identify key activities that should be performed by the company. The proper completion of these functions should require the performance of other, more numerous, secondary activities, described in the following paragraphs. All provisions should be as specific as possible in expressing the parties' intentions; the goal should be to furnish a court with a document that can be used as a yardstick for measuring each party's performance of its obligations.

Computer Operations. The user should describe in detail what will be sent to the computer room, what format the data should be in, what processing is required on the data and in what time frame, and what output should be provided from the computer, including the format and distribution.

Equipment. The present and future hardware configuration should be outlined along with considerations of ownership. The physical environment required for that hardware should be described in detail along with who is responsible for changes in and maintenance of that environment. Naturally, the use and maintenance of the hardware should be laid out in detail.

Software. Each program that the user requires for the performance of the firm's business should be listed along with specifications of how and when such programs can be modified by the facilities management company. Agreements for development of new applications software should list in detail the tasks the software should perform, when implementation should take place, and ownership of the new programs. The maintenance and development of software required for the continued, smooth operation of the computer should be detailed along with responsibility for any processing delays.

Secrecy. The same considerations requiring protection of confidential information by employees require similar protection by facilities management firms. It may be even more important in the facilities management context since the user does not have as much ability to oversee and control the use of the firm's information in the hands of the other company as it does when in the hands of the firm's own employees. Moreover, in the employee context, the law will impose a duty upon the employee not to act negligently or adversely toward the employer's interest, even absent a specific contract provision to that effect. Against the facilities management firm, on the other hand, the law will presume an "arm's-length" bargaining relationship with no duties beyond those spelled out in the agreement.

Predictability of Costs. A very attractive feature of facilities management is the ability to fix data-processing costs over an extended period of time, usually several years. In a facilities management agreement, however, these costs may not be as fixed as they first appear. Most contracts will have some form of adjustment or escalator formula. Unless a company is very careful in structuring the formula, the result could be a service that has neither a fixed nor predictable cost. Common formulas are based on the cost-of-living index and allow adjustments for substantial increases in the use of data-processing equipment.

Two common methods of measuring the volume of data processing are the number of input transactions processed and increased margin usage (based on the usage meter on the hardware). The first is difficult to measure and requires a fairly complex record system. The second has a potential for increasing costs because it rewards inefficiency. It does nothing to discourage poor planning, poor performance, or incompetence, which can increase the amount of rerunning, testing, and processing required to successfully execute application programs.

If a contract is properly worded, the facilities management service assumes the risk of a financial overrun and cannot pass this cost on. That means if the cost of equipment increases significantly or if wages go up substantially, the facilities management company has to bear the additional expense.

It may also be possible to shift expenses arising out of delays in processing to the facilities management. To do this requires a clause detailing the user's responsibilities for getting the information into the proper format for use by the facilities management along with specific time guidelines for processing and receipt of the information generated. This time frame can be the basis for awarding damages or offsetting charges arising from delays in processing.

Performance Standards. Since the success of the user's business will depend upon the facilities management company's successful performance of the required tasks, the user must establish in the contract exactly what successful performance is. In defining this, the user will more than likely discover appropriate criteria for monitoring and evaluating the facilities management company. Some possible measures of performance might include the number of reports distributed on schedule, compliance with a hierarchical listing of processing jobs from most to least critical, and statistics on the number of times each job required processing before being successfully completed.

Systems should be established to perform the measuring according to the agreed-upon standards. A dual monitoring system providing both internal system controls and manually prepared reports offers the best protection for the user. Internal system controls generated by the computer are the most desirable. If carefully designed, they can be the basis for easy resolution of disputes. Manually prepared reports of late output, number of job reruns, and other problems supplement and verify the internal controls. Monitoring of software development may require audits by independent consultants to ensure quality and compatibility with the user's overall system.

Turnover and Turnback Procedures. The successful transition of data processing from the hands of the user to the facilities management company depends on both parties agreeing on the present condition of hardware, software, personnel, and tasks to be performed. Each piece of hardware should be included in the turnover list along with the usage meter reading and information on whether the hardware is owned or leased. All programs that will be handed over to the company and brief descriptions of the functions they perform should also be included. Any documentation put in the hands of the facilities management company should be listed as well. All personnel who will become employees of the company should be listed along with their age, seniority, pay level, pension rates, and other pertinent information. Finally, the functions to be performed by the facilities management company during the transition period should be outlined.

The need for turnback lists can arise under two very different conditions. In the first, the contract has run to term or the parties have mutually agreed to end the contract. In the second, one or both parties may have breached the contract and the user must reassume control over processing. In either event, the procedures and personnel required by the user to reassume control over operations must be specified in detail.

Since facilities management personnel may not wish to join the user's company, provisions should be included in the contract to allow use of these personnel until replacements can be found within a reasonable time. One method is to continue the original agreement on a day-to-day basis using a rate formula on jobs performed.

Because the facilities management usually operates several computer installations, it may furnish excess computer capacity at each site for backup in the event of a computer failure or overload. Similarly, since the facilities management company often provides outside services during slack time, they may acquire hardware having much greater capacity than the user's company needs. In either case, when the user reassumes control, the cost of the excess capacity can be prohibitive.

The user should be alert to changes that have been made to hardware or software for the benefit of the facilities management company. Larger, more expensive hardware may have been acquired to handle the additional load of outside users and may be more expensive than the more modest processing requirements of the user. Software tailored to more general use or a specific configuration of hardware may be of little benefit to the user in the long run. Provisions should be included in the contract for resolving these potential problems.

Yet another important consideration is the protection of proprietary rights. Unless spelled out in detail, the user may be handed a computer without application programs or programs developed for the user may be used by a competitor. Procedures for handling software and business data including labeling, copying, and transferability should be included. The ownership rights to all data, present and future application programs, and systems software should be detailed. Agreement should be reached on the permissible uses of programs developed for the user by the facilities management company.

Specific Contract Provisions. From past litigation, it is possible to highlight a number of common potential pitfalls to avoid in writing the contract agreement. Some specific contract considerations follow.

Control and cooperation clauses work generally to the benefit of the facilities management. Control clauses give the user final responsibility for acts and decisions when in reality the user has little, if any, influence over the operations. Cooperation clauses require both parties to cooperate with each other. Used together, these clauses become escape hatches for facilities management. They may avoid responsibility by claiming the user had final control over all decisions. They may also suggest that the user failed to cooperate by not presenting the material in the proper format or by failing to give more opportunities to correct a program. A more acceptable provision may be to set limits on the user's duty to cooperate by detailing specific dispute resolution procedures, with reasonable and appropriate time limits, to be followed in the event of disagreements about the terms or performance of the contract.

Integration clauses say that the contract is the final and complete expression of the parties' agreement. These clauses prevent the use of past conversations or letters to explain or clarify what the contract meant when it was signed. The court can consider only what is actually in the contract or specifically referred to by the contract. Along with the integration clause is usually a statement that all modifications of the contract must be in writing. Integration clauses can be a real problem because in setting up a facilities management relationship, there will be many contracts, letters, and negotiations that occur over a period of time. As a general rule, if the facilities management firm has made any significant promises or offers that are not included in the contract, the user should strenuously object to the inclusion of an integration clause until and unless those promises are included in the contract. If more than one contract or agreement is made over time, the user should see to it that those agreements are referenced in the final contract so that all of them may be enforced. Whether an integration clause is used or not, if the parties later agree to change or modify any part of their agreement, the change, modification, or addition to the contract should be formalized in writing and signed by both parties, preferably in the same manner and by the same persons as the original contract.

Exculpatory clauses are a third type of clause to watch out for. They disclaim liability on the facilities management's part for anything and everything that may go wrong. These clauses may provide an easy basis for judges to decide cases without having to spend the time and effort to learn what computers, data processing, and facilities management are all about. Exculpatory clauses may be upheld in court even if they prove to be unfair, since the court assumes that businesspeople deal with each other "at arm's length" and that the terms were thus the product of a careful negotiation process culminating in a mutual agreement over terms. A court is reluctant to rewrite such an agreement in the interest of fairness. Exculpatory clauses should not be agreed to in writing unless the user truly intends and agrees to relieve the facilities management firm of liability for its part of the bargain.

CONSULTING AND CONSULTING FIRMS

The decreasing cost of computer hardware coupled with a growing number of software programs tailored to specific business applications is making the use of data-processing equipment more attractive to today's businesses. The shortage of qualified personnel to maintain these computer systems has created a lucrative field for data-processing consultants. Consultants answer the real need of smaller businesses that require computer expertise but only on a part-time basis. Larger companies as well may find consultants' services useful in setting up new systems, modifying old ones, or dealing with particular problems in an existing system. The problem for the businessperson, however, is sorting out from the legitimate consultants those who are either incompetent or otherwise unable to provide the service they advertise or agree to do.[26] In the world of computer consultants, the bargain hunter will very likely become dissatisfied with the services provided. This section examines two areas of concern for a business seeking outside consulting services: determining a consultant's competency and legal remedies for unsatisfactory consulting.

Determining Competency

Two of the most important factors determining the reliability and integrity of a consultant are financial responsibility and previous contract performance.

Financial Responsibility. The financial health of a consultant is important in assessing the firm's ability to provide not only the short-term services contracted for but also future maintenance and new services a business may require. A consultant's financial state may reflect a general attitude toward business relationships.

Most legitimate consultants will show little hesitancy in providing the financial information required to evaluate the firm. Even then, a business may wish to verify this information with outside sources. Such sources might include other customers, the consultant's bank, the consultant's suppliers, credit bureaus, trade press and journals, and financial reporting services.

Previous Contract Performance. The best source of information about a consultant's performance under contract is the consultant's previous customers. The consultant, of course, will probably not tell the user where to find dissatisfied customers, but simply asking around data-processing circles may help to track them down. Interviews with previous customers should probe beyond general comments to specifics about the methods used by the consultant in performing the required services. Working papers, written correspondence, and other notes relevant to the service provided by the consultant are good indications of the level of expertise and professionalism.

The consultant's active and willing participation in contract negotiations for services to be provided shows a responsible approach to the business process, an attitude that more than likely will carry over into the performance of the contract.

Legal Remedies for Unsatisfactory Consulting

Even in the best of circumstances, situations may arise where a business feels that a consultant has unsatisfactorily performed the terms of the contract. Legal remedies may be difficult for the business that engaged the consultant due to the court's view of business contracts being negotiated and agreed to at arm's length by both parties. In the court's view, partners in contract usually agree only to what they want to agree to. This view is especially troublesome to the user in a consultant contract because it may be difficult to specify in a contract exactly what the consultant is expected to do. For example, if a user hires a consultant to aid in the implementation of a computer system, including advising on the selection of suitable hardware and software, the user is essentially gambling that the consultant chosen is qualified to give good advice. It is difficult to pin down desired results in the language of a consultant contract, especially if the user is hiring the consultant precisely because the user does not know the computer field. Even the best consultants will probably not contract to guarantee a successful implementation. In most cases, the best the user can do is contract for the particular consultant's best skill in accomplishing the stated purpose of the contract with the success of the venture riding on the selection of the consultant. This characteristic of the computer consultant profession, that is, the need for reliance on a common standard of competency, has led to the suggestion that consultants should be held liable for "computer malpractice" when their services fall below that standard. In addition, the consultant may be liable for ordinary negligence or tortious misrepresentation. Even if it has been determined that there is an appropriate legal remedy, however, the lack of technical expertise by the judge or jury often works to the consultant's advantage since it is difficult for the noncomputer professional to understand either what was required by the contract or what standard of competency should reasonably be expected of a computer consultant.

Contract. It is somewhat difficult to define in a contract what a consultant will do for the user of a computer system with enough objective certainty to enable a court to enforce the terms of the agreement. It is possible, however, to prescribe some minimal performance requirements capable of court enforcement.

The contract should always be in writing. It should specify the cost of the services or a formula for determining the cost based on the nature of the work to be done. Time limitations should be set for the duration of the contract unless there is to be an ongoing relationship for a particular project, which should also be specified. There should also be a means established to monitor the consultant's progress such as a requirement that the consultant submit periodic written reports to the user. The consultant should identify, with the user's approval, which persons will actually work on the project and give their qualifications. The user should also insert a provision into the contract to permit voluntary termination of the contract if the user is either dissatisfied with the consultant's work or simply decides not to finish the project for whatever reason. This provision may be essential in preventing the user from being obligated to pour more money into what looks like a losing proposition.

Apart from these basic contract considerations, if the user has any definite plans or expectations of what tasks or results the consultant is being hired to accomplish, these should be clearly set forth, as well as specific remedies that will accrue to the user if they are not accomplished by the consultant.

Tort. The law of negligence provides that a defendant may be held liable to a plaintiff for damages caused by the defendant's breach of a duty of care owed to the plaintiff. Negligence law may be especially useful in establishing a consultant's liability since it is independent of the parties' contractual obligations (although the terms of the contract may influence the court's determination of the nature of the duty owed by the consultant). If the consultant fails to exercise the requisite amount of care in protecting the interests of the user, the user may recover the resulting damages from the consultant.

The major difficulty in evaluating the appropriateness of a negligence action against a consultant is determining by what standard of care the consultant's action or lack of action is to be measured. The ordinary negligence standard is the care that an ordinary, reasonable person would have exercised in the same situation as the defendant. This standard is desirable since theoretically the members of a jury made up of ordinary persons can evaluate the appropriateness of a defendant's actions according to their own standards of reasonableness. The law recognizes a higher standard, however, in dealing with defendants who have held themselves out as professionals, that is, as possessing a greater-than-ordinary skill or expertise in a given field. Thus, courts hold doctors, lawyers, and accountants to a higher level of responsibility in dealing with the affairs of their patients and clients. A higher standard is also applied to bank trust departments if they represent that they hold higher-than-average skills in their field.

It has been suggested that similar considerations, such as dependence on a consultant's expertise not available to the layperson, justify the creation of a computer malpractice standard for use against computer professionals.[27] This standard has not been adopted by any court although one judge indicated in a pretrial conference that such a claim would not be ruled out at that stage of the case.[28] Two courts have expressly rejected the opportunity to adopt a malpractice standard.[29] It must be noted that none of the three cases involved a suit against a computer consultant. The first case was a facilities management case, and the other two were actions against computer vendors. There are different considerations in a consultant contract from these cases since the latter involve an agreement between businesspeople, while a consultant generally acts in an advisory and almost representative or fiduciary capacity for the user. Thus, it is still an open question whether a court may in the near future adopt a malpractice standard for computer consultants.

It may be possible in cases of accountants who engage in contracts to provide computer consultant services to hold the consultant-accountant to a higher-than-ordinary standard of skill and expertise, based at least in part on his or her education, specialized experience, and, perhaps most important, professional licensing by the state. If an accountant takes advantage of the accounting position to obtain computer consultant positions, a court may be persuaded to impose the higher standard of competence in judging the accountant-consultant's performance.

Fraud, or deceit, is a tort action that permits a person fraudulently induced to enter a transaction to recover damages against the defrauding party. Five elements must be present in a fraud action. First, there must have been a representation of a false fact. Second, the wrongdoer must have known that he or she was representing a false fact with, third, the intent that someone rely on that misrepresentation. Fourth, that person must have justifiably relied on the false representation and, fifth, suffered actual damage as a result of this reliance.

Probably the most difficult element to prove in a misrepresentation tort action is the second element, that a false fact was *knowingly* represented by the person in question. The courts have, however, eased the burden of such proof by allowing the element to be found when a statement is made without belief in its truth or when it is made recklessly or carelessly without regard to its truth or falsity.

Take the scenario of a business wishing to convert its manual systems to computerized ones. The business seeks a consultant familiar with such transactions. A consultant who represents successful direction of several businesses through similar transitions while in fact being involved with only one in greatly different circumstances may be guilty of fraud. If the consultant made this false representation with the intent that the business rely on this supposed expertise and hire the consultant's services, the first three elements of a fraud action are present. If the business relied on these misrepresentations and in fact hired the consultant with the result that severe financial losses were incurred due to a faulty transition, the remaining two elements exist, and a fraud action may be successfully argued in court.

A business may still have legal recourse if the second element, knowledge of the misrepresentation, cannot be proven in court. A consultant may be subject to a charge of negligent misrepresentation since he or she is in the business of advising others in their dealings with third parties by recommending suitable hardware and software vendors. A consultant holding him- or herself out to the public as an expert should be just that. Even if a consultant honestly believes that he or she possesses the required skills and expertise, the consultant may have been negligent in failing to apply the skill and competence attested to. A business would have to prove the existence of such negligence to the court.

Each case will require a different examination of the facts before a legal opinion regarding the best remedy can be rendered. The best course for a business seeking consulting services is to adequately research the consultant's past performance and construct a detailed and thorough contract for performance.

COURT CASES

Hiring Data-Processing Personnel

There are a number of relevant cases in this area that include labor law, the employee's duty of loyalty, noncompetition clauses, and use of secret information.

Labor Law. The following case illustrates some of the problems that may occur in determining which data-processing personnel may be included in a union's bargaining unit.

Exxon Pipeline Co. v. National Labor Relations Board.[30] Exxon employed oil movement supervisors (OMSs) located at the company's downtown Houston office, who monitored computer-assisted consoles that showed the progress of batches of oil as they flowed through the pipelines according to established schedules. The OMS personnel physically operated the system by remote control, detected breakdowns and other upsets as they showed up on the console, and reacted to correct these breakdowns and minimize losses. When a move was made to unionize Exxon's employees, the NLRB included the OMS personnel in the bargaining unit and an election was held. After Exxon's employees elected the union as their bargaining representative, Exxon refused to bargain with the union contending that the NLRB should not have included the oil movement supervisors in the bargaining unit.

The federal court noted that "it is not responsibility *per se* or exercise of independent judgment in themselves [that qualify individuals as 'supervisors' under the NLRA]. Rather responsibility for directing other *employees* is the critical factor in characterizing someone as a supervisor" (emphasis in original). Thus, although the court acknowledged the great responsibility and discretion vested in the OMS personnel, that was not enough to label them as supervisors.

The employer argued that the OMS personnel should be categorized as supervisors since they "responsibly directed" other personnel, as when problems arose, OMS personnel were authorized to deploy field personnel to correct the problem. Further, argued the employer, the OMSs used independent judgment to determine whether the repair needed to be corrected immediately, even to the extent that field personnel had to work overtime, or whether the problem was minor and could be corrected later. The court disagreed, finding that the OMS simply notified the field that a certain problem existed and had no further authority or responsibility to direct the field personnel in the manner in which repairs were carried out. The court emphasized that the field personnel and OMS personnel were in wholly separate departments with different hierarchies of authority. Whenever the OMS needed to contact a field division, the OMS was not permitted to call on a wage employee until the OMS had been unable to locate a sequence of higher officials in the field division. The court also referred to testimony that someone from the field department participated equally with the OMS in reaching a joint decision about whether a repair should be effected. As a result, the court upheld the NLRB's decision that the oil movement supervisors were not supervisors under the federal labor laws but rather were entitled to all the rights of any employee under the federal labor laws.

The Exxon case illustrates two important points. First, simply because the employer labels a person a supervisor does not mean that the NLRB or courts will adopt that label. The NLRB and courts are perfectly free to conduct their own inquiry into the underlying facts and circumstances to determine whether a particular person or class of personnel are supervisors or employees. Second, a supervisor in the labor law sense must supervise other *people*. It is not enough to supervise a machine even when this supervision affects the work of an entire department of other employees.

Employee's Duty of Loyalty. The case reporters contain several stories of employers who have sued former employees or the new employer of former employees to preserve the value of perceived competitive advantages. One has been selected for purposes of illustration.

Auxton Computer Enterprises, Inc. v. Parker.[31] The defendant in this case, Parker, was employed as a data-processing consultant by Auxton, a firm that provided data-processing consulting services, computer programmers, and analysts on a contract basis. Parker began working for Auxton in 1972 and was assigned to work at various client companies. In 1975, Parker decided to look for another job and contacted several other prospective employers. Parker interviewed with Spiridellis and Associates (called Associates) in January and February 1976, but no job offer was made at that time. On March 18, 1976, a Thursday evening, Spiridellis phoned Parker and asked him if he wanted to go to a technical interview the next day at the offices of Pan American Corporation on behalf of Associates. Associates had been doing consulting work for Pan Am for the preceding six or seven months and had a chance to enlarge their relationship through this technical interview aimed at developing Pan Am's passenger revenue data-processing system. Associates had interviews lined up for five or six other technicians besides Parker. Parker, suffering from a sore throat, did not give Spiridellis a definite answer to his offer and request to appear at the interview. Neither Spiridellis, Parker, nor Associates knew that Auxton was also seeking to obtain the Pan Am contract.

Parker decided to attend the Pan Am interview and called in sick for his work for Auxton. Coincidentally, one of Auxton's marketing representatives was trying to solicit work from Pan Am the day of the interview and learned that Parker was attending an interview there. The following Monday Parker was confronted with the fact that he had been at Pan Am on Friday. Parker initially denied the allegation, later decided to offer his resignation, but instead was terminated summarily by Auxton.

Apparently due to a sense of moral obligation, Spiridellis hired Parker when he learned of Parker's discharge by Auxton. Parker first worked at a designated job site for two or three days, then, after approval from Pan Am, Parker went to work as Associates' employee on the Pan Am job for almost one year.

Auxton sued Parker alleging breach of his duty of loyalty to his employer, interference with Auxton's prospective economic advantage, and unfair competition. Spiridellis and Associates were charged with inducing Parker to violate his duty of loyalty by recruiting him to solicit business for them while aware that Parker was still employed by Auxton. Following a non-jury trial, the court assessed damages of $10,601.38 against all of the defendants but dismissed all counts based upon interference with prospective economic advantage and denied requests for punitive damages.

All of Auxton's claims against Spiridellis and Associates were settled while the appeal was pending. Thus, the appellate court considered only the claims against Parker.

The trial court had accepted Auxton's argument that Parker should have been at work on the day of the interview instead of attempting to secure work for Auxton's competitor. Auxton maintained that by utilizing his talents on behalf of a competitor of his employer and presenting himself as an employee of Associates, Parker acted in callous disregard of his duty to serve his employer with only his employer's interest in mind. The trial court criticized Parker for wanting to "have his cake and eat it as well," finding that the sham excuse of illness not only permitted him to aid himself but also aided the employer's competitor on the employer's time.

The appellate court disagreed, stating that "an employee who is not bound by a covenant not to compete after the termination of employment . . . may anticipate the future termination of his employment and, while still employed, make arrangements for some new employment by a competitor or the establishment of his own business in competition with his employer." The court qualified this statement with the admonition that an employee may not solicit his employer's customers for his own benefit before terminating his employment or do other similar acts in direct competition with the employer's business. Mere planning was not viewed as a breach of an employee's duty of loyalty and good faith to his employer.

The court characterized Parker's actions as simply seeking alternative employment since neither he nor Spiridellis had any knowledge that Auxton would be competing for the same job. The court reasoned that "[if] the right to change jobs is to be meaningful for an employee not under contract for a definite term, it must be exercisable without the necessity of revealing the plans to the employer." In the absence of a covenant not to compete or breach of a confidential relationship, the court found nothing about Parker's conduct so unfair, immoral, or unethical as to make it actionable. Consequently, the judgment against the employee was reversed.

As there was no express contractual duty, the *Auxton* court was reluctant to impose a very vigorous standard of loyalty on an employee. The implication for the employer is to make employment contracts reflect the degree of loyalty expected of the employee from the outset. As is seen in the following cases, courts are more likely to require a higher standard when the employee has contractually submitted to that obligation.

Noncompetition Clauses. Judging from their presence in many former employee cases, covenants not to compete are a common feature of data-processing employee contracts. The treatment of these contract clauses by the courts, however, has been anything but uniform, as discussion of the following cases indicates.

Electronic Data Systems Corp. v. Powell.[32] Powell was employed by EDS from May 1970 to August 1972. Before that time, he had no data-processing experience. While employed by EDS, he worked as a system engineer on a team that developed a system for processing health-care claims involving private or nongovernmental contracts. The EDS system that Powell worked on, the Prepayment Utilization Review, or PPUR, competed with the Model System, a system developed by a governmental agency.

In August 1972, Powell went to work for Systems Resources, Inc. (SRI), a direct competitor of EDS in the health-care-processing field. SRI employed the Model System but was developing a proprietary system for processing business health-care claims, termed the "health insurance system," or HIS. The new HIS system was not based on the government's Model System but rather included automated features and concepts that had previously been unique to EDS in regular business health-care claims processing. SRI had planned the development of the new HIS system before Powell joined them in 1972. Powell made contributions to the HIS system's development, but after suit was filed by EDS, SRI transferred Powell to work in their public utility data-processing area. Even after the transfer, however, Powell made sales presentations on the HIS system on behalf of SRI to two health-care companies, in direct competition with EDS for the companies' business. In addition, Powell was later reassigned to full-time work on a health-care account and was the first person assigned to the HIS project by SRI. Although Powell denied having provided the PPUR documentation to SRI, he admitted that he had shared information about PPUR with another SRI employee. The trial court found, however, that Powell made no material disclosures of information concerning PPUR.

The restrictive covenant in the actual employment contract provided that EDS's computer systems and related data were to remain confidential; EDS retained a proprietary interest in its systems and information; the employee was not to participate in recruiting other EDS employees or in the solicitation of EDS customers and was not to compete with EDS within 200 miles of any city in which it did business until three years after the contract term; and the employee was likewise not to use any method, information, or system developed by EDS in competition with EDS within the same time and territorial limits.

The trial court issued an injunction enforcing the covenants not to compete, defining the word "competing" to effectively restrain Powell from soliciting EDS customers, recruiting EDS employees to work for a competitor, and furnishing information concerning PPUR to others. The appellate court, however, found that the trial court's order did not go far enough to protect EDS's interest in that it "failed to give effect to the covenant not to compete."

The appellate court stated that the test for determining the validity of a covenant not to compete was "whether the restrictions imposed upon the employee are greater than reasonably necessary to protect the business and good will of the employer or impose undue hardships on the employee." Even if such covenants were unreasonable as to time or territory covered, the covenant will not necessarily be void, the court said, but could be enforced by a court order restraining competition to a time and area that is "reasonable under the circumstances." In the EDS case, to give effect to the restrictive covenant, the court found it necessary to bar Powell from participating, directly or indirectly, individually or as an employee of a firm, in any activity involving the development, sale, or operation of electronic data systems for processing health-care claims for three years from August 1972 and within 200 miles of any EDS installation. The court found that no undue hardship would be imposed on Powell by the broadened injunction since he was not required to enter a different type of business but merely to enter a different area of the data-processing business.

The statement of the "reasonableness" standard declared by the EDS court for restrictive covenants appears to be nearly universal in those jurisdictions permitting restrictive covenants, but the effect of the "unreasonableness," that is, for the court to narrow the scope of the restriction when issuing its order, is peculiar to only some courts. The implication for the employer in these jurisdictions is to state the restriction as broadly as could possibly be thought reasonable with relation to the interests to be protected. Then, if the court finds the restriction to be excessive, it can still give effect to the covenant but in a more limited scope. In *EDS v. Powell,* the contract's competition provision was quite explicit in every regard except one very significant one: It neglected to define "compete." The EDS court took a view very favorable to the employer so that the employer essentially won the enforcement of every restriction placed in the covenant. (Indeed, the author of the court's opinion stated that he would have gone even farther to protect EDS's interests.) Another court (such as the EDS trial court) might not have construed the terms so broadly. It is therefore advisable to spell out precisely what the employee is prohibited from doing.

For example, in *Gill v. Computer Equipment Corporation,*[33] the court upheld the following covenant not to compete:

> Each stockholder covenants and agrees that, should he leave the employment of Computer for any reason, he will not compete with Computer for a period of two (2) years following such termination of employment. Competing shall be defined as (1) working in an executive, administrative, sales, or service capacity for any manufacturer which was represented by the [employee's division of the employer firm] during all or any part of the one (1) year period immediately preceding the date of such termination of employment; or (2) working for a sales representative and/or service organization which represents any such manufacturer; or (3) selling or servicing the products of any such manufacturer as an independent representative.

The *Gill* court found the definition of "compete" to be so precise and limited in scope that it enforced the clause even in the absence of any geographic limitation. It should be noted that *Gill* involved a shareholder agreement, which courts are more likely to uphold than pure employee covenants.

Electronic Data Systems Corp. v. Kinder.[34] This case is an example of the drastically different outcomes that may result from having a noncompetition clause case tried in a different court. This case, decided shortly before *EDS v. Powell,* in the same state but by a federal court (applying state law) also involved a health-care system engineer who left EDS to join Systems Resources, Inc. (SRI).

Kinder, the employee, had agreed to the following noncompetition clause in his employment contract with EDS:

> The Employee . . . agrees that during the term of this agreement and for a period of three (3) years thereafter, Employee shall not, directly or indirectly, individually or as an employee, partner, officer, director or stockholder, or in any other capacity whatsoever of any person, firm, partnership or corporation, (i) recruit . . . [or] assist others in recruiting or hiring . . . any person who is, or within the then preceding twelve months was, an employee of EDS . . . , (ii) compete with EDS or any subsidiary or affiliated company within two hundred (200) miles of any city in the United States in which EDS or any subsidiary or affiliated company does business, or (iii) use in competition with an EDS or subsidiary or affiliated company customer, prospective customer, or former customer, any of the methods, information, or systems developed by EDS . . . within two hundred (200) miles of any city where such customer, prospective customer, or former customer does business. Employee further agrees during the same period not to call upon, solicit,

accept employment with, sell or endeavor to sell within the United States any customer, prospective customer, or former customer of EDS or any subsidiary or affiliate company. The term "prospective customer" . . . shall mean such firms as EDS . . . has actively solicited within twelve months prior to the date of termination of Employee's employment hereunder.

While employed by EDS, Kinder, like Powell, worked as a system engineer on a team developing Medicare-payment computer programs. At this time, there were two available methods for processing Medicare claims: the EDS plan and the Model System developed by the government from public information. SRI, EDS's competitor, used the Model System. After joining SRI after April 30, 1972, Kinder worked exclusively on the Model System. EDS brought suit to enforce the terms of its noncompetition agreement. The defendant, Kinder, was able to remove the suit to a federal court. The jury found that Kinder did not disclose EDS information to SRI and did not directly engage in competition with EDS. The jury did, however, find that Kinder had indirectly engaged in competition with EDS as an employee of SRI and that he had assisted SRI in recruiting other EDS employees. The judge adopted the jury's findings except for the finding of indirect competition with EDS. The court reasoned that the term "indirect" meant "not resulting directly from an act or cause, but more or less remotely connected with or growing out of it." Thus, the court stated, to engage in indirect competition with EDS, Kinder must himself be the causal link between the competitor and EDS—"he must personally have some causal connection with the alleged competition. . . . The mere act of entering into an employment relationship with an existing competitor of EDS is not sufficient by itself to constitute indirect competition with EDS by Kinder." Moreover, the court noted, the finding of indirect competition was even further weakened by the fact that Kinder worked exclusively on the EDS plan for EDS but only on the Model System for SRI.

The court went further to hold that even if Kinder had indirectly competed with EDS, the restrictive covenants could not be enforced either because they were unreasonable or because they were not necessary for the protection of EDS's business and good will.

The court noted that the limitation of time, that is, three years from the employment termination date, was quite specific and reasonable. The geographic limitation, however, 200 miles from any city in which EDS or its customers maintained business operations, was deemed "so vague and uncertain that Kinder could not terminate his employment with EDS and have any certainty as to a specific city or town in which he could engage in the data processing of Medicare-payment applications without being in violation of the agreement." The court reasoned that if the covenant were to be enforced according to its terms, if Kinder went into the data processing of Medicare-payment applications anywhere and EDS or a customer should decide to expand into that area, Kinder would be obligated to discontinue his business there. Finding such a restriction to be unreasonable, the court held the noncompetition covenant unenforceable and void.

The court then went even further, stating that an injunction should be issued to enforce a noncompetition covenant (a "harsh remedy") only when necessary to protect the employer's business. Since Kinder's work with SRI was found to be entirely on the Model System while his work with EDS was exclusively on EDS's plan, the court found that to restrain Kinder from working on a publicly available data-processing plan would not lessen the competition facing EDS, the purpose of the covenant.

The standards for validity of the noncompetition clauses applied by each of the *EDS* courts are not at all dissimilar. The difference is in the result arrived at by the court if the covenant is found to be invalid. Recall that in *EDS v. Powell* the court indicated that if a noncompetition clause was unnecessarily broad, the court could simply limit its scope in its injunction order. In that situation, the employer lost nothing by drafting an overly broad restriction on competition. The *EDS v. Kinder* court, on the other hand, found the provision to be absolutely void and unenforceable if unnecessarily broad.

Aside from this difference in outcome, the two *EDS* cases illustrate a dichotomy in definition as well. First, note that although the geographic limitation in each covenant was essentially the same (no competition within 200 miles of any EDS installation or customer), the *Powell* court found it to be reasonable and the *Kinder* court, unreasonable. Second, the courts' respective definitions of "competition" were significant to the different results. The *Powell* court defined competition broadly, taking the view that anything Powell might do for SRI in the health-care field would unavoidably infringe upon EDS's competitive advantage. The *Kinder* court, conversely, required that the employee be the cause of the competition to find a violation of the noncompetition agreement.

The two EDS cases illustrate the need to engage legal counsel familiar with local case law in the field before attempting to limit an employee's ability to compete with the employer at a later date.

Use of "Secret" Information. The definition of "trade secrets" and their use by employees, who may or may not have signed an agreement regulating such use, have also come under scrutiny of the courts, as the following cases illustrate.

Republic Systems and Programming, Inc. v. Computer Assistance, Inc.[35] The court in this 1970 case recognized "the fierce competition for new business and . . . for technically competent personnel" as one of the most salient characteristics of the data-processing services business whose personnel developed "more loyalty to the industry and to the customers than to their employers." In this case, the plaintiff's (Republic's) assistant vice president and manager of the firm's Cheshire, Connecticut, branch office and 20 of the branch office's staff of 25 mailed letters of resignation to Republic's New Jersey home office before joining a newly formed corporation. The resignations were mailed so that the new corporation members could recruit the other members of the staff before Republic's president learned of the situation and could try to counter the group's efforts. The new firm's members began contacting their former Republic customers the following Monday telling the customers of the resignations but assuring them that one way or another each customer's project would be completed by the people who had worked on it before—the new firm offering to complete the projects without pay if necessary. The customers were also asked to keep the new company in mind for any future business. The employees who had been working on projects for Republic customers reported to those projects, with Republic to be paid for the services, until Republic obtained a temporary restraining order against the new company. The order prohibited them from approaching any of Republic's customers with work in progress trying to induce them to change companies, from soliciting any of Republic's employees to disclose information about work in progress or prospective business, from disclosing any such information, from soliciting Republic's employees or inducing any of the former employees to refuse to revoke their resignations, or from engaging directly or indirectly in unfair competition with Republic. After a hearing on the issuance of a permanent injunction, the court found for the new company, dissolving the temporary restraining order and denying Republic's request for a permanent injunction and damages.

The court found that since none of Republic's officers or employees were subject to any employment contract, the term of employment was indefinite so that each employee was entitled to terminate employment at will. Most important to this case, the court held that the employment ended as of the time the letters were placed in the mail even though admittedly done to permit solicitation of employees without the former employer's intervention. Indeed, the court noted that the facts tended to show that the defendants were well aware of the impropriety of soliciting other employees while still in Republic's employ and behaved as they did precisely to avoid such impropriety. The court suggested that the former employees' "lack of forthrightness" was one of the risks of operating without employment contracts. "In view of the widespread tendency toward job switching in these times, especially prevalent in the data-processing services field," reasoned the court, "the evidence does not indicate the use of any . . . unlawful or improper purposes or means" in soliciting Republic's employees.

The court found no evidence that the defendants of the new firm solicited any of Republic's customers before their termination of employment. The court noted that without a restrictive covenant (see the preceding cases), former employees "may immediately and freely compete with their former employers including solicitation of customers." The only exception to this general rule is that a former employee cannot "use trade secrets, or other confidential information . . . acquired in the course of . . . employment, for [the employee's] own benefit or that of a competitor to the detriment of [the] former employer." Republic attempted to use this exception by arguing that its customer lists and other information (for example, clients' authorized agents, pending and potential future projects, and budget range) were confidential. Thus, the court needed to resolve the issue of whether the information taken and used by the new firm constituted trade secrets.

The court ruled that for a customer list to be protected as a trade secret, the compilation of the list must have been the product of "years of business effort and advertising and the expenditure of time and money." In addition, "a substantial element of secrecy must exist, to the extent that there would be difficulty in acquiring the information except by the use of improper means." The court noted the facts that, first, many of Republic's clients were openly listed in Republic's advertising brochures as "representative clients." Second, many of the clients were also seeking bids from Republic's competitors and, third, efforts to keep the names of the others secret were "meager at best." The court again referred to the nature of the computer software business as a whole, noting that anyone with a computer is considered a potential customer and is actively sought by firms like the ones in this case. This observation figured in the court's conclusion that Republic had spent no unusual efforts in cultivating its customer list and that others would not have had great difficulty in acquiring the same information by permissible means.

This case illustrates two significant points for the computer personnel employer. First, little protection against employee desertion may be afforded the employer who neglects to set out contractual obligations of loyalty and confidentiality. Second, the courts will not protect sensitive or confidential information that the employer has not seen fit to protect. Neither of these points presents an insurmountable problem for an employer, but they are problems that must be dealt with by prevention and forethought, as Republic Systems and Programming, Inc., learned through somewhat bitter experience.

Structural Dynamics Research Corp. v. Engineering Mechanics Research Corp.[36] SDRC was engaged in the business of structural analysis and testing including the development of computer programs for that purpose. Kothawala, Surana, and Hildebrand were all employed by SDRC in various technical capacities, and each had signed an employee patent and confidential information agreement. Kothawala also signed an employment agreement.

Surana was responsible for developing a proposed isoparametric structural analysis program for analyzing curved and irregular-shaped elements. Kothawala, who joined SDRC at about this time, anticipated six to 12 months at SDRC's home office in Cincinnati after which time he would assume management responsibility for a Detroit-based SDRC office, although the details of the arrangement were left to be resolved in the future. While in Cincinnati, Kothawala was assigned to supervise and help draft a formal written proposal for Surana's project. No other SDRC employee had any significant knowledge of isoparametric theory or application at the time. The program, named NIESA (for Numerically Integrated Elements for System Analysis), was developed to the point of running test problems. At this time, SDRC concluded that Kothawala lacked the business experience necessary to assume full responsibility for the proposed Detroit office and so proposed that Kothawala be responsible for the Detroit entity's technical consulting but be required to report to Cincinnati management. On December 28, 1972, Kothawala rejected the proposal and asked to be released from his contract effective January 1, 1973. SDRC released him, and Kothawala returned to Detroit where he established EMRC. Hildebrand then also gave notice of immediate resignation and began to work for EMRC as manager of applications. About a week later, Surana also gave notice of resignation but was persuaded to stay long enough to prepare a handwritten description of NIESA and explain it to other SDRC employees. He thereafter joined EMRC as vice president of engineering.

The newly formed company proposed to develop an isoparametric program for American Motors Corp., substantially the same as NIESA. The details of the proposal made it clear that the program proposed, described by EMRC to AMC as "partially finished," was indeed Surana's NIESA project from SDRC. AMC approved the project's funding, and in February 1974, EMRC began marketing its program under the name "NISA." SDRC, previously unaware of EMRC's development activity, speeded up its own development work and marketed NIESA, renamed SUPERB, in April 1974. The two programs were very similar, the basic difference being that NISA was more fully developed with greater analytical capabilities.

SDRC sued EMRC for damages and a permanent injunction on two different theories related to the misappropriation and misuse of the NIESA information: first, that the former employees had committed a breach of trust by using SDRC's trade secrets for their own advantage and, second, that the employees breached a contractual duty not to use or disclose confidential information.

After a cursory but useful review of trade secrecy law, the court turned to the difficult problems presented when the employee charged with taking the alleged trade secret is its actual discoverer or developer. The court recognized first that Surana and Kothawala had not obtained the alleged trade secrets through improper means since they were hired by SDRC for research and development in precisely this field. The court then addressed itself to the question of whether the defendants' subsequent use or disclosure breached a duty of trust owed to SDRC. The court cited legal authority for the proposition that "apart from breach of contract, abuse of confidence, or impropriety in the means of procurement, trade secrets may be copied as freely as devices which are not secret." The court went on to state that if the subject matter of the trade secret is in existence and an employee learns of it in the course of employment in a relationship of confidence, the duty not to use or disclose the secret adversely to the employer arises. But, the court continued, if the subject matter of the trade secret is the product of the employee's creation, development, or innovation, no such duty arises since the employee may have an interest in the secret at least equal to that of the employer or the knowledge has become part of the employee's personal "skill and experience," which are not ownable by the employer. In such a case, found to exist here, the employee is free to use or disclose such information in subsequent employment activity in the absence of any express contractual obligation to refrain from doing so.

This finding led the court to SDRC's second contention: that the employees breached their contractual duty not to disclose or use the information. All three employees had signed an employee patent and confidential information agreement in which they agreed to refrain from disclosing trade secrets and confidential, privileged, or other information either during or subsequent to termination of employment. In addition, the agreement included a non-competition clause prohibiting competition during or for six months after employment with SDRC. Finally, Kothawala had signed a separate employment contract (which he himself had drafted in part) including a one-year restriction on competition with SDRC, as well as an agreement not to disclose at any time any confidential information or trade secrets concerning the business affairs of SDRC.

Since the agreements had been executed in Ohio, the Michigan federal district court hearing the case decided that Ohio law should control rather than Michigan's. This was a disputed issue because Michigan has a statute declaring covenants not to compete, whether "reasonable" or "unreasonable," to be against public policy, illegal, and void. Michigan does, however, sustain the validity of nondisclosure provisions. On this basis, the court concluded that no matter which state's law was to be applied, the result would be the same insofar as breach of the nondisclosure portion of the agreement was concerned. Finding that the misappropriated information did, indeed, constitute SDRC's confidential, trade secret, and proprietary information, the court assessed damages against EMRC of a "reasonable royalty" of 15 percent of EMRC's gross sales and a license fee of $45,000 for use of its programs.

It is again clear from this case that employment contract provisions are critical to the employer's ability to salvage misappropriation losses, especially with regard to the employees who personally develop the information. In addition, the case illustrates that even in a state forbidding the use of noncompetition covenants, covenants against unauthorized use or disclosure may provide a valid alternative means of protection.

Facilities Management

To illustrate the problems that can arise out of a facilities management agreement, one case will be examined in detail. The case is noteworthy in that most of the points covered in this part occurred in this litigation. In this case CT/East (CTE), a facilities management firm, agreed to provide computer services for Financial Services, Inc. (FSI).

CT/East, Inc. v. Financial Services, Inc.[37] CTE and FSI agreed that CTE would operate FSI's computer facility, assume the cost of the computer equipment and operators, provide related programming for the communications network to and from the facility, and provide for keypunch operators who processed the raw data and prepared punch cards for processing. The agreement also provided for employment by CTE of some FSI personnel.

FSI was a service organization that offered its financial customers four basic services—an on-line savings system that provided direct communication between bank tellers and the computer facility at FSI, an off-line system designed for mortgage lenders, a service mortgage system for customers who manage mortgage investments for third parties, and various daily, monthly, and other periodic reports.

The contract set out the initial operations for which CTE was to be paid a fixed price per year on a monthly basis. Adjustments were allowed for economic, tax, machine utilization, and volume considerations. Included in the initial operations was CTE's full responsibility for operations and maintenance of all operational computer programs. In addition, CTE agreed to develop and implement a new mortgage system, to install an on-line savings system, and to schedule development for other smaller input and report programs.

FSI would have most of its programs updated to higher-level languages by CTE. CTE, while expecting to lose money in the beginning, would later use FSI's central computing facility to process the work of other CTE customers during lulls in FSI's processing and thus be able to capitalize on the initial investment.

The contract was very precise and well thought out. It provided for new applications and major changes as the relationship continued. Included were specific lists of equipment turned over and provisions for program development, personnel, confidentiality, and ownership of new application programs developed by CTE. The process by which CTE and FSI made their way into the courtroom illustrates the problems that can arise even with the most detailed contract.

CTE took control of the computer facility in January 1970. It used substantially all of FSI's equipment and computer personnel who worked at FSI's premises 24 hours a day. FSI complained about delays and errors in reports. CTE objected to FSI's delays in presenting final specifications for the proposed new systems. As early as July 1970, CTE's parent corporation, CT, attempted to persuade FSI to renegotiate the agreement after it became clear that CTE would lose a substantial amount of money on the deal. FSI was satisfied that it had a good contract and refused to renegotiate. On August 28, 1970, CT sent FSI a proposal under whose terms FSI would immediately take over control of operations while CTE would complete installation of the on-line savings and mortgage systems by January 1, 1971, and March 1, 1971, respectively. Counterproposals were exchanged resulting in no agreement. Meanwhile, CTE's final development of the new systems was delayed by FSI's continually expanding list of system requirements. The savings system was finally installed by April 1971, in the midst of negotiations for a new contract to redefine the parties' contractual obligations. These negotiations finally broke down in June 1971. CTE then demanded all sums due and owing under the agreement. FSI refused to pay more than a nominal sum. CTE gave written notice to FSI that CTE considered FSI's failure to pay to be a substantial breach of the agreement, giving FSI 10 days to cure its breach before terminating the agreement. This procedure for termination by CTE was authorized by the contract's provisions for termination. FSI responded to CTE's letter by proposing a meeting with CT personnel. This meeting took place on August 4 and failed to resolve the parties' differences. CTE delivered a notice of termination to FSI on August 11, to be effective August 21, and filed suit for the $365,000 that it claimed to be owing under the contract.

On the evening of August 13, Friday, CTE's chief programmer removed a large amount of documentation for the on-line savings system from FSI's facilities, intending to take it to CTE's office on Monday to continue his work since he understood that there was no more test time available to CTE at FSI's facilities. The court noted that although the material may have been the property of FSI, it had always been in CTE's possession and work on it had been performed at both FSI's and CTE's facilities. After discovering the material's disappearance on Saturday and being unable to locate the programmer or his superior, FSI obtained a warrant for the programmer's arrest. The materials were discovered at the programmer's home and returned to FSI on the following Monday. FSI thereupon banned CTE's employees from its premises claiming that CTE's actions had jeopardized FSI's business. The criminal charges against the programmer were later dismissed by the court. FSI responded to CTE's suit by claiming damages of its own, alleging fraud and that CTE's failure to perform services for which FSI had paid entitled FSI to an accounting and return of those payments. The following discussion of some of the major areas of dispute in the case illustrates many of the concepts contained in this part.

The court found that CTE had operated FSI's computer facility from January 1, 1970 to August 16, 1971, keeping track of millions of transactions for about 150 large financial institutions having a million and a quarter accounts and producing the hundreds of daily, periodic, and special reports necessary to FSI's and its customers' businesses. The court acknowledged that in doing all this, there were occasions when things did not "operate to perfection" and that there were delays and errors in furnishing reports and other services. FSI had indicated to the court that delays had occurred because of CTE's lateness, although according to the contract FSI had retained responsibility for lateness resulting from incorrect or late data. The contract required only that CTE "exert every effort to maintain the established data-processing schedule of [FSI's] work." The court could point to no evidence that CTE had not done this nor that FSI had been damaged in any monetary way because of any errors or delays that might have occurred. Moreover, the contract explicitly stated that the contract was to be construed as one for services only (so Uniform Commercial Code implied warranties would not apply—see Part II), specifically excluded any warranties of merchantability or fitness for a particular purpose, and stated that it was not intended that CTE assume FSI's risks of data-processing error. Finding that the great bulk of work contemplated under the fixed price was operational, the court held that CTE had performed its part of the agreement so as to be entitled to the agreed payments under the contract.

Even though the new mortgage and savings systems were not completed on schedule, the court found that the conduct of FSI in making continued changes in the systems' specifications indicated either that the time of performance by CTE was not essential to the agreement or that FSI had waived its right to on-time performance. In either event, since CTE had completely developed and implemented the savings system by the spring of 1971 and the mortgage system had been scheduled for installation in September 1971, the court concluded that the late performance constituted no barrier to CTE's recovery on the contract.

The court also enforced the terms of the contract pertaining to a cost-of-living adjustment of the fixed price, summarily dismissing FSI's "untenable" argument that the adjustment was not billable until 1972. Similarly, the court upheld CTE's entitlement to an upward annual adjustment based on increased volume as measured by CPU meter readings. "No serious dispute" was found to exist about the proper computation of the 1970 adjustment. Since the 1971 records were in FSI's control, no evidence of volume increase was introduced for the eight months of 1971. Although CTE apparently made no claim for a volume increase for 1971, the court indicated that it would have imposed a similar increase for the first seven months of 1971 had CTE requested it.

Similarly, the agreement had stipulated that if FICA payroll taxes increased during the contract's term, FSI would be charged for the additional expense caused by CTE's employment of former FSI personnel transferred to CTE because of the agreement. The court approved CTE's bill to FSI for the undisputed total amount of $925.80.

The contract's provision for early termination of the agreement permitted FSI to terminate the contract for "any business reason" upon six months' written notice and payment of an early termination fee. The termination fee was set up to decline incrementally over the life of the contract from $150,000 in the first year down to none during the fifth year. In addition to this provision, either CTE or FSI was permitted to terminate early if termination was based on the other party's substantial failure to perform the agreement, provided that the terminating party submitted the alleged failure in writing and in full detail to the other party, giving the other party ten days to correct its failure to perform. If the failure was not corrected to the complaining party's satisfaction, that party was required to describe in writing to the other party the full details of the alleged breach. Termination without liability would then be effective ten days later assuming that the alleged failure actually existed as described. Payment for services rendered up to and including the termination was required.

CTE clearly followed the terms of its termination option to the letter. It still, however, tried to argue that FSI had prematurely terminated the agreement by locking out CTE's employees following the "theft" incident. If the court had accepted this argument, CTE would have arguably been entitled to a $100,000 early termination fee. The court held that CTE's termination of the agreement was self-executing as of the date notice was given, August 11. As of that date, only the passing of ten days was required to terminate the agreement and no further action by either party was required. The court concluded that the only course open to CTE for early termination and damages was the one it had followed—termination followed by a lawsuit. CTE's claim for the early termination fee was accordingly rejected.

The contract also provided that after termination of the agreement, CTE would make available whatever necessary data-processing equipment time FSI may desire at CTE's standard rates in effect at that time until FSI could procure and install its own data-processing equipment. The agreement also spelled out requirements for the return of FSI's data by CTE, delivery of a copy of CTE's programs being used to service FSI, to be used by FSI only for its own internal data-processing operations, and CTE's release of FSI's former employees who wish to rejoin FSI.

Both parties agreed that certain equipment leased by CTE from its parent company, CT, remained at FSI for a period of time after the contract's termination. FSI was willing to pay CTE only for its *actual cost* of permitting FSI to use the equipment during this period of time; that is, FSI was willing to reimburse CTE only for its rental payments to CT. CTE argued on the basis of the contract's termination clause that it was entitled to its *standard rate* for FSI's use of the equipment after termination. FSI countered by contending that the contract's provision for payment of CTE's standard rate referred to such equipment and transition services *as FSI may desire*. Since FSI had not specifically *asked* for the use of the equipment but, on the contrary, had tried to obtain equipment from other sources, FSI argued that its liability should be limited to CTE's actual cost of FSI's continued use.

The court viewed FSI's contentions to be "unsupportable and frivolous," finding that FSI had made clear its "desire" by continuing to use CTE's equipment. Moreover, the court noted that in a suit brought by CTE to recover the equipment in October 1971, FSI had successfully defended by claiming that the equipment was absolutely necessary to FSI's ability to service its customers until the equipment could be replaced. CTE was therefore entitled to recover its standard rate for FSI's use of the equipment, totaling $119,144.

Both parties raised claims that were not expressly within the contract. For example, CTE claimed that it was entitled to payment beyond the fixed annual price of $720,000 for excess program maintenance. The contract had provided that as part of the services covered by the fixed price, CTE would furnish special reports and routine program maintenance not to exceed the services of five programmers. CTE claimed that since more than five programmers' time had been expended on routine program maintenance as defined by the contract, FSI should be forced to pay for that additional expense. The court, however, indicated that *even if* CTE had in fact expended excess time on program maintenance (the court was not convinced that it had), the contract's failure to provide explicitly for an upward adjustment of the fixed price in such an event precluded CTE's recovery of any excess payment. The court noted that in other areas in which the parties anticipated additional charges, a standard for billing had been set forth in the contract, such as for any volume increase in machine usage. Without such a provision regarding program maintenance, the court viewed the situation as one in which CTE's costs of performing the contract had simply proven higher than expected. Without a mutual agreement that FSI pay extra for that cost, CTE was not entitled to any additional compensation.

FSI, to a much greater extent, also based several of its claims on alleged promises and expectations that were not reflected in the contract. For example, FSI claimed that CTE had agreed to provide a new off-line savings system as well as an on-line system, each system to serve different FSI customers. The contract, however, mentioned only an on-line system. The court placed a great deal of emphasis, throughout its opinion, on the contract's integration clause, which stated that the entire agreement of the parties was contained in the writing. This clause was used by the court to defeat virtually every one of FSI's claims that CTE failed to fulfill promises not detailed in the agreement. This proved to be very damaging to FSI outside the scope of this lawsuit since it appears that FSI's salespersons had made claims to their own customers of future system capabilities far beyond those detailed in the CTE contract. FSI apparently lost several customers a few months after termination of the CTE contract when FSI failed to deliver its promised system capabilities.

In addition to the contract's integration clause, the exclusion-of-warranties clause and limitation-of-liability clause were relied upon by the court in denying relief to FSI. The exclusion-of-warranties clause has been discussed earlier as it pertained to CTE's performance under the contract. The limitation-of-liability clause provided that CTE would have no liability to

FSI in fact or contract arising out of its performance of the contract except for general damages not to exceed the amount of FSI's payments in the six months prior to the alleged injury or damage.

FSI tried to persuade the court not to apply this exculpatory clause on policy grounds. While FSI conceded that such clauses were normally upheld, FSI argued that since in this case CTE was to completely take over FSI's business operations, CTE should be held to a fiduciary's standard of care. As a fiduciary, it was argued, CTE should be held to a duty to act solely for the interests of its client and not be immunized from damages for its "willful nonperformance."

This constitutes a novel argument based upon the realities of the facilities management situation. The argument recognizes the vulnerability of a client's business operations to another company which in effect possesses the power to make or break the client. Although this theory makes some sense and may have been adopted in another case, the court found FSI's argument "facetious" in this particular case. First, the contract had explicitly provided for FSI's executive control over CTE's operations and implementation of new systems. Second, the evidence showed no willful nonperformance by CTE. Third, the court found no public policy to be adversely affected by permitting such exculpatory clauses to be agreed upon by parties of equal bargaining power.

In the end, the court awarded CTE $446,539. Every one of FSI's counterclaims was rejected. The court commented on the nature of the contract, regarding it a "marriage which should never have taken place." The nature of the contract under which CTE could expect little profit during the initial stages was found to have encouraged FSI to solicit new clients by representing new services and then to demand that CTE install the new system to provide those services. As the court also pointed out, FSI had an agreement that it was reluctant to change in any way, and it was very careful not to terminate the agreement even in the face of what FSI would ultimately describe as CTE's failure to perform. The judge's description of the case seems to be an apt one and probably explains his placing such great emphasis on enforcing the literal terms of the contract. In the face of such a novel business arrangement, difficult to understand in conventional terms, a judge may be understandably reluctant to vary the terms to which the parties have set their signatures.

Now that the smoke of the battle has cleared, it is helpful to step back and see what the final result really is. Did FSI really lose? The answer gained from a reading of the opinion is, probably not. FSI had negotiated a contract under which it could pay a set monthly fee and, instead of concerning itself with the technical details of its computer system, could simply tell CTE what it wanted and leave it to CTE to determine how to do it. Even though the parties at the time of contracting clearly anticipated that new contracts and modifications would be necessary to deal with future data-processing needs, FSI hung on to its old contract despite CTE's efforts to negotiate a new one. Also, even though it lost the lawsuit, FSI was liable only to the extent of its commitment under this contract. The losses that FSI did sustain, that is, its legal costs and loss of customers after termination of the contract, appear to be at least as much FSI's fault as CTE's, brought on by FSI's attempt to get even more out of the contract than CTE had agreed to.

Was there a good contract in this case? To the extent that the contract dealt with the numerous considerations discussed in this part, one would have to answer yes. This contract was very explicit and detailed in defining the obligations of the parties so that the court had very little trouble applying it to the case. From CTE's viewpoint, it was an excellent contract to the extent that they complied explicitly with its terms and they were able to win almost every claim in court (notwithstanding the wisdom of the transaction in the first place). To FSI, the best that can be said is that they got what they bargained for. If FSI really expected that CTE would provide an off-line savings system, that should have been put in the contract. If FSI really intended to hold CTE liable for lateness or other nonperformance, the exculpatory clause and limitation of warranties should not have been agreed to. This case illustrates as well as any that a contract is good only insofar as it reflects the true intentions of the parties.

Consultants

Very few published opinions have been located dealing with suits involving computer consultants. The cases presented here, although not directly relevant to computer consultants, illustrate some legal principles that may be applied to future computer consultant cases.

Alpern v. Hurwitz.[38] Lawrence Hurwitz, an investor with several corporate holdings, hired Alan Alpern, a semiretired lawyer with expertise in corporate fiscal management and control, to act as his financial consultant from August 1972 to April 1975 for $3,000 a month plus expenses. In addition, Hurwitz was to pay Alpern $900 a month as a "contribution towards [Alpern's] maintaining a working facility" in New York City. Hurwitz had a substantial interest in Computer Power International Corporation of which he served as president and Alpern served as a member of the board of directors. In April 1974, the two became involved in a controversy over Hurwitz's use of corporate funds. Hurwitz was able to force Alpern's resignation as a director. Although Alpern continued to send Hurwitz monthly bills under the consultant contract, Hurwitz made no further payments. Hurwitz never gave notice that he was terminating the consulting agreement. In April 1977, Alpern brought suit to recover on the contract.

In evaluating Alpern's claim for his agreed fee, the trial court inferred that the parties had intended the consulting agreement to be performed only as long as a viable confidential relationship existed between them. Finding that the April 1974 incident had "irretrievably ruptured" the agreement, the trial judge dismissed Alpern's complaint with regard to consulting fees.

The appellate court disagreed with the trial court in its interpretation of the contract. The court first stated the general rule that an employment contract for a definite term may not be lawfully terminated by the employer prior to the expiration date without just cause. The court conceded that when a contract creates a close confidential relationship, such as between attorney and client, courts will sometimes read into the agreement a provision that it may be terminated by the employer at any time without cause. But even in the highly confidential relationship of attorney and client, the court continued, such a provision should not be implied when "the attorney has been employed . . . for a fixed period to perform legal services as the need for them may arise." Thus, the trial court erred in implying a provision into the contract that it would automatically terminate if the confidential relationship was destroyed.

After vacating the lower court's determination of that issue, the court concluded that there was no evidence that Hurwitz ever actually terminated Alpern's employment, assuming for the sake of argument that Hurwitz could have lawfully done so. The court remanded the case back to the trial court for evidence on whether there had been a termination of the agreement, suggesting but not definitely concluding that Alpern might be prevented from recovery if the facts showed that both parties mutually abandoned the contract or that Alpern should be denied recovery for some other reason in the interest of fairness. The court approved the trial court's award to Alpern of $21,600 owed toward the maintenance of Alpern's New York apartment.

This case suggests very strongly that the user of a consultant's services should be cautious of fixed-term consulting contracts. The *Alpern* court made no distinction between a consulting contract and a normal employee contract in cases when a fixed term is set and no contract provision is made for early termination. The implication for the client is to include in the contract a clause stating that the proposed relationship is a fiduciary one in which the consultant will at all times act in the client's best interest. To assure that such a relationship can be maintained, the contract should provide that it is terminable at the will of the employer. To do otherwise, as in *Alpern*, may leave a client in a position in which the client is forced to choose among first, retaining and using the services of a consultant who is incompetent or not working in the client's best interests; second, paying the consultant as required by the contract even though the services are not used (as the *Alpern* result suggested); or third, obtaining and paying for the services of a better consultant while continuing to pay off the former consultant's contract. None of these alternatives is attractive.

The *Alpern* case also suggests the desirability of tying a consultant's fees to some measure of work performance rather than using a flat retainer basis. Again, the *Alpern* case represents a "worst case" example of a client remaining obligated to pay the consultant whether any services are rendered during the contract period or not.

Sanitary Linen Service Co. v. Alexander Proudfoot Co.[39] The Alexander Proudfoot Co. contracted to implement a new scheduling system designed to "provide greater control over utilization of man and machine hours and to effect operating economics" for the Sanitary Linen Service Co. Sanitary agreed to give its full cooperation using the full influence of its authority with its personnel to assure maximum results. Sanitary paid Proudfoot a total of $74,200 on the contract over a six-month period. Proudfoot's proposal to Sanitary had estimated that the first year's payroll savings after installation of the scheduling system would total $246,600. Sanitary contended that Proudfoot had also estimated that when 50 percent of the program was completed, the effected savings would exceed the cash outlay. The promised savings never materialized and Sanitary brought suit for damages.

Sanitary contended that it was entitled to damages in the amount of $246,600 for each year after 1964 because savings of that amount had been warranted or guaranteed by Proudfoot. The court rejected this argument, finding the savings figure had been only an estimate of savings if a workable schedule plan had been implemented. The court noted that even if a workable plan had been developed, the calculation of such savings involved so many variable, unpredictable factors that it would be impossible to determine them in advance. The court stated that no warranty could exist for proposed services unless it was clearly stated and assumed by the warrantor. Although the court recognized that "the suggested savings were intended as an inducement, potential savings are not facts to which a warranty may attach but are merely estimates with uncertain reliability." Moreover, the court added that no implied warranties of fitness or merchantability attach to contracts for services. Noting that Sanitary had been in no way damaged by entering into the contract except for the sum paid to Proudfoot, Sanitary should be made whole for not receiving its part of the bargain only to the extent of what was paid to Proudfoot, $74,200.

This case reinforces the recurrent theme of this book; that is, when contracting for computer goods and services, get it all in the contract. This principle has special and critical significance when applied to consultant contracts. Since consultants almost always provide nothing but services, no warranties of actual results will apply unless actually made a part of the contract. Although consultants are likely to predict certain beneficial results from a prospective contract, most consultants, like Proudfoot, will not be willing to guarantee those results. As the court noted in the *Sanitary* case, such results often involve variable factors out of the consultant's control. Even the most competent consultants may quite understandably be unable and unwilling to guarantee success of any project. The *Sanitary* court noted the preposterous results that could have been realized if Sanitary's arguments had been accepted. Such a decision would have implied that Sanitary could have sued Proudfoot for $246,600 at the end of each subsequent year during which Sanitary's contract expectations were disappointed. Such a result would clearly not be within the expectations of a consultant when entering into a contract for services if not expressly warranted.

One course of action for a prospective client is to agree to a contract that permits the client to terminate the contract when dissatisfied with the progress on the project. In this way, the client can at least minimize wasted payments. Another possibility is to negotiate a contract provision for liquidated damages. Such a clause enables the client to obtain a stipulated amount of monetary damages in the event of the consultant's failure to perform adequately under the contract. The liquidated damages amount should be calculated to reflect at least the client's cash outlay, expense of cooperation with the consultant (that is, disruption of ordinary business), and opportunity cost of the wasted investment over the term of the contract. This course of action also calls for a careful statement of what standards will be used to measure the consultant's performance of the contract to justify imposition of the liquidated damages.

IMPLICATIONS FOR ACTION

The decision whether to hire new personnel or a computer service firm or to retrain existing personnel should be made after a detailed analysis of all costs and legal obligations that may result from each option. The employees whose jobs are affected should be consulted about the nature of the work with which they are the most knowlegeable and about their personal feelings toward working with the new computerized system. Labor relations personnel, the personnel department, financial advisors, and system consultants should be made a part of the decision-making team.

Employment contracts should contain noncompetition clauses that are drawn only broadly enough to protect the employer's interest. For example, if the employee's work is in the health-care field, a court may not enforce a clause prohibiting *any* computer work within a particular time and geographic area. The restriction should be set according to the nature of the sensitive information possessed by the employee. If the employee is intimately familiar with customers in a particular locale, the geographical restriction should be stressed. If the employee has access to confidential technical or marketing information, a geographical limitation will do little to protect the employer. In the latter case, time and type of work restrictions will be the most valuable. Many courts will refuse to enforce a covenant without a geographic limitation, however. The employer should avoid drawing the clause so broadly that it deprives the employee of his or her livelihood.

The employer should try to avoid strikes by using collective bargaining agreements that prohibit strikes. The employer should, however, be sure to provide alternative means of settling labor disputes such as establishing specific grievance procedures leading to arbitration or mediation. Contingency plans should nevertheless be drawn up to be followed in the event of a strike, including a list of data-processing priorities and designation of alternative sources of computer time and employees.

An employment contract should clearly state the employee's duty to keep confidential information secret to protect a competitive advantage or to establish a proprietary interest in such information. The employer should be certain to follow and enforce the company's own procedures for labeling and safeguarding information. The contract should also specify whether the employer or employee is to be considered the owner of intellectual discoveries made by the employee while in the company's employ or outline options to purchase employee developments.

The decision whether to enter into a facilities management contract should include an analysis of the loss of flexibility and control over operations and potential personnel staffing problems weighed against the advantages of obtaining specialized computer technology at a fixed cost. Other factors and costs should also be considered such as the need for increased security and insurance effects.

Facilities management firms should be selected only after a thorough investigation of their financial stability and previous contract performance. A facilities management contract should specifically identify those tasks to be performed by the facilities management firm including detailed data-processing procedures; responsibilities for maintaining, selecting, and changing hardware, software, and the necessary environment; and duties of secrecy. To maximize the benefit of the contract, a suitable cost formula must be specified that will keep the cost at predictable levels while encouraging operational efficiency. Standards for successful performance should be agreed upon in advance including both internal system controls and manually prepared reports. Audits by independent consultants may be necessary to oversee the quality of the facilities management's work.

Two critical stages of the facilities management arrangement are the periods for turnover and turnback of the computer operations. These events need to be extremely well thought out and detailed in advance by agreement of the parties, keeping in mind that the termination of the contract may not be on such good terms as the signing of the contract. Comprehensive inventories of hardware and software should be included in the contract's terms and updated throughout the term of the contract. The user should be sure that some provision is made for keeping the computers running during these transitions, specifying employees who will be transferred, and for making available carry-over services by the facilities management on a day-to-day basis if required.

The user should provide in advance that the equipment acquired at termination is efficient for the *user's* purposes. Thus, provision for adjustments in the equipment and software to be transferred should be made. Ownership of application programs and other software developed during the term of the contract should also be established.

General "control and cooperation" clauses should be avoided or at least augmented by specific definition of the user's duty to cooperate with specific dispute resolution procedures. Integration clauses are not necessarily bad as long as the user has been careful to ensure that all claims, promises, and offers relied upon by the user as a reason for entering into the contract are in fact contained in the written contract. Any changes, modifications, or proposals should be in writing and formalized to the greatest extent possible.

Exculpatory clauses can be extremely damaging to the user in a facilities management contract. When an exculpatory clause is given effect by the courts, the result is that the user gives up control of the innermost workings of the corporate management body, but when things go wrong, there is no legal recourse against the facilities management firm because of the courts' presumption that the parties dealt with each other "at arm's length." When signing the contract, each party's intention is to have a successful working relationship with the other. This kind of confidence in the ability to work together should not cause the user to take lightly the impact of an exculpatory clause. The courts do not.

Consultants' financial responsibility and previous contract performance should be investigated before hiring. Even though a consultant undertakes to perform a highly personal service for the user, the courts have not to date regarded the relationship as any more than an arm's-length business relationship. Thus, in arriving at an agreement, care must be taken to reflect the intended nature of the consultant's services. A cost formula should be specified. Some means of monitoring the consultant's work should be established, such as requiring periodic written progress reports. Since the user probably intends that the consultant perform a function for the personal benefit of the user—that is, the consultant has no real stake in the project other than being paid for the work done for the user—the user may want to provide that the user has the right to terminate the contract at will. Then, if for any reason the user is dissatisfied with the consultant's work or with the feasibility of the project itself, the user can bail out without any contractual obligation to pay the consultant for the entire project. If such a provision is inserted, some formula needs to be devised to adequately cover the consultant's investment of time, money, and disruption of his or her schedule to avoid conflict that might lead to, at least, bad will and, at worst, expensive litigation. If any specific results have been promised by the consultant, these should be included in the contract.

Precontract negotiations, proposals, and claims of expertise should be obtained in writing and kept on file in case the user needs to sue for fraud. The consultant's work should be monitored, preferably by some form of written report, to aid a court in determining negligence, that is, whether the level of skill employed by the consultant met the standard to be reasonably expected.

REFERENCES

1. 29 USC 157 (1976).

2. 29 USC 158 (1976).

3. 29 USC 152(3) (1976).

4. 29 USC 152(11) (1976).

5. 596 F.2d 704 (5th Cir. 1979).

6. Ford Motor Co., 66 NLRB 1317 (1946); R. Gorman, *Basic Text on Labor Law* 37 (1976).

7. National Labor Relations Board v. Bell Aerospace Co., 416 U.S. 267 (1974).

8. Ford Motor Co., 66 NLRB 1317 (1946).

9. R. Gorman, *Basic Text on Labor Law* 39 (1976).

10. 607 F.2d 852 (9th Cir. 1979).

11. 29 USC 152(12) (1976).

12. 29 USC 159(b) (1976).

13. Season-All Industries, Inc. v. National Labor Relations Board, 654 F.2d 932, 934 (3d Cir. 1981).

14. *See* R. Bigelow, *Programming Contracts,* CLS 3-4, art. 3 (Bigelow, ed. 1979).

15. 54 Am. Jur. 2d *Monopolies, Restraints of Trade, and Unfair Trade Practices* 511 (1971).

16. *Id.* at 550.

17. *Id.* at 543.

18. *Id.* at 576.

19. *See* Bigelow, *supra* note 14; R. Courtney, Jr., *Commonly Found Deficiencies in the Security of Data Processing Activities,* CLS 2-2, art. 1 (Bigelow, ed. 1979).

20. *See* Part IV's detailed discussion of proprietary protection.

21. *See* Amoco Production Co. v. Lindley, 609 P.2d 733 (Okla. 1980).

22. *Facilities Management,* CLS 3-1, art. 2 (Bigelow, ed. 1979); W. Fenwick, *Facilities Management Contracts,* CLS 3-1, art. 5 (Bigelow, ed. 1979).

23. Annbar Associates v. American Express Co., 565 S.W.2d 701 (Mo. Ct. App. 1978).

24. Laberis, "DPers Chase 'the Blues' EDSF for $18 Million," *Computerworld,* October 4, 1982, p. 1.

25. *See* Computer Sciences Corp. v. National Labor Relations Board, 677 F.2d 804 (11th Cir. 1982).

26. *See* R. Freed, *Evaluating a Consultant's Business Credentials,* CLS 3-4, art. 1 (Bigelow, ed. 1979).

27. *See* E. Saltzberg, *Computer Malpractice,* CLS Newsletter, 1980 Supp. No. 3.

28. F & M Schaefer Corp. v. Electronic Data Systems Corp., 430 F.Supp. 988 (S.D. N.Y. 1977).

29. Triangle Underwriters, Inc. v. Honeywell Corp., 604 F.2d 737 (2d Cir. 1979); Chatlos Systems, Inc. v. National Cash Register Corp., 479 F. Supp. 738 (D. N.J. 1979), *aff'd in part, remanded in part* 635 F.2d 1081 (3d Cir. 1980).

30. 596 F.2d 704 (5th Cir. 1979).

31. 174 N.J. Super. 418, 416 A.2d 952 (1980).

32. 508 S.W.2d 137 (Tex. Civ. App. 1974), 524 S.W.2d 393 (Tex. Civ. App. 1975).

33. 266 Md. 170, 292 A.2d 54 (1972).

34. 360 F. Supp. 1044 (N.D. Tex. 1973).

35. 322 F. Supp. 619 (D. Conn. 1970).

36. 401 F. Supp. 1102 (E.D. Mich. 1975).

37. 5 CLSR 817 (S.D. N.Y. 1975).

38. 644 F.2d 943 (2d Cir. 1981).

39. 304 F. Supp. 339 (S.D. Fla. 1969), *aff'd* 435 F.2d 292 (5th Cir. 1970).

PART IV

Writing Computer Programs For Sale

Outline

INTRODUCTION

As we enter an age when a homemaker or owner of a small business can go to a nearby computer store to select a computer appropriate for his or her needs, the market for computer programming skills can be expected to expand significantly. Two aspects of the law will be of prime importance to the programmer who is considering going into business writing computer programs: the programmer's potential liability for damages caused by errors and omissions and the ability of the programmer to protect the original programs from unauthorized use.

LIABILITY FOR DEFECTIVE PROGRAMS

The major purpose of this book is to offer a general background for computer users of the legal aspects of contracting for computer services and liability for computer-related activity. Only this part takes the opposite approach, incorporating the same legal concepts from the position of an independent writer of computer programs.

The independent programmer who works for profit may be sued by the user on the following grounds: (a) failure to fulfill the terms of the contract (in a breach-of-contract suit); (b) damage resulting from the use of the program (in a negligence or strict liability action); or (c) deliberately misleading the user about the character of the finished program or services to be provided (in a suit for tortious misrepresentation).

In addition, the programmer may be liable to third parties who are injured by the computer user's use of the program (as described in Part VI). If an injured third party sues the computer user for an injury caused by a defective program, the programmer may be brought into the controversy in one of three ways. First, the injured party may sue *both* the user and programmer, leaving it up to the court to decide which (if either) should be held liable. Second, the user may draw the programmer into the suit by a legal procedure called impleader through which the user in effect says that if there is to be any liability of the user to the injured party, the programmer should assume responsibility for it. Finally, the programmer may not be brought into the lawsuit, but if the user is held liable, the user may sue the programmer for indemnification, that is, reimbursement. For the programmer to be held liable in any of the three situations, the user or injured party must show that the injury was in reality caused by the programmer. Thus, the programmer needs to consider all the risks arising from the use of the program (see Part VI), as well as all the legal obligations owed to the computer user (see Parts I and II).

Contract

The programmer's legal obligations can be significantly reduced by engaging in cautious negotiations and by using a carefully drafted contract. This section will discuss both the contract needed to provide program-writing services and contract obligations for the sale of a packaged program. The programmer needs to become familiar with some aspects of contract law pertaining to express and implied warranties, as well as the damages for which he or she may be held liable.

Express Warranties. Express warranties are those promises and affirmations made by the programmer about the nature and quality of whatever the programmer has contracted to provide. The courts will hold the programmer to these promises. If the programmer promised to provide a program that performs six functions and the program ultimately performs five of the promised six, the programmer will be liable to the user in the amount of the value of the promised but undelivered function (plus any consequential damages that might be recoverable; see remedies section).

The most distinctive feature of express warranties is that they are creations of the programmer. To a large extent, the programmer possesses the ability to create, define, and limit his or her contract obligations. The programmer should be realistic in making claims and predictions about the capabilities of the finished program, whether in negotiating a contract for writing a program or in advertising a packaged program for sale.

The programmer can take further measures to protect against liability for express warranties. A wise approach for the programmer would be to put all contracts in writing and include an integration clause stating that the entire agreement of the parties is represented by the writing. This clause may prevent the programmer from being held to informal or hypothetical statements or predictions made during the negotiation stages.

The programmer's ability to limit contract liability is hampered by the reluctance of courts to enforce contract terms that relieve one of the parties of all contract liability. Thus, the programmer should include some express warranties setting out exactly what guarantees the buyer is being given. For example, the programmer may warrant that the program will be error-free for one year. Errors appearing after that time would create no obligation for the programmer to compensate the user for the errors. In addition, the programmer's liability may be expressly limited to replacement or to the price of the program, excluding liability for consequential damages in most cases (see remedies section).

As further protection, the programmer may include a provision that requires the user to perform within a specified time period a prescribed test of the program upon acceptance as a precondition to the express warranty's operation. In situations where the programmer meets with the user to determine the user's needs, the prescribed test should be developed using input that is representative of the user's operations. This process will also encourage the user to provide the programmer with all of the relevant data about the user's information system, the lack of which is a common problem.

In situations where the program is to be sold over the counter, the test may be constructed by the programmer using test data representative of that envisioned for the intended function. Since packaged programs generally require that the user conform the user's information system to the needs of the program, a programmer's liability could be limited through express warranties to errors arising out of use of the program in compliance with detailed instructions as to the data requirements of the system. If a user neglected to conduct the prescribed test before using the program, conducted the test improperly (thus failing to detect obvious errors), or failed to adapt the user's information system to the packaged program's data requirements, the programmer might escape liability under the limited express warranties.

Implied Warranties. If the court finds that the programming contract is for goods, the Uniform Commercial Code will be applied, bringing into play certain implied warranties. If the contract is found to be one for services, some courts will still imply certain warranties under the particular state's contract law, but most will not.

As discussed in Parts I and II, many considerations enter into the question of whether a contract for programming constitutes a contract for goods or for services. If the contract is worded to suggest that providing programming services is the object of the contract where the program is to be tailored to the user's needs, the contract may be deemed to be one for services. In that case, the UCC would not apply, and in most courts no warranties beyond the programmer's express warranties would be implied by law. If, however, the contract describes the number or type of programs or specifies the type of media to be provided, the object of the contract may be found to be the sale of goods, and the UCC's implied warranties of merchantability,[1] fitness for a particular purpose,[2] title, and against copyright or patent infringement[3] would then apply if the programmer is a merchant (is in the business or claims to have skill or knowledge peculiar to the items in question).[4] Thus, when the programmer markets packaged programs, it is much more likely that the sale will be treated as one for goods, invoking the UCC's provisions on implied warranties. The most the programmer can do to limit potential contract liability is assume that the UCC will apply and take steps to limit or avoid liability for any resultant implied warranties.

The implied warranty of merchantability warrants that the program sold is fit for the ordinary purposes for which such programs are used. The program must also pass without objection in the trade under the contract description of the program and conform to any promises or affirmations of fact made on the container or label. (Promises or affirmations on the label may also constitute express warranties.) Thus, the program's quality and usefulness for its intended purpose will be analyzed by the court. If the program falls below the current market standard for such programs or is not usable for its ordinary purposes, the court may find a breach of the implied warranty of merchantability. As the sale of packaged programs to consumers and small businesses becomes more commonplace, the implied warranty of merchantability may serve as an important legal vehicle for ensuring minimum standards of quality.

The implied warranty of fitness for a particular purpose, on the other hand, is of greatest significance to a programmer who, with knowledge of the particular user's needs, supplies a program intended to meet those needs. This warranty states that the goods provided must be fit to be used for the buyer's intended purpose. To establish the warranty, the seller must have reason to know the particular purpose for which the goods are required and that the buyer is relying upon the seller's skill or judgment to furnish suitable goods. When a user goes to a programmer to have software designed for the user's particular information system, the program's failure to adequately serve the system may constitute a breach of the implied warranty of fitness for a particular purpose.

The programmer who regularly deals in computer programs implicitly warrants that the goods delivered are free of the claims of third parties for "infringement or the like." Thus, unless the programmer's contract of sale states otherwise, the programmer will be liable to the buyer for any loss because of copyright or patent infringement. However, the UCC provides one important exception to this implied warranty. If the programmer prepares the program based upon specifications furnished by the buyer, the buyer must hold the seller harmless (that is, buyer takes responsibility) for any infringement arising out of the programmer's compliance with the buyer's specifications. This warranty therefore appears to affect the writer of packaged programs more than the custom programmer.

All three implied warranties may be excluded or modified in the contract by the express agreement of the parties.[5] To exclude or modify the implied warranty of merchantability, the contract language, whether oral or written, must mention "merchantability" and in a written contract that disclaimer must be conspicuous. For example, the exclusion may be in italic, boldfaced type, or underlined and in a noticeable place; it should *not* be in fine print or on the back of the signed portion of the contract. Language that seeks to modify or exclude the implied warranty of fitness for a particular purpose must be in writing and also conspicuous.

Unless the circumstances indicate otherwise, the merchantability and fitness warranties are also excluded by expressions such as "as is," "with all faults," or other language that in common understanding calls the buyer's attention to the exclusion of warranties and makes plain that there is no implied warranty. Note, however, that the qualifying language "unless the circumstances indicate otherwise" suggests that the verbal exclusions just noted would be ineffective if the conduct of the parties is inconsistent with an as-is sale, for example, if actions are undertaken by the programmer to correct deficiencies in the program after delivery to the user. Moreover, to sell computer programs on an as-is basis in the highly competitive, rapid-growth minicomputer industry would probably be nothing short of economic suicide. Therefore, as-is language in a contract for the sale of computer programs is probably not a viable alternative for the independent programmer.

The UCC, providing a better alternative, states that the following language is sufficient to exclude implied warranties of fitness: "There are no warranties that extend beyond the description on the face hereof." This language coupled with an adequate disclaimer of the warranty of merchantability enables the seller to limit the seller's liability to *express* warranties. The programmer thus becomes the final arbiter of his or her own contract liability.

In addition, if the buyer has examined the goods as fully as he or she desired, or has refused to examine the goods, there is no implied warranty as to defects which such an examination should have revealed. This means of excluding implied warranties can be a very powerful one for the programmer who allows the user to try out a program before purchasing it. Once the user buys the program after the trial period, the programmer escapes all liability for defects that the user should have discovered.

Even if the court finds that implied warranties exist, all is not lost for the programmer. If the user has not given the programmer notice of defects within a reasonable time after delivery, the buyer may not lawfully reject the delivered program. Even if the user does give timely notice of defects and the programmer had reasonable grounds to believe the program would be acceptable, the programmer may notify the user of the programmer's intention to cure the defects. The UCC requires that the user give the programmer a further reasonable time (beyond the contract date) to correct the defects.[6]

In addition, the programmer may avoid liability if the user improperly used the program. If the programmer of a packaged program furnishes a test for the user to check out the installed program, the responsibility for errors that should have been detected by the proper running of the test may be placed on the user instead of the programmer. Similarly, if the programmer clearly explains the data requirements of a packaged program but the user neglects to modify the user's information system to meet the program's needs, the user's misuse of the program may preclude the programmer's liability for errors on the basis of implied warranties.

Remedies. The normal monetary remedy for breach of a contract is the difference between the value of what was promised and the value of what was actually delivered. For example, if a promised six-function program was to be provided for $1,000 and the loss of one function reduced the value of the program to, say, $800, the programmer would be liable to the user for $200.

In certain cases, liability for incidental and consequential damages may be imposed. Incidental damages reimburse the user for costs caused by the programmer's breach. Examples might include the costs incurred by the user in the transporting, receiving, inspecting, and caring for rightfully rejected goods; costs incurred to obtain a substitute program; and costs occasioned by delays caused by the breach.[7] Consequential damages, as defined by the UCC, are of two types: first, losses resulting from requirements that the seller had reason to know of at the time of contracting and that could not reasonably be prevented by the buyer or, second, injury to person or property caused by breach of warranty.[8] Consequential damages constitute the greatest risk to the programmer since they may not be foreseeable. Normal compensatory damages are largely a function of the value of the contract, which is known to the programmer, and incidental damages are relatively minor and foreseeable based upon the characteristics of the program, that is, the testing, handling, expenses of replacing the program, and so on. Consequential damages, on the other hand, are more open ended as their amount is determined by whatever actual damages happen to result from the program. For example, if a malfunction of the inventory program caused the user a $10,000 loss due to its inability to fill customer orders, the user might seek to recover $10,000 in consequential damages from the programmer. The user would be unable to do so unless the programmer, at the time of contracting, was specifically aware or should have been aware of the particular risk of loss.

Thus, at least in the case of packaged programs, it is unlikely that consequential damages of the first type (requiring the programmer's knowledge of the user's risks) would be imposed since the programmer is likely to be removed from contact with the needs of the individual user. Furthermore, the UCC provides that the parties may modify or exclude the UCC's contract remedies by agreement. This means that the programmer may limit contract damages by including contract language making the exclusive remedy for breach, for example, return of the goods and refund of the price or correction of the programming errors by the programmer.

There are two caveats to the ability of the programmer to limit liability for contract damages. First, where circumstances cause an exclusive or limited remedy to fail, UCC remedies will be imposed instead.[9] This point is illustrated by the *Chatlos Systems* case[10] in which the contract limited the user's remedy to having any error corrected by the vendor-programmer within 60 days after the programs were furnished. Because four of the six promised functions were never furnished, the court reasoned that the express warranty had failed. Since the purpose of the limited remedy was to correct programming errors soon after delivery, normal UCC remedies were invoked. This case suggests that unless explicitly bargained for, the programmer will not be permitted to escape *all* liability for program errors. The courts will probably require the programmer to include at least some meaningful liability in the contract or else the UCC's normal remedies will be imposed.

Second, the UCC provides that consequential damages may not be limited or excluded if the limitation or exclusion is unconscionable.[11] The courts find unconscionability to exist in contract terms that are determined to be so unfair as to be against public policy. Typically, transactions between businesspersons will not be found unconscionable since it is presumed that the parties are familiar with contract law and in a position to bargain for more favorable terms. The terms of sales to consumers, on the other hand, have been found to be unconscionable when the court has determined that the consumer is at a considerable disadvantage in expertise and bargaining power. As computer use becomes more commonplace, the programmer should be especially careful to identify programs that pose any physical risks to the consumer, such as those controlling automobiles or robotic devices. By writing and selling such programs, the programmer becomes obligated to compensate any person injured by breach of warranties since the UCC presumes that provisions limiting liability for personal injuries are unconscionable.

It should be noted that modern courts are allowing "strangers" to the sale to enforce contract warranties. In the past, the only persons who could sue on a contract's terms were the parties to the contract, that is, those persons in privity of contract with each other. Lack of privity may be of two types: vertical or horizontal. Vertical privity refers to direct dealings in the chain of distribution of the product. In a typical case, the manufacturer sells to a wholesaler who sells to a retailer who sells to the customer. Tradition-ally, the consumer could sue only the retailer since there was no vertical privity with the wholesaler or manufacturer. Some courts have dispensed with the requirement of vertical privity in certain cases, while others have not. Horizontal privity refers to the person who is entitled to sue. Tradi-tionally, only the person who actually bought the product was entitled to sue on the warranties. Recently, courts have been inclined to extend the protections of contract warranties to other persons who may foreseeably be affected by a breach of warranty. The UCC as adopted by many states specifically abandons the requirement of horizontal privity, stating that a seller's warranty extends at least to any natural person who is in the family or household of the buyer or a guest in the buyer's home if it is to be reasonably expected that the person may be affected by the goods and is in fact injured in person by breach of warranty.[12] Other states extend the pro-tection even further to any person (including corporations) who may rea-sonably be expected to be affected by the goods and who is injured (not necessarily in person) by the breach of the warranty. Furthermore, a seller may not alter or exclude this extended protection by contract. The UCC thus makes it clear that programmers will not be able to escape liability for personal injuries, suggesting that programmers use extreme care in developing programs that pose any risk of personal injury.

Summary. A court is likely to consider the writer of packaged programs to be subject to the terms of the UCC concerning the sale of goods. The writer, therefore, needs to be concerned about limiting the operation of implied warranties. This may be done by using the specific contract language required to exclude implied warranties. The programmer should be careful, however, to provide some contractual remedies to the buyer or else the court may impose its own.

Programs written for a specific user are less likely to be subject to the UCC, but application of the UCC is still possible if the court views the supplied programs as goods rather than services. Therefore, care should still be taken to comply with the UCC provisions for excluding or limiting implied warranties yet leaving some remedy to the user.

In either case, the programmer should be especially careful not to create unintended express warranties. Opinions and predictions expressed to the user should be clearly introduced as such before, during, and after the sign-ing of the contract.

Express warranties may be limited to a specific time period. A contract provision requiring an acceptance test by the user may be useful in discov-ering errors early. This gives the programmer the opportunity to correct them before the user has incurred extensive consequential damages for which it will want to be reimbursed. In addition, a test requirement may operate to create defenses against the user since it forces the user to help provide adequate systems data to the programmer and to discover obvious errors. The test provision should be willingly accepted by the user since it gives assurances that a working, worthwhile program will be installed be-fore the contract is performed and payable.

Tort Liability

Recovery in tort is independent of the parties' agreement. It is based on a finding that the programmer's conduct was socially wrongful in some way or public policy requires that the programmer bear the cost of injury. The programmer needs to be aware of three potential areas of tort liability: misrepresentation, negligence, and strict liability.

Misrepresentation. A tortious misrepresentation, or fraud, is committed when a person makes a false statement of fact with the intention that another person act or refrain from acting because of that fact. The other person must detrimentally rely on the statement that induced action or inaction. A programmer could be held liable for false statements made to induce a user to enter into a contract for a computer program. For example, a programmer's false statement that a certain program has been successfully applied by other users might be sufficient ground for a court to find a tortious misrepresentation.[13]

Since the tort of misrepresentation requires a culpable state of mind on the part of the programmer, the conscientious programmer can avoid the charge by not stating to the prospective user *as fact* anything that is not known by the programmer to be true. The programmer's statements of opinions, predictions of success, and intentions should be stated truthfully and always introduced for what they are. False statements about intentions or the probability of success may subject the programmer to liability for any resultant expenses and losses sustained by the user, as well as possible punitive damages for particularly unsavory conduct.

Negligence. The programmer may also be liable in tort for damages caused by a lack of care in writing the program. It is not yet clear exactly what standard of care should be applied to the computer programmer. Although it has been suggested that a programmer should be held to a professional standard of care comparable to medical or legal malpractice, the establishment of that professional standard appears unlikely at the present time. No court has yet actually held a programmer liable for malpractice, although one judge's pretrial ruling suggested the possibility.[14] Until such a time as computer personnel are regulated and licensed to the same extent as other professions, a professional standard appears inappropriate. The programmer is more likely to be judged as an expert layperson in accordance with the programmer's skill and experience.[15]

To be successful in a negligence suit, the injured party will have to make a detailed showing of the manner in which the programmer was responsible for the injury. This burden of proof has two aspects. First, the injured party will have to show that the cause of the injury was in fact a program error as opposed to a data error, hardware defect, or transmission problem. Second, the injured party must demonstrate exactly what the programmer should have done (or not done) to have prevented the injury.

For example, in one case,[16] a court ruled that a bank's computer program inadequately served its intended purpose, to stop payment of customers' checks on request. The bank's procedure required that the customer give the bank the exact amount of the check to be stopped. The bank's computer was programmed to key in on three sets of numbers, or fields, on the bottom of each check: the bank's Federal Reserve number, the customer's account number, and the amount of the check. The computer would pull the check before payment only if every digit on the check matched exactly the numbers on the stop payment order. In this case, the amount of the check on the stop payment order was in error by fifty cents. The computer therefore failed to pull the check and it was paid, contrary to the customer's instructions. The court ruled in favor of the customer, holding that the bank computer system's total reliance on the accuracy of the amount required the bank to assume the risk that its system's inherent limitations would fail to stop a check.

In the computer industry with many newly emerging applications and techniques and few well-defined standards, it is not at all clear how the courts will determine which techniques programmers should or should not have employed in writing a computer program. The court will probably hear conflicting testimony by computer experts, choose which to believe, and decide whether the programmer did what a programmer of similar skill and experience would have done when writing the program. Another possibility is that the court will look at the less technical issues of whether the programmer adequately tested and debugged the program and whether the programmer adequately warned the user of the program's limitations.

The programmer should therefore attempt to provide the best techniques and procedures available (at a reasonable cost) for the particular application. The programmer should adequately test and debug the programs. If the contract allocates responsibility for testing to the user, the court may not hold the programmer negligent if the contract's specifications have otherwise been met. It is certainly to the programmer's advantage to include such a provision in the contract. Nevertheless, because of the programmer's greater experience, some courts may require that the buyer be given more contract protection. Steps should therefore be taken to ensure that the program meets the programmer's own standards of quality beyond what may be required by the contract.

It is also quite likely that a court will consider a programmer to be the party who is best equipped and obligated to identify risks that are inherent in a particular program and perhaps find the programmer negligent if the programmer fails to warn the user of these risks. The programmer can best meet the requirements of a duty to warn by, again, being frank with the user about exactly what the user is and is not paying for in terms of the program's capabilities. If the programmer encountered unforeseen problems in the design of the system or has reservations about any aspect of its operation, the user should be alerted to watch out for problems in that area.

The lack of proximate cause may be asserted as a defense by the programmer if the user's fault can be shown to be an intervening and superseding cause of the injury (see Part VI); that is, the programmer can claim that even though the program may have been negligently written, the injury would not have occurred were it not for the user's negligence as well. This may occur if the programming error would not have caused any damage if the user had not used faulty data. Or, for example, assume a packaged program is sold with explicit instructions on how to test the program. The user, however, neglects to test the program as directed and, as a result, injury occurs either to the user or to a third party (perhaps one of the user's customers). Even though the error in the program was negligently made by the programmer, the programmer may escape liability by arguing that the more direct cause of the injury was the user's failure to test for the error.

If the user is the injured party, the defense of contributory or comparative negligence may be available to the programmer. For example, the failure of the user to test the program, to provide the programmer with the necessary information to adequately tailor the system to the user's operations, to change the user's operations to meet the requirements of a packaged program, and to report suspected errors to the programmer all represent ways in which the user may fail to exercise a reasonable amount of care to protect the user's own interests. In contributory negligence states, the plaintiff cannot recover anything from the defendant if the plaintiff's own negligence contributed to the injury. In comparative negligence states, the plaintiff's damages are reduced by the percentage of fault allocable to the plaintiff (see Part VI on negligence defenses).

The programmer should note that to establish any defense based upon the fault of the user, the programmer must have done everything possible to enable the user to act in the proper way to protect against injuries resulting from the program. Frankness with the user and a concern for having satisfied clients with useful computer programs will go a long way toward protecting the programmer's legal position in defending against a negligence suit.

Strict Liability. Under the law of strict liability, as discussed in Part VI, liability for injuries may be imposed without any showing of fault. The most common application of strict liability is for defective products. If a product was made in a defective manner and causes physical injury to a person or property, the manufacturer is liable without proof of how the manufacturer was negligent or otherwise at fault (although it is still necessary to show that the product was defective in some way).[17]

Strict product liability may affect the programmer in two ways. First, the computer user who uses a computer program in the manufacture of a product may be held liable for a defective product. If the defect was the result of a program error, the programmer may be required to reimburse the user for the judgment against the user. It is therefore extremely important to use the utmost care in developing programs to be used in the design or manufacture of products. In addition, the programmer can attempt to contract out of any obligation to indemnify the user for defective product claims.

The second and more alarming way in which strict liability may affect the programmer is if the courts view the program itself as a product, thereby making the programmer liable for all resulting injuries without a showing of fault. Determining whether the program is a product entails an analysis of the same factors used in determining whether the program is a good for UCC purposes. The strict liability analysis involves three additional social policy considerations, which may lead a court to impose strict liability for program-related injuries.[18]

First, courts consider a stream-of-commerce policy. If the producer places a product in the stream of commerce making it available to the general public, the courts may impose strict liability for defects under two theories. First, since the producer has placed the product on the market to earn a profit, public policy dictates that the producer bear the risk of loss of resulting injuries. Second, placing the product on the market invites the public to use it. Such an invitation implies that the product is safe, and a court may impose strict liability to give effect to the consumer's reasonable expectation of safeness. Thus, the stream-of-commerce policy appears to require strict liability for programs marketed to the general public but not to those sold on a one-to-one basis to the user. The writer of packaged programs should therefore be especially careful in creating programs for off-the-shelf marketing.

The courts also consider the producer's position to control risks. Under this rationale, the courts assume that the producer of the product has specialized knowledge of the product and is therefore in the best position to evaluate and control the product's risks of harm. With strict liability for defects, the producer (the party with superior knowledge of the product) is held responsible for the decision of whether the product is safe enough for use by the public. This policy also appears to dictate strict liability for the writer of packaged programs since the programmer is far more familiar with the strengths and weaknesses of the program placed on the market than is the consumer. On the other hand, if the program is tailored to a specific user, the user normally has been involved in the program's design since the user must specify what the program is to do. Therefore, under the position-to-control-risks rationale, strict liability should probably not be applied to the writer of a program tailored to a particular user.

A third policy, cost spreading, is also a justification for imposing strict liability. When the producer sells the product to a number of users and strict liability is imposed, the costs of the injury become included in the cost of the product. By imposing strict liability, the cost of the injury may be spread over all the buyers of the product. Such a policy is considered socially desirable because the costs of injury are internalized into the price structure, leading to economic efficiency on the theory that the market will not support a product whose costs, including the costs of injury, are greater than its utility value. This final rationale may also be used to hold the writer of ready-to-use packaged programs strictly liable for injuries since it enables the programmer to spread the costs of injuries over the many buyers of the program. It would more than likely not apply to tailored programs since there are no other buyers of the identical program to absorb the costs of the injury.

These policies have been generalized by the courts to apply strict liability to things that would not normally be considered products. For example, the sellers of mass-produced homes[19] and electricity,[20] and an automobile-leasing agency[21] have all been held liable for injuries on the preceding policy grounds. On the other hand, these policies have not led to strict liability against the designer of a chemical plant because the designer's action was highly specialized and there was no impact on the public at large;[22] nor against the landlord of an apartment dwelling because he was not engaged in mass production of such dwellings and was not in a better position to know about and correct the injury-producing condition.[23] Court decisions seem to be consistent in suggesting that the foregoing policies may lead to strict liability for the seller of prepackaged programs but not for the programmer who sells customized programs.

Strict liability has been used as a basis for recovery against the designer of a computerized sawmill.[24] In that case, the designer argued that the deceased mill operator was contributorily negligent in assuming the risk of injury by climbing into a log carrier without checking to see whether the mill was inoperative. The court held that this conduct did not amount to an unreasonable voluntary assumption of the risk *with actual knowledge* of the risk and therefore posed no defense to the designer's liability. Many courts set a similarly stringent standard before a plaintiff's conduct will act as a defense to strict product liability. Programmers should therefore make every feasible effort to make users (and other foreseeably affected persons) *actually aware* of potential dangers of personal injury or property damage.

Insurance[25]

As for other types of business risks, insurance coverage has been made available to cover liability for programmers' errors and omissions. The selection of insurance policies may be a trap for the unwary requiring the advice of legal counsel. As a general matter, the programmer should be hesitant about buying standard policies at lower prices and take care to ascertain the differences in coverage provided by differently priced policies.

In reading an insurance policy, two sections are critical in determining the scope of coverage. First, the insuring agreement sets out the programmer's activity from which the covered liability may arise. Second, the exclusions section specifies types of errors or activities that are not covered. The prospective insured should not assume that merely because an activity is not mentioned in the exclusion section, it is therefore covered. Many policies may limit the scope of coverage, by definition, to the *included* activities.

The terms of an insurance policy should be analyzed with an eye toward the insured's potential liability. Some types of liability may not be covered by a standard errors and omissions policy. For example, a policy may cover only injuries arising out of errors in the technical programming, leaving uncovered the programmer's potential liability for breaches of contract (such as late delivery or incorrect price quotes) or misrepresentations by sales personnel.

Some attention should also be paid to the policy's procedures for allowing a claim. For example, many errors may not be discovered or create any harm to another for a period of years after the error was made. If there is a potential long-term risk in the types of programs written, the programmer should seek a policy with terms allowing claims that arise out of errors that occurred before the policy's termination date but are reported within a reasonable time after the policy's expiration date. In general, the policy should provide an adequate discovery period for the type of potential liability.

A special problem with insurance policy time limits arises in errors and omission coverage for the writer of packaged programs. Many policies may provide a maximum limit *per occurrence* of an error, which places the limit on *all* claims arising out of each error. When a single program containing an error is sold to many different customers, such a limit may be inadequate. The programmer may instead try to obtain a *per claim* limit so that the set policy limit would be payable to *each* claimant. In using deductibles to reduce the cost of the policy, however, the insured may opt for a per occurrence deductible instead of per claim to avoid the expense of cumulative deductibles for each claim arising out of a single error.

As a general matter, the selection of insurance for programmers requires much more than cost appraisal of standard policies. The programmer should, with the assistance of legal counsel, carefully analyze the potential liability risks and bargain for a policy that will adequately meet those risks at a reasonable cost.

PROTECTION OF PROPRIETARY INTERESTS IN COMPUTER PROGRAMS

In writing computer programs, the programmer may employ some measure of creative thinking. The programmer would certainly like to enjoy the fullest possible economic return from this creativity.

The law recognizes the need for economic protection of products derived from innovative thinking to encourage technological development. By permitting the originator to enjoy a limited monopoly for the creation, the law creates an economic incentive for the development of new ways of thinking and encourages the creator to make the innovation available for widespread distribution to the benefit of industry and society. Such a policy, by eliminating the possible duplication of effort by other would-be inventors, promotes social efficiency in technological development.

Legal authorities have had some difficulty, however, in finding the appropriate legal vehicle to protect the economic interests of software developers for their original creations. Uncertainty in the legal community about this issue is of legitimate concern to the programmer. The following discussion examines four existing courses of action that a program writer can take to protect original works: patent, copyright, trade secrecy, and trademark law. Each is directed toward protecting a certain type of proprietary interest. The task at hand is to determine which, if any, is most appropriate for the protection of a creator's interests in the particular type of computer software created.

Patent

Patent law grants the owner of an invention a monopoly over the use, manufacture, and sale of the invention for 17 years.[26] To be patentable, the invention must consist of a "new and useful process, machine, manufacture, or composition of matter, or any new and useful improvement thereof. . . ." [27] Having determined that the invention represents patentable subject matter, the Patent Office (PTO) investigates the invention to determine whether it represents a novel invention, not "obvious at the time the invention was made to a person having ordinary skill in the art. . . ." [28] If so, a patent may be issued to the applicant by the PTO. The decision of the Patent Office is reviewable by the Court of Customs and Patent Appeals (CCPA) and ultimately by the Supreme Court.

A particular patent falls into one of two categories: apparatus patents or process patents. Apparatus patents cover inventions of, for example, a new machine, while a process patent is for a novel transformation of the machine for a particular use. Early software patent applicants were successful in obtaining apparatus patents since the CCPA adopted the view that when combined with the computer, the innovative program, by physically arranging the memory elements differently, in effect created a new patentable machine. [29] Subsequently, however, the attitude of the court changed and the view that a new machine was created by a program came to be regarded as a legal fiction. [30] Software patent applicants also recognized that even if accepted, apparatus claims offered protection for programs only as components of the computer hardware, affording no protection for the programs themselves. [31] As a result of these two factors, applicants began to submit patent claims as new processes instead of apparatuses.

An early Supreme Court opinion defined a patentable process as "a mode of treatment of certain materials to produce a given result. It is an act, or a series of acts, performed upon the subject matter to be transformed and reduced to a different state or thing." [32] Relying on this precedent, the Patent Office announced that software was not patentable based on machine or process claims unless the program transformed the computer into a special-purpose machine. The Patent Office stance followed the so-called "mental steps" doctrine, which held that if a process could be carried out mentally with pencil and paper, it constituted an unpatentable cognitive process. [33]

The CCPA came to the aid of software developers by doing away with the mental steps test as applied by the Patent Office in a 1970 case. [34] The CCPA held that as long as the invention is considered a technological art as defined by the patent laws, the fact that some steps can be carried out mentally does not preclude its patentability. Similarly, the CCPA has refused to permit the Patent Office to reject patent claims simply because they use a computer to perform mechanical tasks. [35] This course taken by the CCPA resulted in the reversal of other decisions of the Patent Office that had denied software patent applications. However, the Patent Office has also frustrated patent applicants on other grounds such as finding that the applicants failed to adequately describe the subject matter to permit duplication by skilled artisans. [36]

The Supreme Court had three opportunities to speak to the basic issues of whether computer software is patentable but refused to do so in each case. Instead, the Court decided each case on grounds that, when taken together, preserved the somewhat confused state of patent law that existed previously and simply appealed to Congress for resolution of the issues. [37]

In 1981, however, the Supreme Court affirmed the CCPA's holdings that claims should not be rejected merely because a computer is involved.[38] Although apparently expressing approval of the CCPA's position that patentability depends on the nature of the overall task being performed independently of the fact that a computer is used for that function, the Court declined to overrule its earlier cases that suggested the inapplicability of patents to computer programs. As a result, conflicts of interpretation still exist between the PTO and CCPA so that the acquisition of a software patent is likely to be a time-consuming and costly legal battle. Consequently, with so many legal questions left unanswered, patent law does not appear to afford trustworthy protection for the originator's rights in computer software except for limited types of cases.

Patents have been upheld by the CCPA for computerized processes that do more than perform a series of mathematical calculations to arrive at some solution. For example, patents have been upheld for a computerized method of translating human languages[39] and for a computerized typesetter.[40] Similarly, a mechanism that altered or repositioned information in a computer's system base was held patentable.[41] Thus, it appears that a program designed to produce some physical result or physical alterations in the computer itself may be patentable. In such cases, patent protection should perhaps be sought since a patent provides more comprehensive coverage than other proprietary protections. The holder of a patent obtains protection of the invention itself and the underlying ideas from both copying and independent discovery by another inventor. Copyright protection, on the other hand, protects only against unauthorized copying of an expression of the program, affording no protection against use of the underlying ideas expressed in another format. Neither copyright nor trade secrecy law prevents another inventor who independently discovers the innovation from using it.

Copyright

The creator of an original work possesses the copyright from the moment the work is fixed in some tangible medium.[42] Certain formalities must be observed, however, to avoid loss of the copyright itself or loss of certain remedies such as the right to sue for infringement. All published, visually perceptible copies of the work must contain a notice of copyright consisting of three parts: first, the symbol © or the word "copyright" or the abbreviation "copr."; second, the year of the work's first publication; and finally, the name of the copyright owner. This notice may be displayed in several ways, including placing it in machine-readable form so that it appears in any printouts of the program or on the user's terminal, or by attaching labels to cartridges, cassettes, or containers holding the copies of the program. If no copyright notice is given, the copyright is not necessarily forfeited, but a person who duplicates a program without notice may be held to be an innocent infringer and therefore not liable for damages to the holder of the copyright for infringement (see the *Data Cash* case in the court cases discussion). Unpublished programs are now also eligible for copyright registration. Although the notice requirement applies only to published copies, it is advisable to include a copyright notice on *all* copies to avoid mistakes.

Registration is not required to establish a copyright since a copyright exists from the moment of creation. Registration is required, however, to obtain the right to sue for copyright infringement. Registration may be accomplished at any time during the term of the copyright by completing a Copyright Office registration form TX, paying a $10 fee, and depositing one visually perceptible copy of the "identifying portion" of a program, either on paper or in microform, with the Copyright Office. The identifying portion consists of either the first and last 25 pages (or equivalent units) of the program if reproduced on paper, or at least the first and last 25 pages (or equivalent unit) if reproduced in microform, together with the page (or equivalent unit) containing the copyright notice, if any. The register of copyrights will, after examining the application and copies to ensure that the work is copyrightable subject matter and that other legal and formal requirements have been met, register the work and send a certificate of registration to the applicant.

The Copyright Office, in its initial treatment of software applications, expressed doubt about the applicability of copyright law to programs because of two important questions: whether a program is the "writing of an author" within the meaning of the Constitution, which authorizes the copyright laws, and whether a reproduction of a program in machine-readable form is a copy that can be accepted for copyright registration.[43] The Copyright Office decided to resolve all doubts in favor of copyright protection and began to accept software for registration in 1964.

It had been hoped that the new Copyright Act of 1976 (Act) would resolve the issues surrounding the Copyright Office's policy of issuing copyrights for software. Instead, the Act expressly left the state of the law on computer software exactly where it was before the new Act.[44] The new Copyright Act did, however, make it easier for software developers to obtain copyrights by dispensing with the requirements of readability and publication, providing that copyright exists in a literary work from the moment it is "fixed in any tangible medium of expression . . . from which [it] can be perceived, reproduced, or otherwise communicated, either directly or with the aid of a machine or device."[45] Moreover, in a 1980 amendment to the Copyright Act, Congress provided that the owner of a copy of a computer program does not infringe a copyright of the program by making a copy in order to use it in a machine or for archival purposes.[46] This amendment makes it clear that Congress intends that copyright law be extended to computer programs. Thus, for the time being, the pressing concern of software developers is not so much whether copyright protection *is available* but whether it is *adequate* to protect the developer's economic interests since copyright law protects only against unauthorized copying, not against unauthorized use of the underlying ideas.

One major problem with seeking copyright protection for computer programs is that even if applied to software, a copyright protects only the right to copy the *expression* of an idea, not the use of the *idea itself*.[47] The Supreme Court illustrated the effect of this reasoning in an early case involving a copyrighted book that outlined a new bookkeeping system and contained suggested forms for implementing the new system.[48] Another author subsequently published different forms, which accomplished the same purpose as the author's. The Supreme Court held that the book author's copyright did not give an exclusive right to make and use all bookkeeping forms utilizing the ideas expressed in the book but only those forms that were actually a part of the book and copyrighted as such.

A related exception to copyright protection was established in *Morrissey v. Procter & Gamble Co.*,[49] which held that since a description of contest rules could be varied only in a slight way and that to allow a copyright on the means of expression would in effect allow a monopoly on the underlying idea, no infringement occurred when the plaintiff's contest rules were used by the defendant. Given the infinite number of ways in which a source program may be written, varying the labeling of variables and sequence of commands, it would seem unlikely that this doctrine could ever be applied to a computer program. But that is exactly what happened in *Synercom Technology, Inc. v. University Computing Co.*,[50] a case involving the alleged theft of the plaintiff's unique input format for a structural analysis computer program by the defendant. The court noted that of the hundreds of programs available for structural analysis, 15 of which were competitive with the plaintiff's, only the plaintiff's and defendant's had the same input formats. The court stated that on a purely statistical basis, the chances of the defendant's arranging the data in an identical order were less than one in three million! The court nevertheless found that because the ideas expressed by the plaintiff's input formats could be expressed only by using the identical arrangement, the defendant's use of the formats did not infringe the plaintiff's copyright since copyright does not extend protection to ideas.

Another problem that arises once copyright protection is recognized for a computer program is whether it applies to the program in all of its modes. If a copyright is obtained on the source copy of a program, is that copyright infringed when another person copies the program in its machine language, or object code, form? In another early case (under the old copyright laws), the Supreme Court ruled that a pianola roll for a player piano was not a copy of the copyrighted music under the copyright law.[51] This case has been construed to stand for the principle that the form of the work must be perceptible to the human eye to be a copy[52] although the new Copyright Act would appear to replace the "eyeability" standard with "tangibility." Analogizing to computer software, copyright protection would arguably not extend to programs in machine-readable form, such as disks, drums, chips, and tapes. Federal courts have reached contrary conclusions on this question. For reasons discussed at length in the court cases section, the more persuasive and most valuable view as legal precedent is that a copyright of the written mode also extends to the machine mode. While these holdings definitely encourage the use of copyright protection for computer programs, reliance is still risky until higher courts or Congress definitively resolve the matter.

Since a copyright protects only against unauthorized copying, no protection is afforded against another person who can accomplish the copyrighted program's innovative end result by using a different program, referred to as a "knock-off" or "reverse engineering." *Stern Electronics, Inc. v. Kaufman*[53] represents an interesting case involving a video game in which a competitor used a knock-off program to create the same visual effects and game sequence as the copyrighted version. In *Stern,* however, the copyright holder had astutely recognized that in marketing a video game, it was the protection of the audiovisual *result* of the program that was critical instead of the *program* itself. Therefore, the owner declined to copyright the printed program as a literary work but instead copyrighted the game's audiovisual scenarios as an audiovisual work. Thus, the owner argued, it did not matter that the alleged infringer had used a different program to achieve the same end result as the owner's game; the duplication of the audiovisual display was sufficient to constitute copyright infringement. The alleged infringer argued that there had been no fixation of the display in a tangible medium of expression and that the work was not original, both contentions calling attention to the fact that the sequence of actions in the display was dependent upon the intervening actions of the player. These contentions and the court's analysis of them are explained in fuller detail in the court cases section, but in short, the court rejected the infringer's arguments and upheld the use of an audiovisual copyright to ward off potential knock-offs.

The *Stern* case result suggests very strongly that copyright protection may result in almost complete protection of a computer innovation whose end product is the unique aspect requiring protection. So long as the program's end product, or visual display, is itself sufficiently original and sufficiently repetitive over the course of each consecutive run to be considered "fixed" to warrant copyright protection of its own, the owner of the copyright can prevent another from using *any program* that produces the same end result. Without this holding from *Stern,* the owner's rights are limited to preventing anyone copying the particular program itself.

It is not at all clear how far a court would go to find an output format copyrightable. Some courts might not have gone as far as the *Stern* court, which explicitly declined to express an opinion about what other types of output might be similarly protected. It is probably safe to assume that at one end of the spectrum, it would be very difficult to convince a court that a printout displaying various forms of statistical tabulations is sufficiently original or sufficiently fixed (since the expression, or output, will vary significantly depending upon the input) to prevent others from making similar printouts. At the other end, an audiovisual game in which the creator conceived the display of a sequence of attacking spaceships, missiles, mountains, and so on to be present with each run of the program and then wrote a program to create the scenes is well within at least the *Stern* court's idea of a copyrightable display. Where the line should be drawn between these two is not at all clear.

Although many more cases must be decided to be absolutely sure about the availability and adequacy of copyright protection for a particular program, the recent trend of computer software cases is very favorable. At a minimum, copyright can prevent unauthorized duplication of a source copy of the program, and respectable authority exists for the conclusion that this protection extends to the object code as well. If the purpose of the program is to create some unique output that is itself copyrightable, under *Stern* the owner may prevent the use of other programs that will create the same output. The *Synercom* case places an outside limit on copyright protection with its holding that if a copyrighted program represents the *only* way to express certain ideas (and the *Synercom* court was very liberal in finding that situation to exist), the copyright may be infringed without liability to the copyright holder.

Trade Secrecy

A trade secret is a "formula, pattern, device, or compilation of information which is used in one's business, and which gives him an opportunity to obtain an advantage over competitors who do not know or use it."[54] The law of trade secrecy is probably the simplest and the most widely used method of protecting software.[55] Ownership of a trade secret gives the owner exclusive rights to its use. Thus, the developer may license another person to use the innovation for some specified purpose, and if the other party violates the agreement by using the innovation for some unauthorized purpose or by disclosing it to unauthorized persons, the developer may sue the licensee for the economic damage caused by the licensee's unauthorized actions. Similarly, if the secret is stolen by unauthorized persons, the developer may sue for damages caused by the misappropriation.

Trade secret protection is preferable to copyright and patent protection for several reasons. First and foremost, there is too much confusion in the legal profession about patent and copyright protection of software for many developers to feel justified in entrusting their competitive advantages to those two forms of protection. Trade secret protection does not require registration or filing with government agencies for its creation and enforceability; rather, protection exists from the time of the innovation's creation and is a natural outgrowth of the developer's desire to protect the investment by keeping it confidential. Patent and copyright law, on the other hand, require the developer to make the development public as a prerequisite to eligibility for protection.

Although trade secret protection may be easily obtained, it may be lost just as quickly. A trade secret exists only as long as it is a *secret;* that is, the developer may be required to go to great lengths to establish and ensure the continued confidentiality of the innovation. In addition, no protection is afforded against the competitor who independently discovers the new development. As a policy matter, widespread trade secret protection may tend to stifle technological development since it encourages jealous safeguarding of software improvements rather than the free interchange of new ideas.

For a time, it was suggested that trade secret protection, a matter of state law, might be preempted by federal patent law. The Supreme Court apparently resolved this question in 1974 when it held that the two forms of protection were not in conflict and therefore trade secret law remains a viable means of protection.[56] It has been similarly held in a recent computer-related case that federal copyright law does not preempt state trade secret law when the allegedly infringed matter has been copyrighted.[57] These are important holdings, since even though patent and copyright law offer protection with the idea that public disclosure will be made, the innovator is still able to retain as trade secrets those aspects of the innovation not directly covered by the patent or copyright, thereby maintaining a further competitive advantage.

For the time being, trade secrecy may be the most desirable form for legal protection of innovative software developments from the viewpoint of developers. This form of protection is not, however, adequate to further the industry goals of encouraging technological development; protection of developers' investments may encourage innovation by individual developers but trade secret protection may also lead to wasteful duplication of effort by software developers attempting to protect their own investments. For this reason, the legal and computer professions continue to search for a meaningful alternative that will incorporate the strengths and minimize the weaknesses of these three existing means of protection.

The Future of Software Protection

In 1974, Congress created the National Commission on New Technological Uses of Copyrighted Works (CONTU) to study the problems associated with protecting proprietary interests in software and to make specific recommendations for legislation that would adequately protect the interests of software developers. The commission recommended that the Copyright Act be amended to expressly permit copyright protection for computer programs representing an author's original creation. The commission did not accept the view that copyright protection should be denied software merely because programs are used in conjunction with machines but rather found software to be analogous to phonograph records or videotapes, which are copyrightable. The commission did not make clear, however, whether copyright of, say, the source phase of a computer program would protect against copying in the assembly or object phases since the CONTU report stated that copyright would *not* protect the electromechanical functioning of a machine. There is also doubt about whether copyright protection would exist for microchips under the CONTU proposal since read only memories (ROMs) that permanently contain a computer program in the object phase might be regarded as part of the machine and thus not copyrightable. (The current state of this issue is treated in detail in the court cases section.)

Thus, although the CONTU proposal would make certain that copyright protection was made available for computer software, it would do nothing to resolve the questions inherent in the application of present copyright protection to software; that is, the protection afforded under the CONTU proposal would still protect only against unauthorized reproduction of a particular mode of the program copy and not provide any protection of the underlying ideas or of the program itself once it is introduced into the machine.

One member of the commission expressed disagreement with the CONTU proposal in a dissenting opinion. Commissioner John Hersey, a Pulitzer Prize-winning author, expressed serious misgivings about the extension of copyright protection to computer software. Commissioner Hersey rejected the analogy to phonograph records or tapes, urging instead that the boundary line for copyright protection be drawn between creations that communicate with humans and those that communicate with machines. Another member recommended distinguishing between programs that *produce* works that themselves qualify for protection and those that are not capable of producing a written work. Thus, a program resulting in a printout would be copyrightable while a program designed only to control a mechanical process would not.

In a subcommittee report preceding CONTU's final report, Commissioner Hersey proposed legislation to create a new hybrid system of protection for computer software. The proposed computer software protection act would give the proprietor of the software the exclusive right to reproduce the software and any original method or process embodied in the software *in any medium,* to sell or lease the software to the public, and to use the software to operate a computer or to authorize another to do any of these things.

Although legal commentators addressing the question generally agree that any method of software protection requires some form of copyright and patent law hybrid,[58] there is still much uncertainty about the specific aspects to be drawn from each: for example, how rigorous the search of "prior art" should be to determine originality (if any), time limits, definition of the required mediums for submission, and whether independent creation should constitute an infringement. Clearly, to develop such a complex hybrid system will require a great deal of further study and the concern of legislators. To date, the Congress has done little to suggest that a solution is forthcoming. The protection afforded by trade secrecy thus remains the most viable option for most software producers.

Trademark Law

Trademark law may provide a more limited, although perhaps more definite, type of protection for innovative software. Trademark law protects the exclusive right of a business to use a word or symbol to distinguish its product from those of competitors. It is based on the policy that it is unfair and wrongful for a competitor to use a trade name developed by another to sell a competing product. Protection of trademarks is also highly desirable as a matter of public policy since it prevents confusion among consumers of the competing products. The value of trademark protection to the innovative programmer is that competitors may be prevented from capitalizing upon the successful marketing of the trademark owner's product or service by using the same name or symbol to identify the competing product. For example, VisiCalc is a very popular program for minicomputers. A competitor may develop another program with the same capabilities as VisiCalc and try to use the term VisiCalc to describe or identify the new program. Trademark protection of the VisiCalc name prevents the competitor from doing so without legal liability to the trademark owner.

Trademark protection and registration is granted upon a determination that an alleged symbol in fact identifies and distinguishes the goods or services of one seller. The alleged unauthorized use of a trademark may be challenged in a trademark infringement lawsuit or in registration proceedings when the applicant's mark is alleged to be similar to a mark already in use by another. In either case, the controlling issue is whether the two uses of the symbol or similar symbols is likely to confuse customers. For example, in *Telemed Corp. v. Tel-Med, Inc.,*[59] Telemed, a computer analysis of electrocardiograms by telephone, was determined by the court to be a descriptive trade name that was *not* entitled to protection against the use of Tel-Med, a noncompeting medical service that disseminated health information to the general public by telephone.

The degree and type of protection provided by a trademark is of a limited nature. Basically, a trademark gives the owner a property right in the symbol or word consisting of the ability to prevent others from using the mark when that use is likely to confuse or deceive. Trademark protection continues for as long as the mark is used to identify and distinguish, not being subject to any term of years limitation as are patents and copyrights. If the owner stops using the mark, the exclusive right to use it may be lost by "abandonment."

Ownership of a trademark is established by the actual use of a symbol on a label or in advertising to identify one's goods or services. No trademark rights exist and no trademark can be registered until it has been used. The reason for this is that a trademark represents nothing in the way of good will or distinguishing character until it is actually used. Each sale under the trademark results in the accrual of greater legal rights in the user of the symbol. Ownership is determined by priority of use, not by priority of creation or registration. The use must be more than a token sale within the corporation or to relatives or friends to establish a priority, and use must be continuous from the first public marketing under the symbol. For example, in the *Stern* case (discussed previously and in the court cases section), the copyright infringer also attempted to establish a superior right to use of the video game's name, Scramble, by showing that the infringer had ordered 10 silk-screen name plates with the name Scramble and affixed five of the plates to five *other* video games *before* the game's true owner began to market the real Scramble. The court rejected this argument, refusing to give effect to the infringer's attempted preemptive use of the trademark.

Whereas use of the symbol in advertising or as a trade name will establish priority sufficient to *prevent another from registering* the symbol, affixation of the symbol to the goods, their containers, their displays or tags or labels is necessary for the first user to *register* the trademark. Thus, in the case of a computer program, the use of the name of a program in an advertising brochure may not entitle the seller to trademark registration, but the sale of a program with the name imprinted on it would (if the product is deemed a good). Affixation occurs for services when the mark is used or displayed in the sale or advertising of services and the services are rendered in commerce. In either event, there is no usage sufficient for registration until there has been an actual sale or transport of the goods in commerce or an actual rendering of the service under the trademark.

Federal registration of a trademark is *prima facie evidence* that the registrant owns the symbol; that is, it entitles the registrant to a presumption that he or she first used the mark and has continued to use the mark since the filing date. If the registrant needs to prove use before the filing date to establish priority, this must be done by "clear and convincing" evidence. Since the owner must use the symbol before registration to create trademark rights, this prior use should be well documented and registration accomplished as soon as possible thereafter to compile a record of continuous use establishing priority.

Licensing Rights in Computer Software

All of the rights discussed in this section—patent, copyright, trade secrecy, and trademark—give *the owner* certain exclusive property rights in an innovation. To gain any financial return on the innovation, the owner must sell those rights to others in whole or in part. This is commonly done by some form of license agreement, a contract that permits the licensee (the one to whom the rights are sold) to exercise specified rights of the owner. The extent of the rights sold may vary tremendously from one license to another. For example, a Japanese developer of a computer program may license an American corporation to exercise all of its rights in the program as the exclusive distributor in the United States or a software house may license the owner of a personal computer to use a single application program only on a particular computer identified by serial number.

The steps taken to protect the owner's proprietary rights will vary somewhat depending on the type of legal protection used. For example, the owner of a trade secret should probably not simply sell a discovery to another without limitation but rather should permit another to use the development or some part of it only for a specified purpose, for a specified time, and under the condition that its confidentiality be maintained. The owner of a copyright will ordinarily not sell an unlimited right to copy a program but will sell a specified number of copies to others, perhaps with the right to make only one backup copy. The copyright owner may further limit the scope of rights sold by stipulating that the copy sold be used only for a specified machine.

All of these provisions for licensing are directed toward the goal of strictly controlling the scope of the owner's rights, which have been placed in the control of others to get the most from the developer's investment. Such provisions are crucial to profitability. Moreover, in some cases, failure to control the scope of use by a licensee may result in forfeiture of the owner's rights to some degree. For example, a trade secret may no longer be secret or a copyrighted program may be copied and passed on to a third party without giving notice of copyright. Thus, *obtaining* the various protections described in this part is only the first step toward protecting an investment in software development. The owner must then take appropriate steps to protect those legal rights by strictly controlling which rights are sold and which are reserved and by getting the best price possible in exchange for those rights.

There are two basic contexts in which the developer may desire to license a software development to another for profit. First, the developer who wants to keep writing programs for a living will want to license the program to a publisher/distributor for marketing rather than get caught up in the business end of the venture. Second, a developer who believes he or she is on to a sure moneymaker may want to pursue its profitability alone. In that case, license agreements may be the legal vehicle by which the developer distributes the programs directly to users of the program.

The first thing a developer decides is precisely what the developer's involvement in the marketing process will be. This decision will affect whether to license to a publisher or to market the program directly. In addition, whichever approach is pursued, the developer must decide what degree of future support and maintenance he or she will provide. Obviously, all of these questions require sound business judgment based on a critical evaluation of the developer's financial status and commitments to other projects as well as of the competitive market. For example, the question of whether the developer can get by with minimal program support will be affected by the availability of similar programs at comparative prices.

Legal advice should be sought in drafting a license agreement since it will form the primary legal basis for deciding potential disputes. The following summary is intended to give the developer an idea of the kinds of clauses that will need to be included in the license so the developer can go to the lawyer having already thought out the parameters of his or her commitments, rights, and responsibilities that allow the developer to profit most from the investment.[60]

The first idea to be clearly expressed in the license is a statement of purpose. The developer should explicitly state that a *license* is being created with a transfer of only those rights specified in the agreement and subject only to the agreement's terms. This idea should be repeated throughout the agreement to prevent the agreement from being misconstrued as a sale of any more rights than the developer intends to give.

The agreement should specify exactly what the developer will be required to provide to the licensee in terms of physical items and future services. For example, will the developer's obligations be satisfied by delivering a tape or disk to the licensee or will the developer assume responsibility for delivering program documentation, source materials, and perhaps even debugging services in the future? Delivery dates should be definitively stated, as well as set time periods during which the licensee will be entitled to test and evaluate the program before acceptance. A duration term for the license and any geographic or market limitations should be agreed upon. The agreement should specify whether the license gives the licensee exclusive rights (subject to time, geographic, or market limitations).

An extremely important topic (which the developer is sure to think of without advice) is the matter of royalties. The agreement should clearly specify not only the amount of the royalties to be paid and their method of calculation but also any other matters that affect the developer's income from the agreement. For example, the parties should agree how many free copies each of the parties is entitled to, whether royalties will be paid on documentation and manuals, whether and in what amounts advances will be permitted, whether a minimum royalty will be paid if the program does not sell, accounting methods, and a timetable for payment.

Legal responsibilities should be clearly allocated between the developer and licensee such as who must bear the cost of any liability for infringements or program defects. Any warranties or disclaimers made by the developer should be clearly and conspicuously set forth. The agreement should designate who is responsible for registering copyrights or trademarks.

As with any other contract, the developer should anticipate that disputes will arise even under the most comprehensive and detailed agreements. The agreement should therefore specify procedures to be followed in the event of disputes. These might include a binding arbitration clause and provision for early termination. The contract should specify what obligations, if any, will extend beyond termination, such as nondisclosure of trade secrets.

COURT CASES

Patent

The uncertainty surrounding the availability of patent protection for innovative computer software is well illustrated by recent decisions of the Court of Customs and Patent Appeals. Three of these decisions are discussed here.

In re Johnson.[61] During 1978, the court decided the case of *In re Johnson,* involving the patentability of a method for removing undesired signal components, or "noise," from seismic data used to locate subterranean petroleum traps. The process used a complex mathematical analysis of the seismic trace to eliminate the noise. The Patent and Trademark Office Board of Appeals (Board) rejected the patent claims, finding that a patent could not be granted for any subject matter that was "algorithmic in character" since, in the Board's view, the claim was merely a special method for solving problems of seismic data and therefore not patentable.

On appeal, the CCPA reversed the Board's decision since the product of the process was found to be the recording of a noiseless seismic trace on a record medium. The court distinguished between the use of mathematical computations simply to arrive at a numerical value, which would not be a patentable process,[62] and the use of mathematical computations to produce a physical result, which would be a patentable process.

The court asserted that patent protection is not made unavailable merely because an element or step contains a natural law or mathematical algorithm. To deny the patent on the basis of the subject matter, the court stated that a two-pronged test must be satisfied to determine whether the claim "preempts" a mathematical algorithm. First, the claim itself must recite "process steps which are themselves calculations, formulae, or equations."[63] If it does not, the subject matter may be patented.[64] If mathematical algorithms *are* contained in the process, however, a second analysis must be made to determine whether the claim *as a whole,* including *all* of its steps, merely recites a mathematical formula or a method of calculation. In the *Johnson* case, the court found that since mathematical computations were part of the claimed process, the second step of the analysis was required. Since the product of the process was found to be a physical seismic trace, the claim represented a patentable process.

In re Walter.[65] In another seismic prospecting case, the CCPA considered the patentability of a process and apparatus for identifying returning scrambled seismic signals with the appropriate original signal, which had been transmitted into the earth. The process used mathematical operations to take the returning jumbled signals, break them down into component segments, and cross correlate each returning signal with its respective original signal. The process converted the seismic waves received at each detecting station into partial product signals.

The Board rejected the patent application on three grounds relating to the process's use of mathematics. First, the Board found that since the process used the radices imposed by the architecture of the computer, the operations performed were mathematical and therefore unpatentable. Second, since the process required the accommodation of the input data to a finite-sized memory requiring the tailoring of the data to the memory's particular architecture, the process again involved mathematics and was therefore unpatentable. Third, the Board found the processing to be directed to the solution of a mathematical problem, unlike the physical transformation involved in *Johnson*.

On appeal from the Board, the court also rejected the patent application but only on the third ground. The court pointed out that if the mere use of mathematics in carrying out a process precluded patentability, all computer-arts inventions would be in effect unpatentable. To illustrate its point, the court cited past cases that had required the issuance of patents for inventions yet would have rejected the patent claims if they had used the Board's reasoning. For example, the court cited cases in which the court had found to be patentable a process using the law of gravity[66] and a mechanism that altered or repositioned information in the computer's system base.[67] The court suggested that, indeed, any process using a timed process step is mathematical in nature and therefore unpatentable under the Board's reasoning. The court stated that the proper course for decision is to concentrate on what the computer is doing, not on how it is being done. Applying this reasoning to the *Walter* case, the court found the process to be directed toward no more than the solution of a mathematical problem even though the solution was specifically applied to seismic prospecting. In so holding, the court rejected the claimant's argument that since the process resulted in the physical changing of the magnetic recording tape, the process should be patentable under *Johnson*. The court specifically stated that there was "nothing necessarily physical about [the partial product signals] beyond the fact that they are held in some physical storage medium." Similarly, the court held that the production of a "simulation" of a physical result did not change the court's characterization of the process's end product as a mathematical, nonphysical result.

Thus, according to CCPA cases *Johnson* and *Walter,* an original apparatus or process performed by a computer may be patented, first, if the process does not involve mathematics. If the process being performed by the computer does include mathematical formulas or computations, the invention is patentable if it is directed at a physical change. Judging from *Walter,* the use of mathematics incident to computer processing (as opposed to carrying out the process by human means) will not automatically disqualify a patent claim at the first step of the analysis. Conversely, the production of a physical result will not qualify an invention at the second step if the process would not have produced a physical result in the absence of a computer. Thus, the CCPA apparently disregards the computer's function in the proposed process, focusing instead on the function that the computerized process is designed to perform. The CCPA's case results suggest that the patentability of a computer-assisted process depends on the patentability of the particular application.

It should also be noted that achieving the protection afforded by the CCPA to the particular application is not a certainty. The cases described indicate the Board's continued resistance to issuing patents for computer claims. Only after time-consuming appeals through the Board and CCPA were the inventors able to resolve the patentability of their respective inventions.

In re Sarkar.[68] A 1978 case, *In re Sarkar,* evidenced a willingness on the part of the CCPA to accommodate the patent applicant's interest in trade secrecy protection while handling the patent appeal. The court ruled that when a patent applicant requested that the appeal proceedings and transcript be kept secret, the court was authorized to do so if the court was satisfied (as it was in *Sarkar*) that the substance of the claim has remained confidential, the request was made at the outset of the case's filing with the court,[69] the claimant has filed no foreign patent applications, the subject matter has not become generally available through the activities of others, and alternative methods of protecting the alleged trade secrets are impractical. The court noted that if it denied confidentiality, inventors might, because of the risk of losing trade secrecy protection, be deterred from seeking patents. As a result, the public might be deprived of knowledge of new inventions. This case is a significant boon to software developers as it prevents developers from having to make an all-or-nothing commitment to patent protection in those cases in which patentability is uncertain.

Copyright/Trademark

The following cases are a sampling of current judicial opinions dealing with the application of copyright law to computer programs. They represent a variety of views on issues which are vitally important to the computer industry. One of these cases also provides a helpful insight into the application of trademark law.

Data Cash Systems, Inc. v. JS & A Group, Inc.[70] This case is an excellent example of legal problems that may be encountered when relying on copyright law for the protection of a computer program. The plaintiff in the case retained an independent consultant to design and develop a program for a computerized chess game, CompuChess, which the plaintiff intended to manufacture and sell. The consultant developed a program whereby the computer would play chess at six levels of difficulty. The program was translated into machine language and used to create an object program in the form of a read-only-memory (ROM) silicon chip, which was installed as part of the computer's circuitry. All copies of the source program contained copyright notices, but neither the marketed game nor the ROM program contained any copyright notice. After the plaintiff filed a copy of the source program with the Register of Copyrights, the plaintiff was issued a certificate of copyright registration. A year after the plaintiff began marketing CompuChess, the defendants began marketing JS & A Computer Chess, which used a ROM identical to the plaintiff's. The manufacturer of the ROM for the plaintiff informed the plaintiff that the company was manufacturing a ROM for another chess game, and when the manufacturer tested the new ROM, at the plaintiff's request, it was found to be identical to the plaintiff's. Investigation revealed that the new ROM was being manufactured by a Hong Kong firm for the defendants. The plaintiff sued the defendants for copyright infringement and unfair competition.

An Illinois federal district court threw out the copyright claim,[71] finding that the copyright laws afforded no protection to programs in their object phase but only to the copyrighted source program (although neither of the parties argued that issue). However, the court determined that a trial was required on the unfair competition claim since it had not been shown how the ROM was duplicated. The plaintiff was permitted to appeal the court's decision before going to trial.

The Seventh Circuit Court of Appeals affirmed the trial court's dismissal of the copyright infringement claim but did not deem it necessary to decide whether the copyright of the source program extended to the ROM. Instead, the court decided that even if the copyright did extend to the ROM, the program had passed into the public domain by virtue of the plaintiff's failure to include a copyright notice with the marketed game, thus destroying any copyright protection of the game against the defendants' use. The plaintiff claimed that no such notice had been included because it did not know that it was possible to read the program from the ROM itself as the defendants had apparently done. The court noted that a copyright notice could have been imprinted on the game board or the printed instructions or could have been included in the program itself so that anyone printing out the contents of the ROM could not miss seeing it (as the plaintiff began to do after discovering the alleged infringement).

The case presents two difficulties with the protection afforded by the copyright laws. As an initial matter, it is important that a notice of copyright be included as a part of the program in all of its modes so that anyone dealing with it will be put on notice of the copyright. Then even after that has been done, the question of whether copyright of one mode extends to all modes still remains unresolved. The *Data Cash* district court judge was clearly of the opinion that copyright protection extended only to the human-readable source copy while the Seventh Circuit judges expressly declined to offer any guidance on that issue.

Tandy Corp. v. Personal Micro Computers, Inc.[72] A judge from the District Court for the Northern District of California (in "Silicon Valley") took the opposite view of the *Data Cash* district judge in this case, holding that a silicon chip ROM *was* a copy of a computer program for copyright purposes. Tandy Corp., the manufacturer of a home computer, alleged that the defendant had duplicated Tandy's ROM silicon chip, which contained the computer's copyrighted input/output program for converting source language to object code. At the pretrial stage, assuming that the defendant had in fact copied the program, it was not clear whether the defendant had copied it from one of Tandy's ROMs or from a printout of the program. If copied from the ROM, it would be necessary to decide whether the ROM was a copy of the copyrighted program such that its unauthorized duplication constituted copyright infringement. If copied from a printout, there was no real doubt that the duplication violated Tandy's copyright.

The *Tandy* court refused to distinguish between the source copy and object mode for copyright purposes, holding that a computer program is a "work of authorship" subject to copyright and that the imprinting of a program onto a silicon chip subjects the imprinted program to copyright laws. In a very well-reasoned opinion, the *Tandy* court expressly rejected the *Data Cash* lower court's finding that the object mode was not protected by copyright.

The *Tandy* case suggests that copyright protection may protect a computer program in all of its forms. The appellate court ruling in *Data Cash* does not necessarily lead to a contrary conclusion since the basis for its denial of copyright protection in that case was lack of notice; that is, the owner failed to comply with the copyright laws, assuming that the copyright extended to the ROM. The *Data Cash* appellate court's failure to follow the *Data Cash* district court's reasoning suggests at least an unwillingness to conclusively rule out copyright protection for the object mode of computer protection and perhaps suggests tacit approval of such protection provided a copyright notice is included. Indeed, it may be inferred that if failure to give a copyright notice with "publication" of the ROM places the program in the public domain, the ROM of necessity must be a copy of the program.[73] Other appellate courts have since agreed with *Tandy* that a program stored in a ROM constitutes a copy of the program for copyright purposes. It must be remembered, however, that even complete application of copyright law to computer programs protects only against unauthorized copying of the expression of a program, not against uses of the underlying ideas in different but similar programs.

Apple Computer, Inc. v. Franklin Computer Corp.[74] A federal district court judge in Pennsylvania handling this case added yet another view on the subject of copyright protection of the object mode of a computer program. Apple sued Franklin, seeking a preliminary injunction restraining Franklin from infringing its copyrights on its computer programs in ROM object code form on silicon chips. The court, in deciding that Apple had not shown a sufficient likelihood of success on its infringement claim to be entitled to the injunction, emphasized the distinction between operating programs and application programs. The present suit involved operating programs which controlled the computer's internal workings, designed only to facilitate the operating of the application program, readable only by a machine or by an expert with patience. Application programs, on the other hand, are designed to perform the task at hand, such as maintaining records, performing calculations, or displaying graphic images, and are written in high-level languages designed to be easily used by the unsophisticated user.

Relying upon Commissioner Hersey's dissenting CONTU report, the court viewed it necessary to draw the copyrightability line between machine communication, which is essentially a part of the machine itself, and human communication suitable for copyright protection. The court also noted the consistency of its position with the Supreme Court's recent holding in *Diamond v. Bradley*[75] that "firmware," a combination of software and hardware that operates together to control a computer, is patentable subject matter as a physical means of operating the machine.

The approach used by the *Apple* district court is an intriguing one and makes a good attempt to reconcile the seemingly contradictory views of other courts. Under this view, video game object code would be copyrightable since its purpose from the outset is to generate human-perceptible images. The court simply disagreed with the *Tandy* court.

The United States Court of Appeals for the Third Circuit disagreed with the lower court, however, and reversed the district court's denial of the preliminary injunction, holding that the denial had been based on an erroneous view of the applicable law. The appellate court rejected in turn the district court's distinction between operating system programs and application programs; the notion that an operating system program is really part of a machine and thus protectable only by patent law, if protectable at all; and the argument that operating systems are uncopyrightable because they are purely utilitarian works, because copyright protection would effectively block the use of the art embodied in its operating systems.

The appellate court left it up to the district court to decide on remand whether some of the programs at issue represented the only way to express the underlying ideas, so the idea and expression were merged as in the *Morrissey v. Procter & Gamble Co.* and *Synercom Technology, Inc. v. University Computing Co.* cases discussed previously in this part. The court indicated that the issue in this regard was not, as Franklin contended, whether there are a limited number of ways to arrange operating systems to enable a computer to run Apple-compatible software, because Franklin's desire to achieve total compatibility with application programs written for the Apple II computer is merely a "commercial and competitive objective which does not enter into the somewhat metaphysical issue of whether particular ideas and expressions have merged." The court instead stated that, for example, if other methods existed as a practical matter for translating source code into object code (the function of one of the operating programs at issue), there would be no merger of idea and expression sufficient to preclude copyright protection of the program.

The district court's approach bears watching as it provides a logically consistent way of dealing with the patent/copyright problems as applied to computer software. It remains to be seen, however, whether lay courts would be able to consistently make the fine distinctions between hardware, software, and firmware as individual cases require, assuming that higher courts or Congress are persuaded to adopt such an approach.

Stern Electronics, Inc. v. Kaufman.[76] This case illustrates creative attempts by both parties to use the copyright and trademark laws to their best advantage. As in most lawsuits, however, one party was successful while the other was not. The case not only illustrates the operation of existing law but also opens new ground in the direction of comprehensive copyright protection for new computer applications.

Stern was the exclusive American distributor of a video game called Scramble, developed by a Japanese corporation, in which the player moved a spaceship through six different scenes encountering enemy missiles and aircraft. Stern's marketing of the game, beginning March 17, 1981, was extremely successful, selling approximately 10,000 units at $2,000 each in the first two months for an initial sales volume of $20 million. Stern brought suit against Kaufman and Omni Video Games, Inc., to prevent Omni from marketing an identical game under the same name.

The Japanese developer of the original game, Konami Industry Co., Ltd., which had licensed the game to Stern, had registered the game's sights and sounds as a copyrighted audiovisual work, submitting to the Copyright Office videotape recordings of the Scramble game both in its attract mode (the display and sounds projected when the machine is not in use) and its play mode. Konami did not register a copyright on the program which, in the form of a programmable read only memory (PROM) silicon chip, created the game on the screen.

Omni, the alleged infringer, claimed that even before Stern's sale of Scramble, Omni had been marketing a line of video game units that could be equipped to play different games by substituting a PROM containing the program for a particular game. Omni claimed that it had intended to label the headboard of each such unit Scramble along with the name of the particular game whose PROM had been inserted into the unit. On December 1, 1980, Omni's president ordered 10 silk-screen Scramble name plates, and before March 17, 1981, the date of Stern's first sale of Scramble, Omni had sold five units of video games labeled Scramble on the headboard but containing games dissimilar to Stern's Scramble. Beginning in April 1981, however, Omni's Scramble not only bore the same name as Stern's but was identical to Stern's in sight and sound. Omni sold this knock-off version of Stern's Scramble for several hundred dollars less than Stern's game.

Stern alleged that Omni was infringing both Konami's audiovisual copyright and trademark of the game. The lower court agreed and issued a preliminary injunction against Omni's copyright infringement and use of the trademark "Scramble." Omni appealed the decision to the Second Circuit Court of Appeals, claiming that the game's sights and sounds were not copyrightable and that Omni had superior rights to the trademark. The appellate court affirmed the lower court's injunction.

Omni argued that Konami was entitled to copyright only the game's written computer program, not the sights and sounds produced by that program. Such a course, the court noted, would have protected Konami from unauthorized duplication of the program itself but would have afforded no protection against writing a different program to produce the same resulting game display as Omni had apparently done. Omni offered two arguments why copyright of the sights and sounds should not be permitted.

First, Omni argued, the audiovisual work was not fixed in any tangible medium of expression as required by the copyright statutes since the sequence of sounds and scenes varied depending on the actions of each player.

The court noted that fixation in a tangible medium of expression was accomplished by imprinting the program onto the PROM. Citing the many aspects of the game's scenery and sequence that remained constant over each play, the court held that "the repetitive sequence of a substantial portion of the sights and sounds of the game qualifies for copyright protection as an audiovisual work."

Second, Omni contended that the game display was not sufficiently original to qualify for copyright protection as an audiovisual work. This contention was divided into two subarguments. First, Omni argued that each play of the game constituted an original work because of the player's participation. Thus, in Omni's view, the videotape of a particular play of the game obtained protection only for that one "original" display. The court rejected this argument on the same basis as the fixation issue, finding sufficient repetition in each game play to prevent treating each play as an original creation. Omni contended that the display was not original because all of its reappearing features are determined by the program previously created by the player. The court rejected this contention also, finding the aural and visual features of the display to be "plainly original variations sufficient to render the display copyrightable even though the underlying written program has an independent existence and is itself eligible for copyright. . . . Moreover, the argument overlooks the sequence of the creative process. Someone first conceived what the audiovisual display would look like and sound like. Originality occurred at that point. Then the program was written."

The court thus recognized that a copyrightable work may be created by computer even though the protected copy may vary substantially depending on different input for each run of the program. Perhaps most important, the holder of such a copyright may prevent others from using different programs to obtain the same result as the copyrighted work. The court limited its holding by indicating that at some point "the repeating sequence of images would form too insubstantial a portion of an entire display to warrant a copyright" and that "a sequence of images (*e.g.,* a spaceship shooting down an attacking plane) might contain so little in the way of particularized form of expression as to be only an abstract idea portrayed in noncopyrightable form. . . ."

Omni also claimed that its use of the trademark "Scramble" in early 1981 before Stern's marketing of the game in March 1981 entitled it to a superior claim to use of the name. Both the lower court and appellate court found that Omni's prior use was not "bona fide" and thus did not entitle Omni to trademark rights in the name. The prior use was viewed to be merely an attempted bad faith "preemptive use" of the mark. Both courts rejected Omni's claim that it had wanted to establish a trade name for a line of separately named interchangeable games in light of the fact that once Omni obtained a knock-off of Stern's Scramble, it used the Scramble name exclusively for that knock-off version. In the words of the lower court judge, "It would be a truly remarkable coincidence if [Omni] independently thought of the name 'Scramble' and then, only a few months later, produced a video game virtually identical to the one bearing the same name. It is more likely that [Omni] sought to appropriate the trademark with the expectation that they would later imitate the audiovisual display." Moreover, the court noted the inequity that would result if Stern, with a large investment in and successful marketing of the game, were to lose the trademark to Omni who had placed the name on five games that were not Scramble and used the mark for a pirated knock-off of Stern's game.

Other video game cases have treated the copyright issues presented by the preceding case in different ways. In a case dealing with the video game Galaxian, the U.S. International Trade Commission (ITC) was called upon to prevent the importation of a knock-off version of the game.[77] The owner of the allegedly infringed work had registered the game's display as an audiovisual work in both of its forms, the attract mode and play mode. The ITC found that since the alleged infringing game copied the unchanging attract mode of the infringed game, it was unnecessary to decide whether the play mode was copyrightable. The ITC thus granted relief to the owner without dealing with the difficult issues dealt with by the *Stern* court.

Atari, Inc. v. North American Philips Consumer Electronics Corp.[78]

Here the Seventh Circuit Court of Appeals faced a similar case involving the popular Pac-Man game. The *Atari* court granted a temporary injunction against the marketing of an imitation Pac-Man game, although in a much narrower fashion than the *Stern* court and in spite of the fact that the infringer differed in some respects from the original. The *Atari* court held that the Pac-Man work was primarily an unprotectable game, noting that to grant a copyright on the game's maze configurations and scoring scheme would amount to impermissible protection of not only the game's *expression* but also the *idea*. The court found, however, that Atari had shown a substantial probability that it would carry its burden of showing infringement at trial based upon the alleged infringer's use of the same basic characters as the original and the reference to the original by retailers and sales clerks promoting the infringing work. Weighing the equities, or fairness, of the situation, the court noted the substantial investment by Atari and irreparable harm that would result from unlawful competition in the fast-paced video game market and granted the pretrial injunction.

Courts are clearly not consistent in their willingness to use copyright law to protect computer programs. Some legal commentators object to copyright protection for computer programs on the grounds that the Copyright Act's requirements of a "copy" and "fixation" are not met. The apparent trend of courts is to act to protect proprietorship in computer software in the face of an unclear statutory framework. This trend, although helpful to the software developer in the short run in and of itself, may prove to be most valuable in motivating a more definite and permanent legislative response to the problem.

Trade Secrecy

The following case is a good illustration of the function of trade secrecy law in protecting proprietary information.

Com-Share, Inc. v. Computer Complex, Inc.[79]

Both the plaintiff and defendant were engaged in the business of offering time-shared computer systems as well as developing and marketing software. The court noted that the time-sharing business was a "fast-moving operation" where technological developments were important in the ability to attract and retain customers. The two parties entered into a technical exchange agreement in 1967 in which each of the parties agreed to provide the other, for the specified term of the agreement, all information concerning hardware and software that came into its legal possession and that related to the operation of an SDS 940 Time-Sharing Computer System (subject to the provision that the exchange of a user's proprietary applications software was subject to the user's express permission). The agreement appears to have been primarily for the defendant's benefit, the plaintiff supplying extensive confidential information to the defendant and furnishing technical training to the defendant's employees. Consistent with the confidentiality of the information to be shared, the agreement stipulated that each party was not to divulge any information supplied by the other without the other's consent, such restrictions to remain in effect for two years after the agreement was terminated. After difficulties arose between the parties, they voluntarily agreed by letter to prematurely terminate the agreement in November 1970, stating that "neither company requires further performance by the other under the said agreement."

On August 5, 1971, the defendant announced an agreement to sell all of its time-sharing assets and good will to Tymshare, Inc. The plaintiff wrote to both the defendant and Tymshare asserting its rights against the defendant's disclosure of its confidential information to Tymshare, and subsequently brought suit to obtain an injunction preventing the disclosure.

In determining the validity of the plaintiff's trade secret claim, the court first determined that the plaintiff had made substantial innovations in the technology available in the public domain and that, even though the defendant made certain technical changes in the software, the plaintiff's unique principles, engineering, logic, and coherence were not altered. The court thus established initially that the ideas in question were indeed the plaintiff's.

The court then analyzed the "secret" nature of the software, finding it "clear that the utmost caution was used by the plaintiff in protecting the secrecy of this software." The court noted that each page of the listings of the plaintiff's systems contained the words "Com-Share, Inc. Company Confidential." In addition, passwords were built into the systems to prevent unauthorized access, and magnetic tapes and symbolics were kept locked when not in use. The court noted that the systems' built-in protections were designed not only to prevent unauthorized access to customers' data bases or specialized technology by other customers but also to prevent employees of the company itself from having unauthorized access and betraying their employer.

The trial court next dealt with contractual issues relating to the parties' agreements, deciding that the plaintiff had substantially performed its part of the agreement and thus came into court with "clean hands" (necessary because an injunction was sought). The court found the nondisclosure provision of the contract to be binding after the termination despite the defendant's argument that the termination agreement ended *all* obligations under the information-sharing agreement (including the duty not to disclose for two years after termination).

Looking to the financial distress of both parties and the competitive harm that would result if Tymshare acquired the plaintiff's information (noting the comparative size advantage of Tymshare, the fact that some of their customers were clients of both companies, and that the plaintiff's standard contracts allowed for cancellation by the user with only 30 days' notice), the court determined that the circumstances justified an injunction against the sale of any of the plaintiff's information.

The *Com-Share* case illustrates the advantages of trade secrecy protection over other forms of proprietary protection. First of all, it is judicially regulated, not statutorily, so that there is a much greater opportunity for a court to consider the equities of the business situation to arrive at a just result. Copyright and patent protection require tailoring the claim to meet the copyright or patent laws and going through the proper procedural steps, the determination of protection resting on the interpretation of the applicable statutes by the agencies and courts. Trade secrecy protection, on the other hand, in most cases will involve the court's giving legal effect to the protection that the proprietor has established for the innovation, permitting more flexibility and control over the information by the proprietor without as much uncertainty over the loss of protection due to the court's interpretations of public law.

On the other hand, trade secrecy protection is not without its costs. First, as a policy matter, the widespread use of trade secrecy protection may hinder general growth in the computer industry by deterring public dissemination of technological advances. On an individual level, the trade secrecy route is an all-or-nothing risk. Once the information is no longer secret, the proprietor has no superior claim to it. The proprietor must take great care to safeguard against unauthorized use and to contract for remedies against authorized users for their unauthorized disclosures. Moreover, even with the greatest precautions, trade secrecy law provides no protection against independent discovery of the innovation.

The uncertainty surrounding patent and copyright protection suggests extreme caution by the programmer, with experienced legal counsel, in selecting the proper course to protect investments in innovative software. Patent law offers the most comprehensive protection once granted, so patent protection should be considered, particularly for software devoted to performing physical functions or processes. Copyright law is easily and inexpensively available for computer programs, but the quality of protection may be inadequate for the interests of the proprietor since some doubt remains whether it extends to machine-readable modes and it does not protect against the borrowing or independent discovery of the underlying ideas. Trade secrecy thus may be the best of the alternatives in many cases until a more acceptable statutory scheme is established by Congress.

IMPLICATIONS FOR ACTION

This section offers suggestions for the computer programmer in the matters of liability and protection of original material.

Liability

The programmer should at all times be truthful and forthright with prospective clients and in advertising packaged programs. Care should be taken to avoid the creation of unintended express warranties or any basis for charges of misrepresentation. Opinions, negotiation offers, and predictions of success should be offered in earnest and introduced as what they are. The programmer should not create the impression of making promises where promises are not intended.

The best available techniques should be used in writing programs. Even when contract language specifies a lesser standard, the programmer should try to create a program that meets his or her own standards of quality. Extreme care should be taken in writing programs whose applications bear the risk of human physical injury.

Contract liability may be limited by providing alternative remedies and placing limits on the time period during which the program is warranted and the types of errors warranted against. All limitations and exclusions of warranties should comply with UCC specifications. The contract must, however, offer some minimal remedy to the user or else the court may supply its own. The rights and obligations of each party should be enumerated as specifically as possible.

A comprehensive initial testing of the program by the user should be provided for in the contract or with the instructions for a packaged program. Such a test may be made part of the terms of an express warranty and be effective in shifting a portion of the duty to discover errors to the user. The user's failure to test when he or she has a duty to do so may be instrumental in shifting responsibility for obvious errors to the user.

The programmer should thoroughly inform the user of any weaknesses of the program. The user should be instructed how to design the information system to best serve the program, particularly with regard to packaged applications.

Liability insurance policies for errors and omissions should be analyzed by the programmer's counsel to assure that they will cover all legal liability that might be incurred. A few more dollars for special coverages may be necessary.

Protection of Original Material

Upon the creation of an innovation in computer software, there are three basic options available to the developer: copyright, patent, and trade secrecy. (A fourth option, with narrower applications, is trademark law). Careful consideration with the advice of counsel experienced in the area should be given to each before commitment to copyright or patent. Secrecy will almost always be a good interim means of protection.

If the innovation relates to a particular machine or controls a purely physical process, patent protection, which provides the most complete protection against unauthorized use of the innovative ideas and independent discovery, may be appropriate. If the "original" aspect of the development is based on an innovative idea or underlying algorithm, however, patent protection may be denied. As a backup, the measures necessary to trade secrecy status described here should be followed as well, and a timely request to the Patent Office that confidentiality be maintained should be made (see discussion of the *Sarkar* case in the court cases section).

Copyright law protects against unauthorized *copying* of an *expression* of the program. Recent court decisions suggest that copyright protection of a program extends to its other modes of expression, that is, to its expression in machine language as well as in source form. Thus, copyright protection may be obtained to prevent unauthorized duplication of, say, a flowchart diagram of the program and probably protects against use of the program in a machine mode. This development encourages the use of copyright protection for computer software, although a program's underlying ideas would not be protected if duplicated and expressed in a different but similar program format. Copyright affords no protection against the unauthorized use of the underlying ideas of the copyright program nor against independent discovery of the innovation.

Alternate programs accomplishing the same purpose as a copyrighted program do not infringe the copyright of the program. Therefore, trade secrecy protection of underlying ideas is still advisable to help prevent knock-off programs from being developed from published, stolen, or misappropriated proprietary information. If a program *creates* a copyrightable work, copyright of the output may entitle the owner to prevent the use of any other program that creates an infringing output (for example, some video games).

Copyright protection requires a notice of copyright on all published copies to prevent the program's passage into the public domain. Notices should also be attached to in-house unpublished copies to avoid mistakes. Notices should be attached by placement in the object code so that copyright notice appears on any printouts or on the user's terminal or by attaching labels to printouts or to the cartridges, cassettes, or containers holding program copies.

Trade secrecy protection appears to be the safest course (except perhaps against knock-off versions of published works) and the one chosen by most developers. In addition to exclusive use, it may be used to fill the gaps of copyright protection and may operate as a backup means of protection if a patent is denied. This course may require elaborate and expensive safeguarding to establish the secret character of the development, such as disclosure only to licensees for only authorized uses, attaching a notice of confidentiality to each page of a program, using fail-safe systems of password access, keeping copies locked up at all times, or translating the program into machine language and keeping the source copy locked up at all times.

If trade secrecy is chosen as the means of protection, the proprietor should be extremely certain to ensure that all licensing agreements establish the confidential nature of the program with specific provisions to safeguard against unauthorized use. Unauthorized disclosure may destroy the secret character of the innovation for all trade secrecy purposes. For that reason, the developer may want to include a provision in the licensing contract that the licensee will be liable to the developer for a breach of confidentiality by the fault of the licensee, perhaps with a set liquidated damages amount or formula for calculation.

A name or symbol used to identify a program on the market may be used to establish trademark protection. This action enables the owner to prevent another from capitalizing on the owner's successful marketing of the trademark-protected product or services by marketing a competing product or service under the same name. Trademark rights attach once the product or service is marketed under the name or symbol but should be registered as soon as possible after the first sale to obtain the right to sue for enforcement of trademark privileges and to be entitled to the earliest possible presumption of trademark use.

REFERENCES

1. UCC 2-314 (1978).

2. UCC 2-315.

3. UCC 2-312.

4. UCC 2-104.

5. UCC 2-316; 2-312(2).

6. UCC 2-508.

7. UCC 2-715(1).

8. UCC 2-715(2).

9. UCC 2-719(2).

10. Chatlos Systems, Inc. v. National Cash Register Corp., 479 F. Supp. 738 (D. N.J. 1979), *aff'd in part, remanded in part* 635 F.2d 1081 (3d Cir. 1980), *remand aff'd* 670 F.2d 1304 (3d Cir. 1982), *cert. dismissed* 102 S.Ct. 2918 (1982).

11. UCC 2-719(3).

12. UCC 2-318.

13. *Cf., e.g.,* Terris v. Cummiskey, 11 A.D.2d 259, 203 N.Y.S.2d 445 (1960), in which a builder of a home was held liable for misrepresentation. He had persuaded the buyer to buy the home by guaranteeing a dry cellar even though the builder was at the time aware of the fact that several of the homes in the area, including some built by him, had water in the cellars.

14. Pretrial Ruling, F & M Schaefer Corp. v. Electronic Data Systems, Civ. No. 76-3982 (S.D. N.Y. 1977). *See* E. Saltzberg, *Computer Malpractices,* CLS Newsletter, 1980 Supp. No. 3; *Computerworld,* Nov. 28, 1977, p. 1.

15. Nycum, "Liability for Malfunction of a Computer Program," 7 Rut. J. of Computers Tech. & L. 1 (1979).

16. FJS Electronics, Inc. v. Fidelity Bank, 431 A.2d 326 (Pa. Super. 1981).

17. Restatement (Second) of Torts 402A (1966).

18. Note, "Negligence: Liability for Defective Software," 33 Okla. L. Rev. 848 (1980).

19. Schipper v. Levitt & Sons, Inc., 44 N.J. 70, 207 A.2d 314 (1965).

20. Ransome v. Wisconsin Electric Power Co., 87 Wis.2d 605, 275 N.W.2d 641 (1979).

21. Cintrone v. Hertz Truck Leasing & Rental Service, 45 N.J. 434, 212 A.2d 769 (1965).

22. La Rossa v. Scientific Design Co., 402 F.2d 937 (3d Cir. 1968).

23. Dwyer v. Skyline Apartments, Inc., 123 N.J. Super 48, 301 A.2d 463 (1973).

24. Holdsclaw v. Warren and Brewster, 45 Or.App. 153, 607 P.2d 1208 (1980) (discussed in Part VI).

25. *See* H. Chadwick, *The Insurance of Electronic Data Processing Operations,* CLS 2-5, art. 1 (Bigelow, ed. 1979); Tangorra, "Insurance Against Disaster," *Datamation,* July 1982, p. 70.

26. *See* 35 USC 154 (1976).

27. 35 USC 101 (1976).

28. 35 USC 103 (1976).

29. *See Ex Parte* King, 146 U.S.P.Q. (B.N.A.) 590 (Pat. Off. Bd. App. 1964); *In re* Prater, 415 F.2d 1378 (C.C.P.A. 1968), *aff'd in part, rev'd in part on rehearing,* 415 F.2d 1393 (C.C.P.A. 1969).

30. *In re* Johnston, 502 F.2d 765, 773 (C.C.P.A. 1974) (Rich, J., dissenting), *rev'd sub nom.* Dann v. Johnston, 425 U.S. 219 (1976).

31. Pope & Pope, "Protection of Proprietary Interests in Computer Software," 30 Ala. L. Rev. 527, 536–537 (1979).

32. Cochrane v. Deener, 94 U.S. 780, 788 (1876).

33. *See In re* Abrams, 188 F.2d 165 (C.C.P.A. 1951).

34. *In re* Musgrave, 431 F.2d 882 (C.C.P.A. 1970).

35. *See In re* Diehr, 602 F.2d 982 (C.C.P.A. 1979), *aff'd sub nom.* Diamond v. Diehr, 450 U.S. 175 (1981); *In re* Bradley, 600 F.2d 807 (C.C.P.A. 1979), *aff'd by an equally divided court sub nom.* Diamond v. Bradley, 450 U.S. 381 (1981).

36. Pope & Pope, *supra* note 31, at 539. *See* 35 USC 112 (1976).

37. *See* Parker v. Flook, 437 U.S. 584 (1978); Dann v. Johnston, 425 U.S. 219 (1976); Gottschalk v. Benson, 409 U.S. 63 (1972); Pope & Pope, *supra* note 31, at 542; "The Protection of Property Rights in Computer Software," 14 Akron L. Rev. 85, 94 (1980).

38. Diamond v. Bradley, 450 U.S. 381 (1981); Diamond v. Diehr, 450 U.S. 175 (1981).

39. *In re* Toma, 575 F.2d 872 (C.C.P.A. 1978).

40. *In re* Freeman, 573 F.2d 1237 (C.C.P.A. 1978).

41. *In re* Bradley, 600 F.2d 807 (C.C.P.A. 1979), *aff'd by an equally divided court sub nom.* Diamond v. Bradley, 450 U.S. 381 (1981).

42. 17 USC Appendix 302 (1976). *See* Gasaway, L. & M. Murphy, "Legal Protection for Computer Programs," CAUSE Monograph Series (1980); D. Remer, *Legal Care for Your Software* (Reading, Mass.: Addison-Wesley, 1982).

43. Copyright Office, *Copyright Registration for Computer Programs,* Copyright Soc'y U.S.A. Bull. 361 (1964).

44. 17 USC Appendix 117 (1976).

45. 17 USC Appendix 102(a) (1976).

46. 17 USC 117 (Supp. V 1981).

47. *See* Mazer v. Stein, 347 U.S. 201, 217 (1954), *reh. den.,* 347 U.S. 949 (1954).

48. Baker v. Selden, 101 U.S. 99 (1879).

49. 379 F.2d 675 (1st Cir. 1967).

50. 462 F. Supp. 1003 (N.D. Tex. 1978); Comment, "Copyright Protection for Computer Programs," 47 Tenn. L. Rev. 787, 798 (1980).

51. White-Smith Music Publishing Co. v. Apollo Co., 209 U.S. 1 (1908).

52. 14 Akron L. Rev., *supra* note 37, at 95.

53. 669 F.2d 852 (2d Cir. 1982). *See also* Atari, Inc. v. North American Philips Consumer Electronics Corp., 672 F.2d 607 (7th Cir. 1982) (owner of registered copyright of video game "audiovisual work" entitled to preliminary injunction against alleged infringing game which played somewhat differently).

54. Restatement of Torts 757 (1939).

55. *See* Milgrim, "Trade Secret Law to Protect Software," in *Computer Software Protection: A Pragmatic Approach* (Computer Law Ass'n, Oct. 15–16, 1981).

56. *See* Kewanee Oil Co. v. Bicron Corp., 416 U.S. 470 (1974).

57. *See* M. Bryce & Associates, Inc. v. Gladstone, 107 Wis.2d 241, 319 N.W.2d 907 (Wis. Ct. App. 1982), *cert. denied* 103 S.Ct. 258 (1982); 17 USC Appendix 301 (1976).

58. *See* Pope & Pope, *supra* note 31; Akron L. Rev., *supra* note 37; Comment, *supra* note 50; Lynch, "Patent Protection Developments Following Bradley & Diehr," in *Computer Software Protection: A Pragmatic Approach* (Computer Law Ass'n, Oct. 15–16, 1981).

59. 588 F.2d 213 (7th Cir. 1978).

60. *See* D. Remer, *Legal Care for Your Software* (1982).

61. 589 F.2d 1070 (C.C.P.A. 1978).

62. *See* Parker v. Flook, 437 U.S. 584 (1978); Gottschalk v. Benson, 409 U.S. 63 (1972).

63. 589 F.2d at 1077.

64. *See In re* Toma, 575 F.2d 872 (C.C.P.A. 1978) (computerized method for translating natural human languages patentable); *In re* Freeman, 573 F.2d 1237 (C.C.P.A. 1978) (computer typesetter patentable).

65. 618 F.2d 758 (C.C.P.A. 1980).

66. *See* Eibel Process Co. v. Minnesota and Ontario Paper Co., 261 U.S. 45 (1923).

67. *See In re* Bradley, 600 F.2d 807 (C.C.P.A. 1979), *aff'd by an equally divided court sub nom.* Diamond v. Bradley, 450 U.S. 381 (1981).

68. 575 F.2d 870 (C.C.P.A. 1978).

69. *See In re* Sackett, 136 F.2d 248 (1943) (motion to seal record for trade secrecy purposes denied when motion made *after* the court's decision).

70. 628 F.2d 1038 (7th Cir. 1980).

71. 480 F. Supp. 1063 (N.D. Ill. 1979).

72. 524 F. Supp. 171 (N.D. Cal. 1981).

73. Baumgarten, "Copyright & Computer Issues—An Overview of Current Problems," in *Computer Software Protection: A Pragmatic Approach* (Computer Law Ass'n, October 15–16, 1981).

74. 545 F. Supp. 812 (E.D. Pa. 1982), *rev'd in part, remanded in part* 714 F.2d 1240 (1983).

75. 450 U.S. 381 (1981).

76. 669 F.2d 852 (2d Cir. 1982). *See also* Midway Mfg. Co. v. Artic Int'l, Inc., 704 F.2d 1009 (7th Cir. 1983).

77. Certain Coin-Operated Audio-visual Games and Components Thereof, ITC Docket No. 337-TA-87, Opinion of June 26, 1981.

78. 672 F.2d 607 (7th Cir. 1982).

79. 338 F. Supp. 1229 (1971), *aff'd* 458 F.2d 1341 (6th Cir. 1972).

PART V

Computer Crime and Privacy

Outline

INTRODUCTION

This part deals with computer crime and information privacy, two legal topics that are quite different conceptually but that have similar practical implications. Both areas require the computer user to exercise strict controls over a system's security and the uses to which the system and its various components are put. To explore these considerations, computer crime and privacy obligations are dealt with in turn. This part ends with a discussion of implications for action drawn from both legal topics.

COMPUTER CRIME

Introduction and Overview

There is no doubt that the computer has created a permanent change of tremendous proportions in our society. In making possible the formerly impossible, the computer has forced us to deal with entirely new situations. We are awestruck as we attempt to grapple with the beginnings of this technological revolution. Our wonder is tempered, however, by the fact that a computer is created and manipulated by human beings who continue to be subject to the foibles of human nature regardless of the "progress" that the computer has laid at our feet.

Criminal activity is as old as civilization, and the advent of the computer age has created new opportunities for crime. Just how prevalent computer crime has become and how much goes undetected is not known, but it is widely believed that only a fraction of such crimes are ever discovered. Furthermore, there is some evidence to suggest that the average computer crime involves greater sums of money than other, traditional crimes.

This part examines the most common forms of computer crime, including those that occur both inside and outside an organization that uses data processing. Legal responses to computer crime on both the state and federal level are then discussed, followed by a survey of relevant cases illustrating the response of courts to the unique issues raised in this new area of the law. It should be noted that the purpose of this part is not to teach criminal law but rather to demonstrate some of the problems that arise in trying to deal with computer crime within the existing legal framework. It is hoped that some basic knowledge of the problem areas of applying the criminal laws to computer crimes will encourage safeguards to prevent computer crime and facilitate a cooperative attitude toward the legal system when a user has been victimized by computer crime.

Definitions. What is meant by the term "computer crime"? There is no consensus on this question although the legal community has been focusing more attention on it through legislation and court opinions. Some authors prefer the term "computer abuse" to computer crime because it encompasses a broader range of illicit activity and because existing laws are not equipped to provide adequate guidance in this emerging area of criminal activity.[1] Others may take the view that computer crime should be defined very narrowly to exclude crimes in which the criminal conduct is the same as that used in noncomputer crimes.[2] According to this view, for example, obtaining money by impersonating a bank officer over the phone and giving a secret code number would not be a pure computer crime, since the real essence of the wrongful conduct by which the crime was perpetrated was an impersonation, not a computer manipulation. According to this view, true computer crimes are so rare that they are almost mythical.

This book takes a broad but pragmatic view toward defining computer crime: A computer crime is simply a criminal act that poses a greater threat to a computer user than to an otherwise similarly situated nonuser. Computer crime, as defined here, consists of two kinds of activity: (a) the use of a computer to perpetrate acts of deceit, theft, or concealment that are intended to provide financial, business-related, property, or service advantages; and (b) threats to the computer itself, such as theft of hardware or software, sabotage, and demands for ransom. Because computer crimes seldom involve acts of physical violence, they are generally classified as white-collar crimes.

Profile of the Computer Criminal. The popular view of the successful computer criminal is interesting and somewhat unsettling. Most companies would be eager to hire personnel who fit this description. Often such people are young and ambitious with impressive educational credentials. They tend to be technically competent and come from all levels of employees, including technicians, programmers, managers, and high-ranking executives. These people are often viewed as heroes challenging an impersonal computer as an opponent in a game. In contrast, the corporate victim of computer crime is not a sympathetic figure. The victim is often seen as one who is caught in a trap of the victim's own creation. Perhaps most unnerving, a commonly held belief is that many computer criminals have been discovered by chance, not by established detection techniques.

Prevalence of Computer Crime. Because so many computer crimes are discovered accidentally, there has been much speculation, and little consensus, about the actual extent of computer crime. Two of the more reputable studies diverge widely in their estimates.

The Stanford Research Institute (SRI) study was funded by grants from the National Science Foundation, the Atomic Energy Commission, and various private organizations. Data for the study on computer abuse were gathered over a four-year period, and results were published beginning in 1973.[3] By far the most ambitious study of its kind ever undertaken, the study initially identified 381 computer abuse cases from official sources, magazines, and newspapers. Admittedly, the accuracy of some stories printed in the popular media is questionable, both with regard to the exact nature of the crime and the amount of money involved. Despite these drawbacks, the study has generally been well received, since imperfect information may be better than none. Even fictitious accounts have some value as they allow us to study the feasibility of such a crime.

Some of the conclusions drawn by the study illustrate the potential dangers of computer abuse. It found that the average loss per crime was $450,000 and speculated that the crimes reported represented only a fraction of the actual total. However, this finding should be balanced by the fact that the number of cases compiled by the Stanford Research Institute was an insignificant percentage of the 100,000 computers in use at the time.

The Government Accounting Office (GAO) made a search among ten federal agencies for incidents of computer crime.[4] Its findings were much more modest than those of the SRI study. The search generated a list of 69 cases. Nine of these were privacy invasion cases that involved no monetary loss. The average dollar loss for those crimes that did involve money was $44,110, a far cry from the SRI's $450,000 figure. In addition, the GAO report stated that 50 of the crimes were committed by technically naive users.

The large differences in the findings of these two reports does not necessarily reflect biases on the part of those collecting data but rather reflects the more fundamental problems of defining computer abuse, estimating unknown incidents, and allowing for inconsistency in media coverage. Simply stated, there is a great deal of mystery surrounding computer crime that defies quantification with any degree of accuracy. What is certain, however, is that computer crime is real, it involves potentially large sums of money, and it is not likely to decrease as use of computers continues to spread rapidly.

The Effect of Media Publicity. Part of the difficulty in assessing the extent and impact of computer crime is due to its widespread and occasionally inaccurate exposure in the media. Newspapers and magazines have focused on incidents of computer abuse for several reasons. The average person (and perhaps the average newspaper reporter) understands little about the complexities of modern computers and therefore is easily intimidated by them. This lack of understanding is often reflected in media reports, which at times tend to exaggerate the severity of a crime. For instance, a story that appeared in the *San Francisco Chronicle* reported how one computer technician was able to gain access to a computer, resulting in unauthorized use of computer time worth "possibly millions." When the case was brought to court, expert testimony put the value of stolen services at $2,000. Of course, the exaggerated version makes the headlines, while the true version often does not get publicized at all.

As we noted, computer abuse also tends to be glamorized. Often the perpetrator is portrayed as an eccentric genius engaged in a Robin Hood-type operation, stealing from a large, impersonal machine, the epitome of the "establishment." Such a point of view, by fostering sympathy for the lone bandit, leads the public to ignore the high cost to society that such crimes exact.

The Vulnerability of the Computer. There are several factors that make a computer an attractive target for criminals. Among them are the speed with which the computer does its work, making many small thefts of a few cents potentially profitable; the invisibility of records stored in a computer's memory; and the use of programmed processing controls, which can be manipulated or bypassed altogether.

Often overlooked is the fact that although the computer is itself a complex machine, many of the processes used with it are relatively simple. There are five key areas in the operation of a computer, all of which are subject to abuse:

a. Input operations may be manipulated to avoid legitimate charges to a user or to cause the computer to print a check in payment for nonexistent services. Fictitious accounts, and even whole companies, have been created in this way.

b. A program controls the computer's operations and if tampered with can benefit the criminal at the expense of the entity that owns the computer. Also, programs themselves are valuable items that are subject to theft.

c. The central processing unit may be exposed to vandalism or destruction. A user's exclusive reliance on it for vital functions makes it a prime target for vandalism or ransom demands.

d. Output, though the least likely target for criminal attack, can still present serious criminal problems. Valuable data, such as mailing lists, can be stolen. The computer output, such as checks, is usually the goal of the criminal who manipulates the system.

e. The communication process is vital to all information flowing in and out of the computer. This data can be intercepted from the lines of communication through wiretapping or the communication facilities themselves can be destroyed.

Types of Computer Crimes

The variety of computer crimes is quite extensive and can be classified into four broad categories: (a) sabotage, (b) theft of services, (c) property crimes, and (d) financial crimes. This section examines each of these categories and gives examples drawn from actual crimes.

Sabotage. This type of computer crime is usually, though not exclusively, directed against computer hardware. Sabotage of computers often resembles traditional sabotage because a computer facility's unique capabilities would not typically be used to carry out the destruction, although sabotage may require some sophistication if computer-assisted security systems must be thwarted or the system is manipulated to do harm to itself.

Computers are targets of sabotage and vandalism especially during times of political activism. Dissident political groups during the 1960s, for instance, conducted assaults on computer installations, often causing extensive damage. Other forms of physical violence have included shooting a computer with a revolver and flooding the computer room. One fired employee simply walked through the data storage area with an electromagnet, thereby erasing valuable company records. A computer's power source can also be the target of a saboteur.

Obviously, these acts of violence do not require any special expertise on the part of the criminal. Sabotage may, however, be conducted by dissatisfied former employees who may put to use some of their knowledge of company operations to gain access to and destroy both hardware and software.

Though computer sabotage is not the type of computer crime that people see as threatening in the same way as if the secrets of the computer were manipulated by a misguided genius, its potential threat should not be taken lightly. The degree of sophistication in a computer crime does not necessarily correlate with the cost of rectifying the damage.

Theft of Services. Computer services may be abused in a variety of ways, depending upon the individual system. Some examples of theft of computer services have involved politicians using a city's computer to conduct campaign mailings or employees conducting unauthorized free-lance services on a company computer after working hours.

Time-sharing systems have been exposed to great amounts of abuse due to inadequate or nonexistent security precautions. It is much easier to gain unauthorized access to a time-sharing system than to a closed system. Though most require passwords to gain access, such a system is only as good as the common sense and caution of its users. A time-sharing system that does not require regular changing of access codes is inviting the theft of valuable computer time. The amazing lack of care exercised by supposedly sophisticated users in this regard made national headlines recently when it was discovered that a group of high school computer buffs in Milwaukee had accessed numerous information systems, including those of banks, hospitals, and even the defense research center in Los Alamos, New Mexico. The students reportedly gained access by using each system's password, some of which had not been changed for years and many of which were obtained from public sources.

Wiretapping is another technique used to gain unauthorized access to a time-sharing system. By "piggybacking" onto a legitimate user's line, one can have free use of the user's privileges whenever the line is not being used by the authorized party.

One of the prime examples of computer services theft took place at the University of Alberta. In 1976, a student at the university undertook an independent study under the supervision of a professor to investigate the security of the university's computer system, a time-sharing system with more than 5,000 users, some as far away as England. After discovering several gaps in the system's security, he was able to develop a program that reduced the possibility for unauthorized use as well as for other tampering. He brought this program to the attention of the computer center, which took no action on the student's recommendations because it was assumed that planned changes in the system would remove security shortcomings. However, the changes were not implemented for another nine months, and during this period, the program was leaked to several students on campus. "Code Green," as the program was nicknamed, was eventually invoked several thousand times.

The university attempted to crack down on the unauthorized users and revoked several students' access privileges. Among these students were two who had been able to manipulate the program to get the computer to display the complete listing of all user passwords, including those at the highest privilege levels. In essence, this gave them unlimited access to the computer's files and programs. These students retaliated against the university administration by occasionally rendering the system inoperable, as well as less harmful acts such as periodically inserting an obscenity into the payroll file. With an unlimited supply of ID's, they were able to escape detection, compiling a library of the computer's programs and even monitoring the implementation of the new security system. The desperate university computer personnel focused exclusively on this situation, keeping a detailed log of all terminal dialogues. This effort led them to a terminal in the geology department one evening, and the students were apprehended.

Though an extreme example, the situation at the University of Alberta shows the extent to which the theft of computer services can be committed in the absence of adequate security measures. Perhaps a more difficult problem exists in dealing with the theft of computer services by employees who are authorized to use the computer for employment purposes. Recent court cases have dealt with the issue of whether an employee's unauthorized use of the employer's computer for personal use constitutes a crime, with varying results.

In *United States v. Sampson,*[5] for example, an employee of a computer service company under contract with NASA was charged with theft of a "thing of value" belonging to the United States[6] after he was discovered using the company computer for his own personal gain. The federal court held that computer time did qualify as a thing of value within the scope of the relevant federal criminal statute.

In *People v. Weg,*[7] a computer programmer employed by a board of education was charged with a misdemeanor of theft of services for allegedly using the board's computer without permission for various personal projects, including calculating a race horse handicapping system and tracing the genealogy of horses that he owned. The statute provided that a defendant had committed a "theft of services" when

> obtaining or having control over labor in the employ of another person, or of business, commercial, or industrial equipment or facilities of another person, knowing that he is not entitled to the use thereof, and with intent to derive a commercial or other substantial benefit for himself or a third person, he uses or diverts to the use of himself or a third person such labor, equipment, or facilities.

The judge dismissed the case, finding that since the computer was owned by the public school board, no "business, commercial, or industrial equipment or facilities of another person" were involved; that is, a school board was not considered to be a business. In addition, the judge ruled that the charges failed to include any factual allegation that the defendant intended to derive a commercial benefit from the services.

Property Crimes. The most obvious computer crime that comes to mind in crimes of property is the theft of computer equipment itself. This has been more common with the increasing miniaturization of computer components and the advent of home computers. Such crimes, like acts of vandalism, are easily absorbed into traditional concepts of crime and present no unique legal problems. More intriguing, and discussed at length in the next section, is the issue of what actually constitutes property in the context of computer crimes. Different courts have come to very different conclusions on this issue.

Computer crimes of property theft frequently involve merchandise of a company whose orders are processed by computers. These crimes are usually committed by internal personnel who have a thorough knowledge of the operation. By manipulating records, dummy accounts can be created causing orders to be shipped to an accomplice outside the organization. Similarly, one can cause checks to be paid out for receipt of nonexistent merchandise.

Theft of property need not be limited to actual merchandise but may also extend to software. Those with access to a system's program library can easily obtain copies for their own use or, more frequently, for resale to a competitor. Technical security measures in a computer installation are of little use when dishonest personnel take advantage of their positions of responsibility.

Commission of property theft is by no means limited to those within the company structure, however. A computer service having specialized programs but poor security may open itself up to unauthorized access by a competitor. All that is necessary is that the outsider gain access to proper codes. This can be done in a number of ways, including clandestine observation of a legitimate user logging on from a remote terminal or use of a remote minicomputer to test for possible access codes.

Financial Crimes. Although not the most common, financial computer crimes are perhaps the most serious in terms of monetary loss. With the projected increasing dependence on electronic fund transfers, implications for the future are indeed ominous.

A common method of committing a financial computer crime involves checks. These mass-produced negotiable instruments can be manipulated in a number of ways. An employee familiar with a firm's operations can cause multiple checks to be made out to the same person. Checks can also be rerouted to a false address or to an accomplice. Such crimes do not seem so incredible when one realizes the scope of *unintentional* mistakes that have been made with computerized checks. For example, the Social Security Administration once accidentally sent out 100,000 checks to the wrong addresses while the system's files were being consolidated.

A form of a financial computer crime that has captured the attention of many authors, but has probably been used much less frequently than one would expect from media discussion, is known as the round-off fraud. In this crime, the thief, perhaps a bank employee, collects the fractions of cents in customers' accounts that are created when the applicable interest rates are applied. These fractions are then stored in an account created by the thief. The theory is that fractions of cents collected from thousands of accounts on a regular basis will yield a substantial amount of money. It has been suggested that in reality, however, round-off schemes may not yield enough money to make all the manipulations and risks worthwhile.[8]

Another type of financial crime involves juggling confidential information within a computer, both personal and corporate. Once appropriate access is gained to records, the ability to alter them can be highly marketable. At least one group operating in California engaged in the business of creating favorable credit histories to clients seeking loans.

By far the most massive fraud of this nature that ever occurred was the Equity Funding fraud, involving $2 billion over a period of ten years. This fraud, too complex to explain briefly in any detail, occurred in three distinct stages. Much of the criminal activity did not involve the company's computer per se, but there is no doubt that the speed of its data-processing facilities made possible the theft of this exorbitant amount of money.

The Equity Funding Corp. of America (EFCA) had four main activities: the sale of investment programs to the public, the financing of its operations, the purchase of mutual fund shares, and the issuing of insurance. The initial phase of the fraud began in 1964 and involved inflating the company's reported earnings, which made its funded life insurance plan more attractive to investors. An individual bought mutual fund shares, then borrowed on them to pay life insurance premiums over a ten-year period. The hope was that the income generated by the mutual funds would cover the cost of borrowing the money and pay for part of the insurance premium. This phase of the fraud emphasized sales appeal at the expense of profitability, and required only manual entries into company books. It involved about $85 million.

The second phase was known as the foreign phase. It consisted of borrowing funds from foreign subsidiaries without recording the borrowing as liabilities on the company records. Between 1968 and 1970 this scheme allowed the apparently fast-growing organization to acquire several banks, insurance companies, and other financial institutions.

Equity Funding had thus grown from a marketing organization to an insurance conglomerate, bringing into play the third phase of the fraud, carried out with the assistance of a computer. To generate short-term cash flow, Equity Funding sold many of its insurance policies to a coinsurer, Pennsylvania Life Insurance Co. By this time, the company was losing substantial amounts of money due to the necessity of servicing fraudulent policies already in existence, so it created wholly fictitious insurance policies and resold them immediately to coinsurers. To maintain profitability, Equity Funding would have had to sell vast amounts of new insurance, which it failed to do.

The company used its computer to create the new policies, mainly in the form of mass-marketing policies not using individual billing. Eventually, 64,000 fraudulent policies were issued. The fact that many of Equity Funding's subsidiaries were audited by unconnected auditing firms made it possible to shift assets from company to company as the need arose. For instance, an asset on the books of one company would not appear as a liability on another.

At the same time, the computer was programmed to fabricate the appropriate number of deaths, cancellations, and lapses that were to be expected from actual policies. Whenever individual audits were requested, the company would claim that the file was temporarily in service, instruct a programmer to prepare a false file overnight, and have it delivered the next morning. Obviously, the computer's speed and great capacity were central to the success of this phase of the fraud.

The fraud, long suspected by some, was finally exposed in 1973 by a surprise audit by examiners sent by the Illinois Insurance Commission. The company officers were caught off guard and were unable to manipulate financial records quickly enough to perpetuate their massive fraud.

Twenty-two people were convicted of federal crimes in this $2 billion fraud and at least 50 civil suits were filed in connection with the ongoing crime. The computer, though instrumental only in the final stages of the fraud, was the means by which Equity Funding was able to obtain most of its illicit funds. Obviously, a fraud of this proportion is not the result of a breach in the security system of a computer but rather was made possible by deliberate corporate policy.[9] The only bodies capable of exposing fraud of this degree are external entities, such as private securities investigators or governmental regulatory agencies, and the process took ten years in this case.

Another celebrated computer crime was that perpetrated by Stanley Mark Rifkin, a computer consultant retained by the Seattle Pacific Bank. Rifkin was able to penetrate the bank's computerized system and transferred $10.2 million to a numbered Swiss bank account. In this case, the media worked both for and against the criminal. Although somewhat glamorizing the criminal as a clever loner swindling a corporate giant, the substantial publicity given to his subsequent attempt to steal an additional $50 million while his case was awaiting trial was also widely reported in the press, quite likely contributing to the judge's uncharacteristically stiff sentence at the end of his trial: eight years in a federal penitentiary.[10]

Finally, one of the more ingenious financial crimes perpetrated through the use of a computer occurred in 1977 at Florida's Flagler Dog Track. The dog-racing odds were figured by computer, and often the races were conducted so quickly that the odds would not be figured completely until after the race was over. A conspiracy was developed whereby an operator of the computer received the race results from an accomplice observing the race. He then stopped the computer program in progress, deducted a number of losers and added a corresponding number to the pool of winners in computer storage. The program was restarted and shortly finished its run. False winning tickets were then printed, also by computer, and were cashed in the next day. Since winners were paid from a pool formed by the losers' money, there was no way to detect the loss. Rather, each winner's share was somewhat less than it should have been.

The examples cited in this section represent some main areas in which computer crime can occur. It is by no means comprehensive, because the possibilities are nearly limitless for one with computer expertise and a fertile imagination. It should also be noted, however, that most of these crimes, many involving extremely large sums of money, could have been prevented or detected earlier through adequate security measures.

Legal Responses to Computer Crime

This section examines how the law on both the state and federal level has handled the growing problem of computer crime. As is true of many facets of the rapidly expanding computer industry, traditional legal principles have frequently been inadequate to cope with the novel legal questions that computer technology raises, causing serious lapses in the law's effectiveness. For convenience, this section has been divided into two subsections: state law and federal law.

State Law. At the outset, it is important to distinguish a criminal prosecution from a civil action. As a general rule, each crime must consist of at least two elements: the commission of an illegal act as defined by the jurisdiction's criminal statutes and the intent to commit such an act. Because criminal acts typically represent a threat to society as a whole, crimes are prosecuted by the state at public expense and involve heavier sanctions than civil remedies, which usually require that an individual merely be compensated for personal loss. Since one's personal liberty is at stake in a criminal trial, all crimes are codified into statutes so that prescribed behavior is made clear enough to presume that an accused person should have known the criminality of his or her alleged acts, and the prosecution's burden of proof (that is, the extent to which the prosecution must persuade the fact finder of the accused's guilt) is generally higher. Many statutes are merely formalized statements of the common law, which has been developed by English and American courts over the years. Although the discussion of criminal offenses will focus on common-law definitions of the crimes, it should be noted that many of the definitions will vary from state to state, depending upon variations in statutes and judicial interpretations.

Prosecuting Computer Crime under Traditional State Criminal Law. Prosecution of many computer-assisted crimes can be subsumed under existing state laws without too much difficulty. The most difficult legal issues concern the illegal theft or use of intangibles, such as data transmissions or computer software. State courts have differed in their interpretations of the proprietary nature of software. This interpretation eventually determines the applicability of a state's larceny and trade secret laws.

The following is a listing of some state computer-related offenses and the elements that the state must prove to get a conviction. Although, again, there are some differences among states in their definitions of these crimes, most of the basic elements are consistent throughout the nation.

Arson poses a serious threat to computer facilities. Such crimes may be political in nature or used to cover the traces of other criminal acts involving the computer, such as the destruction of financial records. The required elements of common-law arson include (a) the malicious (b) burning (c) of the dwelling of another. The intent to burn must be present; accidental blazes do not constitute arson. The extent of burning required is minimal and may consist only of slight charring, though mere discoloration is not enough. The legal definition of "dwelling" is usually broad enough to cover a computer installation since the definition has been expanded in most states to cover any structure of another (or of oneself if there is a public danger).

Burglary can be applied to theft occurring on the physical premises where a computer is housed. Common law elements of this crime are (a) a breaking (b) and entering (c) of a dwelling (d) of another person (e) in the nighttime

(f) with a felonious intent. The breaking does not require actual damage to a building but must be more than entering through an open door or window; one who successfully picks a lock has satisfied this element. The person entering cannot have the authority to do so. If the person is an employee who is authorized to be on the premises, burglary does not apply even if he or she intends to commit a felony. The common law requires that the crime involve a place where another person actually lives. This requirement, as well as the requirement that the act be committed in the nighttime, has been modified by most state burglary statutes.

Several state statutes applicable in the area of computer crime concern offenses against property. The crime most associated with the idea of computer crime is larceny, which can be either a misdemeanor or a felony in most jurisdictions, depending on the value of the property stolen. Six elements must be met in this crime: (a) personal property (not real estate) must be involved; (b) it must belong to another; (c) it must have been taken from the possession of another (d) by trespass (that is wrongfully, without the owner's consent); and (e) it must be carried away (f) with the intent to permanently deprive the owner of its possession. Any type of valuable property that can be moved will qualify, including the tangible expression of intangible property (such as an airplane ticket). The taker must obtain possession by taking the property from the rightful possession of another. Possession does not necessarily mean ownership but must entail more control over the object than mere custody. Thus, an employee entrusted with the custody of a computer system may be authorized to use the system, manipulate and transport components, and so on in the course of employment, but so long as his or her actions are subject to the employer's control, the employer is still in possession of the system. The employee may be guilty of larceny, however, if he or she converts custody to a wrongful possession by removing software without authorization. Also, the taking need not be direct; if a person sells a computer program to another who actually does the taking, the seller will still be guilty of larceny despite the fact that he or she may have never touched the property in question. The taking may also be committed by machine, such as by the filing of false insurance claims processed by computer. Finally, the taking must be done with the intent of permanently depriving the rightful owner of the article. Thus, the mere copying of a computer program may not qualify as larceny (in the absence of a statute covering theft of the ideas contained in the program), since the copier arguably does not necessarily intend to deprive the owner of the program but may be satisfied with sharing the use of the ideas and data contained within it.

Embezzlement was originally created as a crime to cover the deficiencies of the law of larceny. Its elements include (a) a fraudulent (b) conversion (c) of the property (d) of another (e) by a person to whom its possession has been entrusted. Thus, while the larcenist *obtains* possession wrongfully, the embezzler is already in *rightful possession* of the property but at some point decides to wrongfully exert a greater degree of ownership control over the property. Embezzlement may be said to be an offense against ownership, whereas larceny is an offense against possession. Most commonly, the property is in the form of cash, securities, stock, loans, or other financial instruments. A common example of embezzlement is the floating of funds between accounts at different banks. This crime is frequently committed with the use of a computer.

Another gap in the common law of larceny has been filled by the crime of larceny by false pretenses. This crime consists of five elements: (a) there must be a false representation of a material fact made by a wrongdoer (b) which causes the victim (c) to willingly pass title (d) of his or her property to the wrongdoer (e) who knows his or her representations are false and who intends to defraud the victim. A company that misrepresents its financial health by manipulation of computerized records, as in the Equity Funding fraud, is guilty of larceny by false pretenses. A mere expression of opinion that turns out to be wrong is not enough to satisfy the requirements of false pretenses, but an assertion supported by false computer printouts used to induce someone to make an investment does leave one open to charges. A potentially dangerous area is where a computer program is fed faulty or misleading information that later becomes the basis of erroneous recommendations. However, this crime does not generally apply to future predictions; rather, present or past facts must be misrepresented.

Extortion or blackmail statutes exist in most states. The crime is defined as (a) extracting money or other things of value (b) by means of a threat (c) not sufficient for robbery (that is, not a threat of bodily harm in the victim's presence) or (d) a communication for the purpose of such extraction. Though the computer is not usually actively used in such crimes, it may be the victim of threats of sabotage, and extortion should therefore be of some concern to the computer user.

In addition to these well-established common law crimes, more recent trade secrets statutes may apply to certain forms of software abuse. The main distinction between misappropriation of trade secrets and common-law larceny is the former's broader inclusion of intellectual property. One faces several choices when pursuing a criminal prosecution for the theft of a computer program. First, it must be determined whether the state in which the prosecution takes place has a trade secrets law. If it does not, then prosecution under traditional larceny statutes is the only course available.

This leads to the problem of what actually constitutes stolen property. One court has held that a mere copying of a program by use of a remote terminal is not theft because the only thing actually taken was "electronic impulses" (see *Ward v. Superior Court* in the computer crime court cases section). However, if a program in the form of a printout is removed from a computer facility, there is no doubt that a theft has taken place. The question in that case is one of determining the value of the property stolen for purposes of deciding the degree of the crime, for example, whether the theft constitutes a misdemeanor or felony. It has been argued that the value should be limited to the cost of the paper, whereas at least one court has permitted the intangible value of the program to be taken into account.[11] The related issue then arises of how to determine the actual loss to the company. Although the program itself may be of considerable value to a company, copying it does not deprive the company of its use but merely dilutes any advantage that exclusive use of the program gave it over competitors. Placing a value on this diluting effect may be a troublesome issue for the courts.

When prosecuting the theft of a computer program under a state's larceny statute, therefore, the prosecutor should initially emphasize the actual tangible property lost (that is, the paper on which the program is printed), then argue that its value is derived from the printed matter on it.

If a state does have a trade secrets law and the material at issue in the case has not been copyrighted or patented, care must be taken to avoid conflicting with federal copyright and patent laws. Under the preemption doctrine, a federal law will automatically take precedence over a state law in the event of a conflict, and it is not a crime under federal law to copy uncopyrighted matter. The Supreme Court has, however, given state trade secrets laws greater opportunity to be applied as long as they do not conflict with federal laws[12] (see also Part IV on proprietary protection).

Some states do not permit the prosecution of a crime under both a trade secrets statute and a larceny statute. Several states do, however, permit such multiple charges, in which case one might choose to press charges under both laws to maximize the chances for a conviction.

State Computer Crime Legislation. The rapid increase in the incidence of computer crime coupled with the greater publicity given to it by the media have resulted in much hastily drawn legislation on the state level.[13] For this reason, these laws are not without their weaknesses. The greatest problem with computer crime legislation is its overbreadth, both in terms of defining a computer and describing prohibited activities in its use. For instance, Florida's statute defines a computer as an "internally programmed, automatic device that performs data processing." Obviously, such a definition can be extended to pocket calculators, a result not likely intended by the legislature. Other statutes have been drafted ostensibly to make marginally improper acts, such as playing logic games or making Snoopy calendars on an employer's computer, a felony punishable by several years in prison.

The more recent computer crime statutes have attempted to alleviate these problems. For example, California excludes nonprogrammable calculators that cannot be used with external files from its definition of a computer. Likewise, its law has omitted unauthorized use from the definition of a crime. Illinois has made such use a petty offense punishable by a maximum fine of $500. These laws are in sharp contrast to those passed in New Mexico and Rhode Island, which make unauthorized use a felony.

As of 1979, 12 states had passed computer crime legislation. Three of these states, Arizona, Florida, and Virginia, passed their statutes in 1978. The remaining nine states all enacted their respective laws in 1979. They include California, Colorado, Illinois, Michigan, New Mexico, North Carolina, Rhode Island, Tennessee, and Utah. To date, none of these states have conducted any prosecutions under these laws, so their effects, as well as judicial interpretations, are largely unknown.

Tort Remedies. The victim of a computer crime need not always rely exclusively upon a state criminal prosecution for vindication. Tort remedies apply to many offenses that are also punishable by criminal statutes. A tort remedy may provide a very significant means for private prosecution of computer crimes. For example, if a person has stolen funds from a corporation, many prosecutors may be unwilling to spend the time and money necessary to convict the defendant of larceny, particularly when concern is much higher for violent crimes. Whether a criminal prosecution is brought or not, the corporation may sue the defendant for the tort of conversion to recover any amount lost plus possible punitive damages. The victim has one significant procedural advantage in the tort lawsuit as opposed to the criminal prosecution as the victim needs to convince the fact finder of the defendant's guilt only by a preponderance of the evidence standard (that is, more probable than not; more than 50 percent likely), rather than by the rigorous criminal standard of "beyond a reasonable doubt." There are, however, significant limitations to the use of tort remedies for computer crime. First, the same problems of applying legal definitions of "theft," "property," and so on that are present in the computer crime area are also present in the computer tort area. Second, a successful tort lawsuit merely gives the victim a legal right to enforce a debt against the defendant. If the defendant has insufficient assets within a jurisdiction that will honor the court's judgment, the judgment is worthless. This will often be the case since many criminals will have spent the money or converted it into assets that are beyond the jurisdiction of the court. The victim may be able to establish the defendant's guilt by a preponderance of the evidence as a matter of public record, but the victim will have gained no tangible benefit nor will the defendant be punished in any significant way. The tort remedy is nevertheless a viable alternative response to computer crimes that should not be overlooked.

Federal Law. The growth of federal law on computer crime has many parallels with the evolution of state law. The nature of such crimes has stretched traditional federal criminal law to the point where the need for comprehensive federal computer crime law has been recognized by Congress.

The federal criminal code has three jurisdictional bases: (a) federal property as the situs of a criminal act, (b) a weighty federal interest in the protected activity, or (c) crimes involving federally regulated media. For instance, if a state has granted concurrent federal jurisdiction on part of its property, that property would be subject to federal law. This frequently applies to large computer installations under contract to the federal government. Even if such a jurisdictional arrangement does not exist, the second basis may serve to bring federal law into play if federal property, federal officials, or federal functions are associated with the situs or activity. Finally, federally regulated media include the mails, interstate communications facilities, and other activities of interstate commerce. In addition, the tax laws may provide another legal tool for combating computer crime.

Many of the federal laws that can be applied to computer crimes have evolved out of the same common law sources as the state laws previously described. Therefore, a comprehensive discussion of each element is unnecessary. What follows is a listing of various sections of the federal criminal code by general category.

Several federal laws can be applied to computer crimes involving theft and related offenses. Embezzlement or theft of public money, property, or records is prohibited by federal law.[14] Its terms have been liberally construed so that "public property" may include "any thing of value," tangible or intangible. This law can be applied, for example, to any software that is subject to government custody, control, or ownership. Theft of goods moving in interstate commerce[15] and interstate transportation of stolen property[16] can also be applied to certain computer crimes.

Abuse of federal channels of communication has been a crime used to prosecute computer criminals. Specific laws that apply in this area include mail fraud[17] and wire fraud.[18] Prosecutions must be based on some interstate activity such as using a remote terminal in another state to copy a computer program. Several sections of the federal criminal code relate to various national security offenses,[19] including gathering, transmitting, and delivering defense information to a foreign government. Such information is frequently handled and stored by computer. Burglary is a federal offense when committed in a bank,[20] a post office,[21] or interstate carrier facility.[22]

Various sections of the federal criminal code apply to crimes of property destruction. Among those that have some bearing on computer crime are malicious injury to government property;[23] concealment, removal, or mutilation of public records;[24] and destruction of property affecting national security.[25]

Another significant federal tool for detecting and punishing computer crime comes from the Internal Revenue Code. Calculation of a person's income tax begins with a determination of that person's gross income, defined as "all income from whatever source derived" (subject to some specific exclusions).[26] Unlawful gains must be included within the term "gross income."[27] This fact enables the IRS to act to some extent as a national police force authorized to investigate and prosecute organized crime and other unreported monetary gains, even though the commission of traditional crimes cannot be established. The tax laws thus provide a means by which a computer criminal who has successfully dodged the prohibitions of a jurisdiction's criminal statutes (and judicial interpretations of them) may be brought up short for failing to report ill-gotten gains.[28]

The Process of Prosecuting a Computer Crime

To more fully understand the complexities inherent in prosecuting computer crimes, this section outlines the various stages of any state criminal prosecution, with special emphasis on problems unique to computer situations.[29]

Usually, the prosecution process formally begins by obtaining a search warrant after other investigation has identified a suspect. Constitutional protections require that such warrants be supported by *probable cause* that the property to be seized exists and is in the place specified to be searched, that the warrant state specifically the articles to be seized, and that the warrant be approved by an impartial magistrate. The main problem in drafting such a warrant for a search of a computer is how to describe what is to be seized and its specific location. For a program stored within a computer, several facets of computer technology regarding computer memory and the nature of the program stored in the memory may have to be explained to the magistrate. In addition, the form in which the program may be found is often uncertain. It could conceivably be stored within a computer's memory or in the form of keypunched cards, computer printout sheets, or magnetic tape.

Once the warrant is obtained, it is important that an expert accompany the prosecutor to the site of the computer to perform appropriate queries, locate the relevant information, and retrieve it, all without damaging the computer system, since a careless computer search may result in the destruction of the evidence sought.

Other more complex investigative and search and seizure techniques may be called for besides serving a search warrant. The most effective way to uncover some criminal activity may be to program a computer to conduct detailed monitoring of all user activities.

The next stage in the prosecution is charging the accused with a crime. As discussed previously, close examination of the jurisdiction's law is necessary at this point to determine which criminal charges may be justified by the defendant's alleged actions.

Once formal charges have been filed, discovery procedures must be instituted to gather evidence in preparation for trial. This also presents special problems when computers are involved. Again, an expert should be retained to retrieve the necessary information from a system, but even with the assistance of an expert, some needed material may legally be difficult to obtain because of confidentiality violations. An example of this would be personal information contained in the files of the National Crime Information Center, which is accessible only for very limited purposes.

Surprisingly few computer crime cases ever reach the trial stage. This may be due to the generally light sentences that result in this form of white-collar crime, as well as the uncertainty over the legal issues, making out-of-court plea bargaining more attractive. For those cases that do get to trial, considerable time must be spent by attorneys in self-education to make the complex issues understandable to both the judge and jury. Several evidentiary problems arise when computer data is introduced into evidence.

At the conclusion of the trial, sentence must be passed on the convicted computer criminal. Defendants usually receive light sentences because they often have no prior history of criminal behavior, tend to be upper-middle class, and are often well-respected people within their community. Another important influence on a judge's decision may be the amount the defendant has been assessed in a corresponding civil suit for damages. If a high civil judgment has been or is likely to be awarded, a judge may be inclined to give a light or suspended criminal sentence.

Court Cases

Several illustrative cases on computer crime are described.

Hancock v. State.[30] The defendant in this case was employed by Texas Instruments as a computer programmer. Because of strenuous deadlines, he would often take much of his work home with him to be able to continue working into the evening. While at home, he frequently discussed his work with his roommate, an insurance salesman who had ties to Texaco. The defendant suggested that his roommate make contact with Texaco to see whether they would be interested in buying some of Texas Instrument's programs. A meeting was arranged, and the defendant offered 59 programs to Texaco's representative for $5 million. This representative later identified himself as an investigator, and the defendant was indicted for felony theft.

The case is noteworthy because at trial, the defense moved to reduce the charge since the property in question was really worth only the value of the paper upon which the program was printed; Texas Instruments was never fully deprived of the program. In a landmark ruling, the judge held that the value of the property was determined by the information printed out on the paper and not merely by the paper itself.

Ward v. Superior Court.[31] The defendant in this case was employed by the competitor of a company that owned a valuable computer program enabling it to provide a sophisticated remote-plotting service at a much more reasonable cost than could the competitor. The defendant was able to gain access to this program by using a remote terminal and a legitimate user's password, billing number, and an unlisted phone number necessary to complete the log-on procedures. He directed the computer to print a copy of the remote-plotting program. The theft was discovered when a real customer received a bill for the unauthorized use, which was then traced to the defendant.

The defendant was charged under California's trade secrets law, which prohibited, among other things, the theft of an "article" representing a trade secret. Though convicted on other grounds, the judge found the only theft that had taken place was that of the electronic impulses that produced the defendant's copy of the program. These impulses, according to the judge, were not sufficiently tangible to constitute an article within the meaning of the statute.

People v. Home Insurance Co.[32] In this case, the defendant copied confidential hospital records regarding insurance claims. The issue was identical to the one in the previous case: Do electronic impulses constitute tangible property within the meaning of the applicable statute? Citing *Ward*, the Colorado court said they did not, and the charge was dismissed. As a result of this case, however, the deputy district attorney was able to persuade the state legislature to adopt a sweepingly broad definition of property in its computer crime statute to avoid such results in the future.

United States v. Sampson.[33] The defendant was charged with the theft of a "thing of value" belonging to the United States, a federal crime (18 USC 641). The defendant was an employee of a computer service company under contract to NASA. He was discovered using the computer for his own personal gain, and the indictment followed. In another variation of a property issue, the court had to determine whether computer time was a thing of value to make the federal law applicable. It ruled that theft of computer time was indeed covered by the act—a broad interpretation of the statute, which has important implications for the computer industry.

United States v. Jones.[34] This is another instance of a very technical distinction between terms that has important consequences. The defendants here acted as a team to defraud the Whirlpool Corporation through a Canadian company that employed one of the defendants. This corporation, a subsidiary of Whirlpool, managed its billing operation by computer. The defendant worked in this department and was able to divert some invoices that represented accounts payable to a dummy account at the accomplice's address. Five checks totaling more than $130,000 were thus mailed to a Virginia address instead of to the Whirlpool Corporation offices. The defendants were discovered and indicted under a federal false pretenses statute. The defense claimed that the checks that the defendant caused the computer to print were actually forgeries, thus outside the scope of the statute. The court did not agree and held that the checks were not forgeries, but rather valid checks which had been obtained by making false statements of fact to the computer. The indictment was therefore good, and the defendants were subsequently convicted.

These cases demonstrate the difficulty of applying traditional legal concepts to the unique issues raised by computer technology. Such problems are likely to persist in the criminal area, at least until the new state computer laws are tested in court. It remains to be seen whether legal concepts can be applied both flexibly and consistently as incidents of computer crime become more commonplace.

PRIVACY CONCERNS

Introduction and Overview

A social and legal interest in an individual's right of privacy has been recognized in the United States for almost a century. Rapid technological advances in electronic data processing have provided heightened concern for protection of personal information as it is collected, stored, used, and disseminated by public and private information systems.

Legal recognition of an individual's right of privacy has grown significantly in the last 15 years. Computer technology has outpaced the development of the accompanying legal framework, however, so that existing judicial and legislative solutions may be inadequate to protect privacy interests. Issues of information privacy are increasingly being addressed by courts and legislatures, which indicates that a comprehensive scheme of privacy protection may be forthcoming. Internationally, the issue of safeguarding privacy as it relates to transborder data flows is receiving considerable attention, and has serious implications for multinational businesses. It is therefore essential that an organization, in evaluating its information needs, provide the maximum protection for personal information within its control.

This discussion of privacy begins with an overview of the legal concerns that affect a computer user's obligations regarding privacy. Then, various legal vehicles that might be used to enforce privacy interests are examined in greater detail. The section ends with a discussion of methods and safeguards which will serve both the interests of preserving privacy rights and preventing computer crime.

Information Privacy. Before computerized recordkeeping became widespread, most business and government decisions about credit, educational grants, insurance, and employment were based on personal knowledge of the individuals concerned and on limited information obtained from a decentralized system of public records and from friends and associates. To a large extent, the inefficiency of the methods of data collection served to protect the individual's privacy. Recorded personal information was maintained in widely separated manual files and in the memories of those with whom the individual had dealt. It was difficult to compile a detailed dossier on any person.

The rapid growth of computerized information-gathering techniques has, probably justifiably, heightened the public's awareness and fear of possible intrusion into the sphere of personal privacy. Data is easily collected and stored. The ability of information handlers to increase their data collection activities tends to encourage the recording of more and more personal information. Further, computers can transmit data quickly and easily from one location to another. Penetrating a single computerized file may provide a wealth of information about a person, creating a greater incentive for a privacy invader to attempt it. In addition, computers make it possible to compile lists of people connected with various types of activities from widely scattered data, an impossible task with a manual system. Previously unknown relationships may be revealed or inferred from the multisource data systems. The possibility exists that an individual may be tracked from birth to death through a network of information systems operated by government agencies, private organizations, and business entities.

The right of information privacy has evolved as a result of these technological advances. Information privacy is defined as the "claim of individuals, groups, or institutions to determine for themselves when, and to what extent information about them is communicated to others." [35]

At least three separate interests are included in this basic definition. [36] The first aspect of information privacy involves rights of the individual with respect to the collection of data. The expectation of privacy in personal information may be necessarily limited when a person applies for credit, employment, insurance, or government benefits, since the data subject must be willing to provide sufficient personal data for an organization to make decisions responsibly. Information-gathering activities should be restricted, however, to obtain only data that is relevant and necessary to the decisions being made. Methods of collection should be fair and minimally intrusive.

The second aspect of information privacy is concerned with the accuracy of the records maintained. If the individual must relinquish a measure of control over data collection, then he or she should at least be given the opportunity to inspect those records and correct any inaccurate or misleading information contained in them.

A right of confidentiality of the information collected about an individual highlights the third aspect of information privacy. It is perhaps in this area that computer technology poses the greatest threat. A person has a right to know who will have access to the information in the initial data-gathering process and whether the revelations will be disseminated to third parties and for what purposes. The data subject should also be informed that consent is a prerequisite to information transfer. Without such restrictions, an individual may be encouraged to temper his or her personal history, political expression, or social relationships for fear that an unfavorable record image is being presented.

Restoration of a measure of control over quality and quantity of data will, by encouraging people to divulge the information necessary for legitimate purposes, assure fairer treatment of individuals by the decision-making processes of those providing benefits and services, as well as reinforce the individual's sense of personal autonomy and emotional well-being.

Information privacy can best be understood by applying the concept to four systems with great potential for use and abuse of computerized recordkeeping: governmental, personnel, personal, and other information systems. Since the use of information by the government involves legal concerns not present in the private sector, this topic is discussed separately first. Personnel, personal and other information systems are then discussed in the context of use in the private sector, as well as federal and state attempts to regulate the use of personal information in the private sector.

Governmental Information Systems

An enormous amount of personal information is held in computer data banks of the federal government. The collection of taxes, distribution of welfare and social security benefits, supervision of public health, direction of the armed forces, and enforcement of criminal laws require the orderly preservation of great quantities of data. Much of this data is personal and potentially embarrassing or harmful. The individual's challenge to privacy invasion by the federal government may rest on either (or both) of two legal grounds: a violation of the federal constitution or a violation of laws enacted by Congress. Although state laws and constitutional provisions regarding privacy rights may vary considerably, the policy considerations and legal analysis applied will generally be analogous to the discussion of federal governmental law presented here.

Constitutional Law. Privacy as a constitutional right is a somewhat recent development in American law. Although the right is not expressly mentioned in the United States Constitution, the Supreme Court has found that there are several personal interests that should be free from government intrusion. Official recognition of the right of privacy occurred in a 1965 case involving a state's prohibition of birth control counseling.[37] The Supreme Court held that various specific constitutional guarantees created "zones of privacy." Among the privacy-related interests recognized are the First Amendment guarantee of freedom of speech and association, the Fourth Amendment ban on unreasonable searches and seizures, the Fifth Amendment protection against self-incrimination, and the Ninth Amendment pronouncement of additional fundamental rights, which, although not mentioned in the first eight amendments, are still retained by the people. The Court held that "penumbras" emanating from the specific guarantees created the constitutional right of privacy.[38]

Governmental Data Gathering. Although the Supreme Court recognized an implicit right of privacy, the doctrine has generally been confined to personal decisions relating to domestic issues such as marriage, procreation, family life, and education.[39] The Supreme Court has not to date been receptive to the concept of information privacy. Distribution of a flyer among merchants naming an individual as an active shoplifter was held not to violate privacy rights;[40] and in *Whalen v. Roe*,[41] a state's plan for computerizing information on the use of prescription drugs by named individuals was held not to be an unconstitutional invasion of privacy. The Court did take note of the threat posed by large-scale information collection and processing techniques by noting the "potentially embarrassing or harmful" nature of such information collection.

Justice Brennan, concurring in the court's judgment, cautioned that the decision is predicated on the state's legitimate interest in the information and the safeguards employed to protect confidentiality. He expressed concern over the future of computerized data storage:

> . . . the Constitution puts limits not only on the type of information the State may gather, but also on the means it may use to gather it. The central storage and easy accessibility of computerized data vastly increase the potential for abuse of that information, and I am not prepared to say that future developments will not demonstrate the necessity of some curb on such technology.[42]

Lower courts have followed the lead of the Supreme Court in cases involving aspects of information privacy. Although judges consistently voice grave concern about the dangers of "overzealous data collection and instant data retrieval," the courts invariably hold that no constitutional bar exists to the use of such systems by the particular government. Courts have, for example, upheld the constitutionality of a system for centralized data collection on psychiatric outpatients[43] and have upheld the state's disclosure of information on the amount of public funds paid to particular physicians to perform abortions over claims that both the patients' and physicians' privacy rights would be violated.[44] In two Texas cases, the parents of allegedly abused children objected to the input of information about them into the statewide child abuse computer-reporting system (CANRIS).[45] The courts held that such an entry could be made only after a court had made a final determination that the child had been abused by the parents. Since in one case the judge had made only a temporary order leaving custody of the child with the state, the state was not permitted to make a computer entry identifying the parents as abusers of the child.[46] Thus, although the courts exhibited concern that the truth of such sensitive information be judicially determined before entry, they found no constitutional objection to the existence or character of such a centralized, easily accessible information system.

Law Enforcement. The law enforcement area presents another context in which the government's use and possible abuse of a data network containing potentially damaging personal information is subjected to constitutional challenge. Two primary types of cases dealing with the government's use of computers to investigate crime are becoming almost commonplace: those challenging arrests made on the basis of erroneous data in computerized criminal-reporting systems and those challenging the detection of fraud through the use of computer matching programs. To date, these challenges have been generally unsuccessful.

Law enforcement officers routinely run checks on individuals whom the officers have stopped or temporarily detained for even minor traffic violations or suspicious behavior. The officers accomplish these checks through use of a computerized criminal data system that tells the officer by means of a computer printout whether there are, for example, any arrest warrants outstanding on the person, whether the person is a suspected drug dealer, or if the vehicle is listed as stolen.

If an officer searches the vehicle or person or arrests the person on the basis of erroneous information, two results may occur. First, the officer may find nothing in the search or eventually discover that no reason existed for the arrest, and the person will be free to go. If this happens, the only way for the person to seek legal redress for the mistake is to take the initiative to sue the officer, the government if permitted, the police department, or the provider of the computer service (or any combination of those four) for any damages the person has suffered. The lawsuit may be based on the notion that a tort has been committed, such as false arrest, or that the police action abridged the person's civil rights in violation of federal or state statutes. In addition, the Supreme Court has approved the creation of a "constitutional tort," whereby a person injured by unconstitutional actions by state agents may sue the agents for damages even without the aid of a particular statute. If no prosecution has resulted from the erroneous search or arrest, the burden is on the injured party to bring the lawsuit and establish his or her entitlement to damages. As a practical matter, very few of these exonerated persons ever take the opportunity to litigate the propriety of a search or arrest. It is therefore not surprising that relatively few cases are reported in which exonerated persons have sued to redress wrongful searches or arrests based on erroneous computer information.[47]

The second possible scenario is much more frequently reported. When an officer has been alerted by the computer, albeit mistakenly, to the fact that a person is wanted for or suspected of involvement in a crime, the officer may, on the basis of that information and his or her own observations, decide to arrest the individual or search the person and/or vehicle, as in the first situation described. In this situation, however, the officer does find evidence of a crime for which the person is subsequently prosecuted. The accused person will try to prevent the introduction of the incriminating evidence found by claiming that since it was obtained unconstitutionally (that is, without either a warrant or probable cause), it must be excluded from use as evidence in determining the accused's guilt.

Courts deciding probable cause cases involving computer information generally tend to view the information network as a reliable enough source of information to entitle the officer to rely on it in deciding whether a search or arrest is justified. If erroneous data is relied on in making that decision, the accused has a strong argument that the search or arrest was in reality constitutionally unjustified, notwithstanding the fact that the officer found incriminating evidence. In determining whether probable cause existed, however, courts focus on whether, *in the mind of the police officer with his or her skill and expertise,* the officer was justified in believing the accused was guilty of the crime or that the evidence would be found. Thus, it generally does not matter to the court that the information in a given case was wrong so long as the information system is in general considered to be reliable enough to justify the officer's belief in its trustworthiness.[48]

The search and seizure area seems to present a unique situation in which courts have left the risk of computer error with the victim, rather than holding the user responsible for the system's faults. While tort and statutory remedies may be available for the truly innocent victim who brings suit, their effectiveness to deter mistakes, and conceivably intentional abuses in the absence of adequate input and verification safeguards, is uncertain. This trend in cases suggests the possibility that the computer may serve to justify infringements of individuals' most fundamental rights to freedom from search and arrest, the most extreme form of government interference.

In addition to the personal data maintained by federal agencies and bureaus, information systems are maintained by local and state governments and by private concerns. To date, these files are not all interrelated. The possibility of integration does exist, however, because many of the systems use social security numbers as a common means of identification, permitting the various users to link files. The use of a common key provides an easy way to correlate and match scattered bits of data. At present, integration within government programs is becoming commonplace, and proposals for a comprehensive federal information system have been voiced. Computer matching programs aimed at identifying persons illegally receiving welfare benefits have been implemented. The federal government and the state of New York, for example, have both embarked upon massive computerized matching plans with the objective of detecting ineligible welfare recipients. Both systems use social security numbers to cross-check data on various files.

The system used by the Department of Health and Human Services is called Project Match. It seeks to expose lawbreakers by matching state welfare roles with lists of federal employees. Project Match permits transfers of data among four large federal agencies—the Department of Health and Human Services, the Defense Department, the Office of Personnel Management, and the Justice Department. Since all agencies that have welfare recipients on their payrolls are also involved, data is disseminated throughout the federal government.

The major objection to Project Match is that data obtained for one purpose can be used out of context for a different purpose with no opportunity for those affected to control its flow. Since the concept of privacy is defined as control over personal information, this matching system is seen as undermining privacy rights. In addition, computer scanning of files on millions of people to identify those with certain shared characteristics may pose the most dangerous aspect of automated information systems. More and more data linkages can be made from previously unconnected sources. The threat exists (in the extreme) that the boundaries between various data systems may eventually be erased so that a piece of information entering one system is available to other systems, creating one large data network.

On the other hand, matching programs are defended because they save the government money by uncovering illegal welfare recipients. The traditional process of sampling, in which a limited number of files are randomly cross-checked, is more time consuming and less thorough than the computerized matching program. At least as applied to intragovernment linkages, it seems sensible to permit the government to correlate information from its own agencies to prevent fraud upon itself by its own employees.

The New York State Wage Reporting System also aims to expose individuals who illegally collect both paychecks and welfare benefits. This system, however, uses data that all employees, both public and private, are required to supply to the government for deducting and withholding taxes. Critics oppose this program for much the same reasons as Project Match, although this system is arguably even more objectionable, since it extends to private, as well as public, employees. The New York law also authorizes the use of information originally collected to verify eligibility for social service and employment benefits and to establish support obligations.

Although these matching programs have served to remove ineligible recipients from welfare roles and eliminate overpayments, they have also posed serious questions about possible abuses of computer technology.[49] In an ever-increasing number of cases, however, courts have unanimously upheld the use of computer matching programs against constitutional challenges. Some representative cases include a challenge of the use of a matching program as an investigative tool by a grand jury,[50] a lawsuit brought by welfare recipients to block the use of matching programs,[51] and cases in which the program's constitutionality has been questioned in response to criminal charges or benefit reductions.[52]

Federal Statutes. Statutory law on both the federal and state levels has had the greatest impact by far on the government regarding privacy and confidentiality of information. The present statutory approach is an attempt to balance privacy interests with other interests such as the public's right to know, legitimate organizational needs for personal information, administrative costs, and broader societal objectives such as crime control or receipt of benefits. The most significant federal statute enacted in an effort to prevent privacy abuses in the government information systems is the Privacy Act of 1974.[53]

Here is a summary of the major provisions of the Privacy Act of 1974:

A. Coverage of the Act
   1. The act covers records and procedures of federal agencies.
   2. An "agency" is defined as all executive departments, regulatory agencies, government corporations, and certain private corporations under contract with the government.
   3. A "record" is broadly defined as any item or collection of information about an individual maintained by an agency, including education records, financial transactions, criminal or employment history, or medical history, that contains identifying particulars such as social security number or fingerprints.

B. Collection of Data about an Individual

1. Any information that may have an adverse effect on an individual must be collected from him personally "to the greatest practicable extent."
2. The agency must give an individual the following facts:
   a. the authority under which the data is collected;
   b. whether the requested information is voluntary or mandatory;
   c. the principal purposes for which the agency is planning to use the information; and
   d. what can happen to the individual if he or she does not provide the requested information.

C. Types of Records an Agency May Keep

1. An agency may maintain information only if it is relevant and necessary to accomplish an agency purpose required by law.
2. An agency must keep records with such accuracy, relevance, and completeness to ensure fairness to the individual.

D. Disclosure of Information

1. Disclosure other than for routine purposes of the agency is prohibited without the consent of the individual unless covered by one of several exceptions.

E. Disclosure Accountability

1. An agency must record the date, nature, and purpose of each disclosure.
2. Disclosure records must be maintained for five years or the life of the individual record, whichever is longer.
3. Access to disclosure records must be made available to the individual upon request unless connected with law enforcement.
4. An agency must inform those to whom disclosures are made of any disputes or corrections regarding an individual's record.

F. Rules of Conduct

1. An agency must establish rules of conduct for those who work with the information system and inform them of the provisions of the act.
2. Safeguards to ensure security and confidentiality must be implemented.
3. Procedures by which an individual may check and amend his or her record must be established.
4. These rules are to be compiled annually and made available to the public at a low cost.

G. Remedies

1. An agency shown to be in willful violation of the act is subject to criminal fines up to $5,000.

Another significant piece of legislation dealing with the government's use of information is the Freedom of Information Act.[54] The purpose of the FOIA is to make information in the control of government agencies available to the public upon proper request. The lawmakers recognized the threat that such a policy might pose to the privacy of individuals about whom the government possesses information, and consequently provided two exceptions to the general policy of disclosure based upon the personal nature of the information requested. One of these exceptions exempts from disclosure personnel and medical files and similar files the disclosure of which would constitute a clearly unwarranted invasion of privacy. The other exempts investigatory records compiled for law enforcement purposes, but only to the extent that the production of such records would constitute an unwarranted invasion of personal privacy. These exceptions do very little, however, to define the obligations of the government in its handling of potentially sensitive personal information since the significant terminology is largely left undefined. For example, what are "personnel, medical and *other similar* files," what constitutes an "invasion of privacy," and most importantly, when is such an invasion "clearly unwarranted"? The FOIA exceptions do little more than open a door for the government to go to the courts for clarification of its privacy obligations—they do very little to define practical standards for application to disclosure requests.

State Legislation. State privacy legislation regulating governmental recordkeeping practices has not followed any consistent pattern. An individual can expect to receive comprehensive protection in those states enacting laws patterned after the Federal Privacy Act. Omnibus statutes in Arkansas, Connecticut, and Minnesota, for example, broadly regulate state government activities with respect to data collection, accuracy, and confidentiality. In comparison, other states have prohibited the unauthorized release of specific types of sensitive personal information held by state and local agencies. For example, Florida provides for the confidentiality of records of births and of alcoholics in treatment programs; Colorado restricts disclosure of social service records; Maine limits disclosure of arrest records and further provides for access and review of records by the accused or his or her attorney; and finally, New York protects the confidentiality of centrally stored child abuse information.

Private Information Systems

Introduction and Overview. Many areas of the nonpublic use of information possess the potential for serious abuses of privacy rights. The topic is divided for discussion here into three categories: personnel information systems, other business systems, and personal information systems. This section begins with a discussion of these uses of information and then analyzes the availability of legal avenues for redressing privacy violations in the private business sector.

Personnel Information Systems. The expanding interest in information privacy has recently focused on recordkeeping in the employment relationship. The concern is justified and perhaps overdue since the employment record is the most comprehensive data file maintained on most individuals.[55]

Personnel files often include detailed application forms, results of physical and psychological examinations, test scores, periodic performance evaluations, personal references, transfers and promotions, salaries, and disciplinary actions. The system of compiling and storing employee data varies depending on the needs of the organization and its personnel practices.

From the employee's perspective, much of the information stored is highly sensitive. Release of medical records, personal references, psychological tests, performance evaluations, and even salary information are possible sources of personal embarrassment and even economic harm to an individual. As a result of the volume of data collected and its potential for misinterpretation and abuse, the personnel file may pose the greatest modern risk to individual dignity and freedom.

Data processing of personnel information will be increasingly utilized in the 1980s.[56] It is an efficient and inexpensive way to collect and store specific data about all employees, information often required to be kept by statutory mandate such as the Occupational Health and Safety Act and Equal Employment Opportunity Act (Title VII). Employers may argue that computerized recordkeeping to lower storage costs facilitates privacy through built-in security protections and elimination of extraneous data. The danger exists, however, that collection and use of large quantities of personal information will lead to impersonal decision making and dissemination to third parties for purposes unrelated to employment.

The potential privacy abuses of personnel information systems fit into three main categories: intrusive data gathering, use of inaccurate or outdated information, and breach of confidentiality.

Data collection can be burdensome in the quantity and type of information sought and in the method of solicitation. In addition, the individual may not be given the opportunity to exercise informed consent in deciding whether to disclose the requested information. Nowhere are these intrusions more apparent than at the job application stage. Initial data searches may include disclosure of information about arrest and criminal records, pregnancy, drug and alcohol use, psychiatric history, and political activities. The prospective employee may be required to give blank authorization for probing searches into former employment relationships, educational performances, and past credit history. Informing a job applicant of the right not to disclose means little when the consequence of nondisclosure may be unemployment.

Intrusive data gathering leads to the presence of sensitive, often irrelevant, and possibly embarrassing material in the personnel record. Although the existence of the record may be inherently harmful, the crucial issues to the user of the system are the use and dissemination of information already extracted.

At the outset, the user needs to maintain the accuracy of the information—that is, ensure that the information maintained in the system is the same information as that provided. For example, when qualitative data supplied by an individual is changed to numerical data codes for purposes of storage and manipulation in the computer system, many opportunities for error exist (such as from a numerical transposition) with potentially drastic consequences. Safeguards should therefore be built into the system to detect possible errors, such as procedures to double-check entries for accuracy or a program that rejects for manual handling documents that appear to the computer to be outside a preestablished normal range.

Similarly, procedures should be established for updating files quickly when changes, corrections, or deletions are necessary. For example, if a disciplinary probationary period is set by a union contract at a maximum of 90 days, it may be better for the employer to use a computer program that will automatically remove the probation code from an employee's file at the expiration of 90 days after input, rather than require that another entry be made to terminate the probationary status.

Confidentiality is an attribute of information requiring that sensitive data receive protection from improper use, theft, or unauthorized dissemination. Improper use occurs when personal information is used as the basis for an adverse decision about an employee in a way that the individual did not consent to when disclosing. Guarding against theft of sensitive data requires adequate security procedures. Gaining access to personnel files could result in the storage of sensitive data about a colleague on home computers or outright sale for legal, but unauthorized, purposes or for illegal purposes.

Unauthorized data transfers may be made to government or labor officials and private third parties. Disclosure to the first two groups is usually dictated by statute or at least when a demonstrable public need exists. Confidential information is often required to be given in exchange for a right, privilege, or opportunity. Therefore, the harm to the individual must be balanced against the benefits resulting from information release. Inquiries by third parties may seriously breach the employee's expectation of privacy and confidentiality since the data subject has probably not consented to the disclosure, nor perhaps even received notice of it.

In the recent case of *Detroit Edison Co. v. National Labor Relations Board*,[57] the Supreme Court addressed the issue of employment record privacy. Under the National Labor Relations Act, a union is entitled to access to employment record information for collective bargaining purposes and grievance processing. The court recognized that the interests of the union and the employees may be adverse, however, and held that confidentiality of, in this case, standardized test results, is a valid ground for nondisclosure to the union by the employer. This holding was subsequently applied to personnel files in general by an Administrative Law Judge (ALJ) opinion.[58] Although the ALJ's extension does not carry nearly the same weight as the Supreme Court opinion, it indicates that privacy of employment records is receiving judicial notice.

Information received may also be inaccurate or taken out of context by credit bureaus, insurance companies, or mailing firms. A representative case is *Peller v. Retail Credit Co.*[59] An adolescent job applicant was asked to undergo a polygraph examination. The test results falsely indicated use and dealing in illegal drugs. Not only was employment denied, but the retail store employer sold the polygraph results to a credit-reporting agency. Subsequent employment was short-lived since a credit check revealed the polygraph results. This individual was denied employment for several years.

Computerized personnel systems offer maximum efficiency in handling employee information, but may also compound privacy abuses resulting in serious economic and social harm to an individual. Extreme care should be taken in establishing procedures to prevent errors and unauthorized uses.

Other Business Information Systems. It is impossible to capsulize for purposes of this text the number and types of various business contexts in which information privacy needs to be addressed. We live in an age when it is practically impossible to go through life without becoming an entry in some organization's computer. It can be safely said, however, that whenever a business has in its possession information about someone's personal life, that business needs to be concerned about some basic information privacy requirements: that the information gathered is relevant to the organization's particular need and stated purpose for obtaining it, that the information be maintained to ensure its accuracy, and that it be used only for the purposes for which, and by the persons to whom, consent has been given for its use.

As the state and federal government exercise more controls over the use of personal information by private industry, more definite and rigorous standards may be imposed. For example, as discussed in the legislative remedies section, the Congress has imposed minimal information privacy standards for the credit-reporting industry in the Fair Credit Reporting Act. Many lawsuits are now being brought under this act. Businesses need to be alert to new legal developments in the regulation of information privacy. Ideally, private industry could avoid the need for external regulation through self-imposed information privacy policies. As a practical matter, the user who protects privacy interests early on may be able to avoid future changes and attendant disruptions mandated by government regulation.

Personal Information Systems. The proliferation of microcomputers for home use has created a demand for information and services but has also raised unique privacy issues.

Data of practical use for the computer owner can be self-generated. For example, budget and tax information, social engagements, travel plans, and daily routines are easily recorded and stored. The personal system could be a rich source of information about fellow employees, friends, or family.

Additional data bases can be purchased or access gained for a fee. One currently being offered is the New York Times Data Bank. Information is taken from the New York Times and numerous other publications. A subscriber is able to request all information collected on an individual over the last ten years.[60] Public access over telephone lines is currently limited, so the cost is high. Rapid technological advances coupled with an increase in the volume of subscribers will soon lower the service fee for this and similar competing services.

Another multifaceted information system is Viewdata in the United Kingdom.[61] A central computer system stores enormous amounts of data on airline schedules, want ads, education, news, and public welfare. The service is run by the UK Post Office, which also operates the telephone system. A request for a page of this information can be made from a home or business through a small terminal connected to the telephone line. The data is returned over the telephone line to a receiving television set adapted to Viewdata where it is displayed in full color. Use of the telephone line on a per-minute basis determines the fee as in a normal voice transmission.

As technological developments make possible ultimate conveniences such as these services, computer-assisted grocery shopping from the home, or home entertainment systems that permit the consumer to choose his or her entertainment selection for the evening, the cost to the consumer may be more than monetary. With every link between the consumer's personal life and these external services, the consumer permits more and more of his or her personal life to become less and less private.[62] For example, the consumer who enjoys these services has permitted a file to be created that may reveal to outsiders his or her taste in food and entertainment, travel plans, life style, and so on. If the vendor of one of these systems reveals (or permits to be revealed, negligently or otherwise) any of this information to third parties, the consumer may be subjected to increased advertising by mail based on a marketing profile of the consumer's tastes or, in extreme cases, public humiliation.

The use of personal and remote data bases, Viewdata, and other on-line information systems such as electronic funds transfer and electronic mail could have a tremendous impact on privacy as well as on other traditional rights of individuals. Should the system provider be allowed to conduct surveillance on a user at any given point in time? Will records be kept on who accesses what information and the results offered for sale? Should information about people be available through a Viewdata-type system? Once a user is linked into a data base, has the right to keep unrelated transactions private been relinquished? Should law enforcers have access to personally stored data? Such information could reveal much about an individual's or family's communications, shopping patterns, friendships, and financial status. A government agency or private investigator might be able to create a comprehensive investigative dossier by integrating government, personnel, and personal information systems.

As in other areas, it will probably take a while for the laws to catch up with the technology and marketing of these systems. Until trends in the law develop so that one can determine the extent and nature of regulation that is likely, vendors of such systems are advised to keep in mind the potential privacy implications of their services and safeguard against breaches of basic privacy obligations toward their customers. Potential customers of these services should keep in mind the diminished control over personal information that they may experience.

Common Law (Tort) Remedies. Common law can be described as judge-made law, as opposed to laws formulated and passed by legislatures. The common law develops one case at a time; a judge will examine a controversy in the context of similar past disputes in the same jurisdiction (such as the same state) and try to render a decision that is both fair to the individuals involved in the present case and consistent with past cases involving similar issues. In this type of system, change occurs very slowly because judges are generally reluctant to overrule past decisions or to create new legal doctrines.

A personal tort is defined as an injury to the person or to his or her reputation or feelings. The tort action for invasion of privacy has recently evolved from the "right to be let alone" concept. Currently, there are four general categories of invasion of privacy for which an individual may seek relief through tort law: (a) appropriation of a person's name or likeness for economic gain; (b) intrusion upon another's privacy or private affairs; (c) public disclosures of private, embarrassing facts about an individual; and

(d) placement of an individual in an objectionable false light in the public eye.[63] In addition, defamation actions may also relate to an individual's privacy interest in personal information.

Appropriation. The first category, appropriation, normally includes such situations as using a person's photograph, name, or endorsement in an advertisement without that person's authorization, and is not generally applicable to invasions of information privacy. This tort could, however, be committed by the user of an information system who finds the names of celebrities in its customer files and advertises that fact without first obtaining the celebrity's permission.

Intrusion. The second kind of privacy invasion, intrusion, typically involves physical intrusions, wiretapping, surveillance, and inspection of privately held records such as a taxpayer's bank account or personal diary. In addition, objectionable snooping techniques and collection of highly personal information irrelevant to any legitimate business purpose may constitute an intrusion violation of the right of privacy, as noted by one federal court of appeals.[64] An actionable privacy intrusion into personal information systems is a further extension of the common law right of privacy. Data personally collected and stored in a home computer is arguably entitled to the same protection as other privately held records. Further, surveillance of on-line users and unauthorized access to private data bases can be analogized to telephone wiretapping and physical intrusions.

Public Disclosure. This type of privacy tort occurs when "one gives publicity to a matter concerning the private life of another . . . [and] the matter publicized is of a kind that (a) would be highly offensive to a reasonable person, and (b) is not of legitimate concern to the public."[65]

The element that serves as a drawback to computer applicability is the "publicity to" requirement. The private fact must be disclosed to the public at large or to such a significant number of people that it will be regarded as certain to become public knowledge. Information about a person stored and transferred from one government agency to another or from one business to another, even if highly personal, usually includes only a small number of handlers and falls short of being communicated to the public at large.

The advent of the microcomputer with the capability of storing and transferring vast quantities of information may have created situations in which the public disclosure tort is applicable. For example, an individual could collect and retain information files on fellow employees, potential customers, or competitors. It would be an easy task to trade or perhaps even sell these files to others in the business world. This information exchange could conceivably escalate to a point where the information is deemed public knowledge.

False Light. The false-light tort requires unreasonable and objectionable publicity that, although literally true, attributes to an individual characteristics, conduct, or beliefs that are false. For example, if a picture of a teenage girl taken as she was leaning against a lamppost while waiting for a bus is later used to introduce a magazine article entitled "Teenage Prostitution Reaches Epidemic Proportions," then a valid false-light claim could be asserted. The photo represents a true fact, that this girl leaned against this lamppost. The manner in which it is used, however, creates a damaging false impression about her. The false-light claim has relevance in the computer context if literally true data is used in a false or misleading way and meets the public disclosure requirement.

Future Privacy Tort Remedies. The tort recovery for invasion of privacy in its present forms has limited applicability to computerized information systems. Common-law privacy protection has not dealt specifically with personal information held individually or transferred to a small number of persons. Attention to information privacy to date has focused mainly on business and governmental duties.

A new category of privacy tort addressing personal information possession and dispersion has been proposed. In the absence of this new form, a tort claim based upon a strict invasion of information privacy, without the extra elements described here, will be without remedy in the judicial system.

Defamation. The defamation torts also have application to the privacy area when false information about the victim is communicated to another person, if that false information is of a nature that causes damage to the victim or to the victim's reputation. The defamation torts may take various forms, depending upon the jurisdiction. The tort of libel generally refers to a false written communication; slander, to a false oral communication. Particular applications of the defamation torts may be actionable in a jurisdiction, such as slander of credit. Some privileges act as defenses to a charge of defamation, for example, in the employment context. Since defamation involves false statements, truth is also a defense to defamation actions. Safeguards to ensure accuracy of information may thus go a long way toward reducing the chances of defamation liability.

From the view of the consumer, the defamation action does not address privacy concerns per se since it focuses on the wrongfulness of spreading untruths, not of violating privacy interests. On the other hand, in cases in which false information is involved, the defamation action offers an advantage to the victim over the privacy tort as the defamation publication requirement is satisfied by communicating the information to any nonprivileged person; that is, public dissemination of the information is not required as it is in the privacy tort actions discussed previously.

Legislative Remedies. Federal and state lawmakers have already taken steps toward regulating information privacy in the private sector. A few of these efforts are described here. The success or failure of these methods in causing responsible control of personal information will determine the future role of the government in regulating the use of information in the private sector.

Fair Credit Reporting Act. The Fair Credit Reporting Act (FCRA) of 1974[66] represents the most significant federal attempt to regulate information in the private sector. The FCRA applies to any "consumer-reporting agency," defined as any business that regularly engages in assembling or evaluating information on consumers to be furnished to third parties, as well as to users of consumer reports. The FCRA permits an agency to furnish consumer reports only in certain specified situations, for example, according to the consumer's written instructions or to a person that the agency has reason to believe "has a legitimate business need for the information in connection with a business transaction involving the consumer." The act puts limits on the age of the information that can be used in preparing consumer reports and requires disclosure to the consumer whenever a report on the consumer is procured. The FCRA requires agencies to maintain "reasonable procedures" to ensure compliance with the act's requirements about furnishing information only for legitimate purposes and to assure "maximum possible accuracy" of the information about an individual. This reasonableness standard, roughly analogous to the standard applied in negligence actions (see Part VI), is left open to judicial interpretation.[67] The act also sets forth requirements and procedures that consumers may follow to review the nature, substance, and sources of information in the agency's files on the consumer and to contest the accuracy of the information found. Users of consumer reports are required to advise the consumer of adverse decisions and the nature of the information upon which the decision was based. If the decision was based upon a consumer report, the user must supply the consumer with the name of the agency making the report.

If an agency or user negligently violates the act, the consumer may recover any actual damages plus court costs and attorney's fees. If an agency or user willfully violates the act, the consumer may also recover punitive damages from the agency or user.

Other Federal Legislation. The original version of the Privacy Act of 1974 contained provisions that would have made it applicable to private industry. Congress chose, however, to postpone a decision on state and private-sector application until the relationship between individual privacy and information processing could be comprehensively examined. The enacted legislation created the Privacy Protection Study Commission. The commission's study, concluded in 1977, found that any privacy protection policy must have three basic goals: minimizing intrusiveness, maximizing fairness, and operating a legitimate, enforceable expectation of confidentiality where such expectation is warranted.[68]

The committee's legislative recommendations include regulation of information practices of several private industries such as credit-granting institutions, insurance companies, medical care organizations; hiring and promotion practices within the private sector; and disclosure requirements for denial of credit. The proposal does provide some narrow protections in the employment context. If an applicant is denied employment because of a credit report, he or she has a right to learn the "nature and substance" of the file and then may contest the information.

On the whole, this legislation has several weaknesses that illustrate the difficulty of applying privacy legislation to the private sector. It creates a vague and open-ended loophole by permitting disclosure of personal information to anyone with a "legitimate business need." It makes remedies available to consumers who have been subject to adverse decisions but only after sifting through a complicated scheme of rights and responsibilities that most people without legal training would find incomprehensible, and monetary losses may not be substantial enough to warrant hiring an attorney. Finally, the proposal does not require that an individual be permitted to inspect his or her file.

The Family Education and Right to Privacy Act,[69] passed in 1976, regulates the information practices of federally funded educational institutions. Specific rules on the collection of data, the rights of parents and majority-aged students to educational records, and the dissemination of personally identifiable information were established by this act.

The remaining federal law with significance in information protection is the Right to Financial Privacy Act of 1978.[70] This statute permits government access to customer records of financial institutions for law enforcement purposes only.

These recommendations have helped to create interest in privacy legislation at the state level, mainly aimed at the prohibition of unauthorized release of certain types of sensitive information. For the most part, there is a dearth of law that exercises control over private data banks in the United States. The general congressional tone has been one of reluctance to burden the private sector with additional regulations.

State Legislation. The states' regulation of information activities in the private sector has primarily focused on the confidentiality of medical or financial records. Many states have adopted the Uniform Consumer Credit Code, which requires that any disclosures of credit information be in writing, with a copy to the debtor.[71] In the employment area, a job applicant has some specified protections against intrusive collection practices as well. Several states forbid polygraph examinations as an employment prerequisite. In some jurisdictions, an employer may also be prohibited from asking an applicant questions related to physical or psychiatric illnesses or arrests and convictions unless such information bears directly on job performance.

Unfortunately, there are few, if any, restrictions on the internal use of personnel information. The law considers personnel files to be the property of the employer and does not view the employment relationship as one governed by confidentiality.[72] As a result, in the absence of voluntary employer compliance programs, information privacy in the workplace remains largely unprotected.

Multinational Privacy Concerns

The worldwide development of automated information systems has triggered the passage of data protection laws in many countries. With the emergence of international data networks, increased concern has focused on unifying and fortifying national legislation to protect personal information. International agreements are highly important to multinational companies and time-sharing service firms. Such agreements would serve to protect transborder flows of personal data while harmonizing each country's legislation to prevent disruptions in international communication.

The protection of personal information is the basic principle underlying European and American privacy legislation. There are some significant differences,[73] however, which can be summarized as follows:

a. The United States Privacy Act of 1974 regulates information practices of federal agencies only, whereas data protection in Europe provides comprehensive coverage in the public and private sectors.

b. Privacy legislation in Austria, Norway, and Denmark confers rights on organizations ("legal persons"), whereas American and Canadian law focuses on individuals ("natural persons").

c. The form of processing is not mentioned in U.S. privacy laws; hence both automated and manually recorded data are included. In European nations only computerized data is covered by privacy legislation, with the exception of the German Federal Data Protection Law, which addresses automated and manual information systems.

d. Control institutions, such as "commissioners for data privacy" in Germany, have regulatory and precautionary functions for protecting individual freedom. In the United States, on the other hand, one must resort to the judicial system for privacy abuse remedies.

Multinational business communication needs must be reconciled with privacy protection legislation of individual nations. The Organization of Economic Cooperation and Development (OECD) recently approved guidelines for data protection legislation on an international level. This organization, which includes the United States, Canada, Japan, Australia, New Zealand, and European nations, has addressed the scope of coverage and types of privacy protection requirements that member nations would voluntarily comply with. Transfers of information to nations not complying with OECD standards would be restricted. Therefore, the possibility exists that so-called nontariff barriers could be set up, seriously impeding the flow of information within multinational firms.

Designing a system that will satisfy information needs while at the same time recognizing that certain classes of data require protection will be a foremost consideration of multinational businesses in the 1980s.

Court Cases

Jaffess v. Secretary of Health, Education, and Welfare.[74] This case addressed the issue of whether computer matching by government agencies violates the constitutional right of privacy. The case involved a computer comparison of persons receiving veterans' disability benefits against a list of social security recipients. The amount of a veteran's payment is dependent upon annual income from other sources, including social security benefits, so when a computer cross-check revealed that Jaffess had not reported his social security income as required by law, his veteran's benefits were accordingly reduced.

The court rejected the plaintiff's claim of a constitutional guarantee of privacy, finding that right does not prevent intraagency disclosure of information obtained in the course of conducting regular agency functions. It was further noted that disclosure of Jaffess's benefits to the VA under the matching program was clearly warranted in view of the fact that the Veterans Administration is statutorily obligated to take such payments into account when calculating the amount of benefits a disabled veteran may receive. A violation of the privacy right would occur only if the government possessed "highly personal and confidential information which has been given under compulsion of law and with an expectation of privacy and where the disclosure of such information is unnecessary for the advancement or inconsistent with the fundamental purposes for which the data was obtained."

The action was also brought under the Privacy Act of 1974, but the act was not implemented as of the litigation date. It is doubtful that a different result would have occurred, since the computer matching inquiry would almost certainly have been considered to be "relevant and necessary to accomplish an agency purpose required by law," a legitimate use of information under the Privacy Act.

Tureen v. Equifax, Inc.[75] In this case an invasion-of-privacy claim against a consumer investigation and reporting firm was alleged by an individual seeking health insurance benefits. The defendant, Equifax, was employed by the plaintiff's insurance company to investigate the question of whether Tureen was totally disabled and therefore entitled to disability insurance benefits. The files used by the investigation firm contained, or were reported to contain, 23 prior applications for life insurance totaling $10,000,000. The plaintiff claimed that he had applied for life insurance, with a one-half million dollar value, eight to ten times at most. Evidence indicated that the information about which Tureen complained was copied from previous reports in branch office files, which had no record of origin of the information. Tureen asserted that the investigative report caused him great anguish because it made him look like a potential suicide.

The court found for defendant Equifax, holding that neither the intrusion nor the public disclosure torts could be extended in this case because (a) the personal information, properly collected and retained, was relevant to legitimate consumer-reporting business needs and (b) the publicity requirement for the public disclosure tort had not been met. The information never became and was not likely to become public knowledge.

The court noted, however, that Equifax did not utilize computerized record keeping techniques:

> There is no indication in the record that the information about which the plaintiff complains was obtained from or placed in a computer bank or information bureau by means of which it might reasonably be expected to be more widely disseminated. The possible implications of that fact situation, therefore, are not before this court.

It is reasonable to infer then, that the now-prevalent employment of computerized recordkeeping systems could produce a different result in an invasion-of-privacy tort claim.

Thompson v. San Antonio Retail Merchants Association.[76] This case illustrates the application of the Fair Credit Reporting Act to a computerized credit-reporting system. The credit agency, SARMA, utilized a computerized "automatic capturing" feature. Each subscriber to the credit-reporting service used its own terminal to feed identifying information about a particular consumer to SARMA's computer. SARMA's computer then searched its files and displayed to the subscriber the credit history file that most nearly matched the information fed in by the subscriber. The subscriber was left to decide whether it would accept the displayed file as that of the consumer for whom the request had been made. Whenever the subscriber did accept the file as pertaining to its consumer, however, SARMA's computer automatically captured into the file any information from the subscriber's terminal that SARMA did not already have.

This system caused great problems for the plaintiff, William Douglas Thompson, III. The trouble began in November 1974, when a single truck loader, William Daniel Thompson, Jr., residing at 132 Baxter, opened a credit account with a jeweler that ultimately became delinquent and was charged off as a bad debt. His SARMA file, number 5867114, failed to list his social security number, 457-68-5778.

In early 1978, the plaintiff, William Douglas Thompson, III, applied for gasoline and retail store credit cards, listing his social security number as 407-86-4065, his address as 6929 Timbercreek, his occupation as grounds keeper, and his wife as Deborah C. The gasoline company's terminal operator mistakenly accepted file number 5867114, William Daniel Thompson's, as the plaintiff's file. Consequently, SARMA's computer captured the plaintiff's identifying information into its file number 5867114. That file thus became a hybrid of information about the two men. The name on the file remained William Daniel Thompson, Jr., the social security number was the plaintiff's, a former address and employer were William Daniel's, and the wife's name became the name of the plaintiff's wife.

As a result, the plaintiff's applications for both credit cards were denied. Numerous efforts to discover and remedy the problem failed. The retail store was not ultimately informed of the mistake until more than one and a half years after the mistake and then only after the plaintiff's lawsuit had been filed. The trial court found that the denials of credit had been caused by SARMA's failure to follow reasonable procedures to assure the maximum possible accuracy of its files, and awarded the plaintiff $10,000 actual damages plus $4,485 attorney's fees.

The appellate court upheld the trial court's judgment, citing two acts of negligence in SARMA's procedures in preparing the consumer report as determined by a reasonable-person standard. First, the court held that SARMA failed to exercise reasonable care in programming its computer to automatically capture information into a file without requiring any minimum number of points of correspondence between the consumer and the file. Second, SARMA was negligent in failing to use reasonable procedures to discover the disparity in social security numbers, viewed to be "the most important identifying factor for credit reference purposes." In upholding the damages award, the court ruled that even if there are no out-of-pocket expenses caused by the negligence, the consumer is entitled to recover under the act for humiliation and mental distress. The appellate court agreed with the trial court that in this case the humiliation and mental distress had been substantial enough to warrant the $10,000 award.

Thompson illustrates the importance of conscientious system design and operating procedures to prevent legal liability.

IMPLICATIONS FOR ACTION

Introduction

This section provides a brief look at the types of considerations that need to be a part of any computer user's management plan. It is not our intent to exhaustively teach computer security techniques but rather to furnish a starting point for the manager who has not thought much about the topic and a brief outline for the computer professional.

First, a brief introduction to the topic of security is made for each of the legal topics of computer crime and privacy. Then a managerial approach to security techniques is outlined in three separate but related subtopics of personnel practices, system security, and physical security.

Crime and Security. The data-processing specialist has several courses of action available to respond to the growing problem of computer crime. Legally, of course, it is in his or her best interest to keep abreast of the latest developments in the area of computer legislation on both the state and federal level.

The real key to computer crime prevention, however, is adequate security in all aspects of the computer operation. A brief discussion of major areas of effective computer security is appropriate here to show their importance not only for the prevention of crime but also with regard to legal aspects that permit effective investigation, documentation, and eventual prosecution of criminal acts.

An effective security program will not focus on the potential adversary but rather on the data-processing system that is to be protected. One reality that must be accepted from the outset is that 100 percent security is impossible—increased security will only make breaches more difficult, not impossible. Therefore, a security analysis should employ a risk management point of view. Each of the several vulnerable areas in a system need to be evaluated according to (a) cost, (b) probability of loss, and (c) the value of what is to be protected. These factors should then be applied to the system's operating personnel and its physical components.

Data-processing security has two essential functions related to computer crime. First, if computer crime is to be discouraged and eliminated, the security system must be adequate to deter criminal activity by making unauthorized access attempts unprofitable. Second, the anonymous nature of computers compared with manually kept records requires that each use of the system in any of its vulnerable areas be monitored and recorded to enhance traceability and provide essential evidence for prosecution. Though the increasing dependence of society on computer technology may be expected to lead to a corresponding increase in its abuse, such criminal activity can be minimized by focusing appropriate amounts of energy and resources on effective security measures.

Privacy and Security. Although uniform privacy laws may be the ultimate remedy for personal information abuses, the data-processing industry has a current responsibility to establish a fair and open relationship with those persons about whom they collect, store, and transfer data. This is especially important in an era when information has become synonymous with power. Of course, courts and legislatures stand by ready to create and enforce appropriate sanctions on socially unjustifiable uses of information if users do not meet this responsibility voluntarily. It is therefore incumbent upon users to make meaningful efforts to observe at least basic privacy safeguards in the use of their information systems.

Security and privacy, when applied to data processing, are not identical concepts. Computer security represents the technical and administrative means for safeguarding privacy ensuring that

a. only authorized information enters the system;

b. only authorized users have access to the system;

c. only authorized programs are run on the system;

d. only authorized individuals have access to output; and

e. there is no destruction of facilities, information, or programs.

Privacy, on the other hand, involves legal and procedural considerations about how information is used. The privacy of individuals is dependent on the security of computer systems. Elements of privacy protection as outlined by the Privacy Act of 1974 (although applicable only to federal agencies at this time) include provisions that

a. no secret data bases be maintained;

b. data subjects have a right to examine and correct data;

c. data subjects have a right to control the dissemination of data; and

d. record keepers are responsible for required information controls and ratification of data subjects.

There are four main areas in which procedures will have to be developed to ensure that information systems adhere to privacy protection measures:

a. Data collection. An organization must limit information collection to data that is relevant and necessary to accomplish a legitimate business purpose.

b. Data disclosure. A company must check data use and obtain consent from the data subject if use is other than routine; also, dissenting claims of individuals must be forwarded.

c. Disclosure accounting. A log of authorized users must be kept, as well as a record of usage by all nonregular personnel.

d. Right to access. An organization must permit record review upon request and investigate all claims of inaccuracies; also, a statement of unresolved disputes should be included with subsequent record disclosures.

Such measures would conform with the Privacy Protection Study Commission goals of minimum intrusion, maximum fairness, and confidentiality of information in the private sector.

Finally, there is the question of who manages the managers. For the protection of the right of individuals to be free from undue invasions of privacy and confidentiality, there must be a dynamic, positive relationship between managers and those who formulate public policy. Although management has an obligation to respect the wider responsibilities inherent in information processing, those in policy-making positions must keep abreast of the technological complexities and rapidly developing innovations in the field.

Management Practices for Security

Personnel Practices. Effective management practices begin with careful screening of personnel, followed by emphasis during training on the importance of ensuring the accuracy and veracity of data handled and providing measures for effective accountability and auditability of computer functions.

The hiring of personnel must be a carefully considered process. The sensitivity and value of the equipment and data that they will be handling dictates an in-depth screening process. At a minimum, this should include a series of in-depth interviews that emphasizes integrity and trustworthiness as well as needed technical qualifications. References from former employers should be examined and verified.

Once hired, an extensive program of education should be conducted for new employees, underscoring both personnel and physical security. Each employee's role in maintaining confidentiality must be stressed. If challenging unauthorized personnel is to be a part of their function, procedures for doing so should be carefully outlined, with emphasis placed on management support for each action. Fire and breach of security procedures and basic first aid should also be covered.

Personnel organization is an important key to system security. Positions should be organized so that as much separation of responsibility as possible exists. Programmers should not also be operators, and vice versa. Access to information should be on a need-to-know basis only. Production, marketing, personnel, accounting, and financial operations should be separated to the greatest extent practicable.

Finally, a code of ethics should be developed and enforced for all those working in and around the data-processing system. Areas of emphasis in such a code include meaningful definitions of ethical behavior, taking full responsibility for one's work, and protecting confidentiality.

System Security. A completely secure computer system may be impossible, or at least too expensive to be practical. A more intelligent approach to making security decisions is to take measures that will make it unprofitable for a potential perpetrator to intercept transmissions or gain unauthorized access to the system.

System security must emphasize two areas: access controls and record-keeping. If remote terminals are used with the system, three methods of identification should be required: subscription, operator, and terminal. It is important that all such information be recorded to assist in investigation and legal follow-up of security breaches.

There are many examples of specific security measures that can be programmed into a system. A large computer system will often process information of varying degrees of sensitivity, so a firm might consider implementing a hierarchical program, which would allow personnel access only to levels appropriate to their work. Another type of security program is a monitor program, which can be directed to advise supervisory personnel of unauthorized attempts to gain access, coupled with periodic test intrusions to make sure the program is functioning properly. Programs can also be designed to clear a computer's working memory after each use.

Several other methods of providing system security are available. For instance, scrambled storage formats may be used as well as cryptography in the transmission of data. Various user identification methods are possible, including code words, voiceprints, and fingerprints.

Technical safeguards are absolutely essential for maintaining the security of computers. The question is what kind and how much. These decisions are obscured by the fact that private industry does not have the incentive to build in security measures that add to the cost but not to the productivity of information systems. However, as noted previously, such a shortsighted attitude is ultimately bound to be more costly because of industry's increased susceptibility to computer crimes and greater likelihood of government regulations in the area of privacy.

The choice of technical safeguards will depend on the characteristics of the system hardware and software, whether the organization uses a time-sharing or batch system, the sensitivity of the data processed, the nature of the user class, and the type and extent of security measures already in place.

Cost is another important factor. Adequate security can be very expensive, but there are some mitigating factors. For instance, security measures are generally less expensive if they are built into the computer system rather than being added on later. Unfortunately, most earlier computer system designs emphasized reliability, speed, efficiency, and precision; the focus on privacy and security measures is a relatively recent development for those who manufacture computers. However, some of the economic sting of security measures can be reduced by viewing them as an integration of necessary system functions, such as the prevention of computer fraud, waste, and information security for both the employees and the company.

Beyond this, it is crucial that a comprehensive record of the system's operation be kept. Such a record may be kept manually or built into the system, or a combination of both, and should take the form of a log listing authorized users of data, files examined, and any significant events taking place with the central processor.

Physical Security. Developing a program of physical security begins with an assessment of the system's existing strengths and weaknesses. Major exposures or gaps in system security should be identified, including physical access, magnetic volume access, software access, and, in the case of an open installation, remote terminal access.

Physical access to the central processing unit should always be restricted; ideally, only one main entrance should be used. Emergency exits should be equipped with alarms. In addition, equipment should always be locked when not in use and periodic inventories made.

The handling of both input and output should be restricted to only authorized personnel, and a comprehensive recording system should be in place to keep track of data flowing in and out of the data-processing center.

The sophisticated computer criminal will more likely be interested in stealing information stored on magnetic volumes than in stealing computer equipment. Both the volumes and the library in which they are kept should therefore be made as secure as possible. Library security has important legal implications. When prosecuting for a loss, a firm must demonstrate its ownership of information by showing the court that adequate security measures were taken. These measures should ideally be coordinated and implemented by a librarian. Levels of security for magnetic volumes should be assigned, such as secret, confidential, and internal use. Strict access and accountability procedures should be implemented so that all movement of volumes is recorded. A constant updating of the security levels of both the volumes and those persons with access to them should be made, as well as periodic inventories of the library.

REFERENCES

1. *See e.g.,* Kling, "Computer Abuse and Computer Crime as Organizational Activities," 2 Comp. L. J. 403 (1980); D. Parker, S. Nycum, & S. Aura, "Computer Abuse" (Stan. Research Inst. Rep. 1973).

2. *See, e.g.,* Taber, *A Survey of Computer Crime Studies,* 2 Comp. L.J. 275 (1980).

3. D. Parker, S. Nycum, & S. Aura, "Computer Abuse" (Stan. Research Inst. Rep. 1973). *See* Parker, "Computer Abuse Research Update," 2 Comp. L.J. 329, 351 (1980) for a bibliography of the SRI project for 1975–1980. *See also* D. Parker, *Crime by Computer* (1976).

4. General Accounting Office, *Computer Related Crimes in Federal Programs* (1976), reprinted in Problems Associated with Computer Technology in Federal Programs and Private Industry, Computer Abuses, Sen. Comm. on Gov't Operations, 94th Cong. 2d Sess. 71–91 (Comm. Print 1976).

5. 6 CLSR 879 (N.D. Cal. 1978).

6. 18 USC 641 (1976).

7. 113 Misc.2d 1017, 450 N.Y.S.2d 957 (N.Y. City Crim. Ct. 1982). *See also* "Using Computer Time No Crime, Judge Says," 68 ABA J. 671 (1982).

8. Taber, *supra* note 2.

9. *See* Kling, "Computer Abuse and Computer Crime as Organizational Activities," 2 Comp. L.J. 403 (1980).

10. *See* Becker, "Rifkin, A Documentary History," 2 Comp. L.J. 471 (1980).

11. *See* Hancock v. State, 402 S.W.2d 906 (Tex. Crim. App. 1966).

12. *See* Kewanee Oil Co. v. Bicron Corp., 416 U.S. 470 (1974); M. Bryce & Associates,

Inc. v. Gladstone, 107 Wis.2d 241, 319 N.W.2d 907 (Wis. Ct. App. 1982), *cert. denied* 103 S.Ct. 258 (1982).

13. *See* Krieger, "Current and Proposed Computer Crime Legislation," 2 Comp. L.J. 721 (1980); Sokolik, "Computer Crime—The Need for Deterrent Legislation," 2 Comp. L.J. 353 (1980); Note, "Addressing Computer Crime Legislation: Progress and Regress," 4 Comp. L.J. 195 (1983).

14. 18 USC 641 (1976).

15. 18 USC 659 (1976).

16. 18 USC 2314 (1976).

17. 18 USC 1341 (1976).

18. 18 USC 1343 (1976).

19. 18 USC 793–799 (1976).

20. 18 USC 2113(a) (1976).

21. 18 USC 2115 (1976).

22. 18 USC 2117 (1976).

23. 18 USC 1361 (1976).

24. 18 USC 2071 (1976).

25. 18 USC 2153 (1976).

26. 26 USC 61 (1976).

27. James v. United States, 366 U.S. 213 (1961).

28. 26 USC 7201, 7203, 7206, 7207 (1976).

29. *See also* Becker, "The Trial of a Computer Crime," 2 Comp. L.J. 441 (1980); Ingraham, "On Charging Computer Crime," 2 Comp. L.J. 429 (1980).

30. 402 S.W.2d 906 (Tex. Crim. App. 1966).

31. 3 CLSR 206 (Calif. Super. Ct. 1972).

32. 591 P.2d 1036 (Colo. 1979).

33. 6 CLSR 879 (N.D. Cal. 1978).

34. 553 F.2d 351 (4th Cir. 1977).

35. A. F. Westin, *Privacy and Freedom* 7 (1970). *See* A. Miller, *The Assault on Privacy* 25 (1971).

36. Comment, "The Use and Abuse of Computerized Information: Striking a Balance Between Personal Privacy Interests and Organizational Information Needs," 44 Albany L. Rev., 589, 600–602 (1980).

37. Griswold v. Connecticut, 381 U.S. 479 (1965).

38. *Id.,* at 484.

39. *See, e.g,* Roe v. Wade, 410 U.S. 113 (1973).

40. Paul v. Davis, 424 U.S. 693 (1976).

41. 429 U.S. 589 (1977).

42. *Id.,* at 607 (Brennan, J., concurring).

43. Volkman v. Miller, 41 N.Y.2d 946, 363 N.E.2d 355, 394 N.Y.S.2d 631 (1977).

44. State *ex rel.* Stephan v. Harder, 230 Kan. 573, 641 P.2d 366 (1982); Minnesota Medical Association v. State, 274 N.W.2d 84 (Minn. 1978).

45. Brown v. Jones, 473 F. Supp. 439 (N.D. Tex. 1979); Sims v. State Dept. of Public Welfare, 438 F. Supp. 1179 (S.D. Tex. 1977), *rev'd on other grounds sub nom.* Moore v. Sims, 442 U.S. 415 (1979).

46. Brown v. Jones, 473 F. Supp. 439.

47. *See* Oden & Sims Used Cars, Inc. v. Thurman, 165 Ga.App. 500, 301 S.E.2d 673 (1983); Testa v. Winquist, 451 F. Supp. 388 (D. R.I. 1978).

48. *See, e.g.,* People v. Ramirez, 126 Cal.App.3d 33, 178 Cal. Rptr. 529 (1981); State v. Conaway, 319 N.W.2d 35 (Minn. 1982). *Contra,* United States v. Mackey, 387 F. Supp. 1121 (D. Nev. 1975); Martin v. State, 424 So.2d 994 (Fla. Dist. Ct. App. 1983).

49. *See* Langan, "Computer Matching Programs: A Threat to Privacy?" 15 Col. J. of L. and Soc. Prob., 143 (1979).

50. *In re* Grand Jury Subpoenas Issued to United States Postal Service, 535 F. Supp. 31 (E. D. Tenn. 1981).

51. 15,844 Welfare Recipients v. King, 474 F. Supp. 1374 (D. Mass. 1979).

52. Jaffess v. Secretary, Department of Health, Education, and Welfare, 393 F. Supp. 626 (S.D. N.Y. 1975).

53. 5 USCA 552a (West 1977 & Supp. 1983).

54. 5 USCA 552 (West 1977 & Supp. 1983).

55. Department of Labor Hearings on Workplace Privacy, 45 Fed. Reg. 8780 (1980) (statement of Ray Marshall, Secretary of Labor).

56. *See* A. Miller, *supra* note 35, at 36, 90–99; Ware, W., "Privacy and Information Technology—The Years Ahead," in *Computers and Privacy in the Next Decade* 9, ed. by L. Hoffman (New York: Academic Press, 1980).

57. 440 U.S. 301 (1979).

58. Washington Gas Light Co., JD-735-80 (December 17, 1980).

59. 359 F. Supp. 1235 (N.D. Ga.1973).

60. Isaacson, P., "The Personal Computer versus Personal Privacy," in *Computers and Privacy in the Next Decade, supra* note 56, at 35.

61. *Id.,* at 36.

62. *See* Westin, "Home Information Systems: The Privacy Debate," *Datamation,* July 1982, at 100; Washburn, "Electronic Journalism, Computers and Privacy," 3 Comp. L.J. 189 (1982).

63. Restatement (Second) of Torts 652A, at 376 (1977). *See generally* Note, "Computers, the Disclosure of Medical Information, and the Fair Credit Reporting Act," 3 Comp. L.J. 619 (1982).

64. Tureen v. Equifax, 571 F.2d 411, 415–17 (8th Cir. 1978).

65. Restatement (Second) of Torts 652D, at 383 (1977).

66. 15 USCA 1681 (West 1982).

67. *See, e.g.,* Thompson v. San Antonio Retail Merchants Association, 682 F.2d 509 (5th Cir. 1982); Lowry v. Credit Bureau, Inc., 444 F. Supp. 541 (N.D. Ga. 1978); Millstone v. O'Hanlon Reports, Inc., 383 F. Supp. 269 (E.D. Mo. 1974), *aff'd,* 528 F.2d 829 (8th Cir. 1976).

68. Privacy Protection Study Commission, "Personal Privacy in an Information Society," 15–21.

69. 20 USCA 1232g (West 1978 & Supp. 1983). *See* Note, "The Family Educational Rights and Privacy Act of 1974 and College Record Systems in the Future," 3 Comp. L.J. 563 (1982).

70. 12 USCA 3401–3422 (West 1980 & Supp. 1983).

71. Uniform Consumer Credit Code 2.302(1)(b), 3.302(1)(b) (West 1968).

72. Mironi, M., "Confidentiality of Personnel Records: A Legal and Ethical View," 25 Lab. L.J. 270, (1974).

73. Gassmann, J., "Privacy Implications of Transborder Data Flows: Outlook for the 1980s," in *Computers and Privacy in the Next Decade, supra* note 56, at 109, 109–10.

74. 393 F. Supp. 626 (S.D. N.Y. 1975).

75. 571 F.2d 411 (8th Cir. 1978).

76. 682 F.2d 509 (5th Cir. 1982).

PART VI

Systems Design Considerations

INTRODUCTION

The addition of a computer system to an organization inevitably leads to operational and structural changes. This part, viewing the entire user organization as an information system, focuses upon potential legal liabilities not discussed earlier that should be considered when integrating a computer into the existing system.

Those persons responsible for acquiring computer hardware and designing new systems will necessarily be concerned about the added costs and predicted benefits of the new computer systems. These costs and benefits may include the need for personnel changes, alterations in the amount of time required to perform various stages of the information processing, changes in access to information, and the replacement of human decisions by programmed decision making at various management levels. All too often, system designers neglect the legal implications of these organizational changes, resulting in the legal costs of a particular system design going far beyond any revealed by a simple cost–benefit analysis. It is therefore imperative that system designers analyze not only organizational concerns but also the potential legal obligations that the proposed changes may impose on their organization.

This part begins with an overview of the factual settings, often involving multiple legal theories, in which the user's legal obligations to various classes of persons are affected by the acquisition and use of a computer. Then a more detailed look at the particular legal areas affected by computer use is provided. The section concludes with an in-depth look at two cases in which a computer system's design was critical to the user's legal liability and a summary of implications for action to be drawn from the existing law.

LEGAL OBLIGATIONS TO PARTIES

The prospective computer user owes various legal duties to different classes of persons. Some of these duties are created by the user through the company's contracts with various parties, such as employees, customers, shareholders, and creditors. By entering into a contract with another party, the user has bound the company to provide some performance, such as paying a debt or providing a good or service. In the contractual setting, the parties are for the most part free to define the extent and terms of their obligations within the framework of a body of contract law defined by courts and legislatures.

The user has less control over other legal duties that are created and defined by the courts and legislatures. For example, courts have over the years developed a body of tort law, which basically dictates that persons must conduct their affairs to avoid causing unnecessary harm to others. If a user is found to have committed a tort that has injured another person in some way, the user will be required to reimburse the injured party the monetary value of the injury. Suitable insurance policies may be instrumental in meeting tort liabilities if they occur.

In addition, the Congress and state legislatures have created other bodies of law with which the computer user may need to comply. These include state and federal labor laws, banking laws and regulations, securities regulations, antitrust laws, usury laws, and regulation of data communications.

It is probably impossible to enumerate all of the legal obligations that a user may have and that may be affected by implementation of a computer system. Perhaps a worthwhile way to identify the risks associated with the implementation of a computer system is to begin by identifying the persons to whom duties may be owed and only then to evaluate the nature of the particular legal obligation or obligations owed, since several forms of legal liability may arise out of the same circumstances.

This section shows some of the parties to whom the user may owe various legal obligations. The parties are divided into five basic groups: shareholders, employees, customers, other foreseeable private parties, and the government. This analysis will be helpful in identifying the risks of computerization, whatever the legal source of the obligation. The later sections then introduce and explain the particular legal issues involved so that the user may seek to minimize the risks of legal liability that have been identified.

Shareholders

A corporation is a legal "person," which, through its elected officers, acts according to the will of a majority of its shareholders. In most situations, the management and directors of a corporation act in accordance with the desires of the majority of shareholders either because they wish to maintain their positions or because they *are* the majority shareholders. A shareholder usually has the power of a single vote for each share owned, although this may vary depending upon the terms of the corporation's articles of incorporation or bylaws. Thus, a shareholder can attempt to influence management's actions by electing the corporate directors or by voting on resolutions. This voting power may not be very effective, however, in large corporations where most of the shares are in the control of directors or their supporters. In this seemingly hopeless case, the courts allow a disenchanted shareholder to bring a shareholder derivative suit. This remedy enables a minority shareholder to sue the corporate directors and officers on behalf of the corporation for harm done to the corporation as a result of the directors' action or inaction. In these cases, the courts usually impose a standard of care that a reasonably prudent director of a similar corporation would have used under similar circumstances.[1] For example, a corporate director might be held liable for losses suffered by the corporation that result from a refusal to implement a computer system at a time when other similar corporations were doing so. Indeed, it is even possible that a court will find that an organization has a duty to use an available computer to avoid losses even *before* computer use has become customary in the industry.[2] At the other extreme, liability might be imposed for losses suffered by a corporation that overzealously computerized its systems when such action was not warranted by the firm's needs or financial condition.

Directors are ultimately responsible for, and may not delegate, decisions implementing major corporate changes. However, courts are generally very reluctant to second-guess the business judgment of corporate officers and directors, and if directors and officers make conscientious, informed decisions about computer use, they will not likely be held liable to the corporation's shareholders for negligence even if subsequent events prove them wrong.[3]

Employees

The advent of computer-controlled production processes has brought about a need for special consideration of employee safety. Where the danger of human injury exists, systems should be designed that allow for human intervention when and where it is needed. For example, if the production assembly line speed is completely automated and computer controlled, some readily available shut-off device should exist to prevent possible injury to workers.

One tragic case, in which a computer was used to control a saw mill, illustrates this need.[4] The system was designed so that as logs passed through the mill's two saw blades, the blades adjusted to the log size automatically. Each log's size was read by a scanner, which was connected to a computer. The computer then fed information to valves, which used air pressure to move the blades from an open position of just over two feet to any lesser distance down to just under four inches. If the carriage was empty when it passed by the scanner, the computer automatically set the blades to a closed position.

The mill was run by an employee at a remote console. The console had an emergency switch that turned off electricity to the machine but did not shut off the air pressure or the computer. To entirely shut down the mill, the electric circuit breakers and the air pressure had to be switched off and the air cylinders bled.

On the day of the accident, the employee ordered the mill shut down over lunch hour so that the blades could be adjusted. Two workers shut off the electricity but did not turn off the air pressure or bleed the air cylinders. When the employee returned, he crawled between the blades, then had an assistant manually push the log carriage forward. The log scan and computer activated the air cylinders, causing the blades to close and killing the employee.

Although this particular lawsuit was brought against the designer of the system, it nonetheless illustrates the kind of safety considerations required when computerizing a production system. Most states have some form of workers' compensation plan that would determine liability and compensate the employee for workplace accidents. Although the effect of such recoveries upon the employer varies from state to state, the employer will normally be affected in some way, such as an increase in the firm's premiums. Tort remedies are generally barred in lieu of workers' compensation but may be permitted in certain exceptional cases, again depending upon state law. Congress has also instituted laws regulating workplace safety. The Occupational Safety and Health Administration (OSHA) is endowed with considerable power to detect and order remedies for working conditions it has deemed unsafe.[5] Users should attempt to comply with applicable OSHA regulations and do whatever is necessary in excess of those minimums to make their particular workplace environment as safe as possible.

Typically, a computer's initial function in most businesses is the payroll. It is obviously in the best interests of the employer to ensure that the payroll programs function properly, because a faulty payroll system can cause an employee a good deal of trouble for which the employer might be held legally liable. When an employee has performed services for the employer, the employer incurs a contractual duty to pay for those services. It is not difficult to imagine some of the difficulties that may be encountered by an employee who does not receive a paycheck for two or three pay periods. A damaged credit rating or an inability to pay for essential utilities could be sufficient grounds for legal action on the part of the employee.

As an example of the difficulties that might occur because of payroll system problems, consider a case[6] in which two policemen's names were erroneously placed on a computer payroll printout for a department of managerial police employees. The printout error was discovered and corrected within a month. About one year later, though, the printout got into the possession of the patrolmen's union, at which time the two patrolmen first learned of the earlier computer error. The distribution of copies of the printout had an adverse effect on their standing in the union and on their relations with fellow officers. They appeared at length before union leaders to explain the computer error and even offered to take a polygraph test to prove their innocence. After numerous efforts to straighten out the misunderstanding and remove the printout from circulation, the two patrolmen (one of whom attempted unsuccessfully to run for union office) were denied the right to vote in the union election. The mix-up was not settled until the parties took the matter to the state commission. This case clearly illustrates the way in which a relatively minor error, readily found and corrected, admitted to and explained by management on several occasions, still caused confusion, ill feelings, and expensive negotiations and litigation.

Extensive state and federal labor legislation may also affect the user's system design decisions. This is discussed in detail later in this part.

Customers

Having entered into a contractual relationship with a customer, the prospective user is under a legal duty to perform the user's part of the bargain. Failure to perform as required will not be excused by a court merely because the failure was the result of a computer error or breakdown. For example, if a computerized order entry system sends a customer's order to the wrong address because of a programming or data entry error, the user would be just as liable to the customer for breach of contract as if the order had never been shipped at all. In other words, the user will not be allowed to excuse the company's breach of contract by saying, "It's not our fault. The computer did it." Having decided to computerize a function, the user must bear responsibility for that computer's action or inaction to the same degree as if the user's employees committed the breach of contract.

Consider the case of a bank that failed to discover a magnetic encoding error made by another bank on a customer's check. A $45 support check was sent by the county clerk to the authorized person. When she deposited the check with her bank, it was improperly encoded in magnetic ink as $10,045 and credited to her account. The check was then sent to the county's bank where the county's account was charged for the full amount encoded. As a result of the error, the bank paid $10,045 from the customer's account, although the check was for only $45. The bank was held liable to the customer for the amount of the error because it failed to discover the mistake, even though made by the other bank.[7]

The user may also have legal obligations to the firm's customers that arise from the contractual relationship, yet are outside of the particular contract's provisions. The contractual relationship may provide the "duty" element for a tort action (see the discussion of negligence in this part). For example, the user may be held tortiously liable for damage resulting from an unauthorized third party obtaining confidential information about a customer from the user's computer files. Likewise, if the user's credit files were not promptly updated, resulting in an unfavorable and incorrect credit report on the customer, the user might be liable for any damages to the customer's reputation or business or personal interests.

Other Foreseeable Parties

The first three parties described all have some form of formal contractual relationship to the user. The category of other foreseeable parties includes parties who, although they have not dealt directly with the user, may be harmed by the user's acts or omissions. Since contractual liability is consensual, that is, arises only by express agreement of the parties, no contractual liability will normally exist in favor of persons within this group of other foreseeable parties. The primary legal concern to this class of parties will be tort liability, particularly negligence and products liability. Certain legislatively created liabilities may also involve a legal duty to other foreseeable parties, such as liability for securities law violations of duties owed to potential investors.

Government

The state and federal governments have created certain legal obligations that may be owed by the computer user. Some of these obligations are duties created and enforced by the government to provide protection to certain private parties in addition to that provided by the common law. Examples of this category are labor laws designed to create and protect rights of employees, consumer legislation to protect customers, antitrust and monopoly laws designed to prevent undue restraints on competition, securities laws designed to protect investors, and usury laws to protect debtors. This category of governmental obligations may overlap with the categories discussed previously, such as employees or other parties that may foreseeably be harmed by the user's conduct. In other words, even though the government may have framed the law in terms of a duty owed to the government, since the government assumes responsibility for monitoring and enforcing compliance with the law, the obligation may be explained and anticipated by the user by considering it a duty owed to some class of private parties. Indeed, some obligations may be enforceable by both the appropriate governmental agency's action and by a private lawsuit. Other obligations owed to the government arise from the relationship between the user and the government as sovereign, such as the duty to pay taxes, regulation of imports and exports, and controls over transmissions through the airwaves. Although some major governmental obligations are discussed later in this part, others may apply more specifically to the user's particular operations. The user should be sure to analyze the impact of computer changes on its existing obligations to the government.

FORMS OF LIABILITY

Tort Liability

Three types of tort liability are negligence, strict liability, and intentional torts.

Negligence. The law of negligence requires that a person's affairs be conducted in such a manner to avoid carelessly causing harm to others. Negligence law is an important legal vehicle that may hold the computer user liable for harmful effects resulting from the use of a computer. For an organization to be found negligent, the law requires that five elements be present:

a. The organization must have owed the injured party a *duty* of reasonable care to avoid harm.

b. The organization, by some act or omission, must have *breached* the duty owed to the injured party.

c. The act or omission committed by the organization must have been an *actual cause* of the injury to the party.

d. The organization's act or omission must have been a *proximate cause* of the injury to the party.

e. The other party must have been *damaged* by the organization's act or omission.

Historically, courts have been reluctant to impose on persons an absolute duty to prevent harm to anyone else in the entire world. They have therefore imposed liability only for foreseeable injuries to foreseeable persons, that is, those persons to whom (in the court's view) the user should have taken care to avoid causing harm. The duty element helps to accomplish this. The breach element requires the plaintiff (the injured party bringing the lawsuit) to prove that some careless act or omission by the user led to the injury.

The actual cause element requires that the injury complained of be traceable to the breach complained of. Although the foremost legal scholars differ on a proper description of the proximate cause element, this element is basically intended to limit liability to foreseeable types of injuries, that is, those types of injuries the user could foresee would result from the user's particular conduct. The damage element basically states a "no harm, no foul" rule. To recover, the plaintiff must demonstrate some legally recognized injury of some monetary value. Further definition, illustration, and the significance of each of these elements is discussed in the following pages.

Duty. An organization has an obligation to act with reasonable care toward another party if the court finds that it should have considered the risk of harm to that party when deciding whether to act in a particular manner. In the design and implementation of a computer system, there are four parties to whom this duty might be owed: shareholders, employees, customers, and other foreseeable parties. The first three parties—customers, shareholders, and employees—all have some form of formal contractual relationship to the user. The risk of damage to them in the event of computer problems would probably be clearly foreseeable and liability would therefore probably not be denied on the grounds that no duty was owed (unless the contract contained a valid disclaimer or the damage was totally unrelated to the nature of the contractual relationship). Similarly, if foreseeable damage to other foreseeable parties results from the user's negligence, then the user may be liable despite having no formal relationship with the injured party. This additional class of persons is not definable in universal terms. Rather, the definition depends upon the circumstances of each case.

The type of negligence liability familiar to most people arises out of automobile accidents. In a typical auto accident, two complete strangers are involved, yet the party at fault may be held liable for negligence because he or she owes a duty to other travelers to drive carefully. This type of liability was extended in a recent case to hold a motor carrier liable to a motorist's surviving wife for $10,000,000 in punitive damages for negligence.[8] The carrier (North American Van Lines) was found negligent in failing to include in its computer information system a program which would help to detect violations of the Interstate Commerce Commission's "70-hour rule" which prohibits truck drivers from working over 70 hours within an eight-day period. Despite previous government investigations that had pointed out the inadequacies of North American's log book verification procedures, North American had not developed any kind of program for its sophisticated information system that could have easily detected the flagrant falsity of the log book kept by the North American driver, whose fatigue at the wheel caused the accident that resulted in the motorist's death. Whether a business or professional person owes a duty of care to other noncontractual parties may be a more difficult question, however.

For example, although an attorney's preparation of a will is performed under a contract with the person whose estate is to be disposed of, it is certainly foreseeable that the persons named in the will must rely on the attorney's expertise. The very purpose of the attorney's service is to provide a document that will transfer ownership of the deceased's property to the intended persons. Although the attorney involved in the case was not held liable to the persons named in a will when his negligence cost the named beneficiaries their intended inheritance, one court announced a balancing test to determine whether professionals should be held responsible to third parties for negligence. This test includes an analysis of factors such as "the extent to which the transaction was intended to affect the plaintiff, the foreseeability of harm to him, the degree of certainty that the plaintiff suffered injury, the closeness of the connection between the defendant's conduct and the injury, and the policy of preventing future harm." [9]

This type of analysis should be applied to each potential user's operations to determine the scope of the firm's potential negligence liability. Consider, for example, an architectural engineering firm that utilizes a computer for various mathematical calculations and simulations to determine stress requirements and capabilities for a new large public building. The firm should certainly consider the potential for tort liability to thousands of hitherto unknown persons if the calculations are erroneous and cause the building to collapse.

The potential user should therefore take a careful look at the information system being developed and determine which parts of the system could foreseeably be relied upon by third parties. Special attention should be given to minimizing the risk of error in those parts. Even then, the user should estimate the risk of error above and beyond these additional controls and include potential liability of the organization for computer error as a possible cost of the system.

Breach. An organization breaches its duty of reasonable care when it unreasonably acts, or fails to act, in a manner that results in injury to another party to whom a duty of care is owed. The key to the existence of this element in a particular case is the definition of "reasonable care." Although the wording of the standard may vary, the phrase generally is taken to mean the care that an ordinary, prudent person would have exercised under the circumstances. The obvious danger in this admittedly vague standard is that what seems reasonable under the circumstances to the user, system designer, or programmer may not seem reasonable to a judge or jury. As a result, the vagueness of this standard and lack of understanding of computers by lay judges and juries present considerable opportunities for the courts to second-guess the system design decisions of computer users. If a court determines that the system was designed improperly for its purposes, even if the user's computer system works exactly as it was intended, the user may be held liable for damages to another party injured in some way by the system's inadequacies. This was the situation in *FJS Electronics, Inc. v. Fidelity Bank.* [10] The Fidelity Bank's procedure for stopping payment on checks required that a customer give the exact amount of the check to be stopped. The bank's computer was programmed to key in on three sets of numbers, or fields, on the bottom of each check: the bank's federal reserve number, the account number, and the amount of the check. Every digit on the check had to match exactly the stop payment order before the computer would pull the check.

The president of FJS, a customer of the bank, called in a stop payment order on a check in the amount of $1,844.48. Although FJS's president had been instructed to be exact, the actual amount of the check was $1,844.98.

The computer, operating as programmed, failed to catch the check because of the one wrong digit causing a 50-cent discrepancy. The check was paid, and FJS brought suit to recover the $1,844.98 mistakenly paid out of its account.

The applicable banking law stated that a customer may order the bank to stop payment of any item payable on his or her account but the order must be received at such time and in such manner as to afford the bank a reasonable opportunity to act on it.[11] (Note that although this suit was not based upon a negligence theory, the "reasonableness" standard incorporated into the banking law makes the analysis essentially the same.) The bank argued that since its particular procedure for stopping payment required absolute accuracy in the information provided by the customer, the customer's 50-cent error gave the bank no reasonable opportunity to carry out the stop payment. The court refused to accept this argument, holding that the statute was directed at providing a customer service, and when the bank decided to provide this service by a system that relied totally upon the accuracy of the amount, the bank bore the risk that its system would fail to stop a check because of the system's limitations. FJS was therefore awarded damages for its loss.

This case illustrates that the introduction of a computer into a business will not change the duty of reasonable care that a business must follow in its daily affairs. In this case, in the court's view, the computer could have just as easily been programmed to pull checks with a written amount that is within a reasonable range of that stated, or even without regard to the check amount. The pulled checks could have then been hand checked to assure accuracy.

A computer user should try to avoid breaches of duty in the system design area by ensuring that the system designed is adapted to the user's particular needs. The system should be capable of doing all that a court may expect the user to do in the business transactions in which the user engages.

In addition to underlying system design problems, liability may be imposed for computer error if the system does not work as it had been intended. Computer errors are basically caused by faulty data, data encoding errors, program logic, or hardware malfunction. An organization may be found liable for negligence if it is responsible for any one of these. It should therefore initiate procedures to reduce the risks of faulty programming or use of incorrect or obsolete data, as well as exercise care in the selection and maintenance of computer hardware.

In cases where it is particularly difficult for the injured party to prove the manner in which the defendant breached its duty, the courts may insist that the defendant prove the absence of negligence. This doctrine, called *res ipsa locquitur,* is applied only in cases where three elements are present: (a) the event is a kind that does not normally occur in the absence of someone's negligence; (b) it is caused by an agency or instrumentality within the exclusive control of the defendant; and, in contributory negligence states (see defenses subsection), (c) it must not have been due to any voluntary or contributory action on the part of the injured party.[12]

Computer errors would seem to be particularly susceptible to application of the *res ipsa locquitur* doctrine. First, computer errors do not normally occur without someone's negligence, either through data capture, encoding, programming, or in some cases through hardware defects. Second, the computer is most often within the exclusive control of the user. Finally, the injured party will rarely, if ever, have anything to do with the type of negligence that causes computer error.

Essentially, this doctrine simply places the burden on the computer user to disprove any negligence in causing harm to another. Since computer errors rarely occur spontaneously without *someone's* negligence, lifting this burden usually requires proving negligence by another party, such as the programmer, manufacturer, or carrier. Documentation of the program logic and flow of data may be critical to disproving negligence on the part of the user.

Cause in Fact. It is often up to the courts to decide whether the breach complained of was the *actual cause* (cause in fact) of the injury. In general, a "but for" test determines the presence of this element. Thus, where the injury would not have occurred but for the alleged breach, cause in fact is present. This element will be present in most good faith claims.

Cause in fact is especially at issue when two or more parties have been negligent, and it is impossible to determine whose negligence caused the injury. Using a classic case as an example, if two hunters shoot at a quail in the vicinity of their companion, striking their companion with a piece of buckshot, it may be impossible to determine which hunter actually caused the injury. In this situation, most courts will probably hold both hunters jointly liable for the injury. If the problem arose in a computer context, however, it is not clear how the court would decide the issue. Suppose a computer error damaged a third party. Suppose also that both a programming error caused by an independent programmer and a data-entry error made by the corporation can be demonstrated. Deciding which error was the cause in fact of the injury would be the primary issue of the case. If no causal connection could be established between either of the two errors and the damage, it is theoretically conceivable that neither party would be found liable. More likely, a court, in its sense of justice, might use the earlier hunter example and find both parties jointly liable.

Proximate Cause. Proximate cause is used by the courts to set limits on otherwise open-ended liability for errors that occur. If an injury is of a type that would be a foreseeable consequence of the defendant's negligence or if there was a direct causal sequence from the breach to the injury, then the proximate cause element is probably satisfied. Proximate cause is in reality a flexible legal tool that may be argued by either side for opposite results.

For example, the National Crime Information Center (NCIC) computer maintains information that includes the license plate numbers of stolen vehicles. The press reported a case in which a state trooper, acting upon the computer's information that a suspect's license plate was that of a stolen vehicle, shot and killed a young man.[13] The stolen plate was in fact three or four years old and the numbers had since been reissued. Tragically, the computer's data had not been updated. This data error was an *actual cause* of the young man's death since it could probably be shown that the officer would have acted differently *but for* the incorrect information. Whether the error was a *proximate cause* is a tougher question. The NCIC would probably argue that the trooper's intentional conduct was an intervening and superseding cause, which broke the chain of *direct causation* from the data error to the shooting. Therefore, it could be argued, the type of injury complained of (the young man's death) was not a *foreseeable result* of the computer data error.

On the other hand, proximate cause could be established if the court adopted the broader view that the information was used precisely as intended—to guide officers in appropriately handling law enforcement situations. This view, argued by the plaintiff, would assert that the information's use led foreseeably and directly to the wrongful death of the young man, and the NCIC should therefore be held liable for his death. The proximate cause element should lead computer users to ascertain the particular uses to which their computer output will be put and the particular types of damage that may result from errors.

Damage. To hold a defendant liable for negligence, the other party must have been injured by the defendant's failure to exercise reasonable care. Damage need not be physical or even monetary. An injury to one's reputation or credit could be sufficient. The threat of future injury or near-miss situations where injury could have occurred but did not would not be considered damage necessary to sustain an action for negligence.

Defenses. The most effective defense against negligence (assuming that the plaintiff has proven the defendant's negligence) is *contributory negligence*. Simply stated, the injured party will not be allowed to recover anything from the defendant if it can be shown that the injured party's own lack of reasonable care contributed in any way to the injury. This somewhat harsh traditional defense has been modified in most jurisdictions by the adoption of *comparative negligence*. Under comparative negligence, the court determines each party's proportionate fault and allows recovery only for that proportion of damage not caused by the injured party's own negligence. The court would first determine the amount of damage to the injured party, say, $10,000. It would then determine by what proportion each party was at fault. If the court found that the defendant was 75 percent responsible for the injury and the injured party 25 percent, the injured party could recover $7,500 (the total damage, $10,000 − the proportion caused by the injured party, $2,500). This is in stark contrast to contributory negligence, where nothing can be recovered if the injured party is in the least part responsible for the damage.

It is critical to note that the defense of contributory or comparative negligence implies that the injured party, in some way, *caused the actual injury*. It is extremely rare for an injured party to have contributed to a computer error. As stated earlier, computer errors are mistakes caused in data capture or data entry, programming errors, or hardware malfunction. Since the injured party will almost never have anything to do with these mistakes, the only foreseeable way in which an injured party could be contributorily negligent would be if erroneous data had been supplied to the computer user by that party, resulting in erroneous computer output. Although the case involved a contract of deposit between a bank and its customer, consider the previously described case of the bank found liable to its customer for an erroneously encoded check for an illustration of the importance of causation in placing fault for an error.[14] The customer failed to discover the $10,000 error until an audit revealed it more than seven months after the cancelled check and bank statement had been received. The bank contended that the customer, by failing to examine its statement and report the error, had not exercised reasonable care to protect its own interests. (The bank statement had contained a declaration that after 10 days the account would be considered correct.) The court rejected the bank's argument, finding that the customer did have a duty to examine its statement and report errors to the bank, but that the time period during which this must be done was a "reasonable time." In analyzing the case, the court found that nothing the customer could have done, such as immediately inspecting the bank statement, could have prevented the loss to the bank. The bank, by that time, had already made the erroneous payment. The customer could therefore not be denied recovery on the basis of failing to report the error. The customer's negligence had nothing to do with causing the *loss;* it only prevented its *discovery*.

Successfully arguing contributory negligence (in those states where it is still applied) may still not lift the threat of liability off the defendant. A court may attempt to avoid the often harsh effects of contributory negligence by imposing liability if the defendant had the *last clear chance* to avoid the injury. Thus, even if the injured party has helped to cause a computer error, but the user had an adequate opportunity to detect and correct the error, the user may still be held liable.

Another defense to a charge of negligence is arguing that the injured party assumed the risk of injury. This defense is properly applied when having become aware of the risk of injury, a party voluntarily exposes him- or herself to that risk and is ultimately injured. The computer user may be able to take advantage of this defense if the injured party had reason to know the nature and extent of a risk of injury before exposing him- or herself to that risk. This situation may occur with parties to whom the user has a contractual relationship.

In contracting with other businesspersons, a clause limiting the user's liability for errors may help to relieve the user of some liability. Contractual protection of this type is limited in its application, because courts may not favor contract language that seeks to absolve a party from any liability whatsoever, especially in personal injury cases. The court may honor a clause limiting the amount of liability to, say, refund of purchase price, but may not honor a clause by which the other party, who has no or little control over the computer, bears the entire risk of error.

It is important to note that an assumption of the risk must be *voluntary*. Basic contract law assumes that parties negotiate with equal bargaining power or "at arm's length." Courts may find that a party's contractual assumption of the risk is not voluntary if the computer user possessed a good deal more bargaining power than the other party. Particularly in dealing with consumers, clauses contained in form contracts will probably be ineffective in shifting responsibility for a loss away from the computer user.

Strict Liability. In some cases, the courts will hold a party liable for damages to another without the showing of any fault whatsoever. Strict liability attaches most often in products liability cases. A person who is injured by a defective product need not show how the manufacturer was negligent in its manufacture. It is sufficient to show that the manufacturer produced a defective product which injured the consumer. It is therefore essential that a computer user consider the potential costs of its liability to consumers by first, deciding whether to computerize any part of a product design or production process and, second, by designing a system that minimizes the possibility of error.

Intentional Torts. Intentional torts allow recovery for intentional acts committed by the defendant that cause harm to another. The intent required is the intent to do the *act* that results in injury. It does not necessarily imply an intent to do the particular harm caused. Thus, an intentional tort may be committed even though the defendant has no ill will toward the victim and honestly believes him- or herself to be acting lawfully.

This doctrine is illustrated by three cases involving the repossession of automobiles by the same creditor.[15] In all three cases, the creditor's employees relied upon the company's computerized records, despite the owner's contrary versions of the facts (backed up by payment receipts). Even though the creditor's employees acted under the belief that they were correct, based upon the firm's records, their repossession of the automobiles constituted the tort of conversion of property. (It should be noted that conversion is an offense against another's right to *possession* of property. It is committed by a wrongful repossession even though the creditor holds legal title to the property.)

In addition to damages in the amount of the lost property value, the owners were awarded punitive damages. Punitive damages are granted for intentional torts (usually not for mere negligence) when the court hopes to deter similar misconduct by the defendant and others and when mere compensation for the party's injuries is not sufficient punishment commensurate with the defendant's wrongful acts. Punitive damages are normally awarded only in cases where the defendant's actions have displayed either an evil motive or a conscious and deliberate disregard of the interests of others. The latter was found to be present in the repossession cases. The award of punitive damages permits the jury to make an award large enough, in light of the defendant's financial worth, both to punish the defendant and to deter him or her from committing future wrongful acts.[16]

Another case also illustrates the computer user's liability for intentional conduct committed by employees when they improperly relied on a computer system.[17] In this case, a bank's customer, using an automatic teller machine, deposited $608 on January 4. The machine erroneously imprinted the date of March 4 on his deposit slip. During April, the customer received notice of an overdraft, discovered that his March 4 receipt was not reflected in his March bank statement, and so informed the bank. The bank's president and vice president agreed to credit his account, but told him that an investigation would ensue. The customer then went on a vacation, leaving his vacation address and phone number with the bank. A week later, the bank filed criminal charges against the customer for felony theft. The customer was arrested at his vacation address and spent two days in jail.

In late May, both parties discovered the erroneous deposit slip. The bank offered to dismiss the criminal charges but only if the customer released the bank from civil liability. The customer refused to do so and was subsequently acquitted in the criminal case. He then filed suit alleging intentional infliction of emotional distress and abuse of process. The case was eventually settled out of court for $50,521.

As the previous cases illustrate, the computer user may be held liable for the wrongful acts of *employees* acting within the scope of their employment.[18] This fact has serious implications for system design as it becomes very important to have appropriate levels of the management hierarchy taking responsibility for certain nonroutine decisions. In other words, the law will place responsibility for the actions at the highest level; it would be wise for management to do the same to the greatest extent practicable.

Contract

As previously noted in the section on the duties owed to employees and customers, reliance on a computer system does not modify the user's contract obligations. The user is not at the mercy of the computer system in fulfilling the firm's legal obligations. Rather, having implemented a computer system, the user's responsibility extends to the computer's "actions," not just to the actions of the employees. The user must therefore analyze the impact that the computer system will have upon the terms and requirements of the firm's contracts with other parties.

One area of legal liability that has evolved from contract law and has great significance to a manufacturer is warranty law. As discussed generally in Parts I and II, a contract for the sale of goods carries with it certain implied warranties. This is significant to the computer user when evaluating costs of the computer system since these implied warranties may run to parties with whom the user has never dealt.

Traditionally, the only aggrieved party entitled to enforce a contractual obligation against the user would have been the party who entered into that contract with the user. Strangers to the contract could not sue on the contract because they were not in privity with the defendant. Many courts applying the implied warranties provisions of the Uniform Commercial Code have altered or done away with the privity requirement in the area of consumer products in the retail marketing chain. Thus, the consumer of a good that does not meet the standard of merchantability (not fit for the ordinary purpose for which such products are used) is entitled to assert a breach of warranty against the manufacturer even though the consumer never dealt directly with the manufacturer. The importance of this form of liability, paralleling strict products liability discussed previously, is that the user must approach with caution the use of a computer in the design or production of consumer goods, considering the risks of potential liability for unmerchantable products.

Banking Law

Another form of strict liability has been applied in several cases involving banks with computerized check-processing systems. The Uniform Commercial Code provides that a payor bank becomes liable for the amount of a check presented to it if it does not pay or return the check by midnight of the next banking day following the day it is received by the payor bank.[19] Courts have interpreted this provision as imposing strict liability on banks for the amount of checks that are processed late, regardless of whether there is any negligence or injury to the payee.[20] If a bank is late in processing a check, its only defense is to show that the reason for delay fits one of the exceptions provided by the UCC. Thus, delays are excused only if caused by "interruption of communication facilities, suspension of payments by another bank, war, emergency conditions, or other circumstances beyond the control of the bank provided it exercises such diligence as the circumstances require."[21]

Not surprisingly, the widespread reliance by banks on computer processing has led to problems. Processing delays have been the most prevalent problems, and courts have repeatedly refused to find them excusable. In one notable case,[22] a flooded road prevented the use of the normal carrier route, so processed checks were delivered to an airline by a computer center in another city for return delivery to the bank. The airline, for some unknown reason, did not deliver the checks as scheduled and the bank did nothing to determine the reason for the delay. The court found that the bank had not established an acceptable excuse since an alternate ground route would have ensured on-time delivery. The bank was therefore held liable for the amount of the checks. Similarly, another bank was not excused for a delay caused by both an armored car breakdown and a computer breakdown that occurred on the same day.[23] In yet another case,[24] a bank sought to get its delay excused by arguing that a $48,470 check that was presented to it with pencil marks and an encoding error required manual processing. The bank argued that it should be excused for the delay because such a procedure is so "anomalous in today's civilized world." The court found instead that no distinction can be made between those checks that can and cannot be computer processed, since checks are not even required to be written on paper, let alone on a standardized sheet with magnetic ink.

These decisions set the stage for a rare case in which a court excused a computer-related delay.[25] The computer system at issue was newly installed and was paralleled for two weeks by the manual system. The computer became unusable due to a memory error on the first day it operated without the manual system (a Monday morning). The computer manufacturer indicated that repairs would not take long, so the bank took no extraordinary action. However, as repairs went on into the evening (eventually completed early Tuesday), the bank took its checks to a bank with an identical computer, located two and one-half hours away, in accordance with a previously made backup agreement with the other bank. The bank's personnel began processing the checks at 11:30 P.M., but they returned to their own bank to complete the processing when the backup computer was needed by its owner and when they had been notified that repairs had been completed on their own computer. They continued processing the checks at their own bank until another memory error rendered the computer unusable once again. The computer was not available for use until a new memory module was installed on Thursday, two days later. The bank continued to use the backup computer when it was not needed by its owner. The bank fell two days behind as a result of the breakdown, and was not completely caught up again until the next Monday.

The court, excusing the delays, found that the bank had under the circumstances exercised proper diligence in its attempts to remedy the malfunction and in its use of a backup computer. This case, more than any other, illustrates the importance of contingency plans when implementing a new system. Once the system is in operation, the user must be alert to signs of potential malfunction or other disruptions in processing and take immediate action to circumvent delays.

Labor Law

The potential computer user must consider the needs and rights of its labor force before implementing a computer system into its everyday procedures. The user's labor obligations may arise from basically two sources. First, the employer must observe the company's existing contractual obligations to its employees. Second, the employer must observe the federal statutes governing labor relations.

Several arbitration cases illustrate the importance of considering the possible legal interpretation that may be given the union/employer contract before implementing a computer system. The function of arbitrators is to provide a binding resolution of contract disputes by interpreting the contract, resolving any disputes in the facts, and applying the contract to the facts. Thus, while a particular arbitrator's decision in a particular case gives an indication of how other arbitrators *might* decide similar disputes under similar contracts, each case is in effect a clean slate and must be decided on the basis of the particular contract's provisions, the arbitrator's view of the facts, and the bargaining history and past practices of the parties.

In the first case,[26] the employer implemented a computer system in its production planning department for the primary purpose of scheduling production. In designing the system, however, the employer realized that the computer had all of the information necessary to perform the tasks formerly performed by two of its union employees, called box schedulers. The box schedulers had been responsible for determining the size, shape, and weight of articles ordered by a customer, then computing and requisitioning the necessary packaging materials. With the addition of the computer system, the need for these two positions was eliminated. The contract with the union prohibited taking work from union employees and giving it to nonunion personnel, such as those in the planning department. The arbitrator found that the employer had not violated the agreement since the employer had not hired any nonunion personnel to replace union workers. Even though the production planners supplied the computer with the information necessary to do the work of the two employees, there was no taking of work from union employees and giving of it to nonunion ones. The arbitrator indicated that, had the employer used an *additional person* in the planning department to compute the packaging data, there would have been a violation of a collective bargaining agreement. It would thus appear that in similar cases an employee may be replaced by a computer without violating the union contract.

Arbitrators, in three separate cases, confronted the issue of whether the implementation of an optical character recognition (OCR) system, by which nonunion typists could prepare scanner-ready copy for typesetting purposes, violated the provisions of a bargaining agreement providing that such preparation work be given to union personnel.[27] All three arbitrators held that the employer publishers, by permitting nonunion workers to type scanner-ready copy, violated the contractual provisions giving the union jurisdiction over the input, output, and operation of computerized composing room work. This result is not inconsistent with the previously described case (even assuming that the contractual provisions were identical) since the OCR system implemented by the employer gave union employee functions to nonunion employees, not to the computer. These three OCR decisions have significant ramifications for the employer. The new OCR system allowed, for example, the editorial department's typed copy to be read in by the machine and thus eliminated the need for the intermediary keypunch stage that had previously made the copy ready for scanning by the machine. When a union function is eliminated and a technological advance creates a related position that can be filled by nonunion employees, the collective bargaining agreement may require that union employees be offered that function. This situation may require an employer to train union employees (keypunch operators) so that they can replace the nonunion employees (typists) for purposes of doing the disputed work. Clearly, additional costs may be created when an employer is obliged to completely retrain union personnel, where it had been hoped that a much-simplified production scheme would have entirely eliminated one stage of the process.

Consider also the court case in which a railroad's contract with its employees required that "crew boards showing the order in which crews are to go out . . . be maintained."[28] The traditional crew board design, which used color codings and pegs to conspicuously display information about seniority and constantly changing work situations, had been maintained for more than 75 years. The employer decided to eliminate the old crew boards and instead posted an $8\frac{1}{2} \times 14$-inch computer printout at the beginning of each shift that contained the same information as the crew board had displayed. The court found that the change constituted an attempt by the employer "to change the very terms of the contract." The court stated:

> The posting of printouts three times daily is not equivalent to maintaining a crew board as required by the agreement between the parties. This is not to say that the old hand-operated crew board may not be replaced by crew boards that are operated automatically or electronically. However, the essential features of high visibility and accurate reflection of the current situation must characterize any replacement so long as the contract requires crew boards to be maintained.

This case illustrates that the courts will, on occasion, approve or disapprove of the system designer's decisions as to the correct method of computerization. Each employer should therefore consult with a labor lawyer about installation of a new system to ensure that a violation of the labor contract does not occur.

The outcomes of the contract interpretation cases just described depend in large part upon the language of the existing contract being interpreted. Thus, the place for the employer to begin to avoid problems in this area is at the bargaining table. The employer can improve the company's ability to make needed technological changes by bargaining in advance for some form of management rights clause permitting it to do so. The union will certainly not agree to such a clause without some major restrictions or concessions on the employer's part, if at all. For example, the employer may have to agree to some sort of program for rehiring technologically displaced workers or give significant wage and benefit increases in return for such a management rights clause. The existence of some form of contract provision that allows for computerization of current employees' functions will go a long way toward preventing legal problems when implementing a computer system.

Federal labor laws require that the employer bargain in good faith with its employees' union over any proposed changes in the employees' terms and conditions of employment.[29] Thus, if the current employees are represented by a union but the existing contract does not adequately deal with the employer's ability to make computer changes affecting the employees' jobs, then the employer must bargain with the union over any proposed computerization, either as the issue arises during the contract's term or upon expiration of the old contract as part of the negotiations for the new contract.

The requirement of bargaining over changes in employment consists of two parts. First, the employer may have to bargain over *whether* the proposed change will be made at all and if so, *how* it will be made. Second, the employer will always be required to bargain over the *impact* of a proposed change upon the firm's employees.

The Supreme Court has not yet directly ruled on whether the employer has an obligation to bargain over the decision to implement a labor-saving technological advance. In a well-known earlier case, the Supreme Court ruled that an employer had no obligation to bargain over the decision to subcontract certain work of the firm's unionized employees.[30] The most famous and oft-quoted aspect of that case is found in its concurring opinion, in which the justice stated that certain decisions lying within the "core of entrepreneurial control" belonged to management alone with no duty to bargain with the union over the decision. The author of that opinion listed the decision to install labor-saving machinery among the core types of decisions. Although this view has never been explicitly ratified by a majority of the Supreme Court as applied to labor-saving machinery, the present Supreme Court did quote the "core of entrepreneurial control" language with approval in a recent case, holding that the employer had no obligation to bargain over a termination of its operations.[31] It is probably likely that the present Supreme Court would hold in an appropriate case that the employer has the right to make such decisions without bargaining.

Assuming for the sake of discussion that management has the right to decide to implement a labor-saving computer system without bargaining over that decision, two significant limitations should be noted. First, like nearly all other legal rights, this managerial right (if it exists) may be waived or contracted away. If the employer has agreed in the labor contract not to implement such innovations without bargaining or has begun to bargain over the decision but then makes a new decision and refuses to bargain further, the employer would probably be found to have bound the firm to bargain in good faith over the decision.

Second, even if the employer does not have to bargain over the decision itself, the employer is obligated to bargain with the union over the *impact* of the decision to implement a computer system. Thus, if the impact of a computer system is to replace certain employees, the employer will have to bargain with the union about the terms of their replacement. For example, the employer and union may agree upon a system of severance pay, seniority-based "bumping" or training for other positions, and so on.

Even if the company's employees are not currently represented by a union, the employer needs to be sensitive to the company's labor relations climate to prevent future labor law problems. If a technological innovation displaces even one employee at a time when there is a threat of unionization, the employer's implementation of the change may be viewed as an unfair labor practice by the National Labor Relations Board and federal courts if it appears that the change might have been motivated by antiunion sentiment on the part of the employer. For example, federal labor laws prohibit any actions by an employer that are designed to intimidate or coerce employees in the exercise of their rights to organize. If a technological change displaces a union supporter, the NLRB may infer from all of the facts in the case that management is trying to send the message to other employees that union support may lead to replacement by new technologies. This inference would justify a finding that the employer committed an unfair labor practice, and could lead to court-enforced remedies of reinstatement with full back pay or, in extreme cases, an order that the employer begin to bargain with the union that was organizing at the time. Thus, although legal advice should be sought, a general rule of thumb is to refrain from any actions that might adversely affect personnel during a period of union organization.

Even if a union is not currently in operation or organizing among the company's employees, a distant rumor of technological replacement may lead to feelings of insecurity among employees, which, if left unchecked, may lead to a drive for union protection. Whether this is a significant threat and, indeed, whether it is a major concern to the employer at all will depend upon the circumstances surrounding each particular company and its work force. In general, however, the potential user cannot afford to neglect obligations to employees when considering the installation of a new computer system, and labor relations personnel should therefore be given a significant voice in the decision-making process.

There has been some uncertainty in the courts as to whether the new computer personnel should be classified as supervisory, managerial, or confidential employees (see Part III). Generally, supervisory, managerial, and confidential employees do not enjoy the usual protections of the federal labor laws. The classification is made through a case-by-case analysis that focuses on the scope and type of authority, discretion, and use of independent judgment exercised by the employees.[32] A new system may render the old bargaining unit inappropriate. Thus, the system designer is in a position to define the computer personnel's functions so that their susceptibility to union organization can be minimized. Each employer should be aware of the existence of these issues and consult with labor relations personnel and legal advisors about them at the earliest stages of studying any computerization proposal.

Usury

Under state usury laws, a loan contract is void and unenforceable if it charges interest in excess of a prescribed maximum (unless superseded, in particular types of transactions, by federal law). Usury law has been applied to situations in which interest on loans was incorrectly calculated by a computer. In one case,[33] the note and mortgage stated the legal rate of interest at 10 percent, but the monthly balance and interest statements reflected an interest rate in excess of 10 percent. The computer statements showed an interest yield of 10.4712 percent per annum. In addition, the use of a daily interest factor based on a 360-day year instead of a 365-day year produced an annual interest rate of 10.139 percent. The two figures, taken together, produced a simple interest rate of 10.6235 percent. As a result of the error, the lender was unable to recover on the note and mortgage even though the computation was apparently an innocent mistake.

Data Communications

In developing an information system's data transmission specifications, the user must give some consideration to the pertinent government regulations. The Federal Communications Commission (FCC) is currently in a state of flux regarding regulation of data communications. In the past, the FCC has made a distinction between data-processing services and communications services. The latter are regulated, the former are not. There is much controversy about new services that are difficult to classify as one or the other, in particular, some new private line services. For example, Execunet, a switched message service offered by MCI, was found by the FCC to be an unauthorized message toll service and was therefore not allowed to operate for a period of time while the issue continued to be litigated.[34] Future FCC regulations may have a significant effect on competitive pricing and available services. Hence, the system designer should be acquainted with the current regulatory status of various data communications options.

Regulation of data communications may have an effect upon the system designer's decisions about centralization. Although the FCC's regulatory powers extend to interstate transmissions, the states may regulate intrastate communications to the extent that they are not regulated by the FCC. As a result, both state and federal rates and regulations may affect system design as it relates to interstate communications. Of course, the matter of whether information could be transmitted internationally would require investigating the foreign country's regulations as well.

Antitrust Law

Congress has instituted laws and a regulatory framework making it illegal to artificially restrict competition in American markets.[35] Computerized systems possess the potential for violating antitrust laws in given situations. For example, the Justice Department, the agency charged with enforcement of the antitrust laws, may look askance at computerized reservation systems for airlines or hotels that tend to cut out of the relevant market any airline or hotel that is not a member.[36] It may be feasible (and some may argue economically desirable) to create a "perfect market" by use of a computer network to match willing buyers and sellers of services and commodities, yet traditional antitrust thinking would probably prohibit this kind of market manipulation. Before jumping into intercompany computer networks, therefore, the user would be best advised to consult an antitrust lawyer to prevent future legal difficulties.

Securities Law

Congress has instituted several laws, and a regulatory framework to enforce them, to prevent improprieties in the market for publicly traded securities.[37] This area of the law is very complex and may, depending upon its particular circumstances, impose other obligations on a user aside from those discussed here. Two major areas of concern to the corporate computer user whose stock is publicly traded, however, are liability for false statements and trading on inside information.

The securities laws and regulations prohibit the use of "manipulative and deceptive devices," including the making of false statements or misleading omissions of facts, in connection with trading securities,[38] as well as the making of false statements in registration statements filed with the Securities and Exchange Commission (SEC).[39] Violations of these prohibitions may result in criminal prosecution by the SEC, as well as civil liability to private citizens who are damaged by the false or misleading statements. This potential liability is important to the user whose reliance on computerized information systems may result in disclosure of erroneous information. If the erroneous information is of such a character that it would mislead an investor who relied upon it, and especially if the user benefits from that reliance, the user may find that the company is in the position of defending itself against charges of securities violations even though the errors were unintentional.

A similar prohibition under the securities acts is the proscription against trading on the basis of "inside information," that is, information not yet disseminated to the public at large that would be material to investment decisions.[40] To the computer user, this is yet another reason for maintaining strict controls over access to data contained in the information system. If an employee takes advantage of information not available to the public to make a profit in securities trading, the employee may be subjected to civil or criminal penalties. If the user appears to be guilty of complicity in the employee's scheme, the user could be subjected to penalties and, at a minimum, will be forced to suffer considerable disruption of business operations and legal expense as a result of the SEC investigation of the transactions. The user should, to repeat a recurrent theme, be certain to impose adequate controls over investment-sensitive information to ensure its proper use by employees and inform the investment world at large of all pertinent information in the company's possession before taking action in the securities market based upon that information.

INSURANCE

Increased reliance upon a computer system for the performance of key business functions may result in increased risks of loss resulting from business interruption, errors, and various forms of computer fraud. One survey conducted by an insurance group found that 90 percent of all companies that manufacture or depend on electronic systems and experience a serious interruption or injury to their data-processing operations go out of business after the loss.[41] These risks have created the need for insurance policies that will indemnify the user for certain specified types of computer-connected losses. Such policies have recently become available in the insurance market and the feasibility of subscribing to one or more of them should certainly be investigated by users who may be prone to computer-related risks. Normal insurance policies do not generally cover many types of risks that are critical to a computer user, such as mechanical breakdowns or electrical disturbances. A standard property insurance policy may cover only the blank value of computer media, whereas a computer policy is designed to duplicate the lost or damaged software. Three types of insurance coverage have been offered to protect the various aspects of the user's reliance on a computer: business interruption, professional liability, and computer theft and infidelity.[42]

A business interruption policy is designed to minimize the impact of a shutdown on the user's business. The policyholder may receive reimbursement for all or part of the holder's lost earnings during the downtime, in addition to the cost of extraordinary expenses required to keep the computer operations running, such as for rental of an alternate facility.

Professional liability insurance is primarily for those companies that provide data-processing services to their customers. A part of this coverage is to defend the insured when sued for errors and omissions in programming and use of the computer system. Special coverage may have to be negotiated in this area at variable rates, depending on the number and nature of potential risks to other parties who might sue the user for computer errors.

A third type of policy, computer theft and infidelity, covers losses arising from thefts and misuse of information through unauthorized access to the computer.

Before selecting an insurance policy, both a lawyer and a data-processing expert should be consulted to ensure that the policy adequately covers the types of risks that may exist for the user's computer system. Insurance agents in the data-processing market will also help to identify loss potential. The user should pay particular attention to the risks that will be insured and to those that will be specifically excluded. The risks should be clearly defined to avoid interpretive disputes over the policy's coverage when losses do occur. On the other hand, insured risks should not be defined so specifically as to exclude coverage of all unforeseen risks. An appropriate deductible amount should be arrived at to lower premiums, yet it should still be affordable. In any event, insurance should not be viewed as a substitute for careful control over data-processing operations and a security-minded system design, especially since such precautions may provide a basis for lower insurance premiums.

COURT CASES

In this section, cases are presented that demonstrate how design decisions have been evaluated in the courts and how system design may affect the legal rights and obligations of the user. These cases illustrate the importance of informed analysis of the user's needs and comprehensive design to meet those needs.

Utilities Case: Giving Notice by Computer

Public utilities are more intensely regulated and supervised by government than are other business organizations, but in return for this relinquished autonomy, they are allowed by the state to operate as monopolies. Utility companies thus enjoy a position that is unique among capital enterprises.

State law gives both the utility and the customer certain rights and obligations, such as the right of the utility to terminate service only for nonpayment, or "for cause." In practice, these legal responsibilities have resulted in public utilities having to assure that state citizens are not denied fundamental legal rights, such as due process, whereby a citizen is guaranteed administrative recourse when wronged. As illustrated by several cases, including the one discussed in detail here, public utility companies have breached these obligations by failing to respond adequately to disputed billings before they terminate customer services.

Palmer v. Columbia Gas Co.[43] This case was a class action suit brought on behalf of all customers who had, or would in the future have, their gas service involuntarily terminated. A similar case has since been decided, with the same result, by the United States Supreme Court and has thereby become the law of the land.[44]

The Columbia Gas Co. was headquartered in Columbus, Ohio. The litigation involved the area serviced by its Toledo, Ohio, regional office, about 140 miles distant. The computer was located at the Columbus office and it was from there that all bills and notices were mailed (although the envelopes bore the Toledo office return address).

The evidence showed that during any calendar year, between 120,000 and 140,000 shut-off notices were issued for the Toledo area alone, although only about 6,000 actual shut-offs were made. The company normally read the meters every other month, but at times no readings were made for several months at a time. For the periods during which no reading was taken, the bills were estimated by a computer. Usually, the estimates were conservative. Therefore, when an actual reading was taken, the customer might suddenly be faced with a bill many times greater than the usual one. (The court of appeals noted that one customer whose usual bill was $12 was presented with a bill for $197 after an actual reading was taken.)

In these cases, the company made arrangements with the customer that allowed the larger bill to be paid over a period of time. Nevertheless, during this time period the customer continued to receive a monthly shut-off notice that the customer was instructed to ignore and which would not be followed by an actual shut-off. (At least one customer in this situation, after receiving a shut-off notice and another notice instructing her to disregard it, had her service terminated in mid-December, at which time her church pastor intervened on her behalf. The company then acknowledged its error, apologized, and restored service.)

When company employees went out to terminate service, they did not announce their presence to the customer. Usually, the first indication that shut-off had occurred was an increasingly cooler house.

Other mistakes also led to customer hardship. In one case, a customer received a notice on December 30 that service would be terminated if his bill was not paid by January 4. His check, mailed on December 30, was endorsed and cashed on January 3. On January 4, his service was terminated. The company later showed that a company employee had misplaced the record of the payment, leading to the wrongful termination.

The court of appeals termed the situation an "Orwellian nightmare."[45] The district court judge summed up the situation this way:

> The evidence as a whole revealed a rather shockingly callous and impersonal attitude upon the part of the defendant, which relied uncritically upon its computer, located in a distant city, and the far from infallible clerks who served it, and paid no attention to the notorious uncertainties of the postal service.

Although this particular case pertained to a violation of due process in failing to provide proper notice of pending actions by a public entity, in another case a builder was allowed to recover for the damage to his unoccupied house when the electric heat was shut off.[46] The electric company had sent the bills and shut-off notices to the unoccupied house instead of to the builder, and the bills went unpaid as a result. The court held that the company was negligent in relying on its computerized records when simple manual examination of the customer's records would have revealed the actual circumstances. This case suggests that, although a company may computerize its records, it will still be held to a human standard of care in their use.

The district court opinion in *Columbia Gas* suggests that the company's system designer should have given more consideration to the issues of decentralization and to the need for effective human intervention at critical stages of the information process.

The obvious geographic difficulties presented by a system such as Columbia's are many. The whole process depends entirely upon the central computer. It sent the bills, recorded the payments, and issued the shut-off orders to the regional offices. When it sent out a shut-off notice, the customer had five days to make the payment before termination occurred. In many cases, the customer's fate was already sealed with the mailing of the shut-off notice. During that five-day grace period, the payment would have to be sent from the Toledo area to Columbus where it was processed and recorded, after which an order would have to be sent back to the Toledo office to cancel the termination order. That was hardly enough time to prevent improper shut-offs, given the dependability of the U.S. mail service and the company's clerks.

In addition, *Columbia Gas* illustrates a behavioral problem that must be dealt with in system design. The computer notices and orders were considered to be virtually infallible by the company's employees. In the case where the customer's service was terminated on January 4, even though the check was cashed by the company on January 3, the customer contacted the company by telephone and informed them that he had paid the bill. The company employee's reply was, "Tough, pay the bill again." This inefficiency imperiled the health of the customer's seven children, as the house temperature dropped to 45 degrees before service was restored through the intervention of the Board of Community Affairs.

This problem may be dealt with in several ways. The most effective solution, and the one mandated by the courts, is to provide some accessible company official with the authority to override the computer output before critical action is taken. Moreover, the customer must be given adequate notice and the opportunity to be heard and present evidence at a fair and impartial hearing presided over by the company official. As added protection for both the company and customers, employees should be made aware of the possibility of computer error and the attendant need for human intervention.

Columbia Gas illustrates the basic issue in the analysis stage of system development of determining whether a task is suitable for computerization. Programmed decisions are certainly appropriate for some types of routine decisions. It is possible that the shut-off notice function could be handled by a computer in an efficient and accurate manner. However, that particular function obviously needed more flexibility than was provided for by the Columbia Gas system. The courts objected strongly to the "cry wolf" aspect of the shut-off notices. When customers are routinely told to ignore their shut-off notices, the notices no longer serve the purpose for which they were intended—to give notice of impending termination. Shut-off notices should have been issued only in those cases where a termination of service was pending but certainly not in those cases where the customer had made special arrangements to pay overdue balances.

Insurance Case: Waiver by Computer

The utilities case just described suggests a pressing need for the right hand to know what the left hand is doing. This problem is especially acute if a company computerizes certain routine functions but continues to have related tasks performed manually. This situation is illustrated by the case of an insurance company that computerized its issue of policies but kept the management of claims in human hands.

State Farm Mutual Automobile Insurance Co. v. Bockhorst.[47] In this particular instance, an automobile insurance policy lapsed on August 24, 1969, because the insured failed to pay the premiums due. At 12:45 A.M.on October 4, 1969, a Saturday morning, the insured was involved in an accident that resulted in a pedestrian's death. That same morning, after the accident had occurred, he wrote a check to the insurance company large enough to pay a six-months' premium and mailed it to his insurance agent. He then went to see the agent, told him about the accident, and asked if he had received the check. The agent went to the post office that same day and found the insured's check, an accompanying letter requesting reinstatement of the policy, and the company's notice that the premium was due. The agent told the insured that he did not know whether the company would reinstate the policy, but he nevertheless mailed the check and notice to the company's office. He did not, however, include any information about the accident, which had occurred prior to the receipt of payment, nor did he disclose the exact time that he received the check.

The following Monday, the agent notified the company's regional claims adjuster of the accident and the circumstances of payment. After his investigation ended later that day, the adjuster told the agent that he had serious doubts about whether the accident was covered. The adjuster also spoke to the company's claims superintendent, who agreed that the insured would not be covered. The adjuster then notified the superintendent of the policy service division (the division to which the check was mailed) of the uncertainty concerning the insured's coverage.

During the investigation process, the policy reinstatement was being processed through the insurance company's computer as usual. No data on the accident or specific time of payment was input to the computer. Consequently, the computer automatically issued a routine notice of reinstatement effective retroactively as of 12:01 A.M., October 4, 1969 (the date of mailing). The reinstatement was mailed to the insured on October 10, 1969.

One month and eight days later, the company notified the insured that the policy was not effective until the time the premium was actually received by its agent—1:00 P.M.on October 4—well after the accident. The company later refunded the premium and denied coverage of the previously insured party.

The company brought suit in federal court in an attempt to get a declaration of no liability for the claims of the injured third party against the insured. Both the trial court and the appellate court found that the insurance company *was* liable on the grounds that by issuing the retroactively reinstated policy on October 10, after being informed of all the facts, the insurance company had voluntarily and intentionally waived its right to refuse reinstatement of the insurance contract and thereby agreed to extend coverage for the period of time when the accident occurred.

This case illustrates the paramount importance of data integration; that is, when the same information is vital to two or more business functions, steps should be taken to ensure ready access to information necessary for the efficient meshing of related cogs in a business's operations.

The appellate court at the end of its opinion summed up what appears to be the general rule regarding a user's liability for computer error:

> Holding a company responsible for the actions of its computer does not exhibit a distaste for modern business practices. . . . A computer operates only in accordance with the information and directions supplied by its human programmers. If the computer does not think like a man, it is man's fault. The reinstatement of [the insured's] policy was the direct result of the errors and oversights of [the company's] human agents and employees. The fact that the actual processing of the policy was carried out by an unimaginative mechanical device can have no effect on the company's responsibilities for those errors and oversights.

IMPLICATIONS FOR ACTION

Decision to Use

Management personnel at the highest levels of a business should be involved in the decision of whether to implement a computer. The law places responsibility for organizational decisions with the corporate directors, regardless of who actually makes the decision. Thus, the directors may be held liable for any corporate losses resulting from grossly careless decisions.

The decision maker should consider all other organizational concerns that might affect the decision, such as computer use by the firm's competitors, information needs, and government regulations that might affect computer use.

Special attention should be given to using available computers to protect the personal safety of customers and employees. For example, the law may insist that airlines use a computer landing system when one is available that has been shown to prevent injury at a reasonable cost.

The availability of resources such as finances, personnel, and space for an in-house operation needed to support the proposed computer system should be carefully evaluated.

System Design

Proposed functions should be carefully scrutinized to determine whether they are appropriate for computer processing. Some routine transaction processing functions and complex mathematical calculations might demand computer processing; other functions, such as certain customer service tasks and higher-level management decisions, may require greater discretion than a computer can provide.

Programs and operating procedures should be designed to furnish the maximum security against theft and misuse.

The system should ensure that data provided for one function is available for other related functions that require the same data. The law treats the entire organization as one entity; therefore it does not recognize dual information systems within the organization.

The behavioral implications of system design should be given careful consideration. In some routine applications, such as inventory control, it may be correct and even desirable for employees at various management levels to regard the computer output as the ultimate authority. In other applications, employees must be much more flexible and vested with sufficient authority to overrule or modify computer decisions.

Contingency plans should be developed to be used in the event of computer breakdown or other unforeseen difficulties. These alternative plans might include arrangements with the computer manufacturer or another firm to use a backup computer along with contracts for prompt emergency repair service.

Contracts with customers should include disclaimers of or limits to liability for consequential damages and set reasonable time limits in which other parties may report errors.

REFERENCES

1. Jordan, "The Tortious Computer—When Does EDP Become Errant Data Processing?" in CLS 5-1, art. 2 (R. Bigelow, ed. 1979); Awalt, "Corporate Problems," in CLS 2-1, art. 1 (R. Bigelow, ed. 1979).

2. Jordan, *supra* note 1; The T. J. Hooper, 60 F.2d 737 (2d Cir. 1932); American Machinery & Motor Co., v. United Parcel Service, 87 Misc.2d 42, 383 N.Y.S.2d 1010 (N.Y. City Civ. Ct. 1976); Bigelow, "The Accountant's Potential Legal Exposure When Providing Computer Services and Advice," in CLS 5-1, art. 5 (R. Bigelow, ed. 1979).

3. Jordan, *supra* note 1; R. Bigelow and S. Nycum, *Your Computer and the Law* 14–15 (1975).

4. Holdsclaw v. Warren and Brewster, 45 Or.App. 153, 607 P.2d 1208 (1980).

5. 29 USC 651–678 (1976).

6. Boston Police Patrolmen's Association, Inc., 6 CLSR 869 (Mass. Labor Relations Commission 1978).

7. State *ex rel.* Gabalac v. Firestone Bank, 46 Ohio App.2d 124, 346 N.E.2d 326 (Summit County Ct. App. 1975).

8. Torres v. North American Van Lines, Inc., 135 Ariz. 35, 658 P.2d 835 (Ct.App. 1982).

9. Lucas v. Hamm, 56 Cal.2d 583, 364 P.2d 685, 15 Cal. Rptr. 821 (1961), *cert. denied*, 368 U.S. 987 (1962); Nycum, "Liability for Malfunction of a Computer Program," 7 Rut. J. of Comp. Tech. and L. 1, 11 (1979).

10. 288 Pa.Super. 138, 431 A.2d 326 (1981).

11. *See* UCC 4-403(1) (1978).

12. W. Prosser, *Handbook of the Law of Torts*, 214–228 (4th ed. 1971).

13. This situation is described in Bigelow, *supra* note 2. *See also* Testa v. Winquist, 451 F. Supp. 388 (D. R.I. 1978) (action lies against NCIC for false arrest based upon computer error).

14. State *ex rel.* Gabalac v. Firestone Bank, 46 Ohio App.2d 124, 346 N.E.2d 326 (Summit County Ct. App. 1975).

15. Ford Motor Credit Co. v. Hitchcock, 116 Ga.App. 563, 158 S.E.2d 468 (1967); Ford Motor Credit Co. v. Swarens, 447 S.W.2d 53 (Ky. Ct. App. 1969); Price v. Ford Motor Credit Co., 530 S.W.2d 249 (Mo. Ct. App. 1975).

16. *See generally* Prosser, *supra* note 12, at 9–14.

17. Stagg v. Bank of Breckenridge, 22 ATLA L. Rep. 269, 7 CLSR 529 (Summit County Dist. Ct. 1979).

18. Prosser, *supra* note 12, at 12–14.

19. UCC 4-302.

20. *See, e.g.,* First Wyoming Bank v. Cabinet Craft Distributors, Inc., 624 P.2d 227, 231 (Wyo. 1981).

21. UCC 4-108(2).

22. First Wyoming Bank v. Cabinet Craft Distributors, Inc., 624 P.2d 227 (Wyo. 1981).

23. Sun River Cattle Co. v. Miners Bank of Montana N.A., 164 Mont. 237, 521 P.2d 679 (1974).

24. Bank Leumi Trust Co. v. Bank of Mid-Jersey, 499 F. Supp. 1022 (D. N.J. 1980).

25. Port City State Bank v. American National Bank, 486 F.2d 196 (10th Cir. 1973).

26. Reynolds Metals Co., 32 L.A. 249, 6 CLSR 927 (1959).

27. Beacon Journal Publishing Co., 63 L.A. 453, 6 CLSR 556 (1974); Northwest Publications, Inc., 65 L.A. 37, 6 CLSR 533 (1975); Elmira Star-Gazette, 65 L.A. 958, 6 CLSR 515 (1975). *See also* National Labor Relations Board v. Island Typographers, Inc., 705 F.2d 44 (2d Cir. 1983).

28. United Transp. Union, Local 63E v. Penn Central Co., 443 F.2d 131 (6th Cir. 1971).

29. 29 USC 158(a)(5) (1976).

30. Fibreboard Paper Products Corp. v. National Labor Relations Board, 379 U.S. 203 (1964).

31. First National Maintenance Corp. v. National Labor Relations Board, 452 U.S. 666 (1981). *See* National Labor Relations Board v. Island Typographers, Inc., 705 F.2d 44, 50 (2d Cir. 1983).

32. *See, e.g.,* Pezzillo v. General Telephone & Electronics Information Systems, Inc., 414 F. Supp. 1257 (M.D. Tenn. 1976) (employer failed to prove that computer programmers regularly exercised discretion and independent judgment as opposed to job skills; therefore programmers are "employees" under Fair Labor Standards Act).

33. Cagle v. Boyle Mortgage Co., 261 Ark. 437, 549 S.W.2d 474 (1977).

34. Bigelow, "Some Legal and Regulatory Problems of Computers with Communications Capabilities," in CLS 6-1, art. 1, at 23 (R. Bigelow, ed. 1979).

35. *E.g.,* 15 USC 1 *et seq.* (1982).

36. *See Antitrust and Information Technology,* abridged from 1973 COSATI report, "Legal Aspects of Computerized Information Systems," in CLS 7-1, art. 5 (R. Bigelow, ed. 1979). *But see* Glen Eden Hospital, Inc. v. Blue Cross and Blue Shield of Michigan, 555 F. Supp. 337 (E.D. Mich. 1983).

37. *See, e.g.,* 15 USC 78a *et seq.* (1982).

38. 15 USC 78j (1983); 17 CFR 240.10b-5 (1983).

39. 15 USC 78r (1982). *See also* Sirota v. Solitron Devices, Inc., 673 F.2d 566 (2d Cir. 1982).

40. 15 USC 78 (1982); 17 CFR 240.10b-5 (1983). *See e.g.,* Securities and Exchange Commission v. Texas Gulf Sulphur Co., 401 F.2d 833 (2d Cir. 1968), *cert. denied* 394 U.S. 976 (1969).

41. Tangorra, "Insurance Against Disaster," *Datamation,* July 1982, at 70.

42. *Id.*

43. 342 F. Supp. 241 (N.D. Ohio 1972), *aff'd* 479 F.2d 153 (6th Cir. 1973).

44. Memphis Light, Gas & Water Division v. Craft, 436 U.S. 1 (1978). *See also* Pompeii Estates, Inc. v. Consolidated Edison Co., 91 Misc.2d 233, 397 N.Y.S.2d 577 (N.Y. City Civ. Ct. 1977); Bronson v. Consolidated Edison Co., 350 F. Supp. 443 (S.D. N.Y. 1972).

45. A term borrowed from another similar case, Bronson v. Consolidated Edison Co., 350 F. Supp. 443 (S.D. N.Y. 1972).

46. Pompeii Estates, Inc. v. Consolidated Edison Co., 91 Misc.2d 233, 397 N.Y.S.2d 577 (N.Y. City Civ. Ct. 1977).

47. 453 F.2d 533 (10th Cir. 1972).

PART VII

Computer Records In Court

INTRODUCTION

Whenever an organization decides to computerize all or part of its record-keeping system, it should be concerned about its ability to maintain confidence in the records' accuracy and reliability at a reasonable cost. This concern deserves special attention when the records in question have the potential for use in litigation. Courts and governmental agencies have their own notions of what materials are adequate to serve as evidence of a particular fact or transaction. The organization must therefore ensure that its system design and operations meet the courts' requirements for proving the particular facts that might subsequently need to be proved in court, as well as any applicable rules and guidelines of governmental agencies.

In addition, the courts have rules of discovery that determine the rights of a party to obtain information from the opposing party for trial preparation. These rules are important to the computer user, since they in effect make the user's own information system a source of information for the organization's opponent as well.

COMPUTER DATA AND THE COURTS

Offering Computer Records as Evidence

In any particular litigation involving the computer user, the user's attorney will, of course, bear responsibility for getting the necessary facts into evidence. If computer-stored information is essential to the case, the user can make the lawyer's task much easier by devoting some attention to a few principles in the design and operation of the system beforehand.

Admissibility. The main purpose of the courts' evidence rules is to ensure the reliability and credibility of the evidence presented to the judge or jury. The widespread use of computers by businesses and other organizations has forced the courts to determine appropriate guidelines for the use of computer-generated information as evidence. In doing so, the courts attempt to recognize the value of the computer as an efficient record keeper, relied upon extensively by government and industry. On the other hand, the use of a computer printout to prove certain facts unsubstantiated by adequate background and source material to ensure accuracy and authenticity poses a serious risk of abuse and error in the judicial process.

Relevance. The most basic rule of evidence is that only facts that are relevant, or logically pertinent, to the case at hand may be admitted. For example, in a contract action to collect on a retail credit debt, it is necessary to show only that the debtor assumed a contractual obligation to pay for the goods and has not paid it when due. Any evidence offered that does not tend to prove either of these facts is irrelevant so the court will not waste its time or risk undue prejudice to one of the parties by admitting such evidence. Thus, in a retail contract action in which only those two facts are at issue, the creditor would not be permitted to show that the debtor owns a Rolls-Royce but refused to pay a $75 debt. The fact that the debtor owns a Rolls-Royce is irrelevant to the issue and could prejudice the fact finder toward one of the parties.

The system designer should determine which data to be stored by the system may need to be introduced into evidence and for what purpose. In this way, the user can be sure that all information potentially relevant to a lawsuit is available in a form in which it can be used in court. For example, in a system designed to record retail transactions by computer, the information recorded may be used for several purposes, such as customer accounts and inventory control. That information may be significant in a lawsuit to recover the balance due on a credit account. To be useful for this purpose, it is necessary that each transaction's data be identifiable as a single logical computer record, separable from other similar transactions.

For example, in one case where a retailer sued to recover on a customer's credit account,[1] the retailer intended to rely on a computer printout showing the dates, costs, and departments from which the customer's purchases were made, the customer's credit card number, and the current balance. The original invoices had been destroyed after transfer of the information to the computer. The trial judge threw the case out of court, refusing to accept the printout as evidence. The appellate court reversed, however, finding the printout to be as admissible as any other business record (see the subsection on hearsay evidence). The case illustrates a good system design that identified the essential facts that needed to be proved in court. The user's legal counsel should be consulted to aid in identification of the potentially necessary data before changing or implementing the information system.

Foundation. A basic requirement for introducing computer evidence is laying a proper foundation. The purpose of a foundation is basically twofold. First, it will show that the facts to be proved are relevant to the legal issues in the case. Second, it must provide some facts to suggest that the data coming out of the computer accurately reflect the real-world facts that need to be proved. To lay a proper foundation, some qualified person or persons must testify to the workings of the system and precisely how the computer information is related to these real-world facts. The object of this testimony is essentially to show that the computer information is a genuine record of the fact to be proved. The person testifying needs to have a thorough understanding of the system and, most important, be able to explain it to a lay judge and jury.

The foundation testimony should trace the information's path from the event to be proved (or disproved) to the courtroom. This can best be accomplished by establishing:

a. that the persons entering the information had personal knowledge of the event and entered it within a reasonable time after the event;

b. the way in which the data was originally entered into the system and what measures were taken to ensure accuracy;

c. that the data was normally entered in that fashion in the regular course of business;

d. the dependability of the equipment used;

e. the dependability of the programs used;

f. any means employed to ensure proper operation of the system;

g. the manner in which the data was stored and measures taken to prevent loss or alteration of stored data;

h. time and method of preparation of the computer output to be introduced as evidence; and

i. authentication of the particular printout to be introduced (for example, by the preparer or the witness signing and dating it).

The witness used to establish the foundation does not necessarily need to have personal knowledge of the basic data in question or of the system's actual operation, but a witness with such knowledge would be much more persuasive than one without it.

Simple, straightforward system design will aid greatly in laying the proper foundation for admission of computerized information. Such design will serve the dual purposes of, first, making the system easier for employees to understand and thereby providing more qualified and more credible witnesses and, second, making it easier for a judge and jury to understand the system and believe in its reliability. In addition, it will be much easier to establish the existence of a reliable information system *in court* if the user has taken steps to ensure that the system is *in fact* the most reliable system possible for its purposes.

Hearsay Evidence Rule. The need for a proper foundation is especially important in meeting a more specific objection to admissibility, the hearsay evidence rule. This rule provides that a written or oral assertion of a fact other than one made by a witness testifying at trial is not admissible to prove the truth of the matter being asserted. Therefore, if a judge was not persuaded that a printout fell within one of the hearsay rule exceptions, the printout could not be used to prove, say, the status of a customer's account on a particular date. Fortunately, though, most courts are now willing to accept computer-stored evidence under the exception for business records. This is a well-established exception that recognizes business recordkeeping practices as an acceptable means of establishing facts. To qualify as a business record, the evidence must be a record made in the regular course of business, at or near the time of the event recorded; a qualified witness must testify to its identity and method of preparation; and the information's sources and manner of preparation must indicate trustworthiness.

Thus, to be admissible under the business records exception to the hearsay rule, the foundation laid for the evidence should include all of the foundation elements listed previously. To illustrate the importance of the foundation, consider a criminal case[2] in which the state wanted to introduce records from the phone company's call tracer. The court rejected the evidence since there was not enough testimony as to the method of preparation and the meaning of the records for the court to assess the records' trustworthiness. Other courts have required that the particular computing equipment used be recognized as "standard equipment."[3]

It is especially important that the records be input, stored, and prepared in the *regular course of business*. Courts have generally not required that *printout* evidence be prepared at or near the time of the event and in the regular course of business, as long as the underlying information was *entered* at or near the time in the regular course of business[4] and not especially for the purpose of litigation.

Two criminal cases illustrate the importance of the regular-course-of-business requirement. In one case,[5] the prosecution sought to show that a murder victim had no criminal record, based upon a printout from the National Crime Information Center. The court refused to admit the printout since the prosecution failed to show that law enforcement agencies in the particular locales customarily entered arrest information in the NCIC computer. In the other case,[6] however, a car rental company's computerized records were admitted to prove that a particular vehicle was not rented after a certain date and before it was stolen. Note that in both cases, the records were introduced to establish a *negative* fact. In the first, the court was not convinced that if the disputed event had occurred, it would have been recorded in the regular course of business; in the second, the court *was* convinced and the evidence was therefore admissible as an exception to the hearsay rule.

Here again, the courts want to be convinced of the computerized records' authenticity and reliability as business records before they admit them as an exception to the hearsay rule. A showing of the user's own reliance on the records will help to support a finding of admissibility under the business records exception. In addition, the user can enhance the chances of admissibility by establishing and strictly following routine procedures for the processing of information, emphasizing accuracy and security. Several specific suggestions are included in the implications for action section in this part.

It must also be realized that at the same time that the user is urging admissibility, the opponent will fight against it by attempting to destroy the credibility of the user's system. This may be done in a general way by alleging that the system producing the output is unreliable. For example, the opponent may point to a large history of customer billing complaints as evidence of an error-prone system. It is therefore advisable that the user follow up on complaints and try to eliminate possible sources of errors as they occur. The opponent may also try to point out more specific errors in the program or system that produces the output to be introduced as evidence, using its own expert witnesses. The demands imposed by the rules of evidence should not be underestimated by the user when making decisions about system design. The user will certainly be concerned with the reliability of the system for other reasons, that is, to ensure continuous, smooth operations; minimize costly repairs, debugging, and downtime; and reduce the possibility of being held legally liable to others for harm caused by computer error (see Part VI). Note that the design decisions relative to these goals involve a trade-off between cost and the risk of actual error, that is, the user may be willing to risk a higher probability of error, which might never occur, in return for a lower cost. But, under the rules of evidence, the crucial issue is not so much whether an error *actually* occurs but whether there is a significant *risk* of error that would diminish the system's credibility in the eyes of a judge and jury. It is therefore possible that a system may never produce an error, yet be worthless as evidence in a court of law if the opponent can create the impression of substantial risk of error. This suggests that if the user wants the firm's records to be accepted by a court, the user needs to attempt to satisfy the courts' conception of system design reliability rather than be satisfied with some lower standard in return for lower cost.

Best Evidence Rule. The best evidence rule provides that if the terms of a writing are material and need to be proved, the original writing must be produced unless it is unavailable for some reason (other than by the serious fault of the party seeking to admit the evidence).

Computerized records have presented the courts with conceptual difficulties in dealing with this rule. First, a court must determine what constitutes the original: the printout, the machine-stored data, or the source documentation of the data input. Then the court must decide whether a printout is admissible under the rule.

The Federal Rules of Evidence state that a printout shown to reflect the data accurately is an original.[7] There is thus no question about a printout's admissibility under the best evidence rule. However, state courts are in some disagreement on the issue.

Even though a court may find that the printout is not an original, the printout may still be admissible under one of the rule's exceptions. For example, one exception provides that if the original is lost or destroyed, secondary evidence of the contents may be admitted. Therefore, if the court views the source paper records to be the originals and the paper records are destroyed after the data have been entered into the computer, the computerized records are then the best available evidence and therefore admissible. If the court views the original to be the machine-stored data, unintelligible by humans, and the court equates "unintelligibility" with "unavailability," then the printout is, again, the best available evidence of the data and admissible.[8]

Another exception to the best evidence rule provides that a summary of voluminous writings is admissible if the underlying writings could not be conveniently examined in court and the underlying writings are made available to the other party for inspection before trial. The printout may thus be considered to be a "summary" and therefore admissible, whether the originals are considered to be the paper documents or the computer's data base,[9] as long as the opponent is given the opportunity to examine whatever underlying documents or data are available.

The best evidence rule takes on added significance for the user's trial counsel. For example, whenever a witness testifies about the content of a printout, the printout itself must be introduced since it is the best evidence of the actual content.[10] The user's ability to identify and produce the printout referred to by the witness is therefore important.

Statute of Frauds. Each jurisdiction has a statute of frauds providing in effect that contracts of a certain character (for example, sales of real estate, transactions over $500 in value, or contracts taking more than one year to perform) must be evidenced by a signed writing to be enforced.

These statutes may present difficulty in dealing with transactions conducted by computers on behalf of their respective organizations. In the absence of a writing signed by a company representative, purchase orders transmitted and accepted electronically may not be enforceable under the existing statutes. A written confirmation of a prior electronic "agreement" would probably satisfy the statute of frauds once that confirmation is sent, but if a breach occurs between the date of agreement and the date the confirmation is received, the contract would probably be unenforceable. It is likely that in the near future, courts or legislatures will provide that a statute of frauds may be satisfied by transmission of a coded identifier, to be given the legal effect of a signature. This has already been done for transactions to which the Uniform Commercial Code applies, most notably, to the sale of goods. As defined by the UCC, " 'signed' includes any symbol executed or adopted by a party with present intention to authenticate a writing."[11] A " 'writing' includes printing, typewriting or any other intentional reduction to tangible form."[12] Thus, it appears that any computer-transmitted identifier to be printed out at the receiving end would qualify to satisfy the statute of frauds. Similar broad provisions may be in effect for non-UCC transactions as well. System designers contemplating inter-company purchasing systems should be alert to the legal requirements for proving the integrity of their particular transactions in the jurisdictions involved.

Credibility. In general, to be admissible as evidence, the user must present the picture of a reliable information-gathering system, comparable to the reliability of a traditional manual recordkeeping system. It should be kept in mind, however, that admissibility is only a threshold step. Once admitted, the credibility given the evidence by the judge and jury becomes critical to the case's outcome. The design and rigid following of procedures for accuracy and security not only ensure admissibility but also help the judge and jury accept the truth of the evidence presented over the opposing viewpoint, thereby making the strongest case possible for the computer user.

Opposing Computer Records as Evidence

The computer user involved in litigation may resist the discovery and admissibility of computer evidence for two reasons. First, the evidence may be damaging to the user's case. Second, it may consist of confidential or otherwise sensitive material, the disclosure of which may be damaging to the user. Evidence admitted at trial normally becomes a matter of public record. Moreover, even if the information itself is not admitted into evidence, the mere disclosure to the opponent under rules of discovery may be just as damaging.

Admissibility. The same rules of evidence that govern the introduction of computer evidence by the computer user will also apply to that introduced by the user's opponent. Therefore, it is theoretically possible that a computer user may object to the admissibility of information from its own files on the grounds of hearsay or unreliability. It is unlikely, however, that a court would view such an objection favorably since such arguments are inconsistent with the user's own maintenance of and reliance upon the records. Other objections available to the user in such cases are privilege and prejudicial effect.

Privilege. Modern courts in general tend to favor full disclosure of the facts relevant to a case to achieve a fair and informed decision. They do, however, afford protection to some types of information contained in the files of a business or other organization. One type of information so protected is trade secrets. The trade secrets privilege may be invoked against the opponent's attempt to admit the underlying data, the unique organization of the data, or the computer programs that control the data.[13] To establish the existence of a trade secret in any of these circumstances, the user must prove that the information in question was developed at substantial cost, carefully protected from public disclosure, sufficiently novel, and such that it gives the user a competitive advantage that would be lost if the information were made public. The implication for the computer user is to treat confidential information as such, since careful treatment by the user in the past may influence the court's determination of whether the information may be disclosed during litigation.

On the other hand, the trade secret privilege is not absolute even though a trade secret is found to exist. There are a variety of methods by which courts may permit the admission of such evidence but still protect its confidentiality to some degree. For example, the court may issue a protective order, which admits the evidence but orders all of the parties and witnesses to refrain from using or disclosing the secret information outside of the trial; or the court may convene a confidential meeting for the purpose of presenting the disputed evidence, during which the public and nonparty witnesses are excluded; or the evidence may be stored in a sealed record, to be opened only upon an order by the court. In general, if the information is essential to the opponent's case, it may be admitted into evidence in some limited fashion even though it constitutes a trade secret.

Other forms of privilege also exist. State or federal privacy statutes may protect certain personal data from disclosure in civil litigation. Traditional confidential relationships, such as doctor/patient and attorney/client, are also protected. It must be noted, however, that such privileges are seldom absolute. The jurisdiction's statutes and courts almost always provide for disclosure of such information where it is essential to the opponent's case, essential to produce a just result, or may be handled or modified to limit its sensitivity. The computer user should therefore be on notice that by taking steps to ensure the admissibility of evidence for the firm's own purposes, the user may also pave the way for admissibility of adverse information contained in the firm's files.

Prejudicial Effect. If the value of the evidence is found to be outweighed by the risk of unfair prejudice, confusion, or misleading the jury, the court may refuse to admit the evidence. For example, in one case[14] the court found that the jury would not be able to understand the printout without further foundation testimony and so excluded it from evidence. Likewise, conflicting testimony about the meaning and reliability of computer-based evidence may be objected to as confusing. If the court finds that the potential confusion outweighs any relevance to the issues, the evidence may not be admitted by the court. In addition, if an opponent seeks to introduce a large volume of evidence, such as the original records supporting the printouts, the admission of the evidence may be rejected as being overly broad. In other words, the same purpose could be achieved with a lesser and more carefully selected volume of evidence.

Discovery. Rules of discovery enable parties to gain access to information in the possession of the opposing party to aid in their investigation and preparation for trial. Modern courts tend to favor liberal discovery since complete disclosure of facts encourages a result based on the merits of the situation, not on the lawyers' abilities and surprise tactics (sometimes referred to as "trial by ambush"). A more comprehensive knowledge of the facts by both sides also encourages the voluntary settlement of cases out of court, reducing the backlog in the court systems.

A party preparing for litigation must analyze a wealth of information. Of this information, only a relatively small portion may ever be admitted into evidence at trial since major portions of it may be irrelevant or inadmissible. Discovery rules permitting liberal access to information make it possible for the computer user's opponent to obtain and analyze substantial amounts of information about the user's organization, even though the information may not be admissible in court. Rules of discovery may consequently be significant to a computer user, independent of the evidence rules, in making system design decisions.

When an opponent seeks to discover information from an organization that does not utilize a computer, the courts will require the organization to disclose the requested information at its own expense if it is considered to be reasonably relevant to the case. The disclosure may take the form of permitting an examination of the organization's record books, production of management reports, written answers to written questions drafted by the opponent (called interrogatories), or the pretrial questioning and cross-examination of key persons under oath (called depositions). If the burden of producing the information is found by the court to be too great (or the burden is the same for the opponent to gather the information), the court may decide not to force the organization to produce the requested information.

If the organization uses a computer, however, much of the desired information may be readily available from the computer files. Courts have recognized the value of the computer as a discovery tool, in some cases permitting an opponent to obtain machine-readable copies of the user's data and programs. Alternately, if the parties' computers are not compatible or the opponent has no computer, a printout of the machine-readable records may be obtained.

The availability of the requested information in the computer files makes it less likely that the court will deny discovery because of the excessive burden on the user organization. For example, a case is reported in which the computer user was being sued for sex discrimination among its employees.[15] The opponent requested disclosure of a list of all persons who had worked for the user over the past few years in chronological order of the date of hiring, with each employee's gender, record of job assignments, layoffs, termination, hours worked and gross earnings, and so on. The user asked the trial court to require the opponent to gather the information from the employees' employment folders and the user's payroll records since the burden for the opponent would be the same as for the user. The opponent pointed out to the trial court that much of the information was contained in the user's computer payroll system and therefore was more readily accessible to the user than to the opponent. The court agreed with the opponent and ordered the user to supply the requested information. The opponent, after analyzing and organizing the printout information by hand, was able to establish a definite pattern of different treatment based on gender.

Discovery procedures may result in a large financial burden on the computer user. In an early computer discovery case,[16] the user produced 120,000 copies of computer-generated records, which it was ordered to analyze at its own expense to make them intelligible to the opponent.

A recent Supreme Court decision[17] also illustrates the extent of the burden that may be imposed upon a computer user by the discovery rules. In a class action suit, the opponent sought to force the computer user to compile a list of the names and addresses of the other members of the class from computerized records at the user's expense. To do so, the user would have had to sort through a considerable number of paper records, keypunch between 150,000 and 300,000 computer cards, and create eight new programs, at an estimated cost of $16,000. A federal appeals court held that the federal discovery rules authorized the district court to order the user to bear the $16,000 expense in helping to compile the list. The Supreme Court unanimously reversed, refusing to force the user to bear that cost. However, the Court's decision was not motivated by the cost of supplying the information. Rather, the Court reasoned that the requested information was not relevant to the subject matter of the suit but was intended only to satisfy the opponent's duty to notify other members of the class. It thus appears that if the information had been relevant to the subject of the suit, and thus a proper subject for discovery, the Court might have required the user to bear the cost.

Similarly, the Internal Revenue Service satisfied its discovery obligations in one case by providing an opponent with all IRS handbooks documenting its computer operations, as well as statistical analyses of the system's operations and the services of experts familiar with the system.[18] But in another tax case,[19] the same court denied a request that the opponent be given access to an IRS computer center for up to three weeks to evaluate its operations and accuracy, finding the request to be "patently unreasonable" due to its disruptive effect on the IRS computer operations.

As attorneys become more familiar with computers, it can be expected that the user's computer files will be used more and more extensively as a tool for discovery. Although the same privileges discussed earlier are used to resist both discovery and admissibility, the opponent's need for information where no alternate sources exist may still override or limit those privileges. Consequently, if information in the user's possession is crucial to an opponent's case, it is likely that the opponent will be able to force its discovery in some form.

The computer user may arrive at the conclusion that unfavorable information should be kept out of the computer files to thwart discovery. That is not a wise decision, however. There is certainly no need to store adverse information that is not useful to the user in the regular course of business. But neither should the rules of discovery persuade a user to dispense with information that would otherwise be useful if kept in the computer's files. If the information is crucial to an opponent's case, it will probably be discoverable whether contained in the computer files or not. Attempts to impede discovery through system design (a) will probably be unsuccessful and succeed only in escalating the cost of discovery since information will have to be duplicated from other sources; (b) may be expensive and inefficient by depriving the organization of the use of the information in its computer files; and (3) may be found by a court to constitute "bad faith" in the judicial process, tending to prejudice a court against the user from the outset and perhaps resulting in attorney's fees being assessed against the recalcitrant user. For example, in the sex discrimination suit described previously, the court's decision was based in part upon what it found to be bad faith by the user in causing inexcusable delays in discovery.

A better course for the user would be merely to acknowledge the fact that whatever information is available to the company through its computer system may also be made available to an opponent in litigation. The system should therefore be designed independently of this consideration, computerizing information that is needed for business and other reasons (see, for example, the system design considerations contained in Part VI). Rules of discovery permitting access to computer-stored data in lieu of other traditional discovery methods may even be welcomed, since the delivery of a computer tape or printout will be much less disruptive of the user's operations than extensive manual searches and compilations of records, taking of depositions, and so on. Even though substantial burdens of discovery have been imposed on computer users in some cases, use of the simplest system design possible and the ready availability of complete program documentation will greatly reduce the financial and disruptive burdens of court-ordered discovery on the computer user.

GOVERNMENTAL AGENCY REQUIREMENTS

Governmental agencies usually regulate a specific type of activity, such as the Drug Enforcement Administration, Federal Communications Commission, or various environmental control agencies. Some encompass a substantially larger scope of business activity, such as the Federal Trade Commission or, of course, the Internal Revenue Service. Some are created for purposes related to control and administration of the government, such as the General Services Administration or Office of Management and Budget, and affect businesses dealing with the government. But all of them are entrusted with responsibility for collecting and storing voluminous records pertaining to their specific areas of responsibility. The computer user who deals with any of these agencies should give careful attention to their particular recordkeeping requirements.

The agency requirements may be important in several ways. First, a new system design may subject the user to regulation by agencies with whom the user has not had to deal previously. For example, a user's use of microwave or other forms of data communication may force the company to deal with certain requirements of state and federal regulatory agencies. Second, the user must consider the type of various reports that may be required and provide for their preparation when designing the system. This may require the storage of certain data that would not otherwise be stored. Of course, the deadlines for such reports should also be considered in setting up a calendar for the preparation of the various business reports produced from the computer files. In addition, the particular agency requirements may dictate the form in which the information is to be supplied. For example, some smaller agencies may require that a particular form be completed and returned to the agency, putting the burden on the user to organize and reduce the data to the required format. Other larger agencies equipped with data-processing equipment may permit or require supplying machine-readable records. For example, the IRS encourages the use of floppy disks for small business employee reporting, which may become mandatory in the future.

The computer user should therefore consider all the requirements of agencies with which the company deals, or might have to deal with in the future, in making decisions about its method of keeping records.

COURT CASES

Courts usually accept computer evidence when it is the only available evidence on a given point or highly probative of a fact to be proved, assuming the prerequisites to admissibility discussed earlier are complied with; that is, courts are generally willing to assume that if the computerized business records show that a certain transaction occurred, it probably occurred. Most courts would go a step farther and assume that if there is not a record of a transaction, the transaction probably did not occur. They may, however, require more convincing evidence that input procedures are routinely followed in the latter cases requiring proof of a negative fact.

One type of computer record transaction that remains somewhat unsettled by the courts is proof of mailing by computer, particularly as applied to the insurance industry. Bulk mailing is a routine task that lends itself to computerization, and, as one court noted, requiring proof of every computer transaction in each of millions of policies might raise the cost of insurance to prohibitive levels. Confrontations between a computer that "could not stray from its program" and a person who testifies under oath that "I never received it" have elicited varying judicial responses. Two such cases are examined here.[20]

Gulf Coast Investment Corp. v. Secretary of Housing and Urban Development.[21] Gulf Coast held the mortgage on a home owned by Mr. and Mrs. York and required them to purchase a flood insurance policy. Gulf Coast thereafter agreed to pay the renewal premiums from escrow funds. Subsequent to some flood damage to the home, the Yorks' application for flood insurance benefits was denied. Gulf Coast paid the Yorks for their loss and sued the secretary to recover the amount paid. The Federal Emergency Management Agency (FEMA) contended that the policy terminated more than 15 months prior to the flood loss due to nonpayment of the annual renewal premium. Gulf Coast asserted that no termination took place since the defendant had failed to comply with a provision of the policy requiring written notice of termination. It appears that Gulf Coast received a renewal notice and mailed a check to the insurance agent, but the premium was never received by the defendant and so the policy lapsed. Although the court indicated later in its opinion that it did not find that the notice was necessary, the court nevertheless dealt at length with the issue of whether a termination notice had been sent.

An officer of the National Flood Insurance Association testified about the NFIA's computer program for notifying parties with a possible interest in policy renewal. Although she testified that magnetic tapes were kept that showed the work of the computer on a particular day, including the exact form generated, the date, and policy number, no termination notice or computer record of its production was offered into evidence. However, she stated unequivocally that the termination notice to Gulf Coast was generated, because the computer was programmed to produce a termination notice to the servicing company, Aetna Technical Services, only after it produced the Gulf Coast termination notice. She testified that since a notice was sent to Aetna, one must have been sent to Gulf Coast. She testified that approximately one and a half million NFIA policy renewals were processed annually, and she knew of no instance in which the computer omitted a notice or failed to complete a cycle. The computer kept a count of the number of items to anticipate from a given cycle, and the number was routinely verified against the items actually produced. The number of notices was verified again after insertion into envelopes, and the notices were then delivered to the post office and mailed at bulk rates.

The court held that the evidence of the customary and usual computer procedures supported an inference that the termination notice was delivered, since the evidence of the production and receipt of a renewal notice by Gulf Coast and a termination notice by Aetna implied that the usual and customary procedures were followed in this case. The court noted that "the computer was an unimaginative mechanical device that could not stray from its program." This evidence, according to the court, proved a prima facie case of delivery of the termination notice. It was therefore up to Gulf Coast to rebut this proof with evidence of nondelivery.

The court found that Gulf Coast's case for nondelivery was based solely upon the testimony of Gulf Coast's vice president in charge of flood administration, who testified that the Yorks' loan file did not contain a termination notice. This testimony, in the court's view, supported an inference that the notice was not received by Gulf Coast, but in weighing all the evidence on the issue of delivery, Gulf Coast's testimony was entitled to very little weight. First, the vice president was not the custodian of termination notices, and there was no testimony that he had even been employed by Gulf Coast during the time in question. Moreover, Gulf Coast's recordkeeping was deemed inadequate since there was no established procedure for logging in termination notices when received. Finally, the court found that the Yorks' file was not adequately monitored for renewal certificates. Thus, the defendant's prima facie case of delivery was not rebutted by Gulf Coast's evidence of nondelivery.

This case demonstrates the need to convince a court of a computer system's reliability. The court was convinced that a computer was an unimaginative mechanical device that could not deviate from its program. From this basic principle, the computer user's simple explanation of the program structure led the court directly to the conclusion that the notice must have been mailed. For example, since the notice of Aetna could be produced and mailed only after the notice to Gulf Coast was produced and mailed, and since the notice to Aetna was produced and mailed, the notice to Gulf Coast was more likely than not mailed. It should be noted that the alleged recipient in this case did not make a very convincing demonstration of internal management controls. In the absence of such a demonstration and weighed against the strict controls of the sender, the court found it much easier to believe that the alleged notice was lost or misplaced in a bureaucratic office shuffle than that it was never produced or sent at all.

Cox v. Brookings International Life Insurance Co.[22] Mr. and Mrs. Cox applied for and received a life insurance policy on their son, Steven, from Brookings. Mrs. Cox had as a regular practice been responsible for gathering the monthly bills, including insurance premiums, and writing checks to pay them. Upon her death in October 1977, Mr. Cox became the owner of the policy as the sole surviving beneficiary and also assumed responsibility for payment of the family bills, which included premiums on 13 various types of insurance policies. He testified at trial that he depended upon receiving notice from insurance companies that premiums were due in order to know when to pay the premiums. In June 1978 Steven was killed in a car accident. The insurance company refused to pay Mr. Cox's claim, asserting that coverage had lapsed due to nonpayment of the premium, which had been due April 1, 1978. Mr. Cox sued to recover on the policy. At the close of all the evidence, the judge refused to allow the jury to decide the case, directing a verdict for the insurance company. The appeal by Mr. Cox elicited three different responses from the appellate judges on the issue of proof of notice.

The majority of the judges reversed the trial court's holding on the ground that Mr. Cox had presented sufficient evidence of nonreceipt to require the jury to decide the issue. The court noted that the company "went to great lengths" to establish proper mailing. A company official and a mailroom employee testified as to the procedures used, and mail logs that indicated mailing of the notice were introduced. The appellate majority could not say that the trial court erred in finding from the company's evidence that a presumption of delivery existed. The majority noted, however, that Mr. Cox had offered more evidence of nondelivery than a simple denial. He had gone to some lengths to detail his own procedures for handling incoming mail, including bills and premium notices. He also demonstrated that between early February and late June, the time frame of the alleged lapse, he had sent checks in payment of premiums on 13 other policies, five of which were paid during May. Since Mr. Cox presented more evidence than a mere denial of receipt, the majority held that reasonable minds could differ on the issue and that consequently the jury should have been permitted to decide the issue.

One judge agreed with the majority but offered a separate concurring opinion in which he "refused to hypothesize that computers cannot err." Noting that presumptions of law disappear once actual facts are introduced on an issue, the concurring judge pointed to two additional facts in the record that would rebut the company's presumption of proper mailing. First, Mr. Cox had presented the testimony of the company's South Dakota agent, Mr. Roth, described by company officials as one of their top representatives and salesmen. Mr. Roth testified that he had learned from telephone conversations with the home office in Ohio that the company's computer had malfunctioned at about the time when Mr. Cox's premium notice should have been sent out. One of the company's own expert witnesses admitted that the company did not keep the malfunction "as a secret" and, although this expert placed the time frame at a time unrelated to Mr. Cox's policy, there were premiums that were received late, some as late as approximately 75 days.

Second, the concurring judge surmised that human error may have been involved since the quarterly notices, first generated by a computer in Ohio, were then sent to Brookings, South Dakota, and there matched by hand and placed in an envelope to be mailed to policyholders.

In light of all the facts elicited, the concurring judge concluded that the presumption of delivery ceased to exist. The issue of delivery became a factual issue to be decided by the jury. The judge joined the majority opinion "as the human dimension of justice cannot be sacrificed for the ostensible purity of the computer world."

One judge dissented from the result reached by the rest of the court, unpersuaded that Mr. Cox had presented any evidence sufficient to rebut the insurance company's case. This judge viewed the way in which Cox said he handled his incoming mail and the fact that he paid premiums on other policies to be irrelevant, proving "nothing beyond his self-serving statement as to notice." The dissenter also pointed out that the insurance company had also proved that it notified Mr. Cox by a telephone call taken by Steven Cox in addition to the mailed notice.

Concluding that the evidence left no room for reasonable minds to differ, the dissenting judge voted to affirm the trial court's directed verdict. "To hold otherwise," said the judge, "would allow anyone who has let an insurance policy lapse for nonpayment of premium to nevertheless seek recovery from a jury, by simply saying, 'I do not recall getting a notice.' It would thus tend to encourage fraud and destabilize the insurance industry."

These cases point out that admissibility of computer evidence is only the first step. Once admitted, if there is testimony contradicting the computer system, the system itself may in effect be put on trial. The cases also demonstrate the need to identify the facts that may need to be proved in court, in this case proper mailing, and provide procedures to supply a reliable record of those facts, such as by the use of mailing logs.

IMPLICATIONS FOR ACTION

The computer user who may need to use computer-stored information in court should have as a goal the establishment and operation of a system that will give a judge and jury the impression that the user's output could not possibly be wrong. The user should therefore establish procedures and safeguards at every stage of the information processing that seek to identify and eliminate sources of possible error. Any hint of trouble, including suspect output, customer complaints, and so on, should be promptly and thoroughly investigated.

The following are suggestions for system design and operation to eliminate suspicion of a system's reliability as a recordkeeper.[23]

Input

a. The initial input should be based upon personal knowledge where possible.

b. The fewer human handling stages before input, the better. Data errors are more likely during human handling than machine handling.

c. The person making the input should be authorized and bear responsibility for input of the information.

d. Procedures for protecting against error should be implemented and followed to the letter at all times.

e. Error characteristics of the input equipment and media should be carefully evaluated, and the type least prone to error should be selected.

f. If industry standards exist for equipment and procedures, these should be utilized as a minimum.

Storage

a. Error characteristics of the storage media should be evaluated and the least error-prone selected.

b. Standard procedures should be implemented and strictly followed to protect against loss or change of stored data.

c. Security measures, including strict control over persons using the computer, should be maintained; that is, keeping a log of everyone using the equipment.

Operation

a. Programmers should not be allowed to operate the equipment, since it may be inferred that they would know how to manipulate the system to obtain a desired result not in the ordinary course of business.

b. The programs and equipment should, to the greatest extent possible, be thoroughly tested and debugged.

c. If customary standards exist for the equipment and programs used for the application, they should be met.

d. The programmers and operating personnel should be highly qualified.

e. The longer a program has been in use, the better.

f. Complete documentation of the programs should be maintained and organized.

g. The system should be designed to prevent a single error from compounding itself.

h. Operating and maintenance procedures should be established and strictly followed.

Output

a. The output should be verified for accuracy.

b. A regular time and manner of preparation should be followed.

c. Output should be prepared and relied upon by the user in the normal course of business.

REFERENCES

1. Sears, Roebuck & Co. v. Merla, 142 N.J.Super. 205, 361 A.2d 68 (1976).

2. People v. Gauer, 7 Ill.App.3d 512, 288 N.E.2d 24 (1972).

3. Department of Mental Health v. Beil, 44 Ill.App.3d 402, 357 N.E.2d 875 (1976); Railroad Commission v. Southern Pacific Co., 468 S.W.2d 125 (Tex. Civ. App. 1971).

4. *See* United States v. Russo, 480 F.2d 1228 (6th Cir. 1973).

5. Gassett v. State, 532 S.W.2d 328 (Tex. Crim. 1976).

6. United States v. De Georgia, 420 F.2d 889 (9th Cir. 1969).

7. Fed. R. Evid. 1001(3).

8. *See* United States v. Russo, 480 F.2d 1228 (6th Cir. 1973).

9. *See* King v. State *ex rel.* Murdock Acceptance Corp., 222 So.2d 393 (Miss. 1969).

10. State v. Springer, 283 N.C. 627, 197 S.E.2d 530 (1973). *Cf.* United States v. De Georgia, 420 F.2d 889, 894 (9th Cir. 1969).

11. UCC 1-201(39).

12. UCC 1-201(46).

13. Johnston, "A Guide for the Proponent and Opponent of Computer-Based Evidence," 1 Comp. L. J. 667, 686–88 (1979).

14. Huber, Hunt & Nichols, Inc. v. Moore, 67 Cal.App.3d 278, 136 Cal.Rptr. 603 (1977).

15. Ewald, "Discovery and the Computer," in CLS 5-4.4, art. 2 (R. Bigelow, ed. 1979).

16. Lodge 743, International Association of Machinists v. United Aircraft Corp., 220 F. Supp. 19 (D. Conn. 1963), *aff'd* 337 F.2d 5 (2d Cir. 1964), *cert. denied* 380 U.S. 908 (1965).

17. Oppenheimer Fund, Inc. v. Sanders, 437 U.S. 340 (1978).

18. United States v. Liebert, 519 F.2d 542 (3d Cir. 1975).

19. United States v. Greenlee, 380 F. Supp. 652 (E.D. Pa. 1974), *aff'd* 517 F.2d 899 (3d Cir. 1975).

20. *See also* United States v. Roglieri, 700 F.2d 883 (2d Cir. 1983) (proof of mailing insufficient to support conviction of mail theft); Anzalone v. State Farm Mutual Insurance Co., 92 A.D.2d 238, 459 N.Y.S.2d 850 (1983) (insurer failed to prove mailing of cancellation notice).

21. 509 F. Supp. 1321 (E.D. La. 1980).

22. 331 N.W.2d 299 (S.D. 1983).

23. *See* Johnston, supra note 13, at 680–81; Connery and Levy, "Computer Evidence in Federal Courts," 84 Com. L. J. 266, 273 (1979).

PART VIII

Computer
Tax
Considerations

INTRODUCTION

Before procuring, improving, or upgrading a data-processing system, the tax consequences of the transaction should be analyzed. Usually, a tax attorney or a tax accountant can provide the information necessary for a proper analysis. Some of the important tax considerations relevant to the acquisition of computer hardware and especially software are presented in this part.

FEDERAL TAX TREATMENT OF HARDWARE AND SOFTWARE

Federal Taxation and Hardware

Federal taxation of hardware presents relatively few unique tax questions. For tax purposes, hardware is generally treated just as any other tangible personal property and is subject to the relevant rules of cost recovery (formerly depreciation) and investment credit. Particular attention, however, should be focused on the tax consequences of the various procurement methods discussed in Part I (that is, purchase, rent, lease, and service bureaus). For example, a lease agreement between a user and supplier of an EDP system may be viewed by the IRS as essentially a conditional purchase agreement. How the substance of the transaction is viewed under the tax laws will affect such things as business expense deductions, investment credit, and cost recovery. A failure to examine these tax consequences can have a substantial effect on the cash flow of the user's organization, especially when the procurement transaction involves a very expensive EDP system.

Prior to the Economic Recovery Tax Act of 1981 (ERTA), computer hardware was capitalized and its cost deducted through depreciation. Section 167 of the Internal Revenue Code[1] allowed the owner of an asset to claim the asset's depreciation as a deduction against the owner's taxable income. The amount allowed as a deduction was calculated using any one of the several acceptable methods of depreciation (that is, straight line, declining balance, or sum of the years' digits) by which the taxpayer's basis in the asset (cost) less its salvage value was allocated over the asset's useful life.

The user of a business computer often could reap greater economic benefits, however, by leasing, renting, or contracting for computer services and then claiming the full amount of the actual rental or service fees as an ordinary business expense under Section 162. The decision to contract for computer services or short-term rentals posed no real issue as to the deductibility of the expenses. Longer-term purported "leases" were viewed suspiciously by the IRS and courts to the extent that they approached an actual sale to the user.[2] For example, a business desiring to acquire an expensive computer may have found that it did not have enough income to take full advantage of the depreciation and investment tax credit to which it, as owner of the business computer, was entitled. The business might have decided that it could generate larger annual tax deductions under the old laws by paying "rentals" than by depreciating the cost (less salvage value) over the asset's "useful life." This would have been especially true since, given the rapid obsolescence of certain computer models or anticipated changes in the user's computer requirements, the user may not have contemplated actually using the computer for its entire useful life. Thus, rather than being limited to the smaller deductions resulting from allocation of cost over a longer useful life, the lease arrangement provided a means by which the user could accelerate the tax deductions generated by purchase of the computer.

Two approaches could be taken to acquire the lease. First, the user could select the computer it wanted to buy, then locate a third party to buy it with a simultaneous agreement to lease it to the user. Alternatively, the user could buy the computer, then sell it to the third party with a simultaneous lease back to the user (known as a "sale and leaseback"). In either event, both the user and third-party lessor obtained tax advantages. The arrangement, as already indicated, permitted the user to deduct the full amount of the company's rental payments in larger amounts than its depreciation deductions would be if the computer were purchased outright. The lessor gained a steady cash flow from the lease payments but, as the owner of the computer, was entitled to offset that income by the amount of depreciation allowable and investment tax credit. Frequently, the lessor's tax savings could be shared with the user by charging lower rentals than the user's financing would have cost for an outright purchase. This arrangement was permissible, however, only if the lease was actually a lease. In some cases, leases are drafted in such a way that there is very little difference between the result of the lease and the result under an outright financial sale of the computer. For example, if the user had the option to buy the computer at the end of the lease's term for a nominal amount clearly below its value at that time, the IRS might infer that the lease was actually a sale drawn up as a lease solely to avoid having to capitalize the cost at lower tax deductions per year. The user's company would then be treated for tax purposes as if it had purchased the computer outright, its deductions limited to those permitted by the approved depreciation methods.

The enactment of ERTA made sweeping changes in the rules for depreciating business property.[3] Both ERTA and the Tax Equity and Fiscal Responsibility Act of 1982 (TEFRA) made significant changes in the tax treatment of the type of financing lease transactions just described.[4]

ERTA's most radical change consists of the implementation of the Accelerated Cost Recovery System (ACRS) to replace the old useful-life depreciation rules.[5] Under ACRS, the concepts of useful life and salvage value play no part whatsoever. Instead, shorter recovery periods are specified for each type of property, more cost recovery being permitted in the earlier years. The entire cost of personal property (property other than real estate) will generally be recovered over either three or five years. Most business computers will probably have a five-year recovery period, but if the computer is used in connection with research and development, its cost can be recovered over a three-year period.[6] The user may elect to treat each class of property placed in service during a taxable year under either ACRS or under straight-line depreciation with a half-year convention for specified extended recovery periods. For example, if a user acquires a computer with a five-year recovery period for $10,000, the recovery deduction options would be as follows:

Recovery Year	ACRS[7]	Straight-Line 5-Year Period[8]	Straight-Line 12-Year Period[9]	Straight-Line 25-Year Period[10]
1	$ 1,500 (15%)	$ 1,000 (10%)	$ 416 (4.16%)	$ 200 (2%)
2	2,200 (22%)	2,000 (20%)	833 (8.33%)	400 (4%)
3	2,100 (21%)	2,000 (20%)	833 (8.33%)	400 (4%)
4	2,100 (21%)	2,000 (20%)	833 (8.33%)	400 (4%)
5	2,100 (21%)	2,000 (20%)	833 (8.33%)	400 (4%)
6		1,000 (10%)	833 (8.33%)	400 (4%)
.			.	.
.				
.				
12			833 (8.33%)	400 (4%)
13			416 (4.16%)	400 (4%)
.				.
.				
.				
25				400 (4%)
26				200 (2%)
Total Recovery	$10,000	$10,000	≈$10,000	$10,000

Provisions for recapture of cost recovery deductions for personal property remain essentially the same as for recovery for pre-ERTA depreciation. When an asset is sold before the end of its recovery period, if it is sold for more than its adjusted basis (cost minus cumulative cost recovery deductions), then the owner realizes a taxable gain on the sale.[11] Capital gains are taxed at a lower effective tax rate than ordinary income.[12] To the extent that the gain is realized from an asset's cost recovery (or depreciation) deductions, the gain is treated as ordinary income rather than as a capital gain.[13]

For example, suppose that the $10,000 computer in the previous example is sold by the owner after year 2 for $9,000. By this time, the owner has taken a total of $3,700 ($1,500 + $2,200) in cost recovery deductions. This leaves the owner with an adjusted basis of $6,300 in the computer (basis of $10,000 less deductions of $3,700). The owner, on sale of the computer, realizes a taxable gain of $2,700 ($9,000 − $6,300). The owner must determine whether all or part of this gain must be treated as ordinary income rather than as capital gain.

Section 1245 provides that the amount by which the lower of the amount realized or the "recomputed basis" (adjusted basis + recovery or depreciation deductions taken) exceeds the adjusted basis constitutes ordinary income rather than capital gain.[14] In our example, the amount realized is $9,000, which is lower than the recomputed basis of $10,000 ($6,300 + $3,700). Subtracting the adjusted basis of $6,300 from the amount realized of $9,000, we find that the entire gain of $2,700 will be taxed at ordinary income rates.

If the computer had been sold for $11,000 instead of $9,000, then the recomputed basis of $10,000 would be lower than the amount realized ($11,000). In that case, $3,700 ($10,000 − $6,300) of the total $4,700 gain would be treated as ordinary income with the remaining $1,000 gain treated as a capital gain.

Thus, if a computer owner plans to resell a computer in the future at a price substantially higher than its adjusted basis (which is more likely with the implementation of ACRS), the owner may consider the use of a straight-line depreciation method. The straight-line method, which renders smaller annual deductions in the asset's early years, will leave a higher adjusted basis at a given time. Use of the straight-line method will thus serve to avoid larger gains at ordinary income tax rates when disposing of the asset. The choice of which method will yield the best tax results will, of course, depend upon the particular valuation numbers and the plans of the computer user, so a qualified tax attorney or tax accountant should be consulted.

In addition to ACRS, ERTA brought about changes in the investment tax credit (ITC) that may be applied against the owner's taxes during the taxable year in which depreciable property is placed in service.[15] The owner is entitled to an ITC in the amount of 10 percent of the cost of five-year ACRS property or 6 percent of three-year property.[16] If, for example, our $10,000 computer is five-year ACRS property, the owner would be entitled to a $1,000 tax credit in the year of acquisition.

In terms of recapture of the ITC, if the asset is prematurely disposed of, the ITC is "earned" at the rate of 2 percent per year.[17] Thus, if five-year property is disposed of after three years, only 4 percent of the 10 percent ITC is recaptured since 6 percent has been earned. Continuing with our example, if the $10,000 computer were sold at the end of three years, only $400 (4 percent of $10,000) would have to be treated as recaptured ITC. Since the ITC was used to offset the taxes payable in the year of acquisition, this $400 when recaptured must be added to the taxpayer's taxes.

After ERTA, the ACRS plus ITC could have resulted in greater tax benefits than if the asset had been expensed in the year of acquisition.[18] As a result, Congress now requires through TEFRA that the basis of assets must be reduced by one-half of the investment tax credit.[19] Thus, in our example, if a $1,000 investment tax credit is taken, the basis in the computer would have to be reduced by $500 to $9,500. This reduced basis would be used to calculate ACRS deductions and gain or loss upon disposition. If ITC recapture applies, the basis of the property would be increased by one-half of the ITC recapture. The owner can avoid the reduction in basis requirement by electing instead to reduce its ITC by two percentage points, that is, by taking an ITC of only $800 (10 percent − 2 percent = 8 percent × the basis of $10,000) in our example.[20]

In addition, ERTA instituted some "at-risk" rules. Under ERTA, the owner may not deduct losses unless the capital investment risk falls on the owner.[21] If the owner is not personally liable, such as when the asset is merely collateral for a nonrecourse debt with no personal liability on the owner, the owner is not permitted to deduct the losses. The same rule exists with regard to the ITC but subject to a significant exception.[22] If an amount equal to at least 20 percent of the basis (unadjusted for recovery deductions) is at risk and the asset is acquired from a party unrelated to the lender, nonrecourse financing from government agencies, certain unrelated financial institutions, insurance companies, or qualifying pension trusts are treated as at risk capital for ITC purposes.[23]

Both ERTA and TEFRA made substantial changes in the tax treatment of leases used to finance capital assets.[24] Congress recognized the usefulness of lease transactions as a vehicle for distressed businesses to pass ACRS deductions and the ITC on to parties with sufficient tax liability to take full advantage of them. ERTA replaced the IRS's earlier guidelines about whether a lease was really a lease with much more liberal "safe harbor" rules, which, if satisfied, would entitle the lease to tax treatment as a true lease regardless of other factors that might indicate it is really a sale.[25] TEFRA, however, made drastic cutbacks in the advantages and applicability of safe harbor leases and repealed the safe harbor leasing rules altogether for property placed in service after December 31, 1983.[26]

TEFRA did, however, create a new category of leases called "finance leases."[27] Finance leases are leases such as the pre-ERTA leases described earlier, which appear to be bona fide leases in every regard except that the lessee has the option to purchase the leased property at the end of the lease for at least 10 percent of the property's original cost, or the property leased is "limited use" property, which can be used only by the lessee (for example, a computer system tailored to the user's needs).[28] Many of ERTA's safe harbor restrictions were preserved by TEFRA as prerequisites for finance lease tax treatment. The effect of TEFRA's finance lease provisions, effective for leases entered into after December 31, 1983, will probably be to further encourage the use of leasing arrangements by computer users. These provisions should be especially helpful to computer users who do not show sufficient taxable income to take full advantage of cost recovery deductions and the ITC for newly acquired computer systems, since the finance leasing rules permit the user to effectively sell the tax advantages of capital asset ownership to financers and investors within prescribed limitations.

Yet another way in which ERTA benefited the acquirer of a computer system is by offering the buyer of depreciable property the option of "bonus depreciation" during the asset's first year.[29] During 1983, Section 179 entitled the user to expense up to $5,000 of the cost of any property acquired for use in a business that is eligible for the ITC. The limit increases in 1984 to $7,500 and to $10,000 beginning in 1986. No investment tax credit is permitted to be taken for the expensed portion, however. Thus, the user should make the decision of whether to take the expensing option only after weighing the benefits of the extra first-year depreciation against the ITC that must be foregone.

Federal Taxation and Software

In contrast to the relatively routine tax procedures of computer hardware, the taxation of software presents several interesting treatments by the IRS.

Before 1968, the IRS simply allowed the taxpayer to determine the tax treatment of the firm's software (that is, expense when incurred or capitalize and amortize over time).[30] As previously mentioned, the question of whether an item can be expensed and fully deducted immediately or must be capitalized and amortized over a longer period can affect the cash flow of a company. Generally, by expensing and deducting an item immediately, a company needs to generate significantly less cash (new money) each year to pay its creditors than if the company capitalizes and amortizes the item.[31]

In 1969, the New York regional office of the IRS issued a ruling indicating that software should be capitalized, and because it is intangible, no investment tax credit would be allowable.[32] The ruling by the New York regional office of the IRS opened the floodgates for inquiries about the proper tax treatment of software, to which the IRS responded by issuing Revenue Procedure 69-21.[33]

This revenue procedure provides guidelines for the tax treatment of computer software costs. The revenue procedure sets out a definition of software that includes "all programs or routines used to cause a computer to perform a desired task or set of tasks, and the documentation required to describe and maintain those programs." Procedure 69-21 goes on to set out the IRS's treatment of the costs of *developing software, purchasing software,* and *leasing software.*

The tax treatment of the costs of purchased software depends on whether the software is part of a bundled system whose software costs are included in the entire computer system's cost and not separately identified. In a bundled situation, Revenue Procedure 69-21 requires that the software be treated as part of the hardware whereas in an unbundled system the software is considered an intangible asset.

Generally, there are three possible tax treatments for computer software. First, the owner can elect to expense the cost of developing software and therefore deduct its cost as a current expense under Section 174, research or experimental expenditures.[34] Because the development of software is comparable to research and development in its "intellectual property" aspect, the IRS would allow this type of tax treatment. The research and development deduction may not be available, however, when the user contracts to have the software designed by an outside software firm if the user does not bear the risk of the development.[35] For example, if the software firm guarantees a specific result, the user may be forced to capitalize the expenses as a cost of acquiring the software. Second, if the software is purchased separately from the hardware and used in research and development, the software may be treated as an *intangible* asset and eligible for amortization under Section 174[36] and perhaps a tax credit of up to 25 percent under Section 44F, which provides a tax credit for certain increases in research expenses.[37] Third, the software may be capitalized ratably over a period of five years or less.

It should be noted that Revenue Procedure 69-21 requires software, when capitalized, to be amortized on a straight-line basis.[38] The word *ratable* in the procedure lends support to this requirement. The declining balance or sum-of-the-years-digits method of amortization, although more beneficial, cannot be utilized. If an organization is expensing software development costs and then acquires a new computer, Revenue Ruling 71-248 requires the organization to get clearance from the IRS if it plans to treat the expense of software development differently from in the past, that is, to capitalize.[39]

Revenue Procedure 69-21 treats the leasing of software under the income tax regulations for rental.[40] In this case, the taxpayer deducts the lease payments against income under Section 162 as a business expense.[41] It must be noted, however, that like hardware, some software leasing arrangements may be treated as conditional sales (purchase) agreements and subjected to the relevant tax treatments discussed for the purchase of software.[42] An example of a lease agreement that may be considered a purchase would be one whose rental costs are essentially installment payments or where an option to buy the system is included in the agreement.

The previous material dealing with the federal taxation of computer hardware and software is merely a summary of a few of the ways the IRS treats this area. Consultations with a tax lawyer or an accountant specializing in federal taxation should be a prerequisite to decisions involving computer transactions in hardware or software.

STATE AND LOCAL TAXATION

State and local taxation of computer systems presents some interesting situations for computer users. Some of these situations arise in the context of personal property taxes, sales taxes, and use taxes. Since most contracts for the use of data-processing systems contain clauses that pass on all taxes to the user, this is an important area to understand before procuring a system.

State and local taxation of hardware, like federal taxation, is subject to basically the same treatment as other tangible personal property (for example, office equipment). Problems arise in the area of local taxation of software as a result of unbundling. The following material focuses entirely on state and local taxation of software, although it is essential to note that state tax laws will vary considerably and only generalizations are possible here.

State and local taxation of software has spawned considerable litigation. Assessors have claimed software to be tangible, thus taxable. Users have claimed it to be intangible, thus nontaxable. The tangibility issue and others are examined here in an effort to communicate the important distinctions in this troublesome area.

Personal Property Taxes

Personal property taxation is the taxation of personal, as distinguished from real (such as real estate), property. This discussion is limited to the personal property taxation of computer software and will not examine the methods of calculating value of goods for the purposes of personal property taxes.

Generally, most jurisdictions tax tangible personal property (that is, goods) but do not tax intangible personal property (that is, contract rights, copyrights, patents, and so on). It is this dichotomy of tangible versus intangible that has given rise to taxpayer claims that software is intangible and assessors responding that software is tangible.[43] The assessors base their claim on the fact that software is contained on tangible tapes or cards with monetary value.

Since the use of software is continuing to grow at an enormous rate, it is essential that this dilemma be resolved. The legal community may react in three ways. First, some courts have found software to be a type of intellectual property analogous to television rights, literary works, and photographic reproductions. This analogy leads to a determination that software may be intangible and hence not subject to personal property taxes.[44]

The second way has been for courts to hold that software existing on tangible magnetic tapes or punched cards is essentially tangible personal property, thus taxable.[45] The court's analogy in this situation is that a privately commissioned recording with no restrictions on use would have a value more than that of the blank record or tape and should be subject to taxation at its full cash value as tangible personal property.

The third way to handle the tangible versus intangible dilemma is through legislation. California, for example, has designed tax legislation and regulations to deal specifically with computer programs. The California Tax Code basically taxes as personal property the storage media consisting of cards, tapes, and disks that contain the control or basic operational programs (system software).[46] Other software programs (such as application programs) are not taxed.[47] This type of legislation does away with the necessity of defining software as tangible or intangible and instead focuses on what the programs do. Many authorities believe the California legislation should serve as a model for other states to follow in this area. The California code also deals with sales and use taxes on software.

Sales and Use Tax

Whether software is subjected to sales and use taxes hinges on basically the same tangibility criteria as in the property tax situation.[48] Some courts hold that software is not taxable.[49] They suggest that software is intellectual property or services or that it is exempt under state statutes because the software was used in the production of a product.

Some courts have held computer printouts to be tangible items, thus taxable, and others have held the printout to represent a service, thus not subject to state sales tax. This distinction may have important implications for service bureaus. A service bureau is an independent business that supplies data-processing services to others. The transactions between the bureau and its customers must be analyzed carefully to determine what part (if any) is subject to sales tax based on taxing tangible personal property. Some transactions are in the middle of the road, partially taxable as a sale of goods and partially not taxable as a sale of services. Generally, if analysis is done on data, the costs of the analysis may not be taxable. On the other hand, if the transaction merely rearranges and lists data, it will probably be subject to sales tax.[50]

COURT CASES

For a more complete understanding of the property, sales, and use tax treatment of software, it is helpful to consider the following cases.

District of Columbia v. Universal Computer Associates, Inc.[51] Universal purchased from IBM a data-processing unit for $289,836. Included in the sale were the hardware and two sets of punched cards. One set of cards was the standard software program developed by IBM for this particular system. The other set of cards was a special tax program developed by both IBM and Universal personnel. Of the total purchase price, $106,000 was estimated to be the cost of the special tax program. IBM retained title to the standard program, and Universal obtained title to the special tax program. The court concluded that the issue to be decided in this case was whether the two sets of punched cards (the software) represented tangible personal property taxable under personal property tax or whether they represented intangible values not subject to tax.

The court held the software to be intangible property not subject to personal property tax and "that the material of which the punched cards themselves were made was of insignificant value and that it was for the intangible value of the information stored on the cards that the taxpayer had paid IBM." What eventually ends up in the machine is an intangible knowledge, which is not subject to personal property tax. The court analogized computer software with cartoon mats from another case in which the court said that the mats were just the means of selling the services of the artist and not tangible personal property.

Because this system was sold as a bundled system (prior to IBM's 1969 policy of unbundling), the court was also required to determine what portion of the system consisted of hardware (taxable) and software (nontaxable). The court held that the hardware could not represent more than 50 percent of the total system's value, thus upholding the lower court's 50-percent-to-50-percent allocation to hardware and software.

It should be noted that this case came to the United States Court of Appeals, District of Columbia Circuit from the District of Columbia Tax Court. This is significant because the law decided by the particular case only has substantial weight or authority in the District of Columbia. The relative weight of authority of this case in other jurisdictions (states), however, can be estimated only according to that jurisdiction's case law. The case, because decided in the federal court (U.S. Court of Appeals), can be used as a basis for persuasive arguments in other cases in other jurisdictions.

This case does lend significant support to the position that software represents intangible items not subject to personal property taxes. As will be seen in later cases, this case also supports the intangibility of software arguments in sales and use tax situations.

This case also purports to show the relative values of software and hardware to a computer system. Because antitrust law requires that most systems sold today be priced separately for the hardware and software in the procurement agreement, this case can add leverage to the purchaser's insistence that, at most, only 50 percent of the total purchase price should be for the hardware. This may become significant in a situation where the manufacturer or supplier in the procurement agreement lists $70,000 for hardware and $30,000 for software of the total package price of $100,000. In essence, the user will end up paying personal property taxes as well as possibly sales and use taxes on $70,000 because hardware is definitely a tangible item. However, a user relying on this case who successfully allocates half of the price to software in the purchase contract may have to pay taxes only on tangible items of at most 50 percent of the total package price or, as in the example, on $50,000.

Honeywell Information Systems, Inc. v. Maricopa County.[52] The Maricopa County assessor, in assessing the value of computer equipment (held by Honeywell) for personal property taxation, included certain software items in the value. Honeywell paid the taxes under protest, then litigated a series of appeals, first to the State Board of Property Tax Appeals where Honeywell lost, then to the superior court where Honeywell lost again. The issue brought by Honeywell to the Arizona Court of Appeals was whether the value of intangible services such as classroom education, systems support engineeering services, and computer programs, all together called "software," can be included in the overall valuation of 39 pieces of hardware for personal property tax purposes.

The court in this case merely relied on other cases in other jurisdictions, including the previously discussed *District of Columbia v. Universal Computer Associates, Inc.* case, in concluding that software is intangible, thus not subject to a personal property tax. The court relied on Honeywell's estimates that 24.4 percent of the bundled catalog list price was attributable to intangible software services and that the assessor overtaxed Honeywell by that percentage.

The most significant impact of this decision on the computer industry is that it clearly supports the argument that software should be considered intangible, especially in the area of personal property tax.

Greyhound Computer Corp. v. State Department of Assessments and Taxation.[53] In this case, the State Department of Assessments and Taxation assessed four computer systems owned by Greyhound and leased to Bendix Corporation at $1,501,350. The tax court affirmed the assessment, and Greyhound appealed the assessment to the Maryland Court of Appeals. The issue was the extent to which computer software that had been bundled in the cost of the computers purchased by Greyhound from IBM and leased to others is tangible personal property subject to personal property tax.

The lower court noted that hardware is inoperable without the software that is part of the package and that Greyhound did not separately record the values on its books. Therefore, it could not ascertain how much of the purchase price was attributable to tangible items or intangible services. The appellate court held, however, that these costs can be ascertained and separated in some situations, citing California's property tax statute distinguishing between operational and applications software for property tax purposes. Therefore, the court returned the case to the tax court to allow Greyhound to demonstrate which items included in the bundled system's value are tangible and which are intangible.

This case illustrates that some lower courts, if not presented with clear evidence of intangibility of the software at issue, will deem it tangible and thus subject to personal property tax. This case emphasizes the importance of separating the costs of hardware and software in all transactions.

State v. Central Computer Services, Inc.[54] Central Computer Services purchased from University Computing Company a 99-year license for the use of eight programs. The programs were stored on a set of magnetic tapes and punched cards. The programs were used to program Central's computer, which provided data-processing services to several banks. The programs were transfered from the magnetic tapes and punched cards to magnetic disks owned by Central. The cards were then thrown away and the tapes returned to University Computing Company.

Alabama's Department of Revenue sought to impose a use tax assessment of $13,519.91 on Central's transaction for the eight programs.

Central appealed the assessment, claiming that the transaction involved acquiring intangible information and knowledge and not the tangible tapes and cards. The state claimed that since the tapes and cards were tangible and since they were such an important part of the transaction, the transaction should be regarded as involving tangible personal property subject to the use tax.

The trial court as well as the court of civil appeals agreed that the transaction involved intangible software, thus exempting it from the use tax. The Supreme Court of Alabama decided the issue was the same as in the lower courts: whether computer software is tangible personal property subject to state use tax. The court decided, as did the lower courts, that the computer software consisted of intangible personal property exempt from the state use tax. The court reasoned that the programs could have been brought into the state in the mind of an operator or telephoned into Central's computer. The transfer of tangible property (tapes and cards) was deemed to be merely incidental to the purchase of the intangible knowledge stored on that property.

The impact of this case on the computer industry is essentially the same as the previously discussed cases holding software to be intangible for personal property taxation; that is, it adds to the general overall argument that software consists of intangible intellectual material, exempting it from certain taxes on tangible personal property. Here again, the case was decided in a state court, the Supreme Court of Alabama; therefore, it has its greatest authority in Alabama. It should be noted, however, that it adds significantly to the argument for software intangibility in other jurisdictions as well.

The court in this case relied on the previously discussed case, *District of Columbia v. Universal Computer Associates, Inc.*, as well as a Tennessee case, *Commerce Union Bank v. Tidwell.*[55] The Tennessee Supreme Court reasoned as did the Alabama Supreme Court that since the transfer of magnetic tapes or punch cards is incidental to the transaction for the intangible knowledge on the tapes and cards, they are not subject to state sales and use taxes on tangible personal property. Another case from the Supreme Court of Texas, *Bullock v. Statistical Tabulating*,[56] essentially decided the same.

These cases indicate a definite willingness of several state courts as well as a few federal courts to accept the notion that computer software is an intangible item and thus exempt from ad valorem property taxes and sales and use taxes. A user acquiring a computer system should be aware of these tax consequences as they can save an organization a lot of money. It should be noted, however, that the particular statutes and case law of the user's state should be examined for that state's position on the tangibility status of computer software. In addition, merely because some taxpayers have fought and won in court does not mean that all will.

Another sometimes troublesome aspect of sales and use taxes is the treatment of transactions involving computer printouts. Some of the cases decided in this area are examined briefly here.

Accountants Computer Services, Inc. v. Kosydar.[57] This case seems to offer a reasonable explanation as to how the courts (Ohio courts in this case) will review the transactions for sales tax purposes of service bureaus providing customers with computer printouts. The *ACS* case involved three data-processing companies' appeals of sales tax assessments on their work. All three claimed that their work, including the printouts, consisted of intangible personal services, which are excepted from the state sales tax.

The court in deciding the *ACS* case presented a "real-object" test for analyzing transactions involving computer printouts. If the object sought by the buyer was a service, the sales tax would not be applied. If the object sought was the tangible object, however, tax would be applicable to the entire price without any deduction for the service portion.

The *ACS* case with its companions serve as prime examples of how the real-object test will be applied. In situations in which a service bureau collects the raw data from its customers, transcribes the raw data onto punched cards, then sorts, classifies, and rearranges the data with its computer to *provide the customer with a computer printout for that customer's business analysis*, the real object of the transaction was found to be the tangible computer printout. Thus, it will be subject to sales tax.

Four other cases, *Citizens Financial Corp. v. Kosydar*[58], *Lindner Brothers, Inc. v. Kosydar*[59], *Miami Citizens National Bank and Trust Co. v. Lindley*[60], and *Statistical Tabulating Corp. v. Lindley*[61], applied the real-object test set out in the ACS case in deciding that since the transactions' true objectives were for the tangible computer printouts, they were subject to sales tax.

In a situation where a service bureau obtains information from a customer to make a printout to aid the service bureau's professional personnel in analyzing and solving business problems *for the customer*, the real object of the transaction would appear to be the services rendered. The printout could be viewed as merely an inconsequential element of the transaction, thus excepting the costs of the transaction from sales tax.

IMPLICATIONS FOR ACTION

This section briefly summarizes important factors to consider when confronted with a question about the taxation of a computer system.

Computer hardware is treated, for tax purposes, just like any other tangible personal property (for example, typewriters) and is subject to the applicable rules for depreciation, cost recovery, and investment credit. Much thought should be given to tax treatment of pending computer purchases, emphasizing the impact on the company's financial and tax structure.

Computer software for federal tax purposes is controlled by IRS Revenue Ruling 69-21. Again, tax options are a critical topic for consideration in the procurement stages.

State and local taxation of computer systems is a much litigated area; therefore it is important before procuring a system to be well versed in or advised of the status of the statutes and case law in the particular jurisdiction. This will enable the user both to prevent problems or litigation and to save cash by averting an overly zealous tax assessment, especially for computer software. Apportionment of the sales contract purchase price between hardware operations and applications software may be critical.

Service bureau transactions present unique situations for tax assessors, especially involving computer printouts. The way in which an agreement is drafted, for example, with emphasis on either the goods or services aspect of the transaction, may determine its tax status. A review of how tax assessors treat these kinds of transactions may save tax dollars.

REFERENCES

1. IRC 167 (1976 & Supp. III 1979), *amended by* 26 USC 167 (Supp. V 1981).

2. *See, e.g.,* Rev. Rul. 60-122, 1960-1 C.B. 56.

3. *See* Arthur Young & Co., *Economic Recovery Tax Act of 1981, An Analysis of the New Legislation* 15–22 (1981) [hereinafter cited as *Arthur Young, ERTA*].

4. *See id.,* at 26–29; Arthur Young & Co., *Tax Equity and Fiscal Responsibility Act of 1982, An Analysis of the New Legislation and Related Tax Planning Opportunities* 15–17 (1982) [hereinafter cited as *Arthur Young, TEFRA*].

5. IRC 168 (Supp. V 1981), *amended by* Tax Equity and Fiscal Responsibility Act of 1982 (TEFRA), Pub. L. No. 97-248, 1982 U.S. Code Cong. & Ad. News (96 Stat.) 324.

6. IRC 168(c)(2)(A), (B) (Supp. V 1981).

7. IRC 168(b)(1)(A) (Supp. V 1981).

8. IRC 168(b)(3) (Supp. V 1981).

9. *Id.*

10. *Id.*

11. IRC 1001(a) (1976).

12. IRC 1201, 1202 (1976 & Supp. V 1981).

13. IRC 1245 (1976 & Supp. V 1981).

14. *Id.*

15. *Arthur Young, ERTA, supra* note 3, at 23–25.

16. IRC 38(1976), 46 (1976 & Supp. V 1981), *amended by* TEFRA, Pub. L. No. 97-248, 1982 U.S. Code Cong. & Ad. News (96 Stat.) 324.

17. 26 USC 47 (1976 & Supp. V 1981).

18. *Arthur Young, TEFRA, supra* note 4, at 12–13.

19. TEFRA, Pub. L. No. 97-248, 205, 1982 U.S. Code Cong. & Ad. News (96 Stat.) 324, 427–31.

20. *Id.*

21. IRC 465 (1976 & Supp. V 1981).

22. IRC 46(c)(8) (Supp. V 1981).

23. IRC 46(c)(8)(B)(ii), (c)(8)(D) (Supp. V 1981).

24. *Arthur Young, ERTA, supra* note 3, at 26–29; *Arthur Young, TEFRA, supra* note 4, at 15–17.

25. IRC 168(f)(8) (Supp. V 1981).

26. TEFRA, Pub. L. No. 97-248, 208, 1982 U.S. Code Cong. & Ad. News (96 Stat.) 324, 432–42; *Arthur Young, TEFRA, supra* note 4, at 15–17.

27. TEFRA, Pub. L. No. 97-248, 209, 1982 U.S. Code Cong. & Ad. News (96 Stat.) 324, 442–47; *Arthur Young, TEFRA, supra* note 4, at 17.

28. *Arthur Young, TEFRA, supra* note 4, at 17.

29. IRC 179 (Supp. V 1981); *Arthur Young, ERTA, supra* note 3, at 19–20.

30. R. Bigelow, *Federal Software Taxation,* CLS 2-3.2, art. 1 (R. Bigelow, ed., 1979).

31. *Id.,* at 2-5.

32. *Id.,* at 2; 6 CLSR 1087 (1969) (Memorandum to revenue agents).

33. Rev. Proc. 69-21, 1969-2 C.B. 303.

34. IRC 174 (1976); Rev. Proc. 69-21, 1969-2 C.B. 303; Battaglia & Herskovitz, "Organizing a Computer Software Research & Development Program for Top Tax Advantage," 58 J. Tax'n 92 (1983).

35. Battaglia & Herskovitz, *supra* note 34, at 92–94.

36. Rev. Proc. 69-21, 1969-2 C.B. 303.

37. 26 USC 44F (Supp. V 1981).

38. Rev. Proc. 69-21, 1969-2 C.B. 303; Bigelow, *supra* note 30, at 6.

39. Rev. Rul. 71-248, 1971-1 C.B. 55.

40. *See* Treas. Reg. 1.162-11 (1960).

41. IRC 162 (1976).

42. Rev. Rul. 60-122, 1960-1 C.B. 56.

43. *See generally, e.g.,* Bryant & Mather, "Property Taxation of Computer Software," 18 N.Y.L.F. 59 (1972); Heinzman, "Computer Software: Should it be Treated as Tangible Property for Ad Valorem Tax?" 37 J. Tax'n 184 (1972); Rosen, "Computer Software Classed as Intangible Property Is Exempt from State Property Taxes," 58 J. Tax'n 114 (1983); Tunick, "State and Local Taxation of Computer Goods and Services," CLS 2-3.2, art. 3, (R. Bigelow, ed. 1979); Note, "The Revolt Against the Property Tax on Software: An Unnecessary Conflict Growing Out of Unbundling," 9 Suffolk U.L. Rev. 118 (1974); Annot., 82 A.L.R.3d 606 (1978).

44. *See* District of Columbia v. Universal Computer Associates, Inc., 465 F.2d 615 (D.C. Cir. 1972); Honeywell Information Systems, Inc. v. Maricopa County, 118 Ariz. 171, 575 P.2d 801 (Ct. App. 1977); Honeywell Information Systems, Inc. v. Board of Assessment Appeals, 7 CLSR 486 (Colo. Dist. Ct. 1975).

45. *See* County of Sacramento v. Assessment Appeals Board No. 2 *ex rel.* RCA Corp., 32 Cal.App.3d 654, 108 Cal.Rptr. 434 (1973).

46. Calif. Rev. Tax Code, 995, 995.1, 995.2.

47. *Id. See also* Greyhound Computer Corp. v. State Department of Assessments and Taxation, 271 Md. 674, 320 A.2d 52 (1974).

48. *See generally* Tunick, *supra* note 43, at 8–10; Annot., 91 A.L.R.3d 282 (1979).

49. *See* State v. Central Computer Services, Inc., 349 So.2d 1156 (Ala. Civ. App. 1977), *aff'd* 349 So.2d 1160 (Ala. 1977); Commerce Union Bank v. Tidwell, 538 S.W.2d 405 (Tenn. 1976).

50. *See* Accountants Computer Services, Inc. v. Kosydar, 35 Ohio St.2d 120, 298 N.E.2d 519 (1973); Citizens Financial Corp. v. Kosydar, 43 Ohio St.2d 148, 331 N.E.2d 435 (1975); Lindner Brothers, Inc. v. Kosydar, 46 Ohio St.2d 162, 346 N.E.2d 690 (1976); Miami Citizens National Bank and Trust Co. v. Lindley, 50 Ohio St.2d 249, 364 N.E.2d 25 (1977); Statistical Tabulating Corp. v. Lindley, 3 Ohio St.3d 23, 445 N.E.2d 1104 (1983).

51. 465 F.2d 615 (D.C. Cir. 1972).

52. 118 Ariz. 171, 575 P.2d 801 (Ct. App. 1977).

53. 271 Md. 674, 320 A.2d 52 (1974).

54. 349 So.2d 1156 (Ala. Civ. App. 1977), *aff'd* 349 So.2d 1160 (Ala. 1977).

55. 538 S.W.2d 405 (Tenn. 1976).

56. 549 S.W.2d 166 (Tex. 1977).

57. 35 Ohio St.2d 120, 298 N.E.2d 519 (1973).

58. 43 Ohio St.2d 148, 331 N.E.2d 435 (1975).

59. 46 Ohio St.2d 162, 346 N.E.2d 690 (1976).

60. 50 Ohio St.2d 249, 364 N.E.2d 25 (1977).

61. 3 Ohio St.3d 23, 445 N.E.2d 1104 (1983).

Case Supplement

The following table lists recent cases which illustrate the concepts discussed in the text. The outline of this table corresponds to the outline of the text. To find cases which relate to the textual discussion of a topic, simply locate the topic on the outline. Related cases will be listed under that heading.

Edited opinions are provided in the pages following the table. If a case relates to more than one outline topic, cross-references list the case under each appropriate heading. Boldface type indicates the actual opinion entry. Ordinary type indicates a cross-reference to the outline topic under which the actual opinion entry will be found.

An alphabetical index of the cases included in this section or discussed in the previous text follows the last opinion.

PART I:
Acquiring Computer Hardware and Software: Contracting

Diversified Environments, Inc. v. Olivetti Corp. of America, 461 F. Supp. 286 (M.D. Pa. 1978). (See Part I, II.A, Leasing Hardware.)

Schatz Distributing Co. v. Olivetti Corp. of America, 7 Kan.App.2d 676, 647 P.2d 820 (1982). (See Part II, III.B.11, Damages.)

Office Supply Co. v. Basic/Four Corp., 538 F. Supp. 776 (E.D. Wis. 1982). (See Part I, V.B, Negotiating with Sales Personnel.)

Westfield Chemical Corp. v. Burroughs Corp., 6 CLSR 438, 21 UCC Rep. 1293 (Mass. Super. Ct. of Hampden County 1977). (See Part I, IV.E, The Parol Evidence Rule.)

APLications Inc. v. Hewlett-Packard Co., 501 F. Supp. 129 (S.D. N.Y. 1980), aff'd 672 F.2d 1076 (2d Cir. 1982). (See Part II, III.A.2, Misrepresentation.)

G. Implied Warranties

APLications Inc. v. Hewlett-Packard Co., 501 F. Supp. 129 (S.D. N.Y. 1980), aff'd 672 F.2d 1076 (2d Cir. 1982). (See Part II, III.A.2, Misrepresentation.)

Office Supply Co. v. Basic/Four Corp., 538 F. Supp. 776 (E.D. Wis. 1982). (See Part I, V.B, Negotiating with Sales Personnel.)

Uniflex, Inc. v. Olivetti Corp. of America, 86 A.D.2d 538, 445 N.Y.S.2d 993 (1982). (See Part I, II.A, Leasing Hardware.)

Earman Oil Co. v. Burroughs Corp., 625 F.2d 1291 (5th Cir. 1980). (See Part I, IV.A.2, Sales or Transactions.)

Kalil Bottling Co. v. Burroughs Corp., 127 Ariz. 278, 619 P.2d 1055 (Ct. App. 1980). (See Part I, IV.A.2, Sales or Transactions.)

1. Implied Warranty of Merchantability
2. Implied Warranty of Fitness for a Particular Purpose

Westfield Chemical Corp. v. Burroughs Corp., 6 CLSR 438, 21 UCC Rep. 1293 (Mass. Super. Ct. of Hampden County 1977). (See Part I, IV.E, The Parol Evidence Rule.)

Schatz Distributing Co. v. Olivetti Corp. of America, 7 Kan.App.2d 676, 647 P.2d 820 (1982). (See Part II, III.B.11, Damages.)

Chatlos Systems, Inc. v. National Cash Register Corp., 479 F. Supp. 738 (D. N.J. 1979), aff'd in part, remanded in part 635 F.2d 1081 (3d Cir. 1980), remand aff'd 670 F.2d 1304 (3d Cir. 1982), cert. dismissed 102 S.Ct. 2918 (1982). (See Part II, III.B.9, Failure of Essential Purpose.)

Sperry Rand Corp. v. Industrial Supply Corp., 337 F.2d 363 (5th Cir. 1964).   358

H. Remedies of Rejection and Revocation of Acceptance

Sperry Rand Corp. v. Industrial Supply Corp., 337 F.2d 363 (5th Cir. 1964). (See Part I, IV.G.2, Implied Warranty of Fitness for a Particular Purpose.)

Carl Beasley Ford, Inc. v. Burroughs Corp., 361 F. Supp. 325 (E.D. Pa. 1973), aff'd 493 F.2d 1400 (3d Cir. 1974). (See Part II, III.B.1 Rights of Inspection and Rejection.)

PART II:
Computer Systems Failures: Remedies

PART III:
Personnel, Consulting Services, and Facilities Management

PART IV:
Writing Computer Programs For Sale

PART V:
Computer Crime and Privacy

PART VI:
Systems Design Considerations

Memphis Light, Gas & Water Division v. Craft, 436 U.S. 1 (1978).   881

Annbar Associates v. American Express Co., 565 S.W.2d 701 (Mo. Ct. App. 1978). (See Part III, III.A.1, Flexibility and Control.)

Bank Leumi Trust Co. of New York v. Bank of Mid-Jersey, 499 F. Supp. 1022 (D. N.J. 1980). (See Part VI, III.C, Banking Law.)

FJS Electronics, Inc. v. Fidelity Bank, 288 Pa.Super. 138, 431 A.2d 326 (1981). (See Part VI, III.C, Banking Law.)

First Wyoming Bank, N.A. v. Cabinet Craft Distributors, Inc., 624 P.2d 227 (Wyo. 1981). (See Part VI, III.C, Banking Law.)

Ferreira v. Quik Stop Markets, Inc., 141 Cal.App.3d 1023, 190 Cal.Rptr. 778 (1983). (See Part VI, III.B, Contract.)

In re **Daleview Nursing Home v. Axelrod, 91 A.D.2d 1161, 458 N.Y.S.2d 739 (1983).**   885

D.   Other Foreseeable Parties

Testa v. Winquist, 451 F. Supp. 388 (D. R.I. 1978). (See Part V, III.B.1.b, Law Enforcement.)

Holdsclaw v. Warren and Brewster, 45 Or.App. 153, 607 P.2d 1208 (1980). (See Part IV, II.B.3, Strict Liability.)

Sirota v. Solitron Devices, Inc., 673 F.2d 566 (2d Cir. 1982). (See Part VI, III.H, Securities Law.)

Torres v. North American Van Lines, Inc., 135 Ariz. 35, 658 P.2d 835 (Ct. App. 1982). (See Part VI, III.A.1, Negligence.)

City of Chicago v. Roppolo, 113 Ill.App.3d 602, 447 N.E.2d 870 (1983).   886

Glen Eden Hospital, Inc. v. Blue Cross and Blue Shield of Michigan, 555 F. Supp. 337 (E.D. Mich. 1983). (See Part VI, III.G, Antitrust Law.)

E.   Government Obligations

Sirota v. Solitron Devices, Inc., 673 F.2d 566 (2d Cir. 1982). (See Part VI, III.H, Securities Law.)

Glen Eden Hospital, Inc. v. Blue Cross and Blue Shield of Michigan, 555 F. Supp. 337 (E.D. Mich. 1983). (See Part VI, III.G, Antitrust Law.)

III.   FORMS OF LIABILITY
A.   Tort Liability
1.   Negligence

State v. Firestone Bank, 46 Ohio App.2d 124, 346 N.E.2d 326, 5 CLSR 1318 (1975). (See Part VI, III.C, Banking Law.)

Pompeii Estates, Inc. v. Consolidated Edison Co. of New York, 91 Misc.2d 233, 397 N.Y.S.2d 577, 7 CLSR 518 (N.Y. Civ. Ct. 1977).   897

Testa v. Winquist, 451 F. Supp. 388 (D. R.I. 1978). (See Part V, III.B.1.b, Law Enforcement.)

Annbar Associates v. American Express Co., 565 S.W.2d 701

PART VII:
Computer Records In Court

United States v. Russo, 480 F.2d 1228 (6th Cir. 1973).   982

Rogers v. Frank Lyon Co., 253 Ark. 856, 489 S.W.2d 506 (1973).   991

State v. Springer, 283 N.C. 627, 197 S.E.2d 530 (1973). (See Part VII, II.A.1.b, Foundation.)

Department of Mental Health for Use of People v. Beil, 44 Ill.App.3d 402, 357 N.E.2d 875 (1976). (See Part VII, II.A.1.b, Foundation.)

Sears, Roebuck & Co. v. Merla, 142 N.J.Super. 205, 361 A.2d 68 (1976). (See Part VII, II.A.1.b, Foundation.)

Gassett v. State, 532 S.W.2d 328 (Tex. Crim. App. 1976). (See Part VII, II.A.1.b, Foundation.)

Barney v. Cox, 588 P.2d 696 (Utah 1978).   993

Brandon v. State, 272 Ind. 92, 396 N.E.2d 365 (1979).   994

United States v. Vela, 673 F.2d 86 (5th Cir. 1982). (See Part VII, II.A.1.b, Foundation.)

State v. Corrales, 135 Ariz. 105, 659 P.2d 658 (Ct. App. 1982).   996

Anzalone v. State Farm Mutual Insurance Co., 92 A.D.2d 238, 459 N.Y.S.2d 850 (1983). (See Part VII, II.A.1.a, Relevance.)

In re West, 60 N.C.App. 388, 299 S.E.2d 245 (1983). (See Part VII, II.A.1.b, Foundation.)

***In re* Finkelstein, 458 A.2d 326 (Pa. Commw. Ct. 1983).**   996

d.   Best Evidence Rule

United States v. De Georgia, 420 F.2d 889 (9th Cir. 1969). (See Part VII, II.A.1.c, Hearsay Evidence Rule.)

King v. State *ex rel.* Murdock Acceptance Corp., 222 So.2d 393 (Miss. 1969).   997

State v. Springer, 283 N.C. 627, 197 S.E.2d 530 (1973). (See Part VII, II.A.1.b, Foundation.)

Gassett v. State, 532 S.W.2d 328 (Tex. Crim. App. 1976). (See Part VII, II.A.1.b, Foundation.)

Barney v. Cox, 588 P.2d 696 (Utah 1978). (See Part VII, II.A.1.c, Hearsay Evidence Rule.)

Anzalone v. State Farm Mutual Insurance Co., 92 A.D.2d 238, 459 N.Y.S.2d 850 (1983). (See Part VII, II.A.1.a, Relevance.)

2.   Statute of Frauds
(See Part I.IV.D, Statute of Frauds.)

3.   Credibility

King v. State *ex rel.* Murdock Acceptance Corp., 222 So.2d 393 (Miss. 1969). (See Part VII, II.A.1.d, Best Evidence Rule.)

III. GOVERNMENTAL AGENCY REQUIREMENTS

PART VIII:
Computer Tax Considerations

OLIVETTI LEASING CORP. v. MAR-MAC PRECISION CORP.

117 Misc.2d 865, 459 N.Y.S.2d 399

(Supreme Court, Special Term, New York County, Part I, Feb. 12, 1983.)

SKLAR, J.

* * *

A default judgment was entered by plaintiff, Olivetti Leasing Corporation, against defendant, Mar-Mac Precision Corporation, on July 29, 1982 in the sum of $36,559.57. The complaint is grounded on a claimed breach of a contract regarding the lease of certain computer equipment by Olivetti to Mar-Mac.

The action was instituted by service upon the Secretary of State. Mar-Mac was formed more than ten years ago. Its certificate of incorporation gave the name and address of the law firm that handled the incorporation as the address to which the Secretary of State shall mail a copy of any process against Mar-Mac served upon him. [Citation.]

Mar-Mac's counsel in this action states that he has represented the defendant corporation since its inception and that counsel who handled the incorporation only filed the certificate of incorporation.

For some unspecified reason, or for no reason, the address to which the Secretary of State should forward process has never been changed. However, the firm that processed the incorporation has long since dissolved. As a result, Mar-Mac alleges that it never received notice of the service of process and first learned of this action after the default judgment was entered.

PLAINTIFF'S CONTENTIONS

Olivetti does not dispute these facts. Rather, it asserts, in conclusory fashion, that Mar-Mac has not met its burden of demonstrating a meritorious defense and excusable neglect. Olivetti also asserts that Mar-Mac's failure to submit a proposed answer bars this Court from vacating the default judgment.

MERITORIOUS DEFENSE

Two applicable sections of the CPLR authorize the vacating of a default judgment, §§ 5015 and 317. Both sections require that the de-fendant seeking to vacate a default judgment demonstrate a meritorious defense. Contrary to Olivetti's assertion, Mar-Mac has met this burden. Mar-Mac's papers clearly demonstrate that it has been embroiled in an ongoing controversy with Olivetti since it received the leased equipment.

In essence, Mar-Mac claims that the leased equipment failed to perform as promised and that Olivetti has been unable to make it perform, despite many complaints by Mar-Mac.

Olivetti does not now dispute that the software it leased to Mar-Mac failed to perform. However, it argues that since the subject matter of the action involves only the lease of the computer's hardware, Mar-Mac has failed to demonstrate a meritorious defense. Mar-Mac responds with the persuasive argument that it leased the hardware and software as a package and that the failure of one part of the package constitutes a failure of the entire package.

It appears that Mar-Mac has set forth a meritorious defense, thus meeting its burden under either of the two applicable CPLR sections.

* * *

Since Mar-Mac promptly moved to vacate its default and since it has demonstrated a meritorious defense, the default judgment is vacated on condition that the judgment shall stand as security pending the outcome of the action.

SCHEPPS GROCERY CO. v. BURROUGHS CORP.

635 S.W.2d 606

(Court of Appeals of Texas, Houston (14th Dist.), May 20, 1982.)

JAMES, J.

Appellant, Schepps Grocery Company, appeals from a judgment entered in favor of appellee, Burroughs Corporation, for a rebate of an eleven percent (11%) discount given to appellant pursuant to a computer lease agreement providing for an initial term of five (5) years. We affirm.

On March 28, 1972, the parties entered into an "Agreement for Equipment Lease and Maintenance" on a B3506 computer. The lease provided for a monthly charge of $9,902 less an 11% discount for "5 year unlimited use contract" or a total monthly charge of $8,812.78. At that time, Mr. A. I. Schepps, the president of appellant inquired as to what amount of this discount would have to be paid back were the lease terminated before the five year period. After some discussion, Mr. Schepps wrote the following handwritten amendment to the lease:

> Contract signed this date may be cancelled after one year with payback of the 11% discount.
> If contract is cancelled between the 3 year and 5 year a 4% payback of discount will be assessed.
> In either event, interest on these amounts would be assessed.

This handwritten amendment was signed and dated by appellee's representative.

Billing on the subject lease commenced on May 1, 1972. The lease was terminated by appellants on April 1, 1975, thirty-five (35) months after the effective date of the agreement. On April 17, 1975, appellee sent appellant an invoice for payback of the 11% discount or a sum of $35,954.70, "Interest at Current Prime Rate" or a sum of $4,249.98, and sales tax on those items. No part of that invoice was paid. Thereafter, appellee brought suit for the discount "plus interest thereon from April 17, 1975, to date of judgment."

Appellant defended the suit by asserting the affirmative defenses of failure of consideration, breach of warranty and contract, and usury. It also counterclaimed against appellee on the grounds of failure of consideration and usury. At the conclusion of the evidence in the trial, the case was submitted to the jury on special issues. Judgment was entered that appellee recover from appellant $38,954.70, interest thereon at the rate of six percent (6%) per annum from April 17, 1975 to date of judgment or the sum of $14,023.69, and attorney's fees in the sum of $10,100.

Appellant brings forward twenty points of error. Its points of error 1, 2, 3 and 4 concern the defense of failure of consideration. Appellant asserts that the evidence established this defense as a matter of law and that the jury's answers to Special Issue Nos. 3, 4 and 5 were contrary to the great weight and preponderance of the evidence. It further asserts that the trial court erred in granting judg-

ment based on those answers because it had previously ruled that there was a failure of consideration thus making the answers irrelevant, immaterial, and mere surplusage.

During the proceedings on the parties' objections and exceptions to the charge, the court stated: "I find from the preponderance of the evidence that there was failure of consideration." However, the court submitted Special Issue No. 3 which inquired as to whether appellee failed to provide the necessary service and parts to maintain the computer in good operating condition. It is not uncommon for a trial court to change its ruling on a particular issue as it is in the best position to construe its own ruling. In this case, the trial court either mistakenly made this statement or decided there was enough evidence to submit the issue. Appellant relies on *Kunkel v. Poe Land and Development Company*, 393 S.W.2d 191 (Tex.Civ.App.—Corpus Christi 1965, no writ), for the proposition that the issue of failure of consideration is a legal one within the province of the trial court and not the jury. While we do not dispute the correctness of this statement, *Kunkel* is distinguishable because there the issue submitted to the jury inquired as to whether the evidence "constituted failure of consideration." The court held: "It was the duty of the court (not the jury) to determine whether there was a failure of consideration in this case *based upon ultimate facts found by the jury* or conclusively established." 393 S.W.2d at 195. (emphasis ours) Consequently, in the instant case, the court's submission of Special Issue No. 3 was proper.

Appellant further asserts that there was no evidence and insufficient evidence to support the jury's answer to Special Issue No. 3. In considering all the evidence, we find the jury's verdict was not so contrary to the great weight and preponderance of the evidence as to be manifestly unjust. [Citations.] There was testimony to the effect that the service appellee provided appellant was equal to or better than the service rendered by most companies. The evidence showed also that appellee's response time on service calls was two hours and thirty-four minutes compared to a four hour industry standard. The record further reflects that many of the computer's problems were not due to deficiencies in the service but to environmental problems about which appellant was advised. An installation planning manual which was given to appellant specified certain electrical, air-conditioning, heating, space, and cleanliness requirements. Appellee's service manager testified that the environmental site for the computer was never ideal because fluctuations in temperature and humidity affect the memory aspects of the computer. An engineer of appellee also testified that based on the "emergency service request forms" introduced by appellant, the computer in question experienced a 99.1% "up time" at which it was operating at full efficiency and not "down" for problems or repairs. This percentage is well above the industry standard of a 90% "up time." We find the evidence was sufficient to support the jury's verdict that appellee did not fail to provide the necessary service and parts to maintain the computer in good operating condition. Appellant's points of error 1, 2, 3 and 4 are overruled.

Appellant's points of error 5 through 13 concern the handwritten amendment to the lease. Appellant asserts that the trial court erred in ruling that the amendment was unambiguous as a matter of law, in submitting Special Issue No. 1, and in admitting testimony of appellee's company policy. After hearing some testimony in the case, the trial court ruled that the amendment was unambiguous and that the provision for the return of only a 4% payback of discount applied only to the last two years, or after thirty-six months.

The question of whether a contract is ambiguous is a question of law for the court. [Citation.] If a written instrument is so worded that a court may properly give it a certain or definite legal meaning or interpretation, it is not ambiguous. [Citations.] In the instant case, appellant submits that the phrase "between the 3 year and 5 year" means *during* the third year and up to the fifth year. We disagree. In giving these words their ordinary meaning and usage, we find this phrase means that the 4% payback provision will be applicable between the end of the third year or after thirty-six months, and the fifth year. [Citations.] Consequently, we agree with the trial court's ruling that the amendment was unambiguous and that the 4% payback was not applicable in the instant case.

* * *

Appellant complains further of the court's admission of testimony of appellee's company policy. It asserts this evidence was admitted in violation of the parol evidence rule and contra to rules of procedure because appellee did not plead ambiguity so as to allow proof of the parties' intent.

The evidence about which appellant complains was the testimony of a Mr. Scartaccini who worked as an account manager for appellee during the time the lease was in effect. Before the testimony was admitted, the court gave the following admonition:

> I will allow you to question him on his understanding of the company's policy, but not on his understanding of the legal or quasi-legal interpretation of the contract in question. Limit it to that.

As explained by appellee's attorney after appellant's objection, the testimony was offered not to explain the terms of the handwritten amendment but to describe the context in which the agreement was negotiated and to explain why appellee sent the April, 1975 invoice as relevant to appellant's defense of usury. Consequently, we do not consider this testimony as an attempt to explain or supplement the terms of the amendment or an improper comment on the parties' intent. No error was committed by the admission of this testimony.

Appellant's point of error in which it asserts that the handwritten amendment is not a valid and enforceable contract because "there was no meeting of the minds" is also without merit. The amendment was drafted by appellant's own president. Additionally, the Texas Supreme Court has approved Comment B to § 230 of the Restatement of the Law of Contracts which provides in pertinent part:

> In ordinary oral negotiations and in many contracts made by correspondence the minds of the parties are not primarily addressed to the symbols which they are using, but merely to the things for which the symbols stand. Where, however, they integrate their agreement they have attempted more than assent by means of symbols to certain things. They have assented to the writing as the expression of the things to which they agree, therefore the terms of the writing are conclusive, and a contract may have a meaning different from that which either party supposed it to have.

Appellant's points of error 5 through 13 are overruled.

* * *

UNIFLEX, INC. v. OLIVETTI CORP. OF AMERICA

86 A.D.2d 538, 445 N.Y.S.2d 993

(Supreme Court, Appellate Division, First Department, Jan. 14, 1982.)

MEMORANDUM DECISION

Order, Supreme Court, New York County, entered March 12, 1981, which denied defendants' motion to dismiss the complaint and granted plaintiff's cross-motion to dismiss the first and second affirmative defenses, unanimously modified, on the law, to the extent of denying the cross-motion as to the first affirmative defense and reinstating that affirmative defense, and the order is otherwise affirmed, without costs.

On July 29, 1974, Uniflex entered into a five-year lease of an Olivetti computer with National Equipment Rental Ltd. This transaction had been preceded by extensive negotiations between Uniflex and Jerry Shure, allegedly Olivetti's authorized representative, in the course of which extensive representations as to the capabilities of the computer were given to Uniflex. Under the lease, National Equipment Rental Ltd. disclaimed all warranties. However, National's purchase order with Olivetti specifically stated, "You [Olivetti] agreed that you will make available to LESSEE [Uniflex] and will permit LESSEE to enforce against you your standard representations, warranties and service obligations in the same manner as if LESSEE were the purchaser of the EQUIPMENT." The computer never performed the functions desired by Uniflex, despite recurrent service visits over a two-year period. But it was not until September, 1978 that Uniflex brought this action for breach of contract, misrepresentation and/or breach of express warranty, and breach of implied warranty.

Defendants moved to dismiss the complaint for failure to state a cause of action and for summary judgment on the basis of their first affirmative defense, the four-year statute of limitations of U.C.C. § 2–725, and against the third cause of action on the basis of their second affirmative defense, exclusion of implied warranty under U.C.C. § 2–316. Plaintiff cross-moved to dismiss those affirmative defenses. Special Term denied defendants' motion, finding the U.C.C. inapplicable as the transaction was "clearly a lease, not a contract for the sale of goods". It found the purchase order did not impose the obligations of the U.C.C. along with those rights Uniflex obtained by being considered "the purchaser" of the computer. The Court's order granted plaintiff's cross motion and dismissed the two affirmative defenses.

We agree with Special Term's refusal to dismiss any part of the complaint but find at the same time defendants' statute of limitations defense should stand as well. At the outset, we reject defendants' contention that the claims do not state a cause of action on the ground that plaintiff is not in privity with the defendants. Privity of contract is not an element of the second cause of action for misrepresentation. The express statements were made in defendants' active effort to induce Uniflex to lease an Olivetti computer. The requisite privity of contract needed to support the first and third causes of action is provided from two sources. First, it is asserted that plaintiff and Olivetti had a separate agreement, apart from the lease with National, concerning the programming of the computer by its authorized representative, Shure. Second, the above-quoted portion of National's purchase order with Olivetti clearly intended to give Uniflex the rights of a purchaser in certain respects and thus, as a third-party beneficiary of the contract of purchase, Uniflex may pursue the balance of the complaint.

Examining the cross-motion for summary judgment, we find the record seriously deficient. Defendants ask us to apply the four-year statute of limitations of U.C.C. § 2–725 to this lease transaction on the basis of *Industralease v. RME Enterprises*, 58 A.D.2d 482, 396 N.Y.S.2d 427 and *Hertz Commercial Leasing Corp. v. Transportation Credit Clearing House*, 59 Misc.2d 226, 298 N.Y.S.2d 392. However, the leases in those cases were, in reality, sales. In this case, the lease contains no option to purchase, does not appear to provide for a renewal term at a minimal rent and provides for the physical return of the equipment at the end of the five-year initial term. Therefore, defendants have not conclusively demonstrated that this is not a true lease to which the six-year statute of limitations would apply. [Citation.] On the other hand, Special Term erred in dismissing this first affirmative defense. The record indicates National purchased the computer for $12,420, while Uniflex was obligated to pay more than $20,500 rent over the five-year period. While this may be explained on the basis of the cost of programming the computer or on some other ground, it does tend to support defendants' position as to the applicability of U.C.C. § 2-725 and raise an issue of fact as to the nature of the lease. Therefore, the first affirmative defense should be reinstated.

As to the second affirmative defense, it is contended that Olivetti disclaimed any implied warranties. The only basis for this claim we can discern is the above quoted language of the National lease. However, nowhere in the record is there any parol evidence relevant to the meaning of the clause concerning Olivetti's standard "representations, warranties and service obligations" which might indicate incorporation of a disclaimer of implied warranties therein. The quoted clause of the National lease is most reasonably interpreted as only extending rights to lessee Uniflex and not imposing obligations or limiting those rights, which would be the effect of implying from this language an exclusion of warranty. Having failed to support its second affirmative defense with an evidentiary showing against plaintiff's cross-motion to dismiss, we uphold Special Term's action in striking that defense.

**DIVERSIFIED
ENVIRONMENTS, INC. v.
OLIVETTI CORP. OF
AMERICA**

461 F.Supp. 286
*(United States District Court, M. D.
Pennsylvania, Dec. 4, 1978.)*

HERMAN, D. J.

This is an action for damages brought by a lessee of a computerized accounting system manufactured and sold by the Defendant, Olivetti Corporation of America (Olivetti). Plaintiff, Diversified Environments, Inc., (Diversified) alleges that the Olivetti computer that it leased has never been made operational and that Defendant is liable for damages on theories of breach of contract, misrepresentation and breach of express and implied warranties. Olivetti defends on the basis that it has fully performed and alternatively that it was excused from performance because Diversified unreasonably refused to permit it to effectuate its contractual duties. Plaintiff seeks relief for the total payments made under the lease agreement for the computer, the cost of paper products, and other consequential damages. The following are the Court's findings of fact and conclusions of law.

FINDINGS OF FACT

1. Plaintiff, Diversified Environments, Inc., is a Pennsylvania corporation engaged in the selling of temperature and energy control systems with its principal place of business at Camp Hill, Pennsylvania.

2. Defendant, Olivetti Corporation of America, is a Delaware corporation engaged in the business of selling computer services with local business offices in Harrisburg, Pennsylvania.

* * *

4. In July of 1974, Tim L. Fleegal, a sales representative of Olivetti contacted Diversified's President, Charles E. Andiorio, Jr., for the purpose of inducing him to buy or lease a computerized accounting system.

5. Mr. Andiorio subsequently met with Mr. Fleegal and explained in detail the nature of Diversified's business and particularly noted that the most tedious part of his duties was the preparation of specifications to be used in submitting bids on jobs.

6. Mr. Fleegal also met with Mr. Warren Beck, who was primarily responsible for the Plaintiff's accounting system, during July and Mr. Fleegal was made aware of all of the accounting procedures of Diversified and that Diversified's accounting records had to be compatible with Barber-Colman Co., for whom Diversified was a manufacturing representative.

7. Neither Mr. Beck nor Mr. Andiorio were familiar with computer systems and they relied upon Mr. Fleegal's expertise.

8. After Mr. Fleegal became thoroughly familiar with the operations of Plaintiff's business he stated that the Olivetti P–603 Computer System would meet all of the Plaintiff's

requirements and perform all of the functions that were discussed.

9. Mr. Fleegal was only qualified to sell the P–603 Computer System, which was an accounting computer, and not the Olivetti word processing machines.

10. At the time of the discussions, Mr. Fleegal stated to both Mr. Beck and Mr. Andiorio that utilization of the P–603 Computer System would save the Plaintiff both time and expense by reducing manpower and record keeping.

11. Mr. Fleegal represented to Mr. Andiorio that he would only need to push a button and he would have the specifications, that Mr. Andiorio would save half of his time, and that the computer would enable Diversified to do without one of its secretaries.

12. On July 26, 1974, Mr. Fleegal submitted a proposal to Mr. Andiorio and advised that the P–603 accounting computer could effectively meet all of the objectives discussed between the parties.

13. The proposal specifically set forth that the P–603 computer could perform the functions of specification writing, estimating, accounts payable, job cost, prime cost analysis, accounts receivable and check writing.

14. The proposal stated that the total cost of the system was $9,590.00 which included all programming, forms design, initial operator training, delivery and installation of equipment.

15. It further provided:

> in dealing with Olivetti you do business with a firm which herein guarantees in writing the exact performance of the system both machine and program. Only after these assurances have been met can we ship the machine and bill you as a customer. In addition you have my personal assurance and that of the Harrisburg District Management that all of our resources will be employed toward your complete satisfaction in the system.

16. During July or August of 1974, parts of the proposed computer package were demonstrated to Mr. Beck in the Defendant's office, however, at no time were either the specification writing or estimating demonstrated.

17. On August 7, 1974 Mr. Beck signed in two places, on behalf of Diversified, a "Customer Software Acceptance" form provided by Mr. Fleegal.

18. The Customer Software Acceptance form contains three places for signatures and Mr. Beck signed his name after the following statements on the form:

> 1. I agree that the system explained to me with regard to this application is correct in all respects and that any alterations after this date could result in additional charges according to the current published program rates.
>
> 2. This application as described in section 1 has been demonstrated to me in its final programmed form and I accept it as being a complete and workable solution.

19. Mr. Beck did not sign after the third line which stated:

> The program described in section 2 above has now been installed and the relevant personnel have been fully advised of its capabilities. I have received complete program documentation.

20. Mr. Fleegal advised Mr. Beck that Diversified would owe absolutely no financial obligation until the third line of the form was signed and it was this promise that actually prompted Mr. Beck to sign the first two lines of the form.

21. This "Customer Software Acceptance" form was considered by the defendant as an agreement or contract between the parties.

22. After the signing of the form, the computer and various programs were ordered by Mr. Fleegal.

23. Around this same period of time, in July or August of 1974, Mr. Fleegal also assured Mr. Andiorio that Diversified would not be bound to accept the computer unless and until a third signature was placed on the acceptance form as acceptance and approval of the complete system.

24. Mr. Fleegal promised to personally oversee the installation and implementation of the complete computer system and also promised that Plaintiff's operators would be fully trained and if the training proved unsuccessful that Olivetti girls would be available to run the computer.

25. Mr. Fleegal also promised both Mr. Beck and Mr. Andiorio that either he or other Olivetti staff would transfer all the necessary information onto the computer cards and the Plaintiff's only obligation was to show the Olivetti staff where the information that was needed as a data base was stored.

26. Along with the other representations, Mr. Fleegal told Mr. Andiorio that Plaintiff would not owe one cent until the computer was fully in operation and they were completely satisfied.

27. On these conditions, the computer was placed at Plaintiff's business during September of 1974, however, it was not operational at that time.

28. Mr. Fleegal then contacted an equipment leasing company, Equipment Funding, Inc., (Equipment Funding) and made the arrangements for Equipment Funding's purchase of the computer and software, and the subsequent leasing of it to the Plaintiff.

29. Mr. Fleegal received a lease agreement from Equipment Funding and took it to Mr. Beck for his signature on October 3, 197[4].

30. Mr. Beck signed the lease agreement on October 3, 197[4] after Mr. Fleegal assured him that it was just a mere formality, an application for a lease, and that Plaintiff would not be obligated to keep the system or to make any payments until it was completely satisfied.

31. Subsequently, Mr. Beck received a payment or coupon book from Equipment Funding and on approaching Mr. Fleegal, he was told to disregard it as no payments were due until the computer was operative and until they signed the third line of the Software Acceptance form as their acceptance.

32. The lease was not to be effective until an "Acceptance Certificate" was signed by the Plaintiff.

33. In mid-November, Mr. O'Brien, from Equipment Funding, and Mr. Fleegal went to Plaintiff's place of business for the purpose of obtaining execution of the "Acceptance Certificate" and Mr. Beck initially refused to sign the certificate.

34. Mr. Fleegal then induced Mr. Beck to sign the acceptance on the promises that the computer would be running by the first of the year and on the guarantee that the computer system would be acceptable to the Plaintiff.

35. Subsequently, Mr. Fleegal and another Olivetti employee, Barbara Slagle, made several visits to Diversified for the purpose of installation.

35. [sic] Mrs. Slagle, a customer software representative, met with Plaintiff's employee on December 18, 1974 and together they set up the payroll data base and the employee was taught how to update the data.

36. The payroll function was the only function Mrs. Slagle was supposed to teach as Mr. Fleegal was to teach all of the other functions listed in the proposal.

37. Mrs. Slagle incurred no problems in either teaching Plaintiff's employee or in getting the base data for the payroll function.

38. Mr. Fleegal made several visits during the month of December, 1974 for the purpose of training Plaintiff's employee on the numerous other functions, however, he neither transferred the data as previously promised nor was he successful in training the designated employee on any of the other functions.

39. Mr. Fleegal spent a substantial amount of his time during these visits in discussing his religious beliefs with Plaintiff's employees.

40. After receiving complaints from his employees, Mr. Andiorio refused to allow Mr. Fleegal to return to the premises.

41. During Mr. Fleegal's visits at Plaintiff's business in December of 197[4], he never requested any information from Mr. Andiorio with respect to the specification writing or estimating even though the specification writing was to be the primary use of the computer.

42. By January 7, 1975 the only data that had been transferred was the payroll base data and the computer was only capable of being utilized for this minor function at that time.

43. Plaintiff, pursuant to prior representations, in early January, stopped further training and requested the Defendant to remove the computer from their premises as the computer was at that time nearly worthless because data had not been transferred, employees had not been trained, and because Plaintiff was completely unsatisfied with the computer.

44. Defendant refused to remove the machine and by letter of January 20, 1975 District Manager, T. F. Meade, Jr., replied, "The relevant personnel have been trained" and "[o]ur only remaining obligation is to continue to assist you in the fullest implementation of this system which you requested and for which you contracted."

45. Plaintiff continued making the lease payments after consulting with counsel as it did not want to place its credit rating in jeop-

ardy and was advised to institute suit against Olivetti instead.

46. A meeting was subsequently held in February, 1975 with Mr. Meade, Mr. O'Brien, Mr. Andiorio and others in attendance, and Defendant took the position that it had fully performed.

47. No further training was conducted in 1975 and Defendant was not requested by Plaintiff to conduct training during this period.

48. This suit was then filed on April 13, 1976.

49. Subsequent to the institution of this action, Mrs. Slagle returned in December of 1976 to train another employee and to attempt to prepare the computer for Plaintiff's utilization.

50. After one day or a day and one-half this installation attempt was rejected by the Plaintiff on the advice of his employee who was trained in computer systems for the reasons that the P–603 was not compatible with the Barber-Colman bookkeeping system and because use of the accounting computer for specification writing was cost prohibitive.

51. Use of the P–603 computer for specification writing required that the information be placed on cards at the rate of one paragraph per card, which for Plaintiff's needs would have required likely over a thousand cards at two dollars each, and which would have required someone manually to pick the necessary cards out of a file and insert them into the P–603 computer.

52. The P–603 computer was not designed to perform word processing as that required for specifications writing, which was the Plaintiff's primary concern.

53. Expenses incurred by Plaintiff with respect to this transaction include $15,126.00 for payments due under the lease, $145.54 for paper products, and an accountant's bill of $387.50.

DISCUSSION

While a number of the theories raised by the Plaintiff are indeed relevant and applicable to the facts of this case, it is unnecessary to discuss the theories of warranty and misrepresentation as Defendant's breach of its contractual duties is sufficient to impose liability.

The parol evidence rule is clearly inapplicable here as there was no integrated written agreement between the parties that fully and completely stated the entire agreement. [Citations.] The only writings involved are the written proposal and the Customer Software Acceptance form, neither of which completely embody the agreement between the parties. We find that the oral agreement to provide certain services formed part of the contractual relationship and that the oral agreement obligated Defendant to perform the transfer of data, the training of employees, and generally to make the computer functional. These obligations were breached as the base data has only been transferred for the relatively minor payroll function and the only training that has been completed is to this payroll function. Plaintiff's employees have not been trained on the remaining functions, the ones most important to the Plaintiff, and the base data has never been transferred onto the computer cards.

Defendant asserts that it should be excused from performance because the Plaintiff prevented it from performing its obligation. While not totally devoid of merit, this argument fails to relieve the Defendant from liability. As noted in the findings, the computer was installed at Plaintiff's place of business in September of 1974 and the Plaintiff was fully receptive to having the computer made operational until sometime in early January of 1975. Plaintiff assigned an employee for the computer training and Mrs. Slagle encountered no problems in either the training or the transfer of data for the payroll function. The problems arose from Mr. Fleegal's failure to succeed in training the employees on the other numerous functions and failure to transfer the base data as was initially promised and which formed a part of the understanding between the parties. This could have been due to the fact that this was Mr. Fleegal's first sale and his first attempt at training individuals in the use of the computer. Regardless of this, it is clear that no one was trained to perform the other functions and that Mr. Fleegal interfered with Plaintiff's employees to some extent with his religious discussions.

It was only after Defendant's attempts at performance were proving unsuccessful that Plaintiff demanded the computer be removed and training halted. This was reasonable under the circumstances as Defendant had advised Plaintiff numerous times that it had no financial or contractual obligation until they signed the third line of the Customer Software Acceptance form as an indication that they were completely satisfied and that the computer was fully operational. As noted above, the Defendant took the position that it had performed and that the employee of Plaintiff had been trained, which was simply not true. The Plaintiff remained receptive to having its employees trained, even after suit was filed, until it determined that the computer was neither economically feasible nor compatible with other bookkeeping requirements. In short, Plaintiff's refusal to permit training at the two times noted was reasonable under the circumstances and was not a material interference with Defendant's obligation. The argument that it was excused because base data was not supplied is similarly unpersuasive as Mrs. Slagle encountered no such problem, Mr. Fleegal never advised Mr. Andiorio of any uncooperative conduct of his employees, and because the letter of Mr. Meade of January 1975 never raised the problem of obtaining base data. Therefore, no excuse exists for Defendant's non-performance. [Citations.]

Defendant also argues that Plaintiff has failed to join an indispensable party, Equipment Funding, because complete relief cannot be accorded among those already parties. This argument is not valid for at least two reasons. First, complete relief can be accorded between the present parties. Defendant breached its contractual obligation and defendant has made no showing that Equipment Funding is an indispensable party. Second, the Defendant should be estopped from even raising the issue as it was only due to Defendant's misrepresentation that the lease was initially entered and the acceptance certificate signed.

The final argument of the Defendant is that Plaintiff failed to mitigate its damages. While Plaintiff was under an obligation to mitigate damages, it was Defendant's burden to prove that Plaintiff failed in this obligation. [Citations.] Defendant did not present any facts at trial that established a means of mitigation for the Plaintiff. Instead, the evidence showed that Plaintiff tried to return the computer and that after this was rejected by the Defendant,

Plaintiff gave Defendant other opportunities to perform its contractual duties. The breach was material and the measure of damages is that which was caused by the breach. [Citation.] Under the circumstances of this case, the damages are the cost of the computer and paper products, the interest that Plaintiff was obligated to pay under the lease, and the expense incurred for an accountant on the request of Defendant's agent, totalling $15,659.04.

CONCLUSIONS OF LAW

1. A contractual relationship exists between Diversified and Olivetti, part of which is the oral agreement by Olivetti to perform the transfer of all base data and to train Plaintiff's employees.

2. The contractual duty owed to the Plaintiff was breached by the defendant as Defendant substantially failed to carry out its obligations of transferring the base data, of training Plaintiff's employees, and of making the computer system operational.

3. The injury suffered by the Plaintiff due to Defendant's breach is $15,659.04 and judgment will be entered for the Plaintiff in this amount.

An appropriate order will be entered.

NATIONAL BANK OF NORTH AMERICA v. DELUXE POSTER CO., INC.

51 A.D.2d 582, 378 N.Y.S.2d 462, 6 CLSR 261

(Supreme Court, Appellate Division, Second Department, Jan. 26, 1976)

MEMORANDUM

In an action to recover payments due on a lease of computers and computer equipment, plaintiff appeals from an order of the Supreme Court, Nassau County, dated August 15, 1975, which denied its motion for summary judgment.

Order affirmed, with $50 costs and disbursements.

Plaintiff, a New York corporation, is the assignee of a lease entered into between defendant DeLuxe Poster Co., Inc. (DeLuxe), as lessee, and Odyssey Systems, as lessor. The lease concerns computers and computer equipment; it was executed on June 28, 1974. By the terms of the lease, DeLuxe agreed, inter alia, that the lessor would have the right to assign the lease and, further, that it would not assert against any such assignee any defenses, counterclaims or offsets which it might have against the lessor. The lease further provided that it would commence on the date the lessor's acceptance form was signed by the lessee and delivered to the lessor.

Concurrently with the execution of the lease, a separate agreement was executed by the lessor and lessee which provided, inter alia, that the lease would not be effective if certain acceptable and satisfactory equipment were not delivered to the lessee. On July 1, 1974 the lease was assigned to plaintiff pursuant to a written agreement. In addition, an "equipment acceptance notice," signed by DeLuxe, and a written guarantee of the obligations of the lessee, signed by defendants Ross A. Johnson and Willis G. Johnson, were delivered to plaintiff. Plaintiff disclaims any knowledge of the separate agreement which was entered into by the lessor and lessee concurrently with the execution of the lease. Following four months of payments under the lease by DeLuxe to plaintiff, payments ceased. This action followed.

Plaintiff moved for summary judgment relying, inter alia, on the express provision in the lease whereby DeLuxe agreed not to assert against an assignee any defenses, counterclaims or offsets which it might have against the lessor. Plaintiff maintained that it took the assignment for value, in good faith, and without knowledge of any claim or defense, and that therefore it came within the scope of section 9–206 (subd [1]) of the Uniform Commercial Code. Defendants opposed the motion claiming, inter alia, that section 9–206 (subd [1]) offered no protection because the lease never became effective. Defendants relied primarily on the existence of the separate and concurrent agreement between DeLuxe and Odyssey Systems which, they claimed, conditioned the effectiveness of the lease on the delivery and satisfactory operation of certain equipment. They contended that said condition was never complied with.

Special Term denied plaintiff's motion, finding that there is present, inter alia, an issue of fact as to whether the subject lease and guaranty ever came into existence so as to obligate defendants as lessees and guarantors.

We agree with the result reached by Special Term, but find that there can be no question as to the effectiveness of the lease. Section 9–206 (subd [1]) of the Uniform Commercial Code provides that a lessee may agree not to assert against an assignee any claim or defense which he may have against the lessor. It further provides that such an agreement is enforceable by an assignee who takes his assignment for value, in good faith, and without notice of a claim or defense, except as to defenses which may be asserted against a holder in due course of a negotiable instrument under article 3 of the Uniform Commercial Code. Section 9–206 obviates the need for the former practice of protecting banks and finance companies, in the business of purchasing conditional sale contracts and leases, through the use of forms which included negotiable notes. Clearly, the section is intended to give qualified assignees the protection generally accorded to a holder in due course.

Section 3–119 (subd [1]) of the Uniform Commercial Code provides that a holder in due course is not affected by any limitation of his rights arising out of a separate written agreement between the obligor and his immediate obligee, if he had no notice of the limitation when he took the instrument. While the assignee of a lease who can qualify for the special protection afforded by section 9–206 (subd [1]) is not, strictly speaking, a holder in due course, the purpose of that section is best served by giving such an assignee the protection, in full, accorded to a holder in due course. Accordingly, should plaintiff establish that it is entitled to the preferred status accorded certain assignees under section 9–206 (subd [1]), it cannot be affected by any limitation of its rights arising out of a separate written agreement between its assignor and DeLuxe.

However, an issue of fact is presented as to whether plaintiff did, in fact, take its assignment in good faith and without knowledge of any claim or defense. The affidavits submitted by plaintiff are insufficient to sustain its burden of proof. [Citations.]

* * *

CONVOY CORP. v. SPERRY RAND CORP.

601 F.2d 385

(United States Court of Appeals, Ninth Circuit, April 25, 1979.)

GOODWIN, C. J.

After a disappointing performance by a new computer system for the routing, planning, and management of its nationwide automobile transport business, Convoy Corp. sued Sperry Rand for damages. Convoy recovered in a court trial. Sperry Rand appeals, contending that a substantial part (if not the entire amount) of the trial court's judgment is a double recovery. Sperry Rand contends that Convoy recovered the same damages from another supplier of computer services in an out-of-court settlement of another case.

In August, 1969, Convoy entered into a contract with a computer-technology firm known as WOFAC. For $100,000, WOFAC agreed to design for Convoy a computer system for route planning, dispatching and other operations. WOFAC said it had designed for another firm a similar system that could be adapted to Convoy's needs, with a net saving of $215,000 a year for Convoy.

After soliciting bids from various computer manufacturers, Convoy decided in November 1969 to lease the necessary computer equipment from Sperry Rand (Univac). At WOFAC's recommendation, Convoy ordered a 9200 II Univac computer, with two model 8411 discs. Univac told Convoy, however, that the 8411's might not be available by February 1970, the date by which Convoy wished to switch over to computerized routing and dispatching. After examining two design books prepared by WOFAC, Univac told Convoy that two model 8410 discs would adequately perform the job.

On November 14, 1969, Convoy signed a standard Univac lease agreement. The lease had a five-year term, a provision that Univac would service the equipment, and an option to purchase. The lease also provided that Univac would not be liable for "any indirect, special or consequential damages such as loss of anticipated profits or other economic loss." It also contained a provision that Univac's professional personnel would be available to advise Convoy concerning implementation, review, and improvement of existing data processing systems.

In a separate letter, Univac also agreed that "[i]n support of the programming efforts intended by Convoy personnel, Univac programmers under the direction of the assigned project leader will test and debug programs with the intent of providing a satisfactory work load scheduled to coincide with the delivery of the equipment." In December of 1969, Univac and Convoy worked out a division of labor for writing "peripheral" programs necessary to make the system work: Convoy would write four difficult programs, and Univac 17 less difficult ones.

The program writing took more time than anticipated. When the Univac computer was installed on March 12, 1970, the programs were not yet available. There was substantial testimony, and the trial court found, that Univac reneged on its oral promise to have four programmers available to do Univac's share of the programming. Only one programmer from Univac, Lang, was available to Convoy full time, and there was testimony that the work of the part-time help Univac sporadically supplied was incompetent. Before the computer was installed, it also became clear that the programs designed by WOFAC were seriously flawed.

On March 27, 1970, Convoy hired Computer Knowledge Corp. (CKC) to write programs, among them some of the programs that Univac had agreed to write. In May 1970, CKC ran a test on the Univac computer and determined that the 8410 discs were too slow for the job Convoy needed, contrary to the earlier promises of Univac. Lang, the Univac project leader, spent a great deal of his time attempting to make the 8410's work in the Convoy system. As a result, he was unable to write many programs. Ultimately, he failed to make the 8410's work compatibly; a program that was supposed to run in 75 minutes took 13 hours instead.

On May 14, 1970, Convoy again ordered 8411's; Univac represented that the conversion from 8410's would be simple. But it was not. CKC had to be called in to do extensive conversion work; WOFAC also had to convert some programs. It took WOFAC until December 1970 to finish its changeover to programs suitable for the 8411's.

The 8411 equipment arrived in June 1970, but it worked only intermittently. The defects were many, and caused losses of entire days' work. Convoy, CKC, and Lang, spent many hours trying to locate the source of several major problems without success. Finally, in January 1971, a field engineer from Univac's San Francisco operation put the 8411's in operable condition.

When Convoy began using the computer system, it learned that its old, manual system of routing and dispatching had been as efficient as the computer. No substantial savings resulted. In July 1971, Convoy canceled the lease under an arrangement with Univac by which Convoy paid rent on the basis of short-term instead of the original long-term rates.

Convoy then sued WOFAC for $516,129.09, its alleged out-of-pocket costs, more than $1 million in lost profits, and punitive damages, for a total claim of about $2 million. The parties settled the case by a payment by WOFAC to Convoy of $354,500.

Convoy then sued Univac in this action, claiming damages of $216,398.61 for out-of-pocket expenses. All of this amount had been included in the $516,129.09 in out-of-pocket expenses originally claimed against WOFAC in the settled action. As noted, the district court entered a judgment for Convoy in the full amount of its claim and this appeal followed.

I. DOUBLE RECOVERY

It is agreed that all the items of expense claimed as damages in this case were also claimed as damages in Convoy's action against WOFAC, which was settled. Univac argued in the trial court, and again here, that it cannot be held liable for the full amount of these expenses because they were recovered in the settlement with WOFAC. Moreover, Univac argues that the entire $354,500 Convoy gained in that settlement should be set off against Univac's liability of $216,398.61.

Convoy argues that there should be no set-off, since the payment from WOFAC represented, at least in part, a settlement of Convoy's claims for lost profits and punitive damages, which are not at issue in this case. The trial judge held in favor of Convoy, finding that Convoy's settlement did not fully compensate Convoy for its out-of-pocket ex-

penses. Thus, the court held that Convoy was entitled to recover the full $216,398.61 claimed. Moreover, the court held that, because Univac and WOFAC were not joint obligors, Univac would not have been entitled to any reduction of its own liability to Convoy by virtue of the WOFAC settlement, even if the settlement had fully compensated Convoy for its out-of-pocket expenses.

* * *

We have studied the other authorities cited by the parties, and we note that the question is not entirely free from doubt. * * * Univac is liable to Convoy, but its liability is limited to the total provable damages to which Convoy is entitled from both successive, independent wrongdoers, minus the $354,500 received in the settlement from WOFAC. [Footnote.]

The trial court did not find Convoy's total provable damages against the two defendants. It merely stated that the settlement received from WOFAC did not fully compensate Convoy for its out-of-pocket expenses. A remand is therefore necessary for additional factfinding.

II. CAUSATION

Univac also objects to three components of the $216,398.61 judgment, on the ground that there was insufficient evidence to support the implicit finding of the trial court that these components of damage were proximately caused by Univac. These three elements are: $55,549.34 paid to Univac for computer rent and maintenance, $30,513.78 paid to others to rent computer terminals and telephones, and $56,861.85 of the $83,770.52 paid to CKC for programming assistance. Since the meaning of the contract and causation of damages are questions of fact, the trial court's findings of liability on these issues will not be reversed unless they were clearly erroneous. We have carefully examined each component of damages and find no basis for reversal.

Affirmed in part, reversed in part, and remanded.

* * *

CONVOY CO. v. SPERRY RAND CORP.

672 F.2d 781

(United States Court of Appeals, Ninth Circuit, March 26, 1982.)

GOODWIN, C. J.

This court remanded the initial judgment in favor of Convoy Company for a determination whether the judgment, when coupled with a prior settlement, resulted in a double recovery. *Convoy Corp. v. Sperry Rand Corp.,* 601 F.2d 385 (9th Cir. 1979). On remand the district court found that Convoy's total provable damages exceeded the total of the settlement and the judgment and entered judgment in the same amount previously entered.

On appeal Sperry Rand (referred to as Univac) argues that the district court erred by including in the damages (a) prejudgment interest, (b) the cost of salaried supervisors, and (c) the total electronic data processing staff costs. Convoy cross-appeals, arguing that the interest on the judgment should be increased.

After reviewing the record, transcripts, and briefs we conclude (1) that Univac has failed to show that the district court erred as a matter of law; and (2) that any mistake as to the factual computation of damages is harmless because Convoy's total damages would still exceed the amount necessary to avoid a double recovery. It does appear, however, that the district court erred in failing to provide for the increase in legal interest adopted by Oregon in 1979.

In 1969 Convoy entered into a contract with a firm named WOFAC under which WOFAC agreed to design a computerized load makeup and rerouting system for use in Convoy's motor vehicle transport business. Convoy entered into a second contract with Univac under which Univac agreed to provide the computer hardware to be used with WOFAC's software and certain software support.

The system never functioned properly and Convoy withdrew from the project and sued WOFAC for $516,129.09 in out-of-pocket costs and for more than $1,000,000 in lost profits and punitive damages. Convoy settled with WOFAC for $354,500. Convoy then sued Univac for $216,398.61 for out-of-pocket costs. The district court entered judgment for Convoy in the full amount of its claim and Univac appealed.[1]

On appeal this court affirmed in part, reversed in part, and remanded the case. Univac's major contention on appeal was that Convoy was not entitled to a double recovery. The court agreed, but noted that the question of a double recovery was complicated by the fact that (a) Convoy had sought damages for lost profits and punitive damages from WOFAC but not from Univac [footnote] and (b) the settlement with WOFAC had not allocated portions of the total amount to particular claims. The court rejected Univac's argument that the settlement with WOFAC should be applied to offset all of Convoy's claims against Univac. Rather, the judgment approved Convoy's reliance on *Ciluffo v. Middlesex General Hospital,* 146 N.J.Super. 476, 370 A.2d 57 (App.Div.1977), and concluded:

> [W]e believe that the trial court should have applied the principles enunciated in *Ciluffo* to the facts of this case. Univac is liable to Convoy, but its liability is limited to the total provable damages to which Convoy is entitled from both successive, independent wrongdoers, minus the $354,500 received in the settlement from WOFAC.
>
> The trial court did not find Convoy's total provable damages against the two defendants. It merely stated that the settlement received from WOFAC did not fully compensate Convoy for its out-of-pocket expenses. A remand is therefore necessary for additional factfinding. 601 F.2d at 389.

On remand the parties spent considerable court time arguing over the effect of their prior stipulations as to damages. The court found that Convoy's total damages exceeded $570,898.61 (the total of the WOFAC settlement and the prior judgment against Univac), and therefore reentered judgment for Convoy and against Univac for $216,398.61 (the same amount previously awarded) with 6 percent interest from March 26, 1971. In his opinion, the trial judge found that (a) the parties were bound to the agreement in the initial pretrial order that electronics data processing staff costs

---

1. An expanded statement of these facts may be found in this court's opinion on the first appeal. *Convoy Corp.*

v. Sperry Rand Corp., supra, 601 F.2d at 386–8.

for a stated period totaled $88,045.94; but that evidence of such costs for additional periods could be adduced; (b) Convoy was entitled to recover for the hours its salaried personnel spent supervising the computer system and for construction of a new building addition to house the computer operation; (c) Convoy was entitled under Oregon law to interest on the unliquidated damages from the date of the breach of contract to the date of the settlement with WOFAC; and (d) as the out-of-pocket expenses, coupled with interest exceeded $570,898.61, the court did not have to consider Convoy's third element of damages, loss of the benefit of the bargain.

The following issues remain for decision:

(1) Was the trial court's finding that Convoy suffered total provable damages in excess of $570,898.61 reversible error because:
(a) electronics data processing staff costs of $113,095.35 were neither pleaded nor proved by substantial evidence;
(b) salaried supervisory staff costs of $83,281.63 were not allowable as a matter of law, and
(c) interest was not an item of damages within this court's mandate, was on sums not readily ascertainable as to due date or amount, and resulted in an award of interest on interest?

* * *

(2) SALARIED PERSONNEL COSTS

The trial court awarded Convoy $83,281.63 for the cost of the hours its salaried personnel spent supervising the unsatisfactory computer system. The judge explained:

In *Clements Auto Company v. Service Bureau Corp.*, 298 F.Supp. 115, 134 (D.Minn.1969), *aff'd in relevant part*, 444 F.2d 169 (8th Cir. 1971), a case with similar facts, the court permitted the plaintiff to recover for the hours its salaried personnel spent supervising a data processing system because "their services were effectively lost * * * during the time they supervised a system which was of little benefit to the company. * * * " I find that the time spent by salaried employees of Convoy primarily resulted from problems created by the malfunctioning of the computer system and were properly chargeable as an item of damages.

Univac argues that as a matter of law supervisory staff costs cannot be recovered because the plaintiff would have paid the staff's

salary in any event. Univac relies on *AES Technology Systems, Inc. v. Coherent Radiation*, 583 F.2d 933 (7th Cir. 1978), and *Wilson v. Marquette Electronics, Inc.*, 630 F.2d 575 (8th Cir. 1980). These cases, according to Univac, confirm the longstanding rule that plaintiff is not entitled to recover fixed expenses which do not increase by virtue of any wrongful conduct of the defendant.

The cases cited by Univac are distinguishable. The issue is not whether Convoy would have paid the supervisors' salaries if the defendant had not breached the contract, but whether the breach deprived Convoy of the services it paid for. In *AES Technology*, plaintiff sued defendant because the Laser defendant provided did not work at the warranted power output. The Eighth Circuit denied an award for staff salaries because "[p]roblems with the Laser did not prohibit AES employees from working on other projects nor did the problems delay work on the project itself." 583 F.2d at 942. Similarly in *Wilson*, the corporation was denied reimbursement for Dr. Wilson's time because the evidence, although showing that Dr. Wilson lost time from his private practice as a result of defendant's breach, was insufficient to show that the plaintiff corporation paid Dr. Wilson any extra amount or was denied the benefit of his services.

In *Clements Auto Supply*, the court found that the supervisors' services were effectively lost to plaintiff during the time they supervised a system which was of little benefit to the company. In relying on *Clements Auto Supply*, the district court implicitly found that Convoy had lost the benefit of its supervisors' services for the time they spent supervising the computer system. The cases cited by Univac are not directly in point and in any event are not Oregon cases; accordingly, Univac has failed to show that the district court was wrong as a matter of law.

Univac next argues that even if salaries may be included in the computation of damages, the award here was based on incompetent evidence. The trial court held:

Some of the time salaried personnel spent working on the computer were estimates by the employees themselves and were verified by the testimony of people familiar with their work and the amount of time spent on the computer project. They confirmed that the figures used by Convoy were accurate. I find that the evidence was adequate to sustain the amount requested.

Univac suggests that Convoy's proof is no better than testimony such as "if this machine hadn't broken down, I might have made a million dollars last year". It is true that Convoy's evidence was not based on business records. The evidence was, however, based on individual employees' estimates made under oath on how they spent their time. Univac does not suggest that the judge should not have considered Convoy's evidence. Univac offered no evidence to contradict the estimate. The estimate was not a guess of what might have happened, but a legitimate determination of how in fact the supervisors' time was allocated. Under the circumstances (the trial took place ten years after the event), there was sufficient evidence before the court to support its finding.

(3) ELECTRONIC DATA PROCESSING STAFF COSTS

The district court awarded Convoy $113,094.35 for electric [sic] data processing staff costs. This amount was reached by holding Univac to its stipulation in the initial pretrial order that Convoy incurred costs in the amount of $83,045.94 between March 20, 1970, and January 16, 1971, and adding $8,084.02 for pre-March 20 costs and $16,984.39 for post-January 16 costs. The trial court excused Convoy from offering proof of the amounts, explaining:

> Convoy was entitled to use the agreed fact figure contained in the pretrial order. In addition, at the earlier trial on the $516,129 out of pocket expenses then claimed by Convoy, Sperry Rand's trial attorney agreed 'that if witnesses were called, they would testify that there [was] a valid basis for each of the out of pocket expenses.' I therefore relieved Convoy of the necessity of submitting evidence of those expenses. I find that the stipulation, concessions, and the evidence of expenditures incurred both before and after as well as during the period covered by the stipulation amply support the claim of $113,094.35 in item 6.

Univac argues that the district court's ruling was fundamentally unfair because Univac proved at trial that Convoy's total costs for the entire period of time were only $76,710.94 and there is no factual support for the $88,049.94 figure. The amount of $113,094.35 was computed by extracting from the $76,710.94 those costs incurred before and after the period covered by the stipulation and adding those costs to the stipulation's $88,045.94.

Univac correctly describes Convoy's method for computing $113,094.35. Convoy argues this is acceptable because: (a) Univac was properly held to its pretrial stipulation; (b) there was sufficient evidence of the costs incurred before and after the period covered by the stipulation; and (3) the stipulation relieved Convoy of having to present evidence to support the $88,049.94 figure.

Convoy suggests that the initial issue is whether the court abused its discretion by holding Univac to its pretrial order stipulation. Univac argues that the generally applicable rules governing pretrial orders are irrelevant. This argument is not persuasive. In light of the passage of time, the nature of the remand, and the general rule that parties are generally bound by pretrial orders unless they are modified, the trial court could reasonably hold Univac to the stipulated pretrial order.

The second question: If Univac is held to the $88,000, should Convoy be allowed to seek additional damages outside the period covered by the pretrial order. One possible conclusion is that although Convoy in fact may have incurred only $76,710.94 in costs, Univac will not be heard to complain of a larger award when the award is based on Univac's own stipulation and concessions at the previous trial that the out-of-pocket expenses could be established by witnesses if called. Univac has no right to be relieved of a four-year-old stipulation merely because Convoy cannot now substantiate the amounts stipulated.

Even if we held that the finding of EDP staff costs in excess of the costs previously stipulated is unsupported, the difference would be only about $25,000. If the judgment of the district court was correct in all other respects, however, the error would be harmless, because total allowable damages would still exceed the required sum.

* * *

HONEYWELL, INC. v. LITHONIA LIGHTING, INC.

317 F.Supp. 406

(United States District Court, N. D. Georgia, Atlanta Division, Aug. 5, 1970.)

EDENFIELD, D. J.

BACKGROUND

Plaintiff, Honeywell, Inc., is a manufacturer, vendor, and lessor of electronic data processing (computer) equipment. Its home office is in Wellesley Hills, Massachusetts, and it maintains a branch office in Atlanta, Georgia. Defendant is a manufacturer of industrial lighting fixtures. Its office and plant are located at Conyers, Rockdale County, Georgia.

Prior to January, 1966 defendant leased (and later purchased) a "Solid State 90" computer system from Univac Corporation which it used to monitor its accounting, payroll and sales operations. After its acquisition, however, the state of the art in computerization had progressed apace and while it performed and continued to perform its function, this equipment was no longer adequate to achieve defendant's goals, particularly since defendant wished to convert from an "in line" to an "in process" operation; that is, it wished to expand its computer functions beyond mere accounting and sales so as to include its entire manufacturing operation including raw materials, inventory, work in progress, and finished goods.

With this in mind, plaintiff and defendant began negotiations which led to a contract for the leasing by plaintiff to defendant of a Honeywell "200" computer system. Both parties now contend this contract was breached by the other and each seeks damages. The case was tried to the court without a jury for approximately eight trial days, and in the opinion which follows the court now makes its findings of fact and conclusions of law.

TERMINOLOGY

After hearing the evidence in this case the first finding the court is constrained to make is that, in the computer age, lawyers and courts need no longer feel ashamed or even sensitive about the charge, often made, that they confuse the issue by resort to legal "jargon", law Latin or Norman French. By comparison, the misnomers and industrial shorthand of the computer world make the most esoteric legal writing seem as clear and lucid as the Ten Commandments or the Gettysburg Address; and to add to this Babel, the experts in the computer field, while using exactly the same words, uniformly disagree as to precisely what they mean. Such being the state of the art, the court concludes that before even discussing the contract it should make at least a preliminary attempt at computer definitions.

To begin with, an ordinary business computer, properly loaded and set, is intended to perform three basic functions: First, to store and retain within its innards a complete filing system concerning every employee, every bolt, every screw, every purchase, and every sale within a particular business operation, and to furnish, on command, complete and up-to-date information concerning each; second, to receive and record each change in each of these items as they occur, and, third, to perform routine office chores and computations, such as making out payrolls, printing checks, withholding and paying taxes, and reporting inventory. It can also be made to perform more intricate computations, to recite business history and to predict the future if properly loaded and set. Its components are myriad, each identified by a separate English word whose meaning in the industry is wholly unrelated to that contained in the dictionary.

Perhaps the best recognized and most easily understood dichotomy in the trade is between "hardware" on the one hand and "software" on the other, and even here the experts do not always agree as to whether a particular item falls in one category or the other. Generally speaking, "hardware" refers to the naked, tangible parts of the machinery itself, while "software" denotes the information loaded into the machine and the directions given to the machine (usually by card or teleprompter) as to what it is to do and upon what command. "Software" is also frequently used to include "support"—that is, advice, assistance, counseling, and sometimes even expert engineering help furnished by the vendor in loading the machine for a certain program such as inventory control or preparation of payroll.

Preparation of input data and instructions to the machine in setting up a new program is both intricate and time consuming since every bit of information and every instruction has to be put in either by tape or card or, more recently, by a type of machine English called COBOL (Common Business Oriented Language) which the machine can be set to understand. Moreover, since no two businesses operate exactly alike or have exactly the same problems or goals, the program for each has to either be "tailor-made" for that particular business or a program from some related business has to be "modified" to meet its needs.

Since one of the prime functions of a computer is to supply instant information from that stored and kept up to date by the machine an important question arises as to how the material shall be stored and retrieved. Under one system the various items are stored on tapes in sequence. This is called a "sequential" system. Under this system if management wishes to inquire about Item 100 on the tape he has to wait while the machine plays through Items 1 to 99 before it gives him what he wants, and this, of course, is time consuming. Another, more recent, system is referred to as either "direct" access or "random" access. Under this system, which operates on either drums or discs, the machine can be made to go directly to Item 101, or 201 or 301, as the case may be, without first playing the preceding items in sequence. In result, therefore, it is comparable to a selector button on a juke box as contrasted with an entire album on a single long-playing record.

OPINION

Counsel in the case have each provided the court with well over 100 proposed findings and conclusions, many with innumerable subfindings and subconclusions. Were the court to adopt all or any substantial portion of them, this opinion would be rendered unnecessarily long and in many respects utterly incomprehensible. The court has therefore decided to adopt a more summary approach and to discuss, in detail, only those features of the case which it deems controlling.

To summarize these conclusions at the outset, however, the court concludes that the plaintiff, Honeywell, has proved its case and that the defendant has failed to prove either its defense or its counterclaim.

In the period from late 1965, when negotiations began, through August, 1967, when the contract was cancelled by Lithonia, the defendant Lithonia was already a computer user. During this period it had three successive managers of its Electronic Data Processing (EDP) Department—first Corbett, then Kelly, and finally Bowman. All of them were computer experts. The first of these managers, Corbett, was not only experienced, but had been a teacher in the computer field, having used Honeywell equipment in his classrooms. His recommendations to Lithonia management carried great weight, and from the date of the execution of the first contract in January of 1966 until Bowman became EDP manager on July 11, 1967, Lithonia and its Vice President, Creviston, had left it to the determination of Corbett and Kelly as to what equipment was necessary, and all basic company communications to Honeywell about EDP equipment went through these two managers. Corbett had extensive and broad experience in almost every aspect of EDP and with the products of all vendors of computer equipment. He was thoroughly familiar with its capabilities and, in addition, he caused Lithonia to acquire the services of independent experts to evaluate and double-check Lithonia's computer needs and his conclusions. Both he and Kelly knew precisely what Honeywell's equipment would do and both of them, though no longer with Lithonia at the time of trial, have testified that Honeywell's equipment performed exactly as represented. They have also testified unequivocally that Honeywell supplied all support which it promised and that during their tenure in office (from January 1, 1966, into July of 1967) no complaint was ever made to Honeywell about any failure of its equipment or about any breach of its contract.

On September 20, 1967, after Lithonia had cancelled the contract and in response to an inquiry from Honeywell, Mr. Creviston, the Vice President of Lithonia, cited certain alleged defaults upon which Lithonia relied in terminating the contract. The court knows of no better approach to this case than to discuss these complaints one by one.

The first default alleged by Mr. Creviston was "removal by Honeywell of the on-site maintenance engineer without Lithonia's approval." All parties agree that under the contract Honeywell was to furnish a resident on-site maintenance engineer and did furnish one. Later, however, he was removed from the premises. At this time Mr. Kelly was Lithonia's EDP manager, and as to this subject he testified unequivocally and in substance that by the time some of the problems initially encountered had been solved and that Lithonia needed the space occupied by the engineer and that he, Kelly, asked Honeywell for a progressive phase-out of the on-site engineer. At this point performance of the computer had improved measurably and, according to Kelly's testimony, he arranged with Honeywell, with Creviston's approval, to have the maintenance engineer move from the premises and to thereafter be available on an "on call" basis. He testified further that this arrangement was tried and was successful. It also appears without dispute that after the on-site engineer was released neither Kelly nor Creviston nor anyone else from Lithonia ever complained of this change in the arrangement or denied this understanding, and no one ever asserted to Honeywell that it was not fulfilling its obligations in this regard. In fact, no default with respect to the presence of the maintenance engineer was ever claimed by Lithonia until Creviston's letter of September 20, 1967. The court concludes that this alleged claim of default is utterly without merit.

The second default claimed by Lithonia in the letter of September 20, 1967 was "failure of Honeywell's support in that the COBOL Compiler support disc files had not yet been made available." This complaint raises the whole issue as to what Honeywell agreed to supply, and did supply, in terms of "support" and also what it agreed to supply, and did supply, in the field of disc or direct access equipment. In this regard the evidence is almost without dispute: First, that Lithonia knew they were not getting disc equipment; second, that it was not available at the time, either from Honeywell or its competitor, IBM (in this regard an order for such equipment had previously been placed with IBM but was cancelled by Lithonia because IBM could not make delivery for a year and a half); third, that both Corbett and later Kelly did not want either disc or direct access equipment but were convinced that a tape system such as Honeywell supplied would be adequate for their present needs; and fourth, that neither of them knew when, if ever, Lithonia would need such equipment in the future. It also appears that, much later, when [sic] Kelly, after consultation with Creviston, actually placed an order with Honeywell for disc equipment. Creviston cancelled and deleted this item from the order and initialed the deletion. It is true that still later, after both Corbett and Kelly had gone, and after Bowman had taken over as EDP manager, he and Creviston again expressed interest in direct access disc equipment. This was on July 13, 1967. It is clear that Honeywell was apparently eager to sell such equipment to Lithonia at that time and promised to make a presentation to Lithonia on the subject. With this in mind, Creviston and Bowman thereafter went to Honeywell's home office in Wellesley, Massachusetts, to look into the subject, but placed no order. In fact, at this time and on July 20, 1967, Bowman had already decided to do away with Honeywell's equipment and had in fact already placed an order for substitute equipment with IBM. It thus appears that the only order ever placed by Lithonia with Honeywell for a total direct access system using discs was expressly cancelled by Creviston and no subsequent order was ever placed. In this regard it is extremely significant to the court that whereas the previous EDP managers, Corbett and Kelly, had been committed to tape operations as distinguished from disc operations, and whereas they were satisfied in general with the performance of the Honeywell equipment, Bowman, who succeeded them, was familiar with IBM equipment from past experience and that at the first opportunity after becoming EDP manager he deliberately caused Lithonia to switch to IBM. It also very clearly appears that at the time he did so, he was totally unfamiliar with the existing contracts and obligations between Honeywell and Lithonia and that he caused Honeywell's equipment to be thrown out and IBM's equipment to be ordered in utter disregard of these undertakings.

The third default alleged by Lithonia was "failure of support, in that instead of providing an experienced Honeywell analyst to assist in the implementation of the Honeywell package, Honeywell provided only a former IBM programmer, briefly trained in the Honeywell system." Again, however, the testimony is that Honeywell in fact furnished two programmers, together with support personnel. This matter of "packages", or "programs", deserves some further comment. Packages, of course, fall in the area of "software" in computer terminology. They consist of one or more pre-programmed routines or applications that go onto a computer as sort of a base program. As one witness testified, "They are to a computer what a record is to a victrola." There may be one package or program, for example, which is designed to handle payrolls; another may be calculated to solve problems related to inventory; a third may handle accounts payable or receivable. A package, however, as furnished in the computer industry (and many firms in the computer field compile and sell nothing but packages) cannot be made in advance to fit just any business operation. Instead it is either one which has been successfully used in some other related or similar business and which will therefore have to be modified or altered so as to conform to the particular business in which it is to be used, or it has to be made from scratch for a particular operation. At this point it is significant to note that neither in the contract nor in the correspondence nor elsewhere did Honeywell ever agree to furnish any completed packages. What it did agree to do was to make available to Lithonia such related packages as it had for use by Lithonia to the extent that they could be adapted to its operations. Without going into minute detail, the evidence shows that Honeywell furnished to Lithonia innumerable packages which it was free to try to adapt to its various operations. Many of them were in fact used by Lithonia, albeit without complete satisfaction. In this regard the evidence is also clear that in many instances it is simpler to compose a new program tailor-made to suit a particular business than to try to adapt a pre-programmed package from some other business. In this regard Corbett, the original EDP manager, testified categorically that he concluded that many of the packages made available by Honeywell would require too much modification and would result in a patched-up system which would not be as ef-

ficient as a system written especially for Lithonia. He concluded that in the long run he would save more time by writing a new one, with the help of Honeywell. He also discussed this with Creviston and had recommended that Lithonia undertake to write its own program. In short, the evidence shows that all applications packages which had been discussed between the parties and in which Lithonia had expressed interest were made available by Honeywell during the spring and summer of 1966, and prior to the time when Lithonia requested and executed a contract for five years instead of three. Corbett also testified unequivocally that Honeywell's support was adequate and that it made no misrepresentation to him as to its capabilities in this regard.

The fourth default alleged by Lithonia charges "failure to provide a Bill of Materials Processor Package[1] to meet Lithonia's requirements in the manufacturing control area and failure to provide a workable TRIM package." Again, however, Honeywell did not contract to sell or guarantee to furnish any particular completed packages. It was not in the business of selling packages or programs. All it did agree to do was to make available, for Lithonia's consideration and at no charge, such packages or programs as it might have. This it did, but Kelly, who had by that time become EDP manager for Lithonia, concluded that Lithonia could write a Bill of Materials Processor (package) faster than it could modify the packages furnished by Honeywell. The evidence also shows that he did write a Bill of Materials Processor which became operational by March of 1967 and was used through July 1967. He testified that his Bill of Materials Processor contained many errors, not in the machine but in the programming, and that this took more time than he had anticipated. But during this period he never at any time called upon Honeywell for assistance. In fact Kelly testified that his Bill of Materials Processor worked satisfactorily and that he thought it was adequate for Lithonia's needs.

In alleged Default No. Five Lithonia charges a "failure in Honeywell's card reader." With respect to this item, the evidence shows that

---

1. A "Bill of Materials Processor Package" as used here is a software computer program or package applicable in a manufacturing operation intended to keep a complete inventory and list of every component part necessary to build or assemble one (or 500) completed units of the product being manufactured—in the case of Lithonia the product would be lighting fixtures.

Lithonia did have trouble with the card reader and that Honeywell worked upon it. The evidence is that it was erratic but not necessarily unreliable. The evidence also shows that it was finally discovered that the trouble lay in a voltage meter which Lithonia itself had incorrectly wired when the system was installed.

Default No. Six is alleged to be the "improper functions of the COBOL tape compiler resulting in inability to batch-compile programs, resulting in needless, time-consuming delays in implementing new systems and maintaining assisting programs and generation of incorrect instructions by the compiler." With respect to this item it is again necessary to trace a little chronology. When Bowman was employed by Lithonia on April 11, 1966, Kelly was still head of the EDP department and Bowman was materials manager. Part of the material to be used in the COBOL tape compiler had, of course, been prepared by Kelly in his department, but Bowman had likewise had prior COBOL experience and wrote some programs of his own. He had some initial difficulty in doing this but in time became accomplished and adept at using the Honeywell version of the COBOL compiler. Admittedly, it did give some trouble but Kelly testified that he determined the cause to be that Lithonia was attempting to intermix two different programs, one from Kelly's department and one from Bowman's department, and that the compiler would not function properly under such conditions. He testified that he quickly identified the cause and found the solution, which was not to intermix such programs. He testified that these imperfections did not impair or impede Lithonia's progress and that he was able to effectively utilize the compiler.

Finally, in alleged Default No. Seven, Lithonia lists "inability to supply a tested Bill of Materials Processor and COBOL compiler to support disc files." But Honeywell never agreed to furnish a tested Bill of Materials Processor or a COBOL compiler. It did agree to make available such packages, including processor and compiler packages, as it had for consideration by Lithonia. It certainly never agreed to furnish such packages to be used in connection with disc equipment. As previously stated, Lithonia had no disc equipment and wanted none. Both Corbett and Kelly were

committed to tape equipment and had concluded that tape equipment was adequate for their needs. It is true that on two occasions direct access equipment was ordered by Lithonia but in each instance these orders were cancelled by Lithonia itself and Honeywell was still trying to sell Lithonia such equipment at the time the notice of termination was received.

In summary we repeat: the plaintiff proved its allegations; the defendant did not.

DAMAGES

With respect to damages, Lithonia concedes that "The measure of recovery by Honeywell as lessor would be the equivalent of the specified rentals for the remainder of the lease term, less the expense of performance by Honeywell during the remainder of the term as respects the hardware leased and other Honeywell responsibilities under the contract." [Reference.]

Lithonia contends further, however, that any net damage to Honeywell—as computed above—must be reduced by the amount of rentals that might have been obtained from a leasing by Honeywell to someone else. Lithonia recognizes that the burden of showing potential reduction in rentals by such a releasing is upon Lithonia but apparently contends that it has done so since Honeywell disassembled the equipment after its return instead of keeping it intact for sale or lease. If Lithonia had shown that Honeywell had more customers than it could supply from inventory this contention would have merit. However, the evidence shows that Honeywell had more equipment than customers. Furthermore, Lithonia's own witness (who unhesitatingly gave a figure as to what the equipment would have sold for) testified to the effect that there was little or no market for used equipment of this kind.

Lithonia also makes much of the fact that a few components from the Lithonia equipment have been used in equipment supplied to other customers, but there was no evidence to show that Honeywell would not have had an adequate supply of those parts if the Lithonia equipment had not been returned.

Honeywell contends, and the court agrees, it should recover from Lithonia the net profit which Honeywell would have realized on the remainder of the contract, computed by deducting from the gross rental due for the balance of the contract period both the direct costs[2] (maintenance, depreciation, amortization, taxes and insurance) and the indirect costs[3] (marketing support and operating expenses) which Honeywell would have incurred in performing its part of the agreement if no breach had occurred.

Stated in equation form this comes out in dollar amounts as follows: Gross rental due, $315,750—Direct costs, $121,435—Indirect costs $44,393—Profit (damages), $159,922.

Counsel for the plaintiff may present a judgment in accordance herewith.

It is so ordered.

NORTH AMERICAN CORP. v. ALLEN

636 S.W.2d 797
(Court of Appeals of Texas, Corpus Christi, June 24, 1982.)

NYE, C. J.

This is an appeal based upon a written lease agreement between appellant-plaintiff North American Corporation and appellee-defendant Herbert C. Allen, Jr. North American acquired its rights to the lease under an assignment from the original lessor, Optical Scanning Corporation. Under the terms of the lease, Allen was to lease computer equipment for a term of one year and thereafter for successive periods of like duration until terminated at the end of the initial or any renewal contract period by written notice from either party. On July 19, 1976, appellee Allen no-

tified Optical Scanning Corporation of its intent to terminate the lease. The last payment under the lease agreement was made in May of 1976. The equipment was picked up by North American in May of 1978.

Suit was filed by North American on April 4, 1978, for breach of the equipment lease. Damages were sought for past rentals and attorney's fees. Allen counterclaimed for the reasonable rental value of the office suite rented to store the equipment from the time he terminated the lease to the time North American picked up the equipment, and for attorney's fees. The parties stipulated that reasonable attorney's fees for each side would be $1,500. Trial was to the court, which entered a judgment awarding North American rentals in the amount of $359.10 for the months of June and July of 1976, plus $1,500 in attorney's fees. The court also awarded Allen attorney's fees in the amount of $1,500 on his counterclaim but denied any further relief.

On appeal, appellant North American is contending that there is no evidence to support the trial court's judgment that awarded rentals for only the months of June and July of 1976. Appellants argue that, as a matter of law, they are entitled to rentals from June through November of 1976.

In reviewing these points, we find it necessary to determine when the lease agreement took effect. North American contends that the lease agreement began on September 10, 1973, the date of the delivery of the equipment; and since Allen did not give notice until July of 1976, the lease continued for an additional year. Allen contends that the lease agreement became effective in December of 1973, the date when the equipment first be-

---

2. Under "Direct Costs" Honeywell includes:

(1) Maintenance costs of $40,100, computed by figuring the ratio of M200 maintenance expense to H200 revenue income [Lithonia says historical maintenance cost of the Lithonia equipment itself should be used here, but since these costs vary with the age of the equipment, Honeywell's method appears to be more accurate].

(2) Depreciation of the production cost of the Lithonia configuration for remaining life of contract, amounting to $60,625.

(3) Amortization of research and development costs over the remaining life of contract, amounting to $13,132.

(4) Taxes and insurance in the amount of $7,578, computed as the ratio of property taxes and insurance expenses to revenue [Annese, T. p. 521].

3. Under "Indirect Costs" Honeywell includes:

(1) Marketing support costs in the amount of $2,818. This figure represents the cost of manpower support to be furnished during the remainder of the contract life and is based on figures from their marketing personnel section showing that such support requires eight manpower months during the first year after installation of the equipment, 1½ man months the second year, and one-half man months per year after that.

(2) Operating expenses of $31,575, representing the ratio of total operating expenses (excluding marketing expenses, which are incurred prior to, and in early days of, the contract and are written off then) to total revenue of computer division. [Lithonia says no deduction has been made for software expenses saved, but this is included in operating expenses. Annese, T. 572.]

came operational, the date he began making rent payments. North American did not request, nor were any findings of fact or conclusions of law filed. Therefore, if the judgment of the trial court can be upheld on any legal theory that finds support in the evidence, it should be affirmed. [Citations.] On reviewing the record in this case, we find that the trial court, in its judgment, stated "that adequate notice of termination was given on said lease agreement on July 19, 1976." By finding that adequate notice of termination was given, the trial court impliedly found that the lease agreement, which would allow the required 90 days prior notice to cancel the lease, did not begin until December of 1973. North American admitted during oral argument that December of 1973 was the date that the lease began.

Having determined when the lease began, we must next determine if the trial court properly held that appellants were only entitled to rentals for the months of June and July. The lease in question provides that the agreement should be in effect "until terminated at the end of the initial or any *renewal contract period* by written notice by either party to the other, provided such notice is given at least (90) days prior to the end of any such contract period." (emphasis added.) The lease also provided that it was for a term of one year and thereafter for "successive periods of like duration" unless terminated. It is evident after a careful reading of the lease that the lease was renewed each year for a period of *one year* unless terminated 90 days in advance of the expiration of the year lease agreement. While notice of the termination of the lease in this case was timely given, it did not act to shorten the lease period agreed to, i.e., the end of the 1976 contract year. Therefore, the notice of cancellation in July caused the lease to be effective only until December of 1976. Accordingly, appellee breached the contract by not paying the rental fee for the months of June through November of 1976.

The general rule regarding damages when a breach of contract occurs is that the injured party should be compensated for the damages or loss actually sustained. [Citations.] Where it is shown that loss of profits is a natural and probable consequence of the act complained of and the amount due is shown with sufficient certainty, recovery of lost profits should

be permitted. [Citation.] Thus, we agree with appellants and hold that North American is entitled to receive the rents for the entire last year of the rental lease period, i.e., through December of 1976, as the undisputed evidence shows.

Appellee Allen argues that rentals through December of 1976 are not justified. He contends that, since there were no findings of fact or conclusions of law filed, this Court may hold that the trial court impliedly awarded him damages on his counterclaim for storage fees, and the judge then used such award as an offset for any additional past rents that might have been due North American by Allen. We disagree. The final judgment does not mention any relief being granted on appellee's counterclaim. In fact, the trial court's judgment states that "all relief not specifically granted herein is denied." The general rule is that, where a claim is not expressly disposed of by judgment, even though it has been properly placed in issue by the pleading, the judgment will be considered to have denied such claim. [Citations.] Thus, appellee Allen was not granted any relief as to his counterclaim. There is no offset as to past rentals. We sustain appellant's point of error and hold that the judgment of the trial court should have awarded the sum of $2,154.60 for rentals due through November of 1976.

* * *

The judgment of the trial court is reversed and judgment is here rendered that North American recover $2,154.60 in past rentals, together with attorney's fees of $1,500 and interest from date of judgment. Judgment is also here rendered that Allen take nothing as to his attorney's fees on his counterclaim.

Reversed and rendered.

NAPASCO INTERNATIONAL, INC. v. TYMSHARE, INC.

556 F.Supp. 654
(United States District Court, E.D. Louisiana, Feb. 8, 1983.)

CASSIBRY, D. J.

OPINION

This case was heard before the Court sitting without a jury in November of 1982. The action arises out of an attempted installation of an on-line computer system. The plaintiff alleges breach of contract, states that the breach was in bad faith, and seeks compensatory damages. * * *

FINDINGS OF FACT

I.

The plaintiff, Napasco International, Inc. ("Napasco"), is a Louisiana corporation engaged in the manufacturing and distribution of a number of chemical products. The defendant, Tymshare, Inc. ("Tymshare"), a California corporation, is, to quote from its sales proposal to Napasco, "the world's largest independent remote computer services company." That is, Tymshare primarily deals with companies interested in setting up "on-line" systems, in which the companies do not actually have their own computers "in-house"; its wares are, by and large, software.

II.

In early 1980, Napasco was a company with a problem: information. The company's procedure for taking stock of its inventory was time-consuming, its accounting methods inadequate. As a result of these related problems of timeliness and accuracy, Napasco had been consistently over-buying amounts of goods. To end its wasteful overbuying, Napasco contracted with Alexander Grant and Company, an accounting firm, to set up a perpetual inventory control system, one designed to gain "numerical control" over the company's various raw materials and finished goods and to determine if the quantities on hand were proper.

Napasco soon realized, however, that it needed a computer system if the company was to get a handle on its inventory. In addition, by June of 1980, Napasco was seeking to obtain financing from Citicorp Industrial Credit, Inc. ("Citicorp") and one of the prerequisites to such financing was that Napasco provide Citicorp with regular, i.e. timely, financial statements—a task which, under Napasco's manual system, it could not perform. Consequently, with the agreement of Alexander Grant, Napasco contacted Tymshare.

III.

After speaking with a representative of Tymshare from New Orleans, Don Champagne,

who was Napasco's controller during this transaction, ultimately contacted Tymshare's Houston office, which offered a computer system named "MANUFACTS." In July of 1980, Tymshare gave a presentation of the MANUFACTS system at Napasco's office. MANUFACTS was represented to be a complete computer accounting system for a manufacturing concern; one important element of the system was its "integrated" characteristic, meaning that information would flow between modules without the need for separate entry of the same data into each module.

Following the presentation, two Tymshare representatives returned to Napasco's office in New Orleans and conducted a survey in late July. The purpose of the survey, which lasted two or three days, was for Tymshare to become acquainted with Napasco's operation generally in order to prepare a proposal. During the survey, Tymshare was made aware of Napasco's needs and problems with respect to inventory, and of Citicorp's informational demands on Napasco.

IV.

On August 6, 1980, Tymshare presented Napasco with a document entitled "A Proposal to Napasco International, Inc." This impressive document, after extolling the virtues and qualifications of Tymshare, made clear Tymshare's "Software Philosophy":

> * * * to place in [the customer's] hands powerful tools to enable [it] to bring a system online quickly, and to allow [it] to make alterations with ease and convenience as [its] needs change. The software tools we provide are designed to allow non-computer professionals comfortable interaction with their data. * * *

More particularly, the Proposal represented that MANUFACTS' "modular approach" would allow Tymshare

> to tailor the system to NAPASCO's requirements. By using only the modules relevant to your needs, Tymshare can customize the operations and streamline the system. MANUFACTS uses your forms and fits your reporting formats. * * * The reports are available, complete, current, and tailored to each department's specifications.

Finally, the Proposal offered its "Statement of the Problem." Recognizing that Napasco was then using a wholly manual system and that the company needed "an organized and timely flow of relevant data," Tymshare went on in detail:

> The system must address the following functional specifications: a current-value method of inventory valuation; the storage and comparison of historical accounting data; provide an immediate and complete access to the user; offer custom tailoring of the system as company requirements change; mass change on the Bill of Materials for accuracy and timeliness; system security; material resource planning; the ability to produce immediate and efficient reports; track and control transfers of inventory across all locations; work orders; order entries; and a complete interactive capability.

No small task, indeed; nevertheless, "Tymshare has addressed these requirements and can provide a viable solution to each of them." Following some cost adjustments (as reflected in an August 8 letter from Tymshare to Napasco), the Proposal was signed on August 15, 1980.

V.

There followed an ill-fated series of events. Three modules were to be installed first: inventory, accounts receivable, and order entry. Napasco and Tymshare began working together vigorously to prepare the Specification Documents for these three modules. A series of meetings took place in New Orleans, Houston, and Thibodeaux (where Napasco had another plant). After the first of these meetings, Napasco began building its data base. At some point in September or October, Tymshare provided Napasco with a "MANUFACTS Flow Chart," which indicated that the inventory module would be "up and running" in approximately three months, with the accounts receivable and order entry modules to follow one month later.

The meetings would often last for two or three days. Theoretically, the parties were hammering out solutions to the problems they confronted, providing answers to questions, honing the "flexible, customizable" MANU-FACTS for installation-readiness. On October 20, 1980, the first target date for installation of the crucial inventory module was set—January 15, 1981—which comported nicely with the representation of three months in the flow chart.

VI.

At trial, the testimony became very vague and inconclusive about this time period. Problems with the implementation of MANUFACTS were emerging, yet I cannot find clear responses—neither then nor at trial—that addressed these problems. For example, Don Champagne's notes from an early meeting with Tymshare people in Houston reflect that a new cost module, a method of valuing inventory, was being developed by Tymshare. A standard cost system, apparently to be contained in the inventory module, was crucial to Napasco in its efforts to avoid future overpurchasing. However, it does not appear that Napasco pressed this point with Tymshare, for example, as to when the cost system would be ready, how it would calculate costs, or how it would be utilized. Conversely, it does not appear that Tymshare attempted to make any of these details clear. The history of this transaction from mid-November, 1980 until mid-January, 1981 is a chronicle of ill-focused questions and incomplete or avoided answers.

One thing is clear: through November of 1980, Tymshare in no way indicated that the established target dates could not be met.

VII.

In November, Tymshare gave Napasco three Specification Documents, none of which were the inventory module's, and Napasco refused to sign them. Tymshare delivered the Specification Document for the inventory module on December 15. Though rather desperate for the module due to pressure from Citicorp about Napasco's reporting requirements, Napasco did not sign this document either. In a strident letter to Chris Busch, a Tymshare supervisor, Don Champagne explained that the specification did not provide for interbranch transfers of data or for "general ledger and cost accounting interfaces." Instead, it turned out that the inventory module was to be used solely as a perpetual inventory control system, without satisfactorily "integrated" features. The letter added that,

> It is our opinion that you are using this approach as a method of buying time, and that you are unable to deliver the package (a totally integrated system) you sold us on the agreed upon date.

VIII.

During this time, progress had been made toward the installation of the accounts receivable module. As always, however, Napasco's primary concern was the inventory module. After an intensive meeting on January 8, 1981 with Larry Suchor of Alexander Grant and John Dakin of Tymshare, Champagne sent a letter to Dakin that confirmed the needed program changes in the inventory module, and also highlighted some incorrect formulas in the module. By this time, the parties were apparently seeking installation of the module by late February or early March, 1981.

In response to Champagne's letter, Chris Busch informed Napasco that, in both parties' "best interest," installation of the order entry and inventory modules would be discontinued. Some of the reasons were as follows:

—Last night I was told by Product Development that the modifications regarding automatic standard cost journal entries, especially variance accounting, will not be completed until 4th quarter, 1981. * * *
—My management has instructed me to install standard software. * * * As this project has progressed it has become apparent that the majority of changes required by NAPASCO are not merely cosmetic.
—A decision has been made to remove all statistical inventory control parameters. Our new system will be strictly a time-phased planning system using forecasted data rather than historical data as required by an order point system.
—We have been under the impression that Product Development would have the modifications for automatic inventory transfers for inter-divisional sales available by February of 1981. The fact is this feature will not be available any sooner than 4th quarter 1981.
—In order to install the system, my people must make many custom modifications that will not be supported by Product Development. This will cause a maintenance hardship heretofore for both companies.

* * *

—The logistics problems between Houston and New Orleans have proven to be a greater hardship than originally anticipated, given the current software problems.

Tymshare offered to continue installation of the accounts receivable module; however, Napasco elected not to proceed any further

with Tymshare and so informed them on January 28, 1981.

IX.

Shortly thereafter, Tymshare removed the MANUFACTS system from the marketplace. Though there was a great deal of conflicting testimony as to the precise date of this removal, i.e. whether early or late in 1981, the difference was largely semantic: no sales efforts were made after February of 1981, while all research and development stopped in late 1981.

Over the life of MANUFACTS, it seems that seventeen companies used or attempted to use the system. At the time of trial, only two companies were using MANUFACTS; each of these companies uses but one module.

X.

No money was ever paid by Napasco to Tymshare for the MANUFACTS system.

XI.

Napasco filed this lawsuit on June 8, 1981.

CONCLUSIONS OF LAW

I.

Counsel for Tymshare suggested at trial that the parties never entered into a contract, since the existence of the Proposal proves, at most, an agreement to agree and no meeting of the minds ever occurred. This suggestion, quite simply, is not supported by the evidence.

As both parties agreed, the Proposal itself is the best evidence of its terms and conditions. Perhaps "proposal" sounded less binding to Tymshare than "offer to contract"; however, upon consultation of Webster's Dictionary, one discovers that the two are synonymous: a "proposal" is "something proposed for consideration or acceptance; an offer, as of terms or conditions of agreement. * * *" Furthermore, the cover page of the Proposal refers to "the contents of this proposal, contract, and exhibits. * * *" And, finally, the ultimate page of the document is topped with the word "Acceptance." When this document was signed by both parties, they undoubtedly contracted for something.

Tymshare's second contention, however, is that the "something" was too indefinite—in the phraseology of Louisiana law, that the contract lacked a "certain object." [Citation.] [Footnote.] On the contrary, I have no trouble in finding a certain object in this case, for the Proposal fixed that object with admirable certainty. It described the MANUFACTS system. It explained what MANUFACTS would do for Napasco's problems, making clear that these problems had been recognized and then enumerating the "functional specifications" to solve those problems. It detailed the process of installation and defined what Tymshare's and Napasco's duties would be. Finally, the Proposal listed the modules to be installed and itemized the cost of each module, given a hypothetical amount of usage. [Footnote.]

The facts of the instant case are unlike *White Properties, Inc. v. LoCoco,* 377 So.2d 474 (La.App.1979). In *LoCoco,* the plaintiff sued the defendants for breach of contract to purchase a home to be built by the plaintiff. The defendants had agreed to purchase a "3500–4000 sq. ft. single family dwelling to be constructed as per plans to be attached to contract [with] approximate cost for improvement to be $90,000 to $95,000 range." Id. at 475. This agreement was supposed to reflect the defendants' "ideas and needs" that had been expressed at a meeting that day.

In finding a "certain object" to be lacking, the court stated that: "The problem was that the [defendants'] 'ideas and needs' were so vague and nebulous that they never could be captured." Id. at 476. The defendants had, in actuality, *no* house "in mind" when they signed the agreement to purchase; subsequent events had proven as much.

With Napasco (the analogous party to the defendant-purchaser in *LoCoco*) however, its "ideas and needs" were clearly set forth in the Proposal:

> The goal of the controller's office is to implement a cost-effective system that will track materials-flow, streamline the production process, and supply to the marketing and accounting departments an organized and timely flow of relevant data.

Throughout this transaction, the needs of Napasco, together with the "functional specifications" that needed to be addressed, remained constant. That Tymshare could not fill these needs is another matter. To be sure, things did not work out. Yet failures in the physical world are hardly persuasive proof that no "meeting of the minds" ever occurred, or else every time a party could not perform his contractual duties he would have a ready-made line of escape. Louisiana's requirement of a "certain object" cannot have been enacted to create such a "catch-22."

II.

In reliance on the representations made by Tymshare in discussions with Napasco and in the Proposal, Napasco entered into this transaction. Yet Tymshare would have me hold that, because of the many changes requested by Napasco in the "standard" MANUFACTS system, Napasco cannot now recover its damages. The problem with Tymshare's position, however, is that it would require a finding that Tymshare had *no* duty whatsoever to *respond* to Napasco's requested changes. Logic and fairness dictate otherwise.

In fact, Tymshare had a substantial duty to respond. After all, they were ostensibly the experts in this transaction; they knew how their computer system operated, what its capabilities were, and how long requested modifications would take. Or, at least, they should have known. Yet Tymshare's performance in this transaction suggests a company that was unwilling to come to grips with problems of its own; problems in its computer system, in its interbranch communications, and in the training of its applications personnel. While Napasco informed Tymshare of its problems, Tymshare chose not to return the favor.

The most convincing, illustrative evidence of these problems is the January 23, 1981 letter—the letter that breached the contract—from Chris Busch, Tymshare's branch manager in Houston, to Robert Donnes and Don Champagne. First, the letter makes it clear that Tymshare had not disclosed some rather essential elements of information about what MANUFACTS did and did not contain. For example, Busch informed Napasco "a decision" had been made to use only forecasted data rather than historical data in the "new system" (whatever that last phrase means). Yet, in the Proposal, MANUFACTS was going to address "the storage and comparison of historical accounting data." Either MANUFACTS never could or once could but now would not use historical data and, in any event,

Napasco was never apprised of the situation.

Similarly, the Busch letter notified Napasco that "inventory transfers for interdivisional sales" would not be available "any sooner than 4th quarter 1981." The Proposal had represented that MANUFACTS would address the tracking and controlling of "transfers of inventory across all locations," which, within the dates encompassed by the parties' dealings, it simply did not do. The same dichotomy between Tymshare's representation and actual fact existed with respect to a standard cost system.

A concomitant problem with Tymshare's operation can be analogized to the old saw about "the left hand doesn't know what the right hand is doing." In this case, the "left hand" was the MANUFACTS installation group in Houston; the "right hand" was the Products Development group in California. The oral testimony at trial suggested and the Busch letter confirmed that communication between these two branches was, to put it mildly, less than perfect. Apparently, the people in Houston—those involved with Napasco—were never aware of the precise capabilities of MANUFACTS; this lack of awareness engendered an all-too-frequent response by Tymshare representatives: the classic "We'll get back to you on that," or words to that effect.

By the preceding discussion, I do not mean to suggest that the eventual breakdown of this transaction was solely caused by Tymshare. Testimony at trial made clear that Napasco's accounting system was woefully inadequate, that its data compilation was handled somewhat roughly, and that it probably asked for a number of things from MANUFACTS which were either impossible, ridiculously expensive, or far too time-consuming. What I do mean to suggest is that Tymshare was surely not itself blameless and that insofar as Napasco's imperfections and imperceptions were concerned, Tymshare had a duty to alert Napasco to the areas in which Napasco or MANUFACTS was lacking. Not by saying, as Tymshare's representatives did, "I don't know; that may take some time," or "that will cost a bit more," or "you need to enter more data," but

by focusing Napasco on precisely how long a modification would take, how much a modification would cost, and how certain modifications could not be performed because the technology had not been developed in the MANUFACTS system.

Throughout the four-month period from October to January, Tymshare was content, inter alia, to allow the "three-month" representation about installation of the inventory module to remain undisturbed, to leave undefined the distinction between a minor "custom tailoring" and a "major modification." Having done so, and having allowed Napasco to rely on the promises in their contract and to proceed in the belief that the avowed expertise of Tymshare would keep things on a steady course, Tymshare cannot avoid its liability to Napasco for damages. "Sales-puffing" [3] and silence are not defenses, especially not for the party with more information about the proposed system.

III.

Tymshare's breach of the contract with Napasco was an active violation, defined under Louisiana law to be "doing something inconsistent with the obligation it has proposed." [Citation.] [Footnote.] As stated earlier, the inventory module was in many ways the linchpin of this contract and the Busch letter of Janaury 23, 1981 discontinuing installation of that module (as well as order entry) was, quite clearly, an active violation.

> Where a party refuses and does not merely fail or neglect to comply with his contractual obligation, his refusal constitutes an active breach of the contract which relieves the other party of the obligation of continuing to perform the contract. * * * Moreover, a definitive refusal to perform obviates the necessity of a formal putting in default as a prerequisite to recovery by the obligee.

[Citation.]

IV.

Though an active violation, the breach by Tymshare was not in bad faith. In actions for breach of contract, bad faith "is not * * *

---

3. One contention by Tymshare about the flow charts was that they were merely "sales tools." Yet at least two defense witnesses admitted that buyers were expected to rely on the charts. If relied on in good faith by Napasco, as they were, the issue of whether the flow charts were "sales tools" or "potential working documents" seems largely irrelevant.

the mere breach of faith in not complying with the contract, but a designed breach of it from some motive of interest or ill will." [Citation.] There was no evidence to suggest any kind of Machiavellian scheme on Tymshare's part at any time; rather, the evidence established that both parties worked diligently, if not effectively, toward implementation of the MANUFACTS system. Both parties sincerely hoped their efforts would succeed.

V.

It remains for me to determine the correct measure of damages. Article 1934 of the Louisiana Civil Code provides that "the damages due to the creditor for [a contract's] breach are the amount of the loss he has sustained, and the profit of which he has been deprived. * * *" Furthermore, in light of my finding that Tymshare did not act in bad faith, Tymshare "is liable only for such damages as were contemplated, or may reasonably be supposed to have entered into the contemplation of the parties at the time of the contract." Id.

The plaintiff has the burden of proof to show the damages suffered by him as a result of the defendant's breach. An award of damages cannot be based on speculation or conjecture. On the other hand,

> Damages are not rendered uncertain because they cannot be calculated with absolute exactness. It is sufficient if a reasonable basis of computation is afforded, although the result be only approximate. * * *

Eastman Kodak Co. v. Southern Photo Materials Co., 273 U.S. 359, 379, 47 S.Ct. 400, 405, 71 L.Ed. 684 (1926).[5]

VI.

At trial, each party produced an expert on the question of damages. The plaintiff's expert suggested four elements of damage done to Napasco by Tymshare's breach:

1. Loss due to Tymshare's failure to provide a proper inventory control system;
2. Loss due to Tymshare's failure to provide cost control;
3. Loss due to a distress sale of Napasco necessitated by Tymshare's breach; and
4. Out-of-pocket and unreimbursed expenses.

I take these up in turn.

VII.

Napasco's expert valued the cost of on-hand excess inventory as of September 1, 1982 (after deducting the portion financed by Citicorp) at $110,000. This calculation is indefensible: it did not state how much inventory was on hand as of July 1980; it assumed that all excess inventory was wholly unusable; and it contained no definition of excess inventory. Elements of damages need not be proven with "absolute exactness;" neither should a judge simply make up numbers. Tymshare's expert valued this loss at zero and I concur. See *Clements Auto Company v. Service Bureau Corporation,* 444 F.2d 169, 189–90 (8th Cir. 1971) (no recovery for "obsolete" inventory).

VIII.

The second element of damages about which Napasco's expert testified related to recurring costs at Napasco that could have been saved by MANUFACTS. The number chosen was $50,000 per month which, somewhat dismayingly, materialized without any substantiated basis of proof.[6] I assume that some amount of money would have been saved by the installation of MANUFACTS; however, Napasco failed or was unable to specify its recurring costs, did not explain how and in what amount MANUFACTS would have reduced

5. This quotation has been cited with approval in two cases involving the installation of computer systems and the appropriate measure of damages. See *Clements Auto Company v. Service Bureau Corporation,* 444 F.2d 169, 190 (8th Cir.1971); *Chatlos Systems v. National Cash Register Corp.,* 479 F.Supp. 738, 747 (D.N.J. 1979). These cases have proven conceptually useful to me in arriving at the amount of Napasco's damages.

6. Gary Rinck, a certified public accountant, was hired by Napasco to implement a new accounting system after the MANUFACTS deal fell through. He too testified that MANUFACTS could have "easily recognized" $50,000 per

month savings for Napasco; in fact, Napasco's economic expert appears to have based his calculations on Mr. Rinck's figures. However, Mr. Rinck has only been with Napasco since May, 1982—almost a year and a half after the relationship ended between Tymshare and Napasco. And, aside from his temporal remoteness, Mr. Rinck was in no way specific about the recurring costs.

Additionally, Mr. Rinck testified that "these cuts have been made now," suggesting that poor management, as much as the lack of a computer accounting system, was responsible for Napasco's unnecessarily high overhead.

particular costs, and failed to account for the cost of operating MANUFACTS itself.[7] Again, I may not simply hypothecate a number.

IX.

I must also disallow the third component of plaintiff's alleged damages, which concerned the sale of Napasco under "distress conditions." In the first place, the details of the sale were unclear: Napasco's expert reported that "NAPASCO will not survive the sale in its present position as a manufacturer. It will survive only as a distributor." The import of this statement is not at all apparent. Secondly, Tymshare's expert listed ten problems with the conceptual approach utilized by Napasco's expert; suffice it to say that the plaintiff did not provide me with a "reasonable basis" for computation of damages.

Moreover, I do not believe the damages, if any, resulting from a distress sale were contemplated by the parties as that term is used in Louisiana law. In the Proposal, Napasco held itself out to be a "profitable, growing manufacturer and distributor." At the time the contract was made, Tymshare knew or could be expected to have known that Napasco's accounting department was being run inefficiently, that the amount of the loan to be received from Citicorp was linked to the submission of timely financial statements by Napasco, and that Napasco was relying on MANUFACTS to help operations run more smoothly. However, it cannot be argued that Tymshare realized or should have foreseen that failure to implement the MANUFACTS system would result in a distress sale, when no hint had been made of such allegedly dire straits. This is so particularly when the sale occurred (or is about to occur—plaintiff's testimony was in conflict on this point) at least twenty months after the business relationship between Tymshare and Napasco had been terminated.

7. This is not a situation in which "the trial judge is convinced that substantial pecuniary harm has been inflicted, even though its amount in dollars is *incapable of proof.*" 5 A. Corbin, Corbin on Contracts § 1020 (1964) (emphasis added). In such situations, trial judges have more discretion to fashion an appropriate award. Id.

Here, the recurring costs were hardly incapable of proof. At the very least, Napasco could have adumbrated individual areas of such costs, assigned dollar amounts, reduced the total amount by the cost of using MANU-

X.

Turning now to Napasco's out-of-pocket, unreimbursed expenses, I find, with two revisions, that these damages were proven with enough specificity to afford a "reasonable basis of computation." Unlike the alleged recurring costs, these expenses were broken down individually, were confined to an appropriate time period, and were testified to by employees (primarily Don Champagne) who had personal knowledge of the day-to-day life of the transaction. Furthermore, the defendant's expert could point to no *logical* errors in these figures; he simply felt they were not properly supported by documentation.

The time expenses for Napasco employees working with Tymshare are all reasonable, except the percentages of time assigned for Abe Moradian and Robert Donnes. Moradian was the president of Napasco during this period; his only involvement with Tymshare consisted of attending a few meetings and rubber-stamping decisions made by Champagne and Donnes. From the testimony developed at trial, I have concluded that Moradian spent about five per cent of his time in Tymshare; this reduces the recovery for his time to $3,662.00. Secondly, Robert Donnes testified that he spent ten, not fifty, per cent of his time working on Tymshare; his salary expense is thereby reduced to $1,800.00. Thus, the salary expenses for employees working with Tymshare equal $51,374.00.

The travel and entertainment expenses of Champagne and Donnes were documented, the miscellaneous amount of $200 was too small to quibble with. These expenses equal $2,092.04.

Napasco had to expend an additional $7,163.85 to revivify its contract with Alexander Grant for a perpetual inventory control system. There was testimony that numerous forms were printed in connection with the dealings with Tymshare; their cost was val-

FACTS, and arrived at a reasonable figure. Cf. *Clements Auto Company v. Service Bureau Corporation,* 298 F.Supp. 115, 134 (D.Minn.1969) (plaintiff specified increased clerical and supply costs); *Chatlos Systems v. National Cash Register Corp., supra* note 5 at 747 (plaintiff offered exhibits and testimony to show labor costs that would have been saved by computer system's implementation). Instead, plaintiff offered nothing more than a single undocumented, undifferentiated, bulk figure; this offer did not satisfactorily discharge its burden of proof.

ued at $1,000 and uncontradicted by Tymshare witnesses. Next, Napasco had to pay $3,384 to ACA, a service bureau in Chicago, as a start-up fee for the handling of accounts receivable. And, finally, the phone company: $156.75. The total for these expenses is $11,704.60.

XI.

In conclusion, judgment will be entered for the plaintiff awarding compensatory damages in the amount of $65,170.64.

COMPUTER SERVICENTERS, INC. v. BEACON MANUFACTURING CO.

328 F.Supp. 653

(United States District Court, D. South Carolina, Greenville Division, Dec. 9, 1970.)

HEMPHILL, D. J.

This matter is before the court upon the motion of the defendant for summary judgment in accordance with Rule 56, Federal Rules of Civil Procedure. Though the facts are highly disputed between the parties, for the purposes of this motion, they are considered by the court as claimed by the plaintiff, and are so stated below.

In early 1968, Beacon, through John Austin, Vice President of Administration for Beacon and in charge of Beacon's data processing operations, undertook certain negotiations with CSI with a view toward CSI performing data processing operations for Beacon in replacement of such operations then being presently internally performed on Beacon's own computer. On or about March 21, 1968, a written proposal prepared by CSI with a view toward CSI producing certain data processing results for Beacon was delivered to Mr. John Austin by CSI. Thereafter, in April 1968, Mr. Austin allegedly took up the matter in a meeting of the Management Committee of the defendant, at which time he received authority to enter a binding contract for the defendant with the plaintiff according to the terms of the proposal of March 21. Mr. Austin states that as secretary of the Management Committee he took,

signed, and distributed minutes containing the decision and authorization to enter the contract with the plaintiff. Mr. Austin subsequently, on or about April 19, 1968, agreed orally to a contract with the plaintiff in accordance with the terms of the written proposal.

After extensive preparation and acquisition of additional equipment, the plaintiff provided the defendant with data processing services during the months of September, October, and November, 1968. These services were billed to and paid for by the defendant. At some point in November, 1968, the defendant notified the plaintiff that further services were not required, allegedly in breach of the oral contract. The written proposal of March 21 does not make clear what the duration of the contract was to be. However, it does appear, beyond doubt, that the proposed contract was not to be performed within a year. It is also clear that if the proposed contract was in force as alleged, the action of the defendant in November, 1968, or its subsequent conduct constituted a breach.

In early November, 1968, Mr. Austin abruptly left the employ of the defendant. In December, 1968, at the request of the defendant, Mr. Austin attended a meeting with officers of the plaintiff and the defendant. The purpose of that meeting was the resolution of differences that had arisen between the plaintiff and defendant regarding the data processing arrangement. At that time Mr. Austin signed a statement acknowledging that he had entered for the defendant an oral contract embodying the terms of the written proposal of March 21.

The ground for the defendant's motion for summary judgment is that the statute of frauds renders the alleged oral contract unenforceable because it was not to be performed within a year. S.C.Code Ann. Section 11–101(5) (1962). In opposition to the motion, the plaintiff urges first that the applicable statute of frauds is that contained in the Uniform Commercial Code (S.C.Code Ann. Section 10.2–201 (Add. Vol.1966)) and that subsection 3(a) of that section excludes the subject contract from the requirement of a writing. The plaintiff's second argument is that both the minutes of the defendant's Management Committee prepared and signed by the defendant officer Mr. Austin and the acknowledgment of the oral contract signed by Mr. Austin December 7, 1968 are sufficient writings to satisfy the statute of frauds.

I

Article 2 of the Commercial Code deals with "transactions in goods." (S.C.Code Ann. Section 10.2–102 (Add.Vol.1966)). "Goods" as used in the section means "all things (including specially manufactured goods) which are movable at the time of identification to the contract for sale other than the money in which the price is to be paid, investment securities and things in action." (S.C.Code Ann. Section 10.2–105(1) (Add.Vol.1966)). That definition is indeed broad, however, it must be noted that the article deals with, and the definition of goods is cast in terms of, the contract for sale. "Sale" "consists in the passing of title from the seller to the buyer for a price." (S.C.Code Ann. Section 10.2–106(1) (Add. Vol.1966)).

The fact of the matter here is that the alleged contract was simply not for the sale of goods as contended by the plaintiff. [Footnote.] Rather it was that certain services be provided the defendant by the plaintiff. The written proposal states that it is an agreement "for performance of data processing services." The proposal indicated that there would be a separate charge for supplies unless the defendant provided them. The payment contemplated was for the analysis, collection, storage, and reporting of certain data supplied the plaintiff by the defendant. It was not for the sale of goods, and to claim to the contrary strains the imagination. Due to the recent adoption of the Universal [sic] Commercial Code in South Carolina, the courts of this state have not considered the problem. However, the cases generally support the conclusion that the contract here alleged is not within the scope of the Commercial Code.[2]

The plaintiff does not argue nor does the court find that the allegations or performance rendered constitute sufficient part performance to take the contract out of the statute.

[Footnote.] The performance was urged only as being sufficient under Article 2, Section 201(3) (a) to remove the requirements of the Commercial Code.

II

The remaining consideration is whether either or both of the memorandums signed by Mr. Austin satisfy the requirements of the statute of frauds. The minutes of the management committee meeting upon which the plaintiff relies have not been produced and apparently cannot be found. The defendant earnestly contends that such minutes never existed. Be that as it may, the loss of the memorandum, if executed and sufficient to satisfy the statute of frauds, would not change or impair the obligation of the parties. [Footnote.] The deposition of Mr. Austin provides the only substantial account of the minutes relied upon by the plaintiff. From Mr. Austin's testimony it appears that the minutes signed by him constituted, not an agreement or even an offer, but only an authorization to him to enter a contract according to the terms of the March 21 proposal. His testimony was that he subsequently entered the oral contract sued upon.

As understood by this court, a memorandum giving authority to an agent to enter a contract does not meet the requirements of the statute of frauds with regard to a contract subsequently entered by the agent pursuant to that authority. [Footnote.]

Exception to that rule is made where the memorandum granting the agent authority constitutes such an offer as may be accepted by the other party without further agreement. [Footnote.] It appears that the discussion of the contract which took place at the meeting and would have been reflected in the minutes dealt with the savings expected from the proposed arrangement and changes to be brought about by it. The minutes, therefore, could not have been construed as an offer or an acceptance of the plaintiff's earlier offer. It does not appear either that they were intended for communication to the plaintiff or that the plaintiff ever in fact knew of or relied upon them. The minutes, if in fact they existed,

2. *E. g.*, Epstein v. Giannattasio, 25 Conn. Sup. 109, 197 A.2d 342; Stagner v. Staples, 427 S.W.2d 763

(Mo.App.); National Historic Shrines Found. v. Gali, 4 U.C.C.R.S. 71 (N.Y.).

would constitute proof of Mr. Austin's authority to enter the contract sued upon, but could not constitute sufficient memorandum signed by the defendant to satisfy the requirements of the statute of frauds.

The second memorandum claimed by the plaintiff to satisfy the requirement of a writing was executed by Mr. Austin December 7, 1968. That memorandum, signed by Mr. Austin, states that he entered an oral contract for the defendant with the plaintiff according to the terms of the proposal of March 21, 1968, and that all work done by the plaintiff had been to effect performance of that contract. It is well settled that subsequent written acknowledgment signed by the party to be charged on an oral contract is sufficient to satisfy the statute of frauds with respect to that earlier contract. [Footnote.] In order to charge the defendant upon the statement signed December 7, 1968, by Mr. Austin, it must appear that Mr. Austin had authority, actual or ostensible, to bind the defendant and that he acted in pursuance of such authority in signing the memorandum. [Footnote.] From this record it is clear that Mr. Austin had no such authority as of December 1968. He had left the employment of the defendant without notice in early November of that year. He attended the meeting on December 7, at which time he signed the memorandum acknowledging the contract, at the request of the defendant. However, he was summoned by the defendant, not to enter any contract, but to attempt to resolve differences with the plaintiff. The mere summoning of Mr. Austin by the defendant, would not convey to him authority to bind the defendant by his signature and the defendant could not be held bound by his account of what had transpired. The court does not find the defendant's argument to the contrary at all persuasive. The case of Blocker v. Hundertmark, 204 S.C. 269, 28 S.E.2d 855 (1944) is relied upon by the plaintiff to support the proposition that an agent, who within the scope of his authority, makes an oral contract, may after revocation of that authority, execute a memorandum sufficient to bind the principal. The case does not so hold. The court there stated that the evidence indicated that the agent had become the agent for the estate after the death of the original principal. Therefore, the agency continued until the signing of the memorandum by the agent.

Mr. Austin's statement may be a true account of contractual relationship between the parties. Were the requirements of the statute of frauds satisfied, his testimony in that regard should be very persuasive. However, at the time he signed the statement, he had no authority to bind the defendant. It was not done at the instance or with the knowledge of the defendant, but was the voluntary act of Mr. Austin. Therefore, the statement does not satisfy the requirements of the statute of frauds. [Footnote.]

It therefore appears that the defendant's motion for summary judgment must be granted.

And it is so ordered.

EARMAN OIL CO., INC. v. BURROUGHS CORP.

625 F.2d 1291

(United States Court of Appeals, Fifth Circuit, Sept. 19, 1980.)

BROWN, C. J.

Inappropriate for certification because of the unusual posture of the issues and their straightforward, settled nature [footnote], this case takes us down the Florida law spur of *Erie R. R. v. Tompkins*. [Footnote.] A number of questions line the tracks. When is a lease not a lease? What effect should be given to the terms of a contract which was executory and was in a sense not carried out by the parties? How can disclaimers and limitations of liability be unconscionable as a matter of law? To find the answers, we look to Florida's general contract law and to its version of the Uniform Commercial Code, Fla.Stat. §§ 671.101 *et seq.* ("Code" or "U.C.C."). [Footnote.]

A three-party transaction is the subject of this appeal. Earman Oil Company was the user of a Burroughs Model L 8800–100 computer.[4] The supplier of the computer was Burroughs Corporation. The computer was technically sold by Burroughs to the third party—National Equipment Rental Limited (NER). Simultaneously, NER leased the computer to

---

4. The computer, with associated hardware and software, was intended to process Earman's payroll, record

certain of its sales and purchases, and provide accounting information.

Earman. Burroughs sent the computer directly to Earman, which in turn made "rental" payments to NER.

This common arrangement leads to little trouble until the user feels that the computer has, so to speak, gone awry. Then there is litigation.[5] So it is here. Earman, having no recourse against NER, brought claims for breach of implied and express warranties and for tortious misrepresentation against Burroughs. Earman further narrowed these claims in the District Court. That Court rejected the narrowed claims. On appeal, we affirm.

This trouble began in 1975 when Earman and a Burroughs representative agreed that Earman needed a Burroughs computer. For financial reasons, Earman decided not to try to buy the computer outright, however. Instead, the computer was to be sold to a leasing company which would then lease to Earman. First, however, Burroughs had to locate an agreeable leasing company. So Burroughs asked Earman to sign a contract purporting to sell the computer and associated hardware directly to Earman. That "Equipment Sale Contract" (ESC) identified the computer by model type but not by serial number, and showed a price of approximately $26,155.

Five days later, Burroughs had located NER to act as leasing company and Earman signed a lease for the equipment previously designated in the ESC, with the exception of one immaterial item. At the end of the lease, Earman was to redeliver the computer to NER.

NER countersigned the lease seven days later and simultaneously executed a purchase order to Burroughs for the same model computer and associated hardware. The purchase order designated Earman as lessee. A few months later the leased computer was installed. Allegedly there was trouble from the start, which Burroughs attempted to remedy. Many attempts and two years later, Earman brought this suit against Burroughs.

The thrust of Earman's complaint was that Burroughs: (i) breached its oral express warranties; (ii) breached its implied warranties of fitness for a particular purpose and of merchantability; and (iii) tortiously misrepresented the qualities of its computer. In defense, Burroughs asserted that exculpatory provisions of the ESC, signed by Burroughs and Earman, protected Burroughs from liability.

Earman's counterattack was three-pronged. First, Earman argued that the real economic effect of the transactions involving NER was important in determining whether the previously executed ESC could be accorded any significance. If NER was a true lessor and was not acting solely as a financing agent, then the real economic effect of the three-party transaction was a sale by Burroughs to NER. Earman argued that this meant that the ESC must be treated as a nullity and that only the provisions of the purchase order in the sale to NER could be accorded significance. Second, Earman argued that the purchase order contained no effective exculpatory provisions. Asserting that it was a third party beneficiary of the purchase order, Earman concluded that by virtue of the purchase order it could recover against Burroughs on theories of express and implied warranty. Third, Earman contended that even if the restrictions of the ESC were applicable, they were unconscionable and therefore unenforceable.

In order to clarify the legal issues and especially the unconscionability claim, the District Court held a pre-trial hearing. There, the Court first held as a matter of law—though not fact—that the ESC's restrictions were not unconscionable. Second, as a matter of law, the Court held that the exculpatory language of the ESC governed the relationship between Earman and Burroughs. That conclusion was based on two alternative grounds: (i) That the real economic effect of the transaction was a sale between Earman and Burroughs with NER having only a financing interest in the equipment; or (ii) if NER had more than a financing interest, the restrictions of the ESC

5. There have been an enormous number of suits in which disgruntled computer users have attempted to sort out their rights where both computer vendors and so-called lessors have been involved. *See, e. g., Triangle Underwriters, Inc. v. Honeywell, Inc.;* 604 F.2d 737 (2d Cir. 1979): *Chatlos Systems, Inc. v. National Cash Register Corp.;* 479 F.Supp. 738 (D.N.J. 1979); *National Equipment Rental, Ltd. v. Priority Electronics Corp.,* 435 F.Supp.

236 (E.D. N.Y.1977); *Granite Equipment Leasing Corp. v. Acme Pump Co.,* 13 U.C.C.Rep. 707 (Conn.Sup.Ct.1973); *Computer Sciences Corp. v. Sci-Tek, Inc.,* 367 A.2d 658 (Del.Super.1976); *Leasco Data Processing Equipment Corp. v. Starline Overseas Corp.,* 74 Misc.2d 898, 346 N.Y.S.2d 288 (App.T., 1st Dept. 1973); and cases cited below in this opinion.

were nonetheless applicable to Earman's suit as a matter of contract interpretation. Either way, Earman's claims would be subject to defenses based upon the ESC's disclaimers,[6] damage limitations,[7] and integration provisions.[8]

Upon the Court's ruling, Earman was granted a recess in order to consider the situation. Earman's position at the hearing and its interpretation of the issues and facts in the pre-trial stipulation were largely dependent on a favorable ruling with respect to the ESC.[9] Given the adverse resolution of that issue and the unconscionability issue, Earman decided during the recess not to proceed to trial on the remaining factual issues. Without asking the District Court to proceed to trial on unresolved factual issues, Earman requested the entry of final judgment, which was duly granted.

Earman then brought this appeal. Essentially the same three issues considered by the District Court in its pre-trial ruling are contested by Earman.[10] Thus we are asked to determine the real economic effect of the transaction, to decide whether the ESC's exculpatory provisions apply, and to find whether those provisions are unconscionable.

We do not decide whether further fact-finding might permit Earman to prevail. Earman's case below was predicated on a favorable resolution of the issues of law. Except for an ambiguous reference in the conclusion of

its appellate brief [footnote], Earman does not now seek reversal for lack of fact-finding. Furthermore, the factual aspects of Earman's claims were not properly raised in the District Court. To the extent that any are now being raised for the first time on appeal, we will not consider them. [Citation.] We now proceed to the legal issues properly placed before us by Earman.

Earman first urges us to decide whether or not the three-party transaction had the real economic effect of a sale by Burroughs to Earman. In form, the transaction consisted of a sale to NER followed by a lease of the equipment to Earman. Thus, in form there was no *completed* sale of the equipment directly to Earman.

Earman's primary position is that the subsequent sale to NER had real economic substance. Therefore the lease by NER to Earman was not a financing arrangement nor a subterfuge for taking a security interest in the equipment. If a "true" leasing arrangement was involved, then Earman argues that the NER purchase agreement with Burroughs is of greater significance while the earlier executed ESC between Burroughs and Earman becomes insignificant.

If, on the other hand, NER's lease was not a true lease but rather a financing arrangement, Earman acknowledges that there is more precedent for giving effect to the ESC. Nonetheless, Earman asserts that its position is

---

6. No representation or other affirmation of fact not set forth herein, including but not limited to statements regarding capacity, suitability for use, or performance of the equipment shall be or be deemed to be a warranty by Burroughs for any purpose, nor give rise to any liability or obligation of Burroughs whatever.

EXCEPT AS SPECIFICALLY PROVIDED IN THIS AGREEMENT, THERE ARE NO OTHER WARRANTIES EXPRESS OR IMPLIED INCLUDING BUT NOT LIMITED TO ANY IMPLIED WARRANTIES OF MERCHANTABILITY OR FITNESS FOR A PARTICULAR PURPOSE.

7. IN NO EVENT SHALL BURROUGHS BE LIABLE FOR LOSS OF PROFITS OR OTHER ECONOMIC LOSS, INDIRECT, SPECIAL, CONSEQUENTIAL, OR OTHER SIMILAR DAMAGES ARISING OUT OF ANY BREACH OF THE AGREEMENTS OR OBLIGATIONS UNDER THIS AGREEMENT.

BURROUGHS SHALL NOT BE LIABLE FOR ANY DAMAGES CAUSED BY DELAY IN DELIVERY, IN-

STALLATION OR FURNISHING OF THE EQUIPMENT OR SERVICES UNDER THIS AGREEMENT.

8. The Customer agrees that this Agreement constitutes the entire agreement, understanding and representations, expressed or implied, between the Customer and Burroughs with respect to the equipment, and/or related services to be furnished hereunder and that this Agreement supersedes all prior communications between the parties including all oral and written proposals.

9. For example, the pre-trial stipulation indicates that the admissibility of prior representations made by Burroughs would be a question of law which would turn on the applicability of the ESC's integration clause.

10. Conversely, the misrepresentation claim, which was not pressed in the District Court, is likewise not asserted on this appeal. That claim is therefore deemed abandoned. [Citation.] We in any event feel that the misrepresentation claim is in essence a contract-related claim and thus redundant and impermissible. [Citations.]

distinguishable and that the ESC should not apply.[12]

We need not resolve the issue of the transaction's character in order to decide this appeal, however. We find that either resolution of the issue leads to the same disposition of the appeal. We first assume that the lease was a true lease.

I. IF A TRUE LEASE

If the lease was a true lease, Earman argues that the only sale of the equipment was from Burroughs to NER. That contract is set out by NER's purchase order. The purchase order expressly designates Earman as intended lessee. Because Earman is so designated it is persuasively argued that Earman is a third party beneficiary with the right to enforce the provisions of the purchase order. [Citations.]

As third party beneficiary, Earman first argues that it is entitled to enforce the implied warranty rights of NER against Burroughs. Earman recognizes, however, that its implied warranty theory is made difficult by two terms of the NER-Burroughs contract, as set out on NER's purchase order form. One term, left partially uncompleted, was rubber-stamped onto the purchase order by Burroughs:

> By the below signature of buyer, or his authorized representative, the sale of this equipment shall be governed by the terms and conditions contained in agreement Form No. _____, the receipt of copies of which are hereby acknowledged by the buyer. Further, the buyers purchase order printed terms and conditions herein are null and void.
>
> The period of normal maintenance coverage applicable to equipment purchased hereunder is _____ months.

This term is stamped on the face of the purchase order, directly below the description of the equipment purchased. That placement and the fact that the term is rubber-stamped, tends to make the term conspicuous even though the print of the term is smaller than that used in the rest of the purchase order. This term

obviously refers to the ESC, which contains the disclaimers and limitations of liability which seemingly defeat Earman's claims.

Even if for some reason the rubber-stamped term does not apply, another term of NER's purchase order form also indicates that the provisions of the ESC apply to Earman's claims (emphasis supplied):

> You [Burroughs] warrant that EQUIPMENT will comply with all warranties, agreements and representations made by you to LESSEE [Earman], "By your acceptance [Burrough's acceptance] of this order and invoice to us [NER], you agree that you will make available to LESSEE [Earman] and will permit LESSEE [Earman] to enforce against you your *standard* representations, warranties and service obligations *in the same manner as if LESSEE [Earman] were the purchaser of the EQUIPMENT*."

This term is an integral part of the purchase order form, printed in a type size equal to that of other portions of the form.

Earman launches an innovative attack on these two terms. Earman argues that the terms (i) are not conspicuous and (ii) do not mention the word "merchantability." Therefore, under U.C.C. § 2–316(2) [footnote], the terms are insufficient to disclaim (i) all implied warranties and (ii) the implied warranty of merchantability, respectively. Since those implied warranties are not effectively disclaimed, Earman concludes that it may recover as a third party beneficiary of NER's implied warranty rights.

The obvious weakness in Earman's attack is that those terms of the purchase order are not warranty disclaimers in the first place. It is unimportant that the terms may not meet § 2–316(2)'s requirements. Clearly perceived, the second of the terms is an *express* grant of third party beneficiary rights to Earman but conditioned with an incorporation of Burroughs's "*standard* representations, warranties and obligations" (emphasis supplied). The term expressly provides that "all warranties, agreements and representations" made by Burroughs to Earman are to be enforceable

---

12. The available evidence—the circumstances surrounding the transaction and provisions of the lease—suggests that the transaction was a financing arrangement rather than a lease. But there is no evidence re-

lating to the anticipated economic value of the equipment over the term of the lease. Without evidence of this essential factor, we cannot characterize the transaction with certainty. [Citations.]

by Earman. By specifying that Earman was to be treated as a "purchaser" and by referring to Burroughs's "standard" representations, the language itself seemingly incorporates the prior dealings of Burroughs and Earman. Those prior dealings encompass the ESC and its exculpatory provisions. We find that this language is sufficient to condition Earman's third party rights to the terms and conditions of the ESC, which embodies all of the prior dealings of Earman and Burroughs.

Furthermore, the first term, though not filled in, was an obvious attempt to incorporate by reference the terms and conditions of the ESC. The Code provides that a course of dealing between the parties is relevant to the interpretation of uncertain, incomplete terms. [Footnote.] The dealings between Earman, Burroughs, and NER certainly indicate that the incomplete portion of the purchase order was intended to refer to the ESC, thereby incorporating it by reference.

That Earman's third party rights under the purchase order are governed by the ESC's terms and conditions is further supported by a venerable principle of contract law. In a computer lease case almost identical in facts to the instant one, the Kansas Supreme Court stated:

> It is well settled principle of law that where two or more documents are executed by the same parties at or near the same time in the course of the same transaction and concern the same subject matter they will be read and construed together.

Atlas Industries, Inc. v. National Cash Register Co., 216 Kan. 213, 220, 531 P.2d 41, 46–47 (1975) (citing *Topeka Savings Association v. Beck,* 199 Kan. 272, 428 P.2d 779 (1967). The principle applies to documents executed in the course of a transaction even though they are executed days or weeks apart. Florida recognizes this contemporaneous transaction principle. [Citations.]

The documents involved in the instant case were executed over a 12-day period and manifestly concerned the same transaction. Reading the lease, purchase order, and ESC together is therefore appropriate. Although viewed in isolation the ESC was executory,

when it is viewed as part of the entire transaction it is apparent that the ESC's statement of rights and obligations continues to govern Earman's relationship with Burroughs. The purchase order (and even, more obliquely, the lease),[15] incorporates the ESC in the context of defining Earman's rights. Thus the ESC governs Earman's rights with respect to Burroughs.

II. IF A FINANCING ARRANGEMENT

For much the same reasons, no different result is reached if the lease was a financing arrangement rather than a true lease. Again the contemporaneous transaction principle requires that we construe the three documents together. Assuming now that the lease was a financing arrangement, the real economic effect of the transaction was a sale direct from Burroughs to Earman. That effect coalesces with the ESC's express purpose: a sale direct from Burroughs to Earman. The coalescence is all the more reason, under the contemporaneous transaction principle, to give effect to the ESC's unambiguous statement of Earman's rights against Burroughs. As stated by the Kansas Supreme Court, "it would be anomalous if * * * commercial transactions [which are entered into by the device of a lease rather than a sale] were subject to different rules of law than other transactions which tend to have the identical economic result." *Atlas Industries, Inc. v. National Cash Register Co., supra,* 216 Kan. at 218, 531 P.2d at 45. * * *

III. APPLICATION

Subject to Earman's claim of unconscionability, our remaining task is to apply the terms and conditions of the ESC to Earman's breach of warranty claims. The ESC contains an integration provision. *See* note 8 *supra,* for text. We find the integration provision sufficient to prevent the consideration of prior representations by Burroughs. Several other Courts which have construed Burroughs's ESC unanimously agree. *Bakal v. Burroughs Corp.,* 74 Misc.2d 202, 343 N.Y.S.2d 541 (1972); *Investors Premium Corp. v. Burroughs Corp.,* 389

---

15. The lease states that: "Lessee [Earman] shall look to Vendor [Burroughs] for all hardware, software and programming deficiencies, which are not Lessor's [NER's] responsibility."

F.Supp. 39 (D.S.C.1974) (S.C.); *Byrd Tractor, Inc. v. Burroughs Corp.,* Civ.No. 77–30–A (U.S.E.D.Va., Aug. 8, 1977) (Va.). We are therefore confined to the four corners of the ESC (subsequent documents not being inconsistent), the interpretation of which is a matter of law. [Citations.]

The ESC contains terms disclaiming warranties and limiting liability. *See* notes 6 & 7 *supra,* for text. Earman does not argue that these terms are ineffective. The terms are in type larger than the surrounding terms and meet U.C.C. § 1–201(10)'s definition of being "conspicuous." [16] The implied warranties disclaimer includes the word "merchantability." Thus the implied warranties disclaimer fully complies with the requirements of U.C.C. § 2–316(2). [Footnote.] The disclaimer of express warranties also complies with the Code's requirements. U.C.C. § 2–316(1). [Footnote.] Likewise the limitation of liability terms are effective. The ESC included a three-month maintenance and repair warranty. Consequently, the requirements of U.C.C. § 2–719[19] are met. Our resolution of this essentially uncontested point is again supported by other Courts. [Citations.]

Because of the ESC's exculpatory provisions, Earman's claims must fail unless those provisions are unconscionable. It is Earman's last contention that the ESC's exculpatory provisions are unconscionable and therefore recovery against Burroughs is possible.

IV. UNCONSCIONABILITY

Based on the documents and the stipulated and admitted facts, Earman claims that the ESC's exculpatory provisions are unconscionable as a matter of law. [Footnote.] The burden of proof for this affirmative defense is on Earman. [Citation.] Earman contends that there are sufficient facts to show overreaching and unfair conduct by Burroughs, rendering the ESC's provisions unconscionable.

Unconscionability is allegedly shown by the relatively short period between signing of the ESC and the lease; the fact that there were only two or three meetings between Earman and Burroughs's representative prior to the signings; and the fact that Earman was in the business of selling oil and oil products and was therefore presumably unfamiliar with computers. Earman asserts that those bare facts fulfill all but the last two considerations necessary for unconscionability under *Potomac Electric Power Co. v. Westinghouse Electric Corp.,* 385 F.Supp. 572 (D.D.C.1974), *rev'd & remanded on other grounds* 527 F.2d 853 (D.C. Cir.1975) [footnote]: (i) examination of the negotiation process as to length of time in dealing; (ii) the length of time for deliberations; (iii) the experience or astuteness of the parties; (iv) whether counsel reviewed the contract; and (v) whether the buyer was a reluctant purchaser.

The facts asserted by Earman are not sufficient to show unconscionability. The number of meetings between the parties by itself indicates nothing about the length, nature, or fairness of negotiations. The period of time between the signing of documents does not mean that Earman's deliberations concerning the transaction were limited to that period. Nor does Earman's involvement in the oil industry impune the experience or astuteness of its negotiator. Earman has not shown a lack of legal guidance and if anything the record suggests Earman was a willing party to the transaction.

---

16. The Code states:
A term or clause is conspicuous when it is so written that a reasonable person against whom it is to operate ought to have noticed it. * * * Language in the body of the form is "conspicuous" if it is in larger or other contrasting type or color. * * *

19. CONTRACTUAL MODIFICATION OR LIMITATION OF REMEDY

(1) Subject to the provisions of subsections (2) and (3) of this section and of the preceding section on liquidation and limitation of damages,

(a) the agreement may provide for remedies in addition to or in substitution for those provided in this Article and may limit or alter the measure of damages recoverable under this Article, as by limiting the buyer's remedies to return of the goods and repayment of the price or to repair and replacement of non-conforming goods or parts; and

(b) resort to a remedy as provided is optional unless the remedy is expressly agreed to be exclusive, in which case it is the sole remedy.

(2) Where circumstances cause an exclusive or limited remedy to fail of its essential purpose, remedy may be had as provided in this Act.

(3) Consequential damages may be limited or excluded unless the limitation or exclusion is unconscionable. Limitation of consequential damages for injury to the person in the case of consumer goods is prima facie unconscionable but limitation of damages where the loss is commercial is not.

The procedural sort of unconscionability alleged by Earman requires a showing of overreaching or sharp practices by the seller and ignorance or inexperience on the buyer's part, resulting in a lack of meaningful bargaining by the parties. *See generally* J. White & R. Summers, *supra* § 4–3. In commercial settings such as the instant one, businessmen are presumed to act at arms length. [Citations.] Especially in light of that presumption, Earman has fallen far short of proving unconscionability. [Footnote.]

Affirmed.

KALIL BOTTLING CO. v. BURROUGHS CORP.

127 Ariz. 278, 619 P.2d 1055
(Court of Appeals of Arizona, Division 2, Sept. 25, 1980.)

HOWARD, J.

Kalil is a soft drink bottler and distributor. In 1969 it decided to computerize its inventory and accounting operations. On July 16, 1969, Kalil signed an "Equipment Sale Contract", agreeing to purchase a computer and software[1] from Burroughs Corporation for $40,168.96 with a down payment of $1,750. The balance was to be financed by Burroughs according to terms and conditions established by Kalil. Burroughs rejected Kalil's application for credit, but not before the computer was installed. Kalil was unable to secure bank financing and on April 30, 1970, National Equipment Rental, Ltd. (National) purchased the computer and software from Burroughs and leased it to Kalil for 66 months with a monthly rental of $862.40.[2] The down payment which Kalil had paid Burroughs was credited by Burroughs on the purchase price paid by National.

On the face of the contract between Burroughs and Kalil was the following provision:

MAINTENANCE COVERAGE FOR 12 MONTHS APPLIES AS DESCRIBED ON REVERSE SIDE. TERMS AND CONDITIONS ON REVERSE SIDE ARE PART OF *THIS SECURITY AGREEMENT.* (Emphasis added)

The contract terms and conditions specifically warranted the equipment sold to be "free from defects in material and workmanship." The contract stated:

THERE ARE NO UNDERSTANDINGS, AGREEMENTS, REPRESENTATIONS, OR WARRANTIES, EXPRESS OR IMPLIED (INCLUDING ANY REGARDING MERCHANTABILITY OR FITNESS FOR A PARTICULAR PURPOSE), NOT SPECIFIED HEREIN, RESPECTING THIS CONTRACT OR THE EQUIPMENT HEREUNDER. THIS CONTRACT STATES THE ENTIRE OBLIGATION OF SELLER IN CONNECTWITH (SIC) WITH THIS TRANSACTION.

The contract signed by National and Burroughs stated:

All guarantees, warranties and service normally accompanying this equipment are to be extended directly to the consignee [Kalil]. (For convenience we shall call this provision 1)

It also contained the following provision:

Burroughs' acceptance of this order is conditioned upon agreement by the buyer [National] to the standard terms and conditions of Burroughs standard order form for sale of its equipment. Buyer has signified acceptance of this condition through initialing by an authorized representative in margin hereof. Burroughs standard terms and conditions of sale shall prevail. (We shall call this provision 2)

Many problems were encountered by Kalil with the computer system. It malfunctioned and suffered from too much "down time" causing a work backlog at Kalil. Burroughs failed to install all of the programs required in the software addendum to the equipment contract. Sometime in November of 1971 the computer was rendered inoperable for about 10 days which worsened Kalil's already existing backlog. A second machine was installed by Burroughs in an attempt to make Kalil's operations current, but the second machine also suffered from breakdowns.

Finally, when the lease with National expired in 1976, Kalil purchased its own computer from a different manufacturer. In the interim, Kalil had filed this lawsuit on September 11, 1973.

---

1. Software is a computer program encoded on punch cards, tapes or discs or other media in machine-readable form and in written documents in human-readable form.

2. There was no option to purchase in this lease.

Kalil's claims for relief against Burroughs consisted of counts for breach of contract, breach of express warranty, breach of implied warranties of merchantability and fitness for a particular purpose, negligent misrepresentation, fraud, and consumer fraud. All counts except those for fraud and consumer fraud went to the jury which awarded damages to Kalil in the sum of $401,690. Because the jury was given only one form of verdict to use in the event it found for Kalil, we are unable to determine upon which claim or claims Kalil prevailed.

Our review is somewhat frustrated by the posture of the case before the trial court and before us. The theory adhered to by both parties in the trial court and on appeal is that at all times pertinent to the transactions a contract between Kalil and Burroughs was in existence. However, the facts indicate otherwise since the parties' conduct constituted a mutual rescission of the contract when the computer and software was purchased by National and leased to Kalil.[3] [Citations.]

* * * Relying on the case of *Burroughs Corp. v. Chesapeake Petro & Supply Co., Inc.,* 384 A.2d 734 (Md.App.1978), the trial court ruled that the terms and conditions on the reverse side of the "Equipment Sale Contract" were not part of the contract between the parties. The Court of Appeals of Maryland stated that the clause on the front page of the contract, which was the same as the one here, indicated that the terms and conditions on the reverse side were operative only if the document was a security agreement (installment sale contract). We are unable to agree with the reasoning of the Maryland court and find that the trial court erred in its ruling. The "Equipment Sale Contract" was used for both cash sales and installment sales. The parties spent a great deal of time determining whether this was a "security agreement." We need not reach that issue. It does not matter whether the parties called their contract a "security

agreement" or a "spotted elephant". The reverse side contains terms and conditions such as an express warranty, an exclusion of certain other warranties and a provision excluding consequential damages. It defies logic and reason to conclude that these provisions were intended to apply only if the contract was deemed an installment sales contract but not if it were a cash sale. The net effect is that the exclusion of implied warranties on the reverse side of the contract was valid and binding on the parties. Thus, the court erred in submitting the issue of implied warranties to the jury. [Citations.] Furthermore, since the contract specifically negated the alleged misrepresentations, Kalil's claims for negligent misrepresentation, fraud and consumer fraud, based upon statements made prior to the signing of the contract were not actionable because of the parol evidence rule. [Citations.] This leaves Kalil with a claim for breach of the warranty concerning freedom from defects in material and workmanship. This warranty applies both to the computer and the software. There is, therefore, also a claim for breach of contract.

The terms and conditions also contained an agreement by Burroughs to exchange any parts shown to have become defective as a result of wear and tear from normal use during one year from the date of delivery, a provision that limited its responsibility to no more than an exchange of equipment under its warranty, and a clause which provided that the purchaser expressly waived all damages, whether direct, incidental or consequential.

Burroughs contends that this waiver of consequential damages precludes Kalil from recovery on any and all of its counts. Contracts with provisions identical to those before us have been interpreted by other courts as constituting valid exclusions of consequential damages in commercial loss cases [Citations.] A.R.S. Sec. 44–2398(A)(1) and (2) provides that the agreement may limit the buyer's recovery

---

3. This would change the relationship between the parties and require an analysis of the rights and liabilities between them. Kalil is a third-party beneficiary of provision 1 of the National-Burroughs contract but is not bound by provision 2 since it has not agreed to these terms and conditions. Other questions are also raised by this change of legal relationship. What is the effect of the rescission on representations made prior to the Kalil-Burroughs contract? [Citations.]

Do any implied warranties from the manufacturer extend to Kalil, the lessee from National, despite lack of privity of contract thus giving Kalil a claim for commercial loss? See A.R.S. Sec. 44–2335. Sec. 2–318 of the U.C.C., alternatives A, B and C and Comment 3 thereof. [Citations.]

to repair and replacement of non-conforming goods or parts and make this remedy exclusive. However, subsection (B) provides that where the circumstances cause an exclusive or limited remedy to fail of its essential purpose, it is no longer deemed exclusive. In *Beal v. General Motors Corporation*, 354 F.Supp. 423 (D.C.Del.1973) [footnote] the court stated:

> The purpose of an exclusive remedy of replacement or repair of defective parts, whose presence constitute a breach of an express warranty, is to give the seller an opportunity to make the goods conforming while limiting the risks to which he is subject by excluding direct and consequential damages that might otherwise arise. From the point of view of the buyer the purpose of the exclusive remedy is to give him goods that conform to the contract within a reasonable time after a defective part is discovered. When the warrantor fails to correct the defect as promised within a reasonable time he is liable for a breach of that warranty. (Citations omitted) The limited, exclusive remedy fails of its purpose and is thus avoided under Sec. 2719(2), whenever the warrantor fails to correct the defect within a reasonable period. 354 F.Supp. at 426.

We agree with the *Beal* court and find its principles applicable here. Implicit in the terms of the contract is the presumption that the equipment and software could be cured by replacement or repair in the event they became defective. The record reflects sufficient evidence from which a trier of fact could conclude that the Burroughs equipment and program were defective in material and workmanship and that Burroughs could not and did not repair or replace it. In light of *Beal,* we hold that the remedy of repair or replacement is non-exclusive in the instant case.

* * *

Reversed and remanded for a new trial.

LEASCO DATA PROCESSING EQUIPMENT CORP. v. STARLINE OVERSEAS CORP.

74 Misc.2d 898, 346 N.Y.S.2d 288
(Supreme Court, Appellate Term, First Department, July 6, 1973.)

PER CURIAM.

Plaintiff and defendant, two corporate entities, dealing at arm's length through officers and agents (presumably well-advised, alert, knowledgeable business men) negotiated a written contract which by its terms required plaintiff to purchase a *defendant-specified,* sophisticated billing machine from a *defendant-designated* seller of such machines and lease it to defendant for five years and five months at a fixed monthly rental of $274.20 to be paid by defendant, with the option to defendant of renewing the lease at its expiration for a nominal *yearly* rental of $274.20, the same amount as the *monthly* rental during the term. Plaintiff performed all things on its part to be performed and defendant, in full possession and use of the billing machine, regularly paid the monthly rental installments for three years when it defaulted, claiming the machine to have become inoperable.

Plaintiff's action for the rental due for the balance of the term was met with so-called counterclaims and defenses depending for their validity on proof that the transaction was a sale of goods and plaintiff was a merchant dealing in such machines so that the provisions of Article 2 of the Uniform Commercial Code, relating to sales, governed the transaction.

Defendant not only failed to adduce sufficient evidence to sustain its so-called counterclaims and defenses, but the express language of the written agreement contradicts any implications that plaintiff was a "merchant [dealing] in goods of the kind" within the meaning of U.C.C. section 2–104, when it says at paragraph 3, "lessee requests lessor *to purchase the equipment from a seller* and arrange for delivery which shall be deemed complete upon arrival at Lessee's premises * * *" (Emphasis supplied). Defendant's selection of the specified machine was prompted by the recommendation of a friend, in no way connected with plaintiff or the manufacturer. A representative of the manufacturer or merchant dealing in these machines, was consulted by defendant's president before entering into the leasing agreement with plaintiff.

A proper construction of the written leasing agreement must find it to be a "title retention contract and lease * * * intended as security" within the meaning of U.C.C. 9–102(2), designed to afford defendant the advantage of having the possession and use of its own free choice of a particular machine throughout its usable expectancy, by means of long-term installment payments of $274.20 per month without the large, initial outlay of $13,710 necessary to outright purchase.

Section 1–201(37) of the Uniform Commercial Code defines "security interest" as "an interest in personal property * * * which secures payment * * * of an obligation." And goes on to say "whether a lease is intended as security is to be determined by the facts of each case; however * * * an agreement that upon compliance with the terms of the lease the lessee * * * has the option to become the owner of the property * * * for a nominal consideration does make the lease one intended for security."

The lease in this case, as has been noted above, provided the defendant with an option to renew for a trifling yearly rental which for all practical purposes amounts to making defendant owner of the machine at the end of the lease for a nominal consideration until total obsolescence.

Article 2 of the Uniform Commercial Code— (Sales), at section 2–102, expressly excludes from the application of its provisions (sec. 2–101 to and including sec. 2–725 U.C.C.) "any transaction which although in the form of an unconditional contract to sell or present sale is intended to operate only as a security transaction * * *".

The case of Hertz Comm. Leasing Corp. v. Transp. Credit Clearing House Inc., 64 Misc.2d 910, 316 N.Y.S.2d 585 relied on in the dissent, in reversing the result at the Civil Court, 59 Misc.2d 226, 298 N.Y.S.2d 392, implicitly *rejected* the proposition that leases of personal property, similar to the one here in suit, are necessarily or invariably subject to the provisions of Art. 2 of the Uniform Commercial Code—(Sales) and inferentially reiterated the statutory criteria that "whether a lease is intended as security is to be determined by the facts of each case" (U.C.C. 1–201 [37]). In that case, because of the defendant's failure of proof, as here, this court in reversing the denial of plaintiff's motion for summary judgment granted judgment for the plaintiff lessor for the amount of lease-installment payments in default.

Whether or not defendant was subrogated to plaintiff's right of action against the seller of the machine for breach of warranties (un-disclosed to defendant) and, under principles of restitution, (Sec. 50 N.Y.Jurs. Restitution 122, sec. 1 et seq.) is entitled to recover from plaintiff such damages, if any, as plaintiff may have claimed or received by attribution of defendant's loss or injury to plaintiff's right of recovery, are issues which were neither pleaded nor proved, hence are not a proper subject of review on this appeal.

The judgment should be affirmed with $25 costs to respondent.

Judgment affirmed, etc.

LUPIANO, J. (dissenting):

Plaintiff, Leasco Data Processing Equipment Corporation (Leasco), seeks to recover rental due from defendant, Starline Overseas Corp. (Starline), under an agreement whereby it leased a billing machine to Starline. Leasco had purchased this machine from SCM Corp., the manufacturer, and leased it to Starline for a term of 5 years and 5 months with the option of annual renewals. Starline paid for maintenance and service contracts on the machine, although Leasco at all times retained title to said billing machine. Leasco's endorsed complaint alleged default in rental payments by Starline, lessee, and pursuant to clauses dealing with acceleration of payment on default and 20% attorney's fees, demanded $8,884.08 in money damages. Leasco further requested immediate possession of the leased chattel. Starline's answer contains denials of all the allegations except that of the making of the lease and further contains three "affirmative defense(s) and counterclaim(s)", basically founded on fraud and breach of warranty and requesting rescission and damages. At the trial Starline was granted, with Leasco's consent, leave to amend its answer to allege that paragraph 10 of the lease was unconscionable.

Paragraph 10 of the lease provides in pertinent part:

Lessee agrees that its obligations under this lease are absolute, and shall continue in full force and effect regardless of any disability of Lessee to use the equipment because of War, Act of God, government regulation, strike, loss or damage, obsolescence; breach of contract or warranty; failure of or delay in delivery, misdelivery or any other cause, and that its obligations shall not abate due to any claim or set-off against

Lessor. * * * Lessee agrees that Lessor has made no warranties or representations, express or implied with regard to the equipment. * * *

As noted in its opinion, the trial court, after trying the issue of unconscionability *prior* to the remaining issues, found, in light of the evidence presented as to the commercial setting, purpose and effect of the transaction, that paragraph 10 of the lease was not unconscionable.

After resolving the question of unconscionability, apparently without regard to the U.C.C., the court granted plaintiff's motion for a directed verdict and rejected defendant's argument that Article 2 of the Uniform Commercial Code applies to transactions of this nature. The court found defendant's reliance on Hertz Corp. v. Trans Credit House 59 Misc.2d 226, 298 N.Y.S.2d 392 (Civil Ct. 1969), rev'd on other grounds, 64 Misc.2d 910, 316 N.Y.S.2d 585 unfounded.

Finally, the court observed that the defendant made conclusory statements of defect. There was no proof of damages by defendant and there was waiver of defendant's right of rescission.

Defendant's prime objections on appeal are that: (1) The plaintiff, a lessor has the same obligation regarding warranties under the U.C.C. as a merchant does; (2) The plaintiff's attempt to exclude the implied warranty of fitness is invalid because the exculpatory language was not conspicuous; and (3) The Trial Court was not correct in directing a verdict in favor of plaintiff against defendant.

On this appeal, the critical issues are (1) whether under the equipment lease, there were implied warranties with respect to the equipment; (2) assuming such implied warranties, whether the lessor properly excluded them; and (3) whether the lessor breached non-excluded implied warranties.

In resolving these issues, it should be initially noted that the Uniform Commercial Code Article on sales is attended by a penumbra or umbrella of influence in areas of contract law not specifically within the literal definition of sales under U.C.C. § 2–102 (See Murray, "under the Spreading Analogy of Article 2 of the Uniform Commercial Code", 39 Ford.L.Rev. 447, 448). The courts of New York and of sister states have applied Article 2 of the Uniform

Commercial Code to cases involving exclusion of warranties in equipment leases. [Citations.]

U.C.C. Section 2–102 provides:

Unless the context otherwise requires, this Article [Sales] applies to transactions in goods; it does not apply to any transaction which although in the form of an unconditional contract to sell or present sale is intended to operate *only* as a security transaction. * * * [Emphasis supplied].

Official Comment 2 to U.C.C. § 2–313 states:

* * * the warranty sections of this Article are not designed in any way to disturb those lines of case law growth which have recognized that warranties need not be confined either to sales contracts or to the direct parties to such a contract.

With the foundation set forth above, the rationale of the Hertz case *supra* becomes persuasive. The court therein found that:

[a] consideration of the applicable law, and of economic reason, [mandates the conclusion that] Article 2 of the Uniform Commercial Code, *to the extent that its provisions can be considered applicable,* governs the equipment lease before the court. (Hertz *supra,* 59 Misc.2d p. 231, 298 N.Y.S.2d p. 397) [emphasis supplied]

This conclusion was influenced by existing sister-state courts' interpretations of the Code in view of the Code's stated purpose of making uniform the law among the various jurisdictions (see U.C.C. 1-102[2][C]). Additionally, the court noted that it

* * * would be anomalous if this large body of commercial transactions were subject to different rules of law than other commercial transactions which tend to the identical economic result. (Hertz, supra, 59 Misc.2d p. 229, 298 N.Y.S.2d, p. 395).

The instant case involves a lease with provisions analogous to a sale except for the retention of title by the lessor. It clearly warrants recognition and application of the penumbra of protection of the U.C.C. Article on Sales. It was erroneous for the trial court to refuse to apply the rationale of the Hertz case *supra* to the instant litigation on the legally irrelevant basis that the machine in question was purchased by the plaintiff at defendant's request. Moreover, the court relied on the assumption, not supported by the evidence, that the defendant had theretofore satisfied itself independently as to the proper functioning of the machine.

Application of Article 2 of the U.C.C. to the equipment lease in question, impels recognition that Leasco impliedly warranted the merchantability of the billing machine to Starline (see U.C.C. § 2–314).

Concerning the issue of exclusion of implied warranties, the evidence did not indicate that there were defects which an examination ought to have revealed to defendant, nor did it indicate a course of dealing, course of performance or usage of trade which would exclude implied warranties. Consequently, if the implied warranties were excluded, they must have been so excluded under U.C.C. § 2 316(2) or 3(a) which subdivisions require the written exclusion to be conspicuous. U.C.C. § 1–201(10) defines conspicuous as follows:

A term or clause is conspicuous when it is so written that a reasonable person against whom it is to operate ought to have noticed it. A printed heading in capitals (as: NON-NEGOTIABLE BILL OF LADING) is conspicuous. Language in the body of a form is 'conspicuous' if it is in larger or other contrasting type or color. * * *

Clearly the exclusion sentence *submerged* in paragraph 10 is not conspicuous, and, therefore, can not be relied upon to exclude the implied warranties.

In addition, paragraph 10, is, under all the facts and circumstances herein, unconscionable (see U.C.C. § 2–302). In this regard, the Leasco purchase order sent to SCM Corp. is significant. There was uncontroverted testimony on behalf of both *Leasco* and Starline that this document prepared by Leasco and containing a warranty by SCM running to Starline and Leasco was never given to Starline by Leasco. In addition, it appears that Starline knew nothing of this purchase order until the court in January 1972, *recommended* that Starline sue SCM on the warranty contained therein. By virtue of paragraph 10 of the lease, Leasco attempted to compel Starline to pay regardless of whether the machine was operable, or not, and also attempted to exclude all warranties. Clearly the paragraph in the aforementioned context, is unconscionable. Consequently, Leasco, the lessor, did not properly exclude the implied warranties.

Testimony for Leasco established that prior to this suit, Leasco knew that the type of machine delivered to Starline had problems and very often broke down, that Leasco contacted SCM on several occasions to complain that this type of machine broke down very often, and that Leasco brought an action which was ultimately settled, against SCM on the basis of complaints by Leasco's customers about the type of machine involved herein.

Accordingly on the basis of the aforesaid, Starline appears able to assert a viable *defense* to Leasco's action which should be presented to the jury on the basis of Leasco's prior recovery against SCM and on the basis of breach of implied warranty.

Although Starline's *counterclaims* for breach of warranty are barred by the Statute of Limitations, (U.C.C. § 2–725[1]) the counterclaim for rescission is not so barred (CPLR 213[1]). Moreover, under the facts and circumstances herein, Starline has brought its rescission counterclaim in a reasonable time within the statutory period and thus is not barred by laches. [Citation.]

Finally, it must be noted that Starline's *acquiescence* to the "suggestion" of the trial court that it bring an action for breach of warranty against SCM, does not estop Starline from asserting its right of rescission. Where the remedy initially asserted is barred by the Statute of Limitations, the doctrine of election of remedies does not apply to defeat a subsequent inconsistent remedy. [Citation.]

On the record herein, the judgment should be reversed and a new trial ordered as to all the pertinent issues.

TEXTRON, INC. v. TELEOPERATOR SYSTEMS CORP.

554 F. Supp. 315

(United States District Court, E.D. New York, Jan. 10, 1983.)

BRAMWELL, D. J.

On October 29, 1982, plaintiff commenced the instant action by the filing of a summons and complaint along with an application for a temporary restraining order and preliminary injunctive relief. The application for a temporary restraining order was granted conditioned upon the posting of a one million dollar surety bond. On November 10, 1982 the court denied defendants' application to modify the temporary restraining order and continued it in full force and effect.

The hearing on the preliminary injunction was convened on November 17–20, 1982 during which documentary evidence and the testimony of several witnesses was received. Today, pursuant to Rule 52(a) of the Federal Rules of Civil Procedure, the court disposes of that application.

FINDINGS OF FACT

1. Plaintiff, Textron Inc., is a corporation organized under the laws of the State of Delaware, having its principal place of business at 40 Westminster Street, Providence, Rhode Island. Plaintiff conducts its operations in the United States through a number of Divisions. One of these Divisions is the Bridgeport Machines Division (hereinafter referred to as Bridgeport), having its principal place of business located at 500 Lindley Street, Bridgeport, Connecticut. [References.]

2. Defendant, TeleOperator Systems Corp. (hereinafter referred to as T.O.S.) is a corporation organized under the laws of the State of New York, having its principal place of business at 45 Knickerbocker Avenue, Bohemia, New York. [Reference.]

3. Defendant Carl R. Flatau (hereinafter referred to as Flatau), a recognized expert in the field of robotics, is the president and principal stockholder of T.O.S. [References.]

4. For many years Bridgeport has been in the business of making and selling machine tools, such as vertical milling machines. Over the past ten years, it has been making and selling milling machines provided with computer numerical control units (hereinafter referred to as CNC units). Bridgeport manufactures its milling machines at facilities in Bridgeport, Connecticut. It has an operating facility in Horsham, Pennsylvania that develops, designs and manufactures CNC units that are subsequently integrated with various mechanical machines or tools, such as milling machines, at Bridgeport's manufacturing fa-

cilities in Bridgeport, Connecticut. [Reference.]

5. In 1980, Bridgeport became interested in large scale or volume production and sale of robots for industrial uses, such as in the automotive industry. In that regard, Bridgeport became aware of the functional performance requirements or specifications of General Motors Corporation for industrial robots called the PUMA system (programmable universal machine for light assembly). [References.]

6. In furtherance of this goal and, more specifically, in order to ascertain the names of robotics specialists, Gerald McCaul (hereinafter referred to as McCaul), Vice President for Strategic Planning of Bridgeport/Machines travelled around the United States visiting major manufacturers and buyers of robots, attending conferences on robotics and conferring at research universities working in the field. [References.]

7. During the course of these visits faculty members at the Massachusetts Institute of Technology recommended Flatau to McCaul as an outstanding expert in the design of manipulators and robots. [Reference.]

8. Based on these recommendations, McCaul decided to approach T.O.S. and Flatau because of his expertise in the field. In June of 1980 McCaul wrote to Flatau. [References.]

9. Prior to any contact with Bridgeport, T.O.S. was already involved to a considerable degree in the designing of so-called manipulators or manipulator arms adapted for remote but direct operation by human beings in special environments and applications, as distinguished from design work relating to industrial robots that are programmable for automatic operation in connection with the commercial manufacture of other products. [References.]

10. In July 1980, in response to McCaul's letter, Flatau met with McCaul at T.O.S.'s office. At that meeting, Flatau showed McCaul a film about the robotics technology already developed by T.O.S. [References.]

11. The technology displayed in the film and described in finding of fact number 9 was not directly applicable to what Bridgeport was looking for—that is inapplicable for use with industrial robots automatically programmed

to engage in the commercial manufacture of other products. [References.]

12. In the latter half of 1980, Bridgeport initiated discussions with T.O.S. and Flatau about the design capabilities of T.O.S. in the remote manipulator field and possible application of that capability to industrial robot design. During those discussions Bridgeport provided T.O.S. with a copy of the specifications for the aforesaid PUMA system and requested T.O.S. to prepare a proposal for the design of the mechanical features of an industrial robot that would be integrated with a CNC unit developed by Bridgeport to automatically control and program its operation as desired. [References.]

13. Flatau prepared such a design proposal for T.O.S. and submitted it to Bridgeport on January 30, 1981. That proposal expressly contemplated the design of an industrial robot and the fabrication of one prototype, with the specific stated goal of large scale or volume production by Bridgeport. On pages 2 and 3 of the T.O.S. design proposal, Flatau discussed the then "existing state of the art" in the industrial robot field. No mention was made therein of any prior work done by him or T.O.S. in that field. In addition, the T.O.S. design proposal estimated that the design phase would require 600 hours of engineering time, 1600 hours of design time, and 600 hours of drafting time while 2600 hours of machine shop time were estimated for prototype fabrication. The estimated cost was about $250,000. [References.]

14. On pages three and four of the January 30 design proposal, under the heading of "CONTRACTUAL REQUIREMENTS" appeared the following:

1. T.O.S. will perform the work on a cost plus basis.
2. A Progress Payment arrangement is required.
3. A Proprietary Technology Agreement is required. This must address and define the rights of Bridgeport Machines in the design. It also must define the rights of T.O.S. in its own technology.
4. A Hold Harmless Agreement with respect to product liability of Bridgeport Machines sales on the design will be required.
5. T.O.S. also desires other participation in the sale efforts. This would include furnishing of

application engineering services where required. In addition, we seek an arrangement enabling "TOS" to use the production hardware for devices equipped with more advanced features; e.g. force transducers, or intelligent controls for the University Research Market. This could take the form of a Dealership in the Robotics segment of Bridgeport equipment. The main advantages of such an arrangement to Bridgeport Machines would be that a continuous dialogue with advanced developments in the field would be created. As it is expected that the field of Robotics will mature quite rapidly, such a procedure would allow Bridgeport Machines to stay ahead of technological developments in the industrial sector. [Reference.]

15. At a meeting held on February 9, 1981, Bridgeport advised T.O.S. to proceed with the program as outlined in the January 30 design proposal. The substance of this meeting was embodied in a February 10, 1981 letter of intent from Bridgeport to T.O.S. [Reference.]

16. This letter addressed each of the "CONTRACTUAL REQUIREMENTS" embodied in the January 30 T.O.S. design proposal. With respect to requirement Nos. 3 and 5, quoted above, it specifically provided that:

3. TOS will have rights to apply developed technology to noncompetitive applications. Namely, manipulator, this will receive a more finite definition in the future.
5. As discussed, we have a general agreement that TOS participation in some form of the sales effort will be beneficial to both TOS and Bridgeport/Textron. This matter will also receive further definition in the future. [Reference.]

17. On February 16, 1981 Flatau wrote back to Mr. William R. Jahnke (hereinafter referred to as Jahnke), Vice President of Engineering for Textron/Bridgeport acknowledging the February 10 letter and detailing the costs involved in executing the design proposal. The letter indicated the work would be done at cost plus 20 per cent. [Reference.]

18. The February 16 letter from T.O.S. contains no language disagreeing with paragraph 3 of the February 10 Bridgeport letter of intent. Had defendants so disagreed at that time, plaintiff indicated that it would have cancelled the project. [References.]

19. As a result of the agreements embodied in the foregoing exchange of correspondence,

Bridgeport issued, and T.O.S. accepted, its March 16, 1981 Purchase Order, No. 24881, stating in pertinent part:

> Design 5 KG Industrial Articulated Manipulator Arm in general accordance with G.M. specification for programmable universal machine for light assembly, attached, and T.O.S. design proposal dated 30 January 1981. Bridgeport will design a computerized Control for this manipulator on a closely coordinated basis. [References.]

20. The purchase order provided for performance by T.O.S. on a cost plus 20% fee as per the February 16, 1981 letter from Flatau to Jahnke. It also specifically provided on page 6 that:

> Other terms and conditions will be covered in a separate agreement. [Reference.]

21. The purchase order specified a higher upper limit payment by Bridgeport to T.O.S. of $450,000, rather than $250,000 as estimated in the original T.O.S. design proposal, because the purchase order called for assembly and testing of three prototypes, whereas a single prototype was initially contemplated. [Reference.]

22. At no time during the foregoing exchange of correspondence in January–March 1981 did either T.O.S. or Flatau advise Bridgeport or Textron that T.O.S. or Flatau would claim the rights to any inventions and technology developed by T.O.S. for Bridgeport during the course of this business relationship. Furthermore, at no time during this exchange of correspondence did either T.O.S. or Flatau contradict the statement contained in the Bridgeport letter of intent that T.O.S. would only have the limited right to apply technology developed during this business relationship to "noncompetitive applications." Had defendants done so, Bridgeport claims that it would have terminated the project at that time. [References.]

23. By letter of March 18, 1981 from Flatau, T.O.S. submitted to Bridgeport its first invoice and technical progress report for this project, which was given the code name "TIGER" (or sometimes TIGER 5, the "5" standing for the 5 kilogram load the robot was intended to lift). At the end of the progress report, T.O.S. discussed the design configuration it had adopted for the project and further stated:

> The principle for this (configuration) is directly derived from a T.O.S. patented design for manipulators. Use of this patent for TIGER can be obtained by means of a $1 paid license. [References.]

24. The patent referred to in the plaintiff's exhibit seven is United States Patent No. 4,062,455 entitled "REMOTE MANIPULATOR" and granted December 13, 1977, in the name of Carl R. Flatau, as patentee. [References.]

25. In conformity with the March 16, 1981 purchase order all technical drawings prepared by TOS for the TIGER–5 project were on paper bearing the name "Bridgeport ® Textron, Bridgeport Machines Division of Textron Inc.," as well as the following proprietary legend:

> This document/drawing provides information which is proprietary to Bridgeport Machines and is made available to you for the use and maintenance of our products. Any use, reproduction, or dissemination of this information for any other purpose is prohibited without written permission. [References.]

26. When T.O.S. began using the printed Bridgeport drawing paper as described above in late March–early April of 1981, Robert L. Minter, then a designer and later a vice president of T.O.S., explicitly directed Flatau's attention to the aforesaid Bridgeport proprietary legend on the TIGER project drawings and he advised Flatau that, based on his 30 plus years of experience in the design field, the language contained therein meant that Bridgeport owned all rights to the designs embodied in those drawings. Despite being so advised, Flatau told Minter that T.O.S. should continue to use the aforesaid Bridgeport drawing paper forms in the TIGER program. [References.]

27. In April of 1981, Gerald McCaul, then a senior vice president of Bridgeport, felt it incumbent upon him to clarify with Flatau the exact meaning of the words "[o]ther terms and conditions will be covered in a separate agreement" on page six of the March 16, 1981 purchase order. [References.]

28. Accordingly, in April 1981 McCaul gave Flatau a draft purchase order that McCaul had previously prepared outlining in greater detail the relationship of the parties based upon prior discussions between McCaul and

Flatau. In pertinent part, this draft purchase order states as follows:

> T.O.S. will prepare patent applications for processing by Bridgeport for all proprietary technology developed on this purchase order. Bridgeport will grant T.O.S. a royalty free license to utilize these proprietary developments in any non-competitive T.O.S. future designs.
>
> T.O.S. agrees to license Bridgeport on a royalty free basis for any T.O.S. patented earlier developments which are included in this design.
>
> Bridgeport agrees to sell production versions of this device to T.O.S. for modification and resale into the noncompetitive high technology university research market. In return, T.O.S. will keep Bridgeport informed of any interesting and importing [sic] developments from that source for possible production use.
>
> Bridgeport expects to utilize T.O.S's manipulator technology and experience over a five year period for design of volume production based on successful completion of this initial project. Commitment would be for at least as many man hours as realized in the 1981 time period. [References.]

29. When presented with this document by McCaul, Flatau expressed no objections to any of its terms. Moreover, Flatau and McCaul thereafter continued performance under the TIGER–5 program which was paid for in accordance with a system of monthly invoices submitted to Bridgeport. [References.]

30. On June 15, 1981, McCaul forwarded to Flatau the suggested agreement between the parties. Consistent with the language in the letter of intent and the draft purchase order, the suggested agreement contemplated that Bridgeport would own all patentable proprietary technology developed during the TIGER program and that Bridgeport would grant T.O.S. a royalty-free license to utilize such inventions in non-competitive applications. It also granted Bridgeport a royalty-free non-exclusive license for any previously patented T.O.S. developments included in the TIGER design. Furthermore, the agreement provided that Bridgeport would make reasonable efforts to sell production robots to T.O.S. for modification and resale by T.O.S. in the non-competitive university research market and that Bridgeport would make reasonable efforts to utilize T.O.S.'s design services in the future contingent upon successful completion of the initial TIGER project. [References.]

31. T.O.S. and Flatau remained silent with regard to the suggested agreement by Bridgeport except to advise McCaul that the agreement was being considered. Defendants made no objection to its terms. Said proposed agreement was never signed by Flatau or T.O.S. [References.]

32. In February 1982, T.O.S. sent to plaintiff for review a draft agreement, which gave plaintiff "the exclusive use of systems designed under this agreement" and further stated:

> Bridgeport agrees hereby guarantees [sic] an annual minimum business volume of $1,000,000.00 starting in fiscal year 1982, and continuing thereafter at that rate, subject to adjustments for inflation based on the national wholesale index.

This agreement proposed by T.O.S. was never executed by the parties. [References.]

33. Work on the TIGER project continued through the end of 1981. During that time, T.O.S. advised Bridgeport on or about November 6, 1981 that there would be a significant overrun of One Hundred and Eighty One Thousand Five Hundred Dollars ($181,500) on the original purchase order. Bridgeport, on or about December 16, 1981, issued an amendment to increase the amount of the purchase order to Six Hundred and Thirty Thousand Dollars ($630,000). [References.]

34. On February 22, 1982, Bridgeport issued another purchase order to T.O.S., No. 44817, for a robot design capable of lifting 10 kilograms—called the TIGER 10 project. This purchase order called for a maximum payment by Bridgeport to T.O.S. of Two Hundred Thousand Dollars. [References.]

35. During the period February–June 1982 there were additional significant cost overruns by T.O.S. Bridgeport accordingly became increasingly dissatisfied both with the progress and performance of T.O.S. In March or April 1982, Bridgeport advised T.O.S. to cease work on TIGER 10 and to finish its work on the original TIGER 5 since it was felt that the work on the TIGER 10 project would only further delay completion of the original TIGER 5 project. [References.]

36. In addition to the amount in excess of $800,000 plaintiff had paid to defendants, Bridgeport spent approximately $750,000 to

develop a computer numerical control (CNC) to be used in conjunction with the mechanical structures defendants were to be developing. [References.]

37. Bridgeport, even up to the present time, is spending significant sums of money continuing to prepare for manufacture and commercial production of the TIGER robot by designing and building production fixtures therefor, and purchasing tooling and developing manufacturing processes and computer numerically controlled machine programs therefore. [References.]

38. In about May 1982, defendants began to work on designing and developing another industrial robot of their own. Nevertheless, defendants never advised Bridgeport of their work on this other industrial robot, even though they were working on it at the same time they were working on the TIGER project. Moreover, defendants admit there are features in this other robot that are covered by the inventions T.O.S. made for the TIGER robot. [References.]

39. On June 21, 1982, T.O.S. for the first time advised Bridgeport by a letter from Flatau that T.O.S. considered the technology content of the TIGER design depicted in the engineering drawings to be proprietary to it. T.O.S. stated that it planned to prepare and file three United States patent applications directed thereto. [References.]

40. After receiving the June 21, 1982 letter from Flatau, Bridgeport took immediate steps to remove all of its proprietary engineering drawings and materials from T.O.S. and to terminate the relationship. In particular, Bridgeport made two trips to T.O.S., one around the end of June 1982 and the other around the beginning of July 1982 during which Bridgeport, with the knowledge of T.O.S.'s vice president Minter, removed from T.O.S. and took possession of (a) all copies of the engineering drawings for the TIGER program that could be found, as well as the original tracings, (b) the parts to complete the still unfinished second and third prototypes under the original March 16, 1981 purchase order, and (c) the first prototype. Thereafter, Bridgeport confirmed by letter to T.O.S. dated July 22, 1982, that it was cancelling all outstanding purchase orders with T.O.S. [References.]

41. In early July of 1982 the defendants issued a press release announcing "its intention to design, develop and manufacture a line of industrial robots" and citing "the successful development of a new generation of general purpose robots for the nation's leading machine tool manufacturer [Bridgeport]" as a basis for "the company's decision to enter the rapidly growing robot field." The press release also stated that "TOS expects to have a prototype of its first model completed by the end of August." Further, it quoted Flatau as saying: "We are directing our marketing efforts to original equipment manufacturers who may be searching for robot bodies and accessories to complement their product sales." In the July 26, 1982 issue of the publication "Tech Update," an article appeared based on the aforesaid T.O.S. press release. [References.]

42. By letter dated August 11, 1982, Flatau returned to Mr. McCaul of plaintiff a proposed hold-harmless agreement. That agreement was ratified by Flatau conditioned upon plaintiff's ratification of a rider which he attached. That rider provided in pertinent part that:

" * * * Bridgeport must obtain from TOS a license of certain patent and other proprietary rights owned by TOS."

[References.]

43. Upon receipt of the August 11, 1982 rider, Bridgeport immediately denied T.O.S.'s contention that any such license was necessary. It was Bridgeport's position that it had already paid for and owned the inventions and technology developed during the TIGER program and is already licensed under the aforesaid Flatau United States Patent No. 4,062,455 or any other earlier work of T.O.S. or Flatau embodied in the TIGER robot. The parties undertook to resolve this dispute by negotiation and conducted unsuccessful discussions to settle this matter. [References.]

44. On or about October 4, 1982, Bridgeport received a letter from T.O.S. dated October 1, 1982 and signed by Flatau, forwarding copies of portions of the three patent applications referred to in the June 21, 1982 letter from Flatau. The three applications are identified in the October 1, 1982 letter as follows: Serial No. 395,959 entitled "WRIST FOR

MANIPULATOR ARM," filed in July, 1982 and naming Carl R. Flatau and Robert L. Minter as inventors; Serial No. 413,634 entitled "ROBOT FOREARM," filed in September, 1982 and naming Carl R. Flatau as sole inventor; and Serial No. 417,231 entitled "COUNTERBALANCED ROBOT ARM," filed September, 1982 and naming Carl R. Flatau as sole inventor. [References.]

45. The record reveals that the drawings and specifications contained in the aforesaid "ROBOT FOREARM" and "COUNTERBALANCED ROBOT ARM" patent applications were expressly and deliberately based upon the TIGER project work. On the other hand, the drawings and specification for the "WRIST FOR MANIPULATOR ARM" patent application were based upon work done prior to the TIGER project. [References.]

46. On Thursday, October 21, 1982, Bridgeport was advised over the telephone that T.O.S. and Flatau would accept Bridgeport's position with respect to ownership of the technology, and that counsel for T.O.S. would prepare the settlement papers and forward them for Bridgeport's consideration. Those papers were received by Bridgeport's counsel on Monday, October 25, 1982. The papers provided, in pertinent part, that (a) T.O.S. is the owner of all "Technical Information" relating to the TIGER program and (b) T.O.S. is willing to grant Bridgeport only a nonexclusive license that is non-assignable, non-sublicensable and non-transferable. As a result of plaintiff's rejection of this final offer of settlement and T.O.S.'s stated intention in its July, 1982 press release to market the aforesaid "Technical Information" to equipment manufacturers, plaintiff filed the action that brings the parties before the court and seeks immediate injunctive relief to protect its property rights. [References.]

CONCLUSIONS OF LAW

Based on the foregoing events plaintiff argues that a valid and binding contractual relationship arose between the parties and that under that contract the TIGER technology developed by defendants is proprietary to plaintiff with defendants enjoying only a non-exclusive license to use it in non-competitive applications.[1] Moreover, plaintiff contends that it is entitled to a royalty-free non-exclusive license under any patent or proprietary rights developed by defendants prior to the TIGER project but incorporated in it.

Defendants, in sharp distinction, argue that the vesting of such ownership rights to the TIGER technology in plaintiff was conditioned upon plaintiff entering into a long-term business relationship with defendants and that since no such agreement was ever consummated the rights necessarily vest in defendants. In further support of this they argue that prior to his association with plaintiff, Flatau had already made the decision to enter the industrial robotics field and had already developed the concepts necessary to meet the "PUMA" specifications.[2] The question in the case thus resolves itself into one involving whether a contract covering ownership rights to the TIGER technology exists and, if so, what are the parties rights and obligations under it. [Footnote.] The answer to the question necessarily turns on an interpretation of the parties' words and conduct during their rather tortured relationship.

The record reveals that on the basis of defendants' January 30, 1981 design proposal a meeting was convened at T.O.S. on February 9, 1981. Present at the meeting were defendant Carl Flatau, Joseph E. Clancy, President of Bridgeport; William R. Jahnke, plaintiff's Vice-President of Engineering; and Gerald

---

1. Plaintiff defines non-competitive applications to mean (i) robots that are used for work not involving the commercial production of goods for sale, (ii) robots used in unusual environments such as vacuum, nuclear and/or underwater, (iii) robots used for educational or research purposes or (iv) precision mini-assembly robots.

2. The court rejects defendants' attempt to rely upon a purported distinction between an agreement to "design"

and an agreement to "invent" as militating in its favor. It represents the ultimate in exaltation of form over substance. In either case, one employing another person for valuable consideration would fully expect that the fruits of the employees' labor would be property of the employer. Here, to seize on such a meaningless distinction to deprive plaintiff of the benefit of $800,000 in expenditures would be preposterous.

McCaul, plaintiff's Senior Vice-President for Strategic Planning at the time. Among other things, the five point portion of defendants' January 30 proposal entitled CONTRACTUAL REQUIREMENTS was discussed in its entirety. Specifically, items 3 and 5 of this section dealing with a proprietary technology agreement and future sales cooperation between the parties were discussed.

On February 10, 1981, Mr. Jahnke sent Mr. Flatau a letter of intent which expressed plaintiff's willingness to proceed with the TIGER–5 project as outlined in the January 30 proposal. It also addressed the CONTRACTUAL REQUIREMENTS portion of the proposal point by point as discussed at the February 9 meeting. With respect to point three the letter of intent provided that:

> TOS will have rights to apply developed technology to non-competitive applications. Namely, manipulator, this will receive a more finite definition in the future.

[Reference.]

With respect to point five the letter provided that:

> As discussed, we have a general agreement that TOS participation in some form of the sales effort will be beneficial to both TOS and Bridgeport/Textron. This matter will also receive further definition in the future.

[Reference.]

Thereafter, Flatau wrote to Jahnke acknowledging the February 10 letter of intent. With respect to item one of the CONTRACTUAL REQUIREMENTS portion he stated that billing would be on a cost and 20% basis. Pl.Ex. 5. Subsequently, TOS performed by working on the project and submitting monthly invoices and progress reports as per item 2 of the REQUIREMENTS.

Finally, on March 16, 1981, plaintiff forwarded a 6 page purchase order for the design of 3 prototype TIGER–5 robots as per the defendants' January 30 proposal. "TIGER–5" signified a robot with a capacity to handle loads of up to five kilograms. This purchase order reflected billing on a cost plus 20% basis per defendants' February 16 letter. It reflected that drawings were to be on Bridgeport forms. Finally, it reflected that other terms and conditions " *   *   * will be covered in a separate agreement."

Characterizing this purchase order as the " *   *   * only written contract between the parties." (Defendants' proposed Finding of fact 20) and indicating that as such it failed to specifically address the issue of property rights in the TIGER technology or the long term relationship between the parties defendants' come to the conclusion that they, and not plaintiff, are the rightful owners of the technology. The court, however, cannot view the record quite so narrowly and for that reason rejects this rather strained construction of the dealings between the parties. It simply ignores too much of what transpired between the parties and the legal effect of these events.

It is hornbook law that a party can manifest its assent to an offer by silence, or as in this case, silence coupled with performance consistent with the offer. [Citation.] Here, the February 10 letter of intent from plaintiff to defendant Flatau specifically provided that it was a " *   *   * letter of intent to *proceed* with the program as outlined in [the] letter of 30 January 1981." (Emphasis the court's) [Reference.] Flatau himself so viewed the letter and said as much instructing Jahnke to go forward with the job. [Reference.] The situation at hand is made even more compelling as more than silence exists—defendant having acknowledged receipt of the letter of intent in his reply of February 16 without objection. [Reference.]

Specifically, the court finds that the exchange of the January 30 proposal, the February 10 letter of intent, defendants' February 16 response to the letter, and the March 16 purchase order coupled with defendants' performance without objection constituted a legally binding contract. [Citations.] [Footnote.] The correspondence, when taken together, more than adequately set out price, quantity, time for performance, and, significantly, defendants' limited ownership rights in the TIGER technology as applied in the industrial robotics field. It was a contract that was sufficiently definite to be enforced.

As stated above, point three of the February 10 letter of intent embodied an oral understanding reached at the February 9 meeting between the parties—that understanding being that T.O.S. would receive only a non-exclusive license to utilize the TIGER technology in non-competitive applications. Furthermore, Flatau, in his February 16 acknowledgement of the letter of intent nowhere objects to the inclusion of the foregoing language. It was at this point that the court feels the parties' understanding on this point became concretized.

The March 16 purchase order merely served to confirm what had already been agreed to by the parties in correspondence ending on February 16. It was, more than anything else, issued in conformity with this agreement and not as a final memorialization of it. The "other terms and conditions" language on page 6 of the purchase order that defendants' view as crucial to their case would therefore in no way detract from this conclusion. Even if the court were to accept defendants' characterization of the purchase order as "the" controlling document the same conclusion would follow. The letter of intent stated that:

> 3. TOS will have rights to apply developed technology to non-competitive applications. *Namely, manipulator, this will receive a more finite definition in the future.*

(Emphasis the courts)

The only rational interpretation of the "other terms and conditions" language of the purchase order would be that it was applicable to the italicized portion of the foregoing clause and not the first portion dealing with the parties' agreement that TOS's rights in this new technology would be limited. Therefore, it would in no way detracts or alters the agreement that plaintiff would be the rightful owner of the technology. This interpretation is further borne out by the language contained in the April 1981 proposed draft purchase order [Reference.] and the proposed June 15, 1981 agreement [Reference.] providing for T.O.S.'s right to use the TIGER–5 technology in, among other areas, the non-competitive university research market. *See* note 1, *supra.*

Accordingly then the court finds that the parties, via the exchange of correspondence ending on February 16, followed by performance, entered into a contract whereby plaintiff was to acquire exclusive ownership rights in technology developed by Flatau and TOS during the TIGER project with defendants enjoying only a non-exclusive license to use it in non-competitive applications.[5] The court turns now to an examination of the parties' rights to technology developed by Flatau prior to the parties association.

Flatau, in his first invoice and technology progress report of March 18, 1981 offered plaintiff the use of the patented design for manipulators covered under Patent No. 4,062,455 entitled REMOTE MANIPULATOR granted to Flatau on December 13, 1977 for a $1 paid license. [Reference.] The record reveals that the technology covered under this patent was utilized, to some extent, during the course of the TIGER project. In addition, the technology embodied in the patent entitled "WRIST FOR MANIPULATOR ARM" [reference] filed in the name of Flatau and Robert L. Minter in July of 1982 would cover certain of the designs and structures during the TIGER project. This technology was also developed by Flatau prior to his association with plaintiff. [References.] Unlike the case with the ROBOT FOREARM and COUNTERBALANCED ROBOT ARM developed exclusively during the course of the TIGER project, however, there does not appear to have been reached any sort of contractual arrangement with respect to these latter two designs. This conclusion flows from the fact that none of the proposals or counterproposals purportedly dealing with rights to this technology were ever initialled by both sides. [References.] Moreover, the court finds that the language limiting defendants' right to apply "developed technology" in a non-competitive fashion only contemplated technology developed during the TIGER project and thereby wouldn't limit defendants rights to use the WRIST FOR MANIPULATOR ARM or REMOTE MANIPULATOR in any way it saw fit.

Thus, unlike the technology developed for and at the behest of plaintiff this earlier technology did not become the subject of an express understanding followed by performance—rather there was an uncertain performance only from March 1981 to June 1982 unaccompanied by any sort of verbal agreement.

---

5. The court also notes that to the extent the parties never did consummate any arrangement with respect to a long-term association this too was consistent with the contract which contemplated successful completion of the TIGER 5 prototypes. The record reveals that such was not the case—the project going way over budget and producing little in the way of anything usable by plaintiff.

Under the circumstances the court is unable to discern any mutually agreed upon arrangement with respect to these rights. Performance alone is simply not enough absent some sort of document initialled by both sides as was the case with the technology developed during the project. This is especially so since the letter of intent specifically left open the issue of rights to the manipulator technology for more " * * * finite definition in the future." Moreover, McCaul testified that at the time he prepared his proposals in April and June of 1981 he was aware that such loose ends existed. *See* Finding of Fact 27. Accordingly then, the court finds that defendants remain the rightful owners of the disputed technology they developed prior to the TIGER project. Plaintiff, therefore, enjoys ownership in the TIGER technology subject to such preexisting rights of defendants. [Footnote.]

INJUNCTIVE RELIEF

With the foregoing background in mind, the court now turns to an examination of plaintiff's request for preliminary injunctive relief.

In this circuit, a moving party may obtain a preliminary injunction if it establishes

> (a) irreparable harm and (b) either (1) likelihood of success on the merits or (2) sufficiently serious questions going to the merits to make them a fair ground for litigation and a balance of hardships tipping decidedly toward the party requesting the preliminary relief.

Here, Flatau, notwithstanding the parties' February 1981 agreement concerning ownership of the rights to the TIGER technology, and their performance under it, took the position in June and July of 1982 that such technology was proprietary to him. [References.] Consistent with this position Flatau instructed his patent attorney to file three patent applications, *viz,* patent # 395,959 entitled "WRIST FOR MANIPULATOR ARM"; patent # 413,634 entitled "ROBOT FORE-ARM"; and patent # 417,231 entitled "COUNTERBALANCED ROBOT ARM." [References.] The ROBOT FOREARM and COUNTERBALANCED ROBOT ARM patents filed in the name of Flatau in September of 1982 utilized the technical diagrams prepared during and specifically for the TIGER–5 project minus the Bridgeport logo and proprietary legend. [References.] By contrast, the

drawings for the WRIST MANIPULATOR ARM were derived from work done by Flatau prior to the TIGER project. [Reference.]

Under the circumstances, the conclusion is inescapable that Flatau took the position he did knowing full well that he was doing so in derogation of rights he had negotiated away to Bridgeport. Perhaps the most telling indication of Flatau's state of mind at the time was his deliberate and wrongful excising of Bridgeport's proprietary legend at the time he submitted the technical drawing to his patent attorney. [Reference.]

In sum then it is abundantly clear that plaintiff, in this case, enjoys a substantial likelihood of success on the merits having established the existence of a contract granting it property rights in some of the disputed technology and defendants' attempted wrongful appropriation of it.

With respect to irreparable harm plaintiff argues that it will be deprived of valuable "lead time" if defendants are permitted to make use of themselves or disclose to other competitors the technology that is the subject of this suit. Specifically, it argues that it will be deprived of the opportunity to be one of the *initial* entrants into the field of industrial robotics—a field which will no doubt become increasingly competitive with the developing state of the art. The court agrees.

To permit defendants to wrongfully appropriate to their own use a technology which will thrust them into a competitive position they should not rightfully enjoy would inflict on plaintiff damage hardly calculable in dollars and cents. The damage would be inflicted by virtue of a ruinous competition between the parties that the contractual arrangement simply did not contemplate. To be sure, it was only contemplated that TOS would enjoy rights to *non-competitive* applications of the TIGER technology.

CONCLUSION

In sum then, and based upon the foregoing Findings of Fact and Conclusions of Law the court is of the opinion that preliminary injunctive relief with respect to the technology developed by defendants during the TIGER project should be granted. With respect to any technology developed prior to the project but incorporated in it it is denied.

The parties are hereby directed to settle proposed orders of injunction with the court. The bond shall continue in effect.

* * *

So ordered.

CHELSEA INDUSTRIES, INC. v. ACCURAY LEASING CORP.

699 F.2d 58

(United States Court of Appeals, First Circuit, Decided Feb. 3, 1983.)

ALDRICH, C. J.

This is an action brought by Chelsea Industries, Inc. against AccuRay Leasing Corporation seeking a declaration that Chelsea had duly exercised an option to purchase a certain computer system that was under lease to it by the defendant, and for appendant relief. The basic question is the meaning and effect of defendant's December 30, 1974 "policy" letter delivered, the court found, in a "binder [which] included documents entitled Lease Agreement, Operating Results Evaluation [which was an amendment to the lease, and a] Service Maintenance Agreement. * * *" Although defendant's negotiator testified that the binder content was referred to as a "package" by defendant's signing representative, defendant contends that the policy letter was not part of its total contractual obligation. The case was tried to the court which, after a detailed opinion, entered judgment for the defendant. The court found that the letter was not an option, but simply an expression of a possible basis for a future agreement, and that, even if it purported to be an option, it was improperly exercised. We reverse.

Plaintiff comes to this court making three contentions. The first is that it discovered shortly before trial that defendant had defrauded it by intending not to make the agreement plaintiff had understood had been made, and that the court erred in not permitting an amendment of the complaint by adding a count for fraud. The court denied the motion as untimely. The short answer to this is that, as will be developed, post, defendant was bound by the contract in the terms that plaintiff understood. Plaintiff, accordingly, was not defrauded.

Next, the first ground of the complaint as filed is that the policy letter, as an option, was an addendum to, and part of, the lease. The third is that even if not part of the lease, it was part of the total agreement. Since we agree with this last, the addendum issue is superfluous. We shall, however, deal with it, in part because the parties devoted so much time to it, both below and here, and in part because the question of the substantive meaning of the letter is the same in whichever posture it is considered. We begin with the meaning.

The body of the letter reads as follows:

Gentlemen:

Reference: Lease Agreement Number 74–1030
It is the policy of AccuRay Leasing Corporation to provide for the conversion of the leased equipment to a purchase at anytime during the lease agreement. These are converted at the fair market value of the leased equipment. The fair market value is based on the installed value, in the amount included in the lease agreement; but shall not exceed the percentages as indicated below on our eight (8) year lease agreement.

End of Month	% of Installed Price ($793,630.00)
12	92
24	84
36	74
48	63
60	51
72	37
84	22
96	10

It is our policy not to go below 10% of the installed price of the leased equipment. The above schedule is based on receiving full payments during the initial term of the lease agreement.

The installed price includes the equipment price, and the initial services (Installation Supervision, Correlation, Certification, and Initial Systems Engineering) and cable. If any up-dating of the leased equipment is done, the fair market value of the up-date will be added to the conversion price.

In its correspondence rejecting plaintiff's assertion of an option and attempt to exercise it defendant characterized this letter as a "policy * * * to provide for the conversion of leased equipment to a purchase," a "guideline" letter of no legal consequence. In its brief defendant says the letter "merely describes a policy which is hospitable to conversion." The court called the letter a "conversion letter," but came to the same conclusion of emptiness.

> The conversion letter * * * was intended as a statement of policy, describing the conditions under which the parties could agree to a conversion to a purchase if such a purchase was advisable under the existing circumstances.

The court's further findings were:

> The evidence adduced at trial shows that Futura [plaintiff's assignor] wanted an option to purchase, and that AccuRay accordingly provided the letter at the closing.

Viz., Futura wanted an option to purchase, and defendant "accordingly" gave it nothing.

> The conversion letter was the result of negotiations between competent and knowledgeable parties.

Ergo, plaintiff knew it was negotiating for nothing.

In reaching this seemingly anomalous conclusion the court possibly got off on the wrong foot by overlooking an answer by defendant's negotiator, Speedie, a needle in a veritable haystack of a deposition. Although Speedie's examination left it that defendant did not intend to give an enforceable option, there was no contradiction of his testimony of what plaintiff was intended to understand.

Q. Was there an intent on the part of AccuRay to convey to Chelsea and Futura the impression that they were getting a contractual right—by giving them the so-called policy letter?

A. In my judgment, yes.

Mr. Casty, plaintiff's representative, testified that this was what he, in fact, understood. In reporting back to the plant he called it "a side letter of buy out," an exceptionally accurate description. The concept that it was to be read in as an addendum to the lease appears to be plaintiff's counsel's. While the court made unfavorable remarks about Casty, there was no basis for finding him untruthful on this particular point—he could believe what he was intended to believe.

In deciding whether plaintiff received something of consequence, as it contends, or nothing, as defendant claims, there are a number of standard rules of construction. Since the lease states that Ohio law is to govern, we emphasize Ohio cases, but observe that we find no difference between Ohio and Massachusetts, the forum.

The first principle is that there is a normal assumption that a business transaction is not meaningless and that words have a purpose. [Citations.] The next, which needs no citation, is that a contract is what the parties reasonably understand. A corollary to this must be that if one party causes the other to have a particular understanding, that is the contract. "[O]ne is bound, not only by what he subjectively intends, but by what he leads others reasonably to think that he intends." [Citation.] "Knowingly to lead a person reasonably to suppose that you offer and to offer are the same thing." [Citation.] A third principle, not necessary here, but corroborative, is that in case of doubt, an instrument is to be taken against the party that drew it. [Citations.]

These principles would be violated by defendant's construction that the "letter * * * merely describes a policy which is hospitable to conversion." Plaintiff knew from the outset that defendant preferred a sale to a lease; its future interest would be price. There was no need, nor point to "negotiate" for a price policy that defendant could change at will. It would be only natural for plaintiff to believe that an adjustable schedule, addressed to the entire term of the lease, had an affirmative meaning. Defendant's now seeking to label the schedule a discount table overlooks the fact that it was adjustable downward in case of a decline in fair market value. The presence of such detail precisely supported Speedie's concession of what defendant intended plaintiff to understand. At trial Speedie referred to it as a "comfort letter," apparently an accountant's term. A policy changeable at will would be cold comfort—the comfort would last only until plaintiff sought to avail itself of it. We consider plaintiff's understanding far too reasonable for defendant, who intended it, to contend otherwise.

With respect to the fact that defendant was the drafter, while defendant argues at length about the meaning of the word "policy," it cannot avoid the fact that the letter constituted a sufficient expression of its policy at the moment. If it was intended to be no more, it would have been simple to add the universally familiar caveat, "This policy is subject to change without notice." Under the circumstances, weight could be given to the absence of such a clause. "He who speaks should speak plainly or the other party may explain to his own advantage." [Citation.] All defendant can think to say in answer to the assertion that the letter is to be construed against it is that the rule is inapplicable because the letter is unambiguous. Yet in the next breath it argues that plaintiff, being represented by counsel, should have realized the letter was not part of the contract because it was not "executed in the same formal manner as the lease." We decline to accept this reason, but the important fact is that defendant advances such an argument at the same time that it seeks to say the letter was unambiguous.

The upshot is that in response to plaintiff's expressed desire for an option, defendant, as part of the package, informed it of a policy, viz., a willingness to convert on stated terms, over the period of the lease, that plaintiff was intended to believe was firm. Such belief was warranted, with the consequence that defendant was so bound.

A review of the record, disregarding Casty's testimony on other matters, if one wishes, reveals a clear picture. As a matter of general financial policy, defendant initially preferred to sell the system outright, but acceded to plaintiff's request for a lease agreement, which was based on plaintiff's belief that it would get better service. Given a leasing arrangement, defendant wished to be able to deposit the lease with a bank as collateral for a loan, and it was best that the bank be assured of the continuance of plaintiff's obligation for the stated payments. A buy out, particularly if it might be at a reduced price, could reduce the value of the security. From defendant's standpoint, accordingly, the lease should not contain an option. At the same time, plaintiff, who feared the equipment might become obsolete, expressed a strong desire for an option—its second choice after defendant refused it a right of outright termination due to obsolescence. This dilemma defendant solved by leaving the lease clear, and giving plaintiff a letter which it intended plaintiff to believe to be an option, but with the undisclosed intention that it not be. Defendant doubtless felt this to be the best solution. We believe it to be a sharp one—injurious either to the expectations of the plaintiff, or of the bank, depending upon the assignment, if any, in effect, and how the legal issues might be resolved.

In rejecting plaintiff's claim that the letter was to be read as an integral part of the lease the court relied upon what it described as a "classic merger clause."

> The provisions of this Lease Agreement constitute the full and complete agreement between Customer and AccuRay, and any terms or conditions contained in any document not expressly incorporated herein are not part of this Agreement. * * * This Agreement * * * is effective from the date it is accepted by AccuRay and shall remain in full force until terminated as herein provided.

Although, in asserting this clause, defendant peppered the record with objections based on the parol evidence rule (without regard to the fact that this rule, when applicable, is not waived by failure to object [citation]), it cites no authority indicating the rule's relevancy to the present situation. Its, and the district court's, sole reliance is upon a statutory version of the parol evidence rule contained in Ohio Rev.Code § 1302.05. This statute, by its terms, does not apply to a lease which expressly reserves title in the lessor. Section 1302.01, Definitions, subsection (A)(11) provides, " 'Contract' and 'agreement' are limited to those relating to the present or future sale of goods. * * * A 'sale' consists in the passing of title from the seller to the buyer for a price." It is regrettable that counsel should fail to cite to a busy court the material part of a foreign statute.

It is common for a lessor to accept the surrender of a lease, and in such event all its terms are cancelled. [Citation.] There is equally no reason why a lessor cannot later convey the title of the subject matter to the lessee. If he can do so, he can agree to do so. Defendant has confused an entirely separate matter, whether such an undisclosed separate agreement might be invalid against a third party, such as a bank if it, in ignorance thereof, relied on the above-quoted provision in the lease. The lease provided that defendant might assign, and it did, in fact, assign to a New Jersey bank in June, 1976. It notified plaintiff of the assignment, although not, apparently, of its terms. Whether the assignment remained in effect does not appear. Plaintiff properly joined the bank in its complaint. Instead of availing itself of this opportunity to protect its interests, if any, the bank moved to dismiss for improper venue. This motion was granted. Under these circumstances we will not concern ourselves with the bank's possible interests. Defendant has no right, vicarious or otherwise, to assert the bank's interests as a defense to plaintiff's claim against itself.

In fairness, we do not read defendant's brief as making this claim. Rather, it uses the fact that the existence of an option would impair the security value of the lease as showing it had no intention to grant one. That, however, is not the point. The question is not the private intention of the defendant, but what was the understanding of the plaintiff, particularly, in this case, what was the understanding defendant wished it to have. We are back to the beginning. And, since the bank is not concerned, it makes no substantive difference whether the conversion obligation was, technically, a part of the lease, or was a separate part of the package representing defendant's total undertaking. The court held, correctly, that a holding that the letter was not to be read into the lease did not destroy its force as a separate agreement between the parties.

Finally, defendant contends, and the court found, that even if the letter were a valid option, it was not properly exercised. First, defendant claims that plaintiff did not tender in so many dollars. Under the letter, the price was to be determined by a formula related to fair market value. Plaintiff did state, flatly, that it was exercising the option, would pay whatever was the proper figure, and asked defendant its view thereof. Instead of responding to this inquiry in terms, defendant replied that there was no option (and, by obvious implication, no formula) but that it would sell for a certain figure. It made no suggestion that this figure was reached by applying the formula. Now it says that, because plaintiff did not pay, it lost its rights. Defendant sought to bolster this position by offering testimony at the trial—vigorously disputed by plaintiff—that the figure it named was, in fact, less than what the formula would have produced.

Defendant succeeded in persuading the district court. The court said:

> [T]he letter * * * required that the entire price was to be paid in full on the date the conversion took place. Chelsea never made any such tender of performance, nor did it pursue at any time any efforts to determine a fair market value for the system.

In fact, plaintiff having initiated the inquiry there was nothing for it to pursue. The court apparently lost sight of the principle that when a defendant repudiates an agreement by denying there was one, a plaintiff is under no obligation to go further. [Citations.] Having rejected the agreement, defendant's contention that there remained a duty on plaintiff "to cooperate in good faith to establish that [a] lower price would be appropriate" is simply bad law.

The court's refusal to allow the amendment alleging fraud is affirmed. Except for that, the judgment is reversed and the case is remanded for further proceedings consistent herewith.

CITY UNIVERSITY OF NEW YORK v. FINALCO, INC.
93 A.D.2d 792, 461 N.Y.S.2d 830
(Supreme Court, Appellate Division, First Department, April 28, 1983.)

MEMORANDUM DECISION.

* * *

The relevant facts are set forth in correspondence and conversations, between Marie Drobin, Director for Administrative Services of City University of New York (CUNY) and Robert Applegate, Finalco's Director of Remarketing. At issue is whether there was a meeting of the minds so as to create a binding contract for the sale to the corporate defendant of an IBM computer.

Finalco, a Virginia-based corporation, had submitted a bid in the sum of $1,561,570, subject to (1) the computer equipment being dismantled, packed and ready for shipment; (2) the computer being released by February 12, 1979; and (3) the offer being accepted by the close of business on December 18, 1978. Subsequently, the offer was extended by both parties to January 16, 1979, while Finalco's proposed agreement was reviewed by plaintiff's counsel. On January 9, 1979, Finalco withdrew its offer since its customer, to whom Finalco had intended to lease the computer, withdrew its offer. It is alleged that, by reason of Finalco's status as a merchant, its offer was irrevocable within the time stated and its withdrawal prior to January 16th was improper (UCC § 2–205).

At the time plaintiff solicited bids from prospective buyers, including Finalco, the invitation advised that "[o]nce the quotations have been reviewed and the best offer has been determined, the University Computer Center will negotiate with the bidder a sales contract." Finalco was notified that its bid was the highest, whereupon Applegate acknowledged such notice and advised that Finalco was "prepared to meet with you at your earliest convenience to negotiate a sales contract satisfactory to CUNY." Thereafter, Finalco submitted a proposed contract together with a covering letter offering to meet with Drobin "to negotiate a mutually acceptable agreement." The contract form provided that it had been entered into in Virginia, where Finalco was located and would not take effect unless signed by the seller and returned to the buyer. These provisions generated some disagreement since (1) plaintiff considered the transaction to be governed by New York law as the place of formation, and (2) there was an ongoing dispute over the insistence by each party that the other execute the agreement first. Thereafter, Applegate sent Drobin another contract with certain blanks completed but which still contained clauses previously objected to.

On January 9, 1979, when Finalco sought to withdraw its offer, the agreement had not been executed. However, on January 11th, at a time when Drobin was unaware of the withdrawal, she telephoned Applegate and was informed that Finalco had withdrawn from the deal. On January 16th, notwithstanding, Drobin, notified Finalco that CUNY was prepared to sign the agreement in the form which Finalco had submitted to it.

Subsequent to the aborted transaction, plaintiff completed a sale of the computer in the sum of $1,267,000 and, thereafter, brought this action to recover the difference between that price and Finalco's bid.

Special Term, in granting summary judgment dismissing the complaint, held the documentary evidence and the conduct of the parties were sufficient to demonstrate an intention not to be bound until an agreement had been executed and, accordingly, found no binding contract had been entered into. We disagree. On this record, we find the critical issue concerning the intention of the parties poses factual questions inappropriate for summary resolution upon the conflicting affidavits adduced.

Under the Uniform Commercial Code, where the parties intended to enter into a binding commitment, a contract of sale will not fail for indefiniteness, albeit there may exist a dispute as to material terms (UCC § 2–204). [Citation.] The critical determination to be made is whether, on the one hand, the parties intended to be bound without the necessity of executing a formal written agreement or, on the other, they contemplated that such an agreement would be signed before they would be so obligated. The negotiations and discussions, particularly those dealing with which party was to execute the agreement first and whether the contract was governed by New York or Virginia law, lead to questions as to whether the parties intended to be bound only when a formal agreement had been executed. However, this factual determination may not be made on motion for summary judgment, where the function of the court is limited to issue-finding, not issue-determination. [Citations.] Summary judgment is a drastic remedy and should not be invoked where there is any doubt as to the existence of a triable issue [citation] or where the issue is even arguable [citation].

As a result of the extensive negotiations and discussions which took place after submission of Finalco's bid, we cannot hold on this record that the bid was an irrevocable offer for a term certain. Neither may we determine, as a matter of law, that Finalco withdrew from the transaction in advance of any acceptance since, as a merchant, it could not withdraw its offer during the period of time it was to be held open (UCC § 2–205). The factual issues relating to the intention of the parties and whether a binding agreement had been entered into should more appropriately await the trier of the facts.

However, we are in agreement that there is no basis for imposing liability upon defendant Applegate. The record reflects that Applegate was an employee of International Computer Exchange, Ltd. and that Finalco had contracted to retain his services. The record is clear that, in dealing with plaintiff, Applegate appeared and acted as an employee of Finalco, and as an agent for a disclosed principal, personal liability may not be imposed upon him. [Citations.]

All concur except Sandler, J. P. and Alexander, J. who dissent in a memorandum by Alexander, J. as follows:

For the reasons stated at Special Term, I would affirm the award of summary judgment in favor of Finalco.

The conduct of the parties indicates an intent not to be bound until the execution of a signed agreement. City University of New York agreed to sign the agreement and conceded to the terms proffered by Finalco, only after it learned that Finalco had withdrawn its offer. The record clearly demonstrates that there was no meeting of the minds and the application of UCC 2–205 does not require a different result.

STAHL MANAGEMENT CORP. v. CONCEPTIONS UNLIMITED

554 F. Supp. 890

(United States District Court, S.D. New York, Jan. 4, 1983.)

DUFFY, D. J.

Stanley Stahl decided in the Spring of 1979 to spend his vacation in his old home state of Vermont. While there he stopped in to see a neighbor he had known since 1969, Joel Spiro. The conversation between the two men quickly turned to business, and a subject of mutual interest: computers. Stanley Stahl was vice-president of Stahl Management Corporation ("Stahl Management"), a company engaged in managing residential and commercial real estate. Spiro, a defendant herein, operated Conceptions Unlimited ("CU"), another defendant, which was in the business of selling computer hardware, and developing and selling application computer software.[1]

Stahl's interest in computers dated back to early 1978 when he and his brother Michael Stahl, the president of Stahl Management, decided that their company could conduct business more efficiently and profitably if certain information were computerized. In particular, Stahl was interested in computerizing information relating to fuel oil management, building maintenance, service orders, and monthly rent bill mailings. By the time Stahl and Spiro met in 1979, Stahl Management had reviewed several hardware/software packages on the market, and had determined that its requirements could best be met through use of a business application minicomputer system.

The initial conversation between Stahl and Spiro soon led to discussions in greater depth concerning CU's capability to develop the necessary software for Stahl Management. As the Summer of 1979 progressed, Michael Stahl entered the negotiations with Spiro and CU. Finally, in July of 1979, CU provided Stahl Management with a proposal entitled the "Charter." Plaintiff's Exhibit 1. A contract was executed by Michael Stahl and Joel Spiro soon thereafter on September 26, 1979. Plaintiff's Exhibit 2. Under the contract plaintiff was to pay $30,000 for the computer software developed by Spiro and CU. Simultaneously with the contract signing, Spiro signed a letter provided by Stahl stating that all contractual work had to be supervised by Spiro, and that in the event of CU's breach of the contract, Spiro was personally liable for up to $30,000 in damages. Plaintiff's Exhibit 4. Spiro signed the guarantee letter.

The contract provided, *inter alia*, that CU would provide Stahl Management with a two-phase system. Phase I included several functions: a method of recording repair complaints from tenants, an update repair file, a request information function to print various reports on repairs, a purge completed repairs function, a file management function, fuel transactions' programs, and a system for printing rent bills. Phase II, which was only outlined in the contract, required programs concerning accounts receivable, tenants status inquiry and reporting, arrears inquiry and reporting, dis-

---

1. Spiro had begun CU by himself in 1978 and by the   spring of 1979, CU included two other employees.

possession list, vacancy list, and tenant history. The specifics of the Phase II programs were to be worked out after the completion of the Phase I functions. CU also supplied Wang computer equipment to Stahl Management as part of the agreement for an additional cost of $45,500.

The contract stated that the fuel consumption programs of Phase I were due by November 1, 1979. The balance of the Phase I functions were to be provided by March 1, 1980. Phase II functions were to be operational by January 1, 1981. By November 1, 1980, however, Spiro had encountered unforeseen obstacles in attempting to create the fuel consumption program. The programming was proving to be more difficult than he had originally envisioned. Spiro, therefore, notified Stahl Management of his difficulties, and subsequently delivered a revised program in late November. According to plaintiff, this new program did not meet contract specifications; according to defendants, plaintiff requested functions in the program not previously required by the contract. In the ensuing months, Spiro delivered several revamped fuel consumption programs, the last one in March or April of 1980. After this last fuel consumption program delivery, Spiro and CU did nothing further under the contract. Stahl Management brought this suit on March 23, 1981, against the defendants alleging breach of contract, breach of warranty, fraud, and misrepresentation. It is undisputed that Spiro and CU did not deliver the rest of the Phase I programs, nor any of the Phase II programs as required by contract. Thus, because CU failed to complete the contract, the crucial inquiry at a two and a half day bench trial before me was whether CU has a valid defense to its apparent contract breach.

I. CU's DEFENSES

Defendant's two principal defenses at trial were accord and satisfaction[2] and rescission. [Footnote.] I find that defendants have failed to prove either defense.

2. Defendants label one defense novation. [Reference.] Novation, however, involves the substitution of a third-party for one of the original parties to the contract, and an extinguishing of the original duty. [Citation.] Accord and satisfaction, on the other hand, is a new obligation intended to replace the existing one, along with

A. Accord and Satisfaction

An accord and satisfaction is an agreement between two parties under which one party accepts a stipulated performance by the other party in discharge of an unresolved obligation by the latter party. [Citations.] "To establish an accord and satisfaction, [there] must [be] an intention to discharge the old obligation when the new one has been performed." [Citation.] In the instant case, defendants argue that the plaintiff agreed to discharge defendants of their contractual duty to deliver the balance of the Phase I and Phase II programs in return for defendants' supplying all of the "additional" requested functions in the fuel consumption program without any additional compensation. The defendants, however, have the burden of proving their affirmative defense of accord and satisfaction [Citation.], a burden they have not met.

Defendants do not have any written documents to support their defense. [Footnote.] Instead, they rely principally on defendant Spiro's testimony at trial. I found this testimony neither persuasive nor credible. For example, at trial Spiro claimed that this putative agreement was reached at some uncertain date in February. In their post-trial brief, however, the defendants inconsistently now allege that the accord and satisfaction occurred "about December." [Reference.]

Defendants also presented a witness, Lawrence Johnson, a CU employee, in support of their claim that plaintiff agreed to terminate the contract at a meeting in April, 1980. Johnson, however, admitted that termination of defendants' contractual duties was never explicitly or directly discussed during the meeting. He testified that Michael Stahl essentially stated that "we hope it works the way you said it would"; and Spiro replied "you need any help, give me a call." The defendants' presentation of contradictory testimony thus places the entire viability of the defendants' defense in great doubt.

Moreover, common sense suggests that plaintiff would not have agreed to defendants'

the satisfaction of the substituted obligation. [Citation.] Therefore, I will treat defendants' alleged defense as accord and satisfaction, because the absence of a new party precludes the defendants from asserting the defense of novation.

proposal, had it been made as defendants maintain. The fuel consumption program was apparently less than a quarter of the programming due under the contract, yet the alleged agreement did not provide for any rebate of the $30,000 paid by plaintiff.[5] Defendants claim that they provided several "extra" functions in payment for their contractual release. In reality, however, defendants admitted that this amounted to no more than the addition of one data field. Trial Testimony of Defendant Spiro. Spiro claimed at trial that he spent substantially more time programming the fuel consumption program than he had originally anticipated. This does not excuse his attempt to evade his contractual obligations, though it may explain his attempt to avoid them. [Citation.] [Footnote.]

In sum, defendants failed to prove accord and satisfaction by a preponderance of the credible evidence at trial. Therefore, I turn to defendants' second asserted defense: rescission.

B. Rescission

Defendants have claimed, in the alternative, that plaintiff agreed to rescind the original September 26, 1979 contract, and to substitute in its stead the promise to further develop the fuel consumption program. I find that defendants again failed to sustain their burden of proving their asserted affirmative defense.

In the case of both accord and satisfaction and rescission, "[i]t is frequently difficult to determine whether a new agreement is a substituted contract. * * * It is wholly a question of intention, to be determined by the usual process of interpretation, implication, and construction." *S & L Paving Corp. v. MacMurray Tractor, Inc.,* 61 Misc.2d 90, 304 N.Y.S.2d 652, 658 (1969), *quoting* 6 Corbin on

Contracts § 1293 at 190. Defendants have not shown that the parties intended to rescind their original contract. This insufficiency of proof, charted above in discussing defendants' failure to show plaintiff's intention to enter into an accord and satisfaction, is equally applicable here. Equitable considerations further militate against finding rescission. Usually, rescission may be obtained only when it is reasonably feasible to return the parties to their pre-contract status quo. [Citations.] Defendants have made no attempt to return plaintiff to *status quo ante*.[7] In sum, defendants have failed to prove the affirmative defense of rescission.

II. BREACH OF WARRANTY, FRAUD, AND MISREPRESENTATION

Plaintiff also asserts causes of action for defendants' alleged fraud, misrepresentation, and breach of express warranties. At trial, however, plaintiff did not provide sufficient evidence of defendants' intent to prove either fraud or misrepresentation. [Citation.] I have little doubt that initially Spiro did have a good faith belief that he could perform his obligations under the contract. Absent proof of the requisite intent, plaintiff's claims based on fraud and misrepresentation are dismissed. [Citation.]

Plaintiff also asserts a breach of warranty claim against the defendants. This claim relies on the same factual and legal foundation surrounding the plaintiff's claim for breach of contract. Analogously, the damages flowing from this alleged breach would duplicate the breach of contract damages.[8] Therefore, because no duplicative damage award will issue, the only remaining issue is the amount of damages sustained by plaintiff flowing from defendants' breach of contract.

---

5. The fuel consumption program was in use for seventy-seven weeks before Stahl Management discarded it as unusable. It was unable to salvage anything from its nearly $30,000 investment.

7. Arguably, plaintiff's receipt of the upgraded fuel consumption program without additional cost restored it to *status quo ante*. Plaintiff, however, paid the defendants $30,000 and only allegedly received $6,000 worth of extra work. The fuel consumption program—installed for $24,000 if this argument were followed—did little more than mimic plaintiff's manual fuel consumption program. [Reference.] Thus, the substantial financial loss

plaintiff would have sustained had it been asked to rescind the contract makes it both improbable that it would have agreed to such a proposed rescission, and inappropriate to grant rescission.

8. The only potentially different liability for damages surrounds the cost of the hardware purchased for plaintiff by CU. Plaintiff apparently dropped this claim for the cost of the hardware at trial. [Reference.] Furthermore, the hardware malfunction more likely resulted from plaintiff's failure to purchase a service maintenance contract than from any equipment defect.

III. DAMAGES

Plaintiff has claimed $250,000 for breach of contract and $30,000 for breach of warranty. [Reference.]In its "Calculation of Damages", plaintiff's Exhibit 9, plaintiff enumerates $29,986.96 for payments made to CU for the software program, and $48,511.96 for lost employee time in handling the substandard fuel consumption program.

I find first that defendant is liable for the $29,986.96. Plaintiff paid for a package of computer software programs. In return it received one part of that package, and even this part (the fuel consumption program) eventually was discarded as unusable. Defendants failed to perform their contractual duties, and must return plaintiff's payment for the non-delivered goods. N.Y. Uniform Commercial Code §§ 2–713 & 714 (1964). Defendant, therefore, is liable for the $29,986.96 loss suffered by the plaintiff.

Defendant is also liable for plaintiff's lost employee time expended attempting to overcome the difficulties of the delayed and substandard fuel consumption program. *Id.* Michael Stahl testified that Stanley Stahl devoted five extra hours per week in lost time to this contract over a total of 77 weeks. At his $30 hourly rate, the lost employee time for Stanley Stahl was $11,350.00. In addition, Ms. Carmen Fugazy, a temporary employee, spent four weeks inputting back data because of defendant's late delivery of the first fuel consumption program. At her weekly rate of $300, this amounts to $1,200. These amounts are recoverable. Plaintiff also asserts that Al Fugazy, Stahl Management's office general manager, spent an extra five hours per week due to defendants' breach of contract. Fugazy, however, testified at trial that he expended approximately two to three extra hours per week over the 77 week period. At his rate of $15 per hour, and at an average of two and one-half hours extra per week, plaintiff's loss for its employee Al Fugazy amounts to $2,887.50. Therefore, defendant is liable for $15,637.50 in lost employee time. Total damages assessed are $45,624.46.

Interest will run from the date when defendants' breach was clearly established. By April 1980, the defendants had decided not to deliver any further programs required by the contract, and had decided to do no more work on the substandard fuel consumption program. [Reference.] It is reasonable, thus, to begin interest calculations from April 15, 1980.

The defendant CU is liable for the full damages of $45,624.46 plus interest. Defendant Spiro is personally liable for any of these monies CU is unable to pay, up to the maximum amount of $30,000 as set out in the signed personal guarantee. *See* Plaintiff's Exhibit 4.

* * *

FLAMBEAU PRODUCTS CORP. v. HONEYWELL INFORMATION SYSTEMS, INC.

111 Wis.2d 317, 330 N.W.2d 228
(Court of Appeals of Wisconsin, Jan. 18, 1983.)

CANE, J.

Honeywell Information Systems, Inc., appeals from an order for an interlocutory judgment [footnote] extinguishing Flambeau Products Corporation's obligations under installment purchase contracts and dismissing Honeywell's counterclaim for the unpaid portion of the purchase price, plus accrued interest. Honeywell contends that the trial court erroneously held that Honeywell's retention of proceeds from Flambeau's check marked as payment in full constituted an accord and satisfaction. Honeywell also asserts that an accord and satisfaction did not occur because under sec. 401.207, Stats., it reserved its right to full performance of Flambeau's contractual obligations. Because we conclude that an accord and satisfaction was not effected since Honeywell reserved its rights under sec. 401.207, we reverse and remand.

Flambeau contracted to purchase computer equipment and key tapes from Honeywell's Wisconsin office. The purchase contracts provided that Flambeau was to pay the purchase price in monthly installments. Honeywell granted Flambeau the option to prepay its obligations under the contract at any time and established a $14,000 credit for computer programming services that Flambeau could use until October 1, 1976. Flambeau utilized part of this credit prior to its expiration.

Flambeau requested a prepayment quotation from Honeywell for payment as of January 31, 1977. Honeywell quoted $109,412 as the amount of principal and accrued interest due, which Flambeau did not dispute. After receiving this quotation, Flambeau sent a check for $95,412 and a letter addressed to Honeywell to a post office box in Chicago, Illinois, which was a lock box Honeywell had established with the Northern Trust Company. The check was marked as payment in full of Flambeau's obligations under the purchase contracts. The accompanying letter also stated that the check was in full settlement of Flambeau's contractual obligations, and it indicated that a $14,000 deduction for unused programming had been taken from the figure Honeywell had quoted. Although Northern Trust was not authorized to cash checks bearing qualifying notations, it cashed Flambeau's check and deposited the proceeds in Honeywell's account on February 4, 1977.

Honeywell's Wisconsin office did not learn that the check had been tendered and cashed and that Flambeau had sent an accompanying letter until March 11, 1977. On the next business day, Honeywell's Wisconsin office notified Flambeau via letter that the check did not constitute full payment of Flambeau's contractual obligations and that Honeywell did not accept it as such. Honeywell also requested that Flambeau remit the remaining balance plus accrued interest. Honeywell did not return any of the proceeds from the cashed check to Flambeau.

Flambeau sought a declaratory judgment against Honeywell to the effect that Flambeau had no additional obligations to Honeywell and that Honeywell had no security interest in Flambeau's computer equipment. The trial court initially held that Honeywell's retention of the check proceeds constituted an accord and satisfaction, which it could not avoid by a reservation of rights under sec. 401.207, and granted summary judgment to Flambeau. This court reversed the trial court's decision because the record revealed no evidence of a disputed or unliquidated claim between the parties at the time Flambeau sent its check to the lock box at Northern Trust. We therefore held that based on the limited record before us, Flambeau could not claim an accord and satisfaction by virtue of its partial payment of an undisputed debt, and the matter was remanded for trial.

After trial, the trial court found that there was no dispute concerning the amount Flambeau owed to Honeywell prior to the time Flambeau sent the check and letter in which it had claimed an offset. The court nevertheless held that Honeywell's retention of the check proceeds after it became aware of Flambeau's claimed offset and the condition upon which the check had been tendered constituted an accord and satisfaction, and it granted an interlocutory judgment to Flambeau.

Honeywell contends that this court's decision on their previous appeal constituted the law of the case, and that the trial court was therefore required to hold that there had been no accord and satisfaction after it found that there was no prior dispute between the parties. Flambeau argues that its assertion of a claimed offset in the letter accompanying the check rendered Honeywell's claim disputed and unliquidated, and that its payment of an amount it concedes it owed to Honeywell and Honeywell's retention of the proceeds after Honeywell learned of Flambeau's claim constituted an accord and satisfaction. [Citation.]

It is undisputed that Northern Trust, as an agent for Honeywell, had no authority to cash a check marked as payment in full. There is no evidence that Northern Trust had any knowledge of a possible dispute between Flambeau and Honeywell that could be imputed to Honeywell, or that it was authorized to settle an account on Honeywell's behalf. There is also no evidence that Flambeau disputed the amount Honeywell quoted until it sent the check and letter in which it claimed an offset.

Even if Honeywell's retention of the check proceeds for its use after it learned of and disputed Flambeau's right to an offset constituted an accord and satisfaction under common law principles, we conclude that an accord and satisfaction was not effected because Honeywell reserved its right to full performance from Flambeau under sec. 401.207. [Footnote.] Section 401.207 is part of the Uniform Commercial Code, chs. 401–409. Because the controversy between Flambeau and Honeywell involves a commercial transaction for the sale of goods, that transaction is governed by the provisions of the code. Section 402.102, Stats. We are required to liberally construe the provisions of chapters 401–409 to promote their underlying purposes and policies. Section 401.102, Stats.

Section 401.207, Stats., provides:

> Performance or acceptance under reservation of rights. A party who with explicit reservation of rights performs or promises performance or assents to performance in a manner demanded or offered by the other party does not thereby prejudice the rights reserved. Such words as "without prejudice," "under protest" or the like are sufficient.

Wisconsin has not addressed the applicability of sec. 401.207 (U.C.C. § 1–207) to the cashing of a check marked "payment in full" whereby the creditor attempts to reserve his right to recover the balance of his claim not covered by the check. Some jurisdictions have either held or stated by way of dicta that U.C.C. § 1–207 allows a payee in a code-covered transaction to cash a conditional check, retain the proceeds, and avoid the operation of an accord and satisfaction if he explicitly reserves his right to full performance from the payor. [Footnote.] Other jurisdictions have reached the opposite conclusion. [Footnote.] At least one commentator on the Uniform Commercial Code has questioned the applicability of § 1–207 to the conditional check and has relied on the official comment to § 1–207, which states in part: "This section provides machinery for the continuation of performance along the lines contemplated by the contract despite a pending dispute. * * * " Because an accord and satisfaction involves a new contract, it is argued that this is inconsistent with a "performance along the lines contemplated by the contract."[5] [Citation.] Others have recognized, however, that offering a reasonable payment in full satisfaction of an obligation inflicts "commercial torture" on the payee and have concluded that where the payee has explicitly reserved his rights, U.C.C. § 1–207 applies to the conditional check situation. [Footnote.] Although some have criticized this interpretation on the ground that it may discourage settlements and unfairly favor creditors, it is also recognized that the common law doctrine of accord and satisfaction often gives debtors

an unfair advantage over creditors, and that § 1–207 may be an effort to balance the scales. [Citation.]

The Wisconsin Legislative Council's report concerning sec. 401.207 supports a conclusion that the statute applies to the acceptance under protest of a conditional check tendered in a code-covered transaction. The annotation states in part: "Provides a method of procedure whereby one party claiming a right which the other party feels to be unwarranted can make certain that the fact that he proceeds with or promises or assents to performance will not operate as a waiver of his claim to such right. * * * " This conclusion is also bolstered by the 1961 Report of the Commission on Uniform State Laws [footnote], which interpreted U.C.C. § 1–207 as follows: "The Code rule would permit, in Code-covered transactions, the acceptance of a part * * * payment tendered in full settlement without requiring the acceptor to gamble with his legal right to demand the balance of the * * * payment." [Footnote.] It is clear that this interpretation deals with the situation of an offered compromise of a disputed or unliquidated claim and not a liquidated claim, since there never was a risk of losing the right to recover the balance of a liquidated claim by agreeing to accept partial payment. This same interpretation of sec. 401.207 is consistent with the underlying purposes of the Uniform Commercial Code set forth in sec. 401.102[2], Stats. [Footnote.] That it is also commercially reasonable is apparent in this case where Honeywell would otherwise be forced to return $95,412, which Flambeau concedes that it owes, in order to press its claim for $14,000 that it contends is still due under the contracts.

Flambeau argues that even if sec. 401.207 applies in this case, Honeywell failed to reserve its rights under the statute. We disagree. Although Honeywell retained the proceeds after the check was cashed, it sent a letter to Flambeau immediately after it learned of the check and accompanying letter in which Flambeau claimed an offset. In that letter, Honeywell responded to Flambeau's contention that Flambeau had paid off its obliga-

---

5. A problem with this interpretation arises in the case of a full payment check that is tendered during an intermediate stage of performance. The language of the official comment to § 1–207 indicates that the statute

would then apply. It makes little, if any, sense to apply § 1–207 to that situation but not to a conditional check tendered at the end of performance.

tions to Honeywell by stating, "this is not the case." The letter also indicated that Honeywell did not consider the check to be in full payment of the account. The wording was sufficient to put Flambeau on notice that Honeywell protested the amount of the check, and the letter was a proper and explicit reservation of rights within the purview of sec. 401.207. [Citations.] Although the usual method of reserving rights is for the payee to endorse the conditional check with words indicating protest, Northern Trust had already negotiated the check without authorization when Honeywell, the payee, learned of the transaction. A reservation of rights via letter was the only route available to Honeywell, which it immediately pursued. Honeywell therefore explicitly reserved its rights under sec. 401.207, and its retention of the check proceeds did not effect an accord and satisfaction.

Because the trial court held that an accord and satisfaction had occurred, it dismissed Honeywell's counterclaim. We therefore remand for a consideration of the merits of this counterclaim.

Order reversed and cause [sic] remanded.

FOLEY, J. (concurring).

Honeywell's acceptance of Flambeau's check was not an accord and satisfaction. An accord and satisfaction is contractual in nature. [Citation.] It requires consideration. [Citation.] The only possible consideration here was Flambeau's check. As neither party disputed the fact that at least this amount was presently due, the check is not consideration.

DDP MICROSYSTEMS, INC. v. TILDEN FINANCIAL CORP.

88 A.D.2d 875, 451 N.Y.S.2d 778
(Supreme Court, Appellate Division, First Department, June 24, 1982.)

MEMORANDUM DECISION.

Order and Judgment of the Supreme Court, New York County, entered October 26, 1981, which granted plaintiff's motion for summary judgment, denied defendant's cross-motion for summary judgment and awarded judgment for plaintiff in the sum of $10,066.41, is unanimously modified on the law without costs, to

the extent of denying plaintiff's motion for summary judgment and otherwise affirmed.

Defendant Tilden Financial Corporation (Tilden) is engaged in the business of purchasing certain equipment and then leasing it to professional and business entities, who themselves either cannot afford or, for some other reason, choose not to buy the hardware outright. Plaintiff DDP Microsystems, Inc. (DDP) sells small electronic computer systems and services. Plaintiff contends that its president, Richard Bock, was informed by Edward Ingram, one of defendant's salesmen and account executives, that the credit of Weekend Sports Co., Inc. (WESCO), a potential customer of DDP and a proposed lessee of Tilden, had been approved and that plaintiff was authorized to deliver two computer systems to WESCO. After delivery was effected, and Bock had notified Ingram of that fact, Ingram advised him to send an invoice to Tilden. Bock immediately complied and, for three months, received no objections to the bill or the equipment. However, when DDP attempted to collect, defendant refused to pay for the order.

Defendant denies ever entering into a purchase agreement with plaintiff for the computers. Tilden also asserts that since it was never informed of the delivery of the computer systems, it assumed that there had been no such delivery. DDP, moreover, never received an acknowledgment of delivery on defendant's authorized form although plaintiff knew that Tilden would consent to the delivery only if such a procedure were followed. In addition, plaintiff failed to secure the required leasehold agreement and the personal guarantee of the proposed lessee's principal. Defendant further alleges that in the two previous transactions between Tilden and DDP, plaintiff had secured execution of the leases and obtained delivery receipts on forms supplied by defendant. Pursuant to the parties' prior course of dealings, defendant would pay only upon execution of a purchase order, followed by Tilden's approval of the lessee's credit and installation of the equipment by plaintiff, who would then transmit to defendant a delivery receipt prepared by Tilden.

Special Term, in granting summary judgment to plaintiff, based its decision on the fact that defendant was promptly invoiced for the computer equipment and never expressed any objection thereto during the three months that elapsed before the instant action was commenced. However, DDP has not submitted any writing to indicate that a contract of sale had ever been entered into between plaintiff and defendant. Thus, even if it is assumed that defendant's failure to give plaintiff written notice of any objections to the contents of the invoice can be deemed to satisfy the requirements of the Statute of Frauds (UCC section 2–201), and defendant has advanced several arguably meritorious grounds in support of its claim that section 2–201 of the U.C.C. is inapplicable to the instant situation, plaintiff still has the burden of proving the existence of an oral agreement. Since there are a number of unresolved factual and legal issues, both with regard to the alleged oral contract and otherwise, summary judgment was inappropriate.

WESTFIELD CHEMICAL CORP. v. BURROUGHS CORP.

6 CLSR 438, 21 UCC Rep. 1293
(Commonwealth of Massachusetts, Hampden County Superior Court, April 15, 1977.)

GREANEY, J.

This is a suit brought by Westfield Chemical Corporation against Burroughs Corporation alleging breach of contract and breach of express and implied warranties, fraud and negligence in connection with the manufacture, sale and servicing of a Burroughs computer.

On January 28, 1971 the parties entered into a written equipment sales contract,[1] a copy of which is appended to the affidavits. In that contract the seller, Burroughs Corporation, warranted that the equipment was free from defects in material and workmanship and agreed to exchange any defective equipment for a period of one year from delivery. However, the contract expressly and conspicuously disclaimed all express or implied warranties, including any for merchantability or fitness. It also provided that the entire obligation of the seller in connection with the transaction was contained in the contract.

The plaintiff alleges an express warranty by the defendant that the computer would generate efficiency and time savings and was fit for the plaintiff's account system (Declaration, Count I); an implied warranty that the system was fit for the particular use to which it was put by the plaintiff (Declaration, Count III); and a contractual agreement by the defendant to assemble, program, maintain, and service the equipment (Declaration, Count II). The plaintiff also asserts claims that are expressed in tort language, but the underlying allegations in those claims are virtually identical with the assertions contained in the warranty counts (Declaration, Count IV [negligence], Count V [fraudulent inducement]).

This case was heard before the Court on March 23, 1977, pursuant to the defendant's motion under Mass R Civ P 56 for summary judgment. From an examination of the evidentiary material submitted, as well as the issues raised during oral argument, and the briefs, I find that there are no genuine issues of material fact in dispute and that the defendant is entitled to prevail as a matter of law.

First, I find that the disclaimer of implied and express warranties contained in the contract complies with GL c 106, 1–201(10) and is conspicuous. I also find that the disclaimer is valid and effective so as to disclaim all warranties express or implied pursuant to GL c 106, §2–316, and to therefore determine any rights that the plaintiff has to recover for claimed breach of warranties. Other courts have held that identical language in contracts of the defendant in use in other states has

---

1. On the same date, the parties also signed a separate "Application Software Support Contract." The plaintiff at times seems to claim damages caused by an alleged delay in completing the programming called for under this contract, more particularly the so-called "batch ticket program." (Declaration, Count II; Plaintiff's Answers to Interrogatories Propounded by the Defendant, Answers 4(b), (c), 13, and 14(b).

Any such claim is barred by the provisions of that contract which also limits liability and disclaims warranties and representations. But even if these disclaimers and limitations were held ineffective in the circumstances of this case, the most that the plaintiff could recover would be its reasonable damages caused by any alleged delay in the delivery of the program. He cannot thereby acquire any rights to recover for defective machinery, maintenance or repair services covered by the other contract.

effectively disclaimed all express and implied warranties. *Bakal v. Burroughs Corp.*, 343 N.Y.S.2d 541, 74 Misc.2d 202 (1972); *Investors Premium Corp. v. Burroughs Corp.*, Civil No. 72–1526 (D.S.C. Feb. 1, 1974). *See*, GL c 106, §2–719, Official UCC Comment 3 (discussing unconscionability) ("The seller in all cases is free to disclaim warranties in the manner provided in Section 2–316.") The *Investors Premium Corp.* decision, not a decision of record though thoroughly in point here, is attached to defendant's brief, and covers issues germane to those present in this case.

I also find that the plaintiff and the defendant validly agreed upon a limitation of damages as governed by GL c 106, §2–719, and that the defendant is entitled to prevail as a matter of law on any claim for damages other than replacement or repair of defective parts of the computer.

The contract in issue here provides:

> Seller shall deliver, install and service the equipment as promptly as is reasonably possible, but shall not be held responsible for delay in delivery, installation or service, nor in any event under this agreement for more than an exchange of equipment under its warranty, upon return of the equipment to the seller, with seller's prior written consent. (Purchaser hereby expressly waives all damages, whether direct, incidental or consequential.)

GL c 106, §2–719(1) specifically provides that "the agreement may * * * limit or alter the measure of damages recoverable under this Article, as by limiting the buyer's remedies to return of the goods and repayment of the price or to repair and replacement of non-conforming goods or parts. * * * " The purpose of this provision is to leave the parties "free to shape their remedies to their particular requirements and reasonable agreements limiting or modifying remedies are to be given effect." GL c 106, §2–719, Official UCC Comment 1.

GL c 106, §2–719(3) provides:

> Consequential damages may be limited or excluded unless the limitation or exclusion is unconscionable. Limitation of consequential damages for injury to the person in the case of consumer goods is prima facie unconscionable *but limitation of damage where the loss is commercial is not.* (Emphasis added.)

This agreement is not unconscionable. "The principle [of unconscionability] is one of the prevention of oppression and unfair surprise * * * and not of disturbance of allocation of risks because of superior bargaining power." GL c 106, §2–302, Official UCC Comment 1. The majority of contracts held unconscionable have been in the area of consumer transactions. *E.g., Williams v. Walker Thomas Furniture Co.*, 350 F.2d 445 (D.C. Cir. 1965), and this contract is between businessmen acting at presumed arm's length.

Nor has the limited remedy provided by this contract failed of its essential purpose. At any time the plaintiff could have returned any defective part for repair or replacement. *Compare Wilson Trading Corp. v. David Ferguson, Ltd.*, 23 N.Y.2d 398, 244 N.E.2d 685, 297 N.Y.S.2d 108 (1968) (remedy fails of its essential purpose where time for reporting defect was shorter than time reasonably necessary to discover it).

I also find that the contract makes it clear that the seller will provide maintenance coverage for twelve months at no additional cost, but shall not be liable for damages or losses in the rendering of that maintenance. Under these circumstances, the absence of any claim that the seller did not in fact offer "as well trained and competent a staff of service technicians as are available in the industry," the plaintiff cannot recover for damages allegedly caused by delays in rendering of maintenance coverage, and this entitles the defendant to judgment on Count II alleging breach of the maintenance contract.

Furthermore, I find that any alleged misrepresentation concerning the function of the computer related to future performances not susceptible of actual knowledge and cannot serve as a basis for recovery in fraud. *See, Harris v. Delco Products, Inc.*, 305 Mass. 362. The plaintiff is, therefore, barred by GL c 106, §202 from introducing in evidence as to alleged representations made by the seller during the sale negotiations, particularly in view of the clause in the contract limiting the entire obligation of the parties to what appears in the written agreement. The mere characterization of representations as "fraudulent" is insufficient to take them out of the general rule that one is bound by the terms of the written agreement, whether he reads and understands it or not. [Citation.]

Harris v. Delco Products, Inc., supra, in point here on the fraud claims, provides that:

It is well settled in this Commonwealth that the charge of fraudulent intent, in an action for deceit, may be maintained by proof of a statement made, as of the party's own knowledge, which is false, provided the thing stated is not a matter of opinion, estimate, or judgment, but is susceptible of exact knowledge * * * Representations, although false, concerning matters not susceptible of actual knowledge have been held to be nonactionable, at least when made by one not in a fiduciary capacity * * * and it is a general rule that the law refuses to permit recovery in tort for damages resulting from reliance upon false statements of belief, of conditions to exist in the future, or of matters promissory in nature.

This test applies as well to contract actions. *Id.,* at 364.

Any representations made by the defendant here necessarily related to the future. The plaintiff, when asked to give particulars concerning misrepresentations made by the defendant has [answered] in interrogatories:

(a) One such warranty was conveyed by Burroughs proposal date 14 September 1970 signed by Richard Carlson, the substance of which was a substantial man-hour savings. The savings never materialized, and, in fact, operating time exceeded man-hours originally performed manually by Westfield Chemical Corporation. [Reference.]

As is apparent from the affidavit of Julius J. Samal, appended to defendant's motion for summary judgment, man-hour savings are dependent upon such variables as the program actually decided upon, the cooperation and the efficiency of the operators, the caliber of the electrical current supplied to the computer, the volume of business being processed, etc., none of which were susceptible of knowledge when the proposal was written.

When a representation relates to a matter not susceptible of personal knowledge, it cannot be considered as anything more than a strong expression of opinion, notwithstanding it is made positively and as of the maker's own knowledge. The mere fact that it is stated positively cannot make it a statement of fact. The most anyone

can do as to such matters is to express his opinion. It cannot be found, from the single fact that such a statement is untrue, that it was made with fraudulent intent; there must also be evidence that the maker knew it was in some respect untrue, *before there is anything to submit to the jury.* (Emphasis added.) *Harris v. Delco Products, Inc.,* supra, at 366 (1940).

Furthermore, as a matter of law the plaintiff could not have reasonably relied upon such representations. *Harris v. Delco Products, Inc., supra.*

* * * Regardless of what has been said about the matter, or of how strongly the statement has been put, he knows that the speaker cannot actually know what the fact of the matter is, and that, therefore, he is not justified in relying on what can, in its nature, be nothing more than the opinion, however strong, of the speaker on the matter. *Harris v. Delco Products, Inc., supra,* at 367.

This is particularly true where, as here, any statements were made during the early planning stages. *Compare Yerid v. Mason,* 341 Mass. 527 (1960) with *Pietrazak v. McDermott,* 341 Mass. 107 (1960) (stage of completion distinguishing factor where defendants represented that cellars would be dry).

Moreover, the letter dated September 14, 1970 from Richard Carlson clearly states:

This recommendation of Burroughs products is submitted for your consideration and guidance only in the hope that we may be favored with your order. *Since this proposal is preliminary only, the order when issued shall constitute the only legally binding commitment of the parties.* (Emphasis added.)

It should also be noted that this is not a case where the nature of the thing being sold was misrepresented, *City Dodge, Inc. v. Gardner,* 232 Ga. 766, 208 S.E.2d 794 (1974) (dealer represented to consumer that car had never been previously owned), or the nature of the contract being signed was kept from the plaintiff. *Compare Schell v. Ford Motor Co.,* 270 F.2d 384 (1st Cir. 1959) (applying Massachusetts law) (consumer not barred from suing where release saying no representations had been made was characterized as a pass to enter the plant). Other courts have held that the same Burroughs contract barred similar claims couched in the language of fraud and deceit where the claims were "essentially" contract claims. *E.g., Investors Premium Corp. v. Burroughs Corp., supra.*

In summary, the breach of warranty counts fail because of the existence of a complete, conspicuous and valid disclaimer.

The breach of contract count fails because of the limitation of damage clause in the contract which is valid and enforceable and is not claimed to have been breached.

The count claiming fraud fails on the authority of *Harris v. Delco Products Inc., supra,* which I find controls this claim based on the materials submitted.

Finally, the negligent manufacture count fails since it is basically a duplicate of the warranty and contract counts and hence barred by the agreement, and since nothing has been indicated factually to show any triable issue on the negligent manufacture claim.

On the basis of the foregoing, I find this to be an appropriate case for a Rule 56 motion and summary judgment to be entered for the defendant on all counts.

SPERRY RAND CORP. v. INDUSTRIAL SUPPLY CORP.

337 F.2d 363

(United States Court of Appeals Fifth Circuit, Oct. 5, 1964.)

JONES, C. J.

* * * Industrial Supply brought an action for the rescission of its purchase from Sperry Rand, by written agreement, of a record-keeping system and equipment. Breach of an express or implied warranty, or both, was asserted, and a fraud claim was founded on the averment that false representations were willfully, recklessly or negligently made by Sperry Rand. The district court rejected the claim that there had been a breach of an express warranty and found against Industrial Supply on the fraud issue. The court found, however, that there had been a breach of an implied warranty, decreed rescission and entered judgment for Industrial Supply, conditioned upon the return of the equipment, for the purchase price, transportation costs, insurance and interest. Sperry Rand has appealed. Industrial Supply has taken a cross-appeal, contending that its judgment should have included an award for its claims for other items of damage.

Industrial Supply is engaged in the business of selling and distributing steel, pipe, equipment, tools, hardware, and other items to industrial, agricultural and other users, doing a large volume of business throughout a large territory, and having its principal place of business at Tampa, Florida. Sperry Rand, through its Remington Rand Univac Division, is in the business of manufacturing, selling and installing business systems and equipment, including automatic electronic data processing equipment. Industrial Supply, desiring to improve its system of paper work and produce its records faster and more efficiently, invited several makers of electronic processing equipment to make surveys and recommendations. Two responses were made, one of them by Sperry Rand. Conferences were held between representatives of Sperry Rand and Industrial Supply. Sperry Rand made a study of the business procedures of Industrial Supply over a period of about three months. In January 1959, Sperry Rand submitted "A Report Prepared Expressly for Industrial Supply Corp. * * * following a work process survey of your administrative operations, routines, and procedures." The title page of the report, which is sometimes referred to as "the brochure," recited that "It is understood that the recommendations herein are intended only for consideration by your organization and that the detailed operating advantages are obtainable through the integrated utilization of Remington Rand products and services." The brochure listed about seventy procedures, so called, that the RRU (Remington Rand Univac) recommended equipment was intended to execute. Seventeen flow charts were included to show the processes by which the RRU equipment would carry out the procedures. Ten separate items of equipment, having prices ranging from $1,994 for an Alphabetical Punch to $75,000 for a Univac Electronic Computer, were included.

The brochure contained "Recommendations", including the following:

1. We recommend the use of RRU equipment as the one best suited to a tailor made job for your organization.

2. We have demonstrated the fact that through the use of RRU punched card procedures and exclusive equipment features, we can produce your records and reports more economically, faster and accurate than your present operation.

3. We suggest the use of several RRU exclusive machines, namely the Card-O-Matic, the UNIVAC 60 computer, the fast speed Electronic Sorter, the Collating Reproducer, the 100 Sector Alphabetical Printing Tabulator, and other devices incorporated in the equipment for use on your procedures.

The brochure was transmitted to Industrial Supply by a letter signed by two "Univac Representatives" of Sperry Rand. The letter is in the following terms:

We have completed our study of the phases of your organization that you desire to mechanize, and are submitting our proposal applying fully automatic Remington Rand Univac equipment to your procedures in Order Writing, Invoicing, Inventory, Accounts Receivable, Salesman Commissions, Accounts Payable, Back Ordering, and Purchasing Department activity.

Our study disclosed that the use of tabulating equipment suggested in this proposal will produce your records and reports with greater speed, uniformity, accuracy, and economy. Using the principle, developed for the Card-O-Matic Punch, of coding, pricing and punching in one operation, without further verification, and the fast extending, comparing, and punching operations of the Univac 60, you will no doubt be able to absorb increased activity on the suggested equipment for a greater volume of business without an appreciable increase in cost.

We have demonstrated to you our complete interest in formulating, planning, and assisting in installing a system on tabulating equipment tailored to your needs, and your organization's work. Our proposal covers the subject matter thoroughly, but is only the beginning of applying our experience and know how to your routines and procedures.

We wish to thank you and the personnel in your organization, for the help and assistance they gave us to make this proposal possible. We will be indeed proud to accept your signature on the enclosed contract for equipment, and welcome your organization to the large number of satisfied Remington Rand Customers.

In the pocket of the back cover of the brochure were two forms of the agreement between Sperry Rand and Industrial Supply, one being for the use and service of the equipment, which will be referred to as a lease or rental agreement, the other being a contract for the sale of the equipment. The lease agreement, dated April 3, 1959, calling for a rental of $1,980 per month, was executed. The equipment was delivered to Industrial Supply at Tampa, Florida, in July and August, 1959. It was decided by Industrial Supply, on advice of its accountant it appears, that the equipment should be purchased rather than leased. No rental had been paid. During December 1959, the parties entered into the agreement for the sale of the equipment. The final payment of the sales price was made in February, 1960.

The sales agreement contained a warranty clause obligating Sperry Rand to make adjustments during thirty days after installation and to replace defective parts within ninety days from the date of installation. The final paragraph of the agreement provided that the entire agreement was contained in it, and no representation, except when made in writing by a duly authorized officer of RRU, should be deemed to be a part of the agreement. To the extent these clauses are material they will be hereinafter quoted.

Quite some time was spent in preparing to convert the record-keeping procedures of Industrial Supply from methods previously used to the RRU system. Several additional months were spent by Industrial Supply in using or attempting to use the equipment, during which time it expressed to Sperry Rand its dissatisfaction with the equipment and its functioning. Its discontent was indicated by correspondence and in conference with Sperry Rand representatives. In the early part of 1961 Industrial Supply repudiated the transaction and sought the return of the purchase price and redelivery of the equipment. Sperry Rand attributed the failure of the equipment to give satisfaction to the unwillingness of Industrial Supply's personnel to make it operate efficiently and a desire on the part of Industrial Supply's management, for economic reasons, to get out of the deal. This suit followed. The complaint alleges that Sperry Rand made express and implied warranties that the system and equipment were fit and specially tailored for the use intended and required by Industrial Supply. A breach of the warranty was asserted. Rescission was sought and damages were claimed. Sperry Rand asserted that its representatives, who were said by Industrial Supply to have made representations, were only expressing opinions, that Industrial Supply did not rely upon the statements made to it but made its decision to purchase on the basis of its own investigations. Sperry Rand asserted that the equipment fully performed all that had been promised for it.

The district court found that the statements were representations on behalf of Sperry Rand and not merely the opinions of salesmen, and that the equipment was not reasonably fit for the purpose and use for which it was intended and had been recommended. The court held that the applicable law for the interpretation of the contract was the law of New York, where the contract was made. The court concluded that under the New York law the transaction between the parties gave rise to an implied warranty that the equipment was reasonably fit for the purpose required by the purchaser. Under the law of New York, so held the district court, the integration clause does not exclude or preclude the existence of implied warranties. There was, according to the district court's findings and conclusions, a breach of an implied warranty of fitness which entitled the purchaser to rescind the contract of sale, return the equipment and recover the purchase price and incidental charges and expense. A decree was entered in accordance with the findings and conclusions. Sperry Rand has appealed. Industrial Supply has taken a cross-appeal on the ground that it was entitled to a recovery of damages for incidental charges and expenses in an amount greater than the award of the court.

* * *

The appellate courts of Florida with an occasional contribution from this Court, have fully participated in the development of the doctrine of implied warranty of fitness for a disclosed purpose. At common law the doctrine of caveat emptor applies to all sales unless there is an express warranty of the seller or a warranty is implied by operation of law. [Citation.] In an early decision, the Florida Supreme Court quoted from Benjamin on Sales and stated the following rule:

[W]here a person contracts to supply an article in which he deals for a particular purpose, knowing the purpose for which he supplies it and that the purchaser had no opportunity to inspect the article, but relies upon the judgment of the seller, there is an implied condition or "warranty," as it is called, that the article is fit for the purpose to which it is to be applied. Berger v. E. Berger & Co., 76 Fla. 503, 511, 80 So. 296, 299.

The rule was reiterated and the Berger case was cited in the most recent of the Florida implied warranty cases. [Citation.] In Smith v. Burdines, Inc., 144 Fla. 500, 198 So. 223, 131 A.L.R. 115, the same rule was announced, and in its opinion the court stressed the requirements that the seller be possessed of a superior knowledge of the articles sold, that the seller knows of the particular purpose for which the articles are required, that the buyer relies upon the skill and judgment of the seller, and that the seller is aware of such reliance by the buyer. [Citation.] The evidence here clearly establishes the knowledge of Sperry Rand as to the particular purposes for which Industrial Supply desired to purchase the equipment, and the reliance by the buyer upon the judgment of the seller. The admissibility of this evidence, under the parol evidence rule, will be later considered. We accept the determination of the district court that the equipment was not fit and suitable for the intended purpose and that it did not perform the required functions in accordance with the known purpose.

The judicial opinions, in sometimes stating the doctrine of implied warranty, confine it to situations where the buyer lacks an opportunity to inspect the subject matter of the sale. [Citations.] Sperry Rand invokes this restriction upon the rule and stresses the length of time the equipment was in the possession of Industrial Supply under the lease before the purchase was made, and the opportunity which it might have had for further inspection before buying by remaining a lessee for a further period. It is only where an inspection would have revealed to the purchaser that the subject of the purchase was not fit or suitable for the intended purpose that the implied warranty may not be relied upon. [Citations.] Industrial Supply did not know and could not be expected to ascertain, except by use and experiment, the functional abilities and capacities of the electronic equipment, with its transistors, tubes and diodes, its varicolored maze of wiring, its buttons and switches, and the supplementing of machines and devices for the punching of cards and others for the sorting thereof. And, of course, the personnel of Industrial Supply could not be expected to understand the processes by which a set of these modern miracle-makers perform their tasks. Whether the trial use of the equipment was an inspection or its equivalent we need not decide. We see no merit in the contention that the termination of the lease by the purchase of the equipment operated in some fashion as a rejection of the opportunity of continuing the inspection. The substantial rights of the parties, we think, were the same as if there had been no intervening lease. An inspection, if required, could have been made after the sale had been completed as well as before.

By a clause in the sales contract captioned "Warranty" Sperry Rand undertook to make necessary adjustments during a thirty-day period, and to replace broken or defective parts, with some exceptions, during a ninety-day period. The final clause of the contract, designated "General," provided that:

> The entire Agreement between the parties with respect to the subject matter hereof is contained in this Agreement and no representation, except when made in writing by a duly authorized officer of RRU, shall be deemed to be part of this Agreement, nor shall this Agreement be deemed or construed to be modified, amended, rescinded, cancelled or waived in whole or in part, except by a duly executed written agreement of the parties hereto or their lawful successors.

It is urged by Sperry Rand that the express warranties of the sales contract exclude any implied warranties. This contention would be sound if the express warranties were of the same kind as the asserted implied warranty and were inconsistent with it. [Citations.] Here the express warranty is for the making of adjustments and the replacement of broken and defective parts while the asserted implied warranty relates to fitness for use. There is no inconsistency. In such a case the implied warranty is unaffected by the express warranty. [Citation.] * * * The express war-

ranties of the contract are not inconsistent with and do not exclude an implied warranty of fitness for a known purpose.

It is strongly and plausibly argued by Sperry Rand that the integration clause, so called, of the sales contract precludes any recovery by Industrial Supply on an implied warranty. If the general clause had expressly provided that there were no implied warranties the position of Sperry Rand would be sound. [Citation.] But it did not so provide, and while there are authorities holding contra, the majority and, we think, the better reasoned rule is that a contract clause that all agreements are contained in the writing does not operate to bar recovery on an implied warranty of fitness for use. [Citation.]

But, says Sperry Rand, the representations as to fitness for use were written and were excluded as express representations by the integration clause. How, asks Sperry Rand, can there be an actionable implied warranty of fitness for a specific purpose when its representations as to fitness are not actionable because of the integration clause. The question presented is, it seems, a different phrasing of the parol evidence rule. This rule is not procedural but is substantive, and the Florida law will apply. Under the rule, when the parties have reduced their agreement to writing, evidence as to other prior or contemporaneous transactions or undertakings is immaterial with respect to the matters covered by the written contract. [Citations.] As has been said, while there may be a valid express disclaimer of an implied warranty, the right to assert such a warranty is not precluded by express warranties which are not inconsistent, and since the implied warranty arises independently of the contract of sale, it is not to be rejected because of an integration clause. The contention of Sperry Rand has been answered by the Supreme Court of Florida in saying:

> The fact that a contract of sale is in writing does not necessarily exclude warranties that may be implied by law; and where the alleged verbal warranty sought to be established is only what would be implied, evidence thereof does not change the legal effect of the contract, and is therefore admissible. McDonald v. Sanders, 103 Fla. 93, 137 So. 122. Cf. Hoskins v. Jackson Grain Co., Fla., 63 So.2d 514.

The rule that there is no implied warranty of fitness where a known, described and definite article is purchased by its trade name is relied upon by Sperry Rand. There may be some question as to whether the Florida courts would follow this doctrine. [Citations.] Assuming that the Florida courts would apply the rule, we think the situation presented by this case is not within it. The transaction between Sperry Rand and Industrial Supply was not the sale of a single item. It was of the ten items to which reference has been made, incorporated into a system intended to be tailored to the needs of Industrial Supply. The operational functions of these ten machines were keyed together in a manner intended to meet the accounting and record-keeping requirements of the buyer. They were tailored by Sperry Rand's "know how" for the particular needs of Industrial Supply. There is no difference in principle between the incorporating of specifically described machines into an integrated system and the building of a specially designed single piece of equipment for a like purpose. The sale of a group of specifically described machines, which have been combined into an integrated system, specially arranged for the purchaser, is not to be exempted from the otherwise applicable operation of the doctrine of implied warranty on the ground that the machines comprising the system are patented and have been designated by trade names.

It is urged by Sperry Rand that the failure of the equipment to meet the needs of the buyer resulted, not from any inadequacy of the equipment, but because Industrial Supply did not operate the equipment as recommended and planned. The district court found that "Despite reasonable compliance by plaintiff with defendant's original and further recommendations and reasonable efforts by plaintiff to make the system function satisfactorily, the defendant's system continued to be deficient." The district court further found that "During December, 1960, and January, 1961, it first became evident to plaintiff that, notwithstanding any and all reasonable efforts which plaintiff had made and might be expected to make, defendant's system would not function as previously represented by defendant, or as needed by plaintiff in its business. * * * *" No useful purpose would be served by a recital

of the evidence upholding these findings. It is enough to say that they are fully supported and hence are not to be set aside. Rule 52(a), Fed.Rules Civ.Proc., 28 U.S.C.A.

Having reached the conclusion that none of Sperry Rand's assignments of error can be sustained, we turn to the cross-appeal of Industrial Supply. It asserts that the award of damages was insufficient as a matter of law. The district court decreed that the buyer could rescind, return the equipment to the seller and have judgment for the purchase price of the equipment and accessories, for the amounts expended for transportation, and for interest. The court rejected the claims of Industrial Supply for forms and supplies, the travel and moving expense of and the rental of an automobile for Robert C. Castle, an employee hired to supervise the installation and operation of the Univac Card-O-Matic equipment, the salary paid to Castle, part of the salary paid to Henry Gardner, and the salaries of other personnel used on the equipment, construction costs, additional insurance premiums and storage expense. As Industrial Supply states in its brief, "These items were disallowed to plaintiff, not because they had not been expended or incurred, but evidently because the trial judge felt that plaintiff had consumed or otherwise benefited from them." To recover for an asserted loss, the plaintiff has the burden of proving the fact, the cause and the extent of such loss. McCormick on Damages 53, § 14. In a sales warranty case the Supreme Court of Florida has announced these principles:

> It may be stated as a general rule that the party is entitled to compensation for an injury to his person, in his property or in his reputation. There is another general rule that a person is not liable in damages for the remote consequences of his act or conjectural consequences. Damages, to be recovered, must be both the natural and proximate consequence of the wrong complained of. The wrongdoer must answer in damages for those results injurious to other parties which are presumed to have been within his contemplation when the wrong was done. Vaughan's Seed Store v. Stringfellow, 56 Fla. 708, 720, 48 So. 410, 414.

[Citations.]

The arguments made by Industrial Supply in support of the disallowed portion of its claim for damages, set forth in part in the margin,[1] seem to us to demonstrate pretty well the correctness of the district court's conclusion as to the rejected items. While the court found that the equipment did not function as impliedly warranted and hence the buyer was entitled to rescind, nevertheless the equipment was used, some of the supplies were consumed in use, and there was some service rendered by the personnel who worked with the equipment. The evidence does not show the extent of the admitted benefit of the buyer from these payments, and the absence of evidence to prove the damage is not supplied by conjectural assertions regarding loss of business, customer dissatisfaction, and personnel problems. The construction cost of remodeling a room to house the RRU equipment was shown to be $8,324.84. The contractor testified that the only actual permanent improvement to the building was partitions of the value of $400. Whether or not the construction work on the building was a proper item for consideration in determining damages, it can be said that there was no certainty of proof as to the amount of the loss when no salvage credit was

given for a two-ton air-conditioning unit which the contractor had installed. We find no error in the district court's award of damages.

The judgment of the district court is affirmed.

JONES, MORRISON, STALNAKER, P.A. v. CONTEMPORARY COMPUTER SERVICES, INC.

414 So.2d 637

(District Court of Appeal of Florida, Fifth District, June 2, 1982.)

COBB, J.

The issue in this case is whether the trial court committed reversible error by refusing to give a jury instruction requested by the appellant law firm, Jones, Morrison, Stalnaker, P.A. ("Jones"). We hold that it did, and reverse.

The record indicates that Jones purchased a software computer package from the appellee, Contemporary Computer Services, Inc. ("Contemporary"), for $4,000. Alleging the

---

1. "Any thought that plaintiff might have benefited by the use of defendant's equipment or the above enumerated out-of-pocket expenses is dispelled by the failure of the system and the resulting, unmeasured, loss of business, customer dissatisfaction, and personnel problems. These items were not susceptible of proof sufficiently definite to sustain an allowance of damages for loss of profits and employee morale, but they did contribute to the uselessness of defendant's system in plaintiff's business and establish the valueless nature of the unreimbursed out-of-pocket expenses.

"It is undenied that the office equipment or supplies consisting of binders, tabs, forms, racks, files, and envelopes are specially useful to plaintiff only in connection with defendant's system. Gardner referred to them as expendible supplies. * * * The Court may judicially notice that electronic data processing forms and other such supplies are of no value in manually operated record-keeping systems.

"Castle's traveling and moving expense, the travel expenses of other prospective specialists, as well as Castle's salary in his efforts to install and supervise the operation of defendant's system, were obviously of no value to plaintiff, since it derived no value from the system. The same is true of the automobile rented for his use, of the extra personnel employed and of the overtime payments, all of which expenses are attributable only to plaintiff's reasonable efforts to make use of defendant's system.

"Even the calculated portion of Gardner's salary, which was allocated to cover his time consumed as a result of defendant's breach of warranty, should be upheld. Al-

though defendant's right to cross-examine Gardner was reserved, no cross-examination was made as to his allocation of his salary. Thus the account remains unchallenged in the record.

"The requested construction costs were fully explained. A room was altered and remodeled at defendant's specifications, with a large air-conditioning unit as required for the maintenance of special humidity and temperature control, with special bracing to support the heavy weight of the equipment, special wiring and special sound-conditioning, and partitioning. The area had been previously used for dead storage with a window air-conditioner sufficient for personnel comfort. It is now being used as a control room and location for plaintiff's ditto system for which the alterations and remodeling were unnecessary and useless. The requested sum for useless construction costs was part of a larger bill from the contractor. In the contractor's uncontradicted opinion the maximum salvage value, representing what was actually a useful improvement to the building was $400.00.

"One of plaintiff's major complaints is that defendant's heavy and bulky equipment has been occupying valuable space and requiring care, as well as insurance coverage, since rescission on February 1, 1961. Gardner's estimate was that $500.00 per month was the cost of space, protective precautions and insurance premiums totalling $7,000.00 at the time of trial. Despite plaintiff's demand that defendant take over the equipment at the end of January, 1961, and since then defendant has refused to do so. Hence, the storage protective care, and insurance outlays are continuing."

package did not perform as Contemporary had represented, Jones revoked its acceptance of the package and sued Contemporary, demanding a refund of the purchase price, as well as incidental and consequential damages. Contemporary answered Jones' amended complaint, and alleged several affirmative defenses. The case was tried before a jury, which awarded Jones $500 damages on its claim.[1]

At trial, the court refused to give Jones's requested instruction 13, which stated:

> Should you find the Plaintiff entitled to damages, you should award it:
> 1. A refund in full of the purchase price it paid for the computer program and computer language.
> 2. Those reasonable expenses, if any, incurred by Plaintiff as a result of the breach.

The court told Jones's counsel she could tell the jury "what damages you want in your closing arguments." Jones argues that the court's refusal to give this instruction constitutes reversible error.

Jones based its action for purchase price and incidental and consequential damages on section 672.711(1), Florida Statutes (1979), which provides:

> Where * * * the buyer rightfully rejects or justifiably revokes acceptance then with respect to any goods involved, and with respect to the whole if the breach goes to the whole contract (s. 672.612), the buyer may cancel and whether or not he has done so may *in addition to recovering so much of the price as has been paid.* * * * (Emphasis added.)

Jones's requested instruction 13 was therefore a correct statement of the applicable law.

In *Keyes Co. v. Shea*, 372 So.2d 493 (Fla. 4th DCA 1979), the trial court refused to specifically instruct on the proper measure of damages; instead, it instructed the jury to "determine in dollars the total amount of losses which the greater weight of the evidence showed [the plaintiff] sustained as a result of the incident complained of." 372 So.2d at 495. Finding that the instruction "gave the jury no guidance on the proper measure of damage to use in determining their verdict," the Fourth District held the trial court erred "in failing

to adequately and correctly instruct the jury on the proper measure of damages under one of the theories of plaintiff's case." *Id.* In the present case, the general instruction on damages given by the court was similar to the one found deficient in *Keyes:*

> Should you find in favor of Plaintiff, JONES, MORRISON, AND STALNAKER, P.A., you should award Plaintiff such damages as have, from the greater weight of the evidence, been proven to your satisfaction.

Jones's requested instruction 13 would have guided the jury as to the exact damages sought—if the jury concluded Jones had proved its cause of action and that Contemporary had failed with its affirmative defenses, Jones was entitled to recover at least the full purchase price.[2]

Finding Contemporary's arguments on appeal unpersuasive, we conclude the failure to give the requested instruction constitutes harmful error, and reverse and remand for a new trial.

Reversed and remanded.

OFFICE SUPPLY CO., INC. v. BASIC/FOUR CORP.

538 F.Supp. 776
(United States District Court, E. D. Wisconsin, May 3, 1982.)

REYNOLDS, C. J.

This is an action for damages brought pursuant to 28 U.S.C. § 1332. The plaintiff Office Supply Co., Inc. ("Office Supply") is a corporation located in Racine, Wisconsin, which sells office supplies. The defendant Basic/Four Corporation ("Basic/Four") is a California corporation which manufactures and sells computer hardware and software. In 1975, Office Supply purchased computer hardware and leased computer software from Basic/Four. Office Supply claims that the system was defective and caused it to suffer substantial losses. It seeks compensation for "lost customers, income, good will and executive time and incurred additional hardware and software expense, office form expense, personnel expense

---

1. Contemporary counterclaimed for various services; the jury awarded it $950 damages. This award is not a part of the appeal.

2. This assumes the return of undamaged equipment.

and maintenance expense, all to its damage in the sum of $186,000 plus reasonable interest since April, 1975." [Reference.]

* * * For the following reasons the plaintiff's motions will be denied and the defendant's motion for summary judgment will be granted.

THE SUMMARY JUDGMENT MOTIONS

On January 31, 1975, the plaintiff's president, James F. Bruno, signed a contract for the purchase of computer hardware from the defendant and of computer software which was intended to control order processing, inventory control, sales analysis, and accounts receivable.[1] Mr. Bruno mailed the contract to the defendant, and it was accepted by the defendant's assistant treasurer, R. C. Trost, on February 7, 1975. On April 1, 1975, the hardware was installed. In a letter dated May 22, 1975, the defendant advised the plaintiff that the warranty on the hardware would expire on July 1, 1975. The input of data on the software programs took longer to complete, and for a period of time the plaintiff ran parallel operations on the computer and manually as a check on the accuracy of the software applications. In a letter dated October 6, 1975, Mr. Bruno advised Basic/Four:

> All of the applications anticipated by our company in agreeing to acquire our BASIC/FOUR System are complete and the system appears to be satisfactory. This fulfills your contractual obligation.
>
> Although the applications programs appear to be operating satisfactorily, some "defects" might become apparent [sic] later. (Defects might comprise misinterpretation of data, mishandling of a keyboarding error, or a confusing operator instruction—but would not include anything beyond the scope of the system design specification.) It is my understanding that you warrant your programs, when used in accordance with Basic/Four operating instructions, to be free from "defects" for a period of ninety days, and that you will correct such "defects" promptly when they are brought to your attention. [Reference.]

Basic/Four took the position that its warranty on the software expired on January 6, 1976. As to complaints received after that date from Office Supply, it did continue to work with Office Supply in an effort to correct any claimed defects in the computer system. Office Supply also hired Ted Templeton, an independent programmer with a company called Computer Methods, Inc., who was recommended by Basic/Four, to work on its Basic/Four system starting some time after Basic/Four advised that the warranty period was over. The record established that Mr. Templeton made some modifications in the Basic/Four software. He also added at least one new program, the ABC program which involved inventory control, to the system. Starting in January 1978, Office Supply also hired a programmer, Marc Jerome, as a fulltime employee. He found what he claims were three major defects in the software system. The record establishes that two of those defects were in programs which Basic/Four did not supply to the plaintiff. The third defect was in the UJ portion of the Basic/Four accounts receivable program, but there is no evidence that the defect arose in the UJ program until after July 1976, which was after the end of the ninety-day period during which Basic/Four continued to warrant its software applications to be free from defects.

The plaintiff's vice president, David Carlson, testified during his deposition that starting at the end of October 1975 and continuing through early 1978, approximately 20% of the customer accounts were out of balance and the Basic/Four system performed up to 78% of expectation for Office Supply [reference]. Since February 1978, when Marc Jerome finished correcting the defects in the system, Carlson testified that it has performed up to 100% of expectation [reference]. The plaintiff's president, James Bruno, testified that the system only performed up to 50% of expectation prior to 1978 [reference], that the accounts receivable first went out of balance on the October 1975 monthly statement printed during the first week of November 1975 [reference], that it printed through for the first time in February 1976 [reference], but that thereafter the accounts receivable problem continued on an

---

1. The sale of the software was technically in lease form for reasons related to copyright protection. No one has contended that the technical lease arrangement has any significance to application of the UCC.

intermittent basis until it was corrected by Marc Jerome in early 1978 [reference]. Both men testified that there were also problems with the hardware but that those problems were always corrected by Sorbus, a service corporation related to Basic/Four with which Office Supply had a hardware maintenance contract, with only a very few minimal extra charges not covered by the monthly maintenance charges. [References.]

On June 17, 1980, Office Supply commenced its action against Basic/Four.

The portion of the Office Supply-Basic/Four contract dealing with the purchase of the hardware is a straightforward document. It describes on the front of the document the computer model and features and the purchase price. Additional terms and conditions of sale are set forth on the reverse. In relevant part it provides on the reverse that it constitutes the entire agreement and understanding between the parties, that it shall be governed by the law of California, and as to warranties and remedies for breach of warranty:

3. For ninety (90) days after the Equipment is installed * * * the Seller warrants the Equipment to be free from defects in material, workmanship, and operating failure from ordinary use, and the Seller's liability is limited solely to correcting any such defect or failure without charge. * * *

In italic print paragraph 3 also states:

The warranties contained in this Agreement are in lieu of all other warranties, express or implied, including any regarding merchantability or fitness for a particular purpose, arising out of or in connection with any Equipment (or the delivery, use or performance thereof). The Seller will not be liable * * * (b) for loss of profits or other incidental or consequential damages. * * *

The portion of the contract dealing with the lease of the software is not as clearly drafted. On its first page, which is page 3 of the contract, it states:

This Addendum to the Agreement for the Purchase of BASIC/FOUR Equipment, dated as of the 31 day of January 1975, between Basic/Four Corporation and Office Supply Inc. is hereby incorporated therein and made a part thereof.

Page 3 describes the program applications and their price. Additional terms and conditions

are set forth on the reverse side. As to warranties and limitation of remedies, paragraph 3 provides:

The Seller believes that the programming being furnished hereunder is accurate and reliable and when programming accomplishes the results set forth in the "Design Specifications," to be agreed to by the Seller and the Purchaser, such programming will be considered completed.

Paragraph 3 continues in italics:

However, the amounts to be paid to the Seller under this Agreement and this Addendum do not include any assumption of risk, and the Seller disclaims any and all liability for incidental or consequential damages arising out of the delivery, use or operation of the programs provided herein.

If the purchaser, without the written consent of the Seller, makes any modification to the programming or any deviations from the operating instructions or violates the provisions of paragraph 2, all warranties set forth herein cease immediately.

All warranties set forth herein are in lieu of all other warranties, express or implied, including any regarding merchantability or fitness for a particular purpose, arising out of or in connection with any program (or the delivery, use or performance thereof).

The contract also contains a fourteen-page description of the program applications.

The parties agree that the contract is a sales contract, that the choice of law provision which it contains is valid, and consequently that the parties' rights and liabilities are governed by the Uniform Commercial Code ("UCC") as adopted in California. They agree about very little else.

The defendant contends in its motion for summary judgment that this action is barred by the applicable statute of limitations, that the warranty disclaimer and damage limitation provisions in the contract are valid and binding and therefore the plaintiff is entitled to no relief, and that the plaintiff's second cause of action, which is based not on the UCC but on a negligence tort theory, does not state a cognizable claim. The plaintiff's summary judgment motion consists of a denial of each of those contentions and arguments favoring the application of contrary rules of law at the ultimate trial of this action.

Each of the defendant's contentions, along with the arguments as to the applicable legal principles raised by the plaintiff in opposing defendant's summary judgment motion, is discussed separately below.

* * *

(2) Disclaimer of Warranties

The Office Supply-Basic/Four contract specifically provides that it constitutes the entire agreement and understanding between the parties. That being so, parol evidence is not admissible under California law to vary the terms of the agreement. *APLications, Inc. v. Hewlitt-Packard Co.,* 501 F.Supp. 129 (S.D.N.Y. 1980). The language of the contract must be interpreted in an effort to determine the intent of the contracting parties. *S. M. Wilson & Company v. Smith International, Inc.,* 587 F.2d 1363 (9th Cir. 1978).

If there are no exclusions or modifications in the contract, every sales contract governed by the UCC contains an implied warranty of merchantability and, if the seller has reason to know of a particular purpose for which the goods are required, an implied warranty of fitness for a particular purpose. Section 2315, Cal.Comm.Code. Express warranties are created if the seller makes an affirmation of fact or promise to the buyer and the affirmation becomes part of the bargain between the parties. Section 2313, Cal.Comm.Code. Thus, any express warranties must be found in the language of the contract. Implied warranties, in contrast, will be held to exist unless they are specifically excluded.

With regard to the computer hardware, the contract expressly warrants the hardware to be free from defects in material, workmanship, and operating failure from ordinary use for ninety days after installation. [Reference.]

With regard to the computer software, the most reasonable interpretation of the contract is that the same ninety-day warranty of material, workmanship, and operating failure applies, dating from the time when the "programming accomplishes the results set forth in the 'Design Specifications' " [reference], which in this case was on October 6, 1975, when plaintiff's president so advised the defendant.

The plaintiff contends that the language just quoted is a warranty of future performance, and that in fact the programming did not accomplish the desired results until 1978.

Courts have been parsimonious in finding warranties of future performance where there is no explicit language in the contract creating such a warranty. [Citation.] For example, a representation as to the performance ability of an existing product will not be construed as an explicit warranty of future performance ability of the product. [Citation.] Section 2316(1), Cal.Comm.Code, provides in part:

> (1) Words or conduct relevant to the creation of an express warranty and words or conduct tending to negate or limit warranty shall be construed wherever reasonable as consistent with each other. * * *

The first page of the software addendum [reference] provides that it is incorporated within and made a part of the hardware purchase agreement. That agreement contains the ninety-day express warranty provision which, as a result of the incorporation, also applies to the software purchase. In light of the ninety-day express warranty, the most reasonable construction of the software addendum language regarding the results to be accomplished by the programming is that the completion of the programming and installation of all of the bargained-for applications starts the running of the ninety-day warranty period, and not that the applications are warranted to run perfectly once their installation is apparently successfully completed.

The UCC allows contracting parties to exclude or modify all implied warranties. There is no correlative requirement that if implied warranties are excluded, express warranties must be given. Thus it is permissible, for example, to exclude all implied warranties and to provide for a ninety-day express warranty limited to repair or replacement of defective goods. *APLications, Inc. v. Hewlitt-Packard Co.,* supra (ninety-day express warranty on the sale of a computer system under California law). [Citation.]

In order to make an effective waiver of implied warranties, the provisions of § 2316(2), Cal.Comm.Code, must be followed:

> * * * to exclude or modify the implied warranty of merchantability or any part of it the language must mention merchantability and in case of a writing must be conspicuous, and to exclude or modify any implied warranty of fitness the exclusion must be by a writing and conspicuous. * * *

There is no dispute that the language contained in the contract was in this case sufficient to waive all implied warranties. The issue is whether the disclaimer was "conspicuous." Section 1201(10), Cal.Comm. Code, provides:

> (10) "Conspicuous." A term or clause is conspicuous when it is so written that a reasonable person against whom it is to operate ought to have noticed it. A printed heading in capitals (as: NONNEGOTIABLE BILL OF LADING) is conspicuous. Language in the body of a form is "conspicuous" if it is in larger or other contrasting type or color. But in a telegram any stated term is "conspicuous." Whether a term or clause is "conspicuous" or not is for decision by the court.

Basic/Four points out that it disclaimed the implied warranties not once but twice, and that the disclaimers were written in italicized print, in contrast to the regular print used on the rest of the contract. Nevertheless, the disclaimers are not conspicuous. In *Dorman v. International Harvester Company*, 46 Cal.App.3d 11, 120 Cal.Rptr. 516 (1975), the California court of appeals noted that under pre-Code California law, disclaimers of warranty are strictly construed, and, applying the code, it found that an attempted disclaimer written in only slightly contrasting print and without a heading adequate to call the buyer's attention to the disclaimer clause was not effective. That decision controls in this case. The two disclaimers in the Office Supply-Basic/Four contract are on the reverse sides of the first two pages of the contract. They are not positioned close to the buyer's signature line. The contracts are printed on pale green paper and the disclaimers are set forth in print which, although italicized, is only slightly contrasting with the remainder of the contract. There are no headings noting the disclaimers of warranty. Since there is only " 'some slight contrasting set-off' " and there is " 'only a slight contrast with the balance of the instrument,' " [citation], therefore, the disclaimers are not conspicuous.

Discussion of the effectiveness of the disclaimer provisions in the contract does not end with the finding of lack of conspicuousness. In their treatise *Uniform Commercial Code* § 12–5 at 444 (2d ed. 1980), Messrs. White and Summers note "with apprehension" the growing number of cases which hold that if a buyer is actually aware of a warranty disclaimer, then the disclaimer is effective even if not conspicuous. [Citation.] The Official Comment to UCC § 2–316 states that the section is designed "to protect a buyer from unexpected and unbargained language of disclaimer." Pointing to that language, the Court in *Dorman*, supra, 120 Cal.Rptr. at 521–522, indicated that California will follow the trend:

> * * * [W]e must rely predominantly on the official comments to sections 2316 and 1201, subdivision (1), and to foreign law. The official comment to subdivision (10) of section 1201 states that the "test [of conspicuousness] is whether attention can reasonably be expected to be called to [the disclaimer provision]." [Citation.] We must examine this comment in the light of the official comment to section 2316, which states: "This section is designed principally to deal with those frequent clauses in sales contracts which seek to exclude 'all warranties, express or implied.' It seeks to protect a buyer from *unexpected* and unbargained language of disclaimer by denying effect to such language when inconsistent with language of express warranty and permitting the exclusion of implied warranties only by conspicuous language or other circumstances which protect the buyer from surprise." (Emphasis added.) In other words, section 2316 seeks to protect the buyer from the situation where the salesman's "pitch," advertising brochures, or large print in the contract, giveth, and the disclaimer clause—in fine print—taketh away.

The *Dorman* Court also noted that under pre-Code California law as well, a provision disclaiming implied warranties "was ineffectual unless the buyer assented to the provision or was charged with notice of the disclaimer before the bargain was completed." *Id.*, 120 Cal.Rptr. at 521.

James Bruno testified during his deposition taken on November 3, 1980, that before he purchased the Basic/Four system, he spent approximately two months comparing it with other systems [reference], and that he drew up a written comparison of the Basic/Four and Qantel systems, including their guarantees. Basic/Four, 90 days; and Qantel had one year. [Reference.] He read the back of the contract before he signed it, [reference], when he received the contract from Basic/Four he made out a list of questions to ask Basic/Four before signing and one subject on his list was the ninety-day guarantee [reference], and before he signed he showed the warranty provision in the contract to someone he knew in the data processing field [reference]. He discussed the warranties with Basic/Four before signing and tried to have them modified:

Q. Did you read the provisions of the warranty?

A. Yes.

Q. And did you discuss those provisions with Basic/Four, or with someone from Basic/Four?

A. Yes.

Q. And what was said to you about those provisions?

A. That that was the condition that I had to accept.

Q. All right. And was that discussion before or after the contract was signed?

A. I would say before.

* * *

Q. * * * did you call up Darryl Bannister, for example, and say I want to buy this system but I refuse to agree to the warranty provisions in the contract?

A. Well, I argued with him, but it was to no avail. Nothing. [Reference.]

He also was aware of the warranty limitations before he signed the contract:

Q. Well, were you aware of the provisions of that warranty before you signed the contract?

A. That there were limitations?

Q. That there were limitations to the warranty? Were you aware of that?

A. Certainly.

Q. You were?

A. Yes. [Reference.]

That testimony establishes that the warranty disclaimers were neither unexpected nor unbargained for, and that, consequently, under *Dorman,* they should be enforced.

On December 15, 1981, Basic/Four filed its motion for summary judgment. In opposition to the motion, on January 21, 1982, the plaintiff filed an affidavit signed by Mr. Bruno in which he states:

> "3. * * * that there was no statement by the Basic/Four sales executives that they would not stand behind their system after 90 days were up; that affiant did not have these Agreement [sic] reviewed by his attorney, nor was he aware from the documents signed by affiant on 1-31-75 that there were any disclaimers by Basic/Four. * * *"

The plaintiff has offered no explanation of the discrepancy between the affidavit and the deposition testimony. The issue now before the Court, therefore, is whether the discrepancy is sufficient to create a genuine issue of fact for trial as to the plaintiff's awareness of the warranty limitations contained in the contract before it was signed.

* * *

* * * In this case the deposition testimony upon which the defendant relies so clearly indicates that the plaintiff knew of the warranty limitations before the contract was signed, and at a minimum discussed the ninety-day provision with the defendant, that the plaintiff should not now be permitted to compel a trial on the issue by filing an affidavit denying the admissions made during the deposition. I therefore conclude that the record establishes that the plaintiff was aware of the warranty limitations before the contract was signed, that no genuine issue of material fact exists on that point, and that under California law the warranty limitation provisions in the contract are therefore valid.

(3) Limitation of Remedies

In addition to its exclusion of implied warranties, the contract states that the remedy available to Office Supply is limited to repair or replacement of defective parts and that Basic/Four has no liability for incidental or consequential damages.

Section 2316(4), Cal.Comm.Code, provides:

> (4) Remedies for breach of warranty can be limited in accordance with the provisions of this division on liquidation or limitation of damages and on contractual modification of remedy (Sections 2718 and 2719).

Section 2719, Cal.Comm.Code, on contractual modification or limitation of remedies, provides in part:

(1) * * * (a) The agreement may provide for remedies in addition to or in substitution for those provided in this division and may limit or alter the measure of damages recoverable under this division, as by limiting the buyer's remedies to return of the goods and repayment of the price or to repair and replacement of nonconforming goods or parts; and

* * *

(3) Consequential damages may be limited or excluded unless the limitation or exclusion is unconscionable. * * * Limitation of consequential damages where the loss is commercial is valid unless it is proved that the limitation is unconscionable.

Office Supply contends that if the exclusion of warranties clause is found to have been invalid because it was not conspicuous, then the limitation on remedies contained in the contract automatically fails as well and the plaintiff may pursue all of the remedies set forth in the code, including its claims for incidental and consequential damages. The argument is without merit. The Code provisions on limitation of damages are set forth in a separate section from that containing the warranty disclaimer provisions, and the section does not require that a limitation on damages, in order to be effective, be conspicuous. [Citation.]

The plaintiff also contends, first, that the exclusion of incidental and consequential damages was unconscionable, and second, that the limitation of remedy to repair or replacement of defective parts failed to provide the plaintiff with a functioning computer system and therefore the disclaimer is invalid and plaintiff should be able to pursue all of the remedies available under the Code. The defendant argues that the plaintiff modified the software applications without written consent and therefore the warranty is terminated.

As to the modifications which Ted Templeton of Computer Methods, Inc., made to the system and which plaintiff's own programmer, Marc Jerome, made to the system, paragraph 3 (in italics) of the contract at page 4, relating to additional terms and conditions for the purchase of the software, provides in part:

If the purchaser, without the written consent of the Seller, makes any modification to the programming * * * all warranties set forth herein cease immediately.

There is no claim that any of the modifications were made prior to the expiration of the warranty period on January 6, 1976. Therefore, if any defects remained in the system as of that date which Basic/Four had failed to correct under its warranty obligation, plaintiff's subsequent modification of the programs would have no effect on its right to recover for those defects.

As for the limitation of remedies, § 2719(2), Cal.Comm.Code, provides:

(2) Where circumstances cause an exclusive or limited remedy to fail of its essential purpose, remedy may be had as provided in this code.

A repair remedy fails of its essential purpose if the repair is unduly delayed or if there is a total inability to repair:

* * * so long as the buyer has the use of substantially defect-free goods, the limited remedy should be given effect. But when the seller is either unwilling or unable to conform the goods to the contract, the remedy does not suffice. * * * *Chatlos Systems, Inc. v. National Cash Register Corporation (NCR Corporation)*, 635 F.2d 1081, 1085 (3d Cir. 1980).

If a repair remedy fails of its essential purpose, then under § 2714(2), Cal.Comm.Code, the buyer may recover what is the basic measure of damages for breach of warranty under the Code, i.e., "the difference at the time and place of acceptance between the value of the goods accepted and the value they would have had if they had been as warranted."

If a remedy fails of its essential purpose, in addition to breach of the bargain damages allowed under § 2714(2), incidental and consequential damages may also be recovered in a proper case. Section 2714(3), Cal.Comm.Code. If a remedy is limited to repair and consequential and incidental damages are excluded, however, then even if the repair remedy fails of its essential purpose, the buyer is limited to his breach of the bargain damages under § 2714(2) unless he can prove that the exclusion of incidental and consequential damages was unconscionable under § 2719(3), Cal.Comm.Code. In other words, an exclusion of incidental and consequential damages is a contract provision separate and distinct from a limitation of remedy to repair, and must receive separate consideration. [Citations.]

Office Supply has the burden of proving that the exclusion of incidental and consequential damages was unconscionable. Section 2719(3), Cal.Comm.Code. The exclusion is presumed valid in a commercial setting. [Citations.] Among the factors relevant to determining unconscionability are the length of the negotiation process, the length of time the buyer has to deliberate before signing the contract, the experience or astuteness of the parties, whether counsel reviewed the contract, and whether the buyer was a reluctant purchaser. *Earman Oil Company, Inc. v. Burroughs Corporation,* 625 F.2d 1291 (5th Cir. 1980). The commercial setting and the purpose and effect of the allegedly unconscionable clause are also relevant [citation], as is the extent of the seller's default in attempting to fulfill its obligations on a remedy to repair. [Citation.]

Basic/Four argues that summary judgment on the unconscionability issue is appropriate in this case because Office Supply negotiated with a number of computer sellers before settling on Basic/Four, it achieved a price concession on a disc drive from Basic/Four, it viewed several computer systems installed by Basic/Four before deciding to purchase, James Bruno convened a meeting of the board of directors to consider the purchase, and he held the contract for almost a week before deciding to sign it.

The plaintiff, on the other hand, contends that no one at Office Supply had any familiarity with computer systems and consequently Office Supply relied extensively on the claims of the Basic/Four salesmen as to the performance capabilities of the proposed system, and particularly on the "guarantee" made in a presentation to the board of directors that the software system would be "flawless." Office Supply did not have an attorney review the contract.

Mr. Bruno testified during his deposition that in November 1974, Office Supply decided to purchase a mini computer [reference]. Thereafter he primarily on behalf of Office Supply and also David Carlson to some extent spent about two months contacting manufacturers and comparing various systems. In addition to Basic/Four, he looked at Qantel, Wang, Micro Data, and Data Point [references]. He drew up for his own use a written comparison of the Basic/Four and Qantel products and consulted with a computer systems acquaintance at a bank as to what ques-

tions he should be asking [reference]. He attended some systems demonstrations, and for a period Qantel and Basic/Four engaged in an active competition to sell Office Supply a system [references]. As an incentive, Basic/Four offered to give Office Supply a double capacity disc at no extra charge [reference].

After Office Supply decided to buy from Basic/Four, and after Bruno received the contract in the mail from Basic/Four, he showed the contract to someone he knew in the data processing field and prepared a list of questions to ask Basic/Four before signing [reference]. He also attempted to negotiate the warranty provision with Basic/Four but could not obtain any concessions [reference]. After receiving the contract but before signing it, he also convened a meeting of the Office Supply board of directors to consider the Basic/Four offer and to hear a sales presentation from a Basic/Four salesman [references]. The following day Bruno signed the contract and mailed it back to Basic/Four.

The parties in this case did not have equal sophistication in the data processing field, and Basic/Four is a much larger commercial operation. Nevertheless, the plaintiff is also an established commercial operation of significant size, and the plaintiff's president testified during his deposition that he is accustomed to engaging in contract negotiation on behalf of Office Supply. The plaintiff instituted negotiations with Basic/Four and engaged in a two-month period of comparative shopping. Basic/Four was not the only available source of the product which the plaintiff desired, and there was active competition amongst computer manufacturers to sell the plaintiff a system. The plaintiff took its time in deciding to purchase and was not prevented by Basic/Four from thoroughly investigating the system and examining the contract provisions. [Citations.] There was no atmosphere of haste or undue pressure exerted on the plaintiff to compel it to enter into the contract. [Citations.] Furthermore, it is undisputed that during the warranty period Basic/Four did make numerous efforts to repair all defects asserted by the plaintiff to exist in the system, even though the plaintiff contends that the efforts were not successful, and even after the warranty period expired that Basic/Four continued its efforts to resolve any problems raised by the plaintiff. [Citation.]

In a commercial setting a damages limitation clause is presumed to be valid under California law, § 2719(3), and the contracting parties are presumed to act at arms length. [Citation.] Relying upon the deposition testimony of the plaintiff's president, the defendant has presented evidence which, if unrebutted, would establish that the damages limitation clause was not unconscionable under the circumstances of this case. While with respect to the issue of unconscionability a party should be permitted to present evidence as to the commercial setting in which the contract was made and the purpose and effect of the limitation clause [citation], when confronted with a summary judgment motion a party must do more to defeat it than rely upon "the vague hope that something may turn up at trial." [Citations.] In this case, the plaintiff having made no effort to controvert the defendant's proof, summary judgment on the issue of unconscionability is appropriate.

The plaintiff's final hope for the recovery of damages is to prove that the repair and replacement remedy provided for in the contract "failed of its essential purpose," § 2719(2), Cal.Comm.Code, which would entitle plaintiff to present evidence of the difference between what the system was worth at the time it was accepted and what it would have been worth had it been as warranted, § 2714(2), Cal. Comm.Code.

As previously stated, the remedy of repair and replacement is deemed to fail of its essential purpose when the goods which the buyer purchases are not substantially defect free, and in addition the seller is unable or unwilling to conform the goods to the contract. [Citations.]

In *Chatlos,* a UCC case involving a computer sale, the Court found that the repair remedy failed of its essential purpose where the buyer contracted for six software applications to be fully operational within six months after installation and to which a sixty-day repair warranty applied, and after one year only one application was operational, and after one and one-half years less than half the applications were operational. As the court stated at page 1085:

* * * Viewed from the buyer's standpoint, the repair remedy's aim is to provide goods that conform to the contract for sale and do so at an appropriate time. A delay in supplying the remedy can just as effectively deny the purchaser the product he expected as can the total inability to repair. In both instances the buyer loses the substantial benefit of his purchase.

Despite repeated attempts to repair, after a year and a half the seller had been unable to provide to the buyer the product for which the buyer had contracted.

* * *

In this case Office Supply contracted for four software applications and all four of them were installed. [Reference.] On October 6, 1975, Mr. Bruno wrote to Basic/Four that all four of the applications were operational and appeared to be satisfactory. [Reference.] In the first week of November 1975, the October monthly statement of customer accounts in the accounts receivable application printed out of balance. [Reference.] Mr. Carlson testified that as a result of that problem approximately 20% of the accounts receivable were out of balance, and the system was therefore only 78% operational.[4] [Reference.] Basic/Four worked on the problem, which continued through 1975, and finally in February 1976, the monthly statement printed through correctly. [Reference.] Thereafter, both Mr. Bruno and Mr. Carlson testified, the accounts receivable application continued to cause intermittent problems until early 1978 when it was finally corrected by Marc Jerome, Office Supply's own programmer. [Reference.] The accounts receivable problem was, Mr. Bruno testified, the one significant defect left in the system at the expiration of the warranty period on January 6, 1976. [Reference.] Both men testified that while problems occurred with the hardware, the problems were always corrected either by Basic/Four or by Sorbus with a few minimal exceptions pursuant to the maintenance contract. [Reference.]

Marc Jerome prepared a report identifying three significant defects which he found in the software applications when he began work at Office Supply in early 1978. [Reference.] One

---

4. Mr. Bruno testified that between the hardware and software problems, the figure was 50%. He also stated

that the figure was "[j]ust a guess." [Reference.]

was in the ABC program, one in the B0 and B2 programs, and one in the UJ program. [Reference.] Only the UJ program was installed by Office Supply. [Reference.] Furthermore, the defect identified by Jerome in the UJ program, which is part of Basic/Four's accounts receivable software application, did not exist in that program in July 1976, meaning that it must have been introduced into the program after that date. [Reference.] It is not disputed that commencing soon after the warranty period expired and continuing up to the present, both Ted Templeton of Computer Methods, Inc. and Marc Jerome have made extensive modifications to the programs on Office Supply's computer system. Finally, between March 1976 and March 1978, Basic/Four apparently received no complaints from Office Supply about the functioning of the software applications. [Reference.]

The inference suggested by the evidence which has been presented both in support of and in opposition to the summary judgment motion is that while Office Supply may have had problems with the accounts receivable program starting in November 1975 and continuing through early 1978, the problems did not all result from the same defect in the program but rather resulted from at least two different defects, one of which was corrected by Basic/Four before the accounts were printed out in February 1976, and another of which was introduced into the program some time after July 1976. Consequently, the conclusion results that Basic/Four did make the repairs which it was obligated by the contract to make, that the repairs cured the defect then existing in the accounts receivable program, and that Basic/Four did fulfill its warranty obligations during the warranty period. [Citation.]

The underlying purpose of the summary judgment procedure is—

* * * to pierce the pleadings so that the burden and expense of a trial will not be wasted on baseless claims or phantom issues. * * * Accordingly, * * * the party opposing the summary judgment motion does not have the right to withhold his evidence until trial; nor can he demand a trial because of the speculative possibility that a material issue of fact may appear at that time. * * *

[Citations.]

Mr. Bruno and Mr. Carlson testified that the accounts receivable program had problems from November 1975 through early 1978. They admitted that they were unqualified to make a more explicit identification of the cause of the problems or to testify as to whether or not any of the problems might have been caused by Templeton or Jerome and not by Basic/Four. Templeton admitted that he might have made some modifications to the accounts receivable program starting in the spring of 1976. [Reference.] The evidence establishes that the defects which Marc Jerome identified could not have been caused by Basic/Four. Under the circumstances, there exists only the "speculative possibility" that Office Supply could come up with evidence at trial to show that a defect remained in the software at the end of the warranty period. The evidence presently in the record proves otherwise, and the "speculative possibility" is insufficient to justify putting the defendant through the burden and expense of a trial.

(4) Negligence

The plaintiff's second cause of action alleges that Basic/Four was negligent in its manufacture, design, installation, and repair of the computer system and seeks damages caused by that negligence. The cause of action must be dismissed.

Under California law economic losses are not recoverable in tort. The rationale is explained in *S. M. Wilson & Company v. Smith International, Inc.,* supra, at 1376:

Where the suit is between a nonperforming seller and an aggrieved buyer and the injury consists of damage to the goods themselves and the costs of repair of such damage or a loss of profits that the deal had been expected to yield to the buyer, it would be sensible to limit the buyer's rights to those provided by the Uniform Commercial Code. [Citations.] To treat such a breach as an accident is to confuse disappointment with disaster. Whether the complaint is cast in terms of strict liability in tort or negligence should make no difference.

In a somewhat curious way California law achieves this result by limiting the type of losses recoverable under an action in negligence. Economic losses are not recoverable under negligence. *Seely v. White Motor Co.,* 63 Cal.2d 9, 18, 45 Cal.Rptr. 17, 23, 403 P.2d 145, 151 (1965) fixed the rule and it frequently has been followed. * * * It serves to limit the parties' rights to those provided by the Uniform Commercial Code, a body of law specifically designed to deal with commercial disputes between sellers and buyers of goods.

* * *

ORDER

For the foregoing reasons,

It is ordered that the plaintiff's motions to compel discovery and for partial summary judgment are denied.

It is further ordered that the defendant's motion for summary judgment is granted, and that judgment be entered dismissing this action with prejudice and awarding costs to the defendant.

APLICATIONS INC. v. HEWLETT-PACKARD CO.

501 F. Supp. 129
(United States District Court, S. D. New York, Oct. 20, 1980.)

CARTER, D. J.

Defendant Hewlett-Packard Co. ("H-P") moves for summary judgment on the claims of plaintiff APLications, Inc. ("APLications") for fraudulent misrepresentation, negligent misrepresentation, and breach of warranties, express and implied, and on plaintiff's claim for consequential damages. Judgment is granted on the claim for breach of express and implied warranties, but otherwise denied.

FACTS

This matter from the bright new frontier of small-scale computers was previously before this court when plaintiff's motion for summary judgment on its claims was denied [footnote], and the facts may be briefly recounted. H-P developed and marketed the computer language subsystem APL/3000 for use on its HP 3000 Series II computers. APL is prized as a computer language for its elegance and flexibility. (*See e. g.* May 24, 1979, Affidavit of Chester Sherer, Plaintiff's Memorandum in Opposition) However, the language also taxes the computer's resources: theretofore, attempts at adapting APL to small-scale com-

puters had not proven acceptably responsive (*id.,* p. 2), and its use had been confined to larger, more expensive systems. If APL/3000 in fact was able to provide acceptable performance on a less expensive computer, it would constitute an important innovation in the field.

Plaintiff APLications adapts and resells computers, with software of its own design, to the ultimate user of the computer system. When APL/3000 was announced in the fall of 1976, APLications was in the early stages of negotiating the sale of a system to American Field Services ("AFS"). Responding to H-P's announcement and accompanying brochures APLications contacted H-P about using APL/3000 in the proposed system for AFS. Representatives from APLications and AFS met through January of 1977 to negotiate the deal, and representatives of H-P attended a number of these discussions.

On February 1, 1977, APLications and H-P entered into a written "OEM Purchase Agreement" ("Agreement") under which APLications would be entitled to a discount on H-P equipment purchased for adaptation and resale. APLications ordered a 3000/Series II computer in March, 1977, programmed in APL/3000, and other hardware, to be delivered directly to AFS. When the computer was installed and initially tested, however, it was determined that AFS's needs could not be met with the machine as programmed: response time in APL/3000 was unacceptably long. The computer has since been reprogrammed in another language and is now performing acceptably for AFS.

APLications contends that it relied on H-P's claims about APL/3000 performance in contracting with AFS, and in reorienting its business. In APLications' eyes, H-P represented—to the industry in general, and to APLications and AFS in particular—that APL/3000 would provide "fast response even with multiple users" (H-P Brochure, "Total Solution APL," Affidavit of Jean Denver, Ex. A, Defendant's Affidavits in Support of Motion), as was required by AFS. APLications claims to have lost profits on its contract to AFS, as well as on other possible adaptation and resale contracts, and to have suffered damage to its business reputation, which supposedly resulted from its reliance on H-P's representations.

H-P, for its part, insists that its statements about APL/3000 were generalized statements or "puffing," and were not to be relied on. Further, H-P points to the terms of the Agreement, as precluding any warranties that might have been breached, as well as reliance by APLications on other statements.

That Agreement contains the following warranty section:

5. WARRANTY

HP products are warranted against defects in materials and workmanship. This warranty applies for ninety (90) days following delivery. For products installed by HP this warranty period shall commence upon installation or the 31st day following shipment whichever occurs first. During the warranty period, HP will at its option, repair or replace products which prove to be defective.

Necessary travel will be provided at no charge to locations served regularly by transportation within countries where HP has Computer Systems service facilities. However, the following products must be returned to HP at Buyer's expense for warranty repair or replacement: 3070A, 3071A, 2103K, 2649A, and their associated accessories.

NO OTHER WARRANTY IS EXPRESSED OR IMPLIED. HP SPECIFICALLY DISCLAIMS THE IMPLIED WARRANTIES OF MERCHANTABILITY AND FITNESS FOR A PARTICULAR PURPOSE. HP IS NOT LIABLE FOR CONSEQUENTIAL DAMAGES.

Among the other terms and conditions of the Agreement are:

12. MISCELLANEOUS

* * *

b. It is understood and agreed that the attached agreement and exhibits contain the entire understanding between the parties relating to the subject matter hereat and that any representation, promise, or condition not contained herein shall not be binding on either party.

c. The terms and conditions contained in the attached agreement and exhibits shall take precedence over any standard terms and conditions which appear on Buyer's order issued hereunder or any documents incorporated by reference.

* * *

2. The Agreement so states. However, both sides' papers are replete with discussions of New York law. *See*

f. This agreement shall be in all respects governed by the laws of the State of California.

BREACH OF WARRANTIES

APLications argues that the computer was impliedly warranted for merchantability and fitness for the purpose of use by AFS, and that an express warranty was created by H-P's statements. H-P stands on the limitation of warranty in the Agreement and argues that no warranty, express or implied, is enforceable against H-P for plaintiff's losses. As will emerge, the undisputed facts, together with the applicable law, compel judgment for defendant on this issue.

The Agreement proclaims that it shall be governed by the laws of California. (Section 12. f., *supra*) Each party has affirmed this provision,[2] and it is to that law that we turn to resolve this question.

Under California law, as elsewhere, the contract must be interpreted to give effect to the intentions of the parties. [Citations.] When a contract is reduced to writing the parties' intent should be ascertained from the written instrument. [Citations.] for the execution thereof supersedes prior negotiations and stipulations. [Citation.] When the parties agree to a written contract as a "complete and final embodiment of the terms of the agreement," [citation] the writing is an integration of the agreement, and parol evidence may not be used to vary its terms.

Similarly, when only part of the agreement is integrated, parol evidence may not vary that part. [Citation.] The determination as to whether a writing integrates the parties' understanding is for the court. [Citation.]

The Agreement plainly states that it contains the entire understanding between the parties, and plaintiff has raised no genuine issue about the parties' agreement with respect to warranties. There is no dispute that the parties bargained for and signed the Agreement, including the section on warranties; nor is there any question that APLications was aware of the significance of that section and intended it to be a part of the contract. Plaintiff's only suggestion to the

infra, note 4.

contrary comes by way of a remark that the contract "can be construed as one of adhesion." (Plaintiff's Memorandum in Opposition, p. 25) Whatever the truth of that suggestion as a matter of legal possibility, plaintiff has provided no factual predicates for such a construction of this contract.[3] Accordingly, we must regard the Agreement's warranty section as the "complete and final embodiment" of the parties' agreement on warranties and find that the Agreement fully integrated the understanding between them on that issue. Therefore, if the limitations on warranties are effective under the relevant provisions of the California Commercial Code, which govern contracts for sales of goods, no warranties are enforceable against H-P other than those included in the Agreement for defects in materials and workmanship.

With respect to implied warranties, § 2316(2) of the California Commercial Code provides:

> Subject to subsection (3), to exclude or modify the implied warranty of merchantability or any part of it the language must mention merchantability and in case of a writing must be conspicuous, and to exclude or modify any implied warranty of fitness the exclusion must be by a writing and conspicuous. Language to exclude all implied warranties of fitness is sufficient if it states, for example, that "There are no warranties which extend beyond the description on the face hereof."

Clearly, the Agreement's exclusion satisfies all these criteria: it is written and conspicuous, and it mentions merchantability. Indeed, if contracting parties may ever agree under the Code to exclude implied warranties of merchantability and fitness, then the language of the instant provision is surely effective. The implied warranties asserted by plaintiff are not enforceable against H-P, and consequently, defendant's motion must be granted to this extent. [Citation.]

The same result must be reached on the issue of express warranties. Plaintiff does not assert that the computer's material or workmanship were in some way defective. Instead, plaintiff contends that an express warranty was created by defendant's descriptions of the computer. *See Cal.Com.Code* § 2313(1)(a), (1)(b). The Agreement excludes this warranty as well. While there are no particular requirements under the Code to limit express warranties or liability, the Code contemplates that such limitations may be undertaken by the parties. *See id.,* §§ 2316(1), 2316(4), 2719 [Citation.] The instant limitation is categorical and unambiguous, and limitations nearly identical in language to this provision have frequently been upheld. *See e. g. Investors Premium Corp. v. Burroughs Corp.,* 389 F.Supp. 39, 44-45 (D.S.C.1974); *Westfield Chemical Corp. v. Burroughs Corp.,* 21 UCC Rep.Serv. 1293, 1295 (Mass.Super.Ct. Hampden Co.1977); *Bakal v. Burroughs Corp.,* 74 Misc.2d 202, 343 N.Y.S.2d 541 (S.Ct.1972). Therefore, the Agreement effectively excludes the express warranties for which plaintiff contends, and defendant's motion must, in this respect be granted.

FRAUDULENT MISREPRESENTATION

H-P avers that granting summary judgment on the issue of warranties must preclude plaintiff's claim for fraudulent misrepresentation, lest the policies behind the parol evidence rule be frustrated. Defendant also contends that the undisputed facts compel a grant of summary judgment on the question of fraud. While defendant's factual contentions appear in many respects to be convincing, it cannot be concluded that no issues of fact obtain with respect to the claim of fraudulent misrepresentation or that APLications should be precluded from maintaining that claim.

Contrary to defendant's argument (Defendant's Memorandum in Support of Motion, pp. 24-28) the parol evidence rule does not dictate that summary judgment be entered against

---

3. Plaintiff's only allegation in support of this suggestion is the claim that "there was nowhere the same extensive negotiation" as obtained in *American Electric Power Corp. v. Westinghouse Electric Corp.,* 418 F.Supp. 435 (S.D.N.Y.1976) (Carter, J.). Since plaintiff never con-

tends that the parties were in any way prevented from negotiating the terms of the contract to their full satisfaction, the paucity of negotiation indicates that the warranty provision was acceptable to both parties.

plaintiff on the claim of fraud.[4] As this court in *Horwitz v. Sprague,* 440 F.Supp. 1346, 1350 (S.D.N.Y.1977) (Tenney, J.) made clear, fraud is a magic word, and it is

> elementary that any contract can be put aside for fraud. * * * By casting this complaint in tort, *i.e.,* fraud, plaintiff has avoided the perils of the parol evidence rule which would likely bar oral evidence to vary the terms of so explicit an instrument as [is at issue].

See also Plum Tree, Inc. v. N.K. Winston Corp., 351 F.Supp. 80, 85 (S.D.N.Y.1972) (Gurfein, J.):

> The plaintiff sues not for any breach of contract but for injuries suffered as a result of the defendant's conduct which is separate and distinct from the formal contract. Consequently, a party seeking to prove fraudulent inducement may introduce evidence which has the effect of varying the terms of a written contract, the parol evidence rule notwithstanding.

This conclusion is unaffected by the statement in Section 12.b of the Agreement that representations not contained in the Agreement shall not be binding on the parties. In both California and New York, it is clear that a properly maintained action for fraud may overcome the policies behind the parol evidence rule,[5] even with respect to contracts that disclaim reliance on representations not contained in the written instrument.

> It was never intended that the parol evidence rule should be used as a shield to prevent the proof of fraud. * * * And this is true even though the contract recites that all conditions and representations are contained therein.[6] [Citations.]

In sum, plaintiff's cause of action for fraudulent misrepresentation must be evaluated for the purposes of this motion as a separate and distinct claim, summary judgment on breach

---

4. H-P cites a number of cases for the proposition that plaintiff's claim for fraudulent misrepresentation is precluded: *Perma Research and Development Co. v. Singer,* 410 F.2d 572 (2d Cir. 1969); *Investors Premium Corp., supra; Potomac Electric Power, supra;* and *Westfield Chemical Corp., supra.* This contention is without merit. In the first place H-P mistakes the import of these cases: fraud was not properly alleged, and those particular claims were dismissed, but no infirmity was found in maintaining a separate and distinct count for fraudulent misrepresentation together with a count for breach of warranties. In the second place, defendant's contention would elide the distinctiveness of the claims for the sake of the parol evidence rule, ignoring the fact that each action requires particular elements of proof. *See e.g. Ajax Hardware Mfg. v. Industrial Plants Corp.* 569 F.2d 181, 187 (2d Cir. 1977).

5. While the Agreement expressly stipulates that California law shall govern, the parties have referred to New York, as well as California law on fraudulent misrepresentation. For the purposes of this branch of the motion, it is sufficient to note that the conclusions reached are valid regardless of which state's law is ultimately found to govern. The only difference that arises in the case at hand is that New York, but apparently not California, supports a distinction between specific and general disclaimers of reliance. However, as footnote 6, *infra,* makes clear, the conclusions reached herein are in accord with California law, notwithstanding the doctrinal difference just noted.

6. * * * New York cases distinguish between specific and general disclaimers of reliance on representations. [Citations.] A general disclaimer clause, as is found in the Agreement, will not bar an action for fraud in the inducement of a contract. [Citation.]

This conclusion is supported by another line of argument which need only be outlined here. The maxims of contract construction dictate that the provision in the Agreement stating that "any representation * * * not

contained in the Agreement shall not be binding." (Sec. 12.b.) is to be disregarded. The contract is to be construed as a whole. *See e. g. Cal.Civ.Code* § 1641. However, the Agreement cannot be regarded as the whole of the contract. The Agreement sets the conditions under which plaintiff was to place orders for H-P's products, and the discount on those products, but it listed no quantities or prices. Orders by plaintiff were to be placed under the Agreement. *See* March 8, 1977 letter of Kenneth David (Affidavit of John J. Greene III. Ex. C., Defendant's Affidavit in Support). Thus, the Agreement implies that plaintiff's orders under the Agreement are included in the contract as a whole. *See e. g. Cal.Civ.Code* § 1656. The terms of the Agreement imply this as well. Section 12.c., *supra,* contemplates that orders placed under the Agreement might include additional terms or conditions. The disclaimer of any representations that is found in Section 12.b. of the Agreement, then, must be subordinated to the contract as a whole, *see e. g. Cal.Civ.Code* § 1650, and the disclaimer of representations therein disregarded. *Id.* § 1652. Moreover, the Agreement makes no representation or description whatever of H P's products which plaintiff might order, and the particular computer that was in fact ordered (the Model 8, HP 32418A) was not even included in the list of H P products attached to the Agreement. It is patent, then, that at least some representations about H P's product are essential to the contract but are nonetheless not a part of the Agreement. Else, the plaintiff is in the absurd position of contracting to purchase an unidentified, undescribed computer, whose specifications are nowhere stated or referred to in the contract. The Agreement, therefore, is not a complete embodiment of the parties' understanding. *Cal.Civ.Code* §§ 1652, 1653, 1656. Summary judgment on the issue of fraud depends on whether, among the statements made by defendant extrinsic to the Agreement are some of specific material facts on which plaintiff could justifiably rely.

of warranties notwithstanding. That is, plaintiff's claim for fraud must be evaluated in terms of the applicable law concerning the elements of that cause. [Citations.] With respect to those elements, defendant further contends that plaintiff has failed to establish two requisites in particular: defendant contends that the misrepresentations plaintiff alleged defendant to have made were not statements of specific, material facts, and that plaintiff's reliance on these statements was not justified.

However, resolving all ambiguities and drawing all reasonable doubts and inferences in favor of the plaintiff, as we must, *United States v. Diebold, Inc.,* 369 U.S. 654, 655, 82 S.Ct. 993, 994, 8 L.Ed.2d 176 (1962), *Heyman v. Commerce and Industry Insurance Co.,* 524 F.2d 1317 (2d Cir. 1975), material factual issues remain to be resolved at trial. Plaintiff has raised a genuine issue concerning H-P's representation of the capabilities of APL/3000, most significantly concerning the representations in H-P's brochures of the system's responsiveness in a multiple user configuration. By the same token, triable issues arise with respect to plaintiff's reliance on H-P's statements, focusing on APLication's opportunities to test the system's capabilities in a manner adequate to assess its suitability for the contract with AFS.

None of this, of course, is to suggest that plaintiff will necessarily ultimately prevail on the merits. H-P has set forth a detailed and lengthy account of the parties' dealing, and plaintiff's burden at trial appears formidable. For the purposes of this motion, however, the court is bound to accept as true plaintiff's allegations, *Adickes v. Kress & Co.,* 398 U.S. 144, 157, 90 S.Ct. 1598, 1608, 26 L.Ed.2d 142 (1970); *First National Bank of Cincinnati v. Pepper,* 454 F.2d 626, 629 (2d Cir. 1972), and defendant has not demonstrated an absence of material issues of fact genuinely in dispute. Consequently, summary judgment on plaintiff's claim of fraud must be denied. *See American Elec. Power, supra,* 418 F.Supp. at 451-452.

NEGLIGENT MISREPRESENTATION

As defendant acknowledges (Defendant's Memorandum in Support of Motion, p. 49), the essential elements of plaintiff's cause for negligent misrepresentation are the same as for fraud, except that plaintiff need not establish that H-P made false statements with knowledge of their falsity. *E. g. Walters v. Marler,* 83 Cal.App.3d 1, 18, 147 Cal.Rptr. 655, 664-65 (1st Dist. 1978). Defendant's motion for summary judgment on the question of negligent misrepresentation must be denied as well.

DAMAGES

Defendant also argues that under the Agreement and as a matter of law plaintiff may not recover consequential damages. Since summary judgment is granted on the issue of breach of warranties, there is no need to reach the issue of consequential damages under the Agreement. However, if plaintiff's claims for fraudulent misrepresentation is heard at trial, the contractual limitation precluding recovery of consequential damages is ineffective. [Citation.] The Uniform Commercial Code provides in both California and New York that remedies for fraud may include consequential damages, §§ 2-721 and 2-715, with respect to contracts covered by its sections. The issue of consequential damages cannot be resolved at this time, and this branch of defendant's motion is accordingly denied.

It is so ordered.

APLICATIONS, INC. v. HEWLETT-PACKARD CO.

672 F.2d 1076

(United States Court of Appeals, Second Circuit, Feb. 19, 1982.)

PER CURIAM.

In this non-jury action for fraudulent misrepresentation and negligent misrepresentation, tried before Judge Robert L. Carter (S.D.N.Y.), the district court held (1) that no false representations were made and (2) that plaintiff did not rely on the representations that were made. We affirm substantially for the reasons set forth in Judge Carter's memorandum opinion of July 21, 1981.

Appellant bought a minicomputer—the HP APL/3000—from Hewlett-Packard, planning to program the computer in the language "APL" for resale. Hewlett-Packard salesmen made glowing statements about the speed of the machine, and the company's technical brochures reported that tests of the HP APL/3000 showed the machine took less than two seconds to respond when it was hooked up to 12 terminals. Appellant's president and sole shareholder himself tried out the HP APL/3000 and was impressed. When installed, however, the HP APL/3000 proved much slower than its tests indicated. Appellant sued Hewlett-Packard, alleging breach of warranty, fraud and misrepresentation.

Judge Carter granted summary judgment to defendant on the warranty claims because Hewlett-Packard's sale contract contained an express waiver of warranties. 501 F.Supp. 129 (1980). The district court dismissed the tort claims at trial, after the close of the plaintiff's case. Plaintiff appeals, arguing that the district court failed to apply California law, and that its findings of fact were clearly erroneous. We find no merit in either contention.

Reliance on the part of the plaintiff is an essential element of the cause of action for misrepresentation in California as it is elsewhere. *See Civille v. Bullis,* 209 Cal.App.2d 134, 137, 25 Cal.Rptr. 578 (1962). Judge Carter concluded that plaintiff's president and sole shareholder was more knowledgeable in the field of computer science than the representatives of the defendant with whom he dealt and much too knowledgeable to rely on publicity blurbs issued by the defendant. Judge Carter therefore found as a fact that plaintiff did not rely on representations by Hewlett-Packard. The record indicates this finding is not clearly erroneous; the finding is fatal to plaintiff's case no matter what jurisdiction's law is applied.

Affirmed.

BLACK, JACKSON AND SIMMONS INSURANCE BROKERAGE, INC., v. INTERNATIONAL BUSINESS MACHINES CORP.

109 Ill.App.3d 132, 440 N.E.2d 282
(Appellate Court of Illinois, First District, Fourth Division, Sept. 9, 1982.)

JIGANTI, J.

The plaintiff, Black, Jackson & Simmons Insurance Brokerage, Inc. (Black, Jackson), brought this action against the defendants, International Business Machines Corporation (IBM) and Lubin-Bergman Organization, Inc. (Lubin-Bergman). Black, Jackson asserts that its complaint against both defendants is based upon negligent misrepresentations which induced Black, Jackson to purchase a computer from IBM and a software package from Lubin-Bergman. It seeks to recover economic losses in the form of lost profits, salaries, office supplies and accounting and leasing expenses which it incurred as a result of the failure of the system to function as expected. The trial court granted summary judgment in favor of IBM and Lubin-Bergman and against Black, Jackson on the grounds that Illinois law does not permit recovery of purely economic losses in a tort action. A separate count alleging breach of warranty against Lubin-Bergman is still pending in the trial court and is not involved in this appeal.

Black, Jackson makes the following allegations in its complaint. It contacted representatives of IBM to discuss the possibility of using a computer to assist the corporation in its insurance business. IBM recommended that Black, Jackson purchase an IBM System 32 computer and related IBM programs. IBM further recommended that Black, Jackson purchase the necessary software for the computer system from Lubin-Bergman. Representatives of Black, Jackson were taken to Lubin-Bergman's offices and given the opportunity to observe a complete data processing system. Based upon representations that this type of system would be satisfactory for its needs, Black, Jackson entered into contracts with IBM and Lubin-Bergman. In fact, the System 32 computer sold to Black, Jackson had a smaller computer disc and a slower printer and could not interface with the Lubin-Bergman software. Black, Jackson alleges essentially that IBM and Lubin-Bergman were negligent in representing that they were skilled and competent and able to supply Black, Jackson with a suitable data processing system. Black, Jackson's economic losses flow from the inadequacy of this system.

The main issue in this appeal is whether the facts alleged in the case at bar state a cause of action for negligent misrepresentation which will enable Black, Jackson to recover purely economic losses. We do not believe a cause of action is stated.

In *Moorman Manufacturing Company v. National Tank Company* (1982), 91 Ill.2d 69, 61 Ill.Dec. 746, 435 N.E.2d 443, the Illinois Supreme Court recently held that purely economic losses cannot be recovered under claims sounding in tort. The court stated that the law of sales and the law of contracts were well-articulated and sufficient to govern the economic relations between suppliers and consumers of goods. As part of the basis for its opinion, the *Moorman* court adopted the following reasoning from *Seeley v. White Motor Co.* (1965), 63 Cal.2d 9, 18, 403 P.2d 145, 151, 45 Cal.Rptr. 17, 23:

> The distinction that the law has drawn between tort recovery for physical injuries and warranty recovery for economic loss * * * rests * * * on an understanding of the nature of the responsibility a manufacturer must undertake in distributing his products. He can appropriately be held liable for physical injuries caused by defects by requiring his goods to match a standard of safety defined in terms of conditions that create unreasonable risks of harm. He cannot be held for the level of performance of his products in the consumer's business unless he agrees that the product was designed to meet the consumer's demands. A consumer should not be charged at the will of the manufacturer with bearing the risk of physical injury when he buys a product on the market. He can, however, be fairly charged with the risk that the product will not match his economic expectations unless the manufacturer agrees that it will. Even in actions for negligence, a manufacturer's liability is limited to damage for physical injuries and there is no recovery for economic loss alone. *Moorman* at 80-81, 61 Ill.Dec. 746, 435 N.E.2d at 448.

If the courts allow parties to circumvent their contractual remedies by suing in tort, the ability of contracting parties to allocate and bargain for risk of loss will be effectively destroyed and certainty in commercial transactions will be radically undermined. Tort law should thus be reserved to remedy hazards peripheral to the product's function, that is, those which were not in the forefront of the minds of the contracting parties. [Citation.]

Moorman does, however, enumerate certain exceptions to the general rule prohibiting recovery of economic losses in tort, and it is one of these exceptions which forms the basis for the plaintiff's argument on appeal. The *Moorman* court stated that "economic loss is recoverable where one intentionally makes false representations [citation] and where one who is in the business of supplying information for the guidance of others in their business transactions makes negligent representations. (*Rozny v. Marnul* (1969), 43 Ill.2d 54, 250 N.E.2d 656)." (*Moorman* at 88-89, 61 Ill.Dec. 746, 435 N.E.2d at 452.) The plaintiff argues that its cause of action is based upon negligent misrepresentation and therefore falls within the second above-quoted exception to the *Moorman* rule.

In addressing the merits of this argument, it is helpful to examine the situations in which Illinois law has been considered concerning recovery of economic losses in a tort action. For the most part, the cases have relied upon the Restatement (Second) of Torts, section 552 which is entitled "Information Negligently Supplied for the Guidance of Others." Section 552 provides in part as follows:

> One who, in the course of his business, profession or employment, or in any other transaction in which he has a pecuniary interest, supplies false information for the guidance of others in their business transactions, is subject to liability for pecuniary loss caused to them by their justifiable reliance upon the information, if he fails to exercise reasonable care or competence in obtaining or communicating the information. (Restatement (Second) of Torts § 552 (1977).)

The case of *Penrod v. Merrill Lynch, Pierce, Fenner & Smith, Inc.* (1979), 68 Ill.App.3d 75, 24 Ill.Dec. 464, 385 N.E.2d 376, concerned a stockbroker who was alleged to have negligently supplied incorrect information. The *Penrod* court construed section 552 as meaning that "*[i]f it is one's business to supply information* and if that information is negligently supplied * * * the supplier can be liable for the resultant damages." (*Penrod* at 81, 24 Ill.Dec. 464, 385 N.E.2d at 381.) (Emphasis added.) This construction of the tort was followed in *National Can Corp. v. Whittaker Corp.* (N.D.Ill.1981), 505 F.Supp. 147. In *National Can*, the plaintiff, a manufacturer of bottle caps, sued a supplier of compounds used in making the caps based upon negligent misrepresentations concerning the fitness of the compounds. The court held that although an action for negligent misrepresentation is recognized in Illinois, such suits are limited to situations involving one who in the course of his business or profession supplies information for the guidance of others in their business relations with *third parties*. The Illinois Supreme Court in the *Moorman* case confirmed the interpretation of negligent misrepresentation espoused in *Penrod* and *National Can* by specifically limiting the recovery of economic losses in negligent misrepresentation actions to situations in which "*one who is in the business of supplying information* for the guidance of others in their business transactions makes negligent representations." *Moorman* at 89, 61 Ill.Dec. 746, 435 N.E.2d at 452. (Emphasis added.)

In the context of this case, there are two significant features. First, the defendant must supply the information in the course of his business and second, the information must be supplied for the guidance of others in their business transactions. While section 552 of the second Restatement of Torts says that liability arises when one "in the course of his business" supplies false information for the guidance of others, *Moorman* and *Penrod* have construed that section to mean that the defendant must be in the business of supplying information. [Citations.] Neither of the defendants in the case at bar was in the business of supplying information. They were selling merchandise directly to Black, Jackson.

The second significant aspect of this case concerns the requirement that the information supplied shall be "for the guidance of others in their business transactions." That requirement is considered specifically in *National Can*, where the court stated that suits for negligent misrepresentation are limited to situations involving one who in the course of his business or profession supplies information for the guidance of others in their relations with third parties. The information allegedly supplied here by IBM and Lubin-Bergman was not supplied for the guidance of Black, Jackson in its dealings with others.

Black, Jackson makes a claim in its brief that Terry E. Simmons, its president, suffered emotional distress as a result of the computer system's failure. However, it does not appear that Simmons is a party to this action. Although his name appears in a caption of the second amended complaint, he is not identified as a plaintiff in the body, preamble or prayer of the complaint. The only plaintiff in this cause is Black, Jackson and Simmons Brokerage, Inc. A corporation cannot sustain emotional distress.

Accordingly, the judgment of the circuit court is affirmed.

Affirmed.

TRIANGLE UNDERWRITERS, INC., v. HONEYWELL, INC.

457 F. Supp. 765
(United States District Court, E. D. New York, Sept. 18, 1978.)

NICKERSON, D. J.

* * *

Defendant Honeywell, Inc. ("Honeywell"), a Minnesota corporation, develops and sells computer systems. In January 1970, Honeywell's New York office approached plaintiff Triangle Underwriters, Inc. ("Triangle"), a New York corporation, to sell or lease to it Honeywell's H-110 computer system to replace the IBM 360-20 computer then used by Triangle for data processing. The H-110 system is a package consisting of "hardware", or the computer, printer, collator and other equipment, and programming or "software" created for use in connection with the hardware. Honeywell supplies both standard programming aids of general application to its computers and "Custom Application Software" specifically designed for the customer's individual needs.

On March 19, 1970 Honeywell submitted to Triangle a written "Letter and Formal Proposal" (the "Proposal") for the installation of the H-110 system. Triangle alleges that Honeywell warranted that the system was to be "turn-key", with the software prepared and the system ready for immediate functioning. The Proposal sets forth an "implementation plan" reciting the steps to be taken to make the system fully operational within 105 days of approval of the Proposal. Honeywell employees were to install the system and train Triangle employees in its use, whereupon Triangle would take over complete supervision. The Proposal contained no provision requiring Honeywell to update or amend the software after the Triangle employees assumed supervision. A printed lease form for the rental of the hardware was attached to the Proposal. The parties executed the lease on April 3, 1970, and Honeywell began preparation of the "Custom Application Software."

In December 1970 Honeywell advised Triangle that the system was fully operational. Triangle then elected to purchase rather than lease the hardware, and on December 5, 1970 entered into an "Agreement for the Sale of Data Processing Equipment" (the "Agreement") with defendant Honeywell Information Systems, Inc. ("H.I.S."), a separately incorporated division of Honeywell. The system was installed in January 1971, at which time Triangle discontinued the IBM System.

Triangle contends that from the beginning the system failed to function effectively. At that time, according to Triangle, it discovered that various programs did not function as Honeywell had represented they would, that there were "numerous errors" in the programs, and that Honeywell had not "run a proper parallel system during the change-over period."

After the installation in January 1971 the Honeywell personnel attempted to correct the deficiencies in the programs, which under the Agreement should have been functioning properly at the time of installation. Modifications were made by Honeywell in various of the programs, and Honeywell personnel worked on them at the Triangle premises until some time in 1972 when they left.

Triangle brought this diversity action against Honeywell and H.I.S. on August 14, 1975 for damages for loss of business as a going concern, loss of profits, and expenses and special damages. Triangle's complaint contains nine counts alleging, in various forms, negligent or fraudulent inducement to enter into the contract, breach of a contemporaneous oral agreement to prepare custom application software, breach of express and implied warranties, negligence and fraud. The essence of Triangle's claim is that Honeywell failed in January 1971 to supply a fully operational software system to fulfill Triangle's data processing needs and failed thereafter to correct the deficiencies.

* * *

Honeywell urges that the counts are all barred by § 2-725(1) of the U.C.C. which pro-

vides, in pertinent part, "An action for breach of any contract for sale must be commenced within four years after the cause of action has accrued." N.Y.U.C.C. § 2-725(1); Mass.G.L.A. ch. 106 § 2-725(1). This section applies to "transactions in goods", see U.C.C. § 2-102, and a "cause of action accrues when the breach occurs." U.C.C. § 2-725(2).

Honeywell contends that the essence of all the claims, regardless of their various characterizations, is that Honeywell breached a contract for sale of goods, that the alleged breach occurred on the January 1971 date of installation, and that the action brought on August 14, 1975, is therefore barred.

Triangle urges, among other things, that the completed breach of contract did not occur until after Honeywell ceased in 1972 to attempt to correct the deficiencies in the programs.

The date when the breach of contract occurred depends on what the agreement between the parties was. The answers to interrogatories make it manifest that Triangle's claim from the inception of the litigation has been that Honeywell undertook to deliver in January 1971 an entire system, including not only hardware but the programs or "software" to be used in the hardware. The system was to be "turn-key" and ready to function immediately. A breach of that undertaking occurred in January 1971 when Honeywell allegedly delivered a defective system, and Triangle would have been entitled to bring suit forthwith.

Triangle has drawn nothing to the court's attention in the answers to interrogatories or the excerpts from depositions which would justify a finding that less than a full breach of the alleged agreement occurred when the January 1971 delivery was made. It is not suggested by Triangle that Honeywell had a conditional obligation, for example, to deliver a "turn-key" system on a specified date or in the alternative to correct within a period of time a defective system. Triangle throughout has contended that Honeywell's duty to hand over a system fully capable of operation was unconditional. The breach of the alleged contract therefore occurred in January 1971 when Honeywell allegedly failed to perform its obligation.

Triangle contends that the system, which included the software, did not consist solely of "goods" within the meaning of the U.C.C., and that what was sold was predominantly "services". If that were true, not the U.C.C. four year statute of limitations, but the longer six year period applicable to actions on "contracts" generally would apply. New York C.P.L.R. § 213(2). Triangle cites no authority in support of the argument that a data processing system essentially involves the provision of services. The New York courts have not yet considered this question. In *F & M Schaefer Corp. v. Electronic Data Systems Corp.*, 430 F.Supp. 988, 992 (S.D.N.Y.1977) the court found that a data processing system was tangible and hence properly subject to replevin, but there the motion for replevin covered only the documentation. This court must therefore consider the nature of this sale in order to predict how a New York court might characterize the transaction.

The court concludes that a New York court would not find that the H-110 computer system principally consists of "services". The agreement with Honeywell did not contemplate that it would run a data processing service for Triangle but rather that Honeywell would develop a completed system and deliver it "turn-key" to Triangle to operate. After the installation and training period, Honeywell personnel were to withdraw, and Honeywell's major remaining obligation was to be maintenance. Although the ideas or concepts involved in the custom designed software remained Honeywell's intellectual property, Triangle was purchasing the product of those concepts. That product required efforts to produce, but it was a product nevertheless and, though intangible, is more readily characterized as "goods" than "services". Intangibles may be "goods" within the meaning of U.C.C. § 2-106 [Citation.]. The system was subject to sale, and the services provided by Honeywell, design, installation and maintenance, were incidental to that sale. Under these circumstances it is likely that a New York court would hold the sale subject to the U.C.C. statute of limitations.

Triangle suggests that the breach did not occur at the time of delivery and points to subsection (2) of § 2-725 reciting that where a warranty "explicitly extends to future performance of the goods and discovery of the breach must await such performance," the cause of action "accrues when the breach is or should have been discovered." But this subsection is of no help to Triangle. Such a warranty must expressly refer to the future, and the implied warranty alleged by plaintiff by its nature does not do so. Moreover, the express warranty alleged was to install a "turn-key" system fit for the purposes required by Triangle. Even if Triangle had alleged that Honeywell made an express warranty for future performance, the cause of action would accrue no later than the time of discovery. Yet, as noted, Triangle claims knowledge of breaches on the very first day of operations (Plaintiff's Interrog.Resp. 4(c)). Although Honeywell's alleged inability to correct the malfunction developed later, the essence of Triangle's claim is the alleged failure to provide a system operational from installation. That failure is asserted by Triangle to have been apparent in January 1971.

Several of Triangle's claims (Counts I, II and IX) assert that Honeywell defrauded and misled Triangle, and Triangle argues that these claims are governed by the six year statute of limitations applicable to actions for fraud. New York C.P.L.R. § 213(8).

However, in applying statutes of limitations to a complaint in which a claim arising out of one set of facts is based upon a number of different theories, New York courts ordinarily look beyond the form of pleading to the essence or gravamen of the cause of action. [Citations.] In this case it is apparent that Triangle's fraud claims are simply restatements of the breach of contract claim. They therefore should not be treated as separate claims for statute of limitations purposes. Triangle alleges fraudulent or negligent misrepresentation which induced it to enter into the contract (Count I) and to allow the installation of the H-110 system (Count II). The essence of the fraud alleged in the counts is that Honeywell failed to perform its contractual obligations as it represented it would in negotiating the contract. The only other specific allegation of fraud is contained in Count IX and alleges that Honeywell should have known and yet failed to disclose that its system was not properly designed. Although Triangle characterizes this count as fraudulent concealment, it is based on Honeywell's breach of its contractual duty to provide a functional system.

In this case the basic claim is that Honeywell agreed to deliver a working system but failed to live up to its agreement. To permit Triangle to obtain a longer statute of limitations by characterizing the breach of the agreement as "fraud" would be inconsistent with the New York decisions.

Assuming *arguendo* that the counts of the second amended complaint which include allegations of negligence should be considered as tort claims for purposes of the statute of limitations, the counts are, as stated, governed by New York law. [Citation]. The relevant limitations period for negligence claims is three years. New York C.P.L.R. § 214(4). Triangle concedes that as a matter of general New York law a cause of action accrues upon occurrence of the negligent event. If the negligence asserted consisted of failing to design and deliver a working "turn-key" system, the tortious act and the resulting injury took place no later than January 1971.

Triangle urges that the negligence did not end there and that Honeywell's wrong continued during the period in which Honeywell employees attempted to repair the malfunctioning system. The continuous tort theory has primarily been applied in trespass cases where the action complained of is the continued existence of a harmful condition so that the injury did not occur at any particular point in time. *See Holdridge v. Heyer-Schulte Corp. of Santa Barbara*, 440 F.Supp. 1088, 1096 (N.D.N.Y.1977). Here Triangle does not assert that Honeywell continuously made matters worse by its repair efforts from early 1971 to 1972. There is no suggestion that the defective system created a continuing risk during this period. There is no basis for finding a continuous tort.

Alternatively Triangle suggests that Honeywell be considered as having engaged in professional malpractice. In such cases the New York courts have applied the continuous treatment doctrine and held that the statute of limitations does not commence to run until the professional relationship has ended. The doctrine has been extended to non-medical professionals such as lawyers. [Citation.], ac-

countants, [Citation.], and architects [Citation]. The complaint need not formally allege professional malpractice. * * *

This exception to the ordinary limitations period is based on the degree of reliance involved in a professional relationship: a plaintiff should not be expected to interrupt a continuing course of treatment by bringing suit. *Holdridge v. Heyer-Schulte Corp. of Santa Barbara, supra,* 440 F.Supp. at 1099. In the case at bar, however, the necessary continuing professional relationship did not exist. Honeywell was not responsible for the continuous running of a data processing system for Triangle. Honeywell agreed to develop and install a system Triangle could operate. Despite the specialized nature of the computer field Triangle was fully able to and did discover the malfunctioning from the moment of installation. Any continuing relationship between the parties after that time consisted of Honeywell's efforts to repair the system. The effort of a manufacturer to repair a defective product is not the "continuous treatment" contemplated by the professional malpractice cases. Although the *Holdridge* case did extend the doctrine to the manufacturer of a defective medical device, the court reasoned that plaintiff was relying on the professional skill of his doctor and that the limitations period should therefore not begin to run until the physician's underlying treatment had ended. 440 F.Supp. at 1099.

Triangle finally argues that Honeywell is equitably estopped from raising the statute of limitations as a defense. The contention is that Honeywell fraudulently concealed the errors in the system and continued to reassure Triangle and to attempt to repair the system until September 1972.

As stated previously, Triangle's claim of alleged fraud does not state an independent cause of action but is inseparable from the claim of breach of contract. Even if Triangle's allegations are construed as a claim of concealment after installation of the extent of the deficiencies of the system (a construction hardly consistent with Triangle's assertion of its discovery of the defects from the inception), there is no showing that as a result of the concealment Triangle delayed bringing this action.

Triangle also maintains that Honeywell's attempts to repair the system should toll the running of the statute of limitations. This argument has been rejected by the majority of jurisdictions, including New York, [Citation.], and Triangle presents no reason to believe that a higher New York court would rule differently.

Counts I through V alleging breach of contract are barred by the four year statute of limitations. Counts VI through IX alleging negligence are barred by the three year statute of limitations. Honeywell's motion for summary judgment is granted, and the second amended complaint is dismissed.

So ordered.

TRIANGLE UNDERWRITERS, INC., v. HONEYWELL, INC.

604 F.2d 737

(United States Court of Appeals, Second Circuit, July 17, 1979.)

HAIGHT, D. J.

Plaintiff-appellant Triangle Underwriters, Inc. ("Triangle") commenced this action in the United States District Court for the Eastern District of New York against defendants-appellees Honeywell, Inc. ("Honeywell") and Honeywell Information Systems, Inc. ("H.I.S.") to recover damages for the alleged failure of performance of a computer system sold by appellees to Triangle. * * * Triangle's second amended complaint, which forms the subject matter of this appeal, charged in essence that the computer system installed by appellees failed entirely of performance, causing Triangle great damage and its ultimate commercial demise. The complaint alleged causes of action sounding in fraud, breach of contract, and negligence. The district court (Eugene H. Nickerson, *Judge*) granted appellees' motion for summary judgment and dismissed the complaint in its entirety, on the basis that all claims asserted were time barred. 457 F.Supp. 765. This appeal followed. We reverse dismissal of one of the fraud counts, affirm dismissal of the other counts, and remand for further proceedings consistent with this opinion.

I.

In its second amended complaint, Triangle alleged that it was a general agent for many insurance companies, undertaking the placement of casualty insurance from brokers, and assuming responsibility to bind the carriers, bill the brokers, collect the premiums, remit the premiums to the carriers, keep records of payments, extensions, cancellations, credits, remit commissions to brokers, issue policies, and update all records.

Through the arteries of such an insurance organism flow quantities of paper. Triangle relied on computers to process this paper. As of January, 1970, Triangle had for some time been using an IBM 360–20 computer, coordinated with its own programs and manual card system. At that time, the complaint alleges, Honeywell solicited Triangle to replace the IBM equipment with the Honeywell H–110 computer system.

The H–110 system, as described by the district judge, is a package consisting of "hardware," or the core computer, printer, collator, and related equipment; and "software," the designation for programming created for use in connection with the hardware. Honeywell supplied both standard programming aids of general application to its computer, and "Custom Application Software" specifically designed for customer's individual needs.

Honeywell's blandishments bore fruit. On March 19, 1970, after a number of meetings between Honeywell and Triangle representatives, Honeywell sent Triangle a proposal which, in Honeywell's view, "indicates immediate economic and operational benefits will be derived from the installation of a Honeywell 110 Computer System." The proposal contemplated the leasing by Triangle of Honeywell hardware. Honeywell employees were to install the system and train Triangle employees in its use, who would then take over complete operation. Triangle signed the hardware lease on April 3, 1970. Honeywell thereupon began preparation of the "Custom Application Software." In December, 1970, Honeywell advised Triangle that the system was fully operational.

At that point, Triangle elected to purchase rather than lease the hardware. On December 5, 1970, Triangle entered into a contract of sale with defendant-appellee H.I.S., a separately incorporated division of Honeywell. The system was installed in January, 1971, at which time Triangle discarded the IBM system.

The new Honeywell system was brought on line with high anticipation. Triangle's president Robert Weinstein, present at the first computer run, used a poignant analogy: "A new baby was being born, and I was very concerned with the success of that baby and how healthy it was going to be." But the "delivery" gave immediate cause for concern. The system first tried to print out invoices on a summary form. It was immediately apparent that all of the figures in the first batch were wrong. Weinstein testified: "There was literally a scream and I panicked." Honeywell personnel, murmuring reassurances, threw out the first run of invoices and produced a second. This second set was sent out to Triangle's broker-customers. It produced a wave of complaints about billing inaccuracies. These complaints continued every month "for the rest of the time we were in business."[1]

In addition to billings, the system was supposed to produce "runs" on other statistics. The entire system was not run in January of 1971. In addition to the run on billings, there was a monthly run on production from each individual producer; a run on dividends paid by insurance companies to insureds; a run on Triangle's cash receipts, on a daily, weekly and then monthly basis; a renewal record run on a monthly basis; and a cancellation record run. The last-named run was never performed. The cash receipts were run to some extent during the month of January. The renewal records were run in March, April or May. The monthly run by producers was first performed in April. The run on dividends was first attempted perhaps a year after installation. Errors appeared repeatedly in each of these computer runs. [Footnote.]

Subsequent to January, 1971, Honeywell personnel attempted without success to correct the deficiencies in the programs, modifying certain of them. Honeywell personnel worked on the system at the Triangle premises until some time in 1972, when they departed, never to return.

1. The quotations are taken from Weinstein's deposition, A. 483–491.

3. "In industry parlance 'turn-key' is referred to as a System which is pre-prepared and can be virtually plugged right in and ready to function immediately." Triangle's memorandum to district court, Transmittal Document 40 on Record on Appeal.

II.

Triangle filed its initial complaint on August 14, 1975. The second amended complaint contains nine counts. Count I charges Honeywell with fraudulent inducement, in that it falsely represented to Triangle that the H–110 system would be a "turn-key" system,[3] superior to Triangle's present computer in many ways. Count II charges Honeywell with fraud in falsely representing to Triangle that it was ready to install a fully tested and operative system commencing in January, 1971.[4]

Counts III, IV and V allege various contract claims against Honeywell: breach of an oral contract to provide an effective system (III); and breach of express (IV) and implied (V) warranties in the written contract.[5]

Counts VI–IX sound in negligence, asserting various theories against either or both appellees: failure to realize the system was inadequate (VI); negligence in preparation and design of the system (VII); failure to supervise and correct deficiencies in the system (VIII); and wrongful withdrawal of support personnel (IX). These last two counts Triangle characterizes as "computer malpractice."

The district court, applying statutes of limitation derived from New York law, [footnote], dismissed all counts as time barred.

III.

We agree that the contract claims are barred by the applicable statute of limitations.

[1] The district court properly held that the written contract of sale of December 5, 1970 falls within the Uniform Commercial Code ("U.C.C."), § 2–725(1) of which provides:

> An action for breach of any contract of sale must be commenced within four years after the cause of action has accrued.

§ 2–725(2) provides:

> A cause of action accrues when the breach occurs, regardless of the aggrieved party's lack of knowledge of the breach. A breach of warranty occurs when tender of delivery is made, except

4. Count IX also includes general allegations of fraud against both Honeywell and H.I.S. The fraud allegations are considered in greater detail under Point IV, *infra*.

5. Triangle concedes that the claim for breach of an oral contract is merged with claims arising out of the written contract, and no longer presses Count III.

that where a warranty explicitly extends to future performance of the goods and discovery of the breach must await the time of such performance the cause of action accrues when the breach is or should have been discovered.

In the case at bar, the breach of the contract pleaded by Triangle accrued in January, 1971, over four years before suit was commenced in August, 1975. The contract causes of action are accordingly barred by § 2-725(1).

Triangle's second amended complaint alleged that Honeywell represented its system would be a "turn-key" system (Count I), able to "function immediately in place of [Triangle's] present system" (Count II). Count III alleges an oral contract to install a 'turn-key' system that would be capable of operating within a relatively short period of time"; Counts IV and V allege breaches of express and implied warranties to furnish Triangle with a "totally integrated 'turn-key' system which would be fit for the purposes required by the plaintiff in its operations." The negligence counts (see, *e.g.*, Count VII, ¶ 50) define Honeywell's negligence as consisting of "the failure of the System to properly function, all as more specifically set forth in ¶ 15"; ¶ 15, which appears in Count I, charges that "the System and Programs [Honeywell] provided for the plaintiff were not ready for proper installation and use. * * * "

Thus the concept of a system capable of performance as soon as installed runs like a *leitmotiv* through Triangle's several theories of recovery, whether they sound in fraud, contract or negligence. That Triangle conceived of itself as having contracted for a "turn-key" system is evidenced by its simultaneous abandonment of the IBM system, in a step of such technological finality that once the Honeywell system was installed, the IBM data could not be retrieved: "Honeywell's system erased footprints." Small wonder, then, that Triangle gave this response to Honeywell's interrogatory, inquiring as to which of its representations were alleged to be false:

(i) that the defendants' system would be a 'turn-key';

(vi) there would be a very short requirement to run parallel systems because the defendant's system was so well perfected;

(vii) Defendant represented that prior to delivery of the System it would furnish to plaintiff output reports that would be functionally equivalent to all reports being currently run by plaintiff;

(xix) that the defendants' System would be 'turn-key' and function immediately upon installation. [Reference.]

Given this pervasive theory of liability, the system's panic-inducing failure on its very first run, and its inability to function properly at any time after installation in January, 1971, we can only conclude with the district court that the breach occurred when the system was installed and immediately proved itself incapable. Thus Judge Nickerson was right in holding that Triangle was entitled to bring suit for breach of contract "forthwith," and that a complaint filed in August, 1975 was untimely under § 2-725(1).

Triangle argues on appeal that its use of the phrase "turnkey operation" was possibly "ill conceived"; that the phrase does no more than paraphrase Honeywell's fraudulent inducements; and that in fact "Triangle did not contract for a turnkey operation." [Footnote.] This is a wholly unpersuasive effort to reverse course 180 degrees so as to avoid the shoals of the statute of limitations. Triangle's breach of contract claims were founded upon the proposition that Honeywell promised to install a system ready to operate in January, 1971, and failed to do so. The fact that the word "turnkey" does not appear in the written contract is of no significance; it was clearly the governing concept, with which the written contract is wholly consistent. The district judge did not indulge in impermissable fact finding when he so construed the document; he simply read the contract in the light of Triangle's own pleadings and the deposition testimony of its president.

Nor is Triangle's entitlement to sue in January, 1971 affected by the addition of other statistical "runs" to the system subsequent to January. In the first place, the immediate and never-corrected failure of the brokers' billing run furnished adequate grounds for suit by itself. Secondly, most of the additional runs were attempted and found wanting prior to August, 1971, more than four years before commencement of suit.

Triangle argues that the contract was one for services, rather than for the sale of goods; or at least the question presented a triable issue of fact precluding summary judgment. If the contract is properly viewed as one for services, and not for a sale, then the New York statute of limitations is six years, N.Y.C.P.L.R. § 213,[9] and the contract claims would be timely. *Dynamics Corporation of America v. International Harvester Co.,* 429 F.Supp. 341 (S.D.N.Y.1977). But the district court was justified in concluding, as a matter of law, that the contract was one for a sale of goods. A contract is for "service" rather than "sale" when "service predominates," and the sale of items is "incidental." [Citation.] Here precisely the converse is true. Triangle bought Honeywell's equipment in the hope it would outperform IBM's equipment[10]—the essence of the contract was for sale of goods. While certain services by Honeywell were contemplated, the contract remains one for sale if those services were "merely incidental or collateral to the sale of goods," *Dynamics Corporation of America, supra,* at 347, clearly the case here. The contract declares itself unequivocally to be an "Agreement for the Sale of Data Processing Equipment." The district court accurately stated, at 457 F.Supp. 769:

> The agreement with Honeywell did not contemplate that it would run a data processing service for Triangle but rather that Honeywell would develop a completed system and deliver it 'turn-key' to Triangle to operate. After the installation and training period, Honeywell personnel were to withdraw, and Honeywell's major remaining obligation was to be maintenance.

Honeywell's compensation was limited to the purchase price for the hardware; it did not bill for services prior, during or subsequent to installation. These are recognized indicia of a contract for the sale of goods, and not the rendition of professional services. *Aluminum Co. of America v. Electro Flo Corp.,* 451 F.2d 1115, 1118 (10th Cir. 1971).

---

9. § 213 provides:
    The following actions must be commenced within six years:

             *   *   *

    2. an action upon a contractual obligation or liability express or implied, except as provided in article 2 of the uniform commercial code. * * *

10. Triangle's president Weinstein described his company's primary objective in replacing the IBM system with Honeywell's:
    There came a time when we thought we needed faster equipment and the equipment that could give us greater controls than we had had prior thereto.

While Honeywell attempted to repair the H–110 system, New York and other jurisdictions hold that attempts by the seller to remedy defects giving rise to the cause of action do not toll the U.C.C.'s four-year period of limitations. *Thalrose v. General Motors,* 8 U.C.C.Rep.Serv. 1257, *aff'd. without opinion,* 41 A.D.2d 906, 343 N.Y.S.2d 303 (1st Dept. 1973). There is authority to the contrary, see cases cited in *Zahler v. Star Steel Supply Co.,* 50 Mich. App. 386, 213 N.W.2d 269 (1973), but we have no reason to doubt that *Thalrose* states the present rule in New York, and it forecloses Triangle's argument based upon post-failure repair efforts.

Finally, Triangle relies upon the proviso to § 2–725(2) of the U.C.C., which as noted reads:

> * * * A breach of warranty occurs when tender of delivery is made, *except where a warranty extends to future performance of the goods and discovery of the breach must await the time of such performance the cause of action accrues when the breach is or should have been discovered* (emphasis added).

This reliance is misplaced. We perceive nothing in the original proposal or the contract of sale (assuming the former is not merged in the latter) which could constitute "a warranty explicitly extend[ing] to future performance of the goods." But even if such warranty existed, the immediate failure of the system, and attendant manifestations of the defects now complained of, take the case out of the statutory exception.[11]

The district court correctly held that the breach of contract claims were barred by the four year limitations period in the U.C.C., § 2-725(1).

IV.

In addition to contract claims, the complaint also pleads tort claims: some sounding in fraud,

---

11. In *Gemini Typographers, Inc. v. Mergenthaler Linotype Co.,* 48 A.D.2d 637, 368 N.Y.S.2d 210 (1st Dept. 1975), the Court construed § 2-725(2) in a closely analogous situation and said:
    Even assuming, as plaintiff does, that there was a warranty extending to future performance, the statute would still have run. As indicated in the above-quoted statute, a cause of action for breach of warranty of future performance accrues either when the breach is discovered or when it should have been discovered. In the case at bar, the breach was discovered almost immediately upon delivery of the machine and therefore the statute of limitations, even with regard to 'future performance,' began to run from July 1965. 368 N.Y.S.2d at 212.

others in negligence. New York law recognizes the right to plead contract and tort causes of action arising out of a single transaction, although different statutes of limitation may apply to the separate claims. See, e. g., *Sears, Roebuck & Co. v. Enco Associates, Inc.*, 43 N.Y.2d 389, 401 N.Y.S.2d 767, 372 N.E.2d 555 (1977). Triangle's fraud claims are considered under Point V *infra*. Here we consider those claims sounding in negligence.

The statute of limitations in New York for negligence claims is three years. N.Y.C.P.L.R. § 214(4). A cause of action accrues when acts or omissions constituting negligence produce injury. *Schwartz v. Heyden Newport Chemical Corp.*, 12 N.Y.2d 212, 237 N.Y.S.2d 714, 188 N.E.2d 142 (1963), *cert. denied*, 347 U.S. 808 (1963). To the extent that Triangle charges appellees with negligence in the design and installation of the computer system, injury was produced by the system's initial failure in January, 1971. Accordingly the negligence claims are barred by the statute of limitations, unless there is some basis for ascribing actionable negligent conduct on the part of appellees occurring later than August 14, 1972, the complaint having been filed on August 14, 1975.

Triangle argues that there was evidence from which the jury could find that Honeywell's personnel continued to work on Triangle's premises, attempting to improve the performance of the system, through September, 1972.[12] From that evidence, Triangle contends that "it is entirely possible that negligence occurred" at a time within three years of the institution of suit. Accepting that possibility *arguendo*, the fact remains that a cause of action against Honeywell for negligence accrued in January, 1971. Subsequent negligence in respect of efforts to repair or improve the system is cognizable only if Triangle claimed separate injury caused by the negligent repair (e.g., that the repairs made matters worse), which is not alleged here, or if, as Triangle urges, the "continuous treatment" concept, initially applied to actions for medical malpractice, should be extended so as to embrace claims against a manufacturer of machinery. The district court refused to apply the continuous treatment concept to the case at bar. We conclude that it was correct in doing so.

The "continuous treatment" concept was first applied by the New York Court of Appeals in *Borgia v. City of New York*, 12 N.Y.2d 151, 237 N.Y.S.2d 319, 187 N.E.2d 777 (1962), which held that in a suit for malpractice of physicians and nurses in a city hospital, the statute of limitations began to run "at the end of continuous treatment or hospital-patient or physician-patient relationship," and not at the last date of malpractice. The Court in *Borgia* defined "continuous treatment" as:

> * * * treatment for the same or related illnesses for [sic] injuries, continuing after the alleged acts of malpractice, not mere continuity of a general physician-patient relationship. 12 N.Y.2d 157, 237 N.Y.S.2d 322, 187 N.E.2d 779.

The concept is thus a narrow one, proceeding from the sensible propositions that a lay patient is entitled to rely upon the professional skill of his physician, and need not be expected to interrupt a continuing course of treatment by bringing suit.[13]

Since *Borgia*, the continuous treatment concept has been extended by the New York courts to other professions;[14] but each application has depended upon that particular re-

---

12. Triangle brief at 24. The reference to the record is Weinstein's testimony at A. 431–432 that Honeywell personnel worked on the system "up to the installation and for two years approximately thereafter."

13. In *Borgia* Chief Judge Desmond articulated the rationale for the concept:

It would be absurd to require a wronged patient to interrupt corrective efforts by serving a summons on the physician or hospital superintendent, or by filing a notice of claim in the case of a city hospital. 12 N.Y.2d 156, 237 N.Y.S.2d 322, 187 N.E.2d 779.

14. *Attorneys: Grago v. Robertson*, 49 A.D.2d 645, 370 N.Y.S.2d 255 (3rd Dept. 1975), citing *Gilbert Properties v. Millstein*, 33 N.Y.2d 857, 352 N.Y.S.2d 198, 307 N.E.2d 257 (1973), although the Court of Appeals' memorandum in *Gilbert* falls short of a definitive holding on the point;

Siegel v. Kranis, 29 A.D.2d 477, 288 N.Y.S.2d 831 (2d Dept. 1968). *Accountants: Wilkin v. Dana R. Pickup & Co.*, 74 Misc.2d 1025, 347 N.Y.S.2d 122 (Sup.Ct. Allegheny Cty. 1973). *Architects: County of Broome v. Vincent J. Smith, Inc.*, 78 Misc.2d 889, 358 N.Y.S.2d 998 (Sup.Ct. Broome Cty. 1974). *Quaere* whether, quite apart from the questions arising out of the 1975 amendments to the N.Y.C.P.L.R., see text at note 16 *infra*, the Court of Appeals would extend the continuous treatment concept as far as the lower state courts have done. Cf. *Ultramares Corp. v. Touche*, 248 N.Y. 517, 518, 162 N.E. 507 (1928), holding that accounting firms were not subject to the malpractice statute of limitations, which applies only to the misconduct "of physicians, surgeons and others practicing a profession similar to those enumerated."

lationship of trust and reliance that exists between a lay plaintiff and a professional defendant.[15]

Enactments of the New York Legislature in 1975 have given rise to considerable doubt as to whether the continuous treatment concept is now applicable to any area other than medical malpractice. In that year, the Legislature enacted N.Y.C.P.L.R. § 214–a, a new section applying solely to medical malpractice, which provides:

> An action for medical malpractice must be commenced within two years and six months of the act, omission or failure complained of *or last treatment where there is continuous treatment* for the same illness, injury or condition which gave rise to the said act, omission or failure; * * * (emphasis added).

The Legislature also amended N.Y.C.P.L.R. § 214(6), so that the three year limitations period in respect of negligence applies to:

> 6. An action to recover damages for malpractice, *other than* medical malpractice; * * * (emphasis added).

These amendments may reasonably be construed as reflecting the Legislature's intent to limit the "continuous treatment" concept to the relationship from which it sprang, namely, that of patient and physician.[16]

We need not decide that particular point, however, because it is clear that whether or not the 1975 amendments limit the continuous treatment concept to cases of medical malpractice, there is wholly lacking in the case at bar that professional relationship upon which application of the doctrine, in any con-

text, depends. Honeywell manufactured computer equipment and sold it to Triangle. As the district court correctly observed, it was never contemplated that Honeywell would undertake the continuous running of a data processing system for Triangle. Triangle personnel were trained to perform that function, and had no difficulty in observing, and complaining about, the malfunctioning of the system. It is quite true that thereafter Honeywell personnel attempted repairs to the system. However, New York law provides generally that a manufacturer's efforts at repair subsequent to delivery do not extend the contract statute of limitations, *Thalrose v. General Motors Corp., supra*; and we are not inclined to undermine that rule by clothing sellers or manufacturers of machinery in the garb of members of the learned professions.

Triangle stresses that Honeywell knew more about computer equipment than it did, and that Triangle relied upon Honeywell's expertise. But there is nothing novel in this. The manufacturer of a large, complicated, and expensive piece of machinery may be presumed to know more about its workings than the purchaser, at least in most cases. However, to lift the continuous treatment concept from its narrow origin of personal services rendered by a professional defendant to a lay patient or client, and apply it generally to the law of commercial sales, would open Pandora's box, and create uncertainty where well-defined statutes of limitations now offer repose.

We reject Triangle's appeal to the continuous treatment concept, and hold with the district court that the claims sounding in negligence are time barred.

---

15. "The client is hardly in a position to know the intricacies of the practice or whether the necessary steps in the action have been taken. For better or for worse, the client must depend on his attorney to pursue the litigation diligently and according to the rules." *Siegel, supra*, at 288 N.Y.S.2d 835. "* * * generally the client is required to rely almost totally on the professional advice of the architect. He must have confidence in the architect and place his full trust in him." *County of Broome, supra*, at 358 N.Y.S.2d 1002.

Triangle states that the "continuous treatment" doctrine was applied to "non-professionals" in *LeVine v. Isoserve, Inc.*, 70 Misc.2d 747, 334 N.Y.S.2d 796 (Sup.Ct. Albany Cty. 1972); *Colpan Realty Corp. v. Great American Insurance Co.*, 83 Misc.2d 730, 373 N.Y.S.2d 802 (Sup.Ct. Westchester Cty. 1975); and *Holdridge v. Heyer*

Schulte Corp., 440 F.Supp. 1088 (N.D.N.Y.1977). *LeVine* is not a "continuous treatment" case at all; plaintiff sued defendant manufacturer for radiation caused by a defective isotope, and the statute of limitations issue turned on when the damages could reasonably have been discovered. *Colpan* and *Holdridge* hold, on the particular facts presented, that sufficiently close analogies to the attorney-client and physician-patient relationship existed to justify application of the concept.

16. See also the Executive Department's Legislative Memorandum proposing § 214–a, which said of the amendment that it "continues the 'continuous treatment' theory in medical malpractice cases. * * * *" McKinney's Sess. Laws, 1975, p. 1599.

V.

We turn now to Triangle's claims which sound in fraud. The applicable statute of limitations under New York law is six years from commission of the fraud or two years from discovery, whichever is longer. [Citation.] [Footnote.]

Allegations of fraud appear in Counts I, II and IX of the complaint. Count I alleges that on or about January, 1970, defendant Honeywell, Inc. solicited Triangle to replace its IBM system with the Honeywell H–110 system, and, in order to induce Triangle to make such a conversion, fraudulently represented to Triangle the capabilities of its system, Triangle relying upon such representations and entering into the contract, to its ultimate damage.

Count II, also against Honeywell, alleges that on or about December, 1970, Honeywell fraudulently advised Triangle that it was ready to introduce its system into Triangle's operations commencing January, 1971.

Count IX is against both defendants, Honeywell and H.I.S. Its main thrust is the defendants' failure to correct the system and withdrawal from attempting to do so. This is one of the "continuous treatment" counts which we considered under Point IV, *supra*. However, it also contains in ¶ 65 a blanket reference to "material misrepresentations, concealments and mis-statements of facts" fraudulently made by both defendants.

The district court applied to each of these allegations the four year contract statute of limitations, rather than the six year fraud statute, because it concluded that Triangle's fraud claims were "simply restatements of the breach of contract claim," and accordingly "should not be treated as separate claims for statute of limitations purposes." 457 F.Supp. at 770. We hold that, as to the allegation of fraud in the inducement in Count I, this conclusion was erroneous.

Honeywell relies, as did the district court, upon *Brick v. Cohn-Hall-Marx Co.*, 276 N.Y. 259, 11 N.E.2d 902 (1937), for the proposition that in applying statutes of limitation, New York courts look to the essence of plaintiff's claim and not to the form in which it is pleaded. We have no quarrel with the general principle, but the facts in *Brick* were entirely different. *Brick* did not involve a claim of fraud

in the inducement. There the claim was that *after* the parties had entered into a contract regarding royalties for use of a certain type of package, which obligated the defendant to pay 7½ cents for each package sold and to keep accurate books and records showing the number of packages sold by it, and to render verified statements showing its package sales, the defendant "kept false books, rendered false statements and made false statements for which it did not account," thereby avoiding payment of royalties due under the contract. This clearly was a patent effort to disguise the breach of contract claim as one for fraud, in order to take advantage of a longer period of limitations in respect of fraud claims. The Court of Appeals in *Brick*, holding that the claim was time barred for failure to sue within the contract period of limitations, pointed out that:

> The falsity of these statements and the fraud of the defendant according to the allegations amounted to a breach of the contract and was no more or less a breach of the contract than if the defendant had deliberately refused to pay or had neglected to pay. 276 N.Y. at 264, 11 N.E.2d at 904.

"If there were fraud extraneous to the contract," the Court also observed, "a different situation might arise." *Ibid.*

The case at bar does not involve any such attempt to dress up a contract claim in a fraud suit of clothes. The fraud Triangle alleges in Count I consisted of independent false representations, made before there ever was a contract between the parties, which led Triangle to enter into it. In other words, Triangle clearly alleges fraud that was extraneous to the contract, rather than a fraudulent nonperformance of the contract itself.

The allegations in Count I state a claim for fraud in the inducement under New York law. In *Coolite Corp. v. American Cyanamid Co.*, 52 A.D.2d 386, 384 N.Y.S.2d 808 (1st Dept. 1976), plaintiff entered into an agreement with defendant establishing plaintiff as the exclusive distributor of a "light stick" device manufactured by defendant. The complaint alleged that prior to execution of the contract in January of 1971, defendant fraudulently represented to plaintiff that it had fully tested the device, which could be produced in large commercial quantities of merchantable quality. Plaintiff further alleged that it would not have entered into the agreement, but for the fact that throughout the preliminary negotiations, defendant continuously represented that it was capable of mass producing a perfected product. Defendant argued that such statements were merely promises of future action, and did not constitute representations of fact sufficient to sustain a claim in fraud. The court disagreed, holding at 384 N.Y.S.2d 810:

* * * a fair reading of the complaint affords ample basis for concluding Cyanamid's representations, concerning the state of its research and testing and its ability to produce a perfected light stick, when made, were representations of fact and not merely promises of future action. When the complaint and the contract which it incorporates are considered together it is apparent that Coolite claims it was induced to enter into the distributorship agreement because Cyanamid represented that as a result of thorough testing it was then presently able to carry out its contractual commitment to produce commercial quantities of merchantable light sticks and that these representations were knowingly false and untrue when made. Allegations of this character are sufficient to sustain a fraud claim.

While *Coolite* was decided on a motion addressing the sufficiency of the pleadings, rather than on a statute of limitations point, the holding is pertinent to the case at bar because it demonstrates the elements of a claim for fraudulent inducement of a contract under New York law. As to those elements, we perceive no difference between the allegations in *Coolite* and the allegations in Count I of the complaint at bar. It follows that Count I adequately pleads a claim for fraud in the inducement under New York law.[18]

Given that sufficiency of pleading, no reason appears why the fraud period of limitations should not be applied to Count I, although the complaint also contains contract claims which are barred by the shorter limitations period. "Two or more causes of action may arise out of the same transaction with different statutes of limitations, and although one may be barred, the other may be good." *Conklin v. Draper*, 229 App. Div. 227, 241

N.Y.S. 529, 533 (1st Dept. 1930). See also *Sears, Roebuck & Co. v. Enco Associates, supra.*

The six year period of limitations for fraud applies to a claim for fraudulent inducement of contract; "the cause of action accrues when the document is executed and when the party alleging fraud has given consideration and thus suffered damage." *Dynamics Corporation of America v. International Harvester Co., supra,* at 355 (construing New York cases). In the case at bar, the parties first entered into a contractual relationship when Triangle signed the hardware lease (subsequently replaced by the contract to purchase) on April 3, 1970. The time within which to sue on the fraudulent inducement claim could not have commenced to run prior to that date; in consequence the complaint filed in August of 1975 was timely.

This analysis does not apply to the allegations of fraud in Counts II and IX, since they refer to alleged misrepresentations and concealments made after the parties had entered into a contractual relationship with each other. Under the rule in *Brick*, these allegations do not state separate claims for the purposes of the statute of limitations.

Because the district court erred in applying the four year contract statute of limitations to the claim of fraud in the inducement alleged in Count I, the order and judgment dismissing the complaint must be reversed as to that Count, and the case remanded to the district court for trial only of the claim asserted against defendant Honeywell, Inc. in that Count.

The order and judgment below are accordingly reversed with respect to Count I, affirmed as to Counts II through IX and the case remanded to the district court for further proceedings consistent with this opinion.

TRIANGLE UNDERWRITERS, INC., v. HONEYWELL, INC.
651 F.2d 132
(United States Court of Appeals, Second Circuit, Decided June 5, 1981.)

PER CURIAM.

Triangle Underwriters, Inc. (Triangle) appeals from an order of the United States Dis-

---

18. See also *Terris v. Cummiskey*, 11 A.D.2d 259, 203 N.Y.S.2d 445 (3rd Dept. 1960), in which the defendant seller's false statement, prior to the signing of a contract

for sale of a house, that after occupancy the cellar would be dry was held sufficient, together with the other elements of fraud, to constitute fraud in the inducement.

trict Court for the Eastern District of New York, Eugene H. Nickerson, J., granting in part the motion of defendant Honeywell, Inc. for judgment notwithstanding the verdict. Honeywell cross-appeals from that portion of Judge Nickerson's order denying in part Honeywell's motion to set aside the verdict.

In 1975, Triangle commenced the present action in the Eastern District, alleging nine counts of fraud and breach of contract against Honeywell and a related corporation, in connection with installation of a data processing system for Triangle in 1970. The gist of Triangle's complaint was that the system installed by Honeywell was defective, causing substantial damage to Triangle, eventually forcing it out of business in 1975. On Honeywell's motion for summary judgment, the district court dismissed all the counts of Triangle's complaint as barred by the applicable statute of limitations. *Triangle Underwriters, Inc. v. Honeywell, Inc.*, 457 F.Supp. 765 (E.D.N.Y. 1978). This court affirmed the dismissal as to counts two through nine, but reversed and remanded for trial on count one, which alleged fraud in the inducement of the contract. *Triangle Underwriters, Inc. v. Honeywell, Inc.*, 604 F.2d 737 (2d Cir. 1979).

After a trial on the sole remaining count before Judge Nickerson, the jury returned a verdict for Triangle. In response to special interrogatories, the jury found that Honeywell did fraudulently induce Triangle to enter into the contract, and was thereby liable for $1,089,000 in damages proximately caused by this action: $35,000 for the difference between the price Triangle paid for the computer system and its actual value to Triangle; $54,000 for Triangle's hiring of an independent data consultant in 1974; and $1 million for the termination of Triangle's business in 1975. In a memorandum opinion, dated November 26, 1980, Judge Nickerson granted Honeywell's motion to set aside the latter two items of damages (totaling $1,054,000) on the ground that even if the evidence is examined in the light most favorable to the plaintiff, Triangle had not sustained its burden of proving that its hiring of a data consultant and the termination of its business were proximately caused by Honeywell. The district court refused to set aside the jury's finding of fraud on the $35,000 portion of the damage award. This appeal followed.

We affirm the decision of the district court, for the reasons given in Judge Nickerson's opinion.

CARL BEASLEY FORD, INC. v. BURROUGHS CORP.
361 F.Supp. 325
(United States District Court, E. D. Pennsylvania, July 13, 1973.)

LUONGO, D. J.

Carl Beasley Ford, Inc. (Beasley), a Ford dealer, bought from Burroughs Corporation (Burroughs), the manufacturer of the equipment, electronic accounting equipment (E-4000 Series) to produce records required under Beasley's franchise agreement with Ford Motor Company. Contending that the equipment failed to perform as warranted, Beasley instituted this suit to recover the purchase price and consequential damages. The case presents many interesting and novel questions relating to Pennsylvania law under the Uniform Commercial Code, 12A P.S. § 1-101 et seq.

In a bifurcated trial, the issues were submitted to the jury under Federal Rule of Civil Procedure 49(a) for special verdict, and the jury answered interrogatories as follows:

LIABILITY

1. Did the plaintiff and defendant enter into an oral understanding and agreement for the furnishing by defendant to plaintiff of programming for the E-4000 machine purchased by plaintiff?

Yes X   No __

If your answer to #1 is "YES":

2. Did the defendant agree to provide programming which would perform the functions which had been performed by the Reynolds & Reynolds books and produce information necessary to preparation and submission of Ford Financial Reports?

Yes X   No __

3. Did the plaintiff rely on the defendant's skill and judgment in selecting and furnishing suitable programming for the E-4000 accounting machine?

Yes X   No __

4. Did the defendant promise and agree to provide such programming for the E-4000 machine by January 2, 1970?

Yes X   No __

5. Did the defendant provide, by January 2, 1970, programming adequate to accomplish the purposes contemplated by the agreement and understanding between the parties?

Yes __ No X

6. If your answer to #5 is "NO", did defendant provide such programming within a reasonable time after January 2, 1970?

Yes __ No X

If your answer to both #5 and #6 is "NO":

7. Did the plaintiff reject the E-4000 machine within a reasonable time after it knew or should have known that defendant would not provide programming adequate to accomplish the purposes contemplated by the agreement and understanding between the parties?

Yes X No __

8. Did the plaintiff at anytime accept the E-4000 machine and the programs submitted by defendant?

Yes __ No X

9. If your answer to #8 is "YES", specify when.

DAMAGES

1. Is the plaintiff entitled to recover the purchase price of the E-4000 equipment?

Yes X No __

(If your answer is "YES" the parties have agreed that the purchase price is $35,000.)

2. Is the plaintiff entitled to recover interest paid on the loan by which the purchase price was paid?

Yes X No __

(If your answer is "YES", the parties have agreed that the interest paid is $5,600.)

3. Is plaintiff entitled to recover any of the following items as consequential damages. If so, fill in the amount; if not, leave the amount blank.*

(a) Overtime to employes	$ NONE
(b) Extra help	$ 867.50
(c) Accountant's services	$16,840.00
(d) Computer services	$ 6,704.82

4. Is defendant entitled to credit for accounting service fees which would have been paid to Reynolds & Reynolds during 1970 if defendant's equipment had not been purchased?

Yes X No __

---

* In the court's charge, this was changed to the request to write in the word "None".

1. At that time Burroughs' practice was to sell the equipment and the programming under a "bundled" price, i. e. the price for the equipment was the same whether

---

If your answer is "YES", indicate how much credit should be given to defendant. $9,000

By its special verdict, the jury found that the parties had entered into an oral agreement under which Burroughs had agreed to program the equipment by January 2, 1970; that Burroughs had failed to provide, by that date or within a reasonable time thereafter, programs which would perform the functions which had previously been accomplished by Reynolds & Reynolds; that plaintiff had never accepted the equipment and the programming; and that it had rejected the E-4000 within a reasonable time. The jury found that plaintiff was entitled to specific items of damages totalling $56,012.32.

Before the court are Burroughs' motions for judgment n. o. v., or, in the alternative, for a new trial.

FACTS

Viewing the evidence in the light most favorable to the verdict winner, the jury could reasonably have found the following facts:

By a writing dated June 19, 1969 (P-2), Burroughs undertook to sell and deliver to plaintiff an E-4000 electronic accounting machine for $35,000. Not included or referred to in the writing was an oral agreement between the parties that, by January 2, 1970, Burroughs would furnish thirteen programs which would enable the machine to produce accounting records such as had theretofore been produced by Reynolds & Reynolds, records which were required by Beasley for submission to Ford Motor Company under the franchise agreement. The price of the programming service was included in the price of the equipment.[1]

Negotiations for the sale of the machine and for the programming to be furnished were conducted, on Burroughs' behalf, by its salesman, John Cibula. Under Burroughs' practice, salesmen were authorized to enter into such agreements and it was primarily the salesman's responsibility to do the programming, with assistance, where needed, from

---

Burroughs did the programming or not. For anti-trust reasons, this practice was later discontinued by Burroughs and separate prices were quoted for equipment and for programming, and separate agreements entered into. See footnote 4, *infra*.

Burroughs' technical programming personnel.

The equipment was delivered in October, 1969, and the payroll program, the first of the thirteen programs, was installed in November, 1969. Shortly thereafter, Cibula assured plaintiff's general manager that the remaining twelve would be completed and installed in the equipment by January 2, 1970, and that plaintiff should give the required 30 days' notice to cancel its arrangement for the processing of its records by Reynolds & Reynolds as of the end of December, 1969.

Cibula, the salesman who sold the equipment to plaintiff and who was responsible for the programming, left Burroughs during the first week of December. The programming was then taken over by the Zone Sales Manager, Gerald Smyser, and by a salesman for an adjoining territory.

None of the remaining twelve programs was presented (i.e. installed and tested in the equipment) by the agreed date, January 2, 1970. Two programs were submitted in mid-January and additional programs were submitted, at the rate of one or two a month, until June, 1970, when the final program was introduced into the machine. By this time plaintiff had fallen behind in its record keeping and had failed to submit timely reports to Ford Motor Company.

The difficulties did not end with the installation of the thirteen programs. Three of the promised programs were particularly essential to the conduct of plaintiff's business. One of the three related to accounts receivable. In that program it was essential to have an analysis of accounts showing the amount owed by each customer and how much of the balance was current, and how much was 30, 60, 90 and 120 days past due. The program submitted by defendant failed to operate correctly and at times the age analysis showed a portion past due greater than the total amount of the customer's balance. Another program, the general ledger trial balance, was designed to collect all of the accounts and give their monthly and year to date balances. The general ledger trial balance was essential to the preparation of the financial statements which were required to be furnished to Ford Motor Company, on a monthly basis, on or prior to the 10th day of the succeeding month.

The program submitted failed to produce the required year to date figures. The third crucial program which did not operate properly was that relating to new car and truck sales. The program was intended to give the gross profit for each month and inventory information such as types and price of vehicles in stock, and their inventory values. The program was defective in that, from time to time, the machine cleared, eliminating totals, and presenting thereafter a distorted picture of sales, inventory, etc.

As a result of the faulty performance of the E-4000, plaintiff fell far behind in the posting of its accounting records. The office staff began compiling the accounting records by hand. The services of IBM were secured to run the warranty and policy records, car and truck sales, and the general ledger. Burroughs supplied a second E-4000 and plaintiff hired extra personnel to operate the machine. Finally, when all the attempts to catch up failed, plaintiff brought in its accountants to completely reconstruct its accounting records for the calendar year 1970.

Throughout the entire time plaintiff had kept Burroughs advised of the difficulties it was having. Despite substantial efforts by Burroughs' personnel, the difficulties were not corrected. As late as September, 1970, one of the Burroughs' officials assured plaintiff that plaintiff's accounting records would be current by November 1, 1970. When that failed to come to pass, on December 11, 1970, plaintiff's counsel wrote a letter to Burroughs rejecting the E-4000 machine.

MOTION FOR JUDGMENT N.O.V.

At trial, plaintiff sought to impose liability for Burroughs' breach of contract on two theories: (1) Burroughs' failure to deliver the machine and its programs by January 2, 1970, the agreed upon date, or within a reasonable time thereafter, and (2) failure of the programs to perform as agreed.

Burroughs argues that it is entitled to judgment notwithstanding the verdict (a) because plaintiff's payment of the purchase price and subsequent use of the E-4000 machine while adjustments were made constituted a waiver of the lateness claim, and (b) as to the defective programs claim, although plaintiff's proof established that incorrect results were obtained, it failed to show that the incorrect results were caused by faulty programming, rather than by operator error or machine malfunction.[2] Burroughs contends that plaintiff's failure to produce expert testimony attributing the bad results to faulty programming is fatal to plaintiff's claim of breach of contract.

(a) Burroughs' contention that plaintiff waived its claim based on late delivery is governed, generally, by Article 2 of the Uniform Commercial Code, 12A P.S. § 2-101 et seq., and, in particular by §§ 2-602 and 2-606.

§ 2-602, provides in pertinent part:

(1) Rejection of goods must be within a reasonable time after their delivery or tender. It is ineffective unless the buyer seasonably notifies the seller.

§ 2-606, entitled "What Constitutes Acceptance of Goods", provides:

(1) Acceptance of goods occurs when the buyer
* * *
  (b) fails to make an effective rejection (subsection (1) of Section 2-602), but such acceptance does not occur until the buyer has had a reasonable opportunity to inspect them; or
  (c) does any act inconsistent with the seller's ownership; but if such act is wrongful as against the seller it is an acceptance only if ratified by him.

Burroughs argues that, as a matter of law, plaintiff failed to effectively reject the equipment within a reasonable time after delivery, and it must therefore have accepted it within the meaning of § 2-606, thereby waiving any claim of breach for late delivery.

I do not agree that the facts of this case require a finding, as a matter of law, that there was no timely rejection under § 2-602. In speaking to a comparable section (§ 69) of the predecessor Sales Act of 1915, relating to time within which to rescind. Justice Stern in Franz Equipment Co. v. The Leo J. Butler Co., 370 Pa. 459, 467-468, 88 A.2d 702, 707 (1952) stated:

What is a reasonable time within which to give such notice depends upon the circumstances of each case and is a question of law for the court. * * * Here it could not be fairly ascertained

by defendant whether the [machine] fulfilled the requirements of the contract until it had been tested by actual operation. The tests which were employed revealed defects of various kinds, and [buyer] properly gave to the manufacturer the opportunity to make such adjustments, repairs and replacements as might correct them; it was only after all such attempts were ineffectual that defendant became obliged to notify [seller] of its election to rescind the sale. In Kirk Johnson Co., Inc., v. Light, 100 Pa.Super. 425, 427, 428, it was pointed out that where the article sold is a machine which is the subject of adjustment or repair the situation differs from one where defects or breaches of warranty are at once discoverable; it was there said * * * that 'He [defendant] was not bound to rescind the contract and insist on the instrument being removed as long as there was a reasonable likelihood of the plaintiff's being able to overcome the defects, and it desired the chance to do so. Plaintiff's continual attempts to fix the instrument, conformably to its guaranty, did not deprive defendant of his right to rescind as soon as he was satisfied that it could not be made to work satisfactorily.'

[Citations.]

Here the period of adjustment of the programming of the E-4000 equipment took up at least eight months, not an unwarranted amount of time in view of the complexity of the machine. On April 9, 1970, plaintiff wrote a letter (P-3) in which the various deficiencies were identified and warned that the machine would be rejected unless all the enumerated matters were corrected. As late as September 11, 1970, Burroughs notified plaintiff by letter (P-17) that "Burroughs will do all that we can to be of assistance to you in resolving the operating problems of your installation", and on September 14, 1970, Burroughs, also by letter (P-13), assured plaintiff that its accounting would be caught up by November 1. On December 11, 1970, counsel for plaintiff wrote a letter to defendant rejecting the equipment.

* * *

There was no failure to make a timely rejection. As late as September 14, 1970, Burroughs continued to assure plaintiff that matters would be corrected and the work brought

---

2. If it was due to machine malfunction, Burroughs relies on a specific provision in P-2 limiting its liability to

replacement of defective parts.

up to date by November 1, 1970. The notice of rejection, written six weeks after the November 1 date passed, was reasonable. The use of the machine by plaintiff during all the period of "experimentation" did not constitute an acceptance.

(b) Burroughs contends that plaintiff failed to prove that the inaccurate records were caused by programming deficiencies rather than by machine defects or by operator error. In this breach of contract suit, plaintiff might well have carried its burden simply by proving that defendant had promised to produce a result (accounting records suitable for its purposes) and that defendant had failed to do so, leaving it to defendant to establish, as a matter of defense, that the errors were due to plaintiff's own personnel, but plaintiff did not stop there. For example, as to the malfunction of the "aging" aspect of the accounts receivable program, plaintiff presented evidence that after a Burroughs' representative had suggested that the cause was incorrect coding of input cards by plaintiff's employees, the Burroughs representative then coded the cards himself and, nevertheless, the program failed to produce the required aging of accounts. Further, as to the deficiency in the trial balance program, plaintiff presented the testimony of a Burroughs' employee that the program submitted by Burroughs did not include provision for the required "year to date" figures. And with respect to the new car and truck sales program, plaintiff presented testimony, again by a Burroughs' employee (a salesman), that the cause of the difficulty was defective programming. (N.T. 5-42). There was, thus, ample evidence to support the jury's finding that the inaccurate records produced by the Burroughs equipment was caused by deficiencies in the programming.

(c) Burroughs argues that plaintiff was obligated to establish, by expert testimony, that the inaccuracies in the records were attributable to faulty programming. This argument appears to stem from confusing negligence principles with those applicable to breach of contract cases. As noted above, plaintiff's obligation was simply to prove that defendant had agreed to produce a result and had failed to do so. The reasons for the failure, if they were of a nature to absolve defendant, were defendant's burden to establish. If there was

an obligation to produce expert testimony, it was defendant's obligation, not plaintiff's.

The motion for judgment n. o. v. will be denied.

MOTION FOR NEW TRIAL

The various grounds assigned by plaintiff in support of its motion for new trial will be discussed seriatim.

A. The Court erred in permitting the jury to determine what the contract was between the parties.

At trial, plaintiff produced a document entitled "Equipment Sale Contract," dated June 19, 1969 (P-2). This document contained a clause waiving consequential damages. The court, exercising its function to interpret written agreements, ruled that P-2 did not cover programming for the equipment, and so instructed the jury. Burroughs maintains that P-2 constituted the entire agreement between the parties and that it was error to permit the jury to determine whether there was an oral contract for programming and to determine what the terms of the oral agreement were.

The evidence produced in the instant case amply justified submission of the issue to the jury. Where there is a dispute as to which set of several circumstances, some expressed in writing and some oral, constitutes the agreement between the parties, it is the jury's function and not the court's to determine which set of circumstances constitutes the true agreement. [Citations.] Furthermore, as to Burroughs' contention that the agreement covered the programming aspect of the transaction as well as the sale of the machine, this statement from Gianni v. Russell & Co., Inc., 281 Pa. 320, 324, 126 A. 791, 792 (1924) controls:

> In cases * * * where the cause of action rests entirely on an alleged oral understanding concerning a subject which is dealt with in a written contract it is presumed that the writing was intended to set forth the entire agreement as to that particular subject. 'In deciding upon this intent [as to whether a certain subject was intended to be embodied by the writing], the chief and most satisfactory index * * * is found in the circumstances whether or not the *particular element of the alleged extrinsic negotiation is dealt*

with at all in the writing. If it is mentioned, covered, or dealt with in the writing, then presumably the writing was meant to represent all of the transaction on that element; if it is not, then probably the writing was not intended to embody that element of the negotiation.' Wigmore on Evidence (2d Ed.) vol. 5, p. 309 (emphasis in original).

P–2 contained no reference[4] to the terms of a programming agreement. There is no mention that the equipment would produce accounting records required by Ford, that thirteen programs were to be installed, no mention of the purpose for which they were designed and no agreed upon date for completion. These factors provided ample justification for the court's decision to permit the parol evidence relating to the alleged oral understanding. Whatever doubt there was as to correctness of this decision was dispelled when Burroughs' own employees testified that Burroughs' salesmen were instructed not to incorporate programming into written agreements for the sale of equipment, but to enter into instead oral agreements with the purchasers regarding the programming to be provided with the equipment. It was conceded that the equipment without programming was virtually worthless. These admissions by defendant's representatives furnished ample support for the conclusion that the writing did not encompass the entire agreement between the parties, and parol evidence was properly received to establish what the terms of the agreement were. [Citations.]

Burroughs contends that even if there was an oral agreement as to programming, the waiver of consequential damages clause, contained in P–2, must be included as one of the terms of that oral agreement. Burroughs was permitted to argue to the jury that the oral agreement included at least that portion of the writing, but the jury quite apparently rejected the argument. As noted above, where the terms of an oral agreement are in dispute, it is the jury's function to resolve the dispute.

B.   Errors in the Court's treatment of the damage aspect of the case.

The Uniform Commercial Code provides, with respect to remedies for breach of contract, inter alia:

§ 2—711. Buyer's Remedies in General; Buyer's Security Interest in Rejected Goods
(1) Where the seller fails to make delivery or repudiates or the buyer rightfully rejects or justifiably revokes acceptance then with respect to any goods involved, and with respect to the whole if the breach goes to the whole contract (Section 2—612), the buyer may cancel and whether or not he has done so may in addition to recovering so much of the price as has been paid
(a) 'cover' and have damages under the next section as to all the goods affected whether or not they have been identified to the contract
* * *

* * *

§ 2—712. 'Cover'; Buyer's Procurement of Substitute Goods
(1) After a breach within the preceding section the buyer may 'cover' by making in good faith and without unreasonable delay any reasonable purchase of or contract to purchase goods in substitution for those due from the seller.
(2) The buyer may recover from the seller as damages the difference between the cost of cover and the contract price together with any incidental or consequential damages as hereinafter defined (Section 2—715), but less expenses saved in consequence of the seller's breach.

* * *

§ 2—715. Buyer's Incidental and Consequential Damages

* * *

(2) Consequential damages resulting from the seller's breach include

---

4. There was an incidental mention in the printed portion of P–2 to programming. However, it quite clearly had nothing to do with an agreement to provide programming. The printed portion dealt only with buyer's obligation to make payment for the equipment, regardless of delays in delivery or installation, etc. The printed portion in question provided:

The requirement for service on the equipment or the need for an extended period to complete installation of or training on applications and programming on

Seller's equipment shall not justify failure of Purchaser to comply with its payment commitments hereunder. Seller shall deliver, install and service the equipment as promptly as is reasonably possible, but shall not be held responsible for delay in delivery, installation or service, nor in any event under this agreement for more than an exchange of equipment under its warranty, upon return of the equipment to Seller with Seller's prior written consent. (Purchaser hereby expressly waives all damages, whether direct, incidental or consequential.)

(a) any loss resulting from general or particular requirements and needs of which the seller at the time of contracting had reason to know and which could not reasonably be prevented by cover or otherwise; * * *

Burroughs has raised the following issues with respect to damages.

1. *The programming contract must be considered by itself to determine the measure of damages.* At trial, plaintiff disclaimed any recovery for damages based upon defects in the machine itself. Burroughs argues that since the evidence indicated that the price of the machine, including programming, was $35,000, and since no evidence was presented as to the separate price of the programming, and since plaintiff had disclaimed any right to recover for defective equipment, there was no evidence upon which the jury could have arrived at a proper amount of damages for improper programming.

In making this argument, Burroughs has overlooked a very important part of the proof in this case. There was testimony at trial that the E–4000 machine was virtually worthless without proper programming; that, at the time of the sale, Burroughs sold the equipment at a "bundled" price, i. e., the price was the same whether or not the customer had Burroughs do the programming, thus virtually forcing the customer to accept Burroughs' programming.[5] It was quite apparent, therefore, that although two separate agreements were used, one in writing for the physical equipment, and the other oral to cover the programming of the equipment, the two were virtually inseparable insofar as the utility of the equipment was concerned. It appears appropriate, therefore, to allow the return of the entire purchase price as an element of damage for breach of the agreement to furnish proper programming.

Burroughs contends further that the true measure of damages is the cost of securing proper programming of the machine. I have no dispute with that statement of law. [Citations.] The disagreement really arises as to who has the burden of proof in matters relating to mitigation of damages. Plaintiff's evidence established that the equipment was worthless without proper programming; that Burroughs, the manufacturer of the equipment (and presumably "the expert" in the programming of its own equipment) was unable to program it to function properly. Under the circumstances, I believe that it was Burroughs' burden to establish that there were available sources of programming known, or which should have been known, to plaintiff to furnish that which Burroughs had failed to produce (see discussion infra at pp. 19–20). Burroughs produced no such evidence.

2. *Interest as an element of damage.* Burroughs argues that the court erred when it permitted the jury to award, as an element of consequential damage, interest charges paid by plaintiff for the purchase of the E–4000. The matter is not at all free from doubt. I find no authority for the allowance of interest on indebtedness as an element of "price" as that term is used in § 2—711 of the Uniform Commercial Code. See Wagner Tractor, Inc. v. Shields, 381 F.2d 441 (9th Cir. 1967). On the other hand, the nature and price of this equipment was such that "at the time of contracting [Burroughs] had reason to know" that plaintiff would borrow money to purchase this capital item, thereby establishing the interest charge as an item of consequential damage under § 2—715. I am frank to state that there is no evidence in the record establishing what normal business practice and custom is with regard to the purchase of such items, but on balance (and acknowledging reservations) it appears a properly allowable item of consequential damage.

3. *Accounting fees, additional help and computer services.* Because of the inaccuracy and unreliability of the records produced by the

---

5. A practice shortly thereafter abandoned. The antitrust implications of "bundled" pricing had, at about the time of plaintiff's negotiations with Burroughs, resulted in the filing of several suits in which this practice was alleged to be a violation of Section 2 of the Sherman Act, 15 U.S.C. § 2. See Control Data Corp. v. International Business Machines Corp., (3–68 Civ. 312 (D.Minn. Third Division)); Data Processing Financial & General Corp.

v. International Business Machines Corp., (3–69 Civ. 157 (S.D.N.Y. 69 Civ. 19)); Applied Data Research, Inc. v. International Business Machines Corp., (3–69 Civ. 158 (S.D.N.Y. 69 Civ. 1682)); Programatics, Inc. v. International Business Machines Corp., (3–69 Civ. 159 (S.D.N.Y. 69 Civ. 2185)). And see Control Data Corp. v. IBM Corp., 1970 CCH Trade Cases ¶73,297 (D.Minn.1970).

Burroughs equipment, plaintiff brought in its accountants to reconstruct its records and balance sheet for 1970. Some of the records which had been produced by the machine were available to the accountants while they were so engaged, but the equipment itself was not used in any of the reconstruction work. Burroughs argues that its equipment should have been used and that, if it had been, the expense would have been considerably reduced.

In addition, plaintiff hired outside help to get caught up in its record keeping, incurred charges by outside computer firms to perform some of the work which the Burroughs equipment should have performed, and used some of its own personnel on an overtime basis.

Burroughs' basic argument as to all these items, of course, is that consequential damages are barred by reason of the clause in the writing (P–2). Apart from that, its position is essentially that plaintiff failed to prove that it used the most economical means available to undo the harm caused by Burroughs' breach, i. e. that plaintiff had the burden to prove that it had mitigated damages.

Plaintiff was undoubtedly under an obligation to mitigate damages, but it was defendant's burden to prove that plaintiff had failed to do so. [Citations.] Burroughs' contentions as to the unreasonableness of the accountants' fees, as to the lack of necessity for other computer services and outside help, were all submitted to the jury and rejected. Its contention that plaintiff had failed to prove that overtime by its own employees was attributable to Burroughs' breach was apparently accepted by the jury and no award made for that item. All of these items were properly submitted for resolution by the jury and the jury's findings have ample support in the evidence.

4. *The Court erred in permitting proof of damages which were not set forth in plaintiff's pretrial memorandum or its answers to interrogatories.* In its pretrial memorandum, plaintiff claimed (in addition to return of the purchase price) two basic items of damage; loss of profits in its business from lack of proper records; and specific items of expense incurred. At trial, plaintiff abandoned the claim for loss of profits and pursued only the claim for expenses incurred. Burroughs complains that it was prejudiced because plaintiff was permitted to prove expenses in amounts above

and beyond those set forth in the pretrial memorandum. I believe that what was done here was within the allowable range of a trial judge's discretion, see Moore v. Sylvania Electric Products, Inc., 454 F.2d 81, 84 (3d Cir. 1972), particularly in view of the fact that counsel for defendant made no request for postponement of trial to enable him to investigate the additional amounts claimed.

* * *

3. *Deficiency in operating instructions as a basis for breach of contract.* Burroughs' last point is that it was error to charge the jury that a deficiency in instructions could serve as a basis for a breach of contract. Plaintiff's general manager had testified that he did not contend that plaintiff's employees could not operate the equipment because of a lack of an operations manual. Burroughs argues that plaintiff was bound by that testimony and was therefore not entitled to have that issue submitted to the jury.

The questioned submission was made because there was evidence, in defendant's case, which raised serious questions concerning whether the instructions in the manual furnished by Burroughs were sufficient to enable plaintiff's personnel to operate the equipment properly. (See N.T. 5–56; 5–62; 5–72). Under these circumstances I believe the submission was proper under the principle stated in Guenther v. Armstrong Rubber Co., 406 F.2d 1315, 1318 (3d Cir. 1969):

> [A] plaintiff's testimony is not a judicial admission when it * * * relates to an objective matter about which he might honestly be mistaken, * * * where there is other evidence in the case, including the adverse party's, which is more favorable to him, even though it conflicts with his own testimony, since a party may be mistaken in his testimony, like any other witness; in other words, a party is regarded as not bound by his own testimony where there is contradictory evidence or circumstances which the trier of fact might fairly believe.

This is such a case. Plaintiff's general manager was admittedly not an expert in electronic accounting equipment. Ketterman was. The jury was entitled to pass judgment on the adequacy of the instructions notwithstanding plaintiff's testimony.

The motion for new trial will be denied.

NATIONAL CASH REGISTER CO. v. MARSHALL SAVINGS AND LOAN ASSOCIATION

415 F.2d 1131

(United States Court of Appeals Seventh Circuit, Sept. 23, 1969.)

FAIRCHILD, C. J.

Action by The National Cash Register Company against Marshall Savings and Loan Association and its receiver for the purchase price of an electronic data processing system. [Footnote.] Each party moved for summary judgment. The district court entered judgment in favor of National for $655,079.77. Defendants appealed.

Marshall signed an agreement to purchase the "system" April 23, 1962. The agreement said the "system" would consist of a list of tangible components. It is undisputed that all were delivered and physically installed at Marshall before May 18, 1964, except that ten teller's window machines were delivered and physically installed in August, 1964.

It is also undisputed that Marshall's data were never completely converted so that the system could be made ready to carry out its intended functions in Marshall's day to day operations. Marshall employees were to convert the Marshall data, working under supervision to be provided by National. It is conceded that Marshall, rather than National, was responsible for failure to proceed with this task.

New owners took over Marshall in the fall of 1964, the Director of Financial Institutions of Illinois took custody December 31, 1964, and a receiver was appointed April 8, 1965. The system was used, although for very limited purposes, from time to time before and after state custody began.

Defendants' position is that since the data were not converted the purchase price never became due pursuant to the purchase agreement, that since Marshall failed to convert the data National has a cause of action for damages for anticipatory breach, but that National failed in its duty to minimize damages by selling the equipment.

The critical provision of the purchase agreement is: "The Purchaser shall pay National's invoices when rendered, said invoices to be rendered when the System has been delivered, installed and certified by National as being ready for use."

On May 18, 1964, National's service manager sent a letter to the president of Marshall, saying, in part:

This is [to] certify that the above numbered NCR System has been delivered, installed, tested and made available for use, as of this date.

Although the letter used the word "available" rather than "ready", it is clear that the certification called for by the purchase agreement was intended. For the letter went on to explain that the 90 day warranty would become effective with the date of the letter. According to the agreement, the 90 days ran "from the date such equipment has been certified by National as ready for use."

Marshall never rejected nor disputed the May 18 letter. It is true that the ten window machines were an important part of the system and not installed until August, but it appears by affidavit that the former officers of Marshall orally promised a National representative that payment would be made. On November 19, 1964 the new president wrote to National saying that the new owners were attempting to determine the liquidity of Marshall and it would take about thirty days to decide what Marshall would be able to do. "That is, we may determine to either arrange for financing or pay for this equipment in full at that time."

The affidavits indicate a difference of opinion over the meaning of "installed". An officer of Marshall whose duty was to supervise the system, stated that it was "installed". A representative of National, on the other hand, indicated that "installed" includes "that it's actually performing on the application for which it was intended." It could well be argued, that "ready for use" means that the purchaser's data has been converted so that the system could immediately begin day to day operation.

But National, at the time of the transaction, took the position that the system was installed and ready for use when it was physically installed and ready to use as soon as Marshall converted its data. Marshall, by its conduct, so unequivocally accepted the same interpretation of the agreement that it is no longer open to the receiver to advance a different one, even though arguable.

The judgment is affirmed.

CHATLOS SYSTEMS, INC. v. NATIONAL CASH REGISTER CO.

479 F. Supp. 738

(United States District Court, D. New Jersey, Oct. 22, 1979.)

WHIPPLE, D. J.

This case was tried before the Court sitting without a jury during May and June of 1979. The action arises out of the sale, through a leasing arrangement, of computer hardware and software. The plaintiff alleges breach of contract, breach of express and implied warranties, fraudulent misrepresentation, and seeks compensatory and punitive damages.[1] The parties have submitted extensive trial memoranda and proposed findings and conclusions. After careful consideration of all testimony, exhibits admitted into evidence, oral argument, and trial memoranda, the Court hereby adopts the following findings of fact and conclusions of fact pursuant to Fed.R.Civ. Pro. 52.

The plaintiff, Chatlos Systems, Inc. (hereinafter CSI) is a New Jersey corporation engaged in the design and manufacture of cable pressurization equipment for the telecommunications industry. Edward Chatlos is the president of CSI. The defendant, NCR Corporation (hereinafter NCR) previously known as National Cash Register Corporation, is a Maryland corporation having its principal place of business in Dayton, Ohio. NCR designs, manufactures and sells computer systems, programming and services.

* * *

In the spring of 1974 the plaintiff became interested in purchasing a computer system in order to modernize the control of data which had become increasingly difficult since the incorporation of CSI in 1967. Mr. Chatlos made inquiries of several computer companies and was visited by Sam Long, a NCR salesman.

After discussions wherein NCR was apprised of CSI's detailed business history and operations, Mr. Long recommended that CSI acquire a computer known as the NCR 399 Magnetic Ledger Card System (330 MAG).

It was represented that the 399 MAG would provide six functions for CSI through the use of computer programs. The six functions were Accounts Receivable, Payroll, Order Entry, Inventory Deletion, State Income Tax, and Cash Receipts.

On July 11, 1974 Mr. Chatlos in his capacity as chief executive of CSI signed a System Services Agreement for the sale of a 399 MAG. Shortly thereafter he had discussions with a representative of Burroughs Corporation, a major competitor of NCR. In these discussions Mr. Chatlos learned of a more advanced method of storing data than magnetic ledger cards which was known as a disc system. When he brought this information to the attention of Mr. Long, he was told that NCR also sold a disc system which could be utilized with the basic 399 unit. The computer was called the 399/656 Disc System.

It was represented by NCR that the 399/656 Disc would perform the same functions as the 399 MAG. It was further represented that the more advanced system was a good investment for CSI's present and future needs, that it would solve inventory problems, would result in direct savings of labor costs, would be programmed by capable NCR personnel, and would be "up and running"[2] within six months.

In reliance upon these representations CSI entered into the transaction. On July 24, 1974 CSI entered into a System Services Agreement with NCR as part of the transaction. CSI paid $5,621.22 under this agreement. [Reference.] Because both NCR and an independent leasing company disapproved CSI's credit, on February 4, 1975 CSI entered into a leasing arrangement with the Midlantic National

---

1. Though not raised in the pleadings, in posttrial memoranda plaintiff has asserted two additional theories of liability. "Computer malpractice" and strict liability in tort are alleged to have been proven at trial.

The novel concept of a new tort called "computer malpractice" is premised upon a theory of elevated responsibility on the part of those who render computer sales and service. Plaintiff equates the sale and servicing of computer systems with established theories of professional malpractice. Simply because an activity is technically complex and important to the business community does not mean that greater potential liability must attach. In the absence of sound precedential authority, the Court declines the invitation to create a new tort. In view of the findings and conclusions, *infra* the Court deems it unnecessary to rule explicitly on plaintiff's assertion of strict liability in tort.

2. "Up and running" is a trade term which means that the system is fully performing the functions for which it is intended.

Bank whereby CSI agreed to pay $70,162.09 in sixty-six equal payments. [Reference.] This is a common practice in the trade; the computer company sells the system to a bank who in turn leases it to the "purchaser."

On December 11, 1974 the computer hardware was delivered to CSI. At this point Mr. Chatlos, on behalf of CSI, understood that it would take slightly longer, that is three months from the date of delivery, to have the system "up and running." Based upon the representations of NCR, CSI expected the machine to be fully operational by March 1975.

After the hardware was delivered, Frank Hicks, an experienced NCR programmer began learning the CSI payroll program. Though experienced in the 399 unit, Mr. Hicks had not attended the Disc school. He arrived at CSI in January 1975 and attempted to program and install the 399/656 Disc until February 1976. The payroll program became operational in March 1975, yet the State Income Tax programs were not successfully installed until September 1, 1976.

After programming the payroll function Mr. Hicks attempted to install the inventory deletion and order entry programs which involved the use of a procedure known as multiple records per sector. Placing multiple records in a sector means that several pieces of data or information are stored in one sector or section of the disc. Mr. Hicks had problems with the process in that he could not delete one piece of information within the same sector. CSI's business involves the assembly of technical equipment using many component parts. If the information contained in a sector was the existence of several specific parts in inventory, when one part was deleted (because it had been used in the assembly of equipment), the existence of the other parts was also deleted. Thus the functions of inventory deletion and order entry were inoperative.

On January 1, 1976 Richard Moody, Branch Service Manager of NCR's Newark District Office became responsible for the CSI installation. In February 1976 Mr. Moody assigned Pasquale Turi and Edward Tuosto to replace Mr. Hicks at the CSI site. Assurances were given to CSI that the computer would soon be demonstrated. On March 9 and 10, 1976 several NCR system analysts attempted to demonstrate the order entry and accounts receivable functions. This demonstration revealed significant problems with both functions.

On June 7, 1976 CSI asked that the lease be cancelled and the computer removed. NCR asked for additional time to make the 399/656 Disc fully operational and CSI agreed.

In July and August 1976 several meetings took place between NCR and CSI. Two other NCR analysts, Doug Russo and Bob Zebroski began another attempt to program the computer. On August 31, 1976 CSI experienced problems with the payroll function, the only job the computer had been performing. On that same day Mr. Tuosto installed the State Income Tax programs and on September 1, 1976 the problems with it were corrected.

On September 2, 1976 Mr. Moody arrived at CSI and announced that he was ready to install the order entry program. CSI refused. On September 3, 1976 Mr. Chatlos sent a letter to NCR describing the events of that summer and asked to cancel the lease and have the computer removed from the CSI premises. NCR refused stating that it had no ownership rights in the 399/656 Disc because it had been paid by the Midlantic Bank in August 1975.

Though Mr. Hicks worked on the programming problems for over one year, and other NCR personnel attempted to correct them, the 399/656 Disc only performed the payroll function and never performed the other four functions. Moreover, Mr. Chatlos and the other personnel of CSI gave full cooperation to NCR up until September 2, 1976.

This transaction was for the "sale of goods" notwithstanding the incidental service aspects and the lease arrangement; therefore Article 2 of the Uniform Commercial Code, as adopted by the State of New Jersey, is the applicable law. [Citations.] Because of this application and the following conclusions it is unnecessary to consider the common law breach of contract claim.

WARRANTY

Under N.J.S.A. 12A:2–313(1)(a) and (b) express warranties are created by a seller as follows:

> (a) Any affirmation of fact or promise made by the seller to the buyer which relates to the goods and becomes part of the basis of the bargain creates an express warranty that the goods shall conform to the affirmation or promise.

(b) Any description of the goods which is made part of the basis of the bargain creates an express warranty that the goods shall conform to the description.

* * *

Express written warranties were made by NCR in the Equipment Order and Sales Contract where it specifically stated that NCR warranted the described equipment for "12 months after delivery against defects in material, workmanship and operational failure from ordinary use." Furthermore the July 24, 1976 System Services Agreement specifically states, "NCR warrants that the services will be performed in a skillful and workmanlike manner." Though for services, this was part and parcel of the entire transaction for a sale of goods.

Together with the written warranties, Mr. Long, the NCR salesman, made verbal warranties as outlined in the facts. All of these warranties were memorialized in the Purchase Order prepared by the Midlantic National Bank where it is written at paragraph 6:

> Since the above goods [the 399/656 Disc] are purchased by us expressly for the use of the lessee, [CSI] you [NCR] further warrant that the goods are in good working order, fit for the use for which the Lessee intends them, fulfill all representations made by you to Lessee. * * *

[Reference.]

Since the written and verbal representations were obviously a basis of the bargain, it is clear that NCR created express warranties.

Under N.J.S.A. 12A:2–315 an implied warranty of fitness for a particular purpose is created:

> Where a seller at the time of contracting has reason to know of any particular purpose for which the goods are required and has reason to know that the buyer is relying on the seller's skill or judgment to select or furnish suitable goods, there is * * * an implied warranty that the goods shall be fit for such purpose.

---

3. Because it is concluded that NCR breached express warranties and the implied warranty of fitness for a particular purpose, it is unnecessary to discuss and rule upon

NCR states in their trial brief that language in the Equipment Order and Sales Contract and the Systems Services Agreement effectively disclaimed all implied warranties. This argument merits little discussion because in the pre-trial order, by stipulation, NCR agreed they had represented the 399/656 Disc would perform the six functions and that NCR would provide the requisite know-how necessary to put the system into operation. While those stipulations all but admit express warranties, NCR also agreed it had expertise in the computer field and that it recommended the 399/656 Disc for the plaintiff's "express purpose." Furthermore, NCR was well aware that CSI was relying upon NCR's skill and judgment. Nothing was presented at trial to contradict the conclusion that under N.J.S.A. 12A:2–315 there was an implied warranty of fitness for the particular purposes of CSI.

Moreover, CSI having met their burden of proof and based upon the facts outlined, it is clear that NCR breached both express warranties and the implied warranty of fitness.[3] It is unnecessary to outline each breach because the statutory remedies provided in N.J.S.A. 12A:2–714 become applicable after any breach of warranty is established.

REMEDY FOR BREACH OF WARRANTY

Having concluded that NCR breached express and implied warranties, plaintiff is entitled to the remedies as provided in the Uniform Commercial Code as follows:

* * *

(2) The measure of damages for breach of warranty is the difference * * * between the value of the goods accepted and the value they would have had if they had been as warranted, unless special circumstances show proximate damages of a different amount.

(3) In a proper case incidental and consequential damages under the next section [2–715] may also be recovered.

---

whether there existed an implied warranty of merchantability and if so, whether it was breached.

N.J.S.A. 12A:2–714 captioned "Buyer's Damages for Breach in Regard to Accepted Goods."[4]

The Court does not lightly view the admonition of N.J.S.A. 12A:1–106(1) which states that:

> [t]he remedies provided by this Act shall be liberally administered to the end that *the aggrieved party may be put in as good a position as if the other party had fully performed* but neither consequential or special nor penal damages may be had except as specifically provided in this Act or by other rule of law. (emphasis supplied)

A two-step process is necessary in order to fully consider the initial question of damages herein. The first inquiry must be to determine the value of the goods if they had been as warranted. This is not the "market value" since that term is conspicuously absent from § 2–714(2). The appropriate starting place is the $70,162.09 the plaintiff indebted itself to pay the bank for the computer system. It includes the amount the defendant received, the sales tax, together with the interest charges under the lease arrangement.[5] The $5,621.22 paid by the plaintiff for the service contract is added because it was an inseparable element of the entire transaction. The Court finds the total value of the computer system if it had been as warranted to be $75,783.31.

The value of what was accepted must be deducted from the $75,783.31. Plaintiff's expert testified that the value of the hardware presently located at CSI is between $5,000.00 and $7,000.00. Taking the average, the Court finds the present value to be $6,000.00. An additional element must be calculated; the value of the payroll function which plaintiff admits was used from March 1975 until October 1976. Since neither plaintiff nor defendant presented any evidence of this value, the Court will assign a value as follows. The payroll function was one of the six that were promised, therefore, it is reasonable to recognize this benefit as one-sixth of the value if as warranted, or one-sixth of $75,783.31. This equals $12,630.55. The sum of the two adjustments is $18,630.55. When this figure is deducted from $75,783.31 the $57,152.58 result is the amount to which plaintiff is entitled as the direct measure of damages for breach of warranty, before discussion of incidental and/or consequential damages.

NCR maintains that an effective limitation on recovery of consequential damages appears in the System Services Agreement. The written warranties previously discussed conclude that "NCR's obligation is limited to correcting any error in any program as appears within 60 days after such has been furnished." [Reference.] Later language in the System Services Agreement states, "in no event shall NCR be liable for special or consequential damages from any cause whatsoever." These phrases clearly attempt to limit the purchaser's remedy to having any error corrected within sixty days after the appropriate programs are furnished. Since four of the six functions were never furnished, the attempted limitation falls squarely within N.J.S.A. 12A:2–719(2) which provides that:

---

4. CSI attempted to revoke their acceptance by requesting the removal of the computer system in their letters of June 7, 1976 and September 3, 1976. As stated in NCR's responding letter of September 10, 1976:

> * * * the equipment was purchased by your bank who in turn leased it to Chatlos Systems, Inc. Since this was a purchase, NCR has no ownership rights to the equipment and therefore, I cannot have it removed from your premises.

[Reference.]

Because NCR's response was essentially correct, CSI was unable to revoke their acceptance. Thus CSI cannot invoke the remedies of N.J.S.A. 12A:2–712 and 12A:2–713. *See* White and Summers, *Text on The Uniform Commercial Code* (1972) § 10–1, at 306. The appropriate remedy is N.J.S.A. 12A:2–714, the remedy for breach in regard to accepted goods.

5. The total amount of interest charges are included for two reasons. First, any purchaser using credit would have had to pay similar charges to receive the computer system. Secondly, if the interest charges were not included here, they would be proper as consequential damages. As stated in a similar computer case within the Third Circuit:

> [A]t the time of contracting (the defendant) had reason to know that plaintiff would borrow money to purchase this capital item, thereby establishing the interest charge as an item of consequential damage under § 2–715.

Carl Beasley Ford Inc. v. Burroughs Corp., 361 F.Supp. 325, 334 (E.D.Pa. 1973), *aff'd without opinion,* 493 F.2d 1400 (3d Cir. 1974). *See also, Diversified Environments v. Olivetti Corp.,* 461 F.Supp. 286, 292 (M.D.Pa. 1978). The holding in *Carl Beasley Ford, supra* has even greater weight when applied to the facts herein. When NCR refused to extend credit to CSI, plaintiff was forced to seek the lease arrangement.

Where circumstances cause an exclusive or limited remedy to fail of its essential purpose, remedy may be had as provided in this Act.

Uniform Commercial Code Comment 1 following N.J.S.A. 12A:2–719 states:

[I]t is of the very essence of a sales contract that at least minimum adequate remedies be available. If the parties intend to conclude a contract for sale within this Article they must accept the legal consequences that there must be at least a fair quantum of remedy for breach of the obligations or duties outlined in the contract. Thus any clause purporting to modify or limit the remedial provisions of this Article in an unconscionable manner is subject to deletion and in that event the remedies made available by this Article are applicable as if the stricken clause had never existed. Similarly, *under subsection (2), where an apparently fair and reasonable clause because of circumstances fails in its purpose or operates to deprive either party of the substantial value of the bargain, it must give way to the general remedy provision in this Article.* (emphasis supplied)

This reasoning has been adopted by several courts. In *Beal v. General Motors,* 354 F.Supp. 423 (D.Del.1973) a motion to strike allegations of consequential damages was denied, despite an apparently valid exclusive remedy clause. There the district court noted that:

[t]he purpose of an exclusive remedy of replacement or repair of defective parts, whose presence constitute a breach of an express warranty, is to give the seller an opportunity to make the goods conforming while limiting the risks to which he is subject by excluding direct and consequential damages that might otherwise arise. From the point of view of the buyer *the purpose of the exclusive remedy is to give him goods that conform to the contract within a reasonable time after a defective part is discovered. When the warrantor fails to correct the defect as promised within a reasonable time he is liable for a breach of that warranty. * * * The limited, exclusive remedy fails of its purpose and is thus voided under § 2–719(2), whenever the warrantor fails to correct the defect within a reasonable period.* (citations omitted) (emphasis added)

354 F.Supp. at 426. [Citations.]

Because NCR never furnished four of the six promised functions, their attempted lim-

itation of remedy failed of its essential purpose. CSI was thereby deprived of the substantial value of its bargain. For these reasons NCR is liable for consequential and incidental damages as provided for in N.J.S.A. 12A:2–714(3) and defined in N.J.S.A. 12A:2–715.

Though not arising out of the contract, a major limitation does exist on plaintiff's claim for consequential damages. When CSI refused to accept Mr. Moody's offer of September 2, 1976, CSI's claim for consequential damages terminated. Initially CSI asked that the computer system be removed by letter of June 7, 1976. [Reference.] When NCR asked for additional time to make all functions operable, CSI granted them more time. Here CSI was acting in a commercially reasonable manner. During the summer of 1976 NCR was making a renewed effort. New people had been brought in. CSI's own memo of events [reference] shows that by September 1, 1976 the State Income Tax program was installed and operational. When Mr. Moody offered to continue the installation CSI should have accepted.

N.J.S.A. 12A:2–715(2)(a) limits the recovery of consequential damages to situations where they "could not reasonably be prevented by cover[6] or *otherwise.*" (emphasis supplied) CSI was not in a position to "cover" by spending large sums of money for a replacement computer system. Until September 2, 1976 they were relying upon NCR to supply it. However, they could have prevented many of their consequential damages "otherwise", that is by continuing their cooperation. In *Fablok Mills Inc. v. Cocker Machine & Foundry Corp.,* 120 N.J.Super. 350, 294 A.2d 62 *rev'd on other grounds,* 125 N.J.Super. 251, 310 A.2d 491 (App.Div.1973) it was stated that:

In certain situations continued use of [the] goods by the buyer may be the most appropriate means of achieving mitigation, i. e., where the buyer is unable to purchase a suitable substitute for the goods.

125 N.J.Super. at 257–258, 310 A.2d at 494. This was precisely the situation CSI faced. Because they could not reasonably be expected to replace the system in September of 1976, they should have continued their co-

---

6. "Cover" is the term used in the Uniform Commercial Code to describe the purchase of replacement goods by a

buyer where the original goods received do not conform to the contract.

operation by accepting the installation of the other programs.[7]

A time limitation on damages was imposed in *Clements Auto Company v. Service Bureau Corp.*, 444 F.2d 169 (8th Cir. 1971). *Clements* involved a similar factual situation where the district court concluded that fraudulent misrepresentations were made and awarded substantial damages. On appeal the United States Court of Appeals for the Eighth Circuit limited the damages awarded to the time period in which the plaintiff was justified in relying upon the misrepresentations. That is not the situation at bar, however, *Clements* has been relied upon by CSI in support of their various damage claims, while CSI has ignored the time limitation. *Clements* demonstrates that commercially reasonable standards can create a limited time period during which the damages are recoverable. For purposes of this case, all recoverable elements of consequential and incidental damages will be determined from March 1975 (when the system was promised) until September 1976 (when CSI ceased their cooperation), a total of eighteen months when NCR was liable for breach of warranties.

Incidental and consequential damages are defined as follows:

> (1) Incidental damages resulting from the seller's breach include expenses reasonably incurred in inspection, receipt, transportation and *care and custody of goods* rightfully rejected, any commercially reasonable charges, expenses or commissions in connection with effecting cover and *any other reasonable expense incident to the delay or other breach.*
>
> (2) Consequential damages resulting from the seller's breach include:
>
> (a) *any* loss resulting from general or particular requirements and needs of which the seller at the time of contracting had reason to know. * * *

(emphasis supplied) N.J.S.A. 12A:2–715(1) and (2).

[Footnote.]

The plaintiff has offered exhibits and testimony to substantiate their claim for these damages. The first loss to be considered is what plaintiff calls increased labor cost for accounting, inventory, sales, and executive salaries. These costs largely occurred after September 1976 and are disallowed with an important exception. Having found NCR expressly warranted that CSI would save labor costs by implementation of the 399/656 Disc, and that warranty having been breached, it is necessary to compensate plaintiff for the consequential costs.

It was estimated that by implementation of the NCR computer system, CSI would save the cost of two employees whose services would no longer have been needed. NCR knew this was the major reason CSI entered the transaction. The United States Supreme Court has determined that:

> Damages are not rendered uncertain because they cannot be calculated with absolute exactness. It is sufficient if a reasonable basis of computation is afforded, although the result be only approximate. * * *

Eastman Kodak Co. v. Southern Photo Materials Co., 273 U.S. 359, 379, 47 S.Ct. 400, 405, 71 L.Ed. 684 (1926). From the proofs it appears the cost for each employee of this type was $15,000 annually. Therefore plaintiff is entitled to the cost (for eighteen months) for each of the employees receiving $15,000 per year, a total of $45,000.

Plaintiff also seeks damages for executive salaries for the time devoted to working with NCR. These are reasonable with the exception of the time spent by Mr. Chatlos. As Chief Executive Officer he assumed the risk of all corporate problems and is not entitled to reimbursement of compensation by NCR. The expenses for the Plant Operations Manager (12% of salary for twenty-six weeks or $2620.00) and the Chief Bookkeeper (30% of salary for the eighteen month period or $5,107.20) are reasonable. Plaintiff is therefore awarded $7,727.20. *See, Clements Auto Company v. Services Bureau Corp., supra.*

Plaintiff also seeks losses in profits for excesses and deficiencies in inventory. These were a consequence of the failure of the inventory

---

7. The Uniform Commercial Code Comment 2 following N.J.S.A. 12A:2–715(2)(a) further describes the purpose of subparagraph 2 in that it:

carries forward * * * prior uniform statutory provisions as to consequential damages [for] breach of

warranty, but *modifies the rule by requiring first that the buyer attempt to minimize his damages in good faith, either by cover or otherwise.* (emphasis supplied) deletion and order entry functions to operate. This was another major reason CSI entered into the transaction. Plaintiff presented evidence [reference] and testimony to show lost profits because of excess inventory in 1975 totalling $5,080.95. Similarly for 1976 CSI showed a deficiency in inventory causing a profit loss of $3,325.24. When adjusted to include only the eighteen-month period these figures are reduced to $4,234.13 for 1975 and $2,216.83 for 1976, a total of $6,450.96. CSI paid $1,750.00 for a manual inventory system which could not perform the functions as well as a computer system. Plaintiff is entitled to the $1,750.00 in addition to $6,450.96 for profit losses.

CSI will receive the cost of various supplies purchased in an attempt to make the computer function. Evidence disclosed this amount to be $1,433.00. Moreover, plaintiff is entitled to the cost of the space occupied by the machine. Testimony revealed a formula for the annual rental; the cost per square foot multiplied by the measured size of the computer. After adjusting the figure to include only the eighteen months, plaintiff is entitled to $1,197.00.

Plaintiff's requests for the value of the space occupied by Mr. Hicks, cost of the powerline, and for maintenance of the area where the computer was kept, are denied. Mr. Hicks was trying to make it operate, the powerline was needed for the payroll function to be performed, and maintenance would have been done whether the machine worked or not.

FRAUDULENT MISREPRESENTATION

Plaintiff alleged and attempted to prove at trial that NCR made fraudulent misrepresentations in this transaction.[9] It is necessary to consult the common law of New Jersey for consideration of this claim. In *Thomas v. Dur-*

alite Company, 386 F.Supp. 698 (D.N.J.1974), *aff'd in part, rev'd in part on other grounds and vacated,* 524 F.2d 577 (3d Cir. 1974) it was stated that:

> The term fraud is used in New Jersey to designate what is really an action for deceit. *Anderson v. Modica,* 4 N.J. 383, 389, 73 A.2d 49 (1950). There are five necessary elements to maintain an action for deceit in New Jersey:
> (1) a representation by defendant to the plaintiff with intent that the latter party rely upon it;
> (2) knowledge on the part of the defendant that the representation is in fact false;
> (3) belief by the plaintiff that representation is true;
> (4) reliance on such representation; and
> (5) the taking of action and consequent injury.

386 F.Supp. at 718.

Plaintiff attempted to prove that NCR knew the representations they made were false. It was plaintiff's position that NCR knew CSI was an experimental site and wrongfully withheld this information. Plaintiff correctly asserts that under New Jersey law, an affirmative representation is not required to prove fraud. *Weintraub v. Krobatsch,* 64 N.J. 445, 317 A.2d 68 (1974). However, NCR admits CSI was a control site. No evidence was presented to show plaintiff was unaware of this fact.

Plaintiff's own expert testified that 40% of all computer installations fail. It is not unreasonable to view all such installations as somewhat of an experiment. When remembered that CSI itself was engaged in a highly technical business, clearly NCR's representations were not directed to an unsophisticated consumer. One issue at trial was the degree of development of other 399 disc systems at the time of this contract. The plaintiff failed to show the other systems were not operating.[10] Plaintiff did not prove NCR fraud-

---

9. *See generally, Triangle Underwriters Inc. v. Honeywell, Inc.,* 457 F.Supp. 765 (E.D.N.Y. 1978), *aff'd in part, rev'd in part,* 604 F.2d 737 (2d Cir. No. 79–7532, decided July 17, 1979) where fraud allegations were made in a similar factual situation. The district court dismissed the allegations of fraud as "simply restatements of the breach of contract claims." The Second Circuit partially reversed holding that the allegation of fraud in the inducement was extraneous to the contract, while the dismissal of the

other fraud claims was affirmed. *Triangle, supra,* however, involved extensive reliance on the substantive laws of New York.

10. Plaintiff's ex. 25 and ex. 45 list numerous 399 Disc Sites in various parts of the country. Even if similar problems were encountered, all of the listed dates for delivery are prior to March 1975.

ulently represented the state of affairs at the time.

NCR did represent the 399/656 Disc would work and essentially it did not. Plaintiff alleges that NCR knew it would not work and were simply seeking a competitive advantage by installation at CSI. Among the NCR intercompany documents that plaintiff successfully had admitted into evidence was a memo captioned "399 Disc Control Site Selection Guidelines." [Reference.] It contains statements relating to the competitive benefits NCR would enjoy with, "(a) *good* NCR disc installation in this area * * *" (emphasis supplied). This pertained to the CSI site and while it does show NCR was concerned about competitive aspects, it also shows that NCR fully intended the installation to be successful.

NCR made promises they hoped would be fulfilled in the future. However, under New Jersey case law:

> Statements as to future or contingent events, as to expectations and probabilities, or as to what will be or is intended to be done in the future, do not constitute misrepresentations even though they turn out to be false, at least where they are not made with intent to deceive, and where the parties have equal means of knowledge, [citations omitted] or the subject is equally open to the investigation of both, and an examination has not been fraudulently prevented.

Middlesex County Sewer Authority v. Borough of Middlesex, 74 N.J.Super. 591, 605, 181 A.2d 818, 826, aff'd 79 N.J.Super. 24, 190 A.2d 205 (App.Div.1962). Any intent to deceive by NCR is negated by the presence of various NCR employees at CSI throughout. During that time period both parties shared the same intent; to get the system "up and running" as soon as possible. In this way plaintiff would have been satisfied and defendant would have attained their goal of a "good" installation. Had NCR abandoned the project, plaintiff's allegation of fraud may have been sustained, however, after consideration of all testimony and evidence it is concluded that NCR's representations were overly optimistic, not fraudulent.

Because of alleged fraudulent misrepresentation and other theories of liability plaintiff seeks punitive damages. In New Jersey, punitive damages are awarded in the sound discretion of the trier of fact:

> upon a theory of punishment * * * [after taking] into consideration all of the circumstances surrounding the particular occurrence including the nature of the wrongdoing, the extent of the harm inflicted, the intent of the party committing the act, the wealth of the perpetrator, as well as any mitigating circumstances which may operate to reduce the amount of damages.

Leimgruber v. Claridge Associates Ltd., 73 N.J. 450, 456, 375 A.2d 652, 654–655 (1977). Moreover, as indicated by the language in *Leimgruber* above:

> Punitive or exemplary damages have traditionally been reserved for civil wrongs characterized as torts.
>
> * * *
>
> In the absence of exceptional circumstances dictated by the nature of the relationship between the parties or the duty imposed upon the wrongdoer, the concept of punitive damages has not been permitted in litigation involving breach of a commercial contract.

Sandler v. Lawn-A-Mat Chem. & Equip. Corp., 141 N.J.Super. 437, 448–449, 359 A.2d 805, 811 (App.Div.1976).

Since no tort liability has been imposed and in view of the fact that NCR had an employee or employees at CSI for the entire time, the Court fails to find evidence of wrongful intent. Furthermore, in the absence of the plaintiff having established any exceptional circumstances, no basis exists to justify an award of punitive damages.

In conclusion, judgment will be entered for the plaintiff awarding compensatory damages alone in the amount of $120,710.92, as outlined in this opinion and restated in the following chart.

COMPENSATORY DAMAGES

1. For Direct Breach of Warranties:

   a. Value of goods if they had been as warranted:

CSI indebtedness	$70,162.09	
Service Contract	5,621.22	
		$75,783.31

   b. Value of goods accepted:

Hardware	$ 6,000.00	
Payroll Program	12,630.55	
		−$18,630.55
	Sub Total	$57,152.76

2. Consequential Damages:

a.	employee losses	$45,000.00
b.	executive losses	7,727.20
c.	profit losses	6,450.96
d.	manual system cost	1,750.00
e.	supplies	1,433.00
f.	rental space	1,197.00
		$63,558.16

3. Punitive Damages: $ 0.00

Total Damages $120,710.92

Counsel for plaintiff shall submit an appropriate order within five (5) days.

CHATLOS SYSTEMS, INC. v. NATIONAL CASH REGISTER CO.

635 F.2d 1081

(United States Court of Appeals, Third Circuit, Decided Nov. 26, 1980, As Amended Dec. 5, 1980.)

WEIS, C. J.

In this diversity case governed by the Uniform Commercial Code, the district court assessed damages for breach of warranty after finding that the seller's failure to timely program a computer system caused a contractual remedy to fail of its essential purpose. Despite an express provision in the agreement prohibiting recovery of consequential damages, the court also made an award for such losses. Although we accept the determination on the failure of the contractual remedy, we do not agree that the disclaimer of consequential damages is ineffective as a result. We conclude that that clause must be evaluated on its own merits and, in this case, enforced. In addition, we are unable to accept certain trial court determinations on the factors used to compute the other items of damage, and we remand for recalculation.

I

Chatlos Systems, Inc. (Chatlos), filed suit in the New Jersey Superior Court against National Cash Register Corp. (NCR), alleging, *inter alia,* breach of warranty in connection with the sale of a computer system. The case was removed to the United States District Court for the District of New Jersey, and after a bench trial, judgment was entered in favor of the plaintiff for $120,710.92. [Footnote.]

Chatlos designs and manufactures cable pressurization equipment for the telecommunications industry. In the spring of 1974, the company decided to purchase a computer system and contacted several manufacturers, among them NCR. That firm suggested a magnetic ledger card system, but, after further inquiry by Chatlos, agreed to provide the 399/656 disc system, a computer utilizing more advanced technology, as the appropriate model for the customer's need.

This system was designed to provide six functions for Chatlos: (1) accounts receivable, (2) payroll, (3) order entry, (4) inventory deletion, (5) state income tax, (6) cash receipts. NCR represented to Chatlos that the system would solve inventory problems, result in direct savings of labor costs, and be programmed by capable NCR personnel to be "up and running" (in full operation) within six months.

On July 24, 1974 Chatlos signed a system service agreement with NCR as part of the transaction, and the computer hardware was delivered the following December. Because NCR would not extend credit, Chatlos made a leasing arrangement with Midlantic National Bank, agreeing to pay $70,162.09 on a monthly installment basis. This is a common practice in the trade; the computer company sells the system to a bank, which in turn leases it to the customer.

Chatlos understood that the system would be operational about three months after delivery and therefore expected it to be "up and running" by March 1975. An NCR employee began programming in January 1975, but by March, only one of the functions, payroll, was in operation. Efforts to install the inventory deletion and order entry programs were unsuccessful. These functions used multiple records per sector technology the storing of several items of information in one section of a disc. But the NCR programmer was unable to delete any information within the same section without erasing it all. Since Chatlos had purchased the computer to record its extensive parts inventory, the inability to solve the multiple records sector problem posed a major difficulty—the withdrawal of one part in a unit erroneously deleted the entire unit.

One year later the problem persisted. NCR analysts attempted a demonstration of the order entry and accounts receivable functions in March 1976, but significant problems surfaced with both. In June 1976 Chatlos asked that the lease be cancelled and the computer removed, but, at NCR's request, agreed to allow additional time to make the system operational. On August 31, 1976 Chatlos experienced problems with the payroll function, the only operation the computer had been performing properly.

On September 1, 1976 the state income tax program was installed. The next day an NCR representative arrived at the Chatlos plant to install the order entry program. Chatlos refused to allow the work to proceed and again asked NCR to terminate the lease and remove the computer. NCR refused, stating that it had no ownership rights in the system, having been paid by the bank.

The district judge, applying New Jersey law, reasoned that despite the service aspects and lease arrangement, the transaction was for the sale of goods within the meaning of Article 2 of the Uniform Commercial Code. N.J.Stat.Ann. §§ 12A:2-101 to 12A:2-725 (West 1962 & Cum. Supp. 1980). He determined that certain express warranties had been made in various writings executed by the parties.

The court found that NCR had warranted its product for "12 months after delivery against defects in material, workmanship and operational failure from ordinary use," and further that "services [would be] performed in a skillful and workmanlike manner." In addition, there was an oral, express warranty, memorialized in a purchase order prepared by the Midlantic Bank, providing that "since the goods * * * are purchased by us expressly for the use of [Chatlos], [NCR] further warrants that the goods are in good working order, fit for the use [Chatlos] intends them, and fulfill all representations made by [NCR] to [Chatlos]." 479 F.Supp. at 743. The purchase order also provided that Chatlos was "to obtain all the benefits of all warranties." Finally, the court held that since Chatlos's reliance upon the skill and judgment of NCR was known to it, an implied warranty of fitness for Chatlos's particular purposes was created as well. *Id.;* see N.J.Stat.Ann. § 12A:2-315 (West 1962).

Finding that these warranties had been breached, the court looked to U.C.C. § 2-714(2). That section measures damages for breach of warranty as the difference between the value of what was accepted and what was warranted. N.J.Stat.Ann. § 12A:2-714(2), which in this case was determined to be $57,152.76. The court awarded additional damages of $63,558.16 for items such as employee salaries and lost profits, since it concluded that NCR's disclaimer of consequential damages was ineffective.

No evidence of wrongful intent on the part of NCR was found, nor did the plaintiff prove fraudulent misrepresentation. Consequently, a claim for punitive damages was denied.

II

Both parties have appealed, and while they concede the applicability of the U.C.C., each contests liability and damage determinations. We have examined the contentions of the parties with respect to the court's conclusions on warranties, their breach, lack of fraud, and punitive damages. The district court's findings and reasoning on these aspects of the case are not erroneous and will be affirmed.

III

We are unable to concur, however, with the trial court's computation of damages. Accepting the finding that NCR breached its warranties, our next step is to examine the contract and determine whether the parties limited otherwise applicable remedies. U.C.C. § 2-719(1) provides that the parties may so agree. N.J.Stat.Ann. § 12A:2-719(1) (West 1962).

The contract states that services would be performed in a skillful and professional manner, and further provides that NCR's obligation was limited to correcting any "error in any program or routine as appears within 60 days after such has been furnished." Another part of the contract reads: "In no event shall NCR be liable for special or consequential damages from any cause whatsoever." We will discuss these two restrictions separately.

Before a limitation on a party's remedies may be enforced, it must be established that the contract contains "an exclusive or limited remedy." *Id.* § 12A:2-719(1)(b). The agreement here does say that NCR's obligation is "limited." Although an argument might be made that this is not clearly expressed, we will assume *arguendo* that the contract satisfies this Code requirement.

An exclusive or limited remedy, however, must be viewed against the background of U.C.C. § 2-719(2), which provides, "Where circumstances cause an exclusive or limited remedy to fail of its essential purpose, remedy may be had as provided in this Act." N.J.Stat.Ann. § 12A:2-719(2) (West 1962).

This section requires analysis of the applicable remedy so as to determine its essential purpose and whether it has failed of that purpose. Several goals of the limited remedy of repair may be envisioned, but its primary objective is to give the seller an opportunity to make the goods conform while limiting exposure to risk by excluding liability for damages that might otherwise be due. [Citation.] Viewed from the buyer's standpoint, the repair remedy's aim is to provide goods that conform to the contract for sale and do so at an appropriate time. A delay in supplying the remedy can just as effectively deny the purchaser the product he expected as can the total inability to repair. In both instances the buyer loses the substantial benefit of his purchase.

To be effective the repair remedy must be provided within a reasonable time after discovery of the defect. *Id.* [Citation.] [Footnote.] It is not necessary to show negligence or bad faith on the part of the seller. [Citation.] The detriment to the buyer is the same whether the seller diligently but unsuccessfully attempts to honor his promise or acts negligently or in bad faith.

When presented with the question whether an exclusive repair remedy fails of its essential purpose, courts generally have concluded that so long as the buyer has the use of substantially defect-free goods, the limited remedy should be given effect. But when the seller is either unwilling or unable to conform the goods to the contract, the remedy does not suffice. * * *

In this case we consider a product programmed specifically to meet the customer's individual needs. Time was of substantial importance. Chatlos realized that the increasing scale of its operations required computerization and undertook the investment in 1974 because added efficiency was needed at that time. NCR represented to Chatlos that a six-

function system would be up and running by March 1975. Yet, more than a year later, only one of the functions was in operation, and by September 1976, less than half of the desired capability of the system was available to Chatlos.

NCR repeatedly attempted to correct the deficiencies in the system, but nevertheless still had not provided the product warranted a year and a half after Chatlos had reasonably expected a fully operational computer. In these circumstances, the delay made the correction remedy ineffective, and it therefore failed of its essential purpose. Consequently, the contractual limitation was unenforceable and did not preclude recovery of damages for the breach of warranty.

This conclusion, however, does not dispose of the contractual clause excluding consquential damages. U.C.C. § 2-719(2) states that when an exclusive or limited remedy fails of its purpose, remedy may be had as provided in the Act. Recognizing that consequential damages may be a subject of agreement between the parties, § 2-719(3) provides:

> Consequential damages may be limited or excluded unless the limitation or exclusion is unconscionable. Limitation of consequential damages for injury to the person in the case of consumer goods is prima facie unconscionable but limitation of damages where the loss is commercial is not.

N.J.Stat.Ann. § 12A:2-719(3) (West 1962).

Several cases have held that when a limited remedy fails of its purpose, an exclusion of consequential damages also falls [sic], but approximately the same number of decisions have treated that preclusion as a separate matter. New Jersey has not taken a position on this question, so in this diversity case we must predict which view the New Jersey Supreme Court would adopt if the question were presented to it.

It appears to us that the better reasoned approach [footnote] is to treat the consequential damage disclaimer as an independent provision, valid unless unconscionable. This poses no logical difficulties. A contract may well contain no limitation on breach of warranty damages but specifically exclude consequential damages. Conversely, it is quite conceivable that some limitation might be placed on a breach of warranty award, but consequential damages would expressly be permitted.

The limited remedy of repair of a consequential damages exclusion are two discrete ways of attempting to limit recovery for breach of warranty. *See id.* § 12A:2-719(1)(a). [Citation.] The Code, moreover, tests each by a different standard. The former survives unless it fails of its essential purpose, while the latter is valid unless it is unconscionable.[4] We therefore see no reason to hold, as a general proposition, that the failure of the limited remedy provided in the contract, without more, invalidates a wholly distinct term in the agreement excluding consequential damages. The two are not mutually exclusive.

Whether the preclusion of consequential damages should be effective in this case depends upon the circumstances involved. The repair remedy's failure of essential purpose, while a discrete question, is not completely irrelevant to the issue of the conscionability of enforcing the consequential damages exclusion. The latter term is "merely an allocation of unknown or undeterminable risks." U.C.C. § 2-719, Official Comment 3, N.J.Stat.Ann. § 12A:2-719, at 537 (West 1962). Recognizing this, the question here narrows to the unconscionability of the buyer retaining the risk of consequential damages upon the failure of the essential purpose of the exclusive repair remedy.

One fact in this case that becomes significant under the Code is that the claim is not for personal injury but for property damage. Limitations on damages for personal injuries are not favored, but no such prejudice applies to property losses. It is also important that the claim is for commercial loss and the adversaries are substantial business concerns. We find no great disparity in the parties' bargaining power or sophistication. Apparently, Chatlos, a manufacturer of complex electronic equipment, had some appreciation of the prob-

lems that might be encountered with a computer system. Nor is there a "surprise" element present here. [Footnote.] The limitation was clearly expressed in a short, easily understandable sales contract. This is not an instance of an ordinary consumer being misled by a disclaimer hidden in a "linguistic maze." [Citation.]

Thus, at the time the contract was signed there was no reason to conclude that the parties could not competently agree upon the allocation of risk involved in the installation of the computer system.

From the perspective of the later events, it appears that the type of damage claimed here came within the realm of expectable losses. Some disruption of normal business routines, expenditure of employee time, and impairment of efficiency cannot be considered highly unusual or unforeseeable in a faulty computer installation. Moreover, although not determinative, it is worth mentioning that even though unsuccessful in correcting the problems within an appropriate time, NCR continued in its efforts. Indeed, on the date of termination NCR was still actively working on the system at the Chatlos plant. In fact, the trial court thought that Chatlos should have cooperated further by accepting the installation of the programs.[6] This is not a case where the seller acted unreasonably or in bad faith.

In short, there is nothing in the formation of the contract or the circumstances resulting in failure of performance that makes it unconscionable to enforce the parties' allocation of risk. We conclude, therefore, that the provision of the agreement excluding consequential damages should be enforced, and the district court erred in making an award for such losses.

IV

As we said earlier, since there was a breach of warranty, damages were appropriate on that

---

4. Official Comment 1 to U.C.C. § 2-719 states that any clause purporting to limit the remedial provisions in an unconscionable manner is subject to deletion and in that event the remedies made available by the article are applicable as if the stricken clause had never existed.
[Citations.]

6. The court limited Chatlos's award for consequential damages to the period before September 2, 1976, con-

cluding that the buyer had an obligation to minimize his damages in good faith, *see* New Jersey Study Comment 2, N.J.Stat.Ann. § 12A:2-715, at 519-20 (West 1962), and had additional time been granted, the installation might have been completed. Apparently the trial court thought that further tolerance by Chatlos would have been the least expensive variant of cover.

score. The district judge looked to U.C.C. § 2-714(2), which sets out the measure of damages for breach when the claim is for accepted goods,[7] as the difference "between the value of the goods accepted and the value they would have had if they had been as warranted, unless special circumstances show proximate damages of a different amount." N.J.Stat.Ann. § 12A:2-714(2) (West 1962). In applying this provision, the judge first determined the value of the goods had they met the warranty. He discarded "market value" because that term was "conspicuously lacking" from § 2-714, and began with $70,162.09, the amount Chatlos was required to pay the bank. That sum included the amount the defendant received, sales tax, and interest. The court added the $5,621.22 Chatlos paid for the service contract because it was an inseparable element of the entire transaction.

The plaintiff contends that the correct starting point is market value, an amount its expert testified was substantially in excess of the contract price. To use contract price in this case, argues Chatlos, deprives it of the benefit of its bargain.

It is true that § 2-714 does not use the term market value and thus introduces a degree of flexibility into the damage computation. Although fair market value is not referred to in § 2-714, that standard has been employed by some courts [citation] and considered by textwriters as "the most appropriate measure of the value of the goods as guaranteed." J. White & R. Summers, Uniform Commercial Code § 102, at 380 (2d ed. 1980). If the value of the goods rises between the time that the contract is executed and the time of acceptance, the buyer should not lose the advantage of a favorable contract price because of the seller's breach of warranty. Conversely, if the value drops, the seller is entitled to the resulting lower computation.

It may be assumed that in many cases fair market value and contract price are the same, and therefore, if a party wishes to show a difference between the two he should produce evidence to that effect. But here as we read his opinion, the district judge felt compelled

to disregard all considerations of market value. We hold, however, that the court should consider that factor as the starting point.

The court included in the value of the goods as warranted the interest paid to the bank on the purchase price. In the absence of special circumstances, interest is not a proper factor to be considered. Interest represents the cost of the money borrowed to buy the goods because capital was not available to make a cash purchase. If, however, the buyer is awarded lump sum damages, he would be able to make a replacement purchase without borrowing and incurring interest expenses. To the extent, therefore, that the recovery included interest on the original purchase, it would constitute a windfall. With today's rapidly changing interest structures, however, it may be that the buyer can demonstrate some actual loss. We have difficulty envisioning such a scenario, but leave the plaintiff free to present the matter to the district court on remand. [Citation.]

In calculating the other element of the formula, the value of the goods as accepted, $12,630.55 was added to the value of the hardware to compensate for the benefit Chatlos received from using the system's payroll function. The court arrived at this figure by dividing the contract price of the computer system by six, the number of functions to have been provided. Although the benefit Chatlos received should be taken into account, the parties agree that there is no evidence in the record to show that each function had the same value. That issue, too, may be addressed on remand.

The plaintiff's final contention is that it is entitled to prejudgment interest. Because the district judge's opinion does not reveal whether he exercised his discretion in this matter, we intimate no view on the merits of the claim and expect that the court will rule on the issue on remand.

Accordingly, the judgment of the district court will be affirmed insofar as it imposes liability on the defendant to pay damages to the plaintiff. The case will be remanded for a redetermination of the award in accordance with this opinion.

---

7. The district court accepted NCR's position that in September 1976 it no longer had any ownership interest and therefore could not retake the equipment. Thus, Chatlos was unable to revoke its acceptance and could not invoke U.C.C. §§ 2-712 or 2-713.

CHATLOS SYSTEMS, INC.
v. NATIONAL CASH
REGISTER CO.

670 F.2d 1304

*(United States Court of Appeals, Third
Circuit, Decided Jan. 15, 1982, Rehearing
Denied Feb. 11, 1982, Certiorari Dismissed
June 9, 1982, See 102 S.Ct. 2918.)*

PER CURIAM.

This appeal from a district court's award of damages for breach of warranty in a diversity case tried under New Jersey law presents two questions: whether the district court's computation of damages under N.J.Stat.Ann. § 12A:2-714(2) was clearly erroneous, and whether the district court abused its discretion in supplementing the damage award with pre-judgment interest. We answer both questions in the negative and, therefore, we will affirm.

Plaintiff-appellee Chatlos Systems, Inc., initiated this action in the Superior Court of New Jersey, alleging, *inter alia,* breach of warranty regarding an NCR 399/656 computer system it had acquired from defendant National Cash Register Corp. The case was removed under 28 U.S.C. § 1441(a) to the United States District Court for the District of New Jersey. Following a nonjury trial, the district court determined that defendant was liable for breach of warranty and awarded $57,152.76 damages for breach of warranty and consequential damages in the amount of $63,558.16. *Chatlos Systems, Inc. v. National Cash Register Corp.,* 479 F.Supp. 738 (D.N.J.1979), *aff'd in part, remanded in part,* 635 F.2d 1081 (3d Cir. 1980). Defendant appealed and this court affirmed the district court's findings of liability, set aside the award of consequential damages, and remanded for a recalculation of damages for breach of warranty. *Chatlos Systems, Inc. v. National Cash Register Corp.,* 635 F.2d 1081 (3d Cir. 1980). On remand, applying the "benefit of the bargain" formula of N.J.Stat.Ann. § 12A:2-714(2) (Uniform Commercial Code § 2-714(2)) [footnote], the district court determined the damages to be $201,826.50,[2] to which it added an award of pre-judgment interest. Defendant now appeals from these damage determinations,

contending that the district court erred in failing to recognize the $46,020 contract price of the delivered NCR computer system as the fair market value of the goods as warranted, and that the award of damages is without support in the evidence presented. Appellant also contests the award of pre-judgment interest.

Waiving the opportunity to submit additional evidence as to value on the remand which we directed, appellant chose to rely on the record of the original trial and submitted no expert testimony on the market value of a computer which would have performed the functions NCR had warranted. Notwithstanding our previous holding that contract price was not necessarily the same as market value, 635 F.2d at 1088, appellant faults the district judge for rejecting its contention that the contract price for the NCR 399/656 was the only competent record evidence of the value of the system as warranted. The district court relied instead on the testimony of plaintiff-appellee's expert, Dick Brandon, who, without estimating the value of an NCR model 399/656, presented his estimate of the value of a computer system that would perform all of the functions that the NCR 399/656 had been warranted to perform. Brandon did not limit his estimate to equipment of any one manufacturer; he testified regarding manufacturers who could have made systems that would perform the functions that appellant had warranted the NCR 399/656 could perform. He acknowledged that the systems about which he testified were not in the same price range as the NCR 399/656. Appellant likens this testimony to substituting a Rolls Royce for a Ford, and concludes that the district court's recomputed damage award was therefore clearly contrary to the evidence of fair market value— which in NCR's view is the contract price itself.

Appellee did not order, nor was it promised, merely a specific NCR computer model, but an NCR computer system with specified capabilities. The correct measure of damages, under N.J.Stat.Ann. § 12A:2-714(2), is the difference between the fair market value of the goods accepted and the value they would have had if they had been as warranted. Award

---

2. The district court found the fair market value of the system as warranted to be $207,826.50; from this it sub-

tracted its determination of the value of the goods delivered, $6,000.

of that sum is not confined to instances where there has been an increase in value between date of ordering and date of delivery. It may also include the benefit of a contract price which, for whatever reason quoted, was particularly favorable for the customer. Evidence of the contract price may be relevant to the issue of fair market value, but it is not controlling. [Citation.] Appellant limited its fair market value analysis to the contract price of the computer model it actually delivered.[3] Appellee developed evidence of the worth of a computer with the capabilities promised by NCR, and the trial court properly credited the evidence.[4]

Appellee was aided, moreover, by the testimony of Frank Hicks, NCR's programmer, who said that he told his company's officials that the "current software was not sufficient in order to deliver the program that the customer [Chatlos] required. They would have to be rewritten or a different system would have to be given to the customer." Appendix to Brief for Appellee at 2.68. Hicks recommended that Chatlos be given an NCR 8200 but was told, "that will not be done." *Id.* at 2.69. Gerald Greenstein, another NCR witness, admitted that the 8200 series was two levels above the 399 in sophistication and price. *Id.* at 14.30. This testimony supported Brandon's statement that the price of the hardware needed to perform Chatlos' requirements would be in the $100,000 to $150,000 range.

Essentially, then, the trial judge was confronted with the conflicting value estimates submitted by the parties. Chatlos' expert's estimates were corroborated to some extent by NCR's supporters. NCR, on the other hand, chose to rely on contract price. Credibility determinations had to be made by the district judge. Although we might have come to a different conclusion on the value of the equipment as warranted had we been sitting as trial judges, we are not free to make our own credibility and factual findings. We may reverse the district court only if its factual determinations were clearly erroneous. *Krasnov v. Dinan*, 465 F.2d 1298 (3d Cir. 1972.)[5]

Upon reviewing the evidence of record, therefore, we conclude that the computation of damages for breach of warranty was not clearly erroneous. We hold also that the district court acted within its discretion in awarding pre-judgment interest, *Chatlos Systems, Inc. v. National Cash Register Corp.*, 635 F.2d at 1088.

The judgment of the district court will be affirmed.

ROSENN, C. J., dissenting.

The primary question in this appeal involves the application of Article 2 of the Uniform Commercial Code as adopted by New Jersey in N.J.S.A. 12A:2-101 et seq. (1962) to the measure of damages for breach of warranty in the sale of a computer system. I respectfully dissent because I believe there is no probative evidence to support the district court's award of damages for the breach of warranty in a sum amounting to almost five times the purchase price of the goods. The measure of damages also has been misapplied and this could have a significant effect in the

---

3. At oral argument, counsel for appellant responded to questions from the bench, as follows:
> *Judge Rosenn:* Your position also is that you agree, number one, that the fair market value is the measure of damages here.
> *Counsel for Appellant:* Yes, sir.
> *Judge Rosenn:* The fair market value you say, in the absence of other evidence to the contrary that is relevant, is the contract price. That is the evidence of fair market value.
> *Counsel:* That's right.
> *Judge Rosenn:* Now seeing that had the expert or had the plaintiff been able to establish testimony that there were other machines on the market that were similar to your machine—
> *Counsel:* Yes.
> *Judge Rosenn:* That the fair market value of those was $50,000, that would have been relevant evidence but it had to be the same machine—same type machine.

> *Counsel:* Well, I would say that the measure of damages as indicated by the statute requires the same machine—"the goods"—in an operable position.
4. We find the following analogy, rather than the Rolls Royce-Ford analogy submitted by appellant, to be on point:
> *Judge Weis:* If you start thinking about a piece of equipment that is warranted to lift a thousand pounds and it will only lift 500 pounds, then the cost of something that will lift a thousand pounds gives you more of an idea and that may be—
> *Counsel for Appellee:* That may be a better analogy, yes.
> *Judge Weis:* Yes.
5. The dissent essentially is based on disagreement with the estimates provided by Chatlos' expert, Brandon. The record reveals that he was well qualified; the weight to be given his testimony is the responsibility of the fact-finder, not an appellate court.

marketplace, especially for the unique and burgeoning computer industry.[1]

In July 1974, National Cash Register Corporation (NCR) sold Chatlos Systems, Inc. (Chatlos), a NCR 399/656 disc computer system (NCR 399) for $46,020 (exclusive of 5 percent sales tax of $1,987.50). The price and system included:

The computer (hardware)..........$40,165.00
Software (consisting of 6 computer
   programs)[2] 5,855.00
                              —————
                         $46,020.00

NCR delivered the disc computer to Chatlos in December 1974 and in March 1975 the payroll program became operational. By March of the following year, however, NCR was still unsuccessful in installing an operational order entry program and inventory deletion program. Moreover, on August 31, 1976, Chatlos experienced problems with the payroll program. On that same day and the day following NCR installed an operational state income tax program, but on September 1, 1976, Chatlos demanded termination of the lease[3] and removal of the computer.

When this case was previously before us, we upheld the district court's liability decision but remanded for a reassessment of damages, instructing the court that under the purchase contract and the law consequential damages could not be awarded. Consequential damages, therefore, are no longer an issue here.[4]

On remand, the district court, on the basis of the previous record made in the case, fixed the fair market value of the NCR 399 as warranted at the time of its acceptance in August 1975 at $207,826.50. It reached that figure by valuing the hardware at $131,250.00 and the

software at $76,575.50, for a total of $207,826.50. The court then determined that the present value of the computer hardware, which Chatlos retained, was $6,000. Putting no value on the accepted payroll program, the court deducted the $6,000 and arrived at an award of $201,826.50 plus pre-judgment interest at the rate of 8 percent per annum from August 1975.

Chatlos contends before this court, as it had before the district court on remand, that under its benefit of the bargain theory the fair market value of the goods as warranted was several times the purchase price of $46,020. As the purchaser, Chatlos had the burden of proving the extent of the loss. *Council Brothers, Inc. v. Ray Burner Co.*, 473 F.2d 400, 408 (5th Cir. 1973). In remanding to the district court for reassessment of the damages, we did not reject the contract price for the goods sold as the proper valuation of the computer as warranted. We merely corrected the district court's misconception that the language of the New Jersey statute precluded consideration of fair market value. We held that "value" in section 2-714(2) must mean fair market value at the time and place of acceptance.[5] We pointed out:

> *It may be assumed* that *in many cases* fair market value and contract price are the same, and therefore, if a party wishes to show a difference between the two he should produce evidence to that effect.

Chatlos Systems, Inc. v. National Cash Register Corp., 635 F.2d 1081, 1088 (3d Cir. 1980) (emphasis added) *on remand*, No. 77-2548 (D.N.J., filed Mar. 12, 1981). Thus, the sole issue before us now is whether the district court erred in fixing the fair market value of

---

1. Plaintiff's expert, Brandon, testified that generally 40 percent of all computer installations result in failures. He further testified that successful installations of computer systems require not only the computer companies' attention but also the attention of the customers' top management.

2. The six basic computer programs were: (1) accounts receivable, (2) payroll, (3) order entry, (4) inventory deletion, (5) state income tax, and (6) cash receipts. The contract price also included installation.

3. Chatlos decided to lease the system rather than purchase it outright. To permit this arrangement, NCR sold the system to Mid Atlantic National Bank in July 1975 for $46,020, which leased the system to Chatlos. Chatlos made monthly payments to Mid Atlantic in amounts which

would have totaled $70,162.09 over the period of the lease.

4. Besides rejecting the district court's award of consequential damages, this court on the previous appeal disagreed with the district court's starting point of $70,162.22, the amount Chatlos obligated itself to pay the bank, for two reasons: (1) the price Chatlos paid the bank included the bank's finance charges which should have been excluded, and (2) the district court erred in refusing to consider Chatlos' evidence of fair market value, which is the starting point for determining damages under section 2-714(2).

5. August 1975 represents the acceptance date. It is the date the finance company paid NCR and leased the computer system to Chatlos.

the computer system as warranted at the time of the acceptance in August 1975 at $207,826.50.

II.

A.

I believe that the district court committed legal error. The majority conclude that the standard of review of the district court's determination of the fair market value of the goods for the purpose of awarding damages is whether the trial judge's determination of market value is clearly erroneous. I disagree. Had the court merely miscalculated the amount of damages, I might agree with the majority's standard, for then our concern would be with basic facts. Here, however, no evidence was introduced as to the market value of the specific goods purchased and accepted had the system conformed to the warranty. Thus, the matter before us is one of legal error, and our standard of review is plenary. But even under the standard applied by the majority, the district court should be reversed because its determination of market value is not supported by probative evidence.

There are a number of major flaws in the plaintiff's attempt to prove damages in excess of the contract price. I commence with an analysis of plaintiff's basic theory. Chatlos presented its case under a theory that although, as a sophisticated purchaser, it bargained for several months before arriving at a decision on the computer system it required and the price of $46,020, it is entitled, because of the breach of warranty, to damages predicated on a considerably more expensive system. Stated another way, even if it bargained for a cheap system, *i.e.*, one whose low cost reflects its inferior quality, because that system did not perform as bargained for, it is now entitled to damages measured by the value of a system which, although capable of performing the identical functions as the NCR 399, is of far superior quality and accordingly more expensive.

The statutory measure of damages for breach of warranty specifically provides that the measure is the difference at the time and place of acceptance between the value "of the goods accepted" and the "value they would have had if they had been as warranted." [6] The focus of the statute is upon "the goods accepted"—not other hypothetical goods which may perform equivalent functions. "Moreover, the value to be considered is the reasonable market value of the *goods delivered,* not the value of the goods to a particular purchaser or for a particular purpose." *KLPR-TV, Inc. v. Visual Electronics Corp.,* 465 F.2d 1382, 1387 (8th Cir. 1972) (emphasis added). The court, however, arrived at value on the basis of a hypothetical construction of a system as of December 1978 by the plaintiff's expert, Brandon. The court reached its value by working backward from Brandon's figures, adjusting for inflation.

In presenting its case Chatlos developed its expert testimony as though it were seeking "cover" damages—the cost for the replacement of the computer system under section 2-712 of the statute. First, "cover" damages are obviously inappropriate here because both the district court and this court in its earlier decision held that the measure of damages is governed by section 2-714(2).[7] Furthermore, Chatlos did not "cover" in this case and, although there was testimony that it would use an IBM Series 1 mini-computer to perform the NCR 399 functions, the president of Chatlos personally testified that the IBM "wasn't purchased with intent to replace the 399 system at the time of purchase." Second, Chatlos gave no evidence as to the cost of the IBM Series 1 computer system. However, under the applicable section of the statute, 2-714, the measure of damages is specifically confined to "the difference between the value of the *goods accepted* and the value they would have had if they had been as warranted" and does not include "the difference between the cost of *cover* and the contract price" as provided by section 2-712.

---

6. The measure of damages is not an issue. Since Chatlos accepted the computer system, the measure of damages is set out in N.J.S.A. 12A:2-714 "Buyer's Damages for Breach in Regard to Accepted Goods." The relevant subsection is:
    (2) The measure of damages for breach of warranty is the difference * * * between the value of the

goods accepted and the value they would have had if they had been as warranted, unless special circumstances show proximate damages of a different amount.
    Id.
7. "Cover" damages are not available for goods purchased except under the provisions of N.J.S.A. 12A:2-711 and 712 (1962).

Although NCR warranted performance, the failure of its equipment to perform, absent any evidence of the value of any NCR 399 system on which to base fair market value,[8] does not permit a market value based on systems wholly unrelated to the goods sold. Yet, instead of addressing the fair market value of the NCR 399 had it been as warranted, Brandon addressed the fair market value of another system that he concocted by drawing on elements from other major computer systems manufactured by companies such as IBM, Burroughs, and Honeywell, which he considered would perform "functions identical to those contracted for" by Chatlos. He conceded that the systems were "[p]erhaps not within the same range of dollars that the bargain was involved with" and he did not identify specific packages of software. Brandon had no difficulty in arriving at the fair market value of the inoperable NCR equipment but instead of fixing a value on the system had it been operable attempted to fashion a hypothetical system on which he placed a value. The district court, in turn, erroneously adopted that value as the fair market value for an operable NCR 399 system. NCR rightly contends that the "comparable" systems on which Brandon drew were substitute goods of greater technological power and capability and not acceptable in determining damages for breach of warranty under section 2-714. Furthermore, Brandon's hypothetical system did not exist and its valuation was largely speculation.

B.

A review of Brandon's testimony reveals its legal inadequacy for establishing the market value of the system Chatlos purchased from NCR. Brandon never testified to the fair market value which the NCR 399 system would have had had it met the warranty at the time of acceptance. He was not even asked the question. His testimony with respect to the programming or software[9] was developed along the following line:

Q: Mr. Brandon, based upon your knowledge and experience in the field, are you aware of any other vendors in the computer industry who would have been able to supply a system, that is, hardware and software, which would provide the functions that were contemplated by the arrangement between NCR and Chatlos Systems.

* * *

A: Yes, there are a number of other vendors who would have made or could have made comparable systems available whose functions would be identical to those desired by Chatlos or required by Chatlos.

* * *

Q: What, if you know, would have been the price of acquiring that similar system in September of 1976?

* * *

A: I made some estimates of cost of acquiring seven separate application components, the seven to which I have earlier testified. I made those estimates in December, 1978, at which time I estimated the cost to be approximately, in the aggregate, approximately $102,000.

His estimate of the cost of the hardware in 1976 was "in the range of $100,000 to $150,000."

Not only did Brandon not testify in terms of the value of the NCR 399, but he spoke vaguely of "a general estimate * * * as to what the cost might be of, let's say, developing a payroll or purchasing a payroll package today, and installing it at Chatlos." He explained that what he would do, without identifying specific packages, would be to obtain price lists "from the foremost organizations selling packages in our field, in that area," organizations such as Management Science of America in Atlanta, and take their prices for specific packages. When asked what packages he would use for this system, he replied, "I would shop around, frankly." Speculating, he testified, "I think that I would go to two or

---

8. There is evidence that the NCR 399 model had been installed at a number of customer sites prior to the Chatlos installation. *See* plaintiff's Exhibit No. 25.

9. By working backwards and factoring 15 to 20 percent for inflation, Brandon attempted to fix a value on the

software as of September 1976. But under the statute, the valuation date is the "time of acceptance" and it is undisputed that took place over a year earlier—August 1975. The court adjusted for inflation back to August 1975.

three alternatives in terms of obtaining packages."[10] When asked to address himself to the packages that he would provide for this system, he acknowledged that the programs he had in mind were only available "[for] certain types of machines." For example, he conceded that these programs would not be available for the Series 1 IBM mini-computer, "with the possible exception of payroll."

Thus, the shortcomings in Brandon's testimony defy common sense and the realities of the marketplace. First, ordinarily, the best evidence of fair market value is what a willing purchaser would pay in cash to a willing seller. [Citations.] In the instant case we have clearly "not * * * an unsophisticated consumer." *Chatlos Systems v. National Cash Register Corp.*, 479 F.Supp. 738, 748 (D.N.J.1979), *modified*, 635 F.2d 1081 (3rd Cir. 1980), *on remand*, No. 77–2548 (D.N.J., filed Mar. 12, 1981), who for a considerable period of time negotiated and bargained with an experienced designer and vendor of computer systems. The price they agreed upon for an operable system would ordinarily be the best evidence of its value. The testimony does not present us with the situation referred to in our previous decision, where "the value of the goods rises between the time that the contract is executed and the time of acceptance," in which event the buyer is entitled to the benefit of his bargain. *Chatlos, supra,* 635 F.2d at 1088. On the contrary, Chatlos here relies on an expert who has indulged in the widest kind of speculation. Based on this testimony, Chatlos asserts in effect that a multi-national sophisticated vendor of computer equipment, despite months of negotiation, incredibly agreed to sell an operable computer system for $46,020 when, in fact, it had a fair market value of $207,000.

Second, expert opinion may, of course, be utilized to prove market value but it must be reasonably grounded. Brandon did not testify to the fair market value "of the *goods* accepted" had they met the warranty. Instead, he testified about a hypothetical system that he mentally fashioned. He ignored the realistic cost advantage in purchasing a unified system as contrasted with the "cost of acquiring seven separate application components" from various vendors.

Third, in arriving at his figure of $102,000 for the software, Brandon improperly included the time and cost of training the customer's personnel associated with the installation of the system. In a deposition prior to trial, Brandon testified that his valuation of the software included the time necessary to train Chatlos' personnel in the use of the system. On direct examination at trial, he testified that the $102,000 value fixed for software and programming did *not* include the time and cost necessary to train Chatlos' personnel in the use of the system, indicating that the cost of training a customer and his personnel is "definitely" not included in the price of programming and software. When confronted with his prior inconsistent deposition, he conceded that in his estimate of $102,000 "we included the Chatlos time."

Fourth, the record contains testimony which appears undisputed that computer equipment falls into one of several tiers, depending upon the degree of sophistication. The more sophisticated equipment has the capability of performing the functions of the least sophisticated equipment, but the less sophisticated equipment cannot perform all of the functions of those in higher levels. The price of the more technologically advanced equipment is obviously greater.

---

10. The speculative nature of his estimate is revealed by his reply on cross-examination.

> *Q.* Now, your estimate of $103,000 was based on the use of what packages, payroll, accounts receivable, order entry, inventory control etcetera: what packages did you include in your estimate of $102,000?
> *A.* I assumed that we would be able to obtain through competitive bidding packages from vendors in the computer field to meet most of these requirements, if not all of those requirements, and that to the extent that we could not meet the Chatlos requirements they could be modified by a programmer to meet those requirements.
> *Q.* Do you know or did you make an estimate of the purchase price for the various programs that you have

> told us about, packages?
> *A.* I only made estimates, sir, because no decision as to machine is available, therefore, it is impossible to go out and shop for specific packages.
> *Q.* Does the cost of a package depend on the machine?
> *A.* In part.
> *Q.* You estimated a cost of $102,000 but you don't know how much the packages cost, is that right?
> *A.* Well, I did obtain some estimates of packages from, as I mentioned the foremost package sales organization in the country, just so that I would have a basis for making sure that my numbers were not unreasonable.

It is undisputed that in September 1976 there were vendors of computer equipment of the same general size as the NCR 399/656 with disc in the price range of $35,000 to $40,000 capable of providing the same programs as those required by Chatlos, including IBM, Phillips, and Burroughs. They were the very companies who competed for the sale of the computer in 1974 in the same price range. On the other hand, Chatlos' requirements could also be satisfied by computers available at "three levels higher in price and sophistication than the 399 disc." Each level higher would mean more sophistication, greater capabilities, and more memory. Greenstein, NCR's expert, testified without contradiction that equipment of Burroughs, IBM and other vendors in the price range of $100,000 to $150,000, capable of performing Chatlos' requirements, was not comparable to the 399 because it was three levels higher. Such equipment was more comparable to the NCR 8400 series.[11]

Fifth, when it came to the valuation of the hardware, Brandon did not offer an opinion as to the market value of the hypothetical system he was proposing. Instead, he offered a wide ranging estimate of $100,000 to $150,000 for a hypothetical computer that would meet Chatlos' programming requirements. The range in itself suggests the speculation in which he indulged.

III.

The purpose of the N.J.S.A. 12A:2–714 is to put the buyer in the same position he would have been in if there had been no breach. *See* Uniform Commercial Code 1–106(1). The remedies for a breach of warranty were intended to compensate the buyer for his loss; they were not intended to give the purchaser a windfall or treasure trove. The buyer may not receive more than it bargained for; it may not obtain the value of a superior computer system which it did not purchase even though such a system can perform all of the functions the inferior system was designed to serve. Thus, in *Meyers v. Antone*, 227 A.2d 56 (D.C.App.1967), the court held that where the buyers contracted for a properly functioning used oil heating system which proved defec-

tive, they were free to substitute a gas system (which they did), change over to forced air heating, or even experiment with a solar heating plant. "They could not, however, recover the cost of such systems. They contracted for a used oil system that would function properly, and can neither receive more than they bargained for nor be put in a better position than they would have been had the contract been fully performed. *Id.* at 59 (citations omitted).

This court, in directing consideration of fair market value as the starting point in deciding damages noted Chatlos' contention that exclusive use of contract price deprives the dissatisfied buyer of the "benefit of his bargain." We accepted the concept of "benefit of the bargain" and explicated our understanding of the concept as follows:

> If the value of the goods rises between the time the contract is executed and the time of acceptance, the buyer should not lose the advantage of a favorable contract price because of the seller's breach of warranty. Conversely, if the value drops, the seller is entitled to the resulting lower computation.

Chatlos, supra, 635 F.2d at 1088. Ironically, this example of benefit of the bargain is actually based on contract price. If on the date of acceptance the fair market value of the goods has risen or declined from the contract price, that variation must be taken into account in awarding damages. But here plaintiff's market value figures, accepted by the district court on remand, have no connection whatsoever with the contract price.

Although it may be that the "benefit of the bargain" concept is applicable to situations involving other than periodic fluctuations in market prices, the cases cited by *Chatlos* stand only for the premise that the proved market value of the goods in question must be accepted. * * *

Even if we were to accept plaintiff's theory that the value of other systems may be used to establish the value of the specific computer system purchased, the cases cited by Chatlos to support its theory are distinguishable. * * *

---

11. Greenstein testified that NCR had two higher levels of computer equipment between its 399/656 model and

the NCR 8400 series.

Because Brandon's testimony does not support Chatlos' grossly extravagant claim of the fair market value of the NCR 399 at the time of its acceptance, the only evidence of the market value at the time is the price negotiated by the parties for the NCR computer system as warranted.

> There are many cases in which the goods will be irreparable or not replaceable and therefore the costs of repair or replacement can not serve as a yardstick of the buyer's damages. * * * When fair market value cannot be easily determined * * * the purchase price may turn out to be strong evidence of the value of the goods as warranted.

J. White & R. Summers, Uniform Commercial Code § 10–2, at 380 (2d ed. 1980) (footnotes omitted).[Footnote.] [Citation.] In *Long v. Quality Mobile Home Brokers, Inc.*, 271 S.C. 482, 248 S.E.2d 311 (1978), the court applied section 2–714(2) of the U.C.C. to arrive at a measure of damages for breach of warranty. Noting that "value as used in that section meant "fair market value," it asserted that "the cash price paid for goods is prima facie the value of the goods as warranted." *Id.* 248 S.E.2d at 312. *White & Summers, supra,* at 382 also remind us that "the value of goods *as warranted* will seldom be in dispute, for the contract price will be a powerful measure of that end of the formula." (Emphasis added; footnote omitted.)

Thus, where there is no proof that market value of the goods differs from the contract price, the contract price will govern [citation], and in this case that amounts to $46,020. Chatlos has retained the system hardware and the district court fixed its present value in the open market at $6,000. The court properly deducted this sum from the damages awarded.

IV.

Chatlos purchased the NCR payroll program and acknowledged at trial that the program operated fully and satisfactorily beginning February or March 1975 until October 1978 when it discontinued its use. The district court assigned no value to it because there was no evidence of fair market value. However, the law is clear that without evidence of a value other than contract price, that price should be accepted as the fair market value of the payroll program. The parties agreed on a contract price of $1,000 and that sum should be deducted from the measure of damages.

V.

NCR complains that the award of prejudgment interest is impermissible under New Jersey law. On remand, the district court awarded prejudgment interest from August, 1975 but offered no explanation for so doing. Congress has not provided for prejudgment interest but has provided that interest on a money judgment recovered in a district court in a civil case shall be allowed and "shall be calculated from the date of the entry of the judgment, at the rate allowed by State law." 28 U.S.C.A. § 1961 (1959). *See also* Fed.R.App.P. 37.

In *Buono Sales, Inc. v. Chrysler Motors Corp.*, 449 F.2d 715 (3d Cir. 1971), the plaintiff also claimed that it was entitled to prejudgment interest under New Jersey law for a breach of contract. In writing for this court, Chief Judge Seitz stated:

> Under New Jersey law, a successful plaintiff in an action for breach of contract is not entitled to prejudgment interest as a matter of right where damages are unliquidated. Indeed, the rule appears to be that, unless consideration of justice and fair dealing clearly demand a different result, "interest should not be allowed where the damages are unliquidated and not capable of ascertainment by mere computation, or where a serious and substantial controversy exists as to the amount due under a contract." *Jardine Estates, Inc. v. Donna Brook Corp.*, 42 N.J.Super. 332, 341, 126 A.2d 372, 377 (App. Div.1956).

Id. at 723. This case too involves a breach of contract and unliquidated damages. In light of its history and the nature of the very appeal, there can be no doubt that a substantial controversy existed over liability and damages. The trial judge made no finding that considerations of justice and fair dealing demanded an award of prejudgment interest. On the contrary, the judge found that plaintiff had not proved fraud on NCR's part and found that it had acted fairly and in good faith with Chatlos during the entire course of their dealings. When we previously considered the issue of liability, we concluded "[n]o evidence of wrongful intent on the part of NCR was found, nor did the plaintiff prove fraudulent misrepresentation." *Chatlos supra,* 635 F.2d at 1084. We also stated:

> [I]t is worth mentioning that even though unsuccessful in correcting the problems within an appropriate time, NCR continued in its efforts. Indeed, on the date of termination NCR was still actively working on the system at the Chatlos plant. In fact, the trial court thought that Chatlos should have cooperated further by accepting the installation of the programs. This is not a case where the seller acted unreasonably or in bad faith.

Id. at 1087 (footnote omitted).

I have examined the cases cited by Chatlos in support of the award and find them inapposite. Thus, I conclude that under New Jersey law Chatlos is not entitled to prejudgment interest.

VI.

On this record, therefore, the damages to which plaintiff is entitled are $46,020 less $6,000, the fair market value at time of trial of the retained hardware, and less $1,000, the fair market value of the payroll program, or the net sum of $39,020.

Accordingly, I would reverse the judgment of the district court and direct it to enter judgment for the plaintiff in the sum of $39,020 with interest from the date of entry of the initial judgment at the rate allowed by state law.

SUR PETITION FOR REHEARING

The petition for rehearing filed by appellant in the above entitled case having been submitted to the judges who participated in the decision of this court and to all the other available circuit judges of the circuit in regular active service, and no judge who concurred in the decision having asked for rehearing, and a majority of the circuit judges of the circuit in regular active service not having voted for rehearing by the court in banc, the petition for rehearing is denied. Judges Adams, Hunter and Garth would grant the petition for rehearing.

ADAMS, C. J., dissents from the denial of rehearing, and makes the following statement:

> Ordinarily, an interpretation of state law by this Court, sitting in diversity, is not of sufficient

consequence to warrant reconsideration by the Court sitting in banc. One reason is that if a federal court misconstrues the law of a state, the courts of that state have an opportunity, at some point, to reject the federal court's interpretation. [Citation.] In this case, however, the majority's holding, which endorses a measure of damages that is based on what appears to be a new interpretation of New Jersey's commercial law, involves a construction of the Uniform Commercial Code as well. Rectification of any error in our interpretation is, because of the national application of the Uniform Commercial Code, significantly more difficult than it would be if New Jersey law alone were implicated. Moreover, the provision of the Uniform Commercial Code involved here is of unusual importance: the measure of damages approved by this Court may create large monetary risks and obligations in a wide range of commercial transactions, including specifically the present burgeoning computer industry. Because there would appear to be considerable force to the dissenting opinion of Judge Rosenn and because I believe that the principle articulated by the majority should be reviewed by the entire Court before it is finally adopted, I would grant the petition for rehearing in banc.

JAMES HUNTER, III, C. J., and GARTH, C. J., join in this statement.

By the court. RUGGERO J. ALDISERT, C. J.

HORNING v. SYCOM
556 F. Supp. 819
(United States District Court, E.D. Kentucky, Covington Division, Feb. 24, 1983.)

BERTELSMAN, D. J.

This matter is before the court on the defendants' motion to dismiss or transfer in order to give effect to a forum selection clause in the contract between the plaintiffs and defendant for the sale of an office computer. The plaintiffs are Dr. Charles Horning, a solo practitioner dentist, plying his trade in Florence, Kentucky, and his wife, Sandra, who manages the office. The defendants are the members of a limited partnership (hereinafter Sycom), a seller of computer hardware with its principal place of business in Wisconsin; Tandy Corporation, a manufacturer of computer hardware with its principal place of business in Texas; and E.F. Hutton Credit Corporation, holder of leasing documents used to finance the plaintiffs' acquisition of a computer system from Sycom, with its principal place of business in Delaware.

On January 28, 1981, Sycom's local sales representative, Dennis McDonough, whose office is in Cincinnati, and its Eastern Regional Manager, Jerry Conca, whose office is in New York, visited Dr. Horning in his office in Florence and attempted to interest him in installing Sycom's Micro-System Data Plan. Apparently, the plaintiffs were persuaded. After further meetings at their office, on February 25, 1981, McDonough sent them a letter relating that, for a total investment of $16,779, at $348 a month for 84 months, they could obtain a Tandy computer, Sycom's software, and maintenance and assistance in the use of the system from Sycom. On March 4, 1981, Dr. Horning signed a "purchase agreement" within which Sycom promised to license its computer software to Dr. Horning and he promised to buy the hardware.

The plaintiffs' purpose in having the system installed was to assist them in compiling accurate financial data, tax records and patient information. The plaintiffs claim that, from the date of installation, the system never worked properly. Nevertheless, they continued making lease-purchase payments for 10 months, paying approximately one-quarter of the total cost, around $4,000. It is alleged that during this time, the system was not performing as it should have; that the plaintiffs were not being effectively schooled in its use; that Sycom was made aware of this state of affairs; and that Sycom acknowledged that a "communication gap" existed and promised to remedy it. At one point, apparently, when six weeks had elapsed and Sycom had not responded to a service call to its Cincinnati office, the plaintiffs paid an independent computer consultant some $2500 to come in and identify the problems in the system.

Around January of 1982, the plaintiffs ceased making monthly payments on the system. They obtained an attorney and, on April 16, 1982, met with a Sycom representative to discuss solving the problems in the system. When this did not work, in a letter dated July 19, 1982, they asked for recission [sic] of the contract and repayment of the money they had expended. In November of 1982, plaintiffs filed suit in Boone Circuit Court, alleging breach of contract, breach of UCC warranties, negligence and fraud against Sycom and the other defendants. The action was removed to this court. E.F. Hutton has counterclaimed against plaintiffs and cross-claimed against Tandy and Sycom.

Defendants' motion is based on a forum selection clause in the form sales contract, which provides:

(a) This Agreement shall be governed by the laws of the State of Wisconsin and the exclusive jurisdiction for any legal proceeding regarding this Purchase Agreement shall be the State of Wisconsin.

The court has carefully reviewed the file and the memoranda of the parties and finds that this matter may be disposed of without great difficulty.

The motion is controlled by the decision of the Kentucky Court of Appeals in *Prudential Resources Corporation v. Plunkett,* Ky.App., 583 S.W.2d 97 (1979) (Lester, J.). Before applying this decision to the facts before it, this court wishes to make clear that it does not regard the matter as a problem going to federal jurisdiction, but rather as a matter of substantive state contract law. [Citation.]

Turning to the decision of the Kentucky Court in *Prudential Resources,* this court finds that Kentucky has adopted the position of the American Law Institute, as stated in § 80, *Restatement 2d, Conflict of Laws. Prudential Resources, supra,* 583 S.W.2d at 99. That section of the *Restatement* reads:

The parties' agreement as to the place of the action cannot oust a state of judicial jurisdiction but such an agreement will be given effect unless it is unfair or unreasonable.

Judge Lester, speaking for the Kentucky Court, applied the following four factors in determining whether or not to enforce a forum selection clause:

(1) Whether the clause was freely negotiated;

(2) Whether the specified forum is a seriously inconvenient place for trial;

(3) Whether enforcement would contravene a strong public policy of the forum in which suit is brought;

(4) Whether Kentucky has more than a minimal interest in the lawsuit. 583 S.W.2d at 99-100. [Citation.]

The application of all of these factors dictates that the motion herein be denied. The plaintiff, a sole dental practitioner would be seriously inconvenienced by being required to litigate this matter in Wisconsin, whereas the defendant would not be inconvenienced. While the court cannot say that the defendant has engaged in overreaching, it does regard the clause as bordering on unconscionability as applied to the sale of an important piece of office machinery to a small businessman for the substantial purchase price involved. In the opinion of the court, there was a disparity of bargaining power with regard to the particular clause of the contract in question. The forum selection clause is only one of many clauses in the form contract that together represent the best job of boiler-plating since the building of the Monitor.

Finally, the court feels that, in this situation, Kentucky has a substantial interest in the lawsuit, in that it is the policy of Kentucky that its consumers have a local forum to redress grievances against non-resident sellers of products. There is no doubt that far more contacts exist here than would be needed to sustain long-arm jurisdiction. [Citation.] The court feels that, while not totally controlling, Kentucky's long-arm cases may be looked to by analogy when enforcement of forum selection clauses is considered.

For the reasons above stated, the court being advised,

It is ordered that the motion to transfer by the defendants be, and it is, hereby denied.

SCHATZ DISTRIBUTING CO., INC., v. OLIVETTI CORP. OF AMERICA

7 Kan.App.2d 676, 647 P.2d 820
(Court of Appeals of Kansas, July 2, 1982.)

SPENCER, J.

Defendant Olivetti Corporation of America, a manufacturer and distributor of business machines, has appealed from judgment in favor of plaintiff for damages resulting from breach of warranty in the sale to plaintiff of an Olivetti DE-525 computer with related equipment.

Anticipating a substantial increase in its accounts, plaintiff, through its then president Michael Scherzer, commenced negotiations with defendant for the purchase of a computer. A meeting was arranged with Jim Neese, an Olivetti sales representative, at which Robert Wedow, plaintiff's accountant, explained to Neese the contents of a three-page list of functions which plaintiff expected to accomplish by means of a computer, with particular emphasis on general ledger accounting, inventory analysis, route profitability, and container analysis. Neese advised that defendant's DE-525 computer would satisfactorily perform all the functions outlined, and further that plaintiff would "never outgrow" the system. These assurances were also recorded in two items of correspondence directed to Scherzer by Neese during the latter part of 1975.

The sale was accomplished in January and February, 1976, but since plaintiff did not desire to pay the full price at the time of purchase, defendant arranged for a lease purchase agreement with Executive Financial Services, Inc. Defendant then sold the computer directly to that company, which contracted with plaintiff for the purchase of the computer by means of monthly payments. Plaintiff had previously paid defendant $1,000.

The computer remained unused and in August, 1976, Thomas Creach, plaintiff's office manager, scheduled a meeting with Neese, Neese's superior Charles Wildman, and an Olivetti programmer. The purpose of that meeting was to discuss what steps needed to be taken to get the computer into operation. Creach was advised that Olivetti did not have the personnel available to install the software desired, but that Neese would nevertheless seek a competent programming firm on plaintiff's behalf.

In March of 1977, Neese arranged a meeting between Creach and representatives of Information Services International, Jim Burke and Raymond Lear. As a result of this meeting, plaintiff entered into an agreement with Information whereby the latter contracted to program the computer with a "general ledger processing" system for $3,000. Plaintiff made a down payment of $1,500.

To assist Burke in programming the computer, Neese provided several operations manuals for setting up a general ledger system for the DE-525 computer. In order to familiarize himself with the computer and the programs provided, Burke spent several hours working on the DE-525 computer at Olivetti's Kansas City, Missouri, facility. Despite this, Burke was unable to get the computer to function. In an effort to gain additional information, Burke telephoned Olivetti facilities in Denver, Seattle, San Francisco, Atlanta, New Orleans, and New York City, but could not locate anyone with direct experience with the DE-525 and its software manuals. Eventually Burke was successful in contacting a Mr. Valhon, an Olivetti employee in New Orleans. Valhon informed Burke he was preparing to install the same program for a customer in New Orleans and invited Burke to assist. At his own expense, Burke traveled to New Orleans and spent two days assisting Valhon. During the course of their work, Valhon made several handwritten corrections to the operations manuals, and Valhon provided Burke with several discs containing other revisions. Burke returned to Kansas City with this information but still could not get a general ledger program to function on either plaintiff's computer or the DE-525 at the Olivetti facility.

Burke resumed telephoning Olivetti facilities around the country for additional information. As a result, an individual with Atlanta Olivetti referred Burke to Walt Grambling, a former Olivetti employee who had purportedly programmed the system Burke was attempting to install on plaintiff's computer. Burke contacted Grambling at his place of business in North Carolina and arranged for Grambling to travel to Kansas City, where together they worked on plaintiff's computer for two and one-half days without success. At this point Burke offered to refund the $1,500 already paid by plaintiff, but was refused.

Due to the inability to get the computer to work satisfactorily, plaintiff's new president Patrick Scherzer called a meeting with Creach, Neese and Wildman. According to Creach and Scherzer, it was at this meeting that Neese informed them the DE-525 was incapable of performing the functions originally warranted. Neese then suggested that plaintiff sell its computer to a purchaser located by Olivetti for the sum of approximately $10,000

and purchase a new computer from Olivetti. Having paid out approximately $20,000 at the time, with another $11,000 owed on the contract with Executive, Scherzer refused Olivetti's offer. Plaintiff initiated this action on September 28, 1978.

Count II of plaintiff's petition asserted violation of express warranties and the implied warranty of merchantability, as set out in K.S.A. 84-2-313 and 314. It was on this theory the trial court granted relief to plaintiff.

The matter was tried to the court over a two-day period in July, 1980. Judgment was entered on February 3, 1981. At the close of plaintiff's evidence, the trial court ruled in favor of Executive's motion for involuntary dismissal, ordering all sums paid into court to be turned over to Executive. Generally, the findings of fact rendered by the court reflect a wholesale adoption of testimony offered by plaintiff's witnesses on direct examination. The court determined the computer sold to plaintiff was incapable of performing the functions warranted by Olivetti. As to damages, the court held:

5. Plaintiff has been damaged in the full amount of the money it has had to pay to EFS, and in this case is entitled to pre-judgment interest on each payment from the date of said payment to February 1, 1981, at the rate of twelve percent (12%) per annum. That contract required the payment of $529.92 per month, commencing February 13, 1976, for sixty-one (61) months, plus a $1,990.00 payment for the sixty-second (62nd) month, and a payment of $1,024.00 at the outset. No prejudgment interest attaches to any payments made in the future by Olivetti on the EFS contract. Counsel for plaintiff is requested to furnish the amount for inclusion on the journal entry of judgment assessed against Olivetti including the amount of pre-judgment interest which will have accrued as of February 1, 1981, which is declared to be the effective date of this entire judgment. This amount should include all payments made by Schatz to EFS, the North Hills Bank, and the Clerk of the District Court whether paid by Schatz or the First State Bank.

6. Plaintiff is also given judgment versus Olivetti for $1,000.00, the original payment made directly to Olivetti by Schatz, plus prejudgment interest at the rate of twelve percent (12%) per annum from December 23, 1975 to February 1, 1981, and counsel for plaintiff is directed to com-

pute this figure also for inclusion in the journal entry of judgment effective February 1, 1981.

7. Similarly, judgment is entered for plaintiff versus defendant Olivetti for $355.00 paid by plaintiff to Morasch Electric on 2-10-77, for $1,500.00 paid by plaintiff to Information Services International, Inc. (Mr. Burke) on 4-12-77 and for $1,786.02 paid by plaintiff to defendant Olivetti for a maintenance agreement on 5-11-77, all to bear pre-judgment interest at the rate of twelve percent (12%) per annum, and all of which are directed to be computed by plaintiff's attorney as of February 1, 1981, for inclusion in the journal entry of judgment effective as of that date.

8. Plaintiff's request for allowance of damages for loss of use of the computer's services is denied as speculative.

9. I find specifically that defendant breached its express warranty and the implied warranty of fitness for a particular purpose, and that defendant was unjustly enriched. Defendant's claim of lack of mitigation effort on the part of plaintiff is likewise denied. The proposed sale, if it had ever been able to be consummated, was packaged to the purchase of still another Olivetti computer, and it is difficult to understand why the unused DE525 would have lost so much value in such a short period as to bring only $10,000.00. The requirement to mitigate does not require a subsequent sale at any price. Olivetti is directed to pick up its DE525.

The court rendered judgment in the total amount of $47,279.59, including prejudgment interest of $11,339.29.

Initially, defendant challenges the sufficiency of evidence to support a finding of breach of warranty.

> When a verdict or judgment is attacked for insufficiency of the evidence, the duty of the appellate court extends only to a search of the record for the purpose of determining whether there is any competent substantial evidence to support the findings. The appellate court will not weigh the evidence or pass upon the credibility of the witnesses. Under these circumstances, the reviewing court must review the evidence in the light most favorable to the party prevailing below. [Citation.]

[Citation.]

Essentially, defendant complains the evidence does not support the conclusion the computer had "hardware" defects which prevented it from functioning properly. The court determined that not only was the computer

incapable of performing the functions warranted, but "would not function in a much more limited capacity, and was, in fact, worthless." Although no one testified the hardware was malfunctioning, a strong inference tending to prove that fact was created by the testimony of Burke concerning his extensive efforts to program the computer for a single function.

In any case, the gist of the court's decision was that the computer could not perform as warranted. This conclusion is amply supported by the testimony of Rex Babcock, a former Olivetti employee, that even assuming the hardware of the computer was in good order, it simply did not possess the capacity for data storage required to perform the many functions plaintiff desired and which defendant had guaranteed. Additionally, plaintiff's office manager and president testified that Neese admitted the computer lacked the capacity to carry out those functions. Accordingly, we find this issue to be without merit.

It is argued plaintiff is not entitled to recover as damages interest paid on the lease purchase contract. K.S.A. 84-2-714 provides in part:

> (2) The measure of damages for breach of warranty is the difference at the time and place of acceptance between the value of the goods accepted and the value they would have had if they had been as warranted, unless special circumstances show proximate damages of a different amount.
>
> (3) In a proper case any incidental and consequential damages under the next section may also be recovered.

Subsection (2) is generally in accord with the common law concept that damages in case of a breach of warranty are ordinarily the difference between the value of the article delivered and what it would have been worth had it been as warranted. 67 Am.Jur.2d, Sales §§ 740, 741. The court found the computer sold to plaintiff was not functional to any degree and was "worthless." Accordingly, the measure of damages in this case constitutes the difference between zero and the value the computer would have had if it had been as warranted—presumably the agreed upon purchase price. Additionally, the court awarded plaintiff interest which it had paid under the contract with Executive.

K.S.A. 84-2-715 provides in relevant part:

(2) Consequential damages resulting from the seller's breach include
(a) any loss resulting from general or particular requirements and needs of which the seller at the time of contracting had reason to know and which could not reasonably be prevented by cover or otherwise. * * *

As to those losses which are consequential, Official UCC Comment 2 states in part:

Subsection (2) operates to allow the buyer, in an appropriate case, any consequential damages which are the result of the seller's breach. The 'tacit agreement' test for the recovery of consequential damages is rejected. Although the older rule at common law which made the seller liable for all consequential damages of which he had 'reason to know' in advance is followed, the liberality of that rule is modified by refusing to permit recovery unless the buyer could not reasonably have prevented the loss by cover or otherwise.

The common law rule has always been that damages recoverable for breach of contract are limited to those which may fairly be considered as arising, in the usual course of things, from the breach itself, or as may reasonably be assumed to have been within the contemplation of both parties as the probable result of the breach. [Citation.]

Neither party cites authority dealing directly with the issue of whether interest expense may constitute consequential damages. This appears to be a question of first impression in this state. However, in *Coyle Chevrolet Co. v. Carrier*, 397 N.E.2d 1283 (Ind.App.1979), the defendant-automobile company appealed from judgment in favor of plaintiff-buyer on the theory of breach of warranty. Part of the appeal concerned judgment in favor of the buyer for sales tax and finance charges. The court stated:

Coyle fails to comprehend the significance of the evidence relating to the sales tax and finance charge. The sales tax is clearly an incidental damage resulting from expenses 'reasonably incurred in * * * receipt' of the car. *Ind. Code.* 26-1-2-715. [Citation.] We recently held in *Hudson v. Dave McIntire, Inc.* (1979), Ind.App., 390 N.E.2d 179, 184, that finance charges could be included as a consequential damage.
Consequential damages are recoverable when they represent a loss resulting from general

or particular requirements and needs of which the seller at the time of contracting had reason to know. Such damages should be direct, immediate and probable and not speculative. The determination of these damages is a question for resolution by the trier of fact. [Citation.] This is a question of first impression in this state. However, we see no reason why this type of damage could not be assessed as a consequential damage where a buyer presents evidence that the seller had "reason to know" the buyer needed to borrow money in order to complete the purchase. See *Carl Beasley Ford, Inc. v. Burroughs Corporation*, 361 F.Supp. 325 (E.D.Pa.1973), where such damages were awarded. [Citation.]
Further, we note some jurisdictions consider the sales tax and finance charge as part of the price of the goods as warranted. [Citations.] 397 N.E.2d at 1286-87.

Although there is authority to the contrary, [citation], we find the reasoning in *Coyle* accords with the governing principles of the UCC on the subject of consequential damages. It was established by defendant's own witnesses that its agents were aware of plaintiff's need to finance the purchase of the computer. Indeed, defendant's salesman Neese arranged for the sale of the computer through Executive. No reason exists why interest paid Executive should not be considered and assessed as a component of consequential damages.

Defendant next asserts error in awarding prejudgment interest. As a general rule, prejudgment interest is not allowable on a claim for unliquidated damages. This rule is subject to the qualification however, that where necessary to arrive at full compensation, a court may in the exercise of its discretion award interest or its equivalent as an element of damages even where the primary damages are unliquidated. *Lightcap v. Mobil Oil Corporation*, 221 Kan. 448, Syl¶¶ 10, 11, 562 P.2d 1, *cert. denied* 434 U.S. 876, 98 S.Ct. 228, 54 L.Ed.2d 156 (1977). [Citation.]

Here there exist two classifications of damages based on defendant's breach of warranty: (1) The difference at the time and place of acceptance between the actual value of the computer and the value the computer would have had if it had been as warranted (K.S.A. 84-2-714[2]); and (2) consequential damages resulting from seller's breach (84-2-714[3], 715[2][a]).

Although plaintiff claimed as damages under the first classification all moneys paid on the principal of the purchase price, the exact measure of damages could not be ascertained until the court had determined, at the least, the actual market value of the computer. In *Lightcap* the court responded to a substantially similar situation where presented with the question of whether the court had correctly withheld an award of prejudgment interest on royalties due.

> As to the amounts which were determined to be due only when judgment was entered below, we believe the general rule as to unliquidated claims should apply. Apart from the question of liability (one of 'initial impression' as noted by the trial court), the amount due if there was liability was not determined until judgment. The 'market value' of the gas sold was subject to proof at trial by any competent evidence. [Citations omitted.] Here plaintiff chose to rely on the arbitrated value as establishing market value, and that figure was accepted by the trial court in the absence of any other evidence on the issue. *Such a result, however, could not have been foretold before this litigation was well under way, and until that time the total claim was unliquidated.* 221 Kan. at 467, 652 P.2d 1; emphasis added.

Here damages awarded under K.S.A. 84-2-714(2) were unliquidated where the actual value of the computer was uncertain. The trial court should not have awarded prejudgment interest on the principal obligation incurred for the computer.

Items of consequential damages awarded plaintiff, *e.g.*, electrical wiring, maintenance agreement, finance charges, and programming fees, were sums certain in amount with the issue of defendant's liability being the sole determinant of whether they would be allowed or denied in full. Here prejudgment interest was warranted.

Defendant argues plaintiff failed to mitigate damages: (1) by refusing Olivetti's offer to effect a resale of the computer; and (2) in not taking back the $1,500 paid to Burke, as offered. While the first of these arguments was presented to the trial court, the second was not. Thus, whether plaintiff failed in its duty to mitigate damages by refusing Burke's offer to refund programming fees is a matter beyond this court's ability to consider. [Citation.]

In denying defendant's claim that plaintiff failed to mitigate by refusing to offer to effect a resale, the court stated:

> Defendant's claim of lack of mitigation effort on the part of plaintiff is likewise denied. The proposed sale, if it had ever been able to be consummated, was packaged to the purchase of still another Olivetti computer, and it is difficult to understand why the unused DE525 would have lost so much value in such a short period as to bring only $10,000.00. The requirement to mitigate does not require a subsequent sale at any price.

This finding is amply supported by the evidence.

Prejudgment interest was awarded at the rate of 12 percent per annum and it appears the court was in error in doing so. The record reveals that consequential damages allowable in this case were incurred in 1976 and 1977, and accordingly interest on those amounts should have been at the rate of 6 percent per annum to July 1, 1980. [Citations.] From and after July 1, 1980, prejudgment interest should have been assessed at the rate of 10 percent per annum. The judgment as entered should be modified accordingly.

This cause is remanded to the trial court with directions to modify its judgment by (1) deletion of prejudgment interest on the principal of purchase money paid by plaintiff to Executive Financial Services, Inc., and (2) by recomputation and an award of prejudgment interest on consequential damages at rates and in the manner herein set forth. In all other respects, the judgment is affirmed.

PEZZILLO v. GENERAL TELEPHONE AND ELECTRONICS INFORMATION SYSTEMS, INC.

414 F. Supp. 1257

(United States District Court, M. D. Tennessee, Nashville Division, Jan. 15, 1976.)

MORTON, D. J.

FINDINGS OF FACT

1. This action was brought by ten former salaried employees of the defendant under the

provisions of the Fair Labor Standards Act of 1938, 29 U.S.C. § 201 *et seq.*, hereinafter referred to as "the Act," alleging that the defendant knowingly and willfully violated Section 7 of the Act (29 U.S.C. § 207) by failing to compensate them for work in excess of 40 hours per week at one and one-half times their normal hourly rate. Plaintiffs seek the amount of overtime payments due plus an equal amount as liquidated damages and reasonable attorney fees.

2. * * * The defendant is a division of General Telephone and Electronics, Inc. and was, prior to its acquisition by said corporation in 1972, known as P.M.I. (Programming Methods, Inc.).

3. The defendant offers consulting and implementation of data processing services on a contractual basis. Its operation is nationwide with its central office located in New York City. It employs approximately 1,100 persons. The plaintiffs were employed by the defendant to implement computer systems for certain customers according to specifications. They were referred to by the defendant variously as programmer analysts, programmers, and members of technical staff. The overtime violations complained of by the plaintiffs occurred in Miami, Florida, during the years of 1972 and 1973 while the plaintiffs were working on three contracts for defendant (viz., Ryder Truck Rental, General Development Corporation of Miami, Florida, and Dade County, Florida).

4. The individual plaintiffs were employed by the defendant for the periods indicated below in connection with the performance of the three jobs in Miami, Florida:

(a) Lawrence A. Pezzillo—1/10/72 to 9/19/74

(b) Ronald Ray—10/3/72 to 7/26/74

(c) Thomas Kos—6/12/72 to 2/15/75

(d) James Matheson—6/11/73 to 5/22/74

(e) Thomas Papaiski—9/11/72 to 2/28/74

(f) Stanley Walters—6/1/73 to 2/6/74

(g) James Schweizer—7/30/73 to 12/21/73

(h) Jerry Harness—8/2/72 to 2/28/74

(i) Mark S. Cotter—5/14/73 to 4/8/74

Each of the plaintiffs was employed by the defendant on a salary basis at the amounts set forth below:

Plaintiff	Starting Rate	Rate at Termination
(a) Pezzillo	$11,640	$12,640
(b) Ray	10,500	11,500
(c) Kos	11,800	12,900
(d) Matheson	9,000	9,500
(e) Papaiski	12,100	13,900
(f) Walters	11,500	11,500
(g) Schweizer	10,500	10,500
(h) Harness	12,500	14,000
(i) Cotter	12,500	12,500

5. The parties, through their attorneys, have agreed that if defendant is found to be in violation of the Act, the hours worked and hourly rates of the plaintiffs will be stipulated on the basis of the records kept by the parties, and overtime payments will be computed and stipulated.

6. The issues to be decided by the court are whether the work performed by the plaintiffs exempted them from coverage as administrative employees under 29 U.S.C. § 213(a)(1), and whether the defendant in good faith failed to pay the plaintiffs overtime (29 U.S.C. § 259).

7. For the purpose of this litigation, the following descriptions will be helpful:

A computer is a machine with no intelligence and has no independent stimuli. It must be instructed in minute detail as to every activity which it is requested to perform. Each computer is manufactured to accept only specified language, one of which is known as "cobol" (common business oriented language). Through the use of the binary principal, symbols made up of combinations of the figures 0 and 1 are arbitrarily assigned to denote words, numerals, phrases and processes.

By the use of electronic impulses, activated by a device similar to a typewriter, language can be fed into the computer and placed on storage units (magnetic tapes or magnetic disks). On command, by use of the built-in language, the information stored can be selectively combined to produce a defined result, i. e., complete bookkeeping systems, leasing systems, information storage banks, etc.

To accomplish the desired result, a person with knowledge of the computer's capability must design a system for the particular information to be put into the machine, prescribe certain manipulations, and specify the desired result. This requires considerable expertise, discretion, and independent judgment free from immediate direction or supervision.

Once the designer, sometimes called an analyst, determines the system, he usually describes this system in narrative form,[1] commonly referred to as a program narrative or specifications. To further complicate the matter, there is ordinarily an overall system with numerous subsystems. At this point, there exists input of known information, a designation of certain computations or operations, and a desired result narrated by the designer. The next step is to translate the narrative, which is in the English language, into computer language.[2] This portion of the project is referred to as programming. The programmer writes in computer language the commands to the computer to implement the narrative.[3] These commands, once translated into computer language, can be stored on punch cards, the use of which avoids necessity of typing the entire process on each use of the computer.

Once the programming is completed, the system must be tested to determine if the design is effective and has been effectively implemented.

In fact, the program is run through the computer using known sample material or with data which will produce a known result.

The testing is generally called "debugging." The most common errors arise by reason of improper syntax, human errors in detailing the command steps, and logic in design. The correction of syntax and other human errors are discovered by reexamination of the computer command language previously written by the programmer. If there is a defect in the design of the system, the designer must reexamine the design and make the appropriate changes. Of interest is the fact that a programmer does not need the expertise of the designer, need not know the innerworkings of the computer, and can do adequate work with only a general familiarity of its function and a grasp of computer language.

8. *The Ryder Contract.* Ryder Truck Rental decided to change from its computer system to a new data processing system utilizing an IBM 370 computer. It contracted with defendant to furnish certain personnel designated as experienced commercial programmers. One of defendant's vice presidents described the defendant's function as:

> Basically at Ryder we were working in a support capacity with Ryder and IBM and assisting them to go to an on-line third generation computer system.

A complete new system was being established. The design and specifications (program narrative) were developed by analysts employed by Ryder. No specifications were developed by defendant's employees. The specifications were written and the programmer translated the specifications into computer language. The programmer could make suggestions as to possible ways of improving the system. However, any proposed improvements were required to be approved by a Ryder analyst. If problems in design were encountered in the program through testing or otherwise, a Ryder analyst would advise defendant's employees as to what was wrong and how to remedy the problem.

9. *General Development Computer Contracts.* There were two separate phases of work under these contracts.

The first involved the Univac operation at GDC. Certain systems were used in operating the Univac computer. The analyst at GDC had

---

1. A narrative has been defined as a running account of the logical operations occurring in any segment of a program.

2. Computer language might be compared to any foreign language.

3. To illustrate:

Assume one were instructing a baby to eat from a bowl. Instead of placing a spoon in the hand of the baby and demonstrating, through performance, the dipping of the spoon into the bowl, carrying it to the mouth and depositing its contents into the mouth, the instructions to a computer would be more detailed. The possible commands might be:

(1) Raise your right arm to table height

(2) Move your right hand forward 8″
(3) Place your right hand on the spoon
(4) Curl your fingers around the spoon
(5) Raise your right arm 4″
(6) Move your right arm 4″ to the left
(7) Lower your right arm 4″
(8) Tilt the spoon forward 30°
(9) Move the spoon forward 1″
(10) Tilt the spoon upward 30°
(11) Raise your right arm upward 14″
(12) Turn the spoon horizontally 180°
(13) Move your right arm 4″ and simultaneously open your mouth
(14) Rotate the spoon 180°
(15) Move the spoon outward 4″ and return it to the original position.

designed and written a narrative of the programs in use. The defendant, through its personnel, was to check the narrative with the programs in use to ascertain if the narrative was accurate. If the narrative omitted any step actually in use, this step was to be narrated and placed in proper sequence.

The second phase of the work was to convert existing Univac and Honeywell computer systems to an IBM 370/145 system.

Each system had its own language (foreign). These systems were designed and programmed before defendant's employees came on the scene. GDC employees were more experienced and knowledgeable about those systems than were defendant's personnel. The primary function performed by defendant was the translation of the computer language of Univac and Honeywell to cobol, the language used by IBM in IBM 370/145. Thereafter, the translated programs, with adjustments to accommodate the particular peculiarities of the IBM computer, were tested and debugged by defendant's employees.

The project leader on the job (now director of projects) described the GDC project as follows:

A. There were two projects on the General Development job, the Univac and Honeywell conversions.

Q. All right.

A. The Univac system had specifications which included a narrative and flow chart and a Univac program listing. The programmer was given that package, and his job was to write a Cobol program which would give the same answers.

Q. All right, sir. Was the program listing from the Univac system written in machine language, the Univac language?

A. Yes, sir, it was written in a language call PAL.

Q. That's not the same as Cobol or English language?

A. There's a big difference.

Q. All right, and what kind of language were they given on the Honeywell conversion?

A. The Honeywell was a little bit easier in that we were converting Cobol programs on the Honeywell to Cobol programs on IBM.

There was a documentation package prepared that showed the input and output files coming into the program, and if I remember right, there was some sort of brief narrative about what the program did.

Q. Mr. Riley, in developing a new program on the Univac conversion, was there any analytical process required of the programmer?

A. I'm sorry?

Q. Was any analytical process required of the programmer in developing new programs from the old Univac programs?

A. He would have to understand what the program was supposed to do by examining the specifications, yes.

10. *Dade County, Florida, Contract.* The Dade County contract was described by the defendant's project leader as follows:

Q. All right, sir. Now, what was involved in the Dade County job?

A. The Dade County job involved taking the current, a current criminal justice system and converting that from an antiquated teleprocessing monitor that it ran under to a PMI soft ware package called intercom.

Q. What were the programmers on that job given to work from to develop the new programs?

A. As far as I remember, the only documentation they received was the actual program listing of the current system, plus manuals on intercom, and, I believe, there was a—I'm not really sure whether they attended an intercom class or not. They did receive some instructions from PMI personnel who worked with intercom.

Q. And, basically, what were the requirements of the job on Dade County, what were the programmers actually doing?

A. They were taking specific programs, locating the areas in those programs that dealt primarily with the input and output files and input and output messages, extracting all of that information and replacing it with the requirements of intercom.

Q. Was that purely a mechanical process, eliminating the old steps and putting in new ones?

A. It wasn't totally mechanical. There was a lot of mechanical work involved, I guess.

Q. All right, sir, was there some other work involved that was not mechanical?

A. Yes, sir.

Q. What was that?

A. Understanding what the programs were supposed to do, whether they functioned correctly in the current state and cases where they didn't.

One of the plaintiffs gave the following information:

Q. You had the program listing—did you have sample output?

A. Yes, we did.

Q. Was the output supposed to match the existing output?

A. Yes, it was. No—we were given, in some cases we were given new formats to program.

Q. I see, and you had to come up with a program to develop the new format or the new output?

A. The new—a new display screen, yes, sir.

Q. Rather than making a print-out, you were working on a system that displayed on a video display terminal, is that correct?

A. That's right.

Q. Where it shows up on a little tube, I think they call it sometimes?

A. Right.

Q. Mr. Cotter, did you also have to, as a result of this conversion to the intercom system, come up with new data selection or new input to the system?

A. No new input, no.

Q. So, the input was the same?

A. Yes.

Q. All right, sir, were the calls to the data system different because of the intercom system?

A. Yes, that was the—that was what was changed.

Q. That's basically what you were doing?

A. Yes.

Q. A different instruction went to the computer to select the same data?

A. Yes.

Q. When you were required to come up with new output, did you have to come up with new logic for the program to make it come up with the new output?

A. In some cases we had to add small amounts of logic to be compatible with intercom.

Q. I see. And did someone give you that logic or was that a result of your own work?

A. That was taught in the beginning, how we would handle that, and then we programmed it in.

Q. All right. So, as far as actually working on the program, you came up with the new logic yourself?

A. No, the logic was given to us and we applied it to the programs.

Q. I see. It was given to you in the classroom type instruction?

A. Yes.

Q. Who taught that instruction?

A. John Butts.

11. The plaintiffs were designated in the personnel records of the defendants as holding positions on the "Tech Staff." In this capacity, certain of them have received evaluations as to ability which are particularly noteworthy:

> Matheson, Jas K. Unable to perform in a technical capacity required by PMI Brief Evaluation of Employees Ability—Very, very little
>
> Walters, Stanly J Good Programmer
>
> Schweizer, James Reasonable Programmer
>
> Ray, Ronald Starting date—10/3/72 Ron started with PMI with very little experience. Over the past year he has learned a great deal and can now stand on his own in coding and completing programs. He is dependable and tries his utmost to do a good job. His technical ability is limited but does ask for help when he needs it and learns when shown something
>
> Harness, Jerry Competent Cobol programmer
>
> Kos, Thomas Tom is a good Cobol programmer. He has been doing a good job since he has been with the company. At present he shows no signs of wanting or having the ability to advance beyond the programming/analysis stage.

Pezzillo, Lawrence Larry is at best an average programmer. He is careless in the work he does and does not spend the time required to write and complete a good program. * * *

12. The project leader employed by the defendant gave the following testimony.

Q. All right, Mr. Riley, when the programmer is given a specification, is he required to develop the logic for his program from the specification or is that already done for him?

A. By logic, if you mean flow chart, some kind of system that the programmer may have of his own to break down the actual specification, yes, he is.

Q. All right, sir, even if the programmer. * * *

BY THE COURT: Now, wait just a minute, now wait just a minute. The specifications, as I understand it, detail what you expect the programmer to do?

A. Yes, they do.

BY THE COURT: And you are talking— and a flow chart then you are saying is something that the programmer does just to draw himself a kinetic picture rather than a mental picture, is that what you are saying?

A. That's right, he's talking a narrative and drawing a picture from that.

BY THE COURT: And that is for his own benefit?

A. Either for his own benefit or at times it becomes part of the documentation of the system.

BY THE COURT: But that's a matter of convenience as far as the programmer is concerned or is that a requirement?

A. It will vary depending on the organization we work for. There are some places that it is required.

BY THE COURT: So, what he is doing is transforming or translating from the specification a visual chart?

A. Yes, sir.

BY THE COURT: Isn't that mechanical?

A. The drawing of the chart is mechanical.

BY THE COURT: Well, the transferring, it says you go from A to B, so he puts A to B

on a chart. Do not the specifications detail how it goes?

A. The specifications could say go from A to B, but they could say go from A to Z which may involve going through the entire program, depending on the level of detail in the specification.

BY THE COURT: What I'm saying is I am having a little problem on this matter as to whether or not it is mechanical or not mechanical. When you have a specification to say we are going to start at point A and we are going to wind up at point Z and we are going to go from point A to point Z through New York and back to New Jersey and down to Washington and back up to New Jersey and back to Washington and then down to Z. Now, that's all spelled out in the specifications, is it not?

A. If you take the specification that was introduced Friday and you look at it, that's a very detailed specification, and it's very—it's a mechanical process.

BY THE COURT: All right.

A. Not all specifications are that detailed.

BY THE COURT: All right, now, then, do you—are those specifications that say, "We are going from A to Z, and we are not going to tell you anything about how to get there; you are just going to have to get there the best way you can"?

A. That's right.

BY THE COURT: And you turn those over to programmers and not to analysts?

A. Programmers receive them, yes.

BY THE COURT: I beg your pardon?

A. Yes, they are turned over to programmers.

BY THE COURT: And you expect programmers to do the coding and programmers do, they work out the method of getting from A to Z?

A. By whatever means they can.

BY THE COURT: By whatever means they can.

Then they determine whether to go from New Jersey to Washington, back to New Jersey and down to Philadelphia and back—

A. Yes, sir.

BY THE COURT: —by the calls they put in the instructions they put in the computer, is that what you are saying?

A. Yes.

BY THE COURT: Well, then why do you need an analyst?

A. The analyst determines.

BY THE COURT: Because the company can say I want to go from A to Z. Why do they need you?

A. The analyst was the one that determined that you wanted to go from A to Z.

* * *

A. I would say Mr. Kos and Mr. Pezzillo performed some analysis work.

Q. What did they do, systems analyst work?

A. Pardon?

Q. Systems analyst work?

A. Yes.

Q. Wherein did they perform any?

A. Mr. Pezzillo worked on the accounts payable system and assisted Mr. Vajda and Mr. Van in designing part of that system.

Q. All right, now did they—weren't they given programs, the specifications for programs prepared by Mr. Vajda and the systems analyst at Ryder?

A. Yes, they did, they were.

Q. Well, they were given those program specifications for programs to work on, is that right?

A. Yes, they were.

Q. They did not prepare those specifications, did they?

A. No, they didn't.

Q. Well, wherein did they design these specifications, that is what a systems analyst does, is it not?

A. It is part of what he does. I would say after they received the specifications and wrote some of the programs involved in that system, there were some problems in the system, and they assisted Mr. Van and Mr. Vajda in making corrections to that system.

Q. Well, they went to them and consulted with them about problems they found?

A. Yes, they did.

Q. They didn't advise Mr. Vajda how to change the system, did they?

A. I would think they did to a minor degree.

Q. Well, to a minor degree. Well, primarily they were coding and debugging, isn't that right?

A. That was their primary function, yes.

BY THE COURT: Mr.—let me ask this witness a question. Do you know anything about the construction business at all?

A. No, sir, I don't.

BY THE COURT: Well, normally an architect designs a building and he designs the stress. He draws up sections of it. He puts in the streets, mathematical computations. He outlines where the—he outlines basically the type of bathrooms he wants and what have you, and then he turns it over to a draftsman, and the draftsman draws all of the pretty lines, and then he checks out the mathematical computations, and he calls up the architect and says, "Wait a minute, you've made a bust here on the mathematical computations; you added two and two together and got six, so the stress is off"; and then he counts up the number of square feet in the building and says, "Well, wait a minute, the building code says you have to have so many extra bathrooms"; and then he looks at the use of the building and looks at the number of outside lights in the building, outside windows, and he says, "The building code says you have to have so many square feet of windows for so many square feet of building", and he says, "You made a bust on this one. What are we going to do about it?"

The architect says, "You make it conform."

A draftsman is mechanical, he's covered by the Wage and Hour, even though he uses his mind, even though he points out where an architect makes mistakes, he points out where the professional blew it.

Now, then, what is the difference between what I have told you about a draftsman and what these gentlemen did here about your problems?

A. They are similar in that they were given the original outline.

BY THE COURT: And checked up and found out somebody blew it.

A. Yeah.

BY THE COURT: They said, "Look, you blew it."

A. Yes.

BY THE COURT: "And, therefore, since you have blown it, don't you think we had better do something about it?"

A. Yes, and recommend what to do about it.

BY THE COURT: Well, the draftsman said, "We will put more skylights in or we will put more bathrooms in or we will put more outer doors in to comply with the fire code."

Is that what your man does? He said, "If this monster is going to work, we need another step."

A. It's sort of similar, yes.

13. It is generally conceded that the writing of the command orders (translating the narrative from English into computer language—sometimes referred to as decoding) is a mechanical process and as a general rule comprises approximately 20% of a programmer's time in implementing a program. The other approximately 80% is spent in debugging, i. e., discovering and correcting syntax and human errors in translating the narrative to code plus discovering design errors, calling them to the attention of the analyst, and thereafter, at his direction, correcting them. No evidence appears in this record as to what portion of the 80% is normally expended in discovering syntax and human error in the direct translation of the narrative (specifications) to computer language. These are mechanical errors and their discovery and correction are mechanical and nondiscretionary.

14. After the hearing, the defendant introduced the deposition of Dr. William H. Rowan, Jr., a Professor of Systems and Information Science at Vanderbilt University, who testified as an expert in the field of computer sciences. Dr. Rowan, aside from his academic duties, owns a firm which provides data processing services for clients. His firm employs programmers who code and debug and are not paid overtime. Dr. Rowan stated that in his opinion a programmer was not analogous to a draftsman working for an architect, but was instead more like an engineer working as a professional with the architect on the structural aspect of a building. Dr. Rowan considers programmers to be professionals. His explanation for Mr. Vajda's analogy between architect and draftsman and systems analyst and programmer was that Mr. Vajda probably didn't know what an architect did. He finally admitted that architects and engineers were both professionals who used draftsmen to implement their plans and that here his analogy broke down. His opinions are rejected.

15. The defendant contends that its failure to pay overtime to the plaintiffs was based on its good faith belief that they were exempt from coverage. The only live witness from the defendant was Mr. Dennis Riley. He took orders from Mr. Donald Toy in New York, who had general management of the company in the Eastern United States and from Mr. George Langnas, President of the defendant. Mr. Riley had no connection with the Wage and Hour policy of the defendant and had never had any discussion with Mr. Toy as to whether any employees of the company should be paid overtime. The only explanation Mr. Riley could offer as to why the plaintiffs were not compensated for overtime was that he did not know of anyone else in the industry who paid overtime.

The defendant also offered the statement of a representative of the data processing industry submitted at a public hearing in February, 1971, held by the Wage and Hour Division to determine the status of, among others, programmers under the professional, executive administrative exemption (29 U.S.C. § 260). It was stated that the purpose of this exhibit was to show that the defendant followed in good faith the position of the industry contained in the statement that programmers were exempt from coverage as professional or administrative personnel. It is significant that as a result of the public hearing the Wage and Hour Divison determined in December, 1971, that programmers and systems analysts were not professionals (38 C.F.R. § 541.302(h); Fed.Reg. Vol. 36, No. 232, Dec. 2. 1971). It gave as examples of the activities of programmers not requiring the degree of discretion and independent judgment to classify them as administrative, the preparation of flow charts, the preparation of instructions to the operator and debugging the program (38 C.F.R. § 541.207(c)(7)). It is material that the regulations specifically pointed out that the determination of the exemption of programmers as administrative employees is a factual determination. Neither Mr. Toy nor Mr. Langnas, who determined the defendant's personnel and wage policies, appeared as witnesses. Mr. Toy, in his deposition, indicated a familiarity with Wage & Hour regulations. Mr. Toy was not conscious of the defendant ever having received, or having sought, a legal opinion, an administrative determination, or any advice as to the status of its employees relative to the overtime provisions of the Act. The defendant knew that the work of its employees consisted of coding, debugging, preparing flow charts and instructions.

16. Mr. Riley had no responsibility for determining whether the plaintiffs or other employees of the defendant would receive overtime or be treated as exempt from the Act. Neither Mr. Toy, the general manager of the division of the defendant's business in which Mr. Riley and the plaintiffs worked, nor Mr. Langnas, President of the defendant, were offered as witnesses. There is evidence in the record that some other companies did not pay programmers overtime, but there is no credible evidence whatever that the defendant relied on this fact or any other reason in failing to pay the plaintiffs overtime as required by the Act.

17. The defendant has therefore failed to offer any proof that it had a good faith belief based on reasonable grounds which motivated its failure to pay overtime. It is obvious that the data processing industry has attempted and is attempting to convince the Wage and Hour personnel that computer programmers as a group are exempt from the provisions of the Fair Labor Standards Act. The industry has not been successful. Certain regulations, *infra,* spell out the ground rules. However, it appears that defendants have decided to run the risk of detection and to assert that there is enough ambiguity to justify a good faith defense on detection. This court does not agree.

Mr. Riley's testimony, hereinbefore quoted, clearly reflects sufficient knowledge by the defendant. With this knowledge the defendant intentionally elected not to comply with the overtime provisions of the Act. This constitutes a willful violation.

18. The court finds that plaintiffs did not perform services as analysts. Furthermore, the greater part of their work was mechanical and involved the use of practical skills (as distinguished from discretion and independent judgment) acquired in the trade. In fact, the plaintiffs in each of the three contracts were presented with systems previously designed by analysts and plaintiffs merely used their skills in placing the programs in the computer. Thus, there was no exercise of discretion and independent judgment as described in the regulations.

CONCLUSIONS OF LAW

* * *

3. The exemptions from overtime requirements of the Fair Labor Standards Act are set forth in 29 U.S.C. § 213. The pertinent provision is § 213(a)(1) as follows:

§ 541.2 Administrative.
The term "employee employed in a bona fide * * * administrative * * * capacity" in section 13(a)(1) of the act shall mean any employee:
(a) Whose primary duty consists of: * * *
(1) The performance of office or nonmanual work directly related to management policies or general business operations of his employer or his employer's customers. * * *

* * *

(b) Who customarily and regularly exercises discretion and independent judgment; and

* * *

(2) Who performs under only general supervision work along specialized or technical lines requiring special training, experience, or knowledge, or
(3) Who executes under only general supervision special assignments and tasks; and
(d) Who does not devote more than 20 percent * * * of his hours worked in the work-week to activities which are not directly and closely related to the performance of the work described in paragraphs (a) through (c) of this section; and

(e)(1) Who is compensated for his services on a salary or fee basis at a rate of not less than $155 per week. * * *

4. Regulations have been promulgated defining and implementing 29 U.S.C. § 213. Those pertinent appear in Title 29 of the Code of Federal Regulations and are as follows:

§ 541.206 Primary duty.

(a) The definition of "administrative" exempts only employees who are primarily engaged in the responsible work which is characteristic of employment in a bona fide administrative capacity. Thus, the employee must have as his primary duty office or non-manual work directly related to management policies or general business operations of his employer or his employer's customers. * * *

(b) In determining whether an employee's exempt work meet the "primary duty" requirement, the principles explained in § 541.103 in the discussion of "primary duty" under the definition of "executive" are applicable.

§ 541.207 Discretion and independent judgment.

(a) In general, the exercise of discretion and independent judgment involves the comparison and the evaluation of possible courses of conduct and acting or making a decision after the various possibilities have been considered. The term as used in the regulations in Subpart A of this part, moreover, implies that the person has the authority or power to make an independent choice, free from immediate direction or supervision and with respect to matters of significance. (Without actually attempting to define the term, the courts have given it this meaning in applying it in particular cases.) [Citations.]

(b) The term must be applied in the light of all the facts involved in the particular employment situation in which the question arises. It has been most frequently misunderstood and misapplied by employers and employees in cases involving the following: (1) Confusion between the exercise of discretion and independent judgment, and the use of skill in applying techniques, procedures, or specific standards; and (2) misapplication of the term to employees making decisions relating to matters of little consequence.

(c) Distinguished from skills and procedures:

(1) Perhaps the most frequent cause of misapplication of the term "discretion and independent judgment" is the failure to distinguish it from the use of skill in various respects. An employee who merely applies his knowledge in following prescribed procedures or determining which procedure to follow, or who determines

whether specified standards are met or whether an object falls into one or another of a number of definite grades, classes, or other categories, with or without the use of testing or measuring devices, is not exercising discretion and independent judgment within the meaning of § 541.2. This is true even if there is some leeway in reaching a conclusion, as when an acceptable standard includes a range or a tolerance above or below a specific standard.

* * *

(7) In the data processing field a systems analyst is exercising discretion and independent judgment when he develops methods to process, for example, accounting, inventory, sales, and other business information by using electronic computers. He also exercises discretion and independent judgment when he determines the exact nature of the data processing problem, and structures the problem in a logical manner so that a system to solve the problem and obtain the desired results can be developed. Whether a computer programer is exercising discretion and independent judgment depends on the facts in each particular case. Every problem processed in a computer first must be carefully analyzed so that exact and logical steps for its solution can be worked out. When this preliminary work is done by a computer programer he is exercising discretion and independent judgment. A computer programer would also be using discretion and independent judgment when he determines exactly what information must be used to prepare the necessary documents and by ascertaining the exact form in which the information is to be presented. Examples of work not requiring the level of discretion and judgment contemplated by the regulations are highly technical and mechanical operations such as the preparation of a flow chart or diagram showing the order in which the computer must perform each operation, the preparation of instructions to the console operator who runs the computer or the actual running of the computer by the programer, and the debugging of a program. It is clear that the duties of data processing employees such as tape librarians, keypunch operators, computer operators, junior programers and programer trainees are so closely supervised as to preclude the use of the required discretion and independent judgment.

* * *

§ 541.209 Percentage limitations on nonexempt work.

(a) Under § 541.2(d), an employee will not qualify for exemption as an administrative employee if he devotes more than 20 percent * * * of his hours worked on the workweek to nonexempt work; that is, to activities which are not directly and closely related to the performance of the work described in § 541.2(a) through (c).

(b) This test is applied on a workweek basis and the percentage of time spent on nonexempt work is computed on the time worked by the employee.

(c) The tolerance for nonexempt work allows the performance of nonexempt manual or nonmanual work within the percentages allowed for all types of nonexempt work.

* * *

8. The defendant employer has failed to carry its burden of proof to establish that plaintiffs in the work *sub judice* customarily and regularly exercised discretion and independent judgment. On the contrary, the credible evidence clearly establishes that plaintiffs performed work in which they exercised job skill as contrasted to discretion and independent judgment.

9. The defendant employer has failed to carry its burden of proof that plaintiffs met the requirement of 29 C.F.R. § 541.2(d). On the contrary, the credible evidence clearly reflects that more than 20% of the plaintiffs' work time did not fall within the descriptions contained in 29 C.F.R. § 541.2(a) through (c).

10. Pursuant to the provisions of 29 U.S.C. § 216, plaintiffs are entitled to "an additional equal amount as liquidated damages" unless "the employer shows to the satisfaction of the court that the act or omission giving rise to such action was in good faith and that he had reasonable grounds for believing that his act or omission was not a violation. * * *" 29 U.S.C. § 260. The employer has the burden of proof to establish the elements of the escape clause. [Citation.]

As set forth in the findings of fact, *supra,* the employer has not carried this burden and the plaintiffs are entitled to liquidated damages pursuant to § 216.

11. The plaintiffs are entitled to three years unpaid back wages. 29 U.S.C. § 255(a). In *Hodgson v. Hyatt,* 318 F.Supp. 390 (N.D. Fla.1970), the court emphasized that "willful" under § 255.

> * * * must be construed in the civil sense. It therefore applies to violations which are intentional, knowing or voluntary *as distinguished*

from accidental and it is used to characterize conduct marked by careless disregard whether or not one has the right so to act. (emphasis added)

Of interest is the language in the case of *Coleman v. Jiffy June Farms,* 458 F.2d 1139, 1142 (5th Cir. 1972):

> The entire legislative history of the 1966 amendments of the FLSA indicates a liberalizing intention on the part of Congress. Requiring employers to have more than awareness of the possible applicability of the FLSA would be inconsistent with that intent. Consequently, we hold that employer's decision to change his employees' rate of pay in violation of FLSA is "wilful" when, as in this case, there is substantial evidence in the record to support a finding that the employer knew or suspected that his actions might violate the FLSA. Stated most simply, we think the test should be: Did the employer know the FLSA was in the picture? In this case, Trainor knew that the FLSA had to be considered when he ceased to comply with the Act and asked his lawyer if it was permissible to do so. We need not consider today whether the three-year statute of limitations applies in a case where the employer ought to have known of the possible applicability of the FLSA but can demonstrate compellingly that in fact he did not.

The evidence in this case and the findings of fact, *supra,* compel the holding that defendant's violation of the Act was willful as within the context of 29 U.S.C. § 255(a), and that the three year statute of limitations applies.

* * *

The defendant has filed a motion to modify the memorandum opinion of this court filed on January 15, 1976. Two issues are raised in this motion.

(1) The first issue is whether the court's memorandum leaves doubt as to the percentage of work performed by the plaintiffs which could be classified as discretionary or the exercise of independent judgment.

Upon re-reading its memorandum of January 15, the court cannot find any such uncertainty. Nonetheless, the court deems it appropriate to clarify the meaning of the memorandum for defendant's benefit.

The court found and now reiterates that the credible evidence reflects that plaintiffs used 100% of their time in purely mechanical and highly skilled work not qualifying as the use of discretion or the exercise of independent judgment. The defendant has entirely failed to carry the burden of proof to show that plaintiffs would qualify for any exemption from the Fair Labor Standards Act.

(2) The second issue raised in defendant's motion to modify concerns the assessment of liquidated damages. Defendant insists that liquidated damages should not have been assessed against it, alleging that it met its burden of showing good faith under the Portal to Portal Act, 29 U.S.C. § 260. In support of this allegation, defendant asserts industry practice, unsettled issue of law, pay level of plaintiffs, and regulations characterizing the issue of exemption as a factual one.

As indicated in its memorandum of January 15, the court was most reluctant to grant plaintiffs a "windfall," when they were paid as highly skilled artisans. This problem was specifically discussed on pages 16 *et seq.* of the January 15 memorandum, and those comments are incorporated herein.

Notwithstanding the above considerations, the burden of establishing its good faith was on the defendant. The presence of good faith can only be judged by objective standards, and this court considered the following factors in reaching its determination that defendant did not act in good faith:

(a) there was an unsuccessful industrywide attempt to exempt programmers as a class. The failure of this attempt was publicly known in 1971;

(b) regulations were issued on December 2, 1971 [38 CFR 541.207(c)(7) and 541.302(h)] which reflected that the status of programmers was a factual determination in each instance;

(c) the defendant introduced no evidence of a review of the activities of the plaintiffs or persons similarly employed to determine actual work being performed;

(d) the defendant had in its files evaluations for salary adjustment which reflect information sufficient to cause an inquiry;

(e) in addition to failing to make its own investigation, the defendant sought no assessments, evaluations, or opinions from any other source; and

(f) defendant's supervising staff knew or should have known the type of work which was performed by plaintiffs.

The factors cited above have convinced this court that defendant knowingly "took a chance" as the result of a conscious determination to disregard the mandates of the regulations issued pursuant to the provisions of the Fair Labor Standards Act. This constitutes bad faith under the provisions of the Portal to Portal Act. Liquidated damages are thus proper in this case.

An appropriate order will be entered.

UNION OIL COMPANY OF CALIFORNIA, INC. v. NATIONAL LABOR RELATIONS BOARD

607 F.2d 852
(United States Court of Appeals, Ninth Circuit, Oct. 16, 1979.)

KENNEDY, C. J.

The Union Oil Company petitions us for review of a National Labor Relations Board order directing the company to bargain with an employee unit certified by the Board. The Board cross petitions for enforcement of the order. The issue is whether three of the company's computer operators should have been classified as confidential employees by the Board because of their access to restricted company information. We find substantial support for the Board's determination to deny confidential status to the employees, and we conclude the Board's order should be enforced.

In 1976, the Oil, Chemical, and Atomic Workers International Union (Oil Workers) filed a petition seeking to represent the seventeen clerical employees of the company's Wilmington refinery. Three employees were computer operators responsible for both entry and extraction of computer information. The data consist mostly of customer and personnel information, although some data regarding capital and operating expenses are also maintained. Personnel data include actuarial statistics, wage information, and employment history. The employment information is distributed on a limited basis and only five or six supervisorial personnel are authorized to obtain it. The three operators may not extract the information on their own. Some of the information has been supplied to the Oil Workers, either pursuant to contractual requirements or voluntarily by the company.

The three operators are supervised by one Marquardt, but virtually all requests for employee information are made by personnel supervisor Ward Stennet, through his personal secretary. The data are used by Stennet both in the resolution of grievances and in the negotiation of contracts.

The question before this court is whether the Board erred in finding the three computer operators are not confidential employees. On petition for enforcement, the Board's ruling will stand as long as it is not arbitrary, capricious or unsupported by substantial evidence. [Citations.]

The Board has long recognized that employees who have a confidential relationship to management should be excluded from the bargaining unit. *See, e. g., Ford Motor Co.,* 66 N.L.R.B. 1317-1322, 317, 1322 (1946); *The B. F. Goodrich Co.,* 115 N.L.R.B. 722, 724 (1956). [Citation.] The rationale behind this rule is that employees should not be placed in a position which creates a potential conflict between the interests of the employer and the union.

In *B. F. Goodrich, supra,* the Board defined confidential employees as those who "assist and act in a confidential capacity to persons who formulate, determine, and effectuate management policies in the field of labor relations." 115 N.L.R.B. at 724. Under this test the central inquiry is whether the employee is in a confidential work relationship with a specifically identifiable managerial employee responsible for labor policy. Because most employees have an arguably confidential relationship with management, and because an expansive application of the exclusionary rule would deprive many employees of the right to bargain collectively, the Board has narrowly construed the definition of confidential employee. [Citations.]

The company contends that the computer operators had a confidential relationship with Stennet. The record, however, does not support this argument. There was no showing that the computer operators ever dealt with Stennet; indeed, the closest contact that the employees had with Stennet was through his secretary, Ruth Schultz. Since the parties stipulated that Schultz was a confidential employee and that the computer operators perform duties previously done by Schultz, the

company contends that this also demonstrates the existence of a confidential work relationship. We do not agree. The record shows that the duties taken over by the computer operators were purely clerical in nature.

More significant is the fact that the computer operators were under the supervision of Marquardt, who was responsible for computer operations, not labor relations. [Citation.] Because there is substantial evidence that the computer operators acted as record custodians for persons who do not formulate or implement labor policy, we conclude that there is an adequate basis for the Board's ruling.

In a separate line of decisions, the Board has also accorded confidential status to "those employees who, in the course of their duties, regularly have access to confidential information concerning anticipated changes which may result from collective bargaining negotiations." *Pullman Standard Division.* 214 N.L.R.B. 762, 762-63 (1974). The company contends that the computer operators come under the *Pullman Standard* definition of confidentiality because they have access to information that might be used in contract negotiations. This information, it is argued, includes data concerning the refinery's capital and expense budgets as well as individual personnel information. Critical to the Board's decision in *Pullman Standard,* however, was the fact that the employees there had access to the precise labor rates which the employer was willing to agree to in collective bargaining. Premature disclosure of managerial estimates of the results of future contract negotiations, the Board reasoned, would have unduly prejudiced management's bargaining position.

In the case before us, there was no showing that the capital budget indicated the precise labor rates the company would accept, or that it otherwise disclosed the company's bargaining position. The record only indicates that the computer operators have access to personnel or statistical information upon which the company's labor relations policy is based. The Board has consistently held that access to such information is insufficient to establish confidential status. [Citations.] In this regard the Board's ruling is well within the discretion granted it to promulgate standards for effective implementation of the National Labor

Relations Act in the industrial context. [Citation.]

The computer operators have responsibilities similar to those of employees who have been found not to be confidential employees. [Citations.] We conclude, therefore, that substantial evidence supports the Board's conclusion that the computer operators were not confidential employees under the *Pullman Standard* test.

Finally, the company argues that the *Pullman Standard* test is satisfied because the computer operators regularly perform the same duty of running new test programs as those persons classified as confidential employees in *C F & I Steel,* 196 N.L.R.B. 470 (1972). The record does not support this contention. Absent a showing of regular performance as required by *C F & I Steel,* this argument is without merit.

Order enforced.

EXXON PIPELINE CO. v. NATIONAL LABOR RELATIONS BOARD

596 F.2d 704

(United States Court of Appeals, Fifth Circuit, June 11, 1979.)

PER CURIAM.

Exxon Pipeline Company challenges a determination by the National Labor Relations Board in a representation proceeding that the company's "oil movement supervisors" (OMS's), formerly "dispatchers," be classified as employees in a proper collective bargaining unit rather than as unprotected supervisors. The Board cross-applies for enforcement of its subsequent order requiring the company to cease refusing to bargain with the union duly elected by the employees in question. Finding much evidence in the record to support the Board's characterization, we enforce its order.

Exxon Pipeline's business is the operation of about 13,000 miles of pipeline in seven states

as a common carrier of petroleum. It has about 450 employees in the field keeping the pipe in good repair and monitoring the flow of petroleum in certain areas of the pipeline. The rest of the pipeline, about 8,000 miles, is monitored at the company's office in downtown Houston by the oil movements supervisors. These men, operating around the clock in three daily shifts, sit at computer-assisted consoles that show the progress of the various batches of oil as they flow through the pipes according to the schedules prepared by others at the Houston office. The OMS personnel have highly responsible positions; they physically operate the system by remote control to ensure that each batch goes through the proper pipes to the correct destination; they are charged with detecting breakdowns and other "upsets" as they show up on the control panel and with reacting appropriately to minimize loss of oil and to effect the scheduled deliveries. But it is not responsibility per se or exercise of discretion or independent judgment in themselves that signify under section 2(11) [1] of the National Labor Relations Act. Rather, responsibility for directing other *employees* is the critical factor in characterizing someone as a supervisor. [Citations.]

The company asserts that OMS personnel have authority "responsib[ly] to direct" other employees because when they discover an upset in a monitored pipeline the OMS on duty has the authority to deploy the field personnel near the site to correct the problem. The OMS, the company argues, makes an independent judgment whether a problem must be corrected immediately, even to the extent that field employees must work overtime, or whether a problem is minor and may be attended to later. The record amply demonstrates, however, that the OMS does little more than notify the field that a certain problem has occurred and request assistance in remedying it. He has no further authority or responsibility to direct the field personnel in the manner of performing their remedial duties.

---

1. Section 2(11) of the National Labor Relations Act, 29 U.S.C. § 152(11), defines "supervisor" as
   any individual having authority, in the interest of the employer, to hire, transfer, suspend, lay off, recall, promote, discharge, assign, reward, or discipline other employees, or responsibility to direct them, or to adjust their grievances, or effectively to recommend such action, if in connection with the foregoing

the exercise of such authority is not of a merely routine or clerical nature, but requires the use of independent judgment.

The company does not contend that the OMS's have authority to hire, fire or discipline other employees. It argues solely that OMS personnel "responsib[ly] direct" others in the company.

The field personnel are in a wholly separate department of the company and thus function in a different supervisory hierarchy from that of the OMS. The OMS must call on field personnel in a particular sequence required by the lists promulgated for each field division and thus may not usually call on a "wage employee" until he has unsuccessfully attempted to locate the local supervisor. Since it is the "joint mission and objective" of the two parallel departments to move oil through the system, the field employees and their supervisors probably have prior independent authorization to do whatever is necessary in the event of a serious upset, even if overtime results. In addition, there was testimony that someone from the field department participates equally with the OMS in reaching a joint decision as to whether and when a repair will be effected.

These circumstances persuasively distinguish this case from those relied on by Exxon Pipeline. In *Arizona Public Service Co. v. N. L. R. B.*, 453 F.2d 228, 231-32 (9th Cir. 1971), for instance, the systems supervisors had the power to "choose which linemen are to work, when and where." The supervisors there, in great contrast to OMS personnel here, had "clear delegated authority over virtually everybody in the company." *Id*. In *N. L. R. B. v. Detroit Edison*, 537 F.2d 239, 241, 243 (6th Cir. 1976), the supervisors in question issued "literally thousands of instructions" to field personnel. The reviewing court concluded that the instructions, though couched in terms of request, amounted to orders derived from the supervisors' independent judgment. Having no access to the record in that case, we cannot observe the character of those instructions for ourselves. Our careful review of the record herein convinces us that the requests issued by OMS personnel do not amount to supervisory direction of the type required. The OMS's do not "direct appropriate action to remedy

the problem," nor can they "take over any operator under system control that would ordinarily be under local control" any time they see fit. *Id*. Once notified of a suspected problem, the field personnel here are left to their own devices and chain of command in doing what the situation requires. There is, of course, close communication between the two bases of operation so that the OMS will shut down pipelines or pumps as needed and will not restart the system precipitously. But as regards the field employees, the OMS is little more than a night watchman, who can hardly be said to supervise the police when he calls to report and request investigation of the burglary he has just discovered. Accordingly, the order of the Board is hereby enforced.

SEASON-ALL INDUSTRIES, INC. v. NATIONAL LABOR RELATIONS BOARD
654 F.2d 932
(United States Court of Appeals, Third Circuit, Decided July 17, 1981.)

GARTH, C. J.

* * *

B.

Season-All also objected to the Board's determination that its computer programmers were not professional employees as that term is defined in 29 U.S.C. § 152(12).[6] If the computer programmers were professional employees, they could not be included in a bargaining unit with nonprofessional employees unless a majority of such professional employees were to vote for inclusion in such a unit. See 29 U.S.C. § 159(b)(1) quoted *supra* at p. 936 n.1. No such separate election was ever held because the Board concluded that the computer

---

6. The term "professional employee" means—
    (a) any employee engaged in work (i) predominantly intellectual and varied in character as opposed to routine mental, manual, mechanical, or physical work; (ii) involving the consistent exercise of discretion and judgment in its performance; (iii) of such a character that the output produced or the result accomplished cannot be standardized in relation to a given period of time; (iv) requiring knowledge of an advanced type in a field of science or learning customarily acquired by a prolonged course of specialized intellectual instruction and study in

an institution of higher learning or a hospital, as distinguished from a general academic education or from an apprenticeship or from training in the performance of routine mental, manual, or physical processes; or
    (b) any employee, who (i) has completed the courses of specialized intellectual instruction and study described in clause (iv) of paragraph (a), and (ii) is performing related work under the supervision of a professional person to qualify himself to become a professional employee as defined in paragraph (a).

programmers were not professional employees.

The hearing held on April 17, 1979 resulted in an opinion of the Regional Director dated May 16, 1979, which was affirmed by the Board. That opinion states in relevant part:

> The record discloses that computer programming requires special education or training above the high school level of at least two years. However, the Employer does not require a four-year college degree and it is in business education with four courses relating to computer programming. The other two programmers attended one or two year technical schools which prepared them as trainees. The record further reveals that substantial additional time is required before a trainee becomes fully qualified as a programmer.
>
> The record reveals that pursuant to a request for information from any of the employer's departments, the programmers develop computer programs to extract the information from the computer in a useable form. The record indicates that the formulation of such programs requires the exercise of judgment and the programs are developed without supervision.
>
> * * *
>
> While knowledge of the type described in [29 U.S.C. § 152(12)(a)(iv)] [citation] might be desirable for a programmer to have, it is clear that their work does not require it. Further, the record fails to establish that the computer programmers are engaged in other than pure programming activities. Accordingly, inasmuch as the Employer's computer programmers do not satisfy all of the requirements of Section 2(12), I find that they are not professional employees as defined by that Section of the Act. At best, the computer programmers are technical employees. Inasmuch as the parties have agreed to include technical employees, I find that the Employer's computer programmers are appropriately included in the unit.

[Reference.] (footnotes omitted).

While the Board has previously determined that a systems analyst with wide discretion and significant amounts of technical training might be considered a "professional employee" in certain situations [citation] it has generally considered computer programmers to be technical and thus nonprofessional employees. [Citations.]

Here, the Board's factual determination that the computer programmers are not "professional employees" is "supported by substan-

tial evidence on the record considered as a whole" 29 U.S.C. 160(f), and giving our usual deference to the Board's expertise in a classification context, we conclude that the Board did not err in its ruling. [Citations.]

* * *

COMPUTER SCIENCES CORP. v. NATIONAL LABOR RELATIONS BOARD
677 F.2d 804
(United States Court of Appeals, Eleventh Circuit, June 4, 1982.)

HILL, C. J.

This case is before us on a petition by the National Labor Relations Board (NLRB or the Board) for an adjudication that respondent Computer Sciences Corporation (CSC) is in civil contempt of a prior judgment of the former Fifth Circuit granting enforcement of a Board order. That order was issued against CSC's competitor, Federal Electric Corporation (FEC). The current dispute between the Board and CSC centers on whether CSC may properly be bound by the prior judgment since it was neither a party to the unfair labor practice proceeding which gave rise to the Board order nor to the subsequent enforcement proceedings before the Fifth Circuit.

I

FEC provided space shuttle computer support services under a contract with the National Aeronautics and Space Administration (NASA) at Kennedy Space Center. In 1975 the International Alliance of Theatrical Stage Employees and Moving Picture Machine Operators (IATSE) won a representation election conducted among FEC employees. On September 29, 1976, a panel of the former Fifth Circuit enforced a Board order which overruled objections made by FEC to the conduct of the election and which found FEC guilty of an unfair labor practice in its refusal to bargain. [Citation.] The Board's order, as enforced by the court, directed FEC's "officers, agents, *successors,* and assigns" to commence good faith bargaining with the union certified to represent employees in the Commercial Programming Section of FEC's Computations Department. [Citation.]

Following the court's decision, CSC successfully underbid FEC for a contract to provide NASA with shuttle support services. FEC's contract expired on September 30, 1977. On October 1, 1977, CSC, having employed many former FEC commercial programmers, began performing support services. Because FEC and the union had not completed negotiations on a collective bargaining agreement before CSC's takeover, the union requested that CSC bargain with the union. Based on its belief that the union no longer represented a majority of the commercial programmers it employed, CSC refused, and the union filed an unfair labor practice charge with the Board.

Rather than proceeding to adjudicate this charge, the Board instead instituted this civil contempt action against CSC as successor to FEC. Upon CSC's motion to dismiss the contempt petition [footnote], a panel of the former Fifth Circuit ordered CSC to file an answer to the petition and referred the cause to an administrative law judge as special master for an evidentiary hearing. The special master's report found that CSC is a successor to FEC within the scope of the court's prior enforcement decree and recommended that CSC be adjudged in contempt. The purgation order suggested by the special master proposed that CSC fully comply with the decree, set an initial meeting date for bargaining, publicize the contempt adjudication to its bargaining unit employees, file periodic reports with the clerk of this court showing steps toward compliance, and pay the Board's costs, including attorney's fees.

II

CSC raises several arguments against an adjudication of contempt. First, [citation], it contends that Federal Rule of Civil Procedure 65(d) [footnote] precludes contempt sanctions because there is no privity between itself and FEC. CSC also objects that this court is without authority, prior to a Board hearing on the question, to determine whether it is a successor to FEC. [Citation], CSC maintains that a court of appeals may not decide in the first instance whether a bargaining unit remains appropriate—one of the prerequisites to imposition of successorship obligations under the labor laws—[footnote]—because unit determinations lie within the Board's primary ju-

risdiction. In a related argument CSC further contends that it is a denial of due process to impose contempt sanctions upon it in the same proceeding in which it is first determined that the court's prior judgment is binding upon it. [Citation.] Finally, CSC maintains that it is not a "successor" to FEC under the labor law meaning of that term as defined in *NLRB v. Burns International Security Services, Inc.*, 406 U.S. 272, 92 S.Ct. 1571, 32 L.Ed.2d 61 (1972).

We need not address each of the issues CSC raises. Notwithstanding any power this court might have to determine the successorship question as ancillary to enforcement of the prior decree, we deem it unwise for policy reasons to do so in this case. We hold that when a dispute over successorship is bona fide, it is inappropriate for this court to decide it on a contempt application. When the dispute over successorship liability is but a sham, this court may proceed via contempt proceedings.

III

In the context, like that here, of a competitive bidder relationship between the first employer and the alleged successor, *NLRB v. Burns International Security Services, Inc.*, 406 U.S. 272, 92 S.Ct. 1571, 32 L.Ed.2d 61 (1972), established the test for determining when the subsequent employer is a successor bound by the predecessor's obligation to bargain with the union. "[W]here the bargaining unit remains unchanged and the majority of the employees hired by the new employer are represented by a recently certified bargaining agent," the new employer has a duty "to bargain with the incumbent union." *Id.* at 281, 92 S.Ct. at 1579. The first element of the *Burns* test—whether the bargaining unit remains appropriate under the new employer—is an intensely factual inquiry, which may be decisively affected by changes in operational structure or practices under the new employer. [Citations.] In this case, CSC argues that organizational and operational changes implemented among its employees preclude a finding of successorship. It points specifically to the fact that under FEC's operations, commercial programmers and scientific programmers were completely segregated both physically and functionally such that a bargaining unit composed only of commercial programmers was appropriate. Under its policies for providing services, however, CSC cross-trains these two groups, placing them in a single department; maintains the same education and experience requirements, the same salary structure and benefits, and the same career path for both; and provides interaction among these employees. Hence it argues that a unit composed only of commercial programmers is no longer appropriate. Further alleged to be relevant to the unit determination issue is a presumption under Board precedent against a unit of less than all of a company's technical employees who share a community of interest. [Footnote.]

As with the first element of the *Burns* inquiry, the second is also fact-laden, and, again as with the first, it is also the subject of considerable dispute between the Board and CSC. The parties present different figures for assessing whether former FEC bargaining unit employees constitute a majority of the relevant CSC work force.

Reasons akin to those underlying the doctrine of exhaustion of administrative remedies persuade us that it is ill-advised to resolve these highly factual and close issues before the agency possessing expertise in these matters has passed upon the question of continued appropriateness. The policies advanced by requiring exhaustion of administrative remedies prior to judicial review of agency action include more complete development of the factual record by the agency and the observance of administrative autonomy, particularly as to decisions involving the exercise of discretionary powers granted the agency by Congress or requiring the application of special expertise possessed by the agency. [Citation.] From what we have set out above regarding the *Burns* test, it clearly ap-

pears that further development of the factual record in this case would indeed be beneficial. Moreover, we are mindful of the large measure of discretion granted the agency under its statutory authority to make unit determinations, 29 U.S.C. § 159(b), and of the limited role of the courts of appeals in reviewing such determinations. [Citations.] Therefore we believe that any judicial determination of the successorship liability of CSC is better postponed until there has been agency action.[5] In our view this manner of proceeding more fully accords with the congressional distribution of authority between executive agencies and the judicial branch.[6] [Citation.] [Footnote.]

In addition, the interest in uniformity within federal labor law convinces us that we should await agency action. We are concerned that allowing initial court determination of unit questions via contempt proceedings would set courts of appeals on a course of developing their own standards for unit appropriateness—standards which might reflect judgments differing from those of the agency with expertise in labor matters. Just as it is important that the Board itself maintain a consistent approach in its unit determinations [citation], we think it important to avoid divergent administrative and judicial standards for such determinations.

* * *

IV

It appears from what we have set out above, from the special master's report, and from the statements of the Board's counsel that the dispute over successorship in this case is bona fide. Hence we decline for policy reasons to adjudicate CSC's contempt liability. CSC's

---

5. In this case, as we noted above, there is a pending unfair labor practice charge against CSC for its refusal to bargain with the union. The Board hearing on the charge must necessarily entertain the issue of CSC's status as a bona fide successor.

6. We do not commend the Board for resorting first to the courts rather than proceeding on the pending unfair labor practice complaint lodged with it. It is somewhat ironic that we find ourselves issuing such a reprimand, for it is usually the agency which argues against premature judicial intervention and in favor of allowing the administrative process to run its course. At oral argument the Board's counsel confessed that this is the first case in which it has sought to resolve the successorship

issue via judicial contempt proceedings rather than an unfair labor practice proceeding. Motivating the agency's choice was a concern with the rapid turnover of contractors at the Kennedy Space Center and the resultant increased difficulty in enforcing a bargaining obligation. That a contempt proceeding in a court of appeals would prove a more expeditious means of handling the matter is a questionable assumption, given the crowded dockets which have become commonplace. To be sure, the cumbersomeness of the administrative machinery and the process of seeking enforcement in a court of appeals is lamentable. But if a cure is needed, it lies in the streamlining of those procedures by Congress, not in disregard of the machinery currently in place.

motion to dismiss the contempt petition, which has been carried with the case, is granted. The Board's petition for contempt is Dismissed without prejudice to further proceedings before the NLRB.

GILL v. COMPUTER EQUIPMENT CORP.
266 Md. 170, 292 A.2d 54
(Court of Appeals of Maryland, June 30, 1972.)

SMITH, J.

Appellant, Earl F. Gill (Gill), sued appellee, Computer Equipment Corporation (Computer), for breach of contract in allegedly failing to honor an employment contract. A jury returned a verdict in favor of Gill in the amount of $20,000, which was set aside when the trial court entered judgment *n. o. v.* in favor of Computer, the defendant, upon its seasonably filed motion. The second count of Gill's declaration asked for a declaratory judgment that a covenant not to compete was void. The trial court ruled against Gill upon that count also. Gill has filed appeals from both actions of the trial court. We shall affirm.

Gill and B. J. Fadden had been partners in a manufacturers' representative business known as Eastronics. They later incorporated under the name of Eastronics, Inc. In 1969 conversations took place between the executive vice-president of Computer and Messrs. Gill and Fadden culminating in a contract under which shares of Eastronics stock were exchanged for shares of Computer, Gill and Fadden were employed by Computer, provision was made for bonuses to them based upon the earnings of a new division to be known as "Peripheral Systems Division of Computer Equipment" set up to take over the business of Eastronics, an annual salary of $25,000 each was agreed upon as to Gill and Fadden, and each stockholder agreed that "should he leave the employment of Computer for any reason, he [would] not compete with Computer for a period of two (2) years following such termination of employment."

The relationship between the parties terminated when Computer sent Gill a telegram on July 8, 1970, advising that sales were not developing satisfactorily, that Gill's employment was terminated that date "with salary including vacation paid thru end of July," and that his "rights to any future CEC shares earned under terms purchase agreement between CEC and shareholders of Eastronics [would] of course be protected for the term of the agreement." This suit followed on September 2, 1970.

JUDGMENT *N.O.V.*

The jury returned a verdict in the amount of $20,000 in favor of Gill. Gill had sought to prove that the true intent of the agreement between him and Computer was to employ him for a definite term of three years, commencing on May 28, 1969, when the agreement was executed. The trial judge permitted the introduction of testimony of prior discussions between Gill and Computer's representative because he felt that the written agreement was rendered ambiguous by an apparent conflict between two paragraphs. On the motion for judgment *n. o. v.* the court reversed itself, holding that it had erred in permitting admission of this testimony, that the contract was not ambiguous. It further observed:

> However, assuming this evidence had been properly admitted, we think the jury's verdict was wrong because it was against the clear weight of the evidence.

* * *

Section 11.01 of the contract provided that "[e]ffective immediately upon Closing Computer agree[d] to employ each of the Stockholders at an annual salary of $25,000.00, and the Stockholders agree[d] to accept such employment and devote their full time and best efforts thereto." It was silent as to the period of employment. The bonus provision provided for additional shares for Gill and Fadden in Computer based upon the earnings of Peripheral Systems Division "for the calendar years 1969, 1970, and 1971."

The two sections originally regarded as conflicting were § 13.04 and § 13.06 which read:

> 13.04 *Entire Agreement.* This Agreement contains the entire agreement between the parties hereto and supersedes any and all prior agreements, arrangements or understandings between the parties relating to the acquisition of Eastronics by Computer. No oral understand-

ings, statements, promises or inducements contrary to the terms of this Agreement exist. No representations, warranties, covenants or conditions, express or implied, whether by statute or otherwise, other than as set forth herein, have been made by either Stockholders or by Computer. No waiver of any term, provision or condition of this Agreement, whether by conduct or otherwise, in any one or more instances shall be deemed to be or construed as a further or continuing waiver of any such term, provision or condition, or of any other term, provision or condition of this Agreement. This Agreement cannot be changed or terminated orally.

13.06 *Survival of Representations, Etc.* All representations, warranties and covenants made by Stockholders and by Computer (as the case may be) in this Agreement or pursuant hereto, shall be deemed joint and several (except as otherwise expressly stated) and made for the purpose of inducing Computer or the Stockholders (as the case may be) to enter into this Agreement, and shall survive the Closing and remain operative and in full force and effect regardless of any investigations at any time made by or on behalf of the party or parties to whom such representations or warranties are made, and shall not be deemed merged in any document or instrument executed or delivered at the Closing.

On direct examination of Gill there was but a single reference to the term of the employment contract. The record is:

Q. Were there any specifics discussed between you and Mr. Fadden on the one hand and Mr. Gundy and Mr. Moore on the other hand with respect to the term of your employment?

A. Yes, we talked. They illustrated to us the method of remuneration. They proposed a salary of $25,000.00 and illustrated how in the first year and second year and third year the bonus plans would operate.

Then there was some discussion as to the exact number of shares that we were to receive for Eastronics.

At the conclusion of it when we agreed on the number of shares everybody jumped up and I remember very plainly we all shook hands and Mr. Gundy said, "We are glad to have you aboard. We will send you a written contract which will obligate you to us for three years, but we hope you will stay longer than that."

Then the meeting was over.

Q. That was said by Mr. Gundy?

A. That was said by Mr. Gundy to Mr. Fadden and I at the meeting.

Q. And the bonus contingent shares and so on you are relating are the same as set forth in the agreement?

A. Yes.

On cross-examination of Gill the record is in part as follows:

Q. Let's back up a minute.
I believe you testified that you first met Mr. Gundy sometime in 1968; is that correct?

A. Yes.

Q. Now, you say that you came to a meeting of the minds of this merger in New York?

A. Yes.

* * *

Q. How was that meeting of the minds consummated, if you understand what I mean?
How did you know that they knew you had an agreement?

A. Well, we agreed on their number of stock for the exchange of Eastronics and everybody got up and shook hands and Phil said, "Welcome aboard. We will be sending you the contract."

Q. Was there anything in that agreement reduced to writing at that time?

A. No.

Q. Had it been reduced to writing prior thereto?

A. No.

Q. I believe you testified Mr. Gundy shook your hand and said, "Welcome aboard. You are committed to CEC for three years."?

A. He said, "We will be sending you a written contract which obligates you to CEC for a three-year period, but we hope you will stay longer."

Q. Before you said that you had a meeting of the minds?

A. Yes, he had been discussing the three-year period, at least three years, of which there was to be remuneration based upon sales and upon bonuses and shares of stock and so forth.

This seemed to be the culmination of everything.

Q. You say he was discussing remuneration?

A. He very carefully outlined how renumeration was to take place and how to get the shares [in] the first, second and third year.

Q. That deals with the pay-out and compensation for the purchase of Eastronics?

A. Oh, no. That has nothing to do with that. The purchase of Eastronics was incidental to the whole thing. It was us he wanted. This was a method of acquiring us since we had a business.

Q. Prior to Mr. Gundy making this alleged statement and the handshake, was there any specific discussion between you and Mr. Gundy as to the period of your employment with CEC?

A. No, we *assumed* when we were talking and he talked about three years it was three years. We were talking about employment and salaries and bonuses we could earn and we *assumed* we were going to be there to earn them.

Q. Was it your *assumption* prior to that handshake you were being employed for three years?

A. Yes, really, in fact, we had expectations of making more money without CEC at that time and if it hadn't been for the fact we were going to be employed for three years, that we had some degree of security built in at that point of time, we weren't about to take less salary.

* * *

Q. You say that with all this discussion in this hotel room about this three-year period and it was your assumption that related to the terms of employment?

A. Yes, it wasn't all that discussion, it was in the discussion.

Q. When he mentioned the obligation for three years with the handshake was that the first you heard of the three-year employment?

A. No, we had been discussing the employment and the compensation.

Q. Mr. Gill, you remember being deposed in my office on the 22nd of February of this year, don't you?

A. Yes, sir.

Q. I refer you to page 16, the last question.

Question. When did you go to work for them?

Answer. Went to work for them virtually immediately after the agreement in March that we would do this, and, in fact, I remember it very distinctly. We were all in a hotel room, and we spent several hours talking about how we would do it and what we would do, and so forth, and we agreed on the figure of the exchange of stock. And at that point in time everybody stood and shook hands and Phil Gundy said, "Welcome to Computer Equipment Corporation. We'll be sending you a contract. You're obligated to us for three years, but we hope you fellows will stay longer."

Question. Was there any discussion with him about the period of your employment?

Answer. Well, that was the discussion.

Question. Was that all it consisted of?

Answer. That was all it consisted of, and when we got the contract I took it to my attorney and I read it and he read it. And it was his opinion that because of the statements—

I am not going to read his opinion.

It seems at variance with what you are telling us now.

* * *

Q. I would like you to explain, did you mean there was no discussion until the handshake and he said, "Welcome aboard. You are here for three years"?

A. I didn't say that at all. I don't follow what you are trying to get at.

We discussed during the meeting the compensation. They brought up how we were to be compensated over the three-year period and we *assumed* that that was, they were talking about employment for a three-year period.

I don't see what I have just said that is at variance with what you have just read. (Emphasis added.)

At no point was there evidence presented from any source that Computer bound itself to employ Gill and Fadden for a three-year period. The contract sent to them did not call for this. Other parties present even denied Gill's version of what was said. In McCullough Iron Co. v. Carpenter, 67 Md. 554, 11 A. 176 (1887), our predecessors observed:

> There can be no doubt that, in this country, the rule is, an indefinite hiring is *prima facie* a hiring at will. It is also well settled that a hiring at so much a week, month or year, no time being specified, does not, of itself, make more than an indefinite hiring. It is competent for the parties to show what the mutual understanding was, but unless there was a mutual understanding, it is only an indefinite hiring. [Citing authorities.] * * * Now under the law as we understand it to be, if the plaintiff's case rested solely upon his own testimony, there would seem to be no escape from instructing the jury there was no legally sufficient evidence of a contract for a yearly hiring. *Id.* at 557, 11 A. at 178.

As Chief Judge Robinson observed in Baltimore & O. R. R. v. Stewart, 79 Md. 487, 498, 29 A. 964, 965 (1894), "[A party is] in no manner bound by the assumptions or belief of the witness, they are bound by the contract itself, construed by the same rules of law which govern all other contracts." We have nothing offered here to bind Computer other than the assumption of the witness. Accordingly, assuming *arguendo* that the parol evidence was admissible, Gill has failed to establish an employment contract other than a hiring at will. Therefore, Judge Mathias did not err in entering judgment *n. o. v.* in favor of Computer, the defendant.

THE NONCOMPETITIVE AGREEMENT

Section 12.01 of the contract provided:

> 12.01 *Covenant not to Compete.* Each Stockholder covenants and agrees that, should he leave the employment of Computer for any reason, he will not compete with Computer for a period of two (2) years following such termination of employment. Competing shall be defined as (1) working in an executive, administrative, sales or service capacity for any manufacturer which was represented by the Peripheral Systems Division during all or any part of the one (1) year period immediately preceding the date of such termination of employment; or (2) working for a sales representative and/or service organization which represents any such manufacturer; or (3) selling or servicing the products of any such manufacturer as an independent representative.

It will be noted that although no territorial limitation is imposed that competition is defined, in effect, as working for customers of Peripheral Systems Division of the year prior to termination of employment.

Gill cites Ruhl v. F. A. Bartlett Tree Expert Co., 245 Md. 118, 225 A.2d 288 (1967), where [citation] the Court observed that the general rule in Maryland, as in most jurisdictions, is that restrictive covenants in a contract of employment by which an employee as a part of his employment contract agrees not to engage in a competing business or vocation with that of his employer on leaving the employment will be sustained if the restraint is confined within limits which are no wider as to area and duration than are reasonably necessary for the protection of the business of the employer and do not impose undue hardship on the employee or disregard the interest of the public. Gill then goes on to fashion an argument that the clause here is unduly restrictive because it contains no limitation as to area.

Oddly enough, neither party cited Tuttle v. Riggs-Warfield-Roloson, Inc., 251 Md. 45, 246 A.2d 588 (1968). There the employee agreed to "refrain, for a period of two years beginning with the effective date of such termination, from engaging either directly or indirectly, in any insurance activities with *customers* of Riggs-Warfield-Roloson, Inc." (Emphasis added.) The trial court there found that the restrictive covenant was valid, the agreement being reasonable as to time and scope. Judge Marbury said for the Court:

> We agree with the lower court that the agreement in question was a valid and enforceable contract. *Id.* at 49, 246 A.2d at 590.

We see no difference between this case and *Tuttle.* The time is the same in both cases. The scope of the limitation here basically is to customers of Computer in the narrow area in which Gill was employed. Actually this restriction might be more favorable to the employee than that in *Tuttle.* There in a general insurance brokerage business the employee serviced certain accounts already on the books, developed new business from those accounts, and developed new accounts. He was not restricted from dealing only with customers he had formerly served, but "from engaging either directly or indirectly in any insurance activities with customers" of his employer. Computer's activities were not confined to its Peripheral Systems Division. Gill's testimony showed that the larger part of the contact with customers of that division was by him. He was restricted in his employment only as to customers of that division. He was otherwise free to operate whenever and wherever he chose. The restriction was not unreasonable. *Tuttle* is controlling here.

Judgments affirmed; appellant to pay the costs.

REPUBLIC SYSTEMS AND PROGRAMMING, INC. v. COMPUTER ASSISTANCE, INC.

322 F. Supp. 619
(United States District Court, D. Connecticut, Jan. 15, 1970.)

BLUMENFELD, D. J.

In this diversity action, plaintiff seeks damages for and an injunction against allegedly unlawful conduct of two former employees, the competing corporation those former employees organized following their resignation from plaintiff's employ, and another competing corporation, already in existence at the time the events complained of here occurred. Plaintiff complains of the following allegedly unlawful conduct by the defendants: (1) approaching plaintiff's customers to induce them to terminate their contracts with plaintiff and to transfer the work contracted for to defendants; (2) soliciting and inducing plaintiff's employees to resign from plaintiff's employment and enter defendants' employ, and thereafter to refuse to revoke their resignation and return to plaintiff's employ; (3) taking from plaintiff's files documents relating to prospective business and work in progress; (4) appropriating to themselves plaintiff's business and good will.

On December 12, 1969, a temporary restraining order was issued prohibiting defendants from (1) approaching any of plaintiff's present customers for whom plaintiff had work in progress under contract and attempting in any way to induce them to terminate their contracts with plaintiff and transfer the work to defendants; (2) soliciting or inducing any of plaintiff's employees to disclose any information concerning work in progress or prospective business; (3) disclosing any information concerning work in progress or prospective business; (4) soliciting or inducing any of plaintiff's employees to resign from plaintiff's employment; (5) soliciting or inducing any of plaintiff's former employees to refuse to revoke their resignation from plaintiff and to refuse to return to plaintiff's employment; (6) engaging directly or indirectly in unfair competition with plaintiff "in the manner complained of in plaintiff's complaint."

An order to show cause why a preliminary injunction should not issue was filed simultaneously, and a hearing was set for December 19. By agreement of counsel, the hearing on a preliminary injunction was consolidated with the hearing on a final injunction, with only the issue of damages being reserved. At the conclusion of that hearing, defendants having consented, the temporary restraining order then in effect, with the exception of one paragraph, was extended until January 15, 1970. The scope of the permanent injunction sought by plaintiff is somewhat broader than the terms of the temporary restraining order now in effect.

For the reasons set forth more fully herein, the temporary restraining order is dissolved and the applications for preliminary and permanent injunctions are denied.

FINDINGS OF FACT

1. Plaintiff, Republic Systems and Programming, Inc., is organized under the laws of Texas and has a principal place of business in New Jersey. Defendants Vignola and Geddes are citizens of Connecticut and defendants Computer Assistance, Inc. and Computer Assistance of Hartford, Inc. are Connecticut corporations with principal places of business in Connecticut.

2. The amount in controversy exceeds $10,000, exclusive of interest and costs.

3. The business of all the parties may be generally described, as it was by various witnesses, as the data processing services business or the computer software business. In general, the parties are engaged in analyzing

problems which might be solved by the use of computers and other data processing equipment, designing a solution to those problems, and implementing the solution by the use of computer programs on the premises of the client, who in most cases would already own a computer.

4. The computer software or data processing services business is relatively new and rapidly expanding. One of its most salient characteristics is the fierce competition for new business and, of special relevance here, for technically competent personnel.

5. Perhaps because of the keen competition for technically qualified personnel, it is not uncommon for those in this field to move frequently from one employer to another, developing in some instances more loyalty to the industry and to the customers than to their employers.

6. Plaintiff Republic Systems, in addition to its home office in East Orange, New Jersey, has branch offices in Secaucus, New Jersey and Cheshire, Connecticut, the latter being established in 1967.

7. Defendant Andrew Vignola was, prior to December 5, 1969, assistant vice-president of plaintiff and manager of plaintiff's Cheshire office, in charge of the day-to-day operation of plaintiff's business at that office.

8. Defendant Roger Geddes was, prior to December 5, 1969, senior staff manager of plaintiff's Cheshire office, with general supervisory authority over the "technical" staff members there.

9. Prior to December 5, 1969, there were, including defendants Vignola and Geddes, approximately 25 employees at plaintiff's Cheshire office. Among the other 23 were 3 staff managers, 2 account managers, 13 technicians, 2 marketing managers and 1 full-time and 2 part-time secretaries.

10. None of plaintiff's officers and none of its employees at the Cheshire office was bound by an employment contract.

11. In addition to the plaintiff's 3 branch offices listed above, there were at one time 2 other branches, 1 located in New Hampshire and 1 in Old Greenwich, Connecticut, both organized in late 1968.

12. Sometime in March, 1969 plaintiff's New Hampshire and Old Greenwich offices were closed for lack of business.

13. At approximately the same time, March of 1969, defendant Vignola held a meeting at his home attended by defendant Geddes and the three staff managers. At that meeting, the financial straits of plaintiff were discussed, as were alternatives to remaining in plaintiff's employ. Specifically the possibility of leaving plaintiff to form a new company was explored. The discussion included the possibility of asking some of plaintiff's other employees to join them and of securing the business of some of the plaintiff's then present customers.

14. In April of 1969 defendant Vignola again chaired a meeting at his home, this time with defendant Geddes, two of the three staff managers and one of the two marketing managers present. The decision was made to leave the plaintiff and form a new company. A week later, the participants were notified that the whole thing was off.

15. In May of 1969, following these two meetings, Mr. Vignola went to plaintiff's home office in New Jersey to submit his resignation to plaintiff's president. He was unhappy with the company and its performance. After gaining some concessions from plaintiff's president, however, Vignola agreed to stay on at his position. It was agreed that the Cheshire office would become a separate corporation, a wholly owned subsidiary of plaintiff, and that defendant Vignola would be an officer, director, and shareholder in the new company. Some steps were taken to initiate that reorganization, but many more which were contemplated had not been taken by December 5, 1969, when the conduct complained of in this action occurred.

16. Defendant Computer Assistance, Inc. had for some time been a competitor of plaintiff Republic Systems and Programming, Inc. in the computer software business.

17. Sometime in early November 1969 Mr. Thomas McDonagh, president of defendant Computer Assistance, Inc., acting pursuant to rumors of unrest in plaintiff's organization, called defendant Vignola at the latter's home to feel him out as to the extent of his dissatisfaction and as to the chances of getting him to come with Computer Assistance.

18. McDonagh's telephone call precipitated an extended series of further conversations and meetings between him and Vignola at various locations through the balance of the

month. The early conversations might be described as cautious, exploratory, boasting sessions. Later they developed into more substantive discussions of the means by which Vignola might in some capacity join forces with McDonagh if and when he were to leave plaintiff.

19. Among the relevant points of discussion were: (a) Vignola's compensation for joining McDonagh; (b) the possible forms their alliance might take, including (i) installation of Vignola as president of a subsidiary of defendant Computer Assistance, Inc.; (ii) employment of Vignola directly as an employee of McDonagh's, or (iii) formation by Vignola of his own corporation, which would then be merged with Computer Assistance, Inc.; (c) the name of Vignola's separate corporation, if one were to be formed; (d) indemnification by McDonagh of legal expenses incurred by Vignola in the event of suit by plaintiff; (e) the employees of plaintiff Republic's Cheshire office and whether and how they could fit into McDonagh's organization; and (f) Republic's clients and whether Vignola could bring their business to Computer Assistance.

20. At some point late in November, Vignola informed defendant Geddes that he was thinking of leaving plaintiff. Geddes was invited to and did attend the meeting between Vignola and McDonagh on December 1, 1969. His proposed role as a technical manager in McDonagh's organization was discussed. Two of McDonagh's top assistants also joined the discussion group at that point.

21. Prior to the December 1 meeting, attorneys for both Vignola and McDonagh were informed of the pending discussions. They attended the November 26 meeting of the principals and were thereafter active in working out the details of the proposed alliance.

22. In addition to the introduction of defendant Geddes, the December 1 meeting was devoted to organizational problems and the accommodation, without prejudice, of whichever Republic employees chose to follow Vignola and Geddes in resigning from Republic and joining McDonagh's group.

23. On December 3, 1969, Vignola made a final decision to leave plaintiff's employ. That day he informed McDonagh of his decision and that he would probably leave on December 5.

He also informed his attorney of his decision and requested the latter to proceed with drafting papers for a new corporation, to be known as Computer Assistance of Hartford, Inc. Curiously, Mr. McDonagh, director, president and major stockholder of Computer Assistance, Inc., approved of Vignola's use of the obviously similar name, even though at that time there was no agreement to merge the two corporations. Vignola's attorney was also instructed to draft a "merger agreement."

24. On the morning of Friday, December 5, 1969, Vignola picked up the incorporation papers prepared by his attorney, mailed his letter of resignation to plaintiff's president in New Jersey, and went to Republic's office in Cheshire where he found and informed Geddes of his actions. Geddes, who was listed as secretary of the new corporation, readily agreed to resign and join the new venture.

25. The incorporation papers of defendant Computer Assistance of Hartford, Inc. were filed on December 5, 1969.

26. On the afternoon of December 5 and over the weekend, Vignola, Geddes, and their top lieutenants contacted substantially all of plaintiff's Cheshire employees, offered each a job with defendant Computer Assistance of Hartford, Inc. at a salary slightly higher than each was receiving at Republic, and successfully recruited nearly all. The other employees joining the movement agreed to submit their resignations by mail to the home office in New Jersey.

27. At least one of the reasons for choosing the mails to communicate their resignations was to allow time for recruitment of all of plaintiff's employees before plaintiff's president was informed of the situation and could attempt to counteract the efforts of the Vignola group.

28. On the evening of December 5, Vignola and McDonagh executed an agreement to merge their two corporations. The agreement also included terms of compensation for Vignola.

29. On Sunday evening, December 7, plaintiff's president was informed by one of the wavering employees that Vignola had resigned and taken most of the staff with him. He received the letters of resignation in the mail the following day.

30. Of the original 25 employees at plaintiff's Cheshire office on December 4, only five remained by December 9.

31. On Monday, December 8, Vignola and others of his group began to contact customers of Republic for whom they had been doing work at the time of their resignations (or for whom work had been done in the past on a warranty basis). Each of the customers with work in progress was told of the resignations but assured that in one way or another his particular project would be completed by the people who had been working on it as Republic employees. Vignola offered to complete the projects without pay if necessary. He also asked the Republic customers to keep him and his new company in mind for any future business.

32. On Monday evening, Vignola met with Republic's president and offered to complete Republic's work in progress on a subcontract basis. His offer was declined. He did not inform the president of his offer to the customers to complete the work without pay if necessary.

33. Of the 20 employees who shifted to Vignola, 11 had at the time of the resignations been engaged in work in progress for several of Republic's clients. The remainder were apparently then unassigned.

34. During the week of December 8, at the suggestion of Vignola, employees of his who had been working on two of the accounts as Republic employees reported to those projects. Republic was to be paid for their services.

35. On December 12, 1969, the temporary restraining order, described above, was issued. Vignola's employees were then pulled off the Republic jobs to which they had reported.

36. On December 15, 1969, Vignola held a meeting with the 11 employees engaged in work in progress for Republic at the time of their resignations. He told them that because of the temporary restraining order they could not report to Republic's customers as employees of Computer Assistance of Hartford, Inc. He urged them to resign from Computer Assistance of Hartford and return to Republic so that Republic's contracts pending as of December 8 could be completed. He wrote a letter to each of the 11 to that effect and also a letter to Republic outlining the recommendations he had made to those employees.

37. As of the time of the hearing on December 19, 1969, nine of the eleven employees involved in pending contracts had resigned from Computer Assistance of Hartford and returned to Republic's employ for the purpose of completing work in progress.

38. Vignola and/or other members of his group of employees of defendant Computer Assistance, Inc. also contacted, in the early part of the week of December 8, some or all of Republic's prospective customers—that is, those to whom Republic had submitted proposals or who had furnished Republic with specifications by way of invitation of a proposal. These prospects were told of the resignations and the formation of a new corporation. Additionally, those contacted were apparently told that Computer Assistance of Hartford, Inc. would be available to bid on the proposed projects and on any future work.

39. Republic maintained a list of its present and prospective customers. Some of those customers, but not all, were listed as "representative clients" on various advertising brochures.

40. Certain kinds of information about a customer or prospective customer are of particular usefulness to those in the computer software business. Among them are: (a) the name of the person authorized to award contracts for work in this field; (b) the type and timing of any new jobs which might be coming up in the future; (c) the particular area of the client's business in which data processing services were or might be needed; (d) information relative to the amount budgeted by the client for this type of work over a given period of time; and (e) information about the client's own business as that relates to assisting in devising data processing solutions to its problems. Vignola and Republic's other former employees possessed, among them, as much of this kind of information as Republic had with respect to its former, present and prospective customers.

CONCLUSIONS OF LAW AND DISCUSSION

* * *

Solicitation of Employees

2. Plaintiff is not entitled to damages for or an injunction against defendants' solicitation

of its employees to resign from plaintiff's employ, enter defendants', and refuse to revoke their resignations to return to plaintiff. Such solicitation or inducement was not unlawful in the circumstances of this case.

Since none of Republic's officers or employees served pursuant to an employment contract, each was employed for an indefinite term and entitled to terminate the employment relationship at will at any time with or without cause. [Citations.] [Footnote.] Defendants Vignola and Geddes exercised that option on Friday, December 5, 1969, by depositing letters of resignation in the mail to the home office in New Jersey. At that point, they had committed themselves to no longer being employees and were no longer entitled to the benefits of the employment relationship. Similarly, obligations imposed by that relationship terminated at the time the letters were mailed.

Plaintiff urges the court to hold that the fiduciary obligation of these employees to plaintiff persisted until December 8, the date defendants calculated as that on which plaintiff would receive the letters, or at least until December 7, when plaintiff received actual notice of the resignations. However, I do not find that approach consistent with the recognized right in situations like the present of either party to terminate the employment relationship at any time with or without cause. There was no legal obligation to give advance notice of an intention to quit the job.

The evidence indicates that defendants were aware that solicitation of other employees might be inconsistent with the fiduciary obligation they had while they remained as employees [citation] and were careful to terminate their employment before embarking on any such solicitation. It is also apparent that defendants were using the normal delay of the mails, perhaps with the advice of counsel, to give themselves more time in which to maneuver before being challenged by plaintiff's president. Despite the lack of forthrightness thus evidenced, however, the facts of this case do not justify choosing a different time as the point of resignation. [Citation.] One of the risks of operating without employment contracts is that the employee (or employer) will exercise his right to terminate at any time and the crippling weakness of the plaintiff's case lies in the fact that unlike the employer in Sperry

Rand Corp. v. Rothlein, 241 F.Supp. at 554, 559, [D.Conn.1964] it did not have such contracts with its key employees.

Plaintiff urges the court to consider the meetings in March and April of 1969 at Vignola's home, Vignola's aborted resignation in May 1969 and the events of November and December 1969 leading up to the alliance with Computer Assistance, Inc. as a continuous scheme to solicit and induce Republic's employees to resign. This may be a tenable position, but I do not share it. A better view of the evidence is that the March and April meetings, though perhaps related to each other, were unrelated to the difficulty in May and that neither of these incidents was related to the events of November and December, except insofar as each reflects the frailty of employee tenure in this business.

Considering then the defendants' conduct in November and December separately, it is clear that none of the defendants solicited or induced any of plaintiff's employees to resign and join their organization until after their resignations had been mailed on December 5, 1969. Consequently, the applicable legal principles are those relating to the solicitation of employees not under contract by those without fiduciary obligations to the employer. The general rule and the economic and social considerations upon which it rests were expressed by Judge Learned Hand in 1929 as follows:

> So far as we have found, it has never been thought actionable to take away another's employee, when the defendant wants to use him in his own business, however much the plaintiff may suffer. It is difficult to see how servants could get the full value of their services on any other terms; time creates no prescriptive right in other men's labor. If an employer expects so much, he must secure it by contract. [Citation.]

[Citation.] Although no Connecticut cases have been found on this point, it appears that Judge Hand's perceptive analysis is still the prevailing rule absent an unlawful or improper purpose or means in the inducement. See Annot. 24 A.L.R.3d 822 (1969). In view of the widespread tendency toward job switching in these times, especially prevalent in the data processing services field, the evidence does not indicate the use of any such unlawful or improper purposes or means. [Citations.]

Solicitation of Customers and Use of Trade Secrets

3. Plaintiff is not entitled to damages for or an injunction against defendants' solicitation of its present and prospective customers as that solicitation is not unlawful in the circumstances of this case.

The only evidence is that defendants did not solicit plaintiff's present or prospective customers until at least December 8, when they were no longer employees of, or subject to a fiduciary obligation to Republic Systems.[2] Under those circumstances, the rule is that, absent a restrictive covenant (as here), former employees may immediately and freely compete with their former employers, including solicitation of customers. Town and Country House & Homes Serv., Inc. v. Evans, 150 Conn. 314, 317, 189 A.2d 390, 393 (1963).

An exception to this rule is that a former employee cannot "use trade secrets, or other confidential information which he has acquired in the course of his employment, for his own benefit or that of a competitor to the detriment of his former employer." Allen Mfg. Co. v. Loika, 145 Conn. 509, 514, 144 A.2d 306, 309 (1958). [Citations.] Plaintiff attempts to bring this case within that exception by arguing that its customer lists and other kinds of information (see finding of fact #40) about the customers are confidential. There is authority for the proposition that "[i]f in any particular business the list of customers is, because of some peculiarity of the business, in reality a trade secret and an employee has gained knowledge thereof as a matter of confidence, he will be restrained from using that knowledge against his employer." Town & Country, *supra* 150 Conn. at 320, 189 A.2d at 394.

In order to merit the protection afforded for trade secrets, a customer list must consist of customers whose "trade and patronage have been secured by years of business effort and advertising and the expenditure of time and money. * * *" *Id.* at 319, 189 A.2d at 393. Moreover, "a substantial element of secrecy must exist, to the extent that there would be difficulty in acquiring the information except

by the use of improper means." *Id.* [Citation.] Criteria to consider in determining whether given information is a trade secret are:

> (1) the extent to which the information is known outside the business; (2) the extent to which it is known by employees and others involved in the business; (3) the extent of measures taken by the employer to guard the secrecy of the information; (4) the value of the information to the employer and to his competitors; (5) the amount of effort or money expended by the employer in developing the information; (6) the ease or difficulty with which the information could be properly acquired or duplicated by others. Restatement, 4 Torts § 757, comment b. Town and Country, *supra* 150 Conn. at 319, 189 A.2d at 393.

The plaintiff's customer lists do not qualify as trade secrets. Many of the clients were openly listed in plaintiff's advertising brochures as "representative clients." Others were those seeking bids from not only the plaintiff but also from the plaintiff's competitors. Furthermore, efforts to keep the names of the remainder secret were meager at best. In the computer software business, anyone with a computer is considered a potential customer and is actively sought after by firms like those involved here. Even plaintiff's president admitted on the stand that the names of his customers were not the most confidential aspect of his business. There was no indication that the plaintiff expended an unusual amount of effort, time or money in cultivating the trade and patronage of any of its clients or that others would have had great difficulty in acquiring the same information by permissible means.

The same considerations obtain with respect to the other kinds of information about plaintiff's customers (e.g. the name of the person who is authorized to let contracts in data processing services, new jobs coming up, the amount budgeted for these kinds of services, etc.) which plaintiff claims to be confidential. I find that all of the claimed information lacks confidentiality. The evidence indicated that it would be comparatively easy for others to properly obtain it and that plaintiff took scant precautions in guarding its secrecy. [Citations.]

---

2. No customer was brought in to testify to the contrary.

Tortious Interference

The plaintiff also contends that, even in the absence of the use of confidential information, defendants' conduct in this case was tortious. They rely on R an [sic] W Hat Shop, Inc. v. Sculley, 98 Conn. 1, at 14, 118 A. 55, at 59 (1922), wherein the court held:

> The intentional procurement of the breach of an existent contract, if done with knowledge of the contract and without just cause or excuse, makes him who causes the breach liable for the resulting damage, and this is so even though he acted in promoting his own legitimate interests.

But it is clear from what happened here that the motives and methods of the defendants do not fit the thesis that the defendants intentionally sought to procure the breach of any of Republic's contracts with its customers or that any such breach occurred.

Defendants, having resigned, had, absent considerations of confidential information, as much freedom to compete as any other competitor in the field. While that freedom is not absolute, certainly it encompasses informing plaintiff's customers of their resignations from plaintiff's employment and of the formation of a new company, and that the new company would be available for future work. Moreover, it being apparent that plaintiff could not complete the pending contracts without at least hiring a new staff, it was not improper to inform the customer that the former employees would complete the work and that the customer could pay Republic for the services thus performed—that was certainly not a tortious interference with plaintiff's contractual relations with its customers. [Citations.]

CONCLUSION

Since the defendants' solicitation of plaintiff's employees and customers was not unlawful and there has been no tortious interference with plaintiff's business or contractual relations, plaintiff's application for a permanent injunction is denied. The temporary restraining order now in effect is hereby dissolved. No damages are awarded for what has already occurred.

So ordered.

TRILOG ASSOCIATES, INC. v. FAMULARO
455 Pa. 243, 314 A.2d 287
(Supreme Court of Pennsylvania, Jan. 24, 1974.)

MANDERINO, J.

This is an appeal from a decree which permanently enjoined the appellants from engaging in various conduct allegedly in violation of their employment contracts with their former employer, the appellee. The appellants, John D. Famularo, Louis A. Marabella, and Dennis J. Gawrys, were employed in 1967 by the appellee, Trilog Associates, Inc., a corporation engaged in the data processing business. In November of 1969, Gawrys was fired. In April of 1970, Famularo and Marabella simultaneously resigned their employment with Trilog and established their own data processing business under the name of General Data Systems, Ltd. Famularo and Marabella were the principal stockholders and officers of the new business. In June of 1970, Gawrys, who had been fired by Trilog seven months earlier, was hired by General Data Systems, Ltd.

During the time that the appellants worked for Trilog, the Girard Trust Bank of Philadelphia was one of Trilog's clients for whom data processing services were performed involving *shareholders' records*. Famularo, as an employee of Trilog, worked on the Girard Bank project. Marabella did so to a lesser extent. Gawrys did not work on any matters relating to Girard Bank.

In September of 1970, General Data Systems, Ltd., entered into an agreement with the Girard Bank for certain data processing involving *trustees' records*. Shortly thereafter, Trilog filed this action claiming the appellants were violating restrictions in their employment contracts with Trilog. Injunctive relief was granted.

Essentially the injunction enjoined the appellants from: (1) performing computer related services for the Girard Bank or any other customer of Trilog; (2) disclosing or using any confidential information as to Trilog; (3) inducing present employees of Trilog from terminating their employment; (4) inducing former employees of Trilog to break their restrictive employment covenants; (5) inducing any customer of Trilog to violate its contract with Trilog; (6) interfering with Trilog's business relations; (7) keeping any copies of documents generated within Trilog whether authorized by appellants or not and whether obtained as a result of their law suit or not. In addition, Famularo was enjoined from developing or exploiting a shareholders' record system.

The findings of fact in the trial court's opinion are basically as follows:

> While in Trilog's employ * * * Famularo and Marabella had constant contact with those officers of the bank who operated the Corporate Trust Department and became familiar with the operation thereof although they *did not at that time work specifically on the trustees' record system*. However, not only were the two systems in the same department of the bank and under the administration of its one set of managing officers but they used the same computer and the same cage where both corporate shares and debt securities were kept. And *there were instances and circumstances* where the *functions of the two systems overlapped*.

> [W]hile working for Trilog at Girard Trust Bank * * * Famularo and Marabella actually *obtained information* for Trilog *concerning its customer* which * * * they used * * * as the owners of General Data Systems, Ltd. * * *

> [T]he employee *acquired the opportunity to compete with his former employer* on the same premises and with the same management * * * *by virtue of the information concerning that customer's needs and methods which he had accumulated while working for his former employer*. * * * Famularo * * * *sought to oust Trilog* * * * as the contractor engaged in *computerizing and servicing the data processing of* Girard's *shareholders' record system by proposing or at least suggesting, a revision in procedures and computer uses*. * * * Famularo * * * produced a plan envisioning the reorganization of the Corporate Trust Department.

> * * *

> While Trilog *had not been employed* by Girard to perform services *for other than that branch* of the activities of its Corporate Trust Department *known as the shareholders' records system* it was actually having *contact* with the problems of the *closely related trustees' records system*. Thereby its employees Famularo and Marabella came to *know of the existence of that system and its relationship in part with the other system*, combined as the two were in the same depart-

ment under the same management and using the same computer and the same securities cage. The shareholders' records system was staffed by far more employees than the trustees' record system * * * and the physical equipment of the latter, aside from the computer, was smaller and the space occupied by it was less than that of the shareholders' record system. * * * [W]hile the knowledge of * * * Famularo and Marabella * * * *was slight with respect to the trustees' record system*, the possession of such knowledge and of the *considerable amount of information about the Corporate Trust Department* obtained * * * enabled them * * * to acquire the opportunity to augment it when their company sought and obtained employment by Girard * * * also served as a means of approach to, or entree in, to the councils of that bank's officers. * * *

> * * * [Famularo and Marabella had] knowledge of Girard's man-power methods, needs, management, equipment and procedures, all originally obtained at the bank while they were employed by Trilog. * * *

> *Admittedly the information obtained for Trilog while they were its employees was inconsiderable so far as the trustees' records system is concerned and admittedly it was only after they left Trilog that they acquired the additional data necessary to perform their task in computerizing the trustees' records system.* (Emphasis added.)

The relevant provision in Famularo's contract, which differed from the contract provision of the other two appellants, provided:

> [Y]ou are bound to observe Trilog's rights in your work product and Trilog's proprietary and customer information under the common law of unfair competition and * * * it is specifically agreed that you will not, until March 2, 1972, develop or assist in the development or exploitation of any shareholders' record system on your own account or for any other party.

Famularo promised (1) not to engage in unfair competition under the common law and (2) not to develop or assist in the development or exploitation of a shareholders' record system. We conclude that (1) the trial court's findings do not sustain its ultimate conclusion that the first promise was violated and (2) the second promise is void. We shall first discuss Famularo's alleged violation of his promise not to engage in unfair competition. We note that a former employee would have the same obligation under the law of torts even without a contractual provision.

From its findings of fact, the trial court ultimately concluded that Famularo unfairly competed with Trilog by using *confidential* customer information about the Girard Bank with [sic] Famularo had acquired while he was a Trilog employee. We do not agree with the trial court's ultimate factual or legal conclusion. * * *

Some of the trial court's findings are irrelevant on the issue of unfair competition. It may be that Famularo's work in the shareholder's record system at Girard gave him "constant contact" and an "entree" to the bank officers. It may be that Famularo would never have had the "opportunity" to perform services for Girard had he not become known at Girard while working for Trilog. Such facts, however, although they may be relevant in considering a covenant not to compete, are not relevant to the issue of unfair competition. [Citations.]

The trial court had two bases for its finding that Famularo unfairly competed with Trilog: (1) he performed data processing services involving the trustees' record system and (2) he attempted to oust Trilog in its work in the shareholders' record system. As to the first basis for the finding of unfair competition, we point out that Famularo was free to compete and obtain this contract so long as it did not involve the use of *confidential* customer information. [Citation.] Trilog had a contract with Girard to perform work which was limited to the shareholders' records and never performed any work involving trustees' records. It is difficult to see what *confidential* customer information Famularo could have used in his contract with Girard. Although the trial court ultimately concluded that Famularo used *confidential* information, there are no findings which sustain that conclusion. The trial court did find that the trustees' records and the shareholders' records (1) were in the same department; (2) were related in physical location; (3) had the same officers; (4) differed in the number of employees; (5) used the same cage; and (6) overlapped to a minor extent. None of these findings, however, shed any light on what *confidential* customer information was used by Famularo in his contract with Girard. To the contrary, many key findings of the trial court point to exactly an opposite conclusion. The trial court found that (1) Trilog (and, thus,

Famularo) never worked with the trustees' records; (2) Famularo's information was slight as to the trustees' records when he left Trilog; and (3) Famularo only acquired the bulk of his information about the trustees' records after he left Trilog.

General information as distinguished from *confidential* information which Famularo may have obtained about Girard is irrelevant. To enjoin use of information, it "must be the particular secrets of the complaining employer, not general secrets of the trade in which he is engaged. * * *" Macbeth-Evans Glass Co. v. Schnelbach, 239 Pa. 76, 85, 86 A. 688, 691 (1913). Famularo, even before his employment by Trilog, was an experienced computer programmer and surely knew, as does the general public, that banks use data processing services, have computers, and have Corporate Trust Departments which provide a variety of services. Famularo's use of information about Girard, which was generally known or readily and easily available to any Trilog competitor, is not unfair competition. [Citations.]

The second basis for the trial court's conclusion that Famularo unfairly competed rested on the following two findings: (1) Famularo proposed a revision in the shareholders' record system in an attempt to oust Trilog *"at least as to procedure and computer uses"* and (2) Famularo proposed a reorganization of the entire Corporate Trust Department. These two findings, as other findings of the trial court, are not related to the use of any *confidential* customer information. Neither of these proposals were ever implemented. Even if they had been, no *confidential* information was used by Famularo in these proposals.

Girard's Corporate Trust Department used data processing many years before Trilog or Famularo began any work at Girard. The department had used various computer programs which were developed by its own data processing staff and the department had its own computer. Trilog was hired to develop and improve the data processing system for the shareholders' records. The computer program which Trilog developed was in a "computer language" which could not be used in Girard's own computer, and Girard, therefore, had to lease computer time from Trilog for the shareholders' record system. At the time the unimplemented proposals referred to by the trial court were made, Trilog had completed its initial work on the shareholders' record system and had received substantial compensation. Much of its income from Girard, at the time of the above proposals, involved the leasing of Trilog's computer for the shareholders' record system,

Famularo's proposals could have been made by any experienced computer programmer. The proposal to reorganize the Corporate Trust Department involved the converting of all the computer programs of Girard into the same "computer language" so that Girard would not be required to lease outside computer time and, thus, would fully utilize its own computer. No *confidential* information was used or required. Any intelligent and creative programmer, even if he had never worked at Girard, could have made the same recommendations if he had a minimum of general information about data processing in Girard's Corporate Trust Department. If the proposal had been implemented, Trilog, of course, would have been "ousted" and would no longer have been needed to provide leased computer time. But again, we repeat, Famularo was not barred from competing with Trilog or ousting Trilog from its work with Girard. He was only bound not to unfairly compete with Trilog by using *confidential* customer information acquired as a Trilog employee. In Van Products Co. v. General Welding & Fabricating Co., 419 Pa. 248, 262, 213 A.2d 769, 777 (1965), we said:

> It is clear that this jurisdiction affords protection to an employer's confidential customer information. * * * As with any other trade secret, for customer information to be protectible it must be a particular secret of the business, of value to the employer and wrongfully appropriated by the employee.

Girard Bank, as a member of the consuming public, decided that Famularo's talent, knowledge, and experience in the data processing field, would be valuable to them. Famularo, in a free enterprise system, had every right to compete with his former employer and serve Girard so long as he did not do so by unfair competition. In Spring Steels, Inc., v. Molloy, 400 Pa. 354, 363, 162 A.2d 370, 375 (1960), we stated:

> Nor is the fact that the new company may acquire some of the plaintiff's former customers

contrary to law. It is not a phenomenal thing in American business life to see an employee, after a long period of service, leave his employment and start a business of his own or in association with others. And it is inevitable in such a situation, where the former employee has dealt with customers on a personal basis that some of those customers will want to continue to deal with him in his new association.

The trial court's findings do not sustain its ultimate factual conclusion that Famularo used any *confidential* information in competing with Trilog.

What we have said about Famularo's alleged unfair competition would be equally applicable to appellants Marabella and Gawrys. Even though their contracts did not contain any provisions concerning unfair competition, they were still subject to the common law of unfair competition. [Citation.] Marabella as a Trilog employee worked to a lesser extent than Famularo with the shareholders' records at Girard and Gawrys never worked at Girard while he was a Trilog employee. There is no contention that Gawrys had any *confidential* customer information and Marabella's minimal knowledge did not enable him to engage in unfair competition with Trilog by the use of any *confidential* customer information. They, therefore, did not unfairly compete with Trilog.

The second promise that Famularo entered into with Trilog was "not to develop or assist in developing a shareholders' record system for himself or anyone else." This is in effect a covenant not to compete with Trilog in developing shareholders' record systems. The law of restrictive employment covenants applicable to this promise by Famularo is the same law applicable to the promises in the contracts of Marabella and Gawrys. Their contracts provided:

> The employee * * * agrees not to come under the employ of any customer or client of [Trilog], or of any business or individual with which employee has come into contact or acquaintance principally through his * * * employment with [Trilog] for a period of two years after leaving the employ of [Trilog].

The restrictive employment covenants of Famularo, Marabella, and Gawrys are void. The covenants are not bargains "by an assistant, servant, or agent not to compete with his employer, or principal, during the term of the employment or agency or thereafter, *within such territory* and within such time *as may be reasonably necessary* for the protection of the employer or principal, without imposing undue hardship on the employee or agent." Restatement of Contracts § 516(f) (1932) (emphasis added). [Citation.] The promises are unreasonable restraints of trade in that they are "greater than is required for the protection of the person for whose benefit the restraint is imposed" and impose undue hardship "upon the person restricted.* * * " Restatement of Contracts §§ 515(a)–(b) (1932).

The restrictive covenants have no limitation on territory and thus are broader than is necessary for the protection of Trilog. Famularo in effect promised not to practice his profession *anywhere for anyone* in developing a shareholders' record system. His promise is similar to a covenant by an attorney not to try murder cases *anywhere for anyone* because he gained experience in trying murder cases from his former employer, or a covenant by a bricklayer not to build an apartment house *anywhere for anyone* because his former employer gave him his first opportunity to use his bricklaying talent in building an apartment house. Such covenants, unrestricted in territorial application, are not necessary to protect any valid interest of the former employer and are unreasonable restraints of trade. [Citations.]

The covenant entered into by Marabella and Gawrys is, likewise, an unreasonable restraint of trade. That covenant is divisible into two parts: (1) not to come under the employ of any customer or client of Trilog's, and (2) not to come under the employ of any business or individual with which the employee has come into contact or acquaintance principally through his employment with Trilog. Each part is broader than necessary for the protection of the employer's interest and neither are divisible in any way which would allow a narrower restriction to remain intact without a rewriting. [Citations.]

In the first part of the covenant, Marabella and Gawrys promised not to be employed by any customer or client of Trilog. This prohibits them from accepting, with any customer or client of Trilog, *any employment anywhere*. There is no restriction on the kind of employment prohibited or upon the territory covered. By its terms, the promise prevents the employee from accepting employment with a Trilog customer in *any* capacity. It covers employment totally unrelated to whatever work the employee performed for Trilog. Although Marabella and Gawrys worked as data processing employees for Trilog, they are barred from working as janitors, bank managers, truck drivers, doctors, lawyers, or indian [sic] chiefs—for any customer or client of Trilog. Such a covenant is a completely unreasonable restraint of trade and cannot be upheld. Moreover, there is no limitation as to territory. Such a failure to limit the territorial application of the covenant also renders the covenant invalid.

In the second part of the covenant, Marabella and Gawrys promised not to come under the employ of any business or individual with which they came into contact or acquaintance principally through their employment with Trilog. This promise is more unreasonable and burdensome than the first promise. It prohibits, as does the first, *any employment anywhere* and thus is not related to the protection of any reasonable employer interest. Such a covenant is so far-reaching, that it becomes ludicrous. It *bars* Marabella and Gawrys from accepting employment as *bar*tenders in Ireland from the father of the sister-in-law of the aunt of the elevator operator whom Marabella and Gawrys happen to meet in a *bar* in Scranton while on Trilog's business. Such a restraint is illegal. Therefore, we conclude that both parts of the covenant not to compete in the contracts of Marabella and Gawrys are void and will not be rewritten by this Court.

* * *

From our review of the trial court's findings of fact, we must conclude that those findings do not support any aspect of the injunctive relief granted and we, therefore, reverse the trial court's decree.

* * *

EAGEN, J. (concurring).

I am in agreement with the result reached by Mr. Justice Manderino; however, I feel a need to briefly discuss the restrictive employment covenants of Marabella and Gawrys.

"[P]ublic policy permits the enforcement of restrictive covenants only if they are reasonably limited as to duration of time and geographical extent [citations omitted]." Albee

Homes, Inc. v. Caddie Homes, Inc., 417 Pa. 177, 184, 207 A.2d 768, 772 (1965). But, in determining whether a geographic limitation has been delineated by the covenant, it is required that one look at the contract as a whole, as well as the surrounding circumstances. [Citation.] In addition, this Court in Jacobson & Co. Inc. v. International Environment Corp., 427 Pa. 439, 235 A.2d 612 (1967) ruled a court may properly limit the geographic extent of a restrictive covenant.

Mr. Justice Manderino apparently overlooks the above principles, but nonetheless has reached the correct result because the challenged restrictive covenant, in particular its second provision,[1] is too encompassing to be considered a reasonable restraint. Restrictive covenants are reasonable only if they are " 'necessary for the protection of the employer * * * without imposing undue hardship on the employee.' " *Jacobson*, supra, 427 Pa. at 452, 235 A.2d at 620. The particular provision here in question is far too broad to reasonably be "necessary for the protection of" Trilog, as well as being excessively burdensome upon both appellants, Marabella and Gawrys. I, therefore, would invalidate this restrictive covenant, without needing to examine the feasibility of limiting said provision in scope of geographic territory.

AUXTON COMPUTER ENTERPRISES, INC. v. PARKER

174 N.J.Super. 418, 416 A.2d 952
(Superior Court of New Jersey, Appellate Division, May 21, 1980.)

LORA, P. J. A. D.

Plaintiff Auxton Computer Enterprises, Inc. (Auxton) is engaged in the business of providing data processing consulting services and computer programmers as well as analysts on a contract basis to firms seeking such assistance. Defendant Spiridellis and Associates (Associates) is engaged in similar work. Defendant Nikolaos Spiridellis (Spiridellis), the president and principal officer of Associates,

is and was the chief operating officer of that enterprise.

On June 22, 1972 defendant Parker entered Auxton's employ as a data processing consultant, assigned to work at various client-companies by Auxton. While on one such assignment at the American Broadcasting Company in 1975, Parker decided to look for another job and contacted several other prospective employers, including Spiridellis and Associates.

Parker and Spiridellis arranged for an interview, which Parker attended in January 1976 and which had been arranged by one Paul Chu, a former employee of Auxton who had gone to work for Associates. During that meeting Parker was questioned generally concerning his qualifications, and Spiridellis likewise informed Parker of the general operations of Associates.

The interview between Parker and Spiridellis ended favorably, with Spiridellis requesting Parker to return for an interview with one of Associates' senior technicians. That interview subsequently took place in February 1976. However, there was no job offer made to Parker at that time.

On March 18, 1976, a Thursday evening, Parker received a telephone call from Spiridellis, who asked him if he wanted to go for a technical interview the next day, March 19, 1976, at the offices of Pan American Corporation in Rockleigh, New Jersey, on behalf of Associates. Associates, which had been doing data processing consultative work for Pan Am for approximately six or seven months prior thereto, had an opportunity to enlarge their relationship with Pan Am by attending this technical interview with the prospect of providing their services with respect to Pan Am's passenger revenue data processing system which was then being either developed or improved upon. Associates had interviews lined up for five or six other technicians in addition to Parker.

When Spiridellis contacted Parker that evening, Parker, apparently suffering from a sore throat, did not give Spiridellis any definitive answer to his offer and request to have

---

1. The second provision of the restrictive covenant of both Marabella and Gawrys provides:

The employee * * * agrees not to come under the employ * * * of any business or individual with which employee has come into contact or acquaintance principally through his * * * employment with [Trilog]. * * *

him appear in Rockleigh, New Jersey, on March 19, 1976. At the time Spiridellis called Parker, he knew that Parker was employed by plaintiff. However, neither Parker nor Spiridellis nor Associates had any knowledge that plaintiff was also seeking to obtain the Pan Am contract.

Parker subsequently determined to go to the Pan Am interview and called in sick insofar as his work at ABC on behalf of Auxton was concerned. On that day, by sheer coincidence, Lilla Leuchs, a marketing representative of Auxton, was at the offices of Pan Am trying to solicit work for Auxton from Pan Am, and learned that Parker was attending an interview there.

On the following Monday, the interview having taken place on Friday, a representative of Auxton confronted Parker with the fact that he had been at Pan Am the previous Friday. Parker initially denied having been there, but later decided to offer his resignation, which resulted, however, in his being terminated summarily by Auxton.

When Spiridellis learned of Parker's termination, he hired him, apparently due to a sense of moral obligation. Parker initially worked at a designated job site for two or three days, and then, upon receiving favorable approval from Pan Am, Parker went to work as an employee of Associates on the Pan Am job for a period of almost one year.

Auxton brought this claim against Parker, alleging breach of his duty of loyalty to his employer, interference with Auxton's prospective economic advantage and unfair competition. As against defendants Spiridellis and Associates, Auxton alleged that they had induced Parker to violate his duty of loyalty to plaintiff by recruiting him to solicit business for them while aware that Parker was still employed by Auxton. Following a bench trial and accounting of the losses Auxton allegedly sustained by reason of Parker's termination of employment in March 1976, the trial judge assessed damages jointly and severally against all defendants in the amount of $10,601.38. He further ordered that all counts in the complaint based upon alleged interference with prospective economic advantage and all requests for punitive damages be dismissed.

* * *

Appellant Parker contends that the trial judge erred when he found that Parker had breached his duty of loyalty to Auxton. He asserts he was not soliciting Auxton's clients nor forming a rival corporation, but merely seeking other employment, which he had a clear right to do, and hence his conduct did not constitute a breach of duty of loyalty. Auxton, on the other hand, argues that Parker breached his duty of loyalty to Auxton by presenting himself to Pan Am as a representative of Spiridellis and Associates while in the employ of Auxton. It bottoms its position on the fact that Parker should have been at work on March 19, 1976, instead of attempting to secure work for a competitor of Auxton; Parker utilized his talents on behalf of a competitor of his employer, and Parker presented himself as an employee of Associates. Auxton suggests that, cumulatively, Parker's "actions were in callous 'disregard [of] his duty to serve his principal with only his principal's interest in mind.'" (Quoting *Restatement,* Agency 2d, § 394).

The trial judge, while finding that none of the defendants knew that Auxton was soliciting Pan Am's business, found from the "totality of the circumstances" a breach of the duty of loyalty by Parker. In reaching that conclusion, the trial judge reasoned:

> When Parker attended the March 19th interview he was still on Auxton's payroll. I have found that his excuse of illness given to Auxton was a mere sham utilized to permit him not only to aid himself but to aid plaintiff's competitor on plaintiff's time. That is undisputed. He did not resign on the 19th day of March. To use an old expression, he wanted his cake and he wanted to eat it as well. He wanted it both ways that day. The facts show that he continued to work for the plaintiff for approximately an additional week, until he was fired.

An employee who is not bound by a covenant not to compete after the termination of employment, and in the absence of any breach of trust, may anticipate the future termination of his employment and, while still employed, make arrangements for some new employment by a competitor or the establishment of his own business in competition with his employer. The only restriction to such action is that he may not solicit his employer's customers for his own benefit before he has terminated his employment. Nor may he do other similar acts in direct competition with the employer's business. This would constitute a breach of the undivided loyalty which the employee owes to his employer while he is still employed. [Citations.] It is the nature and character of the act performed that will determine if there has been an actionable wrong and whether or not the act has caused some particular injury to the employer. [Citations.] The mere planning, without more, is not a breach of an employee's duty of loyalty and good faith to his employer. [Citations.]

Admittedly, the mere decision to enter into competition may eventually prove harmful to the former employer. However, because of the competing interests of allowing an employee some latitude in switching jobs and at the same time preserving some degree of loyalty owed to the employer while on the job, neither the decision to compete nor the consequent entering into competition alone is actionable. [Citation.] If the right to change jobs is to be in any way meaningful for an employee not under contract for a definite term, it must be exercisable without the necessity of revealing the plans to the employer. [Citation.] It is something more than preparation which is so harmful as to substantially hinder the employer in the continuation of his business. Obviously, each case must be decided upon its own facts; because of the competing interests the actionable wrong is a matter of degree. "No ironclad rules as to the type of conduct which is permissible can be stated, since the spectrum of activities in this regard is as broad as the ingenuity of man itself." [Citation.]

It is clear, then, in light of these general principles, that the employee owes a duty of loyalty to the employer, and the employee must not, while employed, act contrary to the employer's interests. Equally clear is the proposition that the employee is entitled to make "arrangements" for some new employment by a competitor and should be given some latitude in this regard.

In our view, the conduct of Parker, when assessed by the standards set forth above, does not amount to a breach of his fiduciary duty. While the undisputed evidence shows that Parker attended an interview at Pan Am on behalf of Associates at a time when he should have been fulfilling his employment respon-

sibilities to Auxton, his conduct in that regard does not reach that level of impropriety which has heretofore been required when imposing liability for violating the duty of loyalty owed to an employer. Further, the trial judge's finding, which is amply supported by the evidence, that neither Parker, Spiridellis nor Associates knew that Auxton had intention of competing for Pan Am's work or was in fact competing that day for any work from Pan Am, also militates in favor of such a finding. Also significant is that until the time of Parker's termination he had neither accepted nor been offered any position by Associates. Therefore, absent a covenant not to compete or breach of a confidential relationship, liability may not be founded upon these facts for breach of duty of loyalty. Spiridellis did nothing to "pirate" Parker away from plaintiff. Neither Parker nor Spiridellis knew plaintiff was interested in the Pan Am job and this was not an attempt by Parker to solicit business on behalf of Associates. He was simply trying to get a job with Associates, and the latter was trying to get better connected with Pan Am and also considering hiring Parker for the job. We can see nothing so unfair, immoral or unethical about this conduct as to make it actionable.

Having so concluded, and in light of the settlement of the matters in dispute between plaintiff Auxton and defendants Spiridellis and Associates, we need not pass upon the remaining contentions of the parties to the consolidated appeals.

The judgment of the Chancery Division in favor of plaintiff Auxton Computer Enterprises, Inc. and against the defendant David Parker is reversed.

CALSPAN CORP. v. PIECH

91 A.D.2d 844, 458 N.Y.S.2d 211
(Supreme Court, Appellate Division, Fourth Department, Dec. 17, 1982.)

MEMORANDUM.

This is an action seeking damages and other relief from defendants for unfair business practices and breach of an employee's fiduciary duty. Two theories of recovery are advanced by plaintiff: first, it contends that its former employee, defendant Piech, has been guilty of actionable disloyalty to it because he permitted his name and reputation to be used by a competitor, defendant Scipar, Inc., to plaintiff's disadvantage and second, it contends that all the defendants conspired to damage it by the same means and also by misappropriating plaintiff's trade secrets and property. Plaintiff seeks to recover from Piech $16,502.21, the wages it paid him from April 2, 1979, the date when his act of disloyalty occurred, until August 3, 1979, the date when he left plaintiff's employ and started working for defendant Scipar, Inc. It seeks to recover from all defendants the amount of profit defendant Scipar, Inc. earned on a government contract which plaintiff claims rightfully belonged to it and which it would have received but for defendant's wrongful acts. Special Term denied cross motions for summary judgment. As I interpret its decision, it held that plaintiff had no right of recovery on its first theory and that there existed questions of fact preventing summary judgment to either side on the second theory. I agree that plaintiff is not entitled to summary judgment on the causes of action which seek to require defendants to disgorge the contract profits earned. I disagree with Special Term however, that plaintiff has no right to recover wages from Piech. It is entitled to recover on that cause of action because of Piech's disloyalty quite apart from whether he and his codefendants are guilty of misappropriating property or secret information of Calspan. Moreover, I disagree with the majority because I not only believe plaintiff states a cause of action for disloyalty on its first theory, I think it has established its right to recover as a matter of law. Defendant Dr. Piech is an accomplished theoretical physicist and a recognized expert in the field of photometric image processing and analysis. He was employed by Calspan's predecessor in 1967 and continued with the company until his resignation in August, 1979. During that time he conducted numerous sophisticated research programs for various government agencies and he was highly regarded within the intelligence and defense community. Immediately prior to his resignation from Calspan he was serving as the "principal investigator", or senior project scientist, for several research and development contracts awarded to Calspan by the United States Defense Ad-

vanced Research Projects Agency ("DARPA") at the Rome Air Development Center. In March, 1979 DARPA requested Calspan to submit an informal or "unsolicited" proposal for further research designed to extend and integrate existing image processing and material identification techniques into a computerized, unmanned missile identification and guidance system for use with "cruise" missiles. With the approval of Calspan management, such a proposal was prepared by Piech and other Calspan scientists and submitted to DARPA on Calspan's behalf on or about April 10, 1979. The proposal stated that Piech would serve as the project's principal investigator, or project leader, if the contract was awarded to Calspan. For some time prior, however, Piech had been discussing with defendant Kinzly, President of defendant Scipar, Inc. and a former college classmate and co-employee of Piech at Calspan, the possibility of Piech's leaving Calspan and joining Scipar. These discussions came to a head in February and March, 1979 and by letter dated April 2, 1979, Piech formally accepted an offer to join Scipar the following August. Piech testified that at that time he was working on Calspan's proposal for DARPA, and Kinzly knew he was, and that at that time he, Piech, assumed that Scipar intended to bid on the same program and was preparing a competing proposal. In fact, it was his testimony that when he accepted Scipar's job offer, he "assumed" he could be in charge of the DARPA project after it received the contract. When Scipar's proposal was submitted to DARPA on April 4, 1979 it stated that Piech intended to join Scipar in August, 1979 and that "Dr. Piech will serve as Project Engineer for the proposed effort and will be responsible for the day to day performance of the technical effort, including liaison with the government and other contractor personnel." Dr. Piech's letter of April 2 confirming his employment was attached. Piech testified that he knew that his letter of April 2 would be used by Scipar to demonstrate Scipar's "corporate capability", i.e., to prove that Scipar had the technological expertise and personnel to complete the program. Notwithstanding all this, Piech did not inform Calspan until June 25 that he intended to join Scipar August 3 and plaintiff did not learn until September that he had forwarded a commitment letter to Scipar on April 2 or that he acquiesced in use of this letter as part of Scipar's bidding proposals. After plaintiff's and Scipar's proposals had been received by the Defense Department in April, the officer in charge of DARPA contacted Piech and told him that his name appeared on both of them. (At some points during his pre-trial testimony Piech claimed that he did not know that his commitment letter would be used in the Scipar proposal. At the very least he knew it was so used in mid-April, 1979, however, after this conversation). He also told him that plaintiff's proposal was "too high". Piech advised the contract officer that the only way to reduce Calspan's proposal was to remove high cost labor, namely Piech, and a second Calspan proposal was subsequently submitted to DARPA on April 23 with Piech's name removed from it. Scipar was awarded the DARPA contract and executed it August 3, 1979. Piech became associated with defendant Scipar as a Vice-President on the same day. The majority contend that these facts are unresolved because Piech's testimony is uncertain and contradicting on several points. His testimony certainly contains evasions and quibbles but his dissembling should not obscure the fact that he admitted sufficient facts to establish plaintiff's right to recover. Under broadly stated rules of law, an employee may not act in any manner inconsistent with his employment and he is at all times bound to exercise the utmost good faith and loyalty in the performance of his duties. [Citations.] An employee who is faithless is generally disentitled to recover his compensation and it makes no difference that the services were beneficial to the employer or that it suffered no provable damages as the result of the employee's disloyalty. [Citations.] Unless the terms of employment are otherwise, the employee must act solely for the benefit of his employer in all matters connected with the employment. [Citation.] He may not compete with his employer, directly or indirectly, concerning the subject matter of his employment. [Citation.] Notwithstanding these general duties, an employee, while working for another may engage in a variety of activities in preparation for future employment which may result in his competing with his present employer. Special Term held that Piech's conduct here was not actionable because it did not go beyond the permissible stage of preparation. It noted that he was entitled to talk to the co-defendants while employed by plaintiff and to change his employment at will, even by forming or joining a competing business. There can be no argument with that; a substantial body of case law holds as much. What Piech could not do, however, was engage in conduct inconsistent with plaintiff's best interests. Most certainly he could not solicit his employer's customers during his employment [citation], and we should not permit him to do so indirectly, and excuse his conduct in knowingly permitting Scipar to use his name when seeking the same contract his employer was bidding on. Manifestly, Piech was a key part of the DARPA proposal. In this day, when huge sums of government money are available to high technology firms and universities in the form of research and development contracts and grants, the reputation and prestige of company or university employees is not a negligible factor. Since the government is granted discretion in awarding such contracts and grants and it is not required to contract with the lowest responsible bidder, the scientist-personnel available to the bidder may well be the determining factor in deciding which proposal will be accepted. Indeed, it might well be argued that government procurement officers are more concerned with the names and reputations of the people available to the contractor than with the contractor for which they work. Thus, Piech's actions were the full equivalent of direct solicitation of plaintiff's business because while working for plaintiff he allowed his name, his prestige and his rapport with the government procurement officers to be used as a "bidding chip" by a competitor to solicit further business, the extension or refinement of the technical system that the employer was then developing. [Citation.] Indeed defendants engineered the transfer so smoothly that the DARPA program development barely skipped a beat, the execution of the new contract by Scipar and Piech's employment by Scipar occurring the same day. That is not to say that the use of Dr. Piech's name caused plaintiff to lose the contract or defendant Scipar to gain it. That is a matter yet to be proved. But it is not necessary that plaintiff prove Piech's conduct caused actual injury to it to sustain this cause of action. It is enough that his actions were contrary to the best interests of his employer and that they "might work injury * * * or deprive it of profit or advantage which his skill, knowledge and ability might personally bring to it or enable it to realize in the responsible exercise of its power." [Citations.] Defendants contend that there are reasonable and innocent explanations for all of this and that none of it was of much consequence in the bidding process anyway. The majority agree to the extent that they believe bad faith is a necessary element of the cause of action and presents a question of fact. It is difficult to imagine how Piech could have been acting in good faith, but his good or bad faith is immaterial in any event. Piech was obligated to disclose to plaintiff his relationship with Scipar and the use of his name on Scipar's proposal whether his failure to do so was motivated by bad faith or not. [Citations.] Finally, the simple answer to defendant's contention that use of Piech's name was of little consequence is that the government apparently thought the identity of the proposed project leader was important because the bid specifications required that he be named in the proposal. The parties apparently thought it was important because his name was included in both proposals (five times in Scipar's proposal). If more is needed to prove the point, the government contract, when it was awarded, contained a clause stating "In the event that the contractor [Scipar] ceases to furnish the services of Dr. Piech [it] shall immediately notify the contracting officer." I would grant plaintiff partial summary judgment against defendant Piech in the amount of $16,502.21.

MOHAWK DATA SCIENCES CORP. v. INDUSTRIAL COMMISSION OF THE STATE OF COLORADO

660 P.2d 922

(Colorado Court of Appeals, Div. I, Feb. 10, 1983.)

ENOCH, C. J.

Employer, Mohawk Data Sciences Corporation (Mohawk) seeks review of a final order of the Industrial Commission awarding claimant full unemployment compensation benefits pursuant to § 8–73–108(4), C.R.S.1973 (1982 Cum.Supp.). We affirm.

Mohawk was in the business of manufacturing, selling, leasing, and servicing computer equipment. Claimant was a customer service engineer who performed maintenance on equipment purchased or leased from Mohawk.

Mohawk's representative, a company District Service Manager, testified that claimant was discharged because of a "direct conflict with the interests" of Mohawk after Mohawk learned that claimant was working for a competitive company known as M & D Enterprises (M & D). The witness testified that claimant, while still working for Mohawk, was involved in soliciting sales on behalf of M & D to a state agency, one of Mohawk's regular customers. The witness also testified that claimant serviced a customer's equipment on behalf of M & D after the customer terminated its service contract with Mohawk.

On cross-examination, Mohawk's representative confirmed the existence of a "secondary market" for Mohawk's computer equipment. Sellers in the "secondary market" bought old equipment, refurbished it, and sold it to interested customers. The representative further stated that Mohawk was not actively engaged in selling to this market. The witness admitted that, on at least one occasion, he himself had made a profit selling some of Mohawk's equipment in the secondary market. He also admitted that he had a conversation with claimant and claimant's immediate supervisor in which they mentioned that they had some of Mohawk's used equipment for sale. The witness testified that he did not criticize claimant for this activity, or mention that it might constitute a conflict of interest. Finally, the witness stated that he was not aware of any written policy prohibiting employees from selling old equipment in the secondary market.

Claimant admitted that he was employed by M & D while still working for Mohawk, but stated that he did not feel there was any conflict of interest. He testified that M & D only sold equipment in the secondary market, a market in which Mohawk did not participate. Further, he stated that he performed service work for M & D only if the customer had no service contract with Mohawk and the equipment was customer owned. As to the sale of equipment by M & D to the state agency, claimant admitted that he had given M & D's name to the state's purchasing agent. However, this was done after Mohawk's sales force had repeatedly ignored his advice to contact the customer.

Claimant also testified that his activities on behalf of M & D did not constitute a conflict of interest because such activities were common among Mohawk's management personnel. He testified that he worked for Mohawk in Houston between 1975 and 1978, and during that period his supervisor was actively engaged in servicing customer-owned equipment after business hours. And, he stated that Mohawk's witness was actively engaged in secondary market sales and had invited him to solicit customers in exchange for a "kickback." Claimant stated that he was not aware of a company policy prohibiting his activities.

The referee found that Mohawk failed to demonstrate that claimant's independent sales activities in the "secondary market" or his service activities for M & D, were competitive with and therefore damaging to Mohawk. The referee also found that, although claimant's activities were questionable, "company-wide activities of a similar nature" engaged in by managerial personnel made "placement of the burden for the problem" on claimant unreasonable. Consequently, the referee determined that Mohawk was primarily responsible for the separation and awarded full benefits pursuant to § 8–73–108(4), C.R.S.1973. The Commission adopted the findings and conclusions of the referee.

Mohawk contends that the uncontradicted evidence demonstrated that claimant's actions were contrary to the interests of Mohawk, and therefore, the Commission should have reduced claimant's benefits because of "gross misconduct" pursuant to § 8–73–108(3)(c), C.R.S.1973 (1982 Cum.Supp.), or "wilfull neglect or damage to [the] employer's property or interest" pursuant to § 8–73–108(9)(a)(XIII), C.R.S.1973 (1982 Cum.Supp.). We disagree.

Generally, the reason for separation from employment is a question of fact, and the Commission's determination in this regard may not be altered on review, if as in this case, it is supported by the evidence. [Citation.] Contrary to the assertions of Mohawk, the evidence here is conflicting as to whether claimant's activities on behalf of M & D were "damaging" to Mohawk's interests, and the resolution of these conflicts is a matter properly left to the Commission in its fact-finding role. [Citation.]

The determination of whether claimant engaged in "gross misconduct" or "wilfull neglect or damage" to Mohawk's interests is one which requires an examination of the factual context of claimant's activities. [Citation.] The Commission's findings, supported by evidence, that claimant's superiors were engaged in similar activities, militate against the finding of gross misconduct or wilfull neglect or damage to Mohawk. Thus, contrary to Mohawk's contention, the Commission's reliance on § 8–73–108(4) is supported by the evidence, and the fact that the sections cited by Mohawk might have been applicable does not change the result. The Commission is given wide latitude in determining which section of the statute governs a particular set of facts. [Citation.]

We find no merit in the other issues raised by Mohawk.

Order affirmed.

ELECTRONIC DATA SYSTEMS CORP. v. POWELL

508 S.W.2d 137
(Court of Civil Appeals of Texas, Dallas, Feb. 28, 1974.)

BATEMAN, J.

This is an action by appellant to enforce by injunction certain restrictive covenants in an employment contract against its former employee. The employer prevailed below in the hearing for a temporary injunction but, being dissatisfied with the limited scope of the temporary injunction, has perfected this appeal.

Appellee Douglas W. Powell worked for appellant (herein referred to as EDS) from May 1970 until August 1972, after which he went to work for Systems Resources, Inc., (herein called SRI), a competitor of EDS. EDS employs systems engineers who write computer programs for its customers. There are five industry groups which EDS serves, the two which are material here being the health care and public utilities industries. Powell worked in the health care area for EDS as a systems engineer on a team which developed a "system," or series of computer programs for processing health care claims involving private or non-governmental contracts. The health care industry group was subdivided into the private and governmental sectors. The EDS system which Powell helped to develop, referred to as "Prepayment Utilization Review" or "PPUR," competes with the "Model System," which was developed by a governmental agency, and which is employed by Powell's present employer, SRI. However, at the time of trial, Powell was working in the public utilities area for SRI, an area in which EDS did not even have a data processing system when Powell was employed by it.

The restrictive covenant in Powell's contract with EDS included the following limitations: its computer systems and related data were to remain confidential; EDS retained a proprietary interest in its system and information; the employee was not to participate in recruiting other EDS employees or in the solicitation of customers of EDS, and was not to compete with EDS or any subsidiary within 200 miles of any city in which it does business until three years after the contract term; and the employee was not to use any method, information or system developed by EDS in competition with EDS, within the same 200 mile radius and for the same period of time.

The temporary injunction entered by the trial court restrained Powell from recruiting other EDS employees, and from soliciting past, present and prospective customers of EDS, in substantially the same language as the restrictive covenant. It also restrained Powell from competing with EDS within the 200 miles radius and for the same time period mentioned in the contract, but the court defined the word "competing" as:

* * * conduct by Douglas W. Powell involving the design or use, or providing further information to others concerning the design or use of electronic data processing programs or systems for performing, in whole or in part, the function known as prepayment utilization review in processing health care claims as that function was designed to be performed by the

EDS National Regular Business program on August 15, 1972, where such function designed to be performed by the EDS Regular Business program exceed [sic] that which is generally accepted and known in the data processing industry for prepayment utilization review programs.

In effect, the trial court enjoined Powell from competing with the EDS system which he had helped EDS to develop. It is this limitation of the scope of the temporary injunction which appellant complains of on this appeal.

Restrictive covenants in employment contracts by which employees agree not to compete with the former employer after termination of the contract have traditionally been viewed as being in restraint of trade and not enforceable unless the terms are reasonable. The test of reasonableness is whether the covenant imposes upon the former employee an undue hardship or any greater restraint than is reasonably necessary to protect the former employer's business and good will. [Citation.] The reasonableness of the covenant is generally recognized to be a question of law for the court's determination. [Citations.]

The granting or denial of an injunction, and especially a temporary injunction, and the scope of one which is granted, are largely and peculiarly within the broad discretion of the trial court, whose action will not be disturbed on appeal unless a clear abuse of discretion is shown. [Citations.]

From a review of this record, we are unable to say that the trial court abused its discretion in limiting the scope of the injunction as it did here. We cannot say, as a matter of law, that appellant needs a broader temporary injunction to preserve its rights pending a trial on the merits. It must be borne in mind that a temporary injunction is merely a provisional remedy to preserve the subject matter of the controversy pending trial. [Citations.]

The court unquestionably had the power to limit the restrictive covenant to the geographic area in which the employee worked for the employer. [Citations.] We see no reason why this same principle should not apply to a limitation of the covenant as to its subject area as well. [Citation.] Powell worked for EDS on a specialized system for the health care industry. He did not work for it in the public utilities industry area, nor did EDS even have a data processing system for public utilities when Powell worked for it.

Although there is some dispute as to the facts regarding whether the technical expertise is common between systems for health care and systems for public utilities, we do not have to resolve that dispute on this appeal. There is some evidence in this record to support an implied finding of fact that there is not enough similarity between the two systems for EDS to be irreparably injured, if injured at all, by Powell's work in a different system. In reviewing this temporary injunction, we must draw all legitimate inferences from the evidence in the light most favorable to the trial court's judgment. [Citations.] It was not an abuse of discretion for the trial court to conclude, under this record, that an impending irreparable injury was not shown by the appellant. [Citation.]

Appellant argues that Powell should be enjoined from employment with SRI entirely because the injunction is unenforceable as a practical matter so long as his employment continues, since he is "a telephone call away" from SRI's work in the health care area and violation of the injunction would be difficult, if not impossible to detect. However, there was no showing of bad faith on Powell's part, or that his work with SRI was even likely to injure the effectiveness or profitability of the EDS health care system. The appellant's contention is simply that Powell *might* assist SRI in the health care area. Such a *possibility* is not a sufficient ground for extending the scope of an injunction. It is a conjecture by appellant, which is far short of a showing of probable right and probable injury. [Citations.]

No abuse of discretion being shown, the judgment of the court below is affirmed.

ELECTRONIC DATA SYSTEMS CORP. v. POWELL

524 S.W.2d 393

(Court of Civil Appeals of Texas, Dallas, April 11, 1975.)

AKIN, J.

Appellant Electronic Data Systems (hereinafter called EDS) brought suit to enjoin appellee Douglas W. Powell from violating certain restrictive covenants contained in an employment contract between Powell and EDS.

These covenants related to (1) disclosure of EDS business information and secrets; (2) interference in relationships between EDS and its employees; (3) *competition with EDS*; (4) *the use of methods, information or systems developed by EDS or EDS's customers in competition with EDS*; and, (5) contact with EDS's customers.

The district court entered a temporary injunction directing Powell not to interfere with the relationship between EDS and its employees, not to solicit EDS's customers whose contracts had been serviced by Powell, and not to compete with EDS in designated locations by using electronic data processing programs systems developed by EDS not generally known in the data processing industry which are used for performing "the function known as prepayment utilization review in processing health-care claims" (hereinafter referred to as PPUR). EDS appealed the trial court's decree asserting that the relief granted was insufficient to protect its interests. This court affirmed the temporary injunction in Electronic Data Systems Corp. v. Powell, 508 S.W.2d 137 (Tex.Civ.App.—Dallas 1974, no writ), holding that no abuse of discretion was shown.

The case is now before this court on appeal from a permanent injunction entered by the trial court incorporating the identical terms of the temporary injunction. Prior to consideration of EDS's points of error attacking the permanent injunction entered by the trial court, a discussion of the distinction between the review of a temporary injunction and the review of a permanent injunction by an appellate court is necessary. Powell's first counterpoint asserts that the permanent injunction granted by the trial court cannot be disturbed on appeal unless a clear abuse of discretion is shown. We cannot agree.

* * *

* * * We conclude, therefore, that although the trial court's fact findings are subject to review only for legal and factual insufficiency of evidence, the court's construction of restrictive covenants and its determination of the proper remedy for breach of such covenants are matters of law for our decision. * * * We, therefore, overrule Powell's counterpoint.

With this distinction in mind, we have reviewed the facts. The present record contains evidence not before us on the temporary injunction appeal. On that appeal we summarized the evidence as follows:

Appellee Douglas W. Powell worked for [EDS] from May 1970 until August 1972, after which he went to work for Systems Resources, Inc., (hereinafter called SRI), * * * EDS employs systems engineers who write computer programs for its customers. There are five industry groups which EDS serves, the two which are material here being the health care and public utilities industries. Powell worked in the health care area for EDS as a systems engineer on a team which developed a 'system,' or series of computer programs for processing health care claims involving private or non-governmental contracts. The health care industry was subdivided into the private and governmental sectors. The EDS system which Powell helped to develop, referred to as 'Prepayment Utilization Review' or 'PPUR,' competes with the 'Model System,' which was developed by a governmental agency, and which is employed by Powell's present employer, SRI. However, at the time of trial, Powell was working in the public utilities area for SRI, *an area in which EDS did not even have a data processing system when Powell was employed by it.* [Emphasis added.] Electronic Data Systems Corp. v. Powell, *supra.*

At the trial on the merits the evidence showed that SRI was developing a proprietary system for processing regular business health-care claims. The name "health insurance system" (hereinafter referred to as HIS), has been given to this SRI system. This system is not based on the government's "model system." SRI was planning the development of this system before Powell was hired by SRI in August 1972. The HIS system includes automated features and concepts which had been unique to EDS in regular business health-care claims processing system, including PPUR. The record shows conclusively the similarity of features and concepts of the HIS system and EDS National Regular Business System, including features and concepts originally unique to the EDS system. The competition between EDS and SRI in the health-care processing field is direct, wide-spread and "keen."

Powell made contributions to the development of the HIS system. Prior to Powell's EDS employment, he had no data processing ex-perience. After suit was filed, SRI transferred Powell from the health-care field to the *public utility data processing area.* The application for temporary injunction was heard in May 1973, and a temporary injunction was entered in August 1973. In November 1973, Powell made presentations on the HIS system planned by SRI to both the Kansas City Blue Shield and American Health & Life Insurance Company of Baltimore, Maryland. This activity was in direct competition with EDS. EDS also submitted financial proposals to both companies using the EDS proprietary PPUR system.

A significant addition to the record on the previous appeal is evidence that after the temporary injunction hearing Powell again became active in the health-care field. In September 1973, he was reassigned from the SRI utilities project and again began working full time in Dallas with the primary responsibility of servicing the Kansas City Blue Shield account. In January 1974, Powell was the first person assigned by SRI to the HIS project. Although Powell denies responsibility for having produced the SRI documentation for PPUR, he does admit that he "shared" information about PPUR with another SRI employee. This activity was in direct violation of Powell's contract with EDS and in violation of the temporary injunction; although the trial court found that Powell did not make any "material" disclosures of information concerning PPUR.

The trial court limited its permanent injunction as it did also its temporary injunction by defining the word "competing" as:

Conduct by Powell involving the design or use, or providing further information to others on systems for performing in whole or in part, the function known as prepayment utilization review in processing health care claims as that function was designed to be performed by the EDS National Regular Business program on August 15, 1972, where such function designed to be performed by the EDS National Regular Business program exceeds that which is generally accepted and known as the data processing industry for prepayment utilization review program.

Accordingly, the permanent injunction, in effect, restrained Powell from soliciting EDS customers, recruiting EDS employees for a competitor, and from furnishing to others information concerning PPUR, the system which he had helped EDS to develop. The significant question here is whether or not the district court erred in concluding that this relief is all the relief reasonably necessary to protect EDS's business and goodwill. We hold that the permanent injunction granted provides inadequate protection and fails to give effect to the covenant not to compete.

The law in Texas governing restrictive covenants in employment contracts is well settled. The test for determining the validity of this covenant is whether the restrictions imposed upon the employee are greater than reasonably necessary to protect the business and goodwill of the employer or impose undue hardships on the employee. Weatherford Oil Tool Co. v. Campbell, 161 Tex. 310, 340 S.W.2d 950, 951 (1960). Such covenants will not be declared wholly void because they are unreasonable as to time, or as to extent of territory covered, or unreasonable as to both time and territory. Instead, a court of equity will enforce the contract by granting an injunction restraining competition for a time and within an area that is reasonable under the circumstances. Justin Belt Co. v. Yost, 502 S.W.2d 681, 685 (Tex.1973). In determining what is a reasonable restraint under the circumstances, the courts will ordinarily consider the question as one of law. [Citations.]

The permanent injunction granted by the trial court fails to give effect to the covenant not to compete. It grants no more protection than that which EDS is entitled to receive under the common law of trade secrets—the use and disclosure of information not generally known in data processing. Appellant's business of employing systems engineers to write computer programs for its customers is unique and highly specialized. Its training of Powell included specialized information pertaining to its business as distinguished from general skills and knowledge of the trade. Restraining him from using this information is intrinsically unenforceable so long as he is employed by a competing employer in the health-care field. It would indeed be difficult to determine if Powell were imparting his specialized knowledge to SRI until SRI markets a product resembling closely EDS's system.

The evidence on the merits reveals that Powell, by participating in the servicing of SRI medicare contracts, preparing SRI proposals to process health-care claims for potential EDS customers, including a proposal to incorporate utilization review into the system operated by SRI for Kansas City Blue Shield, and participating in the development and marketing of an SRI computer system for processing regular business health-care claims, has violated his covenant not to compete with EDS. All of these activities were admitted by Powell.

It was clearly established that the methods and techniques developed by EDS have resulted from a significant investment of time and money. Even in the best of good faith, a former technical or "creative" employee such as Powell working for a competitor such as SRI can hardly prevent his knowledge or his former employer's confidential methods from showing up in his work. [Citations.] If Powell is permitted to work for SRI in the same area as that in which he was trained by EDS, injunctive relief limited to restraint of imparting such special knowledge as prepayment utilization review, is likely to prove insufficient. The mere rendition of service in the same area would almost necessarily impart such knowledge to some degree in his subsequent employment. Powell cannot be loyal both to his promise to his former employer, EDS, and to his new obligation to his present employer, SRI. [Citation.] In these circumstances, the most effective protective device is to restrain Powell from working in the same computer field in which he was associated while employed by EDS.

EDS also argues that the confidential information and trade secrets of EDS cannot effectively be protected by permitting Powell to continue employment with SRI in the health-care field of data processing. We agree. The record conclusively shows that SRI and Powell failed to disclose at the temporary injunction hearing that Powell was working in the health-care area. If Powell is permitted to continue in the employment of SRI in the health-care field, there is no way to protect EDS's business and goodwill. Powell has disregarded his covenant not to compete since pursuing SRI employment. The evidence shows that Powell is assisting SRI to develop a system incorporating features previously unique to EDS. Both Powell and his SRI supervisor testified that Powell is expected to do anything that needs to be done to help SRI. Powell testified: "[D]ue to the size and nature of SRI, that it's difficult to assign anyone to a project and that be their only work at that time; that an individual has a background in a given area we call upon from time to time to work in that area even though that is not the primary responsibility." This is confirmed by Powell's admission that he "shared" information about PPUR with SRI. Indeed, Powell was part of the SRI–HIS team and has made sales representations describing the HIS system in direct competition to EDS. He has been involved with selecting new personnel for employment on the HIS team and has shared his knowledge with them. Powell has furthermore violated his employment contract with EDS by even recruiting an EDS employee to work for SRI in the HIS program development. The conclusion is inescapable that Powell is totally involved in the development of the SRI–HIS system. Powell cannot help but utilize information from EDS's health-care programs and data systems if permitted to continue in the SRI–HIS systems development effort which parallels EDS's PPUR system. Throughout Powell's employment with SRI, Powell has been actively assisting SRI in the health-care area of data processing in direct competition with EDS, except for a brief period of time after this action was filed. It was only then that Powell was reassigned by SRI to the public utilities field. In view, however, of Powell's above quoted testimony, it is reasonable to conclude that even then Powell was giving assistance to SRI in the health-care area. Mr. Justice Bateman, speaking for this court, in the appeal of the temporary injunction, placed much emphasis on the fact that Powell was working in the public utilities area and not the health-care area. The majority of this court concludes, therefore, that the only effective relief for EDS is to restrain Powell from working in the health-care field for SRI or any other employer that competes with EDS.

Accordingly, we reform the judgment of the district court and add to the definition of "competing" used in the judgment as follows:

> Participating, directly or indirectly, individually or as an employee, partner or officer of any person, firm or corporation in any activity involving the development, sale or operation of electronic data systems for processing health care claims; such shall include working for SRI in the health-care area of data processing.

This restraint will be subject to the restriction of three years from August 1972, and two hundred miles from any EDS installation, as provided in the trial court's judgment.

EDS also contends that the district court erred in finding that any further restraint, other than that granted, would impose upon Powell undue hardship and would be against public policy. We agree. This finding is unsupported in the evidence. In Orkin Exterminating Co. v. Wilson, 501 S.W.2d 408, 411–12 (Tex.Civ.App.—Tyler 1973, writ dism'd), the court stated that "the only hardship that would be suffered by appellees by the enforcement of the restrictive covenant would be that they be required to find other employment in different type businesses." The court found this to be insufficient to prevent enforcement of a covenant not to compete. Here, Powell would not be required to enter a *different type* of business, as in *Wilson*, but will be required to work in a different *area* of the electronic data processing business. The record here discloses that the health-care area of electronic data processing is but a small part of the total field of electronic data processing services.

My learned colleagues are of the opinion that the injunctive relief here granted is all that is reasonably necessary to protect EDS and its business. I respectfully disagree. In order to give EDS effective injunctive relief reasonably necessary to protect its business pursuant to its contract with Powell, I would broaden the injunctive relief to enjoin Powell from working in any capacity for SRI or any other EDS competitor.

Judgment modified and affirmed in part, and reversed and rendered as to costs, all of which, both in the trial court and here, are assessed against Powell.

PERIPHERAL DYNAMICS INC. v. HOLDSWORTH

254 Pa.Super. 310, 385 A.2d 1354
(Superior Court of Pennsylvania, April 13, 1978.)

PER CURIAM.

The six Judges who heard this appeal being equally divided, the order is affirmed.

HOFFMAN, J., concurring.

Appellant contends that the lower court erroneously refused to grant a preliminary injunction enforcing a restrictive employment covenant between appellant and its employee, appellee.[1] I disagree and, therefore, would affirm the lower court.

The following facts were adduced at a hearing before the Court of Common Pleas of Montgomery County pursuant to appellant's request for a preliminary injunction. Appellant, Peripheral Dynamics Inc. (P.D.I.), a corporation located in Montgomery County, is in the business of designing, manufacturing, and selling computer peripheral equipment, specifically card readers, throughout the world. Although hundreds of companies manufacture and deal in other types of computer peripheral devices, appellant P.D.I. is one of the four companies that manufacture peripheral card readers. From August, 1973, until November, 1975, appellee, Joseph H. Holdsworth, served as national or international sales manager. In that capacity, Holdsworth used his expertise in card readers, marketing, and engineering, and travelled throughout the world in an effort to sell P.D.I.'s card readers. Specifically, Holdsworth's job took him throughout the United States, as well as to Europe and Japan.

In May, 1974, Holdsworth submitted his resignation to P.D.I., effective June 13, 1974, in order to accept a similar position with one of P.D.I.'s competitors, Documation, Inc. However, prior to the effective date of his resignation, Holdsworth changed his mind and informed P.D.I. that he would continue as its employee. P.D.I. agreed to retain Holdsworth as an employee, provided that he sign an agreement in which he promised to refrain from working for P.D.I.'s competitors. Holdsworth agreed and in a letter to P.D.I., dated June 7, 1974, he stated that he was withdrawing his resignation and desired to continue his employment with P.D.I. The letter also contained the following provisions:

> 5. For a period ending one year after the end of my employment with PDI, for any reason whatsoever, I shall not either directly or indirectly, as proprietor, partner, stockholder, di-

rector, agent, principal agent, employee, consultant or lender, become associated with Documation, Inc., True Data, Inc., Oki Bridge Data Products, Inc., Mohawk Data Sciences, Inc., or any other person, firm corporation or other entity which manufactures, sells or otherwise deals in computer peripheral card readers.

> 6. In furtherance of, and without in any way limiting the restriction in paragraph 5 above, for the period specified in paragraph 5, I shall not directly or indirectly,

> (a) request any customers of PDI to curtail or cancel their business with PDI;

> (b) solicit, canvas or accept, or authorize any person or entity to solicit, canvas or accept, from customers or potential customers of PDI, any business for myself or for the companies specified in paragraph 5 or for any other person, firm, corporation or other entity which manufactures, sells or otherwise deals in peripheral card readers.

> As used in this paragraph, "potential customer" shall mean possible customers with which PDI has had some business contact.

After signing the letter, Holdsworth continued to work for P.D.I. until November, 1975, when he gave the company notice that he would be leaving. In November, 1975, Holdsworth went to work for True Data, a competitor of P.D.I., in a job involving the sale of True Data card readers.

On January 20, 1976, P.D.I. filed a complaint in equity, requesting a preliminary injunction to enjoin Holdsworth from continuing his employment with True Data and to comply otherwise with the terms of the agreement contained in the letter of June 7, 1974. On January 26, 1976, the Court of Common Pleas of Montgomery County issued a rule to show cause why a preliminary injunction should not be issued and set a hearing for February 10, 1976. However, on February 10, 1976, after a brief discussion with counsel in chambers, the court refused to hold a hearing and denied P.D.I.'s request for a preliminary injunction. P.D.I. appealed to our Court from this order. On April 10, 1976, pursuant to a stipulation among the parties, our Court vacated the lower court's order and remanded the case to the Court of Common Pleas of Montgomery County and directed a prompt

1. The two appellees in this case are Joseph S. Holdsworth, an employee of appellant Peripheral Data, Inc. and True Data, Inc., appellant's competitor for which

Holdsworth went to work after resigning from employment with appellant.

hearing on P.D.I.'s request for a preliminary injunction.

The lower court held hearings on May 13, May 14, and June 7, 1976. At the close of appellant's case, appellees moved to dismiss appellant's request for a preliminary injunction, stating that the motion was in the nature of a demurrer. Appellees maintained that P.D.I. had not met its burden of establishing a restrictive covenant with a geographic limitation and of showing that the covenant, as written, was reasonably related to protecting P.D.I.'s interest. Moreover, appellees urged that the extensive enforcement P.D.I. sought would work a severe hardship on appellee Holdsworth. On June 10, 1976, the lower court granted appellees' motion and entered an order denying the preliminary injunction. This appeal followed.

Appellant contends that the lower court erred in refusing to grant a preliminary injunction to enforce the restrictive employment covenant because the court could have implied a reasonable geographic limitation despite the absence of an explicit geographic limitation. The Majority finds that although the restrictive covenant could have been given a reasonable geographic limitation, appellant did not seek such reasonably limited enforcement. Accordingly, the Majority affirms the lower court's denial of the preliminary injunction. I concur.

* * *

There are four prerequisites which are essential for the issuance of a preliminary injunction:

> * * * first, that it is necessary to prevent immediate and irreparable harm which could not be compensated by damages; second, that greater injury would result by refusing it than by granting it; and third, that it properly restores the parties to their status as it existed immediately prior to the alleged wrongful conduct. * * * Even more essential, however, is the determination that the activity sought to be restrained is actionable, and that the injunction issued is reasonably suited to abate such activity. And unless the plaintiff's right is clear and the wrong is manifest, a preliminary injunction will not generally be awarded. [*Bryant v. Sling Testing and Repair, Inc.*, 471 Pa. 1, 7, 369 A.2d 1164, 1167 (1977).]

In the instant case, after three days of hearings during which it heard the testimony of both Holdsworth and P.D.I.'s corporate president, the lower court refused to grant a preliminary injunction. In its opinion, the court based its refusal to grant equitable relief on the grounds that the injunction sought was not reasonably designed to abate the activity sought to be restrained, working for P.D.I.'s competitor. The court correctly reasoned that in order for a restrictive employment covenant to be enforceable, it must be reasonable in time, reasonable in geographic extent, and reasonably necessary to protect the employer without imposing an undue hardship on the employee. These requirements are the well-established criteria that our courts have used in evaluating the enforceability of restrictive employment covenants. [Citations.] Because the restrictive covenant in question was not geographically limited and P.D.I.'s operations were world-wide in scope, the lower court found it impossible to imply a reasonable geographic limitation. Moreover, because Holdsworth's employment caused him to travel throughout the world, the court reasoned that the restrictive covenant would prevent Holdsworth from working as a salesman of peripheral card readers anywhere in the world. Thus, the court concluded that such a restriction placed an unreasonable hardship on Holdsworth as an employee and, accordingly, it refused to grant the preliminary injunction.

I agree that the record demonstrated a reasonable basis to support the lower court's refusal of a preliminary injunction. At the hearings, P.D.I.'s president conceded that both the corporation's operations and the restrictive covenant were worldwide in scope. Moreover, P.D.I. sought complete enforcement of the covenant. P.D.I.'s president specifically stated that the only two places in which he would not contemplate enforcement were Tibet and the North Pole.

Second, the lower court properly refused to imply a geographic limitation in the absence of an explicit limitation and in the face of P.D.I.'s demand for total enforcement. The lower court correctly distinguished those cases which have implied such geographic limitations. Those cases have involved employment contracts which either defined the geographic scope of the employer's operations or specified the territorial area of the employee's activities. [Citation.] Consequently, the courts could interpret those agreements as implying reasonable geographic limitations in the restrictive covenants. In the instant case, however, the lower court found neither a specific geographic limitation nor other language implying a reasonable geographic limitation. In short, the lower court reasonably determined that the restrictive covenant could not be limited and would have an inordinately harmful impact on appellee Holdsworth.[2] Consequently, the lower court had reasonable grounds for refusing to grant the preliminary injunction.[3]

Because I find that there were apparently reasonable grounds to support the lower court's denial of a preliminary injunction, I would affirm the lower court. Accordingly, I concur.

SPAETH, J., in support of affirmance.

The facts in this case are fully set forth in Judge Van der Voort's opinion in support of reversal and in Judge Hoffman's opinion in support of affirmance. I, too, agree that the case must be affirmed, but for reasons somewhat different from Judge Hoffman's. Judge Van der Voort says that the restrictive covenant could be limited, and proceeds to write limitations into it. Judge Hoffman says that the covenant "could not be limited." In my opinion, the covenant could be limited, but whether to limit it was within the lower court's discretion, and the court's decision not to limit it should not be disturbed.

2. The Dissenting Opinion rewrites the restrictive covenant by limiting its geographic scope to the United States, Europe, and Japan, those places to which Holdsworth travelled most frequently. Even apart from the undue hardship this would work on Holdsworth, there is additional authority contradicting such an approach. In *Reading Aviation Services v. Bertolet* [454 Pa. 488, 311 A.2d 628 (1973)], our Supreme Court recognized the potentially adverse consequences of courts rewriting restrictive employment covenants in order to characterize them as reasonable:

> The objection to such practice is that it tends to encourage employers and purchasers possessing superior bargaining power over that of their employees and vendors to insist upon unreasonable and excessive restrictions, secure in the knowledge that the promise may be upheld in part, if not full. *Reading Aviation Services,* supra, 454 Pa. at 493, 311 A.2d at 630. [Citation.]

3. The lower court's opinion bases its denial of the preliminary injunction exclusively on the fact that the in-

1

I agree with Judge Van der Voort that the scope of a covenant not to compete may be limited by a court to ensure both that the duration and geographical scope of a covenant are reasonable and that the covenant is neither unnecessary for the employer's protection nor unduly burdensome for the employee. It does not follow, however, that this court is the court to impose such limitations. In my opinion, they should be imposed by the lower court, after evidence and findings of fact on such matters as the nature of the business in question and the employee's business experience. * * *

Furthermore, even if the record here were such as to make it appropriate for us to limit the covenant, we should not do so, for the issue of the propriety of an injunction is moot. The covenant provided that "[f]or a period ending one year after the end of my [Holdsworth's] employment with PDI * * * I shall not * * * [enter into various types of employment]". Holdsworth left the employ of PDI in November 1975.

2

Given the lower court's ability to limit the covenant, the question is whether its refusal to do so was error.

It is true, as Judge Van der Voort states, that

> [a] contract between an employer and an employee which contains restrictive covenants against competition by the employee after ter-

junction sought was not reasonably designed to abate the activity sought to be restrained. This is the fourth and most important prerequisite to injunctive relief. [Citation.] Because all four requirements must be satisfied before a court will grant a preliminary injunction, the absence of any of the four requisite elements will preclude the grant of equitable relief. Accordingly, it is unnecessary to evaluate the other prerequisites to a preliminary injunction. However, I note that in three days of testimony, P.D.I. failed to establish any irreparable injury which could not be compensated by damages. P.D.I.'s president testified that since Holdsworth had left P.D.I. to work for True Data, customers had selected True Data card readers over P.D.I. card readers at least five times in five months and that in the six years that the two companies had been in business, this had never happened over a similar time period. However, P.D.I.'s president failed to establish any nexus between these unprecedented purchases and Holdsworth's breach of the restrictive covenant.

mination of his employment, is valid and will be sustained unless the employee proves that the covenant constitutes an unreasonable or illegal restraint of trade. *Seligman and Latz of Pittsburgh, Inc. v. Vernillo*, 382 Pa. 161, 164, 114 A.2d 672 (1955).

[Citations.] Applying this principle here, it would appear that the lower court erred when it granted the employee's motion "in the nature of a demurrer" at the close of the employer's evidence. Since the employee has the burden of proving the covenant unreasonable, should not the court have required the employee to have come forward with evidence?

In considering this question it must be borne in mind that a restrictive covenant is prima facie enforceable only if it is reasonable in time, reasonable in geographic extent, and reasonably necessary to protect the employer without imposing undue hardship on the employee. [Citations.] Here the covenant contained no geographic limitation. Because of this, a prima facie case was not presented, and the burden did not shift to the employee to demonstrate the unreasonableness of the covenant. It was therefore proper, I conclude, for the court to have decided against the employer without requiring the employee to come forward with evidence.

The absence of a geographic limitation did not, however, disable the employer from making out a case—as Judge Hoffman's opinion may suggest. Rather, the employer had at least two possible courses of action open to it.

First, the employer might have attempted to demonstrate to the court that under the factual circumstances of this case the absence of a geographic limitation was not unreasonable.[1] For example, the employer could have attempted to prove that its operations were in fact worldwide, and that during his employment the employee had in fact traveled throughout the world. On such proof it might be found that prima facie, at least, the limitation was not unnecessarily broad, so that the burden would then shift to the employee to show that even so, it was unduly burdensome for him. It may be that it was the employer's intention to proceed in this manner. If so, however, it did not succeed, for instead

of showing that the employee had traveled throughout the world, its evidence showed that he had only traveled in the United States, and parts of Europe and Japan.

Alternatively, the employer might have requested only limited enforcement of the covenant, demonstrating by evidence in support of this request that such enforcement would be reasonable in consideration of the necessities of its business. In such event, too, a prima facie case would have been made out, and the burden would shift to the employee to show that even as limited, the covenant was unduly burdensome for him. Here, however, the employer specifically declined to adopt such a course of action, instead requesting complete enforcement. As Judge Hoffman notes, the president of PDI stated that the only two places that he would not seek enforcement of the covenant were Tibet and the North Pole.

Despite this sweeping request, the court could have looked to all of the surrounding circumstances to judge the reasonableness of the covenant and could have granted partial enforcement. [Citations.]

> The man who wildly claims that he owns all the cherry trees in the country cannot be denied protection of the orchard in his back yard. A restrictive covenant, when it comes under the scrutiny of a court of equity, will be held to reasonable geographical and chronological boundaries, according to the realities of the situation. *Barb-Lee Mobile Frame Co. v. Hoot*, 416 Pa. 222, 224, 206 A.2d 59 (1965).

The point, it seems to me, is that whether to grant protection only as to some of the cherry trees is discretionary. Where, as here, an employer claims protection of all of the trees, the court may decline to give him protection, as to any. [Citation.]

> This sort of gratuitous overbreadth militates against enforcement because it indicates an intent to oppress the employee and/or to foster a monopoly, either of which is an illegitimate purpose. An employer who extracts a covenant in furtherance of such a purpose comes to the court of equity with unclean hands and is, therefore, not entitled to equitable enforcement of the covenant. *Sidco Paper Company v. Aaron*, [465 Pa. 586, 599, 351 A.2d 250, 257 (1976)]

---

1. The lower court reasoned that " * * * Mr. Holdsworth's operations were admittedly worldwide; therefore, the court could not possibly be able to interpret a reasonable geographic limitation." [Reference.] This is a non sequitur.

Affirmed.

VAN der VOORT, J. in support of reversal.

Appellant Peripheral Dynamics, Inc. (P.D.I.) is in the business of manufacturing and selling computer devices known as peripheral card readers. Appellee Joseph S. Holdsworth was employed by appellant from August 1973 until November 1975 as national sales manager. While so employed, appellee traveled throughout the United States, Europe, and Japan, soliciting business for his employer. In May of 1974, appellee resigned to accept a similar position with a rival company; however, prior to the effective date of the resignation, he changed his mind and requested that P.D.I. continue to employ him. P.D.I. agreed, on condition that appellee sign an agreement (in the form of a letter from Holdsworth to P.D.I.) containing the following provision:

> For a period ending one year after the end of my employment with P.D.I., for any reason whatsoever, I shall not either directly or indirectly * * * become associated with Documation, Inc., True Data, Inc., Oki Bridge Products, Inc., Mohawk Data Sciences Inc., or any other person, firm, corporation or other entity which manufactures, sells or otherwise deals in computer peripheral card readers.

The agreement also sought to prevent Holdsworth from soliciting P.D.I.'s customers for the benefit of any competing companies for a period of one year following the cessation of Holdsworth's employment with P.D.I. Mr. Holdsworth signed the agreement and was permitted to remain an employee of P.D.I.

On November 14, 1975, appellee Holdsworth voluntarily terminated his employment with P.D.I. and became an employee of appellee True Data, Inc. P.D.I. filed a complaint in equity to enjoin Holdsworth from continuing his employment with True Data and to otherwise require Holdsworth to comply with the terms of the employment agreement. Hearings were held on May 13 and 14 and June 9, 1976, and a motion in the nature of a demurrer was granted, denying the request for a preliminary injunction. Appeal was taken to our court from the order denying the injunction, appellant arguing that the lower court erred in finding that the restrictive employment covenant contained no geographical limitation and was not susceptible to the imposition of a reasonable geographical limitation, and that the lower court also erred in applying an improper presumption of unreasonableness. This position appears to be valid.

A contract between an employer and an employee which contains restrictive covenants against competition by the employee after the termination of his employment, is valid and will be sustained unless the *employee* proves that the covenant constitutes an unreasonable or illegal restraint of trade. [Citation.] In other words, the burden will be on the party asserting the illegality of the covenant to show how and why it is unlawful. [Citations.] In the case before us, the lower court erroneously placed the burden on plaintiff-employer citing *Reading Aviation Service, Inc. v. Bertolet*, 454 Pa. 488, 311 A.2d 628 (1973) and *Girard Investment Co. v. Bello*, 456 Pa. 220, 318 A.2d 718 (1974) for the proposition that "a restrictive covenant in an employment contract will be presumed to be unreasonable without a geographical limitation." These two cases simply do not stand for the proposition stated. The restrictive covenant in *Reading* had no geographical or time limitation, and the Supreme Court found that the covenant placed an unconscionable burden on the employee's ability to pursue his chosen occupation, with restrictions that were "far greater than * * * reasonably necessary for the protection of the [the employer]." In *Girard*, a chancellor denied a preliminary injunction to enforce a restrictive employment covenant, holding that the general covenant not to compete was not reasonably necessary for the employer's protection, and also that, because of the overly broad geographic limitations, the contract constituted an undue hardship on the employee. The Supreme Court affirmed the chancellor's decision, but on the narrow ground that "under the circumstances, the covenant was not reasonably necessary for the employer's protection. * * *" (The employee had been a branch manager of Girard Investment Co., and had left to start his own concern). Both *Reading* and *Girard* are distinguishable from the case before us, neither case refers to any presumption of unreasonableness, and I believe the lower court erred in applying such a presumption.

Employment contracts containing general covenants by an employee not to compete after the termination of his employment are prima facie enforceable if they are reasonably limited as to time and geographical extent, and they will be deemed "reasonably limited" if the restrictions are reasonably necessary for the protection of the employer while not imposing undue hardship on the employee. [Citation.] In the case before us, appellee Joseph Holdsworth had access to customer lists and information about P.D.I., which could be used by P.D.I.'s competitors. P.D.I. attempted to protect itself by restraining Holdsworth from working for its competitors and using his knowledge and information against P.D.I. for a period of one year. The period of time was reasonable, but other restrictions were too broad. The agreement between Holdsworth and P.D.I. specified that Holdsworth would not associate himself with four named companies (including True Data) "or any other person, firm, corporation or other entity which manufactures, sells or otherwise deals in computer peripheral card readers." The covenant would thus seem to restrict Holdsworth from working in any capacity for any company that dealt in any way with computer peripheral card readers. Furthermore, as the lower court noted, the agreement imposed no geographical limitations. The lower court noted that Holdsworth's operations were "worldwide," and the court therefore ruled that a reasonable geographical limitation could not be imposed by the court. I conclude that the covenant can be limited and, as limited, be enforced.

Mr. Holdsworth testified that his work for P.D.I. took him to Europe and Japan and throughout the United States. It would not be an undue hardship on Mr. Holdsworth to enjoin him from working for a period of one year for the four named P.D.I. competitors in the three geographical areas in which he formerly operated. Mr. Holdsworth did agree in writing, as a condition of his continued employment with P.D.I., not to take advantage for a period of one year of information obtained and contacts made by him while employed by P.D.I. [Footnote.] He should be held to this part of the agreement. It would be unreasonable however, to restrain Mr. Holdsworth from working for *any* company which might deal in some way with peripheral card readers. I would enforce the covenant to the extent that Mr. Holdsworth should be enjoined from working for True Data, Inc., and the three other companies named in the complaint, in Europe, Japan, and the United States, for a period of one year.

I would remand to the lower court in order that a preliminary injunction be issued in accordance with this opinion.

NATIONAL CASH REGISTER CORP. v. ARNETT

554 F. Supp. 1176
(United States District Court, D. Colorado, Jan. 17, 1983.)

CARRIGAN, D. J.

Plaintiff, National Cash Register Corporation, ("NCR"), has moved to dismiss the defendants' first counterclaim. That counterclaim alleges a violation of § 2 of the Sherman Anti-Trust Act, 15 U.S.C. § 2. The issues have been thoroughly briefed and argued.

Plaintiff NCR is a multi-national corporation engaged primarily in the development, marketing and distribution of computer hardware and software. Defendant Arnett was employed by NCR for eight years, principally in the area of research, development and sale of computerized financial systems for use by banks.

In 1980 Arnett left NCR and established the defendant corporation, Creative Financial Systems, Inc. ("Creative"). Creative also is involved in selling software to banks. It competes directly with NCR in this aspect of NCR's business.

During his employment at NCR, Arnett worked on "Banker 79", a confidential computer program licensed to NCR by CT Associates, and on its updated successor system, "Banker 80." The licensing agreement between NCR and CT Associates prohibited NCR from disclosing any aspect of these programs. In its complaint, NCR asserts that Arnett is now marketing programs nearly identical to "Banker 79" and "Banker 80." NCR claims that in so doing, Arnett is breaching his own employment contract, violating his fiduciary duty, wrongfully appropriating the programs, and violating NCR's confidentiality agreement with CT Associates.

Defendants' first counterclaim, the target of the instant motion to dismiss, alleges that the only real purposes of this litigation are "to eliminate the defendant as a competitor, to force discontinuation of the defendant's system and illegally to restrain trade and competition in the area of computer software systems utilized by commercial banks." As grounds for its motion to dismiss this counterclaim, NCR urges that the facts asserted cannot constitute a violation of the anti-trust act. It argues that litigation cannot rise to the level of a Sherman Act violation unless multiple spurious actions are instituted.

The law is clear that in deciding a motion to dismiss, I must construe the factual allegations in the light most favorable to the pleading party, and must deny the motion "unless it appears beyond doubt that the [party whose claims may be dismissed] can prove no set of facts in support of his claim which entitles him to relief." [Citations.]

The general language of the Act itself fails to provide any guidance in deciding whether the conduct alleged in the counterclaim under consideration constitutes monopolization or conspiracy to monopolize. The Act states:

> "Every person who shall monopolize, or attempt to monopolize or combine or conspire with any other person or persons to monopolize any part of the trade or commerce among the several states. * * *" (shall be guilty of a violation of the laws of the United States.) 15 U.S.C. § 2.

There is, however, case law to support the defendants' counterclaim. *Eastern Railroad Presidents Conference v. Noerr Motor Freight, Inc.,* 365 U.S. 127, 81 S.Ct. 523, 5 L.Ed.2d 464 (1961) and *United Mine Workers v. Pennington,* 381 U.S. 657, 85 S.Ct. 1585, 14 L.Ed.2d 626 (1965) developed the "Noerr-Pennington doctrine" that—as a general rule—efforts to influence judicial, legislative or executive action do not violate the anti-trust laws. In balancing the First Amendment freedom of speech against the evils prohibited by anti-trust statutes, the Court resolved the question in favor of the constitutional guarantees.

An exception to the *Noerr-Pennington* holding exists where "concerted effort, ostensibly directed toward influencing government action [is] a mere sham to cover what is actually nothing more than an attempt to interfere directly with the business relation-

ships of a competitor." 365 U.S. at 144. This has become known as the "sham exception."

The question remains: what claims, if proved, would establish a sham? Plaintiff concedes that bad faith litigation may give rise to a § 2 violation, but argues that "bad faith" cannot be shown, absent the filing of multiple lawsuits. This contention evolves from the *Noerr-Pennington* extension in *California Motor Transport v. Trucking Unlimited,* 404 U.S. 508, 92 S.Ct. 609, 30 L.Ed.2d 642 (1972). There, the Supreme Court noted that a pattern of "baseless, repetitious claims" could result in an antitrust violation.

* * *

Recently, Judge Kane of this Court held that one case alone may constitute a violation of § 1 of the Sherman Anti-Trust Act. *Colorado Petroleum Marketers Association v. Southland Corp.,* 476 F.Supp. 373 (D.Colo. 1979). He cited *Lektro-Vend Corp. v. Vendo Co.,* 433 U.S. 623, 97 S.Ct. 2881, 53 L.Ed.2d 1009 (1977), which, while never directly addressing the issue whether a single action can amount to sham litigation, had indicated that vexatious prosecution may be countermanded by instituting an anti-trust action. [Citations.]

In *Colorado Petroleum,* Judge Kane rejected the argument that more than one prior suit is required to establish an anti-trust claim. He interpreted *California Motors* as merely addressing the probative value of having filed only one suit as contrasted to that of having filed many. The number of sham lawsuits filed speaks to the weight of evidence to support the claimed anti-trust violation, not to its existence. [Citation.]

Referring to *California Motors,* Judge Kane stated:

> I am not convinced that the Court intended to give every dog one free bite, thus making it an irrebuttable presumption that the first lawsuit was not a sham regardless of the overwhelming evidence indicating otherwise. Advancing such a holding denigrates the animus of the anti-trust laws. * * *

Colorado Petroleum Marketers Association v. Southland Corp., 476 F.Supp. at 378.

I agree with Judge Kane.

In the instant case, NCR, a long established corporation, has sued a fledgling company seeking to prevent its profiting from the only product it offers. A victory for NCR would put the defendant out of business, thus eliminating a competitor from the marketplace. Defendant claims that the technical proof will show that NCR must have realized that the programs or systems allegedly misappropriated were significantly different from NCR's. If the defendant can prove that assertion, then the conclusion might be drawn that NCR acted with no intent other than to "monopolize part of the trade or commerce among the several states." 15 U.S.C. § 2.

Accordingly, it is ordered that the plaintiff's motion to dismiss the defendant's first counterclaim is denied.

ELECTRONIC DATA SYSTEMS CORP. v. KINDER

360 F. Supp. 1044
(United States District Court, N. D. Texas, Dallas Division, July 12, 1973.)

HUGHES, D. J.

* * *

EDS seeks injunctive relief to specifically enforce paragraph 5 of an employment agreement. Paragraph 5 reads as follows:

The Employee, as consideration of his employment, and in consideration of all the matter contained in the preceding paragraphs, and the information he will obtain as an employee of EDS agrees that during the term of this agreement and for a period of three (3) years thereafter, Employee shall not, directly or indirectly, individually or as an employee, partner, officer, director or stockholder, or in any other capacity whatsoever of any person, firm, partnership or corporation, (i) recruit, hire, assist others in recruiting or hiring, discuss employment with, or refer to others concerning employment, any person who is, or within the then preceding twelve months was, an employee of EDS or any subsidiary or affiliated company, or of any present, prospective or former customer of EDS or any subsidiary or affiliated company, (ii) compete with EDS or any subsidiary or affiliated company within two hundred (200) miles of any city in the United States in which EDS or any subsidiary or affiliated company does business, or (iii) use in competition with an EDS or subsidiary or affiliated company customer, prospective customer, or former customer, any of the meth-

ods, information, or systems developed by EDS or any subsidiary or affiliated company or its customers, prospective customers, or former customers within two hundred (200) miles of any city where such customer, prospective customer, or former customer does business. Employee further agrees during the same period not to call upon, solicit, accept employment with, sell or endeavor to sell within the United States any customer, prospective customer, or former customer of EDS or any subsidiary or affiliated company. The term "prospective customer" as used herein shall mean such firms as EDS or any subsidiary or affiliated company has actively solicited within twelve months prior to the date of termination of Employee's employment hereunder.

Kinder, as his defense, alleges the restrictive covenants in the employment agreement to be unreasonable and in violation of the Anti-Trust Laws of Texas. He further asserts there was fraud in the inducement to enter into the contract. Finally, he counterclaims for overtime wages allegedly due under the Fair Labor Standards Act and a bonus of $2,500.00.

EDS is incorporated under the laws of the State of Texas and has its principal place of business in Dallas, Texas, although it conducts business in at least fifteen states and twenty major cities. It has customers or potential customers in other states. The corporation engages in data processing, computer programming, establishing data processing systems, and other activities related to the computer industry. A major business activity of EDS relates to computer processing of medicare payment applications.

Previously trained in the field of electronic data processing, Kinder was recruited by EDS during the summer of 1969. After discussing with various EDS personnel the organization of the company and the benefits of employment with EDS, Kinder signed an "Employment Agreement" on June 13, 1969, under the terms of which he was employed as a "Systems Engineer" salaried at $11,000.00 per annum.

By agreement with EDS management, Kinder began his employment on September 2, 1969, in the EDS operations center located in Kansas City, Kansas. In November, 1970, Kinder was transferred to Dallas, Texas, and later to California.

As a systems engineer, Kinder worked in a "team" of four to five men engaged in the development of a computer program that would mechanically process applications for payment of medicare claims.

On April 30, 1972, Kinder terminated his employment with EDS. Thereafter, he was employed by Systems Resources, Incorporated (SRI). Before and after Kinder became a SRI employee, SRI was in competition with EDS for the data processing market related to payment of medicare claims.

There are two methods for processing medicare payment claims: (1) the EDS Plan and (2) the Model Plan. The EDS Plan is a processing plan unique to EDS. This plan is specifically designed and programed for the state whose resident applications it processes. Thus, a computer programed under the EDS Plan to process applications of Texas residents would have to be modified to handle applications filed by residents of any other state. During his employment with EDS, Kinder worked on the development of an EDS Plan for Kansas, Texas and California.

The Model Plan is a processing plan devised by the Social Security Administration and is public information available to all persons or companies attempting to process medicare payment claims. When employed by SRI, Kinder worked exclusively on the Model Plan. At no time prior to his employment with SRI did Kinder have any contact with the Model Plan.

At trial a jury was empaneled and requested to answer special issues raised by the parties in their pleadings.

In response to plaintiff's Amended Complaint seeking injunctive relief for alleged violations of paragraph 5 of the EDS-Kinder Agreement, the jury in Special Issue No. 1 found that Kinder since leaving the employment of EDS:

(a) Did not disclose information to his employer relating to computer programs or data systems he learned about while employed by EDS,

(b) Did disclose to his employer the names of EDS Corporation employees,

(c) Did recruit, hire, assist his employer in recruiting or hiring, discussed employment with or referred to his employer for possible employment persons who were or who had been within the immediately preceding 12 months employed by EDS,

(d) Did not as an employee of SRI directly engage in competition with EDS,

(e) Did as an employee of SRI indirectly engage in competition with EDS,

(f) Did not as an employee of SRI directly use in competition with a customer, prospective customer, or former customer of EDS any of the methods, information, or systems developed by EDS,

(g) Did not as an employee of SRI indirectly use in competition with a customer, prospective customer, or former customer of EDS any of the methods, information, or systems developed by EDS, and

(h) Did not call upon, solicit, sell, or endeavor to sell within the United States to any customer, prospective customer, or former customer of EDS.

The findings of the jury on the issues relevant to plaintiff's cause of action are hereby adopted by this court except as to the issue of Kinder's indirect competition with EDS while employed by SRI.

This court specifically rejects that portion of the jury's verdict and holds there has been no indirect competition by Kinder with EDS. In so doing, this court focuses upon the meaning of the term "indirect" in Texas:

* * * circuitous, oblique; as, an indirect road; not leading to an aim or result by the plainest cause or method or by obvious means, but obliquely or by remote means; round-about; not resulting directly from an act or cause, but more or less remotely connected with or growing out of. * * *

Maryland Cas. Co. v. Scharlack, D.C., 31 F.Supp. 931, 933, aff'd, 115 F.2d 719 (5th Cir. 1940).

To engage in indirect competition, Kinder must himself be the causal link between the competitor and EDS. It is not necessary that Kinder himself have initiated the competition, for that would be direct competition. However, he must personally have some causal connection with the alleged competition. In this case, there is not a scintilla of evidence that Kinder engaged in any act, either oral or physical, that could be construed as even inferring that he was engaged or was about to engage in competition with EDS. The mere act of entering into an employment relationship with an existing competitor of EDS is not sufficient by itself to constitute indirect competition with EDS by Kinder.

Moreover, Kinder's work for SRI was in an area of data processing distinct from that *practiced* by EDS. While employed by EDS, Kinder worked on the EDS Plan. While employed by SRI, Kinder worked on the Model Plan. There is no evidence that Kinder promoted, assisted in the promotion, or otherwise solicited any business from any person or corporation described in paragraph 5 by virtue of his previous association with EDS. Second, to constitute "indirect" competition, the employee himself must have a causal connection with the competition that infringes the restrictive covenant at issue. Kinder's employment at SRI was of a purely mechanical nature and totally passive as to the recruitment of additional business and, therefore, lacking in this causal element. Finally, this court notes that SRI and EDS were engaged in competition *before* Kinder became employed by EDS and no evidence was presented that links Kinder to any post-SRI employment competition activity.

This court holds further that even if there were evidence of indirect competition by Kinder with EDS the restrictive covenants contained in paragraph 5 could not be enforced either because they are unreasonable or are not necessary for the protection of EDS' business and good will.

Although the parties to an employment agreement are generally free to draft their own agreement, it is for the courts, as a matter of law, to determine whether covenants of non-competition are reasonably limited as to both time and space and, therefore, enforceable. [Citation.] Weatherford Oil Tool Co. v. Campbell, 161 Tex. 310, 340 S.W.2d 950 (1960). [Citation.]

The restriction as to time in the EDS-Kinder Agreement is quite specific and reasonable: 3 years from the date of termination of employment.

The restriction as to space, however, is unreasonable under the *Weatherford* doctrine which is controlling in this cause. Like the covenants at issue in *Weatherford,* the EDS geographic restrictions on competition appear, at first blush, to be specific and logical. However, further examination shows the 200 mile territory set forth in paragraph 5 to be

so vague and uncertain that Kinder could not terminate his employment with EDS and have any certainty as to a specific city or town in which he could engage in the data processing of medicare payment applications without being in violation of the Agreement. Under paragraph 5, the zone of non-competition is measured from any city in which EDS maintained business operations or in which was located an EDS customer, potential customer, subsidiary, or affiliated company. As the Texas Supreme Court stated in *Weatherford:*

> If petitioner should extend its business operations into such territory, respondents are obligated by their contract to discontinue selling competing merchandise therein for the remainder of the year. Enforcement of the agreement in accordance with its terms would thus effectively prevent respondents from competing with petitioners anywhere in the world for the stipulated period.

161 Tex. 313, 340 S.W.2d at 952.

In view of the foregoing, this court holds the non-competition covenants in paragraph 5 of the EDS-Kinder Agreement to be unreasonable and, therefore, unenforceable and void.

However, even if these covenants were reasonable, this court holds the covenants to be unnecessary for the protection of EDS' business and, therefore, unenforceable.

The remedy of injunctive relief to specifically enforce a covenant of non-competition is a harsh remedy that is utilized only when necessary to protect the business of the employer. As stated by the Texas Supreme Court in *Weatherford:*

> * * * the test usually stated for determining the validity of the covenant as written is whether it imposes any greater restraint than is reasonably necessary to protect the business and good will of the employer.

161 Tex. at 312, 340 S.W.2d at 951.

At trial, there was a plethora of evidence that EDS did not employ the Model Plan in processing medicare payment claims. Moreover, Kinder's work at SRI was exclusively on the Model Plan. At no time did SRI advertise that a former EDS employee was available to work on potential jobs. The Model Plan on which Kinder worked was public information and, therefore, Kinder's work cannot per se be classified as being competitive with EDS.

Therefore, to restrain Kinder from working on a publically available data processing plan is inconsistent with the purpose of the covenants of non-competition. That is, to enjoin Kinder will not lessen the competition facing EDS.

As to Kinder's allegation that the employment contract was void ab initio because of fraud and misrepresentation in the inducement, Kinder is estopped to assert the invalidity of that contract because he received the full benefits thereof. [Citations.]

With respect to the counterclaims of Kinder, the jury in Special Issues No. 2 and 3 found that he was not an administrative employee or professional employee during his tenure with EDS, as those terms are used in the Fair Labor Standards Act.

In Special Issue No. 4, the jury found that EDS acted in good faith in conformity with and reliance upon the Department of Labor regulations pertinent to the Fair Labor Standards Act in not paying Kinder time and a half compensation for overtime hours exceeding 40 hours per work week. In Special Issue No. 5, the jury further found that EDS did not willfully fail to pay Kinder time and a half overtime compensation.

In view of the jury's findings on Special Issues No. 4 and 5, this court holds that Kinder is not entitled to a judgment on his counterclaim for overtime wages.

In Special Issues No. 6 and 7, the jury found that Kinder was promised a $2,500.00 bonus by his supervisors for his work on the EDS regular business team in San Francisco before the completion of the installation of the EDS Regular Business System there.

It is therefore ordered, adjudged and decreed that:

1. Frederick J. Kinder, Jr. be and he is hereby enjoined from the date of entry of this Order through April 30, 1975, from recruiting, hiring, or assisting others in recruiting or hiring, discussing employment with, or referring to others concerning employment, the name or identity of any person who is, or who within the immediately preceding twelve month period was, an employee of EDS or any subsidiary or affiliated company of EDS;

2. A judgment be and the same hereby is entered for Frederick J. Kinder, Jr. against EDS for the sum of twenty five hundred dollars and no/100 ($2,500.00);

3. Each party is to bear his own costs and attorney fees; and,

4. All other relief sought by either party be and the same hereby is denied.

THREE PHOENIX CO. v. PACE INDUSTRIES, INC.

135 Ariz. 113, 659 P.2d 1258
(Supreme Court of Arizona, En Banc, Jan. 12, 1983, Rehearing Denied March 1, 1983.)

HOLOHAN, C. J.

Respondent, Three Phoenix Company, initiated this litigation seeking injunctive and other relief based upon an alleged breach of covenants not to compete by the petitioner, Pace Industries, Inc. Pace moved to dismiss on the grounds that the respondent was not the proper party to enforce the covenants and that the covenants were unenforceable in any event. The trial court treated the motion as one for summary judgment, considered affidavits submitted by respondent, and granted judgment to petitioner Pace.

Three Phoenix appealed. The Court of Appeals reversed the trial court's judgment. *Three Phoenix Co. v. Pace Industries, Inc.,*——Ariz. ——, 659 P.2d 1271 (1 CA-CIV 4773, filed March 10, 1981). We granted the petition of Pace for review. The opinion of the Court of Appeals is vacated.

The essential facts are that Wabash Computer Corporation (Wabash) sought to divest itself of a portion of its computer business. Wabash accomplished the divestiture by selling its single-disc tester business to Three Phoenix and by selling the pack-scan tester business to Pace. Wabash and Three Phoenix entered a written agreement in June 1973. Pace and Wabash entered a written agreement in October, 1973, although it appears that there was an oral agreement prior to that time.

The written agreement between Pace and Wabash contained two covenants which in essence provided that Pace would not compete with Three Phoenix. These covenants stated:

9. *Non-Competition.* BUYER shall not during the term of this agreement within the world manufacture, use, lease, sell or otherwise dispose of any equipment or inventions which would directly or indirectly perform the same operations as said INVENTIONS or be in competition

therewith nor shall BUYER for a period of two (2) years or for so long as they manufacture or sell said INVENTIONS, whichever period is longer, design, manufacture or sell any other equipment or products which were heretofore designed, manufactured or sold by the SELLER INCLUDING THE # SSA AND # SDT FOR THE WINCHESTER DISC which SELLER intended to design, manufacture or sell.

10. *Non-Competition with Three Phoenix Company.* SELLER has sold the following product lines to Three Phoenix Company, an Arizona corporation: the certification equipment, disc memo and TCT-300. BUYER shall not in any way compete with Three Phoenix in said product lines and shall not engage in any business activity with respect to them, including without limitation consulting services, maintenance or the supplying of spare parts.

The trial court found that the covenants at issue were unenforceable because they failed to include any time limit, and the trial court also ruled that the covenants violated the antitrust laws. We believe that it is only necessary for us to address the antitrust issue.

Three Phoenix brought this action to enforce the covenants. We have no difficulty in holding that, if legally enforceable, Three Phoenix as a third party beneficiary could enforce the covenants.

The issues to be resolved are:

1. Did the restrictive covenants contained in the Pace-Wabash agreement constitute a horizontal market division scheme or were they ancillary to an otherwise legitimate transaction?

2. If the restrictions were ancillary to a valid transaction, were they reasonable?

Three Phoenix sought to enforce the covenants, claiming they are ancillary to an otherwise valid transaction (namely, Wabash's sale of its disc-testing technology). If the covenants are in fact ancillary restraints, they will be scrutinized under the so-called rule of reason and enforced if "reasonable."

Conversely, Pace asserts, *inter alia,* that the restrictive covenants constitute a market division scheme between competing firms. As such, the covenants are naked restraints of trade which state and federal antitrust statutes prohibit. Under this view, the rule of *per se* illegality would apply to invalidate the covenants.

The language of the Sherman Act, 15 U.S.C.A. § 1 (and its Arizona counterpart, 14

A.R.S. § 44-1402) paints with a very broad brush, making illegal *every* contract, combination, or conspiracy in restraint of trade. Taken literally, this language would outlaw virtually every commercial contract, since each time a buyer elects to deal with a particular seller the contract limits the freedom of both to deal with others. Consequently, the courts found it necessary to interpret the statutory language in a somewhat looser fashion. [Citation.] Thus, the U.S. Supreme Court adopted the more flexible "rule of reason" for determining whether most business relationships violate the prohibitions of the Sherman Act. *United States v. Topco Associates, Inc.,* 405 U.S. 596, 92 S.Ct. 1126, 31 L.Ed.2d 515 (1972). [Citation.]

* * *

While the Supreme Court applies this approach to most restraints, over time it has delineated certain categories of business activity which are *per se* violative of antitrust law. With respect to these activities, the conclusion of illegality is reached without conducting the *extensive* inquiry into "purpose, power and effect" required under rule of reason analysis.

One such category of *per se* violations is the horizontal market division, *i.e.,* a market division scheme between two or more firms which otherwise would be competitors. Prior to the U.S. Supreme Court's decision in the *Topco* case, there was some dispute as to whether horizontal market division agreements were *per se* illegal, in the absence of other Sherman Act violations such as price fixing. [Citations.]

Topco removed any doubts in this regard, however. In an expansively worded majority opinion, Justice Marshall stated:

One of the classic examples of a *per se* violation of § 1 is an agreement between competitors at the same level of the market structure to allocate territories in order to minimize competition. Such concerted action is usually termed a "horizontal" restraint, in contradistinction to combinations of persons at different levels of the market structure, *e.g.,* manufacturers and distributors, which are termed "vertical" restraints. This court has reiterated time and time again that "[h]orizontal territorial limitations * * * are naked restraints of trade with no purpose except stifling of competition." * * * Such limitations are *per se* violations of the Sherman Act. (citations omitted).

United States v. Topco Associates, Inc., supra,
405 U.S. at 608, 92 S.Ct. at 1133-34, 31 L.Ed.2d
at 525.

Although *Topco* dealt with a horizontal
market division along territorial lines, and
the market division in this case is along product lines, the courts and commentators have
not been willing to make any distinctions between the two types of market division. [Foot-
note.] Both are illegal.

Their reasoning is sound in that the adverse effect on competition is the same whether
the division is along territorial or along product lines. * * *

A covenant not to compete ancillary to an
agreement for the sale of a business or a transfer of business property will be enforced, if the
restraint imposed is no greater than necessary to afford fair protection to the parties,
and if the restraint is partial in nature and
reasonably limited in scope.

The classic covenant not to compete incident to the sale of a business in one restricting
the *seller's* right to compete in order to effectuate a transfer of the good will associated
with the tangible assets sold. The rationale
for upholding such covenants appears in *United
States v. Addyston Pipe & Steel Co.,* 85 F. 271,
280-81 (6th Cir.1898), written by Judge (later
Justice) Taft:

> It was of importance, as an incentive to industry
> and honest dealing in trade, that, after a man
> had built up a business with an extensive good
> will, he should be able to sell his business and
> good will to the best advantage, and he could
> not do so unless he could bind himself by an
> enforceable contract not to engage in the same
> business in such a way as to prevent injury to
> that which he was about to sell.

* * *

> "Many * * * partial restraints on trade are
> perfectly consistent with public convenience and
> the general interest, and have been supported.
> Such is the case of the disposing of a shop in a
> particular place, with a contract on the part of
> the vendor not to carry on a trade in the same
> place. It is, in effect, the sale of a good will, and
> offers an encouragement to trade by allowing a
> party to dispose of all the fruits of his industry."
> (citation omitted).

Thus, even though an ancillary covenant may
produce some division of the markets served,
society's interest in promoting the free trans-

ferability of business assets is sufficient to justify a rule of reason approach in these circumstances.

If we characterize the covenants in the Pace-
Wabash transaction as a horizontal market
division, it is difficult to avoid the conclusion
that these agreements are *per se* antitrust violations and, therefore, unenforceable. On the
other hand, if the covenants come under the
ancillary restraints doctrine, they will be
scrutinized under the rule of reason.

In either case, the inquiry begins with an
examination of the purpose of the restrictive
covenants as well as their probable effect. Even
in *per se* analysis, purpose and effect must be
examined initially in order to determine that
a particular type of behavior falls within its
ambit. While a flat-out market division agreement is subject to the *per se* rule, its applicability is less certain where an arrangement
only tends to work a market division. [Cita-
tion.]

Given the facts of this case, the covenants
in question had the effect of dividing the market between two competitors or, at least, potential competitors. Although the firms were
not necessarily competitors at the time of their
respective acquisitions, the potential for competition between them existed. Antitrust law
reaches agreements not to compete involving
potential as well as actual competitors. [Ci-
tation.] Therefore, it is undisputed that Pace
and Three Phoenix stood in a horizontal relationship to each other.

In addition, Three Phoenix's argument that
the deal actually fostered competition is mistaken. Admittedly, as a result of the transaction there were two entities (Three Phoenix
and Pace) where previously there had been
only one (Wabash). Nevertheless the challenged covenants (if enforceable) would effectively preclude all competition between the
successor firms. Thus, the transaction as Three
Phoenix perceives it, actually would have the
effect of stifling potential competition, rather
than promoting it. It seems equally clear from
the scope of the covenants that the intended
purpose was to do precisely that. They purport
to prohibit Pace from competing by any means
in designated areas of commerce and forbid
Pace's manufacture or sale of certain classes
of products. Thus, even if Pace, by its own
initiative and without the use of anything ac-

quired from Wabash, developed the technology to compete with Three Phoenix, the covenants would bar the competition as well.

Three Phoenix attempts to avoid the *per se* classification by claiming the covenants were ancillary to the sale of a business. A legitimate ancillary restraint is one which is subordinate to (and essential to attainment of) the main lawful purpose of the transaction. The mere fact that the covenants accompanied the sale of a business does not automatically place them in the ancillary restraint category. [Citations.]

To gain ancillary status, the covenants in question must be deemed necessary to effectuate Wabash's divestiture of its computer disc-testing operations. Under this doctrine, the buyer must acquire or the seller must retain an interest which can be protected via the restrictive covenant. In either the buyer-protection or seller-protection situation, the covenant is a necessary incident of the underlying sales transaction. Often the seller of a going concern cannot effectively alienate the intangible property which he has accumulated (in the form of good will) unless his buyer can have a valid, contractual assurance that the seller will not immediately set himself up in competition with the business he just sold. Likewise, the seller may extract from his buyer a promise not to use the assets or technology sold to compete with the seller in the seller's remaining business operations.

Here Wabash (the seller) sought to bind Pace (one buyer) not to compete with Three Phoenix (another buyer). Wabash retained no interest capable of being protected by the covenant with Pace. While Three Phoenix (as a buyer) may have been able to prevent Wabash (as the seller) from competing with it in the single-disc testing business, it could not extract such a promise from Wabash's other purchaser.

The restrictive covenants here were necessary to the sale transaction only in the sense that Three Phoenix had the bargaining power to veto the entire deal if it was unable to obtain the sought-after concessions. This type of necessity is insufficient to invoke the doctrine of ancillary restraints. To find otherwise would enable any entity with sufficient bargaining power to effectively circumvent the antitrust laws by refusing to deal unless the offensive

conduct were incorporated into the transaction.

Three Phoenix further argues that a seller should be permitted to dispose of his business under the most favorable or perhaps the only terms he is able to negotiate. While it may be true that a seller is entitled to strike the best bargain he can, that bargain may not be unlawful. Any business transaction is enhanced substantially by the seller's assurances against competition from a rival firm. This is not enough to change an otherwise unlawful trade restraint into "legitimate" ancillary covenants. The offensive conduct is no less so merely because the potential rivals acquire their interests from the same seller as part of the same or related transactions or because one party refuses to deal unless it can secure an assurance against competition.

Nor can the covenants be justified by the claim that they were necessary to make the single disc-testing business a viable one, *viz,* one better able to compete. Any business would be a more effective competitor with the guaranteed elimination of a potential rival.

* * *

The covenants were not necessary to effect or to give shape to the underlying sale transaction. Rather, the covenants were part of a general scheme to dispose of Wabash's business by carving out separate market preserves for each of the two successor entities. The most compelling evidence of the real purpose of these covenants is their breadth. They foreclose Pace's competition with Three Phoenix in all areas, not only in those areas involving the technology acquired from Wabash.

From the foregoing, it is clear the *per se* rule against horizontal market division, and not the rule of reason, applicable to covenants ancillary to the sale of a business, is appropriate here.

Even assuming the covenants were ancillary to Wabash's sale of its computer disc-testing business, the result would be the same. Under the rule of reason if either the purpose or effect of a practice is sufficiently adverse to competition to outweigh any benefits, the conduct may be deemed unreasonable. [Citation.] Applying the rule of reason, the covenants at issue would be found unreasonable as a matter of law because their restrictions far exceed any measures necessary to protect the interests transferred in the trilateral sale. Accordingly, the covenants may not be enforced.

The judgment of the superior court is affirmed.

DITTMER v. SOURCE EDP, TEXAS, INC.

595 S.W.2d 877

(Court of Civil Appeals of Texas, Dallas, Feb. 19, 1980.)

GUITTARD, C. J.

Defendant Paul Dittmer complains of a temporary injunction restraining him from competing with plaintiff Source EDP, Texas, Inc. in the placement of computer professionals in and within one hundred miles of the city of Dallas. The suit is based on a covenant against competition signed by defendant as an employee of Source EDP, Western Region, Inc., which is alleged to be a "predecessor in interest" of plaintiff Source EDP, Texas, Inc. The question for our decision is whether the trial judge abused his discretion in granting a temporary injunction to preserve the status quo until a trial on the merits. We find no abuse of discretion.

DURATION OF RESTRAINT

One of the grounds defendant advances to show abuse of discretion is that the temporary injunction enables plaintiff to achieve the whole object of its suit without a full hearing. In this connection defendant points out that the covenant runs two years from termination of his employment, which occurred September 1, 1978. Defendant started his own competing business in October 1979, and the temporary injunction was issued November 12, 1979. Defendant acknowledges that trial on the merits is set for January 21, 1980, but he asserts that he has no assurance that the case will be reached for trial on that date. He says he fears that because of other cases set on the same day this trial will be postponed so as to keep the temporary injunction in force for substantially the whole of the remaining period of the covenant, which expires on September 1, 1980.

We do not believe that these circumstances show an abuse of discretion. We commend the trial judge for giving the case precedence by setting the trial on the merits within three months after the suit was filed. Apparently he did so in the light of our decisions [citations], in which we emphasized that an early trial on the merits provides more expeditious relief from a temporary injunction than an interlocutory appeal because of the precedence to which injunction cases are entitled. In view of the expiration of the covenant on September 1, 1980, and the trial court's evident recognition of such precedence, we may presume that the case will be tried on January 21, or as soon after that date as may be consistent with prompt disposition of other cases entitled to similar precedence, and that it will not be postponed for trial of other cases on the docket. Consequently, we have no reason to suppose that the temporary injunction will accomplish substantially the whole purpose of the suit. [Citation.]

* * *

REASONABLENESS OF RESTRAINT

Defendant contends that the restraint enforced by the temporary injunction is unnecessary and unreasonable because he had not been engaged in the business of computer personnel placement during the three years preceding termination of his employment. The evidence shows that in 1975 he was assigned to placement of personnel in finance-related jobs, and, although he continued to supervise employees engaged in placement of computer personnel, he had no more direct contacts with customers in that field.

This change in defendant's duties does not, in our opinion, establish an abuse of discretion in granting the temporary injunction. The judge could reasonably find from the evidence that the defendant's contacts with customers in the computer personnel placement aspect of plaintiff's business were still of sufficient value to constitute protectable assets. Consequently, notwithstanding this change in defendant's duties, we conclude that the temporary injunction is supported by authorities holding that the competitive advantage an employee gains by contacts with his employer's customers justifies enforcement of a reasonable covenant against competition after the employment has terminated. [Citations.]

PROBABLE INJURY

Defendant complains further that the pleading and proof fails to show probable injury from violation of the covenant in that it fails to show an appropriation of plaintiff's protectable interests by defendant. In this connection defendant points out that when he left plaintiff's employment he took with him no list of customers or other proprietary information and made no use of any special methods or secrets. We conclude that the evidence of probable injury, though weak, is sufficient to sustain the trial court's discretion to preserve the status quo until a final trial. The testimony showed that the number of companies operating computer facilities in Dallas and within a hundred miles from it is limited and although lists of such companies are available to anyone, the business of personnel placement in this field is highly competitive and defendant's past contacts with hiring officers of such prospective customers provides a definite competitive advantage. Defendant's testimony shows that he was making calls to some of the same companies that he had solicited when working for plaintiff and that he would continue to do so unless restrained. Consequently, we hold that sufficient probable injury has been shown to justify injunctive relief to preserve the status quo. [Citation.]

EVIDENCE OF OTHER COVENANTS

Defendant complains of the trial court's exclusion of evidence that after he had signed the covenant in question, plaintiff adopted for its employees a standard form of covenant against competition which limited the period of restraint to one year after termination of employment. He insists that this evidence constitutes an admission that the two-year restraint provided by the covenant in question is unreasonable in duration. We do not agree. The evidence shows that defendant was a branch manager in computer personnel placement and not only had made substantial contacts with customers, but had been responsible for developing the business and training

other employees. The excluded evidence had little probative force. Before giving it any weight, the judge would have had to determine whether any other employees who had signed one-year covenants in situations similar to defendant's and why plaintiff had limited duration of their covenants to one year. We hold that the trial judge had discretion to decline to go into these collateral matters at the temporary injunction hearing.

* * *

ON MOTION FOR REHEARING

In his motion for rehearing defendant raises the single contention that the temporary injunction should be reformed to expire on September 1, 1980, or on rendition of final judgment, whichever occurs first. On original submission we declined to reform the injunction on that ground in view of the trial court's evident intent to try the merits at an early date. On reconsideration, however, we conclude that the order is technically in error in that the injunction by its terms could continue beyond the period of the covenant. Consequently, we reform the order in that respect.

* * *

The motion for rehearing is granted and the court's order is reformed so as to limit the duration of the temporary injunction to September 1, 1980, or until rendition of final judgment on the merits, whichever occurs first.

COMPUTER PRINT SYSTEMS, INC. v. LEWIS
281 Pa.Super. 240, 422 A.2d 148
(Superior Court of Pennsylvania, Filed Oct. 10, 1980.)

PRICE, J.

This appeal is from an action in equity by appellee for conspiracy to usurp a corporate opportunity and for conversion of computer programs. The chancellor denied appellee's request for a preliminary injunction restraining appellants from utilizing the computer programs, and on the trial on the merits, he found no support for the conspiracy charge but entered judgment for $18,000, representing the value of the computer programs appropriated by appellants. Appellants now appeal alleging numerous instances of error. Finding no merit to these contentions, we affirm the order in the trial court.

* * * The evidence presented at trial established that appellee is a data processing service company specializing in the field of direct mail advertising and the development of computer programs to accomplish the direct mail requirements of its clients. Appellant David Lewis (Lewis) was an officer of appellee serving as administrative manager and vice-president from May of 1973 until January 1975 and thereafter as its president until May 7, 1976. Appellant C. P. C. Associates, Inc. (CPC) was a customer of appellee from 1973 until May 1976, and appellant Victor Liss (Liss) was CPC's president and one of its principal shareholders. Another individual, Kurt Schneider (Schneider), is the sole shareholder of appellee and also figured prominently in the proof at trial.

From 1973 until 1976, Lewis was extensively involved in the day to day operations of appellee and maintained exclusive control over the management of the CPC account. This control entailed the processing of the monthly direct mailing requirements of CPC and was accomplished by specialized computer programs.[1] In January 1975, Lewis requested permission to make copies of the computer programs used to process the CPC account and to deliver them to CPC as a precaution against fire. Schneider refused this request, stating that it was against company policy to give copies of programs developed by appellee to its customers, which policy served as an inducement to prevent the customers from taking their account to another computer processor.

In or about June of 1975, another company in which Schneider owned 100% of the stock encountered financial difficulties and ceased activity. As a result, Liss became fearful that a similar fate would befall appellee, thus forcing a disruption of CPC's monthly mailing operation. Consequently, Liss informed Lewis that unless CPC could acquire "backup" copies of the computer programs used to process its work, it would take its account to another company. In response, Lewis procured taped copies of the programs along with machine code instructions without informing Schneider and turned them over to Liss in June of 1975. At that time, Liss did not know that it was contrary to appellee's corporate policy for Lewis to supply these items. Liss obtained the items but did not use them and continued to maintain the CPC account with appellee.

In January of 1976, Lewis expressed dissatisfaction with his position with appellee and commenced discussion with Schneider regarding a termination of his employment. In March of that year, he submitted to Schneider his resignation but remained with CPC until May 7, 1976. At or about the beginning of April 1976, Liss discovered for the first time that Lewis was terminating his relationship with appellee. Somewhat concerned, he sought to induce Schneider to retain Lewis by threatening to take his account to a competing computer processor if Lewis was not available to manage the CPC account. Apparently, Liss was concerned that the CPC account would not receive the individualized attention that had been the hallmark during Lewis' tenure with appellee. When these efforts failed, and

---

1. CPC had as clients a number of department and specialty stores located in various portions of the country. These stores wanted to identify individuals who had recently moved to an area in the vicinity of the particular store in order to target those individuals as potential customers. To accomplish this purpose, CPC purchased subscription lists from several magazine publishing companies. Through manipulation of these lists, appellee was able to identify those persons who had recently moved and it therefore was able to print the names of these individuals and mail to them pertinent literature from stores in the area that subscribed to CPC's services. Appellant Liss testified that it was extremely important to

CPC's clients that the mailing be achieved as expeditiously as possible after they learned of the new potential customer in order to contact them before their shopping habits became established and before they were contacted by competing stores. Thus, a rigid timetable for each month's mass mailing was established. As examples of the specialized programs designed to process the CPC account, Schneider testified that an "unduplicating" program was developed to prevent duplicate mailing to individuals who subscribed to more than one magazine and whose name therefore appeared on more than one list, and a zip code program designed to identify those persons who lived within a particular zip code district.

unbeknownst to Schneider, Liss contacted Lewis on April 20, 1976, and agreed to hire Lewis to process the CPC account as an independent consultant. Lewis agreed, and in preparation for this task, he purchased several blank computer tapes. On April 23, 1976, he utilized the facilities of appellee to run a test of the blank tapes to determine that they were in good condition. For some unexplained reason, however, the log that records the use of the computer at appellee's facility was torn so as not to reflect this use by Lewis on April 23, 1976.

On May 1, 1976, Schneider learned for the first time that Lewis was to take over the processing of the CPC account. By correspondence dated May 4 and May 14, 1976, Liss instructed Schneider to relinquish to Lewis the programs and all other material used to process the CPC account. Schneider did not respond to these letters, and on May 17, 1976, a "final settlement" meeting was held, attended by Lewis, Liss and Schneider. At that meeting, Schneider refused to deliver the material and for the first time informed Liss that the programs were the exclusive property of appellee and did not belong to CPC. At no time did either Lewis or Liss reveal that CPC still retained the copies of the programs obtained in June of 1975. After the meeting, Lewis also informed Liss that in his assessment the tapes and other material did not belong to CPC, but Liss responded by telling Lewis "not to worry about it."

The next day, May 18, 1976, Liss turned the backup tapes over to Lewis who secured the services of an independent computer processing company and, with the benefit of the 1975 backup tapes, was able to develop new programs to process the CPC account in time for the direct mailing at the end of May. Shortly thereafter, Schneider learned that the computer at appellee's office had been utilized on April 23, 1976, and that this use was not reflected in the computer log. This, plus the knowledge that Lewis had developed programs to process the CPC account in an extremely short period of time, led Schneider to suspect that Lewis had appropriated copies of the CPC tapes in April 1976 as part of a conspiracy to usurp the CPC account at a time when he still maintained his contacts with appellee and had access to its facilities.

On June 8, 1976, appellee filed suit charging appellants with conversion of the CPC tapes and conspiracy to have Lewis breach his fiduciary duty as an officer of appellee and to usurp appellee's corporate opportunity. The complaint was verified by Schneider and proceeded upon the premise that appellants had been conspiring to divert the CPC account from appellee from the time Lewis first contemplated terminating his employment relationship with appellee in January 1976, until the final negotiations in April 1976, and that Lewis had converted copies of the CPC programs in furtherance of the conspiracy. Not until after the complaint had been filed did Schneider discover the correct account of how CPC had obtained copies of the computer programs. At the termination of trial the chancellor concluded that the evidence was insufficient to support the allegation regarding the usurpation of the corporate opportunity,[2] but entered a verdict on the claim for conversion of the computer programs.

* * *

Appellants Liss and CPC next contend that they are not guilty of conversion because: (1) appellee did not have a proprietary interest in the computer programs; (2) the initial acquisition of the programs from Lewis was innocent and based upon a presumption of apparent authority; and (3) they paid for and thus had an ownership interest in the tapes and all other materials developed by appellee in servicing the CPC account.

In addressing appellant's first claim, the chancellor concluded that appellee had a legally protected interest in the items taken "since the programs represented a substantial investment of time and money by [appellee] and a device of importance to the continuing operation of [appellee's] business." [Reference.] In so ruling, the chancellor rejected appellee's initial claim that the programs were trade secrets, but failed to specify upon what

---

2. The chancellor concluded that even if a conspiracy to usurp the corporate opportunity had existed, it would be of no effect in the instant case since appellee did not have a contract obligating CPC to utilize its services and the value of the CPC account to appellee was only nominal.

basis he concluded they should not be so classified.[3] Instead, the chancellor merely concluded that the programs were general chattels and that appellants should be required to pay for their use under the Restatement of Restitution § 1 (1937): "A person who has been unjustly enriched at the expense of another is required to make restitution to the other."

In this appeal, appellants dispute the conclusions of the chancellor in two respects. First, they allege that computer programs are the type of property that would qualify as trade secrets. [Footnote.] *See University Computing Co. v. Lykes-Youngstown Corp.*, 504 F.2d 518 (5th Cir. 1974); *Telex Corp. v. International Business Machines Corp.*, 367 F.Supp. 258 (N.D.Okl.1973), *aff'd. in part and ref'd. in part*, 510 F.2d 894 (10th Cir.), *cert. dismissed*, 423 U.S. 802, 96 S.Ct. 8, 46 L.Ed.2d 244 (1975); *Electronic Data Systems Corp. v. Kinder*, 360 F.Supp. 1044 (N.D.Tex.1973), *aff'd.*, 497 F.2d 222 (5th Cir. 1974); *Com-Share, Inc. v. Computer Complex, Inc.*, 338 F.Supp. 1229 (E.D.Mich.1971), *aff'd.*, 458 F.2d 1341 (6th Cir. 1972). Second, they challenge the chancellor's conclusion that appellee had a protected property interest in the instant case. Rather, they allege that although the pro-

grams would normally be protected as trade secrets, appellee failed to take adequate precautions to prevent public disclosure by its employees thus precluding continued trade secret protection in the instant case. Unfortunately, appellants failed to specifically allege these challenges in their exceptions to the chancellor's decree and their boiler-plate exception that appellee did not have "any legally protected interests in the computer programs in question" cannot be construed as encompassing the allegations presented in this appeal. Pa.R.C.P. No. 1518.

Moreover, even assuming that the programs would otherwise be protected as trade secrets, appellants' challenge to that continued status on the basis of public disclosure by appellee's officer is misplaced. While continued secrecy is the *sine qua non* to maintenance of trade secret protection [citations], the issue in the instant case is not whether the precautions utilized by appellee were reasonable, but whether a confidential relationship existed such that appellee's officer was prohibited from disclosing the trade secrets revealed by appellee during the confidential employment relationship. If the trade secrets were acquired through breach of that rela-

---

3. Some of the factors to be considered in determining if an item qualifies as a trade secret are listed in the Restatement of Torts § 757, comment *b* (1939):

> (1) the extent to which the information is known outside of his business; (2) the extent to which it is known by employees and others involved in his business; (3) the extent of measures taken by him to guard the secrecy of the information; (4) the value of the information to him and to his competitors; (5) the amount of effort or money expended by him in developing the information; (6) the ease or difficulty with which the information could be properly acquired or duplicated by others.

See Cudahy Co. v. American Laboratories, Inc., 313 F.Supp. 1339 (Neb.1970).

After extensive review of the record, we conclude that the only reasonable basis upon which the programs could be challenged as not being trade secrets is that of public knowledge. Although the testimony at trial on this subject was scarce, it was established that the programming knowledge needed to create these programs was not unique, and that the programs developed to process the CPC account could have been duplicated by any skilled programmer willing to invest approximately four months of work and computer services at a cost of $18,000. Testimony also established that other competitors had developed programs to achieve similar results although special modification of their programs would have been required to process the CPC account.

In light of this evidence, we conclude that although

the "concept" of developing computer programs to expedite direct mail advertising and the computer programming expertise necessary to develop the programs were public knowledge and not subject to trade secret protection, [citations], the specific programs developed by appellee to accomplish this purpose should be afforded such protection. Novelty and uniqueness are not prerequisites for trade secret protection, *see* Restatement of Torts § 757, comment *b* (1939), and "[t]he fact that others might do similar work, if they might, does not authorize them to steal plaintiff's." [Citation.] Rather, the fact that competitors could duplicate the product through investment of their own funds and application of general programming principles does not preclude trade secret protection for one who has invested such effort. *See Telex Corp. v. International Business Machines Corp.*, 510 F.2d 894 (10th Cir.), *cert. denied*, 423 U.S. 802, 96 S.Ct. 8, 46 L.Ed.2d 244 (1975) (computer software). [Citations.]

In light of the considerable investment and the competitive advantage obtained by appellee through development of the computer programs, we conclude that they were trade secrets. Indeed, we note an inconsistency in that the authorities relied upon by the chancellor in concluding that appellee had a protectable interest in the chattels, *Telex Corp. v. International Business Machine[s] Corp., supra*, [citations], all involved trade secrets, yet the chancellor concluded that the computer programs did not enjoy that status.

tionship, appellants would be subject to liability for their unlawful acquisition. Restatement of Torts, § 757 comment, *j* (1939). As stated by our supreme court:

> The duty of the servant not to disclose the secrets of the master may arise from an express contract, or it may be implied from their confidential relations. It is likewise true that other persons who induce such disclosures by an employee, knowing of his contract not to disclose, or knowing that the disclosure is in violation of the confidence reposed in him by his employer, will be enjoined from making use of the information so obtained. Where confidence is reposed, and the employee by reason of the confidential relation has acquired knowledge of trade secrets, he will not be permitted to make disclosure of those secrets to others to the prejudice of his employer. *Macbeth-Evans Glass Co. v. Schnelbach,* 239 Pa. 76, 85-86, 86 A. 688, 691 (1913).

[Citations.] Thus, in light of the reasonable assumption that its employees and officers would abide by their obligation not to disclose its trade secrets, we cannot conclude that appellee's failure to employ more elaborate precautions to prevent disclosure precludes continued attachment of trade secret protection.[5]

Appellants Liss and CPC next contend that they cannot be guilty of converting appellee's computer programs because their initial acquisition of the backup tapes was innocent and without knowledge that it was in violation of appellee's corporate policy. In dismissing this claim, the chancellor relied upon comment *c* to the Restatement of Restitution § 123 (1937) which provides that a party is guilty of conversion if he innocently acquired possession of chattels without giving value and thereafter learns of the superior interest of another but fails to make restitution. While certainly persuasive, we believe that because the programs are trade secrets [footnote], the correct provision is found in Restatement of Torts § 758(b) (1939), which in substance repeats the provisions of § 123 of the Restatement of Restitution and states as follows:

> One who learns another's trade secret from a third person without notice that it is secret and that the third person's disclosure is a breach of his duty to the other, or who learns the secret through a mistake without notice of the secrecy and the mistake,
>
> * * *
>
> (b) is liable to the other for a disclosure or use of the secret after the receipt of such notice, unless prior thereto he has in good faith paid value for the secret or has so changed his position that to subject him to liability would be inequitable.

Thus, while appellants Liss and CPC were not cognizant of the confidential nature of the computer tapes when they initially acquired possession in June of 1975, their use of the programs subsequent to the "final settlement" on May 17, 1976, when such information was made known to them, subjects them to liability for trade secret infringement at that time.

Appellants claim, however, that they fit within the exception in subsection (b) of § 758 in that they "paid value" for the tapes in June 1975 and therefore were entitled to utilize the tapes in processing their work. In this respect, appellants claim that their action in continuing to bring the CPC account (worth approximately $20,000 per month) to appellee subsequent to June 1975 provided consideration for Lewis' business decision to provide Liss and CPC with a backup copy of the programs. While it is true that the business arrangement between appellee and CPC was at will and that CPC was free to place its account with any other computer processor, we do not believe that the agreement between Lewis and CPC in June of 1975 to provide the backup tapes as a means of alleviating Liss' insecurity regarding the continued business operation of appellee served as authorization for CPC to utilize the programs under any other conditions. [Footnote.] [Citations.]

Appellants Liss and CPC also contend that CPC paid value for the programs by reason of the billing procedures utilized by appellee.

---

5. While appellants have drawn our attention to one other case in which a company employed elaborate precautions to prevent unauthorized access to computer programs, *Com-Share, Inc. v. Computer Complex, Inc., supra,* we note that in that case, plaintiff had voluntarily disclosed portions of its programs through a technology pooling agreement. Obviously, this was not the case in the instant proceeding in which the programs were to remain "in house" and appellee could reasonably rely upon the duty imposed on its employees and officers not to reveal confidential information.

In this respect, the chancellor observed that the initial agreement establishing the business relationship between appellee and CPC was loosely structured and did not delineate the rights of the parties to the programs developed in servicing the CPC account. Thus, the terms of the oral agreement must be developed from the probable intent of the parties as evidenced by their course of conduct as reflected in the billing process. [Citations.]

Testimony at trial established that there are two methods in the computer service industry for assessing customers for the cost of developing computer programs. Assessment is made either by a direct charge for the costs incurred in developing the programs or, employing the method utilized by appellee, of not charging for the initial costs of development, but instead charging a premium "running charge" each time the programs must be utilized in processing work for the customer.[8] Under the latter method, the expectation of the service company is that the costs of development will be recovered through the premium charged for each subsequent run.

Appellants Liss and CPC argue that because the CPC account was maintained with appellee for a period of four years, the premium that CPC paid for each computer run was more than sufficient to offset the costs of development and thus CPC had an ownership interest in the programs. We disagree, for as the parties acknowledged, the billing procedure utilized by appellee involved a risk that the customer would not maintain its account with it for a sufficient period of time to permit appellee to recoup the costs of development. Thus, because the initial arrangement served to provide a windfall to appellee, Liss and CPC cannot now reverse their decision post factum upon learning that the decision was not as advantageous as originally contemplated. If Liss and CPC had desired to purchase the programs from appellee, they should have contracted to that effect at the commencement of the business arrangement. Not having done so, they cannot now complain that the billing

procedure used should be construed as vesting an ownership interest on the basis that the total charges ultimately paid would have been sufficient to purchase the programs initially.

Finally,[9] appellants contend that the trial court erred in its assessment of damages. The chancellor determined that appellee had established a conversion of the computer programs in the value of $18,000 and awarded judgment in that amount. In so ruling, he took note of the two measures of damages in an action for conversion: (1) the loss by plaintiff measured by the value of the item converted; and (2) unjust enrichment measured by the value of the converted chattel to the defendants. *See Diesel v. Caputo*, 244 Pa.Super. 195, 366 A.2d 1259 (1976). The chancellor concluded that the $18,000 cost of developing the programs was the proper amount applicable under both theories of recovery. Appellants dispute this conclusion and allege that the evidence was insufficient to establish a proper measure of damages.

First, they contend that $18,000 does not represent the value of appellee's loss because appellee was not actually deprived of the programs and was free to utilize them in serving other customers. We find this contention to be meritless as it ignores the fact that the value to appellee in its exclusive possession of the programs was as a protection for the time and expense it had invested in developing the completed programs. Because of this investment, appellee had a valuable product that it presumably could have sold to other parties, in this case CPC, which desired to obtain the product in its completed form rather than expending its own resources to develop the same product independently. We therefore believe that the evidence supports a determination that appellants' appropriation of the programs resulted in a loss to appellee of an interest in the value of $18,000.

In addition, we believe that appellee presented sufficient evidence to support the conclusion that the value of the programs to appellees was in a similar amount. With the aid

---

8. The chancellor also found that appellee on occasion assessed a $50.00 "single application charge" when an unusual program was required to process the CPC account, but was not utilized on a regular basis in performing the work for CPC.

9. Appellant Liss also contends that he cannot be held

personally liable because he acted at all times in his role as a corporate officer and did not benefit personally from the appropriation of the computer tapes. We find, however, that this issue has not been preserved for appellate review since Liss failed to present it in his exceptions to the chancellor's decree. [Reference.]

of the backup tapes, Lewis was able to design programs to service the CPC account within approximately ten days as opposed to the estimated three weeks to four months that would have been required without the aid of the tapes. By their use, CPC was able to complete its direct mailing for the month of June without interruption of service. Thus, even applying the "standard of comparison" test urged by appellants, *see Telex Corp. v. International Business Machine Corp.*, 510 F.2d 894 (10th Cir.), *cert. dismissed*, 423 U.S. 802, 96 S.Ct. 8, 46 L.Ed.2d 244 (1975), between the cost that CPC would have incurred if it had not utilized the backup tapes, minus the actual costs incurred through their use, the measure of damages would remain $18,000. Moreover, the conflicting testimony of appellants' witnesses regarding the alleged limited use of the backup tapes is an issue of credibility and was for resolution by the chancellor whose finding will not be reversed on appeal. [Citations.]

The order in the trial court is affirmed.

AMOCO PRODUCTION CO. v. LINDLEY

609 P.2d 733

(Supreme Court of Oklahoma, Jan. 15, 1980.)

BARNES, J.

This case centers on the contested ownership of a computer "software" program commonly referred to as the "Lindley System". The "Lindley System" was developed by the Defendant-Appellant while he was in the employ of the Plaintiff-Appellee.

The events leading up to the present litigation began in 1964 upon Lindley's employment with Amoco under a written contract whereby he agreed "to disclose promptly and in writing * * * all inventions or discoveries capable of use in connection with the business of COMPANY * * * and agrees not to disclose same to others, except as required by his employment, without consent of COMPANY." Lindley was employed to do research relating to geological exploration for oil and gas, and he did create various devices, some of which were patented, in keeping with the contract provisions.

Mr. Lindley is a well log analyst by formal training, and therefore his basic research projects were in the area of developing means of using well log data more efficiently and more quickly in the search for hydrocarbons. Well log analysis is a basic tool for engineers and geologists to determine if oil is present in certain geological formations. It is a time-consuming process in a business where it is important to move quickly to ascertain oil prospects in order to obtain leases to the land prior in time to a competitor. The information originally obtained in a well log can be digitized, and once in this format it can be analyzed by a computer. Properly programmed, the computer will analyze well logs in a relatively short period of time. Computer analysis of well logs is a recent innovation and is little developed, so that a company with a good computer "software" system has a competitive advantage within the field of hydrocarbon exploration.

In early 1971, Lindley orally requested permission from Dr. Walton, head of Amoco's Geological Research Department, to develop a general purpose, comprehensive log analysis system with which the data from the operational log digitizer (an invention by Lindley, patented by Amoco) would be analyzed and computed. Lindley's request was denied orally and later in writing by Amoco on the ground that the Company had made a decision to develop another computer program for this purpose [Applications Management System—"A.M.S."] and did not wish to allow development of competing systems within the Company. Lindley then worked on the existing log analysis program during Company time, but on his own time he continued to work on his concept of a computer log analysis. In 1973, Lindley disclosed his work to the A.M.S. team and other members of Amoco's management. Thereafter, Lindley was directed to cease creative work on the system and take the developed concepts and integrate them into Amoco's present system. Lindley did document the existing capabilities of the Lindley System during working hours, for use in the A.M.S. System, but continued working on additional program capabilities on his own time. Amoco officially recognized the Lindley System in 1975, when it was found to be responsible for the location of large hydrocarbon-bearing subsurface geological formations. Ten months later, Mr. Lindley left the Company, due to differences with management over the program.

The procedural history of the case is important to understanding the present appeal. Amoco brought suit in the District Court of Tulsa County against Lindley, asking for specific performance of an employment contract. Amoco asserted that under the terms of the contract any "invention" or "discovery" made by Lindley during his employment, which could be used in its business, was its property and not that of the employee. Amoco also requested injunctive relief to restrain Lindley from divulging Amoco's "trade secret" embodied in the "Lindley System" to third parties.

An ex parte temporary restraining order was issued and, upon hearing, a temporary injunction was issued which precluded the Defendant-Appellant from using any part or portion of the Lindley System, including the concepts thereof, for his own use or benefit, or for the use or benefit of any third party, nor could Lindley divulge the workings of this alleged "trade secret" to third parties.

* * *

II.

The second appeal, which is numbered 51,011, deals with the interlocutory appeal from the entering of the temporary injunction. The Trial Judge made certain findings of fact and law which we will address, and, upon remand of this case for further determination, our findings on the record before us will be conclusive as to those issues found to be decided erroneously.

The Trial Judge, in issuing the temporary injunction, found as a matter of law that the Lindley System was an invention, and that the employment contract governed the rights of the parties to the invention. Since the computer system developed by Lindley was useful in the business of Amoco, the "invention" was solely owned by Amoco.

The appellant, who for the greater part of this litigation has artfully and adeptly represented himself, argues on appeal that the Lindley System is not an invention and is therefore not the property of Amoco under the contract.

The contract provisions[2] do purport to give ownership to the Company of all inventions and discoveries made by an employee while working for Amoco, but the contract is liberally interspersed with language applying to patents, which indicates to us that the "invention" must be an invention which would be considered such under applicable patent law, whether the invention is patented or not.

The Trial Judge was correct in stating that "the right of the employer, if there is any to

2. Contract in pertinent part:
COMPANY hereby engages EMPLOYEE to devote his time, skill, labor and knowledge to the advancement of the COMPANY'S interest by performing such duties as may be assigned to him and in general by aiding to whatever extent he may, consistent with the performance of his specifically assigned duties, in the prosecution of research and technical development and in the making and perfecting of inventions and discoveries capable of use in connection with the business of COMPANY, and its Affiliates, which work EMPLOYEE recognizes as being a material function of COMPANY'S business. * * *

* * *

EMPLOYEE hereby agrees to disclose promptly and in writing * * * all inventions or discoveries capable of use in connection with the business of COMPANY * * * which EMPLOYEE, alone or with others, has made or may make during his employment by COMPANY, and he hereby assigns and agrees to assign all his right, title and interest in and to such inventions or discoveries to COMPANY * * * and agrees not to disclose same to others, except as required by his employment, without consent of COMPANY. EMPLOYEE further agrees that during his employment * * * or at any time thereafter he will on request of COMPANY execute specific assignments to COMPANY * * * of any such inventions or discoveries, made during his employment by COMPANY, applicable to the United States and to any and all foreign countries, as well as execute all papers and perform all other lawful acts which COMPANY deems necessary or advisable for the preparation, filing, prosecution and maintenance of patent applications and patents of the United States and foreign countries and for the transfer of interests therein, including the execution of original, divisional, continuing and reissue applications, preliminary statements, affidavits and concessions, and the giving of testimony with respect to said inventions, discoveries, applications and patents. * * *

COMPANY agrees to consider or have considered with reasonable promptness every invention or discovery submitted in writing by EMPLOYEE and at its option to request specific assignment thereof and of all patent rights thereon applicable to both the United States and foreign countries. COMPANY agrees that if and when it decides to take a specific assignment of any invention or discovery from EMPLOYEE, with or without the filing of a patent application, COMPANY * * * will pay employee Fifty Dollars ($50.00) upon his executing said assignment. * * *

the invention of his employee, springs from the contract of employment * * * because were it otherwise but for an express agreement or implied agreement in the employment relationship, then the employee's invention remains the property of the employee." Thus, the crucial issue is whether this computer software system is an invention. The Trial Judge found that the "software" program was not a discovery. We agree. This is so because discovery is something less than invention, because it does not entail the creative genius which gives birth to an inventive concept; it can result from mere application, industry, or be simply fortuitous. Discovery is finding something unknown, but it is entitled to no more protection than an invention and must meet the same strenuous prerequisites of patentability as an invention. Thus, the law as to invention is equally applicable to discovery.

The trial court, in reaching its decision, relied on the definition of invention from Black's Law Dictionary, which states:

> INVENTION. *In patent law*, the act or operation of finding out something new; the process of contriving and producing something not previously known or existing, by the exercise of independent investigation and experiment. Also the article or contrivance or composition so invented. [Citations omitted.] Black's Law Dictionary, p. 740 (5th Ed. 1979). [Emphasis added.]

The court also relied on a definition of invention found in *General Electric Co. v. Sangamo Electric Co., 174 F. 246, 251 (7th Cir. 1909)*, which states:

> Invention, in the nature of improvements, is the double mental act of discerning, in existing machines or processes or articles, some deficiency, and pointing out the means of overcoming it.

Both definitions are based on patent law; thus it follows that "invention", to be so classified for purposes of determining ownership under the contract, must be patentable whether it is or not. Under the Patent Act of 1952, 35 U.S.C., §§ 100–292 (1976), there are three standards for patentability: (1) containment within the statutory subject matter; (2) novelty; and (3) non-obviousness. [Footnote.] Section 112 of the Act defines the scope of patentability. The requirements are cumulative, and to date no computer program, as such, has

ever been granted a patent. The statute contemplates two types of statutory patents called "apparatus" and "process" patents. The apparatus claims had some success in the patent courts on the theory that if a machine is programmed in a new and unobvious way, it is a machine physically different from a machine without the program. [Citations.] However, later cases have generally found the concept of a novel use of computer hardware, i.e., the "apparatus" claim, to be unavailing. See *Gottschalk v. Benson, 409 U.S. 63, 71, 93 S.Ct. 253, 34 L.Ed.2d 273 (1972)*.

Process claims failed as well; first, by what is called the "mental processes" doctrine, which means if a patent application described a process that could be performed entirely by a mental process or by the additional use of pencil and paper, the patent was rejected because a monopoly could not be granted on a cognitive process. This theory was dropped in *Application of Musgrave, 431 F.2d 882, 57 CCPA 1352 (1970)*, where the court found that to bring a program within the statutory framework, it must be in the field of technology, but this has not aided the patentability of the programs.

Recent United States Supreme Court decisions have denied patents to computer programs. See *Gottschalk, supra,* where the application was denied because the effect would be to give the patent programmer a monopoly on a mathematical formula; and *Dann v. Johnston, 425 U.S. 219, 96 S.Ct. 1393, 47 L.Ed.2d 692 (1976)*, where the application was denied because it involved no novel concept besides a formula.

In *Parker v. Flook, 437 U.S. 584, 98 S.Ct. 2522, 57 L.Ed.2d 451 (1978)*, the Court denied an application of a method to update alarm limits. The Court said at *437 U.S. 584, 594, 98 S.Ct. 2522, 2528, 57 L.Ed.2d 451*:

> Here it is absolutely clear that respondent's application contains no claim of patentable invention. The chemical processes involved in catalytic conversion of hydrocarbons are well known; as are the practice of monitoring the chemical process variable, the use of alarm limits to trigger alarms, the notion that alarm limit values must be recomputed and readjusted, and the use of computers for automatic process monitoring-alarming. Respondent's application *simply provides a new and presumably better method for calculating alarm limit values.*" [Emphasis added.]

The Lindley System, by way of comparison, is not new or novel; it is a combination of two arts—well log analysis and computer programming. The system can do nothing that cannot be done manually; its utility and importance lies in the facts, from evidence presented in the injunction hearing, that it is a better and more efficient way of getting the data sought. The above cited cases show this is simply not enough to make it patentable.

Each of the last Supreme Court patent cases has occasioned submission of amicus curiae briefs in support of patent protection for computer "software", but the Court has consistently stated that its job is to interpret the patent statutory law as it now stands, which admittedly was enacted prior to the advent of computer programs, and if these programs are to be afforded patent protection, it must be provided by legislation. [Citations.]

The Appellee argues that the Lindley System is an invention, regardless of whether patentable or not, and expressly covered by the contract and is thus the property of Amoco. If the Appellee is to prevail, the contract must withstand traditional contract interpretation principles.

The contract is an Oklahoma contract, and our law governing contract interpretation places primary significance on the intent of the parties at the time of contracting, which in this case was 1964. [Citations.] The intention of both parties must be found in the whole contract and a construction given to the contract which will give effect to each provision. [Citation.] The contract can be explained through the circumstances at the time of contracting and subsequently taking into consideration the subject matter thereof. [Citations.]

The hearing on the temporary injunction produced the following relevant evidence as to the contract. It is a fineprint form contract used frequently by Amoco, and it is not confined to those people who work in the research area, who would be most likely to produce "inventions" and "discoveries". The contract is liberally laced with language concerning patents. Of primary importance as to the intent of the parties is Section V, which states in pertinent part:

COMPANY agrees that *if and when* it decides to take a specific assignment of any invention

or discovery from EMPLOYEE *with or without the filing* of a patent application, COMPANY or its nominee will pay to EMPLOYEE Fifty Dollars ($50.00) upon his executing said assignment. [Emphasis added.]

The language is not ambiguous. It contemplates affirmative action on the part of the employer to assert rights to an employee's work product if the employer is to be considered as owning it.

Mr. Lindley was not approached as to ownership until this suit was brought; the Company left the program in his control completely. He was formally denied in writing the right to develop it, with the Company later retrenching when it was proven to be valuable. The manuals of operation were not marked confidential or even numbered to show how many were out and where distributed by Lindley to any employee upon request. This action by Amoco does not show an exercise of dominion over the Lindley System. There is even testimony that the Company was willing to allow their London facility to pay money directly to Lindley if he would enhance the use of the installed Lindley System there.

In *Jamesbury Corp. v. Worcester Valve Co., 318 F.Supp. 1 (D.Mass.1970)*, there was a contract of employment similar to the one in question here, and that Court found at page 8:

[I]n ascertaining the parties' intention in using the word 'invention' in the agreement between Rockford and Freeman, the contract as a whole is, of course, important * * * the term [invention] was used in connection with 'patent applications' and there is nothing in the agreement to indicate that the parties used it in any different sense from that which would constitute an invention under patent law.

This is the same situation involved here. A search of the cases which hold that by express contract an employer is the owner of his employee's invention shows that these cases inevitably deal with patent law and patent applications. [Citations.] This indicates that the law considers an invention to be one which is patentable under patent law and is used in this context in employment contracts which use the term in connection with "patent applications".

Thus, it is concluded that the trial court's conclusion as a matter of law that the "Lindley II System", as testified to in the temporary injunction hearing, satisfies the terminology and definition of "an invention * * * in the law as well as that term is used in connection with the contract", is clearly erroneous and cannot stand. That, however, does not end our inquiry, because the trial court went on to call the system a "trade secret". The reasoning of the court was that if there was a contract giving property rights to Amoco in the invention of its employee, then that invention was a "secret process", which gave Amoco a business advantage, and the common law would entitle the Plaintiff, even in the absence of a contract, to prevent Defendant's disclosure of the "trade secret".

We have previously held herein that the Lindley System is not an invention and cannot be owned by Amoco on that basis. There is no question that under applicable law a computer system could be classified as a "trade secret", which is generally defined as "any formula, pattern, device or compilation of information which is used in one's business, and which gives him an opportunity to obtain an advantage over competitors who do not know or use it." Restatement of Torts, § 757, Comment b, at page 5 (1939). The problem with the trial court's analysis of the Lindley System is that as a matter of law there was insufficient evidence before the court for a finding of trade secret.

In the Restatement of Torts, Comment b, at page 6, it is stated:

> * * * *a substantial element of secrecy must exist*, so that, except by the use of improper means, there would be *difficulty* in acquiring the information. An exact definition of a trade secret is not possible. Some factors to be considered in determining whether given information is one's trade secret are: (1) the extent to which the information is known outside of his business; (2) the extent to which it is known by employees and others involved in his business; (3) the extent of measures taken by him [employer] to guard the secrecy of the information; (4) the value of the information to him and to his competitors; (5) the amount of effort or money expended by him in developing the information; (6) the ease or difficulty with which the information could be properly acquired or duplicated by others. [Footnote.] [Emphasis added.]

The burden of proving these criteria is on the Plaintiff. Like the common law, the contract as it relates to non-disclosure will not aid the Plaintiff here because it deals only with inventions or discoveries made by the Defendant while in the employ of the Plaintiff. The software system is not an invention, so on the sole basis of the contract Mr. Lindley could disclose it, or use it for his own benefit.

The decision of the Trial Judge was based on the contract, and the evidence to support a finding of "trade secret" is simply not in the record. There has to be evidence that indeed the secret was a secret, and that evidence is not before the court. The Lindley System certainly was treated in a much less secretive manner than the Inlan [A.M.S.] System favored by management, as testified to by Amoco's own witnesses. The Inlan user manuals were stamped confidential, numbered, and controlled centrally by management. This was not true of the Lindley System. Trade secret status is difficult to establish and often entails establishing that affirmative and elaborate steps were taken to insure that the secret claimed would remain so. *Telex Corp. v. International Business Machines Corp.*, 367 F.Supp 258 (N.D.Okl.1973), rev'd on other grounds, 510 F.2d 894 (10th Cir. 1975); ComShare, Inc. v. Computer Complex, Inc., 338 F.Supp. 1229 (E.D.Mich.1971).

The Appellee relies on *Sperry Rand Corp. v. Rothlein, 241 F.Supp. 549 (D.Conn.1964)*, to establish that where an employee is hired under an express contract to deliver all inventions to the employer, the employee may not on termination of his employment divulge his employer's trade secret, even when it was created by the employee. The case is distinguishable from this case. There, one of the defendants had approached the plaintiff, Sperry Rand, prior to entering employment with the plaintiff, to try to persuade it to go into the semiconductor business. Sperry Rand liked the defendant's idea and employed him to investigate the economic feasibility of entering the semiconductor area. The defendant submitted recommendations which were adopted by plaintiff, and defendant was put in charge of the operation, in which the plaintiff expended huge sums of money in the development thereof. The defendant's process was later used by defendant and others in direct competition with Sperry Rand. The defendant was methodical and calculating in his resignation from the plaintiff company, taking approximately thirty workers with him into the competing company. In this case, the Court stated at page 565:

> The essential points are that Sperry developed *at its own plant and at great expense* a process for the production of silicon alloy junction transistors which *were superior* to other transistors on the market. It had kept its process secret; no other manufacturer knew the process or used it. As a result Sperry had a distinct competitive advantage. [Emphasis added.]

All these findings by the Court were substantially supported by the evidence before the Court. Such evidence is absent here.

The Appellee also asserts that a computer program conceived and developed by a company is a trade secret protected by law from unlawful use, relying on *University Computing Co. v. Lykes-Youngstown Corp., 504 F.2d 518 (5th Cir. 1974)*. In that case, the parent company had developed and owned a computer program which was pirated away by a subsidiary in a devious manner. There was no question of who owned the program—it was owned by the parent. That is not the situation here. There is no question that a computer program can qualify as a trade secret. The question is, is it one under the circumstances of this case?

In *Structural Dyn. Res. Corp. v. Engineering Mechanics Research Corp., 401 F.Supp. 1102 (E.D.Mich.1975)*, the Court dealt with charges against three former employees of Structural Dynamics Research Corporation [S.D.R.C.] for unfair competition, misappropriation, and misuse of confidential trade secret material and breach of contractual duty not to disclose confidential information. The Court identified the defendants as the discoverers and then commented on the effect this proposition has on the issue of trade secrecy. It stated:

> One argument is that such an employee's skill, experience and knowledge should be protected. Some scholars point out that relief [to a former employer] 'may be denied in cases where the secret has become such an important part of an employee's job skills that he will have difficulty in obtaining a new position if he cannot take it with him.' 401 F.Supp. at 1110, citing Developments in the Law—Competitive Torts, 77 Harv.L. Rev. 888, 949 (1964).

The court then approached the concept of whether a process is a trade secret from the point of view of weighing the fact that in a highly technological society useful knowledge should be disclosed, against the fact that secrecy may favor and motivate inventiveness, with special consideration given to the genuine concern for the technically skilled worker whose job mobility may be diluted if knowledge he acquires is deemed to be a trade secret. The Court noted, in determining the existence of a trade secret which gives rise to either a contractual or fiduciary obligation not to disclose to others or adopt to one's own use, that:

> Vital to a consideration of the creation of duty in such situations is the key question as to *how the person acquiring such trade secret knowledge obtained it*. If the subject matter of the trade secret is in being and an employee learns about it in the course of his employment in a relationship of confidence, the duty not to use or disclose trade secret knowledge adversely to his employer arises. *On the other hand, if the subject matter of the trade secret is brought into being because of the initiative of the employee in its creation, innovation or development even though relationship is one of confidence, no duty arises since the employee may then have an interest in the subject matter at least equal to that of his employer or in any event, such knowledge is a part of the employee's skill and experience.* 401 F.Supp. at 1111. [Emphasis added.]

The Court did find in this case a breach of duty by the defendants on the basis of an exceptionally broad non-disclosure clause in their employment contract, which used the language, "Employee [will not] divulge to any person, firm or corporation * * * any privileged or confidential information, trade secret, or other proprietary information including but not limited to the experimental and research work of the corporation, its methods, formulae, drawings or appliances, imparted or divulged to. * * *" This language was embracive enough to cover the subsequent actions of defendants in setting up a business using a computer system very similar to the one they had created for their former employer. The language of the Amoco employment contract is not so comprehensive.

The above cases point out that in trade secret litigation, courts are looking at the equities of the given set of circumstances out of which the claimed trade secret arises. The courts are then balancing those equities between the right of the company to use its employees and resources to its utmost advantage against the right of the highly developed mind and skill of the employee. Factors to be considered are how many of the innovative elements in the newly developed process are available in the prior art; how closely tied is the development to intrinsic knowledge of the innovator. In other words, is it possible to sort the process from the inner workings of a man's knowledge; did the company treat the innovation with the requisite secrecy to place others on notice of its claim? Other considerations are time and money and company facilities used in its production, and the employer's own knowledge thereof.

The evidence before the Trial Judge as to the existence of a trade secret is at best inconclusive because the Judge relied on the bare definition of trade secret, i.e., "a secret process that gives Amoco a business advantage." It is interesting to note that this case differs from other trade secret cases in that here the employer did not divulge a secret to the employee, and the employer does not even know how the system works without its employee. We therefore hold that the Lindley System is not an invention within the meaning contemplated by the parties to this contract, in light of the considerable "patent application" terminology. Nor is there sufficient evidence in the record, absent the erroneous finding of invention, to show that a trade secret exists which belongs to Amoco.

It may very well be that Amoco intended to cover the contingency of development of computer programs in its form contract, but the fact is it did not. It is a common reality that printed contracts will be construed most strongly against the party who prepared them. [Citation.]

III.

Finally, we address the issue of the propriety of the issuance of the temporary injunction under the above stated circumstances. * * *

Here, we hold that the court below committed a clear mistake of law and has abused its discretion in granting the injunction.

For Amoco to establish a right to this injunctive relief, the burden was on it to show that the Lindley System was its "property" by virtue of the contract, or its "trade secret" by virtue of its actions in so delineating a secret proprietary interest in the system. Amoco never argued that the system was an invention; the Trial Judge merely so held. The present evidence, as stated elsewhere herein, does not establish the existence of a trade secret.

The harm to be occasioned in absence of an injunction must be irreparable to the Plaintiff. Amoco has not shown such harm. It alleges that Lindley is constructing a system for his present employer that will duplicate the Lindley System, while at the same time alleging it does not know what is contained in the Lindley System because Lindley won't divulge this information to it, because of his honest belief that the system is his own property. Amoco's own witnesses testified to the fact that the Lindley System is operational at the present time, but they believe it capable of doing more—just what, they don't know. These statements hardly add to Amoco's claim of ownership, nor do they aid Amoco's claim that Lindley will do them irreparable harm by "duplicating" the Lindley System in the system he was designing for another company. Amoco's witnesses freely admit computer programs in the area of well log analysis are available commercially, that Lindley has incorporated known data in his program, and that it is not new or novel—only better. Amoco withheld any kind of encouragement until the system resulted in large hydrocarbon finds, and it asserted no ownership rights until the gentleman left its employ, taking with him his unique skills and experience. An injunction has the purpose of keeping the status quo and should not give a remedy which can only be done by a trial on the merits.

The rules for injunctive relief against a claim of "trade secret" are stated in 43A C.J.S. Injunctions § 151:

> Injunctive relief against the use of trade secrets is discretionary, and depends on the facts and circumstances of the particular case. On equitable principles and in consideration of public policy, relief by injunction should not be granted *unless the claim that the plan or process is a trade secret* is clearly established. * * * While

injunction may issue before the use or disclosure of a trade secret occurs, *a trade secret will not be protected by an injunction on the mere suspicion or apprehension of an injury.* [Emphasis added.]

Amoco has only a suspicion that Lindley's new system will harm it, nothing more.

Amoco has the burden of showing the need for equitable relief, and its evidence cannot be aided by the erroneous findings of the Trial Judge. Under the circumstances of this case, the Judge has clearly abused his discretion. Even if we could find the evidence supports the issuance of the injunction, it would fail because it is too vague.[5]

The injunction enjoins the employee from divulging the invention "including the concepts thereof". No attempt is made to explain what is meant by the term "concepts". In *Xerox Corporation v. Neises, 31 A.D.2d 195, 295 N.Y.S.2d 717 (1968)*, a case with very similar facts to those present here, the Court stated:

> Moreover, a decree granting injunctive relief, whether temporary or permanent, must define specifically what the enjoined person must or must not do, in language so clear and explicit that a layman can understand what he is expected to do, or refrain from doing, without placing the one enjoined in the position of acting at his peril. [Citations omitted.]

The Court, by failing to define concepts, places the Defendant in the precarious position of acting at his own peril. He can develop his new computer system and hope that a trial on the merits will find that the Lindley II System was his property. But should the trial go the other way, he has expended great energy, time, and financial resources for nothing. His alternative is not to work in the area, and under the undisputed circumstances of this case that is simply inequitable.

In *Superior Oil Co. v. Renfroe, 67 F.Supp. 277 (W.D.Okl.1946)*, a geologist was found guilty of duplicating confidential information of his employer, disseminating them to third parties, and using them for his own profits.

The Court, on the undisputed evidence, did issue a temporary injunction precluding the defendant from use of the ill-gained data, but the Court specifically identified those items and added:

> * * * it being understood that this injunction is not to preclude or hinder the defendant from the practice of his profession, even in the territory involved in this case, so long as he does not use the information, data and maps above described. 67 F.Supp. at 282.

The default judgment is hereby vacated, the injunction is dissolved, and the case is remanded for a trial on the merits as to whether a "trade secret" exists to which the Plaintiff is entitled to claim ownership.

Reversed and remanded with instructions.

STRUCTURAL DYNAMICS RESEARCH CORP. v. ENGINEERING MECHANICS RESEARCH CORP.

401 F. Supp. 1102

(United States District Court, E. D. Michigan, S. D., Sept. 9, 1975.)

FEIKENS, D. J.

I.

Structural Dynamics Research Corporation (SDRC) brought this action against three former employees, Kant Kothawala, Karan Surana and Robert Hildebrand, for unfair competition, misappropriation and misuse of confidential and trade secret material, breach of confidential disclosure agreements and interference with SDRC's customer relations, and against Engineering Mechanics Research Corporation (EMRC) for conspiring with the individual defendants to accomplish the above purposes. It seeks both damages and a permanent injunction.

SDRC is an Ohio corporation with its principal place of business at Cincinnati, Ohio. EMRC is a Michigan corporation with its

---

5. The injunction states in relevant part:
 [D]efendant is temporarily enjoined during pendency of this action, and until final judgment is entered after trial on the merits from using any part or portion thereof for his own benefit, or for the use and benefit of any third party or entity.
  It is further ordered * * * Defendant is * * *

enjoined from making any disclosures to third parties or entities of the confidential information and/or subroutines, including *the concepts thereof* that constitute and comprise the Lindley II Log Analysis System except * * * does not enjoin Defendant from utilizing any part or portion [thereof] that is commercially available. [Emphasis added.]

principal place of business at Southfield, Michigan. Kothawala, Surana and Hildebrand are all residents of Michigan.

* * *

Both SDRC and EMRC are engaged in the business of structural analysis and testing. They are also engaged in the development of computer programs for such purposes for use in their business and for lease to other users.

Kothawala, Surana and Hildebrand were all formerly employed by SDRC in various technical capacities. Kothawala was employed by SDRC between August 3, 1972 and December 31, 1972 as a member of its Technical Staff.[2] Surana worked for SDRC from February of 1970 to January of 1973, initially as a project leader in the computer operations department and later as a member of the Technical Staff. Hildebrand was employed by SDRC as a project manager between August of 1972 and December 31, 1972. Each signed an Employee Patent and Confidential Information Agreement while so employed and, in addition, Kothawala executed an Employment Agreement.

These three individuals are now employed by EMRC. Kothawala is the President and sole shareholder. Surana is Vice-President of Engineering. Hildebrand is Manager of Applications.

Structural analysis involves, generally speaking, the prediction of how a physical structure will react when forces are applied to it. One of the methods used to solve structural analysis problems is a finite element computer program. The technical part of this dispute concerns two such programs. These computer programs are used to obtain an approximation of the reaction of a physical structure when forces are applied to it. This approximation is termed a mathematical model. It simulates actual conditions.

The method involves drafting a model of the structure under analysis. The model is then divided into sections or substructures known as elements. The elements are connected together at points called nodes or nodal points. The nodes are assigned coordinates which specify their location within the structure. The coordinates plus the material properties of the structure, the forces to be applied and the constraints on the structure are written in terms of mathematical equations. The availability of high speed computers permits the rapid solution of these equations in a computer program. The input data is "read" and in practical effect is converted into meaningful data which predicts reactions of the structure with sufficient accuracy to be attractive for commercial use.

The finite element computer programs generally in use prior to 1971 employed primarily straight sided elements such as triangles and rectangles. When the structure involved curved surfaces, straight sided elements had cost and accuracy limitations as a large number of elements were required to approximate the structure's configuration.

Thus, the concept of employing curved and irregular shaped elements and "higher order" elements with different nodal structures termed "isoparametric elements" was under investigation. Isoparametric elements, in a properly designed program, offer substantial advantages over conventional finite element programs since the use of curved and irregular shaped elements permits the user to achieve at least as accurate results at a lower cost due to the reduction of the number of elements necessary to prepare models of a structure to be tested.

SDRC first became interested in isoparametric elements when, in the fall of 1971, Surana and Russell Henke, vice-president of SDRC, attended a conference at Urbana, Illinois, where a number of technical papers were delivered. References to isoparametric elements appeared in some papers. Kothawala, then an employee of General Motors, also attended the conference.

Following the Urbana conference Surana began to investigate isoparametric technology thoroughly, primarily from the literature. Prior to this time Surana did not have a substantial background or knowledge in the field of isoparametric finite element technology. He concluded that an isoparametric program

---

2. The Technical Staff is comprised of employees having significant technical expertise in the various areas of interest to SDRC. These employees provide technical assistance to project engineers and engage in research and development.

would be useful and advantageous to SDRC and so informed SDRC's management. SDRC encouraged Surana to continue his efforts but also required him to devote time to revenue producing projects. In April, 1972 SDRC gave formal recognition to Surana's isoparametric research by the establishment of a time charge account. By that time Surana had reduced to writing certain preliminary equations, computations and sketches necessary to the development of a program. He continued preliminary development work as time permitted until August.

In August of 1972 Kothawala joined SDRC as a member of the Technical Staff. Beginning a year or more prior to his employment, Kothawala and SDRC had discussed this possibility. SDRC wished to open a Detroit office and Kothawala desired a managerial position in a Detroit-based company which he would wholly or partially own. When Kothawala was hired, both parties anticipated that he would assume management responsibility for an SDRC office in Detroit but the details were left for future resolution. It was agreed that Kothawala would spend six to twelve months in Cincinnati to familiarize himself with SDRC's business and procedures.

Hildebrand was also hired in August of 1972 on Kothawala's recommendation. It was anticipated that he would also be involved in the Detroit office.

In August of 1972, shortly after Kothawala started working at SDRC, Surana showed him the results of his investigation concerning an isoparametric element computer program. Kothawala arranged to have Surana's conclusions reviewed by the Technical Staff.

A meeting of the Technical Staff was held on August 14, 1972. Surana explained to them what he had been doing with respect to isoparametric elements and the advantages he believed a program containing such elements would have over one containing conventional elements. At the conclusion of the meeting, this group gave Surana authority to devote all of his time to develop such a program and assigned to Kothawala and Surana responsibility for drafting a formal written proposal. Kothawala was eventually assigned supervisory responsibility for the project.

On August 23, 1972 Kothawala and Surana submitted a formal proposal. It stressed the importance of the proposed program to

SDRC, the advantages and superiority of isoparametric elements, the significance of Surana's technical work to date and the uniqueness of the program. It also contained cost estimates and a timetable for completion. SDRC relied on these representations since no one employed by SDRC at this time other than Surana had any significant knowledge of isoparametric element theory or application.

On October 25, 1972 Kothawala and Surana issued a technical status report. Surana had developed the program to the point of running test problems. Kothawala stated that the program would "revolutionize" SDRC's problem solving ability. SDRC management felt this report established the feasibility of the program.

Surana continued his work on the program throughout the rest of the year. He named the program "NIESA", an acronym for "Numerically Integrated Elements for System Analysis."

During this period Kothawala submitted several plans for opening a Detroit office. These plans were not satisfactory to SDRC and led it to conclude that Kothawala lacked the business experience to assume full management responsibility. After a number of discussions with Kothawala, SDRC submitted a proposal on December 21, 1972 in which the Detroit entity would combine technical consulting and sales activities with Kothawala responsible for the former as a member of the Technical Staff, but reporting to management in Cincinnati. The offer included an increase in salary which would have made Kothawala the second highest paid employee in the company.

On December 28, 1972 Kothawala responded that, while the offer was attractive, he found it unsatisfactory. He requested to be released from his contract effective January 1, 1973. SDRC released him from the contract except for the provisions pertaining to post-termination activities. Kothawala returned to Detroit and established EMRC.

Hildebrand also gave SDRC notice of immediate resignation. He declined SDRC's offer to continue as a project engineer. Instead, he also returned to Detroit and began to work for EMRC as Manager of Applications.

On January 9, 1973 Surana gave notice of his resignation. He refused to reconsider but was persuaded to stay for a brief period during which he prepared a handwritten description of the program's status and he explained the program to other SDRC employees.

Surana at first apparently intended to obtain a university position. However, in late February of 1973 he began to work for EMRC. On March 1, 1973 he was formally hired as Vice President of Engineering at EMRC.

Shortly after Kothawala arrived back in Detroit, he called upon American Motors Corporation (AMC). He had learned of its interest in acquiring structural analysis programs while employed by SDRC. On January 10, 1973 he proposed to develop for AMC a conventional, non-isoparametric, finite element program.

Then, on February 27, 1973, before AMC had acted on this proposal, Kothawala and Surana, who had now joined EMRC, submitted a new proposal for an isoparametric program substantially the same as NIESA in design, element library, solver and basic capabilities. Their proposal repeated the representations made to SDRC as to the uniqueness, superiority and value of an isoparametric element program. The written materials contained a number of paragraphs and a drawing taken from Kothawala's and Surana's August 23, 1972 formal proposal to SDRC.

In order to prepare a recommendation to its management, AMC personnel asked questions regarding specifics of the proposal. Kothawala responded by an undated letter. It is apparent from a comparison of the undated letter with the recommendation of Joseph Balnave, manager of AMC's computer center, written in mid-March, that the undated letter was written between February 27 and mid-March, since Balnave's recommendation of mid-March contains many of the specifics set out in the undated letter. In the undated letter Kothawala stated that the program being offered to AMC was partially finished, 1200 hours having been spent on it already and only 500 hours remaining for completion. Since defendants had not commenced working on the program at that time, it is clear that Kothawala offered American Motors the benefit of the time spent by him and Surana at SDRC. The partially finished program thus is SDRC's NIESA.

In March of 1973 EMRC commenced program development under an informal arrangement. In June formal approval for the funding of the program was obtained from AMC management. The program was completed about November 1, 1973. At that time Kothawala furnished AMC with certain program documentation which he stated was confidential and the property of EMRC. He instructed AMC to keep all aspects of the program in confidence in order to prevent any copying of the documents or program. He also refused AMC's request for a copy of the program code on grounds of confidentiality.

EMRC continued development of the program and added additional capabilities. In February of 1974 EMRC began marketing its program under the name "NISA", an acronym for "Numerically Integrated Elements for System Analysis".

SDRC, previously unaware of defendants' development activity, speeded up its own development work on NIESA. NIESA, renamed SUPERB, was placed on the market in April of 1974.

NISA and NIESA-SUPERB are very similar programs. The basic difference between them is that NISA is more fully developed, having the additional capacity to perform dynamic and heat conduction analysis.[3] These additional capacities were included in Kothawala's and Surana's plan for the development of NIESA at SDRC. Thus, NISA is in a sense the implementation of the plan for development of NIESA.

Mention must also be made of the Ford Door Project. While this is an element of the damages claimed, the court places particular emphasis on what these events reveal as to Kothawala's character and credibility. Since the testimony presented by plaintiff was often directly contrary to that of Kothawala, credibility is extremely important.

Shortly prior to the hiring of Kothawala and Hildebrand, SDRC bid successfully for an experimental testing and analysis project involving a vehicle component of the Ford Motor Company (Ford). Kothawala was assigned supervisory responsibility for the project and Hildebrand was designated project engineer.

Beginning in about November, 1972 Kothawala advised Ford employees having re-

3. NISA's program is usable on different kinds of computers. This was not so as to the NIESA program. In this sense the NISA program is "machine independent".

sponsibility for the project regarding his lack of success in obtaining a satisfactory arrangement for the Detroit operation and indicated that he might resign from SDRC. These communications continued in an increasingly pessimistic vein until Christmas when Kothawala advised these Ford employees of his intent to resign. Kothawala's statements to Ford regarding prospective and actual resignation preceded his notice to SDRC. With increasing intensity as the end of the year approached, Kothawala created concern on the part of the Ford employees while expressing willingness to assume personal responsibility for completion of the project. Kothawala further led Ford employees to believe that the project could not be completed in a timely and efficient manner by SDRC through the use of other employees. By these actions Kothawala intentionally caused concern at Ford for the future of the project and doubt as to SDRC's ability to perform without Kothawala. The Ford employees assumed that SDRC was aware of the prospect of Kothawala's resignation and felt that SDRC was amiss in failing to communicate with them regarding this contingency.

At about the time of their letters of resignation and while still employed by SDRC, Kothawala and Hildebrand collaborated in the preparation of a letter to Ford critical of SDRC's rate structure and working conditions. The clear intent of the letter was to downgrade SDRC and to persuade Ford to transfer the project from SDRC to Kothawala and Hildebrand. Kothawala admittedly requested an SDRC secretary to type the letter but instead she turned it over to SDRC management. The letter was completed and delivered to Ford by Kothawala on January 4, 1973 at which time Kothawala reiterated his request that Ford transfer the project. In spite of this letter to Ford, Kothawala indicated to SDRC in a letter of January 15, 1973 that the Ford project was in excellent condition and that Kothawala and Hildebrand's presence was not necessary for completion of the work.

With these facts before us we turn to the plaintiff's contentions:

II.

Plaintiff SDRC makes three basic arguments:[4]

(a) Breach of trust on the part of the individual defendants (formerly employees of plaintiff) who used for their own advantage trade secrets owned by plaintiff and acquired by the individual defendants in a confidential relationship with plaintiff;

(b) Breach of contractual duty not to use or disclose confidential information;

(c) Unfair competition.

The law of trade secrecy is bottomed on the theory that in certain relationships a general duty of good faith exists owing by one person to another and that liability results because of a breach of this duty. Section 757 of the *Restatement of the Law of Torts* provides the rationale: there is a privilege to compete with others; this includes a privilege to adopt business methods, ideas or processes of manufacture. But limits on competition are necessary to protect the originator of the idea and so advance the progress of science and the useful arts. Thus the patent law prohibits infringement of a patent granted to another and the tort law "prohibits copying the things of another in a manner which creates in the market avoidable confusion of commercial source". The *Restatement, supra,* points out that one who discloses or uses another's trade secret, without privilege to do so, is liable to the other if "(a) he discovered the secret by improper means, or (b) his disclosure or use constitutes a breach of confidence * * *" (*Restatement, supra,* at 1, 2).

A review of the case law indicates considerable overlap in the application of these principles. In an article entitled *Developments in the Law—Competitive Torts*, 77 Harv.L.Rev. 888, 948–49 (1964), a summary appears. It discusses the requirements: "the discoverer[5] must prove that the taking involved improper conduct; that the information was in fact substantially secret and that reasonable efforts were made to keep it so; and that the defendant knew or should have known of the improper taking".

---

4. Plaintiff's contention that defendants interfered with its customer relations and that EMRC acted conspiratorially is dealt with elsewhere in this opinion.

5. "Discoverer" here refers to the person to whom the protection is due.

In any consideration of the policy underpinning the law of trade secrecy one is aware of the need that useful knowledge should be disclosed. In open societies such as ours this need is clearly recognized. It may be that in controlled societies one reason for the apparent lack of development of technology is the restriction on disclosure. But it is also true that some protection favors innovation and that this encouragement to a discoverer or developer enhances a basic human motivation for inventiveness.

What is the law and its policy as to an employee who is himself the discoverer or developer of a claimed trade secret? Here one argument is that such an employee's skill, experience and knowledge should be protected. Some scholars point out [citation] that relief [to a former employer] "may be denied in cases where the secret has become such an important part of an employee's job skills that he will have difficulty in obtaining a new position if he cannot take it with him." They say that courts should balance the competing interests. In *Manos v. Melton*, 358 Mich. 500, 100 N.W.2d 235 (1960) one court did so and concluded that defendant Melton, an experienced plater, was not to be enjoined from using his knowledge and skill in subsequent employment with plaintiff's competitor. It appears he did disclose valuable techniques to his new employer which he and plaintiff Manos had developed earlier while associated together in business. The court not only found that the techniques were not of sufficient originality so as to be trade secrets, but it also rested its decision on the point that this was a part of Melton's skill and knowledge. It noted that Melton had specifically excluded this matter of his skill from incorporation into a non-competition clause in a contract by which he sold his stock in the business to his former associate, Manos.

Manos may well state a current area of concern for the technically skilled employee. The authors suggest that "both industrial society and the employee have an interest in preserving the job mobility of technically skilled employees, who will be less attractive to new employers so far as their acquired skills and knowledge are regarded as trade secrets" [Footnote.] They go on to suggest a second reason, that "if the employee has himself helped to develop the trade secret, this also weighs against protection [to his employer], since he may have some claim to ownership himself". 77 Harv.L.Rev., *supra* at 951.

In this case Surana and Kothawala did not obtain the claimed trade secrets through improper means. In substantial measure they were the developers and innovators of a general purpose isoparametric computer program. They were hired by SDRC for research and development activity in this very field, and the manner of their acquisition of knowledge of this technology can in no sense be said to have been obtained improperly.

Does their subsequent use or disclosure of this technology, assuming it to be a trade secret, breach a duty of trust owed by these individual defendants to plaintiff? The *Restatement, supra*, at 4, suggests this question by its comment: "apart from breach of contract, abuse of confidence or impropriety in the means of procurement, trade secrets may be copied as freely as devices which are not secret".

The relationship giving rise to a duty is not necessarily dependent upon contract; it may be based on agency principles or on specific dealings between parties in which a situation of trust arises and out of which sought-to-be-protected knowledge is acquired. Vital to a consideration of the creation of duty in such situations is the key question as to how the person acquiring such trade secret knowledge obtained it. If the subject matter of the trade secret is in being and an employee learns about it in the course of his employment in a relationship of confidence, the duty not to use or disclose trade secret knowledge adversely to his employer arises. On the other hand, if the subject matter of the trade secret is brought into being because of the initiative of the employee in its creation, innovation or development even though the relationship is one of confidence, no duty arises since the employee may then have an interest in the subject matter at least equal to that of his employer or in any event, such knowledge is a part of the employee's skill and experience. In such a case, absent an express contractual obligation by the employee not to use or disclose such confidential information acquired during his employment adverse to his employer's interest, he is free to use or disclose it in subsequent employment activity.

* * *

While the question is concededly a close one, the court holds that the isoparametric program developed on the initial encouragement—and under the supervision—of Surana and Kothawala falls within the latter category.

Surana and Kothawala do not owe SDRC a duty not to use or disclose its trade secrets by reason of a relationship of confidence in employment. As the substantial developers and innovators of this technology they have an interest in it and unless they expressly contracted with SDRC not to use or disclose such knowledge or information in future employment activity, there is no duty imposed upon them by reason of their employment relationship with SDRC. Nor is such a duty created by any equitable doctrine of quasi-contract; i. e., a contract implied in law.

Accordingly, the court turns to the remaining question. Are there obligations imposed on the individual defendants not to use or disclose confidential information acquired in and during the course of their employment at SDRC because of express contractual agreements into which they entered?

III.

Here, all three individual defendants entered into an Employee Patent and Confidential Information Agreement. In it they agree:

(d) At no time either during his employment, on either a part or fulltime basis with the Company or subsequent to termination of such employment will Employee divulge to any person, firm or corporation, or use (other than as required by the Company in the course of his employment) any privileged or confidential information, trade secret or other proprietary information including but not limited to information relating to the experimental and research work of the Corporation, its methods, processes, tools, machinery, formulae, drawings, or appliances imparted or divulged to, gained or developed by or otherwise discovered by Employee during his employment with the Company.

* * *

(f) Employee will not during the term of his employment directly or indirectly enter into employment or render services to any person, firm or corporation rendering services or handling

products competitive with the Company's services or products or engage as a principal in any such business, and for a further period of six (6) months following the termination hereof, engage as a principal in any business of or with any person, firm or corporation in the United States, one of the major business activities of which is to render services or handle products competitive with the services or products of the Company. To engage as a principal in any business, as used in this paragraph, is defined as owning or having a contractual right to own in the future a profit sharing interest of 5% or more of any such business entity, or acting as an officer, manager or other comparable executive position or serving on the Board of Directors or similar governing body of said entity.

Kothawala also executed a separate employment contract. He himself drafted some of its terms. SDRC had submitted a proposed contract to him. He found it unacceptable, insisted on modifications and then submitted his draft which was executed. It contains the following provisions:

1. Commencing with the date of this contract and continuing for two (2) years thereafter, Kothawala will devote his entire business time, skill, labor and attention to this employment and will not participate as a consultant, or as a part-time employee in any other business during such time except with the express written permission of SDRC. The services which he will perform for SDRC will be those which are prescribed by SDRC. Such services will be performed in such locations as may be required. Kothawala will not for a period of one (1) year after his termination hereunder directly, or indirectly enter into employment or render services to any person, firm or corporation, which, as one of its business activities, engages in competition with SDRC or distributes products in substantial competition with SDRC anywhere in the United States, nor will Kothawala enter into or become interested in any such competitive business as a principal, which for the purposes of the contract, is defined as owning or controlling in excess of 3% of the capital stock or other earning-sharing interest in any such business.

* * *

4. Neither during the period of employment nor at any time thereafter will Kothawala disclose to anyone any confidential information or trade secrets concerning the business affairs of SDRC, including but not limited to information relating to the experimental and research work

of SDRC, their methods, processes, tools, machinery, formulae, drawings, or appliances imparted or divulged to, gained or developed by or otherwise discovered by Kothawala during his employment with SDRC. Upon termination of his employment, Kothawala will return to SDRC all objects, materials, devices or substances including notes, records, drawings, sketches, recordings, descriptions, samples, specimens, prototypes, models, blueprints, analyses, programs, or the like, and including any facsimile, replica, photograph or reproduction thereof, belonging to SDRC or relating to their respective business.

These contracts were entered into in Ohio.

The agreements not to disclose confidential information impose obligations by their clear terms since these undertakings do not exclude information, technology or knowledge which the employee himself discovers, develops or contributes. [Citation.] Thus, if the contracts are valid and enforceable, defendants are under obligations not to use or disclose confidential information gained while employed at SDRC.

Some courts have held that such express contracts create a confidential relationship between employer and employee, breach of which results in liability. They use the doctrine of trade secrets in the decisional process. This court finds such an approach too restrictive, especially in an area of knowledge and rapid technological change such as the computer field.

The express contracts in issue apply not only to trade secrets but also to privileged, proprietary and confidential information. In this they are analogous to the breadth of coverage recognized under agency principles. In *Shwayder Chemical Metallurgy Corp. v. Baum,* 45 Mich.App. 220, 206 N.W.2d 484 (1973) it was held that while the process plaintiff sought to protect was not a trade secret, defendant stood in a fiduciary and confidential relationship to plaintiff, that he breached the duties and obligations arising from that relationship and was therefore liable for damages. [Citation.]

These considerations apply to the express contracts in issue. Defendants are liable for breach of their contracts and are answerable in damages if they used or disclosed confidential information, knowledge or technology gained while employed at SDRC. This is so even though such information, knowledge or technology is not itself a trade secret. [Citation.]

The contracts in issue are valid *in toto* if governed by Ohio law and valid in part if severable under Michigan law. [Footnote.] Ohio permits its courts to enforce covenants not to use or disclose confidential information as well as reasonable covenants not to compete. [Citation.] In Michigan a statute, M.C.L.A. 445.761, declares that covenants not to compete, whether reasonable or unreasonable, are against public policy and are illegal and void. Michigan, however, does recognize and enforce covenants not to use or disclose confidential information. [Citation.]

Whether Michigan or Ohio law applies is a question of conflict of laws. A United States District Court in exercising diversity jurisdiction must follow the forum state's rules. [Citation.] Michigan follows the general rule expressed in the *Restatement of Conflict of Laws* § 332 that the nature, validity, effect and obligation of a contract are governed by the law of the place where the contract was made. [Citations.]

There does not seem to be any dispute as to the place of the making of the contracts and in any event the court finds that they were entered into in Ohio.

* * *

In this type of case, where the place of performance is not focused in any particular state, courts have held that in the absence of evidence to the contrary, the parties intended that the law of the place where the contract was made should govern questions of validity. [Footnote.] [Citations.]

This being so, the law of Ohio would govern questions of validity. A number of factors indicate this to be the correct result: (a) It is in accord with principles stated in the *Restatement of Conflict of Laws* which were recently so forcefully upheld in Michigan in the area of torts. [Citation.] (b) The contracts in issue were made, executed and delivered in Ohio. (c) It would further the presumed intent of the parties, in accordance with traditional contract doctrine, to enter into a valid contract. (d) The employment relationship arose and centered in Ohio. (e) The defendants acquired the confidential information while employed at SDRC's principal place of business in Ohio.

The extent to which an Ohio contract will be enforced in Michigan depends upon the doctrine of judicial comity. [Citation.] Defendants argue that even though the contracts are valid where made, the inclusion of a non-competition clause in each, void under M.C.L.A. 445.761, invalidates the contracts and precludes their enforcement.

This court is unable to perceive any reason why contracts, valid *in toto* where made, should not be enforced as a matter of comity to the extent their provisions do not contravene the public policy of the forum. In *Glucol Manufacturing Company v. Schulist*, 239 Mich. 70, 214 N.W. 152 (1927) the Michigan Supreme Court, in discussing the enforceability of nondisclosure provisions, stated:

> But we agree with the trial court that this statute [M.C.L.A. 445.761] has no application in the instant case. The reason is obvious. Defendant did not agree not to engage in a similar business, but only that he would not use the formulae of his employer, which, he was given to understand, were the property of plaintiff. 239 Mich. at 74, 214 N.W. at 153.

[Citation.]

The public policy of Michigan does not preclude enforcement of use or non-disclosure provisions. The presence of the non-competition provision, while itself unenforceable, does not make the other logically distinct and separate provisions of these contracts unenforceable when these provisions, standing alone, are valid in both states.

This brings the court to the issue of breach.

It is true that initial recognition of the importance of isoparametric elements in a new program, and the feasibility of development of such a program, must be credited to Surana and, to a lesser extent, to Kothawala. However, this information was acquired in the course of their employment and a fulfillment of their specific assigned responsibilities. This information had business value and SDRC had the sole right because of the express contracts to exploit the advantage. SDRC's possession of this information gave it an opportunity to gain an advantage over its competitors who did not have the information. The August 23, 1972 proposal by Kothawala is a significant compilation of marketing and technical planning for the program and this document was therefore proprietary and confidential. The court finds that SDRC relied on the representations of Kothawala and Surana including those contained in the August 23, 1972 document in its decision to devote its resources to the program. SDRC reasonably anticipated that part of its business advantage would flow from its early entry in the market—an advantage recognized by both sides. SDRC did not anticipate that the very employees who extolled the merits of the program and caused SDRC to undertake its development would use the same information to develop a competitive product and achieve the advantage of being first in the market. These actions by defendants breached their contractual obligations not to use or disclose confidential information.

The technical planning and development of NIESA to its stage of development in January, 1973, including the selection of elements, solver routine, organization of sub-routines, coding, and other factors contributing to the efficiency and effectiveness of the program constituted important and confidential information, particularly prior to public release of the program. The technical accomplishments of Surana and Kothawala reflected in their work on NIESA amounted to a compilation of information which gave SDRC a competitive advantage. The existence or availability of abstract technical data does not detract from the confidentiality of the combination of such parts and data into a program of the type under consideration. This was conceded by Kothawala and confirmed by defendants' actions in dealing with the trade when great emphasis was placed by the defendants on the confidential nature of the NISA program and the competitive importance to EMRC in protecting such confidentiality.

The status report prepared for SDRC by Kothawala and Surana in October includes such information and it is likewise confidential and proprietary. This information had value and was confidential to SDRC. Surana's use of this information for defendants' benefit was a breach of his contract. This also holds true with respect to Kothawala who hired Surana and participated in the unlawful use of information obtained at SDRC, and who, as sole shareholder of EMRC, is presently the primary beneficiary of the illicit information.

Confidentiality of information can be determined from the manner in which defendants themselves treated the information prior to the litigation. [Citations.] Here the record is replete with statements by the defendants both to SDRC and to AMC as to the value, uniqueness and confidentiality of the program.

A quantity of documents belonging to SDRC were also found in possession of defendants when this action was commenced. These included:

Internal SDRC documents pertaining to work on the Ford Door Project.

Internal SDRC documents pertaining to the NIESA program including the August 23 and October 25 documents, customer information and prospective research and development activities.

Surana's notes prepared as part of his development work on NIESA. The court finds these notes to have significant value both in the case of NIESA and NISA.

The court does not credit defendants' explanation that these documents were permitted to be taken from SDRC's office. The court finds that they were taken without permission.

At a pretrial conference the court directed defendants to make a copy of the static portion of the NISA code available to plaintiff's counsel and experts pursuant to a protective order. The code which was furnished was dated December, 1974, and reflected many revisions made subsequent to defendants' initial code. Defendants have represented that no prior version of the NISA code remained. Portions of the NISA code were compared to the NIESA code as it existed in January, 1973. On the basis of this comparison, plaintiff's experts, Dr. Anderson of the Department of Aerospace Engineering at the University of Michigan, and Michael Coble, a computer programmer also affiliated with the University, concluded that defendants must have copied from the NIESA code. They made a careful analysis of the two programs and found not only similarity in the overall structure and organization (some which might be explainable on functional grounds) but they found identical segments of code which were solely arbitrary and, most significantly, deviations or quasimistakes which, in their judgment, could only be explained by copying. Victor Nicholas, who completed the development of NIESA-SU-

PERB at SDRC, testified that the input data cards prepared by Surana for NIESA were taken verbatim into NISA. Except for cross-examination, defendants did not address these specifics relied on by the experts, but attributed such similarities as existed to Surana's memory. The court does not accept this explanation. Memory alone cannot explain the specifics which according to the experts do not make sense but are explainable only by copying. The court finds that defendants copied from the physical NIESA code.

The technical and business information which the court has found to have been misappropriated by defendants was treated by SDRC in a manner consistent with the preservation of its confidentiality. Although SDRC did not use the ultimate in policing measures, the professional calibre of its employees, and the nature of its development work made heavy-handed measures unnecessary. Moreover, the confidential nature of development work was specifically called to each employee's attention in his individual confidential disclosure agreement. The court finds that defendants Kothawala and Surana knew that information pertaining to NIESA was confidential and proprietary to SDRC.

SDRC did not disclose confidential information to outside parties in a manner inconsistent with preservation of confidentiality. To the extent that limited disclosure may have been made to representatives of United States Steel Corporation, that company's relationship to SDRC as its largest shareholder and a business partner was not inconsistent with the preservation of confidentiality.

The defendants' main legal defense was that all the information which is included in a computer program such as NIESA is found in the literature and therefore the NIESA program was not unique, was not novel, was not an invention and could not rise to the level of protectable confidential information and/or trade secrets. The court disagrees with the defendants' position. An overwhelming majority of authorities on the subject have ruled that novelty and uniqueness are not a requirement for trade secret protection. [Citations.] These principles apply with equal force to contractual provisions not to disclose or use confidential information. It is unnecessary for the court to determine whether all the ingredients making up the NIESA program and the NISA program are found in the literature, for the combining of all the essential elements into a program which is primarily and exclusively an isoparametric element program was and is a unique and valuable program in the software industry and is within the definition of confidential information.

The court has held that the NISA program of EMRC was developed through the use of the plaintiff's confidential information regarding the NIESA-SUPERB projects. The fact that the NISA program is at a later stage of completion than the status of NIESA at the time that Surana left SDRC or the fact that EMRC may have modified and added additional capabilities than those existing at the time that Surana left is not a defense to this action. There is not requirement that the defendants use the information in exactly the form in which they received it. Furthermore, the court finds that the later stage of development of NISA is directly attributable to the head start that the use of SDRC's confidential information gave to EMRC in its pursuit of the NISA project.

The defendants also contend that SDRC breached its contract of employment with Kothawala by not offering him a job as the manager of an SDRC office in Detroit, and that this breach entitled defendants to use whatever information they had in regard to the NIESA-SUPERB program in developing the NISA program.

The court finds that SDRC acted in good faith in an effort to accommodate their business interests with Kothawala's ambitions and the pertinent provisions of the contract. SDRC did not guarantee Kothawala a management position at any time and certainly not within five months of the execution of the contract.

Finally, the court finds that EMRC, the corporation of which defendant Kothawala is sole shareholder, is the entity through which this confidential information is being purveyed in the marketplace; it is liable with the individual defendants for agreeing with them to carry out this improper purpose.

In view of these findings, it is unnecessary to consider plaintiff's contention as to unfair competition.

IV.

On the Ford Door Project Kothawala and Hil-

debrand are liable for interference with SDRC's customer relations. Their acts in disparaging SDRC's ability satisfactorily to complete the project were the direct cause of Ford's transfer of the project from SDRC to EMRC. Under Michigan law, "an action for damages lies against one who is not a party to a contract but who wrongfully induces a breach or termination thereof". *Wilkinson v. Powe,* 300 Mich. 275, 1 N.W.2d 539 (1942).

The SDRC contract provided for payment to it in the total amount of $47,530. Ford paid SDRC $31,993 for its portion of the work prior to transfer. The balance of $15,337 was paid to EMRC. SDRC's normal profit factor, which the court finds reasonable and appropriate for determining damages on this project, is 20% of $15,337, or $3,107. Kothawala, Hildebrand and EMRC are jointly and severally liable to SDRC for this loss of profit.

SDRC is also entitled to damages for breach of the express contracts. In *University Computing Co. v. Lykes-Youngstown Corp.,* 504 F.2d 518 (5th Cir. 1974), the court considered in detail the approaches used in this area. It concluded that when a defendant had destroyed the value of the information, courts generally attempted to measure the loss suffered by the plaintiff. However, when the secret had not been destroyed, as here, courts attempted to measure the value of the secret to the defendant. This value is measured by the "reasonable royalty" standard. In explaining the standard, the court stated:

> [T]he type of measure [of damages] used by the Court, based on actual sales, has taken many different forms. As the term is presently understood, the 'reasonable royalty' measure of damages is taken to mean more than simply a percentage of actual profits. The measure now, very simply, means '[t]he actual value of what has been appropriated'. [Citation.] When this is not subject to exact measurement, a reasonable estimate of value is used. *University Computing Co. v. Lykes-Youngstown Corp., supra,* at 537.

Here the court notes that defendants have not made a profit. However, this does not preclude SDRC from recovering damages, for when defendants misused confidential information as outlined herein, they bore this risk of failure and must refund for their breaches. [Citations.]

In determining the measure of damages the court should consider the commercial setting of the injury, the likely future consequences of the breach and the nature and extent of the use.

Here EMRC is in direct competition with SDRC in the development and transfer on a commercial basis of computer software and specifically EMRC's offering of its NISA program in competition with SDRC's SUPERB program. EMRC, in offering its NISA program to the market, is offering a computer program which had been planned and partially completed at SDRC; additionally, EMRC used extensive confidential information regarding SDRC's NIESA program in developing NISA. EMRC is using SDRC's confidential information for:

(a) Internal solution of its customers' structural problems which is known in the trade as applications work; and

(b) Transfer, on a commercial basis, of the program for use by third parties either on an in-house or vendor installation basis.

These uses are without SDRC's permission and without compensation to SDRC. Additionally, EMRC was successful in transferring the use of NISA to a number of potential SDRC customers. The court finds that NISA and SUPERB are so similar that if a customer had NISA it would not need SUPERB. Accordingly, SDRC has been damaged and this same type of competition presently continues.

SDRC submitted evidence of the prices it currently charges to its customers and the profit factors SDRC generally experienced in these lines of business. While the court does not doubt that they are reasonable, it finds the profit factor of 20% used by SDRC to be too high for this purpose. The reason is that, while defendants went so far in their misuse of SDRC's confidential information as to copy from NIESA, they also used in some measure their own skill, knowledge and experience in completing the development of NISA. NIESA was only partially completed at the time defendants left SDRC. The evidence does not reveal that any significant work had been done on the dynamic or heat conduction analysis capabilities of NIESA. At EMRC, defendants completed the work on the static analysis capability of NIESA and then added the additional capabilities described above.

The court finds that while defendants used their own experience, skill and knowledge, this was commingled with the confidential information taken from SDRC. Since the defendants through their own actions placed themselves in this position, the court finds that (a) SDRC is entitled to a recovery of a percentage of all EMRC's sales; (b) a "reasonable royalty" in this case is 15% of EMRC's gross sales; (c) this will include, but is not limited to EMRC's use of NISA for the internal solution of its customers' structural problems and use of the program by EMRC's customers on an in-house or vendor installation basis.

This royalty is imposed for the period of time necessary for a competitor to duplicate the program by independent research rather than through the use of confidential information. SDRC presented expert testimony that this period would be two and one-half to four years. The court finds that three years is a reasonable period and will adequately protect SDRC. The period shall begin to run from the time defendants first used SDRC's confidential information. This occurred when they began developing NISA at AMC. The testimony indicated that defendants began its program informally with AMC in mid-March, 1973 and received formal approval in June of 1974. The court concludes that the period for which such damages as herein defined may be collected shall be calculated from March 15, 1973 and continue to March 15, 1976.

SDRC also seeks a license fee of $45,000 for use of its program on an in-house basis by EMRC and AMC for which there are no billings or sales figures. EMRC was permitted the use of AMC's computer facilities free of charge for program development and independent commercial use in return for which EMRC supplied AMC its NISA program without charge.

Ordinarily, an estimate of a reasonable billing could be made from evidence of the expenditures EMRC incurred for development of NISA. EMRC asserted that it had spent $96,986 for salaries of EMRC personnel, $2,145.88 for other expenditures and $223,000 for use of AMC's computer facilities for a total of $322,131.88. [Footnote.] But this is not a completely realistic measure due to unusually high start-up costs. The court concludes that SDRC's license fee, which is reasonable, provides a sounder basis for the award of damages. Therefore, the court concludes that EMRC is also liable to SDRC for $45,000 for the installation of NISA at AMC.

No injunction will be issued since the court finds that compensatory damages are an adequate remedy.

Accordingly, the court herein enters judgment for compensatory damages in favor of the plaintiff as follows:

(a) Defendants EMRC, Kothawala and Hildebrand are jointly and severally liable for plaintiff's loss of profits from the termination of the Ford Door Project which the court has found to be in the amount of $3,107.

(b) Defendants EMRC, Kothawala and Surana are jointly and severally liable for their unauthorized use of SDRC's confidential information in the NISA program for damages of 15% on all sales of EMRC for a period of three years as hereinbefore defined, and additionally for damages of $45,000 as heretofore stated.

* * *

ANNBAR ASSOCIATES v. AMERICAN EXPRESS CO.

565 S.W.2d 701

(Missouri Court of Appeals, Kansas City District, April 3, 1978.)

WELBORN, S.J.P.

Action for damages by hotel owners against operators of reservations service for misrepresentation as to the availability of rooms at plaintiffs' hotel. Upon trial to jury, verdict was for plaintiffs for $25,000 actual damages and for punitive damages of $100,000 against each of the two defendants. Defendants have appealed.

Annbar Associates is a partnership whose members were Mrs. Ann Goldstein and Mrs. Barbara Goldsmith. From 1962 to 1974 the partnership owned the Muehlebach Hotel in Kansas City. Alfred Goldstein, a resident of New York and husband of Ann, managed the partnership affairs. Day to day operation of the hotel was in the hands of a resident manager, Ralph Hitz, Jr., from 1971 through 1973. An assistant manager, Ken Vincent, was in charge of the Muehlebach's reservations department.

American Express Company is a corporation engaged in various activities, including a credit card business. American Express Reservations, Inc., is a wholly owned subsidiary of American Express. It provided a comput-

erized reservation system for member hotels and motels, involving the employment of a telephone reservations service for use by members of the public by means of a toll-free call in making reservations for accommodations at member hotels and motels.

Prior to 1972, the Muehlebach had not honored national credit cards. Mr. Goldstein did not favor their use by the hotel, although Mr. Hitz and Mr. Vincent believed that the hotel should honor them and on several occasions they made such recommendation to Mr. Goldstein. In 1972, Goldstein acceded to Hitz's "pestering" and authorized Hitz to contract for acceptance of American Express credit cards and membership in Reservations Space Bank system.

On May 9, 1972, the Muehlebach entered into separate agreements with American Express and Reservations. The agreement with the former called for the hotel to permit holders of American Express credit cards to charge purchases at the hotel by use of that card. Such charges were to be sold to American Express at a 3½% discount.

The agreement with Reservations set both the terms and conditions of the hotel's membership and use of the Reservations system. Reservations was to be paid a $50 monthly fee plus 5% of the rental for accommodations reserved through the system, subject to a minimum charge of $1.50 for each rental unit.

The Muehlebach began operating under the agreements. In January, 1973, Goldstein, upon reviewing the hotel's monthly operating statement for December, 1972, directed Hitz to cancel both agreements because they were costing too much. Hitz unsuccessfully tried to talk Goldstein out of the action. Hitz then notified the American Express Regional Hotel Sales Manager that the agreements were being cancelled. A written notice to that effect was made by Hitz on February 1, 1973.

The Muehlebach immediately began refusing to accept American Express credit cards. However, Muehlebach reservations personnel were not told of cancellation of the reservations agreement and they continued to receive and accept reservations under the system. The hotel, which experienced a serious "cash crunch" from February to September, 1973, paid none of Reservations' monthly invoices from February to June 8, 1973. As of April

30, 1973, $699.99 was owed on the account. The agreement between Reservations and Muehlebach called for payment of invoices within ten days of receipt. On May 30, 1973, Reservations notified the Muehlebach that because of its delinquency, its Space Bank service had been terminated, effective May 21, 1973. On June 8 and 13, Muehlebach paid the $699.99 owed as of April 30. Charges continued to be made on the basis of reservations made before May 8. As of August 31, 1973, Muehlebach owed $141.73 on the account.

In accordance with Reservations' May 30 notice, the Muehlebach was placed "off-line" and was ineligible to receive reservations through Space Bank. In August, 1973, a reservations clerk at the hotel told Vincent that there had been some confusion about a guest who attempted to obtain a reservation through Space Bank and was told the Muehlebach was filled. The guest then called the hotel directly. Vincent did nothing about the incident. He couldn't imagine that Space Bank would try to turn a person away from the hotel and concluded it was a misunderstanding.

Around the middle of September, the executive assistant in charge of reservations told Vincent that other reservations clerks had found a "very common problem" in this regard. She, Vincent and Hitz discussed the matter, talked to Muehlebach's attorney and decided to make some test calls to Reservations.

Between September 29 and October 22, seventeen calls were made to Space Bank by Muehlebach employees, requesting rooms there on nights when rooms were available. In seven instances, the operator responded that the Muehlebach was "sold out" on the night desired. In two instances, the response was that the Muehlebach was "booked." In six instances, the response was Muehlebach "not available." On the final call on October 22, the response was "Muehlebach not serviced by American Express." In one instance, the reservation was "confirmed."

On October 10, 1973, suit was filed by Muehlebach against American Express, charging that plaintiffs had been deprived of substantial business because defendants had misrepresented to plaintiffs' customers that plaintiffs could not accommodate such customers, when in fact it could have accommodated such customers. The petition stated that damages could not be determined until plaintiffs obtained the records from defendants of the number of such calls, but alleged that damages were at least $1,000.00. The petition also charged that the false advice to customers was deliberate, intentional and malicious and sought punitive damages of $2,500,000.00.

By an amended petition, Reservations was named a party defendant. The amended petition charged that Reservations had given false information to potential Muehlebach customers as "the result of an agreement between it and [American Express], both defendants having conspired together against plaintiff immediately after they were notified on January 30, 1973 that plaintiff was cancelling the agreements previously entered into by plaintiff. * * *" Again the petition prayed for $1,000 actual and $2,500,000 punitive damages. Both defendants filed what were essentially general denials and the case was tried on such pleadings.

A further understanding as to the basis of plaintiffs' claim as well as to the defense offered requires some detail as to the operation of the Space Bank Reservation Service.

The basic instrument of the system was a computer, located in Phoenix, Arizona, in which was stored data concerning all hotels and motels which belonged to the Space Bank system. Telephone calls from persons seeking reservations for accommodations were received by operators, employed by Reservations, located at Memphis, Tennessee. Each of some 200 to 250 operators had a telephone, a computer terminal and a manually operated "microfiche" viewer which displayed microfilmed information covering addresses, rates, types of rooms, etc., of member hotels. Upon receipt of a request for information or for a reservation, the operator would type the request, which would then appear on a cathode ray tube. The operator sends the message to the computer by depressing the "send" key. The computer responds and its response is displayed on the screen.

Operators were instructed to respond to callers in the language in which the reply appeared on the screen.

When the system was originally set up in 1968 it operated on what was known as a "single threading" computer program concept known as Space Bank System I. Under such program, only one message could be handled by the computer at a single time. In 1970, steps were begun to convert to a "multiple threading" system (SBS II), in which a large number of messages could be handled simultaneously by the computer. Design and implementation of the new program took some 2½ years. The new system was considerably more complicated than the old, evidenced by the fact that the program for SBS I required six volumes whereas that for SBS II required 15 to 18 volumes.

One response programmed into SBS I was "Location Not Open." This response indicated that the hotel was not "presently on the Space Bank System." By directive dated April 13, 1972, Harvey Dice, Director of Reservation Services, advised Reservation Managers:

> When this response is received, please advise your Reservation Agents to advise guests that "The Hotel is not being served by Space Bank at the present time."
>
> Agents should not try to guess why the hotel is not being serviced by Space Bank, just state it isn't being serviced.

When SBS II went into operation in February, 1973, the "Location Not Open" response no longer appeared.

According to Robert Vanderven, an employee of American Express who directed the development and maintenance of computer "software," was in charge of the programming for SBS I, and who worked on SBS II, the response "Location Not Open" was not programmed into SBS II. The response "Not Available" was programmed into SBS I to be used whenever a hotel closed out to the system for any reason. The "Location Not Open" applied when the hotel had been "taken off-line." In the SBS II programming, the response "Not Available" was applied in both situations. According to Vanderven, there was no intentional change and if any came about it was "due to an oversight."

On November 16, 1973, following the filing of this action, Dice notified Reservation Managers that on November 24, a new computer response "Not available on system" would be "loaded on our system." One of the situations to which the response applied was when the hotel destination is "closed" because it has

voluntarily removed itself from the system or because it had been removed involuntarily. Operators were directed that when such response appeared, they should inform the caller: "The hotel is not available on our system."

Miss Jane Carlson, who was employed by Reservations as an agent in February, 1972, became a lead agent in July, 1972, and an instructor in April, 1973, testified that reservation agents were instructed to give only the response which appeared on the tube. As lead agent, she monitored responses given by other agents and corrected them when they failed to follow instructions. When the response "Not available" appeared, the agent was directed to say, "I'm sorry that hotel is not available." The agent was directed to offer accommodations at other hotels in the vicinity. According to Miss Carlson, the response "Not available" * * * "meant that I couldn't sell a room." She conceded that a caller might take the response to mean that the hotel had no rooms to sell.

A printout of computer transactions relative to the Muehlebach revealed that between May 23 and October 21, 1973, the computer was accessed for availability checks 487 room nights and attempted sale on 336 room nights.

According to both Vanderven and Miss Carlson, the "not available" response was not applied exclusively to the Muehlebach but was applied equally to any hotel placed "off-line."

Plaintiffs' claim was submitted by the following verdict-directing instruction:

> Your verdict must be for plaintiffs and against both defendants if you believe:
>
> First, employees in charge of the computer installation of the Space Bank were employees of defendant, American Express Company, and
>
> Second, said computer installation in Phoenix, Arizona forwarded the "not available" response to defendant Reservations in Memphis, Tennessee, and
>
> Third, defendant Reservations gave prospective customers of Hotel Muehlebach said "not available" response on dates when rooms in said hotel were available, and
>
> Fourth, said response deprived plaintiffs of business from prospective customers, and
>
> Fifth, as a result of such response, plaintiffs were damaged.

In this court, appellants first complain that the theory of recovery pleaded by plaintiffs was that of conspiracy and that there was no evidence of any agreement or conspiracy between appellants to injure respondents.

Respondents do not rely upon evidence of conspiracy but assert that they were entitled to ignore the conspiracy allegation and proceed against the appellants as joint tort feasors, relying upon such a rule stated in *Gruenewaelder v. Wintermann*, 360 S.W.2d 678, 688[3] (Mo.1962). As appellants' reply brief points out, Gruenewaelder did not involve a petition which alleged conspiracy (360 S.W.2d at 687[2]), so that the statement of the rule relied upon by respondents was purely dictum. Gruenewaelder quoted the rule relied upon from *Medich v. Stippec*, 335 Mo. 796, 73 S.W.2d 998, 1001[3, 4] (1934). In that case there was also evidence to support the conspiracy but the petition also charged wrongful acts to each of the defendants. In this case, the wrongful act charged was misrepresentation by Reservations as to availability of accommodations at the Muehlebach. The only wrong charged against American Express is by way of the conspiracy allegation.

In their brief, respondents assert that the appellants are jointly liable because American Express loaded the false "Not Available" response into the computer and Reservations is liable because it disseminated the false information. Thus, although the rule relied upon by respondents would permit proof of the charge against Reservations without regard to the conspiracy allegation, the same situation does not exist with respect to American Express. However, the only argument advanced here is in favor of a directed verdict as to both appellants. In such circumstances this court would treat the pleading as amended to conform with the proof and deny this allegation of error.

Appellants also argue that a verdict for defendants should have been directed because the evidence showed that the proximate cause of any loss to plaintiffs was their failure to pay their bill. Although the plaintiffs' default may have given rise to a right to cancel the Muehlebach's membership in the system, it did not give defendants a right to provide false information calculated to discourage future transactions between the hotel and its potential customers. That is the essence of the plaintiffs' complaint.

Appellants' second point is directed at the sufficiency of the plaintiffs' verdict-directing instruction, quoted above. Appellants contend that the instruction did not submit elements of an intentional tort and failed to submit essential elements for a claim of tortious interference.

The parties here have not undertaken to categorize the plaintiffs' claim. The respondents describe this action as one charging "a willful tort." However, their verdict-directing instruction makes no reference to any state of mind on the part of the defendants' officers or agents which might be characterized as "willful."

A distinguished writer has stated: "There is no necessity whatever that a tort must have a name." Prosser on Torts (4th ed.) § 1, p. 3 (1971). However, he has provided a fairly extensive categorization of the situations in which the law affords relief for injurious conduct. One of such categories is "Injurious Falsehood." Id., § 128, pp. 915-926. The Restatement recognizes such category of conduct as affording a basis for liability in tort. 3 Restatement of Torts, Second, Ch. 28, §§ 623A-652, pp. 332-403 (1977). The Restatement states the general principle of liability in this area as follows, Id., § 623A, p. 334:

> One who publishes a false statement harmful to the interests of another is subject to liability for pecuniary loss resulting to the other if
> (a) he intends for publication of the statement to result in harm to interests of the other having a pecuniary value, or either recognizes or should recognize that it is likely to do so, and
> (b) he knows that the statement is false or acts in reckless disregard of its truth or falsity.

Prosser describes the wrong of "injurious falsehood" as consisting of "the publication of matter derogatory to the plaintiff's * * * business in general * * * of a kind calculated to prevent others from dealing with him. * * *" Op. cit., § 128, pp. 919-920.

That this is the essential basis of plaintiffs' complaint is clear from the following allegation in their petition:

> By reason of defendant Reservations so misrepresenting to plaintiff's customers that plaintiff could not accommodate such customers, when in fact plaintiff could have accommodated such customers, plaintiff has been deprived of sub-

stantial business and has suffered substantial damage. * * *

In this case, plaintiffs' submission was upon what was, in effect, a strict liability theory for publication of the false information. The Restatement originally adopted this theory of liability. [Citation.] However, the Restatement Second has rejected the strict liability in favor of the view expressed in § 623A, quoted above. Prosser likewise rejects the strict liability theory. [Citation.]

Restatement of Torts Second, § 651, pp. 371-372, states in part:

§ 651. Burden of Proof

(1) In an action for injurious falsehood the plaintiff has the burden of proving when the issue is properly raised.

(a) the existence and extent of the legally protected interest of the plaintiff affected by the falsehood;

(b) the injurious character of the falsehood;

(c) the falsity of the statement;

(d) publication of the falsehood;

(e) that the circumstances under which the publication was made were such as to make reliance on it by a third person reasonably foreseeable;

(f) the recipient's understanding of the communication in its injurious sense;

(g) the recipient's understanding of the communication as applicable to the plaintiff's interests;

(h) the pecuniary loss resulting from the publication;

(i) the defendant's knowledge of the falsity of the statement or his reckless disregard as to its truth or falsity. * * *

§ 652 states in part (p. 375):

§ 652. Function of Court and Jury

* * *

(2) Subject to the control of the court, when the issue arises, the jury determines whether,

(a) the statement complained of was understood by the recipient as disparaging or otherwise injurious;

(b) the statement was understood to be published of and concerning the plaintiff's interest;

(c) the statement was false;

(d) the circumstances were such as to make reliance on the publication by a third person reasonably foreseeable;

(e) the publication caused pecuniary loss to the plaintiff, and if so, its extent;

(f) the defendant had knowledge of the falsity of the statement or acted in reckless disregard of its truth or falsity. * * *

Appellants' complaint that the verdict-directing instruction given in this case failed to require findings upon essential elements of the plaintiffs' case is valid. The tort of injurious falsehood involves, at least, legal malice. [Citation.] As Prosser expresses it (op. cit. pp. 921-922):

* * * There is liability when the defendant acts for a spite motive, and out of a desire to do harm for its own sake; and equally so when he acts for the purpose of doing harm to the interests of the plaintiff in a manner in which he is not privileged so to interfere. There is also liability when the defendant knows that what he says is false, regardless of whether he has an ill motive or intends to affect the plaintiff at all. The deliberate liar must take the risk that his statement will prove to be economically damaging to others; and there is something like the 'scienter' found in an action of deceit. Any of these three is sufficient to constitute 'malice' and support the action. But in the absence of any of the three there is no liability, where the defendant has made his utterance in good faith, even though he may have been negligent in failing to ascertain the facts before he made it."

In this case, respondents produced no evidence of a spite motive, made clear by the abandonment of a conspiracy theory. They produced no evidence of purposeful harm to respondents by appellants. Therefore, the respondents were entitled to succeed in this case only if appellants knew that the "not available" response was false or if appellants acted in "reckless disregard" of the truth or falsity of the "not available" response.

Respondents' verdict-directing instruction failed to submit any such issue to the jury. The instruction assumes that the response was false. That was also a matter which the jury should have been called upon to decide.

Absent proof of responsibility of one defendant for acts of the other, any verdict-directing instruction must require a finding against each defendant of the requisite elements of the offense, if both are to be held liable.

For error in the verdict-directing instruction, the judgment must be reversed.

Appellants contend that their motion for judgment should have been sustained because plaintiffs failed to prove the fact and amount of damages.

Proof of pecuniary loss is an element of a claim for damages for injurious falsehood. Restatement, § 651(h), supra.

> (2) This pecuniary loss may be established by
> (a) proof of the conduct of specific persons, or
> (b) proof that the loss has resulted from the conduct of a number of persons whom it is impossible to identify. Restatement 2d, § 633, p. 355.

Comment (h) to this section states (p. 357):

> h. Widely disseminated injurious falsehood may, however, cause serious and genuine pecuniary loss by affecting the conduct of a number of persons whom the plaintiff is unable to identify and so depriving him of a market that he would otherwise have found. When this can be shown with reasonable certainty, the rule requiring the identification of specific purchasers is relaxed and recovery is permitted for the loss of the market. As in analogous cases involving the loss of profits of an established business, as the result of other torts or of breach of contract, this may be proved by circumstantial evidence showing that the loss has in fact occurred, and eliminating other causes.

In this case, Mr. Hitz testified to two theories of damage. One attributed the decrease of 12,830 room nights for the period in question below that for the comparable period for the preceding year and computed the loss of profits on that basis at some $200,000.00. Rather obviously, the jury rejected that theory. Evidence of damage on this theory is clearly too speculative to admit of a calculation on this ground. Upon proper objection, evidence in support of this theory should not be received on a new trial.

Hitz's second theory was based upon the assumption that the Muehlebach lost 823 room nights, the total nights shown by the computer printout for which reservations had been requested or inquiries made of Space Bank between June 1 and October 31, 1973. He computed a loss of profits for room rental of $16,297, being 90% of the anticipated room rental. He stated that because the hotel staff was already in place, no additional help would have been required, thus justifying his high rate of profit estimate. He also figured what the profit would

have been on food and beverage sales to the lost customers, based upon the percentage which such sales bore to room rentals for the year 1973 and the rate of profit shown for such operations. These computations produced a loss of $8,039 profit on food sales and $3,039 on beverages.

This evidence sufficed to meet plaintiffs' burden in this case. The circumstances here were such as to permit a method of proof of lost profits analogous to that in breach of contract cases. [Citations.]

Defendants did offer an alternative computation, based upon the assumption that the Muehlebach lost 653 room nights during the period it was "off-line." Defendants' computation of profit from such loss of room sales was $11,372.05. No computation was made of loss from food and beverage sales. Defendants also offered evidence concerning changes in the hotel situation in Kansas City which might have affected the Muehlebach operation during the period in question. However, the evidence was not of such a nature as to require a finding as a matter of law that plaintiffs had failed to relate their loss to the actions of defendants complained of.

Appellants contend that the damage instruction was erroneous because of the alteration of MAI 4.01 to permit recovery for damages "sustained as a direct result of the *occurrences* mentioned in the evidence." Appellants contend that the use of the plural rather than the singular "occurrence," as in MAI 4.01 resulted in error because there was evidence of loss of business by the Muehlebach for which the defendants could not have been liable. Specifically, appellants refer to the evidence of increased competition and other factors, alluded to above.

Appellants rely on the Notes on Use to MAI 4.01 which call for a "descriptive term" to be applied to the word "occurrence" when there is evidence that there were more than one occurrence resulting in damage but the defendants were responsible for only one. They state:

> A properly modified MAI 4.01 would have made it clear to the jury that plaintiffs could not be awarded damages for the Muehlebach's entire loss of business as contemplated by Plaintiffs' Exhibit 38.

As above noted, it is abundantly clear that the jury rejected the theory of damages based upon Exhibit 38, in which plaintiffs calculated their loss at in excess of $200,000.00. In this case, the failure to modify MAI 4.01 to direct the jury's attention to the "occurrence" for which the defendants might have been liable may have been at the most harmless error. [Citation.] However, upon a retrial the admonition of the Notes on Use to MAI 4.01 should be heeded.

Appellants attack the submission of the issue of punitive damages, both for lack of evidence to support the submission and for defects in the instruction submitting the issue.

The claimed lack of evidence is directed primarily to the absence of evidence of actual malice. However, the plaintiffs relied upon legal malice in their submission. Missouri, of course, recognizes legal malice as sufficient to support a claim for punitive damages. [Citation.] Appellants offer no authority supporting the disallowance of punitive damages on such basis in an action such as this. [Citation.]

Appellants assert that the evidence showed at most only negligence on their part, insufficient to support a claim for punitive damages. That conclusion is premised primarily upon the defendants' evidence. The jury was not obliged to accept defendants' evidence and this court looks, on this argument, only at the evidence favorable to the jury's action.

The complaint against the form of the plaintiffs' instruction on this issue is meritorious. The instruction given was as follows:

INSTRUCTION NO. 6

If you find the issues in favor of plaintiffs, and if you believe that the conduct of the defendants as submitted in Instruction No. 3 showed complete indifference to or conscious disregard for the consequences to others, you may assess punitive damages in addition to any damages assessed under Instruction No. 5.

If punitive damages are assessed against more than one defendant, the amounts assessed against such defendants may be the same or they may be different. The amount of punitive damages assessed against any defendant may be such sum as you believe will serve to punish that defendant and to deter him and others from like conduct.

This is MAI 10.03 modified by substitution of "conduct of the defendants" for the lan-

guage "conduct of one or more of the defendants" in the first paragraph. MAI 10.03 is designed for use when two or more defendants are involved. The defendants had the right to have their conduct considered separately for the purpose of determining whether or not punitive damages should be awarded. [Citation.] The second paragraph of the instruction as given does accord defendants this right but the alteration of the first paragraph was unauthorized and is a deviation from MAI which is error.

Appellants also contend that the applicable MAI was 10.03, using the language "was willful, wanton or malicious" (MAI 10.01), accompanied by the definition of "malice" in MAI 16.01, rather than the language "showed complete indifference to or conscious disregard for the [consequences to] others" (MAI 10.02). Having concluded that the instruction given was erroneous, this claim of error need not be pursued. However, New Notes on Use to MAI 10.01 and MAI 10.02 (33 Jour.Mo.Bar, p. 453 (1977)), effective January 1, 1978, clearly infer that 10.01 and the alternative language thereof in 10.03 are to be used in cases of "intentional tort," with MAI 10.02 being the appropriate form for submission of punitive damages when the claim for actual damages is submitted on ordinary negligence. [Citation.] That directive would, of course, be applicable upon a new trial of this cause.

* * *

The judgment of the trial court is reversed and the cause is remanded for a new trial on all issues.

CT/EAST, INC. v. FINANCIAL SERVICES, INC.

5 CLSR 817

(United States District Court, S.D. New York, July 28, 1975.)

TENNEY, J.

This is an action arising primarily out of an Agreement for Services (the "Agreement"), which was executed by plaintiff CT/East, Inc. ("CTE") and defendant Financial Services, Inc. ("FSI") on March 9, 1969. [Reference.] The issues were tried to the Court over the period September 24, 1973 to May 2, 1974. The following constitutes the Court's findings of fact and conclusions of law.

PARTIES

CTE is a Delaware corporation, no longer actively engaged in business, which contracted to and furnished computer services to FSI, as will be more fully described hereinafter.

FSI, a New Jersey corporation located in Glen Rock, New Jersey, at all relevant times, was engaged in the business of maintaining customer account records for financial institutions. It offered its customers four basic types of services: an *on-line* savings system providing direct and substantially instantaneous communication between bank tellers and the computer facility at FSI; an *off-line* system designed for savings banks not equipped to operate on the on-line savings system; a *regular mortgage* system, designed for mortgage lenders; and a *service mortgage* system designed for customers who manage mortgage investments for third parties. In the course of performing these basic services, FSI prepared for its customers various daily, monthly, and other periodic reports and performed certain related services such as printing and mailing 1099 forms, printing dividend and other checks, and maintaining Christmas Club account records.

University Computing Company ("UCC"), a Delaware corporation, is named as an additional party defendant in FSI's counterclaims herein. It is the successor by merger of Computer Technology Inc. ("CT"), a Delaware corporation, which was the parent company of CTE.

Plaintiff seeks payment of invoices sent to FSI prior to and at the time of the actual termination of the Agreement on August 16, 1971, plus certain sums allegedly due it on account of FSI's usage of equipment under lease to plaintiff's parent company, CT, after such termination. UCC, as successor to CT, has also asserted a counterclaim against FSI for this equipment cost.

THE AGREEMENT

In brief, the 19-page Agreement provides that, effective January 1, 1970 and for five years thereafter, CTE would operate FSI's computer facility for FSI, assume the cost of the computer equipment and computer operators, and provide related programming services. FSI agreed to retain operating and financial responsibility for the communication network between FSI's bank customers and the computer facilities at FSI, including telephone lines and pick-up and delivery services, and for the key-punch operators at FSI who initially processed the raw data received from customers and prepared punched cards for processing in the computer room. The annual price for services rendered by CTE was set at $720,000, payable monthly in $60,000 installments, and subject to various adjustments. The Agreement also provided for the employment by CTE of certain FSI personnel. Furthermore, as the Court will have occasion to discuss in greater detail hereinafter, the Agreement contained specific provisions for termination of the Agreement.

The negotiations which led to the Agreement commenced in the fall of 1969. Harold Schunke ("Schunke"), the president of FSI, met with William Bird ("Bird"), the president of CTE, at the latter's invitation. The two men were not strangers. For some years before, Bird had been a marketing manager in IBM's New Jersey office and had supervisory responsibility for FSI's account. Bird told Schunke that CTE recently had been formed to provide facilities management services to organizations using computers, whereby CTE would take over the computer facility of the other organization and assume responsibility for operations and programming. Bird suggested that a facilities management arrangement between CTE and FSI would work to both parties' advantage in that CTE could convert all FSI's programs into third generation language[1] in exchange for which CTE would be able to use FSI as a central facility to process the work of other CTE customers when not engaged in FSI work. Bird sug-

---

1. FSI had invested heavily in replacing its "second generation" 1401 equipment with the advent of IBM's "third generation" System 360 computer equipment in the mid-1960s. FSI's programs, however, were still written in 1401 mode, so that it was unable to obtain the benefits of the higher speed and greater capability of the third generation equipment it had installed.

gested that FSI allow CTE to survey the FSI operations. At the end of October, after a second meeting between Bird and Schunke—this time attended by other members of the two companies—CTE sent a survey team, including Ed Devejian (then a CTE employee), to survey FSI's operations for a period of about two weeks.

In November, CTE presented to Schunke and other FSI personnel oral and written proposals for a facilities management contract with CTE, and a letter of intent dated November 21, 1969 was thereafter signed by the parties.

Even though no formal agreement had been signed, CTE assumed management of the computer operations at FSI on December 29, 1969, transferring to its payroll the various computer operators and programmers who had previously been FSI employees and assuming financial responsibility for the computers and related hardware located at FSI. In the meantime, CTE prepared drafts of a proposed agreement, which were reviewed by FSI, its attorneys and accountant. The Agreement, which by its terms became effective as of January 1, 1970, was not executed by CTE until March 6 and by FSI until March 9, 1970.

Although it would appear that FSI has abandoned its claim for rescission based upon alleged misrepresentations, among the issues to be determined is that of fraud by CTE or UCC either in the inducement, or subsequent to execution, of the Agreement. [Reference.] The claim of misrepresentation or fraudulent inducement is based on the fact that Bird, who had made the initial contacts and presentations to Schunke, decided to leave the employ of CTE prior to the signing of the Agreement. The fact that Bird was leaving was communicated to Schunke on March 17, 1970 by David Allen ("Allen"), the vice president of CTE. Allen also told Schunke to consider whether he wanted to cancel the Agreement.

The claim of fraud has no merit. The fact of the matter is that the Agreement contained no provision requiring the continued employment of Bird by CTE.[2] Bird was essentially a salesman and was not involved in operations.

Moreover, instead of acting to rescind after learning of Bird's departure, FSI repeatedly affirmed the Agreement. Indeed, in the second half of 1970, after Allen as well as Bird had left CTE, Schunke repeatedly indicated that he was satisfied with the Agreement and was not interested in changing it. Finally, there was no credible evidence of any plan on the part of CTE not to perform the Agreement prior to the signing thereof. The suggestion that Schunke was compelled to proceed with the Agreement because it was already in operation at the time he learned of Bird's departure, thereby making it impossible to "unscramble the eggs," is completely unconvincing in the light of the evidence.

What must be borne in mind in resolving the issues in this case is the essential nature of the Agreement: it was extremely favorable to FSI in its initial stages. The Agreement had been structured by CTE and FSI to provide a level annual base or "fixed" price, subject to certain specified adjustments, even though both parties were fully aware that CTE's initial actual costs would exceed the annual price so adjusted. That such was the case is supported by the fact that the fee to be paid by FSI for any premature termination by it for any business reason except CTE's substantial failure to perform amounted to $150,000 for termination in the first year and a lesser amount each year thereafter over the term of the Agreement. [Reference.] In addition, six months' notice of termination was required. CTE expected to benefit from the Agreement once FSI's programs had been converted into third generation language by CTE's ability to (a) increase FSI's volume and (b) increase other areas of CTE's business. In other words, it was anticipated that the FSI facility might become sufficiently enlarged and sophisticated to provide services to clients of CTE other than, and in addition to, FSI.

Before discussing, first, CTE's claims and, thereafter, the counterclaims of FSI, it should be noted that much of the evidence offered by FSI and the arguments raised in its voluminous papers herein would only be relevant in the absence of a written agreement between

---

2. Significantly, the Agreement contained a provision relating to FSI employees who were transferred to CTE and who are listed in Attachment D to the Agreement.

Section I, paragraph 6, of the Agreement provided that such employees should not be reassigned to non-FSI activities to the detriment of CTE's services to FSI.

the parties. However, as already mentioned, there was an Agreement,[3] which was never amended and which, moreover, provided as follows:

2. Complete Understanding

The entire agreement between the parties with respect to the subject matter hereof is contained in this Agreement and the attachments hereto. There are no understandings, agreement or representations not specified herein, respecting this Agreement or the services purchased hereunder. Any terms and conditions of any letter, memorandum, purchase order or other instrument issued prior to the Effective Date by Client or CTE in connection with this Agreement which are in addition to or inconsistent with the terms and conditions of this Agreement shall not be binding on CTE or Client. However, the terms of any written amendment or other written agreement between the parties agreed to and accepted by officers of the parties subsequent to the Effective Date of this Agreement shall be binding notwithstanding the fact that they may be in addition to or inconsistent with the terms and conditions of this Agreement.

CTE'S CLAIMS

1. CTE's performance under the Agreement

CTE contends that it performed its obligations under the Agreement, and that, accordingly, it is entitled to payment for the discharge of those obligations pursuant to the terms of the Agreement. We must therefore look to the Agreement to determine what those obligations were.

The Agreement contemplated that CTE would perform certain services, termed "Initial Operations." [Reference.] Those Initial Operations * * * were as follows:

1. CTE will accept full responsibility under Client's executive direction and control, for operation and maintenance of all operational computer programs.
2. CTE will develop, implement and operate a new Mortgage system for System/360 during 1970 under the guidance of Client.
3. CTE will install an on-line Savings system during 1970 capable initially of supporting IBM 1060 terminals. The procurement cost of any available on-line savings package which CTE may obtain will be at CTE's expense. If such

package is used, CTE will make necessary modifications to incorporate Client's control and other management requirements. If Client wishes to utilize terminals other than the IBM 1060, CTE will provide a cost estimate of special equipment required. Any Programming would be provided by CTE as routine program maintenance. [Reference.]
4. A schedule of input to and reports from the system will be mutually developed.

In return, CTE was to receive a "fixed price" per annum, to be invoiced on a monthly basis, modified by certain adjustments and increases relating to economic, tax, machine utilization and volume considerations. [References.] Since the payments called for under paragraphs 9 through 11 exclude "CTE's fixed price," that price is clearly the $720,000 set forth in paragraph 8. [Footnote.]

Before discussing in detail CTE's performance of its obligations, certain observations should be made. First, throughout the trial and in its briefs, FSI relied in great part on representations made prior to the execution of the Agreement or made without time-reference. CTE and FSI certainly contemplated that there would be a substantial improvement in the performance of FSI's data processing requirements over the five-year term of the Agreement. However, it is impossible to conceive that everything was supposed to have been accomplished in the first, or even the second, year of the Agreement. The very use of the words "Initial Operations" is significant. The Agreement clearly contemplates new applications and major changes to those "Initial Operations." For example, Section I, paragraph 4 of the Agreement provides as follows:

4. New Applications and Major Changes

At Client's request, CTE will undertake evaluation of the feasibility and development requirements of new applications or major changes to Client's Initial Operations. CTE will provide such services under a separate development Agreement, the terms of which will permit maximum flexibility of Client's financial and operational commitments and executive discretion.

Furthermore, it was recognized that FSI might require special analyses, new or revised reports, or other special requirements that

---

3. In the Agreement, the term "Client" refers to FSI.

would necessitate an adjustment of established schedules of CTE's services to FSI. Section I, paragraph 9 accordingly provides:

9. *Executive Direction by Client*
From time to time, Client may identify to CTE the key and critical nature of a special analysis, new or revised report, or other special requirement. CTE's Account Director will promptly advise Client's liaison of his plan to respond to such requirement. If, in the sole opinion of Client's liaison, such plan of action is insufficient or otherwise unsatisfactory, CTE agrees to be responsive to a request of the President or other officer of Client. In such event, establishment of new priorities by Client or other regularly scheduled CTE services may be necessary. CTE will promptly advise Client so that Client may make a value-judgment relative to adjustment of established schedules to CTE's services to Client.

Finally, it must be remembered that, while work on the mortgage and savings systems was in progress, CTE was operating and maintaining the operational computer programs, resulting in a substantial increase in sales revenues to FSI and in the savings and mortgage accounts serviced by it, and that FSI never sought to terminate the Agreement for any business reason or for CTE's substantial failure to perform until CTE had taken action to terminate.

(a) Operation and maintenance of all operational computer programs. Under the Agreement, CTE agreed "to accept full responsibility under Client's executive direction and control, for operation and maintenance of all operational computer programs." [References.] To effectuate the foregoing, CTE agreed to provide all equipment necessary to perform such services and to employ certain FSI employees. However, FSI was to continue to provide all personnel and equipment necessary for the preparation, and transmission or delivery of input to CTE's computer system, and for distribution of output from the system. Additionally, FSI remained responsible for communication lines and interface to communication carriers. [References.] CTE was also obligated to take over certain FSI equipment as specified in Attachment E to the Agreement, it being understood that CTE had the right to add additional equipment and larger systems in order to improve CTE's service to

FSI and to allow FSI to expand its business, as well as to allow CTE to support other areas of CTE's business so long as the latter was not disruptive to FSI or did not degrade CTE's services to FSI. [Reference.] Routine program maintenance and special reports were to be handled by CTE as a part of the fixed price of CTE's services, but the level of such efforts was not to exceed five programmers. [Reference.]

In accordance with the foregoing, CTE operated the computer facility at FSI from January 1, 1970 until August 16, 1971. In performing its obligations, CTE employed and utilized substantially the same persons who had previously operated the computers and performed maintenance programming for FSI. [Reference.] It also used the same computer equipment that FSI had used prior to the effective date of the Agreement [reference], namely, three model 360/30 IBM Central Processing Units ("CPU's") and various supporting equipment except that, anticipating the installation of a new savings system and an increased workload for the computers, CTE upgraded the equipment in December 1970 and January 1971 by replacing two of the model 30 machines with more powerful IBM 360/40 CPU's.

CTE's regular work included operating the various FSI systems, preparing daily and periodic reports for FSI's customers, preparing dividend payments, preparing special reports required by FSI's customers and performing other necessary services. To perform these functions, CTE personnel worked at FSI's premises on a full-time basis, virtually around the clock. CTE also furnished the equipment required to run the computer operation at its own expense.

Through the use of the computer equipment, and on a daily basis, CTE kept track of millions of transactions for about 150 large financial institutions having some million and a quarter accounts. It produced the hundreds of voluminous reports that were required each day to keep FSI's bank customers in business, as well as the voluminous periodic and special reports that were required.

In view of all of this, it is not surprising or unexpected that there were occasions when things did not operate to perfection or that there were delays and errors in the furnishing of reports or other services. However, it is important to remember that CTE's performance was only one step in the entire processing sequence. FSI remained responsible for the provision of all personnel and equipment necessary for the preparation and transmission or delivery of input to CTE's computer system and for the distribution of output from the system, which included responsibility for communication lines and interface to communication carriers. In particular, Section II, paragraph 5 of the Agreement provided:

5. *Input*

Client agrees that CTE shall not be responsible for schedule delays, inaccuracies or other consequences when caused by incorrect or incompatible data, lateness in receipt of Client's data, or by failure of machines or personnel under the control of Client. Any punch cards, tapes, discs or other data furnished by Client or Client's customers to CTE must be compatible with CTE's equipment and must be in good condition for machine processing. Under all circumstances, however, CTE will exert every effort to maintain the established data processing schedule of Client's work.

There is no evidence that CTE did not make "every effort to maintain the established data processing schedule of [FSI's] work." Although FSI claims that late deliveries to customers attributable to CTE's delay in performance were a frequent occurrence, it could not produce the records from which such claims could be substantiated. FSI called as witnesses a number of customers who had voiced complaints about the services they had received. Yet neither the witnesses nor any other customers were shown to have terminated business with FSI during CTE's period of performance. Indeed, none of the customer-witnesses terminated with FSI until seven or eight months after CTE had ceased operations under the Agreement and then, only because of FSI's failure to render particular services which FSI had represented would be available under the new systems. This, however, is far different from a charge of operational failure and CTE can hardly be held responsible for FSI's sales talk, particularly if the services with respect to which FSI made the representations were not within the terms of the Agreement. Further, there was no evidence of any refund to any customer or of any bills reduced

for lateness, indicating that, in general, deliveries were timely, and that, when there were late deliveries, the consequences to FSI were minimal.

The evidence shows that, whatever operating problems may have existed, they had no apparent effect upon FSI's customers or revenues during that period. FSI's sales revenues increased from $993,768 in the six-month period ended December 31, 1969 (immediately prior to CTE's takeover) to $1,157,980 in the six-month period ended June 30, 1971 (less than two months prior to termination of the Agreement). The number of savings accounts serviced increased from 989,682 in the year ended June 30, 1969 to 1,860,015 in the year ended June 30, 1971; and the number of mortgage accounts serviced increased from 218,496 to 258,570 during this same period.

Even if there were occasional errors in CTE's performance—and there is little evidence to support this—CTE did not assume FSI's risks. Section III, paragraph 1 of the Agreement is quite specific in this regard:

1. *Warranty*

Both parties agree that this is and shall be construed to be a contract for services only, regardless of the tangible form in which or by which the services may be from time to time presented to Client. The parties contemplate that their cooperation in this Agreement should produce performance of Client's data processing requirements at the lowest feasible rate of error, but it is not the parties' intent that CTE assume Client's risks in this regard, or otherwise be Client's insurer or guarantor in this regard. Accordingly, while CTE undertakes to use its best efforts in performing the services, and in furnishing the goods described in this Agreement, *it is understood that such undertaking is in lieu of all other undertakings, and all warranties, expressed, implied or statutory, as to the services or goods to be provided, including but not limited to any warranty of merchantability or fitness for use for a particular purpose.* (Emphasis in original.)

In sum, there is no substantial dispute that CTE did in fact operate and maintain FSI's operational computer programs for the entire period from January 1, 1970 to the termination of the Agreement on August 16, 1971. And, without minimizing the significance of the work contemplated under the other portions of the Agreement, it must be remembered that the great bulk of the work contemplated was necessarily that of operations. However, the main issues of dispute herein relate to CTE's performance of its obligations under points 2 and 3 of "Initial Operations"—development, implementation and operation of a new mortgage system for System 360 and an on-line savings system capable initially of supporting IBM 1060 terminals to be installed during 1970, which the Court shall now discuss.

(b) Development, implementation and operation of new mortgage system. As has already been stated, CTE also agreed to develop, implement and operate a new mortgage system for System 360 [footnote] during 1970 under the guidance of FSI. It is conceded that the system was not completed in 1970; indeed, it was not completed before the termination of the Agreement in August of 1971. CTE submits various reasons for the failure to complete the system during 1970.

First, it is claimed that FSI assigned a higher priority to the development of other systems not originally contemplated, which in turn forced CTE to defer work on the mortgage system. Among these were an escrow system, developed by CTE at FSI's request in the first half of 1970 to replace an antiquated and inefficient card handling system that FSI had previously used. CTE also worked on the development of a new tax system during this period. Since the Agreement does not define in precise terms what a new mortgage system for System 360 was to incorporate, FSI argues that the escrow and tax systems were intended to be part of the mortgage system. Actually, such systems are without independent value and only tie into the mortgage system as sub-systems to the main mortgage system. To require development of sub-systems before the specifications for the main system had been defined would not appear to be a reasonable exercise of FSI's duty to cooperate with CTE in the successful rendition of the latter's responsibilities. [References.] Indeed, as it turns out, it subsequently became necessary to make changes in the tax and escrow systems to conform to the new mortgage system.

Also, although CTE had assigned a project leader for the new mortgage system, the project leader was not able to accomplish much

during the first half of 1970 because he had been assigned by FSI to work solely on Phase I of the Federal National Mortgage Association's ("FNMA") aggregate exception system of reports by mortgage loan services handling mortgage loans made by FNMA, which was to be completed by April 30, 1970.

There was also delay in the early part of 1970 due to FSI's having considered the purchase by CTE of an existing mortgage system, the "Marc II" (developed and marketed by UCC), to serve as FSI's service mortgage processor. However, FSI rejected this system in April 1970.

Second, some of the delay was attributable to the fact that the parties were unable to define the mortgage system. In July 1970, a UCC employee assigned to work on the new mortgage system visited FSI to review the existing system and thereafter developed flow charts and attempted to resolve various technical and design problems for the new system. Definition of the new system was still continuing in January and February 1971 and FSI was still making comments about changes at the end of June of that year.

Third, CTE did not commence actual work on the mortgage system because, in the summer of 1970, Schunke had stated that the mortgage system was secondary, that emphasis should be put on development of the new savings system, and that the latter should be installed first, since the mortgage system serviced only about a quarter of the number of accounts which would be serviced by the savings system. Accordingly, CTE did not commence actual work on the mortgage system until November 1970.

Fourth, when it was decided late in 1970 to use FSI's existing system as the basis for the new system, FSI's documentation for its existing system was in such poor shape that CTE's efforts to develop a new system were seriously impeded.

Finally, in January 1971, FSI directed that CTE make no program efforts on the mortgage system until FSI had had an opportunity to review the completed system. Whether such directions were complied with or not, it seems clear that the parties continued to be mutually involved in the project. Letters relating to the system were exchanged between the parties as late as January and February 1971, when it was finally agreed that the basis for the new system would be FSI's present system. [References.]

CTE had from four to six persons engaged in work on the mortgage system between November 1970 and May 1971. By July 1971, it had successfully parallel-tested that portion of the regular mortgage system concerned with daily reports, and by the time the Agreement was terminated, it had projected September 10, 1971 as the date by which all programs of the regular mortgage system needed for conversion to the new system would be completed.

Whether CTE performed its obligations with respect to the mortgage system under the circumstances; whether time was of the essence under the Agreement and, if so, whether compliance was waived; and whether, and to what extent, the parties hereto are entitled to recovery must await consideration hereinafter of certain other relevant factors.

However, before proceeding to a discussion of the on-line savings system, brief mention should be made of the charge of $4,800.00 made by CTE in February for services rendered in October and November 1970 in connection with the FNMA aggregate exception system. Mention has already been made of CTE's services in connection with Phase I of this program, for which no separate charge was apparently billed. Although CTE claims that it did not learn of any additional requirements imposed by FNMA until September or October, the Court believes that this was not the case and that, although the FNMA requirements might not be included within the general mortgage system, there was no definite oral or written agreement between CTE and FSI to the effect that completion of the requirements (Phases II and III) would be billed separately. Accordingly, this claim is disallowed.

(c) Installation of an on-line Savings System. As part of the Initial Operations, CTE had also agreed to install an *on-line* savings system during 1970 capable initially of supporting IBM 1060 terminals. In fulfilling this obligation, CTE had the option of procuring at its own expense any available *on-line* savings package, in which event CTE agreed to make the necessary modifications to incor-

porate FSI's control and other management requirements. If FSI, in turn, wished to utilize terminals other than the IBM 1060, CTE was to provide a cost estimate of special equipment required. Finally, any programming "would be provided by CTE as routine program maintenance" pursuant to Section 1, paragraph 2. [Reference.]

Initially, it should be understood that CTE's obligation under the Agreement was limited to the provision of a new *on-line* savings system in 1970, and not a new *off-line* system, as FSI contends. The parties were very familiar with the distinction between an on-line system and an off-line system. FSI attempts to utilize prior discussions between the parties to show that an off-line system was also contemplated for completion *in 1970.* As will appear, the eventual installation of an off-line system was discussed or referred to not only prior to the execution of the Agreement, but also on occasion during the period after its execution. The record, however, is very clear. The contractual commitment under Attachment A of the Agreement was for a new *on-line* savings system. Evaluation of an off-line system, to the extent it was provided for under the Agreement, was to proceed under Section I, paragraph 4, of the Agreement covering "new applications" and "major changes," and was to be covered by a *separate* development agreement.

With the foregoing in mind, we proceed to a discussion of CTE's performance in connection with the new on-line savings system, which was to be capable *initially* of supporting IBM 1060 terminals.

The on-line savings system in operation at FSI in 1969 was an IBM package that had been purchased by FSI in the beginning of 1968. It supported only one type of terminal and was difficult to use in processing large numbers of accounts. Prior to its initial discussions with CTE, FSI had begun to investigate various savings packages then on the market. Among these was a package developed by Financial Data Systems, Inc. ("FDS") known as the St. Louis On-line Financial Package, which contained a series of programs that had been specifically tailored for a St. Louis bank and was subsequently marketed. Documentation and a presentation with respect to the FDS package had been furnished to CTE by FSI in November and December of 1969.

The consensus among the FSI people after viewing the FDS presentation was that the FDS package was basically good, that some things would have to be added and some changes and modifications made, but that if FSI were assured that this would be done, it would be willing to have CTE purchase the system. This explains the language of Attachment A, paragraph 3, of the Agreement that "[t]he procurement cost of any available on-line savings package which CTE may obtain will be at CTE's expense" and that "[i]f such package is used, CTE will make necessary modifications to incorporate Client's control and other management requirements." By the end of January, CTE had decided to purchase the FDS package and, on March 9, 1970, the same date that FSI executed the Agreement, signed a purchase agreement with FDS.

The package did not arrive until April 1970, at which time CTE had an opportunity to study it to determine in what ways it would have to be modified to accord with FSI's needs. FSI, however, did not begin defining its requirements until June or July of 1970. The list of requirements finally submitted by FSI in August 1970 was a staggering one, covering an off-line system, hereinbefore discussed. It closed with the statement "that most of which is required of the new FSI savings system has not been mentioned in this report." [Reference.] FSI was advised in September that the January 1, 1971 completion date originally contemplated could not be met.

It is not disputed that FSI requested many changes during the course of CTE's work on the system. Also, as was the case with the development of the mortgage system, it was difficult to obtain time on the computers at FSI to test the programs being written. FSI had heavy operational requirements in January and February of 1971 which could not be interrupted. Moreover, it would appear that the date of April 19, 1971, when the new system was finally installed, was reached by agreement between the parties in order to permit the testing which FSI desired. As with the mortgage system, determination of whether CTE performed its obligations with respect to the on-line savings system must await consideration of certain other factors relevant thereto.

(d) Equipment Rentals. It will be recalled that Attachment A, paragraph 3, of that part of the Agreement dealing with Initial Operations provided not only that CTE would install an on-line savings system capable initially of supporting IBM 1060 terminals, but also that, if FSI "wishe[d] to utilize terminals other than the IBM 1060, CTE [would] provide a cost estimate of special equipment required." Section II, paragraph 3, of the Agreement provided that FSI was to be responsible for all equipment necessary for transmission of input to and distribution of output from the computer system. Pursuant to those provisions, CTE has made claims for equipment rentals relating to Burroughs and IBM 2980 terminals, for the purchase by CTE of programming ("terminal support") for Olivetti and Burroughs terminals, and for programming for the IBM 2980 terminal.

In early 1970, FSI desired to determine whether Burroughs terminals could be used with the new on-line savings system. Accordingly, on April 9, 1970, CTE advised FSI that it was installing an IBM 2701 at facilities in New York City to test the compatibility of the Burroughs TC/700 with the IBM 360. FSI was also informed that the $445 monthly cost for the IBM 2701 would be billed to FSI as it was incurred. [Reference.] It was estimated that CTE would need the IBM 2701 for two to three months.

CTE charged FSI $1,019.17 for this item, including $171.00 for a data modem, $803.73 for the IBM 2701, plus $44.44 for transportation. [Reference.] It appears the equipment was used for only 13 days and that the revised invoice purporting to reflect this is incorrect since it includes eighteen days in May and an unidentified period in July 1970, plus the $445 (termination cost) allotted to June. The Court computes the corrected amount for the thirteen days plus the termination cost to be $551.88, plus $129.00 for the data modem and $44.44 for transportation, or a total of $725.32. This amount has not been paid.

In December 1970, FSI asked CTE to add to the new on-line savings system the capacity to utilize IBM 2980 terminals. In order to test and use this terminal, a second IBM 2701 adapter was installed by CTE at FSI, remained there through August 1971 and was used to test and communicate with the IBM 2980 terminal, and later, the Burroughs terminal. CTE submitted bills totalling $5,526.49, including one for December 1970.

It appears that the equipment was delivered to CT on November 11, 1970 and was at its Institute of International Education offices until early January. Accordingly, the December billing is improper. However, the total amount claimed would appear to be correct since it includes charges for only seven months. This bill has also not been paid.

(e) Purchase of Terminal Support for Olivetti and Burroughs terminals and programming for the IBM 2980 terminal. At FSI's request, CTE purchased from FDS programming ("terminal support") for Olivetti and Burroughs terminals, and in addition, provided programming for the IBM 2980 terminal.

Terminal support for terminals other than the IBM 1060 terminal specified in the Agreement was the subject of continuing discussions between CTE and FSI during 1970. Discussions about IBM 2980 terminal support were resolved late in December 1970, at which time CTE agreed to furnish the programming for the 2980 terminal, in exchange for which FSI agreed to pay CTE $3,500 in installments of $500, payable in each of the first seven months of 1971. CTE purchased the IBM 2980 terminal support from FDS and installed it at FSI in January 1971. FSI made the first three payments, and tendered the balance of $2,000 on June 29, 1971, subject to conditions which CTE refused to accept. The $2,000 is still due and owing.

At the same time as payment for programming the 2980 terminal was agreed upon (late in December 1970), the parties also agreed that Olivetti and Burroughs terminal programming would be installed by CTE after the new on-line savings system was installed and operating but not before the end of June 1971, since there would be no purpose in considering these terminals if the IBM 2980 and 1060 did not work. In April of 1970, CTE had done some work on the development of the Burroughs terminal with the IBM 360 computer and had established communication between them. In January 1971, following the December 1970 understanding, FSI considered purchasing the Burroughs terminal directly from FDS in order to have the programming operational in April 1971 rather than in June. FSI had told CTE that it wanted

to demonstrate Olivetti and Burroughs terminals at a bank controllers' convention to be held in Philadelphia on May 10-12, 1971, six weeks in advance of the original June deadline. CTE offered to purchase both the Olivetti and Burroughs support from FDS, to install it, and to charge FSI for the purchase price, which was $11,500. FSI agreed, CTE purchased the programming from FDS, and on June 11, 1971, billed FSI for its cost. Although FSI was fully aware that CTE expected to be reimbursed for its purchase of the programming, it rejected CTE's bill on June 29, 1971, after the fact, on the ground that CT was responsible for providing terminal support other than IBM 1060 as part of the fixed price set forth in the Agreement.

This rejection was unjustified. CTE was never obligated to furnish the FDS support modules, nor was it obligated to furnish any other terminal support modules for Burroughs and Olivetti by April 1971. The Agreement provided only that CTE would install an on-line system during 1970 capable initially of supporting IBM 1060 terminals. There was no reference in the Agreement to the year by which other kinds of terminals were to be provided. Additionally, if programming for terminal support was supposed to have been included as program maintenance, it should be remembered that program maintenance was subject to a five-man limit and had already been exhausted.

FSI has objected to technical defects in the Olivetti and Burroughs modules. However, the modules were generally workable and were successfully demonstrated at the controllers' convention. Furthermore, these are the very modules which FSI asked CTE to purchase for it from FDS to meet a new and earlier deadline. CTE is entitled to reimbursement for what it paid FDS, i.e., $11,500.00.

2. Amounts claimed by CTE under the Agreement

As indicated earlier, CTE was to be paid a fixed price annually in exchange for the services it performed for FSI. Additionally, the Agreement provided for various adjustments to the fixed price. Before discussing these adjustments, mention should be made of the $5,000 for March 1970 which, in addition to the total of $180,000 owed CTE for the months of June, July and August 1971, remains unpaid.

At Schunke's request, and in order to assist FSI in satisfying certain of its obligations to IBM, CTE reduced its monthly billing to FSI from $60,000 to $55,000 for the months of January, February and March 1970 and agreed to defer billing the balance of $15,000. In February or March 1971, CTE reminded Schunke of the deferred billing and FSI paid $10,000 of this amount. There is no dispute that the balance of $5,000 is presently due and owing.

(a) Economic Level Adjustment. The Agreement provides for a cost-of-living adjustment to the fixed price based on the percentage of economic change over each calendar year following the effective date of the agreement, as measured by the New York City average consumer price index. [Reference.]

FSI argues that no adjustment was billable until 1972. That contention is plainly untenable and based upon a misconstruction of the Agreement. The adjustment is defined as "an annual adjustment to the annual fixed price of CTE's services," and the "first such annual adjustment will be based on the percentage of economic change over the first calendar year following the effective date of this Agreement [i.e., 1970]. The percentage of annual change, as indicated by the appropriate CPI [Consumer Price Index] will be multiplied by the annual price of CTE's services to arrive at the annual economic level adjustment amount." [Reference.] Schunke confirmed the fact that payments based on adjustments for 1970 were payable in 1971 when he actually paid the initial January, February and March 1971 installments of the 1970 adjustments. Indeed, FSI did not object to the billing until CTE submitted corrected invoices. In March 1971, CTE rendered corrected monthly invoices to FSI reflecting the amount of the 1970 adjustment, including the Volume Adjustment pursuant to Attachment B of the Agreement and the Payroll Tax Adjustment pursuant to Section II, paragraph 10, of the Agreement. Schunke disputed the correctness of the invoices, which showed as due and owing a total monthly amount in the sum of $6,129.44.

While there is evidence that FSI and CTE later agreed on a $6,000 figure, this is denied by FSI. Accordingly, the Court has computed the cost-of-living adjustment pursuant to the terms of the Agreement. The New York City Consumer Price Index as of the end of 1970 was 145.7 and exceeded the December 1969 figure of 136 by 9.7, or 7.13%. The "annual price of CTE's services" for 1970 was the annual fixed price of $720,000, to which 7.13%, or $51,336 (representing the annual adjustment), was to be added to the regular $60,000 monthly payment to be invoiced in monthly amounts of $64,278 pursuant to Section II, paragraph 8, of the Agreement.

The final year of the contract turned out to be the first eight months of 1971, by virtue of the termination of the Agreement on August 16, 1971. Pursuant to Section II, paragraph 8, of the Agreement, the annual adjustment "in the last year of CTE's services" was to be paid in a lump sum, rather than deferred to the following year. The New York City Index as of August 1971 was 151, which exceeded the December 1970 index of 145.7 by 5.3, or 3.7%, and which, when applied to annual monthly payments for the prior year of $64,278 (base price plus adjustment), results in a figure of $2,322 per month, or, for the eight-month period, a total of $18,576. The Court agrees with FSI's interpretation of the Agreement as set forth in its Reply Brief, pp 7-8, but reaches a slightly different figure. However, the result is the same insofar as plaintiff is concerned. The $18,576 represents the adjustment over that for the prior year, which was $4,278 per month, or $34,224 for the eight-month period. Adding this amount to the $18,576.00 results in a total figure of $52,800, as claimed by plaintiff. The Agreement recognizes that, after the first year, the differential factor would be applied to a combination of two figures—the base price of $720,000 and the annual increase for the prior year. It sets a $100,000 limit over the term of the Agreement solely on that part of the increase that is based on the $720,000 figure. Thus, the amounts payable under the formula are $51,336 for 1970 and $52,800 for 1971.

(b) Volume Adjustment. The Agreement also provides for an additional annual adjustment to the fixed price based on the CPU meter recordings compared with those for each subsequent year. [Reference.] Here again, con-

trary to FSI's contentions, payments based on volume increase in 1970 were due in 1971.

No serious dispute exists as to the computation of the amount due, which the Court finds to be $1,620 per month for 1970, or a total of $19,440. There was no evidence showing the amount of volume increase for the eight months of 1971, FSI having taken possession of the material records in August 1971. Although, under the circumstances, a similar monthly charge for at least seven months in 1971 would appear equitable, CTE has made no such request herein.

(c) FICA Payroll Tax Adjustment. Section II, paragraph 10, of the Agreement provided that, if during the term of the Agreement, the payroll tax rates increased over the 1969 rates, then FSI would be charged for the additional expense attributable to CTE's employment of the former FSI personnel transferred to CTE pursuant to Section I, paragraph 6, and Attachment D of the Agreement. There is no dispute that the tax rate increase resulted in a monthly expense charge to FSI of $46.29 for 1970 and the same charge for the eight months of 1971, or a total of $925.80.

Having discussed CTE's claims herein based on the provisions of the Agreement, we next consider CTE's claim for excess program maintenance, for which the Agreement made no specific provision.

3. Claim for Excess Program Maintenance

Section I, paragraph 2, of the Agreement provided that, during the term of the Agreement and as a part of the fixed price of CTE's services, i.e., $720,000 per year, CTE would furnish special reports and routine program maintenance not to exceed five programmers.

Routine program maintenance consisted of correction, modification or enhancement of existing programs and systems. It also included programming, but only to the extent of enhancing an existing system. It did not normally include programming for or development of new systems. However, under paragraph 3 of Attachment A to the Agreement delineating Initial Operations, it was provided that programming on the *on-line* package purchased from FDS and programming to utilize terminals other than the IBM would

be provided by CTE as "routine program maintenance." Such maintenance, however, did not include programming for, or the development of, the new savings system or the new mortgage system.

CTE's claim for excess program maintenance must be denied. There is, first of all, no provision in the Agreement for an upward adjustment of the fixed price in the event that more than five persons were to work on routine program maintenance. The absence of such an adjustment provision stands in marked contrast to the inclusion of similar provisions elsewhere in the Agreement, e.g., the provision relating to volume increase in machine usage. In instances where the parties contemplated additional charges, a standard for the billing was specifically set forth, e.g., the reference to "CTE's standard rates in effect at that time" in connection with transition services to be performed by CTE for FSI upon termination of the Agreement.

The chronology of events relating to CTE's efforts to charge FSI for excess program maintenance is also revealing. It was not until February 10, 1971 that CTE advised FSI that all the program maintenance contracted for had been exhausted and that, commencing as of March or April 1971, FSI would be billed separately for all such services. This was during the period when negotiations for a new agreement or termination of the present agreement were under may [sic], as will be discussed in greater detail hereinafter. No invoices for the excess services were rendered, but on June 10, 1971, following the breakdown of the latest series of negotiations between FSI and CTE, the issue was again raised, CTE threatening to reassign its maintenance programmers to other accounts unless FSI agreed to be billed for their time. However, it was not until August 11, 1971, concurrently with its letter indicating its intention to terminate the Agreement, that CTE sent FSI invoices totalling $87,618.25 covering what it termed as "Maintenance Programming in excess of contract requirements."

CTE attempts to justify this claim on the ground that there was either an implied agreement to pay for those excess services or that there was a quasi-contractual obligation to pay based on the principle of unjust enrichment. It seems clear, however, that there was never any *mutual* agreement that the cost of excess maintenance was not covered by the fixed price. Furthermore, although it is clear that CTE expended more time than had been anticipated in its performance of the Agreement, CTE has not sustained its burden of showing that such excess time was in fact expended on program maintenance.

4. Negotiations Regarding Modification or Amendment of the Agreement

It seems quite clear from the provisions of the Agreement that, in addition to CTE's supplying the services defined above as "Initial Operations," the parties had originally anticipated that there would be modifications or supplements to the Agreement over its five-year term. Thus, at FSI's request, CTE was to "undertake evaluation of the feasibility and development requirements of new applications or major changes" to those "Initial Operations." [Reference.] Such services were to be provided by CTE "under a separate development Agreement" (id.). Furthermore, under Section V, paragraph 2, of the Agreement it was agreed that

> the terms of any written amendment or other written agreement between the parties agreed to and accepted by officers of the parties subsequent to the Effective Date of this Agreement shall be binding notwithstanding the fact that they may be in addition to or inconsistent with the terms and conditions of this Agreement.

Although the parties never entered into any separate written development agreement or amendment to the Agreement, CTE attempted on several occasions to extricate itself from its improvident commitments. As early as July 10, 1970, CT came to FSI to discuss the possibility of renegotiating the Agreement which its subsidiary had executed. At that time, Schunke was advised that CTE was losing a great deal of money under the Agreement and that a new contract should be negotiated. In response, Schunke stated that FSI had a good contract, and that he was not interested in raising his expenses or in renegotiating the Agreement. At this point, however, the idea of turning the operation back to FSI was first raised: CTE would complete the reprogramming of the mortgage and sav-

ings systems while FSI would resume responsibility for operating the computers.

Accordingly, on August 28, 1970, CT sent Schunke a proposed amendment to the Agreement, which provided for the immediate return of the facility to FSI's control and the development and installation by CTE of an on-line savings system and mortgage system by January 1 and March 1, 1971, respectively, in accordance with specifications to be set forth in exhibits to the amendment. The monthly payment due from FSI to CTE under the Agreement was to be reduced by an unspecified amount, and with one exception (CTE was obligated to make necessary corrections with new systems for up to sixty days thereafter), all obligations under the Agreement were to terminate upon installation and delivery of the systems.

In response, FSI forwarded to CT a list of desired changes and additions, including completion of programming for FNMA by October 24, 1970, completion and conversion of the tax system with processing for a sixty-day period, and maintenance for programming for the escrow system for ninety days.

About two weeks later, FSI received a revised draft, dated September 15, 1970, which incorporated a large portion of FSI's suggestions, including specific provisions relating to FNMA, as well as the tax and escrow systems. However, according to FSI, the matter of "hardware" (equipment) which CTE would leave with FSI became a stumbling block.

Meanwhile, on September 11, 1970, CT had written to Schunke claiming that, although CT had attempted to obtain final systems specifications for the FSI savings system for the past three months, FSI had continued to expand its requirements and was now requesting a significant number of items that would not normally be included in that system. CT indicated that it still felt it to be in FSI's best interest to regain control of operations, but that, prior to any alteration of the existing Agreement CTE and FSI would have to agree on the specifications for both the mortgage and savings systems. Schunke responded on September 16, 1970, pointing out that FSI had recently supplied CT with a list of thirty-nine points which FSI desired in the new savings system, most of which had been discussed with CT prior to execution of the

Agreement and others of which had been discussed thereafter as "the need for them became evident." [Reference.] Schunke further stated that FSI did not desire to terminate the contract but that he would consider CT's proposal that operations be returned to FSI as soon as possible, that the system specifications be developed within a week, and that the Agreement be modified accordingly.

Thereafter, FSI inquired of CT what would be required for CTE to continue under the Agreement. CT responded on September 28, 1970, proposing a pricing schedule based on present and anticipated volumes of major applications, with rates to be determined by the estimated costs of the personnel and hardware required to meet service and schedule requirements as of April 1971. CT computed the monthly cost at $72,850, but pointed out that the current Agreement allowed for a monthly increase of approximately $6,150 in 1971, consisting of $3,150 for increased volume of computer usage and an estimated 5%, or $3,000, increase for economic level adjustment, so that the net increase to FSI per month would be $6,700. Schunke responded on October 14, 1970, rejecting that proposal. After reviewing Schunke's rejection, CT wrote FSI on October 23, 1970 outlining the actions it would take to fulfill its contractual obligations, stating that maximum effort would be exerted to complete the new savings system by January 1 and the new mortgage system by March 1, 1971, although indicating that it would be highly inadvisable to implement both systems at the same time. CT also indicated that the use of maintenance support was being recorded and would have to be limited to the amount specified in the Agreement.

Although CT had now indicated that CTE would retain control of the computer operations, negotiations for returning the operation to FSI resumed shortly thereafter at CT's initiative. In response, on November 5, 1970, FSI prepared and forwarded to CT the items it wanted to see in an amendment turning operations back to FSI and, on December 7, 1970, CT sent Schunke a draft providing for the return of the installation to FSI's control on January 1, 1971. The week before Christmas, however, CT advised FSI that, after reconsidering the matter, it had decided that the only way that CTE would be able to complete the new systems would be to maintain control of the personnel and hardware, and that the parties could thereafter discuss turning the operation back to FSI once the new systems were in.

As CT had indicated in its letter of October 23, 1970, to Schunke, it planned to replace two of the 360 Model 30 computers at FSI with faster, more powerful and more expensive 360 Model 40 computers in December 1970 and January 1971, and increase the number of programmers to define and program the new mortgage system. On December 22, CT advised Schunke that, because of the normal heavy production schedule at the end of December, testing time would be minimal, so that CTE's new target date for the on-line savings system would be January 31, 1971.

The next meeting between the parties in regard to the contract took place on February 10, 1971. At this meeting, the parties discussed not only improvement in CTE's performance and in communication between CTE and FSI, but also implementation of the on-line savings system, with all savings banks to be operational by February 22, 1971. At the same time, CTE indicated that there would be a push for a new contract by April 1 or May 1, 1971. With respect to the present Agreement, it was indicated that FSI would be charged for the difference in hardware costs between 1970 and 1971 and for all future hardware added to the system. It was pointed out that FSI owed $15,000 of the $60,000 base monthly payment from the first quarter of 1970 (referred to hereinbefore) and that all maintenance programming had been exhausted so that FSI would thereafter be charged for maintenance programming, commencing March 1 or April 1, 1971. As to the future contract, new provisions regarding charges by CTE were proposed.

In late February 1971, CT attempted to reconcile the differences between the parties. On March 2, 1971, the parties confirmed that CTE and FSI would promptly enter into good faith negotiations to redefine the respective obligations of CTE and FSI in connection with the Agreement and that, on or before April 15, 1971, they would execute a new contract under which CTE would provide computer services to FSI. The on-line savings system had not yet been installed at this time. During the negotiations which followed, FSI received two successive drafts of a proposed new agreement. By this time, the on-line savings system had been installed and was operating. The drafts were reviewed by FSI and found to be unacceptable. No counter-proposals were forthcoming from FSI, and negotiations finally broke down in June 1971.

5. Events Leading to Termination of the Agreement

Following the breakdown of negotiations, CTE notified FSI on June 11, 1971 that it was making demand for all sums then due and owing under the Agreement. By letter dated June 29, 1971, Schunke reminded CTE that, on March 8, 1971, FSI had taken exception to certain invoices and, since "all meaningful discussion concerning a new agreement had ceased," he refused to pay anything more than some $3,600, although the invoices to FSI then totalled approximately $125,000, including the monthly $60,000 payment for June and the $5,000 balance of the monthly charges for the first quarter of 1970. [Reference.]

CTE replied by letter dated July 2, 1971, stating that it felt it imperative to state its position relative to FSI's exception in writing "as required by Paragraph 2, Section IV, Term and Termination" of the Agreement. It then responded to FSI's exceptions to the invoices and its failure to pay, which it characterized as a failure on FSI's part to substantially perform under the Agreement. Referring further to Section IV, paragraph 2b of the Agreement, it advised FSI that it had ten days in which to take steps to cure its failure to pay or to otherwise satisfy CTE, failing which CTE could terminate the Agreement pursuant to paragraph 2c. [Reference.]

Schunke replied by letter dated July 14, 1971, characterizing CTE's letter as "threatening" and as part of an attempt to cause a breach of the Agreement. After responding to CTE's claims with respect to the unpaid invoices, he proceeded, pursuant to Section IV, paragraph 2, of the Agreement, to notify CTE of CTE's substantial failures to perform under the Agreement. These alleged failures, it should be noted, related to installation of the on-line savings system and the new mortgage system and not to operations. Moreover, Schunke was careful to state that such noti-

fication should not "be construed as an election to terminate the agreement at this time" [reference] and suggested a meeting with CT personnel.

The suggested meeting took place on August 4, 1971 at the offices of FSI's New Jersey counsel. FSI presented a document listing what FSI would require if CTE were to turn back operations to FSI: CTE (1) was to furnish FSI with a 1401 equivalent Regular Mortgage System for System 360 by September 15, 1971 "in form to be agreed"; (2) was to furnish FSI with a Mark [sic] II Service Mortgage System for System 360 (previously turned down by FSI as mentioned hereinbefore) and pay $25,000 towards costs of modification; (3) was to pay FSI $35,000 towards the programming cost, and $30,000 towards the de-bugging, on the on-line savings package; (4) was to pay FSI $10,000 to cover certain conversion costs; (5) was to pay and/or credit FSI in the amount of $250,000 to allow it to operate during its period of readjustment; and (6) was to free FSI to assume or reject present hardware leases of CTE as it deemed appropriate.

In the face of these requirements and FSI's failure to make any payments since the token $3,600 payment made in June, CTE delivered to FSI a notice of termination of the Agreement on August 11, 1971, effective August 21, 1971. [Reference.] On the same date, CTE instituted suit against FSI in the Supreme Court of the State of New York, County of New York, seeking recovery of $365,605.59, covering the invoices to which reference has previously been made. The action was removed to this Court in September 1971.

6. CTE's Claim for a Termination Fee

Before discussing CTE's claim of $100,000 as a termination fee, a brief summary of the events of the weekend of August 13, 1971 is in order. First, it should be noted that a considerable amount of the work on the savings system and the mortgage system had been performed at CTE's facilities in New York City and at CT's facilities in Dallas, Texas. Furthermore, although the Agreement was scheduled to terminate in a matter of days, CTE continued to perform its work at FSI.

On the evening of Friday, August 13, 1971, CTE's chief programmer removed a substantial quantity of documentation for the on-line system from FSI's facilities with the intention of bringing it to CTE's New York office on Monday, August 16, to continue his work, since he understood that there was no more test time available to CTE at FSI's facilities. Although this material may have been the property of FSI, it had always been in CTE's possession and work upon it had been performed not only at FSI's facilities, but also at the CTE facilities in New York City.

The fact that the materials were missing was first discovered by an FSI employee on Saturday morning. After being informed, Schunke attempted to reach CTE's chief programmer and the latter's superior. When such attempts failed, Schunke obtained a warrant for the arrest of the programmer. The documentation, which was in clear view at the programmer's home, was recovered and restored to FSI on Monday, August 16, 1971, on which date FSI barred CTE's employees from its premises on the grounds that CTE's actions had jeopardized FSI's business. Criminal charges against CTE's chief programmer were later dismissed for lack of probable cause.

The incident is mentioned herein because it has been blown out of all proportion by FSI and because CTE has attempted to characterize FSI's lock-out of CTE's employees on August 16, 1971 as a termination of the Agreement by FSI, entitling CTE to a termination fee under the provisions of the Agreement.

Provision for premature termination of the Agreement is found in two portions of that instrument, the first of which covers the procedure to be followed in the case of termination by either party, and the second of which establishes a schedule of termination fees to be paid in the event of termination by FSI. The pertinent portion of the Agreement, Section IV, paragraph 2, reads as follows:

2. *Early Termination*

Notwithstanding any of the provisions of the above paragraph, this Agreement may be terminated prior to expiration of its stated term under either of the following conditions:

a. By Client for any business reason upon six (6) months' written notice and payment of an early termination fee as described more fully in Attachment C to this Agreement or

b. By either party based on substantial failure to perform by the other party to this Agreement.

In the case of premature termination for substantial failure to perform under this Agreement, it is agreed that:

a. The party alleging the failure must submit the fact of the alleged failure in writing and in full detail to the other party.

b. The party whose failure is alleged must be allowed a minimum of ten (10) days after receipt of the written notice of alleged failure in which to take steps to cure the failure or otherwise satisfy the complaining party.

c. If the complaining party is not satisfied that the failure has been corrected and that performance is proceeding as promised, the complaining party must describe to the other party the extent of the failure to correct, in writing and in full detail. Assuming the uncured substantial failure in fact existed as described, termination without liability shall be effective ten (10) days after delivery of said writing.

d. Payment will be made in full for all services rendered to and including the date termination is effective, except that payment for those services in question (a through c above) shall be separately negotiated.

Additionally, Attachment C to the Agreement provides as follows:

In the event of premature termination of this Agreement by Client for any business reason except CTE's substantial failure to perform, it is agreed that:

a. The effective date of such premature termination shall be six (6) months following CTE's receipt of Client's written notice of such termination.

b. An early termination fee shall be paid to CTE by Client according to the following schedule:

If effective date of termination is within	Early termination fee shall be
1st contract year	$150,000
2nd contract year	$100,000
3rd contract year	$ 75,000
4th contract year	$ 25,000
5th contract year	NONE

c. The above early termination fees are in addition to the charges for CTE's services under this Agreement through date of termination.

It seems clear from the foregoing that CTE would be entitled to a termination fee only if the Court were to find that FSI terminated the Agreement for any business reason except CTE's substantial failure to perform; if so, the effective termination date would have been six months following CTE's receipt of FSI's notice to terminate. Attachment A has nothing to do with a termination of the Agreement for any reason by CTE; indeed it would appear that, under Section IV, paragraph 2, CTE could not have terminated the Agreement for any business reason (e.g., because it was losing money on the contract) other than FSI's substantial failure to perform.

CTE complied meticulously with the procedure to be followed by a party alleging substantial failure of the other party to perform, as mandated by Section IV, paragraph 2. Thus, as already mentioned, CTE wrote to FSI on July 2, 1971, submitting "the fact of the alleged failure [to perform—i.e., to pay the outstanding invoices] in writing and in full detail." (Section IV, ¶2a.) Pursuant to paragraph 2b, FSI was allowed a minimum of ten days after receipt of the letter of July 2, 1971 "in which to take steps to cure the failure or otherwise satisfy the complaining party." On July 14, 1971, after the ten day period had elapsed, FSI responded by charging CTE with a substantial failure to perform, indicating at the same time that such charges were not to be construed as an election on FSI's part to terminate the contract. There was no indication by FSI of any intent to cure its alleged failure to perform nor was any such intention evidenced at the meeting on August 4, 1971, at which FSI delivered what can only be described as an ultimatum. Accordingly, pursuant to paragraph 2c, CTE sent FSI a termination notice on August 11, to become effective ten days later, i.e., on August 21, 1971. Since there is no serious dispute that the unpaid $60,000 monthly payments and certain other invoices were due and owing, it can be assumed that "the uncured substantial failure in fact existed" and the provision for termination "without liability" was self-executing. No further action on the part of either party was required.

CTE has attempted to characterize FSI's actions on August 16, 1971 as a "termination" of the Agreement and as an attempt by FSI to avoid terminating for a business reason other than a substantial failure to perform, thereby escaping any liability for the termination fee and avoiding the necessity of giving six-months' notice. The Court rejects any such argument. The machinery for termination, which CTE had set in motion, had proceeded to a point where it could only have been brought to a halt, if at all, by FSI's payment of the invoices—not by FSI precipitately locking out CTE's employees. Nor was CTE damaged by the lock-out, since it was entitled to payment in advance for the services rendered in August. Although the Agreement may not have anticipated the breach in the relations between the parties, it is clear and unambiguous and CTE is as bound by its terms, as is FSI. CTE's remedy was the remedy it pursued, i.e., a lawsuit. A termination fee of $75,000, which would have been payable, if at all, six months after August 16, 1971, is not probative of the damages which CTE may have suffered by its own, or even FSI's, termination of a contract, which was concededly unprofitable insofar as CTE was concerned. Accordingly, CTE's claim for a termination fee must be rejected.

7. CTE's Claim for Post-Termination Rental and Related Costs

Section IV, paragraph 3, of the Agreement provides that, after termination of the Agreement, CTE would make available necessary data processing equipment time at CTE's standard rates in effect at that time if FSI so desired. Specifically, paragraph 3 reads as follows:

> 3. Cooperation at Termination
> At termination of this Agreement, CTE will return all Client-supplied data then under the control of CTE which CTE is then using to provide its service to Client and CTE will certify that no copies of such data have been made or retained by CTE; CTE will deliver a copy of all programs received and developed under this Agreement, and a copy of all documentation and operating instructions then being used in serving Client. If CTE-proprietary programs are furnished to Client under the terms of this Paragraph IV-3, Client agrees that such CTE-proprietary programs will be used only by Client in the performance of Client's internal data processing operations. CTE also agrees to withdraw from such space as would be necessary for Client to handle its own data processing operations. CTE will release from CTE obligations any former Client employees whom Client may wish to re-employ and who wish to accept such re-employment; CTE shall perform further transition services for Client as Client may desire, including making available necessary data pro-

cessing equipment time, at CTE's standard rates in effect at that time. Such services will continue to be available until Client can procure and install its own data processing equipment.

The parties have agreed by stipulation [reference] that equipment under lease to CT remained at FSI for certain periods of time after termination of the Agreement. This equipment included two IBM 360/40's, as well as related control units, tape drives and disk drives. All of this equipment was leased by CTE from CT, which charged CTE through inter-company bookkeeping transactions for the lease payments that CT was making to various leasing companies for use of the equipment. In its termination letter of August 11, 1971 [reference], CTE advised FSI that it would "perform further transition services for FSI as FSI may desire, including making available necessary data processing equipment time, at CTE's standard rates in effect at that time" and that such services would be available until FSI could obtain and install its own equipment. Referring again to CTE's standard rates, the letter advised that, since CTE's lease agreements required rental payments in advance, FSI would be required to pay in advance.

With certain exceptions, FSI does not contest the right of CTE to be reimbursed for those sums actually expended for rental of the equipment for the periods indicated in the stipulation. However, because the Agreement and the letter of August 11 refer to the rendition of such transition services "as FSI may desire" and since FSI did not specifically ask for the use of the equipment (in fact, it tried unsuccessfully to obtain equipment from other sources), it argues that it should be limited to payment of CTE's *actual cost,* rather than its standard rate. FSI also contends that one of the 2803 control units, admittedly on FSI's premises during the stipulated period, had not been installed by CTE prior to its departure and was not installed thereafter. It also contests a charge for freight.

FSI's contentions are unsupportable and frivolous. FSI made clear its "desire" by continuing to use CTE's equipment until the dates specified in the stipulation. Indeed, when in October 1971, CTE moved before this Court for partial summary judgment to recover the equipment or the rental therefor, FSI suc-

cessfully resisted both elements of the requested relief, Schunke having represented that, in order to continue servicing the 150 financial institutions which were its customers, the equipment would have to remain until replaced. At CTE's standard rates, the charges for the various items of equipment for the respective periods set forth in the stipulation amount to $119,143.54, which CTE is entitled to recover.

In addition, CTE claims that it suffered foreseeable damage of $32,303.25 caused by FSI's termination of the Agreement. This amount is alleged to be the actual rental cost which CTE had paid for the two IBM 360 Model CPU's after they had been released to CTE by FSI in November and December 1971 until January 1972, when CTE was first able to re-employ them. However, as has been shown, FSI did not terminate the Agreement, nor does the Agreement make provision for any such charge. Accordingly, CTE is not entitled to recover for this claim.

8. Conclusion as to Plaintiff's Claims

Insofar as the unpaid fixed monthly payments, as well as the unpaid adjustments hereinbefore discussed, are concerned it is clear that CTE substantially performed its contractual obligations and is entitled to the payments specified for such services. CTE is also entitled to reimbursement for the equipment rentals and for the terminal support which it furnished, as hereinbefore discussed. The Court reaches this conclusion recognizing that certain work was not completed within the time specified. The Court finds, however, that such failure was due primarily to the attempt by FSI to obtain services which, although they may have been contemplated by the parties, were certainly not intended to be rendered as part of the Initial Operations or within any specified time period. Additionally, there appears to have been a failure on the part of FSI to render the timely and continuing cooperation essential to the effectual rendition of services by CTE [footnote], and a lack of good faith, as evidenced by FSI's failure to agree to modifications of the Agreement which were clearly contemplated by its terms.

The essential nature of the Agreement has been repeatedly referred to herein. First, it was an agreement under which CTE could expect little, if any, profit during the initial stages but could thereafter anticipate revenue from use of the facilities in servicing CTE, in addition to FSI clients. It was therefore to the advantage of FSI to solicit additional clients by representing that it could furnish services above and beyond those specified under the Agreement and by demanding that CTE create the system to furnish those services in advance of the time contemplated.

Secondly, it was an Agreement which FSI was reluctant to change or supplement even in the case of new applications for or major changes in FSI's Initial Operations, and one which it was careful not to terminate even in the face of what it ultimately charged was a failure to perform on the part of CTE.

Finally, it was an Agreement that invited a clash of personalities growing out of the interchange of operating personnel both under the terms of the Agreement and outside of those terms, with the attendant pressure of personal ambition. Schunke recognized this when he testified that "this marriage when it was made created funny situations." [Reference.] Indeed, it was a marriage which should never have taken place. Like many marriages, it was one where great expectations were voiced at the betrothal. However, it was certainly not the expectation of both parties that all the children would be born and all the dreams of wealth or security or success achieved during the first year of the marriage. When one of the parties claimed that such should be the case, disputes arose and the parent of one of the parties was brought in to help ameliorate the situation, only to be later charged with attempting to destroy the marriage. Finally, one of the parties instituted divorce proceedings and in turn was locked out of the house. And that is about the long and short of it.

In summary, I find that the damages recoverable by CTE are as follows:

(a) Fixed monthly payments
for June, July and August 1971 $180,000.00
(b) Balance due on fixed
monthly payment for March 1970   5,000.00
(c) Volume, Cost of Living
and FICA Adjustments relating
to 1970 and due up to August 1971:

Volume	$ 19,440.00	
Cost of Living (1970)	51,336.00	
Cost of Living (1971)	52,800.00	
FICA (1970)	555.48	
FICA (1971)	370.32	
	$124,501.80	
Paid by FSI	1,858.32	122,643.48

(d) Equipment rentals relating
to Burroughs and IBM 2980
terminals   6,251.81
(e) Terminal support for Olivetti,
Burroughs and IBM 2980   13,500.00
(f) Post-termination rentals   119,143.54

Total $446,538.83

DEFENDANT'S COUNTERCLAIMS

FSI has asserted various counterclaims against CTE and against UCC, the successor by merger of CTE's parent company, CT. These seven counterclaims, also characterized as affirmative defenses, can be summarized as follows.

The first counterclaim alleges that the services under the Agreement were performed in a grossly incompetent and improper manner; that, in reliance on CTE's commitment and with CTE's knowledge and consent, FSI advised its customers of its arrangements with CTE and of the expected reprogramming that would allow them to use Burroughs and Olivetti terminals as of January 1971; and that FSI's customers leased or purchased such terminals for delivery on January 1, 1971 in reliance thereon.

It is further alleged that CTE and UCC failed to perform the programming, operations and various other functions required by the Agreement, although FSI repeatedly requested such performance. It is also alleged that CTE and UCC represented to FSI that they were losing large sums of money in the performance of the Agreement, that on numerous occasions they attempted to provoke FSI into terminating the Agreement by failing to properly perfrom and that, on August 11, 1971, CTE intentionally and wrongfully, and at the instigation of UCC, breached the Agreement by serving notice on FSI that it was terminating the Agreement. As a result, FSI alleges that it has been put to additional expense in operating its business and has lost the goodwill of its customers, and will be put to additional expense and further loss of goodwill in the future.

The second counterclaim charges interference by CTE and UCC with FSI and its customers, and by UCC with FSI and CTE. It further charges CTE and UCC with attempting to dissuade persons from entering into the employ of FSI, with attempting to persuade suppliers of defendant to stop dealing with FSI, and finally with interfering with the advantageous relationships between FSI and its suppliers, all in order to make it impossible for FSI to carry on its business.

The third counterclaim charges that FSI paid substantial sums of money to CTE and UCC during the period from March 1970 through May 1971 for programming and other services, which CTE and UCC failed to perform. FSI demands an accounting and return of the amounts paid for services not performed.

The fourth counterclaim deals with the removal by CTE's chief programmer of certain material from FSI's premises over the weekend of August 13 through 16, 1971, referred to hereinbefore.

The fifth counterclaim relates to the departure of Bird from CTE shortly after the execution of the Agreement, charges that his imminent departure was concealed from FSI by CTE, alleges that FSI would not have entered into the agreement had it known that Bird would leave CTE's employ, and that FSI has thereby suffered irreparable damage. That claim has also been discussed.

The sixth counterclaim alleges that, prior to execution of the Agreement and contrary to representations made to FSI, CTE and UCC had decided to control the operation and growth of CTE's business in the east and to reduce expenses by reducing personnel, including those familiar with FSI's operations and the services to be rendered by CTE under the Agreement, but failed to make this known to FSI in order to induce FSI to enter into the Agreement, which FSI would not have done had it known of said decision.

The seventh counterclaim alleges that, in November 1969 and thereafter, prior to the execution of the Agreement, CTE represented that the fee to be received by it from FSI would not exceed the then current cost to FSI of such services, with the exception of a provision in the Agreement whereby the annual fee could be increased up to, but not in excess, of $100,000, and that CTE represented that it intended to perform the services called for by the Agreement for the stated fee. It is further alleged that, on or about March 17, 1970 and in April and May 1970 and thereafter, CTE confirmed such intention in order to induce FSI from terminating the Agreement with CTE for fraudulent failure to disclose to FSI the departure of Bird (Fifth Counterclaim) or its intention not to continue the maintenance of CTE as a growing operation (Sixth Counterclaim). It is also alleged that CTE and UCC decided that they would not perform the services for the fee stated but that, at some future time when FSI would be unable or less able to terminate the Agreement without serious damage to its business, they would obtain a modification of the Agreement to increase the fee, or failing that, would not perform the specified services. Finally, it is alleged that FSI relied on CTE's representations and refrained from terminating the Agreement.

FSI demands judgment dismissing the complaint and recovery against CTE and UCC for both compensatory and punitive damages.

With respect to the second, fourth, and fifth counterclaims, no damages have been proven. With respect to the remaining counterclaims, FSI claims that it is entitled to damages consisting of the following:

(a) The correction of errors in the on-line savings system	$ 49,052.00
(b) The completion of the on-line savings system	93,922.00
(c) The development of an off-line savings system	49,140.00
(d) The development of a mortgage system	126,180.00
(e) Damages resulting from CTE's termination of the Agreement	121,549.00
(f) Recovery of payments made for IBM 2980 support	1,500.00
(g) Loss of revenue from lost customers	207,489.50
(h) Punitive damages	500,000.00
Total	$1,148,832.50

Before discussing whether FSI is entitled to those damages, a few matters should be noted. First, certain well established legal principles to which the Court has referred generally hereinbefore must be borne in mind. The parties are bound by the objective expression of their intent as set forth in the Agreement. The language of the contract, rather than the parties' subjective intent, controls. [Citation.] [Footnote.] A party's subjective view as to his intent or purpose is generally inadmissible to prove the legal meaning and effect of a written contract; the interpretation of such a contract is for the court to decide.

In the instant case, those principles are reinforced by the language of the contract itself. The comprehensive integration clause, i.e., Section V, paragraph 2, of the Agreement, excluding all understandings and agreements with respect to the services to be rendered, has already been referred to and quoted hereinbefore.[8] It specifically relieves the parties of any obligation which might have arisen directly or indirectly from their prior negotiations but which was not contained in their Agreement.

Thus, FSI's numerous claims for services and programming beyond the scope of the Agreement are barred. For example, FSI argued that, from the very beginning, IBM 2980 terminal support was to be part of the on-line system. However, the Agreement specifically provided that the on-line system was to be capable of initially supporting IBM 1060 terminals, and further provided a special procedure to be followed if other terminal support was provided. [Reference.] That same provision precludes FSI's claim that the new savings system was supposed to have been both an on-line system and an off-line system, with each system to serve different FSI customers. As discussed previously, the Agreement clearly specified that the system to be installed by CTE was to be on-line only. Other contentions of FSI which run counter to the clear language of the Agreement, e.g., the periods to be covered by certain adjustments, have also been discussed previously.

Over objection, and despite the Court's repeated reference at trial to the fact that the Agreement constituted the binding contract between the parties, FSI's witnesses testified extensively about negotiations that took place in November and December 1969 and the proposals that CTE made to FSI at that time, some three months before the Agreement was executed. To the extent that FSI has relied upon these negotiations and documentary background in support of its several claims, the cited provision of the Agreement bars their consideration.

This is not to say that the parties did not anticipate that services beyond those specified in the Agreement would be rendered during the five-year term of the Agreement and that there were no discussions regarding such services prior to the execution of the Agreement. However, such services were to be spelled out in subsequent separate agreements. [References.] Thus, when at FSI's request, CTE conducted tests in April and May 1970 to determine whether the Burroughs terminal was compatible with the IBM 360 CPU, it did not assume an obligation to proceed at its own expense and prepare the extensive programming necessary to permit the Burroughs terminal to be used in FSI's operation. However, Burroughs terminal support, as well as the Olivetti terminal support, was subsequently provided pursuant to a *separate price quotation and agreement* between CTE and FSI (which FSI now attempts to disavow on the ground that such support was included in the services to be rendered).

The second matter which should be kept in mind is that CTE undertook "to use its best efforts in performing the services" and such undertaking was to be *"in lieu of all other undertakings and all warranties, express, implied or statutory, as to the services or goods to be provided, including but not limited to any warranty of merchantability or fitness for use for a particular purpose."* [Reference.] (Emphasis in original.) Thus, although CTE un-

---

8. It should be emphasized that, with the possible exception of the alleged fraud regarding Bird's departure (hereinbefore discussed), this is not a case involving any fraudulent misrepresentation on the part of CTE. Were the instant action one for rescission, a claim of fraudulent misrepresentation would permit the introduction of extrinsic evidence despite the merger clause. Mere prom-

issory statements as to what will be done in the future, however, are not actionable, unless the statements are shown to have been made with a preconceived and undisclosed intention of nonperformance, in which case there would have been a misrepresentation of a material existing fact upon which an action for rescission might be predicated.

dertook to use its best efforts to perform the services specified by the Agreement or any future agreement within the specified time schedule, it did not warrant perfect or timely performance. Furthermore; FSI understood that key elements in the successful rendition of the services under "this or any later Agreement is continuing and effective cooperation and liaison between CTE and [FSI] * * * [and] the continuing need for prompt [FSI] executive decisions as required in matters relating to CTE's services." [Reference.]

Finally, it should be observed that CTE's liability is strictly limited under the terms of the Agreement. Section III, paragraph 2, of the Agreement reads as follows:

2. *Liability*

CTE shall have no strict liability in tort and shall not be liable for non-negligent, unintentional errors, or contingencies beyond its control, arising out of its performance under this Agreement. It is understood that notwithstanding the form (contract, negligence or otherwise) in which any legal or equitable action may be brought by Client against CTE, *CTE shall in no event be liable for special, consequential or exemplary damages; CTE's liability,* if any, arising out of or in any way related to its performance under this Agreement *shall be limited to general damages in an amount not to exceed the payments made by Client in the six (6) months preceding the month in which the damage or injury is alleged to have occurred or commenced* (but if this Agreement has not been in effect for six (6) months preceding such date, then six (6) times the average monthly payment in the months preceding such date). (Emphasis added.)

FSI concedes that exculpatory clauses such as this one have generally been upheld when not perceived as adversely affecting the public interest. [Citations.] However, it attempts to distinguish the instant case on the ground that CTE was a fiduciary since the Agreement provided for a complete takeover of its business operations, including the employment of much of its staff, making CTE, in effect, FSI's managing agent. Hence, FSI argues, CTE should be held to the standards of a fiduciary and not be immunized from assessment for consequential or exemplary damages relating to its willful nonperformance.

Such assertions are facetious. First, the Agreement provided for FSI's executive control over and direction regarding CTE's op-

eration and maintenance of all operational computer programs. [References.] Additionally, CTE was to develop, implement and operate the new mortgage system "under the guidance of [FSI]." [Reference.] Second, the record does not support any charge of willful non-performance on the part of CTE, although it does show that FSI willfully ceased making monthly payments to CTE to force CTE to the bargaining table. Finally, it cannot be said that the public interest was adversely affected, since there was no evidence adduced upon which the Court could find or infer that the exculpatory clause resulted from unequal bargaining power on the part of the respective parties.

Accordingly, Section III, paragraph 2, of the Agreement, relieving CTE of liability for special, consequential or exemplary damages, is valid and enforceable and FSI's general damages, if any, are limited to the amount FSI paid during the last six months preceding the month in which the damage is alleged to have occurred. [Footnote.]

We come, then, to a consideration of FSI's claims for damages.

(a) The Correction of Errors in the On-Line Savings System

FSI claims that, after "a portion of the on-line system was implemented in April 1971, a number of problems in the system were discovered in the course of its operation" and that it is therefore entitled to damages for the amount of personnel and computer time already expended and yet to be expended to correct those problems.

The Court disagrees. In the first place, it is misleading to allege that only a portion of the system was implemented in April 1971. All of FSI's on-line customers were converted to the system at that time, although others were to be added from time to time thereafter. [Reference.] By the time the Agreement was terminated, some 240,000 to 250,000 accounts— or about 50,000 more than on the prior system—were being serviced on-line.

The problems which were encountered by FSI were maintenance problems, the type of problems that FSI had worked on prior to CTE's assuming operational responsibilities, and which CTE would have corrected had FSI paid its bills and the Agreement continued. Of these problems, ten arose from April through August 1971, during most of which period CTE was handling maintenance, and only fifteen arose during the balance of 1971. A total of twenty-seven problems arose in 1972, and FSI has even included five which arose in 1973. By November 1973, however, FSI was servicing 540,000 to 550,000 accounts on the on-line savings system. Whether characterized as "consequential" damages or general damages, these claimed damages were incurred by FSI by reason of termination of the Agreement, which termination was to be "without liability" under Section IV, paragraph 2c, of the Agreement. Furthermore, after August 16, 1971, FSI was in charge of operations and no showing has been made that the problems did not arise due to negligence on the part of FSI personnel. Accordingly, this claim for damages is dismissed.

(b) The Completion of the On-Line System

FSI charges that, in October 1970, CTE suspended work on certain modifications which it felt could be implemented after conversion to the new system, and that, consequently the system as installed in April 1971 was only partially completed. Actually, in October 1970, *"[i]n the absence of any guidance from FSI,* one of three priorities [was] assigned [by CTE] to each requirement" of the savings system. [Reference.] (Emphasis added.)

While it is true that the Agreement stated that an on-line savings system was to be installed in 1970, there is evidence that FSI and CTE mutually agreed on the April 1971 installation date, and FSI accepted installation on that date. Nor is there evidence to support a claim that "time was of the essence," i.e., that performance in 1970 was a specific condition of FSI's duty to make payment under the Agreement. The Agreement recognizes that CTE's obligations to conform to any implementation schedule depended on FSI's timely and continuing cooperation. [Reference.] The establishment of new priorities by FSI was contemplated. [Reference.] The delay in delivery resulted both from failure of the parties to define the characteristics of the new system and from the heavy operational requirements at FSI in January and February of 1971, which FSI did not want interrupted. Indeed, FSI had

wanted to delay installation beyond April to permit further testing.

Additionally, while Schunke may have told his customers in sales pitches of the "expected reprogramming that would allow them to use Burroughs and Olivetti terminals as of January 1971" [reference], the fact is that the Agreement makes no specific mention of such terminals.

FSI also complains of, and attributes the delay in performance in part to, CTE's delay in contracting for the purchase of the FDS system. Such contract was signed on the same date as FSI signed the Agreement. Why CTE should have committed itself to such a purchase in advance of entering a binding agreement has never been explained.

FSI also makes reference to a memorandum dated May 3, 1971 sent by CTE to FSI listing "Outstanding enhancements to on-line system" [reference] and alleges that, at the time the Agreement was terminated, most of the items had not been completed. Whether or not most of the items were completed, it is clear that most were *new* enhancements requested by FSI, which lends further support to the conclusion that much of the delay was attributable to the continuing demands by FSI for enhancements to the system.

Finally, it is not disputed that during the months of June, July and August, FSI deliberately withheld any payments for the enhancements requested.

Accordingly, whether considered as general or consequential damages, the claim for failure to complete the on-line savings system is dismissed.

(c) The Development of an Off-Line Savings System

FSI's damages are also based on CTE's failure to reprogram an off-line savings system. As has already been shown, CTE had no obligation under the Agreement to furnish such a system as part of the Initial Operations. Accordingly, whether considered as general or consequential damages, this claim is dismissed.

(d) The Development of a New Mortgage System

FSI also claims as damages the cost of developing a new mortgage system. The Court has already discussed CTE's obligation to provide a new mortgage system for System 360 during 1970, "under the guidance of [FSI]." [Reference.] For reasons already stated regarding the failure to complete the on-line savings system in 1970, time was also not of the essence in connection with the mortgage system, and even if it had been a condition of performance, timely performance was waived by FSI.

FSI's primary concern was with the on-line savings system. It was satisfied with its present mortgage system except that it wanted to increase its ability to bill and expand; indeed, the parties ultimately agreed to use the present system as the basis for the new system. By July 1971, CTE had completed the daily processing portion of the mortgage system and had successfully parallel tested it with the old system. By mid-August, the parties contemplated a mid-September 1971 installation date, with a further 30- to 60-day test period. However, owing to the termination of the Agreement, the system was not installed.

The only "evidence" offered by FSI to support its claim was a mortgage system development cost estimate made by an FSI employee. In view of the substantial work that had already been done on the system, proof of the cost of a *new* system as a measure of damages is completely irrelevant. Moreover, there is no evidence that the system for which the cost estimate was made was the system to which FSI and CTE had agreed. Finally, the record shows that no attempt was made by FSI to obtain a new mortgage system from other sources after termination of the Agreement. Indeed, FSI did not get around to analyzing the portions of the new mortgage system until 1972.

As in the case of the savings system, FSI is again proceeding on the assumption that CTE breached the Agreement, and that the damages claimed flow from that breach. However, as has been shown, CTE terminated the Agreement in the manner provided therein and, therefore, such termination was "without liability." Accordingly, whether characterized as general or consequential damages, the claim must be dismissed.

(e) Damages Resulting from CTE's Termination of the Agreement

FSI contends that CTE wrongfully terminated the Agreement on the basis of ground-less or erroneous invoices. Accordingly, FSI claims damages in the sum of $121,549, representing the projected difference between what FSI would have paid CTE throughout the remaining 3⅓ years of the contract and what it would cost FSI to perform all the functions that CTE would have performed under the Agreement (excluding the cost attributable to new systems development during this same period). As the Court has already indicated, the unpaid invoices were neither baseless nor substantially erroneous. Accordingly, FSI's demand for consequential damages is not only contrary to the terms of the Agreement, but also unsupported by the record and therefore is dismissed.

(f) Recovery of Payments Made for IBM 2980 Support

The Court has already discussed the purchase by CTE of terminal support for terminals other than the 1060 terminal required under the Agreement. There is no question that FSI agreed to pay $3,500, which represented only one-half of CTE's cost in obtaining such support from FDS. In light of the Agreement, CTE could have charged FSI for the full amount. Despite this, FSI paid CTE only $1,500 and now sues to recover that amount. The claim is dismissed without further comment.

(g) Loss of Revenue from Lost Customers

FSI alleges that it lost a number of its customers because of CTE's failure to perform under the Agreement. FSI has arrived, by stipulation, at a figure of $207,489.50 as the anticipated lost revenues which it is entitled to receive from CTE. [Reference.]

In the first place, this is clearly a claim for consequential damages and barred by the Agreement. In the second place, as has been shown, FSI did not lose customers while CTE operated the premises but only began to lose them seven or eight months thereafter. Moreover, the customers' departure is not attributable to CTE's nonperformance. The claim is accordingly dismissed.

(h) Punitive Damages

FSI seeks punitive damages in the sum of $500,000 based on the alleged wrongful removal of certain material from the FSI premises over the weekend of August 14-16, 1971 and CTE's alleged intentional nonperformance under the Agreement. Exemplary damages are not chargeable under the Agreement. [Reference.] In any event, there has not been a sufficient showing to justify such an award either under the law of New Jersey or of New York. This claim also is dismissed.

CONCLUSION

Judgment is accordingly awarded to plaintiff CTE against FSI in the sum of $446,538.83. Defendant FSI's counterclaims against CTE and CT are dismissed as is CT's counterclaim against FSI. Submit judgment on ten (10) days notice.

So ordered.

PROFESSIONAL COMPUTER MANAGEMENT, INC. v. TAMPA WHOLESALE LIQUOR CO., INC.

374 So.2d 626

(District Court of Appeal of Florida, Second District, Aug. 15, 1979.)

HOBSON, J.

Professional Computer Management, Inc. (PCM) appeals from a final judgment entered on a directed verdict in a jury trial and also from a final cost judgment.

PCM contends that the trial court erred in directing a verdict for appellee Tampa Wholesale Liquor Co. (TWL) when the evidence raised factual questions which should have been submitted to the jury. We agree with appellant's argument and reverse the final judgment in favor of TWL.

In March, 1971, the parties entered into a five-year service contract whereby PCM was to provide various accounting services to TWL. The information was generated from documents prepared by TWL employees.[1] The TWL account occupied a major portion of PCM's service capacity and indeed TWL provided leased office space on its premises for PCM's operation.

The contract provided that after the five-year term ending January 31, 1976, either party could terminate by written notice between 90 and 120 days before the end of the term. If neither party gave termination notice, the contract renewed itself for successive one-year periods until terminated. The contract further provided that in the event of termination by TWL, other than for nonperformance by PCM, TWL would pay $3,000 per month remaining in the term.

An additional paragraph stated that the contract could be terminated by either party "for failure of the other to comply with any of its terms, including failure to perform by PCM, which TWL deems unwarranted." In that event the terminating party "shall have no further liability to the other party to make payment hereunder * * * [or] to perform the services required hereunder. * * *"

Over the period of the contract, which was renewed for one-year terms in February 1976 and February 1977, the volume of business handled by PCM on behalf of TWL increased substantially. In April, 1975, TWL requested that PCM acquire a second IBM computer that could be made available to TWL's staff for data processing, independent of the services being performed by PCM under the contract. PCM leased a second computer and billed TWL for one-half of the rental price from July 1975 until contract termination in 1977. TWL regularly paid $750 per month.

Subsequently, increased business needs from TWL and other clients resulted in PCM's need for a larger, more sophisticated computer, which was scheduled for delivery in March 1977 from Sperry Univac. In November, 1976, TWL began negotiations with Sperry Univac and eventually placed an order for a large computer in January, 1977. This computer was identical to the one ordered by PCM. Consequently, PCM cancelled its order with Sperry Univac for the new computer and terminated its lease on the second IBM computer at a cost of $7,117.24.

In March, 1977, PCM entered into an agreement with TWL to continue renting office space and to rent computer time on TWL's

---

1. TWL employees filled out order forms each day showing the exact quantity of each product sold. PCM used these figures to make up "picking lists." These lists were to be prepared by 8 p.m. each evening so that TWL trucks could be loaded for the next day deliveries. In addition, PCM provided accounts receivable, weekly "House Sales" reports which included salesmen's commissions and discounts.

new computer during the evening hours. During this time, TWL found it necessary to run certain tests on its new computer which required the use of key-punch cards previously prepared by PCM. TWL requested the use of these cards and PCM later billed TWL $1,760.64. TWL declined to pay this bill, claiming that the key-punch cards were to be scrapped by PCM in any event and that TWL had already paid for all of the key-punching. PCM claimed that there was an agreement for payment, an allegation denied by TWL.

On May 11, 1977, TWL informed PCM that the service contract would be terminated effective May 26, 1977 "under the provisions of paragraph X of the Agreement for the failure to perform by PCM which Tampa Wholesale Liquor Co., Inc., deems unwarranted."

PCM filed a complaint alleging that TWL had terminated the contract outside the notice period and without cause, thus becoming liable for liquidated damages. PCM further alleged that TWL was in breach of its agreement to pay half the lease cost of the second IBM computer installed at TWL's request. PCM also claimed the unpaid bill of $1,760.64 for the key-punch cards used to test TWL's new computer. The complaint further prayed for injunctive relief to restrain TWL from evicting PCM from its rented office space.

At the jury trial, PCM presented evidence showing that over a period of six years only six to eight errors had been shown which could be traced to PCM employees.[2] Many of the errors or late reports were attributable to TWL employees who either entered incorrect numbers on the handwritten documents or did not deliver the documents to PCM in time for the information to be processed. The record shows that the conversion of information from TWL's manually prepared forms to punch cards over a period of six years exceeded six million key strokes.

TWL's vice president of operations was called by PCM as an adverse witness and testified that PCM's services had been unsatisfactory from the beginning. When asked to identify any specific defaults by PCM in its contract obligations over the period of the con-

tract, he furnished a compilation of eight occasions between January 1st and March 31st, 1977, when PCM had provided a report later than it should have. (One of the incidents involved a report that was eight minutes late.) He admitted that it was possible that the problem was the result of errors committed by TWL employees.

PCM entered into evidence a letter from the president of TWL dated September 5, 1974 and addressed to a business firm considering the use of PCM's computer services. TWL's president stated in the letter that his association with PCM had been "extremely satisfactory." He reported that under the PCM service contract "our data processing costs have been reduced by 30% and more important, our level of efficiency has greatly increased * * * through PCM's in-depth involvement with Tampa Wholesale Liquor and their accessibility as an onsite system. They have from the onset remained trustworthy, reliable, and very responsive to our every request."

At the close of PCM's case, TWL moved for a directed verdict. The trial court granted the directed verdict and entered a final judgment in favor of TWL. The court further awarded costs of $755.48 to TWL. PCM questions the propriety of this award.

In view of the fact that this case comes to us on a judgment from a directed verdict rendered at the close of appellant's case, we must view the evidence in a light most favorable to appellant. * * *

It is clear that there were factual questions in this case which should have gone to the jury. Testimony showed that although there were mistakes made in PCM's reports to TWL, the number of errors was small compared to the millions of separate computer items processed. The problems were often attributable to TWL's employees who either submitted their reports late or entered illegible figures. A jury should determine whether or not PCM breached the contract by failure to perform and if there was a failure to perform, was it reasonably deemed unwarranted by TWL.

Moreover, the question of the agreement to split the rental cost of the second IBM com-

---

2. PCM's key-punch supervisor testified that she maintained a file of invoices on which errors had been called to her attention by TWL. After a period of six years the file contained reports of four key-punch errors. The su-

pervisor noted that she always requested TWL to send her copies of invoices on which errors appeared in order to verify them, but in most instances TWL did not respond.

puter must be considered. PCM presented uncontradicted testimony that the agreement was made between the parties and that for two years, TWL paid half the rental cost. This question should have been presented to the jury for a factual determination as should the issue of the key punch cards.

* * *

For the reasons stated, we hereby reverse the final judgment entered in favor of Tampa Wholesale Liquor, Inc. and the cost judgment and remand this cause for a new trial.

F. & M. SCHAEFER CORP. v. ELECTRONIC DATA SYSTEMS CORP.

430 F. Supp. 988

(United States District Court, S. D. New York, March 28, 1977.)

MOTLEY, D. J.

FINDINGS OF FACT AND CONCLUSIONS OF LAW

On September 7, 1976 the F. & M. Schaefer Corporation (Schaefer) filed this action against Electronic Data Systems Corporation (EDS) alleging breach of contract and a cause of action for rescission of another contract based on EDS' alleged fraudulent misrepresentations. Schaefer prays for $45 million compensatory damages plus punitive damages. EDS answered the complaint on November 11, 1976 and asserted numerous counterclaims against Schaefer. [Footnote.]

On this same day, EDS filed its motion for replevin of Schaefer's data processing system alleging that it had previously developed this system and had turned the system over to Schaefer in stages during 1975 and 1976 pursuant to agreement. Schaefer filed a reply to the motion for replevin on November 15, 1976.

* * *

In 1969 EDS and Schaefer entered into a contract for the development and supply of data processing services. The term of the contract was seven years. Under Phase 1 of this agreement, which was to end in 1972, Schaefer turned over its old data processing system, and while EDS ran this old card system for

Schaefer, EDS developed a more sophisticated, more modern and much faster tape system to meet Schaefer's data processing needs. Under Phase 2 of the contract EDS was to run the newly developed system for Schaefer until May of 1976.

Phase 1 was essentially completed by the end of 1972, but by this time Schaefer was in severe financial difficulty and requested EDS to defer certain required payments for two years, approximately $1,507,000 in development costs and approximately $35,000 in monthly service charges. The result was a new 1973 agreement governing Phase 2 which (although not explicitly) superseded the 1969 agreement.

Under the 1973 contract the following changes, in essence, were made:

1. The original term of the contract would be extended for one and one-half years until the end of December, 1977, as opposed to May, 1976, the original termination date under the 1969 contract.

2. Monthly payments under the 1969 contract were reduced for 1973 and 1974, and these deferred charges were to be recovered by increased monthly payments in 1975 through 1977.

3. Services performed by EDS were to be reduced.

Under the 1973 contract Schaefer could cancel the contract, which by that time was for the running of the data processing system by EDS, and elect to operate its data processing system prior to the December 1977 termination date.

In order to terminate, two conditions had to be met: First, Schaefer had to pay a cancellation fee which was, in essence, the balance of all the deferred payments which otherwise would have been paid in monthly instalments to December, 1977. Second, Schaefer and EDS had to enter into a termination agreement concerning Schaefer's use of the system developed by EDS.

In its main suit Schaefer claims that EDS did not adhere to the contract, and that the system which EDS developed was faulty and caused great damage to Schaefer. Schaefer also claims that EDS fraudulently induced Schaefer to enter into the 1973 agreement. Schaefer seeks rescission of this agreement.

The court finds that Schaefer did turn over its old system to EDS around 1969. During

Phase 1 of the 1969 contract, EDS did develop another system which was different from the one turned over by Schaefer.

Around 1974 Schaefer expressed an interest in cancelling the 1973 agreement and running its own data processing system. In 1975, in accordance with Task Order C of the 1973 contract, EDS did, in fact, begin turning over the new system to Schaefer. The turnover was accomplished in stages so that no continuity would be lost in Schaefer's data processing needs and so that the EDS personnel would have time to train Schaefer's personnel in the operation of the new system. In addition, EDS compiled additional documentation in 1976 which Schaefer had requested.

The turnover was completed in August, 1976. No company other than Schaefer and EDS was responsible for any portion of Schaefer's data processing system. [Footnote.]

During the period of time during which EDS was turning the system over to Schaefer, its agents met with Schaefer's agents. Throughout the course of the several meetings Schaefer's agents asserted on numerous occasions that Schaefer fully intended to pay the cancellation fee of $1,200,933.68 which Schaefer was obligated to pay as a condition of early cancellation under Task Order C and a sliding buy-out schedule which had been agreed upon by the parties, and any monthly charges due.

The court finds that EDS would not have turned over its system if it did not fully expect the payment of the amount of approximately $1,300,000. The court further finds that by early 1976 Schaefer had no intention of paying this cancellation fee, although officers of Schaefer did assure EDS to the contrary. Schaefer's intention was to receive from EDS all necessary materials and instructions for the system and to have its own newly trained personnel run the system and then institute suit against EDS.

In support of its motion for replevin, EDS says that it has a superior possessory right to the system under the 1973 contract because that contract imposed two conditions on Schaefer for early turnover of the system. Schaefer has met neither of these conditions.

First, the court finds that Schaefer has not met the condition that it pay a cancellation fee of approximately $1,300,000 to EDS.

Second, the court finds that Schaefer did not enter into, nor was it willing to enter into the termination agreement specified under paragraph 6 of the 1973 contract regarding confidentiality.

The court, therefore, finds that EDS has made out a *prima facie* case for replevin.

Under *Fuentes v. Shevin*, 407 U.S. 67, 92 S.Ct. 1983, 32 L.Ed.2d 556 (1972), this court is obligated to provide Schaefer with a full and fair hearing before granting EDS's replevin motion. One aspect of this is that Schaefer is entitled to present any good faith defense to the claim of EDS that it has a superior possessory right to the system. We now turn to Schaefer's defenses.

Schaefer claims that the system which EDS turned over to it in 1976 was the same system which Schaefer turned over to EDS in 1969. If EDS did, indeed, turn over the very same system which it had received from Schaefer in 1969, Schaefer would have a good defense to the replevin action.

The court finds from the evidence adduced upon the hearing of the motion for replevin that this is not a good faith defense. The testimony of Schaefer's own personnel leads to the inescapable conclusion that the EDS system is substantially different from Schaefer's old system. Schaefer's own employee, Kenneth Koleman, qualified by Schaefer as an expert, pointed out that the EDS system was a tape system, while the old Schaefer system was a card operated system. From Koleman's description of both systems, the court finds that the tape system developed by EDS is a faster system; that Schaefer's old card system is now obsolete and is not capable of being operated on today's computers without substantial adaptations. The EDS system, the court finds, is a more sophisticated system, in that it uses the language of present day computers as opposed to the language employed with the card system.

Even if the EDS system is no improvement over the old Schaefer system in terms of ultimate reliability and accuracy; even if the EDS system was not worth the millions that Schaefer paid for it; even if the EDS system is peppered with errors (determinations which the court finds unnecessary to reach at this time), the fact remains that the EDS system is not the same one which Schaefer had given to EDS in 1969 and that the EDS system is different in that it is more sophisticated, more modern and faster.

Schaefer says that a defense to EDS's claim for approximately $1,300,000 cancellation fee is that the EDS system was faulty, costing Schaefer over forty-five million dollars in damages. Therefore, Schaefer argues, the $1.3 million claim is more than offset by Schaefer's claims on the merits. This being true, Schaefer continues, the replevin action should be tried in conjunction with the main case, presumably many months from now when discovery in the main action has been completed.

EDS found a Southern District case which reads:

> Even taking defendants' allegations of poor equipment performance as true, defendant fails to state a valid defense to a replevin claim where, as here, performance was not a condition of payment. *Honeywell Information System, Inc. v. Demographic Systems, Inc.*, 396 F.Supp. 273, 275 (1975).

In the instant case adequate performance of the EDS data processing system was not a condition precedent either to the payment of the cancellation fee or the turnover agreement specified in paragraph 6 of the 1973 agreement.

The only case cited by Schaefer which allegedly offers support for its claim that the poor performance of the system is a defense to replevin, supports just the opposite position. *Computer Leasing Company v. Computer and Software, Inc.*, 37 Ohio Misc. 19, 306 N.E.2d 191, 194 (Ohio Ct. of Com.Pleas 1973).

Another defense—and a more weighty one—is that the 1973 contract (under which EDS claims its superior possessory right) was entered into by Schaefer on the basis of fraudulent misrepresentations by EDS, and that the 1973 contract should be rescinded. It would appear initially that if, *arguendo*, the 1973 contract were rescinded due to misrepresentations by EDS, EDS' replevin action would fall, but on further examination this is not the case. Even if the 1973 contract were rescinded, EDS would still have a valid basis for its replevin claim under the 1969 contract, since the deferred payments were due under that contract.

The 1973 contract superseded the 1969 contract by necessary implication, although there is no explicit supersession clause in the 1973 contract. Therefore, if the 1973 contract were

to be rescinded, the parties' relations would then be governed by the 1969 agreement, which had never been formally abrogated. [Citation.]

Under the 1969 agreement the system was to be turned over to Schaefer on the contract's termination in April of 1976. But even if we assume that the 1969 contract is now in effect, the fact remains that Schaefer has not paid the approximately $1.3 million under that very contract. The question, therefore, is whether, although the 1969 contract calls for the transfer of the system to Schaefer in 1976, EDS is obligated to turn over the system when Schaefer owes it approximately $1,300,000.

Under paragraph 2 of the "Ownership, Conversion and Future Operation" section of the 1969 agreement, EDS was required, upon receipt of 12 months' notice of Schaefer's desire to operate its own data processing system, to notify Schaefer of its charge to convert to the computer system selected by Schaefer. In consideration of such charge, EDS was obliged to accomplish such conversion as may be necessary.

Under this paragraph a condition precedent to EDS' turnover of the system is obtainment of a conversion charge from Schaefer. Surely if Schaefer were to be $1.3 million in arrears on its monthly payments at the time that Schaefer wanted to get possession of the system, EDS would be entitled to demand its money before turning over the system. Furthermore, under the default clause of the 1969 contract, EDS could have terminated the agreement if Schaefer had failed to remit the approximately $1.3 million which it owed.

In sum, the court finds that the 1969 contract contains an implied condition precedent that requires Schaefer to pay all monthly charges before it would be entitled to get the system at the termination of the agreement. Thus, even if, *arguendo*, the 1973 contract is deemed rescinded, EDS would still be entitled to possession of the system under the 1969 agreement.

As a further defense, Schaefer claims that the tape reels and notebooks containing instructions and all copies of same are the property of Schaefer, since Schaefer paid for the blank tapes and blank paper and notebook bindings. The court deems this defense frivolous in this action for replevin, even if Schaefer's contentions are true.

Schaefer argues that the system developed by EDS is a body of intangibles, that is, concepts or ideas, and consists wholly of services rendered by EDS. Likening the system to a recorded song for which Schaefer supplied a blank disc, Schaefer says that just as a song cannot be replevied, so software in a data processing system cannot be made the subject of replevin.

The court finds this argument unpersuasive, especially since Schaefer has offered no case under New York law or any other law which holds that a data processing system, being wholly services or intangibles, cannot be made the subject of replevin. This system, the court finds, is quite tangible. [Footnote.]

In addition to tapes, it consists of numerous instructions in notebooks and other documentation, some of which had been physically produced by Schaefer in the courtroom during the course of this hearing. These tapes, notebooks of instructions and other documentation were delivered by EDS to Schaefer during 1975–1976. There may be intangible parts of the system, consisting of the training given Schaefer's employees in how to operate the system, for example, but those intangible parts of the system, if they are part of it at all, are not a part of this motion for replevin. What EDS seeks are the tapes, the instructions, all supporting documentation *and all copies of same.*

EDS having proved a superior possessory interest and Schaefer having failed to offer any good faith defense to a motion for replevin, the motion must be granted.

EDS has also asked for preliminary injunctive relief restraining Schaefer from divulging the system or permitting its use by others. Before the conclusion of the hearing on this motion the parties entered into a stipulation as to confidentiality. There is, therefore, no need for an injunction with respect to confidentiality.

However, in view of the request for equitable relief by EDS, the court is empowered to grant alternative relief to EDS with respect to the system. Under Rule 54(c), Fed.R.Civ.P., a federal court has the power to grant appropriate relief to the winning party even if not demanded in the pleadings. *United States v.*

Maryland Casualty Co., 384 F.2d 303 (2d Cir. 1967); *Lewis v. Dansker*, 68 F.R.D. 184 (S.D.N.Y.1974). The scope and form of the injunction should suit the circumstances of the case and the needs of the public interest. *Bowles v. Leithold*, 60 F.Supp. 909 (E.D.Pa.1945), *aff'd*, 155 F.2d 124 (3d Cir. 1945).

Accordingly, alternatively, Schaefer will be enjoined from using the system unless, pending the outcome of the trial on the merits, it pays EDS the approximate amount of $1,300,000 due it, secured by a bond from EDS to Schaefer for twice that amount to cover any offset or costs to which Schaefer might be entitled. EDS may choose which relief—either replevin or the injunction—it prefers.

* * *

AMENDED FINDINGS OF FACT AND CONCLUSIONS OF LAW

On March 16, 1977 the court made oral Findings of Fact and Conclusions of Law which were formalized in a written opinion filed on March 28, 1977. Upon submission of the parties' proposed order and counter-order, the court has reconsidered the relief which should be granted and hereby amends its prior opinion as follows:

The court will grant the motion for replevin and enter judgment pursuant to Rule 54(b), Fed.R.Civ.P., there being no just reason for delay in the entry thereof, but the same will be stayed under Rule 62(h), Fed.R.Civ.P., on condition that Schaefer pay to EDS $1.3 million, in which event EDS shall post a bond for $2.6 million, all pending final disposition of the action.

SANITARY LINEN SERVICE CO. v. ALEXANDER PROUDFOOT CO.

304 F. Supp. 339, 2 CLSR 225
(United States District Court, S.D. Florida, Miami Division, May 12, 1969.)

ATKINS, D. J.

The plaintiff, Sanitary Linen Service Co. (hereinafter Sanitary), seeks damages in excess of $1,000,000 for breach of contract and express warranty by the defendant, Alexander Proudfoot Company (hereinafter Proudfoot). Proudfoot denies any warranty and asserts Sanitary failed to cooperate and waived any breach by paying Proudfoot after knowledge of the claimed breach. The case was tried without a jury and the Court makes findings of fact and conclusions as set forth in this memorandum.

* * *

Sanitary rents and processes linen to industry and operates a commercial laundry. Besides the Miami plant, Sanitary also operates subsidiary plants in Orlando and Pensacola which were likewise the subject of the contract between the parties.

Proudfoot sells and installs a scheduling system designed to determine work predictability and thereby recover lost time with consequent savings in payroll.

THE AGREEMENT BETWEEN THE PARTIES

After a "no-obligation" survey and analysis[1] of the operations, Proudfoot made a written offer to install a scheduling program at Sanitary's three plants. This proposal, dated March 12, 1964, is Sanitary's Exhibit 4. After a three to four hour discussion between the parties, Sanitary accepted the proposal. The reciprocal obligations of Sanitary and Proudfoot were as follows:

1. Proudfoot agreed to introduce into Sanitary's operations a "worthwhile installation of schedule and method improvements designed to provide greater control over utilization of man and machine hours and to effect operating economies."

2. Sanitary agreed to give its "full cooperation during the course of the program" to assure maximum results.

3. Sanitary also was required to use the full influence of its authority with its personnel "for the successful consummation" of the program.

Proudfoot's undertaking is also reflected in part by the following excerpt from its proposal of March 12, 1964:

Payroll savings during the first year following completion of our installation are estimated to be $246,600.00.[2] Please note that we are not attempting to evaluate in dollars such benefits as improved management controls, volume forecasting, better customer service and other advantages that will accrue.

In the application of our program, we will require the services of one or more members of our staff for a period of ninety-four (94) man weeks at Eight Hundred ($800.00) Dollars per man week net, payable weekly as invoiced.

Should you elect to proceed with this program in phases, a breakdown of savings and man weeks will be as follows:

	Savings	Man-Weeks
Phase A		
Miami	$149,400.00	63
Phase B		
Orlando and		
Pensacola	97,200.00	40.

Sanitary also contends Proudfoot estimated that at about midway through the program—when 50% of the program had been completed—the effected savings would be more than the cash outlay.

It is undisputed that Sanitary paid Proudfoot a total of $74,200 billed over a period of some six months.

Proudfoot sent its operations staff to Florida immediately after the agreement was consummated. Nelson Sidell was installation manager. William Lamdin and John Bagens served as staff members. Chief of the operation was Norman Cabral. When about half of the projected ninety-four weeks had expired, B. B. Goldstein, President of Sanitary, became concerned because he believed no benefits had been received. Proudfoot's own schedule provided that thirty-two employees were to have been eliminated by May 22. [Reference.] Sidell assured him savings were there to be obtained but "just farther away" and that very shortly they would recommend that twenty-six employees in the production department

---

1. Proudfoot presented a list, styled "what we find," of 17 separate deficiencies in Sanitary's operations. [Reference.] William Lamdin, one of the members of the analysis team, testified that he saw a document on March 2 in Miami, the day before he began work on the analysis, which has the same "points" on it except for the reference to "routemen." Lamdin said that he was told by Carlton

West, Chief of the analysis team, to copy this document "by hand so that I'd know what they were looking for during the analysis."

2. While this figure would appear to be based on some exact computation resulting from the survey, the very day the analysis started on March 2, Proudfoot had this sum fixed as its goal. [Reference.]

be released. This was done at the Miami plant the week ending June 5 after a conference with the plant superintendent who selected those to be discharged.

When the layoff was made at Miami Sidell admits that Proudfoot wasn't ready with a "schedule plan." "Reasonable expectancy" (a given worker in a given job), the other element Sidell testified was necessary for success of a Proudfoot installation, was prepared. Forms were also developed for Sanitary's use. But without a schedule plan the program could not be made viable. Lamdin testified Proudfoot was never able to develop an over-all schedule plan that would develop a continuous flow and eliminate lost time. Bagens' testimony is to the same effect. A week after the layoff it was necessary to operate the plant longer hours to get the work out. Employee complaints followed. To remedy the problem, 26 workers had to be re-hired, with Proudfoot's approval, beginning four to six weeks after their discharge.

A similar experience occurred in Orlando. Proudfoot recommended that six positions be eliminated at Orlando in the production department. After they were released, three were restored with Proudfoot's approval. The total to be discharged at the Orlando plant was twenty-four.

Two of Proudfoot's staff (Lamdin and Bagens) assigned to the Sanitary program had had no prior experience in scheduling. This was their first employment by Proudfoot. Nelson Sidell, the installation manager on the Sanitary job, was discharged by Proudfoot in July.

No other "installations" were attempted.

SANITARY GAVE FULL COOPERATION

Proudfoot urges that Sanitary's failure to cooperate was the proximate cause of any failure to install a feasible plan. The evidence preponderates to the contrary.

As early as March 13, 1964, Sanitary scheduled a meeting of key personnel at the Miami plant to introduce the Proudfoot team and to inform its personnel of their purpose and to recommend that the Sanitary "people assist openly and willingly." Mr. S. Kruse, the Executive Vice President of Sanitary, telephoned each of the other plant managers and explained "our project, our presence, and our purpose." Introductions were made at the Orlando and Pensacola locations. Memoranda were placed on the bulletin boards in both English and Spanish so that everyone in the organizations would be aware of the program. [Reference.]

Sanitary hired coordinators and scheduling clerks at Proudfoot's request at a cost of $15,000.00.

Two Miami plant managers were fired and replacements hired at the suggestion of Proudfoot. Numerous meetings with the supervisors were held to accomplish cooperation and to iron out any difficulties.

There were some problems with lower echelon employees. Supervisors were slow in turning in "action needed" reports. But when fluctuations in cooperation occurred Proudfoot went to the next level of command and "got firm, positive action," as described by Sidell.

Proudfoot maintained a weekly "client contact Record and Fever Charts" which reflected the attitude of key personnel. [Reference.] These varied somewhat but in the main they reflected the symbol "G" for "Good."

Proudfoot contends that Sanitary cannot recover because it continued to pay the amounts billed when it knew no savings were being effected. This would have the anomalous effect of denying relief to one who had performed his contract in good faith reliance upon the other party's promise to perform. Proudfoot simply had not produced the expected savings. This in no way can be said to be a breach. Without a breach by Proudfoot, Sanitary was obligated to continue its payments. As noted above Mr. Sidell assured Mr. Goldstein that savings were forthcoming, thus relieving the latter's concern over Proudfoot's failure to produce any savings. Sanitary had no indication that Proudfoot would breach the contract since at all times Proudfoot's employees remained on the job.

DAMAGES RECOVERABLE

The one remaining question is the measure of damages to which Sanitary is entitled. Sanitary contends it is entitled to $246,600 for each of the years subsequent to September,

1964 because this amount was guaranteed or warranted. By implication, Sanitary urges that at the expiration of each year hereafter it would be entitled to file an action for and recover $246,600. At best such savings were only an estimate if a workable schedule plan had been conceived. Other benefits were also suggested in the proposal letter.

Even had such a plan been developed, the elements incident to such savings involved so many variable, unpredictable factors that it would be conjectural to determine them in advance. Nevertheless, Sanitary was at least entitled to have a workable program presented to it for installation. Sanitary has in no way alleged or proved that it has been damaged by entering into this contract with Proudfoot. Sanitary is in no worse position now than it was when Proudfoot first contacted Sanitary except for the sum paid Proudfoot. In fact, the evidence indicates that Sanitary has received some slight benefits from Proudfoot's activities, although none of them can be evaluated by monetary savings. Therefore not having received what it bargained for, Sanitary should be made whole and thus receive the sum paid to Proudfoot, viz., $74,200.

In essence what Proudfoot agreed to furnish was services. There can be no warranty for proposed services unless such was clearly stated and assumed by the warrantor. I find no such statement and assumption on the part of Proudfoot. [Citations.] Warranties deal with facts. Although obviously the suggested savings were intended as an inducement, potential savings are not facts to which a warranty may attach but are merely estimates with uncertain reliability. [Citation.] Likewise, where services are involved, there is no implied warranty of fitness or merchantability. [Citation.]

The Court makes the following findings of fact in supplement to those above:

    A. Proudfoot did not "guarantee" or "warrant" to Sanitary that payroll savings of $246,600 would accrue "during the first year following the completion of our installation."
    B. The figure of $246,600 was an estimate only.
    C. The agreement between the parties contained no provision that by the time one-half of the total fee of $74,200 had been paid by Sanitary, one-half of the estimated savings would be realized.

CONCLUSIONS OF LAW

1. The Court has jurisdiction of the subject matter and the parties.
2. The plaintiff is entitled to recover from the defendant the sum paid, viz., $74,200 plus interest from September 15, 1964 at the statutory rate.
3. Costs will hereafter be awarded as the Court will determine after notice and application.
4. The plaintiff will submit a proposed form of judgment within ten days from date.

SANITARY LINEN SERVICE CO. v. ALEXANDER PROUDFOOT CO.

435 F.2d 292, 2 CLSR 231
(United States Court of Appeals, Fifth Circuit, Nov. 19, 1970.)

BELL, C. J.

This appeal involves a diversity suit having a contractual basis. The district court ruled for the plaintiff on a failure of consideration and restitution theory although not specifically so denominated. 2 CLSR 225. We affirm on the appeal of defendant. The district court denied plaintiff additional damages and a cross-appeal was taken on this ruling. We also affirm on the cross-appeal.

Defendant Proudfoot is an Illinois corporation which devises and installs systems to increase plant efficiency through what is sometimes known in the business world as short interval scheduling. Plaintiff Sanitary operates a commercial laundry service in Miami, Orlando, and Pensacola, Florida. After a two week analysis of Sanitary's operations, a contract was entered into between the parties on March 12, 1964. During a three or four hour meeting between representatives of each, written letter proposal was discussed as well as two other documents entitled "What We Find" and "What We Propose." Following this discussion, Sanitary accepted Proudfoot's proposal and work was to commence on the following day.

The district court made specific findings with reference to the terms of the contract. These are sustained by the record. Proudfoot was to supply a "worthwhile installation of schedule and method improvements designed to provide greater control over utilization of man and machine hours and to effect operating economies." The purpose of the schedule or system, according to Proudfoot's negotiator, was to ferret out and recover lost time in all phases of production, delivery and office work in Sanitary's operations. The benefit would accrue to Sanitary in the form of reduced man-power thus resulting in payroll savings. Sanitary was to use the full influence of management to insure complete cooperation from all employees during the installation of the program. It was also to pay for the service at the rate of $800.00 per man week for 94 man weeks.

Proudfoot immediately commenced work in Sanitary's Miami plant with a three man team. They began gathering all the necessary data to devise their schedule and to institute their program. Basically the idea was to develop reasonable expectancies for the various machines and crews when working under a continuous flow of materials. Then the schedule would be designed to insure that the flow was steady. The result would be the elimination of speed-ups and slow-downs in the work flow thus allowing fewer workers to turn out the finished product.

The gathering of the data and development of the schedule fell behind and Sanitary's management became restless to see some results. Proudfoot's man in charge of the project reassured Sanitary that savings were just around the corner and that they were going to recommend very shortly that 26 persons be eliminated in the ironing department of the Miami plant. On June 5, 1964 this installation was actually accomplished and the people discharged. Proudfoot's former employees who were on the job at the time admitted at the trial that at the time they had not really worked out a schedule and that without it, the layoff would not achieve the desired result. Shortly after the layoff the plant had to operate at longer hours to get out the necessary production. Employee complaints followed. With the approval of Proudfoot's employees, the 26 persons were rehired. Similar difficulty occurred at the Orlando plant. In sum, as the district court found, former employees of Proudfoot, witnesses for Sanitary at the trial, testified that they were unable to develop an over-all schedule plan that would develop a continuous flow and eliminate lost time.

In July the installation manager was discharged by Proudfoot and new personnel placed on the job in an effort to develop a workable program or installation. Further studies were made and plans and forms drawn up, but no further "installations" were attempted. On October 9, 1964, after having collected $74,200, and spent the contemplated time on the Sanitary job, Proudfoot discontinued its efforts. Several contracts were made after this in an effort to have Proudfoot perform. The parties, however, broke off negotiations and this suit followed.

Originally Sanitary was suing on a theory of breach of express or implied warranty in that the savings promised by Proudfoot did not occur. The district judge found that there was no express promise to effect savings and that there is no implied warranty in a contract for services. He did find, albeit in a rather unspecified way, that Sanitary did not receive what they bargained for, i.e., workable system. He then awarded damages to Sanitary in the nature of restitution. According to the court, they paid for a service which they did not get and thus were entitled to have their money back.

Proudfoot argues that the system failed because Sanitary did not cooperate with them in making the employees follow the plan. The record belies this argument. Sanitary fired two plant managers because Proudfoot said that they were not cooperating. They hired scheduling clerks at Proudfoot's request. Management was available for consultation when any signs of non-cooperation on the part of the workers appeared. The findings of the district court to the effect that there was no failure to cooperate on the part of Sanitary are amply supported.

In the final analysis, the question presented is whether a scheduling installation was devised for Sanitary and made operative. After a careful study of the record we conclude, as did the district court, that no scheduling installation as contemplated in the agreement was ever devised or furnished to Sanitary. Thus, as Proudfoot did not produce what they contracted to do, there was a failure of consideration.

The law in Florida on the subject of failure of consideration where services are to be performed was recently stated in Binz v. Helvetia

Florida Enterprises, Inc., Fla. App. 1963, 156 So.2d 703, 704:

> It is axiomatic that where a promise to pay a sum of money is made upon the consideration of a promise to perform certain service, the consideration fails if the services are not performed, and the promise based thereon is discharged.

[Citation.]

· In *Binz*, there was no attempt to render the services bargained for; however, we can detect no difference in that situation and one where the attempt to perform is unsuccessful and the promisee is without fault in the undertaking. Cf. Restatements of Contracts, § 274.

Proudfoot contends that in any event it did provide a workable system since it proved that some savings occurred. This argument stands or falls as the district court found on whether or not Sanitary purchased guaranteed savings. Proudfoot has maintained throughout that what it was selling was services and not results. The district court found that there were some slight benefits from Proudfoot's activities. We conclude that these savings or benefits were not of any consequence in determining whether the service of developing and installing a system was accomplished as promised. They did not rise to the level of preventing the failure of consideration from being material.

The cross-appeal of Sanitary based on the theory of recovering promised savings in the amount of $1,000,000 is without merit.

The judgment of the district court is affirmed.

* * *

IN RE WHITTEMORE v. TAX COMMISSION OF THE STATE OF NEW YORK

92 A.D.2d 1081, 461 N.Y.S.2d 576
(Supreme Court, Appellate Division, Third Department, March 31, 1983.)

MEMORANDUM DECISION.

* * *

In 1976, petitioner filed a New York State unincorporated business tax return but did not pay the tax due, requesting instead that respondent determine whether the activities of his data processing business constituted the carrying on of a business or trade subject to the tax (Tax Law, § 701). During this period, petitioner was self-employed as a systems designer and computer programmer who developed and implemented data processing accounting systems. In addition, he analyzed information produced by the computer for purposes of client consultation. Petitioner was issued a statement of audit changes and a notice of deficiency which determined his liability for unincorporated business taxes upon "business income from data processing" during 1976 to be $271.17, including interest. Petitioner filed for redetermination contending that he was a professional exempt from tax within the definition of subdivision (c) of section 703 of the Tax Law. After a hearing, respondent determined that petitioner's activities "although requiring special knowledge, did not constitute the practice of a profession within the meaning and intent of the Tax Law." In this proceeding, petitioner contends that the record lacks substantial evidence to support the determination.

The determination should be confirmed. When a taxpayer claims the benefit of a statute providing an exemption from taxation, he bears the burden of proving eligibility for the exemption. The statute is construed against him. [Citation.] Section 703 (subd. [c] of the Tax Law exempts from the unincorporated business tax "[t]he practice of law, medicine, dentistry or architecture, and the practice of any *other profession* in which capital is not a material income producing factor * * *" (emphasis added) (see 20 NYCRR 203.11[b][1][i]). In *Matter of Shmaruk v. State Tax Comm.* 79 A.D.2d 832, 435 N.Y.S.2d 142, a case remarkably similar to this case, this court concluded that the term "other profession" in subdivision (c) "does not necessarily embrace computer programming, designing, engineering or consultation" (*id.* at 833, 435 N.Y.S.2d 142). We further noted "[t]hat to be entitled to a 'professional' exemption, the services performed must 'encompass some of the essential characteristics' of the professions of law, medicine, dentistry or architecture." [Citation.] The *Shmaruk* petitioner, who described his activities in the computer field as "advisory, systems design and computer programming" [citation], did not qualify for the exemption. In his brief, petitioner attempts to distinguish *Shmaruk* by characterizing his activities as primarily those of an accountant and thus encompassed within the exemption for "other professionals," [citation], emphasizing his educational background. The issue, however, is not whether the taxpayer is an accountant, but whether the particular activities engaged in constitute the "practice of [a] profession" as opposed to a purely commercial or business enterprise. Notwithstanding petitioner's background, the record demonstrates that his activities were not primarily those of an accountant. At the hearing, petitioner described his business as a "very small amount of general computer consulting work and a lot of what I would call systems design, systems analysis and computer programming work." In a letter introduced at the hearing, he described himself as "a professional systems designer and a senior computer programmer", conceding that only about one third of his work entailed accounting. In our view, petitioner has failed to meet his burden of proving that his activities qualified as a profession within the scope of the exemption. [Citations.] Respondent's determination is reasonable, based upon substantial evidence, and should not be disturbed.

Determination confirmed, and petition dismissed, without costs.

HOLDSCLAW v. WARREN AND BREWSTER

45 Or.App. 153, 607 P.2d 1208
(Court of Appeals of Oregon, March 10, 1980.)

GILLETTE, J.

This is an action for wrongful death brought against the designer of a computerized saw mill. Plaintiff alleged both negligence in the design of the saw mill and strict liability for selling an unreasonably dangerous product. In its answer, defendant alleged contributory negligence and negligent misuse of the product as affirmative defenses. During the course of the trial, the plaintiff abandoned the negligence theory and proceeded only under strict liability. Thereafter, the trial court struck the affirmative defenses from the answer and refused to submit the issue of contributory neg-

ligence to the jury. A verdict was returned in plaintiff's favor. Defendant appeals. We affirm.

Plaintiff's decedent was a mill superintendent employed by Rogge Lumber Sales at their Wallowa mill. The defendant is the manufacturer of the "Maxi Mill," a series of interrelated machines used to cut logs at the Wallowa facility where the deceased was employed. Logs are passed through the "mill's" two saw blades which adjust to the log size automatically. During the operation, the log is "read" by a scanner that is connected to a computer. The computer feeds information to solenoid valves which use air pressure to move the saw blades from an open position of just over two feet apart to any lesser distance down to slightly under four inches. The blades are very large and heavy; the air pressure required to move them is considerable. If the movable carriage is empty when it passes by the scanner, the computer automatically sets the saw blades to a closed position.

During normal operation, the mill is run by a man working at a remote console. An emergency switch on the console shuts off electricity to the machine but does not shut off the air pressure or computer. In order to shut down the mill, not only must the electric circuit breakers be turned off but the air pressure must also be switched off and the air cylinders that move the blades must be bled.

On the day of the accident, the decedent ordered the mill shut down during the lunch hour so that the saw blades on the machine could be adjusted. He left the machine for a short time and, during his absence, two workers shut off the electricity but apparently did not shut off the air pressure or bleed the air cylinders. Upon his return, decedent began working on the machine. He crawled between the saw blades, then had an apprentice manually push the log carriage forward. The log scan and computer activated the air cylinders, the saw blades closed, and he died immediately.

Evidence was presented on the hazards of the machine and safety devices which could have prevented the accident, as well as the decedent's alleged negligent behavior in failing to follow certain safety regulations. This testimony does not concern us in detail. The sole issue to be decided is whether contributory negligence is a defense in a strict liability action so that the issue of comparative fault should have been submitted to the jury.

Both parties rely on the Oregon Supreme Court's recent opinion in *Baccelleri v. Hyster Co.*, 287 Or. 3, 597 P.2d 351 (1979). Defendant maintains that *Baccelleri* holds that contributory negligence is a defense in strict liability actions. Plaintiff argues that the court in *Baccelleri* was referring to only a certain type of contributory negligence, i. e., that which is sometimes called "assumption of risk." We agree with plaintiff.

In 1975, the Oregon legislature abolished the doctrine of assumption of risk, ORS 18.472(2). [Footnote.] At the same time the contributory negligence statute, ORS 18.470, was amended to read as follows:

> Contributory negligence shall not bar recovery in an action by any person or his legal representative to recover damages for death or injury to person or property if the fault attributable to the person seeking recovery was not greater than the combined fault of the person or persons against whom recovery is sought, but any damages allowed shall be diminished in the proportion to the percentage of fault attributable to the person recovering. This section is not intended to create or abolish any defense.

The issue before the court in *Baccelleri* was whether that conduct which is sometimes labeled "assumption of the risk" but which is,

in reality, a species of contributory negligence rather than assumption of risk can be compared in the apportionment of damages. The court held that it could. *Id.*, at 10, 597 P.2d 351.

The court then went on to decide that this form of contributory negligence could also be used for comparison in apportioning damages when the plaintiff is proceeding on the theory of strict liability in tort. *Id.*, at 12, 597 P.2d [351] at 355. The court stated:

> We hold that Oregon statutes provide that comparative fault is applicable in strict liability in tort. Whether defendant has adequately pleaded or proved that *kind* of contributory negligence which can qualify as comparative fault in a strict liability case was not in issue on this appeal. *Ibid.* (Emphasis added.)

We read the court's opinion as referring only to the species of contributory negligence it had considered earlier, *viz.*, assumption of the risk. An examination of prior opinions in this area strengthens our conclusion.

* * *

Having determined that the form of negligence known as "assumption of the risk" may be applied in strict liability actions, we now must determine whether the defenses raised by the defendant in this case and set out here in the margin[3] properly state that theory. They

3. "FOR A FURTHER SEPARATE ANSWER AND DEFENSE, defendant alleges as follows:

I

That all times material hereto Gilbert Wayne Holdsclaw was the person in charge of the mill referred to in plaintiff's complaint and in the course of said employment was charged with the duty of seeing that suitable safety regulations were promulgated and followed in said mill.

II

That at the time of and immediately prior to his death plaintiff's decedent was negligent in certain particulars, each of which was a cause of his death and plaintiff's loss and damage resulting therefrom.

III

Plaintiff's decedent was negligent in the following particulars:
1. In failing to make certain that no employee of the mill would enter a position of danger between the saws without having personally disengaged all power supplies to the equipment and without placing tags on or locking out the power switches and valves so that they could not be disturbed while a workman was within the area of danger from the machinery;
2. In failing to deactivate the pneumatic power supply which propelled the machinery before entering the zone of hazard;

3. In failing to bleed the air supply from the machinery before placing himself between the saws;
4. In failing to keep a lookout for his own safety;
5. In directing another employee to manually override the automatic braking system on the log carriage while he was within the zone of danger;
6. In propelling the log carriage manually past the position of the limit switch which would activate machinery without first disconnecting all sources of power from the machinery and while he was between the saw blades;
7. In failing to tag out power source controls or require others to do so before entering the area of danger.

AND FOR A FURTHER SEPARATE ANSWER AND AFFIRMATIVE DEFENSE to plaintiff's second cause of action, defendant alleges as follows:

I

That plaintiff's decedent's death was caused by his negligent misuse of the machinery in the following particulars:
1. In failing to make certain that no employee of the mill would enter a position of danger between the saws without having personally disengaged all power supplies to the equipment and without placing tags on or locking out the power switches and valves

do not. The first affirmative defense alleges ordinary negligence. The second alleges negligent misuse of the sawmill but it simply restates the same facts set forth in the first defense. Nowhere are the three elements of assumption of risk * * * set out. Defendant's affirmative defenses did not bring it within the ambit of the *Baccelleri* decision. The trial court did not err in striking them.

Affirmed. [Footnote.]

SCOTT v. WHITE TRUCKS
699 F.2d 714
(United States Court of Appeals, Fifth Circuit, March 7, 1983.)

GARWOOD, C. J.

In this Louisiana law diversity suit, plaintiff Scott appeals from a judgment n.o.v. rendered in favor of appellee White Trucks dismissing Scott's products liability claim. [Footnote.] The primary questions are whether there is sufficient evidence to show that the product was defectively designed or manufactured, and if so, whether the defect existed when it left the manufacturer's hands. We hold there is no sufficient evidence to support the jury's findings and affirm the district court's judgment.

I.

White Truck No. 1872, a three-axle tractor, was manufactured for appellee White Trucks by the Freightliner Corporation ("Freightliner") in October 1975. Following the initial promulgation of federal regulations [footnote] requiring such devices, Freightliner equipped its White Freightliner models of the 1800 series with an automatic electronic anti-lock system designed to minimize air brake lockup problems and to enhance vehicle stability and control. Air brakes were placed on the steering axle, as well as the rear axles, of these trucks. Each axle was equipped with a separate anti-lock system. The system was manufactured by Wagner-Electric Corporation.

On October 31, 1975, Truck No. 1872 was sold by White Trucks to Hunsaker Truck Lines ("Hunsaker"). In October 1976, this truck and seven other White trucks of the same model and series, were sold by Hunsaker to Leaseway of Louisiana, Inc. ("Leaseway"), who leased them to Great Atlantic & Pacific Tea Company ("A & P"). Under the lease agreement, Leaseway maintained and repaired the trucks.

Appellant Otis Scott was employed as a truck driver for A & P. On August 17, 1977, about 5:30 a.m. on a wet and rainy dawn near Pascagoula, Mississippi, Scott was driving Truck No. 1872, which was pulling a trailer equipped with a similar braking system, back to New Orleans from Mobile, Alabama. Traffic was heavy, and a car changed lanes in front of Scott. Scott "lightly applied" the brakes, the left front wheel grabbed, the truck swerved to the left, and, as Scott testified, it ran "into the median and mud," he "lost control" and thereupon "it jackknifed." Scott received injuries in the accident.

Scott sued White Trucks and Leaseway, alleging that the truck's braking system was defectively designed or manufactured. The liability issues were tried separately and before the damages issues. After Scott rested, White Trucks moved for a directed verdict, arguing that Scott had produced no evidence of a defect in design or manufacture. The district court denied this motion without prejudice. At the close of all the evidence, White Trucks reurged its motion for a directed verdict, but the district court reserved a ruling on the motion and sent the case to the jury, who found that the braking system in the truck was defectively designed or manufactured, and that the defect was a cause of Scott's accident. The district court then granted White Trucks' motion for directed verdict and rendered a judgment n.o.v. in its favor. The court held that there was no evidence of a defect in the design or manu-

---

so that they could not be disturbed while a workman was within the area of danger from the machinery;

2. In failing to deactivate the pneumatic power supply which propelled the machinery before entering the zone of danger;

3. In failing to bleed the air supply from the machinery before placing himself between the saws;

4. In failing to keep a lookout for his own safety;

5. In directing another employee to manually override the automatic braking system on the log carriage while he was within the zone of danger;

6. In propelling the log carriage manually past the position of the limit switch which would activate machinery without first disconnecting all sources of power from the machinery and while he was between the saw blades;

7. In failing to tag out power source controls or require others to do so before entering the area of danger.

facture of the truck, and that because of the long delay between the sale of the truck to Hunsaker and the accident, Scott had the burden of proving more than just the fact that the accident was caused by the brakes "grabbing."

II.

Under Louisiana law, an individual "who without fault on his part, sustains an injury caused by a defect in the design, composition, or manufacture of" a product rendering it "unreasonably dangerous to normal use," may recover his damages from the maker of the product and "need not prove any particular negligence by the maker in its manufacture or processing; for the manufacturer is presumed to know of the vices in the things he makes, whether or not he has actual knowledge of them." *Weber v. Fidelity & Casualty Insurance Co. of N.Y.*, 250 So.2d 754, 755–56 (La.1971). The plaintiff, however, not only "has the burden of proving that the product was defective" but also that his "injuries were caused by reason of the defect." *Id.* at 755. Moreover, recovery is allowed against the manufacturer only "if the injured person proves * * * that the product was defective when it left the hands of the manufacturer," and "[w]hile the rule [of strict liability] is harsh, liability is not imposed unless the evidence preponderates * * * that the [injury-causing] defect existed when the product left the hands of the manufacturer." *Madden v. Louisiana Power and Light Co.*, 334 So.2d 249, 253, 255 (La.App. 4th Cir.1976). [Footnote.]

Cases involving products manufactured, sold and retained in sealed containers normally present little difficulty in terms of whether a defect existing at the time of injury was also present at the time of manufacture. *Weber.* Even in other circumstances, the abnormal malfunction of a product shortly after manufacture may, whether there is an adequate "accounting" of the use between the manufacture and the accident and evidence tending to negate other causes, give rise to an inference of a defect existing at the time of manufacture. *See e.g., Hunt v. Ford Motor Co.*, 341 So.2d 614, 618 (La.App. 2d Cir.1977) ("considering the well-documented and supported evidence that the steering mechanism 'popped,'

'binded,' and 'hung up' from the time the car was purchased [new by the plaintiff], with no evidence of intervening causation by faulty repairs, other accidents, or the like, it is reasonable to conclude that an unreasonably dangerous defect related to steering existed from the time of manufacture"); *Ned v. Hertz Corp.*, 356 So.2d 1074 (La.App. 4th Cir.), *writ denied*, 359 So.2d 197 (La.1978) (brake repairs performed March 5, vehicle returned to service March 6, accident occurred March 11 when brakes grabbed, as they had earlier that day and on other occasions since repair; these circumstances allow an inference that the brakes were defective on completion of March 5 repairs).

However, the manufacturer is under no duty "to make a product that will last forever or will withstand abuse or lack of maintenance" or that is "foolproof" [citations], nor one whose component "parts do not wear out." [Citations.] And, where a particular defect or dangerous condition is not directly shown to exist at the time of manufacture, and the product abnormally malfunctions, or even is directly shown to have a defective component, on the occasion of an accident occurring a significant time after manufacture, this will not alone authorize a finding that the product was defective while in the manufacturer's hands, if maintenance and employment by intervening owners and users is not adequately accounted for. [Citations.] [Footnotes.]

While language in the [citations] opinions appears to indicate that in those cases the general theory of liability primarily being advanced was one of negligence, rather than strict liability, we do not attach significance to this for present purposes. Some two years before those decisions *Weber* had established the strict liability of manufacturers for injuries caused by defects in product design, composition, or manufacture. Moreover, the questions of whether the product was defective when it left the manufacturer's hands, and of whether such defect caused the injury, are common to both the strict liability and the negligence theories of recovery. The two theories of liability are distinguished not by any difference in those elements, but rather by the fact that in strict liability the plaintiff need not prove that the presence of the injury-causing defect when the product left the manufacturer's hands was due to "any particular negligence by the maker." *Weber*, 250 So.2d at 756.

* * *

III.

There was no testimony as to any examination of Truck No. 1872's brakes following the accident, and the post-accident repairs apparently did not include any maintenance, repair, or replacement of the computer brake system or any other brake work. On July 28, 1977, some three weeks before the accident, Hessler, a Leaseway mechanic, performed a scheduled routine inspection and maintenance on the truck, which included checking the wiring of the brake system. He did not examine the inside of the "box" controlling the automatic brake system. He adjusted the brakes, which was "routine." He did not check the wheels or the brake lining. Apparently he did not perform a road test, stating that though this was sometimes done, "it's not standard." Pullen, Hessler's foreman, testified that Hessler had no computer brake training. Hessler, however, stated that he had "a little bit" of such training from another Leaseway mechanic, who showed him how to "adjust" the brakes but nothing about the computer "box."

No evidence was offered as to any defective component of this truck's braking system, nor as to any flaw in the system's design. The only evidence as to what caused the grabbing of the brakes on this occasion was the testimony of plaintiff's expert witness Doyle, who stated that in his opinion this resulted from the failure of the electronic anti-lock system to release the brake air pressure with sufficient promptness. [Footnote.] There are several difficulties with Doyle's testimony, however.

Doyle identified no defect in the manufacture, composition, or design of the brakes or the anti-lock system, and did not suggest how or for what reason the supposed failure of the anti-lock system to timely reduce the air pressure came about. He did not even see this truck until August 1979 and there is no suggestion in the record that he ever examined either its brakes or anti-lock system, or the brakes or anti-lock system of any other truck of the same model. Further, Doyle's testimony in this regard was given entirely in response to a hypothetical question which assumed that

when the wheel grabbed this caused "a jackknife effect" "which landed Mr. Scott in the neutral ground." On cross-examination, Doyle made it clear that he had simply "answered a hypothetical question" in which he had been asked to assume that Scott "made a * * * light brake application; the left front wheel locked, and it caused him to go into a jackknife." However, the undisputed evidence is that on the occasion in question the truck jackknifed *after* it hit "neutral ground," and *not* before. [Footnote.] This is significant because Hutton, the Freightliner Manager of Product Integrity, testified it was standard to allow a .55-second interval after braking action commenced and before the electronic anti-lock device commenced to release the air pressure on the brakes. [Footnote.] While Doyle would not agree to the .55-second figure, he did not dispute the presence of some such interval or its reasonableness, but rather was of the view that if the lockup was so severe as to produce a jackknife, then it was too long and evidenced a malfunction in the system. [Footnote.] It is plain from Hutton's testimony, undisputed in this regard, that a jackknife could easily have occurred on account of the truck, or its left front wheel, going into the "neutral ground" or median. Accordingly, Doyle's opinion that the electronic anti-lock device malfunctioned, being based on the incorrect assumption that the truck jackknifed *before* it made contact with the median (and hence that the lockup was sufficiently severe to produce a jackknife by itself), affords at best questionable support for plaintiff's case. [Footnote.]

However, even if it be assumed that there is sufficient evidence to establish that the anti-lock system malfunctioned, and was hence in some way defective on the occasion in question, there is nonetheless insufficient evidence that the system was defective when it left White Trucks' hands.

When the accident occurred in August 1977, the truck had been in use for nearly two years. The evidence does not show the mileage at this time, but an A & P Trip Report of February 8, 1977 shows the truck had then been driven 142,016 miles. Leaseway and A & P had owned and used the truck since October 1976, and Leaseway records did not indicate any repairs to the computer brake system between that time and the occurrence of the accident. The Leaseway maintenance system called for routine maintenance and repair, including brake adjustments and checking of the brake air hoses and electrical lines, every 9,000 miles; every 40,000 miles a more thorough checking of the brakes was performed, including matters not performed on the 9,000-mile inspections such as wheel removal and brake liner and bearing inspection. None of these involved maintenance or repair of the computer "box." Pullen, who started to work for Leaseway as a mechanic in January 1977 and became shop foreman there some time after August of that year, testified that while he never looked at the brake system on Truck No. 1872 "carefully," within a month or two after he arrived he had looked at the truck, though not "thoroughly," and did not see "any changes or alteration to the braking system." When the truck was received by Leaseway from Hunsaker in October 1976, it was approximately one year old and had been driven 128,559 miles. There is no evidence concerning either the age or mileage of the seven other model 1800 trucks which Leaseway acquired at the same time from Hunsaker. There is no evidence as to the use of any of these eight trucks by Hunsaker, nor were any Hunsaker maintenance or repair or other records respecting any of these trucks put in evidence or testified about. There is no indication whether any of these eight trucks were inspected when received by Leaseway, or, if so, the results of any such inspection. The earliest Leaseway record concerning Truck No. 1872 (no records concerning any of the other trucks were in evidence) is an A & P "Trip Report" (these forms also functioned as repair orders to Leaseway) of October 27, 1976, noting "Air pressure leak [sic] down while truck is running & low air light come [sic] on. I can't find the leak." [Footnote.]

Hutton testified that the anti-lock system was tested thoroughly, including extensive road tests, by Freightliner and the government, and that it performed satisfactorily. He also testified that the brakes and anti-lock

system on this particular truck were tested axle by axle before sale to Hunsaker and were in good working order.

Scott points to testimony by Hutton that the "computer box" and some other parts of the anti-lock system were to be maintenance-free by the consumer. However, Hutton further testified that other parts of the anti-lock system required maintenance, including "air lines subject to chaffing; ice buildup; * * * electrical connections subject to water corrosion, and other things. * * * There would certainly be maintenance required in the whole system."[14] Similarly, Pullen testified that he had seen instances, at least some before November 1977, where the brakes would be applied on 1800 models and "they don't come off, the brakes remain on." These instances were remedied by replacing the air release valve, Pullen explaining, "You get water in the tanks and they stick on you sometimes and you have to replace them." Accordingly, it is evident that there were several possible causes for the supposed failure of the anti-lock system to function other than a defect in the "computer box."

As to the "computer box" itself, Hutton testified that the trucks were equipped with a warning light in the cab to indicate a malfunction in the electronic computer for the anti-lock system, and if the light came on the consumer should take the truck "to an authorized garage for repair."[15] Pullen testified that when complaints of computer brakes were made the Leaseway mechanics road tested the trucks, but did not take them to "the White office here." Hessler stated, "We usually change the whole box if it's bad" and recalled "at least one" unspecified instance when this was done. Pullen's testimony reflects that before November 1977 Leaseway had no computer-brake trained mechanics. The testimony also shows that there were no manuals or the like made available to the Leaseway mechanics respecting maintenance or repair of the automatic anti-lock system, and there is no evidence to establish that this lack was attributable to White Trucks or Freightliner. Finally, in re-

---

14. This was in addition to the "normal foundation brakes that are there, regardless of whether you have a computer system or not, the brake drums, everything else * * * that's all subject to wear and tear and maintenance." These items were, in effect, part of the computer brake system because "[t]he computer controls part of the brake system, and if anything malfunctions in the brake system, you have a problem."

15. He also observed that "if the truck battery was having low voltage" this could cause the computer to "act erratically." There was no evidence whether or not this would bring on the warning light.

gard to the care and maintenance of the "computer boxes" we must consider the testimony of plaintiff's witnesses Blade and Green.

Blade, an A & P truck driver from some time in 1976 until October 1977, testified that he experienced "grabbing or pulling of the brakes upon application" when driving White Freightliner model 1800 trucks, and that he drove Truck No. 1872 some seven or eight times in 1977, and on application of the brakes "it would have a tendency to pull either to the right or to the left." When this occurred, he would "write it up and turn it in" to Leaseway for them to fix. Sometimes they fixed it, and sometimes they didn't. He did not know what was causing the brake problem or what part of the brakes malfunctioned. The wheels that would lock up were the wheels on the rearmost axle. While he apparently never experienced a jackknife, on one occasion in May 1977, Truck No. 1872's rear wheels locked up so he could not move the truck. A Leaseway mechanic came out and "beat on" the computer box and after "he hit on there a little while" the brakes released, and "then he adjusted them."

Green's testimony reflects that this method of servicing the computer box was not unique. Green was a Leaseway truck mechanic until June 1977, and before coming with Leaseway worked some nine years in the same capacity for Hunsaker. He worked on the same 1800 model trucks at Hunsaker as he did later at Leaseway. It is impossible to determine whether his testimony about the trucks relates to the time he was with Leaseway or with Hunsaker or both. In any event, Green testified on direct examination by Scott's attorney as follows:

Q. Did you ever work on any White Freightliner of the 1800 series that had any lockup problems?

A. Yes, I have.

Q. Could you tell the Jury how that came about, what repair work you did on it?

A. Well, the Freightliner, we would get them running, and we would set them up in the yard and start them up and get them ready for the guys to go, and let them set there running, and they would lock up, there, sitting out in the yard.

Q. Is that normal?

A. To my idea, no. I don't think no brakes just lock up just setting up in the yard.[16]

Q. How did you fix that when they were locked up?

A. Well, I didn't know too much about it. They had the little black box on there, like.

Q. Was that *the computer box?*

A. Right, and that was the only thing that would cause this trouble, because *I would take the top off and bang around on the wires* and tap the box, and a little while the truck would be ready to go.

Q. The brakes would release?

A. The brakes would release.

Q. Were you given any type of manuals to repair—to work with the computer box?

A. No, they never did give us nothing, no literature, no demonstration, no nothing like that.

Q. Did you take any kind of class on how to repair that?

A. No, they had nobody to teach us nothing about that." (Emphasis added.)

Green testified he worked on "practically all" the eight model 1800 trucks for "locking up".

Green's testimony, the substance of which we have outlined, is the only evidence even arguably relating to the truck in question, or the other model 1800 trucks, while they were

---

16. This is to be contrasted to the testimony of plaintiff's expert Doyle that "any air brake truck will have a certain amount of leaks when it's sitting up for a period of time, that they have to crank the truck up and build the air up to release the brakes before they go on a run." Accordingly, the inference from the indicated portion of Green's quoted testimony is that some character of air leak caused the pressure to fall and the fail-safe mechanical system to take over. [Citation.]

Green also stated, in another part of his testimony:
When you start running these things and you hit the

brakes, sometimes it will stop, and sometimes they wouldn't. When you go across the yard and hit the brake, they just lock up and jerk your arm and almost break your arm; when it's right or left.

The failure to stop obviously bespeaks a problem other than that involved here. The pulling to the right or left would not necessarily indicate a failure of the anti-lock system, as it would release both wheels on an axle or neither, unless some other factor, such as a clogged air line, were involved.

with Hunsaker. Yet, as noted, it is impossible to tell whether Green was speaking of the time he was with Leaseway or with Hunsaker or both. Even if he were addressing the time he was with Hunsaker, his testimony clearly furnishes no reasonable basis for concluding that Hunsaker's use, maintenance, and repair were not such as would likely have caused a defect in the automatic anti-lock system or other aspects of the brakes.

Scott stresses the testimony that "practically all" these eight model 1800 trucks had "lockup" problems. There is no evidence, however, that this occurred soon after manufacture, but at most only at some time while owned by Hunsaker. There is nothing to indicate how many such trucks were manufactured by Freightliner, nor the age or mileage of any of these particular eight trucks other than Truck No. 1872, nor the character of use Truck No. 1872 or any of the others had with Hunsaker. We are informed, however, that truck mechanic Green, and those he worked with, had no literature, manuals, training and "no nothing" on this type of braking system, and "didn't know too much about it." We are also informed that Green took the top off the computer box and "bang[ed] around on the wires" on "practically all" of these eight trucks.

Scott also argues that, even aside from claimed defects in the anti-lock system, the brakes on Truck No. 1872 were defective because they were "too strong." Parts of Doyle's testimony can be read as suggesting that front axle brakes could be dangerous without a properly functioning automatic anti-lock system. However, in the absence of proof that the anti-lock system was defective when manufactured, this does not advance Scott's case. Aside from being on the front axle, there is no evidence that the brakes were too strong when manufactured.

We conclude that plaintiff Scott has not carried the burden of proof which Louisiana law places on him to show that either the automatic anti-lock system in particular, or the brakes in general, on Truck No. 1872 were of a defective design, or contained a defect in manufacture or composition, when it left the

hands of White Trucks in October 1975, and that he has not made the showing required by Louisiana law to authorize a *res ipsa loquitur* type inference against White Trucks. While there may be a scintilla of evidence supporting Scott, nevertheless, viewing the evidence as a whole, though in the light and with all reasonable inferences most favorable to Scott, in our opinion reasonable men could not conclude therefrom that it was more probable than not that the August 1977 accident resulted from a defect in Truck No. 1872's brakes or braking system which existed in October 1975 when it left White Trucks' hands.

* * *

Scott also argues that White Trucks is liable on a failure to warn theory. This argument fails for several reasons. To begin with, for recovery to be had on this basis Scott must first show that the truck was unreasonably dangerous as manufactured. We have held no such showing was made. We further observe that Scott's own testimony amply demonstrates that well before the accident he was aware of a propensity on the part of Truck No. 1872 to have its brakes "grab" or "lock," and to pull the truck to one side or the other. Louisiana law does not require a warning to those who are actually aware of the matter.[17] [Citations.] Finally, the truck was equipped with a warning light to signal that the automatic anti-lock system was not properly operating. While Scott testified that the light did not come on on this occasion and he (and others) testified that these lights on the 1800 model trucks at Leaseway did not seem to work as they should, there is no evidence concerning the cause of any such failure or suggesting that it was attributable to a defect existing when this vehicle or any of the others left the hands of White Trucks, rather than to old or faulty bulbs, worn wiring or any other of a number of possible causes. There was no testimony whatever concerning any examination of any of these lights, or what sort of maintenance, replacement, or repair they were supposed to have or did in fact have. [Footnote.] We also note that Doyle's testimony does not criticize Freightliner or White Trucks on

---

17. We do not suggest that Scott's knowledge would defeat recovery if the accident were shown to have been caused by a defect in the braking system (whether of design, composition, or manufacture) existing when the truck left White Trucks' hands. Such knowledge merely defeats lack of warning as an *independent* ground of recovery in the absence of proof that the accident was caused by a defect (in design, manufacture, or composition) present or inherent in the product when it left the hands of the defendant manufacturer.

any failure to warn basis. Accordingly, we reject Scott's claim of recovery on a failure to warn theory.

* * *

The district court's judgment is affirmed.

GOTTSCHALK v. BENSON
409 U.S. 63
(United States Supreme Court, Certiorari to the United States Court of Customs and Patent Appeals, November 20, 1972.)

DOUGLAS, J.

Respondents filed in the Patent Office an application for an invention which was described as being related "to the processing of data by program and more particularly to the programmed conversion of numerical information" in general-purpose digital computers. They claimed a method for converting binary-coded decimal (BCD) numerals into pure binary numerals. The claims were not limited to any particular art or technology, to any particular apparatus or machinery, or to any particular end use. They purported to cover any use of the claimed method in a general-purpose digital computer of any type. Claims 8 and 13[1] were rejected by the Patent Office but sustained by the Court of Customs and Patent Appeals——C. C. P. A. (Pat.)——, 441 F.2d 682. The case is here on a petition for a writ of certiorari. [Citation.]

The question is whether the method described and claimed is a "process" within the meaning of the Patent Act. [Footnote.]

A digital computer, as distinguished from an analog computer, operates on data expressed in digits, solving a problem by doing arithmetic as a person would do it by head and hand. [Footnote.] Some of the digits are stored as components of the computer. Others are introduced into the computer in a form which it is designed to recognize. The computer operates then upon both new and previously stored data. The general-purpose computer is designed to perform operations under many different programs.

The representation of numbers may be in the form of a time series of electrical impulses, magnetized spots on the surface of tapes, drums, or discs, charged spots on cathode-ray tube screens, the presence or absence of punched holes on paper cards, or other devices. The method or program is a sequence of coded instructions for a digital computer.

The patent sought is on a method of programming a general-purpose digital computer to convert signals from binary-coded decimal form into pure binary form. A procedure for solving a given type of mathematical problem is known as an "algorithm." The procedures set forth in the present claims are of that kind; that is to say, they are a generalized formulation for programs to solve mathematical problems of converting one form of numerical representation to another. From the generic formulation, programs may be developed as specific applications.

The decimal system uses as digits the 10 symbols 0, 1, 2, 3, 4, 5, 6, 7, 8, and 9. The value represented by any digit depends, as it does in any positional system of notation, both on its individual value and on its relative position in the numeral. Decimal numerals are written by placing digits in the appropriate positions or columns of the numerical sequence, $i.\ e.$, "unit" (10^0), "tens" (10^1), "hundreds" (10^2), "thousands" (10^3), etc. Accordingly, the numeral 1492 signifies $(1 \times 10^3) + (4 \times 10^2) + (9 \times 10^1) + (2 \times 10^0)$.

The pure binary system of positional notation uses two symbols as digits—0 and 1, placed in a numerical sequence with values based on consecutively ascending powers of 2. In pure binary notation, what would be the tens position is the twos position; what would be hundreds position is the fours position; what would be the thousands position is eights. Any decimal number from 0 to 10 can be represented in the binary system with four digits or positions as indicated in the following table.

| | Shown as the sum of powers of 2 | | | | | |
Decimal	2^3 (8)	2^2 (4)	2^1 (2)	2^0 (1)		Pure Binary
0 =	0 +	0 +	0 +	0	=	0000
1 =	0 +	0 +	0 +	2^0	=	0001
2 =	0 +	0 +	2^1 +	0	=	0010
3 =	0 +	0 +	2^1 +	2^0	=	0011
4 =	0 +	2^2 +	0 +	0	=	0100
5 =	0 +	2^2 +	0 +	2^0	=	0101
6 =	0 +	2^2 +	2^1 +	0	=	0110
7 =	0 +	2^2 +	2^1 +	2^0	=	0111
8 =	2^3 +	0 +	0 +	0	=	1000
9 =	2^3 +	0 +	0 +	2^0	=	1001
10 =	2^3 +	0 +	2^1 +	0	=	1010

1. They are set forth in the Appendix to this opinion.

The BCD system using decimal numerals replaces the character for each component decimal digit in the decimal numeral with the corresponding four-digit binary numeral, shown in the righthand column of the table. Thus decimal 53 is represented as 0101 0011 in BCD, because decimal 5 is equal to binary 0101 and decimal 3 is equivalent to binary 0011. In pure binary notation, however, decimal 53 equals binary 110101. The conversion of BCD numerals to pure binary numerals can be done mentally through use of the foregoing table. The method sought to be patented varies the ordinary arithmetic steps a human would use by changing the order of the steps, changing the symbolism for writing the multiplier used in some steps, and by taking subtotals after each successive operation. The mathematical procedures can be carried out in existing computers long in use, no new machinery being necessary. And, as noted, they can also be performed without a computer.

The Court stated in *Mackay Co. v. Radio Corp.*, 306 U.S. 86, 94, that "[w]hile a scientific truth, or the mathematical expression of it, is not a patentable invention, a novel and useful structure created with the aid of knowledge of scientific truth may be." That statement followed the longstanding rule that "[a]n idea of itself is not patentable." *Rubber-Tip Pencil Co. v. Howard*, 20 Wall. 498, 507. "A principle, in the abstract, is a fundamental truth; an original cause; a motive; these cannot be patented, as no one can claim in either of them an exclusive right." *Le Roy v. Tatham*, 14 How. 156, 175. Phenomena of nature, though just discovered, mental processes, and abstract intellectual concepts are not patentable, as they are the basic tools of scientific and technological work. As we stated in *Funk Bros. Seed Co. v. Kalo Co.*, 333 U. S. 127, 130:

> He who discovers a hitherto unknown phenomenon of nature has no claim to a monopoly of it which the law recognizes. If there is to be invention from such a discovery, it must come from the application of the law of nature to a new and useful end.

We dealt there with a "product" claim, while the present case deals with a "process" claim. But we think the same principle applies.

Here the "process" claim is so abstract and sweeping as to cover both known and unknown uses of the BCD to pure binary conversion. The end use may (1) vary from the operation of a train to verification of drivers' licenses to researching the law books for precedents and (2) be performed through any existing machinery or future-devised machinery or without any apparatus.

In *O'Reilly v. Morse*, 15 How. 62, Morse was allowed a patent for a process of using electromagnetism to produce distinguishable signs for telegraphy. *Id.*, at 111. But the Court denied the eighth claim in which Morse claimed the use of "electro magnetism, however developed for marking or printing intelligible characters, signs, or letters, at any distances." *Id.*, at 112. The Court in disallowing that claim said:

> If this claim can be maintained, it matters not by what process or machinery the result is accomplished. For aught that we now know, some future inventor, in the onward march of science, may discover a mode of writing or printing at a distance by means of the electric or galvanic current, without using any part of the process or combination set forth in the plaintiff's specification. His invention may be less complicated—less liable to get out of order—less expensive in construction, and in its operation. But yet, if it is covered by this patent, the inventor could not use it, nor the public have the benefit of it, without the permission of this patentee. *Id.*, at 113.

In *The Telephone Cases*, 126 U.S. 1, 534, the Court explained the *Morse* case as follows:

> The effect of that decision was, therefore, that the use of magnetism as a motive power, without regard to the particular process with which it was connected in the patent, could not be claimed, but that its use in that connection could.

Bell's invention was the use of electric current to transmit vocal or other sounds. The claim was not

> for the use of a current of electricity in its natural state as it comes from the battery, but for putting a continuous current in a closed circuit into a certain specified condition suited to the transmission of vocal and other sounds, and using it in that condition for that purpose. *Ibid.*

The claim, in other words, was not "one for the use of electricity distinct from the particular process with which it is connected in his patent." *Id.*, at 535. The patent was for that use of electricity "both for the magneto and variable resistance *methods*." *Id.*, at 538. Bell's claim, in other words, was not one for all telephonic use of electricity.

*   *   *

Transformation and reduction of an article "to a different state or thing" is the clue to the patentability of a process claim that does not include particular machines. So it is that a patent in the process of "manufacturing fat acids and glycerine from fatty bodies by the action of water at a high temperature and pressure" was sustained in *Tilghman v. Proctor*, 102 U. S. 707, 721. The Court said:

> The chemical principle or scientific fact upon which it is founded is, that the elements of neutral fat require to be severally united with an atomic equivalent of water in order to separate from each other and become free. This chemical fact was not discovered by Tilghman. He only claims to have invented a particular mode of bringing about the desired chemical union between the fatty elements and water. *Id.*, at 729.

Expanded Metal Co. v. Bradford, 214 U. S. 366, sustained a patent on a "process" for expanding metal. A process "involving mechanical operations, and producing a new and useful result." *id.*, at 385–386, was held to be a patentable process, process patents not being limited to chemical action.

Smith v. Snow, 294 U. S. 1, and *Waxham v. Smith*, 294 U. S. 20, involved a process for setting eggs in staged incubation and applying mechanically circulated currents of air to the eggs. The Court, in sustaining the function performed (the hatching of eggs) and the means or process by which that is done, said:

> By the use of materials in a particular manner he secured the performance of the function by a means which had never occurred in nature, and had not been anticipated by the prior art; this is a patentable method or process. *   *   * A method, which may be patented irrespective of the particular form of the mechanism which may be availed of for carrying it into operation, is not to be rejected as 'functional,' merely because the specifications show a machine capable of using it. 294 U. S. at 22.

It is argued that a process patent must either be tied to a particular machine or apparatus or must operate to change articles or material

to a "different state or thing." We do not hold that no process patent could ever qualify if it did not meet the requirements of our prior precedents. It is said that the decision precludes a patent for any program servicing a computer. We do not so hold. It is said that we have before us a program for a digital computer but extend our holding to programs for analog computers. We have, however, made clear from the start that we deal with a program only for digital computers. It is said we freeze process patents to old technologies, leaving no room for the revelations of the new, onrushing technology. Such is not our purpose. What we come down to in a nutshell is the following.

It is conceded that one may not patent an idea. But in practical effect that would be the result if the formula for converting BCD numerals to pure binary numerals were patented in this case. The mathematical formula involved here has no substantial practical application except in connection with a digital computer, which means that if the judgment below is affirmed, the patent would wholly pre-empt the mathematical formula and in practical effect would be a patent on the algorithm itself.

It may be that the patent laws should be extended to cover these programs, a policy matter to which we are not competent to speak. The President's Commission on the Patent System [footnote] rejected the proposal that these programs be patentable:

> Uncertainty now exists as to whether the statute permits a valid patent to be granted on programs. Direct attempts to patent programs have been rejected on the ground of nonstatutory subject matter. Indirect attempts to obtain patents and avoid the rejection, by drafting claims as a process, or a machine or components thereof programmed in a given manner, rather than as a program itself, have confused the issue further and should not be permitted.
>
> The Patent Office now cannot examine applications for programs because of a lack of a classification technique and the requisite search files. Even if these were available, reliable searches would not be feasible or economic because of the tremendous volume of prior art being generated. Without this search, the patenting of programs would be tantamount to mere registration and the presumption of validity would be all but nonexistent.

It is noted that the creation of programs has undergone substantial and satisfactory growth in the absence of patent protection and that copyright protection for programs is presently available. [*Id.*, at 13.]

If these programs are to be patentable [footnote], considerable problems are raised which only committees of Congress can manage, for broad powers of investigation are needed, including hearings which canvass the wide variety of views which those operating in this field entertain. The technological problems tendered in the many briefs before us [footnote] indicate to us that considered action by the Congress is needed.

Reversed.

APPENDIX TO OPINION OF THE COURT

Claim 8 reads:

The method of converting signals from binary coded decimal form into binary which comprises the steps of

(1) storing the binary coded decimal signals in a re-entrant shift register,

(2) shifting the signals to the right by at least three places, until there is a binary '1' in the second position of said register,

(3) masking out said binary '1' in said second position of said register,

(4) adding a binary '1' to the first position of said register,

(5) shifting the signals to the left by two positions,

(6) adding a '1' to said first position, and

(7) shifting the signals to the right by at least three positions in preparation for a succeeding binary '1' in the second position of said register.

Claim 13 reads:

A data processing method for converting binary coded decimal number representations into binary number representations comprising the steps of

(1) testing each binary digit position '1,' beginning with the least significant binary digit position, of the most significant decimal digit representation for a binary '0' or a binary '1';

(2) if a binary '0' is detected, repeating step (1) for the next least significant binary digit position of said most significant decimal digit representation;

(3) if a binary '1' is detected, adding a binary '1' at the $(i + 1)$th and $(i + 3)$th least significant binary digit positions of the next lesser signif-

icant decimal digit representation, and repeating step (1) for the next least significant binary digit position of said most significant decimal digit representation;

(4) upon exhausting the binary digit positions of said most significant decimal digit representation, repeating steps (1) through (3) for the next lesser significant decimal digit representation as modified by the previous execution of steps (1) through (3); and

(5) repeating steps (1) through (4) until the second least significant decimal digit representation has been so processed.

DANN v. JOHNSTON
425 U.S. 219
(United States Supreme Court, Certiorari to the United States Court of Customs and Patent Appeals, March 31, 1976.)

MARSHALL, J.

Respondent has applied for a patent on what is described in his patent application as a "machine system for automatic record-keeping of bank checks and deposits." The system permits a bank to furnish a customer with subtotals of various categories of transactions completed in connection with the customer's single account, thus saving the customer the time and/or expense of conducting this bookkeeping himself. As respondent has noted, the "invention is being sold as a computer program to banks and to other data processing companies so that they can perform these data processing services for depositors." [Reference.] [Citation.]

Petitioner and respondent as well as various *amici*, have presented lengthy arguments addressed to the question of the general patentability of computer programs. Cf. *Gottschalk v. Benson*, 409 U. S. 63 (1972). We find no need to treat that question in this case, however, because we conclude that in any event respondent's system is unpatentable on grounds of obviousness. 35 U. S. C. § 103. Since the United States Court of Customs and Patent Appeals (CCPA) found respondent's system to be patentable, *Application of Johnston, supra*, the decision of that court is accordingly reversed.

I

While respondent's patent application pertains to the highly esoteric field of computer technology, the basic functioning of his invention is not difficult to comprehend. Under respondent's system a bank customer labels each check that he writes with a numerical category code corresponding to the purpose for which the funds are being expended. For instance, "food expenditures" might be a category coded "123," "fuel expenditures" a category coded "124," and "rent" still another category coded "125." Similarly, on each deposit slip, the customer again through a category code, indicates the source of the funds that he is depositing. When the checks and deposit slips are processed by the bank, the category codes are entered upon them in magnetic ink characters, just as, under existing procedures, the amount of the check or deposit is entered in such characters. Entries in magnetic ink allow the information associated with them to be "read" by special document-reading devices and then processed by data processors. On being read by such a device, the coded records of the customer's transactions are electronically stored in what respondent terms a "transaction file." Respondent's application describes the steps from this point as follows:

> To process the transaction file, the * * * system employs a data processor, such as a programmable electronic digital computer, having certain data storage files and a control system. In addition to the transaction file, a master record-keeping file is used to store all of the records required for each customer in accordance with the customer's own chart of accounts. The latter is individually designed to the customer's needs and also constructed to cooperate with the control system in the processing of the customer's transactions. The control system directs the generation of periodic output reports for the customer which present the customer's transaction records in accordance with his own chart of accounts and desired accounting procedures. [Reference.]

Thus, when the time comes for the bank customer's regular periodic statement to be rendered, the programmed computer sorts out the entries in the various categories and produces a statement which groups the entries according to category and which gives subtotals for each category. The customer can then quickly see how much he spent or received in any given category during the period in ques-

tion. Moreover, according to respondent, the system can "[adapt] to whatever variations in ledger format a user may specify." [Reference.]

In further description of the control system that is used in the invention, respondent's application recites that it is made up of a general control and a master control. The general control directs the processing operations common to most customers and is in the form of a software computer program, *i. e.*, a program that is meant to be used in a general-purpose digital computer. The master control, directing the operations that vary on an individual basis with each customer, is in the form of a separate sequence of records for each customer containing suitable machine-instruction mechanisms along with the customer's financial data. Respondent's application sets out a flow chart of a program compatible with an IBM 1400 computer which would effectuate his system.

Under respondent's invention, then, a general purpose computer is programmed to provide bank customers with an individualized and categorized breakdown of their transactions during the period in question.

II

After reviewing respondent's patent application, the patent examiner rejected all the claims therein. He found that respondent's claims were invalid as being anticipated by the prior art, 35 U. S. C. § 102, and as not "particularly pointing out and distinctly claiming" what respondent was urging to be his invention. § 112.

Respondent appealed to the Patent and Trademark Office Board of Appeals. The Board rejected respondent's application on several grounds. It found first that under § 112, the application was indefinite and did not distinctly enough claim what respondent was urging to be his invention. It also concluded that respondent's claims were invalid under § 101 because they claimed nonstatutory subject matter. According to the Board, computer-related inventions which extend "beyond the field of technology * * * are nonstatutory" [reference] [citations], and respondent's claims were viewed to be "nontechnological." Finally, respondent's claims were rejected on grounds of obviousness. 35

U. S. C. § 103. The Board found that respondent's claims were obvious variations of established uses of digital computers in banking and obvious variations of an invention, developed for use in business organizations, that had already been patented. [Citation.]

The CCPA, in a 3–2 ruling, reversed the decision of the Board and held respondent's invention to be patentable. The court began by distinguishing its view of respondent's invention as a " 'record-keeping *machine* system for financial accounts' " from the Board's rather negative view of the claims as going solely to the " 'relationship of a bank and its customers.' " 502 F.2d, at 770 (emphasis in CCPA opinion). As such, the CCPA held respondent's system was "clearly within the 'technological arts.' " *id.*, at 771, and was therefore statutory subject matter under 35 U. S. C. § 101. Moreover, the court held that respondent's claims were narrowly enough drawn and sufficiently detailed to pass muster under the definiteness requirements of § 112. Dealing with the final area of the Board's rejection, the CCPA found that neither established banking practice nor the Dirks patent rendered respondent's system "obvious to one of ordinary skill in the art who did not have [respondent's] specification before him." 502 F.2d, at 772.

In order to hold respondent's invention to be patentable, the CCPA also found it necessary to distinguish this Court's decision in *Gottschalk v. Benson*, 409 U. S. 63 (1972), handed down some 13 months subsequent to the Board's ruling in the instant case. In *Benson*, the respondent sought to patent as a "new and useful process," 35 U. S. C. § 101, "a method of programming a general-purpose digital computer to convert signals from binary-coded decimal form into pure binary form." 409 U. S., at 65. As we observed: "The claims were not limited to any particular art or technology, to any particular apparatus or machinery, or to any particular end use." *Id.*, at 64. Our limited holding, *id.*, at 71, was that respondent's method was not a patentable "process" as that term is defined in 35 U. S. C. § 100(b). [Footnote.]

The Solicitor of the Patent Office argued before the CCPA that *Benson*'s holding of nonpatentability as to the computer program in that case was controlling here. However, the

CCPA concluded that while *Benson* involved a claim as to the patentability of a "process," respondent in this case was advancing claims as to the patentability of an "apparatus" or "machine" which did not involve discoveries so abstract as to be unpatentable:

> "The issue considered by the Supreme Court in *Benson* was a narrow one, namely, is a formula for converting binary coded decimal numerals into pure binary numerals by a series of mathematical calculations a patentable *process*?" (Emphasis added.) [Quoting *In re Christensen*, 478 F. 2d 1392, 1394 (CCPA 1973).]
>
> [T]he instant claims in *apparatus* form do not claim or encompass a law of nature, a mathematical formula, or an algorithm. 502 F. 2d. at 771 (emphasis in CCPA opinion).

Having disposed of the Board's rejections and having distinguished *Benson* to its satisfaction, the court held respondent's invention to be patentable. The Commissioner of Patents sought review in this Court and we granted certiorari. [Citation.] We hold that respondent's invention was obvious under 35 U. S. C. § 103 and therefore reverse.

III

As a judicial test, "invention"—*i. e.*, "an exercise of the inventive faculty" [citation]—has long been regarded as an absolute prerequisite to patentability. [Citations.] However, it was only in 1952 that Congress, in the interest of "uniformity and definiteness," articulated the requirement in a statute, framing it as a requirement of "nonobviousness." [Footnote.] Section 103 of the Patent Act of 1952, 35 U. S. C. § 103, provides in full:

> A patent may not be obtained though the invention is not identically disclosed or described as set forth in section 102 of this title, if the differences between the subject matter sought to be patented and the prior art are such that the subject matter as a whole would have been obvious at the time the invention was made to a person having ordinary skill in the art to which said subject matter pertains. Patentability shall not be negatived by the manner in which the invention was made.

This Court treated the scope of § 103 in detail in *Graham v. John Deere Co.*, 383 U. S. 1 (1966). There, we held that § 103 "was not intended by Congress to change the general level of patentable invention," but was meant "merely as a codification of judicial precedents * * * with congressional directions that inquiries into the obviousness of the subject matter sought to be patented are a prerequisite to patentability." *Id.*, at 17. While recognizing the inevitability of difficulty in making the determination in some cases, we also set out in *Graham, supra*, the central factors relevant to any inquiry into obviousness; "the scope and content of the prior art," the "differences between the prior art and the claims at issue," and "the level of ordinary skill in the pertinent art." *Ibid.* Guided by these factors, we proceed to an inquiry into the obviousness of respondent's system.

As noted [in Section II], the Patent and Trademark Office Board of Appeals relied on two elements in the prior art in reaching its conclusion that respondent's system was obvious. We find both to be highly significant. The first was the nature of the current use of data processing equipment and computer programs in the banking industry. As respondent's application itself observes, that use is extensive:

> Automatic data processing equipments employing digital computers have been developed for the handling of much of the record-keeping operations involved in a banking system. The checks and deposit slips are automatically processed by forming those items as machine-readable records. * * * With such machine systems, most of the extensive data handling required in a bank can be performed automatically. [Reference.]

It is through the use of such data processing equipment that periodic statements are ordinarily given to a bank customer on each of the several accounts that he may have at a given bank. Under respondent's system, what might previously have been separate accounts are treated as a single account, and the customer can see on a single statement the status and progress of each of his "sub-accounts." Respondent's "category code" scheme [noted in Section I] is, we think, closely analogous to a bank's offering its customers multiple accounts from which to choose for making a deposit or writing a check. Indeed, as noted by the Board, the addition of a category number, varying with the nature of the transaction, to the end of a bank customer's regular account

number, creates "in effect, a series of different and distinct account numbers. * * *" [Reference.] Moreover, we note that banks have long segregated debits attributable to service charges *within* any given separate account and have rendered their customers subtotals for those charges.

The utilization of automatic data processing equipment in the traditional separate account system is, of course, somewhat different from the system encompassed by respondent's invention. As the CCPA noted, respondent's invention does something other than "provide a customer with * * * a summary sheet consisting of net totals of plural separate accounts which a customer may have at a bank." 502 F. 2d. at 771. However, it must be remembered that the "obviousness" test of § 103 is not one which turns on whether an invention is equivalent to some element in the prior art but rather whether the difference between the prior art and the subject matter in question "is a difference sufficient to render the claimed subject matter unobvious to one skilled in the applicable art. * * *" *Id.*, at 772 (Markey, C. J., dissenting).

There is no need to make the obviousness determination in this case turn solely on the nature of the current use of data processing and computer programming in the banking industry. For, as noted, the Board pointed to a second factor—a patent issued to Gerhard Dirks—which also supports a conclusion of obviousness. The Dirks patent discloses a complex automatic data processing system using a programmed digital computer for use in a large business organization. Under the system transaction and balance files can be kept and updated for each department of the organization. The Dirks system allows a breakdown within each department of various areas, *e.g.*, of different types of expenses. Moreover, the system is sufficiently flexible to provide additional breakdowns of "sub-areas" within the areas and can record and store specially designated information regarding each of any department's transactions. Thus, for instance, under the Dirks system the disbursing office of a corporation can continually be kept apprised of the precise level and nature of the corporation's disbursements within various areas or, as the Dirks patent terms them, "Item Groups."

Again, as was the case with the prior art within the banking industry the Dirks invention is not equivalent to respondent's system. However, the departments of the business organization and the areas or "Item Groups" under the Dirks system are closely analogous to the bank customers and category number designations respectively under respondent's system. And each shares a similar capacity to provide breakdowns within its "Item Groups" or category numbers. While the Dirks invention is not designed specifically for application to the banking industry many of its characteristics and capabilities are similar to those of respondent's system. Cf. *Graham*, 383 U. S. at 35.

In making the determination of "obviousness," it is important to remember that the criterion is measured not in terms of what would be obvious to a layman, but rather what would be obvious to one "reasonably skilled in [the applicable] art." *Id.*, at 37. In the context of the subject matter of the instant case, it can be assumed that such a hypothetical person would have been aware both of the nature of the extensive use of data processing systems in the banking industry and of the system encompassed in the Dirks patent. While computer technology is an exploding one, "[i]t is but an evenhanded application to require that those persons granted the benefit of a patent monopoly be charged with an awareness" of that technology. *Id.*, at 19.

Assuming such an awareness, respondent's system would, we think, have been obvious to one "reasonably skilled in [the applicable] art." There may be differences between respondent's invention and the state of the prior art. Respondent makes much of his system's ability to allow "a large number of small users to get the benefit of large-scale electronic computer equipment and still continue to use their individual ledger format and bookkeeping methods." [Reference.] It may be that that ability is not possessed to the same extent either by existing machine systems in the banking industry or by the Dirks system.[3] But the mere existence of differences between the prior art and an invention does not establish

the invention's nonobviousness. The gap between the prior art and respondent's system is simply not so great as to render the system nonobvious to one reasonably skilled in the art. [Footnote.]

Accordingly, we reverse the Court of Customs and Patent Appeals and remand this case to that court for further proceedings consistent with this opinion.

So ordered.

PARKER v. FLOOK
437 U.S. 584
(United States Supreme Court, Certiorari to the Court of Customs and Patent Appeals, June 22, 1978.)

STEVENS, J.

Respondent applied for a patent on a "Method for Updating Alarm Limits." The only novel feature of the method is a mathematical formula. In *Gottschalk v. Benson*, 409 U. S. 63, we held that the discovery of a novel and useful mathematical formula may not be patented. The question in this case is whether the identification of a limited category of useful, though conventional, post-solution applications of such a formula makes respondent's method eligible for patent protection.

I

An "alarm limit" is a number. During catalytic conversion processes, operating conditions such as temperature, pressure, and flow rates are constantly monitored. When any of these "process variables" exceeds a predetermined "alarm limit," an alarm may signal the presence of an abnormal condition indicating either inefficiency or perhaps danger. Fixed alarm limits may be appropriate for a steady operation, but during transient operating situations, such as start-up, it may be necessary to "update" the alarm limits periodically.

Respondent's patent application describes a method of updating alarm limits. In essence, the method consists of three steps: an initial step which merely measures the present value of the process variable (*e. g.*, the tempera-

---

3. The Dirks patent does allow "the departments or other organizational users [*i. e.*, the analogues to bank customers under respondent's invention, to] retain their au- thority over operative file systems" and indicates that "[p]rogramming is very easy and different programs are very easily coordinated."

ture); an intermediate step which uses an algorithm[1] to calculate an updated alarm-limit value; and a final step in which the actual alarm limit is adjusted to the updated value.[2] The only difference between the conventional methods of changing alarm limits and that described in respondent's application rests in the second step—the mathematical algorithm or formula. Using the formula, an operator can calculate an updated alarm limit once he knows the original alarm base, the appropriate margin of safety, the time interval that should elapse between each updating, the current temperature (or other process variable), and the appropriate weighting factor to be used to average the original alarm base and the current temperature.

The patent application does not purport to explain how to select the appropriate margin of safety, the weighting factor, or any of the other variables. Nor does it purport to contain any disclosure relating to the chemical processes at work, the monitoring of process variables, or the means of setting off an alarm or adjusting an alarm system. All that it provides is a formula for computing an updated alarm limit. Although the computations can be made by pencil and paper calculations, the abstract of disclosure makes it clear that the formula is primarily useful for computerized calculations producing automatic adjustments in alarm settings. [Footnote.]

The patent claims cover any use of respondent's formula for updating the value of an alarm limit on any process variable involved in a process comprising the catalytic chemical conversion of hydrocarbons. Since there are numerous processes of that kind in the petrochemical and oil-refining industries [footnote], the claims cover a broad range of potential uses of the method. They do not, however, cover every conceivable application of the formula.

II

The patent examiner rejected the application. He found that the mathematical formula constituted the only difference between respondent's claims and the prior art and therefore a patent on this method "would in practical effect be a patent on the formula or mathematics itself." [Footnote.] The examiner concluded that the claims did not describe a discovery that was eligible for patent protection.

The Board of Appeals of the Patent and Trademark Office sustained the examiner's rejection. The Board also concluded that the "point of novelty in [respondent's] claimed method" [footnote] lay in the formula or algorithm described in the claims, a subject matter that was unpatentable under *Benson, supra*.

The Court of Customs and Patent Appeals reversed. *In re Flook*, 559 F.2d 21. It read *Benson* as applying only to claims that entirely pre-empt a mathematical formula or algorithm, and noted that respondent was only claiming on the use of his method to update alarm limits in a process comprising the catalytic chemical conversion of hydrocarbons. The court reasoned that since the mere solution of the algorithm would not constitute infringement of the claims, a patent on the method would not pre-empt the formula.

The Acting Commissioner of Patents and Trademarks filed a petition for a writ of certiorari, urging that the decision of the Court of Customs and Patent Appeals will have a debilitating effect on the rapidly expanding computer "software" industry,[7] and will require him to process thousands of additional patent applications. Because of the importance of the question, we granted certiorari, 434 U.S. 1033.

III

This case turns entirely on the proper construction of § 101 of the Patent Act, which describes the subject matter that is eligible for patent protection. [Footnote.] It does not involve the familiar issues of novelty and obviousness that routinely arise under §§ 102 and 103 when the validity of a patent is challenged. For the purpose of our analysis, we

---

1. We use the word "algorithm" in this case, as we did in *Gottschalk v. Benson,* 409 U. S. 63, 65, to mean "[a] procedure for solving a given type of mathematical problem. * * *"

2. Claim 1 of the patent is set forth in the appendix to this opinion, which also contains a more complete de-

scription of these three steps.

7. The term "software" is used in the industry to describe computer programs. The value of computer programs in use in the United States in 1976 was placed at $43.1 billion, and projected at $70.7 billion by 1980 according to one industry estimate. [Reference.]

assume that respondent's formula is novel and useful and that he discovered it. We also assume, since respondent does not challenge the examiner's finding, that the formula is the only novel feature of respondent's method. The question is whether the discovery of this feature makes an otherwise conventional method eligible for patent protection.

The plain language of § 101 does not answer the question. It is true, as respondent argues, that this method is a "process" in the ordinary sense of the word.[9] But that was also true of the algorithm, which described a method for converting binary-coded decimal numerals into pure binary numerals, that was involved in *Gottschalk v. Benson.* The holding that the discovery of that method could not be patented as a "process" forecloses a purely literal reading of § 101. [Footnote.] Reasoning that an algorithm, or mathematical formula, is like a law of nature, *Benson* applied the established rule that a law of nature cannot be the subject of a patent. Quoting from earlier cases, we said:

"A principle, in the abstract, is a fundamental truth; an original cause; a motive; these cannot be patented, as no one can claim in either of them an exclusive right." *Le Roy v. Tatham,* 14 How. 156, 175. Phenomena of nature, though just discovered, mental processes and abstract intellectual concepts are not patentable, as they are the basic tools of scientific and technological work. 409 U.S., at 67.

The line between a patentable "process" and an unpatentable "principle" is not always clear. Both are "conception[s] of the mind, seen only by [their] effects when being executed or performed." *Tilghman v. Proctor,* 102 U.S. 707, 728. In *Benson* we concluded that the process application in fact sought to patent an idea, noting that

[t]he mathematical formula involved here has no substantial practical application except in connection with a digital computer, which means

that if the judgment below is affirmed, the patent would wholly pre-empt the mathematical formula and in practical effect would be a patent on the algorithm itself. 409 U.S., at 71–72.

Respondent correctly points out that this language does not apply to his claims. He does not seek to "wholly pre-empt the mathematical formula," since there are uses of his formula outside the petrochemical and oil-refining industries that remain in the public domain. And he argues that the presence of specific "post-solution" activity—the adjustment of the alarm limit to the figure computed according to the formula—distinguishes this case from *Benson* and makes his process patentable. We cannot agree.

The notion that post-solution activity, no matter how conventional or obvious in itself, can transform an unpatentable principle into a patentable process exalts form over substance. A competent draftsman could attach some form of post-solution activity to almost any mathematical formula; the Pythagorean theorem would not have been patentable, or partially patentable, because a patent application contained a final step indicating that the formula, when solved, could be usefully applied to existing surveying techniques.[11]

*   *   *

Yet it is equally clear that a process is not unpatentable simply because it contains a law of nature or a mathematical algorithm. [Citations.] For instance, in *Mackay Radio & Telegraph Co. v. Radio Corp. of America,* 306 U.S. 86, the applicant sought a patent on a directional antenna system in which the wire arrangement was determined by the logical application of a mathematical formula. Putting the question of patentability to one side as a preface to his analysis of the infringement issue, Mr. Justice Stone, writing for the Court, explained:

While a scientific truth, or the mathematical expression of it, is not patentable invention, a

---

9. The statutory definition of "process" is broad. [Citation.] An argument can be made, however, that this Court has only recognized a process as within the statutory definition when it either was tied to a particular apparatus or operated to change materials to a "different state or thing." [Citation.] As in *Benson,* we assume that a valid process patent may issue even if it does not meet one of these qualifications of our earlier precedents. 409 U. S., at 71.

11. It should be noted that in *Benson* there was a specific end use contemplated for the algorithm—utilization of the algorithm in computer programming. [Citation.] Of course, as the Court pointed out, the formula had no other practical application; but it is not entirely clear why a process claim is any more or less patentable because the specific end use contemplated is the only one for which the algorithm has any practical application.

novel and useful structure created with the aid of knowledge of scientific truth may be. *Id.*, at 94.

Funk Bros. Seed Co. v. Kalo Co., 333 U.S. 127, 130, expresses a similar approach:

> He who discovers a hitherto unknown phenomenon of nature has no claim to a monopoly of it which the law recognizes. If there is to be invention from such a discovery, it must come from the application of the law of nature to a new and useful end.

Mackay Radio and *Funk Bros.* point to the proper analysis for this case: The process itself, not merely the mathematical algorithm, must be new and useful. Indeed, the novelty of the mathematical algorithm is not a determining factor at all. Whether the algorithm was in fact known or unknown at the time of the claimed invention, as one of the "basic tools of scientific and technological work," see *Gottschalk v. Benson*, 409 U.S., at 67, it is treated as though it were a familiar part of the prior art.

This is also the teaching of our landmark decision in *O'Reilly v. Morse*, 15 How. 62. In that case the Court rejected Samuel Morse's broad claim covering any use of electromagnetism for printing intelligible signs, characters, or letters at a distance. *Id.*, at 112–121. In reviewing earlier cases applying the rule that a scientific principle cannot be patented, the Court placed particular emphasis on the English case of *Neilson v. Harford* [citation], which involved the circulation of heated air in a furnace system to increase its efficiency. The English court rejected the argument that the patent merely covered the principle that furnace temperature could be increased by injecting hot air, instead of cold into the furnace. That court's explanation of its decision was relied on by this Court in *Morse:*

> It is very difficult to distinguish it [the Neilson patent] from the specification of a patent for a principle, and this at first created in the minds of the court much difficulty; but after full consideration, we think that the plaintiff does not merely claim a principle, but a machine, embodying a principle, and a very valuable one. *We think the case must be considered as if the principle being well known, the plaintiff had first invented a mode of applying it.* * * * 15 How., at 115 (emphasis added). [Footnote.]

We think this case must also be considered as if the principle or mathematical formula were well known.

Respondent argues that this approach improperly imports into § 101 the considerations of "inventiveness" which are the proper concerns of §§ 102 and 103. [Footnote.] This argument is based on two fundamental misconceptions.

First, respondent incorrectly assumes that if a process application implements a principle in some specific fashion, it automatically falls within the patentable subject matter of § 101 and the substantive patentability of the particular process can then be determined by the conditions of §§ 102 and 103. This assumption is based on respondent's narrow reading of *Benson,* and is as untenable in the context of § 101 as it is in the context of that case. It would make the determination of patentable subject matter depend simply on the draftsman's art and would ill serve the principles underlying the prohibition against patents for "ideas" or phenomena of nature. The rule that the discovery of a law of nature cannot be patented rests, not on the notion that natural phenomena are not processes, but rather on the more fundamental understanding that they are not the kind of "discoveries" that the statute was enacted to protect. [Footnote.] The obligation to determine what type of discovery is sought to be patented must precede the determination of whether that discovery is, in fact, new or obvious.

Second, respondent assumes that the fatal objection to his application is the fact that one of its components—the mathematical formula—consists of unpatentable subject matter. In countering this supposed objection, respondent relies on opinions by the Court of Customs and Patent Appeals which reject the notion "that a claim may be dissected, the claim components searched in the prior art, and, if the only component found novel is outside the statutory classes of invention, the claim may be rejected under 35 U. S. C. §101." *In re Chatfield*, 545 F. 2d 152, 158 (CCPA 1976). Our approach to respondent's application is, however, not at all inconsistent as a whole. Respondent's process is unpatentable under § 101, not because it contains a mathematical algorithm as one component, but because once that algorithm is assumed to be within the prior art, the application, considered as a whole, contains no patentable invention. Even though a phenomenon of nature or mathematical formula may be well known, an inventive application of the principle may be patented. Conversely, the discovery of such a phenomenon cannot support a patent unless there is some other inventive concept in its application.

Here it is absolutely clear that respondent's application contains no claim of patentable invention. The chemical processes involved in catalytic conversion of hydrocarbons are well known, as are the practice of monitoring the chemical process variables, the use of alarm limits to trigger alarms, the notion that alarm limit values must be recomputed and readjusted, and the use of computers for "automatic monitoring-alarming." [Footnote.] Respondent's application simply provides a new and presumably better method for calculating alarm limit values. If we assume that that method was also known, as we must under the reasoning in *Morse,* then respondent's claim is, in effect, comparable to a claim that the formula $2\pi r$ can be usefully applied in determining the circumference of a wheel. [Footnote.] As the Court of Customs and Patent Appeals has explained, "if a claim is directed essentially to a method of calculating, using mathematical formula, even if the solution is for a specific purpose, the claimed method is nonstatutory." *In re Richman,* 563 F.2d 1026, 1030 (1977).

To a large extent our conclusion is based on reasoning derived from opinions written before the modern business of developing programs for computers was conceived. The youth of the industry may explain the complete absence of precedent supporting patentability. Neither the dearth of precedent, nor this decision, should therefore be interpreted as reflecting a judgment that patent protection of certain novel and useful computer programs will not promote the progress of science and the useful arts, or that such protection is undesirable as a matter of policy. Difficult questions of policy concerning the kinds of programs that may be appropriate for patent protection and the form and duration of such protection can be answered by Congress on the basis of current empirical data not equally available to this tribunal. [Footnote.]

It is our duty to construe the patent statutes as they now read, in light of our prior precedents, and we must proceed cautiously when we are asked to extend patent rights into areas wholly unforeseen by Congress. As Mr. Justice White explained in writing for the Court in *Deepsouth Packing Co. v. Laitram Corp.,* 406 U.S. 518, 531.

[W]e should not expand patent rights by overruling or modifying our prior cases construing the patent statutes, unless the argument for expansion of privilege is based on more than mere inference from ambiguous statutory language. We would require a clear and certain signal from Congress before approving the position of a litigant who, as respondent here, argues that the beachhead of privilege is wider, and the area of public use narrower, than courts had previously thought. No such signal legitimizes respondent's position in this litigation.

The judgment of the Court of Customs and Patent Appeals is [r]eversed.

APPENDIX TO OPINION OF THE COURT

Claim 1 of the patent describes the method as follows:

1. A method for updating the value of at least one alarm limit on at least one process variable involved in a process comprising the catalytic chemical conversion of hydrocarbons wherein said alarm limit has a current value of

$$B_0 + K$$

wherein B_0 is the current alarm base and K is a predetermined alarm offset which comprises:

(1) Determining the present value of said process variable, said present value being defined as PVL:

(2) Determining a new alarm base B_1, using the following equation:

$$B_1 = B_0(1.0 - F) + PVL(F)$$

where F is a predetermined number greater than zero and less than 1.0:

(3) Determining an updated alarm limit which is defined as $B_1 + K$; and thereafter

(4) Adjusting said alarm limit to said updated alarm limit value. [Reference.]

In order to use respondent's method for computing a new limit, the operator must make four decisions. Based on his knowledge of normal operating conditions, he first selects the original "alarm base" (B_0); if a temperature of 400 degrees is normal, that may be the alarm base. He next decides on an appropriate margin of safety, perhaps 50 degrees; that is his "alarm offset" (K). The sum of the alarm base and the alarm offset equals the alarm limit. Then he decides on the time interval that will elapse between each updating; that interval has no effect on the computation although it may, of course, be of great practical importance. Finally, he selects a weighting factor (F), which may be any number between 99% and 1%,* and which is used in the updating calculation.

If the operator has decided in advance to use an original alarm base (B_0) of 400 degrees, a constant alarm offset (K) of 50 degrees, and a weighting factor (F) of 80%, the only additional information he needs in order to compute an updated alarm limit (UAV), is the present value of the process variable (PVL). The computation of the updated alarm limit according to respondent's method involves these three steps:

First, at the predetermined interval, the process variable is measured; if we assume the temperature is then 425 degrees, PVL will then equal 425.

Second, the solution of respondent's novel formula will produce a new alarm base (B_1) that will be a weighted average of the preceding alarm base (B_0) of 400 degrees and the current temperature (PVL) of 425. It will be closer to one or the other depending on the value of the weighting factor (F) selected by the operator. If F is 80%, that percentage of 425 (340) plus 20% $(1 - F)$ of 400 (80) will produce a new alarm base of 420 degrees.

Third, the alarm offset (K) of 50 degrees is then added to the new alarm base (B_1) of 420 to produce the updated alarm limit (UAV) of 470.

The process is repeated at the selected time intervals. In each updating computation, the most recently calculated alarm base and the current measurement of the process variable will be substituted for the corresponding numbers in the original calculation, but the alarm offset and the weighting factor will remain constant.

IN RE FREEMAN
573 F.2d 1237
(United States Court of Customs and Patent Appeals, March 30, 1978.)

MARKEY, C. J.

Appeal from the decision of the Patent and Trademark Office (PTO) Board of Appeals (board), affirming the rejection of claims 1-10, all of the claims in application serial No. 32,025, filed May 6, 1970, and entitled "Computer Typesetting." We reverse.

THE INVENTION

The subject matter of Freeman's invention is a system for typesetting alphanumeric information, using a computer-based control system in conjunction with a photo-typesetter of conventional design. Freeman's overall scheme is represented by Figure 1 of his application [see next page; art is from the original opinion.]

Input device 140 provides the identities of symbols and alphanumeric characters to be composed and the positional commands for placement of such symbols and characters in the final composition. Although shown in Figure 1 as a keyboard, input device 140 may be a card reader, a magnetic or paper tape reader, or other known input device. Memory 160 stores character specifications and provides computer 100 with detailed information about the exact nature of the characters which may be selected by coded input signals from input device 140. Memory 160 may be part of computer memory 130. Computer 100 represents a broad category of data processors, including general purpose digital computers.

Output unit 170 receives character position signals from computer 100 and generates a permanent record of the desired positional relationship of the characters. As shown in Figure 1, output unit 170 may include a display device, such as cathode ray tube (CRT) 175, and a photographic system, such as camera 176. Output unit 170 may also be a computer microfilm printer, or other means of producing a permanent record.

Freeman's system is especially useful in printing mathematical formulae. Its particular advantage over prior computer-aided

---

* More precisely, it is defined as a number greater than 0, but less than 1.

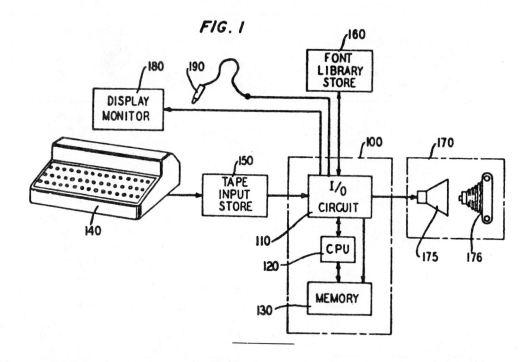

FIG. 1

printing systems is its positioning of mathematical symbols in an expression in accordance with their appearance, while maintaining the mathematical integrity of the expression.

The functioning of appellant's invention is best understood in appellant's example, wherein the objective is the photocomposing of the mathematical expression:

$$Z = \frac{(T + X)^4 + W}{Y + 4} + \int_1^7 h^v dv$$

One embodiment of appellant's invention employs a hierarchical "tree structure" computer storage arrangement. Applied to the above mathematical expression, the hierarchical arrangement produces [the tree structure shown in Figure 3]. [Art is from the original opinion.] Each particular tree structure depends on spatial relationships of the symbols, not on their mathematical meaning, i. e., all symbols, whether characters or operators, are treated in the same way. As in Figure 3 above, the "head" of the tree structure is the symbol at the extreme left of the main line of the formula. New "branches" of the tree are started

by those symbols which begin new lines, above, on, or below the main line of the formula, e. g., exponents and initial symbols of numerators and denominators.

The tree structure storage arrangement is used to determine the sequence, indicated by the circled numbers in Figure 3, in which the symbols of the formula are processed by the "local positioning algorithm" disclosed by appellant. Symbols attached by arrows leading out from a given symbol are called "subordinates" of the given symbol. In Figure 3, for example, the "1," the "7," and the "h" are subordinates of the integral sign.

Another basic feature of appellant's invention is the use of a set of "concatenation points" for each character. Prior art devices, like the typical Linotype machine, employed a rectangular, edge-to-edge concatenation system. Appellant's sets of concatenation points correspond roughly to the eight major compass directions, as shown in [Figure 4]. [Art is from the original opinion.] To form the expression "2†" from the [characters shown in Figure 4], the West concatenation point of the "†" is specified to coincide with the East concatenation point of the "2". A particular advantage of appellant's concatenation point

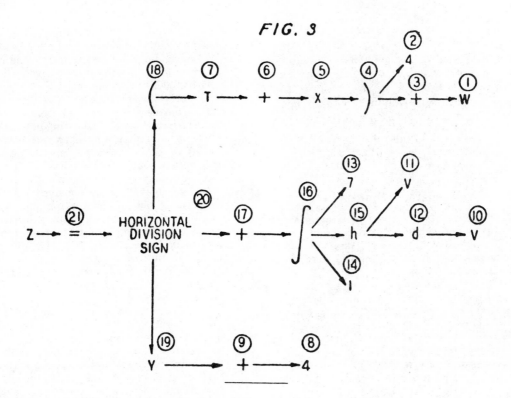

FIG. 3

positioning technique is its applicability to both straight linear text and to subscripts, superscripts, division signs, and integral signs. To form the expression "†²," the Southwest concatenation point of the "small 2" is specified to coincide with the Northeast concatenation point of the "†."

Appellant's local positioning algorithm, using concatenation points to typeset mathematical expressions stored in a hierarchical-tree structure, is disclosed in its simplest form:

(1) Cause an appropriate (specified) concatenation point for subordinates of a given symbol to coincide with appropriate (specified) concatenation points for that given symbol. * * *

(2) The order of symbol processing is as follows:

FIG. 4

N
NW• ┬ •NE
W•   ┼ •E
SW• ┴ •SE
     Ṡ

N
NW•   •NE
W•   •E
SW•   •SE

N
NW•   •NE
W•   •E
SW•   •SE
     Ṡ

(a) Along a given branch of the tree, positioning starts at the righthand end and works back to the left. It should be understood that right and left refer to the structure as shown in FIG. 3 (head at the left). It may be convenient to represent and/or store the structure in a vertical arrangement with the "head" at the top or bottom. In all cases, however, the order of positioning will proceed in a given branch in a direction toward the head of the structure.

(b) If a given symbol along a given branch has subordinate symbols that start new branches, all of these new branches are positioned internally (with respect to the given symbol) before any positioning is performed on the given symbol of the given branch. For example, in FIG. 3, the symbols in the branch started by the left parenthesis "(" that is a subordinate of the horizontal division sign are positioned relative to each other before the local positioning algorithm is applied to any of the symbols on the main (division sign) branch.

In sum, appellant's invention includes three signal-processing steps. First, the input codes are read, and a tree structure of symbols representing the mathematical expression is built. Second, the signals specifying the relative concatenation point positions of the symbols are composed by application of the local positioning algorithm. Third, an image of the expression, with all symbols in proper position, is generated on the CRT or other output device.

THE CLAIMS

Claims 1-7 are apparatus claims:

1. In a computer display system comprising
(A) a display device for generating relatively-positioned symbol images in response to applied sequences of signals specifying the shape and position of said images,
(B) a data processor comprising
(1) means for storing a first plurality of data sequences, each describing individual symbols, and a second plurality of data sequences corresponding to a control program,
(2) means responsive to said control program for nondestructively reading from said means for storing and transferring to said display device selected ones of said first plurality of data sequences,
(3) means responsive to said control program for generating and transferring to said display device data sequences specifying the desired position of at least a first one of said selected data sequences, the improvement comprising
means for storing additional information specifying spatial coordinate positions, relative to a reference point on a corresponding symbol, of a plurality of concatenation points associated with said corresponding symbol, and
means responsive to said control program for generating and transferring to said display device data signals specifying the coincidence of at least one specified concatenation points [*sic*] on adjacent symbols.
2. The system of claim 1 further comprising input means for modifying said control program by providing input data specifying the desired positioning of said images.
3. The system of claim 2 further comprising means for storing said input data in a hierarchical tree structure, the lowest level branch of said structure corresponding to the position of the symbol described by said first one of said selected data sequences, successively higher branches of said structure indicating the position of corresponding symbols relative to the position of the symbol described by said first one of said selected data sequences.

4. The system of claim 3 further comprising editing means responsive to the images generated by said display device and to said control program for modifying the relative position of selected ones of said images.
5. The system of claim 3 [*sic,* 4?] wherein said editing means comprises a light sensitive device for generating signals indicating desired image positions and program controlled means for modifying said data signals specifying the coincidence of concatenation points.
6. A display system comprising
(A) a display device responsive to applied information signals for generating images,
(B) means for storing display information corresponding to a plurality of display entities, said display information comprising entity identification information and information identifying the position of a plurality of concatenation points corresponding to each of said display entities,
(C) programmed controlled means for generating position signals specifying the relative position of selected ones of said display entities by specifying the coincidence of at least one of the concatenation points associated with one of said selected ones of said display entities with appropriate concatenation points associated with adjacent ones of said selected display entities, and
(D) means for applying entity-identification signals and associated position signals to said display device.
7. The system of claim 6 further comprising means responsive to said entity identification signals and said position signals corresponding to said adjacent ones of said selected display entities for testing for lack of a minimum clearance between said selected display entities, and means responsive to said means for testing to modify said position signals when said lack of minimum clearance appears.

Claims 8-10 are method claims:

8. In a computer display system comprising
(A) a display device for generating relatively-positioned symbol images in response to applied sequences of signals specifying the shape and position of said images,
(B) a data processor comprising
(1) means for storing a first plurality of data sequences, each describing individual symbols, and a second plurality of data sequences corresponding to a control program,
(2) means responsive to said control program for nondestructively reading from said means for storing and transferring to said display device selected ones of said first plurality of data sequences.

(3) control means comprising means responsive to said control program for generating and transferring to said display device data sequences specifying the desired position of symbols corresponding to said selected data sequences,

the method of controlling said system comprising the steps of

(A) generating data sequences corresponding to concatenation points associated with each of said symbol images, and

(B) generating data sequences specifying that selected ones of said concatenation points associated with desirably adjacent symbol images should occupy identical spatial positions.

9. The method of claim 8 further comprising the steps of

(A) testing said data sequences specifying the position of said desirably adjacent symbol images for lack of a minimum clearance therebetween, and

(B) modifying said data sequences corresponding to at least one of said concatenation points associated with said desirably adjacent symbol images.

10. The method of claim 8 further comprising the steps of

(A) generating a sequence of input signals representing the desired position of said selected ones of said individual symbols.

(B) generating hierarchically structured signals representing the branches of a tree structure corresponding to the relative position of said selected ones of said individual symbols, higher order signals corresponding to the position of symbols subordinate to symbols represented by lower order symbols

(C) operating sequentially on said hierarchically structured signals to generate said data sequences specifying the desired position of said selected ones of said individual symbols.

BOARD

The examiner rejected claims 1-10 for incom-

2. Responding to appellant's use of the word "synergistically" in describing how his "means" operate, the solicitor states:

However, it is not apparent how appellant's programmed digital computer can produce any *synergistic* result. Instead, the computer will simply do the job it is instructed to do. Where is there any surprising or unexpected result? The unlikelihood of any such result is merely one more reason why patents should not be granted in situations where the only novelty is in the programming of general purpose digital computers. [Citations.]

There being no rejection for anticipation under 35 U.S.C. § 102 or for obviousness under 35 U.S.C. § 103, the relevance of the foregoing escapes us. The cited cases dealt

plete disclosure, under 35 U.S.C. § 112, and claims 8-10 as drawn to nonstatutory subject matter, *i. e.,* "mental steps," under 35 U.S.C. §§ 100, 101. The board reversed both rejections, and entered a new ground of rejection, as authorized by 37 CFR 196(b), rejecting all claims as directed to nonstatutory subject matter under the principles of *Gottschalk v. Benson,* 409 U.S. 63, 93 S.Ct. 253, 34 L.Ed.2d 273, 175 USPQ 673 (1972). [Footnote.]

The board construed the claims "to cover a known program loaded display typesetting device wherein the novelty resides in the program." In applying *Benson,* the board said the improvement covered by the claims appeared to have no substantial practical application except in connection with a digital computer and that the coverage sought "in practical effect would be a patent on the algorithm itself." That claims 1-7 were apparatus claims was dismissed on the view that appellant should not be allowed to claim indirectly what he cannot claim directly with method language.

Neither the examiner nor the board questioned that appellant's invention, as claimed, was new, useful, and unobvious.[2]

ISSUE

The sold issue is whether the systems recited in claims 1-7 and the methods recited in claims 8-10 constitute statutory subject matter under 35 U.S.C. § 101. [Footnote.]

OPINION

THE BOARD'S APPLICATION OF BENSON

The board looked to the "nutshell" holding in *Benson*:

It is conceded that one may not patent an idea. But in practical effect that would be the result

only with the issue of obviousness. Considerations of novelty or obviousness are of no effect whatever in determining whether particular claims define statutory subject matter under 35 U.S.C. § 101.

It disserves the need for clarity in the law, and unjustly skews the judicial process, when the issue presented and considered below is muddied by disinguous presentations relating to new and different issues, and without open admission of that relationship. If the desire to "win" (though the law may lose) be so overwhelming as to impel injection of new and different issues at the appellate level, the candor rightfully expected of all lawyers, government and private, requires that the injection be labeled as such.

if the formula for converting BCD numerals to pure binary numerals were patented in this case. The mathematical formula involved here has no substantial practical application except in connection with a digital computer, which means that if the judgment below is affirmed, the patent would wholly pre-empt the mathematical formula and in practical effect would be a patent on the algorithm itself. [Citation.]

In applying the "principles set down" in *Benson*, the board decided that "the novelty resides in the program," and concluded, without further analysis of the claims themselves, that the results foreseen in the "nutshell" holding would ensue. We disagree with the approach taken and the conclusion reached by the board.

We have indicated the inappropriateness of the "point of novelty" approach in determining whether a claimed invention is statutory subject matter under 35 U.S.C. § 101. See *In re de Castelet*, 562 F.2d 1236, 1240, 195 USPQ 439, 443 (Cust. & Pat.App.1977); *In re Chatfield*, 545 F.2d 152, 158, 191 USPQ 730, 736 (Cust. & Pat.App.1976), *cert. denied*, 434 U.S. 875, 98 S.Ct. 226, 54 L.Ed.2d 155, 195 USPQ 465 (1977). Though the solicitor refers to language appearing in *In re Christensen*, 478 F.2d 1392, 178 USPQ 35 (Cust. & Pat.App.1973), we clarified that language in *In re Chatfield, supra*, 545 F.2d at 158, 191 USPQ at 736:

> Our reference in *Christensen* to the mathematical equation as being "at the point of novelty" does not equate to a holding that a claim may be dissected, the claim components searched in the prior art and, if the only component found novel is outside the statutory classes of invention, the claim may be rejected under 35 U.S.C. § 101. That procedure is neither correct nor within the intent of Congress. * * *

In reversing the examiner, the board considered *In re Christensen, supra*, inapposite because the data here operated upon, *i. e.*, symbols and their concatenation points, were

not in the prior art. "Thus" said the board, "the instant case involves more than the mere practice of an algorithm or formula on data considered to be old and well known."

* * *

The board chose to read *Benson* much too broadly. The solicitor states the PTO's view of the *Benson* holding as being "that a patent should not be granted where the only novelty resides in a program for a general purpose digital computer." That overly broad reading, whatever purpose it may be intended to serve in the PTO, is unjustified. That computer programs are not patentable was neither the holding nor the "thrust" of *Benson. In re de Castelet, supra; In re Chatfield, supra*. Neither this court nor the PTO is at liberty to disregard the words of the Court in *Benson*: "It is said that the decision precludes a patent for any program servicing a computer. We do not so hold." 409 U.S. at 71, 93 S.Ct. at 257, 175 USPQ at 676. [5] Nor is this court or the PTO at liberty to ignore the Court's own characterization of its *Benson* holding: "Our limited holding * * * was that respondent's method was not a patentable 'process' as that term is defined in 35 U.S.C. § 100(b)." *Dann v. Johnston*, 425 U.S. 219, 224, 96 S.Ct. 1393, 1396, 47 L.Ed.2d 692, 189 USPQ 257, 259 (1976).

The fundamental flaw in the board's analysis in this case lies in a superficial treatment of the claims. With no reference to the nature of the algorithm involved, the board merely stated that the coverage sought "in practical effect would be a patent on the algorithm itself." Though the board gave no clear reasons for so concluding, its approach would appear to be that every implementation with a programmed computer equals "algorithm" in the *Benson* sense. If that rubric be law, every claimed method that can be so implemented would equal nonstatutory subject matter under 35 U.S.C. § 101. That reasoning sweeps

---

5. In *In re Chatfield, supra*, 545 F.2d at 156, 191 USPQ at 734, and in *In re Noll*, 545 F.2d 141, 148-49 n. 6. 191 USPQ 721, 726 n. 6 (Cust. & Pat.App.1976), *cert. denied*, 434 U.S. 875, 98 S.Ct. 226, 54 L.Ed.2d 155, 195 USPQ 465 (1977), this court pointed out that the phrase "these programs" in the *Benson* opinion necessarily referred to the specific type of program there involved, not to computer programs in general. Though the present invention is not merely a "program," the solicitor contends that the responsible course would be to deny patents on "software

inventions" until Congress sanctions them. The constitutionally responsible course, however, was stated in *In re de Castelet, supra*, 562 F.2d at 1240, 195 USPQ at 443:

> Absent contrary directions, no basis exists for a moratorium on protection of inventions embodying or using computer programs. Such broad prohibition could subject meritorious statutory inventions to unabatable piracy, and could forestall invention disclosure, the hallmark of the patent system, until Congress chooses to act.

too wide and is without basis in law. The absence, or inadequacy, of detailed claim analysis in the present case is further illustrated by the conclusion that "the novelty resides in the program" when, as here, the claims recite no particular computer program. In the present case, it is not the claims but the *specification* that discloses implementation of the claimed invention with computer programs. [Footnote.]

As a bare minimum, application of *Benson* in a particular case requires a careful analysis of the claims, to determine whether, as in *Benson,* they recite a "procedure for solving a given type of *mathematical* problem." 409 U.S. at 65, 93 S.Ct. at 254, 175 USPQ at 674 (emphasis added).

THE METHOD CLAIMS

Appellant's claims 8-10 define methods of controlling a computer display system. Claim 8 sets forth a process of assigning concatenation points to each character to appear on the display device and specifying which of the concatenation points for adjacent characters will coincide. Claim 9 adds the process limitation of testing and modifying the spatial relationship between adjacent characters to provide minimum clearance therebetween. Claim 10 adds the process limitation of employing a hierarchical tree structure to establish the spatial relationships among a group of characters to appear on the display device.

Determination of whether a claim preempts nonstatutory subject matter as a whole, in the light of *Benson,* requires a two-step analysis. First, it must be determined whether the claim directly or indirectly recites an "algorithm" in the *Benson* sense of that term, for a claim which fails even to recite an algorithm clearly cannot wholly preempt an algorithm. Second, the claim must be further analyzed to ascertain whether in its entirety it wholly preempts that algorithm. We do not reach the second step in this case because method claims 8-10 do not recite an algorithm in the *Benson* sense.

We are not unmindful of the need for clear understanding of the term "algorithm." As we stated in *In re Chatfield, supra,* 545 F.2d at 156 n. 5, 191 USPQ at 734 n. 5:

8. The preferred definition of "algorithm" in the computer art is: "A fixed step-by-step procedure for accomplishing a given result; usually a simplified procedure for

Over-concentration on the word "algorithm" alone, for example, may mislead. The Supreme Court carefully supplied a definition of the particular algorithm before it, i. e., "[a] procedure for solving a given type of mathematical problem." The broader definition of algorithm is "a step-by-step procedure for solving a problem or accomplishing some end." *Webster's New Collegiate Dictionary* (1976). It is axiomatic that inventive minds seek and develop solutions to problems and step-by-step solutions often attain the status of patentable invention. It would be unnecessarily detrimental to our patent system to deny inventors patent protection on the *sole* ground that their contribution could be broadly termed an "algorithm."

Because every process may be characterized as "a step-by-step procedure * * * for accomplishing some end," a refusal to recognize that *Benson* was concerned only with *mathematical* algorithms leads to the absurd view that the Court was reading the word "process" out of the statute.

The manner in which a claim recites a mathematical algorithm may vary considerably. In some claims, a formula or equation may be expressed in traditional mathematical symbols so as to be immediately recognizable as a mathematical algorithm. [Citations.] Other claims may use prose to express a mathematical computation or to indirectly recite a mathematical equation therefor. [Citations.] A claim which substitutes, for a mathematical formula in algebraic form, "words which mean the same thing," nonetheless recites an algorithm in the *Benson* sense. [Citation.] Indeed, the claims at issue in *Benson* did not contain a formula or equation expressed in mathematical symbols. When considered as a whole, each of the claims in *Benson* did, however, recite in prose a formula for converting binary coded decimal numbers into binary numbers. [Footnote.]

The "local positioning algorithm" described in appellant's specification is the order of steps in processing the hierarchical tree structure and spatially relating the various characters to be displayed. Appellant has thus used the term "algorithm" as a term of art in its broad sense, *i. e.,* to identify a step-by-step procedure for accomplishing a given result.[8]

solving a complex problem, also a full statement of a finite number of steps." [Citation.]

The method claims here at issue do not recite process steps which are themselves mathematical calculations, formulae, or equations. Each of claims 8, 9, and 10 merely defines a new, useful, and unobvious process for operating a computer display system. The board, therefore, erred in its reliance on *Benson* as its sole basis for concluding that the present method claims are drawn to nonstatutory subject matter.

The solicitor argues that appellant carries the solution to the algorithm no further than "a fleeting display on a cathode ray tube," and that that step constitutes insufficient "post-solution activity." [Citations.] [Footnote.] The presence or absence of "post-solution activity" was material in *Flook* and *de Castelet* because the claims at issue in those cases recited mathematical equations or calculations as part of the "subject matter as a whole." That factor called the *Benson* holding at least prima facie into play. There being no mathematical calculations, equations, or formulae here, and thus no solution to a mathematical algorithm, no question of "post-solution activity" is present.

THE APPARATUS CLAIMS

Though a claim expressed in "means for" (functional) terms is said to be an apparatus claim, the subject matter as a whole of that claim may be indistinguishable from that of a method claim drawn to the steps performed by the "means." For example, present claim 8 recites process steps of assigning concatenation points to each symbol and specifying which of the concatenation points for adjacent symbols will coincide, and claim 1 merely recites "means for" accomplishing each of these same steps. As another example, claim 3 adds a "means for storing input data in a hierarchical tree structure," paralleling the process step added by claim 10. We agree with the solicitor's contention that if allowance of a method claim is proscribed by *Benson,* it would be anomalous to grant a claim to apparatus encompassing any and every "means for" practicing that very method.[10]

The apparatus claims do not directly or indirectly recite any mathematical equation, formula, or calculation and thus do not preempt the use of any mathematical problem-solving algorithm. It is unnecessary, therefore, to consider the effect of specific apparatus limitations in some of the apparatus claims. [Footnote.]

Because neither the present apparatus claims nor the present method claims recite or preempt a mathematical algorithm as forbidden by *Benson,* both sets of claims are immune from a rejection based solely on the opinion in that case.

Accordingly, the decision of the board, rejecting claims 1–10 under 35 U.S.C. § 101, is reversed.

IN RE SARKAR
575 F.2d 870
(United States Court of Customs and Patent Appeals, May 11, 1978.)

PER CURIAM.

Appellant Sarkar moves the court pursuant to CCPA Rule 5.13(g) to seal the record in Appeal No. 78-554 and to hear oral argument with respect thereto *in camera* so that material disclosed in the involved patent application may be retained, in the event of an adverse decision, as a trade secret. Having considered memoranda stating the views of the parties, the motion is *granted.*

FACTS

February 13, 1978, Sarkar filed with the Clerk of this court the certified transcript of the proceedings in Patent and Trademark Office (PTO) with respect to his pending patent application, which proceedings had culminated in an adverse decision of the Board of Appeals (board), on all pending claims, from which a timely appeal had been taken under 35 U.S.C.

---

10. A claim drawn to new, useful, and unobvious apparatus, specifying what that apparatus is, and not merely what it does, would not, on the other hand, be rejectable on the sole ground that the only presently known use for that apparatus is the practice of an unpatentable method. A claim to a new, useful, and unobvious computer, describing that computer in truly structural terms, would not be rejectable on the ground that the only known use for that computer is the performance of unpatentable methods of calculation. To assert the contrary, on a "preempt an unpatentable method" theory, would deny the incentive of the patent system to research and development in the field of computer-building technology.

§ 141. Sarkar's claimed invention involves a technique for "modeling" a river on a computer so that design requirements of riparian constructions can be accurately predicted. The board held that the claimed method embodying such a technique was not statutory subject matter under 35 U.S.C. § 101 as construed in *Gottschalk v. Benson*, 409 U.S. 63, 93 S.Ct. 253, 34 L.Ed.2d 273 (1972). The controlling legal principles are, as yet, unsettled, and, at this time, the Supreme Court is again considering the status of computer-software inventions as statutory subject matter in *Parker v. Flook, cert. granted,* 437 U.S. 584, 98 S.Ct. 764, 54 L.Ed.2d 780, 196 USPQ 864 (1978).

Concurrent with the filing of the transcript, Sarkar filed with the Clerk of this court the instant motion praying, inter alia, that the record be sealed. Upon receipt of these papers, the Clerk docketed Sarkar's appeal and took steps to preserve the secrecy of the materials contained in the transcript pending disposition of this motion. As a result, the papers constituting the record in this appeal have never been available to the public. [Citation.] In the PTO, they were, presumably, held in confidence in accordance with 35 U.S.C. § 122.

It is alleged that certain mathematical formulae involved in the claimed method have been retained as, and are now, valuable trade secrets, and it is argued that disclosure and attendant loss of such secrets in the course of obtaining judicial review of the PTO decision would be unjust. Attempts to enter into a stipulation with the PTO solicitor whereby an abbreviated record might have been brought publicly before this court have met with no success. Accordingly, relief has been sought under our Rule 5.13(g) which reads:

> (g) *In Camera* Proceeding. In a proper case, where the interests of justice require, and on a convincing showing thereof by motion properly made, the court will sit *in camera,* or seal its record, or both.

The PTO opposes the motion on public policy grounds, saying "A resolution, one way or the other, will have no effect on the Patent and Trademark Office," alleging that the showing made is insufficient to warrant the relief sought. The solicitor notes that Sarkar was granted a license under 35 U.S.C. § 184 to file similar applications abroad and that Sarkar had failed to show that no foreign application filed thereunder was now open to the public. This court's decision in *In re Sackett,* 136 F.2d 248, 30 CCPA 1214, 57 USPQ 541 (1943), is cited for the proposition that the right of public access to court records is paramount to a patent applicant's claim to trade-secret rights.

In reply, Sarkar assures the court that no foreign applications have been filed and that there has been no public disclosure of the alleged trade secrets.

RESOLUTION

This is a case of first impression in this court with respect to which our prior decisions offer no guidance. *Sackett* does not support the proposition urged by the PTO. There, the appellant sought review of a board decision and, *after* the court's decision affirming the board had been rendered, moved the court to seal the record so that the substance of the patent application could be retained as a trade secret. The court denied the motion noting that once appellant had openly and voluntarily brought the alleged invention into the public forum of the court, the court was not (meaning no longer) authorized to protect it as a trade secret. Sarkar's concurrent filing of this motion and the certified transcript effectively avoids the *Sackett* problem.

Any federal court has the *inherent authority* to seal its record when, in the exercise of sound discretion, such action is deemed appropriate. [Citation.] Our Rule 5.13(g) is merely declaratory of this inherent authority never before exercised by this court to protect a trade secret in an ex parte patent appeal.

The determination of what constitutes a "proper case" in which to seal our record requires balancing the triangular interests of the trade secret owner, the court as an institution, and the public. The factors present in this case which lead us to the conclusion that the motion should be granted are:

(1) The substance of the patent application in issue has remained confidential by virtue of the operation of 35 U.S.C. § 122;

(2) The filing of the instant motion *coincided* with the filing of the certified transcript in this court such that the latter was never available to the public;

(3) The motion and supporting memoranda convincingly demonstrate (a) that the appli-

cation in issue contains material susceptible of retention as a trade secret, (b) that such material has, in fact, been so retained, (c) that appellant has filed no foreign patent applications, and (d) that the subject matter has not become generally available through the activities of others;

(4) The merits of appellant's claim of entitlement to patent protection involve unsettled questions of law which are of current concern and the resolution of which is in the public interest;

(5) All less restrictive mechanisms for bringing the dispute before this court while still protecting the alleged trade secrets, e. g., a stipulated statement of facts, an abbreviated record, etc., have been explored and proven impractical; and

(6) The extraordinary action of the court in protecting the substance of the pending application will not be rendered nugatory by the issuance of a patent *regardless* of our holding since there are no allowed claims based on the alleged trade secret pending in Sarkar's application.

We are guided in our determination by the opinion of the Supreme Court in *Kewanee Oil Co. v. Bicron Corp.*, 416 U.S. 470, 94 S.Ct. 1879, 40 L.Ed.2d 315, 181 USPQ 673 (1974), from which we glean the sentiment that, wherever possible, trade secret law and patent law should be administered in such manner that the former will not deter an inventor from seeking the benefit of the latter, because the public is *most* benefited by the early disclosure of the invention in consideration of the patent grant. If a patent applicant is unwilling to pursue his right to a patent at the risk of certain loss of trade secret protection, the two systems will conflict, the public will be deprived of knowledge of the invention in many cases, and inventors will be reluctant to bring unsettled legal questions of significant current interest before this court for resolution. By extending the protection of the court to the *legitimate* trade secret under conditions such as those outlined above, we believe that conflicts between the two systems will be minimized.

It is, therefore, ordered that the motion for *in camera* proceedings and to seal the record is *granted* to the extent that the record, briefs, and other papers in this appeal shall remain confidential and only the parties to this appeal, their counsel, and necessary court personnel shall be permitted to be present at any oral argument. The court reserves the right to articulate the bases of its decision as it deems necessary.

Granted.

IN RE TOMA

575 F.2d 872
(United States Court of Customs and Patent Appeals, May 18, 1978.)

BALDWIN, J.

This appeal is from the decision of the Patent and Trademark Office (PTO) Board of Appeals (board), modified on reconsideration, sustaining the rejection of claims 1, 13, 15-24, 26, 28-36, 40, 41 and 43-56 [footnote] under 35 U.S.C. § 101 as being directed to nonstatutory subject matter. We reverse the rejection of all claims.

THE INVENTION

The invention involves a method of operating a digital computer to translate from a source natural language, e. g., Russian, to a target natural language, e. g., English. The method involves three phases. The dictionary look-up phase establishes the target language meaning of each word in the source text. The syntactical analysis phase identifies syntactical information from the inflection of the word and the position of the word in the source text. The synthesis phase takes the meaning and syntactical information of all of the words of a sentence in the source text and forms a sentence in the target language.

More specifically, the method begins by loading the source text into the memory of a computer. Each source text word is then transformed into a converted source text word. The converted source text word consists of the source text word and coded information. The coded information may include a memory offset address linkage which provides access to a memory location that contains syntactical information and translation for the source text word. The converted source text words which derive from a source text sentence are then synthesized into a target language translation of that sentence. The synthesis correctly establishes both word meaning and the word position in the target language sentence.

An important aspect of the invention is the separate treatment given high frequency versus low frequency words. In order to maximize the effective capacity of the core memory of the computer, the low frequency words carry their translation information along with them, while each of the high frequency words carries a memory offset address linkage which allows easy access to its translation information which is stored in the core memory. Thus, the translation information for frequently used words is held in an easily accessible place in the computer rather than along with every occurrence of the word as is done for low frequency words.

While the above description portrays a human analogy of how the claimed invention functions, it must be understood that, in fact, the actual operation of the process by the computer is quite different. From the time that the source text is converted to machine-readable input data until the time that the machine-readable output data is converted to human-readable translation text, the claimed process proceeds under the control of a computer program. While it is convenient to describe the steps of the program as if they were being performed by a human translator, in fact, nothing of the kind is happening. Rather, the computer is carrying out a series of unthinking, abstract mathematical operations on the abstract values stored in the memory of the computer. The program functions independently of the meaning or significance of the data on which it is acting. The fact that the program is formed in a high level programming language, which makes the program appear to give significance to the machine operation, does not change the fact that the machine is actually carrying out a series of abstract steps which have nothing to do with translating between natural languages. If a different kind of information were fed into the computer, the program used in this invention could conceivably perform a function totally different from translating.

Various claims of appellant recite activity by which information is extracted from the computer. Claims 32 and 36 include "printing out the translation." Claim 51 recites the step

"converting the target language sequence from computer intelligible binary coded signals back to visual indicia." Claims 52 and 53 limit the "converting" step of claim 51 to "printing." Claim 54 recites the step of "converting the proper target language sequence from computer intelligible binary coded signals back to visual indicia." Claims 55 and 56 limit the "converting" step in claim 54 to "printing."

The following claims are representative:

1. A method for translation between source and target natural languages using a programmable digital computer system, the steps comprising:

(a) storing in a main memory of the computer system a source text to be translated;

(b) scanning and comparing such stored source text words with dictionaries of source language words stored in a memory and for each such source text word for which a match is found, storing in a file in main memory each word and in association with each such word, coded information derived from such dictionary for use in translation of such word, the coded information including memory offset address linkages to a memory in the computer system where grammar and target language translations for the word are stored;

(c) analyzing the source text words in its file of words, a complete sentence at a time, and converting the same into a sentence in the target language utilizing the coded information and including the steps of

(1) utilizing the memory offset address linkages for obtaining the target [sic language] translations of words from a memory; and

(2) reordering the target language translation into the proper target language sequence.

32. A method, according to Claim 1, including the steps of analyzing a sequence of words in the source language within phrases and clauses in relation to the target language word sequence, the target language word sequence being expressed symbolically by assigned numbers and printing out the translation taking into consideration each source word.

51. A method for translation between source and target natural languages using a programmable digital computer system, the steps comprising:

(a) converting a source text to be translated from visual indicia to computer intelligible binary coded signals;

(b) storing in a main memory of the computer system the converted source text to be translated;

(c) scanning and comparing such converted source text words with dictionaries of source language words stored in a memory and for each source text word for which a match is found, storing in a file in main memory each word and [sic in] association with each such word, coded information derived from such dictionary for use in translation of each word, the coded information including memory offset address linkages to a memory in the computer system where grammar and target language translations for the word are stored;

(d) analyzing the converted source text words in the file of words, a complete sentence at a time, and converting the same into a sentence in the target language utilizing the coded information and including the steps of

(1) utilizing the memory offset address linkages for obtaining the target language translations of words from a memory; and

(2) reordering the target language translation into the proper target language sequence;

(e) converting the target language sequence from computer intelligible binary coded signals back to visual indicia.

52. The method of claim 51 wherein the last step of converting comprises the step of printing.

THE BOARD

The opinion of the board states that the claimed method is not statutory subject matter under 35 U.S.C. § 101. [Footnote.] The board's position is based on its reading of *Gottschalk v. Benson,* 409 U.S. 63, 93 S.Ct. 253, 34 L.Ed.2d 273, 175 USPQ 673 (1972), and its reading of our early interpretation of *Benson* in *In re Christensen,* 478 F.2d 1392, 178 USPQ 35 (Cust. & Pat.App.1973). Appellant's claimed invention is, according to the board, an algorithm or rule having no substantial practical application except in connection with a digital computer. The board quoted *Benson* for the proposition that such inventions are not patentable subject matter. [Footnote.] Though the board did recognize that appellant's algorithm is far more complex than which was

examined in *Benson,* the board found that *Benson* expressed no limitations on the nature, extent, or complexity of unpatentable algorithms.

On reconsideration, the board considered a very broad, dictionary definition of "algorithm"[4] and concluded that the term is not limited to expressions in mathematical terms but rather includes expressions in natural language. The board argued that the apparent absence of any mathematical notation or activity in appellant's claims did not distinguish appellant's claims from the subject matter in *Benson.*

The board also cited *Christensen* in support of its application of *Benson* to this case. [Footnote.] The only difference the board found between the prior art computer translation method, Oettinger,[6] and the claimed invention was a novel algorithm. The board read *Christensen* for the proposition that such a difference is not sufficient to render a process statutory.

OPINION

* * *

We reject the board's analysis based on *Christensen.* Even if the only novel aspect of this invention were an algorithm, it is not proper to decide the question of statutory subject matter by focusing on less than all of the claimed invention. [Citation.]

Next, we expressly recognize some questions which are not at issue in this case. The examiner and the board do not now directly question whether appellant has invented, properly claimed, and adequately disclosed a computerized method for translating between natural languages. Nor is it directly questioned whether the method is new, useful, and unobvious. The single ground of rejection *articulated by the board* is that the *Benson* holding renders the method unpatentable.

Thus, the main issue in this case is whether

---

4. The board took the following definition from C. Sippl and C. Sippl, Computer Dictionary and Handbook 23 (2d ed. 1972):

algorithm—1. A fixed step-by-step procedure for accomplishing a given result; usually a simplified procedure for solving a complex problem, also a full statement of a finite number of steps. 2. A defined process or set of rules that leads and assures the

development of a desired output from a given input. A sequence of formulas and/or algebraic logical steps to calculate or determine a given task: processing rules.

6. A. Oettinger, *Automatic Language Translation* (Harvard Monographs in Applied Science No. 8, 1960). Oettinger describes a computer-based dictionary which forms a literal, word-for-word translation.

the claims on appeal are rendered nonstatutory by the holding in *Benson.*

In the process of our search for the meaning of *Benson,* we have defined certain classes of claims which are clearly *not* rendered *nonstatutory* by *Benson.* One such class covers those claims which do not directly or indirectly recite a *Benson*-type algorithm. *In re Freeman,* 573 F.2d 1237, —— USPQ —— (Cust. & Pat.App.1978).

In applying the *Freeman* rationale to the case before us, we begin by rejecting the board's definition of algorithm recited in note 4, supra. While we agree with the board that the form in which an "algorithm" is recited, whether algebraic or prose, is of no moment, it is clear to us that the *Benson* Court used the term "algorithm" in a specific sense, namely "a procedure for solving a given type of *mathematical* problem." 409 U.S. at 65, 93 S.Ct. at 254, 175 USPQ at 674 (emphasis added). Using this definition, we have carefully examined the claims in this case and are unable to find any direct or indirect recitation of a procedure for solving a *mathematical* problem.[7] Translating between natural languages is not a mathematical problem as we understand the term to have been used in *Benson.* Nor are any of the recited steps in the claims mere procedures for solving mathematical problems. Since the claims do not directly or indirectly recite an algorithm, the claims cannot preempt an algorithm. We hold, therefore, that the claims in this appeal are not rendered nonstatutory by *Benson.*

There is another issue in this case. The examiner, in his Final Rejection and in his Examiner's Answer, appears to have rejected the claims because a computerized method of translating is not, the examiner submitted, in the "technological arts." The examiner cited *In re Musgrave,* 431 F.2d 882, 57 CCPA 1352, 167 USPQ 280 (1970); *In re Benson,* 441 F.2d 682, 58 CCPA 1134, 169 USPQ 548 (1971), *rev'd sub nom., Gottschalk v. Benson,* 409 U.S. 63, 93 S.Ct. 253, 34 L.Ed.2d 273, 175 USPQ 673 (1972); *In re McIlroy,* 442 F.2d 1397, 58 CCPA 1249, 170 USPQ 31 (1971), for the prop-

osition that all statutory subject matter must be in the "technological" or "useful" arts, and that, as far as computer-related inventions are concerned, *only* those inventions which "enhance the internal operation of the digital computer" are in the "technological" or "useful" arts. The examiner further stated that natural language translation is a "liberal art" and that effecting the translation by means of a machine does not transform the activity into a "technological art." The board's perfunctory treatment of this theory of rejection did not indicate approval or disapproval of it.

First, we hold that the method for enabling a *computer* to translate natural languages *is* in the technological arts, i. e., it is a method of operating a machine. [Footnote.] The "technological" or "useful" arts inquiry *must* focus on whether the claimed subject matter (a method of operating a machine to translate) is statutory, not on whether the product of the claimed subject matter (a translated test) is statutory, not on whether the prior art which the claimed subject matter purports to replace (translation by human mind) is statutory, and *not* on whether the claimed subject matter is presently perceived to be an improvement over the prior art, e. g., whether it "enhances" the operation of a machine. This was the law prior to *Benson* and was not changed by *Benson.*

Second, the examiner has taken language from the cited cases and attempted to apply that language in a different context. *Musgrave, In re Benson,* and *McIlroy* all involved data processing methods useful in a computer, but not expressly limited to use in a computer. Furthermore, all of those cases involved a "mental steps" rejection. The language which the examiner has quoted was written in answer to "mental steps" rejections and was not intended to create a generalized definition of statutory subject matter. Moreover, it was not intended to form a basis for a new § 101 rejection as the examiner apparently suggests. To the extent that this "technological arts" rejection is before us, independent of the rejection based on *Benson,* it is also reversed.

The decision of the board is reversed.

---

7. We do not consider the question whether the mere recitation of a step involving computer activity, but not otherwise reciting an algorithm, "indirectly recites" an algorithm. That issue was neither considered by the board nor argued before us. Furthermore, the question involves factual inquiries which an appellate court is ill-equipped to accomplish.

IN RE JOHNSON
589 F.2d 1070
*(United States Court of Customs and
Patent Appeals, Dec. 7, 1978.)*

BALDWIN, J.

These appeals are from the decisions of the
Patent and Trademark Office (PTO) Board of
Appeals (board) sustaining the rejections of
all claims in three consolidated cases [foot-
note] under 35 U.S.C. § 101 for being directed
to nonstatutory subject matter.[2] We reverse
on all claims.

THE INVENTIONS

The inventions before us involve methods for
removing undesired components (noise) from
seismic data. In seismic prospecting, an acoustic or seismic wave energy source is positioned
either in a relatively shallow shot hole on the
surface of the earth, or is towed a predetermined distance beneath the surface of a body
of water. An acoustic energy impulse of some
preselected wave shape and frequency content
is generated by the seismic energy source. The
acoustic energy generated by the source pen-
etrates through the multiple layers of material comprising the subterranean portion of
the earth in the region being prospected. Since
the speed of sound is generally different in
each layer beneath the surface of the earth,
refractions, reflections, and diffractions of the
acoustic energy occur at the boundary of each
layer. These acoustic energy reflections, refractions, and diffractions cause secondary
acoustic energy waves to return toward the
surface of the earth. At the surface, the returning acoustic energy waves are detected
by a plurality of longitudinally-spaced geophones, hydrophones, or seismic detectors. The
individual seismic detectors are located along
a generally straight line. These detectors generate analog electrical signals or waveforms
which are representative of the arrival of the
acoustic energy waves at the detectors. The
analog waveforms generated by the seismic
detectors are, thus, voltage representations,
generated as a function of time, of the ampli-

tude of reflected, refracted, and diffracted secondary acoustic energy waves arriving at the
surface of the earth.

The secondary waves detected by the seismic detectors are generally amplified and then
recorded or stored in either analog or digital
form on a *record medium* as a function of the
time after the seismic "shot" or energy generation. After amplification and prior to recording, the analog electrical waveform may
be digitized by sampling its amplitude at a
predetermined rate and then recording the
digital amplitude values as a function of time.
A time series of digital numbers representative of the amplitude of the analog waveform
at each detector as a function of time is thus
generated. The recorded representation of
seismic energy at a detector location, whether
it is recorded in analog or digital form, may
be displayed for interpretation in the form of
a "wiggle trace" or plot of the amplitude of
the arriving acoustic energy waves as a function of time for each geophone or seismic detector stationed at a particular surface location. A plurality of such traces forms a record
section of the data. These record sections may
then be processed to interpret the arriving
acoustic energy waves at each seismic detector in terms of the subsurface layering of the
earth structure. This analysis, if performed
properly, can disclose the location of subterranean earth structures or traps which may
contain petroleum deposits. It is quite common for seismic data to be recorded in digital
form as described and for digital data processing equipment (i. e., digital computers) to
be used in the processing of the seismic data
for interpretation in terms of the location of
subterranean structures which may be petroleum traps.

The inventions in each of the three applications in these consolidated appeals deal with
the removal of unwanted seismic signal components or noise present in the recorded seismic data. Noise removal facilitates interpretation of the seismic data and, thereby,
determination of subterranean structure. This
undesired acoustic noise which appears on the

---

2. The Supreme Court handed down its decision in *Parker v. Flook*, 437 U.S. 584, 98 S.Ct. 2522, 57 L.Ed.2d 451,
198 USPQ 193 (1978), after the oral argument of these
appeals. Due to the similarity of issues in *Flook* and the
instant appeals, these appeals were restored to the cal-

endar on July 13, 1978, by an order of this court, and the
parties were requested to file supplementary briefs on
the bearing that decision might have on the issues before
us.

records of seismic data may be caused by a variety of noise sources. One type of noise, called "multiple reflections," involves an "echo" effect caused by hard layers near the surface which "trap" and rebroadcast the primary acoustic energy impulse of the source several times rather than just once. The arrival at the detectors of each repetitive reflection (or re-verberation) causes the detector to perceive nonexistent deep layers, and the echoes mask the true signal. Other sources of noise are electrical interference from power lines or communication systems in use in the vicinity of the seismic exploration and random acoustic energy noise from other energy sources, such as vehicles moving in the region of the seismic exploration. Thus, the removal of noise or undesired signal components from the recorded data representations comprising a seismic record is a problem in the seismic exploration technique practiced in the petroleum industry.

Application serial No. 230,810 (Appeal No. 76-719) is the first-filed application of the three related applications presently on appeal. The invention disclosed in this application comprises a technique for removing unwanted noise components from the seismic traces in a seismic record in which certain conventional seismic data processing techniques, such as the correction for "normal move out" and the "stacking" or adding technique which is applied to Common Depth Point (CDP) seismic data, have already been performed. The invention makes use of the physical principle that, because of the manner in which the seismic data are gathered, closely adjacent detectors should receive reflections of essentially the same wave shape from a given layer. A chronologically small portion of a particular seismic trace (termed a reference trace) is examined and is compared with corresponding portions of spatially adjacent seismic traces in order to define a coherent signal component common to all of the traces being examined. The coherent signal component is then separated from the totality of the recorded seismic data present in the portion of the reference trace being examined, and the remainder is considered noise. The assumption present in such processing is that there should be relatively few abrupt changes in the physical characteristics of the subsurface bed boundaries as a function of horizontal distance. Claim 1 in Appeal No. 76-719 recites:

1. A machine implemented method for enhancing digital data in a seismic record, said data having a coherent signal component comprising a measure of the similarity between spatially related time series data, and a noise [sic noise] component, and for improving the signal to noise ratio thereof, comprising the steps of:

determining, for a search window defined about a selected time on a selected seismic reference trace, the coherent signal associated with said reference trace and a plurality of adjacent seismic traces;

computing, by use of said coherent signal, the component of said coherent signal extant in said reference trace and replacing in time alignment with said reference trace on an output signal record medium, that portion of said reference trace included in said search window with said component of the reference trace comprising said coherent signal portion;

replacing, in time alignment with said reference trace on an output noise record medium, that portion of said reference trace included in said search window, with the remainder of said reference trace which does not comprise said coherent signal portion; and

repeating the above steps for other selected times and other selected reference traces until all data comprising said record is so processed.

Claim 10 in this appeal recites:

10. A machine implemented method for enhancing digital data in a Common Depth Point, moveout corrected and stacked seismic data record, said data having a coherent signal component comprising a measure of the similarity between spatially related time series data, and a noise component, and for improving the signal to noise ratio thereof, comprising the steps of:

determining, for a search window defined about a selected time on a selected seismic reference trace, the shape of the coherent signal associated with said selected reference trace and a plurality of spacewise adjacent seismic traces;

determining, for said search window, the amplitude of said coherent signal;

computing, as a function of the amplitude and shape information pertaining to said coherent signal, the component portion of said selected reference trace corresponding to said coherent signal;

replacing, in time alignment with said selected reference trace, on an output signal record medium the portion of said selected reference trace in said search window, with said coherent signal component portion; and repeating the above steps for other selected times and other selected reference traces until all data comprising said record is so processed.

The remaining independent claim in Appeal No. 76-719 is claim 16 which states:

16. A machine implemented method for enhancing plural raw digital data records, not moveout corrected, said data having a coherent signal component comprising a measure of the similarity between spatially related time series data, and a noise component, and for improving the signal to noise ratio thereof, comprising the steps of:

compiling, from said plurality of raw data records, a synthetic data record of common range traces;

determining, for a search window defined about a selected time on a selected reference trace on said synthetic data record, the shape and amplitude of the coherent signal associated with said reference trace and a plurality of spacewise adjacent seismic traces on said synthetic record;

computing, as a function of the amplitude and shape of said coherent signal, the component portion of said selected reference trace corresponding to said coherent signal;

replacing, in time alignment on said synthetic data record, on an output signal record medium, the portion of said reference trace in said search window, with said coherent signal component portion;

repeating the above steps for other selected times and other selected reference traces until all data comprising said synthetic record is so processed; and

repeating all the above steps for different common shotpoint-detector ranges, thereby enhancing the data on all of said raw data records.

The examiner, by letter of October 24, 1973, found a rejection of claims 1-7, 10, 12 and 14 under 35 U.S.C. § 103 to be overcome by applicants' arguments in an amendment of September 26, 1973, and only the rejection under 35 U.S.C. § 101 was maintained.

The second-filed application in the present appeals (application serial No. 305–386, Appeal No. 76-717), extends the method of the first application to the processing of seismic data in raw form, that is, data upon which "move out" corrections and CDP "stacking" procedures have not been performed. This is accomplished by deriving those segments of spatially related adjacent traces which cor-

respond chronologically to the portion of the reference trace being examined at a given step in processing by projecting the reference trace portion or "window" onto spatially related adjacent traces along a predetermined hyperbolic curve. This hyperbolic projection takes into account the "normal move out" correction which would otherwise be applied to the seismic data prior to its comparison to spatially related traces in order to determine the coherent signal in the technique recited in Appeal No. 76-719. Claim 1 in Appeal No. 76-717 is:

1. A method for enhancing digital seismic data said data having a coherent signal component comprising a measure of similarity between spatially related time series data, and a noise component in unmoved out form, comprising the steps of:

a) determining for a selected time T_R on a selected seismic trace R, the estimated times T_x on one or more additional traces included in the data at which possible events common to a possible event at T_R occur;

b) determining, for a search window having edges equally spaced on either side of times T_R the coherent signal component;

c) computing, by use of said coherent signal component, the component of said coherent signal extant in said selected trace T_R [sic R] with replacing in time alignment with said selected trace on an output signal record medium, that portion of said selected trace T_R [sic R] included in said search window with said component of the selected trace comprising said coherent signal portion; and

d) repeating the recited steps for other selected times and other selected traces until all said seismic data are so processed.

Claim 13 in this appeal recites:

13. A method of enhancing unmoved out seismic data in a gather of common depth point seismogram traces, said data having a coherent signal component comprising a measure of the similarity between spatially related time series data, and a noise component, comprising the steps of:

a) selecting a trace in said gather to function as a reference trace R;

b) selecting a time T_R on said trace R;

c) determining times T_x on one or more traces X included in said gather at which possible events common to a possible event at T_R on trace R occur;

d) cross correlating equal time length trace segments on traces X and R to derive time alignments for producing a coherent signal component segment COH from a segment of said reference trace R;

e) forming said coherent signal component segment COH on an output record medium in time alignment with said reference trace segment; and

f) repeating steps a), b), c), d), and e) with each trace in the gather functioning as the reference trace until all of said gather is processed to form an enhanced gather of coherent seismogram traces on said output record medium.

In a first Office Action, the examiner rejected all of the claims of this application under 35 U.S.C. § 101 and claims 1-4 and 13-15 under 35 U.S.C. § 103 over a combination of references. This § 103 rejection was not repeated after applicants' amendment of December 19, 1973.

The third application concerned in these consolidated appeals (application serial No. 327,267, Appeal No. 76-718), utilizes the same general physical principles for the detection and removal of "multiple" events in a seismic signal trace. The assumption here is that the multiple events have occurred because of the reflection of acoustic energy from the same (or closely adjacent) points on the subsurface boundaries and that the seismic signal or analog waveform produced by such reflections at the surface seismic detectors has the same characteristic shape (although its amplitude may be greatly diminished) after each such multiple reflection or reverberation. Thus, a particular time interval or "window" of a reference seismic trace is examined and compared against the same time duration interval (or window) of the same trace occurring at a later time. The shape of the trace in each of the intervals or time "windows" being examined can, if the assumptions about the nature of the process are valid, be used to extract multiple reflections by defining the existence of such a multiple reflection in the later occurring portion of the trace. With the multiple reflection thus defined, it may be removed from the trace by a subtraction process, thereby leaving the portion or component of the trace which is not attributable to this noise source. Claim 1 in Appeal No. 76-718 is representative:

1. A process for suppressing multiple events in seismic traces comprising the steps of:

a) comparing a first seismic trace segment with a second segment of the same trace to select that portion of the second segment which most closely resembles said first segment;

b) determining the degree of similarity between said selected portion and said first segment; and

c) extracting a part of said selected portion from said first portion, said part being a function of the degree of similarity between said selected portion and said first segment.

The examiner rejected all the claims of this application under 35 U.S.C. §§ 101 and 102, but the board reversed the 102 grounds upon finding that the reference did not suggest or anticipate the limitation that the extracted part be a function of the similarity between the selected portion and the first segment.

THE BOARD

The board, in three separate opinions, affirmed the rejection of all of the claims before us as directed to nonstatutory subject matter under 35 U.S.C. § 101. [Footnote.] It was the board's position that *Gottschalk v. Benson*, 409 U.S. 63, 93 S.Ct. 253, 34 L.Ed.2d 273, 175 USPQ 673 (1972), and *In re Christensen*, 478 F.2d 1392, 178 USPQ 35 (CCPA 1973), preclude a patent grant for any "subject matter which is algorithmic in character." The board found the claims on appeal to be special methods for solving problems involving seismic data and, therefore, algorithms not embraced within 35 U.S.C. § 101.

ISSUE

The sole issue before this court is whether the methods recited in the claims of the three cases constitute statutory subject matter under 35 U.S.C. § 101.

OPINION

Initially, we recognize that the board considered these appeals without the benefit of the Supreme Court's decision in *Parker v. Flook*, supra. While a degree of uncertainty existed concerning the proper interpretation of *Gottschalk v. Benson*, supra, it is clear after *Flook* that the board's conclusion that patent protection is proscribed for all inventions "algorithmic in character" is overbroad and erroneous.

In *Benson,* the Supreme Court determined that the claimed method for converting pure binary numbers to binary coded decimals (BCD) was not patentable subject matter under 35 U.S.C. § 101. The Court set forth its reasons in the following "nutshell" holding: an idea may not be patented and a claim may not issue which would preempt a *mathematical formula.* In the viewpoint of the Court, Benson's claims could not be allowed because to do so would grant him the right to exclude the use of a mathematical formula by others. [Citation.]

In the six years following *Benson,* this Court applied the "nutshell" analysis in a series of cases involving different factual situations. *See, e. g., In re Freeman,* 573 F.2d 1237, 197 USPQ 464 (CCPA 1978); *In re Richman,* 563 F.2d 1026, 195 USPQ 340 (CCPA 1977); *In re de Castelet,* 562 F.2d 1236, 195 USPQ 439 (CCPA 1977); *In re Chatfield,* 545 F.2d 152, 191 USPQ 730 (CCPA 1976), *cert. denied,* 434 U.S. 875, 98 S.Ct. 226, 54 L.Ed.2d 155, 195 USPQ 465 (1977).

It was not until its decision in *Parker v. Flook,* supra, that the Supreme Court again directly spoke on the § 101 issue involving algorithmic type inventions. The claims at issue in *Flook* recited methods of updating alarm limits during the catalytic conversion of petroleum. [Footnote.] The applicant admitted that the novelty of his process rested solely in the mathematical formula for computing the updated alarm limits. The final result of practicing Flook's process as claimed was a number or value to serve as a new alarm limit. This number or value was calculated from previous alarm limits and other data inputs.

The Supreme Court held Flook's process to be a method of calculation and, hence, nonstatutory even though limited to a specific technology and end use. [Citation.] In reaching this decision, the Court simplified the "nutshell" of *Benson* into a single kernel of principle: the discovery of a mathematical formula is not patentable even though the formula is novel and useful. [Citation.] Further, the Court stated that the plain language of 35 U.S.C. § 101 is not to be read literally when determining what is statutory subject matter. [Citation.] This is evidenced by prior judicial decisions which have excised certain categories of invention from the classes of statutory subject matter. [Citations.]

While in *Flook,* the Supreme Court acknowledged [citation] that "[t]he line between a patentable 'process' and an unpatentable 'principle' does not always shimmer with clarity," and, thus, turns on the claimed subject matter of each application, there are significant consistencies evident in the *Benson* and *Flook* opinions. First, the definition assigned in *Benson* to the term "algorithm" was reiterated in *Flook, i. e.,* "a procedure for solving a given type of *mathematical problem.*" [Citation.] [Emphasis added.] Also, the Court, in *Flook,* reiterated that although a law of nature cannot be patented, "a process is not unpatentable simply because it contains a law of nature or a mathematical algorithm." [Footnote.] [Citation.] Additionally, the Court in both *Benson* and *Flook* refused to hold computer programs nonstatutory subject matter per se.[6]

Following the Supreme Court's decision in *Benson,* and before its decision in *Flook,* numerous appeals to this Court necessitated the application of the principles expressed in *Benson* to both apparatus and process claims rejected under 35 U.S.C. § 101. Besides the differing language of the claims in these appeals, the nature of the inventions recited therein varied greatly.

One of these appeals led to our decision in *In re Chatfield,* supra, which set forth certain guidelines for determining whether claims re-

---

6. Numerous legal writers have addressed the question of whether computer programs are patentable under the present statute. *See* Comment, Computer Programs: Should They Be Patentable?, 68 Colum.L.Rev. 241 (1968); Comment, Computer Program Protection: The Need To Legislate A Solution, 54 Cornell L.Rev. 586 (1969); Comment, Computer Program Classification: A Limitation On Program Patentability As A Process, 53 Ore.L.Rev. 501 (1974); Note, Protection of Computer Programs: Resurrection of the Standard, 50 Notre Dame Law., 333 (1974).

The Supreme Court did not definitively answer this question in either *Benson* or *Flook* because it said the issue was more appropriately within the jurisdiction of Congress. [Citations.] The thrust of the *Benson* opinion was that certain claims reciting a mathematical algorithm were not statutory, and the holding in *Flook* was "that a claim for an improved *method of calculation,* even when tied to a specific end use, is unpatentable under [35 USC] § 101." (Emphasis added.) [Citation.]

cite statutory subject matter or mathematical algorithms properly rejectable under the *Benson* principles. In *Chatfield* we indicated that no basis exists in *Benson* or the statute for treating a claimed computer-implemented process differently from a process performed by any other machine system when considering whether statutory subject matter is recited. [Citation.] Judge Rich stated in his dissent that *Benson* applies equally whether an invention is claimed as an apparatus or process, because the form of the claim is often an exercise in drafting. [Citation.] This viewpoint was adopted by this entire Court in *In re Freeman*, supra, 573 F.2d at 1247, 197 USPQ at 472.

Further, this court's opinion in *Chatfield* emphasized that the meaning of the term "algorithm" is no longer in question when we stated:

> The Supreme Court carefully supplied a definition of the particular algorithm before it, i. e., "[a] procedure for solving a given type of mathematical problem." The broader definition of algorithm is "a step-by-step procedure for solving a problem or accomplishing some end." Webster's New Collegiate Dictionary (1976). It is axiomatic that inventive minds seek and develop solutions to problems and step-by-step solutions often attain the status of patentable invention. It would be unnecessarily detrimental to our patent system to deny inventors patent protection on the *sole* ground that their contribution could be broadly termed an "algorithm." [Emphasis in original.]

[Citation.] This court additionally held that each claim must be judged in its entirety when determining whether statutory subject matter is recited. [Citation.] [Footnote.] Therefore, a claim does not recite nonstatutory subject matter merely because an element of a step, when considered out of the context of the rest of the claim, is found to contain a natural law or mathematical algorithm. [Citations.]

In our subsequent decision in *In re Freeman*, supra, we set forth a two-step procedure for analyzing a claim to determine whether or not it preempts a mathematical algorithm. This determination is critical since *Benson* declared claims which preempt mathematical algorithms to be nonstatutory.

The first step of the *Freeman* analysis is to determine whether a method claim directly or indirectly recites "process steps which are themselves calculations, formulae or equations." [Citation.] Only if such steps are recited is the claim to be further analyzed to ascertain whether the claim merely recites a mathematical formula or a method of calculation as in *Benson* and *Flook*. In *Freeman* and the subsequent case of *In re Toma*, 575 F.2d 872, 197 USPQ 852 (CCPA 1978), the steps of the claims did not directly or indirectly recite mathematical calculations, formulae or equations, and hence the second step of the analysis was not reached.

Our decision in *In re Richman*, supra, was handed down between the *Chatfield* and *Freeman* decisions and appears to have foreshadowed the Supreme Court's holding in *Flook*. The claims in *Richman* recited a *method of calculating* an average boresight correction angle within a signal-processing radar apparatus. We held the claims to recite nonstatutory subject matter, not because a mathematical expression appeared in steps of the claims, but because each claim, when considered in its entirety, recited "a method of calculating using a mathematical formula." [Citation.] In *Flook* as in *Richman*, the result of performing the claimed process was a value or number and in each case the claims were held to be nonstatutory recitations of methods for computing the numbers.

Turning to the claims at issue, we must apply the Supreme Court precedents of *Benson* and *Flook* to the three sets of claims on appeal. Initially, we note that there are two important factual distinctions between the claims at issue and the claims in *Flook*. First, in *Flook* the applicant alleged that his claims recited a novel mathematical procedure for computing a number called an alarm limit. The applicants in the instant appeals, however, allege no such novel mathematical procedures and do not seek a patent on a mathematical formula. Second, while the purpose of performing the process in *Flook* was to compute a new value for an alarm limit, the purpose of applicants' methods are to filter out extraneous and erroneous components and to physically record a noiseless seismic trace on a record medium. Any computations required in performing applicants' processes are admitted to be well-known operations mandated by applicants' preference to perform the filtering process with a digital computer.[8] The products produced by applicants' claimed processes are new, noiseless seismic traces recorded on a record medium and not mere mathematical values. Thus, the significant limitations recited in the claims of operating on a recorded, unenhanced, seismic trace to produce and record a new seismic trace lead us to find the claims to recite statutory processes and not methods of calculating as were present in *Flook*.

Finding the claims at issue to be statutory under the *Flook* criterion is not the end of the required analysis, because even though, as has been pointed out, there are significant overlaps between the analyses in the Supreme Court's *Benson* and *Flook* opinions, we still consider it necessary to determine whether the claims recite mathematical algorithms in a nonstatutory manner under the *Benson* "nutshell" holding. We choose to conduct this inquiry with the aid of a two-part analysis as was done in *In re Freeman*, supra. Our search for directly or indirectly recited mathematical algorithms in the instant cases begins by applying the first part of the *Freeman* inquiry to each of the claims before us. In Appeal No. 76-717, step "c" of claim 1 recites "*computing, by use of said coherent signal component, the component of said coherent signal extant in said selected trace.*" (Emphasis ours.) The term "compute" at least suggests the execution of a mathematical algorithm in the form of one or a sequence of mathematical operations, and thus, claim 1 and claims 2-12 which depend therefrom must be subjected to further analysis under the *Benson* and *Flook* precedents.

Claim 13 of Appeal No. 76-717 is the only other independent claim in that case. Step "c" of this claim recites "determining times T_X on one or more traces X included in said gather at which possible events common to a possible event at T_R on trace R occur" and step "d" recites "cross correlating equal time length trace segments on traces X and R to derive time alignments for producing a coherent signal component COH from a segment of said

reference trace R." While "determining" and "cross correlating" are not prima facie mathematical calculations, formulae, or equations, these steps cannot be analyzed in a vacuum. Reference to the specification must be made to determine whether such terms indirectly recite mathematical calculations, formulae, or equations. Although appellants' specification in this case does not equate either the step of "determining" or the step of "correlating" with the execution of a mathematical algorithm, the flow diagrams which form part of the specification disclose explicit mathematical equations which are to be used in conjunction with each of these steps. [Footnote.] Thus, claims 13-17 will also be made the subject of the second *Freeman* inquiry.

Claim 1, the only independent claim in Appeal No. 76-718, recites the steps of "comparing a first seismic trace segment with a second segment of the same trace" and "determining the degree of similarity" between two portions of the seismic trace. Reference to the specification indicates that the step of "determining the degree of similarity" requires the execution of mathematical equations [footnote] and, thus, all of the claims of this case will be further analyzed to determine whether a mathematical algorithm is being preempted.

Appeal No. 76-719 contains three independent claims—claims 1, 10 and 16. Each of these claims includes a step which specifically recites "computing." As we stated in connection with our analysis of claim 1 of Appeal No. 76-717, the term "computing" connotes the execution of one or a sequence of mathematical operations. Since all of the claims of Appeal No. 76-719 either directly or indirectly recite a "compute" step, they too must be analyzed under the second part of the *Freeman* inquiry.

Under the second step of our analysis, we must determine whether each claim as a whole, including *all* of its steps, merely recites a mathematical formula or a method of calculation. This analysis requires careful interpretation of each claim in the light of its supporting disclosure to determine whether or not

---

8. No statutory basis exists for declaring claimed processes nonstatutory merely because they are implemented by a computer system. The Supreme Court has looked to the nature of the invention as recited by the

claims and not to how the process is carried out. We see no reason or precedent for treating a computer implemented process differently than any other machine-implemented process. [Citations.]

it merely defines a method of solving a mathematical problem. If it does not, then it defines statutory subject matter, namely, a "process." [11]

Considering Appeal No. 76-717, claim 1 recites "a selected seismic trace R" having "a coherent signal component" and "a noise component" indicative of a noise event. One or more "additional traces" are chosen which also contain the coherent signal component. The coherent signal (the reference trace without the noise component) is determined and reproduced on an "output signal record medium" in place of the reference trace. Even assuming arguendo that the "computing" step recited in the claim entails performing mathematical calculations, the process is explicitly claimed within the framework of a method for producing an output seismic trace which is different from, and an enhancement of, an input seismic trace. Thus, any calculations which may be performed in practicing the process of claim 1 are but a part of that process which includes the other recited steps.

Claim 13 recites a method for enhancing seismic data which begins with a "reference trace R" (from a gather of seismic data) containing *both* coherent and noise components. By performing the "determining" and "cross correlating" steps set forth in the claim on selected portions of the reference trace and other traces selected from the gather, a coherent (noise-free) signal component segment is *produced* from a segment on the reference trace. This coherent signal segment is then recited to be formed on an "output record medium" in a specific manner. Again, any mathematical operations performed in practicing the method recited in claim 13 are incident to producing a noise-free signal trace from a reference trace, and by no interpretation can claim 13 be construed to be a mere procedure for solving a given type of mathematical problem.

Appellants admitted in their supplemental

brief that any calculations incident to performing the processes claimed in this appeal and Appeal Nos. 76-718 and 76-719 are well known and form no basis for patentability. This is a significant factual distinction from the situation in *Flook* where patentability was predicated upon a particular formula for computing alarm limits and the situation in *Benson* where the claims recited a mathematical algorithm for converting numbers from pure binary to binary coded decimals. It is apparent that any calculations required in practicing the processes appellants recite in claims 1 and 13 result from the selection of a general purpose computer and digital processing techniques to analyze, filter and record the seismic traces instead of using banks of analog filters or other devices. Our decisions in *Chatfield,* supra, and *Deutsch,* supra, held computer-implemented processes to be statutory subject matter, and we reach a similar conclusion with respect to claims 1 and 13. Furthermore, the Supreme Court's decisions in *Benson* and *Flook* support this result because these claims, when considered as a whole, do not merely recite methods of calculations or mathematical formulas.

We see nothing in claims 2-12, which depend from claim 1, or in claims 14-17, which depend from claim 13, which would cause them to be nonstatutory. Since dependent claims, when properly drafted, are by nature less inclusive than their associated independent claims, and since we have found the independent claims to recite statutory processes under 35 U.S.C. § 101, we reverse the board's holding as to claims 1-17 in Appeal No. 76-717.

In Appeal No. 76-718, the process recited by claim 1 begins with a seismic trace and compares a first segment (containing multiple event noise) of the trace with a second segment of the trace to determine the selected portion of the second segment which most closely resembles the first segment. The next

---

11. Again, we note legal precedent which states that the mere presence of a mathematical expression or calculation in an apparatus or process is not sufficient to find the claim, as a whole, to recite nonstatutory subject matter. In *Flook,* the Supreme Court stated "a process is not unpatentable simply because it contains a law of nature

or a mathematical algorithm," supra, 98 S.Ct. at 2526, 198 USPQ 197. In our decision in *In re Chatfield,* supra, we found the dependent claims to recite statutory methods for operating a computer system even though the dependent claims set forth specific formulas for use in implementing the methods.

step recited determines the "degree of similarity" between the first segment and the selected portion. The final step recites "extracting a part of said selected portion from said first portion." If we assume that the determining step is in actuality a mathematical operation performed on the digital representation of the physical seismic trace, the claim when analysed in its entirety still defines a process for producing a segment of a seismic trace, which is free from a multiple noise event, from a segment of the trace which includes the multiple noise event. Thus, while the steps recited in the claim may *include* the execution of a mathematical procedure, it is clear that the claim as a whole defines a sequence of steps for operating upon a seismic data trace to produce a different, noise-free seismic data trace. As is the case in Appeal No. 76-717, we do not find that claim 1 merely recites a mathematical formula or method of calculation and, thus, we conclude claim 1 recites a statutory process. We also find the dependent claims in this case to recite statutory processes under the reasoning set forth with regard to the dependent claims in Appeal No. 76-717.

In Appeal No. 76-719, claim 1, and therefore claims 2-9 dependent thereon, begin with a seismic record having a coherent component and a noise component. One trace is compared with other traces of the record to determine the coherent component and, using the coherent component, the noise component. The coherent component and the noise component are then separately placed on an output signal record medium and an output noise record medium, respectively. The result is a seismic record with the noise removed and a physical record of the noise which has been removed.

Claim 10, and claims 11-15 dependent thereon, begin with a common depth point, moveout-corrected, and stacked seismic data record having a coherent component and a noise component. The shape and amplitude of the coherent signal common to a reference trace and a plurality of other traces are determined. The portion of the reference trace corresponding to the coherent signal is computed and recorded on an output signal record medium.

The analysis of each of the claims in Appeal No. 76-719 necessarily follows the analysis set forth above in Appeal Nos. 76-717 and 76-718. Although the specification makes it clear that the "compute" steps recited in each of the independent claims of this case refer to the execution of mathematical operations on the seismic traces, the claims recite such executions within the framework of a process for filtering out or removing noise from the seismic trace to produce noiseless traces which are recorded on an output signal medium. Each of these independent claims recites processes which include the performance of mathematical calculations as but one of a sequence of substantive steps. The claims in their entireties are not, however, mere procedures for solving mathematical problems. The determination of whether the processes as claimed are statutory requires an analysis of each of the claims as a whole. Appellants do not assert a recitation of a formula or a method of calculation as a basis for patentability of the recited processes, and it is clear that any mathematical operations performed in practicing the processes are incidental to the recited series of steps whereby a seismic data record is analyzed and processed in a specific manner to produce and record a noiseless seismic data record.

As we stated above [reference], appellants' selection of a general purpose computer and digital data processing techniques to implement the processes does not determine whether these claimed processes are statutory. Since the claims before us do not merely recite mathematical formulas or methods of calculation, we reverse the board's decision that claims 1-21 in Appeal No. 76-719 are nonstatutory.

The Solicitor argues in his supplemental brief that the claims at issue are not statutory subject matter because they are computer programs and computer programs are not patentable under *Benson* and *Flook*. This broad statement is not at all germane to the considerations before this court and is an erroneous statement of the law. We stated in *In re Chatfield*, 545 F.2d supra at 155, 191 USPQ at 733, that "the mere labeling of an invention as a computer program does not aid in decision making" and the Supreme Court declined to decide either *Benson* or *Flook* on such broad, non-substantive grcunds but rather considered the specific recitations in the claims. There is no reason for the Solicitor or the PTO to shortcut the analytical framework set forth in

Benson, Flook, and decisions of this Court by relying on unfounded generalities.[12]

Although the board stated that it felt "constrained" by our decision in *In re Christensen*, 478 F.2d 1392, 178 USPQ 35 (CCPA 1973), to find the claims of the three applications nonstatutory, we find the results reached here to be harmonious with our decision in *Christensen*. The claims in *Christensen*, when considered in their entirety, recited data-gathering steps in conjunction with solving a mathematical equation. Such is not the situation with the instant claims, however, which recite statutory methods for producing new and different, noise-free seismic traces from seismic data traces which contain noise.

Because we find each of the claims in all three appeals to recite statutory processes, we reverse the decision of the board in each of the three appeals.

IN RE WALTER

618 F.2d 758

(United States Court of Customs and Patent Appeals, March 27, 1980.)

RICH, J.

This appeal is from the decision of the Patent and Trademark Office (PTO) Board of Appeals (board), affirming the examiner's final rejection of claims 7–14 and 16–18 in application serial No. 303,693, filed November 6, 1972, entitled "Seismic Prospecting System." The sole ground of rejection of the claims is that they are directed to nonstatutory subject matter under 35 U.S.C. § 101. We affirm.

THE INVENTION

Appellant's invention is used in seismic prospecting and surveying. In this field, seismic source waves are generated and transmitted downwardly into the earth. There they are deflected by subsurface formations and anomalies. The deflected waves return to the earth's surface and are detected by transducers, known as geophones, which are distributed on the surface over the area of exploration. The geophones convert the returning mechanical vibrations into electrical signals, which are then recorded on a record medium, such as magnetic tape or chart recorder, for analysis. By studying the records of the deflected waves, analysts are able to make determinations concerning the nature of the subsurface structure of the earth.

Several types of seismic source waves have been used in seismic prospecting and surveying. One type, known as impulse waves, are sharp pulses lasting 0.05 second or less and are generated by a powerful force of short duration, such as an explosion. Another type of seismic source wave, with which appellant's invention is used, are "chirp" signals. A chirp signal is a frequency-modulated continuous wave in which the frequency of vibration is varied as a function of time, usually a linear function, over a substantial period of as much as several seconds. Chirp signals are often referred to as "sweep" signals, since the frequency is swept from one value to another. Chirp signals are generated by mechanical apparatus which vibrates against the surface of the earth.

As a chirp signal travels down into the earth, it is deflected by subsurface features which lie at varying depths and at different distances from the numerous geophones which are set out on the surface. At any given instant, therefore, a single geophone receives portions of the returning chirp signal which have been deflected from different depths and locations. This composite signal is a jumble of different frequency components. Before the results of the survey can be evaluated, the jumbled signal must be broken down into its components and its individual deflected portions identified.

Appellant has invented a method, and apparatus for performing the method, of cross-

---

12. Very simply, our decision today recognizes that modern technology has fostered a class of inventions which are most accurately described as computer-implemented processes. Such processes are encompassed within 35 U.S.C. § 101 under the same principles as other machine-implemented processes, subject to judicially determined exceptions, inter alia, mathematical formulas, methods of calculation, and mere ideas. The overbroad analysis of the PTO errs in failing to differentiate between a computer program, i. e., sets of instructions within a computer, and computer-implemented processes wherein a computer or other automated machine performs one or more of the recited process steps. This distinction must not be overlooked because there is no reason for treating a computer differently from any other apparatus employed to perform a recited process step.

correlating the returning jumbled signal with the original chirp signal which was transmitted into the earth. As a result, the returning signal is effectively unscrambled; each of the trains of waves received at each geophone station is converted to a form equivalent to the type of signal which would have been produced had an impulse-type signal been used in place of the chirp signal. Appellant's claims identify these end products as "partial product signals."

Appellant's method is performed on the record signal made from each geophone. The record signal is sampled and converted to a digital format. It is then divided into segments. Several mathematical operations are performed, including computing Fourier transforms and cross-correlation utilizing the Cooley-Tukey algorithm as modified by Bergland.[1] Appellant's claim 7 is illustrative of his invention:

> 7. In a method of seismic surveying in which a train of seismic source waves is transmitted downwardly into the earth and is there deflected by subsurface formations and in which corresponding trains of seismic waves deflected by such formation are received at geophone stations in a spread at the surface of the earth and wherein;
>
> each train of received seismic waves is converted into a corresponding series of digital sample signals; and
>
> a series of reference signals corresponding to sample of said transmitted seismic waves is developed;
>
> the improved method of correlating said series of sample signals for each geophone station with respect to said series of reference signals that comprises
>
> a) converting said series of sample signals into an augmented series of sample signals divided into N + 1 segments of equal length thereby forming a series of sequential segments S_i of said augmented series, including an empty end segment, where i = 1, . . ., N + 1;
>
> b) forming a Fourier transform FTS_i of each respective series of signals composed of pairs of

successive segments S_i and S_{i+1} of said augmented series, each said Fourier transform being represented by a first series of transform signals.

> c) forming a combined segment of each segment C_j of said reference signals and an empty segment of equal length, where j = 1, . . ., L, each said combined segment comprising a series of signals of double length, where L ≤ N,
>
> d) forming a corresponding Fourier transform FTC_j of each said combined segment, each said latter Fourier transform being represented by a second series of transform signals,
>
> e) forming the non-zero conjugate complex vector products of pairs of the respective Fourier transforms and adding them together in accordance with the following expression:

$$FTP_m = \sum_{j=1}^{N} FTS_{j+m-1} \cdot FTC_j$$

> where N represents the number of segments in the series of reference signals, and

$$0 < j + m - 1 \leq M \leq N$$

> where M is the number of segments to be produced in the cross-correlated result, to produce a series of partial product signals FTP_m where m = 1, 2, . . ., M representative of the Fourier transform of said series of sample signals and said series of reference signals for each said geophone station.[2]

THE REJECTION

In his final rejection, the examiner stated that the claims were directed to the mathematical procedure outlined in the specification for cross-correlating the sets of signals. He found no reason to distinguish between the method and apparatus claims, holding that distinction to be legally immaterial "Where the only mode of practicing an invention is disclosed by way of an algorithm for use in a computer program."

In affirming the rejection, the board agreed that the distinction between method and apparatus claims was of no significance because "It would be anomalous to grant apparatus

---

1. This algorithm is a mathematical procedure, the details of which are not relevant to the issues on this appeal. It is sufficient to note that both the computation of Fourier transforms and the operation of the Cooley-Tukey algorithm are mathematical exercises or algorithms as defined by the Supreme Court in *Parker v. Flook*, 437 U.S. 584, 98 S.Ct. 2522, 57 L.Ed.2d 451 (1978), and *Gottschalk v. Benson*, 409 U.S. 63, 93 S.Ct. 253, 34 L.Ed.2d

273 (1972).

2. Claims 7–9, 13–14, and 16 are method claims. Claims 10–12 and 17–18 are directed to a "system," i. e., apparatus, and are identical in substance to the method claims with the exception that the term "means for" has been inserted in front of each method step to convert the claims from method to apparatus format.

claims encompassing any and every 'means for' practicing the method claimed in the method claims if the latter were nonstatutory. * * *" It therefore addressed both categories of claims in a single discussion.

In analyzing the claims, the board viewed the activity recited in the preambles as being directed to the gathering of data. It found that steps like a) through e) of claim 7 serve to allocate the sample signals to various locations in the computer memory in accordance with the rules built into the programs for producing the end result—"a series of partial product signals * * * representative of the Fourier transform of said series of sample signals and said series of reference signals for each said geophone station," quoting from the last clause of claim 7.

The board stated that practicing the method steps had to include processing the disclosed formulas and operating the computers according to the Cooley-Tukey algorithm as modified by Bergland. After reviewing the definition of the word "algorithm" as used by the Supreme Court in § 101 cases,[3] the board characterized appellant's claims as mathematical exercises giving the following three reasons (bracketed numerals ours):

[1] Steps a)–e), at their most fundamental level as processed in the computer, must necessarily be carried out employing the radix or radices imposed by the architecture of the computer used, binary, binary coded decimal, or the like. It would be difficult, not to say misleading, to characterize such operations as non-mathematical.

[2] At a secondary level, the steps referred to serve to accommodate the input data to a memory, finite in size, requiring the tailoring and configuring of the data to the particular architecture of the memory, note appellant's Figures 13–16 and attendant description, pages 123–139. We think this is a mathematical operation.

[3] Needless to say, the processing incident to the employment of the formulas to which we have referred must also be considered mathematical.

It is also apparent that the processing recited in these steps is directed to the solution of a problem, that of producing a series of partial product signals. Accordingly, we consider appellant's claims to be directed to the processing of an algorithm.

Next, the board addressed the question of preemption of the algorithm, holding that it would be effectively preempted by the claims. Although it recognized that the calculations could be carried out by manual effort, the board found that

* * * the total amount of calculation required for the purposes of producing a practical or useful result would be, we think, so horrendous, and the effort so tedious and time consuming, as to render that alternative (if publicly available), or others like it, to be trivial in consequence.

The board distinguished *In re Johnson* 589 F.2d 1070, 200 USPQ 199 (Cust. & Pat. App.1978), on its facts. According to the board, the method claims in *Johnson*

* * * called for computer programming which improved a signal, i. e., reduced noise, whereas the subject matter at bar purports, as the result of solving a mathematical problem, to produce partial product signals, that is, the method produces a solution.

APPELLANT'S ARGUMENTS

Appellant's main contention is that his claims are not directed to a mathematical procedure but to a method that produces a physical result (the partial product signals) by physical processing of physical signals, all of which are described in mathematical terms, and to apparatus for carrying out special forms of the process.

In furtherance of this argument, appellant asserts that mathematics is an appropriate language to employ for describing inventions, and that programs, algorithms, radices, and calculations have long been commonly employed in inventions.

Appellant also asserts that the PTO has payed [sic] lip service to the proposition that claims are to be considered as entireties but has actually dissected the claims and then ignored the physical aspects or denied that they are physical by calling them mathematical or algorithmic in character.

---

3. *Parker v. Flook*, 437 U.S. at 585 n.1, 98 S.Ct. at 2523;   *Gottschalk v. Benson*, 409 U.S. at 65, 93 S.Ct. at 254.

With regard to the apparatus claims, appellant denies that they encompass any and all means for practicing the process covered by the method claims. Specifically, he argues that the apparatus claims call for the use of a unitary device in which all of the means interact to process the input signals to produce the output signals. He asserts that his method claims refer to steps which may be carried out at different locations, and that, by limiting the apparatus claims to a unitary device, he has avoided the situation where any and all means for practicing the method would be covered by the claims.

In response to the solicitor's argument that the Supreme Court in *Flook*, supra, adopted a "point of novelty" approach to § 101 which supercedes the second step of the analysis this court applies to § 101 cases, *In re Freeman*, 573 F.2d 1237, 197 USPQ 464 (Cust. & Pat. App.1978), appellant relies on the opinion in *Flook* itself to refute that contention. According to appellant, by letting stand its earlier decision in *Mackay Radio & Telegraph Co. v. Radio Corporation of America*, 306 U.S. 86, 59 S.Ct. 427, 83 L.Ed. 506 (1939), the Court recognized that a claim could pass muster under § 101 where the point of novelty resided in a mathematical equation which defined a new relationship between other physical claim elements which were old in the art. On this issue, appellant suggests that any point of novelty approach which may appear in *Flook* be limited to claims where the point of novelty is in calculating without any apparatus at all—the factual setting in *Flook*.

Appellant attempts to distinguish this court's recent cases. *In re Maucorps*, 609 F.2d 481, 203 USPQ 812 (Cust. & Pat.App.1979), and *In re Gelnovatch*, 595 F.2d 32, 201 USPQ 136 (Cust. & Pat.App.1979), relied upon by the solicitor. Appellant's position is that in both of those cases, the end product of the process was merely a number or numbers which had been calculated during the process. In contrast, he asserts that his claims produce a set of physical signals which represent physical phenomena—the characteristics of subterranean geostructure. Thus, rather than performing a nonstatutory process involving the manipulation of mere numbers, appellant states that he performs a statutory process involving the manipulation and processing of actual physical phenomena; two sets of signals are interacted in a particular manner to produce a third set of signals.

In response to a comment by the solicitor that the provision for a magnetic tape recorder in dependent claim 18 comes the closest of any of the claims to assuring that there is a readable output recording or product, appellant makes the following argument. He states that a magnetic tape is a device, and that a magnetic tape on which data are recorded is a different device than a blank tape or a tape containing other data. Turning to language in *Benson*, supra, he urges error in the solicitor's position that such a tape, not eye-readable, is not a proper end result of a patentable process. In *Benson*, the Court stated (409 U.S. at 70, 93 S.Ct. at 256):

> Transformation and reduction of an article "to a different state or thing" is the clue to the patentability of a process claim that does not include particular machines.

Appellant urges that his signals, when recorded on the magnetic tape, cause changes of physical state in the tape and that the tape, after recording, is a new device due to these changes of state. Thus he asserts that his claims define statutory subject matter on the authority of *Benson*.

Finally, while admitting that his claim 12 is not limited to apparatus for seismic prospecting, appellant nonetheless asserts that the claim is limited to a particular art or technology—that of mechanical and electrical correlation of signals—and does not cover pencil-and-paper solutions of mathematical equations. It covers only apparatus for processing signals. Furthermore, with respect to the solicitor's contention that the apparatus claims do not require a unitary device in a geographical sense, appellant points out that the best mode of the invention is disclosed as apparatus which is self-contained within a vehicle during the course of seismic exploration along a line of exploration.

OPINION

The determination of statutory subject matter under § 101 in the field here involved has proved to be one of the most difficult and controversial issues in patent law. The problem here, as we see it, is not one of computer-related inventions per se; it is one of mathematics-related inventions.

In the computer arts, § 101 problems tend to center around the use of mathematics in the claims, which define the invention for which patent protection is sought. This is a natural consequence of the nature of computers. A computer is nothing more than an electronic machine. It is characterized by its ability to process data, usually by executing mathematical operations on the data at high speeds. By virtue of the speed with which computers operate, they are capable of executing complex or otherwise time-consuming calculations in fractions of a second. Their use in technology is analogous to the use of mechanical devices, such as levers, which provide mechanical advantage in inventions of a mechanical nature: they make possible, or practicable, the solution of mathematical problems which are impractical to solve manually due to the inordinate amount of time manual solution would consume.

A computer is not mysterious to one skilled in the art; it is merely a distinct type of machine. It will facilitate understanding the applicability of patent law to computer-arts inventions if it is kept in mind that the issues under § 101 in this area have arisen because the function of the computer has been to perform mathematical operations. The problems revolve about the role of mathematics in the claimed inventions.[4]

It is "clear that a process is not unpatentable [in the sense of not being subject matter within the categories named in § 101] simply because it contains a law of nature or a mathematical algorithm." *Flook*, 437 U.S. at 590, 98 S.Ct. at 2526. It is equally clear, from the

footnote 18 holding in *Flook*, "that a claim for an improved method of calculation, even when tied to a specific end use, is unpatentable subject matter under § 101." [Citation.] Between these reference points a determination must be made with respect to whether a claim, which *recites* mathematical calculations, is directed to statutory subject matter when considered as a whole.

There exists a wealth of precedent, most of it predating the advent of computer technology, which aids in addressing the problem, which, as we have noted, is one of mathematics, not of computers. This precedent has been relied upon by the Supreme Court to answer the difficult questions concerning the statutory nature of computer-arts inventions, and thus remains a source from which to synthesize a reasoned analysis to resolve questions arising under § 101. [Footnote.] No special mode of analysis is required simply because a controversy involves a computer-related invention.

The common thread running through prior decisions regarding statutory subject matter is that a principle of nature or a scientific truth (including any mathematical algorithm which expresses such a principle or truth) is not the kind of discovery or invention which the patent laws were designed to protect. [Citations.] Since a statutory invention may *employ* a scientific truth, a decision as to whether the invention utilizing such truth is statutory must necessarily rest on the relationship which the truth or principle bears to the remainder of the substance of the invention as claimed.

The Supreme Court has given us its interpretation of what that relationship must be for an invention employing a scientific truth

---

4. That the issue of mathematics in claims is at the heart of the controversy in § 101 cases involving computer-related inventions has been explicitly recognized by the Supreme Court in both of the instances in which it has addressed the problem. In *Benson*, supra, the Court stated:

> A procedure for solving a given type of *mathematical problem* is known as an "algorithm." The procedures set forth in the present claims are of that kind; that is to say, *they are a generalized formulation for programs to solve mathematical problems* of converting one form of numerical representation to another. [Citation.] [Emphasis ours.]

Later, in *Flook*, supra, the Court said:

> We use the word "algorithm" in this case, as we did in *Gottschalk v. Benson* * * * to mean "[a] procedure for solving a given type of mathematical prob-

lem." [Citation.]

For the purposes of this opinion, we use the word *algorithm* in the above-defined sense to refer to methods of calculation, mathematical formulas, and mathematical procedures generally. We strongly disagree with the position taken by the PTO, *see* Petition of Commissioner of Patents and Trademarks for Certiorari, *Diamond v. Bradley*, 445 U.S. 926 , 100 S.Ct. 1311, 32 L.Ed.2d 758, that the word *algorithm* as applied by the Supreme Court in § 101 cases is not limited to mathematical algorithms, but extends to the general meaning of the word which connotes a step-by-step procedure to arrive at a given result. [Citation.] Such a proposition, if accepted, would have the effect of totally reading the word "process" out of § 101, since any process is a step-by-step procedure to arrive at a given result.

or principle of nature to be statutory. "Structure created with the aid of knowledge of scientific truth," *Mackay Radio*, 306 U.S. at 94, 59 S.Ct. at 431, is statutory, as is "the application of the law of nature to a new and useful end." *Funk Bros. Seed Co. v. Kalo Inoculant Co.*, 333 U.S. 127, 130, 68 S.Ct. 440, 441, 92 L.Ed. 588. These principles were reaffirmed in *Flook*. [Citation.]

The solicitor has suggested that the Supreme Court has, in *Flook*, adopted a "point of novelty" approach to § 101. Under such an approach, an invention would be nonstatutory if the mathematical algorithm in the claim, as an embodiment of scientific truth, is at the "point of novelty" of the claim.

If this approach were to be adopted it would immeasurably debilitate the patent system. We do not believe the Supreme Court has acted in a matter so potentially destructive. As an illustration of the utter failure of such an approach to resolve these questions, we offer the example of certain improvement inventions, wherein the improvement resides in the application of scientific truth, e. g., mathematical formulae, to previously-known structure or process steps.

Improvement inventions are expressly included within § 101, which provides that "Whoever invents any * * * new and useful *improvement* [of a process, machine, manufacture, or composition of matter] may obtain a patent therefor. * * *" (Emphasis ours.) There is no evidence that Congress intended a different criterion to apply to improvement inventions to determine whether they are statutory. Yet a strict "point of novelty" approach to improvement inventions involving the application of scientific truth as the improvement would effectively place them, as a class, outside the coverage of § 101—and to no purpose.

It is well-settled that a statutory invention will result from the *application* of a scientific truth (law of nature) to an otherwise statutory structure or process. [Citations.] In both *Benson* and *Flook*, the Court again relied on this well-settled precedent.[6]

This principle applies with equal force to basic inventions and improvement inventions. Thus, if an inventor succeeds in applying scientific truth in a specific manner, resulting in the *improvement* of a process, machine, manufacture, or composition of matter, his invention is statutory, subject to the caveat that the underlying subject matter which has been improved *is itself within the bounds of § 101*. [Footnote.]

The solicitor has invited us to reexamine our test in *In re Freeman*, 573 F.2d 1237, 197 USPQ 464, because the second step of the test is alleged to conflict with *Flook*. That step involves examination of the claim "to ascertain whether in its entirety it wholly preempts [the] algorithm." [Citation.]

We find the problem to be one of semantics. We do not read *Flook* as adopting a "point of novelty" test; as we have shown, such a test flies in the fact of Supreme Court precedent reaffirmed in *Flook*, and does violence to the statute.

We have observed that the Court in *Flook* reasoned that a patent claim must be considered as a whole when undergoing analysis under § 101. [Footnote.] The "point of novelty" approach is incompatible with this directive since it necessarily ignores the claim as a whole in order to concentrate on a single claim component. Whatever implication the solicitor may find in *Flook* to support his belief that a "point of novelty" approach was adopted is dispelled by the Court's explicit instructions that, under § 101, a claim must be considered as a whole.

The second step of the *Freeman* test is stated in terms of preemption. We note, however, that *Flook* does not require literal preemption of a mathematical algorithm found in a patent claim. The Court there stated that Flook's claims did not "cover every conceivable application of the formula." [Citation.] Nevertheless, we believe that the *Freeman* test, as applied, is in no way in conflict with *Flook*.

In order to determine whether a mathematical algorithm is "preempted" by a claim under *Freeman*, the claim is analyzed to es-

---

6. In *Flook*, the Court stated that "*Benson* applied the established rule that a law of nature cannot be the subject of a patent." [Citation.] Characterizing its decision in *Flook*, the Court said: "To a large extent our conclusion is based on reasoning derived from opinions written before the modern business of developing programs for computers was conceived." [Citation.]

tablish the relationship between the algorithm and the physical steps or elements of the claim. In *Benson* and *Flook*, no such relationship could be found; the entire claim was, in each case, drawn to the algorithm itself. The preamble in the claim involved in *Flook*, while limiting the application of the claimed method to "a process comprising the catalytic chemical conversion of hydrocarbons," did not serve to render the method statutory because the claim, as a whole, was still directed to the solution of a mathematical problem.

When this court has heretofore applied its *Freeman* test, it has viewed it as requiring that the claim be examined to determine the significance of the mathematical algorithm, i.e., does the claim implement the algorithm in a specific manner to define structural relationships between the elements of the claim in the case of apparatus claims, or limit or refine physical process steps in the case of process or method claims? The point of the analysis is the recognition that "A principle, in the abstract, is a fundamental truth; an original cause; a motive; these cannot be patented," *LeRoy v. Tatham*, 55 U.S. (14 How.) at 175, 14 L.Ed. 367, and that "a hitherto unknown phenomenon of nature" if claimed would not be statutory, but that "the application of the law of nature to a new and useful end," *Funk Bros.*, 333 U.S. at 130, 68 S.Ct. at 441, would be.

While we have *stated* the test in terms of preemption, we have consistently applied it in the spirit of the foregoing principles. Since we have noted that *Flook* does not require literal preemption of a mathematical algorithm by a claim for a finding that the claim is nonstatutory, we thus deem it appropriate to restate the second step of the *Freeman* test in terms other than preemption. Once a mathematical algorithm has been found, the claim *as a whole* [footnote] must be further analyzed. If it appears that the mathematical algorithm is implemented in a specific manner

to define structural relationships between the physical elements of the claim (in apparatus claims) or to refine or limit claim steps (in process claims), the claim being otherwise statutory, the claim passes muster under § 101. If, however, the mathematical algorithm is merely presented and solved by the claimed invention, as was the case in *Benson* and *Flook*, and is not applied in any manner to physical elements or process steps, no amount of post-solution activity will render the claim statutory; nor is it saved by a preamble merely reciting the field of use of the mathematical algorithm.

Various indicia are helpful in determining whether a claim as a whole calls merely for the solution of a mathematical algorithm. For instance, if the end-product of a claimed invention is a *pure number*, as in *Benson* and *Flook*, the invention is nonstatutory regardless of any post-solution activity which makes it available for use by a person or machine for other purposes. If, however, the claimed invention produces a physical thing, such as the noiseless seismic trace in *In re Johnson*, supra, the fact that it is represented in numerical form does not render the claim nonstatutory.[10]

THE "MEANS FOR" APPARATUS CLAIMS

Both the examiner and the board refused to separately consider appellant's apparatus claims because the method and apparatus claims were deemed indistinguishable. This problem arises in computer-arts inventions when the structure in apparatus claims is defined only as "means for" performing specified functions as sanctioned by 35 U.S.C. § 112, sixth paragraph. If the functionally-defined disclosed means and their equivalents are so broad that they encompass any and every means for performing the recited functions, the apparatus claim is an attempt to exalt form over substance since the claim is really

---

10. In *Johnson*, a seismic trace containing superimposed noise was subjected to signal processing by computer. As a result of the processing the unwanted noise component was removed from the trace. In order to make a trace palatable to a computer, it must sometimes be converted to a computer-compatible format. One method of doing this is to sample the amplitude of the signal at regular intervals and convert the resulting amplitude value to a

binary equivalent form. The resulting noiseless trace may also appear in binary form. It nevertheless is the same signal as the "wiggle trace" which it represents, and is not a *pure number*, and unless form is to control over substance, the fact that a process result is stated in computer-compatible form should not be the basis for holding an invention to be nonstatutory.

to the method or series of functions itself. In computer-related inventions, the recited means often perform the function of "number crunching" (solving mathematical algorithms and making calculations). In such cases the burden must be placed on the applicant to demonstrate that the claims are truly drawn to specific apparatus distinct from other apparatus capable of performing the identical functions.

If this burden has not been discharged, the apparatus claim will be treated as if it were drawn to the method or process which encompasses all of the claimed "means." [Citations.] The statutory nature of the claim under § 101 will then depend on whether the corresponding method is statutory.

We agree with the PTO that all of appellant's claims should be treated as method claims. The apparatus claims differ from the method claims only in that the term "means for" has been inserted before each process step to convert the step into the "means" for performing it, wherefore they do not have separate meaning as apparatus claims.

Appellant argues that while the method claims refer to steps which may be carried out at different locations, the apparatus claims are limited to a unitary device in a physical location sense. For support of this proposition, he urges that his patent application be read as a whole, and that, so read, it shows that he is concerned with apparatus which is carried on a single vehicle during the course of seismic exploration. Indeed, his application does disclose this as the best mode for carrying out the invention.

Appellant's *claims*, however, are not limited to a unitary device in any sense. There is no evidence that the best mode contemplated is the only operable mode. In effect, we are asked to read limitations into the claims which are not there. This court will not read limitations into claims merely because they are disclosed in the specification. [Citations.]

THE METHOD CLAIMS

Appellant's claims clearly *recite* mathematical algorithms. The question is whether the claims implement the algorithms in such manner as to render them statutory, since, as we have pointed out, the mere presence of the

algorithms in the claims is not fatal. [Citation.]

We pause to explain a difference between our approach and that of the board, which characterized appellant's claims as mathematical exercises. We have quoted above the three reasons given by the board to support its conclusion. In discussing steps (a) through (e) of the claims, the board stated that at a fundamental level the computer must employ radices imposed by its architecture to manage the data flow and that it "would be difficult, not to say misleading, to characterize such operations as nonmathematical." This statement, if accepted, would suffice to remove all computer-arts inventions from the scope of § 101. It is itself misleading because it ignores what the computer is doing, concentrating instead on how it is being done. [Citation.] One could as easily say that the inclined papermaking wire in *Eibel Process Co. [v. Minnesota and Ontario Paper Co.*, 261 U.S. 45 (1923)], was on a fundamental level, mathematical in nature because it operated according to the law of gravity, which is expressible as a mathematical formula. However, as this court noted *In re Bradley,* 600 F.2d 807, 812, 202 USPQ 480, 485 (Cust. & Pat.App.1979), *cert. granted sub nom. Diamond v. Bradley,* 445 U.S. 926, 100 S.Ct. 1311, 63 L.Ed. 2d 758 (1980), a computer may be retrieving a legal opinion from a computerized legal research service or setting a page from a telephone directory. An overall characterization of these operations as mathematical is too broad because in concentrating on the minutiae, it ignores the whole. Under such reasoning, a timed process step is mathematical in nature because "at a fundamental level" time is *counted* in minutes. We equally reject the board's reasoning with respect to the steps used to accommodate the data to memory requiring the tailoring of the data to the particular computer architecture.

We view only the third reason given by the board as valid and substantial and as directly related to the heart of the § 101 issue as it manifests itself in the computer arts. It relates to the processing of the mathematical algorithms recited in appellant's claims and is the only legitimate basis for the board's rejection.

Appellant's claims, except claims 10–12, are in Jepson [footnote] format. The claim preambles merely set forth the environment in which the improvement operates. They show only the context in which the mathematical exercises in the claims are to be used. In each claim, what is positively claimed, as distinguished from environment, is "the improved method of correlating" (claim 7), or "the improved method of cross-correlating" (claim 16). The same is true of claims 11–12, drafted in illusory apparatus format.

Correlation or cross-correlation is a mathematical exercise which relates two mathematical functions. It remains a mathematical exercise even when verbally tied to the specific end use of seismic prospecting. Although the claim preambles relate the claimed invention to the art of seismic prospecting, the claims themselves are not drawn to methods of or apparatus for seismic prospecting; they are drawn to improved mathematical methods for interpreting the results of seismic prospecting.

The specific end use recited in the preambles does not save the claims from the holding in *Flook*, since they are drawn to methods of calculation, albeit improved. Examination of each claim demonstrates that each has no substance apart from the calculations involved. The calculations are the beginning and end of the claims. Thus, this case falls squarely within the holding in *Flook*, and the claims must be held to be nonstatutory.

Furthermore, the nature of the resulting "partial product signals" is not clear. While these products are termed "signals," there is nothing necessarily physical about them beyond the fact that they are held in some physical storage medium.

Appellant's specification states that these "signals" comprise "a record somewhat similar to that which would have been produced if the original seismic wave had been in the form of an impulse." In *In re Gelnovatch*, supra, a majority of this court affirmed the § 101 rejection of claims to a process invention for determining the component values in a mathematical model of a microwave circuit. Appellant there similarly argued unsuccessfully that his results were the same as if the circuit had been built and real components substituted.

We view the results here as being similar to those in *Gelnovatch*—a simulation of some-thing physical is produced by a process akin to mathematical modeling. Each and every step in these claims involves or intimately relates to mathematical operations; we can view the end product *in this case* only as a mathematical result.

Claim 12, and claims 10 and 11 dependent therefrom, are not presented in Jepson format, but they suffer from a fundamental flaw which places them outside the bounds of § 101. These claims are directed to the process of cross-correlation in the abstract. They are not limited to any particular art or technology, unless pure mathematics is considered as an art or technology. The "signals" processed by the inventions of claims 10–12 may represent either physical quantities or abstract quantities; the claims do not require one or the other. The claims thus dominate the particular method of cross-correlation in any and all arts. They are classic examples of an attempt to embrace the algorithm or scientific truth itself rather than a particular application.

We address another of appellant's arguments to correct a misconception. In arguing the patentability of claim 18 (apparatus format), appellant states that the solicitor was incorrect in his argument that the eye-readability of the tape upon which the "partial product signals" are recorded is in issue.

We find appellant's argument to be without merit and his reliance upon the previously-quoted passage in *Benson* to be misplaced. If § 101 could be satisfied by the mere recordation of the results of a nonstatutory process on some record medium, even the most unskilled patent draftsman could provide for such a step, thus converting a nonstatutory process to a statutory one with relative ease. The fact that a tape containing recorded results is different from a blank tape or a tape containing other results is irrelevant to the inquiry under § 101 where the remaining claim steps provide only for the solution of a mathematical problem.

This case is distinguishable from *In re Johnson*, supra. There the claims were drawn to the enhancement of digital data in seismic records by removing the noise from the physical signals representing physical phenomena. Mathematics were employed to this end. The inventors in that case did not attempt to claim a mathematical exercise or method of calculation. Operation of the claimed process in *Johnson* converted the noise-containing *physical* seismic record present at the start to a new record minus the noise component. Here, appellant claims only an improved mathematical method for cross-correlation.

This case is also distinguishable from our recent *In re Diehr*, 602 F.2d 982, 203 USPQ 44 (CCPA 1979), *cert. granted sub nom. Diamond v. Diehr*, 445 U.S. 926, 100 S.Ct. 1311, 63 L.Ed.2d 758 (1980). There appellants invented a process for molding synthetic rubber articles in which one physical step of the process, maintaining the blank in the mold for the proper period of time, was improved by refining and further defining the step with the aid of mathematics. The improvement yielded a higher quality product over prior processes which did not keep the blank in the mold for a sufficient time or kept it there too long. The equation used in the process remained available for others to use in the rubber-making art as well as other arts; in fact, the equation used had long been in use in rubber-molding processes. The inventors used it to refine a physical step in the process in a manner analogous to the manner in which mathematics and physical laws were employed in the inventions in *Mackay Radio* and *Eibel Process Co.*, supra.

Here appellant claims the mathematical algorithm itself even though most of his claims limit its use to a particular art or technology. This may not be done under the patent law as it now exists.

The decision of the board is *affirmed*.

DIAMOND v. DIEHR

450 U.S. 175

(United States Supreme Court, Certiorari to the United States Court of Customs and Patent Appeals, March 3, 1981.)

REHNQUIST, J.

We granted certiorari to determine whether a process for curing synthetic rubber which includes in several of its steps the use of a mathematical formula and a programmed digital computer is patentable subject matter under 35 U. S. C. § 101.

I

The patent application at issue was filed by the respondents on August 6, 1975. The claimed invention is a process for molding raw, uncured synthetic rubber into cured precision products. The process uses a mold for precisely shaping the uncured material under heat and pressure and then curing the synthetic rubber in the mold so that the product will retain its shape and be functionally operative after the molding is completed. [Footnote.]

Respondents claim that their process ensures the production of molded articles which are properly cured. Achieving the perfect cure depends upon several factors including the thickness of the article to be molded, the temperature of the molding process, and the amount of time that the article is allowed to remain in the press. It is possible, using well-known time, temperature, and cure relationships to calculate by means of the Arrhenius equation[2] when to open the press and remove the cured product. Nonetheless, according to the respondents, the industry has not been able to obtain uniformly accurate cures because the temperature of the molding press could not be precisely measured, thus making it difficult to do the necessary computations to determine cure time. [Footnote.] Because the temperature *inside* the press has heretofore been viewed as an uncontrollable variable, the conventional industry practice has been to calculate the cure time as the shortest time in which all parts of the product will definitely be cured, assuming a reasonable amount of mold-opening time during loading and unloading. But the shortcoming of this practice is that operating with an uncontrollable variable inevitably led in some instances to overestimating the mold-opening time and overcuring the rubber, and in other instances to underestimating that time and undercuring the product. [Footnote.]

---

2. The equation is named after its discoverer Svante Arrhenius and has long been used to calculate the cure time in rubber-molding presses. The equation can be expressed as follows:

$$\ln v = CZ + x$$

wherein ln v is the natural logarithm of v, the total required cure time; C is the activation constant, a unique figure for each batch of each compound being molded, determined in accordance with rheometer measurements of each batch; Z is the temperature in the mold; and x is a constant dependent on the geometry of the particular mold in the press. A rheometer is an instrument to measure flow of viscous substances.

Respondents characterize their contribution to the art to reside in the process of constantly measuring the actual temperature inside the mold. These temperature measurements are then automatically fed into a computer which repeatedly recalculates the cure time by use of the Arrhenius equation. When the recalculated time equals the actual time that has elapsed since the press was closed, the computer signals a device to open the press. According to the respondents, the continuous measuring of the temperature inside the mold cavity, the feeding of this information to a digital computer which constantly recalculates the cure time, and the signaling by the computer to open the press, are all new in the art.

The patent examiner rejected the respondents' claims on the sole ground that they were drawn to nonstatutory subject matter under 35 U. S. C. § 101.[5] He determined that those steps in respondents' claims that are carried out by a computer under control of a stored program constituted nonstatutory subject matter under this Court's decision in *Gottschalk* v. *Benson*, 409 U. S. 63 (1972). The remaining steps—installing rubber in the press and the subsequent closing of the press—were "conventional and necessary to the process and cannot be the basis of patentability." The examiner concluded that respondents' claims defined and sought protection of a computer program for operating a rubber-molding press.

The Patent and Trademark Office Board of Appeals agreed with the examiner, but the Court of Customs and Patent Appeals reversed. [Citation.] The court noted that a claim drawn to subject matter otherwise statutory does not become nonstatutory because a computer is involved. The respondents' claims were not directed to a mathematical algorithm or an improved method of calculation but rather recited an improved process for molding rubber articles by solving a practical problem

---

5. Respondents' application contained 11 different claims. Three examples are claims 1, 2 and 11 which provide:

1. A method of operating a rubber-molding press for precision molded compounds with the aid of a digital computer, comprising:
   providing said computer with a data base for said press including at least,
   natural logarithm conversion data (ln),
   the activation energy constant (C) unique to each batch of said compound being molded, and
   a constant (x) dependent upon the geometry of the particular mold of the press,
   initiating an interval timer in said computer upon the closure of the press for monitoring the elapsed time of said closure,
   constantly determining the temperature (Z) of the mold at a location closely adjacent to the mold cavity in the press during molding,
   constantly providing the computer with the temperature (Z),
   repetitively calculating in the computer, at frequent intervals during each cure, the Arrhenius equation for reaction time during the cure, which is
   $\ln v = CZ + x$
   where v is the total required cure time,
   repetitively comparing in the computer at said frequent intervals during the cure each said calculation of the total required cure time calculated with the Arrhenius equation and said elapsed time, and
   opening the press automatically when a said comparison indicates equivalence.

2. The method of claim 1 including measuring the activation energy constant for the compound being molded in the press with a rheometer and automatically updating said data base within the computer in the event of changes in the compound being molded in said press as measured by said rheometer.

* * *

11. A method of manufacturing precision molded articles from selected synthetic rubber compounds in an openable rubber molding press having at least one heated precision mold, comprising:
   (a) heating said mold to a temperature range approximating a predetermined rubber curing temperature,
   (b) installing prepared unmolded synthetic rubber of a known compound in a molding cavity of predetermined geometry as defined by said mold,
   (c) closing said press to mold said rubber to occupy said cavity in conformance with the contour of said mold and to cure said rubber by transfer of heat thereto from said mold,
   (d) initiating an interval timer upon the closure of said press for monitoring the elapsed time of said closure,
   (e) heating said mold during said closure to maintain the temperature thereof within said range approximating said rubber curing temperature,
   (f) constantly determining the temperature of said mold at a location closely adjacent said cavity thereof throughout closure of said press,
   (g) repetitively calculating at frequent periodic intervals throughout closure of said press the Arrhenius equation for reaction time of said rubber to determine total required cure time v as follows:
   $\ln v = cz + x$
   wherein c is an activation energy constant determined for said rubber being molded and cured in said press, z is the temperature of said mold at the time of each calculation of said Arrhenius equation, and x is a constant which is a function of said predetermined geometry of said mold,
   (h) for each repetition of calculation of said Arrhenius equation herein, comparing the resultant calculated total required cure time with the monitored elapsed time measured by said interval timer,
   (i) opening said press when a said comparison of calculated total required cure time and monitored elapsed time indicates equivalence, and
   (j) removing from said mold the resultant precision molded and cured rubber article.

which had arisen in the molding of rubber products.

The Commissioner of Patents and Trademarks sought certiorari arguing that the decision of the Court of Customs and Patent Appeals was inconsistent with prior decisions of this Court. Because of the importance of the question presented, we granted the writ. [Citation.]

II

* * *

Although the term "process" was not added to 35 U. S. C. § 101 until 1952, a process has historically enjoyed patent protection because it was considered a form of "art" as that term was used in the 1793 Act. [Footnote.] In defining the nature of a patentable process, the Court stated:

> That a process may be patentable, irrespective of the particular form of the instrumentalities used, cannot be disputed * * * A process is a mode of treatment of certain materials to produce a given result. It is an act, or a series of acts, performed upon the subject-matter to be transformed and reduced to a different state or thing. If new and useful, it is just as patentable as is a piece of machinery. In the language of the patent law, it is an art. The machinery pointed out as suitable to perform the process may or may not be new or patentable; whilst the process itself may be altogether new, and produce an entirely new result. The process requires that certain things should be done with certain substances, and in a certain order; but the tools to be used in doing this may be of secondary consequence. Cochrane v. Deener, 94 U. S. 780, 787–788 (1877).

Analysis of the eligibility of a claim of patent protection for a "process" did not change with the addition of that term to § 101. Recently, in Gottschalk v. Benson, 409 U. S. 63 (1972), we repeated the above definition recited in Cochrane v. Deener, adding: "Transformation and reduction of an article 'to a different state or thing' is the clue to the patentability of a process claim that does not include particular machines." 409 U. S., at 70.

Analyzing respondents' claims according to the above statements from our cases, we think

that a physical and chemical process for molding precision synthetic rubber products falls within the § 101 categories of possibly patentable subject matter. That respondents' claims involve the transformation of an article, in this case raw, uncured synthetic rubber, into a different state or thing cannot be disputed. The respondents' claims describe in detail a step-by-step method for accomplishing such, beginning with the loading of a mold with raw, uncured rubber and ending with the eventual opening of the press at the conclusion of the cure. Industrial processes such as this are the types which have historically been eligible to receive the protection of our patent laws. [Footnote.]

III

Our conclusion regarding respondents' claims is not altered by the fact that in several steps of the process a mathematical equation and a programmed digital computer are used. This Court has undoubtedly recognized limits to § 101 and every discovery is not embraced within the statutory terms. Excluded from such patent protection are laws of nature, natural phenomena, and abstract ideas. See Parker v. Flook, 437 U. S. 584 (1978). [Citations.] "A principle, in the abstract, is a fundamental truth; an original cause; a motive; these cannot be patented, as no one can claim in either of them an exclusive right." [Citation.] Only last Term, we explained:

> [A] new mineral discovered in the earth or a new plant found in the wild is not patentable subject matter. Likewise, Einstein could not patent his celebrated law that $E = mc^2$; nor could Newton have patented the law of gravity. Such discoveries are "manifestations of * * * nature, free to all men and reserved exclusively to none." [Citation.]

Our recent holdings in Gottschalk v. Benson, supra, and Parker v. Flook, supra, both of which are computer-related, stand for no more than these long-established principles. In Benson, we held unpatentable claims for an algorithm used to convert binary code decimal numbers to equivalent pure binary numbers. The sole practical application of the algorithm was in connection with the programming of a general purpose digital computer. We defined "algorithm" as a "procedure for solving a given type of mathematical problem," and we concluded that such an algorithm, or mathematical formula, is like a law of nature, which cannot be the subject of a patent.[9]

Parker v. *Flook, supra*, presented a similar situation. The claims were drawn to a method for computing an "alarm limit." An "alarm limit" is simply a number and the Court concluded that the application sought to protect a formula for computing this number. Using this formula, the updated alarm limit could be calculated if several other variables were known. The application, however, did not purport to explain how these other variables were to be determined [footnote], nor did it purport "to contain any disclosure relating to the chemical processes at work, the monitoring of process variables, or the means of setting off an alarm or adjusting an alarm system. All that it provides is a formula for computing an updated alarm limit." [Citation.]

In contrast, the respondents here do not seek to patent a mathematical formula. Instead they seek patent protection for a process of curing synthetic rubber. Their process admittedly employs a well-known mathematical equation, but they do not seek to pre-empt the use of that equation. Rather, they seek only to foreclose from others the use of that equation in conjunction with all the other steps in their claimed process. These include installing rubber in a press, closing the mold, constantly determining the temperature of the mold, constantly recalculating the appropriate cure time through the use of the formula and a digital computer, and automatically opening the press at the proper time. Obviously, one does not need a "computer" to cure natural or synthetic rubber, but if the

computer use incorporated in the process patent significantly lessens the possibility of "overcuring" or "undercuring," the process as a whole does not thereby become unpatentable subject matter.

Our earlier opinions lend support to our present conclusion that a claim drawn to subject matter otherwise statutory does not become nonstatutory simply because it uses a mathematical formula, computer program, or digital computer. In *Gottschalk* v. *Benson* we noted: "It is said that the decision precludes a patent for any program servicing a computer. We do not so hold." [Citation.] Similarly, in *Parker* v. *Flook* we stated that "a process is not unpatentable simply because it contains a law of nature or a mathematical algorithm." [Citation.] It is now commonplace that an *application* of a law of nature or mathematical formula to a known structure or process may well be deserving of patent protection. [Citation.] As Justice Stone explained four decades ago:

> While a scientific truth, or the mathematical expression of it, is not a patentable invention, a novel and useful structure created with the aid of knowledge of scientific truth may be. *Mackay Radio & Telegraph Co.* v. *Radio Corp. of America*, 306 U. S. 86, 94 (1939). [Footnote.]

We think this statement in *Mackay* takes us a long way toward the correct answer in this case. Arrhenius' equation is not patentable in isolation, but when a process for curing rubber is devised which incorporates in it a more efficient solution of the equation, that process is at the very least not barred at the threshold by § 101.

In determining the eligibility of respondents' claimed process for patent protection under § 101, their claims must be considered as a whole. It is inappropriate to dissect the

---

9. The term "algorithm" is subject to a variety of definitions. The petitioner defines the term to mean:

    1. A fixed step-by-step procedure for accomplishing a given result; usually a simplified procedure for solving a complex problem, also a full statement of a finite number of steps. 2. A defined process or set of rules that leads [*sic*] and assures development of a desired output from a given input. A sequence of formulas and/or algebraic/logical steps to calculate or determine a given task; processing rules. [Reference.]

This definition is significantly broader than the definition this Court employed in *Benson* and *Flook*. Our previous decisions regarding the patentability of "algorithms" are necessarily limited to the more narrow definition employed by the Court, and we do not pass judgment on whether processes falling outside the definition previously used by this Court, but within the definition offered by the petitioner, would be patentable subject matter.

claims into old and new elements and then to ignore the presence of the old elements in the analysis. This is particularly true in a process claim because a new combination of steps in a process may be patentable even though all the constituents of the combination were well known and in common use before the combination was made. The "novelty" of any element or steps in a process, or even of the process itself, is of no relevance in determining whether the subject matter of a claim falls within the § 101 categories of possibly patentable subject matter.[12].

It has been urged that novelty is an appropriate consideration under § 101. Presumably, this argument results from the language in § 101 referring to any "new and useful" process, machine, etc. Section 101, however, is a general statement of the type of subject matter that is eligible for patent protection "subject to the conditions and requirements of this title." Specific conditions for patentability follow and § 102 covers in detail the conditions relating to novelty. [Footnote.] The question therefore of whether a particular invention is novel is "wholly apart from whether the invention falls into a category of statutory subject matter." [Emphasis deleted.] [Citations.] The legislative history of the 1952 Patent Act is in accord with this reasoning. The Senate Report stated:

> Section 101 sets forth the subject matter that can be patented, 'subject to the conditions and requirements of this title.' The conditions under which a patent may be obtained follow, and *Section 102 covers the conditions relating to novelty.* S. Rep. No. 1979, 82d Cong., 2d Sess. 5 (1952) (emphasis supplied).

It is later stated in the same Report:

> Section 102, in general, may be said to describe the statutory novelty required for patentability,

and includes, in effect, an amplification and definition of 'new' in section 101. *Id.,* at 6.

Finally, it is stated in the "Revision Notes":

> The corresponding section of [the] existing statute is split into two sections, section 101 relating to the subject matter for which patents may be obtained, and section 102 defining statutory novelty and stating other conditions for patentability. *Id.,* at 17.

[Citation.]

In this case, it may later be determined that the respondents' process is not deserving of patent protection because it fails to satisfy the statutory conditions of novelty under § 102 or nonobviousness under § 103. A rejection on either of these grounds does not affect the determination that respondents' claims recited subject matter which was eligible for patent protection under § 101.

IV

We have before us today only the question of whether respondents' claims fall within the § 101 categories of possibly patentable subject matter. We view respondents' claims as nothing more than a process for molding rubber products and not as an attempt to patent a mathematical formula. We recognize, of course, that when a claim recites a mathematical formula (or scientific principle or phenomenon of nature), an inquiry must be made into whether the claim is seeking patent protection for that formula in the abstract. A mathematical formula as such is not accorded the protection of our patent laws, *Gottschalk* v. *Benson,* 409 U. S. 63 (1972), and this principle cannot be circumvented by attempting to limit the use of the formula to a particular technological environment. *Parker* v. *Flook,* 437 U. S. 584 (1978). Similarly, insignificant post-

---

12. It is argued that the procedure of dissecting a claim into old and new elements is mandated by our decision in *Flook* which noted that a mathematical algorithm must be assumed to be within the "prior art." It is from this language that the petitioner premises his argument that if everything other than the algorithm is determined to be old in the art, then the claim cannot recite statutory subject matter. The fallacy in this argument is that we did not hold in *Flook* that the mathematical algorithm could not be considered at all when making the § 101

determination. To accept the analysis proffered by the petitioner would, if carried to its extreme, make all inventions unpatentable because all inventions can be reduced to underlying principles of nature which, once known, make their implementation obvious. The analysis suggested by the petitioner would also undermine our earlier decisions regarding the criteria to consider in determining the eligibility of a process for patent protection. See, *e. g., Gottschalk* v. *Benson, supra;* and *Cochrane* v. *Deener,* 94 U. S. 780 (1877).

solution activity will not transform an unpatentable principle into a patentable process. *Ibid.*[14] To hold otherwise would allow a competent draftsman to evade the recognized limitations on the type of subject matter eligible for patent protection. On the other hand, when a claim containing a mathematical formula implements or applies that formula in a structure or process which, when considered as a whole, is performing a function which the patent laws were designed to protect (*e. g.*, transforming or reducing an article to a different state or thing), then the claim satisfies the requirements of § 101. Because we do not view respondents' claims as an attempt to patent a mathematical formula, but rather to be drawn to an industrial process for the molding of rubber products, we affirm the judgment of the Court of Customs and Patent Appeals.[15]

It is so ordered.

---

14. Arguably, the claims in *Flook* did more than present a mathematical formula. The claims also solved the calculation in order to produce a new number or "alarm limit" and then replaced the old number with the number newly produced. The claims covered all uses of the formula in processes "comprising the catalytic chemical conversion of hydrocarbons." There are numerous such processes in the petrochemical and oil refinery industries and the claims therefore covered a broad range of potential uses. 437 U. S., at 586. The claims, however, did not cover every conceivable application of the formula. We rejected in *Flook* the argument that because all possible uses of the mathematical formula were not pre-empted, the claim should be eligible for patent protection. Our reasoning in *Flook* is in no way inconsistent with our reasoning here. A mathematical formula does not suddenly become patentable subject matter simply by having the applicant acquiesce to limiting the reach of the patent for the formula to a particular technological use. A mathematical formula in the abstract is nonstatutory subject matter regardless of whether the patent is intended to cover all uses of the formula or only limited uses. Similarly, a mathematical formula does not become patentable subject matter merely by including in the claim for the formula token postsolution activity such as the type claimed in *Flook*. We were careful to note in *Flook* that the patent application did not purport to explain how the variables used in the formula were to be selected, nor did the application contain any disclosure relating to chemical processes at work or the means of setting off an alarm or adjusting the alarm limit. *Ibid.* All the application provided was a "formula for computing an updated alarm limit." *Ibid.*

15. The dissent's analysis rises and falls on its characterization of respondents' claims as presenting nothing more than "an improved method of calculating the time

IN RE BRADLEY

600 F.2d 807
(United States Court of Customs and Patent Appeals, July 5, 1979.)

RICH, J.

This appeal is from the decision of the Patent and Trademark Office (PTO) Board of Appeals (board) affirming the rejection of claims 1–6, all of the claims in appellants' application serial No. 570,331, filed April 21, 1975, for "Switch System Base Mechanism," as being drawn to subject matter which is non-statutory under 35 U. S. C. § 101. We reverse.

THE INVENTION

Appellants' invention is in the field of computer technology. It does not relate to computer applications, i. e., any specific task that a computer is asked to perform, but rather to

that the mold should remain closed during the curing process." [Citation.] The dissent states that respondents claim only to have developed "a new method of programming a digital computer in order to calculate—promptly and repeatedly—the correct curing time in a familiar process." [Citation.] Respondents' claims, however, are not limited to the isolated step of "programming a digital computer." Rather, respondents' claims describe a process of curing rubber beginning with the loading of the mold and ending with the opening of the press and the production of a synthetic rubber product that has been perfectly cured—a result heretofore unknown in the art. [Citation.] The fact that one or more of the steps in respondents' process may not, in isolation, be novel or independently eligible for patent protection is irrelevant to the question of whether the claims as a whole recite subject matter *eligible* for patent protection under § 101. As we explained when discussing machine patents in *Deepsouth Packing Co.* v. *Laitram Corp.*, 406 U. S. 518 (1972):

> The patents were warranted not by the novelty of their elements but by the novelty of the combination they represented. Invention was recognized because Laitram's assignors combined ordinary elements in an extraordinary way—a novel union of old means was designed to achieve new ends. Thus, for both inventions "the whole in some way exceed[ed] the sum of its parts." *Great A. & P. Tea Co.* v. *Supermarket Equipment Corp.*, 340 U. S. 147, 152 (1950). *Id.*, at 521–522 (footnote omitted).

In order for the dissent to reach its conclusion it is necessary for it to read out of respondents' patent application all the steps in the claimed process which it determined were not novel or "inventive." That is not the purpose of the § 101 inquiry and conflicts with the proposition recited above that a claimed invention may be entitled to patent protection even though some or all of its elements are not "novel."

the internal operation of the computer and its ability to manage efficiently its operation in a multiprogrammed format. A multiprogrammed format is one in which the computer is capable of executing more than one program, and thus perform more than one application at the same time, without the need to reprogram the computer for each task it must perform.

Specifically, the invention relates to altering or repositioning information in the computer's system base. The system base of a computer is a fixed area in main memory which acts as the root for all information structures in the computer. In high performance computer systems, it is very advantageous to store portions of the system base in "scratchpad" registers[1] located in the central processing unit (CPU) of the computer rather than in main memory. This greatly enhances the speed of operation of the computer because the access time (the time it takes to retrieve information from a given place) associated with the scratchpad registers is less than that associated with main memory. A problem arises, however, because a programmer may wish to change the positions or content of information in the system base which happens to be located in the scratchpad registers. These registers are "invisible" to the programmer since, unlike main memory, they cannot be accessed by software (computer programs). Prior art systems altered the system base information resident in the scratchpad registers by either reinitializing the system base (completely reloading the system base containing the new information), a process which consumes a considerable amount of time, or by using software which takes advantage of the model-dependent properties of the particular computer. The latter method has the undesirable effect of resorting to reliance on model-dependent software, which is unacceptable to some computer users.

Appellants' invention enables system base information to be altered without having to resort to these techniques and their accompanying drawbacks. They accomplish their result by employing a "firmware" module, consisting of hardware elements permanently programmed with a microcode, which directs the data transfers, between the scratchpad registers and the system base located in main memory, which are necessary to effect the alteration.

Claim 1 is representative of the appealed claims:

> 1. In a multiprogramming computer system having a main memory, a central processing unit (CPU) coupled to said main memory, said (CPU) controlling the state of a plurality of groups of processes being in a running, ready, wait or suspended state, said computer system also having scratchpad registers being accessible to an operating system for controlling said multiprogramming computer system, a data structure for storing coded signals for communicating between said processes and said operating system, and said scratchpad registers, said data structure comprising:
>
> (a) first means in said data structure and communicating with said operating system for storing coded signals indicative of an address for a selected one of said processes;
>
> (b) second means in said first means for storing coded signals indicating priority of said selected one of said processes in relation to others of said processes for obtaining control of said CPU when ready;
>
> (c) third means in said data structure and communicating with said operating system, for storing coded signals indicative of an address for a selected one of said plurality of groups of processes, and,
>
> (d) fourth means coupled to said data structure and said scratchpad registers, for generating signals causing the changing of information in said data structure and said scratchpad registers.

THE REJECTION

The examiner rejected the appealed claims on the authority of *Gottschalk* v. *Benson*, 409 U.S. 63, 93 S.Ct. 253, 34 L.Ed.2d 273, 175 USPQ 673 (1972) (hereinafter *Benson*) before the Supreme Court's decision in *Parker* v. *Flook*, 437 U.S. 584, 98 S.Ct. 2522, 57 L.Ed.2d 451, 198 USPQ 193 (1978) (hereinafter *Flook*). In his final rejection, dated October 27, 1976, the

---

1. A scratchpad register, also known as a scratchpad memory, is a plurality of multibit storage locations, usually located in the central processing unit (CPU) of a computer, used for temporary storage of program information, operands, and calculation results for use by the computer's arithmetic and logic unit, and other information of a temporary nature.

examiner stated that the subject matter "deemed as the invention" is "a data structure" and then made the following analysis:

> The term "data structure" as recited in the claim is comprised of four entities described as "first means", "second means", "third means", and "fourth means." Whether these so called "means" are hardware structure which store coded signals for performing a particular function or whether they refer to coded signals representing computer control words per se, any life which the claim may have in view of that which is admittedly old in the art, resides in the "technique" (page 5, line 4) or "switch-system base instruction" (page 5, lines 13 and 14) for solving the problem of changing information of the system base which is located in scratchpad registers which software cannot access (page 4, line 20). The invention then is embodied in the coded signals representing instructions to the computer, the running process word RPW (first means of claim), priority level indicator word PRI (second means), J Table word and G Table word (third means), and micro-instructions for Figures 15c [sic, 15b] and 15c as found in the central store 1301. The invention resides in a "data structure" or an algorithm designed to control the multiprogramming computer to solve the particular problem indicated.
>
> Under the ruling in *Gottschalk* v. *Benson* [citation], the instant claims, depending upon a program implemented algorithm for patentability, are deemed nonstatutory subject matter.

Appellants requested reconsideration and argued that their claims are directed to data structures in hardware which are "specific new, novel and unobvious [in] arrangement." They asserted that by stating that the invention resided in a "technique", the examiner was clearly disregarding the claims and interpreting the invention strictly on the basis of what is found in the specification, because no "technique" is *claimed*. They stated that even if a technique (i. e., process) were claimed, *Benson* does not render all such inventions nonstatutory, and that their invention does not involve a *mathematical* algorithm. [Footnote.]

In his Answer before the board, the examiner noted that all of the limitations found in claim 1 were old in the art and that the "claim is thus reciting prior art coupled with subject matter which the U. S. Supreme Court has found to be non-statutory in *Benson.*" Appellants responded in their reply brief that it makes no difference whether individual elements are old in the art and that it is the elements in combination which define the invention as a whole.

THE BOARD

The board rendered its decision on September 20, 1978, after the Supreme Court's decision in *Flook*. After incorrectly stating that none of the claims recited the term "firmware,"[3] the board analyzed appellants' claims element by element, concluded that the only novel arrangement of the recited structures resided in the microprogramming "which together with its attendant memory hardware appears to constitute firmware."

Apparently on the basis of *Flook*, the board affirmed the rejection because it was of the opinion that the appealed claims are directed to a method of calculation or mathematical algorithm. The board found the claims similar to the claims at issue in *In re Waldbaum*, 559 F.2d 611, 194 USPQ 465 (Cust. & Pat.App. 1977), which included language characterized by the board as "obviously related to calculating and mathematical problem solving."[4] Although the claims here at issue do not contain similar mathematical language, the board said that this "does not make the functions attendant the 'means' of appellants' claims any less mathematical or less related to an algorithm within the meaning assigned that term by the USSC in *Benson.*"

To support its conclusion that the appealed claims are mathematical in nature, the board relied on a statement in the specification to the effect that all of the data in the computer are in binary form, but may be interpreted as

---

3. Claim 3, as well as dependent claims 4–6, explicitly recites firmware. Firmware is a term of art in the computer field and refers to microinstructions permanently embodied in hardware elements. [Citation.] We need not and do not decide at this time whether firmware *per se* is statutory under 35 U.S.C. § 101 because the invention as a *whole* is not directed thereto. [Citation.]

4. Waldbaum claim I reads in pertinent part:
a method * * * to *count the number* of busy lines * * * *comparing means* * * * *to derive the number of 1's* in said data word. * * * [Emphasis ours.]
It is clear that this claim recites a mathematical algorithm. It solves a mathematical problem, to wit, *counting* a number of busy lines in a telephone system.

binary coded decimal, decimal or alphanumeric. We reproduce the board's reasoning in full:

> Since digital computers normally operate in some numerical radix, binary, binary coded decimal, or the like, we consider the operation of appellants' claimed invention to be mathematical.
>
> Every operation performed in appellants' invention as claimed involves the accommodation of data and instructions to the size of the registers in memory, and to the positional assignment to the registers in memory by the use of some numerical measure or quantity effected by way of electrical signals. In whatever form the instructions employed in appellants' invention are characterized, numerical or otherwise, we think it is accurate to say that the operation of appellants' structure is mathematical and that the instructions constitute a procedure which is algorithmic in character, to the same degree as that of the Waldbaum structure and that satisfactory operation of the apparatus claimed represents the successful solution of a mathematical problem falling within the definition of algorithm supplied in *Benson* and reiterated in *Flook*.
>
> Here the method of calculation is to be used in the internal operation of the computer system and the claims recite such an end use by means of the functions recited for the various means. A claim for an improved method of calculation, even when tied to a specific end use, is unpatentable subject matter under 35 USC 101, *Flook supra*.

In summary, the board stated that the claims are drawn to apparatus in form only, and couple the apparatus (which it asserts is old in the art) "with subject matter, namely, programming, which is nonstatutory under the *Benson, Christensen,*[5] *Waldbaum* and *Flook* cases. * * *"

OPINION

The examiner's basis for the rejection is grounded on the erroneous interpretation of the Supreme Court's decision and opinion in *Benson*, namely, that all computer program or program-related inventions are nonstatutory under § 101. Both the Supreme Court [footnote] and this court [footnote] have thoroughly repudiated this view. Our decision, therefore, is based solely on the analysis made by the board.

The board said that the claims do not *directly* recite a mathematical formula, algorithm, or method of calculation, but, nevertheless, held the claims to be mathematical in nature. As appears from the quoted portion of the board opinion, the board regarded the fact that digital computers operate in some number radix as conclusive on the issue of whether the appealed claims recite a mathematical algorithm in the *Benson* and *Flook* sense. The board did not, however, direct attention to any specific formula it thought is utilized, or to what, if anything, the mathematical calculations alleged to be present in the claims are directed.

We do not agree with the board. We are constrained to reject its reasoning. Such reasoning leads to the conclusion that any computer-related invention must be regarded as mathematical in nature, a conclusion which is not compelled by either *Benson* or *Flook*.

The board's analysis confuses *what* the computer does with *how* it is done. It is of course true that a modern digital computer manipulates data, usually in binary form, by performing mathematical operations, such as addition, subtraction, multiplication, division, or bit shifting, on the data. But this is only *how* the computer does what it does. Of importance is the significance of the data and their manipulation in the real world, i. e., *what* the computer is doing. It may represent the solution of the Pythagorean theorem, or a complex vector equation describing the behavior of a rocket in flight, in which case the computer is performing a mathematical algorithm and solving an equation. This is what was involved in *Benson* and *Flook*. On the other hand, it may be that the data and the manipulations performed thereon by the computer, when viewed on the human level, represent the contents of a page of the Milwaukee telephone directory, or the text of a court opinion retrieved by a computerized law service. Such information is utterly devoid of mathematical significance. Thus, the board's analysis does nothing but provide a quick and automatic negative answer to the § 101 question simply because a computer program is involved.

Appellants have continuously insisted that

5. *In re Christensen*, 478 F.2d 1392, 178 USPQ 35 (Cust. & Pat.App.1973).

they are claiming a new and unobvious combination of *hardware elements*, i. e., a new machine or apparatus. [Footnote.] The issues of novelty and unobviousness [footnote] are not before us, but we agree with appellants insofar as they characterize their invention as a machine or apparatus. The board likewise seems to agree on this point. In its opinion, it identifies all of the "means" of appellants' claim 1 as structural hardware elements, such as registers, portions of main memory and control store,[10] and other computer components. Thus, the claim falls literally within the boundaries of § 101.

Appellants have characterized their combination of hardware elements as a mechanism which enables the computer to alter information in its system base in a manner not previously possible. They are in no way claiming the altered information; in fact, the particular information acted upon by appellants' invention is irrelevant to the operation of the invention itself. We see no difference in this regard, with respect to being within § 101, between appellants' claimed invention and a strictly mechanical adding machine, which is certainly statutory if claimed in a manner which does not embrace any particular calculation that the machine is capable of making.

The PTO regards as significant the fact that firmware is involved in the present invention. In a sense, firmware may be likened to software (computer programs); it is information which has been embodied into hardware by, for example, destroying fusible links in a read only memory (ROM) array. In appellants' invention, the information contained within the firmware, which is located in the control store of the computer, directs the desired information transfers within the system base.

If appellants were claiming the information embodied in the firmware or the firmware itself, per se, a different case would be presented. We express no opinion on the statutory nature of such an invention, a question not before us. Appellants are claiming a combination of hardware elements, one of which happens to be a portion of the computer's control store microprogrammed in a particular manner. It is this subject matter with which we must deal.

From our reading of appellants' specification, their claimed "data structure" is merely that which results from the arrangement of the recited hardware elements in the claimed manner. It is the result of certain structural "means" performing certain recited functions as explicitly sanctioned by 35 U.S.C. § 112, sixth paragraph. We disapprove the board's distillation of appellants' claim down to the information contained in the firmware in order to hold it nonstatutory. The invention is not claimed in that manner, and, in this case, we see no reason to view the claim format as a subterfuge for masking the presence of an essentially nonstatutory invention.

Even though the claimed invention is a machine, we must nevertheless determine whether the claim recites a mathematical algorithm, and, if so, whether it preempts the use of the algorithm. [Citation.] In doing so, we apply the two-step test in *In re Freeman* [573 F.2d 1237 (Cust. & Pat.App.1978)].

When we examine appellants' invention as a whole under the first step of this test, including the information microprogrammed into the firmware element as depicted in Figs. 14(a–i) and 15(b–c), we fail to detect the presence of any *mathematical* algorithm. In altering information in the system base as desired, certain "calculations" are made, such as determining whether a given quantity is equal to zero, or, as noted by the solicitor, multiplying an address in memory by sixteen to arrive at another address. However, it certainly cannot be said that comparing with zero or multiplying by sixteen is preempted by appellants' claims. Furthermore, the presence of these calculations does not transform the invention as a whole into a method of calculation. [Citation.] There is no solution of an equation, such as the new alarm limit in *Flook,* or the equivalent pure binary number, as in *Benson,* present in the computer after the task has been completed. [Citation.]

In summary, we have examined the claims thoroughly and we do not find any mathe-

---

10. The control store of a computer is a plurality of multibit storage locations (memory) containing microinstructions, which, when decoded by appropriate circuitry, pro-

vide control signals which cause specific operations to take place in the computer's CPU.

matical formula or mathematical method of calculation, improved or otherwise, which is either claimed as such or essential to the vitality of the claims. We find that the invention is a combination of tangible hardware elements—a machine—including some hardware elements which contain microprogrammed information termed "firmware." We do not find the invention to be nonstatutory under the authority of *Benson* or *Flook,* or under the authority of our own cases. * * * Therefore, the decision of the board is reversed.

DIAMOND v. BRADLEY

450 U.S. 381
(United States Supreme Court, Certiorari to the United States Court of Customs and Patent Appeals, March 9, 1981.)

PER CURIAM.

The judgment is affirmed by an equally divided Court.

IN RE TANER

681 F.2d 787
(United States Court of Customs and Patent Appeals, June 10, 1982.)

MARKEY, C. J.

* * *

BACKGROUND

I. The Invention

Appellants' invention relates to a method of seismic exploration by which substantially plane or substantially cylindrical seismic energy waves are simulated from substantially spherical seismic waves.

In traditional methods of seismic exploration, seismic sources generate and transmit into the earth seismic energy waves. The waves are propagated through the earth in spherical or near-spherical wavefronts and are reflected by subsurface formations. The reflections return to the earth's surface and are detected by seismic receivers positioned over the area of exploration. The receivers convert the reflections into electrical signals which are then recorded on a record medium, e.g., magnetic tape or chart recorder. The recorded signals contain information on the geological substrata explored. For that information to be meaningful, it must, however, be corrected for various factors, such as spherical divergence of the waves as they are propagated through the substrata.

Appellants' claimed process simulates substantially plane or cylindrical seismic energy waves by summing the reflectional signals of the conventional spherical waves. The composite signal thus represents the response of subsurface formations to plane or cylindrical waves. Claims 1 and 24, the only independent claims, are illustrative:

1. A method of seismic exploration by simulating from substantially spherical seismic waves the reflection response of the earth to seismic energy having a substantially continuous wavefront over an extent of an area being explored having at least one dimension which is large relative to a seismic wavelength, comprising the steps of:
    (a) imparting the spherical seismic energy waves into the earth from a seismic source at a source position;
    (b) generating a plurality of reflection signals in response to the seismic energy waves at a set of receiver positions spaced in an array over an extent having at least one dimension which is large relative to a seismic wavelength; and
    (c) summing the reflection signals to form for the source position a signal simulating the reflection response of the earth to seismic energy having a substantially continuous wavefront over at least one dimension which is large relative to a seismic energy wavelength.

24. A method of seismic exploration by simulating from substantially spherical seismic waves the reflection response of the earth to seismic energy having a substantially continuous wavefront over an extent of an area being explored having at least one dimension which is large relative to a seismic wavelength, comprising the steps of:
    (a) imparting the spherical seismic energy waves into the earth from a set of seismic sources at source positions spaced in an array over an extent having at least one dimension which is large relative to a seismic wavelength;
    (b) generating a reflection signal at a receiver position in response to each of the seismic energy waves; and

(c) summing the reflection signals to form for the receiver position a signal simulating the reflection response of the earth to seismic energy having a substantially continuous wavefront over at least one dimension which is large relative to a seismic energy wavelength.[1]

According to appellants' specification, the combining of signals to simulate plane or cylindrical wavefronts makes possible a reduction in data correction and thereby reduces the expenditures of time and money required for seismic exploration.

II. The Rejections

A. *35 U.S.C. § 101.* In his final rejection, the examiner stated that because appellants' claims define a method of seismic data treatment which is not limited to any apparatus, the claims preempt all implementations of the claimed "mathematical and manipulative" operations upon seismic data, and, as such, fall outside the statutory categories of § 101. In sustaining that rejection, the board undertook to apply the test established by this court in *In re Freeman,* 573 F.2d 1237, 197 U.S.P.Q. 464 (CCPA 1978), as modified by *In re Walter,* 618 F.2d 758, 205 U.S.P.Q. 397 (CCPA 1980). The board found that the claims directly recite a mathematical algorithm, i.e., summing, and that because "there is no close relationship between the algorithm * * * and the other process steps except that the signals to be summed are generated by the precedent process steps," the claims preempt that algorithm. The board concluded therefore that the claims are nonstatutory. That the claims limit the algorithm to geophysical exploration and thus do not literally preempt the algorithm was not in the board's view sufficient to save the claims from characterization as nonstatutory. Citing *In re Christensen,* 478 F.2d 1392, 178 U.S.P.Q. 35 (CCPA 1973), which it viewed as directly on point, the board characterized appellants' claims as directed to the solution of a mathematical equation. In the board's view, the precedent steps merely served to supply the equation with required data and, as in *Christensen,* could not "convert the un-

patentable method to patentable subject matter." [Citation.]

On reconsideration, the board reviewed its decision in light of *Diamond v. Diehr,* 450 U.S. 175, 101 S.Ct. 1048, 67 L.Ed.2d 155, 209 U.S.P.Q. 1 (1981), concluding that its original analysis conformed with *Diehr.* One board member dissented, viewing appellants' claims not "as an attempt to patent the concept of summing signals in general but rather to be drawn to a technique of forming a new type of seismic recording which simulates the response of subsurface formations to cylindrical or plane waves."

B. *35 U.S.C. § 103.* Three references were cited and relied upon by the examiner in making the § 103 rejection:

Smith, Jr. (Smith) 3,256,501   June 14, 1966
Laurent   3,775,737   Nov. 27, 1973
Miller, Dr. G. Kirby, "High Pressure Transducer," *Technical Report GTE Sylvania,* Jan. 10, 1973.

Smith discloses a linear sound source for creating explosive energy along a substantially continuous line to generate either cylindrical or conical seismic waves. Smith teaches that as the length of the source increases, the directivity of wave propagation normal to the line source is enhanced.

Both Miller and Laurent disclose continuous long line seismic cables having a plurality of hydrophones, i.e., seismic receivers, distributed therein at regular intervals. In the Laurent device, approximately 10–50 piezoelectric elements electrically connected in parallel are used as hydrophones.

The examiner rejected appellants' claims as obvious over Miller or Laurent in view of Smith. Treating Miller and Laurent, the examiner stated that "the 'summing' over a hypothetical series of receiver points is inherent in the line sources" of those references and "it is apparent that the continuous line receivers of Miller and Laurent sum * * * the waves received * * * to the extent claimed in simulating a cylindrical wavefront." The examiner relied on Smith for a teaching of the dimensions of a wave source relative to a seismic wavelength.

---

1. If only one dimension is large relative to the seismic wavelength, the "substantially continuous wavefront" referred to in the claims is a cylindrical wavefront; if two dimensions are large, a plane wavefront is simulated.

The board sustained the rejection, agreeing that "a line hydrophone as shown by Miller and Laurent will extend over a number of receiver positions and that the signals detected at various points along the line are inherently summed in the hydrophone."

ISSUES

(1) Whether the method of seismic exploration recited in the claims constitutes statutory subject matter under 35 U.S.C. 101.

(2) Whether certain of appellants' claims were properly rejected under 35 U.S.C. § 103 as obvious from the prior act.

OPINION

I. 35 U.S.C. § 101

The Supreme Court has made clear that not every invention is embraced within the terms of § 101. Excluded therefrom are laws of nature, physical phenomena, and abstract ideas. *See Parker* v. *Flook*, 437 U.S. 584, 98 S.Ct. 2522, 57 L.Ed.2d 451 (1978); *Gottschalk* v. *Benson*, 409 U.S. 63, 93 S.Ct. 253, 34 L.Ed.2d 273 (1973). The Court in *Flook* reiterated, however, that although a law of nature cannot itself be patented, "a process is not unpatentable simply because it contains a law of nature or a mathematical algorithm" [citation], and that the claim must be considered as a whole when undergoing analysis under § 101. [Citation.]

In *Diamond* v. *Diehr, supra,* a mathematical formula was used to control the in-mold time of a claimed molding process. The Court held that although the process for curing synthetic rubber included the use of a mathematical formula and a programmed digital computer, it nonetheless constituted subject matter eligible for patenting under § 101. The Court construed the claims as calling for "nothing more than a process for molding rubber products and not as an attempt to patent a mathematical formula," noting that while an algorithm or mathematical formula, like a law of nature, cannot be the subject of a patent, Diehr sought neither to patent the formula in the abstract nor to preempt its use. [Citation.]

Here, the board characterized the subject matter of appellants' claims as a whole as a "method for calculating (by signal summing) a simulated continuous wavefront reflection response from spherical seismic wave data." As such, the board viewed the claims as merely presenting and solving a mathematical algorithm. We disagree.

Appellants' claims are not in our view merely directed to the solution of a mathematical algorithm. Though the claims directly recite an algorithm, summing, we cannot agree that appellants seek to patent that algorithm in the abstract. Appellants' claims are drawn to a technique of seismic exploration which simulates the response of subsurface earth formations to cylindrical or plane waves. That that technique involves the summing of signals is not in our view fatal to its patentability. Appellants' claimed process involves the taking of substantially spherical seismic signals obtained in conventional seismic exploration and *converting* ("simulating from") those signals into another form, i.e., into a form representing the earth's response to cylindrical or plane waves. Thus the claims set forth a *process* and are statutory within § 101.

Though the board conceded that appellants' process includes conversion of seismic signals into a different form, it took the position that "there is nothing necessarily physical about 'signals' " and that "the end product of [appellants' invention] is a mathematical result in the form of a pure number." That characterization is contrary to the views expressed by this court in *In re Sherwood,* 613 F.2d 809, 204 U.S.P.Q. 537 (CCPA 1980), and *In re Johnson,* 589 F.2d 1070, 200 U.S.P.Q. 199 (CCPA 1978), where signals were viewed as physical and the processes were viewed as transforming them to a different state.

In *Sherwood,* amplitude-versus-time seismic traces were converted into amplitude-versus-depth seismic traces. *Johnson* involved a technique for removing unwanted noise from seismic traces to form noise-free seismic traces. In both cases, this court found that, though appellants' claims recited a mathematical algorithm for manipulating seismic data, the claims were, as a whole, drawn not to a method of solving that algorithm but to a process of converting one physical thing into another physical thing, and in *Sherwood* expressly recognized that "seismic traces are * * * physical apparitions." [Citation.] That those "physical apparitions" may be expressed in mathematical terms is in our view irrelevant.

The board's reliance here on *In re Walter*, 618 F.2d 758, 20 U.S.P.Q. 397 (CCPA 1980) is misplaced. Though *Walter* involved processing of seismic data, the claims there were drawn to "an improved method of correlating" and to "an improved method of cross-correlating," i.e., not to "methods of or apparatus for seismic processing * * * [but rather] to improved mathematical methods of interpreting the results of seismic prospecting." [Citation.]

The board relies too, on this court's decision in *In re Christensen*, supra. The claims there were drawn to a method of determining the porosity of subsurface formations and recited certain data collection steps, all of which were known in the prior art and a mathematical equation to be solved as the final step of the method. This court viewed the issue before it in *Christensen* as a "narrow one, namely, is a method claim in which the point of novelty is a mathematical equation to be solved as a final step of the method, a statutory method?" [Citation.] We concluded that *Gottschalk* v. *Benson*, 409 U.S. 63, 93 S.Ct. 253, 34 L.Ed.2d 273 (1972), required that "the answer is in the negative" pointing to the Court's statement there:

> It is conceded that one may not patent an idea. But in practical effect that would be the result if the formula for converting * * * [BCD numerals to pure binary numerals] were patented in this case. The mathematical formula involved here has no substantial practical application except in connection with a digital computer, which means that if the judgment below is affirmed, the patent would wholly pre-empt the mathematical formula and in practical effect would be a patent on the algorithm itself.
>
> It may be that the patent laws should be extended to cover these programs, a policy matter to which we are not competent to speak. [Citation.]

[Citation.]

Much has transpired in the development of the law in this area since our decision in *Christensen*. Most recently in *Diehr*, the Supreme Court made clear that *Benson* stands

for no more than the long-established principle that laws of nature, natural phenomena, and abstract ideas are excluded from patent protection [citation] and that "a claim drawn to subject matter otherwise statutory does not become nonstatutory because it uses a mathematical formula, computer program, or digital computer." [Citation.] The Court in *Diehr* rejected the "point of novelty" analysis saying "[t]he 'novelty' of any element or steps in a process * * * is of no relevance in determining whether the subject matter of a claim falls within the § 101 categories of possibly patentable subject matter" [citation] and went on to explain that

> when a claim containing a mathematical formula implements or applies that formula in a structure or process, which, when considered as a whole, is performing a function which the patent laws were designed to protect (e.g., transforming or reducing an article to a different state or thing), then the claim satisfies the requirements of § 101. [Citation.]

Accordingly, to the extent that it conflicts with what we say here, *Christensen* is overruled.

II.   35 U.S.C. § 103 [footnote]

In arguing the § 103 question, the Solicitor relies principally on Laurent, maintaining, as did the examiner and the board, that "inherent summing" occurs among the parallel connected elements of Laurent.

We do not agree that the elements of Laurent "inherently" sum. The seismic cable disclosed in Laurent is in effect an elongated single hydrophone, i.e., seismic receiver. The piezoelectric sensing elements are connected in parallel and each receives the same signal. Laurent neither discloses nor suggests isolating or monitoring the signal received at a single sensing position along the length of the seismic cable. In contrast, appellants disclose an array of discrete receivers, each of which samples the reflectional wavefront at a different location along the wavefront. Those discrete signals are then summed to simulate a plane or cylindrical wavefront. Nothing in Laurent suggests an arrangement.

We conclude, therefore, that the board erred in sustaining the rejection under § 103.

Accordingly, the decision of the board is reversed.

IN RE ABELE

684 F.2d 902

*(United States Court of Customs and
Patent Appeals, Aug. 5, 1982.)*

NIES, J.

This appeal is from the decision of the Patent and Trademark Office Board of Appeals (board) affirming the rejection of claims 5–7 and 33–47 [footnote] in their application serial No. 850,892, filed November 15, 1977, for "Tomographic Scanner." The claims stand rejected under 35 U.S.C. § 101 [footnote] as being drawn to nonstatutory subject matter. We *affirm* the rejection of claims 5 and 7, and *reverse* with respect to all remaining claims on appeal.

THE INVENTION

Appellants' invention is in the field of image processing particularly as applied to computerized axial tomography or CAT scans. Specifically, appellants' invention is directed to an improvement in computed tomography whereby the exposure to X-ray is reduced while the reliability of the produced image is improved. Some understanding of tomography, both conventional and computed, is necessary as background for the subsequent analysis of the present invention.

Conventional tomography, also known as laminography, employs the simultaneous movement in opposite directions of an X-ray source and an X-ray film. The method produces a well-defined image of a plane through the body parallel to the plane of the X-ray film. In contrast to an ordinary X-ray, shadows of body structure which lie outside the plane of investigation are blurred so that they do not interfere with a focused image of the plane under investigation. Conventional tomographic systems are not practical when a visualized cross-section transverse to the body axis is desired. Computed tomography was developed to overcome this deficiency among others.

Basically, computed tomography provides an image representing a transverse slice of the body. This slicing is accomplished by rotating an X-ray source and a detection means around the perimeter of the section to be viewed. The source and detection means are placed 180° from each other to allow the detection means to measure the attenuation of the beam as it passes through the plane of interest. When enough measurements have been taken, a computer is implemented to mathematically interpret the data, which is then displayed as a reconstruction of the slice on, inter alia, a television screen for diagnostic purposes. Computed tomography is also useful for looking at only a section of a slice. Thus, if the plane of interest were in the abdomen region of a human, but only the liver were of concern, the computer tomography machine would act in the manner of a conventional tomograph and blur the images outside of this "Region of Interest." It has, however, been necessary that a spread of X-rays "S" be sufficiently wide to subtend the entire body in order to produce an image of the region of interest "R" by this blurring method, as illustrated by the following drawing [art from the original opinion]:

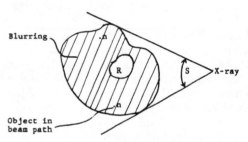

Appellants have discovered that it is unnecessary to expose the body in the above fashion. Rather, they have discovered that the spread of X-ray, S, can be reduced so as to subtend only the region R thus [art from the original opinion]:

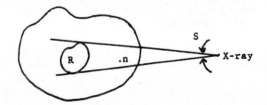

Narrowing the beam is advantageous not only because the exposure of a body to X-ray is thereby reduced but also because computer calculation time to produce the image is shortened inasmuch as the amount of data to be processed is less. However, because fewer data can be collected due to the narrower beam, there is insufficient information to cancel out an object, n, such as a piece of rib, for example, which is in the beam path. Thus, the resultant image shows the region R with an artifact[3] appearing therein due to that object, n [art from the original opinion]:

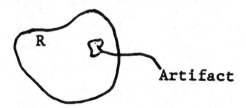

Appellants' invention is directed to an improvement in CAT scan imaging technique whereby the body is exposed to less radiation and, through use of a weighting function in the calculations producing the image, the artifacts are eliminated.

THE REJECTION

The examiner rejected the claims on appeal under the authority of *Parker* v. *Flook*, 437 U.S. 584, 98 S.Ct. 2522, 57 L.Ed.2d 451 (1978). In the final rejection and in the examiner's answer before the board, the examiner construed *Flook* as mandating the following test:

> Taking each claim as a whole, it is assumed, for analysis purposes only, that any mathematical calculation in the claim is part of the prior art. If what is left is new and unobvious, then the claim, taken as a whole, protects more than a mathematical calculation and it is deemed statutory. But if the remainder of the claim is not novel nor unobvious, then the claim, taken as a whole, merely seeks to protect the mathematical calculation and, as such, does not comprise statutory subject matter.

Applying the above test, the examiner determined that, apart from the mathematical calculations, the remaining steps were well known or were "merely a necessary antecedent step to provide values for solving the mathematical equations," and, thus, were directed to nonstatutory subject matter, citing *In re Richman*, 563 F.2d 1026, 195 USPQ 340 (Cust. & Pat.App.1977).

3. The classical determination of computer tomography images may be viewed as the process of solving a large number of simultaneous equations for an equal number of unknown variables. An artifact-free calculation re-

THE BOARD'S DECISION

The board did not address the examiner's contentions, relying instead on *In re Freeman*, 573 F.2d 1237, 197 USPQ 464 (CCPA 1978), as modified by *In re Walter*, 618 F.2d 758, 205 USPQ 397 (Cust. & Pat.App.1980). Without resort to detailed claim language, the board affirmed the rejection under 35 U.S.C. § 101 as follows:

> When the claims are analyzed in [the manner dictated by *Walter*], it is manifest that the mathematical algorithm is not implemented in a manner to define structural relationships between physical elements in the apparatus claims or to refine or limit claim steps in the process claims. The claims do no more than present and solve a mathematical algorithm and are manifestly nonstatutory.

One member dissented with respect to rejection of claims 6 and 33–47 concluding that these claims are directed to "producing a product, an improved tomographic X-ray image," and are, therefore, directed to statutory subject matter citing *Diamond* v. *Diehr*, 450 U.S. 175, 101 S.Ct. 1048, 67 L.Ed.2d 155 (1981).

OPINION

I

A

We agree with the board that a two-part analysis [footnote] is the proper vehicle for resolution of issues here presented under 35 U.S.C. § 101. However, we agree with appellants that the second step of the analysis is not as limited as the board held it to be.

B

In *Gottschalk* v. *Benson*, 409 U.S. 63, 93 S.Ct. 253, 34 L.Ed.2d 273 (1972), the Supreme Court concluded that claims directed to a particular "algorithm," conversion of binary coded decimal numbers to binary numbers, did not define patentable subject matter. In that case the Court defined the term "algorithm" as "[a] procedure for solving a given type of mathematical problem." [Citation.] The Court's holding in *Benson* became the basis for the

quires that a sufficient number of line integral measurements be made to determine the unknown variables at all image points.

first part of the two-part analysis set forth by this court in *In re Freeman*, 573 F.2d 1237, 197 USPQ 464 (Cust. & Pat.App.1978). In *Freeman* [citation], this court concluded:

> As a bare minimum, application of *Benson* in a particular case requires a careful analysis of the claims, to determine whether, as in *Benson*, they recite a "procedure for solving a given type of *mathematical* problem." [Citation omitted. Emphasis in original.]

Hence, the first part of the analysis requires:

> First, it must be determined whether the claim directly or indirectly recites an "algorithm" in the *Benson* sense of that term. * * * [Citation.]

The second part of the *Freeman* analysis is derived from the further holding in *Benson*, 409 U.S. at 72, 93 S.Ct. at 257, that any patent issued in that case "would wholly pre-empt the mathematical formula and in practical effect would be a patent on the algorithm itself." Thus, it was concluded that the presence of an "algorithm" in a claim would not render a claimed invention nonstatutory unless the invention claimed *only* the "algorithm." Stating this conclusion in the language of *Benson*, this court declared:

> Second, the claim must be further analyzed to ascertain whether in its entirety it wholly preempts that algorithm. [Citation.]

This latter step in the *Freeman* analysis was not reached because of this court's conclusion that the claims did not recite an "algorithm." In *In re Toma*, 575 F.2d 872, 197 USPQ 852 (Cust. & Pat.App.1978), the same test was discussed but, again, the second part of the analysis was not reached. Subsequently, the Supreme Court handed down its decision in *Parker* v. *Flook*, 437 U.S. 584, 98 S.Ct. 2522, 57 L.Ed.2d 451 (1978), making clear that the second part of the above analysis was erroneous. The Court held that the claim need "not * * * cover every conceivable application of the formula" to be nonstatutory. [Citation.]

In sum, the Court's decisions have made clear that a claim does not present patentable subject matter if it would wholly preempt an

algorithm, *Benson*, supra, or if it would preempt the algorithm but for limiting its use to a particular technological environment, *Flook*, supra. However, these decisions leave undefined what does constitute statutory subject matter.

In *In re Johnson*, 589 F.2d 1070, 1075, 200 USPQ 199, 205 (Cust. & Pat.App.1978), this court held that, while reciting an algorithm, the claims did not merely define a method of solving a mathematical equation because

> any calculations which may be performed in practicing the process * * * are but a part of the process which includes the other recited steps.
> * * * [They] are *incident* to producing a noise-free signal trace from a reference trace. [Emphasis added.] [Citation.]

This conclusion rests on the premise that an otherwise statutory process remains statutory when implemented by a computer [citation], a premise subsequently approved by the Supreme Court in *Diamond* v. *Diehr*, 450 U.S. 175, 101 S.Ct. 1048, 67 L.Ed.2d 155 (1981). [Citation.]

In *Johnson*, supra, the interrelationship of the algorithm to the remaining limitations of a claim was held to be determinative of whether the claim defined statutory subject matter. Relying on the same reasoning in *In re Walter*, 618 F.2d 758, 205 USPQ 397 (Cust. & Pat. App.1980), the second part of the two-step analysis[5] was defined as follows:

> If it appears that the mathematical algorithm is implemented in a specific manner to define structural relationships between the physical elements of the claim (in apparatus claims) or to refine or limit claim steps (in process claims), *the claim being otherwise statutory*, the claim passes muster under § 101. If, however, the mathematical algorithm is merely presented and solved by the claimed invention, as was the case in *Benson* and *Flook*, and is not applied in any manner to physical elements or process steps, no amount of post-solution activity will render the claim statutory; nor is it saved by a preamble merely reciting the field of use of the mathematical algorithm. [Emphasis added.] [Citation.]

In *Walter*, the claims were directed to a process [footnote] for correlating and cross-correlating signals. All of the claims steps were

---

5. The first part of our analysis was not altered because the definition of an algorithm used by the Court in *Flook* was identical to that used in *Benson*, *Flook*, 437 U.S. at

585 n.1, 98 S.Ct. at 2523 n.1, *quoting Benson*, 409 U.S. at 65, 93 S.Ct. at 254.

algorithm steps for performing the correlation or cross-correlation. There were no limitations in the claims, other than a field of use set forth in the preamble of the claims which stated that the algorithm was for use in connection with seismic surveying. The court concluded that the claims were directed to claiming only the algorithm, were not applied in any manner to any process steps, and were, therefore, directed to nonstatutory subject matter. [Citation.]

Appellants summarize the *Walter* test as setting forth two ends of a spectrum: what is now clearly nonstatutory, i.e., claims in which an algorithm is merely presented and solved by the claimed invention (preemption), and what is clearly statutory, i.e., claims in which an algorithm is implemented in a specific manner *to define structural relationships* between the physical elements of the claim (in an apparatus claim) or to *refine or limit claim steps* (in a process). Appellants urge that the statement of the test in *Walter* fails to provide a useful tool for analyzing claims in the "gray area" which falls between the two ends of that spectrum. We agree that the board's understanding and application of the *Walter* analysis justifies appellant's position. However, the *Walter* analysis quoted above does not limit patentable subject matter only to claims in which structural relationships or process steps are defined, limited or refined by the application of the algorithm.

Rather, *Walter* should be read as requiring no more than that the algorithm be "applied in any manner to physical elements or process steps," provided that its application is circumscribed by more than a field of use limitation or non-essential post-solution activity. Thus, if the claim would be "otherwise statutory," *id.*, albeit inoperative or less useful without the algorithm, the claim likewise presents statutory subject matter when the algorithm is included. This broad reading of *Walter*, we conclude, is in accord with the Supreme Court decisions.

In *Diamond* v. *Diehr*, supra, the Court held that a process for curing synthetic rubber constituted patentable subject matter notwithstanding that the process used an equation

for controlling the in-mold time which was constantly updated by a digital computer. In *Diehr*, were the claim to be read without the algorithm, the process would still be a process for curing rubber, although it might not work as well since the in-mold time would not be as accurately controlled. Hence, the Court concluded that the claimed invention fell within § 101 because it presented "an *application* of a law of nature or mathematical formula to a known structure or process." *Id.* at 187, 101 S.Ct. at 1056 (emphasis in original).[7] [Citation.]

Finally, the purpose of the two-part analysis supports the view taken here. The goal is to answer the question "What did applicants invent?" If the claimed invention is a mathematical algorithm, it is improper subject matter for patent protection, whereas if the claimed invention is an application of the algorithm, § 101 will not bar the grant of a patent.

> In answering that question, [e]ach invention must be evaluated as claimed; yet semantogenic considerations preclude a determination based solely on words appearing in the claims. In the final analysis under § 101, the claimed invention, as a whole, must be evaluated for what it is. [*In re Sarkar*, 588 F.2d 1330, 1333, 200 USPQ 132, 137 (Cust. & Pat.App.1978)(footnote omitted).]

Hence, the analysis "requires careful interpretation of each claim in light of its supporting disclosure. * * *" *In re Johnson*, 589 F.2d at 1079, 200 U.S.P.Q. at 208.

II

In this case, each of the independent claims and, necessarily, each of the dependent claims, includes the limitation "calculating * * * the difference" either as a step in a process or as a means in an apparatus. Accordingly, all of the claims may be directed to nonstatutory subject matter as each presents a mathematical formula or a sequence of mathematical operations. *See,* e.g., *Diehr,* supra, wherein the claims included a limitation requiring "calculating." *Cf. Johnson,* 589 F.2d at 1078, 200 USPQ at 208 (use of term "compute" at least suggests the execution of a mathematical al-

---

7. We do not construe the Court's reference to a *known* structure or process as a limitation. An essential purpose

of the patent laws is to foster the creation of heretofore *unknown* structures or processes.

gorithm). In any event, appellants concede that their claims "implement a mathematical algorithm."

III

A

We now turn to the second part of our analysis to determine whether what is claimed is a statutory process or apparatus or a nonstatutory algorithm.

We begin by contrasting the two broadest process claims, claims 5 and 6:

> 5. A method of displaying data in a field comprising the steps of
> calculating the difference between the local value of the data at a data point in the field and the average value of the data in a region of the field which surrounds said point for each point in said field, and
> displaying the value of said difference as a signed gray scale at a point in a picture which corresponds to said data point.
> 6. The method of claim 5 wherein said data is X-ray attenuation data produced in a two dimensional field by a computed tomography scanner.

We conclude that claim 5 is directed solely to the mathematical algorithm portion of appellants' invention and is, thus, not statutory subject matter under § 101. We reach the opposite conclusion with respect to claim 6.

The method of claim 6, unlike that of claim 5, requires "X-ray attenuation data." The specification indicates that such attenuation data is available only when an X-ray beam is produced by a CAT scanner, passed through an object, and detected upon its exit. Only after these steps have been completed is the algorithm performed,[8] and the resultant modified data displayed in the required format.[9]

Were we to view the claim absent the algorithm, the production, detection and display steps would still be present and would result in a conventional CAT-scan process.

Accordingly, production and detection cannot be considered mere antecedent steps to obtain values for solving the algorithm as in *In re Richman*, cited by the examiner. Indeed, claim 6 presents data gathering steps not dictated by the algorithm but by other limitations which require certain antecedent steps. [Footnote.] It is these antecedent steps that dictate what type of data must be obtained. [Citation.] In any event, we view the production, detection, and display steps as manifestly statutory subject matter and are not swayed from this conclusion by the presence of an algorithm in the claimed method.

In *Flook*, supra, "[t]he patent application did not 'explain how to select * * * any of the variables' " used in the algorithm and, thus, no process other than the algorithm was present. *Diehr*, 450 U.S. at 186 n.10, 101 S.Ct. at 1056 n.10, *quoting Flook*, 437 U.S. at 586, 98 S.Ct. at 2523. *A fortiori*, no process steps to which the algorithm could be applied were present. *Accord, Walter*, supra. In the instant case, claim 6 defines the variables and places the algorithm in a particular relationship to a series of steps in a particular type of process, permitting the algorithm to be applied as a further process step. *In re Taner*, 681 F.2d 787, 790 (Cust. & Pat.App.1982).

The algorithm, when properly viewed, is merely applied to the "attenuation data" to eliminate what would otherwise appear as artifacts upon display of the data in the manner claimed. The algorithm does not necessarily refine or limit the earlier steps of production and detection as would be required to achieve the status of patentable subject matter by the board's narrow reading of *Walter*. What appellants have done is to discover an application of an algorithm to process steps which are themselves part of an overall process which is statutory. Hence, claim 6 cannot be construed as a mere procedure for solving a given mathematical problem. As was the case in

---

8. The algorithm, calculating the difference, is defined in the specification as a Gaussian weighting function which modifies the X-ray attenuation data before it is displayed. It is the weighting that results in removal of the artifacts from the display.

9. While we conclude that the resultant display is an important feature of the claimed invention, because it provides a more useful tool for a doctor's diagnosis, for example, than would numbers alone, we do not rest our

holding with respect to claim 6 on the "non-triviality" of post-solution activity. Even without the final step of displaying the data in a more usable form, "the fact that [the] equation is the final step is not determinative of the section 101 issue." *In re Richman*, 563 F.2d at 1030, 195 USPQ at 343. *Accord, In re Taner*, 681 F.2d 787 (Cust. & Pat.App.1982), *overruling In re Christensen*, 478 F.2d 1392, 178 USPQ 35 (Cust. & Pat.App.1973).

Diehr and *Johnson*, both supra, the algorithm is but a part of the overall claimed process.

We are faced simply with an improved CAT-scan process comparable to the improved process for curing synthetic rubber in *Diehr*, supra. The improvement in either case resides in the application of a mathematical formula within the context of a process which encompasses significantly more than the algorithm alone.

B

We do not reach the same conclusion with respect to claim 5. This claim presents no more than the calculation of a number and display of the result, albeit in a particular format.

The specification provides no greater meaning to "data in a field" than a matrix of numbers regardless of by what method generated. Thus, the algorithm is neither explicitly nor implicitly applied to any certain process. Moreover, that the result is displayed as a shade of gray rather than as simply a number provides no greater or better information, considering the broad range of applications encompassed by the claim. Indeed, this claim does not even attempt to "limit the use of the formula to a particular technological environment," *Diehr*, 450 U.S. at 191, 101 S.Ct. at 1058, as was done in *Flook*, supra. Hence, we view claim 5 as directed merely to a mathematical formula which is not proper subject matter under § 101.

C

Appellants do not argue and, in any event, we see no basis for treating their apparatus claims differently from their method claims.

If the functionally-defined disclosed means and their equivalents are so broad that they encompass any and every means for performing the recited functions, the apparatus claim is an attempt to exalt form over substance since the claim is really to the method or series of functions itself. In computer-related inventions, the recited means often perform the function of "number crunching" (solving mathematical algorithms and making calculations). In such cases the burden must be placed on the applicant to demonstrate that the claims are truly drawn to specific apparatus distinct from other apparatus capable of performing the identical functions.

If this burden has not been discharged, the apparatus claim will be treated as if it were drawn to the method or process which encompasses all of the claimed "means." [*In re Walter*, 618 F.2d at 768, 205 USPQ at 408.]

Thus, claim 7, the apparatus counterpart to claim 5, suffers the same defects as does claim 5.

7. Apparatus for displaying data values representative of values at data points in a two dimensional field comprising:

means for calculating the differences between the local values at each data point and the average value at data points in a limited region of said field surrounding each said data point, and

means for displaying the value of said differences as signed gray scale values at points in a picture which correspond to said data points.

D

What was said about claim 6 applies equally to independent method claim 33 and its apparatus counterpart claim 36.

33. A method of computed tomography comprising the steps of:

measuring the values of the line integrals of an incoherent propagation along a plurality of paths through a region of interest in a body;

calculating, from the values of said integrals at each of a number of reconstruction points in said region of interest, the difference between the local value of a characteristic at said point and the average value of the characteristic in a local region surrounding said point; and

reconstructing a representation of features in said region of interest by displaying the calculated value for each reconstruction point at a point in a picture which corresponds to said reconstruction point.

36. Computed tomography apparatus comprising:

means for measuring the values of the line integrals of an incoherent propagation along a plurality of paths through a region of interest in a body;

calculating means, connected to receive the values of said integrals from said means for measuring and to calculate, at each of a number of reconstruction points in said region of interest, the difference between the local value of a characteristic at said point and the average value of said characteristic in a local region surrounding said point; and

means for reconstructing a representation of features in said region which function to receive said calculated values from said calculating means and to display the calculated value for each reconstruction point at a point in a picture which corresponds to said reconstruction point.

Indeed, the step of "measuring * * * line integrals of an incoherent propagation * * * through * * * a body" explicitly requires the same steps implicit in claim 6, viz., production of a beam and detection of the beam after it is attenuated by passing through a body. Moreover, while the display of claims 33 and 36 is only of a number, we have already disposed of the contention that the last step of a claim may not be a number. *See In re Taner,* supra, *overruling In re Christensen,* 478 F.2d 1392, 178 USPQ 35 (Cust. & Pat.App. 1973). *See also* n.9, supra.

E

In view of our holding with respect to independent claims 33 and 36, the remaining claims, all of which depend from claim 33 or 36, must likewise be proper subject matter for patenting under 35 U.S.C. § 101. The remaining claims on appeal appear in the Appendix for reference purposes.

Modified.

APPENDIX

34. The method of claim 33 wherein said characteristic is a radiation attenuation coefficient.

35. The method of claim 33 wherein said region of interest lies in the body plane and comprises less than the entire area of said body plane.

37. The apparatus of claim 36 wherein said means for measuring comprises tomographic scanner means which function to direct one or more beams of penetrating radiation through said body, to determine the attenuation of said beams within said body, and to sequentially redirect said beams with respect to said region of interest whereby each of the reconstruction points in said region of interest is scanned by said beams from a plurality of different orientations.

38. The apparatus of claim 37 wherein said radiation is X-radiation.

39. The apparatus of claim 37 wherein said region of interest is an area in a plane passing through said body which area includes less than all of a body plane and wherein said scanner beams function to direct and redirect said beams to scan all reconstruction points within said re-

gion of interest from all of said orientations and to scan points in said body plane outside of said region [sic of] interest from less than all of said orientations.

40. The apparatus of claim 39 wherein said calculating means function to calculate the values of said difference by first assigning assumed values of said characteristic to points which are outside said region of interest.

41. The apparatus of claim 40 wherein said assumed values correspond to the value of the characteristic at adjacent reconstruction points at the boundary of said region of interest.

42. The apparatus of claim 36 wherein said calculating means function to calculate the values of said difference in accordance with the formula [formula omitted].

43. The apparatus of claim 42 wherein said calculating means further function to apply a weighting function in said calculations which reduces interpolation errors in said calculation.

44. The apparatus of claim 43 wherein said weighting function is a Gaussian function.

45. The apparatus of claim 36 wherein the calculating means include a general purpose digital computer which includes a stored program which effects the calculation.

46. The apparatus of claim 36 wherein the means for reconstructing includes a display device which displays said calculated values as gray scale values.

47. The method of claim 46 wherein neutral gray represents zero values of said calculated values and wherein shades lighter and darker than neutral gray represent non-zero positive or negative signed values.

MILLER, J., dissenting in part.

I am in substantial agreement with the majority opinion, as I interpret it. However, I would also reverse the rejections under 35 U.S.C. § 101 of claims 5 and 7.

The majority opinion states that each claim as a whole should be examined under 35 U.S.C. § 101 by looking beyond the limitations directed to a mathematical algorithm and determining whether the remainder of the claim is directed to statutory subject matter; if it is, then the mere inclusion of a mathematical formula or algorithm would not require a rejection under 35 U.S.C. § 101.[1] This approach is supported by the Supreme Court's opinion

1. The majority opinion states:
  Were we to view the claim absent the algorithm, the production, detection and display steps would still be present and would result in a conventional CAT-scan process. * * * In any event, we view the produc-

tion, detection, and display steps as manifestly statutory subject matter and are not swayed from this conclusion by the presence of an algorithm in the claimed method.

in *Diamond* v. *Diehr*, 450 U.S. 175, 187, 101 S.Ct. 1048, 1056, 67 L.Ed.2d 155 (1981), in which the Court stated:

> Our earlier opinions lend support to our present conclusion that a claim drawn to subject matter otherwise statutory does not become nonstatutory simply because it uses a mathematical formula, computer program, or digital computer. * * * It is now commonplace that *application* of a law of nature or mathematical formula to a known structure or process may well be deserving of patent protection.

This approach is also supported by prior decisions of this court holding that dependent claims containing mathematical formulae or algorithms do not render nonstatutory the claims from which they depend. *See In re Johnson*, 589 F.2d 1070, 200 USPQ 199 (Cust. & Pat.App.1979); *In re Freeman*, 573 F.2d 1237, 197 USPQ 464 (CCPA 1978); *In re Chatfield*, 545 F.2d 152, 191 USPQ 730 (Cust. & Pat. App.1976).

It is the majority opinion's *application* of this approach to method claim 5 (and apparatus claim 7) that prompts my partial dissent. The claim language involved is: "displaying the [calculated] value * * * as a signed gray scale [*i.e.*, shade of gray] at a point in a picture. * * *[2] " I am persuaded that such a display is essentially different from a display of a number calculated by a mathematical algorithm and that, absent the algorithm, the shade of gray display at a point in a picture is patentable subject matter. Whether display of a number calculated by a mathematical algorithm provides "greater or better information"—a point made by the majority opinion—may be relevant to a rejection under 35 U.S.C. § 103, but its relevance to a rejection under 35 U.S.C. § 101 escapes me. Similarly, the majority opinion's point that claim 5 (and claim 7) "does not even attempt to 'limit the use of the formula to a particular technological environment' " does not appear relevant to the approach supported by *Diamond* v. *Diehr*.

IN RE MEYER

688 F.2d 789

(United States Court of Customs and Patent Appeals, Sept. 16, 1982.)

MILLER, J.

This is an appeal from a decision of the Patent and Trademark Office ("PTO") Board of Appeals ("board") sustaining the examiner's rejection under 35 U.S.C. § 101 of all claims in application serial No. 465,574, filed April 30, 1974, entitled "Process and Apparatus for Identifying Locations of Probable Malfunction." We affirm.

BACKGROUND

Appellants in their brief to this court describe their invention, in pertinent part, as follows:

> The invention is a process and an apparatus for carrying out the process of testing a complex system and analyzing the results of these tests. The process proceeds by (1) dividing the complex system into a plurality of "elements" and (2) associating a factor of *function* or *malfunction* with each of these elements. The factors, which are initialized at the outset, are updated or modified during the course of the process in dependence upon the responses of this system to a series of tests. When the tests have been completed, the resultant factors so produced indicate a measure of probability of function or malfunction of the elements with which they are associated.

> The term "elements" is used * * * to identify any arbitrary subdivision of the complex system. For example, the complex system may be divided into a plurality of volume elements of uniform, or even non-uniform size. Where the complex system is a portion of the nervous system of a human body, each of the volume-elements may contain various neurogenerators and/or portions of neuropathways. Alternatively, each element of the complex system may constitute a "functional component," or a portion or a set of functional components of the system. The term "functional component", as used in the Application and in this Brief, is intended to denote any component of the complex system which is operative to produce, transmit, receive, or store signals or information. In the nervous system, the functional components include the neurogenerators and neuropathways. Thus, the elements into which the nervous system is divided may be individual neurogenerators

---

2. In claim 7, the pertinent language is: "means for displaying the [calculated] value * * * as signed gray

scale [*i.e.*, shade of gray] values at points in a picture. * * *"

and/or neuropathways, or may be portions of sets thereof.

For a given complex system, a table may be compiled of the possible responses or outcomes of the various tests. Each test outcome necessarily falls into one of the following categories:

(a) A specific set of system elements is functioning.

(b) Malfunction is likely to be present in a specific set of system elements; function of another specific set of system elements may also be indicated.

(c) The test outcome has no interpretative significance and no inference can be made concerning function or malfunction of the system elements.

For example, as part of a clinical neurological examination, a patient may be asked to close both his eyes (test). Given this test, the patient may respond in one of three ways (test outcome):

(1) The patient closes both his eyes;

(2) The patient closes his right eye only; or

(3) The patient does not close either eye.

These three test outcomes fall, respectively, into the three categories (a), (b) and (c) described above. Test outcome (1) shows that a specific set of elements (e.g., volume elements containing neurogenerators and pathways) of the nervous system is functioning. Test outcome (2) indicates a malfunction in one or more specific sets of elements (e.g., the volume elements containing those neuropathways leading to the left eyelid). On the other hand, test outcome (2) also shows that certain elements of the nervous system are functioning (e.g., those volume elements containing neuropathways leading to the right eyelid). The test outcome (3) is an example of a response for which no inference can be made. The patient may be deaf, may not understand the language or other unknown factors may be present which remove the interpretative significance of the test outcome.

* * *

A realistic computation of malfunction probabilities for all elements in a complex system, based on a large number of test outcomes, is a rather complex task. This problem may be avoided by using a rather simple algorithm to locate elements of probable func-

tion and malfunction in a complex system.
* * *

Pursuant to the algorithm, each element of the complex system is identified by some suitable code. For the purpose of illustration, let there be K elements designated by numbers $k = 1,\ldots,K$. A "function factor" $NF(k)$ and a "malfunction factor" $M(k)$ are associated with each element k. Initially the function factor $NF(k)$ and the malfunction factor $M(k)$ are set equal to zero for all $K = 1,\ldots,K$. Whenever a test outcome indicates function or malfunction in certain ones of the elements, $NF(k)$ or $M(k)$, respectively, are incremented by some value or set of values for all the elements k involved.

When an element k is described herein as "functioning" or "malfunctioning", it will be understood that, in reality, it is one or more of the functional components contained in the element which is either functioning or malfunctioning.

Each outcome of each test applied to the complex system is also identified by some suitable code. For the purpose of illustration, for all the tests performed let there be a total of I test outcomes considered; these are designated by numbers $i = 1,\ldots,I$.

* * *

For each possible test outcome i in categories (a) or (b) there is a set $F(i)$ of elements k which are functioning and/or a set $M(i)$ of elements k which are malfunctioning. For all values of k in the set $F(i)$ let there be an incrementation factor of probable function $\triangle NF(i,k)$, and for all the values of k in the set $M(i)$ let there be an incrementation factor of probable malfunction $\triangle M(i,k)$. These incrementation factors, as indicated, may be a function of the test outcome i as well as the elements k with which they are associated. If and when the test outcome i should occur, the function factors $NK(k)$ and the malfunction factors $M(k)$ are increased by the incrementation factors $\triangle NF(i,k)$ and $\triangle M(i,k)$ for the elements in the sets $F(i)$ and $M(i)$, respectively.

* * * [T]he algorithm begins by initializing the function factors $NF(k)$ and malfunction factors $M(k)$ to zero for all elements: i.e., $NF(k) = 0$ and $M(k) = 0$ for all $k = 1,\ldots,K$. Thereafter, a series of tests is applied to the

complex system and the test outcomes that occur are read into the computer. Since I is the total number of possible test outcomes considered, the number N of test outcomes that do occur during an entire examination will be less than I.

During or after the examination, the computer compares each of the N test outcomes that have occurred with its prestored data giving the inference, if any, which can be made from each test outcome.

* * *

The output display depends upon the nature of the complex system and the nature of the system elements. The simplest form of output would consist of separate lists of the function factors and the malfunction factors together with the elements with which they are associated. A more informative output would be a video display of the function and malfunction factors (by number or by color) superimposed on an image of the complex system or a particular cross section thereof.

Independent claims 1 (for a process) and 55 (for an apparatus) are representative:

1. A process for indentifying [sic] locations of probable malfunction in a complex system, said process comprising the steps of:

(a) selecting a plurality of elements in the complex system, said elements having known locations;

(b) initializing a factor associated with each of said elements;

(c) testing the complex system for a response, which response, if effective, requires proper functioning of certain said elements, the probable indentity [sic] of at least some of these certain elements being known;

(d) determining whether said response of the complex system was at least partially effective or ineffective;

(e) modifying the factor associated with at least some of said elements known to be possible [sic] involved in the response in accordance with the effectiveness of the response; and

(f) repeating steps (c), (d) and (e) for further responses of the complex system to obtain resultant factors for at least some of said elements.

whereby said resultant factors are indicative of probable malfunction of their associated elements and thereby indicative of probable malfunction at the locations of these elements.

55. Apparatus for indentifying [sic] locations of probable malfunction in a complex system in dependence upon individual responses to a plurality of tests of said system, whereby each response, if effective, requires the proper functioning of certain ones of a plurality of elements of said system, the locations of said plurality of elements and the probable indentity [sic] of at least some of said certain ones of said elements being known, and apparatus comprising, in combination:

(a) means for initializing a factor associated with each of said elements;

(b) means for modifying the factor associated with at least some of said elements known to be possibly involved in a test response, in accordance with the effectiveness of the response, thereby to obtain resultant factors for at least some of said elements which are indicative of probable malfunction of their associated elements and thereby indicative of probable malfunction at the location of these elements; and

(c) means for displaying the resultant factors associated with at least some of said elements.

During oral argument, appellants' counsel explained that a doctor may perform fifty or more tests when conducting a standard neurological examination such as tapping the knee and pricking the skin. According to counsel, doctors know the relationship between these tests, the responses they should receive, and the patient's neurological system. After observing the patient's response indicating that a neurological area or pathway is functioning or malfunctioning, the doctor, utilizing appellants' invention, inputs this information to the computer. The Solicitor characterized the invention, without objection, as a "diagnostic" or "memory" aid for a physician and emphasized that the invention does not conduct a diagnosis in and of itself, but is used by a doctor when performing a diagnosis to store and to accumulate test responses obtained by this standard process of elimination and to narrow the neurological area of possible malfunction. In fact, the Solicitor indicated that these standard tests have been employed for many years and that the more experienced the doctor and the better his memory, the less would be his need (if any) for this invention.

The examiner rejected all claims under 35 U.S.C. § 101 as drawn to nonstatutory subject matter citing *Gottschalk* v. *Benson*, 409 U.S. 63, 93 S.Ct. 253, 34 L.Ed.2d 273 (1972) and *Parker* v. *Flook*, 437 U.S. 584, 98 S.Ct. 2522, 57 L.Ed.2d 451 (1978). In the examiner's view, the claims were drawn not only to an algorithm but to a *mathematical* algorithm which, like any law of nature or scientific truth, "cannot be the subject of a patent." Responding to appellants' arguments that no mathematical formula or expression was recited in the claims, the examiner quoted the following passage from *In re Richman*, 563 F.2d 1026, 1030, 195 USPQ 340, 344 (Cust. & Pat.App.1977):

> That a claim includes a mathematical expression is not determinative. The decisive factor is whether a claimed method is essentially a mathematical calculation. If it is, deletion from the claims of the mathematical formula involved and substitution of "words which mean the same thing" would not transform the claimed method into statutory subject matter.

The board sustained the rejection stating:

> The claims are drawn to a technique of statistical analysis. Data is accumulated from a series of test operations and conclusions are drawn in accordance with a mathematical algorithm. * * *

> * * *

> If we take claim 1 as typical, the first step "selecting" relates to nothing more than the selection of a source for the accumulation of data to be used in the analysis.
> The factor recited in step (b) is a factor which relates to the probability that the particular element is malfunctioning. At the beginning of the test procedure a proper factor would be zero.
> The third step (c), testing for a response, is nothing more than a data gathering step. Such a step cannot make an otherwise nonstatutory claim statutory. *In re Richman*, 563 F.2d 1026, 195 USPQ 340 (Cust. & Pat.App.1977).
> Step (d) provides information that is read into the computer. Step (e) takes place in the computer by a comparison process in which test outcomes are compared with stored data. The computer infers from this comparison that certain elements are functioning or not functioning. Factors are added to the elements designated (step e) in accordance with the results. * * * The process goes on, step (f), and the results are eventually displayed, claim 21 for example. Claim 1 merely says that results are obtained. They are not displayed.
> The process recited is an attempt to patent a mathematical algorithm rather than a process

for producing a product as in *Diamond* v. *Diehr*, [450 U.S. 175, 101 S.Ct. 1048, 67 L.Ed.2d 155 (1981)].

Appellants argue that no mathematical algorithm is claimed, and, even assuming, arguendo, that there is, any such mathematical algorithm is not wholly preempted by these claims. According to the Solicitor, the claims are directed to a mathematical algorithm: steps (a) and (b) are "arbitrary and merely set the stage for the exercise * * * steps (c) and (d) are necessary input producing steps. As recognized by the Board, data gathering steps 'cannot make an otherwise nonstatutory claim statutory.'" Further, according to the Solicitor, step (e) "calls for 'modifying the factor associated with at least some of said elements known to be [possibly] involved in the response in accordance with the effectiveness of the response,' whereas step (f) calls for repetition of steps (c), (d) and (e) for further test results. At the very least, successive incrementation and/or decrementation is involved, *i.e.*, addition and/or subtraction." Having concluded that a mathematical algorithm is involved, the Solicitor argues that the second of the two-part test of *In re Freeman*, 573 F.2d 1237, 197 USPQ 464 (Cust. & Pat.App. 1978), as modified by *In re Walter*, 618 F.2d 758, 205 USPQ 397 (Cust. & Pat. App. 1980), has been satisfied, and, as a consequence, the claims wholly preempt the mathematical algorithm.

OPINION

Both the Senate and the House Committee Reports accompanying the bill that became the 1952 Patent Act indicate that 35 U.S.C. § 101 was intended to encompass a broad range of subject matter. [Citations.] Discoveries not encompassed by 35 U.S.C. § 101—those excluded from subject matter that Congress chose to protect—are narrowly confined.[1] One type of discovery that the Supreme Court has in recent years determined that the Congress did not choose to protect is the mathematical algorithm. *Diamond* v. *Diehr*, 450 U.S. 175, 101 S.Ct. 1048, 67 L.Ed.2d 155 (1981); *Parker* v. *Flook*, 437 U.S. 584, 98 S.Ct. 2522, 57 L.Ed.2d

---

1. The Constitution empowers Congress to protect an inventor's "discoveries." However, Congress has chosen to protect only a "useful process, machine, manufacture,

or composition of matter or any * * * useful improvement thereof." 35 U.S.C. § 101.

451 (1978). This exclusion from protection is consistent with the Court's long-standing exclusion from patentable subject matter of scientific principles, laws of nature, ideas, and mental processes.

Scientific principles, such as the relationship between mass and energy, and laws of nature, such as the acceleration of gravity, namely, a = 32ft./sec.[2], can be represented in mathematical format. However, some mathematical algorithms and formulae do not represent scientific principles or laws of nature; they represent ideas or mental processes and are simply logical vehicles for communicating possible solutions to complex problems. The presence of a mathematical algorithm or formula in a claim is merely an indication that a scientific principle, law of nature, idea or mental process may be the subject matter claimed and, thus, justify a rejection of that claim under 35 U.S.C. § 101; but the presence of a mathematical algorithm or formula is only a signpost for further analysis.

The Supreme Court has recognized that scientific principles and laws of nature, even when for the first time discovered, have existed throughout time, define the relationship of man to his environment, and, as a consequence, ought not to be the subject of exclusive rights of any one person. [Citation.] As the concurring opinion in *O'Reilly* v. *Morse*, 56 U.S. (15 How.) 61, 132–33, 14 L.Ed. 601 (1853) said:

> The mere discovery of a new element, or law, or principle of nature, without any valuable application of it to the arts, is not the subject of a patent. But he who takes this new element or power, as yet useless, from the laboratory of the philosopher, and makes it the servant of man; who applies it to the perfecting of a new and useful art, or to the improvement of one already known, is the benefactor to whom the patent law tenders its protection.

In *Rubber-Tip Pencil Co.* v. *Howard*, 87 U.S. (20 Wall.) 498, 507, 22 L.Ed. 410 (1874), the

Supreme Court stated that "[a]n idea of itself is not patentable, but a new device by which it may be made practically useful is."

In considering a claim for compliance with 35 U.S.C. § 101, it must be determined whether a scientific principle, law of nature, idea, or mental process, which may be represented by a mathematical algorithm, is included in the subject matter of the claim. If it is, it must then be determined whether such principle, law, idea, or mental process is applied in an invention of a type set forth in 35 U.S.C. § 101. This is consistent with *In re Freeman*, 573 F.2d 1237, 197 USPQ 464 (Cust. & Pat. App. 1978), as modified by *In re Walter*, 618 F.2d 758, 205 USPQ 397 (Cust. & Pat. App. 1980),[2] and the more recent decisions by this court in *In re Pardo*, 684 F.2d 912 (Cust. & Pat. App. 1982) and *In re Abele*, 684 F.2d 192 (Cust. & Pat. App. 1982). In *Abele*, this court said that "all of the claims *may* be directed to nonstatutory subject matter as each presents a mathematical formula or a sequence of mathematical operations." At 907. (Emphasis supplied.) And, in order to determine whether they set forth a statutory invention, it is necessary to determine whether the mathematical formula is "applied in any manner to physical elements or process steps" (citing *In re Walter, supra*). At 907.

Appellants' specification and arguments indicate that their invention is concerned with replacing, in part, the thinking processes of a neurologist with a computer. Counsel for appellants acknowledged in oral argument that the claims recite a mathematical algorithm, which represents a mental process that a neurologist should follow.[3] Thus, the decisive question is whether that mental process is applied to physical elements or process steps in an otherwise statutory process, machine, manufacture, or composition of matter, in accordance with 35 U.S.C. § 101. Although the second of the two-part test of *In re Freeman*

---

2. However, the second step in *Freeman*, as modified by *Walter*, is subject to misinterpretation, *see* notes 4 and 5 and accompanying text, *infra*.

3. Appellants' apparatus claims differ from the method claims by reciting "means for" performing the steps set forth in the method claims, and "means for displaying" the results. However, for purposes of section 101, such claims are not treated differently from method claims. As we stated in *In re Pardo*, 684 F.2d 912, 916 n. 6 (Cust.

& Pat. App. 1982):
> Although some of appellants' claims are drawn to a "general purpose data processor of known type operating under the control of a stored program," such claims are treated as indistinguishable from the method claims for purposes of section 101 unless it is demonstrated that the claims are drawn to specific apparatus distinct from other apparatus capable of performing the identical functions. *In re Walter, supra*. [Citation.]

is whether a scientific principle, law of nature, idea or mental process (represented by a mathematical algorithm or formula) is preempted by the claim,[4] this court, in *In re Walter, supra*, modified *Freeman* to require that a positive approach be taken to determine what, as a whole, is claimed, saying:

> Once a mathematical algorithm has been found, the claim *as a whole* must be further analyzed. If it appears that the mathematical algorithm is implemented in a specific manner to define structural relationships between the physical elements of the claim (in apparatus claims) or to refine or limit claim steps (in process claims), the claim being otherwise statutory, the claim passes muster under § 101. [Footnote omitted.]

[Citation.] The above statement from *Walter* complements prior statements by the Supreme Court, but, as with those statements, it was not intended to be the exclusive test for determining the presence of statutory subject matter.[5] A more comprehensive test for cases involving mathematical algorithms is set forth in *In re Abele, supra*, and *Walter* must be interpreted in light of that opinion.

In answering the decisive question, the claims are to be given their broadest reasonable interpretation consistent with the specification. [Citation.] On this basis, we conclude that appellants' independent claims are to a mathematical algorithm representing a mental process that has *not* been applied to physical elements or process steps and is, therefore, not limited to any otherwise statutory process, machine, manufacture, or composition of matter.

* * *

In view of the foregoing, we hold that appellants' claims were properly rejected.[7]

The decision of the board is affirmed.

ORTHOPEDIC EQUIPMENT CO. v. UNITED STATES

702 F.2d 1005

(United States Court of Appeals, Federal Circuit, March 11, 1983.)

PER CURIAM.

Both sides appeal from the judgment of the United States Claims Court in this patent infringement suit. Appellants Orthopedic Equipment Company, Inc. (Orthopedic) and Marriott Corporation (Marriott), plaintiffs in the suit, brought this action pursuant to 28 U.S.C. § 1498 seeking compensation for the unauthorized manufacture or use by or for the United States of a nation-wide material handling system which is alleged to infringe claims 1, 2, 6, and 7 of United States Letters Patent No. 3,304,416 (the Wolf patent), entitled "Business Order Control System Apparatus." They filed administrative claims for compensation with several Department of Defense agencies for infringement of the Wolf patent. The first of these administrative claims was filed in July 1976; none of the claims has ever been denied. The present suit was filed in the United States Court of Claims on May 6, 1977. Then Trial Judge Colaianni, after a trial, issued an opinion and findings holding that the invention set forth in claims 1, 2, 6 and 7 of the Wolf patent would have been obvious within the meaning of 35 U.S.C. § 103 and that the claims were therefore invalid. He either rejected or declined to pass upon other defenses raised by the United States. But he did decide that the plaintiffs were entitled to collect $1,181.25 as part of the reasonable and necessary costs of a certain deposition. The final judgment was that, upon payment by the United States to the plaintiffs-appellants of $1,181.25 as part of those deposition costs, the petition was to be dismissed. Plaintiffs appeal from the determination of invalidity, and de-

---

4. The *Freeman* approach, looking for preemption, has led to a number of "negative" rules for determining the presence of patentable subject matter, such as: mere antecedent data gathering steps do not render the claims statutory [citation]; mere reference to apparatus does not render a claim statutory [citation]; reading out the results of calculations does not render the claim statutory. [Citation.] However, these statements were not intended to be separate tests for determining whether a claim positively recites statutory subject matter.

5. In *Gottschalk* v. *Benson, supra*, the Court stated that

"Transformation and reduction of an article 'to a a different state or thing' is the clue to the patentability of a process claim that does not include particular machines." [Citation.] But the Court also cautioned:

> It is argued that a process patent must either be tied to a particular machine or apparatus or must operate to change articles or materials to a "different state or thing." *We do not hold that no process patent could ever qualify if it did not meet the requirements of our prior precedents.* [Emphasis supplied.] [Citation.]

7. The dependent claims have not been separately argued and, therefore, fall with the independent claims.

fendant appeals from the award of deposition costs and also from the judge's failure to consider, or his rejection of, most of the Government's other defenses.

Because we agree with Judge Colaianni's reasons for his decision that the claims were invalid for obviousness, we confine our discussion of invalidity to those points and do not consider the United States' contentions that invalidity can be reached on other grounds. On the question of obviousness (Part I *infra*) our opinion incorporates, for the most part, Judge Colaianni's opinion. * * *

I—OBVIOUSNESS

Appellants accuse the appellee of infringing claims 1, 2, 6 and 7 of the patent in suit. Claims 1 and 2 are very similar to one another. Likewise, claims 6 and 7 are very similar to each other. The main differences between the claims are the differences which exist between these two similar groups. The parties agreed at trial to treat claims 2 and 7 as representative of their respective groups. This convention will also be followed in this opinion. However, should a peculiar aspect of either claim 1 or claim 6 affect the outcome of the determination of validity, then this fact will be emphasized.

The Claims

Wolf claims 2 and 7, presented in subparagraph form with the sequencing of the claim elements slightly rearranged from the sequencing found in the patent itself,[1] are as follows:

Claim 2

  (a)(1) An electrical system
     (2) for controlling the operation of a business,
  (b)(1) comprising
  (c)(1) a plurality of order stations,
  (d)(1) means
    (2) at each of said order stations
    (3) for generating coded messages corresponding to the orders entered at said station,

  (e)(1) a central station
    (2) connected for control in turn from any of said order stations,
  (f)(1) means
    (2) for programming the operation of each order station to cause the transmission of the messages,
    (3) in orderly fashion,
    (4) to the central station,
  (g)(1) a plurality of work stations
    (2) at which are to be performed respective items of work called for by said messages,
  (h)(1) means
    (2) at said control station
    (3) for recording the messages as received,
    (4) and for computing numerical information
    (5) based on the content of said messages,
  (i)(1) means
    (2) for relaying selected portions of said messages to respective ones of said work stations,
  (j)(1) and means
    (2) at each work station,
    (3) responsive to the relayed message portions,
    (4) for providing a visual display
    (5) of order information pertinent to that work station.

Claim 7

  (a)(1) A remote control
    (2) and computing
    (3) system
    (4) for mercantile operations
  (b)(1) comprising
  (c)(1) work stations,
  (d)(1) at least one order station,
    (2) remote from said work stations,
  (e)(1) and a central station;
  (f)(1) remotely controllable
    (2) order registering equipment
    (3) at said central station
  (g)(1) means connecting
    (2) said order station to said equipment
    (3) to register therein signals representing items of work to be performed;
  (h)(1) automatic means
    (2) associated with said central station
    (3) for translating said signals into a registerable code
    (4) and for appending thereto codes representative of each work item;

---

1. The rearranged sequencing and the subparagraphing is superimposed on the claims of the patent solely for the purpose of facilitating discussions involving the claims. The superimposition permits a precise identification of the various claim elements. It is a more detailed location scheme than the column and line-number scheme which one finds in patents. The rearranged sequencing has no bearing on the patentability of these particular claims. The following shorthand will be used in this opinion: Claim 2(a)(1), or element 2(a)(1), shall refer to subparagraph (a)(1) of claim 2 of the Wolf patent, *i.e.*, "An electrical system."

(i)(1) and a calculator control
(2) led by said automatic means
(3) for registering the items of work and price data individual thereto
(4) and for computing said data to provide an output total;
(j)(1) and means
(2) associated with said central station
(3) for transferring portions of said signals selectively to respective work stations
(4) to control the manifestation thereat of such work items for processing at said stations[,]
(k)(1) apparatus
(2) at each work station
(3) for registering
(4) and intelligibly manifesting
(5) the items of work to be performed, as called for by said signals[.]

The Nonobvious Subject Matter Requirement of 35 U.S.C. § 103

The traditional test, enunciated in *Graham v. John Deere Co.*, 383 U.S. 1, 86 S.Ct. 684, 15 L.Ed.2d 545 (1966), for § 103 nonobviousness requires the factfinder to make several determinations. The test provides:

> Under § 103, the scope and content of the prior art are to be determined; differences between the prior art and the claims at issue are to be ascertained; and the level of ordinary skill in the pertinent art resolved. Against this background, the obviousness or nonobviousness of the subject matter is determined. Such secondary considerations as commercial success, long felt but unsolved need, failure of others, etc., might be utilized to give light to the circumstances surrounding the origin of the subject matter sought to be patented. As indicia of obviousness or nonobviousness, these inquiries may have relevancy. [Citation.]

Scope and Content of the Prior Art Summarized

Much of the prior art in the trial record consists of United States Letters Patent which were considered by the Patent and Trademark Office (PTO) during the prosecution of the Wolf patent. These patents for the most part reside within the art of information processing system hardware. A number of them draw upon the technology found in telephone line-switching devices. The technology embodied in the information processing and telephone

fields tends to evolve rapidly in response to prior and concurrent developments.

The individual patents themselves disclose one or more, but less than all, of the separate Wolf claim elements. Their combined teachings disclose all of the Wolf claim elements. Several of these patents each show how to combine two or more of the Wolf claim elements. They demonstrate the facility with which the various means identified in the Wolf claims can be made to interface with each other in order to form the desired information processing devices.

The Relevant Art of the Invention in Suit

The claims in suit provide a convenient starting point for determining the relevant art. The significant claim elements which combine to form the claims in suit were well-known in the prior art as of the time of the Wolf filing date. Thus nonobviousness of these claims would arise only if they embody a combination of these well-known elements that was not obvious to one of ordinary skill in the art. One factor bearing on the determination of the relevant art is the type of skill required to understand the disclosure of the Wolf patent, which relates to information processing hardware. Beyond a rudimentary knowledge of electromechanical devices, one should be familiar with the workings of information processing systems hardware.

One of skill in the art of designing information processing systems hardware at the time of the Wolf filing date would have been familiar with telephone line-switching technology. This conclusion is apparent from the Andrews-Vibbard[2] disclosure, the Gimpel[3] disclosure, and is consistent with the fact that the technology used for the routing of signals in the early models of information processing systems hardware was borrowed from telephone line-switching technology.

A second factor bearing on the determination of the relevant art is the type of art applied to the claims by the PTO. As already noted, much of this art deals with information processing systems hardware and telephone line-switching technology.

---

2. United States Letters Patent No. 2,977,048.

3. United States Letters Patent No. 2,987,704.

In determining the relevant art of the claims in suit one looks to the nature of the problem confronting the inventor. [Citation.] The appellants' expert, when asked to state the concept embodied in these claims that was not already present in the prior art as of the filing date of Wolf, said:

> The concept of the message identifying an item of work being transmitted through a central station—or is transmitted to a central station, and then the use of the item identifier to route the message onto an appropriate work station with the ability, at the central station, to also perform numerical computations where the—at least some of the operands for that computation are also determined by the item description code entered at the work station, or—at the order station. [Footnote.]

In other words, appellants allege that one source of the patentability of the claims in suit is the way that the apparatus, as defined by the Wolf claims, uses the coded input information to make two separate types of decisions without the aid of direct human intervention at the time when the decisions are made. The first determination involves selecting price information from a data storage apparatus and appending the price information to the item input information. The Wolf system looks at the item code, and based on this code it is able to pick out the price of this item from the price information stored in the memory registers of the central station. It then associates this price information with the item code in all subsequent processing of the item input information. The hardware employed to perform this selection was well-known in the art of information processing systems hardware design as of the filing date of Wolf.

The second determination involves selecting the appropriate route for transmission of the coded input information to the proper work station, as well as to the calculator for numerical computations. The system's route selection is made depending upon the identity of the coded input information. The hardware employed to perform this selection was well-known in the art of designing telephone line-switching hardware.

In view of the foregoing factors, it would seem that one can come no closer to pinpoint-

ing the relevant art of the Wolf claims than by choosing the art of information processing systems hardware. We conclude that the relevant art of the Wolf patent claims resides in the field of information processing systems hardware.

Additional support for this conclusion comes from the fact that the appellants chose as their chief witness a person whose primary experience was in the computer hardware field,[5] which is the major component of information processing systems hardware. Appellants' assertion of warehousing as the relevant art is unpersuasive. In defining the significance of the invention, appellants' chief witness, Mr. Nikolai, relied on his experience in the computer field, not on any expertise in the field of warehousing. In fact, Mr. Nikolai did not possess any expertise in the warehousing art, yet the appellants advanced his testimony in their rebuttal of the appellee's defense of invalidity for lack of nonobviousness of the Wolf claims. If the appellants truly believed that the relevant art was warehousing, it appears reasonable to expect that they would have sought to rebut the defendant's § 103 charge of obviousness in the art of information processing systems hardware by demonstrating the nonobviousness of the claims in the art of warehousing. To do the latter appellants could not advance the testimony of Mr. Nikolai, who was totally unfamiliar with the warehousing art. However, the appellants' choice of Mr. Nikolai was not in fact ill-advised; their actions speak louder than their words in this instance, and their actions bolster the conclusion that the relevant art is in the field of information processing systems hardware.

Section 103 Defense Based on Nelson-Robinson and Andrews-Vibbard

The one of appellee's § 103 defenses that was accepted by the trial judge is based upon the combined teachings of two United States Letters Patents, Nos. 1,974,191 and 2,977,048.

United States Letters Patent No. 1,974,191 entitled, "Merchandise Control System," was filed by Martin L. Nelson and Harold C. Robinson on April 18, 1932 (the Nelson-Robinson patent). It was classified by the PTO in class 178, subclass 4, and issued on September 18,

---

5. Mr. Nikolai testified: "My experience at Univac in the early days involved exposure to digital computer hardware, digital communication hardware."

1934. It was not considered by the PTO during the prosecution of the claims in suit.

The Nelson-Robinson apparatus includes both order stations and work stations. The work stations perform several functions, namely: credit checks, inventory record monitoring, and transaction documentation. Nelson-Robinson envisions a customer bringing merchandise he wants to purchase to a sales clerk at an order station. Attached to the merchandise is a merchandise display card which contains information coded as a pattern of perforations. The sales clerk operates a transmitter which receives the punched merchandise display card together with a sale clerk's card and a cashier's card, each of the three cards containing information in the form of punch codes. The transmitter in effect reads the punched information by completing certain circuits through the punched holes. Electric signals then activate various other devices at the work stations, depending upon the circuit connections made in the transmitter. A printing machine, located at the work station where the credit checks are made, prints out information pertinent to the sales transaction. A punch card machine, located at the inventory record room, punches out an inventory card for the purchased merchandise. Information concerning item description, quantity, and price is transmitted to appropriate adding machines which keep running totals of item quantities and dollar sales volume, and this information can be visually displayed on a printed page.

The Nelson-Robinson apparatus discloses all the elements of the claims in suit except the central station and certain elements associated with the central station. In Wolf's claim 2, for example, the Nelson-Robinson apparatus lacks elements (e), (f), and (h)(3). It also lacks elements (e), (f), (g), (h), (i)(3), and (j)(2) of Wolf's claim 7.

United States Letters Patent No. 2,977,048, entitled, "Automatic Calculator," was filed by Ernest G. Andrews and Edward L. Vibbard on December 17, 1946 (the Andrews-Vibbard patent). It was classified by the PTO in class 235, subclass 162. This is the same class as the Wolf patent, but a different subclass. Andrews-Vibbard issued on March 28, 1961, but was never considered by the Patent Office during the prosecution of the claims in suit.

The Andrews-Vibbard described apparatus is an electrical computing device of some sophistication which has provisions for storing results of intermediate calculations and later accessing those results for use as inputs for further calculations. The input information is coded onto perforated paper tapes. The type of calculation to be performed by the machine, and the timing of this performance in relation to other calculations, is controlled by a separate coded perforated tape called the master control tape. This tape contains the operating commands which permitted the apparatus to perform its basic addition and subtraction operations in a way that enabled it to do multiplication and division calculations, and ultimately to arrive at solutions to ballistic equations.

The Andrews-Vibbard apparatus, though not primarily a data storage or memory device, nonetheless did perform a limited storage function during the course of its calculation procedure. Moreover, as disclosed, the apparatus is capable of storing information on a paper tape for selective accessing by a computing device. The selection process was accomplished by means of telephone line-switching hardware, which Andrews-Vibbard teaches was well-known to those skilled in the art of early information processing systems hardware design. The patent in suit relies on an identical data storage arrangement for its price information. In addition, the Andrews-Vibbard apparatus satisfies all of the central station requirements of the claims in suit. The following claim 2 elements can be found in Andrews-Vibbard: (e), (f), (h), and (i). The following claim 7 elements can be found in Andrews-Vibbard: (e), (f), (g), (h), (i), and (j).

The claims in suit make considerable use of means language which reads broadly on the devices disclosed in the prior art. The structural elements or devices disclosed in the Wolf specification that perform the functions defined in the means portions of the claims were each well-known in the prior art at the time of the Wolf invention,[6] as is amply demonstrated by Nelson-Robinson and Andrews-Vibbard. Thus, the patentability of the claims

---

6. The appellants conceded this fact below:

is not derived from the structural elements disclosed in the specification. The only difference between these references and the claims is that neither reference alone discloses the precise combination of elements claimed in the Wolf patent. Thus, the patentability of the claims must stem from the alleged fact that the specific combination of claim elements in Wolf was not disclosed in the prior art and the additional allegation that the specific combination of claim elements was nonobvious to one of ordinary skill in the art.

The appellants have argued that, not only would one of ordinary skill not know how to arrive at the claimed combination of elements, but that the appellee failed altogether to prove the level of ordinary skill in the art which pertains to the Wolf claims. This deficiency, it is said, makes it impossible to state one way or the other what one of ordinary skill in the art was capable of doing, or why in light of such skill such a person might have found the claimed invention lacking in nonobviousness.

Level of Skill in the Art

Some of the factors which have been considered in evaluating the level of ordinary skill in the art appear in the following excerpt from *Jacobson Bros., Inc. v. United States*, 512 F.2d 1065, 185 U.S.P.Q. 168 (Ct.Cl.1975):

> [T]he various prior art approaches employed, the types of problems encountered in the art, the rapidity with which innovations are made, the sophistication of the technology involved, and the educational background of those actively working in the field are among the factors which will ofttimes aid in developing a picture of what is the level of skill of the ordinary person in an art. Considerations such as commercial success and the failure of others, characterized as "secondary" in *Graham*, are nonetheless invaluable as real-life indicia * * * of the level of skill in the art. * * *

The appellee's proof on the issue of the level of skill in the art consists of the following: (1) The evidence adduced in support of its § 102 defenses (defenses the trial judge prohibited on procedural grounds); (2) the prior art pat-

ents; and (3) the testimony and educational qualifications of the witnesses who were working in the art of information processing systems hardware prior to May 26, 1958.

The evidence adduced in support of the § 102 defenses (the SAGE defense and the Air Force defense)[7] can be probative on the issue of the level of skill in the pertinent art even if it be considered inadequate to establish the existence of a § 102 defense (an issue we do not reach). There is no distinction in this regard between § 102(a) proofs [citation] and § 102(g) proofs. [Citation.] Moreover, *Jacobson, supra*, leaves no doubt about the probativeness of prior art or the educational backgrounds of those working in the field.

In terms of the level of skill in the art at the time of the Wolf filing date, we accept the trial judge's finding that the evidence demonstrated the following facts:—Those skilled in the art were able to coordinate specific input information with related stored data and then route this combined information based upon the original input information. It was within the level of skill in the art to conduct a system capable of performing calculations on the input information before associating it with the related stored data. It was also possible to have the calculations performed on the combined input information and stored data, and then route the calculation results in accordance with the initial input information. The level of skill had reached a point where all of the basic information transfer and manipulation techniques, *e.g.*, accessing stored data from memory devices based on input information, and routing information based upon input information, were completely machine controllable. No human intervention was required in the systems which those skilled in the art of information processing hardware were capable of building at the time of the invention in suit. The advances being made in the level of skill in the art were primarily confined to improving the speed, reliability, and storage and handling capacities of the hardware. Electronic devices were replacing the electromechanical devices. The individuals working in the art were of above average

---

7. SAGE is an acronym for the Semi-Automatic Ground Environment air defense system. The other air force system mentioned is the Air Force's early AUTODIN system

defense. These are both adverted to in more detail in the findings below.

intelligence and educational training. Many possessed advanced university degrees.

The Claims in Suit Lack Nonobviousness

The question of nonobviousness is a simple one to ask, but difficult to answer. The person of ordinary skill in the art at the time of the patentee's invention, which in this case is May 26, 1958, is presumed to have before him all of the relevant prior art. As has been previously explained, the available art shows each of the elements of the claims in suit. Armed with this information, would it then be nonobvious to this person of ordinary skill in the art to coordinate these elements in the same manner as the claims in suit? The difficulty which attaches to all honest attempts to answer this question can be attributed to the strong temptation to rely on hindsight while undertaking this evaluation. It is wrong to use the patent in suit as a guide through the maze of prior art references, combining the right references in the right way so as to achieve the result of the claims in suit. Monday morning quarterbacking is quite improper when resolving the question of nonobviousness in a court of law.

Mr. Bloch, the expert witness engaged by the appellee, testified that the claimed invention would be obvious to one of ordinary skill in the art at the time of Mr. Wolf's invention date. The testimony of this witness on this point consisted of conclusions without supporting explanations. The trial judge considered that the lack of supporting explanations was an omission which detracted from the persuasiveness of the conclusions of Mr. Bloch. Nonetheless, the court below held that the testimony of this witness, when combined with other evidence, was sufficient to constitute a prima facie demonstration of obviousness pursuant to 35 U.S.C. § 103.

In rebuttal of this prima facie demonstration of obviousness, the appellants offered the testimony of Mr. Nikolai, a witness experienced on matters of patentability, though not a person of ordinary skill in the art of information processing systems hardware during the relevant time period. Mr. Nikolai testified that it would not be obvious to one of ordinary skill in the art to combine the Nelson-Robinson apparatus with the Andrews-Vibbard apparatus, both cited by the appellee, to achieve the result of the claims in suit. Building upon this point, appellants allude to the unlikelihood of a retail business using an apparatus like Andrews-Vibbard because of its enormous size, cost, and complexity in comparison to the needs of the retail businessman. However, Mr. Nikolai did not testify that it would not have been obvious to combine the elements found in the disclosures of Nelson-Robinson and Andrews-Vibbard and thereby arrive at the combination of elements recited in the claims in suit. There is a distinction between trying to physically combine the two separate apparatus disclosed in two prior art references on the one hand, and on the other hand trying to learn enough from the disclosures of the two references to render obvious the claims in suit. Mr. Nikolai's testimony touched upon the former, but ignored the latter.

Claims may be obvious in view of a combination of references, even if the features of one reference cannot be substituted physically into the structure of the other reference. [Citation.] What matters in the § 103 nonobviousness determination is whether a person of ordinary skill in the art, having all of the teachings of the references before him, is able to produce the structure defined by the claim. [Citation.] The fact that features of one reference cannot be substituted into the structure of a second reference may indicate that the claims were nonobvious in view of the combined teachings of the two references. But this is not necessarily so. [Citation.] The same can be said regarding a complete mechanical misfit between two separate patented devices when the combination is alleged to demonstrate the obviousness of patent claims. But Mr. Nickolai's testimony does not address these points. Rather, he raises only the point that it was not likely that the Andrews-Vibbard apparatus would be integrated into the Nelson-Robinson apparatus by one of ordinary skill in the art. This may be so for reasons of economic feasibility, but not for any want of technological feasibility. The combination of these two inventions does not make good economic sense, but there is no mismatch between their technologies.

In other words, the fact that the two disclosed apparatus would not be combined by businessmen for economic reasons is not the same as saying that it could not be done because skilled persons in the art felt that there was some technological incompatibility that prevented their combination. Only the latter fact is telling on the issue of nonobviousness.

The failure of appellants to show the existence of a long-felt need for the patented device amply explains why no businessman would undertake to literally combine the Nelson-Robinson and Andrews-Vibbard apparatus. However, this does not indicate any technological incompatibility between these two prior art defenses. Indeed, as the trial judge correctly found, it appears quite feasible both economically and technologically, to combine the *several elements* comprising the Nelson-Robinson and Andrews-Vibbard devices to arrive at the claims in suit. Moreover, it appears that to do so would have been obvious to one of ordinary skill in the art at the time Wolf made his invention.

In sum, Judge Colaianni's conclusion of obviousness, which we accept, rests on the testimony of Mr. Bloch regarding the disclosures of the Nelson-Robinson and Andrews-Vibbard patents, and the exhibits and testimony offered by the appellee in support of its prohibited § 102 defenses. Moreover, the inability of the appellants to effectively undermine the foregoing evidence or to present evidence on such factors as long-felt need, teaching away in the prior art, the failure of others, and commercial success, leaves the appellee's prima facie case of obviousness unshaken.

* * *

Affirmed.

NIES, C. J., concurring.

I agree with the majority that the judgment of the Claims Court that the asserted claims of the Wolf patent are invalid under 35 U.S.C. § 103 should be affirmed. In my view, the majority adopts portions of the trial judge's opinion which are unnecessary to the issues on appeal and, thus, to a great extent the majority's opinion is dictum.

Appellants make no attack on use of Andrews-Vibbard as a prior art reference apart from the fact that it is a large, expensive, and specialized machine which a businessman would not have considered a practical tool to use in connection with selection of the items of merchandise ordered by a customer or for preparing a pricing invoice. I agree with the majority that this argument does not destroy the relevancy of Andrews-Vibbard.

The trial judge found that the apparatus disclosed in Nelson-Robinson and Andrews-Vibbard can be physically combined. Appellants do not show any error in this conclusion. In view of the teachings of these prior art references and the problem confronting the inventor, the trial judge did not err in holding that the subject invention would have been obvious to one of ordinary skill in the art on the record before him.

SYNERCOM TECHNOLOGY, INC. v. UNIVERSITY COMPUTING CO.

462 F. Supp. 1003
(United States District Court, N. D. Texas, Dallas Division, Aug. 24, 1978.)

HIGGINBOTHAM, D. J.

This case presents claims of copyright infringement of instruction manuals and input formats used with a computer program designed to solve engineering problems incident to the analysis of structures. [Footnote.]

The analysis of building structures under anticipated or actual conditions of use including the necessary strength of materials and design has for many years required numerous calculations and hundreds of hours of engineering time in the case of larger structures. Structural analysis is a sufficiently matured science that its analytical discipline calls for numerous essentially arithmetical and rote but time-consuming calculations. The grooved character of the discipline is further reinforced by the circumstance that most structures are made of materials with well known properties.

By the early 1960s, engineers had begun to use computers to perform many of these tasks. Given standardization of engineering principles underlying structural analysis, the relatively rote nature of their application, and the large markets for structural analysis, computer programs for structural analysis followed naturally.[2] A rudimentary knowledge of computers, the history of programs and the necessary tasks in program usage are an essential backdrop to the claims.

THE COMPUTER

We are here concerned exclusively with digital computers.

> A digital computer, as distinguished from an analog computer, operates on data expressed in digits, solving a problem by doing arithmetic as a person would do it by head and hand. Some of the digits are stored as components of the computer. Others are introduced into the computer in a form which it is designed to recognize. The computer operates then upon both new and previously stored data. * * *
> * * * The method or program is a sequence of coded instructions for a digital computer. * * *
> * * * A procedure for solving a given type of mathematical problem is known as an "algorithm." * * * *Gottschalk v. Benson*, 409 U.S. 63, 65, 93 S.Ct. 253, 254, 34 L.Ed.2d 273 (1972).

Most digital computers have five functional components: (1) input; (2) storage of the input by memory; (3) a control unit which receives data from memory and gives instructions for the arithmetic; (4) an arithmetic which carries out the control's commands; and (5) an output capability.

The computer program in a general sense instructs the computer regarding the things it is to do. In the industry, the physical machinery is referred to as hardware and the instructional material as software. In using a program one must have a format for input so that the input of data and the instruction to the computer are compatible with its program.

DEVELOPMENT OF STATISTICAL ANALYSIS PROGRAMS

IBM by the early 1960s had developed a program for use in structural analysis called IBM FRAN (IBM 7090–7094 FRAN Framed Structure Analysis Program). IBM claimed no proprietary interest in FRAN and by 1965 FRAN, together with a "user's manual" prepared by IBM, were in the public domain. Other pro-

grams were also being developed including "STRUDL" developed at MIT, MAGIC, developed by Bell Aerospace, and SAP, developed at Berkeley.

SYNERCOM, THE PLAINTIFF

Synercom, the plaintiff, is a Texas corporation formed in 1969 by James W. Bridges, Evan B. Pappas, and Douglas M. King, all engineers and former employees in Houston of McDonnell Automation Company (McAuto), an engineering consulting firm.

McAuto at one time employed over 100 engineers but by 1969 that number had dropped to about 50. McAuto used the FRAN program developed by IBM and published the "McDonnell FRAN Manual" on August 1, 1965. McAuto claimed no proprietary rights to its manual and made it available to its customers.

McAuto engaged in the "software" end of the computer business, as later did Synercom and EDI, a defendant. The marketing arrangements among an engineering firm, a program seller, and a hardware supplier usually took the form of a market triad. The software peddler would sell to engineers the value of its program which with McAuto was (with some changes to be discussed) the old IBM-created FRAN program. The engineer would be schooled in the usage of the input formats so that he could gather the correct data and collate it for submission to a computer. The program would be stored in the memory of a computer owned by a "hardware company" such as University Computing Company (UCC). UCC would charge the engineering firm for the computer time, remitting part of that fee to the software owner as a royalty for use of the program.

The IBM FRAN program, although the progenitor of the program owned by Synercom (STRAN) was not well received in the marketplace. IBM's incentive to create the program was to generate customers for its computers. FRAN, however, was complex and difficult to use. Marketing the program required training of customer's engineers in its usage, a costly and time-consuming effort. Moreover, a substantial part of FRAN was

---

2. Because there are at least three occasions for analysis [(1) design of a structure; (2) its modification; and

(3) its failure], there is a substantial market for such programs.

usable only with IBM's 7090/7094 computer. McAuto did make changes in assembly language necessary to allow FRAN's use on the faster computers. This increase in speed (and reduced cost) and explanatory material for the using engineer helped but did not solve the problem. McAuto's FRAN remained complex and enjoyed little success in the market.

In May 1969, Bridges, Pappas, and King left McAuto and formed Synercom. This departure was on a friendly basis and Synercom became a customer of McAuto, at least for some services, but a competitor for others, principally the computerized structural analysis market.

SYNERCOM'S PLAN FOR STRAN

Synercom believed that if access to the complex program could be made easier for the user, there was a substantial market for computerized structural analysis. The users of the program were usually design engineers but were often unsophisticated in the mysteries of the programs. Success of the Synercom strategy turned on development of instructional manuals and input formats that gave greater access to the program with less knowledge of the user—the simpler the input methods, the greater the market.

Using the IBM STRAN Manual, the McAuto improvements of that manual and other expert data, Synercom developed a new manual (now in its fourth edition) and new input formats. Unlike McAuto, Synercom has attempted to retain proprietary rights by copyright registration and notice. That effort has spawned this controversy. Synercom also made improvements in the IBM FRAN program (to be discussed in more detail later), but continued to use its solution algorithm.

In November of 1969, Synercom, then six months old, offered STRAN Program on a Control Data Corporation (CDC) 6600 series computer.[3] This first sales effort in the fall of 1969 was launched without a user's manual. By November 1970, Synercom, after considerable work, offered an "expanded" version of STRAN bearing the number 4001–1–1 accompanied by the first edition of the manual and

bearing the notice "(copyright symbol) 1970—Synercom Technology, Inc. All Rights Reserved". The title page of all copies of the "1st Edition" STRAN User's Manual carried the notice "(copyright symbol) 1970—Synercom Technology, Inc. All Rights Reserved". The "1st Edition" STRAN User's Manual was printed in the United States by Gino's Prints, Houston, Texas, and was published (within the meaning of Title 17, U.S. Code) on October 8, 1970. Before preparation of the "1st Edition" STRAN User's Manual, a preliminary draft copy of the manual was prepared by Synercom but all copies bore the notice "(copyright symbol) 1970—Synercom Technology, Inc. All Rights Reserved". It was never publicly distributed. The exact number of the preliminary draft copies is not known, but few were made. Indeed only 120 copies of the "1st Edition" STRAN User's Manual were printed.

The STRAN User's Manual, Second Edition, was printed in the United States by Gallery Printing Company, Houston, Texas, and was published on October 15, 1971. Only 300 copies of the second edition were printed and few were distributed. The title pages all carried the notice "(copyright symbol) Copyright, Synercom Technology, Inc. 1971 All Rights Reserved" and bore the number 401–1–3.

The first printing of the STRAN User's Manual, Third Edition, was printed in the United States by L. R. Golson, Houston, Texas, and published before September 18, 1973. Only 300 copies of the third edition were printed and few were distributed. The title pages of all copies carried the notice "A Synercom Technology, Inc., Program Product 1973 (copyright symbol [sic] 1973 Synercom Technology, Inc. All Rights Reserved" and bore the number 401–1–3. This development of the manual program changes and related efforts required approximately four man years at a cost in the range of $100,000.

The STRAN program (as detailed in the 1973 third edition of the user's manual) and the original FRAN program of IBM as modified by McAuto had substantial differences both in techniques for use and in product. STRAN had a greater analytical capacity such as final stress analysis calculation to deter-

---

3. That version of STRAN was later offered on a Univac Corporation 1108 computer followed by the IBM 360 computer.

mine compliance with applicable codes and specifications. At the same time the input for STRAN was more easily collated resulting in less training time for users. STRAN was also more efficient in its output. For example, FRAN's output could fill boxes with calculations which STRAN could achieve with a few pages.

STRAN's input formats were unique. Many of the same calculations could be made with use of a "post processor" program such as one developed by Rust Engineering of Atlanta, Georgia, and the input task could similarly be accomplished by a "preprocess" program. But the result would be usage of three separate programs to achieve the results STRAN had packaged. Thus one of the improvements was the telescoping of many functions into the single STRAN program. Moreover, STRAN

offered more sophisticated analysis than the combined use of FRAN and a Rust Engineering postprocessing program.

There are hundreds of programs available for structural analysis, and at least fifteen are competitive with STRAN. All but EDI and Synercom have different input formats.

THE FORMATS

Synercom's input formats have nine classes of inputs. Synercom conceived their logic and arranged their sequence. Synercom secured any common-law rights by publishing the input formats with notice of reservation of copyright. In late 1976 Synercom received registrations of its claims to copyright in the input forms. The forms and registration certificates are as follows:

EXHIBIT	FORM TITLE(S)	EXHIBIT	CERTIF. NO.
B	Loan Condition Card Format; Temperature Loan Card Format; LDCOMB Data; End Card	BB	A 811,473
C	UCRANGE Data; AMOD Data	CC	A 811,474
D	Loan Data (1976 publ.)	DD	A 811,475
E	Joint Data (1976 publ.)	EE	A 811,476
F	Loan Data (1970 publ.)	FF	A 811,477
G	Joint Data (1970 publ.)	GG	A 811,478
H	Group Property Data (1976 publication)	HH	A 811,479
I	Job Identification and Heading Information; Options Data (1976)	II	A 811,480
J	Member Data (1970)	JJ	A 811,481
K	Group Property Data (1972 publication)	KK	A 811,482
L	Job Identification and Heading Information; Options Data (1972)	LL	A 811,483
M	Member Data (1976)	MM	A 811,484
N	Section Property Data	NN	A 811,485

The original publications of each consist either entirely or predominately of material that is new and original to Synercom except for two, the Load Data and Joint Data input forms. As to these two, Synercom asserts that their *arrangement* of information is new and original, and they therefore enjoy protection from copying of their unique *arrangement*.

EDI, UCC, AND SACS II

The first efforts of Synercom to market STRAN usage was with Bonner and Moore, Inc., a Houston firm. But by the latter part of 1972, Bonner and Moore had lost interest. John Fowler, while an engineer employed by Boeing Aircraft at its plant in New Orleans, Louisiana, became familiar with a program for structural analysis developed by Boeing called SAMECS. Neither Boeing nor the U. S. government claimed any proprietary rights in the program. When Boeing's New Orleans plant closed in the fall of 1973, Fowler took much of the data regarding SAMECS with him. Fowler, with Dr. David Garland, another former Boeing engineer, then formed EDI.

In the summer of 1974, Bonner and Moore (no longer marketing STRAN with Synercom, who meanwhile had placed STRAN with UCC) acquired an engineering consulting firm in New Orleans and proposed that EDI manage the newly acquired office. The joint effort included development of a structural analysis program to compete with STRAN in the lucrative Gulf Coast market, principally Houston, Texas.

Bonner and Moore told EDI that to be successful in the marketplace its new program called SACS II, must be wholly compatible with the STRAN format. That is, it must be able to receive its data input and allow STRAN users to switch to SACS II with a minimum of training and without loss of data accumulated in stores of key-punched cards, called data decks. EDI's president, Fowler, was not a stranger to STRAN, having obtained a copy of a brochure designed for users of STRAN and earlier printed by Bonner and Moore while Bonner and Moore and Synercom were working together.

By the time EDI entered the market with SACS II, Synercom was enjoying considerable success with STRAN. But that success had required substantial investment in training customers to use STRAN input formats. By that time incurred costs approached $500,000. This cost was perforce reflected in the Synercom price for use of STRAN. Without the cost of developing the input formats or of training customers in their usage, EDI was in position to simply pluck the fruit of Synercom's labors and risks, if SACS II was as good or better than STRAN. An internal memorandum of EDI written in late 1976 reveals EDI's marketing plan, and it was simple.

> MSA (EDI's family of programs) series of programs are "completely compatible with MARCS from Synercom in Houston (our primary competition)." By simply changing to UCC's control cards, a user can switch from MARCS to MSA. Pricing will be established to beat the MARCS

package significantly so this should be an easy market to capture.

The memorandum further noted that EDI's program features "input data transport to MARCS", meaning "no re-evaluation" of the customers (of Synercom) and "no re-formatting of data." EDI then wrote a preprocessing program that made SACS II wholly compatible with the STRAN input formats.

To complete the present alignment of the cast, one more player must be added—UCC. By early 1976, the relationship between Synercom and UCC had deteriorated and in May or June of 1976, UCC sought out EDI, anticipating that Synercom would not renew its contract whose expiration date was near. Thus in the summer of 1976, a new market triad was born—UCC with SACS II being sold by EDI, a marketing effort if not aimed squarely at the old—Synercom accounts included them in its sights.

MANUALS

In the summer of 1975 EDI had distributed its EDI Manual without copyright or other proprietary notice to its customers and potential customers. EDI did not furnish format cards, but its instruction manual which contained mirror images of some of the input cards and instructions effectively enabled a customer to use the STRAN input format. The EDI Manual contained no page numbers and no reference to UCC, but before publication of the EDI Manual, EDI had access to the STRAN User's Manual, Third Edition.

In the latter part of 1976 and after distribution by Synercom of its STRAN User's Manual, Third Edition with copyright notice, EDI published user's manuals for its SACS II program entitled "SACS II CODING INSTRUCTIONS" ("EDI Manual"). Also in the latter part of 1976 UCC distributed user's manuals for EDI SACS II program (hereafter referred to as the "UCC Manual"). The UCC Manual contains on its title page the names and addresses of both UCC and EDI, UCC's designation "UCC 3581" and the publication date of "8–76", *i.e.*, August, 1976. The UCC Manual was published without copyright or other proprietary notice and was distributed by both UCC and EDI to customers and potential customers. The UCC Manual contains page numbers and was physically produced in Texas by UCC from a master provided to it by EDI. Other than for differences in the title pages and the addition of pagination, the UCC Manual is a copy of the EDI Manual. Before publication of the UCC Manual, UCC had access to the STRAN User's Manual, Third Edition.

These facts present four ultimate questions. First, does Synercom hold valid copyrights on its manuals and input cards. Second, has EDI and UCC infringed any of these copyrights. Third, what relief is available. And fourth, have EDI and UCC competed unfairly.

VALIDITY OF COPYRIGHTS

The attack of EDI and UCC at trial was upon "originality" of the manuals and with lesser emphasis they urged that Synercom published without notice before any claim to proprietary rights. Extensive evidence demonstrated that parts of the STRAN manuals contained paragraphs virtually identical to manuals earlier published by McAuto, FRAN, and others. Indisputably parts of the STRAN manual (first edition and brought forward through succeeding editions) were in no sense of the word original with Synercom; but equally undisputed was that substantial parts of all Synercom manuals were original in every sense of the word.

Although originality is judicially imposed gloss upon the copyright statute, its legal force and definition are settled. As stated by Judge Friendly:

> Although "[t]he Copyright Act nowhere expressly invokes the requirement of originality," courts have uniformly inferred this from the constitutional and statutory condition of authorship. * * *
>
> However, originality has been considered to mean "only that the work owes its origin to the author, i.e., is independently created and not copied from other works." *Puddu v. Buonamici Statuary, Inc.*, 450 F.2d 401, 171 U.S.P.Q. 709 (2d Cir. 1971).

Continuing, the court related:

> Originality sufficient for copyright protection exists if the "author" has introduced *any* element of novelty as contrasted with the material previously known to him." (Emphasis added) [Citation.]

EDI's and UCC's effort to defeat proof of originality is confronted by the fact that at least 70% of the prose found in Synercom's manuals is indeed original to Synercom. Although proof of prior art is familiar to patent law, under copyright law the 30% nonoriginal content does not void the copyright as to the 70% or even the 30%, at least as an integrated part of a product whose whole is original. This is not to infer that Synercom's copyright removed the nonoriginal material from the public domain. It is to say that if an assembly of parts— old and new—results in original expression, the whole is protected. In the case at hand, with only approximately 21% of the material in Synercom's STRAN User's Manual, Third Edition being based upon prior material and the remaining 79% being *entirely* original, Synercom has contributed something "recognizably its own" to prior treatments of the same subject. Its copyright is not invalid because some parts of the whole were not independently conceived. Unlike the patent law, originality is not first idea but independent conception. As L. Hand stated it:

> [T]he law imposes no prohibition upon those who, without copying, independently arrive at the precise combination of words or notes which have been copyrighted. *Fred Fisher, Inc. v. Dillingham*, 298 F. 145, 147 (S.D.N.Y.1924).

The requirement of originality is an *a priori* result of protecting expression only by forbidding copying. That is, because the grant of exclusivity to the copyright holder is only of the right to copy the expression, originality can require no more than independent work. But requiring the work to be independent does not deny the role of synergism in protectable expression. As the Ninth Circuit stated in reviewing a copyright contest of a musical piece entitled "Bubbles":

> In fact, "Bubbles" does have a sequence commonly found in other musical pieces. The copyrightability of "Bubbles" is not the four-note sequence, but the fitting together of this sequence with other melodious phrases into a unique composition. *Granite Music Corp. v. United Artists Corp.*, 532 F.2d 718, 721 (9th Cir. 1976).

It follows that the copyright registrations for Synercom's first and second editions which contain only slightly less new matter than the third edition are also valid.

PRIOR PUBLICATION

The allegation that there was a publication authorized by Synercom without notice of claimed copyright is quickly dispatched.

" * * * [P]ublication occurs when by consent of the copyright owner, the original or tangible copies of a work are sold, leased, loaned, given away, or otherwise made available to the general public * * * ." *Bartok v. Boosey & Hawkes, Inc.*, 523 F.2d 941, 945 (1975), quoting 1 M. Nimmer, *The Law of Copyright*, § 49 at 194–95.

Defendants allege four "instances" of authorized publication without copyright notice: Bonner and Moore, Raymond International, Fluor Ocean Services (which purchased Bonner and Moore) and Lawrence Allison. The evidence offered is sparse and equivocal. It never preponderates in defendants' favor. And defendants had the burden of establishing publication, without notice, with the consent or fault of Synercom. [Citations.]

Synercom is said to have authorized Bonner and Moore to publish a brochure (Defendants' Exhibit 20) and the input formats. The court found no credible evidence of this defensive claim, including the uncertain testimony of witness Pye. Moreover, when pressed on cross-examination, Pye conceded that he had no personal knowledge that Synercom authorized Bonner and Moore to print or distribute the brochure. He also lacked personal knowledge as to the number of copies printed. Even his "estimate," which given its basis was little more than speculation, placed the number at only 100. The claim that the brochure was published has a hollow ring when faced with the fact that defendant was less than candid about when and how it came to have the brochure in its possession. Publication by a licensee of "vast numbers of copies without copyright notice may work a forfeiture" if done with full knowledge of a licensor who acquiesces. [Citation.] No such publication occurred here. If contrary to the evidence, the brochures were widely distributed, there would be little reason for EDI's secretive attitude toward its copy. The court is unwilling on this record to find the claimed authorized publication.

Although Synercom did authorize Raymond International and Fluor to make copies for their internal use, there is no evidence of authorized distribution or reproduction without copyright notice. David Engel's testimony when carefully considered was not based upon personal knowledge. In fact, he at one point stated that although he did not know, the forms very likely did have copyright notices on them. [Reference.] Engel did testify that some of the forms now used by Raymond International did not have a Synercom copyright notice, but there is no evidence of probative value that these were for other than internal use or critically that Synercom authorized this deletion.

Proof (by way of the deposition of Robert Jack Herring) that Lawrence Allison was authorized to copy and distribute without notice of copyright was not sufficient. Herring's testimony appears to be regarding his experience at Fluor's Ocean Services, Bonner and Moore's purchaser. Moreover, Herring testified that he had no personal knowledge that Synercom knew " * * * how Fluor was inputting its data to either the STRAN or SACS program * * * ." [Reference.] And that relationship has been otherwise examined and found to be insufficient to support defendants' assertions.

INPUT FORMATS

EDI and UCC here contend that the formats are mere forms not intended to convey information and are not subject to copyright. That these ciphers bear the computer world name of formats is unfortunate because it suggests that they are formats as that term is used in copyright law; they are not.

Certainly blank forms are not the subject of copyright. [Citations.] However, "forms" which communicate information can be the subject of copyright. [Citation.] And code books have received protection. [Citations.] * * *

The litmus seems to be whether the material proffered for copyright undertakes to express. At first glance these input formats are simply devices for the assistance of the user to facilitate his task—forms. On reflection, however, one must conclude that they indeed express ideas. The usage by EDI of the formats (which it contends is not infringing) undercuts its argument that the input formats are not expression. EDI does not furnish card formats to the customer for use; instead it expects the customer to use an 80-column paper, common to the industry. However, in its manual used to instruct users of its SACS II program, it used mirror images of the forms themselves. Their usage only buttresses the reality that these input formats express to the user the sequencing of data for simplified access to the computer programs. The formats by their placement of lines, shaded art, and words tell the user what data to place where and how to do it. It communicates the selection arrangements and the sequence. That was the usage EDI made of it. It follows that the formats are copyrightable if the ideas they express are separable from their expression. This issue is focused by examining the companion question of infringement.

INFRINGEMENT

A. Formats

Closely related to the contention that the formats do not contain expression is the defensive argument that EDI has only used any ideas expressed by the formats. The argument continues that stopping EDI's usage would give the formats patent, not copyright protection. [Footnote.]

EDI was free to "read" Synercom's formats and employ their teaching; it was not free to "copy" the formats and contends that it did not. Thus the issue is whether EDI copied expressed ideas or their expression. EDI put forward an alternative argument that because use of the idea required substantial duplication of Synercom's arrangements and sequencing, copyright protection ought not be allowed.

One can argue that inseparability of idea and expression is here an antinomy. The argument asks if the idea and the usage are not separable, what is the expression?

EDI argues that it did not "copy" the formats, pointing out that it did not even use preprinted formats. EDI instead wrote a preprocessor program to accept Synercom's exact formats. The FORTRAN statements in its preprocessor program are derived directly and precisely from the copyrighted manual card formats. This was not accidental. Independent and coincidentally exact duplication was a statistical improbability. By varying only the order constituent of the format instruction, the manner of communicating with the com-

puter may be expressed in ten factorial (10–9–8–7–6–5–4–3–2–1) [sic]; that is 3,628,800 expressions. It is true that the common engineering problem and common discipline of users would reduce the number of practical variances; regardless before trial ended defendant had conceded that they had indeed done what they set out to do—exactly duplicate. But critically, EDI in doing so, has only appropriated the idea expressed by the formats; that it was deliberate is immaterial.

Title 17 § 1 grants to the copyright owner the exclusive right " * * * (b) to translate the copyrighted work into other language or dialects, or make any other version thereof, if it be a literary work. * * * " Synercom urges that EDI's preprocessor program infringes because it does no more than translate the expression of the formats to a different computer language, unless the subject matter here is not classed as a literary work. The copyright office so classified it although its decision is not determinative.

It has long been the law that " * * * in cases of literary or artistic works, and works of similar character, in which the form, arrangement or combination of ideas represents the product of labor and skilled effort separate and apart from that entailed in the development of the intellectual conception involved, that in such a situation, the medium of expression is entitled to protection by copyright against adoption by another in similar form, arrangement, and combination." *Long v. Jordan*, 29 F.Supp. 287, 288 (N.D.Cal.1939). And writings of an author need not be "tangible to the human eye." *See Goldstein, et al v. California*, 412 U.S. 546, 93 S.Ct. 2303, 37 L.Ed2d 163 (1973) where in deciding that records of artistic performance are under clause 8 of the act, Chief Justice Burger noted that writings " * * * may be interpreted to include any physical rendering of the fruits of creative intellectual or aesthetic labor. * * * " [Citation.]

All of this is clear. The difficult question is whether EDI plagiarized Synercom's idea or its expression. If the idea is the sequence and ordering of data, there was no infringement. If sequencing and ordering of data was, however, expression, it follows that EDI's preprocessor program infringed. As earlier suggested and as will be demonstrated, Synercom's argument is double-edged. If sequencing and ordering is expression, what separable idea is expressed?"

A hypothetical, oversimplified, may serve to illuminate the idea versus expression controversy. The familiar "figure-H" pattern of an automobile stick is chosen arbitrarily by an auto manufacturer. Several different patterns may be imagined, some more convenient for the driver or easier to manufacture than others, but all representing possible configurations. The pattern chosen is arbitrary, but once chosen, it is the only pattern which will work in a particular model. The pattern (analogous to the computer "format") may be expressed in several different ways: by a prose description in a driver's manual, through a diagram, photograph, or driver training film, or otherwise. Each of these expressions may presumably be protected through copyright. But the copyright protects copying of the particular expressions of the pattern, and does not prohibit another manufacturer from marketing a car using the same pattern. Use of the same pattern might be socially desirable, as it would reduce the retraining of drivers. Likewise, the second manufacturer is free to use its own prose descriptions, photographs, diagrams, or the like, so long as these materials take the form of original expressions of the copied idea (however similar they may be to the first manufacturer's materials) rather than copies of the expressions themselves. Admittedly, there are many more possible choices of computer formats, and the decision among

them more arbitrary, but this does not detract from the force of the analogy.

Synercom's argument that the order and sequence of data was the expression, not the idea, has been · rejected.[5] Its acceptance, although answering EDI's claim of noninfringement, would result in a finding that the formats are not proper subjects for copyright protection.

B. Format Copyrightability Revisited

As noted "in cases of literary or artistic works, and works of similar character, in which the form, arrangement, or combination of ideas represents the product of labor and skilled effort *separate and apart from that entailed in the development of the intellectual conception involved*," copyright protection is available. *Long v. Jordan*, 29 F.Supp. 287, 288 (N.D. Cal.1939) (emphasis supplied). Here if order and sequence is the expression, the skilled effort is not separable, for the form, arrangement, and combination is itself the intellectual conception involved. It would follow that only to the extent the expressions involve stylistic creativity *above and beyond* the bare expression of sequence and arrangement, should they be protected. As Mooers states:

Also included in the "expression" is the sequence, choice, and arrangement of descriptive elements. * * * Calvin N. Mooers, *Computer Software and Copyright, Computing Surveys*, Vol. 7, No. 1, March 1975 at p. 50.

---

5. If Synercom's contention were sound (it is not because EDI appropriated ideas, not expression), it would follow that translating the expression of the manual to FORTRAN to another manual equally would be an infringing use. This is true because it is as clear an infringement to translate a computer program from, for example, FORTRAN to ALGOL, as it is to translate a novel or play from English to French. In each case the substance of the expression (if one may speak in such contradictory language) is the same between original and copy, with only the external manifestation of the expression changing. Likewise, it would probably be a violation to take a detailed description of a particular problem solution, such as a flowchart or step-by-step set of prose instructions, written in human language, and program such a description in computer language. But here the similarity to literary translation ends. The preparation of a computer program, in *any* language from a general description of the problem to be solved (as, for example, is contained in the forms and manuals, which prescribe

a problem involving a set of ordered inputs in a particular arrangement which must be accepted by the computer and transmitted to the FRAN program) is very dissimilar to the translation of a literary work, or to the translation of a program from one language to another. In most cases, the formulation of the problem in sufficient detail and with sufficient precision to enable it to be converted into an unambiguous set of computer instructions requires substantial imagination, creativity, independent thought, and exercise of discretion, and the resulting program can in no way be said to be merely a copy or version of the problem statement. The program and the statement are so different, both in physical characteristics and in intended purpose, that they are really two different expressions of the same idea, rather than two different versions of the same expression. Hence EDI's preparation of a FORTRAN preprocessor program from the descriptions contained in the manuals cannot constitute an infringing derivative use provided this was done without copying of the plaintiff's FORTRAN program, as it was.

This is because in the usual case sequence, choice, and arrangement have only stylistic significance, rather than constituting as they would here, the essence of the expression. Finally, Copyright Circular 32 states "Thus, there is no way to secure copyright protection for the idea or principle behind a blank form or similar work, or for any of the methods or systems involved in it." The "idea or principle" behind the forms in question, and the "method or system" involved in them, would be no more or less than the formats. The manuals are copyrightable, but the formats would not be. In sum, if the court is wrong in its finding that order and sequence are expressed ideas, not expressions, its alternative holding is that the formats are not copyrightable.

C. Manuals

There is little question but that EDI and UCC have infringed Synercom's manuals. EDI and UCC have (since the commencement of trial) not seriously contended that its use of the Synercom manuals would not be an infringing use. The battle here was over the validity of the manual's copyrights. Substantial portions of EDI's (and UCC's) manuals are verbatim from the Synercom manual. Some of the Synercom material copied had been in turn copied by Synercom. Nonetheless, some material by UCC and EDI had not been. This question, unlike the others, presents little subtlety.

* * *

RELIEF

Prefatory to a consideration of relief, the following explicit facts are found:

EDI knew before entering the market with its SACS II program that Synercom's STRAN User's Manuals were copyrighted by Synercom.

The infringements by UCC and EDI were willful, deliberate, and for profit. Court action in this dispute was initiated on February 9, 1977, by the filing by EDI, in the United States District Court for the Eastern District of Louisiana, of a complaint (1) seeking a declaratory judgment of invalidity of Synercom's copyrights, (2) alleging "unfair competition" by Synercom, and (3) alleging fraudulent procurement and antitrust violations by Synercom. EDI also sought, unsuccessfully, a temporary restraining order against Synercom.

Substantial parts of the accusations in the action initiated by EDI were groundless. At the ultimate trial on Synercom's request for a permanent injunction, EDI abandoned all allegations of unfair competition, fraud, and antitrust violations, and presented no evidence in their support.

Between its filing of the complaint and trial on the merits, EDI conducted this litigation in a manner calculated to delay hearing on the merits and to increase the costs of litigation to Synercom as much as possible. [Footnote.]

An extraordinary amount of needless discovery was initiated by EDI: substantively thousands of interrogatories, and nearly 30 dispositions [sic]. Additionally, numerous motions without merit were filed by EDI, their purpose being to delay and to increase costs. Throughout EDI steadfastly denied that it ever had access to the Synercom materials, until shortly before trial when it filed its answer to Synercom's First Amended Complaint. Also, until trial, EDI steadfastly maintained (a) that there were no similarities between its manual and Synercom's materials, and (b) if there were, such similarities were "purely coincidental" or because "engineers tend to think alike." EDI knew these contentions were untrue at the time it made them, which coupled with their abandonment before the court, is sufficient to warrant an award of a reasonable attorney's fee to Synercom.

Additionally, officers of EDI executed affidavits to the effect that the Synercom principals had "stolen" their program, documentary materials, that they were trying to "force EDI out of business", that they were making untrue representations to customers and potential customers, and that they were "harassing" EDI's customers. EDI made no such allegations at trial. If this is accepted conduct in the marketplace, it is not in a court of justice.

ORDER

Synercom is now entitled to injunctive relief and further discovery regarding other possible relief. It is ORDERED that the defendants, their agents, servants, officers, and employees, privies, successors, and assigns, and all holding by, through or under them or any of them be and the same are hereby perpetually ENJOINED and RESTRAINED as follows:

All "printed infringing materials" shall mean all printed material derived, directly or indirectly, from Synercom's copyrighted materials, and shall include all user's manuals and other instructional literature for the SACS II program, whether the "UCC Manual" or the "EDI Manual", preliminary draft versions or later versions or copies, abridgments or translations.

1. Defendants EDI and UCC shall hereafter produce no printed infringing materials;

2. Defendants EDI and UCC shall, separately, and within 20 days of the filing of this memorandum and order, account under oath for the production of all printed infringing materials and deliver to Synercom's attorney a list of all entities to which any printed infringing materials have been delivered, and, also recall by written request all printed infringing material and provide Synercom's attorney with copies of all written requests for recall; and

3. Defendants EDI and UCC shall return to Synercom's attorney all recalled printed infringing materials. Defendants shall complete the recall within 60 days of the filing of this order.

* * *

STAY

Enforcement of the order is stayed pending resolution of the unfair competition claim. If Synercom does not wish to pursue the unfair competition claim, the court will entertain an application for stay pending an appeal.

DATA CASH SYSTEMS, INC. v. JS&A GROUP, INC.
480 F. Supp. 1063
(United States District Court, N. D. Illinois, E. D., Sept. 26, 1979.)

FLAUM, D. J.

This action for copyright infringement and unfair competition is brought by the creator of a computer program[1] against the corporations and the officers of these corporations which are allegedly reproducing, importing, distributing, selling, marketing and advertis-

ing copies of plaintiff's computer program. Plaintiff has filed a motion for a preliminary injunction and defendants JS&A Group, Inc. ("JS&A"), Joseph Sugarman ("Sugarman"), and Mary Stanke ("Stanke") have filed a motion for summary judgment. For the reasons set forth below, the motion of defendants JS&A, Sugarman and Stanke for summary judgment is granted on Count I of the First Amended Complaint for Infringement of Copyright and for Unfair Competition (the "First Amended Complaint") and is denied on Count II of the First Amended Complaint and the motion of plaintiff for a preliminary injunction is denied.

Before discussing the facts in this case, it is necessary to set forth what exactly a computer program is. A computer program has been defined generally as a set of precise instructions that tells the computer how to solve a problem. [Citations.] Normally, a computer program consists of several phases which may be summarized as follows. The first phase is the development of a flow chart which is a schematic representation of the program's logic. It sets forth the logical steps involved in solving a given problem. The second phase is the development of a "source program" which is a translation of the flow chart into computer programming language, such as FORTRAN or COBOL. Source programs may be punched on decks of cards or imprinted on discs, tapes or drums. The third phase is the development of an "assembly program" which is a translation of the programming language into machine language, *i.e.*, mechanically readable computer language. Unlike source programs, which are readable by trained programmers, assembly programs are virtually unintelligible except by the computer itself. Finally, the fourth phase is the development of an "object program" which is a conversion of the machine language into a device commanding a series of electrical impulses. Object programs, which enter into the mechanical process itself, cannot be read without the aid of special equipment and cannot be understood by even the most highly trained programmers. [Citations.]

Thus, at some point in its development, a computer program is embodied in material form and becomes a mechanical device which

---

1. In the industry computer programs are collectively known as computer software, as distinguished from computer hardware, *i.e.*, the physical equipment itself. [Citations.]

is engaged in the computer to be an essential part of the mechanical process. At different times, then, a given program is both "source" and "object". The "source program" is a writing while the "object program" is a mechanical tool or machine part.

In this case plaintiff retained an independent consultant, D. B. Goodrich and Associates, to design and develop a computer program for a computerized chess game, CompuChess, which was to be manufactured and sold by plaintiff. From September 1976 to April 1977 D. B. Goodrich and Associates designed and developed the basic instructions which told the computer how to play chess at six different levels of difficulty. This process involved the four phases in the development of a computer program discussed above. The instructions were translated into programming language, the source program, which then was translated into machine language, the assembly program. This assembly program was then used to create the object program, the Read Only Memory (the "ROM"). This ROM was then installed in the computer as part of its circuitry.

Thus, CompuChess is a hand-held computer which uses keyboard and data display devices to input and output information. The human player enters his move on the keyboard device by pressing certain keys and the computer relays its move on the data display device by displaying certain letters and numbers.

In late 1977 plaintiff began to market the CompuChess. No copyright notice appeared anywhere on the ROM, the CompuChess itself, its packaging, or its accompanying literature. The copyright notice did appear, however, on the source program and all copies thereof.[2] In November of 1978 the source program was filed with the Register of Copy-

rights and on November 28, 1978 a Certificate of Copyright Registration was issued to plaintiff.

In late 1978 defendants JS&A, Sugarman and Stanke began marketing the JS&A Chess Computer. The ROM in the JS&A Chess Computer is identical to the ROM in plaintiff's CompuChess.[3] In early 1979 plaintiff filed this action for copyright infringement and unfair competition.

Where, as here, the pleadings, depositions, answers to interrogatories and affidavits show that there is no genuine issue as to any material fact, then summary judgment should go to the party entitled to judgment as a matter of law. However, motions for summary judgment in copyright infringement and unfair competition cases have been generally frowned upon. [Citations.] Nevertheless, such motions may be granted for the defendant in a copyright infringement action if, after assuming copying, the court finds that any similarity between the works is insubstantial or that undisputed facts raise a complete defense as a matter of law. [Citations.]

Since the ROM in the JS&A Chess Computer is identical to the ROM in plaintiff's CompuChess, the court can assume that there was direct copying of plaintiff's ROM. However, the undisputed facts show that defendants JS&A, Sugarman and Stanke have a complete defense as a matter of law with respect to plaintiff's claim of copyright infringement.

Count I of the First Amended Complaint, the count alleging copyright infringement by defendants JS&A, Sugarman and Stanke, is brought under the Copyright Act of 1976, 17 U.S.C. § 101 *et seq.* (App. 1976) (the "1976 Act"). Although this action should be brought under the 1976 Act, the 1976 Act itself does not apply.[4] Section 117 of the 1976 Act states:

---

2. Each and every copy of the source program had printed on it the words "Copyrighted by D. B. Goodrich & Associates" and the date when it was printed out. On November 2, 1978, D. B. Goodrich & Associates, Inc. assigned its copyright to plaintiff.

3. Although defendants JS&A, Sugarman and Stanke do not know how the ROM was manufactured by defendant Novag Industries, Inc., defendants JS&A, Sugarman and Stanke and plaintiff have stipulated that the chess computer program of the JS&A Chess Computer is identical to the chess computer program of plaintiff's CompuChess.

4. Even if the 1976 Act did apply, copying of the ROM would not be actionable. Under the 1976 Act "copies" are defined as

> material objects, other than phonorecords, in which a work is fixed by any method now known or later developed, and from which the work can be perceived, reproduced, or otherwise communicated, either directly or with the aid of a machine or device. The term "copies" includes the material object, other than a phonorecord, in which the work is first fixed. 17 U.S.C. § 101 (App.1976).

While the new definition of copy encompasses works which may be perceived "with the aid of a machine or device," this title [title 17] does not afford to the owner of copyright in a work any greater or lesser rights with respect to the use of the work in conjunction with automatic systems capable of storing, processing, retrieving, or transferring information, or in conjunction with any similar device, machine or process, than those afforded to works under the law, whether title 17 or the common law or statutes of a State, in effect on December 31, 1977, as held applicable and construed by a court in an action brought under this title.

The legislative history for section 117 explains that this section was enacted because the problems in the area of computer uses of copyrighted works are not sufficiently developed for a definitive legislative solution.[5] Thus, the purpose of section 117 is to preserve the *status quo*. It is not intended to cut off any rights that existed on December 31, 1977 or to create new rights that might be denied under the predecessor to the 1976 Act, the Copyright Act of 1909, 17 U.S.C. § 1 (1976) (the "1909 Act"), or under common law principles applicable on December 31, 1977. [Citation.]

Therefore, a court, in deciding the scope of exclusive rights in the computer area, first must determine the applicable law, whether state statutory or common law or the 1909 Act. After determining which law is applicable, the court's decision must depend upon

its interpretation of what that law was on December 31, 1977. [Citation.] If, as of the date of the alleged act of infringement, the computer program allegedly infringed had been neither published nor registered in the copyright office, then the common law copyright rule should be applied. Otherwise, the law under the 1909 Act should be applied. [Citation.]

Prior to the complete revision of the 1909 Act, the American law of copyright had been the subject of a dichotomy between federal and state law. Unpublished works were automatically protected by state law, referred to somewhat inaccurately as common law copyright.[6] Such protection began at the moment of creation and terminated upon publication when common law copyright was lost. Thereafter, protection was available, if at all, only through federal, or as it is generally known, statutory copyright. [Citation.]

The parties have assumed that the ROM is a "copy" of the computer program created by plaintiff within the meaning of both the common law and the 1909 Act.[7] The court does not agree. Both at common law and under the 1909 Act, a "copy" must be in a form which others can see and read.

At common law the author's property in his unpublished work included the right to publish, or to refrain from publishing, at his option, and the right of restraining others from

the court believes that the 1976 Act applies to computer programs in their flow chart, source and assembly phases but not in their object phase, *i.e.*, the ROM, for the following reasons:

(1) Proposed Regulation § 201.20, which sets forth the suggested methods of affixing and positioning the copyright notice on various types of works in order to satisfy the requirement in section 401(c) of the 1976 Act, 17 U.S.C. § 401(c) (App.1976), that the copyright notice "be affixed to the copies in such manner and location as to give reasonable notice of the claim of copyright," states:

(g) Works Reproduced in Machine-Readable Copies. For works reproduced in machine-readable copies (such as magnetic tapes or disks, punched cards, or the like) from which the work cannot ordinarily be visually perceived except with the aid of a machine or device, the following constitute examples of acceptable methods of affixation and position of the notice:

(1) A notice embodied in the copies in machine-readable form in such a manner that on visually perceptible printouts it appears either with or near the title, or at the end of the work;

(2) A notice that is displayed at the user's terminal at sign on;

(3) A notice that is continuously on terminal display;

(4) A permanently legible notice reproduced on a

gummed or other label securely affixed to the copies or to a box, reel, cartridge, cassette, or other container used as a permanent receptacle for the copies. Copyright L.Rep. (CCH) ¶ 14,001 (footnote omitted).

(2) In its object phase, the computer program is a mechanical device which is engaged in the computer to become an essential part of the mechanical process. [Citations.] Mechanical devices which cannot qualify as pictorial, graphic or sculptural works are not writings and may not obtain copyright protection. [Citation.]

5. The National Commission on New Technological Uses of Copyrighted Works was established to recommend, *inter alia*, definitive copyright provisions to deal with these problems. [Citation.]

6. Although the term "common-law copyright" is not technically and strictly accurate, it is useful and suggestive. More accurate is the term "common-law right of first publication." 18 Am.Jur. Copyright & Literary Property § 2 (1965).

7. Since the parties have assumed that the ROM is a "copy" of plaintiff's computer program, they have perceived the issue here to be whether the sale of the CompuChess, which contains the ROM, was a publication of the computer program. Since the court concludes that the ROM is not a "copy" of the computer program, it need not reach this issue.

publishing without his consent. The original manuscript and the incorporeal right of first publication were the private and exclusive property of the author. He had the sole right of first printing and publishing it for sale. Thus, the unauthorized publication of an author's work was a violation of the author's common law right to the "copy". [Citation.]

At common law the noun "copy" signified a tangible object that was a reproduction of the original work. Although any mode of reproduction, whether by printing, writing, photography, or by some other method not yet invented, constituted a copying, to be a "copy" there must have been an appeal to the eye. Thus, the term "copy" has been defined as that which comes so near to the original as to give to every person seeing it the idea created by the original. [Citation.]

That the ROM at common law does not constitute a copy of plaintiff's computer program is supported by the cases which hold that a completed building is not a copy of the architectural plans upon which the building is based. [Citations.] An architectural plan is a technical writing which is capable of being copied only by similar technical writings, *i.e.*, by other plans. A building is the result of plans not a "copy" of them. [Citation.] It follows that at common law a copy of a computer program is another computer program in its flow chart or source phase because these are comparable technical writings. While the ROM is the mechanical embodiment of the source program, it is not a "copy" of it.

This same conclusion is reached under the 1909 Act. The 1909 Act and its predecessors gave authors the exclusive right, *inter alia*, to copy the copyrighted work. 17 U.S.C. § 1(a) (1976). In *White-Smith Music Publishing Co. v. Apollo Co.*, 209 U.S. 1, 28 S.Ct. 319, 52 L.Ed. 655 (1908), the Supreme Court held that a piano roll[8] was not a "copy" of the musical composition recorded thereon and therefore, that the defendant, in making an unauthorized piano roll of plaintiff's musical composition, had not infringed plaintiff's "right to copy". After quoting the definition of copy set

forth in *Boosey v. Whight*, [[1900] 1 Ch. 122], the Supreme Court defined a copy of a musical composition as "a written or printed record of it in intelligible notation". [Citation.] In reaching this result the Court stated:

> It may be true that in a broad sense a mechanical instrument which reproduces a tune copies it; but this is a strained and artificial meaning. When the combination of musical sounds is reproduced to the ear it is the original tune as conceived by the author which is heard. These musical tones are not a copy which appeals to the eye. In no sense can musical sounds which reach us through the sense of hearing be said to be copies as that term is generally understood, and as we believe it was intended to be understood in the statutes under consideration. [Citation.]

Noting that the perforated rolls were parts of a machine which, when duly applied and properly operated in connection with the mechanism to which they were adopted, produced musical tones in harmonious combination, the Supreme Court concluded that they were not "copies" within the meaning of the copyright act then in existence.

Congress in the 1909 Act implicitly adopted the *White-Smith* definition of "copy". [Citation.] Thus, since the ROM is not in a form which one can "see and read" with the naked eye, it is not a "copy" within the meaning of the 1909 Act. In its object phase, the ROM, the computer program is a mechanical tool or a machine part but it is not a "copy" of the source program.[9]

Dicta in *Synercom Technology, Inc. v. University Computing Co.*, 462 F.Supp. 1003 (N.D.Tex.1978), supports this conclusion. There suit was brought for copyright infringement of instruction manuals and input formats used with a computer program designed to solve engineering problems incident to the analysis of building structures.[10] The plaintiff argued that the sequencing and ordering of data was the expression of an idea, not the idea. After rejecting this argument, the court observed that

---

8. A piano roll is a perforated roll of music used in connection with player pianos.

9. A structure is not a copy of the architectural plans upon which the structure is based under the 1909 Act, as at common law. [Citation.] Thus, the conclusion that the ROM is not a "copy" of the source program under the

1909 Act could be supported on that ground also.

10. In using a computer program, it is necessary to have a format for input so that the input of data and the instruction to the computer are compatible with its program. *Synercom Technology, Inc. v. University Computing Co.*, 462 F.Supp. at 1005.

the formulation of the problem [to be solved] in sufficient detail and with sufficient precision to enable it to be converted into an unambiguous set of computer instructions requires substantial imagination, creativity, independent thought, and exercise of discretion, and the resulting program can in no way be said to be merely a copy or version of the problem statement. The program and the statement are so different, both in physical characteristics and in intended purpose, that they are really two different expressions of the same idea, rather than two different versions of the same expression. [Citation.]

Even assuming that the ROM in plaintiff's CompuChess was copied by defendants JS&A, Sugarman and Stanke, the ROM is not a "copy" of plaintiff's computer program and therefore the copying is not actionable. Since a complete defense as a matter of law with respect to plaintiff's claim of copyright infringement exists, the motion of defendants JS&A, Sugarman and Stanke for summary judgment is granted on Count I of the First Amended Complaint.[11]

In Count II of the First Amended Complaint, it is alleged that defendants JS&A, Sugarman and Stanke have engaged in unfair trade practices and unfair competition against plaintiff by importing, distributing, selling, marketing and advertising as its own copies of plaintiff's ROM. [Footnote.] Although the facts are undisputed, defendants JS&A, Sugarman and Stanke have not shown that they are entitled to judgment as a matter of law.

While the rule may once have been otherwise, unfair competition is not confined to the passing off of the goods of one for those of another and the "palming off" theory is no longer the sole and exclusive criterion in determining the right to relief against unfair competition. There may be unfair competition by misappropriation as well as by misrepre-

sentation, that is, the doctrine of unfair competition has been extended to permit the granting of relief in cases where there was no fraud on the public but where one, for commercial advantage, has misappropriated the benefit or property right of another and has exploited a competitor's business values. [Citations.]

* * *

Cases in Illinois indicate that the doctrine of unfair competition has been extended in Illinois to permit relief where one for commercial advantage has misappropriated the property of another. [Citation.] Since the court does not know exactly how the ROM in the JS&A Chess Computer was created,[14] it cannot determine at this time whether defendants' actions constituted unfair competition. Since the undisputed facts presently before the court do not establish that defendants JS&A, Sugarman and Stanke are entitled to judgment as a matter of law, their motion for summary judgment is denied on Count II of the First Amended Complaint.

In order to obtain a preliminary injunction to restrain the unfair competition of defendants JS&A, Sugarman and Stanke, plaintiff must establish a reasonable probability of success on the merits, irreparable injury, the lack of serious adverse effects on others, and sufficient public interest. [Citation.] Here plaintiff has failed to establish any of these four factors.

Firstly, plaintiff has not established that there is a reasonable probability of success on its claim of unfair competition because it can only speculate as to how the ROM in the CompuChess was duplicated. [Footnote.] Thus, at this point in time, the court is unable to determine that there is a substantial likelihood that plaintiff will prevail on the merits.

---

11. Since defendants JS&A, Sugarman and Stanke have a complete defense as a matter of law with respect to plaintiff's claim of copyright infringement, plaintiff's motion for a preliminary injunction to restrain these defendants from infringing plaintiff's copyright is denied.

14. Plaintiff and defendants JS&A, Sugarman and Stanke have stipulated that General Instruments Corporation produces and manufactures the ROM contained in the JS&A Chess Computer, that JS&A obtains the ROM from defendant Novag Industries, Ltd., a foreign corporation with its principal place of business in Hong Kong, and that in May of 1978 General Instruments Corporation manufactured the ROM from a punched paper tape re-

ceived from ASTEC, a Hong Kong company. Plaintiff and defendants JS&A, Sugarman and Stanke speculate that the ROM in plaintiff's CompuChess was unloaded (*i.e.*, plaintiff's ROM was removed from the CompuChess and installed in a computer interface which decoded the ROM). Once the computer had the complete decoding of the ROM, they speculate that either a computer printout could have been furnished to someone who could have made a ROM identical to plaintiff's ROM or that the information from the computer could have been dumped onto a programmable read only memory ("PROM") which could have been furnished to a ROM manufacturer who could have made a ROM containing plaintiff's computer program.

Secondly, plaintiff has failed to show that it will be irreparably harmed if the injunction does not issue. Plaintiff contends that if a preliminary injunction does not issue, it will suffer lost profits, other damages and injury to its good will and business reputation. However, plaintiff has an adequate remedy at law if it has suffered lost profits and other money damages as a result of the actions of defendants JS&A, Sugarman and Stanke. Plaintiff's conclusory statements that its reputation and good will have been damaged do not establish that plaintiff has been irreparably harmed.[16]

Thirdly, the threatened injury to plaintiff may not outweigh the threatened harm to defendants JS&A, Sugarman and Stanke if they are enjoined from reproducing, importing, distributing, selling, marketing and advertising the JS&A Chess Computer. The injury to plaintiff if the preliminary injunction does not issue is a decrease in sales while the injury to defendants JS&A, Sugarman and Stanke if the preliminary injunction does issue is an elimination of sales altogether.

Finally, plaintiff has not convinced the court that the public interest will be served if a preliminary injunction issues. Generally, the public interest is served by freedom of trade and business competition. Absent a showing as to exactly how the ROM in the Compu-Chess was duplicated, this court does not believe it is in the public interest to enjoin defendants JS&A, Sugarman and Stanke from reproducing, importing, distributing, selling, marketing and advertising the JS&A Chess Computer. Therefore, plaintiff's motion for a preliminary injunction to restrain the unfair competition of defendants JS&A, Sugarman and Stanke is denied.

Accordingly, the motion of plaintiff for a preliminary injunction is denied and the motion of defendants JS&A, Sugarman and Stanke for summary judgment is granted on Count I of the First Amended Complaint and is denied on Count II of the First Amended Complaint.

It is so ordered.

DATA CASH SYSTEMS, INC. v. JS&A GROUP, INC.

628 F.2d 1038
(United States Court of Appeals, Seventh Circuit, Sept. 2, 1980.)

NICHOLS, A. J.

This is an appeal from an order of the district court denying plaintiff's motion for a preliminary injunction and granting defendants' motion for summary judgment on Count I of plaintiff's complaint, a claim of copyright infringement. We affirm the result of the district court, but we do so on different grounds. Proceedings on Count II of plaintiff's complaint, a claim of unfair competition, are suspended pending resolution of this appeal.

* * *

Turning to the merits on appeal, we summarize the facts of this case. In 1976, plaintiff contracted with D. B. Goodrich and Associates for the creation of a computer program for a computer chess game. During 1976 and 1977, D. B. Goodrich developed such a program called the "Chess One–Move Calculation" (Program).

The program developed for plaintiff was capable of receiving the player's instructions, determining the computer's possible legal moves, choosing among the permissible moves in accordance with tactical principles, and displaying the computer's move. All of the above could be performed at six different levels of expertise. Needless to say, the development of the "Chess One–Move Calculation" involved considerable human time, effort, and ingenuity.

Typically, a computer program evolves through several stages of development before reaching its final form. Initially, the programmer develops a "flow chart," a schematic representation of the program logic. The next step is to render those instructions into a "source code," a programming language such as FORTRAN or COBOL. The source program is then translated into an assembly language or machine language, a series of "ones" and "zeros."

---

16. The only damages that plaintiff specifically alleges are the decrease in plaintiff's sales since defendants JS&A, Sugarman and Stanke began marketing the JS&A Chess Computer and the refusal of plaintiff's distributors to renew their orders due to competition from defendant JS&A.

Finally, the program is stored in some mechanical medium such as magnetic tape or disk. In this case the final storage medium was in the form of Read–Only–Memory chips (ROM). The ROM is a silicon chip which has been chemically imprinted with tiny switches, an assembly language "one" becoming a connection and a "zero" becoming the absence of a connection.

General Instruments Corporation manufactured the ROM's for plaintiff and they were electrically integrated into plaintiff's game. Marketing of plaintiff's game, CompuChess, began in the fall of 1977 and continued successfully into 1978.

In June of 1978, it came to the attention of plaintiff that a Hong Kong company claimed to be licensed to sell CompuChess at a lower price. Plaintiff learned from General Instruments that it was manufacturing a ROM for another chess game. At plaintiff's request, General Instruments tested the new ROM and found it to be identical to plaintiff's. Upon further inquiry, plaintiff learned that the other chess game was using a ROM made by General Instruments and was being manufactured by Novag Industries of Hong Kong for JS&A Industries to be marketed as JS&A Computer Chess.

Plaintiff's attempts followed to prevent the manufacture and marketing of JS&A Computer Chess. These efforts were unsuccessful.

In late 1978, JS&A began marketing its computer chess. Shortly thereafter, plaintiff filed this suit for copyright infringement and unfair competition. Defendants moved for summary judgment on both counts of plaintiff's petition on April 13, 1979.

The district court granted the motion for summary judgment for defendants on the grounds that the ROM was not a "copy" under the copyright law so that reproduction of the ROM could not be an infringement. The parties had neither briefed nor argued that issue and neither side on appeal defends the district court's position, so we do not consider it further. The parties focused their arguments in the district court and on appeal to whether the program had entered the public domain prior to the duplication, such that plaintiff's copyright had been forfeited. The prevailing party in the lower court may rely on any ground that supports the decision. [Citations.] Since

we find the forfeiture issue dispositive, we do not reach the merits of the district court's decision.

There seems to be no dispute regarding the facts relevant to the issue of whether the program entered the public domain prior to duplication by defendants. The program, in the form of the ROM, was integrated into the CompuChess game, was distributed, and was sold to the general public without restriction in 1977. Over 2,500 CompuChess games were sold that year. Nowhere on the ROM, the game board, the packaging, or the accompanying instructions was there copyright notice. Plaintiff says it did not know that it was possible to read the program, as defendants did, if one had only the ROM. Defendants point out that a purchaser of the CompuChess who removed the ROM and unloaded its contents so as to see a printout of the program would not see a copyright notice because none was there. Plaintiff does not deny this, stating only that the printed readout copies generated by plaintiff and D. B. Goodrich were imprinted with copyright notice. But these were on internal documents and did not inform the public of plaintiff's claim. It does not seem to be denied that a copyright notice could have been placed in the ROM so that one who read out the game could not miss seeing it, and we understand this is now done. Of course a notice on the game board or the printed instructions would have presented no difficulty. Nonetheless plaintiff contends that the program has not entered the public domain.

The first question for decision is whether the applicable law is the Copyright Act of 1909, Act of March 4, 1909, ch. 320, 35 Stat. 1077 (1909 Act), or the Copyright Act of 1976. This new law, Pub.L.No. 94–553, 17 U.S.C. § 101 and ff, had an effective date January 1, 1978. See "Historical Note" before § 101. Plaintiff contends that the applicable law is the 1976 Act. The basis of plaintiff's argument is that if publication of the program occurred at all, it was not until after January 1, 1978. From this premise, plaintiff argues that under the 1976 Act, plaintiff complied with all notice requirements and that even absent notice, publication would not result in forfeiture. Regardless of the merits of plaintiff's characterization of the effect of the 1976 Act, we find that that Act is inapplicable.

The foundation for plaintiff's assertion that the 1976 Act applies is the fact that there is no evidence that the public had seen a printout of the program before it was sent by Novag Industries to General Instruments Corporation in early 1978. For this reason, they argue that there was no publication in 1977 and that, therefore, their common law copyright survived into 1978. Plaintiff would, of course, recognize that if the program went into the public domain prior to January 1, 1978, no copyright protection would be afforded by the 1976 Act. Furthermore, the determination as to whether a work entered the public domain prior to the effective date of the 1976 Act must be made according to the copyright law, common law and statutory, as it existed prior to the 1976 Act. [Citation.]

While there is some philosophical appeal to plaintiff's contention that the absence of copyright notice is irrelevant until someone doesn't see any notice, a proposition akin to the epistemological query after whether a falling tree makes a sound when there is no one to hear it, we cannot accept plaintiff's assertion. While the 1909 Act did not define "publication," the "date of publication" was defined by section 26 of that Act as " * * * the earliest date when copies of the first authorized edition were placed on sale, sold, or publicly distributed by the proprietor. * * * " Act of March 4, 1909, ch. 320, § 62, 35 Stat. 1087. For example, in *Advisers, Inc. v. Wiesen–Hart, Inc.*, 238 F.2d 706 (6th Cir. 1956), *cert. denied*, 353 U.S. 949, 77 S.Ct. 861, 1 L.Ed.2d 858 (1957), the date of publication was the date of distribution of a book to retailers, not four months later when the retailers actually distributed the books to the public. Thus, the focus would seem to be upon the date when the copyright proprietor sacrificed control of the work such that anyone who wished to view the work could do so, not upon when the public actually viewed the work. Plaintiff's argument would make the time of publication hinge on proof of when some member of the public not only could have viewed the program, but also did in fact view it. In 1977, plaintiff sold over 2,500 CompuChess units to the public without restriction. We do not know whether anyone unloaded the ROM and viewed the program during that year. The point is that plaintiff so gave up control that anyone who wished to do so could have seen

the program in 1977, albeit by a technical process of some complexity. We have concluded that there is no legally significant factual difference between 1977 and 1978 as to the states of affairs relative to the dedication issue. Therefore, the determination as to whether there was, in fact, a dedication is to be determined under the law as it existed prior to the 1976 Act.

Under the 1909 Act, statutory copyright could be obtained by publication with notice. Act of March 4, 1909, ch. 320, § 9, 35 Stat. 1077. Of course publication without notice resulted in forfeiture of the copyright. [Citation.] Plaintiff correctly states, however, that a "limited publication" without notice does not divest the proprietor of copyright. [Citation.] Plaintiff asserts that the public distribution of the CompuChess was, at most, a limited publication.

An oft-quoted formulation of the doctrine of limited publication is found in *White v. Kimmel*, 193 F.2d 744 (9th Cir.), *cert denied*, 343 U.S. 957, 72 S.Ct. 1052, 96 L.Ed. 1357 (1952), stating:

> * * * [A] limited publication which communicates the contents of a manuscript to a definitely selected group and for a limited purpose, and without the right of diffusion, reproduction, distribution or sale, is considered a "limited publication," which does not result in loss of the author's common-law right to his manuscript; but that the circulation must be restricted both as to persons and purpose, or it can not be called a private or limited publication. * * * [Citation.]

There is no question but that had the "Chess One–Move Calculation" been marketed in the form of a manuscript, perhaps for home computer enthusiasts to program into their computers, the program would have entered the public domain. In none of the cases discussed by either side was a limited publication found where distribution of printed copies was as unrestricted in scope as to persons and purpose as was the distribution of the CompuChess. [Citations.]

The only way we could find that plaintiff's distribution of CompuChess was a limited distribution of the program would be to find, as urged by plaintiff, that restrictions are to be implied from the nature of the CompuChess.

The core of plaintiff's argument is that at the time the CompuChess was first marketed it was not known by any of plaintiff's officers that the ROM could be copied without obtaining a printout from the plaintiff. They unfortunately relied, as they admit, on their assumption that the ROM was not susceptible of being copied. It is further stressed that plaintiff, upon learning of this possibility, took all reasonable steps to prevent duplication and to inform others of plaintiff's claim. Finally, plaintiff asserts that defendants were not misled by the absence of copyright notice.

In response to plaintiff's assertion that plaintiff did not know that the ROM could be copied directly, it need only be said that dedication is a question of law, not the intent of the proprietor. [Citations.] As to plaintiff's efforts to notify defendants and others of plaintiff's claim, these efforts not only were subsequent to the program's entry into the public domain, but also followed the alleged infringement. Finally, there is no evidence supporting plaintiff's assertion that defendants were not misled by the absence of copyright notice. Furthermore, absence of copyright notice was fatal under the 1909 Act whether or not anyone was misled thereby. [Citation.]

It must be borne in mind that a "limited publication" is really in the eyes of the law no publication at all. Without publication, under the 1909 Act the statutory durational limitations would not start to run. As long as there was no publication, a common law copyright of unlimited duration would be available. Furthermore, statutory copyright limitations would continue to be available to plaintiff at any time plaintiff decided to publish with notice, the time of statutory protection only then starting to run. If the acts the plaintiff admits to effected this result, plaintiff has its cake and eats it too. This would be inconsistent with one of the principles at the heart of copyright law, " * * * [i]n order to induce the author to disclose his work to the public notwithstanding the resulting loss of his common law protection, the statute substitutes new rights, albeit limited in time." A. Latman, the Copyright Law: Howell's Copyright Law Revisited 112 (5th ed. 1979). We conclude that the concept of "limited publication" is not here applicable.

Finally, plaintiff contends that even if there was publication without notice, the absence of notice is excused under section 21 of the 1909 Act. That section provided, in part:

Where the copyright proprietor has sought to comply with the provisions of this title with respect to notice, the omission by accident or mistake of the prescribed notice from a particular copy or copies shall not invalidate the copyright.
* * *

Even if we were to agree with plaintiff that the erroneous belief that the program could not be copied directly from the ROM was the sort of "mistake" contemplated by section 21, we cannot agree that the omission of notice was from a "particular copy or copies" of the program. In no case cited by plaintiff or encountered in our research has section 21 of the 1909 Act been found to prevent divestiture where notice was totally absent from all public copies of a work. Plaintiff cites *Monogram Models, Inc. v. Industro Motive Corp.*, 492 F.2d 1281 (6th Cir.), *cert. denied*, 419 U.S. 843, 95 S.Ct. 76, 42 L.Ed.2d 71 (1974), where model airplane kits were sold without notice affixed to the airplane parts. However, copyright notice did appear on the instruction sheets and containers. In *Herbert Rosenthal Jewelry Corp. v. Grossbardt*, 428 F.2d 551 (2d Cir. 1970), section 21 was held to prevent forfeiture where only five of three hundred pins were marketed with copyright notice obliterated. By contrast, section 21 does not prevent forfeiture where, as here, notice was omitted from all copies. [Citations.]

Plaintiff is not in the position of one the statute in section 21 sought to protect. It did not make an effort to comply and fail, through inadvertence or mistake, to comply completely. It made no effort to comply because it thought it was physically impossible to make a copy. It might, but did not, have provided a notice in case its assumption as to the technical limitations of others proved incorrect. Reliance on a more backward state of the art than the facts would have justified is not a covered case. We cannot award the defendants any accolades for their ethics, but this is not the statutory standard. The arts of the copyist, and his technical resources, were continually advancing in 1909, and have continued since. If Congress had meant to provide that notice would be unnecessary whenever the copyist's techniques were subjectively deemed inadequate to make a copy, it would have said so. We cannot supply the omission.

In conclusion, for the reasons discussed in this opinion, we affirm the district court's grant of summary judgment for defendants and denial of plaintiff's request for injunctive relief. The case is remanded for proceedings on Count II of the complaint.

TANDY CORP. v. PERSONAL MICRO COMPUTERS, INC.

524 F. Supp. 171

(United States District Court, N. D. California, Aug. 31, 1981.)

PECKHAM, C. J.

Plaintiff has sued defendants, stating five causes of action: (1) copyright infringement; (2) unfair competition under federal law, pursuant to 15 U.S.C. § 1125; (3) unfair competition under state law, pursuant to Calif. Business and Prof. Code § 17200 *et seq.*; (4) assumpsit; and (5) interference with prospective advantage (unjust enrichment). The dispute centers around the alleged duplication of a computer program for which the copyright is held by the plaintiff.

Defendants moved to dismiss all of the claims for relief. Their papers, however, focused almost exclusively on the first claim, copyright infringement. They made virtually no attempt to argue their motion as to the other four claims for relief. At the hearing on the motions, the court indicated that it was prepared to deny the motion as it related to counts two through five of the complaint, and counsel for the defendant indicated that they would withdraw the motion as to those four counts. The court will therefore address only the first count of the complaint.

Tandy Corporation, the plaintiff, is the manufacturer of the Radio Shack TRS–80, which is a computer designed for home use. This computer includes what is called an "input-output routine." This is a computer program which tells the computer how to take the information which is put into the computer by an operator in one computer language and translate that information into a more simplified "machine" language which the computer can understand. For obvious reasons, this program is crucial to the operation of the computer, and it is this program which is the subject of the lawsuit. Plaintiff claims that defendants copied that program from the TRS–80, changing only certain items which

specifically identify the program as "Radio Shack" or "Tandy," and then used it in their own computer designed for home use, called the PMC–80.

The basis of this motion to dismiss stems from the method by which this program is placed into and stored in the computer. The technology of computers has reached the point where programs can be imprinted directly onto silicon chips. Those chips are then permanently wired into the computer. This type of information storage is called "Read Only Memory" or "ROM." The defendants contend that ROM chips are not "copies" of the original computer program within the meaning of the federal copyright laws, and that therefore a ROM chip which is a copy of another ROM chip does not infringe the copyright covering the original program. The plaintiff disputes that claim, suggesting that this form of fixation was covered at the relevant time by the copyright laws.

There is no dispute that the court is to initially look to the Copyright Act which was passed by Congress in 1976 and went into effect on January 1, 1978. [Citation.] Looking first to sections 101 and 102 of that Act, 17 U.S.C. § 101, § 102, the court is convinced that under those provisions (1) a computer program is a "work of authorship" subject to copyright, and (2) that a silicon chip is "tangible medium of expression," within the meaning of the statute, such as to make a program fixed in that form subject to the copyright laws.

There can be little doubt that computer programs themselves are among the "works of authorship" covered by the Copyright Act. In fact, the legislative history indicates that Congress understood that computer programs were subject to copyright protection under the law as it existed prior to the 1976 act, as well as under the new statute. [Citation.] The defendants do not appear to dispute this point. Moreover, the statute itself states that works can be "fixed" in "any tangible medium of expression, now known or later developed, from which they can be perceived, reproduced, or otherwise communicated, *either directly or with the aid of a machine or device.*" 17 U.S.C. § 102(a) (emphasis added). If any doubt is left by the wording of the statute, the legislative history makes clear the all-inclusive nature of the definition of "fixed" form:

Under the bill it makes no difference what the form, manner or medium of fixation may be—whether it is in words, numbers, notes, sounds, pictures, or any other graphic or symbolic indicia, whether embodied in a physical object in written, printed, photographic, sculptural, punched, magnetic, or other stable form, and whether it is capable of perception directly or by means of any machine or device "now known or later developed."

[Citation.] The imprinting of a computer program on a silicon chip, which then allows the computer to read the program and act upon its instructions, falls easily within this definition. *But see Data Cash Systems, Inc. v. JS&A Group, Inc.*, 480 F.Supp. 1063, 1066 n.4 (N.D.Ill.1979) (stating in dicta that under the 1976 copyright act, the duplication of a ROM would not be actionable), *affirmed on other grounds*, 628 F.2d 1038 (7th Cir. 1980).

If this was the end of the matter, the court would have no difficulty in resolving the question. However, the 1976 act also contained a section which stated,

Notwithstanding the provisions of sections 106 through 116 and 118, this title does not afford to the owner of copyright in a work any greater or lesser rights with respect to the use of the work in conjunction with automatic systems capable of storing, processing, retrieving, or transferring information, or in conjunction with any similar device, machine, or process, than those afforded to works under the law, whether title 17 or the common law or statutes of a State, in effect on December 31, 1977, as held applicable and construed by a court in an action brought under this title.

[Citation.] Defendants contend that this language requires this court to apply the law as it existed prior to January 1, 1978 to determine whether the ROM chip was a "copy" within the meaning of the copyright laws. Under the law of *White-Smith Publishing Co. v. Apollo*, 209 U.S. 1, 28 S.Ct. 319, 52 L.Ed. 655 (1908), the defendants assert that it cannot be so considered. Plaintiff, on the other hand, argues that section 117 does not require the application of the pre-1978 law to determine whether the ROM chip is a "copy." Moreover, it argues that the evidence developed to date suggests the possibility that the defendants made their copy of the ROM chip by copying a visual or printed display of the program, and

then imprinting it on the chip. Finally, the plaintiff argues that the pre-1978 copyright law would allow this court to find that the ROM chip was a "copy" within the meaning of that law. Because the court is persuaded by the plaintiff's first two assertions, there is no reason for it to reach the last issue.

First, section 117 makes clear on its face that its direction to apply pre-1978 law is not to apply to sections 101 and 102 of the act, which, as previously noted, clearly allows a program in this form to be copyrighted and protected. The legislative history confirms this interpretation. [Citation.] Section 117 modified only sections 106 through 116 and 118, which are the sections concerned with the scope of copyright protection. Defendants correctly pointed out in their papers that it would "not make any logical sense" to suggest that Congress meant, by enacting section 117, to allow computer programs fixed in this manner to be copyrighted, but to then not afford them any protection. [Reference.] The court, however, does not agree with defendants' conclusion therefrom that the court is to look to pre-1978 law, and not to sections 101 and 102 of the 1976 act, to determine whether the ROM chip is a "copy." Instead, the court is convinced that the Congress was only addressing itself in section 117 of the 1976 act to the problems surrounding the input into computers of properly obtained copyrighted materials.

The legislative history and the subsequent revision of section 117 clearly indicates that the Congress was concerned with the issue of the rights of a copyright holder when copyrighted material is inputted into a computer. The House Report indicates that the Congress was uncertain what to do about "computer *uses* of copyrighted works." [Emphasis added.] [Citation.] Moreover, when the section was revised in 1980, the new language defined the extent to which a computer program could be inputted into a computer system by a rightful owner of a copy of the program. [Citation.] Most importantly, the actual language of the original section 117 refers to use of copyrighted material "in conjunction with" computer-type systems.

All of this evidence convinces the court that section 117, as it existed in the 1976 act, was aimed at the problem of copyrighted material inputted into a computer, such as books, magazines, and even computer programs. It was not intended to provide a loophole by which someone could duplicate a computer program fixed on a silicon chip. It did not refer to the unauthorized duplication of a silicon chip upon which a properly copyrighted computer program is imprinted. Such a *duplication* of a chip is not the use of a copyrighted program "in conjunction with" a computer; it is simply the copying of a chip. Moreover, any other interpretation would render the theoretical ability to copyright computer programs virtually meaningless. [Citation.]

The court recognizes that another district court has held differently. *Data Cash Systems, Inc. v. JS&A Group, Inc.*, 480 F.Supp. 1063 (N.D.Ill.1979). However, the Court of Appeals, in considering the same case, noted that neither side had briefed or argued the matter based on the reasoning of the district court, and it explicitly stated that it was not passing on the merits of the district court's ruling. [Citation.] Moreover, it is arguable that the basis upon which the Seventh Circuit affirmed the lower court's decision requires implicitly the rejection of the reasoning relied on by the district judge. [Citation.] This court is not compelled to follow the reasoning of the district court in Illinois, nor are we convinced of the merits of the basis of that decision.

There is an additional reason for rejecting this motion to dismiss. Whatever the merits of the defendants' argument concerning the direct duplication of the silicon chip, the plaintiff has suggested that the evidence may well show that the chip was duplicated by first taking a visual display or printout of the program in question, making a copy of that display or printout, and then having that program imprinted onto a silicon chip. This theory of duplication falls within the pleading of the complaint, which simply indicates that the program imprinted on the plaintiff's ROM chip is duplicated on the defendants' ROM chip. If this method of unauthorized duplication in fact is proved, there can be no doubt that the unauthorized duplication of a visually displayed copy of the program would fall within the reach of the federal copyright laws.

Therefore, for both these reasons, the motion to dismiss is denied.

So ordered.

STERN ELECTRONICS, INC. v. KAUFMAN

523 F. Supp. 635

(United States District Court, E. D. New York, May 22, 1981.)

NICKERSON, D. J.

On November 25, 1980 plaintiff Stern Electronics, Inc. (Stern) filed a complaint alleging that defendants infringed plaintiff's copyrights in its electronic video games "Kamikaze" and "Astro Invaders" by selling a virtually identical video game, "Zygon." On January 19, 1981, following a hearing on Stern's motion for a preliminary injunction, defendants consented to the entry of an order preliminarily enjoining them from infringing plaintiff's copyrights in "Kamikaze" and "Astro Invaders," and instructing them to deliver to the court for impoundment all "Zygon" games under their control.

On April 23, 1981 Stern filed an order to show cause seeking leave to file a supplemental complaint asserting new claims for copyright infringement and false designation of origin against defendants regarding the electronic video game "Scramble." Stern also sought a preliminary injunction to stop defendants from infringing plaintiff's copyright in "Scramble" and from using its "Scramble" trademark.

On May 6, 1981 defendant Omni Video Games, Inc. ("Omni") filed a complaint in the United States District Court for the District of Rhode Island alleging that Stern Electronics, Inc. ("Stern") was infringing Omni's common law trademark rights in the mark "Scramble." On May 8, 1981 Omni moved for preliminary injunctive relief in that case. That motion is apparently still pending.

On May 18, 1981, just prior to the hearing in this court on Stern's motion, defendants filed a cross-motion requesting relief identical to that requested in the District Court for Rhode Island. Stern then filed an order to show cause seeking to restrain Omni from prosecuting its motion for a preliminary injunction in Rhode Island pending final determination of the motion before this court.

I.

Late in 1980 a Japanese corporation, Konami Industry Co., Ltd. ("Konami") devised a new electronic video game named "Scramble." The work was first published in Japan on January 8, 1981 and first came to Stern's attention early that same month at the Amusement Trade Exhibit in London, England. On January 27, 1981 Konami granted an exclusive license to distribute "Scramble" in North and South America to Universe Affiliated International, Inc. ("Universe"), a New Jersey corporation, which simultaneously granted an exclusive sub-license to Stern. Stern began selling "Scramble" in the United States on March 17, 1981.

A Certificate of Copyright Registration for the audiovisual work "Scramble" was issued to Konami on April 14, 1981 by the United States Copyright Office. Documents reciting the exclusive license to Universe and the exclusive sub-license to Stern were recorded with the Copyright Office on April 16, 1981.

Around December 1, 1980 defendant Frank Gaglione, President of Omni, ordered ten silk screen name plates bearing the name "Scramble" from BCA Poster Co. Omni received the name plates on December 15, 1980 and on December 23 began to sell its "Space Guerilla," "Space Carrier," and "Rally-X" video games with headboards bearing the "Scramble" name plates. The invoices indicate that five games were sold before March 17, 1981 bearing the "Scramble" name plate.

Sometime in April 1981, defendant Omni began to sell a video game called "Scramble 2," which, according to Stern, is substantially similar in its audiovisual presentation to Stern's "Scramble." Stern claims that Omni's sale of this game after April 16, 1981 infringes Stern's copyright.

II.

The pattern of conduct alleged in plaintiff's supplemental complaint concerning the electronic video game "Scramble" is similar to that alleged in the original complaint concerning "Kamikaze" and "Astro Invaders." Plaintiff is granted leave to file the supplemental complaint.

III.

For this court to issue a preliminary injunction "there must be a showing of possible irreparable injury *and* either (1) probable suc-

cess on the merits *or* (2) sufficiently serious questions going to the merits to make them a fair ground for litigation *and* a balance of hardship tipping decidedly toward the party requesting the preliminary relief." *Caulfield v. Board of Education of City of New York,* 583 F.2d 605, 610 (2d Cir. 1978) (emphasis in original). "In copyright cases, however, if probable success—a prima facie case of copyright infringement—can be shown, the allegations of irreparable injury need not be very detailed, because such injury can normally be presumed when a copyright is infringed." *Wainwright Securities, Inc. v. Wall Street Transcript Corp.,* 558 F.2d 91, 94 (2d Cir. 1977), *cert. denied,* 434 U.S. 1014, 98 S.Ct. 730, 54 L.Ed.2d 759 (1978).

A. Irreparable Injury

Stern has more than met its burden of showing irreparable injury. "Scramble" is one of the most popular video games ever sold; sales since March 1981 total about twenty million dollars. Counterfeit models (or "knock-ups" as they are known in the industry) can invade this market by selling video games identical to "Scramble" for approximately $650 less per game. Knock-ups pose a substantial threat to the health of the electronic video game industry. Development of a new game requires substantial investment and takes between eight months to a year. However, little expense, time, or initiative is required to reproduce a game's programmed memory. Preliminary injunctive relief is the only effective means of protecting a copyright in a video game since the life span of a successful game is merely six months. If knock-ups dilute a copyright's profitability during that period, a final adjudication in favor of the copyright owner will do him little good. The court finds a strong likelihood of irreparable injury if interlocutory relief is denied.

B. Probable Success on the Merits

If there is a likelihood of irreparable injury, a preliminary injunction is warranted if Stern can show probable success on the merits in its claim of copyright infringement. To prove copyright infringement, Stern must show that it owned a copyright in the audiovisual display in the "Scramble" video game and that Omni copied that display.

1. Ownership of the Copyright. Stern owns a copyright in the "Scramble" audiovisual display if the statutory formalities were complied with in registering for a copyright, the display is an original work of authorship, and the subject matters are "fixed in any tangible medium of expression, now known or later developed, from which they can be perceived, reproduced, or otherwise communicated, either directly or with the aid of a machine or device." 17 U.S.C. §§ 102, 411, 412.

There is no dispute that plaintiff has satisfied the statutory formalities in applying for the copyright. Nor is there any serious dispute that the subject matter is fixed in a computer program stored in a memory device which, by the aid of circuitry, a cathode ray tube, and speakers, can continually reproduce the audiovisual display.

Defendants, however, argue that the "Scramble" audiovisual display is not an original work of authorship. The burden of proving that the audiovisual work is not original falls on the defendants because the Certificate of Registration constitutes prima facie evidence of the validity of the copyright and of the facts stated in the certificate. 17 U.S.C. § 410(c).

Defendants point out that Stern has registered the audiovisual material contained in a videotape and has not registered the underlying computer program which dictates and controls the images and sounds contained in the audiovisual display. Defendants argue that the audiovisual material is not original since it is totally dependent upon the memory device and the underlying computer program. The only original work of authorship, they claim, lies in the computer program, and this has not been registered.

However, copyright protection exists for original "motion pictures and other audiovisual works." 17 U.S.C. § 102(a)(6). " 'Audiovisual works' are works that consist of a series of related images which are intrinsically intended to be shown by the use of machines or devices such as projectors, viewers, or electronic equipment, together with accompanying sounds, if any, regardless of the nature of the material objects, such as films or tapes, in

which the works are embodied." 17 U.S.C. § 101. Stern's video game, "Scramble," falls within this definition, and presents on a screen a series of images projected by a cathode ray tube which depicts a spaceship simultaneously trying to navigate a mountainous airspace, destroy enemy fuel depots, evade deadly ground fire, and prevail in an aerial dogfight, while at the same time watching carefully over a diminishing fuel supply. In essence, the work is a movie in which the viewer participates in the action as the fearless pilot controlling the spaceship.

The popularity of a video game depends on the creativity of its audiovisual display, not on the form of its computer program. Indeed, a potential customer does not care about the computer program except insofar as it affects the audiovisual display.

While the audiovisual display emanates from the computer program, it is senseless to say that therefore the display is not original. An author's work does not become any less original after he has found a means to replicate it.

An audiovisual display is an appropriate subject for a copyright even if the underlying computer program is not copyrighted. The program and the display are quite separate in form and function. The identical audiovisual display may be created from many different computer programs, and a slightly modified computer program may produce a wholly different audiovisual display.

In sum, this court finds that Stern will probably succeed on the merits in showing that it owned a copyright in the audiovisual display of its "Scramble" video game.

2. Copying of a Copyrighted Work. Since it is often difficult to prove by direct evidence that defendant copied a plaintiff's copyrighted work, courts have permitted a finding of copying from evidence that the defendant had access to the copyrighted work and that defendant's work is substantially similar to plaintiff's. [Citation.] Here, Stern has shown access and substantial similarity, and defendants have made no claim of independent creation.

It is undisputed that defendants had access to plaintiff's "Scramble" video game. Gaglione testified that he purchased a "Scramble" video game from a distributor for Omni's corporate purposes.

At the hearing, this court viewed a videotape of plaintiff's "Scramble" and defendants' "Scramble 2." The sequence of images and sounds that appears on the screen when the game has started—the "play mode"—is virtually identical in the two games. The sequence of images that appears on the screen when the game is not being played—the "attract mode"—is slightly different. The Omni game's attract mode uses different wording than Stern's and begins in a different phase. These differences in the attract mode certainly indicate that the games are not identical, but the two games are substantially similar.

The heart of the audiovisual work is the play mode. That is the actual game. The customer pays a quarter to participate in the simulated space battle. The attract mode is merely advertising, designed to attract the bystander to the game and entice him to play it. Even if the attract mode were totally different in the two games, the copying of the play mode would still constitute a copyright infringement. "[I]t is enough that substantial parts were lifted; no plagiarist can excuse the wrong by showing how much of his work he did not pirate." *Sheldon v. Metro-Goldwyn Pictures Corp.*, 81 F.2d 49, 56 (2d Cir.) (L.Hand, J.), *cert. denied*, 298 U.S. 669, 56 S.Ct. 835, 80 L.Ed. 1392 (1936).

This court finds that Stern will probably succeed in showing that defendants copied its audiovisual work in the video game "Scramble," and, consequently, that Stern is entitled to preliminary injunctive relief for copyright infringement.

III. [sic]

Stern and defendants have also moved and cross-moved under 15 U.S.C. § 1125(a) for a preliminary injunction ordering each other to stop infringing their purported trademark in the name "Scramble." Neither plaintiff nor defendants has a registered trademark in the name "Scramble." Each claims that it possesses an exclusive common law trademark in the name.

In deciding whether there has been trademark infringement the court must first determine whether "Scramble" is a distinctive

mark worthy of trademark protection. The word "scramble" has many meanings. In everyday language, it means "to climb or move quickly using one's hands and feet," or "to compete or struggle with others for possession or gain," or "to move in hasty urgency." *The Random House Dictionary of the English Language* 1282 (1967). In military terminology, the word refers to an order to pilots to take off quickly to intercept approaching enemy planes. *Id.*

The word "scramble" is not a valid trademark if it is merely descriptive of the characteristics of the video game and has not acquired secondary meaning. But if the word is suggestive of the nature of the game, it is entitled to trademark protection even without acquiring secondary meaning. [Citation.] The distinction between a mark that is descriptive and one that is suggestive is not always crystal clear. However, Judge Weinfeld has developed a useful standard which the Second Circuit has adopted:

> A term is suggestive if it requires imagination, thought and perception to reach a conclusion as to the nature of goods. A term is descriptive if it forthwith conveys an immediate idea of the ingredients, qualities or characteristics of the goods.

Stix Products, Inc. v. United Merchants & Mfrs., Inc., 295 F.Supp. 479, 488 (S.D.N.Y.1968) *quoted in West & Co., Inc. v. Arica Institute, Inc.*, 557 F.2d 338, 342 (2d Cir. 1977).

Under this standard the mark "Scramble" is more suggestive then descriptive. A prospective customer learning that a video game was called "Scramble" would have no "immediate idea" of the characteristics of the game. At most the word would give a hint that the game may involve aircraft intercepting attack planes and engaging in an air battle. Only by applying imagination could the customer visualize the actual nature of the game.

"Scramble" is therefore a valid mark, and question is who has the right to its exclusive use. Generally, the first person to use a mark "obtains an enforceable right to exclude others from using it, as long as the initial appropriation and use are accompanied by an intention to continue exploiting the mark commercially." *La Societe Anonyme des Parfums Le Galion v. Jean Patou, Inc.*, 495 F.2d 1265, 1271 (2d Cir. 1974).

Clearly Omni preceded Stern in using the name "Scramble"; Omni can document its use as of December 23, 1980 while Stern's first use was on March 17, 1981. Before April 1981, however, Omni used the name only on headboards, and the video games stationed beneath those headboards were not called "Scramble." They were older games already present in the Omni inventory called "Space Guerilla," "Space Carrier," and "Rally-X." The video game called "Scramble 2" was not produced by Omni until after Stern had introduced its original version of "Scramble."

Stern contends that Omni's prior use of the mark "Scramble" was not in good faith and that defendants learned of the development of "Scramble" by Konami and decided to appropriate the mark before the game's introduction into the United States. Stern argues that defendants' limited and calculated efforts to appropriate the trademark are shown by the facts that only the headboards were labeled "Scramble" and that only five of these were shipped before March 17, 1981.

"Determining what constitutes sufficient use for trademark ownership purposes is obviously a case-by-case task. * * * [I]t is important to note expressly that the balance of the equities plays an important role in deciding whether defendant's use is sufficient to warrant trademark protection. * * * " La Societe Anonyme des Parfums Le Galion v. Jean Patou, Inc., 495 F.2d at 1274 n. 11. [Citation.]

This court does not find credible the testimony that defendants decided to use the name "Scramble" before they knew that others had plans to market the new game under the same name. Defendants introduced the name "Scramble" by printing it on headboards attached to video games bearing different names. This practice is likely to confuse customers who can fairly expect that the name on the headboard will match the name of the game. Indeed, Stephen Kaufman, Corporate Vice President of Marketing for Stern, testified that, in his seventeen years of experience in the industry, he had never heard of one name being used to label different amusement games. The most likely explanation for this extraordinary marketing decision is that defendants contrived this usage of the mark solely for trade-

mark maintenance purposes in anticipation of plaintiff's introduction of the "Scramble" video game into the market. Such a contrivance cannot constitute the bona fide usage necessary to sustain a common law trademark. [Citations.]

The plausibility of this explanation is bolstered by evidence that Omni only ordered ten "Scramble" name plates on December 1, 1980 and only shipped five video games bearing a "Scramble" headboard before March 17, 1981. Such a sample is too small to provide any meaningful test of the marketability of the "Scramble" trademark.

Moreover, it would be a truly remarkable coincidence if defendants independently thought of the name "Scramble" and then, only a few months later, produced a video game virtually identical to one bearing the same name. It is more likely that defendants sought to appropriate the trademark with the expectation that they would later imitate the audiovisual display.

In sum, while the court recognizes that defendants first used the mark "Scramble," it finds that defendants' use of the mark was not bona fide.

Both sides have moved for preliminary injunctive relief to protect their alleged interests in the mark "Scramble." Thus, the alternatives open to the court are to deny interlocutory relief and permit both sides to use the mark "Scramble," or to bar one side from further use of the mark.

The first alternative is undesirable. Continued use of the mark by both sides is likely to confuse or deceive operators and consumers, causing injury to the litigants and the purchasing public. One side or the other should be entitled to use the mark. The question is which. The question is certainly serious enough to constitute a fair ground for litigation. Interlocutory relief should therefore be afforded to the side to whom the balance of hardships tips decidedly. That side is Stern's.

Stern has invested a substantial amount of money in developing and marketing its electronic video game "Scramble." Ten thousand units have been sold since the game was introduced to the public in March 1981.

If this court were to enjoin Stern from continuing to use the mark, Stern would have to change the name of the game, market it under a new title, and attempt at considerable cost to re-establish the name recognition it built in the industry within the past two months.

Defendants, on the other hand, will be preliminarily enjoined by this order from infringing Stern's copyright by selling their "Scramble 2" video game. Preliminarily enjoining them from using the mark "Scramble" will not require them to change the name of any video game. Rather, it will merely prevent them from using that mark to identify other games. Such a limitation is unlikely to impose a significant hardship on the defendants.

It is therefore ordered that defendants and their agents, representatives, employees, servants, and assigns are enjoined during the pendency of this action from infringing in any manner plaintiff's copyright in the audiovisual work entitled "Scramble." They are also enjoined during the pendency of this action from further use of the mark "Scramble." Defendants are ordered to deliver up to this court, for impounding during the pendency of this action, all of defendants' "Scramble 2" video games or any other copies of plaintiff's "Scramble" audiovisual work that infringe plaintiff's copyright and are under defendants' control.

The foregoing constitutes the court's findings of fact and conclusions of law.

Issuance of this memorandum and order renders moot plaintiff's motion to enjoin defendants from prosecuting Omni's motion for a preliminary injunction in the United States District Court for the District of Rhode Island. So ordered.

STERN ELECTRONICS, INC. v. KAUFMAN

669 F.2d 852

(United States Court of Appeals, Second Circuit, Jan. 20, 1982.)

NEWMAN, C. J.

This appeal from the grant of a preliminary injunction concerns primarily the availability of copyright protection for the visual images electronically displayed by a coin-operated video game of the sort currently enjoying widespread popularity throughout the country. Omni Video Games, Inc., its distributor, and two of its officers appeal from an order entered May 22, 1981 in the District Court for the Eastern District of New York (Eugene H. Nickerson, Judge), preliminarily enjoining them from infringing the copyright of Stern Electronics, Inc. in the audiovisual work entitled "Scramble" and from making further use of the trademark "SCRAMBLE" in connection with electronic video games. 523 F.Supp. 635. Appellants contend that the visual images and accompanying sounds of the video game fail to satisfy the fixation and originality requirements of the Copyright Act, 17 U.S.C.App. § 102(a) (1976), and that they, rather than appellees, have superior rights to the mark "SCRAMBLE". We reject these contentions and affirm the preliminary injunction.

Video games like "Scramble" can roughly be described as computers programmed to create on a television screen cartoons in which some of the action is controlled by the player. In Stern's "Scramble," for example, the video screen displays a spaceship moving horizontally through six different scenes in which obstacles are encountered. With each scene the player faces increasing difficulty in traversing the course and scoring points. The first scene depicts mountainous terrain, missile bases, and fuel depots. The player controls the altitude and speed of the spaceship, decides when to release the ship's supply of bombs, and fires lasers that can destroy attacking missiles and aircraft. He attempts to bomb the missile bases (scoring points for success), bomb the fuel depots (increasing his own diminishing fuel supply with each hit), avoid the missiles being fired from the ground, and avoid crashing his ship into the mountains. And that is only scene one. In subsequent scenes the hazards include missile-firing enemy aircraft and tunnel-like airspaces. The scenes are in color, and the action is accompanied by battlefield sounds.

The game is built into a cabinet containing a cathode ray tube, a number of electronic circuit boards, a loudspeaker, and hand controls for the player. The electronic circuitry includes memory storage devices called PROMs, an acronym for "programmable read only memory."[1] The PROM stores the instructions and data from a computer program in such a way that when electric current passes through the circuitry, the interaction of the program stored in the PROM with the other components of the game produces the sights and sounds of the audiovisual display that the player sees and hears. The memory devices determine not only the appearance and movement of the images but also the variations in movement in response to the player's operation of the hand controls.

Stern manufactures amusement equipment, including video games, for distribution worldwide. In January 1981 at a London trade exhibit Stern became aware of "Scramble," an electronic video game developed in late 1980 by a Japanese corporation, Konami Industry Co., Ltd. The audiovisual display constituting what Stern alleges is the copyrightable work was first published in Japan on January 8, 1981. Stern secured an exclusive sub-license to distribute the "Scramble" game in North and South America from Konami's exclusive licensee, and began selling the game in the United States on March 17, 1981. Even in the fast-paced world of video games, "Scramble" quickly became a big success. Approximately 10,000 units were sold at about $2,000 each in the first two months for an initial sales volume of about $20 million.

On April 14, 1981, a Certificate of Copyright Registration for the audiovisual work "Scramble" was issued to Konami by the United States Copyright Office, and shortly thereafter documents were filed with the Copyright Office reflecting the license and sub-license to Stern. To satisfy the statutory requirement for deposit of copies of a work to be copyrighted, 17 U.S.C.App. § 408(b) (1976), Konami submitted video tape recordings of the "Scramble" game, both in its "attract mode" and in its "play mode."[2]

Omni alleges that, concurrently with Stern's sales of the "Scramble" game and even earlier, it was endeavoring to sell a line of video game products so constructed that each unit could be equipped for playing different games by substituting a PROM containing the program for a particular game. Omni contends that it planned to market this line of interchangeable games with the label "Scramble" affixed to the headboard of each unit; the name of the particular game was also to be prominently displayed. On December 1, 1980, Omni's president ordered ten silk screen name plates bearing the name "Scramble." Between that date and March 17, 1981, the date of Stern's first sale of its "Scramble" game, Omni sold five units of video games bearing the name "Scramble" on the headboard. In April 1981 Omni began to sell a video game called "Scramble" that not only bears the same name as the "Scramble" game Stern was then marketing, but also is virtually identical in both sight and sound. It sold this copy of Stern's "Scramble" game, known in the trade as a "knock-off," for several hundred dollars less than Stern's game.

1. COPYRIGHT ISSUES

In challenging the preliminary injunction that bars distribution of its "Scramble" game, Omni does not dispute that Konami and its sub-licensee Stern are entitled to secure some copyright protection for their "Scramble" game. Omni contends that Konami was entitled to copyright only the written computer program that determines the sights and sounds of the game's audiovisual display.[3] While that approach would have afforded some degree of protection, it would not have prevented a determined competitor from manufacturing a "knock-off" of "Scramble" that replicates precisely the sights and sounds of the game's

---

1. Memory devices of computers are generally either RAM (random access memory) or ROM (read only memory). RAM, used in most sophisticated computers, is a memory device in which stored information can be changed simply by writing in new information that replaces old information. The stored information in a ROM cannot be changed; it is imprinted into the ROM when the device is manufactured. A PROM is a ROM into which information can be imprinted (programmed) after manufacture; once the information is programmed in a PROM, it

cannot be changed simply by writing in a new program. [Citation.]

2. "Attract mode" refers to the audiovisual display seen and heard by a prospective customer contemplating playing the game; the video screen displays some of the essential visual and sound characteristics of the game. "Play mode" refers to the audiovisual display seen and heard by a person playing the game.

3. Written computer programs are copyrightable as literary works. [Citation.]

audiovisual display. This could be done by writing a new computer program that would interact with the hardware components of a video game to produce on the screen the same images seen in "Scramble," accompanied by the same sounds. Such replication is possible because many different computer programs can produce the same "results," whether those results are an analysis of financial records or a sequence of images and sounds. A program is simply "a set of statements [*i.e.*, data] or instructions to be used directly or indirectly in a computer in order to bring about a certain result," Pub.L.No. 96-517, § 10(a), 94 Stat. 3015, 3028 (1980) (amending 17 U.S.C.App. § 101 (1976)). To take an elementary example, the result of displaying a "4" can be achieved by an instruction to add 2 and 2, subtract 3 from 7, or in a variety of other ways. Obviously, writing a new program to replicate the play of "Scramble" requires a sophisticated effort, but it is a manageable task.

To secure protection against the risk of a "knock-off" of "Scramble" based upon an original program, Konami eschewed registration of its program as a literary work and chose instead to register the sights and sounds of "Scramble" as an audiovisual work. *See* 17 U.S.C.App. § 102(a)(6) (1976). The Act defines "audiovisual works" as "works that consist of a series of related images which are intrinsically intended to be shown by the use of machines, or devices such as projectors, viewers, or electronic equipment, together with accompanying sounds, if any, regardless of the nature of the material objects, such as films or tapes, in which the works are embodied." 17 U.S.C.App. § 101 (1976). Omni contends that Konami is not entitled to secure a copyright in the sights and sounds of its "Scramble" game because the audiovisual work is neither "fixed in any tangible medium of expression" nor "original" within the meaning of § 102(a). Both contentions arise from the fact that the sequence of some of the images appearing on the screen during each play of the game will

vary depending upon the actions taken by the player. For example, if he fails to avoid enemy fire, his spaceship will be destroyed; if he fails to destroy enough fuel depots, his own fuel supply will run out, and his spaceship will crash; if he succeeds in destroying missile sites and enemy planes, those images will disappear from the screen; and the precise course travelled by his spaceship will depend upon his adjustment of the craft's altitude and velocity.

If the content of the audiovisual display were not affected by the participation of the player, there would be no doubt that the display itself, and not merely the written computer program, would be eligible for copyright. The display satisfies the statutory definition of an original "audiovisual work," and the memory devices of the game satisfy the statutory requirement of a "copy" in which the work is "fixed."[4] The Act defines "copies" as "material objects * * * in which a work is fixed by any method now known or later developed, and from which the work can be perceived, reproduced, or otherwise communicated, either directly or with the aid of a machine or device" and specifies that a work is "fixed" when "its embodiment in a copy * * * is sufficiently permanent or stable to permit it to be perceived, reproduced, or otherwise communicated for a period of more than transitory duration." 17 U.S.C.App. § 101 (1976). The audiovisual work is permanently embodied in a material object, the memory devices, from which it can be perceived with the aid of the other components of the game.

We agree with the District Court that the player's participation does not withdraw the audiovisual work from copyright eligibility. No doubt the entire sequence of all the sights and sounds of the game are different each time the game is played, depending upon the route and speed the player selects for his spaceship and the timing and accuracy of his release of his craft's bombs and lasers. Nevertheless, many aspects of the sights and the sequence

---

4. In arguing that the permanent "imprinting" of the computer program in the game's memory devices satisfies the requirement of fixation in a tangible medium, appellees direct our attention to the PROM, which contains, in electronically usable form, the computer program for the game. While the PROM device contains the program specifically written for the "Scramble" game, there are

undoubtedly some items of program stored in memory devices located in other components of the game. Whether located in the PROM prepared for this particular game or elsewhere in the total assembly, all portions of the program, once stored in memory devices anywhere in the game, are fixed in a tangible medium within the meaning of the Act.

of their appearance remain constant during each play of the game. These include the appearance (shape, color, and size) of the player's spaceship, the enemy craft, the ground missile bases and fuel depots, and the terrain over which (and beneath which) the player's ship flies, as well as the sequence in which the missile bases, fuel depots, and terrain appears. Also constant are the sounds heard whenever the player successfully destroys an enemy craft or installation or fails to avoid an enemy missile or laser. It is true, as appellants contend, that some of these sights and sounds will not be seen and heard during each play of the game in the event that the player's spaceship is destroyed before the entire course is traversed. But the images remain fixed, capable of being seen and heard each time a player succeeds in keeping his spaceship aloft long enough to permit the appearances of all the images and sounds of a complete play of the game. The repetitive sequence of a substantial portion of the sights and sounds of the game qualifies for copyright protection as an audiovisual work.

Appellants' claim that the work lacks originality proceeds along two lines. Repeating their attack on fixation, they assert that each play of the game is an original work because of the player's participation. The videotape of a particular play of the game, they assert, secured protection only for that one "original" display. However, the repeated appearance of the same sequence of numerous sights and sounds in each play of the game defeats this branch of the argument. Attacking from the opposite flank, appellants contend that the audiovisual display contains no originality because all of its reappearing features are determined by the previously created computer program. This argument is also without merit. The visual and aural features of the audiovisual display are plainly original variations sufficient to render the display copyrightable even though the underlying written program has an independent existence and is itself eligible for copyright. Nor is copyright defeated because the audiovisual work and the computer program are both embodied in the same components of the game. The same thing occurs when an audio tape embodies both a musical composition and a sound recording. Moreover, the argument overlooks the se-

quence of the creative process. Someone first conceived what the audiovisual display would look like and sound like. Originality occurred at that point. Then the program was written. Finally, the program was imprinted into the memory devices so that, in operation with the components of the game, the sights and sounds could be seen and heard. The resulting display satisfies the requirement of an original work.

We need not decide at what point the repeating sequence of images would form too insubstantial a portion of an entire display to warrant a copyright, nor the somewhat related issue of whether a sequence of images (*e.g.*, a spaceship shooting down an attacking plane) might contain so little in the way of particularized form of expression as to be only an abstract idea portrayed in noncopyrightable form. [Citation.] Assessing the entire effect of the game as it appears and sounds, we conclude that its repetitive sequence of images is copyrightable as an audiovisual display. [Citations.]

2. TRADEMARK ISSUE

Appellants contend that they, rather than appellee, have superior common law rights in the mark "SCRAMBLE" based on their use of the mark in the United States in early 1981, prior to appellants' use. The District Court found that appellants' prior use was not bona fide and that appellee's use entitled it to injunctive relief against appellants' use. We agree.

Though there is no direct evidence that Omni learned of the "SCRAMBLE" mark because of the planned use of the mark by Konami and Stern, that inference was available to the District Court, at least for purposes of considering Stern's entitlement to a preliminary injunction. Omni appears to have attempted only a preemptive use of the mark by ordering just ten name plates with the mark and affixing just five of them to headboards of units of separately named games sold in early 1981. [Citation.] The District Court was entitled to conclude that Omni was simply attaching a secondary label in a bad faith attempt to reserve a mark. [Citations.] Omni's claim that it sought to establish a trade name for its line of separately named, interchangeable games is undermined by the fact that once it secured a "knock-off" of Stern's "Scramble" game, it affixed only the mark "SCRAMBLE", thereby designating the name of the game, and not the line of which it was a part. As Judge Nickerson observed, "[I]t would be a truly remarkable coincidence if defendants independently thought of the name 'Scramble' and then, only a few months later, produced a video game virtually identical to the one bearing the same name. It is more likely that defendants sought to appropriate the trademark with the expectation that they would later imitate the audiovisual display."

Moreover, the equities abundantly justified issuance of an injunction against Omni's use of the mark. Stern has a substantial investment in the mark, having achieved success in the marketplace with its sales of a large number of units bearing the mark. By contrast, Omni has placed the mark on the headboard of five units of games that are not "Scramble" and has used the mark for a "Scramble" game that is a pirated "knock-off" of Stern's game.

The preliminary injunction is affirmed.

ATARI, INC. v. NORTH AMERICAN PHILIPS CONSUMER ELECTRONICS CORP.

672 F.2d 607

(United States Court of Appeals, Seventh Circuit, March 2, 1982.)

WOOD, C. J.

Plaintiffs-appellants Midway Manufacturing Co. ("Midway") and Atari, Inc. ("Atari") instituted this action against defendants-appellees North American Philips Consumer Electronics Corp. ("North American") and Park Magnavox Home Entertainment Center ("Park") for copyright infringement of and unfair competition against their audiovisual game "PAC-MAN." The district court denied plaintiffs' motion for a preliminary injunction, and this appeal followed, 28 U.S.C. § 1292(a)(1).

I. FACTS

Atari and Midway own the exclusive United States rights in PAC-MAN under the registered copyright for the "PAC-MAN audiovisual work." Midway sells the popular coin-operated arcade version, and Atari recently began to market the home video version. As part of its Odyssey line of home video games, North American developed a game called "K. C. Munchkin" which Park sells at the retail level. Plaintiffs filed this suit alleging that K. C. Munchkin infringes their copyright in PAC-MAN in violation of 17 U.S.C. §§ 106, 501 (Supp. I 1977), and that North American's conduct in marketing K. C. Munchkin constitutes unfair competition in violation of the Illinois Uniform Deceptive Trade Practices Act, Ill.Rev.Stat. (Ch. 121½, §§ 311-17 (1980), and the common law. The district court denied plaintiffs' motion for a preliminary injunction, ruling that plaintiffs failed to show likelihood of success on the merits of either claim.

Because this appeal requires us to make an ocular comparison of the two works, we describe both games in some detail.

A. The Copyrighted Work

The copyrighted version of PAC-MAN is an electronic arcade maze-chase game. Very basically, the game "board," which appears on a television-like screen, consists of a fixed maze, a central character (expressed as a "gobbler"), four pursuit characters (expressed as "ghost monsters"), several hundred evenly spaced pink dots which line the pathways of the maze, four enlarged pink dots ("power capsules") approximately located in each of the maze's four corners, and various colored fruit symbols which appear near the middle of the maze during the play of the game.

Using a "joy stick," the player guides the gobbler through the maze, consuming pink dots along the way. The monsters, which roam independently within the maze, chase the gobbler. Each play ends when a monster catches the gobbler, and after three plays, the game is over. If the gobbler consumes a power capsule, the roles reverse temporarily: the gobbler turns into the hunter, and the monsters become vulnerable. The object of the game is to score as many points as possible by gobbling dots, power capsules, fruit symbols, and monsters.

The PAC-MAN maze has a slightly vertical rectangular shape, and its geometric configuration is drawn in bright blue double lines. Centrally located on the left and right sides of the maze is a tunnel opening. To evade capture by a pursuing monster, the player can cause the central character to exit through one opening and re-enter through the other on the opposite side. In video game parlance this concept is called a "wraparound." In the middle is a rectangular box ("corral") which has a small opening on the upper side. A scoring table, located across the top of the maze, displays in white the first player's score on the left, the high score to date in the middle, and the second player's score on the right. If a player successfully consumes all of the dots, the entire maze flashes alternately blue and white in victory, and a new maze, replenished with dots, appears on the screen. When the game ends a bright red "game over" sign appears below the corral.

At the start of the game, the gobbler character is located centrally near the bottom of the maze. That figure is expressed as a simple yellow dot, somewhat larger than the power capsules, with a V-shaped aperture which opens and closes in mechanical fashion like a mouth as it travels the maze. Distinctive "gobbling" noises accompany this action. If fate (or a slight miscalculation) causes the gobbler to fall prey to one of the monsters, the action freezes, and the gobbler is deflated, folding back on itself, making a sympathetic whining sound, and disappearing with a starburst.

The four monster characters are identical except that one is red, one blue, one turquoise, and one orange. They are about equal in size to the gobbler, but are shaped like bell jars. The bottom of each figure is contoured to stimulate [sic] three short appendages which move as the monster travels about the maze. Their most distinctive feature is their highly animated eyes, which appear as large white circles with blue irises and which "look" in the direction the monster is moving. At the start of each play, the monsters are located side-by-side in the corral, bouncing back and forth until each leaves through the opening. Unlike the gobbler, they do not consume the dots, but move in a prearranged pattern about the maze at a speed approximately equal to that of the gobbler. When the gobbler consumes a power capsule and the roles reverse, the monsters

panic: a siren-like alarm sounds, they turn blue, their eyes contract into small pink dots, a wrinkled "mouth" appears, and they immediately reverse direction (moving at a reduced speed). When this period of vulnerability is about to end, the monsters warn the player by flashing alternately blue and white before returning to their original colors. But if a monster is caught during this time, its body disappears, and its original eyes reappear and race back to the corral. Once in the corral, the monster quickly regenerates and reenters the maze to resume its pursuit of the gobbler.

Throughout the play of PAC-MAN, a variety of distinctive musical sounds comprise the audio component of the game. Those sounds coincide with the various character movements and events occurring during the game and add to the excitement of the play.

B. The Accused Work

North American's K. C. Munchkin is also a maze-chase game that employs a player-controlled central character (also expressed as a "gobbler"), pursuit characters (also expressed as "ghost monsters"), dots, and power capsules. The basic play of K. C. Munchkin parallels that of PAC-MAN: the player directs the gobbler through the maze consuming dots and avoiding capture by the monsters; by gobbling a power capsule, the player can reverse the roles; and the ultimate goal is to accumulate the most points by gobbling dots and monsters.

K. C. Munchkin's maze also is rectangular, has two tunnel exits and a centrally located corral, and flashes different colors after the gobbler consumes all of the dots. But the maze, drawn in single, subdued purple lines, is more simple in overall appearance. Because it appears on a home television screen, the maze looks broader than it is tall. Unlike that in PAC-MAN, the maze has one dead-end passageway, which adds an element of risk and strategy.[1] The corral is square rather than rectangular and rotates ninety degrees every two or three seconds, but serves the same pur-

---

1. The K. C. Munchkin home video game has several modes with an almost indefinite variety of mazes. One mode, for example, employs a constantly changing con-

figuration, in another, the player can build his or her own maze, and in yet another, the maze disappears when the gobbler moves.

pose as the corral in PAC-MAN. The scoring table is located below the maze and, as in PAC-MAN, has places on the left and right for scores for two players.[2] But instead of simply registering the high score in the middle, the K. C. Munchkin game displays in flashing pink and orange a row of question marks where the high scorer can register his or her name.

The gobbler in K. C. Munchkin initially faces the viewer and appears as a round blue-green figure with horns and eyes. The gobbler normally has an impish smile, but when a monster attacks it, its smile appropriately turns to a frown. As it moves about the maze, the gobbler shows a somewhat diamond-shaped profile with a V-shaped mouth which rapidly opens and closes in a manner similar to PAC-MAN's gobbler. A distinctive "gobbling" noise also accompanies this movement. When the gobbler stops, it turns around to face the viewer with another grin. If captured by a monster, the gobbler also folds back and disappears in a star-burst. At the start of each play, this character is located immediately above the corral. If successful in consuming the last dot, the munchkin turns to the viewer and chuckles.[3]

K. C. Munchkin's three ghost monsters appear similar in shape and movement to their PAC-MAN counterparts.[4] They have round bodies (approximately equal in size to the gobbler) with two short horns or antennae, eyes, and three appendages on the bottom. The eyes are not as detailed as those of the PAC-MAN monsters, but they are uniquely similar in that they also "look" in the direction in which the monster is moving. Although slightly longer, the "legs" also move in a centipede-like manner as the monster roams about the maze. The similarity becomes even more pronounced when the monsters move vertically because their antennae disappear and their bodies assume the more bell jar-like shape of the PAC-MAN monsters. Moreover, the monsters are initially stationed inside the cor-

ral (albeit in a piggyback rather than a side-by-side arrangement) and exit into the maze as soon as play commences.

K. C. Munchkin's expression of the role reversal also parallels that in PAC-MAN. When the gobbler consumes one of the power capsules, the vulnerable monsters turn purple and reverse direction, moving at a slightly slower speed. If caught by the gobbler, a monster "vanishes": its body disappears and only white "eyes" and "feet" remain to indicate its presence. Instead of returning directly to the corral to regenerate, the ghost-like figure continues to wander about the maze, but does not affect the play.[5] Only if the rotating corral happens to open up toward the monster as it travels one of the adjacent passageways will the monster re-enter the corral to be regenerated. This delay in regeneration allows the gobbler more time to clear the maze of dots. When the period of vulnerability is about to end, each monster flashes its original color as a warning.

There are only twelve dots in K. C. Munchkin as opposed to over two hundred dots in PAC-MAN. Eight of those dots are white; the other four are power capsules, distinguished by their constantly changing color and the manner in which they blink. In K. C. Munchkin, the dots are randomly spaced, whereas in PAC-MAN, the dots are uniformly spaced. Furthermore, in K. C. Munchkin, the dots are rectangular and are always moving. As the gobbler munches more dots, the speed of the remaining dots progressively increases, and the last dot moves at the same speed as the gobbler. In the words of the district court, "the last dot * * * cannot be caught by overtaking it; it must be munched by strategy." At least initially, one power capsule is located in each of the maze's four corners, as in PAC-MAN.

Finally, K. C. Munchkin has a set of sounds accompanying it which are distinctive to the whole line of Odyssey home video games. Many of these sounds are dissimilar to the sounds which are played in the arcade form of PAC-MAN.

C. The Creation and Promotion of the Accused Work

Ed Averett, an independent contractor, created K. C. Munchkin for North American. He had previously developed approximately twenty-one video games, including other maze-chase games. He and Mr. Staup, who is in charge of North American's home video game development, first viewed PAC-MAN in an airport arcade. Later, after discussing the strengths and weaknesses of the PAC-MAN game and its increasing popularity, they decided to commence development of a modified version to add to North American's Odyssey line of home video games. Mr. Averett also played PAC-MAN at least once before beginning work on K. C. Munchkin.

Mr. Staup and Mr. Averett agreed, however, that the PAC-MAN game, as is, could become popular as a home video game, but only if marketed under the "PAC-MAN" name. Thus, as Mr. Averett worked on K. C. Munchkin, North American sought to obtain from Midway a license under the PAC-MAN copyright and trademark. Mr. Staup later learned that the license was not available and so informed Mr. Averett. At that time, Mr. Averett had not yet completed K. C. Munchkin.

When Mr. Averett finished the project, North American examined the game and concluded that it was "totally different" from PAC-MAN. To avoid any potential claim of confusion, however, Mr. Averett was told to make further changes in the game characters. As a result, the color of the gobbler was changed from yellow to its present bluish color. North American also adopted the dissimilar name "K. C. Munchkin" and issued internal instructions not to refer to PAC-MAN in promoting K. C. Munchkin.

An independent retailer in the Chicago area nonetheless ran advertisements in the *Chicago Sun-Times* and the *Chicago Tribune*, describing K. C. Munchkin as "a Pac-Man type game" and "as challenging as Pac-Man." Another printed advertisement referred to K. C. Munchkin as "a PAC-MAN game." Plaintiffs also sent investigators to various stores to purchase a K. C. Munchkin game. In response

to specific inquiries, sales persons in two stores, one being the aforementioned independent retailer, described the Odyssey game as "like PAC-MAN" and as "Odyssey's PAC-MAN."

II. STANDARD OF REVIEW AND PRELIMINARY INJUNCTIONS

This court will not reverse the grant or denial of a preliminary injunction absent "a showing from the totality of the factors that a clear abuse of the trial court's discretion has occurred or that the court's findings were clearly erroneous or represent a certain mistake of law." [Citation.] Four factors enter into the district court's exercise of discretion to grant or deny a preliminary injunction: (1) whether the plaintiff will have an adequate remedy at law or will be irreparably harmed if the injunction does not issue; (2) whether the threatened injury to the plaintiff outweighs the threatened harm the injunction may inflict on the defendant; (3) whether the plaintiff has at least a reasonable likelihood of success on the merits; and (4) whether the granting of a preliminary injunction will disserve the public interest. [Citation.]

The district court concluded only that plaintiffs failed to meet the threshold requirement of showing likelihood of success on the merits. The court thus did not address the other factors in denying plaintiffs' motion. [Citation.] Upon reversing that decision, this court nonetheless may direct that a preliminary injunction be entered if we find from the record that plaintiffs as a matter of law made the requisite showing as to the remaining elements.

Under the circumstances of this case, the determination of copyright infringement (or lack thereof) is predicated upon an ocular comparison of the works themselves and does not involve any material credibility issues. Therefore, this court is in as good a position as the district court to decide that question. [Citations.]

III. COPYRIGHT INFRINGEMENT

To establish infringement a plaintiff must prove ownership of a valid copyright and "copying" by the defendant. *See* 3 M. Nimmer, Nimmer On Copyright § 13.01, at 13-3

(1981) ("Nimmer"). Because direct evidence of copying often is unavailable, copying may be inferred where the defendant had access to the copyrighted work and the accused work is substantially similar to the copyrighted work. [Citation.] The parties stipulated to the validity of plaintiffs' copyright and to access; the district court's ruling turned solely on the question of substantial similarity.

Some courts have expressed the test of substantial similarity in two parts: (1) whether the defendant copied from the plaintiff's work and (2) whether the copying, if proven, went so far as to constitute an improper appropriation. [Citations.] Our analysis focuses on the second part of that test and the response of the "ordinary observer." [Citation.] Specifically, the test is whether the accused work is so similar to the plaintiff's work that an ordinary reasonable person would conclude that the defendant unlawfully appropriated the plaintiff's protectible expression by taking material of substance and value. [Citation.] Judge Learned Hand, in finding infringement, once stated that "the ordinary observer, unless he set out to detect the disparities, would be disposed to overlook them, and regard their aesthetic appeal as the same." [Citation.] It has been said that this test does not involve "analytic dissection and expert testimony" [citation] but depends on whether the accused work has captured the "total concept and feel" of the copyrighted work. [Citation.]

While dissection is generally disfavored, the ordinary observer test, in application, must take into account that the copyright laws preclude appropriation of only those elements of the work that are protected by the copyright. [Footnote.] [Citations.] "It is an axiom of copyright law that the protection granted to a copyrightable work extends only to the particular expression of an idea and never to the idea itself." [Citation.] "Unlike a patent, a copyright gives no exclusive right to the art disclosed; protection is given only to the expression of the idea—not the idea itself." [Citations.] The Copyright Act of 1976 codifies this idea-expression dichotomy. 17 U.S.C.

§ 102(b). [Citation.] Thus, "if the only similarity between plaintiff's and defendant's works is that of the abstract idea, there is an absence of *substantial* similarity and hence no infringement results." [Original emphasis.] [Citations.]

It follows that copyright protection does not extend to games as such. [Citations.] As Professor Nimmer notes, however, "some limited copyright protection is nevertheless available in connection with games. * * * [A] relatively minimal artistic expression, if original, would render copyrightable * * * the pattern or design of game boards and playing cards as pictorial or graphic works." 1 Nimmer § 2.18[H][3], at 2-212. Recognizing this principle, the Second Circuit has held copyrightable as an audiovisual work, see 17 U.S.C. § 102(a)(6), the "repetitive sequence of a substantial portion of the sights and sounds" of a video game called "SCRAMBLE."[7] *Stern Electronics, Inc. v. Kaufman,* 669 F.2d 852, 856 (2d Cir. 1982). [Citations.] This appeal requires us to address the related question of the *scope* of copyright protection to be afforded audiovisual games such as PAC-MAN. To do so, we must first attempt to distill the protectible forms of expression in PAC-MAN from the game itself. [Citation.]

There is no litmus paper test by which to apply the idea-expression distinction; the determination is necessarily subjective. As Judge Learned Hand said, "Obviously, no principle can be stated as to when an imitator has gone beyond copying the 'idea,' and has borrowed its 'expression.' Decisions must therefore inevitably be ad hoc." [Citation.] Courts and commentators nevertheless have developed a few helpful approaches. In *Nichols v. Universal Pictures Corp.,* 45 F.2d 119, 121 (2d Cir. 1930), *cert. denied,* 282 U.S. 902, 51 S.Ct. 216, 75 L.Ed. 795 (1931), Judge Hand articulated what is now known as the "abstractions test":

> Upon any work * * * a great number of patterns of increasing generality will fit equally well, as more and more of the incident is left out. * * * [T]here is a point in this series of abstractions where they are no longer protected,

---

7. But the court carefully limited its holding:
We need not decide at what point the repeating sequence of images would form too insubstantial a portion of an entire display to warrant a copyright, nor the somewhat related issue of whether a sequence of

images (*e.g.,* a spaceship shooting down an attacking plane) might contain so little in the way of particularized form of expression as to be only an abstract idea portrayed in noncopyrightable form. [Citation.] [Citation.]

since otherwise the playwright could prevent the use of his "ideas," to which, apart from their expression, his property is never extended.— Nobody has ever been able to fix that boundary, and nobody ever can. * * * As respects plays, the controversy chiefly centers upon the characters and sequence of incident, these being the substance.

(citations omitted). This "test" has proven useful in analyzing dramatic works, literary works, and motion pictures, where the recurring patterns can readily be abstracted into very general themes.[8]

A related concept is that of idea-expression unity: where idea and expression are indistinguishable, the copyright will protect against only identical copying. [Citation.] *Herbert Rosenthal Jewelry Corp. v. Kalpakian,* 446 F.2d 738 (9th Cir. 1971), presents a good example and discussion of this limitation. Plaintiff charged defendants with copyright infringement of a pin in the shape of a bee encrusted with jewels. The court assumed the validity of plaintiff's copyright, but refused to find substantial similarity:

> What is basically at stake is the extent of the copyright owner's monopoly—from how large an area of activity did Congress intend to allow the copyright owner to exclude others? We think the production of jeweled bee pins is a larger private preserve than Congress intended to be set aside in the public market without a patent. A jeweled bee pin is therefore an "idea" that defendants were free to copy. Plaintiff seems to agree, for it disavows any claim that defendants cannot manufacture and sell jeweled bee pins and concedes that only plaintiff's particular design or "expression" of the jeweled bee pin "idea" is protected under its copyright. The difficulty, as we have noted, is that on this record the "idea" and its "expression" appear to be indistinguishable. There is no greater similarity between the pins of plaintiff and defendants than is inevitable from the use of jewel-encrusted bee forms in both.
>
> When the "idea" and its "expression" are thus inseparable, copying the "expression" will not be barred, since protecting the "expression" in such circumstances would confer a monopoly of the "idea" upon the copyright owner free of the conditions and limitations imposed by the patent law.

[Citations.] "The idea and expression will coincide when the expression provides nothing new or additional over the idea." [Citation.]

In the context of literary works, some courts have adopted a similar *scenes a faire* approach. *Scenes a faire* refers to "incidents, characters or settings which are as a practical matter indispensable, or at least standard, in the treatment of a given topic." [Citations.] Such stock literary devices are not protectible by copyright. [Citation.] Thus, "similarity of expression, whether literal or nonliteral, which necessarily results from the fact that the common idea is only capable of expression in more or less stereotyped form will preclude a finding of actionable similarity." [Citation.] Courts have applied this concept to written game rules [citations] and to the pictorial display of game boards. [Citation.]

As *Kalpakian* and other cases show, that a work is copyrighted says very little about the scope of its protection. But the *Kalpakian* case is nonetheless instructive in that it represents one end of a spectrum of protection. As a work embodies more in the way of particularized expression, it moves farther away from the bee pin in *Kalpakian,* and receives broader copyright protection. At the opposite end of the spectrum lie the "strongest" works in which fairly complex or fanciful artistic expressions predominate over relatively simplistic themes and which are almost entirely products of the author's creativity rather than concomitants of those themes. [Citation.] As one court noted: "The complexity and artistry of the expression of an idea will separate it from even the most banal idea. * * * [T]he scope of copyright protection increases with the extent expression differs from the idea." [Citations.]

Plaintiffs' audiovisual work is primarily an unprotectible game, but unlike the bee pin, to at least a limited extent the particular form in which it is expressed (shapes, sizes, colors, sequences, arrangements, and sounds) provides something "new or additional over the idea." [Citation.] In applying the abstractions test, we find that plaintiffs' game can be described accurately in fairly abstract terms, much in the same way as one would articulate

---

8. One commentator offered a further refinement of this test:

> No doubt the line does lie somewhere between the author's idea and the precise form in which he wrote

it down. * * * [P]rotection covers the 'pattern' of the work * * * the sequence of events, and the development of the interplay of characters. [Citation.]

the rules to such a game. [Citation.] PAC-MAN is a maze-chase game in which the player scores points by guiding a central figure through various passageways of a maze and at the same time avoiding collision with certain opponents or pursuit figures which move independently about the maze. Under certain conditions, the central figure may temporarily become empowered to chase and overtake the opponents, thereby scoring bonus points. The audio component and the concrete details of the visual presentation constitute the copyrightable expression of that game "idea."

Certain expressive matter in the PAC-MAN work, however, should be treated as *scenes a faire* and receive protection only from virtually identical copying. The maze and scoring table are standard game devices, and the tunnel exits are nothing more than the commonly used "wrap around" concept adapted to a maze-chase game. Similarly, the use of dots provides a means by which a player's performance can be gauged and rewarded with the appropriate number of points, and by which to inform the player of his or her progress. Given their close connection with the underlying game, K. C. Munchkin's maze design, scoring table, and "dots" are sufficiently different to preclude a finding of infringement on that basis alone.

Rather, it is the substantial appropriation of the PAC-MAN characters that requires reversal of the district court. The expression of the central figure as a "gobbler" and the pursuit figures as "ghost monsters" distinguishes PAC-MAN from conceptually similar video games. Other games, such as "Rally-X" [9] * * * and North American's own "Take the Money and Run," [10] illustrate different ways in which a basic maze-chase game can be expressed. [Citation.] PAC-MAN's particular artistic interpretation of the game was designed to create a certain impression which would appeal to a nonviolent player personality. The game as such, however, does not dictate the use of a "gobbler" and "ghost monsters." Those characters are wholly fanciful

creations, without reference to the real world. [Footnote.] [Citations.]

North American not only adopted the same basic characters but also portrayed them in a manner which made K. C. Munchkin appear substantially similar to PAC-MAN. The K. C. Munchkin gobbler has several blatantly similar features, including the relative size and shape of the "body," the V-shaped "mouth," its distinctive gobbling action (with appropriate sounds), and especially the way in which it disappears upon being captured. An examination of the K. C. Munchkin ghost monsters reveals even more significant visual similarities. In size, shape, and manner of movement, they are virtually identical to their PAC-MAN counterparts. K. C. Munchkin's monsters, for example, exhibit the same peculiar "eye" and "leg" movement. Both games, moreover, express the role reversal and "regeneration" process with such great similarity that an ordinary observer could conclude only that North American copied plaintiffs' PAC-MAN.

Defendants point to a laundry list of specific differences—particularly the concept of moving dots, the variations in mazes, and certain changes in facial features and colors of the characters—which they contend, and the district court apparently agreed, shows lack of substantial similarity. Although numerous differences may influence the impressions of the ordinary observer, "slight differences between a protected work and an accused work will not preclude a finding of infringement" where the works are substantially similar in other respects. [Citations.] Exact reproduction or near identity is not necessary to establish infringement. "[A]n infringement * * * includes also the various modes in which the matter of any work may be adopted, imitated, transferred, or reproduced, with more or less colorable alterations to disguise the piracy." [Citation.] In comparing the two works, the district court focused on certain differences in detail and seemingly ignored (or at least failed to articulate) the more obvious similarities. The *sine qua non* of the ordinary

---

9. In Rally-X, the object is to guide a car through a maze clearing various check-points (represented by flags) to score points and avoiding collision with a number of pursuit cars. [Citation.]

10. In Take the Money and Run, the player-controlled figure and the pursuit figures are presented as humanoid forms.

observer test, however, is the overall similarities rather than the minute differences between the two works. [Citations.] The nature of the alterations on which North American relies only tends to emphasize the extent to which it deliberately copied from the plaintiffs' work. [Citation.] When analyzing two works to determine whether they are substantially similar, courts should be careful not to lose sight of the forest for the trees.[12] [Citation.]

To assess the impact of certain differences, one factor to consider is the nature of the protected material and the setting in which it appears. [Citation.] Video games, unlike an artist's painting or even other audiovisual works, appeal to an audience that is fairly undiscriminating insofar as their concern about more subtle differences in artistic expression. The main attraction of a game such as PAC-MAN lies in the stimulation provided by the intensity of the competition. A person who is entranced by the play of the game "would be disposed to overlook" many of the minor differences in detail and "regard their aesthetic appeal as the same." [Citation.]

The defendants and the district court order stress that K. C. Munchkin *plays* differently because of the moving dots and the variety of maze configurations from which the player can choose. The focus in a copyright infringement action, however, is on the similarities in protectible *expression*. Even to the extent that those differences alter the visual impression of K. C. Munchkin, they are insufficient to preclude a finding of infringement. "[I]t is enough that substantial parts were lifted; no plagiarist can excuse the wrong by showing how much of his work he did not pirate." [Citation.] Infringement may be found where the

similarity relates to matter which constitutes a substantial portion of plaintiffs' work—*i.e.*, matter which is of value to plaintiffs. [Citations.] It is irrelevant that K. C. Munchkin has other game modes which employ various maze configurations. The only mode that concerns this court is the one that uses a display most similar to the one in PAC-MAN. Other cases similarly have separated the "attract" mode from the "play" mode in comparing two audiovisual games. [Citations.] Moreover, PAC-MAN's distinctive characters alone may constitute material of substantial value. [Citations.]

While not necessarily conclusive, other extrinsic evidence additionally suggests that plaintiffs are likely to succeed on their copyright claim. In promoting K. C. Munchkin, several retailers and sales clerks described that game by referring to PAC-MAN. Comments that K. C. Munchkin is "Odyssey's PAC-MAN" or "a PAC-MAN game" especially reflect that at least some lay observers view the games as similar. [Citations.] Furthermore, North American's direction to Mr. Averett that he make certain superficial changes in the gobbler figure may be viewed as an attempt to disguise an intentional appropriation of PAC-MAN's expression.

Based on an ocular comparison of the two works, we conclude that plaintiffs clearly showed likelihood of success.[13] Although not "virtually identical" to PAC-MAN, K. C. Munchkin captures the "total concept and feel" of and is substantially similar to PAC-MAN. [Citation.] This case is a far cry from those in which the defendant appropriated only the game idea, but adopted its own unique form of expression [citation] or where minor variations or differences were sufficient to avoid

---

12. Many of the differences, such as North American's inability to duplicate some of the more distinctive features of PAC-MAN's monsters, may be due to the lesser capacity of the home video medium. That a work is transfered into a different medium is not itself a bar to recovery. [Citations.] An author has the exclusive right to produce derivative works based on the original work, 17 U.S.C. § 106(2), and that right often can be more valuable than the right to the original work itself. Although dissection and expert testimony is not favored, the judicially created ordinary observer test should not deprive authors of this significant statutory grant merely because the technical requirements of a different medium *dictate* certain differences in expression. Without deciding the question, we note that in some cases it may be important to

educate the trier of fact as to such considerations in order to preserve the author's rights under the Copyright Act. [Citation.] We do not, however, propose that wholly *voluntary* changes in expression be given any less weight by the trier of fact.

13. We do not, however, agree with plaintiffs that PAC-MAN is entitled to broader protection simply because it is an audiovisual work. The case plaintiffs cite for that proposition, *Universal City Studios v. Sony Corp. of America*, 659 F.2d 963 (9th Cir. 1981), in [sic] inapposite. In *Sony*, the Ninth Circuit addressed only the question of whether home video recording is *exempt* from liability for copyright infringement, not whether the test for infringement is any less exacting.

liability because the form of expression was inextricably tied to the game itself. [Citations.]

IV. IRREPARABLE INJURY, BALANCE OF HARDSHIPS, PUBLIC INTEREST

Irreparable injury may normally be presumed from a showing of copyright infringement. [Citation.] Even without the aid of that presumption, plaintiffs clearly have established irreparable harm. The record reveals that Midway's PAC-MAN has become an immensely popular arcade game, sales of which have exceeded $150 million after only one year. In October 1981, Atari had already committed over $1.5 million to the licensing, development, and promotion of its home video version of PAC-MAN, which it intends to put on the market in March 1982. As of the date of the hearing in the district court, Atari had booked orders for PAC-MAN in excess of one million cartridges with a sales value of over $24 million. By marketing K. C. Munchkin, North American jeopardized the substantial investments of Midway and especially Atari. The short-lived nature of video games further underscores the need for a preliminary injunction. [Citations.] Moreover, the Atari and Odyssey game cartridges are not interchangeable. To play K. C. Munchkin, the purchaser must also buy North American's ODYSSEY² game console. The impact of North American's infringement therefore extends even beyond the PAC-MAN game to the whole Atari system.

The balance of hardships and public interest factors do not weigh against the entry of a preliminary injunction. North American's only alleged hardship is the profits it would lose if enjoined from marketing K. C. Munchkin. This argument, however, "merits little equitable consideration." [Citation.] "Advantages built upon a deliberately plagiarized make-up do not seem to us to give the borrower any standing to complain that his vested

interests will be disturbed." [Citation.] This is also not a case in which the plaintiffs' harm would be *de minimis* in comparison to that of the defendants. Finally, a preliminary injunction is necessary to preserve the integrity of the copyright laws which seek to encourage individual effort and creativity by granting valuable enforceable rights. [Citations.] Defendants point to no competing public interest that would be harmed.

V. CONCLUSION

The district court's conclusion that the two works are not substantially similar is clearly erroneous, and its refusal to issue a preliminary injunction constitutes an abuse of discretion. Since this is an interlocutory appeal, however, we are mindful that our holding does not constitute a conclusive adjudication of the merits of plaintiffs' claim. [Citation.] The ordinary observer test should not be applied in a judicial vacuum. Further development of the facts at trial may command a different conclusion.

For the foregoing reasons, we reverse the district court's denial of plaintiffs' motion for a preliminary injunction and direct the district court to enter a preliminary injunction against continued infringement of plaintiffs' copyright.[14]

APPLE COMPUTER, INC. v. FRANKLIN COMPUTER CORP.

545 F. Supp. 812
(United States District Court, E. D. Pennsylvania, July 30, 1982.)

NEWCOMER, D. J.

Plaintiff Apple Computer, Inc., ("Apple") moves for a preliminary injunction restraining defendant Franklin Computer Corp. ("Franklin") from using, copying, selling, or infringing in any other way Apple's registered copyrights on fourteen computer programs that

---

14. A preliminary injunction on the copyright claim eliminates the need to address the district court's ruling on the unfair competition claim. We do note, however, that where the defendants' work is visually similar to the plaintiffs' work, state unfair competition law may prohibit the marketing of defendants' work if it is not clearly labeled to prevent likelihood of confusion as to

source. [Citation.] Moreover, while language such as "like PAC-MAN" or "as challenging as PAC-MAN" might constitute legitimate comparative advertising and not cause confusion, that assessment does not apply with equal force to phrases such as "Odyssey's PAC-MAN" or "a PAC-MAN game." [Citation.]

are contained in or sold with the Apple II personal computer.

I. THE PARTIES

Apple is a California corporation, acknowledged to be a leader in the field of personal computers. It employs approximately 3,000 people and it has sold almost 400,000 computers. Apple had sales of $335,000,000 last fiscal year. Franklin is a Pennsylvania corporation, formed in 1981, with 75 employees. It has sold fewer than 1,000 computers.

For reasons more fully expressed below I have concluded that there is some doubt as to the copyrightability of the programs described in this litigation. Because of this doubt, I find that plaintiff has failed to show a reasonable probability of success on the merits and for that reason, as well as a failure to show irreparable harm, I must deny the motion.

II. THE WORKS

A. The "Computers"

The two machines in this case are the Apple II, made by Apple Computer, Inc., and the Ace 100, made by Franklin Computer Corporation. Both are generally referred to as microcomputers or personal computers because of their size and their ease of use by individuals and small businesses.

Both computers contain a large flat circuit board, called a "mother board". Mounted on this board, forming the electronic circuitry which is the operating center of the computer, are a number of small integrated circuits or chips. These integrated circuits are described herein and are the focus of this lawsuit.

B. The Integrated Circuits: CPU, RAMs, ROMs, PROMs and EPROMs

Personal computers contain a variety of integrated circuits, which are photo-chemically imprinted silicon chips. [Footnote.] Each integrated circuit, or chip, is constructed with a specific size memory or programming capacity. In microcomputers, the capacity of a chip may range from 4,000 bytes (4K of memory) to 64,000 bytes (64K of memory). One

"byte" is one cell or one location point for information to be stored in the chip. In turn, on computers like Apple and Ace, each byte has eight "bits" (Binary digIT) each of which specifies the single value of "0" or "1", negative or positive.

Like all computers, both Apple and Ace have a central processing unit ("CPU") which is the specialized integrated circuit that executes binary programs. The CPU does the primary calculations required of all programs and shifts answers to other parts of the system depending upon the requirements of the program controlling it. On both Apple and Ace, the CPU uses a 6502 microprocessor chip which has a 64K storage capacity.

In addition to the CPU, which does the calculations, computers have internal memories that hold information generated within the computer or entered into the computer from an external source like a floppy disk or keyboard. The information may be stored in a permanent or impermanent ("volatile") form of memory. Some chips store information only as long as the machine is on; these are Random Access Memory chips (RAMs). When the power is turned off, the information stored in these chips is lost.

The information to be stored permanently is held in other chips called Read Only Memory (ROMs). Information stored in ROMs is not lost when the power is turned off. Information is stored in a ROM by destroying the fusible links that make up the structure of each byte, creating the equivalent of on-and-off switches arranged according to the specifications of the program to be imprinted in the ROM. [Footnote.]

For all practical purposes, the information stored in a ROM cannot be changed by the user of a computer. As the name suggests, the ROM contains information that can only be read. Nothing new can be added or "written" onto it. Of the 14 "works in suit," four of them are stored on ROMS.[3]

C. Programs: Software, Interpreters, and Languages

Of signal difficulty in this case is the elasticity

---

3. There has been testimony that the ACE 100 contains EPROMs (Erasable Programmable Read Only Memory) rather than ROMs, but for purposes of this proceeding, the difference is inconsequential. EPROMs perform the same function as ROMs, but the information stored in them can be erased and the chip can be reprogrammed, whereas ROMs are manufactured with a fixed program.

of the word "program." A computer program is a set of serial instructions that directs the computer to perform certain tasks. A user does not instruct the operating center of the machine. The user writes programs that are expressed in "high level" languages resembling English. Depending on the circumstances, one or more special machine "programs" will in turn translate or "interpret" those instructions, given by the user, into a form of instruction that can be executed in the circuitry. At the level of the circuitry, programs are expressed in "low level" languages. At the very lowest level, every program is eventually reduced to "an object code," which is expressed in binary (base 2) numbers, a series of zeroes and ones that represent open and closed switches within the computer's circuits.

Object code is the heart of this case. In a crude way, object code that has been etched onto the ROM architecture can be "read" by an expert with a microscope and patience. However, the object code in either its binary form or in the silicon chip form is not designed to be read by humans. It is the machine's language.

At issue in this case are fourteen "programs" expressed in object code. These programs are either imprinted on the Apple's ROMs or the Ace's EPROM or they are enscribed on floppy disks which allow for easy storage and transmission to the computer's RAMs when the programs are needed.

All of these programs are "operating" programs as opposed to "application" programs. The distinction is based on the breadth of use and the function of the program. An application program has a specific task, ordinarily chosen by the user, such as to maintain records, perform certain calculations, or display graphic images. Application programs are normally written in high level languages which are designed to be easily used by the unsophisticated. An operating program, by contrast, is generally internal to the computer and is designed only to facilitate the operating of the application program.

D. Compatibility and Operating Systems

An operating system that consists of a variety of separate operating programs is in a sense a part of the machine; it provides the func-

tioning system that allows the user to progress in an orderly fashion as he moves through the physical process of keying information into a computer. The operating system instructs the machine how to use this information and receives the solutions to the problems posed. Once in the machine, either permanently implanted as a ROM or entered from a floppy disk, an operating system is very nearly "transparent"; the user is not aware of the work and order of the work it is processing.

Because of the complex relationship between the physical elements of a computer (keyboard, screen, printer, disk drives, etc.) and the logic of the system that is both built into the CPU and added through high level languages, operating systems are critical to personal computers. Without them, every operation would require an impractical number of steps before it could be executed.

The operating system is configured to satisfy the requirements of the physical environment of the computer, especially the structure of the CPU, and to provide easy compatibility with software written in the general market place and with peripherals made by other manufacturers. The present litigation occurs because the Apple computer has stimulated the creation of an extraordinary amount of software and peripheral hardware that is only compatible with Apple. Most of this software and peripheral hardware was designed with Apple's operating system in mind, which means it will not work, except with great difficulty or restructuring, on machines other than those with the particular configuration of operating system and CPU that is found in the Apple.

Amateurs and small businessmen who buy small computers, like Apple, buy it not for its quality, although quality is not unimportant, but for the software and peripherals that are compatible with it. Franklin has "designed" a computer that is Apple-compatible. Essentially that means that the Ace was designed to run most, if not all, of the software written for Apple by hundreds of entrepreneurs and to accept the peripherals manufactured by many others. Apple contends in this suit that Franklin has "stolen" the logic and structure of their system. Franklin contends that Apple has deprived non-Apple owners of the opportunity to take advantage of the wealth of Apple-compatible material that exists in the market place. Franklin's argument is that it has created not an Apple-compatible system but rather a system compatible with Apple-compatible software which must of necessity share a great deal of the essential structure of Apple, especially of the structure of Apple's operating system.

E. The Works in Suit

The works upon which this action is based are in object code, stored in Read Only Memory (ROM) or on floppy disks.

(1) Autostart ROM. The Autostart program, stored in ROM, is a collection of low-level subroutines ("booting" routines) that initiate registers and other circuitry in the Apple II when the power is turned on. It also performs a variety of hardware-oriented functions during operating, so that the machine can accept keystrokes and generate character graphics for video display.

(2) Applesoft. The Applesoft program is Apple's version of BASIC ("Beginner's All-purpose Symbolic Instruction Code"), a higher level programming language that was originally developed at Dartmouth College. The Applesoft program is stored in ROM and is an interpreter program that processes BASIC statements, one statement at a time, and causes the computer to execute those instructions that implement the BASIC statement entered by the user.

(3) DOS 3.3. The DOS 3.3 program is a disk-based, operating systems program. It provides the instructions necessary to control the operation between disk drive and the computer. It controls the reading and writing of the floppy disks and includes several other routines and subroutines, for example, the read-write-track-sector ("RWTS") which puts in sequence all the data transfers. RWTS starts various subprograms that perform certain low level functions such as reading and writing data.

(4) Floating Point BASIC. The Floating Point BASIC is a disk-based version of the Applesoft program. In some modes of the Apple II computer it is loaded into the random-access memory (RAM) of a peripheral card, known as "Language Card," and is there available for the user's programming. Floating Point

BASIC is used in earlier versions of the Apple II computer that do not have the Applesoft program in ROM.

(5) Apple Integer BASIC. The Apple Integer BASIC is a disk-based program and was Apple's first version of BASIC for the Apple II computer. This program implements a simpler version of Apple's Applesoft and Floating Point BASIC programs.

(6) Hello. The Hello program is a disk-based, operating systems program that is used in conjunction with Apple's DOS 3.3 operating system. After start-up, this program is the first program executed each time a floppy disk is "booted up." It determines how much Random Access Memory (RAM) is in the computer and which version of BASIC needs to be loaded into the computer.

(7) Chain. The Chain program is a disk-based operating systems program that is used in conjunction with Apple's DOS 3.3 program. The Chain program allows data to be passed between program segments, only one of which is in the RAM at any given time. The Chain program preserves RAM-based data during the time another program segment is being loaded into RAM.

(8) Copy. The Copy program is a disk-based operating systems program that is used in conjunction with Apple's DOS 3.3 program. The Copy program is a utility program that enables the user to copy programs written in Apple Integer BASIC from one disk to another.

(9) Copy A. The Copy A program is a disk-based operating systems program that is used in conjunction with Apple's DOS 3.3 program. The Copy A program is a utility program that enables the user to copy programs written in Applesoft from one disk to another.

(10) Copy OBJO. The Copy OBJO program contains a file of subroutines used by the Copy and Copy A programs.

(11) Boot 13. The Boot 13 is a disk-based boot program that allows a user to "boot" older versions of the Apple disk operating system when the user has a 16 sector boot ROM on the Controller Card.

(12) MasterCreate. The MasterCreate program is a disk-based, operating systems program. When a floppy disk is first initialized, or formatted, the DOS 3.3 is placed on the disk in a form that is dependent on the amount of RAM available. The MasterCreate program replaces the DOS 3.3 on the disk with a version that is independent of the amount of RAM available.

(13) Apple 13—Sector Boot ROM. The Apple 13—Sector Boot program is in a ROM located on the Disk Controller Card. This boot program initializes numerous circuits in the Controller Card and in the Apple II computer and causes other parts of the disk operating system used for 13 sector formatted disks to load.

(14) Apple 16—Sector Boot ROM. The Apple 16—Sector Boot program is in a ROM located on the Disk Controller Card. This program initializes numerous circuits on the Controller Card and in the Apple II computer and causes other parts of the disk operating system used for 16 sector formatted disks to load.

III. COPYRIGHT LAW

A. The Source of Congressional Power

Congress takes its power in the area of copyright from Art. I, Sec. 8, cl. 8, of the Constitution ("To promote the Progress of Science and useful Arts, by securing for limited Times to Authors and Inventors the exclusive Right to their respective Writings and Discoveries * * * "). From the start, Congress has divided the protection given to authors and inventors, established different criteria for protection, and provided different periods of protection. [Citation.]

The division between the scope of copyright protection and patent protection has been recognized in Section 102 of the 1976 Copyright Law (hereinafter "the Act"). 17 U.S.C. § 102. Section 102(a) restates, with new flexibility, what has been the traditional area covered by copyright: to protect through limited monopoly original works of authorship. [Footnote.] 17 U.S.C. § 102(a). Section 102(b), taken together with the Act's definitions, excludes those areas which, if they are to be protected, may be only through patent law. [Footnote.] 35 U.S.C. § 1, *et seq.* The works in suit are such that they may arguably be entitled to copyright protection or patent protection, both forms of protection or neither. I am asked to consider the motion for preliminary injunction only from the point of view of copyright infringement, yet it is clear that Section 102 must be interpreted in terms of Congress' intent with regard to both copyright and patent, at least as patent law limits the scope of the 1976 Act.[6]

B. The Divided Views of Others.

The problems raised here stem from the fact that there is no clear consensus on how to describe the technology employed in microcomputers. With no clarity there, the application of law to fact becomes unsure. Plaintiff Apple's claim is based on the argument that 1) a computer's operating system is a form of expression, not an idea or process; 2) whether in ROM or on floppy disk, object code or an object program, containing code, is a form of expression and a work of authorship and 3) a ROM is a tangible medium of expression, not a mechanical device. Leaving aside the question of how to describe the computer's technology and the works in suit, plaintiff argues that it was the clear intent of Congress in the

---

6. Plaintiff Apple, relying on *In re Yardley,* 493 F.2d 1389 (C.C.P.A.1974), contends that the scope of copyright is not limited by the scope of patent and that the same thing may receive both copyright and patent protection. I think that this contention is wrong and that plaintiff's reliance on *Yardley* is misplaced. The court in *Yardley,* following the Supreme Court in *Mazer v. Stein,* 347 U.S. 201, 74 S.Ct. 460, 98 L.Ed. 630 (1954), found that the 1909 Copyright Law and the 1952 Patent Law provided for overlapping protection. That analysis applied to this case and the 1976 Act begs the question. Section 102(b) explicitly removes from copyright protection "any idea, procedure, process, system, method of operation * * * " and section 101 explicitly excludes those works whose

"mechanical or utilitarian" function cannot be separated from the work in which it adheres. 17 U.S.C. §§ 101 & 102(b). The test requires both "separability and independence from 'the utilitarian aspects of the article'" H.R.Rep.No. 1476, 94th Cong., 2nd Sess. 55 (1976), U.S.Code Cong. & Admin.News 1976. p. 5659. Neither Section 102(b) nor this test was in the 1909 Copyright Act. In argument, plaintiff has not distinguished the form of the work from its utilitarian purpose. In fact, by arguing that the works in suit are each "literary works" or forms of expression, plaintiff has suggested the opposite: that their function and form are merged because each work as a whole "convey[s] information." [Citation.]

1976 Act and its 1980 Amendment to the Act to protect all computer programs, in whatever form, as if they were a species of "literary works."

Opinion has been divided on how to treat object codes, on the nature of the authorship entailed, and on how to treat ROMs generally. The National Commission on New Technological Uses of Copyright Works (hereinafter

"CONTU") was divided.[7] Judicial opinion has been mixed.[8] *See Data Cash Systems, Inc. v. JS&A Group, Inc.* 480 F.Supp. 1063 (N.D.Ill.1979), *aff'd on other grounds,* 628 F.2d 1038 (7th Cir. 1980); *Tandy Corp. v. Personal Micro Computers, Inc.,* 524 F.Supp. 171 (N.D.Cal. 1981).[9] The legislative history is unclear.[10] Commentators have arrived at different conclusions. [Footnote.]

7. CONTU was established in 1974 to make recommendations to Congress concerning the copyrightability of computer software and other associated programs; it submitted its Final Report in 1978. Final Report, National Commission on New Technological Uses of Copyrighted Works (1978) (hereinafter "Final Report"). The Final Report consisted of a majority statement and separate statements by Commissioner Nimmer (concurring), Commissioner Hersey (dissenting), and Commissioner Karpatkin (dissenting in support of Commissioner Hersey).

The majority in the Final Report appear to be definite in its attitude towards the copyrightability of computer programs. "Flow charts, sources codes, and object codes are works of authorship in which copyright subsists. * * *" Final Report 21. Nonetheless in another passage, the majority observed that "[c]opyright, therefore protects the program so long as it remains fixed in a tangible medium of expression but *does not protect the electro-mechanical functioning of a machine.*" *Id.* 20 (emphasis added). And again later, the majority commented that "[i]f it should prove possible to tap off these [electrical] impulses then, perhaps, the process would be all that was appropriated, and no infringement of the copyright would occur." *Id.* 22 The present case is, of course, focussed exactly on those issues the majority questioned. *See infra* notes 14-15 and accompanying text.

In its summary, CONTU made clear that it had not resolved the issues raised by programs encoded on a ROM.
> It is equally important to note that these recommendations do not deal with each and every technological issue affecting the interests of copyright users and owners. Specific topics may deserve congressional attention * * * (2) protection for topography or layout of microcircuit chips.

* * *

> The question of copyright protection for the topography of microcircuit chips was raised by a manufacturer of these devices too late to be dealt with adequately by the Commission.

Id. 79. *See infra* note 9 for discussion of subsequent congressional investigation of copyright protection for chip topography.

In his concurrence, Commissioner Nimmer suggested that CONTU had gone too far in its views of software copyright protection by extending protection to areas reserved for patent law or areas deliberately left unprotected. *Id.* 26.
> [I]t may prove desirable to limit copyright protection for software to those computer programs which produce works which themselves qualify for copyright protection. * * * A program designed for a computer game would be copyrightable because the out-

put would itself constitute an audiovisual work. On the other hand, programs which control the heating and air-conditioning in a building, or which determine the flow of fuel in an engine, or which control traffic signals would not be eligible for copyright because their operations do not result in copyrightable works. * * *
Id. 27. *See infra* text accompanying notes 18-19.

In his dissent, Commissioner Hersey noted the machine-control character of a computer program. He contended it was neither a "writing" nor a "literary work," since it had no communicative function. *Id.* 27-30. "Communication as we understand it ceases, and * * * 'behavior'—an opening and closing of electronic gates—sets in." *Id.* 37. *See infra* note 14.

8. *Data Cash* is perhaps the most definitive trial court opinion holding that object code in ROM is not copyright protected. Its analysis of the function of object code is persuasive. However, its holding is somewhat weakened by the affirming opinion of the Court of Appeals since it may be read as suggesting that ROMs may be copyright protected if the copyright formalities have been satisfied. *See infra* text accompanying note 18.

In two other cases, a trial court, considering allegations of restraint of trade in the computer field, observed that copyright does not prevent others from copying the material embodiment of the source program that is found in the object program. *In re Data General Corp. Antitrust Litigation,* 490 F.Supp. 1089, 1113 (N.D.Calif.1980), *In re Data General Corp. Antitrust Litigation,* 529 F.Supp. 801, 816 (N.D.Calif.1981). In a somewhat similar question to that raised here, the court in *Synercom Technology, Inc. v. University Computing Co.,* 462 F.Supp. 1003 (N.D.Tex.1978) held that computer input formats were not copyright protected. The court said that "the litmus seems to be whether the material proffered for copyright undertakes to express." *Id.* 1011. "Thus the issue is whether [defendant] copied expressed ideas or their expression." *Id.* 1012.

Tandy Corp. represents the opposite judicial point of view. The facts in *Tandy Corp.* are similar to this case, alleged infringement of ROM object program that consisted of the computer's operating system. Disagreeing with the decision in *Data Cash,* the court held that the program was a work of authorship and that a ROM is a tangible medium of expression under the Copyright Act. [Citation.] More recently in *GCA Corp. v. Chance, et al.* Civ. No. C-82-1062 (N.D.Calif. July 12, 1982), the court followed *Tandy,* holding that object code in a ROM was copyright protected since the source code was copyrighted. However, the court's rather terse analysis provides little guidance.

Apple's position is not implausible. The program of an operating system is, quite conceivably, the expression of an original work that is fixed in the tangible medium of the written program or fixed in the medium that stores it, whether it be disk or ROM. Object code may be said to be the language used by a programmer in the same way Hemingway may be said to have used English to write *For Whom the Bell Tolls*. A ROM may be considered a "tangible medium of expression," fixing an original work much as a book, record or motion picture film fix a literary work, a musical work or a motion picture.[12] 17 U.S.C. § 102(a).

C. Case Law and Copyright Law

All the analysis of the facts in this case depends upon the meaning given to the key words of art used in the Act and defined by the courts. They are: "creativity and originality," "expression and ideas," and "works of authorship".

(1) "Creativity and Originality". From the outset, it is important to recognize that the issues raised here cannot be resolved on the grounds of creativity—the presence or absence of it. Copyright law does not require that the author or artist be exceptionally cre-

---

In the last year, a number of courts have held that a ROM-based object program used to create visual displays in arcade games is properly copyright protected. *Midway MFG. v. Artic International, Inc.,* 547 F.Supp. 999, 211 U.S. P.Q. 1152 (N.D.Ill.1982). [Citation.] *Atari, Inc. v. North American Philips Consumer Electronics Corp.,* 672 F.2d 607 (7th Cir. 1982); *Stern Electronics, Inc. v. Kaufman,* 669 F.2d 852 (2d Cir. 1982); *Atari, Inc. v. Amusement World, Inc.* [547 F. Supp. 222] (D.Md. Nov. 27, 1981); *Midway Manufacturing Co. v. Drikschneider,* 543 F.Supp. 466 (D.Neb.1981); *Williams Electronics, Inc. v. Artic International, Inc.,* Civ. No. 81-1852 (D.N.J. June 24, 1981); *Cinematronics, Inc. v. K. Noma Enterprise Co.,* Civ. No. 81-439 (D.Ariz. May 22, 1981).

9. Congressional intent regarding the copyrightability of object codes and ROMs is not clear. The 1976 Act left intact the case law developed under the 1909 Act. 17 U.S.C. § 117 (1976). See H.R.Rep. 116. The 1980 Amendment to Title 17, P.L. 96-517, incorporated a definition of computer programs, 17 U.S.C. § 101 as amended, and excluded from copyright infringement some forms of copying and adaptation, 17 U.S.C. § 117 as amended. While commentators have been willing to interpret these amendments as extending absolute copyright protection to software. [Citation.] the amendments and subsequent legislative discussions suggest a restrictive reading. In April 1979, Congress held hearings to consider a bill amending the 1976 Act in order to provide copyright protection for imprinted design patterns on semiconductor chips. [Citation.] The question facing the committee was whether chips or integrated circuits are appropriately protected and, if not protected, whether copyright protection should be extended to them through legislation. "In the judgment and practice of the Copyright Office, the configuration of the chip is not [copyrightable]—if you were to depict these patterns on an earlier piece of paper we believe that piece of paper and the drawing is copyrighted, but there are limitations on the rights extended thereby." [Citation.] "[I]t's a question of whether the drawing and the chip are the same thing." [Citations.] A recent House staff report indicated that the debate continues. "The current methods available for protecting

software are patents, copyright, and trade secret law. However, the determination of the best alternative is still under debate. The issue of software protection reflects the problems associated with applying old legal tools to new technologies." [Citation.] "The underlying issue is whether new forms of statutory protection are necessary to insure the continued development of computer software. Congress may wish to consider whether current efforts such as those to amend the Copyright Act of 1976, are sufficient to protect new technologies or whether additional measures should be undertaken. Congress may wish to closely monitor decisions by the Supreme Court in this area in order to assess the need for legislative action." [Citation.]

10. Litigation reflects conflict. The recent increase generally in litigation of the kind represented by this case reflects an increased conflict in the applicability of the copyright law to ROMs and object codes. *See supra* note 8. [Citation.] As one might suspect by the increased litigation, members of the industry appear not to agree on whether the current law covers works like those in suit. * * *

12. Under this definition "copies" and "phonorecords" together will comprise all of the material objects in which copyrightable works are capable of being fixed. The definitions of these terms in section 101 [17 U.S.C. § 101], together with their usage in section 102 [17 U.S.C. § 102] and throughout the bill, reflect a fundamental distinction between the "original work" which is the product of "authorship" and the multitude of material objects in which it can be embodied. Thus, in the sense of the bill, a "book" is not a work of authorship, but is a particular kind of "copy." Instead, the author may write a "literary work," which in turn can be embodied in a wide range of "copies" and "phonorecords," including books, periodicals, computer punch cards, microfilm, tape recordings, and so forth. * * *

H.R.Rep. 53. Section 101, 17 U.S.C., defines "copies" as "material objects * * * in which a work is fixed by any method now known or later *developed * * * from which the work can be perceived, reproduced, or otherwise communicated, either directly or with the aid of a machine or device*," (emphasis added). *See infra* note 21 and accompanying text.

ative or original. In fact, "a modicum of creativity may suffice for a work to be protected." [Citation.] Alternatively, extreme creativity does not in itself make an argument for copyrightability. At issue is only whether the works in suit are the "fixed" expression of an author's "original work." [Footnote.]

Nevertheless, "[i]t is possible to have an 'original work of authorship' without having a 'copy' embodying it, and it is also possible to have a 'copy' embodying something that does not qualify as an 'original work of authorship.'" H.R.Rep. 53. Although there can be a variety of different material embodiments of the work, there can be only one original work.

In the case of computer programs, like those in suit, one must be able to identify the original work that has been embodied. It is not clear whether the program-designer's idea of the operating system program, the source program, or the ROM is the "original work of authorship." It is not surprising that this should be hard to determine, because at each stage major transformations in the structure of the "program" take place. From plaintiff's point of view, the best argument is that the idea of the operating system is the "original work" and that all that follows are copies. The counter-argument that plaintiff must respond to is a technical one that goes to the heart of the technology; in the case of the programs on ROM did the programmer-designer imagine the architectural structure of the ROM, the overlay of micro-switches that would be most economical and efficient for the system, or did he envision the flow chart of operations which the program would perform? If the former, the programmer may be said to have been an engineer designing a utilitarian aspect of the machine. If the latter, the programmer may not be said to have designed the architecture of the chip. *See infra* note 14 and accompanying text.

Apple's argument that its programmers displayed virtuoso skill, if not genius, in developing the programs and the ROMs is not dispositive, even though I tend to agree that the evidence demonstrates their extraordinary skill. In the context of the Copyright Act, an "original" work need not be a work of genius.

(2) "Expression and Ideas". The distinction

between ideas and expression, while not always self-evident, is crucial. An "expression" may, under some circumstances, be said to be the tangible, fixed form of an idea where the expression's purpose is "to convey information." 17 U.S.C. § 101. Such a statutory reading is consistent with both the Act's legislative history, H.R.Rep. 52-53, and case law. Any tangible form can be treated as the constitutional equivalent of "writings" [citation], which are the classic, permanent medium for conveying information and transmitting ideas.

Enlarged as the concept of "writings" now is, it retains its original meaning: to express and communicate. *Baker v. Selden,* 101 U.S. 99, 25 L.Ed. 841 (1879), made the first, and still most notable, statement of this proposition. "The description of the art in a book, though entitled to the benefit of copyright, lays no foundation for an exclusive claim to the art itself. *The object of one is explanation; the object of the other is use. Id.* 105 (an accounting form held not copyrightable, but the explanation of the form was) (emphasis added).

Admittedly, the holding in *Baker* has been somewhat limited after *Mazer v. Stein, see supra* note 6, *see also* 1 Nimmer on Copyright, § 2.18[C], but the underlying perception still retains its vitality. The balance *Baker* presented between "explanation" and "use" is the balance between the material meant to be protected by the copyright clause of the Constitution and that meant to be protected by the patent clause. *Accord Taylor Instrument Companies v. Fawley-Brost Co.,* 139 F.2d 98, 99 (10th Cir. 1943). Following *Baker,* the court in *Taylor* drew the distinction between copyright and patent as between that which "teaches * * * [and] explains the use of the art" and that which "is an essential element of the machine." *Id.* 100. The vitality of *Baker* is found in the distinctions drawn between Section 102(a) and Section 102(b) in the Act, between that work "fixed in a tangible medium of expression" and that which has [sic] its primary function the exploitation or use of an idea. [Citation.]

It is not clear in this case that an operating system in binary code or one represented either in a ROM or by micro-switches are "explanations" under the *Baker-Taylor* doctrine. Equally, it is not clear that object code, which was not designed to be "read" by a human reader and can only be read by an expert with a microscope and patience, is a language of description. It cannot teach. It can be used to control the operation of the computer. For these reasons, it may be more accurate to say that operating systems are an essential element of the machine, if not an essential part of the machine that makes it work. Similarly, it may be more accurate to say that object code in its binary form or chip form is a useful version of the machine's electrical pulse.

(3) "Works of Authorship". Copyright protection subsists only in original works of authorship. 17 U.S.C. § 102(a). Working directly in object code, the programmer appears to think in the manner of a mathematician or engineer, who solves explicit problems that have defined parameters.[14] While it is tempting to treat all computer programs as "literary works," such an analysis may only serve to confuse the meaning of authorship.

The process of constructing a chip is "not so much a work of authorship as the product of engineering knowledge (often skillful and sometimes creative) focused on obtaining a desired function or output. Accordingly, * * * the resulting integrated circuit represent[s] the function desired in the circuit rather than an effort of the type exerted by authors." [Citation.] *See supra* note 9. Hence, it may be more apt to describe an encoded ROM as a pictorial three-dimensional object than as a literary work and to discount the notion of authorship associated with literary or creative works.

Programmers need not write in object code and, most do not, because the computer can make its own "translation" of object code from an original source code.[15] Because this is so, it is argued that the "automatic" translation of source to object code establishes a predictable one-to-one relationship between the two codes that preserves the programmer's original force of authorship. [Citations.]

The reasoning that finds object code a derivative work of source code and thus copyrightable, 17 U.S.C. § 103(a), follows somewhat Judge Hand's in *Reiss v. National Quotation Bureau, Inc.*, 276 F. 717 (S.D.N.Y. 1921) (meaningless code words were copyright protected). [Citation.] According to this reasoning, the programmer meets the standard of authorship when he has created expressions even if the computer is to supply its own "meaning" and its own use. "I can see no reason why [the code] words should not be [writings] because they communicate nothing. They may have their uses for all that, aesthetic or practical, and they may be the production of high ingenuity, or even genius." *Reiss*, 276 F. at 719. [Citation.]

D. The ROM as Three-Dimensional, Pictorial, Graphic or Sculptural Work

It is precisely the problem of description that makes this problem so baffling. The list of comparisons, thanks to ingenious counsel, is

---

14. At the level of the microcode, physical and abstract meet. The microcode controls the actual circuits. * * * Indeed, the physical machine responds only to microcode. It was microcode, at bottom, that caused [the computer] to translate [the division symbol] into microcode. In this sense, the computer chases its tail. * * * Writing microcode, however, is no simple task. The code is by definition intricate. To make the machine execute just one of its two hundred or three hundred basic instructions, the coder usually has to *plan the passage of hundreds of signals through hundreds of gates.* Limited storage space forces the coder to economize—to make one microinstruction accomplish more than one task, for example. At the same time, though, the coder must take care that one microinstruction does not foul up the performance of another.

* * *

Writing microcode is like nothing else in my life. For days there's nothing coming out. * * * [F]inally I get into a mental state where I'm a *microcode-writing machine.* You have to understand the program thoroughly and you have to have thought of all the myriad ways in which you can put your microverbs to-

gether. You have a hundred L-shaped blocks to build a building. You take all the pieces, put them together, pull them apart, put them together. After a while, you're like a kid on a jungle gym. There are all these constructs in your mind and you can swing from one to the other with ease.

T. Kidder, The Soul of a New Machine 97-102 (1981) (quoting program designer) (emphasis added).

15. Programs written in source codes are generally conceded to be copyrightable. [Citations.]

Source codes are mnemonic systems of abbreviating machine instructions. "Typical abbreviations might be HLT for "halt." STA for "store in register A," BR + for "branch if the register is plus," XZJ for "jump if index register is zero." [Citation.] Source programs are placed in the computer through the keyboard, by disk, tape or cards and, then, are converted by the machine into an intermediate assembly language and finally into object code. [Citation.] Although programmers normally write in source code because it can easily be read and corrected, programmers may write directly in object code when it is necessary to have direct control over the architecture of the ROM. *See supra* note 14.

a long one; equally good analogies lead to contradicting results.

ROMs which have interiors etched or designed to incorporate object code in their physical shape may be likened to three-dimensional works of art [citation] and therefore be entitled to copyright protection. [Citation.]

In *Taney [sic] Corp. v. Personal Micro Computers, Inc.*, the court viewed an encoded ROM as being somewhat akin to a three-dimensional object that may not be copied by a noncopyrightholder without infringing on the copyright. *Id.* 173, 175. In this light, a ROM is taken to be a self-contained and clearly fixed form of expression since "*duplication* of a chip is not the use of a copyrighted program 'in conjunction with' a computer; it is simply the copying of a chip." *Id.* 175. This analysis contradicts somewhat the view of the CONTU majority that a "tapped off" ROM may not be protected from copyright infringement. [Footnote.]

On the other hand, ROMs encoded with an object program may be compared to a physical structure with an essentially useful purpose or function, like that of a bridge [citation] or to an architectural work like a house. [Citation.] As such, an object program encoded on a ROM would not be entitled to copyright protection. [Footnote.] * * *

It is possible that this is the situation in the current dispute: neither the Apple nor Franklin ROM is a copy of an "original work" since the plan upon which each is based may be considered to exist separately from the chip that is ultimately constructed. Absent copying, there is no infringement of copyright. [Citation.]

The issue here is, of course, whether the ROM structured with code is a new entity created through the use of the plans, *i.e.*, the program, or whether it incorporates the plan or program in its own structure. If the former, * * * it would not be entitled to copyright protection. If the latter, it might be entitled to protection. But even here, the protection might only extend to the ROM with its interior. It would not cover the object code by itself.

E. The Expression of a Utilitarian Function

Defendants argue that the programmed ROM is an object that merges idea and expression to the point they are indistinguishable [citation] or merges its utilitarian function and expressive purpose so that they too are inseparable. [Citation.] It is this inseparability of function and purpose that the court in *Data Cash* found, where it was held that the ROM at issue was not copyrightable.[18]

The copyright protection available to a ROM is similarly restricted if the ROM is defined as a mechanical device. "In its object phase, the computer program is a mechanical device which is engaged in the computer to become an essential part of the mechanical process." [Citations.] If a ROM is found to be a mechanical device, it loses the protection reserved for writings and expression under copyright. [Citation.] The argument that a ROM is a mechanical device has been made:

> Descriptions and printed instructions tell human beings how to use material or machinery to produce desired results. In the case of computer programs [on the other hand], *the instructions themselves eventually become an essential part of the machinery that produces the results.* They become (in chip or hardware form) a permanent part of the actual machinery. * * * This is a device capable of commanding a series of impulses which open and close the electronic gates of the computer in such order as to produce the desired result.

CONTU, Final Report 28 (Commissioner Hersey dissenting) (emphasis in original)[19] Commissioner Hersey observes that the appropriate analogy to describe a program within the computer is that of a "cam" which, "like a mature computer program, is the objectification of a series of instructions." *Id.* 29-30. While either the cam or the machine-language or binary code may be read by an expert, its purpose is not to serve as a form of human communication. As he wrote, echoing the *Baker-Taylor* doctrine, "[p]rinted instructions explain *how* to do something; programs are *able* to do it." *Id.* 28 (emphasis in original).

---

18. *See supra* note 8.

19. *See supra* note 7.

The argument made by Commissioner Hersey and by defendant Franklin that the ROM is a mechanical device is an argument for its patentability. *See supra* note 6. A ROM may be characterized as firmware, a combination of software and hardware that operates together to control a computer. Certain firmware is protectable under patent law. [Citation.]

The argument for the patentability of the various operating systems in suit may also rest on the view that they are manifestations and implementations of the "useful arts," as the term is understood in patent law, directed to producing a beneficial result. [Citation.] A computer's operating system is, by this view, the means by which a computer is "transformed and reduced to a different state or thing" [citations], although it would have to be shown that its transformed state is specialized and distinct from that of other machines of the same class. I do not, of course, conclude that Apple will be able to satisfy the rather rigorous tests of the patent law.

F. The Test of Communication for Copyright

The *Baker-Taylor* doctrine suggests that the scope of copyright is limited to material that can claim an underlying expressive or communicative purpose. It is a test not easily applied because it raises questions at the very heart of all discussions on the purpose and meaning of language. It is a test not easily satisfied by works, like those in this suit, that are in the form of binary code and electromechanical chips.

Perhaps it is sufficient to say in the context of the present motion for preliminary injunction that no matter how indirect or exotic the form of expression or the medium used, the question must be: is the expression directed to a human audience?

A recent case like *Midway Mfg. Co. v. Artic International, Inc.,* 547 F.Supp. 999, 211 U.S.P.Q. 1152 (N.D.Ill.1982) (ROM containing the code for a visual display held copyrightable) reveals the complexity of the question presented by the present case and the fragile but important distinctions that must be made when considering the copyrightability of object codes.[20] In *Midway,* the object code was the underlying system used by the computer to produce a series of visual images that were meant to be perceived by an arcade game player.

Restricted to these facts, it is not illogical to treat the object code as an "expression * * * which can be perceived, reproduced, or otherwise communicated, either directly or with the aid of a machine or device."[21] 17 U.S.C. § 102(a). The "original work" is the visual display that has been fixed, presumably, first in source code and later in object code. No matter how it has been fixed, its purpose from the outset was to generate an image that could be *perceived* and its goal was to attract and engage a human audience. Such purposes and goals satisfy our conventional expectations of expression.

If the concept of "language" means anything, it means an ability to create human interaction. It is the fixed expression of this that the copyright law protects, and only this. To go beyond the bonds of this protection would be ultimately to provide copyright protection to the programs created by a computer to run other computers. With that, we step into the world of Gulliver where horses are "human" because they speak a language that sounds remarkably like the one humans use. It is an intriguing analogy but false. The logic of the

---

20. *See supra* note 8.

21. It does not distort this phrase to understand it as requiring that the work be perceptible to a human audience and not merely perceptible to a machine. Its plain meaning suggests that machine aid is recognized in this section only if it is capable of aiding human perception and supporting human communication. A similar construction is used in Section 401, "notice of copyright: Visually perceptible copies." It would indeed be a curious interpretation of Section 401 if it were to be read as referring to anything but a copy that can be humanly perceived.

* * * [A] notice of copyright as provided by this section shall be placed on all *publicly distributed copies from which the work can be visually perceived,* either directly or with the aid of a machine or device. 17 U.S.C. § 401. (emphasis added). *See also* Regulations, Office of Copyright.

[T]he Copyright Office will consider registration for a "book" * * * if * * *

(2) The program has been published, with the required copyright notice; that is, *"copies" (i.e., reproductions of the program in a form perceptible or capable of being made perceptible to the human eye) bearing the notice have been distributed or made available to the public.*

[Citations.]

court in *Midway* does not resolve the problem raised in this case.

IV. CONCLUSIONS

The requirements for issuing a preliminary injunction are well known. Plaintiff must show:

    1. A reasonable probability of success on the merits;
    2. Irreparable injury to the plaintiff that exceeds any injury to the enjoined defendant;
    3. The improbability of harm to other interested persons; and
    4. A public interest that would be furthered.

[Citation.]

There is limited evidence as to the last two showings, but, as the foregoing memorandum should make clear, I have considerable doubt about Apple's likelihood of success on the merits. While Apple's arguments are strong, I do not believe that it has shown a reasonable *probability* of success. It is also clear that Apple is better suited to withstand whatever injury it might sustain during litigation than is Franklin to withstand the effects of a preliminary injunction. While I am not prepared to find that the injunction sought by Apple would force Franklin out of business, it would certainly have a devastating effect.

Apple having failed to make the necessary showing, its motion will be denied.

APPLE COMPUTER, INC. v. FRANKLIN COMPUTER CORP.

714 F.2d 1240
(United States Court of Appeals, Third Circuit, Aug. 30, 1983.)

SLOVITER, C. J.

I.

INTRODUCTION

Apple Computer, Inc. appeals from the district court's denial of a motion to preliminarily enjoin Franklin Computer Corp. from infringing the copyrights Apple holds on fourteen computer programs.

* * *

In this case the district court denied the preliminary injunction, *inter alia*, because it

had "some doubt as to the copyrightability of the programs." [Citation.] This legal ruling is fundamental to all future proceedings in this action and, as the parties and amici curiae seem to agree, has considerable significance to the computer services industry. [Footnote.] Because we conclude that the district court proceeded under an erroneous view of the applicable law, we reverse the denial of the preliminary injunction and remand.

II.

FACTS AND PROCEDURAL HISTORY

Apple, one of the computer industry leaders, manufactures and markets personal computers (microcomputers), related peripheral equipment such as disk drives (peripherals), and computer programs (software). It presently manufactures Apple II computers and distributes over 150 programs. Apple has sold over 400,000 Apple II computers, employs approximately 3,000 people, and had annual sales of $335,000,000 for fiscal year 1981. One of the byproducts of Apple's success is the independent development by third parties of numerous computer programs which are designed to run on the Apple II computer.

Franklin, the defendant below, manufactures and sells the ACE 100 personal computer and at the time of the hearing employed about 75 people and had sold fewer than 1,000 computers. The ACE 100 was designed to be "Apple compatible," so that peripheral equipment and software developed for use with the Apple II computer could be used in conjunction with the ACE 100. Franklin's copying of Apple's operating system computer programs in an effort to achieve such compatibility precipitated this suit.

Like all computers both the Apple II and ACE 100 have a central processing unit (CPU) which is the integrated circuit that executes programs. In lay terms, the CPU does the work it is instructed to do. Those instructions are contained on computer programs.

There are three levels of computer language in which computer programs may be written. [Footnote.] High level language, such as the commonly used BASIC or FORTRAN, uses English words and symbols, and is relatively easy to learn and understand (e.g., "GO

TO 40" tells the computer to skip intervening steps and go to the step at line 40). A somewhat lower level language is assembly language, which consists of alphanumeric labels (e.g., "ADC" means "add with carry"). Statements in high level language, and apparently also statements in assembly language, are referred to as written in "source code." The third, or lowest level computer language, is machine language, a binary language using two symbols, 0 and 1, to indicate an open or closed switch (e.g., "01101001" means, to the Apple, add two numbers and save the result). Statements in machine language are referred to as written in "object code."

The CPU can only follow instructions written in object code. However, programs are usually written in source code which is more intelligible to humans. Programs written in source code can be converted or translated by a "compiler" program into object code for use by the computer. Programs are generally distributed only in their object code version stored on a memory device.

A computer program can be stored or fixed on a variety of memory devices, two of which are of particular relevance for this case. The ROM (Read Only Memory) is an internal permanent memory device consisting of a semiconductor "chip" which is incorporated into the circuitry of the computer. A program in object code is embedded on a ROM before it is incorporated in the computer. Information stored on a ROM can only be read, not erased or rewritten.[3] The Ace 100 apparently contains EPROMS (Erasable Programmable Read Only Memory) on which the stored information can be erased and the chip reprogrammed, but the district court found that for purposes of this proceeding, the difference between ROMs and EPROMs is inconsequential. [Citation.] The other device used for storing the programs at issue is a diskette or "floppy disk", an auxiliary memory device consisting of a flexible magnetic disk resembling a phonograph record, which can be inserted into the computer and from which data or instructions can be read.

Computer programs can be categorized by function as either application programs or operating system programs. Application programs usually perform a specific task for the computer user, such as word processing, checkbook balancing, or playing a game. In contrast, operating system programs generally manage the internal functions of the computer or facilitate use of application programs. The parties agree that the fourteen computer programs at issue in this suit are operating system programs. [Footnote.]

Apple filed suit in the United States District Court for the Eastern District of Pennsylvania pursuant to 28 U.S.C. § 1338 on May 12, 1982, alleging that Franklin was liable for copyright infringement of the fourteen computer programs, patent infringement, unfair competition, and misappropriation. Franklin's answer in respect to the copyright counts included the affirmative defense that the programs contained no copyrightable subject matter. Franklin counterclaimed for declaratory judgment that the copyright registrations were invalid and unenforceable, and sought affirmative relief on the basis of Apple's alleged misuse. Franklin also moved to dismiss eleven of the fourteen copyright infringement counts on the ground that Apple failed to comply with the procedural requirements for suit under 17 U.S.C. §§ 410, 411.

After expedited discovery, Apple moved for a preliminary injunction to restrain Franklin from using, copying, selling, or infringing Apple's copyrights. The district court held a three day evidentiary hearing limited to the copyright infringement claims. Apple produced evidence at the hearing in the form of affidavits and testimony that programs sold by Franklin in conjunction with its ACE 100 computer were virtually identical with those covered by the fourteen Apple copyrights. The variations that did exist were minor, consisting merely of such things as deletion of reference to Apple or its copyright notice.[5] James Huston, an Apple systems programmer, concluded that the Franklin programs were "un-

---

3. In contrast to the permanent memory devices a RAM (Random Access Memory) is a chip on which volatile internal memory is stored which is erased when the computer's power is turned off.

5. For example, 8 bytes of memory were altered in the

Autostart ROM program so that when the computer is turned on "ACE 100" appears on the screen rather than "Apple II." The Franklin DOS 3.3 program also had 16 bytes (out of 9000) that allowed use of upper and lower case.

questionably copied from Apple and could not have been independently created." He reached this conclusion not only because it is "almost impossible for so many lines of code" to be identically written, but also because his name, which he had embedded in one program (Master Create), and the word "Applesoft", which was embedded in another (DOS 3.3), appeared on the Franklin master disk. Apple estimated the "works in suit" took 46 man-months to produce at a cost of over $740,000, not including the time or cost of creating or acquiring earlier versions of the programs or the expense of marketing the programs.

Franklin did not dispute that it copied the Apple programs. Its witness admitted copying each of the works in suit from the Apple programs. Its factual defense was directed to its contention that it was not feasible for Franklin to write its own operating system programs. David McWherter, now Franklin's vice-president of engineering, testified he spent 30–40 hours in November 1981 making a study to determine if it was feasible for Franklin to write its own Autostart ROM program and concluded it was not because "there were just too many entry points in relationship to the number of instructions in the program." Entry points at specific locations in the program can be used by programmers to mesh their application programs with the operating system program. McWherter concluded that use of the identical signals was necessary in order to ensure 100% compatibility with application programs created to run on the Apple computer. He admitted that he never attempted to rewrite Autostart ROM and conceded that some of the works in suit (*i.e.*, Copy, Copy A, Master Create, and Hello) probably could have been rewritten by Franklin. Franklin made no attempt to rewrite any of the programs prior to the lawsuit except for Copy, although McWherter testified that Franklin was "in the process of redesigning" some of the Apple programs and that "[w]e had a fair degree of certainty that that would probably work." Apple introduced evidence that Franklin could have rewritten programs, including the Autostart ROM program, and that there are in existence operating programs written by third parties which are compatible with Apple II.

Franklin's principal defense at the preliminary injunction hearing and before us is pri-

marily a legal one, directed to its contention that the Apple operating system programs are not capable of copyright protection.

The district court denied the motion for preliminary injunction by order and opinion dated July 30, 1982. Apple moved for reconsideration in light of this court's decision in *Williams Electronics, Inc. v. Artic International, Inc.*, 685 F.2d 870 (3d Cir.1982), which was decided August 2, 1982, three days after the district court decision. The district court denied the motion for reconsideration. We have jurisdiction of Apple's appeal pursuant to 28 U.S.C. § 1292(a)(1).

III.

THE DISTRICT COURT OPINION

In its opinion, the district court referred to the four factors to be considered on request for a preliminary injunction; a reasonable probability of success on the merits; irreparable injury; the improbability of harm to other interested persons; and the public interest. [Citations.] The court stated it based its denial of the motion on the first two factors. The court held Apple had not made the requisite showing of likelihood of success on the merits because it "concluded that there is some doubt as to the copyrightability of the programs described in this litigation." [Citation.] It also stated that "Apple is better suited to withstand whatever injury it might sustain during litigation than is Franklin to withstand the effects of a preliminary injunction" because an injunction would have a "devastating effect" on Franklin's business [citation], apparently concluding on that basis that Apple had failed to show irreparable harm.

It is difficult to discern precisely why the district court questioned the copyrightability of the programs at issue since there is no finding, statement, or holding on which we can focus which clearly sets forth the district court's view. Throughout the opinion the district court referred to the "complexity of the question presented by the present case" [citation], and the "baffling" problem at issue. [Citation.]

The opinion expresses a series of generalized concerns which may have led the court to its ultimate conclusion, and which the parties and amici treat as holdings. The district court referred to the requirement under the

Copyright Act of finding "original works of authorship", 17 U.S.C. § 102(a), and seems to have found that there was a sufficient "modicum of creativity" to satisfy the statutory requirement of an "original work". [Citation.] The court was less clear as to whether the creation of a computer program by a programmer satisfied the requirement of "works of authorship" [citation] and whether an operating system program in "binary code or one represented either in a ROM or by micro-switches" was an "expression" which could be copyrighted as distinguished from an "idea" which could not be. [Citation.]

Again, although we cannot point to a specific holding, running throughout the district court opinion is the suggestion that programs in object code and ROMs may not be copyrightable. Thus, for example, in a series of discursive footnotes, the district court stated that it found "persuasive" a district court opinion "holding that object code in ROM is not copyright protected" [citation], described an opinion reaching a contrary conclusion as containing "rather terse analysis [which] provides little guidance" [citation], and stated that "Congressional intent regarding the copyrightability of object codes and ROMs is not clear" [citation] and that even among members of the industry it was not clear that the copyright law protects works "like those in suit that are ROM-based." [Citation.]

We read the district court opinion as presenting the following legal issues: (1) whether copyright can exist in a computer program expressed in object code, (2) whether copyright can exist in a computer program embedded on a ROM, (3) whether copyright can exist in an operating system program, and (4) whether independent irreparable harm must be shown for a preliminary injunction in copyright infringement actions.

IV.

DISCUSSION

A. Copyrightability of a Computer Program Expressed in Object Code

Certain statements by the district court suggest that programs expressed in object code, as distinguished from source code, may not be the proper subject of copyright. We find no

basis in the statute for any such concern. Furthermore, our decision in *Williams Electronics, Inc. v. Artic International, Inc., supra*, laid to rest many of the doubts expressed by the district court.

In 1976, after considerable study, Congress enacted a new copyright law to replace that which had governed since 1909. Act of October 19, 1976, Pub.L. No. 94–553, 90 Stat. 2541 (*codified at* 17 U.S.C. §§ 101 *et seq.*). Under the law, two primary requirements must be satisfied in order for a work to constitute copyrightable subject matter—it must be an "original wor[k] of authorship" and must be "fixed in [a] tangible medium of expression." 17 U.S.C. § 102(a). The statute provides:

(a) Copyright protection subsists, in accordance with this title, in original works of authorship fixed in any tangible medium of expression, now known or later developed, from which they can be perceived, reproduced, or otherwise communicated, either directly or with the aid of a machine or device.

Id. The statute enumerates seven categories under "works of authorship" including "literary works", defined as follows:

"Literary works" are works, other than audiovisual works, expressed in words, numbers, or other verbal or numerical symbols or indicia, regardless of the nature of the material objects, such as books, periodicals, manuscripts, phonorecords, film, tapes, disks, or cards, in which they are embodied.

17 U.S.C. § 101. A work is "fixed" in a tangible medium of expression when:

its embodiment in a copy or phonorecord, by or under the authority of the author, is sufficiently permanent or stable to permit it to be perceived, reproduced, or otherwise communicated for a period of more than transitory duration. A work consisting of sounds, images, or both, that are being transmitted, is "fixed" for purposes of this title if a fixation of the work is being made simultaneously with its transmission.

Id.

Although section 102(a) does not expressly list computer programs as works of authorship, the legislative history suggests that programs were considered copyrightable as literary works. [Citation.] Because a Commission on New Technological Uses ("CONTU") had been created by Congress to study, *inter alia*, computer uses of copyrighted works [citation], Congress enacted a status quo provision, section 117, in the 1976 Act concerning such computer uses pending the CONTU report and recommendations.[6]

The CONTU Final Report recommended that the copyright law be amended, *inter alia*, "to make it explicit that computer programs, to the extent that they embody an author's original creation, are proper subject matter of copyright." National Commission on New Technological Uses of Copyrighted Works, *Final Report* 1 (1979) [hereinafter CONTU Report]. CONTU recommended two changes relevant here: that section 117, the status quo provision, be repealed and replaced with a section limiting exclusive rights in computer programs so as "to ensure that rightful possessors of copies of computer programs may use or adapt these copies for their use," *id.*, and that a definition of computer program be added to section 101. *Id.* at 12. Congress adopted both changes. [Citation.] The revisions embodied CONTU's recommendations to clarify the law of copyright of computer software. [Citation.]

The 1980 amendments added a definition of a computer program:

> A "computer program" is a set of statements or instructions to be used directly or indirectly in a computer in order to bring about a certain result.

17 U.S.C. § 101. The amendments also substituted a new section 117 which provides that "it is not an infringement for the owner of a copy of a computer program to make or authorize the making of another copy or adaptation of that computer program" when necessary to "the utilization of the computer program" or "for archival purposes only." 17 U.S.C. § 117. The parties agree that this section is not implicated in the instant lawsuit. The language of the provision, however, by carving out an exception to the normal proscriptions against copying, clearly indicates that programs are copyrightable and are otherwise afforded copyright protection.

We considered the issue of copyright protection for a computer program in *Williams*

Electronics, Inc. v. Artic International, Inc., and concluded that "the copyrightability of computer programs is firmly established after the 1980 amendment to the Copyright Act." [Citation.] At issue in *Williams* were not only two audiovisual copyrights to the "attract" and "play" modes of a video game, but also the computer program which was expressed in object code embodied in ROM and which controlled the sights and sounds of the game. Defendant there had argued "that when the issue is the copyright on a computer program, a distinction must be drawn between the 'source code' version of a computer program, which * * * can be afforded copyright protection, and the 'object code' stage, which * * * cannot be so protected," an argument we rejected. [Citation.]

The district court here questioned whether copyright was to be limited to works "designed to be 'read' by a human reader [as distinguished from] read by an expert with a microscope and patience," 545 F.Supp. at 821. The suggestion that copyrightability depends on a communicative function to individuals stems from the early decision of *White-Smith Music Publishing Co. v. Apollo Co.*, 209 U.S. 1, 28 S.Ct. 319, 52 L.Ed. 655 (1908), which held a piano roll was not a copy of the musical composition because it was not in a form others, except perhaps for a very expert few, could perceive. *See* 1 *Nimmer on Copyright* § 2.03[B][1] (1983). However, it is clear from the language of the 1976 Act and its legislative history that it was intended to obliterate distinctions engendered by *White-Smith*. [Citation.]

Under the statute, copyright extends to works in any tangible means of expression *"from which they can be perceived,* reproduced, or otherwise communicated, either directly or *with the aid of a machine or device."* 17 U.S.C. § 102(a) (emphasis added). Further, the definition of "computer program" adopted by Congress in the 1980 amendments is "sets of statements or instructions to be used *directly or indirectly* in a computer in order to bring about a certain result." 17 U.S.C. § 101 (em-

---

6. Section 117 applied only to the scope of protection to be accorded copyrighted works when used in conjunction

with a computer and not to the copyrightability of programs. [Citation.]

phasis added). As source code instructions must be translated into object code before the computer can act upon them, only instructions expressed in object code can be used "directly" by the computer. [Citation.] This definition was adopted following the CONTU Report in which the majority clearly took the position that object codes are proper subjects of copyright. [Citation.] The majority's conclusion was reached although confronted by a dissent based upon the theory that the "machine-control phase" of a program is not directed at a human audience. *See* CONTU Report at 28–30 (dissent of Commissioner Hersey).

The defendant in *Williams* had also argued that a copyrightable work "must be intelligible to human beings and must be intended as a medium of communication to human beings." [Citation.] We reiterate the statement we made in *Williams* when we rejected that argument: "[t]he answer to defendant's contention is in the words of the statute itself." [Citation.]

The district court also expressed uncertainty as to whether a computer program in object code could be classified as a "literary work."[7] However, the category of "literary works", one of the seven copyrightable categories, is not confined to literature in the nature of Hemingway's *For Whom the Bell Tolls*. The definition of "literary works" in section 101 includes expression not only in words but also "numbers, or other * * * numerical symbols or indicia", thereby expanding the common usage of "literary works." *Cf. Harcourt, Brace & World, Inc. v. Graphic Controls Corp.*, 329 F.Supp. 517, 523–24 (S.D.N.Y.1971) (the symbols designating questions or response spaces on exam answer sheets held to be copyrightable "writings" under 1909 Act); *Reiss v. National Quotation Bureau, Inc.*, 276 F. 717 (S.D.N.Y.1921) (code book of coined words designed for cable use copyrightable). Thus a computer program, whether in object code or source code, is a "literary work" and is protected from unauthorized copying,

whether from its object or source code version. [Citations.]

B. Copyrightability of a Computer Program Embedded on a ROM

Just as the district court's suggestion of a distinction between source code and object code was rejected by our opinion in *Williams* issued three days after the district court opinion, so also was its suggestion that embodiment of a computer program on a ROM, as distinguished from in a traditional writing, detracts from its copyrightability. In *Williams* we rejected the argument that "a computer program is not infringed when the program is loaded into electronic memory devices (ROMs) and used to control the activity of machines." [Citation.] Defendant there had argued that there can be no copyright protection for the ROMs because they are utilitarian objects or machine parts. We held that the statutory requirement of "fixation", the manner in which the issue arises, is satisfied through the embodiment of the expression in the ROM devices. [Citations.] Therefore, we reaffirm that a computer program in object code embedded in a ROM chip is an appropriate subject of copyright. [Citations.]

C. Copyrightability of Computer Operating System Programs

We turn to the heart of Franklin's position on appeal which is that computer operating system programs, as distinguished from application programs, are not the proper subject of copyright "regardless of the language or medium in which they are fixed." [Emphasis deleted.] [Reference.] Apple suggests that this issue too is foreclosed by our *Williams* decision because some portion of the program at issue there was in effect an operating system program. Franklin is correct that this was not an issue raised by the parties in *Williams* and it was not considered by the court. Thus we consider it as a matter of first impression.

---

7. The district court stated that a programmer working directly in object code appears to think more as a mathematician or engineer, that the process of constructing a chip is less a work of authorship than the product of engineering knowledge, and that it may be more apt to describe an encoded ROM as a pictorial three-dimen-

sional object than as a literary work. [Citation.] The district court's remarks relied in part on a quotation about "microcode" [citation]; Apple introduced testimony that none of the works in suit contain "microcode." Moreover, Apple does not seek to protect the ROM's architecture but only the program encoded upon it.

Franklin contends that operating system programs are *per se* excluded from copyright protection under the express terms of section 102(b) of the Copyright Act, and under the precedent and underlying principles of *Baker v. Selden*, 101 U.S. 99, 25 L.Ed. 841 (1879). These separate grounds have substantial analytic overlap.

In *Baker v. Selden*, plaintiff's testator held a copyright on a book explaining a bookkeeping system which included blank forms with ruled lines and headings designed for use with that system. Plaintiff sued for copyright infringement on the basis of defendant's publication of a book containing a different arrangement of the columns and different headings, but which used a similar plan so far as results were concerned. The Court, in reversing the decree for the plaintiff, concluded that blank account-books were not the subject of copyright and that "the mere copyright of Selden's book did not confer upon him the exclusive right to make and use account-books, ruled and arranged as designated by him and described and illustrated in said book." *Id.* at 107. The Court stated that copyright of the books did not give the plaintiff the exclusive right to use the system explained in the books, noting, for example, that "copyright of a work on mathematical science cannot give to the author an exclusive right to the methods of operation which he propounds." *Id.* at 103.

Franklin reads *Baker v. Selden* as "stand[ing] for several fundamental principles, each presenting * * * an insuperable obstacle to the copyrightability of Apple's operating systems." It states:

> *First, Baker* teaches that use of a system itself does not infringe a copyright on the description of the system. *Second, Baker* enunciates the rule that copyright does not extend to purely utilitarian works. *Finally, Baker* emphasizes that the copyright laws may not be used to obtain and hold a monopoly over an idea. In so doing, *Baker* highlights the principal difference between the copyright and patent laws—a difference that is highly pertinent in this case.

[Reference.]
Section 102(b) of the Copyright Act, the other ground on which Franklin relies, appeared first in the 1976 version, long after the decision in *Baker v. Selden*. It provides:

In no case does copyright protection for an original work of authorship extend to any idea, procedure, process, system, method of operation, concept, principle, or discovery, regardless of the form in which it is described, explained, illustrated, or embodied in such work.

It is apparent that section 102(b) codifies a substantial part of the holding and dictum of *Baker v. Selden. See* 1 *Nimmer on Copyright* § 2.18[D], at 2–207.

We turn to consider the two principal points of Franklin's argument.

1. "Process", "System" or "Method of Operation". Franklin argues that an operating system program is either a "process", "system", or "method of operation" and hence uncopyrightable. [Footnote.] Franklin correctly notes that underlying section 102(b) and many of the statements for which *Baker v. Selden* is cited is the distinction which must be made between property subject to the patent law, which protects discoveries, and that subject to copyright law, which protects the writings describing such discoveries. However, Franklin's argument misapplies that distinction in this case. Apple does not seek to copyright the method which instructs the computer to perform its operating functions but only the instructions themselves. The method would be protected, if at all, by the patent law, an issue as yet unresolved. *See Diamond v. Diehr*, 450 U.S. 175, 101 S.Ct. 1048, 67 L.Ed.2d 155 (1981).

Franklin's attack on operating system programs as "methods" or "processes" seems inconsistent with its concession that application programs are an appropriate subject of copyright. Both types of programs instruct the computer to do something. Therefore, it should make no difference for purposes of section 102(b) whether these instructions tell the computer to help prepare an income tax return (the task of an application program) or to translate a high level language program from source code into its binary language object code form (the task of an operating system program such as "Applesoft"). [Citation.] Since it is only the instructions which are protected, a "process" is no more involved because the instructions in an operating system program may be used to activate the operation of the computer than it would be if instructions were written in ordinary English in a manual which described the necessary steps to activate an intricate complicated machine. There is, therefore, no reason to afford any less copyright protection to the instructions in an operating system program than to the instructions in an application program.

Franklin's argument, receptively treated by the district court, that an operating system program is part of a machine mistakenly focuses on the physical characteristics of the instructions. But the medium is not the message. We have already considered and rejected aspects of this contention in the discussion of object code and ROM. The mere fact that the operating system program may be etched on a ROM does not make the program either a machine, part of a machine or its equivalent. Furthermore, as one of Franklin's witnesses testified, an operating system does not have to be permanently in the machine in ROM, but it may be on some other medium, such as a diskette or magnetic tape, where it could be readily transferred into the temporary memory space of the computer. In fact, some of the operating systems at issue were on diskette. As the CONTU majority stated,

> Programs should no more be considered machine parts than videotapes should be considered parts of projectors or phonorecords parts of sound reproduction equipment. * * * That the words of a program are used ultimately in the implementation of a process should in no way affect their copyrightability.

[Citation.]

Franklin also argues that the operating systems cannot be copyrighted because they are "purely utilitarian works" and that Apple is seeking to block the use of the art embodied in its operating systems. This argument stems from the following dictum in *Baker v. Selden*:

> The very object of publishing a book on science or the useful arts is to communicate to the world the useful knowledge which it contains. But this object would be frustrated if the knowledge could not be used without incurring the guilt of piracy of the book. And where the art it teaches cannot be used without employing the methods and diagrams used to illustrate the book, or such as are similar to them, such methods and diagrams are to be considered as necessary incidents to the art, and given therewith to the public; not given for the purpose of publication in other works

explanatory of the art, but for the purpose of practical application.

[Citation.] We cannot accept the expansive reading given to this language by some courts. [Citation.] In this respect we agree with the views expressed by Professor Nimmer in his treatise. *See* 1 *Nimmer on Copyright* § 2.18[C].

Although a literal construction of this language could support Franklin's reading that precludes copyrightability if the copyright work is put to a utilitarian use, that interpretation has been rejected by a later Supreme Court decision. In *Mazer v. Stein*, 347 U.S. 201, 218, 74 S.Ct. 460, 471, 98 L.Ed. 630 (1954), the Court stated: "We find nothing in the copyright statute to support the argument that the intended use or use in industry of an article eligible for copyright bars or invalidates its registration. We do not read such a limitation into the copyright law." *Id.* at 218, 74 S.Ct. at 471. The CONTU majority also rejected the expansive view some courts have given *Baker v. Selden*, and stated, "That the words of a program are used ultimately in the implementation of a process should in no way affect their copyrightability." *Id.* at 21. It referred to "copyright practice past and present, which recognizes copyright protection for a work of authorship regardless of the uses to which it may be put." *Id.* The Commission continued: "The copyright status of the written rules for a game or *a system for the operation of a machine* is unaffected by the fact that those rules direct the actions of those who play the game or *carry out the process.*" *Id.* (emphasis added). As we previously noted, we can consider the CONTU Report as accepted by Congress since Congress wrote into the law the majority's recommendations almost verbatim. [Citations.]

Perhaps the most convincing item leading us to reject Franklin's argument is that the statutory definition of a computer program as a set of instructions to be used in a computer in order to bring about a certain result, 17 U.S.C. § 101, makes no distinction between application programs and operating programs. Franklin can point to no decision which adopts the distinction it seeks to make. In the one other reported case to have considered it, *Apple Computer, Inc. v. Formula International, Inc.*, 562 F.Supp. 775 (C.D.Cal.1983), the court reached the same conclusion which we do, *i.e.* that an operating system program is not *per se* precluded from copyright. It stated, "There is nothing in any of the statutory terms which suggest a different result for different types of computer programs based upon the function they serve within the machine." *Id.* at 780. Other courts have also upheld the copyrightability of operating programs without discussion of this issue. [Citations.]

2. Idea/Expression Dichotomy. Franklin's other challenge to copyright of operating system programs relies on the line which is drawn between ideas and their expression. *Baker v. Selden* remains a benchmark in the law of copyright for the reading given it in *Mazer v. Stein, supra,* where the Court stated, "Unlike a patent, a copyright gives no exclusive right to the art disclosed; protection is given only to the expression of the idea—not the idea itself." 347 U.S. at 217, 74 S.Ct. at 470 (footnote omitted).

The expression/idea dichotomy is now expressly recognized in section 102(b) which precludes copyright for "any idea." This provision was not intended to enlarge or contract the scope of copyright protection but "to restate * * * that the basic dichotomy between expression and idea remains unchanged." [Citation.] The legislative history indicates that section 102(b) was intended "to make clear that the expression adopted by the programmer is the copyrightable element in a computer program, and that the actual processes or methods embodied in the program are not within the scope of the copyright law." [Citation.]

Many of the courts which have sought to draw the line between an idea and expression have found difficulty in articulating where it falls. [Citations.] We believe that in the context before us, a program for an operating system, the line must be a pragmatic one, which also keeps in consideration "the preservation of the balance between competition and protection reflected in the patent and copyright laws." [Citation.] As we stated in *Franklin Mint Corp. v. National Wildlife Art Exchange, Inc.,* 575 F.2d 62, 64 (3d Cir.), *cert. denied,* 439 U.S. 880, 99 S.Ct. 217, 58 L.Ed.2d 193 (1978), "Unlike a patent, a copyright protects originality rather than novelty or invention." In that opinion, we quoted approvingly the following passage from *Dymow v. Bolton,* 11 F.2d 690, 691, (2d Cir.1926):

> Just as a patent affords protection only to the means of reducing an inventive idea to practice, so the copyright law protects the means of expressing an idea; and it is as near the whole truth as generalization can usually reach that, *if the same idea can be expressed in a plurality of totally different manners, a plurality of copyrights may result,* and no infringement will exist.

(emphasis added).

We adopt the suggestion in the above language and thus focus on whether the idea is capable of various modes of expression. If other programs can be written or created which perform the same function as an Apple's operating system program, then that program is an expression of the idea and hence copyrightable. In essence, this inquiry is no different than that made to determine whether the expression and idea have merged, which has been stated to occur where there are no or few other ways of expressing a particular idea. [Citations.]

The district court made no findings as to whether some or all of Apple's operating programs represent the only means of expression of the idea underlying them. Although there seems to be a concession by Franklin that at least some of the programs can be rewritten, we do not believe that the record on that issue is so clear that it can be decided at the appellate level. Therefore, if the issue is pressed on remand, the necessary finding can be made at that time.

Franklin claims that whether or not the programs can be rewritten, there are a limited "number of ways to arrange operating systems to enable a computer to run the vast body of Apple-compatible software". [Reference.] This claim has no pertinence to either the idea/expression dichotomy or merger. The idea which may merge with the expression, thus making the copyright unavailable, is the idea which is the subject of the expression. The idea of one of the operating system programs is, for example, how to translate source code into object code. If other methods of expressing that idea are not foreclosed as a practical matter, then there is no merger. Franklin may wish to achieve total compatibility with independently developed application programs written for the Apple II, but that is a commercial and competitive objective which does not enter into the somewhat metaphysical issue of whether particular ideas and expressions have merged.

In summary, Franklin's contentions that operating system programs are *per se* not copyrightable is unpersuasive. The other courts before whom this issue has been raised have rejected the distinction. Neither the CONTU majority nor Congress made a distinction between operating and application programs. We believe that the 1980 amendments reflect Congress' receptivity to new technology and its desire to encourage, through the copyright laws, continued imagination and creativity in computer programming. Since we believe that the district court's decision on the preliminary injunction was, to a large part, influenced by an erroneous view of the availability of copyright for operating system programs and unnecessary concerns about object code and ROMs, we must reverse the denial of the preliminary injunction and remand for reconsideration.

D.   Irreparable Harm

The district court, without any extended discussion, found that Apple had not made the requisite showing of irreparable harm, stating "Apple is better suited to withstand whatever injury it might sustain during litigation than is Franklin to withstand the effects of a preliminary injunction." [Citation.] In so ruling, the district court failed to consider the prevailing view that a showing of a prima facie case of copyright infringement or reasonable likelihood of success on the merits raises a presumption of irreparable harm. [Citations.] A copyright plaintiff who makes out a prima facie case of infringement is entitled to a preliminary injunction without a detailed showing of irreparable harm. *See 3 Nimmer on Copyright* § 14.06[A], at 14–50, 14–51 & n. 16 (collecting authorities).

The CONTU Final Report recognized that "[t]he cost of developing computer programs is far greater than the cost of their duplication." [Citation.] Apple introduced substantial evidence of the considerable time and money it had invested in the development of the computer programs in suit. Thus even without the

presumption of irreparable harm generally applied in copyright infringement cases, the jeopardy to Apple's investment and competitive position caused by Franklin's wholesale copying of many of its key operating programs would satisfy the requirement of irreparable harm needed to support a preliminary injunction. [Citations.]

In *Kontes Glass Co. v. Lab Glass, Inc.*, 373 F.2d 319, 320–21 (3d Cir.1967), this court appeared to adopt an inverse relationship approach to the irreparable harm issue, suggesting that the strength of the required showing of irreparable injury varies inversely with the strength of plaintiff's showing of a likelihood of success on the merits. [Citation.] In *Kontes*, we were not presented with a case in which copyrighted material central to the essence of plaintiff's operations was concededly copied as we are here. We believe the *Kontes* approach is best suited to those cases where the injury from copying can be fairly considered minimal, limited or conjectural. In those circumstances it provides flexibility in applying the equitable remedy of preliminary injunctions through evaluation of the irreparable harm factor. Normally, however, the public interest underlying the copyright law requires a presumption of irreparable harm, as long as there is, as here, adequate evidence of the expenditure of significant time, effort and money directed to the production of the copyrighted material. Otherwise, the rationale for protecting copyright, that of encouraging creativity, would be undermined. As Judge Broderick stated in *Klitzner Industries, Inc. v. H. K. James & Co.*, 535 F.Supp. [1249, 1259–60 (E.D.Pa.1982)]:

> Since Congress has elected to grant certain exclusive rights to the owner of a copyright in a protected work, it is virtually axiomatic that the public interest can only be served by upholding copyright protections and, correspondingly, preventing the misappropriation of the skills, creative energies, and resources which are invested in the protected work.

Nor can we accept the district court's explanation which stressed the "devastating effect" of a preliminary injunction on Franklin's business. If that were the correct standard, then a knowing infringer would be permitted to construct its business around its infringement, a result we cannot condone. [Citations.]

The size of the infringer should not be determinative of the copyright holder's ability to get prompt judicial redress.

* * *

V.

For the reasons set forth in this opinion, we will reverse the denial of the preliminary injunction and remand to the district court for further proceedings in accordance herewith.

MIDWAY MFG. CO. v. ARTIC INTERNATIONAL, INC.

704 F.2d 1009

(United States Court of Appeals, Seventh Circuit, April 11, 1983.)

CUMMINGS, C. J.

This appeal involves questions regarding the scope of protection video games enjoy under the 1976 Copyright Act, 90 Stat. 2541, 17 U.S.C. § 101 *et seq.*

Plaintiff manufactures video game machines. Inside these machines are printed circuit boards capable of causing images to appear on a television picture screen and sounds to emanate from a speaker when an electric current is passed through them. On the outside of each machine are a picture screen, sound speaker, and a lever or button that allows a person using the machine to alter the images appearing on the machine's picture screen and the sounds emanating from its speaker. Each machine can produce a large number of related images and sounds. These sounds and images are stored on the machine's circuit boards—how the circuits are arranged and connected determines the set of sounds and images the machine is capable of making. When a person touches the control lever or button on the outside of the machine he sends a signal to the circuit boards inside the machine which causes them to retrieve and display one of the sounds and images stored in them. Playing a video game involves manipulating the controls on the machine so that some of the images stored in the machine's circuitry appear on its picture screen and some of its sounds emanate from its speaker.

Defendant sells printed circuit boards for use inside video game machines. One of the circuit boards defendant sells speeds up the rate of play—how fast the sounds and images change—of "Galaxian," one of plaintiff's video games, when inserted in place of one of the "Galaxian" machine's circuit boards. Another of defendant's circuit boards stores a set of images and sounds almost identical to that stored in the circuit boards of plaintiff's "Pac-Man" video game machine[1] so that the video game people play on machines containing defendant's circuit board looks and sounds virtually the same as plaintiff's "Pac-Man" game.

Plaintiff sued defendant alleging that defendant's sale of these two circuit boards infringes its copyrights in its "Galaxian" and "Pac-Man" video games. In a memorandum opinion and order reported at 547 F.Supp. 999 (N.D.Ill.1982), the district court granted plaintiff's motion for a preliminary injunction and denied defendant's motion for summary judgment. The district court's order enjoins defendant from manufacturing or distributing circuit boards that can be used to play video games substantially similar to those protected by plaintiff's copyrights. Defendant appeals from that order on the ground that plaintiff has not shown a likelihood of succeeding on the merits of its claim of copyright infringement. We affirm for the reasons that follow.

Plaintiff claims that its "Pac-Man" and "Galaxian" video games are "audiovisual works" protected under the 1976 Copyright Act. Section 101 of that Act defines audiovisual works as

> works that consist of a series of related images which are intrinsically intended to be shown by the use of machines or devices such as projectors, viewers, or electronic equipment, together with accompanying sounds, if any, regardless of the nature of the material objects, such as films or tapes, in which the works are embodied. 17 U.S.C § 101.

It is not immediately obvious that video games fall within this definition. The phrase "series of related images" might be construed to refer only to a set of images displayed in a fixed sequence. Construed that way, video games

---

1. We described the "Pac-Man" video game in some detail in *Atari, Inc. v. North American Philips Consumer*

Electronics Corp., 672 F.2d 607, 610, 611 (7th Cir.1982).

do not qualify as audiovisual works. Each time a video game is played, a different sequence of images appears on the screen of the video game machine—assuming the game is not played exactly the same way each time. But the phrase might also be construed more broadly to refer to any set of images displayed as some kind of unit. That is how we construed it in *WGN Continental Broadcasting Co. v. United Video, Inc.*, 693 F.2d 622 (7th Cir.1982), where we held that a news program and a thematically related textual display ("tele-text") transmitted on the same television signal but broadcast on different television channels constituted a single audiovisual work. We see no reason to construe it more narrowly here. As we noted there, the legislative history of the Copyright Act of 1976 suggests that "Congress probably wanted the courts to interpret the definitional provisions of the new act flexibly, so that it would cover new technologies as they appeared, rather than to interpret those provisions narrowly and so force Congress periodically to update the act." 693 F.2d at 627.

There is a second difficulty that must be overcome if video games are to be classified as audiovisual works. Strictly speaking, the particular sequence of images that appears on the screen of a video game machine when the game is played is not the same work as the set of images stored in the machine's circuit boards. The person playing the game can vary the order in which the stored images appear on the screen by moving the machine's control lever. That makes playing a video game a little like arranging words in a dictionary into sentences or paints on a palette into a painting. The question is whether the creative effort in playing a video game is enough like writing or painting to make each performance of a video game the work of the player and not the game's inventor.

We think it is not. Television viewers may vary the order of images transmitted on the same signal but broadcast on different channels by pressing a button that changes the channel on their television. In the *WGN* case, we held that the creative effort required to do that did not make the sequence of images appearing on a viewer's television screen the work of the viewer and not of the television station that transmitted the images. Playing a video game is more like changing channels on a television than it is like writing a novel or painting a picture. The player of a video game does not have control over the sequence of images that appears on the video game screen. He cannot create any sequence he wants out of the images stored on the game's circuit boards. The most he can do is choose one of the limited number of sequences the game allows him to choose. He is unlike a writer or a painter because the video game in effect writes the sentences and paints the painting for him; he merely chooses one of the sentences stored in its memory, one of the paintings stored in its collection.

Defendant suggests another reason why plaintiff's video games are not copyright-able—because the printed circuit boards in which the games are fixed are patentable. We reject this argument for the same reason District Judge Decker rejected it. [Citation.] Plaintiff claims copyrights in audiovisual works—the distinctive set of images and sounds stored in its circuit boards. It does not claim copyrights in the design of those circuit boards, so it matters not that those designs may be patentable. Recording images and sounds in circuit boards does not destroy their copyrightability any more than does recording them on rolls of celluloid film. Defendant cites *Apple Computer, Inc. v. Franklin Computer Corp.*, 545 F.Supp. 812 (E.D.Pa.1982), and *The Magnavox Co. v. Mattell, Inc.*, 216 U.S.P.Q. 28 (N.D.Ill.1982) in support of its argument, but those cases are easily distinguished. Both dealt with copyrights in computer programs, not with copyrights in audiovisual works fixed in computer programs. We thus conclude that video games are copyrightable as audiovisual works under the 1976 Copyright Act and we note that every other federal court (including our own) that has confronted this issue has reached the same conclusion. *Williams Electronics, Inc. v. Artic International, Inc.*, 685 F.2d 870 (3rd Cir.1982); *Atari, Inc. v. North American Philips Consumer Electronics Corp.*, 672 F.2d 607, 617 (7th Cir.1982); *Stern Electronics, Inc. v. Kaufman*, 669 F.2d 852 (2nd Cir.1982); *Midway Manufacturing Co. v. Dirkschneider*, 543 F.Supp. 466 (D.Neb.1981). [Citation.]

Defendant next argues that plaintiff's copyrights are invalid because the 1976 Copyright Act does not apply to plaintiff's video games. Section 117 of the 1976 Copyright Act was amended in 1980 to define the exclusive rights of owners of copyrights in computer programs. As originally enacted, Section 117 provided that the 1909 Copyright Act and common law were to govern the rights of a copyright owner "with respect to the use of the [copyrighted] work in conjunction with" computers. Defendant argues that the 1980 amendment does not apply to copyrights, like those of plaintiff, in existence before the amendment took effect and that the original Section 117 requires that we look to the 1909 Act and common law to determine whether the circuit boards defendant manufactures are copies of plaintiff's audiovisual works.

We disagree. Even if the 1980 amendment applies only to copyrights issued after its effective date—an issue we do not decide—the district court properly applied the 1976 Act. The language and legislative history of the 1980 amendment are convincing that original Section 117 was intended only to leave unaltered the existing law governing the exclusive rights of owners of copyrights in computer programs. [Citations.] It was not intended to permit pirating of audiovisual works stored in computers.

Defendant also argues that even if plaintiff's video games are copyrightable, plaintiff's asserted copyrights are invalid because the works they protect were originally published without the notice of copyright required by Section 401 of the 1976 Act. Plaintiff purchased the copyrights it asserts in this suit in 1979 and early 1980 from a Japanese company that invented the video game machines plaintiff now markets. Defendant claims that the Japanese company published in Japan without notice of copyright the audiovisual works stored in these machines before it assigned its copyrights to plaintiff. Even if that is so, however, the copyrights plaintiff purchased from the Japanese company are valid. Plaintiff registered its works in the United States in May and November 1980 (Supp.App. 102, 110)—within five years of the date they were originally published in Japan. Section 405(a)(2) affords a copyright owner five years within which to remedy the omission of a copyright notice from published copies of a work. Defendant does not allege that

plaintiff has omitted to put a notice of copyright on any of the machines plaintiff has distributed in the United States or that its alleged infringement of plaintiff's copyrights was in reliance upon the omission of such notice from those copies originally published in Japan.

The final argument of defendant's that we address is that selling plaintiff's licensees circuit boards that speed up the rate of play of plaintiff's video games is not an infringement of plaintiff's copyrights. Speeding up the rate of play of a video game is a little like playing at 45 or 78 revolutions per minute ("RPM's") a phonograph record recorded at 33 RPM's. If a discotheque licensee did that, it would probably not be an infringement of the record company's copyright in the record. One might argue by analogy that it is not a copyright infringement for video game licensees to speed up the rate of play of video games, and that it is not a contributory infringement for the defendant to sell licensees circuit boards that enable them to do that.

There is this critical difference between playing records at a faster than recorded speed and playing video games at a faster than manufactured rate: there is an enormous demand for speeded-up video games but there is little if any demand for speeded-up records. Not many people want to hear 33 RPM records played at 45 and 78 RPM's so that record licensors would not care if their licensees play them at that speed. But there is a big demand for speeded-up video games. Speeding up a video game's action makes the game more challenging and exciting and increases the licensee's revenue per game. Speeded-up games end sooner than normal games and consequently if players are willing to pay an additional price-per-minute in exchange for the challenge and excitement of a faster game, licensees will take in greater total revenues. Video game copyright owners would undoubtedly like to lay their hands on some of that extra revenue and therefore it cannot be assumed that licensees are implicitly authorized to use speeded-up circuit boards in the machines plaintiff supplies.

Among a copyright owner's exclusive rights is the right "to prepare derivative works based upon the copyrighted work." 17 U.S.C. § 106(2).

If, as we hold, the speeded-up "Galaxian" game that a licensee creates with a circuit board supplied by the defendant is a derivative work based upon "Galaxian," a licensee who lacks the plaintiff's authorization to create a derivative work is a direct infringer and the defendant is a contributory infringer through its sale of the speeded-up circuit board. [Citations.]

Section 101 of the 1976 Copyright Act defines a derivative work as "a work based upon one or more preexisting works, such as a translation, musical arrangement, dramatization, fictionalization, motion picture version, sound recording, art reproduction, abridgment, condensation, or any other form in which a work may be recast, transformed, or adapted." It is not obvious from this language whether a speeded-up video game is a derivative work. A speeded-up phonograph record probably is not. [Citations.] But that is because the additional value to the copyright owner of having the right to market separately the speeded-up version of the recorded performance is too trivial to warrant legal protection for that right. A speeded-up video game is a substantially different product from the original game. As noted, it is more exciting to play and it requires some creative effort to produce. For that reason, the owner of the copyright on the game should be entitled to monopolize it on the same theory that he is entitled to monopolize the derivative works specifically listed in Section 101. The current rage for video games was not anticipated in 1976, and like any new technology the video game does not fit with complete ease the definition of derivative work in Section 101 of the 1976 Act. But the amount by which the language of Section 101 must be stretched to accommodate speeded-up video games is, we believe, within the limits within which Congress wanted the new Act to operate. [Citations.]

Defendant raises other arguments on appeal, all of which we reject for the reasons set forth in District Judge Decker's exhaustive opinion. See 547 F.Supp. at 1005-1012.

Affirmed.

---

1. We use the word "defendant" herein to refer to Com-Share Southern, Inc., prior to the date on which Computer

COM-SHARE, INC. v. COMPUTER COMPLEX, INC.

338 F. Supp. 1229

(United States District Court, E. D. Michigan, S. D., Nov. 22, 1971.)

SMITH, D. J.

The case before us arises out of a dispute between the parties to a contract related to the operation of computers. We have ruled upon (and denied) defendant's motions to dismiss for lack of jurisdiction, for failure to state a claim upon which relief can be granted, and for failure to join an indispensable party. We have heard several days of testimony from the principals, have weighed their respective credibilities, have considered numerous exhibits, and briefs, have heard oral arguments and have considered submitted findings of fact and conclusions of law submitted by both parties. It is our conclusion that the conduct of the defendant has been unconscionable and that a preliminary injunction should issue forthwith for reasons that will be spelled out in detail hereinafter.

Certain background materials are necessary not only to an understanding of the issues (which, legally, are not complicated) but as well to the explanation of certain of the unique meanings given words commonly employed in every day speech. Thus the word "languages", as used in this operation is a collection of programs that individually allow a user to develop programs of his own in a language something like English, but which is susceptible to translation into such computer languages as NEWBASIC, XTRAN, and QED.

The plaintiff, Com-Share, Incorporated, is a Michigan corporation with its principal place of business in Ann Arbor. Defendant,[1] Computer Complex, Inc., is a Delaware corporation, with its principal place of business in Houston, Texas. Computer Complex is the successor to the business, assets, and obligations of Com-Share Southern, Inc., a Texas corporation. It does a continuous and systematic part of its general business within the State of Michigan. Two of the defendant's customers are located within this state. Defen-

---

Complex, Inc., succeeded to Southern's business, and to Computer Complex, Inc., thereafter.

dant derived $4,566 (or 0.2%) of its total revenues from customers in Michigan in 1969, $1,017 (or 0.3%) in 1970, and $66,184 (or 2%) in 1971.

The contract between the parties concerned the business each was engaged in, namely, offering the use of computer systems on a "time sharing" basis. This business and its mechanisms are so set up that different customers can use the computer system simultaneously from their places of business through the use of telephone facilities. Both parties are also engaged in developing and marketing what is known as "software". This word, as here employed, refers to the programs and controls which are used in the computer. It is clear that this business of computer time sharing is a fast moving operation. Developments in the technology and improvements thereof are frequently made and are important not only for the service of existing customers but in attracting potential customers for the systems.

The agreement before us, concerning which the dispute arises, was entered into on February 10, 1967 and denominated "Technical Exchange Agreement". [Footnote.] The negotiations preceding the Technical Exchange Agreement began in or around January, 1967 and were conducted in part by Mr. William D. Mercer, then President of the defendant, who came to Ann Arbor and Detroit for the purpose of these negotiations, which ultimately resulted in the Technical Exchange Agreement. Defendant's stated objective was to obtain workable systems of time sharing software, plaintiff's subsequent new software developments, and all enhancements, and the maintenance of such software. Summarizing briefly, under the Technical Exchange Agreement, so negotiated, plaintiff and defendant agreed to provide to each other during the term of their agreement, all information concerning "hardware" (e. g., specifications, designs, production drawings, changes, improvements, and new designs relating to computer components) and "software" (i. e., programs and controls that are read into a computer) that came into the legal possession of either party and which related to any phase of operating an SDS 940 Time Sharing Computer System, except that the exchange of applications software in any way proprietary to

a user was subject to the express permission of the user. The technology was supplied by magnetic tapes, listings, printouts, and other appropriate transfer media.

From, then, approximately February of 1967 through November 1, 1970, in reliance upon and pursuant to the terms of the Technical Exchange Agreement, plaintiff supplied to defendant, in confidence, from and within the State of Michigan, information, systems software developments and technology called for by the Technical Exchange Agreement, including developments, information, training, knowhow, documents, tapes, tangible things and other technology developed by plaintiff. Such developments and technology as were supplied by defendant to plaintiff under the Technical Exchange Agreement were delivered by defendant to plaintiff in Ann Arbor, Michigan. In addition, certain of the defendant's employees received extensive technical training under the Technical Exchange Agreement at plaintiff's offices in Ann Arbor.

Consistent with the confidential nature of such developments and technology, the Technical Exchange Agreement specifically provided [footnote] as follows:

> Com-Share and Southern [now Computer Complex, Inc.] each agreed not to lease, sell or otherwise divulge to any third party interest, without the prior written consent of the other, any and all systems software developments supplied to it by the other.

Further to safeguard the information and data thus supplied, the Technical Exchange Agreement also provided [footnote] that

> Notwithstanding the expiration or termination of this Agreement, the limitations set forth in Section XI (last paragraph) shall continue for a period of 24 months after such expiration or termination.

Differences having arisen between the parties, they agreed by letter dated November 30, 1970 that the Technical Exchange Agreement was terminated effective as of November 1, 1970. This letter, which was drafted by the defendant, provided in part as follows:

> This letter signifies mutual termination of the Technical Exchange Agreement dated February 10, 1967 between our two companies. This termination shall be effective as of November 1,

1970, as of which date neither company requires further performance by the other under the said agreement.

The prayer for a preliminary injunction before us was triggered in large part by the circumstance that on August 5, 1971, defendant publicly announced that it had entered into an agreement with Tymshare, Inc., a California corporation, to sell substantially all of defendant's assets and goodwill related to its computer time sharing operations to Tymshare, Inc. The obligations of Tymshare, Inc. under this agreement, which is dated August 4, 1971, are subject to certain conditions precedent, including the approval of defendant's shareholders. Defendant's shareholders have not yet approved the sale of the assets to Tymshare, Inc., which corporation, we find, is not an indispensable party which must be joined or in the absence of which this action must be dismissed under Fed.R.Civ.P. 19(a) and 12(b) (7). [Citations.]

The plaintiff, obviously disturbed by the implications of the above with respect to its confidential data, wrote to both defendant and Tymshare, Inc., a letter (August 10, 1971) citing to them the provisions of the paragraphs above quoted of the Technical Exchange Agreement, and stating, in addition, that plaintiff presumed that defendant would not divulge to Tymshare, Inc. any information about or pertaining to the systems software developments which had been supplied to the defendant by the plaintiff. Subsequent thereto, the plaintiff took the action before us. On August 27, 1971 it filed for preliminary and permanent equitable relief. On September 13, 1971 defendant filed motions to dismiss the complaint for failure to state a claim upon which relief could be granted, for lack of jurisdiction, and for failure to join an indispensable party. On October 1, 1971, plaintiff filed its motion for a preliminary injunction restraining and enjoining defendant Computer Complex, Inc., its directors, officers, agents and employees, and all other persons acting in concert with them who receive notice of its order, pending the final determination of this action and thereafter until November 1, 1972, from leasing, selling, transferring, disclosing or otherwise divulging to Tymshare, Inc., its directors, officers, agents, and employees, or to any other third party, any of the systems

software developments and technology supplied by plaintiff to defendant pursuant to the Technical Exchange Agreement.

With reference to the "systems software developments and technology supplied by plaintiff", the record shows that during the period from 1967 to November 1, 1970, plaintiff delivered to defendant, pursuant to the Technical Exchange Agreement, certain magnetic tapes, symbolics, listings, printouts, documents and other items containing or embodying plaintiff's systems software developments and technology as the use of such was made commercially available by plaintiff. Pursuant to the amendment to the Technical Exchange Agreement dated August 3, 1970, plaintiff also delivered to defendant software developments and technology pertaining to the SDS (XDS) 940 computer while such developments and technology were still in the developmental stages prior to their release to plaintiff's customers in a normal time sharing environment. The systems software supplied by plaintiff to defendant under the Technical Exchange Agreement included the following:

(a) The "Monitor" (a collection of programs that combine to control the various operations of the physical hardware devices that comprise the computer) and the "Executive" (a collection of programs that combine to perform administrative functions and interfacing the user to the machine). The "Monitor" and "Executive" programs supplied by plaintiff to defendant were in three separate series: the "C-00" Series, the "T-00" Series and the "W" Series. The "Monitor" and "Executive" programs in the "W" Series were unique and new programs.

(b) The "Languages", which, as we have noted heretofore, is a collection of programs allowing a user to develop programs of his own, in a language which resembles English but which can be translated into language peculiar to the computer, including XTRAN, QED and NEW-BASIC.

These systems software developments and technology so supplied by the plaintiff to the defendant were developed by the plaintiff's Research and Development Division at a cost of some two million dollars to the plaintiff.

Some of the history behind the systems software technology for computer time sharing must be noted at this point since it bears upon defendant's claim that there really isn't anything unique about plaintiff's software. Certain of the original concepts had been developed in 1966 at the University of California in Berkeley in a project called "Project Genie" which had been financed by the Federal Government. The systems software developed in this project was identified as System 1.50 and 1.53 and its principal use was in scientific research rather than for commercial time sharing programs.

Also, representatives of plaintiff, Scientific Data Systems, Inc. (commonly referred to as "SDS" and now wholly owned by Xerox Corporation and referred to as "XDS"), and Tymshare, Inc., assisted by faculty and students from the University of California participated in a joint project in 1966 at the facilities of Tymshare, Inc., in Palo Alto, California, for the purpose of developing a commercial version of the software developed earlier at Berkeley for use on a modified SDS 930 computer (later called a 940 computer after certain hardware modifications were made by Scientific Data Systems). This joint project, which was sponsored by Scientific Data Systems (the manufacturer of the SDS 930 computer) resulted in the development of a more commercially oriented system identified as System 1.82. System 1.82 was available to those firms that participated in the joint project, including plaintiff. Mr. Richard Crandall, now plaintiff's president, participated as an employee of plaintiff in this joint project.

Following Mr. Crandall's return to plaintiff Com-Share, Incorporated, in late 1966, he recruited and assembled a staff of research and development technicians, including Mr. Steven Weiss (later, the principal inventor of the W system technology) and Mr. Ronald Jeffries (later, the inventor of XTRAN), and plaintiff commenced developing and did develop, a number of software systems for use with the SDS 940 computer.

Using separate research and development groups, plaintiff developed software systems along two distinct lines: (1) enhanced versions of System 1.82 (Systems C-00 and T-00) which contained a number of improvements, among the most important of which was the increase in the maximum number of simultaneous users which had theretofore been relatively restricted; and (2) certain totally new software systems, including the W system "Monitor",

the W system "Executive", "XTRAN" and Com-Share's version of the "QED" text editor. A great many smaller routines were also developed. The W system Monitor and Executive permit 34 to 40 simultaneous users as compared to the 8 to 10 simultaneous users possible under System 1.82, the 13 to 15 simultaneous users possible under the C-00 system, and the 20 to 25 simultaneous users possible under the T-00 system.

It is our judgment, upon the record before us, that the W system software, XTRAN and plaintiff's version of the QED were invented by plaintiff's employees based upon new principles and concepts with unique engineering, logic and coherence, and did not embody the technology developed by the University of California staff in Project Genie or that developed in the joint project sponsored by Scientific Data Systems. Moreover, with reference to defendant's argument that the software supplied to it by plaintiff was not secret but "instead, in the public domain", it is necessary to note that the existing software systems which are unique in the computer time sharing industry all contain certain elements which perform similar functions and many utilize certain similar fundamental concepts, of a general nature. This is no more than saying that all have a common concept, and, in the most general sense, a common base. Such is common in all engineering. Thus, the concept of vehicular locomotion, involving in one aspect, the basic principles of the internal combustion engine, is common to snowmobiles, ships, airplanes, and automobiles, but there the similarity stops. The varying systems, as patent lawyers so eloquently demonstrate, differ greatly in the steps taken to accomplish the objective. Similarly here. The specific engineering of these software systems, and their particular underlying technologies and design, together with what has been referred to as their "logic and coherence", as well as their speed, accuracy, cost, and commercial feasibility may differ greatly from system to system. They will and do inevitably reflect the peculiar and unique accomplishments and technical skills of the developers thereof. This, in a nutshell, is what the software systems developed by the plaintiff supplied to the defendant under the Technical Exchange Agreement. And while it is true that defendant may have made certain technical changes in software supplied to it by plaintiff under the Technical Exchange Agreement, the defendant did not alter the unique principles, engineering, logic, and coherence developed by plaintiff into such software systems. This software was supplied to the defendant on magnetic tapes in machine readable form known as "selfills" and "symbolics", referred to as "human readable in printed form."

It is clear that the utmost caution was used by plaintiff in protecting the secrecy of this software. Each page of the listings embodying plaintiff's systems contains the words "Com-Share, Inc. Company Confidential." "Passwords", it was testified, are built into the systems to prevent unauthorized access. Magnetic tapes and symbolics are kept locked when not in use. These protections have been built into the systems themselves, not only in order that no customer can have unauthorized access to any other customer's data base or specialized technology, but also in order that no employee of the company itself can have unauthorized access to any system, and possibly betray his employer and client.

The plaintiff's systems, software development, technology, and their underlying engineering, we find, have been, in fact, kept secret and confidential. Disclosures have been made by the plaintiff only to the defendant, and to plaintiff's foreign licensees. With respect to the "C-00" Series and "T-00" Series software there have been disclosures in isolated instances to certain other firms not in the time sharing business, but such exceptions do not impeach plaintiff's allegations of secrecy. It is clear that plaintiff's software has not been made available to competitor companies in the computer time sharing business.

In the conduct of this business, which it is clear is not static, either as to technologies and operations, certain disputes occurred between the parties as to the performance of their respective obligations to exchange technology thereunder. Defendant complains of plaintiff's failure to furnish symbolics, whereas plaintiff established that up to the date of the termination of the Technical Exchange Agreement the defendant had declined to furnish plaintiff with at least one of its hardware design elements, specifically, the "CCI" communications interface device, which would

have been of material value to the plaintiff. Defendant argues thus that plaintiff has come into Court with "unclean hands." We do not so find. There is nothing here of morally reprehensible conduct, of acts of such nature that good conscience should not permit the plaintiff to be heard. At the most, there were no more than minor breaches of the contract, neither major nor substantial. It is significant that the parties themselves did not regard such failures as existed as having gone to the root of the contract. At no time prior to November 30, 1970 (the date of the termination letter) nor since that date, has either party threatened to rescind or to commence an action for damages under the Technical Exchange Agreement as a result of any such claims of non-performance. In fact, as of August 3, 1970, the plaintiff and defendant entered into a letter agreement clarifying what were considered by the parties to be ambiguities in the Technical Exchange Agreement. Plaintiff delivered to defendant during the term of the Technical Exchange Agreement substantially all of the technology within its possession or control that was within the scope of the Agreement, and there is no evidence of an anticipatory breach thereof by the plaintiff.

We now come to the termination agreement and its bearing upon the contractual obligations of the parties. This termination, by mutual agreement, was evidenced by a letter dated November 30, 1970, prepared by defendant and executed by both parties. The first paragraph of this letter stated as follows:

> This letter signifies mutual termination of the Technical Exchange Agreement dated February 10, 1967 between our two companies. This termination shall be effective as of November 1, 1970, as of which date neither company requires further performance by the other under said agreement.

The defendant argues that the parties intended by this agreement to discharge not only their mutual obligations "to perform under the Technical Exchange Agreement" but also the obligations not to disclose to any third party the software developments supplied to each other by the parties. Thus, it is argued, the very clause designed to prevent disclosure upon termination becomes nugatory upon termination. A more complete exercise in contractual futility would be difficult to find. The purpose behind the non-disclosure provisions is self evident. It is to confine the use of the systems software development, researched and formulated at substantial expense, strictly to the other party, to whom it had been furnished.

The difficulty with defendant's suggested interpretation of the letter, to the effect that it terminates as well the non-disclosure provisions, is simply that it does not say so. An agreement to safeguard sale or disclosure for two years following termination will not be read out of a contract by implication. Nor will it be rendered nugatory by an agreement that there will be no "further" performance under the agreement. Restraint on disclosure is not "further" performance of anything. There can be no "further" performance of a clause that does not come into operation until termination. We find no inconsistency here with the terms of the contract and no ambiguities. But should ambiguity there be, it will be recalled that it was drafted by the same party who now insists that contained within it is a mutually-agreed abrogation of the protective provisions of the contract.

But we are not left solely to the four corners of the instrument. Mr. Crandall, of the plaintiff, took the stand. (It was he who signed the letter on behalf of the plaintiff.) He testified that before he signed the letter he obtained verbal confirmation from Mr. C. H. McCall, then defendant's vice president, that the termination letter did not extinguish the provision of the Technical Exchange Agreement prohibiting the sale, lease or disclosure of the software systems developments or technology supplied by plaintiff to defendant for the 24 month period following the date of termination of the Technical Exchange Agreement.

An affidavit from Mr. McCall was filed in support of defendant's motion to dismiss the failure to state a cause of action, which we denied. In it he does not assert that Mr. Crandall's version of the conversation is in error. Mr. McCall simply doesn't recall any conversation that could be so interpreted. Mr. McCall was not produced at the hearing.

It is our conclusion, having seen and heard the witnesses, received the instruments, and having heard arguments of counsel, that the disclosures we are about to describe, made by

defendant, were in wilful and deliberate violation of the terms of the Technical Exchange Agreement and for the purpose of relieving the dire financial distress in which defendant found itself, all at the expense of the plaintiff. The plaintiff has thus stated a claim upon which relief can be granted under Fed.R.Civ.P. 12(b) (6).

Disclosure by defendant, to its vendee, Tymshare, has already commenced. Early in August, 1971, shortly after the agreement between the defendant and Tymshare, Inc. had been executed, defendant commenced disclosure of software technology to Tymshare and, in fact, some of defendant's employees have been working in the facilities of Tymshare, Inc. to implement the disclosure and transfer of the software to Tymshare, Inc.

The software so disclosed was invented and developed by plaintiff, and is its principal business asset and its principal means of retaining and servicing its existing customers and obtaining new customers. The plaintiff regards, and the Court finds that, its software systems developments as secret, confidential and proprietary in nature. (Other companies in the computer time sharing industry, including Tymshare, Inc., also regard their own software as secret, confidential and proprietary in nature.)

The competitive situation in the time shared computer business has a direct bearing on the remedy sought. The standard contracts which plaintiff has with the users of its time shared computer services are cancellable by the users on 30 days' notice to the plaintiff. Approximately 40% of the plaintiff's gross revenues are derived from ten customers, some of whom are also customers of Tymshare, Inc. Approximately 50% to 55% of plaintiff's revenues are attributable to time sharing services sold to customers in the areas of Chicago, Illinois; Los Angeles, California; San Francisco, California; Washington, D. C.; New York, New York; and Boston, Massachusetts. Tymshare, Inc., is a principal competitor of plaintiff in each of these areas. Defendant is not a competitor of plaintiff in the Chicago, Washington, D. C., and Boston areas, and is not a major competitor of plaintiff in the New York City, Los Angeles and San Francisco areas.

Tymshare, Inc., has revenues of approximately $1,200,000 a month, compared to plaintiff's revenues of approximately $450,000 a month. Tymshare, Inc., has a sales force approximately three times as large as the sales force of plaintiff and a geographic communications coverage that is approximately twice as large as plaintiff's. Tymshare, Inc., presently has 19 XDS 940 computers, as compared to plaintiff's 8 XDS 940 computers. Defendant has 4 XDS 940 computers.

In the event that defendant is permitted to make further disclosure of plaintiff's software to Tymshare, Inc. and in the event that defendant is permitted to transfer title to plaintiff's software to Tymshare, Inc., Tymshare, Inc., in the absence of legal restraint, would have no obstacles to thereafter offering such software to plaintiff's customers.

Both parties assert financial distress. Defendant pleads that should the Court grant the relief requested, it will have to go into bankruptcy. It therefore argues for a money-damage remedy, should plaintiff prevail, though the utility of such a remedy against a financially precariously situated corporation may well be doubtful. Plaintiff, as well, pleads a desperate financial situation, though it does not go to the lengths of asserting impending bankruptcy should relief not be granted. The plaintiff has sustained operating losses every year since its founding in 1966. At the end of its fiscal year ending June 30, 1970, the plaintiff had working capital (i. e., net current assets) of $147,071. At the end of its fiscal year ending June 30, 1971, plaintiff's working capital position was even less favorable. Since June 30, 1970 plaintiff has been unable to obtain bank or venture capital financing, and plaintiff is dependent upon its operating revenues for the survival of its business. The loss of operating revenues would reduce the plaintiff's cash flow and income to the point where plaintiff would not be able to meet its obligations as they become due and would place plaintiff's business in a position of severe financial jeopardy.

It is clear that in the event that plaintiff would lose customers to Tymshare, Inc., as a result of Tymshare, Inc., offering plaintiff's technology to such customers, the loss of revenues and income therefrom in the future could not be accurately ascertained, nor would it be possible to ascertain the loss of revenues and income that might be attributable to plain-

tiff's inability to obtain new customers in the future.

The above generally summarizes the factual situation emerging from several days of testimony and numerous exhibits. The conclusions of law resulting therefrom are clear.

* * *

* * *

As to the relationship between the parties and the materials furnished, under the laws of the State of Texas (governing this contract) the Technical Exchange Agreement established a confidential relationship between plaintiff and defendant. Hyde Corp. v. Huffines, 158 Tex. 566, 314 S.W.2d 763 (1958). The systems software developments supplied by plaintiff to defendant were unique property that constituted trade secrets of plaintiff and were supplied to defendant in confidence under the restraints against sale, lease or disclosure set forth in the Technical Exchange Agreement.

The plaintiff has rendered substantial and satisfactory performance of its obligations under the Technical Exchange Agreement.

There has been no anticipatory breach of the Technical Exchange Agreement by plaintiff. Changes may, indeed, have been necessitated by the nature of the operation but did not alter the unique principles, engineering, logic, and coherence developed by plaintiff into its systems software developments.

With respect to the rights upon termination, the letter dated November 30, 1970, providing for the termination of the Technical Exchange Agreement did not, as we have noted, contain terms inconsistent with the provisions of Section XII, paragraph (e), of the Technical Exchange Agreement and did not supersede or negate the provisions of Section XII, paragraph (e).

The letter dated November 30, 1970 between the plaintiff and the defendant which provided that "termination shall be effective as of November 1, 1970, as of which date neither company requires further performance by the other under the said agreement," is interpreted to mean that as of November 1, 1970 neither plaintiff nor defendant required the other to supply technology to the other under the Technical Exchange Agreement.

The provision in Section XII, paragraph (e), of the Technical Exchange Agreement continuing the restraint against lease, sale or disclosure of systems software developments supplied by plaintiff to defendant for a period of 24 months after termination of the Technical Exchange Agreement, was not extinguished or waived by the termination letter dated November 30, 1970; this provision survives the termination of the Technical Exchange Agreement and is interpreted to mean that defendant is restrained from selling, leasing or disclosing plaintiff's systems software developments to any third party prior to November 1, 1972.

Moreover, as we have previously commented, if there is any ambiguity as to whether the termination letter dated November 30, 1970 extinguished the provisions of Section XII, paragraph (e), the termination letter must be construed against the defendant, the party that drafted the letter, and in favor of the plaintiff. In addition, we state once more that the Court will not imply the waiver of the explicit contractual obligation of defendant to refrain from selling, leasing or disclosing the systems software developments supplied to it by plaintiff for a period of 24 months after termination of the Technical Exchange Agreement.

We are advised that, technically, the sale to Tymshare has not yet been fully consummated. With respect to this sale, it is our legal conclusion that defendant's sale, lease or disclosure prior to November 1, 1972, of the systems software developments and technology supplied by plaintiff to defendant under the Technical Exchange Agreement would constitute a breach of Sections XI and XII(e) of the Technical Exchange Agreement. Such sections of the Technical Exchange Agreement do not permit the sale in their entirety, nor the piecemeal sale, of the systems software developments and technology supplied by plaintiff to defendant under the Technical Exchange Agreement.

The sale prior to November 1, 1972 by defendant to Tymshare, Inc., or to any other third party, of the systems software developments and technology supplied by plaintiff to defendant in confidence and subject to the terms of the Technical Exchange Agreement, would constitute a wrongful disposition of such developments and technology and would unjustly enrich defendant at the expense of plaintiff.

The sale and further disclosure by defendant to Tymshare, Inc. of the systems software developments and technology supplied by plaintiff to defendant under the Technical Exchange Agreement, will if not restrained, cause plaintiff to suffer substantial and irreparable injury, loss and damage to plaintiff's business for which plaintiff will have no adequate remedy at law.

If the sale and further disclosure by defendant to Tymshare, Inc. of plaintiff's systems software developments and technology is not restrained, plaintiff would suffer damages which would be impossible to calculate and which could not be adequately compensated by money damages, and plaintiff's entire business would be placed in a position of severe financial jeopardy.

The sale and further disclosure prior to November 1, 1972 by defendant to Tymshare, Inc., of the systems software developments and technology supplied by plaintiff to defendant should be restrained for the reason that plaintiff's systems software developments and technology are unique property and constitute trade secrets of plaintiff and were supplied by plaintiff to defendant in confidence.

That defendant may be in financial difficulty and may not receive the consideration provided under its August 4, 1971 agreement with Tymshare, Inc., if preliminary relief is granted to plaintiff, does not confer upon it a right to breach its contractual obligation under the Technical Exchange Agreement with plaintiff and cannot prevent the issuance of a preliminary injunction in view of the confidential and secret nature of the plaintiff's systems software developments and technology and the threatened irreparable injury and loss to plaintiff.

In balancing the equities, the threatened irreparable injury and loss to plaintiff that would follow upon the sale and further disclosure of plaintiff's systems software developments and technology by defendant to Tymshare, Inc. outweighs any adverse consequences that might result to defendant by reason of the issuance of the preliminary injunction. We are of the opinion, as well, that there is a reasonable and substantial probability that plaintiff will prevail on the merits.

Defendant has argued that the Court is presented with a *fait accompli,* that the transfer of software to Tymshare and incorporations in its system have already started, that the omelet cannot be unscrambled, that equity never decrees a "vain act" and that it would be a "rather apparent [illusory?] victory for them to get an injunction in this case." Plaintiff, on the other hand, argues that the difficulties in enforcement are not insurmountable, that they are, in effect, those encountered in the usual trade secret, proprietary information, case.

We are not persuaded that modern technology has withered the strong right arm of equity. Moreover, difficulties of enforcement often reflect in direct ratio the recalcitrance or lack thereof in the parties affected by the Court's order. We will not anticipate untoward difficulty. At this moment, the first duty of this Court is to issue a preliminary injunction as the only adequate means of preserving the status quo. This injunction shall provide that, to the extent, if any, that defendant is unwilling or unable to extricate changes made by defendant to any software supplied to it by plaintiff, defendant cannot sell, transfer or disclose the whole or any part of that portion of the technology which defendant cannot or will not separate; that the injunction shall restrain and enjoin defendant, its directors, officers, employees, agents, and all other persons acting in concert with them who receive notice thereof, pending the final determination of this action and thereafter until November 1, 1972, from leasing, selling, transferring or further disclosing to Tymshare, Inc., or to any other third party, any of the systems software developments and technology supplied by plaintiff to defendant pursuant to the Technical Exchange Agreement.

A suitable order may be presented.

WARRINGTON ASSOCIATES, INC. v. REAL-TIME ENGINEERING SYSTEMS, INC.

522 F. Supp. 367
(United States District Court, N. D. Illinois, E. D., Aug. 26, 1981.)

MORAN, D. J.

Plaintiff, Warrington Associates, Inc.

("Warrington"), a designer and marketer of computer software programs for banks and other financial institutions, has filed this action alleging the wrongful appropriation and use of its trade secrets and proprietary materials by defendant, Real-Time Engineering Systems, Inc. ("Real-Time"). More specifically, in its five-count amended complaint, Warrington alleges that Real-Time, individually and in conspiracy with others, misappropriated Warrington's secret computer software programs (Count I), unlawfully interfered with and conspired to breach contractual assurances of confidentiality owed to Warrington (Counts II and III), infringed Warrington's copyrights (Count IV), and engaged in unfair competition (Count V).

Now before the court is what was, initially, Real-Time's motion to dismiss all but the federal copyright claims on the ground that the common law tort counts are preempted by the Copyright Act of 1976, 17 U.S.C. § 101 *et seq.* Both sides, however, have submitted extensive evidence outside the pleadings, as well as legal memoranda raising additional issues and sounding like post-trial briefs. In light of these submissions, pursuant to Fed.R.Civ.P. 12(b), the motion has been regarded as one for summary judgment. Stripped of their hyperbole, the memoranda raise several discrete issues: (1) whether the common law trade secrets claims are preempted by federal law; (2) if they are not, whether Warrington, by securing copyright protection for its User's Manual, has so extensively disclosed its confidential information so as to forfeit any common law protection for those secrets; and (3) whether Real-Time intended to pirate Warrington's materials. Because the court concludes, first, that the trade secrets claims are not preempted, and second, that genuine material issues of fact remain as to Real-Time's intent to misappropriate as well as the extent to which the information was disclosed without assurances of confidentiality, the motion for summary judgment is denied.

A. LEGAL ISSUES: PREEMPTION.

The scope of federal preemption of state law by the Copyright Act is prescribed by that statute itself. In Section 301(b), the Act provides:

Nothing in this title annuls or limits any rights or remedies under the common law or statutes of any State with respect to

* * *

(3) activities violating legal or equitable rights that are not equivalent to any of the exclusive rights within the general scope of copyright as specified by section 106.

An analysis of the interests secured by Copyright and trade secret law makes plain that the claims are not "equivalent" as intended by the Congress. It is well-settled that copyright protection extends not to an idea itself, but rather to the particular *expression* used by its author. [Citations.] In contrast, the protection provided by the common law of trade secret misappropriation extends to the very ideas of the author, subject, of course, to the requirement that the idea has some originality and is as yet undisclosed or disclosed only on the basis of confidentiality. [Citations.] The practical distinction between the two interests is manifest. While disclosure of the expression does not vitiate rights secured by copyright law, that same disclosure may well strip the underlying idea of its confidentiality, and thus its status as a trade secret. To a certain degree the two respective rights in intellectual property interact. To the extent a work has been copyrighted and published, the chances of unprivileged disclosure may increase. But the mere fact that an expression is copyrighted does not, in and of itself, disclose the trade secret or eliminate its mantle of confidentiality.

In light of the analysis expressed above, it is hardly surprising that neither Congress nor the courts have viewed the federal Copyright Act as preempting the common law of trade secret misappropriation. For example, in the legislative history of the Copyright Act, the House Committee Report states:

The evolving common law rights of "privacy," "publicity," and trade secrets, * * * would remain unaffected so long as the causes of action contain elements such as an invasion of personal rights or a breach of trust or confidentiality. * * *

[Citation.]

Both federal and state courts have con-

curred. In an analogous context, the Supreme Court found nothing incompatible between the law of trade secrets and federal patent statutes. *Kewanee Oil Co. v. Bicron Corp.,* 416 U.S. 470, 94 S.Ct. 1879, 40 L.Ed.2d 315 (1974). If anything the congruence and, concomitantly, the likelihood of preemption, between patent and trade secret law is stronger than between trade secret and copyright law. *See also, Synercom Technology, Inc. v. University Computing Co.,* 474 F.Supp. 37 (N.D.Tex.1979), *Compumarketing Services Corp. v. Business Envelope Manufacturers, Inc.,* 342 F.Supp. 776, 777 (N.D.Ill.1972). Finally, whether Wisconsin or Minnesota law is applied [footnote], state law provides an area of protection extending beyond copyright. The highest courts of both states have continued to recognize causes of action for trade secret misappropriation subsequent to the amendment of the federal Copyright Act in 1976. The common law of each of these forums stresses that the trade secrets tort is premised on concepts of breach of trust and confidentiality, and not copying. [Citations.]

Accordingly, the court holds that the Copyright Act does not preempt Warrington's common law tort claims in this action.

B.   FACTUAL ISSUES:
DISCLOSURE, ACCESS AND
INTENT.

As noted above, although the Copyright Act does not preempt Warrington's trade secret claim, the fact that it registered its User's Manual for a copyright might well affect the continued secrecy of the ideas in that manual for which Warrington seeks trade secret protection. However, on the basis of the record before the court, no final determination on this issue can be made at this time. Viewing the evidence favorably to Warrington, deposition testimony permits the inference that Warrington only released the copyrighted manual after receiving assurance of confidentiality from the users. Thus, while Warrington's self-serving declaration that it registered the manual with the Copyright Office as "unpublished" does not, in itself, defeat Real-Time's claim that Warrington's information is in the public domain, the court cannot conclude, as a matter of law, that Warrington's proprietary materials have lost their mantle of confidentiality.[2]

Similarly, summary judgment also is premature with respect to other issues raised by Real-Time. For example, even assuming that Real-Time had access only to Warrington's User's Manual (as opposed to the Operations Manual and computer source tapes), the deposition testimony of Richard Mulligan, Real-Time's President, indicates that the information contained in the User's Manual is of such a highly technical nature that pirating of Warrington's trade secrets may have been possible from this source alone. As such, the fact that Real-Time's access to Warrington's materials was restricted is not determinative on summary judgment.

Finally, genuine issues of fact remain concerning Real-Time's intent to misappropriate Warrington's trade secrets. Admittedly, Warrington has not yet submitted any direct evidence demonstrating Real-Time's actual knowledge of Warrington's nondisclosure agreements. But such evidence hardly is essential to preclude summary judgment here. Mulligan's deposition testimony reveals that the overwhelming industry practice was to make available software packages upon pledges of confidentiality. Mulligan acknowledged at this deposition that Real-Time had never previously been afforded such extensive access to a competitor's materials when it proposed to develop compatible software programs for prospective clients. With these facts in the record, it is not necessary to accept Warrington's rather strident description of Real-Time's deal with the Kellogg Bank as a "kickback" in order to draw the inference that Real-Time nevertheless had notice of the Bank's confidentiality obligations and intended to disregard them. Accordingly, the motion for summary judgment is premature and is denied.

* * *

M. BRYCE & ASSOCIATES, INC. v. GLADSTONE

319 N.W.2d 907

(Court of Appeals of Wisconsin, March 26, 1982.)

RANDA, J.

The plaintiff, M. Bryce & Associates, Inc. (MBA), contends that the defendants, Arthur Young & Co. (Young) and Harley-Davidson Motor Co., Inc. (Harley-Davidson), took and used for their own benefit MBA's "trade secret" contained in a methodology for the design of management information systems— PRIDE (*PR*ofitable *I*nformation by *DE*sign). The jury returned a verdict in favor of MBA and the trial court entered judgment against Young and Harley-Davidson. We affirm.

In May, 1974, Young agreed to assist Harley-Davidson in revamping its internal operating systems. One of the projects was to design a management information systems standards manual (MIS). Harry Mayo (Mayo), Young's employee, and John Chapel (Chapel), Harley-Davidson's employee, were assigned to this project. Both were experienced in MIS design. They began their work in May, 1974.

In June, 1974, Gerald Myers (Myers), a Harley-Davidson employee, suggested that one of the commercially available MIS methodologies, PRIDE, marketed by MBA, be considered. On June 19, 1974, Mayo called Milton Bryce, MBA's president, and arranged for a sales presentation at Harley-Davidson on July 2, 1974.

The demonstration of PRIDE lasted approximately one full day. During the morning session, Bryce explained in general terms what PRIDE could accomplish and how it could benefit the business. Before going into the details of PRIDE at the afternoon session, Bryce required all participants to sign a non-disclosure form. Present at this time were Mayo of Young, and Chapel, Myers, Beach and Bryan of Harley-Davidson. Only Mayo, Bryan and Chapel signed this form. Nonetheless, Bryce

---

2. Real-Time relies heavily on the fact that Warrington provided the Kellogg Bank with a copy of its Manual prior to the execution of certain confidentiality agreements. This fact alone, however, does not prove that the information was no longer confidential or that Warrington failed to take appropriate precautions against disclosure. The evidence indicates that it was the practice in the computer software industry that no manuals were provided absent assurances of confidentiality. It is quite possible that the Bank was given an advance copy of the Manual only upon the understanding that such information was not to be disclosed and in contemplation of the impending execution of the actual nondisclosure agreements.

continued with the afternoon session with the non-signers present.

After the afternoon presentation, employees of both Young and Harley-Davidson were impressed with the PRIDE system. During the next week Young and Harley-Davidson discussed whether Harley-Davidson should purchase PRIDE or stay with the work of Chapel and Mayo. A decision was made not to purchase PRIDE. The reason given for this decision was that PRIDE was not an economical choice in light of the time and effort already invested by Mayo for which Harley-Davidson still would have to reimburse Young.

Mayo and Chapel continued their work on MIS. The final version of their draft manual was submitted in August, 1974. Certain Harley-Davidson personnel were unhappy with the draft and requested changes that were needed to be made. The project was concluded in mid-October, 1974.

Subsequent to the submission of their draft, Mayo and Chapel learned that an independent standards drafting team had been set up at Harley-Davidson and was headed by Stuart Moebus (Moebus). In October, 1974, the Mayo and Chapel version of the manual was given to Moebus who revised it based on his team's independent work. The Harley-Davidson manual was issued in final draft form on January 10, 1975.

MBA filed its complaint in 1975, contending that Young and Harley-Davidson through their agents and employees, Mayo and Chapel, used the information disclosed on July 2, 1974, to duplicate, copy, appropriate and reproduce PRIDE without authorization, license or right, in substantially the same or identical form. MBA requested a permanent injunction and an award of compensatory damages.

Young filed a supplemental counterclaim for declaratory relief alleging there was no trade secret in PRIDE and that MBA did not own its supposed secret because MBA copied the methodology of Bryce's prior employer, Tek-Fax. MBA denied the allegations and asserted the affirmative defense that Young was estopped to attack PRIDE's trade secret status because its employee had signed a non-disclosure form for PRIDE.

Young and Harley-Davidson's motion for summary judgment on the ground that MBA's voluntary election of a federal copyright in the PRIDE manuals precluded any trade secret claim was denied. Young and Harley-Davidson's motion for summary judgment on the ground that the admissions of MBA and its expert witness indisputedly showed that the PRIDE "secret" was not taken or used by Young or Harley-Davidson was also denied. Young and Harley-Davidson successfully moved to strike MBA's affirmative defense of estoppel concerning the supplemental counterclaim. Before the trial court instructed the jury, Young and Harley-Davidson agreed to assume responsibility for all the acts of Chapel and Mayo, and the action against Chapel and Mayo was dismissed.

At the close of the evidence, the case was submitted to the jury on a nine-question special verdict. [Footnote.] Questions 1, 2, 3 and 8 pertained to the "alleged" trade secret and questions 4, 5, 6, and 9 pertained to the non-disclosure agreement. In summary, the jury concluded that (i) MBA had a trade secret; (ii) the trade secret was disclosed in a confidential relationship; (iii) the trade secret was used by both Young and Harley-Davidson; and (iv) the trade secret had not been appropriated by MBA from Tek-Fax. The trial court entered judgment for MBA.

Motions after verdict by Young and Harley-Davidson were filed, briefed, and denied in a 35-page opinion by the trial court. This appeal by Young and Harley-Davidson followed. The following issues are raised on appeal:

1. Did MBA have a trade secret in the three volumes of PRIDE together with Bryce's presention of July 2, 1974, and the Data Management Section of "PRIDE"?

2. Is there credible evidence to support the jury's finding that Young and Harley-Davidson used MBA's trade secret?

3. Did MBA's voluntary use of a copyright notice on the PRIDE manual prevent the state of Wisconsin from applying its trade secret law to bar use by others of the information contained in the work?

4. Is there credible evidence to support the jury's finding that MBA's trade secret was not developed by Tek-Fax and appropriated by MBA?

5. When employees Chapel and Mayo were dismissed from the case pursuant to an agreement between counsel and the trial court that employers Young and Harley-Davidson were re-

sponsible for their employees' acts, were the employers discharged by operation of law?

I. EXISTENCE OF A TRADE SECRET

In *Abbott Laboratories v. Norse Chemical Corp.*, 33 Wis.2d 445, 147 N.W.2d 529 (1967), our supreme court considered the following six factors as being relevant in determining whether the material sought to be protected is a trade secret:

" * * * Some factors to be considered in determining whether given information is one's trade secret are: (1) the extent to which the information is known outside of his business; (2) the extent to which it is known by employees and others involved in his business; (3) the extent of measures taken by him to guard the secrecy of the information; (4) the value of the information to him and to his competitors; (5) the amount of effort or money expended by him in developing the information; (6) the ease or difficulty with which the information could be properly acquired or duplicated by others." *Id.* at 463–64, 147 N.W.2d at 538–39 (quoting Restatement (First) of Torts § 757, comment b (1939)).

* * *

After the jury returned their verdict, the trial court reviewed the evidence and stated its reasons for sustaining the jury's verdict. As to the six factors enumerated in *Abbott*, the trial court found the following facts in support of those six factors:

1) The extent to which the information is known outside of the plaintiff's business is supported by the following evidence:

The people involved in the afternoon session and those involved in the preparation of the standards manual for Harley-Davidson all were impressed with the "PRIDE" material and the information given at the afternoon session to such a degree that one of the defendants himself, "an expert," was willing to pay the $10,000.00 for information. This, inferentially, attests to the fact that the concept was not known; the testimony of Bryce concerning the method in which he protected the confidentiality from getting outside his business; the fact that the product is never sold without the expressed agreement to maintain confidentiality.

The defendants have in a very thorough manner gone over the material presented in the sale literature and the "state of the art" at the time

of the misappropriation and argue that all or any trade secret was known or spelled out by the plaintiff in a public advertisement. [Reference.] This evidence was presented to the jury. The evidence the jury could have believed was that demonstrated to them, the actual portraying of the methodology in the specific case study and the detailed unique uses of the generally known components. Those advertisements could have been interpreted by the jury to define the "what" of "PRIDE" but certainly not the "*how*" and "why" which they found the defendants heard and saw and used.

2) The extent to which it is known by employees and others involved in his business. Here again, Mr. Bryce's testimony is sufficient for the jury to draw reasonable inferences that all employees were informed of the confidential nature of the material with the pledge of keeping it secret.

3) The extent or measures taken by him to guard the secrecy of the information; the signing of the Non-Disclosure Agreement by every person that was at a sales meeting where a secret portion of the sales presentation was made; the testimony concerning Bordens, the fact that their employee was cognizant of the pledge of secrecy; the testimony concerning the July 2, 1974, meeting relating to signing the agreement and the oral warnings; and while one of the parties is alleged not to have signed the agreement, there is evidence that that party was on notice orally. The documents themselves say it. Bryce referred to secrecy a number of times during his presentation. All is sufficient evidence to support a conclusion that that factor was covered.

4) The value of the information to him and to his competitors is supported by the amounts paid for the product and the fact that many knowledgeable people at Harley-Davidson and Arthur Young found it valuable.

5) The amount of effort or money expended by him in developing the information system. The record is replete with evidence, the number of days that he spent in drafting the documents, his wife's work, the efforts in upgrading it and keeping it current to society's needs.

6) The ease or difficulty with which the information could be properly acquire [sic] or duplicated by others. There was a search for a methodology by Dr. DuBois, by Arthur Young, Harry Mayo. There is the cost that was made by Harley-Davidson to develop a manual. Generally, the list of "PRIDE" customers shows the cost and inferentially the difficulty or ease with which an information system would be created, let alone a system that was so highly special-

ized. The jury could draw the inference that because these experts recognized this as a unique contribution, that experienced persons in the data processing industry would have difficulty in acquiring the concepts and implement them as they were done in "PRIDE".

After a thorough review of the record, we agree with the trial court's conclusion that all six factors stated in *Abbott* are sufficiently supported by the evidence. Since the evidence in this case fulfills the criteria necessary to constitute a trade secret, we conclude that, as a matter of law, a trade secret existed.

II. USE OF A TRADE SECRET

Young and Harley-Davidson contend that in order for the jury to have found "use" by Young or Harley-Davidson of MBA's trade secret, Young or Harley-Davidson must be found to have "precisely duplicated" or "copied" MBA's trade secret. We disagree.

Our supreme court has concluded that sec. 757 of Restatement (First) of Torts (1939) is the correct statement of the general law of trade secrets. [Citation.] The trial court, in instructing the jury as to a "use" of a trade secret, quoted directly from comment c of sec. 757. The trial court said:

> To subject a person to liability for use of another's trade secret, there is no requirement that he use it exactly in the form that he received it. He may be liable even if [he] uses it with modification—modifications or improvements upon it affected by his own efforts.
>
> Differences in detail do not preclude liability if substantially the process used by the actor is derived from the other's secret in breach of a relationship of trust and confidence.
>
> The liability is avoided only when the contribution by the other's secret is so slight that the actor's process can be said to be derived from other sources.

We conclude that the trial court's instruction is a correct statement of the law in this area.

The jury found that both Young and Harley-Davidson used MBA's trade secret. The jury's verdict had the approval of the trial court.

* * *

After a review of the record, we agree with the trial court's conclusion that the jury ver-

dict is sustained by the credible evidence. Specifically the trial court found:

> Here the testimony of Dr. DuBois and Dr. Heintz both identify similarities. The exhibits used by Dr. DuBois and the testimony of Mr. Bryce could have been related by the jury to identify the use of the trade secret. Dr. Heintz said, "although not identical, very similar" as he talked of the procedures and techniques which are the trade secret. Heintz leaves the question of the violation of the proprietary nature of "PRIDE" to the jury. Then he suggested that if it were a copying that went into the preparation that he would have to know the experience of the persons, their prior knowledge and the work papers that form the foundation in the preparation of the manual.
>
> There is testimony of similarities in the work papers that relate to periods after June 26th and after July 2nd. There is Bryce's testimony; Mayo's testimony; a reference in the log of John Chapel dated July 16, 1974, concerning Dave Bryan's contribution; the comparison made by Dr. DuBois in the arrow charts, Exhibit 225, which illustrates the comparison of the Data Management Section of "PRIDE" and the forms taken from Harley-Davidson's manual; Dr. DuBois's reference to the real use of the subsystem concept in the implementation of the Harley-Davidson information system. Finally, there is the accidental use of the word "subsystems" by Harley-Davidson in the work papers and the motive of getting the Harley-Davidson manual out as quickly as possible.

III. COPYRIGHT LAW

Because the events in this case occurred prior to January 1, 1978, when a complete revision of the Copyright Act of 1909 took effect, this case is governed by the Copyright Act of 1909. [Footnote.] Under the 1909 Act, "publication" was the central, operative feature of the copyright law. [Citation.] State common-law copyright existed only until the first publication of the work. [Citation.] Federal statutory protection was secured by publishing the work with the appropriate copyright notice. 17 U.S.C. § 10. If the work was published without notice, in most cases the work would irretrievably enter the public domain. [Citation.] The importance of "publication" gave rise to a considerable body of cases deciding whether a work had been "published" in particular circumstances. [Citation.]

In order to mitigate the harsh rule that publication divests common-law rights, courts evolved a distinction between a "general publication" and a "limited publication." Only a general publication would divest common-law rights. [Citation.]

A limited publication has been held to be a publication "which communicates the contents of a manuscript to a definitely selected group and for a limited purpose, and without the right of diffusion, reproduction, distribution or sale. * * *" [Citation.] Both persons and use must be restricted.

In compliance with 17 U.S.C. § 19, MBA placed a copyright notice, the publication date of 1971 and/or 1973, and the identification of MBA as the copyright holder on all its PRIDE manuals and forms. Nevertheless, MBA argues that there was no general publication, notwithstanding its use of the copyright notice.

Bryce testified that customers using PRIDE are allowed unlimited reproduction of PRIDE manuals and forms as long as MBA's copyright notice is included and that MBA cannot account for the number or whereabouts of such copies.[3] When the principal facts and the reasonable inferences are undisputed, as they are here, we are not bound by the findings of the trial court. [Citation.] We conclude that a general publication occurred in the manner in which MBA disseminated its PRIDE manuals and forms. [Citation.]

Further, the limited publication exception arose in circumstances quite different from this case. If the author disseminated his work without a copyright notice and if it was held that a publication had occurred, the author's protection was forfeited. [Citation.] Where finding a general publication would divest the author of the benefit of his work, courts have avoided a complete forfeiture by concluding that a limited publication occurred. [Citations.] Courts were more likely to find a general publication despite less dissemination where the issue was whether a publication was sufficient to invest copyright protection. [Citation.]

The inquiry here is not whether MBA published the PRIDE manuals and forms without any notice and was thereby divested of all copyright protection. Rather the issue here is whether a publication occurred that would invest a federal copyright in the PRIDE manuals and forms and thus accord MBA federal protection. We conclude that such an investiture occurred.

Having concluded that a general publication occurred, we must determine whether MBA's voluntary use of the federal copyright notice on PRIDE's manuals and forms prevent the state of Wisconsin from applying its trade secret law to bar use by others of the information contained in the work.

---

3. Mr. Bryce testified as follows:
Q. Now, when you sold "PRIDE" beginning in 1971, you have allowed all your purchasers to print their own forms haven't you?
A. Yes, sir, as part of our agreement.
Q. And all they need to do is put the copyright symbol on it, that is all that is required of them, isn't it?
A. No, I think if I remember correctly, in our agreement they have to maintain the copyright and a trade mark of "PRIDE".
Q. And you don't know how many of these forms have been printed, do you, by customers?
A. No, sir.
Q. And you don't know where they have been printed, do you?
A. No, sir.
Q. And you don't know where all of these forms exist that were printed, do you?
A. No, sir.
Q. Also your customers are allowed to reprint copies of the M. Bryce & Associates manuals, are they not?
A. Yes.
Q. And you don't know whether any have been reprinted do you?
A. I am sorry, would you repeat that question?
(Whereupon the above pending question was read back by the reporter.)

THE WITNESS: Our manuals have been reprinted by customers.
MR. KLOEHN: Q. You know of some?
A. Yes.
Q. But you don't know of all of them, do you?
A. No, sir.
Q. And you don't know where all of the copies are today?
A. No, sir.
Q. You don't check up on your customers with a careful audit to determine what they are doing with your manuals, do you?
A. We do periodically.
Q. And how do you conduct this audit?
A. We have a form that we send out and we tell them, the manuals we have, our records, and we ask them to account for them.
Q. When did you start doing that?
A. We did that informally almost from the beginning, but we started to formalize it.
Q. By "informal" meaning you called them on the telephone?
A. We called them on the phone.
Q. Now, you simply signed out a form?
A. Our customer base has grown since then.

Young and Harley-Davidson contend that MBA by publishing its PRIDE manual and forms have invoked the federal copyright laws, thus limiting their recovery to a federal copyright infringement claim.

Lawyers and the courts have been plagued by the uncertainty of the interplay between state trade secret law and federal copyright protection. [Citation.] This problem is most evident, as is the case here, where a party has marked trade secret documents with a copyright notice and date of publication.

The 1981 ABA Committee Report, Section of Patent, Trademark & Copyright Law, best summarized this conflict as follows:

> The conflict in the dual use of state trade secret and federal copyright protection stems from the inherent substantive differences between them. Copyright protection is the manifestation of the constitutional power to extend a limited commercial monopoly to creators in order to promote the general public good through the diffusion of knowledge and the concomitant stipulation of progress and competition in a free society. Copyright protection requires the creator to relinquish, however, all rights save for those reserved and enumerated by the Copyright Act, i.e., the control of copying and reproduction of the work. Copyrighting a work therefore results in its divulgation to the public, including the ideas inherently embodied therein, and the public may make "open and free" use of such material within the strictures of the copyright law.
>
> Conversely, secrecy and non-disclosure are the very essence of state trade secret protection. The creator has a right to perpetual protection of the secret as long as secrecy is maintained, but the risks are substantial. Trade secret protection evaporates upon any disclosure, whether intentional or inadvertent. Nor is any protection afforded against any independent development of the same secret by another or "reverse engineering" of it. In summary, a choice is offered—an exclusive federal right for a limited time versus an imperfect state law perpetual remedy. [Citation.]

Although we recognize the conflict between state trade secret law and federal copyright law, we conclude that the state trade secret protection is not preempted. We reach this conclusion on a number of bases.

1. Demarcation between trade secret protection and copyright protection.

The line of demarcation between trade secret and copyright protection is clear. Trade secret law protects content irrespective of form of expression; copyright law protects form of expression but not the underlying ideas. As the United States Supreme Court stated in *Baker v. Selden*, 101 U.S. 99, 103, 25 L.Ed. 841 (1880):

> The copyright of a work on mathematical science cannot give to the author an exclusive right to the methods of operation which he propounds, or to the diagrams which he employs to explain them, so as to prevent an engineer from using them whenever occasion requires. The very object of publishing a book on science or the useful arts is to communicate to the world the useful knowledge which it contains. But this object would be frustrated if the knowledge could not be used without incurring the guilt of piracy of the book. And where the art it teaches cannot be used without employing the methods and diagrams used to illustrate the book, or such as are similar to them, such methods and diagrams are to be considered as necessary incidents to the art, and given therewith to the public; not given for the purpose of publication in other works explanatory of the art, but for the purpose of practical application.

Trade secret law prohibits unauthorized disclosure or use of protected ideas only by persons who are privy to the trade secret by reason of some relationship to the owner which legally limits use or disclosure by them. Copyright law prohibits unauthorized copying by anyone of the form of expression in which the ideas are fixed by the author. [Citation.]

If state trade secret protection was preempted by federal copyright law, MBA would have to turn to the federal copyright law for protection. Since copyright protection covers only the form of expression, its value to MBA in protecting MBA's interests would be limited. Only MBA's PRIDE manuals and forms would be protected but not MBA's methodology which is embodied also in the oral presentation by Bryce. We conclude that such a preemption of trade secret law by federal copyright law incapable of providing equivalent protection would disrupt an area of property protection which has been found to be of great value.

2. The 1976 Copyright Act.

The 1976 Copyright Act, the earlier versions

of the bill and the hearings on the act, make it clear that Congress has not unmistakenly ordained the preemption of trade secrets. [Footnote.]

In order to analyze the bounds of preemption under the 1976 Copyright Act, 17 U.S.C. §§ 102 [footnote], 103 [footnote], and 106 [footnote] (1976) must be considered in conjunction with 17 U.S.C. § 301 (1976). [Footnote.] Section 301 requires that in order for preemption to occur, the following two conditions must coexist: (a) definitions of statutory subject matter of copyright in secs. 102 and 103 are met, and (b) rights equivalent to the exclusive rights of copyright as defined in sec. 106 are violated.

The most troublesome question of preemption is the second condition—whether an "equivalent right" has been violated. The predecessor bill included the following examples of exceptions to preemption in sec. 301(b)(3):

> (3) activities violating legal or equitable rights that are not equivalent to any of the exclusive rights within the general scope of copyright as specified by section 106, including rights against misappropriation not equivalent to any of such exclusive rights, breaches of contract, breaches of trust, trespass, conversion, invasion of privacy, defamation, and deception [sic] trade practices such as passing off and false representation; or S.Rep.No.473, 94th Cong., 1st Sess. 20 (1975).

The hearings on this bill state that these examples:

> are intended to illustrate rights and remedies that are different in nature from the rights comprised in a copyright and that may continue to be protected under State common law or statute. The evolving common law rights of "privacy," "publicity," and *trade secrets*, and the general laws of defamation and fraud, would remain unaffected as long as the causes of action contain elements, such as an invasion of personal rights or a breach of trust or confidentiality, that are different in kind from copyright infringement. [Emphasis added.] [Citation.]

Congress, rather than clearly stating its intent from a positive viewpoint, approached the preemption question from the negative side by providing examples of when preemption would not be found.

This intent is further complicated by the absence from the 1976 Act of those examples which were included in the final draft. This deletion was preceded by a discussion among three congressmen. They agreed that the examples should be deleted but seemed to differ on whether this action was to limit or expand preemption. [Citation.] [Footnote.]

Although confusion arose during the enactment of the 1976 Copyright Act, the thrust of the congressional discussion was in the direction of continued state protection. This is further shown by the Report by the Committee on the Judiciary comments on an amendment which clarifies the law of copyright as it applies to computer software. It stated:

> During the course of Committee consideration the question was raised as to whether the bill would restrict remedies for protection of computer software under state law, especially unfair competition and *trade secret laws*. The Committee consulted the Copyright Office for its opinion as to whether section 301 of the 1976 Copyright Act in any way preempted these and other forms of state law protection for computer software. On the basis of this advice and advice of its own counsel the Committee concluded that state remedies for protection of computer software are not limited by this bill. [Emphasis added.] [Citation.]

This same congressional view can logically be applied to trade secrets other than those embodied in software. We conclude that state trade secret law was not disturbed by the 1976 Copyright Act which specifically contained a preemption section.

3. United States Supreme Court decisions.

In *Sears, Roebuck & Co. v. Stiffel Co.*, 376 U.S. 225, 84 S.Ct. 784, 11 L.Ed.2d 661 (1964), and *Compco Corp. v. Day-Brite Lighting, Inc.*, 376 U.S. 234, 84 S.Ct. 779, 11 L.Ed.2d 669 (1964), the question before the United States Supreme Court was "whether a State's unfair competition law can, consistently with the federal patent laws, impose liability for or prohibit the copying of an article which is protected by neither a federal patent nor a copyright." [Citations.]

In both cases the defendants had copied and marketed plaintiffs' patented light fixtures. The plaintiffs sued on both patent infringement under federal law and unfair competition under state law. The lower courts found the patents invalid in both cases but upheld the unfair competition claims. [Citations.]

The Supreme Court reversed both decisions, holding that if the lower court judgments were allowed to stand:

States could allow perpetual protection to articles too lacking in novelty to merit any patent at all under federal constitutional standards. This would be too great an encroachment on the federal patent system to be tolerated.

* * * [B]ecause of the federal patent laws a State may not, when the article is unpatented and uncopyrighted, prohibit the copying of the article itself or award damages for such copying. [Citations.]

It should be noted that *Sears* and *Compco* did not purport to make any ruling concerning trade secret law. In both cases information—new configuration of plaintiffs' lighting fixtures—had plainly been disclosed to the public by issuance of plaintiffs' patents and by the presence of the lighting fixtures on the open market. The plaintiffs could not have claimed any rights under the law of trade secrets. [Citation.]

Any doubt created by the *Sears/Compco* cases about the continued validity of trade secret law was resolved in favor of state law in *Kewanee Oil Co. v. Bicron Corp.*, 416 U.S. 470, 94 S.Ct. 1879, 40 L.Ed.2d 315 (1974).

In *Kewanee*, petitioner Kewanee Oil Co. was the leading manufacturer of synthetic thallium activated scintellation crystals. The process which enabled Kewanee to grow these crystals with a diameter of 17 inches was the trade secret at issue. Respondents were former employees of Kewanee who had left Kewanee to form their own company and produce the same crystals in breach of an employment agreement not to disclose Kewanee's trade secrets. [Citation.]

The precise preemption issue before the Supreme Court was whether Congress, by carefully setting forth the standards of patentability, intended to preclude state protection for secret processes which fall within the patentable subject matter but which were not patented. [Citation.]

Kewanee held that misappropriation of trade secrets under state law is not preempted because exclusivity was not vested in Congress for discoveries. The court stated: "The only limitation on the States is that in regulating the area of patents and copyrights they do not conflict with the operation of the laws in this area passed by Congress. * * *" [Citation.] The court then went into a detailed analysis of the objectives and effects of trade secret law to show that the federal policy was "not * * * set at naught, or its benefits denied." [Citation.]

The Supreme Court in *Kewanee* has recognized the value of trade secrets. No significant opposition to this aspect of the *Kewanee* decision has been shown by Congress, particularly in view of the statutory evidence that Congress did not intend to preempt trade secret law.

Since no "unmistakable" indication has been given to the contrary by Congress and the weight of the evidence points to the recognition by Congress and other authorities of the value of state protection of trade secrets, we conclude that state trade secret protection has not been preempted by the federal copyright laws.

IV. APPROPRIATION FROM TEK-FAX

Young and Harley-Davidson contend that the jury's finding that PRIDE's trade secret was not developed by Tek-Fax and appropriated by MBA was against the great weight and clear preponderance of the relevant evidence. We disagree.

* * *

The trial court relied on testimony that the relationship between the two systems was like comparing "kindergarten to college" and that "a great deal of difference existed between them." The trial court also noted that Tom Nies, the principal of Tek-Fax, testified that to his knowledge no materials were taken.

We conclude that the jury's verdict is sustained by credible evidence.

* * *

Judgment affirmed.

TELEMED CORP. v.
TEL-MED, INC.

588 F.2d 213

(United States Court of Appeals, Seventh Circuit, Nov. 29, 1978.)

SPRECHER, C. J.

This appeal determines that the word "Telemed" as used in connection with the computer-analysis of electrocardiograms by telephone is a descriptive tradename which in the absence of a showing of secondary meaning is not entitled to protection against the use of "Tel-Med" in a noncompeting medical service.

This is an action for tradename infringement, registered service mark infringement, and dilution of service mark and tradename brought by the plaintiff, Telemed Corporation (plaintiff or "Telemed"), pursuant to the Lanham Act, 15 U.S.C. §§ 1051–1127 (1975) and the Illinois Trademark Act, Ill.Rev.Stats., ch. 140, § 22 (1975), which provides for injunctive relief to protect against dilution of the distinctive quality of the name and mark. * * *

The district court denied injunctive relief to the plaintiff and dismissed its complaint after a bench trial. This appeal followed.

I

In 1969, Telemed initiated a business of providing commercial computer analysis of electrocardiograms (ECGs) accomplished through the use of special transmitting equipment of a highly sophisticated nature which transmits ECG signals from a patient undergoing diagnosis to plaintiff's central computer via the standard telephone system. After the computer, located in Hoffman Estates, Illinois, signals verification of the telephone connection to the transmitter operator at the sending location, it then signals additional verification of the receipt of patient identification and characteristic data. Next, it receives and analyzes the patient's ECG and teletypes the report back to the sender for use by a diagnosing physician. Currently, plaintiff provides in excess of 125,000 analyses each month to some 1,600 licensees throughout the United States, Canada, and Japan. Since its inception Telemed's annual revenues have increased from $2,629 in 1969 to $11,430,619 in 1977.

Telemed's customers comprise a class of highly discriminating purchasers, including doctors, hospitals, clinics, and medical teaching facilities. To attract additional customers, Telemed regularly solicits business through nationwide mass mailings to the medical community, advertisements in medical and computer periodicals, and by maintaining display booths at local, regional, and national medical trade shows and conventions.

On November 1, 1973, Telemed applied for registration of TELEMED as printed in a distinctive computer-readable "optical font." On August 12, 1975, the United States Patent and Trademark Office issued to Telemed Service Mark Registration No. 1,018,226 based on a first use of October 31, 1969, for the TELEMED service mark as appearing in the distinctive, computer recognition style or "optical font" as shown below:

The registration states that the mark applies to the service of "providing of computerized electrocardiogram analyses to hospitals and private physicians."

Between April and August of 1971, the San Bernardino County, California, Medical Society received public funding grants for a feasibility study into the concept of disseminating health information over the telephone to the general public, particularly those in the lower income segments for whom medical information and assistance was neither readily available nor economically feasible. The feasibility study proved fruitful and in April, 1971, a telephone health care program began. Initially the Society used the name "Telemed" to describe its service program. However, in late fall, 1971, it learned of the existence of plaintiff and its prior use of the same name and changed the program name to Tel-Med. At no time, however, did the San Bernardino Medical Society adopt the "optical font," stylized logo used by Telemed.

On June 26, 1972, the San Bernardino Medical Society applied for a United States Trademark registration for the mark "TEL-MED" to identify its health care information service, namely, recorded messages on specific health subjects made available to the public by telephone. Service Mark Registration No. 959,558 was issued on May 22, 1973. Subsequently, the San Bernardino Medical Society transferred the TEL–MED mark to defendant, Tel-Med, Inc. (defendant or "Tel-Med").

Tel-Med has continued the public service program through a process of recording the health care messages on separate cassette-type tapes, each lasting from three to seven minutes. Tel-Med maintains a master library of these tapes from which spinoff cassettes are produced and distributed to various subscribers. In addition to the tapes, subscribers receive publicity leaflets describing both the program and the topics available. While the text of each message is geared to an eighth-grade comprehension level, all are written by recognized medical experts with the final approval of a message being retained by panels of doctors in each local area. The procedure for hearing a message is simple: a person dials the local "Tel-Med" operator and asks for the message either by name or tape number. The operator then inserts the tape into the playback unit and the message is reproduced. Currently, Tel-Med is available in approximately 110 cities. Each month, over 500,000 messages are played to anonymous callers. Over 20 million calls have been received by Tel-Med operators from its inception to the date of trial. The medical community, the general public, and, indeed, the plaintiff itself highly regard Tel-Med's services as being accurate, understandable, and a valuable health maintenance tool.

Telemed is a Maryland corporation with its principal place of business in Hoffman Estates, Illinois. Tel-Med is a non-profit California corporation with its principal place of business in Colton, California. The second defendant, Chicago Medical Society (Society) is a non-profit Illinois corporation with its principal offices in Chicago, Illinois.

Society is a volunteer organization of physicians who pay membership dues which, in the main, comprise its operating budget. Society first learned of the Tel-Med program in 1974. An ad hoc committee of doctor members was formed to study the program, and after various negotiations, Society became a licensed Tel-Med subscriber. The Chicago Tel-Med program began in February, 1976. At that time, Society knew of Telemed's service,

but did not believe there would be a conflict. Society publicizes its Tel-Med program by circulation of brochures to the general public, as well as by coverage in the local media. Most of the promotional costs were underwritten by third parties, such as Blue Cross-Blue Shield. Society's Tel-Med program currently receives between 2,000 and 4,000 calls per week.

In January, 1977, Society learned that Telemed had received a number of phone calls asking for Tel-Med information tapes. Upon investigation, Society discovered that the Tel-Med program was listed in the telephone directory only under Chicago Medical Society in the "C" section and not under the "T's". Society arranged for the program to be listed under the "T's" in the next issue of the telephone directory. Since the issuance of that directory in July, 1977, Telemed has received less than one call per month intended for Society's Tel-Med program.

II

Section 32(1)(a) of the Lanham Act, 15 U.S.C. § 1114(1)(a) (1976) provides, in pertinent part, that:

> Any person who shall, without the consent of the [trademark] registrant—(a) use in commerce any reproduction, counterfeit, copy or colorable imitation of a registered mark in connection with the sale, offering for sale, distribution, or advertising of any goods or services on or in connection with which such use is likely to cause confusion, or to cause mistake, or to deceive * * * shall be liable in a civil action by the registrant. * * *

The term "colorable imitation" includes any mark which so resembles a registered mark as to be likely to cause confusion or mistake or to deceive. 15 U.S.C. § 1127.

For Telemed to prevail in its action for service mark or tradename infringement, it must establish that the infringer uses a mark likely to cause confusion or to deceive in interstate commerce. The same standards apply equally in an action for registered trademark or service mark infringement. 15 U.S.C. § 1053. The term "service mark" means a mark used in the sale or advertising of services to identify the services of one person and distinguish them from the services of others. 15 U.S.C. § 1127.

Employing the basic principles set forth in *Miller Brewing Co. v. G. Heileman Brewing*

Co., 561 F.2d 75, 79 (7th Cir. 1977), *cert. denied*, 434 U.S. 1025, 98 S.Ct. 751, 54 L.Ed.2d 772 (1978), we first must determine where, on the trademark spectrum which ranges through (1) generic or common descriptive and (2) merely descriptive to (3) suggestive and (4) arbitrary or fanciful, the mark "Telemed" falls.

A generic or common descriptive term is one which is commonly used as the name or description of a kind of goods. It cannot become a trademark under any circumstances. A merely descriptive term specifically describes a characteristic or ingredient of an article. It can become a valid trademark by acquiring a secondary meaning, *i. e.*, by becoming "distinctive, as applied to the applicant's goods" (15 U.S.C. § 1052(f)). A suggestive term suggests rather than describes an ingredient or characteristic of the goods and requires the observer or listener to use imagination and perception to determine the nature of the goods. Such a term can be protected without proof of a secondary meaning. An arbitrary or fanciful term enjoys the same full protection as a suggestive term but is far enough removed from the merely descriptive not to be vulnerable to possible attack as being merely descriptive rather than suggestive.

Webster's Third New International Dictionary (1966) contains the following:

tele—see tel-
tel *abbr.* * * * 3. telephone * * *
med. *abbr.* * * * 3. medical; medicine * * *

The Court of Customs and Patent Appeals has given its attention to both elements of the subject mark. In denying registration of "Telecolor" for color television transmitting, the court said in *Columbia Broadcasting System, Inc. v. Technicolor Motion Picture Corp.*, 166 F.2d 941, 944, 35 C.C.P.A. 1019 (1948):

"Tele" is a dictionary term which is defined in substantially the same manner by all the lexicographers. We quote that given by Webster's New International Dictionary, Second Edition, 1932:

"Tele— * * * tel—. Combining form from Greek * * * *far, far off*; as in *tele*graph, *tele*pathy, *tele*phone, etc;—often used in naming or designating devices or instruments, usually electrical, which control or direct the action of distant apparatus (as in telecontrol, a device for regulating different electrical circuits at a distance by means of radio-telegraphy, or which

have a distant recording apparatus (as in tele-anemograph, telebarograph, telebarometer, etc.)."

Even if the word be descriptive to only those skilled in the television art, registration would be deniable. * * *

In determining that "Meds" could be used concurrently with "Med-I-Pax," the court said in *Personal Products Corp. v. Allen Laboratories, Inc.*, 141 F.2d 702, 704–05, 31 C.C.P.A. 889 (1944):

The prefix "Med" in appellee's trademark is, as stated by appellee's witness Griswold, defined by the lexicographers as an abbreviation of the terms "medical" and "medicine." See Funk & Wagnalls New Standard Dictionary, Webster's New International Dictionary, and The Century Dictionary and Cyclopedia. Furthermore, it was conceded by that witness, who, at the time of the taking of his testimony, had been engaged in the manufacture of drugs and pharmaceutical products for more than ten years, that he understood the prefix "Med" to be an abbreviation of "medical" or "medicine." Accordingly, the prefix "Med," as used in appellee's mark, is descriptive of the character or quality of appellee's goods and, therefore, is not the dominant feature of the mark.

* * *

Considering the fact that appellee's "Medicated Vaginal Suppositories" are used for medical treatment and for the prevention, cure, or alleviation of disease, whereas appellant's *unmedicated* tampons are devices used solely for catamenial protection, and considering the differences in the marks of the parties, we are of opinion that the concurrent use of the marks on the goods of the parties would not be likely to cause confusion or mistake in the mind of the public or to deceive purchasers.

Both "Telemed" and "Tel-Med" mean "medicine by telephone" or more broadly "medicine at a distance," which is descriptive of plaintiff's services and also of defendant's services. "[C]ombining two descriptive words to form one new word does not automatically render the new term fanciful." [Citations.]

* * *

To find "Telemed" descriptive of plaintiff's services requires no more imagination than Judge (now Justice) Stevens found necessary to conclude that "Homemakers" as applied to household services is merely a descriptive term. *Homemakers Home and Health Care Services,*

Inc. v. Chicago Home for the Friendless, 484 F.2d 625 (7th Cir. 1973). He said at 628:

> Since there is the greatest likelihood that such [descriptive] terms will form a part of the trade name used by competitors, there is a corresponding probability that the [descriptive] word will not unambiguously advise the public of the source of the goods or services.

* * *

In this case the record showed that the Manhattan Telephone Directory for 1977–78 listed some 254 business names beginning with the prefix "Tele" or "Tel" and the Chicago, Illinois, Telephone Directory for July, 1977 listed some 112 business names in that category. There were 88 such names separating plaintiff Telemed's listing from defendant Tel-Med's listing. The evidence further showed the existence of other programs such as TEL–LAW (for legal information), TEL–ED (for educational information), and TEL–MONEY (for information on money matters), names all obviously adopted with intent to indicate a connection with the telephone. The district court concluded that the evidence adduced at trial demonstrated that plaintiff chose its name and mark to indicate the telephone aspect of its service and its availability to the medical community.[1]

We cannot say that the district court was clearly erroneous in finding that "Telemed" was merely descriptive, particularly in view of FS Services, Inc. v. Custom Farm Services, Inc., 471 F.2d 671, 674 (7th Cir. 1972), where we found the letters "FS" to be descriptive or generic, saying:

> Further, we agree with defendant that the letters FS have come to signify "farm service" or "farm supply," at least to the farmers within the area in which both parties do business. The words "farm service" or "farm supply" are descriptive or generic terms as to which public policy militates against monopolization of use.

Being merely descriptive, the mark "Tele-med" is entitled to protection only if it has acquired a secondary meaning.

III

The district court found that the plaintiff has established "Telemed" as a strong mark and hence protected only when it appears in the distinctive "optical font" typestyle, but that when it appears other than in its optical font logo or simply as a word it is a weak mark. Not only did the plaintiff have the burden of establishing a secondary meaning, but also due to the nature of the mark as a "weak" mark, it had the heavier burden of showing a *strong* secondary meaning.

The connotations this circuit has placed on strong or weak marks was clarified in *Westward Coach Manufacturing Co., Inc. v. Ford Motor Co.*, 388 F.2d 627, 634 (7th Cir.), *cert. denied*, 392 U.S. 927, 88 S.Ct. 2286, 20 L.Ed.2d 1386 (1968), where we said that "[t]he law protects a trademark only if it is, or has become distinctive" and then quoted the following from 3 R. Callman, Unfair Competition and Trade-Marks § 82.1 (2d ed.):

> In essence, the distinctiveness and popularity of the trade-mark will determine its relative strength or weakness and will accordingly define the scope of protection to be accorded the mark against the confusing similarity of others. A mark is strong if it is conspicuously distinctive; it is distinctive if the public has already been educated to accept it as the hallmark of a particular source. Then too, a mark can be distinctive either because it is unique, that is, distinctive in itself, because it has been the subject of wide and intensive advertisement, or because of a combination of both. It seems to follow as a necessary conclusion that the trade-mark has the advantage of strength where its owner has invested a considerable amount in advertising or can point to a long period of time during which his mark was used on a great quantity of articles, as symbolic of his business. * * * If the mark is weak, its protection may have an 'ex-

---

1. The district court found both "Telemed" and "Tel-Med" to be merely descriptive. The court found that TELEMED" was selected as Telemed's name and service mark because it best described the telephone aspect of its service ("tele") and its use by and availability to the medical community ("med"). In addition, the usage of the

aforedescribed "optical font" style distinguished Telemed as a computerized operation." The court also found that "[i]nitially San Bernardino Medical Society adopted and used the name Telemed to identify and describe its service program."

tremely narrow scope'; and may indeed be limited to similar goods similarly marketed. Only the strong mark will be protected against infringements arising out of its use in connection with noncompeting goods.

A mark that is strong because of its fame or its uniqueness is more likely to be associated in the public mind with a greater breadth of products or services than is a mark that is weak because it is very much like similar marks. [Citations.]

Chief Judge Markey of the Court of Customs and Patent Appeals said in *King Candy Co. v. Eunice King's Kitchen, Inc.*, 496 F.2d 1400, 1401 (Cust. & Pat.App. 1974):

> The expressions "weak" and "entitled to limited protection" are but other ways of saying, * * * that confusion is unlikely because the marks are of such non-arbitrary nature or so widely used that the public easily distinguishes slight differences in the marks under consideration as well as differences in the goods to which they are applied, even though the goods of the parties may be considered "related."

Here the mark was neither used for a long period of time nor used in connection with a great quantity of goods and services. Furthermore, the mark merely consisted of the fusion of two extremely common prefixes. As we noted earlier, the words "tele" and "med" are extensively used as a prefix for business and service names. Therefore the mark "Telemed" is not entitled to protection against marks used in related but non-competing services.

* * *

The plaintiff here had the burden of proving a strong secondary meaning of the word "Telemed" in order to merit protection. The district court was "impelled to conclude plaintiff has failed to establish that its tradename or its service mark has attained a strong secondary meaning in the mind of the public."[2]

Inasmuch as the mark for which the plaintiff sought protection is merely descriptive and also weak and inasmuch as the plaintiff did not sustain its burden of proving a strong secondary meaning, it follows that it is unlikely that confusion would result.

The district court found that the attempted demonstration of confusion consisted of a showing by the plaintiff of "occasional superficial confusion" and that of that "most was superficial, trivial, and attributable to the error in the listing of defendants' program in the Chicago telephone directory and not because of any palming off or unfair competition on defendants' part." With plaintiff's 125,000 and defendant's 500,000 telephone calls per month, it is remarkable that only a few times was the wrong number called due to the use of "Telemed" and "Tel-Med." In addition, plaintiff adduced testimony that Telemed salesmen and representatives were questioned on occasion, in regard to defendants' Tel-Med program. However, there was no evidence that any person or corporation ever mistakenly purchased defendants' program while intending to purchase plaintiff's service.

The trial court concluded that defendant's use of the term "Tel-Med" did not constitute a violation of either the service mark or tradename infringement laws as alleged in Counts I and II of plaintiff's complaint and that Telemed's claim under Count III for injunctive relief based on dilution under Ill.Rev.Stat., ch. 140, § 22 (1975) is equally without merit.[3]

The district court's judgment is affirmed.

---

2. The district court found and concluded:
Thus, the critical question becomes whether plaintiff's name and mark, though weak, has attained a strong secondary meaning in the mind of the public. Factors relevant to the issue of whether a name or mark has acquired a secondary meaning are the amount and manner of advertising, volume of sales, length and manner of use, direct consumer testimony and consumer surveys. [Citation.] To this end, plaintiff's evidence evinced a showing that while it expended sums in excess of $1,000,000 on advertising, it nevertheless directed this advertising to a class of highly discriminating purchasers, as hereinbefore set forth. Moreover, plaintiff's business has continued to grow during the period from its inception through the instant litigation. On the other hand, defendants gear their program not to the discriminating professional but rather to the public in general, especially those members in the lower income, less sophisticated "market". Clearly, the parties herein do not compete in the public market place for prospective customers. Having so found, the court is impelled to conclude plaintiff has failed to establish that its tradename or its service mark has attained a strong secondary meaning in the mind of the public.

3. The court also found that the facts did not support a finding that defendants' use of Tel-Med constitutes a deceptive trade practice under Illinois Law [citation] or that Tel-Med was confusingly similar to Telemed.

VITEK SYSTEMS, INC. v. ABBOTT LABORATORIES, INC.

520 F. Supp. 629

(United States District Court, E. D. Missouri, E. D., July 23, 1981.)

REGAN, D. J.

In this action Abbott Laboratories (Abbott) is charged with federal and state trademark infringement and unfair competition by Vitek Systems, Inc. (Vitek), a wholly owned subsidiary of McDonnell Douglas Corporation (McDonnell). The issue is whether Abbott's use of its MS–2 mark either alone or in conjunction with its established corporate logo infringes upon Vitek's AMS mark or results in unfair competition.

Vitek and Abbott are competitors in the manufacture and marketing of automated computerized microbial testing equipment. These instruments which came upon the market relatively recently, are promoted and sold in the same market, namely, clinical laboratories and acute care hospitals. The Vitek instrument was developed by McDonnell in the early 1970s based on the engineering and technology expertise it had gained in the development of a device used on manned space flights. Abbott's microbiology system was developed through its Diagnostic Division, commencing in 1973, working in conjunction with two entrepreneurs who had invented the instrument.

In 1974, following an in-house contest at McDonnell, the name "AutoMicrobic System" was chosen for its instrument. The following year, the MDC (McDonnell) Trademark Committee having decided that the initials "AMS" also be used to identify the instrument, McDonnell filed trademark registration applications on July 9, 1976 for both "AMS" and "AutoMicrobic System." The AMS registration was granted on April 5, 1977.

Theretofore, in April 1974, McDonnell contracted with Fisher Scientific Company (Fisher), a distributor of clinical laboratory products, to market the instrument. During the approximately four years the Fisher contract was in effect, a total of only seven instruments were delivered by McDonnell to Fisher. Fisher did not make any sales, although a very few of the instruments which had been placed with prospective customers for testing and evaluation were ultimately purchased by them.

On June 8, 1977, McDonnell formed Vitek, pursuant to its decision to phase out Fisher as well as the McDonnell identification of the instrument. After Fisher was terminated as the distributor (by mutual agreement), Vitek (to which McDonnell had assigned all its patent and trademark rights relating to the instrument) assumed the marketing functions.

In May, 1976, the McDonnell instrument was first introduced to the trade by Fisher (as the AutoMicrobic System) at a meeting of the American Society of Microbiologists in Atlantic City, New Jersey. A great amount of interest was generated, but no sales resulted. The instrument involved had been "grandfathered" by being hurriedly shipped in interstate commerce to avoid the requirements of the Medical Device Amendments of 1976 (21 U.S.C. § 301 et seq.) which became effective May 28, 1976. However, because most of the test kits utilizable with the instrument required pre-market clearance from the Food and Drug Administration (FDA) under the 1976 Act (a very slow process), the marketability of the instrument was severely limited for some time.

The Distributorship Agreement between Fisher and McDonnell described the product as a "Semi-Automated Microbial Laboratory (SAML) instrument and system." Nowhere in the 41 page Agreement and Exhibit A thereto or in the Supplemental Agreements No. 1 (February 18, 1976), No. 2 (Feb. 27, 1976), No. 3 (April 15, 1976), No. 4 (July 23, 1976), and No. 5 (Nov. 26, 1979), was the product described otherwise. And even in Supplemental Agreement No. 6 (Dec. 26, 1977) in which Vitek (as assignee of McDonnell) first appeared as a party, and in Supplemental Agreement No. 7 (January 26, 1978) the product was still described as a Semi-Automated Microbial Laboratory (SAML) instrument and system. It was not until February 27, 1978, in the preamble to a Memorandum of Understanding relating to a new agreement between Vitek and Fisher, that "AMS" was substituted without explanation for "SAML" and used in the body of the Memorandum.

During Fisher's tenure as exclusive distributor, the marketing of the instrument was handled through its "AutoMicrobic Division."

For the most part, Fisher referred to the instrument as the "AutoMicrobic System." At other times it was referred to as the "AMS AutoMicrobic System." Fisher stressed the merits and benefits of the *"system."* In its advertising and promotion of the instrument, Fisher would on occasions use its own name and logo, frequently in conjunction with the name and logo of McDonnell.

In May, 1978 a year after Vitek was formed, it was decided that with sales being "nil" (in the language of a written "Communications Plan" of Vitek's newly employed Director of Marketing and its Manager of Marketing Services) to de-emphasize McDonnell's relationship with the AutoMicrobic System, including the removal of the name and logo of McDonnell. Pursuant to that decision, a Chicago advertising firm was employed to create a public image of Vitek and its instrument. As the result, emphasis was placed upon the name "AMS" and Vitek as its source beginning in late 1978.

The name "AMS" has been associated over the years with many products and services (of a nature different from the instrument in question). In fact, one of McDonnell's own divisions (the Health Services Division of the McDonnell Douglas Automation Company) for a period of time used and stressed the name "AMS" for its "Account Management System" in dealing with hospitals and other health care institutions until instructed to change the name. Those in charge of the Health Services Division had never heard of Vitek's AMS instrument.

Abbott, a very large company, has been well known for many years in the medical and health field as a purveyor of pharmaceuticals. Beginning in 1963, it decided to diversify into other related health care areas, including the manufacture and sale of diagnostic equipment. The Abbott logo [logo omitted], which was created in the late 1950s, has been used continuously on virtually all its products as well as on its correspondence and its advertising and promotional materials since before 1960. This logo has attained wide recognition as the symbol of Abbott products.

Following a trademark search which indicated that the mark was available, Abbott contemplated the use of the initials "AMS" for its instrument. However, just prior to the

first scheduled trade display of the instrument in May, 1976, when it discovered (from a Fisher mailing) that "AMS" was being used on the McDonnell AutoMicrobic System it decided to forego the use of that name. Abbott's Trademark Department then ascertained that the mark "MS–2" was available for use on the instrument. In the trademark search by an independent firm in connection with that mark no reference to McDonnell or Fisher was found. Abbott had first used the name "MS–2" in 1971 in connection with a cardiscope it produced. This, of course, was long prior to the events in issue in this case.

In November 1976, Abbott applied for registration of its "MS–2" mark. It subsequently developed that in mid-1976 an affiliate of Rohm & Haas Company had filed a trademark registration for the mark "MS–2" for use on a diagnostic spectrophometer, claiming a first use on May 11, 1973. In view of that, Abbott considered for a time changing its mark to "QS–2", but instead negotiated an agreement with Rohm & Haas in early 1977 whereby Abbott was allowed to continue the use of its possibly infringing "MS–2" mark on its instrument with the provision that it would (as it customarily did) display its logo on the instrument and in its literature to distinguish the source of its product from Rohm & Haas.

The Abbott instrument was first displayed in Europe at a trade show in Cambridge, England in September 1976 and in this country at a trade show in Los Angeles, California, during October 1976 as the "Abbott MS–2." The Vitek (then the McDonnell) instrument was displayed at this Los Angeles show as the McDonnell-Fisher "AutoMicrobic System." However, not until May, 1979, was Abbott able to effect any sales of its "MS–2" in this country because the instrument had not earlier been cleared by the FDA for clinical use under the Medical Services Act of 1976.

We are convinced by the great weight of the credible evidence that there is no likelihood of confusion between Vitek's "AMS" mark and Abbott's "MS–2" mark either alone or in conjunction with the Abbott logo. The instruments themselves differ in appearance and are easily distinguishable. Vitek's name appears on the face of its AMS instrument. On the nameplate on the face of the MS–2 instrument, the Abbott name as well as its logo appears. The Abbott mark is commercially displayed only in connection with its corporate name. And when both the logo and the mark appear in proximity, the logo is contrasted in spacing, size, color and style with the mark. On the other hand, the letters of the AMS mark are evenly spaced and are uniform in size, color and style. In addition, one of its four model numbers appears on the Vitek instrument, whereas Abbott shows no model number. The supplies for the two instruments (disposable laboratory cassettes which are a necessary part of their function) are not interchangeable. None of the "disposables" sold by either party can be used on the competing instrument.

It is clear to us that the buyers of these expensive instruments are sophisticated and knowledgeable professionals whose buying process is a long and complex one. These instruments are never sold on a single sales contract, and impulse buying is unknown in this field. [Citation.] One of the marketing methods employed by both Vitek (and its predecessor) and Abbott is to display their products at trade shows in conjunction with meetings of the professionals in the field. At these shows, floor space is assigned to each of the exhibitors. In Abbott's booths, its name and logo are prominently displayed. And Vitek's booths clearly identify its instrument with the Vitek name and logo. Various marketing tools are employed in conjunction with the trade shows to acquaint potential buyers with Abbott's product and to create sufficient interest for further contacts with Abbott. So, too, Vitek's booths, which obviously are unrelated to Abbott's, are operated in much the same manner.

Other marketing methods used by each of the parties are advertisements in technical journals, mailings to potential customers, and direct salesmen's calls. Abbott's advertising of its MS–2 instrument contains its name and telephone number. Similarly, Vitek's advertisements of the AMS clearly identify the source. The Abbott logo appears in each of its advertisements and in the direct mailings, but not in close conjunction with the MS–2 mark. As for the salesmen's calls, most of them are made only after a customer has earlier expressed interest in the product. The customer is apprised of the identity of the manufacturer. The sales presentation by the salesmen typically includes such techniques as an audio-visual display (that specifically mentions the manufacturer's name) and delivery of the instrument to the customer for prolonged demonstration and testing, as well as a written proposal and a cost justification. Vitek, but not Abbott, commonly uses a rental program to give the customer a period of time to evaluate its instrument before the ultimate purchasing decision is made.

A number of persons in the potential customer's institution, including microbiologists, pathologists and laboratory technicians, are usually involved in making recommendations before the final decision to purchase the instrument is made by the administrator or board. The salesman's function is to provide the highly technical information desired by the customer's personnel, as well as to stress the reputation of the manufacturer and its ability to provide on-going service. Typically, five to ten sales contacts extending over a period of time as long as a year or more are required before the instrument is budgeted for purchase and a sale is effected.

Bearing in mind the level of sophistication of the relevant purchasers of these relatively high-priced single purchase instruments, each of which bears the name of the manufacturer, as well as the differences in their appearance, it is inconceivable to us in light of the evidence as a whole that there is any reasonable likelihood of confusion in the mind of a purchaser either as to the source of the product or as to the product itself by reason of the mark adopted and used by Abbott. Whatever "confusion" there might have been was not attributable to the trademarks in issue. [Citation.] We note that, unlike the situation in cases where the defendant has copied the configuration and appearance of the competing product itself [citation] or its advertising materials. Vitek makes no claim that Abbott has done so.

Although contrary to its answers to interrogatories stating that it was aware of no instances of actual confusion, Vitek claimed at trial there were in fact incidents of actual confusion. We find the testimony submitted in support of this claim to be ambiguous at best and not credibly probative of the asserted confusion. Significantly, the surveys conducted by Vitek's advertising agency not only contain no reference whatever to any possible confusion on the part of any potential customer but implicitly assume the absence of confusion. And there is no credible evidence that Vitek or its assignor lost any sale by reason of any customer confusion, nor is there any evidence whatever that any customer purchased an MS–2 instrument believing it was an AMS instrument. Admittedly, there is no contention that Abbott ever attempted to pass off the Vitek instrument as its own.

In the earlier stages of the promotion of the Vitek instrument the name most commonly used for it (and stressed) was "AutoMicrobic System." The initials "AMS" in our judgment were intended simply as an abbreviation or a shorthand way of referring to "AutoMicrobic System." It was not until McDonnell and Vitek realized that Abbott's "MS–2" instrument was a very formidable competitor in the automatic microbiology field that Vitek began to put more and more emphasis on "AMS," its literature referring to the instrument as the "AMS AutoMicrobic System" (usually with the "AMS" in much larger type than the "AutoMicrobic System").

The parties have argued at length the nature of the Vitek marks, that is, whether they are to be considered descriptive, suggestive or arbitrary and fanciful. A descriptive term identifies a characteristic or quality of an article or service. A suggestive term suggests rather than describes some characteristics of the article to which it is applied and requires the consumer to exercise his imagination to reach a conclusion as to the nature of that article. Arbitrary or fanciful terms bear no relationship to the product or service with which they are associated.

Abbott urges that Vitek's mark is descriptive, in which case the burden would be upon Vitek to establish secondary meaning of the mark. "Secondary meaning exists when the trademark is interpreted by the consuming public to be not only an identification of the product, but also a representation of the products' origin." *Scott Paper Co. v. Scott's Liquid Gold, Inc.*, 589 F.2d 1225, 1228 (3 Cir. 1978). As stated in *RJR Foods, Inc. v. White Rock Corp.*, 603 F.2d 1058, 1059 (2 Cir. 1979): "To be entitled to the benefit of the secondary meaning doctrine, a plaintiff must establish that the purchasing public has come to asso-

ciate certain words, symbols, collocations of sales and designs, or other advertising materials or techniques, with goods from a single source." [Citation.]

Vitek contends not only that its marks are not descriptive but that in any event they have acquired a secondary meaning. It is, of course, true, as Vitek points out, that the term "automicrobic" is not to be found in the dictionary. However, those in the relevant field at once and without resort to imagination recognize the term as meaning automated microbiology. So, too, "AMS" as applied to microbiology instruments is obviously recognizable as an abbreviation of "Auto-Microbic System" and so is not an arbitrary or fanciful term.

Factors relevant to the issue of secondary meaning include the amount and manner of advertising, the volume of sales, the length and manner of the mark's use and direct consumer surveys and testimony. Unquestionably, Vitek and McDonnell have expended a very substantial amount for advertising and promoting the AutoMicrobic System (AMS) instrument. However, it was not until late 1978 that the marketing emphasis on the "AMS" mark began. In fact, the market for both the Vitek and Abbott instruments was still in the embryonic stage when this suit was filed, and certainly so at the time Abbott adopted its MS–2 mark. On the other hand, considering the limited number of potential customers for the product, it is clear to us that in spite of the very short period of time the respective instruments were on the market, such customers associated AMS only with Vitek and also associated MS–2 only with Abbott, and in that sense each mark may be said to have a secondary meaning. The buyer's choice was between two different instruments, each of which had its own separate identity and known source. Under no sense of the word was Abbott trading on the Vitek name or "reputation." And since, as we have found, there is no reasonable likelihood of confusion (or actual confusion), the issue of secondary meaning, as such, is mooted.

Vitek has vigorously attacked the bona fides of Abbott in adopting and continuing to use its MS–2 mark both alone and in conjunction with the Abbott logo. We reject this claim and expressly find that the mark was chosen and is used in good faith with no intent to infringe upon the Vitek mark. As we have held supra, no infringement actually resulted from the use of the Abbott mark and logo.

* * *

Having found there is no reasonable likelihood of confusion between the Vitek and Abbott mark nor of any injury to Vitek's "reputation", it follows that * * * Vitek is not entitled to an injunction nor to cancellation of the Abbott trademark registration. We also find no basis in the credible evidence for a finding of unfair competition. Judgment will be entered in favor of Abbott on all counts of the complaint. Defendant has counterclaimed for a declaratory judgment with respect to the validity and scope of the Vitek AMS mark. We find that the mark is valid when applied to microbiology instruments. The judgment will so declare.

* * *

VITEK SYSTEMS, INC. v. ABBOTT LABORATORIES
675 F.2d 190
(United States Court of Appeals, Eighth Circuit, April 13, 1982.)

McMILLIAN, C. J.

Vitek Systems, Inc. (Vitek) appeals from a judgment entered in the District Court [footnote] for the Eastern District of Missouri denying injunctive relief for alleged trademark infringement. Following a bench trial, the district court found that Abbott Laboratories, Inc.'s (Abbott) "MS–2" mark, viewed by itself or in conjunction with Abbott's logo,   , did not infringe upon Vitek's "AMS" mark because there was no substantial likelihood of confusion as to the source of the parties' products. [Footnote.] For reversal Vitek argues that the district court's findings are clearly erroneous. For the reasons discussed below, we affirm.

A complete statement of the facts is set forth in *Vitek Systems, Inc. v. Abbott Laboratories, Inc.*, 520 F.Supp. 629 (E.D.Mo. 1981), and will not be repeated here. The pertinent facts are

as follows. Vitek, a wholly-owned subsidiary of McDonnell Douglas Corp. (McDonnell), and Abbott are competitors in the manufacturing and marketing of automated computerized microbial testing instruments. The market for the instrument consists of approximately 2,000 clinical laboratories and acute care facilities. The cost of the instrument ranges between $26,500 and $74,500. The instruments are marketed through displays at trade shows, journal advertising and direct sales calls. The instruments are never sold on a single sales contact and impulse buying is unknown in the field.

The Vitek instrument was developed in the early 1970s by McDonnell. In 1974, following an in-house contest at McDonnell, the name "AutoMicrobic System" was chosen for the instrument. On July 9, 1976, McDonnell filed trademark registration applications for two marks, "AutoMicrobic System" and "AMS." The "AMS" registration was granted on April 5, 1977.

The Vitek instrument was originally marketed by the Fisher Scientific Company (Fisher). Fisher promoted the instrument primarily under the name "AutoMicrobic System." At other times it was referred to as the "AMS AutoMicrobic System." In its promotional materials Fisher would occasionally use its own name and logo in conjunction with the name and logo of McDonnell.[3]

On June 8, 1977, McDonnell formed Vitek pursuant to its decision to phase out Fisher and McDonnell identification of the instrument. In 1978, Vitek assumed the marketing functions and employed a Chicago advertising firm to create a public image of Vitek and the instrument. As a result, emphasis was placed upon the "AMS" mark beginning in late 1978.

Abbott developed its instrument commencing in 1973. It adopted the mark "MS–2" on September 2, 1976, and filed a trademark registration application in November of that year. However, it developed that in mid-1976 an affiliate of the Rohm & Haas Co. had filed a registration for the "MS–2" mark claiming a first use on May 11, 1973. Abbott then considered changing its mark to "QS–2," but in-

---

3. The Fisher contract was in effect for approximately four years. During that period of time only seven instruments were delivered by McDonnell to Fisher. Fisher did not make any sales, although a few of the instruments which had been placed with prospective customers for evaluation were ultimately purchased by them.

stead negotiated an agreement with Rohm & Haas whereby Abbott was allowed to continue the use of the "MS–2" mark. One provision of the agreement was that Abbott would display its logo on the instrument and in its promotional materials to distinguish the source of its product from Rohm & Haas.

The Abbott instrument was first displayed in this country at a trade show in October 1976. It was displayed as the "Abbott MS–2." The Vitek (then McDonnell) instrument was displayed at the same show under the name "McDonnell-Fisher Auto-Microbic System."

On or about November 5, 1976, counsel for McDonnell wrote a letter to Abbott claiming that Abbott's mark infringed upon the "AMS" mark. Abbott took the position that there was no infringement and informed McDonnell that it was seeking trademark registration of the "MS–2" mark. Abbott continued to use the mark on its instrument and in its promotional material. Vitek then instituted this infringement proceeding in 1980, claiming that there was a likelihood of confusion because consumers would think that the MS–2 had some connection with Vitek and would consider it on that basis.

After a full bench trial the district court held that Vitek had failed to carry its burden of showing a likelihood of confusion as to the source of the product based on the following findings, summarized here: (1) a lack of similarity between the marks; (2) the sophistication of the buyers and the complexity of the sales process; (3) the absence of credible, unambiguous evidence of actual confusion; (4) the fact that the Vitek name and AMS mark were not emphasized until late 1978; and (5) Abbott's adoption and use of the MS–2 mark were done in good faith. On appeal Vitek challenges the findings regarding the similarity of the marks and the evidence of actual confusion.

The essential question in any case of alleged trademark infringement is whether purchasers are likely to be misled or confused as to the source of the different products. [Citation.] The resolution of this issue requires the court to consider numerous factors to determine whether, under all the circumstances, there is a likelihood of confusion. [Citation.] Actual confusion is not essential to a finding of infringement. [Citation.] However, a mere possibility is not enough; "there must be a substantial likelihood that the public will be confused." [Citation.] "Likelihood of confusion is a finding of fact. Therefore, we must uphold the trial court's finding * * * unless it is clearly erroneous." [Citation.]

With the foregoing principles in mind we examine Vitek's arguments. Vitek first argues that the district court erred in not finding that the marks are confusingly similar. It reasons that Abbott's logo, [logo omitted], is an "A" so that the Abbott's mark is actually "AMS–2"—a designation confusingly similar to Vitek's "AMS" mark. In support of its argument Vitek requests this court to take judicial notice of Abbott's 1980 renewal trademark registration in which Abbott's vice-president called the logo a "block A." Vitek reasons that the registration is an admission by Abbott that its logo is an "A" proving that the marks are confusingly similar. [Footnote.] We disagree.[5]

"Similarity of the marks * * * must be considered as they are encountered in the marketplace. Although similarity is measured by the marks as entities, similarities weigh more heavily than differences." [Citation.] The comparison should be made "in light of what occurs in the marketplace," taking into account the "circumstances surrounding the purchase of the goods." [Citation.]

The manner in which Abbott describes its logo for registration purposes carries little weight in determining whether the marks are confusingly similar to the public. The logo is not presented as a block A on the instrument or in Abbott's promotional materials. The district court properly considered Abbott's systematic and continuous use of its logo since the 1950s and found that the logo "has attained wide recognition as the symbol of Abbott Products."[6] *Vitek Systems, Inc. v. Abbott Laboratories, Inc.*, 520 F.Supp. at 631. That

---

5. In essence we conclude that Abbott's logo is not analogous to Gertrude Stein's rose—that is to say, an [logo omitted] is not an A by any other name for purposes of this case.

6. The Abbott logo was created in the late 1950s and has been used continuously on virtually all its products as well as on its correspondence and in its promotional materials since that time.

finding is supported by the testimony of Vitek's own witnesses identifying [logo omitted] as Abbott's logo rather than an "A".

The district court also properly considered the facts that Abbott's logo is displayed only in connection with its corporate name and that when the logo and mark appear in proximity, the logo is contrasted in spacing, size, color and style from the mark. In contrast, the letters of "AMS" are evenly spaced and are uniform in size, color and style. Vitek's name appears on the face of its instrument and Abbott's name, as well as its logo, appears on the nameplate of its instrument. We realize that display of the manufacturer's name is not determinative of the confusion issue. [Citation.] However, in the case of a high-priced, single-purchase article, "there is hardly likelihood of confusion or palming off when the name of the manufacturer is clearly displayed." [Citation.] The district court noted other differences including the contrasting appearance of the instruments and the fact that the purchasers are knowledgeable, sophisticated specialists in their areas. [Citation.] These differences support the district court's rejection of the likelihood of confusion.

Vitek next argues that there was evidence of actual confusion in the record and that the district court's findings in view of that evidence indicates that the district court used an erroneous standard. Much of the evidence was the testimony of Vitek and McDonnell employees and consultants to the effect that customers had told them they were confused by the marks. The district court found that the testimony was "ambiguous at best and not credibly probative of the asserted confusion." *Vitek Systems, Inc. v. Abbott Laboratories*, 520 F.Supp. at 632. On appeal Vitek highlights extracts of various witnesses' testimony to support its argument that the district court's finding is clearly erroneous. After a review of the entire transcript, we disagree.

Seven of Vitek's witnesses were employees or consultants of Vitek and McDonnell. These witnesses testified, in effect, that customers had told them that they were confused by the similarity of the marks. Such testimony was hearsay in nature and the district court properly gave it little weight. [Citations.] In addition, the district court could refuse to credit the uncorroborated testimony of such interested persons. [Citation.]

Vitek also introduced the testimony of three customer witnesses. Our review of the record convinces us that there is substantial evidence supporting the district court's finding that their testimony was not probative of actual confusion. For example, customer Stephen Hnatko was not asked, nor did he indicate, whether he was confused between the two instruments. Customer Connie Brown expressly denied having been confused as to the source of the instruments.[7] "Confusion, in the legal sense means confusion of course." [Citation.] The above testimony does not reveal such confusion.

Customer Rollie Rebulta testified that he used the MS–2 and AMS terms interchangeably during a meeting with Vitek representatives. However, the evidence established that a Vitek representative met with Rebulta and, contrary to company policy, brought up competitive products after Rebulta had already had five earlier meetings with Vitek representatives and had decided to acquire the Vitek AMS. The district court was not required to give weight to confusion created by Vitek.

Vitek also argues that the district court erred in excluding, on hearsay grounds, employee Robert Mattaline's handwritten memorandum of his meeting with a potential customer which allegedly indicates confusion.[8] Vitek argues that the memorandum is admissible under Rule 803(1) Fed.R.Evid., the "present sense impression" exception to the hearsay rule. We disagree. Vitek's offer of proof reveals that Vitek sought to elicit Mattaline's evaluation of the customer's thought process.

---

7. Brown stated as follows:
   Q. Okay. At any point in time, from when you first began considering the Vitek instrument, were you ever confused as to who manufactured that particular instrument?
   A. No.
   [Reference.]

8. The memorandum consists of 19 handwritten pages of illegible notes. Vitek has not summarized the contents of the memorandum in its brief so that the only indication of its contents is the offer of proof made by Vitek's counsel. *See note 9 infra.*

As such, the testimony does fall within the present sense impression exception to the hearsay rule.[9]

The judgment of the district court is affirmed.

GIMIX, INC. v.
JS & A GROUP, INC.

699 F.2d 901

(United States Court of Appeals, Seventh Circuit, Feb. 1, 1983.)

CUDAHY, C. J.

This case comes before us under our jurisdiction over trademarks. [Citations.] Appellant Gimix, Inc. ("Gimix") sued defendants Iwata Electric Co. ("Iwata"), Auto Page, Inc., and JS & A Group, Inc. ("JS & A") for trademark infringement, false advertising, unfair competition, deceptive practices, injury to business reputation, dilution and unjust enrichment. The district court granted the defendants' motion for summary judgment on the grounds that the term in question—"Auto Page"—was generic and thus that Gimix had no protectible rights in it; thus Gimix also did not have standing to raise the false advertising claims. We affirm the district court's order, although we do so on grounds other than those relied on below.

I.

Plaintiff-appellant, Gimix, is a manufacturer of telephone products and computers. In 1975 Gimix began to market an automatic dialing device. The most common use of this device, although not the only use,[1] is to connect an automatic telephone answering service with a paging terminal; the machine responds to a message left with an answering service by automatically dialing a paging terminal, causing it to notify the user, via the user's "beeper," that a message has been left on the

telephone answering machine. Gimix markets this device through dealers, such as telephone stores and answering machine distributors; the machine is also promoted at trade shows.

On April 26, 1976, Gimix applied for a patent on this product, which it described in the application variously as an "automatic dialer" or as an "automatic page." The device has been advertised both under the name of "Gimix Auto Page" and under the name of "Gimix," although only the word "Gimix" was registered as a trademark. Gimix contends that it nonetheless holds trademark rights in the word "Auto Page."

Defendant-appellee Iwata, is a Japanese manufacturer and exporter. In 1977 Iwata conducted a trademark search in preparation for marketing a car theft warning device under the name "Auto Page." In January of 1978, having found no prior or pending registration, Iwata began to advertise its new product under that name. In March of 1978, Iwata filed an application to register "Auto Page" as a trademark for its car theft warning devices; the registration was subsequently granted in January 1980. Defendant Auto Page, Inc. was incorporated in 1979 to act as Iwata's United States distributor for these car theft warning devices.

In May or June of 1980 Iwata also began manufacturing and selling a wireless portable paging system consisting of a short-range transmitter and receiver for use in paging persons inside buildings or within a one-mile radius. The system includes a desk-top transmitter-receiver, a microphone, a CB antenna and portable pocketsize receivers, or "beepers." The desk-top transmitter-receiver has buttons that can be manually pressed to signal the beepers, and the person operating the buttons can communicate with a person carrying a beeper by talking through the micro-

---

9. Vitek's offer of proof states:
   Judge, I make an offer of proof that Exhibit 31 was the recollection of the witness of a meeting he had * * * in which the witness if asked would testify that he *perceived confusion in the witness* because the witness confused the operational characteristics of the instrument that he indicated he was familiar with * * *.
   The other thing he was going—he would testify to

is that the man indicated he knew all about the AMS when, in fact, he had never observed the AMS and was confused as to the fact that it was the Abbott instrument that he had interpreted as being the AMS instrument.
[Emphasis supplied.] [Reference.]

   1. The device apparently can also be manually operated or connected to an alarm system.

phone. Auto Page, Inc. is Iwata's United States distributor for this product, which is also marketed under the name "Auto Page." Defendant JS & A advertises and sells this product of Iwata by mail.

On December 10, 1980, Gimix filed a complaint charging Iwata, Auto Page, Inc. and JS & A with trademark infringement under federal trademark law and at common law, false advertising, unfair competition, deceptive practices, injury to business reputation, dilution and unjust enrichment, and demanded a jury trial. On April 9, 1981, Auto Page, Inc. and Iwata moved for summary judgment on the ground that "Auto Page" was a generic name for the plaintiff's product and thus not an interest protectible at law. Defendants asserted that Gimix' own use of the term in its patent application and in the deposition of Richard Don, Vice-President of Gimix ("Don Deposition"), demonstrated that "Auto Page" was a noun naming the device, rather than a mark referring to its source of origin. They argued, as well, that Gimix would not be able to establish secondary meaning and that there was no likelihood of confusion, since the products were different and non-competing. In response to the motion for summary judgment. Gimix argued that the generic name for its product was an automatic dialer and that confusion was likely because the end result of all the products involved in the lawsuit was the same: paging. To support its contention that the term "Auto Page" was not generic, Gimix adduced evidence that no competing producer of paging devices except the defendant used the term; the evidence consisted of advertisements, listings in the telephone Yellow Pages, and FCC classifications. Gimix also argued that Iwata was estopped to claim that the term was generic by its own application to register the term as a trademark for its car theft warning device. Moreover, Gimix maintained that the test for genericness is public perception and that summary judgment was inappropriate since that test involves subjective reactions and requires purchaser, distributor and user testimony.

On May 21, 1981, the district court denied the defendants' first motion for summary judgment. After a period of additional discovery, a second motion for summary judgment was filed on October 16, 1981. In it Iwata and Auto Page, Inc. not only renewed their argument that "Auto Page" was a generic term but also maintained, alternatively, that it was merely descriptive and thus not a protectible interest, since plaintiff could not meet the burden of establishing secondary meaning. As evidence that the term was used to impart information about the product's function, rather than its origin, defendants proffered Gimix' description in its patent application of the device as an "automatic page," the statement in the Don Deposition that "auto page" "might be a shorter corruption of 'automatic pager'," and various items of promotional literature in which Gimix listed the product as an "auto page." The defendants also maintained in their motion that the evidence about secondary meaning was insufficient as a matter of law since Gimix had not invested an adequate amount of time or effort to develop the term as a distinctive mark. Neither side presented surveys of public reaction on this or any other point.

In its response to the renewed motion for summary judgment, Gimix pointed to the fact that no testimony about secondary meaning in the minds of buyers, dealers and distributors had been advanced by the defendants and asserted that there remained genuine issues of material fact on this as well as on other allegations of the complaint.

On November 24, 1981, JS & A also filed a motion for summary judgment with respect to the false advertising claims, which were based on various statements by it about the cost, range, ownership and other asserted advantages of the Iwata Auto Page system. JS & A maintained that the various statements complained of were not false in relation to the wireless paging system advertised by it and that the statements had no relation whatever to Gimix' product.

On January 13, 1982, Judge Will granted the defendants' motions for summary judgment, finding that the term "automatic page"— and thus also "auto page"—were generic terms for which Gimix could not claim trademark protection. Further, since Gimix had no trademark rights in the term, Judge Will ruled that it had no standing to challenge the accuracy of JS & A's advertising. He nonetheless observed that the claims did not appear to be false. It is this order which is now before us.

II.

Appellant has chiefly taken issue with Judge Will's holding that "Auto Page" is a generic term. Although the issue on appeal has been drawn primarily in terms of genericness because of the district court finding and was briefed largely, although not entirely, in those terms, we may affirm the district court's granting of summary judgment on grounds different from those which formed the basis for its holding. [Citations.] We do so with no prejudice to the parties since those alternate grounds were in fact before the court. [Footnote.]

We will therefore consider the following questions in sequence: First, is Gimix' alleged trademark invalid, as Judge Will held, because it is generic?[3] Second, if "Auto Page" is not a generic term, is it nonetheless unprotectible as merely descriptive of the product's qualities or functions? Third, if "Auto Page" is in fact descriptive, has plaintiff Gimix created a genuine issue of material fact as to whether the term had acquired secondary meaning by long use? Fourth, do any of the false advertising or other claims alleged survive a finding that Gimix' trademark is invalid?

A. Genericness

A generic term is one which is commonly used as the name of a kind of goods. *Miller Brewing Co. v. G. Heileman Brewing Co.*, 561 F.2d 75, 79 (7th Cir.1977), *cert. denied*, 434 U.S. 1025, 98 S.Ct. 751, 54 L.Ed.2d 772 (1978). Unlike a trademark, which identifies the source of a product, a generic term merely specifies the type, or genus, of thing into which common linguistic usage consigns that product. A common source of evidence on genericness is the dictionary. For example, the *Miller* case, the leading Seventh Circuit case on this issue, relied heavily upon the dictionary for its conclusion that "light," or its misspelled equivalent, was a generic term in relation to low-calorie beer. [Citation.]

Gimix here contends that the standard for genericness requires instead direct evidence, such as consumer surveys, of what the public understands by the use of a term, referring us to Learned Hand's famous "test": "What do the buyers understand by the word for whose use the parties are contending?" [Citation.] Gimix points to the fact that the defendants in this case submitted no direct evidence about consumer understanding of the term "Auto Page" and argue that summary judgment is inappropriate where a case thus turns upon an issue of subjective understanding.

Plaintiff's argument in this respect, however, ignores the fact that words may be classified as generic in two distinct ways. A manufacturer may select a word which is already in common use and apply it to his product according to that common meaning; the use of "light" in relation to beer is an example of this first type of generic term. However, a manufacturer may also invent a word which thereafter enters common usage and *becomes* generic. [Citation.] It was this latter process which Judge Hand was discussing in the *Bayer* case: had "aspirin," a coined word, so entered the common understanding as to have become generic and thus no longer subject to exclusivity of use? Evidence of public understanding of the term is clearly critical with respect to this question, in deciding whether a word has degenerated from trademark status into a generic term, a term which the public has "expropriated" for the use of all speakers.

We do not understand either party in this case to argue that "Auto Page" is such a coined word turned generic. In fact, the defendants point to Gimix' use of the term in its patent application, before the public had even been exposed to the product. Thus, the only question here is whether "Auto Page" was a commonly used and commonly understood term prior to its association with the product or products at issue. And the dictionary, with its continuing catalogue of words arriving in and departing from common speech, is an especially appropriate source of evidence about the

---

3. We reject Gimix' initial assertion that the defendants are somehow estopped to claim, or have waived, their defense that "Auto Page" is an invalid trademark by their own registration of the term. We find this claim to be without merit, both because the elements of reliance and injury necessary to estoppel are absent and because there is a strong public interest in permitting challenges to invalidity. Nonetheless our holding here, that "Auto Page" is a descriptive term incapable of being the subject of a valid trademark, may have implications for the validity of the defendants' trademark as well.

meaning attached by a linguistic group to a particular verbal symbol.

Based upon such evidence, we have no difficulty concluding that "Auto Page" is not a generic term. The parties both concede, and our research confirms, that the term does not appear, as such, in any dictionary. Defendants contend, however, that the word is a combination of two generic terms and thus itself generic. The problem with this argument is that both of these terms—"auto" and "page"— are susceptible of multiple meanings, making their combination particularly ambiguous. On the one hand, "auto," from an original Greek root meaning "self," is described by Webster's Third Unabridged Dictionary as having several meanings. It is used as a prefix, which in combination with "mobile" or "motive" means "self-propelling." It may also be an independent word, the short form of "automobile." According to yet another use, "auto" is a prefix which is itself the short form of the word "automatic." The word "page," similarly, is laden with diverse denotations. In its appearance as a noun, it may in modern usage signify a hotel attendant, a small boy dressed up for a wedding, or a leaf of a book. As a verb, "page" may import the actions of summoning someone (over a public address system, for example), or of numbering the pages of a book, or rifling through the pages of a book.

This abundance of meaning leads us to conclude that "Auto Page" cannot be subject to any common public understanding. Although all of the products in this case have been connected by their makers with the term "page" in order to evoke its description of summoning a person, it is not clear that a member of the public would immediately so understand the word. This inherent ambiguity is heightened by the fact that the two manufacturers seem to have used the prefix "auto" according to two different uses: Gimix for its content of "automatic," and Iwata, in the use for which it originally sought and ultimately obtained a trademark, as short for "automobile." It is difficult, indeed impossible, for us to fathom how a word which is alleged by the defendant to identify a genus or species of object can be used, as in this very case, to denote both a device to activate an alarm when a car is broken into and a machine which connects one's answering service to her paging system. Moreover, the evidence that other manufac-

turers and the Federal Communications Commission use a variety of different terms to designate the kind of automatic dialing device marketed by Gimix also persuades us that "Auto Page" is not a generic term.

B. Descriptiveness

Our holding that "Auto Page" is not a generic term does not dispose of the question whether it is a protectible trademark, for a term which is found to be merely descriptive is also incapable of being the subject of a valid trademark. [Citations.] This court has defined such a mark as being one which is "merely descriptive of the ingredients, qualities, or characteristics of an article of trade." [Citation.] Such terms are "unsuited to the function of marks both because they are poor means of distinguishing one source of services from another and because they are often necessary to the description of all goods or services of a similar nature." [Citation.]

Thus our initial inquiry here must be whether the term "Auto Page" is reasonably descriptive of the characteristics of the article in relation to which Gimix asserts a trademark. We hold that it is. As we have already discussed, one common use of the term "page" is to signify an individual whose role it is to summon another person, frequently because that person has received a telephone call. As a verb, "to page" is commonly understood (in a context apart from books) as meaning to locate a person via some sort of signalling system for the purpose of reaching her with an incoming telephone call. "Auto" in all of its manifestations retains some sense of self-activating or self-operating. As a combined term, therefore, "Auto Page" is a very apt description of Gimix' product, which is capable of paging a person in response to the receipt of an incoming telephone call, without the intervention of any independent agent or actor.

The rationale for prohibiting the appropriation of such a descriptive term as a trademark rests upon the equal right of another individual producing and marketing a similar product to describe his or her product with similar accuracy. Were this right not protected by the law, elements of the language could be monopolized in such a way as to impoverish others' ability to communicate. [Citation.] In recognition of the need to protect the language against incremental monopolization, this court has held that the terms "Auto Shampoo" and "Car Shampoo" were merely descriptive of the nature of a product used in cleaning and washing automobiles [citation] and that "Telemed" merely described a process by which electrocardiograms were analyzed by computer over the telephone, *Telemed Corp. v. Tel-Med, Inc.*, 588 F.2d 213 (7th Cir.1978). In like fashion, we hold that "Auto Page" is descriptive of the plaintiff's product here.

C. Secondary Meaning

Having found "Auto Page" to be a merely descriptive term, Gimix' alleged trademark could be upheld only if it were established that the term had acquired secondary meaning in the mind of the public. In other words, although the term's "primary" meaning was merely descriptive, if through use the public had come to identify the term with plaintiff's product in particular, the words would have become a valid trademark. [Citation.]

The factors which this court has indicated it will consider on the issue of secondary meaning include "[t]he amount and manner of advertising, volume of sales, the length and manner of use, direct consumer testimony and consumer surveys." [Citation.]

These factors are relevant because they shed light upon the ultimate issue: how does the public regard the mark in question? [Citation.] Consumer testimony and consumer surveys are the only direct evidence on this question, and the existence of neither has been suggested here. The other factors are relevant in a more circumstantial fashion. Advertising is relevant because it is the means by which a manufacturer establishes its trademark in the minds of consumers as an indication of origin from one particular source; it is especially persuasive if the exposure has been "massive." [Citation.] In this case, however, far from creating an issue of fact as to a massive advertising campaign to establish "Auto Page" in the minds of the public as its exclusive mark, Gimix has failed to counter the impression that it in fact used the term inconsistently. Some Gimix flyers tout the product as "Gimix"; others as "Gimix Auto Page." Moreover, the period of time involved here, from the introduction of plaintiff's product in 1975 until the introduction of Iwata's similar product in 1980, is so brief as to cast serious

doubt upon the very possibility of having established a strong secondary meaning; by way of contrast, the Ever-Ready battery, for example, had been marketed under that name for over fifty years. [Citation.]

The only arguably relevant evidence Gimix has presented on this question is an affidavit and a letter by one dealer, a Mr. Sheldon Epstein, alleging that "Auto Page" was well-known as a trademark for Gimix' product and saying that he thought its use by JS & A was confusing. Even if evidence to this effect were presented at trial, however, it is not probative of a strong connection in the mind of the *consuming public* between the term and its source. Epstein was a Gimix dealer and his affidavit and letter were conclusory in nature and did not adequately place the question of secondary meaning to consumers in issue. Gimix, as the owner of an alleged mark we have found to be descriptive, has the burden of establishing a genuine issue of material fact as to whether its mark has attained secondary meaning in the mind of the public. [Citations.] Gimix has made no showing that sufficiently establishes such an issue of fact. We therefore hold that summary judgment was properly granted.

III.

The other issue argued to us on appeal is Gimix' false advertising claim, which is based on certain statements in the defendants' advertising about the cost, range, ownership, and other advantages of the Iwata Auto Page. From the cases cited in Gimix' brief [citations], we understand plaintiffs to be attempting to raise a claim under Section 43(a) of the Lanham Trademark Act, 15 U.S.C. § 1125(a). This provision reads, in relevant part, as follows:

> (a) Any person who shall * * * use in connection with any goods or services * * * a false designation of origin, or any false description or representation, including words or other symbols tending falsely to describe or represent the same, and shall cause such goods or services to enter into commerce, * * * shall be liable to a civil action * * * by any person who believes that he is or is likely to be damaged by the use of any such false description or representation.

To the extent that Gimix' claim is based on a "false designation of origin," it must fail with our holding that the alleged trademark is invalid as a merely descriptive term. Assuming arguendo that the complaint does state a claim under the "false description" prong of Section 43(a), appellant's argument still must fail as a matter of law. The case before us does not involve a comparative advertising claim in form, since Gimix' product is nowhere named in the defendants' advertising. [Citation.] Even if the misrepresentations covered by the Lanham Act are broader than those involved in a deceptive comparative advertising case, a plaintiff must at least show that the allegedly false or deceptive statements are of a type that are likely to have a direct impact upon sales of its own product. [Citation.] In this case Gimix relies solely upon the contents of the advertisements in question. True or false,[4] misleading or not, this evidence is insufficient to raise an issue under Section 43(a) of the Lanham Act. Appellant has submitted no affidavits, depositions, or other material creating any issue of fact as to likelihood of impact on Gimix' sales or of confusion of customers by the advertisements in question. The defendants' motion for summary judgment was therefore properly granted.

IV.

All of the plaintiff's other claims—infringement, dilution, unfair competition, deceptive practices, injury to business reputation and unjust enrichment—depend upon the allegations of trademark infringement and false advertising discussed above. Since we have held that Gimix does not have a valid trademark in the term "Auto Page" and that Gimix has not made a showing sufficient to create a material issue of fact as to the false advertising claim, summary judgment is appropriate as to all of those related claims as well.

The order of the district court is hereby affirmed.

---

4. The district court persuasively analyzed the advertisements and concluded that they were not false. We see no reason to quarrel with this analysis.

UNIVERSITY COMPUTING CO. v. LYKES-YOUNGSTOWN CORP.

504 F.2d 518

(United States Court of Appeals, Fifth Circuit, Nov. 15, 1974.)

TUTTLE, C. J.

I. FACTS

This case involves three separate claims for damages arising out of a complicated series of transactions between four corporations and a number of their executive officers. The trial lasted three weeks and the record is correspondingly lengthy and complex. We begin by briefly summarizing the critical facts.

A. Joint Venture Agreement Between UCC and LYC.

University Computing Company (UCC), a Texas corporation, and Lykes-Youngstown Corp. (LYC), a Delaware corporation, entered into a written agreement on July 1, 1969 to create jointly a new corporation, to be called Lykes-University Computing Company (Lykes/UCC), which was to offer computer services [1] in the southeastern United States. This enterprise was a new venture for LYC, which is a large diversified holding company active in insurance, shipping and other manufacturing enterprises. UCC was active in other parts of the country, particularly in the southwest, offering essentially the same services as Lykes/UCC was to offer. The joint venture was designed to open new markets for the sale of UCC's computer systems. [Footnote.]

As part of their agreement and pursuant to it, UCC funded early operations of the new corporation, including payrolls, equipment purchases and other expenses. These expenditures totalled $66,647.45.[3] Several UCC employees were hired by the new corporation, including defendant Oliver Shinn who became President of Lykes/UCC.[4] The joint ven-

---

1. Computer services entail both the sale of computer programs to customers who own their own computer equipment, and leasing of time on in-house computers. This latter type of service is referred to as functioning on a "service bureau basis" in the industry.

3. Both parties agree UCC is entitled to $73,312.20 for actual expenditures of $66,647.45 from July 1 to October 7, and an additional 10% of those expenditures pursuant

to the terms of their joint venture agreement as payment for "management services."

4. Shinn at the time of the joint venture was Vice President in charge of sales for UCC. His original contract of employment with UCC provided:

> * * * I agree to hold in confidence all information regarding UCC's business and not to use such information to UCC's damage. * * * For a period of twenty-four (24) months following any termination, I agree not to compete with UCC in any state in which UCC operates a computer center.

The same clause was in all UCC employment contracts.

ture agreement provided UCC was to sell computer "hardware" (i. e., computer equipment) and "software" to the new corporation. UCC was further to receive 10% of the gross disbursements of the new corporation for the first year for "management services." LYC agreed to have its various controlled subsidiaries (with the exception of Youngstown Sheet and Tube Co.) purchase computer services from the new corporation. The agreement did not set forth in any greater detail the manner in which the corporation was to be managed, or by whom.

The new corporation, Lykes/UCC, was chartered in Delaware, and its articles of incorporation provided for a Board of Directors to be composed of four individuals, who then had the option of electing a fifth. This was pursuant to the terms of the joint venture agreement which provided that UCC and LYC would each select two members of the Board of Directors of Lykes/UCC.

By October, 1969, before either party had contributed capital and before stock had been issued, the two original members of the joint venture came to disagree over the day-to-day management of Lykes/UCC. The original intent of the parties is now in dispute, with UCC pointing to the fee for "management services" and other terms of the contract as evidence that it was intended to make operational management decisions, while LYC points to the terms of the contract, provisions of the Delaware Corporation Act and other extrinsic evidence to support its claim that the new corporation was to be wholly independent.

The parties aired their disagreements at a meeting held on September 30, 1969. The outcome of this meeting is now also in dispute. LYC claims UCC agreed to make a final decision, prior to October 7, about remaining in the joint venture and that in a telephone conversation on October 6 both sides agreed to terminate the joint venture. UCC claims the matter was left open at the meeting and thereafter, and that while both sides understood UCC would likely wish to withdraw, the terms of that withdrawal and the amount of compensation for initial expenditures and loss of prospective profits were left unsettled.

On October 7, 1969, a fourth corporation, Lykes-Youngstown Computer Services Corp. (LYCSC) was formed as a wholly owned subsidiary of LYC. Oliver Shinn became President of this corporation; all property formerly owned by Lykes/UCC was taken over by LYCSC, and the new subsidiary of LYC proceeded to enter into the business planned for Lykes/UCC. UCC had no part in the decision to create this fourth corporation, and UCC now claims it wasn't aware of the existence of LYCSC until a story on it appeared in the *Wall Street Journal* on October 14, 1969. It is undisputed that UCC did not authorize the creation of the new corporation, nor did UCC authorize the seizure of all Lykes/UCC's property.

While a draft of a rescission and termination agreement was prepared by UCC following the October 6 telephone conversation, and a copy was sent to LYC for its consideration, it is undisputed that the terms of UCC's withdrawal were unsettled and the parties remained in substantial disagreement over the amount of compensation UCC was to receive. The draft agreement was not signed.

During the period between July 1 and September 30, while the disagreement over the management of Lykes/UCC was developing, Oliver Shinn met twice with executive officers of LYC. UCC claims to have been unaware that these meetings were taking place. In any event, it is undisputed that UCC certainly was unaware of the matters discussed at these meetings. Among these topics discussed were the desirability of Lykes/UCC being independent of UCC and LYC, the burden of paying the 10% management fee owed UCC under the joint venture agreement, and the fact that Shinn was confident the UCC name was unlikely to further sales efforts in the southeast where UCC was virtually unknown. Although one of the meetings Shinn had with LYC executives took place when he was still a Vice President of UCC, Shinn made it clear at the beginning of the meeting that he was there solely on his own behalf, and he felt no loyalty to his employer, UCC.

In preparation for the September 30 meeting between UCC and LYC, Shinn prepared a report which he made available only to LYC on a confidential basis. In that report Shinn demonstrated that for $688,000 LYC could fund a wholly owned subsidiary which would have substantially the same chances for success as the joint venture corporation, to which LYC had committed $500,000 for only half ownership. These secret meetings and the confidential Shinn memo were the primary evidence of LYC bad faith in terminating the joint venture agreement introduced at trial.

B. Misappropriation of AIMES III By LYCSC.

Among the computer systems Lykes/UCC was to market was a retail inventory control system owned by UCC called "AIMES III." (Automated Inventory Management Evaluation System). This system was designed to maintain information on inventory in retail department stores.[5] UCC had previously sold the system to Leonard's Department Store in Fort Worth, Texas, subject to a restrictive use agreement which limited Leonard's to private and confidential use of the system. Leonard's paid $41,700 for the rights to restricted use of AIMES III. Lykes/UCC was to offer this system, as well as several others designed and owned by UCC, to customers in the southeast. The joint venture agreement provided for discount sales of these systems to Lykes/UCC at no more than 20% of UCC's development costs.

Following the incorporation of LYCSC (the newly created subsidiary of LYC), the new corporation proceeded to offer AIMES III to customers. Rather than purchase unrestricted rights to the system from UCC, LYCSC elected to steal the system from Leonard's. In December, 1969, LYCSC bribed an employee of Leonard's for $2500 to deliver a suitcase filled with computer tapes and other materials to an employee of LYCSC. In February, 1970, this same Leonard's employee was paid to fly to Atlanta from Dallas with additional tapes and documents once the materials originally obtained were found to be insufficient to run the system. With the new materials

5. The system was designed to generate reports on volume of inventory, broken down by specific items, and assess the quantity of each item sold for specific reporting periods.

6. By running the programs, LYCSC compiled a complete set of Cobol listings for the system. These listings, using a type of computer language designed to correspond to common business English, showed the various data the system could generate.

7. The system was offered both as "AIMES III" and as "MIMIC" (Maximum Information Through Merchandising Inventory Control), a system represented as having been developed by LYCSC. Rich's Department Store in Atlanta was offered MIMIC for $45,000; Colony Shops in Tampa was offered AIMES III for $42,000; and Technical Resources, a computer consulting firm, was offered MIMIC for restricted use only for $30,000.

and the help of the Leonard's employee in installing the system in the LYCSC in-house computer. LYCSC was able to run the system in its entirety.[6]

After receiving these materials in December, LYCSC attempted to market the AIMES III system. This marketing effort continued until April of the following year. Salesmen for LYCSC made offers to department stores in Atlanta, New Orleans and Tampa, Florida. In addition the system was offered to another computer services firm in Atlanta. While none of these offers was accepted, in several cases detailed sales presentations were made by sales representatives of LYCSC. A brochure was printed by LYCSC to assist the sales effort.[7]

C. Judgment in District Court.

UCC brought this suit against LYC, LYCSC and Oliver Shinn claiming damages under seven Counts. Counts 1 and 2 were combined at trial into a single count against LYC for breach of the joint venture agreement. Count 3 charged a conspiracy among the three defendants to misappropriate UCC's trade secret, AIMES III; Count 4 charged a conspiracy among the three defendants to convert unlawfully AIMES III; Count 5 charged a conspiracy among the three defendants to infringe UCC's common law copyright in AIMES III; Count 6 charged a conspiracy among the three defendants to violate Oliver Shinn's non-competition agreement with UCC; and finally Count 7 charged a conspiracy among the three defendants to induce a breach of the restrictive use agreement between Leonard's and UCC. Plaintiff conceded at trial Counts 3, 4, 5 and 7 all involved essentially the same dam-

The brochure identified the MIMIC system as being a retail merchandising inventory control system owned by LYCSC. LYCSC also occasionally used UCC sales literature after removing the UCC logo from the corner of the printed publications.

A former sales representative of UCC, David Hudson, was hired by LYCSC to direct this sales campaign. Hudson had negotiated the original Leonard's sales agreement when he was with UCC. After joining LYCSC, he arranged the theft and accepted delivery of the AIMES III system. Hudson had been trained by UCC to teach selling techniques, and had even conducted a course for Lykes/UCC sales personnel on techniques to be used in selling AIMES III prior to the termination of the joint venture. At this sales seminar, the sales literature and other publications on the AIMES III system which LYCSC subsequently used in its marketing campaign were distributed.

ages for the misappropriation of the AIMES III system.

The district court granted a directed verdict for defendants on Counts 5 and 7. The remaining counts went to the jury, which returned verdicts against the plaintiff on Counts 4 and 6, against defendant LYC on Count 1 and against all three defendants on Count 3. The jury awarded $172,000 against LYC for its breach of the joint venture agreement (Counts 1 and 2); $220,000 against all three defendants for misappropriation of UCC's trade secret, AIMES III (Count 3); and finally the jury awarded $100,000 in attorneys' fees against LYC on Count 1.

Defendants bring this appeal attacking these verdicts on a number of different grounds. Plaintiff cross-appeals the directed verdict on Count 7, and the verdicts on Counts 4 and 6. We affirm the judgment of the court below on the jury verdict on Count 1 against defendant LYC, and on Count 3 against defendants LYC, LYCSC and Oliver Shinn. We affirm judgment on the jury verdict on Counts 4 and 6 against plaintiff UCC and affirm the directed verdict against plaintiff UCC on Count 7. We reverse and remand for a new trial on the issue of attorneys' fees.

II. BREACH OF THE JOINT VENTURE AGREEMENT BY LYC.

A. Enforceability of the Joint Venture Agreement.

The jury found that LYC breached its July 1 joint venture agreement with UCC by unilaterally terminating the joint venture corporation and appropriating the property and assets of the joint venture corporation for its own use. The defendant first challenges the validity of the July 1 agreement which it was found to have breached. LYC and UCC subsequent to July 1 were unable to agree as to how the agreement allocated management control. UCC claimed the right to make day-to-day operational decisions about such matters as employment, equipment acquisitions, and the like, while LYC claimed Lykes/UCC was intended to be independent of both the members of the joint venture and its President, Oliver Shinn, was to have a free hand in managing the new corporation. LYC's argument is that to the extent the joint venture agreement failed to settle this important question it was deficient.

Under Georgia law [footnote] when the parties fail to agree on some element of a contract which affects the operation of the agreement in some extensive and important way, such a defect cannot subsequently be cured, and the contract is void for indefiniteness. We believe the testimony presented a jury question as to whether the parties agreed over operational control, and whether their July agreement can be so construed. The question whether there was a meeting of the minds of the two parties is essentially a factual one, and this would determine whether the agreement was enforceable. The problem here really is not that the parties had failed to consider and agree on some vital element of the contract, rather it is the parties' dispute as to what their original agreement was.

The record amply supports the jury finding that the contract was enforceable. The written agreement's references to accounting and management services might on its face be ambiguous,[9] but there was sufficient parol evidence for the terms to be understood by the jury as indicating the parties' intent that UCC exercise day-to-day operational supervision over the affairs of the new corporation. Further, the conduct of Oliver Shinn subsequent to his taking the position of President of Lykes/UCC supports this jury finding. Shinn used normal UCC procedures and accounting forms in requesting authorization for purchases, and sought UCC approval of his hiring guidelines. These actions are inconsistent with LYC's claim that he had always been meant to function independently of UCC. Until shortly before the ultimate rift between the parties, when he did in fact begin to act independently— thereby necessitating the September 30 meeting—Shinn performed essentially as a subordinate of UCC's President of the Data Link Division, Karl Young. Young was asked to approve all expenditures, down to so trivial an expenditure as moving expenses for a par-

---

9. The plaintiff claimed the word "management" was intended to mean the right to make decisions, as it normally is taken to mean; the defendants claimed the phrase "management services" had a technical meaning in the computer industry and involved only advice on decisions and routine bookkeeping. The testimony was in conflict as to this question.

ticular employee of Lykes/UCC. There was sufficient evidence that this pattern of conduct was what the parties intended that the jury could conclude the contract was complete and enforceable.

While LYC executives vigorously denied that they had ever agreed to this at trial, UCC executives just as vigorously testified that they had. On this type of factual dispute, concerning primarily the credibility of the witnesses, we are bound by the jury's findings. [Citation.]

* * *

B. Challenges to Jury's Finding LYC Breached the Joint Venture Agreement.

We conclude that there was more than adequate evidence for the jury to find that LYC breached the joint venture agreement with UCC. LYC could be found to have done this by unilaterally terminating Lykes/UCC, the joint venture corporation, and substituting in its place LYCSC, a wholly owned subsidiary which thereupon seized all the assets of Lykes/UCC and entered into the business planned for the joint venture. LYC's defense came down to its claim that UCC unilaterally withdrew from the venture after orally rescinding the agreement over the telephone. The pivotal conversation in LYC's account of events leading up to the dissolution of Lykes/UCC was one between Frank Nemec, then President of LYC, and Karl Young, then President of the Data Link Division of UCC, on October 6. Both men testified at trial, and both recounted substantially different accounts of the conversation—Nemec testifying that Young unconditionally withdraw on behalf of UCC, and Young denying any statement indicating UCC's intention to withdraw until the terms of withdrawal could be negotiated. This factual controversy clearly comes down to the credibility of the two witnesses. We find no reason to upset the jury's finding that Young did not withdraw from the venture and that UCC's intention to withdraw was conditioned upon the two sides coming to terms over the

amount of compensation UCC was to receive.

The evidence the jury received was conflicting. In addition to the direct conflict between Nemec's and Young's versions of the October 6 telephone conversation, there were a number of documents which each side used to support its claim. The documentary evidence was ambiguous, and thus while we don't find any of the evidence offered conclusive on this question, we are satisfied that the jury's decision that UCC did not unilaterally withdraw is permissible in light of all the evidence, and that in unilaterally terminating the joint venture on October 7 LYC breached its agreement with UCC.

C. Damages for Breach of the Joint Venture Agreement.

We finally come to the question of damages. In attacking the verdict of $172,000, LYC claims that there was no substantial evidence to support UCC's claim that in breaching the joint venture agreement LYC appropriated assets and business opportunities belonging to the joint venture without UCC's knowledge or consent. In part this raises again the question of mutual termination of the agreement which we have previously discussed.

We note there can be no doubt that LYCSC, LYC's subsidiary, appropriated the joint venture's property and business. In our view, once the jury found LYC breached the agreement with UCC, it was wholly justified in assessing damages in addition to the $66,647.45 which UCC had expended on behalf of LYKES/UCC before LYC's breach. [Footnote.] At trial UCC proved a variety of damages, including loss of the 10% management fee to October 1, 1970; loss of the 5% management fee for the period thereafter; loss of profits on sales and leases of hardware to Lykes/UCC as provided in the agreement; and finally loss of the opportunity to begin operations in the southeast with the guaranteed flow of revenues from the Lykes subsidiaries obliged to purchase computer services from the new corporation.[17] Together, the amount of damages subject to proof at trial

---

17. UCC took the position at trial that it was entitled to the value of the potentially successful business Lykes/UCC was to enjoy had it been under efficient management. The measure employed by UCC was to value the worth of Lykes/UCC were it to be purchased by a third party. Because UCC had in the past purchased a number of service centers which had on-going accounts, thereby building its business by acquisition. UCC executives testified that the value placed on a functioning service center by a willing purchaser was one to two times its gross annual revenues. Using this measure, UCC placed a total value of 1 or 2 million dollars on the business opportunity LYC appropriated.

on Count 1 totalled well in excess of two million dollars. We find the jury verdict of $172,000 was supported by the record.[18]

III. MISAPPROPRIATION OF UCC'S TRADE SECRET, AIMES III, BY LYC, LYCSC, AND OLIVER SHINN.

The defendants admit that LYCSC paid one Ron Clinton, an employee of Leonard's Department Store in Fort Worth, Texas, $2500 to induce him to steal Leonard's copy of the AIMES III system and deliver the tapes and documents comprising that system to an LYCSC employee. The defendants do not now claim that this conduct was lawful or even defensible.

The defendants do not challenge the finding of the jury that they acted in concert. If the jury finding of misappropriation of AIMES III is thus upheld, all three defendants properly share liability.

A. Legal Standards on Protection of Trade Secrets

A trade secret is protected against illegal appropriation and commercial use by a competitor. The development of this area of the law has been progressive, and most jurisdictions have developed similar standards. [Footnote.] What Georgia law exists in this area seems to follow the Restatement, Torts § 757. [Footnote.] We so held in Water Services, Inc. v. Tesco Chemicals, Inc., 410 F.2d 163 (5th Cir.1969). [Footnote.]

Under the Restatement § 757 formulation, a trade secret is defined as [footnote]:

> Any formula, pattern, device or compilation of information which is used on one's business and which gives him an opportunity to obtain an advantage over competitors who do not know or use it.

18. We reject defendant's argument that the jury should have been charged UCC was entitled only to an accounting for actual expenditures made on behalf of Lykes/UCC. The jury was properly charged that this type of an accounting was proper only if it was to find the two joint venturers had mutually decided to terminate the venture.

The defendant also challenged the admission of certain evidence which it claims was prejudicial. We find none of the evidentiary questions warrant upsetting the jury verdict on Count 1.

24. "The argument of appellee that the improvement dis-

In large measure the requirements simply are that "the parties view the process or device as a secret and that the secret be revealed in confidence. * * *" Water Services, supra, 410 F.2d at 172.

Liability attaches under the Restatement if one, "who discloses or uses another's trade secrets without a privilege to do so * * *

> (a) * * * discovered the secret by improper means
> or (b) his disclosure or use constitutes a breach of confidence reposed in him by the (owner of the secret) in disclosing the secret to him,
> or (c) he learned from a third person with notice of the facts that it was a secret and that the third person's disclosure of it was otherwise a breach of his duty to the (owner of the secret). * * *"

Unlike a patent which is totally protected for the period of time for which it is granted, the protection afforded a trade secret is limited—for it is protected only so long as competitors fail to duplicate it by legitimate, independent research. [Citation.] [Footnote.]

While the defendants in this action have deprecated the value of AIMES III [24] and made an effort at trial to challenge its uniqueness, they do not appeal the finding of the jury that AIMES III was a trade secret within the meaning of the § 757. Certainly it was undisputed that UCC viewed the system as a valuable and unique property, and used great caution in attempting to preserve its confidentiality. LYCSC itself described the system to one potential customer as " * * * the finest automated merchandising system available today," and proceeded to offer it to that customer for $45,000. Evidence was adduced at trial that AIMES III had unique capabilities and features which make it a valuable competitive product.[25] The jury could properly

closed in the patent under consideration was without value, or of only nominal value, was rightly rejected. The appellee, by infringing use, has paid tribute to the utility of the device infringed." Enterprise Manufacturing Co. v. Shakespeare Co., 141 F.2d 916, 920 (6th Cir. 1944).

25. We note that we have held that novelty is not a requirement of a trade secret under Georgia law. [Citation.] This follows the majority rule of the Restatement, Torts, § 759, comment b (1939). While a trade secret need not meet the standards of novelty required of a patented process, the secret must be something other than common knowledge. [Citations.]

find that the AIMES III computer system owned by UCC was a trade secret. The jury further could find that LYCSC's appropriation of the system was unlawful and a knowing violation of Leonard's restrictive use agreement with UCC. The requirements for liability under § 757 were satisfied in this case.

Once having determined that the jury finding that AIMES III was a trade secret wrongfully appropriated by the defendants was proper, the problem remains as to what is the appropriate measure of damages. It seems generally accepted that "the proper measure of damages in the case of a trade secret appropriation is to be determined by reference to the analogous line of cases involving patent infringement, just as patent infringement cases are used by analogy to determine the damages for copyright infringement." International Industries, Inc. v. Warren Petroleum Corp., 248 F.2d 696, 699 (3d Cir. 1957). The case law is thus plentiful, but the standard for measuring damages which emerges is very flexible.

In some instances courts have attempted to measure the loss suffered by the plaintiff. While as a conceptual matter this seems to be a proper approach, in most cases the defendant has utilized the secret to his advantage with no obvious effect on the plaintiff save for the relative differences in their subsequent competitive positions. Largely as a result of this practical dilemma, normally the value of the secret to the plaintiff is an appropriate measure of damages only when the defendant has in some way destroyed the value of the secret. The most obvious way this is done is through publication, so that no secret remains.[26] Where the plaintiff retains the use of the secret, as here, and where there has been no effective disclosure of the secret

through publication[27] the total value of the secret to the plaintiff is an inappropriate measure.

Further, unless some specific injury to the plaintiff can be established—such as lost sales—the loss to the plaintiff is not a particularly helpful approach in assessing damages.

The second approach is to measure the value of the secret to the defendant. This is usually the accepted approach where the secret has not been destroyed and where the plaintiff is unable to prove specific injury. In the case before us, then, the "appropriate measure of damages, by analogy to patent infringement, is not what plaintiff lost, but rather the benefits, profits, or advantages gained by the defendant in the use of the trade secret." International Industries, Inc. v. Warren Petroleum, supra, 248 F.2d at 699. The cases reveal, however, many variations in the way this benefit to the defendant can be measured.

Normally only the defendant's actual profits can be used as a measure of damages in cases where profits can be proved, and the defendant is normally not assessed damages on wholly speculative expectations of profits. Sheldon v. Metro-Goldwyn Pictures Corp., 309 U.S. 390, 60 S.Ct. 681, 84 L.Ed. 825 (1939). Had the defendants here been able to sell the AIMES III system at a profit, our task would be simplified.[28] Because the defendants failed in their marketing efforts, no actual profits exist by which to value the worth to the defendants of what they misappropriated. However, the Supreme Court has held in a patent case that the lack of actual profits does not insulate the defendants from being obliged to pay for what they have wrongfully obtained in the mistaken belief their theft would benefit them. In re Cawood Patent, 94 U.S. 695,

---

26. *See, e.g.,* Precision Plating v. Martin Marietta, 435 F.2d 1262 (5th Cir. 1970), cert. denied, 404 U.S. 1002, 92 S.Ct. 571, 30 L.Ed.2d 556 (1971) where public disclosure of a process was held to constitute a complete destruction of the value of the trade secret.

27. Defendants disclosed the complete system to one Hugh Cort of Technical Resources, Inc., unaware that Cort had been retained by UCC to discover whether LYCSC had in fact stolen the AIMES system. Cort had pledged to retain that information he discovered in confidence. Thus while the defendants' disclosure of the system to him in our view constitutes a "use" of the system, see discussion

p. 541, *infra,* this use did not amount to a form of public disclosure which destroyed the value of the secret to the plaintiff. [Citations.]

28. *See, e. g.,* Westinghouse Electric and Manufacturing Co. v. Wagner Electric and Manufacturing Co., 225 U.S. 604, 32 S.Ct. 691, 56 L.Ed. 1222 where the Court put the burden of proving factors other than the infringed patent caused the profits on the infringer once the plaintiff patentee proved profits were made. *See also* Carter Products, Inc. v. Colgate-Palmolive Co., 214 F.Supp. 383 (D.Md.1963) which awarded plaintiff the profits defendant made by using one of plaintiff's trade secrets.

24 L.Ed. 238 (1877).[29]

The rationale for this seems clearly to be that the risk of defendants' venture, using the misappropriated secret, should not be placed on the injured plaintiff, but rather the defendants must bear the risk of failure themselves. Accordingly the law looks to the time at which the misappropriation occurred to determine what the value of the misappropriated secret would be to a defendant who believes he can utilize it to his advantage, provided he does in fact put the idea to a commercial use. [Footnote.]

This second technique frequently entails using what is called the "reasonable royalty" standard: while the parties to this action agree this is the appropriate standard, they are unable to agree on what the measure entails. Originally this measure was intended to deal with the situation where the misappropriated idea is used either to improve the defendant's manufacturing process, or is used as part of a larger manufactured product. In the early case of Egry Register Co. v. Standard Register Co., 23 F.2d 438 (6th Cir. 1928), a patent infringement case, the defendant manufactured and sold cash registers which in part used a device developed by the plaintiff to roll paper through the machine. The trial court had awarded the plaintiff the total profits the defendant had made on all sales of the machines using this device. The Sixth Circuit Court of Appeals held this measure of damages was inequitable, because the device was only a part of the larger product sold by the defendant. Because no actual apportionment of profits based on what percentage of the success of the marketing of the machines was due to the

plaintiff's device could be shown, the court held the proper measure of damages would be a reasonable royalty on defendant's sales, thereby creating an apportionment of profits based on an approximation of the actual value of the infringed device to the defendant.

The Court explained its new measure in this way:

> To adopt a reasonable royalty as the measure of damages is to adopt and interpret, as well as may be, the fiction that a license was to be granted at the time of beginning the infringement, and then to determine what the license price should have been. In effect, the court assumes the existence *ab initio* of, and declares the equitable terms of, a supposititious license, and does this *nunc pro tunc;* it creates and applies retrospectively a compulsory license. * * *

The Court further held the proper standard would be a willing buyer-willing seller test: " * * * the primary inquiry * * * is what the parties would have agreed upon, if both were reasonably trying to reach agreement." *Egry Register, supra,* at 443.

The language of the *Egry* decision has been often quoted, but the type of measure used by the Court, based on actual sales, has taken many different forms.[31] As the term is presently understood, the "reasonable royalty" measure of damages is taken to mean more than simply a percentage of actual profits. The measure now, very simply, means "[t]he actual value of what has been appropriated." Vitro Corporation of America v. Hall Chemical Co., 292 F.2d 678, 683 (6th Cir. 1961). When this is not subject to exact measurement, a reasonable estimate of value is used. Many different factors are now considered in

29. Defendant's actual profits are now usually only one of a number of elements which can be considered in measuring damages for patent infringement. *See, e. g.,* Activated Sludge v. Sanitary District of Chicago, 64 F.Supp. 25 (N.D.Ill.1946), aff'd Per Curiam 157 F.2d 517 (7th Cir. 1946), cert. denied, 330 U.S. 834, 67 S.Ct. 970, 91 L.Ed. 1281 (1947) where the Court found no actual profits gained by the defendant, yet concluded "[t]he law is not impotent in attempting precise valuation, even though no market value exists and no loss or impairment of sales can be proven." 64 F.Supp. at 27. [Citations.]

31. 35 U.S.C. § 284 (1974) presently provides:
Upon finding for the claimant the court should award the claimant damages adequate to compensate for the infringement, but in no event less than a reasonable royalty for the use made of the invention by the infringer. * * *

The defendants attempt to define reasonable royalty as "a share of the profits on the product received by the owner for permitting another to use property" citing Patterson v. Texas Co., 131 F.2d 998, 1001 (5th Cir. 1942), cert. denied, 319 U.S. 761, 63 S.Ct. 1318, 87 L.Ed. 1712 (1943). [Reference.] As should be clear from our discussion of the development of the "reasonable royalty" measure in the law of ideas, and the gloss placed on this term as it is used in the cases, this standard commercial definition of the word "royalty" has no meaning in measuring damages for misappropriation of a trade secret.

As presently understood in patent law, a reasonable royalty is simply that amount which the trier of facts estimates a person desiring to use a patent right would be willing to pay for its use and a patent owner desiring to license the patent would be willing to accept. [Citations.]

arriving at the "reasonable royalty" in any given case:

> As pointed out in many cases * * * in a case where no established royalty is shown it is for the Court to determine a reasonable royalty which represents the value of that which has been wrongfully taken by the infringer * * * it is sufficient to point out that in making such determination many factors were taken into consideration * * *. In fact, the reasonable royalty was based upon the advantages which would have accrued to (the infringer) had it negotiated a license. * * *

Union Carbide Corp. v. Graver Tank and Manufacturing Co., 282 F.2d 653, 674-675 (7th Cir. 1960), cert. denied, 365 U.S. 812, 81 S.Ct. 692, 5 L.Ed.2d 691 (1961).

One other important variation of this "reasonable royalty" standard is the standard of comparison method, which also attempts to measure the value to the defendant of what he appropriated. As the Court in International Industries, Inc. v. Warren Petroleum Corp., 248 F.2d 696, 699 (3d Cir. 1957) explained this method, relating it to the facts of the case in which the defendant had misappropriated a method of converting dry cargo vessels into ones equipped to transport liquefied petroleum gas, and had actually used the technique to convert one vessel:

> This method contemplates the comparison of the cost of transportation by means of the use of the trade secret with a method of accomplishing the same result which would have been open to defendant had he not appropriated the trade secret.

Occasionally this has been taken to mean the difference in costs to the defendant of developing the trade secret on his own, using the actual development costs of the plaintiff as the complete measure of damages. [Citation.] This measure of damages simply uses the plaintiff's actual costs, and in our view is frequently inadequate in that it fails to take into account the commercial context in which the misappropriation occurred.

In certain cases, where the trade secret was used by the defendant in a limited number of situations, where the plaintiff was not in direct competition with the defendant, where

the development of the secret did not require substantial improvements in existing trade practices but rather merely refined the existing practices, and where the defendant's use of the plaintiff's trade secret has ceased, such a limited measure might be appropriate. In the type of case which we now consider, when the parties were potentially in direct competition and the course of conduct of the defendant extended over a period of time and included a number of different uses of the plaintiff's trade secret, and where the process of developing a computer system was very difficult and required substantial technical and theoretical advances, we believe a broader measure of damages is needed.

This broader measure should take into consideration development costs, but as only one of a number of different factors. We believe this type of measure is appropriate despite the fact that the inclusion of other factors means the final damage figure "need not be as precise as if the actual development costs for the trade secret were itself the measure of damages." Forest Laboratories, Inc. v. Pillsbury Co., 452 F.2d 621, 628 (7th Cir. 1971).

Our review of the caselaw leads us to the conclusion that every case requires a flexible and imaginative approach to the problem of damages. We agree with the Court of Appeals for the Sixth Circuit that "each case is controlled by its own peculiar facts and circumstances" [citation], and accordingly we believe that the cases reveal that most courts adjust the measure of damages to accord with the commercial setting of the injury, the likely future consequences of the misappropriation, and the nature and extent of the use the defendant put the trade secret to after misappropriation. Naturally in some cases the damages will be subject to exact measurement, either because the parties had previously agreed on a licensing price as in Vitro Corp. v. Hall Chemical Co., *supra,* or because some industry standard provides a clear measure.[32] Where the damages are uncertain, however, we do not feel that that uncertainty should preclude recovery; the plaintiff should be afforded every opportunity to prove damages once the misappropriation is shown.

---

32. *See, e. g.,* Carter Products, Inc. v. Colgate-Palmolive Co., 214 F.Supp. 383 (D.Md.1963) where evidence of other royalty rates for use of other of plaintiff's patented processes was held to have been properly considered by the Master, but did not amount to evidence of an established industry royalty.

Certain standards do emerge from the cases. The defendant must have actually put the trade secret to some commercial use. The law governing protection of trade secrets essentially is designed to regulate unfair business competition, and is not a substitute for criminal laws against theft or other civil remedies for conversion. [Footnote.] If the defendant enjoyed actual profits, a type of restitutionary remedy can be afforded the plaintiff—either recovering the full total of defendant's profits or some apportioned amount designed to correspond to the actual contribution the plaintiff's trade secret made to the defendant's commercial success. Because the primary concern in most cases is to measure the value to the defendant of what he actually obtained from the plaintiff, the proper measure is to calculate what the parties would have agreed to as a fair price for licensing the defendant to put the trade secret to the use the defendant intended at the time the misappropriation took place.

In calculating what a fair licensing price would have been had the parties agreed, the trier of fact should consider such factors as the resulting and foreseeable changes in the parties' competitive posture; the prices past purchasers or licensees may have paid; the total value of the secret to the plaintiff, including the plaintiff's development costs and the importance of the secret to the plaintiff's business; the nature and extent of the use the defendant intended for the secret; and finally whatever other unique factors in the particular case which might have affected the parties' agreement, such as the ready availability of alternative processes. Hughes Tool Co. v. G. W. Murphy Industries, Inc., 491 F.2d 923, 931 (5th Cir. 1973).

B. Challenges to Jury Instructions on Measuring Damages.

The district court charged the jury that the following factors should be considered by them in arriving at the proper damages for the defendants' misappropriation of AIMES III: (1) the development costs incurred by the plaintiff; (2) the fees paid by customers of the plaintiff who utilized the system on a service bureau basis; (3) the prices at which the system was leased or sold by the plaintiff for restrictive use; (4) the sale price placed on the system by the defendants; and (5) expert testimony as to what would constitute a reasonable royalty for the rights to unrestricted use of the system. We believe that these factors were proper to be considered by the jury.

The defendants challenge the trial court's charging the jury that they were to find the "reasonable value" of the computer system, arguing that the phrase "reasonable value" is an improper measure of damages, and that the proper measure can only be "reasonable royalty." In our view, the trial court's charge was proper. Naturally we read the charge in its entirety, and we do not believe that the trial court's charge in any way confused the jury as to what damages they were entitled to find. Defendants argue that the word "value" necessarily means the *entire* value of the system, or, in other words, the value of the system *to the plaintiff,* a measure they argue is appropriate only in cases where the secret has been totally destroyed. We believe the meaningful question is not whether the word "value" was used, but whether the jury was properly charged, as they were here, that they could assess damages only for the actual use of the AIMES III system in an amount which would fairly approximate the price the parties would have come to, had the defendant been licensed to use the system as it did.

The court properly concluded its instructions on Count 3 by charging the jury:

> [i]f you should further determine that (the plaintiff, UCC) has sustained any damages, it will be your responsibility to determine from all the evidence in the case what amount would be paid as a reasonable royalty for the unrestricted use of said computer program by a buyer willing, but not compelled to buy, to a seller willing, but not compelled, to sell.

This was an accurate statement of the law.

C. Challenges to Jury's Finding Defendants Put AIMES III to a Commercial Use.

The defendants' position is quite simply that there was no evidence they ever "used" the system, as required by the law on misappropriation of trade secrets, and that accordingly the trial court erred in denying their motion for a directed verdict on Count 3. The defendants place considerable emphasis on the fact that, in their view, the plaintiff lost nothing.

They point to the plaintiff's failure to prove lost profits as grounds for dismissal of plaintiff's claim for damages. In our view the established rule is that the plaintiff is not required to prove lost profits; rather it need only prove misappropriation of its valuable trade secret and prove that it was put to some commercial use.

The defendants claim that their inability to market the AIMES III system should insulate them from liability. While the defendants may be technically liable to the plaintiff under the formulation of § 757 of the Restatement of Torts due to the way they obtained the AIMES III system, they argue damages can be assessed against them only for a limited percentage of actual profits. We reject this view.

While the cases use the term "reasonable royalty" to describe the method of calculating damages, we do not believe the word "royalty" has the talismanic quality the defendants ascribe to it. While in certain cases the reasonable royalty would be a percentage of profits on actual sales, we do not accept the view that this need be the measure in all cases.

Rather the measure should correspond to the nature of the use. In cases where the trade secret was used to improve manufacturing, and subsequently manufactured items were sold at a profit [footnote], it would seem natural and equitable to measure damages based on those sales. But when, as here, the trade secret itself was what was to be sold—unlike any of the other cases we have discussed—we do not believe the same measure should apply.

Superficially the defendants' argument that they did not "use" the AIMES III system seems supported by the cases. Almost without exception prior trade secret cases involved a device or process which was used by the defendant to improve his manufacturing process. Either the idea was some new way to improve manufacturing, or some new device which improved a larger manufactured product. Obviously when a trade secret is "used" in such cases, the use is manifest and extensive. Here the use by the very nature of the misappropriated secret is more subtle. The computer system had value in that it could be sold to customers for their internal use, or it could be used by its owner on a service bureau basis if the owner chose to lease time on its computer to outside clients, and permitted the clients to use the programs. Further, the system had a value in that it represented a technical achievement, some new method of accomplishing the ordering of data to produce useful business reports. Testimony at trial indicated experts in the field of computer technology could be assisted in their experimental work by viewing the systems of others. Given these facts concerning the utility of the AIMES III system, in our view three separate sets of facts established a pattern of use of the system by the defendants which warrants damages for use of the system as if the defendants had been licensed to use it without restrictions.

Because of the earnestness with which this issue is argued by the parties, we feel it is necessary to discuss it in some detail.

First, it is clear that the defendants offered the system to potential buyers. They represented they held rights to the system which entitled them to sell the system to others. In some cases the defendants represented the system to be of their own design, designating the system under the initials MIMIC. In other cases the defendants acknowledged the UCC role in developing the system, but asserted rights to it. We believe this was a "use" which satisfied the requirements of the law on misappropriation of trade secrets.

Defendants claimed that computer service organizations frequently offered systems they did not own. Plaintiff's witnesses who had expertise in the field denied that this was true; defendants produced no examples of marketing campaigns of the type they conducted for systems the seller did not own. While it was shown that occasionally firms would sell systems they were in the process of developing (as indeed UCC had sold the AIMES III system to Leonard's before the research had been completed) clearly this is not the same thing as selling the system another owned. The only other instance of the marketing campaign preceding the seller's obtaining rights to the system was when the owner of the system had explicitly solicited such a campaign. We further believe the jury could find that LYCSC was attempting to sell a system it believed it had in its possession (i. e., the system it had misappropriated) rather than a system it believed it could purchase from UCC. The relations between UCC and the LYC subsidiary grew progressively more strained following what the jury found to have been LYC's breach of the joint venture agreement in October, 1969. The jury could reasonably infer that UCC was unwilling to deal with LYCSC and that LYCSC had no reason to believe that it would be able to purchase a copy of the AIMES III system from UCC after December, 1969; the defendants offered no evidence that they attempted to revive negotiations for purchases of software from UCC during 1970, despite the fact their marketing efforts continued unabated.

Finally, we find it difficult to ignore the fact that in February, months after all negotiations for the purchase of AIMES III ceased, LYCSC was still anxious to obtain the entire system and used Ron Clinton to obtain additional tapes and materials. We accept the jury's finding that LYCSC intended to sell the system it had misappropriated.

While defendants presented testimony at trial attempting to show that LYCSC arranged to steal the system only to guarantee that upon later purchasing the system from UCC they could be assured they received a current copy of the system, this testimony was thoroughly discredited by the fact that undisputed evidence at trial proved that the negotiations with UCC over the purchase of AIMES III ended prior to January, 1970, and that despite this fact LYCSC obtained additional AIMES III materials from Clinton in February, subsequently ran the system in their computer in February, compiled a complete Cobol listing for the system, and continued to offer the system to potential customers until April, 1970. The jury could reasonably reject this defense.

Once having determined this, it seems clear that any misappropriation, followed by an exercise of control and dominion such as an attempted sale (in which lay the principal value the system held for LYCSC), must constitute a commercial use for which damages can be awarded.

Second, LYCSC displayed the component programs and listings of AIMES III to Hugh Cort of Technical Resources, Inc. Once again such conduct indicates a continuing use in that the defendants viewed the system as something they could handle as they wished, without regard to the interest they knew UCC had in maintaining its confidentiality. The ad-

mitted secrets of AIMES III lie in its ability to generate specific reports and in its novel use of certain types of numbers placed on the inventory items (the so-called AIMES numbers) which are used to accomplish the compilation of inventory data. There is evidence in the record which indicates that any expert in computer software who observes the Cobol listings, the reports generated, and the details of the programs of a system of a competitor will gain a commercial advantage from that information. LYCSC thus took upon itself the authority to display all this information to such an expert, knowing that he could potentially use that information to the competitive disadvantage of UCC. We view this as a clear commercial use of the system—but one which has a second facet as well.

LYCSC displayed the various reports, listings and programs described above in the hopes of interesting Technical Resources in jointly developing a type of control system called RANFILE which they believed Technical Resources to be developing. AIMES III thus served the commercial interests of LYCSC and the other defendants in that it was used to prove LYCSC's technical expertise inasmuch as the AIMES III system was represented as being of LYCSC's design and invention.

Finally, there is some evidence that LYCSC had installed the AIMES III system on a service bureau basis. What this would mean is that LYCSC would be equipped to lease time on its in-house equipment and its clients could use the AIMES III system. The evidence of this is indirect, the unobjected to hearsay account of one Herbert Martenson who told of a LYCSC's salesman's claim that this was true. There was, further, clear and undisputed testimony that LYCSC had run the entire system to generate a complete set of Cobol listings after Clinton had delivered the additional tapes to LYCSC in February, 1970. We believe there is evidence from which the jury could reasonably infer that LYCSC had used the system on its computer, and that this constituted a commercial use.

Taken together, these three patterns of usage lead us to the conclusion that the jury could, indeed, find that LYCSC and, through it, the other two defendants, used the AIMES III system as if it had been theirs to do with as they pleased. They ran the tapes, they compiled the listings, they generated several reports, they exposed the secrets of the system to a competitor. In short, they acted as if they owned unrestricted rights to the system. No other pattern of licensing was shown by the defendants which would permit them the complete freedom they had in using the system as they chose. The defendants offered no evidence that under past industry practice the type of agreement the parties would most likely have reached would be some form of royalty on sales, thereby sanctioning this type of unrestricted use by the fictional licensee. We are unprepared to hold that because UCC had in the past refused to sell its rights to the AIMES III system to a competitor, and thus was unable to show past transactions to show how an agreement of this sort would have been reached, it should accordingly be denied damages.

In our view it is precisely in cases where the plaintiff had previously attempted to maintain the complete confidentiality of its trade secret that the lack of evidence of prior industry practice should not unreasonably limit the plaintiff's ability to prove its damages.

D. Challenges to Admission of Evidence on Value of AIMES III

The defendants challenge the method by which UCC proved damages at trial. The only evidence introduced by either side on the question of damages for the AIMES III misappropriation was the expert testimony of one Stan Josephson, who estimated the value of a sale of unrestricted rights to AIMES III at $220,000. Defendants challenge both the expert qualifications of this witness and the legal sufficiency of his testimony. We deal with the first of these issues quickly.

The trial court has substantial discretion over the admission of evidence [citation], and this includes the admission of expert testimony. [Citation.] In the absence of obvious error we will not disturb the ruling of the trial court. We find no error in permitting Josephson to testify as an expert. He was UCC Vice President of Technical Services. He testified he was responsible for developing software systems, pricing them for marketing, and then assisting as technical expert at sales presentations. He testified in pricing a software system he took into account such factors as development costs, the long-term potential for

the system and UCC's sales objectives, as well as such extrinsic facts as the current market for such systems. We find Josephson was properly permitted to testify as to the value placed on the sale of unrestricted rights to the AIMES III system by UCC.

The second challenge to Josephson's testimony involves this colloquy from the record during Josephson's cross-examination:

Q: Now, of course, you understand Mr. Josephson, I take it, that value—when you give an opinion on value, you are talking about what someone is willing to pay. Is that correct?

A: Oh, I wouldn't categorize it as that narrow.

Q: You wouldn't?

A: No. Value I don't think is what someone else will pay.

Q: What—

A: As you stated, I don't believe that value is strictly what someone else is willing to pay.

Q: Well, when you are talking about value here what were you talking about?

A: I'm talking about many things, the value of that particular product, the use that a retail company or data processing firm can make of that product. Many things besides—inherent in value.

Q: Then you were not telling us, arriving at a price at which the willing buyer would buy from a willing seller, that price they would arrive at?

A: What I was telling you, as I testified, was the generally accepted practice within the computer industry for unrestricted use of a valuable computer program.

Q: And that's not what a willing seller and a willing buyer would arrive at as a consequence of a negotiated transaction?

A: No. They're two separate things.

Defendants rightly point to the ambiguity created by Josephson's concession that what he was calculating was something other than what a willing buyer would agree to, which is the proper measure of damages.

In part our decision to sustain the jury verdict, which was heavily dependent on the Josephson testimony in view of the fact they assessed damages of $220,000, the precise estimate he had testified to, is based on our view that the jury was properly instructed in the law governing damages. The verdict of a jury properly instructed in the law clearly resolves ambiguities of this sort in testimony, and the jury had been fully instructed in the willing buyer-willing seller test.

But secondly we believe the ambiguity created by cross-examination was more apparent than real. Naturally, we read Mr. Josephson's testimony in its entirety and we do not find the above-quoted passage so inconsistent with his otherwise legally accurate description of how to calculate the value of unrestricted rights to AIMES III as to justify the jury verdict based on that testimony. Certainly estimating sales price as a function of costs is unexceptionable, and Josephson in our view had the expertise to opine that the proper way to calculate value is to multiply costs by a multiple of 2½.

What the disputed passage amounts to is Josephson's reluctance to claim that the figure he set as the proper sale price was necessarily that which a buyer would agree to. We can understand why he would demur from confidently asserting this is what the parties would agree to, for he had no prior transaction upon which to base his opinion. We believe it wasn't improper for UCC to prove its best estimate of the proper sales price, in part taking into consideration its policy of normally not offering its systems to potential competitors. While a certain amount of speculation is involved in this highly theoretical reconstruction of a sale which never took place, the aggrieved plaintiff must be permitted to present its best evidence on damages and not be foreclosed from seeking damages it deserves due to difficulty in measurement.

While we do not dispute the proper standard to be the "willing buyer-willing seller" test, we do not think a reconstruction of the agreement these two reasonable parties would arrive at can be taken too far. Nor do we feel that a witness as to value must cast his answers in the precise language that the Court uses in charging the jury. Both sides in such a hypothetical transaction have interests they wish to protect; such interests affect the price at which they are prepared to buy or sell—and in cases such as this one, the law is far more concerned with the rights and interests of the aggrieved plaintiff than in the interests of the defendants which they would have tried to protect had they dealt openly with the plaintiff from the beginning. As the Court in the *Egry Register* case acknowledged, the hypothetical agreement "must be modified by the commercial situation" *supra,* 23 F.2d at 443, and where the "willing seller" would have been unwilling to sell but for the theft of his secret, the Court reconstructing the agreement should consider the reasons the seller is unprepared to sell, and take into account such factors as the possible decline in the seller's future competitive posture.

This interest the holder of a trade secret has in retaining his rights to his secret is not a trivial one, and one which we do not intend to minimize. Courts should be reluctant to penalize an aggrieved plaintiff by too unrealistic and sterile a requirement of proving that the defendant *would* have agreed to the price the plaintiff thinks is fair. As in Forest Laboratories, Inc. v. Formulations, Inc., 320 F.Supp. 211, 213 (E.D.Wis.1970), affirmed in part, reversed in part on other grounds, 452 F.2d 621 (7th Cir. 1971), where the president of the plaintiff company was permitted to testify as to what price would have been required for the plaintiff to willingly agree to sell its patented secret, we believe a consideration of plaintiff's interest in protecting its future competitive position is proper, and some consideration must be given to the price at which the seller would be "willing" to deal. In affirming the trial court's assessment of damages in the *Forest Laboratories* case, the Seventh Circuit expressly acknowledged that consideration of such factors as plaintiff's future ability to stay in business is proper. 452 F.2d at 627-628. We fully agree with this approach.

The proper method of fleshing out the dimensions of this hypothetical sale is by cross-examination and rebuttal testimony. The plaintiff fulfills its burden of proving damages by showing the misappropriation, the subsequent commercial use, and introduces evidence by which the jury can value the rights the defendant has obtained. This UCC did; the defendants introduced no evidence on the question of the value of unrestricted rights to AIMES III. The defendants chose to leave Josephson's testimony unchallenged as to how his estimate of value was arrived at, save for their belief his admission he couldn't guarantee a willing buyer would accept the $220,000 figure necessarily destroyed the value of all his testimony.

Because we read the record as presenting a valid issue of damages to the jury, with sufficient evidence by the plaintiff to permit the jury to value the system at $220,000, we cannot now decide that the $220,000 verdict was clearly excessive as defendants argue.

The defendants also attack the basis for Josephson's calculation of total development cost—claiming such factors as marketing expenses and the plaintiff's royalty agreement with the original developer of the system should not have been included as development costs. We believe these were questions for the jury; the defendants did not choose to cross-examine Josephson extensively on this point, nor did they present rebuttal evidence to dispute his inclusion of these amounts. The jury was not obliged to accept Josephson's figures, but we hold they could reasonably do so.

*   *   *

UNITED STATES v. SAMPSON

6 CLSR 879
(United States District Court, Northern District California, April 4, 1978.)

INGRAM, D. J.

Each of defendants have moved to dismiss the Indictment on the ground that it fails to state a criminal offense. The Indictment alleges violations of 18 U.S.C. § 641 which provides as follows, in pertinent part:

Whoever embezzles, steals, purloins, or knowingly converts to his use or the use of another, or without authority, sells, conveys or disposes of any record, voucher, money, or thing of value of the United States or of any department or agency thereof, or any property made or being made under contract for the United States or any department or agency thereof; or

Whoever receives, conceals, or retains the same with intent to convert it to his use or gain, knowing it to have been embezzled, stolen, purloined or converted *   *   *

It is the position of defendants that computer time and computer storage capacity are not property within the meaning of the stat-

ute. Defendants characterize these as being mere philosophical concepts as distinguished from interests capable of being construed as property.

The motions to dismiss are denied. The consumption of its time and the utilization of its capacities seem to the court to be inseparable from the physical identity of the computer itself. That the computer is property cannot be questioned. Thus, the uses of the computer and the product of such uses would appear to the court to be a "thing of value" within the meaning of 18 U.S.C. § 641, sufficient upon which to predicate a legally sufficient indictment.

In *Morisette v. United States,* 342 U.S. 246 (1951) Mr. Justice Jackson stated with respect to conversion as used in the statute:

Conversion may include misuse or abuse of property. It may reach use in an authorized manner or to an unauthorized extent of property placed in one's custody for limited use.

An alleged unconsented appropriation of time and capacity seem to the court to constitute a "use" within the meaning so articulated.

PEOPLE v. WEG

113 Misc.2d 1017, 450 N.Y.S.2d 957
(Criminal Court of the City of New York, Kings County, May 5, 1982.)

JUVILER, J.

This is a written version of an opinion delivered from the bench on April 14, 1982, explaining an order dismissing an information. The information charged the defendant, a computer programmer employed by the Board of Education of the City of New York, with the class A misdemeanor of theft of services (Penal Law sec. 165.15(8)), allegedly committed by using his employer's computer for his own personal benefit without permission.

The defendant has moved to dismiss the information on various grounds, including failure to state a crime, failure to allege facts supporting each element of the crime, and denial of a speedy trial. The motion to dismiss is granted on each of the first two grounds.

The information consists of a complaint sworn to by a detective, and a supporting deposition of another public official. The information alleges:

that on 10/80 thru (*sic*) 6/24/81 * * * the defendant committed the (offense) of: P.L. § 165.15. Theft of Services under the following circumstances:

Deponent states that he is informed by Rolf Moulton—Director of Computer Security in the Department of Education—that during the above period of time, the defendant, having control over computer equipment belonging to the Board of Education, with intent to derive a commercial (*sic*) benefit to himself, diverted the use of said computer equipment to himself in that the defendant used the computer to record and retrieve data for his own personal benefit, none of which data relates to the Board of Education.

Deponent is further informed by David Wolovick—Director of Bureau of Supplies—that the defendant knew he was not entitled to such personal use of Board of Education equipment.

Although the information does not allege the applicable subdivision of section 165.15 of the Penal Law, the parties agree that the prosecution rests on subdivision 8, which provides that a person is guilty of theft of services when:

> *Obtaining or having control over* labor in the employ of another person, or of *business, commercial or industrial equipment or facilities of another person, knowing that he is not entitled to the use thereof, and with intent to derive a commercial or other substantial benefit* for himself or a third person, *he uses* or diverts to the use of himself or a third person *such* labor, *equipment or facilities. (emphasis supplied).*

In order to survive a motion to dismiss for failure to state a crime, an information must allege facts establishing conduct that the penal statute makes criminal. [Citation.] The present information undoubtedly alleges some of the elements of the crime of theft of services: It alleges "control" of "equipment," "use" of it, and knowledge that the use was unauthorized. It also alleges ownership of the equipment by "another person"; "person" is defined in the general provisions of the Penal Law to include "a governmental instrumentality" [citation], a term which covers the Board of Education of the City of New York. [Citation.]

The central issue, however, is whether the computer was "business, industrial or commercial" equipment, within the contemplation of the statute.

The People appropriately conceded during oral argument of this motion that the Board's computer was not "commercial or industrial" equipment, for it was not used for profit in trade or commerce, or in manufacturing, but was used internally by a governmental agency as an administrative tool. [Citations.] The People contend that the computer was "business" equipment, on the theory that the word "business" is not limited to profit-making enterprises or professions, but as the dictionaries indicate also may mean anything that is related to the "role or function" of the equipment's owner, in this case the Board of Education. The defendant contends, on the other hand, that "business" means related to trade, commerce, or pecuniary gain. He argues that because the Board of Education is a public agency, not a private business, and its computer was not rented to outsiders for a fee, the computer was not "business" equipment.

"As a matter of textual analysis either construction is verbally plausible." [Citation.] As one judge noted, "The expression 'business' may be an uncertain one." [Citation.] "Business" can have the broad meaning urged by the District Attorney, as in "the business of learning" or "mind your business," or the narrow one asserted by the defendant, as in "businessman," "business cycle," or "*Business Week*."

No court has construed subdivision 8 of section 165.15. Article 165 contains no definitions. But the available evidence, including the statutory language and context, and the legislative purpose reflected in the legislative history, indicates that section 165.15(8) was intended to apply only to unauthorized use of equipment that is offered for use as a service in a commercial setting, such as for lease or hire, and was not designed to make it a crime for a public or private employee to use his employer's internal office equipment without permission.

The meaning of the word "business" in statutes varies with the purpose of the particular statute. [Citation.] For example, in some laws the term "business" clearly is intended to have its commercial meaning. [Citations.] * * *

In other laws, the context indicates that a broad, noncommercial meaning of "business" is intended. [Citations.]

In the present statute the context is commercial. Words in a statute are to be construed in connection with associated words in the same list. [Citation.] In Subdivision 8 of

Penal Law section 165.15, "business" is used as the first of three similar adjectives ("business, commercial or industrial equipment"), the other two apply to commerce. The crime occurs only when the thief has an intent to derive "a *commercial* or other substantial benefit." The crime is called "Theft of *services*." indicating a legislative purpose of protecting the offering of services to the public, not guarding equipment used internally by an agency or firm; section 165.15 has been construed generally as being aimed only at the supplying of a service, an activity absent here. [Citation.] Moreover, if the adjective "business" were to include everything connected with the role of the Board of Education, as the People contend, the term would be superfluous. "Business, commercial or industrial equipment or facilities of another person" would have the same scope as "equipment or facilities of another person."

Legislative history confirms that subdivision 8 was enacted to protect commercially supplied equipment from tampering or unauthorized use. In *People v. Ashworth*, 220 App.Div. 498, 222 N.Y.S. 24 (4th Dept.), decided before section 165.15 was enacted, the court held that the crime of larceny was not committed by employees of a mill who used the complainant company's machines and workmen without permission to spin wool for sale. The court found that this corrupt use of the mill's labor and equipment was not "property," and therefore could not be the subject of larceny. Subdivision 8 (originally enacted as subdivision 7) was included in the revised Penal Law in 1967 "for the purpose of plugging (this) apparent gap" in the existing law "pointed up" by the decision in *Ashworth*. [Citations.] [Footnote.]

In plugging this gap, however, the drafting Commission rejected broad criminal coverage of the kind urged by the People here. The draftsmen expressly decline "to go to the other extreme of equating services with property and of predicating, whenever possible (mainly in the area of deception), 'theft of service' offenses to those involving thefts of property, or larcenies. Legislation of that character would doubtlessly lead to hosts of 'criminal' charges of a *basically civil nature*" (emphasis supplied). [Citation.]

Moreover, subdivision 8 is derived from a prototype law which was specifically intended to apply only to services offered commercially. Subdivision 8 is closely patterned after subdivision 2 of Section 206.7 of the Model Penal Code, a Section titled "Theft of Labor or Service." [Citation.] The latter provides:

(2) A person commits theft if, having control over the disposition of labor or service of others, to which he is not entitled, he diverts their labor or service to his own benefit or to the benefit of another not entitled thereto.

This provision, like subdivision 8 in our law, was designed to remedy the "inadequacy" of existing law to reach industrial fraud of the kind illustrated by *People v. Ashworth*. [Citation.] It does not apply to the facts alleged in the present information, for "The subsection limits liability to misappropriation of services available for *hire* * * *" *(emphasis in original)*. [Citation.]

Further indication that this was the intended meaning of section 165.15(8) of the Penal Law is the simultaneous enactment in 1967 in the same chapter of a provision in which the term "business" was defined to include noncommercial governmental activity. Article 175 of the revised Penal Law, dealing with false written instruments, includes crimes relating to falsifying "business" records. These records are defined to include all records of a governmental entity reflecting its activity. [Citations.] The absence of a similar definition applicable to section 165.15 indicates that this broad meaning was not intended there; when the word "business" is intended to have a noncommercial meaning in a portion of the Penal Law, the statute says so clearly.

If "business equipment or facilities" in section 165.15(8) had the broad meaning claimed by the People and included any equipment or facilities serving the function of the owner, the enactment of the revised Penal Law in 1967 would have made criminals of the thousands of employees in government and the private sector who make unauthorized use of their employers' computers, word processors, calculators, copying machines, telephones, typewriters, and other equipment or facilities for personal benefit. The Legislature could not have intended such a dramatic change in the criminal law of this State, transforming "basically civil" wrongs to misdemeanors punishable by a year in jail, without giving clearer indication of its novel purpose.

"Although a court must not be overly technical in interpreting penal provisions, penal responsibility cannot be extended beyond the fair scope of the statutory mandate. If there is to be a diametric change in the statute, it should come from the Legislature." [Citation.]

In 1982 the Legislature of the State of New York could reasonably find a need to regulate, even by penal sanction, conduct of the type alleged in this information. Perhaps computers are a special type of expensive, commonly owned equipment so subject to misuse that the Legislature might wish to give their owners special protection.

Extensive literature in the field of computers describes the widespread unauthorized use of this type of equipment. See 37 Record of the Association of the Bar of the City of New York, April 1982, "Selected Materials on Computer Crime," p. 285. Other legislatures have recently addressed this problem. Illinois created the offense of "unlawful use of a computer," which includes any use of a computer without consent, whether or not the computer service is for hire. [Citation.] This Court, however, may not create an offense. Unless Penal Law section 165.15(8) is amended, it will apply only to unauthorized tapping into a computer whose service is for hire.

Even if the People's interpretation of section 165.15(8) were correct, a separate ground for dismissal of the information would be its failure to allege every element of the crime, and failure to allege facts supporting every element of the crime. "(E)very element of the crime" must be "properly recited in the factual part of the information and the accompanying deposition." [Citation.] In addition, "every element of the offense charged must be supported by nonhearsay allegations" of fact. [Citations.]

The information before the Court is the third filed by the People in this action, the first two having been insufficient. The first information was replaced because it failed to allege the element of intent [citation], the second because it was amended without verification.

The present information is defective because, like the first two, it does not allege the element of "business, commercial or industrial equipment"; the information is silent as to which if any of those three categories the complainant's computer was in. Another defect is failure to allege any facts supporting the allegation relating to the element of an intent to derive a "commercial benefit"; no facts are alleged in the information regarding the use to which defendant put the computer. (The defendant's motion to dismiss contains allegations about this, but these are not part of the accusatory instrument). These defects could be corrected by amending the information, if my ruling as to the first ground for dismissal (failure to state a crime) is incorrect. [Citations.]

* * *

UNITED STATES v. JONES
414 F. Supp. 964, 6 CLSR 197
(United States District Court, D. Maryland, May 13, 1976.)

WATKINS, D. J.

Defendant Amy Everston Jones is charged in a ten-count indictment with transportation in interstate commerce of stolen, converted, or fraudulently obtained securities valued at more than $5,000 in violation of 18 U.S.C. § 2314; and with receiving, selling, or disposing of those same securities knowing them to have been stolen, converted, or taken by fraud, in violation of 18 U.S.C. § 2315.

The securities at issue are five checks [footnote], payable to the order of "A. L. E. Jones,"[2] drawn on the Royal Bank of Canada against the account of Inglis, Limited, a Canadian appliance firm. The government alleges that Defendant transported these checks from Canada to Maryland (or that they were sent to her) and that the checks were then deposited in a Maryland bank account.

For purposes of this motion, it is not disputed that these checks were "stolen, converted or taken by fraud." Defendant contends, however, that the Inglis securities are not genuine and are instead forgeries of checks

---

2. "A. L. E. Jones" appears to be the true name of the

Defendant.

of a foreign corporation, to which §§ 2314 and 2315 expressly do not apply. Defendant has, therefore, moved that the instant indictment be dismissed. [Footnote.]

Except for minor differences in punctuation, the exclusionary language referring to foreign securities is the same in the two sections. Section 2314 provides, in pertinent part, as follows:

> This section shall not apply to any falsely made, forged, altered, counterfeited or spurious representation of an obligation or other security of the United States, or of an obligation, bond, certificate, security, treasury note, bill, promise to pay or bank note issued by any foreign government or by a bank or corporation of any foreign country.

Under most circumstances, the issue of genuineness of instruments poses little difficulty; certainly there is no dearth of authority as to what constitutes a forgery at common law and for purposes of the various federal forgery statutes. The circumstances of the instant case, however, are not the usual ones. The Inglis checks were printed by a computer, complete with authorized facsimile signatures, and, it is alleged, were the direct result of tampering by an Inglis employee with data records stored in the computer and with payment data inserted into the computer. Whether or not they can be characterized as "falsely made, forged, altered, counterfeited or spurious" poses an interesting question and one which the Court considers novel in the case law.

The unusual nature of this case requires that the facts be recited in some detail.

Inglis, Limited, is a Canadian company which routinely purchases substantial quantities of household appliances from Whirlpool Corporation, a United States manufacturer. The accounts payable generated by these purchases are processed through a rather complex system at Inglis which in part involves manual accounting techniques but which culminates in the issuance of checks by means of automated electronic data processing equipment.

According to Edward McCormack, comptroller and assistant treasurer of Inglis, the system is initiated by the arrival of invoices and other documents (including warehouse receipts, customs clearing documents, and shipping manifests) associated with a particular purchase or shipment. These materials are collected and matched with records of orders. The information needed to process payment of the account is then extracted from the various documents and written down on an "accounts payable distribution slip." This information includes the invoice number, the date, the amount due, and a vendor code number. The vendor code number is used to identify the payee to the computer, which issues the actual check.

The data thus collected are verified within the accounts payable department, and batches of documents, with verified accounts payable distribution slips attached, are then sent to the keypunch operators. The keypunch operators do not check any of the information given them; they merely take the information necessary to process the payment from the accounts payable distribution slip and prepare it for entry into the computer by transferring it to a computer keypunch card. The data thus processed are entered into the computer and are retained in the computer memory as "open item entries." Periodically, the computer is commanded to execute a "check run" by printing checks for all entries on the "open item" list. The checks are automatically printed by the computer in fully negotiable form, complete with facsimile signatures.

According to the theory advanced by the government, and not disputed by the Defendant for purposes of this motion alone, the checks in question resulted when an alleged confederate of the Defendant, one Michael Everston, tampered with certain of the data being processed through the system described above. At the time of the alleged tampering, Everston was supervisor of the accounts payable department. As such, he was familiar with all aspects of the system, including the verification techniques employed to assure the proper payment of accounts payable.

The first step in the scheme alleged by the government was the creation of an improper vendor code listing in the computer which would have rendered the computer receptive to the insertion of false data at a later time. An exhibit filed at the hearing suggests that this was done by means of an order to change vendor codes and addresses issued on September 3, 1975, allegedly at the direction of Michael Everston. That order contained an instruction to create a new vendor code, 99894, to correspond to "A.L.E. Jones, P.O. Box 123." Creation of this code within the computer's memory ensured that any order to pay code 99894, if properly entered into the computer, would automatically result in the issuance of a check payable to the order of "A.L.E. Jones."

The second step in the scheme involved the entry into the computer of data relating to specific checks to be issued to A.L.E. Jones. According to the government, Everston's supervisory position enabled him to obtain batches of Whirlpool invoices with attached accounts payable distribution slips after the documents had been verified as described above. Then, the government alleges, Everston prepared accounts payable distribution slips like those which had been prepared in his department but bearing the vendor code "99894" instead of the proper vendor code corresponding to Whirlpool.

As the final element in the scheme, the documents and accounts payable distribution slips were allegedly forwarded to keypunch. The data on the accounts payable distribution slips were routinely transferred to keypunch cards. When directed, the computer read the data from the keypunch cards and stored the information in its memory. In due course, when commanded to process a check run, the computer automatically printed checks payable to the order of "A.L.E. Jones" which had been intended to be made payable to the order of Whirlpool Corporation. The government then alleges that the "A.L.E. Jones" checks were sent or given to the Defendant, who, it is charged, deposited them in a bank account in Maryland.

Assuming all of this to be true for purposes of the instant motion only, the question is whether or not checks thus produced can properly be the subject matter of a prosecution under §§ 2314 and 2315.

It has long been settled in this circuit that the terms "falsely made, forged, altered, or counterfeited" as used in § 2314 are substantially synonymous and refer to the crime of forgery. *Greathouse v. United States,* 170 F.2d 512, 514 (4 Cir. 1948). Since § 2315 was enacted at the same time and as part of the same law, the National Stolen Property Act, it seems clear that a single construction would apply to essentially identical language in the two sections. Furthermore, it would seem that the term "spurious" must likewise be considered *ejusdem generis,* since a contrary construction would require the Court either to hold that the exclusionary provision excises from the statutes that which was not included, or to regard the term "spurious" as surplusage.

A forged writing was defined in *Greathouse* as one "which falsely purports to be the writing of another person than the actual maker." [Citation.] It seems apparent from the sources relied upon that this was intended to express the meaning of forgery as it is known at common law. Furthermore, the Supreme Court defined what it termed "the concept of 'federal' forgery" as being no broader than its common law counterpart, in the absence of some contrary indication in the statute or legislative history. *Gilbert v. United States,* 370 U.S. 650, 655, 82 S.Ct. 1399, 1402, 8 L.Ed.2d 750, 754 (1962). Although the Court was there referring specifically to 18 U.S.C. § 495, the construction of § 2314 in *Greathouse* was noted with approval. [Citation.] The area of consideration in this case is thus circumscribed by what would have been a forgery at common law.

In contending the Inglis checks were forgeries, the Defendant has relied principally on those cases which have held that one who obtains a stolen instrument in blank and later completes it, has committed a forgery. [Citation.] Such a scheme would ordinarily constitute forgery, even though the blank is filled with the name of a real person and even if the thief-forger uses his or her own name. [Citations.]

The government urges two alternative theories. First, it is contended, even conceding that the substitution of "A.L.E. Jones" for Whirlpool constituted a false writing, the falsity was in the meaning rather than in the making of the instrument. Thus, the government seeks to bring the instant case within the rule stated by Wharton and quoted by the government in its brief that:

* * * when a person writes a letter or fills out a loan application which he signs with his own name intending that it be accepted as his writing, he is not guilty of forgery because statements contained therein are false and their falsity was known to him. The better view, and

that supported by the majority opinion, is that under the common law under statutes defining forgery is [sic] substantially the language of the common law definitions, the genuine making of an instrument for the purpose of defrauding does not constitute the crime of forgery. In other words, the term 'falsely' as applied to making or altering a writing in order to make it a forgery, does not refer to the contents or the tenor of the writing or to the facts stated therein, but implies that the paper or writing is not genuine, that in itself it is false or counterfeit.

[Citation.] In essence the government argues that the documents in question are genuine, but contain false statements. Furthermore, the government argues, such "genuine" documents would not have been regarded as forgeries at common law even though their execution might have been procured by fraud, citing the following language:

> According to settled authority, it is not forgery to obtain a person's signature to an instrument by means of false and fraudulent representation as to its contents, or as to the purpose for which the instrument is to be used. [Footnote.] Nor is it forgery to fraudulently procure a person's signature to an instrument which has previously been altered without his knowledge.

[Citation.]

Neither the doctrine advanced by the Defendant nor those put forward by the government are apposite to the case at bar.

The cases cited by the Defendant all involve the fraudulent making or alteration of an instrument by one who is a stranger to the instrument. In the instant case, however, the individual who drafted the instrument in a practical sense was Everston, although he employed the computer as the instrumentality by which the checks were physically drawn. Everston, unlike the defendants held to have committed forgery in *Ketchum* [*v. United States*, 327 F.Supp. 768 (D.Md.1971)] and like cases, was authorized for certain purposes to direct the entry of data into the computer and thus initiate the drafting of checks bearing authorized Inglis signatures; although, if the government's theory is correct, Everston was in no way authorized to effect the creation of the particular checks at issue.

Nor do the theories urged by the government provide an answer. The government's contention that the instruments, if genuine, cannot be considered forged merely because they contain false information is correct. [Citation.] Where the falsity in an instrument is in its content, rather than in the manner of making, the instrument is not a forgery. [Citation.] This expression, however, merely restates the venerable rule that a lie will not be considered forgery at common law merely because it is written down; it retains its character as fraud or misrepresentation. For example, it is settled that there is no common law forgery where an agent, in executing a document purportedly authorized by his principal, misrepresents the extent of his authority on the face of the instrument. *Gilbert, supra. See, also, Cunningham v. United States*, 272 F.2d 791, 793-794 (4th Cir.1959), and *Selvidge v. United States*, 290 F.2d 894, 895 (10 Cir.1961). The application of this doctrine, however, presupposes a statement *on the face of the instrument* which is false as to its meaning, and there is no such statement with respect to the Inglis checks.[5] The only words on the checks that can in any way be characterized as false are "A.L.E. Jones," and those words make no assertion, either true or false; their only falsity lies in the fact that their presence on the instruments was unauthorized.

But even assuming that the mere presence of the payee's name on the instrument can in these circumstances be considered an "assertion" capable of characterization as true or false, a premise this Court does not accept, the rule as to falsity of content has no application where the documents were in fact falsely made.

With respect to false making, the government's principal authority is the quotation from Clark and Marshall noted above. That language cannot be applied to the facts of the instant case.

As is apparent from the case authority cited in their treatise, Clark and Marshall were re-

---

5. Quite conceivably the accounts payable distribution slips were false as to meaning, rather than making, and could not themselves be considered forgeries. However, the Court is concerned in the instant case only with the checks. In any event, forgeries or not, the slips could not properly be the basis of a charge under §§ 2314 and 2315 since there is no nexus with interstate commerce as to them.

ferring to situations involving two parties and the reliance by one on fraudulent misrepresentations of another.[6] As with the lie set to writing which does not thereby become forgery, that which is essentially false pretenses or misrepresentation retains its character as such.

In the case at bar, however, there were no fraudulent misrepresentations to any second party and in fact there was no second party to be deceived.

As the government urged at the hearing, the mere fact that a computer was used to print these checks should not be permitted to confuse the matter. The computer was merely an inanimate and obedient instrumentality employed by Everston, who himself accomplished everything necessary to assure the issuance of checks to an unauthorized payee and was, as a practical matter, the drawer of the checks. Like a checkwriting machine or a ball point pen, the computer did exactly what it was told to do by its program and by the data inserted at Everston's command. Likewise, the keypunch operator's function was to follow instructions exactly and to punch into computer cards exactly the information given. It was only by means of this mechanical process that the computer could digest the information; and it is fair to say that the operator, acting routinely, functioned in a sense as an adjunct of the machine. At most, the computer operator was the innocent agent of Everston.

These facts, therefore, describe a one-party transaction without any of the deception described by Clark and Marshall. That deception was rendered unnecessary by the seemingly efficient system devised at Inglis which made it possible for one man to accomplish the entire transaction in essence singlehandedly.

That being the case, it seems plain that the checks fit within the definition of forgery. It has long been the rule that an agent may commit forgery by executing an instrument in disobedience of his instructions, provided that the requisite *mens rea* exists and that the documents so executed have the capacity to defraud. *Selvidge, supra,* at 895. [Footnote.]

Selvidge itself involved a false agency endorsement, as noted above. Such endorsements are now held not to be forgery. The Court noted, however, that the critical factor was the assertion on the face of the instrument that the Defendant was acting as an agent and stated that "if Selvidge had merely endorsed the name of her principal and cashed the checks contrary to her instructions, the crime of forgery would have been complete." [Citation.]

This "rule of general application" is in harmony with the established concept that it is "the giving [to an instrument of] a false appearance of having been executed by [the principal] which makes a man guilty of forgery." [Citation.] In making his own unauthorized act appear to be the act of his principal, the agent commits forgery in the classical sense; he makes a "writing which falsely purports to be the writing of another." [Citation.]

The rule has been most often expressed in the English cases. Typical is the case of *Regina v. Wilson* (1848), 2 Car. & K. 527, 175 Eng.Rep. 219 (Nisi Prius Book 6) in which a clerk was given a check that had been signed but was otherwise blank, with instructions to fill in the check to a certain amount and then to give the proceeds to one Williamson. The clerk instead filled the check out to a larger amount, cashed the check, and converted the proceeds. This was held to be forgery, fourteen judges concurring.

The rule has been stated less often, but with no less authority, in the American cases. It was recognized early in *Ex Parte Hibbs*, 26 F. 421 (D.Or.1886). A postal employee, author-

---

6. It is clear that the two-party situation was the subject matter of the quote from Clark and Marshall. Citation was made therein to *Regina v. Chadwick* (1844). 2 Moody & Robinson 545; there, the question was whether or not the Defendant had induced creditors of his principal to sign a receipt which he had fraudulently altered as to amount. In ruling that this would not have been a forgery, provided the alteration preceded the signature, Baron Rolfe referred to an earlier case in which he had consid-

ered the doctrine generally, that being *Regina v. Collings* (1843), 2 Moody & Robinson 461. In that case, Baron Rolfe stated that it would not be forgery fraudulently to induce a person to execute an instrument based on a misrepresentation as to its contents because, if a charge were permissible, "any party might be indicted for forgery who prevails on a man to execute a deed by misrepresenting its legal effect." [Citation.]

ized to issue money orders when paid for, made out money orders for which no payment had been received and converted the proceeds. This was held to be forgery:

> The instruments set out in these indictments, and of which the prisoner is thereby charged with forging, purport to be postal money orders of the United States. They were issued without authority, and contrary to the prohibition of law. They were falsely made, filled up, signed, stamped, and issued by the prisoner, as upon a state of facts which did not exist, with intent to defraud his employer, the United States. This, in my judgment, was a false making within the statute, and such a false making as constitutes the crime of forgery at common law. The writing is false, because it purports to be what it is not. It purports to be a money order of the United States, issued by its authority, after the receipt by its agent of the sum named therein, on the application of a real person, while in truth and in fact, it was issued without such authority and contrary to law. * * *

Hibbs, supra, at 432.
See, also, Quick Service Box Co. v. St. Paul Mercury Ind. Co., 95 F.2d 15, 17 (7 Cir. 1938) (bookkeeper obtained signatures of his employer to blank checks and, in excess of authority, filled in the blanks and appropriated the proceeds; held, forgery).[8]

This situation must be distinguished, of course, from the cases that deal with agency endorsements such as *Gilbert* and *Selvidge.* The reason for the rule that false agency endorsements are not forgery is that the party who would be defrauded by such a false endorsement would not regard the endorsements as the act of the principal; instead, his reliance would be upon the existence of authority as evidenced by the representation of agency on the instrument. The distinction between the case where the agency is stated on the document and those, such as the case at bar, where there is no such representation and where the party to whom the instrument is given regards it as the act of the principal, is

very clear. It is a "decisive circumstance which compels a different conclusion." [Citation.] That distinction was drawn in *Selvidge* with respect to *Hibbs* and *Quick Service Box,* and was explicitly approved by the Supreme Court in *Gilbert.* [Citation.]

Additionally, the case at bar should be distinguished from those that involved an agent with general authority. A case nearly identical with the instant case, except for that critical factual difference, is *Regina v. Richardson,* (1860), 2 F. & F. 343, 175 Eng.Rep. 1088 (Nisi Prius Book 6). In that case, the Defendant had been employed as a clerk with authority to pay the routine expenses of the business. To that end, he was given control of the cash on hand, into which he was to pay receipts. When necessary, he was authorized generally to cash checks on that account, drawing the money himself and then using it to pay the creditors. On one occasion he cashed such a check and entered into the books a notation that he had used the proceeds to pay a creditor when, in fact, he had converted the funds. This was held not to be forgery, because the Defendant's authority was limited only by the amount in the account; rather than draw checks to the creditors, his function was to cash checks and pay over the cash. In cashing the check at issue, he quite possibly had not exceeded his authority; his crime was misappropriation of the proceeds *after* the check had been cashed, rather than forgery. [Citation.]

Everston, however, had no such general authority to draw checks. His authority was strictly limited by the parameters of the accounts receivable, which were to be satisfied by check rather than out of any cash fund over which Everston had control. Unlike the clerk in *Richardson,* he clearly acted outside the scope of his authority. By executing documents without authority in such a way that they appeared to be the solemn act of his principal, Everston committed forgery, given, of

---

8. The District of Columbia Circuit had likewise declared the rule in *Yeager v. United States,* 59 App.D.C. 11, 32 F.2d 402 (1929). There an employee authorized to endorse checks and deposit them to his employer's account instead endorsed the checks and pocketed the proceeds. This was held to be forgery under the rule cited in *Hibbs.* [Citation.] It may be, as later developed, and

as noted in *Selvidge,* that *Yeager* was wrongfully decided because the endorsement was an agency endorsement, a fact that did not come to light in the case law until some three years after *Yeager* had been decided. [Citation.] However, *Yeager* is still authority, although perhaps no more than dictum, in support of the rule of forgery by an authorized agent.

course, that the government's allegations are true.[9]

Since, under the theory of this transaction advanced by the government, the checks were "forged * * * securit[ies] * * * issued by * * * a bank or corporation of any foreign country," prosecution under §§ 2314 and 2315 is improper, and the indictment must be dismissed.

Accordingly, it is this 13th day of May, 1975, by the United States District Court for the District of Maryland, ordered:

(1) That the motion of the Defendant to dismiss the indictment be, and the same hereby is, granted;

(2) That the indictment in the instant case be, and the same hereby is, dismissed. * * *

* * *

UNITED STATES v. JONES
553 F.2d 351, 6 CLSR 209
(United States Court of Appeals, Fourth Circuit, April 12, 1977.)

FIELD, S. C. J.

A ten-count indictment was returned against Amy Everston Jones, charging her with five counts of transporting in interstate or foreign commerce securities[1] valued at more than $5,000.00 knowing the same to have been "stolen, converted or taken by fraud" in violation of 18 U.S.C. § 2314; and five counts of selling or receiving these same securities knowing them to have been stolen, unlawfully converted or taken by fraud, in violation of 18 U.S.C. § 2315. The defendant moved to dismiss the indictment, contending that the securities involved in the case were forgeries and thus excluded by the limiting language of sections 2314 and 2315.[2] The district court agreed with the defendant and dismissed the indictment. [Footnote.] The Government has appealed. [Footnote.]

The facts, as presented by the Government, were not basically contested by the appellee and "[f]or the purposes of [the motion to dismiss], it [was] not disputed that these checks were 'stolen, converted or taken by fraud.'" [Footnote.] Accordingly, if the securities were not excluded by the limiting paragraphs of sections 2314 and 2315, the acts committed by Jones would constitute indictable offenses.

This is a case of computer abuse, [footnote], involving the input[7] into a computer facility of allegedly altered accounts payable data. The computer crime was perpetrated against a Canadian company, Inglis, Limited, which is a subsidiary of Whirlpool Corporation, a United States corporation. It specifically involved the issuance of five checks to one "A.L.E. Jones"[8] which should have been issued to Whirlpool. It is the Government's theory that the appellee transported or caused these checks to be transported from Canada to Maryland;[9] and

---

9. In holding these checks to be forgeries, the Court expresses no opinion as to any possible questions of civil liability. Those questions involve considerations which are irrelevant in the context of a criminal prosecution, such as any possible fault, estoppel, or application of the impostor rule. [Citation.]

1. The securities here were checks and fall within sections 2314 and 2315. See 18 U.S.C. § 2311.

2. The limiting language of section 2314, basically mirrored in section 2315, provides that:

This section shall not apply to any falsely made, forged, altered, counterfeited or spurious representation of an obligation or other security of the United States, or of an obligation, bond, certificate, security, treasury note, bill, promise to pay or bank note issued by any foreign government or by a bank or corporation of any foreign country.

7. Input refers to data capture, e.g., keypunching, optical character recognition, and the entry of the data into the system in machine-readable form. The possible abuses included in this function are omission of documents, creation of entirely false records, and the altering of amounts, names, and the like, on other authentic documents. [Citation.]

8. "'A.L.E. Jones' appears to be the true name of the defendant." [Citation.]

9. Count One of the indictment is an example of the alleged section 2314 violations:

On or about September 12, 1975, in the State and District of Maryland, Amy Everston Jones, did willfully and knowingly transport and cause to be transported in interstate and foreign commerce from Canada to the State of Maryland, securities and money which were stolen, converted and taken by fraud, to-wit, a check #47456 in the amount of $11,138.04 payable to A.L.E. Jones, drawn on the account of Englis [sic] Limited, then knowing the same to have been stolen, converted and taken by fraud.

then disposed of the checks when they arrived in Maryland.[10]

An understanding of Inglis' accounting system is necessary to explain the scheme devised by the appellee and her cohort, one Michael Everston, who was the supervisor of Inglis' accounts payable department. When payments are made to Inglis' vendors, the supporting documents (invoices and evidence of receipt of goods) are matched in the accounts payable department by the invoice audit clerks. These clerks then attach an accounts payable distribution slip to the supporting documents. At the accounts payable distribution slip level, the clerks record (1) the invoice number, (2) the vendor and/or supplier number, and (3) the amount of the invoice. The clerks then initial as to the recording of that data. The accounts payable distribution slip is attached to the documents to facilitate the preparation and the collection of the data on the supporting documents. The invoice audit clerks then forward the documents to another accounts payable clerk who logs and records the voucher or the accounts payable number. The documents are then transferred to the data processing area where receipt of the documents is noted and they are sent to a key punch operator who sets up cards for the documents. The papers are then picked up by a data control clerk who takes them to a production area for computer processing. Once fed into the computer, it then produces a report called a balancing report which is used to identify all of the invoices in a particular batch. The totals which appear on the balancing report are compared to a taped total which is attached to the group of documents, and this total is then compared against a log maintained by the data processing area. The documents are then sent back to the accounts payable department for a further verification of their accuracy. After the data is entered into the computer, an order is given to the computer to print-out checks, complete with facsimile signatures, payable to the order of the designated payee.

According to the government's testimony

the appellee's accomplice, Everston, directed an accounts payable clerk to set up documents under the name of "A.L.E. Jones" which included a vendor number "98844." He then altered Whirlpool accounts payable documents by changing Whirlpool's vendor number "99900" to "98844" to correspond to the "A.L.E. Jones" account. Through a process of personally reviewing the groups of accounts payable documents, Everston was able to store these altered documents in the Inglis computer. Ultimately, the computer issued checks payable to the account of "A.L.E. Jones" which should have been paid to Whirlpool Corporation. The five checks thus issued resulted in over $130,000.00 being paid to the "A.L.E. Jones" account. Upon receipt of the checks in Maryland the appellee deposited them in a specified account to her credit.

The sole issue is whether the alteration of accounts payable documents fed into a computer which resulted in the issuance of checks payable to an improper payee constituted a "falsely made, forged, altered, counterfeited or spurious" security within the meaning of the exclusionary clauses of sections 2314 and 2315 of Title 18.

In considering the phrase "falsely made, forged, altered, or counterfeited" in the statutory sections the district court correctly noted that the terms "are substantially synonymous and refer to the crime of forgery. *Greathouse v. United States,* 170 F.2d 512, 514 (4 Cir. 1948)." [Footnote.] We also agree with the district court's conclusion that the term "forgery" should be viewed in the light of its common law meaning:

A forged writing was defined in *Greathouse* as one "which falsely purports to be the writing of another person than the actual maker." [Citation.] It seems apparent from the sources relied upon that this was intended to express the meaning of forgery as it is known at common law. Furthermore, the Supreme Court defined what it termed "the concept of 'federal' forgery" as being no broader than its common law counterpart, in the absence of some contrary indication in the statute or legislative history. [Ci-

---

10. Count Six of the indictment is illustrative of the section 2315 violations:

On or about the 12th day of September, 1975, in the State and District of Maryland, Amy Everston Jones, did receive, conceal and dispose of certain securities and money that is, a check #47456 in the amount of

$11,138.04, payable to A.L.E. Jones, drawn on the account of Englis [sic] Limited, which were moving as, were part of, and constituted interstate and foreign commerce from Canada to the State of Maryland, knowing the same to have been stolen, unlawfully converted and taken.

tation.] Although the Court was there referring specifically to 18 U.S.C. § 495, the construction of § 2314 in *Greathouse* was noted with approval. [Citation.] The area of consideration in this case is thus circumscribed by what would have been a forgery at common law. [Footnote.]

However, we disagree with the district court's conclusion that the acts committed by Everston constituted common law forgery. The Supreme Court has noted that " '[f]orgery, or the *crimen falsi,* * * * may with us be defined (at common law) to be, the fraudulent making or alteration of a writing to the prejudice of another man's right. * * *' [Citation.]" [Citation.] Significantly then, "[a]n essential element of the crime of forgery is *making* the false writing. [Emphasis added.] [Citations.] [Footnote.]

In the present case, the district court was of the opinion that Everston, in fact, *made* a false writing because "the individual who drafted the instrument in a practical sense was Everston, although he employed the computer as the instrumentality by which the checks were physically drawn." [Footnote.] We think, however, that the acts of Everston did not constitute the *making* of a *false writing,* but rather amounted to the creation of a writing which was genuine in execution but false as to the statements of fact contained in such writing.[15] The distinction is critical to the sufficiency of the indictment.

In criminal cases the great weight of authority holds false statements in or fraudulent execution of otherwise valid instruments not to be

forgery within its common law or unexpanded meaning. [Citations.]

[Citation.]

The district court was of the opinion that the facts did not warrant the conclusion that false statements appeared on the face of the checks issued by Inglis to "A.L.E. Jones."[16] We cannot agree. The checks state that the designated amount is payable "to the order of A.L.E. Jones," and implicit in such an unconditional order was the existence of an obligation running from Inglis, Limited, to the payee. There was, of course, no such obligation, but as the result of Everston's misconduct the accounting department of Inglis was defrauded into believing that the company owed a bona fide obligation to "A.L.E. Jones" and, accordingly, issued a *genuine instrument containing a false statement of fact as to the true creditor.*[17]

We recognize that, at common law, one need not have physically counterfeited an instrument to be convicted for forgery, *see In re Count De Toulouse Lautrec,* 102 F. 878 (7 Cir. 1900).[18] However, we note that in those circumstances the issuance of the instrument purporting to have legal efficacy *"was neither intended nor issued as such by the purported maker." Id.* at 881 (emphasis added). In the present case, the purported maker, Inglis, *issued* the check and "the instrument [was] of such nature that if not voidable for the defendant's fraud it could have some legal or prejudicial effect upon the signer." [Citation.] We conclude that the crime herein was a fraud or false pretense, and not forgery.

---

15. There is, of course, a valid and recognized distinction between the false making of a writing and the making of a false writing. [Citations.]

16. The district court stated that "[t]he only words on the checks that can in any way be characterized as false are 'A.L.E. Jones,' and those words make no assertion, either true or false; their only falsity lies in the fact that their presence on the instruments was unauthorized." [Citation.] As noted above, we cannot agree with the district court's view on this point.

17. Although the district court correctly notes that reference to the "imposter doctrine" as found in the civil arena would be "irrelevant in the context of a criminal prosecution * * *" [citation], we think the imposter/forger distinction is helpful in deciding that the facts of the present case do not amount to forgery. [Citations.] The annotation draws an interesting distinction between the "imposter/forger" rule and the "defrauder/forger" rule. The case at bar involves the latter doctrine. [Citation.]

18. The Seventh Circuit has capsulated the factual contours of its *Lautrec* decision thusly:

In *Lautrec* a printer retained as samples of his work several interest coupons, the originals of which had been validly issued in connection with certain corporate bonds. The petitioner obtained some of these samples and, although knowing that they were not genuine obligations of the issuing corporations, negotiated them. The petitioner argued that he was not guilty of common law forgery because: 1) the coupons had been lawfully printed and retained; 2) he had obtained the coupons legitimately from a person with authority to distribute them; and 3) he was able to negotiate the coupons without altering them in any way. The court rejected this argument, concluding that forgery was committed when

the accused adopted the otherwise innocent work of the printer for the purpose of defrauding purchasers by selling as genuine an instrument which purported to have legal efficiency, but was neither intended nor issued as such by the purported maker. [Citations.]

[Citation.]

Decisional support for the proposition that the alteration of supporting documents giving rise to the issuance of a bona fide instrument amounts to the crime of false pretenses is found in the Ninth Circuit's decision in *Lemke v. United States,* 211 F.2d 73 (9 Cir.), cert denied, 347 U.S. 1013 (1954). In *Lemke* the court was faced with a situation wherein the manager of a cafeteria, who had previously purchased vegetables from a truck farmer, attempted to have the farmer make out invoices showing the sale to the cafeteria of vegetables which had never been delivered. The manager planned to sign and approve the slips and present them for payment. Under such circumstances the invoices were treated as vouchers authorizing payment to the sellers. Thus, "in ordinary course, the bookkeeper would at the end of the month add the amounts of these vouchers and write a check for the total and deliver it. * * *" [Citation.] The Ninth Circuit held that

> [t]he evidence here was sufficient to show that Lemke had put in motion a procedure which, had it not been interrupted in consequence of the intervention by the officers, would have resulted in $60 being paid by check to Elbert for vegetables never delivered or intended to be delivered. Had Lemke's plan been consummated the Civilian Mess would have been defrauded in consequence of Lemke's false pretenses.

[Citation.] Just as the facts before us indicate that the alteration of supporting documents generated a valid security, so also in Lemke the falsely made invoices would have resulted in the issuance of a valid check. In each instance the pattern of conduct was designed to defraud the company through the use of false pretenses.

Since we conclude that the checks did not fall within the exclusion of the statutes as forgeries, the order of the district court dismissing the indictment must be reversed.

Reversed.

HANCOCK v. STATE

402 S.W.2d 906, 1 CLSR 562

(Court of Criminal Appeals of Texas, April 20, 1966.)

BELCHER, C.

The conviction is for felony theft; the punishment, five years.

The indictment alleged the theft of fifty-nine documents in writing which were computer programs, and that they were taken on or about November 10, 1964, from the possession of Dan Wilkins. The programs were not set out in the indictment but each was sufficiently described for identification.

The appellant, an employee of Texas Instruments Automatic Computer, a corporation (hereinafter referred to as TI), and William Bennett Smith III, an employee of an insurance company, first became acquainted with each other in May, 1964, and on September 1, 1964, began sharing together an apartment in Dallas. The appellant told Smith his job was classified and for security reasons he could not talk about it, but soon they began discussing computers, computer programs, and the value of computers, as the appellant had been a computer operator and was then engaged in writing and re-writing computer programs and was in possession of computer programs; and he told Smith they would be of great value to Texaco, one of TI's clients. Upon appellant's suggestion and offer to finance, Smith agreed to go to Houston and approach Texaco about the purchase of the programs. After a meeting was arranged by telephone with Texaco in Houston for October 16, the appellant gave Smith an index listing all the programs he had and also gave him one program to verify the authenticity of those listed in the index. The appellant gave Smith his walking cane to carry for protection if Texaco tried to take the index and programs from him. After a meeting with two representatives of Texaco, Smith returned to Dallas and told the appellant that the representatives after examining the material, which they said was very valuable, stated that they could not enter into any confidential negotiations. To this report the appellant became very upset, but when nothing developed during the next few days the appellant asked Smith to again contact Texaco, which he did. In a short time, Don Sims, purportedly of Texaco, told Smith by telephone while appellant listened on an extension, that they were interested in the programs, and if Smith would bring them to Houston they would examine them and be in position to begin discussions on the price, and they agreed to meet November 11.

The appellant gave Smith the programs, took him to the airport, and Smith made the contact in Houston with a man using the name of Don Sims, who said he was in the computer department. Smith showed Sims the index and a program, then Sims asked for the other programs and Sims' companion examined each of them. When Sims asked for a price, Smith, believing he was an agent of Texaco, offered to sell the programs for five million dollars. At this time Sims took possession of all the material Smith had and then revealed that his name was Dale Simpson, an investigator, and told Smith he would meet him at a nearby office. Smith immediately telephoned the appellant saying, "We are in a heck of a lot of trouble," and the appellant replied, "Yes, I know it," and Smith returned to Dallas.

Dan Wilkins testified that he was the manager of the Dallas Computer Center of Texas Instruments; that he knew the appellant, who began working at TI as a computer operator and later began writing and rewriting computer programs; and that the programs shown him by Dale Simpson were the same listed in the indictment. It was stipulated that Dan Wilkins had read the indictment in this case, and that the items listed in the indictment were his corporeal personal property and in his care, control, and custody as a manager of TI, and he did not, for those programs listed in the indictment, give permission to remove them from the premises.

Testimony was introduced that each of the programs listed in the indictment had a reasonable market value of more than fifty dollars; that all the programs listed in the indictment had a reasonable market value of approximately two and one-half million dollars; and that the appellant did not have consent to take and appropriate said programs to his own use and benefit.

Testifying in his own behalf, the appellant admitted his employment at TI and that he had been engaged in writing and rewriting computer programs at the time here in question, and that all of the programs listed in the indictment were included in his assignment; that TI wanted to complete the program production schedule as soon as possible, and for appellant to comply with the plan of speedy production he would have to take this material to his apartment and work on it both at home and the office, and Wilkins consented to his work plan; that he began working on the programs at home immediately and con-

tinued until he left TI, and during this period he had at home at least 75 or 100 copies of programs. During this time Smith was present when he worked on programs at home and was aware of and showed interest in the programs. Appellant further testified that the first time he knew he was charged with improperly taking the programs from TI was on November 11, when he was told by a security officer at TI that Smith at that moment was in Houston offering a large number of programs for sale to Texaco, and it appeared he had furnished these programs to Smith; that he was then placed on suspension and it was so emphatic it scared him and he insisted on advising [sic] with an attorney; that when he arrived at the apartment Smith called from Houston saying he was in trouble, and appellant asked him what it was about and Smith replied that he would tell him when he got home; that he never gave Smith any programs or directed him to sell any; that he had missed the programs in question but thought he had misplaced them.

It is contended that the computer programs alleged to have been stolen do not constitute corporeal personal property and were not the subject of theft.

Title 17, Chapter 8 of the Penal Code, entitled Theft In General, in Art 1418, Vernon's Ann PC, defines "property" in part as follows:

> The term 'property,' as used in relation to the crime of theft, includes * * * *all writings of every description, provided such property possesses any ascertainable value.*

It is evident that the computer programs as alleged and the evidence in support thereof show that such property is included and comes within the meaning of the provisions of the statutes defining the offense of theft.

Appellant contends that the trial court erred in permitting the state to prove the contents of the documents as charged in the indictment by oral testimony over his objection that the documents themselves were the best evidence and should be introduced in evidence.

The indictment is in the ordinary form for charging felony theft. None of the computer programs was set out in the indictment, but each of them was sufficiently described for identification. No complaint was made at the trial or on appeal to the sufficiency of the indictment. The computer programs were produced and available during the trial but were not introduced in evidence. Their introduction into evidence in light of the pleadings and the evidence was not required. [Citation.] However, it is pointed out that the state offered the programs several times during the trial to the appellant and his attorney for examination but they never availed themselves of the offer. The programs were also made available to the jury, but for security reasons the state requested that they not be formally introduced in evidence, which request the trial court granted. The testimony of the appellant reveals that he was familiar with each of the computer programs described in the indictment.

It is contended that the testimony of the witness Smith pertaining to the computer programs was not admissible on the ground that they [sic] were illegally obtained by the state.

Dale Simpson, an investigator employed by Texas Instruments and Texaco, testified that after determining that Smith had exhibited and offered for sale computer programs to representatives of Texaco which belonged to TI, he contacted Smith in Houston on November 11; that at the meeting Smith exhibited to Simpson and his companion the computer programs which they examined, and then he (Simpson) identified himself, took possession of the computer programs which are the programs involved herein, and left, taking them to Dallas.

From the facts it is evident that Simpson had reasonable grounds to suppose and believe that the computer programs were stolen, and under Art 325, Vernon's Ann CCP, he had the right to prevent the consequences of theft by taking possession of the programs and delivering them to a peace officer. The programs were legally obtained and were admissible in evidence. [Citation.]

It is insisted that there is no evidence showing the market value of the computer programs in Dallas County.

Robert C. Dunlap, Jr., testified that he had degrees in science and geology and had done graduate work in geophysics and geology at Harvard; that he was vice-president of Texas Instruments and had been employed by them thirty-two years; and that he was president of Geophysical Services, Incorporated. He further testified as follows:

Q. How long have you been associated with the, and connected with the computer aspect of the business?

A. Since it began (ten years ago).

* * *

Q. All right, sir. I'll ask you if you are familiar with the computer programs that are listed in that Indictment?

A. Yes, sir.

Q. Are those computer programs that are listed in that Indictment, are they computer programs of Texas Instruments?

A. Yes, sir.

Q. Now, are there what I would think of as competitors in that field, that is, seismic programs as competitors?

A. Yes, sir. I think we were the first to introduce this type of technology. Other people are working in the area now.

Q. Now, let me ask you this: In the past, have companies or competitors or whatever you want to call it, have they made requests of your organization seeking perhaps to purchase programs from you?

A. Yes, sir.

Q. Would those include the packages or the lists of programs included in the Indictment?

A. Yes, they do.

Appellant's Attorney: Excuse me, Your Honor, I object to that as hearsay.

The Court: Overruled.

Q. Assuming that Texas Instruments, the Science Services Division, assuming that the programs listed in the indictment were going to be sold, what person in the whole Texas Instruments organization would be the one to decide, first of all, what value we ask for?

A. I would be the one.

Q. Now, in relation to these computer programs and the seismic computer programs, is there a market for these—by that, I mean if you were willing to sell them to a willing buyer a willing buyer under no compulsion to buy, I have to state that to you because that's the way the law says it, could you find a buyer— Do you understand my question?

A. I do, and certainly there is a market.

Q. Now, in regards to this Indictment, sir, I'll ask you if each of those programs in that Indictment, thinking about each one of them separately, yet from the standpoint of you as a willing seller under no compulsion to sell and a willing buyer under no compulsion to buy, in order to arrive at a reasonable market value of each one of those programs there separately, a reasonable market value for each one of those, would it be more than $50.00?

A. Yes, sir.

Q. Now, in relation to the entire computer programs, the entire package listed in that Indictment, can you give me any opinion, your own opinion, based upon your knowledge of the business and circumstances—can you give me any opinion what the reasonable market value of all of those programs would be?

A. Yes, sir.

Q. What would that be?

A. A minimum figure would be approximately two and a half million dollars.

Q. Now, is that being conservative?

A. Yes, sir.

On cross-examination Dunlap testified:

Q. Now, you say that there is a market for these programs here in Dallas County?

A. I said there's a market. I am sure there's one in Dallas County.

* * *

Q. These programs, Mr. Dunlap, were developed by the employees of Texas Instruments, right?

A. That is right.

Q. They are for use only by the personnel of Texas Instruments?

A. That's right.

Q. You maintain a degree of secrecy and security concerning these?

A. Yes, sir.

Q. And the fact that these programs, insofar as we know, the fact that these programs are superior to any other programs, that gives you an economic advantage over other competitors?

A. Well, that's our opinion.

Q. Are the contents of these programs known only to the people within the Texas Instruments company?

A. Yes, sir.

* * *

Q. And at times a great deal of money and effort is expended in the development of a program?

A. That's right.

Q. Now, these particular programs listed in this Indictment, insofar as you know, are they unique within this particular field of geophysical use with computers?

A. Insofar as we know.

Dan Wilkins, manager of the computer center for Texas Instruments, testified in part as follows:

Q. Do they (computer programs) have anything to do with operations that Texaco is interested in?

A. Well, yes, Texaco have [sic] purchased from us two of our TIAC computers and they are in the process of trying to find oil with them.

Q. Of the programs that you read in the Indictment, would Texaco have any more interest in those programs than they would in any other programs that you all have out there?

A. Well, at that time, these were—you might say our hottest thing going—they were what we were selling as service with or to Texaco based on the use of these programs.

Q. These are programs listed in the Indictment?

A. Yes, sir.

This evidence was sufficient to authorize a finding that the computer programs as alleged had a market value in excess of fifty dollars each.

The refusal of the trial court to require the state to elect the count upon which it sought a conviction is urged as ground for reversal.

The indictment alleges only one count which includes and describes each of the fifty-nine computer programs. In submitting the case to the jury, the trial court required the jury to find beyond a reasonable doubt that the appellant, either alone or acting together with another as principals fraudulently took the fifty-nine computer programs described in the indictment before they could find him guilty; or if they had a reasonable doubt thereof, to acquit him. In considering the evidence in light of the allegations in the indictment, the motion to elect was properly refused. [Citation.]

The evidence is sufficient to support the conviction and no error appearing, the judgment is affirmed.

* * *

HANCOCK v. DECKER
379 F.2d 552, 1 CLSR 858
*(United States Court of Appeals Fifth
Circuit, June 20, 1967.)*

PER CURIAM.

In this appeal from the denial of a petition for habeas corpus, Robert F. Hancock, the prisoner, contends that he was unlawfully convicted of a felony theft in that the corporeal personal property he was accused of taking did not have a value in excess of $50, as required by Texas law. We affirm.

Hancock, an employee of Texas Instruments Automatic Computer Corporation, photocopied fifty-nine computer programs belonging to his employer. He attempted to sell these to Texaco, one of T. I.'s clients, for five million dollars. At the state trial and in the court below, Hancock, noting that no original documents were removed from the employer's premises, argued that at most he stole $35 worth of paper. He contended that the information contained in the computer programs constitutes trade secrets, not corporeal property worth in excess of $50.

Article 1418 of the Vernon's Ann.Texas Penal Code defines property, for purposes of theft sections, as including "all writings of every description, provided such property possesses any ascertainable value". The Court of Criminal Appeals of Texas held: "[The] computer programs as alleged and the evidence in support thereof show that such property is included and comes within the meaning of the provisions of the statute defining the offense of theft. * * * [The] programs as alleged had a market value in excess of fifty dollars

each." [Citation.] "It is our duty, of course, to accept this state judicial construction of the ordinance [statute]." [Citation.] "Absent the infringement of federal constitutional rights, we are bound by the interpretation made by the [state] court of the criminal statutes of that State." [Citation.] We cannot say that the law, as authoritatively construed by the Texas courts, is so unreasonable or arbitrary as to be violative of due process. See, for example, United States v. Seagraves, 3 Cir. 1959, 265 F.2d 876 holding that certain geophysical maps were "goods, wares, merchandise" of the value of $5000 or more within the meaning of 18 U.S.C. § 2314.

This case is not one in which there was no evidence of the accused having committed the charged offense. [Footnote.] In light of the Texas courts' authoritative construction of pertinent Texas law, there was ample evidence that Hancock committed the offense for which he was indicted.

We have considered all of the appellant's other contentions. They are without merit.

The judgment of the district court is affirmed.

WARD v. SUPERIOR COURT
3 CLSR 206
*(Superior Court of the State of California,
March 22, 1972.)*

SPARROW, J.

FACTS

Defendant Ward, an employee of UCC, a computer service company in Palo Alto, is charged in a two-count Information with the theft on January 19, 1971, of a trade secret belonging to ISD, a computer company in Oakland, in violation of Penal Code Section 499c and 487 (Grand Theft). Both UCC and ISD compete in providing computer services to Shell Development in Emeryville and Aerojet General in Sacramento, among others.

The alleged trade secret is a computer program, Plot/Trans, developed by ISD and valued at $5,000. The program makes it possible to provide a remote plotting service from the ISD Univac 1108 computer, through a CTMC switching attachment, over telephone wires to customers distant from ISD's Oakland office who have a Calcomp plotter and transceiver unit. As of January 19, 1971, only Aerojet had such a transceiver unit and only ISD had the CTMC computer attachment which made it possible automatically to switch telephone calls to and from the remote transceiver unit directly into ISD's Univac computer and its Fastrans memory bank attachment. The Plot/Trans Program eliminates the need for ISD to buy or lease an expensive Calcomp 611 sending unit, and, in conjunction with the CTMC, eliminates the need for a manual magnetic tape exchange of the executive program to be remotely plotted from the computer to the sending unit.

Since competitors of ISD had neither a CTMC nor a program such as Plot/Trans, they could not provide a telephonic remote plotting service without the added expense of securing a Calcomp 611 sending unit and the added time to effectuate a manual tape exchange, both of which the Plot/Trans Program avoided. The evidence clearly indicates that ISD did not sell the details of the Plot/Trans *program* itself but rather sold only the remote plotting *service,* which it made possible. Because of the savings in time and equipment, ISD could provide such a *service* at a lesser cost than its competitors, including UCC.

As of January 19, 1971, the details of the Plot/Trans Program itself were stored in the Fastrans memory bank attached to ISD's Univac computer in two forms: (1) in source code, i. e. man readable symbolics, and (2) in object code, i. e. machine readable symbolics. Access to the details of the Plot/Trans Program in source or object code could be secured at that time by one using a special data phone dial-up who knew three sets of numbers: (1) the unlisted telephone number of the ISD computer, (2) the two-character site code number of any ISD customer, and (3) an account or billing number of that customer. The form in which the details of any computer program comes off the drum of a Univac computer is by way of either a printout or a deck of cards punched out (i. e. computer software).

The evidence indicates that on January 19, 1971, someone using a PT&T data phone dialed

the ISD computer, furnished the Shell Development's site and billing numbers[1] and secured a printout of the source code form of ISD's Plot/Trans Program. (Contemporaneously, the ISD computer in Oakland punched out cards of what had been accessed, together with the time of access.) When the punched out cards were delivered to Shell, and the latter billed for the service, it was learned that Shell had not in fact, accessed the program. A check with the telephone company indicated that the call to the ISD computer at the time in question was from UCC, not Shell. A search warrant was secured and ISD's Plot/Trans Program printout was discovered in defendant Ward's UCC office in Palo Alto.

PENAL CODE SECTION 499C

Insofar as pertinent to this case, Section 499c(b) of the Penal Code provides "Every person is guilty of theft who, with intent to deprive or withhold from the owner thereof the control of a trade secret * * * does any of the following:

(1) Steals, takes, or carries away any article representing a trade secret.

* * *

(3) Having unlawfully obtained access to the article, without authority makes or causes to be made a copy of any article representing a trade secret.

Since the defendant Ward was neither an employee of, nor was he in a fiduciary relationship with ISD, subdivisions 2 and 4 are here inapplicable.

Implicit in the definition of "article" contained in Section 499c(a) is that it must be something *tangible,* even though the trade secret which the article represents may itself be *intangible.* Based upon the record here, the defendant Ward did not carry any tangible thing representing ISD's Plot/Trans Program from the ISD computer to the UCC computer unless the impulses which defendant allegedly caused to be transmitted over the telephone wire could be said to be tangible. *It is the opinion of the Court that such impulses are not tangible and hence do not constitute an*

---

1. At Shell's insistence, it had the same site and billing number at both UCC and ISD, a fact presumably known

to Ward.

"article" within the definition contained in Section 499c(a)(1) as inclusive of "object, material, device or substance or copy thereof, including any writing, record, recording, drawing, sample, specimen, prototype, model, photograph, microorganism, blueprint or map." All of the forging [sic] things are tangible and under the principle of ejusdem generis, telephonic impulses would not constitute an article representing a trade secret.

However, the preliminary transcript does establish probable cause to believe that the defendant Ward, after unlawfully obtaining access to the Plot/Trans Program, did, without the authority of ISD, make a copy thereof through use of the UCC computer and thereafter carried that copy from the UCC computer to his office at UCC, thus providing the asportation required under subdivision (1) of Section 499c(b).

In any event, a violation of Section 499c(b)(3) is established by probable cause to believe that defendant made a copy, consisting of 2 printouts, of the Plot/Trans Program, irrespective of its asportation.

To adopt and expand the library analogy suggested by defense counsel at the preliminary hearing [reference]: ISD had in its computer and Fastrans memory bank a library of computer recorded information, including the Plot/Trans Program which is the subject of the alleged theft. Other than being physically present at the ISD office itself, no one could gain access to this recorded information except by telephone. Telephonic access could lawfully be secured either (1) by a direct leased line from a customer in to the ISD computer, or (2) by an ordinary dial line by a customer using a data phone into the ISD computer provided the customer knew three sets of numbers: (1) The unlisted telephone number of the computer; (2) a two-character site number; and (3) an account number identifying the customer for billing purposes. In other words, the ISD "library" was a private, not a public, library and access thereto was restricted to customers authorized by ISD to use a "library card" consisting of the unlisted telephone number, the site number, and the billing number. Anyone else using this library card to gain access to the library would be doing so unlawfully and without authorization of ISD. And the fact, if it be a fact, that

ISD was negligent in leaving the source code to the Plot/Trans Program in the Fastrans memory bank, as it did on January 19, 1971, so that the program could be accessed and copied by one using the library card without authorization does not make noncriminal that which otherwise would constitute a crime. To adopt defendants' argument would mean that because from the standpoint of maximum security an owner might place his jewelry in a safe, it could never be the subject of a theft if he places it in a less secure location.

The evidence adduced at the preliminary thus established probable cause to believe that:

(1) The Plot/Trans Program is secret in that ISD took measures to prevent it from becoming available to persons other than those selected by ISD to have access thereto for the limited purpose of utilizing the *service* it provided. (No one, not even a customer, was authorized by ISD to access and copy the *program* itself.)

(2) The Plot/Trans Program was not generally available to the public;

(3) Use by ISD of the Plot/Trans Program gave the latter an advantage over competitors including UCC, the employer of defendant, who did not know of or use the program. (Indeed, the evidence establishes that no competitor of ISD at the time of the alleged theft on January 19, 1971, even had the capability of providing a remote plotting service because none had CTMC.)

(4) Defendant Ward on January 19, 1971, used the unlisted telephone number of the ISD computer, together with the Shell Development Company site and billing numbers to access the ISD computer in Oakland from the UCC office in Palo Alto and make a computer printout copy of the Plot/Trans Program through the UCC computer.

(5) The defendant carried the printout copy of the trade secret from the UCC computer to his office, thus providing the asportation required by subdivision (1), or Section 499c(b) (although, as above noted, asportation is not a requirement of subdivision (3); cf. *People v. Dolbeer* (1963) 214 Cal.2d 619).

DEMURRER AND MOTION TO DISMISS

The Legislature specifically states that the purpose of Section 499c of the Penal Code is to "clarify and restate existing law with respect to crimes involving trade secrets and to make it clear that articles representing trade secrets, including the trade secrets representing thereby, constitute goods, chattels, materials and property. * * *"

Mr. Witkin in 1 *California Crimes*, 1969 Supplement, page 155, Section 518 F, notes that the enactment of Section 499c, "brings the wrongful appropriation of any trade secret *within the scope of the crimes of theft and bribery*." (Emphasis added.) A trade secret or an article representing it therefore is now, if it was not previously, "money, goods, chattels, things in action, and evidences of debt." [Citation.]

It follows that a wrongful appropriation of any trade secret, or article representing it, can properly be charged either as (1) a theft of property under Section 487 of the Penal Code, provided the requisite value and intent elements are established, or (2) as a violation of Section 499c of the Penal Code, which neither requires proof of value nor of an intent permanently to deprive. Accordingly, since the elements of the crime set forth under Penal Code Section 487 and 499c are not identical, it is proper to charge both violations in a single Information, notwithstanding each arises out of the same transaction. [Citation.]

The count charging a violation of Penal Code Section 499c states an offense under that section. The record establishes that ISD took "measures to prevent it from becoming available to other than those selected by the owner to have access thereto for limited purposes" within the meaning of Section 499c(a)(3). These measures, as above indicated, consisted of an unlisted telephone number, a two-character site code number, and a billing number, all of which had to be known and used to make the Plot/Trans Program in the ISD computer available to those seeking it. The program is, therefore, presumed to be secret under the definition of "Trade Secret" contained in Section 499c(a)(3). Anyone using these numbers for the purpose of securing access to the Plot/Trans Program without the authority of the owner would be acting unlawfully within the meaning of Section 499c(b)(3). The fact that the owner might have taken additional measures to make the program more secure such as by scrambling or adopting one of the number of other methods testified to by Dr. Chapin is immaterial. Finally, the record establishes that the Plot/Trans Program was not generally available to the public and that its use gave ISD an advantage over competitors such as UCC who, although knowing of the Plot/Trans *service,* did not know or use the *program* itself.

There is probable cause to believe that offenses under Sections 499c and 487 of the Penal Code were committed and the defendant committed them. Accordingly, the motion to dismiss the Information under Section 995 of the Penal Code is denied and the demurrer thereto overruled.

PEOPLE v. CALANDRA
117 Misc.2d 972, 459 N.Y.S.2d 549
(Supreme Court, Criminal Term, New York County, Part 50, Feb. 7, 1983.)

ROTHWAX, J.

The defendants have been charged in a ninety-four count indictment with grand larceny in the second degree [citation]; abstraction * * * of bank funds [citation]; and falsification of bank reports [citation] based upon the alleged diversion by the defendants Calandra and Levine, vice-presidents in the commercial loan department of Chase Manhattan Bank, of eighteen million dollars in Chase funds to the defendants Freedman and Roseman or to entities under their control. The defendants allegedly attempted to portray unlawful transfers as loan transactions in the bank's records, or attempted to conceal the transfers altogether from senior bank officials. The indictment is based upon twenty-nine transactions, of which twenty-one were purported loans made by Calandra and Levine to Freedman, to entities controlled by Freedman or to Freedman surrogates. The remaining transactions include reversals of interest due on several of the loans; substantial overdrafts paid on Freedman's account, and an unconditional guarantee, by Calandra on behalf of Chase, of a loan by the National Bank of North America (NBNA) to a Freedman-Roseman enterprise. All of these alleged transactions were conducted by Calandra and Levine from a branch office of Chase Manhattan located on Court Street in Brooklyn (Kings County). Calandra was the executive lending officer of Chase's eastern district and Levine was his subordinate, responsible for a team of lending officers for the Brooklyn-Staten Island area. The loans were generally negotiated by Freedman in person or through a representative, in Brooklyn, or by telephone from Florida. The loan notes were executed in Brooklyn or were executed in blank elsewhere and were sent to Brooklyn for completion. The Freedman and related corporate accounts were maintained with the Brooklyn branch of Chase Manhattan.

The defendants challenge the court's geographical jurisdiction over these offenses, since the locus of their conduct was primarily in Kings County. [Citation.] If jurisdiction over these offenses is exclusively in Kings County, then the indictment must, of necessity, be dismissed. (*Matter of Steingut v. Gold*, 42 N.Y.2d 311, 316, 397 N.Y.S.2d 765, 366 N.E.2d 854 [1977].) The determination of proper venue is a question of fact, which must be established by a preponderance of the evidence. [Citation.] It is necessary, therefore, to review in some detail the proof before the Grand Jury as to the specific manner in which the transactions alleged in the indictment occurred.

Loans were made by having the customer complete a promissory note which was kept on file at the branch. The loan officer, who approved the loan by countersigning the note, would simultaneously complete a second form (# 179), entitled common credit input form. Contained in this form was the borrower's name, address, the amount of the loan, rate of interest, schedule of repayments and manner in which the loan was to be credited to the borrower. The loan principal could be credited in two ways, either by direct deposit to the borrower's checking account, or by issuing bank checks in the principal amount. The loan officer's signature on the 179 form authorized a loan processing clerk to transcribe the information relevant to the loan from the 179 form to a computer input sheet. The computer input sheets were sent, at the end of each business day, to the bank's central computer operations located at One New York Plaza, in New York County. The information from the input sheets would be entered into the bank's computer, which would then credit the borrower's checking account in the amount of the loan. If the loan principal was delivered by check, the loan clerk would issue the check when he received the 179 form. The checks would subsequently be reacquired by Chase from local banks through the New York

Clearing House Association, or from other banks through the Federal Reserve System. In either case, Chase would exchange an equivalent dollar amount of the depository bank's checks for the face value of the Chase checks. Reacquisition took place in New York County. The reacquired checks were then delivered to Chase's accounting office for debit against Chase holdings.

The 179 form was also used to modify any terms of an original loan, such as the principal amount, interest rate, and frequency of interest payments. The process for modification was the same as for the creation of an original loan. The 179 containing the new or additional information would be completed by the loan officer whose signature authorized a loan clerk to enter the modifications on computer input sheets, subsequently transported to Manhattan and logged into the bank's computer.

In addition to the 179 form, the loan officer was required to complete a customer profile form (# 178) which contained a new borrower's name, financial circumstances and relationship to any existing borrower. This information, when authenticated by the loan officer's signature, was transcribed to input sheets and entered into the bank's central customer information file through the computer terminal in Manhattan. Additional documentation in regard to loans was kept in the credit files maintained at the branch.

Within forty-five days of making a loan, the officer who authorized the loan was required to file a report to higher management regarding the terms of the loan and financial condition of the borrower. Loans in excess of $100,000 but less than $250,000 were reported and reviewed at the district level, which was in Brooklyn. The report of loans in this range was entitled Credit Authorization report. Loans in excess of $250,000 were reported by means of Credit Facility reports, filed periodically in the group headquarters of the commercial loan department, in Manhattan, for review by senior management. The purpose of review was to ensure adherence to the bank's lending policy guidelines at the district level. The credit facility reports were the senior management's only source of information about the loans.

A document similar to the 179 loan form,

entitled new account memorandum, was required to be prepared by the account's relationship officer whenever a checking account was opened at the branch. The memorandum contained the name and address of authorized signatories, and relationship to any existing accounts. This information, when authenticated by the bank officer's signature, was entered into the bank's computerized records in the same manner as information recorded on the 179 form. The branch also maintained signature cards by which to verify the signatures of the authorized signatories.

In the event of an overdraft against a checking account, the relationship officer would receive a computer issued refer card upon which he would indicate whether the draft should be paid or returned. The officer's signature authorized the bank's bookkeeping department in Manhattan, where the cards were sent, to pay or refuse to pay the overdraft and to modify the bank's records accordingly. If the overdraft were paid, the checking account remained unaffected and the amount of funds unavailable would be entered in the bank's accounts receivable records.

The loan guarantee was a letter, similar to a letter of credit, drafted by Calandra in Brooklyn. The purpose of this unique document was to assist a Freedman company, R.S. Grist, to obtain a subsidiary mortgage on Florida real estate known as Holiday Isle, in order to repay an original Chase loan used to purchase the Holiday Isle property. A copy of the letter was delivered to the National Bank of North America (NBNA) in Manhattan first for revisions by NBNA counsel in consultation with Calandra by telephone, and subsequently at the closing when the letter was exchanged for the checks representing the principal paid on the mortgage. No copy of the letter was ever filed with Chase's counsel in Manhattan, as required by bank policy. R.S. Grist defaulted on the mortgage loan to NBNA and NBNA invoked the guarantee by Chase, which Chase honored in the amount of 2.8 million dollars.

LARCENY AND ABSTRACTION

The court has essentially two kinds of geographical jurisdiction; that in which conduct constituting an element or essential result of the crime has occurred within the county [citation], and that which is necessary to protect the People and institutions within the county from conduct occurring elsewhere. [Citations.] There is a third category of jurisdiction, legislatively prescribed, in specific circumstances. [Citations.] In determining whether venue is properly in New York County with respect to the various offenses set forth in the indictment, the court has accepted the factual allegations therein on their face, and has not considered whether the allegations establish the offenses charged.

Venue of the larceny and abstraction [citation] counts is established in New York County based upon the commission, within the County, of an element of the offenses. Twenty-two of the larceny counts relate to loan transactions and one relates to the loan guarantee Calandra made to NBNA. Twenty-one of the abstraction counts relate to loan transactions, five relate to reversals of interest due on loans, one relates to overdrafts paid to balance Freedman's checking account, and one to the loan guarantee to NBNA.

The loan transactions as framed in the indictment are a species of larceny by embezzlement. [Citation.] The bank entrusted control over certain amounts of its money to the defendant officers for a specified purpose, and the officers allegedly converted the money to the unauthorized use and control of their co-defendants, with larcenous intent. [Citations.] Conversion is an essential element of larceny by embezzlement. [Citation.] Conversion of the money, funds, property or credit of a bank to an unauthorized use by an officer of the bank is also an essential element of abstraction [citation], encompassed within the definition of "abstracts or wilfully misapplies." [Citations.] Conversion being an element of proof essential to both crimes, geographical jurisdiction vests in the courts of the county in which the conversion occurred. [Citation.]

In general, conversion is an unauthorized exercise of dominion or control over property by one who is not the owner, which interferes with and is in defiance of the owners possession. [Citation.] In the context of larceny, the interference must be to the degree that the owner is deprived altogether of the economic value of his property. [Citation.] Conversion of the loan principal in the various transactions subject to this indictment, occurred in two ways. In regard to loans in which the principal was credited to the purported borrower's checking account, conversion was accomplished by the computerized transfer of funds from the bank's control to the borrower's. [Citation.] In regard to loans in which the principal was paid to the purported borrower by check, conversion was accomplished by the payment of the face amount of the check upon presentation to Chase Manhattan Bank. Money paid upon the check by previous depository banks was not, in fact, the loan principal since it was not the property of Chase Manhattan. [Citations.] The majority of jurisdictions are in accord that venue attaches in embezzlement prosecutions in the jurisdiction where the assets of the owner corporation were reduced by the act of embezzlement. [Citations.]

The place of conversion, where the purported borrower ultimately obtained control over money belonging to Chase Manhattan Bank, was, in both transactions, New York County. The borrower's account was not credited with the loan principal until the officer's directive to make the loan was entered into the bank's computerized records in Manhattan. The funds of Chase Manhattan represented by checks issued in the amount of the loan principal were not affected until Chase reacquired the checks, by payment through the Federal Reserve System or Clearing House Association in New York County.

Similar considerations support the venue in New York County of the larceny count based upon the loan guarantee given by Calandra to NBNA. The unauthorized guarantee induced a transfer of funds in Manhattan from Chase to NBNA when the guarantee was honored. No Chase asset was exchanged prior to the said transfer, which was a form of asportation. [Citations.] Until the guarantee was honored there was no conversion equivalent to larceny, since the guarantee may have never been invoked. [Citation.]

In those instances of abstraction [citation] based upon reversals of interest due on loans and payments of overdrafts, conversion, in the sense of interference with the bank's possessory interest in its funds or credit, also occurred in New York County. The reversals of interest due were accomplished by directives, in the 179 form, to change interest schedules from monthly to quarterly deductions against the borrower's checking account. The directive was carried into effect when entered into the bank's computer in Manhattan, whereupon any deductions of interest from the borrower's account were either reversed or were aborted. The bank's possession of such money as the interest due represented was accordingly curtailed by acts undertaken in Manhattan pursuant to the Brooklyn directive. Payments of overdrafts were made when the refer card directing that the draft be honored was received by the bank's accounting office in Manhattan. The bank's credit was affected when the money used to satisfy the draft was deducted, by entries in the bank's accounting records, from the bank's general revenue. The exchange of the unauthorized loan guarantee at the Manhattan office of NBNA was a misapplication of Chase Manhattan's credit [citation], which physically occurred in New York County.

FALSIFICATION OF BANK REPORTS

Falsification of bank reports may be committed either by making a false entry or by wilfully omitting to make a true entry in such reports. [Citation.] In either event the entry or omission must be that of a bank employee whose intent is to deceive the bank's officers, examiners, or a public authority in regard to the affairs or condition of the bank. The defendants argue that since, as in the case of forgery, the offense of falsification is complete when the entry is made with the requisite intent, and since all the forms at issue were completed in Kings County, no element of the offense was committed in New York County (see *People v. Schlatter*, 55 A.D.2d 922, 390 N.Y.S.2d 441 [2d Dept. 1977]). The defendants argue further that the prosecution has failed to show a sufficient impact upon New York County as a result of the falsifications alleged in the indictment to warrant an exercise of protective jurisdiction. [Citation.]

The court, however, finds a critical distinction between the forgery charges at issue in *Schlatter, supra,* and the falsification counts here. Of the two types of instrument which may be the subject of forgery [citation], the instruments at issue in *Schlatter* were checks, which "constitute a symbol or evidence of value, right, privilege or identification." The instruments at issue in these falsification counts are "book(s), report(s) or statement(s)" [citation] of the bank, which "recite, embody, convey or record information." [Citation.] This is evident from the statutory requirement that the false entry or wilfull omission must pertain to the "affairs" or "condition" of the bank in a way that tends to deceive those responsible for the bank's administration. The statements subject to falsification must be communicative of information necessary to assess the bank's affairs.

Included within the venue article [citation] is a provision which deems any "written statement made by a person in one jurisdiction to a person in another jurisdiction by means of * * * any * * * method of communication * * * to be made in each such jurisdiction." [Citation.] The documents which are the subject of the falsification counts constituted a "method of communication" among Chase officials in the ordinary course of the bank's business. All of the documents specified in the indictment were written by or at the discretion of the defendant bank officers and the information contained therein authenticated by the officers' signatures. The information contained in the signature cards, credit file memoranda, credit facility reports, and credit authorization forms was communicated among bank officials on the face of the documents themselves. The information contained in the 179 form, the customer profile, and new account memoranda was transposed, once the authorizing signature on the document was verified, to computer input forms which were physically transported to Manhattan where the information was entered in the bank's computerized records. The court finds CPL 20.60, subd. 1 equally applicable to those documents which conveyed information on their face, and those documents which contained information subsequently translated into computer language. Insofar as the computer coded information was transcribed verbatim from a written document, it represented that document in another form. The transmittal of the document in its computer input form was a "method of communication" of the written statements contained in the original.

Therefore, CPL 20.60, subd. 1 establishes jurisdiction in New York County insofar as the documents allegedly falsified were used to convey information from a person in Kings County to a person in New York County, since the documents are deemed to have been made in each jurisdiction. The "making" of the falsified document is, of course, an element of the offense. [Citations.] Insofar as the falsification charges are based upon omissions, the evidence shows that the information allegedly omitted was required by the form of the documents to be reported. Accordingly, the omissions were a form of misrepresentation integral to the written statements and may also be deemed to have been "made" in New York County for purposes of venue.

This reasoning (CPL 20.60, subd. 1) is, of course, inapplicable to any documents which were not communicated from the Kings County branch to the central Manhattan offices of the bank. There was no evidence before the Grand Jury that the signature cards, or credit file memoranda were ever used to convey information outside of the Court Street branch in Kings County. The evidence indicates that the credit files were maintained at the branch and were only reviewed by audits undertaken there. The credit authorization forms completed in regard to loans of less than $250,000 were limited to review at the district level in Brooklyn. Any misrepresentation of information contained in these documents was confined entirely to Kings County. Therefore, the falsification counts based upon these documents are dismissed for lack of sufficient evidence of proper venue. [References.]

Twenty-one of the falsification counts in the indictment are based upon the defendant bank officers' failure "to file" "in the County of New York and elsewhere" internal bank documents including credit facility reports and a copy of the loan guarantee to NBNA. As previously noted, the court accepts this formulation of the offense as legally sufficient [citations] for the limited purpose of assessing proper venue. Credit facility reports were used to report loans in excess of $500,000 to the senior bank management in the commercial loan department's headquarters in Manhattan. The reports were to be submitted within forty-five days of making the loan and periodically thereafter. When not under review, the reports were kept at the branch offices. The use of the words "failed to file" in these counts is ambiguous at best, since the evidence before the Grand Jury established that the defendants completely failed to create the credit facility reports. The loan guarantee was, of course, created but not submitted to the bank's counsel for review as required by bank policy.

It is certain, in any event, that the omission "to file" or to make or create a document may not, like the omission to include information in a completed document conveyed from one county to another, constitute a jurisdictional basis under CPL 20.60, subd. 1, since no "oral or written statement" has been "made" between persons in separate jurisdictions. Although the failure to convey information which is required to be reported under specific circumstances, may be regarded as a "method of communication" that such circumstances do not exist, the statute (CPL 20.60, subd. 1) must be strictly and literally construed. [Citation.]

The counts as framed suggest that the defendants failed to perform a duty imposed by law "which duty was required to be or could properly have been performed" in New York County, in which case venue would properly vest here under CPL 20.40, subd. 3. However, what is made criminal by the falsification statute [citation] is not the failure to file documents as required by bank policy, but the failure to make or create documents or to complete statements in an attempt to deceive the bank's managers. The duty imposed by the statute is "to make * * * true entri(ies) of any material particular(s) pertaining to the business of (the bank) in any book, report or statement of (the bank)." If the credit facility reports had been accurately completed in Brooklyn, but not filed in Manhattan for review as required by bank policy, there would have been no violation of the statute. [Citation.] The duty to make the credit facility reports arose at the Brooklyn branch when loans of the specified amount were made, and the documents were in fact retained at the Brooklyn branch before and after submission to Manhattan for review. Therefore, jurisdiction under CPL 20.40, subd. 3 would vest exclusively in Kings County. [Citation.]

Moreover, falsification [citation] is not a "result" offense [citation], the essential consequence of which may be prosecuted in the county where it occurs. [Citation.] Falsification does not require as an element of the offense that any specific consequence occur as a result of the wilfull misstatements or omissions. Although intent to deceive must be proved, there is no requirement that the bank officers, examiners or public authorities have been deceived in fact. Nor is proof of loss to the bank an element of the offense. [Citation.]

Therefore, the only cogent basis for venue over these falsification counts in New York County is the protective theory of jurisdiction. [Citation.] Jurisdiction may be invoked under this theory when the extraterritorial criminal conduct produces consequences within the county of prosecution, which are not elements of proof of the crime itself, but which so affect the community welfare or governmental processes of the county that prosecution is justified by the need to protect the county's residents. The District Attorney of the county seeking to apply the long arm aspect of criminal jurisdiction must prove to the Grand Jury by a preponderance of evidence that the county meets the criteria of an injured forum: that the extraterritorial conduct was intended to affect the injured county in particular; that the injury to the county was material and subject to proof; and that the injury was not limited to the welfare of a particular person but affected the county's community as a whole. [Citations.] The court accordingly rejects the suggestion that extraterritorial conduct which defrauds a single person within a county is subject to the county's criminal jurisdiction, even though the fraud is not an element of the crime. [Citations.] There is no exception in law where the "person" defrauded is a corporation of whatever size. [Citation.]

The court is also persuaded that the particular injurious effect upon which the county bases its jurisdictional claim must be pleaded in the indictment. One basis for this conclusion is dicta in *Matter of Steingut, supra* (42 N.Y.2d p. 318, 397 N.Y.S.2d 765, 366 N.E.2d 854), in which the court stated in reference to the form of the indictment that "invoking of the extraordinary injured forum jurisdictional statute requires the specification of a * * * concrete and identifiable injury." This conclusion is supported by close scrutiny of the relevant statutory provisions. The Criminal Procedure Law [citation] requires that an indictment recite in each count that the offense "was committed in a designated county." The essence of protective, or particular effect, jurisdiction is that the conduct constituting the offense has occurred outside of the county of prosecution. [Citations.] Therefore, it would appear from an otherwise accurate pleading based upon a protective jurisdictional theory that the courts of the prosecuting county did not have jurisdiction over the offense [citation], unless the facts upon which jurisdiction rests in the prosecuting county are specifically pleaded. It is, of course, no answer to allege that the offense was "committed in" the prosecuting county when in fact only the injurious but nonelemental consequences occurred there.

The Grand Jury presentation in this case failed to establish that New York County's general welfare suffered material injury as a result of the defendants' alleged conduct in failing to file credit facility reports or a copy of the loan guarantee with the Chase Manhattan Bank's central office. Moreover, those falsification counts based upon the failure to file such documents are inaccurate to the extent they allege that the offense occurred "in the County of New York." Since the counts fail to set forth a concrete and identifiable injury to the welfare of New York County as a result of the defendants' extrajurisdictional conduct, the counts are defective. [Citation.] These counts [references] are accordingly dismissed.

The indictment is sustained except to the extent indicated herein. The foregoing constitutes the opinion, decision and order of the court.

UNITED STATES v. HUFF

699 F.2d 1027

(United States Court of Appeals, Tenth Circuit, Jan. 17, 1983.)

SETH, C. J.

The defendants appeal their convictions on five counts of mail fraud in violation of 18 U.S.C. §§ 1341 and 1342. The indictment charged that the defendants engaged in a scheme to defraud customers of Interstate Business Marketing, Inc. Defendant Leland Max Huff incorporated Interstate and was its first president. His sons, John M. Huff and Rick Huff, were officers of the company and trained some of its salesmen. Defendant John C. Huff is not related to the other Huffs; both he and defendant James Nierstheimer were salesmen for Interstate.

The evidence shows that Interstate solicited by means of mass mailings business owners in the West and Midwest that might be interested in selling their businesses. Typically an owner would return a card to Interstate acknowledging that he was interested in selling his business. An Interstate salesman would then go out and call on the business owner. The salesman would explain that Interstate had numerous qualified buyers that were interested in purchasing businesses and would undertake to match the seller's business with buyers who might be interested in purchasing that kind of business in that location.

Interstate placed advertisements in magazines and newspapers stating little more than that it had a large number of businesses for sale and giving an address to which a buyer could write for further information. If a response was received, the prospective buyer was then sent a simple questionnaire asking the general type of business he was interested in operating, his general geographic preference, and the approximate price he was willing to pay. The buyers were then assigned a code number and a computer would match them with every listed business falling within broad categories. The prospective buyers were then sent a xeroxed brochure prepared by Interstate describing each business to which they had been matched, and were advised if interested to contact the sellers directly. The would-be sellers received a list of potential buyers to whom their businesses had been matched, and were advised that the buyers that were interested would contact them. As a practical matter, the listing provided by Interstate made it difficult for the sellers to contact the buyers. In any event, the buyers and the sellers were then to arrange the sale of the business without further assistance from Interstate.

Interstate charged the sellers a nonrefundable fee at the outset for its services, and negotiated a contract with them which provided that the sellers would pay an additional fee if they were to sell their businesses to buyers referred by Interstate. The amount of the fee charged by Interstate was directly related to the asking price of the business.

The indictment returned against the defendants charged that the enterprise failed to qualify its buyers before entering their names into the computer as it had represented to potential sellers, failed to update its buyer list, exaggerated the number and quality of potential buyers, falsely claimed that it would spend hundreds of dollars to advertise individually the seller's business, and falsely represented that Interstate was frequently successful in securing a buyer for a client's business. The evidence showed that in eight years of operation Interstate had been responsible for the sale of only one business while taking in over four million dollars from over two thousand clients. The jury returned guilty verdicts on all counts of mail fraud against all the defendants. The evidence was sufficient to support the verdict.

* * *

We must hold that the record demonstrates that the jury could keep separate the evidence and identity of the defendants and no prejudice is indicated.

Affirmed.

WHALEN v. ROE

429 U.S. 589

(Appeal from the United States District Court for the Southern District of New York, February 22, 1977.)

STEVENS, J.

The constitutional question presented is whether the State of New York may record, in a centralized computer file, the names and addresses of all persons who have obtained, pursuant to a doctor's prescription, certain drugs for which there is both a lawful and an unlawful market.

The District Court enjoined enforcement of the portions of the New York State Controlled Substances Act of 1972 [footnote] which re-

quire such recording on the ground that they violate appellees' constitutionally protected rights of privacy. [Footnote.] We noted probable jurisdiction of the appeal by the Commissioner of Health, 424 U. S. 907, and now reverse. [Footnote.]

Many drugs have both legitimate and illegitimate uses. In response to a concern that such drugs were being diverted into unlawful channels, in 1970 the New York Legislature created a special commission to evaluate the State's drug-control laws. [Footnote.] The commission found the existing laws deficient in several respects. There was no effective way to prevent the use of stolen or revised prescriptions, to prevent unscrupulous pharmacists from repeatedly refilling prescriptions, to prevent users from obtaining prescriptions from more than one doctor, or to prevent doctors from overprescribing, either by authorizing an excessive amount in one prescription or by giving one patient multiple prescriptions. [Footnote.] In drafting new legislation to correct such defects, the commission consulted with enforcement officials in California and Illinois where central reporting systems were being used effectively.[6]

The new New York statute classified potentially harmful drugs in five schedules. [Footnote.] Drugs, such as heroin, which are highly abused and have no recognized medical use, are in Schedule I; they cannot be prescribed. Schedules II through V include drugs which have a progressively lower potential for abuse but also have a recognized medical use. Our concern is limited to Schedule II, which includes the most dangerous of the legitimate drugs. [Footnote.]

With an exception for emergencies, the Act requires that all prescriptions for Schedule II drugs be prepared by the physician in triplicate on an official form. [Footnote.] The completed form identifies the prescribing physician; the dispensing pharmacy; the drug and dosage; and the name, address, and age of the patient. One copy of the form is retained by the physician, the second by the pharmacist,

---

6. The Chairman of the T. S. C. summarized its findings: Law enforcement officials in both California and Illinois have been consulted in considerable depth about the use of multiple prescriptions, since they have been using them for a considerable period of time. They indicate to us that they are not only a useful adjunct to the proper identification of culpable professional and unscrupulous drug abusers, but that they also give a reliable statistical indication of the pattern of drug flow throughout their states: information sorely needed in this state to stem the tide of diversion of lawfully manufactured controlled substances. [Reference.]

[Citations.]

and the third is forwarded to the New York State Department of Health in Albany. A prescription made on an official form may not exceed a 30-day supply, and may not be refilled. [Footnote.]

The District Court found that about 100,000 Schedule II prescription forms are delivered to a receiving room at the Department of Health in Albany each month. They are sorted, coded, and logged and then taken to another room where the data on the forms is recorded on magnetic tapes for processing by a computer. Thereafter, the forms are returned to the receiving room to be retained in a vault for a five-year period and then destroyed as required by the statute. [Footnote.] The receiving room is surrounded by a locked wire fence and protected by an alarm system. The computer tapes containing the prescription data are kept in a locked cabinet. When the tapes are used, the computer is run "off-line," which means that no terminal outside of the computer room can read or record any information. Public disclosure of the identity of patients is expressly prohibited by the statute and by a Department of Health regulation.[12]

Willful violation of these prohibitions is a crime punishable by up to one year in prison and a $2,000 fine. [Footnote.] At the time of trial there were 17 Department of Health employees with access to the files; in addition, there were 24 investigators with authority to investigate cases of overdispensing which might be identified by the computer. Twenty months after the effective date of the Act, the computerized data had only been used in two investigations involving alleged overuse by specific patients.

A few days before the Act became effective, this litigation was commenced by a group of patients regularly receiving prescriptions for Schedule II drugs, by doctors who prescribe such drugs, and by two associations of physicians. [Footnote.] After various preliminary proceedings [footnote], a three-judge District Court conducted a one-day trial. Appellees offered evidence tending to prove that persons in need of treatment with Schedule II drugs will from time to time decline such treatment because of their fear that the misuse of the computerized data will cause them to be stigmatized as "drug addicts."[16]

12. Section 3371 of the Pub. Health Law states:

1. No person, who has knowledge by virtue of his office of the identity of a particular patient or research subject, a manufacturing process, a trade secret or a formula shall disclose such knowledge, or any report or record thereof, except:

(a) to another person employed by the department, for purposes of executing provisions to this article; or

(b) pursuant to judicial subpoena or court order in a criminal investigation or proceeding; or

(c) to an agency, department of government, or official board authorized to regulate, license or otherwise supervise a person who is authorized by this article to deal in controlled substances, or in the course of any investigation or proceeding by or before such agency, department or board; or

(d) to a central registry established pursuant to this article.

2. In the course of any proceeding where such information is disclosed, except when necessary to effectuate the rights of a party to the proceeding, the court or presiding officer shall take such action as is necessary to insure that such information, or record or report of such information is not made public.

Pursuant to its statutory authority, the Department of Health has promulgated regulations in respect of confidentiality as follows:

No person who has knowledge by virtue of his office of the identity of a particular patient or research subject, a manufacturing process, a trade secret or a formula shall disclose such knowledge, or any report or record thereof, except:

(a) to another person who by virtue of his office as an employee of the department is entitled to obtain such information; or

(b) pursuant to judicial subpoena or court order in a criminal investigation or proceedings; or

(c) to an agency, department of government, or official board authorized to regulate, license or otherwise supervise a person who is authorized by article 33 of the Public Health Law to deal in controlled substances, or in the course of any investigation or proceeding by or before such agency, department or board; or

(d) to a central registry established pursuant to article 33 of the Public Health Law. 10 N. Y. C. R. R. § 80.107 (1973).

16. Two parents testified that they were concerned that their children would be stigmatized by the State's central filing system. One child had been taken off his Schedule II medication because of this concern. Three adult patients testified that they feared disclosure of their names would result from central filing of patient identifications. One of them now obtains his drugs in another State. The other two continue to receive Schedule II prescriptions in New York, but continue to fear disclosure and stigmatization. Four physicians testified that the prescription system entrenches on patients' privacy, and that each had observed a reaction of shock, fear, and concern on the part of their patients whom they had informed of the plan. One doctor refuses to prescribe Schedule II drugs for his patients. On the other hand, over 100,000 patients per month have been receiving Schedule II drug prescriptions without their objections, if any, to central filing having come to the attention of the District Court. The record shows that the provisions of the Act were brought to the attention of the section on psychiatry of the New York State Medical Society (App. 166a), but that body apparently declined to support this suit.

The District Court held that "the doctor-patient relationship is one of the zones of privacy accorded constitutional protection" and that the patient-identification provisions of the Act invaded this zone with "a needlessly broad sweep," and enjoined enforcement of the provisions of the Act which deal with the reporting of patients' names and addresses. [Footnote.]

I

The District Court found that the State had been unable to demonstrate the necessity for the patient-identification requirements on the basis of its experience during the first 20 months of administration of the new statute. There was a time when that alone would have provided a basis for invalidating the statute. *Lochner v. New York*, 198 U. S. 45, involved legislation making it a crime for a baker to permit his employees to work more than 60 hours in a week. In an opinion no longer regarded as authoritative, the Court held the statute unconstitutional as "an unreasonable, unnecessary and arbitrary interference with the right of the individual to his personal liberty. * * *" *Id.*, at 56.

The holding in *Lochner* has been implicitly rejected many times. [Footnote.] State legislation which has some effect on individual liberty or privacy may not be held unconstitutional simply because a court finds it unnecessary, in whole or in part. [Footnote.] For we have frequently recognized that individual States have broad latitude in experimenting with possible solutions to problems of vital local concern.[20]

The New York statute challenged in this case represents a considered attempt to deal with such a problem. It is manifestly the product of an orderly and rational legislative decision. It was recommended by a specially appointed commission which held extensive hearings on the proposed legislation, and drew on experience with similar programs in other States. There surely was nothing unreasonable in the assumption that the patient-identification requirement might aid in the enforcement of laws designed to minimize the misuse of dangerous drugs. For the requirement could reasonably be expected to have a deterrent effect on potential violators [footnote] as well as to aid in the detection or investigation of specific instances of apparent abuse. At the very least, it would seem clear that the State's vital interest in controlling the distribution of dangerous drugs would support a decision to experiment with new techniques for control. [Footnote.] For if an experiment fails—if in this case experience teaches that the patient-identification requirement results in the foolish expenditure of funds to acquire a mountain of useless information—the legislative process remains available to terminate the unwise experiment. It follows that the legislature's enactment of the patient-identification requirement was a reasonable exercise of New York's broad police powers. The District Court's finding that the necessity for the requirement had not been proved is not, therefore, a sufficient reason for holding the statutory requirement unconstitutional.

II

Appellees contend that the statute invades a constitutionally protected "zone of privacy."[23]

---

20. Mr. Justice Brandeis' classic statement of the proposition merits reiteration:

To stay experimentation in things social and economic is a grave responsibility. Denial of the right to experiment may be fraught with serious consequences to the Nation. It is one of the happy incidents of the federal system that a single courageous State may, if its citizens choose, serve as a laboratory; and try novel social and economic experiments without risk to the rest of the country. This Court has the power to prevent an experiment. We may strike down the statute which embodies it on the ground that, in our opinion, the measure is arbitrary, capricious or unreasonable. We have power to do this, because the due process clause has been held by the Court applicable to matters of substantive law as well as to matters of procedure. But in the exercise of this high power, we must be ever on our guard, lest we erect

our prejudices into legal principles. If we would guide by the light of reason, we must let our minds be bold. *New State Ice Co. v. Liebmann*, 285 U. S. 262, 311 (dissenting opinion) (footnote omitted).

23. As the basis for the constitutional claim they rely on the shadows cast by a variety of provisions in the Bill of Rights. Language in prior opinions of the Court or its individual Justices provides support for the view that some personal rights "implicit in the concept of ordered liberty" (see *Palko v. Connecticut*, 302 U. S. 319, 325, quoted in *Roe v. Wade*, 410 U. S., at 152), are so "fundamental" that an undefined penumbra may provide them with an independent source of constitutional protection. In *Roe v. Wade*, however, after carefully reviewing those cases, the Court expressed the opinion that the "right of

The cases sometimes characterized as protecting "privacy" have in fact involved at least two different kinds of interests.[24] One is the individual interest in avoiding disclosure of personal matters,[25] and another is the interest in independence in making certain kinds of important decisions.[26] Appellees argue that both of these interests are impaired by this statute. The mere existence in readily available form of the information about patients' use of Schedule II drugs creates a genuine concern that the information will become publicly known and that it will adversely affect their reputations. This concern makes some patients reluctant to use, and some doctors reluctant to prescribe, such drugs even when their use is medically indicated. It follows, they argue, that the making of decisions about matters vital to the care of their health is inevitably affected by the statute. Thus, the statute threatens to impair both their interest in the nondisclosure of private information and also their interest in making important decisions independently.

We are persuaded, however, that the New York program does not, on its face, pose a sufficiently grievous threat to either interest to establish a constitutional violation.

Public disclosure of patient information can come about in three ways. Health Department employees may violate the statute by failing, either deliberately or negligently, to maintain proper security. A patient or a doctor may be accused of a violation and the stored data may be offered in evidence in a judicial proceeding. Or, thirdly, a doctor, a pharmacist, or the patient may voluntarily reveal information on a prescription form.

The third possibility existed under the prior law and is entirely unrelated to the existence of the computerized data bank. Neither of the other two possibilities provides a proper ground for attacking the statute as invalid on its face. There is no support in the record, or in the experience of the two States that New York has emulated, for an assumption that the security provisions of the statute will be administered improperly.[27] And the remote pos-

---

privacy" is founded in the Fourteenth Amendment's concept of personal liberty, id., at 152–153.

"This right of privacy, whether it be founded in the Fourteenth Amendment's concept of personal liberty and restrictions upon state action, as we feel it is, or, as the District Court determined, in the Ninth Amendment's reservation of rights to the people, is broad enough to encompass a woman's decision whether or not to terminate her pregnancy." Id., at 153 (emphasis added). [Citations.]

24. Professor Kurland has written:
> The concept of a constitutional right of privacy still remains largely undefined. There are at least three facets that have been partially revealed, but their form and shape remain to be fully ascertained. The first is the right of the individual to be free in his private affairs from governmental surveillance and intrusion. The second is the right of an individual not to have his private affairs made public by the government. The third is the right of an individual to be free in action, thought, experience, and belief from governmental compulsion. [Citation.]

The first of the facets which he describes is directly protected by the Fourth Amendment; the second and third correspond to the two kinds of interests referred to in the text.

25. In his dissent in Olmstead v. United States, 277 U. S. 438, 478, Mr. Justice Brandeis characterized "the right to be let alone" as "the right most valued by civilized men"; in Griswold v. Connecticut, 381 U. S. 479, 483, the Court said: "[T]he First Amendment has a penumbra where privacy is protected from governmental intrusion." [Citations.]

26. [Citations.] In Paul v. Davis, 424 U. S. 693, 713, the Court characterized these decisions as dealing with "matters relating to marriage, procreation, contraception,

family relationships, and child rearing and education. In these areas, it has been held that there are limitations on the States' power to substantively regulate conduct."

27. The T. S. C.'s independent investigation of the California and Illinois central filing systems failed to reveal a single case of invasion of a patient's privacy. [Citation.]

Just last Term in Buckley v. Valeo, 424 U. S. 1, we rejected a contention that the reporting requirements of the Federal Election Campaign Act of 1971 violated the First Amendment rights of those who contribute to minority parties:
> But no appellant in this case has tendered record evidence. * * * Instead, appellants primarily rely on 'the clearly articulated fears of individuals, well experienced in the political process.' * * * At best they offer the testimony of several minor-party officials that one or two persons refused to make contributions because of the possibility of disclosure. On this record, the substantial public interest in disclosure identified by the legislative history of this Act outweighs the harm generally alleged. 424 U. S. at 71–72 (footnote omitted).

Here, too, appellees urge on us "clearly articulated fears" about the pernicious effects of disclosure. But this requires us to assume even more than that we refused to do in Buckley. There the disclosures were to be made in accordance with the statutory scheme. Appellees' disclosures could only be made if the statutory scheme were violated as described. [Citation.]

The fears of parents on behalf of their pre-adolescent children who are receiving amphetamines in the treatment of hyperkinesia are doubly premature. Not only must the Act's nondisclosure provisions be violated in order to stigmatize the children as they enter adult life, but the provisions requiring destruction of all prescription records after five years would have to be ignored. [Citation.]

sibility that judicial supervision of the evidentiary use of particular items of stored information will provide inadequate protection against unwarranted disclosures is surely not a sufficient reason for invalidating the entire patient-identification program. [Footnote.]

Even without public disclosure, it is, of course, true that private information must be disclosed to the authorized employees of the New York Department of Health. Such disclosures, however, are not significantly different from those that were required under the prior law. Nor are they meaningfully distinguishable from a host of other unpleasant invasions of privacy that are associated with many facets of health care. Unquestionably, some individuals' concern for their own privacy may lead them to avoid or to postpone needed medical attention. Nevertheless, disclosures of private medical information to doctors, to hospital personnel, to insurance companies, and to public health agencies are often an essential part of modern medical practice even when the disclosure may reflect unfavorably on the character of the patient.[29] Requiring such disclosures to representatives of the State having responsibility for the health of the community does not automatically amount to an impermissible invasion of privacy.

Appellees also argue, however, that even if unwarranted disclosures do not actually occur, the knowledge that the information is readily available in a computerized file creates a genuine concern that causes some persons to decline needed medication. The record supports the conclusion that some use of Schedule II drugs has been discouraged by that concern; it also is clear, however, that about 100,000 prescriptions for such drugs were being filled each month prior to the entry of the District Court's injunction. Clearly, therefore, the statute did not deprive the public of access to the drugs.

Nor can it be said that any individual has been deprived of the right to decide independently, with the advice of his physician, to acquire and to use needed medication. Although the State no doubt could prohibit entirely the use of particular Schedule II drugs [citation], it has not done so. This case is therefore unlike those in which the Court held that a total prohibition of certain conduct was an impermissible deprivation of liberty. Nor does the State require access to these drugs to be conditioned on the consent of any state official or other third party.[31] Within dosage limits which appellees do not challenge, the decision to prescribe, or to use, is left entirely to the physician and the patient.

We hold that neither the immediate nor the threatened impact of the patient-identification requirements in the New York State Controlled Substances Act of 1972 on either the reputation or the independence of patients for whom Schedule II drugs are medically indicated is sufficient to constitute an invasion of any right or liberty protected by the Fourteenth Amendment.[32]

*   *   *

29. Familiar examples are statutory reporting requirements relating to venereal disease, child abuse, injuries caused by deadly weapons, and certifications of fetal death. Last Term we upheld the recordkeeping requirements of the Missouri abortion laws against a challenge based on the protected interest in making the abortion decision free of government intrusion, *Planned Parenthood of Central Missouri v. Danforth*, 428 U. S. 52, 79–81.

31. In *Doe v. Bolton*, 410 U. S. 179, for instance, the constitutionally defective statute required the written concurrence of two state-licensed physicians, *other than* the patient's personal physician, before an abortion could be performed, and the advance approval of a committee of not less than three members of the hospital staff where the procedure was to be performed, regardless of whether the committee members had a physician-patient relationship with the woman concerned.

32. The Roe appellees also claim that a constitutional privacy right emanates from the Fourth Amendment, citing language in *Terry v. Ohio*, 392 U. S. 1, 9, at a point where it quotes from *Katz v. United States*, 389 U. S. 347. But those cases involve affirmative, unannounced, narrowly focused intrusions into individual privacy during the course of criminal investigations. We have never carried the Fourth Amendment's interest in privacy as far as the Roe appellees would have us. We decline to do so now.

Likewise the Patient appellees derive a right to individual anonymity from our freedom of association cases such as *Bates v. Little Rock*, 361 U. S. 516, 522–523, and *NAACP v. Alabama*, 357 U. S. 449, 462. But those cases protect "freedom of association for the purpose of advancing ideas and airing grievances" [citation], not anonymity in the course of medical treatment. Also, in those cases there was an uncontroverted showing of past harm through disclosure [citation], an element which is absent here. [Citation.]

IV

A final word about issues we have not decided. We are not unaware of the threat to privacy implicit in the accumulation of vast amounts of personal information in computerized data banks or other massive government files. [Footnote.] The collection of taxes, the distribution of welfare and social security benefits, the supervision of public health, the direction of our Armed Forces, and the enforcement of the criminal laws all require the orderly preservation of great quantities of information, much of which is personal in character and potentially embarrassing or harmful if disclosed. The right to collect and use such data for public purposes is typically accompanied by a concomitant statutory or regulatory duty to avoid unwarranted disclosures. Recognizing that in some circumstances that duty arguably has its roots in the Constitution, nevertheless New York's statutory scheme, and its implementing administrative procedures, evidence a proper concern with, and protection of, the individual's interest in privacy. We therefore need not, and do not, decide any question which might be presented by the unwarranted disclosure of accumulated private data—whether intentional or unintentional —or by a system that did not contain comparable security provisions. We simply hold that this record does not establish an invasion of any right or liberty protected by the Fourteenth Amendment.

Reversed.

BRENNAN, J., concurring.

I write only to express my understanding of the opinion of the Court, which I join.

The New York statute under attack requires doctors to disclose to the State information about prescriptions for certain drugs with a high potential for abuse, and provides for the storage of that information in a central computer file. The Court recognizes that an individual's "interest in avoiding disclosure of personal matters" is an aspect of the right of privacy [citations], but holds that in this case, any such interest has not been seriously enough invaded by the State to require a showing that its program was indispensable to the State's effort to control drug abuse.

The information disclosed by the physician under this program is made available only to a small number of public health officials with a legitimate interest in the information. As the record makes clear, New York has long required doctors to make this information available to its officials on request, and that practice is not challenged here. Such limited reporting requirements in the medical field are familiar [citation] and are not generally regarded as an invasion of privacy. Broad dissemination by state officials of such information, however, would clearly implicate constitutionally protected privacy rights, and would presumably be justified only by compelling state interests. [Citation.]

What is more troubling about this scheme, however, is the central computer storage of the data thus collected. Obviously, as the State argues, collection and storage of data by the State that is in itself legitimate is not rendered unconstitutional simply because new technology makes the State's operations more efficient. However, as the example of the Fourth Amendment shows, the Constitution puts limits not only on the type of information the State may gather, but also on the means it may use to gather it. The central storage and easy accessibility of computerized data vastly increase the potential for abuse of that information, and I am not prepared to say that future developments will not demonstrate the necessity of some curb on such technology.

In this case, as the Court's opinion makes clear, the State's carefully designed program includes numerous safeguards intended to forestall the danger of indiscriminate disclosure. Given this serious and, so far as the record shows, successful effort to prevent abuse and limit access to the personal information at issue, I cannot say that the statute's provisions for computer storage, on their face, amount to a deprivation of constitutionally protected privacy interests, any more than the more traditional reporting provisions.

In the absence of such a deprivation, the State was not required to prove that the challenged statute is absolutely necessary to its attempt to control drug abuse. Of course, a statute that did effect such a deprivation would only be consistent with the Constitution if it were necessary to promote a compelling state interest. [Citations.]

VOLKMAN v. MILLER

52 A.D.2d 146, 383 N.Y.S.2d 95
*(Supreme Court, Appellate Division, Third
Department, May 13, 1976.)*

KOREMAN, P. J.

* * *

The plaintiffs, John Doe, Robert Roe, and
Jane Anonymous (names being fictitious), are
out-patients at the Tremont Crisis Center in
New York City. Plaintiffs Volkman, Snyder
and Dunn are medical doctors enrolled in a
psychiatric residency program at the Tremont
Crisis Center, and plaintiff Felix is a social
worker and administers psychiatric therapy
at that center. The Tremont Crisis Center is
a part of the Bronx State Hospital which is a
facility of the New York State Department of
Mental Hygiene.

The action arises out of the use of a certain
system or procedure established by the Department of Mental Hygiene which requires
departmental personnel to enter information
on forms on all out-patients and to send that
information to Albany to be recorded and stored
in a central computer. The patient's name and
other identifying data is required to be entered on the form as well as a description of
the illness and a diagnosis. In the action,
plaintiffs seek a declaration that the use of
such a centralized computerized system, without adequate safeguards, is violative of section 15.13 of the Mental Hygiene Law, the
doctor-patient privilege [citation], and plaintiffs' constitutional right to privacy. The continued use of such system is sought to be enjoined, and the information already acquired
under the system is sought to be destroyed.
Special Term granted defendants' motion for
summary judgment and dismissed the complaint. This appeal ensued. Plaintiffs contend
that triable issues of fact exist and that these
facts lie within the exclusive control of the
defendants, and, for that reason, urge that
they are entitled to discovery of such facts.

* * *

The question presented on this appeal is
whether summary judgment should have been
granted to the defendants. Basically, complaint is made in this action concerning the
maintenance and keeping by a department of
State government of a central index and storage center of its own records. Plaintiffs are
patients of an out-patient facility of the Department of Mental Hygiene, and members of
the department's medical staff. The complaint
alleges in a conclusory manner that the requirement that the doctors at out-patient psychiatric clinics report information concerning
their patients to include their names and other
identifying data to a central computerized
storage facility is an intrusion upon the constitutional rights of the patients as well as of
the members of defendants' staff. Specifically,
the right of privacy, the patient-physician
privilege, and the right of staff personnel to
practice their profession are alleged to be violated by defendants in the use of the procedure in question.

On this record, it is clear that a defense to
the action was established sufficiently to warrant the court at Special Term, as a matter
of law, in directing judgment in favor of the
defendants. [Citation.] We conclude from the
evidentiary matter submitted in support of
defendants' motion that plaintiffs' cause of action, as alleged, is without merit. In opposition to the motion, plaintiffs have submitted
only an affidavit of their attorney which sets
forth merely arguments without any factual
support of the allegations in the complaint.
Nor have plaintiffs demonstrated that summary judgment should have been denied for
the reason that the facts necessary to justify
opposition to the motion are within the exclusive knowledge of the defendants. In order to
deny the motion on that ground, it must appear from the affidavits in opposition that such
facts may exist but cannot then be stated. [Ci-
tation.] Only in the event that it is persuaded
that the opposing party's reasons for not being
able presently to oppose the motion are adequate, does the court have broad discretion to
determine the further course of the litigation.
[Citation.]

The record in the instant proceeding is bar-
ren of any proof by affidavit or otherwise that
could serve to defeat the motion, and, therefore, Special Term properly granted summary
judgment to the defendants. However, the
complaint in an action for a declaratory judgment should not be dismissed merely because
the plaintiffs are not entitled to the declaration sought by them, but the rights of the parties should be declared with respect to the

subject matter of the litigation. [Citations.] We conclude that the record keeping system established by defendants concerning out-patients of their facility does not constitute a violation of any constitutional rights of the plaintiffs, nor does it violate any statutory requirement. Accordingly, plaintiffs are not entitled to the relief they seek.

The judgment should be modified, on the law, to the extent of directing judgment be entered in favor of the defendants (1) declaring that the plaintiffs' right of privacy, the patient-physician privilege, and the right of staff personnel to practice their profession have not been violated, and (2) that it is proper for the defendants to keep identifying data and information concerning out-patients in a centralized computerized facility, and, as so modified, affirmed, without costs.

* * *

GREENBLOTT, J. (dissenting).

We respectfully dissent from the majority opinion. While we agree that the present action is properly one for declaratory judgment, we do not believe that the complaint should be dismissed or that the system should be declared constitutional.

The majority grant the defendants' motion for summary judgment dismissing the complaint and hold that the challenged system is constitutional. They have apparently done so on the ground that the plaintiffs' affidavit in opposition lacks sufficient "factual support", and from conclusions drawn "from the evidentiary matter submitted" by the defendant. The majority condemns the affidavit of the plaintiffs' attorney submitted in opposition to the motion for a lack of factual support, notwithstanding the plaintiffs' claim that the facts necessary to justify opposition exist within the exclusive control of the defendants. [Citation.] The majority then proceed, apparently on the basis of the defendants' evidence, to rule the system constitutional. There has been no discovery in this case and the factual record before this court is very sparse.

If it is assumed that there are facts sufficient to oppose summary judgment within the exclusive control of the movants, it is not at all clear how the plaintiffs could provide the "factual support" required by the majority. Admittedly, the statute requires the party op-posing summary judgment to convince the court that these facts may exist [citation], but, it is equally clear that summary judgment must be denied when "the facts presented in the pleadings or on a pretrial motion are not sufficient to permit a declaration for either party. * * *" [Citations.] While the plaintiffs' attorney should have obtained affidavits from the parties personally rather than submitting one based on his own information and belief, it does not appear that any plaintiffs' affidavit could have added any significant factual support in opposition to this motion. If discovery is allowed, as requested by the plaintiffs, it would soon become apparent whether these facts exist and a "just, speedy and inexpensive determination" could be secured. [Citation.]

It is clear that the key to summary judgment is issue finding, not issue determination. [Citations.] The majority, however, conclude "from evidentiary matter submitted" by the defendants, that the cause of action is without merit. In addition to issue determination, this result gives conclusive weight to the defendants' affidavits before the plaintiffs have been allowed discovery. It would be an unquestionable denial of justice to force the plaintiffs to wait until a leak in the allegedly confidential system costs them their jobs or worse, or to dissuade a potential patient from seeking needed psychiatric counseling for fear of this computerized system, merely to afford them a factual basis on which to oppose summary judgment. In the interests of justice the motion for summary judgment should be denied, without prejudice to the defendants raising the question anew after discovery has been completed. [Citations.]

We also dissent from the holding of the majority that the challenged system is constitutional. There are insufficient facts contained in the instant record to determine whether the challenged system would pass constitutional muster. It is impossible at the very outset to determine whether the right of privacy has been infringed upon. A critical factual issue in this regard is whether the plaintiffs' decision-making in their personal life (seeking psychiatric treatment) is affected by the challenged system. [Citation.] There is no evidence in the record on this point other than the allegations in the plaintiffs' complaint that their decision-making is being affected.

The majority cannot contend that the plaintiffs have failed to state a cause of action [citations]; nor can they claim that an order allowing discovery would be unprecedented or unreasonable. [Citation.] The majority proceeds, however, to a declaration on the merits holding that the challenged system is constitutional. Such a holding and its *res judicata* effect denies these plaintiffs one of the most basic rights in our jurisprudence—their right to a day in court. Procedural inadequacies should not be held to prejudice those other citizens of the State who deserve the full protection of their Constitution.

The judgment should be reversed, and the case remitted for discovery.

VOLKMAN v. MILLER

41 N.Y.2d 946, 363 N.E.2d 355,
394 N.Y.S.2d 631
*(Court of Appeals of New York,
March 29, 1977.)*

MEMORANDUM.

Prima facie the State has the power to provide a central facility for the storage and retrieval of statistics involving inpatients or outpatients of institutions and facilities owned or operated by the State. On this record there has been no showing that any supervening right has been invaded. [Citations.]

Accordingly, the order of the Appellate Division, 52 A.D.2d 146, 383 N.Y.S.2d 95, is affirmed, with costs.

BROWN v. JONES

473 F. Supp. 439
*(United States District Court, N. D. Texas,
Wichita Falls Division, March 19, 1979.)*

HILL, D. J.

Came on for consideration defendants' motion to dismiss the above-styled cause of action. Having reviewed the motion and the briefs of the parties, the court is of the opinion that, except for the plaintiffs' action based on defendants' threatened use of the Child Abuse and Neglect Report and Inquiry System ("CANRIS"), the motion should be granted.

With respect to the plaintiffs' request for equitable relief based on defendants' use of CANRIS, the court is of the opinion that such relief should be granted.

I. THE FACTS

Plaintiffs bring this action pursuant to 42 U.S.C. § 1983 and seek injunctive relief with respect to a pending state proceeding which was instituted by defendant Helen Hicks ("Hicks") in order to terminate the parent-child relationship existing between plaintiffs and their child, Bryan J. Brown ("child"). Plaintiff Allen Brown ("Mr. Brown") is the natural father of the child and is married to plaintiff Gennie Brown ("Mrs. Brown"), who is not the natural mother of the child. The plaintiffs also have three other children, who are Shelly Denay Brown, a child of Mr. Brown's prior marriage, and Monica Sue Willey and Dewayne Eugene Castleberry, children of the prior marriages of Mrs. Brown. Defendant Hicks is a child welfare counselor of the Wichita County Family Court Services, and defendant Jim Jones ("Jones") is the supervisor of the child welfare unit. Also named as defendants are the Texas Department of Human Resources and the State of Texas. The guardian ad litem of the child has intervened in this action without objection by the parties. The facts which give rise to this lawsuit are summarized in the following manner and are drawn from the pleadings, the stipulations of fact, and the evidence presented at the preliminary injunction hearing.

On November 16, 1978, the child sustained an injury to his head, a subdural hematoma, and was taken to the Sheppard Air Force Base Hospital Emergency Room. He remained confined in various hospitals until approximately a week before Christmas. On November 16 Hicks filed an original petition for the emergency protection of the child in the juvenile court of Wichita County. This petition requested the court to issue an order appointing the child welfare unit as the temporary managing conservator of the child, and the administrator of the hospital as temporary possessory conservator of the child. The order was granted by the court, but no date was set for a hearing on the matter in such order. At the time Hicks filed the petition, she did not have possession of the child, who was confined in the hospital in critical condition, and she did not deliver the child to the court. The plaintiffs were not formally notified about the petition or order, although there is evidence that Mr. Brown had some knowledge of the proceedings.

On the next day, November 17, Hicks appeared before Judge Temple Driver, a state district court judge, and made an oral, unsworn request for an emergency protection order for the other three children. This request was made without notice to the plaintiffs. Judge Driver orally granted the request. At this time, Hicks did not have possession of the children nor did they appear before the court. A written petition requesting an emergency protection order was later filed by Hicks on the same day, and a written order was also entered by Judge Driver. At approximately 3:00 p.m., a hearing was held in Judge Driver's court regarding the emergency protection orders issued for the four children. William Harris was appointed guardian ad litem for the children by the court. Mr. Brown was present at this hearing, but was not allowed to respond to any of Hicks' representations to the court. Mrs. Brown was not present at the hearing since she was confined in a psychiatric ward at that time.

Thereafter, at Hicks' request, Judge Driver on November 21 entered an order allowing release of the medical records of the child to the appropriate representative of the welfare unit. This order was issued without notice to the plaintiffs and without their consent. On November 22 Hicks filed an original petition affecting the parent-child relationship, wherein she sought to terminate the parent-child relationship existing between plaintiffs and their four children. Plaintiffs were served with this petition, and a hearing was set for November 27. By the date of the hearing, plaintiffs answered and raised their objections to the proceedings. At the hearing plaintiffs were also represented by counsel. At the conclusion of Hicks' presentation of evidence, Judge Driver granted plaintiffs' motion to dismiss with respect to the three children other than the child. Judge Driver also acknowledged that the burden of proof would be upon the state. Hicks testified at the hearing that with respect to this case she would make a report of suspected child abuse into the Texas Department of

Public Welfare's computerized child abuse and neglect reporting system, CANRIS. On November 29 Judge Driver entered a temporary order appointing the supervisor of the Wichita County Child Welfare Unit, Jones, as temporary managing conservator of the child, and Juanita and Marvin Brown, the grandparents of the child, as his temporary possessory conservators. On December 19 plaintiffs filed a motion to appoint themselves as co-possessory conservators and to specify visitation privileges. On January 2, 1979, Judge Driver entered an order setting a date for a final hearing on the matter, February 8. On January 3 Judge Driver entered his findings of fact and conclusions of law regarding the November 27th hearing. He found by clear and convincing evidence and by a preponderance of the evidence that for the protection of the child the orders concerning the possessory and managing conservatorships should be continued during the pendency of the cause.

Plaintiffs filed their federal suit on December 20, 1978, and raised numerous objections to the state proceedings involving the child. More specifically, they contend that their constitutional rights of substantive and procedural due process as well as their right of privacy have been violated by defendants' actions: * * * (j) by Hicks' threatened input of the alleged child abuse information into CANRIS absent or contrary to a judicial determination concerning such information. * * * The defendants have moved to dismiss on the grounds that under the doctrine of *Younger v. Harris*, 401 U.S. 37, 91 S.Ct. 746, 27 L.Ed.2d 669 (1971), this court should exercise equitable restraint and refrain from interfering with the pending state proceeding regarding plaintiffs and the child.

II. THE SIMS CASE

In *Sims v. State Department of Public Welfare*, 438 F.Supp. 1179 (S.D.Tex.1977), *prob. juris. noted sub. nom., Moore v. Sims*, 439 U.S. 925, 99 S.Ct. 306, 58 L.Ed.2d 317 (1978), a three-judge court considered the constitutionality of the Texas statutes dealing with summary seizure of children who are subjected to suspected child abuse. Similar to the facts in this case, the plaintiff's children in *Sims* had been seized summarily by a case worker for the county child welfare unit. * * *

* * *

* * * Finally, the court in *Sims* also ruled that the use of the computer reporting service, CANRIS, under § 34.08, absent a judicial determination of abuse or neglect, was an unconstitutional application of that provision.

* * *

IV CANRIS

The last problem to be faced by this court is deciding whether the *Younger* doctrine should be inapplicable in light of plaintiffs' constitutional objections to the use of CANRIS, the child abuse computer reporting system. Unlike plaintiffs' other constitutional challenges, this claim probably cannot be raised in the normal course of the pending state court proceeding since it would not have any relevant bearing on the issues presented to the state trial court. The only certain manner in which the plaintiffs could raise their argument concerning CANRIS would be by way of counterclaim. One seeking redress, however, under § 1983 for deprivation of federal rights need not initiate state proceedings. [Citations.] Another way to argue the point is by stating that the action of the state is multifaceted and only certain parts of that action are "pending" before a state court, as the court in *Sims* did. *Sims* refused to abstain from considering one part of the statutory scheme without considering it in its entirety. Somewhat to the contrary, this court finds under the facts of this case the more appropriate action to be that of deciding the issue presented by the state administrative "action" in using CANRIS and abstaining from interference with the pending state proceeding. [Citation.] The situation is not one where the plaintiff has two constitutional claims, both of which would serve as a basis for federal injunctive relief against a state judicial proceeding, and only one of which can be presented in that state proceeding. Moreover, plaintiffs in their complaint have requested a separate form of relief for defendant Hicks' threatened input of information into CANRIS. Therefore, in light of principles of comity and federalism, the court will decide only those issues raised by the potential or actual use of CANRIS.

At the hearing held in this court, defendant

Hicks, in her testimony, indicated that she had entered information into CANRIS with respect to the suspected abuse of the plaintiffs' children. Before the November 27th hearing, this information was "sanitized," that is, the date [sic] simply reflected the number of children involved, the dates of the alleged abuse, etc., without identifying who allegedly abused the children. After the hearing, Hicks entered a report into CANRIS which stated that the suspected abuse to the child had been validated and gave identifying information concerning the plaintiffs. Apparently, after the state court's dismissal of the action which involved the other three children, Hicks did not make a similar report to CANRIS regarding those children.

In *Sims*, the court found a violation of the parents' rights of due process and privacy whenever the state entered a "validated" report into CANRIS without a judicial determination as to the existence of the abuse or neglect. [Citation.] Obviously, defendant Hicks believed that the order entered on November 29, 1978, was such a judicial determination. The court cannot agree with this conclusion. First, a reading of the state court's findings of fact and conclusions of law does not indicate that the abuse of the child by the plaintiffs has been established. Second, even assuming a judicial determination has been made, such determination is only temporary. No compelling reason can be found for making this type of report into CANRIS absent a final judicial determination on the merits. [Footnote.] Accordingly, the court holds that defendant Hicks should be enjoined from making any report into CANRIS which in any way identifies the plaintiffs as child abusers, and defendants are ordered to immediately remove all such information which is now stored in CANRIS.

* * *

REYNAUD v. SUPERIOR COURT

138 Cal.App.3d 1, 187 Cal.Rptr. 360
(Court of Appeal, First District, Division 2, Dec. 13, 1982.)

SMITH, A. J.

Raymond Lucien Reynaud, M.D., a psychiatrist enrolled as a provider of publicly-funded health services under California's Medi-Cal statute [citation] is accused by information of grand theft [citation] and of 10 counts of presenting false Medi-Cal claims. [Citation.] The evidence introduced against him at preliminary examination included 10 of Reynaud's claims for services to named patients together with related cancelled checks, explanations of benefits and computer compilations, and admissions cards for the patients at the care facilities in which the patients were housed. In the Superior Court Reynaud moved under Penal Code section 1538.5 to suppress these records as evidence. His motion was denied and he seeks review of the denial by petition for a writ of mandate. We issued the alternative writ. At our request the parties have submitted further briefing on issues germane to the propriety of writ review. We conclude that insofar as predicated on search and seizure grounds Reynaud's suppression motion was properly denied. We further conclude that Reynaud has not established that this is a proper case for writ review, at this stage, of his separately argued contentions that use of the records in evidence would violate both his patients' constitutional rights of privacy [citation] and their statutory psychotherapist-patient privileges. [Citation.] Accordingly, we deny the peremptory writ and discharge the alternative writ. Because the privacy and privilege issues are likely to arise in further trial proceedings and have been argued at some length by the parties, we also briefly state our views on the merits of these issues. [Citation.]

Reynaud had filed claims with Medi-Cal for extensive psychiatric services to patients who qualified for Medi-Cal assistance. The patients were developmentally disabled persons who were housed in privately-owned care facilities in the San Jose area under the general supervision of the California Department of Developmental Services. Reynaud filed his claims with a private corporation, Blue Shield, which at the relevant time was a claims processing agent for the state under the authority of the Medi-Cal statute. In accordance with the statute and administrative regulations [citation], each claim disclosed the patient's name, the type of medical services for which the claim was made, dates of service, relevant diagnosis, and certain other information.

Checks (with attached explanations of benefits) were sent to Reynaud by Blue Shield in payment (ultimately from state funds) of these claims; and each claim and its disposition were recorded on a computer compilation referred to as a "UM–150."

In June, 1979, an investigator in the California Attorney General's Medi-Cal Fraud Unit received from a psychiatric social worker in the Department of Developmental Services a complaint that Reynaud had received a Medi-Cal "sticker" (evidence of a patient's eligibility for Medi-Cal) for a patient who was not present at the group session for which Reynaud was collecting stickers. An investigation was initiated in the course of which the Fraud Unit investigators obtained from Blue Shield, by informal request under the terms of the state's contract with Blue Shield and without patient consents or any kind of court order or process, copies of 10 of Reynaud's claims together with related checks, explanations of benefits, and UM–150s. The investigators also inspected patient indices in the possession of the Department of Developmental Services, primarily to help synthesize other information they had received. On the basis of these materials and extensive additional investigation including surveillance of Reynaud over a long period, the state brought felony charges of theft and presenting false Medi-Cal claims against Reynaud.

In the course of the lengthy preliminary examination of these charges, a manager of one of the care facilities, at the request of a Fraud Unit investigator but without subpoena or warrant, brought with her to the hearing several patient "admission cards" each of which identified a patient and gave his or her birthdate, social security number, telephone contact, next of kin, doctor, psychiatrist, dentist, date of admission, burial plan, and other information.

These cards, and the materials retrieved from Blue Shield, were admitted in evidence over objection at the preliminary examination. Reynaud raised a privacy objection to the cards but objected to the Blue Shield records only on relevance and foundational grounds. Reynaud was held to answer.

Reynaud moved in the Superior Court to suppress "all evidence seized and observations made as a result of: (1) unlawful surveillances; and (2) inspection and seizure of records." As developed at the subsequent hearings, his theory was that the surveillances had been rendered unlawful by the asserted impropriety of the antecedent "seizures" of records. In the course of the suppression proceedings Reynaud apparently narrowed his motion to address only the "seizures" of the Blue Shield records, the information on the Department of Developmental Services cards, and the index cards from the care facilities. The motion was denied.

In this court Reynaud focuses primarily on the Blue Shield records and does not renew his contentions with respect to the Department of Developmental Services cards.

* * *

I. PRIVACY

Reynaud contends that the Fraud Unit improperly infringed his patients' inalienable constitutional right of privacy under article I, section 1, of the California Constitution. He argues that the privacy clause "contemplates notice and an opportunity for an adversary hearing at which the opposing interests can be weighed and any compell[ed] disclosure can be narrowly limited" and that for want of such a hearing and a properly drawn subpoena the Fraud Unit investigators obtained the records—in this instance apparently referring exclusively to the Blue Shield records—in violation of the constitutional privacy provision.

We have recognized a nexus between the confidentiality of information derived from psychotherapist-patient communications and the constitutional right of privacy. [Citations.] While the right of privacy is not absolute, it is well established that the propriety of any governmental intrusion upon the right will depend upon a showing that the intrusion was justified by a state need which was compelling not only in the abstract but also when weighed against the privacy rights of the individual and that the scope of the intrusion was no greater than could be justified by the state's need in all the circumstances. [Citations.] The crux of Reynaud's contention is that the Fraud Unit was required to obtain a judicial determination of the propriety of the proposed intrusion at a noticed hearing before it inspected or copied the Blue Shield records.

Generalized, Reynaud's rule would require that whenever the state's authority is to be invoked to obtain information in arguable derogation of an individual's privacy rights, the privacy issues should be fully litigated, with notice to all interested parties, in advance. The undeniable significance of the concept of personal privacy lends philosophical appeal to such a rule, but the rule's breadth and inflexibility would in many applications create practical problems disproportionate to its abstract desirability. The scope of the privacy clause is potentially enormous and the variety of circumstances in which it might be invoked is essentially infinite. To require a noticed preliminary judicial determination whenever privacy rights are arguably involved would severely, and in our view unnecessarily, restrict the state's capacity to conduct legitimate inquiries. Administration of the privacy clause, like the right of privacy itself, should take adequate account of all competing interests in the circumstances of each case.

In general, the state, or a private proponent who invokes the state's authority by judicial process or otherwise, should (whenever individual privacy rights can reasonably be perceived to be involved) make a showing of predominate state need and sufficiently circumscribed means, in a form susceptible to judicial review, before disclosure is compelled whenever reasonably possible and as soon as reasonably possible in any event. The proponent should also obtain an advance judicial determination of the propriety of the inquiry whenever it is reasonable and practical to do so. The proponent should notify the individual of the proposed or accomplished incursion upon his privacy rights whenever and as soon as reasonably and practicably possible. The determination of what is reasonable and practical should be gauged by the circumstances of each case as it arises and should take into account not only the interests of the parties but also the availability and sufficiency of existing procedures.

Thus, in civil litigation the Discovery Act already provides means by which notice must be given, and privacy issues may be fully litigated, before court process to compel discovery will issue. [Citations.] In proceedings in which a state administrative agency is empowered to issue its own subpoenas it is enough that the state incorporate into the subpoena declaration a showing on the privacy issues sufficient to sustain the state's position upon subsequent judicial review. [Citation.] In situations to which search warrant requirements apply, privacy issues are necessarily involved in the advance showing required to be made, in the magistrate's decision to issue the warrant, and in the prompt and detailed subsequent judicial review already provided for by law. [Citation.] Indeed, the Legislature has added to the search warrant provisions a procedure specially designed to protect individual privacy rights where warrants issue for documents particularly likely to contain information subject to those rights. [Citations.]

In the areas of criminal and disciplinary investigation, it has not been the rule that a noticed hearing must be had before disclosure is compelled. The reason seems plain. The state's legitimate interest in obtaining full and accurate information would be unduly compromised, in such situations, by affording direct or indirect advance notice to an inculpated custodian who might be motivated to destroy, conceal, or alter the evidence. These considerations, we take it, led the Legislature to make an exception to the special search warrant procedure referred to above in instances in which the custodian is "reasonably suspected of engaging or having engaged in criminal activity related to the documentary evidence. * * *" [Citation.]

In the circumstances of this action no reasonable occasion for an advance showing concerning, or determination of, patients' privacy rights arose. The Blue Shield records were essentially internal to the state and were based on information disclosed to the state for legitimate purposes. It would have been unreasonable to have required the state to make a formal showing or to seek formal adjudication, or even to perceive a genuine privacy issue, before reviewing its own records for the very purposes for which those records were compiled. We note with approval another court's conclusion that this kind of essentially internal agency investigation of possible fraud on the public "is not the stuff out of which a cause of action for violation of right of privacy grows." [Citation.] The admission cards were brought to court, and first disclosed, in response to informal request. The pending court

proceedings afforded ample opportunity for adjudication.

II. PRIVILEGE

If properly invoked in a proceeding in which testimony can be compelled [citation], the psychotherapist-patient privilege applies to any "confidential communication between patient and psychotherapist. * * *" [Citation.] "Confidential communication" includes a "diagnosis made and the advice given by the psychotherapist" [citation], and we have held that even the identity of the patient may (because of its tendency to disclose, by association with the psychotherapist, the nature of the patient's ailment) come within the privilege. [Citation.] As described in the record the Blue Shield documents reflect identification and diagnostic conclusions necessarily based on presumably confidential [citation] psychotherapist-patient communications and, thus, would be subject to the privilege unless application of the privilege has been waived or is otherwise barred. The holder of the privilege is the patient (or his guardian, conservator, or personal representative), and only he (or they) may waive it. [Citation.] So far as the record shows no patient has either asserted or waived the privilege in this action.

Reynaud did not assert the privilege at the preliminary examination, where the Blue Shield documents were received in evidence over other objections. He raised the privilege in the superior court, and raises it again in this court, as a predicate for his contention that the Blue Shield documents were improperly "seized", but of course at the time the Fraud Unit obtained the documents there was no pending "proceeding" in which the evidentiary privilege could properly have been invoked. The privilege would not, strictly speaking, have applied to that preliminary investigation. We assume, however, that Reynaud will again seek to invoke the privilege at some stage of the trial court proceedings.

Reynaud asserts that he invokes the privilege because he is required to do so by Evidence Code section 1015. But in our view the circumstances that Reynaud would invoke the privilege in criminal proceedings pending against him and that the privilege would have the effect of excluding evidence which would tend to incriminate him, not only release him from his statutory duty but bar him from asserting the privilege. Absent his patients, only Reynaud could say whether the Blue Shield documents (based on information he had communicated to Blue Shield) embodied the substance of confidential communications between his patients and himself. Indeed it is the state's position, necessarily, that at least some of the information Reynaud communicated to Blue Shield was false and had originated with Reynaud himself for the purpose of defrauding Medi-Cal. It would be wholly untenable to require that the trial court rely on Reynaud's statement of the pertinent facts in these circumstances.

A determination that Reynaud should not be authorized to claim the privilege would evoke the statutory requirement that "[t]he presiding officer, on his own motion or on the motion of any party, shall exclude information that is subject to a claim of privilege under [the privilege statutes] if: (1) the person from whom the information is sought is not a person authorized to claim the privilege; and (2) there is no party to the proceeding who is a person authorized to claim the privilege." [Citation.] Although a broad suggestion that circumstances to which this provision would apply vest the court with *discretion* to "protect an absentee holder of the privilege who has not waived it" [citation] appears to conflict with the mandatory language of the provision and has been cogently criticized [citation] and subsequently disregarded [citation], it remains proper for the court to make a preliminary determination whether the information in issue "is subject to a claim of privilege." It is our view that in the circumstances of record, a trial court could properly conclude that a Medi-Cal patient could be deemed to know that for the limited purpose of obtaining public payment for his treatment certain narrowly-circumscribed information concerning him must be communicated to the state and be and remain subject to state audit, that to that extent and for that purpose the patient did not intend his communications to be confidential in the sense requisite to the privilege, and that, therefore, the Blue Shield documents would not in the circumstances be subject to the psychiatrist-patient privilege.

For further proceedings in this action, a more practical alternative suggests itself:

Surely the state should be able to ascertain from the patients, or their personal representatives, whether they would be willing to waive the privilege for the narrow purposes of this action and (if so) to obtain such waivers in appropriate form.

* * *

The peremptory writ is denied. The alternative writ is discharged.

UNITED STATES v. MACKEY

387 F. Supp. 1121
(United States District Court, D. Nevada, Jan. 21, 1975.)

CLARY, S. D. J.

A federal grand jury in the District of Nevada returned a two-count indictment against the defendant, James Owen Mackey, charging him with possession of an unregistered firearm in violation of 26 U.S.C. §§ 5861(c), (d) and 5871. On January 10, 1975 a hearing was held on defendant's motion to suppress evidence seized from him. There is no substantial disagreement as to the events which occurred, and only one question is presented for resolution.

On the evening of October 24, 1974, defendant was attempting to "thumb a ride" along Interstate 15 in an area patrolled by the North Las Vegas Police Department. He was approached by Officers Lathan and Judd who requested that he identify himself. In response, defendant produced a California driver's license. The officers checked the defendant through the National Crime Information Center (NCIC) and learned through their dispatcher that he was wanted in Monterey, California for probation violation. Relying on this information, the officers arrested the defendant and took him to the police station.

Although it was not the usual practice, Officer Judd made a telephone call to the Monterey Police Department to verify defendant's contention that the warrant was no longer outstanding. The Monterey Police Department indicated that it could not verify the warrant at that time because the issuing agency was unknown.[1] Officer Judd then testified that his supervisor directed him to make no further calls, but to follow the usual procedure of sending teletype messages requesting verification of the warrant. The usual procedure also called for the individual in custody to be booked prior to sending the teletypes because of the time factor involved in receiving a reply.

Summarizing the facts in this case as noted above, it clearly appears:

1. On the 24th day of October 1974, defendant as well as other pedestrians were seeking a ride (hitchhiking) along I–15 in the North Las Vegas area and among those interviewed by the North Las Vegas Police was defendant, James Owen Mackey.

2. That he showed them his identification (California driver's license).

3. That his name and description was put on the NCIC computer and the return answer showed an outstanding fugitive warrant for violation of probation out of Monterey, California.

4. That without this false and erroneous information, the officer testified he would not have detained him and would have sent him on his way.

5. That the false and erroneous information furnished by NCIC was the sole cause of his arrest.

6. That the information received was false in that the warrant had been complied with some five months previous to the incident of arrest in this case.

During the booking process, a .12 gauge Taiya Juki Japanese shotgun was found in a duffle bag in defendant's possession. Possession of this weapon is the basis of the federal charges and the evidence which defendant seeks to suppress.

* * *

Defendant's sole contention for excluding the shotgun from evidence is that the NCIC information was inaccurate, and had been inaccurate for five months, when the arrest was

made. The arrest, he argues, was therefore illegal. No challenge has been raised as to the conduct of the officers after the arrest itself. The parties have so stipulated and no evidence to support a contrary position was introduced. Therefore, events subsequent to the arrest may be disregarded in reaching a decision. Assuming, without deciding, for the purpose of this motion that an accurate NCIC report or "hit" is sufficient to establish probable cause for arrest, must evidence otherwise admissible be suppressed because it was seized subsequent to an arrest based solely on NCIC information[2] which was inaccurate when relayed to the arresting officers and which had been so for five months?

After careful consideration of the testimony, arguments of counsel and written briefs, this Court is of the opinion that the arrest of the defendant under the circumstances described constituted a denial of due process of law. The motion to suppress must be granted.

The NCIC is an outgrowth of the Attorney General's congressionally mandated obligation to "acquire, collect, classify, and preserve identification, criminal identification, crime, and other records" and to exchange such information with "authorized officials" on both the federal and state level. [Footnote.] Under the auspices of the Federal Bureau of Investigation, NCIC is to provide computerized information to law enforcement agencies in eight categories including outstanding warrants, stolen vehicles and certain identifiable stolen property. [Footnote.] The information gathered and stored in the computer is not the "property" of the FBI, but of the agencies which submit it originally. [Citations.] This disclaimer of federal "ownership," as well as the need for accuracy, has also been made in a policy statement approved by the NCIC Advisory Policy Board.

In a national system, although individual users are responsible for the accuracy, validity, and completeness of their record entries and their action decisions on positive responses to inquir-

---

1. The issuing agency could have been the Monterey Police Department, The Monterey Park Police or the Monterey Sheriff's Office. The Monterey Police Department reported only that they had no outstanding warrant for the defendant.

2. The Government's contention that the defendant could

have been arrested for hitchhiking, a violation of N.R.S. 484.331, is irrelevant since that was not the offense for which he was arrested. Defendant's exhibit C, the booking sheet, indicates that defendant was initially charged with "Prob. Violation (NCIC)." Additional charges were brought only after the discovery of the shotgun.

ies, more stringent controls with respect to system discipline are required. [Footnote.]

Further, under the heading of Steps to Assure Accuracy of Stored Information, the policy statement provides:

A. The FBI/NCIC and state control terminal agencies will make continuous checks on records being entered in the system to assure system standards and criteria are being met.

B. Control terminal agencies shall adopt a careful and permanent program of data verification including:

1. Systematic audits conducted to insure that files have been regularly and accurately updated.

2. Where errors or points of incompleteness are detected the control terminal shall take immediate action to correct or complete the NCIC record as well as its own state record.[6]

This aspect of the FBI's operation, "storage" of criminal records and information, has been the subject of recent, and potentially far reaching, litigation. In this still nebulous area of the law, some solid areas have nevertheless emerged. The "passive recipient" theory advanced by the government for FBI record keeping has been rejected. [Citations.] Further, while not a guarantor of the absolute accuracy of all its records, the FBI has some duty to insure that the information which it disseminates is accurate [footnote] [citation], and it must remove from its criminal files "arrest records" which the contributing agency has advised it were not reflective of legal arrests. [Citation.]

In Menard v. Mitchell, 139 U.S.App. D.C. 113, 430 F.2d 486 (1970) (*Menard I*), Chief Judge Bazelon noted the consequences of having an "arrest record" with the FBI even if no conviction results:

Information denominated a record of arrests, if it becomes known, may subject an individual to serious difficulties. Even if no direct economic loss is involved, the injury to an individual's reputation may be substantial. Economic losses themselves may be both direct and serious. Opportunities for schooling, employment, or professional licenses may be restricted or non-existent as a consequence of the mere fact of an arrest, even if followed by acquittal or complete

exoneration of the charges involved. An arrest record may be used by the police in determinating whether subsequently to arrest the individual concerned, or whether to exercise their discretion to bring formal charges against an individual already arrested. Arrest records have been used in deciding whether to allow a defendant to present his story without impeachment by prior convictions, and as a basis for denying release prior to trial or an appeal; or they may be considered by a judge in determining the sentence to be given a convicted offender. *Id.* at 490–491 (footnotes omitted).

While analogous to a degree to the cases previously noted, the instant case has significant distinguishing features. First, this is a criminal case with criminal penalties awaiting the defendant if he is convicted. [Footnote.] Second, NCIC is a different type of storage system than the general Identification Division. NCIC appears designed for rapid reference to specific current information while the Identification Division, containing fingerprint and arrest records, is to store information more static in nature. Third, the defendant seeks to suppress evidence obtained as a result of information in the system rather than to expunge the information itself. Finally, the consequences of the dissemination of inaccurate information in this case are more serious than those listed by Chief Judge Bazelon in *Menard I*.

Because of the inaccurate listing in the NCIC computer, defendant was a "marked man" for the five months prior to his arrest, and had this particular identification check not occurred, he would have continued in this status into the indefinite future. At any time, as demonstrated by this situation, a routine check by the police could well result in defendant's arrest, booking, search and detention. Further, there is no evidence to suggest that defendant would not continue to be subject to such humiliation until Monterey police officials cleared the computer of the warrant. [Citation.] Moreover, this could happen anywhere in the United States where law enforcement officers had access to NCIC information. Defendant was subject to being deprived of his liberty at any time and without any legal basis.

---

6. [Citation.] Further, NCIC sends printouts to each contributing agency to verify the accuracy of data on file.

In the case of wanted persons, these printouts are sent every 90 days. [Citation.]

In the words of the District of Columbia court, " * * * there is limit beyond which the government may not tread in devising classifications that lump the innocent with the guilty." [Citation.] In this instance that limit has surely been passed. What was said of the FBI's Identification Division appears true also in the case of NCIC:

> There are no controls on the accuracy of information submitted by the contributing agencies. The Bureau exercises little supervision and control over contributing agency uses of the records the FBI disseminates. We are not now called upon to evaluate these practices of the FBI. However, this case does call upon us to take into account that the FBI's function of maintaining and disseminating criminal identification records and files carries with it as a corollary the responsibility to discharge this function reliably and responsibly and without unnecessary harm to individuals whose rights have been invaded. The FBI cannot take the position that it is a mere passive recipient of records received from others, when it in fact energizes those records by maintaining a system of criminal files and disseminating the criminal records widely, acting in effect as a step-up transformer that puts into the system a capacity for both good and harm. Menard v. Saxbe, 162 U.S.App.D.C. 284, 498 F.2d 1017, 1026 (1974) (footnotes omitted).

The Court finds that a computer inaccuracy of this nature and duration, even if unintended, amounted to a capricious disregard for the rights of the defendant as a citizen of the United States. The evidence compels a finding that the government's action was equivalent to an arbitrary arrest, and that an arrest on this basis deprived defendant of his liberty without due process of law.[9] Once the warrant was satisfied, five months before defendant's arrest, there no longer existed any basis for his detention, and the Government may not now profit by its own lack of responsibility.

This raises the question of the relief to which the defendant may be entitled; a question already answered by the Supreme Court:

> Our decisions recognize no exception to the rule that illegally seized evidence is inadmissible at trial, however relevant and trustworthy the seized evidence may be as an item of proof. Davis

v. Mississippi, 394 U.S. 721, 724, 89 S.Ct. 1394, 1396, 22 L.Ed.2d 676 (1969).

The fact that state officials, on information supplied by NCIC, made the actual arrest and search in no way insulates the federal government. [Citation.]

To conclude, it is not necessary to go beyond the specific facts of this case in order to afford the defendant relief. Therefore, no attempt is made to determine precisely what the responsibility of the United States Government is for the information lodged in NCIC and what specific steps must be taken to insure an acceptable degree of accuracy. The Court has determined, however, that this type of infringement of the rights of the defendant, perpetrated primarily with the assistance of a mindless automation controlled by the government, cannot be tolerated. All evidence seized as a result of defendant's arrest must be suppressed.

JAFFESS v. SECRETARY, DEPARTMENT OF HEALTH, EDUCATION AND WELFARE
393 F. Supp. 626
(United States District Court, S.D. New York, May 6, 1975.)

CANNELLA, D. J.

* * *

The plaintiff, Ira G. Jaffess, is a World War II Navy veteran who has received a disability benefits pension from the Veterans Administration (VA) since 1943. Such benefits are awarded pursuant to 38 U.S.C. § 521 and are based upon the payments formula contained therein. Under the statute, the amount of benefits payable varies depending upon the veteran's annual income from other sources, including income received under the Social Security Act, 38 U.S.C. § 503. A veteran who receives § 521 benefits is obligated by law to report changes in his annual income to the VA. [Citations.] The applicable regulation, 38 CFR § 3.660(a), declares, *inter alia*, that:

---

9. The Court is cognizant of the Fourth Amendment basis for the arguments of counsel, but finds it unnecessary to focus on this line of analysis in order to reach

a decision. Therefore, there is no need to resolve the issue of the status of NCIC as "reliable informant" so as to justify a warrantless arrest and search.

A veteran * * * who is receiving pension * * * must notify the Veterans Administration of any material change or expected change in his income or other circumstances which would affect his entitlement to receive, or the rate of, the benefit being paid. Such notice must be furnished when he acquires knowledge that he will begin to receive additional income at a rate which if continued will cause his income to exceed the income limitation or increment applicable to the rate of the benefit being paid or when his marital or dependency status changes.

In the more recent past, Jaffess has also been receiving disability benefits from the Social Security Administration (SSA), but he has not reported such payments to the VA as required by law. Thus, in effect, he has received in recent years government benefits beyond those to which he was lawfully entitled.

On January 6, 1975, Jaffess received notice from the VA that his benefits under § 521 would be reduced from $143.00 to $6.32 per month because his expected income for 1975 included $2,913 in social security benefits. [Reference.] Such adjustment apparently resulted from a computer comparison of persons who received § 521 benefits with those receiving social security benefits. This survey was performed "in order to locate persons who have failed to report their social security benefits to the VA as required by law," so that an appropriate adjustment of VA benefits could be made. [Citation.] Jaffess, it appears, is exactly the sort of person this computer check was designed to discover.

Given this drastic reduction in his benefits, Jaffess commenced the instant suit to recover $50,000 in damages. His complaint is premised upon the Privacy Act of 1974 [citation], the Freedom of Information Act, as amended, 5 U.S.C. § 552, as well as the constitutionally secured right of privacy. For the reasons which we discuss below, we find each of these grounds to be an insufficient predicate for the relief now sought.

The Privacy Act of 1974 can not serve as basis for the present claim because such law, insofar as it is here relevant, does not become effective until 270 days after December 31, 1974, or September 27th of this year. Similarly, the provisions of the Freedom of Information Act are unavailing to plaintiff as he has failed to exhaust the administrative remedies specified thereunder prior to commencing this action. 5 U.S.C. § 552(a)(6)(C).

Thus, plaintiff's claim resolves itself into one purportedly arising under the right of privacy guaranteed to citizens by the Constitution. In this regard, certain other provisions of the law are to be noted. 42 U.S.C. § 1306(a) prohibits the disclosure of matters concerning social security benefits which are contained in the Department of Health, Education and Welfare files, except in a fashion prescribed by appropriate regulations. The statute was enacted to preserve the privacy of social security recipients and the Secretary, in compliance with the statutory grant, has promulgated certain regulations which both limit the disclosure of information and advance legitimate governmental purposes. [Citation.] With regard to the precise factual contours of this case, 20 CFR § 401.3(f) is particularly pertinent. That regulation states, *inter alia*:

> Disclosure of any such file, record, report, or other paper, or information, is hereby authorized in the following cases and for the following purposes:
>
>   * * *
>
> (f) To any officer or employee of an agency of the Federal Government lawfully charged with the administration of a law providing for public assistance, or work relief, or pension, or retirement, or other benefit payments, only for the purpose of the proper administration of such law, or of the Social Security Act. * * *

Thus, the disclosure of Jaffess' social security benefits to the VA was clearly lawful under the regulation in view of the fact that the VA is obligated by statute to take such payments into account in its determination of benefits under 38 U.S.C. § 521. [Citation.]

This does not end the matter, however, as we recognize that compliance with these statutory and regulatory dictates can not justify conduct which has deprived Jaffess of constitutionally secured privacy rights. However, the short answer to plaintiff's privacy claim is that despite the recognition which courts have given to a constitutional right of privacy in other contexts, *i.e.*, the most intimate phases of one's personal life [citations], the present thrust of the decisional law does not include within its compass the right of an individual to prevent disclosure by one governmental agency to another of matters obtained in the course of the transmitting agency's regular functions. [Citations.] Our research reveals no case in which a right of privacy has been recognized in circumstances such as these.

What we have said *supra* is not intended to minimize the problems presented by the interagency transfer of information within the federal government. Indeed, such activities are the subject of much of the commentary *supra* and fashioning the proper scope of such disclosure was the motivating force behind the newly enacted privacy legislation. [Citation.] Nor do we suggest that a constitutional right of privacy might not be found to exist and appropriate relief granted in instances where the government is possessed of highly personal and confidential information which has been given under compulsion of law and with an expectation of privacy and where the disclosure of such information is unnecessary for the advancement or inconsistent with the fundamental purposes for which the data was obtained. Rather, we hold only that, on the facts of this case, Mr. Jaffess has not been deprived of any constitutionally secured privacy right.

One further thought comes to mind. We recognize that plaintiff will suffer a great economic loss as the result of the reduction of his VA benefits. Unfortunately, this Court is not the forum in which the proper allocation of federal resources for former servicemen is to be decided, but we are sympathetic with the plight of men, like plaintiff, whose VA benefits are reduced to almost nothing when equally vital social security benefits of less than $3,000 a year are received. We urge that this matter be brought to the attention of the Congress and that our legislators seek out an equitable solution to the problem of providing disabled veterans with adequate economic benefits. [Citation.]

* * *

CHILDRESS v. UNITED STATES

381 A.2d 614

(District of Columbia Court of Appeals, Dec. 15, 1977.)

YEAGLEY, A. J.

At 11:15 on the morning of November 18, 1975, plainclothes officers Herman J. Keels and T. J. Jones of the Metropolitan Police observed appellants Michael Childress and Alvin Martin acting in what they considered a suspicious manner, looking into automobiles and apparently casing a bank in the vicinity of the 4500 block of Wisconsin Avenue, N.W. The officers had been assigned to that area because of a high rate of reported burglaries and larcenies from automobiles parked there.

The officers watched as appellants Childress and Martin met appellant Ezekiel Peebles and codefendant Aubrey Martin. After the four men got into the car the officers noted its license number and radioed in for a "tag check." As the officers followed appellants' vehicle in an unmarked car, the police dispatcher responded that there were four traffic warrants outstanding for Childress, the car's owner. The officers lost track of appellants' vehicle in traffic, but relayed the information they had received to similarly assigned plainclothes officers Timothy Leach and Charles Madison.

Shortly after noon, both groups of officers spotted appellants' car as it turned into the campus of Washington Technical Institute in the 4200 block of Connecticut Avenue, N.W. They stopped the car and ordered appellants out. In plain view within the now-unoccupied vehicle police observed a bent coat hanger, screwdriver, wire cutters, and a citizens' band radio and tape player from both of which protruded cut wires.

Police told appellant Childress, the driver, that he was being stopped because of outstanding traffic warrants. In the course of the ensuing conversation, police requested and received appellant Childress' permission to open the trunk, in which they found another citizens' band radio with cut wires, bearing the name and Virginia address of another man. Police arrested appellant Childress on the traffic warrants and appellant Martin after a WALES check revealed an unrelated warrant outstanding for him. Appellant Peebles was allowed to go but was later arrested.

On February 9, 1976, the trial court denied appellants' motions to suppress all evidence seized from the car in the course of appellant Childress' arrest. Eleven days later, a jury found appellants guilty of three counts of petit larceny [citation] and one count of destruction of property. [Citation.]

* * * We affirm.

I.

Appellants first assign error to the trial court's finding that the outstanding traffic warrants justified the stop of appellant Childress' vehicle. Appellants contend, and indeed it is undisputed, that on November 14, 1975, appellant Childress had posted collateral for his outstanding traffic warrants. Appellants argue that as a result the warrants were extinguished and did not exist four days later when appellant Childress' vehicle was stopped. Appellants maintain that appellant Childress' arrest was supported only by the officers' belief that warrants were outstanding for him, was unsupported by independent probable cause, and that all evidence seized thereafter should have been suppressed as the fruit of Childress' illegal arrest.

We hold that, under the circumstances here presented, the police officers' good faith reliance on the radio report and the resultant reasonable belief that valid traffic warrants were outstanding provided probable cause to arrest appellant Childress.

This holding is mandated by our decision in *Patterson v. United States*, D.C.App., 301 A.2d 67 (1973), in which we affirmed appellant's conviction and found that his arrest had been based on probable cause despite the police officer's reliance on what turned out to be misinformation. There, the police radio dispatcher incorrectly informed an officer that the car which appellant was driving was still listed on the department's "stolen sheet." Appellant was arrested and an incidental search uncovered an unlicensed revolver for the possession of which appellant was convicted. We upheld the trial court's refusal to suppress the weapon.

At the outset, we reject appellant's contention that there was no probable cause for his arrest. Although the stolen car bearing the dealer tags in question had been recovered earlier on the day of appellant's arrest, and for some unexplained reason, the police records did not accurately reflect that fact, this does not mean that the officer's action, in reliance on these records, was unreasonable. * * *

Officer Nern was mistaken in his belief that appellant was driving a stolen car. However, at the moment of arrest, he clearly had probable cause to believe a crime had been committed and that appellant was the person who had committed it. [*Id.* at 69.]

Appellants direct our attention to *Whitely v. Warden*, 401 U.S. 560, 91 S.Ct. 1031, 28 L.Ed.2d 306 (1971). In that case petitioner had been arrested by an officer who had relied on a police radio bulletin which stated that a warrant existed for petitioner's arrest. After finding that the warrant itself was invalid because it was unsupported by a proper affidavit, the Court reversed petitioner's conviction and rejected the state's argument that the officer's reasonable reliance on the bulletin furnished probable cause and thus legalized the arrest.

Whitely does not control the instant case, however, because the warrant there under examination, unlike those at issue here and in *Patterson*, was void *ab initio*. [Footnote.] As such, we read *Whitely* to stand for the proposition that the prosecution may not bootstrap itself to a legal arrest and resultant conviction by asserting that police relied reasonably on a warrant that never legally existed. Indeed, we so held in *Sanders v. United States*, D.C.App., 339 A.2d 373, 379 (1975). There, appellant was arrested by District of Columbia police officers acting in reliance on a radio report that an Arlington County, Virginia arrest warrant was outstanding for him. Police learned subsequently that the warrant in question was for another man. We upheld appellant's conviction for the unlicensed carrying of a pistol retrieved from him pursuant to his arrest. We distinguished that situation, in which police relied in good faith on mistaken identity, from *Whitely* in which there was "an infirmity inherent in the foundation of the warrant." *Id.* at 379. In the instant case, there was no such infirmity, and the warrants enjoyed unassailable legal existence, at least until November 14, when appellant Childress posted collateral to satisfy them. Administrative delays attendant to the operation of any metropolitan area police department resulted in failure to remove the satisfied warrants from the computerized "active" list before the officers received the radio dispatch on November 18 that the warrants were outstanding.[3] This combination of reasonable administrative delay and reasonable police reliance on misinformation produced by such a delay presents a situation in which acceptance of appellants' position would do nothing to advance the purposes of the exclusionary rule. [Citation.] There is simply no unlawful or improper police conduct here to deter. Accordingly, we affirm the trial court's determination that probable cause existed to arrest appellant Childress.

* * *

TESTA v. WINQUIST

451 F. Supp. 388
(United States District Court,
D. Rhode Island, May 15, 1978.)

PETTINE, C. J.

Third-party defendants Christine Manfredi, Treasurer of the City of Warwick, and Richard Steiner, a Warwick police officer, move to dismiss the action brought by third-party plaintiffs Carl D. Winquist, Lieutenant of the East Providence Police Department and other unnamed officers of that department. The issues briefed by the parties have only a superficial simplicity that masks complicated and controversial questions concerning the scope of both jurisdiction and causes of action in federal court. After careful analysis of all the pertinent issues, the Court has decided to deny the motion to dismiss.

The primary action is brought by plaintiffs Alfred Testa, Manuel daSilva and Tabco, Inc. against officers of the East Providence police force (hereinafter "third-party plaintiffs") for alleged deprivations of constitutional rights secured by the fourth, sixth and fourteenth amendments. Plaintiffs pend state law claims for detention in violation of R.I.G.L. sec. 12–7–1, malicious prosecution, false imprisonment, libel and slander, trespass and malicious destruction of property. Among the many violations alleged, plaintiffs charge that third-party plaintiffs unlawfully detained them on the night of January 31, 1977. Although both plaintiffs Testa and daSilva were detained overnight, only plaintiff Testa was charged with possession of a stolen vehicle. This vehicle was in fact lawfully purchased in September, 1975. At the police station, plaintiffs' attorney produced the certificate of title, but, according to the complaint, Lieutenant Winquist refused to make any inquiry into its authenticity. Subsequently, both plaintiffs spent the night in jail and their vehicle was seized.[1]

Third-party plaintiffs filed their complaint claiming, in essence, contribution or indemnification from third-party defendants for any liability based on this detention. They allege that, upon observation of suspicious activity at plaintiffs' auto body shop, third-party plaintiffs chased and ultimately stopped plaintiffs in their vehicle. Upon failure to produce proof of ownership, third-party plaintiffs ran a check of the vehicle through the National Computer Information Center (NCIC)

---

3. Justifiable administrative delay distinguishes this case from *United States v. Mackey*, 387 F.Supp. 1121 (D.Nev.1975). There the District Court suppressed evidence seized from a defendant who had been arrested in Nevada solely on National Crime Information Center computer information which stated that he was wanted on an arrest warrant in California. In fact, defendant had complied with this warrant five months earlier. The court found

> that a computer inaccuracy *of this nature and duration,* even if unintended, amounted to a capricious disregard for the rights of the defendant as a citizen of the United States. * * * Once the warrant was satisfied, *five months* before defendant's arrest, there no longer existed any basis for his detention, and the Government may not now profit by its own lack of responsibility. [*Id.* at 1125 (emphasis added).]

In the instant case, collateral was posted, and the warrants were thus satisfied, on Friday, November 14. Appellant was arrested on the following Tuesday, November 18. We find that the four-day delay, two days of which

were attributable to the weekend, does not rise to the level of police administrative negligence fatal to the government in *Mackey,*

1. The other violations alleged include failure to accord procedural rights to plaintiffs during their detention, communication to both the Providence police and the press that plaintiffs were operating a "hot car ring", Lieutenant Winquist's false affidavit in support of a search of plaintiffs' auto body shop, and the subsequent arrest of plaintiff daSilva without probable cause for possession of stolen license plates. The charges against daSilva were later dismissed and the warrant quashed.

It is not clear from the complaint whether plaintiffs complain that the arrest of plaintiff Testa, detention of both plaintiffs and their car and Lieutenant Winquist's failure to investigate the authenticity of plaintiffs' certificate of title were all unlawful. Third-party plaintiffs have brought their complaint on the assumption that plaintiffs do so complain. For purposes of this motion to dismiss, the Court assumes the same.

which reported the vehicle stolen out of Warwick, Rhode Island. The officers then called Richard Steiner of the Warwick police department who confirmed that the vehicle was stolen and still unrecovered. Allegedly pursuant to this information, third-party plaintiffs charged plaintiff Testa with possession of a stolen vehicle. It appears from both the original and third-party complaints that the vehicle had in fact been previously stolen but had been recovered by the insurance company and subsequently sold to plaintiff Tabco, Inc. Pursuant to Rule 14(a) of the Federal Rules of Civil Procedure, third-party plaintiffs impleaded Robert Stevenson, the administrator of the Rhode Island Division, National Computer Information Center, and Richard Steiner, the Warwick police officer who confirmed the vehicle's status, for negligent failure to keep current and accurate records, upon which information third-party plaintiffs allegedly relied in detaining or arresting plaintiffs. Third-party plaintiffs also sue Christine S. Manfredi, in her representative capacity as Treasurer of the City of Warwick.

Third-party defendants Manfredi and Steiner bring this motion to dismiss, claiming that * * * the complaint failed to state a claim on the ground that an intentional tortfeasor (third-party plaintiffs) cannot recover against a merely negligent tortfeasor. * * *

I. THIRD-PARTY PLAINTIFFS' RIGHT TO RECOVER AGAINST THIRD-PARTY DEFENDANTS STEVENSON AND STEINER

Although not explicit, third-party plaintiffs base their claim on both a right of contribution, secured by R.I.G.L. sec. 10–6–1, et seq. (1969), and a right of indemnity, recognized by Rhode Island law. [Citation.] The premise of both these claims is that third-party plaintiffs may be held liable to plaintiffs for wrongdoing that was caused in whole or in part by third-party defendants. Any judgment against third-party plaintiffs should be either shared or borne solely by third-party defendants. Necessarily, without liability to plaintiffs, third-party plaintiffs have no right of recovery against third-party defendants, even though plaintiffs may still have valid claims against third-party defendants.

Because of the circular nature of the parties' liability, the initial focus must be on the circumstances under which third-party plaintiffs could be held liable to plaintiffs. If these circumstances in turn could form the basis for liability against third-party defendants, the motion to dismiss for failure to state a claim must be denied. The motion must be denied unless "it appears beyond doubt that the [third-party] plaintiff can prove no set of facts in support of his claim which would entitle him to relief." [Citation.]

It is well established that a policeman is not liable for a warrantless arrest under sec. 1983 or under the common law tort of false arrest, if the arrest was made in good faith and with probable cause. [Citation.] To escape liability, the policeman must establish both that he in fact believed he had probable cause and that this belief was reasonable. [Citations.] Typically, the policeman is shielded from liability if the basis for his belief in probable cause was a mistake in fact, provided the mistake was reasonable. [Citation.] Reasonableness must be judged in the context of the necessity for on-the-spot judgments by the policeman on the street. [Citation.] The standard reflects a proper balance between the constitutional guarantee of freedom from unreasonable seizures and protection of public safety by the arrest of those persons suspected of criminal activity.

Applying these principles to the skeletal outline of the facts alleged in the complaints, the reasonableness of third-party plaintiffs' belief in probable cause at several points in time is crucial. The initial detention was allegedly based on the computer check and third-party-defendant Steiner's confirmation. Absent allegations that the typical police practice was to make further inquiries or that these sources were notoriously inaccurate, reliance on this information as a basis for probable cause, particularly in combination with the alleged results of their surveillance and observation of suspicious activities, appears reasonable. Thus, if third-party plaintiffs' allegations of fact are true, they would probably not be liable to plaintiffs for the initial detention and, as a consequence, would have no claim against third-party defendants for contribution or indemnity. Because a cautious approach to factual determinations is appropriate when considering a motion to dismiss, without more information, the Court is reluctant to find that, as a matter of law, the reliance was reasonable and dismiss third-party plaintiffs' complaint. Such a determination is more appropriately left to the jury, unless, based on affidavits accompanying a summary judgment motion, it is evident there is no justiciable issue. [Citation.]

In addition, the initial detention or arrest is not the only crucial point in time. Plaintiffs claim that third-party plaintiff Winquist failed to make any inquiry into the authenticity of the certificate of title to the vehicle. Assuming the truth of this allegation, it is certainly conceivable that the previously reasonable reliance is stripped of its reasonableness in light of this prima facie evidence of title and the diminished necessity for quick decisions once at the station house. [Citation.] Thus, third-party plaintiffs could be indeed liable to plaintiffs for illegal arrest following presentation of the certificate of title.

Turning now to the intersection of third-party defendants' liability, the Court concludes that the alleged failure to maintain current and accurate records of stolen automobiles by third-party defendants Stevenson and Steiner could be a concurring proximate cause of plaintiffs' detention, along with third-party plaintiffs' unreasonable reliance on the information furnished. Under Rhode Island tort law, a negligent act continues to be a proximate, concurring cause of the injury if the intervening act was a reasonably foreseeable result of the original negligence. [Citation.] Liability lies even if the intervening cause involved negligence or an intentional tort, provided the intervening act was foreseeable. [Citations.] Reliance, even unreasonable reliance, on the false information stored in the computer or Warwick police records, could be found by a jury to be a *foreseeable* intervening cause that did not supersede or exempt from liability the original negligent maintenance of these record systems.

In Rhode Island, contribution is generally available between joint tortfeasors for negligent acts that are the concurring causes of plaintiff's injury. Third-party defendants urge that contribution is only available to the non-intentional tortfeasor and, thus, third-party plaintiffs charged with false arrest, imprisonment and constitutional wrongs cannot recover against them for their negligent acts. Third-party defendants correctly state the rule in some states which have abrogated the common law prohibition against contribution but still deny the right of contribution to an intentional tortfeasor. [Citation.] However, Rhode Island has adopted, without material alteration, the Uniform Contribution Among Tortfeasors Act which contains no such limitation on the right of contribution between joint tortfeasors, nor makes any distinction between negligent or intentional torts. [Footnote.] [Citation.] The moving party has failed to provide any Rhode Island case law suggesting such a narrow interpretation of the Act, nor has this Court found any. Of course, intentional conduct is more likely to constitute a superseding, unforeseeable cause for which the initial negligent tortfeasor is not liable. But there is no reason to institute a hard and fast rule denying contribution to the party who commits an intentional tort such as false arrest and imprisonment.

Even assuming that contribution is unavailable to the tortfeasor who acts with malicious intent or reckless disregard against the merely negligent tortfeasor, the facts of the instant case do not suggest such a discrepancy in culpability between the joint tortfeasors as to deny contribution. The Court has supposed that third-party plaintiffs may be held liable upon a showing of unreasonable reliance on the computer check and on the Warwick police officer's confirmation. Such reliance is not significantly more culpable than the original negligent failure to maintain accurate records. Although the jury may in fact find that third-party plaintiffs engaged in malicious or reckless conduct which, according to third-party defendants' suggested interpretation, would disentitle them to contribution, the jury *could* properly find liability based solely on unreasonable reliance without any finding of malicious or reckless conduct. Therefore, even if this Court adopted third-party defendants' narrow reading of the contribution statute, dismissal would not be appropriate at this stage of the litigation. [Footnote.]

Though the parties have not raised the following ground for dismissal, the Court deems it worthy of discussion since it directly affects third-party plaintiffs' right to contribution. The right of contribution is premised not only on third-party plaintiffs' potential liability to plaintiffs, but also third-party defendants'. If third-party defendants owed no duty to plaintiffs, then they are not "jointly or severally liable in tort for the same injury" and cannot be required to contribute, R.I.G.L. sec 10–6–2. However, the Court today concludes that both third-party defendants Stevenson and Steiner had a duty to maintain reasonably accurate and current record systems. Mr. Stevenson, administrator of the Rhode Island Division of the National Computer Information Center, had a duty to establish reasonable administrative mechanisms designed to minimize the risk of inaccuracy by requiring that the records be constantly updated. A similar duty with respect to the maintenance of individual criminal record history information has been established by statute, 42 U.S.C. sec. 3771 (1973) and regulations, 28 C.F.R. sec. 20.20 *et seq.* These measures reflect a growing consciousness of the new dangers to personal liberty that "the accumulation of vast amounts of personal information in computerized data banks or other massive government files" presents. [Citation.] The right to be free of unreasonable seizures, constitutionally established since the beginning of our nation, is directly threatened by the careless use or abuse of this new technology. Legal protections must likewise be modernized to meet the new threats. It is now commonplace for the arresting officer to rely on the computer check of the present status of an automobile reported stolen. If the arresting officer is not liable to the arrestee for a false or unconstitutional arrest because his reliance is reasonable, the arrestee's only recourse must be against those in control of the information system that resulted in the unwarranted denial of liberty.

Consistent with the realities of modern day law enforcement, the Fifth Circuit, while granting dismissal against the arresting officer, permitted the arrestee's action to go forward against the federal officer whose misinformation, developed during his investigation, was materially relied upon by the grand

jury returning the indictment. [Citation.] Although in this case the plaintiffs have not sought relief against the third-party defendants, that fact does not abrogate third-party plaintiffs' right to contribution which is presently before us. The Fifth Circuit has also recognized the duty of a sheriff to keep accurate records so as to avoid unlawfully imprisoning the plaintiff. [Citation.] The Circuit Court for the District of Columbia suggested both constitutional and common law dimensions to the protection against inaccurate arrest records, *Tarleton v. Saxbe*, 165 U.S.App.D.C. 293, 507 F.2d 1116 (1974). The Court wrote:

> In the largest sense, both this constitutional issue and the common law principle forbidding defamation of innocent individuals refer to the value of individual privacy. This value, consistently reaffirmed in recent years, serves to insulate individuals from unjustifiable government interference with their private lives. This value finds its most direct expression in the Fourth and Fifth Amendments; it also is reflected in certain aspects of the First Amendment: government collection and dissemination of inaccurate criminal information without reasonable precautions to ensure accuracy could induce a levelling conformity inconsistent with the diversity of ideas and manners which has traditionally characterized our national life and found legal protection in the First Amendment. [Footnotes omitted.] [Citation.]

While the Federal Bureau of Investigation also had a duty to ensure accuracy, the Court in *Tarleton* suggested that the primary responsibility for accuracy was imposed at the state and local level since these agencies were in a better position to verify the information. [Citation.] Similarly, the arresting officer is not in a position to establish the administrative mechanisms that will prevent false arrests based on inaccurate computer checks. The duty to minimize inaccuracies is imposed on the official in control of the system—in this case, third-party defendant Stevenson.

The arresting officer is also not in as good a position as the police department which initially reported the vehicle stolen and where the vehicle was registered to update the status of the vehicle. Particularly since the crime involves an item quintessentially mobile, the primary duty to keep track of the vehicle must fall to the police department that covers the area where the vehicle was registered. Thus, Officer Steiner and his department had the duty to maintain current, accurate records of the previously stolen vehicle.[4]

When breach of this duty to maintain accurate records results in a false or unconstitutional arrest actionable under both Rhode Island and federal law, the arrestee has a cause of action against those who breached this duty. [Citations.] Since the injured party has a cause of action against third-party defendants, third-party plaintiffs have a right to contribution against third-party defendants, should third-party plaintiffs ultimately be found liable to plaintiffs. [Citations.]

Key similarities and distinctions from the common law action for false arrest support this Court's conclusion that third-party defendants' conduct is actionable. The arrestee generally has a claim not only against those who physically arrested him but also against those who actively brought about the arrest. Generally, no liability attaches to merely giving false information which the authorities choose to rely upon as the basis for the arrest. [Citation.] In Rhode Island, a private individual is only liable for knowingly giving false information to the police. [Citation.] The interest in "efficient enforcement of the criminal law" which counsels against extending liability to the good faith private informer [citation] counsels in favor of extending liability here when the state and local law enforcement agencies allegedly fail to establish mechanisms for ensuring accurate records. The special expertise, position of control over systems of information, and public trust that law enforcement agencies possess, justify holding them to a higher standard of accuracy than that applicable to the private individual.

* * *

Third-party defendants' motion to dismiss is denied.

4. It is not clear from the third-party complaint what position Officer Steiner occupies with regard to the Warwick police records. It is also unclear from the papers filed to date whether Officer Steiner inaccurately reported accurate data in the file or whether he accurately

15,844 WELFARE RECIPIENTS v. KING

474 F. Supp. 1374

*(United States District Court,
D. Massachusetts, Aug. 23, 1979.)*

GARRITY, D. J.

* * *

Plaintiffs now seek a preliminary injunction enjoining the defendants from proceeding to redetermine the continuing eligibility of plaintiffs for AFDC benefits based on the 1977 computer match, or, in the alternative, enjoining defendants from redetermining plaintiffs, except upon certain stated conditions. The preliminary injunction would also enjoin defendants from referring any of the plaintiffs to other Bureau of Welfare Auditing, from interviewing or investigating any of the plaintiffs for alleged fraud based on the 1977 computer match and from initiating any recoupment action, except upon certain stated conditions. In view of the extensive briefs filed by both parties and the numerous supporting and opposing affidavits, we conclude that a further hearing would not assist us in resolving the issues. We grant plaintiffs' motion for a preliminary injunction by continuing in effect our April 3, 1979 Temporary Restraining Order dated April 5, 1979, as supplemented in our June 11, 1979 Supplemental Restraining Order and as modified by our July 3, 1979 order, as a preliminary injunction, hereto attached as Appendix A. Insofar as plaintiffs' motion requests preliminary relief not contained in the aforementioned orders of this court, that relief is denied.

* * *

FINDINGS OF FACT

Our statement of the facts dictated at the April 3, 1979 hearing will serve as the findings of fact required by Fed.R.Civ.P., Rule 52, up to the date of that hearing. In addition we find the following:

reported inaccurate data. The answers to these questions could determine whether Officer Steiner is the proper third-party defendant and whether he should prevail on a summary judgment motion.

1. On or about April 17, 1979, after issuance of our April 3, 1979 Temporary Restraining Order, the Department of Public Welfare sent Memorandum AP–79–27 to Assistance Payments Staff informing all staff of the substance of our Order and setting forth procedures to be followed to restore cases to the status quo ante existing prior to the March 19, 1979 notice and related interviewing process. * * *

2. On May 8, 1979, pursuant to our April 3, 1979 Temporary Restraining Order, ¶ 1.b, defendants mailed to each plaintiff a notice intended to undo the effect of the March 19, 1979 notice and interviewing process. * * *

3. About May 17, 1979, defendants conducted a review of each plaintiff's file in order to determine which plaintiffs would be subject to priority redeterminations and/or fraud referrals. * * * This desk review resulted in reducing the total number of recipients subject to redetermination and possible fraud referral to about 6,000.

4. About June 14, 1979, the Department of Public Welfare issued to its Assistance Payments Staff Memorandum AP–79–43 outlining the procedures to be followed in determining the group of about 6,000 recipients who remained after the desk review and in referring members of this group for fraud investigations. * * *

5. Also about June 14, 1979 new redetermination interview notices were mailed to those recipients designated by the AP–79–43 memorandum. * * *

6. The Bureau of Welfare Auditing informed all supervisors by memo dated July 10, 1979 that the Department of Public Welfare would remove all information from DPW case files obtained from client contact related to the computer match. Moreover, by Memorandum AP/ADM–79–28 dated July 16, 1979, the Department of Public Welfare directed all Associate Regional Managers for Assistance Payments, RDCU Managers, CSAO/WSO Directors, and Assistant Directors for Assistance Payments to remove temporarily from a case file any information obtained as a result of client contact related to the Earnings Match before BWA investigators review the file. * * *

7. In response to our July 3, 1979 Order modifying our April 3, 1979 Temporary Restraining Order, defendants have drafted new Bureau of Welfare auditing notices of fraud investigation interviews specifying that "[y]our lack of cooperation with this investigation will not effect [sic] your current eligibility for assistance." * * *

8. Defendants' efforts to separate DPW and BWA activities and records and the very limited scope of examination in DPW interviews demonstrate their good faith in isolating eligibility redeterminations from fraud investigations.

CONCLUSIONS OF LAW

Our conclusions of law include those dictated at the April 13, 1979 hearing and those contained in subsequent orders of this court. Plaintiffs raise a number of additional arguments in support of their request for preliminary relief, the most important of which we address below. The following discussion divides the arguments into two categories, those challenging the conduct of eligibility redeterminations and those challenging the fraud investigations.

DPW ELIGIBILITY REDETERMINATIONS

Plaintiffs continue to insist that, in spite of the substantial modifications that defendants have made in their procedures and the mailing of the May 8, 1979 "curative" notice, defendants are still conducting fraud investigations under the guise of eligibility redeterminations. We do not agree. Contrary to plaintiffs' claim at page 3 of their Reply Memorandum in support of Motion for Preliminary Injunction, the eligibility redeterminations plainly serve a purpose different from that served by fraud investigations. The state has a strong interest not only in identifying and deterring welfare fraud but also in allocating its limited welfare resources to those most in need of assistance. [Citation.] Eligibility redeterminations are the primary vehicle for promoting this allocation goal.

Plaintiffs point out that nearly all remaining 6000 recipients who are subject to eligibility redeterminations are at the same time the focus of possible fraud investigations and that, on defendants' instructions in AP–79–33 and AP–79–43 as well as the affidavit of

Ralph Muller, DPW Deputy Commissioner, it appears that fraud referral forms, so-called FR–1 forms, were prepared for each recipient before any eligibility redeterminations took place. Rather than transforming redeterminations into fraud investigations, the prior preparation of FR–1 forms after a case file review serves further to separate DPW and BWA functions by ensuring that fraud referrals are based only upon information obtained independently of redetermination interviews. Under normal circumstances eligibility redeterminations are not necessarily disguised fraud investigations. [Citation.] In our opinion, the fact that interviewees might also be the focus of a potential fraud investigation prior to redetermination in this case does not change the complexion of the interview process, where the recipient may only be questioned about current employment and income, a social worker may not initiate a collateral investigation without the recipient's consent, and DPW and BWA activities are structurally isolated to the extent they are in this case. [Citations.]

* * *

Plaintiffs also challenge the propriety of conducting redeterminations of current eligibility on the basis of information about a welfare recipient's employment during the last quarter of 1977, about eighteen months prior to his redetermination interview. Based on the June 7, 1979 affidavit of Michael J. Piore and the May 30, 1979 affidavit of Bennett Harrison, both professors of economics specializing in labor economics and employment, plaintiffs contend that because of the high job turnover among the working poor, the chance of a welfare recipient currently working for the employer identified in the 1977 computer match is extremely remote, too small in fact for the computer match information to serve as the trigger for a "special" eligibility redetermination. 45 C.F.R. § 206.10(a)(9) requires in relevant part that "eligibility will be considered or redetermined: * * * (ii) promptly, after a report is obtained which *indicates* changes in the individual's circumstances that *may affect* the amount of assistance to which he is entitled or may make him ineligible, and (iii) periodically, *within agency-established time standards*, but not less frequently than 6

months in AFDC. * * *" (Emphasis added.) And the corresponding state regulation, 6 CHSR III § 303.52, provides that "continuing eligibility of each recipient shall be determined: (a) at least every six months or *more frequently as required* * * * [or] (c) when a CSA/WSO obtains information which *indicates* a change in circumstances which *may affect* eligibility or the amount of assistance." (Emphasis added.)

It is our opinion that the computer match information demonstrating a substantial likelihood of unreported employment in the last quarter of 1977 "indicates" a relevant change in the recipient's current circumstances. Statistical studies provide only limited information. In particular, Mr. Harrison's study, upon which plaintiffs rely, cannot *prove* that there is no chance that a welfare recipient who worked for an employer in late 1977 is still working for the same employer; there is certainly some probability of continuing employment. Moreover, without additional information about the distribution of the data regarding length of employment, not just the averages, we are unable to judge the true significance of Mr. Harrison's results. Indeed, Mr. Piore states in paragraph 5.c of his June 7, 1979 affidavit that "Harrison's results suggest the chances that somebody on welfare in 1977 would be employed in 1979 are about 60%." A sixty percent likelihood is plainly sufficient to "indicate" current unreported employment.

Finally, although we do not suggest that the fact that a recipient may have withheld information in late 1977 proves that he certainly must be withholding information about current employment, we cannot ignore this significant possibility, especially in view of the increased risk of fraud prosecution that might result from a later admission of employment that had previously been withheld. Fear of prosecution would doubtless also make a recipient reluctant to admit current employment during intervening periodic redetermination interviews. Under these circumstances the computer information is sufficiently relevant to current circumstances to trigger a redetermination pursuant to 45 C.F.R. § 206.10(a)(9)(ii) and 6 CHSR III § 303.52(c).

However, even if the requirements of § 206.10(a)(9)(ii) and § 303.52(c) were not met by the computer match, redeterminations would nevertheless be proper under 6 CHSR III § 303.52(a). This regulation gives a great deal of latitude to DPW officials to conduct eligibility redeterminations "as required." Neither the federal nor the state regulations impose an outer limit on the frequency of redeterminations. They specify only when an eligibility redetermination must, not may, be done. Of course, a recipient's being subjected to very frequent eligibility redeterminations without any reasonable basis would present serious Fourteenth Amendment due process and equal protection issues; and less frequent, but groundless, redeterminations might violate 45 C.F.R. § 206.10(a)(10) as being inconsistent with the purposes of the Act. In the instant case, however, there appears to be a reasonable basis to suspect current unreported employment, and plaintiffs have offered no evidence of harassment in the form of repeated redetermination interviews. [Footnote.]

* * *

BWA FRAUD INVESTIGATIONS

Plaintiffs mount a five-prong attack on BWA fraud investigations. They argue that defendants are obligated by the terms of 45 C.F.R. § 235.110(a) to (1) publish methods and criteria for identifying fraud prior to making fraud referrals; (2) to provide advance written notice of a recipient's rights to counsel and to remain silent and of the possible criminal consequences of his cooperation during the interview; (3) to give interviewees advance notice of the specific allegations of fraud that will be the subject of the interview; (4) to establish procedures to provide appointed counsel to those recipients who request it prior to commencing any fraud interviews; and (5) to develop "procedures" for referring cases to a prosecutor in accordance with 45 C.F.R. § 235.110(a)(2) prior to making any such referrals. We discuss each contention briefly.

Plaintiffs' first point cannot withstand a close examination of the relevant regulation. 45 C.F.R. § 235.110(a)(1) requires that a state plan must provide "(a) that the state agency will establish and maintain: (1) methods and criteria for identifying situations in which a question of fraud in the program may exist."

The computer match together with the subsequent case file review is one such "method" and the standards for preparing FR–1 forms outlined at page 2 of the AP–79–33 constitute "criteria." Publication of this method and these criteria in advance of the computer match itself, although advisable, is not required by § 235.110(a)(1), nor any other regulation or statutory or constitutional provision that plaintiffs cite. Moreover, it is doubtful whether plaintiffs have standing to complain of a violation of § 235.110(a)(1), since the duties imposed on the state by that regulation appear to be for the benefit of the federal government as a participant in the AFDC program, not for the benefit of individual recipients. [Citations.]

Plaintiffs also seek to enjoin all fraud investigations until defendants delineate more specific criteria for identifying a "question of fraud" according to the elements of welfare fraud under state law. § 235.110(a)(1) speaks generally of "situations in which a question of fraud may exist" (emphasis added). This language does not appear on its face to require more rigorous standards than defendants have articulated in AP–79–33. [Citation.] Indeed, it would be very difficult for a social worker to screen cases more carefully based on the very limited information about current employment obtained from the redetermination interview and collateral contacts, if any. Fraud investigations instigated only on the basis of information gleaned from computer match studies and case file reviews like those in the instant case are not without precedent. *See, e. g., Greater Cleveland Wel. Rights Org. v. Bauer,* N.D. Ohio 1978, 462 F.Supp. 1313; *Carleson v. Golden Gate Welfare Rights Org.,* 1972, 27 Cal.App.3d 1, 103 Cal.Rptr. 824.

* * *

CONCLUSION

Based on the foregoing, we grant plaintiffs' motion for a preliminary injunction only to the extent that the requested relief has already been granted by our prior orders. The motion is denied in all other respects on the ground that plaintiffs have failed to demonstrate a probability of success on the merits.

APPENDIX A

PRELIMINARY INJUNCTION

GARRITY, D. J.

Upon consideration of memoranda of law, affidavits and exhibits, and on the basis of the findings and conclusions of the court announced April 3, 1979 and of the orders of the court entered April 5, June 11 and July 3, 1979, the defendants, their agents and servants are restrained until further order of this court from:

1. Further interviewing any members of the plaintiff class until defendants fully comply with all regulations and procedures of the Bureau of Welfare Auditing for investigating alleged fraud, or procedures of the Department of Public Welfare for redetermination of current eligibility:

   a. prior to the Bureau of Welfare Auditing again commencing interviews of any members of the plaintiff class, the BWA shall mail revised notices to plaintiffs which rescind all previous notices and state that lack of cooperation with any fraud investigation does not affect current eligibility for welfare assistance, except that where a sanction for failure to cooperate is authorized by normal BWA policies and properly issued regulations and is otherwise consistent with all legal requirements, the notice may contain a reference to that sanction.

   b. prior to the Department of Public Welfare commencing redetermination reviews of current eligibility for welfare assistance of any members of the plaintiff class, it shall determine which members of the plaintiff class are due for redetermination, and shall send notices to each such recipient rescinding the notice of March 19, 1979 and explaining in substance that the purpose of the interview is to redetermine current eligibility only, that no inquiry will be made at the interview into wages earned before 1979 and that the sole documentation relating to verification of wages the recipient must bring to the interview is verification of the previous five weeks of earnings, if any;

2. Failing to vacate or cease all termination, suspension, reduction or other adverse action, including any recoupment action or referral to the Bureau of Welfare Auditing, based upon information from, or actions taken by, any members of plaintiff class subsequent to the March 19, 1979 notice, with respect to those members of the plaintiff class who have been interviewed, terminated, or who have closed out their cases, *provided* that defendants may proceed to redetermine the current eligibility of the members of the plaintiff class or close their cases in accordance with normal procedures for redeterminations and case closings, and may require the cooperation of members of the plaintiff class in verifying any assertion that they were not currently employed at the time of the redetermination interview by the employer(s) named on the Computer Match, after adequate notice to plaintiffs of their rights pursuant to this court order; and

3. Failing to return to each member of the plaintiff class, or in the event that proves impossible to destroy, any information obtained from her or him in connection with the March 19, 1979 notice and related interviewing process which might be used against the recipient in a criminal proceeding in violation of her right against self-incrimination under the Fifth Amendment to the United States Constitution.

Plaintiffs are exempted from the bonding requirements of Rule 65(c).

Dated: September 10, 1979.

PEOPLE v. RAMIREZ

126 Cal.App.3d 33, 178 Cal.Rptr. 529
(Court of Appeal, Second District, Division 3, Nov. 25, 1981.)

LUI, A. J.

STATEMENT OF THE CASE

In an information filed by the District Attorney of Los Angeles County, appellant was charged with possession of phencyclidine, a violation of section 11377, subdivision (a), of the Health and Safety Code.

Appellant was arraigned and entered a plea of not guilty. Appellant's motion to suppress evidence pursuant to Penal Code section 1538.5 was denied. Pursuant to a negotiated disposition, appellant entered a plea of guilty to the charged violation as a misdemeanor pursuant to Penal Code section 17, subdivision (b)(5). Appellant was granted probation for a period of three years on condition that he serve the first 90 days in the county jail, such sentence to run consecutively with any other time appellant was serving. Appellant appeals from the denial of his motion to suppress evidence.

FACTS

On May 29, 1980, at 12:45 a. m., Officer Gary Brown of the City of Montebello Police Department was on patrol in a one-man car traveling eastbound on Whittier Boulevard when he observed two individuals at the front of a closed tire store located in a business district. The store was located about 50 feet from a public sidewalk. The nearest light was about 50 feet from the store.

Brown could see no reason for anyone to be there at that time of the night because all the businesses were closed. The two persons in question were apparently not on a route that would take them to any sidewalk, open business or parked cars. Additionally, Brown was aware of numerous burglaries and window smashings that had occurred continuously during the past three to four months in the immediate area and that the tire store had been the target of a window smashing.

His suspicion aroused, Brown drove up to the individuals and asked what they were doing and received a reply that they were looking for a hamburger stand. Brown had just driven by an open hamburger stand, The Ox, about six blocks away. The individuals, however, told him that they had left the hamburger stand because it was closed. Both individuals did not appear to be carrying tools for window smashing. With his suspicion further aroused by what appeared to be a lie, Brown asked the appellant and his friend for their names and addresses. Appellant verbally indicated his identity but produced no written identification. Brown checked with communications for a warrant check on both appellant and his friend although there was nothing in their behavior which would lead him to believe that a warrant was outstanding on either appellant or his friend. Brown testified that he ran the warrant check to see if appellant was giving him truthful information and to take him to jail if a warrant was outstanding. Appellant also wanted to find out appellant's true identity.

About five minutes after the warrant request was made, but not more than ten minutes from the point of his first questions to the two individuals, Brown received a radio communication indicating that there was a bench warrant outstanding on appellant for possession of phencyclidine. Brown released appellant's companion, arrested appellant and transported him to jail. Brown asked appellant if he could put up the $250 bail but did not inform him that he could secure the services of a bail bondsman if he did not have the cash. When appellant said he could not post bail, Brown conducted a pre-booking search and found the phencyclidine which is the subject matter of the motion to suppress.

Counsel stipulated during the 1538.5 motion that the bench warrant in question issued by the East Los Angeles Municipal Court was recalled in November of 1979 and that Officer Brown had no knowledge of the fact that the warrant had been recalled. The record is silent as to why the warrant was recalled and also lacks any explanation regarding the cause for the delay in entering the recall in the computer system.

APPELLANT'S CONTENTIONS ON APPEAL

Appellant's contentions on appeal are as follows:

1. Appellant's initial detention was unlawful and was of an impermissibly long duration. This requires suppression of subsequently discovered evidence.

2. The bench warrant, which served as a basis for appellant's arrest, had been previously recalled and consequently the evidence discovered pursuant to such arrest must be suppressed.

DISCUSSION

Appellant Was Lawfully Detained For a Reasonable Time

Appellant contends that he was unlawfully detained for an unreasonable length of time by Officer Brown who should have terminated detention once he ascertained that appellant had no devices for burglarizing or vandalizing in his possession.

As stated in *People v. Mickelson* (1963) 59 Cal.2d 448, 450, 30 Cal.Rptr. 18, 380 P.2d 658, it is well-settled that circumstances short of probable cause to make an arrest may still justify an officer's stopping pedestrians or motorists on the street for questioning. (See also

Terry v. Ohio (1968) 392 U.S. 1, 22, 88 S.Ct. 1868, 1880, 20 L.Ed.2d 889.)

Our Supreme Court has recently summarized the rule justifying an investigative stop or detention. "[I]n order to justify an investigative stop or detention the circumstances known or apparent to the officer must include specific and articulable facts causing him to suspect that (1) some activity relating to crime has taken place or is occurring or about to occur, and (2) the person he intends to stop or detain is involved in that activity. Not only must he subjectively entertain such a suspicion, but it must be objectively reasonable for him to do so: the facts must be such as would cause any reasonable police officer in a like position, drawing when appropriate on his training and experience, [citation], to suspect the same criminal activity and the same involvement by the person in question. The corollary to this rule, of course, is that an investigative stop or detention predicated on mere curiosity, rumor, or hunch is unlawful, even though the officer may be acting in complete good faith. [Citations.]

When Officer Brown approached appellant and his companion, he was aware of the fact that the area in which this particular tire store was located was in a high burglary area and that this particular store had been the target of vandalism. The store was set back from the street with no overhead lighting nearby to illuminate the area and there appeared to be no reason for the appellant and his companion to be standing outside the store late at night when it was not on a route that would lead them to any discernible place or innocent activity. Officer Brown approached the appellant and his companion to ascertain what they were doing. The appellant and his companion stated information that the officer had reason to believe was untrue. His suspicions were aroused and he requested that the appellant and his companion identify themselves and where they lived. Appellant produced no written identification but verbally identified himself.

We cannot say that the officer's actions were unreasonable or improper under these circumstances. Given the facts and circumstances set forth above, the officer was justified in at least making an initial inquiry with regard to reasons for the appellant and his companion being at the location. Upon receiving a false response, he had reason to detain the appellant and his companion for a short period of time to verify their identification and to ascertain whether any warrants were outstanding. * * *

Officer Brown made the warrant check in order to verify the identification of the appellant who was unable to document his identification. Consequently, Officer Brown was continuing in his investigation of appellant's identity in making the warrant check which extended the detention time some four to five minutes. * * * We conclude that the trial court's decision in upholding the detention was proper and should be upheld.

The Appellant's Arrest on the Bench Warrant Was Valid In Spite of the Fact that the Warrant Had Been Recalled

We next deal with the difficult question of whether the arrest on the warrant should be validated even though the warrant had in fact been recalled some eight months prior to the arrest. Appellant argues that but for the fact that his name was still mistakenly "on the police computer's wanted list, he would not have been arrested, booked, searched, or charged with any offense."

We do not believe that the deterrent effect of the exclusionary rule would be served by the suppression of the evidence of this case. Here, Officer Brown could not have manufactured the existence of the warrant.[1] There is also no evidence that would justify the belief that the warrant was purposely maintained on the computer system which if true would, in our opinion, justify declaring the arrest invalid for this reason alone.

---

1. Nor is this a question dealing with " 'the manufacture of reasonable grounds for arrest within a police department by one officer transmitting information purportedly received by him from an informer to another officer who had not received such information from the informer, without establishing under oath that the information had in fact been given to any officer by the informer or indeed that there was an informer at all. The possibilities of the phantom informer, if this were to be permitted, are too obvious to need elaboration.' [Citation.]" [Citation.]

Appellant cites by analogy, *Michigan v. DeFillippo* (1979) 443 U.S. 31, 99 S.Ct. 2627, 61 L.Ed.2d 343, and *Jennings v. Superior Court* (1980) 104 Cal.App.3d 50, 163 Cal.Rptr. 691, which deal with the issue of an arrest made in good faith reliance upon an ordinance that is subsequently declared unconstitutional. Although the United States Supreme Court upheld the good faith rule in *DeFillippo,* the Fourth District Court of Appeal in *Jennings* held that the good faith rule was not the appropriate standard under the California Constitution (art. I. § 13). *Jennings* is distinguishable from the facts of the instant case because that decision did not deal specifically with good faith reliance on the existence of an arrest warrant.

In *People v. Marquez* (1965) 237 Cal.App.2d 627, 47 Cal.Rptr. 166, a warrantless arrest followed a traffic stop by officers in which the defendant was operating a car without stoplights and driving without a license. The court in *Marquez* stated: "[I]n determining whether or not an arresting officer acts reasonably in believing that the person arrested committed a felony the court looks only to the facts and circumstances presented to the officer when the arrest was made—not to something later discovered. [Citation.]" *(Id.,* at p. 633, 47 Cal.Rptr. 166.) This good faith rule *viewed as of the time of arrest* was followed in *People v. Honore* (1969) 2 Cal.App.3d 295, 300-301, 82 Cal.Rptr. 639.[2]

Further, in *People v. Knight* (1970) 3 Cal.App.3d 500, 83 Cal.Rptr. 530, defendant Knight was detained on suspicion of auto burglary, without probable cause to arrest. Defendant was later arrested on an outstanding felony warrant which the officers learned of during the detention period as the result of a routine radio check. The outstanding warrant was based on a complaint which was defective because the underlying facts were not set forth in the complaint and the complaint was not

signed by an officer who had personal knowledge of the facts. While it is true that the defective warrant in *Knight* is distinguishable from the warrant in the instant case because it could have been cured by a properly drawn complaint, the thrust of the *Knight* decision is to validate an arrest if based on communications received through official channels. The court stated: "The People cite the line of cases which stand for the proposition that an officer may validly arrest on the basis of requests made through official communication channels such as the police radio. Pointed to is the fact that all the prosecution need show is that the officer who made the request had the required probable cause to do so. [Citation.] It is argued that, since official communication channels are valid conduits of probable cause, where, as here, the officer *initiating the request for an arrest warrant has probable cause for arrest,* and there is thereafter a communication through official channels to arrest on the warrant, the fact the warrant may be invalid for one reason or another should not affect the legality of the arrest. [¶] We conclude that that argument must prevail." [Citation.]

The factual situation in the instant case is analogous to that which existed in *Hill v. California* (1971) 401 U.S. 797, 91 S.Ct. 1106, 28 L.Ed.2d 484, affirming *People v. Hill* (1968) 69 Cal.2d 550, 72 Cal.Rptr. 641, 446 P.2d 521, wherein the police admittedly had probable cause to arrest defendant Hill, proceeded to Hill's address and encountered an individual who professed to be one Miller. The officers nevertheless arrested Miller because of descriptions previously received from various sources and statements made by Miller that he was in actuality Hill. Pursuant to the arrest, the officers searched Hill's house and the fruits of that search were introduced at trial. In affirming, the Supreme Court stated: "The upshot was that the officers in good faith be-

---

2. The question of the validity of an arrest based on the good faith belief of the existence of a warrant was discussed in *People v. Rice* (1970) 10 Cal.App.3d 730, 738, footnote 3, 89 Cal.Rptr. 200, as follows: "However, the officers' belief in the existence of a warrant, while not sufficient in itself to justify the arrest, is of some significance. The fact that the officer had received information from an official source concerning an alleged warrant indicates that the officers' act of going to the residence

was reasonable and not merely the result of some unfounded hunch of the officers that criminal activity might be underway there. A totally different situation would be present if the officers were not acting in response to a communication from another police department but were instead indiscriminately knocking on all doors in the neighborhood until they chanced upon someone engaged in criminal activity."

lieved Miller was Hill and arrested him. They were quite wrong as it turned out, and subjective good faith belief would not in itself justify either the arrest or the subsequent search. But sufficient probability, not certainty, is the touchstone of reasonableness under the Fourth Amendment and on the record before us the officers' mistake was understandable and the arrest a reasonable response to the situations facing them at the time." [Citation.]

Our Supreme Court in *Theodor v. Superior Court* (1972) 8 Cal.3d 77, 100, 104 Cal.Rptr. 226, 501 P.2d 234, discussed the wisdom of the *Hill* decision and stated "[u]nder those circumstances in which an officer makes an arrest without a warrant [citation], he is in essence required to perform two tasks: first, he must ascertain what events have transpired, i. e., what are the facts; second, from those facts he must deduce whether a crime has been committed. It is to this task in a warrantless search or arrest that the probable cause standard usually refers. * * * 'Because many situations which confront officers in the course of executing their duties are more or less ambiguous, room must be allowed for some mistakes on their part. But the mistakes must be those of reasonable men, acting on facts leading sensibly to their conclusions of probability.' * * * [¶] There is no reason to hold an officer to a standard of absolute accuracy in those instances in which the inference-drawing power is reserved for the magistrate who is to issue a warrant, when the officer is only required to reach a reasonable factual deduction in those instances in which he makes the inferences and acts without a warrant. In both cases, the constitutional standard is one of reasonableness."

The policy considerations on this question are clear. Should the court validate an officer's arrest on an outstanding warrant made in good faith even if the warrant is subsequently found to be recalled? Or, should the court look with the benefit of hindsight to invalidate the arrest because the warrant was no longer in existence and the defendant never should have been arrested? We choose to follow the former alternative following the decision in *Marquez* which would validate the arrest made in good faith at the time of the arrest though it is later discovered to have

been factually incorrect. This view is consistent with the decision in *Hill, supra,* by our United States Supreme Court. Consistent therewith, we are of the opinion that the tests and standards should be good faith and reasonableness.

The judgment is affirmed.

IN RE GRAND JURY SUBPOENAS ISSUED TO UNITED STATES POSTAL SERVICE

535 F. Supp. 31
(United States District Court, E. D. Tennessee, N. D., Dec. 10, 1981.)

TAYLOR, D. J.

Grand jury subpoenas were issued to each of the three Postal Service (Service) Section Managers in this District. Each subpoena asks for personnel information and directs that it be placed on a computer tape. The information is apparently sought for a computer matching program to identify any postal employee who might be receiving federally-funded welfare benefits and who might be shown by further investigation to have obtained such benefits by making false or fraudulent statements in violation of 18 U.S.C. § 1001. On November 17, 1981 the Service moved to quash the three subpoenas duces tecum. The requested tapes have been submitted under seal.

The Service contends that the Privacy Act, 5 U.S.C. § 552a(b), prohibits disclosure of the requested information absent a court order and that the subpoenas are not court orders as that term is used in the Privacy Act, 5 U.S.C. § 552a(b)(11) citing primarily *Stiles v. Atlanta Gas Light Co.*, 453 F.Supp. 798 (N.D.Ga.1978), and cases interpreting a similar provision of the Fair Credit Reporting Act (FCRA). The Service asserts that the Department of Justice can obtain the information pursuant to guidelines established by the Office of Management and Budget (OMB), 44 Fed.Reg. 23,138 (1979), and that even if the Court enforces the subpoenas duces tecum the Federal Bureau of Investigation would still be required to follow the guidelines.

The United States Attorney argues in his response that the information is requested by the grand jury, not the Federal Bureau of Investigation or the United States Attorney, and that the grand jury is not an "agency" subject to the Privacy Act and the OMB guidelines. He contends further that a grand jury subpoena is a court order within the meaning of 5 U.S.C. § 552a(b)(11). Alternatively, he moves the Court for an order compelling the Service to comply with the subpoenas. The nature of the investigation in the present case is set forth in an affidavit of the United States Attorney which was submitted under seal.

There is a fairly even split of authority as to whether or not a grand jury subpoena is a court order. The Sixth Circuit has not decided the issue. Judge John Feikens held in an FCRA case that a grand jury subpoena is a court order. *In re TRW, Inc.*, 460 F.Supp. 1007 (E.D.Mich.1978). He reasoned that a grand jury is an arm of the court, standing between the government and the accused and exercising independent judgment. He observed that "If a grand jury could not issue a subpoena without prior authorization by a federal judge a serious problem would arise as to what standard the judge should apply in evaluating the necessity and reasonableness of the requested subpoena." [Citation.] Other courts have agreed. [Citations.] The cases which hold to the contrary do so because a grand jury subpoena "is functionally a tool of the prosecutor, issued at the initiative of the United States Attorney, with no judicial participation." [Citation.] Some courts have adopted that reasoning. [Citations.]

The Court has examined the affidavit of the United States Attorney and is of the opinion that the information sought is relevant to the investigation being conducted by the grand jury. Therefore, the Service must comply with the subpoenas duces tecum. It is, therefore, unnecessary for this Court to express its opinion as to whether or not a grand jury subpoena is a court order.

Although the Court is sympathetic to the concern of the Service that the privacy interests of its employees be protected, the Court holds that the OMB guidelines are inapplicable. A grand jury conducting a criminal investigation is not an "agency" of the government as that term is used in the OMB guidelines. [Citation.]

For these reasons, it is ordered that the motion to quash the subpoenas duces tecum

be, and the same hereby is, denied. It is further ordered that the Service comply with the subpoenas duces tecum and that disclosure and use of the information be limited to the grand jury proceedings and any criminal prosecutions which may follow.

AMERICAN CIVIL LIBERTIES UNION v. DEUKMEJIAN
186 Cal.Rptr. 235
(Supreme Court of California, In Bank, Sept. 27, 1982.)

BROUSSARD, J.

Pursuant to the California Public Records Act (Gov. Code, § 6250 et seq. hereafter the Act) [footnote], petitioner American Civil Liberties Union Foundation of Northern California, Inc. (ACLU) sought to inspect and copy, among other things, certain index cards and computer printouts held by defendant California Department of Justice. The department refused to allow inspection on the ground that the information in question was "intelligence information" exempt from disclosure under section 6254, subdivision (f) of the Act. The ACLU then brought suit to compel production of these records. The trial court, after inspecting the records *in camera*, ruled that data on the cards and printouts should be disclosed with the exception of personal identifiers and information which might reveal confidential sources. Defendants appeal from that decision.

The first issue presented by this appeal is the definition and scope of the exemption for "intelligence information" in section 6254, subdivision (f). We agree with the trial court that this exemption should not be read so broadly as to preclude discovery of any information in intelligence files which relates in some manner to criminal activity. We believe, however, that the court erred in limiting the statutory protection to personal identifiers and material which might disclose confidential sources. The term "intelligence information," even if read narrowly so as to further the Act's objective of expanded public disclosure, should protect information furnished in confidence, even if that information does not reveal the identity of a confidential source. Thus the "intelligence information" exemption severely limits the information subject to disclosure, but does not entirely protect the index cards and printouts.

Secondly, defendants invoke the balancing test of section 6255, asserting that the burden of segregating exempt and non-exempt information outweighs the benefits of disclosure. The issue is close, but after *in camera* inspection of the index cards in question, we conclude that in this case the segregation of personal identifiers, confidential information, and information which might reveal confidential sources will be so burdensome, and will so reduce the utility of disclosing the documents to the ACLU, that the public interest will not be served by requiring disclosure of the index cards. We therefore reverse the trial court's judgment to the extent it compels disclosure of nonexempt information on the cards in question. The computer printouts, on the other hand, contain neither confidential information nor information supplied by confidential sources, but only data derived from public records. Excision of personal identifiers from the printouts would be a relatively simple task. We therefore affirm the portion of the trial court's judgment requiring disclosure of nonexempt information on the printouts.

I.

This case arose when the ACLU, in May of 1976, filed a request under the Act to inspect and copy a number of documents relating to state law enforcement surveillance practices and records. Among those documents were index cards, compiled by a network of law enforcement departments known as the Law Enforcement Intelligence Unit (LEIU), listing persons suspected of being involved in organized crime. Each card lists, among other data, the individual's name, alias, occupation, family members, vehicles, associates, arrests, modus operandi, and physical traits. The subject of a card may be a person suspected of a specific crime; a person suspected of aiding, directly or indirectly, those involved in organized crime; or a person who is "associated" with a principal suspect. "Associates" might be individuals entirely innocent of crime, including family members, business associates, or attorneys of the principal suspects.[2]

The ACLU also sought to inspect and copy computer printouts from the Interstate Organized Crime Index (IOCI). The IOCI printouts, in contrast to the LEIU index cards, contain entries based solely on information that is a matter of public record.[3] Existing IOCI printouts are still being used by law enforcement agencies but no new information is being added to them. The printout entries include, among other information, an individual subject's name, physical characteristics, criminal record, crime-related and noncrime-related associates, occupation, and residence.

The ACLU's objective in seeking disclosure was to determine generally the nature of the information contained on the LEIU cards and stored in the IOCI computers, not to ascertain the entries relating to any particular person. The ACLU, therefore, requested the first 100 cards in alphabetical order in the LEIU index and the first 100 entries in the computer printouts, omitting personal identifiers protected from disclosure by section 6254, subdivision (c).[4] When the department refused to permit inspection, the ACLU, charging that

---

2. The ACLU cites a striking example of the potential for abuse in unmonitored gathering of information by law enforcement agencies. Briefly, former State Senator Nate Holden was listed as one of six "associates" of Black Panther Party member Michael Zinzun on the latter's index card. That card was disclosed in litigation in Chicago and was, therefore, on file in other places outside California. Holden, who had never been arrested or convicted of a crime, had rented a house to Zinzun for about four months.

3. The department's Organized Crime Criminal Intelligence Branch is the coordinating agency not only for the LEIU which produces the index cards, but also for the nationwide computer system which formerly produced the printouts. That system, the IOCI, was originally funded by a grant from the Law Enforcement Assistance Administration (now defunct); one condition of

that grant was that the computer entries be based on information that was a matter of public record.

4. The ACLU's original request included a total of nine items; in addition to the cards and printouts, the ACLU sought disclosure of annual reports submitted to the Legislature by the department's Organized Crime Criminal Intelligence Branch (OCCIB), notes and texts of briefings given to the Legislature, a catalog of OCCIB publications, the OCCIB policy statement with regard to maintenance or establishment of political files, lists of training conferences, a hardware index, and the current issue of various publications. Some of these items were produced voluntarily; others were produced at the order of the trial court; others did not exist or had been discontinued. On appeal, defendants challenged the trial court's order only insofar as it applied to the index cards and printouts.

the department had violated the Act, brought suit to compel disclosure.

At trial, the department claimed the records in question were protected by section 6254, subdivision (f) of the Act, which permits the state to withhold "[r]ecords of complaints to or investigations conducted by, or records of *intelligence information* or security procedures of, the office of the Attorney General and the Department of Justice, and any state or local police agency, or any such investigatory or security files compiled by any other state or local police agency * * * for correctional, law enforcement or licensing purposes. * * *" (Emphasis added.) The department also claimed an exemption under section 6255, which permits an agency to avoid disclosure of materials by showing that "on the facts of the particular case the public interest served by not making the record public clearly outweighs the public interest served by disclosure of the record."

The trial court first rejected the department's claim of exemption under subdivision (f), holding that the "intelligence information" exemption was confined to (1) personal identifiers [footnote], i.e., information which might reveal the names of those who were the subjects of the cards and printouts, and (2) information which might reveal the names of confidential sources who gave the department the card and printout data. The trial court further found that "[p]ublic revelation of the information other than personal identifiers and confidential sources * * * is in the public interest and the public interest weighs in favor of disclosure. Revelation of this information will inform interested members of the public of the type of information which the defendants develop and gather." Although the trial court initially concluded that separation of exempt from nonexempt information on the LEIU cards and the IOCI printouts would be unduly burdensome, on motion to modify the

judgment the court reversed its decision and found that the burden of segregating nonexempt information was outweighed by the public interest in access to that information. The trial court therefore rejected the claimed exemption under section 6255 [footnote] and accordingly entered judgment requiring disclosure, among other matters, of the LEIU index cards and the IOCI printouts, excluding personal identifiers and data which would reveal confidential sources.

II.

The Act, enacted in 1968, replaced a confusing mass of statutes and court decisions relating to disclosure of governmental records. [Citation.] The Act begins with a declaration of rights: "In enacting this chapter, the Legislature, mindful of the right of individuals to privacy, finds and declares that access to information concerning the conduct of the people's business is a fundamental and necessary right of every person in this state." In the spirit of this declaration, judicial decisions interpreting the Act seek to balance the public right to access to information, the government's need, or lack of need, to preserve confidentiality, and the individual's right to privacy. [Citations.]

The Act was modeled on the 1967 federal Freedom of Information Act (81 Stat. 54), and the judicial construction and legislative history of the federal act serve to illuminate the interpretation of its California counterpart. [Citations.] As enacted in 1967, the Freedom of Information Act exempted "investigatory records compiled for law enforcement purposes." [Citation.][7] The California Act, enacted in 1968, elaborated on this exemption, barring disclosure of "[r]ecords of complaints to or investigations conducted by, or records of intelligence information or security procedures of, the office of the Attorney General

---

7. The 1967 federal act contained no express mention of "intelligence information." It did incorporate other statutory exemptions, including a statute (50 U.S.C. § 403(d)(3)) which orders the Director of the Central Intelligence Agency to protect "intelligence sources." The federal courts have construed that enactment to bar disclosure of information relating to national security which could not have been obtained without guaranteeing the confidentiality of the source. [Citation.]

It is unlikely that the California Legislature, when it enacted an exemption for "intelligence information," had in mind protection of information and sources relating to national security. The language of section 6254, subdivision (f) suggests instead that the Legislature considered "intelligence information" a subclassification of the broader exemption for law enforcement investigatory records under the 1967 federal act.

and the Department of Justice, and any state or local police agency, or any such investigatory or security files compiled by any other state or local police agency, or any such investigatory or security files compiled by any other state or local agency for correctional, law enforcement, or licensing purposes. * * * "[8]

When a series of federal decisions held that under the 1967 law all documents in a law enforcement investigatory file were exempt [footnote], Congress amended the Freedom of Information Act to narrow and clarify the exemptions from disclosure. [Citations.] The act, as amended in 1974, limited the exemption to "investigatory records compiled for law enforcement purposes, but only to the extent that the production of such records would (A) interfere with enforcement proceedings, (B) deprive a person of a right to a fair trial or an impartial adjudication, (C) constitute an unwarranted invasion of personal privacy, (D) disclose the identity of a confidential source and, in the case of a record compiled by a criminal law enforcement authority in the course of a criminal investigation, or by an agency conducting a lawful national security intelligence investigation, confidential information furnished only by the confidential source, (E) disclose investigative techniques and procedures, or (F) endanger the life or physical safety of law enforcement personnel; * * *." (5 U.S.C. § 552(b)(7).) Since the 1974 amendments were adopted to reinstate the scope of the exemption as intended in the original act [citation], and since the California law was modeled upon that original act, we may use the amendments to guide the construction of the California Act.

We therefore reject defendants' contention that the "intelligence information" exemption of section 6254, subdivision (f), exempts all information which is "reasonably related to criminal activity." Such a broad exemption would in essence resurrect the federal judicial

doctrine which Congress repudiated in 1974, and which was never part of California law. It would undercut the California decisions which in some circumstances limit the exemption of subdivision (f) to cases involving concrete and definite enforcement prospects. [Footnote.] And most important, it would effectively exclude the law enforcement function of state and local governments from any public scrutiny under the California Act, a result inconsistent with its fundamental purpose.

We believe, however, that the definition adopted by the trial court is too narrow. We do not dispute its exemption of "personal identifiers"; such an exemption would be required, if not by the express terms of the Act, by the right of privacy established in article I, section 1 of the California Constitution. Indeed, in view of the substantial harm that could be inflicted by a public revelation that an individual was listed in an index of persons involved in organized crime, or even listed as an "associate" of someone involved in organized crime, we think the exclusion of personal identifiers must be viewed broadly. Not only names, aliases, addresses, and telephone numbers must be excluded, but also information which might lead the knowledgeable or inquisitive to infer the identity of the individual in question.

We agree also that information which might lead to the disclosure of confidential sources should be exempt from disclosure. The terms of subdivision (f), however, do not protect sources as such, but protect "intelligence information." We thus see no escape from the conclusion that information supplied in confidence is protected by the Act even if the revelation of that information will not necessarily disclose the identity of the source.

We conclude that the "intelligence information" exemption bars disclosure of information that might identify individuals mentioned in the LEIU or IOCI records, that might

---

8. Defendants, claiming that the "intelligence information" exemption was intended to encompass all information on the LEIU index and the IOCI printouts, rely on the fact that state budget bills antedating the Act refer to the California Department of Justice's cooperative information exchange with the FBI. These bills, however, relate not to the indexing systems involved here, but to

the National Crime Information Center telecommunications system which linked existing department records with a federal computer. In any case, proof that the Legislature was aware of an information exchange system does not shed any light on whether it intended to protect all information in that system from disclosure.

identify confidential sources, or that was supplied in confidence by its original source.[11]

The foregoing construction of section 6254, subdivision (f) will bring that exemption into approximate alignment with the exemption in section 552, subdivision (b)(7) of the amended federal act. We recognize, of course, that California has not enacted any amendments to the Act comparable to the 1974 federal amendments, but then the California Legislature faced no overly restrictive court decisions such as those which impelled the federal amendments. As we have explained, the 1974 federal amendments were intended to restate and clarify the original purpose of the federal act, and since that purpose—public access to records except where access must be limited to protect privacy or confidentiality—corresponds to the purpose of the California Act, we believe the two statutes should receive a parallel construction.

Our interpretation of subdivision (f) also derives from the fact that the Act imposes no limits upon who may seek information or what he may do with it. In the present case the ACLU seeks information to test the operation of the LEIU index and the IOCI printouts and to determine if those police intelligence systems are being misused. In other cases, however, information may be sought for less noble purposes. Persons connected with organized crime may seek to discover what the police know, or do not know, about organized criminal activities [citation]; persons seeking to damage the reputation of another may try to discover if he is listed as an organized crime figure or as an associate of such a figure; other persons may simply try to put the state to the burden and expense of segregating exempt and nonexempt information and making the latter available to the public. In short, once information is held subject to disclosure under

the Act, the courts can exercise no restraint on the use to which it may be put [Citation.]

* * *

We therefore conclude that the "intelligence information" exemption bars disclosure to the ACLU of personal identifiers, confidential sources, and confidential information relating to criminal activity. Although much of the information of the LEIU cards and the IOCI printouts is thus exempt from disclosure, the scope of the intelligence information exemption alone thus is insufficient to justify the defendants' blanket refusal of disclosure.

III.

Defendants next argue that in the present case the burden of segregating exempt from nonexempt information is so great, and the utility of disclosing nonexempt information so minimal, that the court should invoke section 6255 to bar any disclosure. [Footnote.] That section states that an agency can justify nondisclosure by showing "that on the facts of the particular case the public interest served by not making the record public clearly outweighs the public interest served by disclosure of the record."

Section 6255 has no counterpart in the federal Freedom of Information Act, and imposes on the California courts a duty which does not burden the federal courts—the duty to weigh the benefits and costs of disclosure in each particular case. We reject the suggestion that in undertaking this task the courts should ignore any expense and inconvenience involved in segregating nonexempt from exempt information. Section 6255 speaks broadly of the "public interest," a phrase which encompasses public concern with the cost and efficiency of government. To refuse to place such items on

---

11. We agree with the trial court that information is not "confidential" in this context unless treated as confidential by its original source. Thus, information does not become confidential because the California Department of Justice and the submitting law enforcement agency agree to treat it as such; it is confidential only if the law enforcement agency obtained it in confidence originally.

Amicus calls our attention to a definition of "confidential information" in the Information Practices Act of 1977. [Citation.] That definition includes as "confidential" all information compiled by law enforcement agencies "for the purpose of a criminal investigation of suspected crim-

inal activities, including reports of informants and investigators, and associated with an identifiable individual." [Citation.] It is not clear, however, if this definition would encompass the LEIU cards or the IOCI printouts, since those materials are not necessarily compiled for the purpose of a current investigation. In any event, Civil Code section 1798.24, subdivision (g), makes it clear that information classed as confidential under the Information Practices Act may still be disclosed pursuant to the California Act; thus, the Information Practices Act definition cannot be used to define an exemption under the California Act.

the section 6255 scales would make it possible for any person requesting information, for any reason or for no particular reason, to impose upon a governmental agency a limitless obligation. Such a result would not be in the public interest. [Footnote.]

After careful examination of the LEIU index cards *in camera*, we conclude that in the present case the public interest predominates against disclosure of the cards. It is clear that the burden of segregating exempt from nonexempt information on the 100 cards would be substantial. The cards do not indicate which material is confidential, might reveal a confidential source, or identify the subject of the report; in many instances defendants would have to inquire from the law enforcement department supplying the information. The utility of disclosure to the ACLU, on the other hand, is questionable: the deletion of personal identifiers will make it impossible for the ACLU to learn if a particular person is improperly listed as an associate of a criminal suspect [citation]; the deletion of confidential information will defeat its efforts to learn if any person is listed on the basis of inaccurate or unsubstantiated rumor.

At best, disclosure of nonexempt information from the cards in question might reveal certain generalities about the records, such as the proportion of persons listed with prior criminal records, the type of criminal activity of which they are suspected, etc. Conceivably such information might help to confirm or allay suspicions concerning the operation of criminal indexing systems. When this marginal and speculative benefit is weighed against the cost and burden of segregating the exempt and nonexempt material on the cards, we conclude that on the facts of this particular case the public interest served by not making the record public clearly outweighs the public interest served by disclosure of the record.[14] We therefore conclude that defendants, relying on section 6255 of the Act, may refuse to disclose the subject index cards of the LEIU.

The IOCI printouts, however, stand on a different footing. All information on the printouts is derived from public records. Information so acquired is not confidential, and the public records in question are not confidential sources. Consequently, the task of segregating exempt material on the printouts reduces to one of excising the personal identifiers. This is a much less onerous burden than the deletion of personal identifiers, confidential information, and confidential sources from the LEIU cards. Weighing the burden of segregation against the benefit of disclosure of the IOCI printouts, the balance tips in favor of disclosure.

The portion of the judgment of the superior court requiring disclosure of the Interstate Organized Crime Index printouts is affirmed. The portion of that judgment requiring disclosure of the Law Enforcement Intelligence Unit index cards is reversed. The cause is remanded to the superior court for further proceedings consistent with this opinion. * * *

RICHARDSON, J., concurring and dissenting.

I concur in the majority opinion to the extent that it reverses that portion of the judgment below which required disclosure of the Law Enforcement Intelligence Unit index cards. I respectfully dissent, however, from the opinion insofar as it affirms the compelled disclosure of the Interstate Organized Crime Index printouts. In my view, both the index cards and the printouts are "intelligence information" which are absolutely exempt from disclosure under state law.

Unlike the federal Freedom of Information Act [citation] and its broadly *qualified* exemption for various investigatory records [citation], the California Public Records Act [citation] on its face contains an *absolute* exemption for "records of intelligence information" of all state and local law enforcement agencies. [Citation.]

---

14. Section 6255 requires the courts to look to "the facts of the particular case" in balancing the benefits and burdens of disclosure under the Act. Thus our decision against requiring disclosure is necessarily limited to the facts of this particular case; in another case, with different facts, the balance might tip in favor of disclosure of nonexempt information on the LEIU cards. If, for example, a person were to seek disclosure of only his own card, the diminished need to delete personal identifiers (the person in question presumably knows his own identity and that of his associates) and the reduced burden of determining confidentiality of sources or information when only a single card is involved might justify a court in requiring disclosure.

The computer printouts at issue here clearly constitute "records of intelligence information" within the meaning of the California act. As the majority explains, these printouts disclose the names, criminal records, physical characteristics, associates, occupations and residences of each person suspected of organized crime activities. Although the printouts are compiled from information contained in various public records, the printouts themselves are used exclusively by law enforcement agencies to assist in their investigations. The majority holds that only the "personal identifiers" contained in the printouts are exempt from disclosure, and it imposes upon the agency the task of excising such personal identifiers from the remaining, discoverable information.

The California act, however, does not call for, or authorize, the disclosure or segregation of the nonconfidential or nonpersonal portion of the intelligence records of law enforcement agencies. Instead, by its terms the act protects the records in toto. On the assumption that plaintiff ACLU is interested merely in the "types of information" gathered by law enforcement agencies, no reason appears why a *blank* form of printout would not suffice. As Justice Paras carefully explained in his opinion for the Court of Appeal in this case, "The [blank] forms, which defendants have not refused to provide, fully describe the 'type of information' involved. Anything more than that is the information itself, which would add nothing but specific data relating to specific people. * * * But the specific data placed into the blank spaces is beyond question 'intelligence information,' expressly excluded by section 6254, subdivision (f), from the scope of section 6253, subdivision (a)."

Agreeing with the foregoing reasoning, I would reverse the judgment in its entirety.

BIRD, C. J., concurring and dissenting.

I respectfully dissent from that portion of the court's decision which denies disclosure of the LEIU cards.

James Madison once said, "A popular Government, without popular information, or the

means of acquiring it, is but a Prologue to a Farce or a Tragedy: or, perhaps both." [Citation.]

Like James Madison, the California Legislature is of the view that "access to information concerning the conduct of the people's business, is a fundamental and necessary right of every person in this state." (Gov. Code, § 6250.) [Footnote.] Thus, the California Public Records Act (or Act) was passed for the precise purpose of "increasing freedom of information" by giving the public "access to information in possession of public agencies." [Citation.] The Act is "intended to be construed liberally in order to further the goal of maximum disclosure in the conduct of governmental operations." (Final Rep., Assem. Statewide Info. Policy Com. [hereafter *Final Report*] (Mar. 1970) p. 145, appen. G, setting forth opn. Cal.Atty.Gen. No. 67/144 (1970).)

In approving the government's efforts in the present case to keep the LEIU cards wholly secret, today's majority concludes that (1) the cards contain much information that is exempt from disclosure under section 6254, subdivision (f); (2) segregation of the exempt material from the nonexempt would be a substantial burden on the government; and (3) this administrative inconvenience justifies withholding even the nonexempt portions of the LEIU cards, pursuant to section 6255.

The first two of these conclusions find no support whatsoever in the record. The government has never sought to demonstrate how much, if any, of the information on the LEIU cards is exempt from disclosure nor what the inconvenience or cost of deleting this information might be. Although the Public Records Act clearly places the burden of justifying nondisclosure on the agency desiring secrecy,[2] a majority of this court somehow waives this requirement and finds in favor of the government on these issues.

The court's third conclusion—that administrative inconvenience is dispositive of these plaintiffs' claim of access to the records of their government—threatens the very foundations of the Act. It represents a major triumph for bureaucratic inertia and secrecy, and it per-

---

2. "*The agency shall justify* withholding any record *by demonstrating* that the record in question is exempt under express provisions of this chapter or that on the facts of the particular case the public interest served by not

making the record public clearly outweighs the public interest served by disclosure of the record." [§ 6255, emphasis added.] [Citations.]

mits—and even encourages— state agencies to undermine the broad disclosure policies of the Act. Yet, as the Court of Appeal has held, the Public Records Act is "suffused with indications of a contrary legislative intent." (*Northern Cal. Police Practices Project v. Craig* (1979) 90 Cal.App.3d 116, 123, 153 Cal.Rptr. 173.)

The federal Freedom of Information Act (or FOIA) [footnote] provides a right of public access to records of federal agencies, and, as today's majority agrees, the state and federal enactments "should receive a parallel construction." [Citation.] However, the majority chooses to ignore the unanimous interpretation of the FOIA that "equitable considerations of the costs, in time and money, of making records available for examination do not supply an excuse for non-production." (See, e.g., *Sears v. Gottschalk* (4th Cir. 1974) 502 F.2d 122, 126, and cases cited.)

I remain unpersuaded.

I.

The California Public Records Act was enacted against a "background of legislative impatience with secrecy in government. * * *" (53 Ops.Cal.Atty.Gen. 136, 143 (1970).) The Legislature had long been attempting to "formulate a workable means of minimizing secrecy in government." (*Id.*, at p. 140, fn. omitted.) The basic law "was vague and had been interpreted by the courts in a restrictive fashion." (*Final Report, supra*, p. 7.)

Moreover, it "appeared * * * to be creating (or perhaps merely reinforcing) an attitude of reluctance on the part of various administrative officials to make records in their custody available for public inspection." (53 Ops.Cal.Atty.Gen., *supra*, p. 143.) Those limited reform efforts that managed to become law—such as the Brown Act of 1953 [footnote] —were insufficient to address the problems. What was needed was a comprehensive statute governing access to information. [Citation.]

Such an enactment was the California Public Records Act. (§§ 6251–6165.) The tone of the Act was set by the broad language used to define "public records." [Citation.] "This definition is intended to cover every conceivable kind of record that is involved in the governmental process and will pertain to any new form of record-keeping instrument as it is developed." (*Final Report, supra*, p. 9.)

Like the federal Freedom of Information Act upon which it was modeled, "the general policy of the [Public Records Act] favors disclosure. Support for a refusal to disclose information 'must be found, if at all, among the specific exceptions to the general policy that are enumerated in the Act.' " (*Cook v. Craig* (1976) 55 Cal.App.3d 773, 781, 127 Cal.Rptr. 712, citation omitted, quoting *State of California ex rel. Division of Industrial Safety v. Superior Court* (1974) 43 Cal.App.3d 778, 783, 117 Cal.Rptr. 726.) The burden of establishing that an exception applies lies with the agency resisting disclosure. [Citation.]

Even where the Public Records Act permits nondisclosure, it does not *require* withholding the requested information. [Citation.] The Act sets forth "the minimum standards" for access to government information, and generally "a state or local agency may adopt requirements for itself which allow greater access to records." [Citations.]

Moreover, the fact that parts of a requested document fall within the terms of an exemption does not justify withholding the entire document. [Citation.] Section 6257 of the Act specifically provides that "[a]ny reasonably segregable portion of a record shall be provided to any person requesting such record after deletion of the portions which are exempt by law."

Relying on the Public Records Act, plaintiff ACLU has sought to examine a random sampling of the LEIU cards[5] maintained by the California Department of Justice (or Department) ostensibly in connection with its function of "[g]athering, analyzing and storing intelligence pertaining to organized crime." [Citation.] The ACLU's concern stems from mid-1970's revelations on the national level of law enforcement abuses in the acquisition and maintenance of information for surveillance purposes. The fears expressed at that

---

5. The ACLU agrees that all information on the LEIU cards which identifies an individual should be deleted prior to disclosure.
The ACLU also sought a similarly edited sampling of

entries in the now-defunct IOCI system. Since I agree with the majority that this information should be released to plaintiff, I do not discuss that aspect of the case further.

time have increased as a result of the Department's recent publication of a report purportedly relating to organized crime and terrorism. [Citation.] The report suggests that the Department views its duty to monitor organized crime activities as covering "activities of domestic extremist groups in the form of rallies and demonstrations." [Citation.]

Thus, the goals of the ACLU suit include testing the degree to which units in the Department of Justice engage in political surveillance under the guide [sic] of obtaining information pertaining to law enforcement and "determining whether the conduct of [the Department] complies with law. * * * "

The Department has refused to disclose any portion of the LEIU cards. It asserts that two provisions of the Public Records Act authorize its actions. Primary reliance is placed on subdivision (f) of section 6254 (Exemption (f)), which permits the withholding of "records of intelligence information * * * of * * * the office of the Attorney General and the Department of Justice, and any state or local police agency. * * * " The Department also seeks to invoke the provision of section 6255 authorizing nondisclosure when "on the facts of the particular case the public interest served by not making the record public clearly outweighs the public interest served by disclosure of the record."

Throughout these proceedings, the Department has taken the position that these exemptions protect the LEIU cards in toto. It has adduced no evidence to establish a confidential source for any specific information on any of the cards. Moreover, while occasionally asserting that segregation of exempt from nonexempt information would be "burdensome," the Department has offered no testimony, affidavit, or other evidence of the extent of this alleged burden.

Following meticulously conducted proceedings *in camera*—including examination of the LEIU cards themselves—the trial court ruled in favor of disclosure except for "those portions [of the cards] which show and disclose personal identifiers and confidential sources." It found that disclosure of the nonexempt material "will inform interested members of the public of the type of information which the [Department] develop[s] and gather[s]." It further found the public interest served by disclosure to be "the need to insure that [the Department is] complying with the Constitution and laws of the United States and the State of California * * * and to defend and protect constitutional rights by guarding against unlawful invasions of privacy and personal security by over-zealous spying, surveillance and covert activities."

I agree with the majority that the trial court's interpretation of the Public Records Act's exemption for "records of intelligence information" was too narrow. Exemption (f) permits withholding not only information which might identify confidential sources but also "confidential information furnished only by the confidential source" to "a criminal law enforcement authority in the course of a criminal investigation." (See 5 U.S.C. § 552(b)(7)(D) [hereafter Exemption 7(D) of the FOIA].)

This conclusion is supported by a close reading of Exemption (f). By the plain wording of the Public Records Act, the Legislature sought to protect confidential "information," not merely the identity of confidential sources. Moreover, in providing within the same subdivision for disclosure of certain facts to victims or their representatives, the Legislature specifically exempted the "statements" and "names and addresses" of confidential informants. This indicates that the Legislature was aware of a distinction between statements and identity and that its choice of the broad term "intelligence information" was intended to encompass more than either of these two ideas separately.

Reading Exemption (f) as protecting confidential sources and information brings this portion of the California Act into close alignment with Exemption 7(D) of the FOIA. [Citation.] I agree that the two exemptions should normally receive a "parallel construction." [Citation.]

However, I am perplexed by one reason tendered by the majority for interpreting Exemption (f) in this fashion. Here, it is asserted that the Public Records Act should be interpreted in light of the "fact" that "information may be sought for less noble purposes" than those of the ACLU in this case. [Citation.] This reasoning is completely untenable.

The majority conjures up the possibility that

a disclosure request may be made for ignoble purposes and yet fails even to consider that bureaucracies may have improper reasons of their own for refusing disclosure.

Secrecy is not required by the Public Records Act; disclosure is virtually always permitted. [Citation.] Thus, it is well recognized that disclosure may be resisted not because of a genuine need for secrecy, but out of fear of "arous[ing] public opinion against the policies the agency is determined to employ." [Citation.] A governmental agency may resist disclosure merely because "from a bureaucratic standpoint, a general policy of relevation [sic] could cause positive harm, since it could bring to light information detrimental to the agency and set a precedent for future demands for disclosure." (*Vaughn v. Rosen,* (D.C.Cir.1973) 484 F.2d 820, at p. 826.) In entirely ignoring these obvious teachings of history, the majority blinds itself to the very need for a Public Records Act in the first place.

Moreover, the majority thwarts one of the Legislature's avowed purposes in passing the Act, i.e., to "invalidate[]" court decisions which had interpreted the prior law "in a restrictive fashion." [Citation.]

In an Attorney General's opinion incorporated into the *Final Report*, it was said to be "clear" that the Act "is intended to be construed liberally in order to further the goal of maximum disclosure in the conduct of governmental operations." (53 Ops.Cal.Atty.Gen., *supra*, at p. 143; *Final Report, supra*, at p. 145.) This source also indicated that the "same historical evidence which compels the conclusion that the * * * Act should be construed broadly also compels the conclusion that [the exemptions] must be construed strictly so as not to interfere with the basic policy of the act." [Citations.]

The federal cases interpreting the FOIA are all in agreement with our Legislature and our Attorney General. The federal courts have universally accepted the proposition that the FOIA "creates a liberal disclosure requirement, limited only by specific exemptions which are to be narrowly construed." (*Bristol-Myers Company v. F.T.C.* (D.C.Cir.1970) 424 F.2d 935, 938, fn. omitted, cert. den., 400 U.S. 824, 91 S.Ct. 46, 27 L.Ed.2d 52.) [Citations.] This, of course, is the very same Freedom of Infor-

mation Act whose "judicial construction and legislative history * * * serve to illuminate the interpretation of its California counterpart." [Citation.]

While I agree with the majority as to the scope of Exemption (f), I cannot subscribe to the dictum which would construe the disclosure provisions of the Act in a one-sided manner, blind to the countervailing considerations. Such statutory construction might accord with those justices' view of good policy, but it does not conform to that which is supposed to be paramount—the Legislature's intent.

II.

Having determined the proper scope of Exemption (f), the majority proceeds to uphold the Department's claim of secrecy under the balancing test of section 6255. [Citation.] It rules that the cost and administrative inconvenience of segregating exempt from nonexempt information on the LEIU cards justify the refusal to disclose any information contained in these public records. This conclusion is absurd. It violates the terms and basic concerns of the Public Records Act, the prior court decisions of this state, the "parallel" Freedom of Information Act and the cases interpreting it, as well as common sense.

It is inconceivable that the Legislature, in enacting the section 6255 balancing test, intended to permit administrative cost and inconvenience to be dispositive of a request for access to public records. Nowhere in section 6255 or the Act as a whole is such an intention manifested.

The specific exemptions of section 6254 are of considerable aid in ascertaining the Legislature's conception of "the public interest served by not making [a] record public * * *," as used in section 6255. [Footnote.] However, none of these provisions displays a solicitude for the inconvenience or cost to bureaucracies of affording access to public records. The concerns articulated relate to protection of personal privacy, confidential information, and agency deliberative processes, not bureaucratic convenience.

Further evidence in this regard can be found in the final sentence of section 6257. There, it is required that "[a]*ny* reasonably segregable portion of a record *shall be provided* * * * after deletion of the portions which are exempt by law." (Emphasis added.) It is difficult to see how the Legislature could have been clearer in requiring the production of *any* such nonexempt material.[7]

The Legislature clearly was aware that some requests for information under the Public Records Act would require an agency to (1) "search for and collect * * * records from * * * establishments that are separate from the office processing the request"; (2) "search for, collect, and appropriately examine a voluminous amount of separate and distinct records"; and (3) consult with "another agency * * * or among two or more components of the agency." (See § 6256.1.) The only concession granted to a bureaucracy by the Legislature in this regard was that such "unusual circumstances" would permit the agency a maximum of 10 extra working days within which to respond to the request. (*Ibid.*) There is not the slightest suggestion that such circumstances ipso facto justify a refusal to disclose.

If any further evidence of legislative intent is necessary, it can be found in section 6250, where the Legislature "declares that access to information concerning the conduct of the people's business is a fundamental and necessary right of every person in this state." Today's majority attributes to the Legislature an intent to permit this "fundamental and necessary right" to be overcome by a mere allegation of bureaucratic inconvenience and cost. Once again, this is patently absurd.

In addition to these direct indications of legislative intent, simple logic and experience dictate that the public's right to know not be overridden by claims of bureaucratic inconvenience. The history of freedom of information laws, both in this state and on a national level, is largely the history of bureaucratic resistance to revealing agency operations. If a disclosure request may be defeated by an agency's showings of administrative cost and burden, then the very foundations of the Public Records Act are undermined.

Initially, uncertainty is injected by this court into an act where clarity was intended. The result will surely be that agencies will be emboldened to resist disclosure requests. This is contrary to the Legislature's intent. Compliance was to be encouraged. The likely result of today's decision is the multiplication of contested court proceedings and the end of voluntary settlements.

Even more important, the bureaucracy—rather than the Legislature, the courts, or the people—will be empowered to determine what records will be revealed. It is the bureaucracy that decides in what form and where to keep its records. By commingling exempt and nonexempt information and spreading out responsibility for the compilation and storage of records, the agency can be assured of a tenable claim of exemption under section 6255. At the very least, already wary agencies are discouraged from creating "internal procedures that will assure that disclosable information can be easily separated from that which is exempt." [Citations.]

Finally, as modern society becomes more complex, so do the issues which confront us and the agencies that are supposed to serve us. At the same time, our demands and expectations of government continue to expand. Thus, colorable claims of administrative burden will increase. As a result, constrained by this court's holding that access to public records may be denied because of bureaucratic burdens, the Public Records Act will be reduced to an anachronism, applicable to trivialities or events no longer important, but incapable of ensuring the public knowledge necessary to the proper functioning of a democracy.

It is, therefore, not surprising that the courts

---

7. The majority opinion hints in a footnote that nonexempt information is not "reasonably segregable" if the burden of segregation is great. [Citation.] This suggestion does not withstand analysis.

The "reasonably segregable" provision of the California Act was lifted nearly verbatim from the federal Freedom of Information Act. [Citation.] The federal provision, in turn, has been interpreted to require disclosure of any nonexempt material "if it is at all intelligible—unintelligibility indicating, of course, that it is not 'reasonably' segregable from the balance." [Citation.]

As will be shown hereafter, the federal cases have uniformly rejected the position of the majority that administrative burden can be dispositive of a disclosure request under the FOIA.

have unanimously taken a position contrary to that of today's majority. "Undoubtedly, the requirement of segregation casts a tangible burden on governmental agencies and on the judiciary. Nothing less will suffice, however, if the underlying legislative policy of the [Act] favoring disclosure is to be implemented faithfully. If the burden becomes too onerous, relief must be sought from the Legislature." (*Northern Cal. Police Practices Project v. Craig, supra,* 90 Cal.App.3d at p. 124, 153 Cal.Rptr. 173.)

The federal cases are in complete accord. "[E]quitable considerations of the costs, in time and money, of making records available for examination do not supply an excuse for non-production." (*Sears v. Gottschalk, supra,* 502 F.2d at p. 126.) "Allowing such a defense would undercut the Act's broad policy of disclosure." (*Ferguson v. Kelly* (N.D.Ill.1978) 455 F.Supp. 324, 326.) Even a cursory sampling of cases involving the Freedom of Information Act reveals that the federal act is used to obtain access to enormous quantities of documents from which an agency must segregate exempt information. The request in the present case for access to 100 small LEIU cards pales by comparison. (See, e.g., *Pratt v. Webster* (D.C.Cir.1982) 673 F.2d 408 [FOIA used to obtain access to edited versions of over 1,000 documents, totalling thousands of pages]; *Reporters Committee for Freedom of the Press v. Sampson* (D.C.Cir.1978) 591 F.2d 944, 949, fn. 17 [FOIA available to obtain access to the "massive volume of materials" in the presidential papers of former President Nixon]; *Diapulse Corp. of Am. v. Food & D. Admin. of Dept. of H.E.W.* (2d Cir. 1974) 500 F.2d 75 [FOIA used to obtain access to thousands of documents, the collection and editing of which would take four to six days].)

These federal practices and cases should be highly persuasive to those members of this court who have signed today's majority opinion. Their opinion is replete with statements acknowledging that the Public Records Act "was modeled upon" the federal act and "should receive a parallel construction." [Citation.] Yet, federal authority is conspicuously absent when they decree that bureaucratic inconvenience may prevail over the people's "fundamental and necessary right" to know.

I am constrained once again to disagree.

III.

Even if the administrative burden to an agency could be dispositive of a request for information under the Act, I would be hard pressed to comprehend the conclusion of the majority that as a matter of law, the LEIU cards are exempt from disclosure. The majority reasons that (1) "much of the information of the LEIU cards * * * is * * * exempt from disclosure"; (2) the "burden of segregating exempt from nonexempt information on the 100 cards would be substantial"; and (3) on balance "the public interest predominates against requiring disclosure" of the nonexempt information. [Citation.] The first two of these conclusions are wholly unsupported by the record; the third is a serious misapplication of the law.

The Department has never even attempted to establish how much, if any, of the information on the LEIU cards is exempt from disclosure under a proper interpretation of Exemption (f). Rather, it has consistently taken the position that all of the information on those cards *per se* constitutes "records of intelligence information." Since this court has correctly rejected this extreme position [citation], I am at a loss to discover the source of its conclusion that "much of the information of the LEIU cards" is exempt under a proper interpretation of Exemption (f). Indeed, the only evidence on this point suggests there is little "intelligence information." A high ranking Justice Department official testified in passing that "L.E.I.U. is just an index anyway * * *. *It does not have hard intelligence.* L.E.I.U. does not contain that." [Footnote.] (Emphasis added.)

There are similar problems with the court's conclusion regarding the "substantial" burden of segregation. Here, at least, the Department has proffered an allegation that segregation is "burdensome," but its claim is conclusory and supported by *no* facts. "[B]are conclusory allegations [do] not suffice to establish an essential fact concerning the applicability of an FOIA exemption." (*Irons v. Bell* (1st Cir. 1979) 596 F.2d 468, 471.) Agency claims that an exemption applies "may or may not be accurate." (*Vaughn v. Rosen, supra,* 484

F.2d at p. 824.) Thus, "courts will simply no longer accept conclusory and generalized allegations of exemptions. * * *" (*Id.* at p. 826, fn. omitted.)

It is the court, not the agency, which finally determines the applicability of an exemption. [Citations.] Without evidence, however, a court obviously cannot make that determination. Neither this court nor the trial court has been presented with such evidence.

Given this state of the record and the fact that the agency bears the burden of establishing the applicability of an exemption [citation], it is hard to fault the trial court for ordering disclosure. How this court manages to arrive at a contrary conclusion as a matter of law remains a mystery.

It bears noting that the interpretation given today to Exemption (f) was not the interpretation used at the trial proceedings below. Moreover, the Department, relying on its erroneous reading of Exemption (f), tendered no evidence as to how much information on the LEIU cards would disclose or is attributable to a confidential source, as this court today construes those terms. The proper disposition of this aspect of the appeal would be to remand the case for further proceedings in light of the interpretation today given Exemption (f) and section 6255.

One final point. The section 6255 balancing test permits the withholding of records only when "the public interest served by not making the record public *clearly* outweighs the public interest served by disclosure of the record." (§ 6255, emphasis added.) The word "clearly" is significant. The Assembly Information Policy Committee itself emphasized the word in its *Final Report*: "A public agency may only refuse to disclose the contents * * * of a public record, if it can * * * show that the public interest *clearly* is on the side of nondisclosure. * * *" [Citation.]

In light of this heavy burden on those who seek to justify nondisclosure, the majority's conclusion that the public interest predominates against disclosure is even more indefensible. It represents no more than lip service to the test of section 6255. It seems to present yet another example of the roughshod manner in which the majority ride over the commands of the Legislature and the "fundamental and necessary right of every person in this state"

to information about his or her government. [Citation.]

STATE v. CONAWAY
319 N.W.2d 35
(Supreme Court of Minnesota, May 14, 1982.)

YETKA, J.

* * *

Defendant is a 54-year-old Bloomington resident who has spent approximately a fifth of his life in jail and who, by his own admission, has been a professional thief most of his adult life.

On August 10, 1979, defendant was having his van repaired at Downtown Chevytown. When it became apparent that the repairs would not be completed that day, Herbert Borreson, the used car manager, who knew defendant as a customer, allowed defendant to take one of the dealership's used cars as a loaner. The loaner was a 1976 maroon-over-white Chevrolet Monte Carlo bearing license plate number ACD 362. Several months earlier, in May, a 1976 black-over-silver Chevrolet had been stolen from the lot. In reporting the car as stolen, Borreson apparently got the inventory index cards for this car and the maroon-over-white car mixed up. He gave police the correct color of the stolen car (black over silver) but the license plate number and vehicle identification number of the maroon-over-white car. Thus, on August 10, when defendant took the loaner home for the weekend, he took home a car which had never been stolen, but which had been listed on police department records and on the state computer as stolen.

On August 13, 1979, Special Agent Robert Bonshire of the FBI, who knew defendant from prior investigations and was acquainted with defendant's record, received a call from a neighbor of the defendant. The neighbor informed him that defendant was now driving a different car. After checking the state computer, which listed the car as stolen, Bonshire contacted Bloomington police.

Bloomington Police Officer James Johnson checked with the state computer and obtained the same information. Reserve officers, acting under Johnson's orders, then checked and learned that the originating agency was the Minneapolis Police Department.

Surveillance of defendant's house was established at 6:00 p.m. on August 13. Minutes later, defendant came out, entered the car, and took an unusual, indirect route to a Perkins Restaurant. Before leaving the restaurant, defendant made at least one telephone call.

After leaving, defendant took a direct route home. Officers Bonshire, Johnson and McComb continued their surveillance and commented that it was unlikely that defendant, an experienced career criminal who knew that at any time the police might be investigating him, would park a known stolen vehicle in his driveway in open view. The officers decided that it was possible that the defendant needed the car available at a moment's notice.

While waiting, the officers made a number of calls concerning the car. Johnson contacted the Minneapolis police, who told him that the car was listed as stolen but that the report listed the car as being black over silver. The officers decided, however, that the report was either incorrect about the car's color or that the car had been repainted. Johnson next contacted a representative of Downtown Chevytown. The representative said he did not believe Downtown Chevytown had any cars listed as stolen at that time and that it was possible the car had been sold to AAA Leasing. Johnson contacted a representative of AAA Leasing, who said that, to the best of his knowledge, AAA had no car similar to the alleged stolen car. Johnson then made a follow-up call to the Minneapolis Police Department and was told that Herbert Borreson or Benneson had filed a report. The officers made a number of attempts to contact him, but were unsuccessful.

At this point, the officers decided to attempt to connect the defendant to the car. In order to do this, the officers planned to contact a marked squad car and have it stop the car as soon as defendant left and to arrest the defendant as he was driving the car.

Shortly after 10:00 p.m., defendant came out, opened the trunk two times, got in the car and left. The officers did not contact the marked squad car, but instead decided to follow defendant. Instead of taking a quick route to downtown Minneapolis, defendant took a slower route using city streets. Once downtown, defendant parked his car and entered Murray's Restaurant.

McComb then contacted Minneapolis police and asked them to make the arrest when defendant came out and re-entered the car. Defendant was stopped around 11:30 p.m. on Second Avenue between Sixth and Seventh Streets.

When he was arrested and told that the car was stolen, defendant responded that the car was a loaner from Downtown Chevytown and that the problem could be straightened out quickly if the police would call Herbert Borreson or Downtown Chevytown. The apparent response of the Minneapolis officer was that it did not matter, that they were arresting him at the request of Bloomington police and that the car was listed as stolen.

An immediate on-the-scene inventory search of the trunk resulted in the discovery and seizure of three plastic garbage bags containing approximately 120 items of clothing, many on hangers with double tags attached, about half of which were later specifically identified as having been stolen (presumably shoplifted) from nine different Twin Cities area stores. The clothes that were specifically identified as having been stolen were valued at approximately $4,500. Police also found a number of gems in a black case in the trunk, as well as gems in an ankle wallet on defendant's person. These gems, which had a retail value of approximately $25,000, were offered into evidence only to connect defendant to the items in the trunk; the state stipulated that defendant had obtained the gems from retail outlets in the normal course of business. Defendant also had $1,000 in traveler's checks on his person.

A warranted search of defendant's house for more stolen property at 6:00 a.m. the following morning failed to turn up any stolen property, but resulted in the discovery of a large number of burglary tools in an old wellroom in the basement and a couple of lock picks upstairs in the living quarters. Items seized from the basement included books showing radio frequencies for various police departments around the country; books containing lock codes; communications equipment, including crystals for frequencies used by certain local police departments; sets of both blank and cut keys; tools a burglar could use; numerous lock picks; a burglar alarm bypass device; and a bulletproof vest. Although many of the items found were a number of years old, the state was able to show that one of the drills was only 2 years old, at the most, and another drill less than 6 months old. The "red boxes" used in the separate prosecution of defendant for telephone fraud were also discovered in the house. Police also took a photograph of defendant's bookshelf, which contained, among other books, a number of books on subjects of interest to the professional criminal.

* * *

On the basis of stipulated evidence, the court denied the suppression motion at the omnibus hearing, stating that probable cause was not defeated because the evidence that indicated to the officers that the car was stolen "preponderated over the evidence to the contrary."

* * *

1. Defendant's contention that the arrest was illegal is a two-part contention. First, he contends that the arrest was not based on probable cause because the police were not entitled to rely on the inaccurate stolen property report. Second, he argues that his arrest was an illegal pretext arrest made solely to make possible a search of the trunk and of defendant's person.

Several points should be noted initially. First, a defendant's "arrest is not justified by what the subsequent search discloses." [Citation.] Second, as both parties admit, if the police did not have probable cause to arrest defendant for the stolen vehicle offense, then everything else falls and the subsequent search was improper. [Citation.]

Addressing the issue of probable cause, under *Whiteley v. Warden*, 401 U.S. 560, 91 S.Ct. 1031, 28 L.Ed.2d 306 (1971), police, in a limited sense, are entitled to act upon the strength of a directive or request from other police officers or other police departments to make an arrest. This means that "the arresting officer is himself not at fault and thus should not be held personally responsible in a civil action for disciplinary proceeding if it turns out that

there was no probable cause at the source." 1 W. LaFave, *Search and Seizure*, § 3.5(b) (1978). However, in the context of a suppression motion, the question is "whether the law enforcement system as a whole has complied with the requirements of the Fourth Amendment, which means that the evidence should be excluded if facts adding up to probable cause were not in the hands of the officer or agency which gave the order or made the request." *Id.*

There are several ways to review the probable cause determination of an arresting officer who has not personally acquired the factual data from which to establish probable cause, but instead has learned of these facts from police communications. The first of these can be referred to as the "collective knowledge" approach; the second approach focuses on the reasonableness of the arresting officer's belief in the information supplied by the police communication. This court adopted the collective approach in *State v. Radil*, 288 Minn. 279, 283, 179 N.W.2d 602, 605 (1970), *cert. denied*, 401 U.S. 921, 91 S.Ct. 910, 27 L.Ed.2d 825 (1971):

> In a metropolitan environment, with many police and fast-moving criminal activities, it is unrealistic to demand that each officer in the department personally know all the facts necessary to justify an arrest. The right to act must be judged by the total knowledge of the police department.

Under the "collective knowledge" approach, the *entire* knowledge of the police force is pooled and imputed to the arresting officer for the purpose of determining if sufficient probable cause exists for an arrest. Should, however, the police network fail to have sufficient collective information to establish probable cause (*e.g.*, the initial arrest warrant is defective), then the arrest is illegal. [Citations.] This "collective knowledge" approach has also been followed in Wisconsin. *Schaffer v. State*, 75 Wis.2d 673, 250 N.W.2d 326 (1977). [Citation.]

The "collective knowledge" approach does not hamper a police force in the completion of its law enforcement duties. [Citation.] Police officers are entitled to act on the strength of information received from the department and may assume at the time of apprehension that probable cause exists. [Citations.] The

Wisconsin court summarized this rule well in *Schaffer* when it said:

An arresting officer may rely on all collective information in the police department, and, acting in good faith on the basis of such information, may assume at the time of apprehension that probable cause has been established. Thus, an officer, such as Vande Berge here, who in good faith relies upon such collective information, is legally justified to make an arrest.

Such legal justification, however, cannot alone constitute probable cause for such an arrest, for it is necessary that the officer's underlying assumption of probable cause be correct.

75 Wis.2d at 676–77, 250 N.W.2d 326 at 329 (citations omitted).

The "collective knowledge" approach does not mean that every time erroneous information is communicated to an officer, a resulting arrest is invalid. When information is reported to an officer which alone would not sustain a finding of probable cause but leads the officer to gather additional information, this newly gathered information can be used to sustain a finding of probable cause if it is *corroborative* of the initially reported information. [Citation.] Moreover, because the facts relied upon turn out to be untrue after the fact does not destroy probable cause. The operative question is whether the police—as a collective body—have knowledge of information that belies probable cause at the time of the arrest. [Citation.]

A review of the evidence on this point is helpful here. It is clear that the license number and VIN (serial number) given of the stolen automobile were those of the 1976 Monte Carlo white with burgundy top found in defendant's possession and that such car had not been stolen. It is also clear that the 1976 Monte Carlo silver with black top which had been stolen was recovered minus its license plates about one week later. There is no information in the transcript indicating how the police identified that car since only the car's color fit the stolen vehicle report information. At any rate, it seems that neither any individual policeman nor the police department as a whole had any basis for determining that the stolen car had been recovered.

Furthermore, witness McComb testified: The colors were somewhat similar in that it was a dark top and a lighter bottom. Awmm, the fact

that it was also from a—a car dealership could have been a mistake in our minds; and we had, aw, in previous experience—or, from previous experience quite often the color that is listed is not always the color, the actual color of the vehicle.

According to a statement of the prosecutor, the property that was in the car was inventoried at the scene of the arrest and the car was then towed to a storage service pursuant to standard procedure.

The purpose of the exclusionary rule is to deter unconscionable invasions of privacy by law enforcement officials in pursuit of their duties. [Citation.] Far from being culpable, the actions of the police department do not even appear to have been negligent. The police had received a report of a stolen vehicle bearing the license number of the car driven by appellant; Borreson had given the wrong license number. That was not the fault of the police, and the police had no reason to question the information. The police records, at the time of the arrest, contained the information that the car driven by appellant was stolen. Thus, there was no information held by the police department that the car thought to be stolen in fact was not. In that context, the police had sufficient collective knowledge to establish probable cause for the arrest.

In addition, the police were aware of the defendant's circuitous route with his car on one of the two trips he took that day from his home; of the telephone call the defendant made from Perkins Restaurant; of the opening of the car trunk in the late evening by defendant; and of defendant's long criminal record. Therefore, the arresting officers had independent corroborative information to establish probable cause. [Citation.] Nor does the color discrepancy, in view of both the officers' explanation and the fact that the license number matched, make the officers' actions unreasonable. This does not appear to be sufficient information to place the officers on notice that the police reports upon which they relied were false.

In light of this evidence, we concur with the trial court's findings that the police acted with probable cause for stopping and arresting the defendant and searching his car.

* * *

ODEN & SIMS USED CARS, INC. v. THURMAN

165 Ga.App. 500, 301 S.E.2d 673
*(Court of Appeals of Georgia,
Feb. 22, 1983.)*

POPE, J.

These appeals arise out of the same lawsuit in which plaintiff Thurman filed an action against defendants Martin Burks Chevrolet, Inc. and Oden & Sims Used Cars, Inc. Plaintiff sought to recover damages against Oden & Sims on a contract claim and against both defendants on a tort claim. The trial court directed a verdict in favor of both defendants as to the tort claim, and the jury returned a verdict of $2,000 in favor of plaintiff against Oden & Sims on the contract claim. The parties adversely affected by these rulings bring these appeals.

CASE NO. 64871

1. Oden & Sims enumerates three errors, the first of which concerns the trial court's denial of its motion for directed verdict and subsequent motion for judgment notwithstanding the verdict. Three grounds are asserted in support of this enumeration. Since our decision as to the first ground is dispositive of this case, we do not reach the merits of the remaining grounds and other enumerations.

Oden & Sims asserts that plaintiff did not meet his burden of proof as to the giving of notice pursuant to Code Ann. § 109A-2-607(3)(a) (now OCGA § 11-2-607(3)(a)), to wit: "Where a tender has been accepted (a) the buyer must within a reasonable time after he discovers or should have discovered any breach notify the seller of breach or be barred from any remedy. * * *" We agree with Oden & Sims that this provision of the Uniform Commercial Code is applicable to this case. [Citations.]

Between a buyer and a merchant seller of goods there is a warranty of title. [Citation.] Plaintiff's contract action against Oden & Sims was for damages for breach of this warranty. A condition precedent to bringing this action was that plaintiff must have notified Oden & Sims of the breach within a reasonable time thereof. [Citations.] The content of the notification needed merely to have been sufficient to have informed Oden & Sims that the trans-action was " 'still troublesome and must be watched.' " [Citation.] Such notification did not need to have been in writing. [Citation.] The record discloses, however, that plaintiff gave no notice whatsoever to Oden & Sims regarding the breach of warranty of title. Plaintiff argues on appeal that even if notice were not given, Oden & Sims had actual knowledge of the breach.

"Section 2-607 [of the UCC] expressly requires notice of 'any' breach. [Official] Comment 4 says that notice 'need only be such as informs the seller that the transaction is claimed to involve a breach.' The express language of the statute and the official comment mandate notice regardless whether either or both parties had actual knowledge of breach. [Cit.]

"We also note that this same result would take place under § 2-607's predecessor, section 49 of the Uniform Sales Act. Judge Learned Hand's oft-quoted words applying section 49 are equally applicable here: 'The plaintiff replies that the buyer is not required to give notice of what the seller already knows, but this confuses two quite different things. The notice "of the breach" required is not of the facts, which the seller presumably knows quite as well as, if not better than, the buyer, but of buyer's claim that they constitute a breach. The purpose of the notice is to advise the seller that he must meet a claim for damages, as to which, rightly or wrongly, the law requires that he shall have early warning.' *American Mfg. Co. v. United States Shipping Board E.F. Corp.,* 7 F.2d 565, 566 (2d Cir.1925, cited with approval in *Columbia Axle Co. v. American Automobile Ins. Co.,* 63 F.2d 206 (6th Cir.1933). [Cits.]

"An examination of the policy reasons which underlie 2-607 further support our view. Notice of breach serves two distinct purposes. First, express notice opens the way for settlement through negotiation between the parties. [Cits.] Second, proper notice minimizes the possibility of prejudice to the seller by giving him 'ample opportunity to cure the defect, inspect the goods, investigate the claim or do whatever may be necessary to properly defend himself or minimize his damages while the facts are fresh in the minds of the parties.' Note, *Notice of Breach and the Uniform Commercial Code,* 25 U.Fla.L.Rev. 520, 522 (1973)."

Standard Alliance Indus. v. Black Clawson Co., 587 F.2d 813, 825-6 (6th Cir.1978), cert. den. 441 U.S. 923, 99 S.Ct. 2032, 60 L.Ed.2d 396 (1979). [Citation.]

Since there was no conflict in the evidence as to plaintiff's failure to give notice pursuant to Code Ann. § 109A-2-607, the trial court erred in denying Oden & Sims' motion for directed verdict and subsequent motion for judgment notwithstanding the verdict. [Citations.] Therefore, the judgment of the trial court is reversed with direction that judgment be entered in accordance with said motions.

CASE NO. 64872

2. Defendants' motion to dismiss this appeal is denied.

3. Plaintiff's first two enumerations of error challenge the correctness of the trial court's directing a verdict in favor of the defendants as to his tort claim. Plaintiff contends that his evidence set forth a cause of action for malicious arrest and/or malicious prosecution against both defendants.

The evidence showed that in November of 1977 defendant Oden & Sims picked up a 1970 Volkswagen from the premises of defendant Martin Burks. On December 15, 1977 Martin Burks reported this vehicle as stolen to the Forest Park Police Department. The Forest Park police then entered the vehicle as stolen into the national and state computer systems. On January 7, 1978 plaintiff purchased the subject vehicle from Oden & Sims for $700 plus title and documentary fees and sales tax of $38. Plaintiff paid $700 in cash at the time of sale but did not pay any of the other charges. At this time plaintiff received a bill of sale and was told that the certificate of title would be mailed to him at a later date.

At approximately 2:30 a.m. on January 23, 1978 plaintiff was arrested by two police officers in Forsyth, Georgia. The reason he was arrested was that he was in possession of the subject vehicle which had been reported as stolen by Martin Burks. He was eventually released from custody at approximately 9:00 a.m. that same day after the Forsyth police had been informed by the Forest Park police that there was insufficient cause to continue holding him. This conclusion by the Forest Park police was based on their investigation which was instigated when the Forsyth police

related that plaintiff had a bill of sale for the vehicle from Oden & Sims. Martin Burks advised the Forest Park police that Oden & Sims might have picked up the subject vehicle by mistake.

Harold R. Oden, co-owner of Oden & Sims, testified that he picked up the subject vehicle from Martin Burks in November of 1977 and that he did not speak with anyone at that time. He explained that the keys were in the automobile at that time and that it was likely parked on the back line with the other wholesale merchandise. He testified that he had given Martin Burks a sight draft in payment for the vehicle a day or two before he picked it up. He was told sometime thereafter by his co-owner Sims that the vehicle had been reported stolen. He then contacted Martin Burks to explain how and why Oden & Sims had the vehicle. Oden & Sims issued a replacement draft to Martin Burks dated January 21, 1978, two days before plaintiff was arrested. Finally, Oden testified that if he had not left a draft with Martin Burks before he picked up the subject vehicle, he would not have had the right to sell it.

We agree with defendants that plaintiff did not establish the tort of malicious prosecution because there was no evidence of a "prosecution" as defined in Code Ann. § 105-805 (now OCGA § 51-7-42). [Citation.] We also agree with defendants that plaintiff did not establish the tort of malicious arrest because plaintiff's arrest was not made under civil process. [Citation.] Nor did plaintiff's evidence make out a case for false imprisonment, there being no evidence that plaintiff's detention was commanded, requested or directed by defendants. [Citations.] Notwithstanding plaintiff's failure to establish his claim under any pertinent theory of intentional tort, we find that he did not set forth sufficient evidence on a theory of negligence to withstand defendants' motions for directed verdict.

A directed verdict should be granted only "[i]f there is no conflict in the evidence as to any material issue and the evidence introduced, with all reasonable deductions therefrom, shall demand a particular verdict. * * *" Code Ann. § 81A-150(a) (now OCGA § 9-11-50(a)). The entire thrust of the complaint in this case is that defendants' actions in regard to the subject vehicle amounted to the tort of negligence by which plaintiff was injured. [Citations.] The evidence produced by plaintiff at trial, as set forth above, certainly did not demand a verdict in favor of defendants on the issue of negligence. [Citations.]

* * *

MARTIN v. STATE
424 So.2d 994
(District Court of Appeal of Florida, Second District, Jan. 12, 1983.)

OTT, C. J.

Kevin Martin appeals his judgment and sentence for possession of heroin, contending that the trial court erred in denying his motion to suppress. We reverse.

On December 4, 1980, the state charged appellant with possession of heroin contrary to section 893.13(1)(e), Florida Statutes (1979). Appellant filed a motion to suppress which was denied by the trial court after a hearing on the motion. Appellant pled *nolo contendere,* reserving his right to appeal the denial of his motion to suppress. The court sentenced appellant to three years probation.

On November 3, 1980, Officer Vaney observed a vehicle run a red light. The officer stopped the vehicle. The driver was unable to produce a driver's license and was thereupon arrested. The officer requested appellant, who was a passenger in the car, for identification. Appellant voluntarily gave the officer his driver's license. The officer called for a computer check on the appellant which indicated an outstanding warrant for appellant's arrest under an Alabama charge. The officer arrested appellant based upon the warrant. The officer then searched appellant and took a brown pouch from his pants pocket. The pouch contained minute particles of residue which subsequently were established as a mixture of cocaine and heroin.

At the suppression hearing, the state conceded all the foregoing facts and that the warrant had been served on appellant on February 6, 1980; that appellant had been incarcerated in Alabama and released on Oc-

tober 16, 1980. The warrant, however, was not removed from the Tampa police computer until the day after appellant was stopped by Officer Vaney and a check of appellant's story proved accurate.

We hold that the trial court improperly denied appellant's motion to suppress. Officer Vaney did not have independent probable cause to arrest appellant. The officer relied solely on erroneous information received by radio that there was an outstanding Alabama warrant for appellant's arrest. The warrant was void at the time appellant was arrested. An otherwise illegal arrest cannot be insulated from challenge by the fact that the executing officer relied on erroneous radio information dispatched by a fellow officer or employee. [Citation.] A void or nonexisting warrant cannot be the basis for a legal arrest and search. [Citation.] Since the contraband was seized pursuant to an unlawful arrest, it should have been suppressed as a fruit thereof. [Citation.]

Based upon the specific facts of this case, we reverse the denial of appellant's motion to suppress and subsequent judgment and sentence for possession of heroin.

MINNESOTA MEDICAL ASSOCIATION v. STATE
274 N.W.2d 84
(Supreme Court of Minnesota, Nov. 24, 1978.)

SHERAN, C. J.

* * *

In June 1977, a Catholic Bulletin reporter requested the Department of Public Welfare to provide him a list of all physicians, clinics, and hospitals that had performed abortions for medical assistance patients in 1976 and 1977 and to disclose the amounts the state had paid each service provider for these procedures. The department agreed to provide the information, which is stored with other data furnished by the providers on computer tapes.[1] The department informed the Bulletin that it

1. To receive payment for services to medical assistance patients, the hospital, clinic, or physician must submit a "Practitioner Invoice" containing information about the patient and the service performed. The invoices are then microfilmed, and the originals are destroyed. The microfilm copies are read by a machine which records the data on master computer tapes. Both the microfilm copies and the tapes are retained by the department. Retrieving the data from the computer rather than allowing access to the microfilm copies protects the confidentiality of the patients since only the specific information sought need be disclosed.

would cost $2,500 to $4,000 to program and run the computer to retrieve the data, but later agreed to furnish it at no cost if the Bulletin would prepare the program.

At that time the Minnesota Medical Association and its president, Dr. Chester Anderson, brought an action for a temporary and permanent injunction to prohibit the department from disseminating the information stored in state computers until administrative regulations governing access to computer-stored information were adopted and complied with, which regulations should require payment of retrieval costs, public hearings prior to dissemination, and protection of patients' and physicians' rights to receive and render medical treatment. On November 23, 1977, a temporary restraining order and order to show cause was issued. On December 14, 1977, a hearing was held on plaintiffs' motion for a temporary injunction—

> * * * restraining and enjoining Defendants, their officers, agents and employees and all persons acting in concert or participation with them from publishing, providing, disseminating or otherwise disclosing data in response to the request of the Catholic Bulletin that it be provided without cost and by use of its own computer program, any data relating to names of service providers and/or medical procedures and amount paid to service providers relating to 'abortions' during 1976 and 1977, including any portions or part thereof, and whether alone or in combination, until the final adjudication of Plaintiffs' claims for relief.

On December 20, 1977, the court issued its order denying the motion. It concluded that, with the exception of Dr. Chester Anderson's claim that providing the information to the Catholic Bulletin without cost would constitute an unlawful expenditure of public funds, the plaintiffs had "no constitutional or statutory right to the relief sought." It held that the information sought was "public" enjoying no classification of "private" or "confidential" under Minn.St. 15.1642, and that the fact that the information was stored on computer tapes does not remove it from the category of "public records" under Minn.St. 15.17. It further held that prohibiting disclosure would impose an unconstitutional prior restraint on publication by the Catholic Bulletin. With respect to Anderson's claim as a taxpayer, the court held that the Catholic Bulletin must pay the cost of providing the data. It ruled, however, that a claim that the department would not charge the full cost was not a ground for injunctive relief since the taxpayer could challenge the reasonableness of the department's charges in a taxpayer suit to recover the sum allegedly due.

Plaintiffs appeal, contending * * * that the use of the state's computers to compile, collate, and correlate the requested data will impair or defeat privacy rights, physicians' rights to administer medical treatment according to their professional judgment, and medical assistance patients' right to a free choice of physicians; that state agencies must adopt rules governing access to computer files before releasing any information stored therein; and that taxpayers may obtain injunctions prohibiting agencies from furnishing services or property until full payment is received.[3]

The issue on appeal from an order denying a motion for a temporary injunction is whether the lower court abused its discretion. [Citation.] In this case, where the lower court determined that the plaintiffs have no right to the relief sought, we confine our review to an examination of this dispositive issue. Appellants claim both statutory and constitutional rights to prevent the requested disclosure. They contend that disclosure is not permitted under the Data Privacy Act and that disclosure would infringe medical assistance patients' right under Minn.St. 256B.01 to free choice of a physician. They and amicus Minnesota Civil Liberties Union also contend that disclosure would infringe physicians' privacy and property rights and medical assistance patients' privacy rights. We find these contentions to be without merit.

I. STATUTORY BASES FOR INJUNCTIVE RELIEF

A. Statutory Classification of the Requested Data

The purpose of Minn.St. 15.162 to 15.169,

---

3. Because the court below ordered the department to assess the full cost of providing the requested information and nothing in the record indicates that the department will not do so, Dr. Anderson's taxpayer claim has been resolved in his favor. Having been granted appropriate relief, he is not in a position to raise this issue on appeal. [Citation.]

known as the Minnesota Data Privacy Act, is to control the state's collection, security, and dissemination of information in order "to protect the privacy of individuals while meeting the legitimate needs of government and society for information." Minn.St. 15.169, subd. 3(3). To accomplish this purpose the law provides for the classification of data on individuals into three categories: "confidential," "private," and "public."

"Confidential data on individuals" is defined as data which is "(a) made not public by statute or federal law applicable to the data and is inaccessible to the individual subject of that data * * *." Minn.St. 15.162, subd. 2a.

"Private data on individuals" is data "which is made by statute or federal law applicable to the data: (a) not public; and (b) accessible to the individual subject of that data." Minn.St. 15.162, subd. 5a.

"Public data on individuals" means "data which is accessible to the public in accordance with the provisions of section 15.17." Minn.St. 15.162, subd. 5b.

These definitions require that classifications as "confidential" or "private" be made by "statute or federal law applicable to the data." [Footnote.]

Appellant cites no statute or federal law which makes the names of those receiving payments for abortion services provided to medical assistance patients or the amount of the payments received "not public." [Footnote.] Therefore, this information is neither "confidential" nor "private." Appellants nevertheless contend that the information is not "public data on individuals" because it does not fall within the definition of "public records" under Minn.St. 15.17.

Minn.St. 15.17 subd. 1, requires all state agencies to "make and keep all records necessary to a full and accurate knowledge of their official activities." The statute then provides that "[a]ll such public records" shall be made on durable paper, but that they may be photographed, photostated, microphotographed, or microfilmed and that the reproductions may be substituted for the originals. Minn.St. 15.17, subd. 4, requires public record custodians to keep the records "easily accessible for convenient use," and provides in part:

* * * Except as otherwise expressly provided

by law, he shall permit all public records in his custody to be inspected, examined, abstracted, or copied at reasonable times and under his supervision and regulation by any person; and he shall, upon the demand of any person, furnish certified copies thereof on payment in advance of fees not to exceed the fees prescribed by law.

Appellants contend that, because the information sought here was stored on computer tapes, it is not a "public record" accessible to the public under § 15.17. Rather, they argue, only the microfilm copies of the practitioner invoices from which the computer tapes are made constitute public records. This argument is without merit.

The requirement of Minn.St. 15.17, subd. 1, that public records be made on durable quality paper does not constitute a definition of public records. Rather, that requirement is imposed on "[a]ll *such* public records." "Such" refers to the sentence immediately preceding, which requires officials to keep "all records necessary to a full and accurate knowledge of their official activities." Thus, whether records are "public records" depends not on the form in which they are kept but on whether they are "necessary to a full and accurate knowledge" of official activities. The form requirements merely ensure that the records are made permanent. The department has complied with this provision by microfilming the practitioner invoices.

Minn.St. 15.17, subd. 4, which grants public access to all public records, "except as otherwise expressly provided by law," places no restrictions on the form in which the records shall be made available other than that they shall be "easily accessible for convenient use." While it provides that "[p]hotographic, photostatic, microphotographic, or microfilmed records shall be considered as accessible for convenient use regardless of the size of such records," it does not proscribe furnishing the records in some other form acceptable to the requester. Therefore, Minn.St. 15.17 does not in any way prohibit the department from releasing data contained in its public records in the form of a computer printout.

Minn.St. 256B.041 provides for the establishment of a system for the centralized disbursement of medical assistance payments to vendors by the commissioner of public welfare. Minn.St. 256B.064 provides for the termination of such payments to vendors of medical care who have been determined to be ineligible for payment. These provisions establish that the records of payments to individual providers of medical care are "necessary to a full and accurate knowledge" of the department's official activities. Without such records it could not be determined whether the department was making payments only to eligible providers or whether the payments made were reasonable for the services provided. Therefore, such records are public records accessible to the public under Minn.St. 15.17, and the information contained in such records is "public data on individuals" under Minn.St. 15.162, subd. 5b.

B. Patients' Right to Free Choice of Physician

Appellants argue that even if the disclosure of the information sought is not proscribed by statute, such disclosure would impair or defeat the statutory right of medical assistance patients to a free choice of physicians. They contend that, if the information is disclosed, fewer doctors will be willing to participate in the medical assistance program and the patients' right to free choice will thereby be impaired. Even if this is true, however, it does not serve as a ground for injunctive relief.

The legislature has provided mechanisms by which the public may be denied access to information controlled by state agencies. It has further determined that public records are to be available to the public "except as otherwise expressly provided by law." Minn.St. 15.17, subd. 4. These provisions evidence a legislative intent to retain full control of public access to information. The power to restrict access is given to administrative agencies only in emergency situations, and even that power is subject to legislative action. No power to restrict access is granted to the courts.

With such a clear statement of legislative intent, appellants' contention that the court should balance the public's statutory right of access against medical assistance patients' statutory right to a free choice of physicians and the effectiveness of the medical assistance program is unacceptable. The legislature has expressly reserved the power to engage in such balancing to itself, and its failure to deny public access to the information sought

here constitutes a legislative determination that the public's right to know outweighs the competing interests of the medical assistance program and its patients.

C. Necessity for Rules and Regulations Governing Access to Computer-Stored Data

Minn.St. 15.1641(e) provides:

> The responsible authority shall establish procedures and safeguards to ensure that all public, private or confidential data on individuals is accurate, complete and current. Emphasis shall be placed on the data security requirements of computerized files containing private or confidential data on individuals which are accessible directly via telecommunications technology, including security during transmission.

Minn.St. 15.1671 provides in part:

> The commissioner [of administration] shall with the advice of the intergovernmental information services advisory council promulgate rules, in accordance with the rulemaking procedures in the administrative procedures act which shall apply to state agencies, statewide systems and political subdivisions to implement the enforcement and administration of sections 15.162 to 15.169.

Appellants argue that since no rules have been adopted as required by § 15.1671, no information stored in the department's computer may be compiled or disseminated to the public. Appellants base their argument on the broad legal principle that important questions of social and political policy should not be decided by administrative agencies on an *ad hoc* basis. Yet, they fail to relate this principle to the facts of this case.

Minn.St. 15.1641(e), quoted above, does not expressly require agencies to implement computer security procedures through rulemaking. The definition of "rule" in Minn.St. 15.0411, subd. 3, of the Administrative Procedures Act specifically excludes "rules concerning only the internal management of the agency or other agencies, and which do not directly affect the rights of or procedure available to the public." The "procedures and safeguards" to ensure the accuracy, completeness, and currency of agency data on individuals concern only the internal management of the agency since they provide guidance to the agency in its collection and storage of information. Therefore, such procedures and safeguards need not be adopted in the manner specified by the Administrative Procedures Act.

Minn.St. 15.1671 requires the commissioner of administration to adopt, in accordance with the Administrative Procedures Act, rules "to implement the enforcement and administration of sections 15.162 to 15.169." The commissioner has not done so. Nevertheless, this failure cannot affect public access to "public" information. Nothing in sections 15.162 to 15.169 purports to govern dissemination of public data. Dissemination is governed by Minn.St. 15.17 to 15.174. Minn.St. 15.171 expressly authorizes the use of "alternative methods for the compilation, maintenance and storage of information contained in [official] records" and provides that such methods must provide for access to the information "by those authorized by law to have access." Since the information sought here is public information, the Catholic Bulletin is authorized to have access to it. Its access is thus determined under the Official Records Act, and the commissioner's failure to promulgate rules under the Data Privacy Act is immaterial. [Citation.]

Because the information sought by the Catholic Bulletin is "public data on individuals" accessible under the Official Records Act, because the statutory right of medical assistance patients has been legislatively subjected to the public's right to information contained in official records, and because the failure of the commissioner of administration to adopt rules under the Data Privacy Act does not affect the public's right to information, appellants have no statutory right to prevent the department from disclosing the requested information.

II. CONSTITUTIONAL GROUNDS FOR INJUNCTIVE RELIEF

Appellants assert that "collection and disclosure of data relating to abortions is constitutionally suspect, and may be sustained only upon a showing that it will be held in confidence and that it will not restrict the physicians' right to exercise of medical judgment or otherwise interfere with a pregnant woman's right to obtain an abortion prior to viability of the embryo." This statement is overly broad and does not correctly state the holding

of the court's decision in *Planned Parenthood of Central Missouri v. Danforth,* 428 U.S. 52, 96 S.Ct. 2831, 49 L.Ed.2d 788 (1976). The amicus brief of the Minnesota Civil Liberties Union provides a better statement of the constitutional issues. The M.C.L.U. contends that disclosure of the names of physicians who performed abortions on medical assistance patients would infringe the privacy rights of both the patients and the physicians.

A. Patients' Right to Privacy

In *Roe v. Wade,* 410 U.S. 113, 93 S.Ct. 705, 35 L.Ed.2d 147 (1973), the court held that a woman has a right of personal privacy that encompasses the decision whether or not to terminate her pregnancy. This right is not absolute, but is subject to the states' compelling interests in the protection of maternal health, medical standards, and prenatal life. The states' interests in maternal health, however, do not become "compelling" until the second trimester, and their interests in prenatal life do not become compelling until the fetus is viable. Thus, a state may not interfere with the patients' and physicians' decision to abort during the first trimester and, during the second trimester, may regulate abortions only in ways reasonably related to the health of the mother. [Citation.]

In *Planned Parenthood of Central Missouri v. Danforth,* 428 U.S. 52, 96 S.Ct. 2831, 49 L.Ed.2d 788 (1976), the court upheld a provision of a Missouri statute that required doctors to make and keep records on all abortions for the use of local, state, and national public health officers. The records were to be confidential and used only for statistical purposes to enhance medical knowledge for the preservation of maternal health. The recordkeeping requirement was challenged on the ground that it constituted an unconstitutional restriction on the patients' abortion decision during the first trimester. The court, however, found that the records served the state's interest in protecting the health of its female citizens and that, because the records were confidential, there was "no legally significant impact or consequence on the abortion decision or on the physician-patient relationship." [Citation.]

Amicus M.C.L.U. contends that the proposed disclosure of the names of physicians who performed abortions will have the legally significant impact not found in *Danforth*. First, there is the danger that patients' names will be accidentally disclosed. Second, any disclosure will have a chilling effect in that women may be prevented from obtaining an abortion by the fear that their names might be accidentally disclosed. Third, a woman may be deterred from seeking an abortion from the doctor named because people might correctly infer the reason she saw that doctor. Fourth, disclosure may cause some doctors to discontinue performing abortions, thus making it more difficult for women to find a willing doctor and infringing their freedom of choice in the selection of a physician. M.C.L.U. also notes that the confidentiality of the physician-patient relationship is protected under state law.

Nevertheless, the M.C.L.U.'s speculations on the possible effects of the disclosure of the doctors' names on women seeking abortions are not sufficient grounds for injunctive relief. Whenever the state acquires confidential information, the possibility of accidental disclosure exists. That possibility is not sufficient to preclude the state from acquiring the information, *Whalen v. Roe,* 429 U.S. 589, 97 S.Ct. 869, 51 L.Ed.2d 64 (1977), and should also not be sufficient to deprive the public of access to other, nonconfidential information. Beyond simply presenting the possibility of accidental disclosure of patients' names, amicus offers nothing to show that the procedures followed by the department in this case are insufficient to protect patient anonymity. Similarly there is no evidence to support the speculation that the mere possibility of disclosure of patient identities, however slight, will be a significant factor in a medical assistance patient's decision not to seek an abortion.

The guilt-by-association argument is also without evidentiary support and appears even less reasonable. The validity of that argument must rest on the assumption that once a doctor is known to have performed abortions, it may be inferred that all, or at least the majority, of his female patients employ him to perform abortions. Only if the doctor provides almost no services except abortions, does such an assumption have merit. In such a case, it is likely that the nature of the doctor's practice would be known even without disclosure

of the department's information. Thus, it is improbable that disclosure will have any significant effect on the inferences that can be drawn from the fact that a woman visits a particular physician.

A "radical restriction in the number of Minnesota physicians willing to perform abortions" resulting from disclosure would present a more difficult problem than the more direct effect on women themselves. Amicus contends that such a reduction would infringe on a woman's right to make an independent abortion decision by making abortions less available. Here again, however, there is no evidence that such a reduction will occur.

Robert G. Randle, director of the Medical assistance division of the state Medicaid program, states in his deposition that disclosure of physicians' names "could have some kind of an impact on participation" of medical providers in the medical assistance program. He goes on to state, however, that his "primary concern was the relationship between the providers and the program." Nowhere does he forecast a "radical restriction" in the number of participating providers.

The affidavit of plaintiff Dr. Chester Anderson states that disclosure of the names of physicians and the nature of the treatments they provided "would also discourage physicians and other medical providers from providing treatment covered by the Medical Assistance program to patients eligible for Medical Assistance and discourage physicians and other medical providers from performing necessary medical procedures which are controversial from a nonmedical point of view." He does not allege any significant reduction in the number of doctors willing to participate in the medical assistance program. Neither Randle nor Anderson offers any support for his speculations.

Morever, it seems unlikely that mere disclosure of the fact that a doctor has performed abortions will cause him to stop providing that service. Once that fact is known, the doctor has little reason to stop. In fact, disclosure could aid women seeking abortions to find a doctor willing to provide the service.

Of course, disclosure may also permit those who oppose abortions to focus pressure on the named doctors to convince them that it would be in their best interests to cease providing the service. The propriety of such action, however, is not before this court, which is concerned on this appeal only with the effect of the disclosure itself.

The United States Supreme Court has indicated that any state action that interferes with a woman's right to make an independent abortion decision or with her physician's exercise of medical judgment constitutes an invasion of her right to privacy, at least during the first trimester of pregnancy. See, *Planned Parenthood of Central Missouri v. Danforth,* where the court stated:

> * * * We naturally assume, furthermore, that these recordkeeping and record-maintaining provisions will be interpreted and enforced by Missouri's Division of Health in the light of our decision with respect to the Act's other provisions, and that, of course, *they will not be utilized in such a way as to accomplish, through the sheer burden of recordkeeping detail, what we have held to be an otherwise unconstitutional restriction.* (Italics supplied.)

The disclosure sought to be prevented in this case would not constitute such an "otherwise unconstitutional restriction." Disclosure places no burden on the doctor, does not destroy the confidentiality of his relationship with patients, and does not restrict his freedom to exercise his medical judgment. Disclosure itself does not have any effect on the moral or ethical considerations that affect his decision whether or not to perform abortions. If anti-abortion factions of the public convince him to stop performing abortions, his decision will be the result of private, not state, actions. Therefore, even if the ultimate consequence of disclosure is a reduction in the number of physicians willing to perform abortions, that reduction will not constitute an unconstitutional infringement of women's rights of privacy.

Plaintiffs thus have failed to establish that failure to grant the requested injunction will result in a deprivation of female medical assistance patients' rights to privacy in making an independent decision to seek termination of pregnancy.

B. Physicians' Right to Privacy

Amicus M.C.L.U. asserts that disclosure will deprive physicians of their rights to both privacy and property. The property right claimed

is "to practice medicine according to his or her best judgment and without undue interference by the state." Whether physicians have the property right claimed, independent of their patients' rights to receive the services involved, has not been decided. [Citation.] Even if such a right exists, as is noted in the preceding section, disclosure itself does not constitute "interference" by the state. Thus, the physician's right to privacy is the only right not derived from the patients that can serve as a ground for injunctive relief.

In *Roe v. Wade,* 410 U.S. 113, 152, 93 S.Ct. 705, 726, 35 L.Ed.2d 147, 176 (1973), the court stated:

> The Constitution does not explicitly mention any right of privacy. In a line of decisions, however, going back perhaps as far as *Union Pacific R. Co. v. Botsford,* 141 U.S. 250, 251, 11 S.Ct. 1000, 35 L.Ed. 734 (1891), the Court has recognized that a right of personal privacy, or a guarantee of certain areas or zones of privacy, does exist under the Constitution. * * * These decisions make it clear that only personal rights that can be deemed 'fundamental' or 'implicit in the concept of ordered liberty' [citation] are included in this guarantee of personal privacy.

Thus, the question presented by the assertion of the physicians' right of privacy is whether the personal right claimed—that is, the right of medical assistance providers to keep the details of their dealings with the department of public welfare from becoming public knowledge—is "fundamental" or "implicit in the concept of ordered liberty."

The right claimed is not, as amicus argues, "the right not to have all their professional and business dealings made public." The department does not propose to disclose "all their professional and business dealings." Only services that are paid for with public funds are involved. The providers contracted with the department to provide medical care to medical assistance patients and were paid by the department for services rendered pursuant to the agreement. The intervenors seek disclosure of information concerning only those services and payments.

Viewed in this manner, the contention that disclosure would infringe the physicians' personal rights of privacy loses much of its force. The public has a right to know about the workings of government. The United States

Supreme Court stated in *Cox Broadcasting Corp. v. Cohn,* 420 U.S. 469, 491, 95 S.Ct. 1029, 1044, 43 L.Ed.2d 328, 347 (1975):

> * * * [I]n a society in which each individual has but limited time and resources with which to observe at first hand the operations of his government, he relies necessarily upon the press to bring to him in convenient form the facts of those operations. Great responsibility is accordingly placed upon the news media to report fully and accurately the proceedings of government, and official records and documents open to the public are the basic data of governmental operations. Without the information provided by the press most of us and many of our representatives would be unable to vote intelligently or to register opinions on the administration of government generally.

In opposition to the public's need for information in this case is the doctors' asserted right to prevent public disclosure of their names. In *Paul v. Davis,* 424 U.S. 693, 713, 96 S.Ct. 1155, 1166, 47 L.Ed.2d 405, 421 (1976), the court held that no personal right of privacy was infringed when a police department distributed a flyer identifying the plaintiff as an "Active Shoplifter" to local businesses. The court stated:

> * * * In *Roe* the Court pointed out that the personal rights found in this guarantee of personal privacy must be limited to those which are 'fundamental' or 'implicit in the concept of ordered liberty' as described in *Palko v. Connecticut,* 302 U.S. 319, 325, 58 S.Ct. 149, 152, 82 L.Ed. 288, 292 (1937). The activities detailed as being within this definition were ones very different from that for which respondent claims constitutional protection—matters relating to marriage, procreation, contraception, family relationships, and child rearing and education. In these areas it has been held that there are limitations on the States' power to substantively regulate conduct.
>
> Respondent's claim is far afield from this line of decisions. He claims constitutional protection against the disclosure of the fact of his arrest on a shoplifting charge. His claim is based, not upon any challenge to the State's ability to restrict his freedom of action in a sphere contended to be 'private,' but instead on a claim that the State may not publicize a record of an official act such as an arrest. None of our substantive privacy decisions hold this or anything like this, and we decline to enlarge them in this manner.

The instant case, like *Paul v. Davis,* involves the disclosure of records of official acts. As previously noted, that disclosure does not restrict the doctors' freedom of action in a private sphere. Moreover, the information to be disclosed cannot be characterized as purely "personal" since it concerns the expenditure of public funds. In *Nixon v. Administrator of General Services,* 433 U.S. 425, 459, 97 S.Ct. 2777, 2798, 53 L.Ed.2d 867, 901 (1977), the court distinguished between the former president's personal matters "for example, 'extremely private communications between him and, among others, his wife, his daughters, his physician, lawyer and clergyman, and his close friends as well as personal diary dictabelts and his wife's personal files' [citation]," and matters relating to acts done in his public capacity. The same distinction can be made between a doctor's private records and the records of the department of public welfare's payments to him. The latter records are not "extremely private communications." It must, therefore, be concluded that disclosure of the information sought here will not infringe physicians' constitutional rights of privacy.

Appellants have failed to establish that they have any statutory or constitutional right to prevent disclosure of the requested information. Since disclosure will not violate appellants' rights, the district court did not abuse its discretion in denying their plea for injunctive relief and its decision is affirmed.

Affirmed.

STATE EX REL. STEPHAN v. HARDER

230 Kan. 573, 641 P.2d 366

(Supreme Court of Kansas, Feb. 17, 1982.)

MILLER, J.

This is an appeal by the State on relation of the attorney general from the decision of the Shawnee district court in a declaratory judgment action. The principal issue is whether the custodian of public records which contain some information made confidential by law is required upon request to disclose nonconfidential information contained therein, under the provisions of the Kansas public records inspection act, K.S.A. 45-201 *et seq.* (Ensley). The trial court, for various reasons, held that the statute does not require disclosure of the data. The attorney general disagrees with that determination; the defendant, Robert C. Harder, Secretary of Social and Rehabilitation Services, and the intervening defendant, the Kansas Medical Society, applaud the court's ruling.

The requests which engendered this litigation were directed to the Secretary. He was asked to disclose the names of physicians and the amounts of public funds paid to each for abortions performed during a particular time period. Had the requests related to any other medical procedure, the legal issues would have been much the same, but public interest would not have been so acute. That interest, however, has no doubt been responsible for the excellent arguments, and the high quality of the briefs furnished by the parties and the *amici curiae*, for which we express our appreciation. There are a number of issues which we will state and discuss during the course of this opinion; a determination of the principal issue, however, will govern public officials in the disclosure or nondisclosure of a broad range of information in addition to the select data targeted here.

At the heart of this controversy is the Kansas public records inspection act. The first three sections were originally enacted in 1957. The first section has since been amended. The fourth section was added in 1978. The act as applicable here, and as presently existing (in the K.S.A. Ensley edition), reads as follows:

K.S.A. 45-201:

(a) All official public records of the state, counties, municipalities, townships, school districts, commissions, agencies and legislative bodies, which records by law are required to be kept and maintained, except those of the district court concerning proceedings pursuant to the juvenile code which shall be open unless specifically closed by the judge or by law, adoption records, records of the birth of illegitimate children, and records specifically closed by law or by directive authorized by law, shall at all times be open for a personal inspection by any citizen, and those in charge of such records shall not refuse this privilege to any citizen.

(b) For the purposes of this act and the act of which this act is amendatory, the term 'official public records' shall not be deemed to apply to personally identifiable records, files, and data which are described in K.S.A. 72-6214 and the accessibility and availability of which is limited by the terms of said section.

(Note: 72-6214 deals with personally identifiable school records, and is inapplicable here.)

K.S.A. 45-202:

In all cases where the public or any person interested has a right to inspect or take extracts or make copies from any such public records, instruments or documents, any such person shall have the right of access to said records, documents or instruments for the purpose of making photographs of the same while in the possession, custody and control of the lawful custodian thereof, or his authorized deputy. Such work shall be done under the supervision of the lawful custodian of the said records who shall have the right to adopt and enforce reasonable rules governing the said work. Said work shall, where possible, be done in the room where the said records, documents or instruments are by law kept, but if the same in the judgment of the lawful custodian of the said records, documents or instruments be impossible or impracticable, then the said work shall be done in such other room or place as nearly adjacent as may be available.

K.S.A. 45-203:

Any official who shall violate the provisions of this act shall be subject to removal from office and in addition shall be deemed guilty of a misdemeanor.

K.S.A. 45-204:

(a) Upon application to the director of accounts and reports and approval by the director of the accounting procedures to be utilized, each state agency which is not otherwise specifically authorized by law is hereby authorized to charge and collect fees for copies made of public documents by xerographic, thermographic or other photocopying process, in order to recover the actual costs incurred, including any costs incurred in certifying such copies, subject to approval of the fees to be charged by the director of accounts and reports. Each state agency shall remit all moneys received by or for it from fees charged for copies of public documents under this act to the state treasurer at least monthly. Upon receipt of each such remittance, the state treasurer shall deposit the entire amount thereof in the state treasury and the same shall be credited to the state general fund, unless otherwise specifically provided by law.

(b) Whenever a state agency is authorized by any other statute to charge fees for copies made of public documents by xerographic, thermographic or other photocopying process, and such fees are not fixed by such statute, the amounts of such fees shall be first approved by the director of accounts and reports in order to recover the actual costs incurred, including any costs incurred in certifying such copies.

(c) As used in this section:

(1) "Public documents" means any document or other record which is required by law to be kept and maintained by a state agency and which is required to be open to inspection by the public under K.S.A. 45-201 or any other document or record which is made available for copying by the state agency.

(2) "State agency" means any state office or officer, department, board, commission, institution, bureau, or any agency, division or unit within any office, department, board, commission or other state authority within the executive department of the state. "State agency" shall not include any agency within the judicial or legislative departments of the state.

Dr. Robert Harder is the Secretary of Social and Rehabilitation Services. In that capacity he is the chief executive of that agency which was created by the legislature to care for the poor and needy in this state. As Secretary, one of his responsibilities is the administration of the Kansas medical assistance program. That program is funded about 50% by the state and about 50% by the federal government, under the Medicaid program. Administration of the Kansas program is subject to both state and federal regulation.

In administering the Kansas medical assistance program, the Secretary, as authorized by K.S.A. 39-708c(s), has entered into agreements with private fiscal agents to perform various functions relating to the claims of "providers," those who provide services to persons entitled to medical assistance under the program. "Providers" include hospitals, clinics, other care facilities, and individual practitioners of the healing arts. Providers submit detailed claim forms to the fiscal agent in order to be paid for their services. These forms include the name and address of the provider, the name and address of the person for whom services are performed, a description of the services performed, and the charges for the services. The claims are examined, reviewed, and when approved are paid by the Department of Administration. During 1977 and through June 30, 1978, the fiscal agent was Blue Cross-Blue Shield of Kansas; since that time, the fiscal agent has been a corporation known as EDS Federal. The records available through June 30, 1978, are in the form of computer tapes prepared by Blue Cross. EDS Federal maintains a special file containing copies of the paper claim forms and payment records for abortion claims as is now required by federal law; it also stores the claims on microfiche; and it enters and stores the data from claim forms on computer tapes. The testimony at trial indicates that the information sought—names of physicians performing abortions and the amount paid to each—is contained within the computerized data prepared and retained by each of the fiscal agents. A program could be designed to retrieve it; preparation of the program would take a specialist about a month to prepare, and would be expensive. Verification of payment may have to be done manually or by a separate program.

Abortions have been provided at state expense since July 1978 only in limited circumstances, where the life of the mother is endangered by the pregnancy or the pregnancy has resulted from rape or incest, since those are the only circumstances in which Medicaid funds may now be utilized to provide abortions. Kansas has not funded abortions other than in those limited areas since the effective date of the federal act so limiting the use of federal funds. The result of this policy change is that there have been very few abortions publicly funded since July 1, 1978, compared to the estimated 2,000 abortions performed at public expense in the fiscal year ending June 30, 1978.

The information sought is not separately maintained by the Secretary or by the fiscal agents; it is in all instances contained within records which also contain the names and addresses of patients for whom the services were provided, and much other extraneous information. It is undisputed that names and addresses of persons receiving medical assistance, the amounts received, the specific medical aid received, and the medical records of those persons, are confidential. [Citations.]

The original requests for information were made to the Secretary by Mrs. Patricia Goodson, a member of the board of directors of Right to Life of Kansas, Inc., an organization which is opposed to abortion. She asked the Secretary repeatedly, both orally and in writing, for the names of the individual physicians who performed abortions at public expense, and the amounts of money paid by the state to each in the year 1977 and subsequent years. Her requests were continuing ones. When the requests were refused, she turned to the attorney general, asking that he enforce the public records inspections act, commonly referred to as the open records law, which she felt made the release of the information mandatory.

The attorney general concluded that the information sought was contained within public records which the Secretary was required by law to keep and maintain, and that Sections 201, *et. seq.,* required that the information be disclosed upon request. He so informed the Secretary. The Secretary responded promptly. He acknowledged that the information could be compiled through a special computer program which would be time consuming and costly (around $2,000), but he suggested that disclosure is not mandated by the statutes; would seriously jeopardize the state's medical assistance program; would constitute an unwarranted invasion of personal privacy; would jeopardize the fragile relationship between SRS and the medical profession and might make such services unavailable in the future; and might result in the identification of recipients. He also suggested that he is not required by the act to compile a special record or listing which, by itself, would not be required or useful to his agency. This action was then filed by the attorney general.

Trial was held on March 13, 1981. Petitioner presented the testimony of the Secretary, an official from the Minnesota department of public welfare, and the manager of EDS Federal in Kansas. The Secretary presented the testimony of three SRS executives, all of whom are familiar with the records and programs of the agency. The intervenor presented the testimony of Mrs. Patricia Goodson, a board member of Right to Life of Kansas, Inc., and Phillip Godwin, M.D., president of the Kansas Medical Society, a member of the Society's Medical Advisory Committee to Welfare, and a participant in the Kansas Medicaid Program.

The trial court set forth his findings of fact, his decision, and his reasons therefore, in a detailed memorandum opinion. He said in part:

> Since all of the data containing the requested information also contains information contain-

ing the identity of Medicaid recipients which is required by law to be kept confidential, the defendant Harder is, in effect, being asked to manufacture a record which does not currently exist in the form that it is requested.

> The requested records are not "public records" which "by law are required to be kept and maintained" within the meaning of K.S.A. 45-201 and therefore, open to inspection by the public.

* * *

> The rationale for the Court's decision in this case is that the Kansas Public Records law, K.S.A. 45-201 requires that records which are required by law to be kept and maintained are public records and available for public inspection unless specifically closed by law. The facts are that in this case all of the records containing the requested information contain material which is required by law to be kept confidential. To provide the requested information, records would have to be manufactured or compiled at no small cost to the public in computer time and staff time.

> It is the opinion of this Court that by enacting K.S.A. 45-201, the Legislature did not intend to require public officials or agencies to compile data or disclose all information in the possession of the agency in response to any public request.

* * *

> Since there is no current Kansas statute which mandates the disclosure of the requested information or requires the defendant, Secretary of SRS, to manufacture records, his refusal to do so was an appropriate exercise of his administrative discretion as Secretary of SRS. Nothing contained in K.S.A. 45-201 requires the creation of a record. The act addresses only those records which are "required by law to be kept and maintained."

Judgment was entered for the Secretary, and the State appeals.

* * *

II.

DOES THE KANSAS PUBLIC RECORDS INSPECTION ACT REQUIRE THE DELETION OF CONFIDENTIAL INFORMATION FROM AN OTHERWISE DISCLOSABLE RECORD?

The attorney general maintains that K.S.A. 45-201 *et seq.* implies a duty on the official

CASE SUPPLEMENT

custodian of public records to delete confidential information from an otherwise non-confidential and disclosable record. The Secretary and the intervenor disagree.

The fundamental rule of statutory construction, to which all others are subordinate, is that the purpose and intent of the legislature governs when that intent can be ascertained from the statute. That intent is to be determined by a general consideration of the whole act. [Citations.]

The first part of the act, Section 201, provides that public records which are by law required to be kept and maintained, with certain exceptions not here material, are to be at all times open for inspection by any member of the public. Section 202 speaks not only of inspection but of the right to take extracts or make copies. Section 203 puts teeth in the act, not only by making violation a misdemeanor, but by making the violator subject to removal from office. The purpose of the legislature is exceedingly clear: To subject to public view and scrutiny all of those records which the law requires public officials to keep. Sunshine is the strongest antiseptic—its rays may penetrate areas previously closed. The legislature must have so intended when it enacted this legislation. This is not to say that *all* documents in public offices are open to inspection; only those required by law to be kept and maintained must be made available. The latter, however, must be open for inspection under penalty of the law.

Since the purpose of the act is to provide public disclosure of certain documents, is deletion of confidential or nondiscoverable information reasonably required of custodial agencies? This court has not previously dealt with this specific question. Most of the courts which have dealt with the issue have interpreted public disclosure laws to require, in the interests of disclosure, that the custodial agency delete excluded information from an otherwise disclosable document pursuant to a request for the disclosable information.

The Georgia open records law, Ga.Code Ann. § 40-2701 *et seq.*, is similar in wording and content to the Kansas act, except that it contains an exclusion for "medical records and similar files, the disclosure of which would be an invasion of personal privacy." The petitioner in *Griffin-Spalding etc. Auth. v. WKEU,*

240 Ga. 444, 241 S.E.2d 196 (1978), sought by mandamus access to certain ambulance records. The custodian of the records, a county hospital authority, contended that the records in issue contained medical information, the disclosure of which was forbidden by statute. The Georgia Supreme Court, in a unanimous opinion, said:

> [W]e do agree with the trial court that the intent of the General Assembly was to afford to the public at large access to public records with the exceptions of certain information which the Act exempts from disclosure. We think Code Ann. § 40-2702 can be read in a way to comport with this intent.
>
> We think Code Ann. § 40-2702 requires a custodian of public records to preserve the confidentiality of information that the public does not have a right to see. The manner of separating this information is left to the discretion of the public agency.
>
> We recognize that this duty places an additional financial burden upon the hospital authority beyond the mere cost of the administrative task itself. Personnel used to separate the information on the forms will be lost from their normal work duties. Additionally, the hospital may be open to added liability from lawsuits by patients for invasion of privacy if a mistake is made in separating the information. However, we think that Code Ann. § 40-2702 provides for this situation. It specifically allows the custodian of the records to charge the individual requesting the information with the cost of providing it. The hospital authority in this case has a right to exact payment for these additional duties and liabilities from the radio station before it releases the information. We do note, however, that this charge must be reasonable. It can only be a reimbursement for costs incurred by the hospital. It may not contain a charge for the hospital services. [Citation.]

The Federal Freedom of Information Act now lists nine exceptions to its disclosure provisions and then states:

> Any reasonably segregable portion of a record shall be provided to any person requesting such record after deletion of the portions which are exempt under this subsection. 5 U.S.C. § 552(b).

This provision was added in 1974 and in effect codified the interpretation given to the act by the federal courts. [Citation.] In *Long v. U.S. Internal Revenue Service,* 596 F.2d 362 (9th Cir. 1979), the court held that under the Federal Freedom of Information Act the deletion of identifying information (names, addresses and Social Security numbers) from certain requested computer tapes was reasonable and did not result in the creation of an entirely new record in response to the request.

Several state courts have recognized a duty under various state disclosure laws to delete exempt materials from an otherwise disclosable record. [Citations.] The cases emphasize the importance of allowing public access to official records.

Three principal cases are relied upon to support the contention that the Secretary should not be required to create a "new record." We find all of them distinguishable on the facts. In *NLRB v. Sears, Roebuck & Co.,* 421 U.S. 132, 95 S.Ct. 1504, 44 L.Ed.2d 29 (1975), the court held that the NLRB could not be required, under the Freedom of Information Act (FOIA) to write an opinion explaining and clarifying a phrase used in one of its earlier opinions. In *Forsham v. Harris,* 445 U.S. 169, 100 S.Ct. 978, 63 L.Ed.2d 293 (1980), the court held that the FOIA did not require a federal agency to request from a privately controlled organization documents which had never been in the federal agency's possession and which had never been agency records. In the same vein, the court in *Kissinger v. Reporters Committee,* 445 U.S. 136, 100 S.Ct. 960, 63 L.Ed.2d 267 (1980), held that the agency was not required, pursuant to an FOIA request, to retrieve for the person making the request, documents which were no longer in its custody. In the case at hand, what is sought is information on records which have not escaped from the Secretary's custody, but which are maintained by contracting parties for agency and official use.

One further issue arises: Are the records which are stored on computer tapes "official public records?" In 1957, when K.S.A. 45-201 was enacted, few computers were in use by either public or private agencies. Since that time, computer usage has mushroomed and it is common knowledge that in many instances the only record maintained is that stored within the computer. We hold that the computer tapes described herein are "official public records."

We have seen that the information requested exists as a part of official public records which are by law required to be kept and maintained. The same records, however, contain information which is by law confidential and may not be released. We think it is far more consistent with the purpose of the Kansas public records inspection act to interpret that act as we now do. We hold that the act implies a duty upon the agency to delete confidential and nondisclosable information from that which may be disclosed, and thus to carry out the act's purpose of making available for public inspection all disclosable parts of the public record. Were this not so, any record which an agency is required by law to keep could be rendered inaccessible to public scrutiny by including confidential material therein.

The disclosure of the information sought, either by deleting confidential information from the existing record or by extracting the requested information therefrom, does not require the "creation" of a new public record.

* * *

IV.

WOULD DISCLOSURE OF THE REQUESTED INFORMATION INFRINGE UPON EITHER THE PHYSICIAN'S OR THE PATIENT'S RIGHT TO PRIVACY?

The privacy claims involve two issues: Whether the requested disclosure will impair a physician's right to personal privacy; and whether such disclosure will infringe a patient's privacy-protected right to make a personal decision to obtain an abortion.

As to the patient's privilege, the United States Supreme Court recognized in *Roe v. Wade,* 410 U.S. 113, 152, 93 S.Ct. 705, 726, 35 L.Ed.2d 147 (1973), that the personal right of privacy encompasses the decision of a woman to terminate a pregnancy. The Medical Society and the *amicus* A.C.L.U. of Kansas contend (1) that disclosure of physicians' names would create the possibility that patients' names might be disclosed; (2) that public knowledge of physicians who perform abortions may deter women from seeking abortions since others might infer that she went to a named physician for that purpose; (3) that disclosure might cause some physicians to discontinue participation in the Medicaid program, thus making it more difficult for some women to obtain an abortion; and (4) that disclosure would invade the physicians' personal right of privacy.

As to the first of these contentions, there is no reason shown by the record to cause this court to suspect that any method employed by the Secretary to delete the confidential information—or to extract the requested non-confidential portions—will be inadequate or ineffective. Similar information was released, under court order, by the Minnesota department of public welfare. Minnesota's assistant commissioner testified in this case that the release of the names of those who performed abortions and the amounts paid did not, to his knowledge, lead to the identification of any recipients. On the record before us we have no reason to expect a different result in Kansas.

Contentions (2) and (3) are, of course, highly speculative. The assistant commissioner from Minnesota testified that he could not ascertain any reduction in the number of providers participating in the program following the release of information; over 95% of the physicians in that state were Medicaid participants. Dr. Godwin, president of the Kansas Medical Society, expressed the opinion that if names of providers who perform abortions are released, there are two possibilities: Those who provide abortions under the Medicaid program would quit doing so; and numerous physicians would drop out of the Medicaid program. Surveys have indicated that a sizeable percentage of Kansas physicians are dissatisfied with the Medicaid program and some are thinking of dropping out. There is, of course, a third possibility: That release of the information would have no discernible effect upon the number of physicians who participate, as was the case in Minnesota. We cannot say, on the basis of this record, that disclosure would have a "legally significant impact" on the abortion decision or on the physician-patient relationship. [Citation.]

We now turn to the matter of the physicians' personal privacy. In *Roe v. Wade*, 410 U.S. 113, 152, 93 S.Ct. 705, 726, 35 L.Ed.2d 147 (1973), the court said that its prior decisions "make it clear that only personal rights that can be deemed 'fundamental' or 'implicit in the concept of ordered liberty,' * * * are included in [the] guarantee of personal pri-

vacy." The physicians here are participating in a publicly funded program. It is difficult to conclude that a physician has a fundamental privacy interest in the facts that a service was performed and public funds were expended in payment. The details of the procedure, the communications between physician and patient, even the identity of the patient and the specific date of the operation, are not sought, and will not be disclosed under the request before us. We have carefully examined the cases relied upon by the Medical Society, but find them distinguishable and unpersuasive. We hold that the public's right to know how and for what purposes public funds are spent is a matter of legitimate public concern, far outweighing any personal privacy right of those providers to whom public funds are disbursed. The fact that public funds were paid to a particular provider for a specified purpose does not give rise to a fundamental personal right of privacy in the recipient. As the United States District Court for the District of Columbia observed in *Public Citizen Health v. Dept. of Health,* 477 F.Supp. 595, 604 (D.D.C.1979). "Practitioners who contract with the government to provide medical services in exchange for * * * payments perform a quasi-public function."

The same issues raised here were presented to the Minnesota Supreme Court and decided adversely to the Minnesota Medical Association, a party, and the Minnesota Civil Liberties Union, *amicus,* in *Minnesota Medical Ass'n v. State,* 274 N.W.2d 84 (Minn.1978). * * *

         * * *

We find that opinion persuasive and well reasoned, and we agree with and adopt the conclusions reached by the Minnesota court.

V.

WHO SHALL BEAR THE EXPENSE OF DELETING THE EXEMPT MATERIAL FROM AN OTHERWISE DISCLOSABLE RECORD?

The information requested may be provided by deletion or extraction. The latter appears to be the customary procedure where the bulk of the data is stored on computer tapes. It will require, however, the creation of a special computer program and, for certain of the time periods, perhaps a certain amount of visual examination of claims and vouchers. The trial court found that the estimated cost of development of the computer program was $2,000 and that would be followed by a computer run costing perhaps $3,600. It is not clear from the record whether this estimate covers recovery of both the Blue Cross and the EDS Federal data, or just the latter. It does not include the individual examination of claim forms and vouchers which may be required. It is clear, however, that we are concerned with a substantial expenditure.

K.S.A. 45-204 does not specifically mention the retrieval of information from computerized records. It does, however, make clear the legislative intent that the state recover the actual costs incurred by state agencies in the furnishing of information to the public pursuant to the Kansas public records inspection act, and that the person seeking information should bear the actual expense. Charging the requesting party with the attendant expense does not appear inconsistent with the purposes of the act, and appears to be the express intent of the legislature. See K.S.A. 45-204(a) and (b). We conclude that the requesting party may be required to make a deposit with the agency, in an amount approved by the director of accounts and reports, before the project is undertaken; and we further hold that the agency shall have a reasonable time to furnish the requested information so that its everyday functions are not impeded or disrupted.

The judgment is reversed.

DETROIT EDISON CO. v. NATIONAL LABOR RELATIONS BOARD

440 U.S. 301

(Certiorari to the United States Court of Appeals for the Sixth Circuit, March 5, 1979.)

STEWART, J.

The duty to bargain collectively, imposed upon an employer by § 8(a)(5) of the National Labor Relations Act [footnote], includes a duty to provide relevant information needed by a labor union for the proper performance of its duties as the employees' bargaining representa-

tative. [Citations.] In this case an employer was brought before the National Labor Relations Board to answer a complaint that it had violated this statutory duty when it refused to disclose certain information about employee aptitude tests requested by a union in order to prepare for arbitration of a grievance. The employer supplied the union with much of the information requested, but refused to disclose three items: the actual test questions, the actual employee answer sheets, and the scores linked with the names of the employees who received them. [Footnote.] The Board, concluding that all the items requested were relevant to the grievance and would be useful to the union in processing it, ordered the employer to turn over all of the materials directly to the union, subject to certain restrictions on the union's use of the information. [Citation.] A divided Court of Appeals for the Sixth Circuit ordered enforcement of the Board's order without modification. [Citation.]

We granted certiorari to consider an important question of federal labor law. [Citation.] This is apparently the first case in which the Board has held that an employer's duty to provide relevant information to the employees' bargaining representative includes the duty to disclose tests and test scores achieved by named employees in a statistically validated psychological aptitude testing program administered by the employer. Psychological aptitude testing is a widely used employee selection and promotion device in both private industry and government. Test secrecy is concededly critical to the validity of any such program, and confidentiality of scores is undeniably important to the examinees. The underlying question is whether the Board's order, enforced without modification by the Court of Appeals, adequately accommodated these concerns.

I

The petitioner, Detroit Edison Co. (hereinafter Company), is a public utility engaged in the generation and distribution of electric power in Michigan. Since about 1943, the Utility Workers Union of America, Local 223, AFL-CIO (Union) has represented certain of the Company's employees. At the time of the hearing in this case, one of the units represented by the Union was a unit of operating and maintenance employees at the Company's plant in Monroe, Mich. The Union was certified as the exclusive bargaining agent for employees in that unit in 1971, and it was agreed that these employees would be covered by a pre-existing collective-bargaining agreement, one of the provisions of which specified that promotions within a given unit were to be based on seniority "whenever reasonable qualifications and abilities of the employees being considered are not significantly different." Management decisions to bypass employees with greater seniority were subject to the collective agreement's grievance machinery, including ultimate arbitration, whenever a claim was made that the bypass had been arbitrary or discriminatory.

The aptitude tests at issue were used by the Company to screen applicants for the job classification of "Instrument Man B." An Instrument Man is responsible for installing, maintaining, repairing, calibrating, testing, and adjusting the powerplant instrumentation. The position of Instrument Man B, although at the lowest starting grade under the contract and usually requiring on-the-job training, was regarded by the Company as a critical job because it involved activities vital to the operations of the plant.

The Company has used aptitude tests as a means of predicting job performance since the late 1920's or early 1930's. [Footnote.] In the late 1950's, the Company first began to use a set of standardized tests (test battery) as a predictor of performance on the Instrument Man B job. The battery, which had been "validated" for this job classification [footnote], consisted of the Wonderlic Personnel Test, the Minnesota Paper Form Board (MPFB), and portions of the Engineering and Physical Science Aptitude Test (EPSAT). All employees who applied for acceptance into the Instrument Man classification were required to take this battery. Three adjective scores were possible: "not recommended," "acceptable," and "recommended." [Footnote.]

In the late 1960's, the technical engineers responsible for the Company's instrumentation department complained that the test battery was not an accurate screening device. The Company's industrial psychologists, accordingly, performed a revalidation study of the tests. As a result, the Personnel Test was

dropped, and the scoring system was changed. Instead of the former three-tier system, two scores were possible under the revised battery: "not recommended" and "acceptable." The gross test score required for an "acceptable" rating was raised to 10.3, a figure somewhat lower than the former score required for a "recommended" but higher than the "acceptable" score used previously.

The Company administered the tests to applicants with the express commitment that each applicant's test score would remain confidential. Tests and test scores were kept in the offices of the Company's industrial psychologists who, as members of the American Psychological Association, deemed themselves ethically bound not to disclose test information to unauthorized persons. [Footnote.] Under this policy, the Company's psychologists did not reveal the tests or report actual test numerical scores to management or to employee representatives. The psychologists would, however, if an individual examinee so requested, review the test questions and answers with that individual.

The present dispute had its beginnings in 1971 when the Company invited bids from employees to fill six Instrument Man B openings at the Monroe plant. Ten Monroe unit employees applied. None received a score designated as "acceptable," and all were on that basis rejected. The jobs were eventually filled by applicants from outside the Monroe plant bargaining unit.

The Union filed a grievance on behalf of the Monroe applicants, claiming that the new testing procedure was unfair and that the Company had bypassed senior employees in violation of the collective-bargaining agreement. The grievance was rejected by the Company at all levels, and the Union took it to arbitration. In preparation for the arbitration, the Union requested the Company to turn over various materials related to the Instrument Man B testing program. The Company furnished the Union with copies of test-validation studies performed by its industrial psychologists and with a report by an outside consultant on the Company's entire testing program. It refused, however, to release the actual test battery, the applicants' test papers, and their scores, maintaining that complete confidentiality of these materials was necessary in order to insure the future integrity of the tests and to protect the privacy interests of the examinees.

The Union then filed with the Board the unfair labor practice charge involved in this case. The charge alleged that the information withheld by the Company was relevant and necessary to the arbitration of the grievance, "including the ascertainment of promotion criteria, the veracity of the scoring and grading of the examination and the testing procedures, and the job relatedness of the test(s) to the Instrument Man B classification."

After filing the unfair labor practice charge, the Union asked the arbitrator to order the Company to furnish the materials at issue. He declined on the ground that he was without authority to do so. In view of the pendency of the charges before the Board, the parties proceeded with the arbitration on the express understanding that the Union could reopen the case should it ultimately prevail in its claims. During the course of the arbitration, however, the Company did disclose the raw scores of those who had taken the test, with the names of the examinees deleted. In addition, it provided the Union with sample questions indicative of the types of questions appearing on the test battery and with detailed information about its scoring procedures. It also offered to turn over the scores of any employee who would sign a waiver releasing the Company psychologist from his pledge of confidentiality. The Union declined to seek such releases.

The arbitrator's decision found that the Company was free under the collective agreement to establish minimum reasonable qualifications for the job of Instrument Man and to use aptitude tests as a measure of those qualifications: that the Instrument Man B test battery was a reliable and fair test in the sense that its administration and scoring had been standardized; and that the test had a "high degree of validity" as a predictor of performance in the job classification for which it was developed. He concluded that the 10.3 score created a "presumption of significant difference under the contract." [Footnote.] He also expressed the view that the Union's position in the arbitration had not been impaired because of lack of access to the actual test battery.

Several months later the Board issued a complaint based on the Union's unfair labor practice charge. At the outset of the hearing before the Administrative Law Judge, the Company offered to turn over the test battery and answer sheets to an industrial psychologist selected by the Union for an independent evaluation, stating that disclosure to an intermediary obligated to preserve test secrecy would satisfy its concern that direct disclosure to the Union would inevitably result in dissemination of the questions. The Union rejected this compromise.

The Administrative Law Judge found that notwithstanding the conceded statistical validity of the test battery, the tests and scores would be of probable relevant help to the Union in the performance of its duties as collective-bargaining agent. He reasoned that the Union, having had no access to the tests, had been "deprived of any occasion to check the tests for built-in bias, or discriminatory tendency, or any opportunity to argue that the tests or the test questions are not well suited to protect the employees' rights, or to check the accuracy of the scoring." The Company's claim that employees' privacy might be abused by disclosure to the Union of the scores he rejected as insubstantial. Accordingly, he recommended that the Company be ordered to turn over the test scores directly to the Union. He did, however, accept the Company's suggestion that the test battery and answer sheets be disclosed to an expert intermediary. Disclosure of these materials to lay Union representatives, he reasoned, would not be likely to produce constructive results, since the tests could be properly analyzed only by professionals. [Footnote.] The Union was to be given "the right to see and study the tests," and to use the information therein "to the extent necessary to process and arbitrate the grievances," but not to disclose the information to third parties other than the arbitrator.

The Company specifically requested the Board "to adopt that part of the order which requires that tests be turned over to a qualified psychologist," but excepted to the requirement that the employee-linked scores be given to the Union. It contended that the only reason asserted by the Union in support of its request for the scores—to check their arithmetical accuracy—was not sufficient to overcome the principle of confidentiality that underlay its psychological testing program. The Union filed a cross exception to the requirement that it select a psychologist, arguing that it should not be forced to "employ an outsider for what is normal grievance and Labor-Management work."

The Board, and the Court of Appeals for the Sixth Circuit in its decision enforcing the Board's order, ordered the Company to turn over all the material directly to the Union. They concluded that the Union should be able to determine for itself whether it needed a psychologist to interpret the test battery and answer sheets. Both recognized the Company's interest in maintaining the security of the tests, but both reasoned that appropriate restrictions on the Union's use of the materials would protect this interest. [Footnote.] Neither was receptive to the Company's claim that employee privacy and the professional obligations of the Company's industrial psychologists should outweigh the Union request for the employee-linked scores.

II

* * *

Two issues, then, are presented on this record. The first concerns the Board's choice of a remedy for the Company's failure to disclose copies of the test battery and answer sheets. The second, and related, question concerns the propriety of the Board's conclusion that the Company committed an unfair labor practice when it refused to disclose, without a written consent from the individual employees, the test scores linked with the employee names.

* * *

B

* * * The Company argues that even if the scores were relevant to the Union's grievance (which it vigorously disputes), the Union's need for the information was not sufficiently weighty to require breach of the promise of confidentiality to the examinees, breach of its industrial psychologists' code of professional ethics, and potential embarrassment and harassment of at least some of the examinees. The Board responds that this information does satisfy the appropriate standard of "relevance" [citation], and that the Company, having

"unilaterally" chosen to make a promise of confidentiality to the examinees, cannot rely on that promise to defend against a request for relevant information. The professional obligations of the Company's psychologists, it argues, must give way to paramount federal law. Finally, it dismisses as speculative the contention that employees with low scores might be embarrassed or harassed.

We may accept for the sake of this discussion the finding that the employee scores were of potential relevance to the Union's grievance, as well as the position of the Board that the federal statutory duty to disclose relevant information cannot be defeated by the ethical standards of a private group. [Citation.] Nevertheless we agree with the Company that its willingness to disclose these scores only upon receipt of consents from the examinees satisfied its statutory obligations under § 8 (a)(5).

The Board's position appears to rest on the proposition that union interests in arguably relevant information must always predominate over all other interests, however legitimate. But such an absolute rule has never been established [footnote], and we decline to adopt such a rule here. [Footnote.] There are situations in which an employer's conditional offer to disclose may be warranted. This we believe is one.

The sensitivity of any human being to disclosure of information that may be taken to bear on his or her basic competence is sufficiently well known to be an appropriate subject of judicial notice. [Footnote.] There is nothing in this record to suggest that the Company promised the examinees that their scores would remain confidential in order to further parochial concerns or to frustrate subsequent Union attempts to process employee grievances. And it has not been suggested at any point in this proceeding that the Company's unilateral promise of confidentiality was in itself violative of the terms of the collective-bargaining agreement. Indeed, the Company presented evidence that disclosure of individual scores had in the past resulted in the harassment of some lower scoring examinees who had, as a result, left the Company.

Under these circumstances, any possible impairment of the function of the Union in processing the grievances of employees is more than justified by the interests served in conditioning the disclosure of the test scores upon the consent of the very employees whose grievance is being processed. The burden on the Union in this instance is minimal. The Company's interest in preserving employee confidence in the testing program is well founded.

In light of the sensitive nature of testing information, the minimal burden that compliance with the Company's offer would have placed on the Union, and the total absence of evidence that the Company had fabricated concern for employee confidentiality only to frustrate the Union in the discharge of its responsibilities, we are unable to sustain the Board in its conclusion that the Company, in resisting an unconsented-to disclosure of individual test results, violated the statutory obligation to bargain in good faith. [Citation.] Accordingly, we hold that the order requiring the Company unconditionally to disclose the employee scores to the Union was erroneous.

The judgment is vacated, and the case remanded to the Court of Appeals for the Sixth Circuit for further proceedings consistent with this opinion.

It is so ordered.

PEOPLE v. HOME INSURANCE CO.

197 Colo. 260, 591 P.2d 1036

(Supreme Court of Colorado, En Banc, March 19, 1979.)

LEE, J.

The People appeal from the dismissal of theft and theft-related charges by the trial court at the close of the prosecution's case. The charges arose from the surreptitious procurement by agents of the insurance company defendants of confidential medical information concerning two patients of a Denver hospital. The trial court granted the dismissal because the medical information obtained was not a "thing of value" as defined in the pertinent statute and therefore was not subject to theft. We affirm.

The defendants hired an injury claims investigative service to obtain medical information reports on two claimants. Through the use of the telephone, an investigator for the

service obtained a verbatim reading of the medical reports which he later transcribed and sent to the defendants. The actual medical records themselves never left the hospital file room; rather, only the medical information contained in the records was thus acquired.

The theft statute, section 18-4-401(1)(a), C.R.S.1973 (1978 Repl. Vol. 8), reads in pertinent part:

A person commits theft when he knowingly obtains or exercises control over anything of value of another without authorization, or by threat or deception, and:

(a) Intends to deprive the other person permanently of the use or benefit of the thing of value. * * *

Crucial to our determination of this case is the definition of "thing of value" contained in section 18-1-901(3)(r), C.R.S.1973 (1978 Repl. Vol. 8):

"Thing of value" includes real property, tangible and intangible personal property, contract rights, choses in action, services, and any rights or use or enjoyment connected therewith.

The People argue that the confidentiality inherent in one's personal medical information is a "thing of value" within the meaning of the theft statute inasmuch as the confidentiality is intangible personal property. We do not agree with this expansive interpretation of the theft statute.

In determining the meaning of criminal statutes, we are guided by the principle that such statutes must be strictly construed in favor of the accused and they cannot be extended either by implication or construction. [Citations.]

As far as we have been able to determine, and no cases have been cited by the People to the contrary, confidentiality has never been considered as intangible personal property. Rather, the term intangible personal property has been held to be property which is merely representative of value, such as certificates of stock, bonds, promissory notes, patents, copyrights, tradebrands and franchises. [Citation.] We, therefore, would have to expand unduly the traditional concept of intangible property if we were to accept the People's contention.

Furthermore, the General Assembly has specifically addressed the violation of analogous privacy interests in the criminal code. Thus, it has authorized criminal sanctions for the theft of trade secrets, section 18-4-408, C.R.S.1973 (1978 Repl. Vol. 8),[1] unauthorized wiretapping of telephone or telegraph communication, section 18-9-303, C.R.S.1973 (1978 Repl. Vol. 8); eavesdropping, section 18-9-304, C.R.S.1973 (1978 Repl. Vol. 8); and unauthorized reading, learning or disclosure of telephone, telegraph or mail messages, section 18-9-306, C.R.S.1973 (1978 Repl. Vol. 8). The foregoing amply demonstrates that the General Assembly has the legislative competence, if inclined to do so, to make illegal the invasion of privacy or confidentiality. The legislature, however, has not chosen to apply criminal sanctions to the invasion of the confidentiality of medical information. We will not now do so by an unwarranted interpretation of the meaning of intangible personal property as it is used in the statutory definition of "thing of value."

In the civil context the legislature has considered the importance of confidentiality of medical information. Section 25-1-802, C.R.S.1973 (1978 Supp.) concerns confidentiality of patient records in the custody of health care facilities. Section 27-10-120, C.R.S.1973, provides that all information obtained in the course of providing services to the mentally ill in state institutions shall be confidential and privileged. Section 25-1-312, C.R.S.1973, makes records of alcoholics compiled at treatment facilities confidential and privileged. Section 24-72-204(3), C.R.S.1973, provides that public records containing medical and psychological data shall not be available for public inspection except in certain prescribed circumstances. The legislature, therefore, has taken specific steps to protect the confidentiality of medical information by creating statutory duties, the breach of which could serve as the basis for a civil remedy. However, the legislature has not imposed criminal penalties for violations of the confidentiality or privilege.

Finally, the acceptance of the People's contention that invasion of the confidentiality of

one's medical records constitutes theft would have far-reaching ramifications. Conceivably, a person who committed one of the four recognized torts for the invasion of privacy[2] could be tried for theft. Also, the breach of one of the recognized privileges (*e. g.*, husband-wife, attorney-client, clergyman-penitent, doctor-patient, accountant-client and psychologist-client, *see* section 13-90-107, C.R.S.1973) might possibly be construed as theft. In our view, such an expansion of criminal liability could not have been intended by the legislature when it adopted the theft statute. Although we agree with the trial court that the defendants' conduct was "reprehensible and outrageous," that conduct simply was not made criminal under the theft statute. Proof of moral turpitude is not alone sufficient to authorize a criminal conviction. [Citation.]

Because of our disposition, it is unnecessary to address the issue of how to calculate the monetary worth of the medical information or the issue of whether the evidence established the element of permanent deprivation.

The judgment is affirmed.

TUREEN v. EQUIFAX, INC.
571 F.2d 411
(United States Court of Appeals, Eighth Circuit, Feb. 21, 1978.)

HUNTER, D. J.

Bernard H. Tureen brought this action for damages resulting from an alleged invasion of his privacy by Equifax, Inc. (hereinafter "defendant"). * * * Defendant appeals from a jury verdict in favor of plaintiff and against defendant in the amount of $5,000. The relevant facts are as follows.

During 1973 and 1974, plaintiff maintained a health insurance policy with the All-American Insurance Company. In 1973, he suffered a heart attack and in July of that year made a claim for health insurance benefits. Again in February of 1974, following a

---

1. Although traditionally there has been a civil remedy for appropriation of trade secrets [citation], the legislature considered the increasing encroachment on this type of confidentiality as warranting criminal penalties.

2. According to *W. Prosser, Torts* § 117 (4th ed. 1971),

the common law tort of invasion of privacy contains four distinct kinds of invasion of four different interests: (1) intrusion upon physical solitude; (2) public disclosure of private facts; (3) false light in the public eye; and (4) appropriation of name or likeness.

second heart attack, plaintiff made a claim of disability. All-American employed defendant to investigate each of plaintiff's claims. Defendant is an independent consumer reporting firm engaged in the business of investigating and providing information upon request to assist merchants, employers, insurers, etc. in making determinations as to whether to extend credit, hire, insure, etc. a given individual. Defendant conducted its investigation of plaintiff's second claim and issued a report to All-American. That report gives rise to this action.

Plaintiff's second claim was received by All-American in the form of a letter from one of plaintiff's employees. Upon receipt of the letter, Raymond Sawaicki, a claims adjuster for All-American, issued a written request, on a standard form supplied by defendant, for defendant to investigate the question of whether or not plaintiff was totally disabled and therefore entitled to disability insurance benefits. The request form consisted of a series of boxes which could be checked as to the type of investigation requested, and a space in which specific investigation instructions could be given. Sawaicki checked the box for a "special health" investigation, and further requested specifically that defendant make a detailed investigation as to plaintiff's business activities in St. Louis, his business holdings and his degree of participation in the management of his businesses in St. Louis and Florida during the period in question.[1]

On the back of the request form was printed information which directed that in the event a special health investigation was called for, it should answer the questions raised in Equifax Form 37 of the claim investigation report. Form 37 contains the following question:

Claim or underwriting history. (Give all claim history. Give life and health underwriting history to life and health accounts only—not to claim or loss accounts. Auto insurance history

may be given to all accounts. If already given, so state: Do not repeat.)

The report submitted to All-American by defendant stated:

FILE DIGEST: A thorough check of our files reveals no previous claim history on Bernard H. Tureen. The last underwriting report was a special life report done on 6-13-68. This report was for Connecticut Mutual Life Insurance Co., 140 Garden St. Hartford, Conn. 06115. The inspection showed Bernard H. Tureen residing at 100 S. New Ballas Road and his occupation was given as President of the American Duplex Corp. 3450 Russell, St. Louis, Mo. Amount applied for was $100,000 and at the time he was carrying $400,000. Beneficiary was the American Duplex Corp. of which he was President. Insurance history indicates we had reported on 23 occasions to various account numbers for life insurance going back to 1949. Total amount applied for for [sic] life was in excess of $10,000,000 * * *. We are not quoting the remainder of the 23 insurance companies due to their age. However, if you desire a supplemental listing of these underwriting reports, please advise and we will put this together for you at a later date.

Upon receipt of defendant's report concerning plaintiff, All-American retained the report in its claim department and did not disseminate it to any other persons.

Plaintiff brought this action originally in two counts, one alleging invasion of his privacy as a result of the investigative report, and the second alleging that the report's statements concerning his past insurance history were libelous. Due to the running of the statute of limitations on libel, that count was dismissed as time-barred, and the case proceeded to trial solely on the issue of invasion of privacy.

At the trial, Robert B. Stinson, defendant's insurance claims supervisor who reviewed the final report prior to its being forwarded to All-American, testified that the Equifax Form 37, containing plaintiff's insurance history, was filled out because a special health report had

---

1. Those instructions read, "Please contact any neighbors or business sources where Mr. Tureen lived in St. Louis to determine if he has been totally disabled from 11/16 to present. Contact the person who is in charge of managing Mr. Tureen's business in St. Louis. Find out if Mr. Tureen has been flying down to St. Louis regarding his business. If he has not, determine who is in charge of his business in his absence, and if he has been calling

or corresponding with Mr. Tureen in regard to his business. Is Mr. Tureen known to have worked in a supervisory capacity, or any sedentary duties during the time which he is claiming total disability? In general, are his activities consistent with those of a totally disabled person? Secure a signed statement from Manager and pursue any leads that you may have."

been requested. He stated that insurance companies often find insurance history helpful and necessary to learn of other carriers with coverage on the same risk. Mr. Sawaicki, who issued the written request to defendant, testified that he did not specifically request a report on plaintiff's past insurance history as a part of the investigation, and that he generally weighs each case as to whether past insurance history will be requested. He stated that All-American did not suspect any fraud or misrepresentation on the part of plaintiff in connection with his claim for disability insurance benefits. Sawaicki further testified that he did intend the investigation of plaintiff's claim to include everything which was included on the request form.

Robert C. Nixon, defendant's employee who investigated and answered the questions contained on defendant's Form 37, testified that he did so by going to defendant's file on plaintiff, pulling the last several insurance reports which had been made, and listing the information contained within the last report. Mr. Nixon stated that prior underwriting history is a standard item routinely reported upon at the request of insurance companies faced with claims.

Over defendant's objection as to relevancy, plaintiff was allowed to testify that he had *not* applied on 23 prior occasions for $10,000,000 worth of life insurance, as stated in defendant's report. Plaintiff asserted that he had made at most eight to ten applications for insurance from 1931 to the date of the trial, and that the total value of all such applications had not been over half a million dollars. He stated that the language of the report caused him great anguish because it made him look like a potential suicide. He also testified that the report had upset him and caused him great concern and loss of sleep.

At the close of all the evidence, defendant filed its Motion for Directed Verdict. Reserving its ruling on defendant's motion, the district court submitted the case to the jury on the following instruction:

Plaintiff, Mr. Tureen, must establish by a preponderance of the evidence: (1) that the information contained in the investigative report stamped March 19, 1974, relating to his past applications for life and health insurance, was not reasonably needed to determine whether the claim for Mr. Tureen's illness was justified; and (2) that defendant's conduct was such that it was offensive, unreasonable, serious and unwarranted to a person of ordinary sensibilities.

Counsel for defendant expressly did not object to the law as expressed in that verdict-directing instruction, but did object that there was no evidence in the record to support the giving of the instruction. The trial court further instructed the jury that:

If you find the issues in favor of the plaintiff then you must award the plaintiff such sum as you find will fairly and justly compensate the plaintiff for any damages you find Mr. Tureen sustained and is reasonably certain to sustain in the future as a direct result of the investigation of the report of March 19, 1974.

Defendant objected to the damage instruction on the basis that there was no evidence of damage to plaintiff, and no evidence of any future damage.

Following the jury's verdict for plaintiff, defendant filed its Motion for Setting Aside Verdict and Judgement in Accordance With Motion for a Directed Verdict or in the Alternative Motion for a New Trial. This timely appeal followed a denial of defendant's motion.

Defendant first contends that the trial court erred in denying defendant's motion for directed verdict at the close of the evidence. We agree.

The origin of the tort of invasion of privacy is commonly traced to an article by Warren and Brandeis in the Harvard Law Review of 1890,[2] which was prompted by the authors' concern with the invasion of privacy by newspapers.[3] Their concern also extended to other aspects of their "modern" society:

2. Warren and Brandeis, The Right to Privacy, 4 *Harv.L.Rev.* 193 (1890).

3. "The press is overstepping in every direction the obvious bounds of propriety and of decency. Gossip is no longer the resource of the idle and of the vicious, but has become a trade, which is pursued with industry as well as effrontery. To satisfy a prurient taste the details of sexual relations are spread broadcast in the columns of the daily papers. To occupy the indolent, column upon column is filled with idle gossip, which can only be procured by intrusion upon the domestic circle." Warren and Brandeis, *supra* at 196.

If we are correct in this conclusion [the existence of a right to privacy based on an inviolate personality], the existing law affords a principle which may be invoked to protect the privacy of the individual from invasion either by the too enterprising press, the photographer, or the possessor of any other modern device for recording or reproducing scenes or sounds.

[Citation.]

The basis of the right of privacy is the right to be let alone. *Barber v. Time, Inc.,* 348 Mo. 1199, 159 S.W.2d 291, 294 (1942). [Citations.] It has been suggested that what is actually involved is "appropriation of an interest in personality * * * which recognizes that the individual does not exist solely for the state or society but has inalienable rights which cannot be lawfully taken from him, so long as he behaves properly." *Barber v. Time, Inc., supra,* 159 S.W.2d at 294.

Missouri law first recognized the tort of invasion of privacy in *Munden v. Harris,* 153 Mo.App. 652, 659-60, 134 S.W. 1076, 1078-79 (1911). That decision also noted the necessity of harmonizing individual rights with community and social interests in establishing conditions of liability for invasion of the right of privacy.

> [I]t ought also to be understood that the right of privacy does not extend so far as to subvert those rights which spring from social conditions, including business relations. By becoming a member of society one surrenders those natural rights which are incompatible with social conditions.

[Citation.] The same concern was reiterated by the Missouri Supreme Court in the leading case of *Barber v. Time, Inc., supra,* 159 S.W.2d at 295-96, and subsequent Missouri cases have involved the balancing of public and private interests. [Citations.]

Dean Prosser has identified and described four generally recognized tort actions for invasion of privacy: intrusion, public disclosure of private facts, false light in the public eye, and appropriation. W. Prosser, *Handbook of of the Law of Torts* § 117, at 833, 834, 837, 839 (4th ed. 1971). The American Law Institute, following Prosser's classifications, has recognized the general principle that the right of privacy is invaded by (1) unreasonable intrusion upon the seclusion of another, (2) appropriation of the other's name or likeness,

(3) unreasonable publicity given to the other's private life, or (4) publicity that unreasonably places the other in a false light before the public. *Restatement (Second) of Torts* §§ 652A-652E (1977). The circumstances presented in this case—investigation of plaintiff by a retail credit company at the request of its client, plaintiff's insurance carrier, and disclosure of certain information about plaintiff to the insurance company—must be examined in connection with two of the above actions: intrusion and public disclosure.

In considering defendant's conduct as an intrusion, this court is aware that proponents for regulation of the consumer reporting industry usually point to insurance investigations as the type of conduct most likely to intrude upon the consumer's right of privacy. [Citation.] Certain objectionable snooping techniques used by consumer reporting companies could be considered an intrusion violative of the right of privacy. [Citations.]

The instant case, however, does not contain evidence of objectionable snooping techniques on the part of defendant. Defendant obtained the information about which plaintiff complains merely by means of searching defendant's own files containing a summary of defendant's own prior reports on plaintiff, hardly an act which intruded in any manner upon plaintiff. Because defendant's technique was not objectionable, any intrusion giving rise to a cause of action for invasion of Mr. Tureen's privacy must stem from the fact that defendant *collected* and *retained* the information concerning plaintiff's past insurance history.

We are not unmindful of the potential for abuse in the collection and retention of consumer reporting information. [Footnote.] We do not rule out the possibility that instances may exist where the collection of highly personal information irrelevant to *any* legitimate business purpose might constitute an invasion of privacy by unreasonable intrusion. [Footnote.] This, however, is not such a case.

In today's mobile society, there is a legitimate business need for consumer reports, which serve such important public functions as minimizing the risks of extending valuable benefits and credit and assisting in detection of fraudulent credit applications and insurance claims. In order to make informed judgments in these matters, it may be necessary for the decision maker to have information which normally would be considered private, provided the information is legitimately related to a legitimate purpose of the decision maker. In such a case, the public interest provides the defendant a shield which is similar in principle to qualified privilege in libel. [Citation.] Some factual situations so clearly and unquestionably do not result in an invasion of privacy that the court should so declare as a matter of law. [Citation.] This is such a case. Because there may be a legitimate purpose for the collection and even the disclosure, in certain circumstances, of an individual's past insurance history,[6] we must conclude as a matter of law from the record before us that defendant did not invade plaintiff's privacy merely by collecting and retaining his past insurance history. [Footnote.]

The fact that information may have been properly collected and retained, however, does not mean that its disclosure by the reporting company was proper.[8] Certainly, indiscriminate publication of private information unrelated to any legitimate public purpose could, and should, give rise to an action for invasion of privacy.

Missouri substantive law, which controls in this diversity action, [citations], specifically recognizes a cause of action in tort for the public disclosure of private facts. [Citations.] Elements of the tort include (1) publication, (2) absent any waiver or privilege, (3) of private matters in which the public has no legitimate concern, (4) so as to bring shame or humiliation to a person of ordinary sensibilities. [Citations.]

Although the parties have directed themselves in this appeal primarily to the question of whether or not there was a public interest in the information disclosed by defendant to All-American Insurance Company, and whether a public interest is required to be present, we need not reach that issue for the reason that the essential element of publication is absent from the evidence in this case. [Footnote.]

The *Restatement (Second) of Torts* § 652D, at 383 (1977), articulates the tort of public disclosure of private facts by stating that "[o]ne who gives *publicity* to a matter concerning the private life of another is subject to liability to the other for invasion of his privacy, if the matter *publicized* is of a kind that (a) would be highly offensive to a reasonable person, and (b) is not of legitimate concern to the public." [Emphasis supplied.] The Comment following § 652D of the *Restatement* identifies the degree of "publicity" required to give rise to an action for invasion of privacy:

> The form of invasion of the right of privacy covered in this Section depends upon publicity given to the private life of the individual. "Publicity," as it is used in this Section, differs from "publication," as that term is used in § 577 in connection with liability for defamation. "Publication," in that sense, is a word of art, which includes any communication by the defendant to a third person. "Publicity," on the other hand, means that the matter is made public, by communicating it to the public at large, or to so many persons that the matter must be regarded as substantially certain to become one of public knowledge. The difference is not one of the means of communication, which may be oral, written or by any other means. It is one of a communication that reaches, or is sure to reach, the public.
>
> Thus it is not an invasion of the right of privacy, within the rule stated in this Section, to communicate a fact concerning the plaintiff's private life to a single person or even to a small group of persons. On the other hand, any publication in a newspaper or a magazine, even of small circulation, or in a handbill distributed to a large number of persons, or any broadcast over the radio, or statement made in an address to a large audience, is sufficient to give publicity within the meaning of the term as it is used in this Section. The distinction, in other words, is one between private and public communication.

[Citation.]

The same conclusion was reached by the

---

6. The evidence in this case, produced by plaintiff's own witnesses, illustrates that prior underwriting history is useful in determining the amount of disability insurance carried by a claimant, in providing leads as to important prior health history and other information, and in detecting suspected fraudulent claims. [Citation.] "There is

no satisfactory, economical substitute for a credit bureau report."

8. Nor does this court express any opinion as to whether defendant has violated any provisions of the Fair Credit Reporting Act, 15 U.S.C. § 1681 *et seq.*

district court in *Wilson v. Retail Credit Co.,* 325 F.Supp. 460, 463 (S.D.Miss.1971), *aff'd,* 457 F.2d 1406 (5th Cir. 1972), an action brought against a reporting agency alleging libel and invasion of privacy with respect to reports made on the plaintiff and his wife. The court, noting that Georgia law recognized the four categories of invasion of privacy, and identifying the tort of public disclosure of private facts as the second of those four categories, quoted an earlier decision by the district court for the Northern District of Georgia in the case of *Peacock v. Retail Credit Co.,* 302 F.Supp. 418 (N.D.Ga.1969), *aff'd,* 429 F.2d 31 (5th Cir. 1970), as follows:

> Plaintiff's attempt to recover under category (2), on the theory that the credit report amounted to a public disclosure of embarrassing private facts about him, must likewise fail, for the simple reason that there has been no "public" disclosure of any information concerning plaintiff. Only clients of Retail Credit have been supplied with this information, and while this limited publication may have resulted in the denial of an insurance policy, or a denial of credit, the court holds that this is not the type of public disclosure required to establish an invasion of privacy under category (2).

Accordingly, the district court held that the defendant was entitled to judgment as a matter of law. Although the decision in *Wilson v. Retail Credit, supra,* was the result of the district court's interpretation of Georgia law, it is in accordance with the generally-held view on this issue, as expressed in the *Restatement (Second) of Torts.*[10]

Missouri law accords. Although the publicity required to constitute the tort of public disclosure of private facts has not specifically been defined in Missouri, each Missouri case has involved publicity in the form of an advertisement [footnote], newspaper [footnote], magazine [footnote], or television [footnote], account, or language spoken to a sizeable group of people in a public place. [Footnote.] Implicit in the language of the cases is the conclusion that invasion of privacy requires publicity in the broad, general sense of the word "public."

Illustrative is the case of *Munden v. Harris, supra,* 134 S.W. at 1077. The Missouri Supreme Court, recognizing for the first time the existence of the right of privacy in Missouri, quoted with approval the language of an earlier New York decision [footnote] in stating that "[t]he so-called right of privacy is, as the phrase suggests, founded upon the claim that a man has the right to pass through this world, if he wills, without having his picture published, his business enterprises discussed, his successful experiments written up for the benefit of others, or his eccentricities commented upon, either in *handbills, circulars, catalogues, periodicals, or newspapers. * * *"* [Emphasis supplied.] Similarly, in *Barber v. Time, Inc., supra,* 159 S.W.2d at 293, 295, the Missouri Supreme Court defined the "limits of decency" in terms of "publicity" given to the intimate details of an individual's life, stated that the plaintiff's previous habits with reference to "publicity" were a factor for the court to consider, and concluded that defendant therein was liable for having caused embarrassing information about the plaintiff to be "circulated generally throughout the community."

The Missouri Supreme Court's decision in *Biederman's of Springfield, Inc. v. Wright,* 322 S.W.2d 892, 895-7 (1959), emphasizes the public aspect of disclosure in an invasion of privacy action in holding that the giving of undue publicity to private debts constitutes an invasion of the debtor's right of privacy. Of particular significance in the *Biederman's* case is the Missouri Supreme Court's reliance on Prosser, *Handbook of the Law of Torts* (2d ed.) § 97 at 641. At page 898 of its opinion, the Court quoted with approval the following language, which echoes the position adopted in the *Restatement of Torts:*

> Except in cases of physical intrusion, it has been held that the tort must be founded upon publicity, in the sense of communication to the public in general or to a large number of persons, as distinguished from one individual or a few.

Our examination of Missouri law, which is in accordance with the view set forth in the

---

10. For example, *Black's Law Dictionary* 1393 (4th ed. 1968), defines "public," in pertinent part: "Pertaining to a state, nation, or whole community; proceeding from, relating to, or affecting the whole body of people or an entire community. Open to all; notorious. Common to all

or many; general; open to common use. [Omitting citations.] Belonging to the people at large; relating to or affecting the whole people of a state, nation, or community, not limited or restricted to any particular class of the community. [Omitting citations.]"

Restatement (Second) of Torts, thus leads to the conclusion that there must be evidence of publicity in the sense of a disclosure to the general public or likely to reach the general public, as opposed to "publication" required in a defamation action, in order for plaintiff to make a submissible case of invasion of privacy by public disclosure of private facts. [Citations.]

In view of the evidence in this case, which reveals only a disclosure by defendant to its client, All-American Insurance Company, without further dissemination of the information about plaintiff,[17] we conclude that the district court erred in denying defendant's motion for directed verdict at the close of the evidence.

We need not, and do not, reach the other issues raised on this appeal.

For the foregoing reasons, the judgment is reversed and the case is remanded to the district court with instructions to enter judgment for defendant.

HEANEY, C. J., dissenting.

I agree with the majority's holding that the collection and retention of the plaintiff's past insurance history by Equifax did not constitute an invasion of his privacy by unreasonable intrusion. There is no substantial evidence that the manner of the procurement of this information constituted an offensive interference with the plaintiff's affairs [footnote], or that the information collected was of such a personal nature or so unrelated to any legitimate business purpose that its collection and retention by Equifax constituted *ipso facto* an invasion of the plaintiff's right to privacy. [Footnote.] [Citations.]

I disagree, however, that there is insufficient evidence of "publicity" to justify submission of the case to the jury under the theory of public disclosure of private facts. As acknowledged by the majority, the common law tort of public disclosure of private facts requires "a communication that reaches, *or is sure to reach,* the public." [Emphasis added.] [Citations.] The likelihood of widespread dissemination can be inferred from the medium employed by the defendant for the particular publication [citations], or from the defendant's action in making private information available to the public where that action is likely to result in the further dissemination of the information. [Citation.][3]

In my view, the collection and retention of personal information about a particular consumer by a commercial information broker such as Equifax makes the dissemination of that information sufficiently likely as to meet any reasonable requirement of "publicity." [Footnote.] Equifax, formerly known as Retail Credit Company, has more than 2,000 locations across the continent and is the largest individual consumer investigative firm in the country. [Footnote.] Approximately 46 million consumer files are maintained by Equifax, and the corporation claims to make some 35 million reports on consumers each year. [Footnote.] Evidence at trial indicated that once a report on a particular consumer is made, a copy of that report is retained in the files of the reporting office for use in later reports about the same individual requested by the same or a different customer.[7] Upon request from another office, a copy of the report is sent to the requesting office for dissemination to its local customers. A copy of the report which

---

17. We note that the evidence reveals that defendant does not operate its business by means of a computer. There is no indication in the record that the information about which plaintiff complains was obtained from or placed in a computer bank or information bureau by means of which it might reasonably be expected to be more widely disseminated. The possible implications of that fact situation, therefore, are not before this court.

3. In *Ind. Foundation, Etc. v. Texas Ind. Acc. Bd.,* 540 S.W.2d 668 (Tex.1976), *cert. denied* 430 U.S. 931, 97 S.Ct. 1550, 51 L.Ed.2d 774 (1977) the court held that where government records containing private information pertaining to individuals are opened to public inspection, the information is sufficiently "publicized" as to give rise to a cause of action for invasion of privacy by public disclosure of private facts. "To hold otherwise would be to

deny an individual any protectable privacy interest in private information disclosed to a governmental unit, if such information would otherwise be 'public information." [Citation.]

7. Not only is potentially adverse information copied by investigators from prior reports, but the reports in which the information was originally contained have often been destroyed, making the original source of the information impossible to ascertain. Evidence in this case indicated that the information about which the plaintiff complains was copied from previous reports in the files of the St. Louis office; that office, however, had no records showing the origin of the information, and when asked whether such information could exist in the files of other offices, the St. Louis branch manager replied that he doubted it.

was the subject of the present suit was sent to the Fort Lauderdale, Florida, branch office, apparently in anticipation of requests for information about the plaintiff in that locale.

The majority cites *Peacock v. Retail Credit Company,* 302 F.Supp. 418 (N.D.Ga.1969), *aff'd,* 429 F.2d 31 (5th Cir. 1970), in support of its holding. In *Peacock,* reports containing private information about the plaintiff were distributed to insurance companies, banks and other businesses requesting such information. The court held that no public disclosure of private information had occurred since "[o]nly clients of Retail Credit have been supplied with this information;" and as assurance against further dissemination, the court cited the presence of a clause in the contract between Retail and its customers, requiring that the information reported and Retail's identity as the source be kept "strictly confidential." [Citation.] I find this analysis wholly inadequate. The dissemination of private information by a commercial credit broker to insurance companies, banks and other customers requesting such information is no less "public" than the posting of a debt in a creditor's shop window. [Footnote.] Nor does the fact that the information in issue in that case had been disseminated to only a few customers, or that the contract between Retail and its customers limited further dissemination by the latter, limit future dissemination by Retail itself in any way or make that dissemination any less likely.

Even if there is substantial evidence tending to show that the elements of a cause of action for invasion of privacy have been met,[9] a verdict in favor of the defendant must be directed if the defendant's conduct serves any basic public interest which outweighs the in-

dividual right infringed. [Citations.] The determination as to what is a matter of sufficient public interest is similar in principle to the determination as to the existence of a qualified privilege in libel. [Citations.]

Most jurisdictions have granted credit bureaus and other consumer investigative agencies a conditional privilege in defamation and invasion of privacy actions under the theory that the information supplied by these companies is useful to society in preventing the improvident extension of credit or the payment of fraudulent insurance claims. [Footnote.] Assuming that such reports would be conditionally privileged under Missouri law,[11] that privilege would not protect the disclosure made here. A conditional privilege extends only to the publication of information which bears upon the public interest which is entitled to protection. [Citation.] The public interest asserted by Equifax—that of determining the validity of the plaintiff's insurance claim—was not served by publication of the fact that the plaintiff had applied for life insurance "in excess of $10,000,000" since 1949. Even if, as urged by Equifax, *current* applications for life insurance might contain relevant medical information bearing on the question of present disability, applications made twenty-five years ago certainly would not.[12]

Consumer reporting has become a multimillion dollar industry,[13] with files maintained on millions of Americans.[14] Justice Douglas, in describing governmental collection and dissemination of personal information, has stated:

> We are rapidly entering the age of no privacy, where everyone is open to surveillance at all

---

9. In addition to publicity, the plaintiff must establish that the defendant's conduct was offensive, unreasonable, serious and unwarranted to a person of ordinary sensibilities. [Citations.] The trial court held that there was sufficient evidence establishing this element to justify submission of the case to the jury. I would agree.

11. The appellate courts of Missouri apparently have not yet addressed the question as to whether consumer investigative agencies should receive the protection of such a conditional privilege. Those cases which have stressed the balancing of the individual right of privacy against community interests have involved freedom of the press. [Citations.]

12. The irrelevance of this information is acknowledged in the report, where, after three insurance carriers are

listed, it is stated that "[w]e are not quoting the remainder of the 23 insurance companies due to their age." The branch manager of the St. Louis office of Equifax testified that underwriting files for life insurance applicants are routinely destroyed after a period of 13 months, five years, or ten years, apparently because any information contained therein would be obsolete. *See also* Fair Credit Reporting Act, 15 U.S.C. § 1681c(a)(1)(6) (1970), which prohibits in most instances the reporting of adverse information which is more than seven years old.

13. Total revenues of Retail Credit Company were $195,262,000 in 1972. FTC, *In the Matter of Equifax, Inc.,* para. 12, at 10 (1977) (initial decision).

14. Credit Data Corporation, the nation's second largest individual consumer reporting firm, maintains files on times; where there are no secrets from government.

* * *

The dossiers on all citizens mount in number and increase in size. Now they are being put on computers so that by pressing one button all the miserable, the sick, the suspect, the unpopular, the offbeat people of the Nation can be instantly identified.

These examples and many others demonstrate an alarming trend whereby the privacy and dignity of our citizens is being whittled away by sometimes imperceptible steps. Taken individually, each step may be of little consequence. But when viewed as a whole, there begins to emerge a society quite unlike any we have seen—a society in which government may intrude into the secret regions of man's life at will.

Osborn v. United States, 385 U.S. 323, 341-343, 87 S.Ct. 429, 439, 17 L.Ed.2d 394 (1966) (Douglas, J., dissenting) (footnote omitted).

In my view, the potential for abuse by the commercial consumer reporting industry is no less real. The dissemination of personal information must be limited to that which serves those legitimate business needs which such companies cite to justify their existence. Otherwise, we may indeed be threatened with the loss of the very core of personal privacy: control over the dissemination of information about ourselves. [Footnote.]

LOWRY v. CREDIT BUREAU, INC. OF GEORGIA

444 F. Supp. 541
(United States District Court, N.D. Georgia, Atlanta Division, Jan. 23, 1978.)

MURPHY, D. J.

This is an action for damages predicated upon defendant's alleged violation of the Fair Credit Reporting Act, 15 U.S.C. § 1681 et seq. Plaintiffs contend defendant violated 15 U.S.C. § 1681e(b) in failing to follow reasonable procedures so as to insure maximum possible accuracy of information about the plaintiffs. Plaintiffs contend defendant violated 15 U.S.C. § 1681i in failing to undertake the reinves-

some 27 million persons and is reportedly adding new files at the rate of one-half million per month. [Citation.] Almost all of Credit Data's operations are computerized, and when asked in 1968 how long it would take before

tigation required after the accuracy of a file is disputed. Plaintiffs contend defendant libelled them in reporting to Decatur Federal Savings and Loan Association that James F. Lowry had once been adjudicated bankrupt.

* * * The facts of this case are that on August 1, 1976, plaintiffs formalized an application with Decatur Federal Savings and Loan Association ("Decatur Federal") for permanent financing of a home plaintiffs had recently constructed. On the loan application, Mr. Lowry listed his name as "James F. Lowry" and his former address as Solana Beach, California.

The loan application was sent to the South Regional Loan Office of Decatur Federal. At this office, Decatur Federal maintains a computer terminal which provides direct access to information stored in the computers of the defendant Credit Bureau on various consumers. This terminal affords Decatur Federal the opportunity to obtain credit information directly and without intervention by Credit Bureau personnel.

In seeking a consumer's credit history, the party desiring the information supplies the computer with as much relevant data as possible about the party as to whom they are inquiring. The computer will then provide the names of parties for whom it has credit histories and with whom there is a programmed minimum of correspondence between the identifying information of the party for whom information is sought and the parties for whom the computer has stored credit information. The computer will not provide the names of any party for whom it has credit information unless there are at least fifty "points" of correspondence between the subject of the inquiry's data and the relevant credit records. The operator chooses the credit histories he or she wishes to review from the computer proffered list of names and the number of "points" of correspondence.

The inquiry by the Decatur Federal operator resulted in the offering of a "James Frank Lowry" of San Francisco, California whose file showed 50 "points" of correspondence. The operator made the independent decision to have

every American's name was listed with the corporation, its president replied, "we regard it as approximately a five-year job." [Citation.]

the computer supply its information on "James Frank Lowry" despite the fact that only the minimum of correspondence had been indicated. The computer disclosed that "James Frank Lowry" of San Francisco, California had been adjudicated bankrupt in 1967.

The facts that the applicant for the insurance, and the plaintiff in this litigation, was named James Francis, and not James Frank Lowry and had listed his prior address as Solano Beach, not San Francisco, California were not enough to dispel the notion that James Francis Lowry was a bankrupt not worthy of credit. Plaintiffs were informed that a problem existed with regard to the issuance of credit to them. Plaintiffs were informed a resolution of the difficulty must come from the Credit Bureau.

On August 19, 1976, Mr. Lowry visited defendant's office in Atlanta, Georgia. During the course of an inquiry which carried through the following day, Mr. Lowry was told by an employee of defendant Credit Bureau that there was indeed a bankruptcy on his record. On Monday, August 23, 1976, an inquiry was begun with the processing of a "request for investigation". The focus of the investigation was plaintiff's contention that he had never filed for bankruptcy nor had he lived at the address indicated for him in San Francisco.

During Credit Bureau's investigation, new reports were sought on "James F. Lowry" from the Credit Bureau's computer banks by Decatur Federal. The reports included the previously noted disclosure of a bankruptcy by a James Frank Lowry. On September 10, 1976, Decatur Federal issued a "decline letter" indicating a denial of plaintiff's loan application.

On September 13, 1976, Mr. Lowry notified Credit Bureau of the denial of his loan application and demanded a correction of his credit report. On October 8, 1976, defendant Credit Bureau notified Decatur Federal that a correction was being made in Mr. Lowry's report. The letter of October 8th suggested Decatur Federal might wish to reconsider Mr. Lowry's application on the basis of the correction. The corrected report included no allegations of bankruptcy.

Plaintiffs were not notified of the correction of the record nor were they informed of the outcome of the investigation they had requested. On December 9, 1976 plaintiffs' attorney was notified that plaintiffs would probably receive their loan if they were to reapply. Plaintiffs were offered a loan commitment on December 13, 1976 with slightly higher closing costs than those apparent on the loan application. The loan was closed on February 7, 1977.

. 1. Plaintiffs contend they have been the victim of a violation of defendant Credit Bureau's duty to insure the maximum possible accuracy of information. The Fair Credit Reporting Act provides in relevant part:

> Whenever a consumer reporting agency prepares a consumer report it shall follow reasonable procedures to assure maximum possible accuracy of the information concerning the individual about whom the report relates. 15 U.S.C. § 1681e(b).

This section imposes an obligation to insure maximum accuracy only in the preparation of a report. The crux of plaintiffs' complaint is the potential for confusion of reports inherent in defendant's computer system. Plaintiffs note the potential for confusion was realized in their case and resulted in at least the delay in the grant of a loan.

Plaintiffs' concern is not accuracy in the preparation of credit reports; plaintiffs' concern is the confusion of those reports. Confusion of reports did result, but that does not provide a basis for a federal claim. This district has previously recognized that "in order to pursue a cause of action predicated upon willful or negligent violation of 15 U.S.C. § 1681e(b), the report sought to be attacked must be inaccurate." [Citations.]

The only inaccuracy in the questioned credit reports arises from the presence of plaintiff James Francis Lowry's social security number in the James Frank Lowry file. As noted by both sides, the plaintiff's social security number appeared with the bankrupt James Frank Lowry's file because the computer was programmed to add the information when Decatur Federal's operator accepted the file of James Frank Lowry the first time. The automatic addition of this information may constitute a violation of the 15 U.S.C. § 1681e(b) obligation to provide the maximum possible accuracy in the preparation of a credit report. Preparation may be viewed as a continuing process and the obligation to insure accuracy arises with every addition of information. Plaintiffs may have difficulty demonstrating the existence of damages sustained as a result of this breach [as required under 15 U.S.C. § 1681o(1)] but at this stage it cannot be said such proof would be impossible.

2. Plaintiffs contend there has been a breach of defendant Credit Bureau's duty to investigate the accuracy of information "in his file". 15 U.S.C. § 1681i(a). Preliminarily, it must be noted that the circumstances of this case indicate the necessity of reading the language "in his file" to include more than just the computer report which a two month investigation discloses to be the only report relevant to the subject of the inquiry. As encountered in this instance, if a party has credit difficulties because of confusion of two similar computer reports, the subject's "file" must be viewed as the totality of the conflicting information which is causing the credit uncertainty. Under this view, and the language of 15 U.S.C. § 1681i(a), a consumer reporting agency is obligated to reinvestigate the accuracy of information as it relates to the subject of the inquiry. The agency's obligations are not terminated by the fact that the information is accurate about someone else if that information is presented in a manner such as to create inaccurate impressions as to the credit history of a particular individual. To permit the activity encountered here to go uncovered would be contrary to the broadly remedial aims disclosed in 15 U.S.C. § 1681.

The Fair Credit Reporting Act creates an obligation to investigate "within a reasonable period". There is no doubt an investigation was undertaken and changes were made. The only issue here is whether 49 days constitutes a "reasonable period" to determine if one party is the bankrupt referred to in a particular credit report. This element of the complaint is not proper for disposition on summary judgment.

3. Plaintiffs allege they were defamed by the order to attribution of a bankruptcy to them. Defendant responds to this contention by noting that the notation of a bankruptcy was clearly attributed to a James F. Lowry who is not the plaintiff.

The review of libel allegations must begin with a widely cited rule of Georgia law: "[t]he defamatory words must refer to some ascertained or ascertainable person, and that person must be the plaintiff." [Citations.] The unquestioned fact is that the defendant's attribution of bankruptcy concerned a James F. Lowry who is not the plaintiff in this case. Defendant Credit Bureau has simply reported the truth of a bankruptcy by an individual with a name similar to that of the plaintiff, and that fact alone is not enough to support the specter of libel.

Georgia courts have noted that language susceptible to but one, non-defamatory meaning is for the court's interpretation. [Citations.] Georgia courts have previously held that a libel does not arise as to a third person when true information is stated as to another party. [Citations.] Plaintiff has not demonstrated the requisite elements under Georgia law.

* * *

5. Accordingly, the motion for summary judgment is denied as to claims premised upon 15 U.S.C. § 1681e(b) and 1681i(a). The motion for summary judgment is granted as to the state law claims of defamation. * * *

THOMPSON v. SAN ANTONIO RETAIL MERCHANTS ASSOCIATION
682 F.2d 509
(United States Court of Appeals, Fifth Circuit, Aug. 13, 1982.)

PER CURIAM.

This case involves the liability of the San Antonio Retail Merchants Association (SARMA) for an inaccurate credit report. Gulf Oil Corporation (Gulf) and Montgomery Ward (Ward's) denied credit to William Douglas Thompson, III, on the basis of erroneous credit information furnished by SARMA. The district court, after a nonjury trial, entered judgment for Thompson in the sum of $10,000 actual damages and $4,485 attorneys' fees. SARMA appeals.

I. BACKGROUND

SARMA provides a computerized credit reporting service to local business subscribers. This service depends heavily upon credit history information fed into SARMA's files by subscribers. A key mechanism used by SARMA to update its files is a computerized "automatic capturing" feature. A subscriber must feed certain identifying information from its own computer terminal into SARMA's central computer in order to gain access to the credit history of a particular consumer. When presented with this identifying information, SARMA's computer searches its records and displays on the subscriber's terminal the credit history file that most nearly matches the consumer. The decision whether to accept a given file as being that of a particular consumer is left completely to the terminal operator.[1] When a subscriber does accept a given file as pertaining to a particular consumer, however, the computer automatically captures into the file any information input from the subscriber's terminal that the central file did not already have.

The disadvantage of an automatic capturing feature is that it may accept erroneous information fed in by subscribers, unless special auditing procedures are built into the system. In the instant case, SARMA failed to check the accuracy of a social security number obtained by its automatic capturing feature. The social security number is the single most important identifying factor for credit-reference purposes. As a result, the computer erroneously began to report the bad credit history of "William Daniel Thompson, Jr.," to subscribers inquiring about "William Douglas Thompson, III."

In November 1974, William Daniel Thompson, Jr., opened a credit account with Gordon's Jewelers (Gordon's) in San Antonio, listing his social security number as 457-68-5778, his address as 132 Baxter, his occupation as truck loader, and his marital status as single. He subsequently ran up a delinquent account of $77.25 at Gordon's that was ultimately charged off as a bad debt. When Gordon's voluntarily reported the bad debt, SARMA placed the information and a derogatory credit rating into file number 5867114, without any identifying social security number.

In early 1978, the plaintiff, William Douglas Thompson, III, applied for credit with Gulf and with Ward's in San Antonio. He listed his

social security as 407-86-4065, his address as 6929 Timbercreek, his occupation as grounds keeper, and his wife as Deborah C. On February 9, 1978, Gulf's terminal operator mistakenly accepted file number 5867114 as that of the plaintiff. SARMA's computer thereupon automatically captured various information about William Douglas Thompson, III, including his social security number, into file number 5867114. At that point, the original file, which was on William Daniel Thompson, Jr., became a potpourri of information on both the plaintiff and the original William Daniel Thompson, Jr. The name on the file remained that of William Daniel Thompson, Jr. The social security number became that of the plaintiff, the current address and employer became that of the plaintiff, a former address and employer became that of William Daniel Thompson, Jr., and the wife's name became that of the plaintiff's wife.

Shortly thereafter, Ward's terminal operator ran a credit check on the plaintiff, was given the garbled data, and accepted file number 5867114 as that of the plaintiff. As a result of the adverse information regarding the Gordon's account, Ward's denied the plaintiff credit. The plaintiff applied for credit at Ward's in May 1979 and was again rejected.

On February 21, 1978, Gulf requested a "revision" of file number 5867114, a procedure which entails a rechecking of information in a file with respect to a particular creditor or creditors. Following its usual procedures, SARMA would call Gordon's to verify in detail the information in the file. Although this was probably done, whoever contacted Gordon's apparently failed to check the social security number of Gordon's delinquent customer and take corrective action when it was received. Instead, the adverse information remained in the file under the plaintiff's social security number after Gulf's revision request, and Gulf denied the plaintiff credit.

The adverse information remained in the plaintiff's file during 1978 and the first five and a half months of 1979. During all of this time the plaintiff thought he had been denied credit from Ward's and Gulf because of a 1976

---

1. The terminal operator has the option of accepting the file as that of the consumer or of requesting the computer to supply the file of the next most likely match. The terminal operator's decision can be made without any minimum number of "points of correspondence" between the subject of inquiry and the relevant credit file.

Texas felony conviction for burglary. He had received a five-year probationary sentence,[2] but subsequently gained fulltime employment and straightened out his life. In June of 1979, plaintiff's wife learned from her credit union in processing an application for a loan that her husband's adverse credit rating resulted from a bad debt at Gordon's. The plaintiff knew he had never had an account at Gordon's so he and his wife went directly to their place of business. After waiting some two hours he was informed that there had indeed been a mistake, their credit record was for William Daniel Thompson, Jr.

The plaintiff and his wife went to SARMA with this information in an attempt to purge the erroneous credit information. They spoke with an individual and showed birth registration and drivers license information revealing his name to be William Douglas Thompson III. The entire process required some three hours. Nevertheless SARMA thereafter mailed appellee a letter addressed to William Daniel Thompson III. Appellee's wife again returned to SARMA. Following this SARMA once again addressed appellee in another letter as William Daniel Thompson III. Appellee again returned to SARMA—yet again SARMA wrote still another letter with the same incorrect name. Further, though SARMA's policy was to send corrections made on a file to any subscribers who had made inquiry about it within the last six months, SARMA failed to notify Ward's of the corrections. The plaintiff filed an action in state court on October 4, 1979. It was not until October 16, 1979, that SARMA informed Ward's of the erroneous credit information.[3] On November 5, 1979, the action was removed to the federal district court. After a bench trial, the district court found that denials of credit to the appellee by Gulf and Ward's were caused by SARMA's failure to follow reasonable procedures to assure the maximum possible accuracy of its files. The district court awarded plaintiff actual damages in the sum of $10,000 plus attorneys' fees in the sum of $4485.

II. THE LIABILITY ISSUE

Under 15 U.S.C. § 1681o of the Fair Credit Reporting Act (Act), a "consumer reporting agency" is liable to "any consumer" for negligent failure to comply with "any requirement imposed" by the Act. [Footnote.] In the instant case, the district court determined that SARMA was liable under section 1681o for negligent failure to comply with section 1681e(b) of the Act, which provides:

> When a consumer reporting agency *prepares* a consumer report, it shall follow *reasonable procedures* to assure *maximum possible accuracy* of information concerning the individual about whom the report relates.

15 U.S.C. § 1681e(b) (emphasis added).

Section 1681e(b) does not impose strict liability for any inaccurate credit report, but only a duty of reasonable care in preparation of the report. That duty extends to updating procedures, because "preparation" of a consumer report should be viewed as a continuing process and the obligation to insure accuracy arises with every addition of information. *Lowry v. Credit Bureau, Inc. of Georgia,* 444 F.Supp. 541, 544 (N.D.Ga.1978). The standard of conduct by which the trier of fact must judge the adequacy of agency procedure is what a reasonably prudent person would do under the circumstances. *Bryant v. TRW, Inc.,* 487 F.Supp. 1234, 1242 (E.D. Mich.1980).

Applying the reasonable-person standard, the district court found two acts of negligence in SARMA's updating procedures. First, SARMA failed to exercise reasonable care in programming its computer to automatically capture information into a file without requiring any minimum number of "points of correspondence" between the consumer and the file or having an adequate auditing procedure to foster accuracy. Second, SARMA failed to employ reasonable procedures designed to learn the disparity in social security numbers for the two Thompsons when it revised file number 5867114 at Gulf's request.

---

2. Appellee was placed on probation and after successfully fulfilling the conditions thereof for over one-half of the probationary period of five years, was permitted to withdraw his plea of guilty, the indictment was dismissed, and the judgment of conviction was set aside.

3. Ward's reprocessed the plaintiff's application for credit, but under new guidelines denied Thompson credit on the basis of a "preliminary score" that did not take into account any information in SARMA's computer file.

This Court can reverse the district court on these findings of fact only if there is a definite and firm conviction that the judgment of the district court is clearly erroneous. [Citations.]

With respect to the first act of negligence, George Zepeda, SARMA's manager, testified that SARMA's computer had no minimum number of points of correspondence to be satisfied before an inquiring subscriber could accept credit information. Moreover, SARMA had no way of knowing if the information supplied by the subscriber was correct. Although SARMA did conduct spot audits to verify social security numbers, it did not audit all subscribers. With respect to the second act of negligence, SARMA's verification process failed to uncover the erroneous social security number even though Gulf made a specific request for a "revision" to check the adverse credit history ascribed to the plaintiff. SARMA's manager, Mr. Zepeda, testified that what should have been done upon the request for a revision, was to pick up the phone and check with Gordon's and learn, among other things, the social security number for William Daniel Thompson, Jr. It was the manager's further testimony that the social security number is the single most important information in a consumer's credit file. In light of this evidence, this Court cannot conclude that the district court was clearly erroneous in finding negligent violation of section 1681e(b).[5] [Citations.]

III. AWARD OF DAMAGES

The district court's award of $10,000 in actual damages was based on humiliation and mental distress to the plaintiff. Even when there are no out-of-pocket expenses, humiliation and mental distress do constitute recoverable elements of damage under the Act. [Citations.] In the instant case, the amount of damages is a question of fact which may be reversed by this Court only if the district court's findings are clearly erroneous. [Citations.]

SARMA asserts that Thompson failed to prove any actual damages, or at best proved only minimal damages for humiliation and mental distress. There was evidence, however, that Thompson suffered humiliation and

embarrassment from being denied credit on three occasions. Thompson testified that the denial of credit hurt him deeply because of his mistaken belief that it resulted from his felony conviction:

> I was trying to build myself back up, trying to set myself up, get back on my feet again. I was working sixty hours a week and sometimes seventy. I went back to school. I was going to school at night three nights a week, four nights a week, three hours a night, and [denial of credit] really hurt. It made me disgusted with myself.
>
> * * * [I needed credit to] be able to obtain things that everybody else is able to obtain, to be able to buy clothes or set myself up where I can show my ability to be trusted.
>
> We didn't even have a bed. It was pretty bad. We were hurting. Everything we had to do, we had to save up and pay cash for strictly. It was just impossible to do it any other way.

Further, the inaccurate information remained in SARMA's files for almost one and one-half years after the inaccurate information was inserted. Even after the error was discovered, Thompson spent months pressing SARMA to correct its mistakes and fully succeeded only after bringing a lawsuit against SARMA. This Court is of the opinion that the trial judge was entitled to conclude that the humiliation and mental distress were not minimal but substantial.

SARMA contends that the instant damage award is excessive when compared to similar cases such as *Millstone,* 528 F.2d at 834-35 and *Bryant,* 187 F.Supp. at 1239-40. In *Millstone,* an insurance company cancelled an automobile insurance policy after a consumer credit report alleged the insured was a political activist disliked by his neighbors. The insurer first cancelled the insured's policy and then reinstated it when an agent discovered the insured was in fact a highly respected assistant managing editor of the *St. Louis Post Dispatch.* Even though the incorrect report involved a mere $68.00 insurance policy, the district court awarded $2500 in actual damages for Millstone's mental anguish over the report. In *Bryant,* an inaccurate credit report was issued on a consumer in connection with a mortgage application for a house purchase. The credit report resulted in denial of the

---

5. Other courts have held that failure to take reasonable action to verify adverse information is a violation of § 1681e. See *Millstone v. O'Hanlon Reports, Inc.,* 383

F.Supp. 269 (E.D.Mo.1974), *aff'd,* 528 F.2d 829 (8th Cir. 1976). [Citations.]

mortgage. The consumer called the inaccuracy to the attention of the credit reporting agency, yet the same inaccurate information was issued in connection with a later mortgage application. A jury determination of $8,000 in actual damages was sustained in that instance. [Citation.] The damage award in the instant case is not so out of line with *Bryant* and *Millstone* as to be clearly erroneous. The case *sub judice* was a trial before the court without a jury. The trial judge was in a position to weigh the credibility of testimony on humiliation and mental distress and, therefore, should be given considerable latitude; it cannot be said that his determination was clearly erroneous.

SARMA finally asserts that Thompson was required to mitigate his damages by first exhausting alternative remedies. SARMA cites section 1681i of the Act which sets forth a procedure for consumers to challenge the completeness or accuracy of any disputed information in this file.[6] The Act, however, does not require that a consumer pursue the remedies provided in section 1681i before bringing suit under section 1681o for violation of section 1681e. If a consumer can prove a violation of section 1681e, he can sue directly on that basis without first exhausting alternative remedies. [Citation.] Thompson was not required to mitigate his damages by formally disputing the accuracy of information contained in his file.

* * *

The judgment of the district court is affirmed.

BOSTON POLICE PATROLMEN'S ASS'N, INC.

6 CLSR 869

(Commonwealth of Massachusetts, April 11, 1978.)

DECISION.

STATEMENT OF THE CASE

On March 9, 1976, the Boston Police Patrol-

men's Association, Inc. (Association) filed a petition for clarification with the Massachusetts Labor Relations Commission (Commission). In substance, the petition alleged that the Association had in its possession certain overtime lists prepared for the Boston Police Department, which appeared to indicate that Patrolman Joseph McNulty and Patrolman Paul Johnston were either assigned to the Special Investigations Unit (SIU) of the Boston Police Department or had performed overtime services for that unit.[1] The petition requested the Commission to investigate the employment status of Patrolmen McNulty and Johnston, and to determine whether they were employed by SIU or performing services for that unit. Both patrolmen denied performing such services and they retained private counsel. On May 24, 1976 the two patrolmen, through their counsel, moved to intervene. The Commission allowed said motion over the objection of the Association. [Footnote.]

* * *

FINDINGS OF FACT

Johnston joined the Boston Police Department on December 28, 1968, and was assigned as a patrol officer in District 15 for approximately 2 years. He was then assigned to the Tactical Patrol Force, where he served for approximately two years before being transferred back to District 15, where he served an additional 1½ years as a patrol officer. In January, 1974 he was assigned to the Planning and Research Division in police headquarters. In March of 1976 he returned to the Tactical Patrol Force where he was serving at the time of the hearing.

McNulty joined the Boston Police Department September 7, 1970. After graduating from the Boston Police Academy he was assigned to District 2. In January, 1974 he was assigned to the Planning and Research Division.

On October 2, 1974, a routine computer print-out was issued which listed the overtime hours for the month of September of police officers assigned to various units in the Police

---

6. Both Gulf and Ward's notified the plaintiff of his right to make a written request from the consumer reporting agency of the reasons for the adverse action.

1. The Special Investigations Unit of the Boston Police Department is an internal anti-corruption unit which was organized in 1973 for the purpose of investigating alle-

gations of police misconduct. In a prior case the Commission excluded SIU employees from the collective bargaining unit represented by the Association, since they spend substantially all of their time investigating other police officers, and their investigations may result in discipline or prosecution of those police officers. [Citation.]

Commissioner's office. This two-page print-out contained the names of Johnston, McNulty, and twenty-two other officers who were assigned to the Planning Research Division, one of the units within the organizational structure which reported directly to the Commissioner's office. Solely because of a computer programming error, both pages of this print-out were labeled "Prepared for Special Investigation Unit." They should have been denominated "Prepared for Commissioner's Office." The Commissioner's office noted the error, and on October 2 or 3, 1974 informed Robert Hunt, a department payroll clerk, of it. Hunt contacted Joseph Sarno, the Director of Data Processing, and John Connor, a systems analyst, and steps were taken to correct the computer error. Although the same error occurred the following month, it was corrected on the routine print-out which was issued on November 29, 1974. From that date on, Johnston and McNulty were correctly listed as being assigned to the Commissioner's office and not to the SIU.

No further notice was taken of this computer error until a year later when the Association came into possession of xeroxed copies of the mistakenly labeled computer print-outs which were produced by the Employer during the course of arbitration proceedings concerning distribution of overtime. John F. Bilodeau, Vice-President of the Association, was involved in the arbitration case and noticed the print-outs which had been erroneously labeled as being prepared for the SIU. Bilodeau discussed the matter with Chester Broderick, Chairman of the Association, and others. He kept a copy of the list in his jacket pocket "for quite some time"; and included a copy in the Association's records. At an open meeting of the Association held in August of 1975 at the University of Massachusetts, Bilodeau was accused of concealing a list of men who were suspected of performing services for the SIU. In response, he removed the xerox copy of the erroneous print-out from his jacket pocket and read the names on the list to the members present. In early September 1975, Bilodeau took down a copy of the same erroneous print-out from a bulletin board in District 5. Someone had written "SIU Rats" in heavy bold print upon the print-out.

In August 1975, McNulty learned of the issuance of the erroneous computer print-out. Johnston heard of it early in September from his brother, who is also a police officer. Shortly thereafter, Johnston heard that the print-out was being circulated throughout the police department. Johnston, McNulty, and certain other officers assigned to the Planning and Research Division, who had been erroneously linked to the SIU by the incorrect heading on the computer print-outs, met together and attempted to find out why their names were on the list, and why it was being circulated among the patrolmen in the department.

Johnston discovered from the payroll clerk, Robert Hunt, that the heading was a computer programming error, and he, McNulty and several others named on the print-out met with Garrett Flanagan, an Association Representative, on September 18, 1975. They decided to send representatives to the Association to see if the matter could be cleared up. Johnston and McNulty were chosen as the group's representatives.

That same afternoon, September 18, 1975, Johnston, McNulty and Flanagan met with Chairman Broderick at the latter's office. Bilodeau joined them about 45 minutes after their arrival. Johnston explained to Broderick how the error had occurred, and that the men had heard that the list was being publicized to the detriment of their reputations. Johnston and McNulty requested permission to explain the occurrence of the computer programming error to the Association's House of Representatives in order to clear up the matter as soon as possible. Broderick told them that, although the Association's by-laws required a one-month waiting period before an individual could address the House of Representatives, he might be able to arrange a meeting with the House of Representatives that very night. Broderick also suggested to Johnston and McNulty that an explanatory call or a letter from Superintendent Paul Russell or someone of Russell's stature in the department might help clear the matter up.

Johnston and McNulty were introduced to the House of Representatives that same night and they made a detailed presentation, explaining the programming error to the delegates present. Thereafter each was questioned individually for approximately 35 to 45 minutes concerning his alleged affiliation with

SIU and his duties in the Planning and Research Division. Both reiterated their lack of any SIU affiliation and Johnston volunteered to take a polygraph test to aid in clearing his name. They also stated that, regardless of who was responsible for the computer error, they wanted the circulation of the list stopped. When the questioning ended Broderick thanked Johnston and McNulty for coming and told them that the House would vote upon what action might be taken.

On September 22, 1975, Johnston and McNulty each were sent the following letter from Frank J. McGee, the attorney for the Association:

> Dear Mr. Johnston:
> The House of Representatives of the Boston Police Patrolmen's Assn., Inc. at its regular scheduled monthly meeting held on September 18, 1975 has instructed me to inform you that you are assigned to the Special Investigative Unit. The House of Representatives has further instructed me to request that you come to the Association and converse with me for the purpose of discussing whether you will go to the Massachusetts Labor Commission for the purpose of disputing the fact that you are assigned to or detailed to the Special Investigative Unit. Further, the House of Representatives has requested that you take action within seven (7) days from your receipt of this letter.
> I wish to advise you that at an earlier meeting of the House of Representatives it was voted that members of the Special Investigative Unit are not only managerial employees but also confidential employees and therefore not members in good standing of the Boston Police Patrolmen's Assn., Inc.
> Trusting that you will contact me at the earliest possible time, I am
> Very truly yours,
> Frank J. McGee
> Attorney for
> Boston Police Patrolmen's Assn., Inc.

Both Johnston and McNulty attempted to contact Attorney McGee several times by telephone and in person but were unable to reach him.

On September 30, 1975, McNulty sent the Association a letter formally announcing his intention to run for Treasurer in the upcoming Association election. The following day he received a reply from Paul J. Whelan, the Association's Secretary, informing him that:

> The Association is unable to accept your letter of intention to seek the office of treasurer. This action is taken because an examination of Association records indicates that you are not a member in good standing as required by Art V, § 4 of the by-laws of the Boston Police Patrolmen's Association, Inc.
> At an earlier meeting of the BPPA House of Representatives it was voted that members of the special investigative unit are not only managerial employees but also confidential employees and therefore not members in good standing of the Boston Police Patrolmen's Association, Inc.
> Very truly yours,
> Paul J. Whelan, Secretary
> Boston Police Patrolmen's Association, Inc.

On October 3, 1975, Johnston and McNulty were informed by letter that Broderick, Bilodeau, and McGee would be at the offices of the Labor Relations Commission on October 16, 1975

> For the purpose of assisting you in filing a petition for clarification of your status as an employee of the Boston Police Department and a member of this bargaining unit.
> If you desire to place such a petition to the State Labor Relations Board, please meet us at the above time and place.
> Sincerely,
> Chester J. Broderick, Chairman
> Boston Police Patrolmen's Association, Inc.

Although Johnston did not receive a copy of the October 3rd letter, Representative Flanagan informed him of the planned October 16th meeting.

Neither Johnston nor McNulty attended the meeting which was called at the Labor Relations Commission on October 16, 1975.[3] However, Johnston sent the following letter to McGee the day before said meeting:

> Dear Mr. McGee:
> I am writing in response to your certified letter #003759, dated September 22, 1975. Im-

---

3. At least eleven of the twelve persons whose names appeared on the erroneous print-out were requested to attend the meeting held at the Labor Relations Commission on October 16, 1975. Only two (Brady and Murray) appeared. A third officer, Carpentino, went to the Commission at a later date in connection with the matter.

mediately following its receipt, I made several attempts to contact you to discuss this matter, but was unable to reach you. During the early part of the week of September 28, 1975 I went to the B.P.P.A. office, but was informed by the secretary that you were tied up in an arbitration hearing. Chairman Broderick was also unavailable at that time. I left my home and work phone number then and on three other occasions to assist you in contacting me. At the time of this writing I have not received a return call or any other communication from you.

Realizing that there appears to be considerable difficulty in reaching you, I have decided it might be more efficient for all concerned to deal with this matter by mail.

I do not understand the statement contained in your letter indicating that the House of Representatives decided that I am assigned to the Special Investigative Unit. To begin with, I was unaware that such a decision was made and secondly, and what perplexes me most, is that this decision was made after I had presented to the House documents which I believed cleared the suspicions surrounding the controversial Computer Print-out.

As I remember, you attended the monthly House of Representatives' meeting on September 18, 1975 and had the opportunity to hear my presentation as well as that of Joseph McNulty's. You may also remember that both Joseph McNulty and I requested the time to address the House not only on our behalf, but also as spokesmen for the other officers assigned to Planning and Research, and Informational Services who were listed on the print-out. Although, it was decided by the House that we could only speak for ourselves, we both stressed the danger of allowing unsubstantiated documents to be circulated throughout the department.

In this particular "Print-Out Incident" the reputations of 11 police officers, all members of the B.P.P.A. have been severely impaired because this print-out implied that they were members of the S.I.U. When McNulty and I went out to the Union Administrators for help we did so with documents, which clearly demonstrated the print-out in question was nothing more than an error in programming. If your letter is to be taken as an indication of the Union Administration's help, then I am safe in assuming both McNulty's and my efforts were in vain.

Your letter makes reference to you and me discussing whether I will go [sic] the Massachusetts Labor Commission for the purpose of disputing the "fact" that I am assigned or detailed to the S.I.U. I believe I have already established that I am not a member of this unit

and therefore, Mr. McGee there is, in my opinion, no need for me to take this action; or for Union funds to be expended in this fashion.

Sincerely,

Paul A. Johnston

Broderick, Bilodeau and McGee were present at the October 16th meeting, and Broderick placed a telephone call to Superintendent Paul Russell. The two men discussed the computer print-out, and Russell informed Broderick that the print-out was erroneous; that the heading was misleading and should not be taken to mean that the men named on the print-out had performed overtime for the S.I.U. Broderick requested a letter from Russell affirming that the men whose names appeared upon the erroneous print-out had never worked for the S.I.U. nor performed overtime services for it. The next day Russell sent Broderick the following letter:

Dear Mr. Broderick:

Pursuant to our telephone conversation of October 16, 1975, enclosed as requested is a copy of the communication from Superintendent Charles T. Cobb, Chief of the Bureau of Administrative Services.

Sincerely,

Paul J. Russell, Superintendent
Office of the Police Commissioner

Cobb's memorandum, which was attached, read as follows:

To whom it may concern:

Due to the fact that a program malfunction occurred on the November overtime, inadvertently several units of the Commissioner's Office were all incorporated as members of the S.I.U.

The following persons are the only patrolmen assigned to the S.I.U.

John Bean
Stanley Gawlinski
Frank Zimmerman

Charles T. Cobb
Superintendent Chief,
Bureau of Administrative Services

On October 29, 1975, the day of the Association's election, Johnston was told by an Association representative manning the ballot box that he would not be permitted to vote. The representative showed him a list denominated "Patrolmen who are ineligible to vote because they have been deemed confidential employees by the department," upon which Johnston's and McNulty's names, as well as the names of eleven other police officers, appeared.

OPINION

During six days of hearings, the Commission heard testimony from Joseph T. Doyle, the now retired Commanding Officer of the SIU; Lieutenant James M. Hayes, the present Commander of SIU; Mark Furstenberg, who was Johnston and McNulty's supervisor and Director of the Planning and Research Division; and Johnston and McNulty themselves. Their testimony encompassed the entire duration of time that the SIU has been in existence, and was clear, unequivocal, and convincing beyond any shadow of doubt. The city produced for the Association's inspection the overtime slips of all persons who had ever worked for the SIU from February 1973 (when it was formed) until the present. The persons responsible for the error in the computer printout admitted responsibility for that error, and explained how it occurred. Based upon the overwhelming totality of the evidence, we conclude, without reservation whatever, that patrolmen Paul Johnston and Joseph McNulty are not and never have been members of the Special Investigation Unit, even temporarily; have never performed any services for the Special Investigation Unit during either regular or overtime hours, with or without compensation; and have never given any information to the special investigation unit, openly, anonymously, or even inadvertently. The appearance of their names upon overtime lists labeled "Prepared for the Special Investigation Unit" was solely the result of a computer programming error and nothing more. They are not managerial or confidential employees who should be excluded from the collective bargaining unit.

BECNEL v. ANSWER, INC.

428 So.2d 539

(Court of Appeal of Louisiana, Fourth Circuit, March 4, 1983.)

AUGUSTINE, J.

Plaintiff, Michele Ann Becnel, sued her former employer, Answer, Inc., for unpaid va-cation wages, as well as penalties and attorney fees, allegedly due under L.S.A.-R.S. 23:632 [footnote] within three days after she was terminated.

Ms. Becnel began employment with Answer, Inc. (a branch of Answer of Iowa) as a telephone operator on May 23, 1978. She continued in their employ without incident until May of 1980, when she was terminated due to the loss of customers and the closing of the downtown New Orleans office. Ms. Becnel was notified of her termination in a letter dated May 14, 1980, signed by her supervisor and the vice-president of the company.

On May 19th, Ms. Becnel wrote a letter to John Lund, the vice-president, demanding "all wages due * * * which includes: gross, net, etc." by May 21, 1980. In addition, the letter indicated that if she was not paid within the 72 hour grace period provided by L.S.A.-R.S. 23:631, her attorney would thereafter handle the matter. The statute provides:

A. Upon the discharge or resignation of any laborer or other employee of any kind whatever, it shall be the duty of the person employing such laborer or other employee to pay the amount then due under the terms of employment, whether the employment is by the hour, day, week, or month, not later than three days following the date of discharge or resignation. Said payment shall be made at the place and in the manner which has been customary during the employment. * * *

B. In the event of a dispute as to the amount due under this Section, the employer shall pay the undisputed portion of the amount due as provided for in Subsection A of this Section.

* * *

On May 23rd, two days beyond the "grace" period, a check was issued to Ms. Becnel totalling $97.04 before deductions, representing regular pay for 29.30 hours worked during the pay period. No other demands were made until Ms. Becnel filed this suit on June 19, 1980, in which she specifically asked for unpaid vacation wages, penalties and attorney fees. Six months later, in December 1980, a check was issued to Ms. Becnel for two weeks vacation totalling $264.00 in gross pay. However, this check was not tendered to Ms. Becnel through her attorney until May, 1981.

After much delay, the trial in this matter was held on October 12, 1981. At that time the trial court findings were:

1. that the defendant paid the salary due within the delay allowed by law;

2. that there was a genuine dispute as to whether plaintiff was entitled to vacation pay;

3. that plaintiff was paid two days late and the court did "not feel that an actual delay of two days would entitle the plaintiff to penalties";

4. that the defendant was agreeable to discussing the matter with a view toward settlement but plaintiff (or her counsel) chose to proceed to trial for penalties and attorney fees;

5. that the plaintiff (or her counsel) sought punitive damages rather than reasonable damages and attorney fees; and the laws of our State do not permit the awarding of punitive damages.

In accordance with the trial court's findings, judgment was rendered in favor of the plaintiff against the defendant awarding $50.00 in penalties for late payment of vacation wages, and $250.00 in attorney fees plus costs. Plaintiff now appeals, alleging that the judgment is inadequate and inconsistent with the evidence, and seeks an increase in the amount of penalties and attorney fees.

Specifically, plaintiff argues that the trial court erred in finding there was a genuinely disputable question of plaintiff's entitlement to vacation wages. She also alleges that the evidence demonstrates bad faith on the part of the defendant in failing to pay her timely. And finally, plaintiff alleges that the trial court erred in its finding that the laws of the State do not permit the award of punitive damages.

I

UNPAID VACATION BENEFITS

All employees of Answer, Inc. received a handbook in which rules and policies were outlined. The vacation policy reads in part:

Full time employees (employee averaging at least 35 hours per week) are entitled to paid vacation as follows:

A. 1. Employee must work one year before any vacation is paid.

2. After one year and up to five years employment, two weeks paid.

3. After five years and up to fifteen years employment, three weeks paid.

4. After fifteen years employment, four weeks paid.

* * *

C. Vacation pay may not be accumulated.

The handbook further provides that the vacation period is from May 1 to October 31, during which only a limited number of employees may be given a vacation during any particular week. If an employee resigns or is dismissed for cause prior to or during vacation, the vacation earnings and other employee benefits will be forfeited.

Ms. Becnel testified that in her first year of employment she took a vacation. According to the policy, then, this was an unpaid vacation. In April 1980, during her second year of employment, Ms. Becnel notified her manager of her intention to schedule a vacation. She testified that although she made several requests for vacation during that time, no approval was ever given by her employer. After May 23, 1980, her vacation would have been forfeited. Ms. Becnel was terminated, however, before her requested two-weeks vacation had been approved. At the time she was terminated, her vacation time had not yet been forfeited under that clause in the policy which prohibits accumulated vacation. Clearly, Ms. Becnel made efforts to take her vacation and would have been entitled to do so had she not been terminated. The defendant admits that she was not terminated for cause, and therefore, that her benefits had not been forfeited under the terms of the policy.

Mr. Bridenstein, Secretary-Treasurer for Answer of Iowa, appeared for the defendant at trial. He testified that all payroll information is kept on a computer and a notation is made as to whether the pay is for regular, overtime, or vacation hours. When an individual takes a vacation, a time sheet is mailed to the main office designating vacation hours. Therefore, the company had at its disposal documentation which would have indicated whether or not plaintiff was entitled to a vacation or vacation pay.

L.S.A.-R.S. 23:631 provides that upon discharge or resignation of any laborer or other employee of any kind, it shall be the duty of the employer to pay the amount then due under the terms of employment. *Berteau v. Wiener Corp.*, 362 So.2d 806 (La.App. 4th Cir.1978), is directly applicable to the present case. In *Berteau*, the plaintiff, after becoming eligible for one week of vacation under the terms of her employer's company handbook, and upon completion of one year of service, was terminated before taking her scheduled vacation.

She thereupon requested her vacation pay, but it was denied.

In deciding that the plaintiff was entitled to vacation pay, this court in *Berteau,* 362 So.2d at 808, said:

> There is jurisprudence in Louisiana to the effect that vacation benefits are included in the definition of the 'amount due under the terms of employment.' The Second and Third Circuits have held that vacation benefits are additional wages and are, therefore, to be included in the amount paid to the employee upon discharge. [citations omitted].

> * * *

> Appellant's right to her vacation had vested under the handbook and her request for its approval, and the company cannot force forfeiture of that right. * * * Mrs. Berteau clearly had a present interest in a vacation benefit and divesting her of this is a forfeiture.

Ms. Becnel met all the requirements imposed by the company handbook with regard to vacation pay. She was not terminated for cause and her eligibility to take a vacation had not yet lapsed under the clause which prohibited accumulation of benefits. Therefore, her right to vacation or vacation pay had vested under the terms of the handbook. Ms. Becnel was clearly entitled to the vacation pay, and the evidence shows that there could have been no reasonable dispute of Ms. Becnel's entitlement to vacation pay.

II

PENALTIES UNDER L.S.A.-R.S. 23:632

L.S.A.-R.S. 23:632 provides in part that:

> Any employer who fails or refuses to comply with the provisions of R.S. 23:631 shall be liable to the employee either for ninety days wages at the employee's daily rate of pay, or else for full wages from the time the employee's demand for payment is made until the employer shall pay or tender the amount of unpaid wages due to such employee, whichever is the lesser amount of penalty wages

> * * *

The jurisprudence of this state is to the effect that statutes which are expressly penal in nature are to be strictly construed. [Citation.] If it is determined that a bona fide dispute as to wages due existed at the time of the refusal or failure to pay, no penalties will be awarded. [Citation.] For the employee to recover, the employer must have been motivated by bad faith or must be found to have acted in an 'arbitrary or unreasonable' manner. [Citation.]

It appears to this court that the actions by the defendant were arbitrary and unreasonable. The defendant unreasonably delayed determining whether or not the plaintiff was entitled to vacation pay. Given the testimony by Mr. Bridenstein, this information was literally at the company's fingertips on the computers at Answer's main office in Iowa. To determine whether a vacation had been taken it was only necessary to review the payroll records of the company for the preceding year.

By way of defense, Mr. Bridenstein testified that during the period in which Ms. Becnel requested to be scheduled for a vacation, the New Orleans office was undergoing changes in management and as a result there is no documentation in the records to support or refute her claim. In addition, defendant argues that due to the flooding in the New Orleans area when the office was moving, many files and records which would have indicated whether Ms. Becnel made any requests for a vacation were destroyed. These arguments lack merit. Whether or not there was documentation of a request for vacation is irrelevant. The defendant could have easily verified through the main office computer that Becnel had not taken a vacation.

Mr. Bridenstein also testified that the company had no idea Ms. Becnel was seeking vacation pay until suit was filed on June 19, 1980. But as we have already stated, the term "wages", under the statute, has been held by the courts in Louisiana to include vacation pay. Therefore, when Ms. Becnel demanded *"all wages"* in the letter dated May 19, 1980, vacation pay was necessarily included.

Even assuming, however, that the defendant was not aware of her demand until June 19, 1980, a check for the vacation pay was not issued until December 19, 1980, six months later. In light of the ready availability of information required to process plaintiff's claim, this six month period was clearly in excess of a reasonable time in which to respond. It has been held that when an employer is merely "negligent" in failing to pay past-due wages, penalty wages will be assessed. [Citations.] In the present case, we find that the defendant's delay in tendering the vacation pay was both unreasonable and negligent.

We find that the actions of the defendant in negligently failing to determine whether the plaintiff was entitled to vacation pay and in unreasonably delaying the tender of the vacation pay until one year after termination constitute bad faith. Since the defendant failed to comply with the statute and offered no reasonable defense on the issue of entitlement, Ms. Becnel should be awarded penalties under the statute.

The trial court found that although the defendant was agreeable to discuss the matter with a view to settlement, plaintiff chose to file suit for the penalties and attorney fees. In *Sifers v. Exxon Corp.*, 388 So.2d 763 (La.App. 4th Cir.1976), this court held that the plain meaning of 'penalty wages' contemplated recovery even if the regular wages initially sought were, in fact, paid after demand but prior to suit. In the present case, payment was made after the institution of the suit but prior to trial, therefore the plaintiff was still entitled to "penalty wages" under the statute.

The statute provides for penalties from the time demand for payment is made until the employer pays the amount due, or ninety days wages at the employee's daily rate of pay, whichever is the lesser amount. Since the employer tendered payment more than ninety days after the request was made, the ninety day penalty would be the lesser amount. The testimony indicated that Ms. Becnel was paid $3.30 per hour, eight hours a day, which computes to a daily rate of $26.40. The penalty of ninety days at a daily rate of $26.40 totals $2,376.00.

* * *

Affirmed and amended.

FORD MOTOR CREDIT CO. v. HITCHCOCK

116 Ga.App. 563, 158 S.E.2d 468,
1 CLSR 893

(Court of Appeals of Georgia, Division No. 2, Oct. 31, 1967.)

Wilma Hitchcock, appellee, brought an action on May 2, 1966, against Ford Motor Credit

Company, appellant, in the Civil Court of Fulton County alleging the following: "3. On or about September 29, 1964, plaintiff purchased a 1964 Volkswagen automobile, and had the same financed through the defendant whereby monthly payments were to be made to the defendant in the amount of $66.45 for a period of thirty-six months. Plaintiff gave defendant a conditional sales contract to secure defendant's interest in the auto.

"4. On March 5, 1966, plaintiff paid the eighteenth payment to defendant, and on April 2, 1966, plaintiff paid the nineteeth payment to defendant.

"5. On or about April 13, 1966, defendant did wilfully, intentionally, and maliciously without cause commit trespass against plaintiff by stealing, taking, and carrying away of her 1964 Volkswagen automobile from her home at the aforesaid address. Defendant sent one of its agents, servants, and employees to plaintiff's home, took possession of the auto, and carried it away to some unknown location. The name of defendant's servant, agent, and employee is not known to plaintiff, but the same is well known to defendant.

"7. Plaintiff avers that there were no monthly payments in arrears at the time the defendant took said auto, and that the defendant took said auto without reason or cause.

"8. At the time of the taking of the auto by defendant, the said auto had a reasonable market value of $1,800 for which plaintiff seeks damages for said amount.

"9. By reason of the fact that the taking of said auto by defendant was wilful, intentional, malicious, and without cause plaintiff seeks $5,000 in exemplary damages against defendant to deter it from repeating the trespass.

"10. Plaintiff avers that defendant acted in bad faith by taking her automobile without cause, and since the taking has refused to return it to the plaintiff. Plaintiff further avers that defendant has been stubbornly litigious and has caused plaintiff unnecessary trouble and expense in prosecuting this suit. By reason of the fact that defendant has acted in bad faith, has been stubbornly litigious, and has caused plaintiff unnecessary trouble and expense of prosecuting this case, plaintiff seeks a reasonable attorney's fee." The prayers were for process, $1,800 damages for the value of the automobile, $5,000 as "exemplary damages," and a reasonable sum as attorney's fees. The defendant's demurrers 10 and 11, as follows, were overruled.

"10. Defendant demurs to and moves to strike that portion of paragraph ten (10) of the plaintiff's petition that reads as follows: 'Plaintiff avers that defendant acted in bad faith by taking her automobile without cause, and since the taking has refused to return it to the plaintiff' upon the grounds that the said portion of said paragraph is vague and indefinite in that it fails to state the date and name of the person who, on behalf of this defendant, refused to return said vehicle to plaintiff.

"11. Defendant demurs to and moves to strike that portion of paragraph ten (10) of the plaintiff's petition that reads as follows: 'Plaintiff further avers that the defendant has been stubbornly litigious and has caused plaintiff unnecessary trouble and expense of prosecuting this case, plaintiff seeks a reasonable attorney's fee' upon the grounds that the said portion of said paragraph is a conclusion of the pleader, unsubstantiated by allegations of ultimate fact." The defendant's original answer, filed on June 3, 1966, denied the material portions of the petition. By amendment on January 17, 1967, the defendant admitted Paragraph 4 of the petition averring payments in March and April of 1966 and admitted that at the time the automobile was repossessed no monthly payments were in arrears and further answered as follows:

"7. That on January 28, 1966, plaintiff and defendant entered into an extention [sic] agreement, a copy of said agreement being attached hereto, marked Exhibit A and made a part thereof.

"8. That due to a clerical error upon the part of an employee of the defendant herein, said agreement was not processed upon the books and records of defendant herein to plaintiff's account.

"9. Defendant admits that plaintiff's account was not delinquent in its monthly installments at the time plaintiff's vehicle was repossessed by defendant, but shows that such repossession was caused by a clerical error in not processing the aforesaid extention [sic] agreement."

The evidence was sufficient to authorize the jury to find the following facts:

Appellee was behind in her payments, and a Mr. Fricks called on appellee, and a monthly payment in arrears was made and the entire contract extended one month. A monetary consideration was paid for the extension. This payment and the extension for one month made the contract current and payable in twenty installments of $66.45 each and one of $57.45, beginning January 29, 1966. A payment of $15.53 (for the extension) was credited to the contract on January 31, 1966, and payments of $66.45 each for February 8, 1966, March 9, 1966, and April 6, 1966. No credit was entered for the payment made at the time of the execution of the extension agreement. Mr. Fricks prepared the necessary forms and these were placed upon the desk of Mr. Trahan, Mr. Fricks' superior, whose duty it was to check the figures and then transmit the form indicating the extension and one payment collected to the home office so that the computer system would reflect this on the account ledger of the appellee. Mr. Trahan checked the form and the matter relating to the extension and initialed it, but failed to send it into the home office. On April 13, 1966, Mr. Fricks sent a Mr. Houston to see the appellee in reference to two payments supposedly past due although the records showed installment payments were made in February, March, and April, 1966. When Mr. Houston arrived at the appellee's home, her son was there and, when informed of the purpose of the visit, that is, either to collect the payments or pick up the automobile, the son showed Mr. Houston two money order receipts and a copy of a cashier's check reflecting the three payments. Mr. Houston then called Mr. Fricks and Mr. Fricks checked the records again and informed Mr. Houston that the account was not current and to pick up the automobile. This was done. The account records at that time did not reflect the extension of the time for payment but did reflect the three payments made after the extension was granted. On April 25, the appellant wrote appellee the following letter: "Your account remains past due for the 2-29-66 and 3-29-66 installments for a total amount due of $176.90 including all charges. Please contact us immediately on receipt of this letter so that we can make definite arrangements towards redeeming this car." As a result of this letter, appellee's husband on April 28 went to see Mr. Trahan, exhibited the evidences of payment to him, insisted that the contract was current, but was told by Trahan that the account was not current and that this sum would have to be paid before they could get the car. The evidence disclosed no express demands upon the appellant for the automobile. Suit was filed against the appellant in June of 1966, and Mr. Fricks testified that he "discovered" on approximately June 24, 1966, that the account ledger did not show the extension of time for payment. Mr. Trahan testified that he "discovered" it sometime prior to August 12, 1966. Neither Mr. Fricks nor Mr. Trahan upon the "discovery" of this fact made any effort to return the automobile to the appellee, but instead the appellant kept said automobile and was in possession of said automobile at the time of trial.

* * *

SYLLABUS OPINION
BY THE COURT

PANNELL, J.

1. The "bad faith" which will authorize recovery of attorney's fees in an action seeking damages and attorney's fees under Code § 20-1404 is "bad faith" in the transaction out of which the cause of action arose. [Citations.]

Where, as here, a petition seeking damages for the alleged wrongful repossession of an automobile alleges that the defendant finance company wilfully, intentionally, and maliciously and without probable cause repossessed the plaintiff's automobile, that there were no monthly payments in arrears and that defendant took the automobile without reason or cause and refused to return it, is a sufficient allegation of facts to support an allegation of bad faith and stubborn litigiousness under Code § 20-1404. The trial court therefore did not err in overruling the demurrer to such allegations in the petition attacking them on the grounds that they were a conclusion of the pleader.

The attorney's fees were eliminated by charge to the jury, and even if the overruling of the demurrer be error, it was harmless.

2. While the allegations of the petition that "since the taking [the defendant] has refused to return it [the automobile] to the plaintiff," the defendant being a corporation, may have been subject to the demurrer that it did not disclose the date or the name of the person who on behalf of the defendant refused to return the automobile to the plaintiff, it appears that the overruling of this demurrer was harmless to the defendant since the defendant had as witnesses at the trial all of its employees with whom the plaintiff or her agents had any conversations or dealings with reference to the matters at issue, and the evidence discloses the defendant never, at any time, offered to return the automobile except upon payment of sums which it was not entitled then to receive.

3. The court gave the following charge: "Now, the plaintiff has sued for the market value of this automobile. This action being in tort, and since the repossession, if wrongful, caused the plaintiff to sustain a total loss of her property right in the automobile, the measure of the actual damages was the market value of her property at the time of the trespass, to which interest could be added. The market value of the plaintiff's property right would be determined by taking the market value of the automobile itself and subtracting therefrom the balance due on the purchase price of the automobile." After some intervening charges he gave the following charge which was objected to: "Notwithstanding the holder of the legal title to personalty may maintain an action in tort for damages to the property, one who is not the holder of the legal title but who is in legal possession of the property having a special interest therein and holding an equitable title thereto as purchaser with part of the purchase money unpaid, may maintain an action in tort to recover for the entire damage to the property, the amount recovered, however, being subject to his own use and that of the holder of the legal title as their respective interests may appear." The ground of objection was that the latter charge was "actually in conflict with" the prior charge, the charge objected to indicating "that plaintiff may recover the entire amount."

The charge objected to was a charge of an abstract principle of law which applies only to cases where such an action is brought by the equitable owner against a third party not the legal title holder. Here the action was against the legal title holder as covered in the first charge. There is no conflict in the charges.

That the latter charge might have been confusing to the jury is not raised by the objection made.

4. "An act of a person, although without legal right or authority, upon the person or property of another, which causes damage, where done in good faith and without willfulness or malice, or such gross neglect as to indicate a wanton disregard for the rights of another, will not authorize the infliction of punitive damages." [Citation.] "To authorize the imposition of punitive damages there must be evidence of willful misconduct, malice, fraud, wantonness, or oppression, or that entire want of care which would raise the presumption of a conscious indifference to consequences. [Citation.]" [Citation.]

Neither the agent of defendant who collected a payment on the contract at the same time he secured the extension agreement, nor the agent who approved these actions and initialed the formal reports thereof, testified or claimed that they forgot about such facts. It follows therefore that the jury was authorized to find that this knowledge, coupled with knowledge that three additional payments had been made, was knowledge that the account was not in arrears at the time the repossession was made on the instructions of one agent and at the time the plaintiff's husband exhibited evidence of payments to the other agent in an attempt to secure a return of the automobile. The jury was authorized to find additionally, therefore, that the repossession was made in bad faith and was wilfully and wantonly made with full knowledge of lack of all probable cause for so doing, and that rather than depend upon their own knowledge they preferred to go by what the computer "told" them. It might be said further that the evidence shows that with the payment, made at the time of the extension agreement, credited to the contract, the contract would not have been in arrears until April 29, 1966, even without the extension, and therefore that the defense, based upon the failure to send in the extension agreement as the cause of the error, is not supported by the evidence. The verdict was authorized by the evidence both for actual and exemplary damages under Code § 105-2002, which provides that "In every tort there may be aggravating circumstances, either in the act or the intention, and in that event the jury

may give additional damages, either to deter the wrongdoer from repeating the trespass or as compensation for the wounded feelings of the plaintiff."

5. The remaining enumerations of error relating to the charges of the court, when the evidence and the charge as a whole are considered, are without merit.

Judgment affirmed.

FORD MOTOR CREDIT CO. v. SWARENS

447 S.W.2d 53, 2 CLSR 347
(Court of Appeals of Kentucky, Oct. 17, 1969.)

REED, J.

The appellee, Swarens, sued the appellant, Ford Motor Credit Company, because Ford wrongfully repossessed his automobile. After a trial before a jury, judgment was entered pursuant to a verdict that Swarens recover from Ford $2,000 compensatory damages and $5,000 punitive damages. The judgment was entered on June 27, 1968. Ford served and filed a motion and grounds for new trial on July 10, 1968. On July 12, 1968, this motion was overruled. Ford appeals. The errors asserted are: the trial judge made comments which were prejudicial because they influenced the jury to make an excessive award; the compensatory damages and the punitive damages are excessive; and the instructions given to the jury by the trial judge were erroneous. It is our conclusion that the question of the excessiveness of damages was not properly preserved for appellate review; that the comments of the trial judge complained of were not prejudicial; and that the instructions were correct. We affirm the judgment.

In February 1963, Swarens purchased a 1962 Ford car from a dealer in Indiana for about $2,300. The unpaid part of the purchase price was the subject of a security agreement that was assigned by the selling dealer to Ford Motor Credit Company. The agreement provided for monthly installment payments to be made to Ford's home office in Michigan. Swarens made the payments as required, but in June 1963, he was visited by employees of Ford's Louisville, Kentucky, collection office. These Ford representatives told Swarens that he was delinquent in his payments. He showed them his cancelled checks which clearly established that he was current in payments. Two months later, the visit, the accusations of delinquency, and the proof to the contrary occurred again. Finally, in October of 1963, the collectors returned for the last time and Swarens, who Ford admits was at all times current in his payments, was tired of their visits; he advised them that he would show them no more records, and while displaying a shotgun, he also strongly suggested that they leave his home. They left, but first reminded him of their experience in the repossession of automobiles and promised him that they would repossess his.

Swarens, who was employed at a plant in Jefferson County, Kentucky, drove to work on December 2, 1963 and parked his car in a lot. After working all day, Swarens returned to the parking lot and found his car missing. He reported this to the police who advised him that Ford has repossessed his car. Swarens hitchhiked home that night.

The next morning Swarens visited the Louisville collection office. Kawa, the office manager of Ford's Louisville collection office, testified concerning what happened on this occasion. According to Kawa, the mistake of Ford was admitted and apologies were made to Swarens. Kawa said that he offered to return the car to Swarens. Kawa admitted, however, that this offer was conditional. The condition was that Swarens accept the car and his out-of-pocket expense necessitated by his trip to the Louisville office, and in consideration of the delivery and payment of expense execute and deliver a release to Ford exonerating Ford from further liability. According to Swarens, he was asked to "sign a blank piece of paper." In any event, Swarens refused Kawa's offer and left without his car. Ford retained the car, and when the next monthly installment payment came due, notified Swarens that he was in default. Apparently, sometime later, Ford sold the car and applied the proceeds to the debt. Swarens waited a considerable time after the loss of his car, but finally brought suit against Ford for the fair market value of the car at the time of its seizure and for punitive damages. The suit was commenced within the statutory period of limitations.

At the trial Ford confessed liability. The only issues tried concerned damages. Ford conceded that both the issues of compensatory damages and punitive damages should be submitted to the jury.

At the outset, we are faced with the undisputed fact that the motion and grounds for new trial alleging excessive damages was neither served nor filed by Ford within the time prescribed by CR 59.02. That rule requires the motion to be served not later than ten days from the date of the judgment. In this instance, the motion was served thirteen days from the date of the judgment. The prescribed ten-day period ended on Monday. The time of service of the motion was on the succeeding Thursday. The trial court did not strike the motion but, nevertheless, overruled it. CR 6.02 specifically provides that a court is not authorized to extend the time prescribed by CR 59.02. The plain purpose of CR 59 and CR 6 is to fix a definite time when judgments become finally effective and free from attack by the methods designated. [Citations.]

In the instance where the motion for new trial is not timely served or filed, the trial court may not exercise any discretion and is obligated to deny the motion for lack of power to grant new trial relief. [Citation.] This conclusion is fortified by the provisions of CR 59.04 as amended effective July 1, 1969. That amendment expanded the authority of the trial court under the circumstances recited in the amendment to grant a motion for new trial for a reason not stated in the motion, but the amendment carefully retained the requirement that in order to be eligible for this relief the moving party must first have served a motion for new trial within the time prescribed by CR 59.02. [Citation.]

We have held that whether damages awarded are excessive may not be considered on appeal if the appealing party has failed to present that question to the trial court. [Citations.] One of the reasons for the rule is that the trial court must be given an opportunity to effectively rule on the issue. Where the trial court is without power to rule on the question, then no effective opportunity to correct any error is afforded on the trial level. In the case before us, if the trial judge had granted the motion for new trial on the ground that the damages awarded were excessive and this determination had been appealed, such action would have been held to be reversible error because the trial court would have acted in a situation in which it had no power. Therefore, we regard the trial judge's action in overruling the motion for new trial equivalent to a finding that the motion had not been timely served or filed, and hence the trial court was without power or opportunity to exercise discretion to afford the relief sought. We, therefore, conclude that we cannot consider the issue of excessiveness of damages awarded on this appeal.

It would seem that since Ford admitted liability, whether the trial judge's oral statements made during the trial were prejudicial could only be tested by determining whether excessive damages were awarded as a result of the statements. We have, nevertheless, examined the two particular incidents involving the witness Kawa about which Ford complains and find that in each instance the judge either merely attempted to prevent inadmissible hearsay evidence or attempted to elicit pertinent facts from an evasive witness. There was nothing in the judge's statements to indicate that he was reflecting on the credibility of the evidence or that he was occupying anything other than a position of impartiality so far as the contentions of the contending litigants were concerned. We reject Ford's assertions of error concerning the statements of the trial judge during the testimony of Kawa. [Citation.]

Ford also complains that the admonition of the trial judge to the jury about the evidentiary significance of a letter, introduced and admitted during the testimony of Kawa, was erroneous. This letter written by Kawa to Swarens recited the events that transpired on the day Swarens visited Ford's Louisville collection office. It omitted any reference to the requirement of a release from Swarens to Ford which Kawa admitted actually occurred. The judge admonished the jury to consider the contents of the letter only "on the question of punitive damages." Ford objected to this admonition on the specific ground that Swarens was seeking compensatory damages for occurrences after the taking of the car and, therefore, the jury had the right to consider this evidence on the issue of compensatory damages. The instruction on compensatory damages given by the trial court limited Swarens' recovery for compensatory damages to the fair market value of the car at the time of its seizure. Ford seized and retained the car and insisted on its retention until Swarens would settle on Ford's terms and execute a release. The only possible evidentiary value of the letter is confined solely to the question of Ford's good faith and lack of wilfulness— the issue of punitive damages. We conclude that Ford was not prejudiced by the trial court's admonition.

Ford's final contention is that the instruction on compensatory damages is erroneous in that it fails to incorporate Ford's offer to return the car. What we have said concerning the contents of Kawa's letter applies equally here. Ford relies on the case of *Kasey v. Hofgesang*, Ky., 333 S.W.2d 262. This authority is not applicable. In the *Kasey* case, a creditor secured by a lien on personal property had a contract right to take possession of the secured property upon default by the debtor. The creditor also had a contract right upon taking possession after a default by the debtor to retain the property "as his own absolutely or sell it to pay said indebtedness." The debtor defaulted. The creditor took possession of the property during the pendency of a suit concerning the debt. One month after the suit was filed the creditor notified the debtor by letter that he was waiving his right to retain possession of the property and that the debtor could use and enjoy the property until the litigation terminated and without prejudice to the rights or claims of the parties in the pending suit. The debtor did not take back the property. When the suit was subsequently decided in favor of the creditor, the debtor contended that the creditor had converted the property unreasonably because the creditor could have sold the property and subjected the proceeds of the sale to the satisfaction of his lien without court action. We rejected the debtor's contention and held that the creditor had acted reasonably under the circumstances. In the instant case, there was no default and there was no unconditional offer to return the property. The instruction on compensatory damages was correct.

Ford explains that this whole incident occurred because of a mistake by a computer. Men feed data to a computer and men interpret the answer the computer spews forth. In this computerized age, the law must require that men in the use of computerized data regard those with whom they are dealing as more important than a perforation on a card. Trust in the infallibility of a computer is hardly a defense, when the opportunity to avoid the error is as apparent and repeated as was here presented.

The judgment is affirmed.

PALMER v. COLUMBIA GAS OF OHIO, INC.

479 F.2d 153

(United States Court of Appeals, Sixth Circuit, May 22, 1973.)

PECK, C. J.

I

The plaintiffs, residential customers of natural gas supplied by the defendant Columbia Gas Company, brought this class action for injunctive and declaratory relief and for damages, alleging that their gas service had been terminated under color of state law in violation of their constitutional right to due process.

The Columbia Gas Company is a large, privately owned, pervasively regulated public utility company. It serves over 140,000 customers in the Toledo, Ohio area [footnote], and all of its billing is handled by computer in Columbus, Ohio. A reading is normally taken from each customer's meter every other month, although on occasion no reading may be taken for a period of many months. When no reading is taken to reflect actual usage, the company's computer estimates usage and calculates an amount which is then billed to the customer. For some reason which is not made clear in the record, the computer usually underestimates in these situations; consequently, when an actual reading is eventually made after a series of several computer estimates, the resulting bill for actual gas consumed can be surprisingly high.[2] In these cases, the customer, especially if poor, often has been unable to pay a bill several times larger than normal.

Whenever a monthly bill is not paid by the customer, the amount is carried forward and added to the customer's next bill. Whenever the second month's bill is not paid by five days after the due date and the amount in arrears is $20 or more, a notice of termination (a "shut-off notice") is sent to the customer:

COLUMBIA GAS
OF OHIO, INC.
701 JEFFERSON AVENUE
TOLEDO OH   43624

PAYABLE AT COMPANY OFFICE

----   GCD LO UN BK ACC# C ∝
               341 13 05 52 2820 3 0 ⊢

----   L3823

RETAIN THIS NOTICE FOR YOUR RECORDS.
PLEASE RETURN THE ENCLOSED CARD
WITH YOUR PAYMENT.

COMPANY OFFICE HOURS:
MONDAY THRU FRIDAY . 9:00 A.M. TO 4:45 P.M.   7152

1042 AVONDALE AV   12
SERVICE ADDRESS

BARBARA BELL
1042 AVONDALE AV
TOLEDO OHIO   43607

FINAL NOTICE

Your account is Past Due.

Unless the Past Due amount is paid, or satisfactory arrangements are made with this office, it will be necessary to discontinue service to you without further notice.

This Past Due amount should be paid at the Local Office. Our servicemen and collection agencies are not authorized to accept such payments.

If payment has been made, please disregard this notice.

If shut-off is necessary, Budget Customer must pay total amount before service is reconnected.	Service will be discontinued if payment is not received by:	Past Due Pay This Amount
	03-10-72	131.26

2. For example, one of the plaintiffs received a series of estimated bills ranging in amount from $10 to $15; after an actual reading was taken, the bill for actual gas consumed was almost $200.

If payment is not made within five days of the issuance of the shut-off notice, an employee of the company called "a collector" [3] goes to the residence and terminates the service. Although this employee is authorized to grant temporary extensions of time in which payment may be made, he is under no obligation to inform the occupants of the premises that he is about to terminate gas service, and he usually will make no contact at all with the occupants, even to verify the correctness of the address.[4]

The evidence established that however imperfect the company's procedure was in theory, in practice it was more so. Significant and tragic mistakes were often made; for example, one witness testified that his gas service was terminated even though he had paid his bill in full upon receipt of a final notice. One of the intervening plaintiffs testified that his gas service was unexpectedly terminated on January 4, even though he had paid his bill, by mail, on December 30. When he contacted the company by telephone and informed them that he had paid the bill, an employee of the company replied: "Tough. Pay the bill again." This customer had seven children, and the temperature in his house dropped to 45 degrees before service was eventually restored through the intervention of the Board of Community Relations.

Additional confusion is introduced into the company's procedures by the fact that when a customer did make special arrangements for deferred payments of a larger than usual bill, a shut-off notice would be sent with each monthly bill, which the customer would be instructed to disregard. For example, one plaintiff testified that after having been billed about $12.00 a month for a series of about 5 estimated bills, she received a bill for actual usage for over $197.00. She made special ar-

rangements to pay this large amount over a period of months, during which time she received a shut-off notice each month and an additional notice requesting that she disregard the shut-off notice. Although she paid the stipulated amount monthly, her service was terminated in mid-December, until, through the eventual intervention of her church pastor, the company acknowledged its mistake, apologized and restored service.

Administrative and clerical errors also resulted in unpleasant surprises for the company's customers. One witness testified that he received on December 30 a notice that his service would be terminated if his bill were not paid by January 4. He mailed his personal check to the company on December 30, which was endorsed by the company and cashed on January 3. Nevertheless, on January 4, his service was terminated. The first that he, his three children, and his pregnant wife learned of the termination was when it started to get cold in the house. The company showed that a clerical employee had misplaced the record of the customer's payment, thereby causing this unwarranted termination.

After two days of hearing what one court has aptly described as a bizarre "Orwellian nightmare," [5] the District Court concluded:

> The evidence as a whole revealed a rather shockingly callous and impersonal attitude upon the part of the defendant, which relied uncritically upon its computer, located in a distant city, and the far from infallible clerks who served it, and paid no attention to the notorious uncertainties of the postal service. *Palmer v. Columbia Gas of Ohio*, 342 F.Supp. 241, 243 (N.D.Ohio 1972).

The Court found that termination procedures of the company constitute action taken under color of state law because an Ohio statute, § 4933.12, O.R.C., authorizes the company to

---

3. The reason for the designation of this employee as such is not clear, since he is not authorized to accept payment or partial payment of a bill.

4. One plaintiff testified that when her gas service was suddenly terminated without notice, the gas company apologized for the mistake and informed her that they had intended to terminate the gas service for another apartment in the same building.

5. *Bronson v. Consolidated Edison of New York*, 350 F.Supp. 443 (S.D.N.Y.1972). In that case, the plaintiff, upset at a sudden and drastic increase in the amount of

her monthly electric bill, caused an investigation to be made which resulted in the discovery by the utility company that her landlord had been diverting current through her meter. Nevertheless, the higher bills continued, and when she refused to pay, the company terminated service. After three weeks without electricity, she paid the bill, and the amount was credited to her account. However, her check was lost by the bank; the bank notified the company that they had not received the check, and the company then re-entered the deficit in the customer's account. At this point, the customer instigated litigation.

enter the premises of a customer who has not paid his bill for the purposes of disconnecting and removing its equipment. [Footnote.] The Court also found that the termination procedures of the company "are clearly offensive to even the most elementary notion of what constitutes due process." [Citation.]

Accordingly, the Court ordered that the company not terminate, interrupt, cut-off or interfere with gas service to any residential customer of the company in its Northwestern District (the Toledo area) except in conformity with the following conditions: Any individual employee of the company charged with the mechanical process of terminating the gas service of any customer must first speak personally with that customer or some responsible adult member of his household[7] and inform him of his intention to terminate gas service to that residence. Should the customer indicate that his account with the company has been paid or that he disputes the amount of the bill, the employee shall not terminate the gas service for at least 24 hours. If the customer fails to contact the company in that time,[8] his service may be terminated without further notice. If the customer is unavailable, the company shall send a notice to the customer via certified mail, return receipt requested, advising him of its intention to terminate service for nonpayment of bills unless, within 24 hours after the company receives the return receipt, the company receives payment or the customer notifies the company that the bill has been paid or that he is engaged in a dispute concerning the account.

If the customer communicates, by telephone or otherwise, with the company's office within 24 hours, the company may take no further action toward termination of service until some officer or employee of the company, no lower in position than Office Manager, Local Manager, or person who performs a com-

parable function, shall have addressed himself to the customer's communication, made inquiry into any factual disputes presented by the customer and made a direct individual response to the customer, explaining in detail the company's position.[9] If the response of the officer does not resolve the dispute as to the amount claimed to be due from the customer, the termination of service shall be stayed upon the giving of bond with good and sufficient surety [footnote] not to exceed the amount in dispute. Further resolution of the dispute may be made either by the action of a higher ranking officer or employee of the company which meets with the satisfaction of the customer or by litigation commenced by the company to collect the amount in dispute.

If the dispute concerns a deficiency which is a result of a series of underestimated bills, service may not be terminated for non-payment of the amount due, but the deficiency must be prorated and billed to the customer in monthly installments not greater than the average monthly amount for that residence for the previous twelve months. These prorated amounts may then be billed to the customer in addition to his regular current charges.

Finally, the Court's order provides that service may be terminated without notice of any kind in an emergency situation where the inhabitants or the public health or safety are threatened; following the correction of the cause of the emergency, service must be restored and terminated only in accordance with the provisions of the Court's order.

* * *

II

STATE ACTION

* * *

---

7. The District Court has ordered the company to make "residence service" of the notice to terminate service for nonpayment. This should be distinguished from "personal service" which would require the company to notify the customer or person who has opened the account. The procedure required by the order of the District Court is similar in operation to the service of process requirements of Federal Rule of Civil Procedure 4(d)(1). [Citation.]

8. The order provides that the employee shall orally advise the customer or adult member of his household

that if he does not, within 24 hours communicate with the company's office, he will thereafter return and terminate the gas service without further notice.

9. If the company makes an oral response to the customer, the company must reduce the response to writing and send a copy to the customer by certified mail, return receipt requested, prior to any termination of service. The Court's order provides that it shall not be interpreted to prohibit the investigation officer from assigning the detailed investigation to one or more of the company's supervisors who report directly to such officer.

In summary, inasmuch as the operations of the appellant company are fully circumscribed by an all-encompassing system of state statutes, city ordinances and the supervision of the state regulatory authority, and inasmuch as the state of Ohio is significantly involved in virtually every one of the company's activities, including the specific activity complained of, the conclusion that the regulatory activities of the state have insinuated it into a position of interdependence with the company so that it must be recognized as a joint participant with the company is inescapable. [Citation.]

III

DUE PROCESS

We now turn to the company's contention that its present practices satisfy the requirements of due process. Like the state action issue, the question of what constitutes due process of law can only be answered in relation to the circumstances of each particular case; due process varies with the subject matter and the requirements of each situation. *Fuentes v. Shevin*, 407 U.S. 67, 82, 92 S.Ct. 1983, 32 L.Ed.2d 556 (1972). "[T]here is no table of weights and measures for ascertaining what constitutes due process." [Citation.]

In considering the kinds of due process protection that might be afforded in any given case, the nature of the affected interest, the manner in which it has been adversely affected, the reasons for which it was affected and the viable alternatives to the challenged procedure must be considered, and the injury complained of must be balanced against the good to be accomplished. [Citation.] " 'Due process' is, perhaps, the least frozen concept of our law—the least confined to history and the most absorptive of powerful social standards of a progressive society." *Griffin v. Illinois*, 351 U.S. 12, 20–21, 76 S.Ct. 585, 591, 100 L.Ed. 891 (1956) (concurring opinion of Mr. Justice Frankfurter). The due process clause requires, as a minimum, that parties whose rights are to be affected are entitled to

be notified of the proposed action, and they are entitled to be heard. [Citation.] It is equally fundamental that the right to notice and to the opportunity to be heard must be granted at a meaningful time and in a meaningful manner. [Citation.] We will first discuss the adequacy of the company's notice procedure.

IV

NOTICE

The company contends that its existing procedures of notifying customers of a proposed termination of service satisfy the requirements of the due process clause of the Fourteenth Amendment. The computer-issued shut-off notice, aside from dates, dollar amounts, account numbers and addresses, informs the customer that his account is past due, and that unless the past due amount is paid, or unless "satisfactory arrangements" are made with the company, the customer's service will be terminated without further notice. He is instructed to pay the past due amount at the local office, and is alerted to the fact that the company's servicemen and collection agencies are not authorized to accept such payments.

The company serves 140,000 customers in the Toledo area, and although the company's computer issues between 120,000 and 140,000 of these notices per year, only about 4% of them are followed by actual terminations.[17] In addition, the company instructs customers to disregard these notices whenever special arrangements for installment payments have been made.[18] Notice must be one which is designed to actually inform the consumer of the proposed termination of service, and the reason for the proposed termination; it must be given sufficiently in advance to permit him adequate opportunity to prepare for and to be present at the hearing. [Citations.]

The company's shut-off notice does not provide the customer with the information he needs to quickly and intelligently take available steps to prevent the threatened termination of service. No mention is made in the notice of the fact that a dispute concerning

17. During December 1971, about 9,000 final notices were issued and about 400 actual terminations were made.

18. One plaintiff testified that, after special arrangements had been made for the payment of her bill, she received a shut-off notice every month accompanied by

another notice requesting her to disregard all other notices. Her gas service was suddenly terminated, apparently in accordance with one of the notices she had been instructed to disregard.

the amount due might be resolved through discussion with representatives of the company, nor is notice given to a customer that special payment programs are available for a customer whose unexpectedly large bill is the result of, among other things, a series of computer underestimates. The single reference to making "satisfactory arrangements" cannot be construed as informing a customer of his right to continued service pending a hearing if he disputes the accuracy of the bill or the propriety of the shut-off notice. In fact, the company's district office manager conceded on cross-examination that the notice does not inform the customer of any rights whatever. In short, the company's termination notice is, in the context of constitutional law, virtually no notice at all. "But when notice is a person's due, process which is a mere gesture is not due process." [Citation.]

The company argues that the personal notice requirement required by the order of the District Court is an unreasonable imposition upon the gas company. We disagree for several reasons. First, it is clear that the flood of final notices sent out by the company was, as the District Court expressed it, "a wolf kind of notice" [19] which does not conform to the constitutional requirements that notice be truly informative and be given at a meaningful time. In addition, the fact that several witnesses testified that they were told by the company to disregard the notices is an additional persuasive factor which supports the District Court's requirement that the company personally contact a resident of the premises prior to actual termination.

The notification required by the District Court's order does not preclude an attempt by the company to contact the customer to ascertain the reason for nonpayment and to determine whether in fact a dispute exists. If there is a dispute, the hearing procedure can come into play and obviate the need for personal notification, which is only required when

the company has proceeded to the stage of actual termination of service. The reasonableness of any notice procedure must be considered in the light of the circumstances of each particular case. [Citations.] Balancing the potential harm to the customer against the inconvenience to the gas company, we cannot say that the notice requirement as established by the order of the District Court is unreasonable or an abuse of discretion.

V

HEARING

"[W]hen a person has an opportunity to speak up in his own defense, and when the State must listen to what he has to say, substantively unfair and simply mistaken deprivations of property interests can be prevented." *Fuentes, supra*, 407 U.S. at 81, 92 S.Ct. at 1994.

The highly computerized collection and termination practices of the company are governed by a singular corporate concern for efficiency and protection of assets. However, the Due Process clause was designed to protect the rights of the citizens from procedures which often serve more to insulate the state from individuals than to serve their needs. The Constitution recognizes higher values than speed and efficiency. [Citation.]

Several factors militate against acceptance of the company's argument that its informal hearing procedures, essentially through the office of its "Urban Affairs Coordinator," satisfy the requirements of due process. Foremost is the fact that the company has no established procedure for resolution of disputes arising from collection and termination activities, nor is there any established procedure for negotiation of partial payment of delinquent accounts in lieu of termination. Appeal to the Urban Affairs Coordinator is an informal procedure of which the customer is not

---

19. In rendering his decision from the bench, the District Judge explained his reasoning:
"Several thousand years ago, I believe there was a writer who told the story about a boy who thought he would cause excitement by crying that the wolf was attacking his flock of sheep. It did cause excitement, but since no wolf was attacking, after he had stirred up excitement a couple of times, when the

wolf really did attack nobody paid any attention to him. So that what we have here is a wolf kind of notice that is very convenient for the computer to issue, but is not, I think, what the statute [O.R.C. § 4933.12] contemplates, which, in my interpretation, is a meaningful notice that applies to the person who is going to be affected by it and will be followed by some action."

informed, either before or after a dispute arises. The Company's notice contains no indication that somewhere within the company's internal framework there lies a procedure which permits a customer to be heard on his complaint. The services of the Urban Affairs Coordinator are available only to those customers who happen to know about them because no advertising of any kind has been utilized by the company to inform its customers of his services, and because the company's employees are not instructed to inform customers of this service. More importantly, in no case does the customer have the right to appeal through the Urban Affairs Coordinator, nor does he have the right to continued service pending the disposition of his grievances. The company's argument that its existing procedures satisfy minimal due process requirements is in essence an attempt to substitute an unsupported assumption of corporate good faith for the guarantees of the due process clause of the Constitution. The mere theoretical possibility of informal resolution cannot serve as a substitute for a mandatory procedural mechanism designed to prevent unjust deprivations of important property interests. "The right to a fair and open hearing is one of the rudiments of fair play assured to every litigant by the Federal Constitution as a minimal requirement." [Citation.]

On the other hand, we conclude that the hearing procedures imposed by the order of the District Court are not unreasonable under the circumstances. The fact that gas service, at least in the context of this case, is a necessity in the ultimate sense that one's life may depend on it[20] goes not toward the question of whether due process attaches but to what type of procedure should be constructed to ensure that one is not wrongfully deprived of its use. [Citation.] Since uncontradicted evidence was introduced from which the District Court concluded that the company's clerical employees were "hostile, arrogant, and unyielding in dealing with consumers," [21] [Citation.] the District Court ordered that a personal hearing be conducted by an employee in a management position, in order to remove the collection-oriented and clerical employees from the decision making procedure. The protection of the individual from the sudden, unexpected and catastrophic consequences of the company's termination procedures is an interest which outweighs any possible loss the company might suffer in complying. If the past due amount is rightly owed, the company has an adequate remedy at law. Any gas consumed pending a pre-termination hearing will be minimal, and must be paid for by the customer.

The company contends that legal remedies are available to the recipient whose service is unjustly terminated. This argument is unpersuasive for several reasons. First, as noted above, during the pendency of such litigation, the customer would be deprived of the use of the gas service. [Footnote.] Secondly, placing such a burden upon the customer to justify or to explain nonpayment of a bill would be violative of the principle that the one asserting something to be due him shall have the burden of legal action and proof. [Citation.] Thirdly, moderate and low income families, whose service is most likely to be terminated for nonpayment[23] are those who will be least likely to be familiar with or to be able to afford the costs of civil litigation.[24] It is simply not

---

20. The District Court found that gas utility service is a necessity of life, the deprivation of which can cause serious emotional and physical damages, especially in Northwestern Ohio in the dead of winter. "A person can freeze to death or die of pneumonia much more quickly than he can starve to death." [Citation.]

21. For example, one witness testified that her gas service was terminated on the day before the due date on the bill; when she inquired of the company representative why she had received no shut-off notice, "she said it was tough." Gas service was not restored to this witness even though the bill was paid in full on the due date, January 13. The entire home was "completely iced over," several windows were broken from the cold and water pipes froze and cracked. The witness, her husband, and her children of eleven months and seven years were unable to live in

the house during this time. When she called the company she was informed that they did not know when her service would be reconnected because they did not make preferences. When she informed the company representative that she had with her an eleven month old baby, the representative told her to run around to keep warm.

23. At least four of the plaintiffs and witnesses who testified at trial were receiving all or some of their support from a welfare system. Similarly, the plaintiff in *Bronson, supra,* was receiving welfare assistance from the Department of Social Services. [Citation.]

24. Amicus Ohio State Legal Services Association asserts that Ohio's legal services programs, which serve only the destitute, operate in only 18 of 88 counties in Ohio.

realistic to assume that anyone who disputes the gas company has the full arsenal of legal remedies available to him; as a practical matter, disputes concerning such relatively small sums are seldom brought to litigation. [Citations.]

In *Fuentes v. Shevin, supra,* the Supreme Court held that the sworn affidavit of a creditor stating that he is entitled to certain goods, accompanied by a bond to indemnify the debtor for wrongful seizure, could not substitute for the due process requirement of a prior hearing because the bare assertion of entitlement tested only the applicant's own belief in his rights. [Citation.] In *Fuentes,* the debtor was permitted to regain possession after seizure by posting a bond, and yet the Supreme Court found that this procedure did not comport with the requirements of due process because "[i]f the right to notice and a hearing is to serve its full purpose, then, it is clear that it must be granted at a time when the deprivation can still be prevented." [Citation.] This minimal protection of the rights of the customer is lacking from the procedures presently employed by the company; the customer does not have the right to post a bond to receive continued service pending a final determination of his dispute. To correct this deficiency, the District Court's order permits the customer to post a bond so that he may receive gas service pending the outcome of litigation commenced by the company should the initial hearing by the company fail to resolve the dispute to the satisfaction of the parties. Similarly, the unsupported conclusory allegation of the company that the bill is past due, based upon the tacit assumption that the party was properly billed, cannot substitute for a procedure allowing the customer to be heard by someone who is in a position to mediate the dispute, and who is at least sufficiently removed from the internal corporate business and affairs which might prejudice a fair decision. [Footnote.]

In summary, the District Court's order, more than anything else, merely formalizes and makes available to every customer of the company informal procedures that the company asserts have always been available. We find

no abuse of discretion in this determination.

VI

* * *

The company also contends that the District Court's order was unreasonable in requiring the use of certified mail as a means of notifying customers of a proposed termination of service. The Court ordered that in the event the collector cannot make personal contact with a responsible adult member of the household, the service must be continued until at least 24 hours after the company's receipt of the return signifying that the customer has been notified in writing by certified mail of the company's intention to terminate service. As concluded above, the evidence showed that the company's practice of giving notice of its intention to terminate service was virtually no notice at all.[26] The evidence also showed that terminations were made without any effort to contact the individuals residing in the residence to be affected. A method of notification must be employed which will actually inform the customer of the company's intention. [Citation.] In addition, the company must be assured that the customer has actually been notified so that, should the customer not notify the company during the 24 hour period [footnote], the company may fairly assume that the customer acknowledges nonpayment and has no dispute concerning the propriety of the billing. In determining the constitutional adequacy of what purports to be notice in any given context, courts look to the practical realities of the circumstances of each particular case. [Citation.] Since the certified mail requirement is not per se unreasonable, and since the District Court's order provides that it may be modified upon good cause shown by the company, we find that this part of the District Court's order does not constitute an abuse of discretion.

* * *

The judgment of the District Court is affirmed.

---

26. Sometimes it actually gave no notice at all. The original plaintiffs, Mr. and Mrs. Morris Palmer, testified that they received no shut-off notice whatsoever from the company and yet their service was terminated for a period of two days.

MEMPHIS LIGHT, GAS & WATER DIVISION v. CRAFT

436 U.S.1
(United States Supreme Court, Certiorari to the United States Court of Appeals for the Sixth Circuit, May 1, 1978.)

POWELL, J.

This is an action brought under 42 U.S.C. § 1983 by homeowners in Memphis, Tenn., seeking declaratory and injunctive relief and damages against a municipal utility and several of its officers and employees for termination of utility service allegedly without due process of law. The District Court determined that respondents' claim of entitlement to continued utility service did not implicate a "property" interest protected by the Fourteenth Amendment, and that, in any event, the utility's termination procedures comported with due process. The Court of Appeals reversed in part. We granted certiorari to consider this constitutional question of importance in the operation of municipal utilities throughout the Nation.

I

Memphis Light, Gas and Water Division (MLG&W) [footnote] is a division of the city of Memphis which provides utility service. It is directed by a Board of Commissioners appointed by the City Council, and is subject to the ultimate control of the municipal government. As a municipal utility, MLG&W enjoys a statutory exemption from regulation by the state public service commission. Tenn. Code Ann. §§ 6–1306, 6–1317 (1971).

Willie S. and Mary Craft, respondents here [footnote], reside at 1019 Alaska Street in Memphis. When the Crafts moved into their residence in October 1972, they noticed that there were two separate gas and electric meters and only one water meter serving the premises. The residence had been used previously as a duplex. The Crafts assumed, on the basis of information from the seller, that the second set of meters was inoperative.

In 1973, the Crafts began receiving two bills; their regular bill, and a second bill with an account number in the name of Willie *C.* Craft, as opposed to Willie *S.* Craft. Separate monthly bills were received for each set of meters, with a city service fee [footnote] appearing on each bill. In October 1973, after learning from a MLG&W meter reader that both sets of meters were running in their home, the Crafts hired a private plumber and electrical contractor to combine the meters into one gas and one electric meter. Because the contractor did not consolidate the meters properly, a condition of which the Crafts were not aware, they continued to receive two bills until January 1974. During this period, the Crafts' utility service was terminated five times for nonpayment.

On several occasions, Mrs. Craft missed work and went to the MLG&W offices in order to resolve the "double billing" problem. As found by the District Court, Mrs. Craft sought in good faith to determine the cause of the "double billing," but was unable to obtain a satisfactory explanation or any suggestion for further recourse from MLG&W employees. The court noted:

> On one occasion when Mrs. Craft was attempting to avert a utilities termination, after final notice, she called the defendant's offices and explained that she had paid a bill, but was given no satisfaction. The procedure for an opportunity to talk with management was not adequately explained to Mrs. Craft, although she repeatedly tried to get some explanation for the problems of two bills and possible duplicate charges. [Citation.]

In February 1974, the Crafts and other MLG&W customers filed this action in the District Court for the Western District of Tennessee. After trial, the District Court refused to certify the plaintiffs' class and rendered judgment for the defendants. Although the court apparently was of the view that plaintiffs had no property interest in continued utility service while a disputed bill remained unpaid, it nevertheless addressed the procedural due process issue. It acknowledged that respondents had not been given adequate notice of a procedure for discussing the disputed bills with management, but concluded that "[n]one of the individual plaintiffs [was] deprived of [a] due process opportunity to be heard, nor did the circumstances indicate any substantial deprivation except in the possible instance of Mr. and Mrs. Craft." [Citation.][4] The court expressed "hope," "whether on the principles of [pendent] jurisdiction or on the basis of a very limited possible denial of due process to Mr. and Mrs. Craft," that credit in the amount of $35 be issued to reimburse the Crafts for "duplicate and unnecessary charges made and expenses incurred by [them] with respect to terminations which should have been unnecessary had effectual relief been afforded them as requested." The court also recommended "that MLG&W in the future send a certified or registered mail notice of termination at least four days prior to termination," and that such notice "provide more specific information about customer service locations and personnel available to work out extended payment plans or adjustments of accounts in genuine hardships or appropriate situations." [Citation.] [Footnote.]

On appeal, the Court of Appeals for the Sixth Circuit affirmed the District Court's refusal to certify a class action, but held that the procedures accorded to the Crafts did not comport with due process. [Citation.]

On July 12, 1976, petitioners sought a writ of certiorari in this Court to determine (i) whether the termination policies of a municipal utility constitute "state action" under the Fourteenth Amendment; (ii) if so, whether a municipal utility's termination of service for nonpayment deprives a customer of "prop-

erty" within the meaning of the Due Process Clause; and (iii) assuming "state action" and a "property" interest, whether MLG&W's procedures afforded due process of law in this case. [Footnote.] On February 22, 1977, we granted certiorari. [Citation.] We now affirm.

* * *

III

The Fourteenth Amendment places procedural constraints on the actions of government that work a deprivation of interests enjoying the stature of "property" within the meaning of the Due Process Clause. Although the underlying substantive interest is created by "an independent source such as state law," federal constitutional law determines whether that interest rises to the level of a "legitimate claim of entitlement" protected by the Due Process Clause. [Citations.]

The outcome of that inquiry is clear in this case. In defining a public utility's privilege to terminate for nonpayment of proper charges, Tennessee decisional law draws a line between utility bills that are the subject of a bona fide dispute and those that are not.

> A company supplying electricity to the public has a right to cut off service to a customer for nonpayment of a just service bill and the company may adopt a rule to that effect. [Citation.] An exception to the general rule exists when

---

4. The District Court's conclusion was advanced with little explanation, other than a reference to MLG&W's credit extension program. In an earlier discussion, the opinion offered a description of the utility's procedures. First, the court listed the steps involved in a termination: (i) Approximately four days after a meter reading date, a bill is mailed to the service location or other address designated by the customer. The last day to pay the net amount would be approximately 20 days after the meter reading date. (ii) Approximately 24 days after the meters are read, a "final notice" is mailed stating that services will be disconnected within four days if no payment is received or other provision for payment is made. (iii) Electric service is then terminated by the meter reader, unless the customer assures him that payment is in the mail, shows a paid receipt, or explains that nonpayment was due to illness. If there is no communication prior to termination, the meter reader or serviceman is instructed to leave a cutoff notice giving information about restoration of service. (iv) Approximately five days after the electric service cutoff, the remaining services are terminated if the customer has not paid the bill or made other arrangements for payment. [Citation.]

The court also noted that on or about March 1, 1973,

MLG&W instituted an "extended payment plan." This generous program allows customers able to demonstrate financial hardship to pay only one-half of a past due bill with the balance to be paid in equal installments over the next three bills. The plaintiffs in this action were participants in the plan. [Citation.]

Finally, the court observed that MLG&W provided a procedure for resolution of disputed bills:

> Credit counselors assist customers who have difficulty with payments or disputes concerning their bills with MLG&W. If those counselors cannot satisfy the customer, then the customer is referred to management personnel; generally the chief clerk in the department; then the supervisor in credit and collection. In addition, a dissatisfied customer may appeal to the Board of Commissioners of MLG&W as to complaints regarding bills, service, termination of service or any other matter relating to the operation of the Division. A customer may, if he so desires, be accompanied by an appropriate representative. The billing of customers, the determination as to when a final notice is sent, and the termination of service [are] governed by policies, rules and regulations adopted and approved by the Board of Commissioners of MLG&W. [Citation.]

the customer has a bona fide dispute concerning the correctness of the bill. [Citations.] If the public utility discontinues service for nonpayment of a disputed amount it does so at its peril and if the public utility was wrong (e.g., customer overcharged), it is liable for damages. [Citation.] *Trigg v. Middle Tennessee Electric Membership Corp.*, 533 S. W. 2d 730, 733 (Tenn. App. 1975). cert. denied (Tenn. Sup.Ct. Mar. 15, 1976). [Footnote.]

The *Trigg* [Tennessee] court also rejected the utility's argument that plaintiffs had agreed to be bound by the utility's rules and regulations, which required payment whether or not a bill is received. "A public utility should not be able to coerce a customer to pay a disputed claim." *Ibid.* [Footnote.]

State law does not permit a public utility to terminate service "at will." [Citation.] MLG&W and other public utilities in Tennessee are obligated to provide service "to all of the inhabitants of the city of its location alike, without discrimination, and without denial, except for good and sufficient cause. [Citation.] and may not terminate service except "for nonpayment of a just service bill." [Citation.] An aggrieved customer may be able to enjoin a wrongful threat to terminate or to bring a subsequent action for damages or a refund. [Citation.] The availability of such local-law remedies is evidence of the State's recognition of a protected interest. Although the customer's right to continued service is conditioned upon payment of the charges properly due, "[t]he Fourteenth Amendment's protection of 'property' * * * has never been interpreted to safeguard only the rights of undisputed ownership." [Citation.] Because petitioners may terminate service only "for cause" [footnote], respondents assert a "legitimate claim of entitlement" within the protection of the Due Process Clause.

IV

In determining what process is "due" in this case, the extent of our inquiry is shaped by the ruling of the Court of Appeals. We need go no further in deciding this case than to ascertain whether the Court of Appeals properly read the Due Process Clause to require (i) notice informing the customer not only of the possibility of termination but also of a procedure for challenging a disputed bill and (ii) " '[an] established [procedure] for resolution of disputes' " or some specified avenue of relief for customers who "dispute the existence of the liability." [Citation.][12]

A

"An elementary and fundamental requirement of due process in any proceeding which is to be accorded finality is notice reasonably calculated, under all the circumstances, to apprise interested parties of the pendency of the action and afford them an opportunity to present their objections." *Mullane v. Central Hanover Trust Co.*, 339 U.S. 306, 314 (1950) (citations omitted). The issue here is whether due process requires that a municipal utility notify the customer of the availability of an avenue of redress within the organization should he wish to contest a particular charge.

The "final notice" contained in MLG&W's bills simply stated that payment was overdue and that service would be discontinued if payment was not made by a certain date. As the Court of Appeals determined, "the MLG&W notice only warn[ed] the customer to pay or face termination." [Citation.] MLG&W also

---

12. The Court of Appeals did refer to its earlier decision in *Palmer v. Columbia Gas of Ohio, Inc.*, 479 F.2d 153 (1973), which approved a comprehensive remedy for a due process violation, including investigation of every communicated protest by a management official, provision of a hearing before such an official, and an opportunity to stay the termination upon the posting of an appropriate bond. [Citation.] These procedures were fashioned in response to findings, based on uncontradicted evidence, of hostility and arrogance on the part of the collection-oriented clerical employees. [Citation.] No such findings were made here, and the Court of Appeals' ruling did not purport to require a similar remedy in this case.

Respondents do request certain additional procedures:

"an impartial decision maker," who may be a responsible company official; "the opportunity to present information and rebut the records presented"; and "a written decision," which apparently can be rendered after termination or payment. [References.] As respondents have not cross-petitioned [citation], we do not decide whether—or under what circumstances—any of these additional procedures may be appropriate. We do note that the magnitude of the numbers of complaints of overcharge would be a relevant factor in determining the appropriateness of more formal procedures than we approve in this case. The resolution of a disputed bill normally presents a limited factual issue susceptible of informal resolution.

enclosed a "flyer" with the "final notice." One "flyer" was distributed to about 40% of the utility's customers, who resided in areas serviced by "credit counseling stations." It stated in part: "If you are having difficulty paying your utility bill, bring your bill to our neighborhood credit counselors for assistance. Your utility bills may be paid here also." No mention was made of a procedure for the disposition of a disputed claim. A different "flyer" went to customers in the remaining areas. It stated: "If you are having difficulty paying your utility bill and would like to discuss a utility payment plan, or if there is any dispute concerning the amount due, bring your bill to the office at * * *, or phone. * * * " [Citation.]

The Court of Appeals noted that "there is no assurance that the Crafts were mailed the just mentioned flyer" [citation], and implicitly affirmed the District Court's finding that Mrs. Craft was never apprised of the availability of a procedure for discussing her dispute "with management." [Footnote.] The District Court's description of Mrs. Craft's repeated efforts to obtain information about what appeared to be unjustified double billing—"good faith efforts to pay for [the Crafts'] utilities as well as to straighten out the problem"—makes clear that she was not adequately notified of the procedures asserted to have been available at the time. [Footnote.]

Petitioners' notification procedure, while adequate to apprise the Crafts of the threat of termination of service, was not "reasonably calculated" to inform them of the availability of "an opportunity to present their objections" to their bills. [Citation.] The purpose of notice under the Due Process Clause is to apprise the affected individual of, and permit adequate preparation for, an impending "hearing." [Footnote.] Notice in a case of this kind does not comport with constitutional requirements when it does not advise the customer of the availability of a procedure for protesting a proposed termination of utility service as unjustified. As no such notice was given respondents—despite "good faith efforts" on their part—they were deprived of the notice which was their due. [Footnote.]

B

This Court consistently has held that "some kind of hearing is required at some time before a person is finally deprived of his property interests." [Citation.] We agree with the Court of Appeals that due process requires the provision of an opportunity for the presentation to a designated employee of a customer's complaint that he is being overcharged or charged for services not rendered. [Footnote.] Whether or not such a procedure may be available to other MLG&W customers, both courts below found that it was not made available to Mrs. Craft. [Footnote.] Petitioners have not made the requisite showing for overturning these "concurrent findings of fact by two courts below. * * * " [Citation.] [Footnote.]

Our decision in *Mathews v. Eldridge*, 424 U.S. 319 (1976), provides a framework of analysis for determining the "specific dictates of due process" in this case.

[O]ur prior decisions indicate that identification of the specific dictates of due process generally requires consideration of three distinct factors: First, the private interest that will be affected by the official action; second, the risk of an erroneous deprivation of such interest through the procedures used, and the probable value, if any, of additional or substitute procedural safeguards; and finally, the Government's interest, including the function involved and the fiscal and administrative burdens that the additional or substitute procedural requirement would entail. [Citation.]

Under the balancing approach outlined in *Mathews*, some administrative procedure for entertaining customer complaints prior to termination is required to afford reasonable assurance against erroneous or arbitrary withholding of essential services. The customer's interest is self-evident. Utility service is a necessity of modern life; indeed, the discontinuance of water or heating for even short periods of time may threaten health and safety. And the risk of an erroneous deprivation, given the necessary reliance on computers [footnote], is not insubstantial. [Footnote.]

The utility's interests are not incompatible with affording the notice and procedure described above. Quite apart from its duty as a public service company, a utility—in its own business interests—may be expected to make all reasonable efforts to minimize billing errors and the resulting customer dissatisfaction and possible injury. [Citation.] Nor should "some kind of hearing" prove burdensome. The opportunity for a meeting with a responsible employee empowered to resolve the dispute could be afforded well in advance of the scheduled date of termination. [Footnote.] And petitioners would retain the option to terminate service after affording this opportunity and concluding that the amount billed was justly due.

C

Petitioners contend that the available common-law remedies of a pretermination injunction, a post-termination suit for damages, and post-payment action for a refund are sufficient to cure any perceived inadequacy in MLG&W's procedures. [Footnote.]

Ordinarily, due process of law requires an opportunity for "some kind of hearing" prior to the deprivation of a significant property interest. [Citation.] On occasion, this Court has recognized that where the potential length or severity of the deprivation does not indicate a likelihood of serious loss and where the procedures underlying the decision to act are sufficiently reliable to minimize the risk of erroneous determination, government may act without providing additional "advance procedural safeguards." [Citations.] [Footnote.]

The factors that have justified exceptions to the requirement of some prior process are not present here. Although utility service may be restored ultimately, the cessation of essential services for any appreciable time works a uniquely final deprivation. [Citation.] Moreover, the probability of error in utility cutoff decisions is not so insubstantial as to warrant dispensing with all process prior to termination. [Footnote.]

The injunction remedy referred to by petitioners would not be an adequate substitute for a pretermination review of the disputed bill with a designated employee. Many of the Court's decisions in this area have required additional procedures to further due process, notwithstanding the apparent availability of injunctive relief or recovery provisions. It was thought that such remedies were likely to be too bounded by procedural constraints and too susceptible of delay to provide an effective safeguard against an erroneous deprivation. [Footnote.] These considerations are applicable in the utility termination context.

Equitable remedies are particularly unsuited to the resolution of factual disputes typically involving sums of money too small to justify engaging counsel or bringing a lawsuit. [Footnote.] An action in equity to halt an improper termination because it is less likely to be pursued [footnote] and less likely to be effective, even if pursued, will not provide the same assurance of accurate decision-making as would an adequate administrative procedure. In these circumstances, an informal administrative remedy along the lines suggested above, constitutes the process that is "due."

V

Because of the failure to provide notice reasonably calculated to apprise respondents of the availability of an administrative procedure to consider their complaint of erroneous billing, and the failure to afford them an opportunity to present their complaint to a designated employee empowered to review disputed bills and rectify error, petitioners deprived respondents of an interest in property without due process of law.

The judgment of the Court of Appeals is affirmed.

IN RE DALEVIEW NURSING HOME v. AXELROD
91 A.D.2d 1161, 458 N.Y.S.2d 739
(Supreme Court, Appellate Division, Third Department, Jan. 27, 1983.)

MEMORANDUM DECISION.

* * *

By letter dated June 22, 1981, petitioner was advised that its Medicaid reimbursement rates for the period 1980–1981 had been retroactively revised downward and that the overpayments would be recouped. The revision resulted from the discovery some seven months earlier that "electronic data processing problems" and other errors in calculation had resulted in higher rates than authorized by the relevant rules and regulations. Petitioner sought to prohibit respondent from making the retroactive revisions and recouping the overpayment. Special Term dismissed the petition, holding that the State could not be precluded from revision or recoupment of unauthorized payments caused by errors of State employees since equitable estoppel does not lie against the State when acting in its governmental capacity. There must be an affirmance.

Where overpayments are the result of errors in computing the rate, respondent may recoup the unauthorized payments. [Citation.] To be contrasted are the cases where the reimbursement rate is properly calculated pursuant to the applicable statute or rules and regulations, but the facility's actual costs are less than those anticipated in the prospectively calculated rates. [Citations.] Thus, where the overpayment results from a mere error in judgment, rather than an erroneous calculation, the commissioner's common-law right of recoupment has been questioned. [Citation.] Here, it is undisputed that the overpayments were due to data processing problems and other errors in calculation, and thus, were not caused by errors in judgment. Accordingly, the overpayments are subject to recoupment. [Citation.]

Petitioner points out that respondent continued to make reimbursement at the mistaken rates during the seven-month period following discovery of the mistake. The underlying cause of the overpayments, however, continued to be the original errors in calculation. There is nothing in the record to suggest that the delay was occasioned by some conscious, judgmental decision on respondent's part to continue paying petitioner at the higher rate.

The decision to recoup was in furtherance of respondent's duty as a public official to protect public funds and ensure that they are expended in accordance with applicable statutes, rules and regulations. Respondent's determination was within his authority and had a rational basis. The judgment dismissing petitioner's application must, therefore, be affirmed.

Judgment affirmed, without costs.

KANE, J., dissenting.

To excuse the State for its errors in this case on the theory that they emanate from "electronic data processing problems" and are mere errors in rate computation, thus rendering the overpayments recoverable, is, in my view, an oversimplification of the problem as well as a violation of respondents' own rules and regulations.

The computer failed to provide the necessary information at the time of the original computation of the 1980 rate, not because the computer made a mathematical error, but because someone failed in the performance of his or her duties, as an employee of the State, to comply with the requirements necessary to determine the proper rate, i.e., give the computer the necessary information. Clearly, this failure to so act was the cause of the problem. I fail to see how such "error" permits an otherwise unauthorized retroactive rate adjustment to become validated under one of the two exceptions provided by the department's rules and regulations. [Citations.] Accountability for loss, under these circumstances, should be assumed by those responsible therefor and not assessed against petitioner. Simple justice demands no less. Furthermore, *Matter of University of Rochester Strong Mem. Hosp. v. Whalen*, 61 A.D.2d 867, 402 N.Y.S.2d 232, mot. for lv. to app. den. 44 N.Y.2d 646, 406 N.Y.S.2d 1026, 378 N.E.2d 126, crucial to the argument advanced by respondents, is not to the contrary. Not only is *Strong* factually distinguishable (the petitioner itself was seeking a prospective rate increase and was provided with an obvious erroneous rate), but the legal principle for which it stands is founded upon errors of commission in the ratemaking process. Here we have a failure to act which, absent proof to the contrary, should be classified as a considered judgment on the part of the State and, thus, retroactive adjustment is prohibited. [Citations.]

Finally, the "error" in failing to notify petitioner of the rate revision for more than seven months after discovery thereof is egregious and inexcusable.

The judgment should be reversed, and the petition granted.

CITY OF CHICAGO v. ROPPOLO

113 Ill.App.3d 602, 447 N.E.2d 870
(Appellate Court of Illinois, First District, Second Division, March 22, 1983.)

DOWNING, P. J.

This action arises from the demolition of the Henry W. Rincker House, a two-story frame residence on Chicago's far northwest side, which had been declared a landmark by the Commission on Chicago Historic and Architectural Landmarks (Landmark Commission).

Plaintiffs, the City of Chicago and a class comprised of all its citizens, brought this action for the imposition of a constructive trust on the property on which the house stood and for damages. The constructive trust was to be measured by the extent of the savings in restoration costs to Anthony Roppolo, the property owner, generated by the house's demolition. In addition to Roppolo, the suit named as defendants the Northwest National Bank of Chicago, as Trustee under Trust Agreement dated March 1, 1978, and known as Trust 4525 (Trustee), Cirro Wrecking Company (Cirro), the wrecking company which performed the demolition, and Lela Cirrincione, the owner of Cirro. After a bench trial, the trial court held that plaintiffs failed to prove any of the defendants guilty of a fraud or that any defendant had breached a fiduciary duty, and that plaintiffs had not proved damages or established their right to a constructive trust. The pertinent evidence, some of which was stipulated to, may be summarized as follows.

In March 1978, defendant Anthony Roppolo and a business partner purchased over five acres of land located at the intersection of Devon, Milwaukee and Nagle Avenues in Chicago. The property was improved with seven structures: two grocery stores, a drug store, a laundromat, a hamburger stand, the Rincker House and the tool shed adjacent to the house. The Rincker House was occupied at the time of purchase, but thereafter vacated and the windows boarded. Roppolo was a 50% owner and agent of the land trust which paid $1,600,000 for the property. In early April of 1978, Roppolo entered into a contract with Joseph Romono to demolish the Rincker House. The application for a demolition permit showed the address of the house as 6366 N. Milwaukee Avenue. The application was processed through the various city departments which must approve any demolition permit. On May 1, 1978, the Commissioner of the Department of Buildings notified Romono that the permit would not be issued. The owners' complaint for a writ of mandamus against the Commissioner was dismissed by the trial court. An

appeal from the trial court's action was dismissed by this court for want of prosecution. In July 1978, the City, with the consent of Roppolo, demolished the shed on said property.

On June 5, 1978, the Landmark Commission voted to begin proceedings to have the property, including the Rincker House, declared an official Chicago landmark. Roppolo was represented during these proceedings by an attorney. On April 10, 1979, the Landmark Commission recommended to the city council that the property, including the Rincker House, be designated as a landmark. On August 10, 1979, the city council passed an ordinance designating the property, including the Rincker House, as a Chicago Historical Landmark.

In April of 1979, Romono, on behalf of Roppolo, applied the second time for a permit to demolish the house. A permit was issued on May 7, 1979 and revoked on the same day by the Commissioner of the Department of Buildings.

On February 29, 1980, Roppolo applied for a zoning amendment in order to develop the tract on which the house stood. Hearings on the proposed amendment were held on July 10, 1980 by the Chicago Plan Commission. The application was modified by the agreement of Roppolo and the Plan Commission to include a provision that Roppolo would retain the house as a designated Chicago Landmark, move it to another part of the tract, and restore and reconstruct the house at the direction of the Landmark Commission. This development was to be known as "Landmark Square." The Plan Commission then approved the modified plan of development.

Prior to July 30, 1980, Roppolo asked Mario Rizzi to inquire of various demolition contractors whether any of them would be willing to apply for a permit to demolish the Rincker House. Rizzi spoke to Cirro. Mrs. Cirrincione, owner of Cirro, agreed to apply for a permit only if the company was given a contract to perform the actual demolition. Roppolo thereupon authorized Rizzi to enter into the contract with Cirro for the demolition of the house. Thereafter, Mrs. Cirrincione began the application process.

On July 30, 1980, Mrs. Cirrincione went to the Permit Control Desk of the City's Department of Inspectional Services, Plans, and Examinations (formerly the Department of

Buildings) with a partially completed application for a demolition permit. Annette Bueck, an employee of the department, made an entry in the permit application received log showing the receipt of a permit application to demolish the building at 6366 N. Milwaukee Avenue. Mrs. Cirrincione then went to the Department of Streets and Sanitation to register the application. That department requires a two-day notice before a sidewalk permit can be issued. No demolition permit can be issued without a sidewalk permit.

Shortly after these preliminary steps in the application process were completed, Alderman Roman Pucinski, in whose ward the property is located, received notice of the application to demolish the structure at 6366 N. Milwaukee. Pucinski telephoned the Permit Control Desk to inquire about the application and was informed that the structure was a landmark and that no permit would be issued. At about the same time, Philip Margolis, a city sidewalk inspector, visited the demolition site. He found no structures bearing the address 6366 N. Milwaukee in the area, then telephoned his office for a more detailed description of the building to be wrecked. Margolis was finally able to determine that the structure to be demolished was a wood-frame structure bearing signs identifying it as a landmark.

Mrs. Cirrincione received an executed contract for the demolition work prior to August 20, 1980. On that date, she went to the demolition site and took the photograph of the structure to be demolished which must accompany all demolition permit applications. This photograph of the house was submitted with the application. It was last seen in the possession of a city employee. It was not produced during pre-trial discovery or at trial. On the same day, Mrs. Cirrincione went to Roppolo's office, showed him the application for the permit and gave him a letter of authorization which required his signature. She also asked him if she should use the 6366 address on the application. She said that she had observed that the addresses of the other buildings on the tract were 6374 through 6382, and that the house must be numbered out of sequence, as the other buildings all stood to the south of the house. She asked Roppolo if the proper house number shouldn't be higher than 6382.

Roppolo stated that the address that should be used was 6366, and then signed the application [footnote] and authorization letter with that address. At the same time, Roppolo provided Mrs. Cirrincione a legal description of the property and the number of water cut-off and dust control permits obtained by Roppolo in his previous attempts to obtain a demolition permit for the house.

Mrs. Cirrincione then went to City Hall. She obtained permits or approvals that were necessary to process the application from the Sewer Department, Streets and Sanitation, the Water Department, the Environmental Control Section, the Flammable Liquid Tank Section, the Zoning Department, and the Map Department. In the Map Department, the location of 6366 N. Milwaukee Avenue was plotted on the official city map. The employees of the Map Department determined that 6366 was not the correct address of the house, then issued a house certificate bearing the address 6384 N. Milwaukee Avenue. It was not unusual for the addresses on applications to be changed in this manner during processing. There was testimony that 6366 N. Milwaukee was the house number affixed to the tool shed which had stood adjacent to the Rincker House until the City caused the shed to be demolished. Mrs. Cirrincione took the house number certificate, the corrected application with other documents to the Demolition Department and received an approval of the permit application.

Mrs. Cirrincione then returned to the Permit Control Desk. She gave all the documents to Helen Cowell, a Department of Inspectional Services employee, who was assigned the duty of processing applications for building and demolition permits at the Permit Control Counter. She calculated the permit fee, had it checked and organized the permit papers. She gave the papers to Annette Bueck, another employee assigned at the counter who passed the papers back to the remote terminal operator, whose terminal is located behind the Permit Control Counter.

The remote terminal operator's job is to type the street address and other information contained on a permit application into the computer. If the address of a designated landmark is entered from the terminal, the computer will buzz and the word "landmark" will appear on the screen. No further information can be entered unless the operator manually overrides the system. If the address entered is not listed as a landmark, all the information from the application can be entered and the computer will print out the permit. On the application at issue, a line had been drawn through the number 6366 and the number 6384 was written above it. The operator entered the 6384 number, and the computer printed out Permit No. B586952, which permit gave Cirro permission to demolish the two-story frame structure at that address.

Five days later, employees of Cirro demolished the Rincker House. The application for a demolition permit was never reviewed by the Landmark Commission.

The Rincker House, built in 1851, was the second oldest building in Chicago, and the oldest example of the "balloon frame" construction method which originated in Chicago. It was also an example of the architectural style known as "carpenter gothic." Signs were attached to the house identifying it as a landmark, with one sign being approximately three feet by four feet. Several witnesses testified that the signs were always attached to the house during the summer of 1980, although other testimony indicated that vandals would occasionally remove the plywood window coverings to which the signs were attached in order to enter the house. Alfred Cirrincione, the bulldozer operator who wrecked the house, testified that he did not see the signs before wrecking the building, and that the plywood window coverings were lying on the ground around the house when he arrived on the site. Two neighbors testified that they had spoken to Alfred after the demolition and that he had made statements indicating that he had been told to expect landmark signs and that he was to ignore them.

Mrs. Cirrincione testified that she had never been told that the building was a landmark, and that she had seen no signs when she had visited the site to take the photograph for the application. She also testified she did not inform anyone at City Hall that the building was a landmark. Mrs. Cirrincione also testified that she called Commonwealth Edison (the electric company) to instruct it to remove its equipment from the site. The electric company maintains a record of customer calls

known as the "terminal transaction record" which memorialized a call on August 21, 1980 at 3:57 p.m. from Mrs. Lee Cirro (Mrs. Cirrincione's business name) from the telephone number of Cirro, who stated, "Cirro Wrecking Co. will be demolishing two-story, green frame building on Monday, 8/25/80 at approximately 8:00 a.m.—requests removal of CECO [Commonwealth Edison Co.] equipment— customer warns there are four buildings on lot—remove equipment from building with Chicago Historical Landmark sign on it."

Testimony on behalf of the City indicated that to reconstruct the Rincker House and move it to a new location on the five-acre site would cost approximately $200,000 to $250,000; that the demolition of the Rincker House had an adverse effect on the neighborhood surrounding the house and resulted in a loss to Chicago's cultural and aesthetic heritage. On the other hand, Roppolo offered the testimony of a real estate appraiser that the demolition of the house had no effect on real estate values in the neighborhood or the City. Roppolo testified that the destruction of the Rincker House and the continuing debt service and attorney fees had cost him $325,000 between the date of demolition and the trial.

Plaintiffs appeal, contending that the proofs presented at trial established that defendants demolished the Rincker House without authority; that defendants are guilty of fraud, and that damages to plaintiffs were proved. Defendants filed a cross-appeal contending, amongst other things, that the trial court erred in not granting a change of venue, in denying their request for a jury trial and other relief.

I.

The foremost issue in this appeal is whether a constructive trust arises by operation of law as the result of the actions, either jointly or severally, of defendants Roppolo, Cirro and Mrs. Cirrincione in demolishing the Rincker House, a Chicago landmark. In order to answer this question, we must first review some general principles of law and then examine the facts in the record.

Plaintiffs say that the defendants without authority wilfully demolished a landmark thereby causing damages. The trial court held that the evidence did not clearly and convincingly prove any of the allegations of the complaint. [Footnote.]

* * *

Plaintiffs claim defendants wilfully, intentionally and without authority demolished a landmark, and that in so doing the defendants are guilty of fraud. In order to determine the validity of plaintiffs' claim, we shall analyze and evaluate the separate conduct of each defendant.

A.

We first consider defendant Roppolo. He was associated with Roppolo-Prendergast Builders, developers and builders, with offices at 6315 North Milwaukee Avenue, Chicago.[3] In March 1978, Roppolo and Prendergast purchased the approximately five acres of real property on which the Rincker House was then located. Title to the property was placed in a land trust with the Northwest National Bank of Chicago, Roppolo and Prendergast each owning 50% beneficial interest. Prendergast is not a party in this litigation and there is nothing in the record to suggest he was more than nominally involved.

About April 3, 1978, shortly after the purchase of the property, Roppolo caused one Joseph Romono to file with the City an application for a permit to wreck a building at 6366 Milwaukee Avenue. The building to be demolished was the Rincker House. On May 1, 1978, the City advised that the demolition permit would not be issued. Thereupon, Roppolo and Prendergast commenced a mandamus action in the circuit court of Cook County which was dismissed on June 16, 1978. An appeal to this court was dismissed for want of prosecution.

On June 5, 1978, proceedings were commenced to designate the Rincker House and the tract of property on which it was located as an official Chicago Historical and Architectural Landmark. Roppolo was represented by an attorney who appeared at the landmark proceedings. After a recommendation by the Landmark Commission on April 10, 1979, the Chicago city council on August 10, 1979, by ordinance, designated the Rincker House as

a Chicago Historical Landmark. Roppolo op posed the designation throughout. He also tes tified that he knew that upon designation c a building as a landmark, thereafter permis sion to demolish the building had to be ob tained from the Landmark Commission. I 1979, signs appeared on the house identifyin it as an "Official Chicago Landmark."

During the pendency of the landmark pro ceedings, Joseph Romono, on behalf of Rop polo, in April 1979 filed with the City a secon application for a demolition permit which wa issued by the City on May 7, 1979 and revoke on the same date.

On February 29, 1980, Roppolo filed wit the City an application for an amendment t its zoning ordinance. Specifically the amenc ment requested approval of a planned deve opment to be called "Landmark Square" an provided for relocating the Rincker House i the corner of the property. It was referred t the Chicago Plan Commission for a publi hearing.

On July 10, 1980, during the course of th Plan Commission public hearings on the pr posed amendments for "Landmark Square Roppolo agreed, through his attorney, to th following language to be included in the a plication:

> 9. Roppolo-Prendergast Builders, Inc. will r tain the Rincker House, a designated Chica Landmark, and will move the House to the lan scaped site designated in the attached site pla Roppolo-Prendergast Builders, Inc. will reco struct the House. The movement, reconstructi and use of the House will be subject to the a proval of the Commission on Chicago Historic Landmarks and may be modified with the a proval of said body;[4]

Notwithstanding all of the preceding a tion, around July 10, 1980, Roppolo autho ized one Mario Rizzi to find a demolition co tractor to apply to the City for a demoliti permit to demolish the Rincker House. Ther is evidence in the record that Roppolo mac the application to protect his legal right Around July 30, 1980, Rizzi secured Mrs. Ci rincione to agree to apply for a permit only

---

3. Roppolo's office was located in the same block as the Rincker House, but across Milwaukee Avenue, a wide, heavily traveled thoroughfare.

4. The dissent notes this agreement does not specifically

state Roppolo would pay the costs of moving and resto ing. Although we agree the word "costs" is not literal included, we fail to understand how the work entailed b such acts can be done without "costs."

there was a contract to demolish the structure. Roppolo agreed to that and authorized a contract with Cirro to demolish the Rincker House. In fact, Roppolo signed a "Letter of Authorization" to Cirro to wreck the building. Thereupon, Mrs. Cirrincione applied to the City for a demolition permit, which application contained the signature of Roppolo as the owner.

During the application procedure, questions were raised as to the exact address of the house. The application, dated July 30, 1980, indicated 6366 N. Milwaukee Ave.[5] Roppolo advised Mrs. Cirrincione to use that number and provided a legal description. During the application processing, the Map Department of the City identified the property as 6384 North Milwaukee Avenue. As the landmark was designated 6366 North Milwaukee, a demolition permit was issued on August 20, 1980, notwithstanding the application to demolish the Rincker House was never submitted to or reviewed by the Landmark Commission prior to the demolition of the house. The application having been issued on Wednesday, August 20, 1980, the Rincker House was demolished about 9 a.m. on Monday, August 25, 1980.

The record clearly established (1) that Roppolo had knowledge the Rincker House was designated a landmark; (2) that Roppolo knew approval by the Landmark Commission was necessary to demolish a landmark; (3) that Roppolo neither applied to the Landmark Commission for approval to demolish or directed Mrs. Cirrincione, on his behalf, to apply; (4) that in consideration for the approval of pending rezoning of the Landmark Square, Roppolo agreed to move and reconstruct the house which, along with the use, would be subject to the approval of the Landmark Commission; (5) that Roppolo in authorizing the demolition promised to comply with the Municipal Code of the City; (6) that there would be a cost to move and reconstruct the Rincker House which would be approximately $200,000 to $250,000; and (7) that application to demolish had been twice refused. Knowing all of the aforesaid, Roppolo nevertheless concealed from the Landmark Commission his

intent to demolish the landmark. Then he caused the action which resulted in the demolition of the Rincker House in violation of his promises, and also in violation of the requirement that the permission of the Landmark Commission was required before demolition would proceed. By so doing, he caused the injury to the City by the unlawful destruction of the landmark.

We consider Roppolo's conduct to have been irresponsible, in utter disregard of the law and his commitments to the City. During the period Mrs. Cirrincione was attempting to secure the permit, she and Roppolo admittedly discussed the address question. Placing that in its best light, it is obvious Roppolo was aware that he had everything to gain and nothing to lose by having Mrs. Cirrincione, as his agent, seek a demolition permit. Immediately following the issuance of the permit, Mrs. Cirrincione called the gas, electric and telephone companies, and went to the Illinois Department of Transportation offices for permits to transfer her equipment from its garage to the property. Yet, Mrs. Cirrincione testified that after obtaining the permit, she never advised Roppolo.

We think the facts clearly indicate Roppolo acted in bad faith in that he used Mrs. Cirrincione to obtain the permit to demolish, knowing that he had a continuing duty to move and reconstruct the landmark. Roppolo knowingly and wilfully triggered the demolition, by agreeing to pay $4,000 to demolish that which he knew he was obligated not to demolish, thereby saving a large amount of money estimated to be approximately $200,000 to $250,000. Roppolo, by using Mrs. Cirrincione, was ready to, and willingly, accepted the benefits of the erroneously issued permit. This is the type of action in which equity, good conscience and the prospective unjust enrichment (by not having to fulfill his obligation) demands the imposition of a constructive trust.

We think the facts as to Roppolo can be characterized as either fraud or constructive fraud. *In re Estate of Neprozatis* (1st Dist.1978), 62 Ill.App.3d 563, 568, 19 Ill.Dec. 470, 378 N.E.2d 1345, this court discussed "fraud" and "constructive fraud." [Citation.] Fraud is a ge-

---

5. The dissent suggests by using the address 6366 "Roppolo was under no duty to disclose more." This disregards his specific duty to the Landmark Commission.

neric term, embracing all multifarious means which human ingenuity can devise, and which are resorted to by one individual to get advantage over another by false suggestions or by suppression of truth, and includes all surprise, trick, cunning, dissembling, and any unfair way by which another is cheated. It comprises all acts, omissions, and concealments involving a breach of a legal or equitable duty and resulting in damage to another. [Citation.]

* * *

Constructive fraud consists in any act of commission or omission contrary to legal or equitable duty which operated to injure another, which if generally permitted would be prejudicial to the public welfare. [Citation.] We think Roppolo's conduct can also be classified as a "constructive fraud."

Roppolo falsely led Mrs. Cirrincione to believe that he was entitled to a demolition permit, falsely induced the City, through Mrs. Cirrincione acting as his agent, to issue a permit to demolish a landmark without the approval of the Landmark Commission, and falsely omitted, through his agent, to advise and inform the city employees of the agreement he had with the City to move and reconstruct the building for which he sought the demolition permit. We think that his acts, and those of his agent, were intended to deceive the city employees for Roppolo's gain and to the detriment of the plaintiffs.

Roppolo failed to act when he had a duty to secure the permission of the Landmark Commission prior to any demolition. By using Mrs. Cirrincione, he was able to conceal the true facts and was the willing beneficiary for his financial gain, of the administrative error which occurred in issuing the permit. The conduct of Roppolo and Mrs. Cirrincione had a detrimental effect upon public interest and public confidence in city government.

Mrs. Cirrincione was acting as agent for Roppolo for the specific purpose of securing the permit and demolishing the building. By failing to disclose to the city employees that the address involved was a landmark, Mrs.

Cirrincione, as Roppolo's agent, concealed a material fact. It is well established that the principal may be liable to third persons for wrongful or tortious acts committed by his agent at his direction or while acting within the scope of his authority. Mrs. Cirrincione's failure to disclose a material fact with intent to mislead in order to obtain the permit amounted to fraudulent concealment. Roppolo cannot hide behind the acts of Mrs. Cirrincione or Cirro. The acts of the agent are imputable to the principal. [Citation.]

As the result of the actions which Roppolo triggered, the Rincker House was demolished. The City was damaged as the result of the destruction of the landmark. The City established the Commission on Chicago Historical and Architectural Landmark for the purpose of, amongst other things, designating buildings having a special historical, community, or aesthetic interest or value as "Chicago Landmarks" to preserve, protect, enhance, rehabilitate and perpetuate the designated landmarks. [Citation.][6] Thus, the City in order to enhance the cultural and historical environment elected to officially designate the Rincker House as a Chicago Landmark. The destruction of the building frustrated the City's action and diminished the cultural and historical quality of the City. It is to be remembered that Roppolo demonstrated his awareness of the benefit of a landmark designation by identifying his proposed redevelopment as "Landmark Square."

B.

Defendant Roppolo argues that the judgment of the circuit court is not against the manifest weight of the evidence. The trial court held that as to all defendants, the evidence failed to prove fraud, a breach of fiduciary duty, a constructive trust or damages of any kind.

It is elementary that a reviewing court will not disturb a trial court's finding and substitute its own judgment unless the holding of the trial court is manifestly against the weight of the evidence. On the other hand, it is our duty as a reviewing court to reverse any judgment wherein the findings are clearly and

---

6. The dissent discusses the financial burden imposed on landowners by the designation of property as a landmark, along with procedures to be followed by the Landmark Commission and city council upon the filing of an

application to alter or demolish a landmark. As no application was ever filed with the Landmark Commission, we question the relevance of that discussion.

palpably against the manifest weight of the evidence. [Citation.] As to the defendant Roppolo, for the reasons set out in this opinion, we find the trial court's findings clearly and palpably against the manifest weight of the evidence.

C.

Defendant Roppolo further urges that he was under no duty to insure that the city's employees properly performed their jobs and followed its own procedures. And, as it issued the permit, the City was estopped from bringing the instant action. [Citation.] Roppolo argues, rather imaginatively that, as he was required by ordinance to apply for a permit, it would be inequitable to impose a constructive trust when the City issued the permit.

Roppolo's estoppel argument is without merit. The Chicago Landmark Ordinance [citation] required the approval of the Landmark Commission in order to obtain a permit. This was not obtained. The fact is the permit was issued by virtue of an incorrect street address being placed on the application in the City Map Department. * * * Estoppel generally arises against a municipality in two situations: (1) where there is a substantial change of position under a permit validly issued which is later revoked due to a subsequent change in the law; or (2) where there has been a substantial change of position under an invalid permit and the party to whom the permit was issued was actively induced or misled by city officers.

As discussed below, we are satisfied beyond any doubt that Mrs. Cirrincione at the time she was processing the application, knew that the building was a landmark. Further, on the morning Mrs. Cirrincione secured the permit, she met with Roppolo across the street from the site and then took a picture of the building. Mrs. Cirrincione, acting for Roppolo, had a duty to secure the Landmark Commission approval. Roppolo had a duty to insure that the Rincker House was not destroyed until the Landmark Commission had approved. To hold otherwise would make a mockery of existing city ordinances. The principle that everyone is presumed to know the law has been the cornerstone of our law far too long to require citation.

It therefore follows that the act of demolition was not induced by the employees of the city and Roppolo stood to gain, rather than lose, by the demolition. We find no basis for applying the estoppel theory.

We therefore reverse the judgment against Roppolo and Northwest and remand the matter to the circuit court of Cook County for trial on the question of damages.

* * *

IV.

CONCLUSION

The judgment of the circuit court of Cook County:

(1) as to defendants Roppolo and Northwest National Bank of Chicago, as Trustee under Trust Agreement dated March 1, 1978, is reversed and remanded for further proceedings in accordance with the views expressed herein. * * *

* * *

STAMOS, J., respectfully dissenting.

The majority holds that the actions of Roppolo prior to the demolition of the Rincker House amount to a fraud and a constructive fraud, and that therefore the trial court erred in refusing to impose a constructive trust on the property where the Rincker House once stood. However, the evidence which was adduced at trial, taken with the stipulations of the parties, is not sufficient to establish a fraud or a constructive fraud. Because plaintiffs did not make out their cause of action, I would hold that the trial court correctly refused to grant the relief that they sought.

* * *

The essential elements of a cause of action for fraudulent misrepresentation are that:

(1) a statement of material fact was made;

(2) the statement was untrue;

(3) the party making the statement knew it was untrue or believed it to be so;

(4) the person to whom the statement was made believed it and relied on it, and was justified in doing so;

(5) the statement was made for the purpose of inducing the other party to act; and

(6) the reliance on the statement by the person to whom it was made caused his injury. [Citations.]

Fraud does not always consist of an affirmative statement of fact; fraud may also consist of the concealment of a material fact accompanied by scienter, deception, and injury. [Citation.] However, where a failure to disclose information is the basis of the cause of action, there must be a duty to speak on the part of the silent party, and an active concealment of the pertinent fact. [Citation.] Additionally, the facts which are not disclosed must not only be known to the silent party, but must be "unknown to or beyond the reach of" the party relying on the silence. [Citations.] Each element of the cause of action for fraud must be proven by clear and convincing evidence. [Citation.]

Constructive fraud differs from actual or intentional fraud in that constructive fraud may be inferred from the facts and circumstances surrounding a transaction regardless of a lack of proof of any actual dishonesty of purpose. [Citation.] Constructive fraud is "often equated with a breach or abuse of a confidential or fiduciary relationship." [Citation.] Where a fiduciary or confidential relationship does not arise as a matter of law, such a relationship must be shown to have existed by clear and convincing evidence. [Citation.] No Illinois cases have made a finding of constructive fraud in the absence of a showing that the parties stood in a confidential relationship. [Citation.] On the contrary, the absence of a fiduciary or a confidential relationship precludes the imposition of liability for a constructive fraud. [Citation.] Before turning to the question of whether Roppolo is guilty of an actual fraud with regard to the demolition of the Rincker House, it need be noted only briefly that there is nothing in the record which would justify a conclusion that Roppolo stood in any type of confidential relationship with the city of Chicago, its employees, or its citizens, and therefore no constructive fraud can be inferred from the circumstances surrounding this case.

The majority refers to several of the acts and omissions of defendants in support of its conclusion that Roppolo's conduct meets the definition of fraud. The acts that the majority characterize as fraudulent are: (1) that Roppolo led Mrs. Cirrincione to believe that he was entitled to a demolition permit; (2) that Roppolo falsely induced the City to issue

the permit; (3) that Roppolo, using Mrs. Cirincione as an agent, omitted to advise the employees of the City of his agreement with the Planning Commission to restore the Rincker House; (4) that Roppolo had the duty to ensure that the Landmark Commission reviewed the application for the demolition permit, and that he failed to do so; and (5) that Mrs. Cirrincione, with the intent to mislead failed to inform the city employees that the application was for a permit to demolish a landmark.

For Roppolo to be guilty of intentional fraud it must be shown that he made some statement with the intent to deceive, and that the statement was relied upon by the City, inducing it to issue the permit. In the alternative, it must be shown that there was a concealment of a material fact which Roppolo had a duty to disclose, that the fact was unknown to the City, and that the City had a right to rely on Roppolo's silence. As was previously noted, each of the necessary elements must have been proved by clear and convincing evidence in order to justify a finding by this court that the verdict of the trial court was against the manifest weight of the evidence.

It cannot be gainsaid that Roppolo, by engaging Mrs. Cirrincione to apply for the permit and by neglecting to tell her that the building was a landmark for which no demolition permit would be issued, set in motion a series of events which led to the unlawful destruction of the Rincker House. It likewise cannot be gainsaid that the circumstances surrounding this case are of the type that naturally raise grave suspicions. However, suspicion is not the standard of proof in any civil or criminal proceeding in our courts, and suspicion is not clear and convincing evidence.

The first act that the majority characterize as fraudulent is Roppolo's failure to inform Mrs. Cirrincione that he was not entitled to a permit to demolish the Rincker House. This failure to speak may or may not amount to fraud on Mrs. Cirrincione. She had made clear to Roppolo, through Rizzi, that she would not go through the application process unless she had a contract to perform the actual demolition. Had the permit been denied, Roppolo would have gained the benefit of Mrs. Cirrincione's efforts on his behalf for the price of executing a contract which could never be performed. However, it is difficult to see how Roppolo's lack of candor with Mrs. Cirrincione translates into a fraud on the City. It must be stressed that the fact that Roppolo made an application for the permit can not be interpreted as a representation to the City that he was "entitled" to approval of the application. This is so because of the procedures which have been formulated by the City for dealing with properties which have been designated as landmarks.

A designation of a property as a landmark imposes a financial burden on the landowner. The landowner can shift some or all of that burden to the City by following the procedures set forth in chapter 21–64.1 of the Municipal Code of the City of Chicago. That section provides that when the Building Department receives an application for a permit to alter or demolish a designated landmark, it shall forward the application to the Landmark Commission. The Landmark Commission then considers the application and approves or disapproves it. A disapproval "shall not be deemed by the applicant for permit as a denial thereof." The Landmark Commission forwards the disapproved application to the Finance Committee of the city council. The Finance Committee must give the application prompt consideration, after which it recommends grant or denial of the application. If the committee decides that the application should be denied, its recommendation on the matter to the full city council must include a report on the ways and means by which the City can arrange to lease or sublease the landmark property, contract with the owner for covenants designed to preserve the landmark, acquire the property by eminent domain, or take other action under Ill.Rev.Stat.1981, ch. 24, par. 11–48.2–2. Courses of action available to the City under that statute include the creation of transferable development rights in favor of the owner of the landmark. After receiving the recommendation of the Finance Committee, the city council must pass an ordinance either approving the issuance of the permit or denying the permit. If the permit is denied, the city council must take one of the actions recommended by the Finance Committee with respect to the property. In short, the City can not deny a permit to demolish a landmark without also taking action which will result

in some form of compensation to the landowner for the burden imposed on him by the landmark designation. The only way to acquire this compensation is to apply for a permit to demolish the landmark. Any owner of a landmark-designated property has the right to apply for a permit to demolish the landmark, and, as is obvious from the foregoing, he is well advised to do so. The mere act of applying for the permit cannot be construed as a representation to the City that the applicant is "entitled" to the issuance of the permit because the Municipal Code encourages him to make the application even if he knows to a certainty that it will be denied. Therefore, it cannot be concluded that Roppolo, by leading Mrs. Cirrincione to believe that he was entitled to a demolition permit, was making any representation which was calculated to deceive the City. It likewise cannot be concluded that Mrs. Cirrincione's belief in that entitlement in any way induced the City to issue the permit, because she would have handled the application process in the same way had she known the true facts and had she been expressly engaged only to begin the process in order to get the application before the city council.

The majority also holds that Roppolo, through Mrs. Cirrincione, falsely induced the City to issue the permit. In this regard, it must be stressed that Roppolo instructed Mrs. Cirrincione to use the 6366 address on the application despite Mrs. Cirrincione's suggestion that that was not the correct street address. This fact was not adduced through testimony at trial, but was stipulated to by the parties. That stipulation is binding on this court, and no inference contrary to the stipulation can be drawn on appeal. [Citation.] It was also stipulated that Roppolo had twice before applied for demolition permits using the 6366 address. Both of those applications were made before the landmark designation. One permit was denied and one was revoked. It can only be concluded that Roppolo knew that a third application using that address would be rejected, but that he caused the permit to bear that address rather than the correct address. The inducement which caused the issuance of the permit was, in fact, not a result of any act of Roppolo's, but resulted from the changing of the address on the application at the direction of city employees. Roppolo's affirmative statements on the face of the application were an inducement to reject rather than to approve the application. The stipulated facts of this case negate any inferences that Roppolo attempted to use deception to induce the City's actions.

The majority also asserts that Roppolo agreed in the application for the permit that all work pursuant to the permit would conform to the Municipal Code, and that therefore he had the duty to secure the approval of the Landmark Commission before demolishing the Rincker House. While it is true that no permit to demolish a landmark can issue without the approval of the Landmark Commission, the Municipal Code does not impose on the applicant the duty of seeking the Commission's review of an application for a permit to alter or demolish a landmark. Chapter 21, section 21–64.1(b) of the Municipal Code provides that "prior to issuing any permit [for the alteration or demolition of a landmark], the Building Department shall forward any application for such permit * * * to the Commission on Chicago Historical and Architectural Landmarks within (7) days of the receipt thereof."

The Building Department clearly has the obligation under the code to process the application in this fashion, and a failure to ensure that the Building Department is doing its job properly can hardly be characterized as a breach of a promise by an applicant for a permit that the work will be performed in compliance with the Municipal Code. The Building Department, by forwarding the application to the Landmark Commission, begins the administrative process which ultimately ends with compensation being paid to the owner of a landmark-designated property. Once the application is made, the process is out of the hands of the applicant. If everyone is presumed to know the law, then it cannot be said that Roppolo acted fraudulently by failing to do something that he knew that the City, and not he, was obliged to do.

The majority also characterizes two omissions of defendants as fraudulent. They are Roppolo's failure to disclose through his agent (Mrs. Cirrincione) that he had an agreement with the Planning Commission to move and restore the Rincker House, and Mrs. Cirrin-

cione's failure to disclose to city employees at the Permit Control desk that the house was a designated landmark.

As has been previously noted, silence can amount to a fraud only when the silent party has a duty to speak. It is difficult to say that such a duty existed with regard to Roppolo's agreement with the Planning Commission. That agreement in no way affected Roppolo's right under the Municipal Code to apply for the permit and receive whatever compensation he might be awarded after the permit was denied. It is significant to note that the agreement with the Planning Commission does not specifically state that Roppolo would pay for the costs of moving and restoring the Rincker House, although it does state that Roppolo's company would perform the work. Therefore, an attempt by Roppolo to have the City assume part, if not all, of the expense of preserving the landmark is not only consistent with his rights under the Municipal Code, but is not in any way inconsistent with his agreement with the Planning Commission. The personnel at the Permit Control desk could not have refused to process the application had they known of that agreement. This is not to say that they might not have processed it with greater care; but the conclusion that a person would have acted differently if a certain fact were known to him is a conclusion that the fact was material. A conclusion that a fact is material is only one element which must be proven to establish fraud. Although the fact may be regarded as material, Roppolo had no duty to disclose it. Additionally, the fact had little relevance to the application process. It must be reiterated that Mrs. Cirrincione was going through the application process in the expectation that she would perform the demolition contract, and that Roppolo was less than candid with her when he avoided informing her that the house was a landmark which was not likely to be demolished, but rather was to be moved and restored. However, it cannot be concluded that those omissions were calculated to deceive the City. It was stipulated between the parties that Roppolo instructed Mrs. Cirrincione to use the 6366 address on the application. By that act, he was providing the City with all the information it needed to determine that the structure was a landmark and that no demolition permit should be issued. Having disclosed all the material facts which were necessary for the City to handle the application correctly, Roppolo was under no duty to disclose more.

The foregoing discussion is equally applicable to the issue of whether Mrs. Cirrincione's failure to tell the city employees that the Rincker House was a landmark was a fraudulent concealment which can be imputed to Roppolo. Additionally, that omission cannot be characterized as a fraudulent concealment because such a concealment must be of a fact which was not only known to the silent party, but which was also unknown or unavailable to the party which relied on the silence. It is evident from the stipulated facts that the City, through its computerized record keeping system, has far superior access to facts concerning the status of any particular piece of property than does the applicant for a building permit. Both the 6366 address and the 6384 address were conspicuously visible on the application, and it would have been a simple matter to enter both addresses in the computer. Indeed, it would have been prudent to do so because the presence of the two addresses should have indicated to a reasonable person that there was some confusion concerning the correct address of the structure to be demolished. Because the facts not expressly disclosed to the City by defendants were readily accessible to the City, the failure to disclose those facts can not be characterized as a fraud. It is also questionable whether the employees of the city department which collects, stores and retrieves the information which the City claims should have been disclosed to those employees could ever be said to have justifiably relied on the silence of an applicant for a permit. Therefore, it cannot be concluded that any of the omissions of defendants were of the type which support a finding that defendants perpetrated a fraud through their silence.

This case presents a set of facts which demand a choice between a determination that a series of unlikely fortuitous accidents and errors occurred and a determination that the destruction of the Rincker House was the result of fraudulent calculation and deception. The latter conclusion would comport with the natural suspicions that any reasonable person would entertain when confronted with the circumstances of this case. Truly, a determination that the destruction of the Rincker House was the result of inexplicable inadvertence rather than fraud seems naive at first blush. However, there is no alternative to that determination in the absence of clear and convincing evidence that a fraud was committed. No matter how suspicious the circumstances surrounding a transaction, the party complaining of the transaction is not released from the obligation to prove the elements of the cause of action.

Therefore, I would affirm.

POMPEII ESTATES, INC. v. CONSOLIDATED EDISON CO. OF NEW YORK, INC.

91 Misc.2d 233, 397 N.Y.S.2d 577, 7 CLSR 518

(Civil Court of the City of New York, Queens County, Trial Term, Part XVI, Aug. 16, 1977.)

POSNER, J.

The "Dawn of the Age of Aquarius" has also ushered in the "Age of the Computer."

There is no question that the modern computer is as indispensable to big business as the washing machine is to the American household. To ask the American housewife to go back to washing clothes by hand is as unthinkable as asking Con Edison to send out its monthly bills by any other method than the computer.

This is an action in negligence by a builder against a public utility for damages sustained as a result of the alleged "wrongful" termination of electricity at an unoccupied one family house (that had recently been constructed by the plaintiff) at 200–15 Pompeii Rd., Holliswood. Sometime in October, 1975, the defendant had installed electric services to the plaintiff's property. On or about Jan. 20, 1976, the defendant terminated such service because of two unpaid bills amounting to $25.11. Since the premises were unoccupied, the lack of electricity caused the motor which operated the heating unit to go off, which resulted in frozen water pipes, which burst and caused $1,030 of proven damages to the premises.

The defendant contends that it followed the mailing requirements of Transportation Corporations Law Section 15 and therefore had no obligation to the plaintiff. The statute reads as follows:

15: Refusal or neglect to pay rent——

1. If any person supplied with gas or electric light by any such corporation shall neglect or refuse to pay the rent or remuneration due for the same or for the wires, pipes or fittings let by the corporation, for supplying or using such gas or electric light or for ascertaining the quantity consumed or used as required by his contract with the corporation, or shall refuse or neglect, after being required to do so, to make the deposit required, such corporation *may discontinue* the supply of gas or electric light to the premises of such person; and the officers, agents or workmen of such corporation may enter into or upon such premises between the hours of eight o'clock in the forenoon and six o'clock in the afternoon, and separate and carry away any meter, pipe, fittings, wires or other property of such corporation, and may disconnect any meter, pipe, fittings, wires or other works whether the property of the corporation or not, from the mains, pipes or wires of the corporation. But the supply of gas or electric lights shall not be discontinued for non-payment of bills rendered for service until and after a five-day written notice has been served upon such person either by delivering the same to such person personally or by mailing the same in postpaid wrapper *addressed to such persons at premises where service is rendered* (emphasis added).

Defendant, through the use of five witnesses, made out a good case proving that the notice to disconnect [reference] was probably mailed even though no witness had actual knowledge of mailing this specific notice. Obviously, it would be overly burdensome, if not impossible, to expect a utility mailing out thousands of disconnect notices a day to be able to prove that each one was individually mailed. The Court of Appeals in *Gardam & Son v. Batterson*, 198 N.Y. 175, 91 N.E. 371, stated: "In the absense of direct proof as to a particular letter being deposited with the Post Office or in a mail-box, the rule requires proof of a course of business or office practice according to which it naturally would have been so deposited."

Accordingly, this court finds that the defendant did comply with the statutory requirement of mailing even though we are also convinced that the plaintiff had never received the notice because an expert witness from the U. S. Postal Department testified that the postal service does not leave mail at an unoccupied address. Unless a statute or the contract between the parties calls for actual notice [citations], proof of mailing is sufficient to prove notice, even though the notice was never received. [Citation.]

While the parties, at the trial and in their memoranda of law devoted considerable time to the issue of "notice," the court finds that this is not the main issue in this case. Let us say that this was a "procedure" hurdle which Con Edison cleared successfully. However, the court has serious doubts as to whether the defendant has cleared the "substantive" hurdle—did it act reasonably or negligently in discontinuing plaintiff's electric service?

Section 15 of the Transportation Corporations Law (*supra*) gives a public utility supplying gas or electric the authority to discontinue the supply of gas or electric for "refusal or neglect to pay rent," and it requires certain notice be given before such action can be taken. Since the language of the statute is discretionary in nature—"may discontinue"—it does not relieve the utility of its common law obligation to exercise ordinary care when a decision to discontinue is made. The defendant's witnesses stated that a customer's file is opened when a new account is established and that all correspondence and other documents involving the customer are included in this file. Defendant's attorney admitted that he had found in such file the original letter from plaintiff requesting the opening of electrical current. This letter is reproduced in its entirety because of its significance to the case:

POMPEII ESTATES INC.
34–34 Bell Blvd.
Bayside, N.Y. 11361
212–631–4466

June 12, 1975

Con Edison
40–55 College Pt. Blvd.
Flushing, N.Y. 11354
Att: Mr. A. Vebeliunas—670–6152

To Whom It May Concern:

Please be advised that there have been no changes in the original Building Plans for the 2 Houses located at the following addresses:

House No. 1—200–15 Pompeii Rd., Holliswood, N. Y.—Lot No. 163.

House No. 2—200–19 Pompeii Rd., Holliswood, N. Y.—Lot No. 160.

Be further advised that the electrical load within the house will be: —6KW Lighting and 3½ Horse Power Air-Conditioning, ¼ Horse Power Blowers, 1.2 KW Dishwashers.

There will be 1–150 AMP—3 wire socket type electric meter for each house.

Sincerely yours,

Pompeii Estates

AT:SWR   Albino Testani—President

Between the date of this letter (June 12, 1975) and the time service was installed (Oct. 24, 1975) four months elapsed. There was no other correspondence; but the plaintiff's witness (Testani) testified that he had numerous conversations with Mr. Vebeliunas on the phone and at the job site. Mr. Vebeliunas, defendant's employee, never appeared in court, even though the case was tried on three separate occasions over a period of two weeks. Though Vebeliunas was defendant's field representative and the only contact plaintiff had with defendant, he was never consulted when the decision was made to discontinue service for the non-payment of the first two months rent. The testimony of defendant's witnesses bore out the fact that said decision was a routine procedure activated by the computer and ordered by a Mr. Chris Hagan. Did defendant produce Mr. Hagan to testify what human input there was to the computer's order? No, like Mr. Vebeliunas, he never graced the courtroom scene. Failure to produce two key witnesses under the defendant's control can only lead to the inference that they would not contradict the plaintiff's contention that defendant acted unreasonably. [Citations.]

Negligence is lack of ordinary care. It is a failure to exercise that degree of care which a reasonably prudent person would have exercised under such circumstances. [Citation.] The statute only requires the notice of discontinuance to be sent to the premises where the service is provided; though, by regulation, the P.S.C. has said that the customer may direct another address for mailing purposes. While the plaintiff's letter (*supra*) does not specifically direct that the mail be sent to 34–34 Bell Boulevard, any reasonably prudent person examining the letter would realize that this is a builder building new homes and that it is not customary for a builder to occupy the homes he builds. Certainly, any reasonably prudent person, if in doubt, would contact Mr. Vebeliunas to ascertain the facts. This is especially so when the termination of service is in the middle of winter and the foreseeable consequences to the heating system and the water pipes are apparent. Where there is a foreseeability of damage to another that may occur from one's acts, there arises a duty to use care. [Citation.] In this instance, a one minute cursory glance at plaintiff's letter (*supra*) would have alerted Mr. Hagan to the fact that there was something unusual in this situation. To the contrary, the computer said, "terminate," and Mr. Hagan gave the order to terminate.

This court finds the defendant liable to the plaintiff for damages in the amount of $1,030, with interest and costs. While the computer is a useful instrument, it cannot serve as a shield to relieve Consolidated Edison of its obligation to exercise reasonable care when terminating service. The statute gives it the discretionary power to do so, and this discretion must be exercised by a human brain. Computers can only issue mandatory instructions—they are not programmed to exercise discretion.

TORRES v. NORTH AMERICAN VAN LINES, INC.

135 Ariz. 35, 658 P.2d 835
(Court of Appeals of Arizona, Division 2, Dec. 1, 1982.)

HOWARD, C. J.

This is an appeal and cross-appeal from a judgment for compensatory and punitive damages awarded to Mrs. Torres for herself and her two minor children, for the death of her husband. The jury assessed $605,000 compensatory damages against both defendants, Formy-Duvall and North American Van Lines. Punitive damages in the sum of $5,000 were assessed against Formy-Duvall, and the sum of $10,000,000 against North American. On motion for new trial, the court ordered a new trial only as to punitive damages conditioned upon the filing by a specified date of a statement by the plaintiffs accepting the sum of $2,500,000 as punitive damages. The court expressly found that the punitive damages were excessive but not the result of bias, passion or prejudice on the part of the jury. Plaintiffs timely filed their notice of acceptance of the remittitur.

Appellants contend on appeal that * * * (2) the evidence was insufficient to support punitive damages inasmuch as North American's conduct was not shown to be either grossly negligent or the cause of any harm to plaintiffs, (3) the punitive damages award against North American was the result of passion or prejudice. * * * The cross-appeal attacks the trial court's reduction in the amount of punitive damages awarded by the jury against North American.

The plaintiffs' decedent was killed when the tractor-trailer, driven by Formy-Duvall for North American, struck the rear end of a vehicle parked in the emergency lane of Interstate 40 near Holbrook, Arizona. In addition to Mr. Torres, two other persons were killed. At the time of the accident, the weather was clear and visibility was good. The road was straight and level and there was clear vision for approximately one mile. The truck was completely in the emergency lane when its brakes were applied and there was no evidence of any evasive action by Formy-Duvall before impact. At the time of impact, the truck was going 65 miles per hour and Formy-Duvall appeared fatigued. The log book which he was required to keep as he went along was approximately two days behind.

Six expert witnesses in accident investigation, reconstruction or analysis testified at trial. All were in agreement that the accident was caused either by fatigue or inattentiveness on the part of Formy-Duvall. All concluded that Formy-Duvall was driving in excess of the lawful speed limit at the time of the collision with their estimates ranging from 65 to 73.9 miles per hour. Formy-Duvall's version was that he observed the vehicle in the emergency lane and as he approached it in a westbound direction, a lady stepped out into his lane and he veered to the right to keep from hitting her. The expert witnesses discredited Formy-Duvall's "pedestrian-in-the-highway" version which indicated that the pedestrian was no more than five feet into the 12.7-foot slow lane, allowing considerable room to maneuver the eight-foot-wide tractor so as to clear the pedestrian instead of hitting a parked car.

North American's liability was predicated not only on a respondeat superior theory but also on the theory that corporate safety policies constituted a wanton disregard for the safety of the public.

North American has some 8,000 drivers on the road. Formy-Duvall was a driver in the High Value Products Division and his cargoes normally consisted of high value electronic goods, such as computers. North American is the number one hauler of this type in the country. Formy-Duvall was regularly assigned to drive goods from the Los Angeles area to the Boston area, an assignment known as the "Boston Turn." He and his nephew, the co-driver, were returning to Los Angeles at the time of the accident. In violation of federal regulations, neither Formy-Duvall nor his nephew kept a log book current during their trip. Although they testified that a notebook was kept in which mileage by state was recorded and all changes in duty status were noted, it was never produced. They filled out the logs at the end of a trip and mailed them to North American headquarters where they were inspected and kept as required by federal regulations.

The log book requirements are part of the federal regulation controlling the hours of service of drivers [citation], which are designed to prevent fatigued drivers from endangering the general public who use the same highways. One important rule is the 70-hour rule which provides that no motor carrier shall permit any driver used by it to remain on duty for a total of more than 70 hours in any period of eight consecutive days. "On duty" time is defined as "all time from the time a driver begins to work or is required to be in readiness to work until the time he is relieved from work and all responsibilities for performing work." In the standard log, on-duty time is the sum of all time shown on both line 3 and line 4. Line 3 shows "driving time" and includes all time spent at the driving controls of a motor vehicle in operation, whereas the line 4 category includes all on-duty time except for actual driving time. Although the regulations include 11 items that must be listed on line 4 time, not one log of Formy-Duvall showed any line 4 time for three months preceding the accident. Thus if on-duty, not driving time is not included in the log, the 70-hour on-duty computation would be based only on line 3 time, i.e., actual driving time.

In 1971, a government safety compliance investigation of North American pointed up the inadequacy of log book verification procedures as to line 4 time. Two safety specialists with the Arizona Department of Public Safety testified that it is impossible for any driver to take a cross-country trip without logging any line 4 time and Arizona Highway patrolmen are instructed to examine a driver's log as to line 4 time. One specialist testified that "if there is no line 4 time, then it is a pretty good indication that there is something amiss." The safety specialist also testified as to the use of fuel purchase receipts and toll receipts to verify the accuracy of log books. In 1964, the federal government accused North American of permitting false logs to be filed. The falsity was discovered primarily through the use of toll receipts. Another investigation was had in 1968 as the result of a letter from a North American driver in which he stated that he had been "pressured by his dispatcher to drive more hours than the regulations tolerated." Approximately 30 false logs were discovered by one verification check.

At the time of this accident in 1979, North American did not use fuel receipts at all to verify log book accuracy and used only certain toll receipts on a spot check basis. One expert based his opinion of North American's safety deficiency on its failure to correct log verification problems that had existed for a number of years. North American has a substantial and sophisticated data processing system and a computer expert testified that it would take a very brief time to set up a program and test it so that North American's computer system could be utilized for log book verification. There was also evidence that North American possesses the personnel and equipment to design and implement an effective dispatch system which would provide a true control of the driver's time. Thus the dispatcher could easily realize that a driver might be approaching the 70-hour limitation of on-duty time in eight consecutive days, and caution him to watch his time.

There was extensive testimony as to the relationship between driver fatigue and traffic accidents. In 1979 and 1980, North American drivers were involved in approximately 1,000 traffic accidents of all types. North American, however, had never attempted to analyze the accident-producing potential of driver fatigue. Although information from each of the accidents involving North American drivers is entered into the company's computerized

data processing system, the computerized information was used only by the company's claims department. Thus North American never availed itself of all the accident data with a view to improving safety measures and reducing accidents.

Dr. Brenner, an expert in safety engineering and fleet safety management, analyzed North American's safety policies and related them to this accident. According to him, danger is the product of its two constituent elements, hazard and risk. Here, the risk was that Formy-Duvall would become inattentive due to fatigue from excessive on-duty hours and the hazard was the potential of harm to people resulting from a collision with a fast-moving tractor and trailer. Dr. Brenner defined safety measures as any action, practice or design alternative that will either reduce or eliminate danger, which in turn means reducing risk or hazard. In his opinion, North American had full knowledge of both the danger and the necessary safety measures. It had been specifically informed that it ought to verify log entries through comparison with toll receipts. It had been investigated for failure to monitor line 4 time. According to Dr. Brenner, its failure to correct the log verification problem over the span of two decades was a key defect in its system. The cost would be minimal where the personnel and computer equipment were already in place. Another key defect in the safety management system was the absence of a trip assignment system to detect and warn drivers who would likely exceed the allowable on-duty hours. He saw no indication of concern as to the possibility that fleet management policies within the company might be defective.

* * *

Appellants' second contention is that the evidence was insufficient to support punitive damages against North American as its conduct was not shown to be either grossly negligent or the cause of any harm to the plaintiffs. We do not agree. First of all, the jury could logically infer from Formy-Duvall's conduct in failing to log line 4 time, not only on this occasion but in the months preceding, that he was attempting to avoid the 70-hour rule. As noted above, the avowed purpose of the federal regulations as to hours of service of drivers is to protect the public traveling on the highways. Formy-Duvall knew this and disregarded the requirements as to log book entries of line 4 time. A jury could logically conclude that this manifested a wanton disregard for the safety of others, that is, gross negligence. Since the jury found Formy-Duvall grossly negligent and awarded punitive damages against him, North American was answerable for punitive damages under the doctrine of respondeat superior. [Citation.]

The issue of punitive damages was also properly submitted to the jury on the theory that North American's failure to police and enforce the 70-hour rule and the federal regulations pertaining thereto, constituted gross negligence. It had been put on notice on several occasions that its drivers were not complying with the regulations. The problem had existed for a number of years and no attempt to take corrective measures had been undertaken. North American's failure to monitor the logs through an appropriate log verification procedure when it had the equipment and personnel to do it expeditiously and without too much additional cost permitted the practice of filing false logs. The company also took no measures, despite the facilities to do so, to establish a proper control of driving time while the drivers were enroute. It should have known that its failure to enforce the 70-hour rule could result in sloppy logging of on-duty time with the concomitant risk of exceeding the time limitation, thus causing fatigue. Submission of the punitive damages issue to the jury was proper.

* * *

The plaintiffs have cross appealed, contending that the trial court abused its discretion by granting a remittitur of $7.5 million from the amount of punitive damages awarded against North American. They recognize that the exercise of the power of remittitur rests in the sound discretion of the trial court. [Citation.] Although the trial court expressly found that the punitive damages awarded by the jury were not the result of passion or prejudice, it did find such award excessive. Of course by ordering a reduction in damages instead of setting aside the verdict, the trial judge determined that the verdict was not the result of passion or prejudice. [Citation.]

The initial responsibility for reducing excessive verdicts is with the trial court. [Citation.] The parties to this appeal have cited numerous cases from our own jurisdiction or others. However, * * * references to verdicts in other cases is a dangerous game. The same principle would apply to punitive damages as no two defendants are alike and no two injuries are alike.

We cannot find that the trial judge abused his discretion in ordering the remittitur. An "abuse of discretion" is discretion manifestly unreasonable, or exercised on untenable grounds, or for untenable reasons. [Citation.] There is no fixed standard for assessment of punitive damages—the touchstone is reasonableness. 25 C.J.S., Damages, § 126(1). We note that the trial judge who granted a remittitur here is no novice in the trial of personal injury cases and is a highly regarded trial judge in this state with vast experience in the trial of personal injury lawsuits. He concluded that $10 million was unreasonable and that $2.5 million was a reasonable sum to achieve the purpose of punitive damages. In order to find that he abused his discretion or acted arbitrarily or capriciously, we must find that under similar circumstances no reasonable trial judge would have ordered a remittitur. [Citation.] This we are unable to do and therefore do not interfere.

Affirmed.

STATE FARM MUTUAL AUTOMOBILE INSURANCE CO. v. BOCKHORST
453 F.2d 533, 3 CLSR 494
(United States Court of Appeals, Tenth Circuit, Jan. 14, 1972.)

MURRAH, C. J.

State Farm Mutual Automobile Insurance Company, a corporation with its principal place of business in Illinois, brought this diversity action for declaratory judgment of nonliability on a policy of automobile insurance which it had issued to Alfred E. Bockhorst, a Kansas resident. The complaint alleged that a third-party defendant was asserting a claim in excess of $10,000, arising out of an automobile accident for which the company would be liable if the policy was in force at the time of the accident. Bockhorst answered and counterclaimed, alleging that the policy was in force at the time he was involved in the accident and covered his collision damages and the asserted liability. * * * This appeal is from a judgment in favor of Bockhorst which we think must be affirmed.

The events leading to this controversy are clearly set forth in the trial court's unchallenged oral findings of fact. The policy in question was originally issued to Bockhorst in December, 1968, through Richard E. Dame, State Farm's local agent in Stafford, Kansas. The policy remained in force until August 24, 1969, when it lapsed as a result of Bockhorst's failure to pay premiums due. At approximately 12:45 a. m. on the Saturday morning of October 4, 1969, Bockhorst was involved in an accident resulting in the death of a pedestrian. Later that same morning he wrote a check payable to State Farm in an amount sufficient to pay a six-months premium on the policy and mailed the check to Dame. Bockhorst then went to see Dame, told him of the accident, and asked if he had received the check. At approximately 1:00 p. m. on the afternoon of October 4, agent Dame went to the local Post Office where he found Bockhorst's letter requesting reinstatement of the policy, together with State Farm's notice that the premium was due and the check in payment of the premium. Dame advised Bockhorst that he was uncertain whether State Farm would reinstate the policy, but he immediately mailed the check and the notice to State Farm's regional office at Columbia, Missouri. He did not, however, include any information concerning the fact that an accident had occurred before he received Bockhorst's payment, or the exact time at which he received the payment.

On the following Monday, Dame notified the State Farm adjuster for his area of Bockhorst's accident and the circumstances of the premium payment. That same day, after investigating the accident, the adjuster advised Dame that he had serious doubts as to whether Bockhorst was covered. Also on that same day the adjuster phoned State Farm's claims superintendent at the Columbia office advising him of the situation and his doubts concerning coverage. The claims superintendent stated that he did not think Bockhorst would be covered. He also informed the superintendent of State Farm's policy service division—the division to which Dame had mailed Bockhorst's

check—that there was a question concerning Bockhorst's coverage.

While the claims division was conducting its investigation Bockhorst's check was received by the policy service division and computerized in accordance with normal business practices. The computer, having no input of facts concerning the accident or the specific time of payment of the premium, automatically issued a notice reinstating Bockhorst's policy of insurance effective, retroactively, as of 12:01 a. m., October 4, 1969. The policy reinstatement was mailed to Bockhorst on October 10, 1969.

One month and eight days later State Farm finally notified Bockhorst that the reinstated policy could not become effective until the time when the company actually received his premium payment through its agent, Dame; that is, at approximately 1:00 p. m. on October 4, some twelve hours after Bockhorst's accident. State Farm subsequently refunded Bockhorst's premium stating that no coverage was available to him. The trial court took the view that by issuing the retroactively reinstated policy on October 10, after being informed of all the facts, State Farm voluntarily and intentionally waived its right not to renew the insurance contract with Bockhorst and agreed to extend coverage for the period of time when the accident occurred.

On appeal State Farm claims that the reinstated policy was void *ab initio* since the occurrence of the contingency insured against was known to Bockhorst when he requested reinstatement and paid his premium. It is also argued that the reinstatement of Bockhorst's policy resulted from the unyielding and unimaginative processes of a computer; hence, State Farm never actually relinquished a known right when in possession of all the facts so as to work a waiver.

State Farm relies primarily on the case of *Matlock v. Hollis*, 153 Kan. 227, 109 P.2d 119 (1941), in support of its claim that the policy was void at its inception since Bockhorst knew of the accident when he paid his premium. We think, however, Matlock and the other cases cited by State Farm involve situations in which the insured not only knew of the occurrence of a prior loss, but fraudulently concealed that information from the insurer until after the policy was issued. In the language of *Matlock*:

" * * * [T]he concealment of the injury went to the very heart of the contract, made it void at its inception, and no one can predicate any rights upon it." [Citation.]

Bockhorst did not conceal any facts concerning his accident from State Farm or any of its agents. Nor was there any evidence of collusion between the company's local agent and the insured which, as a matter of policy, might very well void the contract ab initio. [Citation.] Indeed, the trial court specifically absolved all the parties of any fraud in connection with this case. We are not aware of any rule of contract law or any prevailing concept of public policy which would prevent State Farm from electing to waive its right to refuse renewal of the policy and, with knowledge of an intervening loss, accept a premium tendered for the purpose of reinstating the policy to cover that loss. Although there are apparently no Kansas cases on this precise point, the validity and binding effect of such a waiver has been upheld in several jurisdictions. [Footnote.] Having been made aware of the critical facts when it executed the contract and accepted the premium, State Farm cannot now defend on the ground that the policy was void at its inception. [Citation.]

We also reject State Farm's argument that its actions in this case did not, in fact, establish the requisite elements of a valid waiver. Kansas adheres to the traditional rule that a waiver occurs only when a party in full possession of the facts intentionally relinquishes a known right. [Citations.] Testimony at trial indicated that the division of the company in charge of processing and issuing the reinstated policy did not obtain knowledge of the accident until after Bockhorst's premium payment had been programmed into the computer and could not be removed. State Farm contends that issuance of the reinstated policy was, thus, accomplished without knowledge of all the facts and that, in any event, it was the unavoidable result of the inexorable processes of a computer rather than the intentional relinquishment of a known right.

The trial court's findings of fact leave no doubt that State Farm was in full possession of all relevant information concerning Bockhorst's accident before the notice of reinstatement was actually issued. While there may be some question in Kansas as to whether the knowledge of a local agent such as Dame is sufficient, without more, to impute such knowledge to the insurer [footnote], this poses no problem in the present case since several additional officers and employees, with responsibilities greater than those of a local agent, were fully aware of the facts concerning Bockhorst's accident by October 6. The area claims adjuster investigated the accident and communicated his findings to the superintendent of the claims division at the company's regional headquarters. Though both of these employees expressed doubt as to coverage, the record does not reveal that they ever actually repudiated it or advised Bockhorst that he definitely was not covered before November 18, 1969.

The fact that the company's policy servicing division may not have had knowledge of the accident until after Bockhorst's premium payment was placed in the computer is not controlling. One hand of the company must be charged with what the other hand knows and does. "Knowledge which is sufficient to lead a prudent person to inquire about the matter, when it could have been ascertained conveniently, constitutes notice of whatever the inquiry would have disclosed, and will be regarded as knowledge of the facts." [Citations.]

We also think it clear that, by its act of issuing the reinstated policy to Bockhorst, State Farm intentionally relinquished its right to refuse to extend coverage for a prior loss. The computerized reinstatement of the policy was not unavoidable as State Farm alleges. It is conceded that Bockhorst's premium payment would never have been placed in the computer if agent Dame had included information concerning the accident when he mailed the payment to the company. It is also conceded that if Dame had stated the exact time at which he received the payment the policy would have been reinstated as of that time, rather than 12:01 a. m. In these circumstances the insured should not be charged with the failure to input this critical data.

Holding a company responsible for the actions of its computer does not exhibit a distaste for modern business practices as State Farm asserts. A computer operates only in accordance with the information and directions supplied by its human programmers. If the computer does not think like a man, it is man's fault. The reinstatement of Bockhorst's policy was the direct result of the errors and oversights of State Farm's human agents and employees. The fact that the actual processing of the policy was carried out by an unimaginative mechanical device can have no effect on the company's responsibilities for those errors and oversights. State Farm's reinstatement of Bockhorst's policy while in full possession of information establishing its right to refuse reinstatement constituted a binding waiver, and the reinstated policy effectively extended coverage for the period during which Bockhorst's accident occurred. The judgment is affirmed.

FERREIRA v. QUIK STOP MARKETS, INC.

141 Cal.App.3d 1023, 190 Cal.Rptr. 778
(Court of Appeal, First District, Division 1, April 19, 1983.)

BRENNER, A. J. P. T.

In February 1974, plaintiffs Robert and Kristen Ferreira, husband and wife, purchased a franchise to operate a Quik Stop Market, a convenience grocery and gasoline store. In October 1975, they brought suit against Quik Stop Markets, Inc., the franchisor, seeking damages under several theories: intentional and negligent misrepresentation, breach of the franchise agreement and violation of the Franchise Investment Law. Quik Stop, in turn, cross-complained against the plaintiffs for breach of the franchise agreement. At the conclusion of a lengthy trial, the jury found that defendants had committed no fraud, but awarded plaintiffs $10,000 for breach of contract. The jury further found in favor of Quik Stop on the cross-complaint and awarded Quik Stop $15,616. Judgment was entered in favor of Quik Stop for $5,616.

FACTS

In 1973, plaintiff Robert Ferreira owned and operated two sporting goods businesses—one

in Oakland. He was in the process of selling his partnership interest in the Oakland store. In December 1973, plaintiff learned that a Quik Stop Market on Grand Avenue—just blocks away from his store—was for sale and entered into discussions with the market's owner, Ken Vales. Vales gave plaintiff the quarterly operating statements and monthly purchase records for the market (store No. 46 in the Quik Stop Market chain). Vales told plaintiff how many hours he worked and what his payroll costs were. He showed plaintiff that his net profit from operations was $21,581. Vales also explained that payroll came out of the draw.

Plaintiff Robert Ferreira and his then-fiancee Kristen decided to purchase the market, completed an application, and met with representatives of the Quik Stop Market Company. It is the events at the initial meeting between the Ferreiras and the Quik Stop executives held in January 1974 which form the basis of plaintiffs' claims of fraud.

Plaintiffs presented evidence that Larry Kranich, Assistant Director of Operations, and Joe Yancey, another Quik Stop executive, represented at that meeting that the Quik Stop Market chain was "very successful"; that there had been only one previous failure of a Quik Stop Market;[1] that Quik Stop would provide expert assistance in operating the store whenever needed; that Quik Stop would engage in an advertising campaign to promote Store No. 46; that plaintiffs' expected earnings of $20,000 was a reasonable expectation;[2] that plaintiffs should be able to pay off their $25,000 inventory in 11 months; that other Quik Stop stores were earning net profits of $40,000 per year; that Store No. 46 was one of the best stores in the system.

Yancey and Kranich denied making the alleged statements. Their testimony was supported by testimony of another Quik Stop employee present at the meeting.[3]

In February 1974, plaintiffs purchased the franchise for store No. 46 for $20,000 and began operating the store that same month.

---

1. That failure, coincidentally, was at Store No. 46. Yancey and Kranich attributed the failure to the fact that the store owner was too obese to stock his own shelves.

2. Plaintiffs noted on their application that they expected to earn $20,000 their first year—since Vales' financial statement showed earnings of $21,000.

3. Plaintiffs eventually signed a Franchise Agreement which recited that "there have been no representations or warranties of any kind or nature as to the minimum expected or anticipated profits to be derived from owning and operating this market." Plaintiff Robert Ferreira conceded he saw no financial statements for any other stores.

For the first two weeks, a representative from Quik Stop worked in the store with plaintiffs and showed them how to complete the various financial reports. Quik Stop also redesigned the store, relocating the merchandise, stocking the shelves, and changing price labels. These changes were made because Quik Stop's experts believed they would help increase sales.

In April or May 1974, after plaintiffs had operated the store for three months, plaintiff Robert Ferreira met with Quik Stop representatives to review his performance. The accounting statements showed plaintiffs had suffered a loss of approximately $4,000.[4] Quik Stop suggested that plaintiffs reduce their personnel. Plaintiffs did so—firing all but two employees. For a period of time thereafter, plaintiffs worked extra hours in the store themselves.

The next quarterly operating statement (6/30/74) showed a net profit from operations of $8,327; the remaining statements for 1974 also showed a net profit from operations. What plaintiffs did not understand was that the "net profit from operations" as shown on those statements did not take into account the weekly $400 draw which plaintiffs had been receiving from Quik Stop. Plaintiffs were aware, however, that their draw was an advance—a draw against future profits—and that payroll expenses came out of the draw.

Later in the year plaintiffs began experiencing problems with theft. The Quik Stop area coordinator suggested training the store employees to watch the customers.[5] Eventually, in the summer of the next year, after rampant customer shoplifting continued, Quik Stop redesigned the store—to put the deli case in the front of the store where it could be watched.

Plaintiffs also had problems with over-rings—a method of employee theft—and cash shortages. A tax audit conducted by the Board of Equalization in May 1977 discovered $73,639 in unreported sales for the period of plaintiffs' operation of the store, 1974–1976. By June 1975, Quik Stop recommended to plaintiffs that they sell the store since they were losing so much money.

Indeed, in May 1975, after about 15 months of operation, plaintiffs decided to sell the market, and listed it for sale for $55,000. By this time, plaintiffs were devoting their time and energy to a newly acquired dry cleaning business. Plaintiff Robert Ferreira's brother took over management of the market in July. Still, the problems continued.[6]

In September 1975, Quik Stop discovered an error which had been perpetuated in the accounting statements for Store No. 46. The error first occurred in the March 31, 1974 statement—the first quarter plaintiffs operated the store. Because the gross profits seemed uncommonly low (showing a 9.5 percent loss), the secretary-treasurer of Quik Stop believed the inventory count must be wrong. He manually overrode the computer and used a fictitious figure based on an expected 20 percent gross profit, adding $10,000 to the inventory. Although the inventory was later checked, the $10,000 surplusage added to the records was never removed. This error overinflated the quarterly net profits from operations and was not discovered until September 28, 1975. On September 30, plaintiff Robert Ferreira was informed there was a problem with the inventory adjustment and was invited to a meeting. Plaintiffs did not attend; instead, they immediately filed this action. Eventually, in June 1976, plaintiffs transferred their ownership back to Quik Stop.

At the time of the termination of the franchise agreement, the total amount showing on Quik Stop's records as amounts owed to it by plaintiffs for their inventory, for monthly service fees (a percentage of the gross sales), for advances against profits, and for merchandise and gasoline taken by plaintiffs for their use, but not paid for, was $48,305. This figure was later reduced by $15,000 paid for goodwill when the store was sold to a new owner. In addition, based on the tax auditor's discovery of unreported sales, Quik Stop

---

4. The franchise agreement required the franchisee to maintain a minimum 25 percent gross profit or face cancellation of the franchise.

5. Subsequently—at the end of 1974—the Quik Stop area coordinator helped discover the reason for the disappearance of entire cases of cigarettes.

6. In September 1975, plaintiffs again listed the store for sale—this time for $35,000 above the franchise fees and inventory.

claimed $9,941 in service fees plus the assessed taxes of $4,000. Quik Stop's total claim on its cross-complaint was $52,493.

As noted earlier, the jury found that Quik Stop had made no misrepresentations, had concealed no facts, and had committed no violations of the franchise laws. The jury found only that Quik Stop had breached the franchise agreement by failing to provide accurate accounting statements. The jury further found that plaintiffs owed Quik Stop $15,616 on the cross-complaint.

This appeal by plaintiffs raises three issues: (1) whether certain evidence was erroneously excluded; (2) whether certain instructions were erroneously refused; and (3) whether affidavits by two jurors were admissible to impeach the verdict. For the reasons which follow we find no reversible error in the proceedings and we affirm the judgment.

* * *

II

Among the instructions requested by plaintiffs were two instructions on false promise as a ground of fraud. [Footnote.] The trial court refused to give them, apparently reasoning that no evidence had been presented to support such a theory. The jury was instructed only on intentional misrepresentation, concealment, and negligent misrepresentation as grounds of fraud.

We find no error in the trial court's ruling. Plaintiffs justify their request for such instructions on the failure of Quik Stop to fulfill its promises (1) to come to the aid of a franchise-holder experiencing difficulties with theft, (2) to engage in an advertising campaign to promote plaintiffs' store and (3) to provide accurate accountings of the franchisee's financial condition. Although there was evidence to raise a question of fact whether Quik Stop *fulfilled* its promises, there was no evidence to suggest Quik Stop never *intended* to perform. Indeed, the undisputed evidence established that Quik Stop did post promotional signs in the store windows, did provide some assistance to plaintiffs in their efforts to control theft and did provide monthly financial statements, albeit inaccurate statements. There was simply no evidence to support a finding that Quik Stop had no intention

of carrying out its promises. The instructions on this theory were properly refused. [Citation.]

In any event, even under the instructions given, the jury found that defendants had made no misrepresentations, concealed no facts. The jury necessarily decided against plaintiffs on this issue; there is no likelihood that the jury would have returned a different verdict had it been instructed on the alternate theory of promissory fraud.

* * *

* * * The jury was instructed that Quik Stop could recover, despite its own breach of the franchise agreement, only if Quik Stop substantially performed its obligations. The jury expressly found that Quik Stop *did* substantially perform its contractual promises; that the accounting error did not obviate Quik Stop's substantial performance. We find nothing internally inconsistent about the jury's verdict. Nor was the award of damages to Quik Stop contrary to law or fact. * * *

The judgment is affirmed.

PORT CITY STATE BANK v. AMERICAN NATIONAL BANK, LAWTON, OKLAHOMA

486 F.2d 196, 5 CLSR 357
(United States Court of Appeals, Tenth Circuit, Oct. 23, 1973.)

HILL, C. J.

This appeal is from a judgment entered against appellant Port City State Bank in its suit to collect upon two checks forwarded to appellee and not returned as insufficient before the appropriate midnight deadline. Following a trial without a jury, the United States District Court for the Western District of Oklahoma ruled that the failure to notify of dishonor prior to the deadline was excused in this case by Regulation J of the Federal Reserve Regulations, 12 C.F.R. 210.14, and 12A O.S.A. 4–108(2).

* * *

The record discloses that appellant was the holder of two checks drawn upon the J. H. McClung Coin Shop account with American

National. Both items were forwarded through collecting channels for payment. The first check arrived at American National on Friday, November 28, 1969. That check contained two conflicting amounts: in figures $72,000.00 and in words seventy-two dollars and no/100 dollars. It was processed manually and stamped insufficient funds on Saturday, November 29; however, it was not returned immediately but was placed in Monday's business to determine if any deposits were forthcoming on Monday which would balance the account. Notice of dishonor was given to the last endorser of the check, the Federal Reserve Bank at Oklahoma City, on Wednesday, December 3, and the check was returned to the Federal Reserve on December 4.

The second check, in the amount of $120,377.20, arrived at American National on Tuesday, December 2, 1969. The first notice of its dishonor was by telephone to the Federal Reserve on Friday, December 5; it was returned to the Federal Reserve the same day.

It was stipulated by the parties that the "midnight deadline" for these items as established by Regulation J, 12 C.F.R. 210.12, and 12A O.S.A. 4–103(1) (h) was midnight December 1 for the first check and midnight December 3 for the second check. Additionally, it was stipulated that neither check was dishonored before the applicable deadline.

These facts establish a prima facie case for the application of 12 C.F.R. 210.12 and 12A O.S.A. 4–302(a), both concerning the necessity of fulfilling the midnight deadline, and thus it became the obligation of appellee at the trial to prove an excuse from these provisions under 12 C.F.R. 210.14 [footnote] and 12A O.S.A. 4–108(2). [Footnote.] The latter regulations in essence prevent the operation of the midnight deadline in cases when the delay by the payor bank is caused by the interruption of communication facilities, suspension of payments by another bank, war, emergency condition or other circumstances beyond the control of the bank provided it exercises such diligence as the circumstances require.

In furtherance of its contention, American National presented evidence that prior to December 1, 1969, it had performed its bookkeeping functions by machine posting, a so-called manual system. During 1969, however, a decision was made to implement a computer bookkeeping operation, and a rental agreement was entered into with a large computer company. That lease provided that all repairs and maintenance were the obligation of the computer firm, and American National was not authorized to undertake any such tasks. After the installation of the computer, American National paralleled its manual system with computer operations for approximately two weeks. Finally the decision was made to change over to computer processing beginning on December 1. A last manual posting was made on Saturday, November 29, and the manual bookkeeping equipment was removed from the bank during that weekend.

At approximately 10:00 a.m. on December 1, the first day for use of computer operations, the American National computer developed a "memory error" which rendered it unusable. Though the computer manufacturer indicated repairs would not take "too long," they lasted until late Monday night and the testing procedure extended into the early hours of Tuesday, December 2.

In reliance upon the belief that the computer would be repaired without prolonged delay, American National took no extraordinary steps to process Monday's business during the business day. However, when it became apparent that evening that the computer was not going to be ready immediately, American National decided to utilize an identical computer in a bank which was a trip of some 2½ hours away, in accord with a backup agreement they had made with the other banking institution. Thus at about 11:30 p.m. personnel from American National and the computer company began processing Monday's business on the backup computer and continued processing through the night. This work had proceeded to the point of capturing the items on discs when, because the backup computer was required by its owner and because they were informed their own computer was operational, the American National personnel returned to their bank to complete the work on their own machine. After returning to American National, the work was processed to the point of completing the printing of the trial balances when another memory error developed which again rendered the computer unusable. No further use could be made of the appellee's computer until a new memory module was installed on Thursday, December 4.

Because of the second failure, American National was forced to utilize the backup computer both Wednesday and Thursday during times it was not required by its owner. Monday's business was completed and work was begun on Tuesday's items the evening of Tuesday, December 2. Tuesday's items were not completed until either Wednesday, the third, or Thursday, the fourth. When the second check arrived in Tuesday's business, it was held to determine if a later deposit had balanced the account. Through the use of the backup computer and then its own computer during the next weekend, American National was fully "caught up" by Monday, December 8.

Based upon this evidence, the trial court held that the computer malfunction suffered by American National was the cause of its failure to meet its required midnight deadline on the checks, and that such malfunction constituted both an emergency condition and a circumstance beyond the control of the bank as outlined in 12 C.F.R. 210.14 and 12A O.S.A. 4–108(2). The court further held that the reaction to the situation by American National fulfilled the requirements of diligence imposed by those regulations, and therefore the court entered judgment for American National on both checks.

* * *

Appellant's first contention is that the computer malfunction experienced by appellee was not the cause of the failure to notify on either check and thus could not excuse that lack of action. Though the trial court did not expressly rule upon this causation issue, it impliedly held that the delay in notification was a result of the computer breakdown in both instances, we believe that holding is not clearly erroneous.

As to the first check, it is true that it was processed and stamped insufficient on Saturday, however it was held for Monday's business to allow any deposits made on Monday to balance the account before notice was required. This procedure is reasonable, and only the subsequent computer breakdown prevented timely notice upon the check. In the

case of the second check, appellant contends that problems involved in balancing the "proof batches" caused the delay, not the unavailability of the computer. Such a contention ignores the problems encountered by the bank on Tuesday as a result of the delay in processing Monday's business. Tuesday's work was delayed first by the necessity of driving 2½ hours each day before work could commence, and second by the necessity that Monday's business be completed first. Without doubt, both of these delays resulted from the computer problems at American National.

Further appellant contends that a computer failure, as a matter of law, is not an event which can impose the application of 12A O.S.A. 4–108(2). In our opinion, such a determination is a mixed question of fact and law; however, neither treatment justifies the reversal of the trial court's determination in this case. Factually, it was in no way erroneous to conclude that the malfunction created an emergency condition in the bank and was also a condition beyond the control of the bank. Appellant's argument that in law this malfunction is not included within the prescribed contingencies of § 4–108(2) is without foundation. The statute is clear and unambiguous on its face, and we need not resort to interpretive aids as urged by appellant. Our judgment coincides with that of the trial court that a computer failure such as in this case qualifies for the application of the statute. Additionally, this court has previously indicated that the views of a district judge who is a resident of the state where the controversy arose in a case involving interpretation of laws of that state carries extraordinary persuasive weight on appeal. [Footnote.]

Port City next alleges that the trial court erred in its determination that American National exercised "such diligence" as the circumstances required. Basically, appellant asserts three alternative procedures that American National could have employed, and asserts that if any of these alternatives would have resulted in meeting the deadline, then appellee did not exercise diligence under the circumstances. As the trial court correctly concluded, the statute does not require perfection on the part of appellee, and American National's performance should not be judged on the basis of 20–20 hindsight.

It must first be noted that appellee quickly notified the computer firm of the breakdown, and that company began an immediate repair effort. Further, there was evidence to indicate that such computer breakdowns are generally repaired very quickly. Thus it would appear that appellee was justified in its initial delay in adopting emergency procedures based on its belief such measures would prove unnecessary. Additionally, we must agree with the trial court that appellee's duty under these circumstances was much broader than one requiring merely that it meet its midnight deadline. It was further obligated to keep the bank open and to serve its customers. To abandon the orderly day by day process of bookkeeping to adopt radical emergency measures would have likely prolonged the delay in returning the bank to normal operations.

As to appellant's assertion that appellee should have returned to manual posting, it was shown that the equipment for this procedure was no longer in the bank. Further, no clear evidence was presented to indicate such a procedure would have allowed appellee to fulfill its deadlines if the procedure had been implemented. Any decision to return to manual posting would have to have been made very soon after the discovery of the initial failure. At that time, because of their own experience with computers and the industry history, and also because the manufacturer did not foresee the serious nature of the repairs, American National was justified in believing its computer would be back in service soon. Their delay in commencing emergency operations was reasonable, and these facts prevented a return to manual posting in time to fulfill the deadlines.

As to the possibility of utilizing another backup computer at the regional headquarters of the computer leasing firm, we must agree with the trial court that there was no evidence that this alternative would have proved any more successful than the method actually employed by appellee.

In regard to the last alternative, "sight posting," the evidence is conflicting but sufficient to indicate it is not clear this alternative was so obviously superior as to be mandated under these circumstances. There were differing estimates as to the time required, and it was indicated such a procedure would upset and delay the eventual computer bookkeeping required to return the bank to current status. And as in the consideration of the previous alternatives, it was not clearly demonstrated that this procedure would have allowed American National to meet its deadlines even if it had been adopted.

* * *

Affirmed.

SUN RIVER CATTLE CO. v. MINERS BANK OF MONTANA N.A.
164 Mont. 237, 521 P.2d 679
(Supreme Court of Montana, April 17, 1974.)

PER CURIAM.

This appeal was originally heard on November 27, 1973; an opinion issued January 14, 1974; a rehearing was granted and argued. This opinion replaces that appearing in 31 St.Rep. 44.

This is a case involving three separate plaintiffs and six separate checks. The plaintiffs are cattle raisers and brought this action to recover $74,868.02, plus interest which represents the total of the six checks drawn by Schumacher's New Butte Butchering, hereinafter referred to as New Butte, on its account at Miners Bank of Montana, hereinafter referred to as Miners. One check was payable to Bruce Beck & Son, two to Louis Skaar & Sons, and three to Sun River Cattle Co., who will be referred to hereinafter, respectively, as Beck, Skaar and Sun River individually and as plaintiffs collectively. Each of the checks was accepted by the plaintiff payees in payment for cattle sold and delivered to New Butte. A summary of the history of all six checks is as follows:

The Beck check dated April 28, 1970, was for the amount of $12,478.63. This check was sent by Beck's bank to Miners, stamped "Paid, [sic] run through New Butte's checking account and deducted from the balance on May 11, 1970, (a Monday). The check was reversed and added to the balance on May 13, 1970, and returned to Beck's bank for insufficient funds. The check was sent back to Miners, stamped "Paid", run through New Butte's checking account, deducted from the balance on May 20, 1970, reversed on May 21, 1970, and returned to Beck's bank for insufficient funds. It was then returned to Miners "for collection" June 4, 1970, received by Miners on June 8, 1970, and retained by Miners until July 7, 1970, when it was returned to Beck's bank.

The first Skaar check, dated April 14, 1970, was for the amount of $11,514.74. This check was sent by Skaar's bank to Miners, stamped "Paid", run through New Butte's checking account, deducted from the balance on April 27, 1970, reversed April 28, 1970, and added to the balance and returned to Skaar's bank for insufficient funds on April 28, 1970. The check was sent back to Miners, run through New Butte's checking account and deducted from the balance on May 11, 1970, reversed and added to balance May 13, 1970, and returned to Skaar's bank for insufficient funds. It was returned by Skaar's bank "for collection" on May 15, 1970, received by Miners on May 18, 1970, and retained by Miners until July 27, 1970, when it was returned to Skaar's bank.

The second Skaar check, dated May 4, 1970, was for the amount of $12,434.26. This check was sent by Skaar's bank to Miners, stamped "Paid", run through New Butte's checking account, deducted from the balance on May 12, 1970, reversed on May 13, 1970, and added to the balance and returned to Skaar's bank for insufficient funds. The check was returned by Skaar's bank to Miners "for collection", received by Miners on May 20, 1970, and retained by Miners until July 27, 1970, when it was returned to Skaar's bank.

The first Sun River check, dated April 27, 1970, was for the amount of $12,882.57. This check was deposited in the First National Bank of Great Falls on April 28, 1970, and sent to Miners. It was stamped "Paid May 1, 1970", run through New Butte's checking account and deducted May 1, 1970, (a Friday). The check was reversed and added to the balance on May 4, 1970, (a Monday) and returned to First National Bank of Great Falls. The check was sent back to Miners "for collection" on May 8, 1970, received by Miners on May 11, 1970, and has never been returned.

The second Sun River check, dated May 4, 1970, in the amount of $13,114.23, and the third Sun River check, dated April 1, 1970, (although the invoice for this load of cattle is dated April 28, 1970) in the amount of $12,443.59, were both sent to Miners directly "for collection". The second check was sent on

May 6, 1970, and received by Miners on May 7, 1970, and the third was sent on May 12, 1970, and received by Miners May 13, 1970. These checks have never been returned. None of the checks have been paid.

In 1962 the original transaction between Miners and New Butte took place when Miners loaned New Butte some $289,500. In 1968 refinancing of New Butte became necessary in an amount in excess of Miners' lending capacity.

Refinancing was carried out with two separate loans. One was for $200,000 with Miners having a 30% participation and the remaining 70% spread among seven sister banks. The other was for $100,000, 90% of which was guaranteed by the Small Business Administration (hereinafter referred to as SBA). The loans were made to provide working capital, and to comply with federal regulations as to slaughterhouses.

Miners filed financing statements with the county clerk of Silver Bow County and the secretary of state. A list of equipment was attached to the statement filed with the secretary of state; no such list was attached to the one filed with the county clerk and recorder. No amounts being secured are shown on the statements but Mr. Pitts, Miners' president at the time, stated that they were designed to cover both loans. Witness Pitts testified that the lien of the $200,000 loan was first as to all equipment but that the $100,000 loan was first as to the accounts receivable and inventory.

Miners also took mortgages securing the $200,000 loan as follows: mortgage on New Butte's plant and a mortgage from Harold F. Schumacher and Loretta Schumacher covering their home and personal property. Securing the $100,000 loan Miners took a mortgage from New Butte to Miners covering the plant and equipment and a mortgage from the Schumachers covering their home and personal property.

In each instance the mortgage securing the $200,000 loan was filed first. None of these mortgages has been foreclosed.

Miners also filed a security agreement with the registrar of motor vehicles securing the $200,000 loan and also took an assignment on Schumacher's life insurance as security for the $200,000 loan. The policies were cashed for the cash value.

In December of 1969, New Butte closed down its operation for financial reasons. Operations were resumed in January 1970. At this time a financing firm, Douglas Guardian, with its program of warehousing receipts and accounts receivable financing became involved in cooperation with Miners and New Butte. Advances by Miners under the warehouse receipts plan approximated $390,000. The amounts advanced by Miners under the accounts receivable financing exceeded $400,000. The warehouse receipts program started January 15, 1970, and ended May 22, 1970; the accounts receivable financing covered a period from January 30, 1970 to May 11, 1970.

During the first seven months of 1970, the New Butte checking account was overdrawn in amounts ranging from nominal to as much as $55,000 for all but 87 of those days.

As of May 18, 1970, the $100,000 loan was current in payments. All payments on the $200,000 were made currently through May 28, 1970. On June 2, 1970, the SBA took over the assets of the business. Neither loan was in default at that time. On May 29, and June 1, 1970, Miners' president, Pitts, debited the New Butte account for $12,000 and $9,000 and credited those amounts to the $100,000 SBA loan.

Pitts admitted that he was looking carefully to the account on May 29, 1970, so that he could put in the withdrawal slip for $12,000 and be sure that Miners got ahead of anybody else. He stated that he personally handled the withdrawal.

As to the $9,000 withdrawal, Pitts testified that he kept strict watch of the account and when there was enough deposited, he personally put in a withdrawal slip. On June 18, 1970, Miners credited the $200,000 loan with $4,602, which represented 30% of the total of $15,342 as the result of a sale of equipment by New Butte. The proceeds were not deposited in New Butte's account but were applied directly to the $200,000 loan and that credit was enough to discharge in advance the principal and interest for six months. There was no foreclosure of the security interests nor were the proceeds of the sales placed into New Butte's account.

The bank in this instance knew of the condition of the account of New Butte, it had intimate knowledge of the transactions, it was the "on the ground" representative of the sister banks who shared in the loan and it had more than the usual normal interest in the activities of New Butte.

Plaintiffs brought this action against New Butte and Miners to recover the amounts of the checks plus interest and damages. After a trial without a jury in the second judicial district, Judge James D. Freebourn presiding, found for the plaintiffs against New Butte and found against the plaintiffs and for defendant Miners. Plaintiffs appeal that part of the judgment which exculpated Miners.

Plaintiffs present five issues for review, which are summarized as follows: (1) Whether Miners is liable for holding the Beck check and the first Skaar check past the midnight deadline provided for in section 87A-1-302, R.C.M.1947, and (2) whether Miners is liable for holding all six of the checks past the midnight deadline as provided for in the statute. Plaintiffs' remaining issues involve the question of good faith, which the district court specifically found was exercised by Miners in its dealings with plaintiffs. The question of good faith will be considered in connection with plaintiffs' first two issues.

This case involves sections of the Uniform Commercial Code enacted in Title 87A, R.C.M.1947. The issues presented by plaintiffs are of first impression to this Court, and there are few cases in other jurisdictions which have construed the effect of the sections of the Uniform Commercial Code which are determinative of the issues presented for review.

Plaintiffs' first and second issues raise questions concerning Article 4 of the Uniform Commercial Code. (Hereafter, references to the Uniform Commercial Code will be made by the section number only; the title number will be omitted). Generally plaintiffs argue that Miners is liable for the face amount of the checks for not complying with what is commonly referred to as the "midnight deadline" rule. Defendant argues that with respect to the first issue section 4–108 is an exception to section 4–302 and with respect to the second issue section 4–103 is an exception to section 4–302 and under these sections Miners is not liable. Initially, we will generally discuss the construction of section 4–302, which provides:

In the absence of a valid defense such as breach

of a presentment warranty (subsection (1) of section 87A–4–207), settlement effected or the like, if an item is presented on and received by a payor bank the bank is accountable for the amount of

(a) a demand item other than a documentary draft whether properly payable or not if the bank, in any case where it is not also the depositary bank, retains the item beyond midnight of the banking day of receipt without settling for it or, regardless of whether it is also the depositary bank, does not pay or return the item or send notice of dishonor until after its midnight deadline; or. * * *

The "midnight deadline" is midnight of the banking day following the day of the receipt of the item by the payor bank. Section 4–104(1)(h). A payor bank is a bank by which an item is payable as drawn or accepted. Section 4–105(b). There is no question but that Miners is the payor bank. The checks involved herein are demand items. Section 4–104(1)(g) and section 3–104(1) and (2).

Section 4–302 was construed in the case of *Rock Island Auction Sales v. Empire Packing Co.*, 32 Ill.2d 269, 204 N.E.2d 721, 18 A.L.R.3d 1368, where the Illinois court held that the word "accountable" in the statute is synonymous with "liable". We agree.

Essentially, section 4–302 says that in the absence of a valid defense, a demand item, retained beyond the "midnight deadline" by the payor bank without either paying, returning, or giving notice of dishonor renders the payor bank liable to the payee for the face amount of the item.

In addition, there is a fundamental requirement of good faith under the specific provision of section 1–201(19), which reads as follows:

"Good faith" means honesty in fact in the conduct or transaction concerned."

Furthermore, 1–203 provides:

Every contract or duty within this act imposes an obligation of good faith in its performance or enforcement.

Plaintiffs' first issue concerns the Beck check dated April 28, 1970, and the first Skaar check dated April 14, 1970. These checks were submitted as cash items to Miners on May 11, 1970, and were not returned until May 13, 1970. Plaintiffs contend that because of the delay that Miners violated the "midnight deadline" rule. Facts not heretofore set forth relevant to this issue and undisputed are as follows:

The Computer Corporation of Montana, a data processing company, is a wholly owned subsidiary of Bancorporation of Montana which processed checks for eleven banks in the Bancorporation chain, including Miners. Items to be processed for Miners are sent to Computer Corporation in Great Falls by armored car between 5:00 p. m. and 6:00 p. m. of the day of receipt and are usually back at Miners by 8:00 a. m. the following morning. The checks normally reach Great Falls about 10:30 p. m. On May 11, 1970, the day on which Miners received the checks under discussion, the armored car broke down and did not reach Computer Corporation until 1:30 a. m. the morning of May 12, 1970. Ordinarily the work on Miners' checks would have been processed by 11:30 p. m.; the checks would have started back to Butte by armored car at 4:00 a. m. and have reached Miners at 7:00 a. m.

On the morning of May 12, 1970, the computer malfunctioned, and the checks which would have normally been returned to Miners on the morning of May 12, 1970, did not arrive until 2:30 p. m. that afternoon.

Ken Mahle, vice-president of Miners at the time of the trial, outlined the procedures which were followed each day after the receipt of the checks from the Computer Center. He could not, however, testify as to what occurred on May 12, 1970. There was no testimony as to what actually happened on the day after the checks were received by Miners.

Miners contend that it is this type of situation which section 4–108(2) was intended to cover. Section 4–108(2) provides:

Delay by a collecting bank or payor bank beyond time limits prescribed or permitted by this act or by instructions is excused if caused by interruption of communication facilities, suspension of payments by another bank, war, emergency conditions or other circumstances beyond the control of the bank provided it exercises such diligence as the circumstances require.

The Official Code Comment on this point states:

4. Subsection (2) is another escape clause from time limits. This clause operates not only with respect to time limits imposed by the article itself but also time limits imposed by special

instructions, by agreement or by Federal Reserve regulations or operating letters, clearing house rules or the like. The latter time limits are 'permitted' by the Code. This clause operates, however, only in the types of situation specified. Examples of these situations include blizzards, floods, or hurricanes, and other 'Act of God' events or conditions, and wrecks or disasters, interfering with mails; suspension of payments by another bank; abnormal operating conditions such as substantial increased volume or substantial shortage of personnel during war or emergency situations. *When delay is sought to be excused under this subsection the bank must 'exercise such diligence as the circumstances require' and it has the burden of proof.* (Emphasis supplied.) 3 Anderson, Uniform Commercial Code 191.

The effect of section 4–108(2) is to excuse a payor bank from the standard of strict accountability of section 4–302 and to hold it to a standard of "diligence as the circumstances require". Under section 4–108(2) there must be a showing that the circumstances were beyond the control of the bank and that the bank exercised such diligence as the circumstances require. As the Official Code Comment states, the burden is on the bank.

The district court found that Miners' failure to pay or return the checks or to give notice of dishonor within the prescribed time was due to circumstances beyond its control. The district court also found that Miners exercised the required diligence and that no evidence was introduced showing that Miners failed to exercise due care.

The evidence as to the events in question is undisputed. This Court in *In re Wadsworth's Estate,* 92 Mont. 135, 150, 11 P.2d 788, 792 stated:

* * * But where, as here, there is no dispute as to the facts, this court is in as favorable a position in applying the law as the district court, and in such instances will not hesitate to do so. (Citing authority.) And a judgment or order unsupported by the evidence will be reversed on appeal to this court. (Citing authority.)

The only evidence produced by Miners was what the ordinary operating procedures were.

As we have heretofore stated, Miners had more than the usual normal interest in the activities of New Butte. It necessarily follows that under the circumstances of this case that

the degree of diligence required under 4–108(2) is greater than under normal circumstances.

Miners argues that the testimony of Mahle as to normal operating procedures constitutes a showing of due diligence. While there may be instances where a showing as to what occurs on a normal operating day may constitute a showing of diligence under circumstances where the delay is similar as to the one in the instant case, this case is not one of those instances. Miners' interest in New Butte was more than usual, and a showing of diligence by Miners required more than testimony as to what the normal operating procedures were. Miners' burden under the circumstances of this case is greater for the reason that its relationship and interest in New Butte was significantly more than ordinary. Miners did not meet its burden as imposed by section 4–108(2).

Under the exception of section 4–108(2) the bank must show: (1) A cause for the delay; (2) that the cause was beyond the control of the bank; and (3) that under the circumstances the bank exercised such diligence as required. In the absence of any one of these showings, the excuse for the delay will not apply, and the bank will be held liable under the provisions of section 4–302. Since Miners did not meet its burden, it is therefore liable for the face amount of the Beck check and the first Skaar check under the strict accountability rule of section 4–302.

* * *

STATE EX REL. GABALAC v. FIRESTONE BANK
46 Ohio App.2d 124, 346 N.E.2d 326, 5 CLSR 1318
(Court of Appeals for Summit County, Ohio, Oct. 15, 1975.)

HUNSICKER, J.

This is an appeal from a judgment rendered in favor of Summit County, Ohio, against the Firestone Bank for the sum of $10,000 and costs. The Firestone Bank was a depository for the Summit County clerk of courts alimony and support account. Check 105049 was issued through that account, on December 18, 1972, in the amount of $45. This check was mailed by the clerk of courts to the person authorized to receive it, Leona C. Brechbill, who placed it for deposit with Arlington Trust Co. of Arlington, Virginia. The Arlington Trust Co. improperly encoded this check to read $10,045. This amount was later paid to Mrs. Brechbill.

After encoding the check so that it could be read mechanically instead of by personal examination, The Arlington Trust Co. sent the check for collection to The Riggs National Bank of Washington, D. C., which in turn sent the check to the Federal Reserve Bank of Cleveland. The Federal Reserve Bank sent it to The Firestone Bank for collection or processed it through that bank's account with the Federal Reserve Bank.

On December 29, 1972, The Firestone Bank paid the check by deducting from the alimony and support account the sum of $10,045. This paid check, along with others, was sent to the Summit County clerk on or about January 5, 1973. No examination of the cancelled checks was made by that clerk or his assistants.

An audit of the office of the Summit County clerk was made by the state auditor as required by law. That audit, covering a period from June 1, 1970, through December 31, 1972, reported, on or about August 22, 1973, to The Firestone Bank that check 105049 in the amount of $45, had been paid by The Firestone Bank and charged to the account of the Summit County clerk of courts in the amount of $10,045.

A Firestone Bank officer testified that no checks passing through the clearing process are processed by personal examination. The volume of check writing in modern business requires mechanical examination by means of the modern magnetic tape code system. That system was used in the instant case.

The Firestone Bank also said that the clerk was negligent in failing to examine the cancelled checks herein, which along with others was personally delivered to the clerk's office on or about January 5, 1973, seven and one-half months before notice of the improper payment from the account. This bank statement which was hand delivered contained a printed sentence which stated: "Please examine at once. If no error is reported within 10 days, the account will be considered correct and the checks genuine."

The trial court entered judgment for the plaintiff prosecutor, the appellee herein, who, under the law, was required to prosecute the case on behalf of Summit County.

The defendant Firestone Bank says that the trial court erred in the following respects:

1. * * * [I]n its finding that there was no obligation on the part of plaintiff-appellee to, under the circumstances, exercise reasonable care and promptness to examine its regular monthly statement issued by the bank and to notify the defendant-appellant bank promptly after discovering the erroneous overcharge.

2. * * * [I]n its finding that defendant-appellant failed to exercise ordinary care in processing the check which is the subject of this lawsuit, such conclusion being wholly unsupported by and contrary to the evidence.

3. The decision of the trial court in favor of plaintiff-appellee and against defendant-appellant is not supported by the record and is contrary to law.

Is there a common law duty on the part of a bank customer to examine his monthly bank reconcilement within ten days and report any errors within that period of time to the bank in order to recover for negligence of the bank in making an unauthorized payment out of the customer's account? It is obvious from reading RC 1304.29, that there is no statutory provision, under the facts of this case, which would permit the bank to disclaim liability. The statute talks of: alterations on any item, unauthorized signature, and unauthorized endorsement. The time frame set by the legislature to discover and report these errors is one year and three years, a time longer than the seven and one-half months used by Summit County to notify the bank and much, much longer than the ten days which the bank unilaterally gives its customers to examine the statement for errors.

What happens if the customer is out of town, on a trip overseas, on a cruise, or on an automobile vacation around the United States for more than the ten day bank reconcilement date?

We believe there is a common law duty which devolves upon the customer to examine his bank statement. What the time frame is within which this shall be done, in order to absolve the bank from responsibility for negligence in the handling of the account, is a question of fact that depends on the circumstances which surround each case.

It should be noted here that the day Leona Brechbill secured the $10,045 after a deposit of the check of the clerk of courts in the Arlington Trust Co. is not shown by the evidence. What is shown on the check as an exhibit is the date the check was deposited to the account of Leona Brechbill, to-wit: December 27, 1972. That was the day when the Arlington Trust Co. sent the check through the bank's clearing department to one of its correspondent banks. The check arrived at The Firestone Bank on December 29, 1972.

Two Ohio cases have been brought to our attention but they treat of situations covered by the statutes and a company resolution covering reconcilement. In *White Castle System, Inc. v. Huntington National Bank*, 36 Ohio Law Abs. 253, the court said:

> The law is also equally well recognized that where it is the custom of the bank and known to the customer as in the instant case, for the bank to send out statements at certain intervals, it is the duty of the customer to examine such statements and reconcile the same with their own books, and if there is a variance, report the error within a reasonable time. * * *

The rule there announced was followed in *Portsmouth Clay Products Co. v. National Bank of Portsmouth*, 78 Ohio App. 271.

The loss in the instant case was not due to the negligence of the clerk of courts, for even though he would have discovered the check on January 5, 1973, when checks were delivered to him by The Firestone Bank, the loss had already taken place.

Nothing has been shown in this record that an earlier notice to The Firestone Bank would have prevented the loss of the money herein or would even have reduced the loss. Nothing the clerk of courts would have done after an examination of the checks and the discovery of the over payment to Leona Brechbill would have prevented the several banks in the chain of the clearing process from paying $10,045 to the holder of the check in issue herein after Arlington Trust Co. erroneously encoded it.

If the clerk of courts had notified The Firestone Bank in the ten days, which they say is a reasonable time, that notice would still require the bank to reimburse the clerk for the wrongful payment. In *Faber v. Edgewater National Bank*, 101 N.J. Super. 354, 359, 244 A.2d 339, 342, the court said, in a case involving the payment of a forged check: " * * * * a negligent bank cannot put the loss resulting from a forgery *or the like* onto the customer on the ground the customer also has been negligent." (Emphasis ours.) New Jersey has a statute that requires due diligence in the examination of cancelled checks and due diligence in notifying the bank of any error or irregularities. The Ohio statutes do not extend as far as the New Jersey law. We do say that an unreasonable delay in notifying the bank that an error has occurred which causes a loss to the bank is such negligence on the part of the customer as may result in no recovery being allowed such customer. [Citations.]

There is no showing here that the notice delay caused a loss greater than this bank had sustained when it paid the improperly encoded check. In addition, the statute with reference to forged or altered checks, RC 1304.29, states that a year is a proper period in which to notify the bank for forged or altered checks thus, in effect, establishing that length of time deemed to be reasonable under the circumstances of the instant case.

We have examined all assignments of error and for the reasons set out herein, we reject assigned errors one, two and three. The judgment of the trial court is affirmed.

BANK LEUMI TRUST CO. OF NEW YORK v. BANK OF MID–JERSEY

499 F. Supp. 1022
(United States District Court, D. New Jersey, Oct. 10, 1980.)

ACKERMAN, D. J.

This is a case arising under Articles 3 & 4 of the Uniform Commercial Code, N.J.S.A. 12A:3–101 *et seq.* and 12A:4–101 *et seq.*, and, more particularly, Article 4's "midnight deadline" for the processing of checks, N.J.S.A. 12A:4–302. The focus of the case is the adventures of a certain check, number 1028, drawn on the account of Century Buick, Inc. at the defendant Bank of Mid–Jersey for the amount of $48,470.00, and made payable to Grand Prix, a customer of the plaintiff Bank Leumi Trust Company of New York, Inc. This check was held by Mid–Jersey beyond its midnight deadline. The case is before me today on plaintiff's motion for summary judgment on the first count of its complaint, which I have decided to grant.

Since on a motion for summary judgment the party opposing the motion is entitled to have all factual inferences drawn in its favor [citation], I have analyzed this motion upon the facts as presented by Mid–Jersey in the "Statement of Facts" of its brief opposing Leumi's motion. The facts, therefore, appear as follows:

The check was drawn on October 2, 1978. Grand Prix initially deposited the check in Leumi for collection. It was routed to Mid–Jersey, which returned the check on October 4, 1978, due to insufficient funds in Century Buick's account to cover the check. On October 13, 1978, Century Buick telephoned a stop order on the check to Mid–Jersey. Sometime after October 13, 1978, Grand Prix once again deposited the check at Bank Leumi for collection from Mid–Jersey. When Leumi processed the check on the beginning of its second trip through the collection route it apparently made an error in encoding the computer readable figures that are printed at the bottom right hand corner of most checks that are presented for collection in this day and age. This encoding, along with other modern wonders, speeds the usual check through the usual channels. We are not dealing in this case with the usual check, however, due to Leumi's encoding error. Leumi encoded the check as being for $48,470.72 instead of for an even $48,470 and *no* cents. Leumi noticed this error, however, and crossed out the encoded sum with a lead pencil and with the same pencil, wrote the corrected figure above the one that had been previously encoded. Leumi failed to encode the corrected figure, however, and its pencilled number, while quite legible to the human eye, could not be read by a computer.

So it was that check number 1028 entered the collection channels for a second time, with the rubber stamp scars of its first trip and without a properly encoded sum. It was in this humble state that the check arrived at Mid–Jersey on October 20, 1978, a Friday.

Upon arrival, Mid–Jersey determined that the check could not be processed by its high speed computer system due to the incorrect encoding and accompanying pencil marks. This check, it was determined, would have to be processed by human beings. Mid–Jersey then processed the check, posting it on the next business day, October 23, 1978, a Monday, and returning it on the following day, October 24, 1978, a Tuesday, when it determined that a stop order had been placed by its customer, which, in any event, had insufficient funds in its account to cover the check. This Tuesday return, however, was subsequent to the Bank's usual "midnight deadline," which is created by N.J.S.A. 12A:4–104 and 12A:4–302 and will be discussed in greater detail subsequently. Due to this late return, Leumi made a claim to the Federal Reserve Bank, which had presented the check to Mid–Jersey, for payment pursuant to N.J.S.A. 12A:4–302, which provides for strict liability on the part of the payor bank, in this case Mid–Jersey, to pay the amount of any check held past its midnight deadline. When the Federal Reserve Bank made its usual inquiries about the late return, Mid–Jersey submitted a "Disclaimer of Late Return" in which it denied liability. The Federal Reserve Bank took no further action against Mid–Jersey, but sent Leumi the following debit advice:

> * * * Paying bank has denied the item was returned late. * * * Future action in this matter must be between you and the paying bank.

[Reference.] The debit advice also charged the $48,470.00 back to Leumi in accordance with Federal Reserve Bank procedures.

Accepting all of these facts, Leumi argues that it is entitled to summary judgment because Mid–Jersey held the check beyond its midnight deadline. As I mentioned earlier, N.J.S.A. 12A:4–302 clearly provides that, in the absence of a limited class of valid defenses, a payor bank that holds a check beyond its midnight deadline without either paying or returning it becomes strictly liable to the presenting bank for payment of the check in full. In the present case it is uncontroverted that the check was held beyond the midnight dead line. N.J.S.A. 12A:4–104 defines the midnight deadline as "midnight on [a bank's] next banking day following the banking day on which it received the relevant item. * * * *" The present check was received, according to Mid–Jersey, on Friday, October 20, 1978; Mid–Jersey's next banking day was on Monday,

October 23, 1978 and before the second hand reached 12:01 A.M. on Tuesday, October 24, 1978, its midnight deadline for handling the check had passed. As Mid–Jersey admits, the check was not dishonored until sometime later in the day on Tuesday.

Leumi's argument is a sound one, and they seem to be entitled to payment from Mid–Jersey in accordance with the provisions of N.J.S.A. 12A:4–302. Mid–Jersey, however, has made four arguments in an attempt to avoid the operation of section 4–302. I will discuss these arguments in the order presented in the brief opposing the present motion.

First, Mid–Jersey argues that it is excused from meeting its midnight deadline because the delay was caused by circumstances beyond its control, namely the pencil marks and encoding error on the check. In support of this argument, Mid–Jersey relies on N.J.S.A. 12A:4–l08(2). That section of Article 4 provides that delay past the midnight deadline

> is excused if caused by interruption of communication facilities, suspension of payments by another bank, or, emergency conditions or other circumstances beyond the control of the bank provided it exercises such diligence as the circumstances require.

Mid–Jersey argues that the circumstance that check number 1028 had to be manually processed, instead of being handled by a computer, is so anomalous in "the civilized world today" that it should qualify as "other circumstances beyond the control of the bank." [Reference.] To state this argument is to reject it. Both the Uniform Commercial Code Comment and the New Jersey Study Comment make it clear that this section is designed to permit delay only in extreme situations. In the words of the U.C.C. Comment:

> Examples of these situations include blizzards, floods, or hurricanes, and other "Act of God" events or conditions, and wrecks or disasters, interfering with mails; suspension of payments by another bank; abnormal operating conditions such as substantial increased volume or substantial shortage of personnel during war or emergency situations.

[Citation.] The eventuality of a check being impossible to run through a computer is simply not in this class of events. Moreover, nothing in the Code requires a check to be computer encoded or computer readable. To the contrary, the definition of a check contained in 12A:3–104 does not even require it to be written upon the customary bank form, or even upon paper. Even in what Mid–Jersey calls "the civilized world" a bank must be prepared to handle a check properly even when it is not fit to be run through a computer. The provisions of Article 4 of the Code nowhere make a distinction in time limits between checks that can be computer processed and those that cannot. Certainly nothing in section 4–108(2) can support the construction urged upon this Court by Mid–Jersey.

* * *

Mid–Jersey's final argument is that equitable concerns should bar this Court from granting summary judgment to Leumi. This argument is based on N.J.S.A. 12A:1–103 which provides that

> Unless displaced by the particular provisions of the Act [i. e., the U.C.C.,] the principles of law and equity, shall supplement its provisions.

The simple answer to this argument is that N.J.S.A. 12A:4–302 is a particular provision of the U.C.C. that displaces Mid–Jersey's equitable argument. But even if that were not a sufficient answer, the equities of this case do not favor Mid–Jersey. Leumi's only supposedly inequitable conduct was placing the pencil marks on the check and failing to properly encode the check. These actions neither violated any Code provisions nor created a document that could not be reasonably handled manually. A bank must be prepared to handle checks that are not in perfect computer form and it is not inequitable to expect Mid–Jersey to handle the check in the present case properly.

It is true that granting summary judgment means that Mid–Jersey must pay Leumi $48,470.00. But Mid–Jersey is not without remedies: it may proceed against its customer Century Buick, something it has already attempted to do through a third party complaint in the present action. It is true that $48,470.00 may seem a high price to pay for a day's delay, but it must be remembered that this case only determines which of three innocent parties, the payee Grand Prix, the depository Bank

Leumi, or the payor bank Mid–Jersey, must absorb the loss of Century Buick's wrongful conduct in writing a check on insufficient funds. Article 4 of the U.C.C. provides clear cut rules for deciding who among the innocent parties must absorb the loss created by Century Buick's wrongdoing. If Mid–Jersey had met its midnight deadline it would have passed that loss back to either Leumi or Grand Prix. It failed to do so, therefore the U.C.C. declares that Mid–Jersey must absorb the loss. It is not inequitable to enforce the provisions of the U.C.C. Indeed, it would be inequitable not to do so, because the smooth flow of commerce relies upon the application of the U.C.C., and that flow should not be interrupted by countenancing minor equitable defenses like pencil marks on a check.

Leumi's motion for summary judgment on the first count of its complaint will, therefore, be granted.

FJS ELECTRONICS, INC. v. FIDELITY BANK

288 Pa.Super. 138, 431 A.2d 326
(Superior Court of Pennsylvania, June 19, 1981.)

BROSKY, J.

FJS Electronics, Inc., appellee, brought an action to recover the amount of a check drawn on appellant bank which appellant paid after appellee had requested payment be stopped. The central issue for our determination is whether a bank had a reasonable opportunity to stop payment on a check in the sum of $1,844.98 when the amount given by the customer was $1,844.48, hence, inaccurate. The court below held that an error of $.50 does not deprive the bank of a reasonable opportunity to stop the check. We affirm.

On February 27, 1976, appellee, FJS Electronics, Inc., trading as Multi-Teck (hereinafter Multi-Teck), drew a check in the amount of $1,844.98 on appellant, The Fidelity Bank (hereinafter Fidelity). The number of the check was 896 and the payee was Multilayer Com-

puter Circuits. On March 9, 1976, Mr. Frank Suttill, president of Multi-Teck, called Fidelity on the telephone and requested payment on check number 896 be stopped. Mrs. Roanna M. Sanders took the stop payment order. The amount given by Suttill was $1,844.48; otherwise, the information he provided was essentially correct.[1] A confirmation notice was subsequently sent to Multi-Teck, reciting the inaccurate amount, and Multi-Teck confirmed all the information which it contained. The confirmation notice also contained the request, "PLEASE ENSURE AMOUNT IS CORRECT." (The entire notice was in block letters.)

The parties stipulated the following facts:

6. In March 1976, the Bank used a computer to pull checks on which stop payment request had been made. The computer keyed on the amount of the check which was typed in computer digits by the depository Bank on the bottom of each check.

7. The Bank, except when requested by a customer, did not pre-print nor post-print the number of the check in computer digits on the bottom of the check. Some banks in Philadelphia and other cities did pre-print the number of the check.

8. The Bank's computer was programmed to read three sets of computer digits called "fields" on the bottom of each check: the federal reserve number of the bank, the account number and the amount of the check.

9. The Bank's computer program was designed so that all digits of the amount of the stop payment request had to agree with the computer digits of the amount on the bottom of the check before the check was pulled.

10. The Bank's computer was not programmed to pull checks where there was a discrepancy in a digit of the amount of the stop payment request and the computer digits of the amount on the bottom of the check nor was it designed for stop payment purposes to read the number of the check.

11. The Bank received approximately 100 to 150 stop payment requests a day during 1976.

12. In taking stop payment orders, the Bank tells the customer that every bit of information must be accurate. Mr. Suttill was told that on March 9, 1976.

---

1. The Court below notes that the subsequent written confirmation notice denominated the payee of the check as Multilator, rather than Multilayer, Computer Circuits. On page 2 of its opinion, in footnote 2, the court stated that this "variance would not appear to have mean-

ingful bearing on the principle issue in dispute." We assume, without deciding, that this is correct, and note that this issue is not before us, since the parties have not raised it.

13. The Bank did not tell Mr. Suttill, nor did he request, information as to the procedure whereby the computer pulls checks on which stop payments have been issued.

14. If the computer pulls more than one check where the amount field matches that of the stop payment order, then those checks are compared manually with the stop payment request.

On March 15, 1976, check No. 896 was paid by Fidelity, and Multi-Teck's account was charged. The court below found that this charge resulted in a loss of $1,844.98 to Multi-Teck.

We must decide whether the court below was correct in holding that a customer's error in the amount of a check in a stop payment request does not relieve the bank of liability.

Section 4–403(1) of the Uniform Commercial Code [footnote] addresses the problem of stop payment orders:

> A customer may by order to his bank stop payment of any item payable for his account but the order must be received at such time and in such manner as to afford the bank a reasonable opportunity to act on it. * * *

It is clear that the order here was timely received. The court below determined that even though it contained an error, the order was given in such manner as to give the bank a reasonable opportunity to act. Fidelity, in essence, asserts that the section should be read to require compliance with the procedures of a particular bank, regardless of what they are and regardless of whether the customer has been made aware of them. Fidelity argues that since its technique for ascertaining whether payment had been stopped required absolute accuracy as to the amount of a stopped check, this section would require absolute precision in order for the notice to be reasonable. Such a narrow view is not consistent with the intent being § 4–403, expressed in Comment 2 following the section:

> The position taken by this section is that stopping payment is a service which depositors expect and are entitled to receive from banks notwithstanding its difficulty, inconvenience and expense. The inevitable occasional losses through failure to stop should be borne by the banks as a cost of the business of banking.

Fidelity does not contend that it could not have used a technique which required less precision in the stop payment order. It does not contend that it could not have found the check had it used a more thorough system. It merely asserts that since it chose a system which searched only by amount, notice is not reasonable unless it conforms to the requirements of this system.

Fidelity made a choice when it elected to employ a technique which searched for stopped checks by amount alone. It evidently found benefits to this technique which outweighed the risk that an item might be inaccurately described in a stop order. This is precisely the type of inevitable loss which was contemplated by the code drafters and addressed by the comment quoted above. The focus of § 4–403 is the service which may be expected by the *customer*, and a customer may expect a check to be stopped after the bank is given reasonable notice. A bank's decision to reduce operating costs by using a system which increases the risk that checks as to which there is an outstanding stop payment order will be paid invites liability when such items are paid.

An error of fifty cents in the amount of a stop payment order does not deprive the bank of a reasonable opportunity to act on the order. *See, Elsie Rodriquez Fashions, Inc. v. Chase Manhattan Bank*, 23 U.C.C. Reporting Service 133 (New York Supreme Ct., Trial Division, 1978), holding a bank is liable when a check is paid over a stop order bearing an amount which is in error by ten cents; *Rimberg v. Union Trust Co. of the District of Columbia*, 12 U.C.C. Reporting Service 527 (D.C.Superior Ct. 1973), finding a bank liable for failing to stop a check over an order inaccurate as to amount, where the bank had notice that the amount might be incorrect. *But see* the discussion of necessary information in Hawkland, *Stop Payment Orders Under the Uniform Commercial Code*, 75 Commercial Law Journal 53, 58 (1970), which would require conformity to the system employed by a particular bank.

Appellant further contends that appellee should bear the loss since it failed to ascertain whether check No. 896 had been paid before a replacement check had been issued. While 13 Pa.C.S.A. § 4403(c) places the burden of proof of loss on the customer, the purpose behind this requirement is to prevent unjust enrichment (Comment 8 to § 4–403), and not to impose any additional burden on the customer beyond a showing of loss and payment over a binding stop order. The fact that payment occurred over a binding stop order was addressed above. Appellee's proof that a replacement check was issued and paid satisfied the trial court that a loss had been suffered due to Fidelity's payment of check No. 896. Appellant has made no argument that this loss did not occur.

The order of the court below is affirmed.

FIRST WYOMING BANK, N.A. v. CABINET CRAFT DISTRIBUTORS, INC.

624 P.2d 227

(Supreme Court of Wyoming, Feb. 18, 1981.)

ROSE, C. J.

The Uniform Commercial Code provides that except in certain circumstances a bank is liable for the amount of a check which it fails to timely dishonor. Section 34–21–451, W.S.1977 (U.C.C. § 4–302). In this case, the appellee presented a check payable to itself to the appellant bank. The payor had insufficient funds on deposit with the bank to cover the check. The bank dishonored the check but failed to do so within the time mandated by the Uniform Commercial Code.

Appellee then sued in district court for the face amount of the check, interest and costs. The district court agreed with the appellee that the bank was liable under the Code and gave judgment accordingly. The bank has appealed and argues that its "excuse" for failing to timely dishonor the check is sufficient under the Code to enable it to escape liability. Section 34–21–408(b), W.S.1977 (U.C.C. § 4–108(2)).

We shall affirm the trial court.

The case was tried on stipulated facts. However, before presenting the stipulation, it is appropriate to reproduce the controlling Code provisions.

THE STATUTES

Section 34–21–451 (U.C.C. § 4–302), *supra*, provides:

> (a) In the absence of a valid defense such as breach of a presentment warranty (subsection

(1) of section 4–207 [§ 34–21–426(a)]), a settlement effected or the like, if an item is presented on and received by a payor bank the bank is accountable for the amount of:

> (i) A demand item other than a documentary draft whether properly payable or not if the bank, in any case where it is not also the depositary bank, retains the item beyond midnight of the banking day of receipt without settling for it or, regardless of whether it is also the depository bank, does not pay or return the item or send notice of dishonor until after its midnight deadline; or

> (ii) Any other properly payable item unless within the time allowed for acceptance or payment of that item the bank either accepts or pays the item or returns it and accompanying documents.

The term "midnight deadline" is defined in § 34–21–404(a)(viii), W.S.1977 (U.C.C. § 4–104(1)(h)):

> (viii) 'Midnight deadline' with respect to a bank is midnight on its next banking day following the banking day on which it receives the relevant item or notice or from which the time for taking action commences to run, whichever is later;

Section 34–21–408(b) (U.C.C. § 4–108(2)), *supra*, provides:

> (b) Delay by a collecting bank or payor bank beyond time limits prescribed or permitted by this act or by instructions is excused if caused by interruption of communication facilities, suspension of payments by another bank, war, emergency conditions *or other circumstances beyond the control of the bank provided it exercises such diligence as the circumstances required.* (Emphasis added.) [Footnote.]

In arguing that the delay in dishonoring the check was excusable, appellant bank also relies on 12 Code of Federal Regulations 210.14 which provides:

> If, because of interruption of communication facilities, suspension of payments by another bank, war, emergency conditions or other circumstances beyond its control, any bank (including a Federal Reserve bank) shall be delayed beyond the time limits provided in this part or the operating letters of the Federal Reserve banks, or prescribed by the applicable law of any State in taking any action with respect to a cash item or a noncash item, including forwarding such item, presenting it or sending it for presentment and payment, paying or remitting for it, re-

turning it or sending notice of dishonor or non-payment or making or providing for any necessary protest, the time of such bank, as limited by this part or the operating letters of the Federal Reserve banks, or by the applicable law of any State, for taking or completing the action thereby delayed shall be extended for such time after the cause of the delay ceases to operate as shall be necessary to take or complete the action, provided the bank exercises such diligence as the circumstances require.

The bank points out that under § 34–21–403, W.S.1977 (U.C.C. § 4–103), if not under the supremacy clause of the Federal Constitution, the above regulation is controlling law in Wyoming. We agree that the regulation controls but fail to see how it adds anything to § 34–21–408(b) (U.C.C. § 4–108(2)), *supra*. In light of the stipulated facts to be presented immediately below, it appears that either under the statute or the regulation the bank must show that its delay in dishonoring the check was due to circumstances beyond its control and that the bank exercised such diligence as the circumstances required.

THE FACTS

The stipulated facts are quoted below. As we understand the facts, both parties to this suit have acted in good faith and the plaintiff-appellee has made no showing that it was prejudiced by the untimely dishonor of the check. The untimely dishonor of the check was due to delay in delivering checks from a computer center in Billings, Montana, to the bank in Sheridan. Normally, the same courier delivering the checks to the Montana computer center from Sheridan would have driven them back to Sheridan after the center had processed them. However, after the check in issue had been taken to Billings, the main road between Billings and Sheridan became flooded. Although the courier could have taken an alternate route back to Sheridan, the check was instead given to Western Airlines by the computer center to be placed on the next morning's flight to Sheridan. For unknown reasons Western Airlines failed to deliver the check to Sheridan although it made its usual flight. Western Airline's failure to deliver the check to Sheridan as planned caused the bank to miss its Uniform Commercial Code deadline for dishonoring the check.

STIPULATION OF FACTS BY LITIGANTS

The parties, Cabinet Craft Distributors, Inc., a Montana Corporation, and First Wyoming Bank, N. A. Sheridan, Wyoming, a Wyoming Corporation, by and through their undersigned attorneys enter into the following Stipulations and Admission of Facts for the purpose of simplifying the factual issues to expedite the litigation.

I.

The Defendant, First Wyoming Bank, is the payor bank on a check drawn on account 01–209–2 of Quality Kitchens, a division of Flynn's Inc., for Ten Thousand Dollars ($10,000.00). That check is Plaintiff's Exhibit '1' and is dated May 6, 1978. Plaintiff, Cabinet Craft Distributors, Inc., is the payee pursuant to that check. The parties stipulate that said check shall be admitted in evidence as Plaintiff's Exhibit '1' for all purposes.

II.

Plaintiff's Exhibit '1' was delivered to Jerry Franz of of [sic] Cabinet Craft Distributors, Inc., on May 6, 1978, as partial payment for cabinets and other related kitchen ware sold by Cabinet Craft Distributors, Inc., to Quality Kitchens prior to that date.

III.

Plaintiff's Exhibit '1' was then deposited in the account of Cabinet Craft Distributors, Inc., in the Security Bank of Billings on May 8th, 1978. Security Bank as the depository bank then credited the account of Cabinet Craft Distributors, Inc., in the amount of Ten Thousand Dollars ($10,000.00) and proceeded to send the check throught [sic] the bank collection system.

IV.

Plaintiff's Exhibit '1' was mailed from the Denver Federal Reserve Bank on May 20, 1978, to the Defendant, First Wyoming Bank of Sheridan, for payment.

V.

Plaintiff's Exhibit '1' was received by the First Wyoming Bank of Sheridan, at the office of the bank as a cash item for payment on Monday, May 22, 1978, prior to 3:00 o'clock P.M. On May 22, 1978, the check was sent from the First Wyoming Bank Sheridan, to a computer center in Billings, Montana, run by Data Share, Incorporated, which the First Wyoming Bank uses to process its checks in the normal course of business. The check was taken by Jack Burns, an employee of Robert Collins, who contracts for the First Wyoming Bank as a courier to transport checks to the computer center in Billings. The courier would have left Sheridan [at] approximately 6:00 P.M. on May 22 and arrived in Billings between 8 and 10 P.M. The material would have been processed within an hour or two after its arrival in Billings.

VI.

The computer center printed Plaintiff's Exhibit '2' admitted in evidence for all purposes by stipulation of the parties, which Exhibit is entitled 'Unposted Transaction Journal' and dated May 22, 1978.

VII.

In the Unposted Transaction Journal the catagory [sic] for Reason Not Posted was labeled Non Sufficient Funds due to a hold.

VIII.

In the normal course of business the courier would wait at the computer center until the checks have been processed and then return immediately with the checks and a computer print out to Sheridan showing all the checks processed by the computer center. On May 22, 1978, after the courier had gone through toward Billings, the main road between Sheridan, Wyoming and Billings, was closed due to flooding for a period of several days. If the courier had delivered the checks through Lovell, Wyoming, and come across the Big Horn Mountains it would have been possible to have provided the checks to the First Wyoming Bank during the banking day of May 23, 1978.

IX.

Since the courier did not drive back to Sheridan, Wyoming, from Billings, the checks were placed by Data Share, Incorporated on Western Airlines, which was the normal procedure when the courier could not travel or when for computer reasons it took longer to run the checks than the courier could wait. Data Share turned the checks over to Western Airlines on May 22, 1978, to be taken to Sheridan in the early morning run of Western Airlines on May 23, 1978. The Western Airlines flight did leave Billings and did arrive at Sheridan at 8:13 A.M. but no checks were left in Sheridan for the First Wyoming Bank on May 23, 1978. The reason the checks were not delivered is unknown. Western Airlines destroys all records after one year. On May 25, 1978, the employees of First Wyoming Bank were notified by the First Wyoming Bank in Casper, Wyoming, that the checks had been received in Casper and the checks were subsequently placed on Continental Trailways and were received in Sheridan by Ruth Zimdars of the First Wyoming Bank on May 25, 1978. The Plaintiff's Exhibit '1' was posted out marked insufficient funds on May 25, 1978.

X.

On May 25, 1978, First Wyoming Bank President, Everett Cassidy, made the decision to dishonor the check, which is Plaintiff's Exhibit '1'. First Wyoming Bank employee Mary Seibel placed a stamp on the check showing that it was dishonored for insufficient funds.

XI.

Following the dishonor of the check at the First Wyoming Bank on May 25, 1978, the check was returned through the bank collection system through the Security Bank of Billings, which then reversed the credit placed on the account of the Plaintiff as of June 5, 1978. At all times between the receipt of the check on May 6, 1978, and June 5, 1978, the payee Cabinet Craft had no knowledge that there were insufficient funds to cover the check and the payee was at all times acting in good faith.

XII.

That from the 6th of May, 1978, when the check was received to the 16th of May there were not funds in the account of Quality Kitchens sufficient to pay the check. On the 16th of May, 1978, Tim Flynn deposited a check for Twenty-five Thousand Dollars ($25,000.00) in the account, written on an account in the Stockmen's Bank in Gillette, Wyoming, where he did not have Twenty-five Thousand dollars ($25,000.00) on deposit. On May 22, 1978, after a meeting with Everett Cassidy, the President of the First Wyoming Bank, Tim Flynn made known that the Twenty-five Thousand Dollars ($25,000.00) deposit would not be covered by accounts in the Stockmen's Bank in Gillette. Everett Cassidy therefore from that date ordered a hold placed on all of Tim Flynn's accounts and there were not sufficient funds to pay the face amount of Exhibit '1' at any time. The hold was placed on the account on May 22, 1978.

WYOMING CASE LAW

The only Wyoming case discussing § 34–21–451 (U.C.C. § 4–302), *supra*, is *American National Bank of Powell v. Foodbasket*, Wyo., 493

P.2d 403 and 497 P.2d 546 (1972). (The earlier opinion was withdrawn on rehearing.) The case is not particularly relevant since the check payee in *Foodbasket* was not acting in good faith whereas the payee in the instant case is stipulated to have been acting in good faith.[2]

CASE LAW FROM OTHER JURISDICTIONS

Liability under U.C.C. § 4–302

Courts generally interpret U.C.C. § 4–302 (our § 34–21–451), *supra*, as imposing strict liability upon a bank which fails to dishonor a check in time unless the bank meets its burden of proving a valid defense. In *Sun River Cattle Co., Inc. v. Miners Bank of Mont. N.A.*, 164 Mont. 237, 521 P.2d 679, 684 (1974), reh. den., the Montana Supreme Court spoke of U.C.C. § 4–302 as imposing a "standard of strict accountability" and cited the Official Code Comment for the proposition that the bank has the burden of proving an excuse under U.C.C. § 4–108(2) (our § 34–21–408(b)), *supra*. [Citations.] The United States Tenth Circuit Court of Appeals has said that if it is shown that a check has not been dishonored within the Code time limit, a prima facie case is established for imposing liability on the bank and the bank has the obligation of proving an excuse for untimely dishonor under U.C.C. § 4–108(2) (our § 34–21–408(b)), *supra*. *Port City State Bank v. American National Bank, Lawton, Okl.*, 10 Cir., 486 F.2d 196, 198 (1973). The United States Fifth Circuit Court of Appeals recently said, "Failure * * * to perform these duties within the time limits prescribed [by U.C.C. § 4–302] mandates the imposition of strict liability for the face amount of any late instrument. * * *" [Citation.] The Supreme Court of New Mexico has said, "The liability created by [U.C.C. § 4–302 (our § 34–21–451), *supra*] is independent of negligence and is an absolute or strict liability for the full amount of the items which it fails to return. * * *" [Citation.]

Both the Illinois Supreme Court and the Kentucky Court of Appeals have rejected arguments that a bank which fails to timely dishonor a check under U.C.C. § 4–302 (our § 34–21–451), *supra*, is only liable if the delay in the dishonoring of the check injured the check's payee. [Citations.]

* * *

Thus, since there is no issue of bad faith, our examination of appellant bank's claim of a valid excuse under U.C.C. § 4–108(2) (our § 34–21–408(b)), *supra*, does not entail a consideration of the equities involved. Rather our task is simply to determine whether the record demonstrates a sufficient excuse under the above statute.

CASE LAW FROM OTHER JURISDICTIONS

Excuses under U.C.C. § 4–108(2)

It is obvious that the flooded road between Billings and Sheridan which disrupted the normal procedure for delivery of the check was a "circumstance beyond the control of the bank" as contemplated by § 34–21–408(b) (U.C.C. § 4–108(2)), *supra*. Our inquiry is whether the bank used "such diligence as the circumstances required," in allowing the Montana computer center to give the check to Western Airlines for delivery and in not following up the failure of the airline to deliver the packet on schedule. In answering this question we must consider that the stipulated facts show that the bank had an alternative to using Western Airlines: its courier could have taken a different route. We are also somewhat handicapped by a lack of information. For example, although we know that the bank had previously used the airline's delivery service, we do not know what the airline's previous record for timely deliveries had been. We do not know if the computer center in turning the check over to the airline emphasized the need for a timely delivery. We do not know if the bank could have traced the checks which failed to arrive on the Western Airlines flight and gotten them sooner.

We have found no case involving a claimed

---

2. The Montana Supreme Court has said that U.C.C. § 4–302 (our § 34–21–451), *supra*, is modified by U.C.C. § 1–203 (our § 34–21–122, W.S.1977), which states:

> Every contract or duty within this act [§§ 34–21–101 to 34–21–1002] imposes an obligation of good faith in its performance or enforcement.

Sun River Cattle Co., Inc. v. Miners Bank of Mont. N.A., 164 Mont. 237, 521 P.2d 679, 684 (1974); reh. den. Good

faith is defined in U.C.C. § 1–201(19) (our § 34–21–120(a)(xix), W.S.1977) which provides:

> (xix) 'Good faith' means honesty in fact in the conduct or transaction concerned;

Thus, a bad faith check payee may not demand enforcement of U.C.C. § 4–302 (our § 34–21–451), *supra*.

This analysis by the Montana Supreme Court is sound and consistent with our opinion in *Foodbasket, supra*.

U.C.C. § 4–108(2) (our § 34–21–408(b)), *supra*, excuse identical to the one involved here and only a few cases involving somewhat similar excuses. Surveying the area in 1977 the Kentucky Court of Appeals found "only two cases involving the application of U.C.C. § 4–108 to a payor bank's midnight deadline." *Blake v. Woodford Bank & Trust Co.*, Ky.App., 555 S.W.2d 589, 594 (1977). The two cases found by the Kentucky court are *Sun River Cattle Co., supra*, and *Port City State Bank, supra*. We have not been able to discover any cases in addition to the Kentucky, Montana and Tenth Circuit decisions.

The Montana case is, perhaps, most in point. A bank in Butte, Montana, had its checks processed at a computer center in Great Falls, Montana. In the usual course of business the Butte bank's checks were sent by armored car to Great Falls for processing. Ordinarily, the checks would leave Butte at 5:00 or 6:00 p. m. on the day of receipt, arrive at Great Falls about 10:30 p. m., be processed by 11:30 p. m., be loaded back onto the armored car headed for Butte at 4:00 a. m. and arrive back in Butte at 7:00 a. m. *Sun River Cattle Co., supra*, 521 P.2d at 684.

Unfortunately for the Butte bank, it received some checks on May 11, 1970. That day the armored car broke down and did not reach Great Falls until 1:30 a. m. May 12. Moreover, the computer in Great Falls malfunctioned with the result that the checks were not returned to Butte until 2:30 p. m. on May 12, rather than at 7:00 a. m. on that date. The Butte bank's "midnight deadline" for dishonoring the checks was midnight of May 12. *Id.* and U.C.C. § 4–104(1)(h) (our § 34–21–404 (a)(viii)), *supra*. Thus, even though the armored car and computer breakdowns threw the bank off its normal schedule, it would have been physically possible for the bank to have dishonored the checks by midnight of May 12. The bank was unable to offer an explanation for failing to dishonor the checks by midnight of May 12.

The Montana court said:

Under the exception of section 4–108(2) the bank must show: (1) A cause for the delay; (2) that the cause was beyond the control of the bank; and (3) that under the circumstances the bank exercised such diligence as required. *In the absence of any one of these showings, the excuse for the delay will not apply*, and the bank will be held liable under the provisions of section 4–302. * * * (Emphasis added.) 521 P.2d at 686.

Along these lines our appellee urges that we note that there is no evidence in the record that the appellant bank made any efforts to trace the checks when they did not arrive in Sheridan aboard the Western Airlines flight as scheduled. Perhaps a trace started on the missing checks that morning would have enabled the bank to obtain the checks that day and meet the midnight deadline for dishonoring the insufficient-funds check which is the focus of this appeal.

However, although the appellant does not discuss this case, there is a distinguishing feature about *Sun River Cattle* which favors the appellant's cause. In the Montana case the checks in question were drawn on a business greatly indebted to the Butte bank and in precarious financial shape. The Montana court stated that it was holding the Butte bank to a stricter standard of proof under U.C.C. § 4–108(2), *supra*, than would ordinarily be required. [Citation.]

Our appellant bank relies almost solely on the Tenth Circuit case. *Port City State Bank, supra*. In this case the defendant, American National Bank, failed to timely dishonor two checks submitted to it by Port City State Bank. It was stipulated that the midnight deadlines for the two checks were December 1, and December 3. On December 1, American National computerized its operations and the computer broke down on its inauguration day. Despite assurances from the manufacturer that it could be repaired quickly, the computer was not repaired until late at night. When it became apparent that the computer could not be rapidly repaired, American National decided to use an identical computer in a bank some two and a half hours away, under a previous backup arrangement. Processing of checks was begun at 11:30 p. m. on December 1 on the backup bank's computer. Work was proceeding nicely on the backup computer when American National was notified by the computer manufacturer that its own computer was ready. The American National employees returned to their own bank. American National's computer worked for awhile and then broke down on December 2 and was rendered inoperable until a replacement part was installed on December 4. Because of the second failure of its new computer, American National Bank was again forced to utilize its backup arrangement. However, because of the distance between the American Bank and its backup computer, and the need of American to work around the schedule of the bank which owned the backup computer, American got behind in its processing.

The district court held that the cause of the delay in dishonoring the checks was the computer breakdowns, and the Tenth Circuit, applying its usual appellate rules, concluded that the holding was "not clearly erroneous." [Citation.] The Tenth Circuit also found that American reasonably relied on the assurance of the computer manufacturer that the initial malfunction could be repaired quickly; thus, the Tenth Circuit held that the bank was justified in not using the backup computer earlier. [Citation.] Also, the Tenth Circuit accepted the argument that the bank's duty when the emergency became apparent was to remain open and serve its customers as best it could. "To abandon the orderly day by day process of bookkeeping to adopt radical emergency measures would have likely prolonged the delay in returning the bank to normal operations," the court said. [Citation.]

As pointed out earlier, the Tenth Circuit stated in this case that it was the defendant bank's burden to prove an excuse under U.C.C. § 4–108(2) (our § 34–21–408(b)), *supra*. We agree with our appellee in this case that the Tenth Circuit case is readily distinguishable from the case before us. The defendant bank in the Tenth Circuit case proved to the satisfaction of the trial court that it used the diligence required by the above statute and that its failure to timely dishonor the checks was due to circumstances beyond its control—computer breakdowns. The showing of diligence included proof of utilization of a backup system. In the case before us, there is no showing that defendant-appellant bank used any diligence when the packet of checks failed to arrive as scheduled on the flight from Montana.

The Kentucky case involved a failure to timely dishonor two checks. *Blake, supra.* The two checks in this case were presented for payment to the defendant bank on December 24, 1973, so that under the midnight-deadline rule

the bank was responsible for dishonoring the checks by midnight of December 26, December 25, of course, being a bank holiday. [Citation.] Unfortunately for the bank, it did not send notice that it was dishonoring the checks until December 27. In the trial court the bank sought to justify the delay for several reasons. The bank presented evidence that while it normally processes only 4,200 to 4,600 checks a day, it had 6,995 to process on December 26. The bank had four posting machines but two broke down on December 26, one for two and a half hours and one for one and a half hours. Also, one of the four regular bookkeepers was absent on December 26 and had to be replaced by a less proficient substitute. The bank regularly employed a Purolator courier to pick up checks at 4:00 p. m. and take them to the Federal Reserve bank. Because of the above-described problems, the bank did not have the two checks in question processed on December 26 in time for the Purolator courier. [Citation.]

The trial court found these excuses sufficient under U.C.C. § 4–108(2) (our § 34–21–408(b)), *supra*, to relieve the bank of liability under U.C.C. § 4–302 (our § 34–21–451), *supra*. The Kentucky appellate court reversed. The appellate court focused on additional facts. One of the bookkeepers had in fact discovered that there were insufficient funds to pay the two checks on December 26 after the Purolator courier left. However, because of "the lateness of the hour" there was no responsible bank official on the premises and the bookkeeper merely left the two checks on the desk of the bank official who was supposed to handle insufficient funds checks. [Citation.] Thus, the bank did not send out notice that it was dishonoring the check until the next day.

The Kentucky appellate court concluded:

Even though the bank missed returning the two checks by the Purolator courier, it was still possible for the bank to have returned the checks by its midnight deadline. Under UCC § 4–301(4)(b) [footnote] an item is returned when it is 'sent' to the bank's transferor, in this case the Federal Reserve Bank. Under UCC § 1–201(38) [footnote] an item is 'sent' when it is deposited in the mail. [Citation.] Thus, the bank could have returned the two checks before the midnight deadline by the simple procedure of depositing the two checks in the mail, properly addressed to the Cincinnati branch of the Federal Reserve Bank.

This court concludes that circumstances beyond the control of the bank did not prevent it from returning the two checks in question before its midnight deadline on December 26. The circumstances causing the delay in the bookkeeping department were foreseeable. On December 26, the bank actually discovered that the checks were 'bad,' but the responsible employees and officers had left the bank without leaving any instructions to the bookkeepers. The circuit court erred in holding that the bank was excused under § 4–108 from meeting its midnight deadline. The facts found by the circuit court do not support its conclusion that the circumstances in the case were beyond the control of the bank. [Citation.]

The cases discussed above persuade us that the appellant bank has failed to prove an excuse sufficient under § 34–21–408(b) [U.C.C. § 4–108(2)], *supra*, to enable it to escape liability under § 34–21–451 [U.C.C. § 4–302], *supra*, for its failure to dishonor the check in question by the midnight deadline imposed by the U.C.C.

The judgment of the district court is affirmed.

KNIGHTS OF COLUMBUS
6 CLSR 614, 67 Lab.Arb. 334
(Labor Arbitration Reports, June 17, 1976.)

HOLDEN, A.

ISSUES

The parties did not agree upon the issues to be submitted for decision. This case concerns the question of whether the Order violated the Contract when it unilaterally modified the job content of certain jobs.

BACKGROUND

This case concerns the partial transfer of work from principally the Cash Loan and Surrender Department (hereinafter referred to as CLSD) to other Departments at the Order's National Headquarters. Generally speaking, the partial transfer of work involved the taking of work from higher-graded jobs in CLSD and transferring such work to lower-graded

jobs in other Departments. The Union here vigorously questions the right of the Order to make such work transfers.

Originally, the Cash Loan and Surrender Department had a substantial role in the conservation of outstanding insurance. The role principally had been to try to persuade policyholders to borrow against the equity in their policy rather than to surrender the policy for its cash value.

By memorandum dated July 26, 1974 [reference] Virgil Dechant, Supreme Secretary, notified all Department Heads that a Conservation Division was being established in the Agency Department effective August 15, 1974, and that all insurance conservation work was to be consolidated in the Conservation Division under the supervision of Ernest Slomchinski. With regard to the CLSD this meant that all correspondence pertaining to surrender requests was to be first routed through a Conservation Division in another Department—the Agency Department. Conservation was to make the determination that either a policy be surrendered or a loan be issued against the equity in the policy. After such determination was made, the matter then was to go to CLSD for processing which was one of the functions CLSD had previously performed.

In order to establish a Conservation Division in the Agency Department certain jobs in the CLSD were transferred in full to Conservation, and elements of other jobs in CLSD were also assumed by Conservation.

About the same time as the foregoing memorandum issued, the "Nickerson Report" issued. [Reference.] The Nickerson Report pertained to the impact that the introduction of a computerized data processing system (the Life 70 system) was going to have on various jobs at the National Headquarters. Mr. Nickerson made his projections based on the Order's initial experience with a pilot Life 70 program. [Reference.] According to the Nickerson Report, Life 70 would have a minor change on five jobs and a major change on nine jobs in CLSD which were all the jobs in that Department. The major change apparently was that it would result in diminution of certain calculation functions in CLSD since these were going to be done by machine.

While Life 70 resulted in the diminution of

certain job responsibilities in CLSD, it was the establishment of Conservation in Agency that resulted in the total and partial transfer of jobs from CLSD. Out of fourteen bargaining unit employees assigned to CLSD in July 1974, there are now nine remaining.

There is also a further matter that is important to the background on this problem. Many years ago a comprehensive job evaluation study of jobs at the National Headquarters was made. As time went on, this study became outdated, and, consequently, the parties in their 1969 agreement established the mechanics for updating job descriptions and revising job evaluations. The process, however, languished until the conclusion of an eight week strike in December 1973 at which time the updating and revising process began in earnest. Job evaluation guidelines and forms were adopted shortly after the strike settlement. The process of writing job descriptions to reflect job content and of evaluating jobs was completed in general by March 1974. There remained, however, a dispute over the proper evaluation of some twenty jobs, and this dispute was processed to arbitration.

This, then, provides some of the background against which the instant grievance is to be considered.

POSITION OF THE PARTIES

A. Position of the Union

The Union argues that the partial transfer of job duties from one Department to another has the effect of undermining the long, arduous effort made by the parties to arrive at accurate job descriptions and proper job evaluations. This type of job fragmentation, the Union argues, is precluded by Article XIV, Sec. 2 of the Contract which states that "job evaluation of positions within the bargaining unit will become effective and remain in effect during the term of this Agreement in accordance with the guidelines and findings as adopted by the Joint Job Evaluation Committee." The Union further argues that the power to modify the content of job classifications, referred to in Section 2 of Article XIV, does not give the Order an absolute right to make such modifications but gives the Order the right to make only such good faith, minor modifications as operational efficiency requires. The Union hints that the Order's motive for making the job modifications in CLSD stemmed from the Order's reaction to the eight week strike and an arbitrator's decision involving twenty job evaluations.

The Union also claims that Virgil Dechant, Supreme Secretary of the Order, gave assurances to certain CLSD employees that there would be no division of duties in CLSD and that either the entire job would be transferred from CLSD or there would be no transfer at all.

Also, the Union is very concerned about job security and job satisfaction among its members. It is concerned about the demoralizing effect that job fragmentation has had upon the higher-graded employees since such fragmentation has left these employees with less to do and may eventually cause their jobs to vanish.

For remedy, the Union proposes that the Order cease and desist from such job modifications, including, among other things, the parcelling out of job duties, and that, among other things, all work which has been transferred to other jobs be restored to the jobs from which such work was taken.

B. Position of the Order

The Order does not deny that a partial transfer of job duties from CLSD to other Departments has taken place; however, the Order insists that it has the contractual right to make such unilateral job modifications.

The Order cites the language of Article XIV, Sec. 2 which provides that nothing in that section "shall be deemed to limit the Order's discretion in determining the content of the various job classifications, abolishing existing classifications, establishing new classifications, or from time to time modifying the content of any classification. * * *" The Order asserts that this language is clear, unequivocal and unambiguous on its face, and that under the terms of this section it has the sole right to determine job content as business needs require. The order acknowledges that once it has determined job content, the Union has the right to challenge the accuracy of any job description or the propriety of a labor grade assigned to a particular job (job evaluation).

The Order further contends that the Union sought to change the very language quoted above during the last contract negotiations, and that such change was one of the key issues during the eight week strike, but that the Order successfully resisted any such change.

The Order argues that the job modifications in CLSD were made in good faith and in the interest of business economy and efficiency, and that the record of insurance conservation made over the past few years testifies to the soundness of the business judgment that was made.

The Order also points out that with regard to the Union's concern over job security no one has been laid off as a result of the business decisions that have been implemented over the past few years, and that, in fact, the work force has expanded. The Order further points out that even if modifications of job content warranted downgrading certain jobs, the incumbent's wage rate is protected under the Contract by virtue of a red circling provision.

In sum, the Order asks that the Union's grievance be denied.

ANALYSIS

This analysis must begin with examination of the pertinent contract language. Article XIV, Section 2 provides in relevant part as follows:

> Nothing in this section shall be deemed to limit the Order's discretion in determining the content of the various job classifications, abolishing existing classifications, establishing new classifications or from time to time modifying the content of any classification, subject to (i) the Union's right to request evaluation of the new or changed classification by the Joint Job Evaluation Committee and (ii) arbitration in the event of dispute as to the accuracy of the new or changed job description or its evaluation.

It must be said that this language is plain and unequivocal on its face. It specifies that nothing in Section 2 shall limit the Order's discretion in determining job content or modifying job content.

The evidence showed that prior to the 1973 contract renegotiations, the Order made clear to the Union at a Joint Labor Committee meeting that the Order construed this language to mean that it had the unilateral right to modify job content by making partial transfer of work from one job to another.

The evidence also showed that during the 1973 negotiations the Union sought first to

change and later to water down the nature of this particular right.

* * *

The 1973 negotiations resulted in an eight week strike at the conclusion of which a settlement was reached. The evidence was that the authority of the Order to modify unilaterally job content was one of the issues in this eight week strike. This was evidenced by the fact among others that during the strike the Supreme Knight felt obliged to set forth to the striking employees at some length the Order's position on this particular issue. What prompted such major concern on the Union's part over this issue was its knowledge that the Life 70 system, when fully installed, would have a substantial impact on a sizeable number of jobs. The Union, quite naturally, wanted to limit the Order's right to shape and reshape jobs as a result of the conversion to the Life 70 system, and, consequently, it sought to circumscribe the Order's right to change unilaterally job content.

The evidence further showed that the Order successfully resisted all attempts by the Union to change the language as now contained in Article XIV, Section 2. This particular language was first written into the 1969 contract between the parties and has been carried forward unchanged through all succeeding contracts including the present one.

Thus, this record plainly shows that the clear and unambiguous language of Article XIV, Section 2 has existed since the 1969 contract; that the Union knew prior to the 1973 negotiations how the Order intended to apply this language and that circumstances would soon be arising causing such power to be exercised; that the Union sought to restrict the Order's right to modify unilaterally job content and made this one of the 1973 strike issues; and that the Order successfully resisted all attempts by the Union to change this language. Therefore, it can be conclusively found that nothing in Section 2, Article XIV limits the Order's discretion in determining job content or in modifying job content.

Since nothing in Section 2, Article XIV limits the Order's discretion in this regard, does it follow then that the Order has the unbridled right under the Contract to modify job content for any reason it wishes? The Order takes the position that it has the right to modify jobs as business needs require. This was the same position it took during the 1973 strike. Evidence of this is found in the letter dated November 27, 1973 from the Supreme Knight to the striking employees in which the Order explains its position with regard to Article XIV, Section 2 (formerly Article XV) of the Contract.

> The Order feels that these job descriptions will provide the necessary protection to employees, subject to the right which the Order must have to determine the duties of new jobs or to modify the duties of old jobs as business needs require. The purpose of job description is to clarify, for the benefit of employees and the Order alike, exactly what the present duties of each job are.
>
> The Order is quite willing to see that there will be no unauthorized encroachment on the defined duties of any existing position. However, in the interest of efficient operation and as a necessary part of its management responsibilities, the Order will not relinquish or water down its right and duty to determine job content and to abolish, establish or modify classification.

The Union takes several positions here. First, it argues that the setting of a wage rate for each job classification evidences an agreement as to the wages to be paid in exchange for the work customarily performed in a classification, and that the terms of this bargained-for exchange may not be unilaterally altered. Secondly, the Union argues that while the Order does not have an absolute right to modify job content, it does have the right to make reasonable changes when such changes are made in good faith and motivated by the desire to increase the efficiency of its operation. The Union, however, argues that the modifications made here were not prompted by such factors. Also, the Union argues that the Order does not have the right to make major changes in job content but only minor changes.

With regard to the first Union argument concerning no unilateral modification of the bargained-for exchange, I think it is worth quoting from Arbitrator Howard S. Block in *American Cement Corp.*, 48 Lab.Arb. 72, 76 (1967), wherein he said:

> The impact of a changing technology upon the work force has posed problems to both management and labor not easy of solution. That this issue has been a persistent and vexing one over

the years is indicated by the significant number of arbitration proceedings on this subject dating back to the earliest reported decisions. A review of these decisions reveals that they fall into two fairly distinct categories which seem noteworthy here: (1) One line of cases emphasizes that where a Collective Bargaining agreement sets forth a comprehensive rate structure, the wage rate established for each classification evidences an agreement between the parties as to the wage rate, as well as the classification; these cases then go on to provide that, in general, the terms of this bargained for exchange may not be unilaterally altered. To the extent that some of these decisions regard the classification structure as being unalterably frozen during the life of the Agreement, they do not represent the weight of arbitration authority. (2) A second group of cases holds that the existence in the Agreement of a negotiated rate structure does not guarantee that the classifications will remain unchanged during the term of the Agreement. The reason advanced for this interpretation is that economic necessity in a competitive market makes it essential that management have the degree of flexibility necessary to adapt the work force to changed conditions. Where arbitrators have upheld management's right to eliminate jobs or classifications and reallocate residual job duties, they have stressed that such changes must be made in good faith, based upon factors such as a change in operations, technological improvements, substantially diminished production requirements, established past practice, etc. It is this second line of cases which appears to reflect the present weight of authority on this issue.

Next, with regard to the issue of the partial transfer of work from one job or classification to another job or classification, substantial arbitral authority upholds such work transfers where no restriction on such transfers is found in the contract and where such transfers are made in good faith. Arbitrator Prasow in *Reynolds Metals Co.*, 25 Lab.Arb. 44, 48–49 (1955) stated that "(i)t is a well-established principle in industrial arbitration that management has the right, if exercised in good faith, to transfer duties from one classification to another, to change, eliminate or establish new classifications, unless the Agreement specifically restricts this right." [Citations.]

In the case before me I have been shown no contractual restrictions on the right of management to modify job content, and I have, in fact, been referred to language in Article XIV, Sec. 2, together with the history of negotiations concerning such language, which makes it plain that nothing in Section 2 shall be deemed to limit the Order's right to determine or modify job content.

Also, I have found no provision in the contract which commits the Order to making only minor changes in job content. Article XIV, Sec. 2 indicates that nothing in that Section is to prevent the Order from making thoroughgoing changes, such as abolishing or establishing new job classifications, as well as from making partial changes, such as modifying the content of various job classifications. Since that Section specifies no restraint on total change—job abolition—it would be a tortured construction to infer that there is nonetheless some restraint on partial change—i.e., job modification.

Consequently, I find that the Order has the unilateral right to modify job content in a minor or major way so long as the job modification is made in good faith. Certainly, a showing that changes were made for legitimate business reasons is evidence of the good faith nature of the change.

The question then becomes whether the job modifications made here were made in good faith.

With regard to the diminution in duties stemming from the conversion to the Life 70 system, there is no question that the installation and implementation of the Life 70 system was a legitimate business decision made in the interest of efficiency of operation.

With regard to the diminution in duties due to the partial transfer of work from CLSD to Agency, the record showed that as early as March 1, 1973 [reference], there were some problems in the coordination of insurance conservation work between Agency and CLSD. Then came the memorandum dated July 26, 1974 [reference], which formally established a Conservation Division in the Agency Department effective August 15, 1974, and consolidated all conservation work in the Conservation Division under the supervision of Ernest Slomchinski. This consolidation process required work to be transferred to Conservation not only from CLSD but also from Certificate Service. [Reference.] The logic of placing Conservation under Agency was apparently due in part to the fact that the Order used its field staff—its Agents—to assist in the conservation process by making direct

contact with the insured. [Reference.]

The order also presented some statistical data which tended to suggest that the Order had been successful in recent years in not only significantly increasing its insurance in force but also in conserving existing insurance better than it had in the past.

In short, the record indicated that the establishment of a Conservation Division in the Agency Department was supported by legitimate business considerations.

The Union suggests that the Order's motive for modifying jobs in CLSD may have stemmed from the Order's reaction to the eight week strike in 1973 and to an arbitration decision involving twenty job evaluations. The Union, however, in its brief acknowledged that "we may be accused of speculation" in this regard. There was not sufficient evidence in the record to support this hypothesis, and, therefore, I find this argument to lack merit.

The Union further noted that Virgil Dechant, Supreme Secretary, had given certain assurances to certain CLSD employees that there would be no division of duties in CLSD. As part of these assurances, one Union witness cited the memorandum of July 26, 1974. [Reference.] As already described, this memorandum provided for the establishment of a Conservation Division in Agency and for the consolidation of all conservation duties under Conservation. Suffice it to say that under the circumstances in which the remarks construed to be assurances were made here, such remarks cannot without more be elevated to the status of a binding contractual obligation.

The Union has also expressed throughout the hearings in this case deep concern about the demoralizing effect that job fragmentation has had upon the employees remaining in CLSD since such fragmentation has left these employees with less to do and has raised the spector that eventually their jobs may disappear altogether. While one can readily understand and appreciate the deeply-felt concern expressed here concerning loss of work opportunity, one is bound nevertheless to construe the agreement in a manner which reflects what the parties have negotiated.

Moreover, it must be recognized that no business unless it is dying remains static. An organization must have a certain degree of fluidity and dynamism to service the needs of its customers and to meet the challenges of more efficient operation. Arbitral law generally does not recognize that employees have a proprietary interest in the bundle of components that comprise a job unless such has been specifically negotiated by the parties. While no such interest has been negotiated here and while the Order has the right to determine and modify unilaterally job content, the Union has built into the contract a variety of measures to cushion the impact of change. In addition to the job bidding, bumping and layoff procedures, there is also provision for the red circling of an incumbent's wage rate in the event job modification results in a downgrading of the incumbent's job. Also, where jobs change or are newly-established, the Union has the right, where the parties cannot otherwise agree, to arbitrate the accuracy of job descriptions and/or the values assigned to particular jobs (job evaluation). While the severity of the job dislocations in this case cannot be gainsaid, the existence of contractually-specified dampening effects on such change should not be overlooked.

Thus, in sum, I find that the Order has the unilateral right to modify job content in a minor or a major way so long as the job modification is made in good faith. I further find that the establishment of a Conservation Division in Agency and the consolidation of conservation work thereunder was supported by legitimate business considerations. A bad faith transfer of job duties has not been established here.

AWARD

Therefore, after having considered the evidence and arguments of the parties, including their well-argued briefs, I award as follows:

The Order did not violate the Contract when it unilaterally modified the job content of certain jobs. The Union's grievance dated March 24, 1975 is denied.

DESERT PALACE, INC. v. LOCAL JOINT EXECUTIVE BOARD OF LAS VEGAS

679 F.2d 789
(United States Court of Appeals, Ninth Circuit, June 15, 1982.)

SOLOMON, D. J.

Desert Palace, Inc. (the Hotel), which owns and operates Caesars Palace in Las Vegas, brought this action under Section 301 of the Labor Management Relations Act. 29 U.S.C. § 185, to vacate an arbitration award in favor of the Local Joint Executive Board of the Culinary Workers and Bartenders Locals (the Union). The district court entered summary judgment for the Hotel. The Union appealed. We reverse.

I.

The Hotel has a large showroom where it stages two shows a night featuring well-known entertainers. Before May 18, 1978, patrons made show reservations with a Hotel reservations clerk. The charge for the show was the same for each patron, regardless of the seating location. The price of the show included two or three drinks. The patron could order additional drinks at regular Hotel bar prices. At the end of the show, the cocktail server would give the patron a bill that included the charge for the show plus the charge for the extra drinks. Most patrons gave the server a tip. Patrons usually computed their tips based on the total bill, which averaged about $25 a patron.

Some patrons used tickets, coupons, or package prices to pay for the show. When the ticket, coupon, or package price constituted a "special event" as defined in the collective bargaining agreement, the agreement required the Hotel to pay the cocktail server 15 percent of the charge to the general public for the show.

On May 18, 1978, the Hotel adopted a computerized "Ticketron" system. Under the new system, patrons continued to make reservations through the Hotel reservations clerk, but they paid for the show ticket before instead of at the end of the show. The price of the ticket varied with the location of the table. The price of the ticket did not include drinks. The patron could order drinks at $1.00 instead of the $2.00 to $3.50 charge at the Hotel bars. As a result of this change, the bill presented at the end of the show included only the drinks the patron had ordered. There was evidence that the servers who had formerly averaged $78 to $125 a week in tips were now only averaging from $20 to $25 a week.

The Union, under it's collective bargaining agreement, filed a grievance against the Hotel. The agreement provided a grievance and arbitration procedure for a "dispute or difference of opinion between the Union and the Employer involving the meaning, interpretation, application to employees covered by this Agreement, or alleged violation of any provision of this Agreement."

The Union asserted that ticket sales under the Ticketron system were "special events" that entitled the servers to 15% of the price of show tickets. Pursuant to the provisions of the collective bargaining agreement, when the grievance was not resolved by the parties, it was submitted to arbitration.

The dispute in this case centers on the interpretation of sections 18.01 and 18.03(a) of the collective bargaining agreement. Section 18.03(a) provides:

Cocktail servers serving guests included in a special event * * * show in the main showroom shall be guaranteed a minimum gratuity per person served of fifteen percent (15%) of the then current minimum charge to the general public for the second show.

"Special event" is defined in section 18.01 as:

any event for a person, persons, group or groups, arranged by a travel agent, booking agent, hotel sales representative, convention agent, promotional representative, operator or any other individual or agency where tickets, coupons or package prices for food and/or beverages to be served to patrons of such events are involved and where regular employees of an establishment covered by this Agreement provide such service.

The arbitrator found that Ticketron ticket sales were "special events" that entitled the cocktail servers to the guaranteed 15 percent gratuity under section 18.03(a).

The Hotel then petitioned the arbitrator to clarify or modify the method of calculating the amount of the award. The arbitrator denied the petition. The Union threatened to strike to enforce collection of the award. The Hotel then paid the award in full after the Union stipulated that payment would not prejudice the Hotel's rights to seek judicial review. Thereafter the Hotel stopped using Ticketron.

The Hotel filed this action in the district court against the Union to vacate the award. Both parties moved for summary judgment. After a hearing, the court granted the Hotel's motion and vacated the award. The court held that: (1) the arbitrator's interpretation of

"special event" ignored the plain and unambiguous meaning of the contract language; and (2) the arbitrator's calculation of the amount of the award under section 18.03(a) was based on an implausible interpretation of "minimum charge" and constituted punitive damages. [Citation.] The Union appealed.

II.

* * *

The key question is "whether the arbitrator's interpretation could in some rational manner, be derived from the collective bargaining agreement, viewed in light of its language, its content, and any other indicia of the parties' intention." [Citation.] If, on its face, the award "represents a plausible interpretation of the contract in the context of the parties' conduct", judicial inquiry ceases and the award must be affirmed. [Citation.] The correctness of the arbitrator's reasoning and conclusion "is not relevant to a reviewing court so long as the award complies with these standards." [Citation.]

* * *

The district court concluded that the definition of "special event" in section 18.01 plainly did not include Ticketron sales because: (1) Ticketron sales are not "arranged" within the meaning of section 18.01; (2) the price of a Ticketron ticket does not include "food and/or beverages"; and (3) Ticketron sales are not "special."

In our view, all three of these contract terms are ambiguous and the arbitrator's construction of these terms is plausible.

A. "Arranged"

To be a special event under the collective bargaining agreement, the ticket sale must be "arranged by a travel agent, booking agent, hotel sales representative, convention agent, promotional representative, operator or any other individual or agency." Under the Ticketron system, patrons made reservations through the Hotel reservations clerk. Although the Union argued that "any other individual or agency" is broad enough to include a Hotel reservations clerk, the district court disagreed and interpreted "special event" to mean an event arranged by someone other than the Hotel reservations clerk. [Citation.]

The interpretation disregards the fact that be
fore May 18, 1978 the Hotel treated ticketed
show reservations made through the Hotel reservations clerk as "special events."

B.   "Food and/or Beverages"

The district court held that the "special event"
provision in the collective bargaining agreement applied only when the ticket price included the price of beverages or food. [Cita-
tion.] It is uncertain whether the words "for
food and/or beverages" modify the entire phrase
"tickets, coupons or package prices" or whether
they modify only "package prices." The arbitrator concluded that the price of a ticket need
not include the cost of any food or beverage
for the ticket to fall within the definition of
"special event". He therefore held that a special event included a Ticketron ticket even
though the ticket did not include the cost of
cocktails.

The district court rejected this interpretation. It concluded that to constitute a special
event, a ticket must include the cost of food
or beverages and must also be either complimentary or part of a package price. [Citation.]
Because Ticketron tickets did not include
cocktails and were not complimentary, the
court reasoned, they were not special events.

Far from being the only plausible interpretation, the district court's interpretation is
contradicted by the Hotel itself. The Hotel has
consistently argued that complimentary tickets are specifically excluded from the definition of "special events."

The arbitrator's conclusion that tickets for
special events need not entitle the holder to
food or beverages is a plausible interpretation
of the contract and the court may not substitute its interpretation for that of the arbitrator. It is not the district court's function to
choose among the various interpretations of
a contract as long as the arbitrator's interpretation is plausible.

As an alternative ground, the arbitrator
found that even if the food-or-beverage requirement applied to tickets, Ticketron satisfied the requirement because the Hotel offered drinks to showroom patrons for much
less than the regular Hotel bar prices. Hotel
witnesses testified that the price reduction was
to give showroom patrons "something extra
for their money." The arbitrator could reason-

ably conclude that the ticket was partly "for
* * * beverages" within the meaning of section 18.01 because a Ticketron ticket in effect
entitled the holder to a discount on drinks.

C.   "Special"

The Hotel argues that the parties intended
the "special events" procedure to be an exception to the usual showroom billing procedure.
The Hotel contends that even though Ticketron sales may fall within the literal definition of "special event," it is not plausible to
treat as "special" a billing procedure that applies to every member of the general public
who attends a show.

The arbitrator rejected this interpretation.
He ruled that "special" means special to the
employees, not to the patrons. The arbitrator's
interpretation was based on testimony from
union representatives that the protection of
the tipping potential was a key consideration
in the contract negotiations. The Union accepted lower wages in certain job classifications on the understanding that the tipping
potential of the jobs would be preserved and
that whenever the Hotel deprived the server
of the opportunity to present a check for the
full price of the show, drinks, and other services, the Hotel would guarantee the server
a 15% tip. Ticketron sales are "special" because they are exceptions to the server's general expectation of presenting a check that
includes the price of the show.

The district court held the arbitrator had
modified the contract in applying it to an unforeseen situation, the Ticketron system.

As long as a plausible solution is available
within the general framework of the agreement, the arbitrator has the authority to decide what the parties would have agreed on
had they foreseen the particular item in dispute. [Citation.] In such cases, judicial review
is limited to whether the arbitrator's solution
can be rationally derived from some plausible
theory of the general framework or intent of
the agreement.

We hold that the arbitrator's interpretation that Ticketron sales were "special events"
should be sustained.

III.

A.   Punitive Damages

The arbitrator awarded the servers as a group

$1,477,498 for the period May 18, 1978 to March 14, 1979 and from this amount, the regular servers received an average pay of more than $725 a week.[1]

The district court held that the award was punitive because it awarded the servers approximately seven times the amount of tips they received before Ticketron.[2] Generally, the remedy for breach of a collective bargaining agreement is limited to an award of compensatory damages. Ordinarily, an award that exceeds the monetary loss which an injured party suffered as a result of a contract breach is considered punitive. [Citation.]

The district court assumed that for an award to be compensatory, it must be limited to the tips the servers lost as a result of the Hotel's change to the Ticketron system.

This is incorrect. The arbitrator did not decide that the Hotel breached its contract by instituting the Ticketron system. He found that the breach was the Hotel's refusal to apply section 18.03(a) of the contract to Ticketron sales. By awarding the servers 15 percent of all Ticketron ticket sales, the arbitrator merely restored to the servers the tips they lost when the Hotel refused to honor the 15 percent guaranteed tip provision of section 18.03(a) for Ticketron sales. This award was compensatory and not punitive.

B. Minimum Charge

Section 18.03(a) entitles servers to 15% of "the then current minimum charge to the general public for the second show." At the time the contract was written, all the seats in the showroom were priced the same but under Ticketron the charge for each show varied with the location of the seat. The arbitrator held that the parties intended "minimum charge" to mean the price of the show itself as opposed to the price of the show plus extra drinks.

The district court rejected the arbitrator's interpretation and held that the minimum charge for each show must be the price of the least expensive seat for that show and that the arbitrator's interpretation of "minimum" renders the word meaningless. We disagree.

The arbitrator's interpretation followed the Hotel's own practices in computing gratuities for special events. Both the Hotel's catering manager and its food and beverage director were responsible for the Hotel's practices and interpretation of "minimum charge" for a "special event." Even if we disagree with the arbitrator's interpretation, we are bound by it as long as his "interpretation met the test which the courts must apply in exercising the limited function of review in cases arising from labor arbitration." [Citation.]

We believe that the arbitrator's award drew its essence from the contract and that it was a rational and plausible interpretation of the contract viewed in the light of its language and the conduct of the parties.

The judgment of the district court is reversed and the arbitrator's award is reinstated.

NATIONAL LABOR RELATIONS BOARD v. ISLAND TYPOGRAPHERS, INC.

705 F.2d 44

(United States Court of Appeals, Second Circuit, April 6, 1983.)

MESKILL, C. J.

The National Labor Relations Board (Board), petitions pursuant to section 10(e) of the National Labor Relations Act (NLRA or the Act), 29 U.S.C. § 160(e) (1976), for enforcement of its September 9, 1980 order

---

1. The total amount of the loss and the loss to each server was determined by the parties on the basis of a formula which the arbitrator directed them to follow. They took 15% of the gross amount the Hotel received in Ticketron sales and deducted therefrom $5 a day for each server. They then divided the balance based on the number of days each server worked during the relevant period. The Hotel also deducted the 15% gratuities already paid on "special events".

2. The amount of the award was based in part on uncontroverted evidence that the tip income of the servers before Ticketron averaged from $78 to $125 a week. On

a five-day week, the servers received from $15.60 to $25 a night for two shows, or between $7.80 and $12.50 for each show. The uncontroverted evidence also showed that the servers averaged $5 a night, or $2.50 for each show in tips after Ticketron. The price of the tickets is high and the audience is made up of many high rollers, junketeers and vacationers. Most of the tips are paid in cash and the figures testified to were the figures reported by the servers on their federal income tax returns. Apparently, the Hotel had its reasons for not challenging these figures even though the tip income materially affected the size of the award.

against the respondent, Island Typographers, Inc. (Island or the company). The Board found that Island had violated section 8(a)(1) and (5) of the Act by unilaterally deciding to replace its "hot type" typesetting operation with a "cold type" method of production,[1] and by furloughing its linotypists without giving the Long Island Typographical Union No. 915, International Typographical Union (Local 915) notice or an opportunity to bargain. *See* 29 U.S.C. § 158(a)(1), (5) (1976). The Board also found that the company violated section 8(a)(1) and (3) by failing to present proof of a business motivation to justify its decision to lay off union employees while retaining non-union employees. *See* 29 U.S.C. § 158(a)(1), (3) (1976). Island has cross-petitioned to set aside the Board's order. Based upon our review of the record as a whole, we find that the Board's order is not supported by substantial evidence. Therefore, we deny enforcement. [Citations.]

Island Typographers, Inc. is engaged in the manufacture, sale and distribution of typeset proofs and related products. Since the late 1950s, Island, as a member of a typographical industry employers' association, has had a congenial collective bargaining relationship with Local 915, the union that has represented its journeymen linotypists. Indeed, both Island and Local 915 characterize the history of their collective bargaining relationship as amicable and free from major labor dispute.

Against this backdrop of labor tranquility, representatives from the union and industry met on eight separate occasions during August and September of 1976 to negotiate a new labor agreement. During these sessions, spokesmen for the industry expressed concern over competition from nonunion shops that were using a cost-efficient "cold type" process. The employers proposed that they be given the unilateral authority to replace their "hot type" method of production with the new technology. The union took the position that it would meet separately with each employer to discuss the question of technological innovation. The final contract did not address this issue.[2]

Although one industry association represented the eight employers during contract negotiations with the union, the industry custom was for each employer to sign the final contract. Therefore, in November of 1976, Mr. O'Brien, vice-president of Local 915, visited Island's plant to obtain its signature on the new collective bargaining agreement. Mr. Bjornsen, Island's president, stated that he could not afford to pay the contractual wage scale and refused to sign.

On November 13, 1976, about the same time as O'Brien's first visit, the company posted a letter advising its employees that non-union employers were increasingly using "cold type" equipment and, to remain competitive in the industry, it would be necessary for Island to acquire similar machinery. After the first "cold type" equipment was delivered the company provided its employees with a set of instructions and allowed them to practice on these machines during company time and on their own time.

Mr. O'Brien returned to Island's plant during March of 1977 in a renewed effort to con-

---

1. In previous opinions the Board and the courts have often described the "hot type" and "cold type" processes as follows:

> This [hot type process] is a fairly complicated method whereby skilled composing room employees cast lines of type in molten lead, assemble those lines by hand into a complete page and send the page on to the pressroom where the pressmen * * * make up the press plates which actually print the newspaper.
> * * * "Cold type" is a process by which type is prepared by simply pasting printed material on a mat which in turn is photographed in a manner that transfers the image to a metal plate which when exposed to acid is etched into a finished plate ready for the pressroom. The cold type process eliminates the highly complicated linotype procedure. Consequently, it does not require any of the skilled labor necessary to the hot metal process.

[Citations.]
2. Although the 1976-79 collective bargaining agreement did not cover the employers' decision to switch to cold type, it addressed the effect of that decision by providing that

> [i]n the event of the introduction of any new equipment, machinery or process which replaces or serves as a substitute, for, or evolution of any composing equipment now in use all work within the jurisdiction of the Union will be performed by journeymen and apprentices covered by this Agreement regardless of method, equipment or materials used in the performance of the work.

[Reference.] Because of this provision, which would bring cold type workers within the union pay scale, Bjornsen refused to sign the contract.

vince management to sign the contract. Upon arriving at the premises and observing a "cold type" keyboard there, O'Brien again asked Bjornsen to identify the reasons why Island was unwilling to sign the contract. Bjornsen responded that "he couldn't pay the [union] wage scale to people *who were going to be operating a cold type process.*" [Emphasis added.] In fact, according to O'Brien's testimony, Bjornsen feared "a problem could arise in the future and 'he felt that he couldn't sign the contract and then find he couldn't live within the framework of the contract.' " [Reference.]

In the summer of 1977, the company hired the first of several "cold typists" to operate the new equipment and continued through 1978 to hire new employees skilled in the use of the "cold type" equipment. Local 915 made no objections or inquiries with respect to the new employees. Moreover, despite the existence of a union shop clause in both the expired and new collective bargaining agreements, Local 915 never demanded that the new employees join the union. Over the same period, Island increased its acquisition of "cold type" machinery. In May of 1977, Bjornsen formally notified the president of Local 915 that Island was planning to rent two more "cold type" keyboards. At no time did Local 915 object to or request bargaining about the increasing use of this new technology.

Actions undertaken by the union during this period do reveal, however, that it was cognizant of the threat posed by the movement to the "cold type" process. In fact, during May of 1977, Local 915, purportedly reflecting its concern about the "cold type" employees, proposed an amendment to the collective bargaining agreement designed to create a new classification known as "computer typist." The union also proposed separate wages, hours and working conditions for the new title. The proposal did not, however, contain any request for bargaining about Island's acquisition of new technology, or about the linotypists' adaptation to the new methods of production.

At about the same time the union transmitted a "revised proposal" to Bjornsen [footnote], O'Brien visited the Island plant for the third time. At this meeting he discussed with Bjornsen the "type of equipment * * * in the plant" and "the ability to make adjustments." [Reference.] Bjornsen reiterated his position that he could not afford to pay journeymen's wages for work on cold type equipment. The record contains no evidence that Local 915 initiated any further negotiations or requests for bargaining beyond this point.

In September of 1978, Island laid off one journeyman, and subsequently furloughed two additional employees from this job classification. On December 20, 1978, the union filed its first unfair labor practice charge,[4] alleging that Island violated section 8(a)(1) and (5) of the Act by refusing to bargain with the union over the decision and impact of the change in operation from the "hot type" to the "cold type" process, and 8(a)(1) and (3) of the Act by laying off three journeymen because of their union membership. [Citations.] On June 6, 1979, the union filed a second charge alleging that Island furloughed two more journeymen because of their union membership.

The Board adopted most of the ALJ's findings that Island's actions constituted unfair labor practices,[5] but modified her order in light of the finding that the company had not been shown to have "a proclivity to violate the Act." [Citation.] Despite this qualified finding, the Board ordered Island to (1) bargain upon request concerning its decision to eliminate the hot type operation and to lay off union employees, and (2) offer immediate and full reinstatement to its furloughed employees while making them whole for past loss of earnings.

SECTION 8(A)(5)

Under section 8(a)(5) of the Act, it is an unfair labor practice for an employer to refuse to bargain collectively with the representative of his employees. [Citation.] The duty to bargain

---

4. On December 6 the union's president sent a letter to Island complaining about the failure to sign the contract, the laying off of linotypists, and the inability to reach an "agreement to cover the non-union help working within the jurisdiction of the Union." [Reference.] The Board adopted the finding of the ALJ that this letter contained no request for bargaining. [Reference.]

5. The ALJ found that by acceding to Island's payment of differing wages to linotypists and cold typists, the union abandoned its right to represent the cold type employees. The Board reversed this finding and stated that the facts do not support the conclusion that "the Union effectively abandoned its claims to represent the newly hired cold type employees." [Citation.]

is defined by section 8(d) of the Act as the duty "to meet at reasonable times and confer in good faith with respect to wages, hours, and other terms and conditions of employment." [Citation.] If an employer, while engaged in negotiation with the union, unilaterally changes the "conditions of employment," he violates his statutory duty to bargain in good faith. [Citations.] In this case, the Board found that Island violated section 8(a)(5) by unilaterally deciding to update the plant's technology and by laying off union employees as a consequence of that decision.

Even if we were to agree that Island unilaterally changed the "conditions of employment," we need not necessarily find a violation of section 8(a)(5). An employer cannot be held liable for his failure to bargain over changes in "conditions of employment" if "the union has made a 'clear and unmistakable waiver' of its right to bargain on the issue." [Citations.] On this record it is clear that Local 915 waived both its right to object to Island's decision to adopt the new technology and its right to bargain over the effects of this change on the employees.

A. Notice

A union cannot be held to have waived its right to bargain over a change in working conditions unless it has received timely notice of the employer's proposed change. [Citations.] Here the Board found that Island sufficiently notified Local 915 of its initial introduction of "cold type" machinery into the plant, but violated section 8(a)(5) by failing to *further notify* the union of its intention to abandon the "hot type" process and lay off unit employees. We do not agree.

Between 1976 and 1977, Island made no secret of its financial hardship and inability to continue paying high wages to "hot type" linotypists.[6] At the hearing before the ALJ, Mr. O'Brien testified that Local 915 was fully aware of Island's concerns: "We understand

our employers' position—it's a battle of survival." [Reference.] In order to compete more successfully with non-union shops using the "cold type" process, Island had but one choice, namely, to acquire this new cost-efficient technology. Consistent with this strategy, the company posted a notice in November of 1976 informing its employees that Island would be acquiring a "cold type" machine. [Reference.]

This Court has recognized that plant gossip, "conjecture or rumor is not an adequate substitute for an employer's formal notice to a union of a vital change in working conditions. * * *" [Citation.] Here the employer did not rely on innuendo to inform union employees that management intended to rely increasingly on "cold type" machinery. Rather, in November of 1976, Bjornsen posted documents on Island's premises to afford the union notice of management's plan. In May of 1977, Bjornsen notified the president of Local 915 that Island had decided to rent two more cold type keyboards. [Citation.] We find that these actions constituted sufficiently formal notice to apprise the union of the imminent change in the method of production. [Citations.]

In 1977 Island increased its acquisition of cold type machinery and commenced hiring new employees skilled in its operation. [Footnote.] Throughout this period, Island unequivocally stated that it could not afford to pay a linotypist wage scale "to people who [are] going to be operating a cold type process." [Reference.] Consequently, it must have become apparent to Local 915 that competitive pressures were forcing Island to depend increasingly on "cold type" typesetting.

In finding that Island violated section 8(a)(5), the Board simply assumed that the union did not understand the implications of Island's increasing reliance on the new technology. Such a finding is naive at best. In the last thirty years the typographical industry has witnessed a rapid increase in technological innovation. Both the courts and the Board re-

---

6. At the hearing before the ALJ, Mr. O'Brien testified that:

> [T]he competition between the union plants and the non-union plants was very strenuously [sic] and encompassed the majority of the time we negotiated.

* * *

The employers say that the non-union competition

[by using the cold type process] was working for far less rate of wages than our people were. * * * [Reference.] The ALJ found that "[t]he evidence clearly shows that Bjornsen maintained throughout the period beginning with the introduction of the first cold type machine that he would be unable to pay the contractually mandated wages for work on the cold type process." [Citation.]

gard as common knowledge the fact that employers have achieved substantial cost savings by replacing labor intensive methods of "hot type" linotyping with mechanized "cold type" processes. [Citations.] Given this well-known trend, together with Island's persistent protestations of economic hardship and clear intention to incorporate cold type machinery into its productive process, the union must have recognized the inevitable mechanization of the shop. We believe that Island's statements and actions sufficed to notify Local 915 of the new changes in method of production and their impact on union employees.

B. Waiver

After concluding that the union had formal notice of Island's plans to replace "hot type" methods and personnel with the "cold type" processes, we now turn to the question of waiver. The employer's duty to bargain over the updating of its plant encompasses two distinct issues: (1) the duty to bargain over the *decision* to adopt the new technology, and (2) the duty to bargain over the *impact* of that decision on union members.[8] The Board found that Island violated both duties "by its unilateral action in deciding to terminate the hot type method of production and by its unilateral action in laying off its hot type employees." [Citation.] We believe the evidence in the record as a whole shows that the union "clearly

and unmistakably" waived both bargaining rights.

Between 1976 and 1978, Local 915 never requested that Island bargain over its decision to introduce new cold type machinery into the plant or over the increasing importance of this technology in the production process. Indeed, as early as 1976, the union clearly expressed its indifference to the employer's desire to adopt "cold type" machinery. Mr. O'Brien testified that during the 1976 negotiations he had told the employers that they could "[p]ut any equipment you want in. * * * We don't care." [Reference.]

Furthermore, in order to assuage the employer's anxiety over competitive pressures in the industry, Mr. O'Brien stated, "[d]on't worry about it. If any of you folks want to go to the cold type process, we'll modify the contract with you on an individual basis." [Reference.] These statements are susceptible to only one reasonable interpretation. The union waived its right to bargain over Island's decision to modernize its plant through the introduction of "cold type" machinery.

Moreover, by failing to request bargaining over the impact of this change, Local 915 waived its right to bargain over Island's decision to furlough "hot type" employees. Both the Board and this Court have recognized that a union cannot simply ignore its responsibility to initiate bargaining over subjects of concern and thereafter accuse the employer of

---

8. The courts have drawn a distinction between the employer's duty to bargain over a particular business *decision* that affects unit employees and the duty to bargain over the *decision's effects* on unit employees. [Citation.] Although the courts have generally held that the effect of technological innovation on employees is a mandatory subject of bargaining [citation], they have not yet decided the appropriate treatment to accord the employer's decision to innovate. [Citation.]

At oral argument the Court, *sua sponte*, raised the question of whether the Supreme Court's recent decision in *First National Maintenance Corp. v. NLRB,* 452 U.S. 666, 101 S.Ct. 2573, 69 L.Ed.2d 318 (1981), provides the standard for measuring Island's duty to bargain under section 8(a)(5) of the National Labor Relations Act. In *First National Maintenance,* the Court held that an employer has no legal duty under section 8(a)(5) to bargain with the union over the decision to partially terminate its business but must bargain over the effects of such a decision on the employees' job security. In writing for the majority, Justice Blackmun underscored a particular type of managerial decision: "This decision, involving a change in the scope and direction of the enterprise, is akin to the

decision whether to be in business at all, 'not in [itself] primarily about conditions of employment, though the effect of the decision may be necessarily to terminate employment.'" *Id.* at 677, 101 S.Ct. at 2580 (quoting *Fibreboard Paper Products Corp. v. NLRB,* 379 U.S. 203, 223, 85 S.Ct. 398, 409, 13 L.Ed.2d 233 (1964) (Stewart, J., concurring)). The Court devised a balancing test for dealing with this type of managerial decision: "[I]n view of an employer's need for unencumbered decisionmaking, bargaining over management decisions that have a substantial impact on the continued availability of employment should be required only if the benefit, for labor-management relations and the collective-bargaining process, outweighs the burden placed on the conduct of the business." *Id.* at 679, 101 S.Ct. at 2581.

In this case, Island's decision to update the plant's technology fits within Justice Blackmun's special category of managerial decisions. Thus, ordinarily this Court would rely on the balancing test to determine whether Island violated section 8(a)(5) of the Act. However, as we conclude that the union waived its right to bargain over the decision to update this plant, we need not engage in the *First National Maintenance* analysis.

violating its statutory duty to bargain. [Citations.]

* * *

In this case the union knew as early as the summer of 1977 that Island was replacing its hot type linotyping method of production and hiring skilled cold typists to effectuate the change. Local 915 never requested that Island bargain over this significant change in personnel and method of operation. Rather, in May of 1977, the union initiated negotiations that focused solely on the terms and conditions of the new "cold type" employment. These talks, which ended without agreement in June of 1977, constituted the union's only attempt to bargain over the impact of the switch to the cold type method of production.

If the union officers found Island's technological changes to be unacceptable, it was incumbent on them to act diligently to enforce their bargaining rights. Local 915 was fully aware that the employer intended to hire "cold type" employees by the summer of 1977. Despite this knowledge, the union never requested bargaining about the impact of management's decision until December of 1978, when it filed charges against Island. Given this unexplained lapse, we hold that the union waived its right to bargain over the effects of the change in the method of production.

SECTION 8(A)(3)

In addition to section 8(a)(5), the Board found that Island's acts violated section 8(a)(3) of the Act. This section provides in pertinent part:

(a) It shall be an unfair labor practice for an employer—

* * *

(3) by discrimination in regard to hire or tenure of employment or any term or condition of employment to encourage or discourage membership in any labor organization. * * *

[Citation.] To find a violation of section 8(a)(3), the courts have required a showing that the employer's conduct was motivated by anti-union animus. [Citations.] Here, the Board inferred the requisite anti-union animus from Island's failure to provide proof of a business motive for the firing of union employees while retaining nonunion employees.

We believe the Board's inquiry into motivation was premature. As the Supreme Court stated in *Radio Officers' Union v. NLRB,* 347 U.S. 17, 74 S.Ct. 323, 98 L.Ed. 455 (1954):

The language of § 8(a)(3) is not ambiguous. The unfair labor practice is for an employer to encourage or discourage [union] membership by means of discrimination. Thus this section does not outlaw all encouragement or discouragement of membership in labor organizations; only such as is accomplished by discrimination is prohibited. Nor does this section outlaw discrimination in employment as such; *only such discrimination as encourages or discourages membership in a labor organization is proscribed.* [Emphasis added.]

[Citations.] Moreover, this Court has expressly stated that "it is patent that no inquiry into motivation is necessary unless that conduct is first found to have encouraged or discouraged union membership." [Citation.]

The record indicates that it was the union's failure to organize the "cold type" employees that "discouraged" union membership, *not* the employer's change in its method of production. Both the expired 1973-76 collective bargaining agreement and the proposed 1976-79 agreement contained "union shop" clauses which provided that:

All present employees who are not members of the local Union * * * shall on and after the 31st day following the beginning of their employment or on and after the 31st day following the effective or execution date of this Agreement, whichever is the later, shall become and remain members in good standing of the local Union as a condition of employment.

[Reference.] Consequently, in the summer of 1977, when the cold typists were first hired, the union could have mandated that they join the union. However, Local 915 made no attempt to invoke the union shop agreement. Instead, the union waited for approximately one year and then merely "suggested" that the employees voluntarily join the union. At that time, the union vice-president approached three cold typists and invited them to sign "authorization cards" designating Local 915 as their collective bargaining representative. The employees declined the invitation. The record contains no evidence of any subsequent attempts by the union to include the cold type employees among the ranks of its active members. Given the union's whole-sale failure to invoke the union shop clauses, Local 915 cannot now place the blame on the employer as the party responsible for dis-couraging union membership. It is clear from this record that journeymen were furloughed for a business motive, namely because they were "hot type" operators, not because they were union members.

Moreover, after reviewing this record, we find no substantial evidence of anti-union animus sufficient to support a finding of a section 8(a)(3) violation.[9] The Board expressly found that "it has not been shown that the Respondent has a proclivity to violate the Act or has engaged in such egregious or wide-spread misconduct as to demonstrate a general disregard for employees' fundamental statutory rights." [Citation.] The employer's actions here are consistent with this general pattern; the record shows that Island's deci-sion to shift its mode of production to the "cold type" process was motivated by economic ne-cessity, not by anti-union animus. There is not substantial evidence in the record as a whole to support the Board's finding that Is-land violated section 8(a)(3). [Footnote.]

Accordingly, we deny enforcement of the Board's order.

CAGLE v. BOYLE MORTGAGE CO.

261 Ark. 437, 549 S.W.2d 474
(*Supreme Court of Arkansas, En Banc, Feb. 14, 1977.*)

HOLT, J.

In this foreclosure action brought by the appellee, the appellants interposed the de-fense of usury. The chancellor found the

transaction between the parties was free of usury and, therefore, appellee was entitled to foreclosure. We must agree with appellants' contention that the court erred in so finding.

In December, 1973, the appellants signed a construction note and mortgage in the amount of $28,000, bearing 10% interest per annum, in favor of appellee for the purpose of financing the construction of a residence. Ad-vances or "draws" totaling $22,180 were made from February, 1974, through September, 1974. Subsequently, appellants sought to can-cel the note and mortgage in the local federal court on the basis of usury. Appellee answered and then brought this action in the state court alleging that, despite demand for payment, the balance of $22,180 was due plus interest in the amount of $2,715.81, which represents the legal rate of interest. Appellants defended on the basis that the note and mortgage were usurious since the monthly statements, fol-lowing advances on the loan, showed that ap-pellee had compounded the interest monthly which resulted in exeeding the legal rate of 10% per annum simple interest. Further, the monthly statements reflected that appellee charged a daily rate of interest which also resulted in exceeding the legal rate of inter-est. Admittedly, the note and mortgage are not usurious on their face. No payment was ever made on the indebtedness.

Appellee is a Tennessee corporation which operates in Arkansas and Mississippi with corporate offices in Memphis. Its Arkansas manager, who negotiated the loan with ap-pellants, testified there was never any inten-tion to charge any interest on the loan in ex-cess of the legal rate of interest. Appellant Lloyd Cagle responded by exhibits to his tes-timony which show that the appellee mailed computerized monthly statements to him from its Memphis office. These exhibits on their face show, according to the balance and in-

---

9. In citing the Supreme Court's decision in *NLRB v. Great Dane Trailers, Inc.*, 388 U.S. 26, 87 S.Ct. 1792, 18 L.Ed.2d 1027 (1967), the Board contends that no proof of anti-union motivation is needed to find a section 8(a)(3) violation "if it can reasonably be concluded that the em-ployer's discriminatory conduct was 'inherently destruc-tive' of important employee rights." [Citation.] Here the Board concluded that Island's "inherently destructive" conduct could be inferred from its failure to show a busi-ness motive for the firing of union linotypists while re-taining non-union cold typists. We disagree.

This Court has often recognized that section 8(a)(3) is not violated if the employer can show that legitimate business considerations motivated its "discriminatory" actions. [Citations.] We believe the record contains abun-dant evidence that the competitve pressure of the typo-graphical industry forced Island to rely exclusively on "cold type" machinery and therefore to employ only "cold type" operators. [Citation.]

terest due, that a usurious rate of interest was being charged. It appears from appellants' computation that these exhibits reflect a compounding of interest which yields 10.4712% interest per annum. The exhibits further reflect that by the use of a daily interest factor based on a 360 day year times 365 produces an annual interest rate of 10.139% interest per annum. It appears that when both of these methods are used together it produces a simple interest rate of 10.6235296% per annum. Appellant Cagle testified that he "suspected" a usurious rate was being charged and complained to the Arkansas manager, who replied that he "had nothing to do" with computing the interest and "it all came out of Memphis." The appellee's manager testified that these computer print-outs were inaccurate and eventually he notified the Memphis office to discontinue them. It appears that this occurred about the time these parties were involved in litigation in federal court which, as stated, preceded briefly this state action. He admitted the print-outs computed the interest monthly and the computer was programmed to compound interest on all notes whether in Arkansas or Tennessee. He could not say whether the interest was computed on a monthly or daily basis. It appears undisputed that in a companion transaction the appellee collected a note secured by a mortgage from appellants based upon a computerized monthly statement as here.

Appellee argues that the requisite intent to collect a usurious rate of interest is not shown since the note on its face recites a valid rate of interest, no payment was ever made and the computer print-outs were erroneous. We are not convinced by this argument. There is a "conclusive legal presumption that, in the absence of fraud or mutual mistake, the lender is presumed to know the consequences of its adding an illegally excessive charge." [Citation.] Here there is no evidence of fraud presented and although a mistake in the computer print-out is asserted, it is certainly not a mutual mistake of the parties. We have also said that mere errors in mathematical calculations are not necessarily forgiven, thereby removing the taint of usury. [Citations.]

Here it is also argued that the lender merely made a mistake of facts as to the calculations of interest and since the action is not based on a usurious rate of interest, the note and mortgage should be enforced according to its provisions. We are not persuaded by this argument. *Brooks v. Burgess,* 228 Ark. 150, 306 S.W.2d 104 (1957). There we reiterated:

> It is not necessary for both parties to intend that an unlawful rate of interest shall be charged, but if the lender alone charges or receives more than is lawful, the contract is void.

Here the lender's monthly statements showed a computation of interest above the legal rate of interest. It appears it was not until litigation ensued that the appellee sought to collect its loan free of usury. We are not convinced that appellee's monthly statements were mere mathematical errors in calculations. It is significant that, in a companion transaction with the appellants, the appellee made a loan to them and collected the principal and interest on monthly computerized statements as here. We must hold that the evidence is clear and convincing that the transaction was usurious.

Reversed and remanded for entry of a decree cancelling the note and mortgage.

GLEN EDEN HOSPITAL, INC. v. BLUE CROSS AND BLUE SHIELD OF MICHIGAN

555 F. Supp. 337
(United States District Court, E.D. Michigan, S.D., Jan. 21, 1983.)

GILMORE, D. J.

This is an action by plaintiff alleging that defendant Blue Cross has engaged in anticompetitive activities in violation of Sections 1 and 2 of the Sherman Act, 15 U.S.C. § 1 and § 2. The complaint also includes two pendant state claims alleging a violation of the Michigan Antitrust Law and breach of contract.

Defendant has moved for summary judgment on all counts. For the reasons given below, the motion for summary judgment is granted.

I

Defendant Blue Cross and Blue Shield ("Blue Cross") provides health benefits to individuals ("subscribers") by contracting with hospitals ("providers"). The providers agree to furnish health care services to subscribers in return for direct reimbursement paid by defendant. Hospitals that enter into such contracts are "participating hospitals" and the contract between the provider and Blue Cross is called the "Participating Hospital Agreement." Under this agreement, hospitals are reimbursed for all their reasonable costs, plus an additional 2%. This reimbursement formula has been in effect since 1948.

Plaintiff Glen Eden is a private for-profit psychiatric hospital. Until 1973, Michigan law prohibited Blue Cross from entering into participation agreements with for-profit hospitals such as Glen Eden. [Footnote.]

In 1967, Blue Cross created a special reimbursement mechanism for profit-making hospitals by offering an addendum to its subscriber hospitalization contracts. This addendum, known as the "Non-Participating Psychiatric Hospital" ("NPPH") Rider, provided that, if a subscriber was admitted to a for-profit psychiatric hospital, Blue Cross would pay the hospital's reasonable and customary charge, not to exceed the average per diem payment to participating hospitals.

On December 5, 1969, Glen Eden entered into a contract with Blue Cross, pursuant to the NPPH rider, agreeing to furnish psychiatric care to subscribers covered by the rider in exchange for Blue Cross's agreement to reimburse it for its reasonable and customary charges. The payments to Glen Eden could not exceed the average per diem payment to hospitals operating under the Participating Hospital Agreement. The agreement also provided that either party could terminate the contract on 30 days' notice.

In February 1979, Blue Cross informed Glen Eden that it was terminating the 1969 contract and that Glen Eden could apply for participating hospital status. In its letter of termination, Blue Cross stated that it was terminating the contract because the amended state law would now allow Glen Eden to become a participating hospital, although it did not explain why it waited six years after the

state law was amended to change the contract. [Footnote.]

Glen Eden thereupon filed a suit in Michigan Circuit Court alleging breach of contract. This suit was settled, and by its terms the settlement agreement operated as Glen Eden's application for participating hospital status. The agreement further provided for an interim period of reimbursement which was to extend until June 30, 1980, unless Glen Eden's application as a participating hospital was accepted earlier. Although Blue Cross accepted Glen Eden as a participating hospital on March 26, 1980, Glen Eden refused to sign the Participating Hospital Agreement.[3]

On June 10, 1980, plaintiff commenced this lawsuit alleging that defendant had engaged in a conspiracy to restrain trade in violation of Section 1 of the Sherman Act, 15 U.S.C. § 1, and had conspired to monopolize, attempted to monopolize, and engaged in the unlawful exercise of monopoly power in violation of § 2 of the Sherman Act, 15 U.S.C. § 2.

Count I of the complaint alleges that defendant, acting in concert with co-conspirator hospitals,[4] established and maintained a non-competitive reimbursement mechanism, and used coercion and threats of boycott or refusals to deal to force plaintiff (and other hospitals) to accept the reimbursement system. Plaintiff claims that Blue Cross unlawfully refused to deal with it by terminating the 1969 contract and refusing reimbursement unless it accepted the Participating Hospital Agreement. Plaintiff also alleges that an unlawful refusal to deal was manifested by defendant's refusal to reimburse plaintiff on an experimental basis or to permit plaintiff to have access to defendant's computer. The final contention is that there was an unlawful refusal to deal when defendant declined to approve plaintiff's proposed new facility located in Troy, Michigan.

Count II of the complaint alleges that defendant has attempted and conspired to monopolize, and does monopolize, the health care

---

3. The Court notes here that Glen Eden signed the Participating Hospital Agreement on October 31, 1980, after this Court denied plaintiff's motion for a preliminary injunction. Thus, Glen Eden has been and presently is operating under the "cost plus 2%" reimbursement formula that is applied to all participating hospitals.

4. The complaint does not name any co-conspirators as defendants; however, the plaintiff alleges that other hospitals in competition with plaintiff are among the co-conspirators. [Reference.]

industry in Michigan in violation of Section 2 of the Sherman Act. Here plaintiff claims that defendant has abused this monopoly power and attempted to acquire monopoly power by engaging in refusals to deal, boycotts, and by fixing a non-competitive reimbursement scheme. It is also claimed that defendant has prevented expansion of competing hospitals.

Count III alleges that, as a result of all the above-mentioned activity, defendant has restrained trade in violation of the Michigan anti-trust law, M.C.L.A. § 445.701. Count IV alleges that defendant breached the 1969 contract by failing to properly reimburse plaintiff while that contract remained in effect.

The matter is before the Court upon defendant's motion for summary judgment on all counts. Defendant contends that there is no violation of Section 1 because plaintiff cannot prove the existence of the requisite conspiracy and because there was never any boycott or refusal to deal. Defendant also argues that there can be no Section 2 violation because Blue Cross is not a monopoly and because Blue Cross did not unlawfully exercise or attempt to acquire monopoly power. If Counts I and II are dismissed, Counts III and IV must fall because they are pendant state claims.

II

Section 1 of the Sherman Act prohibits every contract, combination, or conspiracy in restraint of trade. To establish a violation of Section 1, plaintiff must show that there was some kind of concerted action and that this action restrained trade. Defendant contends that plaintiff has not and cannot produce any evidence of a conspiracy of any kind.

The crux of plaintiff's Section 1 claim is that a conspiracy in violation of the Sherman Act exists by virtue of the relationship between Blue Cross and the participating hospitals. Plaintiff contends that Blue Cross's reimbursement policies are controlled by the large participating hospitals and that these hospitals have collectively established a non-competitive reimbursement system. Plaintiff claims defendant has used coercion or boycott to force plaintiff to agree to that reimbursement system.

Plaintiff claims that the acts of defendant violate the antitrust laws under both a *per se* analysis and under the rule of reason. This

Court has previously declined to analyze the case under a *per se* approach. There is nothing in the structure of the reimbursement mechanism discussed below which would justify a finding of a *per se* violation of the Sherman Act. Further, courts that have addressed antitrust complaints involving participation agreements such as this have almost uniformly applied a rule of reason analysis. [Citation.] Therefore, this Court will address this case under the rule of reason. * * *

* * *

In addition to its theory of hospital control of reimbursement policies, Glen Eden advances other theories to support its argument that the requisite conspiracy exists. Glen Eden contends that Blue Cross's termination of the 1969 contract for the purpose of requiring adherence to a price-fixing scheme and its subsequent imposition of the Participating Hospital Agreement provide the necessary contract, combination, or conspiracy. In effect, Glen Eden is alleging that the provider agreement itself can be viewed as a sort of vertical restraint.

Plaintiff relies on *Albrecht v. The Herald Co.*, 390 U.S. 145, 88 S.Ct. 869, 19 L.Ed.2d 998 (1968) for the proposition that an illegal combination was formed when Glen Eden was forced to sign the allegedly illegal Participating Hospital Agreement. *Albrecht* involved an agreement to set the resale price at which goods would be resold to a third party. The plaintiff, a newspaper carrier for defendant Herald, alleged a combination to fix the price charged to customers. The Court in *Albrecht* found that defendant Herald and two other parties had combined to force the plaintiff to conform to the resale price. In a footnote, the court stated that the plaintiff could have claimed a combination between the Herald and himself as of the day he complied with the suggested price.

The Court does not feel that *Albrecht* controls the instant case. *Albrecht* requires more than a unilateral setting of a price or reimbursement formula between a buyer and a seller. It requires some coercive activity or some collaboration with others. [Citation.]

Plaintiff has not suggested any coercive activity that could bring this case within the scope of *Albrecht*. The denial of computer services cannot be characterized as activity to coerce compliance with the allegedly anti-competitive agreement. The computer service is only available to providers that have signed the Participating Hospital Agreement. There is no reason why those services should have been available to Glen Eden before it became a participating hospital. Nor can Blue Cross's refusal to approve plaintiff's proposed new Troy hospital be characterized as the type of coercion necessary under *Albrecht*. Blue Cross has presented deposition testimony that the refusal to certify the Troy facility was based on a mathematical determination of the number of hospital beds in that area. The plaintiff has not produced any evidence refuting that explanation.

Nor has plaintiff been able to point to any collaboration that would bring this case within the *Albrecht* rule. Plaintiff cannot allege that Blue Cross collaborated with its member hospitals unless plaintiff can prevail in its claim that the hospitals really control Blue Cross's action, or that Blue Cross conspired with hospitals to impose this contract on Glen Eden. In a deposition, Mr. Kehoe, Blue Cross Vice-President for Provider Affairs, states that Blue Cross did not consult with anyone when it decided to terminate the 1969 contract and implement the Participating Hospital Agreement. Further, Blue Cross has reviewed all of the minutes of meetings from January 1, 1978 through April 25, 1980 of Blue Cross bodies containing hospital representatives. Glen Eden was discussed only twice during this period. On March 6, 1980, the Hospital Relations Committee voted to recommend Glen Eden for participating status. On March 20, 1980, the Board of Directors approved this application. [Footnote.] Thus, submits defendant, there was no collaboration with hospitals to force plaintiff to sign the Participating Hospital Agreement. Plaintiff has submitted no affidavit or deposition testimony refuting defendant's statements. Therefore, the Court must find that Blue Cross's termination of the 1969 contract and insistance that plaintiff adhere to the terms of the Participating Hospital Agreement were unilateral actions by defendant.

A review of the relevant case law reveals that several courts have considered the legality of provider agreements similar to the one at issue here. The courts have uniformly decided that, absent proof of some boycott or price fixing conspiracy, agreements determining the amount of reimbursement for the provider of services do not constitute vertical restraints of trade under either the rule of reason or a *per se* analysis. [Citations.]

* * *

Therefore, for the reasons given, the motion for summary judgment of dismissal as to Count I of the complaint will be granted.

III

To establish the offense of monopolization under Section 2 of the Sherman Act, plaintiff must show 1) the possession of monopoly power in the relevant market, *and* 2) "the willful acquisition or maintenance of that power as distinguished from growth or development as a consequence of superior product, business acumen, or historic accident". [Citations.]

Glen Eden asserts that Blue Cross possesses monopoly power because it controls approximately 70% of the health care market for eastern Michigan and 64% of the market for the entire State. Blue Cross disputes this definition of the relevant market and contends that the relevant market is defined by hospital revenues derived from Blue Cross. It states that, since only 33% of all hospital patient days are paid for by Blue Cross, there is no monopoly. Glen Eden has conceded the correctness of the 33% figure in its reply memorandum in support of its preliminary injunction motion, where it said, on page 55, "Whereas an average of only 33% of total patients at other participating hospitals are covered by Blue Cross, at Glen Eden the Blue Cross patients constitute 88% of the total."

This Court cannot determine the relevant market in this case based on the unsupported statements of the parties. There has been no clear expert evidence regarding the relevant market, nor any evidence defining the relationship between the health care insurance market and the market for psychiatric services. Nevertheless, plaintiff's claim of monopolization must fail because, even though the relevant market cannot be defined, there is no showing of unlawful acquisition and exercise of monopoly power, if indeed it does exist.

Glen Eden contends that Blue Cross abused its monopoly power by engaging in threats and boycott activities to induce Glen Eden to sign the Participating Hospital Agreement; by refusing to provide access to the computer; and by refusing to participate in the proposed new Troy facility. This Court has already determined that these activities did not amount to a boycott or refusal to deal.

Blue Cross has offered to deal with Glen Eden on the same terms as all other participating hospitals, and since Glen Eden signed and agreed to the Participating Hospital Agreement on October 31, 1980, Blue Cross has in fact been dealing with Glen Eden. Indeed, in its ruling on the motion for preliminary injunction, this Court found that the refusal of Blue Cross to give Glen Eden special treatment did not "suffice as evidence of an attempt to monopolize or eliminate [Glen Eden] from business. * * *" [Reference.]

The antitrust laws do not require a monopolist to accede to each and every demand of its competitors or customers. [Citations.] As the Court noted in *Daily Press Inc. v. United Press International,* 412 F.2d 126, 135 (6th Cir.1969), *cert. den.* 396 U.S. 990, 90 S.Ct. 480, 24 L.Ed.2d 453 (1969):

> As we pointed out before, our case does not even involve a refusal to deal with plaintiff. UPI was willing to deal with plaintiff on the same basis as its other contract customers. Plaintiff * * * wanted a special deal. Failure of UPI to give plaintiff a special deal * * * did not operate to create or attempt to create a monopoly.

Further, a monopolist may lawfully refuse to deal so long as the refusal is unilateral and does not extend or maintain the monopolist's market power. *Official Airline Guides Inc. v. F.T.C.,* 630 F.2d 920 (2d Cir.1980), *cert. den.* 450 U.S. 917, 101 S.Ct. 1362, 67 L.Ed.2d 343 (1981). In *Official Airline Guides,* the Court held that a monopolist publisher of airline guides could arbitrarily exclude certain airlines from its guide. While recognizing that the publisher's refusal to deal adversely affected the excluded airlines, the Second Circuit found the conduct to be lawful because the publisher did not compete in the airlines field and thus the publisher's refusal to deal in no way enhanced its monopoly power. The dealings of Blue Cross with Glen Eden here

in no way extended or enhanced Blue Cross's purported monopoly power. It is not an actual or potential competitor of Glen Eden, so its failure to give Glen Eden a special deal did not affect its market position in any way.

It therefore is clear that Blue Cross has not unlawfully exercised its purported monopoly power with Glen Eden since Blue Cross has offered to do business with Glen Eden on the same terms as with virtually all other hospitals. It is also clear that Blue Cross's actions with respect to Glen Eden in no way enhanced Blue Cross's purported monopoly power.

Glen Eden also claims that Blue Cross has abused its monopoly power through its involvement with member hospitals in setting pricing policies. It is not clear exactly what plaintiff is claiming. It seems to be arguing that a Section 2 violation exists because it is unlawful for a monopolist to use its monopoly power in one market to destroy competition in another. This position is only tenable if there is some link between Blue Cross and the market for psychiatric services. Thus, Glen Eden can only maintain this claim if it can prove that Blue Cross conspired with, or is in fact controlled by, its member hospitals and that these actions have the purpose or effect of affecting competition in the market for psychiatric services. Since this Court has already ruled that the hospitals' power to veto changes in reimbursement policy does not evidence hospital control of Blue Cross, this claim cannot prevail.

Therefore, for all of the reasons given, it appears that there is no basis for this case to proceed on the monopolization claim under Section 2. Therefore, the motion for summary judgment of dismissal as to Count II of the complaint will be granted.

* * *

SIROTA v. SOLITRON DEVICES, INC.
673 F.2d 566
(United States Court of Appeals, Second Circuit, Feb. 19, 1982.)

OAKES, C. J.

This securities class action was tried on the theory that Solitron Devices, Inc. (Solitron), and certain of its officers, aided and abetted by its accountants, Louis Sternbach & Co. (Sternbach), intentionally issued annual reports and financial statements containing materially false misrepresentations of the company's sales, income, and inventories. The plaintiff class, purchasers of Solitron shares on the public market (the American Stock Exchange), received a general verdict and favorable answers to special interrogatories from a jury in the United States District Court for the Southern District of New York, before Charles L. Brieant, Jr., Judge.

* * *

I. FACTS

Solitron, a manufacturer of electronic semiconductors, was subject by virtue of its contracts with the United States government to the Renegotiation Act of 1951, as amended, 50 U.S.C.App. §§ 1211-1233. In 1972 the Eastern Regional branch of the United States Renegotiation Board, which enforces the Act's limits on profits from government contracts, determined that Solitron had realized renegotiable profits of $3.2 million in fiscal year 1967 and $4.4 million in fiscal year 1968.

Solitron, seeking administrative review of the Board's assessment, retained Price Waterhouse & Co. to reexamine its financial statements for 1967 through 1970. Price Waterhouse concluded that those statements, prepared and certified by Sternbach and signed by Benjamin Friedman, Solitron's chief executive officer and largest shareholder, had substantially overstated inventories and sales. In 1973 and 1974 Solitron, seeking to avoid liability for excess profits, disclosed these over-statements to the Renegotiation Board in letters prepared by James S. Trager, a former Sternbach accountant who was then Solitron's assistant treasurer, and James P. Barry, then Solitron's treasurer. In January 1975 the Renegotiation Board issued a final determination that Solitron owed $3.9 million in excess profits from 1967 to 1970, which Solitron is contesting before the Court of Claims. In March 1975 the Securities and Exchange Commission (SEC) brought an action against Solitron for violations of the securities laws, but withdrew the charges the next month pending an investigation by special SEC

counsel, who concluded in June 1978 that Solitron had overstated income, but had not done so fraudulently.

Named plaintiffs Howard Sirota (who purchased Solitron shares on June 1, 1971) and Family Restorations (who purchased Solitron shares on April 7, 1971) filed the instant action in March 1975. They contended that the misrepresentations of fact in the company's 1967-70 financial statements that were revealed in the proceedings before the Renegotiation Board demonstrated that defendants Solitron, Friedman, Trager, Barry, and Sternbach had violated section 10(b) of the Securities Exchange Act of 1934, 15 U.S.C. § 78j, and Rule 10b-5 promulgated thereunder, 17 C.F.R. § 240.10b-5. They complained that inventories had been overstated while consignments had been improperly treated as sales, and that Solitron had failed to provide any reserve for probable refunds to the government of renegotiated profits. Their complaint was consolidated with others against Solitron in February 1976.

* * *

II. DISCUSSION

* * *

B.   Sufficiency of the Evidence

1. Fraud by the Solitron Defendants, 1967-70. The Solitron defendants also appeal from the district court's decision not to set aside the jury's verdict that in the company's financial statements for 1967, 1968, and 1970 they knowingly and materially misrepresented inventories and characterized certain consignments as sales. As the court properly noted, judgment notwithstanding the verdict may be entered only if the evidence, viewed in the light most favorable to the non-movants without considering credibility or weight, reasonably permits only a conclusion in the movants' favor. [Citation.]

a. Inventory Overstatements. It is undisputed that the financial statements for the fiscal years ending 1967, 1968, and 1970 materially overstated inventory. The Solitron defendants argue collectively, however, as they did below to the jury and the court, that the inventory recosting that demonstrated the substantial overstatements was not even possible until Solitron had acquired for the first time a computer capability and a sophisticated inventory costing system based upon newly developed time-and-motion studies recommended by Price Waterhouse in 1972, some two years after the misstatements. They therefore argue that the evidence was insufficient to show scienter, *i.e.,* that there was either actual knowledge of the misrepresentations or a reckless disregard for the representations' truth or falsity. [Citations.]

We agree with Judge Brieant's post-verdict assessment that there was sufficient evidence of scienter on the part of the company and the individual defendants to sustain the jury verdict against the Solitron defendants for 1967, 1968, and 1970. The jury could properly infer intent from subsequent admissions of misrepresentations, coupled with the defendants' continuous intimate knowledge of company affairs. Solitron benefited from overstating its inventory. From 1966 through 1970 its reported earnings per share surged upward 100%, 50%, 33⅓, and 20% respectively. The price of the stock followed the reported earnings, enabling Solitron to make numerous acquisitions [footnote] after a five-for-one split in April 1968. There was direct evidence that Friedman as well as Trager knew that inventory had increased from $1.5 million in 1966 to $2.94 million in 1967, while the inventory-turnover rate declined from 6 times a year to 4.5 times a year; that inventory had increased nearly $5 million in 1968, reducing inventory turnover to less than 2.5 times per year; and that in 1970 inventory had increased by nearly $4 million to $12.5 million, with a turnover rate of only 1.9. The Solitron defendants admitted such overstatements of inventory to the Renegotiation Board in 1974.

There was also direct evidence that accounting procedures at the Riviera Beach, Florida plant, where Solitron carried on its government business, were inadequate to cost inventory accurately. As Barry stated in a letter to renegotiation counsel, the accounting department was "understaffed" and "poorly managed," in keeping with the company's policy at that time: "get the shipment out the back door, get the invoice in the mail to the customer, operate with a minimum overhead, and profits will be generated." Inability to cost

certain "highly reliable" and commercial inventory resulted in overstatements in 1967 of $556,000, in 1968 of $1.35 million, and in 1969 of $904,000: there were also raw-material and piece-part costing and other errors of lesser magnitude. Mathematical calculation and addition errors in the year 1968 amounted to $1.05 million.

* * *

Without the overstatements, not only would the earnings per share have been less during the years 1966 through 1970, but the gradient of earnings growth would have been flatter. Indeed in 1970 there would have been a decline in earnings. There was expert testimony before the jury about the effect that the overstatement of earnings and the gradient of earnings growth have on stock prices generally. Overall, we believe there was substantial evidence to support the jury's verdict that the Solitron defendants all had the necessary scienter; the court's refusal to set aside the verdict was proper.

* * *

GULF COAST INVESTMENT CORP. v. SECRETARY OF HOUSING AND URBAN DEVELOPMENT

509 F. Supp. 1321
(United States District Court, E. D. Louisiana, Sept. 18, 1980.)

SEAR, D. J.

This is an action under a policy of flood insurance issued pursuant to the National Flood Insurance Act of 1968, 42 U.S.C. § 4001 *et seq.* On May 3, 1978, the insureds, Irvin and Bobbie York, sustained flood damage to their Marrero, Louisiana house. After their claim for flood insurance benefits was denied, the Yorks' mortgagee, Gulf Coast Investment Corporation (Gulf Coast), paid them for their loss and sued the Federal Emergency Management Agency (FEMA) [footnote], the present operator of the National Flood Insurance Program (NFIP) for the amount it paid. [Footnote.] In denying the Yorks' claim the defendant contends that their policy terminated more than fifteen months prior to the flood loss due to nonpayment of the renewal premium. Plaintiff asserts that the termination is invalid because the defendant failed to comply with a provision of the policy requiring written notice of termination.

As a condition to financing the purchase of the Yorks' home, their mortgage lender, Gulf Coast, required them to purchase a National Flood Insurance policy. The policy was purchased through Jimmy Phillips (Phillips), an insurance agent for Prudential Property & Casualty Insurance Company (Prudential). The Yorks paid the initial premium of $73.00 and the National Flood Insurance Association (NFIA) [footnote] issued policy number FC 104011908 effective for a one-year term January 21, 1976 to January 21, 1977. Gulf Coast agreed to pay subsequent annual renewal premiums from escrow funds collected with the mortgage payment.

On December 16, 1976, Gulf Coast received a NFIA Form 58 renewal notice covering the York policy which was generated by defendant's computer and dated December 10, 1976. The notice was mailed to Gulf Coast at its correct Houston, Texas mailing address.[4] The renewal notice advised that the insurance on the Yorks' property would expire January 21, 1977, that no further notice would be sent, and that to avoid a lapse in coverage, the renewal premium for the next annual term would have to be received by NFIA prior to the expiration date. It instructed that if the mortgagee was to pay the renewal premium, it should immediately contact the local agent (Phillips), who had been provided a renewal application. Finally, the form stated that if the policy was allowed to expire, the mortgagee would be provided written notice according to the policy conditions. The policy provided that the premium for successive policy terms must be paid prior to the expiration of the then current term, and

> if not so paid, this policy shall then terminate; provided, however, with respect to any mortgagee * * *, this insurance shall continue in force only for the benefit of such mortgagee * * * for 20 days after written notice to the mortgagee * * * of termination of this policy, and then shall terminate. [Footnote.]

Rather than contacting Phillips regarding the renewal application, Gulf Coast mailed him a check [footnote] on January 13, 1977 to pay the premium for the period January 21, 1977 to January 21, 1978; however the defendant never received a renewal premium, so the Yorks' policy lapsed on January 21, 1977.

Richard E. Hulbirt, Gulf Coast's vice president in charge of flood administration, received the Yorks' loan file and testified that no such notice was received and the file did not contain a policy renewal certificate.

After a computer indicated that the policy had lapsed, Gulf Coast attempted to renew the policy for the following coverage year, January 21, 1978 to January 21, 1979.[7] Gulf Coast sent the renewal premium to Prudential on February 14, 1978,[8] more than three weeks after a renewal premium for the January 21, 1978 to January 21, 1979 coverage period would have been due. On February 24, 1978, Prudential returned the payment to Gulf Coast indicating an overpayment remittance on the Yorks' homeowner's policy, which Prudential also issued; Gulf Coast then credited the Yorks' escrow account with an amount equal to the

---

4. The address was provided on the Yorks' Application and Declarations Form. [Reference.]

7. Under cross-examination, Hulbirt testified as follows:

Q. Did Gulf Coast attempt to renew the Yorks' flood insurance policy a second time?
A. Yes, we did.
Q. And why was this? Was it on the basis of having received a policy premium renewal notice?
A. No, it was done from an expiration list, hazard insurance and expiration list, and it came up for renewal and we did not receive a renewal certificate notice therefore we sent our check, which is February 14, 1978 to Pru-Pack [sic].
Q. What expiration list are you talking about?
A. Well, we had—we have a hazard insurance plus

it is separated into a flood expiration—flood insurance. Say, for example, the policy period would have come up for January 21, 1978. We would have found that this policy, or the renewal certificate—renewal certificate notice—apparently had not been received. Therefore we didn't have anything to go on other than what was previously set up on our records as far as a premium.
Q. In other words, your computer told you the policy had lapsed, you better do something.
A. Right.
[Reference.]

8. [Reference.] The payee, Prupac, was Prudential's premium collection agency in Phoenix, Arizona. The $73.00 line item on the gross check referenced the Yorks' loan and initial flood insurance policy numbers.

flood insurance premium. Again the Gulf Coast file does not indicate a renewal certificate for the January 21, 1978 to January 21, 1979 policy period.

On April 6, 1978, almost fifteen months after Gulf Coast sent its first renewal check to Phillips, its accounting department discovered that the check had not cleared its bank and on that date wrote the bank, inquiring about the status of the check. On May 9, 1978, six days after the Yorks' flood loss, Janet Thompson, the Gulf Coast employee primarily responsible for handling flood insurance renewals during the period pertinent to this case, requested a new flood insurance policy from another agent, and a new policy was issued, effective May 27, 1978.

In its effort to prove that it complied with the terms of the insurance contract by giving written notice of termination of the Yorks' policy to Gulf Coast, defendant offered the testimony of Mary Ralston, who served as an officer of the NFIA beginning in 1975, and later as a flood insurance consultant for the Department of Housing and Urban Development. [Footnote.] She testified regarding the program of the NFIA's computer for notifying parties with a possible interest in the policy renewal and that a termination notice dated March 18, 1977 was generated and sent to Aetna Technical Services, Inc. (Aetna), the servicing company in this instance. [Footnote.]

Although Ralston testified that magnetic tapes showing the work of the computer on a particular day, including the exact form generated, the date, and the policy number, were kept,[11] neither a copy of the mortgagee's termination notice nor a computer record of its production were offered into evidence. Nevertheless, Ralston testified she could state unequivocally that the NFIA Form 54 termination notice to Gulf Coast was generated, because the computer was programmed to produce the Form 55 termination notice Aetna received only after it produced Form 54. She

testified that approximately one-and-one-half million NFIP policies are processed through the renewal programs annually, and she knew of no instance in which the computer omitted one of the notices or failed to complete a cycle. The computer kept a count of the number of items to anticipate from a given cycle, and the number was routinely verified against the items actually produced. The number of notices again was verified after insertion into envelopes, and the notices then were delivered by defendant to the post office and mailed at bulk rates.

Following the May 3, 1978 flood, the Yorks reported their flood damage to the local Prudential office, which, in turn, reported it to defendant, whose adjuster estimated the structural damage at $8,503.06. [Footnote.] After defendant denied the claim, Gulf Coast paid the Yorks that amount for their loss [footnote], which it now seeks to recover from defendant.[14]

* * *

The contract provision crucial to determination of this case simply states that the insurance shall continue in force for the mortgagee's benefit for twenty days "after written notice to the mortgagee * * * of termination of this policy." This provision is ambiguous because it could be reasonably construed to mean *either* "after written notice is mailed to the mortgagee" *or* "after written notice is delivered to the mortgagee."

Where statutes require that notice be given the insured before cancellation of an insurance policy is effective, courts frequently hold that a presumption of delivery is raised when the insurer proves proper mailing. *E. g.,* *Broadway v. All-Star Ins. Corp.,* 285 So.2d 536 (La.1973), *construing* La.Rev.Stat. 22:636; *Traders & Gen'l Ins. Co. v. Mallitz,* 315 F.2d 141 (5th Cir. 1963). The purpose of notice provisions, however, is to inform the insured that his policy is being cancelled and to provide him sufficient time to obtain other insurance

---

11. Ralston testified that when the NFIP was taken over by HUD from the NFIA, the tapes were turned over to the Federal Insurance Administrator of HUD, which, in turn, delivered them to its contractor, EDS Federal Corporation. [Citation.] In a colloquy with the Court, defense counsel explained that the magnetic tape, which would show that Gulf Coast's termination notice was generated, "is apparently in cold storage and just can't be retrieved,

and the information which was retrieved did not have those particular factors on it." [Reference.]

14. Plaintiff originally also sought recovery from defendant of $7,015.65 it paid the Yorks for their contents loss; however, defendant's motion for summary judgment on that item was granted prior to trial.

protection. [Citations.] Since an interpretation that permits a deposit in the mails to conclusively terminate coverage undermines the purpose of the notice [citation], the presumption of delivery may be rebutted by "positive evidence of lack of delivery or receipt." [Citations.] These rules have been developed for disputes involving cancellation notices, but they will be applied by analogy to this termination notice dispute, so that a rebuttable presumption of delivery of the termination notice will be raised upon proof of proper mailing.[15]

Both sides had considerable problems of proof on this issue. The bulk of defendant's testimony was devoted to establishing its procedures for handling all renewal and termination notices and the operation of its computer system, rather than the precise procedure followed in this case. Defendant urges that such evidence of the customary and usual computer procedures supports an inference that the termination notice was delivered in this case. Such an inference is permissible, because the evidence of the production and receipt of the renewal by Gulf Coast and the termination notice by Aetna implies that defendant's customary and usual procedure in producing termination notices was adhered to in this case. The computer was an unimaginative mechanical device that could not stray from its program.

On the other hand, the testimony of plaintiff's witness. Hulbirt, that a termination notice was absent from the Yorks' loan file supports an inference that the notice was not delivered to Gulf Coast.[16] Nevertheless, in weighing all the evidence on the issue of delivery, this testimony must be accorded very little weight. Hulbirt was not the custodian of termination notices, and there was no testimony that he was employed by Gulf Coast, particularly in the flood insurance section, prior to April 1, 1978, which was more than a year after the notice normally would have been received. Additionally, Gulf Coast's recordkeeping was inadequate, as there was no established procedure for logging in termination notices when received. Furthermore, the Yorks' file was not adequately monitored for renewal certificates.

In sum, defendant proved a prima facie case of delivery of the termination notice in accordance with the insurance contract, which was not rebutted by plaintiff's evidence of nondelivery.[17] Cf. *United States v. Greenlee,* 517 F.2d 899 (3d Cir. 1975) (jury finding was permissible that evidence of recordkeeping and computer procedures of Internal Revenue Service, together with testimony that no tax return was received from defendant for a particular year, established beyond a reasonable doubt that none was filed, despite self-serving evidence of defendant that he mailed it); *Nichols v. Unity Industrial Life Ins. Co.,* 71 So.2d 604 (La.App. 2d Cir. 1954) (testimony that as a matter of customary and usual policy in the conduct of its insurance business, insurer mailed premium-due notices to all policyholders, was sufficient to prove mailing of a par-

---

15. There is a fundamental difference in meaning between "cancellation" and "termination," which, when used in insurance policies, are terms of art:

"Cancellation" means termination of the policy prior to expiration of the policy period by act of one of the parties to the agreement; "termination" refers to the expiration of the policy by lapse under its own terms.

The very terms of a contract for insurance coverage for a specified term, such as the one here, put the insured on notice that the policy will terminate if the renewal premium is not received prior to expiration of the coverage period. Statutes requiring affirmative cancellation by written notice generally are construed to apply only to cancellation and not to expiration or lapse because of nonpayment of premium, where the policy is for a specified term. [Citations.] Nevertheless, since defendant's duty of providing written notice of termination to the mortgagee is imposed by the contract, the rules of *Broadway* and *Mallitz* will be applied by analogy so that a rebuttable presumption of delivery of notice is raised upon proof of proper mailing.

16. Federal Rule of Evidence 803(7) provides that evi-

dence that a matter is not included in records kept in the course of a regularly conducted business activity, if offered to prove the nonexistence of the matter, is not excluded by the hearsay rule "if the matter was of a kind of which a * * * record * * * was regularly made and preserved, unless the sources of information or other circumstances indicate lack of trustworthiness." As the defendant did not object to plaintiff's evidence of the non-receipt of the termination notice on hearsay grounds, the evidence is treated as properly admitted and given such probative effect and value as it is entitled to. [Citation.]

17. To require defendant to keep readily accessible records of every computer transaction in each of its one-and-one-half million flood insurance policies, or to send notices by certified mail to those with interests in the coverage, in order to defeat the claim of this plaintiff, which did not exercise due diligence in renewing the insureds' policy, might raise the cost of NFIP policies to prohibitive levels, defeating the congressional purpose of providing low-cost insurance to residents of flood-prone areas. *See* 42 U.S.C. §§ 4001, 4002.

ticular notice, in light of lack of evidence of any variation from routine).

Even if defendant had not literally complied with the insurance contract by delivering notice of termination to plaintiff, there is another reason for denying plaintiff recovery. The Yorks' Standard Flood Insurance Policy contained no provision that they be given notice of termination. This suggests that the requirement of notice to the mortgagee and the twenty-day grace period must have been designed to give the mortgagee special protection when payment of the renewal premium was out of its control because it was to be made by the insured. In this case, it was the mortgagee's responsibility to make the renewal payments. Although it had notice the policy would expire if the payment was not timely made, the mortgagee did not fulfill its responsibility. The absence of a termination notice was not the reason the payment was not made; rather, Gulf Coast's inadequate recordkeeping and file review was the cause.

Finally, to allow a one-year flood insurance policy to provide coverage in perpetuity when a mortgagee, which was not diligent in renewing the policy, does not receive a termination notice would serve no public policy. Thus, federal common law must require that the maximum period for which coverage may be extended to a mortgagee who proves non-delivery of a termination notice, under NFIP policy terms like those here, is twenty days from the date when the mortgagee had actual knowledge of expiration. The evidence in this case is that Gulf Coast had actual knowledge the policy lapsed at least by April 6, 1978, when it learned its first renewal premium check had not cleared the bank. Therefore, coverage expired no later than April 27, 1978, prior to the Yorks' flood loss.

Accordingly, plaintiff's claim is dismissed at its cost.

* * *

UNITED STATES v. ROGLIERI

700 F.2d 883

(United States Court of Appeals, Second Circuit, Feb. 15, 1983.)

WINTER, C. J.

Victor Roglieri appeals from a judgment of the United States District Court for the Southern District of New York, Judge Milton S. Pollack, sentencing him to two concurrent three-year prison terms and a $4,000 fine after his conviction by a jury of two counts of possessing checks stolen from the mail in violation of 18 U.S.C. § 1708 (1976). [Footnote.] On appeal, Roglieri argues that the evidence was insufficient to prove the checks were stolen from the mail and that the trial judge incorrectly instructed the jury on the elements of the crime, including aiding and abetting.

We affirm.

BACKGROUND

On September 21, 1981, M & T Chemicals of Rahway, New Jersey, issued a check for $14,355.21 to Amax Copper, Inc. ("Amax"), addressed to P.O. Box # 12038, Church Street Station, New York, New York 10049. On September 25, 1981, Fritzche Dodge Olcott, Inc. issued a check for $52,601.98 to Monsanto Co., addressed to Box 8495, Church Street Station, New York, New York 10049. Neither check was received by the intended recipient.

On October 7 and 9, 1981, respectively, the two checks were deposited in Roglieri's account at the Poughkeepsie Savings Bank. Each was visibly altered with the name "Edward Lynch" typed above the payee company in a different typeface, and each was endorsed by Edward Lynch and Victor Roglieri. Roglieri had opened the account on September 9, 1981, and, until the deposits in question, had kept only a few hundred dollars in it.

Roglieri claimed to have received the checks in question from a man named Edward Lynch, whom he had met a few times over drinks at a Poughkeepsie bar. Although he barely knew Lynch, his address or even his telephone number, Roglieri testified that he agreed to cash the checks in return for some of the proceeds. He then took the checks and deposited them in his own account, and, at Lynch's direction, withdrew portions of the proceeds in cash, which he gave to Lynch.

DISCUSSION

Sufficiency of Evidence

In order to establish a violation of 18 U.S.C. § 1708 (1976), the government must prove that matter was stolen from the mail and that the defendant possessed or received it knowing it had been stolen. However, it is not necessary to prove that the defendant knew the matter was stolen from the mail. [Citation.]

Roglieri concedes the evidence proved that he knowingly possessed stolen checks. He asserts, however, that the evidence was insufficient to establish that the checks were stolen from the mail. * * *

The government may meet its burden as to the element of theft from the mail by proving that an item in a defendant's possession was mailed to but never received by the addressee. As we said in *United States v. Lopez,* 457 F.2d 396, 398 (2d Cir.), *cert. denied,* 409 U.S. 866, 93 S.Ct. 162, 34 L.Ed.2d 114 (1972):

> [A] letter shown to have been "properly mailed and never received by the addressee, but found in quite improper and misusing hands, can be found to have been stolen from the mails in the absence of any other explanation being proffered." * * * When such facts are established it is reasonable to assume that the letter was stolen rather than inadvertently lost or misplaced by postal officials.

In the present case, the corporate cashier of M & T Chemicals, John Abbruzzese, identified the Amax check and testified that the check as issued did not bear the name of Edward Lynch. Abbruzzese also testified that his practice after he received a check from his company's computer room was to pass it to other employees for signature and mailing. Similarly, Edward Cohen, the accounting manager of Fritizche Dodge, testified that the practice of his company is to mail checks such as that issued to Monsanto. There was no particularized evidence of the mailing of either check.

Evidence of non-receipt was provided by officials of the banks which maintained post office lock boxes for the payee corporations at the Church Street Station. John McKay of Amax's bank described his firm's practice of retrieving checks from the post office by messenger. He testified that his bank never received the Amax check because it did not bear a stamp indicating such receipt. Nancy Van Ness, vice-president of the bank which collected checks for Monsanto from the Church Street Station, testified about her firm's practice of retrieval by messenger and stated that the absence of a receipt stamp indicated that

her bank also had never received the Monsanto check. Each bank uses its own employees as messengers to retrieve mail from its Church Street Station lock box.

The evidence both as to mailing and non-receipt of the checks in question proved only the routine practice of the issuer and intended recipients. It did not include direct testimony by someone with personal knowledge of the mailing or non-receipt of the particular checks. Where checks issued by sizeable firms to other similar firms or banks are involved, the existence of evidence other than routine practice would be exceptional. We are not prepared to say that such evidence, which is subject to cross-examination on both the usual procedures and the frequency of lost checks within the particular firm, does not go a long way to proving both the mailing and non-receipt of particular items. *Cf. United States v. Huber,* 603 F.2d 387, 399 (2d Cir. 1979) (absent evidence to the contrary, ordinary practice sufficient to prove mailing for purposes of mail fraud where receipt is conceded), *cert. denied,* 445 U.S. 927, 100 S.Ct. 1312, 63 L.Ed.2d 758 (1980); *United States v. Toliver,* 541 F.2d 958, 966 (2d Cir.1976) (same).

Nevertheless, we are also reluctant to go beyond existing precedent and hold that evidence of routine practice alone proves beyond a reasonable doubt that a particular item was stolen from the mail where large commercial firms are involved at each end of a transaction. None of our prior decisions have gone that far. For example, while *Lopez* held that evidence of mailing and non-receipt would support a finding of theft from the mail, there was direct evidence in the case concerning the mailing and non-receipt of the particular item. Similarly, in *United States v. Indelicato,* 611 F.2d 376 (1st Cir.1979), 68 Treasury checks made out to individual payees were stipulated to have been mailed but not received. Since individuals usually receive mail directly from the Postal Service, evidence of its non-receipt is by its nature particularized. [Citation.] Where firms are involved at both ends of a transaction, however, and evidence of routine practice alone is available, the hands of numerous unidentified persons in accounting offices, mail rooms and messenger services are usually involved and many opportunities for theft exist at various stages in transit other than while in the mail, thus reducing greatly the probability that the actual theft was from the mail. *See United States v. Robinson,* 545 F.2d 301 (2d Cir.1976).

The mail fraud cases cited in the concurring opinion do not, we believe, support the view urged by Judge Cardamone. In both *Huber* and *Toliver,* receipt of the particular items was acknowledged and the only question was whether the mails or some other form of transportation was used. Evidence of a routine practice of mailing such items provides a logical base to conclude that the mails were in fact used on the occasions in question. Theft involving large firms at both ends of a transaction, however, generally entails the disappearance of items at an unknown point in a lengthy chain of custody, of which the Postal Service is only one part. In these circumstances, the conclusion that a particular item was stolen from the mail seems no more plausible than the conclusion that it was stolen elsewhere.

In Roglieri's case, however, there is other evidence to prove that the checks possessed were stolen from the mail. While both checks were mailed from different locations and, if received by the addressees, would have been picked up by different messengers, they were both addressed to boxes in the Church Street Station. This evidence of a common location while in the mail supplies, we believe, sufficient particularized evidence to support a finding that the checks in question were stolen while in the mail. Evidence of routine practice as to mailing by different senders and receipt by different addressees along with a single common location occurring in the mail is enough, absent other circumstances, to allow a jury to find that the checks were stolen from the mail.

Hesitation in reaching this result is caused by *Robinson, supra.* In that case, a number of checks originating in three separate disbursing offices, and of a kind always received by the addressees in the mail, were "laundered" by the defendant. We reversed Robinson's conviction on the grounds that while the evidence surely proved that some of the checks were stolen from the mails, that fact was not proven as to any particular check mentioned in the indictment. That conclusion is in no way inconsistent with our holding here, for *Robinson*

did not involve evidence of a common location in the mail.

Nevertheless, we do rely upon evidence pertaining to both checks to prove the theft of each from the mail, and the following passage in *Robinson* gives us pause:

> Thus, although it may be "most unlikely" that the seven checks would all be stolen from three different disbursement offices and then transported individually to the grocery store, it is not so unlikely that an individual check would be so stolen and so transported. The individual checks, which were the subject of separate counts of the indictment, cannot be lumped together to support the inference urged by the government. With respect to Robinson's guilt or innocence as to any particular check, evidence concerning other checks, whether or not included in the indictment, was merely similar act evidence. Such evidence * * * was not relevant to prove that any particular check covered by the indictment was stolen from the mails. *See* Fed.R.Evid. 404(b). * * * Consequently, in determining whether there was sufficient evidence to support the charge that the checks possessed were stolen from the mails, we cannot draw any inference from the fact that some checks originated from different out-of-state disbursement offices.

Id. at 304. If that passage is taken to mean that Rule 404(b) prohibits use of evidence as to other checks to prove theft from the mail of a particular check, then *Robinson* would preclude the reasoning we follow here. *Robinson* need not be read so restrictively, however, for the evidence of the other checks in the case did not reveal a common location in the mail and was thus insufficient, even if admissible, to support an inference that a particular check was stolen from the mail. *Robinson* can, therefore, be limited to its holding as to the sufficiency of the evidence, and we believe it should. [Footnote.]

In drawing an inference from the circumstances relating to both checks, we in no way undermine either the language or purpose of Rule 404(b). It expressly prohibits use of such evidence to prove character but permits it for the purpose of proving matters such as "motive, opportunity, intent, preparation, plan, knowledge, identity, or absence of mistake or accident." The fact that the two checks negotiated by Roglieri were addressed by different senders to the same postal station, to be picked up by different messengers, is plainly relevant to prove that the best opportunity for someone to have stolen both checks was at that Station.

* * *

Affirmed.

CARDAMONE, C. J., concurring:

I am in agreement with most of the majority's opinion and with the result it reaches in the case, but I cannot agree with its reasoning on the issue of the sufficiency of evidence of customary practices to prove theft from the mail. In the context of mail fraud prosecutions, which necessarily require similar proof of mailing, our Court has repeatedly upheld the use of evidence of routine business practices to establish that on a particular occasion an item had been placed in the mail. *See, e.g., United States v. Huber,* 603 F.2d 387, 399 (2d Cir. 1979), *cert. denied,* 445 U.S. 927, 100 S.Ct. 1312, 63 L.Ed.2d 758 (1980); *United States v. Toliver,* 541 F.2d 958, 966 (2d Cir.1976). We have also held that an addressee's non-receipt may be proven by evidence that an item which is regularly received in the mail did not arrive on the occasion in question. *See, e.g., United States v. Robinson,* 545 F.2d 301, 303-04 (2d Cir.1976). A jury armed only with this type of circumstantial evidence of mailing and non-receipt could infer that an item was properly mailed and not received by the addressee. If the item is then found in improper hands and no other plausible explanation is provided, the jury may conclude beyond a reasonable doubt that the person in whose possession the item was found stole it from the mails. *See United States v. Lopez,* 457 F.2d 396, 398 (2d Cir.), *cert. denied,* 409 U.S. 866, 93 S.Ct. 162, 34 L.Ed.2d 114 (1972). It is true that *Lopez* involved some direct evidence of mailing and non-receipt while we are here faced with circumstantial evidence, but I think that *Lopez* read together with *Huber, Toliver* and *Robinson* can only lead to the conclusion that circumstantial evidence of mailing and non-receipt is sufficient in and of itself to place before the jury the issue of theft from the mail.

It is a fact of modern-day life that sizeable organizations, such as the companies and banks involved in this case, mail and receive through the postal system innumerable items on a daily basis. Checks mailed in large numbers simply cannot be singly recollected. The same is true of checks received in large numbers from the mail. Consequently, the only proof of mailing and non-receipt ordinarily available in cases of this nature will be customary practices. [Citation.] Nothing has been called to our attention indicating abuse by the prosecution or unfairness to defendants in the use of customary business practices to prove mailing and non-receipt. Permitting such proof is a good rule, one which has been established in similar situations, and one that should be maintained.

By holding that evidence of customary practices, without more, is insufficient to establish mailing and non-receipt, my colleagues unnecessarily increase the burden of proof on the government in theft from the mail cases under 18 U.S.C. § 1708. The majority's rationale is based on their concern with the possibility that in cases such as the one before us any of the several hands involved in mailing and receiving the checks had an opportunity to steal them at various non-mail stages in transit from company to company. Thus, the majority concludes that in this instance there is a reduced probability that the theft which occurred was from the mail. But the government, even in criminal cases, need not offer absolute, unequivocal proof beyond all doubt or to a mathematical certainty. If such proof was necessary, circumstantial evidence of the elements of a crime would never be sufficient to establish guilt beyond a reasonable doubt. Circumstantial evidence is intrinsically no different from testimonial evidence. [Citation.] If the evidence of customary practices proffered by the government in this case indicated something other than that the checks were stolen from the mail, it was up to defense counsel to comment on the ambiguity of the government's proof and up to the jurors to decide if that ambiguity raised a reasonable doubt in their minds as to whether the theft was from the mail. In this case the jury concluded that it had no doubt that the checks were stolen from the mail. Unless we are to rule that circumstantial evidence such as customary practices is suspect proof and overrule *Huber, Toliver, Robinson* and *Lopez,* it seems to me that we must conclude that evidence of customary practices is sufficient standing alone to establish mailing and non-receipt and, therefore, to prove theft from the mail beyond a reasonable doubt. It is on this basis that I vote to affirm the judgment of conviction.

ANZALONE v. STATE FARM MUTUAL INSURANCE CO.

92 A.D.2d 238, 459 N.Y.S.2d 850

(Supreme Court, Appellate Division, Second Department, March 14, 1983.)

PER CURIAM.

In this action, plaintiffs, Peter and Betty Anzalone, seek a declaration that the automobile liability policy issued to defendant Ellen Steed by defendant Insurance Company of North America (INA), was in effect on July 18, 1979 when Steed's car collided with that of plaintiffs. INA defends with the claim that Steed's policy was canceled before the accident because she defaulted in her payment of premium installments to the Broadway Bank & Trust Company (the Bank) which had financed the premium. Special Term conducted an evidentiary hearing and decided that the Bank had indeed canceled the policy prior to the accident. Plaintiffs and their own insurer, defendant State Farm Mutual Insurance Company, now appeal, claiming INA failed to prove (1) that Steed signed the premium finance agreement which contained a power of attorney authorizing the Bank to cancel the policy, (2) that the cancellation notice was mailed to Steed, and (3) that Steed defaulted in the payment of premium installments. The appellants also allege that the cancellation was ineffective because Steed was overcharged by the Bank and because it did not return the unearned premiums.

To avoid liability under its policy, INA had the burden of proving cancellation in strict compliance with section 576 of the Banking Law. [Citations.] A premium finance company has the right to cancel the policy it has financed but only if the right is contained in the finance agreement. [Citation.] On this record—and in the absence of any denial from Steed or any contrary evidence [citations]—the authenticity of Steed's signature on the finance agreement may be reasonably inferred from the fact that she paid at least five premium installments. [Citations.]

Proof that the cancellation notice was mailed to Steed was insufficient, however. Bernadette Sudenko, an officer of the Bank in charge of the financing of insurance premiums, testified that the Bank's cancellation notices are produced by computer and placed in envelopes by a clerk who later delivers groups of envelopes to the post office and returns with a mailing sheet stamped by the post office. A mailing sheet, apparently so stamped, and containing 19 names, including Steed's, was received in evidence. Sudenko's testimony demonstrated an office practice and policy followed by the Bank in the regular course of its business. [Citation.] But the office practice "must be geared so as to ensure the likelihood that a notice of cancellation is always properly addressed and mailed." [Citation.] When reliance is placed on a mailing sheet, there must be testimony that an employee normally checks the names and addresses on the envelopes with those on the mailing sheet. [Citations.] Since Sudenko failed to provide such testimony, INA failed to establish that a cancellation notice was mailed to Steed.

Proof that Steed was in default in the payment of any premium installment also was deficient. Sudenko testified that the Bank's computer automatically generates a cancellation notice when there is a default in payment, but she produced no record of Steed's payment history. This failure violates the best evidence rule which requires the production of the original writing or that its absence be satisfactorily accounted for. [Citations.] Moreover, even though computer printouts of Steed's payment record might have been admissible in evidence under the business entry exception of the hearsay rule had a proper foundation been laid [citations] here, no record was offered. Sudenko's testimony concerning Steed's default was inadmissable hearsay.

* * *

In sum, the failure to establish cancellation and premium default mandates reversal and a declaration that the policy issued by INA was in full force and effect on the date of the accident.

* * *

PEOPLE v. GAUER

7 Ill.App.3d 512, 288 N.E.2d 24
(Appellate Court of Illinois, Second District, Sept. 29, 1972.)

ABRAHAMSON, J.

The only question presented here is whether the State laid a proper foundation for the admissibility, as records in the ordinary course of business, of telephone company records on "IBM Trouble Recorder Cards" of telephone calls from defendant's telephone to those of the complaining witnesses. Defendant, who with his wife, was an employee of Illinois Bell Telephone Company ("Illinois Bell") was convicted in a bench trial of disorderly conduct in violation of Section 26-1(a)(2) of the Criminal Code (Ill.Rev.Stat.1969, ch. 38, sec. 26-1(a)(2)) and fined $100. He was charged with disorderly conduct on July 17, 1970, during the course of a strike against Illinois Bell, for making telephone calls to two female employees. Defendant and his wife were observing the strike, whereas the complaining witnesses continued working.

When the calls reached each of the complaining witnesses, no words were spoken by the caller except on one occasion. At that time the witness was unable to identify the voice as that of the defendant, but she was certain it was that of a male.

After several such calls on July 14th and 15th, the complaining witnesses requested that a "trap" or electronic tracer device be placed on their telephone lines. This was done.

One of the complaining witnesses testified that she was an annoyance call specialist and had personal knowledge of what a tracer is, and a general idea of how the tracer works: a trouble recorder is put on the line of the receiving party and "every time a call is ringing on your line a card will click. * * * It gives the location of the calling phone and the time, date and location to the receiving phone."

The State then called a witness who testified that his occupation was keeper of the records for Illinois Bell and that as such he had direct supervision and control of all the records. The records he brought with him pursuant to subpoena were 2 sets of punched "IBM Trouble Recorder Cards", which were business records of Illinois Bell, made in the ordinary course of business at or about the times and dates reflected thereon. He testified that

"* * * our records are reliable, and we place a lot of faith in our records. * * *" Upon that testimony the records were received in evidence, over defendant's objection.

He then testified to what the records reflected, namely, specific completed telephone calls made at various times and dates, including July 17, 1970, from defendant's telephone to those of complaining witnesses.

In the light of the general use of electronic computing and recording equipment in the business world and the reliance of the business world on them, the scientific reliability of such machines can scarcely be questioned. [Citation.] In *People v. Wells*, 80 Ill.App.2d 187, 193-194, 224 N.E.2d 288, testimony and records pertaining to a telephone call tracing device were received in evidence after the witness testified that he was familiar with the equipment and went with the technician as he checked through each stage of the tracing operation, and when it was checked back to the calling telephone. The court there held that the testimony describing the tracing operation was sufficient to show the "circumstantial probability of trustworthiness."

Likewise, in *King v. State ex rel. Murdock Acceptance Corp.*, (Miss.) 222 So.2d 393, and *Transport Indemnity v. Seib*, 178 Neb. 253, 132 N.W.2d 871, cited by defendant, electronic computer print-out sheets were held to be admissible as records in the ordinary course of business. However, both courts pointed out that the method of their preparation was fully testified to and a complete and comprehensive explanation of its meaning was given. In *King* the opinion stresses that the court must be satisfied from the foundation testimony that the sources of information, method and time of preparation were such as to indicate its trustworthiness and justify its admission. We agree.

In the case at bar there was no such testimony on which the admissibility of these records could be predicated. We hold, therefore, that it is necessary to reverse and remand this case for a new trial where competent testimony may be given to justify admission of the records. If an adequate foundation is laid, testimony could be received of earlier telephone calls as evidence of intention or design of the defendant to annoy the complaining witnesses. [Citation.]

For the reasons stated, the judgment of conviction is reversed, and the case is remanded for a new trial.

STATE v. SPRINGER

283 N.C. 627, 197 S.E.2d 530
*(Supreme Court of North Carolina,
July 12, 1973.)*

* * *

The bill of indictment charges that on 28 March 1972 the defendant "did unlawfully, wilfully, and feloniously withhold a Bankamericard Credit Card from the control and possession of Mabel L. Long, the person named on the face of such Credit Card and to whom the Credit Card had been issued. This withholding was done without the consent of the above named Cardholder, to whom such Credit Card has been issued by North Carolina National Bank on September 20, 1971 and which Card was in effect at the time of such withholding, against the form of the statute in such case made and provided and against the peace and dignity of the State."

The State offered in evidence the following exhibits and elicited the following testimony relating thereto:

State's Exhibit No. 1—A Bankamericard with the name Mabel L. Long embossed on it and bearing the number 434 215 027 2369. This card bears the signature of Mrs. Long and she testified she placed it thereon. She testified that she had never given defendant or anyone else permission to use or withhold this card; that she discovered it was missing on 4 February 1972 and reported its loss to North Carolina National Bank the same day. At the time it was lost the balance she owed North Carolina National Bank for use of the card was approximately $7.92. She identified the card by number and by her signature thereon.

State's Exhibit No. 2—A Citgo credit card with the name of Neil E. Bohn embossed on it and bearing the number 190 392 456. Mr. Bohn testified that he used this credit card for four or five months and discovered it missing about the middle of March 1972. He stated that he did not give defendant or any other person permission to have or to use it.

State's Exhibit No. 3—A BP credit card bearing the name Edward Carriker and a number which is not shown in the record. Edward Carriker testified that he and defendant had previously been in business together in the early part of 1971 selling burglar alarms; that he allowed defendant to use his credit cards during that period of time, one of which was a BP credit card, and defendant made arrangements to pay the bill through the oil company; that he does not remember this particular BP card—"I never received this card." Mr. Carriker further testified that defendant "gave me my cards back and I mailed mine back to BP. There is no issue date on that card. I do know that for a period of time he made payments on the BP credit card. * * * To my knowledge I was never issued this card." This witness further stated that during the month of March 1972 he did not give defendant permission to use any BP credit card that previously may have been issued to him.

State's Exhibit No. 4—A Humble Oil and Refining Company credit card bearing the name Richard B. Young and the number 361 113 4580. Mr. Young testified that he held and used this credit card until September or October 1971 at which time he put it away in a large briefcase; that he never knew the card was missing until Humble Oil and Refining advised him that "they had found the credit card"; that he never gave defendant or anyone else permission to use or hold it.

The State's evidence further tends to show that on 29 March 1972 defendant and another man purchased some gas and three cans of Sta-power Oil Cushion from an Esso Service Station in Hickory, totaling $12.50 plus tax, and paid for the purchase with S-4, the Humble Oil and Refining Company credit card issued to Richard Young. Mildred Brittain, one of the station operators, identified S-4 as the card used and testified: "A credit card was handed to the short man which was later known as Lou Kirk or some Kirk. A credit card was handed to him * * * and the signature on the credit card was made by Mr. Kirk. I looked at the signature because the name was in Richard Young and the signature was written R. Young. Mr. Kirk said something about taking some more oil with them because they had just purchased a car that day and it was drinking the oil, and I said, well, I will need to call in. Mr. Springer said, no, we won't need any more oil. * * * I became suspicious and called Humble and they advised me that there was a reward out on the card and not to issue any type of purchase on it and to immediately turn it over so I went ahead and called the police station." Mrs. Brittain further testified that at the time she saw defendant hand this credit card to Kirk "I saw cards. I did not look close enough to see which was any type of cards. I did see more than one. * * * Mr. Springer handed Mr. Kirk one of these cards." Mrs. Brittain identified a can of Sta-power Oil Cushion (S-5) as one of the cans sold to defendant and Kirk on the date in question.

Lt. Hugh Hunt of the Hickory Police Department testified that on 29 March 1972 he was on the lookout for a 1959 Chevrolet, white over blue, Tennessee license number D 1564; that he spotted the car on U.S. 321 Bypass in Hickory and stopped it; that defendant was the operator and, upon request, presented a valid driver's license but was unable to present a registration card; that a man named Louie Kirk was a passenger in the car; that both men were placed in the back seat of the patrol car and taken to the police station; that on the way he glanced at his rear view mirror and saw Louie Kirk passing cards to defendant and saw defendant "put them down between his legs and the next time they were under the seat where Thomas Springer was sitting. Springer didn't take the cards and hold on to them, he put them under the seat of the patrol car. All I could see were that they were credit cards. I couldn't read the number or the names on them." When defendant and Louie Kirk were removed from the patrol car at the police station, the officer looked under the seat and found State's Exhibits 1, 2 and 4. State's Exhibit 3 was taken from defendant's billfold at the police department.

Lt. Hunt searched defendant's car with his permission and found ninety-three quarts of motor oil of various brands, a can of oil softener and a little hand drill.

Fred Holt, a special investigator with Bankamericard, North Carolina National Bank, in Greensboro, testified that when a credit card has been reported lost or stolen he checks to see when it was issued, where it was issued and how many were issued; that this checking is done through North Carolina National Bank's IBM computer and the computer printout shows the official record pertaining to each and every credit card. Over objection, he was permitted to testify that the official computer printout with regard to credit card No. 434 215 027 2369, issued to Mabel L. Long, showed that said card was issued on 15 September 1971; that as of 4 February 1972, the date the card was reported missing, the balance Mrs. Long owed by reason of using said card was $7.12; that the computer printout showed that since 4 February 1972 the Mabel L. Long card had been used seventy-three times in twenty-two North Carolina cities for purchases totaling $1,209.63; that the printout showed the last date the card was used to be 30 March 1972 in connection with a purchase from Shamrock Hardware in Charlotte—at which time defendant was in jail in Hickory, having been arrested and jailed on 29 March 1972 in connection with this case.

Defendant offered no evidence. Defendant's motion for nonsuit was denied. The jury returned a verdict of guilty as charged and defendant was sentenced to a prison term of not less than two nor more than three years. His assignments of error on appeal will be noted in the opinion.

* * *

HUSKINS, J.

Defendant is charged with unlawfully, willfully and feloniously withholding a credit card from Mabel L. Long, the cardholder, in violation of G.S. § 14-113.9(a)(1). That subsection reads as follows:

> § 14-113.9. *Credit card theft.*—(a) A person is guilty of credit card theft when:
> (1) He takes, obtains or withholds a credit card from the person, possession, custody or control of another without the cardholder's consent or who, with knowledge that it has been so taken, obtained or withheld, receives the credit card with intent to use it or to sell it, or to transfer it to a person other than the issuer or the cardholder.

Acts dealing with credit card crimes have been enacted in nearly all states in recent years. In defining credit card theft, the majority of these acts have been drafted with much greater clarity than ours. Georgia and

Virginia have followed our statute almost verbatim. [Citations.]

Our statute almost defies analysis. Apparently, an accused may violate G.S. § 14-113.9(a)(1) in four distinct ways. [Citation.] He may (1) *take,* (2) *obtain,* or (3) *withhold* a credit card from the person, possession, custody or control of another without the cardholder's consent; or (4) he may receive a credit card with intent to use it or sell it or transfer it to some person other than the issuer or cardholder, knowing at the time that the card had been so taken, obtained or withheld. A person violating G.S. § 14-113.9(a)(1) in any of the four enumerated ways is guilty of credit card theft. Of course, a person who commits the acts proscribed by G.S. § 14-113.9(a)(2), (3) and (4) is also guilty of credit card theft.

* * *

Fred Holt, a special investigator with Bankamericard, North Carolina National Bank, in Greensboro, testified that the bank's IBM computer printout is the official record pertaining to credit cards. Over objection, he was permitted to testify that the official computer printout regarding credit card 434 215 027 2369, issued to Mabel L. Long, showed: (1) That said card was issued on 15 September 1971; (2) that as of 4 February 1972 when the card was reported missing Mrs. Long's balance owed was $7.12; (3) that since 4 February 1972 the card had been used seventy-three times in twenty-two North Carolina cities for purchases totaling $1,209.63, which amount is currently due according to the printout; and (4) that said card was last used on 30 March 1972 in connection with a purchase from Shamrock Hardware in Charlotte. Admission of this testimony constitutes defendant's second assignment of error.

Modern business conditions and methods have long since required revision of the rule of evidence formerly observed by the courts limiting proof of business transactions to matters within the personal knowledge of the witness. [Citations.] "The impossibility of producing in court all the persons who observed, reported and recorded each individual transaction gave rise to the modification which permits the introduction of recorded entries, made in the regular course of business, at or near the time of the transaction involved, and au-

thenticated by a witness who is familiar with them and the method under which they are made. This rule applies to original entries made in books of account in regular course by those engaged in business, when properly identified, though the witness may not have made the entries and may have had no personal knowledge of the transactions." *Supply Co. v. Ice Cream Co.,* 232 N.C. 684, 61 S.E.2d 895 (1950).

Few courts have dealt with the use in evidence of business records stored on computers. In *King v. State for Use and Benefit of Murdock Acceptance Corp.,* 222 So.2d 393 (Miss.1969), it was held that printout sheets of business records stored on electronic computing equipment "are admissible in evidence if relevant and material, without the necessity of identifying, locating, and producing as witnesses the individuals who made the entries in the regular course of business if it is shown (1) that the electronic computing equipment is recognized as standard equipment, (2) the entries are made in the regular course of business at or reasonably near the time of the happening of the event recorded, and (3) the foundation testimony satisfies [sic] the court that the sources of information, method and time of preparation were such as to indicate its trustworthiness and justify its admission." [Citations.]

The General Assembly of North Carolina has enacted the following statutes, almost identical, dealing with the subject:

§ 55-37.1. *Form of records.*—Any records maintained by a corporation in the regular course of its business, including its stock ledger, books of account, and minute books, may be kept on, or be in the form of, punch cards, magnetic tape, photographs, microphotographs, or any other information storage device; provided that the records so kept can be converted into clearly legible form within a reasonable time. Any corporation shall so convert any records so kept upon the request of any person entitled to inspect the same. Where records are kept in such manner, the cards, tapes, photographs, microphotographs or other information storage device together with a duly authenticated print-out or translation shall be admissible in evidence, and shall be accepted for all other purposes, to the same extent as an original written record of the same information would have been. [Citation.]

§ 55A-27.1. *Form of records.*—Any records

maintained by a corporation in the regular course of its business, including its books of account and minute books, may be kept on, or be in the form of, punch cards, magnetic tape, photographs, microphotographs, or any other information storage device; provided that the records so kept can be converted into clearly legible form within a reasonable time. Any corporation shall so convert any records so kept upon the request of any person entitled to inspect the same. Where records are kept in such manner, the cards, tapes, photographs, microphotographs or other information storage device together with a duly authenticated readout or translation shall be admissible in evidence, and shall be accepted for all other purposes, to the same extent as an original written record of the same information would have been. [Citation.]

These statutes were designed to give broad legislative approval to the use in evidence of corporate computer records. However, in declaring such computer records admissible in evidence "to the same extent as an original written record of the same information would have been," these statutes do not deal with the special problems of reliability created by the use of computers. [Citation.] We therefore construe them as authorizing the admission of corporate computer records under appropriate safeguards deemed sufficient to render them trustworthy. These statutes do not, and were not designed to, preclude judicial development of workable standards for the admission of computerized business records generally.

The rules of evidence governing the admissibility of computerized business records should be consistent with the reality of current business methods and should be adjusted to accommodate the techniques of a modern business world, with adequate safeguards to insure reliability. We therefore hold that printout cards or sheets of business records stored on electronic computing equipment are admissible in evidence, if otherwise relevant and material, if: (1) the computerized entries were made in the regular course of business, (2) at or near the time of the transaction involved, and (3) a proper foundation for such evidence is laid by testimony of a witness who is familiar with the computerized records and the methods under which they were made so as to satisfy the court that the methods, the sources of information, and the time of prep-

aration render such evidence trustworthy. Computer printout evidence may be refuted to the same extent as business records made in books of account.

Application of the enunciated rule to the case before us impels the conclusion that the computer printout referred to in the testimony of Fred Holt, the special investigator, was inadmissible since no foundation was laid for its admission. In fact, the printout itself was not offered in evidence. Instead, the witness Fred Holt was permitted to testify as to the contents of the printout, and this evidence was likewise inadmissible under the best evidence rule. [Citations.] Admission of this testimony constitutes prejudicial error requiring a new trial.

* * *

DEPARTMENT OF MENTAL HEALTH FOR USE OF PEOPLE v. BEIL

44 Ill.App.3d 402, 357 N.E.2d 875
(Appellate Court of Illinois, Fourth District, Dec. 2, 1976.)

REARDON, J.

This action was brought by the plaintiff, Department of Mental Health, to recover from defendant, Mervin L. Beil, charges for treatment furnished to defendant's wife, Mary Beil. By stipulation the parties agreed that the Beils were married on July 4, 1947, they retained a valid marriage even though Mrs. Beil had filed for divorce on August 16, 1971, and that they lived separate and apart between August 16, 1971 and April, 1974.

During the separation Mrs. Beil was institutionalized in several State mental institutions and incurred the charges in question. The plaintiff assessed these charges against defendant as a "responsible relative" pursuant to the provisions of section 12–12 of the Mental Health Code which provides in part:

Each patient receiving treatment in a mental health program of the Department, and the estate of such patient, is liable for the payment of sums representing charges for treatment of such patient at a rate to be determined by the Department in accordance with this Section. If such patient is unable to pay or if the estate of such patient is insufficient, the responsible relatives are severally liable for the payment of such sums, or for the balance due in case less than the amount prescribed under this Act has been paid. * * *

The rate at which the sums for the treatment of patients in a mental health program of the Department is calculated by the Department is the average per capita cost of the treatment of all such patients, such costs to be computed by the Department on the general average per capita cost of operation of all state hospitals for the fiscal year immediately preceding the period of state care for which the rate is being calculated, except the Department may, in its discretion, set the rate at a lesser amount than such average per capita cost. * * *

The Department may investigate the financial condition of each person liable under this Act, may make determinations of the ability of each such person to pay sums representing treatment charges, and for such purposes may set a standard as a basis of judgment of ability to pay in accordance with Section 12–12.1 of this Act. * * *

Treatment charges assessed against responsible relatives take effect on the date of admission or acceptance of the patient for treatment or as soon thereafter as each responsible relative's financial ability during the period which the patient receives treatment subjects him to liability for charges as required under this Section. * * *

Any person who has been issued a Notice of Determination of sums due as treatment charges may petition the Department for a review of that determination. The petition must be in writing and filed with the Department within 90 days from the date of the Notice of Determination. The Department shall provide for a hearing to be held on the charges for the period covered by the petition. The Department may after such hearing, cancel, modify or increase such former determination to an amount not to exceed the maximum provided for such person by this Section. * * * Any person aggrieved by the decision of the Department upon such hearing may, within 30 days thereafter, file a petition with the Department for review of such decision by the Board of Reimbursement Appeals. The Board of Reimbursement Appeals may approve action taken by the Department or may remand the case to the Director with recommendations for redetermination of charges. Ill.Rev.Stat.1973, ch. 91½, par. 12–12.

The plaintiff sent Notices of Determination of the treatment charges to defendant on November 1, 1971, and February 22, 1974. Both notices apprised defendant of his right to a redetermination of the charges. The defendant never responded to the notices. On June 26, 1974, the plaintiff filed a complaint in circuit court seeking to recover Mrs. Beil's treatment charges incurred between August 16, 1971 and April, 1974. At the ensuing jury trial, the plaintiff offered the testimony of Robert Dewan, a determinations supervisor for the Department of Mental Health, whose duties were to gather financial information on patients and relatives of people in the State hospitals to compute the charges that are due the State of Illinois. The witness testified that as soon as a patient enters a State hospital a fact sheet is made up showing his or her name and address, county, and other personal data of the patient and that information is sent to the determination section of the hospital and the hospital keeps a copy of all these records. The witness stated that he was familiar with investigations into patients' ability to pay for their treatment and this particular type of activity came under his supervision. The witness then stated that when patients are treated or enter a hospital under the supervision of the Department, there is an investigation made in the usual course of business. He stated that the Department sent the questionnaire to the relatives of the patient to ask them for financial information regarding the patient. The Department's witness then stated that the above steps were taken in the case of the patient, Mary P. Beil, and that Mervin Beil, the defendant, filled out a questionnaire in 1965 which did not show that the patient had any assets or income at the time he filled out the questionnaire. The witness also stated that this financial form was filled out as a usual and normal matter in connection with the admission of patients to hospitals under the jurisdiction of the Department. The witness stated that the spouses of patients who are responsible relatives under section 12–12 of the Mental Health Code were notified of treatment charges. Although Mr. Dewan had no personal knowledge of Mrs. Beil or her financial condition, he did testify that the amount owed plaintiff remained unpaid. No testimony was given by this witness as to the operation or capability of the computer machinery. During Mr. Dewan's testimony a computer printout, abstracting Mrs. Beil's hospital attendance record, and the 1965 statement of Mr. Beil regarding his wife's assets were admitted into evidence. Mr. Dewan testified that the records were kept in the regular course of business and described the procedure used to forward hospital records to a central computer. The plaintiff also introduced copies of the Notices of Determination sent defendant on November 1, 1971, and February 22, 1974. The defendant offered into evidence only an affidavit which alleged in part that the Beils had been separated for more than 10 years, that Mrs. Beil willfully failed to support or contribute to their marriage and that section 12–12 was unconstitutional. The trial court refused the affidavit as evidence on the grounds that it included incorrect statements of law and irrelevant statements of fact, and that it only went to the proceedings on the Motion to Dismiss and the Motion for Summary Judgment. Defendant offered no other evidence. The trial court instructed the jury to enter a directed verdict for the plaintiff and judgment was entered against the defendant in the amount of $1,420.78. * * *

* * *

Lastly, defendant attacks the trial court's actions in allowing certain items into evidence. The State introduced into evidence a number of computer printout sheets upon which were recorded an abstract of the attendance record of Mrs. Beil at various State mental institutions. The defendant raised the question of admissibility of these records by a timely and proper objection.

In view of our conclusion that the notices of determination stand as fact unchallengeable in the trial court, the relevancy of these records to the presentation of the State's case is doubtful. It is clear, however, that the State did not meet the foundation requirements for the introduction into evidence of computer generated records. Before such records can be introduced into evidence, it must be shown that the electronic computing equipment is recognized as standard, that the entries are made in the regular course of business at or reasonably near the time of the happening of the event recorded, and that the testimony satisfies the court that the sources of information, method and time of preparation were such as to indicate its trustworthiness and

justify its admission. [Citation.] The foundation related here merely established that the entries were made in the regular course of business. * * * Since plaintiff's case is sufficiently supported without the introduction of the computer records, any error resulting from their admission did not prejudice defendant and is harmless. For these reasons, we affirm the decision of the trial court.

Affirmed.

SEARS, ROEBUCK & CO. v. MERLA
142 N.J.Super. 205, 361 A.2d 68
(Superior Court of New Jersey, Appellate Division, June 7, 1976.)

PER CURIAM.

Plaintiff appeals from an order dismissing its complaint on an alleged book account. Plaintiff claimed that defendant owed it $577.69. The trial judge dismissed the complaint before trial on defendant's motion seeking either more specific answers to her interrogatories or, alternatively, dismissal of the complaint for failure to comply with a prior order for more specific answers.

At the argument of defendant's motion it developed that plaintiff intended to rely at trial on a computer printout of defendant's account, that plaintiff had destroyed the original invoices when the information they contained was transferred to the computer, and that plaintiff was unable to give a description of the goods sold. However, plaintiff stated that the computer printout would show the dates, costs, and departments from which the various purchases were made, the number of defendant's credit card, the payments made on the account, and the balance presently due.

The judge below, expressing a disdain for computer technology, concluded that he would not accept the computer printout as evidence at trial and that this justified dismissal of the complaint without a trial.

We reverse. Under the circumstances here, the judge below erred in entering judgment before trial, thus depriving plaintiff of any opportunity to present its proofs. [Citation.] But beyond that, this action is nothing more than a suit upon a book account where plaintiff seeks to introduce its records under the old "shopbook rule" now expressed in Evid.R.

63(13) which superseded the Business Records as Evidence Act, N.J.S.A. 2A:82–34 *et seq.* [Citation.] We hold that as long as a proper foundation is laid, a computer printout is admissible on the same basis as any other business record.

> The Rules of Evidence Commission of the New Jersey Legislature gave the following illustration of the meaning of Rule 1(13) defining a "writing" as used in the Rules of Evidence: A printout of paper from invisible recordings in a computer is a writing, but proof of suitable safeguards is required.

And the Commission's comment to Rule 63(13) states:

> In combination with Rule 1(13), this rule covers printouts of computer recordings that would otherwise be considered "writings."

Computerized bookkeeping has become commonplace. Because the business records exception is intended to bring the realities of the business world into the courtroom, a record kept on computer in the ordinary course of business qualifies as competent evidence. This result is in accordance with that reached in other jurisdictions. [Citations.] Of course, if the computer printout at issue here is admitted at trial, it will constitute only prima facie evidence of an account stated. Defendant will have the opportunity to refute plaintiff's evidence.

Judgment is reversed and the matter is remanded for further proceedings not inconsistent with the views expressed herein.

GASSETT v. STATE

532 S.W.2d 328
(Court of Criminal Appeals of Texas, Jan. 21, 1976.)

ROBERTS, J.

This is an appeal from a conviction for murder with malice under Arts. 1256 and 1257, V.A.P.C. Trial was before a jury and the jury assessed a punishment of seven years' imprisonment.

This murder grew out of a family dispute. The deceased was a former husband of the appellant's wife and had waged a long, and finally successful, battle for custody of the couple's children. The evidence showed, however, that appellant's wife was illegally retaining custody of one of the children, and this prompted the deceased to make periodic trips into her neighborhood to search for signs of the child. Appellant killed the former husband on one of these periodic surveillance trips into appellant's neighborhood. The defense put great stock in showing the deceased to have a bad reputation as a husband and a father. Appellant's wife testified that the deceased had been arrested or indicted for desertion or non-support in Dallas, Odessa, and Clovis, New Mexico. In rebuttal, the State adduced evidence that appellant's wife was a bad mother. The State also attempted to prove that the deceased did not have the criminal record testified to by his former wife.

In this connection, the State called an investigator from the Dallas district attorney's office who offered testimony that the National Criminal Information Center (N.C.I.C.) computer revealed no record of arrests or indictments concerning the deceased. Appellant objected to this testimony on the grounds that it was hearsay and the proper predicate had not been laid. In this appeal, appellant contends that the proffered testimony, which finally came in over his numerous and thorough objections, was hearsay not within the exceptions to the hearsay rule provided by Arts. 3731a or 3737e, V.T.C.A.

Appellant calls our attention to Sec. 5 of Art. 3731a, which governs admissibility of written statements to the effect that no record of a specified tenor exists. We note, however, that no written record was offered by the State or admitted into evidence by the court. Thus, the provisions of Sec. 5 obviously do not authorize the admission of this evidence. The witness offered oral testimony as to the contents of the N.C.I.C. computer print-out showing the non-existence of any arrests or indictments. Sec. 6 of Art. 3731a permits other methods of proving the lack of an entry in an official record if authorized by statutory or decisional law.

The witness's parol offer constituted common law hearsay. Whether or not it came within the statutory exception to the hearsay rule for business records is a question of first impression in this Court. In fact, our research has revealed no case in which any Texas court has construed Art. 3737e, Sec. 3, V.T.C.A., the law applicable to this case. Nor is there a comparable provision in the federal "business records as evidence" act. [Citation.]

Art. 3737e, V.T.C.A., sets out the well-recognized "business records" exception to the hearsay rule. Subsection 1 thereof states three prerequisites to the introduction of a relevant business record or memorandum: (a) it must have been made in the regular course of business, (b) by an employee or representative with personal knowledge of its contents, (c) at or near the time in question. The record or memorandum may be offered by the entrant, custodian, or other qualified witness, even though he may lack personal knowledge of its contents. [Citations.] "Business" is defined broadly enough in Sec. 4 to include the law enforcement agencies involved herein. [Citation.] Section 3 permits *testimony* as to the absence of such a record or memorandum and would seem to control the situation at bar. The only prerequisite stated in Sec. 3 to the introduction of such testimony showing the non-existence of an act, event, or condition is that the judge must find that such act, event, or condition would otherwise be recorded and preserved in the ordinary course of business at or near the time in question. Presumably the testimony contemplated by Sec. 3 should be given by the "entrant, custodian or other qualified witness" mentioned in Sec. 2.

In the case at bar, the witness did not show that the arrests and indictments which he said did not exist would otherwise have been entered in the computer in the ordinary course of law enforcement business. Without such proof, his testimony would have no probative value at all. [Citation.] In discussing the N.C.I.C. and other computer systems, it has been said:

> The major problems of the developing crime data networks are ones of controlling the accuracy, accessibility, scope and uses of crime information. Much of the basic data in such systems consists of local police reports, arrest records, rap sheets, and court records which are often inaccurate and incomplete. * * * Incomplete information—recording a person's indictment without his subsequent acquittal, for instance, or failing to withdraw an outdated warrant—could subject innocent parties to continued police pickups and interrogations.

* * *

> Crime records in a centralized data network may be subjected to tampering or accidental destruction. * * * '[D]ata saboteurs' could intentionally destroy or obfuscate the computer files on particular criminals or purposefully introduce false information on innocent parties into the system. Poorly trained computer operators or illdesigned systems might inadvertently 'dump' vital data records. Katzenbach, Nicholas de B. and Richard W. Tomc, Crime Data Centers: The Use of Computers in Crime Detection and Prevention, 4 Colum. Human Rights L.Rev. 49, 52–53 (1972).

The chance that law enforcement officials in Odessa and Clovis, New Mexico failed to enter information on arrests of and charges against deceased is not insubstantial. It was not even shown that the N.C.I.C. has computer terminals in Odessa or Clovis. The probative value of the witness' testimony is thus open to serious question. [Citation.]

The witness, an investigator for the district attorney's office, stated that the "normal custodian" of the N.C.I.C. computer terminal was an employee of the sheriff's department who had initialed the print-out from which the witness was testifying. It would appear then that he was not the "entrant or custodian" contemplated by Sec. 2 although the judge might have found that he was an otherwise "qualified witness" to give the testimony. This conclusion would be supported by the fact that the witness had regular access to the N.C.I.C. computer terminal, understood how the N.C.I.C. computer system worked, and knew how to operate the terminal fixture in the sheriff's office. [Citation.] However, it is apparent that the State did not adduce that part of the predicate specifically called for by Sec. 3. The witness' testimony therefore did not comply with the statute and amounted to nothing more than rank hearsay.

It remains to consider the harmfulness of this error. Appellant's defense relied heavily on proving the deceased's bad character. The primary defensive issues were murder without malice and self-defense. The marital and custody disputes between the deceased and appellant's wife were an integral part of the events leading to this killing. Appellant's wife, whose credibility was severely impugned by the erroneously-admitted testimony, was one of appellant's main witnesses. The only other instance in the record in which the State hinted that the deceased had no criminal record was also objected to by the appellant. And an investigator for the district attorney's office apparently quoting from an N.C.I.C. computer print-out would be clothed with much indicia of respectability. We are unable to conclude beyond a reasonable doubt that the error complained of could not have affected the verdict in this case.

The conviction is reversed and the cause remanded.

MORRISON, J., dissenting.

I dissent to my brother Roberts' opinion reversing this conviction on the basis of an incomplete predicate under Sec. 3 of Article 3737e, V.T.C.A.

The testimony showed that the witness had personal knowledge of the existence of a terminal in Odessa and the entry into N.C.I.C. records of all arrests in Odessa. He testified that Dallas County also had a N.C.I.C. computer terminal and the print-out he received that morning was created in the normal course of business. He stated that he had searched the records in the district attorney's office in Dallas County of all complaints in criminal actions filed in Dallas County since 1920. He also searched the records in the identification division of the Dallas County Sheriff's Office, where records are communicated on persons who are arrested anywhere in the country. Without stating what had been said, he testified that he had contacted the police department and records bureau in Clovis, New Mexico. On the basis of this testimony, the witness stated he had no knowledge of any arrests for the deceased.

Under these circumstances, the failure to prove that arrests are entered in N.C.I.C. records in the regular course of business in Clovis, New Mexico, was harmless error.

The judgment should be affirmed.

DOUGLAS, J., dissenting.

* * *

The majority reverses this conviction because of the admission of testimony offered by the State in its attempt to rebut the testimony given by the appellant's wife concerning the deceased's criminal record. The State called an investigator from the district attorney's office who testified that he had received a computer print-out from the National Criminal Information Center (N.C.I.C.) showing that the Center had no record of arrests or indictments relating to the deceased. The appellant objected to this testimony on the grounds that it was based on hearsay, that no proper predicate had been laid for the introduction of the witness' testimony and that the witness was not the custodian of the N.C.I.C. records.

It should not be necessary to decide if the testimony came within the business record exception to the hearsay rule as set out in Article 3737e, V.T.C.A., [more specifically, Section 3 of Article 3737e dealing with testimony as to the absence of any record or memorandum]. This testimony was introduced to rebut the appellant's wife's testimony concerning the indictment and arrest of the deceased for criminal desertion. The wife's testimony itself was not properly admitted. In *Morgan v. State*, 515 S.W.2d 278 (Tex.Cr.App.1974), this Court held that it was not proper for a witness to testify that another was convicted without the records being introduced. Her testimony about indictments had nothing to do with any defensive issue in this case. The witness Messick testified that appellant said that he had seen a man snooping around his property and he chased him and shot the son-of-a-bitch. Appellant made a similar statement to an officer before he was arrested. After appellant testified he stated that he shot Dr. Sollock in self-defense, the court instructed the jury on self-defense. The trial judge was very patient in permitting evidence of several custody trials involving the children of the deceased. If there were indictments they were immaterial to any issue in the case. There was no objection that the witness was being impeached upon on an immaterial matter and appellant points this out in his brief.

Prior acts of violence or misconduct which show the violent character of the deceased can be admitted in certain limited circumstances. [Citation.] In this case, however, the prior record sought to be introduced would not show the violent nature of the deceased. Criminal desertion or nonsupport cannot be characterized as crimes of violence. Such crimes, in and of themselves, could not be said to indicate that the deceased was the aggressor at the time of the killing and should not be admissible. [Citation.] Even if the arrest and indictment did show the violent nature of the deceased more would be required in way of proof than the hearsay testimony of the wife. [Citations.]

In view of the lack of probative value of the wife's testimony [citation] and the amount of other testimony dealing with the violent character of the deceased by Joan Gassett's father, the admission of the testimony concerning the computer print-out, if error, was harmless error. [Citation.][1] The testimony of appellant's wife was rebutted by her own daughter. The daughter testified that Dr. Sollock was not a man of violent character but that her mother was.

There being no reversible error, the judgment should be affirmed.

UNITED STATES v. VELA

673 F.2d 86

(United States Court of Appeals, Fifth Circuit, April 2, 1982.)

CLARK, C. J.

Ricardo "Ricky" Vela assigns a plethora of errors in this appeal from conviction of conspiracy to commit a drug-related offense. After considering each of his arguments, we affirm his conviction. Our resolution of two points he raises is of precedential value. These points are set out in this published opinion. * * *

I. BACKGROUND

On November 12, 1980, a grand jury sitting in the Southern District of Texas' Laredo Division handed down a five-count indictment charging Ricky Vela with: conspiring to possess with intent to distribute cocaine in violation of 21 U.S.C. §§ 846 & 841(a)(1), possession of a small sample of cocaine with intent to distribute it in violation of 21 U.S.C. § 841(a)(1), distribution of that small sample of cocaine in violation of 21 U.S.C. § 841(a)(1), possession of 639.1 grams of cocaine with intent to distribute it in violation of 21 U.S.C. § 841(a)(1), and distribution of 639.1 grams of

cocaine in violation of 21 U.S.C. § 841(a)(1). [Footnote.] Vela was tried before a jury which acquitted him of the four counts alleging substantive offenses, but convicted him of the conspiracy count. He was sentenced by the judge to serve a six-year prison term and fined $10,000.

The government's side of the story, accepted at least in part by the jury, was as follows. Francisco Caballero and Cesar Gutierrez, both of whom appeared as cooperating witnesses for the prosecution, agreed in June 1980 that Caballero would locate a cocaine supplier to meet the needs of a prospective buyer known to Gutierrez. Caballero's supplier was Vela. Gutierrez' buyer was undercover Special Agent Castro of the Drug Enforcement Administration.

Caballero testified that a course of negotiations with Vela over a period of several days culminated in the delivery of a cocaine sample by Vela to him on the afternoon of June 20, 1980, in Laredo, Texas. The sample was promptly taken to Agent Castro and his colleague Agent Gomez by Caballero and Gutierrez. After several unsuccessful attempts, Caballero contacted Vela and announced to Agent Castro that the delivery of the main shipment of cocaine would take place that night. According to Caballero's testimony, he then met with Vela, traveled in Vela's automobile with him to pick up the cocaine, dropped Vela off in Laredo, and returned with the cocaine to meet Gutierrez, Castro, and Gomez. Upon the delivery of the cocaine, Castro and Gomez revealed their previously disguised identities and arrested Caballero and Gutierrez.

The thrust of Vela's defense was that only Caballero, among the prosecution witnesses, testified to direct contacts with him and that his movements during the crucial evening hours of June 20, 1980, were covered by an alibi placing him at the Laredo Civic Center viewing a closed-circuit telecast of the Leonard-Duran prize fight. Vela sought to attack Caballero's credibility by pointing to inconsistencies in his testimony, the fact that Ca-

---

1. The jury had appellant's admission that he killed the deceased. Appellant followed the deceased, curbed his car and shot him. Appellant testified that he ended the custody matter when he killed the deceased. Appellant also admitted that he sent a bill to the wife of the deceased for $160 because he was required to be present at a hearing involving the murder case and he missed a day of driving a truck. This is included to show what the jury had before it to show harmless error.

ballero did not implicate Vela initially, and the sentencing deal between Caballero and the government.

On appeal, Vela sets forth numerous arguments for reversal of his conviction. In this published opinion, we discuss only two of those arguments: first, that the prosecution abused the federal notice-of-alibi rule so as to deny him of a fair trial, and second, that the trial court improperly admitted certain telephone records into evidence.

* * *

III. ADMISSION OF TELEPHONE RECORDS

Vela argues that the district court erred in admitting copies of the telephone bills of Vela, Caballero, and Gutierrez under the business records exception to the hearsay rule because a proper foundation was not laid to support the reliability of Southwestern Bell Company's computer-billing process. We hold that the foundation was adequate to support admissibility under Rule 803(6).[4]

At trial, an employee of Southwestern Bell described as custodian of the records sponsored copies of the telephone bills. He testified that the copies were made from microfiche records prepared by the comptroller's department of the company, that the records were prepared in the usual course of the company's regularly-conducted business activity, and that it was part of that activity to prepare such records. When questioned by Vela's counsel outside of the jury's presence, the employee explained the process by which automatic call

identification equipment registers the dialing of long-distance telephone calls on electronic tapes. The tapes are then transmitted to the comptroller's office where the information is transferred onto billing tapes. Computers are used at two stages: first, in the recording of the initial dialing, and second, in the computation and preparation of bills in the comptroller's office. The testifying employee vouched only for the general reliability of the process. He was unable to identify the brand, type, and model of each computer, or to vouch for the working condition of the specific equipment during the billing periods covered.

The district court admitted the bills under Rule 803(6) declaring that they "would be even more reliable than * * * average business record[s] because they are not even touched by the hand of man." The defense had previously examined the custodian outside of the jury's presence. Before the jury returned, the court advised the defense that it might want to attack the credibility of the bills on cross-examination. However, the defense never cross-examined the telephone company employee in the presence of the jury. Moreover, the defense did not attack the accuracy of the bills during its closing argument. Indeed, the only reference made to the bills during the defense's closing argument is a suggestion that the jury consult the bills for information tending to exonerate Vela.[5]

Vela's central attack on admissibility of the bills under Rule 803(6) is that the prosecution did not lay a satisfactory foundation. Vela does not dispute that insofar as the custodian of the records testified that the records were kept in the regular course of business the dictates

---

4. Federal Rule of Evidence 803(6) provides:

(6) *Records of regularly conducted activity.* A memorandum, report, record, or data compilation, in any form, of acts, events, conditions, opinions, or diagnoses, made at or near the time by, or from information transmitted by, a person with knowledge, if kept in the course of a regularly conducted business activity, and if it was the regular practice of that business activity to make the memorandum, report, record, or data compilation, all as shown by the testimony of the custodian or other qualified witness, unless the source of information or the method or circumstances of preparation indicate lack of trustworthiness. The term "business" as used in this paragraph includes business, institution, association, profession, occupation, and calling of every kind, whether or not conducted for profit.

5. We pretermit the question of whether Vela waived his right to challenge the admission of the telephone bills by relying on them for his own purposes in closing argument. At one point, Vela's attorney referred the jury to Gutierrez' telephone bill, stating "that that guy had been making calls to Brazil, to Chicago the capital of the ganster world; and San Antonio, Nuevo Laredo, Zapata, Hebronville. Many places in Mexico and all over." At another point, the attorney referred the jury to Gutierrez' bill and suggested that a Hebronville number on that bill belonged to Gutierrez' source. Finally, Vela's attorney asked the jury to consult Caballero's telephone bill. Vela's argument on appeal is a classic attempt to eat his cake and have it too.

of Rule 803(6) were satisfied. What Vela does argue is that by failing to establish that the computers involved in the billing process were in proper working order a satisfactory foundation was not made and Vela was denied confrontation rights.

Our review of a trial court's decision to admit business records is a limited one. We test it only for abuse of discretion. *See Rosenberg v. Collins*, 624 F.2d 659, 665 (5th Cir. 1980). While the suggestion has been made that there are unique foundation requirements for the admission of computerized business records under Rule 803(6) [citations], this court has previously held that "computer data compilations * * * should be treated as any other record of regularly conducted activity." *Rosenberg v. Collins*, 624 F.2d at 665. Like the computer records in the *Rosenberg* case, the telephone company's long distance billing records are "sufficiently trustworthy in the eyes of this disinterested company to be relied on by the company in conducting its day to day business affairs." *Id.*

The prosecution laid a proper predicate for the admission of the bills. A telephone company employee explained the precise manner in which the billing data are compiled. The failure to certify the brand or proper operating condition of the machinery involved does not betray a circumstance of preparation indicating any lack of trustworthiness. Fed.R.Evid. 803(6). This court has previously stated that computer evidence is not intrinsically unreliable. [Citations.] Vela's arguments for a level of authentication greater than that regularly practiced by the company in its own business activities go beyond the rule and its reasonable purpose to admit truthful evidence. The court did not abuse its discretion in admitting the bills or deny Vela his confrontation rights. At best, the arguments made go to the weight that should be accorded the evidence, not its admissibility. [Citation.]

IV.   CONCLUSION

The various arguments set forth by Vela, whether considered singly or cumulatively, do not convince us that a reversal is warranted. His conviction is affirmed.

PEOPLE v. JONES
118 Misc.2d 687, 461 N.Y.S.2d 962
(Albany County Court, April 14, 1983.)

HARRIS, J.

The issue presented by the motion of the defendant is whether the results of a breath test performed on an Intoximeter 3000, a device employing infrared and electrical analysis of breath vapors, are admissible as evidence in a prosecution for driving while intoxicated.

A suppression hearing was held at which this Court heard testimony from one of the developers of the instrument, from an official of the Bureau of Municipal Police in the New York State Division of Criminal Justice Services, from a Project Director for the breath alcohol program of the U.S. Department of Transportation involved in the evaluation of breath alcohol test devices for the National Highway Traffic Safety Administration and, for the defendant, from a professor of chemistry at the State University of New York at Albany.

This is a case of first impression and may be of broad impact throughout the State of New York; thus a full exposition of the issues and their resolution is required.

FINDINGS OF FACT

The Intoximeter 3000 is a breath-testing device which utilizes infrared energy and electrical current to detect the presence of ethyl alcohol (ethanol) in the breath of a driver. The device, as are all breath-testing devices, is based upon Henry's Law [footnote] and, unlike more common breath-testers such as the breathalyzer, upon the Beer-Lambert Law of Absorption. [Footnote.]

The Intoximeter 3000 is equipped with an infrared energy source of nichrome (an alloy of nickel, chromium and iron) surrounding a ceramic core. An electric current passing through this source causes two beams of infrared energy to be emitted in the direction of a two-chambered gas cell after reflecting off a collimating mirror. After traversing the gas cell, the infrared beams pass through a narrow band interference filter. This filter permits infrared energy with a wavelength ranging from 3.3 to 3.48 microns to pass through and strike a detector while at the same time blocking energy with wavelengths greater or lesser than that range. Thus the beam of energy striking the detector is modified so that it corresponds to one of the major absorption bands of ethyl alcohol.

The cell through which the infrared beams pass has two chambers. One, the reference cell, contains only room air. The other, the sample cell, contains during a test 900 cubic centimeters of the subject's alveolar air. The device gives a reading of the amount of interfering substance[3] in the subject's breath by comparing the amount of infrared energy striking the detector after the two beams pass through the chambers, one through the sample cell, the other through the reference cell. Otherwise stated, the device compares the amount of infrared energy absorbed by the air from the lungs of the subject with the amount absorbed by the air from the room. If the ratio resulting from that reading (energy absorbed by the alveolar air/energy absorbed by the room air) is greater than one, there is present in the subject's breath some substance which absorbs infrared radiation at 3.39 microns. The amount of interfering substance present is determined by the amount of infrared energy it absorbs. At this point it is impossible to conclude that the absorbing substance is ethyl alcohol because in addition to ethyl alcohol there are other substances which absorb radiation at 3.39 microns.

In order to enable the Intoximeter 3000 to give a specific reading for ethyl alcohol, another device is necessary. Thus the Intoximeter 3000, in addition to its infrared analysis of breath based on the Beer-Lambert Law of Absorption, also contains a semi-conductor (a Taguci sensor) by which it is able to distinguish ethyl alcohol from other substances which absorb infrared radiation in the area of 3.39 microns. [Footnote.]

The Taguci sensor is a semi-conductor device the conductivity of which is influenced by the ambient air in the sample chamber. The conductivity of the semi-conductor varies when there is present in that ambient air an oxidizible vapor such as ethyl alcohol or other hydrocarbon. Programmed into the memory of the computer that is mated to the Intoximeter 3000 are the specific conductivity readings (in amperes) of the sensor when ethyl alcohol is present in the sample chamber at varying levels which correspond to the various blood-alcohol levels. These conductivity readings are predetermined empirically in the laboratory, and are specific for ethyl alcohol. Every other substance that absorbs infrared radiation at a wavelength of 3.39 microns produces a different current in the semi-conductor. The computer incorporated into the device compares the outputs from the infrared sensor (amount of infrared energy absorbed) and the semi-conductor (amperes of electrical current). If the semi-conductor reading does not correspond to that stored in the computer's memory for the blood-alcohol level reported by the infrared sensor, an interferent other than or in addition to ethyl alcohol is present in the subject's breath. The computer performs a calculation to determine the difference between the reading for the blood-alcohol level reported by the infrared sensor and the reading from the semi-conductor sensor, which difference automatically reduces the infrared reading by a corresponding amount. That adjusted amount is reported as the subject's blood-alcohol level.[5]

Operation of the Intoximeter 3000 is relatively simple and requires minimal operator

---

3. By "interfering substance" is meant any substance that absorbs radiation at 3.39 microns, among which are ethyl alcohol and acetone.

5. The Intoximeter 3000 reports all non-ethyl alcohol interfering substances found by the semi-conductor as "acetone", even though there may theoretically be some other interferent present. Acetone not only is the most common interfering substance found in the human body that, like ethyl alcohol, absorbs infrared radiation at a wavelength of 3.39 microns, but is the only such interferent present in the human body (and mostly in diabetics and persons on longstanding stringent diets) in sufficient quantity and with sufficient vapor pressure so as to appear in the breath and register on the Intoximeter 3000.

In the vast multitude of cases, what is reported by the infrared sensor will be ethyl alcohol.

However, the semi-conductor sensor is still always present to take care of the aberrational case and assure that the final reading of the Intoximeter 3000 is purely ethyl alcohol.

The actual identity of the interfering substance reported by the semi-conductor, which realistically will always be acetone, is actually irrelevant because we are only interested in the quantity of the interferent and not its identity.

The above conclusions are supported empirically by numerous laboratory and field tests, not only by the manufacturer but by the National Highway Traffic Safety Administration.

intervention compared with more common breath-testing devices.

Each test commences with a twenty minute waiting period during which the subject is observed to insure that he does not ingest any alcohol, regurgitate or vomit. The operator presses a "start" button and then follows the machine's commands to enter his name and identification number and the subject's name. Following the last entry, the machine automatically blanks and purges to remove any residual alcohol fumes and to take a baseline reading, which ought to read ".00." The machine then commands the subject to blow into the breath tube until the machine indicates that a sufficient sample has been entered. The Intoximeter then reports the subject's blood-alcohol content on its display and proceeds to purge and blank itself. The machine then automatically runs a test with a reference solution, the ethyl alcohol content of which has been previously certified by the State Police Laboratory. Following the test with the reference sample, the machine again purges itself. The operator then presses the "print" key, whereupon the information previously entered and the results of the subject's test, the reference sample test and the blank tests, the latter two being control tests to assure that the machine is functioning properly, are printed along with the times that the tests took place. The operator thus is required merely to type certain minimal information on the machine's keyboard; he does not have to handle ampules of chemicals nor turn dials and levers as with more common breath testing devices.

The machine automatically safeguards against any contaminants in the room air and contains fail-safe devices to abort if there are room temperature or electrical or voltage problems, which rarely occur.

CONCLUSIONS OF LAW

Counsel for the defendant makes two threshold arguments. First, that sections 1193-a and 1194 of the Vehicle and Traffic Law permit only a "chemical test" of the breath, blood, urine, or saliva of a motor vehicle operator for the purpose of determining the alcoholic or drug content of his blood.

The defendant argues the Intoximeter 3000, based as it is on infrared and electrical analysis of a driver's breath, is not a "chemical test" and thus the results of such test are inadmissible.

The defendant's position is unrealistic and unfounded. There is no precedent in the State of New York on this issue, but a similar argument was made and rejected in courts of other states with regard to the Omicron Intoxilyzer (another breath-testing device utilizing infrared theory). In Ohio, a court held that even though the infrared test did not involve an actual chemical reaction, the definition of chemical analysis was broad enough to embrace the infrared process. [Citation.] Similarly, in Delaware, the court held that the Intoxilyzer did perform a chemical analysis as required by State law regardless of the fact that the procedure was purely mechanical. The court concluded the term "chemical test" meant only an "analysis" of the substance being tested—that is, an examination of a substance to determine its component parts and proportions thereof, regardless of the method of testing. [Citation.] This Court likewise concludes that the term "chemical test" as used in Vehicle and Traffic Law 1193-a and 1194 was intended to mean an analysis of the chemistry of the substances therein referred to—breath, blood, urine or saliva—to determine the subject's blood-alcohol content, and was not intended to refer to the method of testing. Thus an analysis of breath as performed by the Intoximeter 3000, which utilizes established principles and laws of physics, is a chemical test within the meaning of that term in Vehicle and Traffic Law 1193-a and 1194. The position advanced by defendant seeks to restrict the meaning of "chemical test" to a process more appropriately called a chemical reaction. There is no authority in the law to require defendant's interpretation. Furthermore, to adopt the defendant's position would be to bind inflexibly the administration of justice to the level of technology extant at the time of the enactment of the statute while technological advances thereafter would be unavailable to law enforcement officials if they did not fall within the terminology of a dated statute. If such a result is not required, it ought not to be adopted.

The defendant's second threshold argument is that the results of the Intoximeter test are inadmissible because the instrument has not been certified or tested by the New York State Department of Health nor has it been listed by the director of the State Police laboratory as a device which meets the criteria of the Department of Health, both of which pre-conditions, the defendant argues, are required by Vehicle and Traffic Law section 1194, subdivision 9.

This Court finds nothing in section 1194, subdivision 9, mandating the Department of Health to establish criteria for breath-alcohol testing devices, let alone conditioning the evidentiary admissibility of the test results of such devices upon their conformance with such criteria. Vehicle and Traffic Law, section 1194, subdivision 9, is concededly inartfully drawn, but in this Court's view its obvious intent and purport was to establish a procedure for issuing permits to qualified test operators so as to establish a presumption that the test was properly given and thus ease at trial the People's burden with respect to establishing a foundation at trial for the admissibility of breath-alcohol test results. Interestingly the subdivision in question specifically provides that it does not prohibit the introduction as evidence of an analysis made by an individual not possessing a permit issued by the Department of Health.

The fact that the Department of Health saw fit to promulgate "regulations", contained in Part 59 of Title 10 of the New York Code of Rules and Regulations, purporting to establish standards respecting the techniques and methods for breath-alcohol testing, is not governing. There is no express provision in the Vehicle and Traffic Law requiring compliance with the Health Department's regulations as a condition for the admission into evidence of breath test results. [Citation.] Rather, the validity of the test and the admission of the test results into evidence should be, and is, determined by their accuracy and reliability as de-

termined by resort to generally accepted scientific standards. [Citation.] Similarly, the absence of compliance with 10 NYCRR 59.4, in that the Intoximeter 3000 is not listed by the Director of the State Police laboratory as a device which meets the criteria of the Department of Health, is not a bar to the admission into evidence of its test results where otherwise not prohibited by law.[6]

Essentially both threshold arguments by the defendant beg the basic question: Can the Intoximeter 3000 reliably and accurately measure the amount of alcohol in a driver's blood through an analysis of the subject's breath?

The law with respect to the admissibility of evidence derived from a scientific test or process has its touchstone in *Frye v. United States*, 293 F. 1013 (D.C.Cir.1923): Is the process "sufficiently established to have gained general acceptance in the particular field in which it belongs." [Citation.]

New York courts have consistently employed the *Frye* criterion to determine the admissibility of scientifically derived evidence. It has served as the basis for excluding the results of lie detection tests conducted with the pathometer [citation], the polygraph [citation], and voice stress analysis. [Citation.] Conversely, *Frye* has been used to sanction the introduction of breathalyzer test results [citation] and automobile speed evidence obtained with radar. [Citation.]

Thus, the inquiry at hand becomes whether the process of analyzing breath by means of infrared energy and electrical current is sufficiently established so as to have gained general acceptance in its field. It is the conclusion of this Court that it has.

The identification of unknown compounds by means of principles of infrared molecular absorption is well-recognized and accepted by the scientific community, as attested to by the defendant's own expert witness. This process, based on the generally-recognized Beer-Lam-

---

6. 10 NYCRR 59.4 lists four criteria for breath-alcohol testing devices. Interestingly the Intoximeter 3000 does, in fact, meet all of these criteria. The device does, in fact, collect and analyze a fixed volume of alveolar breath; it also is capable of analyzing and, in fact, does analyze reference samples of alcohol, and its analysis thereof has been shown to be within one-hundredth of one percent of the certified alcohol content of the reference solution. As

to the final criteria (that the procedure's specificity be adequate and appropriate for the analysis of breath specimens for the determination of alcoholic concentration in traffic law enforcement), that is the very question addressed in the hearings on this motion and in this opinion and which question the Court herein answers in the affirmative.

bert Law of Absorption, supra, has been practically applied in research instruments such as the spectrophotometer. The infrared process incorporated in the Intoximeter 3000, while more restricted and narrower in scope than that of the spectrophotometer, is nonetheless the same process and is capable of detecting the presence and quantity of a certain group of substances, including ethyl alcohol, which have a major infrared absorption band at 3.39 microns. Thus it is the conclusion of this Court that this portion of the Intoximeter 3000 process—relying upon infrared analysis—is based upon generally accepted scientific principles and methods and is sufficiently established and accepted in the scientific community so as to have gained general acceptance in its field.

However, this can not end the discussion. If infrared analysis were the only process incorporated in the Intoximeter 3000, the results of its tests would be inadmissible because the test would lack specificity in light of the numerous substances, in addition to ethyl alcohol, which absorb infrared energy at the wavelength of 3.39 microns.

This lack of specificity in the report of the Intoximeter's infrared sensor is fully compensated for by its semi-conductor sensor. The utility of semi-conductors in electrical devices cannot be gainsaid. They are generally recognized in the scientific community and the electronics industry as being capable of conducting varying rates of electrical current depending upon the environment in which they are located. Thus, as has been empirically demonstrated, a Taguci-type semi-conductor is able to distinguish between the various substances which absorb infrared energy with a wavelength of 3.39 microns by conducting electrical currents of varying strengths depending upon what substances are present in its environment. For each such substance, including ethyl alcohol, the semi-conductor transmits an electrical current of a specific strength which can be empirically predetermined.[7]

Even though the Intoximeter 3000 incorporates two processes which this Court concludes are generally accepted in the scientific community and in their respective fields, it takes the Intoximeter's computer to tie the two separate processes together into a coherent, reliable system for the detection of ethyl alcohol in a subject's breath. During a test, the computer performs the essential function of comparing the semi-conductor reading with that stored in its memory for the quantity of interferent, including ethyl alcohol, reported by the infrared sensor. The computer then makes any necessary reduction in the infrared reading due to the presence of any non-ethyl alcohol interferents. That a computer is capable of performing such tasks is beyond doubt in this technological age.

Dr. Arthur Flores, a chemist and project director for the breath alcohol program of the U.S. Department of Transportation, charged with the duty of evaluating breath alcohol testing devices for the National Highway Traffic Safety Administration, testified that extensive tests were performed on the Intoximeter 3000 in 1980 and 1981 to determine the accuracy and reliability of the machine as evidential breath testers in determining the blood alcohol content of a suspected drunk driver. The machine passed all federal requirements and that fact was published in the Federal Register. This means that the National Highway Traffic Safety Administration will provide federal funds under section 302(a) of the Highway Safety Act of 1966 to assist the states in purchasing the Intoximeter 3000.

The Intoximeter 3000 is used not only in the State of New York, but in the states of Idaho, Wyoming, Wisconsin, and Alaska, and country-wide in England.

For all of the reasons stated above it is the ultimate conclusion of this Court that processes used by and incorporated in the Intoximeter 3000 are generally accepted in the scientific community and in the fields in which they belong, and that the Intoximeter 3000 reliably and accurately detects and measures

---

7. The efficacy of the semi-conductor's ethyl alcohol/acetone discrimination has been demonstrated in the laboratory. Arthur Flores, Project Director for the National Highway Traffic Safety Administration, a witness for the People, testified that as part of his testing of the Intoximeter 3000 for NHTS certification, he tested its acetone

detection feature and found that it operated as described. This conclusion is supported by similar studies done by Intoximeters, Inc., the manufacturer, and by the State of Idaho Department of Health and Welfare, Bureau of Laboratories (as reported in Richard Erwin's *Defense of Drunk Driving Cases*, Chapter 19A, pages 19A–3—19A–5).

the quantity of ethyl alcohol in the blood of a driver to the exclusion of any other substance. Therefore, the defendant's motion to suppress the results of the Intoximeter 3000 test given to him following his arrest for Operating a Motor Vehicle While Under the Influence of Alcohol in violation of Vehicle and Traffic Law section 1192, subdivisions (2) and (3) is denied!

The findings of fact and conclusions of law herein are made upon clear and convincing evidence.

IN RE WEST
60 N.C.App. 388, 299 S.E.2d 245
(Court of Appeals of North Carolina, Jan. 18, 1983.)

On 20 April 1979 the petitioner, Farmer's Home Administration (FHA) filed and served a notice of hearing regarding the right of foreclosure under several deeds of trust from respondents, Ronald S. West and wife, Margie H. West on farmland located in Franklin County, N.C. The Franklin County Clerk of Court entered an order on 17 June 1980 finding that the respondents were in default and ordering that foreclosure be completed and a public sale be conducted on the subject premises. The respondents appealed from this order to the Superior Court.

The matter was heard before Judge Hobgood on 2 November 1981. Edith Shearin, secretary and office assistant in the Franklin County Farmers Home Administration office testified primarily from computerized records centrally maintained in a FHA office in St. Louis, Mo. Ms. Shearin testified, over objections by counsel for the respondents, that Ronald S. West and Margie H. West were in default and delinquent under the terms of their various loan accounts.

At the conclusion of the testimony and final arguments, Judge Hobgood made findings of fact and ordered the foreclosure to be completed. From the entry of this order, respondents appeal.

JOHNSON, J.
The respondents present two related arguments on appeal: (1) the trial court erred in admitting the computerized records of the FHA and testimony of Edith H. Shearin into evidence without proper authentication and foundation; and (2) the trial court erred in ordering the completion of foreclosure upon the computerized records erroneously admitted into evidence.

The trial court found that a valid debt existed, that respondents were in default, that there was a right to foreclosure under the instruments and that proper notice had been given to all parties. The respondents do not contest the central fact that the account was in default under the terms of the notes and deeds of trust held by the petitioner. Rather, they take issue with the introduction into evidence of Ms. Shearin's testimony that respondents were in default and the documents and computerized statements of account under the business records exception to the rule excluding hearsay evidence. We find no error in the admission of this evidence.

In the case of *State v. Springer*, 283 N.C. 627, 197 S.E.2d 530 (1973), the Supreme Court set forth the requirements for authentication of business records stored in electronic computing equipment as a prerequisite for their admission into evidence.

> We therefore hold that printout cards or sheets of business records stored on electronic computing equipment are admissible in evidence, if otherwise relevant and material, if: (1) the computerized entries were made in the regular course of business, (2) at or near the time of the transaction involved, and (3) a proper foundation for such evidence is laid by testimony of a witness who is familiar with the computerized records and the methods under which they were made so as to satisfy the court that the methods, the sources of information, and the time of preparation render such evidence trustworthy.

[Citation.]
The respondents cite *State v. Springer* and rely on that case in support of their contention that the proper foundation for Ms. Shearin's testimony was not provided because she did not testify that she was familiar with the computerized records and methods under which they were made. However, *Springer* is distinguishable in that the Supreme Court held that the testimony of a special investigator was inadmissible because the witness was testifying from computer records without attempting to offer the records themselves into evidence. Further, a proper foundation for this testimony had not been laid.

The record discloses that the computer records were properly authenticated and a proper foundation laid through the testimony of Ms. Shearin. Ms. Shearin testified to the effect that the computer center in St. Louis contained all the business records of the FHA and was the only source of such records. Thus, the first requirement set forth in *Springer*, that the computerized entries be made in the regular course of business was met.

The second requirement of the business records exception requires that computer entries be made at or near the time of the transactions involved. Ms. Shearin testified that the FHA in Franklin County provides information during the course of a loan to the finance office. In turn, the finance office puts that information into the computer terminals. In order to allow the county office to follow the course of the loan, the finance office prepares a transaction record which is sent back to the county office for inclusion in the borrower's file as a management systems card. An overall review of Ms. Shearin's testimony shows that information, payment or other data concerning the loan transaction is systematically forwarded by the Franklin County office to the St. Louis finance office without significant delay. Thus, the requirement that data be computerized at or near the time of the transaction involved is satisfied.

The requirement for laying a proper foundation is the third element of admissibility. A proper foundation must be laid by a witness who is familiar with the computerized records and the methods under which they were made. With regard to witness familiarity, the Court in *State v. Springer, supra,* stated:

> "The impossibility of producing in court all the persons who observed, reported and recorded each individual transaction gave rise to the modification which permits the introduction of recorded entries, made in the regular course of business, at or near the time of the transaction involved, and authenticated by a witness who is familiar with them and the method under which they are made. *This rule applies to original entries made in books of account in regular course by those engaged in business, when properly identified, though the witness may not have made the entries* and may have no personal knowledge of the transactions." (Emphasis added.)

[Citation.] Ms. Shearin has been an employee

of the FHA in Franklin County for sixteen years. She identified the records as FHA loan transaction records. Further, Ms. Shearin is familiar with the respondents' loan accounts and testified about the method by which the finance office in St. Louis obtains the loan account data to put on their computer.

As to the records upon which her testimony is based, Ms. Shearin testified:

> This information that I have today is verified with the finance office in St. Louis, Missouri, by the computer terminal in the Finance Office on each loan account.

After stating that the finance center in St. Louis contains all the Farmers Home records in the United States, Ms. Shearin added:

> Farmers Home Administration of Franklin County provides information to the Finance Office in St. Louis, Missouri, to put on a computer and in turn they set up their computer records in Finance and provide us with a transaction record, which we have today with us in Mr. West's management system card. We have a transaction record for every loan account of Mr. West and this information is a summary of those transaction records as given me by the Finance Office in St. Louis, Missouri.

The testimony of Ms. Shearin demonstrated her knowledge both of the subject records and the method by which the data is gathered and the records made. A sufficient foundation was laid to establish the trustworthiness of the loan records. Respondents have not demonstrated that the records indicating their default under the terms of the loan were not trustworthy or that the computer records were otherwise unreliable on the issue of their default. The fact that Ms. Shearin did not personally enter the information furnished the finance office on their computer bank, nor update and compute the interest on a particular loan herself does not in anyway diminish her ability to authenticate the records and testify to the default under the rule announced in *State v. Springer.* [Citation.] The "business records" exception contemplates exactly the situation presented by this case—the "impossibility of producing in court all the persons who observed, reported and recorded each individual transaction." [Citation.] Therefore, to lay a proper foundation for admission of centrally maintained computerized records, it is wholly unnecessary to produce in court the computer terminal operator who actually entered the data onto the computer terminal.

The trial court properly admitted the FHA computer records and testimony of Ms. Shearin into evidence and properly ordered foreclosure to proceed based upon the evidence received at trial.

Affirmed.

UNITED STATES
v. DE GEORGIA

420 F.2d 889
(United States Court of Appeals, Ninth Circuit, Dec. 11, 1969.)

HAMLEY, C. J.

Richard Allen De Georgia appeals from a judgment of conviction, entered on a jury verdict, for violating 18 U.S.C. § 2312 (Dyer Act). The offense involved a 1968 Mustang automobile allegedly stolen from the Hertz Corporation, in New York City, and thereafter driven to Tucson, Arizona. The car was recovered from De Georgia on September 9, 1968.

* * *

Defendant confessed in writing that he stole the automobile from the vicinity of John F. Kennedy Airport, New York, on or about July 2, 1968.[2] However, a confession does not constitute adequate proof of an element of an offense unless, as to that element, the confession is corroborated by other admissible evidence. [Footnote.] While the Government did produce other evidence designed to corroborate the confession with regard to the element in question, defendant contends that this other evidence was inadmissible hearsay and his trial objection thereto should have been sustained.

The evidence offered by the Government in corroboration of defendant's confession that the Mustang was a stolen vehicle consisted of the testimony of Tony Gratta, the Hertz security manager for the company's New York

zone. Gratta produced documentary evidence establishing that the Mustang was owned by Hertz, that it was rented to Edward P. Sweeney from John F. Kennedy Airport on June 28, 1968, and that Sweeney returned it to a Hertz station at the airport on June 30, 1968.

Gratta testified, in effect, that the vehicle was not rented or leased by Hertz after that date and therefore was a stolen vehicle when it was taken from the Hertz lot at the airport sometime after June 30, 1968. Gratta based his testimony that the Mustang had not been rented or leased by Hertz after June 30, 1968, upon information he obtained from the Hertz master computer control in Gratta's New York office.

According to Gratta, Hertz does not keep a running written business record of its rental and lease transactions but maintains this information in a computer system. Information concerning all automobile rental and lease agreements is fed into computer consoles located at each Hertz terminal and may be retrieved at the master computer control in Gratta's New York office. He explained that, under this system, one can check the master control to determine when and where a particular vehicle was last rented and when it was returned. [Footnote.]

On July 26, 1968, Gratta received information from the Hertz office in Lincoln, Nebraska, that led him to believe that the Mustang might have been stolen. He thereupon checked the master computer control in his office and ascertained that the automobile in question had been returned to the Hertz office at the New York airport on June 30, 1968, and that there was no subsequent rental or lease activity recorded. Gratta testified that this indicated that the vehicle had been stolen.

Counsel for defendant objected to the admission of this evidence upon the ground that it was hearsay. As amplified in his motions for judgment of acquittal and in his briefs on appeal, counsel believes that the evidence was hearsay because it amounted to an assertion by those who placed rental and lease infor-

---

2. At the trial defendant disavowed the confession, stating that he signed it only because law enforcement officers told him that they wanted to "clean up" their books and led him to believe he would be immediately released. Defendant testified that he borrowed the car on July 8,

1968, from a friend who told him that he had leased the vehicle. According to defendant, the friend said defendant could keep the Mustang until December, 1968. Defendant had a prior Dyer Act conviction as a youth offender. The jury apparently did not believe defendant.

mation into the Hertz computer system (and who were not called as witnesses) that no such transaction involving the Mustang occurred after June 30, 1968.[5]

This view finds support in the writings of Professor Wigmore. He has expressed the view that the absence of an entry concerning a particular transaction in a regularly-maintained business record of such transactions, is equivalent to an assertion by the person maintaining the record that no such transaction occurred. 5 Wigmore, Evidence (3d Ed.) §§ 1531, 1556, pages 392, 410.

But, assuming that the evidence was hearsay, this does not conclude the matter. There are many exceptions to the hearsay rule, one of which is the business records exception which, in the federal courts, is legislatively declared in the Business Records Act, 28 U.S.C. § 1732. [Citation.] Professor Wigmore believes that negative testimony of the kind described above, based upon what regularly-maintained business records do not show, is admissible hearsay as a corollary to the exception that records made in the regular course of business are admissible. Wigmore, *ibid.*

A contrary view was stated in Shreve v. United States, 77 F.2d 2, 7 (9th Cir. 1935), as one of several alternative reasons for reversing a district court judgment. We there acknowledged that the decisions were not entirely in accord on the point, but cited decisions from five states in support of the rule against the admission of such negative testimony. No federal decisions were cited. As to one of these states, Vermont, *Shreve* was in error in implying that the then prevailing rule was against admissibility, and in another, California, the rule was later changed in favor of admissibility. [Footnote.] In a third state, Massachusetts, the former rule against admissibility has been somewhat modified, and in a fourth state, New York, the rule against admissibility has been adhered to since Shreve. [Footnote.]

All of the other United States Courts of Appeals which have passed upon the matter have held such evidence admissible. [Footnote.] This is also the rule by statute in at least five states. [Footnote.] This rule of admissibility was proposed in the Uniform Rules of Evidence, Rule 63(14), as drafted by the National Conference of Commissioners on Uniform State Laws, and approved by it at its annual conference in 1953. The Uniform Rules were also approved by the American Bar Association in 1953.

The rule that such evidence is admissible has also been proposed by the Committee on Rules of Practice and Procedure of the Judicial Conference of the United States. In the committee's March 1969 Preliminary Draft of Proposed Rules of Evidence for the United States District Courts and Magistrates, Rule 8–03, "Hearsay Exceptions: Availability of Declarant Immaterial," reads in part:

(a) GENERAL PROVISIONS. A statement is not excluded by the hearsay rule if its nature and the special circumstances under which it was made offer assurances of accuracy not likely to be enhanced by calling the declarant as a witness, even though he is available.

(b) ILLUSTRATIONS. By way of illustration only, and not by way of limitation, the following are examples of statements conforming with the requirements of this rule:

* * *

(7) ABSENCE OF ENTRY IN RECORDS OF REGULARLY CONDUCTED ACTIVITY. Evidence that a matter is not included in the memoranda, reports, records, or data compilations, in any form, of a regularly conducted activity, to prove the nonoccurrence or nonexistence of the matter, if the matter was of a kind of which a memorandum, report, record, or data compilation was regularly made and preserved. [Footnote.]

Regularly-maintained business records are admissible in evidence as an exception to the hearsay rule because the circumstance that they are regularly-maintained records upon which the company relies in conducting its business assures accuracy not likely to be en-

---

5. Counsel did not make any point of the fact that the records examined by Gratta in reaching this conclusion were maintained in a computer system rather than in a running written business record of rental and lease transactions. In any event, paragraph (a) of 28 U.S.C. § 1732, which is the part of the Federal Business Records Act

which concerns us here, does not require that, to be admissible, the record must be in writing. That paragraph involves the admissibility of "any writing *or record*, whether in the form of an entry in a book *or otherwise*, made as a memorandum or record of any act, transaction. * * *" (Emphasis supplied.)

hanced by introducing into evidence the original documents upon which the records are based.

In our view, this same circumstance offers a like assurance that if a business record designed to note every transaction of a particular kind contains no notation of such a transaction between specified dates, no such transaction occurred between those dates. Moreover, in our opinion, that assurance is not likely to be enhanced by the only other means of proving such a negative; that is by bringing into court all of the documents involving similar transactions during the period in question to prove that there was no record of the transactions alleged not to have occurred, and calling as witnesses all company personnel who had the duty of entering into transactions of that kind during the critical period and inquiring whether the witnesses remembered any additional transactions for which no record had been produced.

As applied to the case now before us, this alternative method of proving the negative would have been singularly burdensome and unrewarding. An enormous volume of rental and lease contracts would have had to be brought into court. In addition, the Government would have been required to call as witnesses every Hertz employee who might have consummated a lease or rental of the Mustang during the period between June 30, 1968, the date the car was returned after its last recorded rental, and at least July 26, 1968, the date that Gratta first received information that the car was stolen. These employees would have had to be asked to state from memory whether, out of all of the lease and rental transactions which they had entered into during that time, there was any rental of this particular Mustang. Recourse to the Hertz computer avoided these difficulties.[11]

We are in accord with the rule permitting admission of such hearsay evidence, as formulated in Proposed Rule 8–03(b)(7), quoted above, which rule is supported by the weight of modern authority. With the knowledge and approval of all of the members of the court in active service, we therefore disapprove the holding in *Shreve* that such evidence is inadmissible.

It follows that Gratta's testimony to the effect that the Mustang was a stolen vehicle when it was transported across state lines after July 2, 1968, was properly received in evidence and provides adequate corroboration of defendant's confession to the same effect.

In his reply brief defendant argues, for the first time, that reception of Gratta's testimony violated the best evidence rule which required that the business records be introduced into evidence.

No such objection having been made in the trial court, we decline to consider the contention here.

Affirmed.

ELY, C. J., concurring.

I concur in the majority opinion, but I reemphasize that the appellant, in objecting to the questioned evidence, did not rely upon the best evidence rule. Had an objection been made on this basis, I would be more troubled by admission of this testimony, since the computer print-out sheets could have been made available as evidence that there was no transaction recorded.

Moreover, I wish to add a few cautionary words of my own. As Judge Hamley points out, the business records exception to the hearsay evidence rule is grounded on the probability of accuracy that is provided by the fact that, in the regular course of business, certain records are maintained and relied upon

---

11. While, as stated above, it is immaterial that the business record is maintained in a computer rather than in company books, this is on the assumption that: (1) the opposing party is given the same opportunity to inquire into the accuracy of the computer and the input procedures used, as he would have to inquire into the accuracy of written business records, and (2) the trial court, as in the case of challenged business records, requires the party offering the computer information to provide a foundation therefor sufficient to warrant a finding that such information is trustworthy.

In our case defendant had a full opportunity, upon cross-

examination, to inquire into the company practice of feeding information as to all car rentals and leases into the computer, and as to the accuracy of the computer in retaining and retrieving such information. The Government presented foundation evidence as to input procedures used. While the Government did not produce expert testimony as to the mechanical accuracy of the computer, it did establish that it was sufficiently accurate so that Hertz relied upon it in conducting its business. We need not decide whether this was an adequate foundation, because defendant raised no question in the trial court as to the mechanical accuracy of the computer.

in daily business operations. The Federal Business Records Act was designed to conform this exception to the practices of modern business by eliminating the traditional requirement that the authenticity of the records be established by the personal testimony of their maker.[1] Eliminating this requirement, however, should in no way alleviate the need for proof that the particular records have a high degree of trustworthiness. [Citation.]

The requirement of trustworthiness was, I think, incorporated into the Business Records Act by means of the phrase, "in regular course of * * * business." I believe that this criterion of admissibility is nothing more than an assessment of the probability that records ordinarily made in the regular course of business are likely to be accurate. Thus, it is a prerequisite that a firm foundation of admissibility must be laid by convincing the trial court that the circumstances of the making of the record are such that accuracy is not merely probable, but *highly* probable. [Citation.] This principle becomes even more important when related to the questioned introduction of a summary of that which would be found in the records themselves. [Citation.] In fact, some courts have indicated that summaries are inadmissible unless the basic records are offered into evidence. [Citations.]

The problems concerned with mere summaries of records are likely to increase as electronic data processing equipment increasingly becomes a more normal means of keeping records. Summaries, in the form of print-out sheets, of voluminous data stored in a computer may be a more desirable form of evidence than admission of all the separate documents that were transcribed into the computer. Moreover, when a party seeks to

prove the negative, that mention of a transaction of a specified character cannot be found in the records, then a summary may necessarily suffice. But in order fully to protect the defendant in a criminal case from undue infringement of his right to confrontation of the witnesses, this type of evidence should still be strictly tested. As the Supreme Court has stated, in dealing with hearsay evidence, "The reason for excluding this evidence as an *evidentiary* matter also requires its exclusion as a *constitutional* matter." *Bruton v. United States*, 391 U.S. 123, 136 n. 12, 88 S.Ct. 1620, 1628, 20 L.Ed.2d 476 (1968) (Emphasis in original).

At least one court has recently given careful consideration to the question of whether a computer's print-out sheets constituted admissible evidence. The court noted that the best evidence rule might actually support the use of the computer sheets and concluded,

> * * * we hold that print-out sheets of business records stored on electronic computing equipment are admissible in evidence if relevant and material, without the necessity of identifying, locating, and producing as witnesses the individuals who made the entries in the regular course of business if it is shown (1) that the electronic computing equipment is recognized as standard equipment, (2) the entries are made in the regular course of business at or reasonably near the time of the happening of the event recorded, and (3) the foundation testimony satisfies the court that the sources of information, method and time of preparation were such as to indicate its trustworthiness and justify its admission.

King v. State for Use and Benefit of Murdock Acceptance Corp., 222 So.2d 393 (Miss.1969). The Federal Business Records Act should

---

1. The second paragraph of section 1732(a) provides that
   All other circumstances of the making of such writing or record, including lack of personal knowledge by the entrant or maker, may be shown to affect its weight, but such circumstances shall not affect its admissibility.
The Supreme Court gave this paragraph its proper meaning in *Palmer v. Hoffman*, 318 U.S. 109, 63 S.Ct. 477, 87 L.Ed. 645 (1943). The Court noted that the basis of the exception was circumstances indicating a probability of trustworthiness in any particular case. The Court went on to say,
   Nor is it any answer to say that Congress has provided in the Act that the various circumstances of the making of the record should affect its weight not

its admissibility. *That provision comes into play only in case the other requirements of the Act are met.* [Citation.] (Emphasis supplied). I interpret this language to eliminate the need for bringing into court the maker of the record to show his personal knowledge but not to eliminate the need for laying a convincing foundation for introduction of the records. [Citation.]
   Although I cannot see that the prosecution laid a strong foundation for the introduction of the questioned evidence in this case, there was no objection on the ground that foundation was lacking. The only objection was based on the ground that the evidence was hearsay, and Judge Hamley has explained why that objection was properly overruled.

never be construed as authorizing *carte blanche* admission into evidence of any and all information that can be obtained from the records of a business. It most certainly should not be construed so as to permit the introduction of hearsay record evidence in the nature of opinion or conclusion testimony as distinguished from recordation of facts. It must be remembered, too, that the statute creates an exception to the basic principle that entitles an accused to confront the witnesses against him. In a day when the pace of our technology threatens to exceed the development of rules for governing human conduct, we must be careful to insure that fundamental rights are not surrendered to the calculations of machines. If a machine is to testify against an accused, the courts must, at the very least, be satisfied with all reasonable certainty that both the machine and those who supply its information have performed their functions with utmost accuracy. Therefore, it is essential that the trial court be convinced of the trustworthiness of the particular records before admitting them into evidence. And it should be convinced by proof presented by the party seeking to introduce the evidence rather than receiving the evidence upon the basis of an inadequate foundation and placing the burden upon the objector to demonstrate its weakness. The majority appears to acknowledge this desideratum, but I think the principle deserves more emphasis than that given by the somewhat casual comment made in Footnote 11 of my Brother Hamley's opinion.

RAILROAD COMMISSION v. SOUTHERN PACIFIC CO.
468 S.W.2d 125
(Court of Civil Appeals of Texas, Austin, May 12, 1971.)

O'QUINN, J.

Southern Pacific Transportation Company, formerly Southern Pacific Company, applied to the Railroad Commission for authority to discontinue the company's railroad agency at Elsa, in Hidalgo County, and to transfer that agency's duties to Edinburg, a distance of about twelve miles. In its technical aspects the application sought to discontinue the existing agency, retire the depot, and change appli-

cable tariffs to show Elsa as a non-agency station.

The Railroad Commisson entered an order dated October 22, 1968, denying the application.

Southern Pacific filed suit in district court in Travis County under Article 6453, Vernon's Anno.Civ.Stat., seeking cancellation of the order and authority to discontinue the agency at Elsa. The City of Elsa, Plastics, Inc., R. M. Nelson, Agnew Grain Company, Red Barn Chemicals, Inc., Dixon Concrete Product Company and Elsa Lumber Yard, Inc., intervened and participated in proceedings in court without objection.

After hearing before the court without a jury, the trial court held that the substantial evidence did not support the order of the Railroad Commission and entered judgment setting aside the order.

We reverse the judgment of the trial court and render judgment sustaining the order of the Commission.

The Commission has appealed and brings four points of error. Under the first point contention is made that the trial court erred in admitting in evidence seven exhibits which the Commission asserts "are patent hearsay and not admissible evidence under Article 3737e, Vernon's Anno.Civ.Stat."

The exhibits referred to are briefly described by number and content in the summary which follows. The seven exhibits purport to cover operations of the railroad at Elsa over a period of about two years prior to the hearing. Exhibit 13 is a summary of revenues and expenses for Elsa; exhibit 15 is a summary of train stops at Elsa; exhibit 16 covers the work load of the agent; exhibit 18 reflects carload movements through the station; exhibits 19 and 20 cover revenues from cotton shipments and less than carload shipments, which are not handled by the railroad; and exhibit 21 is an abstract of a large mass of railroad records upon which some of the exhibits mentioned above were founded. This exhibit was prepared by agreement for convenience of the court and of counsel, without waiver by the Commission of the right to object to its admission.

All of the exhibits were introduced through Phil H. Boudreaux, Jr., a witness for the railroad, who for twenty-eight years had been employed by the company, the last twelve years in making cost analyses.

The last named exhibit, No. 21, purports to be an abstract of other evidence of the railroad. The other evidence consisted of a mass of documents, estimated by counsel for the railroad as "four feet by two and a half feet by about three feet," which were made available in court during the latter part of the testimony of Boudreaux and afterwards were admitted in evidence. This bulk of evidence in the main comprised volumes of system-wide computer print-outs. Boudreaux as the witness to testify as to the manner of making the records and as to their accuracy was not certain about how many stations were included in the print-outs, saying, " * * * it is pretty close to sixty stations."

Business records, even when voluminous and massive, are admissible as an exception to the hearsay rule when a proper predicate is established under Article 3737e, Vernon's Anno.Civ.Stat. The party offering any such record must show:

> (a) It was made in the regular course of business;
> (b) It was the regular course of that business for an employee or representative of such business with personal knowledge of such act, event or condition to make such memorandum or record or to transmit information thereof to be included in such memorandum or record;
> (c) It was made at or near the time of the act, event or condition or reasonably soon thereafter. (Sec. 1, Art. 3737e)

The Supreme Court held in 1969 that a tabulated schedule or summary of voluminous records may be admitted, in the discretion of the trial court, to expedite trial and aid of the trier of fact, but that this rule assumes that the records themselves are admissible. [Citation.] The summaries tend to prove nothing except the contents of the records themselves and standing alone the tabulations, or summaries, are hearsay and have no probative value.

Exhibit 21, as noted, was prepared as an abstract of the numerous massive volumes of computer summary sheets. The witness Boudreaux was not qualified as the custodian of the records, nor was he offered as the railroad employee having sufficient knowledge of the

records to prove the legitimacy and accuracy of the computer print-outs.

The railroad offered no witness who was in charge of its data processing department, and under whose supervision the computerized accounting records were maintained, to testify as to the type of computer employed, the permanent nature of record storage, and how daily processing of information to be fed into the computer was conducted, resulting in permanent records of the railroad.

A similar question, although not involving electronically kept records, was met by this Court in *Sherwin-Williams Company v. Perry Company*, 424 S.W.2d 940 (Tex.Civ.App., Austin, 1968, writ ref., n. r. e., per curiam opinion, 431 S.W.2d 310), in which it was held that if the voluminous books and records of plaintiff had been produced in the trial court and offered in evidence, they would have been hearsay as to defendant, but upon proper predicate may have been admissible. The testimony of examiners or auditors as to contents of the books "without this predicate was double hearsay."

In that case, it was observed:

> In this era of big business, voluminous records may well become the rule rather than the exception. It is difficult * * * to believe that where records are an integral part of * * * [plaintiff's] case, that merely by making a welter of records accessible to an opposing party * * * the burden is shifted to the opposing party, making it his duty to cull out any barriers to admissibility that may be inherent therein. These records are hearsay and any testimony rooted therein is hearsay spawned in hearsay.

It was not enough that the railroad hauled a "cartload" of records into the court room and proffered an abstract as proof of facts said to be contained in the records themselves. Exhibit 21 and the records it purports to be based on did not meet the tests required by Article 3737e and the cases decided construing the statute.

Business records kept electronically no doubt have become increasingly prevalent, and although the several facts necessary to show that such records are trustworthy will differ in some details from proof by which reliability of conventional records under the "shop book rule" is established, the basic requirements remain unchanged. The ultimate proof to be established under Article 3737e should be accompanied, in the case of electronic records, by proof that the particular computing equipment is recognized as standard equipment, that the records kept and stored electronically were made in the regular course of business, that they were based on information within the personal knowledge of a person whose duties included the collection of such information, and that the records were prepared by persons who understood operation of the equipment and whose regular duty was to operate it. [Citations.]

In the case before us exhibits 13, 15 and 18 were based wholly or in substantial part upon exhibit 21 which itself was but an abstract of the electronically kept records. Exhibit 16 designed to show work of the agent at Elsa was based on freight waybills and other records of the agent. Exhibits 13 and 18 were based in part on the Elsa waybills, in addition to exhibit 21. Boudreaux testified that waybills were basic railroad documents showing car movements, but waybills and freight bills from Elsa were not offered in evidence. Exhibit 19 pertaining to truck movement of cotton appears to be based on various records not tendered in court by the railroad. Exhibit 20 dealing with less than carload shipments, which are made by truck and not by rail, appears to be grounded on similar records not in court and not offered in evidence. Thus it is seen that the railroad's offers to show revenue and expenses at Elsa, the number of train stops, the work of the agent, carload movements through Elsa, and the revenue derived from truck shipment of cotton and less than carload lots of other cargo were made almost entirely through hearsay evidence improperly admitted by the trial court.

* * *

UNITED STATES v. RUSSO

480 F.2d 1228

(United States Court of Appeals, Sixth Circuit, July 6, 1973.)

LIVELY, C. J.

Appellant, Joseph Russo, is an osteopathic physician licensed to practice in Michigan. He and an associate were charged in a single indictment containing 51 counts of violating the mail fraud statute, 18 U.S.C. § 1341. Count one of the indictment was divided into paragraphs I and II. Paragraph I charged that the two physicians "devised and intended to devise a scheme and artifice to defraud Blue Shield of Michigan, * * * by filing claims for services not performed on patients on dates specified and for obtaining money from such organization by false and fraudulent pretenses and representations well knowing at the time that the pretenses and representations would be and were false when made." Subparagraphs A through G set forth in detail the manner in which the alleged scheme and artifice to defraud was carried out. Paragraph II of Count one then recited that on July 14, 1966 at Detroit in the Eastern District of Michigan the defendant, Joseph Russo, did knowingly and willfully cause Blue Shield of Michigan to mail a check, identified by number, to him in violation of the mail fraud statute. Each of the subsequent 50 counts re-alleged and adopted the allegations of paragraph I of Count one and in its paragraph II charged one or the other of the named defendants with willfully causing a check to be placed in the mail by Blue Shield of Michigan for delivery to that defendant. No conspiracy was charged in the indictment.

The evidence reveals that during the period covered by the indictment which was part of the year 1966, all of 1967 and part of 1968, Dr. Russo leased a group of offices in the basement of a building in a "blue-collar" neighborhood in Detroit. These offices, referred to in the testimony as Dr. Russo's clinic, consisted of four examination rooms, an office and a long hallway where patients waited. Although Dr. Russo was associated with several other doctors in a partnership known as The Midwest Clinical Group, only one of the other members of that partnership practiced in the same building with Dr. Russo and there was no sharing of facilities or personnel by them. The Midwest Clinical Group was a loose sort of arrangement in which each of the partners contributed income for the purpose of maintaining one or more osteopathic hospitals in Detroit. It appears from the testimony that the doctors who belonged to the Midwest Clinical Group had problems obtaining hospital beds for their patients and that it was necessary for them to operate, through the partnership, hospitals known as Palmer East and Palmer West for the treatment of their patients. Although the testimony indicates that the Midwest Clinical Group received a portion of its funds from Dr. Russo, presumably including payments from Blue Shield of Michigan which the indictment charges were procured by fraud, there is no evidence that any other member of the Midwest Clinical group was involved in, or had any knowledge of, the scheme charged in the indictment. The co-defendant, Dr. Lieberwitz, was not a member of the Midwest Clinical Group, but was an employee of Dr. Russo.

The Russo office or clinic was kept open throughout the day until late at night and hundreds of patients were seen in a single day. Most of the time Dr. Russo had at least two other doctors working for him in the clinic and each worked on certain days during the week. The other doctors who worked for Dr. Russo gave him a portion of their gross receipts and paid none of the overhead expenses of the offices. The co-defendant who was indicted and tried with Dr. Russo was a younger osteopathic physician who testified to treating an average of 150 patients per day while working at Dr. Russo's office and who stated that he often stayed until 1:00 or 2:00 o'clock in the morning since the office was never closed as long as there were any patients waiting to be seen. Several of the doctors who had worked at the clinic testified that it was Dr. Russo's office and that when they came to work, all of the patients were Dr. Russo's patients, although after they had been there a while some of the patients became theirs. Several witnesses attributed the large number of daily patients at the Russo Clinic to the fact that it was located in a densely populated section of Detroit where few doctors' offices were situated.

It was testified that Blue Shield of Michigan furnishes to the doctors who practice in that state printed forms known as "Doctor Service Reports" (hereafter DSR). In order to be paid by Blue Shield it is necessary for a doctor to complete a DSR for each treatment and submit it for payment. Each doctor is assigned a provider's code number and this and his name are both imprinted on the DSR's furnished to him by Blue Shield. The DSR is completed by filling in the name of the patient, the name of the subscriber, which might be different from that of the patient, and the address, identification number and certain other statistical data of the subscriber. Often the subscriber is the employer of the patient. In addition, the treating physician must indicate the date of the service and a description of the service rendered together with a diagnosis. Each physician is supplied with a manual containing approximately 8,000 different procedures with a four-digit code number for each such procedure. There is an established fee which Blue Shield agrees to pay for each particular type of medical service under its various contracts, and the amount of its liability is determined by the procedure code number and description of services performed as indicated on the DSR. Not all medical services are covered by Blue Shield and the coverage can vary between contracts of various subscribers.

The prosecution did not contend that the appellant submitted DSR's to Blue Shield for patients that he had not seen on the dates indicated. What was contended was that in many cases the treatment received by the patients was of such a nature that it was not covered by Blue Shield and was not compensable under the particular subscriber contract involved and that if the services actually performed had been disclosed on the DSR, no payment would have been due from Blue Shield. Instead of making a charge to the patient for the actual services which were not compensable under the patient's Blue Shield coverage, it was the contention of the prosecution that the defendants caused a DSR to be prepared showing that some procedure had been followed with the patient which would have been compensable.

The prosecution produced 12 former patients of Dr. Russo and Dr. Lieberwitz who testified concerning their visits to the clinic and the treatment which they received. Some of the testimony related to acts referred to in particular counts of the indictment and some related to similar acts not charged in the indictment. Each of these patients was asked to identify a number of DSR's submitted by Dr. Russo or his co-defendant upon which payment had been received. Each of the witnesses identified his or her signature on the DSR and was then asked about the treatment or services received at the clinic. In each case the treating doctor had reported administering a treatment involving either aspiration of a hematoma or bursa, or arthrocentesis. The aspiration of the bursa was usually described in the DSR's as being applied to one of the shoulders or one of the hips. This procedure involves withdrawal of a fluid from the bursa or hematoma by means of either one or two needles. Arthrocentesis, which is the injection of a steroid or other substance into a joint, was described in the reports as being applied variously to either shoulder, as well as both hips and ankles.

These twelve witnesses testified that they went to the clinic because of colds, bronchitis, low blood pressure, weight loss, a broken finger, backache, hurting in the right side, asthma, kidney infection, and arthritis. Without exception, they testified that the only injections they received from Drs. Russo and Lieberwitz were cold shots and ordinary inoculations in the fleshy part of the hip and arm and that they never received any injections into the shoulder or hip joints. A number of the witnesses testified that they were asked by the doctor before receiving the first treatment whether they were allergic to penicillin. Likewise those patients who actually observed the treatment stated that no fluid of any kind was withdrawn by the doctors. Each of them who was asked estimated that his treatment took a very brief time and except for one witness who had arthritis, the testimony was that none had complaints concerning limbs or joints. Floyd Newkirk, the witness who had arthritis, stated that he received no shots in his shoulder and that no fluid was ever withdrawn during any of his treatment. These witnesses agreed on cross-examination that they felt better after being treated by Dr. Russo's clinic. Ordinary injections of medicines made in a doctor's office are not compensable by Blue Shield. However, both arthrocentesis and aspiration of the bursa and hematoma are considered to be surgical procedures and are covered. The defense produced 101 patient witnesses who described the treatment they received at Dr. Russo's clinic and in many cases they were victims of arthritis and bursitis who were treated by aspiration and arthrocentesis. On cross-examination, a number of these witnesses stated that bursitis and arthritis are very painful and that a person knows it if he has one of these ailments.

In addition to patient witnesses the prosecution produced the Director of Service Review of Blue Shield of Michigan, Charles Smith. Mr. Smith testified that the prime objective of his department is to insure the integrity of the reporting forms (DSR's) submitted to Blue Shield by doctor-providers of care. He stated that this is done by various audits and investigative procedures initiated by his department. He considered the DSR to be the basic document in the claims procedure of Blue Shield. It was described as a perforated carbon form which permits the doctor to retain a copy while submitting the original to Blue Shield for payment. This witness went through the internal billing procedures at Michigan Blue Shield in great detail. It was pointed out that each DSR is examined by several different people to determine that it is complete and proper for payment. If a claims examiner determines that it is in all respects complete and correct the appropriate amount of money for the particular service is recorded and the examiner initials and dates the DSR. From that point the form is taken to the data recording section where the information from it is recorded onto a magnetic tape for further processing.

After this information has been stored on magnetic tape the claim form itself is microfilmed and there is a cross reference made between the information on the magnetic tape to be used by the computer and the microfilm copy of the original document. The original DSR is then destroyed. Each two weeks checks are written by the computer based on the information contained on the magnetic tapes. The computer retrieves all of the payments due each doctor under his provider code number and a check is printed out with a voucher attached which indicates part of the same information which had originally appeared on the DSR. Included are an identification of the patient, the date of treatment and the procedure code number. Each check can include payment for a maximum of 17 claims, each representing a separate DSR filed by that particular doctor-provider. Mr. Smith testified that the checks are distributed to the doctors through the United States mail and that neither Dr. Russo nor the co-defendant had ever received a check in any other manner. The witness described a number of cross-checks and verification procedures followed by Blue Shield of Michigan to insure accuracy. While admitting that a computer output is no better than the information fed into it, he pointed out that two different key punch operators work from each DSR and that the work of each is compared with the other before information is finally put into the computer. This witness stated that since all claims payments are based on the correct processing of DSR's it is essential that reliable procedures be followed.

In addition to describing the general procedures of his employer with respect to processing the payment of claims, this witness offered to testify about particular statistics which had been gathered by Blue Shield concerning Dr. Russo and Dr. Lieberwitz and relating certain of their claims during the period in question to the total claims for the same procedures received by Blue Shield of Michigan during that period of time. In order to qualify this testimony, Francis Mrachina, the vice president of Michigan Blue Shield in charge of all computer functions, testified. He described the computer equipment used by his employer and its particular functions in the claims processing procedures. Among other things he described the verification which takes place of the input from the DSR to the computer and the daily balancing procedures followed by Michigan Blue Shield. He stated that new programs are pretested before adoption for use in the computers of Michigan Blue Shield. This witness then described an annual statistical survey which the company has produced by computer each year since 1967. This is a computer printout which shows the number of claims paid for each of the compensable procedures covered by Blue Shield contracts in Michigan. The witness stated that the annual statistical run is made in the ordinary course of business by Michigan Blue Shield and that it is the basis of a number of decisions which the organization makes in the conduct of its business.

The witness Smith was then recalled and further described the annual statistical report. He pointed out that while there is a difference in charges by participating and non-participating doctors, virtually all of the 10,000 physicians practicing in Michigan in 1967 filed some claims with Blue Shield. The annual statistical report classifies claims paid by medical procedure and not by identifying the doctor who made the claim. The report contains a great deal of other information of a demographic nature which is used by Blue Shield for various accounting and actuarial purposes.

The witness then stated that another group of records relating to individual doctors is made each year by Michigan Blue Shield. These are called doctors' profiles and they are made up by clerical employees under the supervision of Mr. Smith. The profile is a method by which the organization determines what particular procedures have been reported by an individual physician, and paid for, during a given period of time. Each profile relates to only one doctor and lists each procedure for which he was paid during the period of the report and the number of claims paid for each procedure. Mr. Smith testified that in any year his organization would prepare approximately 1,200 individual doctors' profiles. Some of these have been constructed by computer operation and some by hand or manual tabulation. He stated that for the year 1967 manually generated profiles were made for Dr. Russo and Dr. Lieberwitz and he described the verification procedures involved to insure accuracy of the profiles. Two of the clerical employees who had constructed the 1967 profiles on the defendants then described in detail the procedures which they had followed. It was testified that a number of reasons might exist for the selection of a particular doctor for a profile in a given year, including the filing of an unusual number of claims, an exceptionally high income, or complaints from patients or other doctors. It was stated that doctors' profiles are done in the ordinary course of business and are routinely used as part of the auditing procedure of Michigan Blue Shield. The employees who actually constructed the Russo profile described the procedures of verification which they followed in doing this job. It was testified that it took two employees approximately one month to construct the 1967 profiles of Drs. Russo and Lieberwitz. This was done early in the year 1968.

The basic document from which the profiles

were made was the check voucher. The testimony was that each check voucher issued to the doctor being profiled during the period was examined and that a tabulation was made of each procedure for which payment was made in that particular check. Each doctor profile was complete and covered all procedures identified by code numbers, for which he was paid during the year and no particular procedure was pinpointed for inclusion in the profile. After every procedure for which payment had been made during the period of time had been tabulated from each check voucher issued during the period covered by the profile, the total for each procedure was obtained by use of adding machines. Two tapes were run on each item for verification.

The prosecution then sought to introduce the annual statistical report of Michigan Blue Shield for the year 1967 and the doctor profiles for the year 1967 of Dr. Russo and the co-defendant. Both defendants objected and further hearings were held out of the presence of the jury, consisting of legal arguments and further voir dire examination of the witness Smith. It was brought out that the paid claims tape file is the basic computer record for the annual statistical run. The court ruled that the prosecution had sustained its burden of showing that the information supplied by the computer is trustworthy. Counsel for the defendants at this point stated that the objection was to the tabulations or summary of evidence, stating that sufficient ground work had not been laid to permit the introduction of summaries rather than original records. The prosecuting attorney then stated that the vouchers from which the tabulations for the doctors' profiles had been made were then in court along with the doctors' profiles and the annual statistical run for the year 1967 and that they had been available for checking by counsel for the defendants.

The witness Smith was then permitted to testify from the doctors' profiles, stating the number of payments which each defendant received in the year 1967 for each of five separate procedures. This was all admitted over the objection of both defendants. The prosecution then sought to show the total number of claims paid by Blue Shield in 1967 to all the doctors in Michigan, including the defendants, for each of these five procedures. Both

defendants objected on numerous grounds, including the claim that no proof of the number of doctors involved in the survey had been made, that the annual statistical run included many doctors who would never have performed the particular procedures involved in the prosecution because of specialties outside of the area of treatment and the fact that the annual statistical record is a summary based on primary records which were never made available to the defendants.

Out of the presence of the jury the witness Smith again explained now the paid claims tape file is constructed and stored and how information from it is retrieved by the computer. He testified that the paid claims tape file is the best and most accurate record for accounting purposes maintained by the Michigan Blue Shield and that the annual statistical report is based entirely on the paid claims file. He again described how the annual statistical report is balanced to insure its accuracy, and the reliance which the company places on it. The witness stated that the sources of the information contained in the annual statistical report were still available in the form of magnetic tapes and that these tapes are computerized reflections of the original entries in the form of check vouchers. Copies of the check vouchers are maintained along with microfilm copies of the DSR's filed by the various doctors in Michigan. These are the original documents which generate the payments by check with vouchers attached which make up the paid claims file. The annual statistical record for the year 1967 was produced on November 7 and 8, 1968. Following this testimony, the court admitted the 1967 annual statistical record as an original and primary record made and kept in the regular and every day course of business and relied upon by Blue Shield of Michigan. The court ruled that all the objections of the defendants to the annual statistical record went to the weight of this evidence and not to its admissibility.

The jury then returned and the witness Smith introduced the annual statistical run for the year 1967 as an exhibit and described it to the jury. Testifying from this record, Mr. Smith stated the total number of claims paid in the year 1967 by Michigan Blue Shield to all doctors submitting claims for the five medical procedures previously identified as being involved in this prosecution and stated that these totals included claims of the two defendants. This evidence, together with that contained in the 1967 profiles previously introduced, may be tabulated as follows:

Procedure Code Number & Description	Dr. Russo	Dr. Lieber- witz	All Doctors
1046—Initial Arthrocentesis	2,048	817	23,897
1047—Subsequent Arthrocentesis	553	1,749	10,693
1413—Initial Aspiration of Bursa	3,528	613	14,357
1418—Subsequent Aspiration of Bursa	10,079	4,062	17,747
0145—Aspiration of Hematoma	150	613	1,568

Lengthy cross-examination of Smith failed to produce any evidence which reflected on the trustworthiness of the information contained in the annual statistical report.

Other witnesses called by the prosecution were an employee and a former employee of Dr. Russo who described office procedures in handling the DSR's and subsequent steps taken in processing them for submission to Michigan Blue Shield for payment. One employee testified that she had ink stamps made for a number of the procedures including arthrocentesis and aspiration of bursa which came up quite often, as this saved time that would have been required to write out the descriptions of these procedures. She testified that the DSR's were brought to her home by Dr. Russo in batches of approximately 1,000. Another witness for the prosecution was Dr. Richard Thompson, an osteopathic physician who was also team physician for the Detroit Lions. He stated that he conducted a full office and hospital practice in addition to his work with the professional football team and some 20 high schools in the Detroit area. This witness described the medical procedures involved in arthrocentesis, aspiration of bursa, aspiration of hematoma and the preparation required for each of these procedures. He stated that in aspiration of a bursa or hematoma the purpose is to extract fluid and that often two needles are used, one to inject an anesthetic and another larger bored needle to withdraw the fluid. He described the time involved in preparing a patient for these procedures and the various locations where penetration is usually made. He testified that normally an injection of penicillin takes place farther down the arm than an arthrocentesis or aspiration of a shoulder. He said that arthrocentesis in-

volves an actual puncturing of a joint with a needle and this requires insertion directly into the joint. He also testified that he knew of no causal relationship between the common cold and a condition requiring arthrocentesis or an aspiration. It was his testimony that it would be impossible to perform an arthrocentesis of a shoulder joint by inserting a needle in the fleshy or muscular part of the arm. Dr. Thompson testified that in an active practice he and his associate did not have occasion to perform more than 1,000 procedures involving arthrocentesis and aspiration of bursa and hematoma within a period of one year.

Both defendants testified and denied that they had ever discussed the matter of billing Blue Shield for compensable procedures when non-compensable services were performed or that either had ever done this. They stated that every DSR submitted by them correctly reflected the services they had performed. Eight counts of the indictment were dismissed on motion of the prosecution, without objection. The jury found Dr. Russo guilty on all counts in which he was named as the party causing the mailing.

Numerous assignments of error have been made. We will consider several of them separately.

* * *

II. THE COMPUTERIZED STATISTICAL EVIDENCE

Appellant has mounted a broad attack on the admission by the court of the 1967 annual statistical run of Blue Shield of Michigan. In the first place it is claimed that this evidence does not qualify as a business record under 28 U.S.C. § 1732(a), the Federal Business Records Act. That statute establishes the admissibility in federal courts of any writing or record, made as a memorandum or record of an act or transaction, as evidence of such act or transaction if made in the ordinary course of business. This is an exception to the hearsay rule. The uncontradicted testimony of two witnesses established that the 1967 statistical run was a regularly maintained business record of Blue Shield and was made in the ordinary course of business. It was also shown that this record was relied upon by the company in conducting its business, particularly with reference to its auditing and actuarial procedures. The appellant maintains that the annual statistical run is not the record of any act or transaction and that only the original DSR's should have been admitted to prove the "act" of payment for medical procedures.

Computer printouts are not mentioned in the Federal Business Records Act. However, no court could fail to notice the extent to which businesses today depend on computers for a myriad of functions. Perhaps the greatest utility of a computer in the business world is its ability to store large quantities of information which may be quickly retrieved on a selective basis. Assuming that properly functioning computer equipment is used, once the reliability and trustworthiness of the information put into the computer has been established, the computer printouts should be received as evidence of the transactions covered by the input. No evidence was introduced which put in question the mechanical or electronic capabilities of the equipment and the reliability of its output was verified. The procedures for testing the accuracy and reliability of the information fed into the computer were detailed at great length by the witnesses. The district court correctly held that the trustworthiness of the information contained in the computer printout had been established.

The appellant also maintains that the computer printout should not have been received in evidence because it was not prepared at the time the acts which it purports to describe were performed, or within a reasonable time thereafter as required by 28 U.S.C. § 1732(a). However, the evidence clearly shows that a record of payment was made at the time each DSR was paid by Michigan Blue Shield and that this record was referred to as the paid claims file. This file consisted of reels of magnetic tape which reflected every payment to a doctor in the year 1967. Since the computer printout is just a presentation in structured and comprehensible form of a mass of individual items, it is immaterial that the printout itself was not prepared until 11 months after the close of the year 1967. It would restrict the admissibility of computerized records too severely to hold that the computer product, as well as the input upon which it is based, must be produced at or within a reasonable time after each act or transaction to which it relates.

The Federal Business Records Act was adopted for the purpose of facilitating the admission of records into evidence where experience has shown them to be trustworthy. It should be liberally construed to avoid the difficulties of an archaic practice which formerly required every written document to be authenticated by the person who prepared it. [Citations.] The Act should never be interpreted so strictly as to deprive the courts of the realities of business and professional practices. [Citation.]

Appellant insists that the 1967 statistical record was a "summary" which is not admissible, citing *Melinder v. United States*, 281 F.Supp. 451 (W.D.Okl.1968). That case involved an exhibit prepared by an Internal Revenue agent for use at the trial of an income tax case. It was not a record produced in the ordinary course of business and was merely a recapitulation of certain information which had not been introduced to verify it in the case. The annual statistical run of Blue Shield of Michigan is not a summary, since it contains a record of every claim paid by the organization during a given year. The information contained in it is arranged in a predetermined manner and classified according to medical procedures. However, all paid claims are included and all compensable procedures are covered. It is important to distinguish the entire printout of the 1967 annual statistical run from a separate item of evidence consisting of a summary of portions of the printout. The witness Smith did summarize portions of the annual statistical record and did relate these summaries to the individual doctors' profiles of the defendants. Nevertheless, the entire statistical run was produced by the prosecution as a business record prepared in the ordinary course of business long before the time of the trial. Although summaries may or may not be admissible in evidence according to the circumstances of a particular case, we hold that the computer printout offered in evidence in this case was an original record and not a mere summary.

The appellant maintains that no proper foundation was laid for the admission of the 1967 annual statistical record. We disagree. The witnesses Smith and Mrachina were qualified as experts by education, training and experience and they showed a familiarity with the use of the particular computers in question. The mechanics of input control to assure accuracy were detailed at great length as was the description of the nature of the information which went into the machine and upon which its printout was based. In *United States v. De Georgia*, 420 F.2d 889 (9th Cir. 1969), the computerized records of Hertz Corporation were admitted for the purpose of showing that a particular automobile was not involved in any rental or lease activity during a certain period of time. An employee of Hertz was permitted to testify, based on the computer information, that an automobile found in the custody of the defendant at the time of his arrest was stolen from the Hertz lot since it had not been rented or leased. As the opinion points out, the foundation for admission of such evidence consists of showing the input procedures used, the tests for accuracy and reliability, and the fact that an established business relies on the computerized records in the ordinary course of carrying on its activities. The defendant then has the opportunity to cross-examine concerning company practices with respect to the input and as to the accuracy of the computer as a memory bank and retriever of information. The concurring opinion in *De Georgia* emphasizes the necessity that the court "be satisfied with all reasonable certainty that both the machine and those who supply its information have performed their functions with utmost accuracy." [Citation.] This opinion goes on to say that the trustworthiness of the particular records should be ascertained before they are admitted and that the burden of presenting an adequate foundation for receiving the evidence should be on the parties seeking to introduce it rather than upon the party opposing its introduction. We believe that in this case the prosecution proved the essential elements upon which the district court could, and did, conclude that the annual statistical run of Blue Shield of Michigan was a trustworthy record which was entitled to be received in evidence under the Federal Business Records Act. Two well-reasoned state court opinions support this conclusion. [Citations.]

Appellant also complains that he was not given an opportunity to prepare his defense to the computerized material used by the prosecution. In *United States v. Stifel*, 433 F.2d 431 (6th Cir. 1970), cert. denied, 401 U.S. 994, 91 S.Ct. 1232, 28 L.Ed.2d 531 (1971), this Court held that if the Government uses highly sophisticated scientific evidence (in that case, neutron activation analysis) involving time consuming and expensive laboratory tests, it must allow time for a defendant to make similar tests. The Manual for Complex and Multidistrict Litigation deals at some length with the use of computer evidence. Its admissibility is strongly defended where the records have been kept in the regular course of business and its reliability has been demonstrated. The Manual further states:

> It is essential that the underlying data used in the analyses, programs and programming method and all relevant computer inputs and outputs be made available to the opposing party far in advance of trial. This procedure is required in the interest of fairness and should facilitate the introduction of admissible computer evidence. Such procedure provides the adverse party and the court with an opportunity to test and examine the inputs, the program and all outputs prior to trial. [Citation.]

On March 22, 1971 appellant filed a request for particulars in which he sought information about the evidence which would be used in support of the charges against him. On April 27, 1971 the government filed its response and forwarded to the attorneys for appellant a number of documents relating to the request for particulars. At the same time the Assistant U. S. Attorney forwarded to the attorneys for the appellant certain documents, including—"[A] statistical summary for 1967 compiled from the records of Blue Shield of Michigan. It compares the number of claims filed for certain services by the defendants as against the total number filed by all doctors in the State of Michigan." So far as the record shows, no discovery steps were taken by the appellant between the time of the disclosure by the prosecution of the nature of this particular evidence and the beginning of the trial on September 14, 1971 despite the fact that Rule 16(b) Fed.R.Crim.P. provides for discovery and inspection by a defendant in a criminal case. At the trial Charles Smith's testimony compared the number of claims made by Drs. Russo and Lieberwitz for five particular medical procedures with those made by all of the doctors in Michigan. This summary was prepared by the witness from two sources. The number of claims paid to Drs. Russo and Lieberwitz was determined from the individual doctors' profiles prepared for each one of the defendants concerning which there is no contention on appeal. The information as to the total number of claims paid all doctors in Michigan in the five categories of medical procedures was based on the annual statistical run which was offered and accepted in evidence. In view of the enclosure of the identical summary in the letter of April 27, there was no surprise or sudden, unexpected production of this evidence. Mr. Smith was cross-examined vigorously as to the manner in which the annual statistical run was produced.

Furthermore, on the third day of the trial, September 16, 1971, there was a discussion between the court and counsel concerning exhibits. The prosecuting attorney referred to the fact that he had furnished statistics to counsel for the defendant pursuant to the court's pretrial order and stated that statistics showing the volume of claims in certain categories by the defendants would be compared with the total volume of such claims paid to all doctors throughout Michigan. On September 24, 1971 the witness Smith was recalled for the purpose of testifying about individual doctors' profiles and the annual statistical run of his employer. The court recalled to the attorneys that there had been a previous discussion of this offer of proof and that he had requested attorneys to be prepared to offer authority for their positions. When counsel for appellant complained that the information included in the annual statistical run was exclusively in the control of Blue Shield the court reminded him that he had a right to get an order which would have permitted him to go into the plant and study the whole process, and had not done so. The court ruled that the summary evidence offered by the witness Smith could be introduced because the primary evidence upon which the summary was based was in the courtroom and available for inspection and use in cross-examination by appellant. The prosecuting attorney pointed out again that the original of the computer run for the 1967 annual statistical report was available to counsel for the defendants, that the doctors' profiles and the vouchers from which they were constructed were also available for examination by counsel.

In cross-examining the witness Smith on September 28, 1971, the defense for the first time asked about other information that Blue Shield might furnish from its computer for comparison with the statistics included in his testimony. At no time prior to the trial or after the September 14th conference with the court did the defense make any effort to require the prosecution or Blue Shield to make its computers available to the defendants or to an expert employed by them or even to provide other information from the computers which was not then available. The computerized annual statistical run was not introduced into evidence and presented to the jury until September 30, 1971. Defense counsel were given an opportunity to examine the exhibit and to cross-examine both Mr. Smith and Mr. Mrachina extensively concerning it. The prosecuting attorney stated that the reason for introducing the annual statistical run as an exhibit was to provide a foundation for the testimony of Mr. Smith. The court pointed out that the annual statistical run itself was not a summary, but a primary and original record constantly used by the company and was admissible in support of the testimony relating to portions of the exhibit by the person under whose supervision it was prepared.

In *United States v. Kelly*, 420 F.2d 26 (2d Cir. 1969), despite a motion for discovery of scientific tests which would be relied upon, the Government failed to inform the defendant of a neutron activation test which it had performed and the defendant only became aware of it at the trial when the Government sought to introduce its exhibits. The defendant objected and requested a month's continuance in the trial to carry out its own neutron tests. The court held that fairness requires a disclosure, in advance, of the results of a scientific test in order to give the defendant an opportunity to conduct his own tests. The present case differs from *Kelly* in several respects. In the first place, in that case there was a motion for discovery as to scientific tests and secondly, there was a motion for a continuance to permit the defendants to conduct their own tests. Neither of these steps was taken by appellant. We conclude, as did the trial judge, that appellant had ample notice of the nature of the statistical evidence which the prosecution planned to use and chose to attempt to discredit this evidence by means of cross-examination rather than availing himself of discovery and the use of expert witnesses of his own choosing. It was within the discretion of the trial judge to admit the expert testimony of the witness Smith and to permit the introduction of supporting evidence in the form of the annual statistical run after proper foundation had been laid by Smith and the witness Mrachina. Much of the objection to admission of the computerized statistics was held by the trial judge to go to the weight of the evidence rather than its admissibility. This ruling was correct in view of the language contained in 28 U.S.C. § 1732(a)—

> All other circumstances of the making of such writing or record, including lack of personal knowledge by the entrant or maker, may be shown to affect its weight, but such circumstances shall not affect its admissibility.

Appellant also complains that the computerized information did not bear directly on the question of guilt or innocence and encouraged the jury to draw unwarranted inferences. The trial court ruled, and we agree, that the testimony of Smith supported by the computerized statistics, when considered in connection with the testimony of Dr. Thompson, furnished an inference from which the jury could properly conclude that the defendants did not actually perform the extremely large numbers of certain designated medical procedures for which they were paid in the year 1967. It is also contended that the court failed to give a qualifying instruction with respect to the statistical evidence. The record discloses that the court instructed the jury that the sum-

maries prepared by the witness Smith and admitted in evidence were not in and of themselves evidence or proof of any facts and were used only as a matter of convenience. The court further instructed that "If and to the extent that you find they are not in truth summaries of facts or figures shown by the evidence in the case, you may disregard them entirely." The court also gave a comprehensive instruction on the right to draw reasonable inferences from established facts and charged that inference might not be built upon inference. We believe that the instructions, read as a whole, fairly and adequately charged the jury on all of the issues in the case. [Citation.]

* * *

ROGERS v. FRANK LYON CO.
253 Ark. 856, 489 S.W.2d 506
(Supreme Court of Arkansas, Jan. 29, 1973.)

FOGLEMAN, J.

Frank Lyon Company recovered judgment for $2,207.94 in a suit on open account against Robert T. Rogers doing business as Rogers Hardware and Lumber Company. Appellant contends that the judgment is not supported by substantial evidence and that the circuit judge erred in overruling his motion for new trial. We find no reversible error.

Appellee offered numerous appliance shipping orders to sustain its allegations that Rogers was indebted to it in the total sum of $5,679.22 for merchandise sold and delivered to the Rogers Hardware and Lumber Company during 1969 and 1970. These were introduced through Owen Morrow, Manager of Credit Sales for appellee. Appellant argues that appellee failed to meet its burden of proof because the witness had no personal knowledge of the transactions purportedly reflected by those records. The records showed that some of the merchandise was sold to another party, and no proof of actual delivery of the merchandise was offered.

Morrow was the custodian of the records introduced, and stated that he was familiar with the account, which had originated in 1966 or 1967. He testified that the records introduced were kept in the regular course of business. Morrow explained the process followed by appellee in reference to this and other accounts as follows: Each invoice originates from a phone call from Rogers or one of his employees or from Lyon's representative in the territory, and orders were filled by shipping merchandise from Lyon's Fort Smith or Little Rock branch to Rogers Hardware Company. The invoices were supported by "appliance shipping orders" based on these orders and were prepared on multi-copy forms, the original being kept in the Lyon Company files, the first copy accompanying the shipment to the customer, the second kept in the credit files and the third kept in the accounting files. The company's computer then posted each invoice to the purchaser's account and billed the customer at the end of each month. An IBM copy of the invoice was transmitted to the customer on the day following its processing.

Morrow identified an IBM summary of the Rogers account, a copy of which he said was mailed to the customer. Copies of appellee's shipping orders and the computer print-out of the Rogers account showing a balance due amounting to $5,679.22 were admitted into evidence. The last date the records of the Rogers account indicated shipment of merchandise to Rogers was July 7, 1970, and the last credit appearing on the account was for $82.96 entered on March 16, 1971. Morrow also identified a memo from Rogers dated September 15, 1970, and testified that he had no recollection of any item of the account having been questioned by any Rogers employee and that the files did not indicate any such question. One invoice for $1,799.55 dated November 24, 1969, for merchandise shipped to Hiwasse Homes was originally charged to Rogers' account, but for some reason Morrow could not readily explain was transferred to an account of Hiwasse Homes, established February 9, 1970. Other invoices of $199.95 and $1,920, Morrow said, were also transferred to Hiwasse Homes. Morrow stated that Charles E. Sims was credit manager of Frank Lyon Company, and, as such, in charge of the overall extension of credit and collections at the time of the transactions with Rogers, and that he (Morrow) handled distressed accounts and had nothing to do with this account during 1969 and 1970.

Five of the orders totalling $4,665.10 indicated upon their faces that they were for goods sold to Borg-Warner Acceptance Corporation. Morrow had no connection with the shipping department and no personal knowledge of the shipping of the merchandise represented by any of the written orders. His entire testimony was based upon company records. A statement of the account showing a balance due of $2,329.14 was exhibited on cross-examination of Morrow, who said that it was prepared by Sims on August 27, 1970. During cross-examination Morrow also identified a copy of a letter of November 17, 1970, addressed to Rogers, stating that the account amounted to $2,133.40; a computerized statement dated December 24, 1970, reflecting a balance of $1,885.05; and a statement of May 26, 1971, showing a credit balance of $21.20. Morrow explained that one of the Borg-Warner invoices (for $1,265.55) was for merchandise to be sold to Borg-Warner and shipped to Rogers by agreement among the parties, but charged to Rogers when Borg-Warner refused to accept it.

Rogers denied owing appellee for invoices for $203.83, $1,265.55, $404.90 and $169.95, totalling $2,044.23, saying that he had paid Borg-Warner for them but could not say whether he actually received the merchandise or not. Morrow testified that Borg-Warner refused to finance these purchases by Rogers on a floor plan and that the records showed that the merchandise was then charged to Rogers and a corrected billing sent to him.

He explained that the three merchandise orders for a total of $3,919.50 were charged to Hiwasse Homes, after he advised Sims that the refrigerators listed on them had actually been shipped to Hiwasse Homes. He said that Sims left trade acceptances dated July 15, 1970, for this merchandise for signature by Hiwasse Homes and transferred the items to the Hiwasse Homes account in 1969, but it is admitted that the acceptances were never signed and returned to appellee. Morrow testified that the transfer of these charges to the Hiwasse Homes account was made when the trade acceptances were prepared. Rogers stated that these invoices were not again charged to his account until after the suit was filed and denied that he had ever agreed to pay for this merchandise. According to Rogers he was the owner of 54% of the stock of Hiwasse Homes, organized in November of 1969, and Rogers Hardware Company made some sales to Hiwasse Homes in 1970. Each appliance shipping order reflected a date of shipment, and a bill of lading number. Most orders indicated the identity of the carrier.

The records introduced through Morrow were properly admitted in evidence under Ark.Stat.Ann. § 28–928 (Repl. 1962). [Citations.] Morrow's lack of personal knowledge might have affected the weight given his testimony, but not its admissibility. The jury might well have found for appellant on the testimony offered, or returned a verdict for appellee in some lesser amount, but we cannot say that there was no substantial evidence to support the verdict. While we cannot say how the jury arrived at its verdict, it is obvious that it found for Rogers on items totalling $3,471.28, since the verdict was that much less than the amount indicated by the statement on which appellee sought to recover.

* * *

BARNEY v. COX
588 P.2d 696
(Supreme Court of Utah, Dec. 7, 1978.)

HALL, J.

* * *

Appellant's license was suspended after excessive traffic violations under Utah's point system.[1] Subsequently, the suspension was extended [footnote] on two occasions for additional violations, including driving with a suspended driver's license. As provided by statute [footnote], appellant demanded a de novo hearing in district court, to review the suspension of his license. He also sought a declaratory judgment [footnote] that U.C.A., 1953, 41–2–19 (Utah's "point system") is an unconstitutional denial of equal protection of the law. This appeal follows the district court's denial of the relief sought by appellant.

* * *

The other points made on appeal challenge the use of computer printouts as evidence: (1) that they are inadmissible as hearsay; and (2) that even if admissible evidence, proper foundation was not laid for their admission at trial.

As to (1), we hold that computer printouts can be admitted to show a driver's accumulated point totals as an exception to the hearsay rule. One of the exceptions to hearsay rule,[6] provides as follows:

Business Entries and the Like. Writings offered as memoranda or records of acts, conditions or events to prove the facts stated therein, if the judge finds that they were made in the regular course of a business at or about the time of the act, condition or event recorded, and that the sources of information from which made and the method and circumstances of their preparation were such as to indicate their trustworthiness; [Emphasis added.]

Although a government agency is not a private business, it is a business in the sense that it must systematically keep records and make "entries." It is the *type of evidence* which will be excepted from the hearsay rule, not the type of organization (i. e., private or public) that is important. Although relatively few cases have involved this question, the courts have held such evidence admissible over objections that the computer printouts were not the best evidence of the public records in question, or that they violated the hearsay rule. [Footnote.]

As to (2), appellant cites *King v. State*[8] for the proposition that three things must be shown in order to lay a proper foundation for the admission of computer generated evidence:

(1) that the electronic computing equipment is recognized as standard equipment,

(2) the entries are made * * * at or reasonably near the time of happening of the event recorded, and

(3) the foundation testimony satisfies the court that the sources of information, method and time of preparation such as to indicate its trustworthiness and justify its admission.

We are convinced that such a test was met in

---

1. U.C.A., 1953, 41–2–19. "Points" are assessed against a driver for various moving traffic violations. The point level at which the department generally takes suspension action is 200, and at the time of appellant's suspension,

he had accrued a total of 480 points.

6. U.R.E., Rule 63(13). * * *

8. Miss., 222 So.2d 393, 398 (1969).

this instance. Mr. Ernest Kyriopoulos, Chief Driver's License Examiner, testified that the computer was kept in the basement of the capitol building, that certain operators enter the records of conviction under code as soon as they are received and that the entries are verified and audited by another clerk for accuracy. He also testified that the whole process of receiving and storing the driving convictions was done under his control and supervision. After hearing the witness and viewing the printout exhibit, the trial judge held the foundation to be sufficient. We will not reverse that decision absent a clear showing of abuse of his discretionary power. [Footnote.]

The judgment of the lower court is affirmed.

BRANDON v. STATE

272 Ind. 92, 396 N.E.2d 365
(Supreme Court of Indiana, Nov. 7, 1979.)

HUNTER, J.

The defendant, Dennis Michael Brandon, was convicted by a jury of bank robbery, Ind.Code § 35–13–5–1 (Burns 1975), and was sentenced to twenty years in prison. His direct appeal raises the following seven issues:

* * *

4. Whether the court erred in admitting certain evidence and testimony over defendant's objections that they were hearsay;

* * *

A summary of the facts most favorable to the state shows that The National City Bank of Evansville was robbed on the morning of June 9, 1977, by a group of five people, four black men and one black woman. They were all wearing dark clothing and stocking masks. One was armed with a shotgun and the others with revolvers. One of the men jumped over a counter and shouted for the employees to hit the floor. Then the robbers took money out of the tellers' drawers and put it in a brown paper sack.

The main witness for the state, Vicki Myers, was a young white girl who testified that she had driven the "switch" car for the robbers on June 9, 1977, and had been charged with bank robbery as a result. She served a sentence at

the Indiana Girls' School for this incident. Vicki testified that she first met the defendant late in May, 1977, at the apartment of two of her friends who lived on her street in Evansville. These two friends were "T" Tillman Morris and Janice Cooke. Morris was one of the five people subsequently involved in the robbery. Vicki also testified that she saw the defendant on two later occasions when she was visiting Morris's apartment. On one occasion, about a week before the robbery, there were five people present besides herself, Janice Cooke, Tillman Morris, Dave Johnson, Larry James and the defendant. Morris, who was also known as Silas Kelley, asked Vicki if she would drive a switch-over car during the robbery. She said she would do it for the money.

On the day of the robbery Vicki went to Morris's apartment around 7:30 a. m. She saw four handguns, one sawed-off shotgun, ammunition, a pillowcase, and stocking hose laid out on the couch and floor. The five people who participated in the robbery assembled there by 8:30 a. m. Vicki testified that the others involved were Tillman Morris, Rene Jeffries, Larry James, Dave Johnson and the defendant. Vicki drove a car to an apartment complex parking lot. After the robbery, the five persons involved drove to the parking lot where Vicki was waiting. Two of them got into a third car and three of them got into Vicki's car. Defendant was one of the men who got into Vicki's car. The three men got down on the floorboard and instructed Vicki to drive to a certain address on Line Street. There they all went into an upstairs apartment, met the other two robbers and divided up the money.

The defendant put on an alibi defense. He testified that he lived in St. Louis, Missouri, at the time of the incident and was employed at the Bailey and English Mortuary there and was also attending technical school. His employer testified that he did not remember the defendant ever missing work during May or June of 1977. Two of defendant's friends in St. Louis testified that they did not know that the defendant ever left town during those months. The state presented telephone company records that showed there had been a large number of calls from the telephone number of one of the defendant's friends in St. Louis to the number of Janice Cooke's residence in Evansville. There were also telephone records showing several calls from Cooke's number in Evansville to various numbers in St. Louis.

* * *

IV.

Defendant next argues that it was error to admit state's Exhibits Nos. 31A–F which were business office copies of the microfiche records of the telephone company showing all long distance calls charged to a certain number in St. Louis. Defendant claims that these copies were not sufficiently qualified to be admitted under the business records exception to the hearsay rule. Defendant admits that these records are regular business records but argues that they are not the original or first permanent entry and therefore cannot be admitted.

The requisites for admission of a hearsay document offered under the business records exception are set forth in *American United Life Ins. Co. v. Peffley*, (1973) 158 Ind.App. 29, 301 N.E.2d 651, rehearing denied 158 Ind.App. 29, 306 N.E.2d 131:

> A synthesis of the Indiana cases treating what modern authorities call the 'business record' exception to the hearsay rule is that documentary evidence is admissible if identified by its entrant or one under whose supervision it is kept and shown to be an original or first permanent entry, made in the routine course of business, at or near the time of the recorded transaction, by one having both a duty to so record and personal knowledge of the transaction represented by the entry. [Citation.]

The theory behind this rule is that regularly maintained business records are admissible in evidence as an exception to the hearsay rule because the fact that they are regularly maintained records upon which the company relies in conducting its business assures their trustworthiness. The rules of evidence governing the admission of business records are of common law origin and have evolved on a case-by-case basis to keep pace with the technology of current business methods of record keeping. It has already been clearly established in this state that a duplicate of a document is admissible in evidence "to the same extent as an original unless a genuine issue is raised as to the authenticity of the original,

or under the circumstances existing it would be unfair to admit the duplicate as an original." *Wilson v. State*, (1976) Ind.App., 348 N.E.2d 90, 95. Even though the scrivener's quill pens in original entry books have been replaced by magnetic tapes, microfiche files and computer print-outs, the theory behind the reliability of regularly kept business records remains the same and computer-generated evidence is no less reliable than original entry books provided a proper foundation is laid. [Citations.]

We therefore find that our business records exception is sufficiently broad to include within its scope a system of keeping records stored on a computer and electronically printed out on demand. However, before such records can be admitted, it must be shown that the electronic computing equipment is standard, that the entries are made in the regular course of business at or reasonably near the time of the happening of the event recorded, and that the testimony satisfies the court that the sources of information and method and time of preparation were such as to indicate its authenticity and accuracy and justify its acceptance as trustworthy. A similar three-part test has been set out by the Mississippi Supreme Court in *King v. State ex. rel. Murdock Acceptance Corp.*, (1969) Miss., 222 So.2d 393, and is followed in several other jurisdictions. [Citations.]

In the instant case, there was testimony describing the manner in which the telephone calls were recorded on magnetic tape at the time each call was made and how the computer later printed out microfiche records for filing. The customer and business office copies of each bill were then printed out from the microfiche and the business office copy was admitted into evidence at the trial. The witness testified that the computer equipment used was a standard type of computer system and had been used by the company for several years. We find no error in admitting the business office copy of the customer's telephone bill into evidence under the business records exception since a sufficient foundation was laid.

In order to impeach defendant's alibi defense, the state put on the stand, Miss Cheryl Pikoriatis who was the financial aid administrator at Bailey Technical School in St. Louis where defendant claimed he had been enrolled at the time of the crime. Miss Pikoriatis testified that she had searched the enrollment records for certain dates in May and June of 1977, and had not found any record indicating that defendant was enrolled during those times. She further testified that in her capacity as financial aid administrator, all applications for enrollment were processed through her office and that she was one of the keepers of the records.

Defendant contends that this testimony is inadmissible since it is testimony of the negative results of a search of records and is hearsay. However, testimony as to the negative results of a search of regularly kept records has long been recognized as admissible in this state, *Lacey v. Marnan*, (1871) 37 Ind. 168. It has also been well established by the federal rules of evidence and by statute or case law in several other jurisdictions that this type of testimony based upon what regularly-maintained business records do not show is admissible as a corollary of the business records exception. [Citations.]

Since the witness in the instant case was one of the keepers of the records and was testifying about the absence of any records where there normally would have been records had defendant been enrolled in the school, there was no error in admitting this testimony.

* * *

STATE v. CORRALES
135 Ariz. 105, 659 P.2d 658
(Court of Appeals of Arizona, Division 2, Dec. 29, 1982.)

BIRDSALL, J.

Appellant was found guilty after a jury trial of driving while under the influence of intoxicating liquor while his license was suspended, a class 6 felony. He was sentenced to prison for 1.5 years and given credit for time served prior to sentencing. * * *

Counsel for appellant has raised two arguable issues for our attention: (1) whether

the computer printout showing appellant's prior driving record was properly authenticated under Rule 902, Arizona Rules of Evidence, and hence properly admitted, and (2) whether it was error for the trial court to permit, over objection, the testimony of a breathalyzer expert. We see no error and affirm.

The printout itself was certified and the certifying person's signature and status as custodian of the record was attested to by the Assistant Director of the Department of Transportation, Motor Vehicle Division. This certificate bore the seal of the Department of Transportation of the State of Arizona. Compliance with Rule 902, Arizona Rules of Evidence, 17A A.R.S., was therefore accomplished. [Citation.]

* * *

IN RE FINKELSTEIN
458 A.2d 326
(Commonwealth Court of Pennsylvania, April 14, 1983.)

BLATT, J.

Allan L. Finkelstein (appellant) appeals here an order [footnote] of the Court of Common Pleas of Allegheny County dismissing his appeal from the action of the Department of Transportation (DOT) in cancelling his driver's license pursuant to Section 1572 of the Vehicle Code, 75 Pa.C.S. § 1572.[2]

The DOT argued to the trial court that, inasmuch as the appellant's license had been revoked in Georgia, which was his previous state of residence, he should never have received a license here. In support of this contention, the DOT introduced into evidence, over the specific timely objection of the appellant's counsel, a "packet" of documents containing mainly photocopies of computer printouts from the Motor Vehicle Division of the State of Georgia and from the National Drivers Register showing numerous driving violations. It is undisputed that these documents were not

---

2. This section reads:
   The department may cancel any driver's license upon determining that the licensee was not entitled to issuance or that the person failed to give the required or correct information or committed fraud in making

the application or in obtaining the license or the fee has not been paid. Upon the cancellation, the licensee shall immediately surrender the canceled license to the department.

certified or authenticated in any way by officials of the State of Georgia.

* * *

The appellant argues here that the "packet" of documents was inadmissible as hearsay, and because the DOT offered no other evidence in support of its cancellation of the license, the DOT has failed to meet its burden of proof. [Citation.] The appellant cites to Section 5328(a) of the Judicial Code, 42 Pa.C.S. § 5328(a) which provides:

> § 5328. Proof of official records
> (a) Domestic record—An official record kept with the United States, or any state, district, commonwealth, territory, insular possession thereof, or the Panama Canal Zone, the Trust Territory of the Pacific Islands, or an entry therein, when admissible for any purpose, may be evidenced by an official publication thereof or by a copy attested by the officer having the legal custody of the record, or by his deputy, and accompanied by a certificate that the officer has the custody. The certificate may be made by a judge of a court of record having jurisdiction in the governmental unit in which the record is kept, authenticated by the seal of the court, or by any public officer having a seal of office and having official duties in the governmental unit in which the record is kept, authenticated by the seal of his office.

Without the proper certification from the Georgia officials, therefore, the printouts here concerned were clearly written statements, made by an individual who is unavailable to testify and therefore unavailable for cross-examination, and they are offered to prove the truth of the matters asserted therein. [Citation.] And Section 5328 of the Judicial Code, by requiring certification of such records from another jurisdiction, provides a means for rendering them reliable and obviates the need for oral testimony to authenticate the writings.

The DOT, however, did not follow the instructions of Section 5328. And the trial judge was therefore in error in receiving the documents as evidence. As a result the DOT has not met its burden. [Citation.][3] The only unobjectionable evidence in the record is the testimony of the appellant, who merely stated

that he never received notification of license revocation by the State of Georgia, and he therefore assumed that he was eligible for licensure in this Commonwealth. Obviously this does not meet the DOT's burden either, but on the other hand, works to rebut it.

We must, therefore, reverse the order of the trial court.

* * *

KING v. STATE EX REL. MURDOCK ACCEPTANCE CORP.
222 So.2d 393
(Supreme Court of Mississippi, April 21, 1969.)

GILLESPIE, P. J.

This is an appeal by Hershel King from a decree of the Chancery Court of Alcorn County rendered against him in favor of the State of Mississippi for the use and benefit of Murdock Acceptance Corporation. The basis for the suit was a false notarial certificate of acknowledgment to a deed of trust. (There were two deeds of trust, but for the purpose of this opinion the singular is used.) King is a notary public.

The questions are (1) whether Murdock came into equity with unclean hands, (2) whether the evidence was sufficient to justify the finding that the false notarial certificate was the proximate cause of Murdock's loss, and (3) whether business records entered on and printed out by electronic computing equipment were admissible in evidence. * * *

Murdock finances dealers engaged in selling automobiles and mobile homes through the purchase of conditional sales contracts. Serl Anderson was a dealer in mobile homes financed by Murdock. Anderson operated a large distribution center and sold mobile homes through agents at other locations, one of whom was John H. Putt of Corinth, Mississippi. Murdock purchased from Anderson six conditional sales contracts, two of which were cosigned by Putt. Murdock contended that Putt had repossessed the mobile homes described in the contracts. Anderson became a bankrupt and Murdock summoned Putt as a witness at

---

3. In *Schreffler License*, 20 Pa.D. & C.2d 634 (1959), a factually similar case, motor vehicle records from Delaware were ruled inadmissible due to their lack of verification or attestation.

the creditors' meeting. Murdock contended that Putt was liable on the aforementioned six contracts with a total net balance due of about $16,000.

Before the creditors' meeting began, Putt proposed a settlement of Murdock's claim against him and agreed to execute a note to Murdock for $11,000, if Murdock would agree not to call Putt as a witness in the bankruptcy proceeding, and not pursue the makers of the six conditional sales contracts or repossess the mobile homes. As part of this settlement, Putt agreed that the note would be signed by his wife and his parents, J. Harvey Putt and Captola Putt, and it would be secured by a deed of trust on the property belonging to J. Harvey Putt. After investigating the value of the property proposed as security for the $11,000 note, Murdock agreed to the settlement.

Accordingly, the note and the deed of trust were delivered to Murdock and were purportedly signed by John H. Putt and his wife, and J. Harvey Putt and Captola Putt, and the deed of trust securing the note was acknowledged before Hershel King, who entered thereon his certificate of acknowledgment. The deed of trust was placed of record and John H. Putt made several payments, reducing the principal balance to $8,900 at the time this suit was brought. When default was made in the payment of note, Murdock sought to foreclose the deed of trust. J. Harvey and Captola Putt filed suit and enjoined the sale because they had not signed the note and deed of trust and Hershel King's notarial certificate to the acknowledgment on the deed of trust was false. Thereafter, this suit was brought against Hershel King and the surety on his official bond, Hartford Accident and Indemnity Company. At the conclusion of the case the chancellor entered a joint and several decree against Hershel King and Hartford Accident and Indemnity in the amount of $2,000, the amount of the notarial bond, and against Hershel King, individually, for $7,900. King prosecuted this appeal; Hartford Accident and Indemnity Company did not join.

* * *

The argument on the admissibility of Murdock's business records printed out by electronic computing equipment raises a question not heretofore considered by this Court.

The pleadings made an issue as to the balance due Murdock on the six conditional sales contracts and the balance due on the $11,000 note. In order to prove the amount of damages, it was necessary for Murdock to prove the amounts paid on the note.

The balances due on the six conditional sales contracts were proved by the introduction of the original contracts and computer sheets printed out by an electronic data processing machine. These sheets showed in separate columns as to each of the six conditional sales contracts (1) the originating branch office number, (2) the dealer's number, (3) the individual account number, (4) the gross balance due, (5) the due date, (6) the amount paid, (7) the date of payment, and (8) the payment number. The sheet contained a complete record of each account. The sheet showing the record of the account and payments of the $11,000 note contained the same information.

These computer sheets were admitted in evidence after extensive testimony by W. M. Spiller, Assistant Treasurer and Accounting Manager of Murdock, who is in charge of the data processing department at the home office, and under whose supervision the computerized accounting records are maintained. The following is the substance of his testimony. A centralized system of accounting is kept at the home office by use of a Burroughs B–280 computer, standard equipment and recognized as an efficient and accurate machine. All records are maintained by this computer on magnetic tape. The information is fed into the machine by competent and experienced operators. At the beginning of each transaction it is given a number and the essential information is key punched on a card. The card is then verified by another operator. If the card is not punched correctly it will not go through the verifying machine. The card is then fed into the computer and the information is recorded on magnetic tape. This is Murdock's permanent record of the customer's account. The machine also performs other functions not necessary to relate. As payments are made at branch offices each payment is recorded on receipt blocks and these, together with a travel card for each account involved, are sent to the home office where verification is made by the machine. The payment information from receipt block and the travel card is then fed into the computer and recorded on the customer's account. The branch office could reconstruct the account from copies of cash receipt blocks and other records kept in the branch offices. The records sent from branch offices from which the information is taken to feed into the machine are kept for a period of time, then microfilmed and the original destroyed. The company considers the information recorded by the computer on magnetic tape as the permanent records of the history of the customer accounts. The information is received by the home office daily and processed and fed into the machine in the ordinary course of business.

King contends that the computer sheets do not meet the requirements of the shop book rule because the sheets are not the original records, citing *Fatherree v. Griffin*, 153 Miss. 570, 121 So. 119 (1929), where the court held inadmissible a sworn itemized statement of account without producing the books from which the account was made, holding that the books were the best evidence. King also contends that the first permanent record of the customer account is maintained in the branch office, that is, a copy of the "receipt blocks", the original of which is forwarded to the home office.

We find it unnecessary to discuss the "shop book" rule as applied to conventional bookkeeping methods. [Footnote.] We are of the opinion that the chancellor was justified in finding that the records of customer accounts maintained by Murdock would meet the requirements of the shop book rule if conventional books were used instead of a computer. The problem is whether the sheet printed out by the computer is inadmissible because it is not the original record under the rule announced in *Fatherree v. Griffin, supra,* or whether the court should adapt the rule formerly applied to conventional books so as to accommodate the changes involved in electronic data processing. This change has been accomplished by statute in a number of states by adoption of the Uniform Business Records as Evidence Act; however, this Court is not dependent upon legislative action to determine the question before us. The rules of evidence governing the admission of business records are of common law origin and have evolved case by case, and the Court should apply these rules consistent with the realities of current business methods. The law always seeks the best evidence and adjusts its rules to accommodate itself to the advancements of the age it serves. Our decision in this case was foreshadowed in *Grenada Cotton Compress Co. v. Atkinson*, 94 Miss. 93, 47 So. 644 (1908), when this Court extended the shop book rule by holding that where an entry is made by one person in the regular course of business recording an oral or written report made to him by one or more other persons in the regular course of business of a transaction lying in the personal knowledge of the latter there is no objection to receiving that entry, provided the practical inconvenience of producing on the stand the numerous persons thus concerned would in the particular case outweigh the probable utility of doing so. In so holding, the Court, quoting from *Wigmore* said:

> It would seem that expedients which the entire commercial world recognize as safe could be sanctioned, and not discredited, by courts of justice. When it is a mere question of whether provisional confidence can be placed in a certain class of statements, there cannot profitably and sensibly be one rule for the business world and another for the courtroom. The merchant and the manufacturer must not be turned away remediless because methods in which the entire community places a just confidence are a little difficult to reconcile with technical judicial scruples on the part of the same persons who, as attorneys, have already employed and relied upon the same methods. In short, courts must here cease to be pedantic and endeavor to be practical. (94 Miss. at 100, 101, 47 So. at 646; *See also* 5 *Wigmore*, § 1530 (3d ed. 1940).

Transport Indemnity v. Seib, 178 Neb. 253, 132 N.W.2d 871, 11 A.L.R.3d 1368 (1965), was decided on the Uniform Business Records as Evidence Act and the Court said that no particular form of record was required. The Uniform Act does not mention computers or electronic machines. In an annotation following *Seib* it is stated:

> The prognostication seems justified that as business records kept electronically become increasingly prevalent, the legal problems in connection with their use in evidence will resolve themselves into the question whether the proof

offered by the litigant seeking receipt of such records in evidence, as to the manner in which they were prepared and kept, is sufficient to satisfy the pre-electronics requirements as to the admission of business records prepared and kept in conventional forms (journals, ledgers, reports, etc.); that is to say, has it been sufficiently shown that the records kept or stored electronically were made in the regular course of business, that they were based on information within the personal knowledge of one whose duties included the collection of such information, that the records themselves were prepared by those who understood the operation of the equipment and whose regular duty it was to operate it, etc. The only case dealing with the problem at the time this annotation was prepared seems to justify the foregoing speculation. [Citation.]

In *Jones on Evidence*, Fifth Ed., Section 609 (Supp.1968) it is said that "[T]he scientific reliability of such machines [electronic computing equipment], in the light of their general use and the general reliance of the business world on them, can scarcely be questioned."

Records stored on magnetic tape by data processing machines are unavailable and useless except by means of the print-out sheets such as those admitted in evidence in this case. In admitting the print-out sheets reflecting the record stored on the tape, the Court is actually following the best evidence rule. We are not departing from the shop book rule, but only extending its application to electronic record keeping.

In sum, we hold that print-out sheets of business records stored on electronic computing equipment are admissible in evidence if relevant and material, without the necessity of identifying, locating, and producing as witnesses the individuals who made the entries in the regular course of business if it is shown (1) that the electronic computing equipment is recognized as standard equipment, (2) the entries are made in the regular course of business at or reasonably near the time of the happening of the event recorded, and (3) the foundation testimony satisfies the court that the sources of information, method and time of preparation were such as to indicate its trustworthiness and justify its admission.

We are not to be understood as indicating that computer evidence is infallible. Its probative value is the same as conventional books,

and it is subject to refutation to the same extent.

We are therefore of the opinion that the chancellor was correct in all his rulings and his decree is affirmed.

Affirmed.

COX v. BROOKINGS INTERNATIONAL LIFE INSURANCE CO.

331 N.W.2d 299
(Supreme Court of South Dakota, March 23, 1983.)

MORGAN, J.

This appeal arises from an action to recover the proceeds of an insurance contract brought by the beneficiary, Raymond Cox appellant (Cox), against Brookings International Life Insurance Company, appellee (Company). After both sides had rested, the trial court directed a verdict in favor of Company and Cox appeals. We affirm in part, reverse in part, and remand.

In April of 1975, Cox's wife applied for and received a life insurance policy on their son, Steven, from Company. Mrs. Cox had, as a regular practice, assumed the responsibility to gather the monthly bills and write checks for payment of the family expenses, including insurance premiums. Upon her death in October of 1977, Cox succeeded to ownership of the policy as he was the sole surviving beneficiary. From that time he also assumed responsibility for payment of the family bills which included premiums on thirteen various types of insurance policies. Cox testified that he depended upon receiving notice in the mail from the insurance companies that premiums were due in order to know when to pay the premiums. On June 10, 1978, Steven was killed in a car accident. After Cox notified Company of Steven's death, he received a letter from Company advising him that coverage under the policy had lapsed due to nonpayment of the premium which was due on April 1, 1978. Cox initiated this action to recover on the policy and, at trial, at the close of all the evidence on motion of the Company the trial court directed a verdict for Company. This appeal follows.

* * *

The threshold issue on this appeal is whether notice is necessary and if so what constitutes adequate notice to an insured that an insurance premium is due. Company first argues that since the policy of insurance, which contains the premium amounts and the due dates, makes no further provision to require notice to the policyholders, no notice is due because the policy owner has actual knowledge of both the amount and due date thereof. This argument is unsupportable. Insurance companies generally are interested in collecting premiums. They send out notices, usually well in advance of the due date. Such notices almost universally furnish policyholders not only a "tickler" reminder of the upcoming due date but a return envelope properly addressed and a coupon or other memo to be returned with the payment to insure proper accounting.

We note the general rule that the necessity for an insurance company to give notice to an insured of a premium due even absent a policy provision may be based upon the practice of the particular insurer. [Citations.] * * *

The life insurance policy insuring Steven was entered into on April 1, 1975, when Steven was fourteen years of age. The policy provided for quarterly premiums and each quarter Company notified the Cox' in advance that the $10.50 premium would be due. Cox testified at trial that he relied on such notice that a premium due date was forthcoming in order to pay the premium. Accordingly, because Company notified Cox each quarter that the premium on this policy was due, Company was required to continue this practice unless it specifically notified Cox that it would discontinue such notification.

Company next asserts its strongest point, that in fact proper notice of the premium due was given to Cox. This is the view that the trial court adopted in directing the verdict. Company contends that it mailed a premium notice to Cox; however, Cox testified that he did not receive it.

It is well established that proof of mailing by depositing a letter in a proper mail receptacle, properly addressed and stamped, raises a presumption of delivery to the person addressed; however, it is only a rebuttable presumption. [Citations.] At the trial, Company went to great lengths to establish proper mailing. There was testimony from a company of-

ficial and a mailroom employee as to the procedure, and mail logs that demonstrate mailing of the particular piece in question. From the record before us we cannot say that the trial court erred in finding that there was a presumption of delivery. Cox, however, not only testified that he had not received the notice but further went to some lengths to demonstrate his own household procedures for handling incoming mail, including bills and premium notices. Cox also demonstrated that during the period from early February to late June, during which time the lapse occurred, he had sent checks in payment of premiums on thirteen other policies; five of which were paid in the month of May. While concededly the mere denial of receipt alone would not be enough, since Cox presented other substantial evidence we agree with what this court stated in *Bank of Ipswich v. Harding County, Etc. Ins. Co.,* 55 S.D. 261, 225 N.W. 721 (1929):

> This rebuttable presumption, with supporting evidence on behalf of [Company] and denial of receipt with its supporting testimony on the part of [Cox], was such, in our opinion, as to make the question of receipt a subject for the determination of the trier of fact.

55 S.D. at 268, 225 N.W. at 723 (citation omitted).

In reviewing this directed verdict, this court must view the evidence in a light most favorable to Cox. [Citations.] Since there is enough evidence to allow reasonable minds to differ, the directed verdict was inappropriate. The trial court should have permitted the trier of fact to determine the issue of receipt.

* * *

HENDERSON, J., specially concurring.

Computers and organizational procedures in an insurance company, are they infallible? Do computers make mistakes? Are all procedures in insurance companies for mailing out premium notices perfect?

Are we mortals, who invented the computers, enslaved to their supposed correctness? Or do we still have the intellectual right to question their propriety, authenticity, reliability, and the possibility of malfunction?

Well, lo and behold, plaintiff-appellant testified herein concerning the reliability of a computer, which evidence went into the record without objection and before the jury, that defendant-appellee's agent in South Dakota, a Mr. Roth, had expressed that his company's computers had malfunctioned "at that time." "At that time" referred to the approximate time when premium notices were sent out, which included a time-frame germane to appellant's premium notice. Indeed, in its defense testimony, the insurance company shored its case up beautifully with personnel from Ohio that its overall procedures were followed to the proverbial "T." And yes, according to this defense testimony, the computers had safeguards for default provisions, and any malfunction would trigger the computer to recycle and print an entire batch of premium notices. Conclusion: per defense testimony, the computer and all mailing procedures were faultless.

This insurance company, in essence, relied upon its computers, mailing logs, and supposed faultless procedures. Based upon this faultless programming, the trial court determined that the evidence of plaintiff-appellant was not competent or probative, and further determined, by theory, that the South Dakota agent of the insurance company did not have personal knowledge of the Ohio computer operations. The verdict was directed against the plaintiff-appellant for, you see, how could the infallibility of the procedures be questioned? Alas, a human element was in the case for somewhere, somehow, as an agent of the insurance company, Mr. Roth learned of the trouble with the computer operation in Ohio. Oh, woe unto the doctrine of computer infallibility. A key to this is found in the testimony of one of the company's experts who admitted that the company did not keep the malfunction "as a secret." From this same expert witness, came the revelation that there were premiums which the company received late and some were as late as approximately 75 days. Grace periods had to be considered. During this phase of the trial, this company expert attempted to restrict these late premiums to a time unrelated to the plaintiff-appellant's due premium. To repeat: the timetable was germane to plaintiff-appellant's premium via the testimony of the company's licensed agent in South Dakota. Company officials described him as one of their top representatives and salesmen. It developed during the testimony

that Mr. Roth had access to telephone communication with the company and the malfunction being, no secret, became knowledge to him. The malfunction of the computer which processed premiums was knowledge within the company at Ohio and apparently spilled over into its office at Brookings, South Dakota. Thus, in my opinion, the trial court should not have disregarded, in toto, the testimony of Mr. Roth relating to the computer malfunction. It was highly relevant as to the receipt of a premium notice by plaintiff-appellant. A classic question of fact arose and it was for the jury to determine that question of fact and not the trial court. Further, I add that it is altogether conceivable that there was human error for the facts additionally disclose: that the quarterly notices, first generated by a computer in Ohio, were then sent to Brookings, South Dakota, there matched by hand and placed in an envelope, to be then mailed to policyholders such as plaintiff-appellant.

These presumptions of law are based upon hypothesis. I refuse to hypothesize that computers cannot err. That plaintiff-appellant was presumed to have received this premium notice, was surely a rebuttable presumption.

> The presumption of receipt of a letter duly mailed is ordinarily indulged in only when there is an absence of evidence to the contrary. [Citations.]

[Citation.] By a wisp of mental process, these presumptions of law are created. When facts come into evidence to negate the presumption, these presumptions of law, which flit about in theory like a butterfly, lose their credible force, for they cannot contend against reality. In *Matter of Voorhees*, 294 N.W.2d 646, 651 (S.D.1980), I expressed my opinion on presumptions of law and it is applicable to my thoughts herein:

> A presumption is just that: It is like a night bird, that flits about in the twilight and into the dark, but disappears under the light and sunshine of actual facts. The sunshine of the facts probe and reveal more than a presumption of law; we must never lose sight of this.

As the human dimension of justice cannot be sacrificed for the ostensible purity of the computer world, I join the majority opinion.

FOSHEIM, C. J., dissenting.

The trial court correctly directed a verdict for the insurance company. I cannot agree that

Cox presented "other substantial evidence," in addition to his mere denial, that he did not receive notice. How Cox said he handled his incoming mail or that he paid premiums on other policies is irrelevant and proves nothing beyond his self-serving statement as to notice. On the other hand, the insurance company proved, pursuant to the business records statute [footnote], that it notified Cox not only by mail but also by telephone. True, this telephone call was taken by Steven Cox, appellant's son, then 17 years of age. Our service of process statutes, however, allow notice of the commencement of a law suit, for an unlimited amount, by service on a 14 year old. [Citation.] Can we properly demand more regarding an insurance contract which doesn't even require the giving of notice.

The evidence does not leave room for reasonable minds to differ about whether Cox was notified. [Citation.] To hold otherwise would allow anyone who has let an insurance policy lapse for nonpayment of premium to nevertheless seek recovery from a jury, by simply saying, "I do not recall getting a notice." It would thus tend to encourage fraud and destabilize the insurance industry.

HUBER, HUNT & NICHOLS, INC. v. MOORE

67 Cal.App.3d 278, 136 Cal.Rptr. 603
(Court of Appeal, Fifth District, Jan. 27, 1977.)

LORING, A. J.

Huber, Hunt & Nichols, Inc., an Indiana Corporation ("Contractor") filed an action in Santa Clara County against The Fresno City-County Community and Convention Center Authority ("Owner"), the City of Fresno ("City") and County of Fresno ("County") and Richard R. Moore, Robert W. Stevens, Robert W. Stevens Associates and Robert Stevens Associates and Adrian Wilson Associates, a joint venture (collectively "Architects") to recover damages allegedly sustained as the result of the construction of a convention center complex in the City of Fresno. Defendant's motion for change of venue to Fresno County was granted. The demurrer of Architects was sustained as to all causes of action except causes of action seven (Negligence) and ten (In-

demnity). Owner filed a cross-complaint against Robert W. Stevens Associates to recover any moneys owner was obligated to pay Contractor.

* * *

Before defining the issues on appeal, it is first appropriate to consider the factual context out of which these cases arise.

Prior to February, 1962, City decided to build a convention center complex consisting of three buildings connected by one roof—a convention center, a theatre and an ice rink—in the City of Fresno. City entered into a contract with Robert W. Stevens, dba Robert W. Stevens Associates, a licensed architect, to prepare the architectural plans and specifications. Later County joined City in the project and Fresno City-County Convention Center Authority was created by a joint powers agreement between City and County executed under authority of Government Code, chapter 5, article 1, section 6500, et seq.

The architectural contract was assigned by City to Owner. As the magnitude of the project increased, Robert W. Stevens Associates entered into a joint venture agreement with Adrian Wilson Associates, a firm of licensed architects. After nine months of work by the Architects, the plans and specifications were approved and accepted by the Owner, checked and approved by City Building Department, building permits issued and public bids on them requested by the Owner. The bids were opened December 15, 1964 and Contractor's bid of $6,398,000 was the low bid. [Footnote.]

The low bid was approximately one million dollars above the Architects' estimates. Owner was uncertain that it could finance the extra cost so it negotiated with Contractor on 50 or 60 possible modifications or alternatives which would reduce the overall costs of the project. The contract with the possible modifications or alternatives was awarded to Contractor and construction began January 25, 1965. The contract required completion within 500 days.

The contract contained a liquidated damages clause of $200.00 for each day's delay over 500. Owner took possession of the convention center in late September, 1965 before the project was entirely completed.

* * *

Under the proposed contract terms as incorporated in the bid forms, the Contractor was required to carefully examine and familiarize itself with the plans and specifications and site and call the Architects' attention prior to bid to any discrepancies in or omissions from the drawings or specifications and if appropriate, amendments would be issued to all bidders prior to bid. The contract documents contemplated that the Architects' plans or specifications might contain errors or omissions and as interpreted by the parties it provided for a process which would enable the Contractor to obtain additional or supplemental information (information request "I.R.") and propose changes including estimates of the cost and time for performance (change estimate "C.E.") and the Owner to issue change orders ("C.O") which would specify the work to be performed, the price to be paid and the time allowed for the additional or changed work. Each C.O. was approved by the City Council. The form of change orders used included a clause [footnote] in which the Contractor approved the change order and agreed that the sum specified was in complete payment of all work to be performed and materials to be supplied and which approved the time as extended. The Architects were designated in the contract as the sole arbiter regarding disputes which might arise between the Contractor and the Owner during the performance of the work. [Footnote.]

During the course of the work Contractor submitted 103 I.R.s, 187 C.E.s and the parties agreed on 25 C.O.s. However, the 25 C.O.s encompassed 124 C.E.s. The record is not clear as to what happened to the remaining 63 C.E.s, but presumably they were rejected by the Owner. Eight of the C.O.s [footnote] reduced the scope of the work resulting in deductions aggregating $152,544.41. Seventeen of the C.O.s increased or changed the scope of the work which resulted in additional charges to

Owner aggregating $472,652.91. Certain of Contractor's records indicate that as of November 30, 1972, its total costs in connection with the convention center were $6,965,518.00 with an additional $72,500 estimated to complete the work. [Footnote.] Contractor's records [footnote] also indicate that as of November 30, 1972, its cost overrun was $337,505.00 which included a revised fee of $271,365.00.

At trial Contractor claimed that Architects' plans and specifications were negligently prepared, contained errors and omissions, and that as a consequence, Contractor was damaged. At trial Contractor also claimed that the Architects were dilatory and negligent in approving change orders, in approving shop drawings and in the overall supervision of the work, and, as a consequence, the overall project was delayed resulting in damages to Contractor.

Contractor sought to recover from Architects the sum of $732,521.00 which it claimed was its total damage. [Footnote.]

* * *

RULINGS ON ADMISSION OF EVIDENCE

We next consider Contractor's claims of error regarding the rulings of the trial court concerning the admission of evidence.

In its closing brief on appeal Contractor described plaintiff's Exhibit 3 for identification as "* * * the *single* piece of evidence which proved or tended to prove that the effect of the architects' errors and omissions was to increase job costs in the categories used by plaintiff". [Reference.] (Emphasis ours.) In oral argument on appeal, Contractor made the same concession. In view of this concession by Contractor, we first examine the court's ruling excluding plaintiff's Exhibit 3 for identification from evidence. Plaintiff's Exhibit 3 is described in the margin.[12]

---

12. Plaintiff's Exhibit 3 is a computer read out consisting of pages approximating 11″ × 15″ in size which in the aggregate are three inches thick. Each page consists of various columns containing words or figures arranged under the following headings: "Cost Code" (under which appear the numbers for 200 different items), "Description" (under which appear one to three words describing the 200 different items such as "Tectun Decks", "Dasher Board inserts", "Dasher boards" "Insulation AC tile", "Allowances", "Metal Deck and siding", "Steel joists",

"Struct. Steel", "Sheet Metal", "Roofing", "Roof Hatches and vents", "Lath and plaster", "Masonry", "Paving", "Filler Panels", "Millwork", "Misc. Matl", "Commitments", "Backcharge sales" and other words of a similar or dissimilar nature); "Construction Budget"; "Budget Changes" with subheadings "Initial", "Final", "Current Budget"; "Costs" with subheadings "To Date", "To Complete", "Overrun/Underrun"; "Variance" with subheadings "Fm.", "Prev.", "Mo.".

The court concluded that the computer read out (Plaintiff's Exhibit 3) would be unintelligible to the jurors without additional evidence such as oral testimony to explain it. The court indicated that it would permit any qualified witness to testify from the document orally.[13] Counsel for Contractor conceded in the court below that there may be risk of "wrong conclusions * * * about what it shows."

Evidence Code section 350 provides that "[n]o evidence is admissible except relevant evidence." Evidence Code section 352[14] empowers the court to exclude evidence (otherwise admissible) if its probative value is substantially outweighed by the probability that its admission will create substantial danger of confusing the issues or of misleading the jury. Even prior to the adoption of Evidence Code section 352, the trial court had wide discretion in determining the relevance and consequent admission of evidence. [Citations.]

In our view Contractor does not demonstrate here that the trial court abused its discretion in refusing to receive plaintiff's Exhibit 3 for identification in evidence. We have examined plaintiff's Exhibit 3 and we conclude that the document is unintelligible particularly with reference to its possible probative value as to the issues of this case without any oral evidence explaining how it relates to the issues in this case.

Aside from the obvious difficulty that a lay jury would have in reading and understanding such a complex document and correlating it with the issues involved in this case, there was great risk of misinterpretation as counsel for Contractor conceded. For example, we find in examining plaintiff's Exhibit 3 for identification that as of "11/30/72" the total "costs" "to date" were "6,965,518" with "72,500" required "to complete". We also find what appears to be a separate set of calculations entitled "Detail Cost Sheet" which indicates that as of "11/30/72" the "Total Cost to Date" was "$5,828,650.68". One month later on "12/31/72" the total "costs" "to date" were "5,132,173" with "72,500" required "to complete". If a jury were to accept the latter two figures at face value it would appear obvious that Contractor suffered no damage in any manner whatsoever but made a very substantial profit in excess of its "fee" as originally budgeted. Presumably there is an appropriate accounting explanation for these various discrepancies and apparent conflicts, but they illustrate the point that the document was subject to possible mis-

---

13. The court explained to counsel its reasons as follows:
   THE COURT: Well, I'm going to treat this in this manner: assuming that the foundational requirements are testified substantially as outlined by Mr. Rushing, I'm going to admit the computer printout—I'm going to have it marked, rather, as an exhibit for identification. I'm then going to permit the witness to testify from the document. But the document itself, the printout itself, will not be—will not go to the jury. And I do that for this reason; that a lay juror is not qualified, and I so find, to interpret a computer printout; that by allowing that document to go to the jury, that the Court would take the risk that the jury would misinterpret the document, just as the same reasoning that has been applied by the Court with reference to x-ray films, for example.

   * * *

   MR. RUSHING: Let me ask the Court one further question, if I may. May I be permitted, if it is not going to go to the jury, to prepare a chart showing the category of work—categories of work? That I deem relevant.
   THE COURT: Supported by the evidence. I'm not saying it would be admissible in evidence, but there is no reason you couldn't use it in argument.
   MR. RUSHING: Well, I want to use it in my argument. This is not a particularly easy area of the case, I think, for any of us. It's a matter that takes considerable care in going through it. *And if one missteps; and makes sort of a category case about codes and categories, and things like that, you will come*

out wrong in the conclusions about what it shows.
   THE COURT: I don't think I can answer your question until I see what you are offering. (Emphasis ours.)

The court admonished the jury as follows:
   THE COURT: Very well. It is the order of the Court that the exhibit, which has previously been marked as Plaintiff's Exhibit 3 for identification, not be received into evidence. It is further ordered, however, that the Witness, this witness, or any other witness, may refer to the document, and testify concerning matters contained therein, and by reference to the matters contained in the document. I would like to explain, ladies and gentlemen, the reason for my ruling.
   The court finds that this exhibit, which consists of printouts from a computer, is a matter which requires interpretation, and that neither the Court nor the jury is qualified to interpret the documents. And it is necessary, therefore, to have a witness who is qualified to testify concerning the documents and the interpretation of matters contained therein. That is the reason I'm not admitting it into evidence, but am ordering that it may be referred to by this witness and any other qualified witness.

14. Evidence Code section 352 reads as follows:
   The court in its discretion may exclude evidence if its probative value is substantially outweighed by the probability that its admission will (a) necessitate undue consumption of time or (b) create substantial danger of undue prejudice, of confusing the issues, or of misleading the jury.

interpretation without explanatory evidence and they demonstrate the wisdom of the trial court's ruling. We find no prejudice resulting from the ruling with reference to plaintiff's Exhibit 3 for identification in any event inasmuch as the record is clear that Contractor was permitted to produce any qualified witness to testify orally from Plaintiff's Exhibit 3. Contractor did produce a witness—Bruce Bennett, its contractor manager. Bennett attempted to testify from Plaintiff's Exhibit 3 for identification but the sum and substance of his proffered testimony was merely to attribute every cost overrun to the fault of the Architects without discrimination as to other possible causes. He was admittedly compelled to do this because Plaintiff's Exhibit 3 included extra costs within total costs without discrimination or segregation and without explanation as to causation. We note in the margin a colloquy between court and counsel which illustrates the problem.[15] It is manifest that counsel for Contractor merely wanted to dump into the record all data from the computer printout including cost overruns without reference to or any consideration whatsoever of the issue of causation.

We think the wisdom of the trial court's ruling is also illustrated by reference to Appendix A attached to Contractor's opening brief on appeal, a copy of which is appended to this opinion. [Appendix omitted.] Contractor represents to us that the material designated on Appendix A has been extrapolated from plaintiff's Exhibit 3 and Contractor alleges that Appendix A in effect proves Contractor's case. A reference to Appendix A demonstrates the fallacy of Contractor's contention. Take for ex-

ample, item "1525" "Drinking water". A reference to plaintiff's Exhibit 3 for identification indicates that Contractor originally estimated the cost of drinking water at $1,000, but $2,293.00 was expended resulting in an overrun (OR) of $1,293 which Contractor alleges is one item of its damage which it seeks to recover from Architects. In order to arrive at that conclusion, the jury would have to assume at least four elements of proof:

1. That Contractor's original estimate of $1,000 for drinking water was an accurate estimate;

2. That the overrun of $1,293 in the cost of drinking water was proximately caused by errors and omissions in the Architects' plans and specifications;

3. That said errors and omissions in the Architects' plans and specifications were proximately caused by Architects' negligence; and

4. That the overrun of $1,293 was not due to other delays caused by change orders, inclement weather or strikes (of which there were several).

When we consider that Contractor concedes on appeal that it really did not take the time to plan check the plans and specifications prior to bid as it was required to do by the terms of the bid and as it represented to Owner by its bid that it had done, the jury would have been required to assume more than was justified by the facts if it was required to assume that Contractor's original estimate of $1,000 as the cost of drinking water was an accurate estimate. There was substantial evidence in the court below (defendants' witness Clarence Vernon Holder) that Contractor's

---

15. Bennett was testifying regarding the costs of additional footings made necessary because allegedly the plans and specifications did not include specific elevations. The court asked Bennett what figures he was going to give from plaintiff's Exhibit 3. Bennett replied that they would include all of the costs on all footings during a particular month indicating that there "is no way absolutely no way" that he could break out cost data attributable to alleged errors in elevation. A colloquy then ensued during the course of which the following occurred:

THE COURT: All right. As I understand the evidence so far, Mr. Bennett included in each one of these anything that would have exceeded the initial budget.

MR. RUSHING: That's correct.
THE COURT: Isn't that right?
MR. RUSHING: Yes.
THE COURT: All right. Now, don't you have to

show that all of these exceptions were in some way related to the claimed errors and omissions and the requirements contained in IR 10? Doesn't that necessarily follow?

MR. RUSHING: Your Honor, all exceptions?
THE COURT: All extra costs.
MR. RUSHING: Okay.
THE COURT: Doesn't that necessarily follow?
MR. RUSHING: Yes, I mean, that is what we are attempting to do.
THE COURT: But you haven't done it.
MR. RUSHING: I'm painfully aware of it.
THE COURT: And I'm not sure you can. And this IR 10 is only one. It merely points it up, because if the extra costs of lowering the footings referred to in IR 10 are included in the total figures, which we know they are, then they most certainly must be broken out from the total figure.

initial bid on many items of labor or material or both was too low. We note in the margin some of the testimony.[16] When we also consider that eight of the 25 C.O.s were designed to reduce the overall costs of the project, apparently pursuant to the alternatives and changes which Owner negotiated with Contractor before executing the contract, it is manifest that not all delays were attributable to the Architects' alleged negligence. Furthermore some of the delays were caused by Contractor's own mistakes or incompetence.[17] The same fallacy applies to most of the other items of claimed damage as shown by Appendix A. Appendix A demonstrates that Contractor is still, at this late date, oblivious to the basic issue of causation.

We think there is also a fifth element of proof that the jury would have to assume in order to award $1,293 damages to Contractor because of the overrun on the cost of drinking water namely, that the Contractor's damage, if any, *was* not compensated for and *could* not be compensated for by the change order process. On each change estimate Contractor included direct costs of labor and material and a factor for administration and overhead (usually 10% although sometimes 15%) and a factor (usually 10%) for profit. We see no legal reason why Contractor could not include the cost of additional drinking water in effecting a specific change pursuant to a specific change order. Additional drinking water was either a direct cost or an indirect cost of the performances of each change order and in either event the estimated cost should have been included in the change order particularly where Contractor knew that it would be required to

sign an acknowledgement in the nature of an accord and satisfaction on each change order accepting the amount thereof in full satisfaction of the work. * * *

* * *

Contractor's entire attitude in the court below and in this court is that it is entitled to be compensated for all losses sustained over its original estimate. * * * Stated in its simplest form, Contractor's position is that since the plans and specifications contained errors and omissions and the Architects were negligent in supervising the work and there were delays in completing the project and Contractor sustained a loss, Contractor should be made whole by Architects. Contractor apparently does not even make an effort to segregate and give the Architects credit for moneys and time credits (90 days) recouped by Contractor in its settlement with Owner.

Contractor asserted in the court below and here that it was not required to segregate total cost overruns from moneys received from Owner under C.O.s (or by the settlement with Owner) because of the "collateral source" rule. The fallacy of course, is that Owner was not a *collateral* source—it was the primary debtor insofar as Contractor was concerned. After all, it was Owner's building. Owner was not in the position of an insurance company with secondary liability. Contractor apparently seeks a double recovery.

When we try to ascertain precisely what Architects did or failed to do which proximately caused damage to Contractor, Contractor's opening brief on appeal merely refers us to its counsel's closing argument to the jury

---

16.   *Q.* Last item, flat slabs, did you observe any flat slabs at the Convention Center?
   A. Yes, I did.
   Q. All right. I want to ask you to assume that there are 6,167 square feet of these slabs, and that the contractor originally estimated that his costs of doing this work would be fifty cents per square foot, and actual costs of doing the flat slab work was $1.30 per square foot. Can you tell me, first, whether or not you can form any opinion as to the fifty cent estimate?
   A. Yes, I can.
   Q. Can you tell us what the opinion is?
   A. My opinion, the unit is—doesn't properly represent the cost of the work involved.
   Q. All right. In other words, it's too low?
   A. Too low.
   Q. Can you form an opinion with regard to the $1.30 cost of actually doing the work?
   A. I think that is a reasonable unit.

17. For example, one problem which caused delay was the deviation in excess of ¼″ in the face of the risers to which the American Seating Company seats were to be bolted (discussed *infra*) which may well have been caused by the slippage of Contractor's forms for concrete. Another cause of delay was a "rock pocket" found after the forms were removed in concrete arch 56 and which required "repair". The "repair" consisted of demolition of the arch and construction of a new one. This delay was caused solely by Contractor. In various C.O.s, Contractor was granted several extensions due to delays caused by rain and inclement weather and several extensions due to delays caused by strikes. During all of these periods at least a portion of its overhead expenses must have continued. Contractor made no effort to explain or segregate.

in the court below which is appended as an exhibit to its opening brief on appeal. Although such argument does not cite any portions of either the clerk's or reporter's record and therefore does not comply with the rules on appeal [citations], we have nevertheless read the sixty-three page argument in an effort to ascertain precisely what Contractor claims. Apparently it complains of seven specific items of work:

1. The main truss design for the roof of the theatre was defectively designed and had to be firred out two inches, which allegedly delayed the project 75 days;

2. The foundation footings, which were to be "one foot six inches below finished grade or actual grade whichever is lower or as otherwise noted", were inadequately described because there was no specification of precise elevation (presumably above sea level), which allegedly resulted in three weeks delay;

3. The cooling tower footings (for the air conditioning system) were defectively designed and the requisite corrections allegedly delayed the fireproofing of the structural steel;

4. Material originally specified for the ice rink insulation was not available, which required use of a substitute material which was more difficult to use and resulted in alleged delay of two weeks; (In this connection Architects point out that Contractor finished the work in the ice rink one month ahead of Contractor's schedule.)

5. The plans did not adequately describe the location of the speaker grills (for the public address system) and the location of the diffuser lights, which required someone to make a decision on their location with reference to each other;

6. During the course of construction the Architects required the Contractor to produce an "absolutely smooth surface" on the concrete work whereas such requirement appeared only in the "repair" section of the original specifications, which resulted in increased labor costs.

7. The specifications were defective in relation to the concrete work in the arena because they did not specify the permissible deviation or variance on the face of the concrete risers to which the seats were to be bolted but merely specified that the seats to be installed on the risers would be supplied by American Seating Co. American Seating Co. allegedly required a deviation or variance on the face of the concrete risers of not more than ¼ inch. Contractor apparently assumed that a greater deviation or variance would be permitted. After the concrete was poured, Contractor allegedly discovered the American Seating Co. requirement and Contractor was required to begin "bush-hammering" the risers down to meet the required tolerance. The Contractor apparently worked too slowly, was removed from that portion of the project, and was replaced by a substitute contractor (Merritt Strunk). Contractor complains that Architects imposed less stringent tolerance requirements on the substitute contractor, who was permitted to relax the tolerance requirements. Architects reply that any relaxation of tolerance was because of necessity not because of any desire to favor the substitute contractor. There was a conflict in the evidence as to whether the excessive deviation or variance on the face of the concrete risers was due to the alleged fact that Contractor's forms slipped during the pouring of the concrete, rather than any uncertainty over the specification requirements.

We have searched this record (contrary to our obligation as an appellate court) and we have been unable to find any excluded evidence which would have shed any light or provided the jury with any additional information regarding any one of these seven specifications of Architects' neglect, particularly with reference to whether or not they resulted in any damage to Contractor and, if so, how much. We have found no excluded evidence which should have been admitted. Each of the seven specifications was fully litigated. The jury decided against the Contractor on each of the seven specifications. Many of the seven specifications involved actions by the Architects as agents of the Owner in the supervision of the work or as quasi-judicial officers acting as arbiters between Owner and Contractor and would not have been actionable in any event under principles enunciated in *Lundgren v. Freeman* (9th Cir. 1962) 307 F.2d 104 in the absence of pleading and proof of wilful misconduct or malice. Contractor's basic problem here and in the court below was not over any esoteric difference, if any, between a cause of action for Architects' simple negligence and a cause of action for Architects' negligent misrepresentations. Contractor's basic problem stems from a failure of evidence to establish causation—the proximate cause of its loss, if any.

We are not persuaded that any excluded evidence would have supplied the missing element of proof or that it would have produced a different result.

As noted Contractor concedes on this appeal that plaintiff's Exhibit 3 for identification was the *single* piece of evidence which established Contractor's damage. Since, as already noted, we conclude that exhibit 3 was properly excluded from evidence, it would appear from Contractor's own admission that there was no competent admissible evidence which established that Contractor sustained any damage proximately caused by Architects' negligence in preparing the plans and specifications. In our opinion, no miscarriage of justice occurred. Under these circumstances we may not reverse because of the exclusion of evidence. [Citation.] [Footnote.]

* * *

UNITED STATES v. GREENLEE

380 F. Supp. 652
(United States District Court, E. D. Pennsylvania, July 17, 1974.)

BECHTLE, D. J.

The above defendant was charged in a two-count indictment with the willful and knowing failure to file an income tax return, in violation of 26 U.S.C. § 7203. [Footnote.] The case was tried before a jury and on February 22, 1974, a guilty verdict on both counts of the indictment was returned. Presently before the Court is a motion of the defendant for judgment of acquittal or, in the alternative, a new trial. For reasons enumerated hereinafter, the motion will be denied.

Count I of the indictment charged that during the calendar year 1970 Greenlee received a gross income of $44,210.50; that by reason of the receipt of such income he was required

by law to file an income tax return on or before April 15, 1971; and that, well knowing the foregoing facts, the defendant willfully failed to file the tax return as required by law. In support of the allegation that Greenlee failed to file the 1970 tax return, the Government introduced evidence consisting primarily of the testimony of several witnesses employed at the Internal Revenue Service Center in Philadelphia. Essentially, Internal Revenue Service (IRS) employees explained the methods and procedures whereby a tax return is received, handled, recorded, and processed through the computer-based system in operation at the Service Center. The testimony of the above witnesses revealed that upon receipt at the Service Center the return is placed in a batch of 100 other similar returns, given a document locator number, and sent to a tax examiner. The examiner reviews each return in a particular batch and underlines with a pencil several items listed on the return. The complete batch of returns is then furnished to a keypunch operator who records on a magnetic tape the items designated by the examiner. The critical feature of the keypunch process is the recording on the magnetic tape of the taxpayer's Social Security Number, as shown on the gum label that the taxpayer affixes to the return at the time of filing. A second keypunch operator, referred to as a "verifier," repeats the performance of the first operator as a protection against the recordation of incorrect information on the magnetic tape. Once the necessary information from the return is placed on the computer tape, the tape is sent to Martinsburg, Virginia.[2] At the computer center in Martinsburg, the Social Security Number on the tape is checked against the number provided by the Social Security Administration. If a conflict in numbers appears, the tape is returned to the Service Center for correction; otherwise, it is stored in the computers at Martinsburg.

The actual return remains at the Service Center. Upon completion of the above-described keypunch operation, the batch of 100 returns is reassembled. According to the testimony of the IRS employees, every return

---

2. The Internal Revenue Service (IRS) operates a national computer center at this location. The function of the Center is to record and store tax return information

received from the Service Centers throughout the country.

originally contained in the batch must be accounted for in order that the batch be considered complete. Augustus Stewart, Assistant Director of the Philadelphia Service Center, testified that of the approximately 25 million returns handled each year at the Service Center he could not recall one return ever being irretrievably lost from its original batch. Six weeks after the batch is complete, the returns are transported to the Federal Records Center at Wissahickon and Abbottsford Avenues in Philadelphia, where they are kept as a permanent record for seven years and thereafter destroyed.

In addition to the testimony of the IRS employees, the prosecution introduced what was referred to at trial as the taxpayer's transcript of account (G-7) and the certificate of assessments and payments (G-6). The transcript of account, a computer printout, was produced from the information in the computer files of the taxpayer at Martinsburg. The certificate of assessments and payments was a document manually prepared at the Service Center and which reflected information stored on microfilm in Martinsburg. Both documents, which were admitted pursuant to the Federal Business Records Act, 28 U.S.C. § 1732, were introduced to prove that the IRS had no record of a Form 1040 tax return for James W. Greenlee for the tax year 1970.

In summary, the witnesses for the Government testified in detail as to each step in the processing of the return. The various controls and procedures both at the Philadelphia Service Center and at Martinsburg were explained in order to demonstrate the strong improbability that Greenlee's return had been lost or misplaced. Similarly, the systems of cross-checks and verifications in connection with the transmission of information from the tax return to the computer tapes were thoroughly and fully described for the avowed purpose of establishing the accuracy of the documentary evidence introduced at trial, specifically the certificate of assessments and payments and the transcript of accounts.

In addition to proving that the tax return was in fact not filed, the Government must show that the taxpayer *wilfully* failed to file the return on or before the required day. With regard to the issue of willfulness in this case, the prosecution introduced evidence which showed that Greenlee was aware of the filing requirement, had filed returns in previous years, and had no lawful reason for not filing in 1970.

The Government alleged in Count II of the indictment that the defendant received an income of $126,014 during the calendar year 1971; that by reason of such income Greenlee was required to file an income tax return on or before May 19, 1972 [footnote]; and that he willfully and knowingly failed to file the return by the required day.

To prove the contentions outlined in Count II of the indictment, the Government introduced in evidence the envelope in which Greenlee mailed his 1971 tax return. The envelope, postmarked December 28, 1972, was preserved by IRS employees because the return was not timely filed.

It is important to note at this juncture that Greenlee alleged that he mailed the return to the Service Center on December 24, 1972. The defendant claimed that his failure to file by May 19, 1972, was attributable to his constant harassment by local municipal authorities and his personal preoccupation with an investigation by a Federal Grand Jury in connection with his official position as legal counsel for the Philadelphia Redevelopment Authority.

Special Agent David Patella, of the IRS Intelligence Division, testified that an investigation of certain members of the Philadelphia Redevelopment Authority revealed that the IRS had no record of tax returns filed by James W. Greenlee for the calendar years 1970 and 1971. The agent stated that on December 26, 1972, he contacted Greenlee at his office in Philadelphia and requested that Greenlee come to the agent's office to discuss the matter of the 1970 and 1971 tax returns. At approximately 5:00 p. m., the defendant appeared at the agent's office and was advised that the IRS was investigating his apparent failure to file returns for the above-stated years. At this meeting, Greenlee asserted that he had filed the 1970 return on time and that he had filed the 1971 return "last week." On the next day, December 27, 1972, at approximately 5:00 p. m., Greenlee returned to the agent's office and presented Agent Patella with purported copies of the returns that the defendant contended were filed for the two years in question.

The Government offered the testimony of Edward DeLong, Superintendent of Collections, United States Postal Service, who stated that an envelope postmarked December 28 had to have been postmarked at sometime between 9:00 p. m. December 27 and 9:00 p. m. December 28, 1972. DeLong further testified that the earliest possible time that an envelope postmarked December 28 could have been collected by a postman was 5:00 p. m. December 27, 1972. The purpose of DeLong's testimony was to prove that Greenlee filed the 1971 return after his meeting with Special Agent Patella on December 26 and thereby impeach the defendant's testimony that he filed the 1971 return on December 24 and to generally discredit the defendant's entire testimony.

Greenlee testified on his own behalf and claimed that he had timely filed the 1970 tax return. As previously discussed, Greenlee also stated that he filed the 1972 return on December 24, 1972, which testimony appeared to be in conflict with the envelope introduced by the Government.

Ellen Greenlee, the defendant's wife, substantially corroborated the testimony of her husband as to the filing of the return. In addition, a computer expert and 14 character witnesses testified on behalf of the defendant.

DISCUSSION

* * *

2. Motion for Access to Buildings, Places and Documents

Three days before the scheduled trial date [footnote], the defendant filed a discovery motion requesting access to the Mid-Atlantic Service Center of the IRS located at 11601 Roosevelt Boulevard in Philadelphia. Defendant asserted that in order to prepare an adequate defense a qualified expert must have access to the computers, computer programs, and documents used in the collection, storage, and dissemination of information found in an income tax return. Access to the computers and computer-related material was purport-

edly necessary so that the defendant's expert could determine the reliability of the information retrieved from the computers. Prior to trial, the discovery motion was denied.

Greenlee's defense to the charges of failure to file consisted of his testimony that he had filed the tax return for the year 1970 on April 15, 1971, and the suggestion that either the tax return had been lost by the IRS during the processing of the return or the information transmitted from the return to the computer tapes was irretrievably lost in the computer system due to a mechanical malfunctioning or human error. With respect to the 1971 tax return due on or before May 19, 1972, Greenlee contended that he mailed the return on December 24, 1972, two days before his first meeting with Special Agent Patella.[5] Defendant now argues that the computer expert employed by him for trial purposes was unable to effectively testify as to the manner in which his return or the data contained thereon could have been lost by reason of mishandling or malfunction of the computers without seeing the total system in operation.

Rule 9 of the Local Rules of Criminal Procedure requires discovery motions to be filed within fifteen (15) days of the date of arraignment. As previously mentioned [citation], defendant's motion for access was not filed until February 8, 1974, approximately eleven months after arraignment. While the trial court may exercise a reasonable amount of discretion in connection with the filing of pretrial motions beyond the time period provided in the Local Rules of Criminal Procedure, the sound administration of justice and the need for a workable adherence to the discovery rules mandated the denial of defendant's motion. Defendant had almost a full year to prepare to meet the charges set forth in the indictment and to raise any discovery issue deemed appropriate. It was not until three days before the scheduled starting date of this trial that defendant requested an Order granting access to the IRS computers and computer-related materials. Had the Court granted the motion, this case would have had to be continued again for a considerable length of time. The motion

---

5. The Government concedes that Greenlee did file a tax return in December of 1972 for the calendar year 1971. The position of the Government is that the violation of § 7203 consisted of the willful failure to file on or before May 19, 1972, and that the late filing of the return does not negate the operation of the statute.

requested access for a period of time not to exceed three weeks. Analysis of information, the preparation of reports by the defendant's expert, and further argument would have consumed even more time. The Court could not reasonably countenance another delay in the start of the instant case, especially in view of the fact that the motion to inspect pertained only to Count I of the indictment.

Rule 16(b) of the Federal Rules of Criminal Procedure provides that the trial court may order the type of discovery sought in this case "upon a showing of materiality to the preparation of his defense and that the request is reasonable." The sole purpose of such a complex, time-consuming, and burdensome discovery undertaking was to ascertain the relative possibility of the IRS system malfunctioning to such an extent that the proper filing of a return would not be reflected on the computer printouts of the taxpayer's account.

Greenlee was unable before and during trial to make the necessary showing of materiality in order to support the discovery motion. Other than a purported copy of the 1970 return which Greenlee gave to Special Agent Patella, the Court was presented with no documentary or tangible evidence that a return had been filed and possibly lost by the IRS. The Court properly and logically construed the materiality provision of Rule 16(b) to require the defendant to come forward and show, at least *prima facie*, that the 1970 return had been timely filed. [Citation.] The mere allegation that a return was filed does not satisfy the materiality requirement of Criminal Rule 16(b). [Citation.]

Moreover, defendant's request was patently unreasonable. Access to and inspection of the computers and computer programs for a period of two or three weeks would unavoidably result in serious interruption of the operations of the IRS. The inherent unreasonableness of the request is further demonstrated by a consideration of such factors as security, the potential for serious interference with the operation of the Service Center and the overall unmanageability of an inspection of computers and documents by persons thoroughly unfamiliar with the system.

* * *

UNITED STATES v. LIEBERT

519 F.2d 542

(United States Court of Appeals, Third Circuit, June 30, 1975.)

ROSENN, C. J.

Despite more than a decade of experience with expanded pretrial discovery in criminal cases, the extent to which it should be permitted continues to be "a complex and controversial issue." [Footnote.] Whether pretrial discovery may be used to secure extrinsic evidence to impeach the reliability of computer printouts which are the fundament of the prosecution's case presents an issue of first impression.

Defendant, Peter P. Liebert, III, was charged in a three-count information on December 21, 1973, with willfully and knowingly having failed to file his income tax returns for the years 1967 through 1969, in violation of section 7203 of the Internal Revenue Code of 1954 (Code). Liebert was arraigned and pleaded not guilty to the charges. His attorneys have claimed he filed a tax return for each of the three years in question.

I. DISCOVERY MOTIONS

In a failure-to-file prosecution, the Government relies heavily upon a report compiled by the personnel of the appropriate service center that their computers have no record of the receipt of a taxpayer's return for the particular year. In preparation for challenging the reliability and accuracy of the computer report, Liebert filed on January 14, 1974, a motion seeking an order permitting his computer expert access to the Mid-Atlantic Service Center for the purpose of analyzing and testing the Internal Revenue Service's (IRS) data processing systems. After extended proceedings, the district court granted the motion.

On February 28, 1974, Liebert filed a second discovery motion seeking production of all records indicating the number of notices issued by the IRS for the years 1967 through 1973 to taxpayers advising that no tax return had been received. [Footnote.] On October 22, 1974, again after extended proceedings, the district court ordered the Government to furnish Liebert a "mutually agreeable portion of the lists" of the people whom the Government suspected as being probable nonfilers for the years 1970 and 1971.[3] [Citation.]

When the Government refused to produce the lists, the district court on November 26, 1974, dismissed the charges against Liebert. The Government appeals, arguing that the lists are not subject to disclosure under the Code. The Government also contends that even if the lists are not privileged under the Code, the information Liebert desires through the use of the lists may be obtained from alternative sources without invading the privacy of the persons listed. [Footnote.] We find merit in the Government's latter contention, vacate the judgment of the district court, and remand.

An understanding of the nature of the lists in dispute is essential for the proper resolution of the problem confronting us. [Footnote.] The lists are prepared in conjunction with the IRS Individual Master File Delinquency Check Program, which identifies individuals who filed in the previous year but apparently have not filed for the current year, and individuals who have not filed for either the current or the previous years.

About six months after the due date of the return in question, an inquiry is initiated by analyzing the individual master file for taxpayers who have filed in the prior year but apparently not for the current year. Also, certain other documents, such as Social Security Administration wage records and W-2 forms, are compared with the master file to identify possible nonfilers. After the potentially delinquent taxpayers have been identified, wage information for the current year, adjusted gross income from the last return filed, and other criteria are used to determine whether the taxpayer probably was required to file.

Within the limitations of available resources, certain of these apparent nonfilers are selected for contact.[6] As soon as the first notices are sent to the apparently delinquent taxpayers, the service center prepares a listing identifying each nonfiling taxpayer. These listings are the lists in issue in this case. If the taxpayer does not respond satisfactorily to the notice, a taxpayer delinquency investigation is issued and forwarded to the local IRS office where an attempt is made to communicate with the taxpayer either by phone, letter, or in person to resolve the apparent delinquency.

Thus, although the lists are commonly referred to as the lists of nonfilers, that appellation is misleading in two aspects. First, the lists contain names of persons who, in fact, have filed. For example, the return may have been in process at the time the lists were prepared, the taxpayer may have moved and filed in a different service center, or the taxpayer may have married and filed jointly under a different name. Second, the lists contain names of persons who did not file, but were under no duty to do so. Such people may have not earned enough adjusted gross income to be required to file, or indeed may have died during the year.

* * *

III.   RULE 16(b)

Absent any statutory prohibition against the production of nonfiling lists, the authority of the district court to order the production of such lists is governed by Federal Rule of Criminal Procedure 16(b) which provides that "the court may order the attorney for the government to permit the defendant to inspect and copy * * * documents * * * within the possession * * * of the government, upon a showing of materiality to the preparation of his defense and that the request is reasonable." [Footnote.] The use of the permissive term "may" calls for an exercise of discretion and indicates the absence of a hard and fast rule when discovery should be ordered. [Citation.] Thus, a district court's ruling on a discovery motion will be disturbed only for an abuse of discretion. [Citation.]

The nonfiling lists undoubtedly are material to the preparation of Liebert's defense. A

---

3. The lists were not available for 1967 through 1969, the years for which Liebert had been charged with failure to file tax returns. The district court ordered the production of the 1970 and 1971 lists after determining that the system producing these lists had been upgraded since the preparation of the 1967 through 1969 lists. The court

reasoned that if errors existed in the later lists, they in all probability would demonstrate the presence of an equal or greater number of errors in the earlier lists. The Government has not challenged this conclusion on appeal.

6. In 1970, out of 6,000,000 potential nonfilers, 465,000 were selected for contact.

defendant in a criminal trial enjoys the sixth amendment right of being confronted with the witnesses testifying against him and of having compulsory process for obtaining witnesses to testify in his favor. As the Supreme Court only recently noted in rejecting a presidential claim of privilege:

> The ends of criminal justice would be defeated if judgments were to be founded on a partial or speculative presentation of the facts. The very integrity of the judicial system and public confidence in the system depend on full disclosure of all the facts, within the framework of the rules of evidence. To ensure that justice is done, it is imperative to the function of courts that compulsory process be available for the production of evidence needed either by the prosecution or by the defense.

United States v. Nixon, 418 U.S. 683, 709, 94 S.Ct. 3090, 3108, 41 L.Ed.2d 1039 (1974).

Included within the constitutional right of confrontation is the ability through cross-examination to challenge the credibility and reliability of the witnesses testifying against a defendant. [Citations.] A major "witness" confronting Liebert will be computer printouts indicating that the IRS has no record of having received his returns. [Citation.] The introduction of a computer printout is admissible in a criminal trial provided that the party offering the computer information lays a foundation sufficient to warrant a finding that such information is trustworthy and the opposing party is given the same opportunity to inquire into the accuracy of the computer and its input procedures as he has to inquire into the accuracy of written business records. [Citation.]

A party seeking to impeach the reliability of computer evidence should have sufficient opportunity to ascertain by pretrial discovery whether both the machine and those who supply it with data input and information have performed their tasks accurately. [Citations.] The nonfiling lists plainly are outputs of the computer system identifying individuals not filing returns. If an individual who in fact has filed is listed as a nonfiler due to computer error, such error casts doubt on the accuracy and reliability of the records identifying Liebert as a nonfiler. The lists, therefore, may be useful to Liebert in his efforts to impeach the reliability of the computer procedures indicating that he has not filed his returns.

Rule 16(b), however, does not allow discovery merely upon a showing that the requested documents are material to the defendant's preparation for trial; the reasonableness of the discovery request must also be demonstrated. The determination by the district court of the reasonableness of a request requires balancing the interests favoring and opposing discovery. Whether the scales are tipped for or against discovery depends upon where lies the most compelling need. [Citation.]

The interest favoring the discovery request in the instant case is, as just discussed, the usefulness of the nonfiling lists to the preparation of Liebert's defense. Opposing the request are weighty interests—the right of privacy of the individuals named on the lists, and the need to avoid the problems in managing the presentation of evidence developed from the lists.

As aptly described by Mr. Justice Brandeis almost a half century ago, and equally true today, "the right to be let alone [is] the most comprehensive of rights and the right most valued by civilized men." *Olmstead v. United States,* 277 U.S. 438, 478, 48 S.Ct. 564, 572, 72 L.Ed. 944 (1928) (Brandeis, J., dissenting). The district court characterized this right as "elusive," primarily because it believed the information in the lists could be obtained under section 6103(f) by addressing to the IRS numerous inquiries as to whether particular individuals had filed their returns. [Citation.] This characterization, however, disregards the existence of three different facets of individual privacy which may be violated by production of the nonfiling lists, only one of which is infringed to the same degree by subsection (f).

First, the failure of an individual to file a return is revealed by production of the lists. Although an individual may desire to keep such information confidential, the fact of nonfiling is public information under subsection (f).

Second, the production of such lists necessarily would lead to communications from Liebert. His specific purpose in seeking the list is to communicate with individuals named in the lists in a zealous effort to find inaccuracies. This he proposed to do in the face of "[t]he ancient concept that 'a man's home is his castle' into which 'not even the king may enter' has lost none of its vitality. * * *" [Citation.] While courts in some instances have ordered production of lists which might lead to contacts between the parties obtaining, and those named, in the lists, such production has been limited to instances where it advanced an important public interest and where the person contacted probably would not be offended. [Footnote.] Where the contact is likely to prove offensive, the courts vigilantly have safeguarded the privacy of the individual. [Footnote.]

An intrusive communication by a stranger about a failure to file a tax return well may prove disturbing to an individual. Moreover, such contact could prove disturbing apart from tax considerations by reviving dormant unpleasant memories.[16] [Citation.]

Of course, inquiries may be made of individuals about their nonfiling as a result of subsection (f), but the probability of such inquiry is significantly less than through the production of the nonfiling lists. Only 450,000 of the estimated 6,000,000 probable nonfilers are contained in the nonfiling lists, thereby increasing the exposure to contact of the individuals named by a factor of twelve. Moreover, as Liebert recognizes, the identification of all nonfilers under subsection (f) is impractical, requiring culling of names from a phone book or street directory, transmitting the list to the appropriate internal revenue office, and tabulating the answers.[17] As contrasted with this impractical procedure, the easy availability of the names in the nonfiling lists increases the likelihood of contact with such persons.

Third, and most important, the individuals on the nonfiling lists are not just individuals who the IRS believes have not filed, but are individuals who the IRS believes have not filed in violation of their legal obligation. Nothing in subsection (f) authorizes the release of information indicating that the IRS preliminarily suspects an individual of being in violation of the law. Although the great majority of persons on the lists in fact have filed a

return or have legitimate reasons for not doing so, being a suspect under investigation by a government agency is a circumstance which every person except the bizarre would prefer to hold in confidence. The courts have respected this preference. [Citation.]

The other interest opposing discovery is the difficulty in managing at trial the information developed from the lists. Liebert hopes to be able to find persons listed as nonfilers but who in fact have filed, and introduce such evidence to the jury either by calling such persons as witnesses or by cross-examination of the IRS computer-experts. The Government then may assume the burden of rebutting the accuracy of such evidence by attempting to prove that the persons cited by Liebert did not in fact file their returns or were listed as nonfilers for reasons other than computer error. The trial thus is likely to deteriorate into a series of minitrials centered upon the reasons individuals, not defendants in the case, were listed as nonfilers. The chief issue, Liebert's alleged willful failure to file his returns, may be obscured.

Balancing the need for disclosing all relevant information in a criminal proceeding against the need for protecting the privacy of individuals having no connection with it, and the further need for avoiding the potential misuse of such information is a difficult and delicate task. It may well be, as Liebert contends, that absent alternative sources of information and difficulty in managing such information at trial, "[t]he generalized assertion of privilege [based on confidentiality] must yield to the demonstrated, specific need for evidence in a pending criminal trial." [Citations.] * * *

Even when the evidence sought in pretrial discovery is material for the defense of a criminal prosecution, we believe the mantle of the privacy of a person having no connection with the case should not be lifted, at least in the present context, if there are reasonable alternative means of securing the information. [Footnote.] The principle has particular application when the intrusion on privacy runs a risk of being extraordinarily burdensome to

---

16. For example, Liebert might contact a relative of a person whose name appeared on the list as a probable nonfiler because of the death of that individual.

17. It is uncertain whether Liebert would have to mail each name in a separate envelope or could transmit the entire list at once.

the parties and also may tend to obscure the real issue in the case.

The Government, both voluntarily and as a result of the district court's order directing that Liebert's experts have access to the Mid-Atlantic Service Center for the purpose of testing and analyzing the computer facilities, represented to the district court that it would make available to Liebert: (a) all the relevant IRS handbooks documenting the procedures, machine operations, and other relevant information pertaining to its electronic data processing system; (b) statistical analyses relating to the Service's ability to discover and report accurately failures to file returns; (c) an expert familiar with all aspects of the non-filing lists; (d) an expert familiar with all aspects of the processing of work through the Mid-Atlantic Service Center; and (e) an expert who has made studies on the reliability of the Service's data processing systems.[19] The experts may be deposed by Liebert on any subject not concerning confidential data obtained from tax returns filed by taxpayers. Moreover, the Government has offered to allow Liebert's computer experts to run any test on its computer system not unreasonably interrupting the Service Center operations. Finally, the Government has offered to conduct tests demonstrating the retrieval of a number of actual tax returns of taxpayers whose authorizations are obtained.

Such alternatives should provide Liebert with the information necessary to cross-examine the computer testimony confronting him by analyzing the reliability of the computer system in theory and checking the accuracy of the system in fact. Moreover, the alternatives should provide information focusing directly on the credibility of the computer testimony and more likely should develop the facts than the digression sought by Liebert. They should provide evidence adducible at trial in a more manageable manner without the risk of invading the privacy of, or inconveniencing, taxpayers wholly unconnected with the case. The order of the district court directing the production of the nonfiling lists was unreasonable in light of the alternatives offered by the Government.

The judgment of the district court will be vacated and the case remanded with directions to reinstate the information. Upon proper motion by the defendant, the district court should order the Government to produce the materials and experts indicated in this opinion. * * *

OPPENHEIMER FUND, INC. v. SANDERS

437 U.S. 340

(United States Supreme Court, Certiorari to the United States Court of Appeals for the Second Circuit, June 19, 1978.)

POWELL, J.

Respondents are the representative plaintiffs in a class action brought under Fed. Rule Civ. Proc. 23(b)(3). They sought to require petitioners, the defendants below, to help compile a list of the names and addresses of the members of the plaintiff class from records kept by the transfer agent for one of petitioners so that the individual notice required by Rule 23(c)(2) could be sent. The Court of Appeals for the Second Circuit held that the federal discovery rules, Fed. Rules Civ. Proc. 26-37, authorize the District Court to order petitioners to assist in compiling the list and to bear the $16,000 expense incident thereto. We hold that Rule 23(d), which concerns the conduct of class actions, not the discovery rules, empowers the District Court to direct petitioners to help compile such a list. We further hold that, although the District Court has some discretion in allocating the cost of complying with such an order, that discretion was abused in this case. We therefore reverse and remand.

I

Petitioner Oppenheimer Fund, Inc. (Fund), is an open-end diversified investment fund registered under the Investment Company Act of 1940, 15 U.S.C. § 80a-1 *et seq.* (1976 ed.). The Fund and its agents sell shares to the public at their net asset value plus a sales charge. Petitioner Oppenheimer Management Corp. (Management Corp.) manages the Fund's in-

---

19. We assume that the information supplied by the Government will include the number of persons listed as non-

filers due to computer error in 1970 and 1971.

vestment portfolio. Pursuant to an investment advisory agreement, the Fund pays Management Corp. a fee which is computed in part as a percentage of the Fund's net asset value. Petitioner Oppenheimer & Co. is a brokerage firm that owns 82% of the stock of Management Corp., including all of its voting stock. The individual petitioners are directors or officers of the Fund or Management Corp., or partners in Oppenheimer & Co.

Respondents bought shares in the Fund at various times in 1968 and 1969. On March 26, May 12, and June 18, 1969, they filed three separate complaints, later consolidated, which alleged that the petitioners, other than the Fund, had violated federal securities laws in 1968 and 1969 by issuing or causing to be issued misleading prospectuses and annual reports about the Fund. [Footnote.] In particular, respondents alleged that the prospectuses and reports failed to disclose the fact that the Fund invested in "restricted" securities [footnote], the risks involved in such investments, and the method used to value the restricted securities on the Fund's books. They also alleged that the restricted securities had been overvalued on the Fund's books, causing the Fund's net asset value, and thus the price of shares in the Fund, to be inflated artificially. On behalf of themselves and a class of purchasers, respondents sought to recover from petitioners, other than the Fund, the amount by which the price they paid for Fund shares exceeded the shares' value. [Footnote.]

In April 1973, respondents moved pursuant to Fed. Rule Civ. Proc. 23(b)(3) for an order allowing them to represent a class of plaintiffs consisting of all persons who bought shares in the Fund between March 28, 1968, and April 24, 1970. [Footnote.] Relying on *Eisen v. Carlisle & Jacquelin,* 54 F. R. D. 565 (SDNY 1972), respondents also sought an order directing petitioners to pay for the notice to absent class members required by Fed. Rule Civ. Proc. 23(c)(2). On May 1, 1973, however, the Court of Appeals for the Second Circuit held that the District Court in *Eisen* erred in ordering the defendants to pay 90% of the cost of notifying members of a Rule 23(b)(3) plaintiff class. *Eisen v. Carlisle & Jacquelin (Eisen III),* 479 F.2d 1005. Respondents thereupon deposed employees of the Fund's transfer agent, which kept records from which the class members' names and addresses could be derived, in order to develop information relevant to issues of manageability, identification, and methods of notice upon which the District Court would have to pass. These employees' statements, together with information supplied by the Fund, established that the class proposed by respondents numbered about 121,000 persons. About 103,000 still held shares in the Fund, while some 18,000 had sold their shares after the end of the class period. Since about 171,000 persons currently held shares in the Fund, it appeared that approximately 68,000 current Fund shareholders were not members of the class.

The transfer agent's employees also testified that in order to compile a list of the class members' names and addresses, they would have to sort manually through a considerable volume of paper records, keypunch between 150,000 and 300,000 computer cards, and create eight new computer programs for use with records kept on computer tapes that either are in existence or would have to be created from the paper records. [Reference.] The cost of these operations was estimated in 1973 to exceed $16,000.

Having learned all this, and in the face of *Eisen III,* respondents moved to redefine the class to include only those persons who had bought Fund shares between March 28, 1968, and April 24, 1970, *and* who still held shares in the Fund. Respondents also proposed that the class notice be inserted in one of the Fund's periodic mailings to its current shareholders, and they offered to pay the cost of printing and inserting the notices, which was about $5,000. [Reference.] These proposals would have made it unnecessary to compile a separate list of the members of the redefined class in order to notify them. Petitioners opposed redefinition of the class on the ground that it arbitrarily would exclude about 18,000 former Fund shareholders who had bought shares during the relevant period, possibly to their prejudice. They also opposed including the class notice in a Fund mailing which would reach the 68,000 current shareholders who were not class members. This, petitioners feared, could set off a wave of selling to the detriment of the Fund. [Footnote.]

On May 15, 1975, more than six years after the litigation began, the District Court ruled on the motions then pending. *Sanders v. Levy,* 20 Fed. Rules Serv. 2d 1218 (SDNY 1975). The court first held that the suit met the requirements for class-action treatment under Rule 23(b)(3). [Citation.] It then rejected respondents' proposed redefinition of the class because it "would involve an arbitrary reduction in the class." [Citation.] [Footnote.] At the same time, however, the court held that "the cost of culling out the list of class members * * * is the responsibility of defendants." [Citation.] The only explanation given was that "the expense is relatively modest and it is defendants who are seeking to have the class defined in a manner which appears to require the additional expense." [Citation.] Finally, the court rejected respondents' proposal that the class notice be included in a regular Fund mailing. Noting that the mailing would reach many current Fund shareholders who were not members of the class, the District Judge said that his "solution to this problem starts with my earlier ruling that it is the responsibility of defendants to cull out from their records a list of all class members and provide this list to plaintiffs. Plaintiffs will then have the responsibility to prepare the necessary notice and mail it at their expense." [Citation.][7]

On petitioners' appeal, a divided panel of the Court of Appeals reversed the District Court's order insofar as it required petitioners to bear the cost required for the transfer agent to compile a list of the class members' names and addresses. *Sanders v. Levy,* 558 F.2d 636 (CA2 1976). [Footnote.] The majority thought that *Eisen IV, Eisen v. Carlisle & Jacquelin,* 417 U.S. 156 (1974), which had affirmed *Eisen III* in pertinent part, required respondents to pay this cost because the identification of class members is an integral step in the process of notifying them. [Citation.] [Footnote.] On rehearing en banc, however, the Court of Appeals reversed the panel's decision and affirmed the District Court's order by a vote of seven to three. [Citation.] [Footnote.] It thought

that *Eisen IV* did not control this case because respondents might obtain the class members' names and addresses under the federal discovery rules, Fed. Rules Civ. Proc. 26-37. The en banc court further held that although Rule 26(c) protects parties from "undue burden or expense" in complying with discovery requests, the District Court did not abuse its discretion under that Rule in requiring petitioners to bear this expense. [Citation.]

By holding that the discovery rules apply to this case, the en banc court brought itself into conflict with the Court of Appeals for the Fifth Circuit, which recently had held:

> The time and expense of gathering [class members'] names and addresses is a necessary predicate to providing each with notice of the action's pendency without which the action may not proceed. [Citation.] Viewed in this context, it becomes strikingly clear that rather than being controlled by the federal civil discovery rules, identification of absentee class members' names and addresses is part and parcel of rule 23(c)(2)'s mandate that the class members receive "the best notice practicable under the circumstances, including individual notice to all members who can be identified through reasonable effort." *In re Nissan Motor Corp. Antitrust Litigation,* 552 F.2d 1088, 1102 (1977).

In the Fifth Circuit's view, Rule 23(d), which empowers district courts to enter appropriate orders in the handling of class actions, is the procedural device by which a district court may enlist the aid of a defendant in identifying class members to whom notice must be sent. The *Nissan* court found it unnecessary to decide whether *Eisen IV* requires a representative plaintiff always to bear the cost of identifying class members. Since the representative plaintiffs could perform the required search through the defendants' records as readily as the defendants themselves, and since the search had to be performed in order to advance the representative plaintiffs' case, they were required to perform it and thus to bear its cost. [Citation.]

---

7. The court subsequently modified this order to allow the notice to class members who still were Fund shareholders to be inserted in the envelopes of a periodic Fund mailing, "provided that the notices are sent only to class members and that plaintiffs pay in full the Fund's extra costs of mailing, including the costs of segregating the envelopes going to the class members from the envelopes going to other Fund shareholders." At the same time, the

court held that the Fund should bear the identification costs in the first instance, "without prejudice to the right of this defendant, at the conclusion of the action, to make whatever claim it would be legally entitled to make regarding reimbursement by another party." The court denied the Fund's request that respondents be required to post bond for the identification costs.

We granted certiorari in the instant case to resolve the conflict that thus has arisen and to consider the underlying cost-allocation problems. [Citation.]

II

The issues in this case arise because of the notice requirement of Fed. Rule Civ. Proc. 23(c)(2), which provides in part:

> In any class action maintained under subdivision (b)(3), the court shall direct to the members of the class the best notice practicable under the circumstances, including individual notice to all members who can be identified through reasonable effort.

In *Eisen IV,* the Court held that the plain language of this Rule "requires that individual notice be sent to all class members who can be identified with reasonable effort." [Citation.] The Court also found no authority for a district court to hold a preliminary hearing on the merits of a suit in order to decide which party should bear the cost required to prepare and mail the class notice. [Citation.] Instead, it held:

> In the absence of any support under Rule 23, [the representative plaintiff's] effort to impose the cost of notice on [defendants] must fail. The usual rule is that a plaintiff must initially bear the cost of notice to the class. * * * Where, as here, the relationship between the parties is truly adversary, the plaintiff must pay for the cost of notice as part of the ordinary burden of financing his own suit. [Citation.]

*   *   *

The parties in the instant case center much of their argument on the questions whether the discovery rules authorize a district court to order a defendant to help identify the members of a plaintiff class so that individual notice can be sent and, if so, which rule applies in this case. For the reasons stated in Part A below, we hold that Rule 23(d), not the discovery rules, is the appropriate source of authority for such an order. This conclusion, however, is not dispositive of the cost-allocation question. As we explain in Part B, we think that where a defendant can perform one of the tasks necessary to send notice, such as identification, more efficiently than the representative plaintiff, the district court has discretion to order him to perform the task

under Rule 23(d). In such cases, the district court also has some discretion in allocating the cost of complying with its order. In Part C, however, we conclude that the District Court abused its discretion in this case.

A

Although respondents' request resembles discovery in that it seeks to obtain information, we are convinced that it more properly is handled under Rule 23(d). The critical point is that the information is sought to facilitate the sending of notice rather than to define or clarify issues in the case.

The general scope of discovery is defined by Fed. Rule Civ. Proc. 26(b)(1) as follows:

> Parties may obtain discovery regarding any matter, not privileged, which is relevant to the subject matter involved in the pending action, whether it relates to the claim or defense of the party seeking discovery or to the claim or defense of any other party, including the existence, description, nature, custody, condition and location of any books, documents, or other tangible things and the identity and location of persons having knowledge of any discoverable matter. It is not ground for objection that the information sought will be inadmissible at the trial if the information sought appears reasonably calculated to lead to the discovery of admissible evidence.

The key phrase in this definition—"relevant to the subject matter involved in the pending action"—has been construed broadly to encompass any matter that bears on, or that reasonably could lead to other matter that could bear on, any issue that is or may be in the case. [Citation.] [Footnote.] Consistently with the notice-pleading system established by the Rules, discovery is not limited to issues raised by the pleadings, for discovery itself is designed to help define and clarify the issues. [Citation.] Nor is discovery limited to the merits of a case, for a variety of fact-oriented issues may arise during litigation that are not related to the merits. [Footnote.]

At the same time, "discovery, like all matters of procedure, has ultimate and necessary boundaries." [Citation.] Discovery of matter not "reasonably calculated to lead to the discovery of admissible evidence" is not within the scope of Rule 26(b)(1). Thus, it is proper to deny discovery of matter that is relevant only to claims or defenses that have been stricken [footnote], or to events that occurred before an applicable limitations period, unless the information sought is otherwise relevant to issues in the case. [Footnote.] For the same reason, an amendment to Rule 26(b) was required to bring within the scope of discovery the existence and contents of insurance agreements under which an insurer may be liable to satisfy a judgment against a defendant, for that information ordinarily cannot be considered, and would not lead to information that could be considered, by a court or jury in deciding any issues. [Footnote.]

Respondents' attempt to obtain the class members' names and addresses cannot be forced into the concept of "relevancy" described above. The difficulty is that respondents do not seek this information for any bearing that it might have on issues in the case. [Citation.] [Footnote.] If respondents had sought the information because of its relevance to the issues, they would not have been willing, as they were, to abandon their request if the District Court would accept their proposed redefinition of the class and method of sending notice. Respondents argued to the District Court that they desired this information to enable them to send the class notice, and not for any other purpose. Taking them at their word, it would appear that respondents' request is not within the scope of Rule 26(b)(1). [Footnote.]

The en banc majority avoided holding that the class members' names and addresses are "relevant to the subject matter involved in the pending action" within the meaning of Rule 26(b)(1) simply because respondents need this information in order to send the class notice. Tacitly acknowledging that discovery must be aimed at illuminating issues in the case, the

court instead hypothesized that there is "a potential issue in all [Rule 23(b)(3) class-action] litigation whether the required notice has properly been sent. A list of the names and addresses of the class members would of course be essential to the resolution of that issue." [Citation.] But aside from the fact that respondents themselves never pretended to be anticipating this "potential issue," it is apparent that the "potential issue" cannot arise until respondents already have obtained the very information they seek.[19] Nor do we perceive any other "potential issues" that could bring respondents' request within the scope of legitimate discovery. In short, we do not think that the discovery rules are the right tool for this job.[20]

Rule 23, on the other hand, deals comprehensively with class actions, and thus is the natural place to look for authority for orders regulating the sending of notice. It is clear that Rule 23(d) vests power in the district court to order one of the parties to perform the tasks necessary to send notice. [Footnote.] Moreover, district courts sometimes have found it appropriate to order a defendant, rather than a representative plaintiff, to perform tasks other than identification that are necessary to the sending of notice.[22] Since identification simply is another task that must be performed in order to send notice, we agree with the Court of Appeals for the Fifth Circuit that Rule 23(d) also authorizes a district court in appropriate circumstances to require a defendant's cooperation in identifying the class members to whom notice must be sent. [Footnote.] We therefore turn to a consideration of the circumstances in which such an order is appropriate and of how the cost of the defendant's complying with such an order should be allocated.

19. Until respondents obtain the information and send the class notice, no issue can arise as to whether it was sent "properly."

20. We do not hold that class members' names and addresses never can be obtained under the discovery rules. There may be instances where this information could be relevant to issues that arise under Rule 23 [citation], or where a party has reason to believe that communication with some members of the class could yield information bearing on these or other issues. Respondents make no such claims of relevance, however, and none is apparent here. Moreover, it may be doubted whether any of these

purposes would require compilation of the names and addresses of *all* members of a large class. [Citation.] There is a distinction in principle between requests for identification of class members that are made to enable a party to send notice, and requests that are made for true discovery purposes. [Citation.]

22. Thus, a number of courts have required defendants in Rule 23(b)(3) class actions to enclose class notices in their own periodic mailings to class members in order to reduce the expense of sending the notice, as respondents asked the District Court in this case to do. [Citations.]

B

Although the Fifth Circuit held that Rule 23(d), not the discovery rules, authorizes a district court to order a defendant to provide information needed to identify class members to whom notice must be sent, it also suggested that principles embodied in the discovery rules for allocating the performance of tasks and payment of costs might be relevant to a district court's exercise of discretion under Rule 23(d). [Citation.] Petitioners and the en banc dissent, on the other hand, argue that *Eisen IV* always requires a representative plaintiff to pay all costs incident to sending notice, whether he or the defendant performs the required tasks. *Eisen IV* does not compel this latter conclusion, for it did not involve a situation where a defendant properly was ordered under Rule 23(d) to perform any of the tasks necessary to sending the notice.

The first question that a district court must consider under Rule 23(d) is which party should perform particular tasks necessary to send the class notice. The general rule must be that the representative plaintiff should perform the tasks, for it is he who seeks to maintain the suit as a class action and to represent other members of his class. In *Eisen IV* we noted the general principle that a party must bear the "burden of financing his own suit." [Citation.] Thus ordinarily there is no warrant for shifting the cost of the representative plaintiff's performance of these tasks to the defendant.

In some instances, however, the defendant may be able to perform a necessary task with less difficulty or expense than could the representative plaintiff. In such cases, we think that the district court properly may exercise its discretion under Rule 23(d) to order the defendant to perform the task in question. As the *Nissan* court recognized, in identifying the instances in which such an order may be appropriate, a rough analogy might usefully be drawn to practice under Rule 33(c) of the discovery rules.[24] Under that Rule, when one party directs an interrogatory to another party which can be answered by examination of the responding party's business records, "it is a sufficient answer to such interrogatory to specify the records from which the answer may be derived or ascertained and to afford to the party serving the interrogatory reasonable opportunity to" examine and copy the records, if the burden of deriving the answer would be "substantially the same" for either party. Not unlike *Eisen IV*, this provision is intended to place the "burden of discovery upon its potential benefitee." [Footnote.] The holding of *Nissan* represents application of a similar principle, for when the court concluded that the representative plaintiffs could derive the names and addresses of the class members from the defendants' records with substantially the same effort as the defendants, it required the representative plaintiffs to perform this task and hence to bear the cost. [Citation.] But where the burden of deriving the answer would not be "substantially the same," and the task could be performed more efficiently by the responding party, the discovery rules normally require the responding party to derive the answer itself. [Footnote.]

In those cases where a district court properly decides under Rule 23(d) that a defendant rather than the representative plaintiff should perform a task necessary to send the class notice, the question that then will arise is which party should bear the expense. On one hand, it may be argued that this should be borne by the defendant because a party ordinarily must bear the expense of complying with orders properly issued by the district court; but *Eisen IV* strongly suggests that the representative plaintiff should bear this expense because it is he who seeks to maintain the suit as a class action. In this situation, the district court must exercise its discretion in deciding whether to leave the cost of complying with its order where it falls, on the defendant, or place it on the party that benefits, the representative plaintiff. Once again, a rough analogy might usefully be drawn to practice under the discovery rules. Under those rules, the presumption is that the responding party must bear the expense of complying with discovery requests, but he may invoke the district court's discre-

---

24. The analogy to the discovery rules is not perfect, for those rules contemplate that discovery will proceed without judicial intervention unless a party moves for a protective order under Rule 26(c) or an order compelling discovery under Rule 37(a). Rule 23, on the other hand, contemplates that the district court routinely must approve the form of the class notice and order how it should be sent and who should perform the necessary tasks.

tion under Rule 26(c) to grant orders protecting him from "undue burden or expense" in doing so, including orders conditioning discovery on the requesting party's payment of the costs of discovery. The analogy necessarily is imperfect, however, because in the Rule 23(d) context, the defendant's own case rarely will be advanced by his having performed the tasks. [Citation.] Thus, one of the reasons for declining to shift costs under Rule 26(c) usually will be absent in the Rule 23(d) context. [Footnote.] For this reason, a district court exercising its discretion under Rule 23(d) should be considerably more ready to place the cost of the defendant's performing an ordered task on the representative plaintiff, who derives the benefit, than under Rule 26(c). In the usual case, the test should be whether the expense is substantial, rather than, as under Rule 26(c), whether it is "undue."

Nevertheless, in some instances, the expense involved may be so insubstantial as not to warrant the effort required to calculate it and shift it to the representative plaintiff. In *Nissan,* for example, the court did not find it necessary to direct the representative plaintiffs to reimburse the defendants for the expense of producing their files for inspection. In other cases, it may be appropriate to leave the cost where it falls because the task ordered is one that the defendant must perform in any event in the ordinary course of its business.[28] Although we do not attempt to catalogue the instances in which a district court might be justified in placing the expense on the defendant, we caution that courts must not stray too far from the principle underlying *Eisen IV* that the representative plaintiff should bear all costs relating to the sending of notice because it is he who seeks to maintain the suit as a class action.

C

In this case, we think the District Court abused its discretion in requiring petitioners to bear the expense of identifying class members. The records containing the needed information are kept by the transfer agent, not petitioners. Since petitioners apparently have the right to control these records, and since the class

members can be identified only by reference to them, the District Court acted within its authority under Rule 23(d) in ordering petitioners to direct the transfer agent to make the records available to respondents. The preparation of the desired list requires, as indicated above, the manual sorting out of names and addresses from old records maintained on paper, the keypunching of up to 300,000 computer cards, and the creation of new computer programs for use with extant tapes and tapes that would have to be created from the paper records. It appears that neither petitioners nor respondents can perform these tasks, for both sides assume that the list can be generated only by hiring the services of a third party, the transfer agent, for a sum exceeding $16,000. As the expense of hiring the transfer agent would be no greater for respondents, who seek the information, than for petitioners, respondents should bear the expense. [Citation.] [Footnote.]

The District Court offered two reasons why petitioners should pay the transfer agent, but neither is persuasive. First, the court thought that petitioners should bear this cost because it was their opposition to respondents' proposed redefinition of the class and method of sending notice that made it necessary to incur the cost. * * * But it is neither fair nor good policy to penalize a defendant for prevailing on an argument against a representative plaintiff's proposals. If a defendant's argument has merit, it should be accepted regardless of his willingness to bear the extra expense that its acceptance would require. Otherwise, a defendant may be discouraged from advancing arguments entirely appropriate to the protection of his rights or the rights of absent class members.

* * * For these reasons, we hold that the District Court erred in linking the questions of class definition and method of notice to the cost-allocation question.

The second reason advanced by the District Court was that $16,000 is a "relatively modest" sum, presumably in comparison to the Fund's total assets, which exceed $500 million. Although in some circumstances the ability of a party to bear a burden may be a

---

28. Thus, where defendants have been directed to enclose class notices in their own periodic mailings, and the additional expense has not been substantial, representative plaintiffs have not been required to reimburse the defendants for envelopes or postage. [Citations.]

consideration, the test in this respect normally should be whether the cost is substantial; not whether it is "modest" in relation to ability to pay. In the context of a lawsuit in which the defendants deny all liability, the imposition on them of a threshold expense of $16,000 to enable the plaintiffs to identify their own class hardly can be viewed as an insubstantial burden. [Citation.] As the expenditure would benefit only respondents, we think that the amount of money involved here would cut strongly against the District Court's holding, even if the principle of *Nissan* did not control.

The panel dissent and the en banc majority suggested several additional reasons to justify the District Court's order, none of which we find persuasive. Both opinions suggest that the fact that part of these records are kept on computer tapes justifies imposing a greater burden on petitioners than might be imposed on a party whose records are kept in another form. Thus, the panel dissent warned that potential defendants may be tempted to use computers "irretrievably [to bury] information to immunize business activity from later scrutiny" [citation], and the en banc majority argued that even where no bad motive is present, "complex electronic processes may be required to extract information which might have been obtainable through a minimum of effort had different systems been used." [Citation.]

We do not think these reasons justify the order in this case. There is no indication or contention that these petitioners have acted in bad faith to conceal information from respondents. In addition, although it may be expensive to retrieve information stored in computers when no program yet exists for the particular job, there is no reason to think that the same information could be extracted any less expensively if the records were kept in less modern forms. Indeed, one might expect the reverse to be true, for otherwise computers would not have gained such widespread use in the storing and handling of information. Finally, the suggestion that petitioners should have used "different systems" to keep their records borders on the frivolous. Apart from the fact that no one has suggested what "different systems" petitioners should have used, we do not think a defendant should be penalized for not maintaining his records in the form most convenient to some potential future litigants whose identity and perceived needs could not have been anticipated. [Citation.]

Respondents also contend that petitioners should be required to bear the identification expense because they are alleged to have breached a fiduciary duty to respondents and their class. [Citation.] Although we had no occasion in *Eisen IV* to consider this argument [citation], suggestions to this effect have met with trenchant criticism elsewhere. [Footnote.] A bare allegation of wrongdoing, whether by breach of fiduciary duty or otherwise, is not a fair reason for requiring a defendant to undertake financial burdens and risks to further a plaintiff's case. Nor would it be in the interests of the class of persons to whom a fiduciary duty is owed to require them, through the fiduciary, to help finance every suit by one of their number that alleges a breach of fiduciary duty, without regard to whether the suit has any merit.

III

Given that respondents can obtain the information sought here by paying the transfer agent the same amount that petitioners would have to pay, that the information must be obtained to comply with respondents' obligations to provide notice to their class, and that no special circumstances have been shown to warrant requiring petitioners to bear the expense, we hold that the District Court abused its discretion in not requiring respondents to pay the transfer agent to identify the members of their own class. The judgment of the Court of Appeals is reversed, and the case is remanded for further proceedings consistent with this opinion. It is so ordered.

DUNN v. MIDWESTERN INDEMNITY

88 F.R.D. 191

(United States District Court, S. D. Ohio, W. D., Sept. 26, 1980.)

RICE, D. J.

The captioned cause is a civil rights action instituted by a black husband and wife against five insurance companies, and an employee or agent of one of said companies, pursuant to

Title VIII of the Civil Rights Act of 1968, 12 U.S.C. § 3601 *et seq.*, 42 U.S.C. §§ 1981-1982. The case deals with a practice sometimes known as "redlining." Plaintiffs allege that they were denied homeowners insurance on their residence in November and December, 1977, because they are black and because their residence is located in a predominantly black neighborhood. Stated differently, they allege that they were denied coverage because of the defendants' racially discriminatory actions and/or standards.

Pursuant to the Court's instructions at a Pretrial Conference held on July 1, 1980, defendants, Midwestern Indemnity Company (Midwestern), American States Insurance Companies (American States), Commercial Union Assurance Companies (Commercial Union), and The Hartford Insurance Company (Hartford), have submitted memoranda summarizing their objections to the plaintiffs' discovery requests relating to these defendants' computer systems and computer tapes which contain records concerning residential policyholders in the Dayton, Ohio area. Commercial Union also filed a motion for protective order and the Court assumes that the above named defendants join in this motion to the extent of their specific objections to Plaintiffs' Amended Second Interrogatories and Amended Third Request to Produce Documents. Plaintiffs filed a Memorandum Contra Defendants' Memoranda, and the matter came on for an oral hearing on August 11, 1980.

The discovery requests to which the defendants object seek minute information about the defendants' computer capabilities, including information about their computer equipment, raw data, programs and data managements systems, in addition to the production of tapes which contain information about past and present policyholders in the Dayton, Ohio area. In some cases, the information is sought for a specified time period; in others, no time limits are indicated. As Commercial Union has characterized the requests, plaintiffs seek a "roadmap" to each of the defendants' computer systems (doc. #65, at 14).

Plaintiffs seek to prove that the underwriting standards formulated and applied by the defendants are racially discriminatory, and that because of defendants' standards and action, plaintiffs were denied homeowner in-

surance coverage during November and December, 1977. It is plaintiffs' position that the requests are relevant to show that the defendants' practices and standards are racially discriminatory, that is, that the information about their computer capabilities may be helpful to determine whether defendants' practices and standards, which allegedly prevented them from procuring insurance, violate the statutory provisions referred to above.

Plaintiffs offer four purposes for the discovery requests at issue:

> 1. to determine what computer based data possessed by defendants support each of defendants' standards;
> 2. to determine what computer based models and analyses the defendants did construct and were capable of constructing from raw data;
> 3. to determine what computer based capacity each defendant possessed that would:
> (a) justify or determine the validity of their standards;
> (b) assess the impact of those standards of minority and integrated neighborhoods and evaluate the feasibility of less discriminatory alternatives;
> (c) determine whether redlining is local or national in scope, that is, to what extent redlining pervades the industry; and
> (d) the extent to which the data lends itself to model formulation and configurations which are less racially discriminatory; and
> 4. to determine the existence and merits of defendants' potential business judgment defense.

[Reference.]

Midwestern's objections apparently go only to the plaintiff's request for the production of the computer tapes and other documents sought in Plaintiffs' Amended Third Request to Produce Documents. It appears that Midwestern has attempted to respond to the document request at least insofar as it seeks information. It also appears that Midwestern has not submitted objection to Plaintiffs' Amended Second Interrogatories.

The objections that have been raised by the defendants differ to some extent as do their arguments in support of their objections. They are, however, unanimous in their contention that these discovery requests are beyond the scope of discovery under Rule 26(b), Fed.R.Civ.Pro., that is, that the requests are irrelevant to the subject matter of this lawsuit. The other objections may be summarized as follows: 1. all relevant information has been or will be provided; 2. since this action involves only two plaintiffs (a married couple), class action-type discovery should not be allowed; 3. compliance, even if feasible, would be a herculean task that is unduly burdensome and expensive, and entirely disproportionate to the dubious value afforded plaintiffs; 4. the requests are vague and overbroad; 5. in some instances, the requests are unintelligible because plaintiffs have failed to define their terms; and 6. the information sought constitutes trade secrets and proprietary information, the disclosure of which would place defendants at a competitive disadvantage.

The issue of whether the requests are within the scope of discovery under Rule 26(b), Fed.R.Civ.Pro., is a threshold matter. The following discussion will set forth the Court's reasons for concluding that plaintiffs' discovery requests are relevant under Rule 26(b). Thereafter, the Court will address certain other arguments raised by the defendants and will apprise the parties of the manner in which the Court intends to proceed toward final determination of these matters.

The defendants contend that all relevant information pertaining to this action either has been or will be provided to the plaintiffs. In their memoranda, each defendant summarizes the discovery that has been had thus far, which appears to be extensive. Defendants further contend that the information sought in the present interrogatories and document requests has either been provided in another form, or that such information is not discoverable under Rule 26(b).

At the outset, the Court notes that it is persuaded by the argument presented in plaintiffs' memorandum, that computer information and machine records are not *per se* irrelevant. [Reference.] [Citation.] *Manual for Complex Litigation.* 2 Moore's Federal Practice. Although this case has not been designated as "complex litigation," the Fifth Recommendation in the *Manual for Complex Litigation,* clearly indicates that the type of discovery being sought in this case has been contemplated:

> *Fifth Recommendation*: Discovery requests relating to the computer, its programs, inputs and outputs should be processed under methods con-

sistent with the approach taken to discovery of other types of information. [Citation.]

* * *

In many instances it will be essential for the discovering party to know the underlying theory and the procedures employed in preparing and storing machine-readable records. When this is true, litigants should be allowed to discover any materials relating to the record holder's computer hardware, the programming techniques employed in connection with the relevant data, the principles governing the structure of the stored data, and the operation of the data processing system. When statistical analyses have been developed from more traditional records with the assistance of computer techniques, the underlying data used to compose the statistical computer input, the methods used to select, categorize, and evaluate the data for analysis, and all of the computer outputs normally are proper subjects for discovery. [Citation.]

Concluding that the plaintiffs' requests are not *per se* irrelevant, the issue before the Court is whether plaintiffs' interrogatories and document requests are relevant to the subject matter of this lawsuit. Rule 26(b) states that parties may obtain discovery regarding any non-privileged matter relevant to the subject matter of the pending action, and that the information need not be admissible at trial if it appears reasonably calculated to lead to the discovery of admissible evidence. The general discovery provisions of the Federal Rules of Civil Procedure are to be liberally construed. [Citations.] This is especially true in complex civil rights cases. [Citations.] The specific relevancy requirement of Rule 26(b) is likewise given liberal construction. [Citations.]

The Court acknowledges that discovery requests similar to those in the case at bar have been denied by other courts. [Citations.] However, since neither of those courts set forth its reasoning with respect to plaintiffs' computer requests, those authorities are in no way dispositive. This Court must look to the context of this action to determine whether plaintiffs have demonstrated the relevancy of their requests.

Stated in admittedly simplistic terms, plaintiffs are essentially alleging that the racial discrimination which caused them to be unable to procure insurance coverage on their residence in November and December, 1977, may, in some way, be built into the defendants' computer systems. As the Court understands their reasons for the requests at issue, they are seeking to discover either: (1) something in defendants' computer systems that should not be there, but is; or (2) something that is not in their systems, which should be. Although the Court expresses no opinion whatsoever on the merits of plaintiffs' allegations, it can envision several ways in which the alleged flaw may occur. For example, because of a man-made decision, the defendants may have developed or used programs in assessing raw data which contribute to the formulation or application of racially discriminatory standards, or, there may be a field in one or more of the defendants' computer programs or tapes which has influenced a man-made decision, the effect of which is to create a racially discriminatory standard or practice. Other possibilities could probably be suggested.

To the extent that defendants' computer capabilities may foster, contribute to, or reflect the formulation or application of the defendants' underwriting standards, which are the subject matter of this action, the plaintiffs' discovery requests are relevant under Rule 26(b), either because the information sought would be admissible at trial or because said information appears reasonably calculated to lead to the discovery of admissible evidence. Because the production of or access to conventional files and computer print-outs does not provide the information herein sought in another form, the discovery which has thus far been completed is no substitute for the present requests.

Additionally, the Court agrees that the present discovery requests are relevant under Rule 26(6), in order for plaintiffs to adequately prepare to meet a business judgment or necessity defense. Counsel for Midwestern conceded at the oral hearing that Midwestern intends to assert this defense. In response to the Court's direct inquiry about whether Commercial Union intended to waive the defense, counsel for Commercial Union reserved the right to assert the business judgment defense. In the Court's view, this defense is inherent in defendants' case, and counsel would be remiss in not asserting it. Consequently, unless assertion of said defense will in no way be supported by defendants' computer capa-

bilities, the Court is wary of denying plaintiffs' full and adequate discovery of the defendants' computer systems, including access to and information about defendants' computer equipment, raw data, programs, data management systems, and the by-products of their analyses. To deny them this discovery may, in effect, be to deny them their day in Court.

Defendants, in their memoranda and at oral hearing, made much of the fact that this action involves only two plaintiffs who seek redress for a single instance of alleged racial discrimination in the procurement of homeowners insurance. They stress that the plaintiffs seek to discover information that is not confined to the time, locale or individuals herein involved. Basically, they contend that since this is not a pattern of practice case, class action-type discovery should not be allowed in this suit brought by private litigants for a single occurrence. Having reviewed the arguments and authorities of the parties, the Court finds no merit to this objection.

A similar contention was rejected by the Court in *Laufman v. Oakley Building & Loan Co.*, 72 F.R.D. 116 (S.D.Ohio 1976) (Porter, J.), in which a married couple instituted an action under, *inter alia*, 42 U.S.C. §§ 3601, *et seq.*, as the plaintiffs have done in the case at bar. *Laufman* also dealt with "redlining." The plaintiffs alleged "that the defendants refused to lend [them] money to purchase a house in * * * a racially integrated area of Cincinnati, Ohio, because of the racial composition of the neighborhood in which the house is located." *Id.* at 119. Claiming that racial considerations were influential in the denial of their loan application, plaintiffs sought discovery relating to "defendants' loan application and appraisal process." *Id.* at 120. Addressing the contention that class action-type discovery should not be allowed, the Court stated:

> The plaintiffs in this case are entitled to discover facts relating to defendants' policies and practices with respect to transactions similar to the one in question whether the present case is a class action or not, as they may tend to show a pattern of refusal to lend in integrated areas. [Citations.] *Georgia Power v. EEOC*, 412 F.2d 462 (5th Cir. 1962); *Burns v. Thiokol Chemical Corp.* 483 F.2d 300 (5th Cir. 1973).

Id. at 121.

In *Burns v. Thiokol, supra* at 305, the Court states that "[a]ny information relevant—in a discovery sense—to an EEOC investigation is likewise relevant to the private attorney general, either *in his individual role* or in his capacity as the claimed representative of a class," (emphasis added). The import of this analogy is illustrated in *Georgia Power v. EEOC, supra,* where the company contended:

> [T]hat the only relevant data were "the records and information pertaining to Mrs. Adkins, together with such records and information pertaining to the individual who was hired in preference to Mrs. Adkins."

Id. at 468. The Court responded to this contention:

> Certainly this information is relevant, but we cannot agree that it was the only relevant evidence. Discrimination on the basis of race or sex is *class discrimination.* The EEOC cannot reasonably be expected to discern such discrimination by examining data relating to two individuals. To limit the investigation to a single position would in many, if not most, instances severely restrict comparative study of the charged party's hiring practices. Thus we think it clear that information concerning other positions is relevant to the investigation. (Court's emphasis).

Id.

The foregoing authorities lead the Court to conclude that plaintiffs are entitled to the broad discovery sought, not only to information concerning their particular claim, but also to information that may lead them to evidence of a pattern of conduct. Acting as private attorneys general under Title VIII of the Civil Rights Act of 1968, 42 U.S.C. §§ 3601, *et seq.,* they are entitled to information "with respect to transactions similar to the one in question, as they may tend to show a pattern" of refusal to accept insurance applications of black applicants and/or applicants who own homes in predominantly black neighborhoods.

Having determined that the plaintiffs' discovery requests are relevant to the subject matter of this litigation, the Court now turns to defendants' other objections. One of the objections, pressed most fervently by Hartford, is that some of the requests are unintelligible because the plaintiffs have failed to define their terms. In its memorandum, Hartford lists over 30 terms which they claim have no clear and certain meanings. [Citation.] To the extent that plaintiffs have failed to define any terms necessary for defendants to respond to the discovery requests, they are ordered to provide said definitions, WITHIN TEN DAYS FROM DATE OF RECEIPT OF NOTICE OF THIS DECISION.

Defendants Commercial Union, American States and Hartford also object to the plaintiffs' discovery requests on the grounds that compliance, even if feasible, would be a herculean tasks that is unduly burdensome and expensive. Their objections with respect to the time frame of the requests, overbreadth and vagueness seem to be closely intertwined with this objection. Because these objections are, to a certain extent, inter-related, they will be considered together.

Rule 26(c) states that a protective order is available "to protect a party or person from annoyance, embarrassment, oppression, or *undue burden or expense.* * * *" The Court has before it a wide divergence of opinion as to the costs, manpower, and feasibility of complying with plaintiffs' discovery requests. Midwestern, as noted earlier, has apparently completed partial compliance with the plaintiffs' requests and is before the Court only on its objection to the production of computer tapes. Commercial Union has submitted the affidavit of one of its employees, which estimates that compliance would take an estimated 10,000 man-hours at a cost of $375,000 to $500,000. [Reference.] Hartford, in its memoranda, states that the costs "in terms of personnel and computer time and other costs * * * would be immense," but does not venture an estimate. [Reference.] It does, however, estimate that "it would take one full person/year for [it] to do the research and investigation necessary to respond. * * *" [Reference.] American States has not, to the Court's knowledge, ventured any estimates concerning costs and human resources necessary for compliance.

These conflicting contentions with respect to the cost, burden, and feasibility of compliance lead the Court to believe that a final decision on these matters at this time would be premature, if not impossible. Instead, the Court will conduct an evidentiary hearing, after giving counsel for defendants sufficient time to consult their clients and to gather evidence and expert support for their contentions. The primary focus of the hearing will be to determine whether compliance with said requests is merely time-consuming and laborious, or whether it is impossible. The Court wishes to stress that impracticability is not to be equated with impossibility in this context. Other issues to be addressed at the proposed hearing concern what, if any, time constraints should be imposed on plaintiffs' requests which contain no time limits, and whether there is merit to plaintiffs' claim that they need certain information, dating back to January 1, 1970, in order to adequately evaluate trends and experience.

In *Kozlowski v. Sears, Roebuck & Co.*, 73 F.R.D. 73 (D.Mass.1976), the plaintiffs sought discovery concerning accidents similar to the one alleged. Sears resisted compliance on the ground that there was "no practical way for anyone to determine whether there have been any complaints similar to those alleged * * * 'other than [by] going through all of the claims * * * which is the equivalent of an impossible task.' " *Id.* at 76. The Court stated, "[m]erely because compliance with a 'Request for Production' would be costly or time-consuming is not ordinarily sufficient reason to grant a protective order where the requested material is relevant and necessary to the discovery of evidence." *Id.* The Court further stated:

> The defendant may not excuse itself from compliance with Rule 34, Fed.R.Civ.P., by utilizing a system of record-keeping which conceals rather than discloses relevant records, or makes it unduly difficult to identify or locate them, thus rendering the production of documents an excessively burdensome and costly expedition. To allow a defendant whose business generates massive records to frustrate discovery, by creating an inadequate filing system, and then claiming undue burden, would defeat the purposes of the discovery rules. [Citations omitted.]

> * * *

> It is well established that a private corporation cannot avoid producing documents by an allegation of 'impossibility' if it can obtain the requested information from sources under its control. [Citations omitted.]

[Citations.]

The Court recognizes that the problems presented in this case may be more complex or of a different nature than those presented in the above cases. However, the Court agrees with the reasoning in *Kozlowski, supra*. Therefore, it wishes to make clear that it will not be receptive to defendants' impossibility contentions insofar as they are grounded in the peculiar manner in which defendants maintain their computer systems.

The final objection which the Court has not yet addressed concerns defendants' contentions that the information sought constitutes trade secrets and proprietary information, the disclosure of which will cause the defendants competitive disadvantage. The Court has no way of knowing the extent to which compliance with the plaintiffs' discovery requests will require them to divulge trade secrets and proprietary information. However, to the extent that trade secrets and confidential information is requested, the plaintiffs will be required to scrupulously comply with the Stipulation and Protective Order that has been in effect since July 14, 1978. [Reference.] No deviation from this Order will be condoned by this Court.

Counsel listed below will take note that an oral hearing will be had * * * the express purpose for which will be, as previously stated, the taking of testimony, if deemed necessary by counsel, to determine whether compliance with the Plaintiffs' Amended Set of Interrogatories and Amended Third Request to Produce Documents is merely time-consuming and laborious (impracticable) or it is impossible. Other issues to be addressed at this hearing will be what, if any, time constraints should be imposed upon plaintiffs' requests which contain no time limits, whether there is merit to plaintiff's claim that they need certain information, dating back to January 1, 1970, whether the plaintiffs have sufficently defined each and every one of the terms contained in the discovery requests in order to enable the defendants to clearly respond to same (the requirement that plaintiffs define their terms within ten days from date of receipt of notice of this decision will enable the defendants to review the plaintiffs' submission in order to determine whether they clearly state the substance of the information, documents and answers required), and whether the plaintiffs require additional protection, above and beyond the Stipulation and Protective Order, in effect since July 14, 1978, in the providing of discovery of matters that they claim to comprise trade secrets and proprietary information.

EX PARTE ALLSTATE INSURANCE COMPANY
401 So.2d 749

(Supreme Court of Alabama, July 10, 1981.)

TORBERT, C. J.

Plaintiff, Douglas Goulet, insured by Allstate, was seriously injured in an automobile accident with an uninsured motorist on May 12, 1979. Allstate investigated the accident and found it to be a case of liability on the uninsured motorist. A draft for $11,000, the supposed policy limit, was delivered to Goulet's attorney after it was confirmed that his medical expenses exceeded that amount.

Subsequently, Goulet discovered that since there were two cars covered by the same policy, he was entitled to an additional $10,000 in uninsured motorist coverage. In an effort to obtain the additional sum from Allstate, his attorney sent two letters to the Company. Receiving no response to either letter, Goulet filed suit on December 6, 1979, for the additional amount due him and for punitive damages for misrepresentation. After suit was filed, Allstate made an offer of judgment for the additional $10,000 plus $2,500 in court costs and attorney's fees, the expenses entailed by Goulet in obtaining the $10,000.

Goulet refused the offer of judgment, and on May 5, 1980, served the following interrogatory on Allstate:

State the names and present addresses of all persons which fall within the following definition:

Persons who, within the past two years, were paid $10,000 in uninsured motorists benefits pursuant to a policy with your company and who, at the time of said payment, had more than one vehicle listed on the policy which fell within the meaning of the statement on your declarations sheet: "The following coverages and limits applied to each described vehicle as shown below:" (This question does not seek the names and addresses of any persons who were represented by counsel at the time of payment of the $10,000 nor does it seek the names and addresses of any persons who were paid $10,000 as a result of litigation, nor does this definition

seek the names and addresses of any persons who resided outside the state of Alabama at the time of said payment).

On June 12, Allstate having failed to answer the interrogatory, Goulet filed a motion to compel. This motion was granted. Allstate then filed a motion for extension of time, which was also granted.

Ultimately, Allstate responded to Goulet's interrogatory by objecting to it on the grounds that: (1) it was irrelevant and could not possibly lead to the discovery of admissible evidence; (2) it was overly broad, oppressive, and unduly burdensome, extremely expensive, and an abuse of discovery; and (3) to release the information to plaintiff's counsel would violate the privacy interests of Allstate's insureds without their consent. Goulet then filed a motion to compel discovery. In the course of the hearing on Goulet's motion, Allstate offered evidence that answering the interrogatory would require the development of a computer program, the cost of which would exceed $1,000, and an extensive manual search of Allstate's files, since the computer did not possess enough information to narrow the list of insureds to only those who possess the qualifications set out in Goulet's interrogatory. Allstate argued further that since the duty owed to insureds represented by counsel is quite different from that owed to those not so represented, and since Goulet was represented by counsel, the names and addresses of insureds not represented by counsel could have no relevance to Goulet's case. Judge Braxton Kittrell granted the motion and ordered Allstate to answer the interrogatory, and Allstate filed a motion to reconsider, which was denied. Allstate then brought a petition for mandamus to review Judge Kittrell's order denying its motion for reconsideration, alleging that he abused his discretion.

Mandamus is a proper means of review to determine whether a trial judge has abused his discretion in ordering discovery. [Citation.] However, matters resting in the sound discretion of the trial court will not be disturbed on appeal unless there has been a clear abuse of discretion. [Citations.] We cannot say from the evidence presented that there was such a clear abuse of discretion by the trial judge in the case before us. Under Rule 26 of the Alabama Rules of Civil Procedure, parties are entitled to discover "any matter, not privileged, which is relevant to the subject matter involved in the pending action." [Citation.] Furthermore, the Rule provides that "[i]t is not ground for objection that the information sought will be inadmissible at the trial if the information sought appears reasonably calculated to lead to the discovery of admissible evidence." [Citation.] Evidence of similar misrepresentations made to others by the defendant are admissible in a fraud action. [Citation.] Therefore, the information sought, the identity of others who had been paid $10,000 although their policy listed more than one vehicle, could very easily lead to admissible evidence. In the case before us, the trial court determined the interrogatory was proper. "The broad scope given our discovery rules necessarily requires that the trial court be vested with considerable discretion in ruling on such matters." [Citations.] Since we find no abuse of discretion, the petition for writ of mandamus is due to be denied.

REV. PROC. 69-21
1969-2 C.B. 303

SECTION 1. PURPOSE.

The purpose of this Revenue Procedure is to provide guidelines to be used in connection with the examination of Federal income tax returns involving the costs of computer software.

SEC. 2. BACKGROUND.

For the purpose of this Revenue Procedure, "computer software" includes all programs or routines used to cause a computer to perform a desired task or set of tasks, and the documentation required to describe and maintain those programs. Computer programs of all classes, for example, operating systems, executive systems, monitors, compilers and translators, assembly routines, and utility programs as well as application programs are included. "Computer software" does not include procedures which are external to computer operations, such as instructions to transcription operators and external control procedures.

SEC. 3. COSTS OF DEVELOPING SOFTWARE.

.01 The costs of developing software (whether or not the particular software is patented or copyrighted) in many respects so closely resemble the kind of research and experimental expenditures that fall within the purview of section 174 of the Internal Revenue Code of 1954 as to warrant accounting treatment similar to that accorded such costs under that section. Accordingly, the Internal Revenue Service will not disturb a taxpayer's treatment of costs incurred in developing software, either for his own use or to be held by him for sale or lease to others, where:

1. All of the costs properly attributable to the development of software by the taxpayer are consistently treated as current expenses and deducted in full in accordance with rules similar to those applicable under section 174(a) of the Code; or

2. All of the costs properly attributable to the development of software by the taxpayer are consistently treated as capital expenditures that are recoverable through deductions for ratable amortization, in accordance with rules similar to those provided by section 174(b) of the Code and the regulations thereunder, over a period of five years from the date of completion of such development or over a shorter period where such costs are attributable to the development of software that the taxpayer clearly establishes has a useful life of less than five years.

SEC. 4. COSTS OF PURCHASED SOFTWARE.

.01 With respect to costs of purchased software, the Service will not disturb the taxpayer's treatment of such costs if the following practices are consistently followed:

1. Where such costs are included, without being separately stated, in the cost of the hardware (computer) and such costs are treated as a part of the cost of the hardware that is capitalized and depreciated; or

2. Where such costs are separately stated, and the software is treated by the taxpayer as an intangible asset the cost of which is to be recovered by amortization deductions ratably over a period of five years or such shorter periods as can be established by the taxpayer

as appropriate in any particular case if the useful life of the software in his hands will be less than five years.

SEC. 5. LEASED SOFTWARE.

Where a taxpayer leases software for use in his trade or business, the Service will not disturb a deduction allowable under the provisions of section 1.162-11 of the Income Tax Regulations, for rental.

SEC. 6. APPLICATION.

.01 The costs of development of software in accordance with the above procedures will be treated as a method of accounting. Any change in the treatment of such costs is a change in method of accounting subject to the provisions of sections 446 and 481 of the Code and the regulations thereunder.

.02 For taxable years ending after October 27, 1969 the date of publication of this Revenue Procedure, the Service will not disturb the taxpayer's treatment of software costs that are handled in accordance with the practices described in this Revenue Procedure.

.03 For taxable years ending prior to the date of publication of this Revenue Procedure, the Service will not disturb the taxpayer's treatment of software costs except to the extent that such treatment is markedly inconsistent with the practices described in this Revenue Procedure. For the purpose of applying the preceding sentence, the absence of any formal election similar to that required by section 174 of the Code, or the amortization of capitalized software costs over a period other than the five-year period specified in section 174(b) of the Code, will not characterize the taxpayer's treatment of such costs as markedly inconsistent with the principles of this Revenue Procedure.

REV. RUL. 71-177
1971 IRB-15, p. 7

During 1968, a taxpayer purchased a new computer. The cost of the software provided with the computer was not separately stated. In accordance with his consistent practice, the taxpayer capitalized the entire cost of the computer, including the cost of the software provided with it, and deducted depreciation thereon based upon a useful life in excess of four years.

Held, the cost of the computer, in the instant case, includes the cost of the software provided with it for purposes of the depreciation allowed under section 167 of the Internal Revenue Code of 1954 and the investment credit allowed under section 38 of the Code.

REV. RUL. 71-248
1971 IRB-23, p. 9

Advice has been requested as to the proper treatment for Federal income tax purposes of certain software costs under the circumstances described below.

A corporation purchased a computer in 1965 which is still in use. Software costs incurred in connection with that computer have been expensed for both book and Federal income tax purposes.

In 1970, the corporation purchased a new computer which was installed in 1971. The installation of the new computer required the development by the corporation of an entirely new set of software for use with it. Software costs were incurred by the corporation in 1970 in connection with programming the new computer that the corporation desires to defer and amortize. Annual software costs in small amounts will continue to be incurred and deducted with respect to the old computer.

Specifically the question here relates to whether the deferral and amortization of software costs incurred in connection with the new computer would constitute a change in method of accounting requiring the Commissioner's consent.

Section 3.01-1 of Revenue Procedure 69-21, C.B. 1969-2, 303, states that the costs of developing software by a taxpayer (whether or not the particular software is patented or copyrighted) in many respects so closely resemble the kind of research and experimental expenditures that fall within the purview of section 174 of the Internal Revenue Code of 1954 as to warrant accounting treatment similar to that accorded such costs under that section. Accordingly, it was stated that the

Service would not disturb a taxpayer's treatment of costs incurred in developing software where all of the costs properly attributable to the development of software by the taxpayer are consistently treated as current expenses and deducted in full in accordance with rules similar to those applicable under section 174(a) of the Code.

In addition, section 3.01-2 of Revenue Procedure 69-21 states that the Service would not disturb a taxpayer's treatment of costs incurred in its developing software where all of the costs properly attributable to the development of software by the taxpayer are consistently treated as capital expenditures that are recoverable through deductions for ratable amortization, in accordance with rules similar to those provided by section 174(b) of the Code and the regulations thereunder, over a period of five (5) years from the date of completion of such development or over a shorter period where the taxpayer clearly establishes that such costs have a useful life of less than five years.

Section 1.174-3(a) of the Income Tax Regulations permits research and experimental expenditures to be treated on a project by project basis.

Revenue Ruling 68-144, C.B. 1968-1, 85, holds that where a taxpayer had elected to currently expense all research and experimental expenditures with the exception of those on particular projects to which the deferred expense method was elected, it cannot in a later year elect the deferred expense method on new projects unless permission is granted by the Commissioner.

Since, as stated above, the costs of developing software closely resemble the kind of research and experimental expenditures that fall within the purview of section 174 of the Code, such software costs may be treated on a project by project basis. Thus, the corporation which has treated as current deductions the costs of software in connection with the old computer, may capitalize software costs with respect to the new computer *only* where permission is granted by the Commissioner.

An application for permission to change to a different method of treating software costs shall be in writing and shall be addressed to the Commissioner of Internal Revenue, Attention T:I, Washington, D.C. 20024. The application shall include the name and address of the taxpayer, shall be signed by the taxpayer (or his duly authorized representative) and shall be filed not later than the last day of the first taxable year for which the change in method is to apply. The application shall—

(1) State the first year to which the requested change is to be applicable;

(2) State whether the change is to apply to all software costs paid or incurred or only to expenditures attributable to a particular project;

(3) Include such information as will identify the projects to which the change is applicable;

(4) Indicate the number of months selected for amortization of the costs, if any, which are to be treated as deferred expenses;

(5) State that, upon approval of the application, the taxpayer will make an accounting segregation on his books and records of software costs to which the change is to apply;

(6) State the reasons for the change.

DISTRICT OF COLUMBIA v. UNIVERSAL COMPUTER ASSOCIATES, INC.
465 F.2d 615, 3 CLSR 549
(United States Court of Appeals, District of Columbia Circuit, June 15, 1972.)

WILKEY, C. J.

This case comes to us on petition by the District of Columbia for review of the decision of the District of Columbia Tax Court, holding that 50% of the purchase price of the respondent Universal's computer and accompanying "software" is properly allocable to taxable "tangible personal property," and 50% of the purchase price is to be ascribed to non-taxable intangible values. Whatever the complexities of computer science, we think the answer here is clear, in spite of the absence of light from guiding precedent and that the applicable statute [footnote] is vintage 1922.

I.

For the sum of $289,836 Universal bought from IBM a data processing unit. This included the computer machine itself (the hardware) and two sets of punched cards (the software) used to program the computer. One set of the punched cards was the usual standard program developed by IBM for this computer. Another set of punched cards contained a special tax program, developed jointly by personnel of IBM and Universal. Of the total price of $290,000, the sum of $106,000, represents estimates of the cost of the special tax program. To the standard cards usually available with this computer IBM retained title; Universal was not free to transfer these cards or to make available the information contained thereon to third parties. To the special tax program cards and the information contained thereon Universal did obtain title, and was free to transfer or utilize the information in any way it saw fit.

Computers can be programmed by punched cards, electronic tapes, or discs on which the information to be stored in the computer is placed. Or, theoretically, a computer could be programmed originally by an operator working from instructions known only to him, although this would be much more laborious and time-consuming. With this particular model computer the punch cards are fed into the computer, the information contained thereon is recorded in the inner operations of the machine; at the completion of the process the computer is programmed. The cards are then stored separately and have no further use, unless at some future date it becomes necessary to insert the same program into the machine. Once the machine is programmed, then it is ready to be employed in the work for which it was purchased.

The legal issue here is whether the two sets of punched cards (the software) represent tangible personal property and are thus subject to the D.C. personal property tax, or whether they represent intangible values which are not subject to tax. The District of Columbia Tax Court held that the software represented intangible values and was not subject to the personal property tax. Since the computer machine itself unquestionably is tangible personal property and subject to tax, the Tax Court had to make an allocation of values between the hardware (the computer machine) and the software (the intangible value of the information stored on the cards). It allocated 50% each to the hardware and software, thus making the original taxable value of the computer approximately $145,000, to be depreciated at

the usual rate each year after the date of purchase.

II.

We conclude that the District of Columbia Tax Court was correct both as to its determination as to the nontaxability of the intangible values represented by the information stored on the punched cards, and in the allocation of 50% of the value of the whole package to the software.

It appears to us that the material of the punched cards themselves is of insignificant value. It was for the intangible value of the information stored on the cards that Universal paid IBM. How the information was created, who has title to it, and how the information is put to the computer machine—all support this appraisal.

A. The Work of IBM's experts in developing the tax information to be put on the punched tax program cards was estimated to be worth $106,000. The punching of the cards themselves, like the cost of the pasteboard and the feeding of them into the machine, is insignificant compared to the time consumed, the skill used, and the inherent value attached to the process of creating the information. What Universal paid for, what IBM charged for, and the value which is or is not subject to tax, is the intangible value created by the intellectual effort in creating this special tax program to go on the cards.

B. Title to the tax program, the intellectual property designed for Universal specially, and which it helped create, was transferred completely to Universal. On the other hand, title to the standard information customarily used in this model computer machine was retained by IBM; under terms of the contract Universal could not transfer either the information or the cards physically to a third party. The standard information on this set of cards was developed by IBM over a period of years at a cost of many millions of dollars. While the cost of the development is thus not ascertainable individually in relation to Universal, it represents an investment of IBM in an intellectual property, which it licenses users like Universal to employ in the computers IBM sells.

C. The punched cards themselves are placed in the machine and then taken out, and in fact could be returned to IBM. It is the information derived by the machine from the cards which stays in the computer, and which is employed repeatedly by the machine when it is used by Universal. What rests in the machine, then, is an intangible—"knowledge"—which can hardly be thought to be subject to a personal property tax. The only visible evidence of that knowledge, the punched pasteboard, could be stacked in a warehouse, returned to IBM, or destroyed, without interfering with the efficiency of the computer machine to perform its designed function.

We think computer software, then, can be likened to the cartoon mats involved in *Washington Times-Herald v. District of Columbia,* in which this court *en banc* held that cartoon mats which were sold by publishing syndicates to individual newspapers were not tangible personal property for purposes of the D.C. sales tax. Judge Miller expressed the rationale of our court:

> The syndicates sold to the Times-Herald the right to reproduce one time the work of artists who make the drawings. *They simply sold the professional and personal services* of the artists whom they had under contract and in so doing transferred title to the mats, of inconsequential value, from which the drawings could be reproduced. *The price was paid for the artists' work,* i. e., for the right to reproduce the impressions on the mats,—not for the mats themselves. The newspaper bought the creation of the artist—not the material on which it was impressed—and the right to reproduce it. Without that right, the comic strips mats would be entirely worthless. (Emphasis supplied.)[2]

We think that the knowledge stored on computer cards, tapes, or discs is even more demonstrably intangible intellectual property than the right to reproduce from the cartoonist's drawings involved in *Washington Times-Herald.*

While in *District of Columbia v. Norwood Studios* the transfer of films was held subject to the sales tax, it was distinguished from *Washington Times-Herald.* Judge Edgerton said:

> The present case is different. The producer of the films retains no interest in them and im-

posed no restriction on their use. They became the property of [the purchasers] without qualification.[3]

In *Norwood Studios* the purchaser of the films was free to make use of the films as many times as he desired, and to sell the films themselves to third parties. In *Washington Times-Herald* the newspaper acquired the right to reproduce the cartoon only once. In the case at bar Universal can use the information on the standard IBM cards, but cannot divulge the knowledge or transfer the cards to a third party; Universal can transfer the special tax program cards or the knowledge contained thereon to a third party, because it paid IBM for their expert services and Universal's own experts participated in developing the knowledge that went on these particular cards; IBM has no use for them otherwise and attached no limits to the transfer of the knowledge to Universal and its computer. Universal, like IBM with the knowledge on the standard cards, could license others to use the cards, but retain title to and control of them. Thus both type cards, the standard IBM and special tax program owned by Universal are the same type intellectual property as the mats in *Washington Times-Herald.* In all respects we think the case at bar is similar to *Washington Times-Herald* and not to *Norwood Studios.*

That the above is the correct tax treatment is reinforced by two other considerations. Since 1969 IBM has followed the practice of billing software in its sales separately from the sale of hardware in the computer line. More importantly, the Internal Revenue Service has promulgated a specific rule permitting the separation of software and hardware for depreciation purposes, which is precisely the problem involved here with the D.C. personal property tax. [Footnote.] Under IRS rules hardware (the computer machine itself) is depreciated on a regular schedule, while the development of software, such as the tax package here (the intangible knowledge residing in punched cards, tapes or discs) may be taken as a deductible expense in the single year of purchase, much like an expenditure for personal services. The billing by IBM and the

---

2. Washington Times-Herald v. District of Columbia, 94 U.S.App.D.C. 154, 155, 213 F.2d 23, 24 (1954).

3. District of Columbia v. Norwood Studios, Inc., 118 U.S.App.D.C. 358, 359, 336 F.2d 746, 747 (1964).

treatment by Internal Revenue for tax purposes would seem to establish that only the computer machine itself is tangible personal property; the software is intangible knowledge not subject to personal property tax.

III.

Lastly, turning to the 50-50% allocation of the values between the hardware and the software, there is evidence in the record sustaining the Tax Court's determination of this issue. While we have no indication of the value placed by IBM on the computer machine itself and the standard software package in this sale in 1966, we do know that out of the total purchase price of $290,000, it was estimated that $106,000 represented the cost of the services rendered by IBM in the development of the tax program package. There was testimony that hardware in the computer field generally amounts to only about ten or twenty percent of the purchase price; somewhat contradictorily and with a high degree of mathematical uncertainty, there was also testimony that software "in some cases goes up as high as fifty or fifty-five percent of the total purchase price." The record shows that the special software tax package was so important that Universal would not have accepted the computer without it.

Whether the total software be taken as having a value of eighty or ninety percent of the purchase price of $290,000, or the software value be assumed to be fifty or fifty-five percent, or it be calculated that the special tax package (the development costs of which were estimated to be $106,000) plus whatever value can be ascribed to the standard software package would total more than 50% of the entire purchase price, the record shows that the District would be entitled to tax no more than 50% of the package total value as hardware. The record thus can be read to support the Tax Court's 50-50% allocation, which means that respondent Universal must pay a personal property tax based on an initial value of $145,000 for the computer machine itself. With a different set of facts, King Solomon did no better in making a similar choice. [Footnote.]

COUNTY OF SACRAMENTO v. ASSESSMENT APPEALS BOARD NUMBER 2 OF SACRAMENTO COUNTY EX REL. RCA CORP.

32 Cal.App.3d 654, 108 Cal.Rptr. 434
(Court of Appeal, Third District, May 29, 1973.)

DAVID, A. J.

These three consolidated appeals have surfaced out of a procedural morass, involving the assessment and taxation of data processing equipment and systems furnished by contract to the State of California, by RCA Corporation. The State of California, being exempt from taxation [citation] [footnote], the county assessor turned his guns on RCA, asserting that it was liable for personal property taxes upon the systems. [Citation.] After a year's conferences with the company, including inspection of the company's records, locally and in New York, the assessor made an assessment for "escaped property," upon which taxes were levied against RCA in the sum of $546,326.87, and were paid under protest.

Thereafter, application was made by RCA before Assessment Appeals Board No. 2 ("board") for reduction of assessments, asserting that although RCA was legal owner, the transactions with the state were actually conditional sales, though denominated "leases," and hence, under accepted principles, the owner had a taxable interest of zero. Factors of valuation and methods of valuation were the subject of testimony and of discussions at the hearing. At the conclusion of the proceeding, the board filed its opinion on May 8, 1970, determining that the contentions of RCA were correct, that its interest had a zero valuation. Thus, the taxes paid for the tax years 1967–1968, 1968–1969 and 1969–1970 were refunded to RCA. The county counsel advised RCA that no appeal of this ruling would be taken.

Commencing eleven months later, the county in a variety of proceedings, has sought to relitigate the issues, and recover the refund and to block any consideration of like protests of assessments made for the tax years 1970–1971 and 1971–1972 by the assessment appeals board. Since the county anticipated that upon any such hearing the ruling made in reference to the first three years might be repeated, its legal contentions are consonant with its fears. [Footnote.] Thus, when the assessor repeated the assessment of RCA Corporation for the tax year 1970–1971, RCA again sought equalization, resulting in the action of the county successfully seeking a writ of prohibition. This was appealed by RCA and is before us as 3 Civil No. 13523.

Again assessed for the tax year 1971–1972, RCA Corporation made application for reduction of the assessment, which the board refused to hear on advice of the county counsel that it had no jurisdiction. RCA sought a writ of mandate to compel the board to proceed. The general demurrer of the county to the petition was sustained and the proceeding dismissed, which is the basis of RCA Corporation's appeal before us (3 Civil No. 13732).

Our discussion will reveal other legal skirmishes.

It will be helpful to consider the appeals chronologically in reference to the tax years for which assessments were made.

I.

Appeal 3 Civil No. 13800 arises from a judgment of the superior court, dismissing the county's petition for a writ of mandate, to compel Assessment Appeals Board No. 2: (1) to set aside its decision of May 8, 1970; (2) to determine that RCA is the fully-assessable owner of the data processing equipment; and (3) for general relief. [Citation.]

In the petition for mandamus, there were annexed and pleaded by reference the transcript of proceedings before Assessment Appeals Board No. 2, its order of May 8, 1970, and an exemplar of the four contracts between RCA and the State of California (stipulated to be typical). The answer admitted that the complaint properly set forth the proceedings. They therefore are before us: (a) we take judicial notice thereof; (b) a demurrer confesses the facts well pleaded, which also places the documentation before us. [Footnote.]

In the petition for mandate in 3 Civil No. 13800, the county and the board of supervisors assert that:

(1) The relief sought by the taxpayer before the assessment appeals board was the declaration of an "exemption" and that the assess-

ment appeals board has no jurisdiction to consider or grant an "exemption."

(2) That as a matter of law, the assessment appeals board erroneously decided that the contracts with the state were conditional sales contracts, and that RCA Corporation was only security owner, and had no taxable interest; that in law and fact, said agreements were for lease and hire of the data processing equipment, the lessor RCA being properly assessed for their value, no purchase option having been exercised.

(3) That the petitioners did not have a plain, speedy and adequate remedy in the ordinary course of law.

* * *

F. The Lessor May be Fully Assessed on a Lease of Personal Property to an Exempt Governmental Agency.

No provision has been made in California law for assessment and valuation of the separate interests of lessor and lessee, in a lease of personal property. [Citations.]

Only three cases have dealt with the lessor-lessee situation in regard to real property where (as here) the lessee is an exempt governmental agency. In *Orbach's Inc. v. County of Los Angeles* (1961) 190 Cal.App.2d 575, 581, 12 Cal.Rptr. 132, the holder of property on a 99 year lease subleased a portion of the premises to the state, whose possessory interest was exempt from taxation. The taxpayer contended that the value of the possessory interest should have been computed and deducted from the assessment against him for the whole.

It was held that the rental received from the sublease represented the use value of the sublease, and that such value plus the value of the reversion constituted the entire value of the property. The lessor was properly assessed, therefore, for the entire value. [Citation.]

The interest of a lessor of real property to a school district, exempt from taxation has been held to be without taxable value. [Citation.] This was based upon the constitutional language, that property "used" by a school district was exempt from taxation although otherwise only property "belonging" to the state was exempted [citation], and that taxation of the lessor would increase the burdens upon the school district. [Citation.] The *Orbach's* case, therefore, is most nearly parallel to the instant situation.

Because it would be an intolerable burden otherwise to consider each contract, fixing the relationships of lessor-lessee [citations], the assessor may assess one in possession or control of property or the owner. [Citation.] Since the exempt State of California is in possession, the assessor perforce considered the contracts between the parties. The question resolves itself into whether or not they constituted conditional sales to the state, wherein RCA Corporation retained only security ownership with no taxable value; or whether they were what they purported to be, leases of data processing equipment and systems with the right but not the obligation to exercise the stated options to purchase all or any part of the leased equipment.

Nothing in the circumstances under which the agreements were made is tendered to change or alter the plain and unambiguous provisions of the instruments. [Citations.]

The assessment appeals board had testimony before it that RCA, for bookkeeping purposes, depreciation accounts and income tax returns, treated these contracts for leasing and hire as conditional sales contracts. But no ambiguity of the language of the instruments was asserted; and, of course, the State of California, the other party to the contracts, was not before the board.

This was incompetent evidence. No mistake or imperfection of the writing is put in issue; no question of the validity of the instruments is in dispute; there is no ambiguity, no claim of illegality or fraud. [Citation.]

There is no dispute concerning the terms of the agreements. Extrinsic evidence is not permitted to add to , detract from, or vary the terms of these fully integrated agreements. [Citation.]

We therefore are permitted and required to make our own independent determination of the legal effect of these instruments. [Citations.]

RCA Corporation freely admits that the language of the instruments is not of conditional sale but of leasing and hiring. The state has an option to purchase the equipment, or any item of it, for specified list prices, wherein rentals paid are credited to the purchase price.

In this instance, the assessor's valuation of the property for 1970–1971 based on the contract value is $12,149,582.

The criteria for determination seem to be whether or not at the time of entering into the contract there was a fixed intention to buy and sell, whether at that moment the entire obligation to pay arose, payments being on a deferred basis; and where the "purchase" was made subject to a scale of options, whether the investment was such that the lessee was under such an economic compulsion to take up the option that it could be construed to be a certainty.

Although no option has ever been exercised, the contention of RCA Corporation is that the "economic compulsion" upon the state at some time to exercise the option is sufficient to require the construction of the agreements as conditional sales for tax purposes. The very "economic compulsion" which the taxpayer urges has been suspect as a badge of illegality. [Citations.]

Where public agencies are concerned, constitutional and statutory debt limitations have held true conditional sales contracts to be invalid, where the entire consideration to be paid under the contract became a liability upon execution of the agreement and exceeded the constitutional debt limitations.

In a public contract, efforts are made in California to insure that, unlike a general conditional sales contract, every separate payment is supported by its own consideration and is not simply an aliquot part of a total indebtedness, and that such separate payment falls within the budgetary allotment provided for that year or budgetary period. (Dean v. Kuchel (1950) 35 Cal.2d 444, 447, 218 P.2d 521.)

The provisions of the agreements here drafted to avoid the prohibitions of California Constitution, article XVI, section 1, establish conclusively that they are in fact, agreements for lease and hire of the data processing systems, and for associated services; and that the unexercised options to purchase do not transmute the arrangement into a conditional sale. This is true, even though a final payment of $1.00 plus the accrued rentals, exercises an option. In *Lagiss v. County of Contra Costa* (1963) 223 Cal.App.2d 77, 90, 35 Cal.Rptr. 450,

458, it is stated: "In the instant case, the exercise of the option by the County in the final year by the payment of the sum of $1.00 is equivalent to the obtaining of title by the County by the payment of the aggregate rentals provided for in the lease as in the *Dean* case. * * * As pointed out in *Dean,* the vesting of title at the end of the term without the payment of anything other than the rentals under the lease does not disqualify the instrument as a lease for the purpose of the debt limitation." The situation is parallel in the RCA Corporation-state contracts.

Omitting reference to those provisions which RCA Corporation admits characterize the agreements as for "lease" and "hire," the following provisions seem conclusive:

(1) During the term of the agreements, upon the anniversary date, the state may elect to purchase the data processing systems, or any constituent elements thereof, each of which is given a purchase price, with credits given for paid rentals upon the purchase price.

(2) Annual rentals are paid. The anniversary dates of the agreement fall after the period when the state budget is adopted in budget years; and it is expressly provided that the state's monetary obligations are contingent upon budgetary appropriations therefor. [Citation.]

(3) The state does not take any title unless an option is exercised.

(4) The state may unilaterally cancel the agreement as of any anniversary date of its signing, upon 60-days' prior notice. No penalty is imposed upon the state if it chooses to cancel the agreement.

(5) Upon any termination of the agreement (other than if the option is exercised), the lessor, RCA, is to receive back the equipment, and the only obligation of the state is to load it for shipment, as specified.

(6) Paragraph 20 of Rider A provides: "Title to equipment, accessories and devices rented under this contract shall remain with the Contractor. All devices and accessories furnished by the Contractor, except those purchased by the State, shall accompany the equipment when returned to the Contractor."

(7) Except for its own fault or negligence, the state is relieved of all risks of loss or damage to the equipment during periods of transportation, installation and during the entire time the equipment is in the possession of the state.

(8) Rider A, paragraph 7a.(1), provides: "Prior to the exercise of the Option to Purchase the Contractor shall keep the equipment in good condition and shall always be responsive to the maintenance requirements of the State. * * *"

(9) Rider A, paragraph 2, provides:

"a. This contract is effective from the date hereof, and the term of the lease of the equipment is from October 27, 1967, to October 27, 1974, subject to the terms hereof.

"b. Rider B shall designate the installation date, and, if applicable, removal dates of each machine to be leased under this agreement."

The provisions relative to purchase are:

"21. Purchase Option

"a. The State may, at any time following acceptance of the equipment, purchase any or all machines at the Contractor's prices shown on Rider B, less the Purchase Option Allowance associated with that price machine.

"b. The Purchase Option allowance is calculated by multiplying the number of monthly payments paid times $1/84$ of the 'Purchase Price' of the equipment on which the option is being exercised.

"c. The State shall specify by model and serial number the equipment to be purchased. The rental charges shall be discontinued as of the close of business of the day immediately preceding the date of payment of the purchase price.

"d. Upon exercise of the Purchase Option the Contractor agrees to perform Maintenance Service on the equipment involved on terms equal or better than the Contractor's commercial maintenance rates at that time, if requested by the State."

The willingness of RCA Corporation to sell the entire equipment and system at the end of the lease period for rentals paid, if the state exercises the option, does not characterize the entire lease as a sale. The testimony before the assessment appeals board by RCA Corporation representatives was that by the end of the seven-year lease period, there would not be a residual value, considering the rapid advances in data processing technology and equipment producing economic obsolescence, and the cost of removing, transporting and reconverting the equipment.

The same advances in technology, changes in the needs of the state department concerned, the performance record of the equipment, and advantages which might be offered by other systems, possibly could induce the state to require the RCA Corporation to remove its equipment, to make way for other devices. There is no firm commitment otherwise.

The transaction solely was that of leasing and hire, with an option to purchase. [Citations.]

G. The Equalization Procedure is Incomplete and Errors are Noted.

Convinced that the transactions were conditional sales, the board did not complete the equalization process, though evidence was presented by both the assessor and the taxpayer respecting the assessment made. The assessor and the taxpayer were at odds: (1) concerning the residual value of the leased property at the end of the lease upon reversion to the lessor; (2) depreciation; (3) the use of the contract price by the assessor as the basis of valuation without stripping therefrom the portion thereof for the services rendered under the contracts; and (4) the refusal of the assessor to consider sales made of the same systems as "hardware" without the accompanying services. Some of these matters were specified in the opinion and order of the board, dated May 8, 1970.

We concur with the opinion of the board that the assessor was in error when he accepted the full contract price in each case as the basis of valuing the property, including therein the service or "software" intangibles, failing to consider in that regard the out-of-country sales made by RCA stripped of such intangibles. The idea that because these sales were in part for resale by the purchaser, they were on a "sales level" which should not be considered, is patently erroneous. The sales price was not the "book value of the inventory." [Citation.] As operative on the lien dates in question [footnote] Revenue and Taxation Code section 110 established the criteria for *value:* " 'Value,' 'full cash value' or 'cash value' means the amount at which property would be taken in payment of a just debt from a solvent debtor. * * *" It stands to reason that if the only market for a unique system

is wholesale or foreign, it should be considered.

H. Appropriateness of the Remedy.

* * *

As we have determined that Assessment Appeals Board No. 2 did not perform its full duty conformably to law, the writ of mandate should issue from the trial court to order its compliance. [Citations.] The cause should be remanded by the trial court to the assessment appeals board to ascertain the value of RCA Corporation's interest. [Citation.]

RCA Corporation should not be prejudiced by reason of the remand of this matter to Assessment Appeals Board No. 2. After the remittitur and within a reasonable time to be fixed by the trial court, RCA Corporation may redeposit the amount paid under protest on August 31, 1970. It shall have six months after the date of such redeposit to file suit, if any be necessary, to recover the taxes paid under protest. The county shall not be liable to RCA Corporation for interest on all or any part of the sum so paid under protest, except for the period that the same has been held by the county. No penalties are chargeable to RCA Corporation beyond those due, if any, as of the original date of deposit under protest, August 31, 1970.

* * *

GREYHOUND COMPUTER CORP. v. STATE DEPARTMENT OF ASSESSMENTS AND TAXATION
71 Md. 374, 320 A.2d 52, 5 CLSR 615
(Court of Appeals of Maryland, May 29, 1974.)

SINGLEY, J.

In this appeal from the Maryland Tax Court, Greyhound Computer Corporation (Greyhound) challenges an order of the tax court which affirmed an assessment of $1,501,350.00 imposed for the tax year 1970–71 by the State Department of Assessments and Taxation (the Department) on four computer systems owned by Greyhound and leased to Bendix Corporation at Towson, Maryland.[1] A second appeal in the same record is that of LMC Leasing Corporation (LMC) which contests the validity of a similar assessment of $1,932,170.00.[2] Because the issues relating to both cases are identical, this opinion will deal primarily with Greyhound.

The only issue in the case was the extent to which computer software [footnote]—programs, educational services, and systems engineering services—which had been "bundled" in the cost of the computers, purchased by Greyhound or LMC from International Business Machines Corporation (IBM) and leased to others, is tangible personal property, subject to assessment, at full cash value, and taxation under Maryland Code (1957, 1969 Repl.Vol.) Art. 81, §§ 8(2), 14(b)(2). [Footnote.]

Greyhound rests its challenge on three arguments:

(i) Software is not tangible personal property subject to tax;

(ii) The Department may not assess software—having substantial value—as if it were tangible personal property merely because certain elements of the software have been placed upon or relate to certain tangible items like cards or magnetic tapes which have insignificant value; and

(iii) The tax court's finding that "software" was not severable from, and was an integral part of, hardware is unsupported by substantial evidence.

Because we have concluded that there is a legal infirmity in the result reached by the tax court, we shall deal only tangentially with these contentions.

The tax court seems to have had no difficulty in affirming the Department's assessment which had been based on the purchase price paid IBM for a "bundle" of computer hardware and software, less an appropriate allowance for depreciation. The court noted that the data processing equipment—computer hardware—was inoperable without the programming and services—the software—which were a part of the package. The court also found that the value of the software had not been separately recorded on Greyhound's books.

As a result, the only estimate of the value of the software came from Walter Misdom, a consultant in the field of computer market research, who was the only witness. Mr. Misdom testified that when IBM in 1969 abandoned its policy of bundling hardware and some of the software, the sale price of its computer hardware dropped about 3%. However, by utilizing what he estimated IBM's budget allocations for the year 1968 to have been, he concluded that about 33% of the purchase price paid IBM by Greyhound was properly allocable to software. The tax court concluded, however, that the software was simply not severable from the hardware for purposes of assessment.

What is troublesome about this approach is the fact that while a substantial portion of the software is of a tangible nature, i. e., punched cards, magnetic tapes, instructions covering operation or applications, and thus might well be subject to assessment and taxation under Code (1957, 1969 Repl.Vol.) Art. 81, § 8(2), the remainder consists of personal services to be rendered after purchase which were characterized by the tax court in this matter [footnote]:

> SYSTEMS ENGINEERING SERVICES: services provided by the software developer to evaluate and meet the problem solving needs of electronic data processing equipment, including the preparation of feasibility studies, systems analysis and design services, the planning and writing of basic operations programs and application programs, and the debugging testing documentation development and the improvement of these programs.
>
> EDUCATIONAL SERVICES: training and instruction in the use of electronic data processing equipment provided to the user thereof, such as on site education, classroom instructions and educational publications.

---

1. International Business Machines Corporation, the manufacturer of the equipment, had charged Greyhound approximately $2,646,000.00 for both the data processing equipment ("computer hardware"), and the programs and educational and engineering service ("computer software"). When the sale was made, it was the manufacturer's policy to "bundle" the cost of hardware and soft-

ware. This policy was changed, commencing in June of 1969, when some software was "unbundled" from hardware.

2. Both appeals are siblings of State Dep't of Assessments & Taxation v. Greyhound Computer Corp., Md., 320 A.2d 40 (1974) in which the same parties, the same computers, but different issues, were involved.

MAINTENANCE: tests, measurements, replacements, adjustments and repairs intended to keep data processing equipment in satisfactory working condition.

A tenable argument may be made in support of the notion that at least that part of the tangible software which constitutes the operational program, without which a computer cannot operate, may have a value far in excess of that of the cards and tapes themselves, a value which represents large amounts expended by the manufacturer before the sale could take place for research, development, engineering, and the acquisition of expertise and skills. [Footnote.] So much of the software as consists of services to be rendered after the purchase is not only intangible in nature, but is beyond the reach of Code (1957, 1969 Repl.Vol.) Art. 81, § 11(c) [footnote], dealing primarily with the taxation of intangibles, which generally permits only the taxation of bonds, certificates of indebtedness or evidence of debt owned by certain corporations. However, it cannot be ascertained from the record before us that portion of the purchase price attributable to such of the software as is tangible, or that portion attributable to that which is intangible.

The difference between the two categories can best be delineated by a simple illustration. A privately commissioned recording, with no restriction on use, of a symphony played by a noted orchestra, has a value far in excess of that of the plastic disc or tape on which it is recorded, and would be subject to assessment for tax purposes at its full cash value. A privately commissioned performance of the same symphony by the same orchestra, however, although it might entail the same expenditure, would produce nothing tangible that could be reached by a tax on personal property.

Another apt analogy may be found in *Michael Todd Co. v. County of Los Angeles*, 57 Cal.2d 684, 21 Cal.Rptr. 604, 371 P.2d 340 (1962), where the Supreme Court of California held that the assessment, for purposes of a tax on tangible personal property, of the negatives of the motion picture "Around the World In Eighty Days" was not limited to the value of the film on which it had been recorded, in a case where possession of the neg-

ative was coupled with a right of reproduction. [Citations.]

The problem posed by this case is of relatively recent vintage, encountered with increasing frequency in a rapidly expanding field. [Citation.] While most states permit some form of taxation on business personal property, policies with respect to the taxation of intangibles vary widely, because such a tax is less uniformly imposed than a tax on tangibles. [Citation.]

It appears that the few courts which have dealt with the taxation of computer software have rejected the idea that software can be reached by a tax on tangible property, *District of Columbia v. Universal Computer Associates, Inc.*, 465 F.2d 615 (D.C.Cir.1972). [Footnote.] *See also County of Sacramento v. Assessment Appeals Bd.*, 32 Cal.App.3d 654, 671, 108 Cal.Rptr. 434, 446 (1973), where the court remanded the cases in order that revaluations of data processing systems be made for purposes of assessing a property tax against the lessor of those systems, excluding the value of "service or 'software' intangibles."

Since 1972, California has, by statute, provided for the valuation, for tax purposes, of storage media, *i. e.*, punched cards, tapes, discs or drums, for computer programs as if there were no programs on such media except basic operational programs. Cal.Revenue & Taxation Code § 995 (West Supp.1974), provides in part:

> Storage media for computer programs shall be valued * * * as if there were no computer program on such media except basic operational programs. Otherwise, computer programs shall not be valued for purpose of property taxation.

* * *

Application programs, *inter alia*, are specifically exempt from valuation for purposes of property taxation. [Footnote.] [Citation.]

We note that the Internal Revenue Service permits a taxpayer to differentiate between hardware and software for purposes of depreciation. Rev.Proc. 69–21, 1969–2 Cum.Bull. 303, provides in part:

> Sec. 4. Costs of Purchased Software.
> 0.1 With respect to costs of purchased soft-

ware, the Service will not disturb the taxpayer's treatment of such costs if the following practices are consistently followed:

1. Where such costs are included, without being separately stated, in the cost of the hardware (computer) and such costs are treated as a part of the cost of the hardware that is capitalized and depreciated; or

2. Where such costs are separately stated, and the software is treated by the taxpayer as an intangible asset the cost of which is to be recovered by amortization deductions ratably over a period of five years or such shorter period as can be established by the taxpayer as appropriate in any particular case if the useful life of the software in his hands will be less than five years.

This leads us to believe that the tax court erred, as a matter of law, when it decided that the cost of the software was inseparable from that of the hardware, and, on this premise, determined to affirm an assessment based on the aggregate purchase price, less depreciation, which was designed to establish the full cash value mandated by Code (1957, 1969 Repl.Vol.) Art. 81, § 14(b)(2).

We recognize that the burden of showing error in the assessment was Greyhound's. [Citation.] Certainly Mr. Misdom's testimony in this area provided scant predicate for an incisive factual determination. There was testimony, however, that some software can now be purchased separately, so that it may well be possible to establish the cost of a software package comparable to that provided by IBM, and then to allocate that cost between the tangible property which is acquired and the services which are to be rendered.

We shall therefore remand the cases in order to give Greyhound and LMC an opportunity to establish by competent evidence, the cost or value of the several items of software, leaving to the tax court the determination of a proper assessable basis for the tangible software.

Tax Court case TP–C 356, Greyhound Computer Corporation v. State Department of Assessments and Taxation, and Tax Court case TP–C 359, LMC Leasing Corporation v. State Department of Assessments and Taxation, remanded as permitted by Maryland Rule 871 a, without affirmance or reversal, for further proceedings. Costs of this appeal to be paid by appellants.

HONEYWELL INFORMATION SYSTEMS, INC. v. BOARD OF ASSESSMENT APPEALS

7 CLSR 486

(Colorado District Court, 1975.)

McLEAN, D. J.

Honeywell Information Systems, Inc. ("Honeywell") initially brought this action in the District Courts of Arapahoe, Boulder, El Paso and Jefferson and of the City and County of Denver for review under Rule 106 of the Colorado Rules of Civil Procedure and pursuant to the provisions of the Administrative Procedure Act, Title 24, Article 4, CRS 1973. All of Honeywell's complaints sought relief from the order of the Board of Assessment Appeals (the "Board") dated April 1, 1974, which dismissed Honeywell's petition for review of assessments by the assessors of the Counties of Arapahoe, Boulder, El Paso and Jefferson (the "outlying counties") and of the City and County of Denver ("Denver"). In each complaint, Honeywell named several parties as defendants who will here be referred to collectively by the county name only.

Upon the stipulated motion of Honeywell and the outlying counties, resisted by Denver, these several actions were consolidated by order of this Court dated September 10, 1974. That same order struck Denver's first affirmative defense alleging lack of jurisdiction of both the Board and this Court to hear Honeywell's tax appeal.

Honeywell makes essentially three contentions of error:

A. That the Board erred by requiring as the standard of proof demonstration of erroneous assessments by "clear and convincing evidence," Honeywell asserting that the proper standard is "preponderance of the evidence."

B. That the Board erred by dismissing the petition after Honeywell showed by clear and convincing evidence that the cost of intangibles had been included in all of the subject assessments, contrary to law.

C. That the Board erred in failing to require reduction of the outlying counties' assessments by an amount reflecting the discounts routinely granted from the list prices which formed the basis for those assessments.

*   *   *

FINDINGS OF FACT

1. Honeywell manufactures, sells and leases electronic data processing equipment ("computers") throughout the United States and leases computers to users in Denver and the outlying counties. It is those leased computers which are the subject of the counties' assessments.

2. Honeywell, like some other manufacturers and computer leasing companies, includes or "bundles" in the price at which it sells or leases computers an amount which represents the value of custom programs, design and implementation of computer systems, design of storage and data retrieval systems, conversion analysis, consulting, feasibility studies, bid evaluations, technical assistance, computer test time, and education and training (reluctantly referred to collectively as "software"). Not every user receives the same amount of each such type of software assistance but the expenses of each such service incurred by Honeywell were reasonably valued by plaintiff at the hearing before the Board.

3. Honeywell publishes a catalog list price for its computers which includes the cost of providing the specified software. It was the catalog list price which the assessors of the outlying counties used as the starting point for their assessments.

4. The lease income capitalized by the Assessor of Denver also includes the cost of providing the specified software.

5. Honeywell routinely discounts from its catalog list price. The catalog list price is a logical point of beginning to determine actual value of the leased computers in the outlying counties. But, in order to determine market value in the ordinary course of trade, that catalog list price must be reduced by the average amount of discounts regularly granted.

6. Arapahoe, Boulder, and El Paso have reduced their assessments by 3%, 3% and 1%, respectively, for education and training, apparently considering that category of software to be intangible and therefore beyond taxation. But those same counties did not make reductions for any other categories of software. And neither Denver nor Jefferson has reduced its assessment for any software.

7. Honeywell incurred reasonable expenses in the amount of $2,586.83 to bring expert witness Frederic G. Withington to testify in the hearing before the Board.

CONCLUSIONS OF LAW

* * *

B. Intangibles.

1. The Colorado General Assembly, pursuant to power granted it by Article X, Section 17 of the Constitution of Colorado, has by Section 39–9–101(i), CRS 1973, specifically exempted from taxation intangible personal property.

2. This is a case of first impression in this State. The only reported Colorado case in which intangibles have been judicially construed preceded enactment of the aforesaid statutory exemption. *Board of Commissioners of Arapahoe County v. Rocky Mountain News*, 15 Colo.App.189, 61 P. 494 (1900). In that case the Court of Appeals held membership in the Associated Press was not a taxable asset, chiefly because it was not subject to levy and sale in the event of a tax deficiency. Application of that judicial reasoning to the facts here requires a finding that the specified software "bundled" into Honeywell's sale and lease prices constitute non-taxable intangibles.

3. Further, this Court relies upon decisions reported from other jurisdictions which are directly in point and compelling on the issue whether similar software provided by computer leasing companies must be separated from the price of the tangible computers themselves, before that taxable tangible property may itself be assessed. The Maryland Court of Appeals in *Greyhound Computer Corporation v. State Department of Assessment and Taxation*, 71 Md. 374, 5 CLSR 615, 320 A.2d 52 (1974), categorized software there offered by the lessor as systems engineering, education and maintenance and then held that the tax court below had erred, as a matter of law, by deciding that the costs of those services were inseparable from the value of the computers themselves. Honeywell demonstrated clearly and convincingly in the hearing before the Board that its sale and lease prices include the cost of providing those above-specified software categories, but the Board

failed to deduct the costs of such software.

This Court also relies upon *District of Columbia v. Universal Computer Associates*, 3 CLSR 549, 465 F.2d 615 (1972), where the court found, as a matter of law, that punch cards containing a computer program constituted intangible personal property not subject to taxation because they were the embodiment of intellectual effort itself clearly intangible. Other relevant decisions have indicated similar results. [Citation.]

4. Arapahoe and Boulder reduced their assessments 3% for the education and training provided by Honeywell for the sale or lease price. These reductions should not be disturbed. That 1% reduction for education and training made by El Paso remains subject to further review and the order of this Court as set forth below.

5. This Court now holds as a matter of law that the cost of providing custom programs, design and implementation of computer systems, design of storage and data retrieval systems, conversion analysis, consulting, feasibility studies, bid evaluations, technical assistance, computer test time, and education and training, which are provided by Honeywell as part of the price paid for sale or lease of computers, must be separated from and deducted from the valuation of the computers by use of catalog list price or capitalization of lease income in order to determine actual value of the computers themselves.

C. Discounts.

1. Honeywell proved clearly and convincingly before the Board that it routinely discounts from list price. The list price therefore exaggerates market and actual value of the tangible computers.

2. To determine actual value of the leased computers, as required by Section 39–1–103(5), CRS 1973, the assessors of the outlying counties must reduce their respective assessments by an amount reasonably reflecting the discounts routinely granted by Honeywell. This Court holds that an established practice of discounting from catalog list price must be considered whenever such list price is utilized by assessors to determine "market value in the ordinary course of trade" pursuant to Section 39–1–103(5), CRS 1973. In analogous circumstances in *Colorado and Utah Coal Co. v. Rorex*, 149 Colo. 502, 369 P.2d 796 (1962), the Supreme Court held failure of the assessor to consider the factor of obsolescence to be error. Rorex authorizes this Court to require consideration by the assessors of the outlying counties of the practice of discounting in order to determine actual value of the leased computers.

3. Denver is not required to reduce its assessment for discounts granted by Honeywell from list price, because the assessor there determined value from capitalization of actual lease income.

Therefore, it is hereby ordered, adjudged and decreed that:

(a) This consolidated appeal be remanded to the Board to be heard in accordance with the findings of fact and conclusions of law contained herein, no later than 60 days from the date of this order with a written decision to be rendered within 15 days of the last day of such hearing on remand;

(b) The Board shall determine the proper amount by which the assessments of all counties-defendant must be reduced to reflect the cost to Honeywell of providing custom programs, design and implementation of computer systems, design of storage and data retrieval systems, conversion analysis, consulting, feasibility studies, bid evaluations, technical assistance, computer test time, and education and training to users of its computers which are included in the sale and lease prices;

(c) The Board shall determine for those assessments of Arapahoe, Boulder, El Paso, and Jefferson the proper deduction to be made for the discounts from catalog list price routinely granted by Honeywell;

(d) This Court shall maintain jurisdiction over this matter as required to effect its order herein;

(e) The counties-defendant shall pay to Honeywell forthwith a total of $2,586.83 as the costs of expert witness Withington, and interest thereon at the statutory rate shall accrue beginning 30 days from the date hereof; and

(f) The parties herein shall have 10 days within which to file motions for rehearing.

HONEYWELL INFORMATION SYSTEMS, INC. v. MARICOPA COUNTY
118 Ariz. 171, 575 P.2d 801
(Court of Appeals of Arizona, Division 1, Department C, Nov. 15, 1977.)

FROEB, C. J.

In this property tax case, appellant Honeywell Information Systems, Inc. (Honeywell) contends that the Maricopa County Assessor overvalued 39 items of computer equipment for 1973 taxes. Honeywell paid the taxes under protest and appealed the assessment to the State Board of Property Tax Appeals. The Board upheld the valuation fixed by Maricopa County and Honeywell appealed to the Superior Court in accordance with A.R.S. §§ 42–146, 42–151 and 42–152. After presentation of Honeywell's case and prior to appellees' case, the court granted judgment in favor of the appellee taxing authorities and against Honeywell. This appeal followed a denial of a motion for new trial.

The fundamental issue raised by Honeywell concerns the purported taxation of intangible services, such as classroom education, systems support engineering services, and computer programs, collectively known as "software" in the computer industry and discussed more fully in the Appendix. Honeywell contends that software is not taxable in Arizona and that the Assessor's inclusion of software in the overall valuation of the 39 pieces of electronic equipment, known as "hardware," resulted in an excessive assessment. Honeywell also contends that in assessing the software appellees knowingly and intentionally discriminated against it in violation of Ariz.Const. art. 9, § 1 and U.S.Const. amend. XIV, since software is not assessed against other taxpayers similarly situated.

On the other hand, appellees contend that it was not necessary for the trial court and it is not necessary for this court to decide whether software is taxable, because the evidence did not prove that the valuation placed on the 39 pieces of equipment represented anything more than the value of the hardware involved. Appellees argue that the question of taxation of intangibles is, therefore, academic. They further argue that Honeywell never overcame the presumption of correctness of the valuation created by A.R.S. § 42–152(B) because

Honeywell failed to prove the value of each of the 39 pieces of equipment but instead proved only a single valuation covering all of them. Finally, they claim that the discrimination issue is not before the court because it is not properly raised.

TAXABILITY OF SOFTWARE

The Arizona unsecured personal property tax statutes (A.R.S. §§ 42–601 through 42–671) and the general administration of tax statutes (A.R.S. §§ 42–101 through 42–163) do not contain a precise definition of the term "personal property." However, under A.R.S. § 42–201, dealing with real property and secured personal property taxes, "personal property" is defined as "property of every kind, both tangible and intangible, not included in the term real estate." Moreover, in accordance with Ariz.Const. art. 9, § 2, the legislature has provided that all property in the state is subject to taxation except for specific exemptions in A.R.S. § 42–271. Our cases have held that exemption is the exception and not the rule and one claiming an exemption must point to a provision of law to sustain the contention. [Citations.] Nevertheless, while Arizona statutes have long authorized taxation of intangibles, our cases have held that intangibles may not be taxed because the legislature has failed to provide a means of equalization for or collection of a tax against intangibles. [Citations.] While recently there have been several amendments to the taxing statutes, appellees refer us to none which would overcome the impediments to taxing intangibles described in the above cases. Tax statutes are to be strictly construed against the taxing authorities and any ambiguities are to be resolved in favor of the taxpayer. [Citation.]

There is little doubt that computer software is intangible property and, as such, should be excluded in determining the value of tangible computer equipment. While this question is one of first impression in this state, every jurisdiction which has considered the issue agrees. [Citations.]

The issue of property taxation of intangible computer software has been the subject of several articles. [Citations.] In each of these articles the author concludes that property taxation of intangible computer software is unjustified. Ironically, the International Association of Assessing Officers (of which the officials in Maricopa County responsible for the assessment in this case are members) has opined in its valuation guidelines for electronic data processing equipment that "[i]n those valuation cases wherein the prices have not yet been unbundled, in the interest of uniformity the assessor has the duty of taking these intangible services out of the value." [Citation.]

A.R.S. § 42–152(B) creates a factual presumption that the valuation made by the appropriate authority is correct and lawful. The presumption is overcome when evidence contradicting the presumption is received. [Citations.] The taxpayer has the burden of proof. [Citations.] Moreover, the taxpayer must show that the valuation was excessive and demonstrate the full cash value of the property. [Citation.] Generally, proof of excessiveness will be an integral part of the proof of true cash value. [Citation.]

There is no dispute as to the method of valuation used by appellees. Honeywell confined all of its proof in Superior Court to the same method; namely, catalog list price less accumulated depreciation. Honeywell's contention is that appellees erroneously included in their starting point (i. e., bundled catalog list price) the value of certain non-taxable items such as computer application programming, systems support engineering services, and classroom education. Honeywell proved which elements are a part of its bundled catalog list price for a computer system and also what portion of the list price is directly allocable to intangible services. Thus the trial court's conclusion that Honeywell failed to show that appellees' valuation of the equipment in question was excessive is unsupported.

Appellees' main argument is that Honeywell was required to show excessive valuation with respect to each item of electronic data processing equipment in question by an appraisal of the equipment. We reject this. The taxpayer's initial burden is only to prove by competent evidence that the assessor's valuation is excessive. [Citations.] Honeywell proved this and met its burden. There is no requirement that the taxpayer or the assessor must have each item of property inspected and appraised. * * * The test of fair market value is not necessarily what an appraiser thinks

the property is worth but rather what the property would sell for between a willing buyer and a willing seller in an arms-length transaction. The sales price at which the same or similar property is offered for sale is ordinarily viewed as the most significant indicator of fair market value. That is why the appellees themselves relied on sales prices as a method of valuing the property involved here. It is apparent that the argument that proof of sales price is insufficient and that appraisal evidence was necessary is incorrect.

Honeywell proved that the bundled catalog list price used by appellees for valuation purposes is attributable in part to separable intangible software services such as computer application programs, systems support engineering services, and classroom education. Honeywell showed that 24.4% of the bundled catalog list price is attributable to these intangible software services and that the intangible software services were provided to the lessees of the 39 items of equipment. Honeywell's systems support manager in Maricopa County testified that he reviewed all of the time records of his department for the lessees of the equipment and determined that Honeywell had provided 38,712 man-hours of systems support engineering services and 15,340 student hours of classroom educational services from January 1, 1973 through April 30, 1974. The services were provided without separate charge to the customer. If these figures are projected over a hypothetical five-year life of a computer system and standard industry charges for the same type of support and educational services provided by unbundled vendors and independent software suppliers are applied (see Appendix), the result is that Honeywell will have provided $4,560,819 worth of systems support and educational services to the lessees of the equipment in question over the lives of those systems. Since the total bundled catalog list price of the 39 items of equipment is $18,765,603, the mathematical projection reveals that the portion of the overall catalog list price of the 39 items which is attributable to intangible software services is approximately 24.3%, a figure almost identical with that determined by Honeywell on the basis of its nationwide study (see Appendix).

We conclude that Honeywell has proved that the appellees' valuation of the electronic data processing equipment is excessive and that the same evidence would also support a determination of the true cash value of the equipment.

SYSTEMATIC DISCRIMINATION

Honeywell contends that the trial court erred in concluding that it failed to show that appellee taxing authorities had knowingly and systematically discriminated against Honeywell in the valuation of the electronic data processing equipment in question.

Initially, appellees claim that the trial court was barred from consideration of the issue because there is no jurisdiction to consider it in a tax appeal under A.R.S. § 42–151. Honeywell injected the issue into the trial court proceedings by an amendment to its notice of appeal which was granted by the trial court over appellees' objection. We find no error in this. Honeywell could have filed a separate action under A.R.S. § 42–204 raising this issue, and it would have been appropriate for the trial court to consolidate the two cases since the proofs are overlapping.

The evidence offered by Honeywell makes it apparent that appellees knowingly and systematically discriminated against Honeywell by assessing personal property taxes against it on a different and more inclusive basis than other similarly situated taxpayers during the same period (see Appendix). In other words, Honeywell was assessed for the software component and other computer companies were not.

It is well established in Arizona that deliberate and systematic discrimination in the assessment and collection of taxes is unlawful. [Citations.]

The facts clearly show discriminatory taxation. Honeywell markets its computer hardware and its separable software services at a single price. On the other hand, large computer manufacturers, such as IBM and Control Data, market their computer hardware at one price and most of their software services at separately stated prices. In valuing the leased computer equipment of companies such as IBM and Control Data, appellees looked only to the catalog list price of those vendors' computer hardware. Appellees made no attempt to tax the unbundled computer vendors on the value of their software services as in

the case of Honeywell. Indeed, the price catalog used by the County Assessor, *Auerbach's Computer Characteristics*, does not even contain prices for software services unless they are included as part of a single bundled price for the services and hardware together.

The testimony of Robert E. Noble, division head of the appellee Department of Property Valuation reflects this:

Q. (Mr. Reed) What do you understand—strike that.

Do you have an understanding of the phrases bundled and unbundled computer vendors?

A. (Mr. Noble) I think I do.

Q. And if you could, explain for us, sir, what that understanding is.

A. Bundled is a company that offers hardware plus the software as a unit, and the unbundled is they just offer the hardware.

Q. When you say as a unit, do I understand you to mean for a single price?

A. Yes.

Q. Do you understand a company like Honeywell to be a bundled vendor?

A. That is my understanding.

* * *

Q. And in reporting the list price, according to the guide lines that you promulgated, what price should a bundled vendor use?

A. Retail selling price.

Q. And that is the retail selling price for the bundle?

A. Yes.

Q. And what price, according to your guide lines, should an unbundled vendor report?

A. Retail selling price.

Q. And that is the retail selling price for the pieces of equipment?

A. Whatever the unit is.

Q. But for the equipment?

A. Yes.

Q. It is not the hundred dollars a day that he may charge somebody to go to his classroom that he reports, it is only—

A. No. We would never know about it, it would never be reported.

The following exchange took place when Mr. Noble was questioned about potential inequitable taxation of a bundled vendor's software:

Q. (Mr. Reed) In promulgating these guide lines, and in seeing to it that the bundled and the unbundled vendor were taxed the same way, and that is what I understand the duties of equalization to be, is that correct?

A. (Mr. Noble) Yes.

Q. In seeing to it that the bundled and the unbundled vendor are taxed in the same manner, was any effort made in the guide lines you promulgated to see to it, or to require the unbundled vendor to report not only the list price for his equipment but the list price for the classroom education and also the list price for the system support, and finally the list price of the computer programs, or according to your guide lines is the unbundled vendor only required to report the list price for his equipment?

A. Well, the answer to your first question was no. And the second question, he is only to report his original retail selling price.

Q. So when you say the answer to my first question was no and the second was yes—

A. There was no special effort to correct this problem.

Q. Okay. Was there any other kind of effort, special, less than special, a whole bunch less than special, or any kind of effort at all to correct this problem?

A. I think we knew the problem was there, but we just didn't have time to get to it.

Moreover, the testimony of the head of the personal property section of the Maricopa County Assessor's Office shows that the County Assessor not only knew that bundled vendors, such as Honeywell, were being taxed on a more stringent basis than unbundled vendors, such as IBM and Control Data, but, in addition, that the County Assessor's Office supposedly had a policy of not taxing intangible software services. Finally, the evidence indicates that appellees made no effort to assess personal property tax on the value of software services supplied by the many independent software houses and service bureaus operating in Maricopa County. We think the showing of tax discrimination is clear.

DISCOUNTS OFF THE CATALOG PRICE

Honeywell challenged the valuation on the additional ground that the Assessor should have taken Honeywell's established discount policies into consideration before using catalog list prices to determine the full cash value of the equipment for property tax purposes.

Honeywell offered considerable evidence that it publishes discounts for educational and nonprofit technological institutions, for purchasers of certain systems who pay cash within 90 days after purchase and for certain competitive purchasers, such as governmental entities. Honeywell's evidence indicates that the "discounts are available to all commercial customers as well as government customers. They're available to everyone." The testimony at trial dwelled on the 39 individual leases of equipment and whether and to what extent the lessees actually enjoyed a discount of some kind in their contracts with Honeywell. The testimony showed that discounts, other than for cash sales, vary considerably, depending upon the equipment and the customers involved in the transaction. The effect of discount policies and actual discounts given to the lessees involved here, whether they may or may not affect fair market value of the equipment, was not specifically determined by the trial court in its findings of fact and conclusions of law. As this is a factual determination which must be made by the trial court on remand, we will not attempt to evaluate Honeywell's evidence in this respect except to state generally our perception of the relevance of that evidence.

The issue is the correct fair market value of the equipment in question. Honeywell has already presented a prima facie showing that the valuation by the appellees is excessive. Having done so, it must prove the fair market value of the equipment. We have stated it may do this by reference to catalog price, particularly since appellees have used catalog price in their valuation. We have further stated that the catalog price of Honeywell's equipment should be reduced to reflect the value of software included in that price. With respect to discounts, we direct the trial court to consider the proof relating to discounts to determine if the fair market value (full cash value) of the equipment is more correctly arrived at by reducing the catalog price by discounts. Fair market value is best indicated by sales price, not list price. [Citations.] Sales price means *cash* sales price. Fair market value is full *cash* value. Thus, if the equipment involved would change hands between the seller and the buyer for cash at a price less than the unbundled catalog price, the valuation should so reflect. On the other hand, if a seller discounts equipment to a buyer at a price below the fair market value in order to develop its market or gain an entry to the customer's business, it may be that such a discount from the unbundled catalog price would not be reflective of fair market value. We are prepared only to say now that the trial court must weigh and evaluate the proof concerning discounts in order to arrive at its determination of fair market value.

* * *

APPENDIX

A statement of the facts presented by Honeywell in its brief furnishes the background necessary for a general understanding of the technical aspects of the case.

Appellant Honeywell manufactures, sells and leases electronic data processing equipment and also provides its customers a wide range of related services and activities. The electronic data processing industry as a whole is made up of a variety of companies and businesses, large and small, which offer numerous types of products and/or services to users of electronic data processing equipment. These products and services include the electronic data processing equipment itself (often referred to as the computer "hardware") and the professional and technological services, such as classroom education, systems support engineering services, and computer programs (often collectively referred to as the computer "software"). The data processing equipment or so-called "hardware" comprising a data processing unit consists of a central processing unit or main frame and peripherals such as input and output terminals and memory storage devices. Classroom education consists of courses designed to teach the operation and programming of data processing equipment.

Systems support engineering services are provided by personnel who assist the computer user in the programming and usage of the data processing equipment. Computer programs are the instructions which make the data processing equipment perform tasks and include "operational programs" which are the basic functions of the computer and "application programs" which are the particularized instructions adapted for an individual user.

In order to have an effective electronic data processing system, a user must have a central processing unit, input and output consoles, memory devices, as well as educational training, systems support engineering services and both operational and application programs. It is not necessary, however, that all of these products and services be provided to the customer by the same company or supplier and it is often the case that the customer obtains them from different suppliers.

Among the many companies and businesses which make up the electronic data processing industry, some, like Honeywell, offer the full spectrum of products and services; others, who are sometimes referred to within the industry as "software houses" or "service bureaus," provide mostly services such as computer programming, systems support engineering services and classroom education.

At the present time, the electronic data processing industry is dominated by several large companies which manufacture and sell computer hardware as well as provide a full range of programming support and educational services. The principal companies in the industry are IBM Corporation, Honeywell, Sperry-Rand, Burroughs and Control Data Corporation.

The method by which companies in the electronic data processing industry market and sell their products and services differs dramatically. Some companies which provide a full range of products and services choose to market and sell those products and services on a "bundled" basis, while other such companies choose to market and sell their products and services on an "unbundled" basis. A "bundled vendor" is one that charges a single, overall price for the computer hardware and the related software such as classroom education, systems support engineering services and computer application programs. An "unbundled vendor" is one that charges a separate price for the variety of computer hardware and software services which that vendor provides.

There exist varying degrees of bundling and unbundling among vendors in the electronic data processing industry. Typically, the most unbundled of the large computer companies is Control Data which charges a separately stated price for each item of equipment and for the operating programs, for the application programs and for every element of support and educational service. The marketing practices of IBM are somewhat similar, generally charging a single price for the computer hardware and operating programs and charging a separately stated price for each application program and each element of systems support and educational service. The most bundled of the large computer companies is Honeywell. That is to say that Honeywell markets and sells its products and services in such a manner that the customer pays one overall price for the computer hardware and internal operating programs together with the application programs and any systems support engineering services or classroom education which the customer may need during the life of the system.

For the most part, the prices for the various items of computer hardware and computer systems which are offered for sale by the large computer companies are contained in elaborate price lists which are published by the companies themselves. In addition, there are commercial publications, such as *Auerbach's Computer Characteristics*, which contain list prices at which computer companies have announced they will sell their products. The prices contained in the catalogs published by Honeywell (as well as the prices contained in the commercial publications such as *Auerbach's* insofar as they relate to Honeywell) are bundled prices for a complete data processing system, including computer hardware and related application programs, systems support engineering services and classroom education. There are also separate commercial price catalogs which contain data relating to the software services and separate charges of companies like IBM and Control Data who, unlike Honeywell, do not provide software services as part of a single overall price.

The large, unbundled computer companies,

such as IBM and Control Data, in addition to charging a separately stated price for most application programs performed for a customer, charge the customer a separately stated daily or hourly rate for systems support engineering services and classroom education. In the tax year in question (1973), the standard charge to its customers by IBM for systems support engineering services was $33 per hour. So also, the separately stated charge for classroom education within the electronic data processing industry was a standard rate of between $100 and $150 per student per day. Similarly, the typical charge by independent computer service bureaus in Maricopa County in 1973 for systems support engineering services was between $30 and $40 an hour and the typical charge by unbundled vendors and private data processing schools in Maricopa County in 1973 for classroom educational services was between $75 and $150 per student per day. In each instance, the type of systems support and educational services provided by the unbundled vendors and service bureaus at a separately stated price are the same type of systems support and educational services provided by Honeywell as part of its single overall bundled price.

In the case of a typical, complete data processing system, a user who obtains all of his products and services on an unbundled basis will generally spend about 65–70% of the total cost and charges for the system over its life for the computer hardware (including internal operational programs) and the remaining 30–35% of the total cost and charges during the system's life for application programs, systems support engineering services and educational activities. In any given case, however, the percentage of a complete electronic data processing system's cost and charges during the life of the system which is attributable to application programs, systems support engineering services and educational activities will vary considerably depending on the nature of the system and the sophistication of the user.

In 1971, and again in the winter of 1972, auditors for Honeywell conducted studies concerning the portion of Honeywell's bundled catalog list price for its data processing systems which is attributable to intangible items such as application programs, systems sup port engineering services and classroom educational services. In conducting these studies the auditors utilized weekly reports of hours work prepared in the ordinary course of business by Honeywell's field personnel (referred to by Honeywell as the Weekly Activity Reporting System or simply WAR System). From the WAR records, the auditors determined, by reference to 10 separate categories of software services[1] which percentage of the time spent by all of the various types of Honeywell's field personnel was attributable to non-manufacturing, non-sales and marketing, and non-maintenance efforts—or, in other words, which portion of the field personnel time was allocable to software services such as application programming, systems support engineering services and classroom educational services. This information relating to the percentage of time spent by Honeywell field personnel in providing intangible software services was then applied to Honeywell's overall expense figures for its field personnel during the same period of time. Finally, once the portion of field personnel expense attributable to intangible software services was determined, this figure was applied against the dollar volume of Honeywell's net shipments of computer systems during that period as reflected in the Honeywell financial records, which dollar volume of net shipments was arrived at on the basis of bundled catalog list price for all products and services provided by Honeywell during that time period. The results of these studies, taken together, disclosed that 24.4% of the bundled catalog list price for Honeywell's data processing systems is attributable to intangible software services such as application programs, systems support engineering services and classroom educational services.[2] Or, stated conversely, only 75.6% of Honeywell's bundled catalog list price is attributable to computer hardware and operational programs.

In addition to the fact that catalog list price for a Honeywell computer system reflects the bundled price for computer hardware and software services, Honeywell's marketing practices include an established, well-defined and consistent discount policy whereby the catalog list price for a Honeywell computer system is reduced by as much as 20% for certain types of customers such as schools and colleges and purchasers who acquire certain complete lines of Honeywell computer systems. These discount policies are formally published in the various catalogs containing Honeywell list prices. Moreover, the discounts are available to all qualified Honeywell customers, without exception.

In the instant case, Honeywell is the owner of certain electronic data processing equipment which it leased to customers at 39 locations within Maricopa County in 1973. In accordance with the Assessor's policy of tax-

---

1. The ten categories of software services, as defined by Honeywell, are:

1. Custom Programs—The writing (coding) and testing of customized programs is a service, requiring the development or ascertainment of information, and the evaluation of data, in addition to other development skills.

2. Designing and implementing computer systems, (e. g., determining equipment and personnel required and how they will be utilized.)

3. Designing storage and data retrieval systems, (e. g., determining what data communication system and input/output devices are required.)

4. Converting manual systems to automated data processing systems; converting present automated data processing systems to new systems, (e. g., changing a 2nd generation system to a 3rd generation system.)

5. Consulting services, (e. g., study of all or part of a data processing system.)

6. Feasibility studies, (e. g., studies to determine what benefits would be derived if procedures were automated.)

7. Evaluation of bids, (e. g., studies to determine which manufacturer's proposal for computer equipment would be most beneficial.)

8. Providing technical help, analysts and programmers.

9. Computer time required to test programs prior to installation of system.

10. Educational services.

2. With reference to the ten categories of software services set forth in Footnote 1, the individual percentages of bundled catalog list price making up the 24.4% are as follows:

(1) custom programs	.7%
(2) designing and implementing computer systems	2.3%
(3) designing storage and data retrieval systems	2.3%
(4) converting manual systems	9.8%
(5) consulting services	1.3%
(6) feasibility studies	.9%
(7) evaluation of bids	.8%
(8) technical help	.7%
(9) computer test time	2.7%
(10) educational services	2.9%
TOTAL	24.4%

payer self-assessment, Honeywell timely filed its 1973 unsecured personal property tax report, computing the undepreciated value of the equipment by taking the bundled catalog list price and reducing that figure by 24.4% to reflect the value of the intangible software services included in the bundled list price and by an additional 10% to reflect the average of the discounts given by Honeywell under its established discount policy.[3] A standard 5-year depreciation factor for such equipment (mandated by guidelines of the Appellee Department of Property Valuation) was then applied to arrive at the full cash value of the equipment which was reported by Honeywell in its tax return. Honeywell's reported valuation for 1973 was $2,165,587.

The Maricopa County Assessor determined, however, that the electronic data processing equipment in question should be valued at Honeywell's bundled catalog list price less only the appropriate amount of depreciation determined in accordance with Appellees' standard 5-year depreciation formula. Accordingly, the Assessor disallowed Honeywell's deduction from its bundled catalog list price of 24.4% for application programming, systems support engineering services and classroom education as well as Honeywell's deduction from catalog list price to reflect the average of discounts regularly given to its customers. The Assessor then entered his full cash value determination of the equipment in question on the 1973 unsecured personal property tax rolls in the total amount of $3,301,200, with each computer system at the 39 customer locations in question being reflected by a separate tax roll number from 63027 to 63066.

Honeywell paid its 1973 unsecured personal property taxes on the electronic data processing equipment in question timely and under protest. Honeywell appealed the Appellee taxing authority's determination of the full cash value of the equipment to the State Board of Property Tax Appeals and the Board upheld the value placed upon the equipment by Appellee. Upon appeal, the Superior Court entered judgment in favor of Appellees.

ACCOUNTANTS COMPUTER SERVICES, INC. v. KOSYDAR

35 Ohio St.2d 120, 298 N.E.2d 519
(Supreme Court of Ohio, July 3, 1973.)

Each of these cases arises out of a sales and/or use tax assessment made by the Tax Commissioner of the state of Ohio. Each also involves a transaction, in the course of which there is transferred, printed or other productions or reproductions of written or graphic matter. The relevant facts pertaining to each individual case are as follows:

In case No. 72–263, Accountant's Computer Services, Inc. (ACS), a data processing company, receives raw data in the form of punch paper tapes or adding machines tapes upon which are recorded debits and credits which constitute records of current financial transactions of a particular business enterprise.

Thereafter, ACS, on its premises, transcribes the information from the tapes onto key punched cards, and, with the use of data processing machines, it sorts, systematically classifies and rearranges this data.

Print-outs of this rearranged data are furnished to the accountant-customer of ACS and in that form are used by the customer as drafts of financial statements, books of original entry, cash receipt journals, sales journals, cash disbursement journals and general ledgers. Historically, the function above described was a part of the accounting profession. Known as "write-up work," it was performed manually by the accountant or his staff. The print-out, now furnished by ACS, duplicates the accountant's write-up efforts.

The Tax Commissioner assessed the entire charge made by ACS as a sale. ACS appealed to the Board of Tax Appeals, arguing that the assessment was arbitrary, unreasonable, unconstitutional and not according to law in that its "activities constitute a service, and said services are specifically exempt under Sect. 5739.01(B), O.R.C." The board affirmed the assessment order of the Tax Commissioner.

Case No. 72–660, Central Data Systems, Inc. (CDS), also involves a data processing

---

3. The 10% discount figure was subsequently amended   to 8.1% by Honeywell at the trial in the court below.

company. CDS obtains information from its customers for analysis of business problems and the data is furnished by the customer in a continuous ongoing manner.

The activity of CDS is described by the board in its decision, as follows:

The taxpayer is engaged in the business of providing both computing and software (brains and paper) sales and services which fall into four categories: (1) Data Processing is the operator's time, machine time, and the various reports and supplies billed generally on a monthly basis. (2) Key Punching is where the operator's time usually is billed at an hourly rate or 1000 card price. In this procedure the company takes the data, paper, or document, and has it transcribed into punched cards. (3) Systems Design and Programming primarily consists of program and system time by the hour; sometimes on a flat fee. The company's professional workers apply thinking to the customer's present system and then write instructions to automate the systems as in the case of upgrading machines from hand bookkeeping. (4) Contracts, which are not involved herein, are the outside consulting division done almost always at the clients' place of business which is billed for the consultants time only by the hour where no forms are used. Both (3) and (4) are considered software but 3 does provide certain computer printouts in addition to consultation.

* * * The testimony was uncontradicted that the appellant provided its operation on a twenty four hour day, seven day each week basis and that during the audit period appellant had 35 to 40 employees.

Again, the Tax Commissioner assessed the entire charge made by CDS as a sale, and the board, finding that CDS's activities constituted a transfer of tangible personal property which was not eligible for exception under R.C. 5739.01(B) as an inconsequential transfer, affirmed the assessment in its entirety.

In case No. 72–860, Andrew Jergens Company (AJC) contracted with A. C. Neilsen Company, a market research organization whose function is to provide services which consist of compiling statistical data as to the movement of consumer products into and from drug stores, food stores and mass merchandiser stores; to interpret this data in order to determine marketing information as to these products on a national basis and in specific

geographic areas; and to analyze, interpret and present to its customers the statistical information compiled and assist management in making marketing decisions based on this data.

During the audit period, AJC utilized the services of Neilsen with respect to both hand lotions and toilet soaps. As to each of these products, it prescribed specifications for the information it wanted from Neilsen—as to the product class, the particular brands of products within each such class, and the sizes of each such brand. It also prescribed that the information was to be assembled on a nationwide basis and in accordance with specific sales territories. These specifications were changed from time to time during the audit period as to each of the products. The information requested by AJC included information not only as to its own products but also as to products of its competitors.

As an integral part of the service furnished, Neilsen assigned two account executives to AJC's account, whose duty it was to analyze, interpret and present to AJC's management the information developed by Neilsen in a meaningful and useful manner.

Once again, and for the same reasons, the Board of Tax Appeals affirmed the assessment order.

The causes are now before this court upon appeals from the Board of Tax Appeals.

* * *

STERN, J.

The essential issue common to each of these three cases is the applicability of the exception from taxation provided by R.C. 5739.01(B) for items of tangible personal property which are transferred, as an inconsequential element for which no separate charge is made, in conjunction with a transaction which also involves some significant degree of contracted-for service. Resolution of this issue necessitates an examination of the taxing scheme provided by statute in Ohio.

The Board of Tax Appeals, in its decisions, placed controlling weight upon the combined impact of two clauses found in R.C. 5739.01(B), *i. e.*, the amendatory "printed matter" [1] language, and the amendatory "excepting" [2] language following the phrase "Other than as provided in this section, * * *."

The board's argument is summarized by the following language from its decision in these cases: "The prefatory language in the 'personal service transaction' stating 'Other than as provided in this section * * *' *clearly* and *unambiguously dictates* that where a particular transaction is defined as a 'sale' by another phrase of Section 5739.01(B), Revised Code, then the 'personal service transaction' exemption [exception] is not applicable."

The board's decision interprets the language of R.C. 5739.01(B) to require (1) taxation of all transactions involving "printed matter," regardless of inconsequentiality, and (2) that when such "printed matter" is transferred in conjunction with a service transaction the *entire* consideration paid is taxable, including that portion which may clearly and separately have been paid as compensation for the personal service rendered.

We cannot agree that the General Assembly intended such a serious and far-reaching construction of R.C. 5739.01(B), *i. e.*, the imposition of a sales tax on professional, insurance, and personal service transactions, which, inconsequentially or otherwise, involved a transfer of "printed matter." It is our conclusion that the language of the statute neither compels nor alludes to the interpretation given it by the Board of Tax Appeals.

It is important to note that the so-called "personal service exception" language is misnamed, for the "item" which is excepted from taxation by that language is not the service. Rather, it is the "item" of tangible personal property which is transferred, as an inconsequential element for which no separate charge is made, incidental to the performance of a professional, insurance, or personal service transaction. The service never was taxed *per se*, and therefore cannot be excepted.

Essentially, the problem regarding the "printed matter" and the "personal service exception" amendments involves the question of what was the intention of the General Assembly. It should be noted that the "exception" language, as found in the original amendment to R.C. 5739.01(B), read: "Other than as *herein provided,* * * *." (Emphasis added.) (128 Ohio Laws 424.) That language was amended, effective January 10, 1961, to read: "Other than as *provided in this section* * * *." (Emphasis added.) (129 Ohio Laws 974.) It appears, therefore, that the "exception" was to apply to *all* inconsequential transfers of tangible personal property *unless* some other portion of R.C. 5739.01 provided to the contrary. Finding no such provision as to "printed matter," we must conclude that "printed matter" *can* be the subject of such an excepted inconsequential transfer. The General Assembly has merely provided a means whereby it can, if and when it deems it necessary, specifically remove some class of tangible personal property from the breadth of the "exception."

That conclusion is not only called for by a strict interpretation of the statutory language, but it comports with the general intent of the Ohio tax scheme that sales taxes were not intended to be collected where the difficulty would be great compared to the insignificant revenue to be gained. Indeed, even if the language were subject to a different interpretation, the resulting ambiguity, of necessity, need be resolved in favor of the taxpayer, for no tax may be assessed by implication.

Furthermore, the "exception" language is not new to taxation. Prior to its being incorporated in R.C. 5739.01(B) in 1959, similar language was found in R.C. 5739.02(B)(13), to wit: The sales tax did not apply to "Professional, insurance, or personal service transactions which involve *sales* as inconsequential elements, for which no separate charges are made." (Emphasis added.) In the amendatory language in R.C. 5739.01(B), the word

---

1. The 1959 amendment to R.C. 5739.01(B) (128 Ohio Laws 421, 423) specified that the definition of "sale" and "selling" include: " * * * all transactions by which printed, imprinted, overprinted, lithographic, multi-lithic, blueprinted, photostatic, or other productions or reproductions of written or graphic matter are or are to be furnished or transferred."

2. The 1959 amendment to R.C. 5739.01(B) (128 Ohio Laws 421, 424) specifically excepted from taxation: " * * * professional, insurance, or personal service transactions which involve the transfer of tangible personal property as an inconsequential element, for which no separate charges are made."

"sales" was replaced with the words "transfer of tangible personal property * * *," thereby emphasizing that *the exception was to apply not just to transactions involving items defined as sales, but to all transfers of "tangible personal property as an inconsequential element [of a service transaction], for which no separate charges are made."* (Emphasis added.)

Both before and after that amendment, this court has interpreted the applicable language to include potential exception for *all* items of tangible personal property. In *City Blue Printing Co. v. Bowers* (1955), 163 Ohio St. 6, 125 N.E.2d 181, this court considered the personal service exception as then found in R.C. 5739.02(B)(13). The holding therein did not say that all sales of printed matter, however inconsequential, were to be subject to taxation. This is evidenced by the inclusion in the syllabus of distinguishing factual language, and the following language [citation] in that opinion, which provides:

> Although appellant did advise its customers *as to the copying process which was best suited* to their needs, the production of the copies themselves was largely mechanical. The machines or devices employed did the work, and those operating them were not required to be persons of extraordinary ability or expertness. (Emphasis added.)

We conclude that the intent of the General Assembly, in adopting the "printed matter" amendment of 1959, was to incorporate the decision in *City Blue Printing Co., supra,* but we find no reason to believe that they intended to go beyond the holding in that case and make any and all transfers of "printed matter" taxable merely because it is "printed matter."

Accordingly, we reject the argument of the Tax Commissioner as adopted by the Board of Tax Appeals. This is not, however, dispositive of the instant cases, for it must also be determined whether the "exception" language is applicable to any of these three cases.

The problem lies in the fact that most transactions, to at least a limited extent, involve a mixed degree of *some* personal service and the transfer of *some* tangible personal property. No doubt, the difficulty of endeavoring to separate the entire charge in all mixed transactions, and the insignificant dollar amount of tax which would be realized by tax-

ing inconsequential amounts of personal property, prompted the General Assembly to enact the so-called "personal service exception."

On this point, it is worth noting that the law of Ohio is in accord with California law as evidenced by 2 CCH (1972) All-State Sales Tax Reporter, 25–012 [footnote], which provides that, in California, in determining whether a particular transaction involves a sale of tangible personal property *or* the transfer of tangible personal property incidental to the performance of a service, a distinction must be made as to the *true object* of the transaction contract:

> * * * that is, *is the real object sought by the buyer the service per se or the property produced by the service. If the true object of the contract is the service per se, the transaction is not subject to tax even though some tangible personal property is transferred.* (Emphasis added.)

Quoting further, we find that in California:

> * * * *When a transaction is [overall] regarded as a sale of tangible personal property, tax applies to the [entire] gross receipts from the furnishing thereof, without any deduction on account of the work, labor, skill, thought, time spent, or other expense of producing the property.* (Emphasis added.)

Recent cases in Ohio demonstrate that we also tax the *entire* consideration paid in transactions which, of necessity, involved some insignificant and inconsequential amount of personal service, without deducting from the total consideration paid an amount attributed to the inconsequential personal service provided. [Citations.]

This long standing practice acknowledges that: (1) Nearly all transactions are, of necessity, mixed transactions involving at least a slight degree of personal service, and (2) where this degree of personal service is of insignificant consequence, both the practical problem of attributing to such service a percentage of the entire consideration paid, and the insignificant effect it would have on the amount paid in taxes, make such a distinction unreasonable and unnecessary.

This problem was well analyzed in *Goodyear Aircraft Corp. v. Arizona State Tax Comm.* (1965), 1 Ariz.App. 302, 306, 402 P.2d 423, 427, which set forth the following *possibilities* regarding mixed sales of services and property:

> 1. The service is the main item sold and the property sold is incidental thereto and not separately charged. (not a taxable sale as a sale of services.)
> 2. The services and property sold can be readily separated. (one tax exempt and the other taxable.)
> 3. The service sold is incidental to the property and not separately charged. (taxable in gross.)

That court, recognizing that the category into which a vendor falls is a *question of fact* to be determined in light of all the evidence, then stated:

> *When there is a fixed and ascertainable relationship between the value of the article and the value of the service rendered in connection therewith so that both may be separately stated,* then the vendor is engaged in both selling at retail and furnishing services and is subject to the tax as to one and tax exempt as to the other. *Where the property and the services are distinct and each is a consequential element capable of ready separation, it cannot be said one is an inconsequential element within the exemption provided by the statute.* [Citation.]

It can be argued that the cases at hand should be treated as falling into the second of the possibilities set forth above, *i. e.,* separable. However, such an argument needs to be supported by a factual analysis which finds that the property transferred and the personal service rendered are distinct, consequential elements having a fixed and ascertainable relationship between the value of the property and the value of the service rendered, so that both may be separately stated. Cases cannot, however, be so categorized on the theory that no personal service, however inconsequential to the overall transaction, should ever be taxed.

Rice v. Evatt (1945), 144 Ohio St. 483, 59 N.E.2d 927, which is an example of a factual situation falling within the second possibility is readily distinguishable from the three cases at hand. It involved an optometrist who did not separate his charge for professional examination from his charge for glasses and other items of personal property transferred. Two separate and distinct transactions were being performed therein; one, a purely professional service, and the other purely a sale of tangible personal property. However, whether treated as a separable mixed transaction (the second possibility) or as two independent transactions, the fact they were singularly billed was of no consequence. The cases now before us, however, do not fall within this possibility, and cannot be so easily disposed of. Nor was it intended that they be so disposed of.

The General Assembly has long been aware of this court's interpretation of the so-called "personal service exception" language, and of this court's application of the economical and functional inconsequentiality test which, prior to and after the amendment of the "exception" language, was utilized to determine the *true object* of mixed transactions for taxation purposes. Had they wished to effect a change in this manner of taxing insignificant service transactions which, of necessity, occur in conjunction with a consequential sale of tangible personal property, they would have done so.

If the Ohio taxation scheme is to be recognized, the cases we have before us this day must be decided by application of the same tests as have heretofore been used. Having concluded that a sale has occurred, it must then be determined whether a consequential professional, insurance, or personal service is involved. If not, then the exception cannot be available, and the *entire* transaction is taxable. If, however, such a consequential service *is* rendered, then it must further be ascertained whether the transfer of the tangible personal property is an inconsequential element of the transaction. If so, then the "exception" provides that none of the consideration paid is taxable.

To accomplish this, the Tax Commissioner, the Board of Tax Appeals, and this court, as necessary, must examine the *real object sought by the buyer, i. e.,* the service *per se* or the property produced by the service, and determine if it was the buyer's object to obtain an act done personally by an individual as an economic service involving either the intellectual or manual personal effort of an individual, or if it was the buyer's object to obtain only the saleable end product of some individual's skill. [Citation.]

In accordance with the analysis set forth herein, we dispose of each of these cases upon the basis of the particular factual situations in each, as evidenced by the record.

CASE NO. 72–263, ACCOUNTANT'S COMPUTER SERVICE, INC. (ACS).

In case No. 72–263 (ACS), the taxpayer receives raw material and transcribes it onto key punched cards, which, *by the use of a data processing machine*, are sorted, classified and rearranged. This print-out is then *delivered to the supplier of the raw material*, and it is *he* who then studies, alters, analyzes, and adjusts it. No such studying, alterations, analysis, adjustments, or other potentially consequential personal services are contracted for or assumed by ACS.

This lack of a consequential personal service is further evidenced by the fact that the object contracted for was the rearranged form of the raw material, *i. e.*, "write-up work" previously performed manually by the accountant (buyer, in this instance) or his staff, and it was valuable not because it was produced *by* ACS, but merely because it was produced.

The production of this end product was almost entirely accomplished by the data processing machine, and although persons may have special training in operating this machine, their training is not related to the *real object* sought, *i. e.*, the rearrangement of the raw material.

In short, ACS represents a classic example of man's use of his intellectual skill to conceive of a process whereby a task, which heretofore took longer, can now be accomplished in a relatively short time. As a result of this development, ACS can offer for sale the *end product* of this skill, *i. e.*, "write-up work."

We conclude that such a process, at best, represents a mixed transaction in which the limited *personal service* was inconsequential to the object sought and sold. Accordingly, we hold that the *entire* transaction is taxable, with no inconsequential allowance for the insignificant personal service rendered.

CASE NO. 72–660, CENTRAL DATA SYSTEM, INC. (CDS).

The statement of facts, as pertains to case No. 72–660 (CDS), contains an essential added element of utmost importance. That is, CDS obtains information from its clients for *analysis* of business problems. The company's professional workers apply *thinking* to the customer's present system.

It was this *analysis* and *thinking* by individuals skilled in solving business problems that was the *real object* sought in this instance. The data processing machines and their print-outs were used to assist CDS personnel in rendering their personal service, reducing their time spent on manual sorting work so as to allow more time for the application of their skills at solving their client's business problems. The transferred "printed matter," in this instance, was valuable not because it existed, but because it existed as a result of the personal service efforts of CDS personnel.

The personal service was the main item contracted for, and the "printed matter" constituted an inconsequential element for which no separate charge was made. Accordingly, we hold that the sale of the tangible personal property is to be excepted from taxation by R.C. 5739.01(B), resulting in no taxation of any portion of the consideration paid.

CASE NO. 72–860, THE ANDREW JERGENS CO. (AJC).

The third and final case, case No. 72–860 (AJC), is an even clearer example of a transaction in which the *real object* sought was the service *per se*, and not the end product produced by the service. The facts show that AJC contracted with A. C. Neilsen Company, a market research organization, whose function was to provide services which consisted of *compiling statistical data;* to *interpret* this data in order to determine marketing information; to *analyze, interpret* and *present* to its customers (AJC) the statistical information compiled, and to *assist* AJC's *management* in making marketing decisions based on this data. Specific requests were made by AJC, which requests changed from time to time, and two of Neilsen's account executives, whose duty it was to *analyze, interpret* and *present* to AJC's management the information developed by Neilsen in a meaningful and useful manner, were assigned to AJC's account.

Clearly, it was the personal service of Neilsen and its staff which was contracted for in this instance. It was the intellectual and manual personal efforts of employees of Neilsen that was sought by AJC, and not the inconsequential tangible personal property which was transferred, for purposes of communication, as an incidental element without a separate charge. Accordingly, we conclude that, here too, the sale of the transferred tangible personal property is to be excepted from taxation by R.C. 5739.01(B), resulting in no taxation of any portion of the consideration paid.

For the reasons set forth herein, we hold that the decision of the Board of Tax Appeals in case No. 72–263 (ACS) is reasonable and lawful, and therefore is affirmed. In cases Nos. 72–660 (CDS) and 72–860 (AJC), the decisions of the Board of Tax Appeals are unreasonable and unlawful, and therefore are reversed.

CITIZENS FINANCIAL CORP. v. KOSYDAR

43 Ohio St.2d 148, 331 N.E.2d 435
(Supreme Court of Ohio, July 16, 1975.)

This case involving a sales tax assessment against Champion Service Corporation, a wholly-owned subsidiary of appellant, Citizens Financial Corporation, hereinafter, "taxpayer," in the amount of $47,698.21, on transactions between taxpayer and its savings and loan organization customers. The audit period is from July 1, 1967, through August 31, 1969.

Citizens Financial is a data processing company utilizing computer equipment which is made available to the thrift industry (savings and loan associations) and to a small number of commercial accounts. The equipment is used in two ways, designated as the "off-line" method and the "on-line" method.

In the "off-line" method, the tellers at the customer savings and loan manually record the daily deposits and withdrawals, and the recorded transactions are daily delivered to the taxpayer, where the information is converted by the computer into "computer legible media." Subsequently, taxpayer delivers to the customer a "hard copy printout" which provides the customer with an accounting journal of daily transactions, thus updating the individual account records. A fee is charged, based on the number of such accounts each customer maintains in the computer.

The "on-line method" consists of teller use of terminals which are located at the tellers'

windows. Passbooks are placed in the terminals and by means of depression of appropriate keys, the transaction (deposit, withdrawal or loan payment) is transmitted via telephone lines to taxpayer's computers. The computers then make the programmed calculation, printing the transaction on both the customer's passbook and upon a print-out at the terminal. Subsequently, a hard copy journal of transactions is delivered by taxpayer to the customer. A fee is charged, as in the off-line method.

The Board of Tax Appeals affirmed the sales tax assessment and the cause is now before this court upon an appeal as of right.

* * *

PER CURIAM.

Taxpayer's contention with respect to the off-line computerization method is that the "printout" received by the customer is an inconsequential element of a personal service transaction for which no separate charge is made, and is therefore excepted from the sales tax under R.C. 5739.01(B). Taxpayer contends also that the use of its equipment by customers in connection with the on-line method does not constitute a license for such use, but is a part of its programming and related personal service, and such use is an inconsequential element for which no separate charge is made and is excepted from sales tax under R.C. 5739.01(B).

OFF-LINE METHOD.

Accountant's Computer Services v. Kosydar (1973), 35 Ohio St.2d 120, 298 N.E.2d 519, provides the criteria for determining whether a sale of tangible personal property is excepted from taxation under the last sentence of R.C. 5739.01(B). Such sentence reads, in pertinent part (" 'Sale' and 'selling' do not include professional, insurance, or personal service transactions which involve the transfer of tangible personal property as an inconsequential element, for which no separate charges are made." There is no question here that a consequential service was rendered.

Paragraph one of the syllabus in *Accountant's* recites, in part: "If a consequential service is rendered, then it must be ascertained whether the transfer of the tangible personal property was an inconsequential element of the transaction." Paragraph two of the syllabus then leads us to the more specific determination which is necessary for ascertaining whether in a mixed transaction (including both personal service and transfer of tangible personal property), as here, the transfer of tangible personal property is an inconsequential element of the transaction. The test recited in *Accountant's* is whether " * * * the real object sought by the buyer [is] the service *per se* or the property produced by the service." As stated in the syllabus a distinction must be made as to the "*true object* of the transaction contract."

The board concluded that the real object sought by the taxpayer's customers was the property produced, *i. e.*, "hard copy print-outs." There was no claim by taxpayer of being consulted with respect to analysis or problem solving. As noted by the board: " * * * Appellant did sort, classify and arrange the data to conform to the needs of its clients, but it did not advise the clients regarding what direction the clients should take in formulating their approach to the business world." The board correctly resolved the factual determination on the basis of the test set forth in *Accountant's*, and such resolution is supported by the record.

ON-LINE METHOD.

Of relevance here is the first sentence of R.C. 5739.01(B), which reads, in pertinent part, that "sale" shall include all transactions where " * * * a license to use or consume tangible personal property is or is to be granted * * * for a consideration in any manner. * * * " Taxpayer argues, as in the off-line method, that the use of its equipment by its customers is inconsequential as relates to its computer system and programming thereof, and constitutes a personal service transaction under the last sentence of R.C. 5739.01(B) which grants exception for " * * * personal service transactions which involve the transfer of tangible personal property as an inconsequential element, for which no separate charges are made."

The board's decision, supported by the record, reflects mechanized transactions initiated by the customers subsequent to original programming by appellant, so that "[t]he

overall service was not substantially made by the persons rendering the service, and a personal service transaction did not occur. * * * " The board cites *Koch* v. *Kosydar* (1972), 32 Ohio St.2d 74, 290 N.E.2d 847, as to the criteria to be used in determining whether a personal service transaction exists. Further, the record supports the decision of the board in applying the test in *Accountant's*, *supra*, "that the use of appellant's computer system is the real reason for and the true object of the transaction contracts between appellant and its clients."

The decision of the Board of Tax Appeals is neither unreasonable nor unlawful, and is, therefore, affirmed.

BROWN, J., dissenting.

The board's decision in the instant case is both unreasonable and unlawful, and is neither supported by any evidence nor by the board's own finding.

The "personal service exception" contained in R.C. 5739.01(B) excepts from sales taxation any inconsequential transfer of tangible personal property incidental to a personal service transaction. As I indicated in my dissent in *United States Shoe Corp.* v. *Kosydar* (1975), 41 Ohio St.2d 68, 322 N.E.2d 668, this exception must be seriously distorted before it can be construed to impose a tax upon a service transaction.

A transaction which consists of full service data processing of customer furnished information by the use of a computer program is a service transaction not subject to sales tax under the Ohio sales and use tax laws. Although the incidental delivery to the customer of a printed write-out of the data processing result of such a service, for which no separate charge is made, is a transfer of tangible personal property, its presence does not make the *service transaction* taxable. That the service contract is performed by persons rather than machines is of interest, in my view, only to the extent that it bears upon determination as to whether the service performed is personal in nature, thus excepting from taxation the incidental transfer of tangible personal property.

Where the service is "personalized," that is, where the charges are for processing customer furnished information (sales data, payroll data), other states having sales tax statutes similar to Ohio's refer to the contractor as a "service bureau," and in clarifying tax regulations, either except the entire transaction from taxation or outline methods of computing *only* the taxable value of the incidental transfers of tangible personal property. In so doing, they generalize at the outset of each such regulation that charges for processing are *not taxable*, as opposed to stating that they are exempt.

One need not discuss exemption (or exception) where the tax does not apply.

Particularly noteworthy is Regulation 1502 of the Board of Equalization of the Department of Business Taxes of the state of California, which thoroughly and rationally regulates all automatic data processing service and equipment transactions in that state. That regulation provides answers to most of the problems involved in separating the service portion of such contracts from the property transfer portion, when taxable, and outlines methods of determining the value of the taxable portion.

The California regulation is contained in its entirety at pages 4–9 of appendix 2–3.2d of 1 Bigelow, Computer Law Service (1975), State Sales and Use Taxes. That appendix also lists the attitudes of other state tax departments with reference to this problem. There, one finds the following tax department positions, state by state:

Connecticut

"Where a service bureau enters into a contract for the processing of customer-furnished information, by the use of a computer program or through an electrical accounting machine programmed by a wired plug-board, and the output is in part or in whole transferred to the customer in tabulated listing or similar human readable form, the true object of the contract is considered to be the rendition of a service, even though some tangible personal property is incidentally transferred to the client. Such contracts usually provide that the service bureau will receive the customer's source documents, record data in machine readable form, such as in punched cards or on magnetic tape, make necessary corrections, process the information, and then provide tabulated listings or record output onto other

similar media (including payroll check forms or cards or W–2 forms or tax returns. * * *" [Citation.]

Louisiana

"The furnishing for a monthly fee [of] computer printed accounting and accounts receivable and payable reports is a service of a type not subject to Louisiana sales tax." [Citation.]

New York

"Services offered by computer operators, which consist of ' * * * services of collecting, compiling or analyzing information of any kind or nature and furnishing reports thereof to other persons, but excluding the furnishing of information which is personal or individual in nature * * * ' are taxable * * *." [Citation.]

Texas

"Processing of data, performing of accounting services and evaluation of information when the information is supplied by the customer, or gathered for the customer, are services which are not taxed under the sales and use tax." [Citation.]

Virginia

"Service bureaus in general provide tabulated listings developed from the customer's source material and payroll checks and W–2 forms, from payroll records. This is considered a nontaxable service even though some tangible personal property of an inconsequential nature is transferred to the customer." [Citation.]

Washington

Sales of "custom" programs do not constitute " 'sales at retail' but * * * are simply the tangible evidence of a professional service rendered." [Citation.]

Wisconsin

"Processing a client's data. Generally speaking, if a person enters into a contract to process a client's data by the use of a computer program, or through an electrical accounting machine programmed by a wired plugboard, the contracts are non-taxable (except if the contract is in the nature of a lease * * *). Such contracts usually provide that the person will receive the client's source documents, record data in machine readable form, such as in punch cards or on magnetic tape, make necessary corrections, rearrange or create new information as the result of the processing and then provide tabulated listings or record output on other media. This service will be considered nontaxable even if the total charge is broken down into specific charges for each step. The furnishing of computer programs and data by the client for processing under direction and control of the person providing the service is nontaxable even though charges may be based on computer time. The true object of these contracts is considered to be a service, even though some tangible personal property is incidentally transferred to the client." [Citation.]

With regard to Champion's on-line activities for its savings and loan clients, I see no valid basis for holding that such activities constitute a *license to use* Champion's computer, taxable under any part of the sales tax law. This is because Champion did not make such a transfer of possession or use of its computers to its clients or their personnel as is necessary in order to make the transaction taxable under clear statutory language.

I would hold the board's decision both unreasonable and unlawful. The consequences of the majority opinion and the confusion demonstrated by the court in its approach to this problem are regrettable.

LINDNER BROTHERS, INC. v. KOSYDAR

46 Ohio St.2d 162, 346 N.E.2d 691
(Supreme Court of Ohio, May 5, 1976.)

PER CURIAM.

These cases are appeals from decisions of the Board of Tax Appeals affirming a sales and use tax assessment levied against Lindner Brothers, Inc., d.b.a. United Dairy Farmers, and a sales tax assessment levied against American Financial Leasing & Services Co.

A thorough review of the records herein reveals that the activities involved here (primarily integrated data processing services and programming) are substantially identical to the activities considered by this court in *Citizens Financial Corp. v. Kosydar* (1975), 43 Ohio St.2d 148, 331 N.E.2d 435.

As such, the decisions of the Board of Tax Appeals in these cases are affirmed. [Citations.]

William B. Brown and Paul W. Brown, Justices, dissent for the reasons stated by Paul W. Brown in his dissenting opinion in *Citizens Financial Corp. v. Kosydar* (1975), 43 Ohio St.2d 148 at 151, 331 N.E.2d 435.

COMMERCE UNION BANK v. TIDWELL

538 S.W.2d 405
(Supreme Court of Tennessee, June 14, 1976.)

FONES, J.

The sole question presented in this direct appeal is whether computer "software"[1] is tangible personal property and taxable under the State Sales and Use Tax provisions of T.C.A. §§ 67–3001, et seq.

The Chancellor held that the computer software purchased by the plaintiff-appellant did not constitute nontaxable services, but was tangible personal property and subject to taxation. We reverse.

The applicable Code section reads in part as follows:

> 67–3003. *Levy of tax—Rate.*—It is declared to be the legislative intent that every person is exercising a taxable privilege who engages in the business of selling tangible personal property at retail in this state, or who uses or consumes in this state any item or article of *tangible personal property* as defined in this chapter, irrespective of the ownership thereof or any tax immunity which may be enjoyed by the owner thereof, or who is the recipient of any of the things or services taxable under this chapter, or who rents or furnishes any of the things or ser-

---

1. Generally, "hardware" refers to the tangible parts of the computer itself, while "software" refers to information and directions loaded into the machine which dictates different functions for the machine to perform. What triggers these functions are referred to broadly as "pro- grams," and are often accompanied by magnetic tapes and discs, punch cards, manuals, flow charts, and expert engineering assistance to comprise what is known in the industry as computer software.

vices taxable under this chapter, or who stores for use or consumption in this state any item or article of tangible personal property as defined in this chapter, or who leases or rents such property, either as lessor or lessee, within the State of Tennessee. (Emphasis added)

Tangible personal property is defined by T.C.A. § 67–3002(1) as "personal property, which may be seen, weighed, measured, felt, or touched, or is in any other manner perceptible to the senses."

Pursuant to T.C.A. § 67–3003, the Commissioner of Revenue assessed a tax deficiency against appellant in the amount of $26,336.32, which was paid under protest. In this appeal only the amount of $4,094.54 remains at issue which represents the total tax, penalty, and interest assessed on the sales and leases of computer software.

Basically, there are two types of software programs. The first is an operational program which controls the hardware and actually makes the machine run; it is fundamental and necessary to the functioning of the computer hardware itself. Secondly, there is an applicational program which is a type of program designed to perform specific functions, such as preparation of the employee payroll, preparation of a loan amortization schedule, or any other specific job which the computer is capable of performing. Applicational programs instruct the central processing unit of the computer to perform the fundamental computations, comparisons, and sequential steps required to take incoming information and compute the desired output. All of the programs involved in this lawsuit, except two, are of the applicational type.

Rather than develop all of its own programs, appellant purchases specialized programs from outsiders. This is the general practice in the computer field. It appears that some of these programs are standard in their design and may be modified to fit the peculiar application of the individual user, while others are unique. The modifications may be minor or complex, depending on the program and its application, and may be performed by the vendor or the user, or both.

The information contained in these programs may be introduced into the user's computer by several different methods. It could be programmed manually by the originator of the program at the location of the user's computer, working from his own instructions; it could be programmed by a remote programming terminal located miles from the user's computer, with the input information transmitted by telephone; or, more commonly, the computer could be programmed by punch cards, magnetic tapes or discs, containing the program developed by the vendor. Often, accompanying the computer program, the vendor will provide manuals, services, and consultation designed to instruct the user's employees in the installation and utilization of the supplied program.

After a program supplied on punch cards has been placed in appellant's computer, the cards are destroyed. The cards cost about $1.30 per thousand, and approximately 4,000 to 6,000 cards are required for a program. When magnetic tapes are utilized as the transmitting device, they are returned to the vendor after the information contained on them has been stored in appellant's computer. Costs for the tape is approximately $11.00 for a reel of tape 200 feet in length. The total cost for programs purchased by appellant has ranged from $700 to almost $60,000.

Appellant argues that while the intellectual processes may be embodied in tangible and physical material, such as punch cards and magnetic tapes, the logic or intelligence of the program is an intangible property right; and it is this intangible property right which is acquired when computer software is purchased or leased.

Appellee views the purchase of software as analogous to the purchase of a phonograph record or the purchase or lease of a motion picture film. He argues that this case is governed by *Crescent Amusement Co. v. Carson*, 187 Tenn. 112, 213 S.W.2d 27 (1948). [Footnote.] There, a tax was levied on the rental of motion picture films. This Court rejected appellant's contention that the rental of the film is merely the extension of a license to use and exhibit a copyrighted production which amounts only to the use of an intangible property right. The Court then went on to discuss the cohesiveness of tangible goods and the thought processes, skill, and labor that go into the production of those goods:

> There is scarcely to be found any article susceptible to sale or rent that is not the result of

an idea, genius, skill and labor applied to a physical substance. A loaf of bread is the result of the skill and labor of the cook who mixed the physical ingredients and applied heat at the temperature and consistency her judgment dictated. A radio is the result of the thought of a genius, or of several such persons, combined with the skill and labor of trained technicians applied to a tangible mass of substance. An automobile is the result of all these elements, and of patents, etc.; and so on, ad infinitum. If these elements should be separated from the finished product and the sales tax applied only to the cost of the raw material, the sales tax act would, for all practical purposes, be entirely destroyed. The material used in the making of a phonograph record probably costs only a few cents. The voice of a Caruso recorded thereon makes it sell for perhaps a dollar. To measure the sales tax only by the value of the physical material in this phonograph record is to apply an impossible formula. [Citation.]

The examples given in the *Crescent* case differ from the situation in the case at bar in that no product is created. What is created and sold here is information, and the magnetic tapes which contain this information are only a method of transmitting these intellectual creations from the originator to the user. It is merely incidental that these intangibles are transmitted by way of a tangible reel of tape that is not even retained by the user.

In *Crescent* the tax was levied on the rental of a motion picture film. The film is inherently related to the movie; without the film there could have been no movie. Therein lies the crucial difference. Magnetic tapes and cards are not a crucial element of software. The whole of computer software could be transmitted orally or electronically without any tangible manifestations of transmission. [Citation.]

It does not appear that appellee has attempted to tax computer programs purchased by appellant which were transmitted to its computers from outside the State by way of telephone lines. That method of transmission, without question, constitutes the purchase of intangible personal property. The principle is the same, only the method of transmitting the information differs.

Appellee maintains that the sale of a phonograph record, which is taxable as tangible personal property, and the sale of a computer program on a reel of magnetic tape are analogous. One who buys a phonograph record intends to obtain possession of a tangible item. Granted, the sound which emanates from the record when it is played is the object of the purchase; but the purchaser has no other viable method of bringing the music of, say, Caruso into his living room. The phonograph record remains in the possession of the purchaser after its purchase, both during periods of use and non-use.

The instant case presents a different situation. A magnetic tape is only one method whereby information may be transmitted from the originator to the computer of the user. That same information may be transmitted from the originator to the user by way of telephone lines, or it may be fed into the user's computer directly by the originator of the program.

When the information is transferred from the tape to the computer, the tape is no longer of any value to the user; and it is not retained in the possession of the user. The information on the tape, unlike the phonograph record, is not complete and ready to be used at the time of its purchase. It must be translated into a language understood by the computer. Once this information has been translated and introduced into the computer and the tapes returned or the punch cards destroyed, what actually remains in the computer is intangible knowledge; this is what was purchased, not the magnetic tapes or the punch cards. *District of Columbia* v. *Universal Computer Associates, Inc.*, 151 U.S.App.D.C. 30, 465 F.2d 615 (1972). Transfer of tangible personal property under these circumstances is merely incidental to the purchase of the intangible knowledge and information stored on the tapes. *See, Washington Times-Herald, Inc.* v. *District of Columbia*, 94 U.S.App.D.C. 154, 213 F.2d 23 (1954). There the newspaper had purchased from an artist the right to reproduce his cartoons. These cartoons were transferred to the newspaper and were physically embodied in mats which were then used to reproduce the cartoons in the newspaper. The Court held that what the newspaper had purchased was the right to reproduce the cartoons, and not the material upon which the cartoons were impressed.

In a closely analogous [sic], *Dun & Bradstreet, Inc.* v. *City of New York*, 276 N.Y. 198,

11 N.E.2d 728 (1937), the New York Court of Appeals held that financial informational services rendered to clients of Dun & Bradstreet were nontaxable even though reference books containing financial information were delivered to the subscribers. No separate charge was made for the books, and they could not be obtained without subscribing to the service. Also, in that case, as here, the same service could have been rendered without transferring the reference books, but the cost of the service would have been much higher.

We hold that the sale of computer software does not constitute the sale of tangible personal property for the purposes of T.C.A. §§ 67-3001 et seq.

The decree of the Chancery Court of Davidson County is reversed and a decree will be prepared and entered in this Court awarding judgment to appellant for the stipulated sum. Costs are assessed against the Commissioner.

STATE v. CENTRAL COMPUTER SERVICES, INC.

349 So.2d 1160

(Supreme Court of Alabama, Sept. 9, 1977.)

TORBERT, C. J.

This court granted the petition for writ of certiorari in this case because it involved a material question of first impression in this state, that question being whether computer "software" constitutes tangible personal property for purposes of the state use tax as set out in Title 51, section 788, Code of Alabama 1940 (Recomp.1958). The Court of Civil Appeals answered this question in the negative. We affirm.

Central Computer Services, Inc., a subsidiary of Central Bank of Alabama, paid $236,400.00 to University Computing Company of Texas for a ninety-nine year license for the use of eight computer programs. Each program consisted of a set of instructions recorded on magnetic tapes and punched cards. The computer "software" was used to program Central Computer Services' computer which provides data processing services for banks affiliated with Central Bancshares of the South, Inc.

Upon receipt of the "software," Central Computer Services extracted the information contained on the magnetic tapes and punched cards, and transferred the programs to magnetic discs owned by Central Computer Services. The tapes were then returned to University Computing Company and the cards were thrown away.

Pursuant to Title 51, section 788, Code of Alabama 1940 (Recomp.1958), the State Department of Revenue entered a use tax assessment against Central Computer Services in the amount of $13,519.91 for its purchase of the eight computer programs.

Central Computer Services appealed this assessment to the Circuit Court of Jefferson County. That court reversed the assessment, ruling that computer "software" was intangible and that the purchase of such "software" was not subject to the use tax on tangible personal property.

The Court of Civil Appeals, 349 So.2d 1156, sustained this ruling of the trial court, stating that what was purchased by Central Computer Services was the information or knowledge which went into the development of the eight programs and not the magnetic tapes and punched cards themselves. Further, the appeals court noted that the magnetic tapes and punched cards were merely the means by which this information or knowledge was transferred.

The State contends that the Court of Civil Appeals erred when it concluded that the "software" was intangible and thus not subject to the tax. The State argues that the magnetic tapes and punched cards are a necessary, integral part of the computer program and that because these items are tangible, there was a purchase of taxable tangible personal property by Central Computer Services.

The only Alabama case relied upon by the State for its proposition of law that computer "software" is tangible and taxable is *Boswell v. Paramount Television Sales, Inc.*, 291 Ala. 490, 282 So.2d 892 (1973). In that case, this court held that the leasing of movie films and tapes by Paramount, a California corporation, to television stations in Alabama involved the leasing of tangible personal property rather than an intangible right to publish as Paramount argued.

We believe that magnetic tapes and punched

cards are distinguishable from movie films. In *Boswell*, the court noted that the right to publish or broadcast the motion picture was physically inseparable from the movie film itself. The physical presence of the movie film is essential to broadcasting the intangible artistic efforts of the actors. However, in the present case, the physical presence of magnetic tapes and punched cards is *not* essential to the transmittal of the desired information from its creator at University Computing Company to Central Computer Services. Testimony in the present case indicates that this information can also be telephoned to the computer or brought into Alabama in the mind of an employee of University Computing Company.

In summary, we find in the present case that there is an incidental physical commingling of the intangible information sought by Central Computer Services and the tangible magnetic tapes and punched cards themselves. We therefore hold that the essence of this transaction was the purchase of nontaxable intangible information.

As previously stated, this is a case of first impression in Alabama. However, we are not without case authority from other jurisdictions to support our holding that computer "software" is not taxable tangible personal property. Several courts have dealt with this issue in factual situations identical to the one presently before this court.

The Supreme Court of Tennessee recently held that specialized computer "software" purchased by a bank is not tangible personal property subject to that state's use tax in *Commerce Union Bank* v. *Tidwell*, 538 S.W.2d 405 (Tenn.1976). The underlying rationale for that decision was stated by the Tennessee court in the following manner:

> When the information is transferred from the tape to the computer, the tape is no longer of any value to the user; and it is not retained in the possession of the user. The information on the tape, unlike the phonograph record, is not complete and ready to be used at the time of its purchase. It must be translated into a language understood by the computer. Once this information has been translated and introduced into the computer and the tapes returned or the punch

cards destroyed, what actually remains in the computer is intangible knowledge; this is what was purchased, not the magnetic tapes or the punch cards. [Citation.] Transfer of tangible personal property under these circumstances is merely incidental to the purchase of the intangible knowledge and information stored on the tapes. [Citation.]

In *District of Columbia* v. *Universal Computer Associates, Inc.*, 151 U.S.App.D.C. 30, 465 F.2d 615 (1972), the United States Court of Appeals for the District of Columbia held that computer "software" was not subject to the District of Columbia personal property tax on tangible property. Concerning the nature of the "software," that court stated the following:

> * * * It is the information derived by the machine from the cards which stays in the computer, and which is employed repeatedly by the machine when it is used by Universal. What rests in the machine, then, is an intangible— "knowledge"—which can hardly be thought to be subject to a personal property tax. The only visible evidence of that knowledge, the punched pasteboard, could be stacked in a warehouse, returned to IBM, or destroyed, without interfering with the efficiency of the computer machine to perform its designed function. [Citation.]

We hold that computer "software" does not constitute tangible personal property for purposes of Title 51, section 788, Code of Alabama 1940 (Recomp.1958). The decree of the Court of Civil Appeals is hereby affirmed.

MADDOX, J., dissenting.

I cannot distinguish this case from *Boswell* v. *Paramount Television Sales, Inc.*, 291 Ala. 490, 282 So.2d 892 (1973). Central Computer Services, a subsidiary of Central Bank of Alabama, paid $236,400 for a 99-year license for the use of eight computer programs from University Computing Company of Texas. This so-called "application software" is tangible personal property, in my opinion. Such programs can be the subject of theft. *Hancock* v. *State*, 402 S.W.2d 906 (Tex.Cr.App.1955).[1]

The problem we face today of trying to decide whether applications software is "tangi-

---

1. In *Hancock* v. *Decker*, 379 F.2d 552 (5th Cir. 1967), the defendant, on appeal from a denial of a petition for habeas corpus, claimed he had not stolen property of a

value in excess of $50. The Fifth Circuit affirmed the denial of the petition.

ble" or "intangible" is admittedly a difficult one and the problem had its genesis with an "unbundling" announcement made by IBM in 1969, the effect of which is discussed in a Note in the Suffolk University Law Review, Vol. IX, pp. 119–144, entitled, *The Revolt Against the Property Tax on Software: An Unnecessary Conflict Growing Out of Unbundling*.

Prior to 1969, when the industry was in its developmental stages, hardware occupied the center of attention, while software was relegated to an incidental service supplied by the computer manufacturer in support of the hardware. This was perhaps a natural tendency. Laymen could relate quite easily to the physical manifestations of the computer with its crisp modern styling much as they would to a new model automobile. The more sophisticated attempted to understand design features and performance characteristics from the descriptive literature and manuals. However, it was a relatively small group of cognoscenti who understood how to get the computer to do useful work and how to control and maximize its efficiency. Apparently relishing their Merlin-like role, this latter group made little effort to increase understanding, while the others were content to concentrate on other areas.

Two factors contributed to this shortsighted position. First, the emphasis of the industry was clearly on developing a smaller, more reliable computer that consumed less energy and which could be produced at less cost. Thus, in the span of approximately fifteen years, the industry put forth three 'generations' of hardware, each one based on improved technology—vacuum tubes, transistors and integrated circuits. The capacity of the hardware of each generation to digest ever increasing quantities of data resulted in less attention being paid to methods that would increase the efficiency of the successive models of hardware.

The second factor was that in this early period, computer users, as a group apart, were noticeably "clubby" in that they formed associations oriented towards a particular manufacturer's equipment in order to share experiences and discuss problems. A natural offshoot of these associations was the free interchange of computer programs so that the other fellow would not have to "reinvent the wheel." This milieu was in large part due to the fact that the earliest computer applications were in the educational and scientific sectors of the market, which are generally characterized by full and free disclosure and immediate publication.

The start of the development of software as a distinct entity within the industry can be traced to 1969 when IBM announced a comprehensive plan for the separation of prices for its computers and related services including certain types of software. Prior to that time it was standard industry practice to price only the data processing equipment itself (the hardware) and to include, at no additional cost, "a variety of services." Such services, furnished free by the manufacturer, normally included customer engineering—the adaptation of the data processing system to the user's environment both physically, in terms of computer room layout and requirements, and conceptually, in terms of meeting the user's application needs. Maintenance of the equipment and training of the user's personnel were also included in the equipment price. Most importantly, however, both systems and applications software were furnished at no cost. This packaged price policy became known within the industry as "bundled" pricing. Hence, after the 1969 IBM announcement, the price separation of hardware from software and services became known as "unbundling."

The evolution of relative independence for software was hastened by the introduction of third generation hardware (built around integrated circuits) which had the capability of performing multiple tasks simultaneously. This dynamic development intensified the pressure on equipment manufacturers to offer systems software that could optimize the hardware capability. The most important boost forward, however, came from the development of higher level programming languages which permitted "machine independence, or at least, * * * ease of transferability from one computer to another." These languages expanded the effectivity of programming efforts in that programs, formerly written on an individual basis for a particular computer, could now be utilized on many computers—both those within the manufacturer's "family" and those made by competing manufacturers—with minimum modification. In concert, these two developments ushered in the beginning of a software industry. It was now possible for those systems and applications programmers with an entrepreneurial bent to establish themselves in business without being irrevocably tied to one manufacturer's hardware. (footnotes omitted.)

As software assumed an independent posture, a confrontation developed between computer manufacturers and purchasers and local taxing authorities. This case specifically points up the problem.

I candidly admit that some other courts,

when presented with the problem we face here, have classified applications software as "intangibles." The majority opinion naturally cites these cases, and I cannot fault them for this, because they do support the result they reach. But for *Boswell* v. *Paramount Television Sales, Inc.*, supra, I would consider these other cases to be persuasive, too. Even so, I still think those cases from other jurisdictions follow a traditional approach to defining "tangibles" and "intangibles" when we are living in a "computer age." In any event, I believe that *Paramount Television Sales* controls, and that the majority has not adequately distinguished it.

The majority says that in *Paramount* the film was actually brought into the state and that here the "knowledge" could have been (although it was not) transmitted by a telephone line or personnel could have come to Alabama and designed the program. The same could have been true in *Paramount*. We all know that films can be transmitted by telephone lines or radio waves across state lines, also. Likewise, the actors in *Paramount* could come into Alabama and perform and produce the film. Does that make the product produced, the saleable item, an intangible? I think not. Here, the cards and tapes had value because of what was contained on them. In *Paramount*, the film had value because of what was contained on it. In *Paramount*, some type of "hardware" had to be used in order to get the "knowledge" off the film. I cannot distinguish *Paramount*, therefore, as easily as the majority does.

In short, the cards and tapes here, although they require a piece of hardware to use what is contained on them, have tremendous value over and above the cost of the physical tapes and cards. Central Computer Services thought so, too. It paid $236,400 for those cards and tapes.

I would reverse the judgment of the Court of Civil Appeals.

MIAMI CITIZENS NATIONAL BANK & TRUST CO. v. LINDLEY

50 Ohio St.2d 249, 364 N.E.2d 25
(Supreme Court of Ohio, June 22, 1977.)

This is an appeal by the Miami Citizens National Bank and Trust Company of Miami County from a decision of the Board of Tax Appeals which affirmed a sales tax assessment made by the Tax Commissioner. The bank claimed an exception from the sales tax assessment under the "personal service" provision of R.C. 5739.01(B).

The bank installed a data processing system in 1967 for the purpose of doing its own computer work. Eventually it began doing data processing for other banks and provided those banks with various programs which may be summarized as follows:

(1) A demand deposit program consisting of 20 reports;

(2) a savings account program consisting of 10 reports;

(3) an installment loan program consisting of 13 reports;

(4) a variety of other programs, including the special demand deposit balance analysis report, the F.D.I.C. summary of accounts and deposits report, the time certificate of deposit program, the shareholders accounting program, and the Christmas Club accounting program.

(5) a consulting program involving comparative studies, and special programs which include preparation of correspondence to customers of the correspondent banks; and

(6) payroll and sales analysis programs, offered primarily to customers other than correspondent banks.

Many of Miami Citizens' programs were provided to the correspondent banks on a daily basis. Each program customarily consisted of a series of "reports" which reveal considerable information for use by the correspondent bank in making informed management decisions for future operations.

The customer bank paid a set monthly fee per account, depending upon the type of account; *e.g.*, saving accounts are 15 cents per account per month. Miami Citizens also billed separately for changes requested in a particular customer's program. The sales tax was assessed only on charges for "computer printouts," and not for programming time.

* * *

O'NEILL, C. J.

The issue presented to this court is whether Miami Citizens transactions are excepted from the sales tax under the provisions of R.C. 5739.01(B). That statute provides, in pertinent part:

"Sale" and "selling" include all transactions by which title or possession, or both, of tangible personal property, is or is to be transferred * * * for a consideration in any manner * * *. * Other than as provided in this section, "sale" and "selling" do not include professional, insurance, or personal service transactions which involve the transfer of tangible personal property as an inconsequential element for which no separate charges are made.

The controlling law is set forth in the syllabus of *Accountant's Computer Services* v. *Kosydar* (1973), 35 Ohio St.2d 120, 298 N.E.2d 519.

In applying the "real object" test as set forth in the syllabus of *Computer Services, supra*, the Board of Tax Appeals concluded that the true object sought by the taxpayer's customers was the property produced, *i.e.*, the computer program data in printed form. The board consequently held the transactions taxable.

Both parties to the instant action contend that the principles of *Accountant's Computer Services, supra*, as applied to the three cases consolidated in that opinion, are dispositive of the issues herein.

The activities of the appellant are substantially identical to those integrated data processing services considered by this court in *Lindner Bros.* v. *Kosydar* (1976), 46 Ohio St.2d 162, 346 N.E.2d 690. In that case, American Financial Leasing & Service Co. provided valuable services to a bank in a number of fields, including demand deposits, accounting, savings accounts, commercial loan problems, installment loan problems, problems relating to bond portfolio analysis in the trust department, and the problem of maintaining a proper collateral loan program. This court found the transaction taxable upon the authority of *Citizens Financial Corp.* v. *Kosydar* (1975), 43 Ohio St.2d 148, 331 N.E.2d 435; *Federated Department Stores* v. *Kosydar* (1976), 45 Ohio

St.2d 1, 340 N.E.2d 840; and *Accountant's Computer Services, supra*.

This court holds that where a bank uses its management to analyze the business operations of its client correspondent banks and devises programs which organize information taken from clients' records and provide the client with the organized information in computer print-out forms, which reports are necessary to make informed management, operational, auditing, marketing and other business decisions, the true object of the transactions as shown by the record is the receipt of the printed form which contains the computer organized data and therefore such transactions constitute sales of tangible personal property pursuant to R.C. 5739.01(B).

The decision of the Board of Tax Appeals, is, therefore, affirmed.

BROWN, J., dissenting.

I dissent for the reasons given in my dissenting opinions in [citation] and *Citizens Financial Corp.* v. *Kosydar* (1975), 43 Ohio St.2d 148, at page 151, 331 N.E.2d 435.

INTELLIDATA INC. v. STATE BOARD OF EQUALIZATION

139 Cal.App.3d 594, 188 Cal.Rptr. 850
(Court of Appeal, First District, Division 2, Jan. 31, 1983.)

MILLER, A. J.

In this action we consider whether transactions between keypunch service companies and their customers are properly taxable as sales of tangible personal property within the meaning of the California Sales and Use Tax Law. (Rev. & Tax.Code, § 6001 et seq.)[1]

The underlying facts in this case are generally undisputed. Intellidata Incorporated (hereinafter "plaintiff") is a computer service bureau. Among other operations it provides keypunching services for corporations that own their own computer. The keypunching service may be described as follows:

---

* Effective August 27, 1976, R.C. 5739.01(B) was amended to include the following:

The transfer of title or possession or both, of tangible personal property, or the granting of a license to use or consume tangible personal property, by an electronic data processor in conveying the results of the

electronic processing of others' data by such processor is not a sale, and the electronic data processor is deemed to be rendering a service.

1. All code sections will refer to the Revenue and Taxation Code unless otherwise indicated.

Plaintiff's customer delivered raw data such as sales invoices, inventory cards, billings, etc. Plaintiff was instructed on what information from each such business record must be transposed onto computer-readable keypunch cards. The keypunch cards, supplied by plaintiff, come in a standard size and shape and, at the time in question, were universally used in the data processing industry. Data was transposed on to the cards by use of a keypunching machine which has alphabetic letters the same as a typewriter and a numerical keyboard similar to a ten-key adding machine. The skills of a keypunch operator are similar to those of a typist.

After plaintiff's employees keypunched the cards, they were delivered to plaintiff's customers. The customer used the cards to input the information into its computer. After the cards were read by the computer they had no further use to the customer and were usually destroyed or recycled.

Plaintiff purchased the cards and paid the tax on them. However, plaintiff's customers were not billed for the cards used. Plaintiff considered the consumption of the cards to be part of the hourly rate it charged its customers for the service; the cost of the cards constituting approximately two percent of the overall cost to the customer.

After having paid over $10,000 [footnote] to defendant for sales tax on its keypunching services and exhausting its administrative remedies, plaintiff brought the instant action for recovery of the collected sales tax on July 18, 1979. Following a trial before the court in which the parties presented both oral and documentary evidence, the court ruled that plaintiff take nothing by its complaint and this appeal followed.

Plaintiff's principal contention, both at trial and on appeal, is that gross receipts from the sale of keypunching services are exempt from sales tax because the true object of the transactions between plaintiff and its customers are the services rendered by plaintiff and not the media on which the services are delivered.

Pursuant to section 6051 [footnote] a tax is imposed upon each retail sale made in California. This tax is an excise or privilege tax on the retail seller, based on the gross receipts from sales of tangible personal property at retail in the state. Section 6016 defines tangible personal property as " * * * personal property which may be seen, weighed, measured, felt, or touched, or which is in any other manner perceptible to the senses," and section 6012, defining gross receipts and excluded items, states in subdivision (b) "The total amount of the sale or lease or rental price includes all of the following: [¶] (1) Any services that are part of the sale."

The term "sale" generally includes any transfer of title or possession of tangible personal property for a consideration (§ 6006, subd. (a)) and more specifically, "[a] transfer for a consideration of the title or possession of tangible personal property which has been produced, fabricated, or printed to the special order of the customer." (§ 6006, subd. (f).)

Pursuant to section 7051 defendant has adopted various administrative regulations that concern the sales and use tax in specific types of transactions. (Cal.Admin.Code, tit. 18, § 1500 et seq.)

California Administrative Code, title 18, section 1501 states in pertinent part: "Persons engaged in the business of rendering service are consumers, not retailers, of the tangible personal property which they use incidentally in rendering the service. Tax, accordingly, applies to the sale of the property to them. * * * [¶] The basic distinction in determining whether a particular transaction involves a sale of tangible personal property or the transfer of tangible personal property incidental to the performance of a service is one of the true objects of the contract; that is, is the real object sought by the buyer the service per se or the property produced by the service. * * * [¶] Examples of service enterprises and regulations pertaining thereto will be found in regulations which follow."

California Administrative Code, title 18, section 1502 specifically deals with automatic data processing services and equipment. Subsection (2) of subdivision (d) of that section (hereinafter "keypunching regulation") states in pertinent part: " * * * agreements providing solely for keypunching; keypunching and keystroke verification; or keypunching, providing a proof list and/or verifying of data are regarded as contracts for the fabrication of punched cards and sales of proof lists.

Charges therefor are taxable, whether the cards are furnished by the customer or by the service bureau."

Plaintiff contends that defendant, through administrative regulation, has extended the sales tax beyond that which the Legislature has intended. Plaintiff asserts that defendant does not have the right to tax an activity that was not deemed taxable under the enabling statutes. It continues that since keypunching constitutes a nontaxable *service* rather than a taxable sale of keypunch cards, the keypunching regulation must be held an unconstitutional act of legislation. The contention is not persuasive.

The linchpin of plaintiff's argument is that section 6006, subdivision (f), the enabling legislation underlying the keypunching regulation, is inapplicable to keypunch cards since the term "fabricate" cannot include punched cards. The word "fabricate" means "to form by art and labor. * * *" (Webster's Third New International Dictionary (1965) p. 811.) Even the dictionary definition submitted by plaintiff includes "to make." Therefore, we hold that the word "fabricated" as used in section 6006, subdivision (f) must be construed in its broadest sense.

In the instant case plaintiff received raw data from its customer with instructions to transpose the data onto cards that could be read by the customer's computer. Starting with blank keypunch cards plaintiff so altered the cards through the keypunching process that they could be used to transfer the data into the customer's computer. We can only conclude that plaintiff produced tangible property to the special order of its customers pursuant to section 6006, subdivision (f).

This conclusion is consistent with results in similar California cases. In *People* v. *Grazer* (1956) 138 Cal.App.2d 274, 291 P.2d 957, the court held that the transfer of X-ray films and the radiologist's findings which accompanied the films from the radiologist to the physician constituted a taxable sale. In reaching this conclusion the court stated that "the raw materials consumed in producing that which [the physician] ordered may have cost the laboratory only a very small part of the charge made. The expense of the producer of the pictures is almost entirely the cost of the skilled

services of the radiologist and the technicians and the use of equipment which is generally quite costly. But the price charged for all taxable transfers is more often than not largely a charge for services rendered in connection with the tangible object transferred." [Citation.]

The same reasoning was followed in *Albers* v. *State Board of Equalization* (1965) 237 Cal.App.2d 494, 47 Cal.Rptr. 69 where the court held that the work of a commercial draftsman making drawings for architects, engineers and business firms based on specifications and data furnished by customers constituted a sale of tangible personal property within the meaning of section 6006, subdivision (f).

Finally, in *Simplicity Pattern Co. v. State Bd. of Equalization* (1980) 27 Cal.3d 900, 167 Cal.Rptr. 366, 615 P.2d 555 our Supreme Court held that tangible property may be taxed on the basis of its total value even though virtually all of the value is attributed to an intangible element such as intellectual content. In the course of its decision, the Court stated: "Yet by no means does the regulation [section 1501] support plaintiff's broad theory that a sale becomes nontaxable whenever its principal purpose is to transfer the intangible content of the physical object being sold." [Citation.]

Plaintiff cites *Bullock v. Statistical Tabulating Corp.* (1977) 549 S.W.2d 166, a Texas Supreme Court case, for the proposition that keypunching constitutes a service and not a sale of tangible personal property. However, in reaching its conclusion the Texas court noted that decisions from other jurisdictions show a divergence of opinion. [Citation.]

Although the decision of a court in a sister state on a similar statutory provision is ordinarily persuasive, it need not be followed if the reasoning is unsound or contrary to California policy. [Citation.] In California, the evolution of case law dealing with sales tax law leads us to our present conclusion that tangible personal property such as keypunched cards may be taxed on their total value even though their primary value is attributed to an intangible element such as keypunching services.

The judgment is affirmed.

COUNTY OF SAN DIEGO v. ASSESSMENT APPEALS BOARD NO. 2, OF SAN DIEGO COUNTY EX REL. XEROX CORP.

140 Cal.App.3d 52, 189 Cal.Rptr. 145
(Court of Appeal, Fourth District, Division 1, Feb. 18, 1983.)

COLOGNE, A. P. J.

There is a single issue in this case: whether for purposes of property tax valuation of personal property the assessor, using the income approach to valuation, may include in the value of leased equipment at the consumer trade level an amount representing imputed sales tax.

The San Diego County Assessor included an imputed sales tax figure of 5 percent in the March 1, 1974 lien date assessment of copier products manufactured and owned by Xerox Corporation, but leased to various customers in the county. The county's Assessment Appeals Board No. 2 determined the full cash value by deleting the sales tax imputed amount. On the county's petition for writ of mandamus and based on a stipulation of facts, the superior court held it was proper to include the figure for imputed sales tax in the valuation, vacated the appeals board decision, with directions, and ordered Xerox to pay the county $26,944 in taxes refunded to Xerox as a result of the erroneous decision. Xerox appeals.

Leasing is the primary means by which Xerox markets its copier products consisting of office copying and related accessory equipment. Though its leases permit shorter terms, Xerox expects the leases to extend at least six months. The lessee remits to Xerox a monthly rental based on a cost per copy metered by the machine with a minimum rental charge. There are various models of copiers involved and thus the rental amount varies based on model, volume of use and pricing plan pursuant to which the copier is leased.

Xerox pays all personal property taxes and all maintenance costs on the leased copier products. The customer remits a monthly use tax, separately stated on the invoices, with the rental payment to Xerox which in turn remits the tax to the State of California.

Although most of the Xerox copier products

have published selling prices, very few outright sales are made. In San Diego County, Xerox had in excess of 3,000 machines. In the year before March 1, 1974, only five sales were made in San Diego County. Nationwide, it has been estimated Xerox has sold only two-tenths of one percent of all machines manufactured.

The assessor generally utilizes two valuation approaches in valuing property of the type owned by Xerox. The property may be valued by the cost approach to value, based upon the current list price, depreciated on a straight line six-year basis, with sales tax included in the final conclusion. The property may also be valued by the income approach to value, pursuant to which the assessor uses a remaining economic life up to six years, with a two percent salvage value and with sales tax included in the final value. In the year under appeal, 1974, because the number of sales of like equipment was insufficient to make list price a reliable indicator of value, the assessor used a true income approach based upon a capitalization of anticipated net income and the addition of an imputed five percent sales tax to arrive at the full cash value determination. In utilizing this method, the assessor determined the net income that could reasonably be expected to be generated by the property and capitalized the net income (using a factor to include yield, recovery of investment and property taxes) to determine its present worth. To this figure the assessor added five percent as imputed sales tax.

Xerox does not dispute the basic method of valuation of its property, i.e., use of the true income approach at the consumer trade level. The sole issue in dispute is the propriety of the addition of the five percent imputed sales tax to the value determination derived pursuant to an income approach to value as utilized by the assessor. The dollar amount of full cash value determination attributable to the inclusion of sales tax was approximately $278,333.

The essence of the assessment situation involved here, use of the trade level concept in evaluating leased property, is described in the following passage from *Ex-Cell-O Corp. v. County of Alameda*, 82 Cal.App.3d 135, at page 141, 107 Cal.Rptr. 839:

As applied to leased equipment, the trade level

theory is designed to produce equity between taxpayers. If it were not applied, and in the years before it was applied, the taxpayer who owned business equipment would be taxed on the basis of the selling price to him, reduced by such factors as depreciation and obsolescence. But in the case of leased equipment, the taxpayer, in this instance the lessor, would be taxed on the basis of the cost of producing the equipment. The purpose of the assessor is to find the fair market value of any given property in the hands of the person who holds it on the lien date of any year. *By using the trade level concept, the assessor puts all of the identical equipment on the same basis, whether the ultimate user chooses to lease it or to buy it, because its value is the same to all.* [Fn. omitted.] In the case of leased equipment, the assessment is to the lessor and although there may be a contractual arrangement between the lessor and the lessee, this of course has no effect upon the action of the lessor. In the case of man-

ufacturers who do not sell any equipment but only lease it, capitalization of income from the leasing is used to establish value. (Italics added.)[1]

The basic principles of assessment practice applicable to this case are also detailed in *Xerox Corp. v. County of Orange*, 66 Cal.App.3d 746, 136 Cal.Rptr. 583, which rejected an identical attack by Xerox on the inclusion of sales tax in the valuation by five county assessors for the fiscal year ending June 30, 1972. The assessment methods used by the assessors in *County of Orange* differed from the true income method used here. [Citation.] However, the goal the assessors attained, arriving at "full cash value," "market value," or "value" (Cal. Const., art. XIII, § 1, as am. 1962; Rev. & Tax.Code, § 110, as am. Stats.1971, ch. 1542),[2] and in the process including the sales tax figure, was fully approved. It is thus

---

1. In a footnote attending this passage, the court explains the trade level assessment theory and practice further as follows:

> The trade level principle is expressed succinctly in Ehrman & Flavin, Taxing California Property, section 380, page 346, as follows: 'Inventory includes raw materials, work in process, and finished goods. It is taxable in all these stages. Moreover, since goods which are finished to a manufacturer may only be materials to a purchaser, it is apparent that more than one cycle of trade levels may occur between the first processor and the consumer. Unlike the situation in valuing equipment, therefore, the trade level is an important consideration in the proper valuation of inventory, whether the trade level be manufacturing, retail, or consumer. At the consumer level, of course, the property ceases to be inventory. The new regulations issued by the State Board of Equalization on valuation principles and procedures specifically require the assessor to give recognition to trade level and the principle that property normally increases in value as it progresses through production and distribution channels to the consumer level.' In the 1973 Supplement, page 112, the following is added: 'The State Board's rules expressly provide that tangible personal property in the hands of the consumer must be valued in accordance with the comparative sales, cost or income method. An exception, however, is property which the taxpayer leases or rents for a period of less than six months, which is to be valued by reference to the property's cost to the lessor, or the price at which the lessor could be expected to sell it, less his experienced gross profit.'
> A detailed account of the procedure for assessing tangible personal property at the trade level is given in title 18, section 10 of the California Administrative Code.

2. *County of Orange* initially points out:

> *The Constitution of California provided on the lien dates applicable to these proceedings: "All property in the State except as otherwise in this Constitution provided, not exempt under the laws of the United States, shall be taxed in proportion to its value, to be ascertained as provided by law, or as hereinafter provided."*

(Cal. Const., art. XIII, § 1 [as amended in 1962].)

> The legal standard of value in California, which has been described variously as "value," "cash value," and "full cash value," was defined on the lien date in question as: " * * * the amount at which property would be taken in payment of a just debt from a solvent debtor." (Rev. & Tax.Code, § 110 [Stats.1941, ch. 605, § 1, p. 2052].) This has been construed by the California Supreme Court to require that property be assessed at "the price that property would bring to its owner if it were offered for sale on an open market under conditions in which neither buyer nor seller could take advantage of the exigencies of the other. It is a measure of desirability translated into money amounts [citation], and might be called the market value of property for use in its present condition." (*De Luz Homes, Inc. v. County of San Diego*, 45 Cal.2d 546, 562 [290 P.2d 544].) Thus, the standard of value for assessment is market value. Indeed, in amending section 110 of the Revenue and Taxation Code to incorporate the *De Luz* definition of full cash value, the Legislature employed the term "fair market value" as interchangeable with "full cash value." [Citation.]

From the court's reference to the Legislature's adoption of the *De Luz* definition, it becomes clear the 1971 legislation applicable to this case is subject to the same observations. Revenue and Taxation Code section 110, as added by chapter 1542 of the Statutes of 1971 (operative March 1, 1972), reads:

> "Full cash value" or, "market value" or "value" means the amount of cash or its equivalent which property would bring if exposed for sale in the open market under conditions in which neither buyer nor seller could take advantage of the exigencies of the other and both with knowledge of all of the uses and purposes to which the property is adapted and for which it is capable of being used and of the enforceable restrictions upon those uses and purposes.

The statute and the Constitution have since been amended in ways not relevant to the issues in this case.

apparent *County of Orange* furnishes good authority for this case in terms of the principles it states with respect to adding the sales tax figure in arriving at value.

Some of the salient observations in *County of Orange* are, "[f]air market value contemplates a hypothetical transaction between an informed seller, being under no compulsion to sell, and an informed buyer, being under no compulsion to buy." [Citation.] The income approach to appraisal is a valid indicator of value because it recognizes "those market forces that affect the price at which knowledgeable buyers and sellers would arrive in an arm's length transaction." [Citation.]

In the context of property moving through and being assessed at various levels of production or distribution, and with an eye to attaining fair and uniform appraisals, *County of Orange* further observes, "costs incurred in producing and marketing property are elements which in common experience ordinarily determine value" [Citation.] The regulations require assessors to recognize the trade level at which the property is situated on the lien date and "the principle that that property normally increases in value as it progresses through production and distribution channels" [Citation.] and, while property at the ultimate consumer level of trade must under the regulations be valued according to one of the standard methods of appraisal, i.e., comparable sales approach, reproduction or replacement approach, or income approach [citation], the trade level concept is nevertheless useful in assessing leased equipment such as we consider here.

Usefulness of the trade level concept, even when considering the income approach to valuation, derives from the fact "it establishes the trade level at which the property is to be appraised, and it focuses on the elements that help establish the market price." [Citation.] Citing *Ex-Cell-O Corp. v. County of Alameda,* supra, 32 Cal.App.3d 135, 141, 107 Cal.Rptr. 839, the court made this important observation:

> *[T]he trade level theory produces equity between taxpayers by assuring that the taxpayer consumer who owns his equipment will pay the same tax on identical equipment as the taxpayer who leases the equipment to the ultimate consumer. The market value of the equipment is the same*

if the property is held by the ultimate consumer regardless of who pays the tax.

Also, because the consideration of the various levels of production compels an awareness of the costs incurred at each level of production and marketing, the relationship between the costs of preparing and marketing the property and the ultimate market price becomes more apparent. (66 Cal.App.3d at p. 755, 136 Cal.Rptr. 583, italics added.)

In the context of these observations and rules, *County of Orange* considered Xerox' argument that sales tax (and freight or installation charges) are not part of the value in exchange at the consumer trade level. [Citation.] Largely as it does in this case, Xerox in *County of Orange* contended inclusion of the sales tax is improper on the following grounds:

> (1) The sales tax that a seller may collect is not part of the 'price' that the parties would agree upon in the market value approach.
> (2) The sales tax and freight charges are not a part of the 'cost' of the property under the cost method of valuation.
> (3) The inclusion of sales tax is a distortion of the income method of valuation.
> (4) The sales tax is an item in which [Xerox] has no interest.

County of Orange held to the contrary on each point.

Here, under the heading that the assessor's method of valuation was invalid, Xerox argues the assessor's final step of adding imputed sales tax under the apparent theory this is required because the property is at the consumer level, is incorrect because it wrongly confuses the level of trade concept with the income approach method of valuation utilized. Xerox recognizes its equipment here, leased for an indefinite period or longer than six months, must be valued at the highest level of exchange [Citation.] It asserts, however, none of the standard methods of valuation including the income approach is designed to produce "recorded cost" or "cost," in the accounting sense, and it claims the assessor's method assumes the consumer trade level requires a determination of the consumer's book cost as a measure of value.

Xerox is here making a hypertechnical argument which ignores principles enunciated in *County of Orange* concerning the market approach. Particularly, Xerox ignores the hypothetical transaction contemplated in the process of arriving at fair market value [citation], the constitutional need for uniformity and fairness in arriving at an appraisal of the same item of property at the same level of trade [citation], here the consumer level, and the reality that "under the market value concept, where price is the basis of value, the sales tax is an element of value." [Citation.] If the owner of an item of property at the consumer level of trade is subject to application of a sales tax element in the valuation of this property, then the lessor of the same item of property at the same level of trade must be subject to the same sales tax element. Otherwise, uniformity of assessment is demolished.

Xerox claims the assessor's method of capitalization of income, with the addition of sales tax, causes an overvaluation. The income approach results in a valuation figure for "the present worth of a future income stream." [Citation.] As Xerox explains:

> Furthermore, "[t]he amount to be capitalized is the net return which a reasonably well informed owner and reasonably well informed buyers may anticipate on the lien date that the taxable property existing on that date will yield under prudent management and subject to such legally enforceable restrictions as such persons may foresee as of that date." [Citation.] The State Board defines net return as the difference between "gross return" and "gross outgo." Gross return is defined as "any money or money's worth which the property will yield over and above vacancy and collection losses. * * *" Gross outgo means "any outlay of money or money's-worth, including current expenses and capital expenditures (or annual allowances therefor) required to develop and maintain the estimated income." [Citation.]

> The net return is capitalized at a rate that returns to the investor his investment in the property, a return or yield on that investment and expenses such as property taxes that are not properly included in gross outgo. [Citation.] An example of the use of an income approach as applied to leased personal property is set forth in *Assessors Handbook* 571, at pages 91 through 94. Courts may take judicial notice of the Assessors Handbook, which is published by the

State Board to assist assessors in performing their duties. [Citation.]

The assessor's method is straight line declining income method. This method "assumes that the income will decline an equal amount each period. It also provides for equal amortization of the investment each period. The decline in income each period equals the amount amortized times the sum of the yield and tax rates." [Citation.]

By way of example, Xerox illustrates what result it believes application of the Assessor's Handbook method should obtain and what result the assessor's method actually brings. The problem with the latter example is it is founded on an unnecessarily narrow construction of 18 California Administrative Code section 8, subdivision (e), which reads, in part: "Recently derived income and recently negotiated rents or royalties (*plus any taxes paid on the property by the lessee*) of the subject property and comparable properties should be used in estimating the future income. * * *" (Italics added.)

The emphasized phrase is not limited to property taxes as Xerox asserts, but may apply to *any* taxes on the property, including sales or use tax. Moreover, inclusion of sales or use tax in the gross income column does not give rise to the need to wash it out again by also placing it in the gross outgo column.[3] It is not as Xerox asserts, purely a matter of comparing sales or use tax with property tax which is not put into gross outgo because property tax is automatically included in the capitalization rate, or of comparing those taxes with corporate net income tax or corporate franchise tax which are not included in gross outgo because they are provided for in the capitalization rate or by deriving a capitalization rate from actual sales and incomes before income taxes. Nor is it simply a matter of concluding, as Xerox suggests, since the use tax is an expenditure necessary to maintain the income stream, it must under the definition of gross outgo be included in it.

Rather, attention must be given to the unique, key feature of this case, that we are

---

3. Incidentally, there is no mathematical difference in result, due to the assessor's method of capitalizing the present worth of the rental payments and then adding to

that value the present worth of sales tax, rather than capitalizing the taxes paid along with the lessee's rental payments representing the income stream.

dealing with and using figures for leased property and the income to the lessor from that property, all at which is ordinarily the retail trade level. Yet, a valuation at the consumer trade level is what is required. Adjustment to the Assessor's Handbook method of capitalizing income must be made to obtain a valuation at the consumer trade level rather than the retail trade level. Otherwise, nonuniformity of assessment will be the result. The adjustment here made by the assessor was proper to achieve a valuation at the consumer trade level.

Xerox' contention the assessor's reliance on *County of Orange* is erroneous because the case did not involve application of a true income approach does not lead to any conclusion that might be beneficial to Xerox, and thus need not be discussed.

Next, Xerox contends the decision in the *County of Orange* case was erroneous and, to the extent it is relevant to this case, should not be followed. We have examined the discussion, analysis and authorities relied upon in the *County of Orange* case and find it is soundly decided, particularly with respect to the basic assessment principles in connection with the market approach it sets forth and applies. Recognizing *County of Orange* dealt with different appraisal methodology than is involved here, we do not consider its holdings on specific issues tied to those facts to be directly binding. We do not intend to again explore the question of sales tax as an element of value because that point was fully and convincingly decided in *County of Orange*. [Citation.] The sales tax is a part of the "price" for assessment purposes. We have already concluded, as did *County of Orange*, the level of trade concept does support the addition of sales tax. Accordingly, no further discussion of the *County of Orange* case is required.

Judgment affirmed.

STATISTICAL TABULATING CORP. v. LINDLEY
3 Ohio St.3d 23, 445 N.E.2d 1104
(Supreme Court of Ohio, March 2, 1983.)

Appellant, Statistical Tabulating Corporation, was in the business of providing data processing systems and programming services to small and medium-sized businesses. It provided services related to payroll, accounts receivable, general ledger, inventory, billing, and specialized services requested by the customers. When a customer engaged appellant's services, appellant's employees would work with the customer to effectuate a conversion to the automated system and train the customer's personnel. Thereafter, the customer would submit to appellant "source documents," which included invoices and employees' time cards, and which information would be organized and processed by appellant. The appellant employed standard programs, which it would occasionally modify to meet a customer's needs, to process the data and to produce reports or other written documents which were transferred to the customer.

Appellant was issued a tax assessment for sales made from August 1, 1973 through July 31, 1976. The Tax Commissioner affirmed the assessment, but partially remitted the penalty. Upon appeal, the Board of Tax Appeals found that these transactions were sales subject to tax under R.C. 5739.01(B) and affirmed the order of the commissioner.

* * *

PER CURIAM.
The issue raised by this appeal is whether the transactions involved are sales subject to tax as defined by R.C. 5739.01(B), which provides in part:

"Sale" and "selling" include all transactions by which title or possession, or both, of tangible personal property, is or is to be transferred, * * * for a consideration in any manner, whether absolutely or conditionally, whether for a price or rental, in money or by exchange, and by any means whatsoever; * * *. Other than as provided in this section, "sale" and "selling" do not include professional, insurance, or personal service transactions which involve the transfer of tangible personal property as an inconsequential element, for which no separate charges are made. [Footnote.]

In *Accountant's Computer Services v. Kosydar* (1973), 35 Ohio St.2d 120, 298 N.E.2d 519 [64 O.O.2d 72], we set forth the criteria to be used in determining whether a mixed transaction involving both personal services and the transfer of personal property falls within the exception contained in the last sentence of R.C. 5739.01(B), and held at paragraphs one and two of the syllabus:

> 1. * * * If the service rendered is inconsequential, the exception is not available and the *entire* transaction is taxable. If a consequential service *is* rendered, then it must be ascertained whether the transfer of the tangible personal property was an inconsequential element of the transaction. If so, then none of the consideration paid is taxable.
> 2. In determining whether a mixed transaction constitutes a consequential personal service transaction, a distinction must be made as to the *true object* of the transaction contract; that is, is the real object sought by the buyer the service *per se* or the property produced by the service. (Emphasis *sic*.)

Therein, and in later cases applying this test where data processing services were concerned, we held that if the company supplied the print-outs for the customer to use in making management decisions or other purposes, the print-outs are not deemed inconsequential. [Citations.]

The Board of Tax Appeals was " * * * not persuaded by the testimony and other evidence presented that the written material produced by the appellant was an 'inconsequential element' of the transactions." If [sic] found that "[t]he true object of the transaction was the receipt of the written reports, documents, and payroll checks, and as such, taxable." Appellant urges this court to overrule the board's factual determination.

" ' * * * This court traditionally does not substitute its judgment on factual issues for that of the Board of Tax Appeals, and we will not overrule a factual determination by the board unless the record reveals that the determination was unreasonable or unlawful.' [Citation.]" [Citation.]

With this standard of review in mind, we find sufficient evidence in the record to support the board's determination that the written materials supplied by appellant to its customers were not an inconsequential element of the transaction.

The decision of the Board of Tax Appeals being neither unreasonable nor unlawful is hereby affirmed.

Alphabetical
Table of Cases

Index